The Concise Dictionary of English Etymology

The Concise
Dictionary of English
Etymology

Walter W. Skeat

Wordsworth Reference

This edition published 1993 by Wordsworth Editions Ltd,
Cumberland House, Crib Street, Ware, Hertfordshire SG12 9ET.

Wordsworth® is a registered trade mark of
Wordsworth Editions Ltd

ISBN 1-85326-311-7

Printed and bound in Great Britain by Mackays of Chatham PLC.

CONTENTS.

INTRODUCTION.

THE present work is not a mere abridgement of my larger Etymological Dictionary, such as might have been compiled by a diligent book-maker, but has been entirely rewritten by myself; and I have found that the experience gained by writing the larger work has been of considerable assistance to me in making occasional slight improvements. My object has been to produce a convenient hand-book for the use of that increasing number of students who wish to learn the history of the English language, and who naturally desire to have Anglo-Saxon and Icelandic forms presented to them rightly spelt and accentuated, a point which seldom receives sufficient attention.

One distinguishing feature of this abridgement, as well as of my larger Dictionary, is that all the forms cited can actually be found in the usual books of reference, except when marked by an asterisk, in which case they are theoretical.

Conciseness has been attained by presenting the results in the briefest possible form; but I have, at the same time, endeavoured to guard against becoming obscure. In my opinion, the habit, frequently adopted, of citing supposed cognate words (often misspelt) *without saying what their meanings are*, is a very bad one, and leads to guessing and vagueness. It is, accordingly, to be understood that, when I do not give the meaning of cognate words, it is because their sense agrees with that of the English word so nearly as to prevent ambiguity. Thus under *bite*, which is derived from the A. S. *bītan*, to bite, I cite the Dutch, Icelandic, Swedish, Danish, and German forms without explanation, because they all mean precisely the same thing; but the Latin and Sanskrit forms are used with a slight difference of sense; and I accordingly give that sense.

I do not, in general, give the history of the *use* of the word under discussion, unless there is some special point which is necessary to be known for the sake of the etymology. For such history, accompanied by illustrative comments. references, and discussions, I must refer students to the unabridged work.

In the course of writing this abridgement, I have taken occasion to introduce several corrections, which, in the larger work, are only to be found in the Second Edition or in the Supplement.

There is one point to which I wish to draw especial attention. By the advice of a friend, I procured a copy of a Dictionary of English Etymology by the Rev. J. Oswald, written on an unusual but excellent plan. The author arranges all the derivatives of the Latin *cedcre* under the heading of the Latin *cedo*, so that words such as *accede*, *concede, recede, succeed*, are all presented to the eye at a glance. The advantage of such an arrangement is obvious, and I at once determined to adopt it, merely substituting the representative English word *cede* for the Latin *cedo*, and so in other cases. At the same time, I adopted two very considerable improvements : (1) the retention of the alphabetical order for the derived words *accede, concede*, &c., with a cross-reference; and (2) the extension of the principle to words of English and Scandinavian origin. Mr. Oswald gives the words *only* under the primary form, which is a great inconvenience, seeing that this is often precisely what one does not know ; and, just for want of the cross-reference, he omits the derivative *ancestor* altogether. At the same time I have found his book very useful, as far as relates to that part of our language which is of classical origin. With respect to words of Teutonic origin it is practically valueless ; thus the *only* word given under W is the word *wonder*.

But it is precisely with respect to these Teutonic words that most light is desired. Even a school-boy would correctly make out most of the derivatives of *cede* (though he would very likely miss *ancestor* and *decease*), but very few even of our best scholars could correctly draw up the list of words connected with *do*, such as *ado, deed, deem, doff, don, doom, dout, dup, indeed.* This I claim to have done (and in the main correctly) *for the first time*; whilst I also endeavour to emphasise the fact that *deem* is derived from *doom*, and not (conversely) *doom* from *deem*, as is so often ignorantly said by those who have probably *never even heard of* the phonetic laws by which Anglo-Saxon sounds are regulated.

The last remark leads to a principle of the first importance in etymology, viz. that no etymologies can be trusted for a moment unless they can fairly be shewn to be consistent with the ordinary phonetic laws which regulate the various Aryan languages. It is impossible to pursue this matter further in the present brief introduction.; it must suffice to lay down the one great principle which will regulate all future researches, viz. that the right understanding of the vowel-sounds lies altogether at the root of the matter.

As I frequently allude to the ordinary vowel-changes in the course of the work, I may note here those which are the most elementary and common. They ought to be learnt by heart at once.

ANGLO-SAXON. The most usual vowel-change is that produced by the occurrence of an *i* (which very often disappears by a subsequent contraction of the word) in the following syllable. Owing to this, we frequently find that the vowels, as arranged in row (1) below, are changed into the corresponding vowels in row (2).

(1) *a, o, u, ea, eo, á, ó, ú, eá, eó.*

(2) *e, y, y, y, y, æ, é, ý, ý, ý.*

Example:—*fyllan,* to fill, put for *fullian**; from *full,* full.

Moreover, substantives and secondary verbs are often formed from bases seen in the past tense singular, past tense plural, or past participle of a strong verb, rather than from the infinitive mood. Thus *band* and *bend* are from the base seen in the A. S. *band,* pt. t. of *bindan,* to bind ; whilst *bundle* is derived from that which appears in the pp. *bund-en.*

ICELANDIC. This language abounds in somewhat similar vowel changes, but very few of these appear *in English.* But we must not pass over the frequent formation of derivatives from the past tenses (singular or plural) and the past participles of strong verbs. Thus *bait,* Icel. *beita,* lit. 'to cause to bite,' is the causal of *bíta,* to bite; its form may be explained by the fact that the pt. t. of *bíta* is *beit.*

Again, as regards the Romance languages, especially French, it must be borne in mind that they also are subject to phonetic laws. This fact is better known since these laws have been sufficiently illustrated in Mr. Kitchin's translation of Brachet's Historical French Grammar. In particular, I may note that most French substantives are derived from Latin *accusatives*; and that to derive *bounty* from *bonitas* (nom.), or *honour* from Lat. *honor* (nom.), is simply impossible.

It is not a little surprising that many etymological dictionaries entirely ignore these most significant, elementary, and essential facts. A notable and very worthy exception is E. Müller's Etymologisches Wörterbuch der Englischen Sprache.

I subjoin a key to the plan of the work, and a list of abbreviations.

KEY TO THE GENERAL PLAN OF THE DICTIONARY.

§ 1. **Order of Words.** Words are given in their alphabetical order; but such words as are mere derivatives from others are only explained under some more primary form, the cross-reference to which is supplied. Thus *Act* is explained under *Agent,* as stated. If reference be made to *Agent,* it will be found that, after *Agent* has been explained and its root given, all allied words, such as *act, agile, agitate, ambiguous,* &c., follow in alphabetical order. These derived words are marked by having no capital letter, and being set a little further to the right than the rest. If the student has any difficulty in finding a word, owing to the alphabetical order being thus occasionally interrupted, let him keep his eyes *on the words printed in capitals at the head of every column,* which refer to primary words *only.*

§ 2. The words selected. The word-list contains nearly all the words of most frequent occurrence, with a few others that are remarkably prominent in literature, such as *unaneled*. Homonymous forms, such as *bay* (used in *five* senses), are numbered.

§ 3. Definitions. Definitions are omitted in the case of common words; but explanations of original forms are added wherever they seemed to me to be necessary.

§ 4. Language. The language to which each word belongs is distinctly marked, in every case, by means of letters within marks of parenthesis. Here the symbol − is to be read as 'derived from.' Thus *Abbey* is (F.−L.−Syriac); i.e. a French word derived from Latin; the Latin word being, in its turn, of Syriac origin.

The order of derivation is always upward or backward, from early to earlier forms.

The symbol **+** is employed to distinguish forms which are merely *cognate*, and are adduced merely by way of illustrating and confirming the etymology. Thus, *bite* is a purely *English* word, derived from the Anglo-Saxon *bítan*. The other Teutonic forms, viz. the Du. *bijten*, Icel. *bíta*, Swed. *bíta*, Dan. *bide*, G. *beissen*, and the other Aryan forms, viz. Lat. *findere* (base *fid*-) and Skt. *bhid*, to cleave, are merely cognate and illustrative. On this point, there commonly exists the most singular confusion of ideas; and there are many Englishmen who are accustomed to derive English, of all things, from *Modern High German*! I therefore introduce this symbol **+** by way of warning. It has its usual algebraical value of *plus* or *additional*; and indicates 'additional information to be obtained from the comparison of cognate forms.'

§ 5. Symbols of Languages. The symbols, such as F. = French, are not used in their usual vague sense, so as to baffle the enquirer who wishes to find the words referred to. Every symbol has a *special sense*, and has reference to certain books, in one at least of which the word cited may be found, as I have ascertained for myself by looking them all out. I have purposely used, as far as was practicable, cheap and easily accessible authorities. The exact sense of each symbol is given in the list below.

§ 6. Roots. In some cases, words are traced back to their original Aryan roots. The root is denoted by the symbol √, to be read as 'root.' Thus *bear*, to carry, is from √BHAR. A list of roots, with their meanings, is given in the Appendix, p. 587; and a similar list, with fuller explanations and numerous examples, in the Appendix to my larger Dictionary.

§ 7. Derivatives. The symbol **Der.**, i.e. Derivatives, is used to introduce forms related to the primary word. Thus, under *Agent*, I give *Act*, and again, under *Act*, such mere derivatives as *act-ion*, *act-ive*, &c.

LIST OF ABBREVIATIONS.

Arab.—Arabic; as in Richardson's Persian and Arabic Dict., ed. F. Johnson; 1829. See also Devic's Supplement to Littré's F. Dict.

A.S.—Anglo-Saxon; as in the dictionaries by Bosworth, Ettmüller, Grein, Leo, and Lye; and in the Vocabularies edited by T. Wright.

Bavar. — Bavarian ; as in Schmeller's Bayerisches Wörterbuch ; 1827-1837.

Bret.—Breton; as in Legonidec's Bret. Dict., ed. 1821.

C.—Celtic; used as a general term for Irish, Gaelic, Welsh, Breton, Cornish, &c.

Corn.—Cornish; as in Williams' Dict.; 1865.

Dan.—Danish; as in Ferrall and Repp; 1861.

Du.—Dutch; as in the Tauchnitz Dutch Dict. Old Dutch words are from Oudemans, Hexham (1658), or Sewel (1754).

E.—Modern English; as in Webster's Dict.

M.E.—Middle English (English from the thirteenth to the fifteenth centuries inclusive); as in Stratmann's Old English Dict., 3rd edition, 1878.

F.—French. Most of the forms cited are not precisely *modern* French, but from Cotgrave's Dictionary, ed. 1660. This accounts for citation of forms, such as F. *recreation*, without accents; the F. accents being purely modern. See also the dictionaries by Brachet and Littré.

O. F.—Old French; as in the dictionaries by Burguy, Roquefort, or (in some cases) Cotgrave.

Fries.—Friesic; as in Richthofen, 1840.

Gael. — Gaelic; as in Macleod and Dewar, 1839.

G.- German; as in Flügel, ed. 1861.

M. H. G.—Middle High German; as in Wackernagel's Wörterbuch, 1861.

O. H. G.—Old High German; as in the same volume.

Gk.—Greek; as in Liddell and Scott's Lexicon, 1849.

Goth. — Mœso-Gothic; as in Skeat's Glossary, 1868.

Heb. — Hebrew; as in Leopold's Dict., 1872.

Hind.—Hindustani; as in Forbes, Bate, or Wilson's Glossary of Indian Terms.

Icel.—Icelandic; as in Cleasby and Vigfusson, 1874.

Irish.— Irish; as in O'Reilly, 1864.

Ital.— Italian; as in Meadows, 1857.

L.—Latin; as in White and Riddle, 1876.

Low G.—Low German; as in the Bremen Wörterbuch, 1767.

Lith. — Lithuanian; as in Nesselmann's Dict., 1851.

Low L.—Low Latin; as in the Lexicon Manuale (abridged from Ducange) by Maigne d'Arnis, 1866.

M. E.—Middle English; see under E. above.

M. H. G.—Middle High German; see under G. above.

Norw.—Norwegian; as in Aasen's Norsk Ordbog, 1873.

O. F.—Old French; see under F. above.

O. H. G.—Old High German; see under G. above.

O. Sax.—Old Saxon; as in the Heliand, ed. Heyne.

Pers.—Persian; as in Richardson's Arab. and Pers. Dict.; or in Palmer's Pers. Dict., 1876.

Port.—Portuguese; as in Vieyra, 1857.

Prov. — Provençal; as in Raynouard's Lexique Roman, and Bartsch's Chrestomathie Provençale.

Russ.—Russian; as in Reiff's Dict., 1876.

Scand.—Scandinavian; used as a general term for Icelandic, Swedish, Danish, and Norwegian.

Skt.—Sanskrit; as in Benfey's Dict., 1866.

Span. Spanish; as in Meadows, 1856.

Swed.—Swedish; as in the Tauchnitz Dict., or in Widegren.

Swed. dial. — Swedish dialects; as in Rietz (1867).

Teut. — Teutonic; a general term for Dutch, German, and Scandinavian.

Turk. — Turkish; as in Zenker's Dict., 1866-1876.

W.—Welsh; as in Spurrell, 1861.

OTHER ABBREVIATIONS.

acc.—accusative case.
adj.—adjective.
adv.—adverb.
A. V.—Authorised Version of the Bible, 1611.
cf.—confer, i.e. compare.
Ch.—Chaucer.
comp.—comparative.
conj.—conjunction.
dat.—dative case.
Der.—Derivative.
dimin.—diminutive.
f. or fem.—feminine.
frequent.—frequentative.
gen.—genitive case.
i.e.—id est, that is.
inf.—infinitive mood.
interj.—interjection.
lit.—literally.
masc.—masculine.
neut.—neuter.

nom.—nominative case.
obs.—obsolete.
orig.—original, or originally.
pl.—plural.
prep.—preposition.
pres. part.—present participle.
pres. t.—present tense.
pp.—past participle.
prob.—probably.
pron.—pronoun.
prov.—provincial.
q. v.—quod vide = which see.
s. v.—sub verbo = under the word.
pt. t.—past tense.
sb.—substantive.
Shak.—Shakespeare.
sing.—singular.
superl.—superlative.
tr.—translated, or translation.
trans.—transitive.
v. or vb.—verb.

Some of the longer articles are marked off into sections by the use of the Greek letters β, γ. This is merely intended to make matters clearer, by separating the various statements from each other.

Notes at the end of an article are marked off by beginning with the symbol ¶. XIV, XV, XVI, mean that the word was introduced in the 14th, 15th, or 16th century, respectively. Hyphens are freely introduced to shew the *etymological* division of a word. Thus, under *Cede*, the word *concede* is derived from Lat. *con-cedere*; meaning that *concedere* can be resolved into *con-* and *cedere*. This etymological division is often very different from that usually adopted in printed books when words have to be divided; thus, *capacious* can only be divided, etymologically, as *cap-ac-i-ous*, because *cap-* is the root-syllable.

Theoretical forms are marked by italics. Thus, under *other*, the Icel. *antharr** is given as having probably preceded the known form *annarr*; and *anter** as possibly the original form of Lat. *alter*.

The symbols ð and þ are both written for *th*. In Icelandic, þ has the sound of *th* in *thin*, and ð that of *th* in *that*; but the M.E. and A.S. symbols are confused. The M.E. symbol ȝ commonly represents *y* at the beginning of a word, and *gh* in the middle. A.S. short and long vowels, such as *a* and *á*, are as distinct from each other as *ε* and *η*, or *o* and *ω* in Greek.

A CONCISE ETYMOLOGICAL DICTIONARY
OF THE ENGLISH LANGUAGE.

A, indef. art. (E.) See **An.**

A- (1), as in *a-down* = A.S. *ofdúne.* (E.) Here *a-* = A.S. *of*; see **Of, Off.**

A- (2), as in *a-foot.* (E.) Put for *on foot*; see **On.** ¶ This is the commonest value of the prefix *a-*.

A- (3), as in *a-long.* (E.) Here *a-* = A.S. *and-*; see **Along.**

A- (4), as in *a-rise.* (E.) Here *a-* = A.S. *á-*; see **Arise.**

A- (5), as in *a-chieve, a-stringent.* (F.- L.; *or* L.) Here *a* = F. *à* = L. *ad*, to; see **Ad-.**

A- (6), as in *a-vert.* (L.) Here *a-*=L. *a*; see **Ab-** (1).

A- (7), as in *a-mend.* (L.) Here *a-mend* is for *e-mend*; and *e-*=L. *e* or *ex*; see **Ex-.**

A- (8), as in *a-las.* (F.) For *hélas*; see **Alas.**

A- (9), as in *a-byss.* (Gk.) Here *a-* = Gk. *á-* or *áv-*; see **Un-, Abyss.**

A- (10), as in *a-do.* (E.) For *at do*; see **At, Ado.**

A- (11), as in *a-ware.* (E.) Here *a-* = M. E. *y-, i-*, A.S. *ge-*; see **Aware.**

A- (12), as in *a-pace.* (E.) Here *a* is the indef. art.; see **An, Apace.**

A- (13), as in *a-vast.* (Du.) For Du. *houd vast*; see **Avast.**

Ab- (1), *prefix.* (L.) L. *ab*, from; short form *a*; extended form *abs*. Cognate with E. *of*; see **Of.** In F., it becomes *a-* or *av-*; see **Advantage.**

Ab- (2), *prefix.* (L.) Put for L. *ad*, to, when *b* follows; see **Abbreviate.**

Aback. (E.) For *on back.* A.S. *onbæc*; see **A-** (2) and **Back.**

Abaft. (E.) From the prefix *a-* (2), and *b-aft*, short for *bi-aft*, by aft. Thus *a-b-aft* = on by aft, i. e. at the part which lies to the aft. Cf. M. E. *biaften*, Gen. and Exod. 3377; A.S. *beæften.* See **A-** (2), **By,** and **Aft.**

Abandon; see **A-** (5) and **Ban.**

Abase; see **A-** (5) and **Base.** ¶ Sometimes confused with *abash* in M. E.

Abash. (F.) M. E. *abaschen, abaischen, abasen.* = O. F. *esbahiss-*, stem of pres. part. of *esbahir* (F. *ébahir*), to astonish. = O. F. *es-* (=L. *ex*, out, very much); and *bahir*, to express astonishment, a word of imitative origin from the interj. *bah !* of astonishment. ¶ Sometimes confused with *abase* in M. E. See **Bashful.**

Abate; see **Batter** (1). **Doublet,** *bate.*

Abbot. (L.-Syriac.) M.E. *abbot, abbod*, A.S. *abbod.* = L. *abbat-* (nom. *abbas*), an abbot, lit. a father.=Syriac *abba*, a father; see Rom. viii. 15.

abbess. (F. = L. = Syriac.) M. E. *abbesse.* = O. F. *abesse, abaesse.* = L. *abbat-issa.* = L. *abbat-* (as above), and *-issa* = Gk. *-ισσα*, fem. suffix.

abbey. (F.=L.=Syriac.) M.E. *abbeye.* = O. F. *abeie.* = Low L. *abbat-ia.*

Abbreviate; see **Brief.**

Abdicate; see **Diction.**

Abdomen. (L.) L. *abdomen* (stem *abdomin-*), lower part of the belly.

Abduce, Abduction; see **Duke.**

Abed. (E.) For *on bed*; see **A-** (2) and **Bed.**

Aberration; see **Err.**

Abet, to incite; see **Bite.** Der. *bet*, short for *abet*, sb.

Abeyance, expectation, suspension. (F. = L.) F. *abéiance*, suspension, waiting (Roq.) = F. *a*; and *béant*, pres. pt. of O. F. *béer* (F. *bayer*), to gape, expect anxiously. = L. *ad*, at; and *badare*, to gape.

Abhor; see **Horrid.**

Abide (1), to wait for. (E.); see **Bide.**

Abide (2), to suffer for, pay for. (E.) In Sh.; corrupted from M. E. *abyen*, to pay for, lit. to buy up, redeem. = A.S. *ábycgan, ábicgan*, to pay for. See **A-** (4) and **Buy.**

Abject, mean; see **Jet** (1).

Abjure; see **Jury.**

Ablative. (L.) L. *ablatiuus*, lit. taking

away. — L. *ab*, from ; and *latum* (= *tlatum*),
to bear, take, allied to *tollere*, to take. See
Tolerate.

Ablaze. (E.) For *on blaze* ; see **A-** (2)
and **Blaze.**

Able ; see **Habit.** Der. *ability* = L. acc.
habilitatem.

Ablution ; see **Lave.**

Abnegate ; see **Negation.**

Aboard. (E.) For *on board* ; see **A-** (2)
and **Board.**

Abode, sb. ; see **Bide.**

Abolish. (F. — L.) F. *aboliss-*, stem of
pres. pt. of *abolir.* — L. *abolere*, to abolish.

Abominate ; see **Omen.**

Abortion ; see **Orient.**

Abound ; see **Undulate.**

About. (E.)   M. E. *abuten, abouten* ;
A.S. *ábútan, onbútan* ; short for *on-be-útan*,
lit. on-by-outward ; where *útan*, outward, is
from *út*, out. See **A-** (2), **By,** and **Out.**

Above. (E.)   M. E. *aboven, abufen*; A.S.
ábufan, short for *an-be-ufan*, lit. on-by-
upward ; where *ufan*, upward, is extended
from Goth. *uf*, up.   See **A-** (2), **By, Up.**
(A. S. *ufan* = G. *oben.*   A.S. *be-ufan* = Du.
boven.)

Abrade, to scrape off ; see **Rase.** Der.
abrasion.

Abreast. (E.)   Put for *on breast* ; see
A- (2), and **Breast.**

Abridge ; see **Brief.**

Abroach, to set. (E. *and* F.)   Put for
to set on broach ; see **A-** (2) and **Broach.**

Abroad. (E.)   M. E. *abrood*; put for *on
brood* ; lit. on broad ; see **A-** (2) and **Broad.**

Abrogate ; see **Rogation.**

Abrupt ; see **Rupture.**

Abscess ; see **Cede.**

Abscind, Abscissa ; see **Rescind.**

Abscond, to go into hiding. (L.)   L.
abscondere, to hide. — L. *abs*, away ; *condere*,
to hide.   *Condere* is from *con-* (*cum*), together, and *-dere*, to put, allied to L. *dare*,
to give ; see **Date.**

sconce (1), a small fort, bulwark. (Du.
— F. — L.)   Also applied to a helmet, and
even to the head. — O. Du. *schantse* (Du.
schans), a fortress, sconce. — O. F. *esconser*,
to hide, cover ; pp. *escons.* — L. *absconsus*,
used (as well as *absconditus*) as pp. of *abscondere*, to hide (above).

sconce (2), a candle-stick.   (F. — L.)
M. E. *sconce, scons*, a covered light, lantern.
— O. F. *esconse*, a dark lantern (Roquefort).
— L. *absconsa*, a dark lantern (in late L.) ;
from L. *absconsus*, hidden.

Absent. (L.)   XIV cent. — L. *absent* ,
stem of *ab-sens*, being away. — L. *ab-*, away ;
-sens, being, occurring also in *præ-sens.*
Here *-sens* is an older form of *ens*, being,
from √ AS, to be.   See **Present, Sooth.**
Der. *absence*, F. *absence*, L. *absentia.*

Absolute, Absolve ; see **Solve.**

Absorb. (L.)   L. *absorbere*, to suck up.
— L. *ab*, away ; *sorbere*, to sup up. + Gk.
ῥοφέειν, to sup up.   Der. *absorpt-ion*, from
pp. *absorptus.*

Abstain ; see **Tenable.**

Abstemious. (L.)   L.*abstemius*, refrain-
ing from strong drink. — L. *abs*, from ; *te-
mum*, strong drink, whence *temu-lentus*,
drunken.   (√ TAM.)

Abstract ; see **Trace** (1).

Abstruse ; see **Intrude.**

Absurd ; see **Surd.**

Abundance. (F. — L.)   F. *abondance.* —
L. *abundantia.*   See **Undulate.**

Abuse ; see **Use.**

Abut, to project towards.   (F. — L. *and*
G.)   O. F. *abouter*, to thrust towards. — L.
ad, to ; O. F. *boter*, to thrust.   See **A-** (5)
and **butt** (1), s.v. **Beat.**

Abyss, a bottomless gulf. (L. — Gk.)
Milton.   L. *abyssus.* — Gk. ἄβυσσος, bottomless. — Gk. ἀ-, short for ἀν-, neg. prefix ; and
βυσσός, depth, akin to **Bathos.**   See **A-**
(9), **Un-** (1).

Acacia, a tree. (L. — Gk.)   L. *acacia.* —
Gk. ἀκακία, the thorny Egyptian acacia. —
Gk. ἀκίς, a point, thorn.   (√ AK.)

Academy. (F. — L. — Gk.)   F. *académie.*
— L. *academia.* — Gk. ἀκαδήμεια, a grove
where Plato taught, named from the hero
Akademus.

Accede ; see **Cede.**   Der. *access*, *access-ion.*

Accelerate ; see **Celerity.**

Accent ; see **Cant** (1).

Accept ; see **Capacious.**

Access ; see **Cede.**

Accident ; see **Cadence.**

Acclaim ; see **Claim.**

Acclivity. (L.)   XVII cent.   As if from
F. *acclivité*. — L. *accliuitatem*, acc. of *ac-
cliuitas.* — L. *ac-*, for *ad* ; and *cliu-us*, sloping, a slope ; see **Lean** (1).   (√ KLI.)

declivity. (F. — L.)   F. *déclivité*. — L.
decliuitatem, acc. of *de-cliuitas*, a downward slope.

proclivity. (L.)   From L. *procliuitas*,
a downward slope, tendency. — L. *pro-cliuus*,
sloping forward.

Accommodate ; see **Mode.**

Accompany; see Company.

Accomplice; see Ply.

Accomplish; see Plenary.

Accord; see Cordial.

Accost; see Coast.

Account; see Putative.

Accoutre. (F. – L. ?) F. *accoutrer*, formerly also *accoustrer*, to dress, array. Etym. quite uncertain; perhaps (1) connected with F. *couture*, a sewing, *coudre*, to sew, and L. *consuere*, to sew together (Diez); or (2) with L. *cultura*, tillage, culture (Scheler); or (3) with O. F. *coustre*, *coutre*, a sacristan who had charge of sacred vestments, from Low L. *custor** = L. *custos*, a custodian, keeper. (The last is best.)

Accretion; see Crescent.

Accrue; see Crescent.

Accumulate; see Cumulate.

Accurate; see Cure.

Accursed, cursed. (E.) M. E. *acorsien*. A.S. *á-*, prefix; and *cursian*, to curse; see **A-** (4), and Curse.

Accuse; see Cause.

Accustom; see Custom.

Ace, the 'one' on dice. (F. – L. – Gk.) M. E. *as.* – O. F. *as.* – L. *as.* – Gk. *ás*; said to be the Tarentine pronunciation of *eîs*, one. ¶ *Not* cognate with One.

Acephalous, headless. (Gk.) Gk. *ἀκέφαλος*, headless. – Gk. *ά-*, un-; and *κεφαλή*, head, cognate with E. Head.

Acerbity; see Acid.

Ache, a pain. (E.) M. E. *ake*, a better spelling. A.S. *æce, ece*, A.S. Leechdoms, iii. 6. Also M. E. *aken*, vb. pt. t. *ook*; A.S. *acan.* – √AG, to drive, agitate; as in L. *agere*, Icel. *aka* (pt. t. *ók*, pp. *ekit*), to drive. See Agent. ¶ Spelt *ache* by confusion with Gk. *ἄχος*, which is cognate with E. Awe.

Achieve; see Capital (1).

Achromatic, colourless. (Gk.) See **A-** (9) and Chromatic.

Acid, sour, sharp. (F. – L.; or L.) F. *acide.* – L. *ac-idus*, lit. piercing. (√AK, to pierce.) Der. *acid-i-ty*; *acid-ul-at-ed* (L. *acid-ul-us*, dimin. of *acid-us*).

acerbity. (F. – L.) XVI cent. F. *acerbité.* – L. acc. *acerbitatem* (nom. *acerbitas*), bitterness. – L. *acer-b-us*, bitter. – L. *ac-er*, sharp, lit. piercing.

acme, top. (Gk.) Gk. *ἀκμή*, top, sharp edge.

aconite, monk's-hood. (F. – L. – Gk.) F. *aconit.* – L. *aconitum.* – Gk. *ἀκόνιτον*, a plant; so called from growing *ἐν ἀκόναις*,

on steep sharp rocks. – Gk. *ἀκ-ονή*, a whetstone, sharp stone.

acrid, tart. (L.) Coined by adding *-id* to L. *acr-*, stem of *acer*, O. L. *ac-rus*, sharp.

acrimony. (F. – L.) F. *acrimoine.* – L. *acri-mon-ia.* – L. *acri-*, for *acer* (above).

acrobat, a tumbler. (Gk.; or F. – Gk.) F. *acrobate.* – Gk. *ἀκροβάτης*, lit. one who walks on tiptoe. – Gk. *ἄκρο-ν*, a point, neut. of *ἄκ-ρος*, pointed; and *βατός*, verbal adj. of *βαίνειν*, to walk; see Come.

acropolis, a citadel. (Gk.) Lit. 'upper city;' Gk. *ἄκρο-s*, pointed, upper; and *πόλις*, a city; see Police.

acrostic, a short poem in which the initial letters spell a word. (Gk.) Gk. *ἀκροστίχιον.* – Gk. *ἄκρο-s*, pointed, also first; and *στίχ-*, base of *στίχος*, a row, order, line, from √STIGH; see Stirrup.

acumen (L.) L. *ac-u-men*, sharpness, acuteness.

acute. (L.) L. *acutus*, sharp; pp. of *ac-u-ere*, to sharpen.

aglet, a tag of a lace. (F. – L.) Also *ayglet*, Spenser, F. Q. ii. 3. 26. – F. *aiguillette*, dimin. of *aiguille*, a needle. – Low L. *acucula*, dimin. of *ac-us*, a needle, pointed thing.

ague, a fever-fit. (F. – L.) Lit. 'acute' attack. – O. F. *ague*, fem. of *agu* (F. *aigu*), acute. – L. *acuta* (*febris*), acute (fever); fem. of *acutus*; see acute (above).

eager. (F. – L.) M. E. *egre.* – O. F. *egre* (F. *aigre*). – L. *acrem*, acc. of *ac-er*, sharp. Der. *vin-egar*.

exacerbate, to embitter. (L.) From pp. of *ex-acerbare*, to irritate. – L. *ex*, very; *acerbus*, bitter; see acerbity, above. See also Awn, Edge, Egg (2), Eglantine.

Acknowledge. (E.; *with* Scand. *suffix*.) XVI cent. M. E. *knowlechen*; the prefix is due to M. E. *uknowen* (– A.S. *oncnáwan*), with the same sense; hence the prefix is **A-** (2). The verb *knowlechen* is from the sb. *knowleche*, mod. E. *knowledge*; see Knowledge.

Acme; see Acid.

Acolyte, a servitor. (F. – Low L. – Gk.) F. *acolyte*, Cot. – Low L. *acolythus.* – Gk. *ἀκόλουθος*, a follower. – Gk. *ά-*, with (akin to Skt. *sa-*, with); *κέλευθος*, a path; so that *ἀκόλουθος* = a travelling companion.

Aconite; see Acid.

Acorn. (E.) M. E. *acorn.* A.S. *æcern*, fruit; properly 'fruit of the field,' from A.S. *æcer*, a field; see Acre. + Icel. *akarn*, Dan. *agern*, Goth. *akran*, fruit; from Icel.

akr, Dan. *ager*, Goth. *akrs*, a field. ¶ Not from *oak*.

Acoustic. (Gk.) Gk. ἀκουστικός, relating to hearing (or sound). − Gk. ἀκούειν, to hear.

Acquaint. (F.−L.) M. E. *acqueynten*, earlier *acointen*.−O. F. *acointer, acointier*, to acquaint with.−Low L. *adcognitare*, to make known (Brachet). − L. *ad*, to; and *cognitare**, formed from *cognitus*, pp. of *cognoscere*, to know. See **cognisance**, quaint, s.v. **Noble**.

Acquiesce; see **Quiet**.

Acquire; see **Query**.

Acquit; see **Quiet**.

Acre. (E.) M. E. *aker*. A. S. *æcer*.+ Du. *akker*, Icel. *akr*, Swed. *åker*, Dan. *ager*, Goth. *akrs*, G. *acker*, L. *ager*, Gk. ἀγρός, Skt. *ajra*. The orig. sense was either 'pasture,' or 'hunting-ground.' (✓AG.) Der. *acor-n*, q.v.

Acrid, Acrimony; see **Acid**.

Acrobat, Acropolis; see **Acid**.

Across. (E. *and* Scand.) For *on cross*; see **A-** (2) and **Cross**.

Acrostic; see **Acid**.

Act; see **Agent**.

Acumen, Acute; see **Acid**.

Ad-, *prefix*. (L.) L. *ad*, to, cognate with E. **At**. ¶ L. *ad* becomes *ac-* before *c*; *af-* bef. *f*; *ag-* bef. *g*; *al-* bef. *l*; *an-* bef. *n*; *ap-* bef. *p*; *ar-* bef. *r*; *as-* bef. *s*; *at-* bef. *t*.

Adage, a saying. (F.−L.) F. *adage*. −L. *adagium*.−L. *ad*; and *agium*, a saying; cf. *aio*, I say. (✓AGH.)

Adamant. (F. − L. − Gk.) M. E. *adamaunt*, a diamond, a magnet. − O. F. *adamant*.−L. *adamanta*, acc. of *adamas*.− Gk. ἀδάμας, a very hard metal or stone; lit. 'unconquerable.' − Gk. ἀ- (=E. *un-*); and δαμάειν, to conquer, tame; see **Tame**.

diamond. (F.−L.−Gk.) M. E. *diamant*.−O. F. *diamant*, corruption of *adamant*; so also Ital. Span. *diamante*, G. *diamant*.

Adapt; see **Apt**.

Add. (L.) M. E. *adden*.−L. *addere*, lit. to put to.−L. *ad*; and *·dere*, to put = *dare*, to give. (✓DA.) See **Date** (1).

Adder, a viper. (E.) M. E. *addere*; also *naddere, neddere*. [*An adder* resulted from *a nadder*, by mistake.] A.S. *nædre*, a snake.+ Icel. *naðr*, Goth. *nadrs*, G. *natter*, a snake.

Addict; see **Diction**.

Addled, corrupt, unproductive. (E.)

M. E. *adel*, foul, applied to an egg (Stratmann). Orig. 'muddy,' from A. S. *adela*, mud (Grein). Cf. Low G. *adele*, mud.

Address; see **Regent**.

Adduce; see **Duke**.

Adept; see **Apt**.

Adequate; see **Equal**.

Adhere; see **Hesitate**.

Adieu, farewell. (F.) M. E. *a dieu*.− F. *à dieu*, (I commit you) to God.−L. *ad Deum*, to God. See **Deity**.

Adjacent, Adjective; see **Jet** (1).

Adjoin, Adjunct; see **Join**.

Adjourn; see **Diary**.

Adjudge, Adjudicate; see **Judge**.

Adjure; see **Jury**.

Adjust; see **Just**. ¶ Not from O. F. *ajoster*, mod. F. *ajouter*.

Adjutant; see **Aid**.

Administer; see **Minor**.

Admiral. (F.−Arab.) M. E. *admiral*, more often *amiral*.−O. F. *amiral, amirail*, also *amire*; cf. Low L. *admiraldus*, a prince, chief.−Arab. *amīr*, a prince; see **Emir**. The suffix is due to Arab. *al* in *amir-al-bahr*, prince of the sea.

Admire; see **Miracle**.

Admit; see **Missile**.

Admonish; see **Monition**.

A-do, to-do, trouble. (E.) M. E. *at do*, to do; a Northern idiom, whereby *at* was used as the sign of the infin. mood, as in Icel., Swedish, &c. See **Do** (1).

Adolescent; see **Aliment**.

Adopt; see **Optative**.

Adore; see **Oral**.

Adorn; see **Ornament**.

Adown, downwards. (E.) M. E. *adune*. A. S. *of-dúne*, lit. off a down or hill.−A. S. *of*, off; and *dún*; see **A-** (1) and **Down** (2).

Adrift. (E.) For *on drift*; see **A-** (2) and **Drive**.

Adroit; see **Regent**.

Adulation, flattery. (F.−L.) F. *adulation*.−L. acc. *adulationem*, from *adulatio*, flattery.−L. *adulatus*, pp. of *adulari*, to flatter.

Adult; see **Aliment**.

Adulterate, to corrupt. (L.) XVI cent. −L. *adulteratus*, pp. of *adulterare*, to corrupt.−L. *adulter*, an adulterer, a debaser of money.

Adumbrate; see **Umbrage**.

Advance, to go forward. (F.−L.) A mistaken form, in the XVI cent., for M. E. *auancen, avancen*.−F. *avancer*, to go forward or before.−F. *avant*, before.−L. *ab*, from; *ante*, before. See **Ante-, Van, Vamp.**

advantage, profit. (F. – L.) A mistaken form for M. E. *avantage*. – F. *avantage*; formed by suffix *-age* from *avant*, before; see above.

Advent, Adventure; see **Venture.**

Adverb; see **Verb.**

Adverse, Advert, Advertise; see **Verse.**

Advice, Advise; see **Vision.**

Advocate, Advowson; see **Vocal.**

Adze, a cooper's axe. (E.) M. E. *adse*, *adese*. A. S. *adesa*, *adese*, an adze.

Aerial; see **Air.**

Aery, an eagle's nest, brood of eagles or hawks. (F. – Low L.) – F. *aire*, 'an airie or nest of hawkes;' Cot. – Low L. *area*, a nest of a bird of prey; of uncertain origin. ¶ Sometimes misspelt *eyry*, by confusion with M. E. *ey*, an egg.

Æsthetic, tasteful. (Gk.) Gk. αἰσθητικός, perceptive. – Gk. αἰσθομαι, I perceive. (√AW.)

anæsthetic, relieving pain, dulling sensation. – Gk. ἀν-, not; and αἰσθητικός.

Afar. (E.) For *on far*.

Affable; see **Fate.**

Affair, Affect; see **Fact.**

Affeer, to confirm. (F. – L.) O. F. *afeurer*, to fix the price of a thing (officially). – Low L. *afforare*, to fix a price. – L. *af-* (for *ad*); and *forum*, a market.

Affiance, Affidavit; see **Faith.**

Affiliation; see **Filial.**

Affinity; see **Final.**

Affirm; see **Firm.**

Affix; see **Fix.**

Afflict, to harass. (L.) XVI cent. – L. *afflictus*, pp. of *affligere*, to strike to the ground. – L. *af-* (*ad*); and *fligere*, to dash. (√BHLIGH, BHLAGH.) So also *conflict*, from pp. *con-flictus*; *in-flict*; *pro-flig-ate.*

Affluence; see **Fluent.**

Afford. (E.) Corrupted from *aforth*, M. E. *aforthen*, to provide, P. Pl. B. vi. 201. – A. S. *geforðian*, *forðian*, to further, promote, provide. – A. S. *ge-*, prefix; and *forð*, forth, forward; see **Forth.**

Affray, to frighten. (F. – L. and Teut.) XIV cent. M. E. *affrayen*. – O. F. *effraier*, *esfreër*, to frighten. – Low L. *exfrediare*, to break the king's peace, cause an affray or fray; hence, to disturb, frighten. – L. *ex*; and O. H. G. *fridu* (G. *friede*), peace. (See Romania, 1878, vii. 121.) **Der.** *affray*, sb.

afraid, frightened; pp. of **affray.**

Affright; see **Fright.**

Affront; see **Front.**

Afloat. (E.) For *on float.*

Afoot. (E.) For *on foot.*

Afore. (E.) For *on fore*; A. S. *onforan*, afore.

Afraid. (F. – L. *and* Teut.) Pp. of **Affray**, q. v.

Afresh. (E.) For *on fresh* or *of fresh*; see **Anew.**

Aft, After. (E.) A. S. *æft*, *eft*, again, behind; *after*, after, both prep. and adv. + Icel. *aptan*, behind, *aptr*, *aftr*, backwards; Dan. and Swed. *efter*, Du. *achter*, O. H. G. *aftar*, prep. and adv., behind. β. *Af-t* is an extension from Goth. *af*, off; see **Of.** *Af-ter* is a comp. form, like Gk. ἀπω-τέρ-ω, further off; it means more off, further off, hence behind. **Der.** *ab-aft*, q. v.; *after-ward* (see **Toward**).

aftermost, hindmost; a corrupt form, for *aftemost*. (E.) A. S. *æftemest*, Goth. *aftumists*. The Goth. *aft-um-ists* is a double superl. form.

Again. (E.) M. E. *ayein*, A. S. *ongegn*, *ongeán*. – A. S. *on*; and *geán*, again, in return, perhaps connected with *gán*, to go. +Dan. *igien*, Swed, *igen*, again.

against. (E.) Formed with added *t* from M. E. *ayeines*, against; extended from M. E. *ayein*, against, with adv. suffix *-es*. – A. S. *ongedn*, against; the same as A. S. *ongeán*, again; see above. + Icel. *í gegn*, G. *entgegen*, against.

Agate. (F. – L. – Gk.) O. F. *agate*, *agathe*. – L. *achatem*, acc. of *achates*. – Gk. ἀχάτης, an agate; so named from being found near the river *Achates* (Sicily).

Age. (F. – L.) O. F. *aage*, *edage*. – Low L. *ætaticum*. – L. *ætati-*, crude form of *ætas* (short for *æui-tas*), age. – L. *æuum*, life, period. + Gk. αἰών; Goth. *aiws*; Skt. *eva*, course. (√I.)

Agent. (L.) XVI cent. L. *agent-*, stem of pres. pt. of *agere* (pp. *actus*), to do, drive, conduct. +Gk. ἄγειν; Icel. *aka*; Skt. *aj*, to drive. (√AG.) See **Ache.**

act. (L.) M. E. *act*. – L. *actum*, neut. of pp. *actus*, done. **Der.** *act-ion*, *act-ive*, *act-or*; *act-u-al* (L. *actualis*); *act-u-ary* (L. *actuarius*); *act-u-ate* (Low L. *actuare*, to perform, put in action).

agile. (F. – L.) XVI cent. F. *agile*. – L. *agilis*, nimble, lit. easily driven about. – L. *agere*, to drive.

agitate. (L.) L. *agitatus*, pp. of *agitare*, to keep driving about, frequent. of *agere*.

ambiguous, doubtful. (L.) L. *ambiguus*, doubtful, lit. driving about. — L. *amb-*, about; and *agere*, to drive.

co-agulate, to curdle. (L.) L. *coagulatus*, pp. of *coagulare*, to curdle. — L. *coagulum*, rennet, which causes milk to run together. — L. *co-* (*cum*), together; *ag-ere*, to drive.

cogent. (L.) L. *cogent-*, stem of pres. part. of *cogere*, to compel; put for *co-igere* (= *con-agere**), lit. to drive together.

cogitate. (L.) L. *cogitatus*, pp. of *cogitare*, to think; put for *co-agitare**.

counteract. (Hybrid; F. *and* L.) See Counter, and act above.

enact (F. — L.) Sh. — F. *en*, in = L. *in*; and act. Lit. ' to put in act.'

exact (1), precise. (L.) Sh. L. *exactus*, pp. of *exigere*, to drive out, weigh out. — L. *ex*; and *agere*.

exact (2), to demand. (F. — L.) Sh. O. F. *exacter*. — Low L. *exactare*. — L. *ex*, out; and *actum*, supine of *agere*.

examine, to test. (F. — L.) F. *examiner*. — L *examinare*, to weigh carefully. — L. *examin-*, stem of *examen*, the tongue of a balance, put for *exagmen**; cf. *exigere*, to weigh out. — L. *ex*, out; *agere*, to drive.

exigent, exacting. (L.) Stem of pres. pt. of *exigere*. — L. *ex*; and *agere*.

prodigal. (F. — L.) O. F. *prodigal*. — Low Lat. *prodigalis*; due to L. *prodigus*, lavish; put for *prod-agus**. — L. *prod-*, forth; and *agere*.

transact, to perform. (L.) L. *transactus*, pp. of *transigere*. — L. *trans*, beyond; and *agere*.

Agglomerate, to mass together. (L.) Pp. of L. *agglomerare*, to form into a mass. — L. *ag-* = *ad*; and *glomer-*, stem of *glomus*, a mass, ball, clue of thread, allied to *globus*, a globe; see Globe.

Agglutinate; see Glue.

Aggrandise; see Grand.

Aggravate; see Grave (2).

Aggregate; see Gregarious.

Aggress; see Grade.

Aggrieve; see Grave (2).

Aghast, horror-struck. (E.) Misspelt for *agast*, which is short for *agasted*, pp. of M. E. *agasten*, to terrify; Ch. C. T. 2343; Leg. of Good Women, Dido, 245. — A. S. *á-*, prefix; and *gǽstan*, to terrify, torment. β. A. S. *gǽsten*, is from the base *gǽs-* = Goth. *gais-* in *us-gais-jan*, to terrify. (√GHAIS.)

Agile, Agitate; see Agent.

Aglet. (F. — L.) See Acid.

Agnail, (1) a sore beside the nail, (2) a corn on the foot. (E. *or* F. — L.) Two words appear to be confused here; (1) A. S. *angnægl*, a sore by the nail (see A. S. Leechdoms, ii. 81, § 34), with which cf. O. Friesic *ogneil*, *ongneil*, apparently used in a similar sense: this is from a prefix *ang-*, signifying afflicting, paining, and *nail*; see Anger and Nail. (2) O. F. *angonaille*, a botch, sore (Cotgrave); allied to Low L. *anguen*, *anguinalia*, a carbuncle, allied to L. *angina*, quinsy, and *angere*, to choke. (√AGH.)

Ago, Agone, gone away, past. (E.) M. E. *ago*, *agon*, *agoon*, pp. of the verb *agon*, to pass by, pass away. A. S. *ágán*, pp. of *ágán*, to pass away. See A- (4) and Go.

Agog, in eage.ness. (C. ?) Put for *on gog*, in activity, in eagerness? — W. *gog*, activity; *gogi*, to agitate. See A- (2).

Agony. (F. — L. — Gk.) M. E. *agonie*. — F. *agonie*. — L. *agonia*. — Gk. ἀγωνία, orig. a contest. — Gk. ἀγών, contest. — Gk. ἄγειν, to drive. (√AG.)

antagonist, an opponent. (Gk.) Gk. ἀνταγωνιστής, an opponent. — Gk. ἀντ-, for ἀντί, against; and ἀγωνίζομαι, I struggle, from ἀγών, a contest.

Agree; see Grace.

Agriculture. (L.) L. *agricultura*, culture of a field. — L. *agri*, gen. of *ager*, a field; and *cultura*. See Acre and Colony.

peregrination. (F. — L.) F. *peregrination*. — L. *peregrinationem*, acc. of *peregrinatio*, a wandering. — L. *peregrinatus*, pp. of *peregrinari*, to travel. — L. *peregrinus*, foreign, adj. from *pereger*, a traveller, one who passes through a land. — L. *per*, through; *ager*, land, field.

pilgrim. (F. — L.) O. F. *pelegrin**, only found as *pelerin*, a pilgrim; but cf. Ital. *pellegrino*, *peregrino*, a pilgrim. — L. *peregrinus*, a foreigner, stranger; as adj. foreign; see above.

Agrimony, a plant. (F. — L. — Gk.) M. E. *agremoine*, *egremoine*. — O. F. *agrimoine*. — L. *argemonia*, *argemone*. — Gk. ἀργεμώνη. (White, L. Dict.) — Gk. ἀργός, shining.

Aground. (E.) For *on ground*.

Ague. (F. — L.) See Acid.

Ah ! (F. — L.) M. E. *a* ! — O. F. *a* ! — L. *ah* !

Ahead. (E.) For *on head* = *in head*, in a forward direction. See A- (2).

Aid. (F. — L.) M. E. *aiden*. — O. F. *aider*. — Low L. *aitare*, *aiutare*, shortened form of L. *adiutare*, frequent of *adiuuare*, to

assist. – L. *ad*; and *iuuare*, to help, pp. *iutus.* (√YU.)

adjutant, lit. assistant. – L. *adiutant-*, stem of pres. pt. of *adiutare*, to assist.

coadjutor. (L.) XVI cent. – L. *co-*, for *con* = *cum*, together; and *adiutor*, an assistant, from vb. *adiutare*.

Ail. (E.) See **Awe.**

Aim; see **Esteem.**

Air. (F. – L. – Gk.) M. E. *air*, *eir*. – F. *air.* – L. *aër.* – Gk. ἀήρ, air. (√AW, WA).

aerial. (L. – Gk.) Formed with suffix *-al* from L. *aëri-us*, dwelling in the air. – L. *aër*, air. – Gk. ἀήρ (above).

Aisle, the wing of a church. (F. – L.) Better spelt *aile*. – F. *aile*. – L. *ala*, a wing. Prob. for *axla**, dimin. of **Axis.**

Ait. (E.) See **Eyot.**

Ajar. (E.) Put for *a char*, *on char*, on the turn (G. Douglas, tr. of Virgil, b. vii, prol.) – A. S. *on cerre*, on the turn. – A.S. *cyrran*, *cerran*, to turn. See **Char** (2).

Akimbo, in a bent position. (Scand.) M. E. *on*, see **A-** (2); and Icel. *kengboginn*, bent into a crook, from *kengr*, a crook, twist, kink, and *boginn*, bowed, pp. of lost verb *bjúga*, to bow. See **Kink** and **Bow** (1). (Very doubtful.)

Akin, of kin. (E.) For *of kin*.

Alabaster. (F. – L. – Gk.) M. E. *alabastre.* – O. F. *alabastre* (F. *albâtre*). – L. *alabaster*, *alabastrum.* – Gk. ἀλάβαστρον, ἀλάβαστρος. Said to be derived from *Alabastron*, a town in Egypt. (Pliny.)

Alack. (E.?) Prob. a corruption of M. E. *a! lak!* alas! a shame! lit. 'lack.' (It cannot be the same as *alas*.)

Alacrity. (L.) Formed, on a supposed F. model, from acc. of L. *alacritas*, briskness. – L. *alacer*, brisk. (√AL.)

allegro, lively. (Ital. – L.) Ital. *allegro.* – L. *alacrum*, acc. of *alacer*.

Alarm, Alarum; see **Arms.**

Alas! (F. – L.) M. E. *alas.* – O. F. *alas* (cf. F. *hélas*). – O. F. *a*, ah! and *las*, wretched that I am! – L. *ah!* and *lassus*, tired, wretched. (Allied to **Late.**)

Alb, a white vestment. (F. – L.) M. E. *albe.* – O. F. *albe.* – Low L. *alba*; fem. of L. *albus*, white.

album, lit. that which is white. (L.) L. *album*, a tablet, neut. of *albus*.

albumen, white of egg. (L.) L. *albumen oui*, also *album oui*, white of egg. – L. *albus*.

auburn. (F. – Low L.) M. E. *auburne*, *awburne*, orig. citron-coloured or light

yellow. – O. F. *auborne*, *alborne*, blond (Godefroy); regularly formed from Low L. *alburnus*, whitish, light-coloured. Florio explains Ital. *alburno* by 'that whitish colour of women's hair called an *alburn* or *aburn* colour.' Cf. L. *alburnum*, the sap-wood or inner bark of trees (Pliny). – L. *albus*, white.

Albatross, a large sea-bird. (F. – Port. – Span. – Arab. – Gk.) F. *albatros*, formerly *algatros.* – Port. *alcatraz*, a cormorant, albatross; Span. *alcatraz*, a pelican. – Port. *alcatruz*, a bucket, Span. *arcaduz*, O. Span. *alcaduz* (Minsheu), a bucket on a water-wheel. – Arab. *al-qādūs*, the same (Dozy). – Arab. *al*, the; and Gk. κάδος, a water-vessel; see **Cade.** Similarly Arab. *saqqā*, a water-carrier, a pelican, because it carries water in its pouch. (Devic; supp. to Littré.)

Alchemy. (F. – Arab. – Gk.) O. F. *alchemie*, *arquemie*. – Arab. *al*, the; and *kīmyá*, alchemy. – Late Gk. χημεία, chemistry; for χυμεία, a mingling. – Gk. χέειν, to pour out, mix. (√GHU.)

chemist, chymist. (Gk.) Shortened forms of *alchemist*, *alchymist*, formed by dropping the Arab. article *al*.

Alcohol. (F. – Arab.) Arab. *alcool*, formerly also *alcohol*, applied to pure spirit, though the orig. sense was a fine impalpable powder. – Arab. *al*, the; and *kahál*, *kohl*, or *kuhl*, a collyrium, very fine powder of antimony, used to paint the eyebrows with.

Alcoran; see **Koran.**

Alcove, a recess. (F. – Ital. – Arab.) F. *alcove.* – Ital. *alcovo*, the same as Span. *alcoba*, a recess in a room. – Arab. *al*, the; and *qubbah*, *qobbah*, a vault, arch, dome, cupola; hence a vaulted space.

Alder, a tree. (E.) M. E. *alder*, *aller* (*d* being excrescent). – A. S. *alr.* + Du. *els*; Icel. *ölr*; Swed. *al*; Dan. *elle*, *el*; G. *erle*; O. H. G. *elira*; L. *alnus*; Russ. *olekha.* (√AL.)

Alderman. (E.) See **Old.**

Ale. (E.) M. E. *ale.* – A. S. *ealu.* + Icel., Swed., and Dan. *öl*; Lithuan. *alus*; Russ. *ol'*, *olovina.*

Alembic, a vessel for distilling. (F. – Span. – Arab. – Gk.) M. E. *alembyk.* – F. *alambique* (Cot.) – Span. *alambique.* – Arab. *al*, the; and *anbik* (pronounced *ambik*), a still. – Gk. ἄμβιξ, a cup, goblet; cap of a still. – Gk. ἄμβη, ἄμβων, foot of a goblet; allied to L. *umbo*, a boss.

Alert. (F. – Ital. – L.) See **Regent.**

Algebra. (Low L. – Arab.) Low L

algebra, computation. — Arab. *al,* the; and *jabr,* setting, repairing; also, the reduction of fractions to integers in arithmetic; hence, algebra. — Arab. root *jabara,* to set, consolidate.

Alguazil, a police-officer; see **Vizier.**

Algum, sandal-wood. (Heb. — Skt.) In 2 Chron. ii. 8, ix. 10; spelt *almug,* 1 Kings, x. 11. — Heb. *algúmmím,* or (transposed) *almugím*; a borrowed word. — Skt. *valgu-ka,* sandal-wood; where *-ka* is a suffix.

Alien. (F. — L.) M. E. *aliene.* — O. F. *alien.* — L. *alienus,* strange; a stranger. — L. *alius,* other. + Gk. ἄλλος, another; Goth. *alis,* other; see **Else, Allegory.**

alias. (L.) Low L. *alias,* otherwise. — L. *alius.*

alibi. (L.) Low L. *alibi,* in another place. — L. *ali-,* from *alius*; and suffix *-bi* as in *i-bi,* there, *u-bi,* where.

aliquot. (L.) L. *aliquot,* several (hence, proportionate). — L. *ali-us,* other; and *quot,* how many.

alter. (L.) Low L. *alterare,* to alter. — L. *alter,* other. — L. *al-* (as in *al-ius*); with compar. suffix *-ter* (Aryan *-tara*).

altercation, a dispute. (F. — L.) M. E. *altercation.* — O. F. *altercation.* — L. *altercationem,* acc. of *altercatio.* — L. *altercatus,* pp. of *altercari,* to dispute, speak in turns. — L. *alter,* other, another.

alternate. (L.) L. *alternatus,* pp. of *alternare,* to do by turns. — L. *alter-nus,* reciprocal. — L. *alter* (with suffix *-na*).

subaltern, inferior to another. (F. — L.) F. *subalterne,* Cot. — L. *subalternus,* subordinate. — L. *sub,* under; *alter,* another.

Alight. (E.) See **Light** (2).

Alike. (E.) See **Like** (1).

Aliment, food. (F. — L.) F. *aliment.* — L. *alimentum,* food; formed with suffix *-mentum* from *alere,* to nourish. (√ AL.)

adolescent, growing up. (L.) L. *adolescent-,* stem of pres. pt. of *adolescere,* to grow up. — L. *ad,* to; *olescere,* inceptive form of *olēre,* to grow, from *alere,* to nourish.

adult, one grown up. (L.) L. *adultus,* pp. of *adolescere,* to grow up (above).

coalesce, to grow together. (L.) L. *coalescere.* — L. *co-,* for *con = cum,* together; and *alescere,* to grow, frequent. of *alere,* to nourish.

Alive, in life. (E.) For *on live* = in life; see **Life.**

Alkali, a salt. (Arab.) Arab. *al,* the; and *qalí,* ashes of glass-wort, which abounds in soda.

All. (E.) M. E. *al,* sing.; *alle,* pl. — A. S. *eal,* pl. *ealle.* + Icel. *allr*; Swed. *all*; Dan. *al*; Du. *al*; O. H. G. *al*; Goth. *alls,* pl. *allai*; Irish *uile*; W. *oll.*

all, adv., utterly. In the phr. *all-to brake* (correctly *all to-brake*), Judges, ix. 53. Here the incorrect *all-to,* for 'utterly,' came up about A.D. 1500, in place of the old idiom which linked *to* to the verb; cf. '*Al* is *tobroken* thilke regioun,' Chaucer, C. T. 2759. See **To-,** *prefix.*

alder-, prefix, of all. In *alder-liefest* (Sh.); here *alder* is for *aller,* A. S. *ealra,* gen. pl. of *eal,* all.

almighty. (E.) A. S. *eal-mihtig.*

almost. (E.) A. S. *eal-mǽst,* i.e. quite the greatest part, nearly all.

alone. (E.) M. E. *al one* = all one, i.e. by oneself; see **One.**

already. (E.) M. E. *al redi* = all ready.

also. (E.) M. E. *al so,* i.e. quite so.

although. (E.) M. E. *al,* in the sense of 'even;' and *though*; see **Though.**

altogether. (E.) M. E. *al together.*

alway, always. (E.) (1) A. S. *ealne weg,* every way, an accus. case. (2) M. E. *alles weis,* in every way, a gen. case.

as. (E.) Short for *also*; M. E. *also, alse, als, as*; see **So.**

Allay. (E.) See **Lie** (1).

Allege; see **Legal.**

Allegiance; see **Liege.**

Allegory. (F. — Gk.) XVI cent. F. *allegorie.* — L. *allegoria.* — Gk. ἀλληγορία, a description of one thing under the image of another. — Gk. ἀλληγορεῖν, to speak so as to imply something else; Galat. iv. 24. — Gk. ἄλλο-, stem of ἄλλος, other; and ἀγορεύειν, to speak, from ἀγορά, a place of assembly; cf. ἀγείρειν, to assemble. Gk. ἄλλος = L. *alius*; see **Alien.**

Allegro. (Ital. — L.) See **Alacrity.**

Alleluia. (Heb.) See **Hallelujah.**

Alleviate. (L.) See **Levity.**

Alley, a walk. (F. — L.?) M. E. *aley.* — O. F. *alee,* a gallery; 'a participial sb. — O. F. *aler, alier,* to go; F. *aller.* β. The etymology of *aller,* much and long discussed, is not yet settled; the O. F. form is *aner, anner,* equivalent to Ital. *andare,* to go. Perhaps from L. *adnare,* to swim to, come by water, arrive, come; or from *anditare**, put for *aditare,* to approach.

Alliance; see **Ligament.**

Alligator; see Lizard.

Alliteration; see Liniment.

Allocate; see Locus.

Allocution; see Loquacious.

Allodial. (Low L. – O. Low G.) Low L. *allodialis*, from *allodium, alodium*, of which an older form is *alodis*, a free inheritance. (Lex Salica.) It means 'entire property,' from O. Low G. *alód*; where *al* = E. all, and *ód* signifies 'property' or 'wealth.' This O. Low G. *ód* is cognate with O. H. G. *ót*, A. S. *eád*, Icel. *auðr*, wealth.

Allopathy, a treatment by medicines which produce an opposite effect to that of disease. (Gk.) Opposed to *homœopathy*, q. v. – Gk. ἀλλο-, for ἄλλος, other; and παθεῖν, to suffer; see Alien and Pathos.

Allot; see Lot.

Allow (1), to assign, grant; see Locus.

Allow (2), to praise, approve of; see Laud.

Alloy. (F. – L.) See p. 243, l. 4.

Allude, Allusion; see Ludicrous.

Allure. (F. – L. *and* G.) See Lure.

Alluvial. (L.) See Lave.

Ally, Alliance; see Ligament.

Almanac, Almanack. (F. – Gk. ?) F. *almanach* (Cot.) – Low L. *almanachus.* – Late Gk. ἀλμενιχιακόν (Eusebius), almanac (?). ¶ Real origin unknown; *not* of Arab. origin (Dozy).

Almighty. (E.) A.S. *ealmihtig.* From All and Mighty.

Almond. (F. – L. – Gk.) M. E. *almaund.* – O. F. *almandre*, more correctly, *amandre*; the *al* being due to Span. and Arab. influence; mod. F. *amande.* – L. *amygdala, amygdalum*, an almond; whence the forms *amygd'la, amyd'la, amynd'la, amyndra* (see Brachet). – Gk. ἀμυγδάλη, ἀμύγδαλον, an almond.

Almoner; see Alms.

Almost. (E.) A.S. *ealmǽst*; see All.

Alms. (L. – Gk.) M. E. *almesse*, later *almes.* A.S. *ælmæsse.* – Late L. *eleëmosyna.* – Gk. ἐλεημοσύνη, pity; hence alms. – Gk. ἐλεήμων, pitiful. – Gk. ἐλεεῖν, to pity. ¶ Thus *alms* is a *singular* form

almoner. (F. – L. – Gk.) O. F. *almos-nier*, a distributor of alms. – O. F. *almosne*, alms; F. *aumône.* – L. *eleëmosyna*; &c.

eleemosynary, relating to alms. (Low L. – Gk.) Low L. *eleemosynarius*, an almoner; from *eleemosyna* (above).

Almug, the same as Algum, q. v.

Aloe, a plant. (L. – Gk.) L. *aloë* (Pliny). – Gk. ἀλόη; John xix. 39.

Aloft. (Scand.) See Loft.

Alone. (E.) See One.

Along. (E.) See Long (1).

Aloof (Du.) See Luff.

Aloud. (E.) See Loud.

Alp. (L.) L. *Alpes*, the Alps; of Celtic origin. Cf. Gael. *alp*, a high mountain. Der. *trans-alp-ine*, i.e. beyond the Alps.

Alphabet. (Low L. – Gk. – Heb.) Low L. *alphabetum.* – Gk. ἄλφα, βῆτα, the names of α and β, the first two letters of the alphabet. – Heb. *áleph*, an ox, the name of the first letter; and *beth*, a house, the name of the second letter. (Really Phœnician.)

Already. (E.) M. E. *al redy*, quite ready; see All.

Also. (E.) M. E. *al so*, quite so; A. S. *ealswá*; see All.

Altar; see Altitude.

Alter, Altercation, Alternate; see Alien.

Although. (E.) M. E. *al thogh*; see All and Though.

Altitude. (F. – L.) XIV cent. – F. *altitude.* – L. – *altitudo*, height. – L. *altus*, high. (√AR.)

altar. (L.) A. S. *altare*, Matt. v. 24. – L. *altare*, an altar, high place. – L. *altus*.

alto, high voice. (Ital. – L.) Ital. *alto.* – L. *altus*.

contralto. (Ital. – L.) Ital. *contralto*, counter-tenor. – Ital. *contra*, opposite to, and *alto*, high (above).

exalt. (F. – L.) F. *exalter.* – L. *exaltare*, to lift out, exalt. – L. *ex*, out; *altus*, high.

haughty. (F. – L.) Short for M. E. *hautein*, arrogant. – O. F. *hautain*, 'hauty;' Cot. – O. F. *haut*, oldest form *halt*, high. – L. *altus*.

hautboy, a musical instrument. (F. – L. *and* Du.) F. *hautbois.* – F. *haut*, high; *bois*, wood. – L. *altus*, high; Du. *bosch*, wood. See Bush (1). It is a wooden instrument with a high tone. Hence Ital. *oboè*, borrowed from *hautbois*.

Altogether. (E.) M. E. *al together*, quite together. See All.

Alum. (F. – L.) M. E. *alum.* – O. F. *alum*; F. *alun.* – L. *alumen*, alum.

Alway, Always. (E.) See All.

Am. (E.) See Are.

Amain (E.) For *on main*, in strength, with strength; see A- (2) and Main, sb.

Amalgam. (F. – Low L. – Gk.) F. *amalgame*, a mixture, esp. of quicksilver with other metals. Either a corruption or an

alchemist's anagram of *malagma*, a molli-
fying application; perhaps with Arab. *al*
(= the) prefixed. – Gk. μάλαγμα, an emollient. – Gk. μαλάσσειν (for μαλάκ-γειν), to
soften. – Gk. μαλακός, soft. (√MAR.)

Amanuensis. (L.) See Manual.

Amaranth, an unfading flower. (L. –
Gk.) Properly *amarant*, as in Milton; but
-anth is due to confusion with Greek ἄνθος,
a flower. – L. *amarantus*. – Gk. ἀμάραντος,
unfading, or as sb. unfading flower. – Gk.
ἀ-, not; and μαραίνειν, to fade. (√MAR.)

Amass. (F. – L. – Gk.) See **Macerate**.

Amatory. (L.) L. *amatorius*, loving.
– L. *amator*, a lover. – L. *amare*, to love;
with suffix *-tor*. (√KAM.)

    amenity, pleasantness. (F. – L.) O. F.
F. *amenité*. – L. *amœnitatem*, acc. of *amœ-
nitas*. – L. *amœnus*, pleasant. Cf. L. *amare*, to love.

    amiable. (F. – L.) O. F. *aimiable*,
friendly; also loveable, by confusion with
aimable (= L. *amabilis*). – L. *amicabilis*,
friendly. – L. *amicus*, a friend. – L. *amare*.

    amicable. (L.) L. *amicabilis*, friendly;
as above.

    amity. (F. – L.) O. F. *amiste, amisted,
amistiet*. – Low L. *amicitatem*, acc. of *ami-
citas*, friendship. – L. *amicus*, friendly; &c.

    amorous. (F. – L.) O. F. *amoros*; F.
amoureux. – L. *amorosus*. – L. *amor*, love.

    amour. (F. – L.) F. *amour*. – L.
amōrem, acc. of *amor*, love.

    enamour. (F. – L.) O. F. *enamorer*,
to inflame with love. – F. *en amour*, in
love; where F. *en* = L. *in*, in.

    enemy. (F. – L.) M. E. *enemi*. – O. F.
enemi. – L. *in-imicus*, unfriendly. – L. *in*,
not; *amicus*, friendly. – L. *amare*.

    enmity. (F. – L.) M. E. *enmite*. – O.F.
enamistiet. – O.F. *en-* (= L. *in-*), neg.
prefix; and *amistiet*, amity; see **amity**
above.

    inimical. (L.) L. *inimicalis*, extended
from *inimicus*, hostile. – L. *in-*, not; and
amicus, friendly; see **amiable** above.

    paramour. (F. – L.) M. E. *par amour*,
with love; orig. an adverb. phrase. – F. *par
amour*, with love; where *par* = L. *per*.

Amaze; see **Maze**.

Amazon, a female warrior. (Gk.) Gk.
ἀμαζών, one of a warlike nation of women in
Scythia. ¶ To account for the name, the
Greeks said that these women cut off the
right breast to shoot better; from Gk. ἀ-,
not; and μαζός, the breast. Obviously an
invention.

Ambassador, Embassador. (F. –
Low L. – O. H. G.) F. *ambassadeur*. – F.
ambassade, an embassy; prob. borrowed
from Ital. *ambasciata*. – Low L. *ambascia*
(Lex Salica); more correctly *ambactia**; a
mission, service. – L. *ambactus*, a servant,
emissary; Cæsar, de Bell. Gall. vi. 14. –
O. H. G. *ambaht, ampaht*, a servant; cf.
Goth. *andbahts*, a servant. β. The O. H.G.
prefix *am-*, Goth. *and-*, is cognate with L.
ante, Gk. ἀντί, before, in place of; the sb.
baht means a servant, orig. 'devoted.' Cf.
Skt. *bhakta*, devoted; *bhakti*, service.
(Origin of L. *ambactus* disputed.)

    embassy, a mission. (F. – Low L. –
O. H. G.) A F. modification of Low L.
ambascia; as above. Cf. F. *embassade*, Ital.
imbasciata, weakened form of *ambasciata*.

Amber. (F. – Span. – Arab.) M. E.
aumbre. – F. *ambre*. – Span. *ambar*. – Arab.
'*anbar* (pronounced '*ambar*), ambergris, a
rich perfume. ¶ The resinous amber was
so called from a resemblance to ambergris,
which is really quite a different substance.

    ambergris, i.e. gray amber. Called
gris amber in Milton, P. R. ii. 344. The
F. *gris*, gray, is from O. H. G. *grís*, gray;
cf. G. *greis*, hoary.

Ambi-, Amb-, prefix. (L.) L. *ambi-*,
about; cf. Gk. ἀμφί, on both sides, whence
E. prefix *amphi-*. Related to L. *ambo*,
Gk. ἄμφω, both.

Ambient, going about. (L.) See **Itinerant**.

Ambiguous. (L.) See **Agent**.

Ambition. (F. – L.) See **Itinerant**.

Amble. (F. – L.) M.E. *amblen*. – O.F.
ambler, to go at an easy pace. – L. *ambulare*, to walk. β. Perhaps for *amb-bulare*,
to go about; from. *amb-*, about; and *ba-*,
to go, appearing in Gk. βαίνειν, to go; see
Ambi- and **Base** (2).

    ambulance, a moveable hospital. (F.
– L.) F. *ambulance*. – L. *ambulanti-*, crude
form of pres. part. of *ambulare*.

    ambulation, a walking about. (L.)
From L. *ambulatio*, a walking about. – L.
ambulatus, pp. of *ambulare*.

    circumambulate, to walk round. (L.)
L. *circum*, around; and pp. *ambulatus*.

    perambulate, to walk about through.
(L.) L. *per*, through; and pp. *ambulatus*.

Ambrosia, food of the gods. (Gk.)
Gk. ἀμβροσία; fem. of ἀμβρόσιος, lengthened form of ἄμβροτος, immortal. – Gk.
ἀμ- for ἀν- (E. *un-*), and βροτός, a mortal.
Or rather, from Gk ἀ-, not (E. *un-*); and

μβροτός, put for μροτός = μορτός, mortal ;
see **Mortal.** Cf. Skt. *a-mrita,* immortal.
See **Amaranth.**

Ambry, Aumbry, a cupboard ; see
Arms.

Ambulance ; see **Amble.**

Ambuscade, Ambush ; see **Bush** (1).

Ameliorate ; see **Meliorate.**

Amen. (L. – Gk. – Heb.) L. *amen.* –
Gk. ἀμήν, verily. – Heb. *ámen,* verily. so be
it. – Heb. *ámen,* firm, true. – Heb. *áman;*
to confirm ; orig. ' to be firm.'

Amenable ; see **Menace.**

Amend, Amends ; see **Emendation.**

Amenity ; see **Amatory.**

Amerce, to fine ; see **Merit.**

Amethyst, a gem. (L. – Gk.) L. *ame-
thystus.* – Gk. ἀμέθυστος, an amethyst ; so
called because supposed to prevent drunkenness. – Gk. ἀμέθυστος, not drunken. – Gk.
ἀ-, not ; and μεθύειν, to be drunken, from
μέθυ, strong drink ; see **Mead.**

Amiable, Amicable ; see **Amatory.**

Amice, a pilgrim's robe ; see **Jet** (1).

Amid, Amidst ; see **Mid.**

Amiss, adv. See **Miss** (1).

Amity. (F. – L.) See **Amatory.**

Ammonia, an alkali. (L. – Gk. – Egyptian.) A contraction for L. *sal ammoniacum,*
rock-salt. – Gk. ἀμμωνιακίν, sal ammoniac,
rock-salt. – Gk. ἀμμωνιάς, Libyan. – Gk.
ἄμμων, the Libyan Zeus-Ammon ; a word
of Egyptian origin ; Herod. ii. 42. ¶ It is
said that *sal ammoniac* was first obtained
near the temple of Ammon.

ammonite, a fossil shell. (Gk.) Coined
with suffix -*ite* (Gk. -ιτης) from the name
Ammon ; because the shell resembles the
twisted ram's horn on the head of the
image of Jupiter Ammon.

Ammunition. (L.) See **Muniment.**

Amnesty, lit. a forgetting of offences.
(F. – L. – Gk.) – F. *amnestie.* – L. *amnestia.*
Gk. ἀμνηστία, forgetfulness, esp. of wrong.
– Gk. ἄμνηστος, forgotten. – Gk. ἀ-, not ;
and μνάομαι, I remember. (√MAN.)

Among, Amongst. (E.) See **Mingle.**

Amorous. (F. – L.) See **Amatory.**

Amorphous, formless. (Gk.) From
Gk. ἀ-, not ; and μορφ-ή, shape, form.

　metamorphosis, transformation. (L.
– Gk.) L. *metamorphosis.* – Gk. μεταμόρ-
φωσις, a change of form. – Gk. μετά, here
denoting change ; and μορφόω, I form, from
sb. μορφή (above).

　metamorphose, to transform ; a verb
coined from the above sb.

Amount ; see **Mount.**

Amphi-, *prefix.* (Gk.) Gk. ἀμφί, on
both sides, around ; see **Ambi-.**

Amphibious ; see **Biography.**

Amphibrach, a foot in prosody. (Gk.)
The foot composed of a short syllable on
each side of a long one (◡–◡). Gk. ἀμφί-
βραχυς. – Gk. ἀμφί, on both sides ; and
βραχύς, short ; see **Amphi-** and **Brief.**

Amphitheatre. (Gk.) See **Theatre.**

Ample, full. (F. – L.) F. *ample.* – L.
amplus, spacious. β. Perhaps = *ambipulus,*
full on both sides. (√PAR.)

Amputate ; see **Putative.**

Amulet. (F. – L. – Arab.) F. *amulette.*
– L. *amuletum,* a talisman hung round the
neck. Of Arab. origin ; cf. Arab. *himálat,*
a sword-belt hung from the shoulder ;
hamáil or *himáyil,* a sword-belt, also a
small Koran hung round the neck as a
charm ; lit. ' a thing carried.' – Arab. root
hamala, he carried. (Disputed.)

Amuse ; see **Muse** (1).

An, **A,** *indefinite article.* (E.) *A* is
short for *an;* and *an* is an unaccented form
of A. S. *án,* one ; see **One.**

An-, **A-,** *neg. prefix.* (Gk.) Gk. ἀν-,
shorter form ἀ-, cognate with L. *in-,* and
E. *un-* ; see **Un-, In-, A-** (9).

An, if. (Scand.) See **And.**

Ana-, An-, *prefix.* (Gk.) Gk. ἀνα-, ἀν-;
from Gk. ἀνά, upon, on, up, back, again ;
cognate with E. *on* ; see **On.**

Anabaptist ; see **Baptize.**

Anachronism ; see **Chronicle.**

Anaesthetic, rendering insensible to pain.
(Gk.) Coined from Gk. ἀν-, not ; and
αἰσθητικός, full of perception ; see **An-** and
Æsthetic.

Anagram ; see **Grammar.**

Analogy ; see **Logic.**

Analysis. (Gk.) Gk. ἀνάλυσις, a resolv-
ing into parts, loosening. – Gk. ἀναλύειν, to
undo, resolve. – Gk. ἀνά, back ; and λύειν,
to loosen. (√LU.) Der. *analyse,* verb a
coined word.

Anapæst, Anapest, a foot in prosody.
(Gk.) L. *anapæstus.* – Gk. ἀνάπαιστος,
struck back, rebounding ; because it is the
reverse of a dactyl. – Gk. ἀναπαίειν, to strike
back. – Gk. ἀνά, back ; and παίειν, to strike.

Anarchy. (F. – Gk.) See **Arch-,** prefix.

Anathema ; see **Theme.**

Anatomy ; see **Tome.**

Ancestor ; see **Cede.**

Anchor. (L. – Gk.) Better spelt without
the *h.* M. E. *anker.* A.S. *ancor.* – L. *ancora*

(also *anchora*). — Gk. ἄγκυρα, an anchor, lit. a bent hook; cf. Gk. ἀγκών, a bend. (√AK, ANK.)

Anchoret, Anchorite, a recluse. (F. — Low L. — Gk.) F. *anachorete* (Cot.) — Low L. *anachoreta.* — Gk. ἀναχωρητής, one who retires from the world. — Gk. ἀναχωρεῖν, to retire. — Gk. ἀνά, back; and χωρεῖν, to withdraw, from χῶρος, space, room. (√GHA.)

Anchovy, a fish. (Span. — Basque?) Span. *anchova*; cf. Basque *ánchoa, ánchova,* an anchovy. Perhaps 'dried fish'; from Basque *antzua,* dry.

Ancient (1), old. (F. — L.) See Ante-.

Ancient (2), a banner, standard-bearer. (F. — L.) A corruption of *ensign*; see **Sign.**

And. (E.) A.S. *and.* + O. Sax. *ende*; Icel. *enda,* if, moreover (the same word, differently used); O. H. G. *anti*; G. *und.* Prob. related to L. *ante,* Gk. ἀντί, over against.

an, if. (Scand.) Formerly also *and*; Havelok, 2861, &c. This is the Scand. use of the word. *An if* = if if, a reduplication. *But and if* = but if if; Matt. xxiv. 48.

Andante, slowly. (Ital.) Ital. *andante,* moving slowly; from *andare,* to go.

Andiron, a fire-dog. (F.) Not connected with *iron,* but corrupted from M. E. *anderne, aunderne, aundire.* — O. F. *andier*; mod. F. *landier,* put for *l'andier,* where *l'* is the def. art. — Low L. *anderia, andena, andasium,* a fire-dog. Cf. Span. and Port. *andas,* a frame, a bier.

Anecdote; see **Dose.**

Anemone. (Gk.) See **Animal.**

Anent, regarding. (E.) See **Even.**

Aneroid, dry. (Gk.) See **Nereid.**

Aneurism, a tumour due to dilatation. (Gk.) Gk. ἀνεύρυσμα, a widening. — Gk. ἀν-, for ἀνά, up; and εὐρύνειν, to widen, from εὐρύς, wide.

Anew. (E.) See **Now.**

Angel. (L. — Gk.) L. *angelus.* — Gk. ἄγγελος, a messenger. Cf. Gk. ἄγγαρος, a mounted courier, from O. Persian. **Der.** *arch-angel,* q. v., *ev-angel-ist,* q. v.

Anger. (Scand.) M. E. *anger,* often with the sense of vexation, trouble. — Icel. *angr,* grief; Dan. *anger,* Swed. *ånger,* regret. + L. *angor,* a strangling, anguish. (√AGH, ANGH.)

Angina, severe suffering. (L.) See **Anguish.**

Angle (1), a corner. (F. — L.) M. E.

angle. — F. *angle.* — L. *angulus,* an angle. Cf. Gk. ἀγκύλος, bent. (√AK, ANK.)

quadrangle, a square figure. (F. — L.) F. *quadrangle.* — L. *quadrangulum,* neut. of *quadr-angulus,* four-angled; see **Quadrate. Der.** So also *rect-angle, tri-angle.*

Angle (2), a hook, fish-hook. (E.) A. S. *angel,* a fish-hook. + Dan. *angel*; G. *angel.* (√AK, ANK.) **Der.** *angle,* verb, to fish.

Anguish. (F. — L.) M. E. *anguis, angoise.* — O. F. *anguisse*; F. *angoisse.* — L. *angustia,* narrowness, poverty, perplexity. — L. *angustus,* narrow. — L. *angere,* to choke. (√AGH, ANGH.)

angina, acute pain. (L.) L. *angina,* pain, lit. choking. — L. *angere,* to choke.

anxious, distressed. (L.) L. *anxius.* — L. *angere,* to choke, distress. And see **Quinsy.**

Animal. (L.) L. *animal,* a living creature. — L. *anima,* breath, life. (√AN.)

anemone, a flower. (Gk.) Gk. ἀνεμώνη, lit. wind-flower. — Gk. ἄνεμος, wind.

animadvert, to censure. (L.) L. *animaduertere,* to turn the mind to, hence, to criticise. — L. *anim-,* for *animus,* the mind (allied to *anima,* breath); *ad,* to; and *uertere,* to turn (see **Verse**).

animate. (L.) L. *animatus,* pp. of *animare,* to endue with life. — L. *anima,* life. **Der.** *in-animate, re-animate.*

animosity. (F. — L.) F. *animosité.* — L. *animositatem,* acc. of *animositas,* vehemence. — L. *animosus,* vehement, full of mind or courage. — L. *animus,* mind, courage, passion. And see **Equanimity, Magnanimous, Pusillanimous, Unanimous.**

Anise, a herb. (F. — L. — Gk.) M. E. *anese, anys.* — F. *anis* (Cot.) — L. *anisum*; also *anethum.* — Gk. ἄνισον, ἄνησον, ἄνηθον, anise, dill.

Anker, a liquid measure. (Du.) Du. *anker,* the same. + Swed. *ankare*; G. *anker.*

Ankle. (E.) M. E. *ancle, anclowe.* — A. S. *ancleow.* + Dan. and Swed. *ankel*; Icel. *ökkla,* (for *önkla*), *ökli*; Du. and G. *enkel.* Lit. 'a small bend;' cf. Gk. ἀγκών, a bend. See **Anchor.**

Annals. (F. — L.) F. *annales,* pl. sb. — L. *annales,* pl. adj., put for *libri annales,* yearly books, chronicles; from *annalis,* yearly. — L. *annus,* a year.

anniversary. (L.) Put for 'anniversary memorial.' — L. *anniuersarius,* returning yearly. — L. *anni-* (*anno-*), from *annus,* a year; and *uersus*, pp. of *uertere*, to turn (see **Verse**).

annual, yearly. (F. – L.) M.E. *annuel*. – F. *annuel*. – L. *annualis*, yearly. – L. *annus*.

biennial, lasting two years. (L.) Formed as if from *bienni-um*, a space of two years; the true L. word is *biennalis*. – L. *bi-* two; and *annalis*, lasting a year, yearly. – L. *annus*. So also *tri-ennial*, from *tri-* (for *tres*), three; *quadr-ennial*, more correctly *quadri-ennial*, from *quadri-* (for *quadrus*), belonging to four; *quinqui-ennial*, from *quinqui-* (for *quinque*), five; *dec-ennial*, from *dec-em*, ten; *cent-ennial*, from *centum*, a hundred; *mill-ennial*, from *mille*, a thousand, &c.

perennial. (L.) Coined from L. *perenni-s*, everlasting; lit. lasting for years. – L. *per*, through; *annus*, a year.

superannuate. (L.) Formerly (and better) *superannate*. – Low L. *superannatus*, orig. that has lived beyond a year. – L. *super*, beyond; *annus*, a year.

Anneal, to temper by heat. ((1) E; (2) F. – L.) Two distinct words have been confused. 1. M. E. *anelen*, to inflame, kindle, heat, melt, burn. A.S. *onælan*, to burn, kindle; from *on*, prefix, and *ælan*, to burn. Cf. A.S. *æled*, fire. (√ AL.) 2. M. E. *anelen*, to enamel glass. – Prefix *a-* (perhaps = F. *à*, L. *ad*); and O.F. *nealer*, *nieler*, to enamel, orig. to paint in black on gold or silver. – Low L. *nigellare*, to blacken. – L. *nigellus*, blackish; from *niger*, black.

Annex. (F. – L.) F. *annexer*. – L. *annexus*, pp. of *annectere*, to knit or bind to. – L. *an-*, for *ad*, to; and *nectere*, to bind. (√ NAGH.)

connect. (L.) L. *connectere*, to tie together. – L. *con-* '(*cum*), together; and *nectere*, to bind (pp. *nexus*). Der. *con-nex-ion*.

Annihilate. (L.) L. *annihilatus*, pp. of *annihilare*, to reduce to nothing. – L. *an-*, for *ad*, to; and *nihil*, nothing.

Anniversary. (L.) See **Annals**.

Annotate; see **Noble**.

Announce; see **Nuncio**.

Annoy; see **Odium**.

Annual; see **Annals**.

Annul; see **Unit**.

Annular, like a ring. (L.) L. *annularis*, adj.; from *annulus*, a ring; dimin. of *annus*, a year, orig. a circuit.

Anodyne, a drug to allay pain. (L. – Gk.)

XVII cent. Low L. *anodynus*, a drug relieving pain. – Gk. ἀνώδυνος, free from pain. – Gk. ἀνα, not; and ὀδύνη, pain. β. ᾿Ανα is the *full* form of the prefix, as in Zend; ω results from α and ο; ὀδύνη prob. means 'a gnawing,' from ἔδειν, to eat. (√ AD.)

Anoint; see **Unguent**.

Anomaly. (Gk.) Gk. ἀνωμαλία, deviation from rule. – Gk. ἀνώμαλος, uneven. – Gk. ἀνα, not; and ὁμαλός, even, related to ὁμός, one and the same. ¶ See **Anodyne**.

Anon, immediately. (E.) See **One**.

Anonymous; see **Onomatopœia**.

Another. (E.) For *an other*, one other.

Answer. (E.) See **Swear**.

Ant. (E.) M.E. *amte*, short for *amete*. A.S. *æmette*, an emmet, ant. Doublet, *emmet*.

Antagonist; see **Agony**.

Antarctic; see **Arctic**.

Ante-, prefix, before. (L.) L. *ante*, before. Allied to **Anti-**, q. v.

ancient. (F. – L.) With excrescent *t*. M. E. *auncien*. – F. *ancien*. – Low L. *antianus*, old, belonging to former time. Formed with suffix *-anus* from *ante*, before.

anterior. (L.) L. *anterior*, former, more in front, compar. adj. from *ante*, before.

antic, fanciful, odd; as sb. a trick. (F. – L.) Orig. an adj.; and the same as **antique**.

antique, old. (F. – L.) F. *antique*. – L. *antiquus*, also *anticus*, formed with suffix *-icus* from *ante*, before; as *posticus* is from *post*, behind.

Antecedent; see **Cede**.

Antediluvian; see **Lave**.

Antelope. (Gk.) In Spenser, F. Q. i. 6. 26. Said to be corrupted from late Gk. ἀνθαλοπ-, or ἀνθολοπ-, the stem of ἀνθάλωψ or ἀνθόλωψ, used by Eustathius of Antioch to signify 'bright-eyed,' i. e. a gazelle. Coined from Gk. ἀνθεῖν, to sprout, blossom, also to shine; and ὤψ (gen. ὠπός), the eye. See **Anther** and **Optics**. ¶ The word *Dorcas*, the Gk. and Roman name of the gazelle, is from δέρκομαι, I see clearly.

Antennæ, feelers of insects. (L.) L. *antennæ*, pl. of *antenna*, properly the yard of a sail.

Antepenultima; see **Ultimate**.

Anterior; see **Ante-**.

Anthem. (L. – Gk.) See **Phonetic**.

Anther, the summit of the stamen of a flower. (Gk.) From Gk. ἀνθηρός, blooming. – Gk. ἀνθεῖν, to bloom; ἄνθος, a young bud or sprout.

anthology, a collection of choice poems. (Gk.) Lit. a collection of flowers. — Gk. ἀνθολογία, a gathering of flowers. — Gk. ἀνθολογός, flower-gathering. — Gk. ἄνθο-, for ἄνθος, a flower; and λέγειν, to cull.

Anthracite, a kind of hard coal. (Gk.) Gk. ἀνθρακίτης, resembling coals. — Gk. ἀνθρακ-, stem of ἄνθραξ, coal.

Anthropophagi, cannibals. (Gk.) Lit. 'men-eaters.' — Gk. ἀνθρωποφάγος, man-eating. — Gk. ἄνθρωπος, a man; and φαγεῖν, to eat. (√BHAG.) β. Gk. ἄνθρωπος is lit. 'man-like'; from ἀνθρ-, for ἀνδρ-=ἀνερ-, stem of ἀνήρ, a man; and ὤψ (gen. ὠπός), face, appearance; see **Optics.**

Anti-, Ant-, *prefix,* against. (Gk.) Gk. ἀντί, against; allied to L. *ante,* before. Cf. Skt. *anti,* over against, locat. of *anta,* end; see **End.** ¶ In *anti-cipate,* the prefix is for L. *ante.*

Antic. (F. — L.) See **Ante-.**

Antichrist; see **Christ.**

Anticipate; see **Capacious.**

Anticlimax; see **Climax.**

Antidote; see **Dose.**

Antimony, a metal. (Low L.) Low L. *antimonium.* Origin unknown.

Antipathy; see **Pathos.**

Antiphon; see **Phonetic.**

Antiphrasis; see **Phrase.**

Antipodes. (Gk.) Gk. ἀντίποδες, pl., men with feet opposite to ours, from nom. sing. ἀντίπους. — Gk. ἀντί, opposite to; and πούς, cognate with **Foot.**

Antique. (F. — L.) See **Ante-.**

Antiseptic, counteracting putrefaction. (Gk.) Gk. ἀντί, against; and σηπτ-ός, rotten, from σήπειν, to rot.

Antistrophe; see **Strophe.**

Antithesis; see **Theme.**

Antitype; see **Type.**

Antler. (F.) M.E. *auntelere,* put for *aundelere* (?) — F. *andouiller,* the brow-antler or lowest branch of a deer's horn. — O.H.G. *andi,* the forehead; Dan. dial. *and,* Swed. *ænne* (for *ænde*), Icel. *enni* (for *endi*), the forehead. Cf. L. *antiæ,* hair on the forehead. The meaning of the suffix *-ouiller* is unknown. β. Or the M.E. *auntelere* may be right; corresponding to an O.F. *antoillier,* said to have been once in use (Littré). In this case, the O.F. word is supposed to be equivalent to a Low L. *antocularium** ; from *ante,* before, and *oculus,* the eye. ¶ Prob. the *latter.*

Anus, the lower orifice of the bowels. (L.) L. *anus.*

Anvil. (E.) M.E. *anvelt, anfeld.* A.S. *anfilte, onfilti.* — A.S. *an, on,* on, upon; and a verb *fealtan**, not found, but cognate with G. *falzen,* to fit together, allied to *falz,* a groove (Kluge). ¶ Some derive it from *on* and *fealdan,* to fold; however, the O.H.G. *aneualz,* an anvil, is not derived from *ane,* on, and *valdan,* to fold up, but from *falzen,* as above. Cf. L. *incus,* an anvil, from *in,* on, and *cudere,* to strike.

Anxious. (L.) See **Anguish.**

Any. (E.) A.S. *ænig,* any, from *án,* one; see **One.**

Aorta. (Gk.) Gk. ἀορτή, the great artery 'rising' from the heart. — Gk. ἀείρεσθαι, to rise up; ἀείρειν, to raise.

Apace. (E. *and* F.) Put for *a pace,* i.e a foot-pace, where *a* is the indef. art. The phrase has changed sense; it used to mean *slowly* (Chaucer, C. T. 10702); it now means *fast.* See **Pace.**

Apart, Apartment; see **Part.**

Apathy; see **Pathos.**

Ape. (E.) M.E. *ape,* A.S. *apa.* ╬ Du. *aap* ; Icel. *api* ; Swed. *apa* ; Irish and Gael. *apa* ; G. *affe* ; Gk. κῆπος ; Skt. *kapi.* β. The word has lost initial *k,* preserved in Gk. and Skt. only. The Heb. *koph,* an ape, is not Semitic, but borrowed from Skt.

Aperient. (L.) XIV cent. Lit. 'opening.' — L. *aperient-,* stem of pres. pt. of *aperire,* to open. See **April.**

Apex. (L.) L. *apex,* summit.

Aph-, *prefix.* (Gk.) See **Apo-.**

Aphæresis; see **Heresy.**

Aphelion; see **Heliacal.**

Aphorism; see **Horizon.**

Apiary, a place for bees. (L.) L. *apiarium,* neut. of *apiarius,* belonging to bees. — L. *api-,* for *apis,* a bee.

Apiece. (E. *and* F.) Put for *on piece,* where *on* = in. See **Piece.**

Apo-, *prefix,* off. (Gk.) Gk. ἀπό, off, from; cognate with E. *of, off;* see **Of.** It becomes *aph-* before an aspirate.

Apocalypse. (L. — Gk.) M.E. *apocalips* (Wyclif). — L. *apocalypsis.* — Gk. ἀποκάλυψις, a revelation. — Gk. ἀποκαλύπτειν, to uncover, reveal. — Gk. ἀπό, off; and καλύπτειν, to cover. (√KAL.)

Apocope. (L. — Gk.) L. *apocope.* — Gk. ἀποκοπή, a cutting off (of a letter). — Gk. ἀπό, off; and κόπτειν, to hew, cut. (√SKAP.)

Apocrypha; see **Crypt.**

Apogee; see **Geography.**

Apologue, Apology; see **Logic**.

Apophthegm, Apothegm. (Gk.) Gk. ἀπόφθεγμα, a thing uttered, a terse saying. — Gk. ἀπό, off, out; and φθέγγομαι, I cry aloud, utter.

Apoplexy. (Low L. — Gk.) See **Plague**

Apostasy, Apostate; see **Statics**.

Apostle. (L. — Gk.) A. S. *apostol.* — L. *apostolus.* — Gk. ἀπόστολος, one who is sent off. — Gk. ἀπό, off; and στέλλειν, to send.

Apostrophe; see **Strophe**.

Apothecary; see **Theme**.

Apotheosis. (Gk.) See **Theism**.

Appal, to terrify; see **Pall** (2).

Appanage; see **Pantry**.

Apparatus. (L.) See **Pare**.

Apparel; see **Par**.

Appeal, Appellant; see **Pulsate**.

Appear; see **Parent**.

Appease; see **Pact**.

Append; see **Pendant**.

Appertain; see **Tenable**.

Appetite; see **Petition**.

Applaud; see **Plaudit**.

Apple. (E.) M. E. *appel.* A. S. *æppel, æpl.* + Du. *appel*; Icel. *epli*; Swed. *äple*; Dan. *æble*; G. *apfel*; Irish *abhal*; Gael. *ubhall*; W. *afal*; Russ. *iabloko*; Lithuan. *obolys.* Primitive form ABALA; root unknown.

Apply; see **Ply**.

Appoint; see **Pungent**.

Apportion; see **Part**.

Appose, Apposite; see **Pose, Position**.

Appraise, Appreciate; see **Precious**.

Apprehend, Apprentice, Apprise; see **Prehensile**.

Approach (F. — L.) See **Propinquity**.

Approbation, Approve; see **Probable**.

Appropriate. (L.) See **Proper**.

Approximate. (L.) See **Propinquity**.

Appurtenance. (F. — L.) See **Tenable**.

Apricot. (F. — Port. — Arab. — Gk. — L.) Formerly also *apricock*, from Port. *albricoque* directly. Also *abricot.* — F. *abricot*, 'the abricot, or apricock plum'; Cot. — Port. *albricoque.* — Arab. *al barqúq*, where *al* is the def. art. — Mid. Gk. πραικόκιον (Dioscorides); pl. πραικόκια. The pl. πραικόκια was borrowed from L. *præcoqua*, apricots, neut. pl. of *præcoquus*, another form of *præcox*, precocious, early ripe (Pliny; Martial, 13. 46). — L. *præ*, beforehand; and *coquere*, to cook, ripen. See **Precocious** and **Cook**. ¶ Thus the word reached us in a very indirect manner.

April. (L.) L. *Aprilis*; said to be so named because the earth then opens to produce new fruits. — L. *aperire*, to open; see **Aperient**.

Apron. (F. — L.) See **Map**.

Apse. (L. — Gk.) Now used of a recess at the end of a church; formerly *apse, apsis*, a turning-point of a planet's orbit. — L. *apsis*, pl. *apsides*, a bow, turn. — Gk. ἁψίς, a tying, fastening, hoop of a wheel, curve, bow, arch. — Gk. ἅπτειν, to tie, bind, (√AP).

Apt, fit. (F. — L.) XVI cent. — F. *apte.* — L. *aptus*, used as pp. of *apisci*, to reach, get, but really pp. of *apere*, to fit or join together. (√AP).

adapt. (L.) XVI cent. — L. *adaptare.* — L. *ad*, to; and *aptare*, to fit, from *aptus*.

adept, a proficient. (L.) L. *adeptus*, one who has obtained proficiency; pp. of *apisci*, to obtain, frequent. of *apere*, to fit.

attitude. (Ital. — L.) Orig. a painter's term, from Italy. — Ital. *attitudine*, aptness, skill, attitude. — L. *aptitudinem*, acc. of *aptitudo*, aptitude. — L. *aptus*, apt.

inept, foolish. (F. — L.) XVII cent. — O. F. *inepte.* — L. *ineptus*, improper, foolish. — L. *in-*, not; and *aptus*, fit. (Also *inapt*, from *in-*, not, and *apt*.) And see **Option**.

Aquatic. (L.) L. *aquaticus*, pertaining to water. — L. *aqua*, water.

aqua-fortis. — L. *aqua fortis*, strong water.

aquarius. — L. *aquarius*, a water-bearer.

aquarium. — L. *aquarium*, a water-vessel.

aqueduct. — L. *aquæductus*, a conduit; from *aquæ*, of water, and *ductus*, a duct; see **Duct**.

aqueous. As if for L. *aqueus**, adj., a form not used. — L. *aqua*, water.

ewer. (F. — L.) M. E. *ewer.* — O. F. *ewer*, a ewer (A.D. 1360), answering to L. *aquarium*, a vessel for water. — O. F. *ewe*, water; mod. F. *eau.* — L. *aqua*, water.

subaqueous, under water. (L.) L. *sub*, under; *aqua*, water. And see **Ait, Eyot, Island**.

Aquiline, like an eagle. (F. — L.) F. *aquilin*; hence *nez aquilin*, 'a nose like an eagle;' Cot. — L. *aquilinus*, adj. from *aquila*, an eagle.

eagle. (F. — L.) F. *aigle.* — L. *aquila*.

Arabesque. (F. — Ital. — Arab.) XVIII cent. — F. *Arabesque*, Arabian-like; also full of flourishes, like fine Arabian work. — Ital.

Arabesco, where *-esco* = E. *-ish.* — Arab. *'arab*, Arabia.

Arable. (F.—L.) F. *arable.*—L. *arabilis*, that can be ploughed.—L. *arare*, to plough. (√AR). See **Ear** (3).

Arbiter. (L.) In Milton.—L. *arbiter*, a witness, judge, umpire.

arbitrary. (L.) In Milton.—L. *arbitrarius*, capricious, like the decision of an umpire.—L. *arbitrare*, to act as umpire.—L. *arbiter.*

arbitrate. (L.) From pp. of L. *arbitrare*, to act as umpire.

Arboreous, belonging to trees. (L.)—L. *arboreus*, adj. from *arbor*, a tree.

Arbour, a bower. (E.) Confused with *Harbour*, q.v. But the word seems to be really due to M. E. *herbere*, also *erbere*, from L. *herbarium*, a herb-garden, also an orchard. The special sense was due to confusion with L. *arbor*, a tree.

Arc. (F.—L.) XIV cent. = F. *arc.*—L. *arcum*, acc. of *arcus*, a bow, arch, arc.

arcade. (F.—Ital.—L.) F. *arcade.*— Ital. *arcata*, an arched place; fem. of pp. of *arcare*, to arch.—Ital. *arco*, a bow.—L. acc. *arcum* (above).

arch. (F.—L.) A modification of F. *arc*, a bow; like *ditch* for *dyke.*—L. acc. *arcum* (above).

archer. (F.—L.) M. E. *archer.* — F. *archier*, a bow-man.—Low L. *arcarius*, a bow-man; from *arcus*, a bow.

Arcana. (L.) See **Ark**.

Arch (1), a vault, &c. See **Arc.**

Arch (2), roguish, waggish. (L.—Gk.) ' So *arch* a leer;' Tatler, no. 193. Not, as I once thought, from M. E. *argh*, *arwe*, timid, which is represented by Scotch *eerie*. The examples in Murray's Dictionary prove that it is nothing but the prefix **Arch-**, chief (for which see below) used separately and peculiarly. Cf. ' The most *arch* act' in Shak. Rich. III. iv. 3. 2; 'An heretic, an *arch* one;' Hen. VIII. iii. 2. 102. Also ' Byends . . . a very *arch* fellow, a downright hypocrite;' Bunyan's Pilgrim's Progress. A. S. *arce-*, L. *archi-*, Gk. ἀρχι- (prefix).

Arch-, *prefix*, chief. (L.—Gk.) The form *arch-* is due to A. S. *arce-*, as in *arce-bisceop*, an archbishop. This form was borrowed from L. *archi-* = Gk. ἀρχί-, as in ἀρχι-επίσκοπος, an archbishop. — Gk. ἄρχειν, to be first, to rule; cf. Gk. ἀρχή, beginning. Der. *arch-bishop*, *arch-deacon*,

&c.; but, in *arch-angel*, the prefix is *directly* from the Gk., the *ch* being pronounced as *k*.

anarchy. (F.—Gk.) In Milton.—F. *anarchie.*—Gk. ἀναρχία, lack of government. — Gk. ἄναρχος, without a chief. — Gk. ἀν-, neg. prefix; and ἀρχός, a ruler, from ἄρχειν, to rule, be first.

archæology. (Gk.) Coined from Gk. ἀρχαῖος, ancient, which is from ἀρχή, the beginning; and the suffix *-logy*, Gk. -λογια, due to λόγος, discourse, from λέγειν, to speak.

archaic. (Gk.) Gk. ἀρχαϊκός, antique, primitive. — Gk. ἀρχή, a beginning.

archaism. (Gk.) Gk. ἀρχαϊσμός, an antiquated phrase. — Gk. ἀρχαίζειν, to speak antiquatedly. — Gk. ἀρχαῖος, old; &c.

archetype. (F.—L.—Gk.) See **Type.**

archi-, *prefix*, chief. (L.—Gk.) L. *archi-*, for Gk. ἀρχι-, prefix: as above.

archipelago, chief sea, i.e. Aegean sea. (Ital.—Gk.) Ital. *arcipelago*, modified to *archipelago.* — Gk. ἀρχι-, chief; and πέλαγος, sea.

architect. (F.—L.—Gk.) See **Technical.**

architrave. (F.—Ital.—L. and Gk.) In Milton. — F. *architrave.* — Ital. *architrave*, the part of an entablature resting immediately on the column. A barbarous compound; from Gk. ἀρχι-, prefix, chief, principal, and Lat. *trabem*, acc. of *trabs*, a beam. See **Trave.**

archives, s. pl., public records; but properly an *archive* is a place where records are kept.—F. *archif*, pl. *archives*; Cot. — L. *archiuum*, *archium.* — Gk. ἀρχεῖον, a public building, residence of magistrates. — Gk. ἀρχή, a beginning, a magistracy, and even a magistrate.

heptarchy, a government by seven persons. (Gk.) XVII cent. — Gk. ἑπτ-, for ἑπτά, seven; and *-αρχία*, due to ἀρχή, beginning, government.

hierarchy. (F.—Gk.) F. *hierarchie*; Cot. — Gk. ἱεραρχία, power of an ἱεράρχης, a steward or president of sacred rites.— Gk. ἱερ-, for ἱερός, sacred; and ἄρχειν, to rule. ¶ Milton has *hierarch* = Gk. ἱεράρχης.

monarch, a sole ruler. (F.—L.—Gk.) F. *monarque.* — L. *monarcha.* — Gk. μονάρχης, a sovereign, sole ruler. — Gk. μον-, for μόνος, alone; and ἄρχειν, to rule.

oligarchy. (F.—L.—Gk.) F. *oligarchie.* — Low L. *oligarchia.* — Gk. ὀλιγαρχία, government by a few men. — Gk. ὀλιγ-, for ὀλίγος, few, little; and -αρχια, from ἄρχειν, to rule.

patriarch. (F. – L. – Gk.) M.E. *patriarche*, *patriarke*. – O.F. *patriarche*; Cot. – L. *patriarcha*. – Gk. πατριάρχης, the father or chief of a race (applied to a chief of a diocese abt. A.D. 440). – Gk. πατρι-, crude form of πατήρ, a father; and ἄρχειν, to rule. See **Father**.

tetrarch. (L. – Gk.) L. *tetrarcha*. – Gk. τετράρχης, one of four chiefs; Luke, iii. 1. – Gk. τετρ-, for τέτταρες, Attic form of τέσσαρες, four; and ἄρχειν, to rule. See **Four**.

Archer; see **Arc**.

Arctic. (F. – L. – Gk.) XVI cent. – F. *arctique*. – L. *arcticus*. – Gk. ἀρκτικός, near the constellation of the Bear, northern. – Gk. ἄρκτος, a bear. Cognate with L. *ursus*; see **Ursine**.

antarctic. (L. – Gk.) L. *antarcticus*. – Gk. ἀνταρκτικός, southern, opposite to arctic. – Gk. ἀντ-, for ἀντί, opposite to; and ἀρκτικός, arctic. See **Anti-**.

Ardent. (F. – L.) XIV cent. M.E. *ardaunt*. – F. *ardant*, pres. part. of *ardre*, to burn. – L. *ardere*, to burn. Der. *ardour*; O.F. *ardor*, from L. *ardorem*, acc. of *ardor*, a burning, fervour.

arson, incendiarism. (F. – L.) O.F. *arson*, incendiarism. – O.F. *ardoir*, to burn. – L. *ardere*, to burn.

Arduous. (L.) Put for L. *arduus*, steep, difficult, high. ✛ Irish *ard*, high.

Are, pres. pl. of the verb substantive. (E.) This is a Northern form; O. Northumbrian *aron*, as distinguished from A.S. (Wessex) *sindon*. Cf. Icel. *er-u*, they are. Both *ar-on* (put for *as-on*) and *s-ind-on* (put for *as-in-d-on*, in which the *-on* is an A.S. addition) are due to the same Aryan form AS-ANTI, they are, from whence also are Skt. *s-anti*, Gk. εἰσ-ίν, L. *sunt*, G. *s-ind*, Icel. *er-u* (for *es-u*); &c. (✓AS, to be.)

am. O. Northumb. *am*, A.S. *eom*; from the Aryan form AS-MA, I am, where AS is the root 'to be,' and MA is the first pers. pronoun (E. *me*). Hence also Skt. *as-mi*, Gk. εἰ-μί, L. *s-u-m* (for *as-(u)-mi*), Goth. *i-m*, Icel. *e-m*; &c.

art. O. Northumb. *arð*, A.S. *eart*. Here *ar-* answers to ✓AS, and the suffix -ð or -*t* denotes the 2nd pers. pronoun; see **Thou**.

is. A.S. *is*, weakened form of ✓AS. The general Aryan form is AS-TA, i.e. 'is he'; hence Skt. *as-ti*, Gk. ἐσ-τί, L. *es-t*, G. *is-t*, E. *is*. See also **Be**, **Was**.

Area. (L.) XVII cent. – L. *area*, an open space.

Arefaction; see **Arid**.

Arena. (L.) L. *arena*, sand; the sanded space in which gladiators fought. Properly spelt *harena*, and *not* allied to *arere*.

Argent. (F. – L.) White; in heraldry. – F. *argent*. – L. *argentum*, silver; from its brightness. (✓ARG, to shine.) See below.

Argillaceous, clayey. (L.) L. *argillaceus*, adj. from *argilla*, clay, esp. white clay. (✓ARG.) See above.

Argonaut. (L. – Gk.) L. *argonauta*. – Gk. ἀργοναύτης, one who sailed in the ship Argo. – Gk. ἀργώ, the name of Jason's ship (lit. swift, from ἀργός, swift); and ναύτης, a sailor; see **Nautical**.

Argosy, a merchant-vessel. (Dalmatian.) Formerly spelt *aragousy* and *ragusy* (see N. and Q. 6 S. iv. 490; Arber's Eng. Garner, ii. 67, *aragousy* has been found by Dr. Murray). The orig. sense was 'a ship of Ragusa,' which is the name of a port in Dalmatia. The name may have been confused with that of the ship Argo, as explained above. ¶ This result is now certain.

Argue. (F. – L.) M.E. *arguen*. – O.F. *arguer*. – L. *arguere*, to prove by argument, lit. to make clear; cf. *argutus*, clear. (✓ARG, to shine.)

Arid, dry. (L.) XVIII cent. – L. *aridus*, dry. – L. *arere*, to be dry.

arefaction. (L.) XVII cent. Coined from L. *arefacere*, to make dry. – L. *are-re*, to be dry; and *facere*, to make.

Aright. (E.) For *on right*, in the right way.

Arise; see **Rise**.

Aristocracy. (Gk.) Modified from Gk. ἀριστοκρατία, government by the nobles or 'best' men. – Gk. ἀριστο-, for ἄριστος, best; and κρατεῖν, to be strong, govern, from κρατύς, strong. The form ἄρ-ιστος is a superlative from the base ἀρ- seen in ἄρ-τιος, fit, ἀρ-ετή, excellence. (✓ AR, to fit.) **Der.** *aristocrat-ic*; whence *aristocrat*, put for 'aristocratic person.'

autocracy. (Gk.) From Gk. αὐτοκράτεια, absolute or despotic government. – Gk. αὐτο-, for αὐτός, self; and κρατεῖν, to rule, from κρατύς, strong. **Der.** *autocrat*, Gk. αὐτοκράτωρ.

democracy. (F. – Gk.) Formerly *democraty* (Milton). – O. F. *democratie*; Cot. – Gk. δημοκρατεία, popular government, rule by the people. – Gk. δημο-, for δῆμος, a country-district, also the people; and κρα-τεῖν, to rule; as above.

theocracy. (Gk.) Lit. 'government by God;' similarly formed from θεός, God; see **Theism.**

Arithmetic. (F. – Gk.) In Sh. – F. *arithmétique* ; Cot. – Gk. ἀριθμητική, the science of numbers ; fem. of ἀριθμητικός, adj. from ἀριθμός, number, reckoning.

logarithm. (Gk.) Coined from Gk. λογ-, stem of λόγος, a word, a proportion, ratio; and ἀριθμός, a number; the sense being ' ratio-number.'

Ark, a chest, box; hence a large floating vessel. (L.) A.S. *arc,* – L. *arca,* a chest, box. – L. *arcere,* to keep. (√ ARK.)

arcana. (L.) L. *arcana,* secrets, things kept secret. – L. *arcere,* to keep.

Arm (1), part of the body. (E). M.E. *arm.* – A.S. *earm.* ✛ Du. *arm* ; Icel. *armr* ; Dan., Swed., and G. *arm*; Goth. *arms* ; L. *armus,* the shoulder; Gk. ἁρμός, joint, shoulder. (√ AR, to fit.)

Arm (2), to furnish with weapons. (F. – L.) See **Arms.**

Armada, Armadillo, Armament, Armistice, Armour, Army ; see **Arms.**

Arms, s. pl. weapons, (F. – L.) M.E. *armes.* – O.F. *armes,* pl. – L. *arma,* neut. pl., arms, lit. ' fittings.' (√ AR. to fit.)

alarm, a call to arms. (F. – Ital. – L.) M.E. *alarme.* – F. *alarme.* – Ital. *all'arme.* to arms! put for *alle arme.* – Low L. *ad illas armas* ; for L. *ad illa arma,* to those arms! to your arms!

alarum. (F. – Ital. – L.) Merely a Northern E. form of *alarm.*

ambry, aumbry, a cupboard. (F. – L.) M.E. *awmebry, awmery*; Prompt. Parv. ; the *b* is excrescent. – O.F. *armarie,* a repository; properly, for arms; but also a cupboard. – Low L. *armaria,* a cupboard ; *armarium,* a repository for arms. – L. *arma,* arms.

arm (2), verb. M.E. *armen.* – O.F. *armer.* – L. *armare,* to furnish with arms. – L. *arma,* arms.

armada, a fleet. (Span. – L.) Span. *armada,* an armed fleet; fem. of *armado,* pp. of *armar,* to arm. – L. *armare,* to arm.

armadillo, an animal. (Span. – L.) Span. *armadillo,* lit. ' the little armed one,' because of its hard shell. Dimin. of *armado,* pp. of *armar,* to arm; as above.

armament. (L.) L. *armamentum,* an equipment. – L. *armare,* to arm, equip.

armistice. (F. – L.) F. *armistice.* – Low L. *armistitium* *. not used; but the right form. – L. *armi-,* for *arma,* arms ; and *-stitum* for *statum,* supine of *sistere,* to make to stand, cause to be still, causal of *stare,* to stand. (Cf. **Solstice.**)

armour. (F. – L.) M.E. *armour, armure.* – O.F. *armure, armeüre.* – L. *armatura,* armour. – L. *armatus,* pp. of *armare,* to arm.

army. (F. – L.) O.F. *armee,* fem. of pp. of *armer,* to arm. – L. *armare,* to arm.

Aroint thee ! begone ! (Scand.) Corruption of prov. E. (Cheshire) *rynt thee,* i.e. get out of the way (Ray). – Icel. *rýma,* to make room, clear the way. – Icel. *rúmr,* spacious, allied to E. *room.* (A guess.)

Aroma, a sweet smell. (L. – Gk.) Late L. *aroma.* – Gk. ἄρωμα, a spice, sweet herb. Der. *aromat-ic,* from the Gk. stem ἀρωματ-.

Around, prep. and adv. (E. and F. – L.) M.E. *around* ; put for *on round*; see **A-** (2) and **Round.**

Arouse; see **Rouse.**

Arquebus, a kind of gun. (F. – Du.) F. *arquebuse,* 'an harquebuse, or handgun;' Cot. – Walloon *harkibuse,* dialectal variation of Du. *haakbus,* lit. 'a gun with a hook.' The 'hook' probably refers to the bent shape of it; the oldest hand-guns were straight. – Du. *haak,* a hook; and *bus,* a hand-barrel, a gun. See **Hackbut.**

Arrack, an ardent spirit. (Arab.) Arab. 'araq, sweat, juice, essence, distilled spirit. – Arab. root 'araqa, to sweat. ¶ Sometimes shortened to *Rack*; cf. Span. *raque,* arrack.

ratafia, a liquor. (F. – Arab. and Malay.) F. *ratafia*; cf. *tafia,* rum-arrack. – Malay *araq táfia,* the spirit called *tafia*; where *araq* is borrowed from Arab. 'araq.

Arraign; see **Rate** (1).

Arrange; see **Ring.**

Arrant, knavish, notoriously bad. (F. – L.) This word is now ascertained to be a mere variant of *errant* (cf. *parson* for *person*). Chaucer has *theef erraunt,* arrant thief, C. T. 17173; and see Piers Plowman, C. vii. 307. See p. 137, col. 1, s. v. **Errant.**

Arras, tapestry. (F.) So named from Arras, in Artois, north of France.

Array; see **Ride.**

Arrears; see **Rear** (2).

Arrest; see **State.**

Arrive; see **River.**

Arrogate; see **Rogation.**

Arrow. (E.) M. E. *arewe, arwe.* A. S.
arewe ; older form *earh.*+Icel. *ör,* an arrow ; perhaps akin to *örr,* swift.

arrow-root. (E.) So called, it is said,
because the juice of the *Maranta galanga*
was used as an antidote against poisoned
arrows.

Arse. (E.) M. E. *ars, ers.* A. S. *ærs.*

Arsenal. (Span. — Arab.) Span. *arsenal,*
a magazine, dock-yard, arsenal ; longer
forms, *atarazanal, atarazana,* where the *a-*
answers to Arab. *al,* def. article. Cf. Ital.
darsena, a wet dock. — Arab. *dár sinâ'at,*
a house of construction, place for making
things, dock-yard. — Arab. *dár,* a house ;
and *sinâ'at,* art, trade, construction.

Arsenic. (L. — Gk.) Late L. *arsenicum.*
— Gk. ἀρσενικόν, arsenic ; lit. a male principle ; the alchemists had the strange fancy
that metals were of different sexes. — Gk.
ἀρσεν-, stem of ἄρσην, a male.

Arson ; see **Ardent.**

Art (1), 2 p. s. pres. of verb. (E.) See
Are.

Art (2), skill. (F. — L.) M. E. *art.* —
O. F. *art.* — L. *artem,* acc. of *ars,* skill.
(√AR, to fit.)

artifice. (F. — L.) In Milton. — F. *artifice.* — L. *artificium,* a trade, handicraft ;
hence skill. — L. *arti-,* crude form of *ars,*
art ; and *-fic-,* for *facere;* to make. Der.
artific-er, a skilled workman.

artillery. (F. — L.) O. F. *artillerie,*
equipment of war, machines of war, including cross-bows, &c., in early times. —
O. F. *artiller,* to equip. — Low L. *artillare*,
to make machines ; a verb inferred from
the sb. *artillator,* a maker of machines.
Extended from *arti-,* crude form of *ars,* art.

artisan, a workman. (F. — Ital. — L.) F.
artisan. — Ital. *artigiano,* a workman. —
Low L. *artitianus*,* not found, but formed
from L. *artitus,* cunning, artful. — L. *arti-,*
crude form of *ars,* art.

inert. (L.) L. *inert-,* stem of *iners,*
unskilful, inactive. — L. *in,* not ; *ars,* skill.

Artery. (L. — Gk.) L. *arteria,* properly
the wind-pipe ; also, an artery. — Gk. ἀρτη-
ρία, wind-pipe, artery.

Artesian, adj. (F.) *Artesian wells* are
named from F. *Artésien,* adj. formed from
Artois, a province in the north of France,
where these wells were early in use.

Artichoke. (Ital. — Arab.) Ital. *arti-
ciocco,* a corrupt form ; Florio also gives the
spellings *archiciocco, archicioffo* ; also (without the *ar,* which answers to the Arab. def.

art. *al,* the) the forms *carciocco, carcioffo.*
Cf. Span. *alcachofa,* an artichoke. — Arab
al harshaf, an artichoke. ¶ Not Arab.
ar'di shaukl (Diez), which is a corrupt
form borrowed from Italian.

Article, a small item, part of speech.
(F. — L.) F. *article.* — L. *articulus,* a joint,
knuckle, article in grammar ; lit. 'a small
joint.' Dimin. of *artus,* a joint, limb.
(√AR, to fit, join.)

articulate. (L.) L. *articulatus,* distinct ; pp. of *articulare,* to supply with
joints, divide by joints. — L. *articulus,* a
joint (above).

Artifice, Artillery, Artisan ; see **Art.**

As (1), conj. (E.) M. E. *as, als, alse,
also, al so. As* is a contraction of *also.*
(Proved by Sir F. Madden.) See **Also.**

As (2), relative pronoun. (Scand.) Now
vulgar ; but found in M. E. as equivalent
to ' which.' — O. Icel. *es,* mod. Icel. *er,* used
as a relative pronoun. (So given in Icel.
Dict. ; but rather the same as **As** (1).)

Asafœtida, Assafœtida, a gum, (Pers.
and L.) Pers. *âzâd,* the name of the gum ;
the L. *fœtida,* fetid, refers to its offensive
smell. See **Fetid.**

Asbestos, a mineral. (Gk.) Gk. ἄ-
σβεστος, unquenchable ; because it is in-
combustible. — Gk. ἀ-, neg. prefix ; and
-σβεστός, quenchable, from σβέννυμι, I
quench, extinguish.

Ascend ; see **Scan.**

Ascertain ; see **Certain.**

Ascetic. (Gk.) Gk. ἀσκητικός, given to
exercise, industrious ; applied to hermits,
who strictly exercised themselves in religious devotion. — Gk. ἀσκητής, one who
practises an art, an athlete. — Gk. ἀσκεῖν,
to work, exercise ; also, to mortify the
body, as an ascetic.

Ascititious ; see **Science.**

Ascribe ; see **Scribe.**

Ash, a tree. (E.) M. E. *asch.* A. S. *æsc.*
+ Du. *esch* ; Icel. *askr* ; Dan. and Swed.
ask ; G. *esche.*

Ashamed ; see **Shame.**

Ashes. (E.) The pl. of *ash,* which is
little used. M. E. *asche, axe,* sing. ; the
pl. is commonly *aschen, axen,* but in Northern E. it is *asches, askes.* A. S. *æsce,* pl.
æscan, æxan, ascan.+Du. *asch* ; Icel. and
Swed. *aska* ; Dan. *aske* ; Goth. *azgo,* pl.
azgon ; G. *asche.*

Ashlar, Ashler, a facing made of
squared stones, (F. — L.) It consists of
thin slabs of stone for facing a building ;

so called because it took the place of the *wooden* shingles or tiles used for the same purpose. — O. F. *aiseler* (Livre des Rois), extended from O. F. *aiselle, aisiele,* a little board, dimin. of *ais,* a plank. — L. *assis,* sometimes *axis,* a board, plank; whence the dimin. *assula,* a thin piece of wood, a shingle for roofing.

Ashore. (E.) Put for *on shore.*

Aside. (E.) Put for *on side.*

Ask. (E.) M. E. *asken, axien.* A. S. *áscian, áhsian, ácsian*; the last answers to prov. E. *ax.*+Du. *eischen*; Swed. *æska*; Dan. *æske*; G. *heischen.* Cf. Russ. *iskate,* to seek; Skt. *ichchhá,* a wish, desire, *esh,* to search. (√ IS, ISK, to search.)

Askance, obliquely. (Ital. — L.) Spelt *a-scance* by Sir T. Wyat; *ascanche* by Palsgrave, who gives *de trauers. en lorgnant,* as the F. equivalent. Etym. doubtful; but prob. due to Ital. *scansare,* ' to go a-slope or *a-sconce,* or a-skew, to go sidelin;' Florio. — Ital. *s-* (= Lat. *ex,* out of the way); and *cansare,* ' to go a-slope, give place;' Florio. This is derived, according to Diez, from L. *campsare,* to turn round a place, bend round it; allied to W. *cam,* crooked, and Gk. *κάμπτειν,* to bend.

Askew, awry. (Scand.) For *on skew*; a translation of Icel. *á ská,* on the skew; cf. Icel. *skeifr,* skew, oblique; see **Skew.**

Aslant. (Scand.) For *on slant.*

Asleep. (E.) For *on sleep*; Acts xiii. 36.

Aslope. (E.) For *on slope.*

Asp, Aspic, a serpent. (F. — L. — Gk.) F. *aspe, aspic.* — L. *aspidem,* acc. of *aspis.* — Gk. *ἀσπίς* (gen. *ἀσπίδος*), an asp.

Asparagus, a vegetable. (L. — Gk. — Pers. ?) L. *asparagus.* — Gk. *ἀσπάραγος.* Supposed to be of Pers. origin; cf. Zend *çparegha,* a prong; Lithuan. *spurgas,* a shoot (Fick).

Aspect; see **Species.**

Aspen, Asp, a tree. (E.) M. E. *asp,* Chaucer, C. T. 2923; *aspen* is an adj. (like *golden*); and is used for *aspen-tree*; cf. Ch. C. T. 7249. A. S. *æsp, æps.* + Du. *esp*; Icel. *ösp,* Dan. and Swed. *asp*; G. *aspe, äspe*; Lithuan. *apuszis*; Russ. *osina.*

Asperity. (F. — L.) F. *aspérité.* — L. *asperitatem,* acc. of *asperitas,* roughness. — L. *asper,* rough.

exasperate, to provoke. (L.) From the pp. of *ex-asperare,* to roughen, provoke. — L. *ex,* very; *asper,* rough.

Asperse; see **Sparse.**

Asphalt. (Gk.) Gk. *ἄσφαλτος, ἄσφαλτον,*

asphalt, bitumen. Prob. a foreign word; perhaps Phœnician.

Asphodel. (Gk.) Gk. *ἀσφόδελος,* a plant of the lily kind.

daffodil. (F. — L. — Gk.) The *d* is a later addition; perhaps from F. *fleur d'affrodille,* translated ' daffodil-flower.' M. E. *affodille*; Prompt. Parv. — O. F. *asphodile,* also *affrodille,* 'th'affodill, or asphodill flower;' Cot. — L. *asphodelus.* — Gk. *ἀσφόδελος* (above).

Asphyxia, suffocation. (Gk.) Gk. *ἀσφυξία,* a stopping of the pulse. — Gk. *ἄσφυκτος,* without pulsation. — Gk *ἀ-,* not; and *σφύζειν,* to pulsate; cf. *σφυγμός,* pulsation.

Aspire; see **Spirit.**

Ass. (E.) M. E. *asse.* A. S. *assa.* Cf. W. *asyn,* Swed. *åsna,* Icel. *asni,* L. *asinus,* Gk. *ὄνος.* Also Irish *asal,* Du. *ezel,* Dan. and G. *esel,* Goth. *asilus,* L. *asellus.* Prob. of Semitic origin; cf. Heb. *athón,* a she-ass.

easel. (Du.) Du. *ezel,* an ass; also a support, a painter's easel. Prob. borrowed directly from L. *asellus.*

Assail; see **Salient.**

Assassin, a secret murderer. (F. — Arab.) F. *assassin.* From Arab. *hashishin,* drinkers of ' hashish,' the name of a sect in the 13th century; the ' Old Man of the Mountain ' roused his followers' spirits by help of this drink, and sent them to stab his enemies, esp. the leading crusaders. — Arab. *hashísh,* an intoxicating preparation from the *Cannabis indica,* a kind of hemp.

Assault; see **Salient.**

Assay; see **Essay.**

Assemble; see **Similar.**

Assent; see **Sense.**

Assert; see **Series.**

Assess; see **Sedentary.**

Assets; see **Sate.**

Asseverate; see **Severe.**

Assiduous; see **Sedentary.**

Assign; see **Sign.**

Assimilate; see **Similar.**

Assist; see **State.**

Assize; see **Sedentary.**

Associate; see **Sequence.**

Assonant; see **Sound (3).**

Assort; see **Sort.**

Assuage; see **Suasion.**

Assume; see **Exempt.**

Assure; see **Cure.**

Aster, a flower. (Gk.) Gk. *ἀστήρ,* a star. See **Star.**

asterisk (Gk.) Gk. ἀστερίσκος, a little star, also an asterisk *, used for distinguishing fine passages in MSS. — Gk. ἀστερι-, for ἀστερο-, crude form of ἀστήρ, a star.

asteroid, a minor planet. (Gk.) Properly an adj., signifying 'star-like.' — Gk. ἀστερο-ειδής, star-like. — Gk. ἀστερο-, crude form of ἀστήρ, a star: and εἶδ-ος, form, figure.

astrology. (F. — L. — Gk.) F. astrologie. — L. astrologia, (1) astronomy; (2) astrology, or science of the stars. — Gk. ἀστρολογία, astronomy. — Gk. ἀστρο-,· for ἄστρον, a star; and -λογία, allied to λόγος, a discourse, from λέγειν, to speak.

astronomy. (F. — L. — Gk.) F. astronomie. — L. astronomia. — Gk. ἀστρονομία. — Gk. ἀστρο-ν, a star; and -νομία, allied to νόμος, law, from νέμειν, to distribute.

disaster. (F. — L.) O. F. desastre, 'a disaster, misfortune ;' Cot. Lit. 'ill-fortune.' — O. F. des-, for L. dis-, with a sinister or bad sense; and O. F. astre, a star, planet, also destiny, fortune, from L. astrum, a star.

Asthma, difficulty in breathing. (Gk.) Gk. ἄσθμα, panting. — Gk. ἀάζειν, to breathe out. — Gk. ἄειν, to breathe. Cf. Skt. vā, to blow. (√WA.)

Astir. (E.) For on stir; Barbour's Bruce, xix. 577.

Astonish, Astound. (E.; modified by F.) The addition of -ish, as in extingu-ish, is due to analogy with other verbs in -ish. M. E. astonien, astunien, astonen; whence later astony, afterwards lengthened to astonish; also astound, by the addition of excrescent d after n, as in sound, from F. son. As if A. S. ástunian (?), to stun completely, compounded of á-, prefix, and stunian, to stun ; the exact equivalent of the cognate G. erstaunen, to amaze; see A- (4) and Stun. β. Doubtless much confused with, and influenced by, O. F. estonner (mod, F. étonner), to amaze ; this is from Low L. extonare, to thunder out, from ex-out, and tonare, to thunder; see Thunder.

Astray. For on stray; Barbour's Bruce, xiii. 195. See Stray.

Astriction; see Stringent.

Astride. (E.) Put for on (the) stride.

Astringent. (L.) See Stringent.

Astrology, Astronomy; see Aster.

Astute. (L.) L. astutus, crafty, cunning. — L. astus, craft.

Asunder. (E.) For on sunder. A. S. on-sundran, apart. See Sunder.

Asylum. (L. — Gk.) L. asylum. — Gk. ἄσυλον, an asylum ; neut. of ἄσυλος, adj. unharmed, safe from violence. — Gk. ἀ-not ; and σύλη, a right of seizure ; συλάω, I despoil an enemy.

Asymptote, a line which, indefinitely produced, does not meet the curve which it continually approaches. (Gk.) Gk. ἀσύμπτωτος, not falling together, not coincident. — Gk. ἀ-, not ; σύμ, for σύν, together ; and πτωτός, falling, from πίπτειν (pt. t. πέ-πτωκα) to fall. (√PAT.)

At. (E.) M. E. at, A. S. æt. + Icel. at; Goth. at; Dan. ad; Swed. åt; L. ad.

Atheism; see Theism.

Athirst. (E.) M. E. ofthurst, athurst, very thirsty; orig. pp. of a verb. A. S. ofþyrsted, very thirsty; pp. of ofþyrstan, to be very thirsty. — A. S. of-, very (prefix); and þyrstan, to thirst; see Thirst.

Athlete. (L. — Gk.) L. athleta. — Gk. ἀθλητής, a combatant, contender in games. — Gk. ἀθλεῖν, to contend for a prize. — Gk. ἄθλος (for ἄεθλος), a contest; ἆθλον (for ἄεθλον), a prize. See Wed.

Athwart, across. For on thwart, on the transverse, across; see Thwart.

Atlas. (Gk.) Named after Atlas, the demi-god who was said to bear the world on his shoulders; his figure used often to appear on the title-page of atlases. — Gk. Ἄτλας (gen. Ἄτλαντος), prob. 'the sustainer' or bearer, from √TAL, to bear.

atlantic, an ocean, named after Mt. Atlas, in the N.W. of Africa ;. from crude form Ἀτλαντι-.

Atmosphere. (Gk.) Lit. 'a sphere of air round the earth.' Coined from ἀτμό-, for ἀτμός, vapour, air; and Sphere.

Atom; see Tome.

Atone; see One.

Atrocity. (F. — L.) F. atrocité, Cot. — L. atrocitatem, acc. of atrocitas, cruelty. — L. atroci-, crude form of atrox, cruel.

Atrophy. (Gk.) Gk. ἀτροφία, want of nourishment or food, hunger, wasting away of the body, atrophy. — Gk. ἀ-, not ; and τρέφειν (pt. t. τέ-τροφα) to nourish.

Attach, Attack; see Tack.

Attain; see Tangent.

Attaint; see Tangent.

Attar of Roses. (Arab.) Also, less correctly, otto of roses, i.e. perfume. — Arab. 'itr, perfume. — Arab. root 'atara, to smell sweetly.

Attemper; see Temper.

Attempt; see Tenable.

Attend: see Tend.

Attenuate; see Tenuity.

Attest; see Testament.

Attic, a small upper room. (Gk.) It orig. meant the whole of a parapet wall, terminating the upper façade of an edifice. Named from the *Attic* order of architecture; see Phillips, ed. 1706. — Gk. 'Αττικός, Attic, Athenian. Cf. F. *attique*, an attic; *Attique*, Attic.

Attire. (F. — Teut.) M. E. *atir, atyr*, sb.; *atiren, atyren*, verb. — O. F. *atirier*, to adorn (Roquefort). — O. F. *a* (= L. *ad*, prefix); and O. F. *tire*, a row, file (Burguy); so that *atirier* is properly 'to arrange.' Cf. O. Prov. *tiera*, a row (Bartsch). β. From a Low G. form, answering to O. H. G. *ziari*, G. *zier*, an ornament; cf. O. Du. *tier*, 'gesture, or countenance,' i.e. demeanour (Hexham).

tire, to deck. (F. — Teut.) Both as sb. and verb. M. E. *tir, tyr*, sb.; which is nothing but M. E. *atir* with the initial *a* dropped. Thus *tire* is merely short for *attire*, like *peal* (of bells) for *appeal*.

Attitude. (Ital. — L.) See Apt.

Attorney; see Turn.

Attract; see Trace (1).

Attribute; see Tribe.

Attrition; see Trite.

Attune; see Tone.

Auburn. (F. — Low L.) See Alb.

Auction. (L.) L. *auctionem*, acc. of *auctio*, a sale by auction, lit. ' an increase,' because the sale is to the highest bidder. — L. *auctus*, pp. of *augere*, to increase. See **Eke**.

augment. (F. — L.) F. *augmenter*. — L. *augmentare*, to enlarge. — L. *augmentum*, an increase. — L. *augere*, to increase.

august. (L.) L. *augustus*, venerable; whence E. *august*, venerable, and *August*, the month named after Augustus Caesar. — L. *augere*, to increase, magnify.

author. (L.) M. E. *autor, autour*; also *auctor, auctour*. (It does not seem to be used in O. F.) — L. *auctor*, an originator, lit. ' one who makes to grow.' — L. *auctus*, pp. of *augere*, to increase.

auxiliary. (L.) L. *auxiliarius*, helping, assisting. — L. *auxilium*, help. — L. *augere*, to increase.

Audacious. (F. — L.) F. *audacieux*, bold, audacious. — L. *audaciosus**, not found; extended from L. *audaci-*, crude form of *audax*, bold. — L. *audere*, to dare.

Audience. (F. — L.) F. *audience*, ' an audience or hearing; ' Cot. — L. *audientia*, a hearing. — L. *audienti-*, crude form of pres. pt. of *audire*, to hear; cf. L. *auris*, the ear. (√AW.)

audible. (L.) L. *audibilis*, that can be heard. — L. *audire*.

audit. (L.) Perhaps from L. *auditus*, a hearing; but in Webster's Dict. it is said to have arisen from the use of the 3rd pers. sing. pres. *audit*, he hears. — L. *audire*, to hear; whence also *audi-tor*.

auricula, a plant. (L.) L. *auricula*, the lobe of the ear; used to mean the ' bear's ear,' a kind of primrose; see below.

auricular, told in the ear, secret. (L.) Low L. *auricularis*, in the phr. *auricularis confessio*, auricular confession. — L. *auricula*, the lobe of the ear; double dimin. from *auris*, the ear. See **Ear**.

auscultation, a listening. (L.) L. *auscultatio*, a listening. — L. *auscultatus*, pp. of *auscultare*, to listen; contr. form for *ausicul-it-are**, a frequentative form from *ausicula**, old form of *auricula*, the lobe of the ear; double dimin. of *auris*, the ear.

obedient. (F. — L.) O. F. *obedient*. — L. *obedient-*, stem of pres. pt. of *obedire* (O. L. *oboedire*), to obey. — L. *ob-*, near; and *audire*, to hear. Der. *dis-obedient*.

obeisance. (F. — L.) M. E. *obeisance*. — O. F. *obeisance*, later F. *obéissance*, obedience. — L. *obedientia*, obedience; hence, respect. — L. *obedienti-*, stem of pres. pt. of *obedire* (above).

obey. (F. — L.) M. E. *obeyen*. — O. F. *obeir*. — L. *obedire*. Der. *dis-obey*.

oyer, a term in law. (F. — L.) *Oyer and terminer* means, literally, ' to hear and determine.' — Norm. F. *oyer* (F. *ouïr*), to hear. — L. *audire*, to hear.

oyez, oyes, hear ye! (F. — L.) Public criers begin by saying *oyes*, now corrupted into *o yes!* — Norm. F. *oyez*, 2 p. pl. imperative of *oyer*, to hear (above).

scout (1), a spy. (F. — L.) M. E. *scoute*. — O. F. *escoute*, a spy. — O. F. *escouter*, to listen. — L. *auscultare*; see **auscultation** (above).

Auger, a tool for boring holes. (E.) See **Nave** (1).

Aught. (E.) For *a whit*; see **Whit**.

Augment. (F. — L.) See **Auction**.

Augur. (L.) M. E. *augur*. — L. *augur*, a sooth-sayer; said to mean a diviner by the flight and cries of birds. Hence a supposed etymology (not certain) from *auis*, a bird, and *-gur*, telling, allied to *garrire*, to shout.

inaugurate. (L.) From pp. of L. *in-augurare*, to practise augury, to consecrate, begin formally.

August; see **Auction**.

Aunt. (F. – L.) M. E. *aunte*. – O. F. *ante* (mod. F. *t-ante*). – L. *amita*, a father's sister. Cf. Icel. *amma*, a grandmother, O. H. G. *ammâ*, mother, G. *amme*, nurse.

Aureate. (L.) Low L. *aureatus*, gilt, golden; for L. *auratus*, gilded, pp. of *aurare*, to gild. – L. *aurum*, gold; O. L. *ausum*. (✓US.) Der. *aur-elia*, a gold-coloured chrysalis; *aur-e-ol-a*, *aur-e-ole*, the halo of golden glory in paintings; *auri-ferous*, gold-producing, from *ferre*, to bear.

loriot, the golden oriole. (F. – L.) F. *loriot*, corruptly written for *l'oriot*, where *oriot* is another form of *oriol*; see **oriole** (below).

or (3), gold. (F. – L.) In heraldry. F. *or*. – L. *aurum*, gold.

oriel, a recess (with a window) in a room. (F. – L.) M. E. *oriol*, *oryall*, a small room, portico, esp. a room for a lady, boudoir. – O. F. *oriol*. – Low L. *oriolum*, a small room, recess, portico; prob. for *aureolum*, that which is ornamented with gold. – L. *aurum*, gold. ¶ See Pliny, b. xxxiii. c. 3, for the custom of gilding apartments.

oriflamme, the old standard of France. (F. – L.) F. *oriflambe*, the sacred standard of France. – Low L. *auriflamma*, lit. 'golden flame,' because the banner was cut into flame-like strips at the outer edge, and carried on a gilt pole. – L. *auri-*, for *auro-*, crude form of *aurum*, gold; and *flamma*, a flame.

oriole, the golden thrush. (F. – L.) O. F. *oriol*. – L. *aureolus*, golden.

ormolu, a kind of brass. (F. – L.) F. *or moulu*, lit. 'pounded gold '– F. *or*, from L. *aurum*, gold; and *moulu*, pp. of *moudre*, to grind, O. F. *moldre*, which from L. *molere*, to grind.

orpiment, yellow sulphuret of arsenic. (F. – L.) Lit. 'gold paint.' F. *orpiment*. – L. *auripigmentum*, gold paint. – L. *auri-*, for *aurum*; and *pigmentum*, a pigment, paint, from *pingere*, to paint.

orpine, orpin, a kind of stone-crop. (F. – L.) Named from its colour. M. E. *orpin*. – F. *orpin*, 'orpin, or live-long'; also orpiment;' Cot. A docked form of *orpiment* above.

Auricular. Auscultation; see **Audience**.

Aurora, the dawn. (L.) L. *aurora*, the dawn; put for an older *ausosa**.+Gk. ἠώς, Æolic αὔως; Skt. *ushâsâ*, dawn. (✓US.)

Auspice. (F. – L.) See **Aviary**.

Austere. (F. – L. – Gk.) M. E. *austere*. – O. F. *austere*. – L. *austerus*, harsh, severe. – Gk. αὐστηρός, making the tongue dry, harsh. – Gk. αὖος, parched; αὔειν, to parch, dry. See **Sere**.

Austral. (F. – L.; *or* L.) We find F. *australe*, 'southerly'; Cot. – L. *Australis*, southerly. – L. *Auster*, the South wind. (✓US.)

Authentic. (F. – L. – Gk.) M. E. *autentique*, *autentik*. – O. F. *autentique*. later *authentique* (Cot.) – L. *authenticus*, original, written with the author's own hand. – Gk. αὐθεντικός, vouched for, warranted. – Gk. αὐθέντης, one who does things with his own hand. (Of uncertain origin.)

Author. (L.) See **Auction**.

Auto-, prefix. (Gk.) Gk. αὐτο-, crude form of αὐτός, self. Der. *auto-biography*, a biography written by oneself (see **Biography**); *autograph*, something in one's own handwriting, from Gk. γράφειν, to write (see **Graphic**).

automaton, a self-moving machine. (Gk.) Gk. αὐτόματον, neut. of αὐτόματος, self-moving. – Gk. αὐτό-, for αὐτός, self; and a stem *ματ-*, appearing in *ματ-εύω*, I seek after, strive to do. Cf. Skt. *mata*, desired, pp. of *man*, to think. (✓MAN.)

autonomy, self-government. (Gk.) Gk. αὐτονομία, independence. – Gk. αὐτόνομος, free, living by one's own laws. – Gk. αὐτό-, self; and νέμομαι, I sway, from νέμειν, to distribute (see **Nomad**).

autopsy, personal inspection. (Gk.) Gk. αὐτοψία, a seeing with one's own eyes. – Gk. αὐτο-, self; ὄψις, sight (see **Optic**). And see **Aristocracy**.

Autumn. (L.) L. *autumnus*, *auctumnus*, autumn. (Perhaps allied to *augere*, to increase.)

Auxiliary. (L.) See **Auction**.

Avail; see **Valid**.

Avalanche; see **Valley**.

Avarice. (F. – L.) M. E. *auarice* (with *u* for *v*). – F. *avarice*. – L. *auaritia*, greediness. – L. *auarus*, greedy; cf. L. *auidus*, greedy. – L. *auere*, to wish, desire. (✓AW.)

avidity. (F. – L.) F. *avidité*, greediness, eagerness. – L. *auiditatem*, acc. of *auiditas*, eagerness. – L. *auidus*, greedy, desirous.

Avast, stop, hold fast. (Du.) Du. *hou vast*, *houd vast*, hold fast. – Du. *hou*, short form of *houd*, imper. of *houden*, to hold (see **Hold**); and *vast*, fast (see **Fast**).

Avatar. (Skt.) Skt. *avatára*, descent; hence, the descent of a Hindu deity in incarnate form. — Skt. *ava*, down; and *tri*, to pass over, pass.

Avaunt, begone! (F. — L.) Short for F. *en avant*, forward! See **Advance**.

Ave, hail. (L.) Short for *Aue Maria*, hail, Mary (Luke, i. 28). — L. *aue*, hail! imper. sing. of *auere*, perhaps to be pleased, be propitious. Cf. Skt. *av*, to be pleased.

Avenge; see **Vindicate**.

Avenue; see **Venture**.

Aver; see **Very**.

Average; see p. 190, col. 1, l. 27.

Avert; see **Verse**.

Aviary. (L.) L. *auiarium*, a place for birds; neut. of adj. *auiarius*, belonging to birds. — L. *aui-*, for *auis*, a bird.

auspice, favour, patronage. (F. — L.) F. *auspice*, a token of things by the flight of birds, an omen, good fortune. — L. *auspicium*, a watching of birds for the purpose of augury. Short for *auispicium**. — L. *aui-*, for *auis*, a bird; and *spicere*, *specere*, to spy, look into (see **Special**).

bustard, a bird. (F. — L.) Formerly also *bistard* (Sherwood). — O. F. *bistarde*, 'a bustard;' Cot. Mod. F. *outarde*. — L. *auis tarda*, a slow bird (Pliny, N. H. x. 22). Cf. Port. *abetarda*, also *betarda*, a bustard. ¶ Both O. F. *bistarde* and F. *outarde* are from *auis tarda*; in the former case, initial *a* is dropped; in the latter, *outarde* stands for an older *oustarde*, where *ous* = L. *auis*. See **Diez**.

ostrich, a bird. (F. — L. *and* Gk.) M. E. *ostrice*, *oystryche*. — O. F. *ostruce*; mod. F. *autruche*. Cf. Span. *avestruz*, Port. *abestruz*, an ostrich. — L. *auis struthio*, lit. ostrich-bird. Here *struthio* is from Gk. στρουθίων, an ostrich; extended from στρουθός, a bird. And see **Egg**.

Avidity; see **Avarice**.

Avocation. (L.) See **Vocal**.

Avoid. (F. — L.) See **Void**.

Avoirdupois. (F. — L.) Formerly *avoir de pois* (Anglo-F. *de peis*), goods of weight, i. e. heavy articles. — F. *avoir*, goods, orig. 'to have'; *de*, of; O. F. *pois*, *peis*, weight. — L. *habere*, to have; *de*, of; *pensum*, that which is weighed out, neut. of *pensus*, pp. of *pendere*, to weigh. ¶ The F. *pois* is now misspelt *poids*. See **poise**, p. 342, col. 1.

Avouch; see **Vocal**.

Avow, to confess, to declare openly. (F. — L.) See **Vow**, where it is explained that the mod. E. *avow* is rather to be connected with **Vocal**.

Await; see **Wait**.

Awake, Awaken; see **Wake**.

Award; see **Ward**.

Aware; see **Wary**.

Away. (E.) For *on way*, though now often used as if it meant *off* (out of) the way. A. S. *onweg*, away. See **Way**.

Awe. (Scand.) M. E. *aʒe*, *aghe*, *awe*; also *eʒe*, *eghe*, *eye*; all orig. dissyllabic. The latter set are from A. S. *ege*, awe; the former, not from A. S. *oga*, awe (which was also used), but rather from Icel. *agi*, awe, fear; Dan. *ave*.+A. S. *ege*, *oga*; Goth. *agis*, fear, anguish; Irish *eaghal*, fear, terror; Gk. ἄχος, anguish, affliction; L. *angor*, choking, anguish; Skt. *agha*, sin. The orig. sense is 'choking.' (√ AGH.) See **Anguish**. Der. *aw-ful*.

ail. (E.) A. S. *eglan*, to pain. — A. S. *eg-e*, fear, orig. pain (above).

Awkward, clumsy. (Scand. *and* E.) Orig. an adv., signifying 'transversely,' or 'in a backhanded manner.' M. E. *awkward*, *awkwart*; 'awkwart he couth him ta' = he gave him a backhanded stroke, Wallace, iii. 175. β. The suffix *-ward* is E., as in *for-ward*, *on-ward*, &c. The prefix is M. E. *auk*, *awk*, contrary, perverse, wrong; this is a contraction of Icel. *öfug-*, like *hawk* from A. S. *hafoc*. — Icel. *öfugr*, often contracted to *öfgu*, adj., turning the wrong way, back foremost, contrary. γ. Here *öf-* is for *af*, off, from, away; and *-ug-* is a suffix. Cf. O. H. G. *ap-uh*, M. H. G. *eb-ich*, turned away, perverse; from *ap* = G. *ab*, off, away, and the suffix *-uh*. Also Skt. *apák*, *apañch*, turned away; from *ap-*, for *apa*, off, away, and *añch*, to bend, of which an older form must have been *ank*, nasalised for *ak*. δ. Thus the sense of *awk* is 'bent away'; from Icel. *af*, cognate with E. *of*, *off*; and a suffix, from the √ AK, to bend. See **Of**.

Awl. (E.) M. E. *awel*, *aul*, *al*, *el*. A. S. *awel*, also *ǽl*, an awl.+Icel. *alr*; G. *ahle*; Skt. *árá*; lit. 'piercer.' Cf. Skt. *arpaya*, to pierce, causal of *ri*, to go.

Awn. (Scand.) M. E. *agune* (13th cent.), *awene*, *awne*. — Icel. *ögn*, chaff, a husk; Dan. *avne*, chaff; Swed. *agn*, only in pl. *agnar*, husks. + Goth. *ahana*; O. H. G. *agana*; Gk. ἄχνα, chaff. Cf. Gk. ἄχυρον, chaff, husk of corn, L. *acus*, chaff; named from its prickliness; the lit. sense being 'prickle.' (✓ AK.)

Awning. (O.F.?) In Sir T. Herbert's Travels, ed. 1665, p. 8; the proper sense seems to be 'a sail or tarpauling spread above a ship's deck, to keep off the sun's heat.' Not from Pers. *áwan*, *áwang*, anything suspended, *áwangán*, pendulous, hanging; *awnang*, a clothes-line; Rich. Dict. p. 206; but rather from O. F. *auvent*, Low L. *auvanna*, 'a pent-house of cloth before a shop-window;' Cot.

Awry. (E.) For *on wry*, on the twist; Barbour, Bruce, iv. 705. See **Wry.**

Αχο, Αx. (E.) M. E. *ax, ex.* A.S. *eax*, *æx*; O. Northumb. *acasa*, *acase*. + Icel. *öx*, *öxi*; Swed. *yxa*; Dan. *öxe*; Goth. *akwisi*; O. H. G. *acchus*, G. *axt*; L. *ascia*, for *acsia*; Gk. *ἀξίνη*; Russ. *ose*. Cf. Gk. *ὀξύς*, sharp. (✓ AK-S?)

Axiom. (Gk.) XVII cent.— Gk. *ἀξίωμα* (gen. *ἀξιώματος*), worth, quality; in science, an assumption.— Gk. *ἀξιόω*, I deem worthy. — Gk. *ἄξιος*, worthy, worth, lit. 'weighing as much as.'— Gk. *ἄγειν*, to drive; also, to weigh as much as. (✓ AG.)

Axis, axle. (L.) L. *axis*, an axis, axle-tree.+Gk. *ἅξων*; G. *achse*; A.S. *eax*, an axle; Skt. *aksha*, an axle, wheel, cart. (✓ AG, to drive.) See **Axle.**

Axle. (E.) M. E. *axel, exel*; it also means 'shoulder.' A.S. *eaxl*, the shoulder. + Icel. *öxl*, shoulder-joint; *öxull*, axis; Swed. and Dan. *axel*, shoulder, axle; G. *achsel*, shoulder, *achse*, axis. β. The G. *achsel*, O. H. G. *ahsala*, is the dimin. of G. *achse*, O. H. G. *ahsa*. The shoulder-joint

is the axis on which the arm turns. *Axle*, an E. word, is dimin. of the form appearing in L. *axis*; see **Axis.** Der. *axle-tree*, where *tree* is a block of wood.

Ay! interj. (E.) M. E. *ey!* A natural interjection. ¶ The phr. *ay me* is French; O. F. *aymi*, alas for me! Cf. Ital. *ahimé*, Span. *ay di mi*, Gk. *οἴμοι*. See **Ah.**

Ay, Aye, yea, yes. (E.) Spelt *I* in old edd. of Shak. It appears to be a corruption of yea; see **Yea.**

Aye, adv., ever. (Scand.) M. E. *ay.* — Icel. *ei*, ever. + A.S. *á*, ever, also *áwa*; Goth. *aiw*, ever, an adv. formed from *aiws*, an age, which is allied to L. *æuum*, Gk. *αἰών*, an age. Cf. Gk. *αἰεί*, *ἀεί*, ever.

Azimuth. (Arab.) *Azimuthal* circles are great circles on the sphere that pass through the *zenith.* Properly, *azimuth* is a pl. form, answering to Arab. *as-samút*, ways, or points (or quarters) of the horizon; from *al samt*, sing., the way, or point (or quarter) of the horizon. — Arab. *al*, the; und *samt*, a way, quarter, direction; whence also E. *zenith.*

Azote, nitrogen. (Gk.) See **Zoology.**

Azure, blue. (F. — Arab.) M. E. *asur*, *azure.* — O. F. *azur*, azure; a corrupted form, standing for *lazur*, which was mistaken for *l'azur*, as if the initial *l* indicated the def. article.— Low L. *lazur*, an azure-coloured stone, also called *lapis lazuli.* — Arab. *lájward*, lapis lazuli, a blue colour. So called from the mines of Lajward, where the lapis lazuli was found (Marco Polo, ed. Yule).

B.

Baa, to bleat. (E.) In Shak.; an imitative word.

Babble. (E.) M. E. *babelen*, to prate, mumble, chatter. The suffix *-le* is frequentative; the word means 'to keep on saying *ba, ba*,' syllables imitative of a child's attempts to speak. + Du. *babbelen*; Dan. *bable*; Icel. *babbla*; G. *bappeln*; and cf. F. *babiller.*

Babe. (C.?) M. E. *bab*, earliest form *baban.*— W., Gael., Irish, and Corn. *baban*, mutation of *maban*, dimin. of W. *máb*, a son, Gael. and Irish *mac*, a son, from Early W. *maqvi*, a son (Rhys). Or due to infantile utterance.

Baboon. (F. or Low L.) F. *babouin*; we also find M. E. *babion*, *babian*, *babewine.*— Low L. *babewynus*, a baboon (A.D. 1295). Origin uncertain.

Bacchanal. (L.— Gk.) L. *Bacchanalis*, a worshipper of *Bacchus*, god of wine.— Gk. *Βάκχος*, *Ἴακχος*, god of wine. — Gk. *ἰάχειν*, to shout, from the shouting of worshippers at the festival of *Iacchus.* Lit. 'to cry *ἰαχ*!'

Bachelor. (F.— L.) M. E. *bacheler.*— O. F. *bacheler.* — Low L. *baccalarius*, a holder of a small farm or estate, called in Low L. *baccalaria.* Remoter origin unknown, and much disputed. Perhaps from

Low L. *baca*, put for L. *uacca*, a cow. Not from Celtic, viz. W. *bach*, little; as has been wrongly suggested.

Back. (E.) M. E. *bak*. A. S. *bæc.* + Icel. *bak*. **Der.** *a-back*, q. v. ; *back-bite*, M. E. *bakbiten* (P. Pl. B. ii. 80); *back-ward*, M. E. *bacward* (Layam. ii. 578), &c.

Backgammon, a game. (E.) In Butler's Hudibras, c. iii. pt. 2. The sense is 'back-game,' because the pieces, when taken, are put back. See **Game.**

Bacon. (F.—Teut.) M. E. *bacon.*—O. F. *bacon*; Low L. *baco.*—O. Du. *baken*, bacon; from *bak*, a pig. Cf. O. H. G. *pacho*, M. H. G. *bache*, a flitch of bacon.

Bad. (E.) M. E. *badde*. Formed from A. S. *bæddel*, s., a hermaphrodite; and allied to A. S. *bædling*, an effeminate man.

Badge. (Low L.—L.) M.E. *bage*; Prompt. Parv.—Low L. *bagia*, *bagea*, 'signum, insigne quoddam;' Ducange.—Low L. *baga*, a golden ring; also a fetter (hence, probably, anything bound round the arm); also spelt *baca*, a ring, link of a chain.—L. *bacca*, *baca*, a berry; also, a link of a chain. (Doubtful.)

Badger. (F.—L.) Spelt *bageard* in Sir T. More; a nickname for the *brock*. M.E. *badger*, *bager*, a dealer in corn, or, in a bad sense, a stealer of corn, because the animal was supposed to steal corn; so also F. *blaireau*, a badger, lit. 'corn-stealer,' from *blé*, corn. *Badger* stands for *bladger*, answering to a Low L. type *ablataticarius**, due to Low L. *ablatum*, corn. Cf. O. F. *bladier*, 'a merchant, or ingrosser of corn,' Cot., Low L. *bladarius*; from Low L. *bladum*, short for *abladum*, *ablatum*, corn. β. Low L. *ablatum* signifies 'carried corn,' hence 'stored corn;' from. L. *ablatum*, neut. of *ablatus*, carried away.— L. *ab*, away; and *latus*, put for *tlatus*, borne, carried; from √ TAL, to lift. ¶ But Dr. Murray shews that *badger* = animal with a *badge* or stripe.

Badinage, jesting talk. (F.—Prov.—L.) F. *badinage*. — F. *badiner*, to jest. — F. *badin*, adj., jesting. — Prov. *bader* (= F. *bayer*), lit. to gape; hence, to be silly.— Late L. *badare*, to gape; prob. of imitative origin, from *ba*, expressive of opening the mouth. Cf. **Babble.**

Baffle, to foil, disgrace. (Scand.) A Scotch word, as explained in Hall's Chron. Hen. VIII, an. 5. *To baffull* is 'a great reproach among the Scottes;' it means to disgrace, vilify. Lowland Sc. *bauchle*

(XV cent. *bachle*), to vilify.—Lowland Sc. *bauch*, *baugh*, *baach* (with guttural *ch* or *gh*), insufficient, dull (said of tools), sorry, poor, tired, jaded, without animation (Jamieson). — Icel. *bagr*, awkward, clumsy, *bágr*, uneasy, *bágr*, strife; whence Icel. *bægja*, to hinder, oppress. Prob. confused with F. *beffler*, to mock.

Bag. (E.) Put for *balg*. M. E. *bagge*; O. Northumbrian *bælig*, *bælg*, Luke, xvii. 35.+Goth. *balgs*, a wine-skin; G. *balg*, a skin; Icel. *belgr*, a skin, a bag. So also Gael. *balg*, *bolg*, also *bag*, a leathern bag. Lit. 'that which swells out.' (Teut. √ BALG.) See **Bulge.**

bagatelle, a trifle, a game. (F.—Ital.— Teut.) F.*bagatelle*, a trifle.—Ital. *bagattella*, a trifle, dimin. of Parmesan *bagata*, a little property; from Lombard *baga*, a wine-skin, of Teut. origin; see **Bag, baggage** (1).

baggage (1), luggage. (F.—C.) M. E. *baggage*, *bagage*.—O. F. *bagage*, a collection of bundles.—O. F. *bague*, a bundle. Of Celtic origin; Bret. *beac'h*, a bundle, W. *baich*, a burden; Gael. *bag*, *balg*, a wallet; see **Bag.**

baggage (2), a worthless woman. (F.— C.) Corrupted from O. F. *bagasse*, 'a baggage, quean,' Cot. Cf. Ital. *bagascia*, a worthless woman. β. Perhaps orig. a camp-follower, baggage-woman; from O.F. *bague*, a bundle; see **Baggage** (1). γ. Dr. Murray makes it the same as **Baggage** (1), in a depraved sense.

bellows. (E.) M. E. *beli*, *bely*, *below*, a bag, but used in the special sense of 'bellows.' *Bellows* is the pl. of M. E. *below*, a bag, also another form of *belly*; and *belly* is another form of *bag*. Cf. G. *blase-balg*, a 'blow-bag,' a pair of bellows.

belly. (E.) M. E. *bely*. A. S. *belg*, oldest form *bælig*, lit. a bag.+Du. *balg*, the belly; Swed. *bälg*, belly, bellows; Dan. *bælg*, husk, belly; Gael. *bolg*, bag, belly.

bilge. (Scand.) Properly the protuberant part (belly) of a ship or cask; hence the verb to *bilge*, lit. to fill one's belly, to begin to leak, as a ship.—Dan. *bælge*, to swill, Swed. dial. *bälga*, to fill one's belly. Also written *bulge*.

bilge-water. (Scand. *and* E.) Water which enters a ship when lying on her *bilge*, or by her leaking there.

billow, a wave. (Scand.) Icel. *bylgja*, a billow; Swed. *bölja*; Dan. *bölge.*+M. H. G. *bulge*, a billow, a bag. Lit. 'a swell' or surge; cf. Icel. *belgja*, to inflate, puff out.

budge (2), a kind of fur. (F. — C.) *Budge* is lambskin with the wool dressed outwards; orig. simply 'skin.' — F. *bouge*, a wallet, great pouch. — Lat. *bulga*, a little bag, a word of Gaulish origin. — Gael. *bolg*, *balg*, a bag, orig. a skin; see Bag.

budget, a leathern bag. (F. — C.) F. *bougette*, dimin. of F. *bouge*; see budge above.

Bail (1), security; as verb, to secure. (F. — L.) O. F. *bailler*, a law term, to secure, to keep in custody. — L. *baiulare*, to carry a child about, to take charge of a child. — L. *bāiūlus*, a porter, carrier. Cf. also O. F. *bail*, an administrator, from L. *bāiūlus*; hence our phr. 'to be *bail*.'

bailiff. (F. — L.) M. E. *bailif*. — O. F. *baillif*, Cot.; cf. Low L. *bailliuus*. — O. F. *bailler*, to keep in custody.

bailiwick. (F. — L.; *and* E.) From M. E. *bailie*, short for *bailif* (above); and M. E. *wike*, A. S. *wice* or *wice*, an office, duty; hence, 'office of a bailiff.'

Bail (2), a bucket. See Bale (3).

Bails, at cricket. (F. — L.?) O. F. *bailles*, s. pl., in the sense of palisade or barricade; lit. pales or sticks. Perhaps from L. *baculus*, a stick. (Very doubtful.)

Bairn, a child. (E.) See Bear (1).

Bait, to feed. (Scand.) See Bite.

Baize. (F. — L.) See Bay (1).

Bake. (E.) M. E. *baken*. A. S. *bacan*, pt. t. *bóc*, pp. *bacen*. + Du. *bakken*; Icel. and Swed. *baka*; Dan. *bage*; G. *backen*; Gk. φώγειν, to roast. (√ BHAG.)

batch. (E.) A batch is as much as is baked at once; hence, a quantity. M. E. *bacche*, a baking; from *baken*, to bake.

Balance. (F. — L.) M. E. *balance*. — F. *balance*, 'a ballance, pair of weights or ballances;' Cot. Cf. Ital. *bilancia*. — L. *bilancem*, acc. of *bilanx*, having two scales. — L. *bi-*, for *bis*, double, twice; and *lanx*, a dish, platter, scale of a balance.

Balcony. (Ital. — Teut.) See Balk (1).

Bald. (E.) M. E. *balled*, the orig. sense was 'shining, white,' as in ' *bald-faced* stag,' a stag with a white streak on its face. — Gael. and Irish *bal*, *ball*, a spot, mark, speckle (properly a white spot or streak); Bret. *bal*, a white streak on an animal's face; W. *bali*, whiteness in a horse's forehead. Cf. Gk. φαλιός, white, φαλακρός, bald-headed. (√ BHA.)

Balderdash, poor stuff. (Scand.) It formerly meant poor or weak drink. — Dan. *balder*, noise, clatter; and *daske*, to slap, flap. Hence it appears (like *slap-dash*) to

have meant a confused noise; secondarily a hodge-podge (Halliwell); and generally, any mixture. See Bellow and Dash.

Baldric. (F. — O. H. G.) See Belt.

Bale (1), a package; see Ball (2).

Bale (2), evil. (E.) M. E. *bale*. A. S. *bealu*, evil. + Icel. *böl*, misfortune; Goth. *balws* *, in *balwa-wesei*, wickedness; O. H. G. *balo*, destruction. Der. *bale-ful*.

Bale (3), to empty water out of a ship. (Du. ?) XVI cent. It means to empty a ship by means of *bails*, i. e. buckets. Perhaps Dutch; cf. O. Du. *baillie*, a tub (Hexham), Du. *balie*, a tub, *balien*, to bale out. Cf. Swed. *balja*, Dan. *ballie*, G. *balje*, a tub. We find also F. *baille*, a tub, which Littré derives from Bret. *bal*, a pail, though referred by Diez to a dimin. form from Du. *bak*, O. Du. *back*, a trough. (Doubtful.)

Balk (1), a beam, ridge of land. (E.) M. E. *balke*. A. S. *balca*, a heap; which explains *balked* = laid in heaps, 1 Hen. IV, i. 1. 61. + O. Sax. *balko*, a beam; Du. *balk*, a beam, bar; Icel. *bálki*, *bálkr*, a balk, partition; Swed. *balk*, a beam, partition; Dan. *bjælke*, a beam; G. *balken*. Orig. a ridge made by the plough. (√ BHAR.) See Bore (1), Bar.

balcony. (Ital. — Teut.) Ital. *balcone*, *palcone*, orig. a stage. — O. H. G. *palcho*, a scaffold; cognate with O. Sax. *balko*, a beam (above).

balk (2), **baulk**, to hinder. (E.) M. E. *balken*. To put a *balk* or *bar* in a man's way.

bulk (3), the stall of a shop. (Scand.) In Sh. — Icel. *bálkr*, a beam; also, a partition (pronounced with *á* like *ow* in *cow*); see Balk, above. Der. *bulk-head*, a partition.

Ball (1), a dance. (F. — Low L.) F. *bal*. — Low L. *ballare*, to dance. + Gk. βαλλίζειν, to dance.

ballad. (F. — Prov. — Low L.) M. E. *balade*. — O. F. *balade*; F. *ballade*. — Prov. *ballada*, a song for dancing to. — Low L. *ballare*, to dance.

ballet. (F. — Low L.) F. *ballet*, dimin. of *bal*, a dance.

Ball (2), a spherical body. (F. — O. H. G.) M. E. *balle*. — F. *balle*. — M. H. G. *balle*, O. H. G. *pallá*, a ball, sphere. + Icel. *böllr*.

bale (1), a package. (F. — O. H. G.) M. E. *bale*. — F. *bale*, a ball, also a pack, as of merchandise; Cot. The same as F. *balle*, a ball; hence, a round package.

balloon, a large ball. (F. — O. H. G.) Formerly *baloon*, a ball used in a game like football. — O. F. *balon*, ' a little ball, or pack; a football or baloon:' Cot. Mod. F. *ballon*; Span. *balon*; Ital. *pallone*; augmentative form of F. *balle*, &c., a ball.

ballot. (F. — O. H. G.) F. *balloter*, to choose lots. — F. *ballotte*, a little ball used for voting; dimin. of F. *balle*, a ball. And see **Bole, Bowl, Bolt, Bolster, Boil** (2), **Bolled** (under **Bulge**).

Ballad; see **Ball** (1).
Ballast. (Du.) See **Lade** (1).
Ballet. (F. — Low L.) See **Ball** (1).
Balloon, Ballot; see **Ball** (2).

Balm. (F. — L. — Gk.) A modified spelling; M. E. *baume*. — O. F. *bausme*. — L. *balsamum*. — Gk. βάλσαμον, fragrant resin of the βάλσαμος, or balsam-tree. Prob. Semitic; cf. Heb. *básám*, balsam.

balsam. (L. — Gk.) L. *balsamum*; as above.

Baluster, a rail of a stair-case, small column. (F. — Ital. — L. — Gk.) F. *balustre*; *balustres*, ' ballisters, little, round, and short pillars, ranked on the outsides of cloisters, terraces,' &c.; Cot. — Ital. *balaustro*, a baluster; so called from a fancied resemblance to the flower of the wild pomegranate. — Ital. *balausto, balaustra*, the flower of the pomegranate. — L. *balaustium*. — Gk. βαλαύστιον, the flower of the wild pomegranate. Cf. Gk. βάλανος, an acorn. Der. *balustr-ade*, F. *balustrade*, from Ital. *balustrata*, furnished with balusters.

banisters; corruption of *balusters* or *ballisters*.

Bamboo. (Malay.) XVII cent. Malay *bambú*, the same.

Bamboozle, to cajole. (Unknown.)

Ban, a proclamation. (E.) Chiefly in the pl. *banns* (of marriage). M. E. *ban*. A. S. *gebann*, a proclamation (the prefix *ge-* making no difference). Cf. A. S. *ábannan*, to summon, order out. + Du. *ban*, excommunication; *bannen*, to exile; Icel. and Swed. *bann*, Dan. *band*, O. H. G. *ban*, a ban; Icel. and Swed. *banna*, to chide, Dan. *bande*, to curse. Cf. L. *fama*, a rumour. (√ BHA.)

abandon. (F. — Low L. — O. H. G.) M. E. *abandoune*, verb. — F. *abandonner*. — F. *à bandon*, at liberty (Brachet). — L. *ad*, at; Low. L. *band-um*, also *bannum*, an order, decree, from O. H. G. *ban, pan*, a summons, ban (above). Der. *abandonment*.

bandit. (Ital. — O. H. G.) In Sh. —

Ital. *bandito*, outlawed, pp. of *bandire*, to proscribe. — Low L. *bannire*, to proclaim. — O. H. G. *bannan*, to summon; from O. H. G. *ban*, cognate with E. *ban*.

banish. (F. — O. H. G.) M. E. *banishen*. — O. F. *banis-*, stem. of pres. part. of *banir, bannir*, to proscribe. — Low L. *bannire*; as above.

banns. (E.) Merely the pl. of *ban*.

contraband. (Ital. — Teut.) Ital. *contrabbando*, prohibited goods. — Ital. *contra* (= L. *contra*), against; *bando*, a ban, from Low L. *bannum*, a word of Teut. origin.

Banana, the plantain-tree. (Span.) Span. *banana*, fruit of the *banano*; prob. of W. Indian origin.

Band (1), **Bond.** (E.) See **Bind**.
Band (2), a company of men; see **Bind**.
Bandit, a robber; see **Ban**.
Bandog, Bandy, Bandy-legged; see **Bind**.

Bane, harm. (E.) M. E. *bane*. A. S. *bana*, a murderer, bane. + Icel. *bani*; Dan. and Swed. *bane*, death; Goth. *banja*, a wound; Gk. φόνος, murder, φονεύς, a murderer. (√ BHAN.) Der. *bane-ful*.

Bang (1), to beat. (Scand.) In Sh. Dan. *banke*, to beat; O. Swed. *bång*, Icel. *bang*, a hammering. Cf. Skt. *bhanj*, to break.

bungle, to mend clumsily. (Scand.) Swed. dial. *bangla*, to work ineffectually; from Swed. dial. *bunka, bonka*, or *banka*, to strike; see **Bang** (1).

Bang (2), a narcotic drug. (Pers.) Pers. *bang*. Cf. Skt. *bhangá*, hemp; the drug being made from the wild hemp.

Banish. (F. — O. H. G.) See **Ban**.
Banisters, corruption of **Balusters**.

Bank (1), a mound of earth. (E.) M. E. *banke, boncke* (Layamon, 25185). A. S. *banc* (unauthorised). + O. Du. *banck*, a bench; Icel. *bakki* (for *banki*), a bank; O. H. G. *panch*, a bank, a bench. Doublet, *bench*.

bank (2), for money. (F. — Teut.) F. *banque*, a money-changer's table or bench. — O. Du. *banck*, M. H. G. *banc*, a bench, table.

bankrupt. (F. — Ital. — Teut. *and* L.) Modified from F. *banqueroute*, bankruptcy, by a knowledge of the relation of the word to L. *ruptus*, broken. — Ital. *banca rotta*, a broken bench, because the money-changer's bench is said to have broken on his failure. — M. H. G. *banc*, a bench; and L. *rupta*, fem. of *ruptus*, pp. of *rumpere*, to break.

banquet. (F. — Teut.) F. *banquet*, a

feast; lit. a small bench or table; dimin.
of F. *banc.* — M. H. G. *banc,* a bench, table.
bench. (E.) M. E. *benche.* — A. S. *benc.*
+ Du. *bank,* a bench, table, bank for
money; Swed. and Dan. *bänk;* G. *bank.*
Banner, Banneret; see Bind.
Bannock, a cake. (C.) Gael. *bonnach,* a
cake.
Banns, pl. of Ban, q. v.
Banquet. (F. — Teut.) See Bank.
Bantam. (Java.) A fowl from *Bantam,*
in Java.
Banter, raillery. (Unknown.)
Bantling, an infant. (E.) Prob. for
band-ling, one wrapped in swaddling bands;
with double dimin. suffix *-l-ing.* See Bind.
Banyan, a tree. (Skt.) An English,
not a native name for the tree. So called
because used as a market-place for merchants or 'bannyans,' as we termed them;
see Sir T. Herbert, Travels, ed. 1665, pp.
51, 123. — Skt. *banij,* a merchant.
Baobab, a tree. (African.) The native
name in Senegal.
Baptise, Baptize. (F. — L. — Gk.) Formerly *baptise;* M. E. *baptisen.* — O. F. *bap-
tiser.* — L. *baptizare.* — Gk. βαπτίζειν; from
βάπτειν, to dip. Der. *baptist,* Gk. βαπ-
τιστής, a dipper; *baptism,* Gk. βάπτισμα, a
dipping.
anabaptist. (Gk.) One who baptizes
again. Coined from Gk. ἀνά, again; and
baptist.
Bar, a rail. (F. — C.) M. E. *barre.* —
O. F. *barre.* — Bret. *barren,* a bar; *bar,*
branch of a tree; W. *bar,* Gael. and Irish
barra, a bar. (Origin of F. *barre* doubtful.)
barracks. (F. — Ital. — C.) F. *baraque.*
— Ital. *baracca,* a tent for soldiers. Of
Celtic origin; Bret. *bar,* a branch of a
tree; Gael. *barr,* a spike, *barrach,* top-
branches of trees, *barrachad,* a hut or
booth. Cf. Low L. *barræ,* palisades.
barrel. (F. — C.) M. E. *barel.* — O. F.
bareil; F. *baril.* — F. *barrs,* a bar; from
the staves of it. β. That the word is of
Celtic origin is shewn by W. *baril,* Gael.
baraill, Ir. *bairile,* Manx *barrel,* a barrel;
from W. *bar,* &c., a bar. And see below.
barricade. (F. — Span. — C.) F. *barricade.* — Span. *barricada,* a barricade, lit.
one made with barrels full of earth. —
Span. *barrica,* a barrel. — Span. *barra,* a
bar; see barrel.
barrier. (F. — C.) M. E. *barrere.* — F.
barrière. — F. *barrer,* to bar up. — F. *barre,*
a bar.

barrister. (Low L. — C.) A barbarous
word; formed with suffix *-ister* (= Low L.
-istarius) from the sb. *bar.* Spelman gives
the Low L. form as *barrasterius.*
debar. (L. *and* C.) Coined from L. *de,*
from; and *bar.*
embargo. (Span. — C.) Span. *embargo,*
an arrest, a stoppage of ships; lit. a putting a bar in the way. Formed with prefix *em-* (= Lat. *in*) from Span. *barra,* a bar.
embarrass. (F. — C.) F. *embarrasser,*
to perplex; lit. to hinder, put a bar in
one's way. — F. *em-* (= L. *in*), and a stem
barras-, due to *barre,* a bar. β. The stem
barras- can be accounted for by the Prov.
barras, a bar, Span. *barras,* a prison, both
used as singular, though really the pl.
forms of Prov. and Span. *barra,* a bar.
The word is *Southern* F.
Barb (1), hook on an arrow. (F. — L.)
F. *barbe.* — L. *barba,* a beard. Hence O. F.
flesche barbelée, 'a bearded or barbed
arrow;' Cot.
barbel, a fish. (F. — L.) M. E. *bar-
bylle.* — O. F. *barbel,* F. *barbeau.* — L. *bar-
bellus,* dimin. of *barbus,* a barbel. — L.
barba, a beard. ¶ Named from four
beard-like appendages near the mouth.
barber. (F. — L.) M. E. *barbour.* —
O. F. *barbier,* a barber. — F. *barbe,* a beard;
as above. See Beard.
burbot, a fish. (F. — L.) F. *barbote,* a
burbot; named from its small beards on
the nose and chin. — F. *barbe,* a beard.
Barb (2), a horse. (F. — Barbary.) F.
barbe, a Barbary horse; named from the
country.
Barbarous. (L. — Gk.) L. *barbarus.* —
Gk. βάρβαρος, foreign, lit. stammering; a
name given by Greeks to express the
strange sound of foreign languages. Cf. L.
balbus, stammering.
Barbed, as applied to horses; see
Beard.
Barbel, Barber; see Barb (1).
Barberry, Berberry, a shrub. (F. —
Arab.) F. *berberis;* Cot. — Arab. *barbáris,*
the barberry-tree. ¶ The spelling should
be *berbery* or *barbary;* no connection with
berry.
Barbican. (F. — Arab. ?) M. E. *barbican.*
— F. *barbacane,* a barbican or outwork of a
castle; also, a loop-hole; also, an outlet
for water. Perhaps from Arab. *barbakh,*
an aqueduct, a sewer (Devic).
Bard. (C.) W. *bardd,* Irish and Gael.
bard, a poet.

Bare. (E.) M. E. *bar*. A. S. *bær*. +
Icel. *berr*; G. *bar*; Lith. *basas, bosus*, barefooted.

Bargain. (F. – Low L.) M. E. *bargayn*,
sb. – O. F. *bargaigner, barginer*, to chaffer.
– Low L. *barcaniare*, to change about.
Supposed to be from Low L. *barca*, a bark
or ship for merchandise; see **Bark** (1).

Barge; see **Bark** (1).

Bark (1), **Barque.** (F. – Low L. – Gk.
– Egypt.) *Bark* is an E. spelling of F.
barque, a little ship. – Low L. *barca*, a sort
of ship; shorter form of *barica**, dimin. of
baris, a sort of boat (Propertius). – Gk.
βᾶρις, a row-boat. Of Egyptian origin;
Coptic *bari*, a boat.

barge. (F. – Low L. – Gk. – Egypt.)
M. E. *barge*. – F. *barge*. – Low L. *barica**,
dimin. of *baris*; as above.

debark. (F. – Low L.) F. *débarquer*,
formerly *desbarquer*, to land from a ship. –
O. F. *des-* (L. *dis-*), away; and F. *barque*.
So also *embark* (F. *em-barquer*); whence
dis-embark.

Bark (2), the rind of a tree. (Scand.)
M. E. *barke*. – Swed. *bark*; Dan. *bark*;
Icel. *börkr*.

Bark (3), to yelp as a dog. (E.) M. E.
berken. – A. S. *beorcan, borcian*, to bark.
Perhaps allied to *break*, to make a cracking
noise; cf. L. *frag-or*, a crash.

Barley. (E.) M. E. *barli*. – A. S. *bærlic*.
– A. S. *bere*, barley (Low Sc. *bear*); and
-lic, put for *llc*, like. Cf. also Goth.
barizeins, made of barley; L. *far*, corn.
See **Farina, Leek, Garlic**.

barn. (E.) M. E. *berne*. A. S. *bern*,
contr. form of *ber-ern* (Luke, iii. 17). –
A. S. *bere*, barley; and *ern*, a place for
storing, corner.

barton, a court-yard, manor. (E.) O.
Northumb. *bere-tún* (Matt. iii. 12). – A. S.
bere, barley; and *tún*, an enclosure; see
Town.

Barm (1), yeast. (E.) M. E. *berme*.
A. S. *beorma*. + Du. *berm*; Swed. *bärma*;
G. *bärme*. Allied to **Ferment** and **Brew**.

Barm (2), the lap. (E.) See **Bear** (1).

Barn. (E.) See **Barley**.

Barnacle (1), a kind of goose. (Low
L. – C. ?) Dimin. from F. *bernaque* (Cot.),
Low L. *bernaca*. '*Bernacæ*, aues aucis
palustribus similes;' Ducange. Used by
Giraldus Cambrensis, and presumably of
Celtic origin. (See Max Müller, Lectures,
2nd Series.)

Barnacle (2), a sort of shell-fish. (C. ?

or L. – Gk.) Prob. a dimin. from Irish
barneach, a limpet; Gael. *bairneach*, W.
brenig, Bret. *brennik, brinnik*, a limpet;
Corn. *brennic*, limpets, derived by R. Williams from *bron*, the breast, which the
limpet resembles in form. β. Otherwise,
it is a dimin. of L. *perna*, a shell-fish;
pernacula being changed into *bernacula*
(Max Müller, Lectures, ii. 584). L. *perna*
also means a ham, thigh-bone. – Gk. πέρνα,
a ham. γ. Or the same as **Barnacle** (1).

Barnacles, spectacles, orig. irons put on
the noses of horses to keep them quiet.
(C. ?) The sense of 'spectacles' is late,
and due to a jesting allusion. M. E. *bernak*, dimin. *bernakill*. '*Bernak* for hors,
bernakill, Chamus' (i.e. L. *camus*); Prompt.
Parv. I suspect *bernak* (for *brenak*) to be
the same word as *brank* or *branks*; see
Branks. The sense is just the same. We
find *bernac* in O. F. (in an Eng. MS.);
Wright's Vocab. i. 100, l. 3.

Barometer, for measuring the weight of
the air. (Gk.) Gk. βαρο-, for βάρος, weight;
and μέτρον, a measure; see **Metre**.

Baron, a title. (F. – O. H. G.) M. E.
baron. – F. *baron*; older form *ber* (Prov.
bar), the suffix *-on* only marking the acc.
case (Diez). – O. H. G. *bar*, a man, prob. a
porter (cf. G. *frucht-bar*, fruit-bearing).
Perhaps from O. H. G. *beran*, to bear; see
Bear (1). ¶ Uncertain.

Barouche, a carriage. (G. – Ital. – L.)
G. *barutsche*. – Ital. *baroccio, biroccio*, a
chariot, orig. a two-wheeled car. – L. *bi-
rotus*, two-wheeled. – L. *bi-*, double; and
rota, a wheel.

Barracks. (F. – Ital. – C.) See **Bar**.

Barrel. (F. – C.) See **Bar**.

Barren. (F.) M. E. *barein*. – O. F. *ba-
raigne*; F. *brehaigne*, sterile. Of unknown
origin.

Barricade, Barrier, Barrister; see
Bar.

Barrow (1), a burial-mound. (E.) See
Borough.

Barrow (2), a wheel-barrow. (E.) See
Bear (1).

Barter, to traffic. (F.) M. E. *bartɔyn*.
– O. F. *bareter, barater*, 'to cheat, beguile,
also to barter;' Cot. O. F. *barat*, ' cheating, also a barter;' Cot. β. Of doubtful
origin; Diez suggests Gk. πράττειν, πράσσειν, to transact business; but rather Celtic
(Littré). Cf. Bret. *barad*, treachery, Irish
brath, W. *brad*, treachery, Gael. *brath*, advantage by unfair means; Irish *bradach*,

Gael, *bradag*, thievish, roguish; W. *bradu*, to plot.

Barton. (E.) See **Barley.**

Barytes, in chemistry. (Gk.) Named from its weight. — Gk. βαρύτης, weight. — Gk. βαρύς, heavy. See **Grave** (2).

barytone. (Ital. — Gk.) Better *baritone*; a musical term for a deep voice. — Ital. *baritono*, a baritone. — Gk. βαρύ-ς, heavy, deep; and τόνος, a tone; see **Tone.**

Basalt. (F. — L.) F. *basalte.* — L. *basaltes*, a hard kind of marble in Æthiopia. An African word (Pliny).

Base (1), low (F. — L.) M. E. *bass*, *base.* — F. *bas*, m., *basse*, fem. — Low L. *bassus*, low; the same word as L. *Bassus*, proper name, which seems to have meant 'stout, fat,' rather than merely 'low.'

abase. (F. — L.) F. *abaisser, abbaisser*; Cot. — Low L. *abassare*, to lower. — L. *ad*, to; and Low L. *bassare*, to lower, from *bassus*, low. **Der.** *abase-ment.*

basement, lowest floor of a building. (F. — Ital. — L.) Appears in F. as *soubassement*, the basement of a building; formed from *sous*, under, and *-bassement*, borrowed from Ital. *bassamento*, lit. an abasement. — Ital. *bassare*, to lower. — Ital. *basso*, low. — Low L. *bassus.*

bass (1), lowest part in music. (F. — L.) F. *basse*, fem. of *bas*, low. Cf. Ital. *basso.*

bass-relief. (Ital. — L.) Ital. *basso-relievo.* See under **Levity.**

bassoon, a bass instrument. (F. — L.) F. *basson.* — Ital. *bassone*, a bassoon. — Ital. *basso*, bass (above).

debase. (L., and F. — L.) Formed from *base* by prefixing L. *de*, down.

Base (2), a foundation (F. — L. — Gk.) M. E. *bas.* — F. *base.* — L. *basis.* — Gk. βάσις, a going, a pedestal, base. — Gk. base βα-, to go, as in βαίνειν, to go. (√GA.)

basis. (L. — Gk.) L. *basis*, as above.

Basement. (F. — Ital. — L.) See **Base** (1).

Basenet, Basnet; see **Basin.**

Bashful. (F. *and* E.) Put for *abash-ful*; see **Abash.** Prob. by confusion with *abase* and *base.*

Basil, a plant. (F. — L. — Gk.) Short for *basilic.* — F. *basilic*, 'herb basill;' Cot. — L. *basilicum*, neut. of *basilicus*, royal. — Gk. βασιλικός, royal. — Gk. βασιλεύς, a king.

basilica, a large hall. (L. — Gk.) L. *basilica*, fem. of *basilicus*, royal.

basilisk, a fabled serpent. (Gk.) Gk. βασιλίσκος, lit. royal; also a lizard or serpent, named from a spot on the head like a crown. — Gk. βασιλεύς, a king.

Basin. (F. — C.) M. E. *bacin, basin.* — O. F. *bacin*; F. *bassin.* — Gael. *bac*, a hollow; W. *bach*, a hook; Bret. *bak, bag*, a shallow boat.

basenet, basnet, a light helmet. (F. — C.) In Spenser. — O. F. *bacinet*, dimin. of *bacin*; from its shape.

Basis. (L. — Gk.) See **Base** (2).

Bask. (Scand.) M. E. *baske*, to bathe oneself, Palsgrave; and cf. *bathe hire*, to bask herself, Ch. C. T. Nonnes Prestes Tale, 446. — Icel. *baða sik*, to bathe oneself; cf. Icel. *baðast* (for *baðask*), to bathe oneself. Cf. also Swed. dial. *at basa sig i solen*, to bask in the sun, *badfisk*, fishes basking in the sun. See **Bath.** ¶ Formed like **Busk.**

Basket. (C.) M. E. *basket.* — W. *basged*; Corn. *basced*; Irish *basceid*; Gaol. *hascaid*, a basket. Perhaps from W. *basg*, a plaiting.

Bass (1), in music. See **Base** (1).

Bass (2), **Barse, Brasse**, a fish. (E.) M. E. *barse, bace* (with loss of *r*). A. S. *bærs*, a perch. + Du. *baars*; G. *bars, barsch*, a perch.

bream, a fish. (F. — Teut.) M. E. *breem.* — O. F. *bresme* (F. *brème*). — M. H. G. *brahsem* (G. *brassen*); O. H. G. *prahsema*; extended form of G. *bars.*

Bassoon. (F. — Ital. — L.) See **Base** (1).

Bast. (E.) M. E. *bast*; *bast-tre*, a lime-tree. A. S. *bæst*, a lime-tree; whence bast is made. + Icel., Swed., Dan., G. *bast.* Perhaps allied to **Bind.**

baste (3), to sew slightly. (F. — M. H. G.) M. E. *basten.* — O. F. *hastir*, F. *bâtir*, to sew slightly; a tailor's term = M. H. G. *basten*, to bind; orig. to tie with bast. — G. *bast*, bast.

Bastard, an illegitimate child. (F.) M. E. *bastard*, applied to Will. I — O. F. *bastard*, the same as *fils de bast*, lit. 'the son of a pack-saddle,' not of a bed. [The expression *a bast ibore*, illegitimate, occurs in Rob. of Glouc. p. 516.] — O. F. *bast*, a pack-saddle (F. *bât*); with suffix *-ard*, from O. H. G. *hart*, hard, first used as a suffix in proper names and then generally.

Baste (1), to beat. (Scand.) Icel. *beysta*, to beat; Swed. *bösta*, to thump. Cf. O. Swed. *basa*, to strike.

Baste (2), to pour fat over meat. (Unknown.) In Sh. '*To baste*, linire;' Levins, ed. 1570.

Baste (3), to sew slightly. See **Bast.**

Bastile, a fortress. (F.) O. F. *bastille,* a building. — O. F. *bastir* (F. *bâtir*), to build. Origin uncertain; perhaps allied to Baton. **bastion.** (F. — Ital.) F. *bastion.* — Ital. *bastione,* part of a fortification. — Ital. *bastire,* to build; allied to O. F. *bastir.* And see **Battlement.**

Bastinado (Span.) See Baton.

Bastion. (F. — Ital.) See Bastile.

Bat (1), a cudgel. (E.) M. E. *batte.* — A. S. *batt* (Eng. Studien, xi. 65). Cf. Irish *bata, bat,* a staff. Der. *bat-let,* with double dimin. suffix *-l-et.*

Bat (2), a winged mammal. (Scand.) Corrupted from M. E. *bakke.* — Dan. *bakke,* now only in comp. *aften-bakke,* evening-bat. And *bakke* is for *blakke*; Icel. *leðr-blaka,* a 'leather-flapper,' a bat. — Icel. *blaka,* to flutter, flap the wings.

Batch. (E.) See Bake.

Bate (1), to diminish. (F. — L.) Short for abate, by loss of *a*; see Batter (1).

Bate (2), strife. (F. — L.) M. E. *bate*; a clipt form of Debate, in the sense of strife. ¶ So also *fence* for *de-fence.*

Bath. (E.) M. E. *baþ.* A. S. *bæð.* + Icel. *baö*; O. H. G. *pad, bad*; O. Swed. *bad.* The orig. sense was a place of warmth; cf. O. H. G. *bâhen* (G. *bähen*), L. *fouere,* to warm, foment. Allied to Foment and Bake.

bathe. (E.) A. S. *baðian,* to bathe. — A. S. *bæð,* a bath. And see Bask.

Bathos. (Gk.) Lit. depth, sinking. — Gk. βάθος, depth; cf. βαθύς, deep. (√GABH.)

Baton, Batoon, a cudgel. (F.) F. *bâton,* O. F. *baston.* — Low L. *bastonem,* acc. of *basto,* a cudgel. Origin doubtful; connected by Diez with Gk. βαστάζειν. to support.

bastinado. (Span.) From Span. *bastonada,* a beating. — Span. *baston,* a stick = Low L. *bastonem* (above).

batten (2), a wooden rod. (F.) To *batten* down is to fasten with *battens. Batten* is merely another spelling of Baton.

Battalion. (F. — Ital.) See Batter (1).

Batten (1), to grow fat, fatten. (Scand.) See Better.

Batten (2); see under Baton.

Batter (1), to beat. (F. — L.) M. E. *batren.* — F. *battre.* — L. *batere,* popular form of *batuere,* to beat.

abate. (F. — L.) M. E. *abaten.* — O. F. *abatre.* — Low L. *abbattere,* to beat from or down. — L. *ab,* from; and *batere,* for *batuere,* to beat. ¶ Hence *bate,* to beat down; by loss of *a.*

battalion. (F. — Ital. — L.) F. *bataillon,* — Ital. *battaglione,* a battalion. — Ital. *battaglia,* a battle; see **battle** below.

batter (2), a compound of eggs, flour, and milk. (F. — L.) M. E. *batour.* — O. F. *bature,* a beating. — F. *battre,* to beat (above). So called because beaten up.

battery. (F. — L.) F. *baterie, batterie,* 'beating, battery;' Cot. — F. *battre,* to beat.

battle. (F. — L.) M. E. *bataille, bataile.* — O. F. *bataille,* (1) a fight, (2) a battalion. Low L. *batalia,* a fight. — L. *batere,* for *batuere,* to beat.

battledoor. (Prov. — L.) M. E. *batyldoure,* Prompt. Parv. — Prov. *batedor,* Span. *batidor,* a washing-beetle, which was also at first the sense of the E. word. [The corruption to *battledoor* was due to confusion with *battle,* a small bat.] — Prov. *batre,* Span. *batir,* the same as F. *battre,* to beat; with suffix *-dor,* which in Prov. and Span. = L. suffix *-torem,* acc. form from nom. *-tor,* expressing the agent.

combat. (F. — L.) Orig. a verb. — F. *combattre,* O. F. *combatre,* to fight with. — F. *com-* (= L. *com-*), with; and F. *battre,* O. F. *batre,* to fight. Der. *combat-ant* (F. pres. pt.).

debate. (F. — L.) M. E. *debaten.* — O. F. *debatre,* to debate, argue. — L. *de,* down; *batere,* to beat (above).

rebate, to blunt a sword's edge. (F. — L.) O. F. *rebatre,* to beat back again. — F. *re-* (L. *re-*), back; O. F. *batre,* F. *battre,* to beat; see Batter (1) above.

Battlement. (F.) M. E. *batlement, batilment.* No doubt equivalent to an O. F. *bastillement*, from O. F. *bastiller,* to fortify, derivative of O. F. *bastir,* to build. See Bastile.

embattle (1), to furnish with battlements. (F.) M. E. *embattelen.* — O. F. *em-* (= L. *im-*, for *in-*, prefix); and O. F. *bastiller,* to fortify; as above.

Bauble (1), a fool's mace. (C.?; *with* E. *suffix.*) Different from *bauble* (2). M. E. *babyll, bable, babel* (Gower, C. A. i. 224). Named from its swinging motion; cf. M. E. *bablen,* to swing about, as if for mod. E. *bobble*, to keep bobbing, frequent. of *bob*; see Bob.

Bauble (2), a plaything. (F. — Ital.) Corr. from F. *babiole,* a child's toy. — Ital. *babbola,* a toy. — Ital. *babbeo,* a simpleton; cf. Low L. *babulus,* a simpleton. From the uttering of indistinct sounds; cf. Gk. βαβάζειν, to chatter; see **Babble, Barbarous.**

¶ The corruption of F. *babiole* was due to confusion with **Bauble** (1).

Bawd, a lewd person. (F. — G.) See **Bold.**

Bawl. (Scand.) Icel. *baula,* to low as a cow; Swed. *bôla,* to roar; see **Bull, Bellow.**

Bay (1), reddish brown. (F. — L.) M. E. *bay.* — O. F. *bai.* — L. *badius,* bay-coloured.

baize, coarse woollen stuff. (F. — L.) An error for *bayes,* pl. of F. *baye,* 'the cloth called bayes;' Cot. — O. F. *bai,* bay-coloured; as above. From the orig. colour. Cf. Span. *bayo,* bay, *bayeta,* baize; &c.

bayard. (F. — L.) A bay horse; from the colour. The suffix -*ard* is Teutonic.

Bay (2), a kind of laurel; properly, a berry-tree. (F. — L.) M. E. *bay,* a berry. — F. *baie,* a berry. — L. *bucca,* a berry.

Bay (3), inlet of the sea. (F. — L.) F. *baie,* an inlet; O. F. *baee,* a gap. — Low L. *badata,* fem. of pp. of *badare,* to gape.

bay-window, a window in a recess. The word *bay,* opening, came to mean any recess, esp. in a building.

Bay (4), to bark as a dog. (F. — L.) For *abay.* M. E. *abayen.* — O. F. *abbayer;* Cot. — L. *ad,* at; and *baubari,* to yelp. Cf. *bubo,* an owl.

bay (5), in phr. *at bay.* (F. — L.) For *abay.* — F. *abois, abbois; être aux abois,* to be at bay, lit. 'to be at the baying of the dogs.' Pl. of F. *aboi,* the bark of a dog; verbal sb. from F. *aboyer,* O. F. *abbayer,* to yelp, bay.

Bay-window; from **Bay** (3) and **Window.**

Bayonet. (F.) XVII cent. F. *baïonnette; bayonette,* a knife; Cot. Named from *Bayonne* (France), where first made.

Bazaar. (Pers.) Pers. *bâzâr,* a market.

Bdellium. (Heb.) A precious substance. — Heb. *bedôlakh,* bdellium.

Be-, prefix. (E.) A. S. *be-,* prefix; often causative, as in *be-numb,* to make numb. Note also *be-head,* to deprive of the head; *be-set,* to set upon, set round; *be-mire,* to cover with mire; &c.

Be, to exist. (E.) M. E. *been.* A. S. *beón,* to be. + W. *bod,* to be; Russ. *buite;* L. *fore* (pt. t. *fui*); Gk. φύειν; Skt. *bhu.* (√BHU.)

Beach. (Scand. ?) XVI cent. Perhaps from Swed. *backe,* a hill, slope, O. Swed. *backe,* the bank of a river; Dan. *bakke;* Icel. *bakki,* a ridge, bank of a river. Allied to **Bank.**

Beacon. (E.) M. E. *beken.* A. S. *bedcen.*

beck (1), to nod. (F. — C.) F. *becquer,* to bob; Cot. — F. *bec,* beak. See **Peak.** (Misplaced; unless it be used for *beckon.*)

beckon. (E.) M. E. *becnen.* A. S. *bécnan, bedcnian,* to make a sign. — A. S. *bécn, bedcen,* a beacon, token, sign.

Bead. (E.) See **Bid** (1).

Beadle. (F. — O. H. G.) See **Bid** (2.)

Beagle, a dog. (Unknown.) M. E. *begle,* Squire of Low Degree, l. 771.

Beak. (F. — C.) See **Peak.**

Beaker. (O. Low G. — L. — Gk.) M. E. *biker, byker.* — O. Sax. *bikeri;* Icel. *bikarr,* a cup. + Du. *beker;* G. *becher;* Ital. *bicchiere.* β. From Low L. *bicarium,* a wine-cup. — Gk. βῖκος, an earthen wine-vessel; a word of Eastern origin.

pitcher. (F. — O. H. G. — L. — Gk.) The same word. F. *pichier,* 'a pitcher; a Languedoc word;' Cot. — O. H. G. *pechári* (G. *becher*). — Low L. *bicarium;* as above.

Beam (1), a piece of timber. (E.) M. E. *beem.* A. S. *beám,* a tree. + Du. *boom;* G. *baum;* Goth. *bagms.*

beam (2), a ray. (E.) The same word specially used to signify a straight ray. A. S. *byrnende beám,* 'the pillar of fire.'

boom (2), a beam, pole. (Du.) Du. *boom,* a tree, a beam; see **Beam** (1).

bumpkin, a thick-headed fellow. (Du.) — O. Du. *boomken,* a little tree (Hexham); dimin. of *boom,* a tree, a beam, bar. The E. *bumkin* also meant a luff-block, a thick piece of wood (Cotgrave, s. v. *Chicambault*); hence readily applied to a block-head, thick-skulled fellow.

Bean. (E.) M. E. *bene.* A. S. *beán.* + Icel. *baun;* O. H. G. *póna;* W. *ffaen.*

Bear (1), to carry. (E.) M. E. *beren.* A. S. *beran.* + Goth. *bairan;* L. *ferre;* Gk. φέρειν; Skt. *bhri.* (√BHAR.) Der. *up-bear.*

bairn, a child. (E.) M. E. *barn.* A. S. *bearn.* + Icel., Swed., Dan., and Goth. *barn;* Skt. *bhazrna.* Lit. 'that which is born.'

barm, the lap. (E.) M. E. *barm.* A. S. *bearm,* lap, bosom. — A. S. *beran,* to bear.

barrow (2), a wheel-barrow. (E.) M. E. *barowe.* — A. S. *beran,* to bear, carry.

berth, a secure position. (E.) It appears to be the same word as *birth.* Cf. M. E. *birð, berð, burð,* a birth, race, nation, rank, place, station.

bier, a frame on which a corpse is borne. (E.) M. E. *beere, bære.* A. S. *bǽr.* — A. S.

beran, to carry.+Icel. *barar*; L. *feretrum*; Gk. φέρετρον. And see **Brother**.

birth. (E.) M. E. *birð*, *birthe*. A. S. *beorð*; also *gebyrd*, birth.━A. S. *beran*, to bear. Cf. Icel. *burðr*, G. *geburt*.

burden (1), **burthen**, a load carried. (E.) A. S. *byrðen*, a load.━A. S. *bor-en*, pp. of *beran*, to bear.+Icel. *byrðr*, *byrði*; Swed. *börda*; Dan. *byrde*; Goth. *baurthei*; G. *bürde*; Gk. φόρτος.

forbear. (E.) A. S. *forberan*; for the prefix *for-*, see **For-** (2).

overbearing. (E.) Lit. bearing over.

Bear (2), an animal. (E.) M. E. *bere*. A. S. *bera*.+Icel. *bera*, *björn*; O. H. G. *pero*; Skt. *bhalla*.

Beard. (E.) M. E. *berd.* A. S. *beard*. + Du. *baard*; Icel. *barð*, a brim, verge, beak of a ship; Russ. *borodá*; W. *barf*; L. *barba*.

barbed, accoutred; said of horses. (F. ━Scand.) Also *barded*, the better form. ━F. *bardé*, 'barbed as a horse;' Cot.━F. *barde*, horse-armour.━Icel. *barð*, a brim (lit. beard); also a beak or armed prow of a war-ship; whence it was applied to horses. Thus *barbed* is a sort of F. translation of *barded*. See **Barb** (1).

Beast. (F. ━ L.) M. E. *beste.* ━ O. F. *beste* (F. *bête*.)━L. *bestia*, a beast.

bestial. (F.━L.) F. *bestial.*━L. *bestialis*, beast-like.━L. *bestia*.

Beat. (E.) M. E. *beten.* A. S. *beátan.* +Icel. *bauta*; O. H. G. *pózan*, M. H. G. *bózen*. (Teut. √ BUT, to beat.)

abut, to project towards. (F.━G.) In Shak. ━ O. F. *aboter*, *abouter*, to thrust against. ━ F. *a* (= L. *ad*), to; M. H. G. *bózen*, to beat; see butt (1) below.

beetle, a heavy mallet. (E.) M. E. *betel.* A. S. *býtel*, a mallet, beater.━A. S. *beátan*, to beat.

boss, a knob. (F.━O. H. G.) M. E. *bosse*, knob of a buckler.━F. *bosse*, a hump, bump.━O. H. G. *pózan*, to beat; a bump being the effect of a blow.

botch (1), to patch. (O. Low G.) M. E. *bocchen*.━Du. *botsen*, to strike; O. Du. *butsen*, to strike, repair. From the notion of repairing roughly by hammering. Du. *bot-sen* is from the same root as A. S. *beát-an*.

botch (2), a swelling. (F. ━ O. H. G.) M. E. *bocche*.━O. F. *boce*, a boss, botch, boil; F. *bosse*. See **boss** above.

bottle (2), a bundle of hay. (F. ━ O. H. G.) M. E. *botel.*━O. F. *botel*, *botelle*, a small bundle; dimin. of *botte*, a bundle of hay. ━ O. H. G. *pózo*, *bózo*, a bundle of flax; allied to O. H. G. *pózan*, to beat; from the beating of flax.

butt (1), an end, thrust; to thrust. (F. ━O. H. G.) [The senses of the sb. may be referred to the verb; just as F. *bout*, an end, butt-end, depends on *bouter*, to strike.] M. E. *butten*, to push, strike.━O. F. *boter*, to push, butt, strike. ━ M. H. G. *bózen*, O. H. G. *pózan*, to beat. Der. *butt-end*, from O. F. *bot*, F. *bout*, an end (see button below); *butt* (to shoot at), from F. *butte*, the same, allied to F. *but*, a mark, *buter*, to hit. Der. *a-but* (above).

buttock. (F.; *with* E. *suffix*.) M. E. *botok*, *bottok*.━O. F. *bot* (F. *bout*), an end (cf. E. *butt-end*); with dimin. suffix *-ock*; see below.

button. (F. ━ O. H. G.) M. E. *boton*, also, a bud. ━ O. F. *boton* (F. *bouton*), a bud, a button; properly, a round knob pushed out. ━ O. F. *boter*, to push, push out; see butt (1).

debut. (F.━L. *and* O. H. G.) A first appearance in a play. ━ F. *début*, a first stroke, first cast or throw at dice. The orig. sense seems to have been 'a bad aim,' or 'a miss;' it is allied to O. F. *desbuter*, 'to repell, to put from the mark aimed at,' Cot.━L. *dis-*, apart; and F. *but*, a mark; see butt (1) above.

rabbet, to cut the edges of boards so that they overlap and can be joined. (F. ━L. *and* G.) F. *raboter*, to plain, level, or lay even; cf. *rabot*, a joiner's plane, a plasterer's beater. ━ F. *re-*, again; O. F. *aboter*, later *abouter*, to thrust against (E. *abut*.)━L. *re-*, again; *ad*, to; and M. H. G. *bózen*, to beat. See abut, and butt (1) above.

rebut. (F. ━ L. *and* M. H. G.) O. F. *rebouter*, to repulse.━L. *re-*, again; M. H. G. *bózen*, to beat; see Beat (above).

Beatify. (F. ━ L.) F. *béatifier.* ━ L. *beatificare*; to make happy.━L. *beati-*, for *beatus*, pp. of *beare*, to bless, make happy; and *-fic-*, for *facere*, to make. Allied to L. *bene*, well.

beatitude. (F.━L.) F. *béatitude.*━L. *beatitudinem*, acc. from nom. *beatitudo*, blessedness.━L. *beati-*, for *beatus*, blessed; with suffix *-tudo*.

Beau, Beauty. (F.━L.) See **Belle**.

Beaver, (1), an animal. (E.) M. E. *bever*. A. S. *befer*.+Du. *bever*; Icel. *björr*; Dan. *bæver*; Swed. *bäfver*; G. *biber*; Russ.

bobr'; L. *fiber*. Cf. Skt. *babhru*, a large ichneumon.

Beaver (2), **Bever**, lower part of a helmet. (F.) So spelt, by confusion with *beaver-hat*. — F. *bavière*, a child's bib; also, the bever (beaver) of a helmet. — F. *baver*, to slaver. — F. *bave*, foam, slaver. Perhaps Celtic; cf. Bret. *babouz*, slaver.

Becalm, to make calm. See **Be-** and **Calm**.

Because. (E. *and* F. — L.) See **Cause**.

Bechance. (E. *and* F. — L.) See **Chance**, under **Cadence**.

Beck (1), a nod, Beckon; see **Beacon**.

Beck (2), a stream. (Scand.) M. E. *bek*. — Icel. *bekkr*; Swed. *bäck*; Dan. *bæk*; a stream. + Du. *beek*; G. *bach*.

Become. (E.) See **Come**.

Bed. (E.) M. E. *bed*. A. S. *bed*, *bedd*. + Icel. *beðr*; Goth. *badi*; G. *bett*.

bedridden. (E.) M. E. *bedreden*, used in the pl. (P. Pl. B. viii. 85); *bedrede*, sing. (Ch. C. T. 7351.) Corrupted from A. S. *bedrída*, lit. 'a bed-rider;' one who can only ride on a bed, not on a horse. — A. S. *bed*, a bed; and *ríd-a**, one who rides, from *rídan*, to ride.

bedstead. (E.) M. E. *bedstede*. — A. S. *bed*, a bed; and *stede*, a place, station; see **Stead**.

Bedabble, Bedaub, Bedazzle, Bedew, Bedim, Bedizen. See **Dabble, Daub**, &c.

Bedlam. (Palestine.) M. E. *bedlem*, corruption of Bethlehem, in Palestine. Now applied to the hospital of St. Mary of Bethlehem, for lunatics.

Bedouin. (F. — Arab.) F. *bédouin*, a wandering Arab. — Arab. *badawíy*, wild, wandering in the desert. — Arab. *badw*, departing to the desert, leading a wandering life.

Bedridden, Bedstead; see **Bed**.

Bee. (E.) M. E. *bee*. A. S. *beo*, *bí*. + Icel. *bý*; O. H. G. *pía*; Skt. *bha* (rare). Cf. Irish *beach*, a bee.

Beech. (E.) See **Book**.

Beef. (F. — L.) M. E. *beef*. — O. F. *boef*; F. *bœuf*. — L. *bouem*, acc. of *bos*, an ox. + Gael. *bò*, Skt. *go*, A. S. *cú*, a cow; see **Cow**.

beef-eater, a yeoman of the guard. (Hyb.) Lit. 'an eater of beef.' ¶ The usual derivation (from Mr. Steevens' imaginary *beaufetier*, now misspelt *buffetier*), is all sheer invention, and false.

· **bugle** (1), a wild ox; a horn. (F. — L.)

Bugle, a horn, is short for *bugle-horn*; a *bugle* is a wild ox. — O. F. *bugle*, a wild ox. — L. acc. *buculum*, a young ox; double dimin. of *bos*, an ox.

Beer. (E.) M. E. *bere*. A. S. *beór*. + Du. and G. *bier*; Icel. *bjórr*. Probably connected with **Brew**.

Beestings; see **Biestings**.

Beet. (L.) M. E. *bete*. A. S. *bete*. — L. *beta*, beet (Pliny.)

Beetle (1), an insect; see **Bite**.

Beetle (2), a mallet; see **Beat**.

Beetle (3), to jut out, hang over; see **Bite**.

Befall, Befool, Before; see **Fall**, &c.

Beg. (E.) See **Bid** (1).

Beget, Begin; see **Get, Gin** (1).

Begone, Beguile; see **Go, Wile**.

Beguine, one of a class of religious devotees. (F.) Chiefly used in the fem.; F. *béguine*, Low L. *beghina*, one of a religious order, first established at Liége, about A.D. 1207. Named after Lambert Le Bègue, priest of Liége (12th c.). Le Bègue means 'stammerer,' from the verb *béguī*, to stammer, in the dialect of Namur.

Behalf, interest. (E.) See **Half**.

Behave, Behaviour. (E.) See **Have**.

Behead. (E.) See **Head**.

Behemoth. (Heb. — Egypt.) Heb. *behemóth*, said to be pl. of *behemáh*, a beast; but really of Egypt. origin.

Behest, Behind, Behold. (E.) See **Hest, Hind, Hold** (1).

Behoof, advantage. (E.) M. E. *to bihoue*, for the advantage of. A. S. *behóf*, advantage. + O. Fries. *behóf*, Du. *behoef*, advantage; G. *behuf*; Swed. *behof*; Dan. *behov*, need. β. The prefix *be* is A. S. *be*, E. *by*. The simple sb. appears in Icel. *hóf*, moderation, measure; cf. Goth. *gahobains*, temperance, self-restraint. From √KAP, to contain, whence the ideas of moderation, fitness, advantage.

behove, to befit. (E.) A. S. *behófian*, verb formed from the sb. *behóf* above. + Du. *behoeven*, from sb. *behoef*; Swed. *behöfva*; Dan. *behove*.

Belabour, Belay; see **Labour, Lie** (1).

Belch. (E.) M. E. *belken*. A. S. *bealcan*, to belch. Allied to **Bellow**.

Beldam. (F. — L.) See **Belle**.

Beleaguer. (Du.) See **Lie** (1).

Belemnite, a fossil. (Gk.) Gk. βελεμνίτης, a stone shaped like the head of a dart. — Gk. βέλεμνον, a dart. — Gk. βάλλειν, to cast. (√GAR.)

Belfry. (F. – G.) Orig. 'a watch-tower.' Corrupted (partly by influence of *bell*) from M. E. *berfray*, *berfrey*, a watch-tower. – O. F. *berfroit*, *berfreit*, *belefreit*. – M. H. G. *berefrit*, a watch-tower. – M. H. G. *berc-*, for *berg-*, base of *bergen*, to protect; and M. H. G. *frit*, *frid*, a place of security, a tower, the same as G. *friede*, peace; hence the lit. sense is 'a guard-peace,' watch-tower. Allied to Borough and Free.

Belie, Believe. (E.) See Lie (2), Lief.

Bell. (E.) See Bellow.

Belle, a fair lady. (F. – L.) F. *belle*, fem. of F. *beau*, O. F. *bel*, fair. – L. *bellus*, fair, fine; perhaps contr. from *benulus*, dimin. of *benus*, another form of *bonus*, good.

beau, a dressy man. (F.) F. *beau*, fine; as above.

beauty. (F. – L.) M. E. *beaute*. – F. *beauté*, O. F. *beltet*. – Low L. *bellitatem*, acc. of *bellitas*, fairness. – L. *bellus*, fair.

beldam. (F. – L.) Ironically for *beldame*, i. e. fine lady. – F. *belle dame*. – L. *bella*, fem. of *bellus*; and *domina*, lady, fem. of *dominus*, lord.

belladonna. (Ital. – L.) Ital. *bella donna*, fair lady. – L. *bella domina*; as above. A name given to the nightshade, from the use of it by ladies to give expression to the eyes, the pupils of which it expands.

embellish. (F. – L.) M. E. *embelissen*. – O. F. *embeliss-*, stem of pres. pt. of *embellir*, to beautify. – O. F. *em-* (= L. *in*); and *bel*, fair (above).

Belligerent. (L.) See Dual.

Bellow, to make a loud noise. (E.) Extended from M. E. *bellen*, the more usual old form. A. S. *bellan*, to make a loud noise. (√ BHAL.) Cf. Icel. *belja*, to bellow.

bell. (E.) M. E. *belle*. A. S. *belle*, that which makes a loud noise, a bell. – A. S. *bellan*; as above. And see Bull (1).

Bellows, Belly. (E.) See Bag.

Belong, Beloved, Below; see Long, Love, Low.

Belt, a girdle. (E.) M. E. *belt*. A. S. *belt*. **+** Icel. *belti*; Irish and Gael. *balt*, a belt, border; L. *balteus*; O. H. G. *balz*.

baldric, a girdle. (F. – O. H. G.) O. F. *baldric** (not recorded), the older form of O. F. *baldret*, *baldrei*; Low L. *baldringus*. – O. H. G. *balderich*, a girdle; extended from O. H. G. *balz*, a belt.

Bemoan. (E.) See Moan.

Bench. (E.) See Bank.

Bend. (E.) See Bind.

Beneath. (E.) See Nether.

Benediction. (F. – L.) F. *bénédiction*. – L. *benedictionem*, acc. of *benedictio*, a blessing. – L. *benedictus*, pp. of *benedicere*, to speak well, bless. – L. *bene*, well; and *dicere*, to speak (see Diction.)

benison. (F. – L.) M. E. *beneysun*. – O. F. *beneison*. – L. acc. *benedictionem*.

Benefactor. (L.) L. *benefactor*, a doer of good. – L. *bene*, well; and *factor*, a doer, from *facere*, to do.

benefice. (F. – L.) M. E. *benefice*. – F. *bénéfice* (Cot.) – Low L. *beneficium*, a grant of an estate; L. *beneficium*, a well-doing, a kindness. – L. *bene*, well; and *facere*, to do.

benefit. (F. – L.) Modified (badly) from M. E. *bienfet*. – O. F. *bienfet* (F. *bienfait*). – L. *benefactum*, a kindness conferred; neut. of pp. of *benefacere*, to do well, be kind.

Benevolence. (F. – L.) F. *bénévolence* (Cot.) – L. *beneuolentia*, kindness. – L. *beneuolus*, *beniuolus*, kind, lit. well-wishing. – L. *beni-*, for *benus* = *bonus*, good; and *uolo*, I wish (see Voluntary).

Benighted. (E.) See Night.

Benign. (F. – L.) O. F. *benigne* (F. *bénin*). – L. *benignus*, kind; short for *benigenus**. – L. *beni-*, for *benus* = *bonus*, good; and *-genus*, born (as in *indigenus*), from *genere**, old form of *gignere*, to beget.

Benison, blessing; see Benediction.

Bent-grass. (E.) M. E. *bent*. A. S. *beonet*, bent-grass (uncertain.) **+** O. H. G. *pinuz*, G. *binse*, bent-grass.

Benumb, Bequeath; see Nimble, Quoth.

Bequest, Bereave; see Quoth, Reave.

Bergamot, a kind of pear. (F. – Ital.) F. *bergamotte*; Cot. – Ital. *bergamotto*, a pear; also, the essence called bergamot. – Ital. *Bergamo*, a town in Lombardy.

Berry. (E.) M. E. *berie*. A. S. *berige*, *berga* (stem *bes-*). **+** Du. *bes*, *bezie*; Icel. *ber*; Swed. and Dan. *bär*; G. *beere*; Goth. *basi*. Lit. 'edible fruit;' cf. Skt. *bhas*, to eat. **Der.** *goose-berry*, &c.

Berth. (E.) See Bear. (1).

Beryl. (L. – Gk. – Skt.) M. E. *beril*. – L. *beryllus*. – Gk. βήρυλλος; cf. Arab. *billaur*, crystal, beryl. – Skt. *vaidûrya*, orig. lapis lazuli, brought from Vidûra.

brilliant, shining. (F. – L. – Gk. – Skt.) F. *brillant*, pres. part. of *briller*, to glitter; cf. Ital. *brillare*, to sparkle. The orig. sense was to sparkle as a beryl. – L. *beryllus*, a beryl; whence also Low L. *berillus*, an eye-glass, G. *brille*, spectacles.

Beseech, Beseem, Beset, Beshrew, Beside, Besiege; see **Seek, Seem, Sit, Shrew, &c.**

Besom, a broom. (E.) M. E. *besum, besme.* A.S. *besma.*+Du. *bezem*; G. *besen.*

Besot, Bespeak; see **Sot, Speak.**

Best; see **Better.**

Bestead; see **Stead.**

Bestial. (F.–L.) See **Beast.**

Bestow, Bestrew, Bestride; see **Stow, &c.**

Bet, to wager. (F. – Scand.) Short for *abet*, in the sense to maintain, or 'back,' as *abet* is explained in Phillips, ed. 1706. See **Bite.** Der. *bet*, sb.

Betake. (E. *and* Scand.) See **Take.**

Betel, a species of pepper. (Port. – Malayalim.) Port. *betel, betele.* – Malayalim *vettila*, i. e. *veru ila*, mere leaf (Yule).

Bethink, Betide, Betimes, Betoken; see **Think, &c.**

Betray. (E. *and* F. – L.) See **Traitor.**

Betroth. (E.) See **True.**

Better, Best. (E.) 1. From the base BAT, good, was formed Goth. *batiza*, better, A.S. *betera*, M.E. *better.* The A.S. *bet*, M. E. *bet*, is adverbial and comparative. 2. From the same base was formed Goth. *batista*, best, A.S. *betst* (for *bet-est*), M.E. *best.* Similarly Du. *beter, best*; Icel. *betri, bextr*; Dan. *bedre, hedst*; Swed. *bättre, bäst*, G. *besser, best.* Cf. Skt. *bhadra*, excellent; Skt. *bhand*, to be fortunate, make fortunate.

batten (1), to grow fat, fatten. (Scand.) Properly intransitive. – Icel. *batna*, to grow better, recover; cf. *bæta*, trans. to improve. From the base BAT, good. Cf. Goth. *gabatnan*, to profit, avail.

boot (2), advantage, profit. (E.) M.E. *bote, boote.* A.S. *bót*, profit. From the same base. – Icel. *bót*, *bati*, advantage, cure; Dan. *bod*, Swed. *bot*, remedy, G. *busse*, atonement. Der. *boot-less*, profitless.

Between, Betwixt; see **Two.**

Bevel, sloping; to slope, slant. (F.) In Sh. Sonn. 121. – O. F. *bivel*, buvel**, only found in mod. F. *biveau*, and in F. *buveau*, 'a kind of squire [carpenter's rule], having moveable and compasse branches, or the one branch compasse and the other straight; some call it a *bevell*;' Cot. Span. *baivel.* Origin unknown.

Beverage, Bevy; see **Bib.**

Bewail, Beware, Bewilder, Bewitch; see **Wail, Wary, Wild, Witch.**

Bewray, to disclose. (E.) Properly to accuse. M. E. *bewraien, biwreyen*, to dis-

close. A.S. *be-*, prefix (see **Be-**); and *wrégan*, to accuse. Cf. Icel. *rægja* (for *vrægja*), to slander, Swed. *röja*, to discover; O. Fries. *biwrogia*, to accuse; Goth. *wróhjan*, to accuse; G. *rügen*, to censure. β. These are causal verbs, from the sb. seen in Goth. *wrohs*, accusation, Icel. *róg*, a slander.

Bey, a governor. (Turk.) Turk. *bég* (pron. nearly as *bay*), a lord, prince.

Beyond. (E.) See **Yon.**

Bezel, the part of a ring in which the stone is set. (F.) Also spelt *basil*; it also means a sloping edge. – O. F. *bisel*, mod. F. *biseau*, a bezel, basil, slant, sloped edge. Cf. Span. *bisel*, the slanting edge of a looking-glass; Low L. *bisalus*, 'lapis cui duo sunt anguli;' Ducange. (Perhaps from L. *bis*, double; and *ala*, a wing?)

Bezoar, a stone. (F. – Port. – Pers.) O. F. *bezoar*, F. *bézoard.* – Port. *bezoar* (Brachet). – Pers. *pád-zahr*, bezoar; lit. 'poison-expeller,' from its supposed virtue. – Pers. *pád*, expelling; and *zahr*, poison.

Bi-, prefix. (L.) In *bi-as*, the prefix is F., but of L. origin. – L. *bi-*, put for *dui-*, twice. – L. *duo,* two. So also Gk. δι-, Skt. *dvi.* See **Two.**

Bias. (F. – L.) F. *biais*, a slant, slope; hence, inclination to one side. – Low L. *acc. bifacem*, from *bifax*, one who squints or looks sideways (Isidore). – L. *bi-*, double; and *facies*, a face.

Bib. (L.) A cloth for imbibing moisture, from M. E. *bibben*, to drink. – L. *bibere*, to drink. Hence *wine-bibber* (Luke, vii. 34); L. *bibens uinum.*

beverage. (F. – L.) O. F. *bovraige, beuraige.* – O. F. *bevre, boivre*, to drink. – L. *bibere* (above).

bevy. (F. – L.) F. *bevée*, a flock, company. Prob. from O. F. *bevre*, to drink (above). Cf. O. Ital. *beva*, a bevy.

imbibe, to drink in. (F. – L.; *or* L.) F. *imbiber* (16th cent.) – L. *imbibere*, to drink in.

imbrue, embrew, to moisten, drench. (F. – L.) O. F. *embruer*; *s'embruer*, 'to imbrue or bedable himself with;' Cot. – F. *em-* (L. *in*, in); and a causal verb *-bevrer*, to give to drink, turned into *-brever* in the 16th cent., and then into *-bruer*; see F. *abreuver* in Brachet. – O. F. *bevre* (F. *boire*), to drink. – L. *bibere.*

imbue, to cause to drink in, tinge deeply. (L.) L. *im-buere*, to cause to drink in; where *-buere* is a causal form, allied to *bibere*, to drink.

Bible. (F. – L. – Gk.) M. E. *bible.* – F. *bible.* – L. *biblia.* – Gk. βιβλία, collection of writings, pl. of βιβλίον, little book, dimin. of βίβλος, a book. – Gk. βύβλος, Egyptian papyrus; hence, a book.

bibliography. (Gk.) Gk. βιβλίο-, for βιβλίον; and γράφειν, to write.

bibliomania. (Gk.) Gk. βιβλίο-, for βιβλίον; and **Mania.**

Bice. (F.) Properly 'grayish;' hence, grayish blue. – F. *bise,* fem. of *bis,* dusky. Cf. Ital. *bigio,* gray. Origin unknown.

Bicker, to skirmish. (C.) See **Peak.**

Bid (1), to pray. (E.) Nearly obsolete; preserved in *bidding-prayer,* and in to *bid beads* (pray prayers). M. E. *bidden.* A.S. *biddan.* + Du. *bidden*; G. *bitten*; Goth. *bidjan.*

bead. (E.) Orig. 'a prayer;' hence a perforated ball, for counting prayers. M. E. *bede,* a prayer, a bead. A.S. *bed, gebed,* a prayer. – A.S. *biddan,* to pray. + G. *gebet*; Du. *bede, gebed.*

beg. (E.) Frequentative of *bid.* M. E. *beggen.* A.S. *bedecian,* to beg; frequent. of *biddan,* to pray. Cf. Goth. *bidagwa,* a beggar; G. *bettler,* a beggar, from *bitten.*

Bid (2), to command. (E.) M. E. *beden.* – A.S. *beodan,* to command. + G. *bieten*; Goth. *ana-biudan*; Skt. *bodhaya,* to inform, causal of *budh,* to awake, understand. (√BHUDH.) Confused with **Bid** (1).

beadle. (F. – Teut.) M. E. *bedel.* – O. F. *bedel,* F. *bedeau,* a beadle; lit. 'proclaimer,' or 'messenger.' – G. *bieten,* Du. *bieden*; cognate with A.S. *beódan,* to bid. Cf. A.S. *bydel,* a beadle, from *beódan.*

bode, to foreshew. (E.) M.E. *boden, bodian.* – A.S. *bodian,* to announce. – A.S. *boda,* a messenger; *bod,* a message. Cf. Icel. *boða,* to announce; *boð,* a bid, offer.

Bide, to await, wait. (E.) M.E. *biden.* A.S. *bídan.* + Du. *beiden*; Icel. *bíða*; Swed. *bida*; Dan. *bie*; Goth. *beidan*; O.H.G. *pítan.*

abide. (E.) A.S. *ábídan.* The prefix *á* = G. *er-*; see **A-** (4).

abode. (E.) M.E. *abood,* delay, abiding. – A.S. *á-,* prefix; and *bád,* pt. t. of *bídan,* to bide.

Biennial. (L.) See **Annals.**

Bier. (E.) See **Bear** (1).

Biestings, Beestings, the first milk given by a cow after calving. (E.) A.S. *býsting, býst, beóst,* thick milk. + Du. *biest*; G. *biest-milch.*

Bifurcated. (L.) See **Fork.**

Big. (Scand.?) M.E. *big*; also *bigg,* rich (Hampole). Not A.S. Perhaps for *bilg,* the *l* being dropped, as in *bag.* Cf. Icel. *belgja,* to inflate, puff out; Norw. *belga,* to fill one's maw, cram oneself; Swed. dial. *bälgig, bulgig,* big. Prob. related to *bag* and *bulk.* β. Or is it related to Irish *baghach,* Gael. *bagach,* corpulent, bulky, Skt. *bahu,* large?

Bigamy, a double marriage. (F. – L. and Gk.) F. *bigamie.* – Late L. *bigamia*; a clumsy compound from L. *bi-,* double (see **Bi-**), and Gk. -γαμία, from γάμος, marriage. It should rather have been *digamy* (Gk. διγαμία.)

cryptogamia, a class of flowers in which fructification is concealed. (Gk.) Coined from Gk. κρυπτο-, for κρυπτός, hidden (see **Crypt**); and γαμ-εῖν, to marry, from γάμος.

monogamy, marriage with one wife only. (L. – Gk.) L. *monogamia.* – Gk. μονογαμία. – Gk. μονόγαμος, marrying but once. – Gk. μονο-, for μονός, sole (see **Mono-**), and -γαμία, from γάμος.

polygamy, marriage with many wives. (Gk.) Gk. πολυγαμία. – Gk. πολύγαμος, marrying many (see **Poly-**).

Bight, a coil of rope, a bay. (E.) See **Bow** (1).

Bigot, an obstinate devotee to a creed. (F. – Teut.?) F. *bigot,* 'an old Norman word signifying for God's sake, an hypocrite, superstitious fellow;' Cot. Applied by the French to the Normans as a term of reproach (Wace). The supposition that it stands for O.H.G. *bî got* (by God) is, after all, not improbable. It is an older word than *beguine,* with which it seems to have been somewhat confused at a later period.

Bijou, a trinket. (F.) F. *bijou.* Origin unknown.

Bilberry, a whortle-berry. (Scand.) Dan. *böllebær,* a bilberry; prob. a ball-berry, from Icel. *böllr,* a ball, and Dan. *bær,* a berry; see **Ball.** ¶ North Eng. *blea-berry* = *blue-berry*; see **Blue.** In both cases, *-berry* takes the E. form; see **Berry.**

Bilbo, a sword; **Bilboes,** fetters. (Span.) Both named from Bilboa or Bilbao in Spain, famous for iron and steel.

Bile (1), secretion from the liver. (F. – L.) F. *bile.* – L. *bilis.* Der. *bili-ous.*

Bile (2), a boil. (E.) See **Bulge.**

Bilge. (Scand.) See **Bag.**

Bill (1), a chopper, sword, beak. (E.) M. E. *bil,* sword, axe; *bile,* bird's beak.

A. S. *bill*, sword, axe.+Du. *bijl*, Icel. *bíldr*, Dan. *biil*, Swed. *bila*, G. *bille*, an axe. Orig. 'a cutting instrument;' cf. Skt. *bil*, *bhil*, to break, *bhid*, to cleave.

Bill (2), a writing, account; see **Bull** (2).

Billet (1), a note; see **Bull** (2).

Billet (2), a log of wood. (F. – C.) F. *billette*, *billot*, a billet of wood. Dimin. of *bille*, a log, stump. – Bret. *pill*, a stump of a tree; Irish *bille oir*, trunk of a tree; W. *pill*, stem, stock, shaft.

billiards. (F. – C.) F. *billard*, 'a billard, or the stick wherewith we touch the ball at billyards;' Cot. Formed with suffix -*ard* (G. -*hart*) from *bille*, a log, stick, as above.

Billion; see **Million**.

Billow. (E.) See **Bag**.

Bin. (E.) M. E. *binne*. A. S. *binn*, a manger; Lu. ii. 7.+Du. *ben*, G. *benne*, a sort of basket. Perhaps allied to **Bent-grass**.

Binary, twofold. (L.) L. *binarius*, consisting of two things. – L. *binus*, two-fold. – L. *bi-*, double; see **Bi-**.

combine. (L.) L. *combinare*, to unite, join two things together. – L. *com-* (*cum*), together; and *binus*, twofold.

Bind. (E.) M. E. *binden*. A. S. *bindan*. + Du. and G. *binden*; Icel. and Swed. *binda*; Dan. *binde*; Goth. *bindan*; Skt. *bandh*, to bind. (√ BHADH, BHANDH.)

band (1), bond, a fastening. (E.) M. E. *bond*, *band*. – A. S. *bend* (for *bandi*). – A. S. *band*, pt. t. of *binden*.+Du., Icel., Swed., G. *band*; Goth. *bandi*; Skt. *bandha*. Der. *band-age*, *band-box*.

band (2), a company of men. (F. – G.) F. *bande*; Cot. – G. *bande*, a gang, set. – G. *band*, pt. t. of *binden*, to bind.

bandog, a large dog. (E.) Orig. *band-dog*, a dog that is tied up. See Prompt. Parv. p. 43.

bandy, to beat to and fro, contend. (F. – G.) Orig. to *band* (Turbervile). – F. *bander*, 'to bind; also, to bandie, at tennis;' Cot. *Se bander*, to league against. – G. *bande*, a band of men; see **band** (2) above.

bandy-legged, bow-legged. (F. and Scand.) *Bandy* is for F. *bandé*, pp. of *bander*, to bind, also to bend a bow (Cot.); see **bandy** above, and **bend**.

banner. (F. – G.) M. E. *banere*. – O.F. *baniere*; Low L. *banderia*. – M. H. G. *band*, a band, strip of cloth. Der. *banner-et*.

bend, to bow, curve. (E.) M. E. *benden*.

A. S. *bendan*, orig. to string a bow, fasten a band or string to it. – A. S. *bend*, a band, bond; see **band** (1) above.

bodice, stays. (E.) A corruption of *bodies*, which was the old spelling. (Cf. F. *corset*, from *corps*.)

body, the frame-work of an animal. (E.) M. E. *bodi*; A. S. *bodig*.+O. H. G. *potach*; Skt. *bandha*, (1) a bondage, fetter, (2) the body, considered as confining the soul. The orig. sense is 'little bond,' the suffix -*ig* (G. -*ach*) being a diminutive.

bond, a tie. (E.) M. E. *bond*, the same as M. E. *band*; see **band** (1) above.

bundle. (E.) M. E. *bundel*. Dimin. of A. S. *bund*, a bundle. – A. S. *bunden*, pp. of *binden*, to bind. + Du. *bondel*; G. *bündel*.

Bing, a heap of corn; *obs*. (Scand.) In Surrey. – Icel. *bingr*, Swed. *binge*, a heap. ¶ Prob. distinct from *bin*, though perhaps confused with it.

Binnacle, a box for a ship's compass; see **Habit**.

Binocular. (L.) See **Ocular**.

Binomial. (L.) See **Noble**.

Biography. (Gk.) A written account of a life; from βίο-, for βίος, life; and γράφειν, to write. The sb. βίος is allied to **Quick**.

amphibious. (Gk.) Gk. ἀμφίβιος, living a double life, both on land and water. – Gk. ἀμφί, on both sides; βίος, life.

biology. (Gk.) Science of life; from Gk. βίο-, for βίος, life; and -λογία, from λόγος, a discourse.

Biped. (L.) See **Pedal**.

Birch, a tree. (E.) M. E. *birche*. A. S. *beorc*.+Du. *berken-boom* (birch-tree); Swed. and Icel. *björk*; Dan. *birk* (whence North E. *birk*); G. *birke*; Skt. *bhúrja*.

Bird. (E.) M. E. *brid* (the *r* being shifted); A. S. *bridd*, a bird, esp. the young of birds. Perhaps allied to **Brood**.

Birth. (E.) See **Bear** (1).

Biscuit. (F. – L.) See **Cook**.

Bisect. (L.) See **Secant**.

Bishop. (L. – Gk.) See **Scope**.

Bismuth, a metal. (G.) G. *bismuth*; also spelt *wismut*, *wissmut*, *wissmuth*. Origin uncertain.

Bison, a quadruped. (L. – Gk. – Teut.) L. *bison* (Pliny). – Late Gk. βίσων. Not a true Gk. word, but borrowed from Teutonic; O. H. G. *wisunt*, G. *wisent*, a bison; A. S. *wesent*, a wild ox; Icel. *vísundr*.

Bissextile. (L.) See **Sexagenary**.

Bisson, purblind. (E.) In Sh. M. E. *bisen.* A. S. *bisen, bisene,* or *biséne,* blind (Matt. ix. 29). Perhaps from A. S. *bī-,* by, near; and *seón,* to see; cf. A. S. *ge-séne, ge-sýne,* conspicuous; also Du. *bijziend,* short-sighted, G. *beisichtig,* short-sighted.

Bistre, a dark brown. (F. – G.) F. *bistre,* a dark brown. Perhaps from prov. G. *biester,* dark, gloomy, also bistre (Flügel). Cf. Dan. and Swed. *bister,* grim, fierce.

Bit (1) and (2); see Bite.

Bitch. (E.) M. E. *biche, bicche.* A. S. *bicce.* + Icel. *bikkja.*

Bite. (E.) M. E. *biten.* A. S. *bītan.* + Du. *bijten*; Icel. *bíta*; Swed. *bita*; Dan. *bide*; G. *beissen*; L. *findere* (pt. t. *fīdi*), to cleave; Skt. *bhid,* to cleave. (√BHID.)

abet, to incite. (F. – Scand.) M. E. *abet,* sb., instigation. – O. F. *abet,* sb., instigation, deceit; *abeter,* to deceive. – F. *a-* (L. *ad-*); and *beter,* to bait (a bear), orig. to instigate, provoke, from Icel. *beita,* to make to bite; see **bait** below. Der. *bet,* q. v.

bait, to feed. (Scand.) Lit. 'to make to bite;' a *bait* is 'an enticement to bite.' M. E. *baiten, beiten.* – Icel. *beita,* to make to bite, causal of *bíta,* to bite; Swed. *beta,* to pasture; Swed. *bete,* Dan. *bed,* a bait.

beetle (1), an insect. (E.) M. E. *bityl.* A. S. *bītel, bétel, bītela,* lit. 'a biting one.' – A. S. *bīt-an,* to bite; with suffixes *-el* and *-a* (of the agent).

beetle (3), to project over. (E.) We talk of a *beetling* rock, an image suggested by the older term *beetle-browed,* M. E. *bitel-browed,* i. e. having projecting brows, lit. with brows projecting like an upper jaw. The M. E. *bitel* also means 'sharp.' A. S. *bītel,* sharp. – A. S. *bītan,* to bite.

bet, to wager. (F. – Scand.) Short for *abet,* in the sense to maintain or 'back;' see **abet** above. Der. *bet,* sb.

bit (1), a mouthful, small piece. (E.) M. E. *bite* (2 syll.) A. S. *bita,* a morsel. – A. S. *biten,* pp. of *bītan.*

bit (2), a curb for a horse. (E.) M. E. *bitt.* A. S. *bitt*,* only in dimin. *bitol,* a curb. + Du. *gebit*; Icel. *bitill* (dimin.); Swed. *bett*; Dan. *bid*; G. *gebiss.*

bitter. (E.) M. E. *biter.* A. S. *biter, bitor,* lit. 'biting.' – A. S. *biten,* pp. of *bītan.* + Du. *bitter*; Icel. *bitr*; Swed., Dan., G. *bitter.*

bitts, naval term. (Scand.) The *bitts* are two strong posts on deck to which cables are fastened. – Swed. *beting,* a bitt, whence *betingbult,* a bitt-bolt, bitt-pin;

Dan. *beding.* Orig. used on land for tethering horses. Swed. *betingbult,* a peg for tethering, from *beta,* to pasture, bait. So also Dan. *bedingsbolt,* from *bede,* to pasture; see **bait** above.

Bitter, Bitts; see Bite.

Bittern, a bird. (F. – Low L.) The *n* is added. M. E. *bitoure.* – F. *butor,* 'a bittor;' Cot. – Low L. *butorius,* a bittern; cf. L. *butio,* a bittern. Origin uncertain; but prob. from the imitative base BU, to make a booming noise; whence L. *bubare,* *butire,* to cry like a bittern, L. *bubo,* an owl.

Bitumen. (L.) L. *bitumen,* mineral pitch.

Bivalve. (F. – L.) See **Valve.**

Bivouac. (F. – G.) See **Wake.**

Bizarre, odd. (F. – Span.) F. *bizarre,* strange, capricious; orig. ' valiant.' – Span. *bizarro,* valiant, gallant. Perhaps of Basque origin.

Blab, to tell tales. (Scand.) M. E. *blabbe,* a tell-tale; *blaberen,* to babble. – Dan. *blabbre,* to babble; cf. Swed. dial. *blaffra,* G. *plappern,* to babble, prate. Of imitative origin; cf. Gael. *plab,* a soft noise; *plabair,* a babbler; *blabaran,* a stammerer, *blabhdach,* babbling, garrulous.

Black. (E.) M. E. *blak.* A. S. *blac, blæc.* + Icel. *blakkr,* dark. Cf. Du. *blaken,* to burn, scorch. Perhaps orig. 'scorched,' and thus connected with the idea of intense light; cf. L. *flag-rare,* to burn; see **Blink, Bleak, Blank.**

blackguard, a term of reproach. (E. *and* F.) From *black* and *guard.* A name given to scullions, turnspits, and kitchen menials, from the dirty work done by them. See Trench, Select Glossary.

blotch, a dark spot. (E.) Put for *blatch,* to blacken, smut (Rich.). Cf. Wilts. *blatch,* black, sooty. M. E. *blakien,* to blacken (Mätzner). ¶ In the sense of 'pustule,' it seems to be confused with *botch*; but see A. S. *blæc,* A. S. Leechdoms, ii. 8, l. 1.

Bladder. (E.) See Blow (1).

Blade, a leaf, flat of a sword. (E.) M. E. *blade.* A. S. *blæd,* a leaf. + Icel. *blaδ,* Swed., Dan., Du. *blad,* a leaf, blade; G. *blatt.* Prob. allied to Blow (2).

Blain. (E.) See Blow (1).

Blame. (F. – L. – Gk.) See **Blaspheme.**

Blanch (1), to whiten. (F. – O. H. G.) See Blink.

Blanch (2), to blench. (E.) See Blink.

Bland. (L.) L. *blandus,* mild.

blandish, to flatter. (F. – L.) M. E. *blandisen.* – O. F. *blandis-,* stem of pres. part. of *blandir,* to flatter. – L. *blandiri,* to caress. – L. *blandus.*

Blank, Blanket. (F. – O. H. G.) See **Blink.**

Blare. (E.) See **Blow** (1).

Blaspheme, to speak injuriously. (L. – Gk.) L. *blasphemare.* – Gk. βλασφημεῖν, to speak ill of. – Gk. βλάσφημος, adj., speaking evil. – Gk. βλασ- for βλαψ-, from βλάψις, damage, βλάπτειν, to hurt; and φήμη, speech, from φημί, I say; see **Fame.**

blame, vb. (F. – L. – Gk.) M. E. *blamen.* – O. F. *blasmer,* to blame. – L. *blasphemare,* to speak ill, also to blame. – Gk. βλασφημεῖν (above).

Blast. (E.) See **Blow** (1).

Blatant. (E.) See **Bleat.**

Blaze (1), and (2). See **Blow** (1).

Blazon (1), and (2). See **Blow.** (1)

Bleaberry; see **Bilberry.**

Bleach, Bleak (1), and (2). See **Blink.**

Blear one's eye, to deceive. (Scand.) In Sh. To *blear* is to *blur,* to dim. – Swed. dial. *blirra; blirra sojr augu,* to quiver (make a dimness) before the eyes, said of a haze caused by the heat of summer; cf. Swed. dial. *blira,* Swed. *plira,* to blink with the eyes. + Bavarian *plerr,* a mist before the eyes.

blear-eyed, dim-sighted. (Scand.) M.E. *bler-eyed.* – Dan. *pliiröiet,* blear-eyed, blinking; from *plire, blire,* to blink. (Dan. *öie,* eye; *öiet,* eyed.) Cf. Swed. *plira,* O. Swed. *blira,* to blink; Swed. dial. *blura,* to blink, partially close the eyes, like a near-sighted person. Perhaps allied to **Blink.**

blur, to stain; a stain. (Scand.) Properly 'to dim;' metaphorically, 'to deceive.' We find: '*A blirre,* deceptio; *to blirre,* fallere;' Levins (1570). See above.

Bleat. (E.) M.E. *bleten.* A.S. *blætan,* to bleat as a sheep. + Du. *blaten.* Cf. Gk. βληχάομαι, I bleat, βληχή, a bleating. Allied to **Blow** (1).

blatant, noisy, roary. (E.) Spenser has '*blatant* beast;' F. Q. vi. 12 (heading). It merely means *bleating;* the suffix *-ant* is a fanciful imitation of the F. *-ant* of the pres. part. Cf. M. E. *bletende,* bleating, Wyclif, Tobit, ii. 20.

Bleb, Blob, a small bubble or blister. (E.) Cf. M. E. *blober,* a bubble on water; *blubber,* a bubble. By comparing *blobber, blubber,* with *bladder,* with much the same meaning, we see the probability that they

are formed from the same root, and signify 'that which is blown up,' from the root of **Blow** (1).

blubber, a bubble; fat; swollen; to weep. (E.) The various senses are all explained by the verb *to blow.* Thus *blubber,* a bubble, is an extension of *blob,* 'that which is blown out;' the *blubber* of the whale consists of bladder-like cells filled with oil; *blubber-lipped,* also *blobber-lipped, blaberlypped,* means 'with swollen or blown out lips.' Lastly, *blubber,* to weep, M. E. *bloberen, blubren,* meant orig. to bubble; Gawain and Grene Knight, 2174. (See Curtius, on the stems φλοι, φλα.) See also **Bubble.**

Bleed. (E.) See **Blow** (2).

Blemish. (F. – Scand.) See **Blue.**

Blench. (E.) See **Blink.**

Blend, to mix together, confuse. (E.) M. E. *blenden.* A. S. *blandan,* to blend; cf. also *blendan,* to make blind. + Icel. and Swed. *blanda,* Dan. *blande,* O.H.G. *plantan,* to mix.

blind. (E.) M. E. *blind;* A. S. *blind.* The orig. sense is 'confused.' + Icel. *blindr;* Swed., Dan., G. *blind.*

blindfold, verb. (E.) M.E. *blindfolden,* verb (Tyndale); corruption of *blindfelden* (Palsgrave), where the *d* is excrescent. The true word is *blindfellen,* to 'fell' or strike blind, Ancren Riwle, p. 106. – A. S. *blind,* blind; and *fellan,* to strike (see **Fall**.)

blunder, to flounder about, err. (Scand.) M. E. *blondren,* to pore over a thing. Formed (as a frequentative) from Icel. *blunda,* to doze, slumber; Swed. *blunda,* to shut the eyes; Dan. *blunde,* to nap. Cf. Icel. *blundr,* Dan. and Swed. *blund,* a doze, a nap. From the sense of 'confusion.'

blunt, dull. (Scand.) M. E. *blunt, blont,* dull, dulled. Allied to Icel. *blunda,* Dan. *blunde,* to sleep, doze (above).

Bless. (E.) See **Blow** (2).

Blight. (E.) See **Blink.**

Blind, Blindfold. (E.) See **Blend.**

Blink, to wink, to glance. (E.) M.E. *blenken,* commonly 'to shine.' Not found in A.S., which has only the form *blícan,* but it probably existed, as there are rather numerous related forms. + Du. *blinken,* to shine; Dan. *blinke;* Swed. *blinka.* Allied to A. S. *blícan,* O. H. G. *blíchen,* to shine; Gk. φλέγειν, to burn, shine; Skt. *bhráj,* to shine. (√ **BHARG.**)

blanch (1), to whiten. (F.—O. H. G.) From M. E. *blanche*, white. — F. *blanc*, white; see **blank** below.

blanch (2), the same as *blench* (below).

blank, white. (F.—O. H. G.) In Milton, P. L. x. 656.—F. *blanc*.—O. H. G. *blanch*, white. From *blinchen**, to shine (mod. G. *blinken*); allied to O. H. G. *blîchen*, to shine.

blanket. (F.—O. H. G.) Orig. of a white colour. M. E. *blanket*.—O. F. *blanket* (F. *blanchet*), dimin. from *blanc*, white; see above.

bleach. (E.) Orig. 'to become pale;' M. E. *blechen*, Ancren Riwle, p. 324, l. 1. A. S. *blǽcan*.—A. S. *blǽc*, *blác*, shining, pale. See **bleak** below. + Icel. *bleikja*; Du. *bleeken*; G. *bleichen*.

bleak (1), orig. pale. (E.) M. E. *bleik*. A. S. *blǽc*, *blác*, shining; allied to *blícan*, to shine.+Icel. *bleikr*; Du. *bleek*; G. *bleich*.

bleak (2), a fish; from its pale colour.

blench, to shrink from. (E.) Sometimes *blanch*. M. E. *blenchen*, to turn aside. A. S. *blencan*, to deceive, orig. 'to make to blink,' to impose on; thus to *blench* is the causal verb, 'to make to blink;' but it was confused with *blink*, to wink, hence, to flinch.

blight, to blast. (E.) From the same root as A. S. *blícan*, to shine; cf. *blícettan*, to shine, glitter. We find M. E. *blichening*, blight, allied to Icel. *blíkna*, to become pale, from the same root. Cf. also Swed. *blicka*, to lighten, *blixt*, lightning, Du. *bliksem*, lightning. And cf. A. S. *áblicgan*, to amaze, from the same root.

Bliss. (E.) See **Blithe.**

Blister. (E.) See **Blow** (1).

Blithe. (E.) M. E. *blithe*. A. S. *blîð*, *blîðe*, sweet, happy.+O. Sax. *blîði*, bright, glad; O.H.G. *blîði*, glad; Goth. *bleiths*, merciful, kind.

bliss. (E.) M. E. *blis*. A. S. *blis*, *bliss*; contr. from A. S. *blîds*, *blîðs*, happiness, lit. blitheness.—A. S. *blîð* (above).+ O. Sax. *blizza*, *blîdsea*, happiness.

Bloat, to swell. (Scand.) We now generally used *bloated* to mean 'puffed out' or 'swollen,' as if allied to *blow*. The sense is rather 'effeminate,' and it is connected with Icel. *blautr*, soft, effeminate, imbecile, *blotna*, to become soft, lose courage. Cf. Swed. *blöt*, Dan. *blöd*, soft, pulpy, mellow. Allied also to Lat. *fluidus*; Gk. φλύειν, to swell, overflow.

bloater, a prepared herring. (Scand.)

A *bloater* is a cured fish, cured by smoke; but formerly a 'soaked' fish. — Swed. *blötfisk*, soaked fish; from *blöta*, to soak, steep; from *blöt*, soft (above).

Blob, a bubble. (E.) See **Bleb.**

Block, a large piece of wood. (C.) M.E. *blok*.—W. *ploc*, a block; Gael. and Irish *ploc*, a block, round mass, stump, plug. Cf. Irish *blogh*, a fragment, O. Irish *blog*, a fragment. Hence also Du. *blok*, Dan. *blok*, Swed. *block*, O. H. G. *bloch*; cf. Russ. *plakha*. Doublet, *plug*. Der. *block-ade*.

bludgeon, a cudgel. (C.) Irish *blocan*, dimin. of *ploc*, a block; Gael. *plocan*, a mallet, bludgeon, club, dimin. of *ploc*, a block; W. *plocyn*, the same.

plug. (Du.—C.) O. Du. *plugge*, Du. *plug*, a peg, bung. Of Celtic origin.— Irish *pluc*, *ploc*, a block, plug, bung, Gael. *ploc*, a block, club, plug, bung, W. *ploc*, a block, plug.

Blond. (F.) A late word.—F. *blond*, m. *blonde*, fem. 'light yellow;' Cot. Referred by Diez to Icel. *blandinn*, mixed; cf. A. S. *blonden-feax*, having hair of mingled colour, gray-haired. See **Blend.**

Blood, Bloom, Blossom. See **Blow** (2).

Blot (1), a spot. (Scand.) M.E. *blot*, *blotte*. — Icel. *blettr*, a stain (stem *blat*-); Dan. *plet*, a spot, stain; *plette*, to spot.

Blot (2), at backgammon. (Scand.) A *blot* is an 'exposed' piece. — Dan. *blot*, bare, naked; whence *give sig blot*, to lay oneself open, expose oneself; Swed. *blott*, naked; *blotta*, to lay oneself open. + Du. *bloot*. naked, *blootstellen*, to expose; G. *bloss*, naked. Allied to Icel. *blautr*, soft; see **Bloat.**

Blotch, a dark spot. (E.) See **Black.**

Blouse, a loose outer garment. (F.) F. *blouse*, a smock frock; O. F. *bliaus*, *bliaus*, properly pl. of *bliaut*, *blialt* (mod. F. *blaude*), formerly a rich vestment, of silk, embroidered with gold. Low L. *blialdus*. Probably Pers.; cf. Pers. *balyád*, a plain garment, *balyár*, an elegant garment.

Blow (1), to puff. (E.) M. E. *blowen*. A. S. *bláwan*.+G. *blähen*; L. *flare*. (✔ BHLA.)

bladder. (E.) M. E. *bladdre*. A. S. *blǽdr*, a blister, lit. 'a blowing out.'+Icel. *blaðra*, a bladder, watery swelling; Swed. *bläddra*, bubble, blister, bladder; O. H. G. *plâtará*. Cf. A. S. *blǽd*, a blast, blowing; L. *flatus*, breath. (From BHLAD, extended from BHLA.)

blain, a pustule. (E.) M. E. *blein*. A. S. *blégen*, a boil.+Du. *blein*; Dan. *blegn*. (From a base BHLAG.)

blare, to make a loud noise. (E.) M.E. *blaren, bloren*; also *blasen* (Ch.), an older form. See **blaze** (2) below.

blast, a blowing. (E.) M. E. *blast*. A.S. *blǽst*, a blowing; cf. Icel. *blástr*, a breath. From **blaze** (2) below.

blaze (1), a flame. (E.) M.E. *blase*. A.S. *blǽse*, a flame; in comp. *bǽl-blǽse*, a bright light. Cf. Icel. *blys*, Dan. *blus*, a torch. (From the root of *blow*.)

blaze (2), to proclaim, noise abroad. (E.) Mark, i. 45. M. E. *blasen*. A.S. *blǽsan*, to blow (Lye). + Icel. *blása*, to blow, blow a trumpet, sound an alarm; Swed. *blåsa*, to sound; Dan. *bläse*, Du. *blazen*, to blow a trumpet; G. *blasen*. (Hence *blast, blare, blason*.)

blason (1), a proclamation. (E.) Hamlet, i. 5. 21; Shak. Son. 106. A corruption from *blaze* (2), M. E. *blasen*, to proclaim; due to confusion with *blazon* (2) below, which was misused in place of *blaze* (2).

blazon (2), to pourtray armorial bearings. (F.—G.) M. E. *blason, blasoun*, a shield; whence *blazon*, verb, to describe a shield.—F. *blason*, a coat of arms, orig. a shield (Brachet). A still older sense is 'fame,' preserved in Span. *blason*, honour, glory, heraldry, blazonry, *hacer blason*, to blazon, *blasonar*, to blason, brag, boast.—G. *blasen*, to blow the trumpet, as done by heralds, to proclaim a victor's fame; see **blaze** (2) above. (See Scheler.)

blister, a little bladder on the skin. (E.) M. E. *blister*. Not found in A. S.; but cf. O. Du. *bluyster*, a blister (Kilian, Hexham); also Icel. *blástr*, a blowing, blast of a trumpet, swelling, mortification (in a medical sense). Also Swed. *blåsa*, a bladder, blister. Allied to *blast*, from root of *blow*; just as *bladder* is from the same root.

blurt, to utter rashly. (E.) The Scotch is *blirt*, to make a noise in weeping. Extended from M. E. *bloren, bleren*, to make a loud noise; the same as **blare** above.

bluster, to blow noisily, swagger. (Scand.) A frequentative form; from Icel. *blástr*, Swed. *blåst*, blast, wind, tempestuous weather; see **blast** above.

Blow (2), to bloom, flourish as a flower. (E.) M. E. *blowen*. A.S. *blówan*. + Du. *bloeijen*; G. *blühen*; L. *florere*; see **Flourish**.

bleed, to lose blood. (E.) M.E. *bleden*. A. S. *blédan*; formed by vowel-change (*ó* to *œ=é*) from A.S. *blód*; see **blood** below.

bless, to consecrate, &c. (E.) The orig. sense must have been 'to consecrate by blood,' i.e. either by sacrifice or by the sprinkling of blood, as the word can be fairly traced back to *blood*. M.E. *blessen*. A.S. *blétsian*, also *blédsian*, *bloedsian* (Matt. xxv. 34, xxvi. 26), which can only be from *blód*, blood, by the usual vowel-change from *ó* to *œ* or *é*. (Sweet; Anglia, iii. 156.) See below.

blood. (E.) M. E. *blod, blood*. A.S. *blód*, the symbol of 'blooming' or 'flourishing' life.—A. S. *blówan*, to bloom. + Du. *bloed*, Icel. *blóð*, Swed. *blod*, Goth. *bloth*; G. *blut*. Hence *bleed, bless*; as above.

bloom, a flower. (Scand.) M. E. *blome*; not in A.S.—Icel. *blóm, blómi*, a flower; Swed. *blomma*; Dan. *blomme*.+Du. *bloem*; Goth. *bloma*; L. *flos*; see **Flower**.

blossom. (E.) M. E. *blosme*, also *blostme*. A.S. *blóstma*, a blossom; from A. S. *bló-wan*, with suffixes -*st* and -*ma*; cf *bla-st* from *blá-wan*, to puff. + Du. *bloesem*; M. H. G. *bluost, blüst*.

Blow (3), a stroke, hit. (E.) M. E. *blowe*. Not in A.S.; but we find O. Du. strong verb *blouwen* (pt. t. *blau*), to strike, dress flax by beating. Allied to G. *bläuen*, to beat. Also to Goth. *bliggwan* (*blingwan*), to strike; L. *fligere*, to beat down, *flagellum*, a scourge. (√BHLAGH, to beat.) See **Afflict, Flagellate**.

Blubber. (E.) See **Bleb**.

Bludgeon. (C.) See **Block**.

Blue, a colour. (F.—O. H. G.) M. E. *blew, bleu*.—O. F. *bloi*, later *bloe, bleu*, blue. —O. H. G. *bldo*, blue, livid.+Icel. *blár*, livid; Swed. *blå*, Dan *blaa*; also Lat. *flauus*. Der. *blaeberry* or *bleaberry* (from Icel. *blár*).

blemish, to stain. (F.—Scand.) M. E. *blemisshen*. — O. F. *blemis-*, stem of pres. part. of *blemir, blesmir*, to wound, stain.— O. F. *bleme, blesme*, wan, pale. — Icel. *bláman*, the livid colour of a wound.— Icel. *blár*, livid, blue. The orig. sense of O. F. *blemir* was 'to beat black and blue.'

Bluff, downright, rude. (Du. ?) A *bluff* is a steep headland. It appears to be Dutch. O. Du. *blaf*, flat, broad; *blaffaert*, one having a broad flat face, also, a boastei (Oudemans); *blaf van het voor-hooft*, 'the flat of a forehead' (Hexham); *blaffen, bleffen*, to mock (id.).

Blunder. (Scand.) See **Blend.**

Blunderbuss, a short gun. (Hyb.) In Pope. Formerly spelt *blanterbusse, plantierbusse* (Palmer); i.e. 'a gun on a rest.' — L. *plantare*, to plant (see **Plant**); and Du. *bus*, a gun, orig. a box, barrel; see **Box** (1).

Blunt. (Scand.) See **Blend.**

Blur, a stain. (Scand.) See **Blear.**

Blurt. (E.) See **Blow** (1).

Blush. (E.) M. E. *bluschen, blusshen*, to glow. A. S. *blyscan*, used to translate L. *rutilare*, to shine (Mone, Quellen, 355). Extended from A. S. *blýsan*, only in comp. *áblýsian, ablísian*, to blush; from A. S. *blys* (*blýs*?) in *bæl-blys*, lit. 'a fire-blaze.' ✠ Du. *blozen*, to blush, from *blos*, a blush; Dan. *blusse*, to flame, glow, from *blus*, a torch; Swed. *blossa*, to blaze, from *bloss*, a torch. Prob. allied to **Blaze.**

Bluster. (Scand.) See **Blow** (1).

Boa, a large snake. (L.) L. *boa* (Pliny); perhaps allied to *bos*, an ox; from its size.

Boar, an animal. (E.) M. E. *bore, boor*. A. S. *bár*. ✠ Du. *beer*; M. H. G. *bér*; Russ. *borov'*. Perhaps orig. 'wild beast,' like **Bear** (2).

Board. (E.) M. E. *bord*. A. S. *bord*, board, side of a ship, shield. ✠ Du. *bord*; Icel. *bord*, plank, side of a ship; G. *bord*; Goth. *-baurd* in *fotu-baurd*, a foot-stool. Cf. Irish, Gael., W., and Corn. *bord*, a board. ¶ The sense 'side of a ship' explains *star-board, lar-board, on board, over-board*. Der. *board*, to live at table; from *board*, a table.

border, an edge. (F. — O. Du.) M. E. *bordure*, Ch. — F. *bordure*. — Du. *boord*, border, edge; orig. the same word as Du. *bord*, a board; see above.

Boast. (E.?) M. E. *bost*, W. *bost*, a bragging; Corn. *bost*; Irish and Gael. *bosd*, boast, vain-glory. But prob. E.

Boat. (E.) M. E. *boot*. A. S. *bát*. ✠ Icel. *bátr*; Swed. *båt*; Du. *boot*; Russ. *bot'*; W. *bad*; Gael. *báta*, a boat. β. The orig. boat was prob. a *bat*, i.e. stick, branch, stem of a tree; cf. Gael. and Irish *bata*, staff, stick, pole, branch, bat. See **Bat.**

boat-swain. (E.) Lit. 'boat-lad;' A. S. *swán*, Icel. *sveinn*, a lad.

Bob, to jerk. (C.?) Perhaps imitative. Or altered from Gael. *bog*, to bob, agitate; Irish *bogaim*, I bob, wag, toss. See **Bog.**

Bobbin, a wooden pin on which thread is wound; round tape. (F.) Formerly *bobin*. — F. *bobine*, 'a quil for a spinning wheele, a skane;' Cot. Orig. uncertain; perhaps Celtic. Cf. Irish and Gael. *baban*, a tassel, fringe, short pieces of thread; Gael. *babag*, tassel, cluster.

Bode. (E.) See **Bid** (2).

Bodice. (E.) See **Bind.**

Bodkin, orig. a small dagger. (C.) M. E. *boydekin*, Ch. — W. *bidogyn, bidogan*, a dagger, poniard; dimin. of *bidog*, a dagger; cf. W. *pid*, a tapering point. Cf. Gael. *biodag*, Irish *bideog*, a dagger.

Body. (E.) See **Bind.**

Bog. (C.) Irish *bogach*, a bog, from *bog*, soft; cf. Irish *bogaim*, I shake; a *bog* being a soft quagmire. So also Gael. *bogan*, a quagmire; *bog*, soft, moist; *bog*, to soften, also to agitate.

Boggle, to start aside, swerve for fear. (C.?) Prob. coined from prov. E. *boggle, bogle*, a spectre. Cf. W. *bwg*, a goblin; *bwgwl*, a threat, *bygylu*, to threaten; *bwgwth*, to scare. See **Bug** (1).

Boil (1), verb. (F. — L.) See **Bull** (2).

Boil (2), a tumour. (E.) See **Bulge.**

Boisterous. (E.) Lengthened from M. E. *boistous*, Ch.; lit. 'noisy.' From E. *boist, bost*, noise. See **Boast.**

Bold. (E.) M. E. *bold, bald*; A. S. *beald, bald*. ✠ Icel. *ballr*; Du. *bout*; O. H. G. *pald, bald*; cf. Goth. *balthaba*, adv., boldly.

bawd. (F. — G.) M. E. *baude*, Ch. — O. F. *baud*, gay, wanton. — O. H. G. *bald*, bold, free.

Bole. (Scand.) See **Bulge.**

Bolled, swollen. (Scand.) See **Bulge.**

Bolster, Bolt (1). See **Bulge.**

Bolt (2), **Boult**, to sift meal. (F. — L. — Gk.) Spelt *boulte* in Palsgrave. — O. F. *bulter*; mod. F. *bluter*; oldest form *buleter*, a corruption of *bureter*, to sift through coarse cloth. — O. F. *buire* (F. *bure*), coarse woollen cloth. — Low Lat. *burra*, coarse red cloth. — Lat. *burrus*, reddish. — Gk. πυρρός, reddish. — Gk. πῦρ, fire. See **Fire.**

bureau. (F. — L. — Gk.) F. *bureau*, a desk, writing-table; so called because covered with brown baize. — F. *bureau*, O. F. *burel*, coarse woollen stuff, russet-coloured. — O. F. *buire* (F. *bure*) coarse red cloth. — L. *burrus*; as above.

Bomb, Bombard. (F. — L. — Gk.) See **Boom** (1).

Bombast, orig. cotton-wadding; hence, padding, affected language. (Ital. — L. —

Gk.) Milanese *bombás*, Ital. *bombagio*, cotton wadding. — Low L. *bombax*, cotton; put for L. *bombyx*. — Gk. βόμβυξ, silk, cotton. ¶ Prob. Eastern; from Pers. *bandash*, carded cotton.

bombazine, bombasine, a fabric of silk and worsted. (F. — L. — Gk.) F. *bombasin.* — Low L. *bombacynus*, made of cotton. — Low L. *bombax*, cotton; see above.

Bond. (E.) See **Bind.**

Bondage, servitude. (F. — Scand.) See **Boor.**

Bone. (E.) M. E. *boon*; A.S. *bán*.+ Du. *been*; Icel. *bein*; Swed. *ben*; Dan. *been*; O. H. G. *pein, peini.*

bonfire. (E.) Orig. a bone-fire. ‘*Bane-fire*, ignis ossium;’ Catholicon Anglicanum, A.D. 1483; where *bane* is the Northern form of *bone*.

Bonito, a kind of tunny. (Span. — Arab.) Span. *bonito.* — Arab. *baynis*, a bonito.

Bonnet. (F. — Low L. — Hind.?) F. *bonnet.* — Low L. *bonneta* (A.D. 1300), the name of a stuff of which bonnets or caps were made. Perhaps Hindustani; cf. Hind. *bandt*, woollen cloth; Rich. Dict. p. 290.

Bonny, fair. (F. — L.) From F. *bonne*, fair, fem. of *bon*, good. — L. *bonus*, good; O. L. *duonus.*

boon, good. (F. — L.) In the phr. ‘*boon* companion.’ — F. *bon*, good.

bounty, orig. goodness. (F. — L.) M. E. *bountee.* — O. F. *bonteit.* — L. acc. *bonitatem*, from *bonitas*, goodness. — L. *bonus.*

Bonze, a priest. (Port. — Japanese.) Port. *bonzo.* — Jap. *bonzo*, a religious man.

Booby. (Span. — L.) Span. *bobo*, a block-head, booby (related to F. *baube*, stammering). — L. *balbus*, stammering; hence stupid. Cognate with Gk. βάρβαρος; see **Barbarous.**

Book. (E.) M. E. *book*; A.S. *bóc*, of which the orig. sense was a beech-tree. The orig. ‘books’ were pieces of writing scratched on a beechen board.+Du. *boek*; Icel. *bók*; Swed. *bok*; Dan. *bog*; G. *buch*; also L. *fagus*, a beech, Gk. φηγός, a beech. (√BHAG.)

beech. (E.) A.S. *béce*, a beech; *bécen*, adj., beechen; both derivatives (by change from *ó* to *é*) from the older form *bóc* above.

buckwheat. (E.) Lit. beech-wheat; from the resemblance of its seeds to the mast of the beech-tree. The form *buck* is Northern. So also Du. *boekweit*, buckwheat; G. *buchweizen.* See **Book.**

Boom (1), to hum. (E.) M. E. *bommen*; not found in A.S. +Du. *bommen*, to boom, to give out a hollow sound like an empty barrel. An imitative word; allied to L. *bombus*, Gk. βόμβος, a humming.

bomb, a shell for cannon. (F. — L. — Gk.) F. *bombe.* — L. *bombus*, a humming noise. — Gk. βόμβος, the same.

bombard. (F. — L. — Gk.) The verb is from E. *bombard*, a great gun; Sh. — F. *bombarde*, a cannon; extended from F. *bombe.* Der. *bombard-ier*, F. *bombardier* (Cot.)

bound (1), to leap. (F. — L. — Gk.) F. *bondir*, to bound; but orig. to resound. — L. *bombitare*, to resound. — L. *bombus*, a humming sound. — Gk. βόμβος, the same. Der. *re-bound* (F. *rebondir*).

bumble-bee. (E.) Cf. O. Du. *bommelen*, to buzz, frequent. of *bommen*, to boom; see **Boom** (1).

bump (2), to boom as a bittern. (C.) W. *bwmp*, a hollow sound; hence *aderyn y bwmp*, a bittern.

bumper, a drinking-vessel. (F. — L. — Gk.) A corruption of *bombard*, used in the same sense (Temp. ii. 2), a jocular word; it orig. meant a kind of cannon; see **bombard** above.

Boom (2), a pole. (Du.) See **Beam.**

Boon (1), a petition. (Scand.) M. E. *bone*, Ch. — Icel. *bón*, Dan. and Swed. *bön*, a petition. + A.S. *bén* (whence *bene* in Wordsworth). Perhaps allied to **Ban.**

Boon (2); see **Bonny.**

Boor, a peasant. (Du.) Du. *boer*, a peasant, lit. ‘tiller of the soil.’ — Du. *bouwen*, to till. + A.S. *búan*, to till, to dwell, whence *búr, gebúr*, a peasant (only preserved in *neigh-bour*). So also G. *bauen*, to till; whence *bauer*, a peasant. (√BHU.)

bondage, servitude. (F. — Scand.) M. E. and F. *bondage*, servitude; the sense being due to confusion with the verb *to bind*. But it orig. meant the condition of a *bond-man*, called in A. S. *bonda*, a word borrowed from Icel. *bóndi*, a husband-man. And *bóndi = búlandi*, a tiller; from Icel. *búa*, to till, prepare, cognate with A.S. *búan.*

bound (3), ready to go. (Scand.) In ‘the ship is *bound* for Spain,’ &c. Formed, with excrescent *d*, from M. E. *boun*, ready, Ch. C. T. 11807. — Icel. *búinn*, prepared; pp. of *búa*, to till, prepare.

bower, an arbour. (E.) M. E. *bour*,

A. S. *búr*, a chamber. – A. S. *búan*, to dwell.
+Icel. *búr*, a chamber.

busk (1), to get oneself ready. (Scand.)
Icel. *búask*, to get oneself ready. – Icel.
búa, to prepare ; and *-sk*, put for *sik*, oneself ; see **bound** (3) above.

by-law, a law affecting a township.
(Scand.) Formerly also *birlaw*, *burlaw*.
– Icel. *bœjar-lög*, a town-law, by-law ;
from *bœjar*, gen. of *bœr* or *byr*, a town,
village (from *búa*, to dwell) ; and *lög*, a
law. So also Dan. *by-lov*, town-law, similarly compounded.

byre, a cow-house. (E.) M. E. *byre*, in
Mätzner, s. v. *bire*. A. S. *býre*, pl., dwell-
ings ; in Sweet, O. E. Texts. – A. S. *búr*, a
bower. Cf. Icel. *búr*, a pantry ; Dan. *buur*,
a bird-cage.

husband ; see under **House.**

neighbour. (E.) Lit. one who dwells
near. A. S. *neáhbúr*, *neáhgebúr*. – A. S.
neáh, nigh ; and *búr*, *gebúr*, a peasant,
dweller.+G. *nachbar*, similarly formed.

Boot (1), a covering for the foot. (F.–
L. – Gk.) See **Butt** (2).

Boot (2), advantage. (E.) See **Better.**

Booth. (Scand.) M. E. *bothe*. – Icel.
búð, a booth, shop ; Swed. *bod*, Dan. *bod*.
+G. *bude*. So also Gael. *buth*, Irish *both*,
boith, W. *bwth*, a hut. Allied to Skt. *bha-
vana*, a house. (√BHU.)

Booty. (F. – Low G.) Formerly spelt
butin. – F. *butin*, 'a booty, prey ;' Cot.
– Du. *buit* ; cf. Icel. *býti*, Dan. *bytte*,
Swed. *byte*, exchange, barter ; also booty,
spoil ; Icel. *býta*, to divide, deal out ;
so that the orig. sense of *booty* was
'share.'

Borage. (F. – Low L.) Formerly *bour-
age*. – F. *bourrache*. – Low L. *borraginem*,
acc. of *borrago*, borage ; prob. named from
its roughness. Perhaps from Low L. *borra*,
burra, rough hair (whence F. *bourre*, Ital.
borra) ; see **Burl.**

Borax. (Low L. – Arab. – Pers.) Low L.
borax ; also *boracum*. – Arab. *búráq*. – Pers.
búrah, borax (Vullers).

Border, an edge. (F. – O. Du.) See
Board.

Bore (1), to perforate. (E.) M. E. *borien*,
A. S. *borian*.+Du. *boren* ; Icel. *bora* ; Swed.
borra ; Dan. *bore* ; G. *bohren* ; L. *forare*.
(√BHAR, to cut.) See **Perforate,
Pharynx.**

bore (2), to worry. Merely a metaph.
use of the verb above ; Hen. VIII, i. 1. 128.
And see **Burin.**

Bore (3), a tidal surge in a river. (Scand.)
Icel. *bára*, a billow caused by wind. Cf.
Swed. dial. *bår*, a mound.

Boreas, the north wind. (L. – Gk.) L.
Boreas. – Gk. Βορέας, Βορρᾶς, the N. wind.

Borough. (E.) M. E. *burgh*, *borgh* ;
also *borwe*. A. S. *burh*, *burg* (gen. and
dat. *byrig*), a fort. – A. S. *burg-on*, pt. pl.
of *beorgan*, to protect ; cognate with Goth.
bairgan, to hide, keep, L. *farcire*, to stuff.
(√BHARGH.) + Du. *burg* ; Icel. *borg* ;
Swed. and Dan. *borg* ; G. *burg* ; Goth.
baurgs.

barrow (1), a burial-mound. (E.) Put
for *berrow* (like *parson* for *person*, &c.)
M. E. *bergh*, *beoruh*, a hill, mound. – A. S.
beorg, *beorh*, a hill, grave-mound. – A. S.
beorgan, to hide, protect ; see **bury** below.

borrow. (E.) M. E. *borwen* ; A. S.
borgian, lit. to give a pledge. – A. S. *borg*,
borh, a pledge. – A.S.*borg-en*, pp. of *beorgan*,
to keep, protect.

burgess. (F. – M. H. G.) M. E. *bur-
geys*. – O. F. *burgeis*. – Low Lat. *burgensis*,
belonging to a fort or city. – Low Lat.
burgus, a fort. – M. H. G. *burc* (G. *burg*) ;
cognate with A. S. *burg* above.

burgher. (E.) Formed by adding *-er*
to *burgh* = *borough.*

burglar. (F. – G. and L.) O. F. *burglar* (a law-term) a house-breaker, lit.
'borough-thief.' – F. *bourg* (from G. *burg*),
a town ; and O. F. *leres*, a robber, from
Lat. *latro* ; see **Larceny.**

burgomaster. (Du.) Du. *burgemeester*,
a town-master. – Du. *burg*, cognate with
E. *borough* ; and *meester*, a master, from
O. F. *meistre* ; see **Master.**

burial. (E.) M. E. *buriel*, *biriel*, a
tomb ; also spelt *beriels*, *biriels*. – A. S.
byrgels, a tomb. – A. S. *byrgan*, to bury ;
see **bury** (1).

burrow, a shelter for rabbits. (E.)
M. E. *borwgh*, a cave, shelter ; merely a
varied spelling of *borough* above. Der.
burrow, verb.

bury (1), verb. (E.) M. E. *burien*. –
A. S. *byrigan*, *byrgan*, to bury, hide in the
ground. Formed (by change of *o* to *y*)
from *borg-en*, pp. of *beorgan*, to hide, protect (as above).

bury (2), a town. (E.) In *Canter-bury*,
&c. – A. S. *byrig*, dat. of *burh*, a borough.

Bosom. (E.) M. E. *bosom*. A. S. *bósm*.
+ Du. *boezem* ; G. *busen*.

Boss, a knob. (F. – O. H. G.) See **Beat.**

Botany. (F. – Gk.) F. *botanique*, orig.

an adj. – Gk. βοτανικός, belonging to plants. – Gk. βοτάνη, a herb. – Gk. βόσκειν, to feed.

Botch (1). to patch. (O. Low G.) See **Beat**.

Botch (2), a swelling. (F. – G.) See Beat.

Both. (Scand.) M. E. *baþe*, Scot. *baith.* – Icel. *báðir*, both, dual adj. ; Dan. *baade* ; Swed. *báda*. ✛ G. *beide* ; Goth. *bajoths*. Allied to A. S. *bá*, both ; Lat. *-bo* in *ambo* ; Gk. *-φω* in *ἄμ-φω* ; Skt. *-bha* in *u-bha*, both. Icel. *-ðir* is for *ðeir*, they.

Bother, v. and sb. (C.) In Swift. – Irish *buaidhirt*, sb., trouble ; *buaidhrim*, I disturb ; cf. *buair*, to vex, trouble. So some say ; but the sounds do not agree. Cf. *pother*.

Bots, small worms. (C.) Gael. *botus*, a belly-worm ; *boiteag*, a maggot.

Bottle (1), a hollow vessel. (F. – Low L. – Gk.) M. E. *botel.* – F. *bouteille.* – Low Lat. *buticula*, dimin. of *butica*, a kind of vessel. – Gk. βύτις, βοῦτις, a flask. Perhaps allied to Butt (2) and Boot (1).

butler. (F. – Low L. – Gk.) M. E. *boteler*, one who attends to bottles ; from M. E. *botel*, a bottle ; see above.

buttery, a place for provisions, esp. liquids. (F. – Low L. – Gk.) A corruption of M. E. *botelerie*, a butlery, properly a place for a butler ; from M. E. *boteler*, a butler ; see above. (Thus *buttery* = *bottlery*.) Confused with the word *butter*.

Bottle (2), a bundle of hay ; see Beat.

Bottom. (E.) M. E. *botum*, *bothom*. A. S. *botm*. ✛ Du. *bodem* ; Icel. *botn* ; Swed. *botten* ; Dan. *bund* ; G. *boden* ; Lat. *fundus* ; Gk. πυθμήν ; Vedic Skt. *budhna*, depth, ground. Allied to Irish *bonn*, sole of the foot ; Gael. *bonn*, sole, bottom ; W. *bon*, base, stock. See **Fundament**.

Boudoir. (F. – C. ?) F. *boudoir*, a private room for a lady ; lit. a place to sulk in. – F. *bouder*, to sulk. Perhaps Celtic ; cf. W. *pwdu*, to pout, sulk ; see Pout (1).

Bough. (E.) M. E. *bough*. A. S. *bóg*, *bóh* ; of which the orig. sense was 'an arm.' ✛ Icel. *bógr*, Swed. *bog*, Dan. *bov*, the shoulder of an animal, hence the bow (shoulder) of a ship ; G. *bug* ; Gk. πῆχυς, the fore-arm ; Skt. *báhus*, the arm, allied to *bahu*, large.

bow (4), the bow of a ship. (Scand.) Lit. the 'shoulder' of a ship. – Icel. *bógr*, as above. Der. *bowline*, attached to the 'side' or 'shoulder' of a sail.

Bought. the same as Bout. See Bow (1).

Boulder, a large stone. (Scand.) Swed. dial. *bullersteen*, a large rolling stone ; so called from its rolling down stream with a crash. – Swed. *bullra*, to thunder, roar ; and *steen*, a stone ; see **Bellow** and **Stone**. Danish puts *ld* for *ll*, and has *buldre*, to roar, *bulder*, a crash.

Bounce, to jump up quickly. (O. Low G.) M. E. *bunsen*, to beat. – Low G. *bunsen*, to beat, knock at a door ; Du. *bonzen*, to bounce, throw. From Du. *bons*, a bounce, thump ; cf. G. *bumps*, bounce ; Icel. *bops*, bump! imitative of the sound of a blow. See Bump (1).

Bound (1), to leap. (F. – L. – Gk.) See Boom (1). Der. *re-bound*.

Bound (2), a boundary. (F. – C.) M. E. *bounde*, Ch. ; with excrescent *d*, as in *soun-d*. – O. F. *bonne*, a boundary ; also spelt *bodne* (Burguy) ; Low Lat. *bodina* (contr. form *bonna*), a bound, limit. – Bred. *bôden*, a thicket, tuft of trees ; *bôd*, a tuft of trees ; cf. Irish *bot*, a cluster, a bunch. Thus the orig. *bound* was a tuft of trees or a thicket. Der. *bound-ary* (for *bound-er-y*).

bourn (1), a boundary. (F. – C.) In Sh. – F. *borne*, a bound ; corrupted from O. F. *bonne*, a boundary, as above.

Bound (3), ready to go. (Scand.) See Boor.

Bounden, the old pp. of Bind. As in 'bounden duty.'

Bounty. (F. – L.) See Bonny.

Bouquet. (F. – Low G.) See Bush.

Bourd, a jest ; to jest. (F. – Teut. ?) M. E. *bourde*, sb. ; *bourden*, v. – F. *bourde*, a game ; *bourder*, to play. Etym. doubtful ; but F. *bourder* prob. = O. F. *bohorder*, to tourney, joust with lances, hence, to amuse oneself. – O. F. *bohort*, a mock tournament ; supposed to stand for *bot-horde*, i.e. a beating against the hurdles or barriers of the lists. – O. F. *bot-er*, to beat ; and *horde*, a hurdle. – M. H. G. *bôzen*, to beat (O. H. G. *pôzan*) ; and M. H. G. *hurt*, a hurdle ; see Beat and Hurdle.

Bourn (1), a boundary. (F. – C.) See Bound (2).

Bourn (2), **Burn**, a stream. (E.) M. E. *bourne*. A. S. *burna*, a fountain, stream, well. (√BHUR ?) ✛ Icel. *brunnr* ; Swed. *brunn* ; Dan. *brönd* ; G. *brunnen* ; Goth. *brunna*, a spring, well ; cf. Gk. φρέαρ, a well.

Bouse, Bouze, Boose, to drink deeply. (Du.) See Box (1).

Bout, a turn. (Scand.) See Bow (1).

Bow (1), to bend. (E.) M. E. *bowen, bogen, bugen.* A. S. *búgan.* + Du. *buigen*; G. *beugen*; Goth. *biugan*; Skt. *bhuj,* to bend; Lat. *fugere,* to turn to flight, give way; Gk. φεύγειν, to flee. (√BHUGH.)

bow (2), a bend. (E.) From the verb.

bow (3), a weapon to shoot with. (E.) M. E. *bowe.* A. S. *boga,* a bow; because it is *bent* or *bowed.*+Du. *boog*; Icel. *bogi*; Swed. *båge*; Dan. *bue*; O. H. G. *pogo.*

bight, a coil of rope, a bay. (E.) M. E. *bight.* A. S. *byht,* as in *wæteres byht,* a bight (bay) of water (see Grein).—A. S. *bug-on,* pt. pl. of *búgan,* to bow, bend.

bout, a turn. (Scand.) Also *bought,* Spenser, F. Q. i. 1. 15.—Dan. *bugt,* a bend, a turn; also a bight or bay; cognate with A. S. *byht* above; see **bight.**

bow-window. (E.) A window of semi-circular form; not the same as *bay-window.*

buxom. (E.) M. E. *boxom, buhsum*; the old sense was obedient, obliging, good-humoured. Lit. '*bow-some.*'—A. S. *búg-an,* to bow, bend, obey; and *-sum,* suffix, as in *win-some.* And see **Bugle** (2).

Bow (4), the 'shoulder' of a ship. (Scand.) See **Bough.**

Bowel. (F.—L.) M. E. *bouele.*—O. F. *boël*; (mod. F. *boyau*).—Lat. acc. *botellum,* a sausage, intestine; dimin. of *botulus,* a sausage.

Bower, an arbour. (E.) See **Boor.**

Bowl (1), a round wooden ball. (F.—L.) See **Bull** (2).

Bowl (2), a drinking-vessel. (E.) See **Bulge.**

Bow-window; see **Bow** (1).

Box (1), the name of a tree. (L.) M. E. *box*; A. S. *box.* — Lat. *buxus,* the box-tree. +Gk. πύξος, the box-tree.

box (2), a chest or case to put things in. (L.) M. E. *box*; A. S. *box.*—L. *buxum,* anything made of box-wood; hence, a box. —Lat. *buxus,* the box-tree. (Hence a *box* at a theatre; a shooting-*box*; a Christmas *box* or present; &c.)

bouse, boose, to drink deeply. (Du. —L.) Spelt *bouse* in Cotgrave (s. v. *boire*). —O. Du. *buysen,* 'to drinke great drafts,' Hexham.—O. Du. *buys,* Du. *buis,* a tube, pipe, &c.; also the tap of a barrel; allied to Du. *bus,* a box, urn, barrel of a gun; borrowed from Latin, like E. *box.*

bush (2), the metal box in which an axle works. (Du.—L.) Du. *bus,* a box; see **bouse,** above.

bushel, a measure. (F.—Low. L.—Gk.) See **Pyx.**

Box (3), to fight with fists; a blow. (Scand.) M. E. *box,* sb.—Dan. *baske,* to slap, strike; *bask,* a slap, thwack; allied to Swed. *basa,* to whip, flog, beat (Ihre). Cf. *pash.*

Box (4), in phr. 'to box the compass.' (Span.) Span. *boxar,* to sail round an island (Meadows); O. Span. *boxo,* a circuit (Meadows).

Boy. (O. Low G.) M. E. *boy.* Preserved in E. Friesic *boi, boy,* a boy (Koolman); allied to O. Du. *boef,* a boy, Du. *boef,* a knave.+Icel. *bófi,* a knave; G. *bube,* a boy; Lat. *pupus,* a boy. See **Pupil.**

Brabble, to quarrel. (Du.) Du. *brab-belen,* to stammer, confound; whence *brab-beltaal,* foolish talk. See **Blab, Babble.**

Brace, orig. a firm hold. (F.—L.) From the notion of embracing.—O. F. *brace,* the two arms (Bartsch); hence a measure of 5 feet, formed with extended arms (Cot.); and hence, a grasp.—Lat. *brachia,* pl. of *brachium,* the arm.+Irish *brac,* W. *braich,* the arm; Gk. βραχίων.

bracelet. (F.—L.) F. *bracelet*; dimin. of O. F. *bracel,* an armlet (Bartsch.)—L. *brachile,* an armlet.—L. *brachium,* an arm.

branch. (F.—C.) M. E. *branche.*—F. *branche.*—Bret. *branc,* an arm; allied to Lat. *brachium,* an arm, a branch.

embrace. (F.—L.) O. F. *embracer,* to grasp in the arms.—O. F. *em-,* for *en* (= L. *in*); and *brace,* the grasp of the arms; see **Brace.**

Brach, a kind of hunting-dog. (F.—L.) M. E. *brache.*—O. F. *brache* (F. *braque*).— O. H. G. *bracco* (G. *brack*), a dog that hunts by the scent.

Brackish. (Du.) Du. *brak,* briny, nauseous.—Du. *braken,* to vomit. Prob. allied to **Break.**

Bracken, fern. (E.) See **Brake** (2).

Bracket, a corbel. See **Breeches.**

Bract. (L.) Lat. *bractea,* a thin plate or leaf of metal.

Brad. (Scand.) M. E. *brod.* — Icel. *broddr,* a spike; Swed. *brodd,* Dan. *brodde,* a frost-nail.

Brag. (C.) See **Break.**

Bragget. (W.) M. E. *braget.* — W. *bragot,* a kind of mead; allied to Irish *bracat,* malt liquor. — W. *brag,* malt; Irish and Gael. *braich,* malt, fermented grain. The Gael. *braich* is from Gael. *brach,* to *brew*; allied to E. **Brew.**

Brahman, Brahmin. (Skt.) Skt. *bráhma*na, a brahman, holy man. — Skt. *brahman*, prayer; also the unknown god. Supposed to mean 'support ;' from *bhri*, to bear; see **Bear** (1).

Braid, to weave. (E.) M. E. *breiden*. A.S. *bregdan, bredan*, to brandish, weave, braid.+Icel. *breg'ða*, to brandish, turn about, change, start, braid, &c. ; hence *brag'ð*, a sudden movement.

Brail, a ligature ; see **Breeches.**

Brain. (E.) M. E. *brayne*. A.S. *bregen, brægen*, the brain.+Du. *brein*.

Brake (1) ; see **Break.**

Brake (2), bush, fern. (E.) A.S. *bracce*, fern.+Low G. *brake*, willow-bush. Prob. so called because growing on rough or *broken* ground ; cf. G. *brach*, fallow, unploughed.

bracken, fern. (E.) A.S. *braccan*, pl. of *bracce*, fern.+Icel. *burkni* (allied to *brok*, sedge, rough grass) ; Swed. *bräken*, Dan. *bregne*, fern.

Bramble. (E.) M. E. *brembil*. A.S. *bremel, brembel*.+Du. *braam*, a blackberry ; Swed. *brom-bär*, Dan. *brom-bær*, G. *brom-beere*, a blackberry. (√ BHRAM.)

Bran. (C.) M. E. *bran*. — W. *bran*, Irish *bran*, husk, chaff. So also F. *bren* ; from Bret. *brenn*, bran.

Branch. (F. — L.) See **Brace.**

Brand, Brandish, Brandy; see **Burn.**

Branks, a punishment for scolds. (C.) See Jamieson. — Gael. *brangus* (O. Gael. *brancas*), a sort of pillory ; Gael. *brang*, Irish *brancas*, a halter.+Du. *pranger*, pincers, barnacle, collar ; G. *pranger*, a pillory ; Du. *prangen*, to pinch.

Bran-new. (E.) See **Burn.**

Brass. (E.) M. E. *bras*. A.S. *bræs*. Derived from the verb seen in Icel. *brasa*, to harden by fire ; Swed. *brasa*, to flame ; Dan. *brase*, to fry. **Der.** *braz-en*, A.S. *bræsen*.

brasier, brazier, a pan to hold coals. (F. — Scand.) F. *braisiere*, a camp-kettle. — F. *braise*, live coals. — Swed. *brasa*, fire, allied to *brasa*, to flame ; see above.

braze (1), to harden. (F. — Scand.) K. Lear, i. i. 11. It merely means to harden ; it is the verb from which *brass* is derived, not vice versa. — F. *braser*, to solder. — Icel. *brasa*, to harden by fire.

braze (2), to ornament with brass. (E.) In Chapman, tr. of Homer, Od. xv. 113. In this sense, it is E., and derived from *brass*, sb. 'Aero, ic *brasige*' ; Ælfric.

breeze (3), cinders. (F. — Scand.) O.F. *brese*, spelt *breze* in Cot., the old form of F. *braise*, live coals ; see **brasier** above.

Brat, a child. (C.) So named from its pinafore ; it also meant a rag, clout, or (in derision) a child. — W. *brat*, a rag, pinafore ; Gael. and Irish *brat*, a cloak, rag.

Brattice, a fence of boards in a mine. (F. — Teut. ?) M. E. *bretasche, bretasce, brutaske*, a parapet, battlement. — O. F. *breteschè*, a small wooden outwork, battlement ; cf. Prov. *bertresca*, Ital. *bertesca*, the same. A difficult word ; prob. formed from G. *brett*, a plank.

buttress, a support, in architecture. (F. — Teut.) M. E. *boteras* ; Palsgrave has *bottras, butteras*. Orig. a plural form, as if for *butterets*. — O. F. *bouteres*, pl. of *bouteret*, a prop. — F. *bouter*, to thrust, prop. Cotgrave also has *boutant*, a buttress, from the same verb ; see **Butt** (1), p. 34, col. 2, l. 5. (Misplaced.)

Bravado. (Span.) See **Brave.**

Brave. (F.) F. *brave*, 'brave, gay, fine, proud, braggard, valiant ;' Cot. The same as Ital., Span., and Port. *bravo*. Etym. unknown ; none of the explanations are satisfactory ; the Bret. *brav*, O. Swed. *braf*, appear to be borrowed from F. Cf. Bret. *braga*, to strut about, Gael. *breagh*, fine ; see **Brag.**

bravado. (Span.) Altered from Span. *bravada*, 'a bravado ;' Minsheu's Span. Dict. — Span. *bravo*, brave.

bravo, a daring villain. (Ital.) Ital. *bravo*, brave ; as a sb., a cut-throat, villain.

bravo! well done. (Ital.) Ital. *bravo*, brave ; used in the voc. case.

Brawl (1), to quarrel. (C.) M. E. *braulen*. — W. *brawl, brol*, a boast ; *brolio*, to boast ; *bragal*, to vociferate ; cf. Irish *bragaim*, I boast, bounce, bully. Prob. allied to **Brag.**

Brawl (2), a sort of dance. (F. — Teut.) See **Burn.**

Brawn, muscle. (F. — O. H. G.) M. E. *braun*, muscle, boar's flesh. — O. F. *braon*, a slice of flesh ; cf. Prov. *bradon*, the same. — O. H. G. *brádon*, acc. of *bráto*, M. E. *bráte*, a slice of flesh for roasting. — O. H. G. *prátan* (G. *braten*), to roast. ¶ The orig. sense was merely 'muscle ;' the restriction to that of 'boar's flesh' is accidental.

Bray (1), to bruise. (F. — G.) See **Break.**

Bray (2), to make a roaring noise. (F. — C.) See **Break.**

Braze, (1) to harden; (2) to ornament with brass; see **Brass.**

Breach. (E.)   See **Break.**

Bread. (E.)   M. E. *breed.*   A. S. *bredd.* Prob. allied to **Brew,** because fermented. Cf. A. S. pt. t. *bréd-w.* + Du. *brood;* Icel. *braud;* Swed. and Dan. *bröd;* G. *brod.*

Breadth. (E.)   See **Broad.**

Break. (E.)   M. E. *breken;* pt. t. *brak;* pp. *broken.*   A. S. *brecan,* pt. t. *bræc,* pp. *brocen.* + Du. *breken;* Icel. *braka,* to creak; Swed. *braka,* to crack; Dan. *brække;* Goth. *brikan;* G. *brechen;* Lat. *frangere.* (√BHRAG.) The orig. sense is to break with a noise, to crack.

brag, to boast. (C.)   W. *bragio,* to boast; Irish *bragaim,* I boast.   Allied to Gael. *bragh,* an explosion. (√BHRAG.)

braggart, a boaster. (F. – C.)   F. *bragard.* – Bret. *braga,* to strut about; cognate with W. *bragio,* to boast; see above.

brake (1), a machine for breaking hemp; a name for various mechanical contrivances. (O. Low G.)   M. E. *brake.* – Low G. *brake,* a flax-brake; O. Du. *braecke,* 'a brake to beat flax;' Hexham. – Du. *breken,* to break; see **Break.**

bray (1), to bruise, pound. (F. – G.) M. E. *brayen.* – O. F. *breier* (F. *broyer*). – G. *brechen,* to break; see **Break.**

bray (2), to make a roaring noise. (F. – C.)   F. *braire* (Low Lat. *bragire, bragare*). Of Celtic origin; cf. W. *bragal,* to vociferate; Gael. *bragh,* a burst, explosion; see **brag** above.

breach. (E.)   M. E. *breche,* a fracture. – A. S. *brece,* as in *hláf-gebrece,* a piece of bread. – A. S. *brecan,* to break, ¶ Or O. F. *breche,* a breach. – G. *brechen.*

brick. (F. – O. Du.)   F. *brique,* a brick; also a fragment, bit. – O. Du. *bricke,* a brick; orig. a fragment. – Du. *breken,* to break.   Der. *brick-bat* (see **Bat**).

Bream, a fish. (F. – O. H. G.)   See **Bass** (2).

Breast. (E.)   See **Burst.**

Breath. (E.)   M. E. *breeth, breth.* A. S. *bræd.* + G. *brodem, broden, brodel,* steam, vapour, exhalation.

Breech. (E.)   See **Breeches.**

Breeches, Breeks. (E.)   A double plural, the form *breek* being, in itself, a pl. form.   A. S. *bréc,* breeks; pl. of *bróc,* with the same sense. + Du. *broek,* a pair of breeches; Icel. *brók* (pl. *brækr*); M. H. G. *bruoch;* Gael. *brog,* a large shoe, *briogais,* breeches. Cf. L. *braccæ,* a word of Celtic origin.

bracket, a corbel, &c. (F. – C.)   Formerly spelt *bragget,* as in Minsheu, ed. 1627.   So named from the resemblance to the front part of a pair of breeches, as formerly made. – F. *braguette,* 'a codpiece,' Cot. (the front part of a pair of breeches); the allied Span. *bragueta* also meant a projecting mould in architecture, a bracket or corbel.   Dimin. of O. F. *brague,* 'a kind of mortaise,' Cot.; from *bragues,* breeches; so also Span. *bragueta* is the dimin. of Span. *bragas,* breeches. – L. *braccæ;* of Celtic origin; Bret. *bragez,* breeches.

brail, a kind of ligature or fastening. (F. – C.)   O. F. *braiel,* a cincture; orig. for fastening up breeches; dimin. of F. *braie,* breeches. – L. *bracca,* Bret. *bragez,* as above.

breech. (E.)   M. E. *breech,* properly breeks, or the covering of the hinder part of the body. – A. S. *bréc,* pl. of *bróc;* see above.

brogues, coarse shoes. (C.)   Gael. and Irish *brog,* a shoe, legging; see **Breeches.**

Breed. (E.)   See **Brood.**

Breeze (1), a gadfly. (E.)   Also *brizze, brimsey.* – A. S. *brimse,* a gadfly, named from its humming. + Du. *brems;* G. *bremse* (from M. H. G. *bremen,* to hum); Skt. *bhramara,* a large black bee (from Skt. *bhram,* to hum, whirl, fly about as insects).   Cf. Lat. *fremere.*

Breeze (2), a strong wind. (F.)   Formerly *brize.* – O. F. *brise,* used by Rabelais in the same sense as F. *bise,* the N. wind; cf. Span. *brisa,* Port. *briza,* the N. E. wind; Ital. *brezza,* a cold wind.   Orig. unknown.

Breeze (3), cinders. (F. – Scand.)   See **Brass.** ¶ Quite distinct from prov. E. *briss,* dust, F. *bris,* rubbish, whence F. *débris;* see **Debris.**

Breve, Breviary; see **Brief.**

Brew. (E.)   M. E. *brewen.*   A. S. *brebwan,* pt. t. *bredw,* pp. *gebrowen.* + Du. *brouwen;* G. *brauen;* Icel. *brugga;* Swed. *brygga;* Dan. *brygge.* (√ BHUR, to boil, ferment.)

brewis, pottage. (F. – M. H. G.)   M. E. *browes.* – O. F. *brows,* a pl. form; from a sing. *brou,* broth. – Low Lat. *brodum,* broth. – M. H. G. *brot,* broth; cognate with E. **Broth;** see below.

brose, pottage. (C.)   Gael. *brothas,* brose.   From the same root as E. **Brew.**

broth. (E.)   A. S. *broð.* – A. S. *bro-wen,* pp. of *brebwan,* to brew. + Icel. *broð;* M. H. G. *brot;* cf. G. *gebräude,* as much as is brewed at once.   And see **Bread.**

Briar, Brier. (E.) M. E. *brere*. A.S.
brĕr.+Gael. and Irish *preas*, a bush, briar.

Bribe. (F.–C.) M. E. *bribe.*–O. F.
bribe, a piece of bread given to a beggar;
Picard *brife*, a fragment of bread.–Bret.
brĕva, to break; cp. W. *briw*, broken,
briwfara (= *briw bara*), broken bread,
from *briwo*, to break. Allied to Brick and
Break.

Brick. (F.–O. Du.) See Break.

Bride. (E.) M. E. *bride*; also *birde*,
brude, *burde*. A. S. *brýd*, a bride. Prob.
allied to Irish *bru*, the womb, Gk. βρύειν,
to teem. + Du. *bruid*; Icel. *brúðr*; Swed.
and Dan. *brud*; G. *braut*; Goth. *bruths*.

bridal. (E.) Formerly *bride-ale*, a bride-
feast. A.S. *brýd-ealo*, a bride-ale, bride-
feast.–A.S. *brýd*, bride; and *ealo*, ale,
also a feast; see Ale.

bridegroom. (E.) For *bridegoom*; the
second *r* is intrusive. A. S. *brýd-guma*, lit.
bride-man; where *guma* is cognate with L.
homo, a man; see Homage. + Du. *bruide-
gom*; Icel. *brúðgumi*; Swed. *brudgumme*;
Dan. *brudgom*; G. *bräutigam*, O. H. G.
brútegomo.

Bridge. (E.) M. E. *brigge, brugge.* A.S.
brycg.+Icel. *bryggja*; Swed. *brygga*; Dan.
brygge, a pier; G. *brücke.* Allied to Icel.
brú, Dan. *bro*, a bridge, pavement; O.
Swed. *bro*, a paved way.

Bridle. (E.) M. E. *bridel.* A. S. *bridel.*
+ Du. *breidel*; M. H. G. *brítel, brittil*
(whence F. *bride*). Perhaps allied to
Braid.

Brief (1), short. (F.–L.) M.E. *bref.*
– F. *bref.* – L. *breuis*, short. + Gk.
βραχύς, short.

brief (2), a writ, &c. (F.–L.) F.
brief, a brief; Cot. The same as F. *bref*
above; from its being in a short form.

abbreviate. (L.) L. *abbreuiatus*, pp.
of *abbreuiare*, to shorten.–L. *ab-*, put for
ad, to; and *breuis*, short.

abridge. (F.–L.) M.E. *abregen.*–
O. F. *abregier*, another form of *abrevier*, to
shorten.–L. *abbreuiare*; see above.

breve. (Ital.–L.) Orig. a *short* note;
now the longest in use.–Ital. *breve*, brief.
–Lat. *breuis*, short. Der. *semi-breve.*

brevet. (F.–L.) F. *brevet*, 'a brief,
breviate, little writing;' Cot. Dimin. from
bref, brief.

breviary. (F.–L.) F. *bréviaire.*–L.
breuiarium, a summary.

brevity. (F.–L.) F. *briĕveté.*–L. acc.
breuitatem, shortness.–L. *breuis*, short.

Brig, Brigade; see Brigand.

Brigand. (F.–Ital.) F. *brigand*, a
robber.–Ital. *brigante*, an intriguer, robber;
orig. pres. part. of *brigare*, to strive after.–
Ital. *briga*, strife, quarrel, trouble. Orig.
uncertain.

brig; see brigantine (below).

brigade. (F.–Ital.) F. *brigade*, a crew,
troop.–Ital. *brigata*, a troop; orig. fem. of
pp. of *brigare*, to strive, fight, as above.

brigandine, a kind of armour. (F.–
Ital.) F. *brigandine*, a kind of armour,
worn by brigands.–F. *brigand*, a robber;
see above.

brigantine, brig, a ship. (F.–Ital.)
Brig is merely short for *brigantine.*–F.
brigantin, a kind of ship.–Ital. *brigantino*,
a pirate-ship.–Ital. *brigante*, a robber.

Bright. (E.) M.E. *bright*. A. S. *beorht.*
+ Icel. *bjartr*; M. H. G. *berht*; Goth.
bairhts, shining. Allied to Skt. *bhrāj*, to
shine; L. *flag-rare*, to flame. (√ BHARG,
to blaze.) See Flame.

Brill, a fish. (C.) Corn. *brilli*, mackarel,
contr. form of *brithelli*, pl. of *brithel*, a
mackarel, a spotted fish.–Corn. *brith*,
speckled. Cf. Irish and Gael. *breac*, speckled.
The *brill* is minutely spotted with white.

Brilliant, shining; see Beryl.

Brim. (E.) M.E. *brim.* A.S. *brim*,
surf, surge on the shore. + Icel. *brim*, surf,
G. *brame*, border, M. H. G. *brem*, border;
Skt. *bhrimi*, a whirl-pool, from *bhram*, to
whirl. The *brim* of the sea is its margin,
where the *surf* is heard to roar; cf. L.
fremere. (√ BHRAM.)

Brimstone, Brindled, Brine; see
Burn.

Bring. (E.) A. S. *bringan*, pt. t. *brang*;
also *brengan*, pt. t. *brohte.* (Mod. E. retains
only the weak pt. t. *brought.*) + Du.
brengen; G. *bringen*; Goth. *briggan*
(written for *bringan*), pt. t. *brahta.* (An extension from √ BHAR, to bear.)

Brink. (Scand.) M. E. *brink.* – Dan.
brink, verge; Swed. *brink*, descent or slope
of a hill; Icel. *brekka* (=*brenka*), a slope,
crest of a hill; allied to Icel. *bringa*, a
grassy slope, orig. the breast. Cf. W.
bryncu, a hillock, *bryn*, a hill, *bron*, the
breast.

Brisk. (C.) W. *brysg*, quick; Gael.
briosg, quick, lively. Allied to Gael. *briosg*,
to start with surprise, leap for joy; Irish
briosg, a start, a bounce.

Brisket. (F.–C.) O.F. *brischet* (Brachet,
s.v. *brechet*); *brichet*, 'the brisket, or breast-

piece' [of meat], Cot. Mod. F. *brechet.* — Bret. *bruched,* the breast ; spelt *brusk* in the dialect of Vannes.

Bristle. (E.) M. E. *bristle, berstle, birstle* ; dimin. of A. S. *byrst,* a bristle. + Du. *borstel* ; Icel. *burst* ; Swed. *borst* ; G. *borste.* Allied to Skt. *bhrishti,* pointed.

Brittle. (E.) M. E. *britel, brotel, brutel.* Formed, with suffix *-el* (= A. S. *-ol*), from A. S. *brut-on,* pl. of pt. t. of *breótan,* to break ; whence also *bryttan,* to break (secondary verb). It means 'fragile.' Cf. Icel. *brjóta,* Swed. *bryta,* Dan. *bryde,* to break.

Broach. (F. — L.) See **Brooch.**

Broad. (E.) M. E. *brood.* A. S. *brád.* + Du. *breed* ; Icel. *breiðr* ; Swed. and Dan. *bred* ; Goth. *braids* ; G. *breit.*

breadth. (E.) The final *-th* is late ; the M. E. form is *brede* ; Ch. — A. S. *brædu,* breadth. — A. S. *brád,* broad. + Icel. *breidd* ; Goth. *braidei* ; G. *breite* ; Du. *breedte.*

Brocade, Broccoli, Brochure ; see **Brooch.**

Brock, a badger. (C.) A. S. *broc.* — W., Corn., and Bret. *broch* ; Irish, Gael., and Manx *broc,* a badger. Named from his white-streaked face ; cf. Gael. *brocach,* speckled, grayish, as a badger ; *brucach,* spotted ; Gael. and Irish *breac,* W. *brech,* speckled.

Brocket. (F. — L.) See **Brooch.**

Brogues. (C.) See **Breeches.**

Broider, to adorn with needlework. (F. — C. ?) [In 1 Tim. ii. 9, *broidered* is put for *broided,* old form of *braided.*] Formerly *broder,* Judg. v. 30 (Bible of 1551). — F. *broder,* 'to imbroyder,' Cot. Perhaps Celtic ; from Bret. *brouda,* to pierce, also to embroider, *broud,* a spike, goad ; W. *brodio,* to embroider ; Gael. *brod,* a goad. β. It has been confused with F. *border,* 'to border, also to imbroyder,' Cot., Span. and Port. *bordar,* to embroider, which seem rather to be connected with F. *bord,* the edge of a garment ; see **Border.** Der. *em-broider.*

Broil (1), to fry, grill. (F. — Teut. ?) M. E. *broilen.* — O. F. *bruiller,* to boil, roast (Roquefort). Prob. a frequent. form of O. F. *bruir,* to roast (Burguy) ; mod. F. *brouir.* Perhaps of Teut. origin ; cf. Du. *broeijen,* to foment, hatch eggs, grow very hot ; G. *brühen,* to scald. ¶ We also find Gael. *bruich,* to boil, roast ; Irish *bruighim,* I boil.

Broil (2), a tumult. (F. — Teut. ?) F. *brouiller,* to jumble, confuse, confound.

Perhaps related to G. *brudeln, brodeln,* to bubble (whence to give off steam, confuse) ; G. *brodel, brodem,* vapour, allied to E. **Breath** (Scheler). Cf. F. *brouillard,* a mist, fog. ¶ We also find W. *broch,* tumult, *brochell,* a tempest ; Gael. *broighleadh,* turmoil, *broiglich,* noise (perhaps unrelated).

Broker. (E.) See **Brook** (1).

Bronchial. (Gk.) Gk. βρόγχια, neut. pl., the ramifications of the windpipe. — Gk. βρόγχος, the windpipe ; cf. βράγχος, a gill. Allied to Gk. βράχειν, to roar. Der. *bronch-itis* ; from βρόγχος.

Bronze. (F. — Ital. — Teut.) See **Brown.**

Brooch. (F. — L.) Named from the pin which fastens it. M. E. *broche,* a pin, peg, brooch. — F. *broche,* a spit, point. — Low L. *brocca,* a pointed stick. — L. *broccus,* a sharp tooth, point. Cf. Gael. *brog,* to goad, *brog,* an awl ; W. *procio,* to stab.

broach. (F. — L.) M. E. *setten on broche* = to set a-broach, tap liquor. — F. *mettre en broche,* to tap, by piercing a barrel. — F. *brocher,* to pierce. — F. *broche,* 'a broach, spit,' Cot. ; see above.

brocade. (Span. — L.) Span. *brocado,* brocade ; orig. embroidered, the pp. of a verb *brocar** (not used) answering to F. *brocher,* 'to broach, also, to stitch . . . with great stitches,' Cot. — Low L. *brocca,* L. *broccus* ; see **Brooch.**

broccoli. (Ital. — L.) Ital. *broccoli,* sprouts ; pl. of *broccolo,* a sprout. Dimin. of *brocco,* a skewer, a shoot, stalk. — L. *broccus,* a point.

brochure, a pamphlet. (F. — L.) F. *brochure,* a few leaves stitched together. — F. *brocher,* to stitch ; see **brocade.**

brocket, a red deer two years old. (F. — L.) F. *brocart,* the same ; so called because he has but one tine to his horn. — F. *broche,* a spit, also, a tine of a stag's horn ; see **Brooch.**

Brood. (E.) M. E. *brod.* A. S. *bród* (rare) ; 'hi *bréðað* heora *bród*' = they nourish their brood ; Ælfric's Hom. ii. 10. + Du. *broed* ; G. *brut.* Perhaps it means 'that which is hatched by heat ;' allied to **Brew** ; cf. W. *brwd,* warm.

breed. (E.) M. E. *breden.* A. S. *brédan,* to produce a brood, nourish. — A. S. *bród,* a brood. (So also *feed* from *food* ; by change from *ó* to *é*.)

Brook (1), to endure, put up with. (E.) M. E. *broken, brouken.* A. S. *brúcan,* to use, enjoy ; which was the orig. sense. + Du. *gebruiken,* Icel. *brúka,* G. *brauchen,*

Goth. *brukjan*, to use; L. *frui*, to enjoy; Skt. *bhuj* (for *bhruj*), to enjoy. (✓ BHRUG.)

broker. (F.—Lat.) M. E. *brocour*, an agent, witness of a transaction. Anglo-F. *brocour*, an agent; orig. a 'broacher' or seller of wine.—Late L. *broccator*, one who broaches.—L. *broccus*; see Brooch. (Misplaced.)

Brook (2), a small stream. (E.) M. E. *brook*. A. S. *bróc*. + Du. *broek*, G. *bruch*, a marsh. (✓ BHRAG.)

Broom. (E.) M. E. *brome*, broom. A. S. *brôm*, the plant broom; hence a besom made from twigs of it. + Du. *brem*. Allied to Bramble.

Brose, Broth; see Brew.

Brothel. (E.; *confused with* F.—Teut.) 1. M. E. *brothel*, a lewd person, base wretch. —A. S. *broð-en*, pp. of *breóðan*, to perish, become vile; whence also *âbroðen*, degenerate, base. Hence was made *brothelhouse*, a house for vile people (Dryden), afterwards contracted to *brothel*. 2. Orig. distinct from M. E. *bordel*, which was used, however, in much the same sense.—O. F. *bordel*, a hut, orig. of boards.—O. Du. (and Du.) *bord*, a plank, board; see Board.

Brother. (E.) M. E. *brother*. A. S. *bróðor*. + Du. *broeder*; Icel. *bróðir*; Goth. *brothar*; Swed. and Dan. *broder*; G. *bruder*; Gael. and Ir. *brathair*; W. *brawd*; Russ. *brat'*; Lat. *frater*; Gk. φρατήρ; Skt. *bhrâtri*. The Skt. *bhrâtri* is from *bhri*, to support, maintain; orig. to bear. (✓ BHAR.)

Brow. (E.) M. E. *browe*. A. S. *brú*, *breáw*. + Du. *braauw*; Icel. *brún*, eyebrow, *brá*, eye-lid; M. H. G. *brá*, eye-lid; Russ. *brove*; Gael. *brá*; Bret. *abrant*; Gk. ὀφρύς; Pers. *abrú*; Skt. *bhrú*. Orig. the eye-lid; named from twitching; cf. Goth. *brahw*, the twinkling of an eye. (✓ BHUR.)

Brown. (E.) M. E. *broun*. A. S. *brún*. + Du. *bruin*; Icel. *brúnn*; Swed. *brun*; Dan. *bruun*; G. *braun*. From the same root as Burn.

bronze. (F.—Ital.—Teut.) F. *bronze*. —Ital. *bronzo*, bronze; cf. *abbronzare*, to scorch. Allied to *bruno*, brown, whence *brunezza*, swarthiness, *brunire*, to burnish. —G. *braun*, brown; see above.

bruin. (Du.) In Reynard the Fox, the bear is called *bruin*, i.e. brown.—Du. *bruin*, brown.

brunette. (F.—G.) F. *brunette*, fem.

of *brunet*, brownish. — M. H. G. *brún*, brown.

burnish, to polish. (F.—G.) M. E. *burnisen*; also *burnen*. — O. F. *burnir*, *brunir* (pres. part. *burnis-ant*), to embrown, to polish.—O. F. *brun*, brown.—M. H. G. *brún*, brown.

Browze. (F.—M. H. G.) A corruption of *broust*.—O. F. *brouster* (F. *brouter*), to nibble off young shoots.—O. F. *broust* (F. *brout*), a sprig, shoot, bud.—M. H. G. *broz*, a bud; Bavar. *brosst*, *bross*, a bud; see Brush.

Bruin. (Du.) See Brown.

Bruise. (F.—Teut.? or C.?) M. E. *brusen*, *brisen*.—O. F. *bruiser*, *briser*, to break. Either from M. H. G. *bresten* (G. *bersten*), to burst (Diez); or of Celtic origin, as seen in Gael. *bris*, to break, Ir. *brisim*, I break. ¶ Not from A. S. *brýsan*, which seems to be allied to A. S. *breótan*, to break.

Bruit, a rumour. (F.—C.?) F. *bruit*, a noise.—F. *bruire*, to make a noise. Perhaps of Celtic origin; cf. Bret. *bruchellein*, to roar as a lion; W. *broch*, din, tumult. Cf. Gk. βρυχάομαι, I roar. β. Scheler derives F. *bruire* from L. *rugire*, to roar, with prefixed *b*.

Brunette; see Brown.

Brunt; see Burn.

Brush. (F.—Teut.) M. E. *brusche*, a brush; also brush-wood, which is the older sense, the orig. brush being made of twigs. —O. F. *broce*, F. *brosse*, brushwood; also, later, a brush.—Low L. *brustia*, *bruscia*, a thicket. Derived by Diez from O. H. G. *brusta*, G. *borste*, a bristle; but rather from Bavar. *brosst*, *bross*, a bud, M. H. G. *broz*, a bud; see Browze.

Brusque, rough in manner. (F.—Ital.) F. *brusque*.—Ital. *brusco*, sharp, tart, sour, applied to fruits and wine. Origin uncertain.

Brute. (F.—L.) F. *brut*, fem. *brute*.— L. *brutus*, stupid.

Bryony. (L.—Gk.) L. *bryonia*.—Gk. βρυωνία, βρύωνη, bryony.—Gk. βρύειν, to teem, grow luxuriantly.

Bubble. (Scand.) Swed. *bubbla*, Dan. *boble*, a bubble; also Du. *bobbel*, a bubble, *bobbelen*, to bubble. A dimin. form; probably put for *blobble*, a dimin. of *blob*, a bubble; see Bleb.

Buccanier. (F.—West Indian.) F. *boucanier*, a pirate.—F. *boucaner*, to broil on a sort of wooden gridiron.—F. *boucan*, a wooden gridiron, used by cannibals for broiling men and animals. The word *boucan* is said to be Caribbean, and to mean 'a place where meat is smoke-dried.'

Buck (1), a male deer, goat. (E.) M. E. *bukke*. A.S. *bucca*, a he-goat. + Du. *bok*, Icel. *bukkr*, Swed. *bock*, a he-goat; Dan. *buk*, a he-goat, ram, buck; G. *bock*, W. *bwch*, Gael. *boc*, Irish *boc*. Also Skt. *bukka*, a goat.

buckram, a coarse cloth. (F. — M.H.G.) M. E. *bokeram*. — O. F. *boucaran* (F. *bougran*), a coarse kind of cloth; Low L. *boquerannus*. — Low L. *boquena*, goat's skin. — M. H. G. *boc*, a he-goat.

butcher. (F. — G.) M. E. *bocher*. — F. *bocher*, orig. one who kills goats. — O. F. *boc* (F. *bouc*), a goat. — G. *bock*, a goat.

Buck (2), to steep clothes in lye. (C.) M. E. *bouken*. — Gael. *buac*, dung used in bleaching, lye in which clothes are washed; Irish *buac*, lye. Orig. cow-dung; from Gael. and Irish *bo*, a cow; see **Cow**.

Bucket. (E.) M. E. *boket*. Formed with dimin. suffix *-et* from A. S. *búc*, a pitcher. Cf. Gael. *bucaid*, Irish *buicead*, a bucket.

Buckle. (F. — L.) M. E. *bokel*. — O. F. *bocle* (F. *boucle*), the boss of a shield, a ring, a buckle. — Low L. *bucula*, the boss of a shield; *buccula*, visor of a helm, boss of a shield, buckle. — Lat. *buccula*, the cheek, dimin. of *bucca*, the cheek.

buckler. (F. — L.) M. E. *bokeler*. — O. F. *bocler* (F. *bouclier*), a shield; so named from the boss on it; see above.

Buckram; see **Buck**.

Buckwheat; see **Book**.

Bucolic, pastoral. (L. — Gk.) L. *bucolicus*. — Gk. βουκολικός, pastoral. — Gk. βουκόλος, a cowherd. — Gk. βοῦ-s, an ox; and κέλλειν, to drive.

Bud. (E.?) M. E. *budde*, a bud; *budden*, to bud. Not found in A. S. Cf. Du. *bot*, a bud; *botten*, to bud, sprout. Prob. allied to **Beat**; see button under **Beat**.

Budge (1), to stir; see **Bull** (2).

Budge (2), a kind of fur; see **Bag**.

Budget, a leathern bag; see **Bag**.

Buff, the colour of dressed buffalo-skin. (F. — L.) F. *buffle*, a buffalo. — L. *bufalus*; see below.

Buffalo. (Span. — L. — Gk.) Span. *bufalo*, *buffalo*, orig. a kind of wild ox. — L. *bufalus*, also *bubalus*. — Gk. βούβαλος, a buffalo, wild ox, antelope. (Not a true Gk. word.)

Buffer (1), and (2); see **Buffet** (1).

Buffet (1), a blow; to strike.   (F.) M. E. *boffet*, *buffet*, a blow, esp. on the

cheek. — O. F. *bufet*, a blow, dimin. of *bufe*, a blow, esp. on the cheek; cf. *bufer*, *buffer*, to puff out the cheeks, also to buffet; mod. F. *bouffer*. Prob. of imitative origin, allied to *pouffer*, to puff; see **Puff.**

buffer (1), a foolish fellow. (F.) Orig. a stammerer; hence a foolish fellow. M. E. *buffen*, to stammer. — O. F. *bufer*, to puff out the cheeks (hence, to puff or blow in talking).

buffer (2), a cushion, to deaden concussion. (F.) Lit. 'a striker;' from M. E. *buffen*, to strike, orig. to buffet on the cheek; see **Buffet.**

buffoon. (F.) F. *bouffon*, a buffoon, jester, one who made grimaces. — F. *bouffer*, to puff.

Buffet (2), a side-board. (F.) F. *buffet*, a side-board. Origin unknown.

Bug (1), a spectre. (C.) In Sh. — W. *bwg*, a hobgoblin, spectre; Gael. and Ir. *bucan*, a spectre. + Lithuan. *baugus*, terrific, from *bugti*, to terrify, allied to Skt. *bhuj*, to bow, turn aside; see **Bow** (1).

bug (2), an insect. (C.) So named because an object of terror, exciting disgust.

bug-bear. (C. *and* E.) A supposed spectre in the shape of a bear.

Bugle (1), a wild ox; see **Beef.**

Bugle (2), a kind of ornament. (M.H.G.) Low L. *bugoli*, pl., the name of a kind of ornaments (A.D. 1388). Dimin. of M.H.G. *bouc*, *boug*, an armlet, large ring, ring-shaped ornament. — M. H. G. *biegen*, to bend, bow; cognate with **Bow** (1).

Build. (Scand.) M. E *bulden*. Late A.S. *byldan*, to build. — A. S. *bold*, a house, which appears to be of Scand. origin, and formed by adding *d* to Icel. *ból*, a house, farm. The word is really Scand. O. Swed. *bylja*, to build (Ihre). — O. Swed. *bol*, a house, dwelling; Icel. *ból*, a house, Dan. *bol*, a small farm. Formed (like A. S. *búr* = E. *bower*) from Icel. *búa*, O. Swed. *bo*, to live, abide, dwell; cf. Skt. *bhū*, to be. See **Be.**

Bulb. (F. — L. — Gk.) F. *bulbe*. — L. *bulbus*, a bulb. — Gk. βολβός, a bulbous root, onion.

Bulge. (Scand.) A rather late word. Of Scand. origin; Swed. dial. *bulgja*, to swell out; *bulgin*, swollen, pp. of a strong verb which occurs as A. S. *belgan* (pp. *bolgen*), orig. to swell, but only used in the sense to swell with anger. So also Icel. *bólginn*, swollen, angry. (✓BHALGH, to swell.)

boil (2), a small tumour. (E.) M. E.

byle. A. S. *byl,* or *býle,* a boil, swelling.**+** Du. *buil;* Icel. *bóla,* Dan. *byld,* G. *beule.* Cf. Goth. *ufbauljan,* to puff up.

bole, stem of a tree. (Scand.) M. E. *bol.* — Icel. *bolr, bulr,* the trunk of a tree, stem; Swed. *bål;* Dan. *bul.* From its roundness.

bolled, swollen. (Scand.) Icel. *bólginn,* swollen, pp. of a lost verb; Dan. *bullen,* swollen, *bulne,* to swell; Swed. *bulna,* to swell.

bolster. (E.) A. S. *bolster;* with suffix *-ster* as in *hol-ster;* from its round shape. **+**Icel. *bolstr;* O. H. G. *polstar.*

bolt, a stout pin of iron, an arrow. (E.) M. E. *bolt.* A. S. *bolt,* only in the sense of catapult for shooting bolts; but properly a round pin, and named from its roundness. **+**O. Du. *bolt,* Du. *bout;* G. *bolzen.*

bowl (2), a drinking-vessel. (E.) M. E. *bolle.* A. S. *bolla,* a bowl; from its roundness.**+**Icel. *bolli;* M. H. G. *bolle.* See **Ball.**

bulk (1), size. (Scand.) M. E. *bolke,* a heap. — Icel. *bálki,* a heap; O. Swed. *bolk;* Dan. *bulk,* a lump. Cf. Swed. *bulna,* to swell.

bulk (2), the trunk of the body. (Du.) In Sh. — O. Du. *bulcke,* thorax (Kilian); Du. *buik.* Cf. Icel. *búkr,* the trunk; Swed. *buk,* Dan. *bug,* G. *bauch,* the belly (which have prob. lost an *l*). The Gael. *bulg* means (1) trunk of the body (2) lump, mass; see **bulk** (1).

bulwark. (Scand.) Dan. *bulværk,* Swed. *bolverk;* cf. Du. *bolwerk,* G. *bollwerk* (whence F. *boulevard*). Compounded of Dan. *bul,* trunk of a tree, log, Icel. *bulr, bolr,* the stem of a tree; and Dan. *værk,* Swed. *verk,* a work. Lit. 'log-work,' or 'bole-work;' see **bole** above. See also under **Ball** (1) and **Bag.**

Bulk (3), a stall of a shop; **Bulkhead;** see **Balk** (1).

Bull (1), male of the cow. (E.) M. E. *bole, bule.* Not found in A. S., but the dimin. *bulluca,* a bullock, occurs. Prob. 'the bellower;' see **Bellow. +** Du. *bul;* Icel. *boli;* G. *bulle;* Lithuan. *bullus.* Der. *bull-ock,* A. S. *bulluca,* as above.

Bull (2), a papal edict. (L.) M. E. *bulle.* — Lat. *bulla,* a bubble, boss, knob, leaden seal or an edict; a bull (in late Latin).

bill (2), a writing, account. (L.) Low L. *billa,* a writing; the dimin. is *billeta, bulleta,* shewing that *billa* is a corruption of Lat. *bulla,* a papal bull, &c.; see **Bull** (2) above.

billet (1), a note. (F.—L.) F. *billet.*

—Low L. *billeta,* dimin. of *billa,* a writing; see **bill** (2) above.

boil (1), to bubble up. (F.—L.) O. F. *boillir,* to boil (F. *bouillir*). — L. *bullire,* to bubble up, boil. — L. *bulla,* a bubble; see **Bull** (2) above.

bowl (1), a round ball. (F. — L.) F. *boule,* a bowl to play with. — Lat. *bulla,* a boss, knob, &c.

budge, to stir. (F.—L.) F. *bouger,* to stir; the same as Ital. *bolicare,* to bubble up.—L. *bullire;* see **boil** (1) above. Cf. Span. *bullir,* (1) to boil, (2) to stir.

bullet. (F.—L.) F. *boulet,* dimin. of F. *boule,* a ball; see **bowl** (1) above.

bulletin. (F.—Ital.—L.) F. *bulletin,* a ticket. — Ital. *bullettino,* a safe-conduct, pass, ticket. Dimin. of *bulletta,* a passport, lottery ticket, dimin. of *bulla,* a seal, bull.—L. *bulla;* see **Bull** (2) above.

bullion. (F.—L.) F. *bouillon,* a stud; but the O. F. *bullione* meant a mint, and Low L. *bulliona, bullio* meant a mass of metal.—Low L. *bullare,* to stamp, mark with a seal.—L. *bulla,* a seal; see **Bull** (2).

ebullition, a boiling over. (F. — L.) O. F. *ebullition.*—L. acc. *ebullitionem;* a coined word, from *ebullitus,* pp. of *e-bullire,* to bubble up; see **boil** (1) above.

parboil. (F.—L.) It now means 'to boil insufficiently,' by confusion with *part.* The old sense is 'to boil thoroughly.'—O. F. *parbouillir,* to cook thoroughly (Roquefort).—Low L. *parbullire,* L. *perbullire,* to boil thoroughly.—L. *per,* through; and *bullire;* see **boil** (above).

Bullace, wild plum. (C.) M. E. *bolas.* — Gael. *bulaistear,* a bullace; Irish *bulos,* a prune; Bret. *bolos, polos,* bullace.

Bullet, Bulletin, Bullion; see **Bull** (2).

Bully, a noisy rough fellow. (O. Low G.) In Sh.—O. Du. *bollaert,* 'a jester or a gyber,' Hexham; Low G. *bullerjaan, bullerbäk,* in Hamburgh *bullerbrook* (cf. E. *bully-rook*), a boisterous fellow. So also Swed. *bullerbas,* a noisy fellow; *buller,* clamour; *bullra,* to make a noise. Allied to **Bull** (1), **Bellow,** and **Boulder.**

Bulrush. (Scand. *and* E.) M. E. *bulrysche,* Prompt. Parv., p. 244, col. 2. Lit. 'stem-rush;' from its stout stem. **—** Dan. *bul,* stem, trunk; see **bole,** under **Bulge.**

Bulwark. (Scand.) See **Bulge.**

Bum, contracted form of **Bottom.** (E.) So also O. Friesic *boden,* bottom, became N. Friesic *bóm.*

bum-bailiff, under-bailiff. (E. *and* F.)

A slang term. Todd quotes passages to shew that it arose from the pursuer catching at a man by the hinder part of his garment.

Bumble-bee, a bee that booms or hums. See Boom (1).

Bumboat. (E.) From *bum* and *boat.* Orig. a scavenger's boat on the Thames (A. D. 1685); afterwards used to supply vegetables to ships.

Bump (1), to thump; a blow. (C.) W. *pwmpio,* to thump; *pwmp,* a lump; Corn. *bom, bum,* a blow; Gael. and Irish *beum,* a stroke, also to strike. The senses are : (1) to strike, (2) a blow, (3) the effect of a blow. See Bunch.

Bump (2), to boom. (C.) See Boom (1).

Bumper. (F. ‒ L. ‒ Gk.) See Boom (1).

Bumpkin. (Du.) See Beam.

Bun. (F. ‒ Scand.) O. prov. F. *bune, bugne,* a cake, kind of fritters; the same as F. *bigne,* a swelling or bump due to a blow (Burguy), whence mod. F. *beignet,* a fritter. ' *Bignets,* little round loaves or lumps,' &c.; Cot. ‒ Icel. *bunga,* a convexity; *bunki,* a bunch; see Bunch.

bunion. (Ital. ‒ Scand.) A late word. ‒ Ital. *bugnone,* a round lump, boil, blain; augmentative of *bugno,* the same; cf. O. F. *bugne, bune,* a swelling; see Bun.

Bunch. (Scand.) M. E. *bunche.* ‒ Icel. *bunki,* a heap, pile; Dan. *bunke,* a heap. ‒ O. Swed. *bunga,* to strike; Swed. dial. *bunga,* to bunch out. Cf. Du. *bonken,* to beat; W. *pwng,* a cluster; and see Bump (1).

Bundle. (E.) See Bind.

Bung. (C. ?) Perhaps Celtic; W. *bwng,* an orifice, also a bung; O. Gael. *buine,* a tap, spigot; Irish *buinne,* a tap, spout.

Bungalow, a Bengal thatched house. (Pers. ‒ Bengalee.) Pers. *bangalah,* of or belonging to Bengal, a bungalow; Rich. Dict. p. 293. From the name *Bengal.*

Bungle. (Scand.) See Bang (1).

Bunion. See Bun.

Bunk, a wooden case or box, berth. (Scand.) Cf. O. Swed. *bunke,* the planking of a ship, forming a shelter for merchandise, &c. (Ihre); the usual sense of Swed. *bunke* is a heap, pile, something prominent; see Bunch.

Bunt, the belly of a sail. (Scand.) It answers in form to Dan. *bundt,* Swed. *bunt,* a bundle, a bunch; from the pp. of the verb to Bind. But the right words for 'bunt' are Dan. *bug,* Swed. *buk,* Du. *bögt,* from the verb to Bow.

Bunting (1), a bird. (E. ?) M. E. *bunting;* also *buntyle* (=*buntel*), Lowl. Sc. *buntlin.* Origin unknown.

Bunting (2), a thin woollen stuff for flags. (F. ‒ L. ‒ Gk.) Lit. 'sifting-cloth'; from M. E. *bonten* (=*bulten*), to sift; see Bolt (2).

Buoy. (Du. ‒ L.) Du. *boei,* a buoy; also a shackle, a fetter. ‒ Low L. *boia,* a fetter, clog. ‒ L. *boiæ,* pl. a collar for the neck, orig. of leather.

Bur, Burdock; see Burr.

Burbot, a fish; see Barb (1).

Burden (1), a load; see Bear (1).

Burden, (2), the refrain of a song. (F. ‒ Low L.) F. *bourdon,* a drone-bee, humming of bees, drone of a bagpipe; see Cot. ‒ Low L. *burdonem,* acc. of *burdo,* a drone. Prob. of imitative origin; cf. Lowland Sc. *birr,* to make a whizzing noise, E. *buzz.*

Bureau. (F. ‒ L. ‒ Gk.) See Bolt (2).

Burganet, a helmet. (F.) F. *bourguignote,* 'a burganet,' Cot. So called because first used by the Burgundians. ‒ F. *Bourgogne,* Burgundy.

Burgeon, a bud. (F. ‒ Teut.) F. *bourgeon,* a young bud. Lengthened from Languedoc *boure,* a bud, eye of a shoot (Diez). ‒ M. H. G. *buren,* O. H. G. *purjan,* to raise, push up, push out. ‒ M. H. G. *bor, por,* an elevation; whence G. *empor* (=*in por*), upwards.

Burgess, Burgher, Burglar, Burgomaster, Burial; see under Borough.

Burin, an engraver's tool. (F. ‒ Ital. ‒ G.) F. *burin.* ‒ Ital. *borino.* Prob. from M. H. G. *boren* (G. *bohren*), to bore; see Bore (1).

Burl, to pick knots and loose threads from cloth. (F. ‒ L.) To *burl* is to pick off *burls.* M. E. *burle,* a knot in cloth. ‒ Languedoc *bouril,* an end of thread in cloth; dimin. of F. *bourre,* a flock or lock of wool or hair. ‒ Low L. *burra,* a woollen pad; allied to L. *burræ,* refuse, trash, Low L. *reburrus,* rough, as if from a L. *burrus**, rough. See Burr.

Burlesque, comic. (F. ‒ Ital. ‒ L.) F. *burlesque.* ‒ Ital. *burlesco,* ludicrous. ‒ Ital. *burla,* waggery, a trick. A dimin. from L. *burra,* rough hair, also a jest (Ausonius). See Burl.

Burly. (C.; *with* E. *suffix.*) M. E. *burli, burliche, borli.* Formed by adding the suffix -*ly* (A. S. -*líc*) to the base of Gael. and Irish *borr, borr-a,* a knob, bunch, grandeur, greatness, whence also Irish *borr-ach,* a proud man, Gael. *borr-ail*, swaggering, boastful. See **Burr**.

Burn (1), verb. (E.) M. E. *bernen*; also *brennen*. A. S. *beornan, byrnan, brinnan*, strong verb, pt. t. *bearn, bran*, pp. *bornen, brunnen*; also *bernan, bærnan, brennan*, weak verb. **+** Icel. *brenna*, Dan. *brænde*, Swed. *bränna*; G. *brennen*; Goth. *brinnan*. Perhaps allied to Lat. *feruere*, to glow.

brand, a burning piece of wood, scar of fire, a sword. (E.) M. E. *brond*, A. S. *brand*, a burning, a sword; from the pt. t. of A. S. *beornan*. **+** Icel. *brandr*, a fire-brand, sword-blade (from its flashing); Swed. and Dan. *brand*, fire-brand, fire; M. H. G. *brant*, a brand, sword.

bran-new. (E.) Short for *brand-new*, i.e. new from the fire.

brant-fox, brant-goose or **brent-goose.** The prefix is Scand., as in Swed. *brandräf*, a brant-fox, *brandgås*, a brent-goose. The orig. sense is 'burnt,' with the notion of redness or brownness.

brandish. (F. — Scand.) M. E. *braundisen*. — F. *brandiss-ant*, pres. pt. of *brandir*, to brandish a sword. — Norman F. *brand*, a sword. — Icel. *brandr*; see **brand** above.

brandy. (Du.) Formerly *brand-wine, brandy-wine*; whence *brandy*. — Du. *brande-wijn*, also *brandtwijn*, brandy; lit. burnt wine. — Du. *brandt*, for *gebrandet*, burnt; and *wijn*, wine; see **Burn**.

brawl (2), a sort of dance. (F. — Scand. or Teut.) 'A French *brawl*,' L. L. L. iii. 9. — F. *bransle*, 'a totter, swing, ... *brawl* or dance,' Cot. — F. *bransler*, to reel; mod. F. *branler*. Allied to O. F. *brandeler* (Littré), *brandiller*, to wag, shake (Cot.), frequentative forms of F. *brandir*. See **brandish** above.

brimstone, sulphur. (E.) M. E. *brimston, bremstoon*, also *brenstoon* (Wyclif). — M. E. *brenn-en*, to burn, and *stoon*, stone. So also Icel. *brennisteinn*, brimstone.

brindled, brinded, streaked. (Scand.) Icel. *brönd-*, as in *bröndóttr*, brindled, said of a cow. — Icel. *brandr*, a brand, flame, sword. Thus *brinded = branded*.

brine. (E.) M. E. *brine*. A. S. *bryne*, salt liquor; a particular use of *bryne*, a scorching; from the burning taste. — A. S. *brunn-en*, pp. of *beornan*, to burn. **+** O. Du. *brijne*; whence Du. *brem*, pickle.

brunt, shock of an onset. (Scand.) M. E. *brunt*, an attack. — Icel. *bruna*, to advance with the speed of fire, as in battle.

— Icel. *bruni*, burning, heat. — Icel. *brunnum*, pt. pl. of *brenna*, to burn.

Burn (2), a brook; see **Bourn** (2).

Burnish; see **Brown**.

Burr, Bur. (E.) M. E. *burre*, knob on a burdock; *borre*, roughness in the throat. Not in A. S. **+** Swed. *borre*, a sea urchin; *kardborre*, a burdock; Dan. *borre*, burdock. Cf. Gael. *borra*, a knob, *borr*, to swell. Der. *bur-dock*.

Burrow; see **Borough**.

Bursar. (L. — Gk.) See **Purse**.

Burst. (E.) M. E. *bersten, bresten*, pt. t. *brast*. A. S. *berstan*, to burst asunder, break; str. vb. **+** Du. *bersten*; G. *bersten*; Icel. *bresta*; Swed. *brista*; Dan. *briste*. Cf. Gael. *brisd*, to break.

breast. (E.) M. E. *breast*. A. S. *brebst*. **+** Du. *borst*; Icel. *brjóst*; Swed. *bröst*; Dan. *byst*; G. *brust*; Goth. *brusts*. The O. H. G. *prust* means (1) a bursting, (2) a breast; the orig. sense is a bursting forth, from the swelling of the female breast.

Bury (1), to hide; (2) town; see **Borough**.

Bush (1), a thicket. (Scand.) M. E. *busch, busk*. — Dan. *busk*, Swed. *buske*, a bush, shrub. **+** Du. *bosch* (whence F. *bois*); O. H. G. *busc*; G. *busch*.

ambuscade. (Span. — Low L. — Teut.) Span. *ambuscado, emboscada*, an ambush. Orig. pp. of *emboscar*, to set in ambush. — Low Lat. *imboscare*, lit. to set in a bush or thicket. — L. *im-*, for *in*, in; and Du. *bosch*, Dan. *busk*, a bush, thicket.

ambush. (F. — Low L. — Teut.) Formerly *embush*. — O. F. *embuscher, embuissier*, to set in ambush. — Low L. *imboscare*; as above.

bouquet. (F. — Low L. — Teut.) F. *bouquet*; O. F. *bosquet*, orig. 'a little wood,' dimin. of O. F. *bos* (F. *bois*), a wood. — Low L. *boscum, buscum*, a wood. — Du. *bosch*, a wood, or O. H. G. *busc*.

Bush (2); see **Box** (1).

Bushel, a measure; see **Pyx**.

Busk (1), to get oneself ready. (Scand.) See **Boor**; and compare **Bask**.

Busk (2), a support for a woman's stays. (F.) F. *busque*, 'a buske, or buste;' Cot. Also spelt *buste*. It seems to be the same word as **Bust**, q.v.

Buskin. (Du.) Put for *bruskin*. O. Du. *brooskens*, buskins (Sewel); from O. Du. *borseken*, a little purse. — O. F. *borse*; see **Purse**.

Buss, to kiss. (G.; *confused with* F. — L.) The old word was *bass*. — F. *baiser*, to kiss. — Lat. *basium*, a kiss. Confused with O.

and prov. G. (Bavarian) *bussen*, to kiss;
cf. Gael. and W. *bus*, mouth, lip.

Bust. (F.—Ital.) F. *buste.*—Ital. *busto*,
the bust, trunk of human body, stays.—
Low L. *bustum*, the trunk of the body.
Etym. uncertain.

Bustard. (F.—L.) See **Aviary.**

Bustle. (Scand.) Icel. *bustla*, to bustle,
splash about as a fish. Cf. Dan. *buse*, to
bounce, pop; Swed. dial. *busa*, to strike,
thrust. Prob. allied to **Busy.**

Busy. (E.) M. E. *bisy*. A. S. *bysig*,
active; whence *bysgu*, exertion. + Du.
bezig, busy. Cf. **Bustle.**

But (1), prep. and conj., except. (E.)
See **Out.**

But (2); see **Butt** (1), **Butt** (2).

Butcher: see **Buck** (1).

Butler; see **Bottle** (1).

Butt (1), an end, to thrust ; see **Beat.**

Butt (2), a large barrel. (F.—L.—Gk.)
We find A. S. *bytt*; but our mod. word is
really F.—O. F. *boute*, F. *botte*, 'the vessel
which we call a *butt*,' Cot.—Low L. *butta*,
a cask.—Gk. βῦτις, βοῦτις, a flask ; of uncertain origin.

  boot (1), a covering for the leg and
foot. (F.—G.) O. F. *boute*, F. *botte*, (1)
a butt, (2) a boot ; the same word as the
above ; from their former shape.

Butter. (L.—Gk.) M. E. *botere*; A. S.
buter, butera.—L. *butyrum.*—Gk. βούτυρον,
butter; lit. ox-cheese.—Gk. βοῦ-s, an ox;
and τυρόs, cheese. ¶ Really Scythian; the
Gk. sense is a forced one.

butterfly. (E.) A. S. *buttor-fleóge*, lit.
butter-fly. So called from its excrement
resembling butter, as shewn by the O. Du.
boter-schijte, a butterfly, lit. butter-voider
(Kilian). + Du. *botervlieg*; G. *butter-
fliege.*

Buttery; see **Bottle** (1).

Buttock, Button; see **Beat.**

Buttress; see **Brattice,** p. 49, col. 2.

Buxom; see **Bow** (1).

Buy. (E.) M. E. *buggen, biggen.* A. S.
bycgan, to purchase. + Goth. *bugjan.*
Der. *abide* (2), q. v.

Buzz. (E.) An imitative word; cf. Lowl.
Sc. *bizz*, to hiss; Ital. *buzzicare*, to hum,
whisper.

Buzzard. (F.—L.) M. E. *bosard, busard*,
an inferior kind of falcon.—F. *busard.*—
F. *buse*, a buzzard; with suffix -*ard.*—Low
L. *busio* = L. *buteo*, a sparrow-hawk.

By, prep. (E.) M. E. *bi*. A. S. *bí, big.*
+ Du. *bij*; G. *bei*; Goth. *bi.* Cf. Skt.
abhi, Gk. ἀμφί.

By-law, a law affecting a township.
(Scand.) See **Boor.**

Byre, a cow-house. (E.) A Northern E.
derivative of *bower*; see p. 46, col. 1, l. 14.

C.

Cab (1); see **Caper** (1).

Cab (2), a Heb. measure. (Heb.) Heb.
qab, the 18th part of an ephah. The literal
sense is 'hollow;' cf. Heb. *qâbab*, to form
in the shape of a vault; see **Alcove.**

Cabal. (F.—Heb.) Orig. 'a secret.' F.
cabale, 'the Jewes Caball, a hidden science;'
Cot.—Heb. *qabbâláh*, reception, mysterious
doctrine.—Heb. *qâbal*, to receive; *qibbel*,
to adopt a doctrine.

Cabbage (1); see **Capital** (1).

Cabbage (2), to steal. (F.) F. *cabasser*,
to put into a basket.—F. *cabas*, a basket;
of unknown origin.

Cabin. (C.) M. E. *caban.*—W. *caban*,
a booth; dimin. of *cab*, a booth made with
rods set in the ground and tied at the top;
Gael. and Irish *caban*, a booth, hut, tent.
(Hence also F. *cabane.*)

  cabinet. (F.—C.) F. *cabinet*, dimin.
of F. *cabane*, a cabin; a word of Celtic
origin, as above. And see **Gabardine.**

Cable, a rope; see **Capacious.**

Caboose, the cook's cabin on board ship.
(Du.) Formerly *camboose.* — Du. *kom-
buis*, a cook's cabin; also 'the chimney in
a ship,' Sewel. A jocular word; it means
lit. 'dish-pipe;' from Du. *kom*, a dish,
and *buis*, a pipe; with reference to the
cook's dishes and chimney. (Hence also
Dan *kabys*, Swed. *kabysa*, caboose.)

Cabriolet; see **Caper** (1).

Cacao, a tree. (Span.—Mexican.) Span.
cacao; from the Mexican name of the fruit
of the tree whence chocolate is made.
¶ Not the same as *cocoa.*

chocolate, a paste made from cacao.
(Span.—Mex.) Span. *chocolate.*—Mex. *cho-
colatl*, chocolate, Clavigero, Hist. Mex. i. 433.

Cachinnation. (L.) L. acc. *cachinna-
tionem*, loud laughter.—L. *cachinnare*, to
laugh. Cf. **Cackle.**

Cack, to go to stool. (L.) M. E. *cakken.*
—L. *cacare.*

Cackle. (E.) M. E. *kakelen*, a frequentative form. Not in A. S. + Du. *kakelen*; Swed. *kackla*; Dan. *kagle*; G. *gackeln*. The sense is 'to keep on saying *kak*;' cf. *gabb-le*, *gobb-le*.

Cacophony, a harsh sound. (Gk.) Gk. κακοφωνία, a harsh sound. — Gk. κακόφωνος, harsh. — Gk. κακό-s, bad ; and φων-ή, sound. Der. *cacophonous* (Gk. κακόφωνος).

Cad, a low fellow. (F. — L.) See under Capital.

Cadaverous; see Cadence.

Caddy, a small box for tea. (Malay.) Better spelt *catty*. A small package of tea, less than a half-chest, is called in the tea-trade a *caddy* or *catty*. — Malay *katí*, a catty, a weight equal to 1⅓ lb. avoirdupois. This weight is also used in China and Japan, and tea is often made up ·in packages containing one catty.

Cade, a barrel, cask. (L.) L. *cadus*, a barrel, cask.+Gk κάδος, a cask.

Cadence, a fall of the voice. (F. — L.) M. E. *cadence*. — F. *cadence*, 'a cadence, just falling of words;' Cot. — Low L. *cadentia*, a falling. — L. *cadent-*, stem of pres. pt. of *cadere*, to fall. + Skt. *çad*, to fall.

accident, a chance event. (F. — L.) F. *accident*, 'an accident;' Cot. — L. *accident*, stem of pres. pt. of *accidere*, to happen. — L. *ac-* (for *ad*) ; and *cadere*, to fall. Der. *accidence*, F. *accidence*, L. *accidentia*.

cadaverous, corpse-like. (L.) L. *cadauerosus*. — L. *cadauer*, a corpse. — Lat. *cad-ere*, to fall, fall dead.

caducous, falling. (L.) L. *caducus*, falling. — L. *cadere*, to fall.

cascade. (F. — Ital. — L.) F. *cascade*. — Ital. *cascata*, a waterfall ; orig. fem. pp. of *cascare*, to fall. Put for *casicare**. — L. *casare*, to totter. — L. *casum*, sup. of *cadere*, to fall.

case (1), an event. (F. — L.) M.E. *cas*. — F. *cas*. — L. acc. *casum*, a fall, a case. — L. *casus*, pp. of *cadere*.

casual. (F. — L.) F.*casuel*. — L.*casualis*, happening by chance. — L. *casu-*, crude form of *casus*; see case. So also *casu-ist*.

chance, hap. (F. — L.) M.E. *chaunce*. — O. F. *chaance*. — Low L. *cadentia*, a falling, a chance; see Cadence. Der. *be-chance*, *mis-chance*.

coincide, to agree with. (L.) L. *co-* (for *con-* = *cum*, with), and *incidere*, to fall upon ; see incident ·below.

decadence, decay. (F. — L.) F. *décadence*. — Low L. *decadentia*, decay. —

L. *de*, down ; *cadentia*, a falling ; see Cadence.

decay, to fall into ruin. (F. — L.̓) O. F. *decaer*. — O. F. *de-* ; and *caer*, to fall. — L. *de*, down ; and *cadere*, to fall.

deciduous, falling off. (L.) L. *deciduus*, that falls down. — L. *decidere*, to fall down. — L. *de*, down ; and *cadere*.

escheat. (F. — L.) M. E. *eschete* (also *chete*), a forfeit to the lord of the fee. — O.F. *eschet*, rent, that which falls to one, pp. of *eschevir* (F. *échoir*). — Low L. *ex-cadere*, to fall in with, meet. — L. *ex*, out ; and *cadere*, to fall. Hence *cheat*.

incident. (F. — L.) F.*incident*, 'an incident;' Cot. — L. *incident-*, stem of pres.pt. of *incidere*, to fall upon. — L.*in*, on ; and*cadere*.

occasion. (F. — L.) — F. *occasion*. — L. acc. *occasionem*. — L. *oc-* (for *ob*, at) ; and *cas-us*, pp. of *cadere*, to fall.

occident, west. (F. — L.) O. F. *occident*, west. — L. *occident-*, stem of pres. pt. of *occidere* ; see occasion (above).

Cadet; see Capital.

Cæsura. (L.) L.*cæsura*, a cutting ; a pause in a verse. — L. *cæs-us*, pp. of *cædere*, to cut.

circumcise. (L.) L. *circumcis-us*, pp. of *circumcidere*, to cut round. — L. *circum*, round ; and *cædere*, to cut.

concise. (F. — L.) F. *concis*. — L. *con-cisus*, brief, cut short ; pp. of *concidere*. — L. *con-* (for *cum*, together) ; and *cædere*, to cut. Der. *concis·ion*.

decide. (F. — L.) F. *décider*. — L. *decidere*, pp. *decisus*, to cut off, decide. — L. *de*, down ; and *cædere*, to cut. Der. *decis-ion* (from pp. *decisus*).

excision (F. — L.) F. *excision*, 'a destroying;' Cot. — L. acc. *excisionem*, a cutting out, a destroying. — L. *excisus*, pp. of *ex-cidere*, to cut out.

incise, to cut into. (F. — L.) F. *inciser*. — L. *incisus*, pp. of *in-cidere*, to cut into.

precise. (F. — L.) O. F. *précis*, strict. — L. *præcisus*, cut off, concise, strict; pp. of *præ-cidere*, to cut off.

Note also suffix *-cide* in *homi-cide*, *sui--cide*, *infanti-cide*, &c. ¶ Here probably belong *chisel*, *scissors*, q. v.

Caducous; see Cadence.

Caftan, a Turkish garment. (Turk.) Turk. *qaftán*, a dress.

Cage; see Cave.

Cairn, a pile of stones. (C.) Gael., Irish, W., Bret. *carn*, a crag, rock; also a pile of stones. Gael. *cairn*, gen. of *carn* ; *carn*, verb, to pile up.

Caitiff; see **Capacious**.

Cajole; see **Cave**.

Cake, see **Cook**.

Calabash. (Port. *or* Span. — Arab.) Port. *calabaça*, a gourd; Span. *calabaza*. Lit. 'dried gourd.' — Arab. *qar'*, a gourd; and *aybas*, dry.

Calamity. (F. — L.) F. *calamité*. — L. acc. *calamitatem*, a misfortune.

Calash, a sort of carriage. (F. — G. — Slavonic.) F. *calèche*. — G. *kalesche*. — Pol. *kolaska*, a small carriage, dimin. of *kolasa*, a carriage; Russ. *koliaska*, a carriage. — Pol. and Russ. *kolo*, a wheel. (√ KAL.)

Calcareous, Calcine, Calculate; see **Calx**.

Caldron, Cauldron. (F. — L.) O. F. *caldron* * (prob. Picard), given only in the form *chaldron*, mod. F. *chaudron* (Ital. *calderone*, Span. *calderon*), a vessel for hot water. — L. *caldus*, contr. form of *calidus*, hot. — L. *calere*, to be hot. + Skt. *çrá*, to boil.

calenture, a feverous madness. (F. — Span. — L.) F. *calenture*. — Span. *calentura*. — L. *calent-*, stem of pres. pt. of *calere*, to be hot.

caloric. (F. — L.) F. *calorique*. — L. *calor*, heat. — L. *calere*, to be hot.

calorific, making hot. (L.) L. *calorificus*, making hot. — L. *calori-*, crude form of *calor*, heat; and *-fic-*, for *facere*, to make.

caudle, a warm drink. (F. — L.) O. F. *caudel, chaudel*, a sort of warm drink. — O. F. *chaud, chald*, hot. — L. *caldus*, for *calidus*, hot.

chafe, to warm by friction, vex. (F. — L.) M. E. *chaufen*, to warm. — O. F. *chaufer* (F. *chauffer*), to warm; cf. Prov. *calfar*, to warm. — Low L. *caleficare*, to warm. — L. *calefacere*, to warm, make to glow. — L. *cale-re*, to glow; *facere*, to make.

chaldron, a coal-measure. (F. — L.) O. F. *chaldron*, orig. a caldron; see **Caldron**.

scald (1), to burn. (F. — L.) M. E. *scalden*. — O. F. *escalder* *, later form *eschauder*, to scald (F. *échauder*). — L. *excaldare*, to wash in hot water. — L. *ex*, out, very; and *caldus* = *calidus*, hot.

Calendar; see **Calends**.

Calender, a machine for pressing cloth; see **Cylinder**.

Calends. (L.) L. *calendæ*, s. pl., the first day of the (Roman) month. Orig. obscure; but certainly from O. Lat. *calare* (or *calere* *), to proclaim. + Gk. καλεῖν, to summon.

calendar. (L.) L. *calendarium*, an account-book kept by money-changers; so called because interest was due on the *calends* (1st day) of each month; also, a calendar. — L. *calendæ*, calends.

conciliate. (L.) Pp. of L. *conciliare*, to bring together, conciliate. — L. *concilium* (below).

council. (F. — L.) F. *concile*. — L. *concilium*, an assembly called together. — L. *con-* (*cum*), together; and *calare*, to summon.

intercalate, to insert. (L.) From pp. of L. *inter-calare*, to proclaim that a day has been inserted in the calendar, to insert.

reconcile. (F. — L.) O. F. *reconcilier*. — L. *re-*, again; *conciliare*; see **conciliate** (above).

Calenture; see **Caldron**.

Calf. (E.) M. E. *kalf*. A. S. *cealf*. + Du. *kalf*; Icel. *kálfr*; Swed. *kalf*; Dan. *kalv*; Goth. *kalbo*; G. *kalb*. Þer. *calve*, A. S. *cealfian*.

Caliber, Calibre, bore of a gun. (F.) F. *calibre*, size of a bore. Etym. unknown. Perhaps from L. *quá librá*, with what weight (Diez); or from Arab. *qálib*, a form, mould, model, Rich. Dict. p. 1111 (Littré).

calipers, compasses. (F.) Put for *caliber-compasses*, i.e. compasses for measuring diameters; see above.

caliver, a sort of musket. (F.) Named from its *caliber* or bore; see Kersey's Dict.

Calico, cotton-cloth. (E. Indian.) Named from *Calicut*, on the Malabar coast, whence it was first imported.

Calif, Caliph. (F. — Arab.) F. *calife*, a successor of the prophet. — Arab. *khalifa*, successor. — Arab. *khalafa*, to succeed.

Caligraphy, Calligraphy, good writing. (Gk.) Gk. καλλιγραφία. — Gk. καλλι-, prefix (from καλός, good, fair); and γράφειν, to write.

calisthenics, callisthenics, graceful exercises. (Gk.) From Gk. καλλισθεν-ής, adorned with strength. — Gk. καλλι- (for καλός, fair); and σθέν-ος, strength.

calomel, a preparation of mercury. (Gk.) Coined to express a *white* product from a *black* substance. — Gk. καλό-s, fair; and μέλ-as, black.

Calipers; see **Caliber**.

Calisthenics; see **Caligraphy**.

Caliver; see **Caliber**.

Calk, Caulk. (F. — L.) M. E. *cauken*, to tread. — O. F. *cauquer*, to tread; to tent a wound with lint. — L. *calcare*, to tread, force down by pressure. — L. *calc-*, stem of *calx*, the heel; see **Heel**.

inculcate. (L.) From pp. of L. *inculcare*, lit. to tread in, hence, to enforce by admonition. — L. *in*, in; *calcare*, to tread.

Call. (E.) A. S. *ceallian*; cf. *hilde-calla*, a herald.+Du. *kallen*; Icel. and Swed. *kalla*; Dan. *kalde*; O. H. G. *challon*. (√ GAR.)

recall. (L. *and* E.) From L. *re-*, back; and *call*.

Callous, hard. (F.—L.) F. *calleux*.— L. *callosus*, thick-skinned.—L. *callus*, *callum*, hard skin.

Callow, unfledged, bald. (E.) M. E. *calu*, *calewe*. A. S. *calu*, bald.+Du. *kaal*, bald; Swed. *kal*; G. *kahl*; L. *caluus*; Skt. *khalati*, bald-headed. (√ SKAR.)

Calm. (F.—Gk.) F. *calme*, adj. Allied to Prov. *chaume*, the time when the flocks rest; F. *chômer* (formerly *chaumer*), to rest from work.—Low L. *cauma*, the heat of the sun (whence, time for rest).—Gk. *καῦμα*, heat.—Gk. *καίειν*, to burn. Der. *be-calm*.

Calomel. (Gk.) See **Caligraphy.**

Caloric, Calorific; see **Caldron.**

Calumny. (F.—L.) F. *calomnie*.—L. *calumnia*, false accusation. — L. *calui*, *caluera*, to deceive.

challenge. (F.—L.) M. E. *chalenge*, *calenge*, often in the sense 'a claim.' — O. F. *chalonge*, *calenge*, a dispute, claim; an accusation.—L. *calumnia*; see above.

Calvo; see **Calf.**

Calx. (L.) L. *calx*, stone, lime (stem *calc-*); in late L., a calx. + W. *careg*, stone.

calcareous. (L.) Should be *calcarious*. —L. *calcarius*, pertaining to lime. — L. *calc-*, stem of *calx*.

calcine. (F.—L.) F. *calciner*.—Low L. *calcinare*, to reduce to a calx.—L. *calc-*, stem of *calx*.

calculate. (L.) L. *calculat-us*, pp. of *calculare*, to reckon by help of small pebbles.—L. *calculus*, pebble; dimin. of *calx*.

causeway, a paved way, raised way. (F.—L.) An extension (with addition of *way*) of *causey*, M. E. *causee*.—O. F. *caucie* (=mod. F. *chaussée*, Prov. *causada*, Span *calzada*)=Low L. *calciata*, put for *calciata uia*, a paved way.—Low L. *calciatus*, pp. of *calciare*, to make a roadway with mortar containing lime. ¶ Or from Low L. *calceatus*, trodden down.

chalk. (L.) M. E. *chalk*. A. S. *cealc*. —L. *calc-*, stem of *calx*, lime.

Calyx. (L.—Gk.) L. *calyx*.—Gk. *κάλυξ*, a covering, calyx (or cup) of a flower. (√ KAL.)

Cam; see **Comb.**

Cambric. (Flanders.) Named from *Kamerijk*, also called *Cambray*, a town in Flanders, where it was first made.

Camel. (F. — L. — Gk. — Heb.) M. E. *camel*, *camail*, *chamel*.—O. F. *camel*, *chamel*. —L. *camelus*.—Gk. *κάμηλος*.—Heb. *gámál*. Cf. Arab. *jamal*.

camelopard, a giraffe. (L.—Heb. *and* Gk.) Formerly *camelopardalis*. — L. *camelopardalis*.—Gk. *καμηλοπάρδαλις*, giraffe; partly like a camel, partly like a pard.— Gk. *κάμηλο-s*, a camel (Heb. *gámál*); and *πάρδαλις*, a pard; see **Pard.**

camlet, a stuff. (Arab.) Formerly *camelot*, supposed to be named from containing *camel's* hair. Really from Arab. *khamlat*, *khamalat*, camlet; Rich. Dict. p. 628.

Camellia. (Personal name.) A plant named after Geo. Jos. Kamel, a Moravian Jesuit, who described the plants in the island of Luzon.

Camelopard; see **Camel.**

Cameo. (Ital.) Ital. *cammeo*, a cameo, precious stone carved in relief. Origin unknown.

Camera. (L.) L. *camera*, a chamber; hence *camera obscura*, a dark chamber, box for photography; see **Chamber.**

Camlet; see **Camel.**

Camomile; see **Chamomile.**

Camp. (L.) We find F. *camp* (Cot.); but the E. word was prob. taken directly from L. *campus*, a field, ground held by an army. + Gk. *κῆπος*, a garden.

campaign, orig. a large field. (F.— L.) F. (Picard) *campaigne*, *campagne*, an open field.—L. *campania*, open field.—L. *campus*, a field. (Also spelt *champaign*, and even *champion* in old authors.)

campestral, growing in fields. (L.) L. *campestr-is*, growing in fields.—L. *campus*, a field.

champagne. (F.—L.) A wine named from *Champagne* in France, which means 'a plain;' see below.

champaign, open country. (F.—L.) In Sh. F. *champaigne*, of which the Picard form was *campaigne*; see **campaign.**

champion. (F.—L.) O. F. *champion.* —Low L. *campionem*, acc. of *campio*, a combatant.—Low L. *campus*, a duel, combat; a peculiar use of L. *campus*, a field.

decamp, to depart. (F.—L.) F. *décamper*; O. F. *descamper*, orig. to remove a camp. — L. *dis-*, away; and *campus*, a field, later, a camp.

encamp. (F. — L.) Coined from *en-* (=F. *en*, L. *in*); and *camp*; hence 'to form into a camp.'

scamp. (F. — Ital. — L.) Formerly a vagabond, or fugitive. — O. F. *escamper*, *s'escamper*, to flee. — Ital. *scampare*, to escape, decamp. — L. *ex*, out; and *campus*, battle-field. **Der.** *scamp-er*, to run or flee away.

shamble, to walk awkwardly. (Du. — F. — Ital. — L.) Du. *schampelen*, to stumble, trip, also to decamp. — O. F. *s'escamper*, to decamp; as above.

Campaign, Campestral; see Camp.

Campanula. (L.) Lit. 'a little bell;' dimin. of Low L. *campana*, a bell. Hence also *campani-form*.

Camphor. (F. — Arab. — Malay.) Formerly spelt *camphire* (with an inserted *i*). — F. *camphre*, 'camphire;' Cot. — Low L. *camphora* (whence the form *camphor*). — Arab. *káfúr*, camphor; cf. Skt. *karpúra*, camphor. — Malay *kápúr*, lit. chalk; *kápúr Barús*, chalk of Barous, a name for camphor. *Barous* is in Sumatra.

Can (1), I am able. (E.) A.S. *can*, *cann*, 1st and 3rd persons sing. pres. of *cunnan*, to know. The pres. t. *can* is really an old pt. t.; the same peculiarity occurs in Du. *kunnen*, Icel. and Swed. *kunna*, Dan. *kunde*, to know, to be able; G. *können*, to know. β. The pt. t. is *could*, with intrusive *l*; M.E. *coude*, A.S. *cúðe*; cf. Goth. *kuntha*, Du. *konde*, G. *könnte*; shewing that A.S. *cúðe* (for *cunðe**) has lost an *n*. γ. The pp. *couth*, A.S. *cúð*, known, only survives in *uncouth*, which see below. (√GAN.)

con (1), to enquire into, observe. (E.) M.E. *cunnien*, to examine. — A.S. *cunnian*, test, seek to know; a desiderative form from *cunnan*, to know. **Der.** *ale-conner*, i. e. ale-tester.

cuddle. (E.) Put for *couth-le*, frequent. form of M.E. *kuþþen* (*kuththen*), to be familiar, embrace. — A.S. *kúð*, known, familiar; see Can, § γ.

cunning, adj. (E.) Orig. pres. pt. of M.E. *cunnen*, to know.

cunning, sb. (Scand.) Modified from Icel. *kunnandi*, knowledge. — Icel. *kunna*, to know. See Can (1).

ken, to know. (Scand.) M.E. *kennen*. — Icel. *kenna*, Swed. *känna*, Dan. *kiende*, to know; so also G. *kennen*, A.S. *cennan*,

Goth. *kannjan*. Causal form of *cunnan*, to know, derived from *can* by vowel-change of *a* to *e*.

kith, kindred, acquaintance. (E.) M. E. *cúððe*, kith. A. S. *cýððe*, native land, kindred. — A.S. *cúð*, known, pp. of *kunnan* to know.

kythe, to make known. (E.) A.S. *cýðan*, to make known. — A.S. *cúð*, known (above).

uncouth. (E.) A. S. *uncúð*, orig. unknown; hence, strange, odd. — A. S. *un-*, not; and *cúð*, known, pp. of *cunnan*, to know. And see Know.

Can (2), a drinking-vessel. (E.) A. S. *canna*, *canne*. ♣ Du. *kan*; Icel. *kanna*; Swed. *kanna*; Dan. *kande*; G. *kanne*, a tankard, mug. (Apparently a true Teut. word.)

Canal. (F. — L.) F. *canal* (whence also Du. *kanaal*.) — L. *canalis*, a channel, trench; orig. a cutting. Cf. Skt. *khan*, to dig, pierce; *khani*, a mine. (√SKA.)

channel. (F. — L.) M. E. *chanel*, *canel*. — O. F. *chanel*, *canel*, a canal. — L. *canalis*; as above.

kennel (2), a gutter. (F. — L.) A corruption of M. E. *canel*, a channel; see above.

Canary, a bird, a wine, a dance. (Canary Islands.) All named from the *Canary* islands.

Cancel; see Cancer.

Cancer. (L.) L. *cancer*, a crab; also an 'eating' tumour. ♣ Gk. καρκίνος, Skt. *karkata*, a crab; cf. Skt. *karkara*, hard. Named from its hard shell.

cancel. (F. — L.) F. *canceler*. — Law L. *cancellare*, to cancel a deed by drawing lines across it. — L. *cancellus*, a grating, pl. *cancelli*, lattice-work; dimin. of *cancer*, a crab, whence pl. *cancri*, sometimes used to mean lattice-work.

canker. (L.) L. *cancer*, a crab, a cancer; hence that which corrodes.

chancel. (F. — L.) So called because orig. fenced off by a latticed screen. — O. F. *chancel*, an enclosure fenced off with an open screen. — Low L. *cancellus*, a chancel, screen; L. *cancellus*, a grating; see cancel (above).

chancellor. (F. — L.) O.F. *chancelier*. — Low L. acc. *cancellarium*, a chancellor; orig. an officer who stood near the screen before the judgment seat. — L. *cancellus*, a grating; see chancel (above).

chancery. (F. — L.) For *chancelry*. M. E. *chancelerie*. — O. F. *chancellerie*. —

Low L. *cancellaria*, the record-room of a *cancellarius*; see chancellor.

Candelabrum; see Candid.

Candid. (F.-L.) F. *candide*, white, fair, sincere. - L. *candidus*, white, shining. - L. *candēre*, to shine. - L. *candēre**, to set on fire (in comp. *in-cendere*). + Skt. *chand*, to shine.

candelabrum. (L.) A candle-holder; from *candela*; see candle below.

candidate. (L.) L. *candidatus*, white-robed; because candidates for office wore white. - L. *candidus*, white.

candle. (L.) A.S. *candel*. - L. *candela*, a candle. - L. *candēre*, to glow.

candour. (F.-L.) F. *candeur*. - L. acc. *candorem*, brightness (hence, sincerity).

cannel-coal. (L. *and* E.) Lit. a 'candle-coal;' because it burns brightly. Prov. E. *cannel*, a candle; see candle.

censer. (F.-L.) Short for *incenser*. - F. *encensoir*. - Low L. *incensorium*, a vase for incense. - Low L. *incensum*; see incense (2) below.

chandelier. (F.-L.) O. F. *chandelier*, a candle-holder. - Low L. *candelaria*, a candle-stick. - L. *candela*; see candle.

chandler. (F.-L.) O. F. *chandelier*, a chandler. - Low L. *candelarius*, a candle-seller. - L. *candela*; see candle. Der. *corn-chandler*, where *chandler* merely means seller, dealer.

incandescent, glowing hot. (L.) From stem of pres. pt. of *in-candescere*, to glow; where *candescere* is the inceptive form of *candere*, to glow.

incendiary. (L.) L. *incendiarius*, setting on fire. - L. *incendium*, a burning. - L. *incendere*, to set on fire. - L. *in*, upon; and *candēre**, to burn; see Candid.

incense (1), to inflame. (L.) L. *incensus*, pp. of *incendere*, to set on fire; see above.

incense (2), smell of burnt spices. (F.-L.) F. *encens*, incense, burnt spices. - L. *incensum*, that which is burnt; neut. of pp. of *incendere*, to set on fire (above).

kindle (1), to inflame. (Scand. - E. - L.) From Icel. *kyndill*, a candle, torch. Borrowed from A. S. *candel*, a candle (as in *candelmæsse*, Candlemass, whence Icel. *kyndillmessa*). - L. *candela*.

Candy, to crystallise. (F. - Ital. - Pers.) F. *se candir*, ' to candie;' Cot. - Ital. *candire*, to candy. - Ital. *candi*, candy; *zucchero candi*, sugar-candy. - Pers. and Arab. *qand*, sugar-candy; whence Arab.

qandí, made of sugar. The word is Aryan (Pers.) ; cf. Skt. *khándava*, sweetmeats, *khanda*, a broken piece. Der. *sugar-candy*, Ital. *zucchero candi*.

Cane. (F. - L. - Gk.) M. E. *cane, canne*. - F. *canne*. - L. *canna*. - Gk. *κάννα*, *κάννη*, a reed. Cf. Heb. *qáneh*, reed ; Arab. *qanát*, cane.

canister. (L. - Gk.) L. *canistrum*, a reed basket. - Gk. *κάναστρον*, the same. - Gk. *κάνη* = *κάννη*, a reed.

cannon. (F. - L. - Gk.) F. *canon*, orig. a gun-barrel. - L. *canna*, a reed ; see Cane.

canon. (L. - Gk.) A.S. *canon*. - L. *canon*, a rule. - Gk. *κανών*, a rod, rule. - Gk. *κάνη* = *κάννη*, a (straight) cane.

Canine. (L.) L. *caninus*, belonging to a dog. - L. *canis*, a dog ; see Hound.

kennel (1), a house for dogs. (F. - L.) M. E. *kenel*. A Norman form of O. F. *chenil*, a kennel. - Norman F. *ken*, O. F. *chen* (F. *chien*), a dog, from L. acc. *canem*, a dog ; with suffix *-il* = L. *-ile*, as in *ou-ile*, a sheep-fold.

Canister; see Cane.

Canker; see Cancer.

Cannel-coal; see Candid.

Cannibal. (Span. - W. Indian.) Formerly *canibal*. - Span. *canibal*, corruption of *Caribal*, a Carib, native of the Caribbean Islands. The W. Indian word *carib* means 'brave.'

Cannon; see Cane.

Canoe. (Span. - W. Ind.) Span. *canoa*; orig. a Caribbean word for ' boat.'

Canon; see Cane.

Canopy; see Cone.

Cant (1), to sing in a whining way, whine. (L.) L. *cantare*, to sing ; frequent. of *canere*, to sing. So also Gael. *cainnt*, talk ; from *can*, to sing, say. *Cant* was at first a beggar's whine ; hence, hypocrisy ; see recant.

accent. (F. - L.) F. *accent*. - L. acc. *accentum*, a tone. - L. *ac-* (for *ad*) ; and *cantus*, a singing. - L. *cantus*, pp. of *canere*.

canorous, tuneful. (L.) L. *canorus*. - L. *canere*, to sing ; see above.

canticle. (L.) L. *canticulum*, a little song ; dimin. of *canticum*, a song ; dimin. of *cantus*, a song.

canto. (Ital. - L.) Ital. *canto*, a singing, section of a poem. - L. acc. *cantum*, a singing, song.

canzonet. (Ital. - L.) Ital. *canzonetta*, dimin. of *canzone*, a hymn, song. - L. *can-*

tionem, acc. of *cantio*, a song. — L. *cantus*, pp. of *canere*, to sing.

chant. (F. — L.) F. *chanter*. — L. *cantare*, to sing; frequent. of *canere*. Der. *chant-ry*, M. E. *chaunterie*; *chanti-cleer*, M. E. *chaunte-cleer*, clear-singing.

descant. (F. — L.) Orig. a variation in a song. — O. F. *descant*, a kind of song. — O. F. *des-* (= L. *dis-*), apart; and *cant* (= L. *cantus*), a song.

enchant. (F. — L.) F. *enchanter*, to charm. — L. *incantare*, to repeat a chant. — L. *in-*, upon; and *cantare*; see Cant (1).

incantation. (L.) L. *incantatio*, an enchanting. — L. *incantare*; see above.

incentive. (L.) L. *incentiuus*, striking up a tune, inciting. — L. *incentus*, unused pp. of *incinere*, to sound an instrument. — L. *in*, into; and *canere*, to sound.

precentor. (L.) L. *præcentor*, the leader of a choir. — L. *præ*, before; and *cantor*, a singer. — L. *cantare*, to sing; see Cant (1).

recant. (L.) L. *recantare*, to sing back, echo; also to recant, recall. — L. *re-*, back; and *cantare*, to sing.

Cant (2), an edge; as verb, to tilt. (Du.) Du. *kant*, an edge, corner. + Dan. and Swed. *kant*, edge; G. *kante*, a corner. ¶ All from L. *canthus* = Gk. κάνθος.

canteen. (F. — Ital. — G.) F. *cantine*. — Ital. *cantina*, a cellar, cool cave (hence the sense of vessel for liquids). Orig. 'a little corner.' — G. *kante*, a corner.

cantle, a small piece. (F. — Teut.) O. F. *cantel*, a small piece, a corner; dimin. from G. *kante*, a corner; see Cant (2) above.

decant. (F. — Ital. — L. *and* G.) F. *décanter*, to pour out wine. — Ital. *decantare*, to tilt a vessel on its edge. — L. *de*, down; and G. *kante*, a corner, edge. Der. *decant-er*, wine-vessel.

scantling, a cut piece of timber, a pattern. (F. — Teut. ; *with* L. *prefix*). From O. F. *eschantillon*, 'a small cantle, scantling, sample;' Cot. — O. F. *es-*, prefix, L. *ex*; *cantel*, a cantle; see **cantle** (above).

Canteen, Cantle; see Cant (2).

Canter, an easy gallop. (Proper name.) Short for *Canterbury* gallop, the pace at which pilgrims rode thither.

Canticle, Canto; see Cant (1).

Canton, a region. (F. — Low L.) F. *canton* (Ital. *cantone*). — Low L. *cantonum*, *canto*, a region, province. Origin doubtful. ¶ *Canton* (in heraldry), a corner of a

shield, is from F. *canton*, a corner, Low L. *canto*, a squared stone; from G. *kante*, a corner; see Cant (2).

Canvas. (F. — L. — Gk.) M. E. *canevas*. F. *canevas*. — Low L. *canabacius*, hempen cloth. — L. *cannabis*, hemp. — Gk. κάνναβις, hemp. Cf. Skt. *çama*, hemp; see **Hemp**.

canvass. (F. — L. — Gk.) Orig. to sift through *canvas*; hence to sift, examine. — O. F. *canabasser*, to canvass, to sift out.

Canzonet; see Cant (1).

Caoutchouc. (F. — Carib.) F. *caoutchouc*; orig. a Caribbean word.

Cap; see **Cape** (1).

Capable; see below.

Capacious, able to contain. (L.) Coined from L. *capaci-*, crude form of *capax*, able to hold. — L. *capere*, to hold, contain; see **Have.** (√KAP.)

accept. (F. — L.) F. *accepter*. — L. *acceptare*, frequent. of *accipere*, to receive. — L. *ac-* (= *ad*); and *capere*.

anticipate. (L.) L. *anticipare*, to take beforehand. — L. *anti-*, before; and *capere*, to take.

cable. (F. — L.) M. E. *cable*. — O. F. *cable*. — Low L. *capulum*, *caplum*, a strong (holding) rope. — L. *capere*, to hold.

caitiff. (F. — L.) M. E. *caitif*. — O. F. *caitif*, a captive, a wretch (F. *chétif*). — L. *captiuus*; see **captive** below.

capable. (F. — L.) F. *capable*. — Low L. *capabilis*, comprehensible; afterwards, able to hold. — L. *capere*, to hold.

capsule, seed-vessel. (F. — L.) F. *capsule*, a small case. — L. *capsula*, dimin. of *capsa*, a case; see **case** (2) below.

captious. (F. — L.) F. *captieux*, cavilling. — L. *captiosus*. — L. *captio*, a taking, a sophistical argument. — L. *captus*, pp. of *capere*, to hold.

captive. (L.) L. *captiuus*, a captive. — L. *captus*, pp. of *capere*, to take.

captor, capture; from L. pp. *captus*.

case (2), a receptacle. (F. — L.) O. F. *casse*. — L. *capsa*, a box, cover. — L. *capere*, to hold.

casement, frame of a window. (F. — L.) Short for *encasement*, that which encases or encloses. From *encase* (below); with suffix -*ment*.

cash, coin. (F. — L.) Orig. a till or box to keep money in. — F. *casse*, a case; see **case** (2) above. Der. *cash-ier*, sb., one who keeps a money-box or cash.

casket, a small box. (F. — L.) Corrupted from F. *cassette*, 'a small casket;' Cot.

Dimin. of F. *casse*, a case, box; see **case** (2) above.

catch. (F.—L.) Picard *cachier*, variant of O. F. *chacier*, to hunt, chase; hence to catch. It answers to Ital. *cacciare*, Low L. *caciare*, put for *captiare*,* extended form of L. *captare*, to catch.—L. *captus*, pp. of *capere*, to seize. ¶ We even find O. Du. *kaetsen*, to catch, borrowed from Picard *cachier*. Doublet, *chase* (1).

cater, to buy provisions. (F.—L.) Formed as a verb from M. E. *catour*, a buyer of provisions (whom we should now call a *cater-er*). *Catour* is short for *acatour*, formed from *acate*, a buying, purchase, Ch. prol. 573.—O. F. *acat* (mod. F. *achat*), a buying. — Low L. *acaptum*, a purchase (A.D. 1118); put for *accaptum*.—Low L. *accaptare*, to purchase (A. D. 1000), frequent. of *accipere*, to receive, also to buy; see **accept** above.

chase (1), to hunt after. (F.—L.) O.F. *chacier*, *chacer*, to pursue; see **catch** above.

chase (2), to enchase; short for *enchase*, which see below.

chase (3), a printer's frame. (F.—L.) F. *châsse*, a shrine.—L. *capsa*, a box; see **case** (2) above.

conceit. (F.—L.) M. E. *conceit*.—O. F. *conceit*, pp. of *concevoir*, to conceive; see below.

conceive. (F.—L.) M. E. *conceuen*.—O. F. *concever*, *concevoir*.—L. *concipere*, to conceive.—L. *con-* (=*cum*, together); and *capere*, to hold.

conception. (F.—L.) F. *conception*.—L. acc. *conceptionem*.—L. *conceptus*, pp. of *concipere*; see above. Der. *pre-conception*.

deceive. (F.—L.) O. F. *decever*, *decevoir*.—L. *decipere*, to take away, deceive.—L. *de*, away; and *capere*, to take. Der. *deceit*, from O. F. *deceit*, pp. of *decever*.

deception. (F.—L.) O. F. *deception*.—L. acc. *deceptionem*.—L. *deceptus*, pp. of *decipere*, to deceive; see **deceive**.

encase. (F.—L.) O. F. *encaisser*, 'to put into a case;' Cot.—F. *en*, in (L. *in*); and O. F. *caisse*, *casse*, a case; see **case** (2) above.

enchase. (F. L.) O. F. *enchasser*, 'to enchace or set in gold,' Cot. Hence to *emboss*.—F. *en*, in (L. *in*); and *chasse*, the same as *casse*, a case; see **case** (2) above.

except, to exclude. (F.—L.) F. *excepter*, to except; Cot.—L. *exceptare*, frequent. of *excipere*, to take.—L. *ex*, out; *capere*, to take. Der. *except*, prep.; &c.

imperceptible. (F.—L.) From *im-* = *in*, not; and *perceptible*; see below.

inceptive. (L.) Coined from L. *inceptus*, pp. of *incipere*, to begin; see below.

incipient. (L.) L. *incipient-*, stem of pres. pt. of *incipere*, to begin. — L. *in*, upon; *capere*, to lay hold of.

intercept. (F.—L.) F. *intercepter*.—L. *intercept-us*, pp. of *intercipere*, lit. to catch between.—L. *inter*, between; *capere*, to take.

occupy. (F.—L.) M. E. *occupien*. F. *occuper*.—L. *occupare*, to lay hold of.—L. *oc-* (=*ob*, near); *capere*, to seize. Der. *pre-occupy*.

perceive. (F.—L.) O. F. *percever*.—L. *percipere*, to apprehend.—L. *per*, thoroughly; *capere*, to seize.

perception. (F.—L.) F. *perception*.—L. acc. *perceptionem*. — L. *perceptus*, pp. of *percipere*; see above.

precept. (F.—L.) O. F. *precepte*.—L. *præceptum*, a prescribed rule.—L. *præceptus*, pp. of *præcipere*, to take beforehand, give rules.—L. *præ*, before; *capere*, to take. Der. *precept-or*.

purchase, verb. (F.—L.) M. E. *purchasen*, *purchacen*. — O. F. *purchacer*, to pursue eagerly, acquire, get.—O. F. *pur* (F. *pour*), from L. *pro*; and O. F. *chacer*; see **chase** (1) above.

receive. (F.—L.) O. F. *recever*, *recevoir*.—L. *recipere*, to take back.—L. *re*, back; *capere*, to take.

receptacle. (F.—L.) F. *réceptacle*.—L. *receptaculum*, a place to store away.—L. *recept-us*, pp. of *recipere*; see above.

reception. (F.—L.) F. *réception*.—L. acc. *receptionem*, a taking back.—L. *recept-us*; as above.

recipe. (L.) L. *recipe*, take thou; imp. of *recipere*; see **receive**.

recipient. (L.) L. *recipient-*, stem of pres. pt. of *recipere*; see **receive**.

sash (1), a case or frame for panes of glass. (F.—L.) Corruption of F. *chassis*, 'a frame of wood for a window;' Cot.—O. F. *chasse* (F. *châsse*), a case, shrine. — L. *capsa*, a case. See **chase** (3) and **case** (2) above.

scaffold. (F.—L. *and* Teut.) M. E. *scafold*. — O. F. *escafalt*,* only found as *escafaut*, mod. F. *échafaud*, a scaffold. Short for *escadafalt* (Burguy), corresponding to Span. and Ital. *catafalco*, a funeral canopy, also a stage, scaffold. β. The former part of the word occurs in O. Span.

catar, to see, view, from L. *captare*, to strive after, watch, observe, frequent. of *capere*, to seize. The latter part is the same as Ital. *balco*, a stage, of Teut. origin; see **Balk**. The lit. sense is 'view-balk,' i.e. a stage to see from.

susceptible. (F.—L.) F. *susceptible.*— L. *susceptibilis*, ready to receive.—L. *suscipere*, to receive.—L. *sus-* (for *sub-s*), under; and *capere*, to take.

Caparison; see **Cape** (1.)

Cape (1), a covering for the shoulders. (F.—Low L.) O. F. *cape.*—Low L. *capa*, a cape (Isidore of Seville); whence also Prov., Span., Port. *capa*, Ital. *cappa*, A.S. *cæppe*, Du. *kap*, G. *kappe*, Icel. *kápa*, &c.

cap, head-covering. (Low L.) A.S. *cæppe.*—Low L. *cappa*, the same as *capa*, orig. a cape; see above.

caparison, trappings of a horse. (F.— Span.—Low L.) O.F. *caparasson.*—Span. *caparazon*, cover for a saddle; augmentative from Span. *capa*, a cloak, cover.— Low L. *capa*, a cape; as above.

capuchin, hooded friar, hood. (F.— Ital.—Low L.) F. *capucin.*—Ital. *cappucino*, a small hood, hence a hooded friar; dimin. of *cappuccio*, a cowl.—Ital. *cappa*, a cape; see **Cape** (1).

chapel. (F.—L.) O.F. *chapele.*—Low L. *capella*, orig. a shrine in which was preserved the *capa* or cope of St. Martin (Brachet). — Low L. *capa*, *cappa*, cape, hooded cloak; as above.

chaperon. (F.—L.) F. *chaperon*, a protector; orig. a kind of hood.—F. *chape*, a cope.—Low L. *capa*; as above.

chaplet. (F.—L.) M. E. *chapelet.*— O. F. *chapelet*, a head-dress, wreath.—O.F. *chapel*, head-dress. — O. F. *chape*, a cope; see **chaperon.**

cope (1), a hood, cape. (F.—Low L.) M. E. *cope*, variant of *cape*, a cape; see **Cape** above. (For the *o*, cf. Icel. *kápa*.)

escape. (F. — L.) M. E. *escapen.* — O. F. *escaper* (F. *échapper*), to escape, lit. to slip out of one's cape.—L. *ex cappá*, out of one's cape; see **Cape** (1) above.

scape; short for *escape* (above).

Cape (2), headland; see **Capital.**

Caper (1), to dance about. (Ital.—L.) Formerly *capreole* (Sir P. Sidney).—Ital. *capriolare*, to skip as a goat.—Ital. *capriolo*, a kid; dimin. of *caprio*, wild-goat; cf. *capra*, she-goat.—L. *capra*, she-goat; cf. *caper*, he-goat.

cab, cabriolet. (F.—Ital.—L.) *Cab*

is short for *cabriolet.*—F. *cabriolet*, a cab; from its supposed lightness.—F. *cabriole*, a caper, leap of a goat; formerly *capriole*; see **capriole** below.

capricorn. (L.) L. *capricornus*, horned goat. — L. *capri-=capro-*, stem of *caper*, goat; and *corn-u*, a horn.

capriole, a peculiar frisk of a horse. (F.—Ital.—L.) F. *capriole*; see Cot.— Ital. *capriola*, the leap of a kid; see **Caper** above.

Caper (2), the flower-bud of a certain plant. (F.—L.—Gk.—Pers.) O. F. *capre* (F. *câpre*),—L. *capparis.* — Gk. κάππαρις, caper-plant; its fruit. — Pers. *kabar*, capers.

Capercailzie. (Gael.) Here *z* = 3 = *y*. —Gael.*capull-coille*, great cock of the wood; lit. horse of the wood.—Gael. *capull*, a horse (see **Cavalier**); *coille*, *coill*, wood.

Capillary, like hair. (L.) L. *capillaris* adj., from *capillus*, hair. Perhaps allied to *cap-ut*, the head.

dishevel. (F.—L.) O. F. *discheveler*, 'to dischevell,' i.e. to disorder the hair; Cot. — O. F. *des-* (L. *dis-*), apart; *chevel* (F. *cheveu*), a hair, from L. acc. *capillum.*

Capital (1), chief. (F.—L.) F. *capital.* —L. *capitalis*, belonging to the head.—L. *capit-*, stem of *caput*, the head; see **Head.**

achieve. (F.—L.) M. E. *acheuen.*— O. F. *achever*, lit. to bring to a head.— O. F. *a chef*, to a head.—L. *ad caput* (the same). **Der.** *achieve-ment.*

cabbage (1), a vegetable. (F.—Ital.— L.) O.F. *choux cabus*, 'a cabbidge,' Cot. (lit. 'round-headed cabbage;' we have dropped *choux*). The F. *cabus*, round-headed, is from Ital. *capuccio*, a little head, dimin. of *capo*, head.—L. *caput*, head.

cad. (F. — L.) Short for Lowl. Sc. *cadie*, an errand-boy, boy; see Jamieson. —F. *cadet*; see **cadet.**

cadet, orig. a younger son. (F.—L.) F. *cadet*, a younger brother; Prov. *capdet*. *Capdet* is a Gascon form=Low L. *capitellum* (by a habit of Gascon, which puts *t* for *ll*; P. Meyer); lit. a little (younger) head, dimin. from L. *caput*, a head.

cape (2), a headland. (F. — Ital. — L.) F. *cap.*—Ital. *capo*, head, headland.—L. *caput*, head.

capital (2), stock of money. (F.—L.) F. *capital.*—Low L. *capitale*, wealth; neut. of *capitalis*, chief; see **Capital** (1),

capital (3), head of a pillar. (Low L. —L.) Low L. *capitellus*, head of a pillar; dimin. from L. *caput*, head.

capitation, poll-tax. (F.–L.) F. *capitation*. – Low L. acc. *capitationem*, poll-tax. – L. *caput*, poll, head.

capitol. (L.) The temple of Jupiter, at Rome, called *Capitolium*. – L. *capit-*, stem of *caput*, a head; but the reason for the name is obscure; see Smith, Class. Dict.

capitular, relating to a chapter. (L.) Low L. *capitularis*, adj. of *capitulum*, a chapter of a cathedral, or a chapter of a book; see chapter below.

capitulate. (L.) Low L. *capitulatus*, pp. of *capitulare*, to divide into chapters, also to propose terms (for surrender). – Low L. *capitulum*, a chapter; see chapter below. **Der.** *re-capitulate*.

captain. (F.–L.) M. E. *capitain*. – O. F. *capitain*. – Low L. *capitaneus*, *capitanus*, a leader of soldiers. – L. *capit-*, stem of *caput*, head.

cattle. (F.–L.) M. E. *catel*, property; hence, live stock, cattle. – O. F. *catel*. – Low L. *capitale*, capital, property; see capital (2) above.

chapiter, the capital of a column. (F. –L.) O. F. *chapitel* (F. *chapiteau*), the same. – L. *capitellum*, the same; dimin. of *caput*, a head.

chapter, a division of a book, synod of clergy. (F.–L.) M. E. *chapitre*, also *chapitel*. – F. *chapitre*, corruption of an older form *chapitle*. – L. *capitulum*, a chapter of a book (little head); also, in late L., a synod; dimin. of *caput*, a head.

chattels. (F.–L.) Pl. of M. E. *chatel*, property, also cattle. – O. F. *chatel* = O. F. *catel*, property; see cattle above.

chief. (F. – L.) M. E. *chef*, *chief*. – O. F. *chef*, *chief*, the head. – L. *caput*, head. **Der.** *ker-chief*, q. v.

chieftain. (F.–L.) O. F. *chevetaine*. – Low L. *capitaneus*, *capitanus*, a captain; see captain above.

corporal (1), a subordinate officer. (F.–Ital.–L.) A corrupt form of F. *caporal*. – Ital. *caporale*, a chief, corporal of a band. – Ital. *capo*, head. – L. *caput*.

decapitate. (L.) From pp. of Low L. *decapitare*, to behead. – L. *de*, off; and *capit-*, stem of *caput*, head.

hatchment, escutcheon of a deceased person. (F.–L.) Corruption of *ach'ment*, shortened form of *achievement*.

occiput. (L.) L. *occiput*, back of the head. – L. *oc-* (for *ob*), over against; and *caput*, head.

precipice. (F.–L.) O. F. *precipice*. –

L. *præcipitium*, a falling headlong down; a precipice. – L. *præcipiti-*, crude form of *præceps*, headlong. – L. *præ*, before; and *capiti-*, cr. form of *caput*. **Der.** *precipitate*, from L. *præcipitare*, to cast headlong.

sinciput. (L.) The fore part of the head; lit. 'half head.' – L. *sinciput*, half the head. – L. *semi-*, half; and *caput*; see also Capsize.

Capitation, **Capitol**, **Capitular**, **Capitulate**; see above.

Capon. (L. – Gk.) A. S. *capun*. – L. acc. *caponem*, from nom. *capo*. – Gk. κάπων, a capon. (√SKAP.)

Caprice. (F. – Ital. –L.?) F. *caprice*. – Ital. *capriccio*, a whim. Perhaps from Ital. *capra*, a she-goat; so that *capriccio* might mean a frisk like a goat's; see Caper (1). ¶ Or *capriccio* = *capo-riccio*, a bristling of the hair; from *capo*, head, *riccio*, a bristling.

Capricorn, **Capriole**; see Caper (1).

Capsize, to upset. (Span.?–L.) Perhaps from Span. *capuzar*, to sink (a ship) by the head; allied to *cabecear*, to nod the head, pitch as a ship does. – Span. *cabeza*, the head, fore part of a ship; a derivative of L. *caput*, the head; see Capital (1).

Capstan. (F. – Span –L.?) F. *cabestan*. – Span. *cabestrante*, *cabrestante*, an engine to raise weights. Etym. uncertain: but Minsheu's Span. Dict. (1623) has *cabrestante* as the form, and Monlau's Etym. Span. Dict. (1881) has *cabria*, a crane, and suggests Span. *cabra estante*, a fixed (permanent) goat; since the Span. *cabra* means (1) goat, (2) a machine for throwing large stones. Here Sp. *cabra* = L. *capra*, a she-goat; see Caper (1); and *estante* = L. *stantem*, acc. of *stans*, standing, from *stare*, to stand.

Capsule; see Capacious.

Captain; see Capital.

Captious, **Captive**; see Capacious.

Capuchin; see Cape (1).

Car. (F.–C.) M. E. *carre*. – O. F. *car* (F. *char*), a car. – L. *carrus*, a car; of Gaulish origin. – Bret. *karr*, a chariot; W. *car*, O. Gael. *cár*, Irish *carr*. (√KAR.)

career. (F.–C.) F. *carrière*, a road; also a horse-race, running of horses, career; O. F. *cariere*, a road. – O. F. *carier*, to carry. – O. F. *car*, car; see above.

cargo. (Span.–C.) Span. *cargo*, freight, load; cf. *cargare*, to load. – Low L. *carricare*, to load a car; see charge below.

caricature. (Ital. – C.) Ital. *cari-*

catura, a satirical picture ; so called because exaggerated or 'overloaded.' — Ital. *cari-care,* to load, burden. — Low L. *carricare,* to load a car ; see **charge.**

carrack. (F. — C.) O. F. *carraque,* a ship of burden. — Low Lat. *carraca,* the same. — Low L. *carracare, carricare,* to load ; see **charge.**

carriage. (F. — C.) M. E. *cariage,* that which is carried about (as in Bible, A. V.) — O. F. *cariage* ; from *carier,* to carry ; see below. ¶ Its modern use is due to confusion with *caroch,* a vehicle (Massinger) = Ital. *carroccio,* a chariot, augmentative of *carro,* a car.

carry. (F. — C.) O. F. *carier.* — O. F. *car,* a car ; see **Car.**

cart. (C.) A. S. *cræt* (for *cært*). — W. *cart,* a wain ; Gael. and Irish *cairt* ; dimin. of W. *car,* Irish *carr* ; see **Car.**

charge. (F. — C.) F. *charger,* to load. — Low L. *carricare,* to load a car. — L. *carrus,* a car, a Gaulish word ; see **Car.** Der. *charg-er,* a dish or horse, because carrying a burden.

chariot. (F. — C.) F. *chariot* ; O. F. *charete.* — Low L. *carreta,* a small car, dimin. of *carrus,* a car ; see **Car.**

supercargo. (L. ; *and* Span. — C.) From L. *super,* above ; and Span. *cargo,* a freight. Suggested by Span. *sobrecargo,* a supercargo ; where *sobre* = L. *super.*

surcharge, sb. (F. — L. *and* C.) F. *surcharge,* an over-charge. — F. *sur* (= L. *super*), above ; and **charge** (above).

Caracole. (F. — Span. — C. ?) F. *caracol, caracole,* a snail ; whence *faire le caracole,* applied to a manœuvre by soldiers, and to turns made by a horse. — Span. *caracol,* a snail, winding staircase, turning about (from the snail-shell's spiral form). Perhaps of Celtic origin ; cf. Gael. *carach,* circling, winding, from *car,* a turn, twist.

Carat. (F. — Arab. — Gk.) F. *carat,* a very light weight. — Arab. *qirrát,* a pod, husk, carat, 24th part of an ounce. — Gk. κεράτιον, fruit of the locust-tree ; also, a carat ; lit. 'a small horn.' — Gk. κερατ-, stem of κέρας, a horn ; see **Horn.**

Caravan. (F. — Pers.) F. *caravane.* — Pers. *karwán,* a caravan, convoy.

caravansary. (Pers.) Pers. *karwán-saráy,* an inn for caravans. — Pers. *karwán,* caravan ; *saráy,* public building, inn.

van, a covered waggon for goods. (F. — Pers.) Short for *caravan,* like *bus* for *omnibus.*

Caraway, Carraway. (Span. — Arab.) Span. *al-carahueya,* a caraway ; where *al* is merely the Arab. .def. art. — Arab. *karwiyá-a, karawíyá-a,* caraway-seeds or plant. Cf. Gk. κάρος, κάρον, cumin.

Carbine. (F. — Gk.) Formerly *carabine, carabin,* which meant (not a musket, but) the man who carried it, a musketeer. — F. *carabin,* 'an arquebuzier ;' Cot. Corrupted from O. F. *calabrin,* a light-armed soldier, orig. a soldier who worked one of the old war-engines. — Low L. *chadabula, cadabula,* a destructive war-engine. — Gk. καταβολή, overthrow, destruction. — Gk. καταβάλλειν, to cast down, strike down with missiles. — Gk. κατά, down ; βάλλειν, to cast. (Cf. F. *accabler,* also from *cadabula.*)

Carbon. (F. — L.) F. *carbone.* — L. acc. *carbonem,* a coal.

carbonado, broiled meat. (Span. — L.) Span. *carbonado,* meat broiled over coals. — Span. *carbon,* coal ; see above.

carbuncle. (L.) L. *carbunculus,* (1) a small coal, (2) a carbuncle, gem, from its glowing. Double dimin. of L. *carbo,* coal.

Carcanet. (F. — C.) Dimin. of F. *carcan,* a collar of jewels, or of gold. — Bret. *kerchen,* the bosom, circle of the neck ; also *kelchen,* a collar. — Bret. *kelch,* a ring.

Carcase, Carcass. (F. — Ital. — Pers.) M. E. *carcays.* — O. F. *carquasse,* a dead body. — Ital. *carcassa,* a kind of bombshell, a shell ; closely allied to *carcasso,* also *turcasso,* a quiver, case (the body being likened to a shell or case). Corrupted from Low L. *tarcasius,* a quiver. — Pers. *tarkash,* a quiver. (See proof in Littré that F. *carquois* and *carcasse* are the same word.)

Card (1), piece of pasteboard. (F. — Gk.) Corruption of F. *carte,* 'a card,' Cot. — Low L. *carta* ; L. *charta.* — Gk. χάρτη, a leaf of paper. Der. *card-board.*

carte, a bill of fare. (F. — Gk.) Chiefly in the F. phr. *carte blanche,* lit. white paper. — Low L. *carta* ; see **Card** above.

cartel. (F. — Ital. — Gk.) F. *cartel.* — Ital. *cartello,* lit. a small paper ; dimin. of *carta,* paper, bill ; see above.

cartoon. (F. — Ital. — Gk.) F. *carton.* — Ital. *cartone,* lit. a large paper ; from *carta,* as above.

cartouche, cartridge. (F. — Ital. — Gk.) *Cartridge* (with intrusive *r*) is for *cartidge,* corrupt form of *cartouche.* — F. *cartouche,* a roll of paper. — Ital. *cartoccio,* a roll of paper, cartridge. — Ital. *carta,*

paper; Low L. *carta*; see Card above.
¶ The *cartridge* took its name from the paper in which it was rolled up.

cartulary, a register. (Low L. – Gk.) Low L. *cartularium, chartularium*, a register. – Low L. *chartula*, a document; dimin. of *charta*, a paper; see Card above.

chart. (L. – Gk.) L. *charta*, a paper. – Gk. χάρτη; as above.

charter. (F. – L. – Gk.) M. E. *chartre*. – F. *chartre*. – Low L. *chartula, cartula*, a small paper or document; see cartulary (above).

Card (2), an instrument for combing wool. (F. – L.) F. *carde*. – Low L. *cardus*, L. *carduus*, a thistle; for wool-combing. – L. *carere*, to card wool.

Cardinal. (L.) L. *cardinalis*, principal, chief; orig. relating to the hinge of a door. – L. *cardin-*, stem of *cardo*, a hinge.

Care. (E.) M. E. *care*. A. S. *caru, cearu*, anxiety. +O. Sax. *kara*, sorrow; Icel. *kæri*, murmur; O. H. G. *chara*, a lament. (✓ GAR.) ¶ No connection with L. *cura*!

cark, anxiety. (F. – C.) Confused with *care*; but really = *kark*, Norman form of *charge*, i. e. a load.

chary, careful, cautious. (E.) M. E. *chari*. A. S. *cearig*, full of care, sad. – A. S. *cearu, caru*, care. *Chary* meant (1) sorrowful, (2) heedful.

Careen. (F. – L.) Lit. 'to clean the keel;' hence to lay a ship on its side. – F. *carine, carène*, keel. – L. *carina*, keel.

Career; see Car.

Caress. (F. – Ital. – L.) F. *caresse*, a fondling. – Ital. *carezza*, a caress, fondling. – Low Lat. *caritia*, dearness. – L *carus*, dear.

charity. (F. – L.) O. F. *charitet*. – L. acc. *caritatem*, dearness. – L. *carus*, dear. ¶ Not allied to Gk. χάρις.

cherish. (F. – L.) O. F. *cheris-*, stem of pres. pt. of *chérir*, to hold dear. – F. *cher*, dear. – L. *carus*.

Carfax. (F. – L.) M. E. *carfoukes*, a place where four roads meet. – O. F. pl. *carrefourgs*, the same. – L. acc. *quatuor furcas*, four forks. – L. *quatuor*, four; and *furca*, a fork. See Fork.

Cargo, Caricature; see Car.

Caries. (L.) L. *caries*, rottenness.

Cark. See under Care (above).

Carmine. (Span. – Arab. – Skt.) Span. *carmin*, short form of *carmesin*, crimson. – Span. *carmes*, kermes, crimson dye. – Arab. and Pers. *qirmiz, qirmizī*, crimson. – Skt. *krimija*, produced by an insect (viz.

the cochineal insect). – Skt. *krimi*, a worm; *jan*, to produce. (See Cochineal, Worm.)

crimson. (F. – Arab. – Skt.) M. E. *crimosin*. – O. F. *cramoisin, cramoisyne* (see *cramoisi* in Littré). – Low L. *cramoisinus*, also *carmesinus*, crimson. – Arab. and Pers. *qirmizī*; see above.

Carnage; see below.

Carnal. (L.) L. *carnalis*, fleshly. – L. *carn-*, stem of *caro*, flesh. +Gk. κρέας; Skt. *kravya*, raw flesh.

carnage. (F. – L.) F. *carnage*, flesh-time, slaughter of animals. – Low L. *carnaticum*, a tribute of animals; cf. *carnatum*, time for eating flesh. – L. *carn-*, stem of *caro*, flesh.

carnation. (F. – L.) F. *carnation*, flesh colour (Littré). – L. acc. *carnationem*, fleshiness. – L. *carn-*, stem of *caro*.

carnival. (F. – Ital. – L.) F. *carnaval*, Shrovetide. – Ital. *carnevale, carnovale*, the last three days before Lent. – Low. L. *carnelevale, carnelevamen*, removal of flesh, Shrovetide. – L. *carne-m*, acc. of *caro*, flesh; and *leuare*, to lift, remove, take away; from *leuis*, light.

carnivorous. (L.) L. *carniuorus*, flesh-eating. – L. *carni-*, crude form of *caro*, flesh; and *uor-are*, to devour.

carrion. (F. – L.) M. E. *caroigne*, a carcase. – O. F. *caroigne*; Low L. *caronia*, a carcase. – L. *caro*, flesh.

charnel. (F. – L.) Properly an adj., containing carcases, as in *charnel-house*. – O. F. *charnel*, adj. carnal; as sb. a cemetery. – L. *carnalis*; see Carnal above.

incarnadine, to dye of a red colour. (F. – Ital. – L.) F. *incarnadin*, carnation colour (Cot.) – Ital. *incarnadino*, carnation colour (Florio); also spelt *incarnatino*. – Ital. *incarnato*, incarnate; also, of flesh colour. – L. *incarnatus*, pp. of *incarnare*, to clothe with flesh (below).

incarnation. (F. – L.) F. *incarnation*. – L. acc. *incarnationem*, embodiment in flesh. – L. *incarnatus*, pp. of *incarnare*, to clothe with flesh. – L. *in*, in; and *carn-*, stem of *caro*, flesh.

Carob-tree, the locust-tree. (Arab.) Arab. *kharrúb*, bean-pods.

Carol, a song. (F. – C.) Formerly, a kind of dance. – O. F. *carole*, a (singing) dance. Of Celtic origin; cf. Bret. *koroll*, a dance, movement of the body in cadence; Manx *carval*, a carol; Corn. *carol*, a choir, concert; W. *carol*, a song, *coroli*, to move in a circle, dance; Gael. *carull*, melody, carolling. ¶ But these Celtic words are now thought to be borrowed from F. or E. True origin unknown.

Carotid, adj. (Gk.) Gk. καρωτίδες, s. pl., the two great arteries of the neck; it was thought that an alteration in the flow of blood through them caused stupor. — Gk. καρόω, I stupefy; κάρος, stupor.

Carousal, (1) a drinking-bout; (2), a pageant. (1. F. — G.; 2. F. — Ital.) 1. Sometimes from the verb *carouse* below. 2. But, in old authors, *cárousél* means a sort of pageant, of which some kind of chariot-race formed a principal part; Dryden, Virgil, Æn. v. 777. — F. *carrousel*, a tilting-match. — Ital. *carosello*, corrupt form of *garosello*, a tournament. — Ital. *garoso*, quarrelsome; *gara*, a strife.

Carouse. (F. — G.) F. *carous*, 'a carrouse of drinke,' Cot. — G. *garaus*, right out; used of emptying a bumper. — G. *gar*, quite; and *aus*, out. (Raleigh even writes *garouse*; directly from G. *garaus*.) Der. *carous-al*, but only in one sense of that word; see above.

Carp (1), a fish. (E.) M. E. *carpe*. Not in A.S. +Du. *karper*; Icel. *karfi*; Dan. *karpe*; Swed. *karp*; G. *karpfen*; late Lat. *carpa* (whence F. *carpe*, &c.).

Carp (2), to cavil at. (Scand.) M. E. *carpen*, which often merely means to talk, say. — Icel. *karpa*, to boast; Swed. dial. *karpa*, to boast, talk much. ¶ The present sinister sense is due to confusion with L. *carpere*, to pluck.

Carpenter. (F. — C.) O. F. *carpentier* (F. *charpentier*). — Low L. *carpentarius*, from *carpenta*, to work in timber. — L. *carpentum*, a carriage; a word of Celtic origin. — Gael. and Irish *carbad*, a carriage, chariot, litter; Irish *carb*, a basket, litter, carriage, plank; Gael. *cairb*, chariot, ship, plank.

Carpet. (F. — L.) O. F. *carpite*. — Low L. *carpita*, *carpeta*, a kind of thick cloth; dimin. of *carpia*, lint. — L. *carpere*, to pluck, pull to pieces (lint being made of rags pulled to pieces); cf. F. *charpie*, lint.

Carrack, Carriage; see Car.

Carrion; see Carnal.

Carronade, a sort of cannon. (Scotland.) So named because made at *Carron*, in Stirlingshire.

Carrot. (F. — L.) F. *carote*, *carotte*. — L. *carota*. Perhaps borrowed from Gk. καρωτόν, a carrot.

Carry, Cart; see Car.

Carte, Cartel; see Card (1).

Cartilage. (F. — L.) F. *cartilage*, gristle. — L. *cartilaginem*, acc. of *cartilago*. Der. *cartilagin-ous*.

Cartoon, Cartouche, Cartridge, Cartulary; see Card (1).

Carve. (E.) M. E. *keruen*. A. S. *ceorfan*. + Du. *kerven*; Icel. *kyrfa*; Dan. *karve*; Swed. *karfva*; G. *kerben*, to notch, cut.

Cascade; see Cadence.

Case (1), an event; see Cadence.

Case (2), a box; see Capacious.

Casemate. (F. — Ital.) F. *casemate*, a loop-hole in a fortified wall. — Ital. *casamatta*, a chamber built under a wall or bulwark, to hinder those who enter the ditch to scale the wall of a fort. It seems to mean 'dark chamber.' — Ital. and L. *casa*, house, cottage, room; and Ital. *matta*, fem. of *matto*, orig. mad, but the Sicilian *mattu* means 'dim.'

Casement, Cash; see Capacious.

Cashier (1); one who attends to cash payments; see cash, under Capacious.

Cashier (2), to dismiss from service. (G. — F. — L.) G. *cassiren*, to cashier; merely borrowed from F. *easser*, 'to breake, burst, .. also to casseere, discharge;' Cot. (G. words, borrowed from F., end in -*iren*.) — L. *cassare*, to annul, discharge. — L. *cassus*, void, null.

Cashmere, a rich stuff. (India.) So called from the vale of *Cashmere*, in India. Also spelt *cassimere*, *kerseymere*.

Casino, a room for dancing. (Ital. — L.) Ital. *casino*, dimin. of *casa*, a cottage, house. — L. *casa*, a cottage.

cassock, a vestment. (F. — Ital. — L.) F. *casaque*. — Ital. *casacca*, an outer coat; a jocular word; from *casa*, a house; see above.

chasuble, a vestment. (F. — L.) F. *chasuble*. — Low L. *casabula*, a little house; hence, a mantle. — L. *casa*, a cottage.

Cask. (Span. — L.) Span. *casco*, a skull, sherd, coat of an onion; also a cask of wine, a casque or helmet. The orig. sense is 'husk;' cf. Span. *cascara*, peel, rind, shell, Port. *casca*, rind. — Span. *cascar*, to burst open; formed (as if from Lat. *quassicare* *) from an extension of L. *quassare*, to break, burst; see Quash.

casque, a helmet. (F. — Ital. — L.) F. *casque*. — Ital. *casco*, a helmet, headpiece; the same as Span. *casco* above.

Casket; see Capacious.

Casque; see Cask.

Cassia, a species of laurel. (L.—Gk.—Heb.) L. *casia, cassia.*—Gk. κασία, a spice like cinnamon.—Heb. *qetsī'ōth*, in Ps. xlv. 9, a pl. form from *qetsī'āh*, cassia-bark.—Heb. root *qātsa'*, to cut; because the bark is cut off.

Cassimere; see Cashmere.

Cassock; see Casino.

Cassowary, a bird. (Malay.) First brought from Java. Littré (s. v. *casoar*) gives the Malay name as *kassuwaris.*

Cast. (Scand.) Icel. *kasta,* to throw; Swed. *kasta*; Dan. *kaste.* Prob. allied to L. *gerere,* to heap up. Der. *re-cast.*

Caste, a breed, race. (Port.—L.) Port. *casta,* a race, orig. a 'pure' breed; a name given by the Port. to classes of men in India.—Post. *casta,* fem. of *casto,* pure.—L. *castus,* pure, chaste.+Gk. καθαρός.

castigate. (L.) L. *castigatus,* pp. of *castigare,* to chasten; lit. 'to keep pure.'—L. *castus,* chaste.

chaste. (F. — L.) O. F. *chaste.* — L. *castus*; see Caste.

chasten. (F.—L.) Used in place of M. E. *chasty* or *chastien*; see chastise.

chastise. (F. — L.) M. E. *chastisen*; shorter form *chastien.*—O. F. *chastier.*—L. *castigare*; see castigate above.

incest, impurity. (F.—L.) M. E. *incest.*—F. *inceste,* sb.—L. *incestus,* unchaste.—L. *in,* not; *castus,* chaste.

Castle. (L.) A. S. *castel.*—L. *castellum,* dimin. of *castrum,* a fortified place. Der. *castell-an,* O. F. *castelain, chastelain,* the keeper of a *chastel* or castle; also *châtelaine* (fem. of F. *châtelain* = O. F. *chastelain*), now applied to a lady's chain or 'keeper' of keys, &c.

chateau. (F.—L.) F. *château,* O. F. *chastel.*—L. *castellum,* as above.

Castor. (L. — Gk.) L. *castor.* — Gk. κάστωρ, a beaver. But of Eastern origin; Malay *kastúri,* Skt. *kastúri,* musk; Pers. *khaz,* beaver.

castor-oil. Named from some resemblance to *castoreum,* 'a medicine made of the liquor contained in the little bags that are next the beaver's groin.' Kersey. But it is really a vegetable production.

Castrate. (L.) L. *castratus,* pp. of *castrare,* to cut.

Casual; see Cadence.

Cat. (E.) A. S. *cat.* + Du., Dan. *kat,* Icel. *köttr,* Sw. *katt,* G. *kater, katze,* L. *catus,* W. *cath*; Ir. Gael. *cat,* Russ. *kot',*

koshka, Arab. *qitt,* Turk. *kedi.* (Prob. Eastern.)

caterpillar. (F.—L.) M. E. *catyrpel*; corruption of O. F. *chatepeleuse,* a weevil; a fanciful name, really meaning 'hairy she-cat.'—O. F. *chate,* a she-cat; and *peleuse,* hairy.—L. *catus,* cat; *pilosus,* hairy, from *pilum,* hair.

caterwaul. (E.) M. E. *caterwawen*; coined from *cat,* and *wawen,* to make a wailing noise.

catkin. (E.) A loose spike of flowers resembling a cat's tail; hence called a *cat-kin,* i. e. little cat.

kitten. (E.; *with* F. *suffix.*) M. E. *kitoun,* where the suffix *-oun* is F., suggested by F. *chatton,* a kitten. *Kit* is a weakened form of *cat,* appearing in the true E. form *kit-ling,* and in (obs.) *kittle,* to produce kittens.

Cata-, *prefix.* (Gk.) Gk. κατά, down, thoroughly.

Cataclysm, deluge. (Gk.) Gk. κατακλυσμός, a dashing over, flood.—Gk. κατά, down; κλύζειν, to dash, wash, as waves.

Catacomb. (Ital.—Gk.) Ital. *catacomba,* a sepulchral vault.—Low L. *catacumba.*—Gk. κατά, down; κύμβη, a cavity, hollow place.

Catalepsy, a sudden seizure. (Gk.) Formerly *catalepsis.*—Gk. κατάληψις, a grasping, seizing.—Gk. κατά, down; λαβ-, base of λαβεῖν, aor. inf. of λαμβάνειν, to seize.

Catalogue. (F.—Gk.) F. *catalogue.*—Low Lat. acc. *catalogum.*—Gk. κατάλογος, a counting up, enrolment.—Gk. κατά, fully; λέγειν, to say, tell; see Logic.

Catamaran, a sort of raft. (Tamil.) In Forbes, Hindustani Dict., ed. 1859, p. 280, we have '*katmaran,* a raft ..; the word is orig. Tamil, and means *tied logs.*'

Cataplasm, a poultice. (F.—L.—Gk.) F. *cataplasme.*—L. *cataplasma.*—Gk. κατάπλασμα, a plaster, poultice.—Gk. καταπλάσσειν, to spread over.—Gk. κατά, fully; and πλάσσειν, to mould; see Plaster.

Catapult. (Low L. — Gk.) Low L. *catapulta,* an engine for throwing stones.—Gk. καταπέλτης, the same.—Gk. κατά, down; πάλλειν, to swing, hurl.

Cataract. (L.—Gk.) L. *cataracta,* Gen. vii. 11.—Gk. καταρράκτης, as sb., a waterfall; as adj. broken, rushing down. Prob. allied to καταρρήγνυμι, I break down; the 2 aor. κατερράγην was used of the rushing down of waterfalls and storms.—Gk. κατά, down; ῥήγνυμι, I break.

Catarrh. (Low L. – Gk.) Low L. *catarrhus.* – Gk. κατάρροος, a flowing down (of rheum), a cold in the head. – Gk. κατά, down; and ῥέειν, to flow.

Catastrophe. (Gk.) Gk. καταστροφή, an overturning, sudden turn. – Gk. κατά, down; στρέφειν, to turn.

Catch. (F. – L.) See Capacious.

Catechise. (Low L. – Gk.) Low L. *catechizare.* – Gk. κατηχίζειν, to catechise, instruct; lengthened form of κατηχέειν, to din into one's ears, lit. 'to din down.' – Gk. κατ-ά, down; ἠχή, a sound, ἦχος, a ringing in the ears; see Echo.

Category, a class. (Gk.) Gk. κατηγορία, an accusation; but in logic, a predicament or class. – Gk. κατηγορεῖν, to accuse. – Gk. κατ-ά, down, against; ἀγορεύειν, to declaim, address an assembly, from ἀγορά, an assembly.

Cater; see Capacious.

Caterpillar, Caterwaul; see Cat.

Cathartic, purging. (Gk.) Gk. καθαρτικός, purgative. – Gk. καθαίρειν, to cleanse, purge. – Gk. καθαρός, pure; see Caste.

Cathedral. (L. – Gk.) L. *cathedralis ecclesia* = a cathedral church, or one which has a bishop's throne. – Low L. *cathedra,* a throne. – Gk. καθέδρα, a seat. – Gk. καθ-, for κατά, down; and ἕδρα, a seat, chair, from ἕζομαι (= ἑδ-γομαι), I sit; see Sit.

chair. (F. – L. – Gk.) M. E. *chaire, chaere.* – O. F. *chaiere, chaere.* – Low L. *cathedra,* a throne, raised seat, chair; see above.

chaise, a light carriage. (F. – L. – Gk.) F. *chaise,* a Parisian modification of F. *chaire,* a pulpit, orig. a seat.

Catholic. (L. – Gk.) L. *catholicus* (Tertullian). – Gk. καθολικός, universal. – Gk. καθόλ-ου, adv., on the whole, in general. – Gk. καθ-, for κατά, according to; and ὅλου, gen. of ὅλος, whole.

Catkin; see Cat.

Catoptric; see Optic.

Cattle; see Capital.

Caudal, belonging to the tail. (L.) L. *cauda,* the tail.

coward. (F. – L.) Norm. F. *couard,* a hare, F. *couard,* a coward; cf. Ital. *codardo,* a coward. Named from the 'bob-tailed' hare. – O. F. *coe* (Ital. *coda*), a tail. – L. *cauda,* a tail.

cue, the same as queue (below).

queue, a tail. (F. – L.) F. *queue,* a tail. – L. *cauda* (above).

Caudle; see Caldron.

Caul, a net, covering, esp. for the head. (F. – C.) O. F. *cale,* 'a kind of little cap;' Cot. – Irish *calla,* veil, hood, cowl; Gael. *call,* the same.

Cauldron; see Caldron.

Cauliflower; see Cole.

Caulk; see Calk.

Cause. (F. – L.) F. *cause.* – L. *causa, caussa,* a cause.

accuse. (F. – L.) F. *accuser.* – L. *accusare,* to lay to one's charge. – L. *ac-* (for *ad*), to; and *causa,* a suit at law, a cause. Der. *accus-at-ive,* the case expressing the *subject* governed by the trans. verb.

because, for the reason that. (E. *and* F.) Formerly written *be cause, bi cause,* i. e. by the cause.

excuse. (F. – L.) F. *excuser.* – L. *excusare,* to release from a charge. – L. *ex,* out; and *causa,* a charge, a cause.

recusant, opposing an opinion. (F. – L.) F. *récusant,* 'rejecting,' Cot.; pres. pt. of *récuser.* – L. *recusare,* to reject, oppose a cause or opinion. – L. *re-,* back from; and *causa.*

ruse, a trick. (F. – L.) F. *ruse,* a trick. – F. *ruser,* to beguile; contr. from O F. *reüser,* to refuse, recoil, escape, dodge. – L. *recusare,* to refuse; see above.

Causeway; see Calx.

Caustic. (L. – Gk.) L. *causticus.* – Gk. καυστικός, burning. – Gk. καίειν (fut. καύσω), to burn.

cauterise. (F. – Low L. – Gk.) F. *cautériser.* – Low L. *cauterizare,* to sear. – Gk. καυτηριάζειν, to sear. – Gk. καυτήριον, a branding-iron. – Gk. καίειν, to burn.

holocaust. (L. – Gk.) L. *holocaustum,* Gen. xxii. 8. – Gk. ὁλόκαυστον, a sacrifice burnt whole; neut. of ὁλόκαυστος, burnt whole. – Gk. ὅλο-s, whole; and καίειν, to burn.

Caution: see Caveat.

Cavalier. (F. – Ital. – L.) F. *cavalier,* a horseman. – Ital. *cavaliere,* the same. – Ital. *cavallo,* a horse. – L. acc. *caballum,* a horse; nom. *caballus.*

cavalcade. (F. – Ital. – L.) F. *cavalcade.* – Ital. *cavalcata,* a troop of horsemen; orig. fem. of pp. of *cavalcare,* to ride. – Ital. *cavallo,* a horse; as above.

cavalry. (F. – Ital. – L.) O. F. *cavallerie.* – Ital. *cavalleria,* cavalry. – Ital. *cavaliere,* a knight; see Cavalier.

chevalier. (F. – L.) F. *chevalier,* a horseman. – F. *cheval,* a horse. – L. acc. *caballum,* a horse (above).

chivalry. (F. – L.) M. E. *chivalrie.* – O. F. *chevalerie,* horsemanship, knighthood. – F. *cheval,* a horse. – Low L. acc. *caballum,* a horse.

Cave. (F. – L.) M. E. *caue.* – O. F. *cave, caive,* a cave. – L. *cauea,* a cave, a cage. – L. *cauus,* hollow. (√KU.) Der. *cav-ity; cav-ern* (L. *cauerna*).

cage. (F. – L.) F. *cage.* – L. *cauea,* a cave, den, cage; as above.

cajole. (F. – L.) O. F. *cageoler,* to chatter like a bird in a cage; hence to flatter, coax (Roquefort). Coined from F. *cage,* a cage; see above.

concave (L.) L. *concauus,* hollow. – L. *con-* (*cum*), with, together; *cauus,* hollow.

excavation. (F. – L.) F. *excavation.* – L. acc. *excauationem,* a hollowing out. – L. *excauatus,* pp. of *excauare,* to hollow out. – L. *ex,* out; *cauare,* to hollow, from *cauus.*

gabion. (F. – Ital. – L.) F. *gabion,* a gabion, large basket filled with earth. – Ital. *gabbione,* a gabion; augment. of *gabbia,* a cage, also spelt *gaggia,* and allied to Span. *gavia,* a cage (in the nautical sense, a cage to which shrouds are fastened). – L. *cauea,* a hollow place, cage, den, coop; see Cage.

gaol, jail, a cage, prison. (F. – L.) O. F. *gaole* (F. *geôle*), a prison, bird-cage. – Low L. *gabiola,* a cage, dimin. of *gabia,* a cage, corrupt form of *cauea*; see cage above.

Caveat, a caution. (L.) L. *caueat,* lit. let him beware. – L. *cauere,* to beware.

caution. (F. – L.) F. *caution.* – L. acc. *cautionem,* heed. – L. *cautus,* pp. of *cauere,* to beware. Der. *pre-caution.*

Caviare, roe of the sturgeon. (F. – Ital. – Turk.) F. *caviar.* – Ital. *caviaro.* – Turk. *havyár, hâvyár,* caviare.

Cavil. (F. – L.) O. F. *caviller.* – L. *cauillari,* to banter; hence to wrangle, object to. – L. *cauilla, cauillus,* a jeering, cavilling.

Caw. (E.) An imitation of the cry of the crow or daw. Cf. Du. *kaauw,* Dan. *kaa,* a jackdaw: see Chough.

Cease; see Cede.

Cedar, a tree. (L. – Gk.) A. S. *ceder.* – L. *cedrus.* – Gk. κέδρος.

Cede. (L.) A late word. – L. *cedere,* to go, to come, to yield (allied to *cadere,* to fall).

abscess (L.) L. *abscessus,* a gathering of humours into one mass; lit. a going

away. – L. *abscessus,* pp. of *abs-cedere,* to go away.

accede. (L.) L. *accedere,* to come towards, assent to. – L. *ac-* (*ad*), to; *cedere,* to come.

access. (L.) From the pp. *ac-cessus.* Der. *access-ion, access-or-y,* &c.

ancestor. (F. – L.) M. E. *ancessour,* whence *ances-t-or,* with excrescent *t* after *s.* – O. F. *ancessour.* – L. acc. *antecessorem,* a predecessor, fore-goer. – L. *ante,* before; and *cess-us,* pp. of *cedere,* to go.

antecedent. (L.) L. *antecedent-,* stem of pres. part. of *ante-cedere,* to go before.

cease. (F. – L.) F. *cesser.* – L. *cessare,* to loiter, go slowly, cease; frequent. of *cedere,* to yield, go away, go.

cessation. (F. – L.) F. *cessation.* – L. acc. *cessationem,* a ceasing. – L. *cessatus,* pp. of *cessare* (above).

cession. (F. – L.) F. *cession.* – L. acc. *cessionem,* a yielding. – L. *cessus,* pp. of *cedere,* to yield.

concede. (L.) L. *con-cedere,* to retire, yield. Der. *concess-ion* (from pp. *concessus*).

decease. (F. – L.) M. E. *deces.* – O. F. *deces* (F. *décès*), death. – L. acc. *decessum,* departure, death. – L. *decessus,* pp. of *de-cedere,* to depart.

exceed. (F. – L.) O. F. *exceder.* – L. *ex-cedere,* lit. to go out.

excess. (F. – L.) O. F. *exces.* – L. acc. *excessum,* lit. a going out or beyond. – L. *excessus,* pp. of *ex-cedere.*

incessant, ceaseless. (L.) L. *incessant-,* stem of *incessans,* unceasing. – L. *in-,* not; *cessans,* ceasing, pres. pt. of *cessare,* to cease; see cease (above).

intercede. (F. – L.) F. *interceder.* – L. *inter-cedere,* lit. to go between; hence, to mediate. Der. *inter-cession,* &c.

precede. (F. – L.) O. F. *preceder* (F. *précéder*). – L. *præ-cedere,* to go before. Der. *preced-ent, pre-cession.*

predecessor. (L.) L. *prædecessor.* – L. *præ,* before; *decessor,* one who retires from an office, from *decessus,* pp. of *de-cedere,* to depart.

proceed. (F. – L.) O. F. *proceder.* – L. *pro-cedere,* to go before or forward. Der. *process* (mod. F. *procès*); *process-ion.*

recede. (L.)' L. *re-cedere,* to go back.

recess. (L.) L. *recessus,* a retreat. – L. *recessus,* pp. of *re-cedere.*

retrocession. (L.) Coined (with suffix *-ion*) from L. *retrocess-us,* pp. of *retro-cedere,* to go backwards.

secede. (L.) L. *se-cedere*, to go apart, withdraw. Der. *secess-ion*.

succeed. (F.—L.) F. *succéder*; Cot. — L. *succedere* (pp. *successus*), to follow after.—L. *suc-* (*sub*), next; *cedere*, to go, come. Der. *success*, O. F. *succes*, L. *successus*, result, from pp. *successus*.

Ceil, Ciel, to line the inner roof of a room. (F.—L.) Hence the sb. *ceil-ing* or *ciel-ing*. M. E. *celen*, to ceil; from the sb. *syle* or *cyll*, a canopy. — F. *ciel*, a canopy; the same word as *ciel*, heaven. [Cf. Ital. *cielo*, heaven, a canopy, a cieling.]—L. *cælum*, heaven. + Gk. κοῖλος, hollow. (√KU.) ¶ Not to be confused with E. *sill*, nor with *seal*; nor with *seel* (F. *siller*); nor with L. *celare*, to hide. The L. *cælare*, to emboss, seems to have some slight influence on the word, but did not originate it.

celestial. (F. — L.) F. *célestiel*.—L. *cælesti-s*, heavenly.—L. *cælum*, heaven.

Celandine, a plant. (F.—Gk.) F. *célidoine*; Low L. *chelidonium*. — Gk. χελιδόνιον, swallow-wort.—Gk. χελιδον-, stem of χελιδών, a swallow. (The *n* is intrusive.)

Celebrate. (L.) L. *celebratus*, pp. of *celebrare*, to frequent, to solemnise, honour. — L. *celeber*, frequented, populous.

Celerity. (F.—L.) F. *célérité*.—L. acc. *celeritatem*, speed.—L. *celer*, quick. (√KAL.)

accelerate. (L.) L. *acceleratus*, pp. of *accelerare*, to quicken. — L. *ac-* (for *ad*); and *celer*, quick.

Celery. (F.—L.—Gk.) F. *céleri*, introduced from the Piedmontese Ital. *seleri*. — L. *selinon*, parsley (with change from *n* to *r*). — Gk. σέλινον, a kind of parsley.

Celestial; see Ceil.

Celibate. (L.) The orig. sense was 'a single life;' it was afterwards an adj., and again a sb., meaning 'one who is single.' — L. *cælibatus*, sb. celibacy, single life. — L. *cælib-*, stem of *cælebs*, single, unmarried. Der. *celibac-y* (for *celibat-y*).

Cell. (L.) M. E. *celle*.—L. *cella*, small room, hut. Cf. *celare*, to hide. (√KAL.)

cellar. (F.—L.) M. E. *celer*.—O. F. *celier*.—L. *cellarium*, a cellar.—L. *cella*.

conceal. (L.) L. *concelare*, to hide. — L. *con-* (*cum*); and *celare*, to hide.

occult. (F. — L.) F. *occulte*. — L. *occultus*, pp. of *occulere*, to cover over, conceal. —L. *oc-* (for *ob*); and obs. L. *calere**, to hide, allied to *celare*, to hide.

Cement. (F.—L.) O. F. *cement*.—L. *cæmentum*, rubble, chippings of stone;

hence, cement. Perhaps for *cædimentum**, from *cædere*, to cut.

Cemetery. (L.—Gk.) Low L. *cæmeterium*.—Gk. κοιμητήριον, a sleeping-place, cemetery.—Gk. κοιμάω, I lull to sleep; in pass., to fall asleep. Allied to κεῖμαι, I lie down. (√KI.)

coma. (Gk.) Gk. κῶμα, a deep sleep. —Gk. κοιμάω, I lull to sleep (above).

Cenobite. (L. — Gk.) L. *cænobita*, a member of a (social) fraternity (Jerome). — L. *cænobium*, a convent. — Gk. κοινόβιον, a convent. — Gk. κοινόβιος, living socially. — Gk. κοινό-s, common; βίος, life.

Cenotaph. (F.—L.—Gk.) O. F. *cenotaphe*. — L. *cenotaphium*. — Gk. κενοτάφιον, an empty tomb. — Gk. κενό-s, empty; τάφ-ος, a tomb.

Censer; see Candid.

Censor. (L.) L. *censor*, a taxer, valuer, assessor, critic. — L. *censere*, to give an opinion, appraise.

censure. (L.) L. *censura*, orig. opinion. — L. *censere* (above).

Cent, a hundred, as in *per cent*. (L.) In America, the hundredth part of a dollar. —L. *centum*, a hundred; see Hundred.

centenary. (L.) L. *centenarius*, relating to a hundred.—L. *centenus*, a hundred (usu. distributively).—L. *centum*.

centennial. (L.) Coined to mean happening once in a century.—L. *cent-um*, hundred; *ann-us*, a year.

centesimal. (L.) L. *centesim-us*, hundredth.—L. *cent-um*, hundred.

centigrade. (L.) Divided into a hundred degrees.—L. *centi-*, for *centum*, hundred; *grad-us*, a degree; see Grade.

centipede, centiped. (F.—L.) F. *centipède*.—L. *centipeda*, a many-footed (lit. hundred-footed) insect.—L. *centi-*, for *centum*, hundred; and *ped-*, stem of *pes*, foot.

centuple. (L.) L. *centuplex* (stem *centuplic-*), a hundredfold. — L. *centu-m*, hundred; *plic-are*, to fold.

centurion. (L.) L. acc. *centurionem*, a captain of a hundred.—L. *centuria* (below).

century. (F.—L.) F. *centurie*. — L. *centuria*, a body of a hundred men; number of one hundred.—L. *centu-m*, hundred.

quintal, a hundred - weight. (F. — Span. — Arab. — L.) F. *quintal* (Cot.) —Span. *quintal*. — Arab. *qintár*, a weight of 100 lbs.—L. *centum*, a hundred.

Centaur. (L. — Gk.) L. *Centaurus*.— Gk. κένταυρος, a centaur, a creature half man and half horse.

centaury, a plant. (L. – Gk.) L. *centaurea*. – Gk. κενταυρίη, centaury; a plant named from the *Centaur* Chiron.

Centenary, Centennial, Centuple, Centurion, &c.; see Cent.

Centre, Center. (F. – L. – Gk.) F. *centre*. – L. *centrum*. – Gk. κέντρον, a spike, goad, prick, centre. – Gk. κεντέω, I goad on.

centrifugal, flying from a centre. (L.) L. *centri-* = *centro-*, crude form of *centrum*; and *fug-ere*, to fly.

centripetal, tending towards a centre. (L.) L. *centri-* (above); *pet-ere*, to seek.

concentre, to draw to a centre. (F. – L. – Gk.) F. *concentrer*. – L. *con-* (*cum*), together; and *centr-um*, a centre. Der. *concentr-ic*, *concentr-ate* (modern).

eccentric, departing from a centre, odd. (F. – L. – Gk.) F. *excentrique*. – Late L. *eccentricus*. – Gk. ἔκκεντρ-ος, out of the centre. – Gk. ἐκ, out; κέντρον, centre.

Ceramic, relating to pottery. (Gk.) Gk. κέραμ-ος, potter's earth.

Cere, to coat with wax. (L.) L. *cerare*, to wax. – L. *cera*, wax. + Gk. κηρός, wax.

cerecloth. (L *and* E.) Lit. a waxed cloth.

cerement. (L.) From *cere*, to wax; with suffix *-ment* (L. *-mentum*).

ceruse, white lead. (F. – L.) O. F. *ceruse*. – L. *cerussa*, white lead. – L. *cera*, wax.

Cereal, relating to corn. (L.) L. *cerealis*. – L. *ceres*, corn.

Cerebral, relating to the brain. (L.) L. *cerebr-um*, the brain. Cf. Gk. κάρα, head.

saveloy, cervelas, a kind of sausage. (F. – Ital. – L.) Formerly *cervelas* (Phillips). – F. *cervelat, cervelas*. – Ital. *cervelata, cervelatta*, a saveloy; from its containing brains. – Ital. *cervello*, brain. – L. *cerebellum*, dimin. of *cerebrum*, brain.

Cerecloth, Cerement; see Cere.

Ceremony. (F. – L.) M. E. *ceremonie*. – F. *cérémonie*. – L. *cærimonia*, a ceremony, rite. +Skt. *karman*, action, rite. (√ KAR.)

Certain. (F. – L.) O. F. *certein, certain*. – L. *cert-us*, sure; with suffix *-anus*. Allied to L. *cernere*, to discriminate; Gk. κρίνειν, to separate, decide.

ascertain. (F. – L.) The *s* is added. – O. F. *acertainer, acertener*, to make certain. – F. *a* (=L. *ad*, to); and *certain*, certain (above).

certify. (F. – L.) M. E. *certifien*. – F. *certifier*. – Low L. *certificare*, to make sure. – L. *certi-*, for *certo-*, crude form of *certus* (above); and *-fic-*, for *fac-ere*, to make.

Cerulean, azure. (L.) L. *cæruleus, cærulus*, blue. Perhaps for *cælulus**, from *cælum*, sky.

Ceruse, white-lead; see Cere.

Cervical, belonging to the neck. (L.) L. *ceruic-*, stem of *ceruix*, neck.

Cervine, relating to a hart. (L.) L. *ceruin-us*. – L. *ceru-us*, a hart; see Hart.

Cess, an assessment; short for assess.

Cessation, Cession; see Cede.

Cess-pool. (C. ?) Also spelt *sess-pool, sus-pool*. Prov. E. *suss, soss*, hogwash, mess, puddle; prob. from Gael. *sos*, any unseemly mixture of food, a coarse mess. Perhaps allied to Gael. *sugh, sogh*, moisture, W. *sug*, moisture, W. *soch*, a drain. *Pool* is originally a Latin word; see Pool. ¶ Or for (*se*)*cess-* or (*re*)*cess-pool*?

Cetaceous, of the whale kind. (L. – Gk.) L. *cete, cetus*. – Gk. κῆτος, a sea-monster.

Chafe; see Caldron.

Chafer, Cockchafer. (E.) A. S. *ceafor*, a kind of beetle. +Du. *kever* : G. *käfer*.

Chaff. (E.) A. S. *ceaf*, later *chæf*, husk of grain. +Du. *kaf*; G. *kaff*. ¶ The verb *to chaff* = *to chafe*, i.e. to vex.

chaffinch, a bird. (E.) I.e. *chaff-finch*; it frequents barn-doors.

Chaffer; see Cheap.

Chaffinch; see Chaff.

Chagrin. (F. – Turk. ?) F. *chagrin*, melancholy. Diez identifies it with F. *chagrin*, shagreen, a rough stuff taken as the type of corroding care; see Shagreen.

Chain. (F. – L.) O. F. *chaine, chaëne*. – L. *catena*, a chain.

chignon. (F. – L.) Hair twisted; another spelling of F. *chaînon*, a link. – F. *chaîne*, O. F. *chaine*, a chain (above).

concatenate. (L.) L. *concatenatus*, pp. of *concatenare*, to link together. – L. *con-* (*cum*), together; and *catena*, a chain.

Chair, Chaise; see Cathedral.

Chalcedony, a kind of quartz. (L. – Gk.) L. *chalcedonius*, Rev. xxi. 19. – Gk. χαλκηδών, Rev. xxi. 19; a stone found at *Chalcedon*, on the coast of Asia Minor.

Chaldron; see Caldron.

Chalice, a cup. (F. – L.) O. F. *calice* (dialectally, *chalice*). – L. *calicem*, acc. of *calix*, a cup. Allied to *calyx*, but not the same word.

Chalk; see Calx.

Challenge; see Calumny.

Chalybeate. (L. – Gk.) Used of water

containing iron. Coined from L. *chalyb-s*, steel. — Gk. χάλυψ (stem χαλυβ-), steel; named from the *Chalybes*, a people of Pontus, who made it.

Chamber. (F. — L.) F. *chambre*; O. F. *cambre*. — L. *camera*, *camara*, a vault, vaulted room, room. (√ KAM.)

chamberlain. (F. — O. H. G. — L.) F. *chamberlain*, O. F. *chambrelenc*. — O. H. G. *chamerlinc*, M. H. G. *kamerlinc*, one who has the care of rooms; formed with suffix *-l-inc* (the same as E. *-l-ing*), from L. *camera* (above).

comrade. (Span. — L.) Span. *camarada*, a company; also an associate, comrade. — Span. *camara*, a chamber, cabin. — L. *camera* (above).

Chameleon. (L. — Gk.) L. *chamæleon*. — Gk. χαμαι-λέων, lit. a ground-lion, dwarf-lion; a kind of lizard. — Gk. χαμαί, on the ground (also dwarf, in comp.); and λέων, lion.

chamomile. (Low L. — Gk.) Low L. *camomilla* (*chamomilla*). — Gk. χαμαίμηλον, lit. ground-apple, from the apple-like smell of the flower. — Gk. χαμαί, on the ground (see above); μῆλον, apple.

Chamois. (F. — G.) F. *chamois*. — M. H. G. *gamz* (G. *gemse*), a chamois. ¶ Borrowed from some Swiss dialectal form. **shammy,** a kind of leather. (F. — G.) Orig. *chamois* leather; see Blount and Phillips. See above.

Champ, to eat noisily. (Scand.) Formerly *cham* or *chamm*. — Swed. dial. *kämsa*, to chew with difficulty. Cf. Icel. *kiaptr*, jaw.

Champagne, Champaign, Champion; see Camp.

Chance; see Cadence.

Chancel, Chancery; see Cancer.

Chandler, Chandelier; see Candid.

Change. (F. — L.) F. *changer*; O. F. *changier*. — Low L. *cambiare*, to change (Lex Salica). — L. *cambire*, to exchange.

exchange. (F. — L.) O. F. *eschange*, sb.; *eschanger*, vb., to exchange. — O. F. *es-* (= L. *ex*); and F. *changer*, to change (above).

Channel; see Canal.

Chant; see Cant (1).

Chaos. (Gk.) L. *chaos*, Lat. spelling of Gk. χάος, chaos, abyss, lit. a cleft. — Gk. χα-, base of χαίνειν, to gape.

chasm. (L. — Gk.) L. *chasma*, a gulf. — Gk. χάσμα, a yawning cleft. — Gk. χα- (above).

Chap (1), to cleave, crack, Chop, to cut.

(E. ?) M. E. *chappen*, *choppen*, to cut; hence, to gape open like a wound made by a cut. Not found in A. S. + O. Du. *koppen*, to cut off; *kappen*, to cut; Swed. *kappa*, Dan. *kappe*, to cut; G. *kappen*, to cut, lop. Cognate with Gk. κόπτειν, to cut, Church Slav. *skopiti*, to cut. (√ SKAP.) See Capon.

chip. (E.) Dimin. form of *chap* or *chop*; hence, to cut a little at a time.

chop, the same as Chap above.

chump, a log. (Scand.) — Icel. *kumbr*, *tré-kumbr*, a log of wood; from Icel. *kumbr*, nasalised form of *kubbr*, a chopping. — Icel. *kubba*, to chop; allied to E. *chop*. Der. *chump-end*, i. e. thick end.

Chap (2), **Chapman;** see Cheap.

Chapel, Chaperon; see Cape (1).

Chapiter; see Capital.

Chaplet; see Cape (1).

Chaps, Chops, the jaws. (Scand.) A South E. variety of North E. *chafts* or *chaffs*, jaws (Cleveland Gloss.). — Icel. *kjaptr* (*pt* pron. as *ft*), the jaw; Swed. *käft*, Dan. *kiæft*, jaw, chops. Allied to A. S. *ceaft*, jowl, Gk. γαμφαί, Skt. *jambha*, jaws; and see Jowl.

Chapter; see Capital.

Char (1), to turn to charcoal. (E.) To *char* is simply to turn; wood turned to coal was said to be *charred*. M. E. *cherren*, *charren*, to turn; A.S. *cerran*, to turn. — A. S. *cerr* (also *cierr*, *cyrr*), a turn. + Du. *keer*, a turn, time, *keeren*, to turn; O. H. G. *chér*, a turning about, G. *kehren*, to turn. Hence *char-coal*, i. e. *charr'd* coal.

char (2), a turn of work. (E.) Also *chare*, *chore*, *chewre*; M. E. *cher*, *char*, orig. a turn, hence, a space of time, turn of work, &c. Hence *char-woman*, a woman who does a turn of work. See Ajar.

Char (3), a fish. (C.) Named from its red belly; [the W. name is *torgoch*, red-bellied, from *tor*, belly, and *coch*, red.] — Gael. *ceara*, red, from *cear*, blood; Irish *cear*, red, also blood. Cf. E. *gore*.

Character. (L. — Gk.) L. *character*. — Gk. χαρακτήρ, an engraved or stamped mark. — Gk. χαράσσειν, to furrow, scratch, engrave.

Charade. (F. — Prov. — Span. ?) F. *charade*, introduced from Provençal (Brachet); Languedoc *charrade*, idle talk (Littré). Prob. from Span. *charrada*, speech or action of a clown. — Span. *charro*, a clown, peasant.

Charcoal; see Char (1).

Charge, Chariot; see **Car.**

Charity; see **Caress.**

Charlatan. (F. — Ital.) F. *charlatan.* — Ital. *ciarlatano,* a mountebank, great talker, prattler. — Ital. *ciarlare,* to prattle. — Ital. *ciarla,* prattle. Prob. of imitative origin.

Charlock, a kind of wild mustard. (E.) Prov. E. *carlock.* — A. S. *cerlic*; the latter syllable means 'leek;' origin of *cer-* unknown.

Charm. (F. — L.) M. E. *charme,* sb. — O. F. *charme,* an enchantment. — L. *carmen,* a song, enchantment. (√ KAS.)

Charnel; see **Carnal.**

Chart, Charter; see **Card** (1).

Chary; see **Care.**

Chase (1), (2), (3); see **Capacious.**

Chasm; see **Chaos.**

Chaste, Chasten, Chastise; see **Caste.**

Chasuble; see **Casino.**

Chat, Chatter. (E.) M. E. *chateren,* also *chiteren,* to chatter, twitter; frequentative form of *chat.* An imitative word; cf. Du. *kwetteren,* to warble, chatter, Swed. *kvittra,* to chirp; Skt. *gad,* to recite, *gada,* speech.

Chateau; see **Castle.**

Chattels; see **Capital.**

Chatter; see **Chat.**

Chaw; see **Chew.**

Chaws, old spelling of **Jaws**; see **Chew.**

Cheap, at a low price. (L.) Not E., but L. M. E. *chep, cheep,* barter, price; always a sb. Hence *good cheap,* in a good market (F. *bon marché*); whence E. *cheap,* used as an adj. A. S. *ceáp,* price; whence the verb *cedpian,* to cheapen, buy. So also Du. *koop,* a bargain, whence *koopen,* to buy; G. *kauf,* purchase, whence *kaufen,* to buy; Icel. *kaup,* Swed. *köp,* Dan. *kiöb,* a purchase; Goth. *kaupon* (weak vb.), to traffic. But all these words are borrowed from L.; in particular, the O. H. G. *choufo,* a huckster, is merely L. *caupo,* a huckster. Cf. Gk. κάπηλος, a peddler, Russ. *kupite,* to buy.

chaffer. (L. *and* E.) The verb is from the M. E. sb. *chapfare,* also *chaffare,* a bargaining. — A. S. *ceáp,* a bargain (see above); and *faru,* a journey, also business; see **Fare.**

chapman, a merchant. (L. *and* E.) The familiar *chap* is merely short for *chapman.* — A. S. *ceápman,* a merchant. — A. S. *ceáp,* price, barter (see above); and *man,* a man.

chop (2), to barter. (O. Du.) M. E.

copen (Lydgate). — Du. *koopen,* to buy; the same as A. S. *ceápian,* to cheapen; see **Cheap** above.

cope (2), to vie with. (Du.) Orig. to cheapen, barter, bargain with; M. E. *copen* (as above).

keep, to regard. (L.) Not E., but L. M. E. *kepen.* A. S. *cépan,* also *cýpan,* orig. to traffic, sell, also to seek after, store up, keep. This verb is a mere derivative of A. S. *ceáp,* barter, price; see above.

Cheat, to defraud. (F. — L.) *Cheat* is merely short for *escheat*; cf. M. E. *chete,* an escheat (Prompt. Parv.). The *escheaters* were often *cheaters*; hence the verb. See *escheat,* entered under **Cadence.**

Check, a sudden stop, repulse. (F. — Pers.) M. E. *chek,* a stop; also check ! in playing chess. The word is due to the game, which is very old. The orig. sense of *check* was 'king!' i.e. mind the king, the king is in danger. — O. F. *eschec,* 'a check at chess-play,' Cot. — Pers. *sháh,* a king, king at chess; whence *sháh-mát,* checkmate, lit. 'the king is dead,' from *mát,* he is dead. Similarly we have F. *échec,* a check, repulse, defeat, pl. *échecs,* chess; Ital. *scacco,* a square of a chess-board, also a check, defeat. See chess below.

checker, chequer, to mark with squares. (F. — Pers.) To mark with squares like those on a chess-board. M. E. *chekker, chekere,* a chess-board. (Hence *The Checkers,* an inn-sign.) — O. F. *eschequier,* a chess-board, also, an exchequer. — O. F. *eschec,* check ! at chess; see above.

checkers, chequers, an old name for the game of check, from draughts; from the *checker* or chess-board; see above.

check-mate. (F. — Pers.) From Pers. *sháh mát,* the king is dead; see **Check.**

cheque. (F. — Pers.) A pedantic spelling of *check,* from confusion with *exchequer*; it is really a name given to a draft for money, of which one keeps a memorandum or *counter-check.*

chess, the game of the kings. (F. — Pers.) A corrupted form of *checks,* i.e. kings; see **Check** above. — O. F. *eschecs,* chess; really the pl. of *eschec,* check, orig. 'king.' ¶ From Pers. *sháh,* a king, were formed O. F. *eschec,* F. *échec,* E. *check,* Ital. *scacco,* Span. *xaque, jaque,* Port. *xaque,* G. *schach,* Du. *schaak,* Dan. *skak,* Swed. *schack,* Low Lat. *ludus scaccorum* = game of checks, or of kings.

exchequer, a court of revenue. (F. —

Pers.) M. E. *eschekere.* — O. F. *eschequier,* a chess-board ; hence a checkered cloth on which accounts were reckoned by means of counters. — O. F. *eschec,* check ; see **Check.**

Cheek. (E.) M. E. *cheke, cheoke.* — A. S. *ceáce,* cheek.+Du. *kaak,* jaw, cheek ; Swed. *kek,* jaw. Allied to **Jaw.**

Cheer. (F. — L. — Gk.) M. E. *chere.* orig. the mien ; hence ' to be of good *cheer.'* — O. F. *chere,* the face. — Low. L. *cara,* face. — Gk. *κάρα,* the head. Der. *cheer-ful,* &c.

Cheese. (L.) M. E. *chese.* A. S. *cése, cýse.* — L. *caseus,* cheese ; whence other forms are borrowed.

Chemise. (F. — L. — C. ?) F. *chemise.* — Late L. *camisia,* a shirt, thin dress. Prob. Celtic ; cf. O. Irish *caimmse,* shirt.

Chemist, Chymist ; short for *alchemist* ; see **Alchemy.**

Cheque, Chequer ; see **Check.**

Cherish ; see **Caress.**

Cherry. (F. — L. — Gk.) M. E. *cheri,* a mistake for *cheris,* the final *s* being mistaken for the pl. inflexion. — O. F. *cerise.* — L. *cerasus,* a cherry-tree. — Gk. *κέρασος,* a cherry-tree ; usually said to come from *Cerasos,* in Pontus ; a story which Curtius doubts.

Chert, a kind of quartz. (C. ?) The Kentish form is *chart,* rough ground. Probably from Irish *ceart,* a pebble ; cf. Gael. *carr,* a shelf of rock, W. *careg,* stone.

Cherub. (Heb.) The true pl. is *cherubim.* — Heb. *k'rúv* (pl. *k'rúvim*), a mystic figure.

Chervil, a plant. (L. — Gk.) A.S. *cærfille.* — L. *cærefolium* (Pliny). — Gk. *χαιρέφυλλον,* chervil, lit. pleasant leaf. — Gk. *χαίρ-ειν,* to rejoice ; *φύλλον,* leaf.

Chess ; see **Check.**

Chest. (L. — Gk.) M.E. *cheste, chiste.* A.S. *cyste.* — L. *cista.* — Gk. *κίστη,* a chest, box (whence G. *kiste,* &c.)

cist, a sort of tomb. (L. — Gk.) L. *cista* ; as above.

cistern. (F. — L. — Gk.) F. *cisterne.* — L. *cisterna,* a reservoir for water. — L. *cista* (above).

Chestnut, Chesnut. (F. — L. — Gk.) *Chesnut* is short for *chestnut,* which is short for *chesten-nut,* nut of the *chesten,* which is the old name of the tree, called in M. E. *chestein.* — O. F. *chastaigne* (F. *châtaigne*). — L. *castana,* chestnut-tree. — Gk. *κάστανον,* a chestnut ; chesnuts were called *κάστανα,* or *κάρυα Κασταναῖα,* from

Κάστανα, Castana, the name of a city in Pontus where they abounded.

Cheval-de-frise, an obstruction with spikes. (F.) Lit. ' horse of Friesland,' a jocular name ; the pl. *chevaux-de-Frise* is commoner.

Chevalier ; see **Cavalier.**

Chew, Chaw. (E.) M. E. *chewen.* A. S. *ceówan,* to chew, eat. + Du. *kaauwen* ; G. *kauen* ; Russ. *jevate.* Der. *chaw,* sb., a jaw ; now spelt *jaw.*

Chicanery. (F. — Pers. ?) F. *chicanerie,* wrangling, pettifogging ; Cot. — F. *chicaner,* to wrangle ; orig. to dispute in the game of the mall or *chicane* (Brachet). This sb. *chicane* is from the medieval Gk. *τζυκάνιον,* a word of Byzantine origin (id.). Prob. from Pers. *chaugán,* a club, bat.

Chicken. (E.) Sometimes shortened to *chick* ; but the M. E. word is *chiken.* A. S. *cicen* (for *cycen**, not found) ; prob. dimin. of *cocc,* a cock (cf. *kitten* from *cat*). So also Du. *kieken, kuiken,* a chicken, appears to be a dimin. from O. Du. *cocke,* a cock ; cf. E. *chuck,* a chicken (Shak.), and G. *küchlein,* a chicken. ¶ More likely, not an exact dimin. of *cocc,* but from the same imitative base ; see **Chuck** (2).

Chicory, a plant, succory. (F. — L. — Gk.) F. *chicorée.* — L. *cichorium.* — Gk. *κιχώριον, κιχώρη,* succory. β. *Succory* is a corrupter form of the word, apparently for *siccory* or *cichory,* from L. *cichorium.*

Chide. (E.) M. E. *chiden.* A. S. *cídan,* to chide, brawl.

Chief, Chieftain ; see **Capital.**

Chiffonier, a cupboard. (F.) Lit. a place to put rags in. — F. *chiffonier,* a ragpicker, also a cupboard. — F. *chiffon,* a rag. Orig. unknown.

Chignon ; see **Chain.**

Chilblain ; see **Cool.**

Child. (E.) M. E. *child.* A. S. *cild.* Allied to Du. and G. *kind,* a child, Goth. *kilthei,* the womb. (√GA.) See **Chit, Kin, Chill** ; see **Cool.**

Chime ; see **Cymbal.**

Chimæra, Chimera. (L. — Gk.) L. *chimæra.* — Gk. *χίμαιρα,* a she-goat ; also a fabulous monster, with a goat's body. — Gk. *χίμαρος,* he-goat. + Icel. *gymbr,* young ewe-lamb.

Chimney. (F. — L. — Gk.) F. *cheminée,* ' a chimney ;' Cot. — Low L. *caminata,* provided with a chimney ; hence, a chimney. — L. *caminus,* a fire-place. — Gk. *κάμινος,* oven, fire-place.

Chimpanzee, an ape. (African.) I am informed that the name is *tsimpanzee* in the neighbourhood of the gulf of Guinea.

Chin. (E.) M. E. *chin*. A. S. *cin*. **+** Du. *kin*, Icel. *kinn*, Dan. *kind*, Swed. *kind*; Goth. *kinnus*, the cheek; G. *kinn*, cheek; L. *gena*, cheek; Gk. γένυς, chin; Skt. *hanu* (for *ganu*), jaw.

China. (China.) Short for *china-ware*, or ware from *China*. The name of the people was formerly *Chineses*; we have dropped the final *s*, and use *Chinese* as a pl.; hence *Chinee* in the singular, by a second dropping of *se*.

Chincough, whooping-cough. (E.) Put for *chink-cough*; cf. Scotch *kink-cough*, *kink-host* (*host* means *cough*). A *kink* is a catch in the breath, nasalised form of a base KIK, to gasp. **+** Du. *kinkhoest*; O. Du. *kichhoest*; Swed. *kikhosta*, chincough, *kikna*, to gasp; G. *keichen*, to gasp. Cf. **Cackle** and **Choke**.

Chine. (F.—O. H. G.) O. F. *eschine* (F. *échine*), the back-bone.—O. H. G. *skiná*, a needle, prickle (G. *schiene*, a splint). For the sense, cf. L. *spina*, a thorn, spine, backbone.

Chink (1), a cleft. (E.) Formed by adding *k* to M. E. *chine*, a cleft, rift.—A. S. *cínu*, a chink.—A. S. *cínan*, to split (strong vb.). **+** Du. *keen*, a chink, also a germ; *kenen*, to bud; cf. G. *keimen*, to bud. (Germinating seeds make a crack in the ground.)

Chink (2), to jingle. (E.) An imitative word; cf. *clink*, *clank*; and see **Chincough**.

Chintz. (Hindustani—Skt.) Hind. *chhínt*, spotted cotton cloth, named from the variegated patterns on it; *chhít*, chintz, also a spot.—Skt. *chitra*, variegated, spotted.

Chip; see **Chap** (1).

Chirography, handwriting. (Gk.) Gk. χειρογραφεῖν, to write with the hand.—Gk. χειρο-, crude form of χείρ, the hand; γράφειν, to write. (√GHAR.) Cf. *chiro-mancy*, fortune-telling by the hand; *chiro-pod-ist*, one who handles (and cures) the feet.

chirurgeon, the old spelling of *surgeon*. (F.—Gk.) F. *chirurgien*, 'a surgeon;' Cot.—F. *chirurgie*, surgery.—Gk. χειρουργία, a working with the hands, skill with the hands, art, surgery.—Gk. χειρο-, crude form of χείρ, the hand; and ἔργειν, to work.

surgeon, contracted form of *chirur-*

geon; see above. **Der.** *surgical*, short for *chirurgical*; *surgery*, corruption of M. E. *surgen-rie* (=*surgeon-ry*); cf. F. *chirurgie*.

Chirp. (E.) Also *chirrup*. M. E. *chirpen*. Also M. E. *chirken*, *chirmen*, to chirp. The forms *chir-p*, *chir-k*, *chir-m* are from an imitative base KIR, to coo; cf. Du. *kirren*, to coo; Skt. *gir*, the voice; L. *garrire*, to chatter. (√GAR.)

Chirurgeon; see **Chirography**.

Chisel. (F.—L.) M. E. *chisel*.—O. F. *chisel*, *cisel* (F. *ciseau*). Cf. Low L. *cisellus*, scissors (A. D. 1352). O. F. *cisel* answers to Low L. *cæsillus* * or *cæsellus* *, not found, but a mere variant of L. *cisorium*, a cutting instrument (Vegetius); see Scheler's note to Diez.—L. *cæs-um*, supine of *cædere*, to cut; whence also late L. *incisor*, a carver, cutter; see **Cæsura**.

scissors. (F.—L.) The mod. E. *scissors* is a corrupt spelling, due to confusion with Low L. *scissor* (from *scindere*, to cut), which, however, only means a man who cuts, a butcher, a tailor, and has, in fact, nothing at all to do with the word. The old spelling was *sizars*, *cizars*, or *cizers*; and this again was adapted (by putting the E. suffix *-ers* in place of F. *-eaux*) from F. *ciseaux*, ' sizars, or little sheers;' Cot. This F. *ciseaux* = cutters, pl. of *ciseau*, a chisel. Thus, etymologically, E. *scissors* = *cisers* = *cisels*, pl. of *cisel* = *chisel*.

Chit, a shoot, sprig; a pert child. (E.) The true sense is a shoot, or bud; hence, a forward child. Put for *chith*. A. S. *cíð*, a germ, sprig, sprout. Allied to Goth. *keian*, *uskeian*, to produce a shoot; also to E. *child*, *kin*. (√CI, for GA.)

Chivalry; see **Cavalier**.

Chlorine, a pale green gas. (Gk.) Named from its colour.—Gk. χλωρ-ός, pale green. (√GHAR.)

chloroform. (L. *and* Gk.) The latter element relates to *formic* acid, an acid formerly obtained from red ants.—L. *formica*, an ant.

Chocolate; see **Cacao**.

Choice; see **Choose**.

Choir; see **Chorus**.

Choke. (E.) M. E. *chowken*, *cheken*, *cheokien*. A. S. *cèocian*; only in the derivative *áceócung*, to translate L. *ruminatio*, which the glossator hardly seems to have understood. **+** Icel. *koka*, to gulp, *kýka*, to swallow, from *kok*, the gullet. Allied to **Cough**, and **Chuck** (2).

Choler, the bile, anger. (F.—L.—Gk.)

Anger was supposed to be due to excess of bile. M.E. *coler.* — O. F. *colere.* — L. *cholera*, bile; also cholera, bilious complaint. — Gk. χολέρα, cholera; χολή, bile; χόλος, bile, wrath. See **Gall**.

cholera. (L. — Gk.) L. *cholera*, as above. And see **Melancholy**.

Choose. (E.) M. E. *chesen, chusen*. A. S. *ceósan*, to choose (pt. t. *ceás*). + Du. and G. *kiesen*, Goth. *kiusan*; allied to L. *gustare*, to taste, Gk. γεύομαι, I taste, Skt. *jush*, to relish. (√GUS.) See **Gust**.

choice. (F. — Teut.) Not E. M. E. *chois.* — O. F. *chois* (F. *choix*). — O. F. *choisir, coisir*, to choose. Of Teut. origin; cf. Goth. *kiusan*, to choose.

Chop (1), to cut; see **Chap** (1).

Chop (2), to barter; see **Cheap**.

Chops; see **Chaps**.

Chord. (L. — Gk.) L. *chorda*. — Gk. χορδή, the string of a musical instrument, orig. a string of gut, related to χολάδες, guts.

cord. (F. — L. — Gk.) M. E. *corde.* — F. *corde.* — Low L. *corda*, a thin rope; the same as L. *chorda*; see above. Der. *cord-age* (F. *cordage*); *cord-on* (F. *cordon*); *cord-elier* (F. *cordelier*, a twist of rope, also a Gray Friar, who used such a twist, from *cordeler*, to twist ropes.)

monochord, a musical instrument with one string. (Gk.) Gk. μονό-s, single; χορδή, chord.

Chorus. (L. — Gk.) L. *chorus*, a band of singers. — Gk. χορός, a dance, a band of dancers or singers. Der. *chor-al, chor-ister*.

choir. (F. — L. — Gk.) The *choir* of a church is the part where the *choir* sit. Also spelt *quire*; M. E. *queir, quer.* — O. F. *choeur*, 'the quire of a church, a troop of singers;' Cot. — L. *chorum*, acc. of *chorus* (above.)

Chough, a bird. (E.) M. E. *chough*. A. S. *ceó*. Named from *cawing*; see **Caw**. + Du. *kaauw*, Dan. *kaa*, Swed. *kaja*, a jackdaw.

Chouse, to cheat. (Turk.) To act as a *chouse* or cheat. Ben Jonson has *chiaus* in the sense of 'a Turk,' with the implied sense of 'cheat;' Alchemist, i. 1. The allusion is to a Turkish *chiaus* or interpreter, who committed a notorious fraud in 1609. — Turk. *chá'ush*, a sergeant, macebearer, Palmer's Pers. Dict.; *cháush*, a sergeant, herald, messenger, Rich. Dict. p. 534. Or (mediately) from O. Ital. *ciaus*.

Chrism; see below.

Christ, the anointed one. (L. — Gk.) A. S. *Crist.* — L. *Christus*. — Gk. χριστός, anointed. — Gk. χρίω, I rub, anoint. Allied to L. *fricare*, Skt. *ghrish*, to rub, grind. (√ GHAR.) Der. *Christ-ian, Christ-endom*, &c.; *Christ-mas* (see **Mass**); *antichrist*, opponent of Christ (from Gk. ἀντί, against; see 1 John, ii. 18).

chrism, holy unction. (F. — L. — Gk.) Also spelt *chrisome*, whence *chrisome-child*, a child wearing a *chrisome-cloth*, or cloth which a child wore after holy unction. — O. F. *cresme*, 'the crisome, ór oyle,' Cot. — Low L. *chrisma*, holy oil. — Gk. χρῖσμα, an unguent. — Gk. χρίω (as above).

Chromatic, relating to colours. (Gk.) Gk. χρωματικός, adj. — Gk. χρωματ-, stem of χρῶμα, colour; allied to χρώς, skin.

achromatic, colourless. (Gk.) Gk. ἀχρώματ-os, colourless. — Gk. ἀ-, not; χρωματ- (as above).

chrome, chromium. (Gk.) A metal; its compounds exhibit beautiful colours. — Gk. χρῶμ-α, colour.

Chronicle. (F. — Low L. — Gk.) M. E. *cronicle*, with inserted *l*; also *cronike, cronique.* — O. F. *cronique*; pl. *croniques*, chronicles, annals. — Low L. *chronica*, fem. sing.; put for neut. pl. — Gk. χρονικά, pl., annals. — Gk. χρονικός, adj. from χρόνος, time. Der. *chron-ic* (= χρονικός).

anachronism, error in chronology. (Gk.) Gk. ἀναχρονισμός. — Gk. ἀναχρονίζειν, to refer to a wrong time. — Gk. ἀνά, up, back (wrong); χρόνος, time.

chronology, science of dates. (Gk.) From χρόνο-s, time; λόγ-os, discourse; see **Logic**.

chronometer, time-measurer. (Gk.) From χρόνο-s, time; μέτρον, measure; see **Metre**.

synchronism, concurrence in time. (Gk.) Gk. συγχρονισμός. — Gk. σύγχρονος, contemporaneous. — Gk. συγ-, for σύν, together; χρόνος, time.

Chrysalis, the form taken by some insects. (Gk.) Gk. χρυσαλλίς, the goldcoloured sheath of butterflies, chrysalis. — Gk. χρυσό-s, gold; see **Gold**.

chrysolite, a yellow stone. (L. — Gk.) L. *chrysolithus*, Rev. xxi. 20. — Gk. χρυσόλιθος. — Gk. χρυσό-s, gold; λίθος, stone.

chrysoprase. (L. — Gk.) L. *chrysoprasus*, Rev. xxi. 20. — Gk. χρυσόπρασος, a yellow-green stone. — Gk. χρυσό-s, gold; πράσον, a (green) leek.

Chub, a fish. (Scand.) Named from its fatness; cf. Dan. *kobbe*, a seal, prov. Swed. *kubbug*, chubby, fat, from Swed. *kubb*, a block, log. — Prov. Swed. *kubba*, to lop, chop; allied to E. *chop*; and see **Chump**, under **Chap** (1).

chubby, fat. (Scand.) Prov. Swed. *kubbug* (above).

Chuck (1), to strike gently, toss. (F. — Teut.) Formerly written *chock* (Turberville). — F. *choquer*, to give a shock, jolt. — Du. *schokken*, to jolt, shake; allied to E. *shock* and *shake*.

Chuck (2), to chuck as a hen. (E.) An imitative word; Ch. has *chuk* to express the noise made by a cock; C. T. 15180. Cf. *cluck*. Der. *chuck-le*, in the sense 'to cluck.'

Chuck (3), a chicken. A variety of *chick*, for *chicken*. See above.

Chuckle. (E.) To *chuckle* is to laugh in a suppressed way; prob. related to *choke* rather than to *Chuck* (2).

Chump, a log; see **Chap** (1).

Church. (Gk.) M. E. *chirche, chireche*. A. S. *cyrice, cirice*, later *circe* (whence E. *kirk*). — Gk. κυριακόν, a church, neut. of κυριακός, belonging to the Lord. — Gk. κύριος, a lord, orig. mighty. — Gk. κῦρος, strength. (√KU.) The Icel. *kirkja*, G. *kirche*, &c. are borrowed from A. S.

Churl. (E.) M. E. *cherl, cheorl*. A. S. *ceorl*, a man. + Du. *karel*, Dan. Sw. Icel. G. *karl*.

Churn; see **Corn** (1).

Chyle, milky fluid. (F. — L. — Gk.) F. *chyle*. — L. *chylus*. — Gk. χυλός, juice. — Gk. χύ-ω, I pour. (√GHU.)

chyme, liquid pulp. (L. — Gk.) Formerly *chymus*. — L. *chymus*. — Gk. χυμός, juice. — Gk. χύ-ω; as above.

Chymist; see **Alchemist**.

Cicatrice, scar. (F. — L.) F. *cicatrice*. — L. *cicatricem*, acc. of *cicatrix*, a scar.

Cicerone. (Ital. — L.) Ital. *cicerone*, a guide; orig. a Cicero. — L. acc. *Ciceronem*, proper name.

Cider. (F. — L. — Gk. — Heb.) It merely means strong drink. M. E. *sicer, cyder*. — F. *cidre*. — L. *sicera*. — Gk. σίκερα, strong drink. — Heb. *shékár*, strong drink. — Heb. *shâkar*, to be intoxicated.

Cieling; see **Ceil**.

Cigar, Segar. (Span.) Span. *cigarro*; orig. a kind of tobacco from Cuba.

Cinchona, Peruvian bark. (Span.) Named after the countess of *Chinchon*,

wife of the governor of Peru, cured by it A.D. 1638. (Should be *chinchona*.)

Cincture. (L.) L. *cinctura*, a girdle. — L. *cinctus*, pp. of *cingere*, to gird.

enceinte, pregnant. (F. — L.) F. *enceinte*. — L. *incincta*, lit. girt in, said of a pregnant woman, fem. of pp. of *in-cingere*, to gird in.

precinct. (L.) Low L. *præcinctum*, a boundary. — L. *præcinctus*, pp. of *præcingere*, to gird about.

shingles, an eruptive disease. (F. — L.) Called *zona* in Latin, from its encircling the body like a belt. — O. F. *cengle* (F. *sangle*), a girth. — L. *cingulum*, a belt. — L. *cingere*, to gird.

succinct, concise. (L.) L. *succinctus*, pp. of *succingere*, to gird up, tuck up short. — L. *suc-* (*sub*), up; *cingere*, to gird.

Cinder. (E.) Misspelt for *sinder* (by confusion with F. *cendre* = L. *cinerem*; see **Cinerary**). A. S. *sinder*, scoria, slag. + Icel. *sindr*; Swed. *sinder*; G. *sinter*, dross; Du. *sintels*, cinders. ¶ The A. S. *sinder* occurs in the 8th century.

Cinerary, relating to the ashes of the dead. (L.) L. *cinerarius*. — L. *ciner-*, stem of *cinis*, dust, ashes of the dead. + Gk. κόνις, dust; Skt. *hana*, a grain.

Cinnabar, Cinoper. (Gk. — Pers.) Gk. κιννάβαρι, vermilion. From Pers. *zinjarf, zingafr*, red lead, vermilion, cinnabar.

Cinnamon, a spice. (Heb.) Heb. *qinnámón*; said to be of Malay origin.

Cipher. (F. — Arab.) O. F. *cifre* (F. *chiffre*), a cipher, zero. — Arab. *sifr*, a cipher. Der. *de-cipher* (L. *de*, in the verbal sense of *un-*; and *cipher*); cf. O. F. *dechiffrer*, 'to decypher,' Cot.

zero. (Ital. — Low L. — Arab.) Ital. *zero*, short for *zefiro*. — Low L. *zephyrum* (Devic). — Arab. *sifr* (above).

Circle. (L.) A. S. *circul*. — L. *circulus*, dimin. of *circus*, a ring, circle; see **Ring**. Der. *en-circle, semi-circle*; and see *circum-*.

circus, a ring. (L.) L. *circus* (above).

research. (F. — L.) Compounded of *re-*, again, and *search* (below).

search, to explore. (F. — L.) M. E. *serchen, cerchen*. — O. F. *cercher* (F. *chercher*). — L. *circare*, to go round; hence, to explore. — L. *circus*, a ring (above).

Circuit; see **Itinerant**.

Circum-, *prefix*, round. (L.) L. *circum*, around, round; orig. acc. of *circus*, a circle; see **Circle**. Der. *circum-ambient* (see **Amble**); *-cise* (see **Cæsura**); *-ference* (see **Fertile**); -*flex* (see **Flexible**); -*jacent* (see **Jet** (1)); -*locution* (see **Loquacious**); -*scribe* (see **Scribe**); -*spect* (see **Species**); -*stance* (see **State**); -*vallation* (see **Wall**); -*volve* (see **Voluble**). Also *circum-fluent, circum-navigate*.

Circus; see **Circle**.

Cirrus, a fleecy cloud, tendril. (L.) L. *cirrus*, a curl, curled hair. Allied to *circus*.

Cist; see **Chest**.

Cit, Citadel; see **Civil**.

Cite, to summon, quote. (F.—L.) F. *citer*. — L. *citare*, frequent. of *ciere*, to rouse, excite, call. + Gk. κίω, I go. (√KI.) See **Hie**. Der. *ex-cite, in-cite, re-cite.*

resuscitate, to revive. (L.) L. *resuscitatus*, pp. of *resuscitare*, to revive. — L. *re-*, *sus-*, and *citare*, to rouse.

Cithern, Cittern, a kind of guitar. (L.—Gk.) Also M.E. *giterne*; from O. Du. *ghiterne*, a guitar. The *n* is excrescent, as in *bitter-n*; the true form is *cither* or *citer*, A.S. *cytere*. — L. *cithara*. — Gk. κιθάρα, a kind of lyre or lute.

guitar. (F.—L.—Gk.) F. *guitare.*— L. *cithara*; as above.

Citizen; see **Civil**.

Citron. (F.—L.—Gk.) F. *citron.*— Low L. acc. *citronem.* — L. *citrus*, orange-tree. — Gk. κίτρον, a citron; κιτρία, citron-tree.

City; see **Civil**.

Civet. (F. — Arab.) F. *civette*, civet; also the civet-cat; borrowed from medieval Gk. ζαπέτιον (Brachet). — Arab. *zabád*, civet.

Civil. (L.) L. *ciuilis*, belonging to citizens. — L. *ciuis*, a citizen. Allied to E. **Hive**. (√KI.) Der. *civil-ise, civil-i-an.*

cit; short for citizen (below).

citadel. (F.—Ital.—L.) F. *citadelle.*— Ital. *citadella*, a small town, fort; dimin. of *cittade* = *cittate* (*città*), a city. — L. *ciuitatem*, acc. of *ciuitas*, a city. — L. *ciuis*, a citizen (above).

citizen. (F.—L.) M.E. *citezein*, where *z* is corruptly written for ȝ (*y*); Chaucer has *citiȝen* (=*citiyen*), tr. of Boethius, p. 14.— O.F. *citeain* (F. *citoyen*); formed from O.F. *cite* (*cité*) by help of the suffix -*ain* = L. -*anus*; see below.

city. (F.—L.) M.E. *cite, citee.*—O.F. *cite* (F. *cité*).—L. *citatem*, short for *ciuitatem*, acc. of *ciuitas*; see **citadel**.

Clack. (E.) M.E. *clacken*. Allied to

Crack. + Icel. *klaka*, to chatter; Du. *klakken*, to clack, crack : Irish *clag*, to din; Gk. κλάζειν, allied to κράζειν, to make a din.

clang, to resound. (L.) L. *clangere*, to resound; whence *clangor*, a loud noise. + Gk. κλαγγή, a clang; allied to κλάζειν (above). Der. *clang-or*.

clank. (E.) Nasalised form of **Clack**.

click. (E.) Weakened form of **Clack**.

clinch, clench, to rivet. (E.) M.E. *clenchen, klenken*, to strike smartly, to make to clink; causal of *klinken*, to clink.

clink. (E.) Nasalised form of **Click**.

clinker, a hard cinder. (Du.) Du. *klinker*, a clinker, named from the tinkling sound which they make when they strike each other. — Du. *klinken*, to clink; cognate with E. *clink*.

clique, a gang. (F.—Du.) F. *clique*, a gang, noisy set.—O.F. *cliquer*, to click, make a noise. — Du. *klikken*, to click, clash; also to inform, tell; cf. Du. *klikker*, a tell-tale.

cloak, cloke. (F.—C.) M.E. *cloke.*— O.F. *cloque, cloche.*—Low L. *cloca*, a bell; also a horseman's cape, which resembled a bell in shape; see below.

clock. (C.) The orig. sense was 'bell;' bells preceded clocks for notifying times.— Irish *clog*, a bell, clock; *clogaim*, I ring or sound as a bell.—Irish *clagaim*, I clack, make a noise; *clag*, clapper of a mill. So also Gael. *clog*, a bell, clock; W. *cloch*, a bell, &c. The Irish *clag* is cognate with E. **Clack**. The G. *glocke* is a borrowed word ; so also Du. *klok*, &c.

cluck. (E.) M.E. *clokken*, to cluck as a hen; a mere variant of **Clack**. + Du. *klokken*, Dan. *klukke*, G. *glucken*; L. *glocire*.

Claim, to demand, call out for. (F.—L.) O.F. *claimer, clamer.*—L. *clamare*, to call out; from O.L. *calare*, to proclaim; cf. Gk. καλεῖν, to summon. (√KAR.) Der. *ac-claim, de-claim, ex-claim, pro-claim, re-claim*; also (from pp. *clamatus*) *ac-clamat-ion, de-clamat-ion, ex-clamat-ion, pro-clamat-ion, re-clamat-ion*.

clamour. (F.—L.) M.E. *clamour.*— F. *clamour.*—L. acc. *clamorem*, an outcry. —L. *clamare* (above). Der. *clamor-ous*.

Clamber; see **Clamp**.

Clammy, viscous. (E.) From A.S. *clám*, clay; confused with an adj. *clam*, sticky; with which cf. Du. *klam*, clammy, moist.

Clamour; see **Claim**.

Clamp. (Du.) XVI cent.—Du. *klampen*, to clamp, grapple, also to board a ship; *klamp*, a holdfast.+ Dan. *klampe*, to clamp, *klamme*, a cramp-iron; Swed. *klamp*, the same; Icel. *klömbr*, a smith's vice; G. *klampe*, a clamp. (Teut. base KLAMP; M. H. G. *klimpfen*, to press tightly together; allied to Cramp.)

clamber, to climb by grasping tightly. (Scand.) M. E. *clameren*, *clamberen.* — Icel. *klambra*, to pinch closely together; Dan. *klamre*, to grip firmly; see above. Allied to Climb.

clasp, vb. (E.) M. E. *claspen*, *clapsen.* The base is KLAPS, extended from KLAP, whence KLAMP; see Clamp.

club (1), a heavy stick. (Scand.) M. E. *clubbe.* — Icel. *klubba*, *klumba*, a club; Swed. *klubb*, a club, log. lump; Dan. *klub*, club, *klump*, lump. A mere variant of *clump* below.

club (2), an association. (Scand.) XVII cent. Lit. 'a clump of people.' — Swed. dial. *klubb*, a clump, lump, also a knot of people (Rietz). See above.

clump, a mass, block. (Scand.) XVI cent. Not in A. S. —Dan. *klump*, Swed. *klump.* + Du. *klomp*, G. *klump*, a clump, lump, log; Icel. *klumba*, a club. All from *klump-*, base of pp. of M. H. G. *klimpfen*, to press tightly together.

Clan. (Gael.—L.) Gael. *clann*, offspring, children; Irish *cland*, *clann*, descendants, a tribe.—L. *planta*, a scion; see Plant.

Clandestine. (F.—L.) F. *clandestin.* —L. *clandestinus*, secret, close. Allied to *clam*, secretly.

Clang, Clank; see Clack.

Clap. (E.) M. E. *clappen.* [We only find A. S. *clæppetung*, a pulsation; Wright's Voc. i. 45.] The orig. sense is to make a noise by striking. + Icel. *klappa*, Swed. *klappa*, Dan. *klappe*, Du. *klappen*, M. H. G. *klaffen*, to pat, clap, prate, make a noise. Allied to Clack, Clatter.

Claret, Clarify, Clarion; see Clear.

Clash. (E.) A variant of Clack; cf. *crash.*

Clasp. (E.) See Clamp.

Class. (F.—L.) F. *classe*, a rank.—L. acc. *classem*, a class, assembly, fleet. (√ KAL.)

Clatter. (E.) A frequentative of *clat*, which is a form of Clack. A. S. *clatrung*, a clattering. + Du. *klateren*, to clatter.

clutter (1), a noise, din. (E.) A mere variant of Clatter.

Clause. (F.—L.) F. *clause.*—L. *clausa*, as in *clausa oratio*, an eloquent period; hence *clausa*, a period, a clause. — L. *clausus*, pp. of *claudere*, to shut. (√ SKLU.)

cloister. (F.—L.) M. E. *cloister.* — O. F. *cloistre* (F. *cloître*).—L. *claustrum*, lit. enclosure.—L. *claus-us* (above).

close (1), to shut in. (F.—L.) M. E. *closen.*—O. F. *clos*, pp. of O. F. *clore*, to shut in.—L. *clausus*, pp. of *claudere* (as above). Der. *dis-close*, *en-close*, *in-close.*

close (2), shut up. (F.—L.) M. E. *clos*, *cloos.*—O. F. *clos* (as above).

closet. (F.—L.) O. F. *closet*, dimin. of *clos*, an enclosed space.—O. F. *clos*; see close (1).

conclude. (L.) L. *concludere*, to shut up, close, end.—L. *con-* (*cum*), together; and *-cludere* = *claudere*, to shut. Der. *conclusion.* Similarly *ex-clude*, *in-clude*, *pre-clude*, *se-clude*; whence *in-clus-ive*, *pre-clus-ion*, *se-clusion* (from pp. *-clusus* = *clausus*).

recluse. (F.—L.) M. E. *recluse*, orig. fem.—O. F. *recluse*, fem. of *reclus*, pp. of *reclorre*, to shut up.—L. *recludere*, to unclose; but in late Lat. to shut up.

sluice, a flood-gate. (F.—L.) O. F. *escluse*, 'a sluce, floudgate;' Cot. — Low L. *exclusa*, a flood-gate; lit. shut off (water); pp. of *ex-cludere*, to shut out.— L. *ex*, out; *claudere*, to shut.

Clavicle, the collar-bone. (F.—L.) F. *clavicule*, the collar-bone.—L. *clauicula*, lit. a small key; dimin. of *clauis*, a key. Allied to *claudere*; see Clause.

clef, a key, in music. (F.—L.) F. *clef*. — L. acc. *clauem*, a key.

conclave. (F.—L.) F. *conclave*, a small room (to meet in).—L. *conclaue*, a room; later, a place of assembly of cardinals, assembly. Orig. a locked up place. —L. *con-* (*cum*); *clauis*, a key.

Claw. (E.) M. E. *clau*, *clee.* A. S. *cláwu*; also *clá*, *cleó*, a claw.+Du. *klaauw*, Icel. *kló*, Dan. *klo*, Sw. *klo*, G. *klaue.* Allied to Clew; from a Teut. base KLU — Aryan GLU. Cf. *glue.*

Clay. (E.) M. E. *clai*, *cley.* A. S. *clæg.* + Du. and G. *klei*, Dan. *klæg.* Prob. allied to Cleave (2).

clog, a hindrance. (E.) Allied to Lowl. Sc. *clag*, to bedaub with clay, hinder, obstruct; Dan. *klæg*, *kleg*, loam, also as adj., loamy. Perhaps a Scand. form.

Claymore; see Gladiator.

Clean. (E.) M. E. *clene.* A. S. *cláene*,

clear, pure.+Irish and Gael. *glan*, W.*glain*, *glan*, clear, bright.

cleanse. (E.) A. S. *clǽnsian*, to make clean.—A.S. *clǽne*, clean.

Clear. (F.—L.) M. E. *cleer, cler.*—O. F. *cler, clair.*—L. *clarus*, bright, clear, loud.

claret. (F.—L.) Orig. a clarified wine. M. E. *claret.*—O. F. *claret, clairet.*—Low L. *claretum.* wine clarified with honey.—L. *clarus*, clear.

clarify. (F.—L.) O. F. *clarifier.*—L. *clarificare*, to make clear.—L. *clari-*, for *claro-*, crude form of *clarus* ; and *-fic-*, for *facere*, to make.

clarion. (F.—L.) M. E. *clarioun.*—O. F. *clarion*, claron* (F. *clairon*), a clear-sounding horn.—L. *clari-* (as above).

declare. (F.—L.) O. F. *declarer.*—L. *declarare*, to make clear, declare.—L. *de*, fully, *clarus*, clear.

glair, the white of an egg. (F.—L.) M. E. *gleyre.*—O. F. *glaire.*—L. *clara.* fem. of *clarus*, bright ; Low L. *clara oui*, the white of an egg.

Cleave (1), to split. (E.) Strong verb. A. S. *cleófan*, pt. t. *cleáf*, pp. *clofen* (= E. *cloven*).+Du. *kloven*, Icel. *kljúfa* (pt. t. *klauf*), Swed. *klyfva*, Dan. *klöve*, G. *klieben*. (Teut. base KLUB; cf. Gk. γλύφειν, to hollow out.)

cleft, clift. (Scand.) The old spelling is *clift.*—Icel. *kluft*, Swed. *klyft*, Dan. *klöft*, a cleft, chink, cave.—Icel. *klufu*, pl. of pt. t. of *kljúfa* (above) ; cf. Swed. *klyfva*, to cleave.

clove (2), a bulb or tuber ; a weight. (E.) A.S. *cluf*, in *cluf-wyrt*, butter-cup (bulb-wort).—A. S. *cluf-on*, pt. t. pl. of *cleófan*, to cleave.

Cleave (2), to stick. (E.) Weak verb. The correct pt. t. is *cleaved*, not *clave*, which belongs to the verb above. A. S. *clifian, cleofian*, pt. t. *clifode.*+Du. *kleven*, Swed. *klibba sig*, Dan. *klæbe*, G. *kleben*, to adhere, cleave to. (Teut. base KLIB.)

cliff, a steep rock, headland. (E.) A. S. *clif*, a rock, cliff.+Du. and Icel. *klif*. Cf. G. and Dan. *klippe*, Swed. *klippa*, a crag. Orig. sense prob. 'a climbing-place,' a steep ; see **Climb, Clip.** ¶ It *cannot* be allied to *cleave* (1).

Clef; see **Clavicle.**

Cleft; see **Cleave** (1).

Clematis, a plant. (Gk.) Gk. κληματίς, brush-wood, creeping-plant.—Gk. κληματ-, stem of κλῆμα, a shoot, twig.—Gk. κλάειν, to break off, prune.

Clement. (F.—L.) F. *clement.*—L. *clementem*, acc. of *clemens*, mild.

Clench; see **Clack.**

Clerk. (F.—L.—Gk.) A. S. and O. F. *clerc.*—L. *clericus.*—Gk. κληρικός, one of the clergy.—Gk. κλῆρος, a lot ; in late Gk., the clergy, whose portion is the Lord, Deut. xviii. 2, 1 Pet. v. 3.

clergy. (F.—L.) M. E. *clergie*, often 'learning.'—O. F. *clergie*, as if from L. *clericia** ; mod. F. *clergé*, from Low L. *clericatus*, clerkship.—Low L. *clericus*, a clerk.

Clever. (F.—L.; *confused with* E.) In Butler's Hudibras (1663). It took the place of M. E. *deliver*, quick, nimble, Ch. prol. 84.—O. F. *delivre*, free, prompt, alert; compounded from L. *de*, prefix, and *liber*, free ; see **Deliver.** But apparently confused with M. E. *cliver*, a claw, also as adj. ready to seize, allied to **Climb, Cleave** (2). ¶ Not from A. S. *gleáw*, M. E. *gleu*, skilful ; still less from G. *klug* !!

Clew, Clue, a ball of thread. (E.) M.E. *clewe.* A.S. *cliwe*, short form of *cliwen*, a clew. +Du. *kluwen*; whence *kluwenen*, to wind on clews (E. *clew* up a sail); M. H.G. *kluwen.* Allied to L. *glo-mus*, a clew.

Click; see **Clack.**

Client. (F.—L.) F. *client*, a suitor.—L. *clientem*, acc. of *cliens* = *cluens*, orig. a hearer, one who listens to advice; pres. pt. of *cluere*, to hear. (√ KRU.)

Cliff; see **Cleave** (2).

Climate. (F.—Gk.) M. E. *climat.*—F. *climat.*—Gk. κλιματ-, stem of κλίμα, a slope, zone, region of the earth, climate.—Gk. κλίνειν, to lean, slope ; see **Lean.**

climacter, a critical time of life. (F.—Gk.) F. *climactere*, adj. ; whence *l'an climactere*, 'the climatericall (*sic*) year; every 7th, or 9th, or the 63 yeare of a man's life, all very dangerous, but the last most ;' Cot.—Gk. κλιμακτήρ, a step of a ladder, a dangerous period of life.—Gk. κλῖμαξ, a ladder, climax; see below.

climax, the highest degree. (Gk.) Gk. κλῖμαξ, a ladder, staircase, highest pitch of expression (in rhetoric).—Gk. κλίνειν, to slope. Der. *anti-climax.*

clime. (L.—Gk.) L. *clima*, a climate. —Gk. κλίμα ; see **Climate.**

Climb. (E.) M. E. *climben*, pt. t. *clomb.* A. S. *climban*, pt. t. *clamb*, pl. *clumbon.*+Du. *klimmen*, M. H. G. *klimmen.* (Teut.

base KLAMB); allied to **Clip, Cramp.**
And see **Clamber.**

Clime; see **Climate.**

Clinch; see **Clack.**

Cling. (E.) M. E. *clingen*, to become stiff, be matted together. A. S. *clingan* (pt. t. *clang*, pp. *clungen*), to dry up, shrivel up.+Dan. *klynge*, to cluster; cf. *klumpe*, to clot.

Clinical. (F. − L. − Gk.) F. *clinique*, 'one that is bedrid;' Cot. − L. *clinicus*, the same. − Gk. κλινικός, belonging to a bed, a physician; ἡ κλινική, his art. − Gk. κλίνη, a bed. − Gk. κλίνειν, to lean; see **Lean.**

Clink, Clinker; see **Clack.**

Clip. (Scand.) M. E. *klippen.* − Icel. *klippa*, Swed. *klippa*, Dan. *klippe*, to clip, shear hair. The orig. sense was 'to draw tightly together,' hence 'to draw together the edges of shears;' cf. A. S. *clyppan*, to embrace. Allied to **Clamp, Cleave** (2).

Clique; see **Clack.**

Cloak, Clock; see **Clack.**

Clod; see **Clot.**

Clog; see **Clay.**

Cloister, Close, Closet; see **Clause.**

Clot. (E.) M. E. *clot, clotte*, a ball, esp. of earth, allied to *clote*, a burdock. A. S. *cláte*, a burdock, orig. a bur.+Du. *kluit*, a clod, *kloot*, a ball; Icel. *klót*, Swed. *klot*, Dan. *klode*, a ball, globe, G. *kloss*, a clot, clod. Allied to L. *glo-bus, glo-mus.*

clod. (Scand.) Dan. *klode*; Dan. form of Icel. *klót*, Swed. *klot* (above).

clutter (2), to coagulate. (E.) M. E. *cloteren*, to form clots, frequent. form of a verb from the sb. *clot.*

Cloth. (E.) M. E. *cloth, clath.* A. S. *cláð.*+Du. *kleed*, Icel. *klæði*, Dan. *klæde*, Swed. *kläde*; G. *kleid*, a dress. **Der.** *clothes*, A. S. *cláðas*, pl. of *cláð.*

clothe, to cover with a cloth. (E.) M. E. *clothen, cluthen*, pt. t. *clothede* or *cladde*, pp. *clothed* or *clad.* Formed from A. S. *cláð.*+Du. *kleeden*, from *kleed*; so also Icel. *klæða*, Dan. *klæde*, Sw. *kläda*, G. *kleiden.*

Cloud. (E.) M. E. *cloude*, orig. a mass of vapours; the same word as M. E. *clude*, a mass of rock. A. S. *clúd*, a round mass, mass of rock, hill. Allied to *clew*, q. v., and to L. *glo-mus* (whence E. *con-glo-mer-ation*).

Clough, a hollow in a hill-side. (E.) M. E. *clow, clew, cleuch.* Allied to Icel. *klofi*, a rift in a hill-side, from *kljúfa*, to cleave; see **Cleave** (1).

Clout, a patch. (C.) M. E. *clout.* A. S.

clút, a patch. − W. *clwt*, Corn. *clut*, a patch, clout; Ir. and Gael. *clud*, the same.

Clove (1), a kind of spice. (F. − L.) M. E. *clow* (the change to *clove*, in the XVIth cent., may have been due to confusion with Span. *clavo*.) − F. *clou*, a nail; *clou de girofle*, 'a clove,' Cot.; from the resemblance to a nail. Cf. Span. *clavo*, a nail, also a clove. − L. *clauum*, acc. of *clauus*, a nail.

cloy. (F. − L.) Orig. to stop up, hence, sate. O. F. *cloyer*, 'to cloy, stop up,' Cot.; a by-form of F. *clouer* (O. F. *cloer*), to nail, fasten up. [A horse pricked with a nail, in shoeing, was said to be *cloyed*.] − O. F. *clo*, F. *clou*, a nail, as above.

Clove (2), a bulb; see **Cleave** (1).

Clover. (E.) M. E. *claver.* A. S. *clæfre*, trefoil.+Du. *klaver*, Swed. *klöfver*, Dan. *klöver*, G. *klee.* ¶ The supposed connection with *cleave* (1) is very doubtful.

Clown. (Scand.) Icel. *klunni*, a clumsy, boorish fellow; Swed. dial. *klunn*, a log, *kluns*, a clownish fellow; Dan. *klunt*, a log; cf. Dan. *kluntet*, clumsy. Allied to **Clump.** The orig. sense is 'a log.' See **Clumsy.**

Cloy; see **Clove** (1).

Club (1), a stick; see **Clamp.**

Club (2), an association; see **Clamp.**

Cluck. (E.) See **Clack.**

Clue; see **Clew.**

Clump; see **Clamp.**

Clumsy. (Scand.) From M. E. *clumsed, clomsed*, benumbed; benumbed fingers are clumsy. This is the pp. of *clomsen*, to benumb, or to feel benumbed. − Swed. dial. *klummsen*, benumbed (Rietz); cf. Icel. *klumsa*, lock-jaw. From the Teut. base KLAM, KRAM, to pinch, whence also **Clamp, Cramp.** Cf. Du. *klemmen*, to pinch, *kleumen*, to be benumbed, *kleumsch*, numb with cold.

Cluster, a bunch. (E.) A. S. *cluster*, *clyster*, a bunch. Allied to Icel. *klastr*, a bunch, *klasi*, a cluster; Dan. and Swed. *klase*, a cluster. We also find Swed. dial. *klysse*, the same as *klifsa*, a cluster, from *klibba*, to cleave, stick to. This links it to **Cleave** (2).

Clutch; see **Latch.**

Clutter (1), a din; see **Clatter.**

Clutter (2), to clot; see **Clot.**

Clutter (3), a confused heap; to heap up. (W.) W. *cludair*, a heap, pile; *cludeirio*, to heap up.

Clyster. (L. − Gk.) L. *clyster*, an injection into the bowels. — Gk. κλυστήρ, a clyster, syringe. — Gk. κλύζειν, to wash. + L. *cluere*, to wash. (✓ KLU.) ·

Co-, prefix. (L.) L. *co-*, together; used for *con-* (= *cum*), together, before a vowel. Hence *co-efficient, co-equal, co-operate, co-ordinate*. See others below; and see **Con-**.

Coach. (F. — Hung.; *or* F. — L. — Gk.) F. *coche*, ʻa coach;ʼ Cot. Etym. disputed ; it was said, as early as A.D. 1553, to be a Hungarian word ; from Hung. *kocsi*, a coach, so called because first made at a Hung. village called *Kotsi* ; see Littré, and Beckmann, Hist. of Inventions. Still, it seems to have been confused with F. *coche*, a kind of boat (E. *cock-boat*), see Littré. This is derived from L. *concha*, a shell, conch ; see **Conch**.

Coadjutor ; see **Aid**.

Coagulate ; see **Agent**.

Coal. (E.) M. E. *col*. A. S. *col*. + Du. *kool*, Icel. Swed. *kol*, Dan. *kul*, G. *kohle*. Cf. Skt. *jval*, to blaze.

collier. (E.) M. E. *colier* ; from M. E. *col*, coal. Cf. *bow-yer, saw-yer*.

Coalesce ; see **Aliment**.

Coarse ; see **Current**.

Coast. (F. — L.) M. E. *coste*. — O. F. *coste* (F. *côte*), a rib, slope of a hill, shore. — L. *costa*, a rib.

accost, to address. (F. — L.) O. F. *accoster*, to come to the side of. — Low L. *accostare*. — L. *ac-* (*ad*) ; and *costa*, rib, side.

costal, relating to the ribs. (L.) From L. *costa*, a rib.

cutlet. (F. — L.) F. *cotelette*, a cutlet ; formerly *costelette*, a little rib ; dimin. of *coste*, rib (above).

Coat ; see **Cot**.

Coax. (C. ?) Formerly *cokes*, vb., from *cokes*, sb., a simpleton, dupe. Perhaps from W. *coeg*, vain, foolish, *coegyn*, a conceited fellow ; Corn. *coc*, vain, foolish, O. Gael. *coca*, void, *goigean*, a coxcomb. See **Cocker, Cog** (2).

Cob (1), a round lump, knob. (C.) As applied to a pony, it means short and stout. M. E. *cob*, a head, a person. — W. *cob*, a tuft, a spider, *cop*, a tuft, top ; *copa*, crown of the head.

cobble (2), a small round lump. (C.) M. E. *cobylstone*, a cobble-stone. Dimin. of W. *cob*, a tuft (above).

cobweb. (C. *and* E.) From W. *cob*, a spider ; or short for M. E. *attercop-web*, where *attercop*, a spider, means ʻpoison-bunch,ʼ from A. S. *átor*, poison, and *coppa*, a head, tuft, borrowed from W. *cob, cop*, as before.

Cob (2), to beat. (C.) W. *cobio*, to thump ; cf. *cob*, a bunch.

Cobalt, a mineral. (G. — Gk.) G. *kobalt*, cobalt ; a nickname given by the miners, because considered poisonous ; better spelt *kobold*, meaning (1) a demon, (2) cobalt. — Low L. *cobalus*, a mountain-sprite, demon. — Gk. κόβαλος, a rogue, goblin.

goblin. (F. — L. — Gk.) O. F. *gobelin*. — Low L. *gobelinus*, dimin. of Low L. *cobalus* (above).

Cobble (1), to patch up ; see **Couple**.

Cobweb ; see **Cob** (1).

Cochineal. (Span. — L. — Gk.) Span. *cochinilla*, cochineal (made from insects which look like berries). — L. *coccinus*, of a scarlet colour. — L. *coccum*, a berry ; also kermes, supposed to be a berry. — Gk. κόκκος, a berry, cochineal.

Cock (1), a male bird. (E.) M. E. *cok*. A. S. *cocc* ; from the birdʼs cry. ʻCryde anon *cok! cok!*ʼ Ch. C. T. Nunʼs Priestʼs Tale, 456. Cf. Gk. κόκκυ, the cry of the cuckoo ; W. *cog*, a cuckoo.

cock, the stop-cock of a barrel, is the same word. So also G. *hahn*, (1) a cock, (2) a stop-cock.

cockade, a knot of ribbon on a hat. (F.) F. *coquarde*, fem. of *coquard*, saucy ; also *coquarde, bonnet à la coquarde*, ʻany bonnet or cap worn proudly,ʼ Cot. Formed with suffix *-ard* from F. *coq*, a cock (from the birdʼs cry).

cockatoo, a kind of parrot. (Malay.) Malay *kakatúa*, a cockatoo ; from the birdʼs cry ; cf. Malay *kukuk*, crowing of cocks, *kakak*, cackling of hens. Skt. *kukkuta*, a cock.

cockloft, upper loft. (E. *and* Scand.) From *cock* and *loft*. So also G. *hahnbalken*, a roost, cockloft ; Dan. *loftkammer*, a loft-chamber, room up in the rafters.

coquette. (F.) F. *coquette*, ʻa pratling or proud gossip,ʼ Cot. ; fem. of *coquet*, a little cock, dimin. of *coq*, a cock. Cf. prov. E. *cocky*, i.e. strutting as a cock.

coxcomb. (E.) A fool, named from his *cockʼs comb*, or foolʼs cap, cap with a cockʼs crest.

cuckold. (F. — L.) M. E. *kokewold, kukeweld, cokold* ; but the final *d* is excrescent, perhaps by confusion with the A. S. suffix *-weald* (M. E. *-wold*) seen in *thresh-wold*, a threshold, &c. — O. F. *coucoul*, a cuckold (Roquefort); later *coucou*; orig. a cuckoo, secondly, a man whose wife is unfaithful. (There are endless allusions to the comparison between a cuckoo and a cuckold; see Shak. L. L. L. v. 2. 920, &c.) — L. *cuculum*, acc. of *cuculus*, a cuckoo (below).

cuckoo. (F. — L.) F. *coucou*. — L. *cuculum*, acc. of *cuculus*, a cuckoo; from the bird's cry. **+** Gk. κόκκυξ, a cuckoo; κόκκυ, its cry; Skt. *kokila*, a cuckoo. Cf. *cock, cockatoo.* And see **Coo.**

Cock (2), a pile of hay. (Scand.) Dan. *kok*, a heap; Icel. *kökkr*, lump, ball; Swed. *koka*, clod of earth.

Cock (3), to stick up abruptly. (C.) Gael. *coc*, to cock; as in *coc do bhoineid*, cock your bonnet; *coc-shronach*, cock-nosed.

Cock (4), part of the lock of a gun. (Ital.) Ital. *cocca*, the notch of an arrow; whence *coccare*, to fit an arrow on the bowstring (E. *cock* a gun, by the transference to guns of the old archery term); cf. Ital. *scoccare*, to let fly, let off an arrow. The Ital. *cocca* was confused with F. *coq*, a cock, whence the G. phrase *den Hahn spannen*, to cock a gun. Origin of Ital. *cocca* (= F. *coche*) unknown; but see **Cog.**

Cock (5), a boat; see **Conch.**

Cockade, Cockatoo; see **Cock** (1).

Cockatrice; see **Crocodile.**

Cocker, to pamper. (C. ?) M. E. *cokeren*. — W. *cocri*, to fondle, indulge; *cocr*, a coaxing, fondling. Perhaps allied to W. *coeg*, Corn. *coc*, vain, foolish.

Cockle (1), a sort of bivalve. (C.) M. E. *cokel*, dimin. of *cock*, a cockle (P. Plowman, C. x. 95). A. S. *sǽ-cocca*; (where *sǽ = sea*). — W. *cocs*, cockles; cf. Gael. *cogan*, a husk, small bowl, Gael. *cochull*, Irish *cochal*, a husk, shell of a nut, hood. The orig. sense was probably ' shell;' cf. L. *cochlea*, a snail, allied to *concha*, a shell; see **Conch.** And see below.

Cockle (2), a weed among corn. (C.) A. S. *coccel*, tares. — Gael. *cogall*, tares, husks, cockle; *cogull*, corn-cockle; *cogan*, a loose husk; Irish *cogall*, corn-cockle, beards of barley. The orig. sense was prob. ' husk.' See above.

Cockle (3), to be uneven, shake up and down. (C.) The same as prov. E. *coggle*, to shake. — W. *gogi*, to shake; *gog*, a toss of the head; Irish *gog*, a nod, *gogach*, reeling, wavering.

Cockney, an effeminate person. (E.)

From M. E. *cokenay*, a foolish person, Ch. C. T. 4206. Lit. ' cock's (i. e. yolkless) egg.' Cf. M. E. *ey*, A. S. *ǽg*, egg.

Cocoa (1), the cocoa-nut palm-tree; see **Conch.**

Cocoa (2); corrupt form of **Cacao.**

Cocoon; see **Conch.**

Cod (1), a fish. (E. ?) Spelt *codde* in Palsgrave. Perhaps named from its rounded shape; cf. O. Du. *kodde*, a club (Hexham); and see below. Der. *cod-ling*, a young cod; M. E. *codlyng.*

Cod (2), a husk, bag, bolster. (E.) Hence *peas-cod*, husk of a pea. A. S. *codd*, a bag. **+** Icel. *koddi*, pillow; *koðri*, scrotum; Swed. *kudde*, a cushion.

coddle, to pamper, render effeminate. (E.) Orig. to castrate; but confused with *cadeler*, ' to cocker.' Cot. See p. 578.

codling, codlin, a kind of apple. (F.) Cf. prov. E. *codlings*, green peas, properly ' young pods;' also A. S. *cod-æppel*, a cod-apple, a quince.

Code, a digest of laws. (F. — L.) F. *code*. — L. *codicem*, acc. of *codex*, a tablet, book.

codicil. (L.) L. *codicillus*, a codicil to a will; dimin. of *codex* (stem *codic-*).

Codling; see **Cod** (1), **Cod** (2).

Coerce. (L.) L. *coercere*, to compel. — L. *co-* (*cum*), together: *arcere*, to enclose, confine, allied to *arca*, a chest; see **Ark.**

Coffee. (Turk. — Arab.) Turk. *qahveh.* — Arab. *qahweh*, coffee.

Coffer. (F. — L. — Gk.) M. E. *cofre.* — O. F. *cofre*, also *cofin*, a chest. — L. acc. *cophinum.* — Gk. κόφινος, a basket.

coffin. (F. — L. — Gk.) Orig. a case, chest. — O. F. *cofin*, as above. (Doublet of *coffer.*)

Cog (1), a tooth on a wheel-rim. (C.) M. E. *cog.* — Gael. and Irish *cog*, a mill-cog; W. *cocos, cocs*, cogs of a wheel.

Cog (2), to trick. (C.) W. *coegio*, to make void, trick. — W. *coeg*, empty, vain; see **Coax.**

Cogent, Cogitate; see **Agent.**

Cognate; see **Natal.**

Cognisance, Cognomen; see **Noble.**

Cohabit; see **Habit.**

Cohere; see **Hesitate.**

Cohort; see **Court.**

Coif, Quoif, a cap. (F. — G. — L.) O. F. *coif, coiffe*; Low L. *cofia*, a cap. — M. H. G. *kuffe, kupfe*, a cap worn under the helmet. Allied to **Cuff** (2) and **Cup.**

Coign; see **Coin.**

Coil (1), to gather together; see **Legend**.

Coil (2), a noise, bustle. (C.)· Gael. *goil*, rage, battle; Irish *goill*, war, fight; Gael. *coileid*, stir, noise. — Irish *goil*, to boil, rage.

Coin. (F. — L.) M. E. *coin*. — O. F. *coin*, a wedge, stamp on a coin, a coin (stamped by means of a wedge). — L. *cuneum*, acc. of *cuneus*, a wedge. Allied to **Cone**.

coign. (F. — L.) F. *coing*, *coin*, a corner; lit. a wedge (as above).

cuneate, wedge-shaped. (L.) L. *cuneus*, a wedge; with suffix *-ate*.

quoin, a wedge. (F. — L.) The same as F. *coin*; see **Coin** (above).

Coincide; see **Cadence**.

Coit; see **Quoit**.

Coke, charred coal. (Unknown.) ' *Coke*, pit-coal or sea-coal charred ;' Coles, 1684. Etym. unknown.

Colander, Cullender, a strainer. (L.) Coined from L. *colant-*, stem of pres. part. of *colare*, to strain. — L. *colum*, a sieve.

culvert, an arched drain. (F. — L.) Formed, with added *t*, from O. F. *couleuëre*, ' a channel, gutter,' Cot. — F. *couler*, to trickle. — L. *colare*, to strain, drain (above).

percolate, (L.) From pp. of L. *percolare*, to filter through.

Cold; see **Cool**.

Cole, Colewort, cabbage. (L.) For -*wort*, see **Wort**. M. E. *col*, *caul*. A. S. *caul*, *cawel*. — L. *caulis*, a stalk, cabbage. + Gk. καυλός, a stalk ; κοῖλος, hollow. (√ KU.)

cauliflower. (F. — L.) Formerly *collyflory*. From M. E. *col* (O. F. *col*), a cabbage; and *flory*, from O. F. *flori*, *fleuri*, pp. of *fleurir*, to flourish, from L. *florere*; see **Flourish**. The O. F. *col* = L. acc. *caulem*, from *caulis* (above).

kail, kale, cabbage. (C.) Northern E. — Gael. and Ir. *cal*, Manx *kail*, W. *cawl*. Cognate with L. *caulis*.

Coleoptera, sheath-winged insects. — Gk. κολεό-s, a sheath ; πτερ-όν, a wing.

Colic; see **Colon**.

Coliseum; see **Colossus**.

Collapse; see **Lapse**.

Collar. (F. — L.) M. E. *coler*. — O. F. *colier*, a collar. — L. *collare*, a band for the neck. — L. *collum*, the neck. + A. S. *heals*, G. *hals*, the neck.

collet, the part of the ring in which the stone is set. (F. — L.) F. *collet*, a collar. — F. *col*, neck. — L. *collum*, neck.

colporteur. (F. — L.) F. *colporteur*, one who carries things on his neck and shoulders. — F. *col*, neck; and *porteur*, a carrier; see **Port** (1).

decollation, a beheading. (F. — L.) O. F. *decollation*. — Low L. acc. *decollationem*. From pp. of *decollare*, to behead. — L. *de*, off; *collum*, the neck.

Collateral; see **Lateral**.

Collation; see **Tolerate**.

Colleague; see **Legal**.

Collect; see **Legend**.

College; see **Legal**.

Collet; see **Collar**.

Collide; see **Lesion**.

Collier; see **Coal**.

Collocate; see **Locus**.

Collodion, a solution of gun-cotton. (Gk.) Gk. κολλώδ-ης, glue-like. — Gk. κόλλ-α, glue; -ειδης, like, from εἶδος, appearance.

Collop, a slice of meat. (E. ?) M. E. *coloppe*. Cf. Swed. *kalops*, O. Swed. *kollops*, slices of beef stewed ; G. *klopps*, a dish of meat made tender by beating. From the verb seen in E. *clop* = *clap*, to make a noise ; Du. *kloppen*, G. *klopfen*, to beat. Allied to **Clap**.

Colloquy; see **Loquacious**.

Collusion; see **Ludicrous**.

Colocynth, Coloquintida, pith of the fruit of a kind of cucumber. (Gk.) From the nom. and acc. cases of Gk. κολοκυνθίς (acc. κολοκυνθίδα), a round gourd or pumpkin.

Colon (1), a mark (:) in writing and printing. (Gk.) Gk. κῶλον, a clause ; hence a stop marking off a clause.

Colon (2), part of the intestines. (Gk.) Gk. κῶλον, the same.

colic. (F. — L. — Gk.) Short for *colic pain*. — F. *colique*, adj. — L. *colicus*. — Gk. κωλικός, suffering in the colon. — Gk. κῶλον.

Colonel, Colonnade; see **Column**.

Colony. (F. — L.) F. *colonie*. — L. *colonia*, a colony, band of husbandmen. — L. *colonus*, a husbandman. — L. *colere*, to till.

agriculture. (L.) L. *agri-cultura*, culture of a field ; see **Acre**.

cultivate. (L.) L. *cultiuatus*, pp. of *cultiuare*, to till. — Low L. *cultiuus*, fit for tilling. — L. *cultus*, pp. of *colere*, to till.

culture. (F. — L.) F. *culture*. — L.

cultura, orig. fem. of fut. part. of *colere*, to till.

Colophon, an inscription at the end of a book, with name and date. (Gk.) Late L. *colophon*. — Gk. κολοφών, a summit; hence, a finishing stroke. Allied to **Column**.

Coloquintida; see **Colocynth**.

Colossus. (L. — Gk.) L. *colossus*. — Gk. κολοσσός, a large statue. Der. *coloss-al*, i. e large.

coliseum, the same as *colosseum*, a large amphitheatre at Rome, in which stood a *colossal* statue of Nero. The Ital. word is *coliseo*.

Colour. (F. — L.) M. E. *colour*. — O. F. *colour* (F. *couleur*). — L. acc. *colorem*, from *color*, a tint. (√ KAL.)

Colporteur; see **Collar**.

Colt. (E.) A. S. *colt*, a young camel, young ass, &c. + Swed. dial. *kullt*, a boy, *kull*, a brood. Perhaps allied to *child*.

Columbine, a plant. (F. — L.) O. F. *colombin*. — Low L. *columbina*, a columbine; L. *columbinus*, dove-like; from a supposed resemblance. — L. *columba*, a dove. See **Culver**.

Column, a pillar, body of troops. (F. — L.) L. *columna*, a pillar; cf. *columen*, *culmen*, a summit; *collis*, a hill; *celsus*, high. (√ KAL.)

colonel. (F. — Ital. — L.) Sometimes *coronel*, which is the Span. spelling; whence perhaps the pronunciation as *kurnel*. — F. *colonel*, *colonnel*. — Ital. *colonello*, a colonel; lit. a little column. The colonel was he who led the company at the head of the regiment. Dimin. of Ital. *colonna*, a column. — L. *columna* (above).

colonnade. (F. — Ital. — L.) F. *colonnade*. — Ital. *colonnata*, a range of columns. — Ital. *colonna*, a column (above).

Colure, one of two great circles on the celestial sphere. (L. — Gk.) So called because a part of them is always beneath the horizon. The word means docked, clipped. — L. *colurus*, curtailed; a colure. — Gk. κόλουρος, dock-tailed, truncated; a colure. — Gk. κόλ-ος, docked, clipped; and οὐρά, a tail.

Com-, prefix. (L.) Put for *cum*, with, together; when followed by *b*, *f*, *m*, *p*. See **Con-**. Der. *com-mix*, where *mix* is E.; and see below.

Coma; see **Cemetery**.

Comb. (E.) A. S. *camb*, a comb, crest,

ridge. + Du. *kam*, Icel. *kambr*, Dan. Swed. *kam*; G. *kamm*.

cam. (Scand.) Dan. *kam*, comb, also a ridge on a wheel, cam, or cog.

oakum, tow from old ropes. (E.) A. S. *ácumba*, tow. (For the letter-change, cf. E. *oak*=A.S. *ác*.) Lit. 'that which is combed out.' — A.S. *á-*, prefix (Goth. *us*, out); *cemban*, to comb, *camb*, a comb; see **A-** (4). Cf. O. H. G. *ácambi*, tow; of like origin.

unkempt, i. e. uncombed; for *un-kemb'd*. — A. S. *cemban*, to comb; formed (by vowel-change of *a* to *e*) from *camb*, a comb.

Comb, Coomb, a dry measure. (L. — Gk.) A. S. *cumb*, a cup. — Low L. *cumba*. — Gk. κύμβη, a bowl, hollow vessel.

Combat; see **Batter** (1).

Combe, a hollow in a hill-side. (C.) W. *cwm*, Corn. *cum*, a hollow, dale; Irish *cumar*, a valley. (√ KU.)

Combine; see **Binary**.

Combustion. (F. — L.) F. *combustion*. — L. acc. *combustionem*, a burning up. — L. *combust-us*, pp. of *com-burere*, to burn up. — L. *com-*, for *cum*, together; *burere* *, to burn, orig. *purere* *.

Come. (E.) A. S. *cuman*, pt. t. *cam*, pp. *cumen*. + Du. *komen*, Icel. *koma*, Dan. *komme*, Sw. *komma*, Goth. *kwiman*, G. *kommen*, L. *uen-ire* (*guen-ire* *), Gk. βαίν-ειν (*gwaίνειν* *); Skt. *gam*, to go, *gá*, to go. (√ GA.)

become. (E.) A. S. *becuman*, to arrive, happen, turn out, befall. + Goth. *bi-kwim-an*; cf. G. *be-quem*, suitable, becoming.

comely. (E.) A. S. *cymlíc*, comely. — A. S. *cyme*, suitable, from *cuman*, to come; and *líc*, like.

income, gain, revenue. (E.) Properly that which *comes in*; from *in* and *come*. So also *out-come*, i. e. result.

welcome. (Scand.) Icel. *velkominn*, welcome, in greeting, properly a pp. — Icel. *vel*, the same as E. *well*; and *kominn*, pp. of *koma*, to come; so also Dan. *vel-kommen*, Swed. *väl-kommen*.

Comedy. (F. — L. — Gk.) O. F. *comedie*, 'a play;' Cot. — L. *comœdia*. — Gk. κωμῳδία, a comedy. — Gk. κῶμο-ς, a banquet, festal procession; ῳδή, ode, lyric song; a comedy was a festive spectacle, with singing, &c. The Gk. κῶμος meant a banquet at which guests reclined; from κοιμάω, I lull to rest; cf. κοίτη, a bed. And see **Ode**.

comic (L. – Gk.) L. *comicus.* – Gk. κωμικός, belonging to a κῶμος, as above.

encomium, commendation. (L. – Gk.) Latinised from Gk. ἐγκώμιον, neut. of ἐγκώμιος, laudatory, full of revelry. – Gk. ἐν, in; κῶμος, revelry.

Comely; see Come.

Comet. (F. – L. – Gk.) O. F. *comete.* – L. *cometa.* – Gk. κομήτης, long-haired; a tailed star, comet. – Gk. κόμη, hair. +L. *coma*, hair. ¶ Also A. S. *cometa* = L. *cometa.*

Comfit; see Fact.

Comfort; see Force (1).

Comic; see Comedy.

Comity, urbanity. (L.) L. *comitatem,* acc. of *comitas*, urbanity. – L. *comis,* friendly.

Comma. (L. – Gk.) L. *comma.* – Gk. κόμμα, that which is struck, a stamp, a clause of a sentence, a comma (that marks the clause). – Gk. κόπτειν, to hew, strike. (√SKAP.)

Command; see Mandate.

Commemorate; see Memory.

Commence; see Itinerant.

Commend; see Mandate.

Commensurate; see Measure.

Comment; see Mental.

Commerce; see Merit.

Commination; see Menace.

Commingle. (L. *and* E.) From Com- and Mingle.

Comminution; see Minor.

Commiserate; see Miser.

Commissary, Commit; see Missile.

Commodious; see Mode.

Commodore; see Mandate.

Common. (F. – L.) M. E. *commun, comoun.* – O. F. *commun.* – L. *communis,* common, general. – L. *com-* (*cum*), together with; and *munis*, obliging, binding by obligation (Plautus). (√MU, to bind.) Der. *commun-ion, commun-ity.*

commune, verb. (F. – L.) M. E. *comunen.* O. F. *communier,* to communicate, talk with. – L. *communicare.* – L. *communis,* common.

communicate. (L.) L. *communicatus,* pp. of *communicare* (above). Der. *excommunicate.*

Commotion; see Move.

Commute; see Mutable.

Compact; see Pact.

Company. (F. – L.) M. E. *companye.* O. F. *companie* (cf. also O. F. *compain,* a companion, O. F. *companion* (F. *compagnon*), a companion). – Low L. *companiem,* acc. of *companies*, a taking of meals together. – L. *com-* (*cum*), together; and *panis*, bread; see Pantry. Der. *companion* = O. F. *companion.* Also *accompany,* O. F. *accompaignier*, from F. *a* (= L. *ad*) and *compaignier*, to associate with, from *compaignie,* company.

Compare; see Pare.

Compartment; see Part.

Compass; see Patent.

Compassion, Compatible; see Patient.

Compeer; see Par.

Compel; see Pulsate.

Compendious; see Pendant.

Compensate; see Pendant.

Compete; see Petition.

Compile; see Pill (2).

Complacent; see Please.

Complain; see Plague.

Complaisant; see Please.

Complement, Complete; see Plenary.

Complex, Complexion; see Ply.

Complicate, Complicity; see Ply.

Compliment, Compline; see Plenary.

Comply; see Plenary.

Component; see Position.

Comport; see Port (1).

Compose; see Pose.

Composition, Compost, Compound; see Position.

Comprehend; see Prehensile.

Compress; see Press.

Comprise; see Prehensile.

Compromise; see Missile.

Comptroller; see Rotary.

Compulsion; see Pulsate.

Compunction; see Pungent.

Compute; see Putative.

Comrade; see Chamber.

Con (1), to scan; see Can (1).

Con (2), short for *contra*, against. (L.) In the phrase 'pro and con.'

Con-, *prefix.* (L.) Put for *com-* (*cum*), with, when the following letter is *c, d, g, j, n, q, s, t*, or *v*. Before *b, f, m, p*, it is *com-*; before *l, col-*; before *r, cor-*.

Concatenate; see Chain.

Concave; see Cave.

Conceal; see Cell.

Concede; see Cede.

Conceit; see Capacious.

Conceive, Conception; see Capacious.

Concentre; see Centre.

Concern, vb. (F—L.) F. *concerner.*—L. *concernere,* to mix; in late Lat., to belong to, regard.—L. *con-* (*cum*), with; and *cernere,* to separate, decree, observe. + Gk. κρίνειν, to separate, decide; Skt. *krî,* to pour out. (√SKAR.)

decree. (F.—L.) M. E. *decree.*—O. F. *decret.*—L. *decretum.*—L. *decretus,* pp. of *de-cernere,* to decree, lit. to separate.

decretal. (L.) Low L. *decretale,* a pope's decree; neut. of *decretalis,* containing a decree.—L. *decretum* (above).

discern. (F.—L.) O.F. *discerner.*—L. *dis-cernere,* to distinguish.

discreet, prudent. (F.—L.) O. F. *discret.*—L. *discretus,* pp. of *dis-cernere* (above). Der. *discret-ion.*

discriminate. (L.) L. *discriminatus,* pp. of *discriminare,* to separate.—L. *discrimin-,* stem of *discrimen,* a separation.—L. *dis-cernere* (pt. t. *discre-ui*), to distinguish.

excrement. (L.) L. *excrementum,* refuse, ordure.—L. *excre-tum,* supine of *ex-cernere,* to separate.

excretion. (F.—L.) O. F. *excretion*; formed from L. *excretus,* pp. of *ex-cernere* (above).

secret. (F.—L.) M. E. *secre, secree.*—O. F. *secret* (fem. *secreie*).—L. *secretus,* secret, set apart; pp. of *se-cernere,* to separate. Der. *secrete,* verb, from L. *secretus*; *secret-ion.*

secretary. (F.—L.) F. *secretaire.*—Low L. *secretarium,* acc. of *secretarius,* a confidential officer. — L. *secret-us,* secret (above).

Concert, to plan with others, arrange. (F.—L.) (Quite distinct from *consort.*) See Series.

Concession; see Cede.

Conch, a marine shell. (L. — Gk.) L. *concha.*—Gk. κόγχη (also κόγκος), a cockle-shell. + Skt. *çankha,* a conch. Der. *conchology* (from κόγκο-s).

cock (5), cock-boat, a small boat. (F. — L. — Gk.) O. F. *coque,* a kind of boat, orig. a shell. — L. *concha* (above). We also find Du. Dan. *kog,* Icel. *kuggr,* prob. borrowed from Corn. *coc,* W. *cwch,* a boat, which are allied to L. *concha.* Der. *cox-swain* (*cock-swain*).

cocoa, coco, cocoa-nut palm. (Port.) Port. and Span. *coco,* a bugbear, an ugly mask to frighten children; hence applied to the - cocoa-nut on account of the monkey-like face at the base of the nut.

The orig. sense of *coco* was skull, head; allied to F. *coque,* shell.—L. *concha* (above).

cocoon, case of a chrysalis. (F.—L.—Gk.) F. *cocon,* a cocoon; from *coque,* a shell.—L. *concha* (above). And see Coach.

Conciliate; see Calends.

Concise; see Cæsura.

Conclave; see Clavicle.

Conclude; see Clause.

Concoct; see Cook.

Concomitant; see Itinerant.

Concord; see Cordial.

Concourse; see Current.

Concrete; see Crescent.

Concubine; see Covey.

Concupiscence; see Cupid.

Concur; see Current.

Concussion; see Quash.

Condemn; see Damn.

Condense; see Dense.

Condescend; see Sean.

Condign; see Dignity.

Condiment. (L.) L. *condimentum,* seasoning, sauce.—L. *condire,* to season, spice. (Orig. unknown.)

Condition; see Diction.

Condole; see Doleful.

Condone; see Date (1).

Condor, a large bird. (Span.—Peruvian.) Span. *condor.*—Peruv. *cuntur,* a condor.

Conduce, Conduct, Conduit; see Duke.

Cone. (F. — L. — Gk.) F. *cone.* — L. *conus.*—Gk. κῶνος, a cone, peak, peg. + L. *cuneus,* a wedge; A. S. *hân,* a hone. (√KA.)

canopy. (F.—Ital.—L.—Gk.) Should be *conopy*; but we find F. *canopé,* borrowed from Ital. *canopè.* (Also F. *conopée.*)—L. *conopeum,* Judith, xiii. 9.—Gk. κωνωπεῖον, an Egyptian bed with mosquito curtains (hence, any sort of hangings). — Gk. κωνωπ-, stem of κώνωψ, a mosquito, gnat; lit. 'cone-faced' or 'cone-headed,' from the shape of its head.—Gk. κῶνο-s, a cone; and ὤψ, face, appearance, from Gk. base ΟΠ, to see (see Optics).

Coney; see Cony.

Confabulate; see Fate.

Confection; see Fact.

Confederate; see Federal.

Confer; see Fertile.

Confess; see Fame.

Confide; see Faith.

Configuration; see Figure.

Confine; see Final.

Confirm; see Firm.

Confiscate; see Fiscal.
Conflagration; see Flagrant.
Conflict; see Afflict.
Confluent; see Fluent.
Conform; see Form.
Confound; see Fuse (1).
Confraternity; see Fraternal.
Confront; see Front.
Confuse, Confute; see Fuse (1).
Conge, Congee; see Permeate.
Congeal; see Gelid.
Congenial, Congenital; see Genus.
Conger, a sea-eel. (L.) L. *conger*, a sea-eel. + Gk. γόγγρος, the same.
Congeries, Congestion; see Gerund.
Conglobe, Conglomerate; see Globe.
Conglutinate; see Glue.
Congratulate; see Grace.
Congregate; see Gregarious.
Congress; see Grade.
Congrue, to agree, suit. (L.) L. *con-gruere*, to suit. (Root uncertain.) Der. *congru-ent*, from the pres. pt.; *congru-ous*, L. *congruus*, suitable; *congru-i-ty*.
Conjecture; see Jet (4).
Conjoin, Conjugal, Conjugate; see Join.
Conjure; see Jury.
Connect; see Annex.
Connive. (F. — L.) F. *conniver*. — L. *conniuere*, to close the eyes at, overlook. — L. *con-* (*cum*), together; and the base *nic-*, to wink; cf. *nic-tare*, to wink. (√NIK.)
Connoisseur; see Noble.
Connubial; see Nuptial.
Conquer; see Query.
Consanguineous; see Sanguine.
Conscience; see Science.
Conscionable, Conscious; see Science.
Conscript; see Scribe.
Consecrate; see Sacred.
Consecutive; see Sequence.
Consent, -serve; see Sense, Serve.
Consider; see Sidereal.
Consign; see Sign.
Consist; see State.
Console; see Solace.
Consolidate; see Solid.
Consonant; see Sound (3).
Consort; see Sort.
Conspicuous; see Species.
Conspire; see Spirit.
Constable; see Itinerant.
Constant; see State.
Constellation; see Stellar.
Consternation; see Stratum.

Constipate; see Stipulation.
Constitute; see State.
Constrain; see Stringent.
Construe; see Structure.
Consul. (L.) L. *consul*, a consul. Etym. doubtful; perhaps from *consulere*, to consult; see below.
Consult. (F. — L.) F. *consulter*. — L. *consultare*, to consult; frequent. form of *consulere*, to consult. Root uncertain.
  counsel. (F. — L.) M. E. *conseil*. — O. F. *conseil*. — L. *consilium*, deliberation. — L. *consulere*, to consult.
Consume; see Exempt.
Consummate; see Sub-.
Consumption; see Exempt.
Contact, Contagion; see Tangent.
Contain; see Tenable.
Contaminate; see Tangent.
Contemn. (F. — L.) F. *contemner*. — L. *contemnere*, to despise. — L. *con-* (*cum*), with, wholly; *temnere*, to despise.
  contempt. (F. — L.) O. F. *contempt*. — L. *contemptus*, scorn. — L. pp. *con-temptus*.
Contemplate; see Temple (1).
Contemporaneous; see Temporal.
Contend; see Tend (1).
Content; see Tenable.
Contest; see Testament.
Context; see Text.
Contiguous; see Tangent.
Continent; see Tenable.
Contingent; see Tangent.
Continue; see Tenable.
Contort; see Torture.
Contour; see Turn.
Contra-, *prefix*. (L.) L. *contra*, against. Compounded of *con-*, for *cum*, with; and *-tra*, related to *trans*, beyond. Der. *contra-distinguish*, &c.; and see Contrary.
  counter-, *prefix*. (F. — L.) F. *contre*, against. — L. *contra* (above).
  encounter. (F. — L.) O. F. *encontrer*, to meet in combat. — F. *en*, in; *contre*, against. — L. *in*, in; *contra*, against.
  rencounter, rencontre. (F. — L.) F. *rencontre*, a meeting. — F. *rencontrer*, to meet. — F. *re-*, again; *encontrer*, to meet (above).
Contraband; see Ban.
Contract; see Trace (1).
Contradict; see Diction.
Contralto; see Altitude.
Contrary. (F. — L.) F. *contraire*. — L. *contrarius*, contrary; formed (with suffix *-arius*) from *contra*, against; see Contra-.
Contrast; see State.

Contravene; see Venture.

Contribute; see Tribe.

Contrite; see Trite.

Contrive; see Trover.

Control; see Rotary.

Controversy; see Verse.

Contumacy. (L.) Englished from L. *contumacia*, obstinacy. — L. *contumaci-*, crude form of *contumax*, stubborn; supposed to be allied to *contemnere*; see Contemn.

Contumely. (F. — L.) F. *contumelie*. — L. *contumelia*, insult, reproach; prob. allied to *contumacia*; see Contumacy.

Contuse, to bruise severely. (L.) L. *contusus*, pp. of *contundere*, to bruise severely. — L. *con-* (*cum*), with, much; and *tundere*, to strike. + Skt. *tud*, to strike; Goth. *stautan*, to strike. (√ STUD.)

obtuse, blunt. (F. — L.) O. F. *obtus*, 'dull;' Cot. — L. *obtusus*, blunted, pp. of *ob-tundere*, to beat against. And see Pierce.

Convalesce; see Valid.

Convene, Convent; see Venture.

Converge; see Vergo (2).

Converse, Convert; see Verse.

Convex; see Vehicle.

Convey; see Viaduct.

Convince; see Victor.

Convivial; see Victuals.

Convoke; see Vocal.

Convolve; see Voluble.

Convoy; see Viaduct.

Convulse, to agitate violently. (L.) L. *conuulsus*, pp. of *conuellere*, to pluck up, convulse. — L. *con-* (*cum*), with, severely; *uellere*, to pluck (of uncertain origin).

revulsion. (F. — L.) F. *revulsion*, 'a plucking away; also the drawing of humours from one part of the body to the other;' Cot. — L. *reuulsionem*, acc. of *re-uulsio*, a plucking back. — L. *reuulsus*, pp. of *re-uellere*.

Cony, Coney, a rabbit. (E.; or F. — L.) M. E. *coni*; also *conyng*. Most likely a French word rather than E. Anglo-F. *conin*, *conil*. — O. F. *connin*, *connil*. — L. *cuniculus*, a rabbit; a word of uncertain origin.

Coo. (E.) A purely imitative word; also spell *croo*. Cf. *cuckoo*, *cock*.

Cook. (L.) M. E. *coken*, to cook; A. S. *côc*, a cook. — L. *coquere*, to cook; *coquus*, a cook. + Gk. πέπτειν, Skt. *pach*, to cook. (√ KWAK, orig. KAK.)

biscuit, a kind of cake. (F. — L.) F. *biscuit*, lit. twice cooked. — F. *bis* (L. *bis*), twice; and *cuit*, cooked, from L. *coctus*, pp. of *coquere*, to cook.

cake. (Scand. — L.) M. E. *cake*. — Icel. and Swed. *kaka*; Dan. *kage*; so also Du. *koek*, G. *kuchen*, a cake, clearly allied to G. *küche*, cooking, *kochen*, to cook. All from L. *coquere*, to cook. (Doubtful).

concoct. (L.) L. *concoctus*, pp. of *con-coquere*, to cook together, boil together, digest.

decoct. (L.) L. *decoctus*, pp. of *de-coquere*, to boil down.

kitchen. (L.) M. E. *kichene*. A. S. *cicen* (put for *cycen*). — L. *coquina*, a kitchen. — L. *coquere*, to cook; see Cook (above).

precocious. (L.) Coined from L. *præcoci-*, crude form of *præcox*, prematurely ripe. — L. *præ*, before; *coquere*, to cook, to ripen.

Cool. (E.) A. S. *côl*, cool. + Du. *koel*; Dan. *köl*, G. *kuhl*. Allied to Gelid.

chilblain. (E.) A *blain* caused by *chill*.

chill, cold. (E.) Properly a sb. A. S. *ciele*, *cyle*, chilliness; cf. A.S. *célan*, to cool; A. S. *côl*, cool. + Du. *kill*, a chill; Swed. *kyla*, to chill; L. *gelu*, frost.

cold. (E.) M. E. *cold*, *kald*, adj., A.S. *ceald*, adj. + Icel. *kaldr*, Swed. *kall*, Dan. *kold*, Du. *koud*, Goth. *kalds*, G. *kalt*. Cf. L. *gelidus*, cold.

keel (2), to cool. (E.) To *keel* a pot is to keep it from boiling over, lit. to cool it. — A. S. *célan*, to cool; see Chill (above).

Coolie, Cooly, an East Indian porter. (Hind. — Tamil.) Hind. *kúlí*, a labourer, porter, cooley (Forbes). — Tamil *kúli*, daily hire or wages; a day-labourer (Wilson).

Coomb; see Comb.

Coop. (L.) M. E. *cupe*, a basket. A. S. *cýpa*. — L. *cupa*, a tub; whence also Du. *kuip*, Icel. *kúpa*, tub, bowl, G. *kufe*, tub, vat, coop. Cf. Skt. *kúpa*, a pit, hollow. (√ KU.) Der. *coop-er*, tub-maker.

cowl (2), a vessel carried on a pole. (F. — L.) M. E. *coul*. — O. F. *cuvel* (*cuveau*), a little tub; dimin. of *cuve*, a vat, tub. — L. *cupa* (above).

goblet. (F. — L.) F. *gobelet*, 'a goblet;' Cot. Dimin. of O. F. *gobel*, a cup. — Low L. *cupellum*, acc. of *cupellus*, a cup; dimin. of L. *cupa*, a vat.

Co-operate, Co-ordinate; see Operate, Order.

Coot. (C.) M. E. *cote, coote,* a water-fowl; A. S. *cýta,* a kind of bird; Du. *koet,* a coot. Prob. Celtic. — W. *cwtiar,* a coot, lit. a bob-tailed hen, from *cwta,* shoit, bob-tailed, and *iar,* a hen; *cwtiad,* *cwtyn,* a plover. Gael. *cut,* a bob-tail. — W. *cwtau,* to shorten, dock; see Cut.

Copal. (Span. — Mexican.) Span. *copal.* — Mex. *copalli,* resin.

Cope (1), a cape; see Cape (1).

Cope (2), to vie with; see Cheap.

Copious; see Optative.

Copper, a metal. (Cyprus.) M. E. *coper.* — Low L. *cuper,* L. *cuprum,* a contraction for *Cuprium æs,* Cyprian brass. — Gk. Κύπριος, Cyprian; Κύπρος, Cyprus, whence the Romans got copper.

copperas, sulphate of iron. (F. — L.) M. E. *coperose.* — O. F. *coperose (couperose)*; cf. Ital. *copparosa.* — L. *cupri rosa,* rose of copper, a translation of Gk. χάλκ-ανθος, brass-flower, copperas.

cupreous, coppery. (L.) L. *cupreus,* adj. of *cuprum.*

Coppice, Coppy, Copse, a small wood. (F. — L. — Gk.) *Coppy* is short for *coppice,* and *copse* is contracted. — O. F. *copeiz;* Low L. *copecia,* underwood frequently cut, brushwood. — O. F. *coper* (F. *couper*), to cut. — O. F. *cop* (F. *coup*), a stroke. — Low L. *colpus,* L. *colaphus,* stroke, blow. — Gk. κόλαφος, a blow.

recoup, to diminish a loss. (F. — L. *and* Gk.) Lit. to secure a piece or shred. — F. *recoupe,* a shred. — F. *recouper,* to cut again. — L. *re-,* again; and F. *couper,* to cut (above).

Copulate; see Couple.

Copy; see Optative.

Coquette; see Cock (1).

Coracle, a light wicker boat. (W.) W. *corwgl, cwrwgl,* coracle; dimin. of *corwg,* a trunk, *cwrwg,* a boat, frame. So Gael. *curachan,* coracle; from *curach,* boat of wicker-work, Ir. *corrach.*

Coral. (F. — L. — Gk.) O. F. *coral.* — L. *corallum, corallium.* — Gk. κοράλλιον, coral.

Corban, a gift. (Heb.) Heb. *qorbán,* an offering to God, in fulfilment of a vow. Arab. *qurbán,* a sacrifice.

Corbel. (F. — L.) O. F. *corbel,* a little basket, a corbel (in architecture). [Distinct from O. F. *corbel,* a raven.] — Low L. *corbella,* little basket. — L. *corbis,* basket.

corvette, a small frigate. (F. — Port. — L.) F. *corvette.* — Port. *corveta;* Span.

corbeta, a corvette. — L. *corbíta,* a slow-sailing ship of burden. — L. *corbis,* basket.

Cord; see Chord.

Cordial. (F. — L.) F. *cordial,* hearty. — L. *cordi-,* crude form of *cor,* heart; with suffix *-alis;* see Heart.

accord. (F. — L.) O. F. *acorder,* to agree. — Low L. *ac-cordare,* to agree; used for L. *con-cordare* (below). Der. *according, accord-ing-ly,* &c.; *accord-ion,* from its sweet sound.

concord. (F. — L.) F. *concorde.* — L. *concordia,* agreement. — L. *concord-,* stem of *con-cors,* agreeing. — L. *con-* (*cum*); *cor* (stem *cord-*), the heart.

concordant. (F. — L.) F. *concordant,* pres. pt. of *concorder,* to agree. — L. *concordare,* to agree.

concordat. (F. — Ital. — L.) F. *concordat,* an agreement. — Ital. *concordato,* a convention, thing agreed on, esp. between the pope and F. kings; pp. of *concordare,* to agree. — L. *concordare* (above).

core. (F. — L.) M. E. *core,* heart (of fruit). — O. F. *cor, coer,* heart. — L. *cor,* heart.

courage. (F. — L.) F. *courage,* O. F. *corage;* formed with suffix *-age* (L. *-aticum*) from O. F. *cor,* heart (above). Der. *en-courage.*

discord. (F. — L.) O. F. *descord, dis-cord,* variance. — L. *dis-cordia,* variance; cf. *concord* (above).

quarry (2), a heap of slaughtered game. (F. — L.) M. E. *querre.* — O. F. *curee, cuiree,* intestines of a slain animal, the part given to hounds; so called because wrapped in the skin. — F. *cuir,* a skin, hide. — L. *corium,* hide. *Not* allied to L. *cor.* (Misplaced.)

record. (F. — L.) M. E. *recorden.* — O. F. *recorder.* — L. *recordare, recordari,* to recall to mind. — L. *re-* again; *cord-,* stem of *cor,* heart.

Cordwainer, shoemaker. (F. — Span.) M. E. *cordwaner,* a worker in *cordewane,* i.e. leather of Cordova. — O. F. *cordouan,* Cordovan leather. — Low L. *Cordoa,* Cordova in Spain (L. *Corduba*).

Core; see Cordial.

Coriander. (F. — L. — Gk.) F. *coriandre.* — L. *coriandrum.* — Gk. κορίαννον, κόριον, coriander. The leaves are said to have a strong bug-like smell; from Gk. κόρις, a bug.

Cork. (Span. — L.) Span. *corcho,* cork. — L. *corticem,* acc. of *cortex,* bark.

Cormorant, a bird. (F.-L.) The *t* is excrescent. - F. *cormoran*; the same as Port. *corvomarinho* (sea-crow), cormorant. -L. *coruus marinus*, sea-crow. Perhaps confused with L. *coruus*, a crow, and Bret. *morvran*, a cormorant (from *mor*, sea, and *bran*, a crow).

Corn (1), grain. (E.) A. S. *corn*.+Du. *koren*, G. Icel. Dan. Swed. *korn*, Goth. *kaurn*, L. *granum*, Russ. *zerno*; see Grain. (√ GAR.)

churn. (Scand.) Icel. *kirna*, Swed. *kärna*, Dan. *kierne*, a churn; from O. Swed. *kerna*, Swed. *kärna*, Dan. *kierne*, to churn; cf. Du. and G. *kernen*, to churn. Orig. to curdle, turn to a curd or 'kernel;' cf. Icel. *kjarna*, Swed. *kärna*, Dan. *kierne*, kernel, pith, core, Du. and G. *kern*, grain, kernel; closely allied to Corn.

kernel. (E.) A.S. *cyrnel*, a grain; dimin. of A.S. *corn*, a grain (with the usual change from *o* to *y*). And see churn above.

Corn (2), a hard excrescence on the foot. (F.-L.) F. *corne*, a horn, horny swelling. (Cot.)-Low L. *corna*; L. *cornu*, a horn; see Horn.

cornea, horny membrane in the eye. (L.) L. *cornea*, fem. of *corneus*, horny.-L. *cornu*, a horn.

cornel, a shrub. (F.-L.) F. *cornille*, a cornel-berry; *cornillier*, cornel-tree. - Low L. *corniola*, cornel-berry; *cornolium*, cornel-tree. - L. *cornus*, a cornel-tree; from the hard, horny nature of the wood. - L. *cornu*, a horn.

cornelian, a kind of chalcedony. (F.-L.) Formerly *cornaline*. - F. *cornaline*, 'the cornix or cornaline, a flesh-coloured stone;' Cot. Cf. Port. *cornelina*; Ital. *corniola*.-L. *cornu*, horn; in allusion to the semi-transparent appearance. ¶ Altered to *carnelian* in E., and *carneol* in G., from a popular etymology which connected it with L. *carn*-, stem of *caro*, flesh. Cf. onyx = Gk. ὄνυξ, finger-nail.

corner. (F.-L.) O. F. *corniere*. - Low L. *corneria*, corner, angle. - Low L. *corna*, angle.-L. *cornu*, horn, projection.

cornet. (F.-L.) M. E. *cornet*, a horn; also a troop of horse (accompanied by a cornet or bugle); also an officer of such a troop.-F. *cornet*, *cornette*, dimin. of F. *corne*, a horn; see Corn.

cornucopia. (L.) For *cornu-copiæ*, horn of plenty.

unicorn, one-horned animal. (F.-L.)

F. *unicorne*. - L. *uni*-, for *unus*, one; *cornu*, horn.

Cornice, Corolla, Corollary; see Crown.

Coronation, Coroner, Coronet; see Crown.

Corporal (1); see Capital.

Corporal (2), belonging to the body. (L.) L. *corporalis*, bodily.-L. *corpor*-, stem of *corpus*, the body. Der. (from L. *corpor*-) *corpor-ate*, *corpor-e-al* (L. *corpore-us*), &c.

corps, corpse, corse, a body. (F.-L.) Here *corps* is mod. F.; *corse* is from *corpse* by loss of *p*. M. E. *corps*.-O. F. *corps, cors*, the body.-L. *corpus*.

corpulent. (F.-L.) F. *corpulent*. - L. *corpu-lentus*, fat.-L. *corpu-s*.

corpuscle. (L.) L. *corpus-cu-lum*, double dimin. of *corpus*.

corset. (F.-L.) F. *corset*, a pair of stays; dimin. of O. F. *cors*, body; see corps.

corslet. (F.-L.) F. *corselet*, 'a little body,' Cot.; hence body-armour. Double dimin. of O. F. *cors*, body; see corps.

incorporate. (L.) L. *incorporatus*, pp. of *in-corporare*, to furnish with a body; hence to form into a body.

Corroct; see Regent.

Correlate; see Tolerate.

Correspond; see Sponsor.

Corridor; see Current.

Corroborate; see Robust.

Corrode; see Rodent.

Corrugate; see Rugose.

Corrupt; see Rupture.

Corsair; see Current.

Corset, Corslet; see Corporal (2).

Cortege; see Court.

Cortex, bark. (L.) See Cork.

Coruscate. (L.) From pp. of L. *coruscare*, to glitter.

Corvette; see Corbel.

Cosmic, relating to the world. (Gk.) Gk. κοσμικός, adj., from κόσμος, order, also the world, universe.

cosmetic, that which beautifies. (Gk.) Gk. κοσμητικός, skilled in adorning; whence also F. *cosmétique*.-Gk. κοσμέω, I adorn.-Gk. κόσμος, order, ornament. Also *cosmo-gony*, *cosmo-graphy*, *cosmo-logy*, *cosmo-polite* (citizen of the world, Gk. πολίτης, a citizen).

Cossack, a light-armed S. Russian soldier. (Russ. - Tatar.) Russ. *kozake*, *kazake*; said to be of Tatar (Tartar) origin.

Cost; see State.

Costal; see Coast.

Costermonger. (F. *and* E.) Formerly *costerd-monger* or *costard-monger*, a seller of *costards* or apples. [The suffix *-monger* is E.; see **Monger**.] M.E. *costard*, an apple, where the suffix *-ard* is F.; prob. from O.F. *coste*, F. *côte*, a rib; cf. F. *fruit côtelé*, ribbed fruit (Hamilton). [Etym. doubtful.]

Costive; see **Stipulation**.

Costume; see **Custom**.

Cot, a small dwelling; **Cote**, an enclosure. (E.) M.E. *cote*. A.S. *cote*, a cot, den; Northumbrian *cot*. ✚ Du. *kot*, Icel. *kot*, cot, hut; prov. G. *koth*, cot. Der. *cott-age* (with F. suffix); *cott-ar* or *cott-er*; *sheep-cote*.

coat. (F.—G.) M.E. *cote.*—O.F. *cote* (F. *cotte*); Low L. *cota*, a coat, also a cot. —M.H.G. *kotte*, *kutte*, a coarse mantle, lit. 'covering;' allied to A.S. *cote*, a cot, orig. 'covering.'

coterie, a set of people. (F.—Teut.) F. *coterie*, a set of people, company; allied to O.F. *coterie*, servile tenure (Littré); Low L. *coteria*, a tenure by cottars who clubbed together.—Low L. *cota*, a cot.—Du. *kot* (above).

cotillon, cotillion, a dance for 8 persons. (F.—M.H.G.) F. *cotillon*, lit. a petticoat; see Cotgrave. Formed, with suffix *-ill-on*, from O.F. *cote*, a coat, frock; see **coat** (above).

Cotton (1), a downy substance. (F.—Span.—Arab.) M.E. *cotoun.*—F. *coton.* —Span. *coton*, *algodon*, cotton (where *al* is the Arab. art.).—Arab. *qutn*, *qutun*, cotton.

cudweed, a plant. (F.—Span.—Arab.; *and* E.) Also called *cotton-weed*, of which *cudweed* is a contraction.

Cotton (2), to agree. From a technical use of Cotton (1); see **Nares**.

Cotyledon, seed-lobe. (Gk.) Gk. κοτυληδών, a cup-shaped hollow. — Gk. κοτύλη, a hollow vessel, cup. (✓KAT?)

Couch; see **Locus**.

Cough. (O. Low G.) M.E. *coughen*, *cowhen*. [The A.S. word is *hwóstan*.] Cf. Du. *kugchen*, to cough; M.H.G. *kuchen*, G. *keichen*, *keuchen*, to gasp. From an imitative base KUK, to gasp; see **Chincough**.

Could; see **Can** (1).

Coulter, part of a plough. (L.) M.E. *colter*. A.S. *culter.*—L. *culter*, a coulter, knife, lit. a cutter. ✚ Skt. *karttarí*, scissors, from *krit*, to cut. (✓KART.)

cutlass. (F.—L.) F. *coutelas*, 'a cuttelas, or courtelas, or short sword;' Cot.

(Perhaps borrowed from Ital. *coltellaccio*, 'a curtleax,' Florio; which is, at any rate, the same word.)—O.F. *coutel*, *cultel* (F. *couteau*), a knife; cf. Ital. *coltello*, knife. —L. acc. *cultellum*, a knife; dimin. of *culter* (above). ¶ The F. *-as*, Ital. *-accio* = L. *-aceus*; but F. *çoutelas* was actually turned into E. *curtleaxe*! Yet a *curtleaxe* was a sort of *sword*!

cutler. (F.—L.) M.E. *coteler.*— O.F. *cotelier.*—Low L. *cultellarius*, knife-maker. —L. *cultellus*, a knife (above).

Council; see **Calends**.

Counsel; see **Consult**.

Count (1), a title; see **Itinerant**.

Count (2), to compute; see **Putative**.

Countenance; see **Tenable**.

Counter-, prefix; see **Contra-**.

Counteract; see **Agent**.

Counterfeit; see **Fact**.

Countermand; see **Mandate**.

Counterpane (1); see **Quilt**.

Counterpane (2), counterpart of a deed; see **Pane**.

Counterpoint; see **Pungent**.

Counterpoise; see **Pendant**.

Counterscarp, -sign, -tenor; see **Scarp, Sign, Tenable**.

Countervail; see **Valid**.

Country. (F. — L.) M.E. *contree.*— O.F. *contree* (=Ital. *contrada*).—Low L. *contrada*, *contrata*, a region, lit. that which lies opposite; a translation of G. *gegend*, country, lit. opposite, from *gegen*, opposite. —L. *contra*, opposite; see **Contra-**.

County; see **Itinerant**.

Couple. (F. — L.) O.F. *cople*, later *couple.* — L. *cõpula*, a bond, band, that which joins; short for *co-ap-ula**.—L. *co-* (*cum*), together; and O.L. *apere**, to join, preserved in the pp. *aptus*; see **Apt**.

cobble (1), to patch up, mend. (F.— L.) O.F. *cobler*, *coubler*, to join together, another form of O.F. *copler*, the same.— O.F. *cople*, a band (above).

copulate. (L.) From pp. of L. *copulare*, to join.—L. *copula*, a band (above).

Courage; see **Cordial**.

Courier, Course; see **Current**.

Court (1), a yard; royal retinue, judicial assembly. (F.—L.) M.E. *cort*, *curt.* — O.F. *cort*, *curt* (F. *court*), a court, a yard, also a tribunal.—Low L. *cortis*, a courtyard, court, palace. —L. *corti-*, crude form of *cors*, also spelt *cohors*, a hurdle, enclosure, cattle-yard, court, also a cohort, or band of soldiers.—L. *co-* (*cum*), together; and *hort-us*, a garden, garth, yard, cognate with E. *garth* and *yard*. (√GHAR.)

cohort, a band of soldiers. (F. – L.) F. *cohorte.* – L. acc. *cohortem*, from *cohors* (above).

cortege. (F. – Ital. – L.) F. *cortége*, a train, retinue. – Ital. *corteggio*, a retinue. – Ital. *corte*, a court. – Low L. *cortis*; see Court (1) above.

court (2), to seek favour. (F. – L.) From the sb. *court*; hence to practise arts in vogue at court.

courteous, of courtly manners. (F. – L.) M. E. *corteis*, seldom *corteous*. – O. F. *corteis*, courteous. – O. F. *corte*, a court.

courtesan. (Span. – L.) Span. *cortesana*; fem. of *cortesano*, one belonging to the court. – Span. *cortes*, courteous; from *corte*, court. – Low L. *cortis* (above).

courtesy. (F. – L.) M. E. *corteisie*. – O. F. *corteisie*, courtesy. – O. F. *corteis*, courteous; see **courteous**.

courtier. (F. – L.; *and* E.) From *court*; with E. suffix *-ier*, as in *coll-ier*, *bow-yer*, &c.

curtain. (F. – L.) M. E. *cortin.* – O. F. *cortine.* – Low L. *cortina*, a small court, a rampart or 'curtain' of a castle, a hanging curtain round an enclosure. – Low L. *cortis* (above).

curtsey, an obeisance (F. – L.) The same word as *courtesy*, a courtly act.

Court cards; a corruption of *coat cards*, pictured cards, the old name.

Courteous, &c.; see **Court**.

Cousin. (F. – L.) M. E. *cosin.* – O. F. *cosin* (F. *cousin*). – Low L. *cosinus*, contr. form of L. *consobrinus*, the child of a mother's sister, a cousin. – L. *con-* (*cum*), together; *sobrinus*, for *sos-brinus** or *sos-trinus,** from *sostor** (later *sosor**, *soror*,) a sister; see Schleicher, Compendium, 3rd ed. p. 432.

cozen. (F. – L.) To *cozen* is to act as *cousin* or kinsman, to sponge upon, beguile. – F. *cousiner*, to call cousin, to sponge, live on other people; see Hamilton and Cotgrave. – F. *cousin*, a cousin (above).

Cove, a nook. (E.) A. S. *cófa*, a chamber, a cave. + Icel. *kofi*, a hut; G. *koben*, a cabin. ¶ Distinct from *cave*, *coop*, *alcove*.

Covenant; see **Venture**.

Cover, to hide. (F. – L.) O. F. *covrir* (*couvrir*). – L. *coöperire*, to cover. – L. *co-* (*cum*), wholly; *operire*, to shut, hide.

coverlet. (F. – L.) M. E. *coverlite.* – O. F. *covrelit* (*couvre-lit*), a bed-cover. –

O. F. *covrir*, to cover; *lit*, a bed (= L. acc. *lectum*, from *lectus*, a bed).

covert. (F. – L.) O. F. *covert*, pp. of *covrir*, to cover (above).

curfew. (F. – L.) O. F. *covrefeu* (F. *couvrefeu*), a fire-cover, covering of fires, time for putting out fires. – O. F. *covrir*, to cover; *feu*, fire (= L. *focum*, acc. of *focus*, hearth, fire); see **Focus**.

discover. (F. – L.) M. E. *discoueren.* – O. F. *descouvrir*, to uncover, disclose. – O. F. *des-* (L. *dis-*), apart; *couvrir*, to cover (above).

kerchief. (F. – L.) M. E. *curchief*, *couerchef.* – O. F. *covrechef*, lit. a head-covering. – O. F. *covrir*, to cover; *chef*, the head; see **chief**, under **Capital**.

Covet; see **Cupid**.

Covey. (F. – L.) O. F. *covee*, a brood of partridges; fem. of pp. of *cover* (F. *couver*), to hatch, sit. – L. *cubare*, to lie down, sit. + Gk. κύπτειν, to bend. (√KUP.)

concubine. (F. – L.) O. F. *concubine.* – L. *concubina.* – L. *con-* (*cum*), together; *cubare*, to lie.

incubate. (L.) From pp. of L. *in-cubare*, to sit on eggs to hatch them.

incubus. (L.) L. *incubus*, a nightmare. – L. *in-cubare*, to lie upon.

incumbent. (L.) L. *incumbent-*, stem of pres. pt. of *in-cumbere*, to recline on, rest on or in (remain in); where *cumbere* is a nasalised form allied to *cubare*, to lie down. So also *pro-cumbent*, prostrate; *re-cumbent*, lying back upon; *suc-cumb*, to lie under, yield to.

Cow (1), female of the bull. (E.) A. S. *cú*; pl. *cý*, whence M. E. *ky*, and the double pl. *ky-en = kine*. + Du. *koe*, Icel. *kýr*, Swed. Dan. *ko*, G. *kuh*, Irish and Gael. *bó*, L. *bos* (gen. *bou-is*), Gk. βοῦς, Skt. *gu*. (√GU.) See **Beef**, **Buck** (2).

cowslip, a flower. (E.) M. E. *cousloppe*. A. S. *cú-sloppe*, *cú-slyppe*, lit. cow-slop, i. e. a piece of dung. (Other A. S. names of plants are of a very homely character.) Cf. *oxlip*.

kine, cows. (E.) A *double* pl., made by adding *-n*, short for *-en* (A. S. *-an*), to M. E. *ky*, A. S. *cý*, cows. The A. S. *cý*, pl. of *cú*, a cow, is formed by vowel-change from *ú* to *ý*.

Cow (2), to dishearten. (Scand.) Icel. *kúga*, to tyrannise over; Dan. *kue*, to coerce, subdue.

Coward; see **Caudal**.

Cower. (Scand.) M. E. *couren.* – Icel.

kúra, Dan. *kure,* to doze, lie quiet; Swed. *kura,* to doze, roost, settle to rest (as birds). Cf. Goth. *kwairrus,* gentle.

Cowl (1), a monk's hood. (L.) M. E. *couel, cuuel.* A. S. *cufle,* a cowl; cf. Icel. *kufl, kofl,* cowl. — L. *cucullus.* (√SKU.)

Cowl (2), a vessel carried on a pole; see **Coop.**

Cowry, a small shell used for money. (Hind.) Hind. *kauri,* a small shell (*Cypræa moneta*) used as coin in the lower provinces of India; Bengali *kori* (Wilson).

Cowslip; see Cow.

Coxcomb; see Cock (1).

Coxswain; see cock (5), under Conch.

Coy; see Quiet.

Cozen; see Cousin.

Crab (1), a shell-fish. (E.) A. S. *crabba.* + Icel. *krabbi,* Swed. *krabba,* Dan. *krabbe,* Du. *krab,* G. *krabbe.* Cf. Gk. κάραβος, prickly crab, beetle, L. *scarabæus,* beetle. (√SKAR.)

crabbed, peevish, cramped. (E.) From *crab,* sb.; i. e. crab-like, snappish or awkward. Cf. Du. *krabben,* to scratch, *kribben,* to be peevish; Icel. *krabba,* to scrawl.

crayfish. (F.—O. H. G.) A misspelling of M. E. *crevise.* — O. F. *crevise, escrevisse* (*écrevisse*). — O. H. G. *crebiz,* G. *krebs,* a crab; allied to G. *krabbe* (above).

Crab (2), a kind of apple. (Scand.) Swed. *krabbäple,* a crab-apple; perhaps allied to Crab (1); i. e. pinching, sharp, sour.

Crabbed; see Crab (1).

Crack. (E.) A. S. *cearcian,* to crack, gnash noisily.+Du. *kraken,* to crack, creak; G. *krachen;* Gael. *crac,* a fissure, *cnac,* a crack, to crack. Imitative, like *crake, creak, croak, crash, gnash, knock.* (√GARK.)

cracknel. (F.—Du.) Formerly *crakenel,* corruption of F. *craquelin,* a cracknel. Named from its crispness. — Du. *kraken,* to crack.

crake, corncrake, a bird. (E.) From its noise; M. E. *craken,* to cry out. Allied to *crack, croak.*

crash. (Scand.) Swed. *krasa,* Dan. *krase,* to crackle, Swed. *slå in kras,* Dan. *slaae i kras,* to break to shivers. Allied to *crack, craze.*

craze. (Scand.) M. E. *crased,* i. e. *cracked.* — Swed. *krasa,* Dan. *krase,* as above; whence also F. *écraser;* see above.

creak. (E.) M. E. *kreken.* Allied to *crake, crack.* Cf. Du. *kriek,* a cricket, F.

criquer, to creak, allied to *craquer,* to crack.

cricket (1), an insect. (F. — Teut.) M. E. *criket.* — O. F. *crequet, criquet,* cricket. — O. F. *criquer,* to creak, rattle, chirp. — Du. *kriek,* a cricket; *krikkrakken,* to rattle. Cf. L. *graculus,* jackdaw.

croak. (E.) A.S. *crácian,* to croak; allied to *crake, crack.* And see Crow.

Cradle. (C.) A. S. *cradol.* — Irish *craidhal,* Gael. *creathall,* a cradle, a grate; cf. W. *cryd,* cradle, Irish *creathach,* a hurdle; L. *crates,* a hurdle. See Crate, Hurdle.

Craft, skill. (E.) A. S. *cræft.* + Du. *kracht,* Icel. *kraptr, kraft,* Swed. Dan. G. *kraft,* force. Allied to Cramp. Der. *handi-craft.*

Crag. (C.) W. *craig,* Gael. *creag,* crag, rock; W. *careg,* Gael. *carraig,* rock, cliff. — Gael. *carr,* a rock.

Crake; see Crack.

Cram. (E.) A. S. *crammian,* to stuff. + Icel. *kremja,* Swed. *krama,* Dan. *kramme,* to squeeze. Allied to Cramp.

Cramp. (E.) M. E. *crampe,* a cramp, spasm; cf. A. S. *crompeht,* crumpled (base KRAMP). + Swed. Du. *kramp,* Dan. *krampe,* G. *kramf,* cramp; G. *krampfen,* to cramp, squeeze. [Lost strong verb *crimpan* *, pt. t. *cramp* *, pp. *crumpen* *.] And see Clamp, Cram.

crimp, to wrinkle. (E.) Weakened form of Cramp. + Du. *krimpen,* Swed. *krympa,* to shrink, Dan. *krympe sig sammen,* to shrink oneself together; G. *krimpen,* to crumple. Der. *crimp-le.*

crumple. (E.) M. E. *cromplen,* to wrinkle; frequentative of Cramp.

Crane, a bird. (E.) A. S. *cran.*+Du. *kraan,* Icel. *trani* (for *krani*), Swed. *trana,* Dan. *trane,* G. *kran-ich;* W. *garan,* Gk. γέρανος, a crane, also a crane for raising weights. Cf. L. *grus.* (√GAR.)

cranberry. (E.) I. e. *crane-berry;* so also G. *kranbeere;* Dan. *tranebær* (from *trane = krane,* as above); Swed. *tranbär.*

Cranium. (L. — Gk.) L. *cranium.* — Gk. κρανίον, skull; allied to κάρα, head.

pericranium, the membrane that surrounds the skull. (L. — Gk.) L. *pericranium.* — Gk. περικράνιον, neut. of περικράνιος, surrounding the skull. — Gk. περί, round; κρανίον, skull.

Crank (1), a bend. (E.) M. E. *cranke.* (Teut. base KRANK, to twist, parallel to Cramp.) Cf. Du. *kronkel,* a little bend, *kronkelen,* to wrinkle, turn, wind.

crank (2), easily upset, as a boat. (E.) I. e. easily bent or twisted aside. Cf. Du. *krengen*, to careen a boat; Swed. *kränga*, Dan. *krænge*, to heel over; see **cringe** below.

crank (3), lively. (E.) The same word, from the metaphor of an unsteady boat.

cringe. (E.) A. S. *cringan, crincan,* to sink in battle, fall beneath the foe. Put for *crink,* weakened form of *crank.*

crinkle. (E.) M. E. *crinkled, crencled,* twisted. A frequent. form of *crink,* which is a weakened form of *crank.*

Cranny. (F. – L.) M. E. *crany*; made by adding E. *-y* to F. *cran,* a notch. – L. *crena,* a notch.

crenate, notched. (L.) From L. *crena,* a notch.

crenellate. (Low L. – F. – L.) From pp. of Low L. *crenellare,* to furnish with battlements. – O. F. *crenel,* a battlement; dimin. of O. F. *cren,* F. *cran,* a notch (above).

Crants, a garland. (O. Du.) O. Du. *krants,* Du. *krans,* a garland, wreath. **+** Dan. *krands,* Sw. *krans,* G. *krantz.*

Crape; see **Crisp.**

Crash; see **Crack.**

Crasis; see **Crater.**

Crass. (L.) L. *crassus,* thick, dense.

grease. (F. – L.) M. E. *grese, grece.* – O. F. *gresse,* fatness. – O. F. *gras,* fat. – L. *crassus* (above).

Cratch; see **Crib.**

Crate. (L.) L. *crates,* a hurdle; hence a wicker case, &c. (√KART.)

grate (1), a framework of iron bars. (Low L. – L.) M. E. *grate.* – Low L. *grata,* a grating; also *crata,* a grating. – L. *crates,* a hurdle.

grill, to boil on a gridiron. (F. – L.) F. *griller,* to broil. – F. *gril,* 'a gridiron,' Cot.; O. F. *greïl, grail.* – L. *craticulum,* for *craticula,* a small gridiron (whence F. *grille,* a grating). – L. *crates* (above).

Crater. (L. – Gk.) L. *crater,* a bowl, a crater. – Gk. κρατήρ, a large bowl in which things were mixed. – Gk. κεράννυμι, I mix (base κρα-).

crasis. (Gk.) Gk. κρᾶσις, mixing; hence, contraction. – Gk. κεράννυμι (above).

Cravat. (F. – Austrian.) F. *cravate,* (1) a Croatian, (2) a cravat. *Cravats* were introduced into France in 1636, as worn by the *Croatians,* who were called in F. *Croates* or *Crovates* or *Cravates.* *Croatia* is a province of Austria.

Crave. (E.) A. S. *crafian,* to crave,

ask. **+** Icel. *krefja,* Swed. *kräfva,* Dan. *kræve,* to demand; Icel. *krafa,* a demand.

Craven. (F. – L.) The oldest form is M. E. *cravant,* with the sense of beaten, foiled, or overcome. Mr. Nicol has conclusively shown that it is a clipped form of O. F. *cravanté,* pp. explained by Cotgrave by 'oppressed, foiled.' It is the pp. of O. F. *cravanter,* to break, oppress = Low L. *crepantare**, formed from *crepant-,* stem of pres. pt. of *crepare,* to crack, break. Cf. Span. *quebrantar,* to crack, break.

Craw, crop of fowls. (Scand.) Dan. *kro,* Swed. *kräfva,* Swed. dial. *kroe,* the craw. Allied to Du. *kraag,* G. *kragen,* neck, collar.

Crawfish, the same as **Crayfish.**

Crawl. (Scand.) Icel. *krafla,* to paw, crawl; Swed. *krafla,* to grope, *kräla,* to crawl; Dan. *kravle,* to crawl. Frequentative from Teut. base KRAP, to seize, grasp, hence, to grope; see **Cramp.**

Crayfish; see **Crab** (1).

Crayon; see **Cretaceous.**

Craze, Creak; see **Crack.**

Cream. (F. – L.) O. F. *cresme* (*crème*); Low L. *crisma.* – L. *cremor,* thick broth, thick juice from soaked corn.

Crease (1), a wrinkle. (C. ?) Bret. *kriz,* a crease, wrinkle; *kriza,* to crease, fold garments; W. *crych,* a wrinkle, *crychu,* to rumple. ¶ Hardly from Swed. *krus,* a curl, *krusa,* to curl; for which see **Gooseberry.**

Crease (2), **Creese,** a dagger. (Malay.) Malay *krîs,* 'a dagger, kris, or creese'; Marsden.

Create. (L.) From pp. of L. *creare,* to make. **+** Skt. *krî,* to make. Der. *creat-ure,* O. F. *creature,* L. *creatura.* And see **Crescent.**

creole, one born in the W. Indies, but of European blood. (F. – Span. – L.) F. *créole.* – Span. *criollo,* a negro corruption of *creadillo,* dimin. of *criado,* one educated, instructed, or brought up; hence a child of European blood. *Criado* is pp. of *criare,* to create, also, to educate. – L. *creare,* to create, make.

procreate. (L.) L. *procreatus,* pp. of *procreare,* to generate. – L. *pro,* before, forth; *creare,* to produce.

recreation. (F. – L.) F. *recreation.* – L. *recreationem,* acc. of *recreatio,* orig. recovery from illness (hence, amusement). – L. *recreatus,* pp. of *recreare,* to revive, refresh. – L. *re-,* again; *creare,* to make.

Creed. (L.) M. E. *crede*; A. S. *creda*.—L. *credo*, I believe; the first word of the creed. + O. Irish *cretim*, I believe; Skt. *çraddadhāmi*, I believe. (√ KRAT.) **Der.** *cred-ence* (O. F. *credence*, L. *credentia*); *cred-ible*; *credit* (L. pp. *creditus*); *cred-ulous* (L. *credulus*), &c. And see **Miscreant.**

grant. (F. — L.) M. E. *graunten.* — O. F. *graanter, graunter*, later spelling of *craanter, creanter*, to caution, assure, guarantee; whence the later senses, to promise, yield; Low L.*creantare*, put for *credentare**. —L. *credent-*, stem of pres. pt. of *credere*, to trust.

recreant. (F. — L.) O. F. *recreant*, faint-hearted; pres. pt. of *recroire*, to believe again, also to give up, give back (hence, to give in). — Low L. *re-credere*, to believe again, recant, give in.

Creek. (E.) A.S. *crecca*, a creek. + Du. *kreek*; Icel. *kriki*, a crack, nook. The orig. sense is 'a bend,' as in Swed. dial. *armkrik*, bend of the arm. Allied to **Crook**, q. v.

crick, a spasm or twist in the neck. (E.) M E. *crykke*; also used in the sense of 'bend.' Merely a variant of **creek** (above).

Creep. (E.) M. E. *crepen*; A. S. *creópan*. + Du. *kruipen*, Icel. *krjúpa*, Swed. *krypa*, Dan. *krybe*, to crawl. (Base KRUP.) Allied to **Cramp**.

cripple. (E.) M. E. *crepel, crupel*; O. Northumb. *crypel*, Luke, v. 24. Lit. 'a creeper.' — A.S. *crup-*, stem of pl. of pt. t. of *creópan* (pt. t. *creáp*); with suffix *-el* of the agent. + Du. *kreupel*, Icel. *kryppil*, Dan. *kröbling* (from *krybe*, to creep), G. *krüppel*.

Cremation, burning. (L.) L. *cremationem*, acc. of *crematio*; from pp. of *cremare*, to burn.

Crenate, Crenellate; see **Cranny.**

Creole; see **Create.**

Creosote, a liquid distilled from tar. (Gk.) Lit. 'flesh-preserver.' — Gk. κρέω-s, Attic form of κρέας, flesh; and σωτ-, short for σωτ-ήρ, preserver, from σώζειν, to preserve.

Crescent. (L.) The 'increasing' moon. —L. *crescent-*, stem of pres. pt. of *crescere*, to grow, increase (pp. *cre-tus*), inchoative form from *cre-are*, to make; see **Create.**

accretion. (L.) L. *accretionem*, acc. of *accretio*, an increase. — L. *accretus*, pp. of *ac-crescere*, to grow to (*ac-* = *ad*).

accrue, to come to by way of increase.

(F. — L.) O. F. *accreu*, pp. of *accroistre* (*accroître*), to increase. — L. *ac-crescere* (above). See **Crew** below.

concrete, formed into one mass. (L.) L. *concret-us*, pp. of *con-crescere*; to grow together.

decrease. (F. — L.) O. F. *decrois*, sb., a decrease; from *decroistre*, vb., to decrease. — L. *de-crescere*, to diminish (pp. *decre-tus*).

decrement. (L.) L. *decrementum*, a decrease. — L. *decre-tus*, pp. of *de-crescere*.

excrescence. (F. — L.) O. F. *excrescence.* — L. *excrescentia*, an outgrowth. —L. *excrescent-*, stem of pres. pt. of *excrescere*, to grow out.

increase. (F. — L.) M. E. *incresen*, *encresen*. — F. *en* (L. *in*); and O. F. *creisser*, Norman F. *creser*, usually *croistre* (F. *croître*), to grow; from L. *crescere*.

increment. (L.) L. *in-crementum*, an increase; cf. *decrement* above.

recruit. (F. — L.) F. *recruter*, to levy troops (Littré). An ill-formed word, from *recrute*, mistaken form of *recrue*, fem. of *recrû*, pp. of *recroître*, to grow again. *Recrue*, as a sb., means 'a levy of troops,' lit. 'new-grown.' — L. *re-crescere*, to grow again.

Cress. (E.) M. E. *cres*, also *kers* (by shifting of *r*). A.S. *cærse, cerse, cressæ*. + Du. *kers*, Swed. *krasse*, Dan. *karse*, G. *kresse*.

Cresset; see **Cruse.**

Crest. (F. — L.) O. F. *creste.* — L. *crista*, a comb or tuft on a bird's head, crest.

Cretaceous, chalky. (L.) L. *cretaceus*, adj. from *creta*, chalk.

crayon. (F. — L.) F. *crayon*; extended from F. *craie*, chalk. — L. *creta* (above).

Crevice, Crevasse. (F. — L.) M. E. *crevice, crevase, crevasse.* — O. F. *crevasse*, a rift. — O. F. *crever*, to burst asunder. — L. *crepare*, to crackle, burst.

decrepit. (L.) L. *decrepitus*, noiseless, creeping about like an old man, aged. — L. *de*, away; *crepitus*, noise, orig. pp. of *crepare* (above).

discrepant, differing. (F. — L.) O. F. *discrepant.* — L. *discrepant-*, stem of pres. pt. of *dis-crepare*, to differ in sound; lit. to crackle apart.

Crew. (F. — L.) Formerly *crue*, short for *accrue*, a re-inforcement. — O. F. *accreue*, increase; orig. fem. of pp. of *accroistre*; see top of this column.

Crib, a manger. (E.) A.S. *crib.* + O. Sax. *kribbia*, Du. *krib*, Icel. Swed. *krubba*, Dan. *krybbe*, G. *krippe*, crib. **Der.** *crib*, verb, to put by in a crib, purloin; *cribb-age*, where *crib* is the secret store of cards.

cratch, a crib, manger. (F.–O. Sax.) M. E. *crecche.*–O. F. *creche* (*crèche*); Prov. *crepcha.*–O. Sax. *kribbia* (above).

Crick; see **Creek.**

Cricket (1), insect; see **Crack.**

Cricket (2), game; see **Crook.**

Crime. (F.–L.) F. *crime.*–L. *crimen*, an accusation, fault (stem *crimin-*) Der. *crimin-al, crimin-ate*; hence *re-criminate.*

Crimp; see **Cramp.**

Crimson; see **Carmine.**

Cringe, Crinkle; see **Crank.**

Crinoline, a lady's stiff skirt. (F.–L.) F. *crinoline,* (1) hair-cloth, (2) crinoline. –F. *crin* (L. acc. *crinem*), hair; and *lin,* flax, hence cloth, from L. *linum,* flax.

Cripple; see **Creep.**

Crisis; see **Critic.**

Crisp, wrinkled, curled. (L.) A. S. *crisp.*–L. *crispus,* curled.

crape. (F. – L.) F. *crêpe,* formerly *crespe,* 'frizzled, crisped, crisp;' Cot. From its wrinkled surface.–L. *crispus.*

Critic. (Gk.) Gk. κριτικός, able to discern; cf. κριτής, a judge.–Gk. κρί-νειν, to judge. Der. *crit-erion,* Gk. κριτήριον, a test; *dia-critic,* from Gk. διακριτικός, fit for distinguishing between.

crisis. (Gk.) Gk. κρίσις, a discerning, a crisis.–Gk. κρί-νειν, to judge.

Croak; see **Crack.**

Crochet; see **Crook.**

Crock, a pitcher. (C.) A. S. *crocca.*– Gael. *crog,* Irish *crogan,* W. *crochan,* a pitcher, pot. Cf. Corn. *crogen,* a shell. So also Du *kruik,* Icel. *krukka,* Swed. *kruka,* Dan. *krukke,* G. *krug*; prob. all of Celtic origin.

crucible. (Low L.–F.–C.) Low L. *crucibolus,* a melting-pot, also a cresset (see **Cruse**). – O. F. *cruche,* an earthen pitcher, crock. Of Celt. origin; see Icel. *krukka,* &c., above.

Crocodile. (F.–L.–Gk.) F. *crocodile.* –L. *crocodilus.*–Gk. κροκόδειλος, a lizard, a crocodile.

cockatrice. (F.–Low L.–L.) By confusion with *cock,* it was said to be a monster hatched from a cock's egg; also confused with *crocodile.*–O. F. *cocatrice,* a crocodile, by confusion with Low L. *cocodrillus,* put for *crocodilus*; but more correctly *caucatrice,* an ichneumon that 'tracked out' crocodiles' eggs.–L. *cal-catrix,* the 'tracker'; a translation of

Gk. ἰχνεύμων. ¶ The result of numerous fables.

Crocus. (L. – Gk.) L. *crocus.* – Gk. κρόκος, crocus, saffron. Cf. Arab. *karkam,* saffron.

Croft. (E. ? or C. ?) A. S. *croft,* a field. + Du. *kroft.* Perhaps of Celtic origin; cf. Gael. *croit,* hillock, croft, small piece of arable ground, *cruach,* a hill, heap.

Cromlech. (W.) W. *cromlech,* a flag-stone laid across others.–W. *crom,* crooked; *llech,* flat stone.

Crone, an old woman. (F.–L.) Tusser has *crone,* an old ewe. Prob. from Picard *carone,* carrion; whence O. Du. *karonie, kronie,* an old sheep. See p. 69, col. 2, l. 30. Der. *cron-y,* orig. an old gossip.

Crook, a hook, bend. (E.) M. E. *crok* (Ancren Riwle); prob. E.+O. Du. *kroke,* Du. *kreuk,* Icel. *krókr,* Swed. *krok,* Dan. *krog,* hook, bend, angle. Also Gael. *crocan,* a crook, W. *crwca,* crooked; W. *crwg,* a crook. (√ SKARK.) See **Cross.**

cricket, a game. (E.) The game succeeded a kind of hockey, played with a hooked stick. Dimin. of A. S. *cricc,* a staff; see **crutch** below.

crochet. (F.–Teut.) F. *crochet,* a little hook; dimin. of *croc,* a crook.–Icel. *krókr,* a hook (above).

crosier. (F. – Teut.) M. E. *crocer, croser,* &c. Formed, with suffix *-er,* from M. E. *croce,* in the same sense of 'bishop's staff.'–O. F. *croce,* 'a crosier,' Cot.; mod. F. *crosse*; Low L. *crocia.*–O. F. *croc,* a crook; see **crochet** above. ¶ Not from *cross,* to which it is only *ultimately* related.

cross. (C.–L.) M. E. *crois, cros* (both are used).–O. Irish *cros*; cf. Prov. *croz,* a cross.–L. *crucem,* acc. of *crux,* a cross, orig. a gibbet (from its 'bent' arm); allied to W. *crog,* a cross, *crwg,* a crook, Gael. *croich,* a gibbet; W. *crogi,* Gael. *croch,* to hang. See **Crook** above. Der. *a-cross.*

cross, adj. (F.–L.) Orig. transverse, from the shape of a cross; hence peevish.

crotchet, in music. (F.–Teut.) F. *crochet,* 'a small hook, a quaver in music;' Cot. (I suppose the *hooked* mark now called a quaver was once called a crotchet.) See **crochet** above.

crouch. (E.) M. E. *crouchen,* allied to *croken,* to bend; from M. E. *crok,* a crook.

crucial. (F.–L.) F. *crucial,* 'crosslike;' Cot. — L. *cruci-*, crude form of *crux*; see cross.

crucify. (F. — L.) O. F. *crucifier*. — Low L. *crucificare**, put for L. *crucifigere* (pp. *crucifixus*), to fix on a cross. — L. *cruci-*, crude form of *crux*; *figere*, to fix; see Fix. Der. *crucifix, -ion*.

cruise. (Du. — F. — L.) Du. *kruisen*, to cruise, cross the sea. — Du. *kruis*, a cross. — O. F. *crois*, a cross; see cross.

crusade. (F. — Prov. — L.) F. *croisade*, an expedition in which men bore the badge of the cross. — Prov. *crozada*. — Prov. *croz*, cross. — L. *crucem*, acc. of *crux*.

crutch. (E.) M. E. *crucche*; allied to A. S. *cricc* (better *crycc*), a crutch, staff; orig. a 'hooked' stick. + Du. *kruk*, Swed. *krycka*, Dan. *krykke*, G. *krücke*.

encroach. (F. — L. *and* Teut.) Lit. to hook away, catch in a hook. — F. *en*, in; *croc*, a hook; cf. F. *accrocher*, to hook up. — L. *in*, in; and O. Du. *kroke*, Icel. *krókr*, &c.; see Crook.

excruciate, to torture. (L.) From pp. of L. *excruciare*, to torment greatly. — L. *ex*, very; *cruciare*, to torture on a gibbet, from *cruci-*, crude form of *crux*, a cross.

Crop. (E.) A. S. *cropp*, the top of a plant, the craw of a bird; orig. a bunch. [Hence the verb to *crop*; to cut off the tops; and hence *crop*, a harvest.] + Du. *krop*, G. *kropf*, bird's crop; Icel. *kroppr*, a hunch; Swed. *kropp*, Dan. *krop*, trunk of the body. Cf. W. *cropa*, Gael. and Ir. *sgroban*, bird's crop. [To *crop out* is to bunch out.]

croup (2), hinder part of a horse. (F. — Teut.) F. *croupe*, crupper; orig. protuberance. — Icel. *kroppr*, a hunch (above).

crupper. (F. — Teut.) F. *croupiere*. — F. *croupe* (above).

group. (F. — Ital. — G.) F. *groupe*. — Ital. *groppo*, a knot, heap, group. — G. *kropf*, a crop, wen on the throat, orig. a bunch (above).

Crosier; see Crook.

Cross, Crotchet; see Crook.

Croton, plant. (Gk.) Gk. κρότων, a tick, which the croton-seed resembles.

Crouch; see Crook.

Croup (1), a disease. (E.) Lowland Sc. *croupe, crope*, to croak, make a harsh noise. — A. S. *hrópan*, to cry out. + Icel. *hrópa*, Goth. *hropjan*, Du. *roepen*, G. *rufen*. The A. S. form might also be *gehrópan*; the *c* is due to *h* or *ge-*

Croup (2); see Crop.

Crow, vb. (E.) A. S. *cráwan*, to crow. + Du. *kraaijen*, G. *krähen*; allied to *crake*, *croak*. (√GAR.) Der. *crow*, A. S. *cráwe*, a bird (croaker); *crow-bar*, bar with a crow-like beak.

Crowd (1), to push, throng. (E.) A. S. *crúdan**, pt. t. *creád*, to push; whence *croda, gecrod*, a crowd, throng.

Crowd (2), a fiddle. (W.) M. E. *croude*. — W. *crwth*, a trunk, belly, crowd, violin, fiddle; Gael. *cruit*, harp.

rote (2), an old musical instrument. (F. — G. — C.) O. F. *rote*, a kind of fiddle; answering to O. H. G. *hrotá, rotá*, a rote; Low L. *chrotta*. Of Celtic origin. — W. *crwth*, a violin; Gael. *cruit*, a harp.

Crown. (F. — L.) M. E. *corone, coroune* (whence *croune*). — O. F. *corone* (F. *couronne*). — L. *corona*, a wreath. + Gk. κορωνίς, κορωνός, curved; Gael. *cruinn*, W. *crwn*, round. Allied to Curve, Circle.

cornice. (F. — Ital. — L. — Gk.) F. *corniche*. — Ital. *cornice*. — Low L. *cornicem*, acc. of *cornix*, a border, short for *coronix*, a square frame. — Gk. κορωνίς, curved; as sb., a wreath, cornice.

corolla. (L.) L. *corolla*, dimin. of *corona*.

corollary. (L.) L. *corollarium*, a present of a garland, a gratuity; also, an additional inference. — L. *corolla* (above).

coronal, a crown. (F. — L.) Properly an adj. — F. *coronal*, adj. — L. *coronalis*, belonging to a crown. — L. *corona*.

coronation. (L.) Late L. acc. *coronationem*, from pp. of *coronare*, to crown. — L. *corona*.

coroner. (L.) Also *crowner*; both forms are translations of Low L. *coronator*, a coroner; lit. one who crowns, also, a crown-officer. — L. *coronare*, to crown (above).

coronet. (F. — L.) Dimin. of O. F. *corone*, a crown; see Crown.

Crucial, Crucify; see Crook.

Crucible; see Crook.

Crude. (L.) L. *crudus*, raw. Allied to Raw.

cruel. (F. — L.) O. F. *cruel*. — L. *crudelis*, cruel; allied to *crudus*, raw (above).

Cruet; see Cruse.

Cruise; see Crook.

Crumb. (E.) A. S. *cruma*. (The final *b* is excrescent.) From an old verb appearing in prov. E. *crim*, to crumble bread, allied to Crimp, Cramp. + Du. *kruim*, Dan. *krumme*, G. *krume*, a crumb; allied to M. H. G. *krimmen*, to pinch, tear.

Der. *crumb-le,* verb; cf. Du. *kruimelen,* G. *krümeln,* to crumble.

Crumple; see Cramp.

Crunch. (E.) An imitative word.

Crupper; see Crop.

Crural. (L.) L. *cruralis,* belonging to the leg. — L. *crur-,* stem of *crus,* the leg.

Crusade; see Crook.

Cruse, a small pot. (Scand.) M. E. *cruse.* — Icel. *krús,* a pot; Swed. *krus,* Dan. *kruus,* a mug; Du. *kroes,* cup, pot, crucible; M. H. G. *krúse,* mug. Prob. allied to Crock.

cresset. (F. — Lat.) M.E. *cresset,* a light in a cup at the top of a pole. — O. F. *crasset,* a cresset; lit. 'cup for holding grease.' — L. *crassus;* see Crass. Confused with O.F. *creuset,* a little cruse ; from O. Du. *kruyse* (above).

cruet. (F. — Teut.) Allied to F. *creuset,* 'a cruet,' Cot. Of Teut. origin ; see above.

Crush. (F. — Teut.) O. F. *cruisir, croissir,* to crack, break. — Swed. *krysta,* Dan. *kryste,* to squeeze; Goth. *kriustan,* to gnash with the teeth, *krusts,* gnashing of teeth.

Crust. (F. — L.) O. F. *cruste* (F. *croûte*). — L. *crusta,* crust of bread. Cf. Gk. *κρύος,* frost; see Crystal.

custard. (F. — L.) Put for *crustade,* by shifting of *r*; compare *buskin* (for *bruskin*). Formerly *custade, crustade,* and orig. used with the sense of 'pasty.' — O.F. *croustade,* a pasty. — L. *crustata,* fem. pp. of *crustare,* to encrust. — L. *crusta,* a crust.

Crutch; see Crook.

Cry; see Querulous.

Crypt. (L. — Gk.) L. *crypta.* — Gk. *κρυπτή,* a vault, hidden cave; orig. fem. of *κρυπτός,* hidden. — Gk. *κρύπτειν,* to hide.

apocrypha. (Gk.) Lit. 'hidden things,' books of the Old Testament not commonly read. — Gk. *ἀπόκρυφα,* neut. pl. of *ἀπόκρυφος,* hidden. — Gk. *ἀπο-κρύπτειν,* to hide away.

grot. (F. — L. — Gk.) F. *grotte,* a cave. — Low L. *grupta, crupta ;* L. *crypta* (above).

grotesque. (F. — Ital. — L. — Gk.) F. *grotesque,* ludicrous. — Ital. *grotesca,* curious painted work, such as was employed on the walls of grottoes. — Ital. *grotta* (below).

grotto. (Ital. — L. — Gk.) Better *grotta.* Ital. *grotta;* the same as F. *grotte* (above).

Crystal. (F. — L. — Gk.) Formerly *cristal.* — O. F. *cristal.* — L. *crystallum,* crystal. — Gk. *κρύσταλλος,* ice, crystal. — Gk. *κρυσταίνειν,* to freeze. — Gk. *κρύος,* frost.

Cub. (C.) Irish *cuib,* a cub, whelp; from *cu,* a dog. See Hound.

Cube. (F. — L. — Gk.) F. *cube.* — L. acc. *cubum.* — Gk. *κύβος,* a cube, die.

Cubit. (L.) L. *cubitus,* an elbow, bend; the length from the elbow to the middle finger's end. Allied to L. *cubare,* to lie down, recline ; see Covey.

Cuckold, Cuckoo; see Cock (1).

Cucumber. (L.) The *b* is excrescent; M. E. *cucumer.* — L. *cucumerem,* acc. of *cucumis,* a cucumber. Prob. from *coquere,* to ripen ; see Cook.

Cud. (E.) M. E. *cude, code, quide.* That which is chewed. Perhaps from the same base as A. S. *ceówan,* to chew ; but *not =* pp. *chewed,* because the verb was orig. strong. Cf. *suds,* allied to *seethe.*

quid, a mouthful of tobacco. (E.) Merely another form of *cud;* M. E. *quide* (above).

Cuddle; see Can (1).

Cudgel. (E.) M. E. *kuggel.* A. S. *cycgel;* in Gregory's Pastoral Care, ed. Sweet, p. 297.

Cudweed; see Cotton (1).

Cue; see Caudal.

Cuff (1), to strike. (Scand.) Swed. *kuffa,* to thrust, push, also to cuff (Ihre). Cf. Goth. *kaupatjan,* to strike with the hand.

Cuff (2), part of the sleeve. (L.) M. E. *cuffe, coffe.* Late A. S. *cuffie,* a kind of cap (Leo). + M.H.G. *kupfe, kuppe, kuffe,* a coif ; see Coif. Of Lat. origin.

Cuirass. (F. — Ital. — L.) Formerly *curace.* — O. F. *cuirace* (F. *cuirasse*). — Ital. *corazza,* a cuirass; Low L. *coratia.* Formed from *coracius**, put for L. *coriaceus,* leathern. — L. *corium,* leather (whence F. *cuir,* leather). + Lith. *skurà,* Gk. *χόριον,* a hide. (√ SKAR.)

excoriate. (L.) Erom pp. of L. *excoriare,* to strip off skin. — L. *ex,* off ; *corium,* hide, skin (above).

scourge. (F. — L.) O. F. *escorgie* (F. *écourgée*), a scourge. Cf. Ital. *scuriata,* O. Ital. *scoriata,* a scourging, *scoriare,* to whip. The Ital. *scoriata* answers to L. *excoriata,* lit. flayed off, hence a strip of leather for a whip, a thong; pp. of *excoriare,* to flay off (above).

Cuisses, pl. (F. — L.) O. F. *cuissaux,* armour for the thighs. — F. *cuisse,* thigh. — L. *coxa,* hip.

Culdee. (C.) Gael. *cuilteach,* a Culdee; Irish *ceilede,* a Culdee, a servant of God, from Ir. *ceile,* servant; and *dé,* gen. of *dia,* God.

Culinary. (L.) L. *culinarius*, belonging to the kitchen. — L. *culina*, kitchen.

Cull; see **Legend.**

Cullender; see **Colander.**

Cullion, a wretch. (F. — L.) A coarse word. F. *couillon* (Ital. *coglione*). — L. *coleus*.

Culm. (L.) L. *culmus*, a stalk; allied to *calamus*, a stalk. See **Haulm.**

Culminate. (L.) From pp. of L. *culminare*, to come to a top. — L. *culmin-*, stem of *culmen* (=*columen*), a top. See **Column.**

Culpable. (F. — L.) O. F. *culpable*, *colpable* (F. *coupable*). — L. *culpabilis*, blameworthy. — L. *culpare*, to blame. — L. *culpa*, a fault.

culprit. (L.) In Dryden. A corruption of *culpate*, i. e. an accused person. — L. *culpatus*, pp. of *culpare* (above). ¶ The *r* is inserted, as in *cart-r-idge*, *part-r-idge.*

exculpate. (L.) From pp. of L. *exculpare*, to clear of blame.

inculpate. (L.) From pp. of Low L. *in-culpare*, to bring blame upon.

Culter; see **Coulter.**

Cultivate, Culture; see **Colony.**

Culver. (E.) A. S. *culfre*, a dove.

Culverin. (F. — L.) Corrupt form, for *culevrin *.* — O. F. *couleuvrine*, a culverin; a piece of ordnance named from its long shape, like a snake. — O. F. *couleuvrin*, adder-like. — L. *colubra, coluber*, an adder.

Culvert; see **Colander.**

Cumber; see **Cumulate.**

Cumin, Cummin, a plant. (L. — Gk. — Heb.) M. E. *comin.* A. S. *cumin*, *cymen.* — L. *cuminum*, Matt. xxiii. 23. — Gk. *κύμινον.* — Heb. *kammón*, cumin.

Cumulate. (L.) From pp. of L. *cumulare*, to heap up. — L. *cumulus*, a heap. (√KU.)

accumulate. (L.) From pp. of L. *ac-cumulare*, to amass; (*ac-* = *ad*).

cumber. (F. — L.) M. E. *combren.* — O. F. *combrer*, to hinder. — Low L. *cumbrus*, a heap; corruption of L. *cumulus*, a heap. Thus *cumber* = to put a heap in the way. Der. *en-cumber*, from O. F. *encombrer*, to encumber, load.

Cuneate, wedge-shaped. (L.) With suffix *-ate*, from L. *cune-us*, a wedge. Allied to **Cone.** Der. *cunei-form*; i. e. wedge-shaped. See **Coin.**

Cunning, sb. and adj.; see **Can** (1).

Cup. (L.) A. S. *cuppe*, a cup. — L. *cupa*, a tub; in late L., a drinking-vessel; whence also Du. Dan. *kop*, F. *coupe*, &c.

+ O. Slav. *kupa*, Gk. *κύπελλον*, a cup. *κύπη*, a hollow; Skt. *kúpa*, a hollow.

cupboard. (L. *and* E.) M. E. *cupborde*, orig. a side-board for holding cups; Allit. Poems, B. 1140; Morte Arth. 206.

cupola. (Ital. — L.) Ital. *cupola*, a dome; from its shape. — Low L. *cupa*, a cup.

Cupid, god of love. (L.) L. *cupido*, desire. — L. *cupere*, to desire. + Skt. *kup*, to become excited. Der. *cupid-i-ty*, F. *cupidité*, from L. *cupiditas.*

concupiscence. (F. — L.) F. *concupiscence.* — L. *concupiscentia*, desire. — L. *concupiscere*, to desire; inceptive form of *concupere.*

covet. (F. — L.) M. E. *coueiten.* — O. F. *coueiter* (F. *convoiter*). Cf. Ital. *cubitare* (for *cupitare*), to covet. Formed, as if from L. *cupiditare**, from *cupidus*, desirous of. — L. *cupere*, to desire (above).

Cupola; see **Cup.**

Cupreous; see **Copper.**

Cur. (Scand.) M. E. *curre.* — Swed. dial. *kurre*, a dog. + O. Du. *korre*, a house-dog. Named from growling. — Icel. *kurra*, to murmur, grumble.

Curate; see **Cure.**

Curb; see **Curve.**

Curd. (C.) M. E. *curd, crud.* — Irish *cruth, gruth*, Gael. *gruth*, curds. Cf. W. *crwd*, a round lump.

Cure. (F. — L.) O. F. *cure.* — L. *cura*, attention. ¶ *Not* allied to *care.*

accurate. (L.) ' From pp. of L. *ac-curare*, to take pains with; (*ac-* = *ad*).

assure. (F. — L.) M. E. *assuren.* — O. F. *aseürer*, to make secure. — O. F. *a* (=L. *ad*); *seür*, sure; see sure below.

curate. (L.) Low L. *curatus*, a priest, curate; *curatum beneficium*, a benefice with cure of souls. — L. *cura*, cure.

curious. (F. — L.) O. F. *curios.* — L. *curiosus*, attentive. — L. *cura*, attention.

ensure, to make sure. (F. — L.) Compounded of F. *en* (L. *in*), in; and O. F. *seür*, sure; see sure (below).

proctor. (L.) M. E. *proketour*; short form of *procuratour.* — O. F. *procurator.* — L. acc. *procuratorem*; see below.

procurator. (L.) L. *procurator*, a manager, deputy. — L. *pro-curare*; see below.

procure. (F. — L.) F. *procurer.* — L. *pro-curare*, to take care of, manage.

proxy. (Low L. — L.) Short for *procuracy.* — Low L. *procuratia*, used for L.

procuratio, management. — L. *procurare*, to manage (above).

scour. (F. — L.) O. F. *escurer*, to scour. Cf. Span. *escurar*, O. Ital. *scurare*, to scour, rub up. — L. *excurare*, to take great care of. — L. *ex*, very; *curare*, to take care, from *cura*, care.

secure. (L.) L. *se-curus*, free from anxiety. — L. *se-*, apart from; *cura*, anxiety.

sicker, siker, certain, secure. (L.) M. E. *siker*. Borrowed from L. *securus*, secure; whence also O. Fries. *siker, sikur*, Du. *zeker*, G. *sicher*, O. H. G. *sichur*, Swed. *säker*, Dan. *sikker*, W. *sicr*. See **secure** (above).

sinecure. (L.) For *sine curâ*, without cure of souls.

sure. (F. — L.) O. F. *seür* (F. *sûr*), earliest form *segur*. — L. *securus*; see **secure** above. Doublet, *secure*.

Curfew; see **Cover.**

Curious; see **Cure.**

Curl, sb. (O. Low G.) M. E. *crul* (with shifting of *r*). — O. Du. *krul*, a curl, *krullen*, to curl; Dan. *krölle*, a curl, Swed. *krullig*, curly. Prob. O. Du. *krullen* is short for *kreukelen*, to crimp, crumple, from *kreuk*, a crook; see **Crook.**

Curlew, a bird. (F.) O. F. *corlieu*, 'a curlue;' Cot. Cf. Ital. *chiurlo*, a curlew, *chiurlare*, to howl, Swed. *kurla*, to coo; so that it is named from its cry.

Curmudgeon. (E. *and* F.) Formerly *corn-mudgin* (Phil. Holland); it means a hoarder of corn, hence a stingy fellow. *Mudgin* is for *mudging*, pres. pt. of *mudge*, to hoard, also spelt *mooch* (M. E. *muchen*), to skulk; from O. F. *mucer*, to hide, to lurk (of unknown origin).

Currant. (F. — L. — Gk.) Formerly *raysyns of corouns.* — F. *raisins de Corinthe*, 'currants,' Cot. Hence *currant* is a corruption of *Corinth* (L. *Corinthus*, Gk. Κόρινθος).

Current, running, flowing. (F. — L.) M. E. *currant*, O. F. *curant*, pres. pt. of *curre, corre* (F. *courir*), to run. — L. *currere*, to run. **+** Skt. *char*, to move. (√KAR.)

coarse, rough. (F. — L.) Formerly *course*, an adj. which arose from the phrase *in course* to denote anything of an ordinary character; cf. mod. E. *of course*. See **course** (below).

concourse. (F. — L.) F. *concours.* — L. *concursus*, a running together. — L. *concursus*, pp. of *con-currere*, to run together.

concur. (L.) L. *con-currere*, to run together, agree.

corridor. (F. — Ital. — L.) F. *corridor.* — Ital. *corridore*, a swift horse; also, a long (running along) gallery. — Ital. *correre*, to run. — L. *currere*, to run.

corsair. (F. — Prov. — L.) F. *corsaire.* — Prov. *corsari*, one who makes the course (*corsa*). — Prov. *corsa*, a course, cruise. — L. *cursus*, a course; *cursus*, pp. of *currere*.

courier. (F. — L.) F. *courier*, a runner. — F. *courir*, to run. — L. *currere*.

course. (F. — L.) F. *course.* — L. *cursum*, acc. of *cursus*, a course; from pp. of *currere*. Der. *cours-er*, a swift horse.

curricle. (L.) L. *curriculum*, a running; also, a light car. — L. *currere*, to run.

cursive. (L.) Low L. *cursivus*, flowing; said of hand-writing. — L. *curs-us*, pp. of *currere*, to run.

cursory. (L.) Low L. *cursorius*, hasty. — L. *cursori-*, crude form of *cursor*, a runner. — L. *curs-us* (above).

discourse. (F. — L.) O. F. *discours*, sb. — L. *discursus*, a running about; also, conversation. — L. *discursus*, pp. of *dis-currere*, to run about.

discursive. (L.) From pp. *discursus*.

excursion. (L.) L. *excursionem*, acc. of *excursio*, a running out. — L. *excursus*, pp. of *ex-currere*, to run out.

incur. (L.) L. *in-currere*, to run into, run upon, befall.

incursion. (F. — L.) F. *incursion.* — L. *incursionem*, acc. of *incursio*, an inroad. — L. *incursus*, pp. of *in-currere*, to run into, attack.

intercourse. (F. — L.) Modified from F. *entrecours*, intercourse, commerce. — Low L. *inter-cursus*, commerce; lit. a running between or amongst.

occur. (F. — L.) F. *occurrer.* — L. *occurrere*, to run to meet, occur; (*oc-* = *ob*.)

precursor. (L.) L. *præ-cursor*, a fore-runner; see **cursory** (above).

recourse. (F. — L.) F. *recours.* — L. *recursum*, acc. of *recursus*, a running back; from pp. of *re-currere*, to run back.

recur. (L.) L. *re-currere*, to run back, recur.

succour. (F. — L.) M. E. *socouren.* — O. F. *sucurre* (Burguy). Mod. F. *secourir.* — L. *suc-currere*, to run under or to, run to help, aid (*suc-* = *sub*).

Curry (1), to dress leather. (F. — L. *and* Teut.) O. F. *conroier, conreier* (Burguy), later *conroyer, courroier*, to curry, dress leather, orig. to prepare. — O. F. *conroi*, gear, preparation. A hybrid word; made by prefixing *con-* (=L. *con-*, *cum*) to O. F. *roi*, order (Ital. *-redo* in *arredo*, array). β. This O. F. *roi* is of Scand. origin; from Dan. *rede*, order, also to set in order, Icel. *reiδi*, tackle. Precisely the same O. F. *roi* helps to form E. *ar-ray*; see **Array.** ¶ To *curry favour* is a corruption of M. E. *to curry favel*, to rub down a horse; *Favel* was a common old name for a horse.

Curry (2), a seasoned dish. (Tamil.) From Tamil *kari*, sauce (Yule); not from Pers. *khur*, meat, relish.

Curse. (E.) A.S. *cursian*, verb; *curs*, sb., an imprecation. **Der.** *ac-cursed*, from M. E. *acorsien*, to curse extremely, where the prefix *a-* = A. S. *á-*, very; see **A-** (4).

Cursive, Cursory; see **Current.**

Curt. (L.) L. *curtus*, short, cut short. See **Short.** (√ SKAR.)

curtail. (F.—L.) It has nothing to do with *tail*; but is a corruption of the older form *curtal*, verb, to dock; from the adj. *curtal*, having a docked tail (All's Well, ii. 3. 65). — O. F. *courtault*, later *courtaut*, 'curtall, being curtalled;' Cot. The same as Ital. *cortaldo*, 'a curtall, a horse sans taile,' Florio. Formed, with suffix *-ault* (=Ital. *-aldo*, Low L. *-aldus*, from G. *wald*, power), from O. F. *court*, short. — L. *curtus*, short (as above).

Curtain; see **Court.**

Curtleaxe; see **Coulter.**

Curtsey; see **Court.**

Curve, a bent line. (L.) L. *curuus*, bent. + Gk. κύρτος, bent. Allied to **Circle.** **Der.** *curv-at-ure*, L. *curuatura*, from pp. of *curuare*, to bend; from *curuus*.

curb. (F.—L.) M. E. *courben*, to bend. F. *courber*, to bend, bow. — L. *curuare* (above).

curvet. (Ital.—L.) Ital. *corvetta*, a curvet, leap, bound. — O. Ital. *corvare* (now *curvare*), to bend, crook, stoop, bend about. — L. *curuare*, to bend.

incurvate, to crook. (L.) From pp. of L. *in-curuare*, to bend into a curve.

kerbstone. (F.—L.; *and* E.) Here *kerb* is for *curb*; so called because the stone *curbs* the stone-work or keeps it in its place; or from its being, as round a well, on a *curved* edge.

Cushat, the ring-dove. (E.) A.S. *cusceote,* a wild pigeon.

Cushion; see **Quilt.**

Cusp. (L.) L. *cuspis*, a point.

Custard; see **Crust.**

Custody. (L.) L. *custodia*, a keeping guard. — L. *custodi-*, crude form of *custos*, a guardian; lit. 'hider.' Cf. Gk. κεύθειν, to hide. See **Hide.** (√ KUDH.)

Custom. (F. — L.) M. E. *custume*. — O. F. *custume, costume*; Low L. *costuma*. The Low L. *costuma* (as in other cases) is due to neut. pl. *consuetumina*, from a sing. *consuetumen*, a word used in place of L. *consuetudo*, custom (Littré). — L. *consuetus*, pp. of *consuescere*, to accustom, inchoative form of *consuere*, to be accustomed. — L. *con-* (*cum*), together, very; *suere*, to be accustomed (Lucretius). *Suere* is prob. from *suus*, own; so that *suere* = to make one's own, have it one's own way.

accustom. (F.—L.) O. F. *estre acostumé,* to be accustomed. — F. *a* (for L. *ad*); O. F. *costume,* custom (above).

costume. (F.—Ital.—L.) O.F. *costume,* a costume. — Ital. *costume.* — Low L. *costuma* (as above). Doublet of *custom*.

desuetude, disuse. (L.) L. *desuetudo,* disuse. — L. *desuetus,* pp. of *de-suescere,* to grow out of use, opposed to *con-suescere* ; see **Custom.**

Cut. (C.) M. E. *cutten,* a weak verb. — — W. *cwtau,* to shorten, dock; compare W. *cwtws,* a lot, with M. E. *cut,* a lot (Ch. C. T. 837). So also Gael. *cutaich,* to shorten, cut short. Cf. also W. *cwt,* a tail; Gael. and Ir. *cut,* a short tail; Corn. *cut,* short. See **Coot.**

Cuticle. (L.) L. *cuticula,* double dimin. of *cutis,* hide, skin. See **Hide.** (√ KU, SKU.) **Der.** *cut-an-e-ous,* from *cut-is*.

Cutlass, Cutler; see **Coulter.**

Cutlet; see **Coast.**

Cuttle, a fish. (E.) Formerly *cudele*. A.S. *cudele,* a cuttle-fish. Altered to *cuttle* by the influence of G. *kuttelfisch*.

Cycle. (F.—L.—Gk.) F. *cycle.* — L. *cyclum,* acc. of *cyclus.* — Gk. κύκλος, a circle, cycle. + Skt. *chakra,* a wheel, circle. Allied to **Curve, Circle.** **Der.** *cyclone* = Gk. κυκλῶν, whirling round, pres. pt. of κυκλόω, I whirl round; *epi-cycle*; *bi-cycle.* Also *en-cyclo-pædia,* instruction in the circle of sciences; from Gk. ἐγκυκλοπαιδεία, put for ἐγκύκλιος παιδεία, circular or complete instruction (see **Pedagogue**). Also. *encyclical,* circular, from Gk. ἐγκύκλι-ος, circular; used of an epistle which goes round to many.

Cygnet, a young swan. (F. — L.) Dimin. of O. F. *cigne,* a swan. Strangely enough, th:s O. F. word is *not* from L. *cycnus,* a swan; but the oldest O. F. spelling was *cisne,* 'from Low L. *cecinus,* a swan. See Diez; 4th ed. p. 714.

Cylinder. (F. — L. — Gk.) O. F. *cilindre,* later *cylindre.* — L. *cylindrus.* — Gk. κύλινδρος, a roller, cylinder. — Gk. κυλίνδειν, to roll; from κυλίειν, to roll. Cf. Russ. *kolo,* a wheel. (√ KAL.)

calender, a machine for smoothing cloth. (F. — L. — Gk.) 'Calender, to press linen;' Bailey. — F. *calendrer,* to smooth linen; *calandre,* sb., a calender. — Low L. *celendra,* a calender; corruption of L. *cylindrus,* a roller (as above). Der. *calender,* a smoother of linen, a mistaken form for *calendrer.*

Cymbal. (F. — L. — Gk.) M. E. *cimbale.* — O. F. *cimbale.* — L. *cymbalum.* — Gk. κύμβαλον, a cymbal; named from its cuplike shape. — Gk. κύμβη, a cup. + Skt. *kumbhá,* a jar. Allied to **Cup**; and see **Comb** (2). (√ KUBH.)

chime, sb. (F. — L. — Gk.) M. E. *chimbe,* of which the orig. sense was cymbal; hence the chime or ringing of a cymbal. Shortened from F. *chimbale,* dialectal form of O. F. *cimbale* (above). Der. *chime,* verb.

Cynic, lit. dog-like. (L. — Gk.) L. *cynicus.* — Gk. κυνικός, dog-like, a Cynic. — Gk. κυν-, stem of κύων, a dog; see **Canine.**

cynosure. (L. — Gk.) L. *cynosura,* the stars in the tail of the constellation of the Lesser Bear; one of these is the Pole-star, or centre of attraction to the magnet. — Gk. κυνόσουρα, the Cynosure, tail of the Lesser Bear; lit. 'dog's tail.' — Gk. κύνος, gen. of κύων, a dog; οὐρά, a tail.

quinsy. (F. — Gk.) Formerly *squinancy.* — O. F. *squinancie* (16th cent.); also *squinance,* 'the squinancy or squinzie;' Cot. Formed with prefixed *s* (= O. F. *es-,* L. *ex,* very) from Gk. κυνάγκη, lit. a dog-throttling, applied to a bad kind of sore throat. — Gk. κύν-, stem of κύων, a dog; ἄγχ-ειν, to choke.

Cypress (1), a tree. (F. — L. — Gk.) M. E. *cipres.* — O. F. *cypres,* later *cyprés.* — L. *cyparissus, cupressus.* — Gk. κυπάρισσος, cypress-tree.

Cypress (2), a kind of crape. (F. — L.) Palsgrave explains F. *crespe* by 'a cypress for a woman's neck'; Cot-grave has '*crespe,* cipres, cobweb lawn.' The origin of *cypress* is doubtful; but it occurs as *cipres, cypirs* in P. Plow-man, and we find *kirsp,* fine linen, in Dunbar. Hence it is prob. corrupted from O. F. *crespe,* crape. See p. 101, col. 1, l. 23. ¶ Or from the isle of *Cyprus.*

Cyst, a pouch (in animals) containing morbid matter. (L. — Gk.) Formerly written *cystis.* — Late L. *cystis.* — Gk. κύστις, a bag, pouch. — Gk. κύειν, to contain. (√ KU.)

Czar, the emperor of Russia. (Russ. — L.) Russ. *tsare* (with *e* mute), a king. Cor-rupted from L. *Cæsar.* ¶ This has been disputed; but see Matt. xiii. 24 in Schleicher, Indogermanische Chrestoma-thie, p. 275, where O. Slav. *cesarstvo* occurs for mod. Russ. *tsarstvo,* kingdom. Der. *czarowitz,* from Russ. *tsarevich,* czar's son.

D.

Dab (1), to strike gently. (E.) M. E. *dabben;* also *dabbe,* a blow. Not in A. S. + O. Du. *dabben,* to pinch, fumble, dabble; G. *tappen,* to grope, prov. G. *tappe,* fist, blow. See **Tap.**

dabble. (E.) To keep on dabbing; frequent. of *dab.* + O. Du. *dabbelen,* to fumble, dabble; frequent. of O. Du. *dabben* (above).

Dab (2), expert. (L. ?) Supposed to be a corruption of *adept.*

Dabble; see **Dab** (1).

Dab-chick; see **Dive.**

Dace; see **Dart.**

Dactyl. (L. — Gk.) L. *dactylus,* the metrical foot marked − ∪ ∪. — Gk. δάκτυλος, a finger, a dactyl. See **Toe.**

date (2), fruit of the palm. (F. — L. — Gk.) M. E. *date.* — O. F. *date* (F. *datte*), a date. — L. *dactylum,* acc. of *dactylus.* — Gk. δάκτυλος, a date. Prob. *not* allied to δάκτυλος above, but of Semitic origin.

Dad. (C.) W. *tad,* Irish *daid,* Bret. *tat, tad,* father. + Gk. τάτα, Skt. *tata,* dad.

Daffodil; see **Asphodel.**

Dagger. (C.) M. E. *daggere;* allied to

daggen, to pierce. – W. *dagr*, Irish *daigear*, a dagger; O. Gael. *daga*, a dagger, pistol; Bret. *dag, dager* (whence F. *dague*).

Daggle; see Dew.

Daguerrotype. (F. *and* Gk.) Formed by adding *-o-type* to F. *Daguerre*, a personal name, the inventor (A.D. 1838).

Dahlia. (Swed.) Named after *Dahl*, a Swedish botanist.

Dainty; see Dignity.

Dairy; see Dike.

Dais; see Disc.

Daisy; see Day.

Dale, a valley. (Scand.) M. E. *dale*. – – Icel. *dalr*, Dan. Swed. *dal*, a dale. + Du. *dal*; Goth. *dals*; G. *thal*.

dell, a dale. (E.) M. E. *delle*. A. S. *del*, dat. *delle*; Cartularium Saxon. i. 547, ii. 71.

dollar. (Du. – G.) Du. *daalder*, a dollar. Adapted and borrowed from G. *thaler*, a dollar. The G. *thaler* is short for *Joachimsthaler*, a coin made from silver found in *Joachimsthal* (Joachim's dale) in Bohemia, ab. A.D. 1518.

Dally; see Dwell.

Dam (1), a mound, bank against water. (E.) A. S. *damm*, only in the derived verb *for-demman*, to dam up.+Du. *dam*, Icel. *dammr*, Dan. *dam*, Swed. *damm*, M. H. G. *tam*, G. *damm*, a dam, dike. Goth. *faurdammjan*, to dam up.

Dam (2), a mother; see Domain.

Damage; see Damn.

Damask. (Syria.) M. E. *damaske*, cloth of Damascus. Heb. *dmeseq*, damask, *Dammeseq*, Damascus (Gen. xiv. 15). Der. *damask-rose*; *damask-ine*, to inlay with gold (F. *damasquiner*).

damson. (Syria.) F. *damaisine*, a Damascene plum. – F. *Damas*, Damascus.

Dame; see Domain.

Damn, to condemn. (F. – L.) M. E. *damnen, dampnen*. – F. *damner*. – L. *damnare*, to condemn, fine. – L. *damnum*, loss, fine, penalty.

condemn. (L.) L. *con-demnare*, to condemn wholly, pronounce to be guilty.

damage. (F. – L.) M. E. *damage*. – O. F. *damage* (F. *dommage*); cf. Prov. *damnatje*, answering to Low L. *damnaticum**, harm; we find Low L. *damnaticus*, condemned to the mines. – L. *damnatus*, pp. of *damnare* (above).

indemnify, to make damage good. (L.) Ill coined. – L. *in-demni-s*, unharmed, free from loss; and *-fic-are*, for *facere*, to make.

indemnity. (F. – L.) F. *indemnité*. –L. acc. *indemnitatem*. – L. *in-demni s*, unharmed, free from loss (*damnum*).

Damp. (E.) Cf. M. E. *dampen*, to suffocate. Not in A. S. + Du. *damp*, vapour, steam; Dan. *damp*, G. *dampf*, vapour; Swed. *damb*, dust. Allied to Gk. τύφος, vapour, Skt. *dhûpa*, incense. (√DHU.) See Dust.

Damsel; see Domain.

Damson; see Damask.

Dance. (F. – O. H. G.) M. E. *dauncen*. – O. F. *danser*. – O. H. G. *dansón*, to drag along, trail. – O. H. G. *dinsen*, to drag, draw; allied to E. Thin.

Dandelion; see Dental.

Dandle. (E.) Cf. prov. E. *dander*, to wander idly; Lowl. Sc. *dandill*, to go about idly. Frequent. form from a low G. base DAND, to trifle; cf. O. Du. *danten*, to trifle, O. F. *dandiner*, 'to look like an ass;' Cot. + G. *tändeln*, to toy, trifle, play, dandle, lounge; from O. H. G. *tant*, a trifle, G. *tand*, a toy. Cf. O. Ital. *dandolare*, 'to dandle or play the baby,' Florio; *dandola*, a toy; words of Low G. origin.

dandy. (F. – O. Low G.) F. *dandin*, 'a meacock, noddy, ninny;' Cot. From the O. Low G. base above.

Dandriff, scurf on the head. (C.) Formerly *dandruffe*. – W. *ton*, skin, peel; whence *marwdon* (= *marw*, dead, *ton*, skin), scurf, dandriff; Bret. *tañ*, scurf. The second syllable may be accounted for by W. *drwg*, Gael. *droch*, Bret. *droug*, bad; the guttural becoming *f*, as in *rough*, &c.

Dandy; see Dandle.

Danger; see Domain.

Dangle; see Ding.

Dank; see Dew.

Dapper. (Du.) Orig. good, valiant; hence brave, fine, spruce. XV. cent. – Du. *dapper*, brave. + O. H. G. *taphar*, weighty, valiant, G. *tapfer*, brave; Goth. *gadobs*, fitting, from *gadaban*, to befit, to happen, befall. Russ. *dobrui*, good.

Dapple; see Deep.

Dare (1), to venture. (E.) M. E. *dar*, I dare; pt. t. *dorste, durste*. A. S. *ic dear*, I dare; *he dear*, he dare; pt. t. *dorste*; infin. *durran*. + Goth. *dars*, I dare, *daursta*, I durst, infin. *daursan*; O. H. G. *tar*, I dare, infin. *turran*. Gk. θαρσεῖν, to be bold, θρασύς, bold; Skt. *drish*, to dare. (√DHARS.)

Dare (2), a dace; see **Dart**.

Dark. (E.) M. E. *derk*. A. S. *deorc*.
Perhaps allied to Du. *donker*, Swed. Dan.
G. *dunkel*, Icel. *dökkr*, dark. Der. *dark-
some*.

darkling, in the dark. (E.) Formed
with adv. suffix *-ling*, as in *flat-ling*, M. E.
hedling (headlong), A. S. *bæc-ling*, backwards.

Darling; see **Dear**.

Darn. (C.) W. *darnio*, to break in
pieces, also to piece; *darn*, a piece, fragment, patch; Corn. *darn*, Bret. *darn*, a
fragment, piece. Prob. from √DAR, to
tear.

Darnel. (F. – Teut.) M. E. *darnel, der-
nel*. From an O. F. word, now only
preserved in Rouchi *darnelle*, darnel (Grand-
gagnage); named from its stupefying quali-
ties. Cf. Rouchi *daurnise, darnise*, tipsy,
giddy; O. F. *darne*, stupefied (Roquefort).
From a Teut. base seen in O. Du. *door*,
Dan. *daare*, G. *thor*, a fool, Swed. *dåra*, to
infatuate; see **Daze**.

Dart. (F. – O. Low G.) M. E. *dart*. –
O. F. *dart* (F. *dard*). Of O. Low G.
origin; A. S. *daroð*, a dart, Swed. *dart*, a
dagger, Icel. *darraðr*, a dart. Cf. A. S.
derian, to injure.

dace. (F. – O. Low G.) Formerly *darce*.
– O. F. *dars*, nom. case of the word also
spelt *dart*, meaning (1) a dart, (2) a dace.
The fish is also called a *dart*, from its swift
motion.

dare (2), a dace. (F. – O. Low G.) F.
dard, a dart (as above).

Dash. (Scand.) M. E. *daschen*. – Dan.
daske, to slap, Swed. *daska*, to beat; we
speak of water *dashing* against rocks.

Dastard; see **Daze**.

Date (1), a given point of time. (F. – L.)
M. E. *date*. – F. *date*, date. – Low L. *data*,
a date; L. *data*, neut. pl. of *datus*, given,
dated. – L. *dare*, to give. + Gk. δίδωμι,
give; δοτός, given; Skt. *dadâmi*, I give;
Russ. *darite*, to give. (√DA.)

condone (L.) L. *condonare*, to remit,
pardon. – L. *con-* (*cum*), wholly; *donare*,
to give; see donation (below).

die (2), a small cube for gaming. (F. –
L.) Used as sing. of M. E. *dys*, more usually
dees, dice. – O. F. *dez*, dice, pl. of *det*, a
die (F. *dé*). Cf. Prov. *dat*, Ital. *dado*, Span.
dado, a die. – Low L. *dadus* (orig. *datus*), a
die, lit. a thing given or shewn, i. e. thrown
forth. – L. *datus*, pp. of *dare*, to give.

donation. (F. – L.) F. *donation*. – L.

acc. *donationem*, a gift, from pp. of *donare*,
to give. – L. *donum*, a gift. + Gk. δῶρον,
a gift. (√DA, to give.)

dowager, a widow with a jointure. (F.
– L.) Coined from *dowage*, an endowment.
Again *dowage* is coined (with suffix *-age*)
from F. *dou-er*, to endow. – L. *dotare*, to
endow. – L. *dot-*, stem of *dos*, a gift, dowry.
Allied to *dare*, to give. Der. *en-dow*, from
F. *en* and *douer*.

dower, an endowment. (F. – L). M. E.
dower. – O. F. *doaire*, later *douaire*. – Low
L. *dotarium*. – L. *dotare*, to endow (above).
Der. *dowr-y*, short for *dower-y*.

edition. (L.) L. *editionem*, acc. of
editio, a publishing. – L. *editus*, pp. of
edere, to give out, publish. – L. *e*, out;
dare, to give. Der. *edit*, a coined word.

pardon, forgiveness. (F. – L.) M. E.
pardoun. – F. *pardon*, sb – F. *pardonner*,
to forgive. – Low L. *per-donare*, to remit a
debt, pardon; see Donation (above).

perdition. (F. – L.) F. *perdition*. – L.
acc. *perditionem*, utter loss. – L. *perditus*,
pp. of *perdere*, to lose. – L. *per*, thoroughly; *dare*, to give.

reddition, a restoring. (F. – L.) F.
reddition. – L. *redditionem*, acc. of *redditio*,
a restoring. – L. *reddere*, to give back. – L.
red-, back; *dare*, to give.

render. (F. – L.) M. E. *rendren*. – F.
rendre. – L. *reddere* (above).

rendezvous. (F. – L.) F. *rendezvous*,
'a rendevous, place appointed for the
assemblie of souldiers;' Cot. – F. *rendez
vous* = L. *reddite uos*, render yourselves;
imperative pl.

rent (2), annual payment. (F. – L.)
M. E. *rente*. – F. *rente*. Cf. Ital. *rendita*,
rent. – Low L. *rendita**, nasalised form of
L. *reddita*, fem. of pp. of *reddere*, to render;
see render (above).

surrender. (F. – L.) F. *surrendre*, to
give up. – F. *sur* (= L. *super*), above;
rendre, to render; see render (above).

tradition. (L.) L. *traditio*, a surrender, a tradition (Col. ii. 8). – L. *traditus*,
pp. of *tradere*, to deliver. – L. *tra-*, for
trans, across; *-dere*, for *dare*, to give.

traitor. (F. – L.) O. F. *traiteur, traï-
tor*. – L. *traditorem*, acc. of *traditor*, a
betrayer. – L. *traditus* (above).

treason. (F. – L.) M. E. *traison*. –
O. F. *traison*. – L. acc. *traditionem*; see
tradition (above).

Date (2), a fruit; see **Dactyl**.

Daub. (F. – L.) M. E. *dauben*. – O. F.

dauber, to plaster; answering to an older form *dalber**. — L. *dealbare*, to whiten, plaster. — L. *de*, down, very; *albare*, to whiten, from *albus*, white; see Alb. Cf. Span. *jalbegar* (= *dealbicare**), to plaster. (Not from 'W. *dwb*, Gael. and Ir. *dob*, plaster.) Der. *be-daub*.

Daughter. (E.) M. E. *doghter, dohter.* A. S. *dóhtor*. ✛ Du. *dochter*, Dan. *datter, dotter*, Swed. *dotter*, Icel. *dóttir*, Goth. *dauhtar*, G. *tochter*, Russ. *doche*, Gk. θυγάτηρ, Skt. *duhitri*. The Skt. *duhitti* seems to have meant 'milker' of the cows; from *duh* (= *dhugh*), to milk.

Daunt. (F. — L.) M. E. *daunten.* — O. F. *danter*; also *donter*. — L. *domitare*, to tame, subdue; frequent. of *domare*, to tame; see **Tame.**

indomitable. (L.) Coined from *in-*, not; *domitare*, to subdue (above).

Dauphin; see **Dolphin.**

Davit, a support for ships' boats. (Heb.?) Formerly spelt *David*, as if from a proper name (A.D. 1626).

Daw. (E.) From the noise made by the bird; cf. *caw*. ✛ O. H. G. *táha*, a daw; dimin. *tahele* (now G. *dohle*), a daw; whence Ital. *tacca*, a daw (Florio). Der. *jack-daw.*

Dawn; see **Day.**

Day. (E.) M. E. *day, dai, dæi.* A. S. *dæg*, pl. *dagas*. ✛ Du. Dan. Swed. *dag*, Icel. *dagr*, G. *tag*, Goth. *dags*. ¶ In no way allied to L. *dies.*

daisy. (E.) M. E. *dayësyě* (4 syllables). A. S. *dæges edge*, eye of day, i. e. sun, which it resembles.

dawn. (E.) M. E. *dawnen*; also *dawen*, of which *daw-n-en* is an extension. — A. S. *dagian*, to become day, dawn. — A. S. *dag-*, stem of *dæg.*

Daze. (Scand.) M. E. *dasen*, to stupefy. — Swed. *dasa*, to lie idle; Icel. *dasask*, to be wearied, lit. to daze oneself, where *-sk* is the reflexive suffix. The orig. sense is to be stupid, to doze; see **Doze.**

dastard. (Scand.; *with* Scand. *suffix*.) M. E. *dastard*; where *-ard* is a F. suffix, as in *dull-ard, slugg-ard*. — Icel. *dæstr*, exhausted, pp. of *dæsa*, to be out of breath; *dasaðr*, exhausted, weary, pp. of *dasask*, to be weary (above). Cf. Icel. *dasi*, a lazy fellow, O. Du. *dasaert*, a fool. The orig. sense is 'sluggard.'

dazzle, to confuse. (Scand.) From *daze*; with frequent. suffix *-le*. Der. *be-dazzle.*

De- (1), *prefix.* (L.; *or* F. — L.) L. *de*, down, away, from, very; hence sometimes F. *dé-*, O. F. *de-*.

De- (2), *prefix.* (F. — L.) F. *dé-*, O. F. *des-* ; from L. *dis-*; see **Dis-.**

Deacon. (L. — Gk.) M. E. *deken.* A. S. *diacon*. — L. *diaconus*. — Gk. διάκονος, a servant, a deacon. (√DI.)

diaconal, belonging to a deacon. (F. — L. — Gk.) F. *diaconal.* — Low L. *diaconalis*, from L. *diaconus* (above).

Dead; see **Die** (1).

Deaf. (E.) M. E. *deef.* A. S. *dedf.* ✛ Du. *doof*, Dan. *döv*, Swed. *döf*, Icel. *daufr*, Goth. *daubs*, G. *taub*. Orig. ' obfuscated ;' allied to Gk. τῦφος, smoke, darkness, stupor. (√DHU.)

Deal (1), a share. (E.) M. E. *deel.* A. S. *dál*, a share. ✛Du. *deel*, Dan. *deel*, Swed. *del*, Icel. *deilð*, Goth. *dails*, G. *theil.*

deal (2), to divide, distribute. (E.) M. E. *delen.* A. S. *dǽlan.* — A. S. *dál*, a share (above). ✛ Du. *deelen*, Dan. *dele*, Swed. *dela*, Icel. *deila*, Goth. *dailjan*, G. *theilen*; all from their respective sbs. (above).

dole, a portion. (E.) Dialectal variant of *deal* (1). M. E. *dole, dale.* A. S. *dál, gedál*, a portion; variant of A. S. *dǽl* (above).

ordeal, a severe test, judgment by fire, &c. (E.) M. E. *ordal.* A. S. *ordél, ordál*, a dealing out, judgment, decision. — A. S. *or-*, prefix, out; *dél, dál*, a dealing; see **dole** (above). The prefix *or-* = Du. *oor-*, G. *ur-*, Goth. *us-*, out. ✛Du. *oordeel*, G. *urtheil*, judgment; similarly compounded.

Deal (3), a thin board. (Du.) Du. *deel*, a plank. ✛G. *diele*; see **Thill.**

Dean; see **Decemvir.**

Dear. (E.) M. E. *dere.* A. S. *debre, dýre*, dear, precious. ✛Dan. and Swed. *dyr*, dear, costly, Icel. *dýrr*, dear, precious; G. *theuer.*

darling. (E.) M. E. *derling.* A. S. *debrling*, a favourite. — A. S. *debr-e*, dear; with double dimin. suffix *-l-ing.*

dearth, scarcity. (E.) M. E. *derthe*, dearness; hence, dearth. Not in A. S.; but formed as *heal-th, warm-th*, &c.✛Icel. *dýrð*, value; from *dýrr* (above).

Death; see **Die** (1).

Debar; see **Bar.**

Debase; see **Base.**

Debate; see **Batter** (1).

Debauch. (F. — L. *and* Teut.) O. F. *desbaucher* (F. *débaucher*), ' to debosh, mar, seduce, mislead ;' Cot. Diez supposes that the orig. sense was 'to entice away from a workshop;' it is certainly derived from the O. F. prefix des- (L. dis-), away, and O. F. bauche, explained by Roquefort as 'a little house,' and by Cotgrave as 'a course of stones or bricks in building.' Cf. F. embaucher, to use in business, employ, esbaucher, to rough-hew, frame. The orig. sense of bauche was prob. 'balk,' i.e. beam, hence frame of a building, course in building, small building, &c. ; of Teut. origin ; see Balk.

Debenture; see Habit.

Debilitate; see Habit.

Debonair. (F.) M.E. debonere, debonaire; put for de bon aire, lit of a good mien. —L. de, of; bon-us, good ; and aire, mien (=Ital. aria), a word of uncertain origin, occurring in the E. phr. 'to give oneself airs.'

Debouch. (F. — L.) F. déboucher, to uncork, to emerge from; hence, to march out of a narrow pass. — F. dé (=O. E. des-=L. dis-), away ; and bouche, mouth, opening, from L. bucca, mouth.

disembogue, to flow into the sea, as a river. (Span. — L.) Span. desembocar, to disembogue. — Span. des- (L. dis-), apart; and embocar, to enter the mouth, from em- (L. in), into, and boca (L, bucca), mouth.

embouchure. (F. — L.) F. embouchure, the mouth or opening (of a river). — F. emboucher, to put to the mouth. — L. in, in; bucca, the mouth.

Debris, broken pieces. (F. — L. and Teut.) F. débris, fragments. — O. F. desbriser, to rive asunder. — O. F. des-(=L. dis-), apart ; and M. H. G. bresten, to break, cognate with E. Burst.

Debt; see Habit.

Debut; see Beat.

Decade. (F. — Gk.) F. decade, 'a decade,' Cot.; i.e. an aggregate of ten. — Gk. δεκάδα, acc. of δεκάς, a company of ten. — Gk. δέκα, ten ; see Ten.

decagon. (Gk.) Named from its ten angles. — Gk. δέκα, ten; γων-ία, a corner, angle, allied to γόνυ, knee ; see Knee. Der. hen-decagon (ἔν, one, ἔνδεκα, eleven) ; do-decagon (δώδεκα, twelve).

decahedron. (Gk.) Named from its ten sides or bases. — Gk. δέκα, ten : ἔδρ-α, a base, lit. 'seat,' from ἔδ-ος, a seat ; see Sit. Der. do-deca-hedron (Gk. δώδεκα, twelve).

decalogue. (F. — L. — Gk). F. deca-logue. — L. decalogus. — Gk. δεκάλογος, the ten commandments. — Gk. δέκα, ten ; λόγος, a speech, saying ; see Logic.

decasyllabic, having ten syllables. (Gk.) Gk. δέκα, ten ; συλλαβή, a syllable. Der. hen-decasyllabic (Gk. ἔνδεκα, eleven).

Decamp; see Camp.

Decanal; see Decemvir.

Decant; see Cant (2).

Decapitate ; see Capital.

Decay ; see Cadence.

Decease ; see Cede.

Deceive ; see Capacious.

Decemvir, one of ten magistrates. (L.) L. decemuir, one of the decemuiri, or ten men joined in a commission. — L. decem, ten (see Ten); and uir, a man (see Virile).

dean. (F. — L.) M. E. deen. — O. F. deien (F. doyen). — L. decanus, one set oven ten soldiers, or over ten monks, a dean.

decanal. (L.) Belonging to a dean. — L. decan-us (above).

decennial, belonging to ten years. (L.) Coined from L. decenn-alis, of ten years. — L. dec-em, ten ; annus, a year.

decimal. (F. — L.) O. F. decimal. — Low L. decimalis, belonging to tithes. — L. decima, a tithe ; fem. of decimus, tenth. — L. decem, ten.

decimate. (L.) From pp. of L. decimare, to select every tenth man, for punishment. — L. decem, ten.

dime, the tenth part of a dollar. (F. — L.) F. dime, O. F. disme, tenth. — L. decimus, tenth. — L. decem.

decussate, to cross at an acute angle. (L.) From pp. of L. decussare, to cross, put into the form of an X. — L. decussis, a coin worth ten asses (as-es), and therefore marked with X, i.e. ten. — L. decem, ten; assi-, crude form of as, an ace ; see Ace.

denary, relating to tens. (L.) L. denarius, containing ten. — L. de-ni (=dec-ni), pl. ten by ten. — L. dec-em, ten. Hence denier, L. denarius, piece of ten (as-es).

Decent. (F. — L.) F. decent. — L. decent-, stem of pres. pt. of decere, to become, befit ; cf. decus, honour.

decorate. (L.) From pp. of decorare, to adorn. — L. decor-, stem of decus, honour, ornament.

decorum. (L.) L. decorum, seemliness ; neut. of decorus, seemly. — L. decor-, stem of decor, seemliness, allied to decus (above). **Der.** in-decorum.

Deception; see Capacious.

Decide; see Cæsura.

Deciduous; see Cadence.

Decimal, Decimate; see Decemvir.

Decipher; see Cipher.

Deck, to cover. (O. Du.) Du. *dekken*, to cover; *dek*, a cover, a ship's deck. Cognate with E. Thatch, q. v.

Declaim; see Claim.

Declare; see Clear.

Declension, Decline; see Incline.

Declivity; see Acclivity.

Decoct; see Cook.

Decollation; see Collar.

Decompose; see Pose (1).

Decorate, Decorum; see Decent.

Decoy; see Quiet.

Decrease; see Crescent.

Decree; see Concern.

Decrement; see Crescent.

Decrepit; see Crevice.

Decretal; see Concern.

Decry; see Querulous.

Decussate; see Decemvir.

Dedicate; see Diction.

Deduce, Deduct; see Duke.

Deed; see Do (1).

Deem; see Do (1).

Deep, profound. (E.) M. E. *deep*. A. S. *deóp*.+Du. *diep*, Dan. *dyb*, Swed. *diup*, Icel. *djúpr*, G. *tief*, Goth. *diups*. (Teut. base DUP.)

dapple, a spot on an animal. (Scand.) Icel. *depill*, a spot, dot; a dog with spots over the eyes is also called *depill*. The orig. sense is 'a little pool,' from Norweg. *dapi*, a pool. Allied to Dan. dial. *duppe*, a hole where water collects, E. *dub*, a pool; and to E. *deep*, *dip*.

depth, deepness. (Scand.) Icel. *dýpð*, depth; from *djúpr*, deep. + Du. *diepte*; Goth. *daupitha*.

dibber, dibble, a tool for setting plants. (E.) Formed with suffix *-er* or *-le* of the agent, from prov. E. *dib*, to dip, hence to make holes in earth, weakened form of **dip** (above).

dimple, a small hollow. (Scand.) Nasalised form of Norweg. *depil, dipel*, a pool; dimin. of *dapi*, a pool; see **dapple** above. Cf. Swed. dial. *depp*, a pool.

dingle. (Scand.) Formerly *dimble*, variant of *dimple* (above).

dip, to plunge, immerge. (E.) M. E. *dippen*. A. S. *dyppan*, later *dippan*; causal form from *dýpan*, to plunge in, formed (by vowel-change from *eó* to *ý*)

from *deóp*, deep (above). + Dan. *dyppe*, to dip. Compare Dive.

Deer. (E.) M. E. *deer*, an animal. A. S. *deór*, a wild animal. + Du. *dier*, Dan. *dyr*, Swed. *djur*, Icel. *dýr*, Goth. *dius*, G. *thier*, L. *fera*, Gk. θήρ, a wild beast. Der. *wilder-ness*, q. v.

Deface; see Face.

Defalcate; see Falchion.

Defame; see Fame.

Default; see Fallible.

Defeasance, Defeat; see Fact.

Defecate; see Fæces.

Defect; see Fact.

Defend. (F. — L.) M. E. *defenden*. — O. F. *defendre*. — L. *defendere*, to defend, lit. strike down or away. — L. *de*, down; *fendere**, to strike, only in comp. *de-fendere*, *of-fendere*. Cf. G. θείνειν, to strike. (√ DHAN.)

defence. (F. — L.) M. E. *defence*. — O. F. *defense*. — L. *defensa*, a defending (Tertullian). — L. *defens-us*, pp. of *defendere* (above).

fence. (F. — L.) Short for *defence*, i. e. a guard.

fend. (F. — L.) Short for *defend*, to ward off. Der. *fend-er*, (1) a metal guard for a fire, (2) a buffer to deaden a blow.

offence. (F. — L.) O. F. *offence, offense*. — L. *offensa*, an offence; orig. fem. of pp. of *of-fendere*, to dash against.

offend. (F. — L.) M. E. *offenden*. — F. *offendre*. — L. *of-fendere*, to dash or strike against, injure (*of-* = *ob-*).

Defer (1) and (2); see Fertile.

Deficient; see Fact.

Defile (1), to pollute. (F. — L.; *confused with* L. *and* E.) M. E. *defoulen*, to trample under foot; later spelling *defoyle*; see Foil (1). This word is obsolete, but it suggested a hybrid compound made by prefixing L. *de*, down, to the old word *file*, to defile (Macb. iii. 1. 65). = A. S. *fýlan*, to defile, make foul, formed (by vowel-change of *u* to *y*) from A. S. *fúl*, foul; see Foul.

Defile (2), to pass along in a file; see File (1).

Define; see Final.

Deflect; see Flexible.

Deflour; see Floral.

Defluxion; see Fluent.

Deforce; see Force.

Deform; see Form.

Defraud; see Fraud.

Defray; see Fragile.

Defunct; see Function.

Defy; see Faith.

Degenerate; see Genus.

Deglutition; see Glut.

Degrade, Degree; see Grade.

Dehiscent, gaping. (L.) L. *dehiscent-*, stem of pres. pt. of *dehiscere*, to gape open. — L. *de*, down; *hiscere*, to gape. Allied to Yawn.

Deify; see Deity.

Deign; see Dignity.

Deity. (F. — L.) M. E. *deite*. — O. F. *deite*. — L. *deitatem*, acc. of *deitas*, deity, Godhead. — L. *dei-*, for *deus*, God; cf. *diuus*, godlike. + A. S. *Tīw*, a god (whence E. *Tues-day*), Icel. *tívi*, a god, O. H. G. *Ziu*, god of war, W. *duw*, Gael. and Ir. *dia*, Gk. Ζεύς (stem ΔIϜ), Jupiter, Skt. *deva*, a god, *daiva*, divine. (√DIW.) See Tuesday.

adieu. (F. — L.) F. *à dieu*, to God, a commendation, used as a farewell saying. — L. *ad Deum*, to God.

deify. (F. — L.) M. E. *deifyen*. — O. F. *deifier*, 'to deifie,' Cot. — Low L. *deificare*. — L. *deificus*, accounting as gods. — L. *dei-*, for *deus*, a god; and *-fic-*, for *facere*, to make. Der. *deificat-ion*, due to pp. of *deificare*.

deist. (L.) From L. *de-us*; with suffix *-ist*.

deuce (2), an evil spirit, devil. (F. — L.) M. E. *deus*, used interjectionally, like mod. E. *deuce!* (Havelok). — O. F. *Deus!* O God! a common exclamation. — L. *Deus*, O God, voc. of *deus* (above). Similar corruptions in sense, esp. from good to bad, are common. So also Du. *deus*.

jovial. (F. — L.) O. F. *jovial*, sanguine, lit. born under the lucky planet Jupiter. — L. *Iouialis*, pertaining to Jupiter. — L. *Ioui-*, crude form of O. Lat. *Iouis*, Jove, whence L. *Ju-piter* (= Jove-father). *Iouis* stands for *Diouis*, allied to *deus*, god; cf. Gk. Διός, gen. case of Ζεύς. And see Diurnal.

Deject; see Jet (1).

Delay; see Tolerate.

Delectable; see Delicate.

Delegate; see Legal.

Delete, to erase. (L.) L. *deletus*, pp. of *delere*, to destroy. Root uncertain.

indelible. (F. — L.) Put for *indeleble*. — O. F. *indelebile*, 'indelible;' Cot. — L. *indelebilis*, indelible. — L. *in*, not; *delebilis*, destructible, from *delere*, to destroy.

Deleterious. (Gk.) Low L. *deleterius*;

for Gk. δηλητήριος, noxious. — Gk. δηλητήρ, a destroyer. — Gk. δηλέομαι, I harm, injure. See Tear. (√ DAR.)

Delf. (Du.) Earthenware first made at *Delft*, a town in S. Holland, about A. D. 1310.

Deliberate; see Librate.

Delicate, dainty, refined. (L.) L. *delicatus*, luxurious; allied to *delicia*, pleasure, delight. — L. *delicere*, to amuse, allure. — L. *de*, away; *lacere*, to entice.

delectable. (F. — L.) Late M. E. *delectable*. — F. *delectable*. — L. *delectabilis*, delightful. — L. *delectare*, to delight; frequent. of *de-licere*, to allure.

delicious. (F. — L.) M. E. *delicious*. — O. F. *delicieus*. — Low L. *deliciosus*, pleasant. — L. *delicia*, pleasure (above).

delight. (F. — L.) Misspelt for *delite*. M. E. *deliten*, verb. — O. F. *deliter*, *deleiter*. — L. *delectare*; see delectable.

dilettante, a lover of the fine arts. (Ital. — L.) Ital. *dilettante*, lit. 'delighting in.' — Ital. *dilettare*, to delight. — L. *delectare*, to delight; see delectable.

elicit, to coax out. (L.) From pp. of E. *e-licere*, to draw out by coaxing. — L. *e*, out; *lacere*, to entice. And see Lace.

Delineate; see Line.

Delinquent; see Licence.

Deliquesce; see Liquid.

Delirious. (L.) A coined word, from L. *delirium*, madness, which is also adopted into English. — L. *delirus*, mad; lit. 'going out of the furrow.' — L. *de*, from; and *lira*, a furrow.

Deliver; see Liberal.

Dell; see Dale.

Delta. (Gk.) Gk. δέλτα, the letter Δ; answering to Heb. *daleth*, the name of the 4th letter of the alphabet; orig. 'a door of a tent.' Der. *deltoid*. (Orig. Phœnician.)

Delude; see Ludicrous.

Deluge; see Lave.

Delve, to dig. (E.) M. E. *deluen*. A. S. *delfan*, pt. t. *dealf*, pp. *dolfen*. + Du. *delven*; M. H. G. *telben*. Extension from the base DAL, a dale. See Dale.

Demagogue. (F. — Gk.) F. *démagogue*. — Gk. δημαγωγός, a popular leader. — Gk. δῆμ-os, people; ἀγωγός, leading, from ἄγ-ειν, to lead.

Demand; see Mandate.

Demarcation; see Mark (1).

Demean; see Menace.

Demented; see Mental.

Demerit; see Merit.

Demesne; see Domain.

Demi-, half. (F. — L.) O. F. *demi*, half. — L. *dimidius*, half. — L. *di-* = *dis-*, apart; *medius*, middle; see Medium.

Demise; see Missile.

Democracy; see Aristocracy.

Demolish; see Mole (3).

Demon. (F. — L. — Gk.) O. F. *demon.* — L. *dæmon.* — Gk. δαίμων, a god, genius, spirit. (√ DA.)

Demonstrate; see Monition.

Demoralise; see Moral.

Demur. (F. — L.) O. F. *demeurer, demourer*, to tarry; hence, to hesitate. — L. *de-morari*, to delay fully.

Demure; see Moral.

Demy; a spelling of *demi-*.

Den. (E.) M. E. *den*; A.S. *denn*, a cave, allied to *denu*, a valley.+O. Du. *denne*, G. *tenne*, floor, threshing-floor, cave.

Denary; see Decemvir.

Dendroid. (Gk.) Gk. δένδρο-ν, a tree; -ειδης, like, from εἶδος, form, shape.

Denizen; see Interior.

Denominate, Denote; see Noble.

Denouement; see Node.

Denounce; see Nuncio.

Dense. (L.) L. *densus*, thick. + Gk. δασύς, thick. Der. *con-dense.*

Dent; see Dint.

Dental. (L.) Formed from L. *dent-*, stem of *dens*, a tooth, cognate with E. Tooth.

dandelion, a flower. (F. — L.) F. *dent de lion*, tooth of a lion; named from the jagged leaves. — L. *dent-em*, acc. of *dens*, tooth; *de*, prep.; *leonem*, acc. of *leo*, lion.

dentated, furnished with teeth. (L.) L. *dentatus*, toothed. — L. *dent-*, stem of *dens*.

denticle, a little tooth. (L.) L. *denticulus*, double dimin. of *dens*.

dentifrice, tooth-powder. (L.) L. *dentifricium* (Pliny). — L. *denti-*, crude form of *dens*; *fric-are*, to rub.

dentist. (L.) Coined from L. *dent-*, stem of *dens*.

dentition. (L.) L. *dentitionem*, acc. of *dentitio*, cutting of teeth. — L. *dentitus*, pp. of *dentire*, to cut teeth. — L. *denti-*, crude form of *dens*.

indent, to cut into points like teeth. (Low L.) A law term. — Low. L. *indentare*, to notch. — L. *in*, in; *dent-*, stem of *dens*, a tooth. Der. *indenture*; so called because duplicate deeds were cut with notched edges to fit one another.

Denude; see Nude.

Denunciation; see Nuncio.

Deny; see Negation.

Depart; see Part.

Depend; see Pendant.

Depict; see Picture.

Depilatory; see Pile (3).

Depletion; see Plenary.

Deplore. (F. — L.; *or* L.) O F. *deplorer.* — L. *deplorare*, to lament over. — L. *de*, fully; *plorare*, to wail, weep, make to flow, allied to *pluuia*, rain.

explore. (F. — L.) F. *explorer.* — L. *explorare*, to search out, lit. to make to flow out. — L. *ex*, out; *plorare*, to make to flow.

implore. (F. — L.) F. *implorer.* — L. *implorare*, to implore. — L. *im-* = *in*, on, upon; *plorare*, to wail.

Deploy; see Ply.

Deponent; see Position.

Depopulate; see Popular.

Deport; see Port (1).

Depose; see Pose.

Deposit, Depot; see Position.

Deprave. (F. — L.) M. E. *deprauen.* — O. F. *depraver.* — L. *deprauare*, to make crooked, distort, vitiate. — L. *de*, fully; *prauus*, crooked, depraved.

Deprecate; see Precarious.

Depreciate; see Precious.

Depredate; see Predatory.

Depress; see Press.

Deprive; see Private.

Depth; see Deep.

Depute; see Putative.

Derange; see Ring (1).

Dereliction; see Licence.

Deride; see Ridiculous.

Derive; see Rivulet.

Derm, skin. (Gk.) Gk. δέρμα, skin. — Gk. δέρειν, to flay; cognate with E. Tear, vb.

epidermis, cuticle. (L. — Gk.) L. *epidermis.* — Gk. ἐπιδέρμις, upper skin. — Gk. ἐπί, upon; δέρμ-α, skin.

pachydermatous, thick-skinned. (Gk.) Gk. παχύ-ς, thick; δερματ-, stem of δέρμα, skin. Παχύς is allied to πήγνυμι, I fix; see Pact. And see Taxidermy.

Derogate; see Rogation.

Dervis, Dervish, a Persian monk, ascetic. (Pers.) Pers. *darvísh*, poor; a dervish, who professed poverty.

Descant; see Cant (1).

Descend; see Scan.

Describe, Descry; see Scribe.

Desecrate; see Sacred.

Desert (1), a waste; see Series.

Desert (2), merit, **Deserve**; see Serve.

Deshabille; see Habit.

Desiccate; see Sack (3).

Desiderate; see Desire.

Design; see Sign.

Desire, to long for. (F.–L.) O. F. *desirer, desirrer.*–L. *desiderare,* to long for, regret, miss. Perhaps (like *considerare*) allied to *sidus,* a star, as if to turn the eyes from the stars, to regret, miss.

desiderate. (L.) L. *desideratus,* pp. of *desiderare* (above).

Desist; see State.

Desk; see Disc.

Desolate; see Sole (3).

Despair; see Desperate.

Despatch, Dispatch; see Pedal.

Desperate, hopeless. (L.) L. *desperatus,* pp. of *desperare,* to lose all hope.–L. *de,* from; *sper-,* from *spe-,* crude form of *spes,* hope. (√SPA.)

despair. (F. – L.) M. E. *despeiren, desperen.*–O. F. *desperer,* to despair.–L. *desperare* (above).

desperado, a desperate man. (Span.– L.) Span. *desperado.*–L. *desperatus,* pp. of *desperare* (above).

prosper. (F.–L.) O. F. *prosperer.*–L *prosperare,* to be prosperous.–L. *prosper,* prosperous, according to one's hope.–L. *pro,* for, according to; *sper-,* from *spes,* hope.

prosperous. (L.) L. *prosperus,* another form of *prosper,* adj.

Despise, Despite; see Species.

Despoil; see Spoil.

Despond; see Sponsor.

Despot, a tyrant. (F.–L.–Gk.) O. F. *despote.*–Low L. *despotus.*–Gk. δεσπότης, a master. The syllable *ποτ-* is allied to Gk. πόσις, husband, Skt. *pati,* lord, and to Potent. Origin of δεσ- unknown.

Desquamation, a scaling off. (L.) L. *de.* off; *squama,* a scale.

Dessert; see Serve.

Destine, Destitute; see State.

Destroy; see Structure.

Desuetude; see Custom.

Desultory; see Salient.

Detach; see Tack.

Detail; see Tailor.

Detain; see Tenable.

Detect; see Tegument.

Detention; see Tenable.

Deter; see Terror.

Deterge, to wipe off. (L.) L. *detergere,* to wipe off.–L. *de,* off; *tergere,* to wipe.

Deteriorate. (L.) L. *deterioratus,* pp. of *deteriorare,* to make worse.–L. *deterior,*

worse. Formed from *de,* away, from; with comp. suffixes *-ter-ior.* (So also *in-ter-ior* from *in.*)

Determine; see Term.

Detest; see Testament.

Dethrone; see Throne.

Detonate, to explode. (L.) L. *detonatus,* pp. of *detonare,* to explode.–L. *de,* fully; *tonare,* to thunder. (√STAN.)

Detour; see Turn.

Detraction; see Trace (1).

Detriment; see Trite.

Detrude; see Intrude.

Deuce (1), two; see Dual.

Deuce (2), a devil; see Deity.

Devastate; see Vast.

Develop; see Envelop.

Deviate; see Viaduct.

Device; see Divide.

Devil. (L.–Gk.) A. S. *deóful, deófol.*–L. *diabolus.*–Gk. διάβολος, the slanderer, the devil. – Gk. διαβάλλειν, to throw across, traduce, slander.–Gk. διά, through, across; βάλλειν, to throw; see Belemnite.

diabolical. (L.–Gk.) L. *diabolic-us,* devilish. – Gk. διαβολικός, devilish. – Gk. διάβολος, the devil (above).

Devious; see Viaduct.

Devise; see Divide.

Devoid; see Void.

Devoir; see Habit.

Devolve; see Voluble.

Devote; see Vote.

Devour; see Voracity.

Devout; see Vote.

Dew. (E.) M. E. *deu, dew.* A. S. *dedw,* dew.+Du. *dauw,* Icel *dögg* (gen. *döggvar*), Dan. *dug,* Swed. *dagg,* G. *thau.* Perhaps allied to Skt. *dháv,* to run, or *dháv,* to wash.

bedew, to cover with dew. (E.) From *dew,* with prefix *be-.*

daggle, to moisten, wet with dew or spray. (Scand.) Frequentative verb from Swed. *dagg,* Icel. *dögg,* dew. Cf. Icel. *döggva,* to bedew.

dank, moist. (Scand.) M. E. *dank,* wet (esp. with ref. to *dew*).–Swed. dial. *dank,* marshy ground; Icel. *dokk,* a pool. Nasalised form from Swed. *dagg,* dew, Icel. *dögg,* dew.

Dexter. (L.) L. *dexter,* on the right hand side, right.+Gk. δεξιός, right, Skt. *dakshina,* on the right or south, Goth. *taihswa,* right hand, W. *deheu,* right, southern, Gael. and Irish *deas* (the same). The Skt. *dakshina* is orig. 'clever;' cf. Skt. *daksha,* clever, *daksh,* to suit.

Dey, a governor of Algiers. (Turk.) Turk. *ddi*, a maternal uncle; afterwards, an officer, chieftain.

Di-, prefix, twice, double. (Gk.) Gk. δι-, for δίς, twice. + L. *bis, bi-*; Skt. *dvis, dvi-*. Allied to **Two**.

Dia-, prefix. (Gk.) Gk. διά, through, between, apart; allied to **Di-**, and to **Two**. ¶ In nearly all words beginning with *dia-*, except *diamond,. diaper, diary*.

Diabetes, a disease accompanied with excessive discharge of urine. (Gk.) Gk. διαβήτης. – Gk. διαβαίνειν, to stand with the legs apart. – Gk. διά, apart; βαίνειν, to go; see **Come**.

Diabolical; see **Devil**.

Diaconal; see **Deacon**.

Diacritic; see **Critic**.

Diadem, a fillet, crown. (F. – L. – Gk.) M.E. and O.F. *diademe*. – L. *diadema*. – Gk. διάδημα, a fillet. – Gk. διά, apart, round; δέ-ω, I bind, allied to Skt. *dá*, to bind (whence *dáman*, a garland). (√ DA.)

Diæresis; see **Heresy**.

Diagnosis; see **Gnome**.

Diagonal. (F. – L. – Gk.) F. *diagonal*. – L. *diagonalis*, running from corner to corner. – Gk. διαγώνιος (the same). – Gk. διά, through, between, across; γωνία, an angle, bend, from γόνυ, knee; see **Knee**.

Diagram; see **Grammar**.

Dial; see **Diary**.

Dialect, Dialogue; see **Logic**.

Diameter; see **Metre**.

Diamond; see **Adamant**.

Diapason, a whole octave, harmony. (L. – Gk.) L. *diapason*, an octave, concord of a note with its octave. – Gk. διαπασῶν, concord of first and last notes of an octave, lit. 'through all' the notes. – Gk. διά, through; πασῶν, gen. pl. fem. of πᾶς, all (χορδῶν being understood); see **Pan-**, prefix.

Diaper; see **Jasper**.

Diaphanous; see **Phantom**.

Diaphoretic, causing perspiration. (L. – Gk.) L. *diaphoreticus*, sudorific. – Gk. διαφορητικός (the same). – Gk. διαφόρησις, perspiration. – Gk. διαφορεῖν, to carry off (by perspiration). – Gk. διά, through; φέρειν, to bear; see **Bear**.

Diaphragm, a dividing membrane. (F. – L. – Gk.) O.F. *diaphragme*. – L. *diaphragma*. – Gk. διάφραγμα, partition, midriff. – Gk. διά, between; φράγνυμι, φράσσω, I fence in, enclose. (√ BHARK.)

Diarrhœa; see **Rheum**.

Diary. (L.) L. *diarium*, a daily allowance, also a diary. – L. *dies*, a day. (√ DIW.)

adjourn, to put off till another day. (F. – L.) O.F. *ajorner*, properly to draw near to day, to dawn. – O.F. *a* (= L. *ad*), to; Low L. *diurnare* *, from *diurnus*, daily. – L. *dies*, a day.

dial. (L.) M.E. *dial*. – Low L. *dialis*, relating to a day; hence a plate for shewing the time of day. – L. *dies*, day.

diurnal. (L.) L. *diurnalis*, daily. – L. *diurnus*, daily. – L. *dies*, a day.

journal. (F. – L.) Properly an adj., signifying 'daily.' – F. *journal*, daily. – L. *diurnalis*, daily; see diurnal.

journey. (F. – L.) M.E. *iournee*, a day's travel. – F. *journée*, a day, orig. a day's work; = Low L. *diurnata* *. – L. *diurnus*, daily. – L. *dies*, a day.

sojourn, to dwell. (F. – L.) O.F. *sojorner, sojourner*. – L. *sub*, under; *diurnare*, to stay.

Diastole; see **Stole**.

Diatonic; see **Tone**.

Diatribe. (L. – Gk.) L. *diatriba*, a place for learned disputations (hence a dispute, invective); an extension of the sense of Gk. διατριβή, a wearing away of time, waste of time, discussion. – Gk. διατρίβειν, to waste time, to discuss. – Gk. διά, thoroughly; τρίβειν, to rub, waste away; allied to L. *terere*, to rub; see **Trite**.

Dibber, Dibble; see **Deep**.

Dice, pl. of *die*; see **Date** (1).

Dicotyledon, a plant with two seed-lobes. (Gk.) From Gk. δι-, double; κοτυληδών, a cup-shaped hollow, from κοτύλη, a cup.

Dictate; see **Diction**.

Diction, talk. (F. – L.) F. *diction*. – L. *dictionem*, acc. of *dictio*, a saying. – L. *dictus*, pp. of *dicere*, to say, appoint; allied to *dicare*, to tell, publish. + Gk. δείκνυμι, I shew; Skt. *diç*, to shew; Goth. *gateihan*, to announce, G. *zeigen*, to accuse, point out. (√ DIK.)

abdicate. (L.) From pp. of L. *abdicare*, to renounce. – L. *ab*, from; *dicare*, to proclaim.

addict. (L.) L. *addictus*, pp. of *addicere*, to adjudge, assign to.

condition. (F. – L.) F. *condition*. – L. *conditionem*, acc. of *conditio*, a late spelling of *condicio*, a covenant, condition. – L. *con-* (for *cum*), together; *dic-are*, to proclaim (or from the same root).

contradict. (L.) L. *contradictus*, pp. of *contra-dicere*, to speak against.

dedicate, to devote. (L.) L. *dedicatus*, pp. of *de-dicare*, to devote.

dictate. (L.) L. *dictatus*, pp. of *dictare*, to dictate, frequentative of *dicere*, to say. Der. *dictat-or*.

dictionary. (L.) Low L. *dictionarium*, formed from *diction-*, stem of *dictio*, a saying, word. See Diction.

dight, adorned. (L.) *Dight* as pp. is short for *dighted*, from the obs. verb *dight*, to arrange, prepare, M. E. *dihten*, to prepare. A. S. *dihtan*, to set in order, arrange; borrowed from L. *dictare*, to dictate, prescribe; see dictate.

ditto. (Ital. – L.) Ital. *ditto*, that which has been said. – L. *dictum*, neut. of pp. of *dicere*, to say.

ditty. (F. – L.) M. E. *ditee*. – O. F. *dite*, a kind of poem. – L. *dictatum*, a thing dictated; neut. of *dictatus*, pp. of *dictare*; see dictate.

edict. (L.) L. *edictum*, neut. of pp. of *e-dicere*, to proclaim.

index. (L.) L. *index* (stem *indic-*), a discloser, something that indicates. – L. *indicare*, to point out (below).

indicate. (L.) From pp. of L. *indicare*, to point towards, point out.

indict. (F. – L.) For *indite* (which is the French spelling), and so pronounced.

indiction, a cycle of fifteen years. (L.) F. *indiction*, a cycle of taxes or tributes arranged for fifteen years; the lit. sense is merely 'appointment.' – L. *indictionem*, acc. of *indictio*, an appointment, esp. of a tax. – L. *indictus*, pp. of *in-dicere*, to appoint, impose a tax.

indite. (F. – L.) O. F. *indicter*, to indict, accuse; also spelt *inditer*. – Low L. *indictare*, to point out, frequent. of *indicare*, to point out. (Doubtless confused with the closely related L. *indictus*, pp. of *indicere*.)

interdict. (L.) Law L. *interdictum*, a kind of excommunication; L. *interdictum*, a decree. – L. *interdictus*, pp. of *interdicere*, to pronounce a judgment between two parties.

preach. (F. – L.) M. E. *prechen*. – O. F. *precher, prescher* (*prêcher*). – L. *prædicare* (below).

predicate. (L.) From pp. of *prædicare*, to publish, proclaim, declare.

predicament. (L.) L. *prædicamentum*, a term in logic, one of the most general classes into which things can be divided. – L. *præ-dicare* (above).

predict. (L.) L. *prædictus*, pp. of *præ-dicere*, to say beforehand, foretell. See also Benediction, Benison, Avenge, Judge, Malediction, Malison, Valediction, Verdict, Vindicate.

Didactic, instructive. (Gk.) Gk. διδακτικός, instructive. – Gk. διδάσκειν, to teach (= διδακ-σκειν*). + L. ·docere, to teach. (√DAK.)

Didapper, Divedapper, a bird; see Dive.

Die (1), to lose life. (Scand.) M. E. *dien, deyen*. – Icel. *deyja*; Swed. *dö*, Dan. *döe*, to die. + Goth. *diwan*, M. H. G. *touwen*.

dead. (E.) M. E. *deed*. A. S. *dedd*, dead. + Du. *dood*, Dan. *död*, Swed. *död*, Icel. *dauðr*, Goth. *dauths*. The Goth. *dau-ths* is formed with weak pp. suffix *-ths* from *dau*, pt. t. of strong verb *diwan*, to die.

death. (E.) M. E. *deeth*. A. S. *deáð*. + Du. *dood*, Dan. Swed. *död*, Icel. *dauði*, Goth. *dauthus*, G. *tod*. The Goth. *dauthus* is formed with suffix *-thus* from *dau*, pt. t. of the strong verb *diwan*, to die.

Die (2), a small cube for gaming; see Date (1).

Diet (1), regimen. (F. – L. – Gk.) M. E. *diete*. – O. F. *diete*, daily fare. – Low L. *dieta, diæta*, a ration of food. – Gk. δίαιτα, mode of life, diet.

Diet (2), an assembly. (F. – L. – Gk.) O. F. *diet*, 'a diete, parliament,' Cot. – Low L. *diæta*, a public assembly; also a ration of food, diet. – Gk. δίαιτα, a mode of life, diet; see Diet (1). ¶ The peculiar use of the word was due to a popular etymology which connected *diæta* with *dies*, a day; we even find *diæta* used to mean 'a day's journey;' Ducange.

Differ; see Fertile.

Difficulty; see Fact.

Diffident; see Faith.

Diffuse; see Fuse (1).

Dig; see Dike.

Digest; see Gerund.

Dight; see Diction.

Digit, a finger, figure. (L.) L. *digitus*, a finger; hence a figure, from counting on the fingers. + Gk. δάκτυλος, A. S. *tá*; see Dactyl, Toe. (√DAK, to take (Curtius).)

Dignity. (F. – L.) M. E. *dignitee*. – O. F. *digniteit*. – L. *dignitatem*, acc. of *dignitas*, worthiness. – L. *dignus*, worthy; allied to *decet*, it is fitting; see Decent.

condign, well-merited. (F. – L.) O. F. *condigne*. – L. *condignus*, very worthy. – L. *con-* (*cum*), very; *dignus*, worthy.

dainty, a delicacy. (F. – L.) M. E. *deintee*, orig. a sb., a pleasant thing. – O. F. *daintie* (i. e. *daintié*), agreeableness. – L. acc. *dignitatem* ; see **Dignity**. ¶ The O. F. *daintie* is the true popular O. F. form ; *digniteit* is a pedantic form ; cf. O. F. *dain*, old spelling of *digne*, worthy.

deign. (F. – L.) M. E. *deignen*. – O. F. *deigner*, *degner*, to deign. – L. *dignari*, to deem worthy. – L. *dignus*, worthy.

dignify. (F. – L.) O. F. *dignifier*. – Low L. *dignificare*, to make worthy. – L. *digni-*, for *dignus*, worthy; *-ficare*, for *facere*, to make.

disdain, sb. (F. – L.) M. E. *disdeyn*. – O. F. *desdein*, sb. – O. F. *desdegner*, to disdain. – O. F. *des-* (L. *dis-*), apart ; *degner* (L. *dignari*), to think worthy, from *dignus*, worthy.

Digress ; see **Grade**.

Dike, a trench, trench and embankment, bank. (E.) M. E. *dik*, also *dich* (= mod. E. *ditch*). A. S. *díc*. ✛ Du. *dijk*, Icel. *díki*, Dan. *dige*, Swed. *dike*, G. *teich*, pond, tank, Gk. τεῖχος, wall, rampart, Skt. *dehí*, rampart. All from √ DHIGH, to knead, form, mould ; as in Goth. *digan*.

dairy. (Scand.) M. E. *deyerye*, a room for a *deye*, i. e. a milk-woman, farm-servant. – Icel. *deigja*, Swed. *deja*, a maid, dairy-maid, who was also the bread-maker; the orig. sense is ' kneader of dough.' – Icel. *deig*, Swed. *deg*, dough ; see **dough** below.

dig. (E.) M. E. *diggen*; weakened form of *dikien*. A. S. *dícian*, to make a dike. – A. S. *díc*, a dike (above).

ditch. (E.) M. E. *dich*, *diche*; weakened form of M. E. *dik*, a dike; see **Dike** above.

dough. (E.) M. E. *dah*, *dogh*. A. S. *dáh*. ✛ Du. *deeg*, Dan. *deig*, Swed. *deg*, Icel. *deig*, Goth. *daigs*, a kneaded lump, G. *teig*. The Goth. *daigs* is from *digan*, to knead; see **Dike** above. (And see **Lady**.)

Dilacerate ; see **Lacerate**.

Dilapidate ; see **Lapidary**.

Dilate ; see **Tolerate**.

Dilemma ; see **Lemma**.

Dilettante ; see **Delicate**.

Diligent ; see **Legend**.

Dill, a plant. (E.) M. E. *dille*. A. S. *dile*. ✛ Du. *dille*, Dan. *dild*, Swed. *dill*, G. *dill*.

Dilute ; see **Lave**.

Dim. (E.) M. E. *dim*. A. S. *dim*, dark. ✛ Icel. *dimmr*, M. H. G. *timmer*, dim ; Swed. *dimma*, a fog, haze. Cf. O. Sax. *thim*, dim, G. *dämmerung*, dimness, L. *tenebræ*, darkness, Skt. *tamas*, gloom.

Dime; see **Decemvir**.

Dimension; see **Measure**.

Diminish; see **Minor**.

Dimissory; see **Missile**.

Dimity, a white stuff. (L. – Gk.) Low L. *dimita*, silks woven with two threads. – Gk. δίμιτος, made with a double thread. – Gk. δι-, double; μίτος, a thread of the woof.

Dimple; see **Deep**.

Din, clamour. (E.) M. E. *dine*, *dune*. A. S. *dyn*, *dyne*; *dynnan*, to resound. ✛ Icel. *dynr*, Swed. *dån*, Dan. *dön*, noise; Skt. *dhuni*, roaring, a torrent, *dhvani*, a din, *dhvan*, to resound.

Dine. (F.) M. E. *dinen*. – O. F. *disner*, F. *dîner*, to dine. – Low L. *disiunare*, short for *dis-ieiunare*. to break one's fast. – L. *dis-* ; and *ieiunus*, fasting. (Romania, viii. 95.)

dinner. (F.) M. E. *diner*; from O. F. *disner*, to dine; the infinitive mood being used as a sb.

Ding, to throw violently, beat. (E.) M. E. *dingen*, pt. t. *dang*, pp. *dungen* ; a true E. strong verb; though not found in A. S. ✛ Icel. *dengja*, Dan. *dænge*, Swed. *dänga*, to bang; all weak verbs.

dangle, to swing about. (Scand.) Dan. *dangle*, Swed. dial. *dangla*, to swing about ; cf. Swed. and Icel. *dingla*, Dan. *dingle*, to swing about; frequentative forms from *ding* (pt. t. *dang*), to throw about.

dingy, dirty. (E.) Orig. soiled with dung. A. S. *dingiung*, a dunging ; from *dung*, dung ; so also Swed. *dyngig*, dungy, from *dyng*, dung; see below.

dung. (E.) A. S. *dung*; orig. that which is thrown away; from the pp. of **Ding**. ✛ Swed. *dynga*, dung ; Dan. *dynge*, a heap, mass; G. *dung*.

Dint, a blow, force. (E.) M. E. *dint*, *dunt*; also *dent*. A. S. *dynt*, a blow. ✛ Icel. *dyntr*, a dint, *dynta*, to dint ; Swed. dial. *dunt*, a stroke; *dunta*, to strike.

dent, mark of a blow. (E.) Orig. 'a blow ;' M. E. *dent*, variant of *dint* (above).

Diocese. (F. – L. – Gk.) M. E. *diocise*. – O. F. *diocese*. – L. *diœcesis*. – Gk. διοίκησις, administration, a province, diocese. – Gk. διοικέω, I keep house, govern. – Gk. δι- (for διά), throughout; οἰκέω, I dwell, from οἶκος, a house; see **Wick**, a town.

Dioptrics; see **Optic**.

Diorama, a scene seen through a small

opening. — Gk. δι- (for διά), through; ὅραμα, a sight, from ὁράω, I see.

Dip; see **Deep**.

Diphtheria. (Gk.) From Gk. διφθέρα, leather; from the leathery nature of the false membrane formed in the disease. — Gk. δέφειν, to prepare leather.

Diphthong, a union of two vowel-sounds in one syllable. (F. — Gk.) Formerly *dipthong* (Ben Jonson). — O. F. *dipthongue*. — Gk. δίφθογγος, with two sounds. — Gk. δι- (for δίς), double; φθόγγος, sound, from φθέγγομαι, I cry out.

Diploma. (L. — Gk.) L. *diploma*, a document conferring a privilege. — Gk. δίπλωμα, a thing folded double; also, a licence, diploma (prob. orig. folded double). — Gk. δι- (δίς), double; -πλόος, folded. Der. *diplomat-ic*, from διπλωματ-, stem of δίπλωμα.

Diptera, two-winged insects. (Gk.) From Gk. δι- (δίς), double; πτερόν, a wing, from πέτομαι, I fly.

Diptych, a double-folding tablet. (L. — Gk.) Low L. pl. *diptycha*. — Gk. δίπτυχα, a pair of tablets; neut. pl. of δίπτυχος, folded in two. — Gk. δι- (δίς), double; πτύσσειν, to fold.

Dire. (L.) L. *dirus*, fearful. **+** Gk. δεινός, dreadful; allied to δέος, fear.

Direct, Dirge; see **Regent**.

Dirk, a dagger. (C.) Irish *duirc*, a poniard.

Dirt. (Scand.) M. E. *drit* (with shifted *r*). — Icel. *drit*, dirt, excrement of birds; *drita*, to void excrement. **+** O. Du. *driet*, sb., *drijten*, vb.

Dis-, *prefix*. (L.) L. *dis-*, apart; cf. Gk. δι-, apart; see **Di-**. Hence O. F. *des-*, which sometimes becomes *dis-* in E., and sometimes *de-*, as in *de-feat*. The prefix *dis-* commonly expresses the reversal of an act, somewhat like the E. verbal prefix *un-*. For most words beginning with this prefix, see the simpler forms. For example, for *dis-abuse*, see *abuse*; and so on.

Disaster; see **Aster**.

Disburse; see **Purse**.

Disc, Disk, a round plate. (L. — Gk.) L. *discus*, a quoit, a plate. — Gk. δίσκος, a quoit. — Gk. δικεῖν, to cast, throw.

· dais, a raised floor in a hall. (F. — L. — Gk.) Now used of the raised platform on which the high table in a hall stands. Properly, it was the table *itself*; but was also used of a canopy over a seat of state, or of the seat of state. M. E. *deis, deys*. —

O. F. *deis, dois*, a high table. — L. *discus*, a quoit, platter; in late L., a table. — Gk. δίσκος (above).

desk, a sloping table. (L. — Gk.) M E. *deske, desk*, a variant of *dish* or *disc*. — L. *discus*, a disc (above).

dish, a platter. (L. — Gk.) M. E. *disch*. A. S. *disc*, a dish. — L. *discus*, a quoit, platter (above).

Discern; see **Concern**.

Disciple. (F. — L.) O. F. *disciple*. — L. *discipulum*, acc. of *discipulus*, a learner. — L. *discere*, to learn; allied to *docere*, to teach; see **Docile**. Der. *discipl-ine*, O. F. *discipline*, L. *disciplina*, learning.

Disclose; see **Clause**.

Discomfit. (F. — L.) M. E. *discomfit* (Bruce). — O. F. *disconfit*, discomfited, pp. of *desconfire*, 'to discomfit, vanquish,' Cot. — O. F. *des-* (L. *dis-*); and *confire*, to preserve, make ready, from L. *con-ficere*, to preserve; see **Fact**.

Disconsolate; see **Solace**.

Discord; see **Cordial**.

Discount; see **Putative**.

Discourse; see **Current**.

Discover; see **Cover**.

Discreet; see **Concern**.

Discrepant; see **Crevice**.

Discriminate; see **Concern**.

Discursive; see **Current**.

Discuss; see **Quash**.

Disdain; see **Dignity**.

Disease; see **Ease**.

Disembark; see **Bark** (1).

Disembogue; see **Debouch**.

Disgrace; see **Grace**.

Disguise; see **Wise** (2).

Disgust; see **Gust** (2).

Dish; see **Disc**.

Dishevel; see **Capillary**.

Disinterested; see **Interest** (1).

Disk; see **Disc**.

Dislocate; see **Locus**.

Dismal. (F. — L.?) In old books, the usual phr. is '*dismal* days,' which prob. refers to tithing-time. — O. F. *dismal*, adj. — L. *decimalis*, relating to tithes. — L. *decima* (O. F. *disme*), a tithe. — L. *decem*, ten. ¶ Or else '*dismal* days' = O. F. *dis mal*. — L. *dies mali*, evil days.

Dismantle; see **Mantle**.

Dismay; see **May** (1).

Dismiss; see **Missile**.

Disparage, Disparity; see **Par**.

Dispatch: see **Pedal**.

Dispel; see **Pulsate**.

Dispense; see Pendant.

Disperse; see Sparse.

Display; see Ply.

Disport; see Port (1).

Dispose; see Pose.

Disposition; see Position.

Dispute; see Putative.

Disquisition; see Query.

Disruption; see Rupture.

Dissect; see Secant.

Dissemble; see Similar.

Disseminate; see Seminal.

Dissent; see Sense.

Dissertation; see Series.

Dissident; see Sedentary.

Dissipate. (L.) From pp. of L. *dissipare*, to disperse. — L. *dis-*, apart; and O. L. *supare*, to throw; we find also *insipare*, to throw into.

Dissociate; see Sequence.

Dissolute, Dissolve; see Solve.

Dissonant; see Sound (3).

Dissuade; see Suasion.

Distaff. (E.) A distaff is a *staff bedizened* with flax, ready to be spun off. 'I *dysyn* a *dystaffe*, I put the flaxe upon it to spynne;' Palsgrave. M. E. *distaf, dysestaf*. A.S. *distæf*. The A.S. *distæf* stands for *dise-stæf**, where *stæf* = E. staff, and *dise** = Low G. *diesse*, the bunch of flax on a distaff. See Dizen.

Distain; see Tinge.

Distant; see State.

Distemper; see Temper.

Distend; see Tend.

Distich, a couplet. (L. – Gk.) L. *distichus, distichon*. — Gk. δίστιχον, a couplet (in verse); neut. of δίστιχος, having two rows. — Gk. δι- (δίς), double; στίχος, a row, allied to στείχειν, to go. (✔STIGH.)

Distil; see Still (2).

Distinguish, to mark off. (F. – L.) O. F. *distinguer*, to distinguish; the suffix *-ish* has been added by analogy, and cannot be accounted for in the usual way. — L. *distinguere*, to mark with a prick, distinguish (pp. *distinctus*). — L. *di-* (for *dis-*), apart; *stinguere** (not in use), to prick, allied to Gk. στίζειν, to prick, and E. *sting*. (✔STIG.) See Instigate.

   distinct. (F. – L.) O. F. *distinct*. — L. *distinctus*, distinguished; pp. of *distinguere*.

   extinguish. (L.) Coined, with suffix *-ish*, from L. *extinguere*, better *exstinguere* (pp. *extinctus, exstinctus*), to quench. — L. *ex*, out; *stinguere**, to prick, also to extinguish. Der. *extinct* (from pp *extinctus*).

instinct. (F. – L.; *or* L.) F. *instinct*. sb. – L. *instinctum*, acc. of *instinctus*, an impulse. – L. *instinctus*, pp. of *in-stinguere*, to goad on.

prestige. (F. – L.) F. *prestige*, an illusion, fascination, influence due to fame. – L. *præstigium*, a deception, illusion, jugglery. – L. *præstig-*, base of *præstinguere*. to obscure, also to deceive.

Distort; see Torture.

Distract; see Trace (1).

Distrain, Distress; see Stringent.

Distribute; see Tribe.

District; see Stringent.

Disturb; see Turbid.

Ditch; see Dike.

Dithyramb, a kind of hymn. (L. – Gk.) L. *dithyrambus*. — Gk. διθύραμβος, - a hymn in honour of Bacchus.

Dittany, a plant. (F. – L. – Gk.) M. E. *dytane*. – O. F. *dictame*. – L. *dictamnum*, acc. of *dictamnus*. – Gk. δίκταμνος, dittany; named from Mount *Dictè* in Crete, where it grew.

Ditto, Ditty; see Diction.

Diuretic; see Urine.

Diurnal; see Diary.

Divan, a council-chamber, sofa. (Pers.) Pers. *díván*, a tribunal; Arab. *daywán*, a royal court, tribunal, council of state.

Divaricate; see Varicose.

Dive. (E.) M. E. *diuen, duuen* (*u* = *v*). A.S. *dýfan*, to drive, weak verb; allied to *dúfan*, strong verb (pt. t. *deáf*, pp. *dofen*), to plunge into.+Icel. *dýfa*, to dive, dip. Allied to Deep.

   dabchick. (E.) For *dap-chick*; see below.

   didapper, a bird. (E.) Short for *divedapper*. Cf. A.S. *dúfedoppa*, a pelican. Here *dapper* (= A.S. *doppa*) means a dipper or diver; and *dive-dapper* = dive-diver, a reduplicated word.

   dove, a bird. (E.) A.S. *dúfa*, lit. a diver. – A.S. *dúfan*, to plunge into. + O. Sax. *dúva*, Goth. *dubo*, G. *taube*, a dove, lit. diver. So also L. *columba*, a dove, is the same as Gk. κολυμβίς, a diver, sea-bird. First applied to sea-gulls, &c.

   dovetail, to fasten boards together. (E.) From *dove* and *tail*; from the shape of the fitted ends of the board (◁).

Diverge; see Verge (2).

Diverse, Divert; see Verse.

Divest; see Vest.

Divide. (L.) L. *diuidere*, to divide, separate (pp. *diuisus*). – L. *di-* (*dis-*), apart;

and *uidere* *, a lost verb, prob. meaning 'to know.' (√ WID.) Der. *divis-ion* (from the pp.).

device, a plan. (F. − L.) M. E. *deuise.* − O. F. *devise*, a device, also a division. − Low L. *diuisa*, a division ; also a judgment, device ; orig. fem. of pp. of *diuidere* (above).

devise, to plan. (F. − L.) M. E. *deuisen.* − O. F. *deviser.* − O. F. *devise*, sb. (above).

subdivide. (L.) L. *sub*, under ; and *diuidere*, to divide. Der. *subdivision* (from the pp.).

Divine. (F. − L.) O. F. *divin.* − L. *diuinus*, divine, god-like ; allied to *diuus*, godlike, *deus*, god ; see **Deity.**

Divorce ; see **Verse.**

Divulge ; see **Vulgar.**

Dizen, to deck out. (E.) To *dizen* was orig. to furnish a distaff with flax, hence to deck out. See **Distaff.** Der. *be-dizen.*

Dizzy ; see **Doze.**

Do (1), to perform. (E.) M. E. *don.* A. S. *dón*, pt. t. *dyde*, pp. *gedón* ; the orig. sense is ' put ' or ' place.' + Du. *doen*, O. H. G. *tuan*, G. *thun* ; Gk. τί-θη-μι, I put, Skt. *dhâ*, to place. (√ DHA.)

ado, to-do, trouble. (E.) Formerly *at do*, i.e. to do. In Northern E., *at* was used (like *to*) to express the gerund. Thus *much ado* = much to do, a great trouble. It is a Scand. idiom.

deed. (E.) M. E. *deed.* A. S. *dǽd*, lit. ' a thing done.' + Du. Dan. *daad*, Swed. *dåd*, Icel. *dáð*, Goth. *gadeds*, G. *that*, O. H. G. *tat.* Der. *mis-deed.*

deem. (E.) M. E. *demen.* A. S. *déman*, to judge, give a doom. − A. S. *dóm*, a doom ; see **doom** (below).

doff, to put off clothes. (E.) Short for *do off*, i.e. put off.

don, to put on. (E.) Short for *do on*, i.e. put on.

doom, a judgment, decision. (E.) M. E. *dom.* A. S. *dóm*, lit. a thing set or decided on ; from *dón*, to set, do ; see **Do** (above). + Swed. Dan. *dom*, Icel. *dómr*, Goth. *doms*, O. H. G. *tuom*, Gk. θέμις, law (from τίθημι, I set). Der. *deem* (above).

doomsday. (E.) A. S. *dómes dæg*, day of doom or judgment.

dout, to extinguish. (E.) Short for *do out*, i.e. put out.

dup. (E.) Short for *do up*, i.e. lift up (a latch).

indeed, in fact, truly. (E.) Put for *in deed*, i.e. in fact ; see **deed** (above).

Do (2), to be worth, be fit, avail. (E.) In the phr. ' that will *do*.' Prov. E. *dow*, to avail ; M. E. *duȝen.* A. S. *dugan*, to avail, be worth. + Du. *deugen*, Dan. *due*, Swed. *duga*, Icel. *duga*, Goth. *dugan*, G. *taugen*, to avail, be worth. (√ DHUGH.)

doughty. (E.) M. E. *duhti*, valiant. A. S. *dyhtig*, valiant. − A. S. *dugan*, to be worth, be strong (above). + Dan. *dygtig*, Swed. *dugtig*, Icel. *dygðugr*, G. *tüchtig* ; similarly formed from the verbs above. And see **Dog-cheap.**

Docile. (F. − L.) F. *docile.* − L. *docilis*, teachable. − L. *docere*, to teach. Cf. Zend *dá*, to know ; Gk. δεδαώς, taught. (√ DAK.) Allied to **Disciple** and **Didactic.**

doctor. (L.) L. *doctor*, a teacher. − L. *docere*, to teach.

doctrine. (F. − L.) F. *doctrine.* − L. *doctrina*, lore, learning. − L. *docere*, to teach.

document. (F. − L.) F. *document.* − L. *documentum*, a proof. − L. *docere*, to teach, shew.

Dock (1), to curtail. (C. ?) Perhaps from W. *tocio*, to clip, dock ; cf. *tocyn*, a short piece.

docket, a label, ticket. (C. ?) Properly a brief abstract. From the verb *dock*, to curtail (make a brief abstract).

Dock (2), a plant. (C. ?) A. S. *docce* ; but prob. borrowed from Celtic. − Gael. *dogha*, a burdock ; Irish *meacandogha*, a great burdock, where *meacan* means a tap-rooted plant, as a carrot. Der. *bur-dock.*

Dock (3), a basin for ships. (Du. − Low L. − Gk. ?) O. Du. *dokke*, a harbour (so also Dan. *dokke*, Swed. *docka*, G. *docke*). − Low L. *doga*, a ditch, canal ; also a cup. − Gk. δοχή, a receptacle. − Gk. δέχομαι, I receive. ¶ History obscure.

Docket ; see **Dock** (1).

Doctor, Doctrine, Document ; see **Docile.**

Dodecagon, Dodecahedron ; see **Decade.**

Dodge, to go hither and thither, to quibble. (E.) Orig. to walk unsteadily, hence to go from side to side as if to escape ; allied to prov. E. *dade*, to walk unsteadily, Scotch *daddle*, *doddle*, to waddle, *dod*, to jog, *dodge*, to jog along, *dodgel*, to hobble, North E. *dad*, to shake, *dodder*, to shake, totter, *dadge*, *dodge*, to walk clumsily. Cf. A. S. *dydrian*, to lead hither and thither.

Dodo, an extinct bird. (Port.) Port. *doudo*, silly, foolish ; the bird being of a clumsy make. Said to be borrowed from E. **Dolt.**

Doe. (E.) M. E. *doo.* A. S. *dá.*+Dan. *daa*; Swed. *dof-*, in *dofhjort*, a buck.

Doff. (E.) See Do (1).

Dog. (E.) M. E. *dogge.* A. S. *docga.* + Du. *dog*, Swed. *dogg*, a mastiff; Dan. *dogge*, a bull-dog. Der. *dog*, verb, to track, follow as a dog; *dogg-ed*, sullen.

Dog-cheap, very cheap. (Scand.) Swed. dial. *dog*, very; as in *dog lat*, extremely idle. —Swed. *duga*, to be fit (=A. S. *dugan*); see Do (2). So also Low G. *döger*, very much, from *dögen*, to avail.

Doge; see Duke.

Doggerel, wretched poetry. (Unknown.) M. E. *dogerel*, Ch. C. T. 13853. Origin unknown.

Dogma, a definite tenet. (Gk.) Gk. δόγμα, an opinion (stem δογματ-). — Gk. δοκέω, I am of opinion. Allied to Decorum. Der. *dogmat-ic*, *dogmat-ise.*

doxology. (L. – Gk.) L. *doxologia.* — Gk. δοξολογία, an ascription of praise. — Gk. δοξο-, for δόξα, glory, orig. a notion; λέγειν, to speak.

Doily, a small napkin. (Personal name.) Formerly we read of '*doily* stuff,' and '*doiley* petticoats.' Said to be named after 'the famous *Doily*;' Spectator, no. 283, Jan. 24, 1712. Mentioned in Dryden's Kind Keeper (1679).

Doit, a small coin. (Du.) Du. *duït*, a doit.

Dole; see Deal (1).

Doleful, sad. (Hybrid; F. – L. *and* E.) The suffix -*ful* is E. M. E. *doel, duel, dol* (Scotch *dool*), sorrow, grief. — O. F. *doel, dol* (F. *deuil*), grief; verbal sb. of O. F. *doloir*, to grieve. — L. *dolium*, in *cor-dolium*, grief of heart. — L. *dolere*, to grieve.

condole. (L.) L. *con-dolere*, to grieve with.

dolour. (F. – L.) M. E. *dolour.* — O. F. *doleur.* — L. *dolōrem*, acc. of *dolor*, grief. — L. *dolere*, to grieve.

indolence. (L.) From L. *indolentia*, freedom from pain; hence, ease, idleness. —L. *in*, not; *dolent-*, stem of pres. pt. of *dolere*, to grieve.

Doll. (Du. *or* Gk.) (1) Perhaps from O. Du. *dol*, a whipping-top; Du. *dollen*, to sport, be frolicsome. Hence perhaps 'a plaything.' See **dally**, under Dwell. (2) Otherwise, from *Doll*, for *Dorothy*; a familiar name, of Gk. origin. ¶ History obscure.

Dollar; see Dale.

Dolour; see Doleful.

Dolphin, a fish. (F. – L. – Gk.) M. E.

dolphine. – O. F. *daulphin* (now *dauphin*). – L. *delphinum*, acc. of *delphinus*, a dolphin. – Gk. δελφιν-, stem of δελφίς, a dolphin.

dauphin. (F. – L. – Gk.) F. *dauphin*, a dolphin (as above). A title of the eldest son of the king of France, who took it from the province of *Dauphiny*; and the province had formerly had several lords named *Dauphin.*

Dolt; see Dull.

Domain. (F. – L.) O. F. *domaine.* – L. *dominium*, a lordship. – L. *dominus*, a lord; allied to L. *domare*, to tame, subdue; see Tame.

dam (2), a mother, applied to animals. (F. – L.) The same word as *dame* (below).

dame. (F. – L.) M. E. *dame.* – O. F. *dame*, a lady. – L. *domina*; fem. of *dominus* (above).

damsel. (F. – L.) M. E. *damosel.* – O. F. *damoisele*, a girl, fem. of *damoisel*, a young man, squire, page. – Low L. *domicellus*, a page, short for *dominicellus**, double dimin. of *dominus*, a lord. (Pages were often of high birth.)

danger. (F. – L.) M. E. *daungere*, power, esp. power to harm. – O. F. *dangier* (F. *danger*), also *dongier* (XIII cent.), absolute power, irresponsible authority. This answers to a Low L. type *domniarium**, *dominiarium**, not found, but regularly formed from Low L. *dominium*, power, authority. – Low L. *domnus*, L. *dominus*, a lord (as above).

demesne. (F. – L.) Formerly *demain*, and merely another spelling of *domain* (above).

dominate. (L.) From pp. of *dominari*, to be lord over. – L. *dominus*, a lord.

domineer. (Du. – F. – L.) O. Du. *domineeren*, to feast luxuriously; but merely borrowed from O. F. *dominer*, to govern, rule. – L. *dominari*, to be lord over (above).

dominical. (F. – L.) O. F. *dominical.* – Low L. *dominicalis*, belonging to the Lord's day, or to the Lord. – L. *dominus*, a lord.

dominion. (Low L.) Low L. *dominionem*, acc. of *dominio*, lordship; allied to Low L. *dominium*, lordship. – L. *dominus.*

domino. (Span. – L.) Span. *domino*, a masquerade-dress; orig. a master's dress. – Span. *domine*, a master, teacher. – L. *doninus.* Der. *dominoes*, s. pl., a game.

don (2), a Spanish title. (Span. – L.) Span. *don*, sir. – L. *dominum*, acc. of *dominus.*

donna. (Ital. — L.) Ital. *donna.* — L. *domina,* fem. of *dominus.*

duenna. (Span. — L.) Span. *dueña,* a married lady, duenna. — L. *domina* (above).

dungeon, donjon. (F. — L.) M. E. *dongeon.* — O. F. *donjon,* the chief tower of a castle. — Low L. *domnionem,* acc. of *domnio,* a dungeon-tower, chief-tower, shortened from *dominio,* properly dominion, feudal power; see dominion (above).

Dome. (F. — Low L. — Gk.) O. F. *dome.* — Low L. *doma,* a house; Prov. xxi. 9 (Vulgate). — Gk. δῶμα, a house; cf. δόμος, a building. (√DAM.) See **Timber.**

domestic. (F. — L.) F. *domestique.* — L. *domesticus,* belonging to a household. — L. *dom-us,* a house.

domicile. (F. — L.) O. F. *domicile,* a mansion. — L. *domicilium,* a habitation. — L. *domi-,* for *domus,* a house; and *-cilium,* allied to *celare,* to hide (see **Cell.**)

Dominate, Domineer; see **Domain.**
Dominical, Dominion; see **Domain.**
Domino, Don (2); see **Domain.**
Don (1), to put on clothes; see **Do** (1).
Donation; see **Date** (1).
Donjon; see **dungeon, s. v. Domain.**
Donkey; see **Dun** (1).
Doom, Doomsday; see **Do** (1).

Door, a gate. (E.) M. E. *dore.* A. S. *duru.* + Du. *deur,* Dan. *dör,* Swed. *dörr,* Icel. *dyrr,* Goth. *daur,* G. *thür, thor,* L. *fores* (plural), Gk. θύρα, Skt. *dvára, dvár.*

Dormant, sleeping. (F. — L.) F. *dormant,* pres. pt. of *dormir,* to sleep. — L. *dormire,* to sleep. + Skt. *drá,* to sleep.

dormer-window. (F. and E.) A *dormer* was a sleeping-room; formed from F. *dormir* (above).

dormitory. (L.) L. *dormitorium,* a sleeping-chamber; neut. of *dormitorius,* adj., belonging to sleeping. — L. *dormitor,* a sleeper. — L. *dormire,* to sleep.

Dormouse. (Scand. and E.) Lit. a 'doze-mouse.' M. E. *dormous.* The prefix is Prov. E. *dor,* to sleep, as in *dorrer,* a sleeper (Halliwell). — Icel. *dúr,* benumbed, very sleepy, *dúrr,* slumber, *dúra,* to sleep. Cf. Icel. *dús,* a dead calm; and see **Doze.**

Dorsal. (F. — L.) F. *dorsal,* belonging to the back. — Low L. *dorsalis.* — L. *dorsum,* the back.

endorse. (F. — L.) Formerly *endosse.* O. F. *endosser,* to put on the back of. — F. *en,* on; *dos,* the back, from L. *dorsum.*

Dose. (F. — Gk.) O. F. *dose,* a quantity of medicine given at once. — Gk. δόσις, a giving. — Gk. δίδωμι (base δο-), I give. (√DA.)

anecdote. (F. — Gk.) F. *anecdote.* — Gk. ἀνέκδοτος, unpublished; hence an unpublished story, story in private life. — Gk. ἀν-, not; ἐκ, out; and δοτός, given, from δίδωμι, I give.

antidote. (F. — L. — Gk.) F. *antidote.* — L. *antidotus,* a remedy. — Gk. ἀντίδοτος, a remedy; a thing given as a remedy. — Gk. ἀντί, against; δοτός, given, from δίδωμι, I give.

Dot. (Du.) Du. *dot,* a little bundle of spoilt wool, &c., good for nothing. Cf. Swed. dial. *dott,* a little heap, small lump; from the str. vb. *detta,* to drop.

Dote. (E.) M. E. *dotien, doten,* to be foolish (Layamon). + O. Du. *doten,* to dote, mope; Du. *dutten,* to doze; Icel. *dotta,* to nod with sleep, M. H. G. *túzen,* to mope.

dotage. (E.; with F. suffix.) M. E. *dotage;* from M. E. *dot-en;* with F. suffix *-age* (L. *-aticum*).

dotard. (E. with F. suffix.) From *dote,* with F. suffix *-ard* (O. H. G. *hart*).

Double, Doublet; see **Dual.**
Doubloon, Doubt; see **Dual.**
Douceur; see **Dulcet.**
Douche; see **Duke.**
Dough; see **Dike.**
Doughty; see **Do** (2).

Douse, to immerge. (Scand.) Allied to Swed. *dunsa,* to plump down, fall clumsily, Dan. *dundse,* to thump. — Swed. dial. *duns,* a din. — Swed. dial. *duna,* to make a din; see Din. Hence to *douse* is prob. to fall plump in, as in Butler, Hudibras, pt. ii. c. 1. 502.

Dout; see **Do** (1).
Dove, Dovetail; see **Dive.**
Dowager, Dower; see **Date** (1).

Down (1), soft plumage. (Scand.) M.E. *down.* — Icel. *dúnn,* Swed. *dun,* Dan. *duun,* down. + Du. *dons,* down. Allied to Dust. (√DHU.)

Down (2), a hill. (C.) A. S. *dún,* a hill. — Irish *dún,* a fortified hill, fort; Gael. *dun,* W. *din,* a hill-fort. + A. S. *tún;* see **Town.**

down (3), prep. and adv. (E. and C.) A corruption of *adown* = A. S. *ofdúne* = off the hill, downwards. — A. S. *of,* off; *dúne,* dat. of *dún,* a hill; see **Down** (2).

dune, a low sand-hill. (C.) M. E. *dune;* the same word as *down* (above).

Dowse (1), to strike in the face. (Scand.) M. E. *duschen,* to strike. — Norweg. *dusa,* to break, cast down from. Cf. O. Du. *doesen*, to strike, E. Fries. *dössen*, to strike. Compare *dash*.

Dowse (2); see **Douse**.

Dowse (3), to extinguish. (E.) A. S. *dwæscan*, to extinguish.

Doxology; see **Dogma**.

Doxy; see **Duck** (3).

Doze. (Scand.) Icel. *dúsa*, to doze; Swed. dial. *dusa*, Dan. *döse*, to doze, mope. Allied to A. S. *dwæs*, stupefied; and prob. to E. *dor-mouse*.

dizzy. (E.) M. E. *dysy*. A. S. *dysig*, dizzy; allied to A. S. *dwæs*, stupefied.+O. Du. *duyzigh*, dizzy; allied to *dwaas*, foolish; Dan. *dösig*, drowsy, *döse*, to doze.

Dozen; see **Dual**.

Drab (1), a slut. (C.) Irish *drabog*, Gael. *drabag*, a slut; Gael. *drabach*, dirty. —Irish *drab*, a spot, stain.

drivel. (C.; *with* E. *suffix*.) M. E. *driuelen*; earlier form *drauelen*, a frequent. form from Irish *drab*, a spot, stain. (Prob. confused with *dribble*.)

Drab (2); see **Drape**.

Drachm; see **Dram**.

Draff, dregs. (E.) M. E. *draf* (Layamon). **+** Du. *draf*, hogswash; Icel. *draf*, Swed. *draf*, Dan. *drav*, dregs. Cf. Gael. and Irish *drabh*, draff; allied to **Drab** (1).

Draft, Drag; see **Draw**.

Dragoman, an interpreter. (Span. — Gk. — Arab.) Span. *dragoman*. — Late Gk. δραγούμανος, an interpreter. — Arab. *tarjumán*, an interpreter, translator; see **Targum**.

Dragon. (F. — L. — Gk.) F. *dragon.* — L. acc. *draconem*, from nom. *draco.* — Gk. δράκων, a dragon, lit. ' seeing ;' from his supposed sharp sight. — Gk. δρακ-, base of δέρκομαι, I see.

dragoon. (F. — L. — Gk.) F. *dragon*, a dragoon ; so called because the dragoons orig. had a *dragon* on their standard (see Rob. of Glouc. p. 303 ; &c.).

tarragon, a plant. (Span. — Pers. — Gk.) Span. *taragontia* (whence F. *targon*).— Pers. *tarkhún*, dragon-wort. — Gk. δράκων, a dragon.

Drain. (E.) A.S. *drehnigean, drenian*, to drain away, strain off, Matt. xxiii. 24.

Drake, male of the duck. (E.) A contraction of *ened-rake* or *end-rake*, a masc. form of A. S. *ened*, a duck. *Endrake* became *drake* by loss of *en-*.+Icel. *önd*, a duck; O. Icel. *andriki*, a drake; Swed. *and*, duck, *anddrake*, drake; Dan. *and*,

duck, *andrik*, drake; G. *ente*, duck ; *enterich*, drake. β. The A. S. *ened* is cognate with L. *anas* (stem *anat-*), a duck ; the suffix is allied to Goth. *reiks*, ruling, mighty, and to *-ric* in *bishop-ric*.

Dram, Drachm. (F. — L. — Gk.) O. F. *drame, drachme*, ' a dram, eighth part of an ounce ;' Cot. — L. *drachma*. — Gk. δραχμή, a handful, a drachma, used both as weight and coin ; cf. δράγμα, as much as one can grasp. — Gk. δράσσομαι, I grasp.

Drama. (L. — Gk.) L. *drama*. — Gk. δρᾶμα (stem δράματ-), an act, a drama. — Gk. δράω, I perform. (√ DAR.) **Der.** *dramat-ic* (from δραματ-) ; &c.

drastic, effective. (Gk.) Gk. δραστικός, effective. — Gk. δράω, I perform.

Drape, to cover with cloth. (F. — Teut.) F. *draper*, to make cloth. — F. *drap*, cloth ; Low L. *drappus*. Prob. from Icel. *drepa*, to beat (from the fulling process) ; see **Drub**. **Der.** *drap-er*, *drap-er-y*.

drab (2), dull brown. (F. — Teut.) The colour of undyed cloth. — F. *drap* (above).

Drastic; see **Drama**.

Draw. (E.) M. E. *drawen*. A.S. *dragan* (by change from *g* to *w*). **+** Du. *dragen*, Icel. Swed. *draga*, Dan. *drage*, Goth. *dragan*, G. *tragen*, to pull along, carry. Allied to Skt. *dhrágh*, to lengthen, to exert oneself. (√ DHARGH.)

drag. (E.) M. E. *draggen* ; properly the weak or causal form from A.S. *dragan*. So also Swed. *dragg*, a drag, grapnel ; whence *dragga*, to drag.

draggle. (E.) Frequentative of *drag*.

draught, draft. (E.) *Draft* is a phonetic spelling. M. E. *draught, draht.* From A.S. *drag-an* ; with suffixed *t*.**+** Du. *dragt*, a load, from *dragen*, to carry ; Dan. *dragt* ; Icel. *dráttr*, a draught of fishes.

drawl. (E.) Frequentative of *draw*; parallel to *draggle*.

dray. (E.) A.S. *dræge*, that which is drawn ; as in *dræge-net*, a draw-net. **+** Swed. *drög*, a sledge, dray.

dredge (1), a drag-net. (F. — Du.) O.F. *drege*, oyster-net. — Du. *dregnet*, a drag-net ; from *dragen*, to draw (above).

dregs, lees. (Scand.) Pl. of M. E. *dreg*, mire ; we also find M. E. *dregges*, dregs. — Icel. *dregg*, pl. *dreggjar*, dregs ; Swed. *drägg*. — Icel. *draga*, to draw, extract.

Dread, vb. (E.) A. S. *drædan, on-drædan*, to dread, fear.

Dream (1), a vision. (E.) M. E. *dreem*.

A. S. *dreám*, a sweet sound, harmony; also joy, glee, happiness; hence 'a dream of bliss.' **+** O. Sax. *dróm*, joy, dream; Du. *droom*, Icel. *draumr*, Dan. Swed. *dröm*, G. *traum*. Allied to **Drum, Drone**.

dream (2), to dream. (E.) A. S. *drý-man*, *dréman*; formed from *dreám*, sb., by change of *eá* to *ý* (as usual). **+** G. *träumen*; from *traum*.

Dreary, Drear. (E.) *Drear* is short for *dreary*. M. E. *drery*. A. S. *drebrig*, sad; orig. 'gory;' formed with suffix *-ig* from A. S. *drebr*, gore. — A. S. *drebsan*, to drip. **+** Icel. *dreyrigr*, gory, from *dreyri*, gore; G. *traurig*, sad, orig. gory, from O. H. G. *trôr*, gore.

drizzle, to rain slightly. (E.) Formerly *drisel* or *drisle*, to keep on dripping. Frequent. form of A. S. *drebsan*, to drip (above). Cf. Dan. *drysse*, to fall in drops.

dross, dregs. (E.) M. E. *dros*, properly 'sediment.' A. S. *dros*; also *drosn*, lit. 'that which falls down.' — A. S. *drebsan*, to drip, also to fall down. **+** Du. *droesem*, dregs, G. *drusen*, lees.

drowse, drowze, to be sluggish. (E.) Formerly *drouse*. A. S. *drúsian*, to be sluggish. — A. S. *drebsan*, to mourn; also to drip, to fall. Der. *drowz-y*.

Dredge (1), drag-net; see **Draw**.

Dredge (2), to sprinkle flour on meat. (F. — Prov. — Ital. — Gk.) To *dredge* is to sprinkle, as in sowing *dredge* or mixed corn. — O. F. *dragée*, mixed corn; also a sweetmeat, sugar-plum. — Prov. *dragea*. — Ital. *treggea*, a sugar-plum. — Gk. τράγημα, something nice to eat. — Gk. τρήγειν (2 aor. ἔτραγον), to gnaw; allied to τρύω, I rub.

Dregs; see **Draw**.

Drench; see **Drink**.

Dress; see **Regent**.

Dribble; see **Drop**.

Drift; see **Drive**.

Drill (1), to pierce, to train soldiers; see **Through**.

Drill (2), to sow corn in rows. (E.) The same as *drill*, to trickle, which stands for *trill*, to trickle, shortened form of *trickle*; see **Trickle**. (Prob. confused with W. *rhillio*, to put into a row, drill, from W. *rhill*, a row, short for *rhigol*, a groove, trench, dimin. of *rhig*, a groove.)

Drilling, a coarse cloth used for trousers. (G. — L.) Corrupted from G. *drillich*, ticking, huckaback. — L. *trilic-*, stem of *trilix*, having three threads. — L. *tri-*, from *tres*, three; *licium*, a thread. See **Three**.

Drink. (E.) A. S. *drincan*, pt. t. *dranc*, pp. *druncen*. **+** Du. *drinken*, Icel. *drekka*, Swed. *dricka*, Dan. *drikke*, Goth. *drigkan* (=*drinkan*), G. *trinken*.

drench, verb. (E.) M. E. *drenchen*. A. S. *drencan*, causal of *drincan*; hence 'to make drink.' **+** Du. *drenken*, Icel. *drekkja*, Swed. *dränka*, G. *tränken*.

drown. (E.) M. E. *drownen*, *druncnen*, *druncnien*. A. S. *druncnian*, to be drowned; to sink. — A. S. *druncen*, pp. of *drincan*. **+** Swed. *drunkna*, from *drucken*, drunken; Dan. *drukne*, from *drukken*, drunken.

drunkard. (E. ; *with* F. *suffix*.) From A. S. *drunc-*, base of pp. of *drincan*; with F. suffix *-ard* (G. *hart*).

drunken, drunk. (E.) A. S. *druncen*, pp. of *drincan*, to drink.

Drip; see **Drop**.

Drive. (E.) M. E. *driuen*. A. S. *drífan* (pt. t. *dráf*, pp. *drifen*). **+** Du. *drijven*; Icel. *drífa*, Swed. *drifva*, Dan. *drive*, Goth. *dreiban*, G. *treiben*. (Base DRIB.)

drift. (E.) M. E. *drift*. Formed from *drif-*, base of pp. of *drífan*; with suffix *-t*. **+** Du. *drift*, Icel. *drift*, Swed. *drift*, G. *trift*. Der. *a-drift* = on the drift; see **A** - (2).

drove. (E.) M. E. *drof*. A. S. *dráf*, a drove. From *dráf*, pt. t. of *drífan*.

Drivel; see **Drab** (1).

Drizzle; see **Dreary**.

Droll. (F. — Du. — Scand.) F. *drole*, 'a pleasant wag;' Cot. — Du. *drollig*, odd, strange. — Dan. *trold*, Swed. *troll*, Icel. *troll*, a hobgoblin, merry imp.

Dromedary. (F. — L. — Gk.) M E. *dromedarie*. — O. F. *dromedaire* (older form *dromedarie**). — Low L. *dromadarius*. — L. *dromad-*, stem of *dromas*, a dromedary. — Gk. δρομαδ-, stem of δρομάς, fast running. — Gk. δραμεῖν, to run. **+** Skt. *dram*, to run.

Drone (1), to hum. (E.) M. E. *dronen*, *drounen*. Not in A. S. **+** Du. *dreunen*, Icel. *drynja*, Swed. *dröna*, Dan. *dröne*, to drone, roar, &c. Cf. Goth. *drunjus*, a sound, Gk. θρῆνος, a dirge; Skt. *dhran*, to sound. (√ DHRAN.)

drone (2), a non-working bee. (E.) M. E. *dran*. A. S. *drán*. **+** Dan. *drone*; Swed. *drönare*, lit. 'hummer;' Icel. *drjóni*, M. H. G. *treno*, Gk. θρῶναξ. (From the *droning* sound it makes.)

Droop; see below.

Drop, sb. (E.) M. E. *drope*, sb.; hence *dropien*, *droppen*, verb. — A. S. *dropa*, sb.; *dropian*, verb. These are from the pp. *drop-en* of the strong verb *dreópan*, to drop, drip. **+** Du. *drop*, sb., Icel. *dropi*, Swed. *droppe*, Dan. *draabe*, G. *tropfe*.

dribble. (E.) Put for *dripple*, frequent. form of *drip*.

drip. (Scand.) M. E. *dryppen*. **–** Dan. *dryppe*, to drip; *dryp*, a drop. **–** Icel. *drop-i∂*, pp. of *drjúpa*, to drip. **+** A.S. *dreópan* (above).

droop, to sink, fail. (Scand.) M. E. *droupen*. **–** Icel. *drúpa*, to droop; weak verb, from *drjúpa*, strong verb, to drip. Cf. 'I am ready to *drop*,' i. e. I *droop*.

Dropsy; see **Hydra**.

Drosky, a kind of carriage. (Russ.) Russ. *drojki*, a low four-wheeled carriage (the *j* sounded as in French).

Dross; see **Dreary**.

Drought; see **Dry**.

Drove; see **Drive**.

Drown; see **Drink**.

Drowse, Drowze; see **Dreary**.

Drub, to beat. (E.) Prov. E. *drab*, to beat. A secondary verb, due to A. S. strong vb. *drepan* (pt. t. *dræp*), to beat. **+** Icel. *drepa*, to kill, slay; Swed. *drabba*, to hit, *dräpa*, to kill; Dan. *drabe*, to kill, G. *treffen*, to hit. (Base DRAP.) See **Drape**.

Drudge. (C.) M. E. *druggen*, vb.; of Celtic origin; cf. Irish *drugaire*, a drudger, drudge, slave.

Drug, Drugget; see **Dry**.

Druid, a priest of the ancient Britons. (C.) Irish *druidh*, an augur, Gael. *druidh*, W. *derwydd*, a druid.

Drum. (E. ?) Prob. E.; not found earlier than the XVI cent. **+** Dan. *drum*, a booming sound, Icel. *þruma*, to rattle; Du. *trom*, Dan. *tromme*, G. *trommel*, a drum. Cf. **Drone** (1).

Drunkard, Drunken; see **Drink**.

Drupe; see **Dryad**.

Dry. (E.) M. E. *druȝe*. A. S. *dryge*. **+** Du. *droog*, dry; G. *trocken*, dry.

drought. (E.) M. E. *drogte*, *drougte*; better *drouhthe* (P. Plowman). A. S. *drugaðe*, drought. **–** A. S. *drugian*, to dry; *dryge*, dry. **+** Du. *droogte*, drought; from *droog*, dry. (It should rather be *droughth*.)

drug. (F. **–** Du.) M. E. *drogge*, *drugge*. **–** O. F. *drogue*, a drug. **–** Du. *droog*, dry; the pl. *droogen*, lit. dried roots, was used in the special sense of 'drugs;' see **Dry**. Der. *drugg-ist*.

drugget. (F. **–** Du.) O. F. *droguet*, 'a kind of stuff that's half silk, half wool;' Cot. Dimin. of *drogue*, a drug (above), also

used in the sense of rubbish, vile stuff; from the coarseness of the material.

Dryad, a nymph of the woods. (L. **–** Gk.) L. *Dryad-*, stem of *Dryas*, a wood-nymph. **–** Gk. δρυαδ-, stem of δρυάς, the same. **–** Gk. δρῦ-s, a tree; see **Tree**.

drupe, a fleshy fruit containing a stone. (F. **–** L. **–** Gk.) F. *drupe*. **–** L. *drupa*, an over-ripe olive. **–** Gk. δρύππα, an over-ripe olive; allied to δρυπετής, meaning either (1) *ripened* on the tree (from πέπτειν), or (2), *falling* from the tree (from πίπτειν).

hamadryad, a wood-nymph. (L. **–** Gk.) L. *hamadryad-*, stem of *hamadryas*. **–** Gk. ἁμαδρυάς, a wood-nymph; the life of each nymph depended on that of the tree to which she was attached. **–** Gk. ἅμα, together with; δρῦ-s, tree.

Dual, consisting of two. (L.) L. *dualis*, dual. **–** L. *duo*, two; see **Two**.

belligerent, waging war. (L.) L. *belligerant-*, stem of *belligerans*, carrying on war. **–** L. *belli-*, for *bellum*, war; *gerens*, pres. pt. of *gerere*, to carry (see **Jest**). *Bellum* is for O. L. *duellum*; see **duel** below.

deuce (1), a two, at cards. (F. **–** L.) F. *deux*, two. **–** L. *duos*, acc. of *duo*, two.

double. (F. **–** L.) O. F. *doble*, later *double*. **–** L. *duplus*, lit. twice-full. **–** L. *du-o*, two; *-plus*, allied to *plenus*, full.

doublet. (F. **–** L.) M. E. *dobbelet*. **–** O. F. *doublet*, an inner (double) garment. **–** F. *double*, double (above).

doubloon. (F. **–** Span. **–** L.) F. *doublon*. **–** Span. *doblon*, a coin, the *double* of a pistole. **–** Span. *doblo*, double. **–** L. *duplus* (above).

doubt. (F. **–** L.) M. E. *douten*. **–** O. F. *douter*. **–** L. *dubitare*, to be of two minds; allied to *dubius*, doubtful; see **dubious** (below).

dozen, twelve. (F. **–** L.) O. F. *dosaine* (F. *douzaine*), a dozen. **–** O. F. *doze* (F. *douze*), twelve; with suffix *-aine* (L. *-aneus*). **–** L. *duodecim*, twelve. **–** L. *duo*, two; *decem*, ten.

dubious. (L.) L. *dubius*, doubtful, moving in two directions. **–** L. *du-o*, two.

duodecimo. (L.) *In duodecimo* = with 12 leaves to the sheet. **–** L. *duodecimo*, abl. of *duodecimus*, twelfth. **–** L. *duodecim*, twelve; see **dozen** above.

duel. (Ital. **–** L.) Ital. *duello*, a duel. **–** L. *duellum*, a fight between two men. **–** L. *du-o*, two.

duet. (Ital. **–** L.) Ital. *duetto*, music for two. **–** Ital. *due*, two. **–** L. *duo*, two.

duodenum, the first of the small intestines. (L.) Late Lat. *duodenum*, so called because about 12 finger-breadths long. — L. *duodeni*, twelve apiece, distributive form of *duodecim* ; see dozen (above).

duplicate, two-fold. (L.) L. *duplicatus*, pp. of *duplicare*, to double. — L. *duplic-*, stem of *duplex*, two-fold (below).

duplicity. (F. — L.) Lit. doubleness. — F. *duplicité*. — L. acc. *duplicitatem*. — L. *duplici-*, crude form of *duplex*, twofold. — L. *du-o*, two ; *plic-are*, to fold.

indubitable. (F. — L.) F. *indubitable*. — L. *indubitabilis*, not to be doubted. — L. *in*, not ; *dubitabilis*, doubtful, from *dubitare*, to doubt ; see doubt (above).

rebel. (F. — L.) The verb is from the sb., and the sb. was orig. an adj. M. E. *rebel*, adj., rebellious. — F. *rebelle*, rebellious. — L. *rebellem*, acc. of *rebellis*, renewing war. — L. *re-*, again ; *bellum*, war = O. L. *duellum*, war ; see duel (above). Der. *rebel*, sb. and verb ; *rebell-ion*, &c.

redoubtable. (F. — L.) O. F. *redoubtable*, terrible. — O. F. *redouter*, later *redoubter*, to fear. See Re- and Doubt.

Dub, to confer knighthood by a stroke. (E.) M. E. *dubben*. A. S. *dubban* ; A. S. Chron. an. 1086. + O. Swed. *dubba*, E. Fries. *dubben*, to strike, beat. ¶ Sometimes derived from O. F. *dober*, to dub ; but this is of Scand. or Low G. origin. Perhaps A. S. *dubban* was also of Scand. origin. Cf. Dab.

Dubious ; see Dual.

Ducal, Ducat ; see Duke.

Duchess, Duchy; see Duke.

Duck (1), a bird; see Duck (2).

Duck (2), to dive, bob the head. (E.) M. E. *duken, douken*. Not in A. S. + Du. *duiken*, to stoop, dive ; Dan. *dukke*, Swed. *dyka*, G. *tauchen*, to plunge, dive.

duck (1), bird. (E.) M. E. *doke, duke*. Lit. ' diver ;' the suffix *-e* represents A. S. *-a*, suffix of the agent. From the verb above. + Dan. *dukand*, lit. diving duck ; Swed. *dykfågel*, diving fowl. Der. *duck-l-ing*, with double dimin. suffix.

Duck (3), a pet, darling. (O. Low G.) E. Friesic *dok, dokke*, a doll ; Dan. *dukke*, doll, puppet ; Swed. *docka* ; M. H. G. *tocke*, a doll, term of endearment.

doxy. (O. Low G.) Cf. E. Fries. *doktje*, dimin. of *dokke*, a doll (above). Prob. introduced from the Netherlands.

Duck (4), light canvas. (Du.) A nautical word. — Du. *doek*, linen cloth, canvas. + Dan. *dug*, Swed. *duk*, Icel. *dúkr*, G. *tuch*.

Duct, Ductile ; see Duke.

Dudgeon (1), resentment. (C.) W. *dychan*, a jeer ; *dygen*, malice, dudgeon. Cf. W. *dygas*, hatred ; Corn. *duchan*, grief.

Dudgeon (2), haft of a dagger. (Unknown.) *Dudgeon-hafted* means that the haft was curiously worked or ornamented ; *dudgin* means covered with waving marks. Etym. unknown.

Due ; see Habit.

Duel ; see Dual.

Duenna ; see Domain.

Duet ; see Dual.

Duffel, coarse woollen cloth. (Du.) Du. *duffel* ; so called from *Duffel*, a place near Antwerp.

Dug, a teat. (Scand.) Allied to Swed. *dägga*, Dan. *dægge*, to suckle. Cf. Skt. *duh*, to milk.

Dugong, a sea-cow. (Malay.) Malay *dúyóng*, a sea-cow.

Duke, a leader. (F. — L.) M. E. *duk*. — O. F. *duc*. — L. *ducem*, acc. of *dux*, a leader. — L. *ducere*, to lead. (√DUK.)

abduction. (L.) L. *abductionem*, acc. of *abductio*, a leading away. — L. *ab-ducere*, to lead away (whence also E. *abduce*).

adduce. (L.) L. *ad-ducere*, to lead to ; hence, to bring forward.

conduce. (L.) L. *con-ducere*, to draw together towards, lead to.

conduct. (L.) Low L. *conductus*, defence, protection, guard, escort. — L. *conductus*, pp. of *con-ducere* (above).

conduit. (F. — L.) M. E. *conduit*. — O. F. *conduit*, a conduit. — Low L. *conductus*, a defence, escort ; also, a canal.

deduce. (L.) L. *de-ducere*, to bring down ; (hence, to infer).

deduct. (L.) Orig. to derive from. — L. *de-ducere*, to bring down.

doge, a duke of Venice. (Ital. — L.) Ital. *doge*, prov. form of *doce**, a duke. — L. *duc-em*, acc. of *dux*, a leader.

douche, a shower-bath. (F. — Ital. — L.) F. *douche*, a shower-bath. — Ital. *doccia*, a conduit, water-pipe. — Ital. *docciare*, to pour ; equivalent to Low Lat. *ductiare**, derivative of L. *ductus*, a duct ; see duct.

ducal. (F. — L.) F. *ducal*, adj. from *duc* ; see Duke.

ducat, a coin. (F. — Ital. — L.) O. F. *ducat*. — Ital. *ducato*, a ducat, also a duchy ; named from *ducatus* (duchy of Apulia) in the legend upon it ; see duchy below.

duchess. (F. — L.) F. *duchesse*, O. F. *ducesse*, fem. of *duc*, duke ; see Duke.

duchy. (F. – L.) F. *duché*. – Low L. *ducatum*, acc. of *ducatus*, a dukedom. – L. *duc-*, stem of *dux*, a duke.

duct, a conduit-pipe. (L.) L. *ductus*, a leading (hence, a duct). – L. *ductus*, pp. of *ducere*, to lead.

ductile. (F. – L.) F. *ductile*, malleable. – L. *ductilis*, easily led. – L. *duct-us*, pp. of *ducere* (above).

educate. (L.) L. *educatus*, pp. of *educare*, to educate. – L. *e-ducere*, to bring out.

educe. (L.) L. *e-ducere*, to bring out.

induce. (L.) L. *in-ducere*, to lead to.

induct. (L.) L. *induct-us*, pp. of *in-ducere*, to bring in.

introduce. (L.) L. *intro-ducere*, to bring in. Der. *introduct-ion* (from the pp.).

produce, vb. (L.) L. *pro-ducere*, to bring forward. Der. *product-ive*, *-ion* (from the pp.).

product, sb. (L.) L. *productus*, produced; pp. of *producere* (above).

redoubt, an intrenched place of retreat. (F. – Ital. – L.) F. *redoute*, formerly *redote* (Littré), redoubt. – Ital. *ridotto*, a place of retreat. – Ital. *ridotto*, *ridutto*, pp. of *ridurre*, to bring home. – L. *re-ducere*, to bring back.

reduce. (L.) Orig. to bring back. – L. *re-ducere*, to bring back. Der. *reduction* (from the pp.).

seduce, to lead astray. (L.) L. *se-ducere*, to lead aside. Der. *seduct-ion* (from the pp.).

subdue. (F. – L.) M. E. *soduen* (afterwards altered to *subdue* for clearness). – O. F. *souduire*, to seduce; but the orig. sense must have been to subdue. – L. *sub-ducere*, to bring under.

superinduce. (L.) L. *super*, beyond; and *in-ducere*, to induce.

traduce, to defame. (L.) L. *tra-ducere*, to lead over, transport, also, to defame. Here *tra-* = *trans*, across.

Dulcet, sweet. (F. – L.) O. F. *doucet* (Cot.), of which an older spelling must have been *dolcet** (Ital. *dolcetto*). – O. F. *dulce*, fem. *dols* (F. *doux*), sweet. – L. *dulcis*, sweet.

douceur. (F. – L.) F. *douceur*, lit. sweetness (hence, pleasant gift). – L. *dulcorem*, acc. of *dulcor*, sweetness. – L. *dulcis*, sweet.

dulcimer. (Span. – L.) Roquefort has F. *doulcemer* (undated); it must be borrowed from Span. *dulcemele*, a dulcimer;

named from its sweet sound. – L. *dulce melos*, sweet sound; see **Melody**.

Dull, stupid. (E.) M. E. *dul*. A. S. *dol*, foolish; put for *dwol**; cf. *gedwol-god*, a false god, idol. – A. S. *dwol-*, base of pp. of strong vb. *dwelan*, to err, be stupid. + Du. *dol*, mad; Goth. *dwals*, foolish, G. *toll*, mad. (√DHWAR.) See **Dwell**.

dolt, a stupid fellow. (E.) M. E. *dult*, blunt; extended from M. E. *dul*, dull (above).

Dumb. (E.) M. E. *domb*. A. S. *dumb*, mute. + Du. *dom*, Icel. *dumbr*, Swed. *dumb*, Dan. *dum*, Goth. *dumbs*, G. *dumm*. Goth. *dumbs* is allied to Goth. *daubs*, deaf; see **Deaf**. Der. *dumm-y* (= *dumb-y*).

Dump, an ill-shapen piece. (E. ?) Prov. E. *dump*, a clumsy lump, a bit; *dumpy*, short and thick. Lowl. Sc. *dump*, to beat, strike with the feet; Swed. dial. str. vb. *dimpa* (supine *dumpit*), to fall down plump. Cf. Du. *dompneus*, a great nose; Icel. *dumpa*, to thump; and cf. **Thump**.

dumpling, a kind of pudding. (E. ?) A small solid ball of pudding; *dump-l-ing* is a double dimin. of *dump* (above).

Dumps, melancholy. (Scand.) Swed. dial. *dumpin*, melancholy, orig. pp. of *dimba*, to steam, reek; Dan. *dump*, dull, low. + Du. *domp*, damp, hazy, G. *dumpf*, damp. Allied to **Damp**; cf. 'to *damp* one's spirits.'

Dun (1), brown. (C.) A. S. *dunn*, dark. – Irish and Gael. *donn*, brown; W. *dwn*, dun, dusky.

donkey. (C.) Double dimin. with suffix *-k-ey* (= Lowl. Sc. *-ick-ie*, as in *horsickie*, a little-little horse, Banffsh.) from *dun*, familiar name for a horse, from its colour (Romeo, i. 4. 41). ¶ So also M. E. *don-ek*, a hedge-sparrow, from its colour.

Dun (2), to urge for payment. (Scand.) Cf. M. E. *dunning*, a loud noise; to *dun* is to thunder at one's door. – Icel. *duna*, to thunder; *koma einum dyn fyrir dyrr*, to make a din before one's door; Swed. *dåna*, to make a noise. Allied to **Din**.

Dunce, a stupid person. (Scotland.) From the phr. 'a *Duns* man,' i.e. a native of *Dunse*, in Berwickshire. In ridicule of the disciples of John *Duns* Scotus, schoolman, died A. D. 1308. ¶ Not to be confused with John Scotus Erigena, died A. D. 875.

Dune, a low sand-hill; see **Down** (2).

Dung; see **Ding**.

Dungeon; see **Domain**.

Duodecimo, Duodenum; see **Dual**.

Dup; see **Do** (1).

Dupe, a person easily deceived. (F.) F. *dupe,* a dupe. The O. F. *dupe* meant a hoopoe; whence *dupe,* a dupe, because the bird was easily caught. (So also Bret. *houperik,* a hoopoe, a dupe.) Perhaps of imitative origin.

Duplicate, Duplicity; see **Dual.**

Durance, Duration; see **Dure.**

Durbar, a hall of audience, levee. (Pers.) Pers. *darbár,* a prince's court, levee; lit. 'door of admittance.' = Pers. *dar,* door (= E. *door*); and *bár,* admittance.

Dure, to last. (L.) L. *durare,* to last. = L. *durus,* hard, lasting. + Irish and Gael. *dur,* firm; W. *dir,* sure. Cf. Gk. δύναμις, force. Der. *dur-ing,* orig. pres. pt. of *dure; dur-able,* &c.

　　durance, captivity. (F. = L.) The orig. sense was long endurance of hardship. = F. *durer,* to last; with suffix *-ance;* see above.

　　duration. (L.) A coined word; from the pp. of L. *durare,* to last.

　　duress, hardship. (F. = L.) M. E. *duresse.* = O. F. *duresce.* = L. *duritia,* harshness. = L. *durus,* hard, severe.

　　endure. (F. = L.) M. E. *enduren.* = F. *endurer.* = F. *en* (L. *in*); and *durer* (L. *durare*), to last.

　　indurate, to harden. (L.) From pp. of L. *in-durare,* to harden.

　　obdurate. (L.) L. *obduratus,* pp. of *ob-durare,* to harden. = L. *ob;* and *durus,* hard.

Dusk, dim. (E.) Properly an adj. M. E. *dosk,* dark, dim; *deosc,* the same. Prob. allied to A. S. *deorc,* dark. + Swed. dial. *duska,* to drizzle; *duskug,* misty. Der. *dusk,* sb.; whence *dusk-y,* adj.

Dust. (E.) A. S. *dust.* + Du. *duist,* Icel. *dust,* dust, Dan. *dyst,* meal. Cf. G. *dunst,* vapour, fine dust. Allied to L. *fu-mus,* smoke, Skt. *dhú-li,* dust. (√DHU.)

Dutch, belonging to Holland. (G.) Properly applied to the Germans. = G. *Deutsch,* German; lit. belonging to the people; M. H. G. *diut-isk,* where the suffix *-isk* = E. *-ish,* and *diut* is cognate with A. S. *þeód,* Goth. *thiuda,* a people, nation. (√TU.)

Duty; see **Habit.**

Dwale; see **Dwell.**

Dwarf. (E.) M. E. *dwerg, dwergh;* the

f represents the guttural. A. S. *dwerg, dweorg,* a dwarf. + Du. *dwerg,* Icel. *dvergr,* Swed. Dan. *dverg,* G. *zwerg.* Cf. Vedic Skt. *dhvaras,* a (female) evil spirit. (√DHWAR.)

Dwell. (E.) M. E. *dwellen,* to linger. A. S. *dwellan,* only in the active sense to retard, also to seduce. Causal of A. S. *dwelan* (pt. t. *dwæl,* pp. *dwolen*), to be torpid or dull, to err. + Icel. *dvelja,* to dwell, delay, orig. to hinder; Swed. *dväljas,* to dwell (reflexive); Dan. *dvæle,* to linger; M. H. G. *twellen,* to hinder, delay. (√DHWAR.) And see **Dull.**

　　dally, to trifle. (E.) Prov. E. *dwallee* (Exmoor Scolding). M. E. *dalien,* to play, trifle. Allied to A. S. *dweligan,* to err, be foolish, O. Northumb. *duoliga, dwoliga,* the same, Mark, xii. 27. And see **Dull.**

　　dwale, deadly nightshade. (E.) Named from its soporific effects. A. S. *dwala,* an error, stupefaction. = A. S. *dwelan* (above). + Dan. *dvale,* stupor, *dvaledrik,* a soporific, 'dwale-drink.'

Dwindle. (E.) The frequent. form of M. E. *dwinen,* to dwindle, A. S. *dwinan,* to dwindle, languish. + Icel. *dvina, dvina,* Swed. *tvina,* to dwindle, pine away.

Dye, to colour; a colour. (E.) M. E. *deyen,* vb.; *deh,* sb. A. S. *deágian, deágan,* verb, to dye; from *deág, dedh,* sb., dye, colour. Perhaps allied to **Dew.**

Dyke; see **Dike.**

Dynamic, relating to force. (Gk.) Gk. δυναμικός, powerful. = Gk. δύναμις, power. = Gk. δύναμαι, I am strong; see **Dure.** (√DU.)

　　dynasty, lordship. (Gk.) Gk. δυναστεία, lordship. = Gk. δυνάστης, a lord. = Gk. δύναμαι, I am strong.

Dysentery, disease of the entrails. (L. = Gk.) L. *dysenteria.* = Gk. δυσεντερία. = Gk. δυσ-, prefix, with a bad sense; ἔντερα, pl., the inwards, bowels, from ἐντός, within, ἐν, in; see **Interior.**

Dyspepsy, indigestion. (L. = Gk.) L. *dyspepsia.* = Gk. δυσπεψία. = Gk. δύσπεπτος, hard to digest. = Gk. δυσ-, prefix, with a bad sense; πέπτειν, to cook, digest; see **Cook.** Der. *dyspeptic* (from δύσπεπτος).

E.

E-, prefix; see **Ex-.**

Each, every one. (E.) M. E. *eche, elch.* A. S. *ælc,* each. Supposed to stand for *ǽlc,* short for *á-líc* or *á-ge-líc,* i.e. aye-like (ever-

like). + Du. *elk,* each; O. H. G. *eógalíh,* M. H. G. *iegelich,* G. *jeglich.* See **Aye.**

Eager; see **Acid.**

Eagle; see **Aquiline.**

Eagre, tidal wave in a river. (E.) A.S. *eágor-, égor-,* in comp. *eágor-stréam,* ocean-stream.+Icel. *ægir,* ocean.

Ear (1), organ of hearing. (E.) M. E. *ere.* A.S. *eáre.* + Du. *oor,* Icel. *eyra,* Swed. *öra,* Dan. *öre,* G. *ohr,* Goth. *auso,* Russ. *ucho,* L. *auris,* Gk. *ovs.* Allied to Skt. *av,* to be pleased, L. *audire,* to hear. (√AW.)

earwig, an insect. (E.) A.S. *eár-wicga,* lit. ear-runner, from its being supposed to creep into the ear. A.S. *wicg,* a horse, or a runner; allied to **Wag.**

Ear (2), spike of corn. (E.) M.E. *er.* A.S. *ear* (pl.); Northumb. *eher.*+Du. *aar,* Icel. Dan. Swed. *ax* (for *ahs*), Goth. *ahs,* G. *ähre.* Allied to **Awn.** (√AK.)

Ear (3), to plough. (E.) M.E. *eren.* A.S. *erian,* to plough. + Icel. *erja,* Goth. *arjan,* Irish *araim,* I plough, L. *arare,* Gk. *ἀρόω,* I plough. (√AR.)

Earl. (E.) M.E. *erl.* A.S. *eorl.* + Icel. *jarl,* O. Sax. *erl,* a man.

Early; see **Ere.**

Earn. (E.) M.E. *ernien.* A.S. *earnian.* + G. *ernten,* to reap, from *ernte,* harvest, from O.H.G. *arnén,* to reap, earn. β. From the sb. seen in O. H. G. *erin,* Goth. *asans,* a harvest. (√AS.)

Earnest (1), seriousness. (E.) Properly a sb., as in 'in earnest.' M.E. *ernest,* sb. A.S. *eornest,* sb.+Du. *ernst,* sb.; G. *ernst.* (Base ARN.)

Earnest (2), a pledge. (F.–L.) The *t* is added. M. E. *ernes*; also spelt *erles, arles,* Dimin. of O. F. *erres, arres,* pl.– L. *arrha.*–Gk. *ἀρραβών,* a pledge.

Earth. (E.) M.E. *erthe.* A.S. *eorðe.* + Du. *aarde,* Icel. *jörð,* Dan. Swed. *jord,* Goth. *airtha,* G. *erde.* Cf. Gk. *ἔρα,* earth.

Earwig; see **Ear** (1).

Ease. (F.) M. E. *ese.*–O. F. *aise,* ease. Cf. Ital. *agio,* Port. *azo,* ease. Orig. unknown.

disease. (F.) O. F. *des-aise,* want of ease.–O. F. *des-* (L. *dis-*); *aise,* ease.

Easel; see **Ass.**

East, the quarter of sun-rise. (E.) M.E. *est.* A.S. *eást,* adv., in the east; *eástan,* from the east. + Du. *oost,* sb., Icel. *austr,* Dan. *öst,* Swed. *östan,* G. *osten, ost.* Also L. *aur-ora,* dawn, Gk. *ἠώς, ἔως, αὔως,* dawn, Skt. *ushas,* dawn. (√US.)

easter. (E.) M. E. *ester.* A.S. *eástor-,* in comp.; pl. *eástro,* Easter.–A.S. *Eástre,* a goddess whose festivities were in April. Allied to *East*; from the increasing light and warmth of spring.

sterling. (E.) M. E. *sterling,* a sterling coin; named from the *Esterlings* (i. e. easterlings, men of the east); this was a name for the Hanse merchants in London, temp. Henry III.–M. E. *est,* east. See **East.**

Eat. (E.) M.E. *eten.* A.S. *etan.*+Du. *eten,* Icel. *eta,* Swed. *äta,* Dan. *æde,* Goth. *itan,* G. *essen,* L. *edere,* Gk. *ἔδειν,* Skt. *ad,* to eat. (√AD.) See **Tooth.**

etch, to engrave with acids. (Du.–G.) Du. *etsen,* to etch. – G. *ätzen,* to corrode, etch; the causal of G. *essen,* to eat.

fret (1), to eat away. (E.) A.S. *fretan,* short for *for-etan,* to devour entirely. + Goth. *fra-itan,* to devour entirely; Du. *vreten,* G. *fressen* (=*ver-essen*).

orts, remnants, leavings. (E.) M. E. *ortes.* From A.S. *or-,* out (what is left); *etan,* to eat. Proved by O. Du. *orete,* a piece left after eating, Swed. dial. *oräte, uräte,* refuse fodder. The same prefix *or-* occurs in *or-deal*; for which see **Deal.**

Eaves, the clipped edge of a thatched roof. (E.) M. E. *euese*; pl. *eueses* (= *eaveses*). A.S. *efese,* a clipped edge of thatch; whence *efesian,* to shear. + Icel. *ups,* Swed. dial. *uffs,* Goth. *ubizwa,* a porch, from the projection of the eaves; O. H. G. *opasa.* Orig. sense 'that which projects or is over;' allied to **Over.** Der. *eaves-dropper,* one who stands under droppings from the eaves, a secret listener.

Ebb. (E.) M.E. *ebbe.* A.S. *ebba,* ebb of the tide. + Du. *eb, ebbe,* sb., Dan. *ebbe,* sb. and vb., Swed. *ebb,* sb. Allied to **Even.**

Ebony, a hard wood. (F.–L.–Gk.– Heb.) Formerly *ebene.*–O. F. *ebene,*ebony. –L. *hebenus, ebenum.*–Gk. *ἔβενος, ἐβένη.* – Heb. *hovním,* pl., ebony wood; prob. a non-Semitic word.

Ebriety, drunkenness. (F.–L.) F.*ebrieté.* –L. acc. *ebrietatem.*–L. *ebrius,* drunken. Der. *in-ebriate,* to make drunken.

sober. (F.–L.) M. E. *sobre.*–F. *sobre.* L. *sobrium,* acc. of *sobrius,* sober.–L. *so-* =*se-,* apart, hence, not; *ebrius,* drunk. Der. *sobriety,* F. *sobrieté,* L. acc. *sobrietatem.*

Ebullition; see **Bull** (2).

Eccentric; see **Centre.**

Ecclesiastic. (L.–Gk.) Low L. *ecclesiasticus.* – Gk. *ἐκκλησιαστικός,* belonging to the *ἐκκλησία,* i.e. assembly, church.– Gk. *ἔκκλητος,* summoned,–Gk. *ἐκκαλέω,* I call forth.–Gk. *ἐκ,* out; *καλέω,* I call.

Echo. (L.–Gk.) M. E. *ecco.*–L. *echo.* –Gk. *ἠχώ,* a sound, echo; cf. *ἦχος, ἠχή,* a ringing noise. Der. *cat-ech-ise,* q. v.

Eclat; see **Slit.**

Eclectic; see **Logic.**

Eclipse. (F. — L. — Gk.) M. E. *eclips, clips.* — O. F. *eclipse.* — L. *eclipsis.* — Gk. ἔκλειψις, a failure, esp. of light of the sun. — Gk. ἐκλείπειν, to leave out, suffer eclipse. — Gk. ἐκ, out; λείπειν, to leave.

ellipse. (L. — Gk.) Formerly *ellipsis.* — L. *ellipsis.* — Gk. ἔλλειψις, a defect, an ellipse of a word; also, an oval figure, because its plane forms with the base of the cone a less angle than that of a parabola. — Gk. ἐλλείπειν, to leave in, leave behind. — Gk. ἐλ-, for ἐν, in; λείπειν, to leave. **Der.** *elliptic-al,* adj., Gk. ἐλλειπτικός.

Eclogue; see **Logic.**

Economy. (F. — L. — Gk.) Formerly *œconomy.* — O. F. *œconomie.* — L. *œconomia.* — Gk. οἰκονομία, management of a household. — Gk. οἰκο-, for οἶκος, a house; and νέμειν, to deal out. See **Wick** (?) and **Nomad.**

ecumenical, general. (L. — Gk.) Low L. *œcumenicus.* — Gk. οἰκουμενικός, universal. — Gk. οἰκουμένη (sc. γῆ), the inhabited world, fem. of οἰκούμενος, pres. pt. pass. of οἰκέω, I inhabit. — Gk. οἶκος, a house.

Ecstasy; see **Statics.**

Ecumenical ; see **Economy.**

Eddy. (Scand.) Icel. *iða,* an eddy, whirl-pool; cf. *iða,* to whirl about; Swed. dial. *iða, idd,* Dan. dial. *ide,* the same. Formed from Icel. *ið-,* A. S. *ed-,* Goth. *id-,* back; only found as a prefix.

Edge. (E.) M. E. *egge.* A. S. *ecg,* an edge, border. + Du. *egge,* Icel. Swed. *egg,* Dan. *eg,* G. *ecke.* Cf. L. *acies,* Gk. ἀκίς, a point, Skt. *açri,* edge, corner. (√ AK.)

egg (2), to instigate. (Scand.) M. E. *eggen.* — Icel. *eggja,* to goad on. — Icel. *egg,* an edge (point).

Edible, eatable. (L.) Low L. *edibilis.* — L. *edere,* to eat; see **Eat.**

esculent, eatable. (L.) L. *esculentus,* fit for eating. — L. *escare,* to eat; from *esca,* food. Put for *edca*.* — L. *edere,* to eat.

obese, fat. (L.) L. *obesus,* (1) eaten away, wasted; (2) fat, lit. 'that which has devoured.' — L. *obesus,* pp. of *obedere,* to eat away. — L. *ob*; *edere,* to eat. **Der.** *obes-i-ty.*

Edict; see **Diction.**

Edify. (F. — L.) O. F. *edifier.* — L. *ædificare,* to build (hence, instruct). — L. *ædi-,* crude form of *ædes,* a building, orig. a hearth; *-fic-,* for *facere,* to make. (√ IDH.) **Der.** *edifice,* F. *edifice,* L. *ædificium,* a building; *ed-ile,* L. *ædilis,* a magistrate who had the care of public buildings.

Edition; see **Date** (1).

Educate, Educe; see **Duke.**

Eel. (E.) M. E. *el.* A. S. *ǽl.* + Du. *aal,* Icel. *áll,* Dan. *aal,* Swed. *ål,* G. *aal.* Allied to L. *anguilla,* an eel, *anguis,* Gk. ἔχις, Skt. *ahi,* a snake. (√ AGH.)

Efface; see **Face.**

Effect; see **Fact.**

Effeminate; see **Feminine.**

Effendi, sir, master. (Turkish — Gk.) Turk. *éfendi,* sir. — Mod. Gk. ἀφέντης, for Gk. αὐθέντης, a despotic master, ruler; see **Authentic.**

Effervesce; see **Fervent.**

Effete; see **Fetus.**

Efficicacy, Efficient; see **Fact.**

Effigy; see **Figure.**

Efflorescence; see **Floral.**

Effluence; see **Fluent.**

Effort; see **Force.**

Effrontery; see **Front.**

Effulgent; see **Fulgent.**

Effuse; see **Fuse** (1).

Egg (1), the oval body whence chickens, &c. are hatched. (Scand.) M. E. *eg,* pl. *egges.* — Icel. *egg,* Dan. *æg,* Swed. *ägg.* + A. S. *æg* (= M. E. *ey*); Du. *ei,* G. *ei,* Irish *ugh,* Gael. *ubh,* W. *wy,* L. *ouum,* Gk. ᾠόν. Allied to L. *auis,* a bird.

Egg (2), to instigate; see **Edge.**

Eglantine. (F. — L.) F. *églantine,* O. F. *aiglantine, aiglantier,* sweet-briar. — Low L. *aculent-us*,* prickly (not found), from L. *aculeus,* a prickle, dimin. of *acus,* a needle; see **aglet,** under **Acid.** (√ AK.)

Egotist, Egoist, a self-opinionated person. (L.) Coined from L. *ego,* I ; see **I.**

Egregious; see **Gregarious.**

Egress; see **Grade.**

Eh! interj. (E.) M. E. *ey.* A. S. *á, ed.* Cf. Du. *he!* G. *ei!*

Eider-duck. (Scand.) The E. *duck* is here added to Icel. *æðr,* an eider-duck (*æ* pronounced like *i* in *time*). + Dan. *ederfugl* (eider-fowl), Swed. *eider.* **Der.** *eider-down,* Icel. *æðardún.*

Eight. (E.) M. E. *eighte.* A. S. *eahta.* + Du. *acht,* Icel. *átta,* Dan. *otte,* Swed. *átta,* Goth. *ahtau,* G. *acht,* Irish *ocht,* Gael. *ochd,* W. *wyth,* L. *octo,* Gk. ὀκτώ, Skt. *ashtan.* **Der.** *eigh-teen,* A. S. *eahtatýne*; *eigh-ty,* A. S. *eahtatig*; *eigh-th,* A. S. *eahtoða.*

Either. (E.) M. E. *either, aither*; also *auther, other.* A. S. *ǽgþer,* contracted form of *ǽghwæþer.* Comp. of *á-ge-hwæþer*; where *á* = aye, *ge* is a prefix, and *hwæþer* =

whether. **+** Du. *ieder*, G. *jeder*, O. H. G. *eówedar*.

or (1), conj., offering an alternative. (E.) Short for *other*, *outher*, *auther*, the M. E. forms, which also answer to Mod. E. *either*. Hence *either* and *or* are doublets.

Ejaculate, Eject; see **Jet** (1).

Eke (1), to augment. (E.) M. E. *eken*. A. S. *écan.*+Icel. *auka*, Swed. *öka*, Dan. *öge*, Goth. *aukan* (neuter), L. *augere*. (√ WAG.)

eke (2), also. (E.) M. E. *eek*, *eke*. A. S. *eác.* **—** Du. *ook*, Icel. *auk*, Swed. *och* (and), Dan. *og* (and), G. *auch*. All from the verb above.

nickname. (E.) M. E. *nekename*, also *ekename* ; (*a nekename* = *an ekename*). See Prompt. Parv.; cf. L. *ag-nomen* (*ag-* = *ad*), G. *zuname*. From *eke* and *name.* + Icel. *auknafn*, Swed. *öknamn*, Dan. *ögenavn*, an eke-name, nickname.

Elaborate; see **Labour**.

Eland, a S. African antelope. (Du. **—** Slavonic.) Du. *eland*, an elk. Of Slav. origin; cf. Russ. *olene*, a stag; see **Elk**.

Elapse; see **Lapse**.

Elastic. (Gk.) Formerly *elastick*, i.e. springing back. Coined from Gk. ἐλάω = ἐλαύνω, I drive (fut. ἐλάσ-ω).

Elate; see **Tolerate**.

Elbow, the bend of the arm. (E.) M. E. *elbowe*. A. S. *elboga.* **—** A. S. *el-*, signifying ' elbow ;' and *boga*, a bow, a bending (see **Bow**). A. S. *el-* is allied to Goth. *aleina*, a cubit, L. *ulna*, Gk. ὠλένη, Skt. *aratni*, the elbow. (√ AR and √ BHUG.)+Du. *elleboog*, Icel. *aln-bogi*, Dan. *al-bue*, G. *ellenbogen*. See **Ell**.

Eld, old age, **Elder** (1), older; see **Old**.

Elder (2), a tree. M. E. *eller*. A. S. *ellen*, *ellern.*+Low G. *elloorn*. ¶ Distinct from *alder*.

Eldest; see **Old**.

Elect; see **Legend**.

Electric. (L. **—** Gk.) Coined from L. *electrum*, amber, which has electric properties. **—** Gk. ἤλεκτρον, amber, also shining metal ; allied to ἠλέκτωρ, gleaming, Skt. *arch*, to shine. (√ ARK.)

Electuary, a kind of confection. (F. **—** L.) M. E. *letuarie.* **—** O. F. *lectuaire*, *electuaire.* **—** L. *electuarium*, a medicine that dissolves in the mouth. Perhaps for *elinctarium* *, from *elingere*, to lick away, or from Gk. ἐκλείχειν (the same).

Eleemosynary; see **Alms**.

Elegant; see **Legend**.

Elegy, a funeral ode. (F. **—** L. **—** Gk.) O. F. *elegie.* **—** L. *elegīa.* **—** Gk. ἐλεγεία, fem. sing., an elegy ; orig. neut. pl. of ἐλεγεῖον, a distich (of lament). **—** Gk. ἔλεγος, a lament.

Element. (F. **—** L.) O. F. *element.* **—** L. *elementum*, a first principle.

Elephant. (F. **—** L. **—** Gk. **—** Heb.) M. E. *olifaunt.* **—** O. F. *olifant*, *elephant.* **—** L. *elephantem*, acc. of *elephas.* **—** Gk. ἐλέφας, an elephant. **—** Heb. *aleph*, *eleph*, an ox.

Elevate; see **Levity**.

Eleven. (E.) M. E. *enleuen*. A. S. *endlufon.* + Du. *elf*, Icel. *ellifu*, Dan. *elleve*, Swed. *elfva*, Goth. *ainlif*, G. *elf*. β. The best form is the Goth. *ain-lif*, where *ain* = one ; and *-lif* = Lithuan. *-lika* (in *vënolika*, eleven). Lith. *lika* means ' remaining.'

Elf. (E.) M. E. *elf*. A. S. *ælf.*+Icel. *álfr*, Dan. Swed. *alf*, G. *elf*. **Der.** *elf-in*, adj.; for *elf-en* *.

oaf, a simpleton. (Scand.) Prov. E. *auf*, an elf. **—** Icel. *álfr*, an elf. Chaucer uses *elvish* in the sense of ' simple.'

Elicit; see **Delicate**.

Elide; see **Lesion**.

Eligible; see **Legend**.

Eliminate; see **Limit**.

Elision; see **Lesion**.

Elixir. (Ar. **—** Gk.) Arab. *el iksír*, the philosopher's stone; where *el* is the definite article. **—** Gk. ξηρόν, dry (residuum).

Elk, a kind of deer. (Scand.) Icel. *elgr*, Swed. *elg*, an elk.+M. H. G. *elch*, Russ. *olene*, a stag; L. *alces*, Gk. ἄλκη, Skt. *rishya*, a kind of antelope (Vedic *riçya*).

Ell. (E.) M. E. *elle*, *elne*. A. S. *eln*, a cubit. + Du. *elle* ; Icel. *alin*, the arm from the elbow to the tip of the middle finger; Swed. *aln*, Dan. *alen*, Goth. *aleina*, G. *elle*, ell; L. *ulna*, elbow, cubit; Gk. ὠλένη, elbow. *Ell* = *el-* in *el-bow*.

Ellipse; see **Eclipse**.

Elm, a tree. (E.) A. S. *elm.*+Du. *olm*, Icel. *álmr*, Dan. *alm*, Swed. *alm*, G. *ulme* (formerly *elme*), L. *ulmus*. (√ AL.)

Elocution; see **Loquacious**.

Elongate; see **Long**.

Elope; see **Leap**.

Eloquent; see **Loquacious**.

Else, otherwise. (E.) A. S. *elles*, adv.; from base *el-*, signifying ' other.' **+** Swed. *eljest*, Goth. *aljis*; allied to L. *alias*, and to **Alien**.

Elucidate; see **Lucid**.

Elude; see **Ludicrous**.

Elysium, a heaven. (L. **—** Gk.) L.

elysium.—Gk. ἠλύσιον, short for ἠλύσιον πεδίον, the Elysian field (Od. 4. 563).

Emaciate; see **Meagre**.

Emanate. (L.) L. *emanatus*, pp. of *emanare*, to flow out.—L. *e*, out; *manare*, to flow.

Emancipate. (L.) From pp. of L. *emancipare*, to set free.—L. *e*, out; *mancipare*, to transfer property.—L. *mancip-*, stem of *man-ceps*, lit. one who takes property in hand or receives it.—L. *man-us*, hand; *capere*, to take; see **Manual, Capacious.**

Emasculate; see **Masculine**.

Em-, *prefix.* (F.—L.) F. *em-* = L. *im-*, for *in*, in, before *b* and *p*. Hence *em-balm*, to anoint with balm; *em-bank*, to enclose with a bank, cast up a bank; *em-body*, to invest with a body, &c.

Embargo; see **Bar.**

Embark; see **Bark** (1).

Embarrass; see **Bar.**

Embassy; see **Ambassador.**

Embattle; see **Battlement.**

Embellish; see **Belle.**

Ember-days. (E.) M. E. *ymber*, as in *ymber-weke.* A. S. *ymbren, ymbryne*, a due course, circuit, or period; the ember-days are days that *recur* at each of the four seasons of the year. The A. S. *ymb-ryne* is lit. 'a running round.'—A. S. *ymb*, round (= G. *um*, L. *ambi-*); and *ryne*, a run, course (see **Run**). ¶ Quite distinct from G. *quatember*, corrupted from L. *quatuor tempora*, four seasons.

Embers, ashes. (E.) M. E. *emeres.* A. S. *æmyrian*, embers. + Icel. *eimyrja*, Dan. *emmer*, M. H. G. *eimurja*, embers.

Embezzle, to filch. (F.—L.) Formerly *embesile, embesell*; no doubt the same as the obsolete verb *imbecill*, to weaken, enfeeble, diminish, subtract from. A shop-boy *embezzles* or diminishes his master's store imperceptibly by repeated filching. The verb is from the adj. *imbecile*, formerly *imbécile*; see **Imbecile.**

Emblem. (F.—L.—Gk.) O. F. *embleme.* —L. *emblema.*—Gk. ἔμβλημα, a thing put on, an ornament.—Gk. ἐμ- = ἐν, in, on; βάλλειν, to throw, to put. See **Belemnite.**

Embolism. (F.—Gk.) O.F. *embolisme.* —Gk. ἐμβολισμός, an intercalation or insertion of days, to complete a period.—Gk. ἐμ- = ἐν, in; βάλλειν, to cast.

Emboss (1), to adorn with bosses or raised work. (F.—L. *and* G.) From **Em-**, prefix; and **Boss.**

Emboss (2), to enclose or shelter in a wood. (F.—L. *and* Teut.) O. F. *embosquer*, to shroud in a wood.—O. F. *em-* = L. *in*, in; O. F. *bosc*, a wood; see **bouquet**, under **Bush** (1).

Embouchure; see **Debouch.**

Embrace; see **Brace.**

Embrasure. (F.) F. *embrasure*, an aperture with slant sides.—O. F. *embraser*, to slope the sides of a window.—O. F. *em-* = L. *in*, in; O. F. *braser*, 'to skue, or chamfret,' Cot. (Of unknown origin.)

Embrocation, a fomenting. (F.—Low. L.—Gk.) O. F. *embrocation.*—Low L. *embrocatus*, pp. of *embrocare*, to foment.—Gk. ἐμβρυχή, a fomentation.—Gk. ἐμβρέχειν, to soak in.—Gk. ἐμ- = ἐν, in; βρέχειν, to wet, soak.

Embroider; see **Broider.**

Embroil; see **Broil** (2).

Embryo. (F.—Gk.) Formerly *embryon.* —O.F. *embryon.*—Gk. ἔμβρυον, the embryo, fœtus.—Gk. ἐμ- = ἐν, within; βρύον, neut. of pres. pt. of βρύειν, to be full of a thing.

Emendation. (L.) Coined from the pp. of L. *emendare*, to free from fault.—L. *e*, free from; *mendum*, a fault.

amend. (F.—L.) M. E. *amenden.* — F. *amender.*—L. *emendare* (above).

amends. (F. — L.) M. E. *amendes*, sb. pl.—O. F. *amende*, reparation.—O. F. *amender* (above).

mend. (F.—L.) M. E. *menden*, short for M. E. *amenden*, to amend, by loss of *a*; see **amend** (above).

Emerald, a green gem. (F.—L.—Gk.) M. E. *emeraude.* — O. F. *esmeraude.* — L. *smaragdum*, acc. of *smaragdus.*—Gk. σμάραγδος, an emerald. Cf. Skt. *marakata* (the same).

smaragdus. (L.—Gk.) L. *smaragdus* (above).

Emerge; see **Merge.**

Emerods; see **Hemorrhoids.**

Emery, a hard mineral. (F.—Ital.—Gk.) Formerly *emeril*; XVII cent. = O. F. *emeril, esmeril.* = Ital. *smeriglio.* — Gk. σμῆρις, σμύρις, emery.—Gk. σμάω, I rub.

Emetic. (L.—Gk.) L. *emeticus.*—Gk. ἐμετικός, causing sickness. = Gk. ἐμέω, I vomit; see **Vomit.**

Emigrate; see **Migrate.**

Eminent, excellent. (L.) L. *eminent-*, stem of pres. pt. of *e-minere*, to project, excel.—L. *e*, out; *minere*, to project.

imminent, near at hand. (L.) L. *imminent-*, stem of pres. pt. of *im-minere*,

to project over. — L. *im-* = *in*, upon ;
minere, to project.

prominent, projecting, forward. (L.)
L. *prominent-*, stem of pres. pt. of *prominere*, to project forward.

Emir, a commander. (Arab.) Arab. *amír*,
a nobleman, prince. — Arab. root *amara*,
he commanded. Der. *admir-al*, q. v.

Emit; see Missile.

Emmet, an ant. (E.) M. E. *amte*,
amote. A. S. *æmete*, an ant. ⊕ G. *ameise*,
an ant. Doublet, *ant*, q. v.

Emollient ; see Mollify.

Emolument ; see Mole (3).

Emotion ; see Move.

Emperor ; see Pare.

Emphasis ; see Phase.

Empire ; see Pare.

Empiric, a quack doctor. (F. — L. —
Gk.) O. F. *empirique.* — L. *empiricus.* —
Gk. ἐμπειρικός, experienced ; also one of a
certain set of physicians. — Gk. ἐμ- = ἐν,
in ; πεῖρα, a trial, allied to πόρος, a way,
and to E. Fare.

Employ; see Ply.

Emporium, a mart. (L. — Gk.) L.
emporium. — Gk. ἐμπόριον, a mart ; neut. of
ἐμπόριος, commercial. — Gk. ἐμπορία, commerce, ἔμπορος, a traveller, merchant. —
Gk. ἐμ- = ἐν, in ; πόρος, a way ; see Em-
piric.

Empty, void. (E.) M. E. *empti.* A. S.
æmtig, lit. full of leisure. — A. S. *æmta*,
æmetta, leisure.

Empyrean, Empyreal, pertaining to
elemental fire. (L. — Gk.) Adjectives
coined from L. *empyræ-us*, Gk. ἐμπύρ-
αιος, extended from ἔμ-πυρος, exposed to
fire. — Gk. ἐμ- = ἐν, in ; πῦρ, fire ; see Fire.

Emu, a bird. (Port.) Port. *ema*, an ostrich.

Emulate. (L.) From pp. of L. *æmulari*,
to try to equal. — L. *æmulus*, striving to
equal.

Emulsion, a milk-like mixture. (F. —
L.) O. F. *emulsion* ; formed from L.
emuls-us, pp. of *e-mulgere*, to milk out. —
L. *e*, out ; *mulgere*, to milk, allied to
Milk.

En-, *prefix*. (F. — L.) F. *en-* = L. *in-*,
in ; sometimes used with a causal force, as
en-case, *en-chain*, &c. See Em-.

Enact; see Agent.

Enamel. (F. — O. H. G.) M. E. *en-
amaile.* — F. *en* (= L. *in*), on ; *amaile*, put
for O. F. *esmail*, enamel (= Ital. *smalto*),
from O. H. G. *smalzjan*, to smelt. See
Smelt, verb, and Smalt.

Enamour ; see Amatory.

Encamp ; see Camp.

Encase ; see Capacious.

Encaustic, burnt in. (F. — L. — Gk.)
O. F. *encaustique.* — L. *encausticus.* — Gk.
ἐγκαυστικός, related to burning in. — Gk. ἐν,
in ; καίω, I burn. See Calm.

ink. (F. — L. — Gk.) M. E. *enke.* —
O. F. *enque* (F. *encre*). — L. *encaustum*, the
purple ink used by the later Roman em-
perors ; neut. of *encaustus*, burnt in. — Gk.
ἔγκαυστος, burnt in. — Gk. ἐν, in ; καίω, I
burn. (Cf. Ital. *inchiostro*, ink.)

Enceinte ; see Cincture.

Enchant ; see Cant (1).

Enchase ; see Capacious.

Encircle ; see Circle.

Encline ; see Incline.

Enclitic. (Gk.) Gk. ἐγκλιτικός, en-
clining ; used of a word which leans its
accent upon another. — Gk. ἐγκλίνειν, to
lean upon, encline. — Gk. ἐν, on ; κλίνειν, to
lean ; see Lean (1).

Enclose ; see Clause.

Encomium ; see Comedy.

Encore, again. (F. — L.) F. *encore*
(= Ital. *ancora*), again. — L. *hanc horam*,
for *in hanc horam*, to this hour ; see
Hour.

Encounter ; see Contra-.

Encourage ; see Cordial.

Encrinite, the stone lily. (Gk.) Coined
from Gk. ἐν, in ; κρίνον, a lily ; with
suffix -ιτης.

Encroach ; see Crook.

Encumber ; see Cumulate.

Encyclical, Encyclopædia ;   see
Cycle.

End, sb. (E.) M. E. *ende.* A. S. *ende*,
sb. ⊕ Du. *einde*, Icel. *endi*, Sw. *ände*, Dan.
ende, Goth. *andeis*, G. *ende*, Skt. *anta*, end,
limit. ¶ Hence the prefixes *ante-*, *anti-*,
an- in *an-swer*.

Endeavour ; see Habit.

Endemic, peculiar to a district. (Gk.)
Gk. ἔνδημ-ος, belonging to a people. —
Gk. ἐν, in ; δῆμος, a people ; see De-
mocracy.

Endive, a plant. (F. — L.) F. *endive.* —
L. *intubus*.

Endogen ; see Genesis.

Endorse ; see Dorsal.

Endow ; see dowager, under Date (1).

Endue, to endow. (F. — L.) An older
spelling of *endow*; XVI cent. — O. F. *en-
doer* (later *endouer*), to endow (Burguy). —
L. *in* ; and *dotare*, to endow, from *dos*

(stem *dot-*), a dowry.   See **Endow.**
¶ Distinct from *indue.*
Endure; see **Dure.**
Enemy; see **Amatory.**
Energy. (F. – Gk.)   O. F. *energie.* – Gk. ἐνέργεια, vigour, action. – Gk. ἐνεργός, at work. – Gk. ἐν, in; ἔργον, at work; see **Work.**
Enervate; see **Snare.**
Enfeoff, to invest with a fief; see **Fief.**
Enfilade; see **File** (1).
Engage; see **Gage.**
Engender; see **Genus.**
Engine; see **Genus.**
Engrain; see **Grain.**
Engrave; see **Grave** (1).
Engross; see **Gross.**
Enhance, to advance, augment. (F. – L.)   M. E. *enhansen.*   [Of O. F. origin; but the word is only preserved in Provençal.] – O. Prov. *enansar*, to further, advance (Bartsch). – O. Prov. *enans*, before, rather. – L. *in ante*, in front of, before; see **Advance.** ¶ The *h* is an English insertion.
Enigma. (L. – Gk.)   L. *ænigma.* – Gk. αἴνιγμα (stem αἰνίγματ-), a riddle, dark saying. – Gk. αἰνίσσομαι, I speak in riddles. – Gk. αἶνος, a tale, story.   Der. *enigmatic* (from the stem).
Enjoin; see **Join.**
Enjoy; see **Gaud.**
Enlighten; see **Light** (1).
Enlist; see **List** (1).
Enmity; see **Amatory.**
Ennui; see **Odium.**
Enormous; see **Normal.**
Enough. (E.)   M. E. *inoh, enogh*; pl. *inohe, enoghe.*   A. S. *genóh, genóg*, pl. *genóge*, sufficient. – A. S. *genéah*, it suffices. + Icel. *gnógr*, Dan. *nok*, Swed. *nog*, Du. *genoeg*, G. *genug*, Goth. *ganohs.*   The *ge-* is a mere prefix. (√NAK.)
Enquire; see **Query.**
Ensample; see **Exempt.**
Ensign; see **Sign.**
Ensue; see **Sequence.**
Ensure; see **Cure.**
Entablature; see **Table.**
Entail; see **Tailor.**
Enter. (F. – L.)   M. E. *entren.* – O. F. *entrer.* – L. *intrare*, to go into. – L. *in*, in; and √TAR, to cross, overstep; cf. L. *trans*, across, Skt. *trí*, to cross.   See **Trans-.**   Der. *entr-ance.*
Enterprise; see **Prehensile.**
Entertain; see **Tenable.**
Enthusiasm; see **Theism.**

Entice. (F.)   M. E. *enticen.* – O. F. *enticer, enticher*, to excite.   Origin unknown.
Entire; see **Tangent.**
Entity, being. (L.)   A coined word, with suffix *-ty* from L. *enti-*, crude form of *ens*, being; see **Essence.**
Entomology; see **Tome.**
Entrails; see **Interior.**
Entreat; see **Trace** (1).
Enumerate; see **Number.**
Enunciate; see **Nuncio.**
Envelop. (F. – L. *and* Teut.)   M. E. *envolupen.* – O. F. *envoluper*, later *enveloper*, to wrap in, wrap round, enfold. – F. *en* (= L. *in*), in; and a base *volup-*, to wrap, of Teut. origin; this base is perfectly represented by M. E. *wlappen*, to wrap, which is merely another spelling of **Wrap.**   And see **Lap** (3).   Der. *envelope*, sb.
develop, to unfold, open out. (F. – L. *and* Teut.)   F. *développer*, O. F. *desveloper.* – O. F. *des-* (= L. *dis-*), apart; and the base *velop-* or *volup-* (above).
Environ; see **Veer.**
Envoy; see **Viaduct.**
Envy; see **Vision.**
Epact. (F. – Gk.)   O. F. *epacte*, an addition, the epact (a term in astronomy). – Gk. ἐπακτός, added. – Gk. ἐπάγειν, to bring in, add. – Gk. ἐπ-, for ἐπί, to; and ἄγειν, to lead, bring.   (√AG.)
Epaulet; see **Spade.**
Ephah, a Hebrew measure. (Heb. – Egypt.)   Heb. *éphâh*, a measure; of Egyptian origin; Coptic *épi*, measure.
Ephemera, flies that live for a day. (Gk.)   XVI cent. – Gk. ἐφήμερα, neut. pl. of ἐφήμερος, lasting for a day. – Gk. ἐφ- = ἐπί, for; ἡμέρα, a day.   Der. *ephemer-al*, adj., *ephemer-is* (Gk. ἐφημερίς, a diary).
Ephod, part of the priest's habit. (Heb.)   Heb. *éphód*, a vestment. – Heb. *áphad*, to put on.
Epi-, *prefix.* (Gk.)   Gk. ἐπί, upon, to, besides; spelt *eph-* in *eph-emeral*, *ep-* in *ep-och*, *ep-ode.*
Epic, narrative. (L. – Gk.)   L. *epicus.* – Gk. ἐπικός, narrative. – Gk. ἔπος, word, narrative, song; see **Voice.**
Epicene, of common gender. (L. – Gk.)   L. *epicænus.* – Gk. ἐπί-κοινος, common. – Gk. ἐπί; κοινός, common.
Epicure, a follower of Epicurus. (L. – Gk.)   L. *Epicurus.* – Gk. Ἐπίκουρος; lit. 'assistant.'
Epicycle; see **Cycle.**
Epidemic, affecting a people. (L. – Gk.)

Formed from L. *epidemus*, epidemic. – Gk. ἐπίδημος, among the people, general. – Gk. ἐπί, among; δῆμος, people. See **Endemic.**

Epidermis; see **Derm.**

Epiglottis; see **Gloss** (2).

Epigram; see **Grammar.**

Epilepsy. (F. – L. – Gk.) O. F. *epilepsie*, 'the falling sickness;' Cot. – L. *epilepsia.* – Gk. ἐπιληψία, ἐπίληψις, a seizure. – Gk. ἐπιλαμβάνειν, to seize upon. – Gk. ἐπί, on; λαμβάνειν, to seize. **Der.** *epileptic* (Gk. ἐπιληπτικός).

Epilogue; see **Logic.**

Epiphany; see **Phantom.**

Episcopal. (F. – L. – Gk.) O.F.*episcopal.* – L. *episcopalis*, belonging to a bishop. – L. *episcopus*, a bishop. – Gk. ἐπίσκοπος, an over-seer, bishop. – Gk. ἐπί, upon; σκοπός, one that watches. (√SPAK.) See **Scope.**

Episode, a story introduced into another. (Gk.) Gk. ἐπείσοδος, a coming in besides. – Gk. ἐπ- (ἐπί), besides; εἴσοδος, an entrance, εἰσόδιος, coming in, from εἰς, in, ὁδός, a way.

Epistle; see **Stole.**

Epitaph. (F. – L. – Gk.) F. *epitaphe.* – L. *epitaphium.* – Gk. ἐπιτάφιος, upon a tomb. – Gk. ἐπί, on; τάφος, a tomb.

Epithalamium, a marriage-song. (L. – Gk.) L. *epithalamium.* – Gk. ἐπιθαλάμιον, bridal song. – Gk. ἐπί, upon, for; θάλαμος, bride-chamber.

Epithet; see **Theme.**

Epitome; see **Tome.**

Epoch. (L. – Gk.) Low L. *epocha.* – Gk. ἐποχή, a stop, pause, fixed date. – Gk. ἐπ- (ἐπί), upon; ἔχειν, to hold, check. (√SAGH.)

Epode; see **Ode.**

Equal. (L.) L. *æqualis*, equal. – L. *æquus*, just, exact. Cf. Skt. *eka*, one.

adequate. (L.) L. *adæquatus*, pp. of *adæquare*, to make equal to. – L. *ad*, to; *æquus*, equal.

equanimity, evenness of mind. (L.) From L.*æquanimitas*, the same. – L.*æquanimis*, of even temper, kind. – L. *æqu-us*, equal; *animus*, mind.

equation, a statement of equality. (L.) L. acc. *æquationem*, an equalising; from pp. of *æquare*, to make equal. – L. *æquus*, equal.

equilibrium, even balancing. (L.) L. *æquilibrium.* – L. *æquilibris*, evenly balanced. – L. *æqui-*, for *æquus*, even; *librare*, to balance; see **Librate.**

equinox. (F. – L.) F. *équinoxe.* – L. *æquinoctium*, time of equal day and night. – L. *æqui-*, for *æquus*; *noctĭ-*, crude form of *nox*, a night; see **Night.**

equipollent, equally potent. (F. – L.) O. F. *equipolent.* – L. *æquipollent-*, stem of *æquipollens*, of equal power. – L. *æqui-*, for *æquus*; *pollens*, pres. pt. of *pollere*, to be strong.

equity. (F. – L.) O. F. *equité.* – L. *æquitatem*, acc. of *æquitas*, equity. – L. *æquus*, equal.

equivalent. (F.–L.) O. F. *equivalent.* – L. *æquiualent-*, stem of pres. pt. of *æquiualere*, to be of equal force. – L. *æqui-* (*æquus*); *ualere*, to be worth; see **Value.**

equivocal. (L.) Formed from L. *æquiuoc-us*, of doubtful sense. – L. *æqui-* (*æquus*); *uoc-*, stem of *uox*, voice, sense; see **Voice. Der.** *equivoc-ate*, to speak doubtfully. ¶ So also *equi-angular*, *equi-multiple*, &c.

iniquity, vice. (F. – L.) M. E. *iniquitee.* – F. *iniquité.* – L. *iniquitatem*, acc. of *iniquitas*, injustice. – L. *in*, not ; *æquitas*, equity; see **equity** (above).

Equerry, an officer who has charge of horses and stables. (F. – O. H. G.) Properly *equerry* means a stable, and mod. E. *equerry* stands for *equerry-man.* – F. *écurie*, O. F. *escurie*, a stable; Low L. *scuria*, a stable. – O. H. G. *skûra, skiura* (G. *schauer*), a shelter, stable. (√SKU.) ¶ Spelt *equerry* to make it look as if allied to *equine.*

Equestrian; see **Equine.**

Equilibrium; see **Equal.**

Equine. (L.) L. *equinus*, relating to horses. – L. *equus*, a horse. + Gk. ἵππος, ἵκκος; Skt. *açva*, lit. 'runner.' (√AK.)

equestrian. (L.) Formed from L. *equestri-*, crude form of *equester*, belonging to horsemen. – L. *eques*, a horseman. – L. *equus*, a horse.

Equinox; see **Equal.**

Equip, to furnish, fit out. (F. – Scand.) O. F. *equiper, esquiper*, to fit out. – Icel. *skipa*, to set in order, allied to *skapa*, to shape. Allied to **Shape. Der.** *equip-age*, *-ment.*

Equipollent, Equity; see **Equal.**

Equivalent, Equivocal; see **Equal.**

Era. (L.) L. *æra*, an era, fixed date. From a particular sense of *æra*, counters (for calculation), pl. of *æs*, brass, money.

Eradicate; see **Radix.**

Erase; see **Rase.**

Ere, before. (E.) M. E. *er.* A. S. *ǽr*, soon, before; prep. adv. and conj. **+** Du. *eer*, Icel. *ár*, O. H. G. *ér*, G. *eher*; Goth. *air*, adv., early, soon. **¶** A positive, not a comparative, form.

early, soon. (E.) M. E. *erly.* A. S. *ǽrlíce*, adv.; from *ǽrlíc**, adj., not used.— A. S. *ǽr*, soon; *líc*, like.

erst, soonest. (E.) M. E. *erst.* A. S. *ǽrest*, superl. of *ǽr*, soon.

or (2), ere. (E.) M. E. *or, er, ar*, various forms of *ere.* A. S. *ǽr* (above). (In the phrases *or ere, or ever*.)

Erect; see **Regent**.

Ermine, a beast. (F. — O. H. G.) M. E. *ermine.* — O. F. *ermine* (F. *hermine*).— O. H. G. *harmín*, ermine-fur (G. *ermelin*). — O. H. G. *harmo*, an ermine. **+** A. S, *hearma*; Lithuan. *szarmú.* **¶** Littré approves the derivation from *Armenius mus*, an Armenian mouse; cf. *Ponticus mus*, an ermine.

Erode; see **Rodent**.

Erotic. (Gk.) Gk. ἐρωτικός, relating to love. — Gk. ἐρωτι-, crude form of ἔρως, love.

Err, to stray. (F. — L.) M. E. *erren.*— O. F. *errer*. — L. *errare*, to wander (for *ers-are* *). **+** G. *irren*, to stray, Goth. *airzjan*, to make to stray. (√AR.)

aberration. (L.) From L. acc. *aberrationem*, a wandering from; from pp. of *ab-errāre*, to wander from.

erratum, an error. (L.) L. *erratum*, neut. of pp. of *errare*, to make a mistake.

erroneous, faulty. (L.) Put for L. *erroneus*, wandering. — L. *errare* (above).

error. (F. — L.) M. E. *errour.* — L. *errōrem*, acc. of *error*, a mistake. — L. *errare* (above).

Errand. (E.) M. E. *erende.* A. S. *ǽrende*, a message, business. **+** Icel. *eyrendi, örendi*, Swed. *ärende*, Dan. *ærende*; O. H. G. *árunti*, a message. The form of the word is that of an old pres. pt.; perhaps 'a going,' from √AR, to go.

Errant, wandering. (F. — L.) F. *errant*, pres. pt. of O. F. *errer, eirer*, to wander. — L. *iterare*, to travel. — L. *iter*, a journey.

Erst; see **Ere**.

Erubescent; see **Ruby**.

Eructate. (L.) From pp. of L. *eructare*, to belch out. — L. *e*, out; *ructare*, to belch; allied to *rugire*, to bellow. (√RU.)

Erudite; see **Rude**.

Eruption; see **Rupture**.

Erysipelas, a redness on the skin. (L.

— Gk.) L. *erysipelas.* — Gk. ἐρυσίπελας, redness on the skin. — Gk. ἐρυσι-, for ἐρυθ-ρός, red; πέλλα, skin.

Escalade; see **Scan**.

Escape; see **Cape** (1).

Escarpment; see **Sharp**.

Escheat; see **Cadence**.

Eschew; see **Shy**.

Escort; see **Regent**.

Esculent; see **Edible**.

Escutcheon; see **Esquire**.

Esophagus, gullet. (L. — Gk.) Late L. *æsophagus.* — Gk. οἰσοφάγος, the gullet, lit. conveyer of food. — Gk. οἴσ-ω, I shall carry, from a base οἰ-, to carry (Skt. *ví*, to drive) ; φαγ-, base of φαγεῖν, to eat.

Esoteric. (Gk.) Gk. ἐσωτερικός, inner; hence, secret. — Gk. ἐσώτερος, inner, comp. of ἔσω, adv., within; from ἐς = εἰς, into, prep. Opposed to *exoteric*.

Espalier; see **Spade**.

Especial; see **Species**.

Esplanade; see **Plain**.

Espouse; see **Sponsor**.

Espy; see **Species**.

Esquire, a shield-bearer. (F. — L.) M. E. *squyer.* — O. F. *escûyer, escuier*, a squire.— Low L. *scutarius*, a shield-bearer. — L. *scut-um*, a shield, cover (F. *écu*). (√SKU.) Doublet, *squire*.

escutcheon, scutcheon, a painted shield. (F. — L.) Formerly *scutchion, scuchin*; XVI cent. — O. F. *escusson*, the same; answering to a Low L. acc. *scutionem* *, extended from L. *scutum*, a shield.

Essay, Assay, an attempt, trial. (F.— L. — Gk.) O. F. *essai*, a trial. — L. *exagium*, a trial of weight. — Gk. ἐξάγιον, a weighing. — Gk. ἐξάγειν, to lead out, export goods. — Gk. ἐξ, out; ἄγειν, to lead. (√AG.)

Essence, a quality, being. (F. — L.) F. *essence.* — L. *essentia*, a being. — L. *essent-*, stem of old pres. part. of *esse*, to be; see *entity*.

quintessence, pure essence. (F. — L.) Lit. 'fifth essence.' — L. *quinta essentia*, fifth essence (in addition to the four elements).

Establish, Estate; see **State**.

Esteem, to value. (F. — L.) O. F. *estimer.* — L. *æstimare*, O. L. *æstumare*, to value. Allied to Sabine *aisos*, prayer, Skt. *ish*, to desire. (√IS.)

aim, to endeavour after. (F. — L.) M. E. *eimen.* — O. F. *aesmer, esmer*, to estimate, aim at, intend. — L. *ad*; and *æstimare*, to estimate.

estimate. (L.)   From pp. of L. *æsti-mare*, to value (above).

Estrange; see **Exterior**.

Estuary, mouth of a tidal river. (L.) L. *æstuarium*, the same. — L. *æstuare*, to surge, foam as the tide.—L. *æstus*, heat, surge, tide. (√ IDH.)

Etch; see **Eat.**

Eternal. (F. — L.)   M. E. *eternel.* — F. *eternel.*—L. *æternalis*, eternal.—L. *æternus*, lit. lasting for an age; put for *æui-ternus*. —L. *æui-*, for *æuum*, an age. See **Age.**

Ether, pure upper air. (L.—Gk.) L. *æther.* — Gk. αἰθήρ, upper air; from its glowing.—Gk. αἴθειν, to glow. (√ IDH.)

Ethic, relating to custom. (L. — Gk.) L. *ethicus*, moral. — Gk. ἠθικός, moral.— Gk. ἦθος, custom, moral nature; cf. ἔθος, manner, custom. ✛ Goth. *sidus*, G. *sitte*, custom; Skt. *svadhā*, self-will, strength, from *sva*, self, *dhā*, to place.

Ethnic, relating to a nation. (L.—Gk.) L. *ethnicus.*— Gk. ἐθνικός, national. — Gk. ἔθνος, a nation.

Etiquette; see **Stick** (1).

Etymon, the true source of a word. (L.—Gk.)   L. *etymon.*—Gk. ἔτυμον; neut. of ἔτυμος, real, true.—Gk. ἐτεός, true. Allied to **Sooth.**

etymology. (F. — L. — Gk.)   O. F. *etymologie.* — L. *etymologia.* — Gk. ἐτυμο-λογία, etymology. — Gk. ἐτυμο-s, true; -λογία, account, from λέγειν, to speak.

Eu-, prefix, well. (Gk.)   Gk. εὖ, well; neut. of ἐύς, good, put for ἐσ-υς*, real, from √ AS, to be.

Eucharist, the Lord's Supper, lit. thanksgiving.   (L.—Gk.)   L. *eucharistia.*—Gk. εὐχαριστία, a giving of thanks. — Gk. εὖ, well; χαρίζομαι, I shew favour, from χάρις, favour. (√ GHAR.)

Eulogy; see **Logic.**

Eunuch, one who is castrated. (L.— Gk.)   L. *eunūchus.* — Gk. εὐν-οῦχος, a chamberlain; one who had charge of sleeping apartments.—Gk. εὐνή, a couch; ἔχειν, to keep, have in charge.

Euphemism, a softened expression. (Gk.) Gk. εὐφημισμός, the same as εὐφημία, the use of words of good omen.—Gk. εὖ, well; φημί, I speak. (√ BHA.)

Euphony. (Gk.)   Gk. εὐφωνία, a pleasing sound.—Gk. εὔφωνος, sweet-voiced.— Gk. εὖ, well; φωνή, voice. (√ BHA.)

Euphrasy, the plant eye-bright. (Gk.) Supposed to be beneficial to the eyes; lit. ' delight.' — Gk. εὐφρασία, delight. — Gk.

εὐφραίνειν, to delight, cheer. — Gk. εὖ, well; φρεν-, base of φρήν, midriff, heart, mind.

Euphuism, affectation in speaking. (Gk) So named from a book *Euphues*, by J. Lyly (1579). — Gk. εὐφυής, well-grown, excellent. — Gk. εὖ, well; φυή, growth, from φύομαι, I grow. (√ BHU.)

Euroclydon, a tempestuous wind. (Gk.) Gk. εὑροκλύδων, supposed to mean ' a storm from the east.'—Gk. εὖρο-s, S. E. wind; κλύδων, surge, from κλύζειν, to surge, dash as waves.

Euthanasia, easy death. (Gk.)   Gk. εὐθανασία, easy death; cf. εὐθάνατος, dying well. — Gk. εὖ, well; θανεῖν, to die.

Evacuate; see **Vacation.**

Evade, to shun. (F.—L.)   F. *evader.*— L. *euadere* (pp. *euasus*), to escape.—L. *e*, away; *uadere*, to go.   Der. *evas-ion* (from the pp.)

invade. (F. — L.)   F. *invader.* — L. *in-uadere* (pp. *in-uasus*), to enter, invade. —L. *in*, in; *uadere.*   Der. *invas-ion.*

pervade. (L.)   L. *per-uadere*, to go through.

Evanescent; see **Vain.**

Evangelist, writer of a gospel. (F.— L.—Gk.)   O. F. *evangeliste.*—L. *euangel-ista.*—Gk. εὐαγγελιστής.—Gk. εὐαγγέλιον, a reward for good tidings, gospel.—Gk. εὖ, well; ἀγγελία, tidings, from ἄγγελος, a messenger; see **Angel.**

Evaporate; see **Vapour.**

Evasion; see **Evade.**

Eve, Even, the latter part of the day. (E.)   *Eve* is short for *even*; (for *evening*, see below). M. E. *eue, euen.* A. S. *æfen, éfen.* ✛ O. Sax. *āvand*, Icel. *aftan*, Swed. *afton*, Dan. *aften*, G. *abend.* Supposed to mean the 'after' part of the day; allied to Aft. Cf. Skt. *apará*, posterior; *apará sandhyá*, evening twilight. Der. *even-tide*, A.S. *æfentíd.*

evening, even. (E.)   M. E. *euening.* A.S. *æfnung*, put for *æfenung**; formed from *æfen*, even, with suffix *-ung.*

Even, level. (E.)   M. E. *euen (even).* A.S. *efen, efn.*✛Du. *even*, Icel. *jafn*, Dan. *jævn*, Swed. *jämn*, Goth. *ibns*, G. *eben.*

anent, regarding, with reference to. (E.)   M. E. *anent, anentis*; older form *anefent*, where the *t* is excrescent. A.S. *anefen, onefen*, near; also written *anemn.* —A.S. *on*, on; *efen*, even. Hence *onefn* = even with, on an equality with.✛G. *neben* (for *in eben*).

Ever. (E.)   M. E. *euer (ever).* A.S.

æfre, ever. Related to A. S. *áwa*, Goth. *aiw*, ever. Der. *ever-lasting*, *ever-more*.

every, each one. (E.) M. E. *eueri*, *euerich*. – A. S. *æfre*, ever; *ælc*, each (Sc. *ilk*). *Ever-y = ever-cach*; see Each.

everywhere. (E.) M. E. *euerihwar*. – A. S. *æfre*, ever; *gehwar*, where. The word really stands for *ever-ywhere*, i. e. *ever-where*; *y*- is a mere prefix (= *ge*-).

Evict; see Victor.

Evident; see Vision.

Evil. (E.) M. E. *euel*. A. S. *yfel*, adj. and sb. ✛ Du. *euvel*, G. *übel*, Goth. *ubils*, Icel. *illr*, adj.; Swed. *illa*, Dan. *ilde*, ill, adv.

ill. (Scand.) Icel. *illr*, cognate with A. S. *yfel*; it is a contracted form.

Evince; see Victor.

Eviscerate; see Viscera.

Evoke; see Vocal.

Evolve; see Voluble.

Ewe. (E.) M. E. *ewe*. A. S. *eowu*, a female sheep. ✛ Du. *ooi*, Icel. *ær*, M. H. G. *ouwe*, Lithuan. *avis*, a sheep, Russ. *ovtsa*, L. *ouis*, Gk. *ŏïs*; Skt. *avi*, a sheep, orig. 'a pet,' from *avis*, devoted, attached. (√AW.)

Ewer; see Aquatic.

Ex-, E-, *prefix*. (L.) L. *ex*, *e*, out. ✛ Gk. *ἐκ, ἐξ,* out; Russ. *iz*', out.

Exacerbate; see Acid.

Exact, (1) precise, (2) to demand; see Agent.

Exaggerate; see Gerund.

Exalt; see Altitude.

Examine; see Agent.

Example; see Exempt.

Exasperate; see Asperity.

Excavation; see Cave.

Exceed; see Cede.

Excel, to surpass. (F. – L.) O. F. *exceller*. – L. *excellere*, to raise; to surpass. – L. *ex*, out; *cellere* *, to drive, only in compounds. Allied to Celerity.

Except; see Capacious.

Excerpt, a selected passage. (L.) L. *excerptum*, an extract; neut. of pp. of *excerpere*, to select. – L. *ex*, out; *carpere*, to cull. See Harvest.

scarce. (F. – L.) M. E. *scars*. – O. F. *escars*, *eschars*, scarce, scanty, niggard (F. *échars*). – Low L. *scarpsus*, short form of *excarpsus*, used as a substitute for L. *excerptus*, pp. of *excerpere*, to select (above). Thus the sense was picked out, select, scarce.

Excess; see Cede.

Exchange; see Change.

Exchequer; see Check.

Excise, a tax; see Sedentary.

Excision; see Cæsura.

Exclaim; see Claim.

Exclude; see Clause.

Excommunicate; see Common.

Excoriate; see Cuirass.

Excrement; see Concern.

Excrescence; see Crescent.

Excretion; see Concern.

Excruciate; see Crook.

Exculpate; see Culpable.

Excursion; see Current.

Excuse; see Cause.

Execrate; see Sacred.

Execute; see Sequence.

Exegesis, exposition. (Gk.) Gk. *ἐξήγησις*, interpretation. – Gk. *ἐξηγεῖσθαι*, to explain. – Gk. *ἐξ*, out; *ἡγεῖσθαι*, to guide, from *ἄγειν*, to lead. (√AG.)

Exemplar, Exemplify; see Exempt.

Exempt, freed. (F. – L.) O. F. *exempt*; whence *exempter*, to exempt, free. – L. *exemptus*, pp. of *ex-imere*, to take out, deliver, free. – L. *ex*, out; *emere*, to take. (√AM.)

assume. (L.) L. *assumere* (pp. *assumptus*), to take to oneself. – L. *as-*, for *ad*, to; *sumere*, to take, which stands for *sub-imere* *, from *sub*, under, secretly, and *emere*, to take. Der. *assumpt-ion* (from the pp.).

consume. (L.) L. *consumere*, lit. to take wholly. – L. *con-* (*cum*), together, wholly; *sumere*, to take, for which see above. Der. *consumpt-ion* (from the pp.).

ensample. (F. – L.) M. E. *ensample*. – O. F. *ensample*, corrupt form of *example*, *exemple*. – L. *exemplum*, a sample, pattern. – L. *eximere*, to select a sample. – L. *ex*, out; *emere*, to take.

example. (F. – L.) O. F. *example*. F. *exemple*. – L. *exemplum* (above).

exemplar. (F. – L.) M. E. *exemplaire*. – O. F. *exemplaire*. – L. *exemplarium*, late form of *exemplar*, a copy (to which the mod. E. word is now conformed). – L. *exemplaris*, adj., serving as a copy. – L. *exemplum*; see ensample above. Der. *exemplar-y* (= O. F. *exemplaire*).

exemplify, to shew by example. (F. – L.) A coined word; as if from F. *exemplifier* *. – Low L. *exemplificare*, properly 'to copy out.' – L. *exempli-*, for *exemplum*, a copy; *facere*, to make.

impromptu, a thing said off hand. (F. – L.) F. *impromptu*. – L. *in promptu*, in readiness; where *promptu* is abl. of *promptus*, a sb. formed from *promere*, to bring forward; see **prompt** (below).

peremptory, decisive. (F. − L.) F. *peremptoire*. − L. *peremptorius*, destructive, decisive. − L. *peremptor*, a destroyer. − L. *peremptus*, pp. of *per-imere*, to take away entirely, destroy. − L. *per*, utterly; *emere*, to take.

premium. (L.) L. *præmium*, profit; lit. 'a taking before;' put for *præ-imium* *. − L. *præ*, before; *emere*, to take.

presume. (F. − L.) M. E. *presumen*. − O. F. *presumer*. − L. *præ-sumere*, to take beforehand, presume, imagine. − L. *præ*, before; *sumere*, to take; see **assume** above. Der. *presumpt-ion*, &c. (from the ˙pp.).

prompt. (F. − L.) F. *prompt*. − L. *promptum*, acc. of *promptus*, *promtus*, brought to light, at hand, ready, pp. of *promere*, to bring forward. − L. *pro*, forward; *emere*, to take, bring.

ransom, redemption. (F. − L.) M. E. *ransoun* (with final *n*). − O. F. *raenson*, later *rançon*, a ransom. − L. *redemptionem*, acc. of *redemptio*, a buying back. − L. *redemptus*, pp. of *redimere*, to redeem; see **redeem** below. Doublet, *redemption*.

redeem, to atone for. (F. − L.) F. *redimer*, 'to redeem;' Cot. − L. *redimere*, to buy back. − L. *red-*, back; *emere*, to take, purchase. Der. *redempt-ion* (from the pp. *redemptus*).

resume, to take up again. (F. − L.) F. *resumer*. − L. *resumere*. − L. *re-*, again; *sumere*, to take; see **assume** (above). Der. *resumpt-ion* (from pp. *resumptus*).

sample. (F. − L.) M. E. *sample*. − O. F. *essemple*, *example*; see **ensample** above.

sampler. (F. − L.) O. F. *examplaire* (XIV cent.), the same as *exemplaire*, a pattern; see **exemplar** above.

sumptuary, relating to expenses. (L.) L. *sumptuarius*, adj. from *sumptu-s*, expense. See below.

sumptuous, costly. (F. − L.) F. *somptueux* (Cot.) − L. *sumptuosus*, costly. − L. *sumptus*, expense. − L. *sumptus*, pp. of *sumere*, to take, use, spend; see **assume** (above).

Exequies; see **Sequence**.

Exercise, sb. (F. − L.) M. E. *exercise*. O. F. *exercice*. − L. *exercitium*, exercise. − L. *exercitus*, pp. of *exercere*, to drive out of an enclosure, drive on, set at work. − L. *ex*,

out; *arcere*, to enclose; see **Ark**. Der. *exercise*, vb.

Exert; see **Series**.

Exfoliate; see **Foliage**.

Exhale. (F. − L.) F. *exhaler*. − L. *exhalare*, to breathe out. − L. *ex*, out; *halare*, to breathe.

inhale. (L.) L. *in-halare*, to breathe in, draw in breath.

Exhaust. (L.) L. *exhaustus*, pp. of *exhaurire*, to draw out, drink up. − L. *ex*, out; *haurire*, to draw water.

Exhibit; see **Habit**.

Exhilarate; see **Hilarity**.

Exhort; see **Hortatory**.

Exhume; see **Humble**.

Exigent; see **Agent**.

Exile; see **Sole** (1).

Exist; see **State**.

Exit; see **Itinerant**.

Exodus, departure. (L. − Gk.) L. *exodus*. − Gk. ἔξοδος, a going out. − Gk. ἐξ, out; ὁδός, a way, a march. (√ SAD.)

Exogen; see **Genesis**.

Exonerate; see **Onerous**.

Exorbitant; see **Orb**.

Exorcise. (L. − Gk.) Late L. *exorcizare*. − Gk. ἐξορκίζειν, to drive away by adjuration. − Gk- ἐξ, away; ὁρκίζειν, to adjure, from ὅρκος, an oath.

Exordium. (L.) L. *exordium*, a beginning. − L. *exordiri*, to begin, to weave. − L. *ex*; and *ordiri*,˳to begin, weave.

Exoteric, external. (Gk.) Gk. ἐξωτερικός, external. − Gk. ἐξωτέρω, more outward, comp. of adv. ἔξω, outward, from ἐξ, out.

exotic, foreign. (L. − Gk.) L. *exoticus*. − Gk. ἐξωτικός, outward, foreign. − Gk. ἔξω, adv., outward, from ἐξ, out.

Expand, Expanse; see **Patent**.

Expatiate; see **Space**.

Expatriate; see **Paternal**.

Expect; see **Species**.

Expectorate; see **Pectoral**.

Expedite; see **Pedal**.

Expel; see **Pulsate**.

Expend; see **Pendant**.

Experience, Expert; see **Peril**.

Expiate; see **Pious**.

Expire; see **Spirit**.

Explain; see **Plain**.

Expletive; see **Plenary**.

Explicate, Explicit; see **Ply**.

Explode; see **Plaudit**.

Exploit; see **Ply**.

Explore; see **Deplore**.

Exponent; see **Position**.

Export; see Port (1).
Expose; see Pose (1).
Exposition; see Position.
Expostulate; see Postulate.
Expound; see Position.
Express; see Press.
Expulsion; see Pulsate.
Expunge; see Pungent.
Expurgate; see Pure.
Exquisite; see Query.
Extant; see State.
Extasy; see Statics.
Extempore; see Temporal.
Extend; see Tend.
Extenuate; see Tenuity.

Exterior, outward. (F.—L.) Formerly *exteriour*.—O.F. *exterieur*.—L. *exteriorem*, acc. of *exterior*, outward, comparative of *exterus* or *exter*, outward.—L. *ex*, out; with compar. suffix *-ter* (= Aryan *-tar*).

estrange, to make strange. (F.—L.) F. *estranger*, to make strange.—F. *estrange*, strange.—L. *extraneum*, acc. of *extraneus*, foreign, on the outside.—L. *extra*, without; see extra below.

external, outward. (L.) From L. *extern-us*, outward, extended form from *exterus*, outward (above).

extra. (L.) L. *extra*, beyond, beyond what is necessary; put for *exterâ = exterâ parte*, on the outer side, where *exterâ* is the fem. abl. of *exterus*; see Exterior.

extraneous. (L.) L. *extraneus*, external; extended from *extra* (above).

extreme. (F.—L.) O.F. *extreme*.—L. *extremus*, superl. of *exterus*, outward; see Exterior (above).

extrinsic, external. (F.—L.) It should rather be *extrinsec*.—O.F. *extrinseque*, outward.—L. *extrinsecus*, adv., from without.—L. *extrin* (=*extrim**), adverbial form from *exter*, outward; and *secus*, beside; so that *extrin-secus* = on the outside. *Secus* is allied to *secundum*, according to, from *sequi*, to follow; see Sequence.

strange, foreign, odd. (F. — L.) O.F. *estrange*; see estrange (above).

Exterminate; see Term.
External; see Exterior.
Extinguish; see Distinguish.
Extirpate. (L.) From pp. of L. *extirpare*, to root out, better spelt *exstirpare*, to pluck up by the stem. — L. *ex*, out; *stirps*, *stirpes*, the stem of a tree.
Extol; see Tolerate.
Extort; see Torture.
Extra, Extraneous; see Exterior.
Extract; see Trace (1).
Extraordinary; see Order.
Extravagant; see Vague.
Extravasate; see Vase.
Extreme; see Exterior.
Extricate; see Intricate.
Extrinsic; see Exterior.
Extrude; see Intrude.

Exuberant. (L.) From stem of pres. pt. of L. *exuberare*, to be fruitful or luxuriant.—L. *ex*; and *uberare*, to be fruitful, from *uber*, an udder, fertility; see Udder.

Exude; see Sudatory.
Exult; see Salient.

Exuviæ, cast skins of animals. (L.) L. *exuuiæ*, things stripped off.—L. *exuere*, to strip off.

Eye. (E.) M.E. *eye*, *eighe*; pl. *eyes*, *eyen* (whence *eyne*). A.S. *éage*, pl. *éagan*. +Du. *oog*, Icel. *auga*, Dan. *öie*, Swed. *öga*, Goth. *augo*, G. *auge*, Russ. *oko*, L. *oculus* (dimin. of *ocus**); O. Gk. ὄκκος; Skt. *aksha*. (√AK.) Der. *dais-y*, q.v.; *wind-ow*, q.v.

eyelet-hole. (F.—L.; and E.) *Eyelet* is put for O.F. *oeillet*, 'a little eye, an oilet hole,' Cot.; dimin. of O.F. *oeil*, from L. *oculum*, acc. of *oculus*, eye.

Eyot, a little island. (Scand.) Also spelt *ait*, *eyet*, *eyght*. From M.E. *ei*, an island=Icel. *ey*, an island; with dimin. suffix *-et*, as in *helm-et*. The A.S. form is *igoð*, *igeoð*; where *ig* is cognate with Icel. *ey*; see Island.

Eyre; see Itinerant.
Eyry, a nest; see Aery.

F.

Fable; see Fate.
Fabric. (F. — L.) F. *fabrique*.—L. *fabrica*, workshop, fabric.—L. *fabri-*, for *faber*, a workman.—L. *fa-*, to put, do, make (as in *fa-c-ere*, to make), with suffix *-ber* of the agent. (√DHA.) Der.

fabric-ate, from pp. of L. *fabricari*, to construct.

forge. (F.—L.) O.F. *forge*, a workshop.—L. *fabrica*, a workshop (above). Der. *forge*, vb.

Façade; see Face.

Face. (F.–L.) F. *face.*–L. *faciem,* acc. of *facies,* the face, appearance. (√ BHA.)

deface. (F. – L.) M. E. *defacen.* – O. F. *desfacer,* to deface, disfigure. – O. F. *des-* (= L. *dis-*), apart; *face,* face (above).

efface. (F.–L.) F. *effacer.*–F. *ef-* = L. *ef-,* for *ex,* out; and *face* (above).

façade, face of a building. (F.–Ital.– L.) F. *facade* (Cot.)–Ital. *facciata,* face of a building. – Ital. *faccia,* face. – L. *faciem,* acc. of *facies,* face.

superficies. (L.) L. *superficies,* surface, outer face.–L. *super,* above; *facies,* face.

surface. (F. – L.) F. *surface,* upper face.–F. *sur,* above; *face,* face.–L. *super,* above; *facies,* face.

Facetious. (F. – L.) F. *facetieux* (Cot.)–O. F. *facetie,* 'witty mirth,' id. – L. *facetia,* wit; common in pl. – L. *facetus,* courteous; orig. fair, allied to L. *facies.*

Facile; see **Fact.**

Fact, a deed, reality. (L.) L. *factum,* a deed; orig. neut. of *factus,* pp. of *facere,* to make, do. (√ DHA.)

affair. (F.–L.) M. E. *affere.*–O. F. *afeire, afaire,* a business; orig. *a faire,* i. e. (something) to do.–L. *ad,* to; *facere,* to do.

affect. (L.) L. *affectare,* to apply oneself to (hence, to act upon); frequent. of *afficere,* to aim at, treat.–L. *af-* = *ad,* to; *facere,* to do, act. **Der.** *dis-affect.*

comfit, sb. (F.–L.) Formerly *confit, confite.*–O. F. *confit,* lit. confected, prepared; pp. of *confire.*–L. *conficere,* to put together. –L. *con-* (*cum*), together; *facere,* to make.

confect, to make up into sweetmeats. (L.) L. *confectus,* pp. of *conficere,* to put together, make up (above). **Der.** *confect-ion, confect-ion-er.*

counterfeit, imitated. (F.–L.) M. E. *counterfeit.*–O. F. *contrefait,* pp. of *contrefaire,* to imitate.–F. *contre,* over against, like; *faire,* to make.–L. *contra,* against; *facere,* to make.

defeasance, a rendering null. (F.–L.) O. Norman F. law-term *defeasance,* a rendering void.–O. F. *defaisant,* pres. part. of *defaire, desfaire,* to render void.–O. F. *des-* (L. *dis-*), apart; *faire* (L. *facere*), to make.

defeat. (F.–L.) M. E. *defaiten,* to defeat.–O. F. *defait, desfait,* pp. of *defaire, desfaire,* to render void (above).

defect. (L.) L. *defectus,* a want.–L. *defectus,* pp. of *deficere,* to fail, orig. to undo. – L. *de,* down; *facere,* to make. **Der.** *defect-ion.*

deficient. (L.) From stem of pres. pt. of *deficere,* to fail (above).

deficit, lack. (L.) L. *deficit,* it fails; 3 p. s. pres. of *deficere* (above).

difficulty. (F.–L.) M. E. *difficultee.* –O. F. *difficulte.*–L. *difficultatem,* acc. of *difficultas* (put for *difficilitas**), difficulty. –L. *difficilis,* hard.–L. *dif-* (for *dis-*), apart; *facilis,* easy; see **facile** (below).

discomfit. (F.–L.) O. F. *desconfiz,* pp. of *desconfire,* 'to discomfit, defeat,' Cot.–O. F. *des-* (= L. *dis-*), apart; *confire,* to preserve, prepare; see **comfit** above.

effect. (F. – L.) O. F. *effect.* – L. *effectum,* acc. of *effectus,* an effect. – L. *effectus,* pp. of *efficere,* to work out. – L. *ef-* = *ex,* out, thoroughly; *facere,* to do.

efficacy, force, virtue. (L.) L. *efficacia,* effective power. – L. *efficac-,* for *efficax,* efficacious.–L. *efficere* (above).

efficient. (L.) From stem of pres. pt. of *efficere,* to work out (above).

facile, easy to do. (F.–L.) F. *facile.* –L. *facilis,* i. e. do-able.–L. *facere,* to do.

fac-simile. (L.) Short for *factum simile,* made like.–L. *factum,* neut. of pp. of *facere,* to make; *simile,* neut. of *similis,* like; see **Similar.**

faction. (F.–L.) F. *faction,* a sect. – L. *factionem,* acc. of *factio,* a doing, taking part, faction.–L. *factus,* pp. of *facere,* to do.

factitious. (L.) L. *factitius,* artificial. – L. *factus,* pp. of *facere,* to make.

factotum. (L.) A general agent.–L. *fac-ere totum,* to do everything.

faculty, facility to act. (F.–L.) M. E. *facultee.*–F. *faculté.*–L. *facultatem,* acc. of *facultas* (= *facilitas**), facility.–L. *facilis,* easy; see **facile** above.

fashion. (F.–L.) O. F. *faceon, fachon,* make, shape.–L. *factionem,* acc. of *factio,* a making; see **faction** above.

feasible, easy to be done. (F. – L.) [Better *feisable.*]–O. F. *feisable, faisable,* 'feasible, doable;' Cot. – O. F. *fais-ant,* pres. part. of *faire,* to do.–L. *facere,* to do.

fetich, fetish, an object of superstitious worship. (F. – Port. – L.) F. *fétiche.* – Port. *feitiço,* sorcery, lit. artificial; also, a name given by the Port. to the roughly made idols of Africa.–L. *factitius,* artificial. –L. *fact-us,* pp. of *facere,* to make.

feat, a deed well done. (F.–L.) M. E. *feet, feite.*–O. F. *fait.*–L. *factum,* a deed; see **Fact.**

feature, make, form. (F.–L.) M. E.

feture. – O. F. *faiture*, fashion. – L. *factura*, work, formation. – L. *factus*, pp. of *facere*, to make.

fiat, a decree. (L.) L. *fiat*, let it be done. – L. *fio*, I become; used as pass. of *facere*, to do.

infect, to taint. (F. – L.) M. E. *infect*, as pp.; also *infecten*, verb. – O. F. *infect*, infected. – L. *infectus*, pp. of *in-ficere*, to put in, dye, stain. – L. *in*, in; *facere*, to put.

perfect. (F. – L.) M. E. *perfit*, *parfit*. – O. F. *parfit*, *parfeit* (F. *parfait*). – L. *perfectus*, pp. of *per-ficere*, to complete.

prefect, a governor. (F. – L.) M. E. *prefect*. – O. F. *prefect* (F. *préfet*). – L. *præfectus*, one set over others; pp. of *præ-ficere*, to set before. – L. *præ-*, before; *facere*, to make.

proficient. (L.) L. *proficient-*, stem of pres. pt. of *pro-ficere*, to make progress, advance. – L. *pro*, forward; *facere*, to make.

profit. (F. – L.) M. E. *profit*. – F. *profit*. – L. *profectum*, neut. of *profectus*, pp. of *proficere*, to make progress, be profitable (above).

refection, refreshment. (F. – L.) F. *refection*, a repast. – L. acc. *refectionem*, lit. a remaking. – L. *refectus*, pp. of *reficere*, to remake, restore. – L. *re-*, again; *facere*.

suffice. (F. – L.) From F. *suffis-*, base of *suffis-ant*, pres. pt. of *suffire*, to suffice. – L. *sufficere*, to supply. – L. *suf- = sub*, under; *facere*, to make, put.

sufficient. (L.) From the stem of pres. pt. of L. *sufficere*, to suffice (above).

surfeit, sb. (F. – L.) O. F. *surfait*, *sorfait*, excess; orig. pp. of *sorfaire*, to augment, exaggerate. – L. *super*, above; *facere*, to make.

Fade; see **Fatuous**.

Fadge, to turn out, succeed. (E.) M. E. *faggen** (not found). A. S. *fægian*, to fit. Allied to **Pact**. (✓ PAK.)

Fæces. (L.) L. *fæces*, dregs; pl. of *fæx*, the same. Der. *fec-ulent*, L. *fæc-u-lentus*, adj. from *fæx*.

defecate. (L.) From pp. of *defæcare*, to free from dregs. – L. *de-*, out; *fæc-*, stem of *fæx* (above).

Fag, to drudge. (E. ?) 'To *fag*, deficere;' Levins (1570). The orig. sense is 'to droop.' Perhaps a corruption of *flag*; see **Flag** (1); and see below.

Fag-end, remnant. (E. ?) In Massinger, Virg. Mart. ii. 3. Perhaps for *flag-end* = loose end; see above.

Faggot, Fagot. (F. – L. ?) F. *fagot*,

'a fagot, a bundle of sticks;' Cot. (1) Perhaps from L. *fac-*, stem of *fax*, a torch; cf. *facula*, a little torch. (2) Or, since the Ital. form is *fangotto*, perhaps from Icel. *fanga*, an armful; see **Fang**.

Fail; see **Fallible**.

Fain. (E.) M. E. *fayn*. A. S. *fægen*, glad. + O. Sax. *fagan*, Icel. *feginn*, glad. Allied to **Fadge**. (✓ PAK.)

fawn (1), to cringe to, rejoice servilely over. (Scand.) Icel. *fagna*, to rejoice, welcome one; allied to *feginn*, fain.

Faint; see **Figure**.

Fair (1), pleasing, beautiful. (E.) M. E. *fayr*, A. S. *fæger*, fair. + Icel. *fagr*; Dan. *feir*, Swed. *fager*, Goth. *fagrs*, fit, O. H. G. *fagar*; Gk. πηγός, firm. (✓ PAK.)

Fair (2), a holiday. (F. – L.) M. E. *feire*. – L. *feria*, a holiday, later, a fair; commoner as pl. *feriæ*, put for *fes-iæ**, feast-days; allied to **Feast**.

Fairy; see **Fate**.

Faith. (F. – L.) M. E. *feith*; also *fay*. Slightly altered from O. F. *feid*, *fei*, faith. – L. *fidem*, acc. of *fides*, faith. + Gk. πίστις, faith. (✓ BHIDH, from BHANDH.)

affiance. (F. – L.) O. F. *afiance*, trust; of. *affier*, *ufier*, to trust (whence E. *affy*). – O. F. *a* (L. *ad*), to; and *fidant-*, stem of pres. pt. of Low L. *fidare*, to trust, from L. *fidere*, to trust. Cf. Low L. *fidantia*, a pledge.

affidavit, an oath. (L.) Low L. *affidauit*, 3 p. s. pt. t. of *affidare*, to pledge. – L. *af- = ad*, to; Low L. *fidare*, for L. *fidere*, to trust.

confide. (L.) L. *confidere*, to trust fully. – L. *con-* (*cum*), fully; *fidere*, to trust.

defy. (F. – L.) M. E. *defyen*. – O. F. *defier*, *deffier*, *desfier*, orig. to renounce one's faith. – Low L. *diffidare*, to renounce faith. – L. *dif-*, for *dis-*, apart; *fidare*, for *fidere*, to trust.

diffident. (L.) L. *diffident-*, stem of *diffidens*, pres. pt. of *diffidere*, to distrust. – L. *dif- = dis-*, apart; *fidere*, to trust.

fealty, true service. (F. – L.) O. F. *fealte*, *feelteit*, fidelity. – L. *fidelitatem*, acc. of *fidelitas*, fidelity; see below.

fidelity. (F. – L.) F. *fidelité*. – L. *fidelitatem*, acc. of *fidelitas*, faithfulness. – L. *fideli-*, crude form of *fidelis*, faithful. – L. *fides*, faith.

fiducial, shewing trust. (L.) From L. *fiducia*, trust. – L. *fidere*, to trust.

infidel. (F. – L.) O. F. *infidele*, 'infidell;' Cot. – L. *infidelis*, faithless. – L. *in*, not; *fidelis*, faithful.

perfidious. (L.) From L. *perfidiosus*, treacherous. — L. *perfidia*, treachery. — L. *perfidus*, treacherous. — L. *per*, away (cf. Skt. *pard*, from) ; *fides*, faith.

Falchion, a sword. (Ital. — L.) Ital. *falcione* (*ci* pron. as *ch*). — Low L. *falcionem*, acc. of *falcio*, a bent sword. — L. *falci-*, crude form of *falx*, a sickle.

defalcate, to abate, deduct. (L.) From pp. of Low L. *diffalcare*, to abate, deduct, take away. — L. *dif-* = *dis-*, apart ; Late L. *falcare*, to cut with a sickle, from L. *falx* (stem *falc-*), a sickle.

falcon. (F. — L.) M. E. *faucon*. — O.F. *faucon, faulcon.* — Late L. *falconem*, acc. of *falco*, a falcon, so named from its hooked claws. — L. *falc-*, stem of *falx*, a sickle.

Faldstool ; see Fold.

Fall, to drop down. (E.) M. E. *fallen.* A. S. *feallan.*+Du. *vallen*, Icel. *falla*, Dan. *falde* (for *falle*), Swed. *falla*, G. *fallen* ; L. *fallere*, to deceive, *falli*, to err ; Gk. σφάλλειν, to cause to fall, trip up ; Skt. *sphal*, to tremble. (√SPAR.) ¶ Grimm's law does not apply, because an initial *s* is lost in Teut. and Latin. Der. *be-fall*, from A.S. *be-feallan*, to fall out, happen.

fell (1), to cause to fall. (E.) A. S. *fellan*, causal of *feallan*, to fall. So also Du. *vellen*, Dan. *fælde*, Swed. *fälla*, Icel. *fella*, G. *fällen* ; all causal forms.

Fallible. (L.) L. *fallibilis*, liable to err. — L. *falli*, to err ; *fallere*, to deceive ; cognate with E. *fall*, q. v.

default. (F. — L.) See fault (below).

fail. (F. — L.) *faillir.* — L. *fallere*, to beguile ; *falli*, to err.

fallacy. (F. — L.) Formed by adding *-y* to M. E. *fallace*, a fallacy, deceit. — F. *fallace.* — L. *fallacia*, deceit. — L. *fallac-*, stem of *fallax*, deceitful. — L. *fallere*, to deceive.

false. (F. — L.) M. E. *fals.* — O. F. *fals* (F. *faux*). — L. *falsus*, false ; pp. of *fallere*, to deceive.

falter, to totter, stammer. (F. — L.) M. E. *faltren*, to totter ; frequentative from a base *falt-.* — O. F. *falter**, to fail ; not recorded ; but see fault below.

faucet, a spigot, vent. (F. — L.) O. F. (and F.) *fausset*, a faucet ; *faulset*, Cot. — O. F. *faulser*, to falsify, forge ; also *faulser un escu*, to pierce a shield, hence, to pierce. — L. *falsare*, to falsify. — L. *falsus*, false.

fault. (F. — L.) Formerly *faut*. M. E. *faute.* — O. F. *faute*, a fault. (Span. and Ital. *falta*, a defect.) — O. F. *falter**, not found, but answering to Span. *faltar*, Ital.

---

faltare, to lack ; frequent. form of L. *faltere*, to fail. Der. *de-fault* (*de-* = O. F. *de-* = L. *dis-*).

refel. (L.) L. *refellere*, to shew to be false, refute. — L. *re-*, again ; *fallere*, to deceive.

Fallow (1), orig. 'harrowed ;' of land. (E.) A. S. *fælging*, fallow-land. — A. S. *fealh*, a harrow.

Fallow (2), used with reference to colour. (E.) A. S. *fealu, fealo*, pale red, yellowish. + Du. *vaal*, Icel. *fölr*, pale, G. *fahl*, pale, also *falb*, L. *pallidus*, Gk. πολιός, gray, Skt. *palita*, gray. See Pale.

False, Falter ; see Fallible.

Fame, report. (F. — L.) F. *fame.* — L. *fama*, report. — L. *fari*, to speak ; see Fate.

confess. (F. — L.) O. F. *confesser.* — L. *confessus*, pp. of *confiteri*, to confess. — L. *con-* (*cum*), fully ; *fateri*, to acknowledge, from L. *fat-um*, supine of *fari*, to speak.

defame. (F. — L.) * M. E. *defamen, diffamen.* — O. F. *defamer*, to take away a man's character. — L. *diffamare*, to spread a bad report. — L. *dif-*, for *dis-*, apart ; *fama*, a report.

infamy. (F. — L.) F. *infamie.* — L. *infamia*, ill fame. — L. *in-*, not, bad ; *fama*, fame.

profess. (F. — L.) We find M. E. *professed*, pp., Englished from O. F. *profes*, masc., *professe*, fem., professed. — L. *professus*, pp. of *profiteri*, to avow. — L. *pro*, forth ; *fateri*, to speak ; see confess (above).

Family. (F. — L.) F. *famille.* — L. *familia*, a household. — L. *famulus*, a servant, Oscan *famel* ; from Oscan *faama*, a house. Cf. Skt. *dhāman*, a house. (√DHA.) Der. *famili-ar* (L. *familiaris*).

Famine. (F. — L.) F. *famine.* — Low L. *famina**, unrecorded, but plainly an extension from L. *fames*, hunger. Cf. Skt. *hâni*, privation, want. (√GHA.) Der. *fam-ish*, formed (by analogy with *languish*, &c.) from L. *fam-es*, hunger.

Fan, an instrument for blowing. (L.) A. S. *fann.* — L. *uannus*, a fan (cf. F. *van*) ; see below. Allied to Skt. *vâta*, wind, from *vâ*, to blow. (√WA.)

van (2), a fan for winnowing. (F. — L.) In Milton, P. L. ii. 927. — F. *van*, 'a vanne ;' Cot. — L. *uannus* (above).

Fanatic ; see Fane.

Fancy ; see Phantom.

Fane, a temple. (L.) L. *fanum*, a temple ; supposed to be derived from L. *fari*, to speak (hence, perhaps, to dedicate).

fanatic, religiously insane. (F. — L.)

F. *fanatique.* – L. *fanaticus*, (1) belonging to a temple, (2) inspired by a divinity, enthusiastic. – L. *fanum*, a temple.

profane, impious. (F. – L.) F. *profane.* – L. *profanus*, unholy; lit. before (i. e. outside of) the temple. – L. *pro*, before; *fanum*, a temple.

Fanfare, a flourish of trumpets. (F. – Span. – Arab.) F. *fanfare*. – Span. *fanfarra*, bluster, vaunting. – Arab. *farfár*, loquacious. Der. *fanfarr-on-ade*, bluster.

Fang, a talon, claw. (E.) A.S. *fang*, lit. a seizing. – A.S. *fangan* *, to seize, only used in the contracted form *fón* (pt. t. *feng*, pp. *gefangen*).+Du. *vangen*, to catch; Icel. *fá* (cf. *fang*, sb., a catch of fish), Dan. *faae*, Swed. *få*, Goth. *fahan*, G. *fangen*, to catch; *fang*, sb., a catch, also a fang. (√ PAK.)

Fantasy; see Phantom.

Far. (E.) M.E. *fer*. A.S. *feor*.+Du. *ver*, Icel. *fjarri*, Swed. *fjerran*, adv., Dan. *fjern*, G. *fern*; Goth. *fairra*, adv. Allied to Gk. πέραν, beyond; Skt. *paras*, beyond, *para*, far. (√ PAR.) The comp. *farther* is a corruption of M.E. *ferrer* (i.e. *far-er*); due to confusion with *further*, comp. of **Forth.**

Farce. (F. – L.) The orig. sense is 'stuffing;' hence, a jest inserted into a comedy. – F. *farce*, stuffing, a farce. – F. *farcer*, to stuff. – L. *farcire*, to stuff.+Gk. φράσσειν, to shut in.

force (2), to stuff fowls. (F. – L.) corruption of *farce*, to stuff (above). Der. *force-meat*, a corruption of *farced meat* or *farce-meat*.

Fardel, a pack, bundle. (F. – Arab.) M.E. *fardel*. – O.F. *fardel* (F. *fardeau*). Dimin. of F. *farde*, a burden, now 'a bale' of coffee. Prob. from Arab. *fardah*, a package (Devic).

furl, to roll up a sail. (F. – Arab.) Formerly spelt *furdle*, *farthel*, to roll up in a bundle. From *fardel*, a bundle (above).

Fare, to travel, speed. (E.) A.S. *faran*, to go, travel.+Du. *varen*, Icel. Swed. *fara*, Dan. *fare*, G. *fahren*, Goth. *faran*, to go; Gk. πορεύομαι, I travel. Cf. L. *experior*, I pass through, Skt. *pri*, to bring over. (√ PAR.) Der. *fare-well*, i.e. may you speed well; *thorough-fare*, a passage through; *wel-fare*, successful practice or journey.

ferry, verb. (E.) M.E. *ferien*. A.S. *ferian*, to convey across. – A.S. *faran*, to go.+Icel. *ferja*, to carry; causal of *fara*, to go; Goth. *farjan*, to travel by ship.

ford. (E.) M.E. *ford*; also *forth*. A.S.

ford, a ford, passage. Allied to A.S. *faran*, to go; and to *frith*; see below.

frith, firth, an estuary. (Scand.) M.E. *firth*. – Icel. *fjörðr*, a firth, bay; Dan. *fiord*, Swed. *fjärd*, the same; L. *portus*, a haven, Gk. πορθμός, a ferry. Allied to *ford* (above).

Farina, ground corn. (L.) L. *farina*, meal. – L. *far*, a kind of grain; allied to Barley. Der. *farinaceous*, L. *farina-ce-us*.

farrago. (L.) L. *farrago*, mixed food for cattle, a medley. – L. *far*, grain, spelt.

Farm; see Firm.

Farrier; see Ferreous.

Farrow, to litter pigs. (E.) From the sb. *farrow*, a litter of pigs. – A.S. *fearh*, a pig; pl. *fearas*.+M.H.G. *varch*, a pig; G. *ferk-el*; L. *porcus*; see Pork.

Farther; see Far.

Farthing; see Four.

Farthingale; see Verdant.

Fascinate. (L.) From pp. of L. *fascinare*, to enchant.

Fascine, a bundle of rods. (F. – L.) O.F. *fascine*. – L. *fascina*, a bundle of twigs. – L. *fascis*, a bundle.

Fashion; see Fact.

Fast (1), firm. (E.) A.S. *fæst*.+Du. *vast*, Dan. Swed. *fast*, Icel. *fastr*, G. *fest*. Cf. Gk. ἔμ-πεδος, fast, steadfast. Allied to **Foot.** Der. *fast* (2), *fast* (3).

fast (2), to abstain from food. (E.) A.S. *fæstan*, orig. to make fast, observe, be strict; from *fæst* (above). + Du. *vasten*, Dan. *faste*, Swed. and Icel. *fasta*, G. *fasten*.

fast (3), quick. (Scand.) A peculiar use of *fast* (1) above; this use is Scand. Cf. Icel. *drekka fast*, to drink hard, *sofa fast*, to be fast asleep, *fastr í verkum*, hard at work; &c. It means firm, close, urgent, quick.

fasten. (E.) A.S. *fæstnian*, to make fast or firm. – A.S. *fæst*, firm.

fastness. (E.) M.E. *festnes*, *fastnesse*, orig. strength. – A.S. *fæstness*, the firmament, orig. that which is firm. – A.S. *fæst*, firm.

Fastidious. (L.) L. *fastidiosus*, disdainful. – L. *fastidium*, loathing; perhaps put for *fastutidium* * (Vaniček). – L. *fastu-s*, arrogance; *tædium*, disgust; so that *fastidium* = arrogant disgust.

Fastness; see Fast.

Fat (1), gross. (E.) A.S. *fæt*.+Du. *vet*, Dan. *fed*, Swed. *fet*, Icel. *feitr*. Cf. Skt. *pīvan*, fat.

Fat (2), a vat; see Vat.

Fate, destiny. (F.—L.) M. E. *fate.*— O. F. *fat.* (not common).—L. *fatum,* what is spoken ; neut. of pp. of *fari,* to speak.+ Gk. φημί, I say, Skt. *bhásh,* to speak ; A. S. *bannan* ; see Ban. (√ BHA.)

affable. (F.—L.) F. *affable.*—L. *affabilis,* easy to be spoken to.—L. *af-=ad,* to ; *fari,* to speak.

confabulate. (L.) From pp. of L. *confabulari,* to talk together. — L. *con-* (*cum*), with ; *fabulari,* to converse, from *fabula,* a discourse ; see **fable** (below).

fable, a story. (F.—L.) F. *fable.*—L. *fabula,* a narrative. — L. *fa-ri,* to speak, tell.

fairy. (F.—L.) M. E. *faerie, fayrye,* enchantment. [The mod. use of the word is improper ; *fairy*=enchantment, the right word for 'elf' being *fay.*]—O. F. *faerie,* enchantment.—O. F. *fae,* a fay ; see below.

fay, a fairy. (F.—L.) F. *fée,* O. F. *fae,* a fay. Cf. Port. *fada,* Ital. *fata,* a fay.— Low L. *fata,* a fate, goddess of destiny, a fay.—L. *fatum,* fate (above).

ineffable. (F.—L.) F. *ineffable.* — L. *ineffabilis,* unspeakable. — L. *in,* not ; *ef-* (for *ex*), out ; *fa-ri,* to speak.

infant. (L.) L. *infant-,* stem of *in-fans,* not speaking, hence, a very young babe.— L. *in-,* not ; *fans,* pres. pt. of *fari,* to speak.

infantry. (F.—Ital.—L.) F. *infanterie.* —Ital. *infanteria,* foot-soldiers ; orig. a band of 'infants,' as young men were called. —Ital. *infante,* an infant.—L. *infantem,* acc. of *infans* (above).

nefarious. (L.) L. *nefarius,* impious. —L. *nefas,* that which is unlawful.—L. *ne,* not ; *fas,* law, from *fari,* to speak, declare.

preface. (F.—L.) O. F. *preface.* — Low L. *præfatium*,* not found, put for L. *præfatum,* a preface, neut. of *præ-fatus,* spoken before.

Father. (E.) M. E. *fader.* A. S. *fæder.* (The spelling with *th* approaches the Icelandic.)+Icel. *faðir,* Du. *vader,* Dan. Swed. *fader,* Goth. *fadar,* G. *vater,* L. *pater,* Gk. πατήρ, Pers. *pidar,* Skt. *pitri.* (√ PA.)

Fathom. (E.) M. E. *fadme.* A. S. *fæðm,* the space reached by the extended arms, a grasp, embrace.+Du. *vadem,* Icel. *faðmr,* a fathom, Dan. *favn,* Swed. *famn,* an embrace, G. *faden.* Allied to **Patent.** (√ PAT.)

Fatigue, sb. (F.—L.) O. F. *fatigue* ; from *fatiguer,* to weary. — L. *fatigare,* to weary.

Fatuous. (L.) L. *fatuus,* silly, feeble.

Der. *in-fatuate,* from pp. of L. *infatuare,* to make a fool of.

fade, vb. (F.—L.) From F. *fade,* adj., unsavoury, weak, faint. —L. *fatuus,* foolish, tasteless.

vade, to fade. (F.—L.) A weakened form of **fade** (above).

Fauces. (L.) L. *fauces,* pl., the upper part of the throat.

Faucet, Fault ; see **Fallible.**

Faun ; see **Favour.**

Fauteuil ; see **Fold** (1).

Favour, sb. (F.—L.) O. F. *faveur* = L. *fauorem,* acc of *fauor,* favour.—L. *fauere,* to befriend.

faun, a rural (Roman) deity. (L.) L. *faunus.* —L. *fauere,* to be propitious.

favourite. (F. — L.) Orig. fem. of F. *favori,* favoured.

Fawn (1) ; see **Fain.**

Fawn (2), a young deer ; see **Fetus.**

Fay ; see **Fate.**

Fealty ; see **Faith.**

Fear. (E.) M. E. *feer.* A. S. *fǽr,* a sudden peril, danger, fear. Orig. used of the peril of travelling.—A. S. *faran,* to go, travel. + Icel. *fár,* harm, G. *gefahr,* danger.

Feasible ; see **Fact.**

Feast ; see **Festal.**

Feat ; see **Fact.**

Feather. (E.) M. E. *fether.* A. S. *feðer.* + Du. *veder,* Dan. *fiæder,* Swed. *fjäder,* Icel. *fjöðr,* G. *feder,* L. *penna* (for *pet-na**), Skt. *patra.* See **Pen.** (√ PAT.)

Feature ; see **Fact.**

Febrile ; see **Fever.**

February. (L.) L. *februarius,* the month of expiation.—L. *februa,* neut. pl., a festival of expiation on Feb. 15. — L. *februus,* cleansing ; *februare,* to expiate.

Feculent ; see **Fæces.**

Fecundity ; see **Fetus.**

Federal. (F.—L.) F. *fédéral.* Formed, with suffix *-al,* from L. *fœder-,* stem of *fœdus,* a treaty. Akin to *fides,* faith.

confederate. (L.) L. *confœderatus,* united by a *covenant,* pp. of *con-fœderare.* —L. *con-* (*cum*), together ; *fœder-,* crude form of *fœdus,* a treaty.

Fee, a grant of land, property, payment. (E.) M. E. *fee.* A. S. *feoh, feó,* cattle, property. + Du. *vee,* Icel. *fé,* Dan. *fæ,* Swed. *fä,* Goth. *faihu,* G. *vieh,* O. H. G. *fihu,* L. *pecus* : Skt. *paçu,* cattle. (√ PAK.) See **Pecuniary.**

fellow, a partner. (Scand.) M. E.

felawe. — Icel. *félagi,* a partner in a ' félag.'
— Icel. *félag,* companionship; lit. a laying
together of property. — Icel. *fé,* property;
lag, a laying together, a law; see **Law.**

Feeble. (F. — L.) M. E. *feble.* — O. F.
foible, standing for *floible*,* as shewn by
Ital. *fievole* (= *flevole*), feeble; since Ital.
fi = fl. — L. *flebilis,* doleful; hence, weak. —
L. *flere,* to weep. Allied to **Fluent.**

foible, a weak point in character. —
O. F. *foible* (above).

Feed; see **Food.**

Feel. (E.) M. E.. *felen.* A. S. *félan.* +
Du. *voelen,* G. *fühlen.* Perhaps allied to
Palpable.

Feign; see **Figure.**

Feldspar; see **Field.**

Felicity. (F. — L.) O. F. *felicite.* — L.
acc. *felicitatem.* — L. *felici-,* crude form
of *felix,* happy, fruitful; allied to **Fetus.**

Feline. (L.) L. *felinus,* belonging to
cats. — L. *felis,* a cat; lit, 'the fruitful;'
allied to **Fetus.**

Fell (1); see **Fall.**

Fell (2), a skin. (E.) M. E. *fel.* A. S.
fel, fell. + Du. *vel,* Icel. *fell,* Goth. *fill,*
M. H. G. *vel,* L. *pellis,* Gk. πέλλα, skin.
Doublet, *pell.*

film, a thin skin. (E.) A. S. *film*; O.
Fries. *film.* Extended from the base *fil-* in
A. S. *fel,* skin, Goth. *fill,* skin.

Fell (3), cruel, dire. (E.) A. S. *fel,* in
comp. *welfel* = fierce for slaughter, &c. +
O. Du. *fel,* wrathful; whence O. F. *fel,*
cruel. + Dan. *fæl,* hideous, grim, horrid.

Fell (4), a hill. (Scand.) M. E. *fel.* —
Icel. *fjall, fell,* a hill; Dan. *field,* Swed.
fjäll, a fell. Orig. an open down; allied
to **Field.**

Felloe; see **Felly.**

Fellow; see **Fee.**

Felly, Felloe, part of a wheel-rim. (E.)
M. E. *felwe.* A. S. *felga,* a felly. So
named from the pieces being put together;
from A. S. *feolan, fiolan,* orig. *filhan,* to
stick, cleave to, allied to Goth. *filhan,* to
hide. + Du. *velg,* Dan. *fælge,* G. *felge.*

Felon, a wicked person. (F. — Low L. —
C. ?) M. E. *felun.* — O. F. *felon,* a traitor.
— Low L. *felonem,* acc. of *felo, fello,* a traitor, rebel. Prob. Celtic. Cf. Gael. *feallan,* a
traitor, Bret. *falloni,* treachery; Irish and
Gael. *feall,* to betray, deceive, allied to L.
fallere, to deceive.

Felt. (E.) M. E. *felt.* A. S. *felt.* + Du.
vilt, G. *filz*; Gk. πίλος, felt; cf. L. *pileus,*
a felt hat.

filter, to strain. (F. — O. Low G.) F.
filtrer, to strain through felt. — Du. *vilt,*
felt; originally spelt *filt.*

Felucca, a ship. (Ital. — Arab.) Ital.
feluca. — Arab. *fulk,* a ship. (See Devic.)

Female; see below.

Feminine. (F. — L.) O. F. *feminin.* —
L. *femininus,* womanly. — L. *femina,* a
woman. (Perhaps allied to **Fetus.**)

effeminate. (L.) From pp. of L.
effeminare, to make womanish. — L. *ef-,* for
ex, thoroughly; *femina* (above).

female. (F. — L.) Put for *femell,* by
confusion with *male.* M. E. *femele.* — O. F.
femelle. — L. *femella,* a young woman;
dimin. of *femina,* a woman.

Femoral, belonging to the thigh. (L.)
L. *femoralis*; adj. from *femor-,* base of
femur, thigh.

Fen, a bog. (E.) M. E. *fen.* A. S. *fenn.*
+ Du. *veen,* Icel. *fen,* Goth. *fani,* mud.
Cf. L. *palus,* a marsh. And see **Vinewed.**

Fence; short for *defence*; see **Defend.**

Fend; short for **Defend,** q. v.

Fennel, a plant. (L.) M. E. *fenel.* A. S.
finol, finugle. — L. *fœniculum,* fennel;
double dimin. of *fenum,* hay.

fenugreek. (L.) L. *fenum Græcum.*

Feoff; see **Fief.**

Ferment; see **Fervent.**

Fern. (E.) A. S. *fearn.* + Du. *varen*;
Skt. *parna,* a wing, feather, leaf, plant, the
orig. sense being 'feather.'

Ferocity. (F. — L.) F. *ferocité.* — L. acc.
ferocitatem, fierceness. — L. *feroci-,* crude
form of *ferox,* fierce. — L. *ferus,* fierce, wild.
Allied to **Deer.**

fierce. (F. — L.) M. E. *fers.* — O. F.
fers, fiers, old nom. of O. F. *fer, fier,*
fierce. — L. *ferus,* wild.

Ferreous. (L.) L. *ferreus,* made of
iron. — L. *ferrum,* iron.

farrier. (F. — L.) Formerly *ferrer,* a
worker in iron. — F. *fer,* iron. — L. *ferrum.*

ferruginous. (L.) L. *ferruginus,* same
as *ferrugineus,* rusty. — L. *ferrugin-,* stem
of *ferrugo,* rust of iron. — L. *ferrum.*

Ferret (1), an animal. (F. — Low L. —
C. ?) O. F. *furet,* a ferret. — Low L. *fure-
tus, furectus,* a ferret; also *furo.* Said to
be from L. *fur,* a thief; more likely from
Bret. *fûr,* wise, W. *ffur,* wise, wily, crafty,
ffured, a wily one, a ferret.

Ferret (2), a kind of silk tape; see
Floral.

Ferruginous; see **Ferreous.**

Ferrule, a metal ring at the end of a

stick. (F.−L.) Corrupted spelling (due to confusion with *ferrum*, iron) of the older form *verril*; XVI cent. − O. F. *virole*, a ferrule; Low L. *virola*, the same. From L. *uiriola*, a little bracelet; dimin. of *uiria*, an armlet.−L. *uiere*, to twist, plait. (√WI.) Allied to **Withy**.

Ferry; see **Fare**.

Fertile. (F.−L.) F. *fertile*.−L. *fertilis*, fertile.−L. *ferre*, to bear; allied to **Bear** (1).

  circumference. (L.) L. *circumferentia*, boundary of a circle.−L. *circumferent-*, stem of pres. pt. of *circum-ferre*, to carry round.

  confer. (F.−L.) F. *conferer*.−L. *conferre*, to bring together, collect, bestow.

  defer (1), to delay. (F.−L.) M. E. *differren*. − O. F. *differer*, to delay. − L. *differre*, to bear different ways, delay.−L. *dif-*, for *dis-*, apart; *ferre*, to bear.

  defer (2), to lay before, submit oneself. (F.−L.) O. F. *deferer*, to admit or give way to an appeal.−L. *de-ferre*, to bring down, bring before one.

  differ. (L.) L. *differre*, to carry apart, to differ.−L. *dif-*, for *dis-*, apart; *ferre*, to bear.

  infer, to imply. (F.−L.) F. *inferer*. −L. *in-ferre*, to bring in, introduce.

  offer. (L.) A. S. *offrian*.−L. *offerre*, to offer.−L. *of-*, for *ob*, near; *ferre*, to bring. Der. *offer-t-or-y*, from F. *offertoire*, L. *offertorium*, a place to which offerings were brought.

  prefer. (F.−L.) O. F. *preferer*.−L. *præ-ferre*, to set in front, prefer.

  proffer. (F.−L.) O. F. *proferer*, to produce, adduce. − L. *pro-ferre*, to bring forward.

  refer, to assign. (F.−L.) O. F. *referer* (F. *référer*).−L. *re-ferre*, to bear back, relate, refer.

  suffer. (F.−L.) M. E. *soffren*, *suffren*. −O. F. *soffrir* (F. *souffrir*).−L. *sufferre*, to undergo.−L. *suf-* (*sub*), under; *ferre*, to bear.

  transfer. (F.−L.) F. *transférer*. − L. *trans-ferre*, to convey across.

Ferule, a rod or bat for punishing children. (L.) Formerly *ferula*.−L. *ferula*, a rod.−L. *ferire*, to strike. + Icel. *berja*, to strike.

  interfere. (F. − L.) Formerly *enterfeir*, to dash one heel against the other (Blount). − F. *entre*, between; *ferir*, to strike.−L. *inter*, between; *ferire*, to strike.

Fervent, hot, zealous. (F.−L.) O. F. *fervent*.−L. *feruent-*, stem of pres. pt. of *feruere*, to boil. Allied to **Brew**. Der. *fervour*, from O. F. *ferveur* = L. . acc. *feruorem*, heat; *fervid*, from L. *feruidus*.

  effervesce. (L.) L. *efferuescere*.−L. *ef-*, for *ex*, out; *feruescere*, to begin to boil, inceptive of *feruere*, to boil.

  ferment. (L.) L. *fermentum* (short for *ferui-mentum*), leaven.−L. *feruere*, to boil.

Festal. (L.) A late word, coined (with adj. suffix *-al*) from L. *fest-um*, a feast, orig. neut. of *festus*, bright, joyful. (√BHA.)

  feast. (F.−L.) M. E. *feste*.−O. F. *feste* (F. *fête*).−L. *festa*, lit. festivals, pl. of *festum* (above).

  festival. (F.−Low L.−L.) Properly an adj.−O. F. *festival*, festive.−Low L. *festiualis*.−L. *festiuus* (below).

  festive. (L.) L. *festiuus*, belonging to a feast.−L. *festum*, a feast.

  fête. (F.−L.) Mod. F. *fête*, the same as O. F. *feste*; see **feast** (above).

Fester, to rankle; see **Food**.

Festive; see **Festal**.

Festoon. (F.−L.) F. *feston*, a garland, festoon.−Low L. *festonem*, acc. of *festo*, a garland. Usually derived from L. *festum*, a feast; but it is quite as likely to be from Low L. *festis* (O. F. *fest*, F. *faîte*), a top, ridge, from L. *fastigium*, a top.

Fetch. (E.) M. E. *fecchen*, pt. t. *fehte*, *fehte*. A. S. *feccan*, to fetch, Gen. xviii. 4; Luke xii. 20. Prob. *feccan* is a later form of *fetian*, to fetch (Anglia, vi. 177).−A. S. *fæt*. a pace, stem, journey. (√PAD.) Der. *fetch*, sb., a stratagem.

Fête; see **Festal**.

Fetich, **Fetish**; see **Fact**.

Fetid. (F. − L.) O. F. *fetide*. − L. *fetidus*, *fœtidus*, stinking.−L. *fœtere*, to stink. Allied to **Fume**.

Fetlock, **Fetter**; see **Foot**.

Fetus, offspring. (L.) L. *fetus*, a bringing forth, offspring.−L. *feuēre* *, an obsolete verb, to generate, produce; allied to *fu-i*, I was; see **Future**, **Be**.

  effete, exhausted. (L.) L. *effetus*, weakened by having brought forth young. −L. *ef-*, for *ex*, out; *fetus*, that has brought forth, pp. of *feuēre* (above).

  fawn (2), a young deer. (F. − L.) O. F. *fan*, *faon*, earlier *feön*, a fawn; answering to a Low L. form *fetonus* * (not found). −L. *fetus*, *fœtus*, offspring.

fecundity. (F.—L.) O. F. *fecondité* (Cot.)—L. acc. *fecunditatem*, fruitfulness. —L. *fe-cundus*, fruitful; allied to *fetus*, offspring. And see **Feline.**

Feud (1), hatred; see **Foe.**

Feud (2), a fief; see **Fief.**

Fever, a kind of disease. (L.) M. E. *feuer* (*fever*). A.S. *fefer*, *fefor*; see Matt. viii. 15.—L. *febris*, fever, lit. a 'trembling.' Cf. A. S. *bifian*, G. *beben*, to tremble.

febrile, relating to fever. (F.—L.) F. *febrile.*—L. *febri-s*, fever; with suffix *-lis.*

feverfew, a plant. (L) A.S. *feferfuge.* — L. *febrifuga*, fever dispelling. — L. *febri-s*, fever; *fugare*, to put to flight.

Few. (E.) M. E. *fewe.* A. S. *fed*, pl. *feáwe.* + Icel. *fár*, Dan. *faa*, Swed. *få*, Goth. *faws*, L. *paucus*; Gk. παῦρος, small.

Fey, doomed to die. (E.) A.S. *fǽge*, doomed to die. + Icel. *feigr*, Du. *veeg*; G. *feig*, a coward; Swed. *feg*, Dan. *feig*, cowardly.

Fiat ; see **Fact.**

Fib. (F. — L.) A weakened and shortened form of *fable*, q. v.

Fibre. (F.—L.) F. *fibre.*—L. *fibra*, a thread.

Fickle. (E.) M. E. *fikel.* A.S. *ficol* ; orig. an adj. from *fic*, sb., fraud.

Fiction ; see **Figure.**

Fiddle, a violin. (L.) A.S, *fiðele*, Icel. *fiðla*, Dan. *fiddel*, Du. *vedel*, G. *fiedel.* Apparently borrowed from L. *uitula*, *uidula*, a viol ; see **Viol.**

Fidelity ; see **Faith.**

Fidget. (Scand.) A dimin. form of *fidge*, to be continually moving up and down, spelt *fike* in North of England, M. E. *fiken*, to fidget, to hasten. — Icel. *fika*, to climb up nimbly, as a spider ; Swed. *fika*, to hunt after, Norw. *fika*, to take trouble, *fika etter*, to hasten after, pursue.

Fiducial ; see **Faith.**

Fie. (Scand.) M. E. *fy.*—Icel. *fý*, *fei*, fie ! ; Dan. *fy*, Swed. *fy*, fie ! Cf. G. *pfui*, Lat. *phui*, *phy*, Skt. *phut*, expressions of disgust.

Fief, land held of a superior. (F. — O.H.G.) O.F. *fief*, formerly spelt *fieu* (Scheler).— O. H.G. *fihu* (mod. G. *vieh*), cattle, property; cognate with E. *fee*, q. v.

enfeoff, to endue with a fief. (F. — L. and O. H. G.) The spelling is Norman F.; formed from F. *en* (= L. *in*), in ; and *fief*, a fief (above). See below.

feoff, to invest with a fief. (F. — O. H. G.) Norman F. *feoffer*, O. F. *fiefer*, verb from F. *fief*, a fief (above). Der. *feoffee*, i. e. *fief-é*, where *-é* is the suffix of the pp.

feud (2), a fief. (Low L. — F. — O. H. G.) Low L. *feudum*, a Latinised form of O.F. *fieu*, also spelt *fief* (above). Der. *feud-al*, adj.

Field. (E.) M. E. *feld.* A.S. *feld.* + Du. *veld*, Dan. *felt*, Swed. *fält*, G. *feld*; cf. Russ. *pole*, a field. Allied to **Fell** (4).

feldspar, a kind of mineral. (G.) Corrupted from G. *feldspath*, lit. field-spar.

fieldfare, a bird. (E.) A.S. *feldefare*, lit. 'field-traveller;' see **Fare.**

Fiend. (E.) M. E. *fend.* A.S. *fiónd*, *feond*, lit. 'a hating one,' an enemy, the enemy; orig. pres. part of *feón*, *feógan*, to hate. + Du. *vijand*, Dan. Swed. *fiende*; Icel. *fjándi*, pres. pt. of *fjá*, to hate; Goth. *fijands*, from *fijan*, to hate; G. *feind.* (√ PI.) See **Foe.**

Fierce ; see **Ferocity.**

Fife. (F.—O.H.G.) F. *fifre.*—O. H. G. *pfifa*, G. *pfeife*, a pipe.—O. H. G. *pfifen*, to blow, whistle. See **Pipe.**

Fig. (F.—L.) F. *figue.*—L. *ficum*, acc. of *ficus*, a fig.

Fight. (E.) M. E. *fihten*, *fehten*, verb. A.S. *feohtan*, to fight ; *feohte*, a fight + Du. *vechten*, Dan. *fegte*, Swed. *fäkta*, G. *fechten*, to fight.

Figure. (F.—L.) F. *figure.*—L. *figura*, a thing made.—L. *fingere* (base *fig-*), to make, fashion, feign. + Gk. θιγγάνειν, to handle, Skt. *dih*, to smear (√ DHIGH.) Der. *dis-figure*, *pre-figure*.

configuration. (F.—L.) F. *configuration* ; from acc. of L. *configuratio*, a conformation. — L. *configuratus*, pp. of *configurare*, to put together.—L. *con-* (*cum-*); *figurare*, to fashion, from *figura* (above).

effigy. (L.) Short for *effigies*, an image. —L. *effig-*, base of *effingere*, to form. — L. *ef-*, for *ex*; *fingere*, to form.

faint. (F. — L.) M. E. *feint.* — O. F. *feint*, weak, pretended ; orig. pp. of *feindre*, to feign.—L. *fingere*, to form, feign.

feign. (F.—L.) M. E. *feinen.* — O. F. *feindre.*—L. *fingere* (above).

fiction. (F.—L.) F. *fiction.*—L. *fictionem*, acc. of *fictio*, a feigning.—L. *fictus*, pp. of *fingere.*

figment. (L.) L. *figmentum*, an invention.—L. *fig-*, base of *fingere.*

transfigure. (F.—L.) F. *transfigurer.*

—L. *transfigurare,* to change the figure or appearance. **—** L. *trans,* across (implying change); *figura,* figure.

Filament; see **File** (1).

Filbert, fruit of hazel. (F.**—**O. H. G.) Formerly *philiberd* (Gower); short for *Philiberd* or *Philibert nut,* from the proper name *Philibert*; (S. Philibert's day is Aug. 22).**—**O. H. G. *fili-bert,* very bright; from *fili* (G. *viel*), greatly, *bert, berht,* bright. ¶ Called in Germany *Lambertsnuss* (S. Lambert, Sept. 17); prob. from the time of year of nutting.

Filch. (Scand.) Extended from M. E. *felen,* to conceal.**—**Icel. *fela,* to hide, bury. **+**Goth. *filhan,* to hide.

File (1), string, line, order. (F. **—** L.) O. F. *file*; allied to F. *fil,* a thread. **—** L. *filum,* a thread.

defile (2), to march in a file. **—** F. *défiler,* to defile.**—**F. *dé-*=O. F. *des-*=L. *dis-,* apart; *filer,* to spin threads, from L. *filum.* Der. *defile,* sb.

enfilade, a line or straight passage. (F. **—** L.) F. *enfilade,* a long string (of things).**—**F. *enfiler,* to thread.**—**F. *en-*=L. *in,* in; *fil,* a thread, from L. *filum.*

filament. (F.**—**L.) O. F. *filamen.* **—** L. *filamentum,* thin thread.**—**Low L. *filare,* to wind thread.**—**L. *filum.*

filigree. (Span. **—** L.) Formerly *filigrane*; XVII cent. **—** Span. *filigrana,* filigree-work, fine wrought work.**—**Span. *fila,* a thread or row, *filar,* to spin; *grano,* grain or texture; so called because the chief texture of it was wrought in silver wire. From L. *filum,* thread; *granum,* grain.

fillet. (F. **—** L.) M. E. *fillet.* **—** O. F. *filet,* dimin. of *fil,* a thread.**—**L. *filum.*

profile. (Ital. **—** L.) Ital. *profilo,* a sketch of a picture, outline (Florio).**—**L. *pro,* before, in front; *filum,* a thread (Ital. *filo,* thread, line). ¶ The mod. F. *profil* is also from Ital. *profilo.*

purl (3), to form an edging on lace, invert stitches in knitting. (F. **—** L.) Frequently misspelt *pearl.* Contraction of *purfle.* **—** F. *pourfiler,* to purfle, embroider on an edge.**—**F. *pour* (L. *pro*), confused (as often) with F. *par* (L. *per*), throughout; *fil,* a thread.

File (2), a steel rasp. (E.) A.S. *feól.* **+** Du. *vijl,* Dan. *fiil,* Swed. *fil,* G. *feile,* Russ. *pila,* a file, sharp tool.

Filial. (L.) From L. *fili-us,* a son; *filia,* daughter; orig. infant; cf. L. *felare,* to suck. (✓DHA.)

affiliation. (F.**—**L.) F. *affiliation,* an adoption as a son. **—** Low L. acc. *affiliationem.***—**L. *af-*=*ad,* to; *filius,* a son.

Filibuster; see p. 156, col. 1, l. 4.

Filigree; see **File** (1).

Fill; see **Full** (1).

Fillet; see **File** (1).

Fillibeg, Philibeg, a kilt. (Gaelic.) Gael. *feileadh-beag,* the modern kilt.**—**Gael. *filleadh,* a fold, plait, from the verb *fill,* to fold; and *beag,* little, small.

Fillip, to strike with the finger-nail, when jerked from the thumb. (E.) Another form of *flip*; see **Flippant.**

Filly; see **Foal.**

Film; see **Fell** (2).

Filter; see **Felt.**

Filth; see **Foul.**

Fin. (E.) A.S. *fin,* a fin. **+** Du. *vin,* Swed. *fena,* Dan. *finne,* L. *pinna.*

Final. (F.**—**L.) O. F. *final.***—**L. *finalis,* final.**—**L. *finis,* end.

affinity. (F. **—** L.) F. *affinité.* **—** L. *affinitatem,* acc. of *affinitas,* nearness.**—**L. *affinis,* near, bordering on.**—**L. *af-,* for *ad,* near; *finis,* boundary, end.

confine, to limit. (F.**—**L.) F. *confiner,* to keep within limits. **—** F. *confin,* near.**—**L. *confinis,* bordering on.**—**L. *con-* (*cum*), with; *finis,* boundary.

define. (F.**—**L.) O. F. *definer,* to define, conclude. **—** L. *definire,* to limit. **—** L. *de,* down; *finire,* to end, from *finis,* end.

finance, revenue. (F.**—**L.) O.F. *finance.* **—** Low L. *finantia,* payment. **—** Low L. *finare,* to pay a fine. **—** Low L. *finis,* a settled payment, a *finish* or end, i.e. final arrangement; L. *finis,* end.

fine (1), exquisite, thin. (F.**—**L.) O.F. *fin,* witty, perfect.**—**L. *finitus,* well rounded or ended, said of a sentence (Brachet); orig. pp. of *finire,* to end.**—**L. *finis.*

fine (2), a tax. (Law L.) Law L. *finis,* a fine; a final arrangement; L. *finis,* end. See **finance** above.

finial. (L.) A coined word; from L. *finire,* to finish.**—**L. *finis,* end.

finical. (F.**—**L.) A coined word; extended from **fine** (1) above.

finish, vb. (F.**—**L.) M. E. *finischen.***—**O. F. *finiss-,* base of pres. pt. of *finir,* to finish.**—**L. *finire,* to end.**—**L. *finis.*

finite, limited. (L.) L. *finitus,* pp. of *finire,* to end, limit. **—** L. *finis.* Der. *infinite, in-finit-esimal.*

refine. (F.**—**L.) Coined from *re-* and *fine* (1), but imitated from F. *raffiner,* to

refine, comp. of L. *re-*, again, L. *af-* = *ad*,
to, and F. *fin*, fine. Der. *refine-ment*; cf.
F. *raffinement*.

superfine. (F. – L.) From L. *super*,
above; and *fine* (1).

Finch, a bird. (E.) M.E. *finch*. A.S.
finc.+Du. *vink*, Dan. *finke*, Swed. and G.
fink; W. *pinc*, a chaffinch. Cf. Gk. σπίγγος, σπίζα, a finch; prov. E. *spink*. Der.
chaf-finch, q. v., *bull-finch*, &c.

Find. (E.) A.S. *findan.* + Du. *vinden*,
Dan. *finde*, Swed. and Icel. *finna* (= *finda*),
Goth. *finthan*, G. *finden*. Allied to L. *petere*,
to seek after; see **Petition**. (√ PAT.)

foundling, a deserted child. (E.) M.E.
fundling; formed with suffix *-l-ing* from
A.S. *fund-en*, pp. of *findan*.

Fine (1) and (2); see **Final**.

Finger. (E.) A.S. *finger.*+Du. *vinger*,
Icel. *fingr*, Dan. Swed. G. *finger*, Goth.
figgrs (= *fingrs*). Prob. allied to **Fang**;
(*finger* = catch-er).

Finial, Finical, Finish; see **Final**.

Fir, a tree. (E.) M.E. *fir*; A.S. *furh*.
+Icel. *fura*, Dan. *fyr*, Swed. *fura*, G.
föhre, W. *pyr*. The same as L. *quercus*,
an oak.

Fire. (E.) A.S. *fyr*. + Du. *vuur*, Icel.
fyri, Dan. and Swed. *fyr*, G. *feuer*, Gk. πῦρ.
Cf. Skt. *pávana* (= *púana*), purifying, also
fire. (PU.) See **Bolt** (2).

Firkin; see **Four**.

Firm. (F. – L.) M.E. *ferme.* – O.F.
ferme. – L. *firmus*, steadfast. Cf. Skt.
dhara, preserving. (√ DHAR.)

affirm. (F. – L.) M.E. *affermen.* –
O.F. *afermer*, to fix. – L. *af-* = *ad*, to; *firmare*, to fix, from *firmus*.

confirm. (F. – L.) M.E. *confermen.* –
O.F. *confermer.* – L. *con-firmare*, to make
firm, strengthen.

farm. (F. – L.) M.E. *ferme.* – F.
ferme, a farm (12th cent.). – Low L. *firma*,
a fixed rent, a farm; fem. of L. *firmus*,
durable. (From the *fixed* rent.)

firmament, celestial sphere. (F. – L.)
O.F. *firmament.* – L. *firmamentum*, a support, also, expanse of the sky. – L. *firmare*,
to strengthen; from *firmus*.

in-firm. (L.) L. *in-firmus*, not strong,
weak. Der. *infirm-ar-y*, *infirm-i-ty*.

Firman, a mandate. (Pers.) Pers. *far-
mán*, a mandate, order.

First; see **Fore**.

Firth; see **Fare**.

Fiscal, pertaining to the revenue. (F. –
L.) O.F. *fiscal.* – O.F. *fisque*, the public

purse. – L. *fiscus*, a basket of rushes, also a
purse.

confiscate, to adjudge to be forfeit.
(L.) L. *confiscatus*, pp. of *confiscare*, to
lay by in a coffer, to confiscate, transfer to
the prince's privy purse. – L. *con-* (*cum*);
fiscus, a purse.

Fish. (E.) A.S. *fisc.*+Du. *visch*, Icel.
fiskr, Dan. and Swed. *fisk*, G. *fisch*, L.
piscis, W. *pysg*, Bret. *pesk*, Irish and Gael.
iasg (for *piasg*).

Fissure. (F. – L.) O.F. *fissure.* – L.
fissura. – L. *fissus*, pp. of *findere*, to cleave.
+Skt. *bhid*, to cleave; A.S. *bítan*, to bite.
(√ BHID.) And see **Vent** (1).

Fist. (E.) M.E. *fist*, *fest*, *fust*. A.S.
fýst.+Du. *vuist*, G. *faust*, Russ. *piaste*.
Allied to L. *pugnus*, Gk. πυγμή, fist.

Fistula, a deep, narrow abscess. (L.)
From the shape; L. *fistula*, a pipe.

Fit (1), to suit; as adj., apt. (Scand.)
M. E. *fitten*, to arrange. – Icel. and Norw.
fitja, to knit together; Swed. dial. *fittja*, to
bind together. + Goth. *fetjan*, to adorn,
deck. Allied to **Fetch**.

Fit (2), a part of a poem, attack of illness. (E.) M.E. *fit*. A.S. *fit*, a song, a
struggle.+Icel. *fet*, a pace, step, foot (in
poetry), fit (of a poem). Allied to **Fetch**
and **Fit** (1).

Fitch, the same as **Vetch**, q. v.

Fitchot, **Fitchew**, a pole-cat, (F. –
O. Du.) *Fitchew* is corrupted from O F.
fissau, a polecat. – O. Du. *fisse*, a polecat ;
from the smell. Cf. Icel. *físa*, to make a
smell; see **Foist**.

Fitz, son. (Norm. F. – L.) Formerly
fiz (with *z* as *ts*). – O.F. *fiz* (with *z* as *ts*) ;
also *filz*, *fils*. – L. *filius*, a son.

Five. (E.) M.E. *fif*; sometimes *fiue*,
as a plural. A.S. *fif* (for *finf* *).+Du.
vijf, Dan. Swed. *fem*, Icel. *fimm*, Goth.
fimf, G. *fünf*, W. *pump*, L. *quinque*, Gk.
πέμπε (also πέντε), Skt. *pañchan*. (Base
KANKAN.) Der. *fif-th*, A.S. *fifta*; *fifteen*, A.S. *fiftyne*; *fif-ty*, A.S. *fiftig*.

Fix. (F. – L.) O.F. *fixe*, fixed. – L. *fixus*,
fixed; pp. of *figere*, to fix. Cf. Gk. σφίγγειν, to compress.

affix. (F. – L.) M. E. *affichen.* – O.F.
aficher. – O. F. *a*, to (L. *ad*) ; *ficher*, to fix,
answering to Low L. *figicare* *, developed
from *figere*, to fix. ¶ So also *pre-fix*, *suffix* (i.e. sub-fix), *trans-fix*.

Fizz. (Scand.) Icel. *físa*, Dan. *fise*;
with the same sense as L. *pedere*.

Flabby; put for *flappy*; see **Flap**.

Flaccid. (F. – L.) F. *flaccide.* – L. *flaccidus,* limp. – L. *flaccus,* flabby.

Flag (1), to droop, grow weary. (E.) Weakened form of *flack,* to hang loosely; M. E. *flakken,* to flap about. From the base *flac-* of A. S. *flac-or,* flying, roving. + Icel. *flakka,* to rove; *flaka,* to flap; *flögra,* to flutter; G. *flackern,* to flutter.

flicker, to flutter. (E.) Frequent. form of *flick,* weakened form of M. E. *flakken* (above).

flag (2), an ensign. (Scand.) Dan. *flag,* Swed. *flagg,* a flag; from base of Icel. *flögra,* to flutter (above).

flag (3), a reed; the same word as *flag* (2); from its waving in the wind.

Flag (4), **Flagstone,** a paving-stone; see Flake.

Flagellate. (L.) From pp. of L. *flagellare,* to scourge. – L. *flagellum,* dimin. of *flagrum,* a scourge. (✓ BHLAG.)

flail. (F. – L.) O. F. *flael* (F. *fléau*), a flail, scourge. – L. *flagellum* (above).

Flageolet; see Flute.

Flagitious. (L.) L. *flagitiosus,* shameful. – L. *flagitium,* a disgraceful act. – L. *flagitare,* to act with violence. Allied to **Flagrant.**

Flagon; see Flask.

Flagrant, glaring, as a fault. (F. – L.) O. F. *flagrant,* properly burning. – L. *flagrant-,* stem of pres., pt. of *flagrare,* to burn. + Gk. φλέγειν, to burn; Sk. *bhráj.* (✓ BHARG.)

conflagration. (F. – L.) F. *conflagration.* – L. acc. *conflagrationem,* a great burning. – L. *con- (cum),* together; *flagrare,* to burn.

flambeau. (F. – L.) F. *flambeau,* a link, torch; dimin. of O. F. *flambe,* a flame; see flame.

flame. (F. – L.) O. F. *flame, flamme;* also *flambe.* – L. *flamma* (=*flag-ma*), a flame; from the base *flag-,* to burn; cf. *flagrare.* See Flagrant.

flamen. (L.) L. *flāmen,* a priest of Rome. Prob. for *flag-men* *, he who burns the sacrifice.

flamingo. (Span. – Prov. – L.) Span. *flamenco,* a flamingo; but said to be a Provençal word. The F. form is *flamant,* lit. 'flaming,' but it was certainly confused with F. *Flamand,* a Fleming, whence the peculiar form of the Span. word seems to be due. Still, the etymology is certainly from L. *flamma,* a flame; from the flame-like colour of the bird.

Flail; see Flagellate.

Flake, a thin slice. (Scand.) Norw. *flak,* a slice, an ice-floe; cf. Icel. *flakna, flagna,* to flake off, Swed. *flaga,* a flake. Allied to **Flay.**

flag (4), a paving-stone. (Scand.) Icel. *flaga,* a flag or slab of stone; Swed. *flaga,* a flake. A weakened form of **flake.**

flaw, a crack. (Scand.) M. E. *flawe.* – Swed. *flaga,* a crack, flaw, also, a flake (as above).

flitch, side of bacon. (E.) M. E. *flicche.* A. S. *flicce.* + Icel. *flikki,* a flitch; *flik,* a flap, tatter. Orig. a thin slice; weakened form of **Flake.**

floe, a flake of ice. (Dan.) Dan. *flage;* as in *iis-flage,* an ice-floe, lit. 'ice-flake.'

Flambeau, Flame; see Flagrant.

Flamen, Flamingo; see Flagrant.

Flange; see below.

Flank, the side. (F. – L.) F. *flanc,* lit. the 'weak' part of the body. – L. *flaccus,* soft; with inserted *n* as in *jongleur* from *ioculatorem;* see Flaccid. ¶ Cf. G. *weich,* softness; also, the side.

flange. (F. – L.) The same as prov. E. *flanch,* a projection; which, again, is a weakened form of *flank;* hence it means 'a rim projecting on one side.'

flunkey, a footman. (F. – L.) Modern. From F. *flanquer,* to flank, run by the side of, support, be at hand. – F. *flanc,* side.

Flannel. (W.) Prov. E. *flannen,* a better form. – W. *gwlanen,* flannel, from *gwlan,* wool. Allied to **Wool.**

Flap, to beat with the wings. (E.) M. E. *flappen,* to beat; not in A.S. A variant of *flack,* to beat; see **Flag** (1). + Du. *flappen,* to flap. Der. *flabby* (flappy).

Flare; see below.

Flash, to blaze. (Scand.) Swed. dial. *flasa,* to burn violently; Icel. *flasa,* to rush, *flas,* a swift rushing.

flare. (Scand.) Norweg. *flara,* to blaze; the same as Swed. dial. *flasa* (above).

Flask. (Low L.?) A.S. *flasc;* we also find Icel. *flaska,* Dan. *flaske,* Swed. *flaska,* G. *flasche;* but hardly a Teut. word. – Low L. *flasca,* a flask; cf. also W. *fflasg,* Gael. *flasg.* Remoter origin uncertain.

flagon. (F. – Low L.) O. F. *flacon,* another form of *flascon.* – Low L. *flasconem,* acc. of *flasco,* a flask. – Low L. *flasca* (above).

Flat. (Scand.) M. E. *flat.* – Icel. *flatr,* Swed. *flat,* Dan. *flad.*

Flatter. (O. Low G.) M. E. *flateren;*

a frequent. form.—O. Du. *flatteren*, to flatter (Hexham). Cf. the base *flak-*, seen in O. Swed. *fleckra*, to flatter, Swed. dial. *fleka*, to caress; cf. M. E. *flakken*, to move to and fro; see **Flag** (1).

Flatulent, windy. (F.—L.) F. *flatulent*. — Low L. *flatulentus*. — L. *flatus*, breath.—L. *flare*, to blow; see **Blow** (1).

inflate. (L.) From pp. of L. *in-flare*, to blow into, puff up.

Flaunt, to display ostentatiously. (Scand. ?) It seems to have been particularly used of the display of fluttering plumes, &c.—Swed. dial. *flanka*, to waver; allied to *flakka*, to waver, answering to M. E. *flakken*; see **Flag** (1).

Flavour. (Low L.—L.) The sense of taste or scent seems to have been adapted from the older sense of 'hue' or 'appearance.'—Low L. *flauor*, golden coin, yellowness.—L. *flauus*, yellow, gold-coloured.

Flaw; see **Flake**.

Flax, a plant. (E.) A. S. *fleax*.+ Du. *vlas*, G. *flachs*. Allied to Goth. *flahta*, a plaiting, Gk. πλέκειν, to weave.

Flay, to strip off skin. (E.) M. E. *flean*. A. S. *fledn*, to flay.+ Icel. *flá*, pt. t. *fló*, pp. *fleginn*. Allied to **Flake**, q. v.

Flea; see **Fly**.

Fleam, a lancet, see **Phlebotomy**.

Fleck, a spot. (Scand.) M. E. *flek*.— Icel. *flekkr*, a spot; *flekka*, to stain; Swed. *fläck*, a spot.+Du. *vlek*, G. *fleck*. From the base FLAK, to strike, dab; cf. L. *plaga*, a blow. (√ PLAK.)

Flection; see **Flexible**.

Fledge, Flee; see **Fly**.

Fleece. (E.) M. E. *flees*. A. S. *flýs*.+ Du. *vlies*, G. *fliess*. Cf. **Flesh**.

Fleer, to mock. (Scand.) M. E. *flerien*. —Norw. *flira*, to titter, giggle; also spelt *flisa*; Swed. *flissa*, to titter.

Fleet (1), a number of ships; see **Float**.

Fleet (2), a creek; see **Float**.

Fleet (3), swift; **Fleet** (4), to move swiftly; see **Float**.

Flesh. (E.) M.E. *flesch*. A. S. *flæsc*, flesh. +Icel. *flesk*, bacon; Dan. *flesk*, Swed. *fläsk*, bacon; G. *fleisch*. Prob. allied to **Flake**.

Fleur-de-lis; see **Floral**.

Flexible. (F. — L.) F. *flexible*. — L. *flexibilis*, easily bent.—L. *flexus*, pp. of *flectere*, to bend. Der. *in-flexible*.

circumflex. (L.) L. *syllaba circumflexa*, a syllable marked with a circumflex (ˆ) or 'bent' mark.—L. *circumflexus*, pp. of *circumflectere*, to bend round.

deflect. (L.) L. *de-flectere*, to bend down or aside.

flection, a bending. (L.) Better *flexion*; from L. acc. *flexionem*, a bending. —L. *flexus*, pp. of *flectere*. So also *flex-or*, *flex-ure*.

flinch. (F. — L.) A nasalised form of M. E. *flecchen*, to flinch, waver. — O. F. *flechir*, to bend, ply, go awry or aside, flinch.—L. *flectere*, to bend.

inflect, to modulate the voice, &c. (L.) L. *in-flectere*, lit. to bend in.

reflect. (L.) L. *re-flectere*, lit. to bend back, hence to return rays, &c.

Flicker; see **Flag** (1).

Flight; see **Fly**.

Flimsy, weak, slight. (W. ?) Prob. from W. *llymsi*, sluggish, spiritless, flimsy. (For *fl* = W. *ll*, see *flummery*.)

Flinch; see **Flexible**.

Fling. (Scand.) Swed. *flänga*, to use violent action, romp, race about; *i fläng*, at full speed (taking one's fling); O. Swed. *flenga*, to strike.+ Dan. *flenge*, to slash; *i fleng*, indiscriminately. Allied to **Flicker** and **Flag** (1).

Flint. (E.) A. S. *flint*.+ Dan. *flint*; Swed. *flinta*; Gk. πλίνθος, a brick.

Flippant. (Scand.) *Flippant* is for *flippand*, the O. Northern pres. pt.; *flippand* = prattling, saucy.—Icel. *fleipa*, to prattle; Swed. dial. *flepa*, to talk nonsense; cf. Swed. dial. *flip*, the lip. Weakened form of **Flap**.

Flirt. (E.) Often written *flurt*, meaning to mock, gibe, scorn; Lowl. Sc. *flird*, to flirt. A. S. *fleard*, a piece of folly; *fleardian*, to trifle; cf. Swed. *flärd*, artifice.

Flit; see **Float**.

Flitch; see **Flake**.

Float, to swim on a liquid surface. (E.) M. E. *floten*; also *fleten*. The form *float* is due to the sb. *float*, from A. S. *flota*, a ship. The verb is properly *fleet*, A. S. *fleótan*; cognate with Icel. *fljóta*, G. *fliessen*, to float, flow. We find, however, the (derived) verb *flotian*, A. S. Chron. an. 1031 (Laud MS.). (√ PLU.)

afloat (E.) M. E. *on flote*, i.e. on the float.

fleet (1), a number of ships. (E.) M. E. *flete*, a fleet. A. S. *fleót*, a ship; the collective sense is later.—A. S. *fleótan*, to float.

fleet (2), a creek, bay. (E.) Cf. *Fleet* Ditch; *fleet* is a shallow creek, channel. M. E. *fleet*. A. S. *fleót*, a bay of the sea (where ships *float*).

fleet (3), swift. (E.) From A. S.

fleótig, swift; allied to *fleótan*, to float; see **flit** below.

fleet (4), to move swiftly. (E.) M. E. *fleten*, to float, swim; A.S. *fleótan*, the same; see **Float** (above).

flit, to remove from place to place. (Scand.) M. E. *flitten*.—Swed. *flytta*, to flit, remove; Dan. *flytte*; causal of Swed. *flyta*, Dan. *flyde*, to float.

flotsam, goods lost in shipwreck, and floating on the waves. (Law F. —Lat.) An O. F. law-term, formerly *flotson* (Blount). A. F. *floteson*.—Low L. *fluctationem*, a floating.—L. *fluctus*, a wave. Confused with E. *float*. Cf. **Jetsam**.

flutter, to flap the wings. (E.) M. E. *floteren*, to fluctuate. A.S. *flotorian*, to float about.—A. S. *flot*, the sea; *flota*, a ship.—A S. *flot-*, stem of *flot-en*, pp. of *fleótan*, to float.

Flock (1), a company of sheep, &c. (E.) M. E. *flok*. A.S. *flocc*. + Icel. *flokkr*, Dan. *flok*, Swed. *flock*. Perhaps a variant of **Folk**.

Flock (2), a lock of wool. (F.—L.) O. F. *floc*.—L. *floccus*, a lock of wool. Cf. Lithuan. *plaukas*, hair.

Floe; see **Flake**.

Flog, to beat. (L.) A late word; and a mere abbreviation of *flagellate*, q. v.

Flood; see **Flow**.

Floor. (E.) A. S. *flór*. + Du. *vloer*, G. *flur*, W. *llawr*, Bret. *leur*, Irish *lar* (= *plar*).

Floral, pertaining to flowers. (L.) *floralis*, belonging to *Flora*, goddess of flowers.—L. *flor-*, stem of *flos*, a flower; cf. *florere*, to flourish, allied to **Blow** (2).

deflour, deflower. (F.—L.) M. E. *deflouren*.—O. F. *defleurer*.—Low L. *deflorare*, to gather flowers.

efflorescence. (F.—L.) F. *efflorescence*, lit. ' a flowering.' From L. *efflorescere*, inceptive form of *ef-florere*, to blossom out. (L. *ef-* = *ex*).

ferret (2), a kind of silk tape. (Ital.— L.) Ital. *fioretto*, a little flower, also ferret; dimin. of *fiore*, a flower.—L. *florem*, acc. of *flos*, a flower.

fleur-de-lis, flower of the lily. (F.) O. F. *fleur de lis*. Here *lis* = Low L. *lilius*, corrupt form of L. *lilium*, a lily; see **flower** and **lily**.

florid. (L.) L. *floridus*, lit. abounding with flowers; hence rosy.—L. *flori-*, crude form of *flos*, a flower.

florin, a coin. (F.—Ital.—L.) M. E. *florin* (about A. D. 1337).—O. F. *florin*, a florin.—Ital. *fiorino* (= *florino*), a coin of Florence, so called because it bore a lily, the symbol of that town.—Ital. *fiore*, a flower; see **ferret** (2) above.

floscule. (L.) L. *flosculus*, a little flower; double dimin. of *flos*.

flour, finer part of meal. (F.—L.) Short for ' flower of wheat.'—F. *fleur*, short for *fleur de farine*, flour; see **flower** below (which is a doublet).

flourish, vb. (F.—L.) M. E. *florisshen*. —O. F. *fleuriss-*, stem of pres. pt. of *fleurir*, to flourish.—L. *florescere*, inceptive form of *florere*, to blossom.

flower, sb. (F.—L.) M. E. *flour*.—O.F. *flour* (F. *fleur*).—L. *florem*, acc. of *flos*.

inflorescence, mode of flowering. (F. —L.) F. *inflorescence*. From the pres. pt. of L. *in-florescere*, to burst into blossom.

Florid, Florin, Floscule; see **Floral**.

Floss; see **Fluent**.

Flotilla. (Span.—L.) Span. *flotilla*, a little fleet; dimin. of *flota*, a fleet, cognate with O. F. *flote*, a fleet of ships, a crowd of people. This O. F. *flote* (fem.) is closely allied to L. *flot* (masc.), a wave; from L. *fluctus*, a wave; see **Fluent**. β. At the same time, the sense seems to have been affected by Du. *vloot*, Icel. *floti*, a fleet.

Flotsam; see **Float**.

Flounce (1), to plunge about. (Swed.) Swed. dial. and O. Swed. *flunsa*, to plunge; allied to **Flounder** (1).

Flounce (2), a plaited border on a dress. (F.—L. ?) Changed from M. E. *frounce*, a plait.—O. F. *fronser, froncer*, to gather, plait, wrinkle; *fronser le frônt*, to knit or wrinkle the forehead. Prob. from Low L. *frontiare**, not found, but regularly formed from *fronti-*, crude form of *frons*, forehead; see **Front**.

Flounder (1), to flounce about. (O. Low G.) XVI cent. Nasalised form of Du. *flodderen*, to dangle, flap, splash through mire. Cf. Swed. *fladdra*, to flutter.

Flounder (2), a fish. (Scand.) Swed. *flundra*, Dan. *flynder*, Icel. *flyðra*. Prob. from *floundering* about; see above.

Flour, Flourish; see **Floral**.

Flout; see **Flute**.

Flow, to stream. (E.) A.S. *flówan*. + Du. *vloeijen*; Icel. *flóa*, to flood; L. *pluit*, it rains; Russ. *pluite*, to float; Gk. πλέειν, Skt. *plu*, to float, swim. (√PLU.)

flood. (E.) A. S. *flód*, a flood; from *flówan* (above). **+** Du. *vloed*, Icel. *flód*, Swed. Dan. *flod*, Goth. *flodus*, a river, G. *fluth*. And see Float.

Flower; see Floral.

Fluctuate; see Fluent.

Flue (1), a chimney-pipe; see Flute.

Flue (2), light floating down. (F.—L. ?) Also called *fluff*; cf. prov. E. *fluke*, waste cotton. Prob. a mere corruption of *flock* (2), q. v.; whence also Low G. *flog*, flue.

Fluent. (L.) From stem of pres. pt. of L. *fluere*, to flow. Cf. Gk. φλύειν, to swell, overflow.

affluence. (F.—L.) F. *affluence*.—L. *affluencia*, abundance.—L. *affluent-*, stem of pres. pt. of *af-fluere*, to flow to, abound. (L. *af-* = *ad*).

confluent. (L.) From stem of pres. pt. of *con-fluere*, to flow together. So also *conflux*, from the pp. *confluxus*.

defluxion. (L.) From acc. of L. *de-fluxio*, a flowing down.

effluence, a flowing. (L.) From the pres. pt. of *ef-fluere*, to flow out.

fluctuate, to waver. (L.) From pp. of *fluctuare*, to float about.—L. *fluctus*, a wave.—L. *fluctus*, old pp. of *fluere*, to flow.

fluid. (F. — L.) O. F. *fluide*. — L. *fluidus*, flowing. — L. *fluere*, to flow.

floss, untwisted silken filaments. (Ital. — L.) Ital. *floscio*, Venetian *flosso*, soft, weak; *floscia seta*, floss silk.—L. *fluxus*, fluid, loose, lax.

fluor, fluor-spar, a mineral. (L.) The L. *fluor* (lit. a flowing) was formerly in use as a term in alchemy and chemistry. —L. *fluere*, to flow.

flush (1), to flow swiftly. (F.—L.) Cf. *flusch*, a run of water (G. Douglas).—F. *flux*, 'a flowing, a flux, also a *flush* at cards;' Cot.—L. *fluxus*, a flowing; from the pp. of *fluere*, to flow.

flush (3), level. (F. ?—L. ?) This seems to be a derived sense; it meant in full flow, full; hence level.

flux. (F.—L.) O. F. *flux*, a flux.—L. *fluxum*, acc. of *fluxus*, a flowing; orig. pp. of *fluere*, to flow.

influence. (F.—L.) O. F. *influence*, a flowing in, esp. used of the influence of planets.—Low L. *influentia*.—L. *influent-*, stem of pres. pt. of *in-fluere*, to flow into.

influenza. (Ital.—L.) Ital. *influenza*, influence, also used of a severe catarrh. A doublet of influence (above).

influx. (L.) L. *in-fluxus*, a flowing in; see flux (above).

superfluous. (L.) L. *super-fluus*, over-flowing.—L. *super*, over; *fluere*, to flow.

Fluke (1), a fish. (E.) M. E. *fluke*. A. S. *flóc*, a kind of plaice. **+** Icel. *flóki*, a kind of halibut.

Fluke (2), part of an anchor. (Low G. ?) Also spelt *flook*.—Low G. *flunk*, a wing; cf. Swed. *ankarfly*, the fluke of an anchor. Prob. allied to fly. A *fluke* (at billiards) is a *flying* stroke; cf. Du. *vlug*, quick, G. *flug*, a flight.

Flummery, a light food. (W.) W. *llymru, llymruwd*, flummery, sour oatmeal boiled and jellied. — W. *llymrig*, crude, raw; *llymus*, sharp, tart. — W. *llymu*, to sharpen; *llym*, sharp.

Flunkey; see Flank.

Fluor; see Fluent.

Flurry, hurry. (Scand.) Swift has *flurry*, a gust of wind.—Swed. *flurig*, disordered, dissolute; *flur*, disordered hair, whim; Norweg. *flurutt*, shaggy, disordered.

Flush (1), to flow swiftly; see Fluent.

Flush (2), to blush, redden. (Scand.) M. E. *flushen*, to redden (with anger).— Swed. dial. *flossa*, to burn, flare; Norweg. *flosa*, passion, vehemence. Allied to Flash.

Flush (3), level; see Fluent.

Fluster, to heat with drinking, confuse. (Scand.) Icel. *flaustra*, to be flustered; *flaustr*, fluster, hurry. Allied to Flush (2) and Flash.

Flute, a musical pipe. (F. — L.) O. F. *flaute, fleute*, a flute; *flauter*, to blow a flute, answering to a Low L. *flatuare* (not found), to blow a flute, from L. *flatus*, a blowing. — L. *flare*, to blow; see Flatulent.

flageolet, a sort of flute. (F. — L.) O. F. *flageolet*, dimin. of *flageol*, with the same sense — Low L. *flautiolus* (not found), dimin. of Low L. *flauta*, a flute (= O. F. *flaute* above).

flout, to mock. (Du. — F. — L.) Borrowed from Du. *fluyten*, to play the flute, also to jeer.—O. Du. *fluyt* (Du. *fluit*), a flute; borrowed from F.

flue (1), an air-passage, chimney-pipe. (F.—L.) A mere corruption of *flute*; in Phaer's Virgil, x. 209, we find *flue*, to translate L. *concha*, a sea-shell trumpet.

Flutter; see Float.

Flux; see Fluent.

Fly, to float in air. (E.) M. E. *flegen*, pt. t. *flew*. A. S. *fleógan*, pt. t. *fleáh*. **+** Du.

vliegen, Icel. *fljúga*, Dan. *flyve*, Swed. *flyga*, G. *fliegen*. Cf. L. *pluma*, a feather. (√PLU.)   Allied to **Flow**.

filibuster, a freebooter. (Span. – E. – Du.) Span. *filibuster*, a mere corruption of E. *freebooter*. – Du. *vrijbuiter*, a freebooter. – Du. *vrijbuiten*, to rob, plunder. – Du. *vrij*, free; *buit*, booty, plunder. (Misplaced.) See **Booty**.

flea. (E.) M. E. *flee*, pl. *fleen*. A.S. *fleá*, *fleó*, a flea.+Du. *vloo*, Icel. *fló*, G. *floh*, Russ. *blocha*. Lit. 'a jumper.' Cf. Skt. *plu*, to swim, to fly, also to jump.

fledge, to furnish with feathers. (Scand.) The pp. *fledged* is now substituted for M. E. *flegge*, ready to fly. – Icel. *fleygr*, able to fly. – Icel. *fleygja*, to cause to fly, causal of *fljúga*; see **Fly**. Der. *fledge-ling*.

flee, to escape. (Scand.) Icel. *flýja*, *flæja*, to flee, pt. t. *flýði* (= E. *fled*); Swed. *fly*, Dan. *flye*, to flee. Allied to Icel. *fljúga*, to fly.

flight, act of flying. (E.) A.S. *flyht*, allied to *flyge*, flight. – A.S. *flug-*, base of pl. of pt. t. of *fleógan*, to fly. So also Swed. *flykt*, G. *flucht*.

Foal. (E) M. E. *fole*, A.S. *fola*. + Du. *veulen*, Icel. *foli*, Dan. *fole*, Swed. *fåle*, Goth. *fula*, G. *fohlen*, L. *pullus*, young of an animal, Gk. πῶλος. (√ PU.)

filly, a female foal. (Scand.) Icel. *fylja*, a filly, from *foli*, a foal; Dan. *föl*, from *fole*; Swed. *föll*, from *fåle*. + G. *füllen*.

Foam. (E.) M. E. *fome*. A. S. *fám*.+ Prov. G. *faum*; L. *spuma*. Allied to **Spume**.

Fob, watch-pocket. (O. Low G.) An O. Low G. word, only preserved in the cognate H. G. (Prussian) *fuppe*, a pocket; for which see Bremen Wört. i. 437.

Focus, a point where light-rays meet. (L.) L. *focus*, a hearth; hence, a centre of fire. Cf. Gk. φῶς, light. (√ BHA.)

fuel. (F.–L.) M. E. *fewell* (Barbour). O. F. *fouaille*, only found in *fouailler*, a wood-yard; Low L. *foallia*, fuel. – Low L. *focale*, fuel. – L. *focus*, a hearth.

fuse (2), **fusee** (1); see **fusil** (1) below.

fusil (1), a light musket. (F.–L.) Orig. not the musket itself, but its fire-lock; also spelt *fusel*, *fusee*, *fuse*. ' *Fuse*, *fusee*, or *fusel*, a pipe filled with wild fire, and put into the touch-hole of a bomb;' Kersey (1715). – O. F. *fusil*, 'a fire-steele for a tinder-box;' Cot. – L. *focile*, a steel for kindling fire. – L. *focus*, a hearth; Der. *fusil-eer*.

Fodder; see **Food**.

Foe. (E.) M. E. *foo*, A.S. *fáh*, *fá*; allied to *feogan*, to hate, and to Goth. *fijan*, to hate. (√ PI.)   Allied to **Fiend**.

feud (1), hatred. (E.) M. E. *fede*. A.S. *fǽhð*, enmity. – A. S. *fáh*, hostile (above). Modified in spelling by confusion with *feud* (2).+G. *fehde*, hatred; Goth. *fijathwa*, hatred.

Fœtus; see **Fetus**.

Fog. (Dan.) Dan. *fog*, as in *snee-fog*, a blinding fall of snow; cf. *fyge*, to drift (as snow).+Icel. *fok*, spray, snow-drift, *fjúk*, snow-storm; from *fok-inn*, pp. of strong vb. *fjúka*, to be tossed by wind, drift.

Foible; see **Feeble**.

Foil (1), to defeat. (F. – L.) M. E. *foylen*, to trample under foot. – O. F. *fouler*, to trample on, also to oppress, foil, overcharge extremely (Cot.). – Low L. *fullare*, *folare*, to full cloth; see **Full** (3). Der. *foil*, a blunt sword, so called because 'foiled' or blunted; *foil*, a defeat.

Foil (2), to set-off; see **Foliage**.

Foin, to thrust with a sword. (F.–L.) Obsolete. Lit. 'to thrust with an eel-spear.' – O. F. *fouine*, an eel-spear. – L. *fuscina*, a trident.

Foison; see **Fuse** (1).

Foist, to intrude surreptitiously. (O. Du.) O. Du. *vysten*, 'to fizzle,' i.e. to break wind noiselessly, which is also the orig. sense of *foist*; allied to O. Du. *veest*, 'a fizzle' (Sewel). So also Dan. *fiis*, the same, from *fise*, to fizz; see **Fizz**.

Fold (1), to double together. (E.) M.E. *folden*, A. S. *fealdan* (pt. t. *feóld*), to fold. +Dan. *folde*, Swed. *fälla* (=*fälda*), Icel. *falda*, Goth. *falthan*, G. *falten*. Allied to Gk. πλέκειν, to weave. (√PLAK.) Der. *fold*, sb., a plait; *-fold*, suffix, as in *two-fold*, &c.

faldstool, a folding-stool. (Low.L.– O. H.G.) Low L. *faldistolium*. – O.H.G. *fald-an*, to fold; *stual* (G. *stuhl*), a stool.

fauteuil, an arm-chair. (F. – Low L.– O.H. G.) F. *fauteuil*, O. F. *fauldetueil* (Cot.) – Low L. *faldistolium* (above).

Fold (2), a pen for sheep. (E.) A. S. *fald*, also *falod*, *falud*. Not connected with *fold* (1), but with Icel. *fjöl* (gen. *fjalar*), a board.

Foliage, a cluster of leaves. (F.–L.) Modified from O.F. *feuillage*, from O. F. *feuille*, a leaf. – L. *folia*, pl. of *folium*, a leaf.+Gk. φύλλον, leaf.

exfoliate. (L.) From pp. of L. *ex-*

foliare, to strip off leaves; from *ex*, off, *folium*, leaf.

foil (2), a set-off, as in setting a gem. (F. – L.) O. F. *feuille*, a leaf, 'also the foyle of precious stones;' Cot. See above.

folio. (L.) From the L. phr. *in folio*, where *folio* is the abl. of *folium*, a leaf, sheet.

perfoliate. (L.) Coined from L. *per*, through ; *folium*, a leaf.

trefoil. (F. – L.) O. F. *trefoil*. – L. *trifolium*, lit. 'three-leaf.' – L. *tri-*, allied to *tres*, three ; *folium*, a leaf.

Folk, a crowd of people. (E.) A. S. *folc.*+Icel. *fôlk*, Dan. Swed. *folk*, Du. G. *volk*, Lithuan. *pulkas*, a crowd, Russ. *polk'*, an army. Allied to **Flock**; and prob. to **Full.**

Follicle, seed-vessel. (F. – L.) O. F. *follicule*, little bag. – L. *folliculus*, double dimin. of *follis*, a bag.

Follow. (E.) M. E. *folwen*. A. S. *fylgan*, *fyligan*, weak verb, to follow. + Du. *volgen*, Icel. *fylgja*, Dan. *fôlge*, Swed. *fôlja*, G. *folgen*.

Folly ; see **Fool.**

Foment. (F. – L.) O. F. *fomenter*. – L. *fomentare*. – L. *fomentum*, short for *fouimentum*, a warm application, lotion. – L. *fouere*, to warm.

Fond, foolish. (Scand.) M. E. *fond*, more commonly *fonn-ed*, pp. of *fonnen*, to act as a fool, from the M. E. sb. *fon*, *fonne*, a fool. – Swed. *fåne*, a fool ; Icel. *fåni*, a standard, metaphorically, a buoyant person. Allied to G. *fahne*, standard, L. *pannus*, a bit of cloth. Thus *fon-d* = flag-like. See **Pane.** Der. *fond-le*, verb.

Font (1), basin of water. (L.) A. S. *fant*. – L. *fontem*, acc. of *fons*, a fount. Allied to **Found** (2). (√ GHU.)

fount (1), a spring. (F. – L.) O. F. *funt* (F. *font*). – L. *fontem* (above). Der. *fount-ain*, O. F. *funtaine*, Low L. *fontana*.

Font (2), **Fount**, an assortment of types; see **Found** (2).

Food. (E.) M. E. *fode*. A. S. *fôda*, what one eats. (√ PA.) Allied to **Pasture.**

feed, to take food, give food. (E.) M. E. *feden*. A. S. *fêdan* ; put for *fœdan*, by vowel-change from *ô* to *œ = ê*.

fester, a sore. (F. – L.) O. F. *festre*, also spelt *fistle*, an ulcer ; *festrir*, to fester (in Godefroy, O. F. Dict.). – L. *fistula*, a running sore. ¶ Misplaced; not from A. S. *fêstrud*, fostered.

fodder, food for cattle. (E.) M. E. *fodder*. A. S. *fôdor, fôddor* ; extended form of *fôda*, food.+Du. *voeder*, Icel. *fôðr*, Dan. Swed. *foder*, G. *futter*.

forage, fodder, chiefly obtained by pillage. (F. – Low L. – Scand.) M. E. *forage*. – O. F. *fourage*. – O. F. *forrer*, to forage. – O. F. *forre* (F. *feurre*), fodder. – Low L. *fodrum*, fodder. – Dan. and Swed. *foder* (above).

foster, to nourish. (E.) A. S. *fôstrian*, vb. – A. S. *fôstor*, nourishment ; allied to *fôda*, food. + Icel. *fôstr*, nursing, *fôstra*, to nurse ; Swed. *fostra*, Dan. *fostre*, to rear, bring up.

Fool, a jester. (F. – L.) O. F. *fol* (F. *fou*), a fool. – L. *follis*, a wind-bag ; pp. *folles*, puffed cheeks, whence the term was easily transferred to a jester. Cf. *flare*, to blow. Der. *be-fool*.

folly. (F. – L.) M. E. *folye*. – O. F. *folie*, folly. – O. F. *fol* (above).

fools-cap, paper so called from the water-mark on it.

Foot. (E.) M. E. *fot, foot*, pl. *fet, feet*. A. S. *fôt*, pl. *fêt*.+Du. *voet*, Icel. *fôtr*, Dan. *fod*, Swed. *fot*, Goth. *fotus*, G. *fuss*, L. *pes* (stem *ped-*), Gk. πούς (stem ποδ-), Skt. *pad*, *pâd*. (√ PAD.)

fetlock. (Scand.) Orig. the 'lock' or tuft of hair behind a horse's pastern-joint. The syllable *lock* = Icel. *lokkr*, A. S. *locc*, a lock of hair. *Fet-* is allied to Icel. *fet*, a pace, step, *feti*, a pacer (used of horses) ; and to Icel. *fôtr*, a foot (above).

fetter, a shackle. (E.) M. E. *feter*. A. S. *fetor*, a shackle for the foot ; allied to *fôt*, foot.+Icel. *fjôturr*, G. *fessel*, L. *pedica* or *com-pes*, Gk. πέδη. Der. *fetter*, vb.

Fop, a coxcomb. (Du.) From Du. *foppen*, to prate, cheat ; *fopper*, a wag ; *fopperij*, cheating (= E. *foppery*).

For (1), prep., in place of. (E.) Orig. a prep. A. S. *for*, for ; also, before that ; allied to A. S. *fore*, before that, for ; see **Fore.** + Du. *voor*, Icel. *fyrir*, Dan. *for*, Swed. *fôr*, G. *für*.

For- (2), *prefix*. (E.) *For-* has usually an intensive force, or preserves something of the sense of *from*, to which it is nearly related. (Quite distinct from *fore-*). A. S. *for-* ; Icel. *for-, fyrir-*, Dan. *for-*, Swed. *fôr-*, Du. G. *ver-*, Goth. *fra-, fair-*, Skt. *parâ-*. The Skt. *parâ* is an old instrumental sing. of *para*, far ; hence the orig. sense is 'away.' Der. *for-bear, for-bid, for-fend, for-go* (misspelt *fore-go*), *for-get, for-give,*

for-lorn, for-sake, for-swear; see **Bear,
Bid,** &c.

For- (3), *prefix.* (F. – L.) Only in *for-
close* (misspelt *foreclose*), *for-feit,* which see.

Forage; see **Food.**

Foraminated, perforated. (L.) From L.
foramin-, stem of *foramen,* a small hole. –
L. *forare,* to bore; see **Bore.**

Foray, Forray, a raid for foraging.
Foray, forray are old Lowl. Scotch spellings of **Forage,** q. v., under **Food.**

Forbear. (E.) From **For-** (2) and
Bear. A. S. *forberan.*

Forbid. (E.) From **For-** (2) and
Bid (2). A. S. *forbeódan.* + G. *verbieten.*

Force (1), 'strength. (F. – L.) M. E.
force, fors. – O. F. *force.* – Low L. *fortia,*
strength. – L. *forti-,* crude form of *fortis,*
strong. (√ DHAR.)

comfort, vb. (F. – L.) M. E. *conforten,*
later *comforten.* – O. F. *conforter,* to comfort. – Low L. *con-fortare,* to strengthen.

deforce, to dispossess. (F. – L.) Legal.
– O. F. *deforcer,* to dispossess (Low L.
difforciare). – O. F. *de-* = *des-* = L. *dis-,*
away; and F. *force* (above).

effort. (F. – L.) F. *effort,* an effort;
verbal sb. from F. *s'efforcer,* to endeavour.
– F. *ef-* (= L. *ex*); and *force,* force.

fort. (F. – L.) O. F. *fort,* sb., a fort;
a peculiar use of F. *fort,* adj., strong. – L.
acc. *fort-em,* strong.

fortalice, small fort. (F. – L.) O. F.
fortelesce, Low L. *fortalitia*; see **fortress**
below.

forte, loud. (Ital. – L.) Ital. *forte.* –
L. acc. *fort-em,* strong.

fortify. (F. – L.) O. F. *fortifier,* to
make strong. – L. *forti-,* crude form of
fortis; *-ficare,* for *facere,* to make.

fortitude. (L.) L. *fortitudo,* strength.
– L. *forti-s,* strong.

fortress. (F. – L.) M. E. *fortresse.* –
O. F. *fortesce, fortelesce.* – Low L. *forta-
litia,* a small fort. – Low L. *fortis,* a fort;
L. *fortis,* strong.

Force (2), to stuff fowls; see **Farce.**

Force (3), **Foss,** waterfall. (Scand.)
Dan. *fos,* Icel. *foss, fors,* a waterfall.

Forceps, pincers. (L.) L. *forceps,* orig.
used for holding hot iron. – L. *for-mus,* hot;
capere, to hold.

Ford; see **Fare.**

Fore, in front, coming first. (E.) A. S.
fore, for, before, prep.; *fore, foran,* before,
adv. + Du. *voor,* Icel. *fyrir,* Dan. *för,* Swed.
för, G. *vor,* Goth. *faura,* L. *pro,* Gk. πρό,

Skt. *pra.* The orig. sense is 'beyond;'
allied to **Far.** Der. *fore-arm, -bode, -cast,
-castle, -date, -father, -finger, -foot, -front,
-go* (in the sense 'to go before' only),
*-ground, -hand, -head, -judge, -know, -land,
-lock, -man, -noon, -ordain, -part, -rank, -run,
-see, -ship, -shorten, -show, -sight, -stall*
(A. S. *fore-steall,* sb. lit. 'an obstructing'),
*-taste, -tell, -thought, -token, -tooth, -top,
-warn*; all easily understood.

afore. (E.) A. S. *onforan,* adv., in
front.

before. (E.) M. E. *bifore.* A. S. *be-
foran, biforan,* prep. and adv. – A. S. *be-,*
bi- (E. *by*); *foran,* before.

first. (E.) A. S. *fyrst* (= *for-est*), the
correct superl. of *fore,* with vowel-change
of *o* to *y.* + Icel. *fyrstr*; Dan. Swed. *förste.*

former, more in front. (E.) Not
early; XVI cent.; a false formation, to
suit M. E. *formest,* i. e. foremost; see
below. Formed by adding *-er* to the base
form- of A. S. *form-a,* first, really a superl.
form, precisely equivalent to L. *primus,*
where *-m-* is an Aryan superl. suffix.

foremost, most in front. (E.) A double
superl., the old superl. form being misunderstood. Formed by adding *-est* to
A. S. *form-a,* foremost, first; this gave
formest, often written *fyrmest*; which was
turned into *foremost* by confusion with *most*!
See below.

forward. (E.) M. E. *forward.* A. S.
foreweard, adj. – A. S. *fore,* before; *-weard,*
suffix; see **Toward.** Der. *forward-s,*
M. E. *forwardes,* where *-es* is the suffix of gen.
case, used adverbially. And see **Further.**

Foreclose, to preclude, exclude. (F. – L.)
Better spelt *forclose.* – O. F. *forclos,* pp. of
forclorre, to exclude, shut out. – O. F. *for-,*
from L. *foris,* outside; and *clorre,* to shut,
from L. *claudere.* See **Forfeit** and **Close.**

Forego, to relinquish; see **Forgo.**

Foreign. (F. – L.) The *g* is wrongly
inserted. M. E. *foraine, foreyne.* – O. F.
forain, alien, strange. – Low L. *foraneus,*
adj., from L. *foras,* out of doors, adv. with
acc. pl. form, allied to L. *fores,* doors; cf.
L. *forum,* a market-place, and E. *door.*

Foremost; see **Fore.**

Forensic, belonging to law-courts. (L.)
Coined from L. *forens-is,* belonging to the
forum. – L. *forum,* market-place, meeting-
place; orig. a vestibule or door-way. Allied to L. *fores,* and E. *door.*

forest. (F. – L.) O. F. *forest.* – Low L.
foresta, a wood. *forestis,* open space of

hunting-ground. (Medieval writers oppose the *forestis*, open hunting-ground, to the *parcus*, enclosed park.) — L. *foris*, out of doors; adv. allied to L. *fores*, doors. **Der.** *forest-er*, also spelt *forster, foster*.

Forfeit, a thing forfeited or lost by misdeed. (F. — L.) M. E. *forfete*; whence *forfeten*, verb. — O. F. *forfait*, a crime punishable by fine, a fine; also a pp. of *forfaire, forsfaire*, to trespass. — Low L. *forisfactum*, a trespass, fine; orig. pp. (neut.) of *forisfacere*, to trespass, lit. 'to do beyond.' — L. *foris facere*, to do or act beyond or abroad; from *foris*, out of doors; and *facere*, to do. See **Foreclose**.

Forfend, Forefend, to avert. (Hybrid; E. *and* F.) M. E. *forfenden*. An extraordinary compound of E. *for-*, prefix, with *fend*, a familiar abbreviation of *defend*. See **For-** (2) and **Defend**; also **Fend, Fence**.

Forge; see **Fabric**.

Forget. (E.) From **For-** (2) and **Get**. A. S. *forgitan*.+Du. *vergeten*, G. *vergessen*.

Forgive. (E.) From **For-** (2) and **Give**. A. S. *forgifan*.+Du. *vergeven*, G. *vergeben*.

Forgo, Forego, to give up. (E.) Better *forgo*. A. S. *forgán*, to pass over. From **For-** (2) and **Go**.

Fork. (L.) A. S. *forc*. — L. *furca*, a fork.

bifurcated, two-pronged. (L.) Low L. *bifurcatus*, pp. of *bifurcari*, to part in two directions. — L. *bi-furcus*, two-pronged; from *bi-s*, double; *furca*, a fork.

Forlorn, quite lost. (E.) M. E. *forlorn*. A. S. *forloren*, pp. of *forleósan*, to lose utterly; from *for-*, prefix, and *leósan*, to lose; see **For-** (2) and **Lose**. So also Dan. *forloren*, Du. and G. *verloren*, similarly compounded.

Form. (F. — L.) O. F. *forme*. — L. *forma*, shape. (√DHAR.) O. F. *forme* also means 'a bench,' like E. *form*.

conform. (F. — L.) F. *conformer*. — L. *con-formare*, to fashion like.

deform. (F. — L.) M. E. *deformen*, chiefly in pp. *deformed*. — O. F. *defforme*, adj., deformed, ugly. — L. *deformis*, ugly. — L. *de*, away; *forma*, shape, beauty.

formula, a prescribed form. (L.) L. *formula*, dimin. of *forma*, a form.

inform, to impart knowledge to. (F. — L.) F. *informer*. — L. *in-formare*, to put into form, mould; also, to tell, inform.

reform. (F. — L.) F. *reformer*, to shape anew. — L. *re-*, again; *formare*, to form.

transform. (F. — L.) F. *transformer*. — L. *trans-formare*, to change the shape of. Also *uni-form, multi-form*, &c.

Former; see **Fore**.

Formic, pertaining to ants. (L.) L. *formica*, an ant.

Formidable, causing fear. (F. — L.) F. - *formidable*. — L. *formidabilis*, terrible. — L. *formidare*, to dread; *formido*, fear.

Formula; see **Form**.

Fornicate. (L.) From pp. of L. *fornicari*, to commit lewdness, seek a brothel. — L. *fornic-*, base of *fornix*, a vault, arch, brothel.

Forsake. (E.) M. E. *forsaken*. A. S. *forsacan*, to neglect, orig. to contend against, or oppose. — L. *for-*, prefix; and *sacan*, to contend, whence the E. sb. *sake*. See **For-** (2) and **Sake**. So also Swed. *försaka*, Dan. *forsage*.

Forsooth. (E.) M. E. *for sothe*, for a truth. A. S. *for sóðe*; where *for*=for, and *sóðe* is dat. of *sóð*, truth; see **Sooth**.

Forswear. (E.) From **For-** (2) and **Swear**. A. S. *forswerian*.

Fort, Fortalice; see **Force** (1).

Fortify, Fortitude; see **Force** (1).

Forth, forward. (E.) M. E. *forth*. A. S. *forð*, adv.; extended from *fore*, before; see **Fore**. + Du. *voort*, from *voor*; G. *fort*, M. H. G. *vort*, from *vor*.

Fortnight; see **Four**.

Fortress; see **Force** (1).

Fortuitous; see below.

Fortune. (F. — L.) F. *fortune*. — L. *fortuna*, chance. — L. *fortu-*, allied to *forti-*, crude form of *fors*, chance; orig. 'that which is brought,' from *ferre*, to bring; see **Fertile**.

fortuitous. (L.) L. *fortuitus*, casual. — L. *fortu-* (as above).

Forty; see **Four**.

Forward; see **Fore**.

Fosse. (F. — L.) F. *fosse*. — L. *fossa*, a ditch. — L. *fossa*, fem. of *fossus*, pp. of *fodere*, to dig.

fossil, petrified remains obtained by digging. (F. — L.) O. F. *fossile*, 'that may be digged;' Cot. — L. *fossilis*, dug up. — L. *foss-us*, pp. of *fodere* (above).

Foster; see **Food** (and **Forest**).

Foul. (E.) M. E. *foul*. A. S. *fúl*. + Du. *vuil*, Icel. *fúll*, Dan. *fuul*, Swed. *ful*, Goth. *fuls*, G. *faul*. Akin to **Putrid**. (√PU.)

filth, foul matter. (E.) A. S. *fýlð*. — A. S. *fúl*, foul (by vowel-change of *ú* to *ý*)

foumart, a polecat. (E. *and* F.) M. E. *fulmart*; comp. of M. E. *ful*, foul (as above), and O. F. *marte, martre*, a marten; see **Marten**.

Found (1), to lay a foundation; see **Fund**.

Found (2), to cast metals. (F. – L.) O. F. *fondre.* – L. *fundere*, to pour, cast metals. (√GHU.)

font (2), **fount**, an assortment of types. (F. – L.) O. F. *fonte*, a casting of metals. – O. F. *fondre*, to cast (above). And see **Fuse** (1).

Founder; see **Fund**.

Foundling; see **Find**.

Fount (1), a spring; see **Font** (1).

Fount (2); see under **Found** (2).

Four. (E.) M. E. *feower, fower, four*. A. S. *feōwer*. + Icel. *fjórir*, Dan. *fire*, Swed. *fyra*, Du. *vier*, Goth. *fidwor*, G. *vier*, W. *pedwar*, Gael. *ceithir*, L. *quatuor*, Gk. τέτταρες, τέσσαρες, πίσυρες, Russ. *chetvero*, Skt. *chatvar*. (Aryan type, *kwatwar*.) Der. *four-th*, A. S. *feórþa*; *four-teen*, A. S. *feówertýne*; *for-ty*, A. S. *feówertig*.

farthing, fourth part of a penny. (E.) M. E. *ferthing*. A. S. *ferþing, feorðing*, older form *feorþling.* – A. S. *feórð-a*, fourth; with double dimin. suffix *-l-ing*.

firkin, the fourth part of a barrel. (O. Du.) From Du. *vier*, four; with suffix *-kin* (as in *kilder-kin*) answering to the O. Du. double dimin. suffix *-k-en* (G. *-ch-en* in *mädchen*).

fortnight, two weeks. (E.) M. E. *fourte-night*; also *fourten night.* – M. E. *fourten*, i. e. fourteen; *night*, old pl., i. e. nights. A. S. *feówertýne niht*. So also *sennight = seven night*.

Fowl. (E.) M. E. *foul*, A. S. *fugol*, a bird. + Du. *vogel*, Icel. *fugl*, Dan. *fugl*, Swed. *fågel*, Goth. *fugls*, G. *vogel*.

Fox. (E.) A. S. *fox*. + Du. *vos*, Icel. *fox, fóa*, Goth. *fauho*, G. *fuchs*.

foxglove. (E.) A. S. *foxes glofa*, i. e. fox's glove; a fanciful name.

vixen. (E.) M. E. *vixen, fixen*, a she-fox; answering to A. S. *fyx-en*, made from *fox* by vowel-change of *o* to *y*, with fem. suffix *-en*; precisely as A. S. *gyden*, a goddess, from *god*, a god.

Fracas. (F. – Ital. – L.) F. *fracas*, a crash. – F. *fracasser*, to shatter. – Ital. *fracassare*, to break in pieces. – Ital. *fra*, prep., among; and *cassare*, to break (imitated from L. *interrumpere*). *Cassare* = L. *quassare*, to shatter; see **Quash**.

Fraction, Fracture; see **Fragile**.

Fractious, peevish. (E.) A prov. E. word, from North. E. *fratch*, to squabble, chide; the same as M. E. *fracchen*, to creak as a cart. ¶ Not from L. *frangere*.

Fragile. (F. – L.) F. *fragile.* – L. *fragilis*, easily broken. – L. *frag-*, base of *frangere*, to break.

defray. (F. – L.) O. F. *defrayer*, to pay expenses. – O. F. *de-* (= L. *dis-*); *frait*, expense (pl. *fraits* = mod. F. *frais*); from Low L. *fractum*, acc. of *fractus*, expense (Ducange). The Low L. *fractus* is from L. *fractus*, pp. of *frangere*, to break.

fraction. (F. – L.) F. *fraction.* – L. acc. *fractionem*, a breaking. – L. *fractus*, pp. of *frangere*, to break.

fracture. (F. – L.) O. F. *fracture.* – L. *fractura*, a breach. – L. *fractus*, pp. of *frangere*, to break.

fragment. (F. – L.) F. *fragment.* – L. *fragmentum*, a broken piece. – L. *frag-* (base of *frangere*); with suffix *-mentum*.

frail. (F. – L.) M. E. *freel.* – O. F. *fraile*, brittle. – L. *fragilem*, acc. of *fragilis*; see **fragile** above.

frangible. (L.) Late L. *frangibilis*, breakable; a coined word. – L. *frangere*, to break.

infraction, violation of law. (F. – L.) F. *infraction.* – L. acc. *infractionem*; a weakening, breaking into. – L. *infractus*, pp. of *in-fringere* (below).

infringe. (L.) L. *in-fringere*, to break into, violate law.

irrefragable, not to be refuted. (F. – L.) F. *irrefragable.* – L. *irrefragabilis*, not to be withstood. – L. *ir-* (= *in*, not); *re-frāgari*, to oppose, thwart; from *re-*, back, and (probably) L. *frag-*, base of *frangere*, to break. (For the long *a*, cf. L. *suffrāgium*, prob. from the same root.)

refract, to bend back rays of light. (L.) L. *refractus*, pp. of *re-fringere*, to bend back. Der. *refract-or-y*, a mistaken form for *refractary*, from L. *refractarius*, stubborn, obstinate. Also *refrangible*, a mistaken form for *refringible*.

refrain (2), the burden of a song. (F. – L.) F. *refrain*; so also Prov. *refranhs*, a refrain, *refranher, refrenher*, to repeat. So called from frequent repetition; the O. F. *refreindre*, to pull back, is the same word as Prov. *refrenher*, to repeat; both are from L. *refringere*, to break back (pull back, hence, come back to, repeat). The word is rather Prov. than F.

Fragrant. (F.–L.) F. *fragrant.*–L. *fragrantem*, acc. of *fragrans*, pres. pt. of *fragrare*, to emit an odour.

Frail ; see **Fragile.**

Frame, to construct. (E.) M. E. *fremen.* A. S. *fremman*, to promote, effect, do, lit. to further.–A. S. *fram*, strong, good, lit. forward.–A. S. *fram*, prep., from, away ; see **From.** + Icel. *fremja*, to further, from *framr*, adj., forward, *fram*, adv., forward, allied to *frá*, from. Der. *frame*, sb.

Frampold, quarrelsome. (C.) Obsolete. Also *frampald.*–W. *ffromfol*, passionate ; from *ffromi*, to fume, fret, *ffrom*, testy.

Franc, Franchise ; see **Frank.**

Frangible ; see **Fragile.**

Frank, free. (F.–Low L.–O. H. G.) O. F. *franc* ; Low L. *francus*, free. – O. H. G. *franko*, a free man, a Frank. The *Franks* were a Germanic people.

franc, a French coin. (F.–G.) M. E. *frank.*–O. F. *franc* ; named from its being *French*, i. e. Frankish.

franchise. (F.–G.) M. E. *franchise.* – O. F. *franchise*, privileged liberty. – O. F. *franchis-*, stem of pres. pt. of *franchir*, to free.–O. F. *franc*, free (above). Der. *dis-franchise, en-franchise.*

frankincense. (F.–G. *and* L.) O. F. *franc encens*, pure incense ; see **Frank** (above) and **Incense.**

franklin, a freeholder. (F.–G.) M. E. *frankelein.*–O. F. *frankeleyn* (= *francheleyn*) ; Low L. *franchilanus.* – Low L. *francus*, free ; see **Frank** (above). The suffix is from O. H. G. *-linc* (= E. *-l-ing* as in *dar-ling*) ; precisely as in *chamberlain.*

Frantic ; see **Frenzy.**

Fraternal. (F. – L.) O. F. *fraternel.* –Low L. *fraternalis*, the same as L. *fraternus*, brotherly. – L. *frater*, cognate with E. **Brother.**

fraternity. (F.–L.) O. F. *fraternite.* –L. acc. *fraternitatem*, brotherhood.–L. *fraternus*, brotherly.–L. *frater*, brother. Der. *con-fraternity.*

fratricide (1), murderer of a brother. (F.–L.) O. F. *fratricide.*–L. *fratricida*, a brother-slayer.–L. *fratri-*, crude form of *frater* ; *-cida*, a slayer, from *cædere*, to kill ; see **Cæsura.**

fratricide (2), murder of a brother. (L.) From L. *fratri-cidium*, the killing of a brother.

friar. (F. – L.) M. E. *frere.* – O. F. *frere, freire*, lit. a brother. – L. *fratrem*, acc. of *frater.*

Fraud. (F. – L.) O. F. *fraude.* – L. *fraudem*, acc. of *fraus*, deceit, guile. Cf. Skt. *dhúrta*, fraudulent ; *dhvri*, to bend. (√ DHWAR.)

defraud. (F.–L.) O. F. *defrauder.*– L. *de-fraudare*, to deprive by fraud.

Fraught, to lade a ship. (Scand.) We now use *fraught* only as a pp. M. E. *frahten, fragten*, only in the pp. *fraught.* –Swed. *frakta*, to fraught or freight, from *frakt*, a cargo ; Dan. *fragte*, from *fragt*, a cargo. + Du. *bevrachten*, from *vracht* ; G. *frachten*, from *fracht.* Origin uncertain.

freight, a cargo. (F.–O. H. G.) A curious spelling of F. *fret*, the freight of a ship, the *gh* being inserted by confusion with *fraught* above.–F. *fret*, 'the fraught or freight of a ship, also, the hire that's paid for a ship ; ' Cot. – O. H. G. *freht*, orig. 'service,' whence use, hire. This O. H. G. *freht* is thought to be the same as G. *fracht*, a cargo.

Fray (1), an affray. (F.–L.) Short for *affray*, or *effray*, orig. 'terror,' as shewn by the use of *fray* in the sense of terror, Bruce, xv. 255. See **Affray.**

Fray (2), to terrify. (F.–L.) Short for *affray* ; see **Affray.**

Fray (3), to rub away ; see **Friction.**

Freak (1), a whim, caprice. (E.) A quick movement ; from M. E. *frek*, quick, vigorous.–A. S. *frec*, bold, rash. + Icel. *frekr*, voracious ; Swed. *fräck*, impudent ; Dan. *fræk*, audacious, G. *frech*, saucy, O. H. G. *freh*, greedy.

Freak (2), to streak. (Scand.) A coined word ; short for *freckle* below.

freckle, a small spot. (Scand.) We find both *frekell* and *freken* or *frakn.*– Icel. *freknur*, pl., freckles ; Swed. *fräkne*, Dan. *fregne*, a freckle. Cf. Gael. *breac*, Gk. περκνός, Skt. *pṛiçni*, variegated, spotted. Allied to **Fleck.**

Free. (E.) M. E. *fre.* A. S. *freb.* + Du. *vrij*, Icel. *frí*, Swed. Dan. *fri*, Goth. *freis*, G. *frei.* Orig. acting at pleasure, rejoicing ; allied to Skt. *priya*, beloved, agreeable ; also to E. **Friend.** Der. *free-dom*, A. S. *freódóm.*

Freeze. (E.) M. E. *fresen.* A. S. *frebsan* ; pp. *froren.*+Icel. *frjósa*, Swed. *frysa*, Dan. *fryse*, Du. *vriezen*, G. *frieren*, L. *prurire*, to itch, originally to burn (cf. *pruina*, hoarfrost), Skt. *plush*, to burn, (√ PRUS.)

frore, frozen. (E.) A. S. *froren*, pp. of *freósan* (above).

frost. (E.) M. E. *frost, forst*; A.S.
forst (for *frost*). – A.S. *freósan* (pp. *froren*,
for *frosen*).+Du. *vorst*, Icel. Dan. Swed.
G. *frost*; Goth. *frius*.

Freight; see **Fraught**.

Frenzy. (F. – L. – Gk.) M. E. *frenesye*.
– O. F. *frenaisie*. – L. *phrenesis*. – Late
Gk. φρένησις = Gk. φρενῖτις, inflammation of
the brain. – Gk. φρεν-, base of φρήν, midriff,
heart, senses.

frantic. (F. – L. – Gk.) M. E. *frenetik*,
shorter form *frentik*. – O. F. *frenatique*. –
L. *phreneticus, phreniticus*, mad. – Gk.
φρενιτικός, mad, suffering from φρενῖτις
(above).

Frequent. (F. – L.) O. F. *frequent*. –
L. *frequentem*, acc. of *frequens*, crowded,
frequent; pres. part. of a lost verb *frequĕre*,
to cram, allied to *farcire*, to cram; see
Farce.

Fresh. (E.) M. E. *fresh*, also *fersh*.
A. S. *fersc*. Here *fersc* (= *far-isc* *) orig.
meant ' moving ' or ' on the move,' used of
fresh water, as opposed to stagnant water.
– A. S. *faran*, to move, travel; see **Fare**.
+Icel. *ferskr*, fresh, *frískr*, brisk; Swed.
Dan. *frisk*, Dan. *fersk*, Du. *versch*, G. *frisch*,
M. H. G. *virsc*.

afresh. (E.) For *on fresh* or *of fresh*;
cf. *anew*.

fresco. (Ital. – O. H. G.) A painting
on *fresh* plaster. – Ital. *fresco*, cool, fresh.
– O. H. G. *frisc* (G. *frisch*).

frisk, to skip about. (F. – Scand.)
From the adj. *frisk*, brisk. – O. F. *frisque*,
' friske, blithe, brisk ;' Cot. – Icel. *frískr*,
frisky; Swed. *frisk*, fresh, also lively, Dan.
frisk, hale; all cognate with E. *fresh* (above).

refresh. (F. – L. *and* G.) M. E. *re-
freschen*. – O. F. *refreschir*; Cot. – L. *re-*,
again; O. H. G. *frisc* (G. *frisch*), cognate
with E. *fresh*.

Fret (1), to devour; see **Eat**.

Fret (2), to ornament, variegate. (E.)
M. E. *fretien*. A. S. *frætwan*, to adorn;
from *frætwe*, ornament. Root unknown.

Fret (3), a kind of grating. (F. – L.)
Common in heraldry. – O. F. *frete*, a ferrule;
frettes, pl., an iron grating (Diez); *fretter*,
to hoop; *fretté*, fretty (in heraldry). Cf.
Span. *fretes*, frets (in heraldry); Ital. *fer-
riata*, an iron grating. – F. *ferrer*, to hoop
with iron. – F. *fer*, iron. – L. *ferrum*, iron.

fret (4), a stop on a musical instrument.
(F. – L.) *Frets* are bars across the neck
of the instrument; the same word as
fret (3).

Friable, easily crumbled. (F. – L.) O.F.
friable. – L. *friabilis*. – L. *friare*, to rub,
crumble. Allied to **Grind**.

Friar; see **Fraternal**.

Fribble, to trifle. (F.) Prob. for *fripple*;
from O. F. *fripper*, to rub up and down, to
wear to rags. See **Frippery**.

Fricassee, a dish of fowls cut up. (F.
– Ital.?–L.?) F. *fricassée*, a fricassee; fem.
of pp. of *fricasser*, to fricassee, also, to
squander money. A fricassee is made of
chickens, &c. cut up into small pieces. I
suspect it to have been borrowed from
Ital. *fracassare*; to break in pieces. See
Fracas. ¶ Origin doubtful.

Friction. (F. – L.) F. *friction*. – L.
acc. *frictionem*, a rubbing. – L. *frictus*,
contr. pp. of *fricare*, to rub; allied to
friare, to rub; see **Friable**.

fray (3), to wear away by rubbing. (F.
– L.) O. F. *frayer*, to grate upon. – L.
fricare, to rub.

Friday. (E.) A.S. *frige-dæg*; where
frige is gen. of *frigu*, love, also the goddess
of love. Allied to **Friend**. (√PRI.)

Friend. (E.) M. E. *frend*. A.S. *freónd*,
orig. ' loving,' pres. pt. of *freón, freógan*, to
love.+Du. *vriend*; Icel. *frændi*, from *frjá*,
to love; Dan. *frænde*, Swed. *frände*. G.
freund; Goth. *frijonds*, a friend, pres. pt.
of *frijon*, to love. Cf. Skt. *pri*, to love.
(√PRI.) Der. *friend-ship*, A. S. *freónd-
scipe*.

Frieze (1), a coarse woollen cloth. (F.
– Du.) F. *frize, frise*, ' frise ;' Cot.; also
drap de frise, i.e. cloth of Friesland. – Du.
Vriesland, Friesland, *Vries*, a Frieslander,
belonging to Friesland. So also *cheval de
Frise*, a horse of Friesland; whence *chevaux
de Frise*, spikes to resist cavalry, a jesting
term.

Frieze (2), part of the entablature of a
column. (F.) O. F. *frize*, ' the cloth called
frize; also the broad and flat band that's
next below the cornish [cornice], or between it and the architrave ;' Cot. Span.
friso, a frieze; cf. Ital. *fregio*, a fringe,
lace, border, ornament. Origin much
disputed.

Frigate. (F. – Ital.) O. F. *fregate*, ' a
frigate ;' Cot. – Ital. *fregata*, a frigate.
Origin uncertain.

Fright. (E.) M. E. *fryght*. A.S. *fyrhto,
fyrhtu*, fright; *fyrht*, timid.+O. Sax. *foroht,
forht*, Dan. *frygt*, Swed. *fruktan*, G. *furcht*,
Goth. *faurhtei*, fright, *faurhts*, fearful.
Root unknown.

affright, to frighten. (E.) The double *f* is a modern mistake. M. E. *afright*, pp. affrighted. — A.S. *áfyrhtan*, to terrify; where the prefix *á* = G. *er-*; see A- (4).

Frigid. (L.) L. *frigidus*, cold, adj. — L. *frigēre*, to be cold. — L. *frigus*, cold, sb. +Gk. *ῥῖγος*, cold.

frill, a ruffle on a shirt. (F. — L.) Orig. a term in hawking; a hawk *ruffling* its feathers, from feeling *chilly*, was said to *frill*. — O. F. *friller*, to shiver with cold. — O. F. *frilleux*, chilly. — Low L. *frigidulosus** *, coined from L. *frigidulus*, chilly, dimin. form of *frigidus* (above).

refrigerate. (L.) From pp. of L. *refrigerare*, to make cool again. — L. *re-*, again; *frigerare*, to cool, from *frigus*, cold.

Fringe, a border of loose threads. (F. — L.) M. F. *fringe*. — O. F. *frenge** * (not found), oldest form of F. *frange*, fringe; the Wallachian form is *frimbie*, put (by metathesis) for *fimbrie** *. — L. *fimbria*, fringe; allied to *fibra*, a fibre; see Fibre.

Frippery, worn-out clothes, trash. (F.) Stuff sold by a *fripier*. — O. F. *fripier*, 'a fripier, or broker, trimmer up of old garments, and a seller of them so mended;' Cot. — O. F. *fripper*, to rub up and down, wear to rags. Origin unknown.

Frisk; see **Fresh**.

Frith, Firth; see **Fare**.

Fritter; see **Fry** (1).

Frivolous, trifling. (L.) L. *friuolus*, silly. The orig. sense seems to have been 'rubbed away;' hence *friuola* meant broken potsherds, &c. — L. *friare, fricare*, to rub; see **Friable**.

Friz, Frizz, to curl, render rough. (F. — Du. ?) O. F. *frizer*, 'to frizle, crispe, curle;' Cot. [Cf. Span. *frisar*, to frizzle, raise the nap on frieze, from *frisa*, frieze.] Similarly the F. *frizer* is from *frise, frize, friese*; see **Frieze** (1). Der. *frizz-le*, frequent. form; in commoner use.

Fro; see **From**.

Frock. (F. — Low L.) M. E. *frok*. — O. F. *froc*; Low L. *frocus*, a monk's frock, also spelt *floccus* (Ducange). Prob. so called because woollen; see **Flock** (2). ¶ So Diez; but Brachet derives it from O. H. G. *hroch* (G. *rock*), a coat.

Frog (1), an animal. (E.) M. E. *frogge*. A. S. *froga, frocga*. Also A. S. *frox*, a frog, Icel. *froskr*, Du. *vorsch*, G. *frosch*.

Frog (2), a substance like a fork in a horse's foot. (E. ?) It is shaped like a fork; perhaps a corruption of *fork*, q. v. Yet it was certainly supposed to mean *frog* (though it is hard to see why) because it was also called a *frush*, i. e. M. E. *frosh*, A. S. *frox*, a frog. See above.

Frolic, adj., sportive. (Du.) XVI cent. Orig. an adj. — Du. *vrolijk*, frolic, merry. +G. *fröhlich*, merry. Formed with suffix *-lijk* (= E. *like, -ly*) from the O. Sax. *frâh*, O. Fries. *fro* (= G. *froh*), merry. Der. *frolic*, sb. and verb.

From, away, forth. (E.) A. S. *from, fram*. + Icel. *fram*, forward, distinguished in use from *frá*, from; Swed. *fram*, Dan. *frem*, O. H. G. *fram*, forth; Goth. *fram*, from; *framis*, adv., further. Allied to **Far**, **Fare**. (√PAR.)

fro. (Scand.) The Scand. form. = Icel. *frá*, Dan. *fra*, from.

froward, perverse. (E.) M. E. *froward*, commonly *fraward* (Northern). A. S. *fromweard*, only in the sense 'about to depart;' but we still keep the orig. sense of *from-ward*, i. e. averse, perverse. (Cf. *wayward*, i. e. away - ward.) And see **Toward**.

Frond, a branch. (L.) L. *frond-*, stem of *frons*, a leafy branch.

Front. (F. — L.) M. E. *front*, forehead. — O. F. *front*, forehead, brow. — L. *front-em*, acc. of *frons*, forehead, brow. Allied to **Brow**.

affront. (F. — L.) M. E. *afronten*. — O. F. *afronter*, to confront, oppose face to face. — O. F. *a* (L. *ad*), to; *front*, forehead, face (above).

confront. (F. — L.) F. *confronter*, to bring face to face. — F. *con* = L. *con-* (*cum*), together; *front*, face (above).

effrontery. (F. — L.) XVIII cent. — F. *effronterie*, 'impudency;' Cot. — O. F. *effronté*, shameless. — O. F. *ef-* = L. *ef-* (L. *ex*); *front*, face.

frontal, a band worn on the forehead. (F. — L.) O. F. *frontal*. — L. *frontale*, an ornament for a horse's forehead. — L. *front-*, stem of *frons*, forehead.

frontier. (F. — L.) O. F. *frontiere*. — Low L. *fronteria, frontaria*, border-land. — L. *front-*, stem of *frons* (above).

frontispiece. (F. — L.) Misspelling of *frontispice*. — O. F. *frontispice*, 'the frontispiece or fore-front of a house;' Cot. — Low L. *frontispicium*, a front view. — L. *fronti-*, crude form of *frons*; *specere*, to see; see **Species**.

frontlet. (F. — L.) For *frontal-et*, dimin. of **frontal** (above).

frounce, to wrinkle, curl, plait. (F.—
L.) The older form of *flounce*; see
Flounce (2).

Frontier, Frontispiece; see **Front.**

Frore, Frost; see **Freeze.**'

Froth. (Scand.) M. E. *frothe.* — Icel.
froða, frauð, Dan. *fraade,* Swed. *fradga,*
froth, foam on liquids.

Frounce; see **Front.**

Froward; see **From.**

Frown. (F.—Scand.) M. E. *frounen.*—
O. F. *frogner,* only in comp. *refrogner,* to
frown, lower, look sullen. Cf. Ital. *in-
frigno,* frowning, Ital. dial. (Lombardic)
frignare, to whimper, make a wry face.
Of Scand. origin; cf. Swed. dial. *fryna,*
Norw. *fröyna,* to make a wry face; Swed.
flina, to giggle. Compare E. *fleer.*

Fructify; see **Fruit.**

Frugal, thrifty. (F.—L.) F. *frugal.*—
L. *frugalis,* economical; lit. belonging to
fruits. — L. *frug-i,* frugal; orig. dat. of
frux, fruits of the earth. Allied to **Fruit.**

Fruit. (F.—L.) M. E. *fruit.*—O. F.
fruit.—L. *fructum,* acc. of *fructus,* fruit.
—L. *fructus,* pp. of *frui* (=*frugui**), to
enjoy; allied to **Brook** (1). (✓BHRUG.)

fructify. (F.—L.) F. *fructifier.*—L.
fructificare, to make fruitful.—L. *fructi-,*
for *fructus,* fruit; -*ficare,* for *facere,* to
make.

fruition. (F. — L.) O. F. *fruition,*
enjoyment. Coined as if from L. *fruitio.*
—L. *fruit-us,* the same as *fructus,* pp. of
frui, to enjoy.

frumenty, furmety, wheat boiled in
milk. (F.—L.) O. F. *froumenté,* 'furmen-
tie, wheat boyled;' Cot. Lit. made with
wheat; the suffix -*é* = L. -*atus,* made with.
—O. F. *froument,* wheat.—L. *frümentum,*
corn (from the base *frü* = *frug*).

Frustrate, to render vain. (L.) From
pp. of L. *frustrari,* to render vain.—L.
frustrá, in vain; orig. abl. fem. of obsolete adj. *frustrus* (= *frud-trus*), deceitful.
Allied to **Fraud.**

Frustum, a piece of a cone or cylinder.
(L.) L. *frustum,* a piece cut off. Cf. Gk.
θραῦσμα, a fragment, from θραύειν, to break
in pieces.

Fry (1), to dress food. (F.—L.) M. E.
frien.—O. F. *frire.*—L. *frigere,* to roast.
+ Gk. φρύγειν, to parch; Skt. *bhrajj,* to
fry. (✓BHARG.)

fritter, a kind of pancake. (F.—L.)
M. E. *frytowre, fritoure.* [Cf. F. *friteau,*
'a fritter,' Cot.]—O. F. *friture,* a frying,

dish of fried fish (also a fragment, Shak).
—O. F. *frit,* fried. — L. *frictus,* pp. of
frigere (above).

Fry (2), spawn of fishes. (Scand.) M. E.
fri. — Icel. *fræ, frjó,* spawn, fry; Dan.
Swed. *frö.* + Goth. *fraiw,* seed.

Fuchsia, a flower. (G.) Named after
L. *Fuchs,* German botanist, ab. 1542.

Fudge. (F.—Low G.) Prov. F. *fuche,
feuche* (Hécart).—Low G. *futsch*! begone!

Fuel; see **Focus.**

Fugitive. (F.—L.) O. F. *fugitif.*—L.
fugitiuus, fleeing away. — L. *fugit-um,*
supine of *fugere,* to flee. + Gk. φεύγειν,
to flee; Skt. *bhuj,* to bend, turn aside,
(✓BHUGH.) Der. *centri-fugal,* q. v.;
febri-fuge, fever-few.

fugue, a musical composition. (F.—
Ital.—L.) F. *fugue.*—Ital. *fuga,* a fugue,
lit. a flight.—L. *fuga,* flight.

refuge. (F. — L.) M. E. *refuge.*—F.
refuge. — L. *refugium,* an escape. — L.
re-fugere, to flee back.

refugee. (F.—L.) F. *refugié,* pp. of
se refugier, to take refuge. — F. *refuge*
(above).

subterfuge. (F.—L.) F. *subterfuge,*
'a shift;' Cot.—Low L. *subterfugium.*—
L. *subter-fugere,* to escape by stealth.

Fugleman, the leader of a file. (G.)
Put for *flugleman.*—G. *flügelmann,* the
leader of a wing or file of men.—G. *flügel,*
a wing, dimin. of *flug,* wing, from *fliegen,*
to fly; *mann,* a man. See **Fly.**

Fugue; see **Fugitive.**

Fulcrum, a point of support. (L.) L.
fulcrum, a support.—L. *fulcire,* to prop.
Cf. Skt. *dhru,* to stand firm.

Fulfil; see **Full.**

Fulgent, shining. (L.) From stem of
pres. pt. of L. *fulgere,* to shine. + Gk.
φλέγειν, to burn; Skt. *bhráj,* to shine.
(✓BHARK.) Der. *ef-fulgent* (*ef-* = L. *ex*);
re-fulgent.

fulminate, to thunder, hurl lightning.
(L.) From pp. of L. *fulminare,* to thunder. — L. *fulmin-,* stem of *fulmen,* a thunder-
bolt (=*fulg-men*).—L. *fulgere,* to shine.

Fuliginous, sooty. (L.) L. *fuliginosus,*
sooty. — L. *fuligin-,* stem of *fuligo,* soot.
Allied to **Fume.**

Full (1), complete. (E.) A. S. *ful.*+Du.
vol, Icel. *fullr,* Dan. *fuld* (for *full*), Swed.
full, Goth. *fulls,* G. *full,* Skt. *púrna,* Gk.
πλήρης, L. *plenus.* (✓PAR.)

fill, verb. (E.) A. S. *fyllan*; formed
from *ful* by vowel-change from *u to y.*+

Du. *vullen,* Icel. *fylla,* Dan. *fylde,* Swed. *fylla,* Goth. *fulljan,* G. *füllen.*

fulfil. (E.) M. E. *fulfillen.* A. S. *fulfyllan.* — A. S. *ful,* full; *fyllan,* to fill.

fulsome, cloying. (E.) M. E. *fulsum,* from M. E. *ful,* full; with suffix *-sum* (= E. *-some* as in *winsome.*) And see **Plenary.**

Full (2), to whiten cloth, bleach. (L.) Only (in *this* sense) in sb. *full-er,* a bleacher. A. S. *fullere,* a bleacher. — A. S. *fullian,* to bleach. — Low L. *fullare,* (1) to cleanse clothes, (2) to full cloth. — L. *fullo,* a fuller, bleacher. Perhaps allied to *in-fula,* a white fillet. (See below.)

Full (3), to full cloth, felt. (F. — L.) O. F. *fouler,* 'to full, or thicken cloath in a mill;' Cot. Also spelt *fouler,* to trample on. — Low L. *fullare,* (1) to cleanse clothes, (2) to full. — L. *fullo,* a fuller. (See above.) ¶ The senses of *full* (2) and *full* (3) should be kept distinct; the sense of felting is due to the washing of clothes by trampling on or beating them.

Fulminate; see **Fulgent.**

Fulsome; see **Full** (1).

Fulvous, Fulvid, tawny. (L.) From L. *fuluus,* tawny, *fuluidus,* somewhat tawny.

Fumble, to grope about. (Du.) XVI cent. — Du. *fommelen,* to fumble. + Swed. *famla,* Dan. *famle,* Icel. *fálma,* to grope about; due to the sb. appearing as A. S. *folm,* the palm of the hand, L. *palma;* see **Palm.**

Fume. (F. — L.) O. F. *fum.* — L. *fumum,* acc. of *fumus,* smoke. + Skt. *dhūma,* smoke. (√DHU.) Allied to **Dust.**

fumigate. (L.) From pp. of L. *fumigare,* to fumigate. — L. *fum-,* for *fumus,* vapour; *-igare,* for *agere,* to drive about.

fumitory, a plant. (F. — L.) Formerly *fumiter.* — F. *fumeterre,* fumitory (put for *fume de terre*). — L. *fumus de terrâ,* smoke from the earth; so named from the smell.

perfume, vb. (F. — L.) F. *parfumer,* to perfume, lit. to smoke thoroughly. — L. *per,* thoroughly; *fumare,* to smoke, from *fumus.*

Fun, merriment. (C.) XVIII cent. — Irish *fonn,* delight, pleasure, a tune, song; Gael. *fonn.* ¶ Distinct from *fond.*

Funambulist, a rope-dancer. (Span. — L.) Formerly *funambulo.* — Span. *funambulo,* a funambulist. — L. *fun-is,* a rope; *ambul-are,* to walk; see **Amble.**

Function, performance, office. (F. — L.) O. F. *function.* — L. acc. *functionem,* performance. — L. *functus,* pp. of *fungi* (base

fug), to perform, orig. to use. + Skt. *bhuj,* to enjoy, use.

defunct, dead. (L.) L. *defunctus,* i.e. having fully performed the course of life, pp. of *defungi,* to perform fully. — L. *de;* and *fungi* (above).

perfunctory. (L.) L. *perfunctorius,* carelessly done. — L. *perfunctus,* pp. of *perfungi,* to perform fully, complete.

Fund, a store. (F. — L.) O. F. *fond,* 'a bottom, a merchant's stock;' Cot. — L. *fundus,* bottom; cognate with E. **Bottom.**

found (1), to lay the foundation of. (F. — L.) M. E. *founden.* — O. F. *fonder.* — L. *fundare,* to found. — L. *fundus* (above).

founder, to go to the bottom. (F. — L.) M. E. *foundren,* said of a horse falling. — O. F. *fondrer,* in comp. *afondrer* (obsolete), *effondrer,* to fall in (still in use); orig. to sink in. — F. *fond,* bottom. — L. *fundus,* bottom.

fundament, base. (F. — L.) M. E. *fundement.* — O. F. *fondement,* foundation. — L. *fundamentum,* foundation. — L. *fund-are;* see **found** (1) above.

profound, deep. (F. — L.) F. *profond.* — L. *profundum,* acc. of *profundus,* deep. — L. *pro,* forward, hence downward; *fundus,* bottom. Der. *profund-ity,* F. *profondité.*

Funeral, relating to a burial. (L.) Low L. *funeralis,* adj., from L. *funer-,* base of *funus,* a burial. Der. *funere-al,* from L. *funereus,* funereal.

Fungus, a spongy plant. (L. — Gk.) L. *fungus* (put for *sfungus*). — Gk. σφόγγος, Attic form of σπόγγος, a sponge; see **Sponge.**

Funnel. (F. — L.) M. E. *fonel.* Prob. from an O. F. *fonil*, preserved in Bret. *founil,* a funnel, and short for *enfonil*. — L. *infundibulum.* a funnel.

Fur. (F. — O. Low G.) M. E. *forre.* — O. F. *forre, fuerre,* a sheath, case; cf. Span. *forro,* lining for clothes, Ital. *fodero,* lining, fur, scabbard. — Goth. *fodr,* scabbard, orig. 'protection;' Icel. *fôðr,* lining; allied to G. *futter,* which (like Icel. *fôðr*) also means 'fodder.' Allied to **Fodder;** the senses of feeding and protecting being connected.

Furbelow, a flounce. (F.) Prov. F. *farbala,* a flounce, in the dialect of Hainault (Diez); the usual form is F. Span. Ital. Port. *falbala,* a flounce. Origin unknown.

Furbish, to polish, trim. (F. — O. H. G.) O. F. *fourbiss-,* stem of pres. pt. of *fourbir,*

to furbish, polish. — O. H. G. *furpjan*,
M. H. G. *vürben*, to purify, clean, rub
bright.

Furl; see **Fardel**.

Furlong; see **Furrow**.

Furlough, leave of absence. (Du. —
Scand.) Also spelt *furloe*. — Du. *verlof*,
leave, furlough; borrowed from Dan. *for-
lov*, Swed. *förlof*, leave. Cf. G. *verlaub*,
furlough; also Dan. *orlov*. β. As to the
prefix, Du. G. *ver-*, Dan. *for-* are the same
as E. *for-*; whilst Dan. *or*=Goth. *us*, out.
The syllable *lof* is Icel. *lof*, (1) praise, (2)
leave, the same as G. *lob*, praise, allied to
E. **Lief.**

Furmety; see **Frumenty**.

Furnace, an oven. (F.—L.) M. E. *for-
neis.*—O. F. *fornaise.*—L. *fornacem*, acc. of
fornax, an oven. — L. *fornus*, an oven;
allied to *formus*, warm. Cf. Skt. *gharma*,
warmth, glow. Allied to **Glow.**

Furnish, to fit up, equip. (F.—O.H.G.)
O. F. *furniss-*, stem of pres. pt. of *fournir*,
to furnish, of which an older spelling is
fornir, the same word as Prov. *formir*,
fromir. — O. H. G. *frumjan*, to provide,
furnish. — O. H. G. *fruma*, utility, profit,
gain; cf. G. *fromm*, good. Allied to **Former**; and cf. **Frame.**

perform, to achieve. (F. — O. H. G.;
with L. *prefix*.) Corrupted from M. E.
parfournen, later *parfourmen*. — O. F. *par-
fournir*, 'to perform;' Cot. — L. *per*, thoroughly; and O. F. *fournir*, to furnish,
provide (as above).

veneer, to overlay with a thin slice of
wood. (G. — F.—O. H. G.) G. *furniren*,
to furnish or provide small pieces of wood,
to veneer. — F. *fournir*, to furnish; a word
of G. origin; see above.

Furrow. (E.) M. E. *forwe*. A. S. *furh*,
a furrow. ✚ G. *furche*, a furrow. Cf. L.
porca, a ridge between two furrows.

furlong, ⅛th of a mile. (E.) A.S. *fur-
lang*, orig. a furrow-long, or the length of a
furrow.—A. S. *furh*, a furrow; *lang*, long.

Further. (E.) Really the comp. of
fore, but usually misunderstood as comp.
of *forth*. M. E. *furðer*. A. S. *furður*,
furðor, further. — A. S. *for-e*, adv., before;
with comp. suffix *-ðor* (Aryan *-tar*). ✚ Du.
vorders, adv., further; comp. of *vor*, before,
with comp. suffix *-der-s*; O. H. G. *furdor*,
from O. H. G. *furi*, before. So also Gk.
πρότερος, comp. of πρό. Der. *further*, verb,
A. S. *fyrðran*, formed from *furðor* by
vowel-change of *u* to *y*.

furthest, a mistaken form, made as the
superl. of *forth*, and due to a mistaken etymology of *further*. The true superl. of *fore*
is *first*.

Furtive. (F. — L.) O. F. *furtif*, fem.
furtive. — L. *furtiuus*, stolen, secret. — L.
furtum, theft.—L. *furari*, to steal.—L. *fur*,
a thief.✚Gk. φώρ, a thief, allied to φέρειν,
to bear, carry (away). (√ BHAR.)

Fury. (F. — L.) F. *furie*. — L. *furia*,
rage.—L. *furere*, to rage. (√ BHUR.)

infuriate. (Ital.—L.) Ital. *infuriato*,
pp. of *infuriare*, to fly into a rage.—Ital.
in furia, 'in a fury, ragingly;' Florio.—
L. *in*, in; *furia*, rage (above).

Furze. (E.) M. E. *firse*. A. S. *fyrs*. ✚
Gael. *preas*, a briar.

Fuscous, brown. (L.) L. *fuscus*, brown.

obfuscate, to darken. (L.) From pp.
of L. *ob-fuscare*, to obscure. — L. *ob*; and
fuscus, brown.

Fuse (1), to melt by heat. (L.) A late
word. Due to *fus-ible* (in Chaucer), *fus-ion*,
in Sir T. Browne. — L. *fusus*, pp. of *fundere*,
to pour, melt. Allied to Gk. χέειν, Goth.
giutan, to pour. (√ GHU.) Der. *fus-ible*
(from O. F. *fusible*); *fus-ion*.

confound. (F.—L.) F. *confondre*.—L.
con-fundere, to pour together, confound.

confuse. (L.) M. E. *confus*, used as a
pp. in Chaucer. — L. *confusus*, pp. of *con-
fundere* (above).

confute. (F. — L.) F. *confuter*. — L.
confutare, to cool by mixing cold water
with hot, to allay, also to confute. — L.
con- (cum), together; *fut-is*, a water-vessel
to pour from, from the base *fu-*, to pour.
See **refute** below.

diffuse. (L.) L. *diffusus*, pp. of *dif-
fundere*, to shed abroad; (L. *dif-*=*dis-*,
apart).

effuse. (L.) L. *effusus*, pp. of *ef-fun-
dere*, to pour out. (L. *ef-*=*ex.*)

foison, plenty. (F.—L.) O. F. *foison*,
abundance. — L. *fusionem*, acc. of *fusio*, a
pouring out, hence profusion. — L. *fusus*,
pp. of *fundere*, to pour.

fusil (3), easily molten. (L.) L. *fusi-
lis*, easily molten.—L. *fusus*, pp. of *fundere*.

futile, vain. (F. — L.) F. *futile*. — L.
fūtilis, that which easily pours forth, also
vain, empty, futile; put for *fud-tilis*.—L
fud-i, pt. t. of *fundere*, to pour.

infuse. (F. — L.) F. *infuser*.—L. *in
fusus*, pp. of *in-fundere*, to pour in.

profuse, lavish. (L.) L. *profusus*, pp
of *pro-fundere*, to pour forth.

refund, to repay. (L.) L. *re-fundere*, to pour back, also to restore, give back.

refuse, to deny a request. (F. – L.) M. E. *refusen.* – O. F. *refuser* (the same as Port. *refusar*, Ital. *refusare*, to reject). It answers to a Low L. type *refusare**, formed as a frequentative of *refundere*, to pour back, also to restore, give back (whence to reject). β. We may also note E. *refuse*, sb., O. F. *refus*, refuse, of which the orig. sense was probably dross to be re-fused. In any case, the etymology is from *re-*, back, and *fundere*, to pour.

refute, to oppose, disprove. (F. – L.) F. *refuter*. – L. *refutare*, to repel, rebut. The orig. sense was prob. 'to pour back;' see confute above.

suffusion. (F.–L.) F. *suffusion.* – L. *suffusionem*, acc. of *suffusio*, a pouring over. – L. *suffusus*, pp. of *suf-fundere*, to pour over. (L. *suf* = *sub*, under, also over.)

transfuse. (L.) L. *transfusus*, pp. of *trans-fundere*, to pour out of one vessel into another.

Fuse (2), **Fusee** (1); see Focus.

Fusee (2), a spindle in a watch. (F.–L.) O. F. *fusée*, orig. a spindleful of thread. – Low L. *fusata*, the same; fem. of pp. of *fusare*, to use a spindle. – L. *fusus*, a spindle.

fusil (1), a spindle, in heraldry. (L.) Dimin. of L. *fusus*, a spindle.

Fusil (1), a light musket; see Focus.

Fusil (2), a spindle; see Fusee (2).

Fusil (3), easily molten; see Fuse (1).

Fuss, haste, flurry. (E.) The sb. corresponding to M. E. *fus*, adj., eager; A. S. *fús*, eager, prompt. + Icel. *fúss*, eager for, willing; O. II. G. *funs*, ready, willing.

Fust (1), to become mouldy; see below.

Fust (2), the shaft of a column. (F. – L.) In Kersey (1715). – O. F. *fust*, a trunk. – L. *fustem*, acc. of *fustis*, a cudgel, thick stick.

fust (1), to become mouldy. (F. – L.) In Hamlet, iv. 4. 39. Coined from *fusted* or *fusty*, answering to O. F. *fusté*, 'fusty, tasting of the cask,' Cot. – O. F. *fuste*, a cask, orig. a stock, trunk, log. – L. *fustem* (as above).

fustigate, to cudgel. (L.) From pp. of L. *fustigare*, to cudgel. – L. *fust-*, stem of *fustis*, a cudgel; *-igare*, for *agere*, to drive, wield.

Fustian, a kind of coarse cloth. (F. – Ital. – Low L. – Egypt.) M. E. *fustane*; also *fustian.* – O. F. *fustaine.* – Ital. *fustagno*; Low L. *fustaneum.* – Arab. *fustát*, another name of Cairo, in Egypt, whence the stuff first came. ¶ Introduced through Genoese commerce.

Fustigate; see Fust (2).

Fusty; see fust (1), under Fust (2).

Futile; see Fuse (1).

Futtocks, certain timbers in a ship. (E.) '*Futtocks*, the compassing timbers in a ship, that make the breadth of it;' Kersey (1715). Called *foot-stocks* in Florio, s. v. *stamine*. The first syllable is for *foot*; *futtocks* is thought to be for *foot-hooks*, but perhaps *futt-ocks* = *foot-ocks* (cf. *bull-ock*). Bailey gives the form *foot-hooks*.

Future, about to be. (F. – L.) O. F. *futur*, fem. *future*. – L. *futurus*, about to be; fut. part. from *fui*, I was; allied to Be. (√BHU.)

Fuzzball, a spongy fungus. (E.) Cf. prov. E. *fuzzy, fozy*, light and spongy; Du. *voos*, spongy.

G.

Gabardine, Gaberdine. (Span. – C.) Span. *gabardina*, a coarse frock. Extended from Span. *gaban*, a great coat with a hood, allied to Span. *cabaza*, the same, and Span. *cabaña*, a cabin. Of Celtic origin; see Cabin.

Gabble, to prattle. (Scand.) Frequent. of M. E. *gabben*, to lie, delude. – Icel. *gabba*, to mock; *gabb*, mockery. Cf. Irish *cab, gob*, the mouth. Allied to Gobble, Gape.

Gabion; see Cave.

Gable, a peak of a house-top. (F. –

M. H. G. – C.) M. E. *gable*. – O. F. *gable*; Low L. *gabulum*. – M. H. G. *gabele*, G. *gabel*, a fork; *gebel* (G. *giebel*), a gable. + Icel. *gafl*, Dan. *gavl*, Swed. *gafvel*, a gable, *gaffel*, a fork, Goth. *gibla*, a gable, Du. *gevel*. But it seems to be of Celtic origin; cf. Irish *gabhal*, a fork, gable, Gael. *gobhal*, W. *gafl*, a fork; see Gaff.

Gaby; see Gape.

Gad (1), a wedge of steel; see Goad.

Gad (2), to roam; see Goad.

Gaff, a light fishing-spear, a sort of boom. (F. – C.) A ship's *gaff* is named from the *forked* end against the mast; the fishing spear is hooked.—O. F. *gaffe*, a gaff, iron hook. Of Celtic origin.—Irish *gaf, gafa*, a hook, W. *caff*, a grasp, grapple, fork, *gafael*, a hold. From Irish *gabh*, to take, cognate with L. *capere*, to take. And see **Gable**. (√KAP.) **Der.** *gavelock* (obsolete), a spear, W. *gaflach*.

javelin. (F.—C.) O. F. *javelin*, 'a javeling,' Cot.; allied to *javelot*, 'a gleave, dart,' id. Most likely orig. a pointed weapon with a forked end, such as could be made of a branch of a tree.—Bret. *gavl*, a place where a tree forks, Irish *gaf, gafa*, a hook, *gabhla*, a spear, *gabhlan*, a fork of a tree; Gael. *gobhlan*, a prong; W. *gafl*, a fork, *gaflach*, a dart. (Irish *bh* as *v*.)

Gaffer; see **Grand**.

Gag. (C. ?) M. E. *gaggen*, to suffocate. —W. *cegio*, to choke; *ceg*, the mouth.

Gage (1), a pledge. (F.—L.) M. E. *gage*.—F. *gage*, verbal sb. from *gager*, to pledge.—Low L. *uadiare*, to pledge.—Low L. *uadium*, a pledge.—L. *uadi-*, crude form of *uas*, a pledge. **+** A. S. *wed*, a pledge. See **Wed**; and see **Wage**.

engage. (F.—L.) O. F. *engager*, to bind by a pledge.—F. *en* (L. *in*), in; *gage*, as above. **Der.** *dis-engage*.

Gage (2), to gauge; see **Gauge**.

Gain (1), profit. (Scand.) M. E. *gain*. —Icel. *gagn*, gain, advantage; Swed. *gagn*, profit, Dan. *gavn*.

gain (2), to win. (Scand.) Really from the sb. above. 'Yea, though he *gaine* and cram his purse with crowns;' and again, 'To get a *gaine* by any trade or kinde;' Gascoigne, Fruits of War, st. 69 and st. 66. But doubtless influenced by F. *gagner*, which it strikingly resembles both in form and sense. This F. *gagner*, O. F. *gaagnier* (Ital. *guadagnare*), is from O. H. G. *weidanjan* = *weidenôn*, to pasture, which was the orig. sense of the F. word; from O. H. G. *weida* (G. *weide*), pasture-ground. **Der.** *re-gain*.

Gainly; see **Ungainly**.

Gainsay, to speak against. (E.) The prefix is A. S. *gegn*, against, whence E. **Again, Against**.

Gait. (Scand.) A peculiar use of M. E. *gate*, a way; see **Gate**.

Gaiter, a covering for the ankle. (F.— Teut.) F. *guêtre*, formerly *guestre*. The spelling with *gu* shews the word to be Teutonic (*gu* = G. *w*). Allied to M. H. G. *wester*, a child's chrisom-cloth, lit. a covering; Goth. *wasti*, clothing; see **Vest**.

Gala; see **Gallant**.

Galaxy, the milky way. (F.—L.—Gk.) M. E. *galaxie*.—O. F. *galaxie*.—L. *galaxiam*, acc. of *galaxias*.—Gk. γαλαξίας, milky way.—Gk. γαλακς- for γαλακτ-, stem of γάλα, milk. See **Lacteal**.

Gale. (Scand.) From Dan. *gal*, furious; Norweg. *ein galen storm*, a furious storm, *eit galet veer*, stormy weather. Cf. Icel. *galinn*, furious, from *gala*, to enchant, storms being raised by witches.

Galeated, helmeted. (L.) L. *galeatus*, —L. *galea*, a helmet.

Galiot; see **Galley**.

Gall (1), bile. (E.) M. E. *galle*. A. S. *gealla*. **+** Du. *gal*, Icel. *gall*, Swed. *galla*, Dan. *galde* (for *galle*), G. *galle*, L. *fel*, Gk. χολή. Allied to **Yellow** and **Green**.

Gall (2), to rub a sore place. (F.—L.) O. F. *galler*.—O. F. *galle*, a galling, itching.—L. *callus*, hard thick skin; Late L. *callus*, itch. See **Callous**.

Gall (3), a gall-nut. (F.—L.) O. F. *galle*.—L. *galla*, a gall-nut, oak-apple.

Gallant, gay, splendid, brave. (F.— M. H. G.) O. F. *gallant*, better *galant*, with one *l*. Orig. pres. part. of O. F. *galer*, to rejoice.—O. F. *gale*, shows, mirth, festivity. (Cf. Ital. Span. Port. *gala*, festive attire.) Perhaps from M. H. G. *wallen*, O. H. G. *wallôn*, to go on pilgrimage.

gala. (F.—Ital.—M. H. G.) F. *gala*, borrowed from Ital. *gala*, festive attire; whence *di gala*, merrily; cf. *galante*, gay, lively. See above.

gallery. (F.—Ital.—M. H. G.) O. F. *gallerie, galerie*, a gallery to walk in, also diversion, mirth.—Ital. *galleria*; Low L. *galeria*, a long portico, gallery.—Low L. *galare*, to rejoice, amuse oneself; the same as F. *galer* (above).

galloon. (F. *or* Span.—O. H. G.) F. *galon*, 'galloon-lace;' Cot. Also Span. *galon*, galloon, orig. finery for festive occasions.—F. and Span. *gala*, festivity (above).

Galleon; see **Galley**.

Gallery; see **Gallant**.

Galley, a low-built ship. (F.) M. E. *galeie*.—O. F. *galie*; Low L. *galea*, a galley. Orig. unknown.

galleon, a large galley. (Span.) Span. *galeon*, a galleon.—Low L. *galea*, a galley.

gallias, a sort of galley. (F.—Ital.) O. F. *galeace*.—Ital. *galeazza*, a heavy galley.—Ital. and Low L. *galea* (above).

galliot, small galley. (F.) O. F. *galiote*; Low L. *galeota*, small galley.

Galliard, a lively dance. (Span.—C. ?)
Span. *gallarda* (with *ll* as *ly*), a kind of
lively Spanish dance. —Span. *gallardo,* gay,
lively. The O. F. *gaillard* meant valiant
or bold ; perhaps of Celtic origin ; cf. Bret.
galloud, power, *galloudek,* strong, W. *gallad,*
able, *gall,* energy.

Gallias ; see **Galley.**

Galligaskins, large hose or trousers.
(F. — Ital. — L.) Corruption of F. *gar-
guesques, greguesques,* 'slops, gregs, gallo-
gascoins, Venitians ;' Cot. — Ital. *Grechesco,*
Greekish. — Ital. *Greco,* a Greek. — L.
Græcus, Greek. The name was given to a
particular kind of hose worn at Venice.

Gallinaceous. (L.) L. *gallinaceus,*
belonging to poultry. — L. *gallina,* a hen.
— L. *gallus,* a cock.

Galliot ; see **Galloy.**

Gallipot, a small glazed earthen pot.
(Du.) Corruption of O. Du. *gleypot,* a
gallipot or glazed pot. — O. Du. *gleye,*
shining potter's clay ; cf. N. Friesic *glöy,*
shining, allied to G. *glatt,* smooth, polished,
and to E. *glad.* And see **Pot.**

Gallon. (F.) M. E. *galon, galun.* —
O. F. *gallon, jalon,* a gallon ; orig. 'a large
bowl ;' augmentative form of the word
which appears as mod. F. *jale,* a bowl.
Orig. unknown. Cf. **Gill.**

Galloon ; see **Gallant.**

Gallop. (F. — O. Flemish.) M. E. *galop-
en* ; also spelt *walopen.* — O. F. *galoper.* —
O. Flem. *walop,* a gallop. The word is
due to a resemblance between the sound
made by a galloping horse and that made
by the boiling of a pot. — O. Fries. ·and
O. Sax. *walla* or *wallan,* to boil ; perhaps
with the addition of Flem. and Du. *op*
(= E. *up*). Allied to E. *well,* verb, to
spring up as water. Cf. E. *wal-k,* and Skt.
valg, to gallop, from the same root.
(√WAR.)

Gallow, to terrify. (E.) King Lear, iii.
2. 44. A. S. *gælwian,* to terrify ; in comp.
ágælwian.

Galloway, a nag, pony. (Scotland.)
Named from *Galloway,* Scotland.

Gallowglass, a heavy-armed foot-soldier. (Irish.) Ir. *galloglach,* a servant, a
galloglass. Lit. 'foreign soldier.' — Ir. *gall,*
foreign ; *oglach,* youth, soldier.

Gallows. (E.) M. E. *galwes,* pl. A. S.
galga, gealga, cross, gibbet ; whence mod.
E. *gallow,* the *s* being a sign of the pl. form.
+ Icel. *gálgi,* Dan. Swed. *galge,* Du. *galg,*
Goth. *galga,* a cross, G. *galgen.*

Galoche, a kind of shoe. (F. — Low L.
— Gk.) F. *galoche.* — Low L. *calopedia*
(see Brachet), a clog, wooden shoe. — Gk.
καλοπόδιον, dimin. of καλόπους, καλάπους, a
shoemaker's last. — Gk. κᾶλο-ν, wood ; πούς,
a foot.

Galore, in plenty. (C.) Irish and Gael.
go leor, gu leor, sufficiently ; from *leor,*
sufficient. The particle *go* or *gu* converts
.an adj. into an adv.

Galvanism. (Ital.) Named from *Gal-
vani* of Bologna, Italy ; about A.D. 1791.

Gambado ; see **Gambol.**

Gamble ; see **Game.**

Gamboge. (Asiatic.) A corruption of
Cambodia, in the Anamese territory, whence
it was brought about A.D. 1600.

Gambol, a frisk, caper. (F. — Ital. — L.)
Formerly *gambold, gambauld, gambaud.* —
O. F. *gambade,* 'a gamboll ;' Cot. — Ital.
gambata, a kick. — Ital. *gamba,* the leg ;
the same as F. *jambe,* O. F. *gambe,* Late L.
gamba, a joint of the leg. The true form
of the base is *cump-* (Diez), corresponding
to Greek καμπή, a bending, with reference
to the bend of the leg. Cf. Gael. and W.
cam, crooked.

  gammon (1), the preserved thigh of a
hog. (F. — L.) O. F. *gambon* (F. *jambon*),
a gammon ; from O. F. *gambe,* leg.

  jamb, side-post of a door. (F. — L.) F.
jambe, a leg, also a jamb (see Cotgrave).
See **Gambol.**

Game. (E.) M. E. *game,* also *gamen.*
A. S. *gamen,* sport. + Icel. *gaman,* Dan.
gammen, O. Swed. *gamman,* O. H. G. *gaman,* joy, mirth.

  gamble. (E.) A late word, put for
gamm-le or *gam-le,* a frequent. form which
has taken the place of M. E. *gamenen,* to
play at games. — A. S. *gamenian,* to play
at games ; from *gamen,* a game.

  gammon (2), nonsense ; orig. a jest.
(E.) M. E. *gamen,* a game (above). And
see **Backgammon.**

Gammer ; see **Grand.**

Gammon (1), preserved thigh of a hog ;
see **Gambol.**

Gammon (2), nonsense ; see **Game.**

Gamut. (F. — Gk. ; *and* L.) Comp. of
O. F. *game, gamme,* and *ut.* Here *gamme*
represents the Gk. γάμμα (γ), because the
musical scale was represented by *a, b, c, d,
e, f, g,* the last being *g*=γ. *Ut* is the old
name for *do,* the 1st note in singing, because it began an old hymn to St. John,
' *Ut* queant laxis,' &c., used in learning

singing. *Gamut* is the scale, from γ (*g*) to *ut* (*a*).

Gander; see **Goose**.

Gang (1), a crew; see **Go**.

Ganglion, a tumour on a tendon. (L. — Gk.) L. *ganglion*. — Gk. γάγγλιον.

Gangrene, a mortification of the flesh. (F. — L. — Gk.) O. F. *gangrene*. — L. *gangræna*. — Gk. γάγγραινα, an eating sore. — Gk. γραίνειν, γράειν, to gnaw. (√ GAR.)

Gannet; see **Goose**.

Gantlet (1); see **Gauntlet**.

Gantlet (2), **Gantlope**, a military punishment. (Swed.) Formerly *gantlope*; corrupted by confusion with *gauntlet*. Again, *gantlope* is a corruption of Swed. *gatlopp*, lit. 'a running down a lane;' to run the gantlope is to run between two files of soldiers, who strike the offender as he passes. — Swed. *gata*, a lane, street (see **Gate**); and *lopp*, a running, from *löpa*, to run, cognate with E. *leap*.

Gaol, Jail; see **Cave**.

Gape. (E.) A. S. *geápan*, to open wide; from *geáp*, wide. + Du. *gapen*, Icel. and Swed. *gapa*, Dan. *gabe*, G. *gaffen*. Cf. Skt. *jabh, jambh*, to gape.

gaby, a simpleton. (Scand.) Icel. *gapi*, a heedless man; cf. *gapamuðr* (lit. gapemouthed), the same. — Icel. *gapa* (above).

gap. (Scand.) M. E. *gappe*. — Icel. and Swed. *gap*, a gap, abyss. — Icel. and Swed. *gapa* (above). And see **Gabble**.

Gar (1), **Garfish**, a fish. (E.) A fish with slender body and pointed head. From A. S. *gár* (or Icel. *geirr*), a spear; cf. **Garlic**. So also *pike*.

Gar (2), to cause. (Scand.) Icel. and Swed. *göra*, Dan. *gjöre*, to make, cause; lit. to make ready. — Icel. *görr*, ready; see **Yare**.

Garb (1), dress. (F. — O. H. G.) In Shak. — O. F. *garbe*, a garb, good fashion. — O. H. G. *garawen*, M. H. G. *gerwen*, to get ready. — O. H. G. *garo*, ready; cognate with E. *yare*; see **Yare**.

Garb (2), a sheaf. (F. — O. H. G.) An heraldic term. — F. *garbe*. — O. H. G. *garba*, a sheaf.

Garbage; see **Garble**.

Garble, to select for a purpose; hence, to corrupt an account. (F. — Span. — Arab.) Orig. to pick out, sort, sift out. — O. F. *garbeler** (not found), the same as *grabeller*, to garble spices, or sort them out, orig. to sift. The same as Span. *garbillar*, Ital. *garbellare*, to garble or sift wares. — Span. *garbillo*, a coarse sieve. — Pers. *ghar-*

bíl, Arab. *ghirbál*, a sieve; Arab. *gharbalat*, sifting, searching.

garbage, refuse. (F. — Span. — Arab.) Prob. for *garble-age*; see above. Cf. F. *grabeau*, refuse of drugs (Littré).

Garboil, a commotion. (F. — L.) O. F. *garbouil*, 'a garboil, hurliburly;' Cot. Cf. Span. *garbullo*, a crowd; Ital. *garbuglio*, a garboil, disorder. From L. *garr-ire*, to prattle, chatter; and *bullire*, to boil, bubble, boil with rage. Thus the sense is 'a noisy boiling,' i. e. a hubbub. Florio has Ital. *garabullare*, to rave. See **Jar** (1).

Garden. (F. — O. H. G.) M. E. *gardin*. — O. F. *gardin* (F. *jardin*). — O. H. G. *gartin*, gen. and dat. of *garto*, a yard, cognate with E. **Yard**, q. v. (The gen. appears also in O. H. G. *gartin-are*, a gardener.)

Gargle, Gargoyle; see **Gorge**.

Garish; see **Gaze**.

Garland. (F. — Teut. ?) M. E. *gerlond*. — O. F. *garlande*. Cf. Span. *guirnalda*, Ital. *ghirlanda* (whence mod. F. *guirlande*), a garland. Prob. formed, with suffix -*ande*, from M. H. G. *wierelen**, a supposed frequentative of *wieren*, to adorn, from O. H. G. *wiara*, M. H. G. *wiere*, refined gold, fine ornament.

Garlic; see **Gore** (3).

Garment; see **Garnish**.

Garner, Garnet; see **Grain**.

Garnish. (F. — O. Low G.) Also *warnish*. — O. F. *garnis-, warnis-*, stem of pres. pt. of *garnir, warnir*, to warn, avert, fortify, garnish; all from the notion of 'wariness' or protection (hence decoration). From an O. Low G. source; O. Fries. *wernia*, to give a pledge, A. S. *wearnian*; see **Warn**.

garment. (F. — O. Low G.) M. E. *garnement*. — O. F. *garnement, garniment*, a robe (defence). — O. F. *garnir* (above).

garniture. (F. — O. Low G.) F. *garniture*, garnishment. — Low L. *garnitura*. — Low L. *garnitus*, orig. pp. of *garnire*, to adorn, which is merely a Latinised form of F. *garnir* (above).

garrison. (F. — O. Low G.) Confused with M. E. *garisoun, warisoun*, a reward; but the true form is M. E. *garnison, warnison*, provision, stores, supply. — O. F. *garnison*, store, supply. — O. F. *garnis-ant*, pres. pt. of *garnir*, to supply, garnish (above). And see **Warisoun**.

Garret. (F. — G.) M. E. *garite*. — O. F. *garite*, place of refuge, watch-tower. — O. F. *garir, warir*, to preserve. — O. H. G. *warjan*, to defend. Allied to **Wary**.

Garrotte; see Garter.

Garrulous. (L.) L. *garrulus*, talkative. — L. *garrire*, to chatter. (√ GAR.)

Garter. (F. — C.) O. F. *gartier* (North of France, Hécart), spelt *jartier* in Cotgrave (F. *jarretière*). — O. F. *garret* (F. *jarret*), the ham of the leg; a dimin. form. — Bret. *gar*, W. *gar*, shank of the leg; Irish *cara*, leg.

garrote, garrotte. (Span. — C.) Span. *garrote*, a cudgel, tying a rope tight, strangling by means of an iron collar. Formed, with dimin. suffix *-ote*, from Span. *garra*, a claw, talon, clutch, grasp. — Bret., W., and Corn. *gar*, the shank of the leg.

Gas. (Du.) The Belgian chemist Van Helmont (died A.D. 1644) invented two terms, *gas* and *blas*, the latter did not come into use. He seems to have been thinking of Du. *gheest*, spirit, volatile fluid (E. *ghost*), and of Du. *blazen*, to blow.

Gasconade, boasting. (Gascony.) F. *gasconnade*, boasting; said to be a vice of Gascons; at any rate named from them.

Gash, to hack, cut deeply. (F. — Low L.) Formerly *garsh, garse*. — O. F. *garser*, to scarify, pierce with a lancet. — Low L. *garsa*, scarification, by making incisions in the skin; called in Gk. ἐγχάραξις. Perhaps corrupted from χάραξις, an incision.

Gasp. (Scand.) Icel. *geispa*, Swed. *gäspa*, Dan. *gispe*, to yawn. Certainly from an old form *gapsa**, extension of *gapa*, to gape; see Gape. (Cf. M. E. *clapsen*, to clasp, E. *aspen* from A. S. *æps*.)

Gastric, belonging to the belly. (L. — Gk.) L. *gastricus*; from a crude form *gastro-*. — Gk. γαστρό-, crude form of γαστήρ, the belly.

Gate (1), a door, hole, opening. (E.) M. E. *gate, yate*. A. S. *geat*, a gate, opening. + Du. *gat*, a hole, opening, gap; Icel. *gat*, an opening. The orig. sense was access, or 'a way to *get* in;' from A. S. *gæt*, pt. t. of *gitan*, to get; see Get.

gate (2), a street. (Scand.) Common in the North; it also means 'a way.' — Icel. *gata*, Swed. *gata*, a way, path, street, lane; Dan. *gade*; cf. Goth. *gatwo*, G. *gasse*. — Icel. *gat*, pt. t. of *geta*, to get; see above. β. Compare G. *gasse*, a street, derived from O. H. G. *kezzan*, to get. Frequently fancied to be allied to the verb *to go* (which is impossible), from its use in the phrases *to gang one's gate* = to go one's way, &c.; we might as well derive *way* from *go*, for the like reason! γ. *Gate* (1)

answers to Teut. type GATA, but *gate* (2) to Teut. type GATWA (Fick, iii. 98); they are closely allied.

gait, manner of walking. (Scand.) A particular use of M. E. *gate*, a way; see gate (2) above. See also Gantlet (2).

Gather. (E.) M. E. *gaderen*. A. S. *gædrian, gaderian*, to collect, get together. — A. S. *gader*, together; also *gador, geador*. — A. S. *gæd*, a company, society (whence also A. S. *gædeling*, a comrade). Allied to Good. + Du. *gaderen*, to collect, from *gader*, together; cf. *gade*, a spouse, G. *gutte*, a husband.

together. (E.) M. E. *togedere*. — A. S. *tó-gædre, tó-gædere*. — A. S. *tó*, to; *gador, gader*, together (above).

Gaud, a show, ornament. (L.) M. E. *gaude*. — L. *gaudium*, gladness, joy; hence, an ornament. — L. *gaudere*, to rejoice (base *gau-*, as in *gauisus sum*, used as pt. t.) + Gk. γαίειν, to rejoice; γαῦρος, proud. Der. *gaud-y*, adj. See below.

enjoy, to joy in. (F. — L.) M. E. *enioien*. — F. *en* (L. *in*); F. *ioie, joie*; see joy (below).

jewel, a valuable ornament. (F. — L.) M. E. *iowel, iuel*. — O. F. *joel, jouel* (later *joyau*), dimin. of F. *ioie*, used in the sense of trinket; see joy (below). ¶ Early misunderstood, and wrongly Latinised as *iocale*, as if it were a derivative of *iocus*, which is not the case.

joy. (F. — L.) M. E. *ioye*. — O. F. *ioye, joye*; oldest form *goye* (F. *joie*); cf. Ital. *gioja*, joy, also a gaud, jewel, Span. *joya*, a gaud. — L. *gaudia*, neut. pl., afterwards turned into a fem. sing. — L. *gaudere*, to rejoice (above).

rejoice. (F. — L.) M. E. *reioisen*. — O. F. *resjois-*, stem of pres. pt. of *resjoir* (mod. F. *réjouir*), to gladden, rejoice. — L. *re-*, again; F. *esjoïr*, to rejoice, from *ex*, much, very, and *gaudere*, to rejoice.

Gauge, Gage, to measure the content of a vessel. (F. — Low L.) Spelt *gage* in Shak. — O. F. *gauger*, later *jauger*, 'to gage,' Cot. — O. F. *gauge** (not found), old form of *jauge*, 'a gage, instrument wherewith a cask is measured;' Cot. Low L. *gaugia* (A.D. 1446). Doubtless allied to F. *jale*, a large bowl; see Gallon.

Gaunt, thin, lean. (Scand.) An East-Anglian word, and therefore presumably Scand. Also spelt *gant* (1691). Cf. Norweg. *gand*, a thin stick, a tall and thin man, an overgrown stripling (Aasen);

Swed. dial. *gank*, a lean, half-starved horse (Rietz).

Gauntlet. (F. – Scand.) O. F. *gantelet*, a double dimin. of *gant*, a glove. – O. Swed. *wante*, a glove; Dan. *vante*, a mitten, Icel. *vöttr* (stem *vant*-), a glove. +Du. *want*, a mitten. Prob. from Wind, verb.

Gauntlet; see **Gantlet** (2).

Gauze, a thin silken fabric. (F. – Palestine.) O. F. *gaze*. Cf. Low L. *gazzatum*, gauze; *gazetum*, wine from Gaza. Named from *Gaza*, in Palestine, whence it was first brought.

Gavelkind, a sort of tenure. (E.) M. E. *gauelkynde*; answering to an A. S. form *gafol-cynd**. – A. S. *gafol*, tribute (a word of uncertain origin); and *cynd*, kind, sort, condition. ¶ Prob. *not* of Celtic origin, as is sometimes said.

Gavotte, a dance. (F.) O. F. *gavote*, orig. a dance of the *Gavotes*, or people of *Gap*, a place in the department of the Upper Alps (France).

Gawk, a simpleton, orig. a cuckoo. (E.) M. E. *gowke*. A. S. *geác*, a cuckoo. + Icel. *gaukr*, Dan. *giög*, Swed. *gök*, a cuckoo; G. *gauch*, a cuckoo, simpleton.

Gay. (F. – M. H. G.) O. F. *gai*. – M. H. G. *gæhe* (G. *jähe*), quick; hence, lively. Orig. 'full of go.' – M. H. G. *gán* (G. *gehen*), to go. See **Go.**

jay, a gay bird. (F. – M. H. G.) O. F. *jay*, also *gai*, a jay (F. *geai*). Cf. Span. *gayo*, a jay, *gaya*, a gay stripe on cloth. Named from its *gay* plumage; see above.

Gaze. (Scand.) M. E. *gasen*. – Swed. dial. *gasa*, to gaze, stare at. Cf. Goth. *us-geisnan*, to be amazed. Allied to **Aghast**, q. v.

garish, staring, showy. (Scand.) From the verb *gare*, to stare, variant of *gaze*; see above. Cf. M. E. *gauren*, to stare, Chaucer, C. T. 5332, 14375.

Gazelle, an animal. (F. – Arab.) Formerly *gazel*. – O. F. *gazel*, *gazelle*. – Arab. *ghazál*, a wild goat, gazelle.

Gazette. (F. – Ital.) O. F. *gazette*, an abstract of news, issued at Venice. – Ital. *gazzetta*, a gazette; the orig. sense is either (1) a magpie, from Ital. *gazzetta*, a magpie, dimin. of *gazza*, a magpie, whence it may have meant 'tittle-tattle;' or (2) a *very* small coin (perhaps paid for the privilege of reading the news), from Ital. *gazzetta*, a coin less than a farthing, probably from Gk. γάζα, a treasury. The reader may choose.

Gear, dress, harness, tackle. (E.) M. E.

gere. A. S. *gearwe*, fem. pl., preparation, dress, ornament. – A. S. *gearo*, ready; see Yare. And see **Gar** (2), **Garb** (1).

Ged, a fish; see **Goad.**

Gelatine; see **Gelid.**

Geld, to emasculate. (Scand.) M. E. *gelden*. – Icel. *gelda*, Dan. *gilde*, Swed. *gälla* (for *gälda*). Perhaps related to Goth. *giltha*, a sickle. Der. *geld-ing*, from Icel. *gelding*, the same.

Gelid, cool. (L.) L. *gelidus*. – L. *gelu*, frost. Allied to Cool.

congeal. (F. – L.) F. *congeler*. – L. *con-gelare*, to cause to freeze together.

gelatine. (F. – L.) F. *gélatine*, a kind of jelly. – L. *gelatus*, pp. of *gelare*, to freeze. – L. *gelu*, frost.

jelly. (F. – L.) Formerly *gelly*. – F. *gelée*, 'gelly;' Cot. Orig. fem. of pp. of *geler*, to freeze. – L. *gelare* (above).

Gem. (F. – L.) M. E. *gemme*. – F. *gemme*. – L. *gemma*, a bud; also a gem, jewel.

Gemini. (L.) L. *gemini*, twins; pl. *geminus*, double.

gimbals, a contrivance for suspending a ship's compass, to keep it horizontal. (F. – L.) Formerly *gimmals*; also called *gemmow* or *gemmow-ring*, a double ring, with two or more links. The forms *gem-mow* and *gimmal* correspond to O. F. *gemeau*, masc., and *gemelle*, fem., a twin. – L. *gemellus*, a twin, a dimin. form of L. *geminus*, double.

Gender (1), sex; see **Genus.**

Gender (2), to engender; see **Genus.**

Genealogy; see **Genesis.**

General, Generate; see **Genus.**

Generic, Generous; see **Genus.**

Genesis, creation. (L. – Gk.) L. *genesis*. – Gk. γένεσις, origin, source. Allied to γένος, race; see **Genus.** (√ GAN.)

endogen, a plant that grows from within. (Gk.) From Gk. ἔνδο-ν, within; γεν-, base of γίγνομαι, I am born, allied to γένος, race.

exogen, a plant that increases outwardly. (Gk.) From Gk. ἔξ-ω, outside, from ἐξ, out; and γεν- (as above).

genealogy. (F. – L. – Gk.) M. E. *genealogie*. – O. F. *genealogie*. – L. *genealogia*. – Gk. γενεαλογία, an account of a family, pedigree (1 Tim. i. 4.) – Gk. γενεά, birth (allied to γένος); and -λογία, an account, allied to λόγος (see Logic).

Genet, an animal. (F. – Span. – Arab.) F. *genette*, 'a kind of weesell;' Cot. – Span. *gineta*. – Arab. *jarneit* (Dozy).

Genial; see **Genus.**

Geniculate, jointed. (L.) In botany. From L. *geniculum*, a little knee, joint in a plant; double dimin. of *genu*, a knee. Allied to Knee.

genuflection, genuflexion, a bending of the knee. (F.—L.) F. *genuflexion*. — Late L. acc. *genuflexionem*. — L. *genu*, knee; *flex-us*, pp. of *flectere*, to bend.

Genital, Genitive, Genius; see Genus.

Gennot; see Jennet.

Genteel; see Genus.

Gentian, a plant. (F.—L.) O.F. *gentiane*.—L. *gentiana*; named after *Gentius*, an Illyrian king, abt. B.C. 180.

Gentile, Gentle; see Genus.

Gentry, Genuine, see Genus.

Genuflection; see Geniculate.

Genus, kin. (L.) L. *genus* (stem *gener-*), kin, race.+Gk. γένος, race.+A.S. *cyn*, kin. See **Kin**. (√GAN.)

congenial, kindred. (L.) Coined from L. *con-* (*cum*), with; and *genial*, adj. from *genius*; for which see below.

congenital. (L.) Coined by adding *-al* to the obs. word *congenite* (XVII cent.)—L. *congenitus*, born with.—L. *con-* (*cum*), with; *genitus*, born, pp. of *gignere*, to produce.

degenerate. (L.) From pp. of L. *degenerare*, to become base. — L. *degener*, adj., base.—L. *de*, down; *gener-*, stem of *genus*, race (above).

engender, to breed. (F.—L.) M.E. *engendren*.—O.F. *engendrer*.—L. *ingenerare*, to produce.—L. *in*, in; *generare*, to breed, from *gener-*, crude form of *genus* (above).

engine. (F.—L.) O.F. *engin*, a tool. —L. *ingenium*, natural capacity, also, an invention.—L. *in*, in; *genius*; see genius (below).

gender (1), kind. (F. — L.) M.E. *gendre* (with excrescent *d*).—O.F. *genre*, kind. —L. *genere*, abl. case of *genus*, kind, kin. ¶ The unusual deriv. from the abl. case is due to the common phrases *genere natus*, *hoc genere*, *omni genere*; so also Ital. *genere*, kind.

gender (2), to produce. (F. — L.) M.E. *gendren*; a clipped form of *engendren*; see engender above.

general, relating to a genus, common. (F.—L.) O.F. *general*. — L. *generalis*, belonging to a *genus* (stem *gener-*). Hence *general*, sb., a leader; *general-issimo*, from Ital. *generalissimo*, a supreme commander, with superl. suffix *-issimo*.

generate. (L.) From pp. of L. *generare*, to produce. —L. *gener-*, stem of *genus*.

generic, pertaining to a genus. (L.) Coined from L. *generi-*, crude form of *genus*.

generous. (F.—L.) O.F. *generous*, later *genereux*.—L. *generosus*, (properly) of noble birth.—L. *gener-*, crude form of *genus*.

genial. (F. — L.) O.F. *genial*. — L. *genialis*, pleasant; adj. from *genius*; see genius (below).

genital. (F. — L.) O.F. *genital*. — L. *genitalis*, generative. —L. *genitum*, supine of *gignere*, to beget.

genitive. (F.—L.) O.F. *genitif.*—L. *genitiuus*, belonging to birth, applied in grammar to a certain case of nouns.—L. *genitum* (above).

genius, inborn faculty. (L.) L. *genius*, the tutelar spirit of any one; also wit, lit. 'inborn nature.' Allied to *genus*.

genteel. (F. — L.) M.E. *gentil*. — L. *gentilis*, belonging to the same clan, a gentile (afterwards applied to mean wellbred, &c.).—L. *genti-*, crude form of *gens*, a clan, tribe. Allied to *genus*.

gentile. (F. — L.) O.F. *gentil*. — L. *gentilis* (above).

gentle. (F.—L.) O.F. *gentil* (above).

gentry. (F.—L.) M.E. *gentrie*, high birth; corruption of M.E. *gentrise*, the same. — O.F. *genterise*, another form of *gentilise*, rank (=Low L. *gentilitia**).— L. *gentilis*; see genteel above.

genuine. (L.) L. *genuinus*, of the true *genus* or stock.—L. *genus*.

gin (2), a trap, snare. (F.—L.) M.E. *gin*, short for M.E. *engin*, a contrivance; see engine above. Prob. confused with Icel. *ginna*, to dupe.

indigenous, native. (L.) L. *indigenus*, native.—L. *indi-* =O. Lat. *indo*, within; and *gen-ui*, pt. t. of *gignere*.

ingenious. (F. — L.) F. *ingenieux* (Cot.) — L. *ingeniosus*, clever.—L. *ingenium*, natural capacity; see engine above.

ingenuous. (L.) L. *ingenuus*, inborn, free-born, frank.—L. *in*, in; *gen-ui*, pt. t. of *gignere*, to beget.

progenitor. (F.—L.) Formerly *progenitour*. — F. *progeniteur*. — L. *progenitorem*, acc. of *progenitor*, an ancestor.— L. *pro*, before; *genitor*, a parent, from the supine of *gignere*, to beget.

progeny. (F.—L.) O.F. *progenie*.— L. *progeniem*, acc. of *progenies*, lineage, offspring.—L. *pro-*, forth; *gen-us*, kin.

regenerate. (L.) From pp. of *regenerare*, to produce anew.

Geography. (F. – L. – Gk.) O. F. *geographie.* – L. *geographia.* – Gk. γεω-γραφία, lit. earth-description. – Gk. γεω- = γηιο-, for γήιος, relating to γῆ, earth; -γραφία, description, from γράφειν, to write. Cf. Skt. *go*, the earth.

apogee, point of the moon's orbit furthest from the earth. (Gk.) From Gk. ἀπό, away from; γῆ, earth.

geometry. (F. – L. – Gk.) O. F. *geometrie.* – L. *geometria.* – Gk. γεωμετρία, land-measurement. – Gk. γεω- (as above); -μετρία, measurement, from μετρέω, I measure, μέτρον, a measure; see **Metre**.

georgic. (L. – Gk.) L. *georgicus*, relating to husbandry. – Gk. γεωργικός, the same. – Gk. γεωργία, tillage. – Gk. γεω- (as above); ἔργειν, to work. See **Work.**

perigee, point of the moon's orbit nearest the earth. (Gk.) From Gk. περί, about, here 'near;' γῆ, earth.

Geranium, a plant. (L. – Gk.) L. *geranium*, Latinised from Gk. γεράνιον, a geranium or crane's bill (from the shape of the seed-pod). – Gk. γέρανος, a crane; allied to **Crane.**

Gerfalcon; see **Gyrfalcon.**

Germ, a seed. (F. – L.) F. *germe.* – L. *germen* (stem *germin-*), a sprout, germ. Der. *germin-ate* (from the stem).

german, germane, akin. (F. – L.) *Cousins-german* are cousins having the same grandfather. Formerly spelt *germain.* – O. F. *germain.* – L. *germanum*, acc. of *germanus*, fully akin. Allied to **Germ.**

Gerund, a part of a Lat. verb. (L.) L. *gerundium*, a gerund. – L. *gerundus*, that which is to be done or carried on; fut. part. pass. of *gerere*, to carry on, perform, bring. (√GAS.)

congeries, a mass of particles. (L.) L. *congeries*, a heap. – L. *con-gerere*, to bring together.

congestion, accumulation. (L.) From L. acc. *congestionem.* – L. *congestus*, pp. of *con-gerere* (above).

digest, to assimilate food. (L.) M. E. *digest*, used as a pp. = digested. – L. *digestus*, pp. of *di-gerere*, to carry apart, separate, dissolve, digest.

exaggerate. (L.) From pp. of L. *exaggerare*, to heap up, amplify. – L. *ex*, very; *agger*, a heap, from *ag-* = *ad*, to, *gerere*, to bring.

gestation, the carrying of the young in the womb. (F. – L.) O. F. *gestation.* – L. acc. *gestationem*, a carrying. – L. *gestatus*, pp. of *gestare*, to carry, frequent. form of *gerere*, to bring.

gesticulate, to make gestures. (L.) From pp. of *gesticulari*, to make mimic gestures. – L. *gesticulus*, a gesture, double dimin. of *gestus*, a gesture. – L. *gestus*, pp. of *gerere*.

gesture. (L.) Low L. *gestura*, a mode of action. – L. *gestus*, pp. of *gerere*.

jest, a joke. (F. – L.) Orig. a story, merry tale. M. E. *geste*, a story. – O. F. *geste*, an exploit, romance, tale of exploits. – L. *gesta*, put for *res gesta*, a thing done, an exploit. – L. *gesta*, pp. of *gerere*.

register. (F. – L.) F. *registre*, 'a record;' Cot. – Low L. *registrum*, more correctly *regestum*, a book in which things are recorded (L. *regeruntur*). – L. *regestum*, neut. of pp. of *re-gerere*, to bring back, record.

suggestion. (F. – L.) F. *suggestion.* – L. acc. *suggestionem.* – L. *suggestus*, pp. of *suggerere*, to bring under, supply, suggest. – L. *sug-* (for *sub*), under; *gerere*, to bring.

Get. (E.) M. E. *geten*, pt. t. *gat*, pp. *geten.* A. S. *gitan*, pt. t. *gæt*, pp. *giten*, to get, obtain. + Icel. *geta*, Goth. *gitan*; L. *-hendere* (base *hed*), in *prehendere*, to seize; Gk. χανδάνειν (base χαδ), to seize. (√GHAD.)

beget. (E.) A. S. *bigitan*; see **Be-.**

forget. (E.) A. S. *forgitan*; see **For-** (2).

Gewgaw, a plaything, specious trifle. (E.) Formerly *gugaw*, corruption of M. E. *giuegoue* (= *givegove*, a gewgaw), Ancren Riwle, p. 196. Cf. North E. *giffgaff*, mutual donation and reception. A reduplicated form of A. S. *gifu*, a gift, from *gifan*, to give. *Gewgaw* was orig. a small gift, a present, toy, trifle, &c. See **Give.**

Geysir; see **Gush.**

Ghastly, terrible. (E.) M. E. *gastly.* A. S. *gástlíc*, ghostly, allied to Goth. *us-gaisjan*, to terrify. See **Aghast.** Allied words are *gasted*, terrified, K. Lear, ii. 1. 57, *gastness*, Oth. v. 1. 106.

Gherkin, small cucumber. (Du. – Gk.) Short for *agherkin.* – Du. *agurkje*, a gherkin (of which an older form was doubtless *agurken* * (= *agurk-ken*), because O. Du. used the dimin. suffix *-ken* where mod. Du. uses *-je*. Without the final *n*, we have Du. *agurke* (Sewel). The word is thus based upon a form *agur**, due to a word appearing as Low L. *angurius*; from Gk. ἀγγούριον, a water-melon.

Ghost, a spirit. (E.) M. E. *gost, goost*. A. S. *gást*. **+** Du. *geest*, G. *geist*. Allied to Goth. *us-gaisjan*, to terrify, and to E. **Ghastly.** -

Ghoul, a kind of demon. (Pers.) Pers. *ghôl*, an imaginary sylvan demon.

Giant. (F. — L. — Gk.) M. E. *geant, geaunt.* — O. F. *geant.* — L. *gigantem*, acc. of *gigas.* — Gk. γίγας (stem γιγαντ-), a giant. (✔ GAN.) **Der.** *gigant-ic*, from L. *gigant-*, stem of *gigas* (above).

Giaour, an infidel. (Turk. — Arab.) *Giaour* is an Ital. spelling usual among the Franks of the Levant (Byron); Turk. *jawr*, better *káfir.* — Arab. *káfir*, an infidel.

Gibberish, idle talk. (E.) Formed from the old vb. *gibber*, to gabble, frequent. of *gibe*, q. v. Compare *jabber*, and *gabble*.

Gibbet. (F.) M. E. *gibbet, gibet.* — O. F. *gibbet* (F. *gibet*), a gibbet. Prob. allied to O. F. *gibet*, a large stick, perhaps a dimin. of O. F. *gibbe*, a sort of arm, an implement for stirring up earth. Root unknown; prob. allied to **Jib** (3).

Gibbon, a kind of ape. (Unknown.) Cf. F. *gibbon*, in Buffon.

Gibbous, humped, swelling. (F. — L.) F. *gibbeux.* — L. *gibbosus*, humped (whence the E. *gibbose*). — L. *gibba*, a hump, hunch; cf. *gibbus*, bent. Allied to Skt. *kubja*, hump-backed.

Gibe, Jibe, to mock. (Scand.) From Swed. dial. *gipa*, to gape, also to talk foolishly and rashly (Rietz); cf. Icel. *geipa*, to talk nonsense, Icel. *geip*, idle talk. Hence **Gibberish**, q. v.

Giblets, the internal eatable parts of a fowl, removed before cooking. (F.) M. E. *gibelet.* — O. F. *gibelet*, which, according to Littré, answers to mod. F. *gibelotte*, stewed rabbit. Of unknown origin, not necessarily related to F. *gibier*, game. Cf. Gael. *giaban*, a fowl's gizzard.

Giddy. (E.) M. E. *gidi*, adj. Formed from A. S. *giddian*, to sing, be merry; so that the orig. sense of *giddy* was mirthful. — A. S. *gid, gidd, gied*, a song, poem, saying.

Gier-eagle, a kind of eagle. (Du. *and* F.) The first syllable is from Du. *gier*, a vulture; cf. G. *geier*, M. H. G. *gír*, a vulture. See **Gyrfalcon.**

Gift; see **Give.**

Gig, a light carriage, light boat. (Scand.)

In Shak., a *gig* is a boy's top. M. E. *gigge*, apparently a whirling thing, Ch. Ho. Fame, iii. 852 (whence E. *whirligig*). Prob. of Scand. origin; cf. Icel. *geiga*, to take a wrong direction, to rove at random, *gjögra*, to reel, stagger; allied to **Jig.**

jig, a lively tune or dance. (F. — M. H. G.) O. F. *gige, gigue*, a fiddle, dance. — M. H. G. *gíge* (G. *geige*), a fiddle. Prob. from the rapid motion of the player, and allied to **Gig.**

Gigantic; see **Giant.**

Giggle, to titter. (E.) A weakened form of M. E. *gagelen*, to cackle, or 'gaggle;' where again *gaggle* is a weakened form of **Cackle.** Cf. Icel. *gagl*, a goose, G. *kichern*, to giggle.

Giglet, Giglot, a wanton woman. (Scand.) Dimin. of *gigle*, a flirt, used by Cotgrave (s. v. *gadrouillette*). — Icel. *gikkr*, a pert person, Dan. *giek*, a wag. Perhaps allied to **Gig.**

Gild; see **Gold.**

Gill (1), organ of respiration in fishes. (Scand.) M. E. *gille.* — Dan. *giælle*, Swed. *gäl*, a gill; Icel. *gjölnar*, pl., gills. Cf. Icel. *gin*, mouth. Allied to **Yawn.** (✔GHI.)

Gill (2), a ravine, chasm. (Scand.) Also *ghyll.* — Icel. *gill, geil*, ravine. (✔GHI.) Allied to **Gill** (1).

Gill (3), with *g* soft, a quarter of a pint. (F.) M. E. *gille.* — O. F. *gelle*, a sort of wine-measure, Low L. *gella*; Low L. *gillo*, a wine-vessel. Allied to F. *jale*, a large bowl; see **Gallon.**

Gill (4), with *g* soft, a woman's name, a pitcher, ground-ivy. (L.) Short for *Gillian*, i. e. L. *Juliana*, a fem. name due to L. *Julius*; see **July. Der.** *flirt-gill* or *gill-flirt.*

jilt, a flirt. (L.) Formerly *jillet*, dimin. of *jill*, a flirt, orig. *Jill* or *Gillian*, a personal name (as above).

Gillyflower, a flower. (F. — L. — Gk.) Formerly *gilofer, geraflour*. Corrupted from O. F. *giroflée*, 'a gilloflower;' Cot. From F. *clou de girofle*, the same. — Low L. *caryophyllum*, Latinised from Gk. καρυόφυλλον, a clove tree, lit. 'nut-leaf.' — Gk. κάρυο-ν, a nut; φύλλον, leaf.

Gimbals; see **Gemini.**

Gimlet, Gimblet; see **Wimble.**

Gimmal-ring; see **Gemini.**

Gimp; see **Wimple.**

Gin (1), to begin. (E.) Obsolete; often needlessly written *'gin*, as though *be-* were omitted. M. E. *ginnen.* A. S. *ginnan,* to begin, commonly *on-ginnan* (pt. t. *ongann,* pp. *ongunnen*). + Goth. *ginnan,* in the comp. *du-ginnan,* to begin. (√GHAN.)

begin. (E.) M. E. *beginnen.* A. S. *beginnan*; from *ginnan,* with prefix *be-* = E. *by*; see By. + Du. G. *beginnen.*

Gin (2), a trap, snare; see **Genus.**

Gin (3), a kind of spirit; see **Juvenile.**

Ginger, the root of a certain plant. (F. — L. — Gk. — Skt.) M. E. *ginger, gingeuere* (= *gingevere*). — O. F. *gengibre* (F. *gingembre*). — L. *zingiber.* — Gk. ζιγγίβερις. — Skt. *çriñgavera,* ginger; lit. 'horn-shaped,' from the horns on it. — Skt. *çriñga,* a horn; *vera,* a body.

Gingerly; see **Go.**

Gingham, a kind of cotton cloth. (F.) Modern. — F. *guingan*; corruption of *Guingamp*; the name of a place in Brittany where such fabrics were made.

Gingle; the same as **Jingle.**

Gipsy; the same as **Gypsy.**

Giraffe, a long-legged animal. (F. — Span. — Arab. — Egypt.) F. *giraffe.* — Span. *giraffa.* — Arab. *zaráf, zaráfat.* From Egypt. *soraphé,* i. e. long neck (Mahn).

Gird (1), to enclose, bind round. (E.) M. E. *gurden, girden.* A. S. *gyrdan,* to gird. + Du. *gorden,* Icel. *gyrða,* to gird (cf. *gerða,* to fence in), Dan. *giorde,* G. *gürten.* Cf. Goth. *bi-gairdan,* to begird. Allied to **Garth, Garden,** and **Yard.** (√GHAR.)

girdle. (E.) A. S. *gyrdel,* that which girds. — A. S. *gyrdan,* to gird. + Du. *gordel,* Icel. *gyrðill,* Swed. *gördel,* G. *gürtel.*

girth. (Scand.) M. E. *gerth.* — Icel. *gjörð,* a girdle, girth; *gerð,* girth round the waist; Dan. *giord.* + Goth. *gairda,* a girdle.

Gird (2), to jest at; see **Yard.**

Girdle, Girth; see **Gird** (1).

Girl. (O. Low G.) M. E. *girl, gerl, gurl,* often used to mean 'a boy'; a child. Formed, as a dimin., from O. Low G. *gör,* a child. Cf. Swiss *gurre, gurrli,* a depreciatory term for a girl (Sanders, Ger. Dict.).

Gist; see **Jet** (1).

Gittern; see **Cithern.**

Give. (E.) M. E. *geuen, yeuen* (Southern), *giff* (Northern); pt. *yaf* or *gaf,* pp. *yiuen, gifen, youen.* A. S. *gifan,* pt. t. *geaf,* pp. *gifen.* + Du. *geven,* Icel. *gefa,* Dan. *give,* Swed. *gifva,* Goth. *giban,* G. *geben.*

gift. (E.) M. E. *gift, yift.* — A. S. *gift,* a gift (rare); common in the pl. *gifta,* nuptials. — A. S. *gifan,* to give. + Icel. *gift,* Du. *gift,* G. *-gift* (in *mit-gift,* a dowry). Der. *gift-ed.*

Gizzard. (F. — L.) M. E. *giser* (the *d* being added). — O. F. *gezier, jugier, juisier* (F. *gésier*). — L. *gigerium,* only in pl. *gigeria,* cooked entrails of poultry.

Glabrous, smooth. (L.) From L. *glaber,* smooth.

Glacial, icy. (F. — L.) F. *glacial.* — L. *glacialis,* icy. — L. *glacies,* ice. Allied to L. *gelu,* cold; see **Gelid.**

glacier, a mountain ice-field. (F. — L.) F. *glacier* (a Savoy word). — F. *glace,* ice. — L. *glaciem,* acc. of *glacies,* ice.

glacis, smooth slope. (F. — L.) F. *glacis.* — O. F. *glacer,* to cover with ice. — F. *glace* (above).

Glad. (E.) A. S. *glæd,* shining, bright, cheerful, glad. + Du. *glad,* smooth, bright, Icel. *glaðr,* bright, glad, Dan. Swed. *glad,* G. *glatt,* smooth, polished. Cf. Russ. *gladkie,* even, smooth. Orig. sense 'shining,' or 'bright.' (√GHAR.)

glade, an open space in a wood. (Scand.) The orig. sense was an opening for light, passage through a wood. — Icel. *glaðr,* bright, shining. Cf. Swed. dial. *glad-yppen,* completely open, said of a lake whence the ice has all melted away. Also Norweg. *glette,* a clear spot among clouds.

Gladiator, a swordsman. (L.) L. *gladiator.* — L. *gladius,* a sword.

claymore, a Scottish broadsword. (Gael.) Gael. *claidheamh mor,* a great sword. Here *claidheamh* is cognate with W. *cleddyf, cleddeu,* a sword, and with L. *gladius.* The Gael. *mor,* great, is allied to W. *mawr,* L. *magnus,* great.

glaive, a sword. (F. — L.) O. F. *glaive.* — L. *gladium,* acc. of *gladius,* a sword.

Glair, white of an egg; see **Clear.**

Glaive; see **Gladiator.**

Glance, a swift dart of light, quick look. (Scand.) — Swed. *glans,* lustre, whence *glänsa,* to shine; Dan. *glands,* lustre, gloss, whence *glandse,* to glaze. + Du. *glans,* G. *glanz,* splendour. β. The Swed. *glans,* put for *glants*, is from the pt. t. *glant* of the strong verb *glinta,* to shine, still found in Swed. dialects (Rietz). See **Glint.**

Gland, a fleshy organ in the body, secreting fluid. (F. — L.) O. F. *gland,* lit. an acorn (hence a kernel, gland). — L. *glandem,* acc. of *glans,* an acorn. + Gk. βάλανος, an acorn; from βάλλειν, to cast, let fall. (√GAL.) Der. *gland-ers,* a disease of glands.

Glare, to shine brightly. (E.) M. E. *glaren* ; cf. A. S. *glær,* a pellucid substance, amber. **+** Du. *gloren,* to glimmer, M. H. G. *glosen,* to glow. Allied to **Glass.** Cf. Dan. *glar,* glass.

Glass. (E.) A. S. *glæs.***+**Du. *glas,* Dan. *glas, glar,* Swed. *glas,* O. Swed. *glær,* Icel. *gler, glas,* G. *glas.* Orig. sense ' shining.' See **Gleam.** (✓ GHAR.)

 glaze, to furnish with glass. (E.) M.E. *glasen.* **-** M. E. *glas,* glass.

Glaucous, grayish blue. (L. **-** Gk.) L. *glaucus.* **-** Gk. γλαυκός, gleaming, blueish.

Glaze ; see **Glass.**

Gleam, a beam of light. (E.) A.S. *glǽm* ; cf. A. S. *glimo,* the same.**+**O. Sax. *glímo,* brightness. Allied to Gk. χλι-αρός, warm ; Skt. *ghri,* to shine. (✓ GHAR.)

 glimmer, verb. (Scand.) M. E. *glimeren.* **-** Dan. *glimre* ; cf. *glimmer,* sb., glitter ; Swed. dial. *glimmer,* verb, *glimmer,* sb., glitter. Frequent. of Dan. *glimme,* Swed. *glimma,* to shine. **-** Swed. dial. *glim,* a glance ; closely allied to **Gleam.**

 glimpse, a slight gleam. (Scand.) Formerly *glimse* ; M. E. *glimsen,* to glimpse ; formed with suffix *-s-* from Swed. dial. *glim,* a glance (above).

Glean. (F. **-** Teut.) M. E. *glenen.* **-** O. F. *glener, glaner* (F. *glaner*), to glean ; Low L. *glenare* (A. D. 561). **-** Low L. *glena, gelina, gelima,* a handful. Of Teut. origin ; best preserved in A.S. *gilm,* a handful, whence prov. E. *yelm,* to provide handfuls of straw ready for a thatcher. **¶** We also find the form *gleame* (Levins), also spelt *gleme* ; this is likewise due to A.S. *gilm,* but is a purely E. word.

Glebe, soil. (F. **-** L.) O. F. *glebe,* ' glebe, land belonging to a parsonage;' Cot. **-** L. *gleba,* soil, a clod of earth. Allied to **Globe.**

Glede (1), a kite (bird) ; see **Glide.**

Glede (2), a glowing coal ; see **Glow.**

Glee, joy, singing. (E.) A. S. *gleó, gleow, gliw,* joy, mirth, music. **+** Icel. *glý,* glee, gladness ; Swed. dial. *gly,* mockery.

Glen, a narrow valley. (C.) Gael. and Irish *gleann,* W. *glyn,* a valley, glen.

Glib (1), smooth, voluble. (Du.) Du. *glibberig,* slippery, *glibberen,* to slide. **-** Du. *glippen,* to slip away. Allied to **Glide.**

Glib (2), a lock of hair. (C.) Irish and Gael. *glib,* a lock of hair.

Glib (3), to castrate. (E.) The same as *lib,* with prefixed *g-* = A. S. *ge-,* a common

prefix. Cognate with Du. *lubben,* to castrate, O. Du. *luppen.* See **Lop.**

Glide. (E.) M. E. *gliden,* pt. t. *glood.* A. S. *glídan.* **+** Du. *glijden,* Dan. *glide,* Swed. *glida,* G. *gleiten.* Allied to **Glad.**

glede (1), a kite, a bird so called. (E.) M. E. *glede.* A.S. *glida,* a kite, lit. ' glider,' from its smooth flight. **-** A.S. *glid-,* base of pp. of *glídan,* to glide.

Glimmer, Glimpse ; see **Gleam.**

Glint ; see **Glitter.**

Glisten, Glister ; see **Glitter.**

Glitter. (E.) M. E. *gliteren,* to shine. Cf. Icel. *glitra,* to glitter, frequent. of *glita,* to shine ; Swed. *glittra,* to glitter ; *glitter,* sb., a sparkle. Cf. O. Sax. *glítan,* G. *gleissen,* to shine. (✓ GHAR.)

 glint, to shine, glance. (Scand.) Swed. dial. *glinta,* to shine ; nasalised from Icel. *glita,* to shine.

 glisten, glister, to glitter. (E.) Extended from base *glis-* of M. E. *glisien,* to shine. A. S. *glisian**, only in the comp. *glisnian,* to shine. We also find M. E. *glisteren, glistren,* to glitter. Cf. Du. *glin-steren,* to glitter.

Gloat ; see **Glow.**

Globe. (F. **-** L.) O. F. *globe.* **-** L. *globum,* acc. of *globus,* a ball ; cf. *glomus,* a ball, clue, *gleba,* a clod. Allied to **Clew.**

 conglobe, to form into a globe. (L.) L. *con-globare.* **-** L. *con-* (*cum*), with ; *globus,* a globe. And see below.

Glomerate. (L.) From pp. of *glomerare,* to collect into a ball. **-** L. *glomer-,* stem of *glomus,* a ball or clew of yarn. See **Globe.**

 conglomerate. (L.) From pp. of *con-glomerare,* to wind into a ball, heap together.

Gloom ; see **Glow.**

Glory. (F. **-** L.) M. E. *glorie.* **-** O. F. *glorie* (F. *gloire*). **-** L. *gloria.***+**Gk. κλέος, Skt. *çravas,* Russ. *slava,* glory. (✓ KRU.)

Gloss (1), lustre ; see **Glow.**

Gloss (2), a commentary, explanation. (F.**-**L.**-**Gk.) M. E. *glose.* **-** O. F. *glose,* ' a glosse,' Cot. **-** L. *glossa,* a difficult word requiring explanation. **-** Gk. γλῶσσα, the tongue, a tongue, language, word needing explanation. **Der.** *gloss,* verb.

glossary. (L. **-** Gk.) L. *glossarium,* a glossary ; formed with suffix *-arium* from L. *gloss-a* (above).

glossographer. (Gk.) Coined from *glosso-,* put for Gk. γλῶσσα, a hard word ; γράφειν, to write.

glottis. (Gk.) Gk. γλῶττις, the mouth

of the windpipe. — Gk. γλῶττα, Attic form of γλῶσσα, the tongue. **Der**. *epi-glottis*.

gloze, to interpret, flatter. (F. — L. — Gk.) M. E. *glosen*, to make glosses. — M. E. *glose*, a gloss; see **Gloss**.

Glove. (E.) A. S. *glóf*, a glove; cf. Icel. *glófi*, prob. borrowed from A. S. *glóf*. Perhaps from *g-* (put for *ge-*), prefix; and Icel. *lófi*, Goth. *lofa*, the palm of the hand. **Der** *fox-glove*.

Glow. (E.) M. E. *glowen*. A. S. *glówan*, to be ardent, to shine brightly. + Icel. *glóa*, Dan. *gloe*, to glow, stare, Swed. *glo*, to stare, Du. *gloeijen*, G. *glühen*. Cf. Skt. *gharma*, warmth. (√ GHAR.)

glede (2), a glowing coal. (E.) A. S. *glēd* (where *ē* is from *ó*, by vowel-change). — A. S. *glówan*, to glow.

gloat, to stare, gaze with admiration. (Scand.) Formerly *glote* (XVI cent.) — Icel. *glotta*, to grin, smile scornfully; Swed. dial. *glotta*, *glutta*, to peep, connected with Swed. dial. *gloa*, to glow, stare; cf. Swed. *glo*, to stare, Dan. *gloe*, to glow, to stare.

gloom. (E.) A. S. *glóm*, gloom, twilight. + Swed. dial. *glåmug*, staring, woful, wan, from the vb. *glo*, *gloa*, to glow, shine, stare.

gloss (1), lustre. (Scand.) Icel. *glossi*, a blaze, *glys*, finery; Swed. dial. *glåsa*, a glowing, *glossa*, to glow; extended from Swed. dial. *gloa*, Icel. *glóa*, to glow.

glum, gloomy. (Scand.) M. E. *glommen*, to look gloomy. — Swed. dial. *glomma*, to stare, from *gloa*, to stare; cf. Swed. *glåmug*, gloomy; and see **Gloom**.

Gloze; see **Gloss** (2).

Glue. (F. — L.) O. F. *glu*. — Low L. *glutem*, acc. of *glus* (gen. *glutis*), glue; allied to L. *gluten*, glue, *glutus*, tenacious.

agglutinate. (L.) From pp. of *agglutinare*, to glue together. — L. *ag-* (= *ad*), to; *glutin-*, stem of *gluten*, glue.

conglutinate. (L.) From pp. of L. *con-glutinare*, to glue together; see above.

glutinous, gluey. (L.) L. *glutinosus*, sticky. — L. *glutin-*, stem of *gluten*, glue.

Glum; see **Glow**.

Glume, a floral covering of grasses. (L.) L. *gluma*, a husk, hull. — L. *glubere*, to peel, take off the husk.

Glut, to swallow greedily. (L.) L. *glutire*, *gluttire*, to swallow; cf. *gula*, the throat. + Skt. *grī*, to devour, *gal*, to eat. (√ GAR.)

deglutition, swallowing. (L.) From

L. *de*, down; *glutitus*, pp. of *glutire*, to swallow.

glutton. (F. — L.) M. E. *gloton*. — O. F. *gloton*. — L. acc. *glutonem*, a glutton. — L. *glutire*, to devour.

Glutinous; see **Glue**.

Glutton; see **Glut**.

Glycerine, a viscid fluid, of sweet taste. (F. — Gk.) F. *glycérine*; from Gk. γλυκερός, sweet; from Gk. γλυκύς, sweet. (√ GAR.)

Glyptic, relating to carving in stone. (Gk.) Gk. γλυπτικός, carving. — Gk. γλυπτός, carved. — Gk. γλύφειν, to hollow out, engrave. Allied to **Grave** (1).

Gnarl, to snarl, growl. (E.) Frequentative of *gnar*, to snarl, an imitative word. + Du. *knorren*, Dan. *knurre*, to growl, Dan. *knarre*, to creak; Swed. *knorra*, G. *knurren*, to growl, G. *knarren*, to creak. Allied to **Gnash**.

Gnarled, knotty, twisted. (E.) *Gnarled* is full of gnarls, where *gnar-l* is a dimin. of *gnar* or *knar*, M. E. *knarre*, a knot of wood. See **Knurr**.

Gnash. (Scand.) M. E. *gnasten*, to gnash the teeth. — Swed. *knastra*, to crash (between the teeth); Dan. *knaske*, to gnash; Icel. *gnastan*., sb., a gnashing, *gnesta*, a crack. + G. *knastern*, to crackle. Cf. Gael. *cnac*, to crack, crash; allied to **Crack**.

Gnat. (E.) A. S. *gnæt*. Said to be named from the whirring of the wings; cf. Icel. *gnata*, to clash, *gnat*, clash of weapons.

Gnaw. (E.) M. E. *gnawen*, pt. t. *gnew*, *gnow*. A. S. *gnagan*, to gnaw; put for *ge-nagen**, the *ge-* being a prefix. + Du. *knagen*, O. Icel. *knaga*, mod. Icel. *naga*, Dan. *gnave*, Swed. *gnaga*. Without the *g*, we have G. *nagen*, Dan. *nage*, to gnaw, Swed. *nagga*, prov. E. *nag*, to worry. See **Nail**.

nag (2), to worry, tease. (Scand.) Swed. *nagga*, to nibble, peck; Dan. *nage*, Icel. *naga*, to gnaw; see above.

Gneiss, a rock. (G.) G. *gneiss*.

Gnome, a kind of sprite. (F. — Gk.) F. *gnome*, a gnome; a word due to Paracelsus. — Gk. γνώμη, intelligence, from the notion that gnomes could reveal secret treasures. — Gk. γνῶναι, to know. (√ GAN.)

diagnosis, scientific determination of a disease. (Gk.) Gk. διάγνωσις, a distinguishing. — Gk. διά, between; γνῶσις, enquiry, from γνῶναι, to know.

gnomon, index of a dial. (L. — Gk.) L. *gnomon*. — Gk. γνώμων, an interpreter (one who knows), the index of a dial. — Gk. γνῶναι (as above).

gnostic, one of a certain sect. (Gk.) Gk. γνωστικός, wise, good at knowing. — Gk. γνωστός, from γνωστός, known. — Gk. γνῶναι, to know.

prognostic, a presage. (F. — L. — Gk.) F. *prognostique*; Cot. — L. *prognosticon*. — Gk. προγνωστικόν, a token of the future. — Gk. πρό, before; γνωστικός, good at knowing (above).

Gnu, a kind of antelope. (Hottentot.) Found in S. Africa. Said to belong to the Hottentot language.

Go, to move about, proceed, advance. (E.) M. E. *gon, goon*. A. S. *gán*, a contracted form of *gangan*, to go. ╋ Du. *gaan*, Icel. *ganga*, Dan. *gaae*, Swed. *gå*, Goth. *gaggan* (put for *gangan*), G. *gehen*.

begone, beset. (E.) *Woe begone* = beset with grief. M. E. *begon*, pp. of *begon*, to beset. — A. S. *bigán, begán, bigangan*, to go about (surround, beset). — A. S. *bi-, be-*; *gán*, to go. The prefix *bi-* = E. *by*. ¶ In the phr. '*begone!*' we really use *two* words, i.e. *be gone*.

gang (1), a crew of persons. (Scand.) Icel. *gangr*, a going; also, a gang (as *þjófagangr*, a gang of thieves); from Icel. *ganga*, to go.

gang (2), to go. (Scand.) Icel. *ganga*, to go; see Go above.

gingerly, with soft steps. (Scand.) Properly with tottering or slow steps. — Swed. dial. *gingla, gängla*, to go gently, totter; frequent. form from Icel. *ganga*, to go. ¶ It appears to have been oddly confused with *ginger*!

Goad. (E.) M. E. *gode*. A. S. *gád*. Apparently put for *gasd**; cf. Icel. *gaddr*, a goad (apparently put for *gasdr**), Goth. *gazds*, a goad. ╋ L. *hasta*, a spear. See **Yard.**

gad (1), a wedge of steel, goad. (Scand.) M. E. *gad*, a goad. — Icel. *gaddr*, a goad, spike, sting; cognate with A. S. *gád* (above).

gad (2), to ramble idly. (Scand.) In Levins. Lit. to run like cattle stung by flies. — Icel. *gadda*, to goad. — Icel. *gaddr* (above).

ged, the fish called a pike. (Scand.) Icel. *gedda*, Swed. *gädde*, a ged; allied to *gaddr*, a goad. Named from the sharp thin head; it is therefore also called *pike*.

Goal, the winning-post in a race. (F. — O. Low G.) Formerly *gole*. ╸ F. *gaule*, a

pole, big rod; in O. F. spelt *waule*. — O. Fries. *walu*, North Fries. *waal*, a staff. ╋ Icel. *völr*, Goth. *walus*, a staff. Orig. a round stick, and named from its roundness; cf. Russ. *val'*, a cylinder. Allied to **Volute**, and to **Wale.**

Goat. (E.) M. E. *goot*. A. S. *gát*. ╋ Du. *geit*, Dan. *ged*, Swed. *get*, Icel. *geit*, G. *geiss, geisse*, Goth. *gaitsa*, L. *hædus*.

Gobbet, a mouthful, a small piece. (F. — C.) M. E. *gobet*, a small piece. — O. F. *gobet*, a morsel of food (see Littré). Dimin. of O. F. *gob*, a gulp (in swallowing). — O. F. *gober*, to devour. — Gael. *gob*, beak, bill, mouth; Irish *gob*, mouth, beak; W. *gwp*, head and neck of a bird.

gobble. (F. — C.) Frequentative, with suffix -*le*, from O. F. *gober*, to devour (above).

job (1), to peck, as a bird. (C.) M. E. *iobbyn*, to peck. From Gael. and Irish *gob*, the beak (above).

job (2), a small piece of work. (F. — C.) Also spelt *gob*, a portion, lump, job of work (Halliwell). — O. F. *gob*, lit. a mouthful, also a lump, portion. — Gael. and Irish *gob*, the mouth (above).

Gobelin, a French tapestry. (F.) Named from Giles *Gobelin*, wool-dyer of Paris, about A.D. 1520–30.

Goblet; see **Coop.**

Goblin; see **Cobalt.**

Goby, a fish. (L. — Gk.) For L. *gobius*, orig. applied to the gudgeon. — Gk. κωβιός, a kind of fish, gudgeon, tench.

gudgeon. (F. — L. — Gk.) M. E. *gojone*. — F. *goujon*. — L. *gobionem*, acc. of *gobio*, a by-form of *gobius* (above).

God. (E.) A. S. *god*. ╋ Du. *god*, Icel. *guð*, Dan. *gud*, Swed. *gud*, Goth. *guth*, G. *gott*. ¶ *Not* allied to *good*, adj.

goddess. (E.; *with* F. *suffix*.) M. E. *goddesse* (*godesse*). Made from *god* by adding the O. F. suffix -*esse* (= L. -*issa* = Gk. -ισσα).

godfather. (E.) M. E. *godfader*, father in baptism; from *god* and *fader*.

godhead. (E.) M. E. *godhed*, also *godhod*; the suffix answers to A. S. *hád*, office, state, dignity; see -**hood** (suffix).

goodbye, farewell. (E.) A familiar, but meaningless, contraction of *God be with you*, the old form of farewell (very common).

gospel, the life of Christ. (E.) M. E. *gospel*. A. S. *godspell*. — A. S. *god*, God, i.e. Christ; *spell*, a story. Lit. 'narrative of God,' i.e. life of Christ. ¶ Early misunderstood as meaning *good spell*, as if meant for a translation of Gk. εὐαγγέλιον ; but this seems a mistake; for the E. word was early introduced into Iceland in the form *guðspjall* (where *guð-* = god, as distinguished from *góð-* = good), and into Germany as O. H. G. *gotspell* (where *got* = god, as distinguished from *guot*, good). And see below; where *gos-* again = *god*.

gossip. (E.) Now a crony; formerly a sponsor in baptism. M. E. *gossib*, also *godsib*, lit. ' related in god.'—M. E. *god*, god ; *sib*, related, from O. Northumb. *sibbo*, pl. relatives, allied to Goth. *sibja*, relationship, G. *sippe*, affinity, *sippen*, kinsmen. Cf. Skt. *sabhya*, fit for an assembly, trusty, from *sabhá*, an assembly.

Godwit, a bird ; see **Good**.

Goggle-eyed, having rolling and staring eyes. (C.) M. E. *gogil-eyid*. ' They giggle with their eyes hither and thither ;' Holinshed, Descr. of Ireland, c. 1.—Irish *gogor*, light (in demeanour), lit. wavering, *gogach*, wavering, reeling, Gael. *gogach*, nodding, fickle ; from Irish and Gael. *gog*, to nod, move slightly. Clearly shewn in Irish and Gael. *gogshuileach*, goggle-eyed, having wandering eyes, from *gog*, to move slightly, and *suil*, a glance.

Goitre ; see **Guttural**.

Gold. (E.) A. S. *gold*. + Du. *goud* (for *gold*), Icel. *gull*, Swed. Dan. *guld*, G. *gold*, Goth. *gulth*, Russ. *zlato*, Gk. χρυσός, Zend *zaranu*, Skt. *hirana*. (√ GHAR.) Allied to **Yellow**. Der. *mari-gold*.

gild, to overlay with gold. (E.) M. E. *gilden*. A. S. *gyldan*, to gild (Ettmüller); cf. A. S. *gylden*, golden. Formed (by regular change from *o* to *y*) from *gold*, gold.

Golf, a game. (Du.) First mentioned A. D. 1538. The name is from that of a Du. game played with club and ball.—Du. *kolf*, a club used to strike balls with. + Icel. *kólfr*, clapper of a bell, *kylfa*, a club; Dan. *kolbe*, butt-end of a weapon, *kolv*, bolt, shaft, arrow, Swed. *kolf*, butt-end, G. *kolbe*, club, mace, knob.

Golosh ; the same as **Galoche**.

Gondola. (Ital.—Gk.) Ital. *gondola*, dimin. of *gonda*, a boat.—Gk. κόνδυ, a drinking vessel ; from the shape.

Gonfanon, Gonfalon, a kind of banner. (F.—M. H. G.) M. E. *gonfanon*.—O. F. *gonfanon*.—M. H. G. *gundfano*, lit. ' battle-flag.'—M. H. G. *gund, gunt*, battle; *fano* (G. *fahne*), a banner, flag. Here *gunt* is allied to A. S. *guð* (for *gunð**), battle,

war, and to Skt. *han*, to kill. *Fano* is allied to **Vane**.

Gong. (Malay.) Malay *agóng* or *góng*, the gong, a sonorous instrument.

Good. (E.) M. E. *good*. A. S. *gód*. + Du. *goed*, Icel. *góðr*, Dan. Swed. *god*, Goth. *gods*, G. *gut*. Allied to Russ. *godno*, suitably, *godnuii*, suitable. Der. *good-s*, s. pl., i. e. good things, property ; *good-will*, &c. Also *good-man*, i. e. master of the house, *good-wife*, mistress of the house.

godwit, a bird. (E.) Lit. ' good creature.' A. S. *gód wiht*, a good wight, good creature (*wiht* being often applied to animals and birds). See **Wight**.

Goodbye ; see **God**.

Goodman ; see **Good**.

Goose, a bird. (E.) A. S. *gós*, pl. *gés* (the long *o* is due to loss of *n*, and *gós* = *gans**). + Du. *gans*, Dan. *gaas*, Swed. *gås*, Icel. *gás*, G. *gans*, L. *anser*, Gk. χήν, Skt. *hamsa*, Russ. *gus'*. (√ GHA, GHAN ?)

gander. (E.) M. E. *gandre*. A. S. *gandra*, also spelt *ganra* (the *d* being, in fact, excrescent). + G. *gänserich* (= *gänser-ich*). From the base *gan-* or (in G.) *gans-*.

gannet, Solan goose, a sea-fowl. (E.) A. S. *ganot*. + Du. *gent*, a gander ; M.H.G. *ganze*, a gander. From a base *gan-*.

goshawk. (E.) Lit. ' goose-hawk.' A.S. *góshafuc*.—A.S. *gós*, goose ; *hafuc*, hawk.

gosling. (E.) Formed from A.S. *gós*, goose (M. E. *gos*), with double dimin. suffix *-l-ing*. And see **Gossamer**.

Gooseberry. (F.—M. H. G. ; *and* E.) In Levins. Put for *grooseberry* (as *gaffer* is for *graffer*). The *r* is retained in North. E. *grosers*, gooseberries ; Burns has *grozet*, a gooseberry. (The suffix *-berry* is English.) —O. F. *grose**, *groise**, a gooseberry, not recorded, but occurring not only in the O. F. dimin. form *groisele, grosele*, a gooseberry, but also in Irish *grois-aid*, Gael. *grois-eid*, W. *grwys*, a gooseberry, all borrowed from M. E. The spelling *groisele* is as old as the 13th century (Bartsch). β. The orig. O. F. *groise** or *grose** was borrowed from M. H. G. *krûs*, curling, crisped, whence G. *krausbeere*, a cranberry, a rough gooseberry. Cf. Swed. *krusbär*, a gooseberry, from *krus*, crisp, curled, frizzled. The name was first given to the rougher kinds of the fruit, from the curling hairs on it ; similarly, Levins gives the Lat. name as *uua crispa* (frizzled grape).

Gopher, a kind of wood. (Heb.) Heb. *gópher*, a wood; perhaps pine or fir.

Gorbellied, Gorcrow; see Gore (1).

Gordian. (Gk.) Only in the phr. '*Gordian* knot,' i. e. intricate knot. Named from the Phrygian king *Gordius*, who tied it. An oracle declared that whoever loosed it should reign over Asia. Alexander cut the knot, and applied the oracle to himself.

Gore (1), clotted blood. (E.) It formerly meant filth. A. S. *gor*, filth, dirt. + Icel. *gor*, gore; Swed. *gorr*, dirt.

gorbellied, having a fat belly. (E.) Compounded of E. *gore*, lit. filth, dirt (also the intestines); and *belly*. So also Swed. dial. *gårbälg*, a fat paunch, from *går*, dirt, contents of the intestines, and *bälg*, belly.

gorcrow, carrion-crow. (E.) I. e. *gore-crow*; see above.

Gore (2), a triangular piece let into a garment, a triangular slip of land. (E.) M. E. *gore*, A. S. *gára*, a spear, projecting piece of land; from *gár*, a spear. Named from the shape. So also Icel. *geiri*, a triangular slip of land, from *geirr*, a spear; G. *gehre*, a wedge, gusset, gore; Du. *geer*, a gusset, gore.

Gore (3), to pierce. (E.) From *gár*, a spear (with the usual change from *á* to long *o*).

garlic, a plant. (E.) A. S. *gárléac*, lit. 'spear-leek.'—A. S. *gár*, a spear (above), *léac*, a leek, plant.

Gorge, the throat, a narrow pass. (F.—L.) O. F. *gorge*, throat.—Low L. *gorgia*, the throat; also *gorga, gurga*, variants of L. *gurges*, a whirl-pool, hence (in late L.) the gullet, from its voracity. Cf. L. *gurgulio*, gullet. + Skt. *gargara*, a whirlpool. (√GAR.)

gargle. (F.—L.) Modified from O. F. *gargouiller*, 'to gargle;' Cot. — O. F. *gargouille*, the weasand of the throat, also a gargoyle, or mouth of a spout. Formed from *gorge*, the throat (above). So also Span. *gargola*, a gargoyle; Ital. *gargozza, gorgozzo*, gullet, from *gorga*, the throat.

gargoyle, a spout. (F.—L.) O. F. *gargouille* (above).

gorgeous, showy, splendid. (F.—L.) O. F. *gorgias*, 'gorgeous;' Cot. The O. F. *gorgias* also meant a gorget; the sense of 'gorgeous' was orig. proud, from the swelling of the throat in pride. Cotgrave gives F. *se rengorger*, 'to hold down the head, or thrust the chin into the neck, as some do in pride, or to make their faces look the

fuller; we say, to bridle it.' Hence the derivation is from F. *gorge*, throat.

gorget, armour for the throat. (F.—L.) From *gorge*, i. e. throat.

gurgle, to purl. (Ital.—L.) In Spenser, Thestylis, 3. Imitated from Ital. *gorgogliare*, to purl, bubble, boil; *gorgoglio*, gurgling of a stream.—Ital. *gorgo*, a whirl-pool.—L. *gurges*, whirlpool; cf. *gurgulio*, gullet.

Gorgon, a monster. (L.—Gk.) L. *Gorgon, Gorgo*.—Gk. Γοργώ, the Gorgon.— Gk. γοργός, fearful.

Gorilla, a kind of large ape. (O. African.) An old word revived. In the Periplus of Hanno, near the end, some creatures are described 'which the interpreters called *Gorillas*.'

Gormandise; see Gourmand.

Gorse. (E.) Formerly *gorst*. — A. S. *gorst*, gorse.

Goshawk, Gosling; see Goose.

Gospel; see God.

Gossamer. (E.) M. E. *gossomer, gosesomer*, lit. 'goose-summer.' The prov. E. name (in Craven) is *summer-goose*. Named from the downy appearance of the film. Also called *summer-colt* (Whitby); also *summer-gauze* (corruptly). Cf. G. *sommerfäden* (lit. summer-threads), gossamer; Du. *zomerdraden*, Swed. *sommertråd*, the same. But in G. it is also called *mädchensommer*, lit. Maiden - summer, *der alte Weiber sommer*, the old women's summer. It would appear that *summer* is here used in the sense of 'summer-film,' so that *gossamer* = goose-summer-film. (Better spelt *gossomer* or *gossummer*).

Gossip; see God.

Gouge, hollow-bladed chisel. (F.—Low L.) F. *gouge*. — Low L. *guvia* (Span. *gubia*).

Gourd. (F.—L.) F. *gourde*, formerly *gouhourde* and *cougourde* (Cot.)—L. *cucurbita*, a gourd.

Gourmand, a glutton. (F.) F. *gourmand*, 'a glutton, gormand, belly-god;' Cot. Etym. unknown; but perhaps of Scand. origin, and really for 'gore-man;' see Gore (1), Gorcrow, &c. Der. *gormandise* (for *gourmand-ise*).

Gout (1), a drop, disease. (F. — L.) M. E. *goute*, a disease supposed to be due to defluxion of humours. — O. F. *goute, goutte*, a drop.—L. *gutta*, a drop.

gutter. (F.—L.) M. E. *gotere*.—O. F. *gutiere, goutiere* (Littré, s. v. *gouttière*, a gutter). Esp. used for catching drops from the eaves of a roof. – L. *gutta*, a drop.

Gout (2), taste; see **Gust** (2).

Govern. (F. – L. – Gk.) M. E. *gouvernen*. – O. F. *governer*. – L. *gubernare*, to steer a ship, rule. – Gk. κυβερνᾶν, to steer.

Gowan, a daisy. (Gael.) Gael. and Irish *gugan*, a bud, flower, daisy.

Gown, a loose robe. (C.) M. E. *goune*. – W. *gwn*, a loose robe; Irish *gunn*, Gael. and Corn. *gun*; Manx *goon*.

Grab, to seize. (Scand.) Swed. *grabba*, to grasp. Allied to **Gripe.**

Grace. (F. – L.) O. F. *grace*. – L. *gratia*. – L. *gratus*, dear, pleasing. Allied to Gk. χαρά, joy, χάρις, favour, Skt. *hary*, to desire, and to E. **Yearn.** (√GHAR.) **Der.** *dis-grace*.

agree, to accord. (F. – L.) O. F. *agreer*, to receive favourably. – O. F. *a gre*, favourably. – O. F. *a* (L. *ad*), according to; *gre, gret*, pleasure, from L. *gratum*, neut. of *gratus* (above). **Der.** *dis-agree*.

congratulate. (L.) From pp. of L. *congratulari*, to wish much joy. – L. *con-* (*cum*), with; *gratulari*, to wish joy, from adj. *gratus*.

grateful, pleasant. (Hybrid; F. – L. and E.) The first syllable is from O. F. *grat*, pleasing, from L. *gratus*; with E. suffix *-ful*.

gratify. (F. – L.) O. F. *gratifier*. – L. *gratificare, gratificari*, to please. – L. *grati-*, for *gratus*, pleasing; and *-ficare*, for *facere*, to make. **Der.** *gratific-at-ion*.

gratis, freely. (L.) L. *gratis*, adv., freely; put for *gratiis*, abl. pl. of *gratia*, grace; see **Grace.**

gratitude. (F. – L.) F. *gratitude*. – Low L. *gratitudinem*, acc. of *gratitudo*, thankfulness. – L. *gratus*, pleasing.

gratuitous, freely given. (L.) L. *gratuitus*, freely given. From *gratus*.

gratuity, a present. (F. – L.) O. F. *gratuité*, 'a free gift;' Cot. – Low L. *gratuitatem*, acc. of *gratuitas*. – L. *gratuitus* (above).

gratulate, to congratulate. (L.) From pp. of L. *gratulari*, to wish a person joy. As if from an adj. *gratulus**, joyful; from L. *gratus*, pleasing.

ingratiate, to commend to the favour of. (L.) Coined from L. *in*, in; *gratia*, favour, grace.

ingrate, ungrateful. (F. – L.) F. *ingrat*. – L. *in-gratus*, not pleasing.

Grade, a degree. (F. – L.) F. *grade*, a

degree. – L. *gradum*, acc. of *gradus*, a degree, step. – L. *gradi* (pp. *gressus*), to step, walk, go. (√GARDH.)

aggress, to attack. (F. – L.) F. *aggresser*. – L. *aggressus*, pp. of *aggredi* (= *ad-gradi*), to assail.

congress, a meeting together. (L.) L. *congressus*. – L. *congressus*, pp. of *con-gredi*, to meet together.

degrade. (F. – L.) O. F. *degrader*, to deprive of rank or office. – L. *degradare*, the same. – L. *de*, from; *gradus*, rank.

degree. (F. – L.) O. F. *degre, degret*, a step, rank; orig. a step *down* (used of stairs). – L. *de*, down; *gradus*, a step.

digress, lit. to step aside. (L.) L. *digressus*, pp. of *digredi* (= *dis-gradi*), to go aside.

egress, a going out. (L.) L. *egressus*. – L. *egressus*, pp. of *e-gredi*, to go out.

gradient, a gradually rising slope. (L.) L. *gradient-*, stem of pres. pt. of *gradi*, to walk, advance.

gradual, advancing by steps. (L.) Orig. *gradual*, sb., a service-book called in Lat. *graduale*, and in E. *gradual* or *grayl*. – Low L. *gradualis*, only in neut. *graduale*, a service-book of portions sung *in gradibus*, i. e. on the steps (of the choir). – L. *gradu-s*, a step.

graduate. (L.) Low L. *graduatus*, one who has taken a degree. – L. *gradu-s*, degree.

grail (1), a gradual, a service-book. (F. – L.) M. E. *graile, grayle*. – O. F. *greël*. – Low L. *gradale*, also called *graduale*; see **gradual.**

grallatory. (L.) A term applied to wading birds. – L. *grallator*, a walker on stilts. – L. *grallæ* (short for *gradulæ*), stilts. – L. *gradus*, a step.

ingredient, that which enters into a compound. (F. – L.) F. *ingredient* (the same). – L. *ingredient-*, stem of pres. pt. of *in-gredi*, to enter upon, begin (hence to enter into). – L. *in*, in; *gradi*, to go.

ingress. (L.) L. *ingressus*, an entering. – L. *ingressus*, pp. of *in-gredi* (above).

progress, advancement. (F. – L.) O. F. *progrez* (F. *progrès*). – L. *progressum*, acc. of *progressus*, an advance. – L. *progressus*, pp. of *pro-gredi*, to go forward.

regress, return. (L.) L. *regressus*, sb. – L. *regressus*, pp. of *re-gredi*, to go back. – L. *re-*, back; *gradi*, to go.

retrograde, going backward. (L.) L. *retrogradus*, adj., used of a planet. – L.

retro-gradi, to go backward. Hence *retro-grade,* verb.

    retrogression. (L.) Coined from pp. of L. *retro-gradi* (above).

    transgression. (F. – L.) F. *transgression.* – L. acc. *transgressionem,* a passage across, in late Lat. a transgression. – L. *transgressus,* pp. of *trans-gredi,* to go across.

Gradient, Graduate; see **Grade.**

Graft, Graff; see **Graphic.**

Grail (1); see **Grade.**

Grail (2), the Holy Dish at the Last Supper. (F. – L. – Gk.) The etymology was very early falsified by an intentional change from *San Greal* (Holy Dish) to *Sang Real* (Royal Blood, perversely taken to mean Real Blood). – O. F. *graal, greal, grasal,* a flat dish; with numerous other forms, both in O. F. and Low L. It would appear that the word was corrupted in various ways from Low L. *cratella,* a small bowl, dimin. of *crater,* a bowl; see **Crater.**

Grail (3), fine sand. (F. – G.) In Spenser, F. Q. i. 7. 6; Vis. Bellay, st. 12. – O. F. *gresle,* lit. hail (F. *grêle*). – G. *gries,* sand-stone; allied to **Grit.**

Grain. (F. – L.) M. E. *grein.* – O. F. *grain.* – L. *granum,* a grain, corn. Cognate with E. **Corn.** (√GAR.)

    engrain, ingrain, to dye of a fast colour. (F. – L.) M. E. *engreynen,* to dye *in grain,* i. e. of a fast colour. Coined from F. *en* (L. *in*); and O. F. *graine,* 'the seed of herbs, also grain, wherewith cloth is died *in grain,* scarlet die, scarlet in graine;' Cot. From L. *granum.*

    garner. (F. – L.) M. E. *garner.* – O. F. *gernier,* variant of *grenier,* a granary. – L. *granaria,* a granary. – L. *granum,* corn.

    garnet. (F. – L.) M. E. *garnet,* also spelt *granat.* – O. F. *grenat,* 'a precious stone called a granat or garnet,' Cot.; Low L. *granatus.* So called from its resemblance to the seeds of the pomegranate, or *malum granatum,* lit. seeded apple. – L. *granum,* a grain, seed.

    granary, store-house for grain. (L.) L. *granaria;* see **garner** above.

    grange, a farm-house. (F. – L.) O. F. *grange,* a barn, a farm-house. – Low L. *granea,* a barn. – L. *granum,* corn.

    granite, a hard stone. (Ital. – L.) Ital. *granito,* granite, speckled stone. – Ital. *granito,* pp. of *granire,* to reduce to grains

(hence, to speckle). – Ital. *grano,* a grain. – L. *granum,* a grain.

    granule, a little grain. (L.) L. *granulum,* dimin. of *granum.*

    grenade, a war-missile. (F. – Span. – L.) Formerly also *granado,* which is the Span. form. Named from its likeness to a pomegranate, being filled with combustibles as that is with seeds. – O. F. *grenade,* 'a pomegranet, a ball of wild-fire;' Cot. – Span. *granada,* the same; *granado,* full of seeds. – L. *granatus,* full of seeds. – L. *granum.* Der. *grenad-ier.*

Grallatory; see **Grade.**

Gramercy; see **Grand.**

Gramineous. (L.) From L. *gramin-,* stem of *gramen,* grass. (√GAR.)

Grammar. (F. – L. – Gk.) M. E. *grammere* – O. F. *gramaire* (XIII cent.) – Low L. *grammaria*,* not found, but regularly formed from Low L. *gramma,* a letter of the alphabet. – Gk. γράμμα, a letter. – Gk. γράφειν, to write. See **Graphic.**

    anagram, a change in a word due to transposition of letters. (F. – L. – Gk.) F. *anagramme.* – L. *anagramma.* – Gk. ἀνάγραμμα. – Gk. ἀνά, up, here used distributively; γράμμα, a letter of the alphabet (above).

    diagram. (L. – Gk.) L. *diagramma,* a scale, gamut (hence, sketch, plan). – Gk. διάγραμμα, a figure, plan, gamut. – Gk. διαγράφειν, to mark out by lines, describe. – Gk. διά, through; γράφειν, to write.

    epigram, a short poem. (F. – L. – Gk.) F. *epigramme.* – L. *epigramma.* – Gk. ἐπίγραμμα, an inscription, epigram. – Gk. ἐπιγράφειν, to inscribe. – Gk. ἐπί, upon; γράφειν, to write.

    grammatical. (F. – L. – Gk.) F. *grammutical;* from L. *grammaticus,* grammatical. – Gk. γραμματικός, versed in one's letters. – Gk. γραμματ-, stem of γράμμα, a letter.

Grampus; see **Grand.**

Granary; see **Grain.**

Grand, great. (F. – L.) O. F. *grand.* – L. *grandem,* acc. of *grandis,* great. Prob. allied to **Grave.**

    aggrandise. (F. – L.) F. *aggrandis-,* stem of pres. pt. of *aggrandir,* to enlarge. Put for *agrandir* (with one *g*). – F. *a* (for L. *ad*); and *grandir* (L. *grandire*), to increase, from *grand,* great (above).

    gaffer, an old man, grandfather. (F. – L.; *and* E.) Put for *gramfer,* West E. form of *grand-father.*

    gammer, an old lady, grandmother.

(F. – L.; *and* E.)   Put for *grammer*, West. E. form of *grand-mother*.

gramercy, thanks. (F. – L.)   Formerly *graund mercy*, Chaucer, C. T. 8964. – F. *grand merci*, great thanks; see **Grand** and **Mercy**.

grampus, a large fish. (Ital. *or* Span. – L.)   Spelt *grampasse*, A.D. 1655.   A corruption, either of Ital. *gran pesce* or Span. *gran pez*, i.e. great fish. – L. *grandis piscis*, great fish.

grandee, a Spanish nobleman. (Span. – L.)   Span. *grande*, great; also, a nobleman. – L. *grandem*, acc. of *grandis*, great.

grandeur, greatness. (F. – L.)   F. *grandeur*; formed with suffix *-eur* (L. *-orem*), from *grand*, great.

grandiloquent, pompous in speech. (L.)   Coined from L. *grandi-*, crude form of *grandis*, great; and *loquent-*, stem of pres. pt. of *loqui*, to speak.   The true L. form is *grandiloquens*.

Grange, Granite; see **Grain**.

Grant; see **Creed**.

Granule; see **Grain**.

Grape. (F. – M. H. G.)   O. F. *grappe*, 'bunch, or cluster of grapes;' Cot.   [In E., the sense has changed, from cluster to single berry.]   The orig. sense of *grappe* was 'a hook,' then clustered fruit. – M. H. G. *krapfe*, O. H. G. *chrapho*, a hook. – M. H. G. *kripfen*, to seize, clutch; see **Cramp**.   The senses of 'hook' and 'cluster' result from that of 'clutching.'

grapnel, a grappling - iron. (F. – M. H. G.)   M. E. *grapenel*. Dimin. of O. F. *grappin*, a grapnel. – O. F. *grappe*, a hook (above).

grapple, to clutch. (F. – M. H. G.)   Properly to seize with a grapnel. – O. F. *grappil*, sb., 'the *grapple* of a ship;' Cot. – O. F. *grappe*, a hook (above).

Graphic, descriptive, pertaining to writing. (L. – Gk.)   L. *graphicus*, belonging to painting or drawing. – Gk. γραφικός, the same. – Gk. γράφειν, to write.   Allied to **Grave** (1).

graft, graff, to insert buds on a stem. (F. – L. – Gk.)   *Graft* is a corrupt form for *graff*, and due to confusion with *graffed*, pp.   Shak. has pp. *graft*, Rich. III, iii. 7. 127.   M. E. *graffen*, to graff, from *graffe*, sb. – O. F. *graffe*, a sort of pencil, also a slip for grafting, because it resembled a pointed pencil in shape. – L. *graphium*, a style to write with. – Gk. γραφίον, γραφείον, the same. – Gk. γράφειν, to write.

programme, program. (F. – L. – Gk.)   Now spelt as if from F. *programme*; formerly *programma* (1706), from L. *programma*. – Gk. πρόγραμμα, a public notice in writing. – Gk. πρό, beforehand; γράμμα, from γράφειν, to write.

Grapnel, Grapple; see **Grape**.

Grasp. (E.)   M. E. *graspen*, used in the sense 'to grope.'   Put for *grapsen* (like *clasp* = M. E. *clapsen*), an extension from a base *grap-*, closely allied to **Grope**, q. v.

Grass. (E.)   M. E. *gras*, *gres*, also *gers*. A.S. *gærs*, *græs*. + Du. Icel. Goth. G. *gras*; Swed. and Dan. *gräs*.

graze (2), to feed cattle.   M. E. *grasen*, vb. – M. E. *gras*, grass (above).   Der. *graz-i-er* (cf. *bow-y-er*, *law-y-er*).

Grate (1), a framework of iron bars; see **Crate**.

Grate (2), to rub, scrape. (F. – Scand.)   O. F. *grater* (F. *gratter*); Low L. *cratare*. – Swed. *kratta*, Dan. *kratte*, to scrape.

Grateful, Gratify; see **Grace**.

Gratis, Gratitude; see **Grace**.

Gratuitous, Gratulate; see **Grace**.

Grave (1), to cut, engrave. (E.)   M. E. *grauen*.   A.S. *grafan*, pt. t. *gróf*. + Du. *graven*, Dan. *grave*, Icel. *grafa*, Swed. *grafva*, Goth. *graban*, G. *graben*, Gk. γράφειν, L. *scribere*.   (√ SKARBH.)   Der. *grave*, sb., a thing cut or dug out.

engrave. (Hybrid; F. *and* E.)   From E. *grave*, with prefix *en-* (F. *en*, L. *in*); suggested by F. *engraver*, in which *graver* is of Teut. origin.

groove. (Du.)   Du. *groef*, *groeve*, a grave, a channel, a groove. – Du. *graven* (above).

grove, a collection of trees. (E.)   M. E. *groue* (with *u* = *v*). – A. S. *gráf*, a grove; properly a glade.   Allied to **Grave** (1).

Grave (2), sad. (F. – L.)   F. *grave*. – L. *grauem*, acc. of *grauis*, heavy. + Gk. βαρύς, Skt. *guru*, heavy.

aggravate. (L.)   From pp. of L. *aggrauare*, to add to a load. – L. *ag-* (= *ad*), to; *grauare*, to load, from *grauis*, heavy.

aggrieve. (F. – L.)   M. E. *agreuen*. – O. F. *agrever*, to overwhelm. – O. F. *a*, to; *grever*, to burden. – L. *ad*, to; *grauari*, to burden, *grauare*, to weigh down, from *grauis*, heavy.

grief. (F. – L.)   M. E. *grief*, *gref*. – O. F. *grief*, *gref*, burdensome, sad, heavy. – L. *grauis*.   Der. *grieve*, vb., O. F. *grever*, L. *grauare*, to burden; from *grauis*.

Gravel. (F. – C.)   M. E. *grauel*. – O. F. *gravele*, dimin. of O. F. *grave*, gravel.   Of

Celtic origin ; cf. Bret. *grouan*, gravel,
Corn. *grow*, gravel, W. *gro*, pebbles.

Gravy ; see **Greaves** (1).

Gray. (E.) M. E. *gray*, grey. A. S.
grǽg.+Du. *graauw*, Icel. *grár*, Dan. *graa*,
Swed. *grå*, G. *grau*, L. *rauus*, Gk. γραῖος,
aged, gray.

Graze (1), to scrape slightly. (F.?—L.?)
Formerly *grase*. Apparently a coined
word, founded on *rase*, i.e. to scrape ; the
initial *g* may have been suggested by the
verb to *grate*. See **Rase**. (Doubtful.)

Graze (2) ; see **Grass**.

Grease ; see **Crass**.

Great. (E.) M. E. *gret*, greet. A. S.
greát.+Du. *groot*, G. *gross*.

　groat, a coin worth 4*d.* (Du.) M. E.
grote.—O. Low G. *grote*, a coin of Bremen ;
meaning 'great,' because large in comparison with the copper coins (*Schwaren*)
formerly in use there ; cf. Du. *groot*, great,
cognate with E. *great*.

Greaves (1), **Graves**, sediment of melted
tallow. (Scand.) O. Swed. *grefwar*, dirt ;
ljus-grefwar, lit. 'light-dirt,' refuse of tallow in candle-making ; Swed. dial. *grevar*,
pl., greaves. + Low G. *greven*, greaves, G.
griebe.

　gravy. (Scand.) Formerly *greavy*, orig.
an adj. formed from *greave* (for *greaves*),
refuse of tallow. Hence *gravy* is (1)
tallowy, (2) fat, gravy.

Greaves (2), leg-armour. (F.) O. F.
greves, 'boots, also greaves ;' Cot. Cf.
Span. *grebas*, greaves, pl. of *greba*.—O. F.
greve, the shank, shin. Origin unknown.

Grebe, a bird. (F.—C.) F. *grèbe*.
Named from its crest.—Bret. *krib*, a comb,
kriben, a tuft of feathers on a bird's head.
So also Corn. and W. *crib*, comb, crest,
Corn. *criban*, W. *cribyn*, a crest, tuft.

Greedy. (E.) A. S. *grǽdig*, grédig. +
Du. *gretig*, Icel. *grǻðugr*, Dan. *graadig*,
Goth. *gredags* ; Skt. *gridhra*, greedy, from
gridh, to be greedy. (√GARDH.) Der.
greed, hunger ; answering to Icel. *grǻðr*,
Goth. *gredus*, hunger.

Green. (E.) M. E. *grene*. A. S. *gréne*.
+ Du. *groen*, Icel. *grænn*, Dan. Swed. *grön*,
G. *grün*, Gk. χλωρός, Skt. *hari*, green or
yellow. (√GHAR.) Allied to **Yellow** and
Grow. *Green* is the colour of *growing*
herbs. Der. *greens*, pl. sb.

Greet (1), to salute. (E.) M. E. *greten*.
A. S. *grétan*, to visit, address. + Du.
groeten, G. *grüssen*.

Greet (2), to cry, weep. (E.) M. E.

greten. A. S. *grǽtan*, grétan. + Icel.
gráta, Dan. *græde*, Swed. *gråta*, Goth.
gretan. Cf. Skt. *hrad*, to sound, roar.

Gregarious. (L.) L. *gregarius*, belonging to a flock.—L. *greg-em*, acc. of *grex*, a
flock.

　aggregate. (L.) From pp. of L. *ag-
gregare*, to collect into a flock.—L. *ag-* (for
ad), to ; *greg-*, stem of *grex*, a flock.

　congregate. (L.) From pp. of L.
con-gregare, to collect into a flock.

　egregious, excellent. (L.) L. *egregius*,
chosen out of a flock, excellent.—L. *e*,
out ; *greg-*, stem of *grex*, a flock.

　segregate, to separate from others.
(L.) From pp. of *se-gregare*, to set apart
from a flock.—L. *se-*, apart ; *greg-*, stem of
grex.

Grenade ; see **Grain**.

Grey ; the same as **Gray**.

Greyhound. (Scand.) M. E. *greihound*.
—Icel. *greyhundr*, a greyhound. — Icel.
grey, a dog ; *hundr*, a hound. The Icel.
grey is also used *alone* in the same sense of
greyhound ; cf. *greybaka*, a bitch. ¶ Not
allied to *gray*, which is spelt *grár* in
Icelandic.

Griddle, a pan for baking cakes.
(F. — L.) Also *girdle*. M. E. *gredil*.
— O. F. *gredil* (Moisy, Dict. of Norman patois) ; also *grëil* (Godefroy). —
Low L. *craticulum*, L. *craticula*, dimin.
of *cratis*, a hurdle. Der. Hence M. E.
gredire, a griddle, afterwards turned into
gridiron, by confusion with M. E. *ire* =
E. *iron*.

Gride, to cut through. (E.) See **Yard** (2).

Grief, **Grieve** ; see **Grave** (2).

Griffin, **Griffon**. (F. — L. — Gk.) Better *griffon*. M. E. *griffon*. — F. *griffon* ;
formed from Low L. *griffus*, a griffon. —
L. *gryphus*, extended form of *gryps*, a
griffon. — Gk. γρύψ (stem γρυπ-), a griffon,
a fabulous animal supposed to have a
hooked beak. — Gk. γρυπός, curved, hook-
beaked.

Grig, a small eel, a cricket. (Scand.)
Weakened form of *crick*, still preserved in
crick-et ; cf. Lowl. Sc. *crick*, a tick, louse.
—Swed. dial. *krik*, *kräk*, a creeping creature. — Swed. dial. *kräka*, to creep ; cf. G.
kriechen, to creep. ¶ In phr. 'as merry
as a *grig*,' grig is for *Greek* (Troil. i. 2.
118) ; *Merygreek* is a character in Udall's
Roister Doister ; from L. *græcari*, to live
like Greeks, i. e. luxuriously.

Grill ; see **Crate**.

Grim, fierce. (E.) A. S. *grim*; allied to *gram*, fierce, angry, furious. **+** Icel. *grimmr*, grim, *gramr*, angry; Dan. *grim*, grim, *gram*, angry; G. *grimm*, fury, *gram*, hostile. Allied to Gk. χρόμη, χρόμος, noise. (√GHARM, from √GHAR.)

Grimace. (F.—Scand.) F. *grimace*, 'a crabd looke,' Cot.—Icel. *grima*, a mask, hood; whence *grimumaðr*, a man in disguise. A *grimace* disguises the face. Cf. A.S. *grima*, a mask. Perhaps allied to Grin.

Grimalkin, a cat. (E.; *partly* O. H. G.) Prob. for *gray Malkin*, the latter being a cat's name. *Malkin = Mald-kin*, dimin. of *Mald = Maud*, i.e. Matilda; from O. H. G. *Mahthilt*. Here *maht* = might; *hilt* means battle.

Grime. (Scand.) Swed. dial. *grima*, a smut on the face; Dan. *grim, griim*, lampblack, soot, grime; Icel. *grima*, a disguise, mask. Allied to Grimace.

Grin, to snarl, grimace. (E.) M. E. *grennen*. A. S. *grennian*, to grin. **+** Du. *grijnen*, to weep, fret; Icel. *grenja*, to howl, Dan. *grine*, to grin, simper, Swed. *grina*, G. *greinen*. Allied to Groan, and to Grim.

Grind. (E.) A. S. *grindan*, pt. t. *grand*, pp. *grunden*. Allied to L. *fri-are*, to rub, Gk. χρί-ειν, to graze, Skt. *ghrish*, to grind. (√GHAR.)

grist, a supply of corn to be ground. (E.) A. S. *grist*. From the base *gri-* of *grind*; cf. *blast* from *blow*.

gristle. (E.) A. S. *gristle*, cartilage; allied to *grist*, and A.S. *gristbitian*, to gnash the teeth. From the base of *grind*, with reference to the necessity of crunching it if eaten. So also Du. *knarsbeen*, gristle, from *knarsen*, to crunch.

Gripe. (E.) A. S. *grípan*, pt. t. *gráp*, pp. *gripen*, to seize. **+** Du. *grijpen*, Icel. *grípa*, Swed. *gripa*, Dan. *gribe*, Goth. *greipan*, G. *greifen*, Russ. *grabite*, Skt. *grah* (Vedic *grabh*), to seize. (√GARBH.) Allied to *grab, grasp*.

grip, sb. (E.) M. E. *gripe*. A. S. *gripe*, a grip; from the pp. of *grípan* (above).

grope. (E.) A. S. *grápian*, to seize, handle; hence, to feel one's way.—A. S. *gráp*, pt. t. of *grípan* (above). See Grasp.

Grisette, **Grisled**; see Grizzly.

Griskin. (Scand.) The lit. sense is 'little pig,' now spine of a hog. Dimin. from M. E. *gris*, a pig.—Icel. *gríss*, a young pig; Dan. *griis*, Swed. *gris*, pig. **+** Gk. χοῖρος, a young pig.

Grisly, terrible. (E.) A. S. *gryslíc*,

terrible. Formed with suffix *-líc* (like) from *grosen* * = *groren*, pp. of *greósan*, to afflict with horror. Allied to G. *grausig*, causing horror, and to Gruesome.

Grist, Gristle; see Grind.

Grit, coarse sand. (E.) Formerly *greet*. A. S. *greót*, grit. **+** O. Fries. *gret*, Icel. *grjót*, G. *gries*. (From a base GRUT.)

groats, grain of oats. (E.) M. E. *grotes*. A. S. *grátan*, pl. groats, A. S. Leechdoms, iii. 292. Allied to Grit.

grout, coarse meal; **grouts**, dregs. (E.) M. E. *grut*. A. S. *grút*, coarse meal. **+** Du. *grut*; Icel. *grautr*, porridge, Dan. *gröd*, Swed. *gröt*, boiled groats; G. *grütze*, groats; Lithuan. *grudas*, corn; L. *rudus*, rubble.

gruel. (F.—O. Low G.) O. F. *gruel* (F. *gruau*).—Low L. *grutellum*, dimin. of *grutum*, meal.—O. Low G. and Du. *grut*, grout (above).

Grizzly, Grizzled, grayish. (F.—M. H. G.) From M. E. *grisel*, a gray-haired man. ─ F. *gris*, gray. ─ M. H. G. *grís*, gray; cf. G. *greis*, a gray-haired man.

grisette, a gay young Frenchwoman of the lower class. (F.—M. H. G.) F. *grisette*; named from the cheap gray dress' which they used to wear. ─ F. *gris*, gray (above).

Groan. (E.) M. E. *gronen*. A. S. *gránian*, to groan. Allied to Grin.

Groat; see Great.

Groats; see Grit.

Grocer; see Gross.

Grog, Grogram; see Gross.

Groin, the fork of the body, where the legs divide. (Scand.) The same as prov. E. *grain*, the place where the branch of a tree forks, the groin.—Icel. *grein*, a branch, arm; Dan. *green*, Swed. *gren*, branch, arm, fork. **Der.** *groin-ed*, having angular curves that *fork off*.

Groom. (E.) Prob. for *goom*. We find, indeed, O. Du. *grom*, Icel. *gromr*, a boy, lad; but these have no obvious etymology, and may be the same as O. Du. *gom*, Icel. *gumi*, a man. If the *r* can thus be disposed of, the etym. is from A. S. *guma*, a man, allied to Icel. *gumi*, Goth. *guma*, L. *homo*, a man. In the comp.' *bride-groom*, it is quite certain that the *r* is intrusive; see Bridegroom.

Groove; see Grave (1).

Grope; see Gripe.

Gross. (F.—L.) O. F. *gros* (F. *grosse*), gross, great.—L. *grossus*, fat, thick.

engross, to write in large letters, to occupy wholly. (F. – L.) The former (legal) sense is the older. From F. *en gros,* in large, i. e. in large characters. – L. *in,* in; *grossus,* large.

grocer. (F. – L.) Formerly *grosser* or *engrosser,* a wholesale dealer. – O. F. *grossier,* a wholesale dealer. – O. F. *gros,* great (above). Der. *grocer-y,* formerly *grossery.*

grog, spirits and water. (F. – L.) Short from *grogram*; it had its name from Admiral Vernon, nicknamed *Old Grog,* from his *grogram* breeches (ab. A. D. 1745); he ordered the sailors to dilute their rum with water.

grogram, a stuff. (F. – L.) Formerly *grogran,* so called from its coarse grain. – O. F. *grosgrain,* grogram. – O. F. *gros,* coarse; *grain,* grain.

Grot, Grotto, Grotesque; see Crypt.

Ground. (E.) A. S. *grund.* (Very likely from A. S. *grund-en,* pp. of *grindan,* to grind; the orig. sense being fine dust.) + Du. *grond,* Icel. *grunnr,* Dan. Swed. G. *grund*; Lithuan. *gruntas.* Cf. Irish *gruntt,* ground, base.

groundling, a spectator in the pit of a theatre. (E.) From *ground,* with double dimin. suffix *-l-ing,* with a contemptuous force.

grounds, dregs. (C.) This peculiar sense appears to be Celtic. – Gael. *grunndas,* lees; from *grunnd,* bottom, ground; Irish *gruntas,* dregs, from *grunnt,* the bottom. So called from being at the bottom.

groundsel, a small plant. (E.) Also *groundswell* (Holland's tr. of Pliny). A.S. *grundeswelge,* lit. 'ground-swallower,' i. e. abundant weed. – A. S. *grund,* ground; *swelgan,* to swallow.

groundsill, threshold. (E.) From *ground* and *sill,* q. v. Also spelt *grunsel* (Milton).

Group; see Crop.

Grouse, a bird. (F.) *Grouse* appears to be a false form, evolved from the old word *grice,* which seems to have been taken as a pl. form (cf. *mouse, mice*). – O. F. *griesche,* gray, speckled; *perdrix griesche,* the gray partridge, *poule griesche,* 'a moorhen, the hen of the *grice* or moorgame;' Cot. The oldest form is *greoches* (13th cent., in Littré, s. v. *grièche*). Perhaps *grouse* may answer to this O. F. *greoches.* Origin unknown.

Grout; see Grit.

Grove; see Grave (1).

Grovel, to fall flat on the ground. (Scand.) Due to M. E. *groveling,* properly an adv., signifying flat on the ground; also spelt *grofling, groflinges,* where the suffixes *-ling, -linges* are adverbial; cf. *head-long, dark-ling.* – Icel. *grúfa,* in phr. *liggja á grúfu,* to lie grovelling, *symja á grúfu,* to swim on the belly; cf. also *grúfa, grúfla,* to grovel; Swed. dial. *gruva,* flat on one's face, *ligga á gruve,* to lie on one's face. Perhaps allied to Groove.

Grow. (E.) A. S. *grówan,* pt. t. *greów,* pp. *grówen.* + Du. *groeijen,* Icel. *gróa,* Dan. *groe,* Swed. *gro.* Esp. to produce shoots, as herbs; allied to Green. Der. *grow-th,* from Icel. *gróðr,* growth.

Growl, to grumble. (Du.) Du. *grollen,* to grumble. + G. *grollen,* to rumble; Gk. γρυλλίζειν, to grunt, γρῦ, grunting. Allied to Grumble.

Grub, to grope in dirt. (E.) M. E. *grobben.* Prob. allied to A. S. *grápian,* to grope; see Grope. ¶ Not allied to grave (1).

Grudge, to grumble. (F. – Teut.) M. E. *grochen, grucchen,* to murmur. – O. F. *grocer, groucer,* to murmur. Of Teut. origin; cf. Icel. *krutr,* a murmur, G. *grunzen,* to grunt. Clearly *gru-dge, gru-nt, grow-l* are all from the same imitative base; cf. Gk. γρῦ, a grunt.

Gruel, see Grit.

Gruesome, horrible. (Scand.) Dan. *gru,* horror; with suffix *-som,* as in *virk-som,* active. Cf. Dan. *grue,* to dread, *gruelig,* horrid. + Du. *gruwzaam,* G. *grausam.* Allied to O. Sax. *gruri,* A. S. *gryre,* horror, and to E. Grisly.

Gruff, rough, surly. (Du.) Du. *grof,* coarse, loud, blunt. + Swed. *grof,* Dan. *grov,* G. *grob,* coarse.

Grumble, to murmur. (F. – G.) F. *grommeler* (Cot.) – O. and prov. G. *grummelen,* to grumble; frequent. of *grummen, grommen,* to grumble (Du. *grommen*). Allied to G. *gram,* anger, *grimmen,* to rage; and to E. Grim.

Grume, a clot of blood. (F. – L.) Rare. O. F. *grume,* a clot. – L. *grumus,* a little heap.

Grunsel; see Groundsill.

Grunt. (E.) M. E. *grunten*; extension of A.S. *grunian,* to grunt. + Dan. *grynte,* Swed. *grymta,* G. *grunzen*; so also L. *grunnire,* Gk. γρύζειν. All imitative; cf. Gk. γρῦ, the noise made by a pig.

Guaiacum, a kind of resin, from lignum vitæ. (Span. — Hayti.) Span. *guayaco, guayacan,* lignum vitæ. From the language of Hayti.

Guano. (Span. — Peruv.) Span. *guano, huano.* — Peruv. *huanu,* dung.

Guarantee, Guaranty; see **Warrant.**

Guard; see **Ward.**

Guava. (Span. — W. Ind.) Span. *guayaba;* no doubt borrowed from the W. Indies.

Gudgeon; see **Goby.**

Guelder-rose. (Du.) Here *guelder* stands for *Gueldre,* the F. spelling of the province of *Gelderland* in Holland.

Guerdon, recompense. (F. — O. H. G. and L.) O. F. *guerdon.* (Ital. *guidardone.*) — Low L. *widerdonum,* a singular compound of O. H. G. *widar,* back, again, and L. *donum,* a gift. The word is really a half-translation of the true form O. H. G. *widarlón,* a recompense. Here *widar =* G. *wieder,* back again; and *lón* is cognate with E. *loan.* So also A. S. *wiðer-leán,* a recompense, lit. ' back-loan.'

Guerilla, Guerrilla, irregular warfare; see **War.**

Guess. (Scand.) M. E. *gessen.* Dan. *gisse,* Swed. *gissa,* to guess. + Du. *gissen,* Icel. *giska.* Allied to Dan. *gjette,* to guess; the Icel. *giska* stands for *git-ska**, i. e. to try to get, from *geta,* to get. Thus *guess* is the desiderative of *get ;* see **Get.**

Guest. (E.) M. E. *gest.* A. S. *gæst, gest, gast.* + Icel. *gestr,* Dan. *giest,* Swed. *gäst,* Du. *gast,* Goth. *gasts,* G. *gast* ; L. *hostis,* a stranger, also an enemy. (√ GHAN.) Allied to **Hostile.**

Guide. (F. — Teut.) M. E. *gyden* (also *gyen*). — O. F. *guider,* to guide. Cf. Ital. *guidare,* Span. *guiar.* The *gu* (for *w*) shews the word to be of Teut. origin; it must be from a source allied to Goth. *witan,* to watch, observe, and to A. S. *witan,* to know. The orig. sense was ' to shew ;' cf. Icel. *viti,* a leader, signal, A. S. *witan,* to observe. Allied to **Wit.**

guy-rope, guy, a guide-rope, used to steady a weight in heaving. (Span. — Teut.) Span. *guia,* a guy-rope, guide. — Span. *guiar,* to guide (above).

Guild, Gild. (E.) The spelling *guild* is as false as it is common. M. E. *gilde.* — A. S. *gild,* a payment ; whence *gegilda,* a member of a gild. — A. S. *gildan,* to pay, yield ; see **Yield.**

Guile ; see **Wile.**

Guillotine. (F.) Named after a physician, *J. I. Guillotin,* died A. D. 1814. First used, 1792.

Guilt, crime. (E.) M. E. *gilt.* A. S. *gylt,* orig. a fine for a trespass ; hence, a trespass. Allied to A. S. *gildan* (pt. t. pl. *guldon*), to pay, yield ; see **Yield.**

Guinea. (African.) First coined of African gold from the *Guinea* coast, A.D. 1663. Der. *guinea-fowl.* ¶ The *guinea-pig* is from S. America ; so that it may mean *Guiana pig.*

Guise ; see **Wise,** sb.

Guitar ; see **Cithern.**

Gules ; see **Gullet.**

Gulf. (F. — Gk.) Formerly *goulfe.* — F. *golfe.* — Late Gk. κόλφος, a variant of Gk. κόλπος, the bosom, also, a deep hollow, bay, creek. Der. *en-gulf.*

Gull (1), a bird. (C.) Corn. *gullan,* a gull ; W. *gwylan.*

gull (2), a dupe. (C.) The same ; from the notion that a *gull* was a stupid bird.

Gullet, the throat. (F. — L.) M. E. *golet.* — F. *goulet* (Cot.) ; dimin. of O. F. *gole, goule* (F. *gueule*), the throat. — L. *gula,* the throat. (√ GAR.)

gules, red. (F. — L.) M. E. *goules.* — F. *gueules,* gules, red ; answering to Low L. *gulæ* (pl. of *gula*), meaning (1) mouth, (2) gules. Prob. from the colour of the open mouth of the heraldic lion. — L. *gula,* the throat.

gully, a channel worn by water. (F. — L.) Formerly *gullet.* — F. *goulet,* ' a gullet, a deep gutter of water ;' Cot. The same word as **gullet** (above).

Gulp. (Du.) Du. *gulpen,* to swallow eagerly. — Du. *gulp,* a great billow, wave, draught, gulp. Perhaps borrowed from O. F. *golfe ;* see **Gulf.**

Gum (1), flesh of the jaws. (E.) M. E. *gome.* A. S. *góma,* jaws, palate. + Icel. *gómr,* Swed. *gom,* G. *gaumen,* palate. (√ GHA.)

Gum (2), resin of certain trees. (F. — L. — Gk.) M. E. *gomme.* — F. *gomme.* — L. *gummi.* — Gk. κόμμι, gum. (Prob. of Egyptian origin ; Coptic *komē.* gum.)

Gun. (C. ?) M. E. *gonne.* — W. *gwn,* a bowl, a gun (in the latter sense as early as the 14th cent.) Of obscure origin ; perhaps orig. the ' bowl ' of a war-engine, in which the missile was placed.

gunwale, upper edge of a ship's side. (G. *and* E.) See *gunwale* or *gunnel* in Kersey (1715). A *wale* is an outer timber on a ship's side ; and the *gun-wale* is a *wale* from which *guns* were pointed. A *wale* is a ' beam;' see **Wale**.

Gurgle; see **Gorge**.

Gurnard, Gurnet, a fish. (F. – L.; with Teut. *suffix*.) *Gurnard* is the better and fuller form. The word means ' a grunter,' from the sound which the fish makes when taken out of the water. – O. F. *grongnard* (F. *grognard*), grunting, grunter, whence O. F. *gournauld, grougnaut*, gurnard (Cot.) – O. F. *grogn-er*, to grunt ; with suffix *-ard* (= G. *hart*). – L. *grunnire*, to grunt; see **Grunt**.

Gush. (Scand.) Icel. *gusa*, to gush; allied to the strong verb *gjósa* (pt. t. *gauss*), to gush. Allied to Icel. *gjóta*, to pour, Goth. *giutan*, L. *fundere*. Cf. Du. *gudsen*, to gush. (√ GHU.) See **Gut**, **Geysir**.

geysir (Icel.) Icel. *geysir*, lit. 'gusher.' – Icel. *geysa*, to gush; allied to *gjósa* (above).

gust (1), a sudden blast, gush of wind. (Scand.) Icel. *gustr*, *gjósta*, a gust. – Icel. *gjósa*, to gush (above). So also Swed. dial. *gust*, stream of air from an oven.

Gusset. (F. – Ital.) F. *gousset*, ' a gusset,' Cot. Also ' the piece of armour by which the arm-hole is covered,' id. Named from its supposed resemblance to a husk of a bean or pea; dimin. of F. *gousse*, husk of bean or pea. – Ital. *guscio*, a shell, husk; of unknown origin.

Gust (1), a blast; see **Gush**.

Gust (2), relish, taste. (L.) L. *gustus*, a tasting; cf. *gustare*, to taste. (√ GUS.) Allied to **Choose**.

disgust, vb. (F. – L.) O. F. *desgouster*, ' to distaste, loath;' Cot. – O. F. *des-* (= L. *dis-*), apart; *gouster*, to taste, from L. *gustare* (above).

goût (2), taste. (F. – L.) F. *goût*, taste. – L. *gustus* (above).

ragout. (F. – L.) F. *ragoût*, a seasoned dish. – F. *ragoûter*, to coax a sick man's appetite. – F. *re-*, again ; *a*, to ; *goûter*, to taste. – L. *re-* ; *ad* ; *gustare*.

Gut, the intestinal canal. (E.) (The word is allied to M. E. *gote*, prov. E. *gut*, a channel.) M. E. *gutte*. A. S. *gut* ; pl. *guttas* ; orig. ' a channel.' – A. S. *gut-*, stem of pt. t. pl. of *geótan*, to pour. (√ GHU.) + Swed. *gjuta*, a mill-leat, Dan. *gyde*, a lane, O. Du. *gote*, a channel, G. *gosse*, a drain. ¶ No connection with *gutter*.

Gutta-percha. (Malay.) The spell-

ing *gutta* is due to confusion with L. *gutta*, a drop, with which it has nothing to do. – Malay *gatah, guttah*, gum, balsam ; *percha*, the name of the tree producing it.

Gutter; see **Gout** (1).

Guttural. (F. – L.) F. *guttural*. – L. *gutturalis*, belonging to the throat. – L. *guttur*, the throat. Perhaps allied to *gutta*, a drop; see **Gout** (1).

goitre. (F. – L.) F. *goître*, a swelled throat. – L. *gutter*, debased form of *guttur*, throat.

Guy, Guy-rope; see **Guide**.

Guzzle. (F.) O. F. *gouziller*, to swill down, swallow greedily (in the compound *des-gouziller*, Cot.) Allied to F. *gosier*, the throat, Ital. *gozzo*, the crop of a bird, throat. Remoter source unknown.

Gymnasium. (L. – Gk.) L. *gymnasium*. – Gk. γυμνάσιον, an athletic school, where men practised naked. – Gk. γυμνά-ζειν, to train naked, exercise. – Gk. γυμνός, naked. Der. *gymnast* = γυμναστής, a trainer of athletes; *gymnast-ic*.

Gypsum. (L. – Gk. – Pers.) L. *gypsum*, chalk. – Gk. γύψον *, not found, by-form of γύψος, chalk. Prob. from Pers. *jabsín*, lime, Arab. *jibs*, plaster, mortar.

Gypsy. (F. – L. – Gk. – Egypt.) Spelt *gipsen*, Spenser, M. Hubbard, 86. Short for M. E. *Egypcien*. – O. F. *Egyptien*. – Late L. *Ægyptianus*; from L. *Ægyptius*, an Egyptian. – Gk. Αἰγύπτιος. – Gk. Αἴγυπτος, Egypt. ¶ The supposition that they came from *Egypt* was false; their orig. home was India.

Gyre, circular course. (L. – Gk.) L. *gyrus*. – Gk. γῦρος, ring, circle. Der. *gyr-ate*, from pp. of L. *gyrare*.

gyrfalcon, gerfalcon, bird of prey. (F. – Gk. ? *and* L.) Formerly *gerfaulcon*; *girefaucon* (used by Trevisa to translate L. *gyrofalco*). Modified from O. F. *gerfault*, a gyrfalcon. – Low L. *gerofalco*, better *gyrofalco*, i. e. a falcon that flies in gyres. – L. *gyrus*, a gyre ; *falco*, a falcon. ¶ Others make *gero-* stand for M. H. G. *gîr* (G. *geier*), a vulture; which is allied to E. *yearn*. (See Kluge.)

Gyves, fetters. (C.) M. E. *giues, gyues*. Of Celtic origin; cf. W. *gefyn*, Gael. *geimheal* (*mh* = *v*), Irish *geimheal, geibheal*, a fetter, gyve, bondage, captive. – Irish *geibhim*, I get, obtain, *gabh*, I take; cf. L. *capere*.

H.

Ha, interj. (E.) An exclamatory sound. Cf. O. Fries. *haha,* to denote laughter; G. *he.*

Haberdasher, a seller of small wares. (F.—Scand.) So named from his selling a stuff called *hapertas* in O. F.; see Liber Albus, ed. Riley, pp. 225, 231.—O. Icel. *hapurtask,* things of small value (Gudmundus Andreæ). I suspect that the true sense was 'pedlars' wares,' named from the haversack in which they were carried; from Icel. *haprtask, hafrtask,* a haversack; orig. a bag for oats. — Icel. *hafr,* oats; *taska,* a pouch (cf. G. *tasche,* a pouch). See **Haversack.**

Habergeon; see **Hauberk.**

Habiliment; see **Habit.**

Habit, practice, custom, dress. (F.—L.) O. F. *habit,* a dress, a custom.—L. *habitum,* acc. of *habitus,* a condition, dress.—L. *habitus,* pp. of *habere,* to have, keep.

able, having power, skilful. (F.—L.) M. E. *able;* also *hable.*—O. F. *habile, able, abel,* able. — L. *habilis,* easy to handle, active. — L. *habere.* Der. *abil-i-ty* (from L. acc. *habilitatem*).

average, a proportionate amount. (F. — L.) 'Average (L. *averagium,* from *averia,* i.e. cattle) signifies service which the tenant owes the king or other lord, by horse or ox, or by carriage with either,' &c.; Blount's Law Dict., ed. 1691. —O. F. *aver* (F. *avoir*), to have, also, as sb., goods, property; hence, cattle. — L. *habere,* to have, possess. ¶ This form (*average*) was afterwards confused with F. *avaris, avarie,* damage of goods (later, proportion or average of payment for damage). (Arab. *'awâr,* a fault, defect, *zâti 'awâr,* spoilt merchandise, merely introduce a form borrowed from Late Lat. *averia.*)

binnacle, a box for a ship's compass. (Port.—L.) A singular corruption of the older word *bittacle,* by confusion with *bin,* a chest. — Port. *bitacola,* a bittacle (i.e. binnacle); Vieyra. Cf. Span. *bitacora,* F. *habitacle,* the same. The Port. *bitacola* stands for *habitacola**, the first syllable being lost.—L. *habitaculum,* a little dwelling, i.e. 'the frame of timber in the steerage of a ship where the compass stands' (Bailey), and prob. (at first) a shelter for the steersman. — L. *habitare,* to dwell, frequent. of *habere.*

cohabit. (L.) L. *co-habitare,* to dwell together with; see **habitation** below.

debenture, acknowledgment of a debt. (L.) Formerly *debentur* (Bacon). — L. *debentur,* lit. 'they are due,' because such receipts began with the words *debentur mihi* (Webster); pr. pl. pass. of *debeo,* I owe; see **debt** (below).

debilitate. (L.) From pp. of L. *debilitare,* to weaken. — L. *debilis,* weak; put for *de-hibilis**, i.e. not active. — L. *de,* away, not; *habilis,* active; see **able** (above).

debt. (F.—L.) A bad spelling of *dett.* M. E. *dette.* — O. F. *dette* (afterwards misspelt *debte*). — L. *debita,* a sum due; fem. of *debitus,* owed, pp. of *debere,* to owe. *Debere = de-hibere**, i.e. to have away, have on loan. — L. *de,* down, away; *habere,* to have. Der. *debt-or,* M. E. *dettur,* from O. F. *deteur,* L. acc. *debitorem.*

deshabille, careless dress. (F. — L.) F. *déshabille,* undress. — F. *déshabiller,* to undress. — F. *dés* (L. *dis-*), apart, away, un-; *habiller,* to dress; see **habiliment** (below).

devoir, duty. (F.—L.) M. E. *deuoir.* —O. F. *devoir, dever,* to owe. — L. *debere,* to owe; see **debt** (above).

due. (F.—L.) M. E. *dewe.*—O. F. *deu,* masc., *deue,* fem.; pp. of *devoir,* to owe (above).

duty. (F. — L.) M. E. *duetee,* in the sense 'debt due.' A coined word, formed by analogy with E. words in *-ty* (of F. origin), from the adj. *due* (above).

endeavour, to attempt. (F. — L.) Coined from the M. E. sb. *dever, devoir,* duty, with F. prefix *en-* (=L. *in*). Due to the old phr. 'to do his *dever'* = to do his duty (Ch. C. T. 1600); see **devoir** (above).

exhibit, to shew. (L.) L. *exhibitus,* pp. of *ex-hibere,* to hold forth.

habiliment, dress. (F.—L.) F. *habillement,* clothing.—F. *habiller,* to clothe, orig. 'to get ready.' — F. *habile,* ready. — L. *habilis;* see **able** (above).

habitable. (F. — L.) F. *habitable.*— L. *habitabilis,* that can be dwelt in. — L. *habitare,* to dwell, frequent. of *habere.*

habitant. (F.—L.) F. *habitant,* pres. pt. of *habiter,* to dwell. — L. *habitare,* frequent. of *habere.*

habitat, the natural abode of a plant. (L.) L. *habitat*, it dwells (there) ; pres. s. of *habitare*, to dwell (above).

habitation, abode. (F.—L.) F. *habitation*. — L. acc. *habitationem*. — L. *habitatus*, pp. of *habitare*, to dwell, frequent. of *habere*.

habitude. (F.—L.) F. *habitude*, custom. — L. *habitudo*, condition. — L. *habitu-m*, supine of *habere*.

inhabit. (F. — L.) F. *inhabiter*.—L. *in-habitare*, to dwell in; see habitation (above).

inhibit, to check. (L.) L. *inhibitus*, pp. of *in-hibere*, to keep in, hold in.

prebend. (F. — L.) O. F. *prebende* (F. *prébende*). — L. *præbenda*, a payment, stipend from a public source ; orig. fem. of fut. part. of *præbere*, to afford, give. —L. *præ*, before, *habere*, to have ; whence *præhibere*, contr. to *præbere*. **Der.** *prebend-ar-y*.

prohibit, to check. (L.) L. *prohibitus*, pp. of *pro-hibere*, to hold before one, put in one's way, prohibit.

provender. (F. — L.) The final *r* is an F. addition, as in *lavender* ; it is prob. due to M F *provende*, a trisyllabic word. — F. *provende*, 'provender, also, a prebendry;' Cot. — L. *præbenda*, a payment ; in late L., an allowance of provisions, also a prebend ; see prebend (above).

Habitable, **Habitant**, &c.; see Habit.

Hack (1), to cut, mangle. (E.) M. E. *hakken*. A.S. *haccian*, in the comp. *tô-haccian*. + Du. *hakken*, Dan. *hakke*, Swed. *hacka*, G. *hacken*, to chop, hack.

haggle (1), to hack awkwardly, mangle. (E.) A weakened form of *hackle*, frequent. of *hack*, to cut.

hash, a dish of meat cut into slices, &c. (F.—G.) O. F. *hachis*, hash. — F. *hacher*, to hack.—G. *hacken*, to hack (above).

hatch (3), to shade by minute lines, crossing each other. (F.—G.) F. *hacher*, to hack, also to hatch or engrave; see above.

hatchet. (F. — G.) M. E. *hachet*.—F. *hachette*, dimin. of *hache*, an axe. — F. *hacher*, to cut.—G. *hacken*, to cut.

Hack (2) ; see Hackney.

Hackbut. (F. — Du.) Also *hagbut*.—O. F. *haquebute*, 'a haquebut, a caliver' (i. e. a sort of musket) ; Cot. So called from the bent form of the gun ; the bent stock was a great improvement on the orig. straight one. A corruption of Du.

haakbus, an arquebus; due, apparently, to some confusion with O. F. *buter*, to thrust. —Du. *haak*, hook; *bus*, gun. See Arquebus.

Hackle (1), **Hatchel**, an instrument for dressing flax; see heckle, under Hook.

Hackle (2); see Hook.

Hackney, **Hack**, a horse let out for hire. (F.—Du.?) M. E. *hakeney*. — O. F. *haquenee*, 'an ambling horse;' Cot. (Cf. Span. *hacanea*, Ital. *chinea*, short for *ac-chinea*, the same.) — O. Du. *hackeneye*, a hackney (Hexham). Of obscure origin; but prob. from Du. *hakken*, to hack, chop, and *negge*, a nag. Perhaps Du. *hakken* may have meant 'to jolt ;' cf. Swed. *hacka*, to hack, hew, chatter with cold, stammer, stutter. ¶ *Hack* is short for *hackney*, and quite a late form ; hence *hack*, verb, i. e. to use as a hack or hackney.

Haddock, a fish. (E. ?) M. E. *haddoke* (15th cent.) Orig. doubtful ; the Irish for ' haddock ' is *codog*.

Hades, the abode of the dead. (Gk.) Gk. ᾅδης, ἅιδης (Attic), ἀΐδης (Homeric), the nether world. 'Usually der. from *a*, privative, and ἰδεῖν, to see [as though it meant ' the unseen '] ; but the aspirate in Attic makes this very doubtful;' Liddell and Scott.

Hæmatite, **Hæmorrhage** ; see Hematite.

Haft ; see Have.

Hag. (E.) M. E. *hagge* ; with same sense as A. S. *hægtesse*, a witch, a hag. + G. *hexe*, M. H. G. *hacke*, a witch, O. H. G. *házissa* [prob. short for *hagazissa*], a witch. Most likely from A. S. *haga*, a hedge, bush ; it being supposed that witches were seen in hedges by night. See Haggard (1) below. ¶ We may particularly note Du. *haagdis*, *haagedis*, a lizard (plainly from Du. *haag*, a hedge), which strikingly resembles A. S. *hægtesse*. Cf. *urchin*.

haggard (2), lean, meagre. (E.) Orig. *hagg-ed*, i. e. hag-like, from *hag*. 'The ghostly prudes with *hagged* face,' Gray, A Long Story, near end. Misspelt by confusion with the word below.

Haggard (1), wild, said of a hawk; see Haw.

Haggard (2), lean ; see Hag.

Haggle (1), to mangle; see Hack (1).

Haggle (2), to be slow in making a bargain. (E.) In Cotgrave, s. v. *harceler*. Doubtless a weakened form of *hackle* ; frequent. of *hack* (1), to hew, cut, hence to mangle, stammer, and so to wrangle, cavil. This appears more plainly by Du. *hakkelen*, 'to hackle, mangle, faulter,' i.e. stammer (Sewel); *hakketeren*, to wrangle, cavil. It is ultimately the same word as **Haggle** (1).

higgle, to bargain. (E.) From *haggle*. Or due to O. Du. *heukelaar*; see Hawker.

Hagiographa, holy writings. (Gk.) Gk. ἁγιόγραφα (βιβλία), books written by inspiration. — Gk. ἅγιο-s, holy; γράφ-ειν, to write.

Ha-ha, Haw-haw; see Haw.

Hail (1), frozen rain. (E.) M. E. *haghel*, *hayl*. A.S. *hagal*, *hagol*. **+** Icel. *hagl*, Du. Dan. Swed. G. *hagel*. Cf. Gk. κάκληξ, a round pebble.

Hail (2), to greet; see Hale (1).

Hail! (3) an exclamation; see Hale (1).

Hair. (E.) M. E. *heer*. A.S. *hár*, *hér*. **+** Du. *haar*, Icel. *hár*, Dan. *haar*, Swed. *hår*.

Hake, a fish; see Hook.

Halberd; see Helm (1).

Halcyon, a king-fisher; as adj. serene. (L. — Gk.) *Halcyon* days = calm days; it was supposed that the weather was calm when king-fishers were breeding. — L. *halcyon*, *alcyon*, a king-fisher. — Gk. ἀλκυών, ἀλκυών, a king-fisher. Allied to L. *alcedo*, the true L. name.

Hale (1), whole. (Scand.) M. E. *heil*. — Icel. *heill*, Dan. *heel*, Swed. *hel*, hale. Cognate with A.S. *hál*, whole, Goth. *hails*, Gk. καλός, fair. See **whole** (below).

hail (2), to greet. (Scand.) M. E. *heilen*; a verb coined from Icel. *heill*, hale (above); this word is common in greeting persons, as *far heill* = farewell, *kom heill*, welcome, hail! The Scand. verb is Icel. *heilsa*, Swed. *helsa*, Dan. *hilse*, to greet.

hail (3), an exclamation. (Scand.) Icel. *heill*, hale, sound; used in greeting; see above.

halibut, holibut, a fish. (E.) So called because excellent eating for holidays; the lit. sense is 'holy (i. e. holiday) plaice.' From M. E. *hali*, holy (see holy), and *butte*, a plaice (Havelok, l. 759). So also Du. *heilbot*, halibut, from *heilig*, holy, *bot*, a plaice; Swed. *helgflundra*, a halibut, from *helg*, holidays, *flyndra*, a flounder.

hallow, to sanctify. (E.) M. E. *halwen*, *halewen*, *halowen*. A.S. *hálgian*, to make holy, from *hálig*, holy; see holy (below).

hallowmass, feast of *All Hallows*, i. e. All Saints. (Hybrid; E. *and* L.) Short for *All Hallows' Mass*, mass (or feast) of All Saints. Here *hallows'* is the gen. of *hallows*, pl. of M. E. *halowe* or *halwe*, a saint = A.S. *hálga*, a saint, def. form of the adj. *hálig*, holy; see holy (below), and **Mass**.

heal. (E.) M. E. *helen*. A.S. *hǽlan*, to make whole; formed from *hál*, whole, by the usual change from *á* to *ǽ*; see whole (below).

health. (E.) A.S. *hǽlð*, health; from *hál*, whole; see heal above.

holiday, a festival. (E.) Put for *holy day*.

hollyhock, a kind of mallow. (Hybrid; E. *and* C.) M. E. *holihoc*, i. e. holy hock. A.S. *holihocce*, the same. Compounded of *holy*, and a word *hock*, meaning 'mallow,' borrowed from Celtic. We find W. *hocys*, mallows, *hocys bendigaid*, hollyhock, lit. 'blessed mallow,' where *bendigaid* = L. *benedictus*. So called because indigenous to Palestine, the Holy Land.

holy, sacred. (E.) [This word is merely the M. E. *hool*, whole, with suffix *-y*; and therefore closely allied to *hale*.] M. E. *holi*, *holy*. A.S. *hálig*, holy; from A.S. *hál*, whole. The orig. sense was 'perfect' or 'excellent.' **+** Du. *heilig*, holy, from *heel*, whole; so also Icel. *heilagr*, *helgr*, from *heill*; Dan. *hellig*, from *heel*; Swed. *helig*, from *hel*; G. *heilig*, from *heil*. See whole (below), and Hale (above).

wassail, a festive occasion, festivity. (E.) Orig. a pledge or wishing of health at a feast. The A.S. form was *wes hál*, lit. 'be whole;' where *wes* is the imper. of *wesan*, to be; and *hál* is the E. *whole*. But the Scand. (Icel.) *heill* has been substituted, in this expression, for the A.S. *hál*, causing a jumble of dialects.

whole. (E.) M. E. *hole* (without *w*). A.S. *hál*, whole. Cognate with Hale (1), Goth. *hails*, Gk. καλός.

Hale (2), Haul, to drag, draw violently. (F. — Scand.) M. E. *halien*, *halen*. — F. *haler*, to haul a boat, &c. (Littré). — Icel. *hala*, Swed. *hala*, Dan. *hale*, to hale, haul. **+** A.S. *holian*, *geholian*, to acquire, get; G. *holen*, to fetch, haul; L. *calare*, to summon. (√KAR.)

halliard, halyard, a rope for hoisting sails. (F. — Scand. *and* E.) Short for *hale-yard*, because it *hales* the *yards* into their places.

Half. (E.) M. E. *half*. A.S. *healf*. **+** Du. *half*, Icel. *hálfr*, Swed. *half*, Dan *halv*, Goth. *halbs*, G. *halb*. Allied to

A. S. *healf*, sb., Icel. *hálfa*, Goth. *halba*, G. *halb*, side. Der. *halve*, verb.

behalf, interest. (E.) Formerly in the M. E. phrase *on my behalue* = on my behalf, on my side; substituted for the A. S. phr. *on healfe*, on the side of, by confusion with *be healfe*, used in the same sense. From A. S. *healf*, sb., side (above). *Be* = by, prep.

Halibut; see **Hale**.

Hall. (E.) M. E. *halle*. A. S. *heall*, *heal*, a hall, orig. a shelter. − A. S. *hæl*, pt. t. of *helan*, to hide. + Du. *hal*, Icel. *hall*, *höll*, O. Swed. *hall*. Allied to **Cell**. (√KAL, KAR.)

Hallelujah, Alleluia, an expression of praise. (Heb.) Heb. *halelú jáh*, praise ye Jehovah. − Heb. *halelú*, praise ye (from *halal*, to shine, praise); *jáh*, God.

Halliard, Halyard; see **Hale** (2).

Halloo, Halloa, a cry to call attention. (E.) M. E. *halow*. A. S. *ealá*, interj. (very common). Prob. often confused with **Holla**, q. v.

Hallow, Hallowmass; see **Hale**.

Hallucination, wandering of mind. (L.) L. *hallucinatio*, a wandering of the mind. − L. *hallucinari, allucinari, alucinari*, to wander in mind, dream, rave.

Halm; see **Haulm**.

Halo, a luminous ring. (L. − Gk.) L. acc. *halo*, from nom. *halos*. − Gk. ἅλως, a round threshing-floor, in which the oxen trod out a circular path. (√WAL, WAR.) Allied to **Voluble**.

Halser; see **Hawser**.

Halt, lame. (E.) M. E. *halt*. A. S. *healt*. + Icel. *haltr*, Dan. Swed. *halt*, Goth. *halts*, O. H. G. *halz*. Der. *halt*, verb, A. S. *healtian*.

Halt! (F. − G.) F. *halte*. − G. *halt*, hold! **Halter**. (E.) M. E. *halter* (an *f* has been lost). A. S. *healfter, hælftre*, a halter. + O. Du. and G. *halfter*.

Halyard; see **Hale** (2).

Ham. (E.) M. E. *hamme*. A. S. *hamm*. + Prov. G. *hamme*. Lit. 'bend of the leg;' allied to W. *cam*, bent, L. *camurus*, crooked. (√KAM.) Allied to **Gammon** (1), **Gambol**.

Hamadryad; see **Dryad**.

Hamlet; see **Home**.

Hammer. (E.) A. S. *hamor*. + Icel. *hamarr*, Dan. *hammer*, Swed. *hammare*, Du. *hamer*, G. *hammer*. Thought to be allied to Russ. *kamene*, a stone, Skt. *açman*, a stone, thunderbolt.

Hammercloth. (Du. *and* E.) The cloth which covers a coach-box; lit. cover-cloth; adapted from Du. *hemel*, heaven, also a cover, tester, canopy. 'Den hemel van een koetse, the seeling of a coach;' Hexham. Dimin. of A. S. *hama*, Icel. *hamr*, a covering. (√KAM.) Allied to **Chamber**.

Hammock, a slung net for a bed. (W. Ind.) Formerly *hamaca*; Span. *hamaca*. A West Indian word.

Hamper (1), to impede. (E.) M. E. *hamperen, hampren*; a variant of *hamelen* (later *hamble*), to mutilate, esp. used of 'expedition,' i. e. the cutting out of the ball of a dog's fore-foot, to *hamper* him from pursuing game. A. S. *hamelian*, to maim. + Icel. *hamla*, G. *hammeln*, to maim; allied to Goth. *hamfs*, maimed, Gk. κωφός, blunt, dumb, deaf. (√SKAP.)

Hamper (2), a kind of basket. (Low L. − F. − G.) Formerly spelt *hanaper*. − Low L. *hanaperium*, orig. a vessel to keep cups in. − O. F. *hanap* (Low L. *hanapus*), a drinking-cup. − O. H. G. *hnapf*, M. H. G. *napf*, a cup. + A. S. *hnæp*, Du. *nap*, a cup, bowl.

hanaper, old form of **Hamper** (above). Hence *Hanaper office*, named from the basket in which writs were deposited.

Hand. (E.) A. S. *hand, hond*. + Du. *hand*, Icel. *hönd*, *hand*, Dan. *haand*, Swed. *hand*, Goth. *handus*, G. *hand*. Lit. 'seizer;' from *hanth*, base of Goth. *hinthan*, to seize.

handcuff. (E.) A *cuff* for the *hand*; but really an adaptation of M. E. *handcops*, a handcuff. − A. S. *handcops*, a handcuff. − A. S. *hand*, hand; *cops*, a fetter.

handicap, a race for horses of all ages. (E.) From *hand i' cap*, hand in the cap, a method of drawing lots; hence, a mode of settlement by arbitration, &c.

handicraft. (E.) A. S. *handcræft*, a trade; the *i* being inserted in imitation of *handiwork* (below).

handiwork. (E.) M. E. *handiwerc*. A. S. *handgeweorc*. − A. S. *hand*, hand; *geweorc*, the same as *weorc*, work. The *i* is due to A. S. *ge*.

handle. (E.) A. S. *handlian*; formed with suffix *-l* and causal *-ian* from *hand*, hand. So also Du. *handelen*, Icel. *höndla*, Dan. *handle*, Sw. *handla*, G. *handeln*, to handle, or to trade. Der. *handle*, sb.

handsel, hansel, first instalment of a bargain. (Scand.) Icel. *handsal*, the conclusion of a bargain by shaking hands; lit.

' hand-sale ;' so also Dan. *handsel*, Swed. *handsöl*, a handsel. See **Sale**.

handsome. (E.) M. E. *handsum*, orig. tractable, or dexterous.—A. S. *hand*, hand ; -*sum*, suffix, as in *wyn-sum*, winsome.+Du. *handzaam*, tractable, serviceable.

handy (1), dexterous. (E.) M. E. *hendi* (never *handi*). A. S. *hendig*, skilful ; formed from *hand*, hand, with suffix -*ig* and vowel-change. + Du. *handig*, Dan. *hændig*, *behændig*, Swed. *händig*, dexterous ; Goth. *handugs*, clever.

handy (2), near. (E.) M. E. *hende*. A. S. *gehende*, near, at hand.—A. S. *hand*, hand.

Hang, to suspend, to be suspended. (E.) The original strong verb was transitive ; the weak verb intransitive ; they are now mixed up. The weak verb is from A. S. *hangian*, pt. t. *hangode*, to hang down (intr.); derived from the base of the A. S. strong verb *hón* (contracted form of *hangan*), pt. t. *héng*, pp. *hangen*.+Icel. *hengja*, weak verb, from *hanga* (pt. t. *hékk*, for *hénk**, pp. *hanginn*) ; G. *hängen*, weak verb, from G. *hangen* (pt. t. *hing*, pp. *gehangen*). Allied to L. *cunctari*, to delay, Skt. *çank*, to hesitate. (√KAK.)

hank, a parcel of skeins of yarn. (Scand.) Icel. *hanki*, a hasp, clasp, *hönk*, *hangr*, a hank, coil ; Swed. *hank*, a string, G. *henkel*, a handle, ear of a vessel. The orig. sense seems to have been 'a loop' to hang up by. From the verb above.

hanker, to long after. (E.) Cf. prov. E. *hank*, to hanker after, of which it is a frequent. form ; cf. the phr. ' to *hang* about.' From the verb above. Verified by O. Du. *hengelen*, to hanker after (from *hangen*) ; O. Du. *honkeren* (Du. *hunkeren*), to hanker after.

hinge. (Scand.) M. E. *henge*, that on which the door hangs ; from M. E. *hengen*, to hang.—Icel. *hengja*, to hang (above).

Hanseatic, pertaining to the Hanse towns in Germany. (F.—O. H. G.) O. F. *hanse*, the hanse, i. e. society of merchants. —O. H. G. *hansa* (G. *hanse*), an association ; cf. Goth. *hansa*, A. S. *hós*, a band of men. (About A.D. 1140.)

Hansel; see **Handsel**.

Hansom, a kind of cab. (E.) From the name of the inventor (no doubt the same word as *handsome*).

Hap. (Scand.) M. E. *hap*. —Icel. *happ*, hap, chance, good luck ; cf. A.S. *gehæp*, fit. The W. *hap* must be borrowed from E. Der. *happ-y*, i. e. lucky ; *hap-less*, i. e.

luckless ; *hap-ly*, by luck (*happily* is used in the same sense).

happen. (Scand.) M. E. *happenen*, *hapnen*, extended from *happen*, i. e. to hap. From the sb. above.

mishap. (Scand.) M. E. *mishappen*, verb, to fall out ill ; from **Mis-** (1) and **Hap**.

perhaps. (L. *and* Scand.) A clumsy hybrid compound.—L. *per*, by (as in *perchance*, where *per* is, strictly, F. *par*) ; *haps*, pl. of *hap*.

Harangue; see **Ring**.

Harass. (F.) O. F. *harasser*, to tire out, vex, disquiet. Perhaps from O. F. *harer*, to set a dog at a beast.—O. H. G. *haren*, to call out, cry out (hence cry to a dog). (√KAR.)

Harbinger; see **Harbour**.

Harbour, shelter. (Scand.) M. E. *herberwe*.—Icel. *herbergi*, a harbour, lit. 'army-shelter.'—Icel. *herr*, an army ; *barg*, pt. t. of *bjarga*, to shelter ; O. Swed. *härberge*, an inn, from *hær*, army, *berga*, to defend ; O. H. G. *hereberga*, a camp, lodging, from O. H. G. *heri* (G. *heer*), an army, *bergan*, to shelter (whence F. *auberge*, Ital. *albergo*). (√KAR ; and see **Borough**.) Der. *harbour*, verb.

harbinger, a forerunner. (F.—O.H.G.) M. E. *herbergeour*, one who provided lodgings for a man of rank.—O. F. *herberg-er*, to lodge, to harbour ; with suffix -*our* (L. -*atorem*).—O. F. *herberge*, a lodging, harbour.—O. H. G. *hereberga* (above).

Hard. (E.) A.S. *heard*.+Du. *hard* ; Icel. *hardr*, Dan. *haard*, Swed. *hård*, Goth. *hardus*, G. *hart*. Perhaps allied to Gk. κρατύς, strong.

hardy, stout, brave. (F. — O. H. G.) M. E. *hardi*.—O. F. *hardi*, brave ; orig. pp. of *hardir*, lit. to harden. — O. H. G. *hartjan*, to harden, make strong.—O. H. G. *harti* (G. *hart*), hard (above).

Hare. (E.) A.S. *hara*.+Du. *haas*, Dan. Swed. *hare*, Icel. *héri*, G. *hase*, W. *ceinach* (Rhys), Skt. *çaça*, orig. *çasa*, a hare. The Skt. word means 'jumper,' from *çaç* (for *ças*), to jump, leap along.

harebell. (E.) From *hare* and *bell*. (Other derivations are fables.)

harrier (1). (E.) Formerly *harier*; from *hare*. Cf. *bow-yer* from *bow*.

Harem, set of apartments for females. (Arab.) Also *haram*. = Arab. *haram*, women's apartments, lit. 'sacred,' or 'prohibited.'—Arab. root *harama*, he prohibited (because men were prohibited from entering).

Haricot (1), a stew of mutton, (2) kidney bean. (F.) F. *haricot*, 'mutton sod with little turneps,' &c.; Cot. The sense of 'bean' is late; that of 'minced mutton with herbs' is old. The oldest spelling is *herigote*, 14th cent. Origin unknown.

Hark! see **Hear**.

Harlequin. (F.) F. *arlequin, harlequin*, a harlequin; cf. Ital. *arlecchino*, a buffoon, jester. The Ital. word seems to be derived from F.; the O. F. phrase was *li maisnie hierlekin* (Low L. *harlequini familias*), a troop of demons that haunted lonely places. This I believe to be derived from O. Fries. *helle kin* (A. S. *helle cyn*, Icel. *heljar kyn*), i. e. the kindred- of hell, host of hell, troop of demons. The change from *hellequin* to *harlequin* arose from a popular etymology which connected the word with *Charles Quint*; Max Müller, Lect. ii. 581.

Harlot. (F. — Teut.) Orig. used of either sex, and not always in a very bad sense; equiv. to mod. E. 'fellow;' Ch. C. T. 649. — O. F. *herlot, arlot*, a vagabond; Prov. *arlot*, a vagabond; Low L. *arlotus*, a glutton. Of disputed origin; prob. from O. H. G. *karl*, a man. Hence also *carlot*, As You Like It, iii. 5. 108, and the name *Charlotte*.

Harm, sb. (E.) M. E. *harm*. A. S. *hearm*, grief, also harm.+Icel. *harmr*, grief, Dan. *harme*, wrath, Swed. *harm*, anger, grief, G. *harm*, grief, Russ. *srame*, shame; Skt. *çrama*, toil, from *çram*, to be weary. (√ KARM.) **Der.** *harm*, verb.

Harmony, concord. (F. — L. — Gk.) M. E. *harmonie*. — F. *harmonie*. — L. *harmonia*. — Gk. ἁρμονία, a joint, proportion, harmony. — Gk. ἁρμός, a joining. — Gk. ἄρειν, to fit. (√ AR.)

Harness; see **Iron**.

Harp. (E.) M. E. *harpe*. A. S. *hearpe*. +Du. *harp*, Icel. *harpa*, Swed. *harpa*, Dan. *harpe*, G. *harfe*. Perhaps allied to L. *crepare*, to crackle; if so, it meant 'loud-sounding.'

harpsichord. (F. — Teut. *and* Gk.) Formerly *harpsechord*, with intrusive *s*. — F. *harpechord*, 'a harpsichord,' Cot. From Teutonic and Greek; see **Harp** and **Chord**.

Harpoon. (F. — L.) Formerly also *harpon*, which is the F. spelling. — F. *harpon*, a cramp-iron, a grappling-iron; whence also Du. *harpoen*. — O. F. *harpe*, a dog's claw or paw; cf. *se harper*, to grapple. Cf. also Span. *arpon*, a harpoon, *arpar*, to

claw, rend; Ital. *arpagone*, a harpoon, *arpese*, cramp-iron; *arpino*, a hook. The Ital. *arpagone* is plainly from L. acc. *harpagonem*, a hook, grappling-iron; so also L. *harpaga*, hook, *harpax*, rapacious. All from Greek; cf. Gk. ἁρπαγή, a hook, ἅρπαξ, rapacious, ἅρπη, a bird of prey; from ἁρπ-, base of ἁρπάζειν, to seize, cognate with L. *rapere*. See **Harpy**.

Harpsichord; see **Harp**.

Harpy. (F. — L. — Gk.) O. F. *harpie*. — L. *harpyia*, usually in pl. *harpyiæ*. — Gk. pl. ἅρπυιαι, lit. 'spoilers.' — Gk. ἁρπ-, base of ἁρπάζειν, to seize, cognate with L. *rapere*. See **Rapacious**.

Harquebus; see **Arquebus**.

Harridan, a jade, a worn-out woman. (F.) A variant of O. F. *haridelle*, 'a poor tit, leane ill-favored jade,' Cot.; i. e. a worn-out horse. Prob. from O. F. *harer*, to set on a dog, hence to vex; see **Harass**.

Harrier (1), a hare-hound; see **Hare**.

Harrier (2), a kind of buzzard; see **Harry**.

Harrow, sb. (E.) M. E. *harwe*. Not found in A. S.+Du. *hark*, a rake; Icel. *herfi*, Dan. *harv*, a harrow; Swed. *harka*, a rake, *harf*, a harrow; G. *harke*, a rake.

Harry, to ravage. (E.) M. E. *harwen, herien, herzien*. A. S. *hergian*, to lay waste, as is done by an army. — A. S. *herg-*, base of *here*, an army.+Icel. *herja*, to ravage, from *herr*, army; Dan. *hærge*, from *hær*. The sense of *here* is 'destroyer.' (√ KAR.)

harrier (2), a kind of buzzard. (E.) I. e. *harry-er*, because it destroys small birds. And see **Heriot**.

Harsh. (Scand.) M. E. *harsk*. — Dan *harsk*, rancid; Swed. *härsk*, rank, rancid, rusty. + G. *harsch*, harsh, rough. Cf. Lithuan. *kartus*, harsh, bitter (of taste); Skt. *krit*, to cut.

Hart. (E.) M. E. *hart*. A. S. *heort, heorot*.+Du. *hert*, Icel. *hjörtr*, Dan. *hiort*, Swed. *hjort*, G. *hirsch*, O. H. G. *hiruz*. Allied to L. *cervus*, W. *carw*, a hart, horned animal; cf. Gk. κέρας, a horn. See **Horn**.

Harvest. (E.) A. S. *hærfest*, autumn; orig. 'crop.' + Du. *herfst*, G. *herbst*, autumn; Icel. *haust*, Dan. Swed. *höst* (contracted forms). Allied to L. *carpere*, to gather. (√ KARP, for SKARP.)

Hash; see **Hack** (1).

Hasp. (E.) A. S. *hæpse*, bolt, bar of a door.+Icel. *hespa*, Dan. Swed. G. *haspe*, hasp. Lit. 'that which fits;' cf. A. S. *gehæp*, fit; see **Hap**.

Hassock. (C.) M. E. *hassok*, orig. coarse grass or sedge, of which the covering of hassocks was made. — W. *hesgog*, adj., sedgy, from *hesg*, s. pl., sedges; cf. W. *hesgyn*, a sieve, *hesor*, a hassock, pad. Allied to Irish *seisg*, a sedge, bog-reed.

Hastate, spear-shaped. (L.) L. *hastatus*, spear-like. — L. *hasta*, a spear. Allied to **Goad**.

Haste, verb and sb. (Scand.) O. Swed. *hasta*, to haste, *hast*, haste; Dan. *haste*, to haste, *hast*, haste. ╋ O. Fries. *hast*, sb., Du. *haasten*, G. *hasten*, vb., Du. *haast*, G. *hast*, sb. Allied to Skt. *çaç* (for *ças*), to jump; see **Hare**. (√ KAS.) Der. *hast-en*, XVI cent.

Hat. (E.) A. S. *hæt*.╋Icel. *hattr*, Swed. *hatt*, Dan. *hat*. Cf. L. *cassis*, a helmet. (√ SKAD.)

Hatch (1), a half-door. (E.) M. E. *hatche*; a *hatch* also meant a latch of a door, North E. *heck*. A. S. *haca*, bolt or bar of a door; also *hæcce*, a hook.╋Du. *hek*, fence, rail, gate, Swed. *häck*, coop, rack, Dan. *hæk*, *hække*, rack. Allied to **Hook**. The orig. sense was prob. a latch or a catch of a door; hence, various modes of fastening. Der. *hatch-es*, pl. sb., a frame of cross-bars over an opening in a ship's deck; *hatch-way*.

hatch (2), to produce a brood by incubation. (E.) From the coop or *hatch* in which the mother-bird sits. Thus Swed. *häcka*, to hatch, from *häck*, a coop; Dan. *hækkebuur*, a breeding-cage, from *hække*, a rack.

Hatch (3), to shade by lines, in engraving; **Hatchet**, axe; see **Hack** (1).

Hatches; see **Hatch** (1).

Hatchment, escutcheon; see **Capital** (1).

Hate, sb. (E.) M. E. *hate*. A. S. *hete*, hate; the mod. E. sb. takes the vowel from the verb *hatian*, to hate.╋Du. *haat*, Icel. *hatr*, Swed. *hat*, Dan. *had*, Goth. *hatis*, G. *hass*, hate. Cf. W. *cas*, hate, *casau*, to hate. (√ KAD.)

hatred. (E.) M. E. *hatred*, *hatreden*. The suffix is A. S. *-ræden*, law, mode, condition, state, as in *hiw-ræden*, a household; and see *kindred*.

Hauberk, a coat of ringed mail. (F. — O. H. G.) M. E. *hauberk*. — O. F. *hauberc*. — O. H. G. *halsberc*, lit. neck-defence. — O. H. G. *hals*, neck; *bergan*, to protect. See **Collar** and **Bury**.

habergeon, armour for neck and breast. (F. — O. H. G.) M. E. *habergeon*, *hauber-*

ioun. — O. F. *hauberjon*, a small hauberk; dimin. of *hauberc* (above).

Haughty; see **Altitude**.

Haul; see **Hale** (2).

Haulm, Halm, stalk. (E.) A. S. *healm*. ╋ Du. *halm*, Icel. *hálmr*, Dan. Swed. *halm*; Russ. *soloma*, straw; L. *culmus*, stalk, Gk. κάλαμος, reed. Allied to **Culminate**.

Haunch, hip, bend of the thigh. (F. — O.H.G.) F. *hanche*, also *anche*. — O. H. G. *enchá*, *einchá* (also *ancha*, acc. to Diez), the leg, joint of the leg; whence O. H. G. *enchila*, ankle. Orig. 'bend;' cf. Gk. ἀγκή, bent arm; allied to **Ancle**.

Haunt, to frequent. (F.) M. E. *hanten*, *haunten*. — O. F. *hanter*, to haunt, frequent. Origin disputed.

Hautboy; see **Altitude**.

Have. (E.) M. E. *hauen*, pt. t. *hadde*, pp. *had*. A.S. *habban*, pt. t. *hæfde*, pp. *gehæfd*. ╋ Du. *hebben*, Icel. *hafa*, Swed. *hafva*, Dan. *have*, Goth. *haban*, G. *haben*; L. *capere*, to seize. (√ KAP.) Allied to **Capacious**.

behave. (E.) I. e. to *be-have* oneself, or control oneself; from *have* with prefix *be-*, the same as prep. *by*.

behaviour. (E.; *with* F. *suffix*.) Formed abnormally, from the verb to *behave*. It was often shortened to *haviour*, and seems to have been confused with F. sb. *avoir*, (1) wealth, (2) ability. Cf. Lowl. Sc. *havings*, (1) wealth, (2) behaviour.

haft, handle. (E.) A. S. *hæft*, a handle. — A. S. *haf-*, base of *habban*, to have, hold. ╋Du. *heft*, Icel. *hepti* (pron. *hefti*), G. *heft*, a handle. Lit. 'that which is held.'

haven, harbour. (E.) A. S. *hæfene*. ╋ Du. *haven*, Icel. *höfn*, Dan. *havn*, Swed. *hamn*, G. *hafen*, a harbour. Lit. 'that which holds.' From the base of the verb *to have*.

Haversack, soldier's provision - bag. (F. — G.) F. *havresac*. — G. *habersack*, *hafersack*, lit. 'oat-bag.' — G. *haber*, *hafer*, oats; *sack*, a sack. See **Haberdasher**.

Havoc, destruction. (F.) It appears to be put for *havot*. — O. F. *havot*, plunder; whence *crier havot*, E. 'cry havoc' (Godefroy). Cf. O. F. *haver*, to hook up; and G. *Haft*, seizure. Prob. from G. *heben*, to heave. ¶ The W. *hafoc*, destruction, is almost certainly borrowed from E. See **Hawk**.

Haw, a hedge; hence, berry of hawthorn.

(E.). M. E. *hawe*, a yard, named from the fence round it. A. S. *haga*, an enclosure, yard.+Icel. *hagi*, Swed. *hage*, enclosure; Dan. *have*, garden; Du. *haag*, G. *hag*, hedge. Allied to **Cincture**. (√ KAK.) **Der.** *haw-haw*, a sunk fence (a reduplicated form); *haw-thorn*.

haggard (1), wild, said of a hawk. (F.–G.) O.F. *hagard*, wild; esp. used of a wild falcon, lit. hedge-falcon. Formed, with suffix *-ard* (of G. origin), from M.H.G. *hag* (G. *hag*), a hedge (above).

hedge. (E.) A.S. *hecg*; a secondary form from *haga*, a haw.+Du. *hegge*, *heg*; from *haag*, a haw; Icel. *heggr*, a kind of tree used in hedges, from *hagi*, haw.

Hawk (1), a bird of prey. (E.) M. E. *hauk*, *hauek* (=*havek*). A. S. *hafoc*, *heafoc*, a hawk.+Du. *havic*, Icel. *haukr*, Swed. *hök*, G. *habicht*, O.H.G. *hapuh*. Prob. 'a seizer;' allied to E. *have*, L. *capere*; see **Have**.

Hawk (2), to carry about for sale. (O. Low G.) A verb formed from the sb. *hawker*; see **Hawker**.

Hawk (3), to clear the throat. (W.) W. *hochi*, to hawk; *hoch*, the throwing up of phlegm.

Hawker, pedlar, (O. Low G.) Introduced from the Netherlands; Du. *heuker*, a hawker, O. Du. *heukeren*, to hawk, sell by retail; *heukelaar*, a huckster. So also Dan. *höker*, a chandler, huckster, *hökre*, to hawk; Swed. *hökeri*, higgling, *hökare*, a chandler, cheesemonger. See further below.

huckster. (O Low G.) M. E. *hukstere*, *hucster*. Imported from the Netherlands; the suffix *-ster* is still commoner in Du. than in E. Formed with this fem. suffix (for which see **Spinster**) from Du. *heuker*, a hawker, O. Du. *hucker*, a stooper, bender, one who stoops, also a huckster. β. The *hawker* or *huckster* was so named from his bowed back, bent under his burden; from O. Du. *hucken*, to stoop under a burden. Cf. Icel. *hokra*, to go bent, crouch, also to live as a small farmer; Icel. *húka*, to sit on one's hams, Low G. *huken*, to crouch; Skt. *kuch*, to bend. Allied to **Hook**, **Hug**.

Hawse, Hawse-hole. (Scand.) *Hawse* is a round hole through which a ship's cable passes, so called because made in the 'neck' of the ship.—Icel. *háls*, *hals*, the neck; also, part of a ship's bows. +A. S. *heals*; Du. G. *hals*; cf. L. *collum*.

Hawser, a tow-rope. (F.–L.) From the O. F. vb. *haulser*, to raise; also, to tow a boat.—Low L. *altiare*, to elevate. —L. *altus*, high. See **Altitude**. Cf. O. Ital. *alzaniere*, 'a halsier [hawser] in a ship' (Florio); from *alzare*, to raise. ¶ Not allied to **Hoist**.

Hawthorn; see **Haw**.

Hay. (E.) M. E. *hey*. A.S. *heg*.+Du. *hooi*, Icel. *hey*, Dan. Swed. *hö*, Goth. *hawi*, grass; G. *heu*. Properly 'cut grass;' from the verb to *hew*; see **Hew**.

Hazard. (F.–Span.–Arab.–Pers.) F. *hasard*.—Span. *azar*, a hazard; the orig. sense must have been 'a die;' cf. O. Ital. *zara*, a game at dice.—Arab. *al zdr*, lit. the die (Devic).—Pers. *zdr*, a die (Zenker); *al* being the Arab. def. art.

Haze, a mist. (Scand.?) Perhaps from Icel. *höss*, gray, dusky; allied to A.S. *hasu*, a dark gray colour. It may have been applied to dull gray weather. (Doubtful.)

Hazel. (E.) M.E. *hasel*. A.S. *hæsel*. + Du. *hazelaar*, Icel. *hasl*, *hesli*, Dan. Swed. *hassel*, G. *hasel*, L. *corulus*, W. *coll*. Root unknown.

He. (E.) A.S. *hé*; gen. *his*, dat. *him*, acc. *hine*. Fem. sing. nom. *heó*, gen. dat. *hire*, acc. *hí*; neut. sing. nom. *hit*, gen. *his*, dat. *him*, acc. *hit*. Pl. (all genders), nom. acc. *hig*, *hí*, gen. *hira*, *heora*, dat. *him*, *heom*. + Du. *hij*, Icel. *hann*, Dan. Swed. *han*. Allied to Gk. ἐκεῖνος, κεῖνος, that one. (Base KI.)

hence. (E.) M.E. *hennes*, older form *henne* (whence *henne-s* by adding adv. suffix *-s*). A.S. *heonan*, for *hinan*✱, adv., closely allied to A.S. *hine*, masc. acc. of *hé*, he.

her. (E.) M.E. *hire*; from A.S. *hire*, gen. and dat. of *heó*, she. **Der.** *her-s*, M.E. *hires* (XIV cent.); *her-self*.

here. (E.) M.E. *her*, *heer*. A.S. *hér*, adv.; from the base of *hé*, he. + Du. *hier*, Icel. *hér*, Dan. *her*, Swed. *här*, G. *hier*, Goth. *her*.

hither. (E.) M.E. *hider*, *hither*. A.S. *hider*, *hiðer*. From the base of *he*, with Aryan suffix *-tar*. So also Icel. *héðra*, Goth. *hidre*, L. *citra*.

it. (E.) M.E. *hit*. A.S. *hit*, neut. of *he*. + Icel. *hit*, neut. of *hinn*; Du. *het*, neut. of *hij*. The old gen. case was *his*, afterwards *it*, and finally *its* (XVII cent.).

Head. (E.) M.E. *hed*, *heed*, *heued* (=*heved*). A.S. *heafod*. + Du. *hoofd*, Icel. *höfuð*, Dan. *hoved*, Swed. *hufvud*, Goth.

haubith, **G.** *haupt*, **O. H. G.** *houbit*, **L.** *caput*; allied to Gk. κεφαλή, head, Skt. *kapála*, skull. Doublet, *chief*. Der. *be-head*.

headlong, rashly, rash. (E.) M. E. *hedling*, *heuedling*, *hedlinges*. Thus the suffix is adverbial, answering to A. S. suffix *-l-unga*, really a double suffix. Cf. A. S. *grund-lunga*, from the ground, *eall-unga*, entirely, *fær-inga*, suddenly.

Heal, Health; see Hale (1).

Heap, sb. (E.) M. E. *heep*. A. S. *heáp*, a heap, crowd. **+** Du. *hoop*, Icel. *hópr*, Dan. *hob*, Swed. *hop*, G. *haufe*, O. H. G. *hufo*, Lithuan. *kaupas*, a heap. Der. *heap*, verb.

hope (2), a troop. (Du.) Only in the phr. 'a forlorn hope,' i. e. troop. — Du. *verloren hoop* = lost band, where *hoop* = E. *heap* (above). 'Een *hoop krijghsvolck*, a troupe or band of souldiers;' Hexham. (Now obsolete in Dutch.)

Hear. (E.) M. E. *heren*, pt. t. *herde*, pp. *herd*. A. S. *hýran*, *héran*, pt. t. *hýrde*, pp. *gehýred*. **+** Du. *hooren*, Icel. *heyra*, Dan. *höre*, Swed. *höra*, Goth. *hausjan*, G. *hören*. (Not allied to ear.)

hark, hearken. (E.) M. E. *herken*, also *herknen*. A. S. *hýrcnian*, to hearken; an extended form from *hýran*, to hear. Cf. G. *horchen*, from *hören*.

hearsay. (E.) From *hear* and *say*, the latter being in the infin. mood. Cf. A. S. *hé secgan hýrde* = he heard say (Beowulf).

Hearse. (F. — L.) M. E. *herse*, hearse. The orig. sense was a triangular harrow, then a triangular frame for supporting lights at a church service, esp. at a funeral, then a funeral pageant, a bier, a carriage for a dead body. All these senses are found. — O. F. *herce*, a harrow, a frame with pins on it. (Mod. F. *herse*, Ital. *erpice*, a harrow.) — L. *hirpicem*, acc. of *hirpex*, a harrow.

rehearse. (F. — L.) M. E. *rehersen*. — O. F. *reherser*, *rehercer*, to harrow over again; hence, to go over the same ground. — L. *re-*, again; O. F. *hercer*, to harrow, from *herce*, sb. (above).

Heart. (E.) M. E. *herte*. A. S. *heorte*. **+** Du. *hart*, Icel. *hjarta*, Swed. *hjerta*, Dan. *hierte*, Goth. *hairto*, G. *herz*, Irish *cridhe*, Russ. *serdtse*, L. *cor* (crude form *cordi-*), Gk. καρδία, κῆρ, Skt. *hrid*, *hridaya*. Lit. 'that which quivers;' cf. Gk. κραδάειν, to quiver, throb; Skt. *kurd*, to jump.

heart's-ease, a pansy. (E.) Lit. *ease of heart*, i. e. giving pleasure.

hearty. (E.) M. E. *herty*; also *hertly*; from M. E. *herte*, heart.

Hearth. (E.) M. E. *herth*, *herthe*. A. S. *heorð*. **+** Du. *haard*; Swed. *härd*, a hearth, a forge, G. *herd*. Cf. Goth. *haurja*, burning coals.

Heart's-ease, Hearty; see Heart.

Heat; see Hot.

Heath. (E.) M. E. *heth*. A. S. *hæð*. **+** Du. G. *heide*, Icel. *heiðr*, Dan. *hede*, Swed. *hed*, Goth. *haithi*, a waste; W. *coed*, a wood; L. *-cetum*, a pasture (in *bu-cetum*, cow-pasture).

heathen, a pagan. (E.) Orig. a dweller on a heath. A. S. *hæðen*, adj. from *hæð*, a heath. Similarly L. *paganus* meant (1) a villager, (2) a pagan. So also G. *heiden*, a heathen, from *heide*, a heath.

heather. (E.) Lit. *heath-er*, i. e. inhabitant of the heath.

hoiden, hoyden, a romping girl. (O. Du.) Formerly applied to males, and meaning a rustic. — O. Du. *heyden* (Du. *heiden*), a heathen; also, a gipsy, vagabond. — O. Du. *heyde*, a heath. See Heath. ¶ The W. *hoeden* is borrowed from English.

Heave. (E.) M. E. *heuen* (= *heven*). A. S. *hebban*, pt. t. *hóf*, pp. *hafen*. **+** Du. *heffen*, Icel. *hefja*, Swed. *häfva*, Dan. *hæve*, Goth. *hafjan*, G. *heben*.

heavy. (E.) Hard to heave, weighty. M. E. *heui* (= *hevi*). A. S. *hefig*, heavy, hard to heave. — A. S. *hef-*, stem formed from *hebban* (pt. t. *hóf*), to heave. **+** Icel. *höfigr*, heavy; from *hefja*, to heave.

heft, a heaving. (E.) In Wint. Tale, ii. 1. 45. Formed from *heave*, just as *haft* from *have*.

upheave. (E.) To heave up.

Heaven. (E.) M. E. *heuen* (= *heven*). A. S. *heofon*, *hefon*. **+** O. Icel. *hifinn*; O. Sax. *hevan*. (Perhaps related to *heave*, but the connection has not been made out; or allied to G. *himmel*.)

Heavy; see Heave.

Hebdomadal; see Heptagon.

Hebrew. (F. — L. — Gk. — Heb.) F. *hébreu* (*hébrieu* in Cotgrave). — L. *Hebræus*. Gk. Ἑβραῖος. — Heb. *'ivrî*, a Hebrew (Gen. xiv. 13), a name given to Israelites as coming from E. of the Euphrates. — Heb. *'âvar*, he crossed over.

Hecatomb. (F. — L. — Gk.) F. *hecatombe*. — L. *hecatombē*. — Gk. ἑκατόμβη, a sacrifice of a hundred oxen. — Gk. ἑκατόν, a hundred; βοῦς, ox.

Heckle, Hackle, Hatchel; see **Hook**.

Hectic, continual, as a fever. (F. – Gk.)
F. *hectique* (as if from Low L. *hecticus**).
– Gk. ἑκτικός, hectic,' consumptive. – Gk.
ἕξις, a possession; also, a habit of body.
– Gk. ἕξ-ω, fut. of ἔχειν, to have, hold.
(√ SAGH.)

Hector, a bully. (Gk.) From Gk. *Hector*,
Ἕκτωρ, the celebrated hero of Troy. Lit.
' holding fast; ' from ἔχειν, to hold.

Hedge; see **Haw**.

Heed, vb. (E.) M. E. *heden*. A. S. *hédan*,
pt. t. *hédde*. Formed as if from sb. *hód**,
care (not found) ; though we find the corresponding G. sb. *hut*, O. H. G. *huota*, care.
+ Du. *hoeden*, from *hoede*, care; G. *hüten*,
from *hut* (O. H. G. *huota*), care. Prob.
allied to **Hood**.

Heel (1), part of the foot. (E.) A. S.
héla, heel. + Du. *hiel*, Icel. *hæll*, Dan. *hæl*,
Swed. *häl*. Allied to L. *calx*, Lithuan.
kulnis, heel ; and to L. *-cellere*, in *per-cellere*,
to strike, drive.

Heel (2), to lean over, incline. (E.)
Corrupted from M. E. *helden*, *hilden*, to incline on one side. A. S. *heldan*, *hyldan*, to
tilt, incline ; cf. *niðer-heald*, bent downwards. + Icel. *halla* (for *halda*), to heel
over (as a ship), from *hallr* (for *haldr*),
sloping ; Dan. *helde*, to tilt, from *held*, a
slope ; Swed. *hälla*, to tilt.

Heft; see **Heave**.

Hegira. (Arab.) Arab. *hijrah*, separation ; esp. used of the flight of Mohammed from Mecca, on the night of Thursday,
July 15, 622 ; the era of the Hegira begins
on July 16. Cf. Arab. *hajr*, separation.

Heifer. (E.) M.E. *hayfare*, *hekfere*. A.S.
heáhfore, a heifer. – A. S. *heáh*, high, full-
grown ; *-fore*, cogn. with Gk. πόρις, a heifer.

Heigh-ho. (E.) An exclamation ; *heigh*,
a cry to call attention ; *ho*, an exclamation.

Height; see **High**.

Heinous. (F. – O. Low G.) M. E. *heinous*, *hainous*. – O. F. *hainos*, odious ;
formed with suffix *-os* (L. *-osus*) from *hair*,
to hate. From an O. Low G. form, such
as Goth. *hatjan*, to hate ; allied to **Hate**.

Heir. (F. – L.) M. E. *heire*, *heir*, also
eyr. – O. F. *heir*, *eir*. – L. *heres*, an heir,
allied to *herus*, a master. (√ GHAR.)
¶ The O. F. *heir* is either from L. nom.
heres, or for *herem*, a mistaken form of
acc. *heredem*. Der. *heir-loom*, where *loom*
signifies ' a piece of property,' but is the
same word as E. *loom*. See **Loom** (1).

hereditary, adj. (L.) L. *hereditarius*.

– L. *hereditare*, to inherit. – L. *heredi-*,
crude form of *heres*, an heir.

heritage. (F. – L.) O. F. *heritage*.
Formed, with suffix *-age* (= L. *-aticum*),
from O. F. *heriter*, to inherit. – L. *hereditare*, to inherit (which seems to have been
corrupted to *heritare**). See above.

inherit. (F. – L.) Coined from L. *in*,
in ; and O. F. *heriter* (above).

Heliacal, relating to the sun. (L. – Gk.)
Late L. *heliacus*. – Gk. ἡλιακός, belonging
to the sun. – Gk. ἥλιος, sun (see Curtius).

aphelion, the point in a planet's orbit
farthest from the sun. (Gk.) Coined from
Gk. ἀπ-, for ἀπό, from ; ἥλιος, the sun.

heliotrope, a flower. (F. – L. – Gk.)
F. *heliotrope*. – L. *heliotropium*. – Gk. ἡλιο-
τρόπιον, a heliotrope, lit. ' sun-turner; '
from its turning to the sun. – Gk. ἥλιο-s,
sun ; τροπ-, base allied to τρέπειν, to turn ;
see **Trope**.

perihelion, the point of a planet's
orbit nearest the sun. (Gk.) Gk. περί,
round, near ; ἥλιος, the sun.

Helix, a spiral figure. (L. – Gk.) L.
hĕlix, a spiral. – Gk. ἕλιξ, a spiral, a twist.
– Gk. ἑλίσσειν, to turn round. Allied to
Volute. (√ WAR.)

Hell. (E.) M. E. *helle*. A. S. *hel*, gen.
helle ; orig. ' that which hides,' from A. S.
helian, to hide, secondary verb formed
from *helan* (pt. t. *hæl*), to hide. + Du. *hel*,
Icel. *hel*, G. *hölle*, Goth. *halja*. Allied to
Cell, **Conceal**.

Hellebore. (F. – L. – Gk.) Also *ellebore*. – O. F. *ellebore*. – L. *helleborus*. – Gk.
ἑλλέβορος, the name of the plant.

Helm (1), an implement for steering a
ship. (E.) Orig. the tiller or handle.
A. S. *helma*. + Icel. *hjálm*, a rudder ; G.
helm, a handle. Allied to **Haulm**.

halberd, **halbort**, a kind of pole-axe.
(F. – M. H. G.) O. F. *halebarde*. – M. H. G.
helmbarte, later *helenbarte*, mod. G. *helle-
barte*, an axe with a long handle, from
M. H. G. *halm*, a helve (helm), or handle ;
though it seems to have been popularly
interpreted as an axe for splitting a *helm*,
i. e. helmet. β. The origin of O. H. G.
parta, G. *barte*, a broad axe, is obscure ;
see **Partisan** (2).

helve, a handle. (E.) M. E. *helue*
(= *helve*). A. S. *hielf*, also *helfe*, a handle.
+ O. Du. *helve*, handle, M. H. G. *halp*,
handle ; allied to **Helm** (1) above.

Helm (2), armour for the head. (E.)
M. E. *helm*. A. S. *helm* ; lit. ' a covering; '

from *helan*, to cover. **+** Du. *helm*; Icel. *hjálmr*, Dan. *hielm*, Swed. *hjelm*, G. *helm*, Goth. *hilms*, Russ. *shleme*, Lithuan. *szalmas*. (**√** KAR.) Der. *helm-et*, dimin. form. Allied to Hell.

Helminthology, history of worms. (Gk.) Coined from Gk. ἕλμινθο-, crude form of ἕλμινς, a worm; -λογία, a discourse, from λέγειν, to speak. The sb. ἕλμινς, also ἕλμις, means 'that which curls about;' allied to Helix.

Helot, a (Spartan) slave. (L. – Gk.) L. pl. *Helotes*, from Gk. εἵλωτες, pl. of εἵλως, a helot, bondsman; said to have meant an inhabitant of *Helos* (a town of Laconia), enslaved by the Spartans.

Help, sb. (E.) M. E. *helpen*, pt. t. *halp*, pp. *holpen*. A. S. *helpan*, pt. t. *healp*, pp. *holpen*. **+** Du. *helpen*, Icel. *hjálpa*, Dan. *hielpe*, Swed. *hjelpa*, Goth. *hilpan*, G. *helfen*. Allied to Skt. *kalpa*, able, able to protect, Lithuan. *szelpti*, to help. (**√** KARP.) Der. *help*, sb., A. S. *helpe*; *help-mate*, a mistaken use of *help meet* (Gen. ii. 18).

Helve; see Helm (1).

Hem (1), border. (E.) A. S. *hemm*, *hem*. Allied to G. *hamme*, a fence, hedge. (**√** KAM.) Der. *hem*, verb, to enclose within a border, hem in; cf. G. *hemmen*, to restrain, from *hamme*, a fence.

Hem (2), a slight cough to call attention. (E.) An imitative word; allied to Hum.

Hematite, an ore of iron. (L. **–** Gk.) Named from the red colour of the powder. **–** L. *hæmatites*. **–** Gk. αἱματίτης, blood-like. **–** Gk. αἱματ-, stem of αἷμα, blood.

hemorrhage, a great flow of blood. (F. **–** L. **–** Gk.) O. F. *hemorrhagie*. **–** L. *hæmorrhagia*. **–** Gk. αἱμορραγία, a violent bleeding. **–** Gk. αἷμο-, for αἷμα, blood; ραγ-, base of ῥήγνυμι, I burst, break; the lit. sense being a bursting out of blood.

hemorrhoids, **emerods**, painful bleeding tubercles on the anus. (F. – L. – Gk.) F. *hemorrhoïde*, sing., a flowing of blood. **–** L. *hæmorrhoides*, pl. of *hæmorrhois*. **–** Gk. αἱμορροΐδες, pl. of αἱμορροΐς, adj., liable to a flow of blood. – Gk. αἷμο-, put for αἷμα, blood; ῥέειν, to flow, cognate with Skt. *sru*, to flow; see Stream.

Hemi-, half. (Gk.) From a Lat. spelling of Gk. ἡμι-, half, cognate with L. *semi-*, half; see Semi-. Der. *hemi-sphere*, &c.

hemistich, a half-line in poetry. (L. **–** Gk.) L. *hemistichium*. **–** Gk. ἡμιστίχιον,

a half verse. **–** Gk. ἡμι-, half; στίχος, a row, verse.

megrim, a pain affecting one side of the head. (F. **–** L. **–** Gk.) F. *migraine*, 'the megrim;' Cot. **–** Low L. *hemigranea*, megrim. **–** Gk. ἡμικράνιον, half of the skull. **–** Gk. ἡμι-, half; κρανίον, cranium.

Hemlock. (E.) M. E. *hemlok*, *humlok*. A. S. *hemlic*, *hymlice*. The origin of *hem* is unknown; the second syllable is a weakened form of A. S. *léác*, a leek, plant; as in *gar-lic*, *char-lock*.

Hemorrhage, **Hemorrhoids**; see Hematite.

Hemp, a plant. (L. **–** Gk. **–** Skt.) M. E. *hemp* (short for *henep*). A. S. *henep*, *hænep*. Borrowed at a very early period from L. *cannabis*, so that the word suffered consonantal letter-change. **–** Gk. κάνναβις. Skt. *çana*, hemp (or rather, from an older form of this word). So also Du. *hennep*, Icel. *hampr*, Dan. *hamp*, Swed. *hampa*, G. *hanf*; all from L. *cannabis*.

Hen. (E.) A. S. *henn*, *hen*, *hæn*; a fem. form (by vowel-change) from A. S. *hana*, a cock, lit. 'a singer,' from his crowing; cf. L. *canere*, to sing. **+** Du. *hen*, fem. of *haan*, a cock; Icel. *hæna*, f. of *hani*; Dan. *höne*, f. of *hane*; Swed. *höna*, f. of *hane*; G. *henne*, f. of *hahn*. (**√** KAN.)

Hence; see He.

Henchman, a page, servant. (E.) Formerly *henseman*, *henshman*; cf. *Hinxman* as a proper name. Prob. for *hengest-man*, i. e. groom; from M. E. *hengest*, A. S. *hengest*, a horse. Cf. Du. and G. *hengst*, Dan. *hingst*, a horse, Icel. *hestr*, a horse. ¶ Or borrowed from Du. *hengst*.

Hendecagon; see Decade.

Hep, hip; see Hip (2).

Hepatic, relating to the liver. (F. **–** L. **–** Gk.) O. F. *hepatique*. **–** L. *hepaticus*. **–** Gk. ἡπατικός, belonging to the liver. **–** Gk. ἡπατ-, crude form of ἧπαρ, the liver. **+** L. *iecur*, Skt. *yakrit*, the liver. Der. *hepatica*, liver-wort, a flower.

Heptagon, a plane seven-sided figure. (Gk.) Lit. 'seven-angled.' **–** Gk. ἑπτά, seven; γωνία, an angle, allied to γόνυ, knee. See Seven and Knee.

hebdomadal, weekly. (L. **–** Gk.) L. *hebdomadalis*. **–** Gk. ἑβδομαδ-, stem of ἑβδομάς, a week. **–** Gk. ἑπτά, seven.

heptahedron, a solid seven-sided figure. (Gk.) From Gk. ἑπτά, seven; ἕδρα, a base, seat (allied to E. Sit).

heptarchy; see Arch-, *prefix*.

Her; see **He**.

Herald. (F.—O. H. G.) M. E. *herald.*
—O.F. *heralt* (Low L. *heraldus*). —O.H.G.
herolt (G. *herold*), a herald; also O.H.G.
Heriold, Hariold, as a proper name. Put
for *hari-wald,* i.e. army-strength, a name
for a warrior, esp. for an officer.—O. H. G.
hari, an army (G. *heer*) ; *wald, walt,*
strength (G. *gewalt*). The limitation of
this name to a herald seems to have been
due to confusion with O. H. G. *foraharo,*
a herald, from *forharen,* to proclaim (allied
to Gk. *κῆρυξ*).

Herb. (F.—L.) M. E. *herbe.*—F. *herbe.*
— L. *herba,* grass, fodder, herb; prob.
allied to O. L. *forbea,* Gk. *φορβή,* pasture,
Skt. *bharb,* to eat.

Herd (1), a flock. (E.) M. E. *heerde.*
A. S. *heord, herd, hyrd,* (1) care, custody,
(2) a herd, flock, (3) family. **+** Icel. *hjörð,*
Dan. *hiord,* Swed. *hjord,* G. *heerde,* Goth.
hairda.

herd (2), one who tends a herd. (E.)
Usually in comp. *shep-herd, cow-herd,* &c.
M. E. *herde.* A. S. *heorde, hirde,* keeper of
a herd; from A.S. *heord,* a flock. (The
final *-e* marks the agent). **+** Icel. *hirðir,*
Dan. *hyrde,* Swed. *herde,* G. *hirt,* Goth.
hairdeis ; all similarly derived.

Here; see **He**.

Hereditary; see **Heir**.

Heresy. (F.—L.—Gk.) M. E. *heresye.*
—O.F. *heresie.*—L. *hæresis.*—Gk. *αἵρεσις,*
a taking, choice, sect, heresy.—Gk. *αἱρεῖν,*
to take. Der. *heretic,* L. *hæreticus,* Gk.
αἱρετικός, able to choose, heretical (from
the same verb).

aphæresis, the taking away of a letter
or syllable from the beginning of a word.
(Gk.) Gk. *ἀφαίρεσις,* a taking away.—Gk.
ἀφ-, for *ἀπό,* away; *αἵρεσις,* a taking (above).

diæresis, a mark (") of separation.
(L. — Gk.) L. *diæresis.*—Gk. *διαίρεσις,* a
dividing.—Gk. *δι-ά,* apart; *αἵρεσις,* a taking
(above).

synæresis, the coalescence of two
vowels into a diphthong. (L. — Gk.) L.
synæresis. — Gk. *συναίρεσις,* a taking together.—Gk. *σύν,* together; *αἵρεσις,* a taking.

Heriot, a tribute paid to the lord of a
manor on the decease of a tenant. (E.)
A. S. *heregeatu,* lit. military apparel;
hence, equipments which, after the death
of a vassal, escheated to his lord; afterwards extended to include horses, &c.—
A. S. *here,* an army; *geatu, geatwe,* apparel,
adornment. See **Harry.**

Heritage; see **Heir**.

Hermaphrodite, an animal or plant of
both sexes. (L.—Gk.) L. *hermaphroditus.*
— Gk. *ἑρμαφρόδιτος* ; coined from *Ἑρμῆς.*
Mercury (representing the male) and
Ἀφροδίτη, Venus (representing the female
principle).

hermeneutic, explanatory. (Gk.) Gk.
ἑρμηνευτικός, skilled in interpreting.—Gk.
ἑρμηνευτής, an interpreter; also *ἑρμηνεύς,*
the same. Supposed to be from *Ἑρμῆς,*
Mercury, the tutelary god of skill.

hermetic. (Gk.) Low L. *hermeticus,* relating to alchemy ; coined from *Hermes,*
from the notion that the great secrets of
alchemy were discovered by *Hermes Trisme-
gistus.*—Gk. *Ἑρμῆς,* Mercury. **¶** *Hermetically* was a term in alchemy ; a glass bottle
was *hermetically* sealed when the orifice
was fused and then closed against any
admission of air.

Hermit. (F.—L.—Gk.) [M. E. *here-
mite,* directly from L. *heremita.*]—F. *her-
mite.*—Low L. *heremita,* more commonly
eremita. — Gk. *ἐρημίτης,* a dweller in a
desert.—Gk. *ἐρημία,* a desert.—Gk. *ἐρῆμος,*
deserted, desolate. Der. *hermit-age.*

Hern; see **Heron**.

Hernia. (L.) L. *hernia,* a kind of
rupture.

Hero. (F.—L.—Gk.) O.F. *heroë.*—L.
heroëm, acc. of *heros,* a hero.—Gk. *ἥρως,* a
hero, demi-god. **+** Skt. *vira,* a hero; L.
uir ; A. S. *wer.* Allied to **Virile.** Der.
hero-ic, O. F. *heroïque,* L. *heroïcus.*

heroine. (F.—L.—Gk.) F. *heroïne.*
L. *heroïne.*—Gk. *ἡρωΐνη,* fem. of *ἥρως,* a
hero.

Heron, Hern, a bird. (F.—O. H. G.)
M. E. *heroun, hairon, hern.*—O. F. *hairon*
(F. *héron,* Ital. *aghirone*). — O. H. G.
heigir, heiger, a heron; with suffixed *-on*
(Ital. *-one*). Prob. named from its harsh
voice; cf. G. *häher,* a jack-daw (lit.
'laugher'), prov. E. *heighaw,* a wood-
pecker, Skt. *kakk,* to laugh. (√ KAK.)
+ Swed. *häger,* Icel. *hegri,* Dan. *heire,* a
heron.

heronshaw, hernshaw, a young
heron ; also a heronry. (F.—O. H. G.)
1. Spenser has *herneshaw,* a heron; this is
M.E. *heronsewe,* a young heron *(still
called *heronsew* in the North). It answers
to an O. F. *herounceau*,* later form of
herounçel, a young heron (Liber Custumarum, p. 304), dim. of *hairon* ; cf.
lionçeau, lioncel, a young lion. The

usual form is F. *héronneau*, O. F. *hairon-neau*. 2. But *heronshaw*, a heronry, is compounded of *heron*, a heron, and *shaw*, a wood; Cotgrave has ' *haironniere*, a heron's neast, a herneshaw, or shaw of wood wherein herons breed.'

Herring, a fish. (E.) M. E. *hering*. A. S. *hærincg*, *hæring*. Prob. so named from appearing in large shoals; from A. S. *here*, a host, army; see **Harry**. + Du. *haring*, G. *häring*.

Hesitate. (L.) From pp. of L. *hæsitare*, to stick fast; intensive form of *hærere*, to stick. + Lithuan. *gaiszti*, to tarry. (√ GHAIS.)

adhere. (L.) L. *ad-hærere*, to stick to.

cohere. (L.) L. *co-hærere*, to stick together (pp. *cohæsus*). Der. *cohes-ion*, *cohes-ive*.

inherent. (L.) L. *inhærent-*, stem of pres. pt. of *in-hærere*, to stick in. Hence *inhere*, as a verb.

Hest, a command. (E.) M. E. *hest*, the final *t* being excrescent, as in *whils-t*, *amongs-t*, &c. A. S. *hǽs*, a command. – A. S. *hátan*, to command. So also Icel. *heit*, a vow, from *heita*, to call, promise; O. H. G. *heiz* (G. *geheiss*), a command, from *heizan* (G. *heissen*), to call, bid, command. Cf. Goth. *haitan*, to call, name.

behest. (E.) M. E. *behest*. From A. S. *behǽs*, a command (see above); formed from *hǽs* by help of the prefix *be-* (by).

hight, was or is called. (E.) The only E. verb with a *passive* sense; *he hight* = he was named. M. E. *highte*; also *hatte*, *hette*. A. S. *hátte*, I am called, I was called; pt. t. of A. S. *hátan* (1) to call (2) to be called, be named. So also G. *ich heisse*, I am named; from *heissen*, to call, bid. β. Best explained from Goth. *haitan*, to call, pt. t. (active) *haihait*, pres. tense (passive) *haitada*, I am called; as in ' Thomas, saei *haitada* Didymus' = Thomas, who is called Didymus, John xi. 6.

Heteroclite, irregularly inflected. (L. – Gk.) L. *heteroclitus*. – Gk. ἑτερόκλιτος, otherwise (i.e. irregularly) inflected. – Gk. ἕτερο-s, another; -κλιτος, formed from κλίνειν, to lean (hence, to vary as a case -does).

heterodox, of strange opinion, heretical. (Gk.) Gk. ἕτερο-s, another; δόξ-α, opinion, from δοκεῖν, to think.

heterogeneous, dissimilar in kind. (Gk.) Gk. ἕτερο-s, another; γέν-os, kind, kin, sort.

Hew. (E.) M. E. *hewen*. A. S. *heáwan*, to cut. + Du. *houwen*, Icel. *höggva*, Swed. *hugga*, Dan. *hugge*, G. *hauen*; Russ. *kovate*, to hammer, forge. Allied to L. *cudere*, to beat. (√ KU.)

hoe. (F. – G.) Formerly *how*. – F. *houe*, a hoe. – O. H. G. *houwa* (G. *haue*), a hoe, lit. a hewer. – O. H. G. *houwan*, to hew (above).

Hexagon, a plane six-sided figure. (L. – Gk.) L. *hexagonum*. – Gk. ἑξάγωνος, six-cornered. – Gk. ἕξ, six; γωνία, an angle, from γόνυ, a knee.

hexameter. (L. – Gk.) L. *hexameter*. – Gk. ἑξάμετρος, orig. an adj., i. e. having six measures or feet. – Gk. ἕξ, six; μέτρον, a measure, metre.

Hey, interj. (E.) M. E. *hei*, *hay*; a natural exclamation. + G. and Du. *hei*.

heyday (1), interj. (G. *or* Du.) Also *heyda* (Ben Jonson). Borrowed either from G. *heida*, hey there! hallo! or from Du. *hei daar*, hey there! The G. *da*, and Du. *daar*, both mean ' there.'

Heyday (2), frolicsome wildness; see **High**.

Hiatus, a gap. (L.) L. *hiatus*, a gap; from pp. of *hiare*, to gape. Allied to **Yawn** and **Chasm**.

Hibernal, wintry. (F. – L.) F. *hibernal*. – L. *hibernalis*, wintry. – L. *hibernus*, wintry; allied to *hiems*, winter. Also to Gk. χι-ών, snow, Skt. *hi-ma*, frost. (√ GHI.) Der. *hibern-ate*.

Hiccough, Hiccup, Hicket, a spasmodic inspiration, with closing of the glottis, causing a slight sound. (E.) The spelling *hiccough* seems to be due to a popular etymology from *cough*, certainly wrong; no one ever so pronounces the word. Properly *hiccup*, or, in old books *hicket* and *hickock*, which are still better forms. *Hick-et*, *hick-ock*, are diminutives of *hick* or *hik*, a catch in the voice, imitative of the sound. Cf. ' a *hacking* cough; ' and see **Hitch**. + Du. *hik*, the hiccough, *hikken*, to hiccough; Dan. *hikke*, sb. and vb.; Swed. *hicka*, sb. and vb.; Bret. *hik*, *hak*, a hiccough; W. *ig*, a sob, *igio*, to sob. And cf. **Chincough**.

Hickory, a. N. American tree; origin unknown.

Hidalgo, a Span. nobleman of the lowest class. (Span. – L.) Span. *hidalgo*; an ironical name, lit. ' son of something,' not a nobody. – Span. *hijo*, son; *de*, of; *algo*, something. – L. *filium*, acc. of *filius*, son (whence O. Span. *figo*, later *hijo*) ; *de*, of ; *aliquod*, something.

Hide (1), to cover. (E.) M. E. *hiden*, *huden*. A. S. *hýdan*. + Gk. κεύθειν, to hide. (√SKU.)

hide (2), a skin. (E.) M. E. *hide*, *hude*. A. S. *hýd*, the skin, i. e. ' cover ; ' allied to A. S. *hýdan* (above). + Du. *huid*, Icel. *húð*, Dan. Swed. *hud*, O. H. G. *hût*, G. *haut*, L. *cutis*, Gk. κύτος, σκύτος, skin, hide. (√SKU.)

hide (3), to flog. (E.) Colloquial ; to ' skin' by flogging. So also Icel. *hýða*, to flog, from *húð*, skin.

Hide (4), a measure of land. (E.) Estimated at 120 to 100 acres, and less ; (Low L. *hida*.) A. S. *híd*, a contracted form ; the full form is *hígid*. *Hígid* and *hiwisc* were used in the same sense, to mean enough land for one family or household. They are probably closely allied words, and therefore allied to *hind* (2) ; for *hiwisc* is merely the adj. formed from *hiw-a*, a domestic, one of a household ; see **Hind** (2). ¶ Not connected with **Hide** (1).

Hideous, ugly. (F. – L. ?) M. E. *hidous*.– O. F. *hidos*, *hidus*, later *hideux*, hideous ; the earliest form is *hisdos*. The prob. original is L. *hispidosus*, roughish ; from *hispidus*, rough, shaggy.

Hie, to hasten. (E.) M. E. *hien*, *hyen*, *hizen*. A. S. *higian*, to hasten. Allied to Gk. κίειν, to go, L. *ciere*, to summon ; see **Cite**. (√KI.)

Hierarchy ; see **Arch-**, prefix.

Hieroglyphic. (L. – Gk.) L. *hieroglyphicus*, symbolical. – Gk. ἱερογλυφικός, relating to sacred writings. – Gk. ἱερό-s, sacred ; γλύφειν, to hollow out, engrave, incise. See **Glyptic**.

hierophant, a priest. (Gk.) Gk. ἱεροφάντης, teaching the rites of worship. – Gk. – ἱερό-s, sacred ; φαίνειν, to shew, explain.

Higgle ; see **Haggle** (2).

High (E.) M. E. *heigh*, *hey*, *hy*. A. S. *heáh*, *héh*. + Du. *hoog*, Icel. *hár*, Swed. *hög*, Dan. *höi*, G. *hauhs*, G. *hoch*. The orig. sense is bent, hence rounded, noblike, as a mound or hill. Cf. G. *hügel*, a bunch, knob, hillock, Skt. *kucha*, the female breast. (√KUK.)

height. (E.) A corruption of *highth* (Milton) ; but we find M. E. *highte* as well as *he3þe* (*heghthe*). A.S. *heáh$u*, *héh$u*, height.– A. S. *heáh*, *héh*, high (above). + Du. *hoogte*, Icel. *hæð*, Swed. *höjd*, Dan. *höide*, Goth. *hauhitha*.

heyday (2), frolicsome wildness. (E.) The ' *heyday* of youth' means the ' *high day* of youth.' The spelling *hey* is a preservation of M. E. *hey*, the usual spelling of *high* in the 14th century.

highland. (E.) From *high* and *land* ; cf. *up-land*, *low-land*.

how (2), a hill. (Scand.) M. E. *hogh*. Icel. *haugr*, a hill ; Swed. *hög*, a mound ; Dan. *höi*, a hill.– Icel. *hár*, Swed. *hög*, Dan. *höi*, high ; see **High**.

Hight ; see **Hest**.

Hilarity, mirth. (F. – L. – Gk.) F. *hilarité*. – L. acc. *hilaritatem* ; from *hilaris*, adj. cheerful, also spelt *hilarus*. – Gk. ἱλαρός, cheerful. ¶ *Hilary* Term is so called from the festival of St. Hilary (L. *Hilaris*), Jan. 13.

exhilarate, to cheer. (L.–Gk. ; *with* L. *prefix*.) From pp. of L. *ex-hilarare*, to gladden greatly. – L. *ex*, very ; *hilaris*, glad (above).

Hilding ; see **Hind** (3).

Hill. (E.) M. E. *hil*, *hul*. A. S. *hyll*. + O. Du. *hil*; L. *collis*, a hill ; Lithuan. *kalnas*, a hill. Allied to **Culminate**. Der. *down-hill*, *up-hill*.

Hilt, sword-handle. (E.) A. S. *hilt*. + Icel. *hjalt*, O. H. G. *helza*. ¶ *Not* allied to *hold*.

Him ; see **He**.

Hin, a liquid measure. (Heb.) Heb. *hín*, a hin ; said to be of Egyptian origin.

Hind (1), female of the stag. (E.) A. S. *hind*. + Du. *hinde* ; Icel. Dan. and Swed. *hind*, M. H. G. *hinde*, O. H. G. *hintâ*, a doe. Perhaps ' that which is caught by hunting ; ' allied to **Hand**.

Hind (2), a peasant ; see **Hive**.

Hind (3), adj. in the rear. (E.) We now say ' *hind* feet ; ' but the older form is ' *hinder* feet.' We even find M. E. *hynderere* (as if hinder-er).– A. S. *hindan*, adv. at the back of, *hinder*, adv. backwards. + Goth. *hindar*, prep. behind ; *hindana*, beyond ; G. *hinter*, prep. behind, *hinten*, adv. behind. Extended from A. S. *hine*, hence ; from *hi-*, base of *he* ; see **He**.

behind. (E.) A. S. *behindan*, adv. and prep., after. – A. S. *be-*, prefix (E. *by*) ; *hindan*, adv. (above).

hilding, a base wretch. (E.) Short for prov. E. *hilderling* or *hinderling*, a wretch. From M. E. *hinderling*, base. From A.S. *hinder*, adv., backwards, with suffix *-l-ing*.

hinder. (E.) M. E. *hindren.* A. S. *hindrian,* to put behind, keep back. — A. S. *hinder, hindan* (above). Der. *hindr-ance* (for *hinder-ance*).

hindmost. (E.) Corruption of *hind-mest,* by confusion with *most. Hindm-est* is formed with suffix *-est* from A.S. *hindema,* hindmost, itself a superl. form with suffix *-ma* (as in L. *opti-mus*). **+** Goth. *hindu-mists,* hindmost (= *hindu-m-ists,* with double superl. suffix).

Hinge; see Hang.

Hint; see Hunt.

Hip (1), the haunch. (E.) M. E. *hupe.* A. S. *hype.* **+** Du. *heup,* Icel. *huppr,* Dan. *hofte,* Swed. *höft,* Goth. *hups,* G. *hüfte,* O. H. G. *huf.* Orig. 'a bend' or 'a hump;' cf. Gk. κυφός, bent, κῦφος, a hump, κύπτειν, to bend. (√KUP.) Allied to Heap.

Hip (2), **Hep,** fruit of the dog-rose. (E.) M. E. *hepe.* A. S. *heópe,* a hip; *heópbrymel,* a hip-bramble. **+** M. II. G. *hiefe,* O. H. G. *hiufo,* a bramble-bush.

Hippish. (Gk.) Short for *hypochondriacal,* adj. of **Hypochondria,** q. v. Hence *hippish = hyp-ish.* The contraction was prob. suggested by *hipped,* foiled, which may well have been due to the phr. 'to have on the *hip,*' Merch. Ven. i. 3. 47, iv. 1. 334.

Hippopotamus. (L. — Gk.) L. *hippopotamus.* — Gk. ἱπποπόταμος, the river-horse of Egypt. — Gk. ἵππο-s, horse; ποταμό-s, river. Gk. ἵππος is cognate with L. *equus;* see Equine. ποταμός is fresh water, allied to Potable.

Hire, sb. (E.) M. E. *hire.* A. S. *hýr,* hire, wages. **+** Du. *huur,* Swed. *hyra,* Dan. *hyre,* G. *heuer,* hire, rent.

Hirsute; see Horrid.

His; see He.

Hiss. (E.) M. E. *hissen, hisshen.* A. S. *hysian,* to hiss. **+** O. Du. *hisschen.* An imitative word.

hist, an interjection enjoining silence. (E.) A mere variant of *hush* or *hiss.* Cf. Dan. *hys,* silence! *hysse,* to hush. Milton has *hist =* silenced, hushed, Il Pens. 55.

hush. (E.) M. E. *hushen,* to make silent; whence pp. *husht,* silenced. A purely imitative word, allied to *hiss.*

whist, a game requiring silence. (E.) From the use of the word *whist* to enjoin silence; Chaucer has *whist,* 'silenced' or 'quiet'; tr. of Boethius, b. ii. met. 5, l. 1341. Also called *whisk;* from Swed. *hviska,* to whisper; see Whisper.

Histology, the science treating of the structure of tissues of plants, &c. (Gk.) Gk. ἱστό-s, a web (hence tissue); -λογια, discourse, from λέγειν, to speak. Gk. ἱστό-s (also a mast) is allied to ἵστημι, to set, place. (√STA.)

History. (L. — Gk.) M. E. *historie.* — L. *historia.* — Gk. ἱστορία, a learning by enquiry, information. — Gk. ἱστορ-, stem of ἵστωρ, ἴστωρ, knowing; put for ἰδ-τωρ*. — Gk. ἰδ-, base of εἰδέναι, to know. (√WID.) Allied to Wit.

story (1). (F. — L. — Gk.) M. E. *storie.* — O. F. *estoire, estore* (and prob. *estorie**), a history, tale. — L. *historia* (above).

Histrionical, relating to the stage. (L.) From L. *histrionicus,* relating to an actor. L. *histrioni-,* crude form of *histrio,* an actor. Prob. 'one who made others laugh;' cf. Skt. *has,* to laugh, *hasra,* a fool.

Hit, to light upon, strike, attain to. (Scand.) M. E. *hitten.* — Icel. *hitta,* to hit upon; Dan. *hitte.* Clearly assimilated from *hinta**, cognate with Goth. *hinthan,* to catch, as in *frahinthan,* to seize. See Hunt.

Hitch, to move by jerks, catch slightly. (E.) M. E. *hicchen,* to move, remove. Cf. Lowl. Sc. *hatch, hotch,* to move by jerks. A weakened form from a base HIK, expressing convulsive motion, as in *hiccough.* ¶ Not allied to *hook.*

Hithe, Hythe, a small haven. (E.) M. E. *hithe.* A. S. *hýð,* a haven. Lit. 'a shelter;' allied to Hide (1) and Hide (2). (√SKU.)

Hither; see He.

Hive, a house for bees. (E.) A.S. *hýf, hýfe,* earliest form *hýfi,* a hive. Orig. 'a cup'; co-radicate with L. *cupa;* see Cup. ¶ Not allied to A.S. *híwan,* domestics (as said in the first edition).

hind (2), a peasant. (E.) The final *d* is excrescent. M. E. *hine,* a domestic. A. S. *hína**, a domestic, unauthenticated as a nominative, and really a gen. pl., so that *hína* stands for *hína man* = a man of the domestics; cf. *hína ealdor* = elder of the domestics, a master of a household. *Hína = híwna,* gen. pl. of *híwan,* domestics (above).

Ho, Hoa, a call to excite attention. (E.) A natural exclamation. Cf. Icel. *hó!* ho! *hóa,* to shout out ho!

Hoar, white. (E.) M. E. *hoor.* A. S. *hár.* **+** Icel. *hárr,* hoar. Cf. Skt. *çára,* variegated in colour, also used of hair mixed with gray and white. **Der.** *hoar-y,* a later form; *hoar-frost.*

hoarhound, horehound, a plant. (E.) The true *hoarhound* is the white, *Marrubium vulgare.* The final *d* is excrescent. A.S. *hárhúne,* also called simply *húne.* — A.S. *hár,* hoar; *húne,* i.e. strongly scented; cf. L. *cunila,* Gk. κονίλη, a species of origanum, Skt. *knúy,* to stink.

Hoard; see **House.**

Hoarding, a kind of fence; see **Hurdle.**

Hoarhound; see **Hoar.**

Hoarse, having a rough, harsh voice. (E.) The *r* is intrusive, but sometimes occurs in M.E. *hors,* properly *hoos,* hoarse. A.S. *hás,* hoarse. + Icel. *háss,* Dan. *hæs,* Swed. *hes,* Du. *heesch,* G. *heiser.*

Hoary; see **Hoar.**

Hoax; see **Hocus.**

Hob (1), Hub, the nave of a wheel, part of a grate. (E.) The true sense is 'projection;' the *hob* of a fire-place was orig. 'the raised stone on either side of the hearth between which the embers were confined' (Webster). Closely related to **Hump,** which is merely the nasalised form of it. **Der.** *hob-nail,* a nail with a projecting head.

Hob (2), a clown, rustic, a fairy. (F. — O.H.G.) 'Elves, *hobs,* and fairies;' Beaumont and Fletcher, Mons. Thomas, iv. 6. *Hob* was a common personal name, a corruption of *Robin* (like *Hodge* from *Roger*). The name *Robin* is F., and is a mere corruption of *Robert,* a name of O.H.G. origin. **Der.** *hob-goblin;* see **Goblin.**

Hobble; see **Hop (1).**

Hobby (1), an ambling nag; see **Hop (1).**

Hobby (2), a kind of falcon; see **Hop (1).**

Hobgoblin; see **Hob (2).**

Hobnail; see **Hob (1).**

Hobnob, Habnab, with free leave, at random. (E.) Compounded of *hab* and *nab,* to have or not to have, hence applied to taking a thing or leaving it, implying free choice, and hence a familiar invitation to drink, as in 'to *hob-nob* together.' *Hab* is from A.S. *hæbban,* to have; *nab* is from A.S. *næbban,* put for *ne hæbban,* not to have; see **Have.**

Hock (1); see **Hough.**

Hock (2), a wine. (G.) For *Hochheim,* the name of a place in Germany, on the river Main, whence the wine comes. It means 'high home.'

Hockey, a game; see **Hook.**

Hocus-pocus, a juggler's trick, a juggler. (Low L.) As far as it can be said to belong to any language, it is a sort of Latin, having the L. termination *-us.* But it is merely an invented term, used by jugglers in performing tricks; see Todd's Johnson.

hoax. (Low L.) Short for *hocus,* i.e. to juggle, cheat.

Hod, a kind of trough for carrying bricks. (E.) A prov. E. form of *hold;* see **Hold.** In Linc. and York. *hod* means 'hold' or 'receptacle'; as in (Whitby) *powder-hod,* powder-flask; *cannle-hod,* candlestick. ¶ Not from F. *hotte,* as said.

Hodge-podge; see **Hotchpot.**

Hoe; see **Hew.**

Hog. (E.) M.E. *hogge,* 'maialis, est enim porcus carens testiculis'; Cathol. Anglic. p. 187. From the verb *hack* (Scotch *hag*), to cut. Cf. *hog-sheep,* one clipped the first year.

Hogshead. (O. Du.) More correctly, *ox-head.* An adaptation of O. Du. *okshoofd,* *oxhoofd,* a hogshead; of which, however, the lit. sense is *ox-head.* So also Dan. *oxhoved,* O. Swed. *oxhufwud,* an ox-head, also a hogshead. No doubt the cask was at first named from the device or brand of an 'ox-head' upon it.

Hoiden, Hoyden; see **Heath.**

Hoist, to heave. (O. Du.) The final *t* is due to the pp. *hoist,* used for *hoised.* The verb is really *hoise.* (Cf. *graft* for *graff.*) — O. Du. *hyssen;* Du. *hijsschen,* to hoise (*y* sounded as E. long *i*). + Dan. *heise, hisse;* Swed. *hissa,* to hoist (whence F. *hisser*). ¶ *Not* allied to F. *hausser,* to elevate.

Hold (1), to keep. (E.) A.S. *healdan.* + Du. *houden,* Icel. *halda,* Swed. *hálla,* Dan. *holde,* Goth. *haldan,* G. *halten.* **Der.** *hold,* sb.; also *be-hold,* with prefix *be-* (E. *by*); *up-hold.*

upholsterer. (E.) Lengthened from *upholster,* put for *uphold-ster,* another form of *upholder,* which was formerly used of a dealer in furniture, lit. one who *holds up* to sale.

Hold (2), the 'hold' of a ship; see **Hole.**

Hole. (E.) M.E. *hole, hol.* A.S. *hol,* a cave. + Du. *hol,* Icel. *hol,* Dan. *hul,* Swed. *hål,* G. *hohl.* Cf. Goth. *us-hulon,* to hollow out. β. Prob. A.S. *hol* is from *hol-en*, pp. of str. vb. *helan*, to cover; see **Hell**. Not allied to Gk. κοῖλος, hollow.

hold (2), the cavity of a ship. (Du.) Put for *hole*, with excrescent *d*, due to confusion with the verb to *hold*. — Du. *hol*, a hole, cave, esp. used of the hold of a ship (Sewel).

hollow. (E.) M. E. *holwe*, adj. A. S. *holh*, sb. a hollow place, also spelt *holg*. Extended from A. S. *hol*, a hole, cave.

Holibut, Holiday; see **Hale** (1).

Holla, Hallo, stop! wait! (F.) Not the same word as *halloo*, to shout; but differently used in old authors. See Oth. i. 2. 56; As You Like It, iii. 2. 257.—F. *holà*, 'an interjection, hoe there;' Cot.—F. *ho*, interj.; and *là*, there (=L. *illac*). ¶ The form *hallo* is due to a confusion with *halloo*.

Holland, Dutch linen. (Du.) From *Holland*, the name of the country. So also *hollands*, spirits from Holland.

Hollow; see **Hole**.

Holly. (E.) M. E. *holin*; so that an *n* has been dropped. A. S. *holen*, *holegn*, holly. ✛ W. *celyn*, Corn. *celin*, Bret. *kelen*, Gael. *cuilionn*, Irish *cuileann*, holly. Cf. also Du. *hulst*, G. *hülse*, holly, O. H. G. *húlis* (whence F. *houx*).

holm-oak, the evergreen oak. (E.) Here *holm* is a contraction of M. E. *holin*, à holly. '*Holme*, or holy [holly];' Prompt. Parv.; and see Way's note. The *Quercus ilex* is a most variable plant; the leaves are sometimes as prickly as a holly.

Hollyhock; see **Hale** (1).

Holm, an islet in a river, flat land by a river. (E.) M. E. *holm*. A. S. *holm*, orig. a 'mound.'✛Icel. *hólmr*, *hólmi*, *holmr*, an islet, flat meadow; Dan. *holm*, Swed. *holme*, G. *holm*, hill, island, Russ. *kholm'*, a hill, L. *culmen*, hill-top. Allied to **Culminate**.

Holm-oak; see **Holly**.

Holocaust; see **Caustic**.

Holster, a leathern case for a pistol. (Du.) Du. *holster*; lit. a cover. Allied to A. S. *heolstor*, a case, covering, Icel. *hulstr*, sheath, Goth. *hulistr*, a veil. The verb is Du. *hullen*, Icel. *hylja*, Goth. *huljan*, to cover; from the strong verb seen in A.S. *helan* (pp. *holen*), to cover. (✓KAL, KAR.) ¶ The suffix -*ster*= -*s-ter*, a double suffix; see **Spinster**.

holt, a wood. (E.) M. E. and A.S. *holt*. ✛ Du. *hout*, O. Du. *holt*; Icel. *holt*, G. *holz*; so also W. *celt*, a covert, from *celu*, to hide. Orig. 'covert;' from the same root as the above.

housings, trappings of a horse. (F.— Teut.) The old form was *houss*; -*ings* has been added.—F. *housse*, a coverlet, 'a foot-cloth for a horse;' Cot. Low L. *hucia*, *husia*, *hussia*, the same; also *hulcia*, *hul-citum*.—Du. *hulse*, a husk, shell (hence, a cover, as in Du. *hulsel*, a woman's head-attire). From the verb seen in O. H. G. and Du. *hullen*, to cover; see **Holster** above.

hull (1), husk. (E.) M. E. *hule*. A. S. *hulu*, a husk, lit. 'covering;' from the same root as **Holster**.

hull (2), body of a ship. (E.) Lit. 'the shell' of a ship, and the same word as the above. Or prob. Dutch; from Du. *hol*, hold. '*Het* hol *van een schip*, the ship's hold or hull'; Sewel. See **Hold** (2).

husk, shell. (E.) M. E. *huske*. This word has lost an *l*, preserved in the cognate languages. The A.S. has only the allied word *hulc*, a hut. ✛ Du. *hulse*, a husk; Swed. *hylsa*; M. H. G. *hulsche*, G. *hülse*. From the verb seen in Du. *hullen*, Goth. *huljan*, to cover; see **Holster**.

Holy; see **Hale** (1).

Homage; see **Human**.

Home. (E.) M. E. *hoom*. A. S. *hám*. ✛ Du. *heim*; Icel. *heimr*, a village; Dan. *hiem*, Swed. *hem*, G. *heim*; Goth. *haims*, a village; Lithuan. *kèmas*, a village, Gk. κώμη, a village. (✓KI.)

hamlet. (F.—O. Low G.) M. E. *hame-let*, dimin. of O. F. *hamel* (F. *hameau*), a hamlet. Formed, with dimin. suffix -*el*, from O. Fries. *ham*, a home, dwelling.

Homer, a large measure. (Heb.) Heb. *chómer*, a homer, also a mound (with initial *cheth*).—Heb. root *chámar*, to undulate, surge up.

Homicide; see **Human**.

Homily; see **Homogeneous**.

Hominy, maize prepared for food. (W. Indian.) W. Indian *auhúminea*, parched corn.

Hommock; see **Hump**.

Homœopathy; see **Homogeneous**.

Homogeneous, of the same kind throughout. (Gk.) Englished from Gk. ὁμογενής, of the same race.—Gk. ὁμο-s, same (cognate with E. **Same**), and γένος, a race (cognate with E. **Kin**). So also *homo-logous*, corresponding, from λόγος, a saying, λέγειν, to say; *hom-onymous*, like in sound, from ὄνυμα, a name.

homily. (L.—Gk.) L. *homilia*.—Gk. ὁμιλία, a living together; also converse, instruction, homily. — Gk. ὕμιλος, a throng, concourse. — Gk. ὁμ-ός, like, same, together, cógnate with E. **Same**; and ἴλη, εἴλη, a crowd, from εἴλειν, to compress, shut in. (√WAR.)

homœopathy. (Gk.) Englished from Gk. ὁμοιοπάθεια, likeness in feeling or condition. — Gk. ὁμοιο-s, like; παθεῖν, aorist infin. of πάσχειν, to suffer. See **Same** and **Pathos**. And see **Homily**.

Hone. (E.) A.S. hán, a hone, (with change from á to long o, as in bán, bone). + Icel. hein, Swed. hen; Skt. çána, a grind-stone, from ço, to sharpen; Gk. κῶνος, a cone, peak. See **Cone**.

Honest; see **Honour**.

Honey. (E.) M.E. huni. A.S. hunig. + Du. honig, Icel. hunang, Dan. honning, Swed. honing, G. honig. Perhaps orig. 'grain-like,' or like broken rice; cf. Skt. kana, grain, broken rice.

honeycomb. (E.) A.S. hunigcamb, a honey-comb; where comb is the usual E. word, though the likeness to a comb is rather fanciful.

honeysuckle. (E.) Lye gives A.S. hunigsucle, unauthorised; but we find A.S. hunigsúge, privet, similarly named. From A.S. súgan, to suck.

Honour. (F.—L.) O.F. honur.—L. honōrem, acc. of honor, better honos, honour.

honest. (F.—L.) O.F. honeste (F. honnête).—L. honestus, honourable; put for honas-tus*, from honas*, orig. form of honos, honour.

Hood, covering. (E.) A.S. hód.+Du. hoed, G. hut, O.H.G. huat, hót, a hat. Cf. Gk. κοτύλη, a hollow vessel. (√KAT.) Allied to **Cotyledon**.

hoodwink. (E.) To make one wink or close his eyes, by covering him with a hood.

-hood, -head, suffix. (E.) A.S. hád, state, quality; cognate with Goth. haidus, manner, way.

Hoof. (E.) M.E. hoof, huf; pl. hoves. A.S. hóf. + Du. hoef, Icel. hófr, Dan. hov, Swed. hof, G. huf, Russ kopuito, Skt. çapha.

Hook. (E.) M.E. hok. A.S. hóc. + Du. haak, Icel. haki, Dan. hage, Swed. hake, G. haken. Allied to Gk. κύκλος, a circle, Skt. kuch, to bend. And see **Hatch** (1).

hackle (2), any flimsy substance unspun, as raw silk. (Du.) So named from its appearance, as if it has been hackled; see **heckle** (below).

hake, a fish. (Scand.) Norw. hakefisk, lit. 'hook-fish;' from the hooked under-jaw.

heckle, hackle, hatchel, an instrument for dressing flax or hemp. (Du.) Du. hekel, a heckle; dimin. of haak, a hook (above). + Dan. hegle, from hage; Swed. häckla, from hake; G. hechel, the same as häkel, a little hook, dimin. of haken, a hook.

hockey, a game. (E.) Also called hookey, because played with a hooked stick.

huckle-bone, the hip-bone. (E.) Huckle is the dimin. of prov. E. huck, a hook. A huckle is a 'small joint.' Cf. Skt. kuch, to bend.

Hookah, Hooka. (Arab.) Arab. huq-qa, a casket; also, a pipe for smoking.

Hoop (1), a pliant strip of wood bent into a band. (E.) M.E. hoop, hope. A.S. hóp. + Du. hoep. Cf. also Icel. hóp, a bay, from its circular form, prov. E. hope, (1) a hollow, (2) a mound, according as the curvature is concave or convex. Cf. Skt. chápa, a bow, Gk. κάμπτειν, to bend. Allied to **Hoop** (1), **Hump**.

Hoop (2), **Whoop,** to call out, shout. (F.—Teut.) M.E. houpen, to shout. — O.F. houper, 'to hoop unto;' Cot. Of Teut. origin; cf. Goth. hwopjan, to boast.

hooping-cough, a cough accompanied by a hoop or convulsive noisy catch in the breath. (Formerly called chincough.)

Hoopoe, the name of a bird. (L.) L. upupa, a hoopoe; the initial h is due to the F. huppe, also derived from upupa.+ Gk. ἔποψ, a hoopoe. Of imitative origin. ¶ The F. huppe, a tuft of feathers, is from huppe, a hoopoe (from its tufted head); not vice versâ.

Hoot. (Scand.) M.E. houten. — O. Swed. huta, to hoot. — Swed. hut! interj. begone! of onomatopoetic origin. So also W. hwt! Irish ut! expressions of dislike.

hue (2), clamour, outcry. (F.—Scand.) In the phr. 'hue and cry.' M.E. hue, a loud cry. = O. F. huer, to hoot. = O. Scand. huta, to hoot (above).

Hop (1), to leap on one leg. (E.) M.E. hoppen, huppen. A.S. hoppian, to leap, dance.+Du. hoppen, Icel. hoppa, Swed. hoppa, Dan. hoppe, G. hüpfen. The orig. sense is 'to go up and down.' (√KUP.) Der. hopp-er (of a mill); hopp-le, a fetter for horses; hop-scotch, a game in which children hop over scotches, i.e. lines scored on the ground.

hobble, to limp. (E.) M. E. *hobelen.*
Really for *hopp-le* ; frequentative of *hop.*+
Du. *hobbelen,* prov. G. *hoppeln.*

hobby (1), **hobby-horse,** a toy like a
horse, ambling nag, a favourite pursuit. (F.
— O. Low G.) Corruption of M. E. *hobin,* a
nag.— O. F. *hobin,* ' a hobby ;' Got.— O. F.
hober, ' to stirre, remove from place to
place ;' Cot. — O. Du. *hobben,* to toss,
move up and down ; weak form of *hoppen,*
to hop. Cf. Dan. *hoppe,* a mare ; N. Fries.
hoppe, a horse (in children's language).

hobby (2), a small falcon. (F.— O.
Low G.) Obsolete. M. E. *hobi, hoby.*
Closely allied to O. F. *hobreau* (= *hob-er-el*),
' the hawke tearmed a hobby ;' Cot.— O. F.
hober, to stir, move about (see above).

Hop (2), a plant. (Du.) Introduced
from the Netherlands ab. 1524.— Du. *hop,*
hop.+ G. *hopfen,* hop. We also find Icel.
humall, Swed. Dan. *humle,* O. Du. *hommel*
(whence late L. *humulus*) ; prob. allied
words.

Hope (1), expectation. (E.) M. E. *hope.*
A. S. *hopa,* hope ; whence *hopian,* to hope.
+Du. *hoop,* Dan. *haab,* Swed. *hopp,* M.H.G.
hoffe, sb. ; whence Du. *hopen,* Dan. *haabe,*
Swed. *hoppas,* G. *hoffen,* to hope. Perhaps
allied to L. *cupere,* to desire.

Hope (2), a troop ; see **Heap.**

Horde, a wandering tribe. (F. — Turk.—
Tatar.) F. *horde.*— Turk. *ordú,* a camp. —
Tatar *úrdú,* a royal camp, horde of Tatars
(Tartars) ; see Pavet de Courteille, p. 54.

Horehound ; see **Hoar.**

Horizon. (F. — L. — Gk.) F. *horizon.*
— L. *horizon* (stem *horizont-*). — Gk.
ὁρίζων, the bounding or limiting circle ;
orig. pres. pt. of ὁρίζειν, to limit.— Gk.
ὅρος, a boundary. **Der.** *horizont-al.*

aphorism, a definition. (Gk.) Gk.
ἀφορισμός, a definition.— Gk. ἀφορίζειν, to
define, limit. — Gk. ἀφ-, for ἀπό, off ; ὁρίζειν,
to limit.

Horn. (E.) A. S. *horn.* + Icel. Dan.
Swed. G. *horn* ; Du. *horen,* Goth. *haurn,*
W. Gael. Irish *corn,* L. *cornu.* Allied to
Gk. κέρ-ας, a horn. (√ KAR.)

hornet, a kind of large wasp. (E.) So
called from its resounding hum. A. S.
hyrnet, a hornet.— A. S. *horn* (with the
usual vowel-change from *o* to *y*).

Horologe, Horoscope ; see **Hour.**

Horrible ; see **Horrid.**

Horrid. (L.) Spenser has it in the
sense of ' rough ;' F. Q. i. 7. 31. — L. *horridus,* rough, bristly. — L. *horrere,* to bristle ;

also to dread, with reference to the bristling
of the hair through terror. Cf. Skt. *hrish,*
to bristle, esp. as a token of fear or of
pleasure. (√ GHARS.)

abhor. (L.) L. *ab-horrere,* to shrink
from through terror.

hirsute. (L.) L. *hirsutus,* bristly,
rough. Allied to L. *horrere* (Skt. *hrish*), to
bristle (above).

horrible. (F. — L.) O. F. *horrible*:
— L. *horribilis,* dreadful.— L. *horrere,* to
dread (above).

horrify. (L.) Coined, by analogy
with F. words in *-fy,* from L. *horrificare,*
to cause terror.— L. *horri-,* for *horrere,* to
dread ; *-ficare,* for *facere,* to make.

horror, dread. (L.) L. *horror.* — L.
horrere, to dread (above).

ordure, excrement. (F.— L.) F. *ordure.*
— O.F. *ord* (fem. *orde*), filthy, foul, ugly,
frightful.— L. *horridus,* rough, frightful.

Horse. (E.) M. E. *hors.* — A.S. *hors,*
pl. *hors,* it being a neut. sb.+Icel. *hross,*
hors, Du. *ros,* G. *ross,* O.H.G. *hros.* Lit.
' a runner ;' cf. L. *currere,* to run.

Hortatory, full of encouragement. (L.)
As if from L. *hortatorius**, coined from
hortator, an encourager. — L. *hortari,* to
encourage ; prob. allied to L. *horior,* I
urge.

exhort. (F.— L.) O. F. *exhorter.*— L.
ex-hortari, to encourage greatly.

Horticulture, gardening. (L.) Coined
from L. *horti,* gen. case of *hortus,* a garden ;
cultura, cultivation ; see **Culture.** L.
hortus is allied to E. *yard* (1).

Hosanna, an expression of praise. (Gk.
— Heb.) Gk. ὡσαννά.— Heb. *hôshî'áh nná,*
save, we pray.— Heb. *hôshî'a,* to save (from
yásha') ; and *ná,* a particle signifying entreaty.

Hose. (E.) M. E. *hose,* pl. *hosen.* A.S.
hosa, pl. *hosan,* hose, stockings.+Du. *hoos,*
Icel. *hosa,* Dan. *hose,* G. *hose.* Cf. Russ.
koshulia, a fur jacket. **Der.** *hos-i-er* (cf.
bow-yer, law-yer).

Hospice, Hospitable, Hospital ; see
Host (1).

Host (1), one who entertains guests.
(F.— L.) M. E. *host, hoste.*— O. F. *hoste.*
Cf. Port. *hospede,* a host, guest. — L.
hospitem, acc. of *hospes,* (1) a host,
(2) a guest. The base *hospit-* is short
for *hosti-pit-,* where *hosti-* is the crude
form of *hostis,* a guest, an enemy, see
Host (2) ; and *pit-* means ' lord,' being
allied to L. *potens,* powerful ; cf. Skt. *pati,*

a **master, governor, lord**; see **Possible.**
Thus . *hospes* = *hostipets* *, guest-master, a
master of a house who receives guests. Cf.
Russ. *gospode*, the Lord, *gospodare*, a
governor, prince, from *goste*, a guest, and
-*pode* (=Skt. *pati*), lord. *Der. host-ess*,
from O. F. *hostesse*, 'an hostesse;' Cot.

hospice. (F. – L.) F. *hospice.* – L.
hospitium, a house for guests. – L. *hospiti-*,
crude form of *hospes* (above).

hospitable. (F. – L.) F. *hospitable.*
From Low L. *hospitare*, to receive as
a guest. – L. *hospit-*, stem of *hospes*
(above).

hospital. (F. – L.) M. E. *hospital.* –
O. F. *hospital.* – Low L. *hospitale*, a large
house, a sing. formed from L. pl. *hospitalia*,
apartments for strangers. – L. *hospit-*, stem
of *hospes* (above).

hostel, an inn. (F. – L.) O. F. *hostel.* –
Low L. *hospitale*; see **hospital** above.

hostler, ostler. (F. – L.) Orig. the
innkeeper himself, and named from his
hostel (above).

hotel, an inn. (F. – L.) Mod. F. *hôtel*,
the same as O. F. *hostel*; see **hostel** above.

spittle (2), a hospital. (F. – L.) M. E.
spitel. – O. F. *ospital, hospital*; see **hospital** (above).

Host (2), an army. (F. – L.) The orig.
sense is 'enemy' or 'foreigner.' M. E.
host, ost. – O. F. *host*, a host, army. – L.
hostem, acc. of *hostis*, an enemy (orig. a
stranger, a guest); hence, a hostile army,
a host. + Russ. *goste*, a guest, stranger;
A. S. *gæsi*; see **Guest. Doublet**, *guest.*

Host (3), the consecrated bread of the
eucharist. (L.) L. *hostia*, a victim in a
sacrifice; O. Lat. *fostia*, lit. 'that which
is slain.' – L. *hostire*, O. Lat. *fostire*, to
strike. (√ GHAS.)

Hostage; see **Sedentary.**

Hostel, Hostler; see **Host** (1).

Hot. (E.) M. E. *hoot* (with long *o*).
A. S. *hát*, hot. + Du. *heet*, Icel. *heitr*, Swed.
het, Dan. *hed*, G. *heiss.* Allied to Icel.
hiti, heat, Goth. *hais*, a torch, Lithuan.
kaitra, heat. (√ KI ?)

heat. (E.) M. E. *hete.* A. S. *hǽtu*,
hǽto; formed from *hát*, hot, by the usual
vowel-change. + Dan. *hede*, Swed. *hetta.*
We also find A. S. *hǽtan*, verb, to heat.

Hotch-pot, Hodgepodge. (F. – Du.)
Hodgepodge is a corruption of *hotchpot*, a
confused medley. – F. *hochepot*, a medley.
– O. Du. *hutspot* (lit. shake-pot), hodge-
podge, beef or mutton cut into small

pieces. – O. Du. *hutsen, hotsen*, to shake;
pot, a pot. See **Hustle** and **Pot.**

Hotel; see **Host** (1).

Hottentot, a native of the Cape of
Good Hope. (Du.) A name given them
by the Dutch, in derision of their speech,
which sounded like stammering, or a repetition of the syllables *hot* and *tot. En* is
Dutch for 'and;' hence Du. *hot en tot* =
'hot' and 'tot.' Cf. Du. *hateren*, to
stammer, *tateren*, to tattle.

Houdah, Howdah, a seat fixed on an
elephant's back. (Arab.) Arab. *hawdaj*, a
litter carried by a camel, a seat placed on
an elephant's back.

Hough, Hock, the joint in the hind-leg
of an animal, between knee and fetlock; in
man, the back part of the knee-joint. (E.)
Now usually *hock*; formerly *hough.* M. E.
houch. A. S. *hóh*, the heel. + Icel. *há*, the
hock; Dan. *ha.* Cf. Du. *hak*, the heel, L.
coxa, the hip, Skt. *kaksha*, an arm-pit.
Der. hough, verb, also spelt *hox.*

Hound, a dog. (E.) A. S. *hund.* + Du.
hond, Icel. *hundr*, Dan. Swed. G. *hund*,
Goth. *hunds.* Allied to L. *canis*, Gk.
κύων (gen. κυνός), Skt. *çvan*, a dog; also
to Irish *cu*, W. *ci*, a dog, Russ. *suka*, a
bitch.

Hour. (F. – L. – Gk.) O. F. *hore* (F.
heure). – L. *hora.* – Gk. ὥρα, a season,
hour. Prob. allied to Skt. *yátu*, time.
(√ YA, from √ I, to go.)

horologe, a clock. (F. – L. – Gk.)
O. F. *horologe* (later *horloge*). – L. *horolo-
gium*. – Gk. ὡρολόγιον, a sun-dial, water-
clock. – Gk. ὡρο-, for ὥρα, hour; -λογιον,
teller, from λέγειν, to tell.

horoscope. (F. – L. – Gk.) F. *horoscope.* – L. *horoscopus*, a horoscope, from
horoscopus, adj., observing the hour. – Gk.
ὡροσκόπος, observing the hour (also as sb.).
– Gk. ὡρο-, for ὥρα, hour; σκοπεῖν, to consider, allied to σκέπτομαι, I consider; see
Sceptic.

Houri, a nymph of Paradise. (Pers.)
Pers. *húrí*, one virgin of Paradise, *húrá*,
húr, a virgin of Paradise, black-eyed
nymph. Cf. Arab. *hawrá*, fem. of *ahwar*,
having fine black eyes.

House. (E.) M. E. *hous.* A. S. *hús.* +
Du. *huis*, Icel. *hús*, Dan. *huus*, Swed. *hus*,
Goth. *hus*, G. *haus.* Cf. Skt. *kosha, koça*,
a coop, a sheath, an abode.

hoard, a store. (E.) A. S. *hord.* + Icel.
hodd, G. *hort*, Goth. *huzd.* The Goth.
form shows that the orig. sense was 'a

thing housed,' from Goth. *hus*, a house (above).

husband. (Scand.) Icel. *húsbóndi*, the master of a house, the goodman; short for *húsbúandi*.— Icel. *hús*, house; *búandi*, dwelling in, pres. pt. of *búa*, to dwell; see **Boor**. Der. *husband-man*, *husband-ry*.

hussif, a case for needles, thread, &c. (Scand.) The final *f* is due to confusion with *huswife*, for which see **hussy**, below. — Icel. *húsi*, a case, as in *skærishúsi*, a scissors-case. — Icel. *hús*, a house.

hussy, a pert girl. (E.) Short for *hus-wife*, which is put for *house-wife* (like *husband* for *house-band*).

hustings. (Scand.) The mod. use is incorrect; it is properly *husting*, sing., and means a council, an assembly for the choice of a candidate. M. E. *husting*. A. S. *hústing*.— Icel. *húsþing*, a council, meeting. — Icel. *hús*, a house; *þing*, a thing, also an assembly; see **Thing**. Cf. Swed. and Dan. *ting*, the same as Icel. *þing*; and the Swed. form better accounts for the E. form.

huswife. (E.) I. e. *house-wife*.

Housel, the eucharist. (E.) The orig. sense is 'sacrifice.' M. E. *housel*. A. S. *húsel*.+ Goth. *hunsl*; sacrifice. (Root uncertain.)

Housings; see **Holster**.

Hovel, a small hut. (E.) M. E. *hovel*, *hovil*; dimin. of A. S. *hof*, *hofa*, a house. + Icel. *hof*, temple, hall; G. *hof*, yard, court.

hover. (E.) A frequentative of M. E. *houen* (= *hoven*), to stay, tarry, wait, orig. to dwell, a verb formed from A. S. *hof*, a house, dwelling (above). Cf. O. Fries. *hovia*, to receive into one's house; O. Du. *hoven*, to entertain, lodge. ¶ The W. *hofio*, to hover, is borrowed from M. E. *houen*.

How (1), in what way; see **Who**.

How (2), a hill; see **High**.

Howdah; see **Houdah**.

Howitzer, a short cannon. (G. — Bohemian.) Borrowed from G. *haubitze*, a howitzer; formerly spelt *hauffnitz*.— Bohemian *haufnice*, orig. a sling for casting a stone; Jungmann, Bohem. Dict. i. 662.

Howl. (F. — L.) M. E. *houlen*.— O. F. *huller*.— L. *ululare*, to shriek, howl.— L. *ulula*, an owl; see **Owl**. So also G. *heulen*, to howl; from *eule*, an owl.

Hox, to hamstring; see **Hough**.

Hoy (1), a kind of sloop. (Du.) Du.

heu, *heude*, a flat-bottomed merchant-ship; Flemish *hui*, a hoy.

Hoy (2), stop! (Du.) Du. *hui!* hoy! come! well! Allied to **Ho**.

Hoyden, Hoiden; see **Heath**.

Hub, a projection; the same as **Hob** (1).

Hubbub; see **Whoop**.

Huckaback, a sort of linen cloth. (Low G.?) The orig. sense was prob. 'pedlar's ware;' cf. Low G. *hukkebak*, G. *hucke-back*, pick-a-back. See **Hawker**.

Hucklebone; see **Hook**.

Huckster; see **Hawker**.

Huddle. (E.) M. E. *hoderen*, *hodren*, which is an equivalent form, meaning to huddle together, as under a covert or shelter. Frequentative of M. E. *huden*; to hide; see **Hide**. It seems also to have been confused with Du. *hoetelen*, Swed. *hutla*, Dan. *hutle*, to bungle, which are allied to **Hustle**, q. v.

Hue (1), show, appearance, colour. (E.) M. E. *hewe*. A. S. *hiw*, *heow*, *heb*, appearance. + Swed. *hy*, skin, complexion, Goth. *hiwi*, form, show.

Hue (2), clamour; see **Hoot**.

Huff, to puff, bluster, bully. (E.) The old sense is to puff, blow hard; hence to bluster, vapour. An imitative word, like *puff*. Cf. Lowl. Sc. *hauch*, a forcible puff, *hech*, to breathe hard; G. *hauchen*, to breathe. ¶ To *huff*, at draughts, simply means 'to blow;' it was customary to *blow upon* the piece removed; cf. Lowl. Sc. *blaw*, to blow, also to huff at draughts; Dan. *blæse en brikke*, to huff (lit. blow) a man at draughts.

Hug, to embrace closely. (Scand.) The orig. sense was to squat, or cower down. Palsgrave has: 'I *hugge*, I shrink in my bed. It is good sport to see this little boy *hugge* in his bed for cold.' Of Scand. origin; cf. Dan. *sidde paa hug* (lit. to sit in a hook), to crouch down; Swed. *huka sig*, to crouch down; Icel. *húka*, to sit on one's hams. So also O. Du. *huken*, G. *hocken*, to couch, Skt. *kuch*, to bend. Allied to **Hook**.

Huge, vast. (F. — Teut.?) M. E. *huge*, *hogge*. An initial *a* has dropped.— O. F. *ahuge*, huge, vast (12th cent.). Prob. from the old form of mod. G. *erhöhen*, to exalt, increase, which is from *hoch* (M. H. G. *houch*), high; see **High**.

Huguenot, a French protestant. (F. — G.). F. *huguenot*; named from some person of the name of *Huguenot*, who was doubtless conspicuous as a reformer. This name was in use two centuries at least before the Reformation, and is a dimin. of F. *Hugues*, Hugh (like *Jeannot* from *Jean*). — M. H. G. *Húg*, Hugh, lit. a thoughtful man. — O. H. G. *hugu*, thought; allied to L. *cogitare*, to think. ¶ See 15 false etymologies of this word noted by Scheler.

Hulk, a heavy ship. (Low L. - Gk.) M. E. *hulke*. — Low L. *hulka*, better *hulcus*, *holcas*, a kind of ship. — Gk. ὁλκάς, a ship which is towed, also a heavy ship, merchantman. — Gk. ἕλκειν, to draw, drag. + Lithuan. *welku*, I pull. (√WARK.) Der. *hulking*, i. e. bulky, unwieldy. ¶ Distinct from M. E. *hulke*, A. S. *hulc*, a hovel.

Hull (1), a husk; see Holster.

Hull (2), body of a ship; see Holster.

Hum (1), to buzz. (E.) M. E. *hummen*; an imitative word. + G. *hummen*, Du. *hommelen*, to hum.

hum (2), to trick, cajole. (E.) A particular use of *hum*, to buzz; it also meant to utter a sound expressive of contempt (Cor. v. 1. 49); also to applaud; see Richardson and Todd's Johnson. Hence it meant to flatter, cajole, trick. So also Port. *zumbir*, to buzz, *zombar*, to jest; Span. *zumbar*, to hum, also to jest. Der. *hum*, sb., a hoax.

humblebee, a humming-bee. (E.) From the verb *humble*, put for *hummle*, frequentative of *hum*. Cf. Du. *hommel*, a humble-bee, from *hommelen*, to hum; G. *hummel*, a humble-bee, from *hummen*, to hum.

humbug, a hoax, piece of trickery. (E.) '*Humbug*, a false alarm, a bugbear,' Dean Milles MS. (cited in Halliwell). 'Drolleries, bonmots, and *humbugs*;' about A. D. 1740. Compounded of *hum*, hoax, and *bug*, a spectre, ghost, bugbear; the orig. sense being 'sham bugbear'; see hum (2) and bug. Der. *humbug*, verb.

humdrum, dull, droning. (E.) Compounded of *hum*, a buzzing noise, and *drum*, a droning sound; see Drum.

Human. (F. - L.) Formerly *humaine*. — O. F. *humain*, 'humane, manly;' Cot. — L. *humanus*, human. — L. *homo*, a man; lit. 'a creature of earth,' from *humus*, ground; see Humble.

homage. (F. - L.) M. E. *homage*. — O. F. *homage*, the service of a vassal to his lord. — Low L. *homaticum*, the service of a vassal or man. — L. *hom-o*, a man.

homicide, man-slaughter, also a manslayer. (F. - L.) F. *homicide*, meaning (1) manslaughter, from L. *homicidium*; (2) a

man-killer, from L. *homicida*. — L. *hom-o*, a man; *-cidium*, a killing, or *-cida*, a slayer, from *cædere*, to kill.

humane. (L.) Directly from L. *humanus*, (1) human, (2) kind.

ombre, a game at cards. (F. — Span. — L.) F. *hombre*. — Span. *juego del hombre*, lit. 'game of the man.' — L. *hominem*, acc. of *homo*, a man.

Humble. (F. — L.) F. *humble*. — L. *humilem*, acc. of *humilis*, humble, lowly, near the ground. — L. *humus*, the ground. Cf. Gk. χαμαί, on the ground, Russ. *zemlia*, earth, land.

exhume, to disinter. (L.) Coined from *ex*, out of; *humus*, the ground.

humiliate. (L.) From pp. of L. *humiliare*, to humble. — L. *humilis*, humble (above).

humility. (F. — L.) M. E. *humilitee*. — O. F. *humiliteit*, humility. — L. *humilitatem*, acc. of *humilitas*, humility. — L. *humilis*, humble.

Humble-bee, Humbug; see Hum (1).

Humdrum; see Hum (1).

Humeral, belonging to the shoulder. (L.) Low L. *humeralis*, belonging to the shoulder. — L. *humerus*, the shoulder; better *umerus*. + Gk. ὦμος, Goth. *amsa*, Skt. *amsa*, the shoulder.

Humid, moist. (F. — L.) F. *humide*. — L. *humidus*, better *umidus*, moist. — L. *humere*, *umere*, to be moist; cf. *uuens*, *uuidus*, *udus*, moist. Gk. ὑγρός, moist. (√UG, for WAG.)

humour, orig. moisture. (F. — L.) See Trench, Select Glossary, and Study of Words. The four *humours*, according to Galen, caused the four temperaments of mind, viz. choleric, melancholy, phlegmatic, and sanguine. — O. F. *humor* (F. *humeur*). — L. *humorem*, acc. of *humor*, moisture. — L. *humere*, to be moist (above).

Humiliate, Humility; see Humble.

Hummock; see Hump.

Hump, a lump, bunch, esp. on the back. (E.) '*Hump*, a hunch, or lump,' *Westmoreland*;' Halliwell. Not found in M. E. It is a nasalised form of *heap*, and from the same base as *heap* and *hop* (1); see Hop (1). Cf. Gk. κύφος, a hump, Lithuan. *kumpas*, hunched, Skt. *kubja*, hump-backed. Parallel to *hunch*, q. v.

hummock, hommock, a mound, hillock, rounded mass. (E.) It appears to be merely a dimin. of *hump*; put as if for *hump ock**. Cf. *hill-ock* from *hill*.

Hunch, a hump, round mass. (E.) A nasalised form of *hook*, q. v. Cf. G. *hucke*, the bent back, *höcker*, a hunch on the back. And cf. Skt. *kuñch*, to bend, with *kuch*, to bend.

Hundred. (E.) M. E. *hundred*. A. S. *hundred*; a compound word. — A. S. *hund*, a hundred; and *réd*, *réd*, speech, discourse, but here used in the early sense of 'reckoning' or rate, to denote the rate of counting. Cf. Icel. *hund-rað*, hundred, *átt-ræðr*, eighty, *tí-ræðr*, a hundred (ten-rate). This suffix is allied to **Read**, q. v. β. The A. S. *hund* is cognate with L. *centum*, answering to an Aryan form KANTA, short for DAKANTA, i. e. tenth, as appears from Goth. *taihun-taihund*, a hundred (lit. tententh). In fact *hund* = *t-enth* without the *t*, just as L. *centum* is for *de-centum*. See **Ten.**

Hunger. (E.) A. S. *hungor*. + Icel. *hungr*, Swed. Dan. *hunger*, Du. *honger*, G. *hunger*; Goth. *huhrus*, hunger. Prob. allied to Skt. *kuñch*, to contract; so that *hunger* denotes the feeling of being shrunk together.

Hunt, to chase wild animals. (E.) M. E. *hunten*. A. S. *huntian*, to capture. Allied to Goth. *hunths*, captivity, which is from *hunthans*, pp. of *hinthan*, to seize, capture (pt. t. *hanth*). Thus the Teut. base is HANTH, to seize. Cf. Skt. *çátaya*, to fell, to drive, causal of *çad*, to fall. (√KAD.)

hint, a slight allusion. (E.) *Hint* is properly 'a thing taken' or caught up; short for M. E. *hinted*, pp. of *hinten* or *henten*, to seize. — A. S. *hentan*, to seize, hunt after; from the Teut. base HANTH (above). ¶ Or from Icel. *ymta*, to mutter.

Hurdle. (E.) M. E. *hurdel*. A. S. *hyrdel*; a dimin. from an A. S. base *hurd-*, not found; but see the cognate words. + Du. *horde*, Icel. *hurð*, G. *hürde*, M. H. G. *hurt*, a hurdle; Goth. *haurds*, a door. Cognate with L. *crates*, a hurdle, Gk. κάρταλος, a (woven) basket. Cf. Skt. *krit*, to spin, *chrit*, to connect. The sense is a 'woven' thing. (√ KART.) **Doublet,** *crate*.

hoarding, a kind of fence. (F. — Du.; or Du.) Not old. Either from Du. *horde*, a hurdle, or from F. *horde*, a palisade, barrier, which is the same word.

Hurdygurdy, a kind of violin, played by turning a handle. (E.) A derisive name, from the grating sound. Cf. Lowl. Sc. *hurr*, to snarl, *gurr*, to growl. 'Som vseþ

strange wlaffyng, chytering, *harryng and garryng*' = some people use a strange babbling, chattering, snarling and growling; Spec. of English, ed. Morris and Skeat, p. 241, l. 163. Formed on the model of *hurly-burly*. See **Hurry.**

Hurl; see **Hurt.**

Hurlyburly, a tumult. (F. — L.; *and* E.) A reduplicated word, the second syllable being an echo of the first. The simple form *hurly* is the original; see 'K. John, iii. 4. 169. — F. *hurler*, to howl, yell ; a corruption of *huller*, to howl ; see **Howl.** So also Ital. *urlare*, *ululare*, to howl ; L. *ululare*, to howl.

Hurrah; see **Huzzah.**

Hurricane, whirlwind. (Span. — Caribbean.) Span. *huracan*. — Carib. *huracan* (Littré).

Hurry. (Scand.) Not allied to *harry*. Formed from an older word *hurr*; so also *scurr-y* from 'skir*. M. E. *horien*, to hurry (Allit. Poems, ed. Morris, B. 883). — O. Swed. *hurra*, to swing, whirl round ; Swed. dial. *hurra*, to whirl, whence *hurr*, sb. hurry, haste. Cf. Dan. *hurre*, to hum, whir; Icel. *hurr*, a noise. Allied to **Whir**, being an imitative word.

Hurst, a wood. (E.) M. E. *hurst*; A. S. *hyrst*. + M. H. G. *hurst*, a shrub, thicket. Lit. 'interwoven thicket;' allied to **Hurdle.**

Hurt, to dash against, to harm. (F. — C.) M. E. *hurten*, *hirten*, (1) to push, dash against ; (2) to injure. — O. F. *hurter* (F. *heurter*), to strike or dash against. Of Celtic origin ; W. *hyrddu*, to ram, push against, *hwrdd*, a push, a thrust, *hwrdd*, a ram ; Corn. *hordh*, a ram ; Manx *heurin*, a he-goat.

hurl, hurtle. (F. — C.; *with* E. *suffix*.) *Hurl* is short for *hurtle*; and *hurtle*, i. e. to keep on dashing against, is the frequentative of *hurt*, in the old sense of 'dash against.' See *hurtleth* = pushes down, Chaucer, C. T. 2618, where some MSS. have *hurteth*; also *hurlid*, Wyclif, Luke, vi. 49, in six MSS., where seventeen MSS. have *hurtlid*.

Husband; see **House.**

Hush; see **Hiss.**

Husk; see **Holster.**

Husky, hoarse. (E.) Corrupted from *husty* or *hausty*, by confusion with the commoner word *husk*. '*Haust*, a dry cough ;' Coles (1684). From M. E. *hoost*, *host*, a cough. A. S. *hwósta*, a cough. + Du. *hoest*, Icel. *hósti*, Dan. *hoste*, Swed.

hosta, G. *husten*, a cough. Allied to Skt. *kása*, a cough. (√KAS.)

Hussar. (Hungarian.) So called because Mathias Corvinus, king of Hungary and Bohemia, raised a corps of horse-soldiers in 1458, by commanding that *one* man should be chosen out of *twenty*, in every village. — Hung. *huszar*, twentieth; from *husz*, twenty (Littré, Scheler).

Hussif, Hussy, Hustings; see **House.**

Hustle, to jostle. (Du.) Put for *hutsle*. — Du. *hutselen*, to shake up and down, huddle together; frequent. of O. Du. *hutsen*, Du. *hotsen*, to shake. See **Hotchpot.** Cf. Lowl. Sc. *hott*, to move by jerks, *hotter*, to jolt.

Hut. (F. — O. H. G.) M. E. *hotte*. — F. *hutte*, a cottage; Cotgrave. — O. H. G. *hutta* (G. *hütte*), a hut. ✚ Swed. *hydda*, a hut. Cf. Skt. *kuti*, a hut; from *kut*, to bend (hence to cover).

Hutch, a box. (F. — Low L.) M. E. *huche*, *hucche*. — F. *huche*, a hutch, bin. — Low L. *hutica*, a hutch, box; of unknown origin. Prob. Teutonic; cf. O. H. G. *huatan* (G. *hüten*), to take care of. See **Heed.**

Huzzah (G.), **Hurrah** (Scand.) *Huzzah* is the older form; also written *huzza*. G. *hussa*, huzzah! So also Swed. and Dan. *hurra*, hurrah! Cf. Dan. *hurre*, to hum, buzz. See **Hurry.**

Hyacinth, a flower. (F. — L. — Gk.) F. *hyacinthe*. — L. *hyacinthus*. — Gk. ὑάκινθος, an iris, larkspur (not our hyacinth).

jacinth, a precious stone. (F. — L. — Gk.) O. F. *jacinthe*. — L. *hyacinthus*, a jacinth. — Gk. ὑάκινθος, a jacinth; Rev. xxi. 20.

Hyæna; see **Hyena.**

Hybrid, mongrel. (L. — Gk.?) L. *hibrida*, *hybrida*, a mongrel, a hybrid. Usually derived from Gk. ὕβριδ-, stem of ὕβρις, insult, wantonness, violation.

Hydra, a water-snake. (L. — Gk.) L. *hydra*. — Gk. ὕδρα, water-snake. — Gk.ὕδ-ωρ, water. Cf. Skt. *udras*, a water-animal, otter. A. S. *oter*. **Doublet,** *otter*. And see **Water.**

dropsy; see **hydropsy** (below).

hydrangea, a flower. (Gk.) A coined name, referring to the cup-form of the capsule, or seed-vessel. From Gk. ὕδρ-, for ὕδωρ, water; ἀγγεῖον, a vessel.

hydraulic, relating to water in motion. (F. — L. — Gk.) F. *hydraulique*. — L. *hydraulicus*. — Gk. ὑδραυλικός, belonging to a

water-organ. — Gk. ὑδραυλις, an organ worked by water. — Gk. ὑδρ-, for ὕδωρ, water; αὐλός, a pipe, tube (from the base α√, to blow; see **Air**).

hydrodynamics, the science relating to the force of water in motion. (Gk.) Gk. ὕδρο-, for ὕδωρ, water; and E. *dynamics*, a word of Gk. origin; see **Dynamics.**

hydrogen, a very light gas. (Gk.) The name means 'generator of water.' — Gk. ὕδρο-, for ὕδωρ, water; and the base γέν-, to produce; see **Genesis.**

hydropathy, the water-cure. (Gk.) Gk. ὕδρο-, for ὕδωρ, water; πάθ-ος, suffering, endurance of treatment; see **Pathos.**

hydrophobia, fear of water. (Gk.) Coined from Gk. ὕδρο-, for ὕδωρ, water; φόβος, fear. (√BHA.)

hydropsy, dropsy. (F. — L. — Gk.) Formerly *dropsie* or *ydropsie*; the form *dropsie* being due to loss of *y*-. — O. F. *hydropisie*. — L. *hydropisis*, *hydropisia*. — Late Gk. ὑδρώπισις*, not found, from Gk. ὕδρωψ, dropsy, extended from ὕδρο-, for ὕδωρ, water. Der. *dropsi-c-al*.

hydrostatics, the science which treats of fluids at rest. (Gk.) Gk. ὕδρο-, for ὕδωρ, water; and **Statics,** q. v.

Hyena, Hyæna, a sow-like quadruped. (L. — Gk.) L. *hyæna*. — Gk. ὕαινα, a hyena; lit. 'sow-like.' — Gk. ὕ-ς, a sow, cognate with E. **Sow;** with fem. adj. suffix -αινα.

Hymen. (L. — Gk.) L. *hymen*. — Gk. ὑμήν, the god of marriage.

Hymn. (F. — L. — Gk.) M. E. *ympne* (with excrescent *p*). — O. F. *ymne* (later *hymne*). — L. *hymnum*, acc. of L. *hymnus*. — Gk. ὕμνος, a song, festive song, hymn.

Hypallage, an interchange. (L. — Gk.) L. *hypallage*. — Gk. ὑπαλλαγή, an interchange, exchange. — Gk. ὑπ-ό, under; ἀλλαγή, change, from ἀλλάσσειν, to change, which from ἄλλος, another. See **Alien.**

Hyper-, prefix, denoting excess. (L. — Gk.) L. *hyper-*, for Gk. ὑπέρ, above, beyond, allied to L. *super*. Hence *hyperbaton*, a transposition of words from natural order, lit. 'a going beyond' (from βαίνειν, to go); *hyper-borean*, extreme northern (from βορέας, north wind); *hyper-bole*, exaggeration, Gk. ὑπερβολή (from βάλλειν, to throw, cast).

Hyphen, a short stroke (-) joining two parts of a compound word. (L. — Gk.) L. *hyphen*, for Gk. ὑφέν, lit. 'under one.' — Gk. ὑφ-, for ὑπό, under; ἕν, neut. of εἷς, one.

Hypo-, prefix. (Gk.) Gk. ὑπό, under; cognate with L. *sub.*

Hypochondria, a mental disorder inducing melancholy. (L. — Gk.) Named from the spleen (which was supposed to cause it), situate under the cartilage of the breast-bone. — L. *hypochondria*, s. pl. — Gk. ὑποχόνδρια, s. pl., the parts beneath the breast-bone. — Gk. ὑπό, under; χόνδρος, a corn, grain, gristle, cartilage of the breast-bone. **Der.** *hipp-ish*, q. v.

Hypocrisy, pretence to virtue. (F. — L. — Gk.) O. F. *hypocrisie.* — L. *hypocrisis*, 1 Tim. iv. 2. — Gk. ὑπόκρισις, a reply, answer, playing a part on a stage, acting of a part. — Gk. ὑποκρίνομαι, I reply, play a part. — Gk. ὑπό, under; κρίνομαι, I contend, middle voice of κρίνω, I judge. See **Critic. Der.** *hypocrite*, F. *hypocrite*, L. *hypocrita*, Gk. ὑποκριτής, a dissembler, Matt. vi. 2.

Hypogastric, belonging to the lower part of the abdomen. (F. — L. — Gk.) O. F. *hypogastrique.* — Late L. *hypogastricus*, belonging to the lower part of the belly. — Gk. ὑπογάστριον, lower part of the belly; see **Hypo-** and **Gastric.**

Hypostasis. (L. — Gk.) L. *hypostasis.* — Gk. ὑπόστασις, a standing under, groundwork, subsistence, substance, a Person of the Trinity. — Gk. ὑπό, under; στάσις, a standing, from √STA, to stand. See **Statics.**

Hypotenuse. (F. — L. — Gk.) Also *hypothenuse* (badly). — F. *hypotenuse.* — L. *hypotenusa.* — Gk. ὑποτείνουσα, the subtending (line); fem. of pres. part. of ὑποτείνειν, to subtend, lit. to stretch under. (√TAN.)

Hypothec, a kind of mortgage. (F. — L. — Gk.) Englished from O. F. *hypotheque*, a mortgage. — L. *hypotheca* (the same). — Gk. ὑποθήκη, lit. 'under prop;' a pledge, mortgage. — Gk. ὑπό, under; θη-, as in τί-θη-μι, I place. (√DHA.)

hypothesis, a supposition. (L. — Gk.) L. *hypothesis.* — Gk. ὑπόθεσις, a placing under, supposition. — Gk. ὑπό, under; θέσις, a place; from the same root as the above.

Hyssop, a plant. (F. — L. — Gk. — Heb.) M. E. *ysope.* — O. F. *hyssope.* — L. *hyssopus.* — Gk. ὕσσωπος, an aromatic plant (not our hyssop). — Heb. *ēzôbh*, a plant (not exactly known what plant).

Hysteric, convulsive, said of fits. (F. — L. — Gk.) O. F. *hysterique.* — L. *hystericus.* — Gk. ὑστερικός, suffering in the womb; hysterical. — Gk. ὑστέρα, the womb. Prob. from Gk. ὕστερος, latter, lower, comparative from the Aryan base UD, out; see **Out.**

I.

I, nom. case of first pers. pronoun. (E.) M. E. (Northern) *ik*, *i*; (Southern) *ich*, *uch*, *i.* A. S. *ic.* + Du. *ik*, Icel. *ek*, Dan. *jeg*, Swed. *jag*, Goth. *ik*, G. *ich*, W. *i*, Russ. *ia*, L. *ego*, Gk. ἐγώ, ἐγών, Skt. *aham*. (Aryan form, AGAM.) ¶ *Me* is from a different base.

I-, neg. prefix; see **In-** (3).

Iambic, a certain metre, a short and a long syllable (◡-). (L. — Gk.) L. *iambicus.* — Gk. ἰαμβικός. — Gk. ἴαμβος, an iambic foot, iambic verse, lampoon. So called from use in satiric poetry. — Gk. ἰάπτειν, to throw, cast (hence attack). Allied to **Jet** (1).

Ibex, a genus of goats. (L.) L. *ibex.*

Ibis, a bird. (L. — Gk. — Egypt.) L. *ibis.* — Gk. ἶβις, an Egyptian bird. Of Egypt. origin; cf. Coptic *hippen* (Peyron).

Ice. (E.) M. E. *ys*, *iis.* A. S. *ís.* + Du. *ijs*, Icel. *íss*, Dan. *iis*, Swed. *is*, G. *eis.* (√IS, to glide.) Cf. Icel. *eisa*, to go swiftly, Skt. *ísh*, to hasten. **Der.** *ice-berg*, quite a modern word; the latter element is the Du., Swed., and G. *berg*, a mountain; cf. Du. *ijsberg*, Swed. *isberg*, Dan. *iisberg*, G. *eisberg*, an ice-berg; (prob. a Dan. word). Also *ice-blink*, Dan. *iisblink*, a field of ice, from Dan. *blinke*, to gleam.

icicle. (E.) M. E. *isikel*, *iseyokel*; from M. E. *ys*, ice, *ikil*, a point of ice. — A. S. *ís-gicel*, an icicle; also written *íses gicel*, where *íses* is the gen. case. *Gicel* is a dimin. form, meaning 'a small piece of ice;' cf. Irish *aigh*, Gael. *eigh*, icê. + Icel. *íss-jökull*, though *jökull* is gen. used by itself in the sense of icicle, and is a dimin. of *jaki*, a piece of ice; Low G. *is-hekel*, *isjäkel.*

Ichneumon. (L. — Gk.) L. *ichneumon.* — Gk. ἰχνεύμων, an ichneumon (lizard); lit. 'a tracker,' because it tracks out (and devours) crocodiles' eggs. — Gk. ἰχνεύειν, to track. — Gk. ἴχνος, a footstep.

Ichor, the juice in the veins of gods. (Gk.) Gk. ἰχώρ, juice; allied to ἰκμάς, moisture. Cf. Skt. *sich*, to sprinkle, wet. (√ SIK.)

Ichthyography, description of fishes. (Gk.) Gk. ἰχθύο-, crude form of ἰχθύς, a fish; γράφειν, to describe. So also *ichthyology*, from λόγος, a discourse, λέγειν, to speak.

Icicle ; see **Ice**.

Iconoclast, a breaker of images. (Gk.) Coined from Gk. εἰκόνο-, for εἰκών, an image; κλάστης, a breaker, from κλάειν, to break.

Icosahedron, a solid figure with twenty equal faces. (Gk.) From Gk. εἴκοσι, twenty ; ἕδρα, a base, lit. a seat, from the base ἑδ-, to sit ; see **Sit**.

Idea. (L. – Gk.) L. *idea*. – Gk. ἰδέα, the look or semblance of a thing, species (hence, notion). – Gk. ἰδεῖν, to see. (√ WID.) See **Wit**.

idol. (F. – L. – Gk.) O. F. *idole*. – L. *idolum*. – Gk. εἴδωλον, an image, likeness. – Gk. εἴδομαι, I appear, seem ; ἰδεῖν, to see. (√ WID.) **Der.** *idolatry* (corruption of *idolo-latry*), from O. F. *idolatrie*, Low L. *idolatria*, shortened form of *idololatria*, from Gk. εἰδωλο-λατρεία, service to idols (where λατρεία, service, is from λατρίς, a hired servant, λάτρον, hire). Hence *idolater*, &c.

idyl, idyll, a pastoral poem. (L. – Gk.) L. *idyllium*. – Gk. εἰδύλλιον, a short descriptive poem. – Gk. εἶδος, form, shape, figure. – Gk. εἴδομαι, I appear (see above).

Identical, the very same. (L.) Formerly *identic*, *identick*. Formed as if from Low L. *identicus**, adj. suggested by L. *identitas* ; see **Identity**.

identity, sameness. (F. – Low L. – L.) F. *identité*. – Low L. acc. *identitatem*, sameness. – L. *identi*-, occurring in *identidem*, repeatedly ; with suffix -*tas*. – L. *idem*, the same. – L. *i*-, and -*dem* ; from Aryan pronominal bases **I** and **DA**.

Ides, the 15th day of March, May, July, October ; 13th of other months. (F. – L.) F. *ides*. – L. *idus*, ides.

Idiom, peculiar mode of expression. (F. – L. – Gk.) F. *idiome*. – L. *idioma*. – Gk. ἰδίωμα, an idiom, peculiarity of language. – Gk. ἰδιόω, I make my own. – Gk. ἴδιος, own. Allied to Skt. *svayam*, self (Curtius).

idiosyncrasy, peculiarity of temperament. (Gk.) Gk. ἴδιο-s, own ; σύγ-κρασις, a blending together, from σύγ- (= σύν), together, κρᾶσις, a mingling. See **Crasis**.

idiot. (F. – L. – Gk.) F. *idiot*. – L. *idiota*, an ignorant, uneducated person. – Gk. ἰδιώτης, a private person ; hence, one who is inexperienced (1 Cor. xiv. 16). – Gk. ἰδιόω, I make my own. – Gk. ἴδιος, own.

Idle. (E.) M. E. *idel*. A. S. *idel*, vain, empty, useless. ╋ Du. *ijdel*, vain ; Dan. *idel*, Swed. *idel*, mere ; G. *eitel*, vain, trifling. The orig. sense seems to have been 'clear' or 'bright ;' cf. Gk. ἰθαρός, clear, pure (as a spring). (√ IDH.)

Idol, Idyll ; see **Idea**.

If, conj. (E.) M. E. *if*, A. S. *gif*. ╋ Icel. *ef*, *if*, O. Fries. *ief*, *gef*, *of*, O. Sax. *ef* ; Goth. *iba*, *ibai*, perhaps. We also find Goth. *jabai*, if (compounded of *jah*, and, *ibai*, perhaps) ; with which cf. Du. *of*, if, or, whether, G. *ob*, whether. Also O. H. G. *ibu*, if, lit. 'on the condition,' dat. of *iba*, condition, stipulation. β. The E. *if*, Icel. *ef*, Goth. *ibai*, O. H. G. *iba*, are from a Teut. type EBAI, dat. of EBA, stipulation, doubt, seen in O. H. G. *iba* (as above) ; cf. L. *op*-, in *op-inus*, imagining, *op-inari*, to suppose. Prob. from √ AP, to obtain.

Ignition, a setting on fire. (L.) F. *ignition*. As if from L. *ignitio** (not used). – L. *ignitus*, pp. of *ignire*, to set on fire. – L. *ignis*, fire. ╋Skt. *agni*, fire. Hence also *ignis fatuus*, a vain fire ; *igne-ous*, adj.

Ignoble, Ignominy, Ignore ; see **Noble**.

Iguana, a kind of American lizard. (Span. – W. Indian.) Span. *iguana*. Of Caribbean origin.

Il- (1), put for *in*-, prefix, from L. *in*, prep., when *l* follows. Exx.: *il-lapse*, *illusion*, &c.

Il- (2), put for *in*-, negative prefix when *l* follows. Exx.: *il-legal*, *il-legible*, *il-legitimate*, *il-liberal*, *il-limitable*, *il-literate*, *illogical* ; for which see *legal*, *legible*, &c. And see *illicit*.

Iliac, pertaining to the smaller intestines. (F. – L.) F. *iliaque*, belonging to the flanks. Formed from L. *ilia*, s. pl., flanks, groin. See also **Jade** (2).

Iliad, an epic poem. (L. – Gk.) L. *Iliad*-, stem of *Ilias*, the Iliad. – Gk. Ἰλιάδ-, stem of Ἰλιάς, the Iliad. – Gk. Ἴλιος, Ilios, the city of Ilus, commonly known as Troy. – Gk. Ἶλος, Ilus, grandfather of Priam, and son of *Tros* (whence *Troy*).

Ill ; see **Evil**.

Illapse ; see **Lapse**.

Illation, an inference. (F. – L.) F. *illation*. – L. acc. *illationem*, a bringing in, inference.—L. *il-* (for *in*), not; *latus* (= *tlatus*), borne, brought (=Gk. τλητός), from √TAL, to lift. See **Tolerate**.

Illicit, unlawful; see **Licence**.

Illision, a striking against; see **Lesion**.

Illude; see **Ludicrous**.

Illuminate; see **Lucid**.

Illusion; see **Ludicrous**.

Illustrate. (L.) From the pp. of *illustrare*, to throw light upon.—L. *il-*, for *in*, upon; *lustrare*, to shine. See **Lucid**.

Illustrious. (F.—L.; *or* L.) A badly coined word; either from F. *illustre*, or from the L. *illustri-s*, bright, renowned. (Imitation of *industrious*.) β. The origin of *illustris* is disputed; the prefix *il-* = *in*, upon; *-lustris* is either allied to L. *lustrum*, a lustration, from √LU, to wash; or it stands for *lu-c-stris* *, from the base *luc-*, light, as in **Lucid**, q. v. The latter is more likely.

Im- (1), prefix (F.—L.; *or* E.) 1. In some words, *im-* is put for *em-*, the O. F. form of L. *im-*, prefix. This prefix stands for L. *in*, in, before *b*, *m*, or *p*. 2. Or it is substituted for E. *in*, as in *im-bed*, for *in-bed*.

Im- (2), prefix. (L.) L. *im-*, put for *in-*, in, when *b*, *m*, or *p* follows.

Im- (3), prefix. (F.—L.; *or* L.) Negative prefix; put for L. *in-*, not. Exx.: *im-material*, *im-mature*, *im-measurable*, *im-memorial*, *im-moderate*, *im-modest*, *im-moral*, *im-mortal*, *im-movable*, *im-mutable*, *im-palpable*, *im-parity*, *im-partial*, *im-passable*, *im-passive*, *im-patient*, *im-peccable*, *im-penetrable*, *im-penitent*, *im-perceptible*, *im-perfect*, *im-perishable*, *im-personal*, *im-pertinent*, *im-perturbable*, *im-piety*, *im-pious*, *im-placable*, *im-polite*, *im-politic*, *im-ponderable*, *im-possible*, *im-potent*, *im-practicable*, *im-probable*, *im-proper*, *im-provident*, *im-prudent*, *im-pure*; for which see *material*, *mature*, &c.

Image, a likeness, statue. (F.—L.) F. *image*.—L. *imaginem*, acc. of *imago*, a likeness. Formed, with suffix *-ago*, from *im-itari*, to imitate; see below.

imagine. (F.—L.) F. *imaginer*, to think.—L. *imaginari*, to picture to oneself, imagine.—L. *imagin-*, stem of *imago*, an image, picture; see above.

imitate. (L.) From pp. of L. *imitari*, to imitate; frequentative of *imare* *, not found.

Imbecile, feeble. (F.—L.) Formerly rare as an adj.; but the verb *imbécil*, to enfeeble, was rather common.—O. F. *imbecille*, 'feeble;' Cotgrave.—L. *imbecillem*, acc. of *imbecillis*, feeble. (Root unknown.) Hence probably E. *embezzle*, q. v.

Imbibe, to drink in; see **Bib**.

Imbricated, bent and hollowed like a gutter-tile. (L.) Botanical. From pp. of L. *imbricare*, to cover with a gutter-tile.—L. *imbric-*, stem of *imbrex*, a gutter-tile.—L. *imbri-*, crude form of *imber*, a shower of rain. ✚ Gk. ὄμβρος, a shower; Skt. *ambhas*, water, *abhra*, a rain-cloud.

Imbrue, Embrew, to moisten, drench. (F.—L.) See **Bib**.

Imbue, to cause to drink, tinge. (L.) See **Bib**.

Imitate; see **Image**.

Immaculate; see **Maculate**.

Immediate; see **Medium**.

Immense; see **Measure**.

Immerge; see **Merge**.

Immigrate; see **Migrate**.

Imminent; see **Eminent**.

Immit; see **Missile**.

Immolate, to offer in sacrifice. (L.) From pp. of L. *immolare*, to sacrifice, lit. to throw meal upon a victim.—L. *im-* (for *in*), upon; *mola*, meal, cognate with E. **Meal** (1).

Immunity, freedom from obligation. (F.—L.) F. *immunité*, immunity.—L. *immunitatem*, acc. of *immunitas*, exemption.—L. *immunis*, exempt from public services.—L. *im-* (for *in*), not; *munis*, serving, obliging (whence also *communis*, common.) (√MU.)

Immure; see **Mural**.

Imp, a graft, offspring, demon. (Low L.—Gk.) Formerly in a good sense, meaning a scion, offspring. M. E. *imp*, a graft on a tree; *impen*, to graft. Shortened from Low L. *impotus*, a graft (Lex Salica); whence also Dan. *ympe*, Swed. *ympa*, G. *impfen*, O. H. G. *impitón*, to graft. — Gk. ἔμφυτος, engrafted, James, i. 21. — Gk. ἐμφύειν, to implant. — Gk. ἐμ-, for ἐν, in; φύειν, to produce, from √BHU, to be; see **Be**. ¶ We find A.S. pl.*impan*; from Low L.

Impact; see **Pact**.

Impair, to make worse, injure, weaken. (F.—L.) M. E. *empeiren*.—O. F. *empeirer*, later *empirer*, 'to impaire,' Cot.—Low L. *impeiorare*, to' make worse. — L. *im-*, for *in*, prep., with intensive force; and *peior*, worse, a comparative form from a lost positive.

Impart; see **Part**.

Impassive; see Patient.
Impawn; see Pane.
Impeach, Impede; see Pedal.
Impel; see Pulsate.
Impend; see Pendant.
Imperative, Imperial; see Pare.
Impertinent; see Tenable.
Impervious; see Viaduct.
Impetus; see Petition.
Impinge; see Pact.
Implement; see Plenary.
Implicate, Imply; see Ply.
Implore; see Deplore.
Import, Importable; see Port (1).
Importune; see Port (2).
Impose; see Pose (1).
Imposition; see Position.
Imposthume, an abscess. (F.–L.–
Gk.) Better *apostume*, as in Cotgrave.–
O. F. *apostume*, ‘an apostume, an inward
swelling full of corrupt matter.’ A still
better spelling is F. *aposteme*, also in Cot-
grave.– L. *apostema*.– Gk. ἀπόστημα, a
standing away from, hence, a separation of
corrupt matter.– Gk. ἀπό, away; στη-, base
of ἵστημι, I set, place, stand. (√STA.)
Impostor; see Position.
Impoverish; see Pauper.
Imprecate; see Precarious.
Impregnable; see Prehensile.
Impregnate; see Natal.
Impress; see Press.
Imprint; see Press.
Imprison; see Prehensile.
Impromptu; see Exempt.
Impropriate; see Proper.
Improve; see Probable.
Improvise; see Vision.
Impudent, shameless. (F.–L.) F. *im-
pudent*.– L. *impudent-*, stem of *impudens*,
shameless.– L. *im-*, for *in*, not; *pudens*,
modest, pres. pt. of *pudere*, to feel shame.
Impugn; see Pugilism.
Impulse; see Pulsate.
Impunity; see Pain.
Impute; see Putative.
In, prep. (E.) A.S. *in.* + Du. *in*, Icel.
í, Swed. Dan. *i*, Goth. *in*, G. *in*, W. *yn*,
O. Irish *in*, L. *in*, Gk. ἐν, ἐνί. *In* is a
weakened form of *en*, as in Gk. ἐν; the
Gk. ἐνί seems to be a locative case, and
is further related to Gk. ἀνά, E. *on*; see
On. (Pronom. base ANA.) Der. *inn-er*,
A.S. *innera*; *in-most*, A.S. *innemest* (i.e.
inne-m-est, a double superl. form). The
form *innermost* is also a corruption of
A.S. *innemest*. Also *in-ward*, *there-in*,

where-in, *with-in*, *in-as-much*, *in-so-much*,
in-ter-, *in-tro-*. And see inn (below).
inn, sb. (E.) M.E. *in*, *inn*.–A.S. *inn*,
in, sb.–A.S. *in*, *inn*, adv., within, indoors.
–A.S. *in*, prep., in (above). + Icel. *inni*,
an inn; *inni*, adv., indoors.
inning. (E.) Properly the securing or
housing of grain, from *inn*, verb, due to
inn, sb., above. Hence *innings*, as a term
at cricket, invariably used in the plural,
because the side which is *in* consists of
several players.
In- (1), prefix. (E.) In some words, it
is only the prep. *in* in composition. Exx.:
in-born, *in-breathe*, *in-bred*, *in-land*, &c.
In- (2), prefix. (L.) In some words, it is
the L. prep. *in* in composition. Exx.: *inaugurate*, *in-carcerate*, &c. Sometimes, it
has passed through French; as *in-dication*,
&c. ¶ It becomes *il-* before *l*, *im-* before
b, *m*, and *p*, *ir-* before *r*.
In- (3), negative prefix. (L.; *or* F.–L.)
From L. neg. prefix *in-*, cognate with E.
neg. prefix *un-*; see Un- (1). ¶ It becomes
i- before *gn*, as in *i-gnoble*; *il-* before *l*;
im- before *b*, *m*, and *p*; *ir-* before *r*. Der.
in-ability, *in-accessible*, &c., &c.; for which
see *able*, *access*, &c.
Inane, empty, silly, useless. (L.) L.
inanis, void, empty. Root unknown. Der.
inan-i-ty.
inanition, exhaustion from lack of food.
(F.–L.) F. *inanition*, ‘an emptying;’
Cot. From the pp. of *inanire*, to empty;
from *inanis* (above).
Inaugurate; see Augur.
Incandescent; see Candid.
Incantation; see Cant (1).
Incarcerate, to imprison. (L.) L. *in*,
in; and *carceratus*, pp. of *carcerare*, to im-
prison, from *carcer*, a prison.
Incarnadine; see Carnal.
Incarnation; see Carnal.
Incendiary, Incense; see Candid.
Incentive; see Cant (1).
Inceptive; see Capacious.
Incessant; see Cede.
Incest; see Caste.
Inch, the twelfth part of a foot. (L.)
M.E. *inche*. A.S. *ynce*.–L. *uncia*, an
inch; also an ounce; orig. a small weight.
Cf. Gk. ὄγκος, bulk, weight.
ounce (1), twelfth part of a pound. (F.
–L.) O.F. *unce*.–L. *uncia* (above).
uncial, large, applied to letters. (L.)
L. *uncialis*, adj. from *uncia*, inch. (From
the size of the letters.)

Incident; see **Cadence.**

Incipient; see **Capacious.**

Incise; see **Cæsura.**

Incite; see **Cite.**

Incline, to lean towards. (F.—L.) F. *incliner.*—L. *inclinare.*—L. *in*, towards; *clinare**, to lean, cognate with E. **Lean** (1), q. v. (✓ KRI.) Doublet, *encline.*

declension. (F.—L.) O. F. *declinaison*, used for the 'declension' of a noun.— L. *declinationem*, acc. of *declinatio*, declination, declension.—L. *declinatus*, pp. of *declinare* (below).

decline. (F.—L.) O. F. *decliner.*—L. *de-clinare*, to lean or bend aside from.

encline. (F.— L.) M. E. *enclinen.*— O. F. *encliner.*—L. *inclinare*; see **Incline.**

recline. (L.) L. *re-clinare*, to lean back, lie down. See also **Acclivity.**

Inclose, Include; see **Clause.**

Incognito; see **Noble.**

Income; see **Come.**

Incommode; see **Mode.**

Incorporate: see **Corporal** (2).

Increase, Increment; see **Crescent.**

Incubate, Incubus; see **Covey.**

Inculcate; see **Calk.**

Inculpate; see **Culpable.**

Incumbent; see **Covey.**

Incur, Incursion; see **Current.**

Incurvate; see **Curve.**

Indeed; see **Do** (1).

Indemnify, Indemnity; see **Damn.**

Indelible; see **Delete.**

Indent: see **Dental.**

Index, Indicate; see **Diction.**

Indict, Indiction; see **Diction.**

Indigenous; see **Genus.**

Indigent, destitute. (F.—L.) F. *indigent.*—L. *indigent-*, stem of pres. part. of *indigere*, to be in want.—L. *ind-*, for *indo* or *indu*, an O. Lat. extension from *in*, in (cf. Gk. ἔνδον, within); *egere*, to want, be in need; cf. L. *indigus*, needy. Cf. Gk. ἀχήν, poor, needy (Theocritus). (✓ AGH.)

Indigo, a blue dye. (F.—Span.—L.— Gk. — Pers. — Skt.) F.*indigo.*—Span.*indico.* —L. *indicum*, indigo; neut. of *Indicus*, Indian (hence Indian dye).—Gk. ἰνδικόν, indigo; neut. of Ἰνδικός, Indian. — Pers. *Hind*, India; a name due to the river Indus. —Skt. *sindhu*, the river Indus; a large river. — Skt. *syand*, to flow. ¶ The Persian changes *s* into *h*.

Indite; see **Diction.**

Indolence; see **Doleful.**

Indomitable; see **Daunt.**

Indubitable; see **Dual.**

Induce, Induct; see **Duke.**

Indue (1), to invest or clothe with, supply with. (L.) In Spenser, F. Q. iii. 6. 35.—L. *induere*, to put into, put on, clothe with. The prefix is rather *ind-* than *in* (for this prefix see **Indigent**); cf. *ex-uuiæ*, spoils, *ind-uuiæ*, clothes. See **Exuviæ.**

Indue (2), a corruption of **Endue**, q. v.

Indulgence. (F.—L.) F. *indulgence.* —L. *indulgentia.*—L. *indulgent-*, stem of pres. pt. of *indulgere*, to be courteous to, indulge. (Of unknown origin.)

Indurate; see **Dure.**

Industry. (F.—L.) F. *industrie.*—L. *industria.*—L. *industrius*, diligent. Origin uncertain; perhaps from O. Lat. *indo*, within, and *stru-ere*, to arrange, build; see **Structure.**

Inebriate; see **Ebriety.**

Ineffable; see **Fate.**

Inept; see **Apt.**

Inert; see **Art** (2).

Inexorable; see **Oral.**

Infamy; see **Fame.**

Infant, Infantry; see **Fate.**

Infatuate; see **Fatuous.**

Infect; see **Fact.**

Infer; see **Fertile.**

Inferior. (F.—L.) O. F. *inferieur.*— L. *inferiorem*, acc. of *inferior*, lower, comp. of *inferus*, low, nether. Strictly, *inferus* is itself a compar. form, answering to Skt. *adhara*, lower, from *adhas*, adv., underneath. low, down.

infernal. (F. — L.) F. *infernal.* — L. *infernalis*, belonging to the lower regions. — L. *infernus*, lower; extended from *inferus* (above).

Infest, to harass. (F.—L.) F. *infester.* —L. *infestare*, to attack.—L. *infestus*, attacking, hostile. *Infestus = infedtus**; from *in*, against; and *fed-*, base of *fendere*, to strike, as seen in *of-fendere, de-fendere.*

Infidel; see **Faith.**

Infinite; see **finite**, under **Final.**

Infirm, Infirmity, Infirmary; see **Firm.**

Inflate; see **Flatulent.**

Inflect; see **Flexible.**

Inflict. (L.) L. *inflictus*, pp. of *infligere*, to inflict, lit. to strike upon.—L. *in*, upon; and *fligere*, to strike. (✓ BHLAGH.) See **Afflict.**

Inflorescence; see **Floral.**

Influence, Influenza, Influx; see **Fluent.**

Inform; see Form.

Infraction, Infringe; see Fragile.

Infuriate; see Fury.

Infuse; see Fuse (1).

Ingenious, Ingenuous: see Genus.

Ingle, fire. (C.) Gael. and Irish *aingeal*, fire; but prob. borrowed from *igniculus*, dimin. of L. *ignis*, fire. See Ignition.

Ingot, a mass of unwrought metal. (E.) M. E. *ingot*, Chaucer, C. T. 16677, &c., where it means a mould for molten metal. But the true sense is 'that which is poured in,' a mass of metal.—A. S. *in*, in; and *got-en*, poured, pp. of *geótan*, to pour, fuse metals. Cf. Du. *ingieten*, Swed. *ingjuta*, to pour in. Also Du. *gieten*, G. *giessen*, Icel. *gjóta* (pp. *gotinn*), Dan. *gyde*, Swed. *gjuta*, Goth. *giutan*, to pour, shed, fuse; cognate with L. *fundere*. (√ GHU.) Hence F. *lingot*, put for *l'ingot*. ✠ G. *einguss*, a pouring in, also an ingot.

Ingrain; see Grain.

Ingratiate; see Grace.

Ingredient, Ingress; see Grade.

Inguinal, relating to the groin. (L.) L. *inguin-*, stem of *inguen*, the groin.

Inhabit; see Habit.

Inhale; see Exhale.

Inherent; see Hesitate.

Inherit; see Heir.

Inhibit; see Habit.

Inimical; see Amatory.

Iniquity; see Equal.

Initial; see Itinerant.

Inject; see Jet (1).

Injunction; see Join.

Injure; see Jury.

Ink; see Encaustic.

Inkle, a kind of tape. (F.—L.) In the Prompt. Parv. (1440) we find, '*Lynyolf*, or *inniolf*, threde to sow wythe, *lynolf*.' This shews that the M. E. *liniolf* sometimes appeared without the initial *l*. This is allied to O. F. *lignel*, *lignioul*, *ligneul*, thread, esp. shoemaker's thread; called in English *lingel*, *lingle*. We may conclude that *inkle* is a corrupt form of *ingle*, which again is the word *lingle* without its initial *l* (mistaken for the French def. article *l'*). Cf. F. *lingot*, an ingot, from E. *ingot*, where the *l* has, contrariwise, been supplied. The O. F. *lignel* is from *ligne*, thread.—L. *linea*, fem. of *lineus*, hempen, flaxen.—L. *linum*, flax. See Linen.

Inkling, a hint, intimation. (Scand. ?) M. E. *inkling*, a whisper, murmur, low speaking. Alexander, when in disguise, feared he was discovered, because he 'herd a *nyngkiling* of his name,' Allit. romance of Alexander, 2968; where *a nyngkiling* stands for *an yngkiling*. 'To *incle* the truthe' = to hint at the truth, Alisaunder (in app. to Wm. of Palerne), 616. I suspect it to be corrupted from Dan. *ymte*, to murmur, mutter, an iterative verb from *ymja*, to mutter, hum (of imitative origin); so also Icel. *ymta*, to mutter.

Inn; see In.

Innate; see Natal.

Innings; see In.

Innocent, Innocuous; see Noxious.

Innovate; see Now.

Innuendo; see Nutation.

Inoculate; see Ocular.

Inordinate; see Order.

Inquest, Inquire; see Query.

Inscribe; see Scribe.

Inscrutable; see Scrutiny.

Insect; see Secant.

Insert; see Series.

Insidious; see Sedentary.

Insignia; see Sign.

Insinuate; see Sinus.

Insipid; see Sapid.

Insist; see State.

Insolent. (F.—L.) M. E. *insolent*.—F. *insolent*, saucy.—L. *insolent-*, stem of *insolens*, not customary, unusual, insolent.—L. *in*, not; *solens*, pres. pt. of *solere*, to be accustomed, be wont.

Inspect; see Species.

Inspire; see Spirit.

Inspissate, to make thick. (L.) From pp. of L. *inspissare*, to thicken.—L. *in*, in; *spissus*, thick, dense.

Instance; see State.

Instead; see Stead.

Instep, the upper part of the foot, where it rises to the front of the leg. (E.) Formerly *instup* and *instop* (Minsheu). The probability is that *instep* is a corruption, and that the true etymology is from *in* and *stoop*, i. e. 'the in-bend' of the foot.

Instigate; see Stimulate.

Instil; see Still (2).

Instinct; see Distinguish.

Institute; see State.

Instruct, Instrument; see Structure.

Insular. (L.) L. *insularis*, insular.—L. *insula*, an island. Prob. from L. *in salo* = in the main sea, where *salo* is abl. of L. *salum*, the main sea, cognate with Gk. σάλος, surge, swell of the sea. Allied to Swell.

isle, an island. (F. – L.) O. F. *isle* (F. *île.*) – L. *insula,* an island (above).

isolate, to insulate. (Ital. – L.) Suggested by Ital. *isolato,* detached, used as a term in architecture. – Ital. *isola,* an island. – L. *insula,* an island.

Insult; see **Salient.**

Insurgent, Insurrection; see Regent.

Intaglio; see **Tailor.**

Integer; see **Tangent.**

Intellect, Intelligence; see **Legend.**

Intend, Intense; see **Tend** (1).

Inter; see **Terrace.**

Inter-, *prefix,* amongst. (L.) L. *inter,* among; a comparative form, answering to Skt. *antar,* within; closely allied to Interior, q. v.

Intercalate; see **Calends.**

Intercede; see **Cede.**

Intercept; see **Capacious.**

Intercourse; see **Current.**

Interdict; see **Diction.**

Interest (1), profit, advantage. (F. – L.) O. F. *interest* (F. *intérêt*), an interest in a thing, interest for money. – L. *interest,* it is profitable; 3 pers. sing. of *interesse,* to concern, lit. 'be among.' – L. *inter,* among; *esse,* to be. See **Inter-** and **Essence.**

interest (2), to engage the attention of another. (F. – L.) A curious word; formed (by partial confusion with the verb above) from the pp. *interess'd* of the obsolete verb to *interess,* used by Massinger and Ben Jonson. – O. F. *interessé,* 'interessed, or touched in;' Cot. – L. *interesse,* to concern (as above). Der. Hence *dis-interested,* from the verb *disinterest,* orig. a pp. and put for *disinteress'd.*

Interfere; see **Ferule.**

Interior. (L.) L. *interior,* comp. of *interus,* within. *In-terus* itself was orig. a comparative form, answering to Skt. *antara,* interior. The positive is the L. *in,* in; see **In.**

denizen, a naturalised citizen, inhabitant. (L.) Formerly *denisen.* – O. F. *deinzein* (also *denzein*), used in the Liber Albus to denote a trader *within* the privilege of the city franchise, as opposed to *forein.* Formed by adding the suffix *-ein* (= L. *-anus*) to O. F. *deinz,* now spelt *dans,* within. – L. *de intus,* from within. – L. *de,* from ; *intus,* within, allied to interior (above).

entrails, the inward parts. (F. – L.) O. F. *entrailles,* intestines. – Low L. *intra-*

lia, also (more correctly) *intranea,* entrails. – L. *interanea,* entrails, neut. pl. of *interaneus,* inward, adj., from *inter,* within.

internal. (L.) Coined from L. *internus,* inward; extended from *inter-,* inward; see **interior** (above).

Interjacent, Interjection; see **Jet** (1).

Interloper; see **Leap.**

Intermit; see **Missile.**

Internal; see **Interior.**

Internecine, thoroughly destructive. (L.) L. *internecinus,* thoroughly destructive. – L. *internecio,* utter slaughter. – L. *inter,* thoroughly (see **White**); and *necare,* to kill.

Interpellation; see **Pulsate.**

Interpolate; see **Polish.**

Interpose; see **Pose** (1).

Interposition; see **Position.**

Interpret, to explain. (F. – L.) M. E. *interpreten.* – F. *interpreter.* – L. *interpretari,* to expound. – L. *interpret-,* stem of *interpres,* an interpreter, properly an agent, broker. The latter part of the word is related rather to Gk. φράζειν (= φράδ-γειν), to speak, than to Gk. πράττειν, πράσσειν, to do.

Interregnum; see **Regent.**

Interrogate; see **Rogation.**

Interrupt; see **Rupture.**

Intersect; see **Secant.**

Intersperse; see **Sparse.**

Interstice; see **State.**

Interval; see **Wall.**

Intervene; see **Venture.**

Intestate; see **Testament.**

Intestine. (F. – L.) F. *intestin,* adj., 'intestine, inward;' Cot. – L. *intestinus,* inward. Formed from L. *intus,* within, cognate with Gk. ἐντός, within; extended from L. *in,* in.

Intimate (1), to announce, hint. (L.) From pp. of L. *intimare,* to bring within, to announce. – L. *intimus,* inmost, superl. corresponding to comp. *interior;* see **Interior.**

intimate (2), familiar. (L.) This form is due to confusion with the word above. It is really founded on O. F. *intime,* 'inward, secret, deer, entirely affected;' Cot.; from L. *intimus* (above).

Intimidate; see **Timid.**

Into, prep. (E.) M. E. *into ;* orig. two words. A. S. *in tó,* in to, where *in* is used adverbially, and *tó* is a preposition; see **In** and **To.**

Intone, to chant. (Low L. – L. *and* Gk.)

Low L. *intonare*, to sing according to tone.
— L. *in tonum*, according to tone; where
tonum is acc. of *tonus*, borrowed from Gk.
τόνος; see Tone.

Intoxicate. (Low L. — L. *and* Gk.)
From pp. of Low L. *intoxicare*, to make
drunk. — L. *in*, into; *toxicum*, poison,
borrowed from Gk. τοξικόν, poison for
arrows. Gk. τοξικόν is der. from τόξον, a
bow, of which the pl. τόξα is used to mean
arrows.

Intrepid; see Trepidation.

Intricate, perplexed, obscure. (L.)
From the pp. of L. *intricare*, to perplex. —
L. *in*, in; *tricæ*, pl. sb., hindrances, vexa-
tions, wiles.

extricate. (L.) From pp. of L. *ex-
tricare*, to disentangle. — L. *ex*, out of;
tricæ, impediments.

intrigue, to form secret plots. (F. — L.)
F. *intriguer*, formerly spelt *intriquer*, 'to
intricate, perplex, insnare;' Cot. — L. *intricare* (above).

Intrinsic; see Sequence.

Introduce; see Duke.

Introspection; see Species.

Intrude, to thrust oneself into. (L.)
L. *intrudere*, to thrust into. — L. *in*, in,
into; *trudere* (pp. *trusus*), to thrust. Allied to Threaten.

abstruse. (L.) L. *abstrusus*, difficult,
concealed; pp. of *abs-trudere*, to thrust
away.

detrude. (L.) L. *de-trudere*, to thrust
down.

extrude. (L.) L. *ex-trudere*, to thrust
out.

obtrude. (L.) L. *ob-trudere*, to thrust
against.

protrude. (L.) L. *pro-trudere*, to
thrust forth.

Intuition; see Tuition.

Intumescence; see Tumid.

Inundation; see Undulate.

Inure; see Operate.

Invade; see Evade.

Inveigh; see Vehicle.

Inveigle. (Unknown.) In Spenser, F. Q.
i. 12. 32. Orig. unknown. ¶ It can
hardly be from F. *aveugler*, to blind; yet
we find *aveugle*, to cajole, seduce, A.D.
1547, in Froude's Hist. v. 132; and A.D.
1543, State Papers, ix. 247.

Invent; see Venture.

Inverse, Invert; see Verse.

Invest; see Vest.

Investigate; see Vestige.

Inveterate; see Veteran.

Invidious; see Vision.

Invite. (F. — L.) F. *inviter*. — L. *invitare*, to ask, request, invite. Origin uncertain. Doublet, *vie*, q. v.

Invocate; see Vocal.

Invoice; see Viaduct.

Invoke; see Vocal.

Involute, Involve; see Voluble.

Iodine, an elementary body. (Gk.)
Named from the violet colour of its vapour.
— Gk. ἰώδ-ης, contr. form of ἰοειδής, violet-
like; with suffix *-ine*. — Gk. ἴο-ν, a violet;
εἶδ-ος, appearance.

Iota. (Gk. — Heb.) Gk. ἰῶτα, the smallest
letter of the Gk. alphabet. — Heb. *yôd*, the
smallest letter of the Heb. alphabet, with
the power of *y*. (Of Phœnician origin.)

jot. (L. — Gk. — Heb.) Englished from
L. *iota*, Matt. v. 18 (Vulgate). — Gk. ἰῶτα
(above).

Ipecacuanha, a medicinal root. (Port.
— Brazilian.) Port. *ipecacuanha* (Span.
ipecacuana). From the Brazilian name of
the plant; Guarani *ipĭ-kaa-guaña*. *Ipĭ =
peb*, small; *kaa*, plant; *guaña*, causing
sickness.

Ir- (1), *prefix*. (L.; *or* F. — L.) Put for
L. *in*, in, prep., when *r* follows.

Ir- (2), *prefix*. (L.; *or* F. — L.) Put for
L. neg. prefix *in-*, when *r* follows.

Ire. (F. — L.) F. *ire*. — L. *ira*, anger.

irascible. (F. — L.) F. *irascible*. — L.
irascibilis, choleric, from *irasci*, to become
angry. — L. *ira*, anger.

Iris, a rainbow. (L. — Gk.) L. *iris*. —
Gk. ἶρις, a rainbow. Der. *irid-esc-ent*,
irid-ium, from *irid-*, stem of L. *iris*.

orris, a plant. (Ital. — L. — Gk.) Formerly *orice*, *oris*. These are E. corruptions
of O. Ital. *irios* (Ital. *ireos*). — O. Ital. *irios*,
'oris-roote,' Florio. Modified from L. *iris*,
above.

Irk, to weary. (Scand.) M. E. *irken*,
to tire. — Swed. *yrka*, to urge, enforce, press,
press upon; cognate with L. *urgere*, to urge.
See Urge. (√WARG.)

Iron, a metal. (E.) M. E. *iren*, also *ire*.
A. S. *íren*, older form *ísen*, iron, both adj.
and sb.+Du. *ijzer*, Icel. *járn* (contr. from
O. Icel. *ísarn*), Dan. Swed. *jern*; O. H. G.
isarn, G. *eisen*; Goth. *eisarn*, sb. (whence
eisarnein, adj.). And cf. W. *haiarn*, Irish
iarann, Bret. *houarn*, iron. β. The Teut.
forms exactly correspond to an adj. form
from *ice*; perhaps *iron* was named from its
smooth hard surface when brightened.

harness. (F.—C.) The old sense was 'armour.' O. F. *harnas, harnois*, armour. —Bret. *harnez*, old iron ; also, armour.— Bret. *houarn* (pl. *hern*), iron ; cognate with W. *haiarn*, Irish *iarann*, iron.

ironmonger, a dealer in iron goods. (E.) From *iron* and *monger* ; see Monger.

Irony. (F.—L.—Gk.) F. *ironie* (Minsheu).—L. *ironia*.—Gk. εἰρωνεία, dissimulation, irony. — Gk. εἴρων, a dissembler, talker, one who says less than he thinks or means.—Gk.εἴρειν, to say, talk. (√WAR.)

Irradiate; see Radius.

Irrefragable; see Fragile.

Irrigate, to water. (L.) From pp. of L. *irrigare*, to flood.—L. *in*, upon ; *rigare*, to wet, moisten. Allied to Rain.

Irritate. (L.) From pp. of L. *irritare*, to snarl greatly (as a dog), to provoke, tease. A frequentative of *irrire, hirrire*, to snarl as a dog ; which is prob. an imitative word.

Irruption; see Rupture.

Is; see Are.

Isinglass, a glutinous substance made from a fish. (Du.) A corruption of O. Du. *huyzenblas*, mod. Du. *huizenblas*, isinglass, lit. 'sturgeon-bladder,' whence isinglass is obtained. (So also G. *hausenblase*, sturgeonbladder, isinglass.) — Du. *huizen*, a sturgeon ; *blas*, a bladder, from *blasen*, to blow.

Island. (E.) The *s* is inserted by confusion with F. *isle*. M. E. *iland*. A. S. *īgland*.—A. S. *īg*, an island ; *land*, land. The A. S. *īg* is also written *ieg, ēg* (cf. *Angles-ey*) ; cognate with Icel. *ey*, Dan. Swed. *ö*, island ; G. *aue*, meadow near water. Fick gives the orig. Teut. form as AHWIA, belonging to water, an adj. formed from AHWA, water, represented by A. S. *ēd*, O. H. G. *aha*, Goth. *ahwa*, a stream, allied to L. *aqua*, water. Thus *i-land* = water-land.

Isle; see Insular.

Isochronous, performed in equal times. (Gk.) Gk. ἴσο-s, equal ; χρόνος, time (see Chronicle).

isosceles, having two equal legs or sides, as a triangle. (L.—Gk.) L. *isosceles*. — Gk. ἰσοσκελής, isosceles. — Gk. ἴσο-s, equal ; σκέλ-ος, a leg, side of a triangle.

Isolate; see Insular.

Issue; see Itinerant.

Isthmus, a neck of land connecting á peninsula with the mainland. (L.—Gk.) L. *isthmus*.—Gk. ἰσθμός, a narrow passage ; allied to ἴθμα, a step. (√I, to go.)

It; see He.

Italics, a name for letters printed thus— *in sloping type.* (L.) Named from Aldo Manuzio, an *Italian*, about A.D. 1500.—L. *Italicus*.—L. *Italia*, Italy.

Itch. (E.) M. E. *iken, icchen*, fuller form *ʒiken* (*yiken*). A. S. *giccan*, to itch.+ Du. *jeuken*, G. *jucken*, to itch.

Item, a separate article or particular. (L.) L. *item*, likewise ;. in common use for enumerating particulars ; closely allied to *ita*, so. Cf. Skt. *ittham*, thus, *iti*, thus.

iterate, to repeat. (L.) From pp. of L. *iterare*, to repeat.—L. *iterum*, again ; a compar. form (with suffix *-tar*) from the pronominal base I, as in *i-tem, i-ta*.

Itinerant, travelling. (L.) From pres. part. of O. Lat. *itinerare*, to travel.— L. *itiner-*, stem of *iter*, a journey.—L. *it-um*, supine of *ire*, to go. (√I, to go.)

ambient, going about. (L.) L. *ambient-*, stem of pres. part. of *amb-ire*, to go about.

ambition. (F.—L.) F. *ambition*.—L. *ambitionem*, acc. of *ambitio*, a going round, esp. used of going round to solicit votes ; hence, a seeking for preferment.—L. *ambitum*, supine of *amb-ire*, to go about (but note that *ambĭtio* retains the short *i* of *ĭtum*, the supine of the simple verb).

circuit. (F.—L.) F. *circuit*.—L. acc. *circuitum*, a going round.—L. *circumitus*, pp.of *circumire* (also *circuire*), to go round. —L. *circum*, round ; *ire*, to go.

commence. (F.—L.) F. *commencer*. (Cf. Ital. *cominciare*.)—L. *com-* (for *cum*), together ; *initiare*, to begin ; see initiate below.

concomitant, accompanying. (F.—L.) Suggested by the F. sb. *concomitance*, Low L. *concomitantia*, a train, suite.—L. *con-* (for *cum*), together ; *comitari*, to accompany, from *comit-*, stem of *comes*, a companion ; see count (1) below.

constable, a peace-officer. (F. — L.) O. F. *conestable* (F. *connétable*).—L. *comes stabuli*, lit. 'count of the stable,' a title of a dignitary of the Roman empire and afterwards in use among the Franks. See count (1) below ; and see Stable.

count (1), a title of rank. (F—L.) The orig. sense was 'companion.'— O. F. *conte*, also *comte* (which is better).—L. *comitem*, acc. of *comes*, a companion (stem *com-it-*).—L. *com-* (for *cum*), together ; and *it-um*, supine of *ire*, to go. Der. *count-ess* ; also *count-y* (below).

county, orig. a province governed by a

count. (F.—L.) M. E. *countee.*—O. F. *comte* (i.e. *com-té*), a province.—Low L. *comitatum*, acc. of *comitatus*, a county (though the old meaning was a company or suite).—L. *comit-*, stem of *comes*, a count; see above.

exit. (L.) L. *exit*, i.e. 'he goes out,' used as a stage direction; 3rd pers. s. pres. of *ex-ire*, to go out.

eyre, a circuit. (F.—L.) M. E. *eire*, circuit, esp. of a judge.—O. F. *eire*, journey, way.—L. *iter*, a journey; see Itinerant (above).

initial, pertaining to the beginning. (L.) L. *initialis*, adj. from *initium*, a beginning. —L. *initus*, pp. of *in-ire*, to go in, to enter into or upon.

initiate, to begin. (L.) From pp. of L. *initiare*, to begin.—L. *initium* (above).

issue, progeny, result. (F.—L.) M. E. *issue*, sb.—O. F. *issuë*, 'the issue, end, event;' Cot. Fem. of *issu*, pp. of *issir*, to depart, go out.—L. *ex-ire*, to go out.

obit, a funeral rite. (F.—L.) O.F. *obit*.—L. acc. *obitum*, a going to or down, downfall, death.—L. *obitum*, supine of *ob-ire*, to go near.

perish. (F.—L.) M. E. *perischen.*—F. *periss-*, stem of pres. pt. of *perir*, to perish. —L. *per-ire*, to come to naught, perish; where *per-* is used with a destructive force (like E. *for-* in *for-do*).

prætor, pretor, a Roman magistrate. (L.) L. *prætor*, lit. a goer before, leader; put for *præ-itor*.—L. *præ*, before; *itor*, a goer, from *ire*, to go.

preterite. (F.—L.) M. E. *preterit.*— O. F. *preterit*, m., *preterite*, fem.—L. *præteritus*, pp. of *præter-ire*, to pass by.

sedition. (F.—L.) O.F. *sedition.*—L. acc. *seditionem*, a going apart, dissension,

mutiny.—L. *sed-*, apart; *it-um*, supine of *ire*, to go.

sudden. (F.—L.) M. E. *sodain.*—O. F. *sodain*, *sudain* (F. *soudain*). Cf. Ital. *subitaneo*, *subitano*, sudden.—Low L. *subitanus**, put for L. *subitaneus*, sudden, extended from *subitus*, sudden, lit. that which has come stealthily, orig. pp. of *subire*, to come or go stealthily.

trance. (F.—L.) F. *transe*, 'a trance, or swoon;' Cot. Lit. a passing away (from consciousness).—L. acc. *transitum*, a passing away; see transit (below).

transient. (L.) From *transient-*, supposed stem of L. *transiens*, passing away, though the real stem is *transeunt-*; pres. pt. of *trans-ire*, to pass across or away.

transit. (L.) L. *transitus*, lit. a passing across.—L. *transitum*, supine of *trans-ire*, to pass across.

Ivory. (F.—L.) M. E. *iuorie* (=*ivorie*). —O. F. *ivurie*, later *ivoire*.—L. *eboreus*, adj., made of ivory.—L. *ebor-*, stem of *ebur*, ivory. Perhaps allied to Skt. *ibha*, an elephant.

Ivy, an evergreen. (E.) A. S. *ifig.* + O. H. G. *ebah*. Perhaps allied to L. *apium*, parsley, a word borrowed from Gk. ἄπιον (whence prob. G. *epheu*, *eppich*).

Iwis, certainly. (E.) M. E. *ywis*, *iwis*. A. S. *gewis*, adj., certain (whence *gewislíce*, adv., certainly). + Du. *gewis*, adj. and adv.; G. *gewiss*, adv. Cf. Icel. *viss*, certain, sure. Allied to **Wit**. (√WID.) ¶ The M. E. prefix *i-* (A. S. *ge-*) is sometimes written apart from the rest of the word, and with a capital letter. Hence, by the mistake of editors, it has been printed *I wis*, and explained as 'I know.' This is the origin of the fictitious word *wis*, to know, given in some dictionaries.

J.

Jabber, to chatter. (Scand.) Formerly *jaber* and *jable*, weakened forms of *gabber* and *gabble*, which are frequentative forms from the base *gab-*, as seen in Icel. *gabba*, to mock. Cf. Du. *gabberen*, to jabber. See Gabble.

Jacinth; see Hyacinth.

Jack (1), a saucy fellow, sailor. (F.—L. —Gk.—Heb.) M. E. *Jacke*, *Jakke*, often used as a term of reproach, as in '*Jakke* fool,' Chaucer, C. T. 3708. [Really from F. *Jaques*, but it is remarkable that *Jack* was

generally used formerly (as now) as a substitute for *John*.]—F. *Jaques.*—L. *Jacobus*. —Gk. Ἰάκωβος.—Heb. *Ya'aqôb*, Jacob; lit. one who seizes by the heel.—Heb. root *'áqab*, to seize by the heel, supplant. ¶ The name was extended to denote various implements, such as a *smoke-jack*, a *boot-jack*; so also *Jack-o'-lent*, *Jack-o'-lantern*, *Jack-pudding*, *Jack-an-apes* (=*Jack o'-apes*, with inserted *n* to prevent hiatus).

jack (2), a coat of mail. (F.—L.—Gk. —Heb.) O. F. *Jaque*, 'James, also a Jack, or coat of maile;' Cot. Cf. Ital. *giaco*, a coat of mail, Span. *jaco*, a soldier's jacket, G. *jacke*, a jacket. Of obscure origin; but prob. due to the *Jacquerie*, or revolt of the peasantry nicknamed *Jacques Bonhomme*, A. D. 1358; and hence due to F. *Jaques*, James; see above.

jacket, a short coat. (F.—L.—Gk.—Heb.) O. F. *jaquette*, a jacket; dimin. of O. F. *jaque*, a jack of mail (above).

jacobin. (F.—L.—Gk.—Heb.) M. E. *jacobin*. —F. *jacobin*.—Low Lat. *Jacobinus*, adj., formed from *Jacobus*, and applied to a friar of the order of St. Dominick. See **Jack** (1). β. Hence one of the *Jacobin* club in the French Revolution, which first met in the hall of the *Jacobin* friars in Paris, Oct. 1789. Also the name of a hooded (friar-like) pigeon.

jacobite, an adherent of James II. (L.—Gk.—Heb.) From L. *Jacob-us*, James.

jockey, one who rides a race-horse. (F.—L. — Gk.—Heb.) A North. E. pronunciation of *Jackey*, dimin. of *Jack* as a personal name.

Jackal, a kind of wild animal. (Pers.) Pers. *shaghál*. Cf. Skt. *çrigála*, a jackal, a fox.

Jacket, Jacobin, Jacobite; see **Jack**.

Jade (1), a sorry nag, an old woman. (Unknown.) Cf. Lowland Sc. *yaud, yawd*, a jade. Of unknown origin; perhaps from Icel. *jalda*, a mare; prov. Swed. *jäldä*, a mare (Rietz).

Jade (2), a hard dark-green stone. (Span.—L.) The jade brought from America by the Spaniards was called *piedra de ijada*, because it was believed to cure pain in the side; for a similar reason it was called *nephritis* (from Gk. νεφρός, kidneys). — Span. *ijada*, the flank. — Span. *ijar*, the flank; cf. Port. *ilhal, ilharga*, the flank, side. — L. *ilia*, pl., the flanks.

Jag, a notch, tooth. (C.) Irish *gag*, a cleft, from *gagaim*, I split, notch; W. *gag*, Gael. *gag*, an aperture, cleft, chink; Gael. *gag*, to split, notch.

Jaguar, a beast of prey. (Brazil.) '*Jagua* in the Guarani [Brazilian] language is the common name for tygers and dogs; the generic name for tygers is *jaquareté*;' Clavigero, Hist. of Mexico, tr. by Cullen, ii. 318.

Jail; see **Cave**.

Jalap, the root of a plant. (Mexican.) Named from *Jalapa* or *Xalapa*, in Mexico.

Jam (1), to press, squeeze. (Scand.) The same word as *cham*, to chew, to champ; prov. E. *champ*, to tread heavily, also to chew; so also *champ*, hard, firm, i. e. *chammed* or pressed down. See **Champ**.

jam (2), a conserve of fruit. (Scand.) A soft substance, like that which is chewed. 'And if we have anye stronger meate, it must be *chammed* afore by the nurse, and so put into the babes mouthe;' Sir T. More, Works, p. 241 *h*. See above.

Jamb, side-post of a door; see **Gambol**.

Jangle, to sound discordantly. (F.—O. Low G.) M. E. *janglen*.—O. F. *jangler*, to jangle, prattle. Of O. Low G. origin; cf. Du. *jangelen*, to importune, frequent. of *janken*, to howl, yelp. An imitative word; cf. L. *gannire*, to yelp.

Janizary. (F.—Turk.) O. F. *Janissaires*, 'the Janizaries;' Cot. Of Turk. origin; it means 'new soldiers;' from Turk. *yeñi*, new; and *cheri*, soldiery. *Cheri* is for *cherik*, a troop; of Pers. origin (Zenker).

January. (L.) Englished from L. *Ianuarius*, a month named from the god Janus, who was supposed to have doors under his protection; cf. L. *ianua*, a door.

Japan, a name given to certain kinds of lacquered work. (Japan.) Named from the country. Der. *japan*, verb, to polish.

Jar (1), to make a harsh noise. (E.) It stands for an older form *char*, only found in the derivative *charken*, to creak (Prompt. Parv.) Again, *char* is from a Teut. base KAR, corresponding to Aryan base GAR, as seen in L. *garrire*, to prate, croak; see **Garrulous**.

jargon, a confused talk. (F.—L.?) F. *jargon*, orig. the chattering of birds, jargon. Cf. Span. *gerigonza*, jargon. Prob. from an extension of the base of L. *garrire*, to prate, croak; cf. M. E. *charken*, to creak (above).

Jar (2), an earthen pot. (F. — Pers.) O. F. *jare*, 'a jarre;' Cot.—Pers. *jarrah*, a jar; cf. Pers. *jurrah*, a little cruse, or jar.

Jargon; see **Jar** (1).

Jargonelle, a kind of pear. (F.—Ital.—Pers.?) F. *jargonelle*, a kind of pear, very stony (Littré); formed (acc. to Littré) from F. *jargon*, a yellow diamond, small stone. — Ital. *giargone*, a sort of yellow diamond. Perhaps from Pers. *zargún*, gold-coloured; from *zar*, gold (Devic).

Jasmine, Jessamine, a plant. (F.—Pers.) F. *jasmin.* (So also Span. *jazmin.*) — Pers. *yásmín,* jasmine; *yásamín,* jessamine.

Jasper, a precious stone. (F.—L.—Gk. —Arab.) O. F. *jaspre* (Littré), an occasional spelling of *jaspe,* a jasper. — L. *iaspidem,* acc. of *iaspis.*—Gk. ἴασπις.—Arab. *yasb, yasf, yashb,* jasper; whence Pers. *yashp, yashf,* jasper. Cf. Heb. *yáshpheh,* a jasper.

diaper, figured linen cloth. (F.—Ital. —L.—Gk.—Arab.) From O.F. *diapré,* diapered; from the verb *diaprer,* to diaper, or ' diversifie with flourishings ; ' Cot. The verb is formed from O. F. *diaspre,* later *diapre,* a jasper, a stone much used for ornamental jewellery. — O. Ital. *diaspro,* a jasper (Petrarch). — L. *iaspidem,* acc. of *iaspis,* a jasper; cf. prov. Ital. *diacere,* put for L. *iacere,* to lie (Diez). — Gk. ἴασπις (above).

Jaundice. (F.—L.) M. E. *iaunis ;* the *d* being excrescent. — F. *jaunisse,* yellowness; hence, the jaundice.—F. *jaune* (oldest spelling *jalne*), yellow. — L. *galbinus,* greenish yellow. — L. *galbus,* yellow. Allied to **Yellow.**

Jaunt, to ramble. (Scand.) The same as Lowl. Sc. *jaunt,* to jeer; whence *jaunder,* to go about idly. — Swed. dial. *ganta,* to play the buffoon, sport, jest; O. Swed. *gantas,* to toy.—Swed. dial. *gant,* a buffoon, fool; *gan,* droll. Cf. Icel. *gan,* frantic gestures. Der. *jaunt,* sb., an excursion.

Jaunty, Janty, fantastical. (F.—L.) Prob. short for *jantyl,* old spelling of *gentle* or *genteel.* But obviously confused with the verb *jaunt,* to stroll about (above).

Javelin; see **Gaff.**

Jaw. (E.) Formerly *chaw* ; see **Chew.**

Jay; see **Gay.**

Jealous; see **Zeal.**

Jeer, to mock, scoff; see **Shear.**

Jehovah. (Heb.) Heb. *yahóváh,* or, more correctly, *yahaveh,* God; see article on *Jehovah* in Dict. of the Bible.

Jejune, hungry, meagre. (L.) L. *ieiunus,* fasting, hungry, dry.

Jelly; see **Gelid.**

Jennet, Gennet, a small Spanish horse. (F. — Span. — Arab.) O. F. *genette,* ' a genet, or Spanish horse;' Cot. — Span. *ginete,* a nag; but orig. ' a horse-soldier.' Of Moorish origin; traced by Dozy to Arab. *zenáta,* a tribe of Barbary celebrated for its cavalry.

Jenneting, a kind of early apple. (Unknown.) Spelt *ginniting* in Bacon, Ess. 46. Origin unknown; the ' etymology' from ' *June-eating*' is a miserable jest; Bacon says they come in *July.* But see p. 579.

Jeopardy; see **Joke.**

Jerboa, a rodent quadruped. (Arab.) Arab. *yarbú',* (1) the flesh of the back or loins, an oblique descending muscle, (2) the jerboa, from the use it makes of the strong muscles in its hind legs, in taking long leaps.

Jerk. (E.) We find *jerk, jert,* and *gird* all used in much the same sense, orig. to strike with a lash, whip, or rod. *Jerk* appears to be a mere variant of *jert* or *gird* ; M. E. *girden,* to strike. See **gird** (2), given under **Yard** (2).

Jerked beef. (Peruvian.) A singular corruption of *charqui,* the S. American name for ' jerked' beef, or beef dried in a particular way. It appears to be a Peruvian word ; see Prescott, Conquest of Peru, c. v.

Jerkin, a jacket, short coat. (Du.) Dimin. of Du. *jurk,* a frock (Sewel), by help of the once common Du. dimin. suffix *-ken,* now supplanted by *-je* or *-tje.* Cf. *fir-kin, kilder-kin.*

Jersey, fine wool, a woollen jacket. (Jersey.) From *Jersey,* one of the Channel Islands.

Jessamine; see **Jasmine.**

Jesses; see **Jet** (1).

Jest; see **Gerund.**

Jesuit; see below.

Jesus, the Saviour. (L. — Gk. — Heb.) L. *Iesus.* — Gk. Ἰησοῦς. — Heb. *Yéshú'a,* Jeshua (Nehem. viii. 17) ; contr. form of *Yehóshu'a,* Jehoshua (Numb. xiii. 16) ; signifying saviour, lit. ' help of Jehovah.'—Heb. root *yásha',* to be large, to save. Der. *jesu-it,* one of the society of Jesus.

Jet (1), to throw out, fling about, spout. (F.—L.) Formerly, to *jet* was to strut about. M. E. *ietten,* to strut. — O. F. *jetter, jecter, getter,* to throw, fling. push forth. — L. *iactare,* to fling ; frequent. of *iacere,* to throw. Allied to Gk. *láπτειν,* to throw (whence *iambic*). Der. *jet,* sb. formerly in the sense of guise or fashion, &c.

abject, mean, lit. cast away. (L.) L. *abiect-us,* pp. of *ab-icere,* to cast away.

adjacent, near to. (L.) From stem of pres. pt. of *ad-iacère,* to lie near. *Iacère,* to lie, is formed from *iacere,* to throw.

adjective. (L.) A grammatical term,

lit. 'put near to' the noun substantive. — L. *adiect-us*, pp. of *adicere*, to put near. — L. *ad*, near; *iacere*, to throw, put.

amice, a pilgrim's robe. (F. — L.) F. *amict*, 'an amict, or amice;' Cot. We also find O. F. *amis*, *amicte*. — L. *amictus*, a garment thrown round one. — L. *am*-, for *amb*-, *ambi*-, around; *iacere*, to cast.

circumjacent, lying near. (L.) From stem of pres. part. of *circum-iacēre*, to lie around; see **adjacent** (above).

conjecture. (F. — L.) F. *conjecture*. — L. *coniectura*, a guess. — L. *coniectus*, pp. of *con-icere*, to throw or put together.

deject, to cast down. (L.) From pp. of *de-icere* (*dejicere*), to cast down.

ejaculate, to jerk out an utterance. (L.) From pp. of L. *eiaculare*, to cast out. — L. *e*, out; *iaculum*, a missile, from *iacere*, to cast.

eject. (L.) From pp. of L. *eicere*, to cast out. — L. *e*, out; *iacere*, to cast.

gist, the pith of a matter. (F. — L.) The *gist* is the point wherein the matter lies. — O. F. *gist* (mod. F. *gît*), it lies; whence the proverb 'c'est là que *gît* le lièvre,' that is where the difficulty is, lit. 'that's where the hare lies.' From the F. verb *gesir* (now *gésir*), to lie. — L. *iacēre*, to lie. (O. F. *gist* = L. *iacet*.)

inject. (L.) From pp. of L. *in-icere*, to cast in, throw into; (*icere* = *iacere*).

interject. (L.) From pres. pt. of L. *inter-iacēre*, to lie between.

interjection. (F. — L.) F. *interjection*, an interjection, a word *thrown* in to express emotion. — L. acc. *interiectionem*, a throwing between, insertion, interjection. — L. *interiectus*, pp. of L. *inter-icere*, to cast between; (*icere* = *iacere*).

jesses, straps round a hawk's legs. (F. — L.) A corruption of O. F. *jects* or *gects*. — O. F. *gect*, a cast; *les jects d'un oyseau*, 'a hawkes Iesses;' Cot. — O. F. *gecter*, to cast. — L. *iactare*, to cast; see **Jet** (above).

jetsam. (F. — L.) An old term in Law F. for things thrown overboard from a wrecked vessel. — A. F. *jetteson*, a casting. — L. acc. *iactationem*. — L. *iactare*, to cast.

jetty, a kind of pier. (F. — L.) O. F. *jettée*, a cast, throw, ' also a jetty or jutty;' Cot. Orig. fem. of pp. of O. F. *jetter*, to throw; see **Jet** (above).

joist, one of a set of timbers to support the boards of a floor. (F. — L.) Some-

times called *jist* (with *i* as in *mice*). M. E. *giste*. — O. F. *giste*, a bed, couch, place to lie on, a joist; because these timbers support the floor. — O. F. *gesir* (F. *gésir*), to lie, lie on. — L. *iacēre*, to lie.

jut, to project. (F. — L.) Merely a corruption of *jet*; in the same way a *jetty* or pier was formerly called a *jutty*; see **jetty** (above).

object. (F. — L.) F. *objecter*. — L. *obiectare*, to throw against, oppose; frequent. of *ob-icere* (*obiicere*), to cast towards.

project, sb., a plan. (F. — L.) O. F. *project* (F. *projet*), a project, purpose. — L. *proiectum*, acc. of *proiectus*, pp. of *pro-icere* (*projicere*), to fling forth; also (in late Lat.) to purpose, plan.

reject. (F. — L.) O. F. *rejecter* (16th cent.; F. *rejeter*; oldest spelling *regeter*). — O. F. *re*-, back; *geter*, *getter*, to throw; see **Jet** (above).

subjacent. (L.) From stem of pres. pt. of L. *sub-iacēre*, to lie under.

subject. (F. — L.) M. E. *suget*, *subjet*. — O. F. *suiet*, *suiect* (later *subiect*), mod. F. *sujet*), a subject. — L. *subiectus*, pp. of *sub-icere*, to put under, subject; (*icere* = *iacere*).

trajectory, the curve which a projectile describes. (F. — L.) Suggested by F. *trajectoire*, 'casting;' Cot. Formed as if from L. *traiectorius* *, belonging to projection. — L. *traiectus*, pp. of *traicere* (= *tra-jicere*), to throw across, fling. — L. *tra*-, for *trans*, across; *iacere*, to cast. Der. *traject* (F. *traject*, a ferry), the right reading for *tranect*, Merch. Ven. iii. 4. 53.

Jet (2), a black mineral. (F. — L. — Gk.) O. F. *jet*, *jaet*, also *gayet*, *gagate*, jet. — L. *gagatem*, acc. of *gagates*, jet. — Gk. γαγάτης, jet; so called from Γάγας, Γάγγαι, a town and river in Lycia, in the S. of Asia Minor.

Jetsam, Jetty; see **Jet** (1).

Jew. (F. — L. — Gk. — Heb.) M. E. *Iewes*, pl., Jews. — O. F. *Juis*, pl., later *Juifs*, pl. — Late L. *Judæus*, a Jew. — Gk. Ἰουδαῖος, an inhabitant of Ἰουδαία, Judæa. — Heb. *Yehûdâh*, Judah, son of Jacob, lit. 'illustrious.' — Heb. root *yâdâh*, to throw, praise, celebrate. Der. *Jew-ry*, M. E. *Jewerie*, O. F. *Juierie*, lit. a Jews' district; also *Jews'-harp*, a name given in derision, with reference to the harp of David.

Jewel; see **Gaud**.

Jib (1), the foremost sail in a ship. (Dan.) So called because easily shifted from side to side; see **jib** (2) below.

jib (2), to shift a sail from side to side.

(Dan.) '*Jib*, to shift the boom-sail from one side of the mast to another;' Ash (1775). Also spelt *jibe*, *gybe*.— Dan. *gibbe*, to jibe, jib; Swed. dial. *gippa*, to jerk up. Allied to Swed. *guppa*, to move up and down; and to E. *jump*. ¶ The form *gibe* answers to Du. *gijpen*, to turn suddenly, said of a sail.

jib (3), to move restively, as a horse. (F.—Scand.) O. F. *giber*, to struggle with the hands and feet (Roquefort); whence O. F. *regiber* (F. *regimber*), to kick as a horse. — Swed. dial. *gippa*, to jerk up (above).

Jibe, the same as **Gibe**, q. v.

Jig; see **Gig**.

Jilt; see **Gill** (4).

Jingle, to clink. (E.) M. E. *ginglen*; a frequentative verb from the base *jink*, allied to *chink*; see **Chink** (2). Also allied to **Jangle**.

Job (1), to peck with the beak; see **Gobbet**.

Job (2), a small piece of work; see **Gobbet**.

Jockey; see **Jack** (1).

Jocose, **Jocular**; see **Joke**.

Jocund. (F. — L.) M. E. *joconde*. — O. F. *joconde**, pleasant, only recorded in the derivatives *jocondeux*, adj., *jocondité*, sb. (Roquefort). — L. *iucundus*, pleasant; orig. helpful. — L. *iuuare*, to help; see **Adjutant**.

Jog, to push slightly, jolt. (C.) M. E. *ioggen*.—W. *gogi*, to shake, agitate; Gael. *gog*, a toss of the head; Irish *gogaim*, I nod, gesticulate. Cf. also W. *ysgogi*, to wag, stir, shake, E. *shog*; allied to **Shake**. Hence *a-gog*, q. v.

John Dory, the name of a fish. (F.—L.) *John dory* is the vulgar name of the fish called the *dory*. *John* appears to be a mere sailor's prefix, like the *jack* in *jackass*; it can hardly be from an alleged F. *jaune dorée*, which would be tautological nonsense. *Dory* is borrowed from F. *dorée*, a dory; lit. 'gilded,' *dorée* being the fem. of the pp. of *dorer*, to gild. — L. *deaurare*, to gild. — L. *de auro*, of gold; see **Aureate**.

Join. (F.—L.) O. F. *joindre*.—L. *iungere* (pp. *iunctus*), to join. (√YUG.) Allied to **Yoke**.

adjoin, to lie next to. (F.—L.) O.F. *adjoindre*.—L. *ad-iungere* (pp. *adiunctus*), to join to. Der. *adjunct*, from the pp.

conjoin. (F. — L.) O. F. *conjoindre*. — L. *con-iungere* (pp. *coniunctus*), to join

together. Der. *conjunct-ion*, *conjunct-ive*, from the pp.

conjugal, relating to marriage. (F.— L.) F. *conjugal*.—L. *coniugalis*, also *coniugialis*, adj. — L. *coniugium*, marriage. — L. *coniugare*, to unite in a yoke.—L. *con-*, together; *iugare*, to connect, from *iugum*, a yoke.

conjugation. (L.) From L. *coniugatio*, a conjugation (Priscian); lit. a yoking together. — L. *coniugatus*, pp. of *con-iugare*, to yoke together (see above).

enjoin, to bid. (F. — L.) O. F. *enjoindre*.—L. *iniungere*, to bid, ordain, orig. to join into.—L. *in*, in; *iungere*, to join.

injunction, command. (L.) From L. *iniunctio*, an order. — L. *iniunctus*, pp. of *iniungere*, to bid; see **enjoin** (above).

joint. (F. — L.) O. F. *joinct*, *joint*, a joint, sb.—O. F. *joinct*, *joint*, pp. of *joindre*, to join; see **Join** (above).

jugular, pertaining to the side of the neck. (L.) From L. *iugul-um*, or *iugul-us*, the collar-bone, which joins the neck and shoulders; dimin. of *iugum*, a yoke.

junction, a joining. (L.) From L. *iunctio*, a joining. — L. *iunctus*, pp. of *iungere*, to join.

juncture, a union, a critical moment. (L.) The sense 'critical moment' is astrological, from the 'union' of planets. — L. *iunctura*, a joining. — L. pp. *iunctus* (above).

junta, a council. (Span. — L.) Span. *junta*, a congress; a fem. form of *junto* (below).

junto, a knot of men, a faction. (Span. — L.) Span. *junto*, united, conjoined. — L. *iunctus*, pp. of *iungere*, to join.

rejoin. (F. — L.) Lit. to join again; in legal language, to answer to a reply.— F. *rejoindre*.—L. *re-iungere*, to join again. Der. *rejoinder*, which is the F. infin. mood used as a sb., as in the case of *attainder*.

subjoin. (F.—L.) F. *subjoindre* (Cot.) — L. *sub-iungere*, to join beneath, annex, subjoin.

subjugate, to bring under the yoke. (L.) From pp. of L. *subiugare*, vb. — L. *sub iugo*, under the yoke.

subjunctive. (L.) L. *subiunctiuus*, lit. joining on at the end, from the use of the subjunctive mood in dependent clauses. — L. *subiunctus*, pp. of *subiungere*, to subjoin; see **subjoin** (above).

Joint; see **Join**.

Joist; see **Jet** (1).

Joke, a jest. (L.) From L. *iocus*, a jest, game.

jeopardy, hazard. (F. — L.) M. E. *jupartie*, later *jopardye, jeopardie*. — O. F. *jeu parti*, lit. a divided game; a game in which the chances were equal, hence, a risk, hazard. — Low L. *iocus partitus*, the same; also an alternative. — L. *iocus*, a game; *partitus*, pp. of *partiri*, to part, divide, from *parti-*, crude form of *pars*, a part. ¶ The diphthong *eo* = F. *eu*; cf. *people* (= F. *peuple*).

jocose, merry. (L.) L. *iocosus*, sportive. — L. *iocus*, sport.

jocular. (L.) L. *iocularis*. — L. *ioculus*, a little jest, dimin. of *iocus*, a jest.

juggler. (F. — L.) M. E. *iogelour*. — O. F. *jogleor, jogleres*; later *jongleur*. — L. *ioculator*, a jester. — L. *ioculari*, to jest. — L. *ioculus*, a little jest, dimin. of *iocus*, joke.

Jole; see **Jowl.**

Jolly; see **Yule.**

Jolly-boat; see **Yawl.**

Jolt; see **Jowl.**

Jonquil, kind of narcissus; see **Junk** (2).

Jordan, a pot. (L. — Gk. — Heb. ?) M. E. *iordan* (*jordan*), Chaucer, C. T. 12239. Short for *Jordan-bottle*; it was customary for pilgrims to bring home water from the river Jordan, and a *jordan* was orig. a bottle, not a pot (Bardsley, Halliwell). — L. *Iordanes*. — Gk. 'Ιορδάνης. — Heb. *Yardén*, i.e. 'flowing down.'

Jostle; see **Joust.**

Jot; see **Iota.**

Journal, Journey; see **Diary.**

Joust, Just, to tilt. (F. — L.) O. F. *jouster*, to tilt. — Low L. *iuxtare*, to approach (hence to approach with hostile intent, as in tilting). — L. *iuxta*, close to, hard by (whence O. F. *jouste*, close to). β. The form *iuxta* is short for *iug-is-tá*, fem. abl. of the superlative form of L. *iug-is*, continual. From the base *iug-* of *iungere*, to join. (√YUG.)

jostle, justle, to push against. (F. — L.; with E. *suffix*.) A frequent. form, with suffix *-le*, from M.E. *jousten*, to tilt, push against.

Jovial; see **Deity.**

Jowl, Jole, the jaw or cheek. (E.) M. E. *jolle*; all the forms are corruptions of M. E. *chol, chaul*, which is a contraction of M. E. *chauel* (*chavel*), the jowl. — A. S. *ceaft*, the jaw; pl. *ceaflas*, the jaws, chaps. Allied to **Chaps**, q. v. ¶ The successive spellings are A. S. *ceaft, chæfte* (Layamon), *chauel, chaul, chol, jole, jowl* (all found).

jolt, to jerk. (E.) From *joll*, verb, to knock the *jole* or head; cf. As You Like It, i. 3. 39.

Joy; see **Gaud.**

Jubilation, a shouting for joy. (L.) From L. *iubilatio*, sb. — L. *iubilatus*, pp. of *iubilare*, to shout for joy. — L. *iubilum*, a shout of joy. ¶ Quite distinct from *jubilee*.

Jubilee, a season of great joy. (F. — L. — Heb.) M. E. *jubilee*. — O. F. *jubilé*, 'a jubilee;' Cot. — L. *iubilæus*, the jubilee (Levit. xxv. 11); masc. of adj. *iubilæus*, belonging to the jubilee (Levit. xxv. 28). — Heb. *yôbel*, a blast of a trumpet, shout of joy. ¶ Distinct from the word above.

Judge. (F. — L.) F. *juge*. — L. *iudicem*, acc. of *iudex*, a judge, lit. 'one who points out law.' — L. *iu-s*, law; *dicare*, to point out. See **Jury** and **Diction.**

adjudge. (F. — L.) M. E. *adiugen*; also *aiugen* (= *ajugen*). — O. F. *ajuger*, to decide. — L. *adiudicare*, to award. — L. *ad*, to; *iudicare*, to judge, from *iudic-*, stem of *iudex*, a judge (above).

adjudicate. (L.) From pp. of L. *adiudicare* (above).

judicature. (F. — L.) F. *judicature*. — Low L. *iudicatura*, office of a judge, judgment. — L. *iudicatus*, pp. of *iudicare*, to judge. — L. *iudic-*, stem of *iudex*, a judge.

judicial. (F. — L.) O. F. *judiciel*. — L. *iudicialis*, pertaining to courts of law. — L. *iudicium*, a trial. — L. *iudici-*, crude form of *iudex*, a judge.

judicious. (F. — L.) F. *judicieux*; as if from a L. form *iudiciosus**. — L. *iudici-*, crude form of *iudex*.

prejudge. (F. — L.) O. F. *prejuger*. — L. *præ-iudicare*, to judge beforehand.

prejudice. (F. — L.) O. F. *prejudice*. — L. *præ-iudicium*, a judicial examination, previous to a trial, also a prejudice; see *judicial* (above).

Jug, a kind of pitcher. (Heb.) Drinking-vessels were formerly called *jacks, jills*, and *jugs*, all of which represent Christian names. *Jug* and *Judge* were usual as pet female names, sometimes equivalent to *Jenny* or *Joan*; see *Jannette, Jehannette* in Cotgrave. But they can hardly represent *Joanna*; I suppose they stand for *Judith*, once a common name; see Gen. xxvi. 34.

Juggler; see **Joke.**

Jugular; see **Join.**

Juice. (F. — L.) M. E. *iuce, iuse*. — O. F. *jus*, juice, broth. — L. *ius*, broth; lit. 'mixture.' ✛ Skt. *yúsha*, soup. (√ YU.)

Jujube, a fruit. (F.—L.—Gk.—Pers.)
O. F. *jujubes*, pl. (Cot.)—L. *zizyphum*, a
jujube; fruit of the tree called *zizyphus*.—
Gk. ζίζυφον, fruit of the tree ζίζυφος.—
Pers. *zayzafún, zízfún, zízafún*, the jujube-
tree.

Julep, a drink. (F.—Span.—Pers.) F.
julep.—Span. *julepe*.—Pers. *juláb*, julep, a
sweet drink; from *guláb*, rose-water, also
julep.—Pers. *gul*, a rose; *áb*, water.

July. (L.) Englished from L. *Iulius*, a
month (formerly called *Quinctilis*) named
after Julius Cæsar, who was born in July.

Jump (1), to leap, spring, skip. (Scand.)
Swed. dial. *gumpa*, to spring, jump, wag
about; allied to Swed. *guppa*, to move up
and down; Dan. *gumpe*, to jolt. ＋ M. H. G.
gumpen, to jump, *gumpeln*, to play the
buffoon; *gempeln*, to jump, prov. G.*gampen*,
to jump, hop, sport (Schmeller), Prob.
allied to **Jib** (2).

jumble, to mix together confusedly.
(Scand.) We also find M. E. *jombren*, Ch.
Troil. ii. 1037; and *jumper*, to mix har-
moniously (More). In fact, *jumb-le, jombren, jump-er* are all frequentative forms of
the verb to *jump*, used transitively. Thus
jumb le = to make to jump, jolt together,
make a discord; or, otherwise, to shake
together, make to agree. See **Jump** (1).

jump (2), exactly, pat. (Scand.) From
the verb above, used in the sense to agree
or tally, esp. in the phr. *to jump with*.
'They *jump* not;' Oth. i. 3. 5; cf. Tam.
Shrew, i. 1. 295.

Junction, Juncture; see **Join**.

June. (L.) Englished from L. *Junius*,
the name of the month and of a Roman
gens or clan. Prob. allied to **Juvenile**.

Jungle. (Skt.) Skt. *jangala*, adj., dry,
desert; hence *jungle* = waste land. ¶ The
Skt. short *a* sounds like *u* in *mud*.

Junior, Juniper; see **Juvenile**.

Junk (1), a Chinese vessel. (Port.—
Chin.) Port. (and Span.) *junco*, a junk.—
Chinese *chw'an*, a ship, boat, bark, junk;
Williams, Chinese Dict. p. 120. Hence also
Malay *ajóng*, a junk.

Junk (2), pieces of old cordage. (Port.
—L.) Port. *junco*, a rush; also junk, as a
nautical term; i. e. rush-made ropes.—L.
iuncum, acc. of *iuncus*, a rush. ¶ *Junk*
also means salt meat, tough as old ropes.
(But *junk*, a lump, is for *chunk*.)

jonquil, a flower. (F.—L.) F.*jonquille*;
named from its rush-like leaves.—F. *jonc*,
a rush.—L. *iuncus*, a rush.

junket, a kind of sweetmeat. (Ital.—
L.) Orig. a kind of cream-cheese, served
up on rushes, whence its name. Ital.
guincata, a kind of cream-cheese on rushes,
also a junket (Florio).—Ital. *giunco*, a
rush.—L. *iuncum*, acc. of *iuncus*, a rush.

Junta, Junto; see **Join**.

Juridical; see **Jury**.

Jurisdiction, Jurist; see **Jury**.

Jury, a body of sworn men. (F.—L.)
F. *jurée*, a jury, a company of sworn men;
orig. the fem. pp. of *jurer*, to swear.—L.
iurare, to swear, bind by an oath. ＋
Skt. *yu*, to bind. (√YU.)

abjure. (L.) L. *ab-iurare*, to deny, lit.
to swear away from.

adjure. (L.) L. *ad-iurare*, to swear to.

adjust (1), to fit exactly. (F. — L.)
From F. *adjuster*, 'to adjust, place justly;'
Cot.—L. *ad*, to; *iustus*, just, exact; see
just below.

conjure. (F.—L.) M. E. *coniuren*.—
F. *conjurer*.—L. *con-iurare*, to swear together, combine by oath.

injure. (F. — L.) F. *injurier*. — L.
iniuriari, to harm.—L. *iniuria*, harm.—
L. *iniurius*, wrong.—L. *in-*, not; *iuri-*,
crude form of *ius*, law, right.

juridical, pertaining to courts of law
or to a judge. (L.) From L. *iuridic-us*,
relating to the administration of justice.—
L. *iuri-*, crude form of *ius*, law; *dicare*, to
proclaim. See *just* (1) below.

jurisdiction. (F.—L.) F.*jurisdiction*.
—L. *iurisdictionem*, acc. of *iurisdictio*, administration of justice.—L. *iuris*, gen. of
ius, law (see *just* (1) below); and see
diction. ¶ So also *juris-prudence*.

jurist, a lawyer. (F.—L.) F. *juriste*
(Cot.)—Low L. *iurista*, a lawyer.—L. *iur-*,
stem of *ius*, law; with suffix -*ista* (=Gk.
-ιστης.

juror, one of a jury. (F.—L.) Imitated
from F. *jureur*, a swearer, a juror.—L.
iuratorem, acc. of *iurator*, one who swears.
—L. *iurare*, to swear; see **Jury** (above).

just (1), upright. (F.—L.) M. E. *Iust*.
—F. *juste*.—L. *iustum*, acc. of *iustus*, just,
according to right. — L. *ius*, right, that
which is fitting; cf. Skt. *yu*, to join.
(√YU.)

justice. (F. — L.) F. *justice*. — L.
iustitia, justice; Low L. *iustitia*, a tribunal, a judge.—L. *iusti-*, for *iustus*, just;
see *just* (1) above.

justify. (F. — L.) F. *justifier*. — L.
iustificare, to shew to be just.—L. *iusti-*.

for *iustus*, just; *-ficare*, for *facere*, to make.

objurgation. (F.—L.) F. *objurgation*. —L. acc. *obiurgationem*, a chiding. —L. *obiurgatus*, pp. of *obiurgare*, to chide. —L. *ob*, against, *iurgare*, to sue, chide, which stands for *iurigare**, from *iur-*, stem of *ius*, law, and *-igare*, for *agere*, to drive.

perjure. (F.—L.) F. *parjurer*. —L. *per-iurare*, to forswear.

Jury-mast, a temporary mast. (F.—L.) Short for *ajury-mast*; where *ajury* = O. F. *ajurie*, aid, succour (Godefroy). From L. *adiutare*, to aid; see **Aid**. Cf. M. E. *iuwere*, assistance; Prompt. Parv.

Just (1), **Justice**, **Justify**; see Jury.

Just (2), to joust; see **Joust.**

Justle; see **Joust.**

Jut; see **Jet** (1).

Juvenile, young. (F.—L.) F. *juvenile*. —L. *iuuenilis*, youthful. —L. *iuuenis*, young. See **Young.**

gin (3), a kind of spirit. (F.—L.) Short for *geneva*, a corruption of F. *genevre*, juniper. —L. acc. *iuniperum*; see **juniper** below.

junior, younger. (L.) L. *iunior*, comp. of *iuuenis*, young (short for *iuuenior**).

juniper, an evergreen shrub. (L.) L. *iuniperus*, a juniper, lit. 'youth-renewing,' because it is evergreen. —L. *iūni-* = *iuueni-*, crude form of *iuuenis*, young; *parere*, to produce (see **Parent**).

Juxtaposition; see **Position.**

K.

Kail, Kale; see **Cole.**

Kails, ninepins. (Du.) Formerly also *keyles*; see *quille* in Cotgrave. These *kails* were cone-shaped. —Du. *kegel*, a pin, kail; *mid kegels spelen*, to play at ninepins.+ Dan. *kegle*, a cone; *kegler*, nine-pins; Swed. *kegla*, a pin, cone; G. *kegel* (whence F. *quille*). Apparently a dimin. of Du. *keg*, *kegge*, a wedge; but Icel. *kaggi* means a keg.

Kaleidoscope, an optical toy. (Gk.) From Gk. καλ-ός, beautiful; εἶδο-s, form; σκοπ-εῖν, to behold; because it enables one to behold beautiful forms.

Kalendar; see **Calends.**

Kangaroo, a quadruped. (Australian.) The native Australian name.

Kayles; see **Kails.**

Kedge (1), to warp a ship. (Scand.) Swed. dial. *keka*, to tug at anything tough, work continually, drag oneself slowly forward, drive softly. To *kedge* is to drag a ship slowly forward, by help of a kedge-anchor, against tide. Hence *kedg-er*, *kedge-anchor*.

Kedge (2), **Kidge**, brisk, lively. (Scand.) An East-Anglian word. M. E. *kygge*, *kydge*. —Icel. *kykr*, corrupter form of *kvikr*, quick, lively; see **Quick.** Cf. G. *keck*, the same.

Keel (1), the bottom of a ship. (E. *or* Scand.) The form answers to A. S. *ceól*, a ship (= Icel. *kjóll*); but it has been confused with Icel. *kjólr*, Dan. *kjöl*, Swed. *köl*, the keel of a ship.+G. Du. *kiel*, a keel.

keelson, kelson, a piece of timber next a ship's keel. (Scand.) Formerly *kelsine* (Chapman). —Swed. *kölsvin*, Dan. *kjölsviin* (Norweg. *kjölsvill*), a keelson.+ G. *kielschwein*. Lit. 'keel-swine;' but this can hardly have been the orig. sense. A better sense is given by Norw. *kjölsvill*, where *svill* answers to G. *schwelle*, E. *sill*; see **Sill.** This suffix, not being understood, may easily have been corrupted to *swine*, and afterwards, in English, to *-son*.

Keel (2), to cool; see **Cool.**

Keelson; see **Keel** (1).

Keen, sharp. (E.) M. E. *kene*. A. S. *céne*; where *é* is due to an older *ó*; the orig. sense is 'knowing' or wise, or able. +Du. *koen*, bold, daring; Icel. *kænn* (for *kænn*), wise, also able; G. *kühn*, bold, O. H. G. *chuoni*. The Teut. base is KONYA, able, from Teut. base KANN, to know; see **Can** (1).

Keep; see **Cheap.**

Keg, a small cask. (Scand.) Formerly also *cag*. —Icel. *kaggi*, a keg; Swed. *kagge*, Norweg. *kagge*, a keg, a round mass or heap. Prob. named from its roundness. Cf. Gk. γογγύλος, round.

Kelp, calcined ashes of sea-weed. Origin unknown. (Also spelt *kilp*).

Ken; see **Can** (1).

Kennel (1); see **Canine.**

Kennel (2); see **Canal.**

Kerbstone, i.e. curb-stone; see **Curve.**

Kerchief; see **Cover.**

Kermes, the dried bodies of insects used in dyeing crimson. (Arab. —Skt.) See **Crimson.**

Kern (1), **Kerne**, an Irish soldier. (Irish.) Irish *ceatharnach*, a soldier.

Kern (2); see **Quern**.

Kernel; see **Corn**.

Kersey; coarse woollen cloth. (E.) Named from *Kersey* (an A. S. word), a village three miles from Hadleigh, in Suffolk, where a woollen trade was once carried on. ¶ Not from *Jersey*, which is also used as the name of a material.

Kerseymere, a twilled cloth of fine wool. (Cashmere.) A corruption of *Cashmere* or *Cassimere*, by confusion with *kersey* above.

Ketch, a small yacht or hoy. (Turkish.) Corrupted from Turk. *qāîq*, *qâîq*, a boat, skiff (whence also Ital. *caicco*, F. *caique*). ¶ The Du. *kits*, F. *caiche*, a ketch, are borrowed from E.

Kettle. (L.) M. E. *ketel*, A. S. *cetel*; not an A. S. word, but borrowed from L. *catillus*, a small bowl (whence also Goth. *katils*, Du. *ketel*, G. *kessel*, &c.). Dimin. of *catinus*, a bowl, deep vessel for cooking food. Allied to Gk. κότυλος, a cup; see **Cotyledon**.

Kex, hemlock, a hollow stem. (C.) M. E. *hex*. — W. *cecys*, pl., hollow stalks, hemlock, allied to *cegid*, hemlock; Corn. *cegas*, hemlock. +L. *cicuta*, hemlock. ¶ *Kex* = *kecks*, and is properly a plural form.

Key. (E.) M. E. *keye*. A. S. *cæg*, *cæge*, a key.+O. Fries. *kai*, *kei*, a key.

Khan, a prince. (Pers.—Tatar.) Pers. *khân*, lord, prince; of Tatar origin. Cf. *Chingis Khan*, i. e. great lord, a Tatar title (Chaucer's *Cambuscan*).

Kibe, a chilblain. (E.) W. *cibwst*, chilblains; explained by Pugh as standing for *cib-gwst*. — W. *cib*, a cup; *gwst*, a humour, malady, disease; hence 'a cup-like malady,' from the rounded form. The E. word has preserved only the syllable *cib*, rejecting the latter syllable. Prob. allied to **Cup**.

Kick. (C.) M. E. *kiken*. — W. *cicio*, to kick; Gael. *ceig*, to kick. O. W. *cic*, a foot.

Kickshaws, a dainty dish. (F.—L.) A sing. sb.; the pl. is *kickshawses*. (Shak.) A curious corruption of F. *quelque chose*, something, hence, a trifle, a delicacy. Spelt *quelquechose* by Dryden.—F. *quelque chose*. — L. *qual-is*, of what sort, with suffix *-quam*; *causa*, a cause, a thing.

Kid, a young goat. (Scand.) M. E. *kid*. — Dan. *kid*, Swed. *kid*, Icel. *kiδ*, a kid.+ G. *kitze*. Allied to **Chit**, **Child**. (√GI, for √GA.)

kidnap, to steal young children. (Scand.) *Kid*, in thieves' slang, means a child; *nap* is our *nab*. — Dan. *kid*, a kid; *nappe*, to nab; see **Nab**.

Kidney. (Scand.) Corruption of M. E. *kidnere*, *kidneer*; *nere* is also used alone. 1. Here *kid* is a corruption of *quid* or *quith*; cf. prov. E. *kite*, the belly, which is the same word. — Icel. *kviδr*, womb, Swed. *qved* (A. S. *cwiδ*), the womb; this word is cognate with Skt. *jathara*, the belly, womb, Gk. γαστήρ. 2. M. E. *nere* is also a Scand. word. — Icel. *nýra*, Dan. *nyre*, Swed. *njure*, a kidney; cognate with Du. *nier*, G. *niere*, and allied to Gk. νεφρός, kidney.

Kilderkin. (Du.) A corruption of O. Du. *kindeken*, also *kinneken*, the eighth part of a vat. The lit. sense is 'little child,' because the measure is a small one as compared with a tun, vat, or barrel. Formed, with dimin. suffix *-ken* (now nearly obsolete), from Du. *kind*, a child, cognate with E. **Child**, q. v. The mod. Du. name is *kinnetje*, by substitution of *-tje* for *-ken*.

Kill. (Scand.) M. E. *killen*, more commonly *cullen*. The old sense was merely to strike. 'We *hylle* of thin heued'—we strike off thy head; Allit. Poems, B. 876. — Icel. *kolla*, to hit on the head, harm; from *kollr*, top, head, pate; Norweg. *kylla*, to poll trees, from *koll*, top, head, crown, poll. So also Du. *kollen*, to knock down; *kol*, a knock on the head.

Kiln. (L.) A.S. *cyln*, also *cylene*; merely borrowed from L. *culina*, a kitchen (hence, a drying-house). See **Culinary**.

Kilt. (Scand.) The sb. is derived from the verb. *kilt*, to tuck up.—Dan. *kilte*, to truss, tuck up; Swed. dial. *kilta*, to swaddle. Again, this verb is from the sb. seen in Swed. dial. *kilta*, the lap, Icel. *kjalta*, lap (whence *kjöltu-barn*, a baby in the lap), Goth. *kilthei*, the womb. Allied to **Child**. From the sense of womb or lap we pass to that of swaddling a child and of kilting or tucking up clothes.

Kimbo; see **Akimbo**.

Kin, genus, race. (E.) M. E. *kin*, *kun*. A.S. *cynn*, orig. a tribe.+Icel. *kyn*, kin, Du. *kunne*, sex; Goth. *kuni*, tribe. Allied to **Genus**. (√GAN.)

kind (1), adj., natural, loving. (E.) M. E. *kunde*, *kinde*. A. S. *cynde*, natural, in-born; allied to Goth. *kunds*, born. Allied to **Kin**. (√GAN.)

kind (2), sb., nature, sort. (E.) M. E. *kund*, *kind*. A.S. *cynd*, *ge-cynd*, nature;

due to the adj. above. **Der.** *kind-ly*, natural.

kindle (2), to bring forth young. (E.) M. E. *kindlen*; from the adj. now spelt *kind*; see above. We find also M. E. *kindel*, sb., a progeny, from the A. S. *cynd*, nature, or from the adj. *cynde*, natural.

kindred. (E.) The former *d* is excrescent. M. E. *kinrede.*—A. S. *cyn*, kin; *-ræden*, a suffix signifying law, state, condition (so also *hat-red* from *hate*). *Ræden* is allied to the verb *to read.*

king, a chief ruler. (E.) A. S. *cyning*, a king; lit. 'belonging to the tribe,' or 'son of the tribe;' hence, elected by the tribe.—A. S. *cyn*, a tribe, kin; with suffix *-ing*, as in *Ælfred Æþelwulfing* = Ælfred the son of Æthelwulf.+O. Sax. *kuning*, from *kuni*, tribe; O. Fries. *kining*; Icel. *konungr*; Swed. *konung*; Dan. *konge*; Du. *koning*; G. *könig*, O. H. G. *chuning* (from O. H. G. *chunni*, a tribe, race).

kingdom. (E.) M.E.*kingdom*; not really a compound of *king* and suffix *-dom*, but an easy substitution for M. E. *kinedom*, A. S. *cynedóm*, a kingdom. The A. S. *cyne* signifies 'royal,' very common in composition, and is allied to A. S. *cyn*, a tribe. The substitution of *kingdom* for A. S. *cynedóm* makes little practical difference; see **king** above.

Kindle (1), to inflame; see **Candle.**

Kindle (2), to bring forth young; see **Kin.**

Kindred; see **Kin.**

Kine, cows; see **Cow.**

King, Kingdom; see **Kin.**

Kink, a twist in a rope. (Scand.) A Northern word. — Swed. *kink*, Norweg. *kink*, a twist in a rope. (So also Du. *kink*.) Allied to Norweg. *kika*, *kinka*, to writhe, Icel. *kikna*, to sink at the knees under a burden, Icel. *keikr*, bent back. (Teut. base KIK, to bend.)

Kipper, to cure salmon. (Du.) This meaning is an accidental one, arising from a habit of curing *kipper-salmon*, i. e. salmon during the spawning season, which were cured because of inferior quality. A salmon, after spawning, was called a *kipper* (Pennant). The lit. sense is 'spawner.'—Du. *kippen*, to hatch; also to catch, seize.+ Icel. *kippa*, Swed. dial. *kippa*, Norweg. *kippa*, to snatch.

Kirk, a church. (Scand.—E. — Gk.) M. E. *kirke.*—Icel. *kirkja*; borrowed from A. S. *cirice*, *circe*, a church. See **Church.**

Kirtle, a sort of gown or petticoat. (E.

or Scand.) M. E. *kirtel.* A.S. *cyrtel*, a tunic.+Icel. *kyrtill*, Dan. *kiortel*, Swed. *kjortel*; evidently dimin. forms. Prob. a dimin. of *skirt*; cf. Icel. *skyrta*, Dan. *skiorte*, Swed. *skjorta*, a shirt, skirt. The loss of *s* may have been due to L. *curtus*, short, which is from the same root as *skirt* and *short*; see **Skirt, Shirt, Curt.** Cf. Du. *kort*, G. *kurz*, short.

Kiss, a salute with the lips. (E.) The vowel *i* is due to the *verb*, which is formed from the *sb.* by vowel-change. M. E. *coss*, sb., a kiss; whence *kissen*, verb. A.S. *coss*, sb.; whence *cyssan*, verb.+Du. *kus*, Icel. *koss*, Dan. *kys*, Swed. *kyss*, G. *kuss*, a kiss. Allied to Goth. *kustus*, a proof, test, L. *gustus*, a taste. The Goth. *kustus* is from *kiusan*, to choose. A kiss is a gust or taste, or something choice. Allied to **Choose** and **Gust.**

Kit (1), a milk-pail, tub; also, an outfit. (O. Low G.) M. E. *kit.*—O. Du. *kitte*, a tub; Du. *kit.* Cf. Norweg. *kitte*, a combin.

Kit (2), a small violin. (L. — Gk.) Short for A. S. *cytere*, a cittern; from L. *cithara*; see **Cithern.**

Kit (3), a brood, family, quantity. (E.) A variant of *kith.* 'The whole *kit*' = the whole kith. See under **Can** (1).

Kit-cat, Kit-kat, the name given to portraits of a particular size. (Personal name.) The size adopted by Sir G. Kneller for painting members of the *Kit-Kat* club, which used to meet at a house kept by *Christopher Kat* (Haydn). *Kit* is for *Christopher* (Gk. Χριστο-φόρος, lit. 'Christ-bearing').

Kitchen; see **Cook.**

Kite, a bird, a toy for flying. (E.) M. E. *kite.* A.S. *cýta*, a kite.

Kith; see **Can** (1).

Kitten; see **Cat.**

Knack, a snap, dexterity, trick. (E.) Imitative, like **Knap.** Cf. Gael. *cnac*, Irish *cnag*, a crack, *cnagaim*, I knock, strike; W. *cnec*, a snap. It meant (1) a snap, (2) a snap with the finger or nail, (3) a jester's trick, piece of dexterity, (4) a joke, trifle, toy, &c.

knag, a knot in wood, peg. (C.) M. E. *knagge*, a peg, a knot in wood. — Irish *cnag*, a knob, peg, *cnaig*, a knot in wood; Gael. *cnag*, knob, pin, peg. Cf. W. *cnwc*, a lump. Just as E. *bump*, a swelling from a blow, is from the verb to *bump*, so *knag*, orig. a bump, knob, is from Irish *cnag-aim*,

I **knock**, strike, Gael. *cnag*, to crack, snap the fingers, knock, W. *cnocio*, to knock. See **Knack** above.

knick-knack, a trick, trifle, toy. (E.) A reduplication of *knack*, in the sense of trifle, toy. Cf. Du. *knikken*, to snap, weakened form of *knakken*, to crack; a word of Celtic origin.

knock, to strike, rap. (E.) M. E. *knocken*. A.S. *cnucian*. Gael. *cnac*, to crack, *cnag*, to knock; Irish *cnagaim*, I knock; W. *cnocio*, to knock; Corn. *cnoucye*, to knock. An imitative word, closely allied to **Knack**.

knoll (1), a hillock. (C.) M. E. *knol*. A.S. *cnol*. (So also Du. *knol*, a turnip, from its roundness, Dan. *knold*, a knoll, Swed. *knöl*, a bump, G. *knollen*, a knoll, clod, lump); a word of Celtic origin. ‒ W. *cnol*, a knoll, hillock; a dimin. form. The orig. is seen in Gael. *cnoc*, a hill, knoll, hillock, Irish *cnoc*, a hillock, a turnip.

knuckle, the projecting joint of the fingers. (C.) M. E. *knokil*; cf. O. Fries. *knokle*, Du. *knokkel*, Dan. *knokkel*, G. *knöchel*, a knuckle. A dimin. form; the shorter form appears in Swed. *knoge*, a knuckle, Du. *knoke*, a bone, knuckle, knot of a tree, G. *knochen*, a bone; words of Celtic origin. ‒ W. *cnwc*, a lump, bump, Gael. *cnag*, a knob, Irish *cnag*, a knob; see **knag** (above).

noggin, a wooden cup. (C.) Irish *noigin*, Gael. *noigean*, a noggin. The word has lost an initial *c*; cf. Gael. *cnagan*, a little knob, a peg, an earthen pipkin, Irish *cnagaire*, a noggin. Named from its round form, or from knotty wood; cf. Gael. *cnagaidh*, bunchy; Irish *cnag*, a knock, blow, bump, *cnaig*, a knot in wood.

nudge, a slight push. (E.) Lowl. Sc. *nudge*, to push, strike, strike with the knuckles. A derivative of **Knock** (above). Cf. Dan. *knuge*, to press, Swed. *knoge*, a knuckle.

Knacker, a dealer in old horses. (Scand.) It formerly meant a saddler and harness-maker (Ray). ‒ Icel. *hnakkr*, a saddle.

Knag; see **Knack**.

Knap, to snap. (Du.) Du. *knappen*, to snap, crack, crush, eat (whence *knapper*, hard gingerbread, a lie). Cf. Dan. *kneppe*, to snap; Swed. *knep*, a trick. A parallel word to *knack*, and of imitative origin. Gael. *cnap*, to strike, beat, thump; Irish *cnapaim*, I strike. See **Knop** (below).

knapsack. (Du.) Du. *knapzak*, a knapsack, lit. a provision-bag. ‒ Du. *knap*, eating, *knappen*, to crush, eat (a word of Celtic origin, as above); *zak*, a sack (a word of Hebrew origin); see **Sack**.

knapweed, knopweed, a weed with a hard head or *knop*; see **knop** (below).

knave, a boy, servant, sly fellow. (E.; *perhaps* C.) M. E. *knaue* (*knave*), a boy, servant. A.S. *cnafa*, older form *cnapa*, a boy. (So also Du. *knaap*, a lad, servant; Icel. *knapi*, servant-boy; G. *knabe*, boy.) All of Celtic origin (the Celtic boys being servants to the Teutons); cf. Gael. *cnapach*, a youngster, a stout smart boy, orig. an adj. signifying knobby, lumpy, stout; from the sb. *cnap*, a knob. We may therefore regard it as ultimately a derivative of *knop*; see below.

knob, a weakened and later form of *knop*.

knop, a bump, protuberance, boss. (E.) M. E. *knop*, a rose-bud; *knap* is also a hill-top (whence *Nab Scar*). A.S. *cnæp*, a hill-top (so also Du. *knop*, a knob, bud, Icel. *knappr*, Dan. *knap, knop*, Swed. *knopp, knop*, G. *knopf*, all in the sense of knob, button, stud). We may also compare Gael. *cnap*, a knob, button, boss, stud, hillock, also a slight blow; from the verb *cnap*, to thump, beat (hence, to raise a bump); W. *cnap*, a knob; Irish *cnap*, knob, bunch, hillock, from *cnapaim*, I strike. See **Knap** (above).

nap (2), the roughish surface of cloth. (E.) M. E. *noppe*, nap, orig. a little *knop* or knob on cloth, which was cut away with little nippers, thus leaving what we now call *nap*. The same as *knop*.

nape, the joint of the neck behind. (E.) M. E. *nape*, of which the orig. sense was ‘knob,’ as applied to the slight projection at the back of the head, above the neck. The same word as *knap* or *knop*.

Knave; see under **Knap**.

Knead, to mould by pressure. (E.) M. E. *kneden*. A.S. *cneden* (pt. t. *cnæd*, pp. *cnoden*), a strong verb, to knead. +Du. *kneden*, Icel. *knoða*, Swed. *knåda*, G. *kneten* (all from Teut. base KNAD). Allied to Russ. *gnetate, gnesti*, to press, squeeze.

Knee. (E.) M. E. *kne*, pl. *knees*; also *cneo*, pl. *cneon*. A.S. *cneow, cneó*. + Du. *knie*, Icel. *kné*, Dan. *knæ*, Swed. *knä*, G. *knie*, Goth. *kniu*. +L. *genu*, Gk. γόνυ, Skt. *jánu*. (Aryan GANU, knee.) See **Genu-flection, Pentagon**, &c.

kneel, to fall on the knees. (Scand.) M. E. *knelen*. — Dan. *knæle*; formed from *knæ*, knee.

Knell, Knoll, to sound as a bell, toll. (E.) M. E. *knillen*. A. S. *cnyllan*, to knock, beat noisily. + Du. *knallen*, to give a loud report, Dan. *knalde*, to explode; Swed. *knalla*, to resound, G. *knallen*, to make a loud noise, Icel. *gnella*, to scream. Words of imitative origin, to denote a loud noise; cf. Du. *knal*, Dan. *knald*, Swed. *knall*, G. *knall*, a loud noise.

Knick-knack; see **Knack**.

Knife; see **Nip**.

Knight, a youth, servant, man-at-arms. (E.) M. E. *knight*. A. S. *cniht*, a boy, servant. + Du. *knecht*, a servant; Dan. *knegt*, man-servant, knave (at cards); Swed. *knekt*, soldier, knave (at cards); G. *knecht*. β. Perhaps *cniht* = *cyn-iht**, belonging to the kin or tribe; cf. Gk. γνήσιος, legitimate, from γένος, kin; see **Kin**.

Knit; see **Knot**.

Knob; see **Knap**.

Knock, Knoll (1), a hillock; see **Knack**.

Knoll (2); see **Knell**.

Knop; see **Knap**.

Knot. (E.) M. E. *knotte*. — A. S. *cnotta*, a knot. + Du. *knot*; Icel. *knútr*; Dan. *knude*; Swed. *knut*; G. *knoten*. + L. *nodus* (for *gnodus*). See **Node**.

   knit. (E.) A. S. *cnyttan*, to form into a knot, to knot; formed (by vowel-change of *o* to *y*) from *cnotta*, a knot. + Icel. *knýta*, from *knútr*, sb.; Dan. *knytte*, from *knude*; Swed. *knyta*, from *knut*.

noddle, the head. (E.) M. E. *nodle*,

nodil, the noddle. Dimin. of *knod*, a word lost in M. E., but the same as O. Du. *knodde*, a knob (Hexham), Icel. *knútðr*, a knob, bail, G. *knoten*, a knot, knob. This is a mere variant of *knot*.

Knout, a scourge. (Russ. — Scand.) Russ. *knute*, a whip, scourge. — Icel. *knútr*, a knot.

Know, to be assured of. (E.) M. E. *knowen*. A. S. *cnáwan* (pt. t. *cneów*, pp. *cnáwen*). + Icel. *kná*, O. H. G. *chnáan*. Further allied to Russ. *znate*, to know; L. *noscere* (for *gnoscere*); Gk. γι-γνώσκειν; Skt. *jná*, to know. (All from a base GNÂ, a secondary form of GAN, to know.)

   knowledge. (E.; *with* Scand. *suffix*.) M. E. *knowlege*, *knauleche*. The suffix *-leche* is a weakened form of *-leke*, answering to Icel. *-leikr*, *-leiki*, Swed. *-lek*, a suffix used for forming abstract nouns. Cf. Icel. *kær-leikr*, Swed. *kär-lek*, love, Icel. *sann-leikr*, truth, *heilag-leiki*, holiness. The A. S. spelling of this suffix is *-lác*, and it occurs in E. *wed-lock*; it is the same as A. S. *lác*, a game, sport, play; see **Lark** (2).

Knuckle; see **Knack**.

Knurr, Knur, a knot in wood, wooden ball. (O. Low G.) M. E. *knor*. Not in A. S. — O. Du. *knorre*, a hard swelling, knot in wood. + Dan. *knort*, a knot; G. *knorren*, a lump. See **Gnarled**.

Koran, sacred book of the Mohammedans. (Arab.) Arab. *qurán*, reading, a legible book, the Koran. — Arab. root *qara-a*, he read. (The *a* is long.)

   alcoran; the same word with the Arab. def. art. *al* (the) prefixed.

Kythe; see **Can** (1).

L.

Label; see **Lap** (2).

Labial. (L.) Late L. *labialis*, pertaining to the lips. — L. *labium*, the lip. See **Lap** (1), **Lip**.

   labellum, a pendulous petal. (L.) L. *labellum*, dimin. of *labium*, a lip.

   labiate. (L.) A botanical term. — L. *labi-um*, a lip; with suffix *-ate* (L. *-atus*).

Laboratory; see **Labour**.

Labour, toil. (F. — L.) M. E. *labour*. — O. F. *labour* (later *labeur*). — L. *labōrem*, acc. of *labor*, *labos*, toil. Allied to *robur*, strength. (√RABH.)

   belabour. (F. — L.; *with* E. *prefix*.)

Coined by prefixing E. *be-* (= *by*) to E. *labour*, a word of F. origin (above).

   elaborate. (L.) L. *elaboratus*, pp. of *elaborare*, to labour greatly. — L. *e*, out, greatly; *laborare*, to work, from *labor*, labour.

   laboratory. (L.) Formerly *elaboratory* (Blount). — O. F. *elaboratoire* (Cot.). Formed from L. *elaboratus*, pp. of *elaborare*, to elaborate, work out.

   laborious. (F. — L.) M. E. *laborious*. — F. *laborieux*. — L. *laboriosus*, toilsome. — L. *labori-*, crude form of *labor*, labour.

Laburnum, a tree. (L.) L. *laburnum*, in Pliny, xvi. 18. Perhaps = *alburnum*.

Labyrinth, a maze. (F. — L. — Gk.) F. *labyrinthe*. — L. *labyrinthus*. — Gk. λαβύρινθος, a maze, a place full of lanes or alleys. Put for λαϝύρινθος; from λαϝρα, usually λαύρα, a lane.

Lac (1), a resinous substance. (Pers.— Skt.) Pers. *lak*, *luk*, gum-lac, whence crimson lake is obtained for dyeing. — Skt. *lákshá*, lac; put for *raktá*, lac. — Skt. *rakta*, pp. of *rañj*, to dye, colour, redden; cf. Skt. *ranga*, colour, paint. Der. *gum-lac*, *shel-lac*.

lacquer, **lacker**, a sort of varnish. (F. —Port.— Pers.—Skt.) F. *lacre* (Cot.).— Port. *lacre*, sealing-wax. — Port. *laca*, gum-lac. — Pers. *lak*, gum-lac (above).

lake (2), a crimson colour. (F. — Pers. —Skt.) F. *laque* (Cot.) — Pers. *lák*, lake. — Pers. *lak*, gum-lac (above).

Lac (2), a hundred thousand. (Hind.— Skt.) A *lac* of rupees = 100,000 rupees. — Hindustani *lak* (also *lákh*), a lac. — Skt. *laksha*, a hundred thousand; apparently with reference to the number of lac-insects in a nest; see Lac (1).

Lace, a cord, tie. (F. — L.) M. E. *las*, *laas*. — O. F. *las*, *laqs*, a snare, noose. — L. *laqueus*, a noose, snare, knot. Allied to L. *lacĕre*, to allure; cf. E. *elicit*, *delight*.

lasso, a rope with a noose. (Span.— L.) O. Span. *laso* (Minsheu); mod. Span. *lazo*, F. *lacs*; see above. ¶ The E. word is from Mexican Span., with *s* = E. *ss*; the Span. *lazo* has *z* sounded as voiceless *th*.

latchet, a little lace, thong. (F.—L.) M. E. *lachet*. — O. F. *lacet*, a lace; dimin. of *laqs*, a lace; see above.

Lacerate, to tear. (L.) From pp. of L. *lacerare*, to tear. — L. *lacer*, mangled, torn. **+** Gk. λακερός, torn; λακίς, a rent; Skt. *vraçch*, to tear. (✓ WRAK.)

dilacerate. (L.) From pp. of L. *di-lacerare*, to tear asunder.

Lachrymal, **Lacrimal**, pertaining to tears. (L.) The spelling *lachrymal* is bad. — L. *lacryma*, better *lacruma*, *lacrima*, a tear; O. L. *dacrima*, a tear. Cognate with Gk. δάκρυ, a tear, and E. *tear*; see Tear (1). Der. (from L. *lacrima*) *lachrymose*, tearful; *lachrymatory*, a tear-bottle.

Lack (1), want. (O. Low G.) The old sense is often 'failure' or 'fault.' M. E. *lak*, *lac*. Not in A. S. — Du. *lak*, blemish, stain; *laken*, to blame. Cf. Icel. *lakr*, defective, lacking. Perhaps allied to **Leak**.

lack (2), to be destitute of. (O. Low G.) M. E. *lakken*; weak verb; from *lak*, sb. See above.

Lacker; see Lacquer, under Lac (1).

Lackey, **Lacquey**, a footman, menial attendant. (F. — Span. ? — Arab. ?) From O. F. *laquay*, 'a lackey, footboy;' Cot. There was also an O. F. form *alacay*; Littré shews that, in the 15th cent., a certain class of soldiers (esp. crossbow-men), were called *alagues*, *alacays*, or *lacays*. (The prefix *a-* is prob. due to Arab. *al*, the def. article.) Prob. from Span. *lacayo*, Port. *lacaio*, a lackey; Port. *lacaia*, a woman-servant in dramatic performances. — Arab. *luka'*, worthless, servile; as a sb., a slave; *lak'á*, fem., mean, servile. Cf. *lakú'*, *lakî'*, servile, *lakâ'i*, slovenly. ¶ This is a guess; it is much disputed; Diez connects it with Ital. *leccare*, G. *lecken*, to lick.

Laconic, brief and pithy. (L. — Gk.) L. *Laconicus*, Laconian. — Gk. Λακωνικός, Laconian. — Gk. Λάκων, a Laconian, Spartan. These men were celebrated for their brief and pithy locution.

Lacquer; see Lac (1).

Lacteal, relating to milk. (L.) From L. *lacte-us*, milky. — L. *lact-*, stem of *lac*, milk. **+** Gk. γαλακτ-, stem of γάλα, milk. Root unknown.

lettuce, a succulent plant. (F. — L.) M. E. *letuce*. — O. F. *laictuce**, *laituce**, not recorded, old form of *laictuĕ* (Cot.), mod. F. *laitue*, lettuce. — L. *lactuca*, lettuce; named from its juiciness. — L. *lact-*, stem of *lac*, milk.

Lad, a youth. (C.) M. E. *ladde*. — Irish *lath*, a youth, champion; W. *llawd*, a youth. Allied to Irish *luth*, nimble, active, Gael. *laidir*, strong, *luth*, strength; and to Goth. *jugga-lauths*, a young man (from *liudan*, to grow).

lass, a girl. (C.) Contracted from W. *llodes*, a girl, fem. form of *llawd*, a lad.

Ladanum; see Laudanum.

Ladder. (E.) M. E. *laddre*. A. S. *hlæder*, a ladder. **+** Du. *ladder*, ladder, rails of a cart; O. H. G. *hleitra*, G. *leiter*, a ladder.

Lade (1), to load. (E.) Formerly a strong verb; we still use the pp. *laden*. M. E. *laden*. A. S. *hladan* (pt. t. *hlód*, pp. *hladen*), meaning (1) to load, heap up, heap together, (2) to draw out water, lade out, drain. **+** Du. *laden*, Icel. *hlaða*, Dan. *lade*, Swed. *ladda*, Goth. *hlathan* (in *af-hlathan*), G. *be-laden*, to lade. (Teut. base

HLATH, to lade). Allied to Russ. *klade*, a load.

ballast, a load to steady a ship. (Du.) From Du. *ballast*, ballast. + Dan. *ballast*, *baglast*; Swed. *barlast*, O. Swed. *ballast*. The Dan. *baglast*, lit. ' back-load,' is a late form due to popular etymology ; the older Dan. form was *barlast*. Again, both Dan. and Swed. *barlast* are corruptions of O. Swed. *ballast*. So also E. Fries. *ballast*, lit. ' unprofitable load ' (Koolman). — Du. *bal-*, evil (as in *bal-dadd*, evil deed) ; *last*, load. See **Bale** (2), and **last** (4), below.

lade (2), to draw out water, drain. (E.) The same word as **Lade** (1).

ladle, a large spoon. (E.) M. E. *ladel*; so named from being used for dipping out or *lading* water from a vessel ; from M. E. *laden*, to lade out ; see above.

last (4), a load, large weight, ship's cargo. (E.) M. E. *last*. A. S. *hlæst*, a burden. Formed from A.S. *hladan*, to lade, load. + Icel. *hlass*, a cart-load, from *hlaða* ; Dan. *last*, cargo, from *lade* ; Swed. Du. and G. *last*, a burden.

load, a burden. (E.) The sense of ' burden' seems to be due to the verb **Lade** (1) above; a confusion caused by the use of *lead*, verb, in the sense ' to carry.' Really = **Lode**, q. v.

Lady; see **Loaf**.

Lag, late, sluggish. (C.) W. *llag*, slack, loose, sluggish ; Corn. *lac*, loose, remiss. + L. *laxus*, lax ; see **Lax**, **Languid**.

Lagoon; see **Lake** (1).

Laic; see **Lay** (3).

Lair, den ; see **Lie** (1).

Laity; see **Lay** (3).

Lake (1), a pool. (L.) A. S. *lac*. — L. *lacus*, a lake. + Gk. λάκκος, a hollow, hole, pit, pond.

lagoon. (Ital. — L.) Ital. *lagone*, a pool; also *laguna*. The former is an augmentative of L. *lacus*; the latter is from L. *lacuna*, extended from *lacus*.

loch, a lake. (Gaelic) Gael. *loch*, a lake. + W. *llwch*, Corn. *lo*, Bret. *louch*; L. *lacus*.

lough, a lake. (Irish). Irish *loch*; the same as Gael. *loch* (above).

Lake (2), crimson ; see **Lac** (1).

Lama (1), a high priest. (Thibetan). We speak of the *grand lama* of Thibet, i. e. chief or high priest (Webster).

Lama (2) ; see **Llama**.

Lamb. (E.) M. E. *lamb*, *lomb*. A. S. *lamb*. + Du. *lam*, Icel. *lamb*, Dan. *lam*, Swed. and G. *lamm*, Goth. *lamb*, a young sheep.

Lambent, flickering. (L.) ' A *lambent* flame.' — L. *lambent-*, stem of pres. pt. of *lambere*, to lick, sometimes applied to flames. + Gk. λάπτειν, to lick. Allied to **Lap** (1).

lamprey, a fish. (F. — L.) O.F. *lamproie* (Ital. *lampreda*). — Low L. *lampreda*, better spelt *lampetra*. Lit. ' licker of rocks,' because the fish cleaves to them. — L. *lamb-ere*, to lick ; *petra*, a rock ; see **Petrify**.

Lame, disabled, esp. in the legs. (E.) M. E. *lame*. A. S. *lama*. + Du. *lam*, Icel. *lami*, Dan. *lam*, Swed. *lam*, G. *lahm*. The orig. sense is bruised, maimed ; from a base LAM, to break. Cf. Russ. *lomate*, to break ; Icel. *lama*, to bruise ; prov. E. *lam*, to bruise.

Lament, vb. (F. — L.) F. *lamenter*. — L. *lamentari*, to wail. — L. *lamentum*, a mournful cry ; from the base *la-*, to utter a cry ; cf. *la-trare*, to bark. Cf. also Russ. *laiate*, to bark, scold ; Gk. ράξειν, to bark. (√RA.) Der. *lament*, sb.

Lamina. (L.) L. *lamina*, a thin plate of metal.

Lammas; see **Loaf**.

Lamp. (F. — L. — Gk.) O. F. *lampe*. — L. *lampas*. — Gk. λαμπάς, a torch, light. — Gk. λάμπειν, to shine. (√LAP, RAP.)

lantern. (F. — L. — Gk.) M. E. *lanterne*. — F. *lanterne*. — L. *lanterna*, *lāterna*; a lantern (not a true L. word). *Lanterna* = *lamterna* * = *lampterna**, borrowed from Gk. λαμπτήρ, a light, torch. — Gk. λάμπειν, to shine. ¶ Sometimes spelt *lanthorn*, because *horn* was used for the sides of lanterns !

Lampoon; see **Lap** (1).

Lamprey; see **Lambent**.

Lance. (F. — L.) F. *lance*. — L. *lancea*. + Gk. λόγχη, a lance. Der. *lance*, verb, to pierce ; *lanc-er*.

lancegay, a kind of spear. (F. — L.; and F. — Span. — Moorish). Obsolete. A corruption of *lance-zagaye*, compounded of *lance* (as above), and F. *zagaye*, a kind of Moorish pike. The latter word answers to Span. *azagaya* (= *al zagaya*), where *al* is the Arab. def. article, and *zagaya* is an O. Span. word for ' dart,' of Moorish origin. So Port. *azagaia*, whence E. *assegai*.

lanceolate, lance - shaped. (L.) L. *lanceolatus*, furnished with a spike. — L. *lanceola*, a spike ; dimin. of *lancea* (above).

lancet. (F. — L.) M. E. *launcet*. — O. F. *lancette*, dimin. of *lance*, a lance (above).

lanch, another spelling of *lance*, verb, to pierce; also of *launch* (below).

launch, lanch, to hurl a spear, send (a ship) into the water. (F. – L.) M. E. *launcen*, to hurl. – F. *lancer*, to hurl, fling, dart, also to prick, pierce. – F. *lance*, a lance (above).

Land. (E.) M. E. *land, lond.* A. S. *land.* **+** Du. Icel. Dan. Swed. Goth. G. *land.* Der. *up-land, out-land-ish.*

landau, a kind of coach. (G.) Said to be named from *Landau*, a town in Bavaria. *Land* is cognate with E. *land*; G. *au* is cognate with *i-* in M. E. *i-land*; see Island.

landgrave, a count of a province. (Du.) Du. *landgraaf.* – Du. *land*, land; *graaf*, a count. Der. *landgrav-ine*, from Du. *landgravin*, fem. of *landgraaf*; see **Margrave.**

landrail, a bird; see Rail (3).

landscape. (Du.) Formerly *landskip*; borrowed from Dutch painters. – Du. *landschap*, a landscape, a province. – Du. *land*, land; and *-schap*, a suffix corresponding to E. *-ship* in *friend ship*, derived from the verb which we spell *shape.* ¶ The Du. *sch* sounds to us more like *sk* than *sh*; hence our spelling with *sc.*

lansquenet, a German foot-soldier, a game at cards. (F. – G.) F. *lansquenet*, 'a lance-knight [a misspelling] or German footman;' Cot. – G. *landsknecht*, a foot-soldier. – G. *lands*, put for *landes*, gen. of *land*, country; *knecht*, a soldier (E. *knight*). Thus *lansquenet = land's-knight*; orig. a soldier from the Low Countries.

Lane. (E.) M. E. *lane, lone.* A. S. *láne, lone*, a lane. **+** O. Fries. *lona, lana*, Du. *laan*, a lane, narrow passage.

Language; see Lingual.

Languish. (F.–L.) M. E. *languishen.* – F. *languiss-*, stem of pres. part. of *languir*, to languish. – L. *languere*, to be weak. Allied to Gk. λαγγάζειν, to slacken, loiter, λαγαρός, slack; Icel. *lakra*, to lag; and to **Lag.** (√ LAG.)

languid. (L.) L. *languidus*, feeble. – L. *languere*, to be languid or weak.

languor, dulness. (F. – L.) M. E. *languor.* – F. *langueur.* – L. *languōrem*, acc. of *languor.* – L. *languere* (above).

Laniard; see Lanyard.

Laniferous, wool-bearing. (L.) From L. *lana*, wool; *ferre*, to bear.

Lank, slender, thin. (E.) M. E. *lank.* A. S. *hlanc*, slender. The orig. sense was prob. 'bending;' see **Link** (1).

Lansquenet; see Land.

Lantern; see Lamp.

Lanyard, Laniard, a certain small rope in a ship. (F. – L.?) Formerly spelt *lannier*, the final *d* being excrescent. – O. F. *laniere*, 'a long and narrow band or thong of leather;' Cot. Orig. uncertain; prob. Latin; yet it is difficult to connect it with L. *lanarius*, woollen, or with *laniarius*, belonging to a *lanius*, i. e. butcher.

Lap (1), to lick up with the tongue. (E.) M. E. *lappen.* A. S. *lapian*, to lap. **+** Icel. *lepja*, Dan. *labe*, O. H. G. *laffan*, to lap up. **+** W. *llepio*, L. *lambere*, Gk. λάπτειν, to lap with the tongue. (Base LAP.) Allied to *lambent, labial*, and *lip.*

lampoon. (F. – Teut.) F. *lampon*, orig. a drinking-song; from the exclamation *lampons!* = let us drink (Littré). – F. *lamper*, nasalised form of O. F. *lapper*, to lap up; of Teut. origin.

Lap (2), the loose part of a coat, an apron, part of the body covered by an apron, a fold. (E.) M. E. *lappe.* A. S. *lappa*, a loosely hanging portion. **+** Du. *lap*, Dan. *lap*, Swed. *lapp*, G. *lappen*, a patch, shred, rag. Cf. Icel. *lapa*, to hang down; Skt. *lamb, ramb*, to hang down. (√ RAB). Allied to Lobe, Limbo, Lapse, Limp (1).

label, a small slip of paper, &c. (F. – O. H. G.) M. E. *label.* – O. F. *label*, a label (in heraldry); mod. F. *lambeau.* Orig. 'a small flap' or shred. – O. H. G. *lappa*, G. *lappen*, a patch, shred, rag (above). ¶ So also *lap-el*, a flap of a coat, dimin. of E. *lap*; *lapp-et*, also dimin. of E. *lap*; whence also the verb *to lap over.*

Lap (3), to wrap. (E.) M. E. *lappen*, also *wlappen*, another form of *wrappen*; see **Wrap.** Quite distinct from *lap* (2). The form *wlappen* explains *de-velop, en-velop.*

Lapidary, one who sets precious stones. (L.) Englished from L. *lapidarius*, a stonemason, a jeweller. – L. *lapid-*, stem of *lapis*, a stone. Allied to Gk. λέπας, a bare rock, λεπίς, a flake, λέπειν, to peel. See **Leaf.**

dilapidate, to pull down stone buildings, to ruin. (L.) From pp. of L. *dilapidare*, to scatter like stones. – L. *di-*, for *dis*, apart; *lapid-*, base of *lapis*, a stone.

Lapse. (L.) From L. *lapsare*, to slip, frequent. of *labi* (pp. *lapsus*), to glide, slip, trip. (√ RAB.) Allied to **Lap** (2).

collapse, to shrink together, fall in. (L.) First used in the pp. *collapsed*, Englished from L. *collapsus*, pp. of *collabi*, to fall together. = L. *col-* (for *con-*, i.e. *cum*), together; *labi*, to slip.

elapse, to glide away. (L.) From L. *elapsus*, pp. of *e-labi*, to glide away.

illapse, a gliding in, a sudden entrance. (L.) L. *illapsus*, sb. a gliding in. = L. *il-* (for *in*), in; *lapsus*, a gliding, from pp. of *labi*.

relapse, to slide back into a former state. (L.) From L. *relapsus*, pp. of *re-labi*, to slide back.

Lapwing; see **Leap**.

Larboard. (E. *or* Scand.?) Cotgrave has: '*Babort*, the larboard side of a ship.' The M. E. spelling appears to be *ladlebord*, if, indeed, this be the same word; see Allit. Poems, ed. Morris, C. 106. This possibly answers to Icel. *hlaða*, to take in sail (properly to lade), Swed. *ladda*, to lade. But it is very uncertain. The word *board* means 'side of a ship,' as in *star-board*. ¶ The F. *babort*, *babord* = G. *back-bord*, where *back* (lit. back) is 'forecastle,' orig. placed on the left side (Littré).

Larceny, robbery. (F. = L.) The *-y* is an E. addition. = O. F. *larrecin* (F. *larcin*), larceny. = L. *latrocinium*, robbery; formed with suffix *-cinium* (as in *tiro-cinium*) from *latro*, a robber. Allied to Gk. λάτρις, a hireling, used in a bad sense; the base appears in Gk. λαϝ, to get, seen in ἀπο-λαύ-ειν, to get, enjoy; cf. L. *lu-crum*, gain. See **Lucre**.

Larch, a tree. (F. = L. = Gk.) O. F. *larege*, 'the larch;' Cot. = L. *laricem*, acc. of *larix*, a larch. = Gk. λάριξ, a larch.

Lard. (F. = L.) O. F. *lard.* = L. *larda*, *larida*, lard, fat of bacon. Cf. Gk. λαρός, nice, λαρινός, fat. **Der.** *lard-er*, from O. F. *lardier*, a tub to keep bacon in, hence a room in which to keep bacon and meat. Also *inter-lard*.

Large. (F. = L.) F. *large.* = L. *largus*, great.

largess, a liberal gift. (F. = L.) F. *largesse*, bounty. = Low L. *largitia**, not found, put for L. *largitio*, a bestowing. = L. *largitus*, pp. of *largiri*, to bestow. = L. *largus*, large, liberal.

Lark (1), a bird. (E.) Another form is *lavrock* (Burns). M. E. *larke*, also *lave rock*. = A. S. *láwerce*, later *láuerce*, *láferce*. + Icel. *lævirki*, a lark; Low G. *lewerke*, O. H. G. *lerehha*, G. *lerche*, Du. *leeuwrik*, Swed. *lärka*, Dan. *lærke*. β. The Icel. *lævirki* = worker of craft, from *læ*, craft, *virki*, worker; so also A. S. *láwerce* = *láw-*

*werca**, worker of guile. The name points to some superstition which regarded the bird as of ill omen.

Lark (2), a game, fun. (E.) The *r* is intrusive, the spelling being phonetic; it should rather be *laak* (*aa* as *a* in father). M. E. *lak*, *lok*; (Northern) *laik*. A. S. *lác*, sport, play, contest. + Icel. *leikr*, Swed. *lek*, Dan. *leg*, Goth. *laiks*; cf. Goth. *laikan*, to skip for joy. **Der.** *wed-lock*, *know-ledge* (where it is a suffix).

Larum; short for **Alarum**.

Larva. (E.) L. *larua*, a ghost, a mask; used as a scientific name for a caterpillar.

Larynx. (L. = Gk.) L. *larynx.* = Gk. λάρυγξ (gen. λάρυγγ-ος), throat, gullet, larynx. **Der.** *laryng-itis*.

Lascar, a native E. Indian soldier. (Pers.) Pers. *lashkarí*, a soldier; *lashkar*, an army.

Lascivious. (L.) Corrupted from L. *lasciuus*, lustful. Cf. Russ. *laskate*, to caress, Skt. *lash*, to desire, *las*, to embrace. (√RAS.)

Lash (1), to bind firmly together. (Du.) Du. *lasschen*, to join, scarf together; *lasch*, a piece, joint, seam. So also Swed. *laska*, Dan. *laske*, to scarf, Swed. Dan. *lask*, a scarf, joint. The verb is from the sb., which further appears in Low G. *laske*, a flap, G. *lasche*, a flap, groove for scarfing timber. The orig. form was prob. LAKSA, with the sense of flap; see below.

Lash (2), a thong, stripe. (O. Low G. *or* Scand.) M. E. *lasshe*, the flexible part of a whip; cf. Low G. *laske*, a flap (see the word above). *Lash* in the sense of thong is from its use in lashing or binding things together; Swed. *laska*, to stitch. The verb *lash*, to scourge, is to use a *lash*.

Lass; see **Lad**.

Lassitude, weariness. (F. = L.) F. *lassi-tude.* = L. *lassitudo*, weariness. = L. *lassus*, wearied; put for *lad-tus**, and allied to E. **Late**.

Lasso; see **Lace**.

Last (1), latest; see **Late**.

Last (2), a wooden mould of the foot for a shoemaker. (E.) M. E. *last*, *lest*. A. S. *lást*, *ledst*, a foot-track, path, trace of feet (whence the mod. sense follows). + Du. *leest*, a last, form; Icel. *leistr*, the foot below the ancle; Swed. *läst*, Dan. *læst*, G. *leisten*, a shoemaker's last; Goth. *laists*, a foot-track. The standard form appears in Goth. *laist-*; with orig. sense 'foot-track;' from Goth. *lais*, I know (find or trace out),

pt. t. of *leisan*, to find out. Akin to **Learn.**
(Base LIS.)

last (3), to endure. (E.) M.E. *lasten*,
lesten ; A.S. *lǽstan*, to observe, perform,
last ; orig. ' to follow in the track of ; '
from *lást*, a foot-track (above). + Goth.
laistjan, to follow after, from *laists* ; G.
leisten, to follow out, from *leisten*, sb.

Last (4), a burden ; see **Lade** (1).

Latch, a catch, fastening. (E.) M.E.
lacche, a latch, from *lacchen*, to catch.—
A.S. *læccan*, to seize, catch hold of.

clutch, to seize. (E.) M.E. *clucchen*, to
clutch ; from the sb. *cloche* (also *clouche*,
cloke), a claw, talon. This sb. is allied to
M.E. *cleche*, a hook, crook, *clechen* (pt. t.
clauchte), to catch, seize. This verb *clechen*
is from A.S. *gelæccan* (pt. t. *gelæhte*), to
catch, seize, formed from *læccan* (above) by
prefixing *ge-* (a common prefix).

Latchet ; see **Lace.**

Late. (E.) M.E. *lat* ; comp. *later*, *latter*,
superl. *latest*, *latst* (Ormulum, 4168), *last*.
A.S. *læt*, slow, late. + Du. *laat*, Icel. *latr*,
Dan. *lad*, Swed. *lat* ; Goth. *lats*, slothful,
G. *lass*, weary ; L. *lassus* (for *lad-tus* *),
weary. From the verb to *lat*, i. e. let go,
let alone ; *late* means neglected, slothful,
slow. See **Let** (1).

latter, another form of *later* (above).

last (1), latest ; contracted form of *latest.*

lot (2), to hinder. (E.) M.E. *letten* ;
A.S. *lettan*, to hinder, make late. — A.S.
læt, late, slow. + Du. *letten*, from *laat* ;
Icel. *letja*, from *latr* ; Goth. *latjan*, to
tarry, from *lats*, slothful.

Lateen ; see **Latin.**

Latent, hidden. (L.) L. *latent-*, stem of
pres. pt. of *latere*, to lie hid. + Gk. λανθάνειν (base λαθ), to lie hid. (√ RADH.)
See **Lethe.**

Lateral. (L.) L. *lateralis*, belonging
to the side. — L. *later-*, stem of *latus*, side.

collateral. (L.) Late L. *collateralis*,
side by side.— L. *col-* (= *com-* = *cum*), with ;
lateralis (above).

quadrilateral. (L.) From L. *quadri-
later-us*, four-sided. — L. *quadri-*, for *quadrus*, belonging to four ; *lateralis*, adj.
(above) ; see **Quadrate.**

Lath. (E.) North E. *lat.* M. E. *latte.*
A.S. *lættu*, a lath ; pl. *lætta.* + Du. *lat* ;
G. *latte* (whence F. *latte*).

latten, a mixed metal, bronze. (F. —
G.) M.E. *latoun.* — O. F. *laton* (F. *laiton*),
latten. — G. *latte*, a lath, thin plate ; because this metal was hammered out into

thin plates. Cf. Port. *lata*, tin-plate, *latas*,
laths.

lattice. (F. — G.) Formerly *lattis.* M.E.
latis. — F. *lattis*, lath-work, lattice-work.
— F. *latte*, a lath. — G. *latte*, a lath.

Lathe (1), a machine for turning wood,
&c. (Scand.) Icel. *löð* (gen. *lað-ar*), a
smith's lathe. Perhaps for *hlöð*, and from
hlaða, to lade ; cf. A. S. *hlæd-weogl*, a wheel
of a well, for drawing water ; see **Lade** (2).

Lathe (2), a division of a county. (E.)
A.S. *láð*, *léð*, a lathe, province ; Thorpe,
Ancient Laws, i. 184, 455.

Lather. (E.) M.E. *lather.* A.S. *leðor*,
lather ; whence *léðrian*, to anoint. + Icel.
lauðr, froth, foam ; soap. Allied to **Lye**
and **Lave.** (Base LU.)

Latin. (F.—L.) F. *Latin.* — L. *Latinus*,
belonging to *Latium.* Der. *latim-er*, an
interpreter ; put for *Latiner.*

lateen, triangular, applied to sails.
(F. — L.) F. *latine*, as in *voile latine*, a
lateen sail ; *latine* is the fem. of *Latin*,
Latin (Roman).

Latitude, breadth. (F. — L.) M. E.
latitude. — F. *latitude.* — L. *latitudo* (stem
latitudin-), breadth. — L. *latus*, broad ;
short for O. L. *stlatus* = *stratus*, spread out,
pp. of *sternere*, to spread ; see **Stratum.**
(√ STAR.)

Latten ; see **Lath.**

Latter ; see **Late.**

Lattice ; see **Lath.**

Laud, to praise. (L.) M.E. *lauden.* —
L. *laudare*, to praise. — L. *laud-*, stem of
laus, praise.

allow (2), to approve of. (F. — L.)
M. E. *alouen.* — O. F. *alouer*, later *allouer*,
to approve of. — L. *allaudare.* — L. *al-* (for
ad), to ; *laudare*, to praise.

Laudanum. (L. — Gk. — Pers.) Now
a preparation of opium, but formerly applied to a different drug. '*Laudanum*,
Ladanum, *Labdanum*, a sweet-smelling
transparent gum gathered from the leaves
of *Cistus Ledon*, a shrub, of which they
make pomander, it smells like wine mingled
with spices ; ' Blount, 1674. (Laudanum
has a like strong smell).—L. *lādanum*, *lē-
danum*, resin from the shrub *lada* (Pliny).
— Gk. λήδανον, λάδανον (same). — Gk.
λῆδον, a shrub. — Pers. *lādan*, the gum-
herb lada (Richardson).

Laugh. (E.) M.E. *laughen*, *lehghen.*
A.S. *hlehhan*, *hlihan* (pt. t. *hlōh*), to
laugh. + Du. *lagchen*, Icel. *hlæja*, Dan. *lee*,
Swed. *le*, G. *lachen*, Goth. *hlahjan* (pt. t.

hloh). (Base HLAH = Aryan KARK; cf.
Gk. κρώζειν, to caw, L. *crocitare, glocire,*
E. *crake, creak, crack, clack, cluck,* &c.)
Der. *laughter,* A.S. *hleahtor.*

Launch; see **Lance.**

Laundress; see **Lave.**

Laurel. (F. — L.) M. E. *lorel, lorer,*
laurer. — F. *laurier.* — L. *laurarius*,* not
found, formed from L. *laurus,* a laurel-
tree.

   laureate. (L.) L. *laureatus,* crowned
with laurel. — L. *laurea,* fem. of *laureus,*
adj. formed from *laurus* (above).

Lava; see **Lave.**

Lave, to wash. (F. — L.) F. *laver.* —
L. *lauare.* ✛ Gk. λούειν, to wash. (Base
LU.) **Der.** *lav-er,* O. F. *lavoir,* a washing-
pool (Cot.); *lav-at-or-y,* F. *lavatoire,* L.
lauatorium, neut. of *lauatorius,* adj., belonging to a washer.

   ablution. (F. — L.) F.; from L. acc. *ab-*
lutionem, a washing away. — L. *abluere,* to
wash away. — L. *ab,* away; *luere,* to wash
(closely allied to *lauare*).

   alluvial, washed down, applied to soil.
(L.) L. *alluui-us,* alluvial. — L. *al-* (= *ad*),
to, in addition; *luere,* to wash.

   antediluvian, before the flood. (L.)
L. *ante,* before; *diluuium,* deluge; see **de-**
luge (below).

   deluge. (F. — L.) O. F. *deluge.* — L.
diluuium, a washing away. — L. *di-luere,*
to wash away.

   dilute. (L.) L. *dilutus,* pp. of *di-luere,*
to wash away, also to mix with water.

   laundress, a washerwoman. (F.—L.)
Formed by adding F. suffix *-ess* to M. E.
launder or *lavander,* a washerwoman. —
O. F. *lavandiere,* 'a launderesse or washing-
woman;' Cot. — Low L. *lauanderia* (same).
— L. *lauand-us,* fut. pass. part. of *lauare,*
to wash. **Der.** *laundr-y = launder-y.*

   lava. (Ital.—L.) Ital. *lava,* a stream
(esp. of molten rock). — L. *lauare,* to wash,
lave.

lavender, a plant. (F. — Ital. — L.)
M. E. *lavendre,* the *r* being an E. addition.
— F. *lavande,* lavender; Cot. — Ital. *la-*
vanda, lavender; used for being laid in
freshly washed linen. — Ital. *lavanda,* a
washing. — L. *lauare,* to wash.

   lotion, a washing, external medicinal
application. (L.) L. *lotion-em,* acc. of
lotio, a washing. — L. *lotus,* pp. of *lauare,*
to wash.

Lavish, profuse, prodigal. (E.) Formerly
spelt *lavish, laves*; also *lavy.* Formed

with suffix *-ish* (A. S. *-isc*) from the obsolete verb *lave,* to pour out, lade out
water; M. E. *lauen,* to bale out water,
whence the *metaphorical* use of *lauen,* to
give bountifully. 'He *lauez* hys gyftez' =
God *lavishes* His gifts; Allit. Poems, A.
607. It answers to A.S. *lafian, gelafian*
(a doubtful word in Beowulf, ed. Grein,
2722); Du. *laven,* G. *laben,* to refresh.
Cf. Gk. λαπάζειν, to empty out. ¶ The
word is almost certainly E., but was prob.
early confused with *lave.* **Der.** *lavish,* vb.

Law; see **Lie** (1).

Lawn (1), a space of grass - covered
ground, a glade. (F. — G. *or* C.) M. E.
laund (the *d* has been dropped). — O. F.
lande, 'a land or laund, a wild, untilled,
shrubby, or grassy plain;' Cot. Cf. Ital.
and Span. *landa,* a heath. β. Of disputed
origin; referred by Littré to G. *land* (= E.
lana), open country; and by Diez to Bret.
lann, a bushy shrub, of which the pl.
lannon means 'waste lands.' Perhaps it
comes to the same thing; for E. and G.
land may be the same as Irish *lann,* an
(enclosed) piece of land, if the sense of
'enclosure' be not original. Cf. W. *llan,*
Gael. *lann,* an enclosure, piece of land.

Lawn (2), fine linen. (F. place-name.)
Richardson supposes it to be a corruption
of O. F. *linon,* 'a fine, thin, or open-waled
linnen; also lawn;' Cot. But this seems
impossible. Nor can it well be from
Span. *lona,* coarse sail-cloth. Palsgrave
has *Laune lynen,* prob. for *Lan lynen,*
where *Lan* is the 16th cent. spelling of
Laon, to the N.W. of Rheims. *Lawn*
was also called 'cloth of Remes,' i. e.
Rheims; see Baret's Alvearie. (A likely
guess.)

Lawyer; see **Lie** (1).

Lax, slack. (L.) L. *laxus,* slack, loose.
Allied to **Lag.**

   laxative, loosening. (F.—L.) F. *lax-*
atif. — L. *laxatiuus,* loosening. — L. *laxatus,*
pp. of *laxare,* to loosen. — L. *laxus,* lax.

   lazy, slow, slothful. (F.—L.) We find
the verb to *laze.* '*S'endormir en sentinelle,*
to *laze it,*' &c.; Cot. The *-y* is an E. adj.
addition, as in *shin-y, murk-y*; and *laze* is
from M. E. *lasche, lache, lashe,* slow (Palsgrave, Chaucer). — O. F. *lasche* (F. *lâche*),
'slack, loose, . . weak, faint, . . remisse,
slow,' &c.; Cot. — Low L. *lascus*,* not
found, a corrupt pronunciation of L. *laxus,*
lax, loose; cf. Ital. *lasco,* lazy.

   lease (1), to let a tenement. (F.—L.)

F. *laisser*, to let go. – L. *laxare*, to slacken, let go. – L. *laxus*, loose.

lessee. (F. – L.) O. F. *lesse* (*lessé*), pp. of *lesser*, later *laisser*, to let go (lease).

leash, a thong to hold in a dog. (F. – L.) M. E. *lees*. – O. F. *lesse* (F. *laisse*), a leash. – Low L. *laxa*, a thong, a loose rope. – L. *laxus*, slack. ¶ A *leash* of three was the number usually leashed together.

relax. (L.) L. *relaxare*, to relax. – L. *re-*, again; *laxare*, to slacken.

release. (F. – L.) M. E. *relessen*, *relesen*. – O. F. *relessier* (F. *relaisser*), to relax. – L. *relaxare*, to relax (above).

Lay (1), to place; see Lie (1).

Lay (2), a song, poem. (F. – C.) M. E. *lai*. – O. F. *lai*, said to be a Breton word. Not preserved in Breton, but it answers to Irish *laoi*, *laoidh*, a song, poem, Gael. *laoidh*, a verse, hymn, sacred poem; cf. W. *llais*, a voice, sound. Perhaps these Celtic words are allied to A. S. *leóð*, G. *lied*, a song; Goth. *liuthon*, to sing.

Lay (3), pertaining to the laity. (F. – L. – Gk.) M. E. *lay*. – O. F. *lai*, secular. – L. *laicus*. – Gk. λαικός, belonging to the people. – Gk. λαός (Attic λεώς), the people.

laic. (L. – Gk.) L. *laicus* (above).

laity, the lay people. (F. – L. – Gk.; with F. *suffix*). A coined word; from *lay*, adj. (above); cf. *gaie-ty* from *gay*, &c.

Layer; see Lie (1).

Lazar, a leper. (F. – L. – Gk. – Heb.) M. E. *lazar*. – L. *lazare*. – L. *Lazarus*. – Gk. Λάζαρος, the name of the beggar in Luke, xvi. 20; contracted from Heb. name *Eleasar*. – Heb. *El'áaár*, he whom God helps. Der. *lazar-etto*, a plague-hospital, Ital. *lazzaretto*.

Lazy; see Lax.

Lea, Lay, Ley, a meadow. (E.) M. E. *lay*, *ley*, untilled land. A. S. *leáh*, *leá* (gen. *ledge*), a lea; cf. *Hæd-leáh*, i. e. Hadleigh. Cognate with prov. G. *loh*, a morass, low plain, Low G. *loge*, Belg. *loo* as in *Water-loo*; also with Lithuan. *laukas*, an open field, L. *lucus*, a glade, open space in a wood. (✔ RUK.) Orig. 'a clearing.' Allied to Lucid.

Lead (1), to conduct; see Lode.

Lead (2), a metal. (E.) M. E. *leed*. A. S. *ledd*.+Du. *lood*, Swed. *lod*, Dan. *lod*, G. *loth*, M. H. G. *lôt*.

Leaf. (E.) M. E. *leef*, pl. *leues* (= *leves*). A. S. *ledf*, neut., pl. *ledf*.+Du. *loof*, foliage; Icel. *lauf*, Swed. *löf*, Dan, *löv*, Goth. *laufs*, G. *laub*. Orig. a strip or scale, thin slice;

allied to Russ. *lepeste*, a leaf, Lithuan. *lápas*, a leaf, Gk. λέπος, a scale; Russ. *lupite*, to peel, Lith. *lupti*, to strip.

lobby, a small hall, passage. (Low L. – G.) Prob. from an O. F. *lobie**, not recorded. – Low L. *lobia*, a portico, gallery, covered way. – M. H. G. *loube*, an arbour, bower, open way up to the upper story of a house (as in a Swiss *châlet*); mod. G. *laube*, a bower. Orig. made with foliage. – M. H. G. *loub* (G. *laub*), a leaf (above).

lodge, a small house, cot, resting-place. (F. – G.) M. E. *loge*, *logge*. – O. F. *loge*; cf. Ital. *loggia*, Low L. *lobia*, a gallery. – O. H. G. *loubá*, M. H. G. *loube*, an arbour (above).

League (1), an alliance; see Ligament.

League (2), about three miles. (F. – L. – C.) O. F. *legue* (Roquefort); F. *lieue*. – Low L. *lega*, *leuca*; L. *leuca*, a Gallic mile; a word of Celtic origin. Cf. Bret. *leò*, *lev*, a league; also *leu* (in Vannes).

Leaguer, a camp; see Lie (1).

Leak. (Scand.) M. E. *leken*. – Icel. *leka*, to drip, dribble, leak as a ship; Swed. *läcka*, Dan. *lække*.+Du. *lekken*, G. *lecken*, to leak, drop; A. S. *leccan*, to wet. (Base LAK.) ¶ The mod. E. word is Scand.; not from A. S. *leccan*. Der. *leak*, sb., from Icel. *leki*, a leak. We also find A. S. *hlece*, leaky.

Leal, loyal; see Legal.

Lean (1), to incline, stoop. (E.) M. E. *lenen*. A. S. *hlænan*, to make to lean, weak verb; cf. A. S. *hlinian*, to lean, weak verb.+Dan. *læne*, Swed. *läna*, causal forms; G. *lehnen*, intrans.+L. *-clinare*, in *inclinare*, to incline; Gk. κλίνειν, to cause to lean, make to bend. (✔ KRI.)

lean (2), slender, frail. (E.) M. E. *lene*. A. S. *hlæne*, lean; orig. bending, stooping, hence thin; cf. L. *decliuis*, declining. – A. S. *hlænan*, to lean (above).

Leap. (E.) M. E. *lepen*, pt. t. *leep*, pp. *lopen*. A. S. *hleápan*, pt. t. *hleóp*, to run, jump.+Du. *loopen*, Icel. *hlaupa*, Dan. *löbe*, Swed. *löpa*, Goth. *hlaupan*, G. *laufen*, chiefly in the sense 'to run.'

elope, to run away. (Du.) From Du. *ontloopen*, to evade, elope, run away; by substituting the familiar prefix *e-* for Du. *ont-*. This prefix = G. *ent-* = A. S. *and-*; see Answer. Du. *loopen*, to run, is cognate with *leap* (above).

interloper, an intruder. (L. *and* Du.) Lit. 'a runner between;' coined from L. *inter*, between; and Du. *looper*, a runner, from *loopen*, to run.

lapwing, a bird. (E.) M. E. *lappe-winke*. A. S. *hléapewince*, lit. 'one who turns about in running.' — A. S. *hleáp-an*, to run; *wince**, one who turns; see **Winch**.

orlop, a deck of a ship. (Du.) Formerly *orlope* (Phillips). Contracted from Du. *overloop*, a running over, a deck of a ship, an orlope (Sewel). So called because it traverses the ship. — Du. *over*, over; *loopen*, to run; see **elope** (above).

Learn. (E.) M. E. *lernen*. A. S. *leornian*. +G. *lernen*, to learn. From Teut. base LIS, to find out; whence also A. S. *léran* (G. *lehren*), to teach. And see **Last** (2).

lore, learning. (E.) M. E. *lore* (= *loor*). A. S. *lár*, lore. This answers to a Goth. form *laisa** (not found), from Goth. *lais*, I have found out, pt. t. of *leisan*, to find out; see **Last** (2). [The change from *s* to *r* is common; see *iron*, *hare*.] + Du. *leer*, G. *lehre*, O. H. G. *léra*, doctrine; of similar origin.

Lease (1), to let tenements; see **Lax**.

Lease (2), to glean. (E.) M. E. *lesen*. A. S. *lesan*, to gather. + Du. *lezen*, to gather, to read; G. *lesen*; Goth. *lisan*, pt. t. *las*, to gather.

Leash. (F. — L.); see **Lax**.

Leasing, a falsehood; see **Loose**.

Least; see **Less**.

Leather. (E.) M. E. *lether*. A. S. *leðer*. + Du. *leder*, Icel. *leðr*, Dan. *læder*, Swed. *läder*, G. *leder*, leather. Der. *leather-n*.

Leave (1), to quit; see **Live**.

Leave (2), permission; see **Lief**.

Leaven; see **Levity**.

Lecher; see **Lick**.

Lectern, **Lecturn**, a reading-desk. (Low L. — Gk.) Corrupted from Low L. *lectrinum*, a reading desk, pulpit; we find M. E. *leterone*, *lectorne*, *lectrone*, *lectrun* (Prompt. Parv.). — Low L. *lectrum*, a pulpit. — Gk. λέκτρον, a couch; also a rest or support for a book. Akin to Gk. λέχος, a couch, bed; cf. L. *lectus*, a couch. Allied to **Lie** (1). ¶ Observe that it has no connection with *lecture*.

Lection, **Lecture**; see **Legend**.

Ledge, **Ledger**; see **Lie** (1).

Lee, a sheltered place; part of a ship away from the wind. (Scand.) M. E. *lee*, shelter. — Icel. *hlé*, lee (of a ship); Dan. *læ*, Swed. *lä*. + Du. *lij*; A. S. *hleó*, *hleow*, a covering, a shelter, whence prov. E. *lew*, warm, also a shelter. See **Lukewarm**. ¶ The peculiar use is Scand.; yet the

pronunciation *lew-ard*, for *lee-ward*, preserves the E. *lew*.

Leech (1), a physician. (E.) M. E. *leche*. A. S. *léce*, one who heals; cf. A. S. *lácnian*, to heal. + Icel. *læknir*, Dan. *lœge*, Swed. *läkare*, Goth. *leikeis*, a leech; Icel. *lœkna*, Dan. *lœge*, Swed. *läka*, Goth. *leiki-non*, to heal.

leech (2), a blood-sucking worm. (E.) A. S. *léce*, lit. 'the healer;' the same word as the above.

Leech (3), **Leach**, the border or edge of a sail at the sides. (Scand.) Icel. *lík*, a leech-line; Swed. *lik*, Dan. *lig*, a bolt-rope. + O. Du. *lyken*, a bolt-rope (Sewel).

Leek. (E.) M. E. *leek*. A. S. *leác*. + Du. *look*, Icel. *laukr*, Dan. *lög*, Swed. *lök*, G. *lauch*. Der. *gar-lic*, *char-lock*, *hem-lock* (latter syllable).

Leer, a sly look. (E.) The verb is a development from the sb., which is an old word. M. E. *lere*, the cheek, face, complexion, mien; usually in a good sense, but Skelton has it in a bad sense. A. S. *hleór*, the cheek; hence, the face, look, mien. + Icel. *hlýr*, the cheek. ¶ Allied to Du. *loeren*, to peep, peer, which is quite distinct from Du. *loeren*, to lurk. See **Lower** (2).

Lees, dregs of wine. (F.) Pl. of a sing. form *lee*, not used. — F. *lie*, 'the lees;' Cot. Low L. *lia*, pl. *liæ*, lees (10th cent.). Origin unknown.

Left, the weaker hand. (E.) M. E. *left*, *lift*, *luft*. A. S. *left*; Mr. Sweet points out that 'inanis, *left*,' occurs in a gloss (Mone, Quellen, i. 443), and that the same MS. has *senne* for *synne* (sin); so that *left* is for *lyft*, with the sense 'worthless' or 'weak;' cf. A. S. *lyft-ádl*, palsy. + North Fries. *leeft*, *leefter hond*, left hand; O. Du. *luft*, *lucht*, left. β. The form of the base is LUB; prob. allied to **Lop**. ¶ *Not* allied to L. *læuus*, Gk. λαιός.

Leg. (Scand.) M. E. *leg* (pl. *legges*). — Icel. *leggr*, a leg; Dan. *læg*, the calf of the leg; Swed. *lägg* (the same).

Legacy; see **Legal**.

Legal, pertaining to the law. (F. — L.) F. *legal*. — L. *legalis*, legal. — L. *leg-*, stem of *lex*, law, cognate with E. *law*. β. The lit. sense is 'that which lies,' that which is fixed; cf. Gk. κεῖται νόμος, the law is fixed, from κεῖμαι, I lie. (√LAGH.)

allege. (F. — L.) M. E. *alegen*, *aleggen*. — F. *alleguer*, 'to alleadge,' Cot. — L. *allegare*, to send, dispatch; also to bring

forward, mention. — L. *al-* (for *ad*), to ; *legare*, to send, appoint, from *leg-*, stem of *lex*, law.

alloy, a due proportion in mixing metals. (F. — L.) Formerly *allay* ; M. E. *alay.* — O. F. *alay, aley, alloy.* — O. F. *aleier, alcyer*, to combine. — L. *alligare*, to bind together ; see **ally**, p. 249, col. 2, l. 18. The O. F. *alei,* sb., became *aloi*, and was misunderstood as being *à loi* = L. *ad legem*, according to rule or law. (Misplaced.)

colleague, a partner. (F. — L.) F. *collegue.* — L. *collēga*, a partner in office. — F. *col-* (= *con-*, for *cum*), with ; *legare*, to send on an embassy ; see **legate** (below).

college, an assembly, seminary. (F. — L.) F. *college.* — L. *collegium*, society of colleagues or persons. — L. *collega*, a colleague (above).

delegate, a chosen deputy. (L.) L. *delegatus*, pp. of *de-legare*, to depute, appoint.

leal, loyal, true. (F. — L.) M. E. *lel.* — Norman F. *leal*, O. F. *leial*, legal, hence, just, loyal. — L. *legalis*, legal. **Doublets**, *legal, loyal.*

legacy. (L.) M. E. *legacie* ; a coined word (as if = L. *legatiu **, not found) from L. *legatum*, a bequest, neut. of pp. of *legare*, to appoint, bequeath ; see below.

legate, a commissioner. (F. — L.) M. E. *legate.* — O. F. *legat*, a pope's ambassador. — L. *legatus*, a deputy ; pp. of *legare*, to appoint. — L. *leg-*, stem of *lex*, law.

legatee. (L. ; *with* F. *suffix*.) A barbarous word ; coined from L. *legat-us*, appointed, with F. suffix *-é* (= L. *-atus*).

legislator. (L.) L. *legislator*, a proposer of a law. — L. *legis*, gen. of *lex*, a law ; *lator*, a proposer, lit. bringer, from *latum* (= *tlatum*), to bear, bring, from √TAL ; see **Tolerate**. Der. *legislate*, &c.

legist. (F. — L.) O. F. *legiste* (F. *légiste*). — Low L. *legista*, one skilled in the laws. — L. *leg-*, stem of *lex*, law (with Gk. suffix *-ista* = ιστης).

legitimate. (L.) Low L. *legitimatus*, pp. of *legitimare*, to declare to be lawful. — L. *legitimus*, according to law. — L. *legi-*, crude form of *lex*, law ; with suffix *-ti-mus.*

loyal, faithful. (F. — L.) F. *loyal* (Cot.). — L. *legalis*, legal (hence just, loyal) ; see **Legal** (above).

relegate, to consign to exile. (L.) From pp. of L. *-re-legare*, to send away, remove.

Legend, a marvellous story. (F. — L.)

M. E. *legende.* — O. F. *legende*, a legend, story. — Low L. *legenda*, a legend ; L. *legenda*, neut. pl. things to be read. — L. *legendus*, fut. pass. part. of *legere*, to read, orig. to gather, collect. +Gk. λέγειν, to tell, speak. (Base LAG.)

coil (1), to gather together. (F. — L.) ' *Coiled* up in a cable ;' Beaumont and Fletcher. — O. F. *coillir*, to collect. — L. *colligere* ; see **collect** below.

collect, vb. (F. — L.) O. F. *collecter*, to collect money (Roquefort). — Low L. *collectare* (the same), from *collecta*, a collection, orig. fem. of pp. of *colligere*, to collect. — L. *col-* (= *con-* — *cum*), with ; *legere*, to gather.

collect, sb. (L.) Low L. *collecta*, a collection in money, an assembly for prayer, hence a short prayer ; see the word above.

cull, to collect, select. (F. — L.) M. E. *cullen.* — O. F. *coillir, cuillir*, to collect ; see **coil** (1) above.

diligent, industrious. (F. — L.) O. F. *diligent.* — L. *diligent-*, stem of *diligens*, careful, diligent, lit. loving (fond) ; pres. pt. of *diligere*, to love, select, lit. choose between. — L. *di-* (= *dis-*), apart ; *legere*, to choose.

elect, chosen. (L.) L. *electus*, pp. of *eligere*, to choose out. — L. *e*, out ; *legere*, to choose.

elegant, choice, neat. (F. — L.) O. F. *elegant.* — L. *elegant-*, stem of *elegans*, tasteful, neat. — L. *e*, out ; *leg-*, base of *legere*, to choose.

eligible. (F. — L.) F. *eligible.* — Low L. *eligibilis*, fit to be chosen. — L. *eligere*, to choose ; see **elect** above.

intellect. (F. — L.) O. F. *intellect.* — L. *intellectus*, perception, discernment. — L. *intellectus*, pp. of *intelligere*, to discern. — L. *intel-*, for *inter*, between ; *legere*, to choose.

intelligence. (F. — L.) F. *intelligence.* — L. *intelligentia*, perception. — L. *intelligent-*, stem of pres. pt. of *intelligere*, to discern, understand (above).

intelligible. (F. — L.) F. *intelligible.* — L. *intelligibilis*, perceptible to the senses. — L. *intelligere*, to discern (above).

lection, a reading, portion to be read. (L.) From L. *lectio*, a reading. — L. *lectus*, pp. of *legere*, to read.

lecture, a discourse. (F. — L.) F. *lecture*, a reading. — Low L. *lectura*, a commentary. — L. *lectus*, pp. of *legere*, to read.

legible, readable. (F. ‒ L.) O. F. *legible.* ‒ L. *legibilis,* legible. ‒ L. *legere,* to read.

legion, a large body of soldiers. (F. ‒ L.) M. E. *legioun.* ‒ O. F. *legion.* ‒ L. *legionem,* acc. of *legio,* a Roman legion, body of from 4200 to 6000 men. ‒ L. *legere,* to gather, select a band.

legume, a pod. (F. ‒ L.) F. *légume,* pulse, a pod. ‒ L. *legumen* (stem *legumin-*), pulse, bean-plant; applied to a crop that can be picked (not cut). ‒ L. *legere,* to gather. Der. *legumin-ous.*

lesson. (F. ‒ L.) M. E. *lesson.* ‒ F. *leçon.* ‒ L. *lectionem,* acc. of *lectio,* a reading; see **lection** (above). Doublet, *lection.*

neglect. (L.) L. *neglectus,* pp. of *negligere,* to neglect (put for *nec-ligere*). ‒ L. *nec,* nor, not, contr. form of *neque*; *legere,* to gather, select.

negligence. (F. ‒ L.) F. *negligence.* ‒ L. *negligentia,* carelessness. ‒ L. *negligent-,* stem of pres. part. of *negligere,* to neglect (above).

predilection, a choosing beforehand. (L.) From L. *præ,* before; *dilectio,* choice, from *di-ligere,* to choose; see **diligent** (above).

recollect, to remember. (F.‒L.) Lit. 'to gather again;' from *re-* (prefix) and *collect*; see **collect** (above).

select, choice. (L.) L. *selectus,* pp. of *seligere,* to choose. ‒ L. *se-,* apart; *legere,* to pick, choose. Der. *select,* verb.

Legerdemain; see **Levity.**
Leger-line; see **Levity.**
Legible, Legion; see **Legend.**
Legislator, Legist; see **Legal.**
Legitimate; see **Legal.**
Legume; see **Legend.**
Leisure; see **Licence.**
Leman, Lemman; see **Lief.**
Lemma, an assumption. (L.‒Gk.) L. *lemma.* ‒ Gk. λῆμμα, a thing taken; in logic, a premiss taken for granted. ‒ Gk. εἴ-λημμαι, perf. pass. of λαμβάνειν, to take (base λαβ-); cf. Skt. *rabh,* to take. (√ RABH.)

dilemma, a perplexity. (L.‒Gk.) L. *dilemma.* ‒ Gk. δίλημμα, a double proposition or argument in which one is caught between two difficulties. ‒ Gk. διαλαμβάνομαι, I am caught between. ‒ Gk. διά, between; λαμβάνειν, to take, catch.

Lemming, Leming, a kind of Norwegian rat. (Norweg.) Norweg. *lemende*; also occurring as *lemming, limende,* &c. Cf. Swed. *lemel,* a lemming. Origin obscure; Aasen derives it from Norweg. *lemja,* to strike, beat, maim, lit. 'lame,' and explains it to mean 'destroying;' from the destruction committed by them; see **Lame.** But the word may be Lapp; the Lapp name is *loumek.*

Lemon. (F. ‒ Pers.) Formerly *limon.* ‒ F. *limon.* ‒ Pers. *límún, límúná,* a lemon, citron.

Lemur, a nocturnal animal. (L.) L. *lemur,* a ghost; so nicknamed by naturalists from its nocturnal habits.

Lend; see **Loan.**

Length; see **Long.**

Lenient, mild. (L.) From pres. part. of L. *lenire,* to soothe. ‒ L. *lenis,* soft, mild.

lenity. (L.) Englished from L. *lenitas,* mildness. ‒ L. *lenis* (above).

relent. (F. ‒ L.) Altered from F. *ralentir,* to slacken, to relent (cf. L. *relentescere,* to slacken). ‒ F. *ra-,* put for *re-a-* (L. *re-ad*); L. *lentus,* slack, slow, allied to *lenis,* gentle (above).

Lens, a piece of glass used in optics. (L.) So called from the resemblance of a double-convex lens to the shape of the seed of a lentil. ‒ L. *lens,* a lentil.

lentil, a plant. (F.‒L.) M. E. *lentil.* ‒ O. F. *lentille.* ‒ L. *lenticula,* a little lentil; double dimin. of *lenti-,* crude form of *lens,* a lentil.

Lent, a fast of 40 days, beginning with Ash-Wednesday. (E.) The fast is in spring-time; the old sense is simply spring. M. E. *lent, lenten.* A. S. *lencten,* the spring; supposed to be derived from *lang,* long, because in spring the days lengthen; this is possible. ✚ Du. *lente,* spring; G. *lenz,* O. H. G. *lenzin, lengizen.* Der. *lenten,* adj., from A. S. *lencten,* sb.

Lentil; see **Lens.**

Lentisk, the mastic-tree. (F. ‒ L.) F. *lentisque.* ‒ L. *lentiscum, lentiscus,* named from the clamminess of its resin. ‒ L. *lentus,* sticky, pliant. See **Lenient.**

Leo, a lion. (L. ‒ Gk.) L. *leo.* ‒ Gk. λέων, a lion. We also find Du. *leeuw,* G. *löwe,* Russ. *lev',* Lithuan. *lévas, lavas,* a lion. Cf. Heb. *lábí',* a lion.

leopard. (F.‒L.‒Gk.) O. F. *leopard.* ‒ L. *leopardus.* ‒ Gk. λεόπαρδος, a leopard; supposed to be a mongrel between a pard (panther) and a lioness. ‒ Gk. λεο-, for λέων, a lion; πάρδος, a pard.

lion. (F. – L. – Gk.) F. *lion.* – L. *leo-nem*, acc. of *leo*; see Leo (above).

Leper. (F. – L. – Gk.) The sense has changed; *lepre* formerly meant the disease itself; and what we now call a *leper* was called a *leprous man.* 'The *lepre* of him was clensid;' Wyclif, Matt. viii. 3.– F. *lepre*, 'a leprosie;' Cot. – L. *lepra.* – Gk. λέπρα, leprosy; so called because the skin scales off. – Gk. λέπρος, scaly, scabby. – Gk. λέπος, a scale.– Gk. λέπειν, to peel. +Russ. *lupite*, Lithuan. *lùpti*, to peel. (√ LAP.)

lepidoptera, a term applied to insects whose wings are covered with scales. (Gk.) Gk. λεπίδο-, crude form of λεπίς, a scale; πτερά, pl. of πτερόν, a wing (allied to E. *feather*).

leprosy. (F. – L. – Gk.) A coined word, from the adj. *leprous*; which is from F. *lepreux*=L. *leprosus*, afflicted with *lepra*, i.e. leprosy (above).

Leporine, belonging to a hare. (L.) L. *leporinus*, adj., from *lepori-*, crude form of *lepus*, a hare.

leveret. (F. – L.) O.F. *levrault*, 'a leveret, or young hare;' Cot. The suffix *-ault*=Low L. *-aldus*, from O. H. G. *wald*, power, common as a suffix. The base *levr-* is from L. *lepor-*, stem of *lepus*, a hare.

Leprosy; see Leper.

Lesion, an injury. (F. – L.) F. *lesion*, hurt; Cot. – L. *læsionem*, acc. of *læsio*, an injury. – L. *læsus*, pp. of *lædere*, to hurt.

collide. (L.) L. *collidere*, to dash together. – L. *col-* (=*con-*=*cum*), together; *lædere*, to strike, hurt. Der. *collis-ion* (from pp. *collis-us*).

elide. (L.) L. *e-lidere*, to strike out. Der. *elis-ion* (from pp. *elis-us*).

illision, a striking against. (L.) From L. *illisio*, a striking against. – L. *illisus*, pp. of *illidere*, to strike against. – L. *il-* (for *in*), upon; *lædere*, to strike.

Less, smaller. (E.) Used as comp. of *little*, but from a different root. M. E. *lessè, lassè*, adj.. *les*, adv. A. S. *læssa*, less, adj.; *læs*, adv.+O. Fries. *lessa*, less. β. The positive appears in Goth *las-iws*, feeble; Icel. *lasinn*, feeble, ailing, *lasna*, to decay. Der. *less-er*, a double comp.; *less-en*, verb.

least. (E.) M.E. *lestè*, adj., *lest*, adv. A.S. *læsast*, whence *læst* by contraction; a superlative form from the same base *las-*.

lest, for fear that, that not. (E.) Not for *least*, but due to A.S. phrase δỹ *læs* δe

= for the reason less that; wherein δỹ (for the reason) was soon dropped, and *læs* δe coalesced into *lest.* Here *læs*=less, adv.; and δe is the indeclinable relative.

nevertheless; see Never.

-less, suffix; see Loose.

Lessee; see Lax.

Lesson; see Legend.

Lest; see Less.

Let (1), to permit. (E.) M. E. *leten*, strong verb, pt. t. *lat, leet*, pp. *laten, leten.* A.S. *lǽtan, létan*, pt. t. *lét, leót*, pp. *lǽten.* + Du. *laten* (*liet, gelaten*); Icel. *láta* (*lét, látinn*); Dan. *lade*, Swed. *låta*, Goth. *letan* (*lailot, letans*); G. *lassen* (*liess, gelassen*). From the same base as Late. (Base LAT.)

Let (2), to hinder; see Late.

Lethal, deadly. (F. – L.; *or* L.) F. *lethal*,'deadly;' Cot. – L. *lethalis*, for *letalis*, mortal.– L. *letum*, death.

Lethe, oblivion. (L. – Gk.) L. *lethe.* – Gk. λήθη, a forgetting; the river of oblivion. – Gk. λαθ-, base of λανθάνειν, to lie hid; see Latent. (√ RADH.)

lethargy, a heavy sleep. (F.–L.–Gk.) O. F. *lethargie*, a lethargy; Cot.– L. *leth-argia*. – Gk. ληθαργία, drowsiness. – Gk. λήθαργος, forgetful. – Gk. λήθη, oblivion (above).

Letter; see Liniment.

Lettuce; see Lacteal.

Levant, Levee; see Levity.

Level; see Librate.

Lever; see Levity.

Leveret; see Leporine.

Leviathan. (L. – Heb.) Late L. *le-viathan*, Job xl. 20 (Vulgate). – Heb. *livyâthân*, an aquatic animal, dragon, serpent; named from its twisting itself in curves. – Heb. root *lâvâh*, to cleave; Arab. root *lawa'*, to bend, whence *lawá*, the twisting or coiling of a serpent.

Levigate, to make smooth. (L.) Out of use.– L. *leuigatus*, pp. of *leuigare*, to make smooth. – L. *lēu-is*, smooth; *-ig-*, for *agere*, to make. Cf. Gk. λεῖος, smooth.

Levite, one of the tribe of Levi. (L. – Gk. – Heb.) L. *Leuita.* – Gk. Λευΐτης, Lu. x. 32. – Heb. *Levi*, one of the sons of Jacob.

Levity, lightness, frivolity. (L.) From L. *leuitas*, lightness. – L. *lĕuis*, light. Allied to Light (2).

alleviate. (L.) From pp. of Low L. *alleuiate*, used for L. *alleuare*, to lighten. L. *al-* (for *ad*), to; *leuare*, to lift, lighten, from *leuis*, light.

elevate. (L.) From pp. of L. *e-leuare*, to lift up.

leaven, ferment. (F.–L.) M.E. *leuain*. –F. *levain*.–L. *leuamen*, an alleviation; here used in the orig. sense of 'that which raises.'–L. *leuare*, to raise. – L. *leuis*, light.

legerdemain, sleight of hand. (F.–L.) O.F. *legier de main*, lit. light of hand. Cf. Ital. *leggiere, leggiero*, light. The O.F. *legier* answers to a Low L. form *leuiarius**, made by adding *-arius* to L. *leui-s*, light. F. *de*=L. *de*, of. F. *main*=L. *manum*, acc. of *manus*, a hand.

leger-line, ledger-line, in music, a short line added above or below the staff. (F.–L.) Properly *leger-line*; where *leger*=F. *léger* (formerly *legier*), light; because these lines are small and short. See the word above.

levant, the E. of the Mediterranean Sea. (Ital.–L.) Ital. *levante*, E. wind, eastern country or part (where the sun rises). –L. *leuant-*, stem of pres. part. of *leuare*, to raise; whence *se leuare*, to rise.–L. *leuis*, light.

levee, a morning assembly. (F.–L.) Misused for F. *le lever* (Littré).–F. *lever*, to raise; see **levy** (below).

lever. (F.–L.) M.E. *levour*.–F. *leveur*, a raiser, lifter.–L. *leuatorem*, acc. of *leuator*, a lifter.–L. *leuare*, to lift.–L. *leuis*, light.

levy, the act of raising men for an army; the force raised. (F.–L.) F. *levée*, 'a levy, or levying of an army;' Cot. Fem. of pp. of *lever*, to raise.–L. *leuare*, to raise.–L. *leuis*, light.

relevant. (F.–L.) The orig. sense is 'helpful;' hence, of use for the matter in hand.–F. *relevant*, pres. part. of *relever*, to raise up, assist, help.–L. *re-leuare*, to raise again.

relieve. (F.–L.) M.E. *releuen* (=*releven*).–F. *relever*, to raise up, relieve.–L. *re-leuare*, to raise again. Der. *relief*, M.E. *relef*, O.F. *relef* (F. *relief*), a sb. due to the verb *relever*.

Lewd, ignorant, base. (E.) M.E. *lewed*, ignorant. A.S. *lǽwede*, adj., ignorant, hence lay, belonging to the laity; the orig. sense was enfeebled, as it is the pp. of *lǽwan*, to weaken, enfeeble. A more usual sense of *lǽwan* is to betray; cf. Goth. *lewjan*, to betray, from *lew*, an occasion, opportunity. The train of thought runs thus: occasion, opportunity, betrayal, en-

feeblement, ignorance, baseness, licentiousness.

Lexicon. (Gk.) Gk. λεξικόν, a dictionary; neut. of λεξικός, adj., belonging to words.–Gk. λέξι-s, a saying.–Gk. λέγ-ειν, to speak; see **Legend**.

Ley, a meadow; see **Lea**.

Liable; see **Ligament**.

Lias, a formation of limestone. (F.–C.?) F. *lias*, formerly *liais, liois*, a hard free-stone. Prob. from Bret. *liach, leach*, a stone; cf. Gael. *leac*, W. *llech*, a flat stone; see **Cromlech**.

Lib; see **Lop**.

Libation, the pouring forth of wine in honour of a deity. (F.–L.) F. *libation*. –L. acc. *libationem*.–L. *libatus*, pp. of *libare*, to taste, sip, pour out.+Gk. λείβειν, to pour out, shed, offer a libation. Cf. Skt. *rī*, to distil. (√RI.)

Libel; see **Library**.

Liberal. (F.–L.) M.E. *liberal*.–O.F. *liberal*.–L. *liberalis*, befitting a free man, generous.–L. *liber*, free. Allied to *libet*, it pleases, it is one's pleasure; Skt. *lubh*, to desire.

deliver. (F.–L.) O.F. *delivrer*, to set free.–Low L. *deliberare*, to set free.–L. *de*, from; *liberare*, to free, from *liber*, free.

liberate. (L.) From pp. of L. *liberare*, to set free.–L. *liber*, free.

libertine. (L.) Cf. Acts, vi. 9. – L. *libertinus*, adj., belonging to a freed man, also sb., a freed man; later applied to denote the licentious liberty of a certain sect (Acts, vi. 9).–L. *libertus*, a freed man. –L. *liber*, free.

liberty. (F.–L.) M.E. *libertee*.–F. *liberté*.–L. *libertatem*, acc. of *libertas*, freedom.–L. *liber*, free.

livery, a delivery, a thing delivered, uniform allowed to servants. (F.–L.) M.E. *liuere* (=*liveré*, three syllables).–F. *livrèe*, 'a delivery of a thing that is given, the thing so given, a livery;' Cot. Orig. fem. of pp. of *livrer*, to deliver, give freely.–L. *liberare*, to set free, give freely; see **liberate** (above).

Libidinous, lustful. (F.–L.) F. *libidineux*.–L. *libidinosus*, lustful.–L. *libidin-*, crude form of *libido*, lust, pleasure.–L. *libet*, it pleases. Cf. Skt. *lubh*, to desire. Allied to **Liberate**.

Library. (F.–L.) F. *librairie*. – L. *libraria*, a book-shop; fem. of *librarius*, belonging to books.–L. *libr-*, stem of *liber*, a book, orig. the bark of a tree (the

earliest writing material). Cf. Gk. λεπις,
a scale, rind.

libel, a written accusation. (L.) M. E.
libel, a brief piece of writing.— L. *libellus,*
a little book, a notice (Matt. v. 31) ; dimin.
of *liber,* a book (above).

Librate, to balance, be poised, move
slightly when balanced. (L.) The verb is
rare, and due to the sb. *libration* (Kersey).
— L. acc. *librationem,* a poising.— L. *libra-
tus,* pp. of *librare,* to balance.— L. *libra,* a
balance, a level; also a pound of 12 oz.+
Gk. λίτρα, a pound of 12 oz.

deliberate, carefully weighed and considered. (L.) L. *deliberatus,* pp. of *deliberare,* to consult. — L. *de,* thoroughly;
librare, to weigh, from *libra,* a balance.

level, an instrument for determining
that a thing is horizontal. (F. — L.) M. E.
liuel, leuel (*livel, level*). — O. F. *livel,* later
spelling *liveau*; mod. F. *niveau,* a level.
— L. *libella,* a level; dimin. of *libra,* a
balance.

Licence, License, leave, abuse of freedom. (F. — L.) M. E. *lycence.*— F. *licence.*
— L. *licentia,* freedom to act.— L. *licent-,*
from *licēre,* to be allowable, orig. 'to be
left free.' It is the intrans. form connected
with L. *linquere,* to leave. (√ RIK.) Der.
licence, more usually *license,* verb.

delinquent, failing in duty. (L.) L.
delinquent-, stem of pres. pt. of *delinquere,*
to omit, to omit one's duty.— L. *de,* away,
from; *linquere,* to leave.

dereliction, complete abandonment.
(L.) L. acc. *derelictionem,* complete neglect.— L. *derelictus,* pp. of *derelinquere,* to
forsake.— L. *de,* from; *re-linquere,* to leave
behind.

illicit, unlawful. (F. — L.) F. *illicite,*
'illicitous;' Cot.— L. *illicitus,* not allowed.
— L. *il-* (for *in-*), not ; *licitus,* pp. of *licēre,*
to be allowed.

leisure, freedom from employment. (F.
— L.) M.E. *leyser.*— O. F. *leisir* (F. *loisir*),
leisure ; orig. an infin. mood, meaning 'to
be permitted.'— L. *licere,* to be permitted.
¶ The spelling is bad; it should be *leiser*
or *leisir; pleasure* is in the same case.

licentiate, one who has a grant to
exercise a profession. (L.) Englished from
Low L. *licentiatus,* pp. of *licentiare,* to
licence. — L. *licentia,* licence; see **Licence**
(above).

licentious. (F. — L.) F. *licencieux.*—
L. *licentiosus,* full of licence.— L. *licentia,*
licence (above).

relic, a memorial. (F. — L.) Chiefly in
the pl.; M. E. *relikes.*— F. *reliques,* s. pl.
'reliques ;' Cot.— L. *reliquias,* acc. of *reli-
quiæ,* pl. remains.— L. *re-linquere,* to leave
behind.

relict, a widow. (L.) L. *relicta,* fem.
of *relictus,* pp. of *re-linquere* (above).

relinquish. (F. — L.) O. F. *relinquis-,*
from vb. *relinquir.* — L. *re-linquere.*

reliquary, a casket for relics. (F. — L.)
F. *reliquaire,* 'a casket wherein reliques
be kept;' Cot. — Low L. *reliquiarium*
(same). — L. *reliquia-,* crude form of *reli-
quiæ,* relics ; see **relic** (above).

Lichen, a moss. (L. — Gk.) L. *lichen.*
— Gk. λείχην, lichen, tree-moss ; also, an
eruption on the skin. Generally connected
with Gk. λείχειν, to lick up; from its en-
croachment. Cf. Russ. *lishai,* a lichen, a
tetter.

Lich-gate; see **Like** (1).

Lick, to lap. (E.) M. E. *likken.* A.S.
liccian.+Du. *likken,* G. *lecken,* Goth. *bi-
laigon* (be-lick), Russ. *lizate,* L. *lingere,* Gk.
λείχειν, Skt. *lih, rih,* to lick. (√ RIGH.)

lecher. (F. — G.) M. E. *lechur, lechour.*
— O. F. *lecheor,* lit. one who licks up, a man
addicted to gluttony and lewdness.— O. F.
lecher (F. *lécher*), to lick — O. H. G.
lechón (G. *lecken*), to lick (above).

relish, to taste with pleasure. (F. — L.
and G.) O. F. *relecher,* to lick over again.
— F. *re-,* again; *lecher,* to lick.— L. *re-,*
again; O. H. G. *lechón,* to lick (above).

Licorice, Liquorice. (F. — L. — Gk.)
M. E. *licoris.* — O. F. *licorice*,* not recorded. later *liquerice,* 'lickorice ;' Cot.—
L. *liquiritia,* liquorice; a corrupted form
of the true spelling *glycyrrhiza* (Pliny,
Nat. Hist. xxii. 9. 11).— Gk. γλυκύρριζα,
liquorice, lit. 'sweet root.'— Gk. γλυκύ-s,
sweet ; ρίζα, root. See **Dulcet** and **Wort.**

Lictor; see **Ligament.**

Lid, a cover. (E.) M. E. *lid.* A. S.
hlid, a lid.— A. S. *hlid-en,* pp. of *hlídan,*
to cover.+Du. *lid,* a lid ; Icel. *hlíð,* a gate,
gateway, gap, breach ; M. H. G. *lit, lid,* a
cover (obsolete). Cf. Gk. κλισιάς, a folding door, gate ; allied to κλίνειν, to lean.
(√ KRI.)

Lie (1), to rest, abide. (E.) A strong
verb. M. E. *liggen, lien,* pt. t. *lay, ley,*
pp. *leien, lein.* A. S. *licgan,* pt. t. *læg,* pp.
legen.+Du. *liggen,* Icel. *liggja,* Dan. *ligge,*
Swed. *ligga,* G. *liegen,* Goth. *ligan,* Russ.
lejate ; Lat. base *leg-* (in *lectus,* bed) ; Gk.
base λεχ- (in λέχος, bed). (√ LAGH.)

allay, to assuage. (E.) M. E. *alaien*, in Gower, C. A. iii. 11, 273. A. S. *ālecgan*, to lay down, lay aside. — A.S. *ā*, prefix (answering to Goth. *us-*, G. *er-*); *lecgan*, to lay; see **lay** below. ¶ It seems to have been confused (in sense and writing, if not in speech) with M. E. *aleggen*, to alleviate, from O. F. *aleger* = Low L. *alleuiare*, to alleviate; see **alleviate** under **Levity**. But the *form* and *sound* remain truly English.

belay, to fasten a rope. (Du.) Du. *be-leggen*, to overlay, also to belay a rope. — Du. *be-* (same as E. *be-*); *leggen*, to lay, cognate with E. *lay*.

beleaguer, to besiege. (Du.) Du. *be-legeren*, to besiege. — Du. *be-* (same as E. *be-*); *leger*, a camp, encamped army; see **lair** (below). +G. *belagern*, from *lager*, a camp; Swed. *belägra*; Dan. *belægge*, also *beleire*.

lair, den or retreat of a wild beast. (E.) M. E. *leir*. A.S. *leger*, a lair, couch, bed. — A.S. *leg-en*, pp. of *licgan*, to lie down, rest. + Du. *leger*, a bed, lair, from *liggen*; G. *lager*, O. H. G. *legar*, a couch, from O.H.G. *liggan*, to lie; Goth. *ligrs*, a couch. **Doublet**, *leaguer* (below).

law, a rule of action, edict. (E.) M. E. *lawe*. A.S. *lagu* (not common; the usual A. S. word is *æ*). The sense is 'that which lies,' or is fixed (cf. Gk. νόμος, the law is fixed, from κεῖμαι, I lie). — A.S. *læg*, pt. t. of *licgan*, to lie.+O. Sax. *lag*; Icel. *lög*, pl. but in sing. sense, a law, from *lag*, a stratum, order; Swed. *lag*; Dan. *lov*. Cf. L. *lex*. **Der.** *law-y-er* (cf. *saw-y-er*).

lay (1), to cause to lie down, set. (E.) M. E. *leggen*, pt. t. *leide*, pp. *leid*. A.S. *lecgan*, pt. t. *legde*, pp. *gelegd*; causal of *licgan*, to lie.+Du. *leggen*, Icel. *leggja*, Dan. *lægge*, Swed. *lägga*, G. *legen*, Goth. *lagjan*.

layer, a stratum, tier, bed. (E.) E. *lay-er*, that which lays; but almost certainly an ignorant substitution for M. E. *leir*, a lair, couch, place for lying down in; hence a bed, stratum, &c. See **lair** (above).

leaguer, a camp. (Du.) In All's Well, iii. 6. 27. — Du. *leger*, a lair, a camp. See **lair** (above).

ledge, a slight shelf, ridge. (Scand.) Cf. Norfolk *ledge*, a bar of a gate, rail of a chair. Of Scand. origin; allied to Swed. *lagg*, the rim of a cask, Icel. *lögg*, the ledge or rim at the bottom of a cask; Norweg. *logg* (pl. *legger*), the lowest part of a vessel. Cf. also Norw. *lega*, a couch, lair, bed,

support on which anything rests. All from Icel. *liggja*. Swed. *ligga*, Dan. *ligge*, to lie. The sense is 'support.'

ledger, a book in which a summary of accounts is preserved. (Du.) Formerly *ledger-book*. (We also find *leger ambas-sadors*, i.e. such as *remained* for some time at a foreign court.) A *ledger-book* is one that lies always ready. — Du. *legger*, one that lies down (the nether mill-stone is also so called). — Du. *leggen*, to lie, a common corruption of *liggen*, to lie (like *lay* for *lie* in English). Similarly, in Middle-English, a large book was called a *liggar* (that which lies), because not portable. ¶ Confused with O. F. *legier*, light; Howell uses *leger-book* for 'portable book,' which is just contrary to the usual sense. See **ledger** in Richardson.

log (1), a block, piece of wood. (Scand.) Icel. *lág*, a felled tree, log; Swed. dial. *lāga*, a felled tree, a tree that has been blown down. So called from its *lying* on the ground, as distinguished from the living tree. — Teut. base LAG, to lie. **Der.** *logg-ats*, a sort of game with bits of wood; *log-wood*, so called because imported in *logs*, also called *block-wood* (Kersey).

log (2), a piece of wood with a line, for measuring the rate of a ship. (Scand.) Swed. *logg*, as a sea-term; whence *log-lina*, a log-line, *log-bok*, a log-book, *logga*, to heave the log; Dan. *log*, *log-line*, *log-bog*, *logge*, vb. Variant of the word above.

logger-head, a dunce, a piece of timber (in a whale-boat) over which a line is passed to make it run more slowly. (Scand. and E.) A similar formation to *blockhead*.

low (1), humble, inferior. (Scand.) M. E. *louh*, also *lah*. — Icel. *lágr*, low; Swed. *låg*, Dan. *lav*. The orig. sense is that which lies down, or lies low (as we say); from Icel. *lág-*, stem of pt. pl. of *liggja*, to lie. **Der.** *be-low* (= by low); also *lower*, verb, i. e. to let lower, from *low-er*, comparative of *low*, adj.

rely, to repose on, trustfully. (L. *and* E.) A barbarous compound. Lit. 'to lie back, lie against.' From L. *re-*, prefix, back (as in *re-cline*); E. *lie*, to rest. **Der.** *reli-ance*, with F. suffix.

Lie (2), to tell a falsehood. (E.) M. E. *lighen*, pt. t. *leh*, pp. *lowen*. A.S. *leógan*, pt. t. *leág*, pp. *lugen*. + Du. *liegen*, Icel. *ljúga*, Dan. *lyve*, Swed. *ljuga*, Goth. *liugan*, G. *lügen*. Cf. Russ. *lgate*, *luigate*, to lie; *loje*, a lie. (Base LUG.)

Lief, dear. (E.) M. E. *leef*. A. S. *leóf*.
+Du. *lief*, Icel. *ljúfr*, Swed. *ljuf*, Goth.
liubs, G. *lieb*. Cf. Russ. *lioboi*, agreeable,
liobite, to love; L. *lubet*, *libet*, it pleases;
Skt. *lubh*, to desire. (√LUBH.)

believe. (E.) M. E. *beleuen* (*beleven*).
Here the prefix *be-* (by) is substituted for
the older prefix *ge-*. A. S. *gelýfan*, to believe, lit. to esteem dear.－A. S. *ge-*, prefix;
leóf, dear (above). + Goth. *galaubjan*, to
believe, from *liubs*, dear; G. *glauben*,
O. H. G. *galaupjan*, to believe, from G.
lieb (O. H. G. *liup*), dear.

leave (2), permission, farewell. (E.)
'To take *leave*'=to take permission to
go. 'By your *leave*'=by your permission.
M. E. *leue* (*leve*). A. S. *leáf*, permission.
From the same root as A. S. *leóf*, dear,
pleasing. The orig. sense was pleasure;
hence a grant, permission.+Du. *-lof*, as in
oor-lof, permission, *ver-lof*, leave; Icel. *leyfi*,
leave, *lofan*, permission, *lob* (1) praise, (2)
permission; Dan. *lov*, Swed. *lof*, praise,
leave; G. *ur-laub*, *ver-laub*, leave, *er-
lauben*, to permit, *lob*, praise.

leman, lemman, a sweetheart. (E.)
M. E. *lemman*, also *leofman*.－ A. S. *leóf*,
dear; *mann*, a man or woman. (Short
for *lief-man*.) And see **Furlough**.

Liege, faithful, subject. (F.－O. H. G.)
The sense has been altered by confusion
with L. *ligatus*, bound. In old use, we
could speak of 'a *liege* lord' as meaning a
free lord, in exact opposition to the imported notion. M. E. *lige*, *lege*; *lege
poustee*=free sovereignty, Bruce, v. 165.－
O. F. *lige*, *liege*, *liege*, *leal*; a *liege* lord
was a lord of a free band, and his *lieges*
were privileged free men, faithful to him,
but free from other service. － O. H. G.
ledic, *lidic* (G. *ledig*), free, esp. from all
obligations of service; the orig. sense was
'going where one likes.'－O. H. G. *lidan*,
to depart, take one's way, cognate with
A. S. *lídan*, to travel. Cf. Icel. *lidugr*,
free, from *lída*, to travel; O. Du. *ledig*,
free. And see **Lode**.

allegiance, the duty of a subject to
his lord. (F.－O. H. G.) M. E. *alegeaunce*.
Formed from F. *a* (=L. *ad*), to; O. F.
ligance, homage, from O. F. *lige*, *liege*,
liege (as above).

Lieger, Leiger, an ambassador; see
Ledger, under **Lie** (1).

Lien; see **Ligament**.

Lieu, Lieutenant; see **Locus**.

Life, Lifeguard; see **Live**.

Lifelong; see **Live**.

Lift (1), to raise; see **Loft**.

Lift (2), to steal. (E.) We speak of
a *shop-lifter*, a thief; see Shak. Troil. i.
2. 109. Properly, the verb should be *liff*.
An E. word, but only preserved in Gothic.
Cf. Goth. *hlifan*, to steal; *hliftus*, a thief.
Cognate with L. *clepere*, to steal. Goth.
hliftus=Gk. κλέπτης, a thief.

Ligament, a band, the membrane con-
necting the moveable bones. (F. － L.)
F. *ligament*.－L. *ligamentum*, a tie, band.
－L. *liga-re*, to tie; with suffix *-mentum*.

alligation, a rule in arithmetic. (L.)
From L. *alligatio*, a binding, band.－L.
alligatus, pp. of *alligare*, to bind; see **ally**
(below).

ally, to bind together. (F.－L.) M. E.
alien.－O. F. *alier*, to bind up.－L. *al-
*(=ad), to; *ligare*, to bind. Dor. *alliance*, M. E. *aliaunce*.

league (1), a bond, alliance. (F.－L.)
F. *ligue*, 'a league;' Cot.－Low L. *liga*, a
league.－L. *ligare*, to bind.

liable, responsible. (F.－L.) Formed,
with suffix *-able*, from F. *li-er*, to tie.－L.
ligare, to tie.

lictor, an officer in Rome. (L.) L.
lictor, i. e. 'binder;' either from the fasces
or 'bound' rods which he bore, or from
binding culprits. Allied to *ligare*, to bind.

lien, a legal claim, charge on property.
(F.－L.) F. *lien*, a band, or tie, anything
that fastens or fetters.－L. *ligamen*, a tie.－
L. *ligare*, to tie.

ligature, a bandage. (F.－L.) F. *ligature*, a tie, bandage.－L. *ligatura*, a binding.
－L. *ligatus*, pp. of *ligare*, to tie.

oblige, to constrain. (F. － L.) F.
obliger. － L. *ob-ligare*, to bind together,
oblige.

rally (1), to re-assemble. (F.－L.) F.
rallier.－F. *re-*, again; *allier*, to ally; see
ally (above).

Light (1), illumination. (E.) M. E.
light. － A. S. *leóht*, light. + Du. and G.
licht, Goth. *liuhath*, light. The *t* is
a suffix; cf. L. *lux* (stem *luc-*), light,
Gk. λευκ-ός, white, Skt. *ruch*, to shine.
(√RUK.)

enlighten, verb. (E.; *with* F. *prefix*.)
Coined with F. prefix *en-* (L. *in*), compounded with *lighten*, verb; see below.

lighten (1), to illuminate, flash. (E.)
I. INTRANS., to shine as lightning; 'it
lightens.' M. E. *lightenen*, more correctly
light-n-en, where the *-n-* is formative,

and gives the sense 'to become light.' **2. Trans.** This is only the intrans. form incorrectly used with a trans. sense. The correct trans. form is simply *to light* = A. S. *leóhtan*, from *leóht*, sb.

lightning, an illuminating flash. (E.) Formed with suffix *-ing* from M. E. *lightnen*, to lighten (above).

Light (2), not heavy. (E.) M. E. *light*. A. S. *leóht*, adj. (put for *líht**).+Du. *ligt*, Icel. *léttr*, Dan. *let*, Swed. *lätt*, Goth. *leihts*, G. *leicht*, O. H. G. *líhti*. Allied to L. *leuis*, Gk. ἐλαχύς, Skt. *raghu*, light. (Ground-form RAGHU; √RAGH.)

alight (1), to descend from. (E.) M. E. *alihten*, to alight from horseback; which stands for *of-lihten*, the prefix *a-* being = A. S. *of*. The simple form *líhtan* occurs in A. S., derived from *líht** = *leóht*, light. See **light** (3) below.

alight (2), to light upon. (E.) M. E. *alihten*, standing for *on-lihten*, the prefix *a-* being = A. S. *on*. See above.

light (3), to alight, settle, descend. (E.) M. E. *lihten*. A. S. *líhtan*, verb, to alight from, lit. to make light, relieve a horse of his burden. — A. S. *leóht*, light (above). The sense 'to descend upon' (the earth) is secondary, due to the completed action of descending from a horse.

lighten (2), to alleviate. (E.) The *-en* is merely formative, as in *strength-en.* — A. S. *líhtan*, to make light. — A. S. *leóht*, light.

lighten (3), to alight on. (E.) Extended from **light** (3) above.

lighter, a boat for unlading ships. (Du.) Borrowed from Du. *ligter*, a lighter, i. e. unloader. — Du. *ligt*, light.

lights, lungs. (E.) So named from their lightness. So also Russ. *legkoe*, lights; from *legkii*, light.

Lighten (1), to flash, **Lightning**; see **Light** (1).

Ligneous, woody. (L.) L. *ligneus*, wooden. — L. *lignum*, wood,

lign-aloes, a kind of tree. (L. *and* Gk.) A sort of translation of L. *lignum aloës*, lit. 'wood of aloes.' *Aloës* is gen. of *aloë*, from Gk. ἀλόη, aloe. See **Aloe**.

Ligule; see **Lingual**.

Ligure, a precious stone. (L. — Gk.) L. *ligurius*. — Gk. λιγύριον, a sort of gem (amber or jacinth); Exod. xxviii. 19.

Like (1), similar. (E.) M. E. *lyk*, *lik*. A. S. *líc*, commonly *ge-líc*. + Du. *ge-lijk*, Icel. *líkr*, *g-líkr*, Dan. *lig*, Swed. *lik*, Goth.

ga-leiks, G. *g-leich*, O. H. G. *ka-líh*. β. Lit. 'resembling in form,' and derived from the sb. meaning 'form, shape,' viz. A. S. *líc*, form, body, Icel. *lík*, Goth. *leik*, form, body, Du. *lijk*, a corpse, Dan. *lig*, Swed. *lik*, a corpse, G. *leiche*, O. H. G. *líh*.

alike, similar. (E.) M. E. *alike*, *olike*. A. S. *onlíc*, like; from *líc*, like, with prefix *on-* = *on*, prep.

lichgate, a churchyard gate. (E.) So called because a corpse (in a bier) may be rested under it. The former syllable is M. E. *lich*, a corpse, but orig. the living body; from A. S. *líc*, a body; see **Like** (1).

like (2), to be pleased with. (E.) The construction has altered; M. E. *liketh*, it pleases, is impersonal, as in mod. E. *if you like* = if it may please you. — A. S. *lícian*, to please, lit. to be like or suitable for. — A. S. *líc*, *ge-líc*, like; see **Like** (1). + Du. *lijken*, to suit; Icel. *líka*, to like; Goth. *leikan*, to please (similarly derived).

liken, to compare. (Scand.) M. E. *liknen*, to liken; but the true sense is intransitive, viz. to be like. — Swed. *likna*, (1) to resemble, (2) to liken, from *lik*, like, Dan. *ligne*, the same, from *lig*, like.

Lilac, a shrub. (Span. — Turk. — Pers.) Span. *lilac*. — Turk. *leilaq*, a lilac. — Pers. *lílaj*, *lílanj*, *lílang*, of which the proper sense is indigo-plant. The initial *l* stands for *n*, and the above forms are from *níl*, blue, whence *nílak*, blueish. The plant is named from the blueish tinge on the flowers in some varieties.

Lily, a plant. (L. — Gk.) A. S. *lilie*. — L. *lilium*. — Gk. λείριον, a lily.

Limb (1), a member, branch of a tree. (E.) M. E. *lim*. A. S. *lim*. + Icel. *limr*, Dan. Swed. *lem*.

limber (2), part of a gun-carriage consisting of two wheels and a shaft. (Scand.) From prov. E. *limbers*, *limmers*, thills or shafts, the *b* being excrescent. Further, *limm-er-s* is a *double* plural; as appears by the derivation. — Icel. *limar*, boughs, branches (hence, shafts), pl. of *lim*, foliage, closely related to *limr*, a limb.

Limb (2), the edge or border of a sextant, &c. (L.) L. *limbus*, a border, edging, edge.

limbo, limbus, the borders of hell. (L.) The orig. phrase is *in limbo*, where *limbo* is the abl. case of *limbus*, a border; the *limbus patrum* was a supposed place on the border of hell, where the patriarchs abode till Christ's descent into hell.

Limbeck, the same as **Alembic.**

Limber (1), flexible, pliant; see **Limp** (1).

Limber (2); see **Limb** (1).

Limbo, Limbus; see **Limb** (2).

Lime (1), bird-lime, mortar. (E.) M. E. *lym, liim,* viscous substance. A. S. *līm,* bitumen, cement. **+** Du. *lijm,* Icel. *līm,* Dan. *liim,* Swed. *lim,* glue; G. *leim,* glue; L. *limus,* slime. (√ RI.)

Lime (2), a tree; see **Lind.**

Lime (3), a kind of citron. (F. – Pers.) F. *lime.* – Pers. *līmū,* a lemon, citron. See **Lemon.**

Limit. (F. – L.) F. *limite,* a limit. – L. *limitem,* acc. of *limes,* a boundary; akin to *limen,* a threshold. Cf. L. *limus,* transverse.

eliminate. (L.) From pp. of L. *ēliminare,* to get rid of. – L. *ē,* forth; *limin-,* stem of *limen,* a threshold (above).

lintel, the headpiece of a door. (F. – L.) M. E. *lintel.* – O. F. *lintel* (F. *linteau*). – Low L. *lintellus,* a lintel, put for *limitellus*,* dimin. of L. *limes* (stem *limit-*), a boundary; see **Limit** (above).

preliminary, introductory. (F. – L.) Coined from *pre-,* prefix, before; and O. F. *liminaire,* 'set before the entry of, dedicatory,' Cot. From L. *liminaris,* adj., coming at the beginning or threshold. – L. *limin-,* crude form of *limen,* threshold (above).

Limn, to paint; see **Lucid.**

Limp (1), flaccid, pliant. (E.) A nasalised form of a base LIP, a weakened form of LAP, as seen in E. *lap,* a flap; see **Lap** (2). Allied words are Icel. *limpa,* limpness, weakness; Bavarian *lampecht,* flaccid, down-hanging, from the verb *lampen,* to hang loosely down; Skt. *lamba,* depending, *lamb,* to hang down. Cf. W. *lleipr,* flabby, *llibin,* limber, drooping, *llipa,* limp. (√ RAB, RAMB.)

limber (1), flexible. (E.) Closely allied to *limp* (above); put for *limper*.* The suffix *-er* is adjectival, as in A. S. *fæger,* fair, and in E. *bitt-er.*

Limp (2), to walk lamely. (E.) In Shak. Mer. Ven. iii. 2. 130. We find A. S. *lemp-healt,* adj., halting; and a cognate form in M. H. G. *limphin,* to limp. More likely allied to *limp* (1) than to *lame.*

Limpet, a small shell-fish. (F. – L.) Formerly *lempet* (Phillips, 1706). A. S. *lempedu,* orig. a lamprey, which also

sticks to rocks. – Low L. *lemprida,* for L. *lampedra,* a lamprey. See **Lamprey,** s. v. **Lambent.** Cf. '*Lemprida,* lenpedu;' Wright's Vocab. 438. 17.

Limpid, pure, bright. (F. – L.) F. *limpide.* – L. *limpidus,* clear. Allied to **Lymph**; also to Gk. λαμπρός, bright, λάμπειν, to shine.

Linch-pin, a pin to fasten a wheel on an axle. (E.) Formerly *lins-pin,* lit. 'axle-pin.' – A. S. *lynis,* an axle-tree.**+**Du. *luns,* a linch-pin, Low G. *lunse,* G. *lünse,* a linch-pin.

Lind, Linden, the lime-tree. (E.) The true form of the sb. is *lind,* and *lind-en* is the adj. from it. Hence *lind-en tree* = *lind*; the same thing. M. E. *lind.* A. S. *lind,* the tree; also a shield, commonly of this wood. The wood is white, smooth, and easily carved; we may therefore connect it with G. *gelind, gelinde,* smooth, Icel. *linr,* smooth, soft, L. *lentus,* pliant, A. S. *līðe* (for *linðe **), pliant. **+** Du. *linde,* Icel. Dan. Swed. *lind,* G. *linde.*

lime (2), the linden tree. (E.) *Lime* is a corruption of *line,* as in Shak. Temp. v. 10; and *line* is a corruption of *lind* (above); the lengthening of *i* being due to loss of *d.*

Line, a thread, thin cord; also a stroke, row, rank, verse (L.; *or* F. – L.). In the sense 'cord,' we find A. S. *līne,* directly from L. *linea.* In the other senses, it is from F. *ligne,* also from L. *linea.* β. The L. *linea* meant orig. a string made of flax, being fem. of adj. *lineus,* made of flax. – L. *līnum,* flax. Cf. Gk. λίνον, flax. Dor. *out-line.*

delineate. (L.) From pp. of L. *delineare,* to sketch in outline. – L. *de,* down; *lineare,* to mark out, from *linea,* a line.

lineage. (F. – L.) F. *lignage,* a lineage. – F. *ligne,* a line, rank. – L. *linea,* a line (above).

lineal. (L.) L. *linealis,* belonging to a line. – L. *linea,* a line.

lineament, a feature. (F. – L.) F. *lineament,* Cot. – L. *lineamentum,* a drawing, delineation. – L. *lineare,* to draw a line. – L. *linea,* a line.

linear. (L.) L. *linearis,* belonging to a line. – L. *linea,* a line.

linen, cloth made of flax. (L.) Used as a sb., but really an old adj.; the old sb. being M. E. *lin,* A. S. *līn,* flax. – L. *linum,* flax. (Cf. *gold-en* from *gold.*) See **linseed** (below).

lining. (L.) Formed, with suffix *-ing*, from the verb *to line*, i.e. to cover the inside of a garment with *line*, i.e. linen; see **linen** (above).

linnet, a bird. (F.—L.) M. E. *linet*.— F. *linotte*, 'a linnet,' Cot. Named from feeding on flax-seed and hemp-seed (cf. G. *hänfling*, a linnet, from *hanf*, hemp.)—F. *lin*, flax.—L. *linum*, flax. See p. 579.

linseed, flax seed. (L. *and* E.) From M. E. *lin*=A. S. *lín*, flax, borrowed from L. *linum*, flax; and E. *seed*.

linsey-woolsey, made of linen and woollen mixed. (L. *and* E.) Made up from M. E. *lin*, linen, and E. *wool*. See **linen** (above).

lint, scraped linen. (L.) Shortened from L. *linteum*, a linen cloth; neut. of *lin-teus*, linen.—L. *linum*, flax.

Ling (1), a fish; see **Long.**

Ling (2), heath. (Scand.) M. E. *lyng*.— Icel. *lyng*, ling, heather; Dan. *ling*; Swed. *ljung*.

Linger; see **Long.**

Lingual, pertaining to the tongue. (L.) Coined from L. *lingua*, the tongue, O. Lat. *dingua*. Cognate with E. *tongue*.

language. (F.—L.) M. E. *langage*.— F. *language*.—F. *langue*, the tongue.—L. *lingua*, tongue.

ligule, a strap-shaped petal. (L.) In botany.—L. *ligula*, a little tongue, also spelt *lingula*, dimin. of *lingua*, tongue.

linguist, one skilled in languages. (L.) From L. *lingua*, tongue, language; with suffix *-ista* (=Gk. *-ιστης*).

Liniment, salve, ointment. (F.—L.) F. *liniment*.—L. *linimentum*, ointment.—L. *linere*, to smear; cf. Skt. *lí*, to melt, *ri*, to ooze. (√RI.)

alliteration, repetition of letters. (L.) Coined from L. *al-* (=*ad*), to; and *litera*, a letter; see below.

letter, a character. (F.—L.) M. E. *lettre*.—F. *lettre*.—L. *litera*, a letter; so called because smeared on parchment and not cut on wood.—L. *litus*, pp. of *linere*, to besmear; see **obliterate** (below).

literal. (F.—L.) O. F. *literal*.—L. *literalis*, according to the letter.—L. *litera*; see **letter** (above).

literature. (F.—L.) F. *literature*.— L. *literatura*, scholarship.—L. *literatus*, learned, skilled in letters.—L. *litera*, a letter; see **letter.**

obliterate. (L.) From pp. of L. *obliterare*, to efface.—L. *ob*, over; *litera*, a

letter, orig. 'a smear;' see **letter** (above).

Lining; see **Line.**

Link (1), a ring of a chain. (E.) A. S. *hlence*, a link. + Icel. *hlekkr* (for *hlenkr*,* by assimilation); Dan. *lænke*, Swed. *länk*; G. *gelenk*, a joint, link, ring. Perhaps allied to **Ring.**

Link (2), a torch; see **Linstock.**

Linnet, Linseed; see **Line.**

Linsey-woolsey; see **Line.**

Linstock, Lintstock, a stick to hold a lighted match. (Du.) Formerly *lintstock*. —Du. *lontstok*, 'a lint-stock,' Sewel.—Du. *lont*, a match; *stok*, a stick (see **Stock**). + Dan. *lunte-stok*; from *lunte*, a match, *stok*, a stick. ¶ E. *lint* is substituted for Du. *lont* by confusion with *lint*, scraped linen.

link (2), a torch. (Du.) A corruption of *lint*, as it appears in *lint-stock* (above). Cf. Lowl. Sc. *lunt*, a torch, Du. *lont*, a match, Dan. *lunte*, Swed. *lunta*.

Lint; see **Line.**

Lintel; see **Limit.**

Lion; see **Leo.**

Lip. (E.) M. E. *lippe*. A. S. *lippa*, *lippe*, the lip. + Du. *lip*, Dan. *läbe*, Swed. *läpp*, G. *lippe*, *lefze*. + L. *lab-rum*, *labium*, lip; Gael. *liob*, Lithuan. *lupa*, Pers. *lab*, lip. Orig. 'the lapper;' see **Lap** (1). Cf. L. *lambere*, to lick.

Liquefy, Liquescent; see **Liquid.**

Liquid, moist. (F.—L.) F. *liquide*.— L. *liquidus*, moist.—L. *liquere*, to be wet. Cf. Skt. *rí*, to ooze. (√RI.)

deliquesce, to become liquid. (L.) L. *de-liquescere*, to become liquid; see **liquescent** (below).

liquefy, to become liquid. (F.—L.) F. *liquefier* (see Cot.). As if from L. *liquefi-care*,* to make liquid; but we only find L. *liquefieri*, to become liquid.

liquescent, melting. (L.) L. *liquescent-*, stem of pres. part. of *liquescere*, inceptive form of *liquere*, to be wet.

liquidate, to make clear; hence, to clear off an account. (L.) From pp. of Low L. *liquidare*, to clarify, make clear.— L. *liquidus*, liquid, clear.

liquor, moisture, strong drink. (F.—L.) M. E. *licour*, *licur*.—O. F. *liqeur*, later *liqueur*, moisture.—L. *liquōrem*, acc. of *liquor*, moisture.—L. *liquere*, to be moist. ¶ Now accommodated to L. spelling; we also use mod. F. *liqueur*.

Liquorice; see **Licorice.**

Lisp. (E.) M. E. *lispen*, *lipsen*. — A. S.

wlispian*, to lisp, not found; regularly formed from A. S. *wlisp*, adj., lisping, imperfect in utterance. **+** Du. *lispen*, Dan. *læspe*, Swed. *läspa*, G. *lispeln*. (Imitative.)

Lissom; see **Lithe.**

List (1), a border of cloth, selvage. (E.) M. E. *list*. A. S. *list*. **+** Du. *lijst*, Icel. *listi*, Dan. *liste*, Swed. *list*, G. *leiste*, O.H.G. *lísta*. (The *i* was orig. long.)

　　enlist, to enter on a list. (F. **–** G.; *with* F. **–** L. *prefix*.) Coined by prefixing F. *en* (L. *in*) to the word below.

list (2), a catalogue. (F. **–** G.) F. *liste*, a list, roll; also, a list or selvage. It meant (1) a strip, (2) a roll or list of names. **–** G. *leiste*, O. H. G. *lísta*, a border; see **List** (1).

List (3); see **Lists.**

List (4), to choose, have pleasure in; see **Lust.**

List (5), to listen; see below.

Listen. (E.) We also find *list*: also M. E. *lust-n-en* and *lust-en*, the former being deduced from the latter by a formative *n*, as in Goth. *full-n-an*, to become full. **–** A. S. *hlystan*, to listen to. **–** A. S. *hlyst*, hearing; from a base HLUS, as in A S. *hlos-nian*, to hearken. Cf. Icel. *hlusta*, to listen, from *hlust*, the ear; W. *clust*, the ear; also L. *clu-ere*, Gk. κλύ-ειν, to hear, Skt. *çru*, to hear. (√KRU.)

Listless; see **Lust.**

Lists, ground enclosed for a tournament. (F. **–** L.) M. E. *listes*, s. pl., the lists. The *t* is excrescent; and *liste* stands for *lisse**. **–** O. F. *lisse* (F. *lice*), 'a list or tiltyard;' Cot. Cf. Ital *liccia*, Span. *liza*, Port. *liça*, a list for tilting. **–** Low L. *liciæ*, s. pl., barriers; *liciæ duelli*, the lists. Apparently allied to L. *licium*, a thread, a small girdle. (Perhaps a space roped in.)

Litany, a form of prayer. (F. **–** L. **–** Gk.) M. E. *letanie*, afterwards altered to *litanie*. **–** O. F. *letanie*. **–** L. *litania*. **–** Gk. λιτανεία, a prayer. **–** Gk. λιταίνειν, to pray. **–** Gk. λίτομαι, I beg, pray, λίτη, prayer, entreaty.

Literal, Literature; see **Liniment.**

Litharge, protoxide of lead. (F. **–** L. **–** Gk.) M. E. *litarge*. **–** F. *litharge*, 'litargie, white lead;' Cot. **–** L. *lithargyrus*. **–** Gk. λιθάργυρος, lit. 'stone-silver.' **–** Gk. λίθ-ος, a stone; ἄργυρος, silver; see **Argent.**

lithography, writing on stone. (Gk.) Coined from Gk. λίθο-s, a stone; γράφειν, to write.

lithotomy, cutting for stone. (L. **–** Gk.)

L. *lithotomia*. **–** Gk. λιθοτομία. **–** Gk. λίθο-s, stone; τομ-, for ταμ-, base of τέμνειν, to cut; see **Tome.**

Lithe, pliant, flexible, active. (E.) M. E. *lithe*. A. S. *líðe*, *líð*, gentle, soft (put for *linðe**, the long *i* being due to loss of *n*). **+** G. *gelinde*, O. H. G. *lindi*, soft, tender; L. *lentus*, pliant. Allied to Icel. *linr*, L. *lenis*, soft. **Der.** *lissom*, i. e. *lithe-some*.

Lithography, Lithotomy; see **Litharge.**

Litigation, a contest in law. (L.) From L. *litigatio*, a disputing. **–** L. *litigatus*, pp. of *litigare*, to dispute. **–** L. *lit-*, stem of *lis*, strife; *-igare*, for *agere*, to carry on. L. *lis*=O. Lat. *stlis*, allied to E. **Strife.**

litigious, contentious. (F. **–** L.) It also once meant debateable. **–** F. *litigieux*, 'debatefull;' Cot. **–** L. *litigiosus*, adj., from *litigium*, contention. **–** L. *litigare*, to dispute (above).

Litmus, a kind of dye. (Du.) Corrupted from Du. *lakmoes*, a blue dye-stuff. **–** Du. *lak*, lac; *moes*, pulp. **+** G. *lackmuss*, litmus; from *luck*, lac, *mus*, pulp. See **Lac.**

Litter (1), a portable bed. (F. **–** L.) M. E. *litere*. **–** O. F. *litiere*. **–** Low L. *lectaria*, a litter. **–** L. *lectus*, a bed. (Base LAGH.) Allied to **Lectern.**

litter (2), materials for a bed, heap of straw to lie on, confused mass of things scattered. (F. **–** L.) The same word, applied to a straw bed for animals, &c.

litter (3), a brood. (F. **–** L.) Really the same word as the last, and not to be connected (as in Vigfusson) with Icel. *látr*. See the various senses of M. E. *lytere* in the Prompt. Parv., and cf. F. *accoucher*, E. 'to be in the straw.'

Little.- (E.) M. E. *litel*, *lutel*. A.S. *lytel*, little; we also find the shorter form *lyt*. **+** Du. *luttel*, little, *lutje*, a little; Icel. *lítill*, also *lítt*, adv.; Dan. *liden*, also *lille* (= *litle**); Swed. *liten*, Goth. *leitils*, O.H.G. *luzil*. All from the base LUT, to deceive; cf. A.S. *lytig*, deceitful, *lot*, deceit; Goth. *liuts*, deceitful, *luton*, to betray; oldest sense to stoop; see **Lout.** The old sense 'base' or 'mean' is still in use. ¶ Not allied to *less*.

Littoral, belonging to the sea-shore. (L.) L. *littoralis*, adj., from *littus* or *litus* (stem *litor-*), sea-shore.

Liturgy, public prayer. (F. **–** L. **–** Gk.) O. F. *liturgie*, *lyturgie*. **–** Low L. *liturgia*. **–** Gk. λειτουργία, public service. **–** Gk. λεῖτο-s, public; ἔργον, work, cognate with

E. *work.* Λεῖτος, also λέϊτος, is from Gk.
λεώς, λαός, the people; see **Lay** (3).

Live (1), to exist. (E.) M. E. *liuien*
(*livien*). A. S. *lifian*, to live, dwell; orig.
sense to remain, be left behind.+Du. *leven*,
to live; Icel. *lifa*, to be left, to live; Dan.
leve, Swed. *lefva*, Goth. *liban*, to live; G.
leben, to live, O. H. G. *liban* (whence G.
b-leiben), to remain. (Base LIB.)

    leave (1), to forsake, quit. (E.) M. E.
leuen (*leven*). A. S. *læfan*, to leave a heritage, leave behind one; from *láf,* a heritage,
that which is left or remains.— A. S. *lifian*,
to remain (above). + Icel. *leifa*, to leave,
from *leif*, heritage, which from *lifa*, to be
left. Cf. Goth. *laiba*, a remnant, from
liban, to be left, to live. ¶ Not allied to
Gk. λείπειν (Curtius, Fick).

    life. (E.) M. E. *lif, lyf*; gen. *lyues*,
dat. *lyue* (*live*). A. S. *líf*, gen. *lífes*, dat.
lífe, pl. *lífas*. From the base of A. S. *lifian*,
to remain; see **Live** (above). + Icel. *líf*,
lífi, Dan. *liv*, Swed. *lif*, O. H. G. *líp*, life
(whence G. *leib*, the body).

    lifeguard. (E.) From *life* and *guard.*
¶ Not from G. *leibgarde*, a body-guard,
which is only a cognate word, with the orig.
sense of ' life-guard,' from O. H. G. *líp*, life.

    lifelong; better **livelong** (below).

    live (2), adj., alive. (E.) Short for
alive, which is not a true orig. adj.; but
due to the phrase *a liue* (*a live*)=A.S. *on
lífe*, in life, hence, alive. *Life* is the dat.
case of *líf*, life; hence the *i* in *live* is long.

    livelihood. (E.) Corruption of M. E.
liuelode (*livelode*), i.e. life-leading, means of
living; older spelling *liflode, liflade*. From
A. S. *líf*, life; *lád*, a leading, way, provisions to live by, a course, a lode; see
Lode.

    livelong, long-lasting. (E.) The same
as *life-long*, i. e. long as life is; but *livelong*
is the older spelling.

    lively. (E.) M. E. *lifly*, i.e. life-like.

    Liver. (E.) M. E. *liuer* (=*liver*). A. S.
lifer. + Du. *lever*, Icel. *lifr*, Dan. *lever*,
Swed. *lefver*, G. *leber*. Cf. Russ. *liver'*,
the pluck of animals. Perhaps allied to
lobe.

    Livery; see **Liberal.**

    Livid, discoloured. (F.—L.) F. *livide*.
— L. *liuidus*, blueish. — L. *liuēre*, to be
blueish.

    Lizard, a four-footed reptile. (F. — L.)
M. E. *lesarde.* — F. *lesard, lezard.* — L. *lacerta*, a lizard.

    alligator. (Span. — L.) Lit. ' the

lizard.' — Span. *el lagarto*, the lizard, i. e.
the great lizard.— L. *ille*, he, that; *lacerta*,
a lizard.

    Llama, a quadruped. (Peruvian.) *Llama*
is a Peruvian word, meaning ' flock ; '
Prescott.

    Lo, behold! (E.) M. E. *lo.* A. S. *lá*, an
interjection. It seems to have been confused with *lóc*, i. e. look thou; though the
vowel is different.

    Loach, Loche, a small fish. (F.) F.
loche, ' the loach,' Cot. Span. *loja, locha*.
Origin unknown.

    Load, a burden; see **Lade.**

    Load-star, Load-stone; see **Lode.**

    Loaf. (E.) M. E. *lof, loof.* A. S. *hláf.*
+Icel. *hleifr*, Goth. *hlaifs, hlaibs*, G. *laib*.
+ Lithuan. *klēpas*, bread, Russ. *khleib'*,
bread.

    lady. (E.) Lit. ' loaf - kneader.' A.S.
hláfdige, a lady. — A.S. *hláf*, a loaf; and
(probably) A. S. *dæge*, a kneader, from the
root seen in Goth. *digan*, to knead; see
Dike, and see **Dairy.** ¶ *Lady* was specially used to mean the Virgin Mary; hence
lady-bird, lady's-slipper, &c.

    lammas, a name for Aug. 1. (E.)
A. S. *hláf-mæsse*, lit. ' loaf-mass ; ' later
spellings *hlammæsse, lammasse*. A loaf
was on this day offered as a first-fruits of
harvest. See **Mass** (2).

    lord, a master. (E.) Lit. ' loaf-keeper.'
A. S. *hláford*, a lord; (probably) for *hláf-
weard **, a loaf-ward; see **Ward.** ¶ The
etymology from *hláf*, loaf, and *ord*, a point
(hence a crust of bread), is ridiculous.

    Loam, clay. (E.) M. E. *lam.* A. S.
lám. + Du. *leem*, G. *lehm*, O. H. G. *leim*.
Akin to **Lime** (1).

    Loan, a lending, money lent. (E.) M. E.
lone (=*láne*). This corresponds to the
rare A. S. *lán*, commonly written as *lǽn*,
a loan. (We have a similar double form
in *dál*, dole, *dǽl*, deal.)+Du. *leen*, a grant,
fief; Icel. *lán*, a loan, *lén*, a fief; Dan.
laan, Swed. *lån*, a loan; G. *lehn, lehen*,
a fief. β. All from the verb seen in A. S.
líhan (pt. t. *láh*), to grant, Icel. *ljá*, G.
leihen, to lend; akin to L. *linquere* (pt. t.
liqui), Gk. λείπειν, Skt. *rich*, to leave.
(√ RIK.)

    lend. (E.) The final *d* is excrescent.
M. E. *lenen.* A. S. *lǽnan*, to lend.— A.S.
lǽn, a loan (above).+Icel. *lána*, from *lán*;
Dan. *laane*, from *laan*; Swed. *läna*, from
län, a fief; G. *lehnen*, from *lehn.*

    Loath. (E.) M. E. *loth.* A. S. *láð*,

hateful, orig. painful. — A. S. *láð*, pt. t. of *líðan*, to travel, experience, suffer. + Icel. *leiðr*, Dan. Swed. *led*, odious; O. H. G. *leit*, odious, orig. painful, from O. H. G. *lîdan*, to travel, suffer (G. *leiden*). Akin to **Lode**. Der. *loath-ly, -some*; also *loathe*, verb.

Lobby; see **Leaf**.

Lobe, flap of the ear, &c. (F. — Low L. — Gk.) F. *lobe*. — Late L. *lobus*. — Gk. λοβός, a lobe of the ear or liver; cognate with **Lap** (2). (√ RAB.)

Lobster; see **Locust**.

Local, Locate; see **Locus**.

Loch; see **Lake** (1).

Lock (1), a fastening. (E.) M. E. *loke*. A. S. *loca*, a fastening. + Icel. *loka*, a lock; Swed. *lock*, a lid; G. *loch*, a dungeon. From Teut. base LUK, to fasten, as in Icel. *lúka*, to shut, Goth. *galukan*, to shut up.

locket, a little gold case worn as an ornament. (F. — Scand. *or* E.) Orig. a fastening (Hudibras, pt. ii. c. i. 808). — F. *loquet*, the latch of a door, dimin. of O. F. *loc*, a lock, which is borrowed from Icel. or E.

Lock (2), a tuft of hair or wool. (E.) M. E. *lok*. A. S. *locc*. + Du. *lok*, Icel. *lokkr*, Dan. *lok*, Swed. *lock*, G. *locke*. Orig. 'a curl;' cf. Icel. *lykkr*, a loop, bend, crook.

Locket; see **Lock** (1).

Lockram, a kind of cheap linen. (F. — Bret.) F. *locrenan*, a sort of unbleached linen; named from the place where it was made, viz. *Loc-Renan*, or *S. Renan*, near Quimper, in Brittany. — Bret. *Lok-Ronan*, cell of St. Ronan; from Bret. *lôk*, a cell.

Locomotion; see **Locus**.

Locus, a place. (L.) L. *locus*, a place; O. Lat. *stlocus*, a place; prob. allied to E. *stall*. (√ STAR.)

allocate, to set aside. (L.) From pp. of Low L. *allocare*, to allot. — L. *al-* (= *ad*), to; *locare*, to place, from *locus*.

allow (1), to assign, grant. (F. — L.) F. *allouer*, to let out for hire, assign for an expense. — Low L. *allocare*, to allot (above).

collocate, to place together. (L.) From pp. of *col-locare*, to place together.

couch, to lay down, place, set. (F. — L.) M. E. *couchen*, to set, arrange. — O. F. *coucher*, *colcher*, to place. — L. *collocare*, to put together (above). Der. *couch*, sb., a place on which one is *couched* or laid.

dislocate, to put out of joint. (L.)

From pp. of L. *dis-locare*, to put out of place.

lieu, place, stead. (F. — L.) F. *lieu*. — L. *locum*, acc. of *locus*, a place.

lieutenant, a 'locum tenens,' deputy, &c. (F. — L.) F. *lieu tenant*. — L. *locum-tenent-*, stem of *locum tenens*, one who hold's another's place. — L. *locum*, acc. of *locus*, a place; *tenens*, pres. pt. of *tenere*, to hold.

local. (F. — L.) F. *local*. — L. *localis*, belonging to a place. — L. *locus*, a place.

locate, to place. (L.) From pp. of L. *locare*, to place. — L. *locus*.

locomotion, motion from place to place. (L.) Coined from *loco-*, crude form of *locus*, a place; and *motion*.

Locust, a winged insect. (L.) M. E. *locuste*. — L. *locusta*, a shell-fish, also a locust.

lobster, a kind of shell-fish. (L.) A. S. *loppestre*, a corrupter form of A. S. *lopust*, a corruption of L. *locusta*, (1) a lobster, (2) a locust. It was perhaps confused with Dan. *loppe*, a flea (lit. a jumper), as though *loppestre* meant jumper; but the true A. S. form of 'leap' is *hleápan*.

Lode, a vein of ore, a water-course. (E.) The true sense is 'course.' A. S. *lád*, a way, course, journey. — A. S. *láð*, pt. t. of *líðan*, to travel, go. + Icel. *leið*, lode, way, course, from *líða*, to go; Swed. *led*, a course. (Base LITH.) Der. *lode-star* (below). ¶ And see **load**, p. 236, col. 1.

lead (1), to conduct. (E.) M. E. *leden*, pt. t. *ladde*, pp. *lad*. — A. S. *lǽdan*, to lead. — A. S. *lád*, a course, way (above). + Icel. *leiða*, from *leið*; Swed. *leda*, from *led*; G. *leiten*, Du. *leiden*.

lodestar, loadstar, the polar star. (E.) Lit. 'way-star,' star that guides; see **Lode** above.

lodestone, loadstone, a magnet. (E.) Compounded of *lode* and *stone*, in imitation of *lodestar*; it should rather have been *lead-stone*, since it means a stone that leads or draws, not a stone to guide.

Lodge; see **Leaf**.

Loft, an upper room. (Scand.) M. E. *loft*, properly 'air;' the peculiar sense is Scand. — Icel. *lopt* (pron. *loft*), (1) air, sky, (2) an upper room; Dan. Swed. *loft*, a garret. Allied to A. S. *lyft*, air, sky, Goth. *luftus*, Du. *lucht* (for *luft* *), G. *luft*, the air.

aloft, in the air. (Scand.) Icel. *á lopt* (pron. *loft*), aloft, in the air. Here prefix *a-* = Icel. *á-* = A. S. *on*, in.

lift (1), to elevate. (Scand.) M. E. *liften.* — Icel. *lypta* (pron. *lyfta*), to lift, exalt in air, from *lopt*, air; Dan. *löfte*, from *loft*; Swed. *lyfta*, from *loft.* (The *i = y*, mutation of *o*.) Der. *up-lift.*

Log (1), a block of wood; see **Lie** (1).

Log (2), a piece of wood with a line, for measuring the rate of a ship; see **Lie** (1).

Log (3), a liquid measure. (Heb.) In Lev. xiv. 10. — Heb. *lóg*, a liquid measure, 12th part of a *hin*; orig. 'a basin.'

Logarithm; see **Arithmetic.**

Loggerhead; see **Lie** (1).

Logic, the science of reasoning correctly. (F. — L. — Gk.) O. F. *logique.* — L. *logica*, put for *ars logica*, logic art. — Gk. λογική, put for λογική τέχνη, logic art; where λογική is fem. of λογικός, reasonable. — Gk. λόγος, a speech. — Gk. λέγειν, to say. + L. *legere*, to speak; see **Legend.**

analogy, proportion. (F. — L. — Gk.) F. *analogie.* — L. *analogia.* — Gk. ἀναλογία, equality of ratios. — Gk. ἀνά, upon, throughout; -λογία, a form made by adding the suffix -ια to λόγ-ος, a word, statement, from λέγειν, to speak.

apologue, a fable, story. (F. — Gk.) F. *apologue.* — Gk. ἀπόλογος, a story, fable. — Gk. ἀπό, from; λόγος, speech.

apology, a defence. (L. — Gk.) L. *apologia.* — Gk. ἀπολογία, a speech made in defence. — Gk. ἀπό, off; and λόγος, speech, from λέγειν, to speak.

catalogue, a list set down in order. (F. — L. — Gk.) F. *catalogue.* — L. *catalogus.* — Gk. κατάλογος, a counting up, enrolment. — Gk. κατά, fully; λόγος, account.

decalogue. (F. — L. — Gk.) F. *decalogue.* — L. *decalogus.* — Gk. δεκά-λογος, the ten commandments. See **Decade.**

dialect, a variety of a language. (F. — L. — Gk.) F. *dialecte.* — L. *dialectos.* — Gk. διάλεκτος, discourse, language, dialect. — Gk. διαλέγομαι, I discourse. — Gk. διά, between; λέγειν, to speak.

dialogue, a discourse. (F. — L. — Gk.) F. *dialogue.* — L. *dialogus.* — Gk. διάλογος, a conversation. — Gk. διαλέγομαι, I discourse (above).

eclectic, choosing out; hence, a philosopher who selected doctrines from various sects. (Gk.) Gk. ἐκλεκτικός, selecting; as sb. an Eclectic. — Gk. ἐκλέγειν, to select. — Gk. ἐκ, out; λέγειν, to choose.

eclogue, a pastoral poem. (L. — Gk.) L. *ecloga* (the F. word was *églogue*). — Gk.

ἐκλογή, a selection, esp. of poems. — Gk. ἐκ-λέγειν, to choose out.

epilogue. (F. — L. — Gk.) F. *epilogue.* — L. *epilogus.* — Gk. ἐπί-λογος, a concluding speech.

eulogy, praise. (L. — Gk.) From L. *eulogium.* — Gk. εὐλογίον, also εὐλογία, praise, lit. good speaking. — Gk. εὐ, well; λέγειν, to speak.

monologue, a soliloquy. (F. — Gk.) F. *monologue*, properly 'one that loves to hear himself talke;' Cot. — Gk. μονόλογος, speaking alone. — Gk. μονό-s, alone; λέγειν, to speak.

prologue, a preface. (F. — L. — Gk.) F. *prologue.* — L. *prologus.* — Gk. πρό-λογος, a fore-speech.

syllogism, a reasoning from premises. (F. — L. — Gk.) F. *syllogisme.* — L. *syllogismus.* — Gk. συλλογισμός, a reasoning. — Gk. συλλογίζομαι, I reckon together, reason. — Gk. συλ- (= συν), together; λογίζομαι, I reckon, from λόγος, discourse, reasoning.

So also all words in -*logy*, the chief being *astro-logy*, *bio-*, *chrono-*, *concho-*, *doxo-*, *entomo-*, *etymo-*, *genea-*, *geo-*, *meteoro-*, *minera-*, *mytho-*, *necro-*, *noso-*, *ornitho-*, *osteo-*, *patho-*, *philo-*, *phraseo-*, *phreno-*, *physio-*, *psycho-*, *tauto-*, *theo-*, *zoo-logy*; see these in their due places.

Loin; see **Lumbar.**

Loiter; see **Lout.**

Loll, to lounge about. (O. Low G.) M. E. *lollen.* — O. Du. *lollen*, to sit over the fire; the orig. sense was prob. to doze; allied to **Lull.**

Lollard, a name given to the followers of Wyclif. (O. Du.) It was confused with M. E. *loller*, i. e. one who lolls, a lounger, lazy fellow; see **Loll** above; but the words are prob. related. Latinised as *Lollardus* from O. Du. *lollaerd*, (1) a mumbler of prayers and hymns, (2) a Lollard, lit. 'God-praiser' or 'singer;' first applied to a sect in Brabant. Formed with suffix -*aerd* (same as E. -*ard* in *drunk-ard*) from O. Du. *lollen*, *lullen*; to sing; see **Lull.**

Lone, short for *alone*; see **One.**

Long (1), extended. (E.) M. E. *long.* A. S. *lang*, *long.* + Du. *lang*. Icel. *langr*, Dan. *lang*, Swed. *lång*, Goth. *laggrs* (= *langrs*), G. *lang*; L. *longus.* Allied to M. H. G. *lingen*, to go hastily, Skt. *iaṅgh*, to jump over, surpass, *raṅgh*, to move swiftly. The orig. sense had reference to the length of the stride in running. (√RAGH.)

along, lengthwise of. (E.) M. E. *along.* A. S. *andlang*, along, prep. with gen.— A. S. *and-*, prefix (allied to Gk. ἀντί, Skt. *anti*, over against); *lang*, long. The sense is 'over against in length.'+G. *entlang*, *along*. See **A-** (3) and **Long**.

belong, to pertain to. (E.) M. E. *belongen*; from *be-*, prefix, and A. S. *langian*, to long after; see **long** (2) below. Cf. Du. *belangen*, to concern.

elongate, to lengthen. (L.) From pp. of L. *elongare*, to remove.—L. *e*, out; *longus*, long (above).

length. (E.) M. E. *lengthe.* — A. S. *lengð*.—A. S. *lang*, long.+Du. *lengte*, from *lang*; Dan. *længde*, from *lang*; Swed. *längd*, Icel. *lengd.* **Der**. *length-en.*

ling (1), a fish. (E.) M. E. *lenge*; answering to A. S. *lenga**, put for *langa*, 'the long one,' def. form of *lang*, long. Cf. A. S. *lengu*, length. Named from its long slender shape.+Du. *leng*, a ling, from *lang*; Icel. *langa*, from *langr*; Norw. *langa*, *longa*, a ling; Swed. *långa*; G. *länge*, a ling, also called *längfisch*, long fish.

linger, to tarry. (E.) Frequent. form of M. E. *lengen*, to tarry.—A. S. *lengan*, to prolong, put off.—A. S. *lang*, long. Cf. Icel. *lengja*, to lengthen, Du. *lengen*, to lengthen, G. *verlängern*, to prolong.

long (2), to desire, yearn; also to belong. (E.) M. E. *longen.* A. S. *langian*, to lengthen, also to long after, crave, long. —A. S. *lang*, long. The orig. sense is to become long, hence to stretch the mind after, to crave; also to apply, belong. **Der**. *be-long.*

longevity, length of life. (L.) From L. *longæuitas*, long life.—L. *long-us*, long; *æuitas*, usually *ætas*, age, from *æui-*=*æuo-*, crude form of *æuum*, life; see **Age.**

longitude. (F.—L.) F. *longitude.*— L. *longitudo*, length; in late Lat., the longitude of a place.—L. *longi-*=*longo-*, crude form of *longus*, long; with suffix *-tu-do.* **Der**. *longitudin-al*, from stem *longitudin-.*

lunge, a thrust, in fencing. (F.—L.) Formerly *longe.* The E. *a longe* is a mistaken substitute for F. *allonge* (formerly *alonge*), a lengthening; i.e. an extension of the body in delivering the thrust. — F. *allonger*, to lengthen (formerly *alonger*).— F. *a* (=L. *ad*), to; *longare**, only used in *e-longare*, to lengthen, from *longus*, long.

oblong, long from side to side. (F.—L.) F. *oblong.*—L. *ob-longus*, long across.

prolong, to continue. (F.—L.) M. E.

prolongen.—F. *prolonger.*—L. *prolongare*, to prolong. — L. *pro-*, forward; *longus*, long. **Doublet**, *purloin.*

purloin, to steal. (F.—L.) O. F. *purloigner*, *porloigner*, to prolong, retard, delay (hence to keep back, detain, filch).— L. *pro-longare*, to prolong (above).

Loo, a game at cards. (F.) Formerly called *lanterloo.* — F. *lanturelu*, *lanturlu*, interj., nonsense! fudge!, also a game at cards. The expression was orig. the refrain of a famous vaudeville (ab. 1640), afterwards used to give an evasive answer. Being purposely nonsensical, it admits of no further etymology.

Loof; see **Luff.**

Look, to see. (E.) M. E. *loken.* A. S. *lócian*, to look.+M. H. G. *luogen*, to mark, behold, said to mean orig. 'to look through a hole,' to peep; from M. H. G. *luoc*, G. *loch*, a hole. Allied to **Lock**. ¶ Distinct from Skt. *lok*, to see.

Loom (1), a machine for weaving cloth. (E.) M. E. *lome*, a tool, implement. A. S. *ge-lóma*, a tool, implement, instrument. **Der**. *heir-loom*, where *loom* meant any implement, hence a piece of furniture.

Loom (2), to appear faintly or at a distance. (F.—L.) The orig. sense is to glimmer, shine faintly. M. E. *lumen*, to shine. — O. F. *lumer*, to shine, give light (Cotgrave). — L. *luminare*, to shine. — L. *lumen*, light. See **Luminous**. ¶ O. F. *lumer* is preserved in F. *allumer.* Cf. also Icel. *ljóma*, to gleam.

Loon (1), **Lown**, a base fellow. (O. Low G.) Put for *loum**, *lowm**; whence M. E. *lowmyshe*, *lownyshe*, and Lowl. Sc. *loamy*, dull, slow.—O. Du. *loen*, a lown, also *lome*, slow, inactive. That *m* is the older letter appears from Du. *lummel*, Dan. *lömmel*, Swed. *lymmel*, G. *lümmel*, a lown, lubber. Allied to O. H. G. *luomi*, drooping, mild, M. H. G. *luomen*, *lómen*, to droop. Perhaps allied to **Lame.**

Loon (2), a water-bird, diver. (Scand.) A corruption of the Shetland name *loom.*— Icel. *lómr*, Swed. Dan. *lom*, a loon. Prob. the same word as the above, from the awkward motion of diving-birds on land; cf. *booby*, *gull*, *goose*, *owl*, &c.

Loop. (C.) Irish and Gael. *lub*, a loop, bow, staple, noose, orig. a bend.—Irish and Gael. *lub*, to bend. **Der**. *loop-hole.*

Loose, slack. (Scand.) M. E. *lous*, *los*; it is difficult to account for the vowel-sound, but Prof. Zupitza shews (in Anglia, vii. 152) that it is due to the Scand. form.

The true M. E. form is *lees*, answering to A. S. *leás*, (1) loose, (2) false. ▬ Icel. *lauss*, Swed. Dan. *lös*, loose; O. Sax. *lôs*, O. Du. *loos*, (1) loose, (2) false (where mod. Du. has *los*, loose, *loos*, false); G. *los*, loose; Goth. *laus*, empty, vain. (Base LUS, to lose.)

leasing, falsehood. (E.) M. E. *lesing*. A. S. *leásung*, falsehood; from *leás*, false (above). Cf. Icel. *lausung*, falsehood; Du. *loos*, false.

-less, suffix. (E.) The true sense is loose, i. e. freed from ; *faith-less* = free of faith, loose from faith. A. S. *-leás*, suffix, the same word as *leás*, loose. So also G. *-los*.

loose, loosen, verb. (E.) The true form is *loose*, later *loosen* by analogy with *strengthen*, &c. M. E. *losen*, *lousen* (where *n* is merely the sign of the infinitive). ▬ A. S. *losian*, to lose, also trans. to set free. ▬ A. S. *los*, loss, destruction; allied to A. S. *leás*, false, vain, loose ; see **loose** above. Other languages derive the verb directly from the adj. ; thus Du. *lossen*, Icel. *leysa*, Swed. *lösa*, Dan. *löse*, G. *lösen*, Goth. *lausjan*, to loosen, are derived (respectively) from Du. *los*, Icel. *lauss*, Swed. and Dan. *lös*, G. *los*, Goth. *laus,* loose, vain.

lose. (E.) There are two M. E. forms, viz. *losien* and *lesen* (the latter being obsolete). 1. M. E. *losien* is from A. S. *losian*, to become loose, escape, sometimes to lose ; from A. S. *los*, loss ; see above. 2. M. E. *lesen* is from A. S. *leósan*, strong verb, to lose (pt. t. *leás*, pp. *loren*). This is cognate with Du. *liezen*, only in comp. *ver-liezen*, G. *lieren*, only in comp. *ver-lieren*, Goth. *liusan*, only in *fra-liusan*, to loose. (Teut. base LUS; cf. LU, as in L. *lu-ere*, Gk. λύ-ειν, to set free.) **Der.** *lorn*, lost, A. S. pp. *loren*; also *forlorn*, q. v.

loss, sb. (E.) M. E. *los*. A. S. *los*, destruction. Allied to **lose** (above).

louse, an insect. (E.) M. E. *lous*, pl. *lys*. A. S. *lús*, pl. *lýs* (lice). ✛ Du. *luis*, Dan. *luus*, Swed. *lus*, Icel. *lús*, G. *laus*. The orig. sense is 'destroyer;' from the base LUS ; see **Loose** (above). Cf. Goth. *lausjan*, to make of none effect.

Loot, plunder. (Hindi. ▬ Skt.) Hindi *lút* (with cerebral *t*), loot, plunder. The cerebral *t* shews that *r* is elided. ▬ Skt. *lotra*, shorter form of *loptra*, booty, spoil. ▬ Skt. *lup*, to break, spoil; allied to L. *rumpere*, to break. See **Rupture**. (√RUP.) *Loot* = that which is *robbed*.

Lop. (O. Du.) O. Du. *luppen*, to maim,

castrate, mod. Du. *lubben.* Cf. Lithuan. *lùpti*, to peel.

lib, to castrate. (Du.) Du. *lubben*, as above. **Der.** *g-lib*, verb, the same (obsolete) ; cf. O. Du. *gelubt*, 'gelt,' Hexham.

Loquacious, talkative. (L.) Coined from L. *loquaci-*, crude form of *loquax*, talkative. ▬ L. *loqui*, to speak. ✛ Russ. *reche*, to speak ; Skt. *lap* (for *lak*), to speak. (√RAK.)

allocution, an address. (L.) From L. *allocutio*, an address. ▬ L. *al-* (for *ad*), to; *locutio*, a speaking, from *locutus*, pp. of *loqui*, to speak.

circumlocution. (L.) L. *circumlocutio*, a periphrasis. ▬ L. *circumlocutus*, pp. of *circum-loqui*, to speak in a roundabout way.

colloquy. (L.) From L. *colloquium*, conversation. ▬ L. *col-loqui*, to converse with, lit. to speak together.

elocution. (L.) From L. *elocutio*, clear utterance. ▬ L. *elocutus*, pp. of *e-loqui*, to speak out.

eloquent. (F. ▬ L.) M. E. *eloquent.* ▬ O. F. *eloquent.* ▬ L. *eloquent-*, stem of pres. pt. of *e-loqui*, to speak out or clearly.

obloquy, calumny. (L.) L. *obloquium*, contradiction. ▬ L. *ob-loqui*, to speak against.

prolocutor, the chairman of a conference. (L.) L. *prolocutor*, an advocate. ▬ L. *prolocutus*, pp. of *pro-loqui*, to speak in public.

soliloquy. (L.) Late L. *soliloquium*, a speaking to oneself (Augustine). ▬ L. *soli-*, for *solus*, alone ; *loqui*, to speak.

ventriloquist. (L.) Coined, with suffix *-ist* (L. *-ista*, Gk. -ιστης), from L. *ventriloquus*, a speaker from the belly, a ventriloquist. ▬ L. *uentri-*, crude form of *uenter*, the belly ; *loqui*, to speak.

Lord; see **Loaf.**

Lore; see **Learn.**

Loriot; see **Aureate.**

Lorn, lost. (E.) A. S. *loren*, pp. of *leósan*, to lose ; see **lose**, under **Loose.**

Lory, a bird of the parrot kind. (Malay.) Also called *lury*. ▬ Malay *lúri*, *núri*, a lury or lory.

Lose, Loss; see **Loose.**

Lot, a portion, share. (E.) M. E. *lot*. A. S. *hlot*, also *hlýt*, a lot, share. ▬ A. S. *hlut-on*, pl. of pt. t. of *hleótan* (pt. t. *hleát*), to obtain by lot. ✛ Du. *lot*; Icel. *hluti*, from str. vb. *hljóta*, to obtain by lot; Dan.

lod, Swed. *lott,* G. *loos,* Goth. *hlauts,* a lot. (Base HLUT.)

allot, to assign a portion to. (L. *and* E.) A barbarous compound. – L. *al-,* for *ad,* to, before *l*; and E. *lot.*

loto, lotto, a game. (Ital. – Teut.) F. *loto*; an F. form of the Ital. *lotto,* a lottery, a word of Teut. origin; see Lot.

lottery. (E.; *with* F. *suffix.*) In Levins, ed. 1570. Formed by adding *-ery* to E. *lot*; cf. *brew-ery, fish-ery.* (The F. *loterie* is borrowed from English.)

Loth; see Loath.

Lotion; see Lave.

Loto, Lotto, Lottery; see Lot.

Lotus, the Egyptian water-lily. (L. – Gk.) L. *lotus, lotos.* – Gk. λωτός, (1) the Gk. lotus, (2) the Cyrenean lotus, the eaters of which were called *lotophagi,* (3) the lily of the Nile.

Loud. (E.) M. E. *loud.* A. S. *hlúd.* + Du. *luid,* G. *laut,* L. *-clutus,* in *in-clutus,* renowned; Gk. κλυτός, renowned; Skt. *çruta,* heard, from *çru,* to hear. (√KRU.)

aloud, loudly. (E.) M. E. *a loude,* i. e. with (lit. in) a loud voice. Here *a* is for *on* – in; see A- (2): and *loude* is the dat. case of the adj. *loud* (above). Cf. M. E. *lud* = A.S. *hlýd,* a din; from A.S. *hlúd,* loud.

Lough; see Lake (1).

Lounge, to loll about. (F. – L.) The verb is formed from a sb., being a corruption of *lungis,* an idle fellow or lounger, not an uncommon word in the 16th and 17th centuries. – F. *longis,* an idle, drowsy, and stupid fellow (Cot.). Littré supposes that this sense of *longis* was due to a pun, having reference to L. *longus,* long, hence a long and lazy man; for, strictly speaking, *Longis* is a proper name, being the O. F. form of L. *Longius* or *Longinus,* the name (in the old mysteries) of the centurion who pierced the body of Christ. This name first appears in the apocryphal gospel of Nicodemus, and was doubtless suggested by Gk. λόγχη, a lance, in John, xix. 34.

Louse; see Loose.

Lout, a clown. (E.) The lit. sense is 'stooping,' from M. E. *louten,* to stoop, bow. – A. S. *lútan,* to stoop. + Icel. *lútr,* stooping, bent (which prob. suggested our use of the word), from *lúta,* to stoop; cf. Swed. *luta,* Dan. *lude,* to stoop, lean. Allied to Little.

loiter, to delay. (Du.) M. E. *loitren.* – O. Du. and Du. *leuteren,* to linger,

loiter, trifle. O. Du. *loteren,* to delay, deceive, vacillate. Perhaps allied to Lout (above). ¶ But Koolman, in his E. Friesic Dict., connects it with Late. Cf. Icel. *lötra,* to loiter; from *latr,* late, lazy.

Louver, Loover, an opening in the roofs of ancient houses. (F. – L.) M. E. *lover,* used to translate O. F. *louvert* in the Romance of Partenay, 1175. – O. F. *louvert,* an opening; put for *l'ouvert*; from *le,* def. article, and *ouvert,* open; see Overt.

Lovage, an umbelliferous plant. (F. – L.) O. F. *levesche, luvesche* (Wright's Voc. i. 139). Cf. Ital. *levistico,* lovage. – L. *ligusticum,* lovage, a plant of *Liguria.* – L. *Ligusticus,* belonging to *Liguria,* a country of Cisalpine Gaul.

Love, affection. (E.) M. E. *loue (love).* A.S. *lufu,* love. + G. *liebe*; Russ. *liobov'*; Skt. *lobha,* covetousness. Closely allied to Lief. (√LUBH.) Der. *love,* verb; *be-love,* first appearing in M. E. *bilufien,* to love greatly.

Low (1), humble; see Lie (1).

Low (2), to bellow. (E.) M. E. *lowen.* A. S. *hlówan,* to bellow, resound. + Du. *loeijen,* O. H. G. *hlôjan.* (Base HLA, of imitative origin.)

Low (3), a hill. (E.) In place-names. A. S. *hláw, hlǽw,* a hill; properly a slope. + Goth. *hlaiw,* a grave; *hlains,* a hill; Lat. *cliuus,* a hill. Allied to Lean (1).

Low (4), flame. (Scand.) Icel. *log,* flame; cf. L. *lux.* Allied to Lucid.

Lower (1), to let down. (E.) From *low-er,* comparative of adj. *low.*

Lower (2), to frown. (E.) A variant of *leer.* M. E. *louren, luren,* to lower, frown, leer; which may be directly deduced from M. E. *lure,* the face, mien. This is a rare word, but we find: 'Hire *lure* lumes liht' = her face shines bright, Wright's Spec. of Lyric Poetry, p. 52. Allied to A. S. *hleór,* the cheek, face; see Leer. Cf. O. Du. *loeren,* 'to leere, to frowne,' Hexham.

Loyal; see Legal.

Lozenge, a rhombus; a small cake of flavoured sugar, &c., orig. of a diamond shape. (F.) Formerly *losenge,* esp. a shield of a diamond shape (in heraldry). – O. F. *losenge, lozenge* (F. *losange*), a lozenge. Origin disputed. Cf. Span. *losanje,* a lozenge, rhombus; prob. from *losa,* a square stone for paving (whence *losar,* to pave). Perhaps from L. *laud-,* stem of *laus,* praise; for we find Span. *lauda,* a tomb-stone with an epitaph (Diez).

Lubber, a dolt. (C.) M. E. *lobre, lobur,* also *loby* (a looby). – W. *llob,* a dolt, lubber, *llabi,* a stripling, looby. Cf. *lob* in Shakespeare, M. N. D. ii. 1. 16. Allied to **Lap** (2), **Limp, Lobe,** &c. And see *lump.*

Lubricate, to make slippery. (L.) From pp. of L. *lubricare,* to make slippery. – L. *lubricus,* slippery.

Luce, a fish, the pike. (F.–L.) O. F. *lus,* a pike, Cot. – L. *lucius,* a fish (perhaps the pike).

Lucid, bright. (L.) L. *lucidus,* bright. – L. *lucere,* to shine; cf. *lux,* light. ⊹ Gk. λευκός, white, Skt. *ruch,* to shine. Allied to **Light** (1). (√RUK.) **Der.** *luci-fer,* i. e. light-bringer, morning-star, from *ferre,* to bring.

elucidate. (L.) From pp. of Low L. *elucidare,* to make clear. – L. *e,* out, very; *lucid-us,* lucid, clear.

illuminate, to enlighten. (L.) From pp. of L. *illuminare,* to throw light upon. – L. *il-* (for *in*), upon; *lumin-,* stem of *lumen,* light; see **luminary** (below). ¶ We also use *illumine, illume,* from F. *illuminer* = L. *illuminare.*

illustrate, to throw light upon. (L.) From pp. of L. *illustrare,* to throw light upon. – L. *il-* (for *in*), upon; *lustrare,* to enlighten; see **lustre** (1) below.

limn, to illuminate, paint. (F.–L.) M. E. *limnen,* contracted form of *luminen,* to illuminate (Prompt. Parv.). Again, *luminen* is for *enluminen.* – O. F. *enluminer,* to illuminate, burnish, limn. – L. *illuminare;* see **illuminate** (above).

lucubration, a production composed in retirement. (L.) Properly, a working by lamp-light; from L. *lucubratio,* the same. – L. *lucubratus,* pp. of *lucubrare,* to bring in lamps, to work by lamp-light. – L. *lucubrum,* prob. a faint light; at any rate, obviously formed from *luc-,* stem of *lux,* light; cf. *lucere,* to shine.

luminary, a bright light. (F. – L.) O. F. *luminarie,* later *luminaire,* a light, lamp. – L. *luminare,* a light; neut. of *luminaris,* light-giving. – L. *lumin-,* stem of *lumen,* light. *Lūmen = luc-men**; from *lucere,* to shine.

luminous, bright. (F.–L.) F. *lumineux.* – L. *luminosus,* bright; from *lumin-,* stem of *lumen,* light (above).

lunar. (L.) L. *lunaris,* adj. from *luna,* moon. L. *lūna = lucna*,* giver of light. – L. *lucere,* to shine. **Der.** *lun-ette, inter-lunar;* and see below.

lunatic. (F. – L.) F. *lunatique.* – L. *lunaticus,* mad; lit. affected by the moon. – L. *luna,* moon.

lustre, (1), splendour. (F. – L.) F. *lustre.* – Low L. *lustrum,* a window; cf. L. *lustrare,* to shine. Prob. from a lost adj. *lustrus** (put for *luc-strus**), shining; and so from *lucere,* to shine.

lutestring, a lustrous silk. (F. – Ital. – L.) A curious corruption of *lustring,* a sort of shining silk (Kersey). – F. *lustrine,* lutestring, lustring. – Ital. *lustrino,* lustring, tinsel; from its gloss. – L. *lustrare,* to shine; see above.

lynx, a keen-sighted quadruped. (L. – Gk.) M. E. *lynx.* – L. *lynx.* – Gk. λύγξ, a lynx; allied to λύχνος, a lamp, and named from its bright eyes. Cf. Skt. *ruch,* to shine, *loch,* to see. Cognate forms are A. S. *lox,* Swed. *lo,* G. *luchs,* a lynx.

pellucid. (F. – L.) F. *pellucide.* – L. *pellucidus* (= *per-lucidus**), transparent.

sublunar, under the moon, earthly. (L.) Coined from L. *sub,* under; and E. *lunar* (above).

translucent, allowing light to pass through. (L.) L. *translucent-,* stem of pres. pt. of *trans-lucere,* to shine through.

Luck, fortune. (O. Low G.) Not found in A. S.; but we find O. Fries. *luk,* Du. *luk, ge-luk,* good fortune, happiness. ⊹ Swed. *lycka,* Dan. *lykke,* G. *glück* (for *ge-lück*). Orig. 'favour' or enticement; from Teut. base LUK, to allure, appearing in Du. *lokken,* Swed. *locka,* Dan. *lokke,* G. *locken,* O. H. G. *lucchen,* to entice, allure.

Lucre, gain, profit. (F.–L.) F. *lucre.* – L. *lucrum,* gain. Allied to Irish *luach,* price, wages, G. *lohn,* reward, Gk. λεία, booty, Russ. *lovite,* to take as booty. (√LU.) **Der.** *lucr-at-ive,* F. *lucratif,* L. *lucratiuus,* from pp. of *lucrari,* to gain, from *lucrum,* gain.

Lucubration; see **Lucid.**

Ludicrous, laughable. (L.) L. *ludicrus,* done in sport. – L. *ludi-,* for *ludus,* sport. – L. *ludere,* to play.

allude. (L.) L. *alludere,* to laugh at, allude to (pp. *allusus*). – L. *al-* (= *ad*), at ; *ludere,* to sport. **Der.** *allus-ion.*

collude, to act with others in a fraud. (L.) L. *colludere* (pp. *collusus*), to play with, act in collusion with. – L. *col-* (= *con-* = *cum*), with ; *ludere.* **Der.** *collus-ion.*

delude. (L.) L. *de-ludere* (pp. *delusus*), to mock at, cajole. **Der.** *delus-ion.*

elude, to avoid slily. (L.) L. *e-ludere*

(pp. *elusus*), to mock, deceive. **Der.**
elus-ory.

illude, to deceive. (L.) L. *il-ludere*, to
mock at; (*il-* = *in*).

illusion. (F. — L.) F. *illusion.* — L.
acc. *illusionem.* — L. *illusus*, pp. of *illudere*
(above).

prelude, an introduction. (F. — L.)
O. F. *prelude*, 'a preludium, preface, pre-
amble;' Cot. — Late L. *præludium.* — L.
præludere, to play beforehand, give a
prelude. — L. *præ*, before; *ludere*, to play.

Luff, **Loof**, to turn a ship towards the
wind. (E.) From M. E. *lof*, a contrivance
for altering a ship's course; see Layamon,
iii. 476. It seems to have been a sort of
large paddle, used to assist the helm in
keeping the ship right. Prob. named from
the resemblance of a paddle to the palm of
the hand; cf. Lowl. Sc. *loof*, Goth. *lofa*,
palm of the hand. Cf. also Du. *loef*, Dan.
luv, Swed. *lof*, weather-gage; Dan. *luve*, to
luff; and perhaps Bavarian *laffen*, blade of
an oar, flat part of a rudder.

aloof, away. (Du.; *perhaps* E.) Put for
on loof; which answers to Du. *te loef*, to
windward. Cf. Du. *loef houlden*, to keep
the luff or weather-gage, Dan. *holde luven*,
to keep to the windward; which suggested
our phrase 'to hold aloof,' i.e. to keep
away (from the leeward shore or rock).

Lug, to drag. (Scand.) Swed. *lugga*, to
pull by the hair; from *lugg*, the forelock.
Lugg is prob. allied to Swed. *lock*, a lock
of hair; see **Lock** (2). So also Norw.
lugga, to pull by the hair, from *lugg*, hair
of the head. Also cf. O. Low G. *luken*, to
pull, pull by the hair; A.S. *lyccan*, to pull
up weeds; Dan. *luge*, to weed. (√ RUG.)
Der. *lugg-age*, with F. suffix as in *baggage*.

lugsail, a sort of square sail. (Scand.
and E.) Prob. from the verb to *lug*; the
sail is easily hoisted by a pull at the rope
attached to the yard. **Der.** *lugg-er*, a ship
furnished with lugsails.

Lugubrious, mournful. (L.) From L.
lugubris, mournful. — L. *lugere*, to mourn.
Cf. Gk. λυγρός, sad, λοιγός, destruction.
(√ RUG.)

Lukewarm, partially warm. (E.) M. E.
luke, *leuk*, tepid. (*Luke-warm* = warm-
warm.) Extension of M. E. *lew*, tepid.
'Thou art *lew* [one MS. *lewk*], nether cold
nether hoot;' Wyclif, Rev. iii. 16. Allied
to A. S. *hleó*, *hleów*, a shelter, mod. E. *lee*;
see **Lee.** Cf. Icel. *hláka*, a thaw, *hlána*,

to thaw, *hlær*, *hlýr*, warm, *hljja*, to shelter.
+ Du. *leukwarm*; G. *lauwarm*.

Lull, to sing to rest. (Scand.) M. E.
lullen. — Swed. *lulla*, Dan. *lulle*, to hum, lull.
+ O. Du. *lullen*, to sing in a humming
voice. From the repetition of *lu lu*, in
lulling children to sleep. This is a drowsier
form of *la! la!* used in cheerful singing;
see **lollard.**

Lumbar, relating to the loins. (L.) L.
lumbaris, adj.; whence *lumbare*, an apron
(Jerem. xiii. 1). — L. *lumbus*, the loin. +
A. S. *lendenu*, pl., the loins, Du. *lendenen*,
pl.; Swed. *länd*, Dan. *lend*, loin; G. *lende*,
haunch.

loin. (F. — L.) M. E. *loine.* — O. F.
logne, also *longe.* — Low L. *lumbea**, not
found, fem. of an adj. *lumbeus**, from L.
lumbus, loin.

lumbago, pain in the loins. (L.) L.
lumbago, pain in the loins. — L. *lumbus.*

sirloin, **surloin.** (F. — L.) M. E. *sur-
loyn*; XV cent. — O. F. *surlonge* (14th
cent.), the surloin. — F. *sur*, upon, above;
longe, loin (above). ¶ The story about
turning the *loin* into *sir-loin* by knighting
it is mere trash.

Lumber (1), useless furniture. (F. — G.)
The *lumber-room* was orig. *Lombard-
room*, where the Lombard broker bestowed
his pledges. Cf. *Lombardeer*, a broker,
Lombard, a bank for usury or pawns;
Blount. — F. *Lombard*, a Lombard (who
acted as pawn-broker in the 14th century).
— G. *Langbart*, Long-beard; a name given
to the men of this tribe.

Lumber (2), to make a great noise.
(Scand.) In Palsgrave. A frequent. verb
of Scand. origin. — Swed. dial. *lomra*, to
resound; from Swed. *ljumm*, a great noise,
Icel. *hljómr*, a sound, a tune. From Teut.
base HLU, to hear; whence also E. *loud*,
and Goth. *hliuma*, hearing. (√ KRU.)

Luminary, **Luminous**; see **Lucid.**

Lump. (Scand.) M. E. *lompe*, *lumpe.* —
Swed. dial. and Norw. *lump*, a block,
stump, piece hewn off a log. Cf. Du.
lomp, a rag, lump, *lomp*, clumsy. Allied
to **Lubber**, and **Lap** (2).

lunch, a large piece of bread, &c.
(Scand.) *Lunch*, 'a gobbet, or peece;'
Minsheu. A variant of *lump*, like *hunch*
for *hump*, *bunch* for *bump.*

luncheon, **lunch**, a slight meal.
(Scand.) *Lunch* is now used as short for
luncheon, though *luncheon* itself is an extension from *lunch*, a lump. Cot. gives F.

caribot, 'a *lunchion*, or big piece of bread,' &c.; also '*horion*, a cuff, thump, also a *luncheon* or big piece.' *Lunchion* appears to be for *lunshin*, as in 'a huge *lunshin* of bread,' Thoresby to Ray (1703), which is prob. merely short for *lunchin*(*g*). At any rate, it is clearly from *lunch*, a large piece (above). ¶ Quite distinct from *nuncheon*, given under **Noon**.

Lunar, Lunatic; see **Lucid**.

Lung. (E.) M. E. *lunge*, pl. *lunges*, *longes*. A.S. *lunge*, pl. *lungan*.+Du. *long*, Icel. *lungu*, pl., Dan. *lunge*, Swed. *lünga*, G. *lunge*, pl. Allied to A.S. *lungre*, quickly (orig. lightly), also to Gk. ἐλαχύς, Skt. *laghu*, light. The *lungs* are named from their lightness; see **Long, Light** (2).

Lunge; see **Long**.

Lupine, a kind of pulse. (F.–L.) F. *lupin*.–L. *lupinum*, a kind of pulse; orig. neut. of *lupinus*, wolfish, though the reason is not clear.–L. *lupus*, a wolf; see **Wolf**.

Lurch (1), to lurk, steal, **Lurcher**, a dog; see **Lurk**.

Lurch (2), the name of a game. (F.– L.?) 'To leave in the *lurch*' is due to an old game.–F. *lourche*, 'the game called lurche, or lurch in a game; *il demoura lourche*, he was left in the lurch;' Cot. The initial *l* is for *le*, def. art.; Cot. also gives *ourche*, 'the game at tables called lurch.' Cf. O. F. *ourcel*, *orcel*, a little vase (Roquefort); whence I think it likely that *ourche* meant 'a pool' in a game. Perhaps from L. *urceus*, a pitcher, vase.

Lurch (3), to devour; *obsolete*. (L.) 'To *lurch*, devour, or eate greedily;' Baret. – Late L. *lurchare*, *lurcare*, to devour greedily. Prob. confused with *lurch* (1).

Lurch (4), a sudden roll sideways. (Scand.?) '*A lee lurch*, a sudden roll (of a ship) to the leeward;' Webster. Obscure; perhaps merely *lurch* (1) or *lurk* in the sense to stoop or duck like one who skulks; see **Lurk**.

Lure, a bait. (F.– G.) M. E. *lure*.– O.F. *loerre*, *loirre*, later *leurre*, 'a faulconer's lure;' Cot. – M. H. G. *luoder* (G. *luder*), a bait, decoy, lure. Perhaps from *lud*, pt. t. of *laden*, to invite.

allure, to tempt by a bait. (F.– L. *and* G.) From F. *a leurre* = to the bait or lure. – L. *ad*, to; M. H. G. *luoder* (above).

Lurid, wan, gloomy. (L.) L. *luridus*, pale yellow, wan. Perhaps allied to Gk. χλωρός, green; see **Chlorine**.

Lurk, to lie in wait. (Scand.) M. E.

lurken, *lorken*; which stands for an older *lusken** (not found). – Swed. dial. *luska*, Dan. *luske*, to lurk, sneak, listen; cf. O. Du. *luschen*, to lurk, G. *lauschen*, to listen. We also find Swed. *lura*, Dan. *lure*, to lurk; G. *lauern*, Icel. *hlöra*, to listen. (Base HLU = √ KRU.) Allied to **Listen**.

lurch (1), to lurk, dodge, pilfer. (Scand.) A weakened form of **Lurk**. The senses are (1) to lie in wait, lurk, (2) to pilfer, steal. Der. *lurch-er*, 'one that lies upon the lurch, or upon the catch, also a kind of hunting-dog;' Phillips.

Lury; see **Lory**.

Luscious, delicious. (E.; *with* F. suffix.) Also *lushious* (Spenser); *lussyouse* (Palsgrave). *Lussyouse* is prob. for *lusti-ous**, of which it is an easy corruption; formed by adding *-ous* to E. *lusty*, pleasant, delicious, which is the usual old meaning. Shak. has *lush* (short for *lush-ious*) where Chaucer would have said *lusty*; hence the singular result that Shak. uses *both* words at once: 'How *lush* and *lusty* the grass looks;' Temp. ii. 1. 52; see **Lust**.

Lust. (E.) The usual old meaning is pleasure. A.S. *lust*, pleasure. + Du. *lust*, Icel. *lyst*, *losti*, Dan. *lyst*, Swed. and G. *lust*, Goth. *lustus*, pleasure. Der. *lust-y*, formerly 'pleasant.' And see *luscious*.

list (4), to please. (E.) M. E. *lusten*, *listen*; 'if thee *lust*' = if it please thee, Ch. C. T. 1185. A. S. *lystan*, to desire, used impersonally. – A. S. *lust*, pleasure (above).+Du. *lusten*, Icel. *lysta*, Dan. *lyste*, Swed. *lysta*, Goth. *luston*, G. *gelüsten*; all from the sb.

listless, careless. (E.) Put for *lustless*; Gower has *lustles*, C. A. ii. 111. From *lust* (above).

Lustration; see **Lustre** (2).

Lustre (1), splendour; see **Lucid**.

Lustre (2), **Lustrum**, a period of five years. (L.) L. *lustrum*, an expiatory sacrifice; also a period of five years, because every five years a lustrum was performed. The orig. sense is 'a purification;' from *luere*, allied to *lauare*, to cleanse, purify; see **Lave**.

lustration, a purification by sacrifice. (L.) From L. *lustratio*, an expiation. – L. *lustratus*, pp. of *lustrare*, to purify. – L. *lustrum*, an expiatory sacrifice (above).

Lute (1), a musical instrument. (F.– Arab.) M. E. *lute*.– F. *lut* (Cotgrave), mod. F. *luth*. We also find Prov. *laut*, Span. *laud*, Port. *alaude*, Ital. *liuto*, Du. *luit*, Dan. *lut*,

G. *laute.* The Port. form shews the Arab. origin; since *a-* is for *al*, the Arab. def. art. — Arab. *'úd*, wood, timber, a staff, stick, wood of aloes, lute, or harp.

Lute (2), a kind of loam. (F. — L.) O. F. *lut*, clay, loam. — L. *lutum,* mud, that which is washed down. — L. *luere*, to wash. Allied to **Lave.**

Lutestring; see **Lucid.**

Luxury. (F. — L.) M. E. *luxurie.* — O. F. *luxurie* (?), F. *luxure.* — L. *luxuria,* luxury. — L. *luxus,* pomp, excess, luxury. Perhaps allied to **License.**

-ly, a common suffix. (E.) A. S. *líc,* adj. suffix; *-líce,* adv. suffix; from *líc,* like; see **Like.**

Lye, a mixture of ashes and water, for washing. (E.) M. E. *ley.* A. S. *leáh.* + Du. *loog,* G. *lauge,* O. H. G. *louga,* lye. Allied to Icel. *laug,* a bath; also to L. *lauare,* to wash. (Base LU.)

Lymph, a colourless fluid. (L.) L. *lympha,* water, lymph, also a water-nymph. The spelling with *y* is prob. due to a supposed connection with Gk. νύμφη, a nymph (prob. false). It is rather allied to **Limpid.**

Lynch, to punish by mob-law. (E.) From *John Lynch,* a farmer (17th cent.; Haydn). The name is from A.S. *hlinc,* a ridge of land. See **Link** (1).

Lynx; see **Lucid.**

Lyre. (F. — L. — Gk.) F. *lyre.* — L. *lyra.* Gk. λύρα, a lyre, lute. **Der.** *lyr-ic.*

M.

Macádamise, to pave a road with small broken stones. (Gael. *and* Heb.; *with* F. *suffix.*) Named after Mr. John *Macadam,* A. D. 1819. *Macadam* = son of Adam. — Gael. *mac,* son; Heb. *ádám,* a man, from root *ádam,* to be red.

Macaroni, Maccaroni; see **Macerate.**

Macaroon; see **Macerate.**

Macaw, a kind of parrot. (Caribbean.) Said to be the native name in the Antilles (Webster).

Mace (1), a kind of club. (F. — L.) O. F. *mace, mache* (F. *masse*). — L. *matea*,* a beetle, only preserved in dimin. *mateola,* a little beetle. Cf. Skt. *math,* to churn, crush, kill.

Mace (2), a kind of spice. (F. — L. — Gk. — Skt. ?) F. *macis,* mace. It seems to have been confused with O. F. *macer,* which ' is not mace, as many imagine, but a reddish, aromaticall, and astringent rind of a certain Indian root;' Cot. Both prob. from L. *macer,* macir, i.e. the ' rind of a great root,' which beareth the name of the tree itself,' Holland, tr. of Pliny, xii. 8. — Gk. μάκερ; doubtless of Eastern origin. Cf. Skt. *makura,* a bud, a tree (Mimusops elengi), Arabian jasmine.

Macerate, to soften by steeping. (L.) From pp. of L. *macerare,* to steep; frequent. from a base *mac-.* + Russ. *mochite,* to steep; Gk. μάσσειν, to knead; Skt. *mach,* to pound. (√ MAK.)

amass, to heap up. (F. — L. — Gk.) F. *amasser,* to heap up. — F. *à masse,* into a mass. — L. *ad,* to; *massa,* a mass; see **mass** (below).

macaroni, maccaroni. (Ital. — L.) O. Ital. *maccaroni,* ' a kinde of paste meate;' Florio. Prob. from O. Ital. *maccare,* 'to bruise, batter, to pester,' Florio; i.e. to reduce to pulp. — L. *mac-,* base of *macerare,* to macerate. **Der.** *macaronic,* i. e. in a confused or mixed state (applied to a jumble of languages).

macaroon. (F. — Ital. — L.) F. *macaron,* pl. *macarons,* ' macarons, little fritterlike buns, . . also the same as macaroni;' Cot. — Ital. *maccaroni* (above). ¶ Now applied to a kind of biscuit.

mass (1), a lump. (F. — L. — Gk.) F. *masse.* — L. *massa* (hardly a true L. word, but taken from Gk.) — Gk. μᾶζα, a barley cake; allied to μάγμα, any kneaded mass. — Gk. μάσσειν, to knead (above). **Der.** *mass-ive, mass-y;* also *a-mass* (above).

maxillar, maxillary, belonging to the jawbone. (L.) L. *maxillaris,* adj., from *maxilla,* jaw-bone. — L. *macerare,* to chew.

Machine. (F. — L. — Gk.) F. *machine.* — L. *machina.* — Gk. μηχανή, a device, machine; cf. μῆχος, means. (√ MAGH.) Allied to **Make.**

mechanic, pertaining to machines. (F. — L. — Gk.) M. E. *mechanike,* in the sense ' mechanic art.' — O. F. *mechanique,* mechanical. — L. *mechanica.* — Gk. μηχανική, science of machines. — Gk. μηχανή (above).

Mackerel; see **Maculate.**

Mackintosh, a waterproof overcoat. (Gael.) Gael. *Mack-intosh,* the name of the inventor.

Macrocosm, the whole universe. (Gk.) Gk. μακρό-s, long, great ; κόσμος, the world. Cf. *microscosm.*

Maculate, to defile. (L.) From pp. of L. *maculare,* to spot. — L. *macula,* a spot, dimin. of a form *maca*,* not used. Prob. from √ MAK, to pound, bruise ; see **Macerate.** Der. *immaculate,* orig. a pp.

mackerel, a fish. (F. — L.) O. F. *makerel* (F. *maquereau*). Lit. ' stained ' fish ; from the dark blotches on them. — L. *maca*,* a stain, preserved in Span. *maca,* a stain, bruise on fruit, and in L. *macula,* a small stain ; see above.

mail (1), steel network for armour. (F. — L.) O. F. *maille,* mail, also a mesh of a net. — L. *macula,* a spot, speck, hole, mesh of a net ; see **Maculate.**

Mad. (E.) The vowel was formerly long. M. E. *maad, made.* — A.S. *ge-mǽd, ge-maad,* in a gloss ; hence *mád-mŏd,* madness (Grein). + O. Sax. *ge-mēd,* foolish ; O. H. G. *gi-meit,* vain ; Icel. *meiddr,* pp. of *meiða,* to maim, hurt ; Goth. *ga-maids,* maimed. The orig. sense seems to be ' severely injured ; ' the prefix *ge-, gi-, ga-* is unessential. ¶ Not allied to Ital. *matto,* for which see **Mate** (2).

Madam, my lady. (F. — L.) F. *madame,* i. e. *ma dame,* my lady. — L. *mea domina,* my lady ; see **Dame.**

mademoiselle, miss. (F. — L.) F. *ma,* my ; *demoiselle,* damsel ; see **Damsel.**

madonna, my lady. (Ital. — L.) Ital. *na,* my ; *donna,* lady, from L. *domina* ; see **Dame.**

monkey, an ape. (Ital. — L.) Corrupted from O. Ital.· *monicchio,* 'a pugge, a munkie, an ape ; ' Florio. Dimin. of O. Ital. *mona, monna,* 'an ape, a munkie, a mun-kie-face ; also a nickname for women, as we say gammer, goodie ; ' Florio. *Monna* is a familiar corruption of *madonna,* i.e. my lady, mistress ; Scott introduces *Monna Paula* in the Fortunes of Nigel. See above.

Madder, a plant. (E.) M. E. *mader, madir.* A. S. *mæderu, madere.* + Icel. *maðra,* Du. *meed.* Cf. Skt. *madhura,* sweet, tender ; whence fem. *madhurá,* the name of several plants.

Mademoiselle, Madonna ; see **Madame.**

Madrepore, coral. (F. — Ital. — L. *and* Gk.) F. *madrépore.* — Ital. *madrepora.* The lit. sense is ' mother-stone,' a fanciful

name, due to the existence of such terms as *madre-selva,* honeysuckle (lit. mother-wood), *madre-bosco,* woodbine (lit. mother-bush), *madre-perla,* mother of pearl. Here *madre* ·is from L. *matrem,* acc. of *mater,* mother ; see **Mother.** *Pora* is from Gk. πῶρος, a light friable stone,· also a stalactite. ¶ But the word has certainly been *understood* (prob. *misunderstood*) as connected with *pore,* whence numerous scientific terms such as *cateni-pora, tubi-pora, denti-pora, gemmi-pora.* ' Scientific ' etymology is usually clumsy, and frequently wrong. We may conclude that E. *pore* has been substituted for Gk. πῶρος, by confusion.

Madrigal, a pastoral song. (Ital. — L. — Gk.) Ital. *madrigale,* a short song, pastoral ditty ; put for *mandrigale*.* Florio also gives *mardriale, mandriano,* a herdsman, also a madrigal. — Ital. *mandra,* a herd, flock. — L. *mandra,* a stall, stable. — Gk. μάνδρα, a fold. + Skt. *mandurā,* stable ; from *mand,* to sleep. (The suffix *-ig-ale* = L. suffix *-ic-alis.*)

Magazine. (F. — Ital. — Arab.) F. *magazin* (F. *magasin*). — Ital. *magazzino,* a storehouse. — Arab. *makházin,* pl. of *makhzan,* a storehouse. — Arab. *khasn,* a laying up in store.

Maggot, a grub. (W.) M. E. *magot, magat.* — W. *maceiad, macai,* a maggot ; cf. *magiaid,* grubs. Allied to W. *magiad,* breeding, *magad,* a brood ; from *magu,* to breed. Cf. Bret. and Corn. *maga,* to feed.

Magi, priests of the Persians. (L. — Gk. — Pers.) L. *magi,* pl. — Gk. μάγοι, pl. of μάγος, a Magian, one of a Median tribe ; also an enchanter, properly a wise man who interpreted dreams. The orig. sense was prob. great, from Zend *maz,* great, allied to L. *magnus,* Gk. μέγας. Der. *mag-ic,* short for *magic art* ; *mag-ic-i-an.*

Magistrate ; see **Magnitude.**

Magnanimity, Magnate ; see **Magnitude.**

Magnesia ; see **Magnet.**

Magnet, the lodestone. (F. — L. — Gk.) M. E. *magnete.* — O. F. *magnete*,* a variant of O. F. *manete* (13th cent.). — L. *magnetem,* acc. of *magnes,* put for *Magnes lapis* = Magnesian stone, the lodestone. — Gk. Μάγνης (stem Μαγνητ-), also Μαγνήτης, Μαγνήσιος, belonging to Magnesia, in Thessaly ; whence λίθος Μαγνήσιος (or Μαγνήτης), Magnesian stone, lodestone, also a kind of silver. Der. *magnesia,* an old name (in Chaucer,

C. T. 16923) for a mineral brought from Magnesia; now differently applied.

Magnificent, Magnify, Magniloquence; see Magnitude.

Magnitude, greatness. (L.) L. *magnitudo*, size. – L. *magnus*, great. + Gk. μέγας, great; Skt. *mahant*, great; A. S. *micel*. See **Mickle**.

magistrate. (F.–L.) F. *magistrat*, a magistrate, ruler.–L. *magistratus*, (1) a magistracy, (2) a magistrate.–L. *magister*, a master. L. *mag-is-ter* is a double compar. form, from *mag-nus*, great.

magnanimity, greatness of mind. (F.–L.) F. *magnanimité*. – L. acc. *magnanimitatem*.–L. *magnus*, great; *animus*, mind.

magnanimous, high-minded. (L.) L. *magnanimus*.–L. *magnus*, great; *animus*, mind.

magnate, a great man, noble. (F.–L.) F. *magnat*.–L. *magnatem*, acc. of *magnas*, a prince.–L. *magnus*, great. ¶ *Magnate* is due to the use of L. *magnas* in Hungary and Poland.

magnificent. (L.) L. *magnificent-*, stem of *magnificens*, lit. doing great things, hence, grand.–L. *magni-*, for *magnus*, great; *-ficens*, for *faciens*, doing, from *facere*, to do.

magnify. (F.–L.) M. E. *magnifien*.– F. *magnifier*.–L. *magnificare*, lit. to make large.– L. *magni-*, for *magnus*, great; *-ficare*, for *facere*, to do.

magniloquence. (L.) L. *magniloquentia*, elevated language. – L. *magni-*, for *magnus*, great; *loquent-*, stem of pres. pt. of *loqui*, to speak; see **Loquacious**.

main (2), adj., chief, principal. (F.– L.) O. F. *maine*, *magne*, chief.–L. *magnus*, great. ¶ Distinct from *main*, sb., which is of A. S. origin.

majesty. (F.–L.) M. E. *magestee*.– O. F. *majestet* (F. *majesté*).–L. *maiestatem*, acc. of *maiestas*, dignity, honour. Here *māies* = *mag-ias* * = *mag-yans* *, formed from the base of *mag-nus*, great, by help of the Aryan comparative suffix *-yans*.

major, a title of rank. (L.) L. *maior*, greater; comparative of *magnus*, great. **Der.** *major-domo*, imitated from Span. *mayor-domo*, a house-steward.

master. (F.–L.) M. E. *maister*. – O. F. *maistre*. – L. *magistrum*, acc. of *magister*, a master; see **magistrate** (above). **Der.** *master-y*, O. F. *maistrie*.

maxim, a proverb. (F. – L.) F.

maxime.– L. *maxima*, put for *maxima sententiarum*, an opinion of the greatest importance, chief of opinions, hence a maxim. Orig. fem. of *maximus*, greatest, superlative of *magnus*, great.

maximum. (L.) Neut. of *maximus*, greatest (above).

mayor. (F.–L.) M. E. *maire*. – F. *maire*.– L. *maiorem* (shortened to *mai'rem*), acc. of *major*, greater; see **major** (above). ¶ *Mayor* is the *Spanish* spelling, introduced in the middle of the 16th century.

merino, a variety of sheep. (Span.– L.) Span. *merino*, roving from pasture to pasture.–Span. *merino*, an inspector of sheep walks.–Low L. *majorinus*, a majordomo, steward of a household; cf. Low L. *majoralis*, a head-shepherd. From L. *maior*, greater; see **major** (above).

miss (2), a young woman. (F.–L.) A contraction of *mistress*; Evelyn's Diary, Jan. 9, 1662. See below.

mister, mr., a title of address. (F.– L.) A corruption of *master*, due to the influence of *mistress*, which is an older word; see below.

mistress, a lady of a household. (F,– L.) O. F. *maistresse*, 'a mistress, dame;' Cot. (F. *maîtresse*.) Fem. of O. F. *maistre*, a master; see **master** (above).

Magnolia. (F.) A genus of plants named after Pierre *Magnol*, of Montpellier, in France; died A. D. 1715.

Magpie, a bird. (F.–L.–Gk.; *and* F. –L.) Also called *magot-pie*, *maggoty-pie*. *Mag* is short for *Magot* = F. *Margot*, a familiar form of F. *Marguerite*, also used to denote a magpie. This is from L. *Margarita*, Gk. μαργαρίτης, a pearl; cf. Pers. *murwárid*, a pearl. *Pie* = F. *pie*, from L. *pica*, a magpie; see **Pie** (1).

Mahogany, a tree. (W. Indian.) The native S. American name (Webster).

Mahometan; see **Mohammedan**.

Maid, Maiden; see **May** (1).

Mail (1), steel network; see **Maculate**.

Mail (2), a letter-bag. (F.–O. H. G.) M. E. *male*.–O. F. *male* (F. *malle*), a bag, wallet. – O. H. G. *malaha*, a leathern wallet.+Gael. and Irish *mala*, a bag; Gk. μολγός, hide, skin.

Maim, a bruise, hurt. (F.–C.?) Also spelt *mahim* in Law-books (Blount). M. E. *maim*. – O. F. *mehaing*, 'a maime, or abatement of strength by hurts received;' Cot. Cf. Ital. *magagna*, a defect, blemish. Orig. uncertain; perhaps from Bret. *machañ*, mutilation, *machaña*, to mutilate (unless this be borrowed from F.).

Main (1), strength; see **May** (1).

Main (2), chief, principal; see **Magnitude.** .

Maintain; see **Manual.**

Maize, Indian corn. (Span. – W. Indian.) Span. *maiz.* – W. Indian *mahiz, mahis*, in the language of the isle of Hayti.

Majesty, Major; see **Magnitude.**

Make. (E.) M. E. *maken.* A. S. *macian*, pt. t. *macode*, to make.+G. *niachen.* (From base MAK, allied to MAG.) Allied to *machine*; and to **May** (1).

match (1), an equal, a contest, marriage. (E.) M. E. *macche, mache*, orig. a comrade. – A. S. *mæcca*, commonly *gemæcca*, a comrade, companion, spouse; from the more · original form *maca*, a companion. See further below.

mate (1), a companion, comrade, equal. (E.) M. E. *mate*, a corruption of the older form *make*, a companion, which is the commoner form. (So also *bat*, a mammal, from M. E. *bak*; and esp. note O. Fries. *matia* (for *makia* *), to make, which is a related word.) – A. S. *maca*, a companion; also *gemaca.* + Icel. *maki*, Swed. *make*, Dan. *mage*, O. Sax. *gimako*, a mate, comrade; but O. Du. *maet*, Du. *maat*, a mate, with *t* as in English, doubtless an O. Friesic form. β. All closely related to the adj. seen in Icel. *makr*, suitable, M. H. G. *gemach*, suitable; and further to A. S. *macian*, to make, because a thing is suitable by being *made* so. ¶ *Mate*, as used by sailors, is prob. Dutch.

Mal-, *prefix*, bad. (F. – L.) F. *mal.* – L. *malus*, bad; see **Malice**.

Malachite; see **Mallow.**

Malady, Malapert, Malaria; see **Malice.**

Male; see **Masculine.**

Malediction, Malefactor, Malevolent; see **Malice.**

Malice, ill will. (F. – L.) M. E. *malice.* F. *malice.* – L. *malitia*, badness. – L. *malus*, bad.º Allied to Gk. μέλας, black; Skt. *mala*, dirty, *malina*, dirty, sinful, bad, Irish *maile*, evil. (√MAR.)

malady. (F. – L.) F. *maladie.* – F. *malade*, sick; oldest spelling *malabde.* Cf. Prov. *malaptes, malaudes*, sick. – L. *male habitus*, out of condition (hence sick, ill); cf. *male habens*, sick, Matt. iv. 24 (Vulgate). – L. *male*, badly, from *malus*, bad; *habitus*, pp. of *habere*, to have; see **Habit.** ¶ Not

from *male aptus* (Diez); this would mean 'foolish.'

malapert, saucy. (F. – L.) O. F. *mal apert.* – O. F. *mal*, ill; *apert*, open, also expert, ready, skilful. The sense is 'badly expert,' i. e. mischievous. – L. *male*, badly; *apertus*, pp. of *aperire*, to open; see **Aperient.**

malaria, noisome exhalation. (Ital. – L.) Ital. *mal'aria*, for *mala aria*, bad air. – L. *mala*, fem. of *malus*, bad; and Ital. *aria*, air; see **Debonair.**

malediction, a curse. (F. – L.) ΄F. *malediction.* – L. acc. *maledictionem*, a curse. – L. *maledictus*, pp. of *maledicere*, to speak evil of. – L. *male*, adv., evilly; *dicere*, to speak. So also *male-factor*, an ill-doer, from *factor*, a doer; from *facere*, to do. So also *malevolent*, lit. wishing ill; from *uolent-*, stem of *uolens*, pres. pt. of *uelle*, to will, to wish.

malign, unfavourable. (F. – L.) O. F. *maling*, fem. *maligne* (F. *malin*). – L. *malignus*, ill-disposed, put for *mali-genus* *, ill-born (like *benignus* for *beni-genus* *). L. *mali-*, for *malus*, bad; *gen-*, base of *gignere*, to produce; see **Genus.**

malinger, to feign sickness. (F. – L.) Coined from F. *malingre*, adj., diseased, formerly ugly, loathsome (Cot.). – F. *mal*, badly; O. F. *haingre, heingre*, thin, emaciated. – L. *male*, adv., badly; *ægrum*, acc. of *æger*, sick, ill (whence O. F. *haingre* with added *h* and *n*).

malison, a curse. (F. – L.) O. F. *malison*, older form of *malediction*; see malediction above. (So also *benison* for *benediction*.)

maltreat. (F. – L.) F. *maltraiter*, to treat ill. – L. *male*, ill; *tractare*, to handle, treat; see **Treat.**

malversation. (F. – L.) F. *malversation*, 'misdemeanor;' Cot. (Hence fraudulent behaviour.) – F. *malverser*, to behave ill. – L. *male*, ill; *uersari*, to be engaged in, from *uersare*, frequent. form of *uertere*, to turn; see **Verse.**

maugre, in spite of. (F. – L.) The proper sense is 'ill will,' as in P. Plowman, B. vi. 242. – O. F. *malgre, maugre, maulgre*, lit. ill will; but also with sense 'in spite of.' – O. F. *mal*, ill; *gre, gret*, a pleasant thing. – L. *malus*, bad; *gratum*, neut. of *gratus*, pleasing.

Malign, Malinger, Malison; see **Malice.**

Mall (1), a large wooden hammer. (F. –

L.) M. E. *malle*. — O. F. (and F.) *mail*, 'a mall;' Cot. — L. *malleum*, acc. of *malleus*, a hammer. (√MAR.)

mall (2), the name of a public walk. (F. — Ital. — G. *and* L.) In *Pall Mall*, and the *Mall* in St. James's Park. Named from O. F. *pale-maille*, because the game so called was played there; this game of *pall-mall* was like the modern *croquet*, which is imitated from it. — O. Ital. *palamaglio*, 'a stick with a mallet at one end,' for playing the game of pall-mall; Florio. Also spelt *pallamaglio*; lit. 'mallet-ball.' — Ital. *palla*, a ball; *maglio*, a mall. A hybrid word. — O. H. G. *pallâ*, M. H. G. *balle*, G. *ball*, a ball; L. *malleum*, acc. of *malleus*, a hammer. See **Ball**.

malleable. (F. — L.) O. F. *malleable*, 'malleable, hammerable, pliant to the hammer;' Cot. From obs. L. *malleare* *, to hammer, of which the pp. *malleatus* occurs. — L. *malleus*, a hammer.

mallet, a small mall. (F. — L.) . M. E. *maillet*. — F. *maillet*, 'a mallet;' Cot. Dimin. of F. *mail*; see **Mall** (1) above.

maul, to beat grievously. (F. — L.) M. E. *mallen*, to strike with a mall, or mace; from M. E. *malle*, sb. a mall, mace; see **Mall** (1) above.

Mallard; see **Masculine**.

Malleable, Mallet; see **Mall**.

Mallow, a plant. (L.) M. E. *malwe*. — A. S. *malwe*; borrowed from L. *malua*, a mallow. + Gk. μαλάχη (= *mal-ua-ka* *), a mallow; named from its emollient properties; cf. Gk. μαλάσσειν, to make soft, μαλακός, soft, mild. (√MAR.)

malachite, a green stone. (Gk.) Named from its colour, which resembles that of mallow-leaves. Formed with suffix *-ites* (Gk. -ιτης) from μαλάχ-η, a mallow.

mauve, mallow colour. (F. — L.) F. *mauve*, a mallow. — L. *malua*, a mallow.

Malmsey, a strong sweet wine. (F. — Gk.) A corruption of M. E. *malvesie*, malmsey. — O. F. *malvoisie*, 'malmesie;' Cot. From *Malvasia*, now called *Napoli di Malvasia*, a town on the E. coast of Lacedæmonia in Greece.

Malt; see **Melt**.

Maltreat, Malversation; see **Malice**.

Mamaluke, Mameluke, an Egyptian light horse-soldier. (F. — Arab.) F. *Mamaluc*; Cot. — Arab. *mamlûk*, a purchased slave or captive, lit. 'possessed.' — Arab. root *malaka*, he possessed.

Mamma. (E.) Better *niama*; put for *ma ma*, a mere repetition of *ma*, an infantine syllable. Many other languages have something like it; cf. F. *maman*, Span. Du. and G. *mama*, Ital. and L. *mamma*, a child's word for mother.

Mammalia, the class of animals that suckle their young. (L.) From L. *mammalis* (neut. pl. *mammalia*), belonging to the breasts. — L. *mamma*, the breast.

mammillary, pertaining to the breasts. (L.) From L. *mammillaris*, adj., formed from L. *mamma*, the breast.

Mammon. (L. — Gk. — Syriac.) L. *mammona*. — Gk. μαμωνᾶς, Matt. vi. 24. — Syr. *mamônâ*, which occurs in Chaldee Targums, and in the Syriac version of St. Matthew, and means 'riches.' Cf. Heb. *matmôn*, a hidden treasure, from *tâman*, to hide.

Mammoth. (Russ. — Tatar.) Russ. *mumunt'*, a mammoth, species of elephant. — Siberian *mammont*. From Tatar *mamma*, the earth; because the Siberian peasants thought the animal burrowed in the earth like the mole, as they could not otherwise account for the finding of the remains of these animals.

Man. (E.) M. E. *man*. A. S. *mann*. + Du. *man*, Icel. *man*, *maðr*, Swed. *man*, Dan. *mand*, Goth. *manna*, G. *mann*; L. *mâs* (for *mans*), a male, Skt. *manu*, a man. (√MAN.)

manikin, manakin, a dwarf, small man. (Du.) O. Du. *manneken* (Hexham); double dimin. of Du..*man*, a man.

mankind, the race of men. (E.) A. S. *mancynn*, mankind. — A. S. *man*, man, *cynn*, kind, race; see **Kin**.

Manacle, Manage; see **Manual**.

Manatee, a sea-cow. (Span. — W. Indian.) Span. *manati*, a sea-cow. From the name of the animal in the language of Hayti.

Mandarin, a Chinese governor of a province. (Port. — Malay. — Skt.) Not a Chinese, but Malay word (through the Portuguese). — Port. *mandarim*, a mandarin. — Malay *mantri*, a counsellor, minister of state. — Skt. *mantrin*, a counsellor; *mahâmantrin*, the prime minister. — Skt. *mantra*, advice, counsel. — Skt. *man*, to think. (√MAN.) ¶ Or directly from Skt.

Mandate, a command. (F. — L.) O. F. *mandat*. — L. *mandatum*, a charge. — L. *mandatus*, pp. of *mandare*, to enjoin; lit. to put into one's hand. — L. *man-us*, hand; *dare*, to give; see **Manual** and **Date**.

command. (F. — L.) O.F. *commander*, *comander*. — L. *commendare*, to entrust to;

in late L., to command. **–** L. *com-* (for *cum*), together; *mandare*, to put into the hands of.

commend. (L.) L. *commendare*, to entrust or commit to (above).

commodore, the commander of a squadron. (Span. **–** L.) Short for Span. *comendador*, lit. a commander. **–** Span. *comendar*, to charge, command. **–** L. *commendare* (above).

countermand, to revoke an order. (F. **–** L.) F. *contremander*, to recall a command. **–** F. *contre* (= L. *contra*), against; *mander* (= L. *mandare*), to command.

demand. (F. **–** L.) F. *demander*, to demand, require. **–** L. *de-mandare*, to entrust; in late L., to demand.

maundy Thursday, the day before Good Friday. (F. **–** L.; *and* E.) *Maundy* is M. E. *maundee*, a command, used with esp. reference to the text '*Mandatum nouum*,' John, xiii. 34. The 'new commandment' is 'that ye love one another;' but in old times it was, singularly enough, applied to the particular form of devotion to others exemplified by Christ, when washing his disciples' feet (on the first *Maundy Thursday*). See my note to P. Plowman, B. xvi. 140. This M. E. *maundee* = O. F. *mandé*, that which is commanded; from L. *mandatum*, a mandate, command. ¶ Spelman's guess, that *maundy* is from *maund*, a basket, is as false as it is readily believed.

recommend, to commend to another. (F. **–** L.) From **Re-** and **Commend**; imitated from F. *recommander*, 'to recommend;' Cot.

remand, to send back. (F. **–** L.) F. *remander*. **–** L. *re-mandare*, to send back word.

Mandible, a jaw. (L.) L. *mandibula*, jaw. **–** L. *mandere*, to chew.

mange, scab or itch in dogs. (F. **–** L.) Made out of adj. *mangy*, an older word. **–** F. *mangé*, eaten, fed on; pp. of *manger*, to eat. **–** L. *manducare*, to eat. **–** L. *manducus*, a glutton. **–** L. *mandere*, to chew.

manger, a feeding-trough. (F. **–** L.) F. *mangeoire*. **–** F. *manger*, to eat (above).

Mandrake, a narcotic plant. (L. **–** Gk.) Short for *mandragora*, Othello, iii. 3. Cf. F. *mandragore*, Ital. and Span. *mandragora*. **–** L. *mandragoras*. **–** Gk. μανδραγόρας, the mandrake.

Mandrel, the revolving shank in which turners fix their work in a lathe. (F. **–** Gk.?) From F. *mandrin*, a punch, a mandrel.

Prob. from Gk. μάνδρα, an enclosed space, sheepfold, also used to mean 'the bed in which the stone of a ring is set,' much like E. *mandrel*. See **Madrigal**.

Mane. (E.) A. S. *manu*; Icel. *man-ar*, gen. of *mön*, a mane; Swed. and Dan. *man.*╋ Du. *maan*, O. Du. *mane*, G. *mähne*, O. H. G. *mana*. Cf. W. *myngen*, mane, from *mwn*, neck; Irish *muince*, collar, from *muin*, neck; Skt. *manyá*, the tendon forming the nape of the neck; L. *monile*, neck-lace. Orig. sense 'hair on the neck.'

Manege, the same as **Manage**; s.v. **Manual**.

Manganese, a metal. (F. **–** Ital. **–** Gk.?) An old term, newly applied. '*Manganese*, so called from its likeness in colour and weight to the *magnes* or loadstone, is the most universal material used in making glass;' Blount, ed. 1674. **=** O. F. *manganese*. **–** Ital. *manganese*, 'a stuffe or stone to make glasses of; also, a kind of mineral stone;' Florio. Of uncertain origin; perhaps allied to *magnesia*; see **Magnet**.

Mange, Manger; see **Mandible**.

Mangle (1), to mutilate. (Perhaps F. **–** C.) In Sir T. More, Works, p. 538. We find Anglo-F. *mahangler*, to maim; in Langtoft's Chron. i. 254. Frequent. form of O. F. *mahaigner*, to maim. **–** O. F. *mehaing*, a maim, hurt. See **Maim**.

Mangle (2), a roller for smoothing linen; to smooth linen. (Du. **–** Low L. **–** Gk.) Borrowed from Du. *mangelen*, to mangle, roll with a rolling-pin; *mangel-stok*, a rolling-pin, cylinder for smoothing linen. The corresponding Ital. word is *mangano*, 'a kind of presse to presse buckrom;' Florio. Both Du. and Ital. words are from Low L. *manganum, mangona*, a military instrument for throwing stones, worked with an axis and winch. Indeed, the Ital. *mangano* also means a mangonel. **–** Gk. μάγγανον, a machine for defending forts, also the axis of a pulley. Allied to **Machine**.

mangonel, a war-engine. (F. **–** Low L. **–** Gk.) O. F. *mangonel* (later *mangonneau*), a mangonel. **–** Low L. *mangonellus*, dimin. of *mangona* (above).

Mango, a fruit. (Malay.) Malay *mañggá*, the mango-fruit.

Mangonel; see **Mangle** (2).

Mania, frenzy. (L. **–** Gk.) L. *mania*. **–** Gk. μανία, frenzy, orig. mental excitement; cf. μένος, mind. (√ MAN.) Der. *mania-c*, F. *maniaque*.

Manifest; see Manual.
Manifold; see Many.
Manikin; see Man.
Maniple, Manipulate; see Manual.
Mankind; see Man.
Manna. (L. — Gk. — Heb.) L. *manna.*
— Gk. μάννα. — Heb. *mán*, manna. β.
Hardly from Heb. *mán hu*, what is this?
Exod. xvi. 15; but from *mán*, (it is) a
gift; cf. Arab. *mann*, favour, also manna.
Manner, Manœuvre; see Manual.
Manor, Manse; see Mansion.
Mansion. (F. — L.) O. F. *mansion*, a
dwelling-place. — L. *mansionem*, acc. of
mansio, an abiding, abode. — L. *mansus*,
pp. of *manere*, to remain, dwell. + Gk.
μένειν, to stay, remain. (√ MAN.)

    manor, (formerly) a residence for a
nobleman. (F. — L.) O. F. *manoir*, a mansion. — O. F. *manoir, maneir*, to dwell. —
L. *manere* (above).

    manse, a clergyman's house, in Scot-
land. (L.) Low L. *mansa*, a farm, dwelling.
— L. *mansus*, pp. of *manere* (above).

    mastiff. (F. — Low L. — L.) O. F.
mastif*, not found, but prob. a variant
of O. F. *mastin* (F. *mâtin*), 'a mastive;'
Cot. The Low L. form would be *mas-
tinus**, doubtless short for *masnatinus**,
i. e. house-dog; from Low L. *masnata*, a
household; see **menagerie** (below).

    menagerie, a place for keeping wild
animals. (F. — L.) F. *ménagerie*, orig. a
place for keeping *household* animals (Brachet). — F. *ménager*, to keep house. — F.
ménage, O. F. *mesnage*, a household. — O. F.
mesnee, meisnee, maisnee, a family; the
same word as Low L. *maisnada, maisnada*,
musnata, Ital. *masnada*, a family (answering to a Lat. type *mansionata**). — L. *man-
sion-*, stem of *mansio*, an abiding, abode;
see **Mansion** (above).

    menial, one of a household, servile.
(F. — L.) Properly an adj.; M. E. *meyneal*,
as 'her *meyneal* chirche'=the church of
their household, Wyclif, Rom. xvi. 5. —
O. F. *mesnee, meisnee*, a household (as
above), whence M. E. *meinee, mainee*, a
household, troop, retinue, once a common
word; with suffix *-al.*

    messuage, a dwelling - house with
offices. (F. — L.) M. E. *mesuage*. — O. F.
mesuage, a manor-house; Low L. *messua-
gium, mansagium*. — Low L. *masa, massa*,
mansa, a farm, dwelling; see **manse**
(above). Thus *messu-age* stands for *mans-
age.*

permanent. (F. — L.) F. *permanent.*
— L. *permanent-*, stem of pres. pt. of *per-
manere*, to endure, lit. abide through.
    remain. (F. — L.) From the F. impers.
verb *il remaint*, it remains. [The infin.
remaindre is preserved in E. *remainder.*]
— L. *remanet*, it remains; *remanere*, to remain. — L. *re-*, back; *manere*, to remain.
    remnant. (F. — L.) M. E. *remanaunt.*
O. F. *remanent*, a residue. — L. *remanent-*,
stem of pres. pt. of *remanere*, to remain.
Mantel; see below.
Mantle, a cloak, covering. (F. — L.)
M. E. *mantel.* — O. F. *mantel*, later *manteau*,
'a cloke, also the mantle-tree of a chimney;' Cot. — L. *mantellum*, a napkin, also
a covering; cf. L. *mantile*, a towel. We
also find Low L. *mantum*, a short cloak,
whence Ital. and Span. *manto*, F. *mante*,
a mantle. **Der.** *mantle*, vb., to form a
covering upon, to gather a scum on a surface.

    mantel, a shelf over a fire-place. (F. —
L.) The same word as the above; in old
fire-places, it projects like a hood, to catch
the smoke. **Der.** *mantel-shelf, -piece.*

    Mantua, a lady's gown. (Ital.) '*Man-
toe or Mantua gown*, a loose upper garment,' &c.; Phillips (1706). *Manto* is
from Ital. *manto*, a mantle (see **Mantle**);
but *Mantua gown* must refer to *Mantua* in
Italy, though this connection may have
arisen from mere confusion. **Der.** *mantua-
maker.*

Manual, done by the hand. (F. — L.)
Formerly *manuel.* — L. *manualis*, adj, from
manus, the hand. (√ MA.)

    amanuensis, one who writes to dic-
tation. (L.) L. *amanuensis.* — L. *a manu*,
by hand; with suffix *-ensis.*

    maintain, to keep in a fixed state, sup-
port. (F. — L.) M. E. *maintenen.* — F.
maintenir. — L. *manu tenere*, to hold in
the hand; or more likely (in late L.) to
hold by the hand, to abet. — L. *manu*,
abl. of *manus*, hand; *tenere*, to hold; see
Tenable.

    manacle, a handcuff. (F. — L.) M. E.
manacle, also *manycle.* — F. *manicle.* — L.
manicula, dimin. of *manica*, a long sleeve,
gauntlet, handcuff. — L. *manus.*

    manage, government of a horse, con-
trol, administration. (F. — Ital. — L.) Orig.
a sb., but now superseded by *management.*
See Rich. II. iii. 3. 179. — O. F. *manege*,
'the manage, or managing of a horse;' Cot.
— Ital. *maneggio*, 'a managing, a hand-

ling;' Florio. — Ital. *mano*, the hand. — L. *manus*. Der. *manage*, verb.

manege, control of horses. (F. — Ital. — L.) The same word as the above.

manifest, apparent. (F. — L.) F. *manifeste*. — L. *manifestus*, evident. The lit. sense is 'struck by the hand,' hence palpable. — L. *mani-*, for *manus*, hand; *-festus* (= *fend-tus**), pp. of the obsolete verb *fendere*, to strike, occurring in *de-fendere*, *of-fendere*; cf. *infestus*, *infensus*, hostile. (√ DHAN.)

manifesto, a written declaration. (Ital. — L.) Ital. *manifesto*, sb. — Ital. *manifesto*, adj., manifest. — L. *manifestus* (above).

maniple, a handful, small band of men, priest's scarf. (L.) L. *manipulus*, a handful, a wisp of straw used as an ensign, a band of men round such an ensign. — L. *mani-*, for *manus*, hand; *-pulus*, lit. filling, from √ PAR, to fill.

manipulate, to handle. (L.) A coined word, and ill coined. Cf. L. *manipulatim*, adv., by troops; but it was rather made directly out of the sb. *manipulus* (above).

manner, way. (F. — L.) M. E. *manere*. — O. F. *maniere*, manner, habit. — O. F. *manier*, adj., habitual; allied to *manier*, verb, to handle, wield. — F. *main*, the hand. — L. *manus*.

manœuvre. (F. — L.) F. *manœuvre*, properly, handiwork. — Low L. *manuopera*, also *manopera*, a working with the hand. — L. *manu*, abl. of *manus*, hand; *operari*, to work, from *opera*, work; see **Operate**.

manufacture. (F. — L.) F. *manufacture*, also *manifacture*, lit. a making by the hand. — L. *manu*, abl. of *manus*, hand; *factura*, a making, from *facere*, to make.

manumit, to release a slave. (L.) L. *manumittere* (pp. *manumissus*), to release, lit. to send away from one's hand. — L. *manu*, abl. of *manus*, hand; *mittere*, to send; see **Mission**. Der. *manumission*.

manure. (F. — L.) Formerly simply 'to till,' or to work with the hand; Othello, i. 3. 328. A contracted form of *manœuvre*; which see above.

manuscript, written by the hand. (L.) Properly an adj., but also as a sb. — Low L. *manuscriptum*, a thing written by the hand. — L. *manu*, abl. of *manus*, hand; *scriptum*, neut. of pp. of *scribere*, to write; see **Scribe**.

Manufacture, Manumit, Manure, Manuscript; see **Manual**.

Many. (E.) M. E. *many*, *moni*. A. S. *manig*, *mænig*, *monig*, many. + Du. *menig*; Dan. *mange*, Swed. *månge*, Icel. *margr* (with change of *n* to *r*), Goth. *manags*, G. *manch*, O. H. G. *manac*. (Teut. base MANAGA.) Allied to Irish *minic*, Gael. *minig*, W. *mynych*, frequent, Russ. *mnogie*, pl. many; and prob. to Skt. *mańkshu*, much, *maksha*, a multitude. Der. *manifold*.

Map. (F. — L.) The oldest maps represented the world, and were called *mappemounde*. This is a F. form of *mappa mundi*, map of the world. L. *mappa* meant a napkin, hence a painted cloth.

apron. (F. — L.) Formerly *napron*. — O. F. *naperon*, a large cloth; augmentative form of O. F. *nape*, a cloth (F. *nappe*). — Low L. *napa*, corruption of L. *mappa*, a napkin, cloth.

napery, linen for the table. (F. — L.) O. F. *naperie*. — Low L. *naparia*, the office in a household for keeping table-linen. — Low L. *napa*, a cloth (above).

napkin, a small cloth. (F. — L.; with E. suffix.) M. E. *napekin*, also *napet*, both dimin. forms of O. F. *nape*, a cloth (above).

Maple, a tree. (E.) M. E. *maple*, *mapul*. A. S. *mæpel*, *mapul*; whence *mapulder*, a maple-tree (where *der* is for *trebw*, tree).

Mar, to injure. (E.) M. E. *merren*. A. S. *merran*, in comp. *åmerran*, *åmyrran*, to dissipate, waste, lose, hinder; also *mirran*, to impede; cf. *gemearr*, an impediment. + O. Du. *merren*, Du. *marren*, to retard; O. H. G. *marrjan*, to hinder, vex. (√ MAR.)

marline, a small cord used for binding ropes. (Du.) Du. *marlijn*, also *marling*, a marline. — Du. *marren*, to bind, tie; and *lijn* (*ling*), from F. *ligne*, a line. See *moor* (2) below; and **Line**. Der. *marline-spike*.

moor (2), to fasten up a ship. (Du.) Du. *marren* (O. Du. *maren*), to tie, bind, moor a ship; also to retard. Cognate with E. *mar* (above).

Maranatha, our Lord cometh. (Syriac.) Syriac *måran athå*, our Lord cometh.

Maraud, to wander in quest of plunder. (F. — O. H. G.?) F. *marauder*, 'to play the rogue, beg;' Cot. — F. *maraud*, a rogue, vagabond. Etym. disputed. Perhaps from O. F. *mar-ir* (F. *marrir*), of which one sense was to stray, wander, lose one's way.

Cf. Prov. *marrir*, to lose one's way. The F. *marrir* is from O. H. G. *marrjan*, to hinder, cognate with E. **Mar**. The suffix *-aud* = Low L. *-aldus* = O. H. G. *-wald*, a common suffix.

Maravedi, a very small coin. (Span. = Arab.) Span. *maravedi*, the smallest Spanish coin; so called because first struck during the dynasty of the *Almoravides* at Cordova, A.D. 1094-1144. Cf. Port. *maravedim*, *marabitino*, a maravedi. = Arab. *Murábitín*, the name of the above-mentioned dynasty.

Marble. (F. = L.) M. E. *marbel*; also *marbre*. = O. F. *marbre*. = L. *marmorem*, acc. of *marmor*, marble, considered as a masc. sb.; but it is commonly neuter. + Gk. μάρμαρος, a glistening white 'stone, from μαρμαίρειν, to sparkle; cf. μαῖρα, dog-star, lit. 'sparkler.' (√MAR.) See *marmoset*.

Marcescent, withering. (L.) L. *marcescent-*, stem of pres. pt. of *marcescere*, inceptive form of *marcere*, to wither, lit. to grow soft. (√MAR.)

March (1), a border; see **Mark** (1).

March (2), to walk with regular steps. (F. = L.? or G.?) F. *marcher*, to march. Of disputed origin; perhaps from a Low L. *marcare**, to beat (hence to tramp), from *marcus*, a hammer (Scheler). β. Or from F. *marche*, a frontier, as in the O. F. phrase *aller de marche en marche*, to go from land to land, to make expeditions (Diez). See **Mark** (1).

March (3), a month; see **Martial**.

Marchioness; see **Mark** (1).

Mare. (E.) M. E. *mere*. A. S. *mere*, fem. form of *mearh*, a horse. + Icel. *merr*, fem. of *marr*, a steed; Dan. *mär*, Swed. *märr*, Du. *merrie*; G. *mähre*, O. H. G. *merihá*, fem. of O. H. G. *marah*, a battle-horse. Cognate with (or borrowed from) Irish and Gael. *marc*, W. and Corn. *march*, a horse, a stallion.

marshal, master of the horse. (F. = O. H. G.) Lit. 'horse-servant,' a groom; it rose to be a title of honour. = O. F. *mareschal* (F. *maréchal*), 'a marshall, a farrier,' Cot. = O. H. G. *marascalh*, lit. horse-servant, a groom. = O. H. G. *marah*, a horse; *scalh*, a servant; cf. Goth. *skalks*, a servant.

Margin. (L.) L. *margin-*, stem of *margo*, 'a border, brink; cognate with **Mark** (1).

Margrave; see **Mark** (1).

Marigold, a plant. (Heb. *and* E.) Compounded of *Mary* (from the Virgin Mary) and *gold* (from its colour).

Marine. (F. = L.) F. *marin*. = L. *marinus*, belonging to the sea. = L. *mare*, sea; cognate with **Mere** (1). Der. *marin-er*.

maritime, pertaining to the sea. (F. = L.) F. *maritime*. = L. *maritimus*, formed with suffix *-timus* from *mari-*, crude form of *mare*, sea.

Marish, a marsh; see **Mere** (1).

Marital; see **Masculine**.

Maritime; see **Marine**.

Marjoram, a plant. (F. = L. = Gk.) M. E. *majoran* (without *r*). = F. *marjolaine*, of which an older form must have been *marjoraine**. Cf. Ital. *majorana*, Span. *mayorana*, Port. *maiorana*, marjoram, Low L. *majoraca*; variously corrupted from L. *amaracus*. = Gk. ἀμάρακος, marjoram.

Mark (1), a stroke, outline. (E.) M. E. *merke*. A. S. *mearc*, mark, bound, border. + Du. *merk*, Icel. *mark*, Swed. *märke*, Dan. *mærke*, M. H. G. *marc*, a mark; M. H. G. *marke*, O. H. G. *marcha*, a march, boundary; Goth. *marka*, confine, coast; L. *margo*, border. (√MARG.)

demarcation. (F. = L. *and* M. H. G.) F. *démarcation*. = L. *de*, down; and *marquer*, to mark, a word of German origin; see **mark** (2) below.

march (1), a border, frontier. (E.) M. E. *marche*. = A. S. *mearc*, a mark, boundary.

marchioness. (Low L. = G.) The proper F. form is *marquise*; the E. *marchioness* answers to Low L. *marchionissa*, formed with fem. suffix *-issa* (Gk. -ισσα) from Low L. *marchionem*, acc. of *marchio*, a prefect of the marches. = Low L. *marcha*, a boundary. = O. H. G. *marcha*, a boundary (above).

margrave, a lord of the marches. (Du.) Du. *markgraaf*, a margrave. = Du. *mark*, a boundary, march; *graaf*, a count. So also G. *markgraf*. (That the word is Du. appears from the fem. form *margravine*, which answers to Du. *markgravin*, not G. *markgräfinn*.)

mark (2), a coin. (E.) M. E. *marc*, A. S. *marc*, a mark, coin; a particular use of A. S. *mearc*, a mark, stamp, &c. + G. *mark*, a weight of silver, a coin; Icel. *mörk*.

marque, letters of. (F. = G.) A *letter of marque* was a permission by a ruler to make reprisals on the country of another ruler; it had particular reference to the catching of a foreigner within the *march* or limit of one's own country. — O. F. *marque*, a boundary. — M. H. G. *marke*, a boundary; see **Mark** (1) above.

marquee, a large tent. (F. — G.) Put for *marquees*; the *s* being dropped because it was thought to be a plural form. An E. spelling of F. *marquise*, a large tent; orig. a tent for a marchioness or lady of rank. — F. *marquise*, a marchioness, fem. of *marquis*, a marquis; see **marquis** below.

marquess. (Span. — Low L. — G.) Span. *marques*, a marquis; see above.

marquetry, inlaid work. (F. — M. H. G.) F. *marqueterie*, inlaid work. — F. *marqueter*, to inlay, diversify, orig. to mark slightly with spots; iterative form of *marquer*, to mark. — F. *marque*, a mark. — M. H. G. *mark*, G. *marke*, a mark.

marquis. (F. — Low L. — G.) M. E. *markis*. — O. F. *markis*, later *marquis*, 'a marquesse, governour of a frontire town;' Cot. — Low L. *marchensis*, a prefect of the marches. — O. H. G. *marcha*, a march or boundary.

remark, to take notice of. (F. — L. *and* Teut.) F. *remarquer*, to mark, note, heed. — L. *re-*, again; *marquer*, to mark, from *marque*, sb. a mark; see **Mark** (above).

Mark (2), a coin; see **Mark** (1).

Market; see **Merit**.

Marl, a rich earth. (F. — L.) O. F. *marle* (F. *marne*). — Low L. *margila*, dimin. of Low L. *marga*, marl (Pliny).

Marline; see **Mar**.

Marmalade; see **Mellifluous**.

Marmoset, a small American monkey. (F. — L.) Much older than the discovery of America; M. E. *marmosette*, a kind of ape (Maundeville, p. 210). — O. F. *marmoset*, F. *marmouset*, 'the cock of a cistern or fountain, any antick image from whose teats water trilleth, any puppet or antick;' Cot. Thus it meant a grotesque creature, orig. a grotesque ornament on a fountain. Formed, by a Parisian change of *r* to *s*, as in *chaise* for *chaire*, (a chair), from Low L. *marmoretum*, a thing made in marble, applied to fountains. [Thus the *rue des marmousets* in Paris was called in Low Latin *vicus marmoretorum*; Littré.] — L. *marmor*, marble; see **Marble**. ¶ This seems to be quite correct; at the same time, the transference in sense from 'drinking-fountain' to 'ape' was certainly helped on by confusion

with F. *marmot*, 'a marmoset, or little monkey;' which is, again, quite a different word from E. *marmot* (see below).

Marmot, a mountain-rat. (Ital. — L.) Ital. *marmotto*, a marmot. From the Romansch (Grison) name *murmont*; O. H. G. *murmunto*, *muremunto*, a marmot. — L. *mur-*, stem of *mus*, mouse; and *mont-*, stem of *mons*, mountain. Thus the sense is 'mountain-mouse.' (See Diez.)

Maroon (1), brownish crimson. (F. — Ital.) F. *marron*, a chestnut (hence, chestnut-colour. — Ital. *marrone*, a chestnut (of unknown origin).

Maroon (2), to put ashore on a desolate island. (F. — Span. — L. — Gk.) F. *marron*, adj. fugitive, applied to a fugitive slave who takes refuge in woods and mountains. [Hence E. *maroon*, to treat as a fugitive, cause to be fugitive.] A clipped form of Span. *cimarron*, wild, unruly, lit. living in the mountain-tops. — Span. *cima*, a mountain-top. (So also Ital. and Port. *cima*, F. *cime*.) The O. Span. *cima* also meant a sprout, twig (Diez). — L. *cyma*, a young sprout. — Gk. κῦμα, anything swollen, a wave, a young sprout. ¶ *Negro cimarron* or *cimarron* was an every-day phrase for a fugitive slave hidden in the mountains, in Cuba, about A.D. 1846.

Marque, letters of; see **Mark** (1).

Marquee, Marquess, Marquetry, Marquis; see **Mark** (1).

Marrow, pith. (E.) M. E. *marow*, *mary*. A. S. *mearh*. + Du. *merg*, Icel. *mergr*, Swed. *merg*, Dan. *maro*, G. *mark*, O. H. G. *marag*; also W. *mer*, Corn. *maru*. Further allied to Russ. *mozg'*, Zend *mazga*, marrow; Skt. *majjan*, marrow of bones, pith of trees.

Marry; see **Masculine**.

Marsh; see **Mere** (1).

Marshal; see **Mare**.

Marsupial. (L. — Gk.) Applied to animals that carry their young in a sort of pouch. — L. *marsupium*, a pouch. — Gk. μαρούπιον, a little pouch, dimin. of μάρσυπος, a bag.

Mart, put for *market*; see **Merit**.

Marten, a kind of weasel. (F. — Low L. — Teut.) Short for *martern* (16th cent.); where the final *n* is added, as in *bitter-n*. Older forms *marter*, *martre*. — F. *martre*. — Low L. *marturis*. Of Teut. origin; cf. Du. *marter*, G. *marder*, a marten; A. S. *meardh*, Icel. *mörðr*, Swed. *mård*, Dan. *maar* (for *maard**), a marten.

Martial, brave. (F.—L.) F. *martial.*—
L. *Martialis*, dedicated to *Mars*, god of
war.

march (3), the name of a month. (L.)
Low L. *Marcius*, L. *Martius*, the month
dedicated to *Mars.*

Martin, a bird. (F.) F. *martin*, (1) a
proper name, Martin, (2) the same name
applied to various birds and animals. Thus
martin-pêcheur is a king-fisher; *oiseau de
S. Martin* is the ring-tail. (Cot.) A nickname, like our *robin, jenny-wren*, &c.; so
that the bird is named after *Martin* as a
proper name.

martinet, a strict disciplinarian. (F.)
So called from a F. officer named *Martinet*
(temp. Louis XIV); dimin. form of *Martin.*

martinmas, martlemas, the feast
of St. Martin; Nov. 11 (F. and L.)
Martlemass is a corrupt form of *Martin-
mass*; occ **Mass** (2).

martlet, a kind of bird, martin. (F.)
A corruption of M. E. *martnet*, short for
martinet. — F. *martinet*, 'a martlet or
martin;' Cot. Dimin. of F. *Martin.*

Martinet; see **Martin.**

Martingale, a strap fastened to a
horse's girth to hold his head down. (F.)
Also applied to a short spar, in ships,
under the bowsprit; but this is only due to
a supposed resemblance to a horse's martingale.—F. *martingale*, 'a martingale for
a horse;' Cot. The term arose (as Littré
says) from an oddly made kind of breeches,
called *chausses à la martingale* (Rabelais).
So also Span. *martingal*, Ital. *martingala*,
an old kind of breeches or hose.—F.
Martigal (pl. *Martigaux*), inhabitants of
Martigues in Provence (Ménage). For the
intrusive *n*, cf. *passenger, messenger.*

Martinmas, Martlet; see **Martin.**

Martyr. (L.—Gk.) A S. *martyr.*—L.
martyr.—Gk. μάρτυρ, μάρτυς, a witness, lit.
one who remembers, records, or declares.
Cf. Skt. *smri*, to remember. (√SMAR.)

Marvel; see **Miracle.**

Masculine. (F.—L.) F. *masculin.*—
L. *masculinus*, lengthened from *masculus*,
male.—L. *mas-*, stem of *mās*, a male.
Allied to **Man.**

emasculate, to deprive of virility.
(L.) From pp. of L. *emasculare.*—L. *e*,
away from; *masculus*, male.

male. (F.—L.) O. F. *masle* (later
male); F. *mâle.*—L. *masculus*, male (above).

mallard, a wild drake. (F.—L.) M. E.
malard. — O. F. *malard*; formed, with

suffix *-ard* (of G. origin, from G. *hart*,)
from O. F. *male*, male (above). The
suffix *-ard* was particularly applied to males,
so that the idea of 'male' appears twice.

marital, belonging to a husband. (F.
—L.) F. *marital.* — L. *maritalis*, adj.
formed from *maritus*, a husband. This
is a masc. sb. made to accompany L.
marita, a woman provided with a husband.
—L. *mari-*, crude form of *mas*, a man,
husband; see **Masculine** (above).

marry. (F.—L.) M. E. *marien.* — F.
marier. — L. *maritare*, to marry. — L. *maritus*, a husband; see **marital** (above).

Mash, to beat into a mixed mass. (E. or
Scand.) A *mash* is properly a mixture;
and to *mash* was, formerly, to mix. We
find A. S. *max-wyrte*, mash-wort, new
beer; so that the word may be English:
but it is commoner in Scandinavian. Cf.
Swed. dial. *mask*, Swed. *mäsk*, brewer's
grains, whence *mäska*, to mix, Dan. and
North Fries. *mask*, grains, mash, Dan.
mæske, to mash, fatten pigs with grains. +
G. *meisch*, a mash, *meischen*, to mash.
The sb. form appears to be the original.
Perhaps allied to **Mix.** Cf. also Gael.
and Irish *masg*, to mix, infuse, steep;
Lithuan. *maisz-yti*, to stir things in a pot,
from *misz-ti*, to mix.

mess (2), a mixture, disorder. (E. or
Scand.) A corruption of the older form
mesh, which again stands for *mash*, sb.
Cf. *mash*, vb. (above). '*Mescolare*, to
mixe, to *mash*, to *mesh*;' Florio. '*Mesco-
lanza*, a medlie, a *mesh*, a mixture;' id.

Mask, Masque, a disguise for the face;
masked entertainment. (F.—Span.—Arab.)
The sense of 'entertainment' is the true
one; the sense of 'disguise' is secondary.
'A jolly company in maner of a *maske*,'
F. Q. iii. 12. 5. 'Some haue I sene
daunce in a *maske*;' Sir T. More, Works,
p. 1039. More uses *maskers* in the sense
of 'visors' (correctly, according to the
Spanish use).—F. *masque*, a mask, visor;
a clipped form, due to F. vb. *masquer*, really
short for *masquerer**; the fuller form comes
out in O.F. *masquarizé*, masked, *masquerie,
masquerade*, 'a mask or mummery;' Cot.
—Span. *mascara*, a masker, a masquerader;
also a mask.—Arab. *maskharat*, a buffoon,
jester, man in masquerade, a pleasantry,
anything ridiculous. — Arab. root *sakhira*,
he ridiculed. ¶ Fully proved; other etymologies are worthless. Der. *masquerade*,
F. *masquerade*, Span. *mascarada.*

Mason. (F. – Low L. – G. ?) O. F. *masson*; F. *maçon*. – Low L. *macionem*, acc. of *macio*, a mason; we also find the forms *machio*, *macho*, *maco*, *mactio*, *mattio*, *matio*. Perhaps from M. H. G. *mezzo*, a mason, whence G. *steinmetz*, a stonemason; allied to O. H. G. *meizan*, to hew, cut (whence G. *meissel*, a chisel). + Icel. *meita*, to hew, Goth. *maitan*, to hew, cut, a strong verb. (Base MIT.)

Masque; see **Mask.**

Mass (1), a lump; see **Macerate.**

Mass (2), the celebration of the Eucharist; see **Missile.**

Massacre. (F. – O. Low G. ?) F. *massacre*, a massacre; *massacrer*, to massacre. Of disputed origin; it is prob. due to Low G. *matsken*, to cut, hew, Du. *matsen*, to maul, kill. Cf. G. *metzelei*, a massacre; from *metzeln*, frequent. of *metzen*, to cut, kill. And see **Mason.**

Mast (1), a pole, to hold the sails of a ship. (E.) M. E. *mast.* A. S. *mæst*, stem of a tree, bough, mast. + Du. *mast*, Swed. and Dan. *mast*, G. *mast*.

Mast (2), fruit of beech-trees. (E.) The orig. sense is ' edible fruit,' used for feeding swine. A. S. *mæst*, mast. + G. *mast*, mast; *mästen*, to fatten. Prob. allied to **Meat.**

Master, Mastery; see **Magnitude.**

Mastic, Mastich, a kind of gum resin. (F. – L. – Gk.) F. *mastic*, 'mastich, a sweet gum,' Cot. – L. *mastichē.* – Gk. μαστίχη, the gum of the tree σχῖνος, called in Latin *lentiscus.* So called because used for chewing in the East. – Gk. μαστ-, base of μάσταξ, mouth, μαστάζειν, to chew; cf. Gk. μασάομαι, I chew.

masticate. (L. – Gk.) From pp. of L. *masticare*, to chew, quite a late word; properly, to chew mastic. – L. *mastichē*, mastic (above). ¶ The true L. word for to chew is *mandere.*

moustache, mustache. (F. – Ital. – Gk.) F. *moustache*. – Ital. *mostaccio*, 'a face, a snout, a mostacho;' Florio. – Gk. μύσταϰ-, stem of μύσταξ, the upper lip, a moustache, Doric form of μάσταξ, the mouth, upper lip (above).

Masticate; see **Mastic.**

Mastiff; see **Mansion.**

Mastodon, an extinct elephant. (Gk.) Named from the nipple-like projections on its molar teeth. – Gk. μαστ-ός, the female breast; ὀδον-, short for ὀδοντ-, stem of ὀδούς, a tooth; see **Tooth.**

Mat. (L.) M. E. *matte.* A. S. *meatta.* – L. *matta* (Low L. *natta*), a mat; whence Du. *mat*, G. *matte*, F. *natte*, &c.

Matador, the slayer of the bull in a bull-fight. (Span. – L.) Span. *matador*, lit. slayer. – Span. *matar*, to kill. – L. *mactare*, to kill, orig. to honour by a sacrifice. Cf. Skt. *mah*, to honour. (√MAGH.)

Match (1), an equal, a contest; see **Make.**

Match (2), a prepared rope for firing a cannon. (F. – L. – Gk.) M. E. *macche.* – O. F. *mesche*, *meiche* (F. *mèche*), wick of a candle, match to fire a gun, ' match of a lamp;' Cot. – Low L. *myxa**, not found (but = Gk. μύξα); Low L. *myxus*, the nozzle of a lamp, through which the wick protrudes; also, a wick. – Gk. μύξα, the nozzle of a lamp; the more original senses being (1) mucus (2) nostril. Allied to **Mucus.** Der. *match-lock*, the lock of a gun holding a match; hence, the gun itself.

Mate (1), a companion; see **Make.**

Mate (2), to check-make, confound. (F. – Pers. & Arab.) From the game of chess. *Check-mate* means 'the king is dead.' – O. F. *eschec et mat*, check-mate; Cot. [Here *et* is not wanted.] – Pers. *shāh māt*, the king is dead, check-mate. – Pers. *shāh*, king (see **Check**); *māt*, he is dead, from Arab. root *māta*, he died. Cf. Heb. *mūth*, to die. ¶ Hence Turk. and Pers. *māt*, astonished, confounded, amazed, receiving check-mate; O. F. *mat*, 'mated, quelled, subdued,' Cot.; M. E. *mate*, confounded, Ital. *matto*, fond, mad.

Material; see **Matter.**

Maternal. (F. – L.) F. *maternal.* – Low L. *maternalis.* – L. *maternus*, belonging to a mother. – L. *mater*, mother; cognate with **Mother.**

matricide, murderer of a mother. (F. – L.) F. *matricide*, adj., ' mother-killing;' Cot. – L. *matricida*, a matricide. – L. *matri-*, crude form of *mater*, mother; *cædere*, to slay; see **Cæsura.** ¶ We also used *matricide* to represent L. *matricidium*, the slaying of a mother.

matriculate, to enrol in a college. (L.) From pp. of Low L. *matriculare*, to enrol, a coined word. – L. *matricula*, a register; dimin. of *matrix* (stem *matric-*), meaning (1) a breeding animal, (2) womb, matrix, (3) a public register, roll, list, lit. parent-stock. See **matrix** (below).

matrimony. (F. – L.) O. F. *matrimonie.* – L. *matrimonium*, marriage, lit.

motherhood. — L. *matri-*, crude form of *mater*, mother; with suffix *-monio-* (Aryan *-man-ya*).

matrix, the womb, cavity or mould. (L.) L. *matrix*, a breeding animal, the womb. — L. *matri-*, crude form of *mater*, mother.

matron, a married woman. (F. — L.) F. *matrone*. — L. *matrona*; extended from *matr-*, stem of *mater*, a mother.

Mathematic, pertaining to the science of number. (F. — L. — Gk.) O. F. *mathematique*. — L. *mathematicus*. — Gk. μαθηματικός, disposed to learn, belonging to the sciences, esp. to mathematics. — Gk. μαθηματ-, stem of μάθημα, a lesson. — Gk. μαθή-σομαι, future of μανθάνειν, to learn.

Matins, Mattins; see **Mature**.

Matricide, Matrimony; see **Maternal**.

Matter (1), substance. (F. — L.) M. E. *matere*, *materie*. — O. F. *matere*, *matiere* (F. *matière*). — L. *materia*, stuff, materials, useful for building, &c. (√ MA.) Cf. Skt. *mâ*, to measure, also (when used with *nis*), to build.

material, substantial. (F. — L.) O. F. *materiel*. — L. *materialis*, adj., formed from *materia* (above).

matter (2), pus, a fluid in abscesses. (F. — L.) Really the same word as matter (1); see Littré, s. v. *matière*, § 8.

Mattins; see **Mature**.

Mattock. (C.) A.S. *mattuc*. — W. *matog*, a mattock, hoe; cf. Gael. *madag*, a pick-axe. + Russ. *motuika*, Lithuan. *matikkas*, a mattock.

Mattress. (F. — Arab.) O. F. *materas* (now *matelas*). Cf. Span. *al-madraque*, a mattress; where *al* is the Arab. def. art. — Arab. *matrah*, a situation, place, a place where anything is thrown; this word came to mean also anything hastily thrown down, hence, something to lie upon, a bed (Devic). — Arab. root *taraha*, he threw prostrate.

Mature, ripe. (L.) L. *maturus*, ripe. Supposed to be from a lost sb. allied to Lithuan. *metas*, a period; so that the sense is 'completed as to period,' fully mature; cf. Lithuan. *matóti*, to measure. Allied to **Mete**.

matins, mattins, morning prayers. (F. — L.) F. *matins*, a pl. sb. from F. *matin*, morning, orig. an adj. — L. *matutinum*, acc. of *matutinus*, adj., belonging to the morning. Cf. Ital. *mattino*, morning. — L. *Matuta*, the goddess of dawn, as if from a masc. *matutus**, with the sense of 'early,' or 'timely;' allied to *maturus*, mature.

matutinal, pertaining to the morning. (L.) L. *matutinus*, adj. (as above).

Matutinal; see **Mature**.

Maudlin, sickly sentimental. (F. — L. — Gk. — Heb.) Orig. 'shedding tears of penitence,' like Mary Magdalen. From M.E. *Maudelein*, the same as *Magdelaine*. — O.F. *Magdeleine*. — L. *Magdalene*. — Gk. Μαγδαληνή, i. e. belonging to Magdala; Luke, viii. 2. — Heb. *migdol*, a tower; whence *Magdala* as a proper name.

Maugre; see **Malice**.

Maul, to disfigure; see **Mall** (1).

Maulstick, a stick used by painters to steady the hand. (G.) G. *malerstock*, lit. 'painter's stick.' — G. *maler*, a painter, from *malen*, to paint; *stock*, a stick. *Malen* was orig. to mark, from G. *mahl*, O. H. G. *mâl*, a mark, mole; see Mole (1) and **Stock**.

Maundy Thursday; see **Mandate**.

Mausoleum, a magnificent tomb. (L. — Gk.) L. *mausoleum*, a splendid tomb, orig. the tomb of Mausolus. — Gk. Μαυσωλεῖον; from Μαύσωλος, Mausolus, a king of Caria.

Mauve, the name of a colour; see **Mallow**.

Mavis, the song-thrush. (F. — C.) M.E. *mavis*. — F. *mauvis*, a throstle; cf. Span. *malvis*, a thrush. — Bret. *milfid*, *milvid*, a mavis, also *milchouid* (at Vannes). Cf. Corn. *melhues*, O. Corn. *melhuet*, a lark.

Maw, stomach. (E.) M.E. *mawe*. A.S. *maga*. + Du. *maag*, Icel. *magi*, Swed. *mage*, Dan. *mave*, G. *magen*. (Perhaps from √ MAGH.)

Mawkish; see **Moth**.

Maxillar, Maxillary; see **Macerate**.

Maxim, Maximum; see **Magnitude**.

May (1), I am able, I am free to do. (E.) Pres. t. *may*, pt. t. *might*; the infin. (not in use) should take the form *mow*. M. E. *mowen*, infin.; pres. t. *may*; pt. t. *mighte*. A.S. *mugan*, to be able; pres. t. *mæg*; pt. t. *mihte*. (Here *mæg* was once the pt. t. of a strong verb.) + O. Sax. *mugan*, pres. *mag*, pt. *mahta*; Icel. *mega*, pres. *mâ*, pt. *mátti*; Du. *mogen*, pres. *mag*, pt. *mogt*; Dan. pres. *maa*, pt. *maatte*; Swed. pres. *mâ*, pt. *mâtte*; G. *mögen*, pres. *mag*, pt. *mochte*; Goth. *magan*, pres. *mag*, pt. *mahta*. + Russ. *moche*, to be able; cf. L. *magnus*, great; Gk. μέγας, great; L. *mactus*, honoured; Gk. μηχανή, means; Skt. *mah*, to honour. (√ MAGH.)

dismay, to discourage. (F.—L. *and* O. H. G.) O. F. *desmayer* (Palsgrave), and exactly the same as Span. *desmayar*, to dismay, terrify. The O. F. *desmayer* was early supplanted by *esmayer* in the same sense, which only differed in substituting the prefix *es-* (L. *ex*) for *des-* (L. *dis-*). The latter part (*-mayer*) of these words is from O. H. G. *magan* (G. *mögen*), to have power, be able. Hence *desmayer* and *esmayer*, at first in the intrans. sense to lack power, faint, be discouraged, but afterwards, actively, to discourage. Cf. Ital. *smagare* (put for *dis-magare**), to lose courage, also to dismay (Florio).

maid, maiden. (E.) M. E. *mayde*, merely short for earlier *maiden*, *meiden*. A. S. *mægden*, a maiden; short for *mægeð-en***, dimin. form of *mægeð*, a maiden. Again, *mæg-eð* is allied to *magu*, a son, a kinsman, and to *mæg*, *mæge*, a maiden (answering to later M. E. *may*). *Mægeð* answers to Goth. *magaths*, a virgin, maid, and *magu*, a son or kinsman, to Goth. *magus*, Icel. *mögr*, a boy, orig. 'a growing lad,' one increasing in strength. From Teut. base MAG, to have strength. **Der.** *maiden-hood*, also spelt *maiden-head*.

main (1), sb. strength. (E.) M. E. *main*. A. S. *mægen*, strength.+Icel. *megin*, strength. From Teut. base MAG (above).

mickle, great. (E.) M.E. *mikel*, *mukel*, *michel*, *muchel*.—A. S. *mycel*, *micel*.+Icel. *mykill*, *mikill*, Goth. *mikils*, Gk. μεγάλη, great. From the same base.

might (1), strength. (E.) M. E. *miȝt*. A. S. *miht*, *mæht*, *meaht*.+Du. *magt*, Icel. *máttr*, Dan. Swed. *magt*, Goth. *mahts*, G. *macht*. (Teut. base MAH-TA.)

might (2), pt. t. of *may*. (E.) See **May** (1) above.

more. (E.) This does duty for two distinct M. E. words, viz. (1) *mo*, more in number, (2) *more*, larger. α. The former is from A. S. *má*, more in number, prob. orig. an adv. form, like G. *mehr*, Goth. *mais*, L. *magis*; from an Aryan form MAG-YANS, where -YANS is a comparative suffix. β. The latter is from A. S. *mára*, greater, cognate with Icel. *meiri*, Goth. *maiza*, a double compar. form; from Aryan MAG-YANS-RA. ¶ The notion that *mo* is a positive form is quite wrong; the positive forms are *much*, *mickle*, *many*.

most. (E.) M. E. *most*, *meste*. — A. S. *mǽst*.+Icel. *mestr*, G. *meist*, Goth. *maists*; from an Aryan form MAG-YANS-TA,

where -YANS is a comparative, and -TA a superlative suffix; cf. Gk. μέγ-ισ-τος.

much. (Scand.) M. E. *moche*, *miche*, *muche*, adj., which only differs from M. E. *mochel*, *michel*, *muchel* (A. S. *mycel*) by the final *l*. Not in A. S.; but suggested by Icel. *mjök*, adv., much; allied to A. S. *myc-*, base of *mycel*, great. ¶ Cf. A. S. *lyt*, used as well as *lytel*, little.

May (2), the fifth month. (F.—L.) O.F. *Mai*. — L. *Maius*, May; the month of 'growth.' (√MAGH.)

Mayor; see **Magnitude.**

Maze. (Scand.) M. E. *mase*; we also find M. E. *masen*, to confuse. Of Scand. origin; cf. Norweg. *masa-st* (where *-st* is reflexive), to lose one's senses and begin to dream, *masa*, to pore over a thing, also to prate, chatter; Icel. *masa*, to prate, chatter; Swed. dial. *masa*, to bask in the sun, to be lazy, lounge about. Cf. E. *in a maze* = in a dreamy perplexity. The orig. sense seems to have been 'to be lost in thought,' dream or pore over a thing, whence the idea of 'perplexity' for the sb.

amaze, to astound. (E. *and* Scand.) Formerly *amase*; we find M. E. *amased* = bewildered, perplexed. — A. S. *á-*, prefix (= G. *er-*, Goth. *us-*); and M. E. *masen*, to bewilder, orig. to be perplexed, from the Scand. source indicated above.

Mazer, a large drinking-bowl. (Scand.) M. E. *maser*. — Icel. *mösurr*, a maple-tree, spotted wood; whence *mösur-bolli*, a mazer-bowl, so called because made of maple-wood. The maple-wood was called *mösurr* or 'spot-wood' from its being covered with spots; but the word for spot is only preserved in other languages, as in M. H. G. *mase*, a spot, and in E. *measles*, which is borrowed from Dutch; see below.

measles, a contagious fever accompanied by small red spots on the skin. (Du.) 'Rougeolle, the *meazles*;' Cot. M. E. *maseles* (14th cent.) — Du. *maselen*, measles; also called *masel-sucht*, 'measell-sicknesse,' Hexham. The lit. sense is 'small spots;' cf. O. Du. *maesche*, *masche*, *maschel*, 'a spot, blot,' Hexham. The orig. word occurs in M. H. G. *mase*, O. H. G. *másá*, a spot. ¶ Wholly unconnected with M. E. *mesel*, a leper, which merely meant orig. 'a wretch,' from O. F. *mesel*, L. *misellus*, from L. *miser*, wretched.

Me. (E.) A. S. *mé*; also *mec*, in the accusative only.+Du. *mij*; Icel. *mér*, dat., *mik*, acc.; Swed. Dan. *mig*; Goth. *mis*, dat.; *mik*, acc.; G. *mir*, dat.; *mich*, acc.; Corn. and Bret. *me*; Irish, Gael. W. *mi*; L. *mihi*, dat.; *me*, acc.; Gk. μοί, ἐμοί, dat.; μέ, ἐμέ, acc.; Skt. *mahyam*, *me*, dat.; *mám*, *má*, acc. (Base MA.)

mine (1), belonging to me. (E.) M. E. *min*, pl. *mine*; often shortened to *my*. A. S. *min*, poss. pron. (declinable), from *mín*, gen. of 1st pers. pronoun. + Goth. *meins*, poss. pron.; from *meina*, gen. case of 1st pers. pronoun; so in other Teut. tongues.

my. (E.) M. E. *mi*, *my*; short for *min* (above), by loss of final *n*. Der. *my-self*, M. E. *mi-self*, formerly *me-self*.

Mead (1), a drink made from honey. (E.) M. E. *mede*. A. S. *medu*.+Du. *mede*, Icel. *mjöðr*, Dan. *miöd*, Swed. *mjöd*, G. *meth*, W. *medd*, Lith. *middus*, Russ. *med'*, Gk. μέθυ; Skt. *madhu*, sweet, also as sb., honey, sugar. Cf. Lith. *medùs*, honey.

metheglin, mead. (W.) W. *meddyglyn*, mead, lit. mead-liquor. — W. *medd*, mead; *llyn*, liquor.

Mead (2), **Meadow**, a grass-field; see Mow (1).

Meagre, thin. (F. − L.) M. E. *megre*. − F. *maigre*.−L. *macrum*, acc. of *macer*, thin, lean; whence Icel. *magr*, Dan. Swed. G. *mager*, thin, were borrowed at an early period. Cf. Gk. μικρός, small.

emaciate. (L.) From pp. of L. *emaciare*, to make thin. − L. *e*, very; *maci-*, base of *macies*, leanness; cf. *macer*, lean.

Meal (1), ground grain. (E.) M. E. *mele*. A. S. *melu*, *melo*. + Du. *meel*, Icel. *mjöl*, Dan. *meel*, Swed. *mjöl*, G. *mehl*. All from Teut. base MAL, to grind, as in Icel. *mala*, Goth. *malan*, O. H. G. *malan*, to grind. (√ MAR.)

Meal (2), a repast. (E.) M. E. *mele*. A. S. *mæl*, (1) a time, portion of time, stated time, hence a common meal at a stated time, not a hastily snatched repast. + Du. *maal*, (1) time, (2) meal; Icel. *mál*, measure, time, meal; Dan. *maal*, Swed. *mål*, measure, meal; Goth. *mel*, a time; G. *mahl*, a meal, *mal*, time. (√ MA.)

Mean (1), to have in the mind, intend. (E.) M. E. *menen*. A. S. *mænan*, to intend. + Du. *meenen*, Dan. *mene*, Swed. *mena*, G. *meinen*. All from the sb. seen in O. H. G. *meina*, thought, allied to *minni*, memory. Allied to **Mind**. (√ MAN.)

Mean (2), sordid. (E.) M. E. *mene*.

A. S. *mæne*, wicked. − A. S. *mán*, iniquity. + Icel. *meinn*, mean, hurtful, from *mein*, a hurt, harm; M. H. G. *mein*, false (cf. G. *mein-eid*, perjury). Perhaps allied to Goth. *gamains*, common, A. S. *gemæne*, common, general; but this is doubtful. (√ MI ?)

Mean (3), **Means**; see **Medium**.

Meander, a winding course. (L. − Gk.) L. *Mæander*. − Gk. Μαίανδρος, a winding stream; Pliny, v. 29.

Measles; see **Mazer**.

Measure. (F. − L.) M. E. *mesure* − O. F. *mesure*. − L. *mensura*, measure. − L. *mensus*, pp. of *metiri*, to measure. (√MA.) Allied to **Mete**.

commensurate. (L.) From pp. of L. *commensurare*, to measure in comparison with, a coined word. − L. *com-* (for *cum*, with); *mensura*, a measure (above).

dimension. (F. − L.) O. F. *dimension*. − L. acc. *dimensionem*, a measuring. − L. *dimensus*, pp. of *di-metiri*, to measure off.

immense. (F. − L.) F. *immense*. − L. *immensus*, immeasurable. − L. *im-*, for *in-*, not ; *mensus*, pp. of *metiri*, to measure.

mensuration, measuring. (L.) From L. *mensuratio*, a measuring. − L. *mensuratus*, pp. of *mensurare*, to measure. − L. *mensura*, measure; see **Measure** (above).

Meat. (E.) M. E. *mete*. A. S. *mete*. + Du. *met*, Icel. *matr*, Dan. *mad*, Swed. *mat*, Goth. *mats*, O. H. G. *maz*, food. Cf. L. *mandere*, to chew.

Mechanic; see **Machine**.

Medal; see **Metal**.

Meddle; see **Miscellaneous**.

Mediate; see **Medium**.

Medic, a kind of clover. (L. − Gk.) L. *medica*. − Gk. Μηδική, Median grass; fem. of Μηδικός, belong to *Media*.

Medicine, a remedy. (F. − L.) O. F. *medecine*. − L. *medicina*. − L. *medicus*, a physician. − L. *mederi*, to heal. (Base MADH; √ MA.) Cf. Zend *madh*, to treat medically. Der. *medical*, Low L. *medicalis*, from *medicus* (above); *medicate*.

meditate. (L.) From pp. of L. *meditari*, to ponder ; a frequent. verb, supposed to be from the same base as *mederi*, to heal (above).

remedy. (F. − L.) M. E. *remedie*. − O. F. *remedie* *, only found as *remede*, mod. F. *remède*. − L. *remedium*, a remedy; that which heals again. − L. *re-*, again; *mederi*, to heal.

Medieval, **Mediocre**; see **Medium**.

Meditate; see Medicine.

Mediterranean; see Medium.

Medium. (L.) L. *medium*, the midst, also a means; neut. of *medius*, middle. Allied to Mid.

demi-, half. (F. − L.) O. F. *demi*, half. − L. *dimidius*, half. − L. *di-* (= *dis-*), apart; *medius*, middle.

immediate, without intervention or means. (F. − L.) O. F. *immediat.* − O. F. *im-* (for L. *in*), not; *mediatus*, pp. of L. *mediare*, to be in the middle. − L. *medius*, middle.

mean (3), intermediate. (F. − L.) O. F. *meien* (F. *moyen*). − L. *medianus*, extended form from *medius*, middle. **Der. mean**, sb., common in pl. *means*.

mediate, adj., acting by or as a means. (L.) Rare. − L. *mediatus*, pp. of *mediare*, to be in the middle. − L. *medius*, middle. **Der.** *mediat-ion*, *mediat-or*.

medieval, relating to the middle ages. (L.) Also written *mediæval*. Coined from L. *medi-us*, middle; *æu-um*, age; see **Age**.

mediocre, middling. (F. − L.) F. *médiocre*. − L. *mediocrem*, acc. of *mediocris*, middling; extended from *medi-us*, middle. (Cf. *fer-ox*, from *fer-us*.)

mediterranean, inland, said of a sea. (L.) L. *mediterrane-us*, situate in the middle of the land. − L. *medi-us*, middle; *terra*, land; see **Terrace**.

meridian, pertaining to mid-day. (F. − L.) O. F. *meridien*. − L. *meridianus*. − L. *meridies*, mid-day; corrupted from *medidies* *. − L. *medi-us*, mid; *dies*, day.

mezzotinto, a mode of engraving. (Ital. − L.) Ital. *mezzo tinto*, half tinted. − Ital. *mezzo*, mid; *tinto*, pp. of *tingere*, to tint. − L. *medius*, mid; *tingere*, to dip, dye.

mizen, mizzen, a sail in a ship. (F. − Ital. − L.) O. F. *misaine*, explained by Cotgrave as 'the foresaile of a ship.' − Ital. *mezzana*, 'a sail in a ship called the poop or misen-saile;' Florio. Cf. Ital. *mezzano*, 'a meane man, between great and little;' id. The orig. sense seems to have been ' of middling size,' without reference to its position. − Low L. *medianus*, middle, of middle size (whence also F. *moyen*, E. *mean*). − L. *medius*, middle.

moiety, half. (F. − L.) F. *moitié*, a half. − L. *medietatem*, acc. of *medietas*, a middle course, a half. − L. *medius*, middle.

Medlar. (F. − L. − Gk.) The name of a tree, bearing fruit formerly called *medies*. M. E. *medler*, the tree, also called *medle-tree*. *Medle* stands for *mesle*. − O. F. *mesle*, a medlar; whence *meslier*, the tree. − L. *mespilum*. − Gk. μέσπιλον, a medlar.

Medley; see Miscellaneous.

Medullar, belonging to the marrow. (L.) L. *medullaris*, adj. − L. *medulla*, marrow. Prob. allied to *med-ius*, middle.

Meed. (E.) M. E. *mede*, *meed*. − A. S. *méd*, older form *meord* (with *r* for older *s*). **+** G. *miethe*, hire; Goth. *mizdo*, Russ. *mzda*, Gk. μισθός, pay.

Meek. (Scand.) M. E. *meke*, *meek* ; spelt *meoc*, Ormulum, 667. − Icel. *mjúkr*, soft, agile, meek, mild ; Swed. *mjuk*, Dan. *myg*, soft; Du. *muik*; Goth. *muks* *, in comp. *muka-modei*, gentleness.

Meerschaum; see Mere (1).

Meet (1), fitting; see Mete (1).

Meet (2), to encounter; see Moot.

Megatherium, a fossil quadruped. (Gk.) Lit. 'great wild beast.' − Gk. μέγα-s, great ; θηρίον, dimin. of θήρ, a wild beast. See **Deer**.

megalosaurus. (Gk.) Lit. 'great lizard.' − Gk. μεγάλο-, crude form extended from μέγα-s, great ; σαῦρος, a lizard.

Megrim; see Hemi-.

Melancholy, sadness. (F. − L. − Gk.) Supposed to be due to an excess of 'black bile.' M. E. *melancholie.* − O. F. *melancholie.* − L. *melancholia.* − Gk. μελαγχολία, melancholy. − Gk. μελάγχολος, jaundiced. − Gk. μέλαν-, stem of μέλας, black ; χολή, bile, gall. Cf. Skt. *mala*, dirty, *malina*, black; and see **Gall**.

Melilot; see Mellifluous.

Meliorate, to make better. (L.) From pp. of Low L. *meliorare*, to make better. − L. *melior*, better. **+** Gk. μᾶλλον, rather, comp. of μάλα, adv., very much.

ameliorate. (F.−L.; *with* L. *suffix*.) Formed with suffix *-ate* (= L. *-atus*) from F. *ameliorer*, to better, improve. − F. *a* (= L. *ad*), in addition; *meliorer* (= Low L. *meliorare*), to make better (above).

•Mellifluous, sweet. (L.) Lit. 'flowing sweetly,' 'flowing like honey.' − L. *melli-*, crude form of *mel*, honey; *-fluus*, flowing, from *fluere*, to flow; see **Fluent**. Cf. Gk. μέλι, Goth. *milith*, honey, Irish *mil*, honey.

marmalade. (F. − Port. − L. − Gk.) O. F. *marmelade*, Cot. − Port. *marmelada*, orig. a conserve of quinces. − Port. *marmelo*, a quince. — L. *mĕlimēlum*, lit. honey-apple ; also a quince. — Gk. μελίμηλον, a sweet apple, apple grafted on a quince. — Gk. μέλι, honey; μῆλον, an apple ; see **Melon**.

melilot, a plant. (F. — L. — Gk.) O. F. *melilot.* — L. *melilotos.* — Gk. μελίλωτος, μελίλωτον, a kind of clover, named from the honey in it. — Gk. μέλι, honey; λωτός, lotus, clover.

mildew. (E.) M. E. *meldew.* A. S. *meledeáw, mildeáw*, lit. honey-dew. — A. S. *mele, mil*, allied to L. *mel*, honey; *deáw*, dew. So also Irish *milceog*, mildew; from *mil*, honey.

molasses, syrup made from sugar. (Port. — L.) It should rather be *melasses.* — Port. *melaço*, molasses ; cf. Span. *melaza* (same). — L. *mellaceus*, made with honey. — L. *mel*, honey.

Mellow, fully ripe. (E.) M. E. *melwe*, orig. soft, pulpy. By the frequent substitution of *l* for *r*, it stands for A. S. *mearu*, soft, tender ; as to the vowel, cf. E. *belch* = A. S. *bealcian*. **+** Du. *murw*, soft, *mollig, malsch*, soft; O. H. G. *maro*, soft. Allied to **Mollify**. (√MAR.)

Melodrama. (F. — Gk.) Formerly *melodrame.* — F. *mélodrame*, acting, with songs. — Gk. μέλο-s, a song; δρᾶμα, an action, drama ; see **Drama**.

melody. (F. — L. — Gk.) F. *melodie.* — L. *melodia.* — Gk. μελῳδία, a singing. — Gk. μελῳδός, adj. musical. — Gk. μέλ-ος, a song ; ῳδή, a song, ode ; see **Ode**.

Melon, a fruit. (F. — L. — Gk.) O. F. *melon.* — L. *melonem*, acc. of *melo*, an apple-shaped melon. — Gk. μῆλον, an apple, also applied to other fruits. Cf. L. *mālum*, an apple, prob. borrowed from Gk.

Melt. (E.) M. E. *melten*, pt. t. *malt*, pp. *molten.* — A. S. *meltan*, pt. t. *mealt.* Allied to Skt. *mridu* (base *mard*), O. Slavonic *mladu*, soft. (√MAR.)

malt, grain steeped in water. (E.) M. E. *malt.* A. S. *mealt*, malt. — A. S. *mealt*, pt. t. of *meltan*, to melt, hence to steep, soften. **+** Icel. Dan. G. *malt* ; O. H. G. *malz*, malt, also soft, allied to Skt. *mridu*, soft (above).

milt (1), the spleen. (E.) M. E. *milte.* A. S. *milte.* **+** Du. *milt*, Icel. *milti*, Dan. *milt*, Swed. *mjälte*, the spleen ; G. *milz*, milt. From the verb to *melt* in the sense to digest; cf. Icel. *melta*, (1) to malt (2) to digest.

Member. (F. — L.) F. *membre.* — L. *membrum*, a member. Cf. Skt. *marman*, a member, a joint.

membrane. (F. — L.) F. *membrane.* — L. *membrana*, a skin covering a member of the body, a membrane. — L. *membrum.*

Memento; see **Mental**.

Memory. (F. — L.) M. E. *memorie.* — O. F. *memorie* *, not recorded; also *memoire.* — L. *memoria*, memory. — L. *memor*, mindful, remembering. This L. *memor* appears to be a reduplicated form (like *me-min-i*, I remember); cf. Gk. μέρ-μερ-ος, anxious, μέρ-ιμνα, care, thought. Allied to Skt. *smri* (base *smar*), to remember. (√SMAR.)

commemorate. (L.) From pp. of L. *commemorare*, to call to mind. — L. *com-* (for *cum*), together ; *memor*, mindful.

memoir, a record. (F. — L.) Commoner in the pl. *memoirs.* — O. F. *memoires*, notes for remembrance, records ; pl. of *memoire*, memory (above).

remember. (F. — L.) O. F. *remembrer.* — L. *rememorari*, to remember. — L. *re-*, again ; *memorare*, to make mention of, from *memor*, mindful.

reminiscence. (F. — L.) F. *reminiscence.* — L. *reminiscentia*, remembrance. — L. *reminiscent-*, crude form of pres. pt. of *reminisci*, to remember. — L. *re-*, again ; and base of *me-min-i*, I remember ; see **Memory** (above).

Menace. (F. — L.) O. F. *menace.* — L. *minacia*, a threat. — L. *minaci-*, crude form of *minax*, full of threatenings, also, projecting forward. — L. *minæ*, things projecting forward, hanging over and ready to fall, hence threats. — L. *minere*, to project, jut out.

amenable, easy to lead. (F. — L.) From F. *amener*, to lead to, bring to. — F. *a*, to ; *mener*, to conduct, drive. — L. *ad*, to ; Low L. *minare*, to conduct, lead about, also to drive out, chase away. — L. *minari*, to threaten. — L. *minæ*, threats (above).

commination, a threatening, denouncing. (F. — L.) F. *commination.* — L. acc. *comminationem*, a threatening. — L. *comminatus*, pp. of *com-minari*, to threaten.

demean (1), to conduct; *reflex.*, to behave. (F. — L.) M. E. *demenen.* — O. F. *demener*, to conduct, guide, manage. — O. F. *de* (= L. *de*), down, fully; *mener*, to conduct; see **amenable** (above).

demean (2), to debase, lower. (F. — L.) The same word as the above; but altered in sense owing to an obvious (but absurd) popular etymology which allied the word to E. *mean*, base.

demeanour. (F. – L.) M. E. *demenure* (15th cent.); a coined word, from M. E. *demenen*, to demean, behave; see **demean** (1).

mien, look. (F. – Ital. – L.) F. *mine*, 'the look;' Cot. – Ital. *mina* (Scheler, Littré), the same as O. Ital. *mena*, 'behauiour, fashion, carriage of a man;' Florio. – Low L. *minare*, Ital. *menare*, to lead, conduct. – L. *minari*, to threaten; see **amenable** (above).

mine (2), to excavate. (F. – L.) F. *miner*. – Low L. *minare*, to lead, conduct; hence to follow up a lode, or vein of ore; see **mien** (above).

mineral. (F. – L.) F. *mineral*, 'a minerall;' Cot. – F. *miner*, to mine (above). Cf. Span. *minera*, a mine.

promenade, a walk. (F. – L.) Formed with Prov. suffix *-ade* (= L. *-ata*) from O. F. *promener*, to walk. – Low L. *prominare*, to drive forwards. – L. *pro*, forwards; Low L. *minare*, to drive, lead; see **mien** (above).

Menagerie; see **Mansion**.

Mend; see **Emendation**.

Mendacity. (L.) From L. *mendacitas*, falsehood. – L. *mendaci-*, crude form of *mendax*, false, allied to *mentiri*, to lie, orig. to think out, devise; cf. *commentum*, a device. Allied to **Mental**.

Mendicant, a beggar. (L.) L. *mendicant-*, stem of pres. pt. of *mendicare*, to beg. – L. *mendicus*, beggarly, poor.

Menial; see **Mansion**.

Meniver, Miniver, a fur; see **Various**.

Menses. (L.) L. *menses*, monthly discharges; pl. of *mensis*, a month. Allied to **Month**. (√MA.)

menstruous. (L.) L. *menstruus*, monthly. – L. *mensis*, a month.

menstruum. (L.) Low L. *menstruum*, a solvent; a word in alchemy; from the notion of some connection of its action with the phases of the moon.

Mensuration; see **Measure**.

Mental. (F. – L.) F. *mental*. – Low L. *mentalis*, mental. – L. *ment-*, stem of *mens*, mind. (√MAN.)

comment. (F. – L.) F. *commenter*. – L. *commentari*, to consider, make a note on. – L. *commentus*, pp. of *comminisci*, to devise. – L. *com-* (= *cum*), with; *-min-*, to think, as in *me-min-i*, I remember, and allied to *mens*, mind.

demented, mad. (L.) Pp. of the old verb to *dement*. – L. *dementire*, to be out of one's senses. – L. *de*, from; *menti-*, crude form of *mens*, mind.

memento, a memorial. (L.) L. *memento* (Luke, xxiii. 42), remember me; imp. of *memini*, I remember, from the base *-min-*, to think.

mention, a notice. (F. – L.) F. *mention*. – L. acc. *mentionem*. – L. *menti-*, crude form of *mens*, mind.

Mentor, an adviser. (Gk.) Gk. Μέντωρ, Mentor (Homer, Od. ii.); the sense is 'adviser,' and it is equivalent to L. *monitor*. See **Monition**.

Mephitis, a pestilential exhalation. (L.) L. *mephitis* (Virgil).

Mercantile, Mercenary; see **Merit**.

Mercer, Merchant; see **Merit**.

Mercury, Mercy; see **Merit**.

Mere (1), a lake. (E.) M. E. *mere*. A. S. *mere*, a lake. + Du. *meer*; Icel. *marr*, sea; G. *meer*, lake; Goth. *marei*, Russ. *moré*, Lithuan. *marés*, W. *môr*, Gael. Irish *muir*, L. *mare*, sea. The orig. sense is 'dead,' hence a pool of stagnant water, also the waste of ocean; cf. Skt. *maru*, desert, from *mri*, to die. Allied to **Mortal**.

marish, a marsh. (F. – O. Low G.) O. F. *maresqs*, *marez*, a marsh; Low L. *mariscus*. [We also find M. E. *marais*, a marsh; Low L. *marensis*.] – Low G. *marsch*, a marsh, cognate with E. *marsh* (below).

marsh, a swamp. (E.) M. E. *mersch*. A. S. *mersc*, a marsh; short for *mer-isc*, lit. mere-ish, i.e. full of meres or pools. – A. S. *mere*, a mere, lake.

meerschaum, a substance used for making pipes. (G.) G. *meerschaum*, lit. sea-foam (because it is white and light). – G. *meer*, lake, sea; *schaum*, foam, lit. scum; see **Scum**.

mermaid. (E.) M. E. *mermaid*. – A. S. *mere*, lake; *mægden*, maiden.

Mere (2), pure, simple. (L.) L. *merus*, pure, unmixed (as wine). Allied to Skt. *marichi*, a ray of light. (√MAR, to shine.)

Meretricious; see **Merit**.

Merge, to sink, plunge under water. (L.) L. *mergere*, to dip. + Skt. *majj*, to dip, bathe.

emerge, to rise from the sea, appear. (L.) L. *e-mergere*, to rise out.

immerge, to plunge into. (L.) L. *immergere* (pp. *im-mersus*), to plunge into. Der. *immers-ion*.

submerge, to plunge under water. (F. — L.) F. *submerger.* — L. *submergere.*

Meridian; see **Medium.**

Merino; see **Magnitude.**

Merit, excellence, worth. (F. — L.) M. E. *merite.* — O. F. *merite.* — L. *meritum*, a thing deserved; orig. neut. of *meritus*, pp. of *merere*, to deserve, orig. 'to receive as a share;' allied to Gk. μέρος, a share, μείρομαι, I receive a share.

amerce, to fine. (F. — L.) O. F. *amercier*, to fine. — O. F. *a* (= L. *ad*), to; *mercier*, to pay, acquit, but usually to thank; cf. Low L. *merciare*, to fix a fine. — O. F. *mercit* (F. *merci*), thanks, pardon. — L. *mercedem*, acc. of *merces*, reward, wages, also detriment, trouble, pains, (passing into the sense of 'fine'). — L. *merc-*, stem of *merx*, merchandise, traffic. — L. *merere*, to gain, buy, purchase.

commerce, traffic. (F. — L.) F. *commerce.* — L. *commercium*, trade. — L. *com-* (= *cum*), with; *merci-*, crude form of *merx*, merchandise (above).

demerit, ill desert. (F. — L.) Also merit, in a *good* sense; Cor. i. 1. 276. — O. F. *demerite*, desert; also a fault, demerit. — Low L. *demeritum*, a fault; from pp. of Low L. *demerere*, to deserve (in a *good* sense). — L. *de*, fully; *merere*, to deserve.

market. (F. — L.) O. F. *market**, not recorded; also *markiet*, *marchet*; (F. *marché.*) Cf. Prov. *mercatz*, Ital. *mercato*, a market. — L. *mercatus*, traffic, also a market (whence G. *markt*. &c.) — L. *mercatus*, pp. of *mercari*, to trade; see **mercantile** (below).

mart, a shortened form of *market*. (F. — L.) In Hamlet i. 1. 74. Prob. influenced by Du. *markt*, market (of Latin origin). See above.

mercantile, commercial. (F. — L.) F. *mercantil*, 'merchantly;' Cot. — Low L. *mercantilis.* — L. *mercant-*, stem of pres. pt. of *mercari*, to trade. — L. *merc-*, stem of *merx*, merchandise. — L. *mer-ere*, to gain, buy, purchase; see **Merit.**

mercenary. (F. — L.) F. *mercenaire.* — L. *mercenarius*, older form *mercennarius*, a hireling. Put for *merced-narius**; from *merced-*, crude form of *merces*, pay; see **amerce** (above).

mercer. (F. — L.) F. *mercier*, lit. 'a trader.' — Low L. *mercerius*, a trader. — L. *merc-*, stem of *merx*, merchandise.

merchandise. (F. — L.) M. E. *mar-*

chandise. — F. *marchandise*, merchant's wares. — F. *marchand*, a merchant (below).

merchant. (F. — L.) M. E. *marchant.* — O. F. *marchant* (F. *marchand*). — L. *mercant-*, stem of pres. pt. of *mercari*, to trade; see **mercantile** (above).

mercury, quicksilver. (F. — L.) M. E. *mercurie*, quicksilver, named after the planet Mercury. — O. F. *Mercurie* (a Norman form); F. *mercure.* — L. *Mercurium*, acc. of *Mercurius*, Mercury, god of traffic. — L. *merc-*, stem of *merx*, merchandise.

mercy. (F. — L.) F. *merci*; O. F. *mercit.* — L. *mercedem*, acc. of *merces*; see **amerce** (above).

meretricious, alluring by false show. (L.) L. *meretricius*, pertaining to a courtesan. — L. *meretrici-*, crude form of *meretrix*, a courtesan. — L. *merere*, to gain, receive hire.

Merle, a blackbird. (F. — L.) O. F. *merle.* — L. *merula*, a blackbird.

merlin, a kind of hawk. (F. — L.?) M. E. *merlion.* — O. F. *esmerillon*, *emerillon*, 'the hawk termed a marlin;' Cot. Cf. Ital. *smerlo*, a kind of hawk. Prob. from L. *merula*, a blackbird; the initial *s* being unoriginal (Diez).

Mermaid; see **Mere** (1).

Merry. (C.) M. E. *merie.* A. S. *merg*, merry. Not a Teutonic word. — Irish and Gael. *mear*, merry, sportive. — Gael. *mir*, to play, sport; cf. Gael. *mireagach*, merry, playful.

mirth. (C.) M. E. *mirthe.* A. S. *myrgð*, *mirhð*, *mirigð*, mirth. — A. S. *merg*, merry; of Celtic origin (as above).

Mesentery. (L. — Gk.) L. *mesenterium.* — Gk. μεσεντέριον, a membrane in the midst of the intestines. — Gk. μέσ-ος, middle, cognate with L. *medius*, ἔντερον, entrail. See **Mid** and **Entrail.**

Mesh, the opening between the threads of a net. (E.) M. E. *maske.* A. S. *max* (= *masc**, by the common interchange of *sc* and *cs = x*); cf. A. S. *mæscre*, a mesh, dimin. form. + Du. *maas*, Icel. *möskvi*, Dan. *maske*, Swed. *maska*, G. *masche*, W. *masg.* Orig. sense 'a knot,' from the knots in a net; cf. Lithuan. *mazgas*, a knot, *mazgtas*, a knitting-needle, allied to *megsti*, verb (pres. t. *mezg-u*), to knot, weave nets.

Mesmerise, to operate on the nervous system of a patient. (G.) Named from *Mesmer*, a German physician (about 1766).

Mess (1), a portion of food; see **Missile.**

Mess (2), a mixture; see **Mash.**

Message, Messenger; see **Missile**.

Messiah, the anointed one. (Heb.) Heb. *máshíakh*, anointed. — Heb. *máshakh*, to anoint.

Messuage; see **Mansion**.

Meta-, prefix. (Gk.) Gk. μέτα, prep., among, with, after; as a prefix, it commonly signifies 'change.' **+** Goth. *mith*, A. S. *mid*, G. *mit*, with.

Metal. (F. – L. – Gk.) M. E. *metal*. – O. F. *metal*. – L. *metallum*, a mine, metal. – Gk. μέταλλον, a cave, mine, mineral, metal. Allied to μεταλλάω, I search after, explore. β. The prefix is μετ-ά, after; the base ἀλ- in ἀλ-λάω is supposed to be identical with the base ἐρ- in ἔρ-χομαι, I go, come; from √ AR, to go. Cf. Skt. *ri* (for *ar*), to go, meet; *richchha* or *archchha*, to go. The orig. sense was prob. 'a place to go about in,' a gallery or mine; later, a mineral.

medal. (F. – Ital. – L. – Gk.) O. F. *medaille*. – Ital. *medaglia*; Low L. *medalia*, *medalla*, a small coin. – L. *metallum*, metal (above).

metallurgy, a working in metals. (F. – L. – Gk.) O. F. *metallurgie*. – Low L. *metallurgia** (not recorded, but it must have existed as a transcription from the Gk.). – Gk. μεταλλουργός, adj., working in metals. – Gk. μέταλλο-ν, metal; ἔργον, work; see **Work**. ¶ L. *u* = Gk. *ov* = *oe*.

mettle, spirit, ardour. (F. – L. – Gk.) Another spelling of *metal*; in Shakespeare, no distinction is made between the two words in old editions, either in spelling or in use (Schmidt). With special allusion to the *metal* (or *mettle*) of a sword-blade.

Metamorphosis; see **Amorphous**.

Metaphor. (F. – L. – Gk.) F. *metaphore*, 'a metaphor;' Cot. – L. *metaphora*. – Gk. μεταφορά, a transferring of a word from its literal signification. – Gk. μεταφέρειν, to transfer. – Gk. μετά, signifying 'change;' φέρειν, to bear; see **Bear** (1).

Metaphrase; see **Phrase**.

Metaphysics; see **Physic**.

Metathesis; see **Theme**.

Mete, to measure. (E.) M. E. *meten*. A. S. *metan*, to measure. **+** Du. *meten*, Icel. *meta* (to value), Swed. *mäta*, Goth. *mitan*, G. *messen*. Cf. L. *modus*, measure, *metiri*, to measure, Skt. *má*, to measure. (√ MA.)

meet (1), fit. M. E. *mete*. A. S. *gemet*, meet, fit (the prefix *ge-* making no difference). – A. S. *metan*, to mete (above). **+** G. *mässig*, frugal; from *messen*, to mete.

Metempsychosis; see **Psychical**.

Meteor. (F. – Gk.) O. F. *vneteore*, 'a meteor;' Cot. – Gk. μετέωρον, a meteor; neut. of adj. μετέωρος, raised above the earth, soaring in air. – Gk. μετ-ά, among; ἐώρα, αἰώρα, anything suspended, from ἀείρειν, to lift.

Metheglin; see **Mead** (1).

Methinks; see **Think**.

Method. (F. – L. – Gk.) O. F. *methode*, 'a method;' Cot. – L. *methodus*. – Gk. μέθοδος, an enquiry into, method, system. – Gk. μεθ-, for μετ-ά, among, after; ὁδός, a way: the lit. sense is 'a way after,' a following after. (√ SAD.)

Metonymy; see **Onomatopoeia**.

Metre, Meter, rhythm, verse. (F. – L. – Gk.) M. E. *metre*. – F. *metre*, 'meeter;' Cot. – L. *metrum*. – Gk. μέτρον, that by which anything is measured, a rule, metre. Lit. 'measure;' cf. Skt. *má*, to measure. (√ MA.) Der. *baro-meter*, *chrono-meter*, *geo-metry*, *hexa-meter*, *hydro-meter*, *hygro-meter*, *penta-meter*, *thermo-meter*, *trigono-metry*, *tri-meter*, &c.

diameter, the line measuring the breadth across or thickness through. (F. – L. – Gk.) O. F. *diametre*, 'a diameter;' Cot. – L. *diametros*. – Gk. διάμετρος. – Gk. διά, through; μετρεῖν, to measure, from μέτρον, a measure.

perimeter, lit. 'the measure all round.' (L. – Gk.) L. *perimetros*. – Gk. περίμετρος. – Gk. περί, round; μέτρον, a measure.

symmetry. (F. – L. – Gk.) F. *symmetrie*; Cot. – L. *symmetria*. – Gk. συμμετρία, due proportion. – Gk. σύμμετρος, of like measure with. – Gk. συμ- (= σύν), with; μέτρον, a measure.

Metropolis, a mother city. (L. – Gk.) L. *metropolis*. – Gk. μητρόπολις, a mother-state; the city of a primate. – Gk. μήτρο-, for μήτηρ, a mother; πόλις, a city. See **Mother** and **Police**.

Mettle; see **Metal**.

Mew (1), to cry as a cat. (E.) M. E. *mawen*; a word of imitative origin. **+** Pers. *maw*, Arab. *mua*, mewing of a cat. Der. *mewl*, from F. *miauler*, to mew.

mew (2), a sea-gull. (E.) M. E. *mawe*. A. S. *mǽw*, a mew. **+** Du. *meeuw*, Icel. *már*, Dan. *maage*, Swed. *måke*, G. *möwe*. From the *mew* or cry of the bird.

Mew (3), a cage for hawks, &c.; **Mews**, pl. of *mew*; see **Mutable**.

Mewl; see **Mew** (1).

Mews; see **Mutable**.

Mezzotinto; see **Medium**.

Miasma, pollution, infectious matter. (Gk.) Gk. μίασμα, a stain. — Gk. μιαίνειν, to stain.

Mica, a glittering mineral. (L.) *'Mica,* a crum, little quantity of anything that breaks off; also, a glimmer, or cat-silver, a metallick body like silver, which shines in marble,'&c.; Phillips (1706). — L. *mīca,* a crumb; cf. F. and Span. *mica,* mica. But it seems to have been applied to the metal from a notion that this sb. is related to L. *mīcare,* to shine, which is not the case.

Mich, to skulk, play truant. (F.) M. E. *michen;* also *moochen, mouchen.* — O. F. *mucer, mucier,* later *musser,* to hide, conceal (hence to skulk). Origin unknown. Der. *mich-er, mich-ing* (Shak.); also *cur-mudgeon,* q. v.

Michaelmas, the feast of St. Michael. (F. — Heb.; *and* L.) M. E. *michelmesse;* where *Michel* = F. *Michel,* from Heb. *Mikhdel,* lit. 'who is like unto God?' The suffix *-mas* = M. E. *messe* = A. S. *mæsse;* from L. *missa*; see mass (2), s. v. **Missile**.

Mickle, great; see **May** (1).

Microcosm, a little world. (F. — L. — Gk.) F. *microcosme.* — L. *microcosmus.* — Gk. μικρόκοσμος, a little world. — Gk. μικρό-s, little, for σμικρός, little; κόσμος, world; see **Cosmetic**.

microscope, an instrument for viewing small objects. (Gk.) Gk. μικρό-s, little; σκοπ-εῖν, to see; see **Scope**.

Mid, middle. (E.) M. E. *mid.* A. S. *mid, midd,* adj. + Du. Dan. Swed. *mid-* (in compounds); Icel. *miðr,* Goth. *midja,* O. H. G. *mitti,* L. *medius,* Gk. μέσος, Æolic μέσσος, Skt. *mádhya,* adj., middle. (Base MADHYA, from MADH-.) See also **Medium**.

amid, amidst, in the middle of. (E.) *Amids-t* is lengthened from M. E. *amiddes.* Again, *amidde-s* was due to adding the adv. suffix *-s* to *amidde* = A. S. *on middan,* in the middle; where *middan* is the dat. of *midde,* sb., the middle. — A. S. *mid, midd,* adj., middle. *Amid* = A.S. *on middan* (as before).

middle, adj., intervening; also as sb. (E.) M. E. *middel,* adj.; *middel,* sb. A.S. *middel,* sb. — A.S. *midd,* adj., middle; with suffix *-el* = Aryan *-ra.* + Du. *middel,* adj. adv. and sb.; G. *mittel,* sb., means; O. H. G. *mittil,* adj. Cf. Icel. *meðal,* prep. among. Der. *middl-ing*; *middle-most,* an ill-coined

superlative, on the model of *after-most, foremost.*

midriff, the diaphragm separating the heart from the stomach, &c. (E.) M. E. *midrif.* A. S. *midrif* (for *midhrif*). — A. S. *mid,* middle; *hrif,* the belly. + O. Fries. *midref*; from *mid,* middle, *ref, rif,* the belly.

midship, short for *amid-ship*; hence *midship-man.*

midst, the middle. (E.) *In middest,* Spenser, F. Q. vi. 3. 25; formed, with added *t,* from M. E. *in middes,* equivalent to *amiddes*; see amid (above).

midwife. (E.) M. E. *midwif*; rarely *medewif,* from a false etymology which connected it with M. E. *mede* or *meed,* reward. — A. S. *mid,* prep., together with; *wíf,* a woman. Thus the lit. sense 'a woman who is with another,' a helper. Cf. A. S. *mid-wyrcan,* to work with. So also Span. *co-madre,* lit. 'co-mother,' a midwife. Cf. Du. *medehelpen,* to assist (from *mede,* with, *helpen,* to help); G. *mithelfer,* a helper with, assistant.

Middle; see **Mid**.

Midge. (E.) M. E. *migge, mygge.* A.S. *micge,* properly *mycge,* a midge, gnat + Du. *mug,* Low G. *mugge,* Swed. *mygg,* Dan. *myg,* Icel. *mý,* G. *mücke.* Teut. type MUG-YA, prob. 'buzzer;' cf. L. *mug-ire,* to low; Gk. μύζειν, to mutter; Skt. *muj,* to sound. ¶ Distinct from L. *musca,* a fly.

mugwort, a flower. (E.) A. S. *mucg-wort,* i. e. midge-wort. (Cf. *flea-bane.*)

Midriff, Midst, Midwife; see **Mid**.

Mien; see **Menace**.

Might (1), strength; see **May** (1).

Might (2), pt. t. of **May** (1), q. v.

Mignonette; see **Mind**.

Migrate. (L.) From pp. of L. *migrare,* to wander; allied to *meare,* to go.

emigrate. (L.) From pp. of L. *e-migrare,* to wander forth.

immigrate. (L.) From pp. of L. *im-migrare,* to migrate to. (*Im-* = *in,* in.)

transmigration. (F. — L.) F. *trans-migration.* — L. acc. *transmigrationem,* orig. a removing from one country to another. — L. *trans-migrare,* to migrate across.

Milch; see **Milk**.

Mild. (E.) M. E. *mild, milde.* A. S. *milde.* + Du. *mild,* Icel. *mildr,* Dan. Swed. G. *mild*; Goth. *milds,* only in *un-milds,* without natural affection. Allied to Lithuan. *melas,* dear, Russ. *miluii,* amiable, kind, *miloste,* kindness, Gk. μείλιχος, mild, Skt.

mᵣilámi, I am gracious, mᵣilíkam, pity. (Base MARL.)

Mildew; see **Mellifluous.**

Mile. (L.) M. E. *mile.* A. S. *mil.* — L. pl. *milia,* commonly *millia,* a Roman mile. — L. *mille,* sing., a thousand; whence *mille passuum,* a thousand paces, a Roman mile.

billion; see **million** (below).

milfoil, yarrow. (F. — L.) Lit. 'thousand-leaf.' — F. *mille,* thousand; *feuille,* leaf. — Low L. *millefolium,* milfoil; L *mille,* thousand; *folium,* leaf; see **Foil** (2).

millennium, a thousand years. (L.) L. *millennium.* — L. *mille,* thousand; *annus,* year; see **Annual.**

million, a thousand thousand. (F. — L.) F. *million*; Low L. *millio,* lit. ' great thousand,' an augmentative form. — L. *mille,* thousand. **Der.** Hence *b-illion, tr-illion, quadr-illion* are formed, by a sort of analogy, in order to express shortly the ideas of *bi-million, tri-million,* &c.

Milfoil; see **Mile.**

Militate, to contend. (L.) From pp. of L. *militare,* to serve as a soldier. — L. *milit-,* stem of *miles,* a soldier.

militia, troops. (L.) L. *militia,* (1) warfare, (2) troops. — L. *milit-,* stem of *miles,* a soldier.

Milk. (E.) M. E. *milk.* A. S. *meolc, meoluc* (put for *milc* *). + Du. *melk,* Icel. *mjólk,* Dan. *melk,* Swed. *mjölk,* Goth. *miluks,* G. *milch.* Teut. type MELKI; from the base MALK, to stroke, preserved in G. *molk,* pt. t. of *melken,* to stroke a cow, milk; allied to Gk. ἀμέλγειν, L. *mulgere,* to milk, Skt. *mrij,* to wipe, rub, stroke. (√ MARG.)

milch, milk-giving. (Scand.) Icel. *milkr, mjólkr,* adj., milk-giving; from *mjólk,* milk. So also G. *melk,* adj., milch.

milksop, an effeminate man. (E.) M.E. *milksoppe,* Ch. C. T. 13916. Lit. ' bread sopped in milk;' hence a soft fellow. — M. E. *milk,* milk; *soppe,* a sop; see **Sop.**

milt (2), soft roe. (Scand.) A corruption of *milk,* due to confusion with *milt* (1). — Swed. *mjölke,* milt, from *mjölk,* milk ; Dan. *fiskemelk,* soft roe of fishes, lit. ' fish-milk.'

Mill; see **Molar.**

Millennium; see **Mile.**

Millet, a plant. (F. — L.) F. *millet.* — L. *milium,* millet (whence A.S. *mil,* millet). + Gk. μελίνη, millet.

Milliner. (Ital. ?) Formerly also *millaner.* Disputed; but almost certainly

Milaner, a dealer in goods brought from *Milan,* in Italy.

Million; see **Mile.**

Milt (1), the spleen; see **Melt.**

Milt (2), soft roe; see **Milk.**

Mimic. (L. — Gk.) L. *mimicus,* farcical. — Gk. μιμικός, imitative. — Gk. μῖμος, an imitator, actor, mime. (√ MA.)

Minaret, a turret on a mosque. (Span. — Arab.) Span. *minarete,* a high slender turret. — Arab. *manárat,* a lamp, lighthouse, minaret. — Arab. *manár,* candle-stick, lamp, light-house. Allied to Arab. *nár,* fire. + Heb. *manóráh,* a candle-stick; from *núr,* to shine.

Mince, to cut up small. (E.) A. S. *minsian,* lit. to be small; hence to make small. — A. S. *min,* small. + Du. *min,* less; L. *min-or,* less. See **Minor.** ¶ We also find F. *mincer,* to mince, from *mince,* small, of Teut. origin. The F. word no doubt affected the E. one; the root is the same either way. **Der.** *mince-pie,* formerly *minced-pie,* i. e. pie of minced meat.

minnow, a small fish. (E.) M. E. *menow.* A. S. *myne,* a minnow. — A. S. *min,* small. ¶ We find another form, viz. M. E. *menuse,* a small fish; from O. F. *menuise,* small fish, due to L. *minutus,* minute, small. The root is the same either way.

Mind. (E.) M. E. *mind.* A. S. *gemynd,* memory. — A. S. *munan,* to think; *gemunan,* to remember (whence *gemynd* by the usual change of *u* to *y*). + Icel. *minni* (for *mindi* *), memory, Dan. *minde,* Goth. *gamunds,* memory. Allied to L. *mens* (stem *ment-*), mind; see **Mental.** (√ MAN.)

mignonette, a plant. (F. — G.) F. *mignonette,* dimin. of *mignon,* darling; see **minion** (below).

minikin, a little darling. (Du.) Used by Florio, to translate Ital. *mignone.* Du. *minnekyn,* a cupid (Sewel); O. Du. *minneken,* my darling, dimin. of *minne,* love (Hexham). + O. H. G. *minna,* love (see below).

minion, a favourite. (F. — O. H. G.) F. *mignon,* sb., a favourite. — F. *mignon,* adj., minion, dainty, also pleasing, kind. — M. H. G. *minne,* O. H. G. *minne,* memory, love (whence *minnesinger* = singer of love). Closely allied to E. *mind.*

minx, a pert wanton woman. (Low G.) Not from *minikin,* as I once thought ; but = Low G. *minsk,* (1) masc. a man, (2) neut. a pert female. Cf. G. *mensch.*

remind, to bring to mind again. (L. *and* E.) From **Re-** and **Mind**.

Mine (1), belonging to me ; see **Me**.

Mine (2), to excavate ; see **Menace**.

Mineral ; see **Menace**.

Minever, Miniver ; see **Various**.

Mingle, to mix. (E.) A frequentative form of *ming*, to mix (Surrey) ; M. E. *mengen, mingen*, to mix. A. S. *mengan*, to mix, to become mixed ; a causal verb. — A. S. *mang*, a mixture, usually *gemang, gemong*, a mixture, crowd, assembly.+Du. *mengelen*, to mingle, from *mengen*, to mix ; Icel. *menga*, G. *mengen*, to mingle. Prob. allied to **Many**.

among, amongst. (E.) The earliest M. E. form is *amonge*, whence *amonges* with added *s* (a common adverbial suffix) ; and hence *amongs-t* with excrescent *t*. — A. S. *onmang*, prep., among. — A. S. *on*, In ; *mang*, a mixture, crowd (above).

monger, a dealer, trader. (E.) Hence *iron-monger, coster-monger*. M. E. *monger*, A. S. *mangere*, a dealer, merchant. — A. S. *mangian*, to traffic, lit. ' to deal in a mixture of things ; ' variant of *mengan*, to mix. — A. S. *mang*, a mixture. Cf. Du. *mangelen*, to barter.

mongrel, an animal of a mixed breed. (E.) Spelt *mungril* in Levins (1570). It stands for *mong-er-el**, i. e. a small animal of mixed breed ; cf. *cock-er-el, pick-er-el* (small pike). — A. S. *mang*, a mixture.

Miniature, a small painting. (Ital. — L.) Ital. *miniatura*, a miniature. — Ital. *miniato*, pp. of *miniare*, to dye, paint, ' to colour or limne with vermilion or red lead ; ' Florio. — L. *minium*, cinnabar, red lead ; said to be of Iberian origin.

Minikin ; see **Mind**.

Minim ; see **Minor**.

Minion ; see **Mind**.

Minish, Minister ; see **Minor**.

Miniver ; see **Various**.

Minnow ; see **Mince**.

Minor, less. (L.) L. *min-or*, less ; the positive form occurs in A. S. *min*, Irish *min*, small. + Icel. *minnr*, Goth. *minniza*, less. (✓ MI.) See **Mince**.

administer. (L.) L. *administrare*, to minister to. — L. *ad*, to ; *ministrare*, to serve, from *minister*, a servant ; see minister (below).

comminution, a reduction to small fragments. (L.) Formed from L. *comminutus*, pp. of *com-minuere*, to break into small pieces ; see minute (below).

diminish, to lessen. (F. — L.) Coined from L. *di-* (=*dis*), apart, and E. *minish* ; in imitation of L. *diminuere*, to diminish (below).

diminution. (F. — L.) F. *diminution*. — L. acc. *diminutionem*, diminution. — L. *diminutus*, pp. of *diminuere*, to lessen. — L. *di-* (=*dis*), apart ; *minuere*, to lessen.

minim, a note in music ; $\frac{1}{60}$th of a drachm (F. — L.). O. F. *minime*, lit. very small. — L. *min-ima*, very small ; superl. allied to *min-or*, less (above).

minish, to lessen. (F. — L.) M. E. *menusen*. — F. *menuiser*, to minish (answering to Low L. *minutiare**). — L. *minutus*, small ; see minute (below).

minister. (F. — L.) M. E. *ministre*. — F. *ministre*. — L. acc. *ministrum* ; nom. *minister*, a servant. L. *min-is-ter* is a double comparative form (Aryan *min-yans-tara**) from the base *min-*, small ; see **Minor** (above).

minstrel. (F. — L.) M. E. *ministral*, or *menestral*. — O. F. *menestrel, menestral*. — Low L. *ministralis*, a servant, retainer, hence one who played instruments or acted as jester. — L. *minister*, a servant (above). **Der.** *minstrel-cy*, M. E. *minstralcie*.

minuet, a dance. (F. — L.) So called from the small steps taken in it. — F. *menuet*, ' smallish, little, pretty ; ' Cot. Dimin. of F. *menu*, small. — L. *minutus* ; see minute (below).

minus, less. (L.) Neut. of *minor*, less.

minute. (L.) M. E. *minute*, sb. — L. *minuta*, a small part ; orig. fem. of *minutus*, small, pp. of *minuere*, to make small. — L. *min-*, small ; base of *min-or*, less.

mystery (2), **mistery**, a trade, handicraft. (F. — L.) The *mystery plays* (better spelt *mistery plays*) were so called because acted by craftsmen ; from M. E. *mistere*, a trade, craft, Ch. C. T. 615. — O. F. *mestier*, a trade, occupation (F. *métier*). — L. *ministerium*, employment. — L. *minister*, a servant ; see minister (above).

Minster ; see **Mono-**.

Minstrel ; see **Minor**.

Mint (1), a place where money is coined ; see **Monition**.

Mint (2), a plant. (L. — Gk.) A. S. *minte*. — L. *menta, mentha*. — Gk. μίνθα, mint.

Minuet, Minus, Minute ; see **Minor**.

Minx ; see **Mind**.

Miocene, less recent. (Gk.) Gk. μείο-, for μείων, less ; καιν-ός, new, recent.

Miracle. (F. – L.) F. *miracle.* – L.
miraculum, a wonder. – L. *mirari*, to
wonder at. – L. *mirus*, wonderful. **+** Skt.
smaya, wonder, from *smi*, to smile. Allied
to **Smile**.

admire. (F. – L.) F. *admirer.* – L. *ad-
mirari*, to wonder at. – L. *ad*, at; *mirari*,
to wonder (above).

marvel. (F. – L.) M. E. *mervaile.* –
F. *merveille*. – L. *mirabilia*, neut. pl.
wonderful things. – L. *mirabilis*, wonderful.
– L. *mirari*, to wonder (above).

mirage. (F. – L.) F. *mirage*, an optical illusion. – F. *mirer*, to look at. – L.
mirari (above).

mirror. (F. – L.) M. E. *mirour.* –
O. F. *mireör*, later *miroir*, a looking-glass,
mirror (answering to a Low L. *miratorium*).
– Low L. *mirare*, to behold; L. *mirari*.

Mirage; see **Miracle**.

Mire. (Scand.); see **Moss**.

Mirror; see **Miracle**.

Mirth; see **Merry**.

Mis- (1), prefix. (E. *and* Scand.) The
A. S. *mis-* occurs in *mis-dĕd*, a mis-deed,
and in other compounds. It answers to
Du. Dan. Icel. *mis-*, Swed. G. *miss-*, Goth.
missa-, with the sense of 'wrong.' Allied
to **Miss** (1). Der. *mis-become*, *-behave*,
-believe, *-deed*, *-deem*, *-do*, *-give*, *-lay*, *-lead*,
-like, *-name*, *-shape*, *-time*, *-understand*.
Also prefixed to words of F. and L. origin,
as in *mis-apply*, *-calculate*, *-carry*, *-conceive*,
-conduct, *-construe*, *-date*, *-demeanour*, *-em-
ploy*, *-fortune*, *-govern*, *-guide*, *-inform*,
-interpret, *-judge*, *-place*, *-print*, *-pronounce*,
-quote, *-represent*, *-rule*, *-spend*, *-term*, *-use*,
&c. Also to Scand. words, as in *mis-call*,
-hap, *-take*.

Mis- (2), prefix. (F. – L.) The proper
spelling is M. E. *mes-*, as in *mes-chief*,
mischief. The same as O. F. *mes-*, Span.
menos-, from L. *minus*, less; with the
sense of 'bad.' Frequently confused with
the prefix above both in F. and E. Der.
mis-adventure (q. v.), *-alliance*, *-chance* (q.
v.), *-chief* (q. v.), *-count* (q. v.), *-creant*
(q. v.), *-nomer* (q. v.), *-prise* (q. v.)

Misadventure. (F. – L.) O. F. *mesa-
venture*; see **Mis-** (2) and **Adventure**.

Misanthrope. (Gk.) Gk. μισάνθρωπος,
adj. hating mankind. – Gk. μισ-εῖν, to hate,
from μῖσ-ος, hatred; ἄνθρωπος, a man. Der.
misanthrop-ic, *-ist*, *-y* (Gk. μισανθρωπία).

Miscellaneous, various. (L.) L. *mis-
cellaneus*. – L. *miscellus*, mixed. – L.
miscere, to mix. Allied to **Mix**.

meddle. (F. – L.) M. E. *medlen*, simply in the sense 'to mix.' – O. F. *medler*,
meller, *mesler*, to mix. (F. *mêler*). – Low
L. *misculare*, to mix; cf. L. *miscellus*,
mixed. – L. *miscere*, to mix.

medley, confusion, mixture. (F. – L.)
M. E. *medlee*. – O. F. *medle*, *melle*, *mesle*,
(fem. *medlee*, *mellee*, *meslee*), pp. of the
verb *medler* (above). The fem. form
medlee = F. *mêlée*.

promiscuous, mixed, confused. (L.)
L. *promiscuus*, mixed. – L. *pro-*, forward
(here of slight force); *miscere*, to mix.

Mischance. (F. – L.) M. E. and O. F.
meschance; from **Mis-** (2) and **Chance**.

Mischief. (F. – L.) M. E. *meschief.* –
O. F. *meschief*, a bad result. Cf. Span.
menos-cabo, diminution, loss. From **Mis-**
(2) and **Chief**.

Miscount. (F. – L.) O. F. *mesconter*;
from **Mis-** (2) and **Count**.

Miscreant, a wretch. (F. – L.) Orig.
an unbeliever, infidel. – O. F. *mescreant*,
misbelieving;' Cot. Here *mes-* = . L.
minus; see **Mis-** (2). *Creant* is from L.
credent-, stem of pres. pt. of *credere*, to
believe. Cf. Ital. *miscredente*, misbelieving;
and E. *re-creant*.

Miser, a niggard. (L.) Also 'a wretch;'
Spenser, F. Q. ii. 1. 8. – L. *miser*, wretched.
Cf. Ital. and Span. *misero* (1) wretched, (2)
avaricious.

commiseration. (F. – L.) F. *commiseration.* – L. acc. *commiserationem*, part of
an oration intended to excite pity. – L.
commiserari, to excite pity. – L. *com-*
(= *cum*), with; *miserari*, to pity. – L.
miser.

miserable. (F. – L.) F. *miserable.* –
L. *miserabilis*, pitiable. – L. *miserari*, to
pity. – L. *miser*, wretched.

Mishap; see **Hap**.

Misnomer, a misnaming. (F. – L.) It
answers to an old Law-French *mesnommer*,
to misname; used as a sb. with the sense
'a misnaming.' – O. F. *mes-*, badly; *nommer*, to name. See **Mis-** (2) and **Noun**.

Misprise, **Misprize**, to slight. (F. –
L.) In As You Like It, i. 1. 177. –
O. F. *mespriser*, 'to disesteem, contemn;'
Cot. – O. F. *mes-*, badly; Low L. *pretiare*,
to prize, esteem, from L. *pretium*, price.
See **Mis-** (2) and **Price**.

Misprision, a mistake, neglect. (F. – L.)
O. F. *mesprison*, 'misprision, error, offence;'
Cot. Cf. F. *méprise*, a mistake. – O. F.
mes-, badly, ill; Low L. *prensionem*, acc.

of *prensio* (short for L. *prehensio*), a seizing,
taking, apprehending, from L. *prehendere*;
to take. ¶ Quite distinct from *misprise*.
Miss (1), to fail to hit. (E.) M. E.
missen. A. S. *missian* (or *missan*), to
escape one's notice (rare); from an old sb.
misse*, signifying 'failure' or 'error,' which
is still preserved in the prefix *mis*-, wrong;
see **Miss** (1). β. Further, *misse* = mid-se**,
from a base MID, occurring in A. S.
mídan, to conceal, avoid, escape notice
(as well as in G. *meiden*, O. H. G. *mídan*,
to avoid, a strong verb). + Du. *missen*,
Icel. *missa*, Dan. *miste* (= *mid-se* ?), Swed.
missa (= *mid-sa* ?), O. H. G. *missan*, to
miss; also Du. *mis*, Icel. *mis*, adv. amiss;
also Du. *mis-*, Icel. *mis-*, Dan. *mis-*, Swed.
G. *miss-*, wrongly; Goth. *misso*, adv.,
interchangeably. All'ed to Skt. *mithas*,
interchangeably, *mithyá*, falsely, amiss.
(√MIT.) Der. *miss*, sb., a fault, M. E.
misse, Will. of Palerne, 532; *miss-ing*.

amiss, adv. wrongly. (E. *or* Scand.)
M. E. *on misse*, i. e. in error. — Icel. *á mis*,
amiss. — Icel. *á* (= A. S. *on*), in; *mis*, adv.,
wrongly (due to an older lost sb.).

Miss (2), a young woman; see **Magnitude**.

Missal; see **Missile**.

Missel-thrush; see **Mist**.

Missile, a weapon that may be thrown.
(L.) Properly an adj., 'that may be
thrown.' — L. *missilis*, that may be thrown.
— L. *missus*, pp. of *mittere*, to throw, send.
+ Lithuan. *metu*, I throw; Russ. *metate*,
to throw; cf. Skt. *math*, to churn, agitate.
(√MAT.)

admit, (L.) L. *ad-mittere*, to send to;
pp. *admissus*. Der. *admiss-ion*.

commissary, an officer to whom
something is entrusted. (L.) Low L.
commissarius, a commissary. — L. *commissus*, pp. of *committere*, to commit; see
below.

commit, to entrust to. (L.) L. *committere*, to send out, begin, entrust,
consign; pp. *commissus*. — L. *con-* (= *cum*),
with; *mittere*. Der. *commiss-ion*, F. *commission*, L. acc. *commissionem*, perpetration.

compromise, a settlement by concessions. (F. — L.) F. *compromis*, 'a compromise, mutual promise;' Cot. Orig. pp.
of F. *compromettre*, 'to put unto compromise;' Cot. — L. *com-promittere*, to make a
mutual promise. — L. *com-* (*cum*), mutually;
promittere, to promise; see **promise**
(below).

demise, transference, decease. (F. — L.)
O. F. *demise*, *desmise*, fem. of pp. of
desmettre, to displace, dismiss. — L. *dimittere*; see dismiss (below).

dimissory, giving leave to depart. (L.)
L. *dimissorius*, giving leave to go before
another judge. — L. *dimissus*, pp. ¯of
di-mittere, to send away.

dismiss, to send away. (F. — L.) A
coined word; suggested by F. *desmettre*,
pp. *desmis*, 'to displace, dismiss;' Cot.
The true L. form is *di-mittere*, to send away.

emit, to send forth. (L.) L. *e-mittere*,
to send forth; pp. *emissus*. Der. *emiss-ion*,
emiss-ary.

immit, to inject. (L.) In Kersey (1715).
L. *im-mittere*, to send into; pp. *immissus*;
where *im-* = L. *in*, in. Der. *immiss-ion*.

intermit, to interrupt, cease awhile.
(L.) L. *inter-mittere*, to send apart, interrupt; pp. *intermissus*. Der. *intermiss-ion*,
F. *intermission*, L. acc. *intermissionem*.

mass (2), the celebration of the Eucharist. (L.) M. E. *messe*. A. S. *mæsse*, (1)
the mass, (2) a church-festival. — Low L.
missa, (1) dismissal, (2) the mass. Usually
said to be from the phr. *ite missa est* (go,
the congregation is dismissed) used at the
end of the service; in any case, the derivation is from L. *missus*, pp. of *mittere*, to
send away. ¶ For the change of vowel
from *i* to *æ*, cf. Icel. *messa*, Swed. *messa*,
Dan. G. *messe*, O.H.G. *messa* as well as
missa, all in the sense of 'mass;' also Du.
mis, mass. And see **missal** (below).
Der. *Candle-mas*, *Christ-*, *Hallow-*, *Lam-*,
Martin-, *Michael-mas*, which see.

mess (1), a dish of meat, portion of
food. (F. — L.) M. E. *messe*. — O. F. *mes*,
a dish, course at table (now spelt *mets*,
badly). Cf. Ital. *messo*, a course at table.
— O. F. *mes*, that which is sent, pp. of
mettre, to send. — L. *mittere*, to send; in
late Lat., to place.

message. (F. — L.) F. *message*. — Low
L. *missaticum*, a message. — L. *miss-us*, pp.
of *mittere*, to send. Der. *messenger*, with
inserted *n*, put for M. E. *messager*, formed
from *message* with suffix *-er*.

missal, a mass-book. (L.) Low L.
missale, a mass-book. — Low L. *missa*,
mass; see **mass** (2) above.

mission. (L.) [The O. F. *mission*
merely means 'expence;' Cot.]. — L. acc.
missionem, acc. of *missio*, a sending. — L.
miss-us, pp. of *mittere*, to send.

missive. (F. — L.) O. F. *missive*, 'a

letter sent;' Cot. Coined from L. *miss-us*, pp. of *mittere*.

omit, to neglect. (L.) L. *o-mittere*, (pp. *omissus*), lit. 'to let go.' Put for *om-mittere** = *ob-mittere**. **Der.** *omiss-ion*, from F. *omission*, 'an omission,' from L. acc. *omissionem*.

permit. (L.) L. *per-mittere* (pp. *per-missus*), to let pass through, lit. send through. **Der.** *permiss-ion*.

premiss, premise. (F.–L.) Better *premiss* than *premise*.–O. F. *premisse* (F. *prémisse*), in use in the 14th century (Littré). – L. *præmissa* (*sententia* being understood), a premiss, lit. that which is sent before or stated beforehand. Fem. of *præmissus*, pp. of *præmittere*, to send before. **Der.** *premis-es*, s. pl. the adjuncts of a building, first stated in full, in a lease, and afterwards referred to as the *premises*; or otherwise, due to the custom of beginning leases with *premises* setting forth the names of the grantor and grantee of the deed. Also *premise*, verb, with accent on *i*.

pretermit, to omit. (L.) L. *præter-mittere*, to allow to go past. **Der.** *preter-miss-ion*.

promise, an agreement to do a thing. (F.–L.) Formerly *promes*.–F. *promesse*, 'a promise;' Cot.–L. *promissa*, fem. of *pro-missus*, pp. of *pro-mittere*, to send or put forth, to promise. **Der.** *promiss-o-ry*.

remit, to abate. (L.) L. *re-mittere* (pp. *remissus*), to send back, slacken, abate. **Der.** *remiss*, adj., from pp. *remissus*; *remiss-ion*.

submit. (L.) L. *sub-mittere*, to let down, submit, bow to (pp. *submissus*). **Der.** *submiss-ion, submiss-ive*.

surmise, an imagination, guess. (F.– L.) O. F. *surmise*, an accusation, charge; orig. fem. of *surmis*, pp. of *surmettre*, to put upon, lay to one's charge.–F. *sur*, above; *mettre*, to put.–L. *super*, above; *mittere*, to send, put.

transmit. (L.) L. *trans*, across; *mittere*, to send. **Der.** *transmiss-ion* (from pp. *missus*).

Mission, Missive; see **Missile**.

Mist. (E.) A.S. *mist*, gloom, darkness. **+** Icel. *mistr*, Du. Swed. *mist*, mist; G. *mist*, dung (the same word); Goth. *maih-stus*, dung. Formed, with suffixed *-st*, from the base MIG (Aryan MIGH), as seen in Lithuan. *migla*, Russ. *mgla*, Gk. ὀμίχλη, mist, Skt. *mih-ira*, a cloud, *megh-a*, a cloud. Cf. Skt. *mih*, to sprinkle, to urine;

L. *mingere*, Du. *mijgen*, Icel. *miga*, A. S. *mígan*, all with sense of L. *mingere*. The orig. sense of *mist* is urine; hence wetness.

missel-thrush, mistle-thrush. (E.) So called from feeding on the berries of the mistletoe; from A. S. *mistel*, mistletoe. **+** G. *misteldrossel*, mistle-thrush.

mistletoe. (E.) A final *n* has been lost. A. S. *misteltán*. – A. S. *mistel*, also used alone in the sense of mistletoe; *tán*, a twig. *Mistel* is from A. S. *mist*, mist, which in O. Du. had the sense of 'glue' or bird-lime, and in G. has the sense of dung. Thus the sense is 'birdlime-twig.' The A. S. *tán*, twig, is the same as Icel. *teinn*, Du. *teen*, Goth. *tains*, Dan. *teen*, Swed. *ten*, twig, spindle. **+** Icel. *mistelteinn*, mistletoe.

mizzle, to rain in fine drops. (E.) Formerly *misle*, put for *mist-le**, frequentative form of *mist*, to form vapour constantly. For the loss of *t*, cf. pronunciation of *whistle*, *glisten*, *listen*, &c.

Mistake, to err. (Scand.) Icel. *mistaka*, to take by error, make a slip. – Icel. *mis-*, wrongly; *taka*, to take. See **Mis-** (1) and **Take.**

Mister; see **Magnitude.**

Mistletoe; see **Mist.**

Mistress; see **Magnitude.**

Mite (1), an insect. (E.) M. E. *mite*. A.S. *mite*, a mite.**+**Low G. *mite*, O. H. G. *mîzâ*, a mite. The word means 'cutter,' i.e. biter; from Teut. base MIT, to cut, as in Goth. *maitan*, Icel. *meita*, to cut.

mite (2), a very small portion. (Du.) M. E. *mite*. – O. Du. *mijt*, *mite*, a very small coin, a mite. Lit. 'cut small;' from Teut. base MIT, to cut (above).

Mitigate. (L.) From pp. of L. *miti-gare*, to make gentle. – L. *mit-is*, gentle; *-igare*, for *agere*, to make.

Mitre, a head-dress, esp. for a bishop. (F.–L.–Gk.) O.F. *mitre*.–L. *mitra*, a cap.–Gk. μίτρα, a belt, girdle, head-band, fillet, turban.

Mitten. (F.–G. or C. ?) M. E. *mitaine*. –O. F. *mitaine*, 'a mittain, winter-glove;' Cot. Disputed; either from M. H. G. *mittemo*, middle, orig. 'mid-most,' as if the sense were 'half-glove;' or of Celtic origin. We find Gael. *miotag*, Irish *miotog*, a mitten; Gael. and Irish *mutan*, muff, thick glove; Irish *mutog*, a stump, a hand or glove without fingers.

Mix, to mingle. (E.) Put for *misk*, like *ax* for *ask*. A. S. *miscan*, to mix (not

borrowed from Latin, but allied to it). **+**
G. *mischen*, W. *mysgu*, Gael. *measg*, Russ.
mieshate, Lithuan. *maiszyti*, L. *miscere*, Gk.
μίσγειν, to mix. Cf. Skt. *miçra*, mixed.
Base MIKSH, from √ MIK, as in Gk. μίγ-
νυμι, I mix. Der. *mash*, q. v.

mixture. (L.) L. *mixtura*, a mixture.
- L. *mixtus*, pp. of *miscere*, to mix (above).
Mizen, Mizzen; see **Medium**.

Mizzle; see **Mist**.

Mnemonics, the science of aiding the
memory. (Gk.) Gk. μνημονικά, mnemonics;
neut. pl. of μνημονικός, belonging to memory.**-** Gk. μνημονι-, crude form of μνήμων,
mindful. **-** Gk, μνάομαι, I remember. (√
MAN.)

Moan, sb. (E.) M. E. *mone*, corresponding to A. S. *mán*, wickedness, of which the
orig. sense seems to have been a hurt or
sore. Hence was formed A. S. *mǽnan*, to
moan, lament, M. E. *menen*, to lament,
now obsolete, its place being supplied by
the form of the sb., used as a vb. A. S.
mán is cognate with Icel. *mein*, a hurt,
sore, Dan. *meen*, defect, blemish, harm.
(√ MI.) Der. *bemoan*, vb., substituted for
M. E. *bimenen*, A. S. *bi-mǽnan*, to bemoan.

Moat. (F.**-**Teut.) M. E. *mote.*-O. F.
mote, an embankment, dike. [As in the case
of *dike*, the same word means either the
trench cut out or the embankment thrown
up, or both together.] The same word as
F. *motte*, 'a clod, lump, sodd, turfe, little
hill, butt to shoot at;' Cotgrave. Cf. also
Ital. *motta*, a heap of earth, also a hollow,
trench (like E. *moat*), Span. *mota*, a mound;
Romansch *muotta*, rounded hill. Of Teut.
origin; from Bavarian *mott*, peat; cf. Du.
mot, dust of turf. Prob. allied to **Mud**.

Mob (1), a disorderly crowd. (L.); see
Move.

Mob (2), a kind of cap. (Du.) From
Du. *mopmuts*, a woman's night-cap (where
muts means cap); O. Du. *mop*, a woman's
coif. Prob. allied to **Muff** (1).

Mobile; see **Move**.

Moccasin, Mocasin, a shoe of deer-
skin. (N. American Indian.) From the
Algonquin *makisin* (Webster).

Mock, to deride. (F. **-** Teut.) M. E.
mokken. **-** O. F. *mocquer*, later *moquer*.**-**
G. *mucken*, to grumble; O. Swed. *mucka*,
O. Du. *mocken*, to mumble. Cf. Ital.
mocca, 'a mowing mouth,' *moccare*, 'to
mocke,' Florio. Cf. Gk. μῶκος, mockery,
L. *maccus*, a buffoon, Gael. *mag*, W. *mocio*,
to mock, deride. (Imitative base MAK or

MUK, from √ MU, to mutter). See
Mope, Mow (3).

Mode. (F.**-**L.) F. *mode.*-L. *modum*,
acc. of *modus*, measure, manner, way. Allied to **Mete**.

accommodate. (L.) From pp. of L.
accommodare, to fit, suit, adapt. **-** L. *ac-*
(= *ad*), to ; *commodus*, fit ; see below.

commodious. (L.) Low L. *commo-
diosus*, useful. **-** L. *commodus*, fit, suitable.
- L. *com-* (= *cum*), with; *modus*, measure.

incommode. (F.**-**L.) F. *incommoder*,
to hinder. **-** L. *incommodare*, to hinder. **-**
L. *in*, not ; *commodus*, fit ; see above.

model. (F.**-**Ital.**-**L.) O. F. *modelle.*
- Ital. *modello*, 'a model, frame, mould;'
Florio. From dimin. of L. *modulus*, a
standard, measure, which is again a dimin.
of *modus*, measure. Der. *re-model.*

moderate, temperate. (L.) From pp.
of L. *moderari*, to regulate. From a stem
moder-us*, *modes-us**, extended from *modus*, a measure.

modern. (F. **-** L.) F. *moderne.* **-** L.
modernus, belonging to the present mode ;
extended from a stem *moder-us** (above).

modest, moderate, chaste, decent. (F.
- L.) F. *modeste.* **-** L. *modestus*, moderate,
lit. 'keeping within measure.' From a
stem *modes-**, with suffix *-tus*; see **moderate** (above).

modicum, a small quantity. (L.) Neut.
of L. *modicus*, moderate. **-** L. *modus.*

modify. (F. **-** L.) F. *modifier.* **-** L.
modificare.-L. *modi-*, for *modus*, measure,
moderation ; *-ficare*, for *facere*, to make.

modulate, to regulate. (L.) From
pp. of L. *modulari*, to measure by a standard. **-** L. *modulus*, dimin. of *modus*, a
measure.

mood (2), manner, grammatical form.
(F. **-** L.) Another spelling of **mode**
(above). ¶ Distinct from *mood* (1).

mould (2), a model, form. (F. **-** L.)
M. E. *molde*, with excrescent *d*. **-** O. F.
molle (F. *moule*), a mould ; earliest spelling
modle. **-** L. *modulum*, acc. of *modulus*,
dimin. of *modus*, a measure.

Model, Moderate; see **Mode**.

Modern, Modest, Modicum; see
Mode.

Modify, Modulate; see **Mode**.

Mogul, a Mongolian. (Mongolia.) Pers.
Moghól, a Mogul; another form of *Mongol*.

Mohair, cloth of fine hair. (F.**-**Arab.)
A sophisticated spelling (by confusion with
hair) of O. F. *mouhaire*, *mouäire*, *mohère*

(F. *moire*). – Arab. *mukhayyar*, a kind of coarse camlet or hair-cloth.

moire, watered silk. (F. – Arab.) An altered form of *mohair*, used in a changed sense.

Mohammedan. (Arab.) A follower of *Mohammed.* – Arab. *muhammad*, praiseworthy. – Arab. *hamada*, he praised.

Mohur, a gold coin. (Pers.) Pers. *muhr*, *muhur*, a gold coin worth 16 rupees (Wilson).

Moidore ; see Monition.

Moiety ; see Medium.

Moil, to toil, drudge ; see Mollify.

Moire ; see Mohair.

Moist ; see Must (2).

Molar, used for grinding. (L.) L. *molaris*, adj., from *mola*, a mill. Cf. *molere*, to grind. (√MAR.)

mill. (L.) M. E. *miln*, *myln*, *mulne*; whence *mille*, *mulle*, by loss of *n*. A. S. *myln*, *mylen*. – L. *molina*, a mill, extended from *mola*, a mill.

mullet (2), a five-pointed star. (F. – L.) O. F. *molette*, a rowell, whence it came to mean the 'mullet' of heraldry ; also O. F. *mollette*, 'a mullet, rowell of a spur ;' Cot. Dimin. from L. *mola*, a mill, whence Ital. *molla*, a mill-stone, mill-wheel, clock-wheel with cogs.

Molasses ; see Mellifluous.

Mole (1), a spot or mark on the body. (E.) M. E. *mole*. A. S. *mál*, a spot (whence *mole* by the usual change from *á* to long *o*). + Dan. *maal*, Swed. *mål*, G. *maal*, Goth. *mail*, a spot. Allied to L. *macula*, a spot. (√MAK.) See Maculate. Der. *maulstick*, q. v.

mould (3), a spot. (E.) Put for *mole*. 'One yron *mole* defaceth the whole peece of lawne,' Lyly, Euphues, p. 39. This is now called *iron-mould* (with added *d*). We also find M. E. *moled*, spotted ; hence mod. E. *mouldy* (in some senses) ; by confusion with *mould* (1).

Mole (2), an animal ; see Mould (1).

Mole (3), a breakwater. (F. – L.) F. *mole.* – L. *molem*, acc. of *moles*, a great heap.

demolish. (F. – L.) O. F. *demoliss-*, inchoative base of *demolir*, to demolish. – L. *demoliri*, *demolire*, to pull down. – L. *de*, from ; *moles*, heap.

emolument, gain. (F. – L.) F. *emolument.* – L. *emolumentum*, what is gained by labour. – L. *emoliri*, to work out, accomplish. – L. *e*, out, greatly ; *moliri*, to work, from *moles*, heap, also effort.

molecule, an atom. (L.) Formerly *mole-*

cula; Bailey. Coined from L. *moles*, a heap ; the true form would have been *molicula*.

molest, to annoy. (F. – L.) F. *molester.* – L. *molestare.* – L. *molestus*, troublesome, formed with suffix *-tus*, from a stem *moles-*, extended from *mol-*, stem of *molis*, a heap, also labour.

Molecule, **Molest** ; see Mole (3).

Mollify, to soften. (F. – L.) O. F. *mollifier.* – L. *mollificare.* – L. *molli-s*, soft ; *-ficare*, for *facere*, to make. (√MAR.)

emollient, softening. (F. – L.) O. F. *emollient.* – L. *emollient-*, stem of pres. pt. of *emollire*, to soften. – L. *e*, out, very ; *mollire*, to soften, from *molli-s*, soft.

moil, to toil, drudge. (F. – L.) Formerly *moile*, to defile with dirt ; later *moil*, 'to dawbe with dirt, to drudge ;' Phillips. The older sense was to dirty, hence to drudge, from the dirt consequent on toil. Spenser has *moyle*, to wallow, Hymn of Heav. Love, st. 32. Still earlier, we have M. E. *moillen*, to moisten, wet. – F. *moiller*, *moiler* (Littré), later *mouiller*, to wet, moisten ; orig. sense, to soften, which (in the case of clay) is effected by wetting it. This verb answers to a Low L. *molliare**, to soften ; not used. – L. *molli-s*, soft, Thus the senses were, to soften, moisten, dirty, soil oneself, drudge. ¶ Prob. confused, in former days, with prov. E. *moil*, a mule, or with L. *moliri*, to strive ; but these words are really quite independent.

mollusc. (F. – L.) F. *mollusque.* – L. *mollusca*, a soft-shelled nut ; which some molluscs were supposed to resemble. – L. *moll-is*, soft.

Molten, old pp. of Melt, q. v.

Moly, a plant. (L. – Gk.) L. *moly.* – Gk. μῶλυ ; Homer, Od. x. 305.

Moment ; see Move.

Monad ; see Mono-, prefix.

Monarch ; see Arch-, prefix.

Monastery ; see Mono-.

Monday ; see Moon.

Monetary, **Money** ; see Monition.

Monger, **Mongrel** ; see Mingle.

Monition, a warning, notice. (F. – L.) F. *monition.* – L. acc. *monitionem.* – L. *monitus*, pp. of *monere*, to advise, lit. to make to think. (√MAN.)

admonish. (F. – L.) M. E. *amonesten* ; so that *admonish* is a corruption of the older form *amonest*. 'I *amoneste* or warne ;' Wyclif, 1 Cor. iv. 14. – O. F. *amonester* (later *admonester*), to advise. – Low L. *admonitare*, afterwards *admonistare*, frequent.

of *admonere*, to advise. — L. *ad*, to ; *monere*, to advise. **Der.** *admonit-or-y* (from pp. *admonitus* of *admonere*).

demonstrate. (L.) From pp. of L. *demonstrare*, to shew fully. — L. *de*, down, fully ; *monstrare*, to shew, from *monstrum*, a portent. See **monster** (below).

mint (1), a place where money is coined. (L.) M. E. *mint*, *mynt*. A. S. *mynet*, borrowed from L. *moneta*, (1) a mint, (2) money. *Moneta* was a surname of Juno, in whose temple at Rome money was coined ; the lit. sense is ' warning one.' — L. *monere*, to warn.

moidore, a Portuguese gold coin. (Port. — L.) See Bailey's Dict. — Port. *moeda d'ouro*, a moidore, £1 7s.; lit. 'money of gold.' — L. *moneta*, money; *de*, of ; *aurum*, gold. See **money** (below).

monetary, relating to money. (L.) L. *monetarius*, lit. belonging to a mint. — L. *moneta*, (1) a mint, (2) money.

money. (F. — L.) M. E. *moneie*. — O. F. *moneie* (F. *monnaie*). — L. *moneta*, (1) mint, (2) money ; see **mint** (above).

monster, a prodigy. (F. — L.) F. *monstre*. — L. *monstrum*, a divine omen, portent, warning. (Put for *mon-es-trum* *.) — L. *mon-ere*, to warn.

monument, a memorial. (F. — L.) F. *monument*. — L. *monumentum*, a memorial. — L. *monu-*, for *moni-*, seen in *moni-t-us*, pp. of *monere*, to advise, remind ; with suffix *-men-tum*.

muster. (F. — L.) M. E. *moustre*, a muster of men, lit. display. — O. F. *mostre*, another form of *monstre*, ' a pattern, also a muster, view, shew ;' Cot. The same word as F. *monstre*, a monster ; see **monster** (above).

premonish, to warn beforehand. (F. — L.) Coined from *pre-*, before ; and *monish*, a corrupted form of M. E. *monesten*, to warn, Wyclif, 2 Cor. vi. 1. See **admonish** above. **Der.** *premonit-or-y*, from L. *præmonitor*, one who warns beforehand.

remonstrate. (L.) From pp. of Low L. *remonstrare*, to expose, to produce arguments against. — L. *re-*, again ; *monstrare*, to shew, from *monstrum*, a portent ; see **monster** (above).

summon. (F. — L.) O. F. *somoner* (Roquefort), early altered to *semoner* and *semondre* (F. *sémondre*), to summon. — L. *summonere* ; to remind privily. — L. *sum-* (for *sub*), under, privily ; *monere*, to remind. ¶ Formerly confused with A. S. *samnien*,

to gather together; but this word soon went out of use.

summons, sb. (F. — L.) M. E. *somouns*, from the orig. form (*somonce* *) of F. *semonce*, ' a warning, summons,' Cot.; which was orig. the fem. of the pp. of O. F. *somoner* (above). ¶ Thus the final *s* in *summons* has nothing to do with L. *summoneas*, as some have imagined.

Monk ; see **Mono-**.

Monkey ; see **Madam**.

Mono-, *prefix*, sole. (Gk.) Gk. μόνο-ς, single.

minster. (L. — Gk.) A. S. *mynster*; a shortened form of L. *monasterium* ; see **monastery** (below).

monad, a unit, &c. (L. — Gk.) L. *monad-*, stem of *monas*, a unit. — Gk. μονάς, a unit. — Gk. μόνος, alone.

monarchy ; see **Arch-**, prefix.

monastery. (L. — Gk.) L. *monasterium*. — Gk. μοναστήριον, a minster. — Gk. μοναστής, dwelling alone, a monk. — Gk. μονάζειν, to be alone. — Gk. μόνος, alone. **Der.** *monast-ic*, from Gk. μοναστικός, living in solitude.

monk. (L. — Gk.) M. E. *monk*. A. S. *munec*. — L. *monachus*. — Gk. μοναχός, adj., solitary ; sb. a monk. — Gk. μόν-ος, alone.

monochord ; see **chord**. So also *mono-cotyledon*, *mon-ocular*, &c. ; see **ocular**, **ode**, **logic**, **syllable**, **tone**.

monopoly, exclusive sale. (L. — Gk.) L. *monopolium*. — Gk. μονοπώλιον, right of monopoly ; μονοπωλία, monopoly. — Gk. μόνο-ς, sole ; πωλεῖν, to sell, barter, connected with πέλειν, to be busy.

Monsoon, a periodical wind. (Ital. — Malay. — Arab.) Ital. *monsone*. — Malay *músim*, a season, monsoon, year. — Arab. *mawsim*, a time, season. — Arab. *wasm* (root *wasama*), marking.

Monster ; see **Monition**.

Month ; see **Moon**.

Monument ; see **Monition**.

Mood (1), disposition of mind. (E.) Prob. sometimes confused with *mood* (2), but properly distinct. M. E. *mood*, mind, also temper, anger, wrath. A. S. *mód*, mind, feeling, heart. + Du. *moed*, courage ; Icel. *móðr*, wrath, moodiness ; Dan. Swed. *mod*, G. *muth*, courage; Goth. *mods*, wrath. Cf. Gk. μέμαα, I strive after. Perhaps allied to **Mind**. **Der.** *mood-y*, A. S. *módig*.

Mood (2), manner, grammatical form; see **Mode**.

Moon. (E.) M. E. *mone*. A. S. *móna*,

a masc. sb. **+** Du. *maan*, Icel. *máni*, Dan. *maane*, Swed. *måne*, Goth. *mena*, G. *mond*, O. H. G. *máno*, Lithuan. *ménū*, Gk. μήνη. Allied to Skt. *mâsa*, a month. Lit. the 'measurer' of time. (√ MA.)

monday. (E.) M. E. *monenday*, later *moneday*, *monday*. A. S. *mônan dæg*, day of the moon; where *mônan* is the gen. of *môna*, moon.

month. (E.) M.E. *moneth*, later *month*. A.S. *mónað*, a lunation; from *móna*, moon. **+**Du. *maand*, Icel. *mánuðr*, Dan. *maaned*, Swed. *månad*, G. *monat*, G. *menoths*, a month. Allied to Lithuan. *ménesis*, Russ. *miesiats'*, L. *mensis*, Irish and W. *mis*, Gael. *mios*, Gk. μήν, Skt. *mâsa*, a month. (√ MA.)

Moor (1), a heath. (E.) M. E. *more*. A. S. *mór*.**+**Icel. *mór*, moor, peat; O. Du. *moer*, moor, mud; *moerlandt*, peaty land; Dan. *mor*, G. *moor*. Prob. allied to **Mire** and **Moss**.

morass, a bog. (Du.) Du. *moeras*, marsh, fen; O. Du. *moerasch*, adj., belonging to a moor, from the sb. *moer*, moor, mud. Cf. G. *morast* (for *morask* *), Swed. *moras*, Dan. *morads*, a morass. ¶ Distinct from *marsh*.

Moor (2), to fasten up a ship; see **Mar**.

Moor (3), a native of N. Africa. (F.— L.—Gk.) O. F. *More*, 'a Moor;' Cot.— L. *Maurus*.—Gk. Μαῦρος, a Moor. Cf. Gk. μαῦρος, ἀμαυρός, dark. **Der.** *black-moor*, corruption of *blackmoor* (Minsheu), i. e. *black Moor*.

morocco, a fine kind of leather. (Morocco.) Named from *Morocco*, in N. Africa; which was named from the *Moors* dwelling there.

morris, morris-dance. (Span.—L.— Gk.) The dance was also called a *morisco*, i. e. a Moorish dance. — Span. *Morisco*, Moorish.—Span. *Moro*, a Moor.—L. *Maurus* (above).

Moose, the American elk. (W. Indian.) The native W. Indian name; 'Knisteneaux *mouswah*, Algonquin *monse* [*mouse*?], Mackenzie;' cited in Webster.

Moot, to discuss a point. (E.) Chiefly used in phr. 'a *moot* point.' Minsheu gives *moot* as a verb, to discuss. The proper sense of *moot* is 'meeting,' as in *moot-hall*, hall of assembly; hence to *moot* is to discuss at a meeting, and 'a *moot* point' is one reserved for public discussion. M. E. *motien*, to discuss, also to cite. A. S. *métian*, to cite to a meeting; from A. S.

mót, a meeting, also spelt *gemót*, esp. in phr. *witena gemót* = meeting of wise men, parliament.**+**Icel. *mót*, M. H. G. *móz*, a meeting.

meet (2), to encounter, find, assemble. (E.) M. E. *meten*. A. S. *métan*, to find, meet. Formed, with the usual vowelchange from *ó* to *é*, from A. S. *mót*, a meeting, assembly (above). **+** Icel. *mæta*, *mœta*, from *mót*; Goth. *gamotjan*, Swed. *möta*, Dan. *möde*, to meet.

Mop (1), an implement for washing floors. (F.— L.) In a late ed. of Florio's Ital. Dict., *pannatore* is explained by 'a maulkin, a *map* of rags or clouts to rub withal.' Halliwell gives *mop*, a napkin; *Gloucestershire*. Origin disputed; but clearly from O. F. *mappe*, a napkin (afterwards turned into *nappe*.) — L. *mappa*, a napkin. See **Map**. Some suppose *mop* to be of Celtic origin; we find W. *mopa*, *mop*, a mop; Gael. *moibeal*, Irish *moipal*; but it is probable that these are from English.

Mop (2), a grimace; to grimace. (Du.) The same word as *mope* (below).

mope, to be dispirited. (Du.) The same word as *mop*, to grimace; cf. 'in the *mops*,' i. e. sulky (Halliwell).—Du. *moppen*, to pout, be sulky. A variant of *mock*, q. v. And see *mow* (3).

Moraine, a line of stones at the edges of a glacier. (F.— Teut.) F. *moraine*; cf. Ital. *mora*, a pile of rocks. — Bavarian *mur*, sand and broken stones, fallen from rocks in a valley; the lit. sense, being 'crumbled material.' Cf. G. *mürbe*, soft, O. H. G. *muruwi*, brittle. (√ MAR.) Allied to **Mould** (1).

Moral. (F.— L.) F. *moral*.—L. *moralis*, relating to conduct.—L. *mor-*, stem of *mos*, a manner, custom.

demoralise, to corrupt in morals. (F. —L.) Mod. F. *démoraliser*.— F. *dé-* (= O.F. *des* = L. *dis-*), apart; *moral*, moral (above); with suffix *-ise* (= F. *-iser* = Gk. ιζειν).

demure. (F.— L.) O. F. *de murs*, i. e. *de bons murs*, of good manners. — L. *de*, of; *mores*, manners, pl. of *mos* (above).

morose. (L.) L. *morosus*, self-willed; (1) in a good sense, scrupulous; (2) in a bad sense, peevish. — L. *mor-*, stem of *mos*, (1) self-will, (2) custom, use. ¶ Confused with L. *mora*, delay, in the 17th cent.

Morass; see **Moor** (1).

Morbid; see **Mortal**.

Mordacity, sarcasm. (F.— L.) Little used. — F. *mordacité*.—L. acc. *mordacitatem*, from *mordacitas*, power to bite.—L. *mor-*

daci-, crude form of *mordax*, biting. — L. *mordere*, to bite. (√SMARD.)

morsel, a mouthful, small piece. (F. —L.) M. E. *morsel*. — O. F. *morsel* (F. *morceau*). Cf. Ital. *morsello*. Dimin. from L. *morsum*, a bite. — L. *morsus*, pp. of *mordere* (above).

remorse. (F. —L.) O. F. *remors*; Cot. —Low L. *remorsus*, remorse. — L. *remorsus*, pp. of *re-mordere*, to bite again, to vex. See also **Muse** (1).

More; see **May** (1).

Morganatic; see **Morn**.

Morion, an open helmet. (F. — Span.) F. *morion*. — Span. *morrion*; cf. Port. *morrião*, Ital. *morione*, a morion. The word is Spanish, if we may accept the prob. derivation from Span. *morra*, the crown of the head. Cf. Span. *morro*, anything round; *moron*, a hillock. Perhaps from Basque *murua*, a hill, heap (Diez).

Mormonite. (E.) The *Mormonites* are the followers of Joseph Smith, who in 1827 said he had found the book of *Mormon*. Invented; but we may call the word E., as used by English-speaking people.

Morn. (E.) M. E. *morn*, a Northern form. Short for M. E. *morwen*, Ancren Riwle, p. 22. A. S. *morgen*, whence *morwen* by the usual change of *g* to *w*. +Du. Dan. G. *morgen*; Icel. *morginn*, Swed. *morgon*. Cf. Lithuan. *merkti*, to blink, Gk. μαρμαίρειν, to glitter. Orig. sense prob. 'dawn.'

morganatic. (Low L. — G.) Coined from G. *morgen*, here short for *morgengabe*, lit. morning-gift, orig. a present made to a wife on the morning after marriage, esp. if the wife were of inferior rank. Hence used to denote such a marriage.

morning. (E.) Short for *morwening*, Ch. C. T. 1064; formed from M. E. *morwen* (above) by adding the substantival (not participial) suffix *-ing* (=A.S. *-ung*).

morrow. (E.) M. E. *morwe*, from the older form *morwen* (above), by loss of final *n*. Thus M. E. *morwen* gave rise (1) to *morrow*, by loss of *n*; (2) to *morn*, by loss of *w*, and contraction. Der. *to-morrow* = A.S. *tō morgene*, i. e. for the morrow, where *tō* is a prep. (E. *to*), and *morgene* is dat. case of *morgen*.

Morocco; see **Moor** (3).

Morose; see **Moral**.

Morphia, Morphine, the narcotic principle of opium. (Gk.) From Gk. Μορφεύς, Morpheus, god of dreams; lit. 'shaper,' i. e. creator of dreams. — Gk. μορφή, a shape,

form; prob. from μάρπτειν, to seize, grasp. Der. *meta-morph-osis*, *a-morph-ous*.

Morris-dance; see **Moor** (3).

Morrow; see **Morn**.

Morse, a walrus. (Russ.) Russ. *morj*'; where the *j* is sounded as F. *j*. Perhaps from Russ. *moré*, the sea; cf. Russ. *morskaia korova*, the sea-cow, another name for the morse. See **Mere** (1).

Morsel; see **Mordacity**.

Mortal, deadly. (F.—L.) F. *mortal*. — L. *mortalis*, adj.; from *mort-*, stem of *mors*, death. From L. *mor-i*, to die; cf. Skt. *mṛi*, to die, *mṛita*, dead. (√MAR.) Der. *im-mortal*.

morbid, sickly. (F.—L.) F. *morbide*. —L. *morbidus*, sickly. —L. *morbus*, disease. Allied to *mor-i*, to die.

mortgage, a kind of security for debt. (F. — L.) O. F. *mortgage*, lit. a dead pledge; because, whatever profit it might yield, it did not thereby redeem itself, but became dead or lost to the mortgagee on breach of the condition. — F. *mort*, dead; *gage*, a pledge. — L. *mortuus*, dead, pp. of *mori*, to die; *gage*, a pledge; see **Gage** (1). Der. *mortgag-ee*, where *-ee* answers to the F. *-é* of the pp.

mortify. (F. — L.) O. F. *mortifier*. — L. *mortificare*, to cause death. — L. *morti-*, crude form of *mors*, death; *-ficare*, for *facere*, to make.

mortmain. (F.—L.) Property transferred to the church was said to pass into *mort main*, lit. 'dead hand,' because it could not be alienated. — L. *mort-uus*, dead; *manum*, acc. of *manus*, hand.

mortuary, belonging to the burial of the dead. (L.) Chiefly in the phr. 'a *mortuary* fee,' which was also called *mortuary* for short. — Low L. *mortuarium*, neut. of *mortuarius*, belonging to the dead. — L. *mortu-us*, dead; pp. of *mori*, to die.

murrain, cattle-disease. (F.—L.) M.E. *moreine*. — O. F. *moreine**, not found; closely allied to O. F. *morine*, a carcase of a beast, also a murrain. Cf. Span. *morriña*, Port. *morrinha*, murrain. — O. F. *morir* (F. *mourir*), to die. — L. *mori*, to die.

Mortar (1), **Morter**, a vessel in which substances are pounded with a pestle. (L.) M. E. *morter*. A. S. *mortere*. — L. *mortarium*, a mortar. Cf. L. *martulus*, a hammer. — √MAR, to pound.

mortar (2), cement. (F.—L.) M. E. *mortier*. — O. F. *mortier*, 'morter;' Cot. — L. *mortarium*, mortar; lit. stuff pounded together; a different use of the word above.

Mortgage, Mortify; see Mortal.

Mortise, a hole in a piece of timber to receive the tenon. (F.) Spelt *mortesse* in Palsgrave. — F. *mortaise*, 'a mortaise in a piece of timber;' Cot. Cf. Span. *mortaja*, a mortise. Orig. unknown; Devic suggests Arab. *murtazz*, fixed in the mark (said of an arrow), very tenacious (said of a miser).

Mortmain, Mortuary; see Mortal.

Mosaic; see Muse (2).

Moslem, a Mussulman. (Arab.) Arab. *moslim*, 'a musulman, a true believer in the Mohammedan faith;' Richardson. Cf. Arab. *musallim*, one who acquiesces. A *mussulmán* is one who professes *islám*, i. e. submission to the will of God and to the orthodox faith. — Arab. *salama*, to submit. ¶ The E. words *moslem, mussulman, islam,* and *salaam* are all from the same Arab. root *salama*, to submit.

mussulman, a true believer in the Mohammedan faith. (Pers. — Arab.) Pers. *musulmán*, an orthodox believer. — Arab. *moslim, muslim* (above).

Mosque, a Mohammedan temple. (F. — Span. — Arab.) F. *mosquée*; Cot. — Span. *mezquita*, a mosque. — Arab. *masjad, masjid*, a temple, mosque. — Arab. root *sajada*, to adore, prostrate oneself.

Mosquito, a gnat. (Span. — L.) Span. *mosquito*, a little gnat; dimin. of *mosca*, a fly. — L. *musca*, a fly. Cf. Gk. μυῖα, Lithuan. *musé*, a fly.

musket. (F. — Ital. — L.) O. F. *mousquet*, a musket, orig. a kind of hawk (another sort of gun was called a *falconet*, another a *saker*, a kind of hawk). — Ital. *mosquetto*, a musket, orig. a kind of hawk, so called from its small size. Dimin. of Ital. *mosca*, a fly. — L. *musca*, a fly.

Moss. (E.) M. E. *mos*; cf. A. S. *meôs*. + Du. *mos*; Icel. *mosi*, moss, also a moss or moorland; Dan. *mos*; Swed. *mossa*; G. *moos*, moss, a swamp, M. H. G. *mos*, allied to M. H. G. *mies*, O. H. G. *mios*, moss. Allied to Russ. *mokh'*, moss, L. *muscus*, moss. ¶ Note E. *moss* in sense of bog, moorland; hence *moss-trooper*.

mire, deep mud. (Scand.) M. E. *mire, myre*. — Icel. *mýrr*, mod. *mýri*, a bog; Swed. *myra*, Dan. *myre, myr*, a bog. + O. H. G. *mios*, M. H. G. *mies*, moss, swamp. From a Teut. type MEUSA, mire; derived from MUSA, i. e. moss (Fick). See above.

mushroom. (F. — O. H. G.) M. E.

muscheron. — O. F. *mouscheron, mousseron*, a mushroom; extended from F. *mousse*, moss. — O. H. G. *mos* (G. *moos*), moss (above).

Most; see May (1).

Mote, a particle of dust, speck. (E.) M. E. *mot*. A. S. *mot*, a mote.

Motett; see Motto.

Moth. (E.) M. E. *mothe*. A. S. *moðe, mohðe*. + Du. *mot*, Icel. *motti*, G. *motte*, a moth; Swed. *mått*, a mite. β. We also find A. S. *maðu*, a maggot, Du. G. *made*, a maggot, Goth. *matha*, a worm; this last form appears to be from the verb *to mow*, i. e. to cut, as if the sense were 'cutter.' Cf. O. H. G. *mádári*, a mower.

mawkish, squeamish. (Scand.; *with E. suffix.*) The older sense is loathsome, lit. 'maggoty.' Formed, with E. suffix *-ish*, from M. E. *mawk, mauk*, a maggot, a contracted form of M. E. *maðek*, a maggot. — Icel. *maðkr*, Dan. *maddik*, a maggot (whence Norw. *makk* = E. *mawk*). Dimin. of the form which appears as A. S. *maðu*, Du. G. *made*, maggot (above).

Mother (1), a female parent. (E.) M. E. *moder*. A. S. *móder, módor*, a mother; the change from *d* to *th* seems due to Scand. influence. + Du. *moeder*, Icel. *móðir*, Dan. Swed. *moder*, G. *mutter*, Irish and Gael. *mathair*, Russ. *mate*, Lithuan. *moté*, L. *mater*, Gk. μήτηρ, Skt. *mátá, mátri*. β. All formed with Aryan suffix *-tar* (of the agent) from √MA, orig. to measure; cf. Skt. *má*, to measure. Orig. sense uncertain; prob. 'manager' of the household.

mother (2), hysterical passion. (E.) In King Lear, ii. 4. 56. Spelt *moder* in Palsgrave; and the same word as the above. + Du. *moeder*, a mother, womb, hysterical passion; cf. G. *mutterbeschwerung*, mother-fit, hysterical passion.

Mother (3), lees, sediment; see Mud.

Motion, Motive; see Move.

Motley, of different colours. (F. — G.) M. E. *mottelee*, Ch. C. T. 273. — O. F. *mattelé*, 'clotted, curdled;' Cot. Cf. O. F. *mattonné*, as in *ciel mattonné*, 'a skie full of small curdled clouds;' id. [Thus the orig. sense of *motley* was merely 'spotted.'] — Bavarian *matte*, curds (Schmeller). Der. *mottl-ed*, put for O. F. *mattelé* above, by substituting the E. pp. suffix *-ed* for the F. pp. suffix *-é*.

Motto. (Ital. — L.) Ital. *motto*, a saying, a motto. — L. *muttum*, a murmur, muttered sound; cf. L. *mutire*, to murmur. (√MU.) Allied to Mutter.

motet, motett, a short piece of sacred music. (F.—Ital.—L.) F. *motet*, 'a verse in musick;' Cot. — O. Ital. *mottetto*, 'a dittie, a witty saying;' Florio. Dimin. of *motto*, a saying (above).

Mould (1), earth. (E.) M. E. *molde*. A. S. *molde*, dust, soil, earth.+Du. *mul*, Icel. *mold*, Dan. *muld*, Swed. *mull* (for *muld**), mould; Goth. *mulda*, dust; G. *mull*, prov. G. *molt*, mould. The lit. sense is 'crumbled.'—√MAL, to crumbre; MAR, to pound. Der.*mould-er*, to crumble; also *mould-y* (which seems to have been confused with **Mole** (1), q. v.).

mole (2), an animal. (E.) *Mole* is a shortened form of the old name *moldwarp*, (Hen. IV. iii. 1. 149;) lit. 'the animal that casts up mould.' M. E. *moldwerp*; from *mold*, mould, *werpen*, to throw up. See **Warp.**+Du. *mol*, short for O. Du. *mol-worp* ; Icel. *moldvarpa*, a mole.

mulled, applied to ale or wine. (E.) *Mulled ale* is a corruption of *muld-ale* or *mold-ale*, a funeral ale or feast. M. E. *molde-ale*, a funeral feast; from *molde*, the earth of the grave, and *ale*, a feast (as in *bride-ale*). The sense being lost, *mulled* was thought to be a pp., and a verb *to mull* was evolved from it.

Mould (2) ; see **Mode**.

Mould (3), in *iron-mould*; see **Mole** (1).

Mouldy; see **Mole** (1), **Mould** (1).

Moult; see **Mutable.**

Mound, an earthen defence, a hillock. (E.) M. E. *mound*, a protection. A. S. *mund*, protection, chiefly as a law-term; but also *mund-beorg*, a protecting hill, a mound. + O. Fries. *mund*, O. H. G. *munt*, a protector; cf. G. *vormund*, a guardian. Prob. from √MAN, to jut out (L. *e-min-ere*) ; and so allied to *mount*.

Mount (1), a hill. (L.) A. S. *munt*.— L. *mont-*, stem of *mons*, a hill. — √MAN, to jut out (see word above).

amount, to mount up to. (F.—L.) O. F. *amonter*, to amount to. — O.F. *a mont*, towards a mountain or large heap. — L. *ad*, to ; *montem*, acc. of *mons* (above).

mount (2), to ascend. (F.—L.) F. *monter*.—F. *mont*, a hill. [The verb is due to O. F. *a mont*, up-hill.] — L. *montem* (above). See **paramount** (below).

mountain. (F.—L.) O. F. *montaine* (F. *montagne*). — Low L. *montana*, a mountain.—L. *montana*, neut. pl. mountainous regions; from *montanus*, adj. from *mons*, a mountain.

mountebank, a quack doctor. (Ital. —L. *and* G.) Lit. one who *mounts a bench*, to proclaim his nostrums. — Ital. *montambanco*, a mountebank ; O. Ital. *monta in banco*, the same. — Ital. *montare*, to mount; *in*, on; *banco*, a bench. Here *montare* is the same word as F. *monter*; *in* = L. *in*, on ; and *banco* is from O. H. G. *banc*, a bench ; see **Bank** (2).

paramount, of the highest importance. (F.—L.) O. F. *par amont*, at the top, above, lit. 'by that which is upwards.'—L. *per*, by ; *ad montem*, to the hill, upwards; where *montem* is acc. of *mons*, a hill.

remount, to mount again. (F.—L.) F. *remonter*.—F *re-*, again ; *monter*, to mount (above).

surmount. (F.—L.) F. *surmonter*.— F. *sur* (L. *super*), above; *monter*, to mount; see mount (2) above.

tramontane, foreign to Italy. (F.— Ital.—L.) F. *tramontain*. — Ital. *tramontano*, living beyond the mountains. — L. *tra-*, for *trans*, beyond; *mont-*, stem of *mons*, mountain.

Mourn. (E.) M E. *mournen*. A. S. *murnan*, *meornan*, to grieve.+Icel. *morna*, Goth. *maurnan*, O. H. G. *mornén*. Extended from base MUR, as seen in G. *murren*, Icel. *murra*, to murmur, growl ; see **Murmur.**

Mouse. (E.) M. E. *mous*. A. S. *mús* (pl. *mýs*). + Du. *muis*, Icel. *mús*, Dan. *muus*, Swed. *mus*, G. *maus*, Russ. *muish'*, L. *mus*, Gk. μῦς, Pers. *mūsh*, a mouse; Skt. *músha*, a rat, a mouse. Lit. 'a stealing animal.'—√MUS, to steal; Skt. *mush*, to steal. See **Muscle** (1).

Moustache, Mustache; see **Mastic.**

Mouth. (E.) M. E. *mouth*. A. S. *múð*. + Du. *mond*, Icel. *munnr* (= *mundr**), Dan. *mund*, Swed. *mun*, G. *mund*, Goth. *munths*.

Move. (F.—L.) M. E. *mouen* (*u* = *v*). — O. F. *movoir* (F. *mouvoir*).—L. *mouere*, to move, pp. *motus*. + Skt. *mīv*, to push. (√MU.)

commotion. (F.—L.) F. *commotion*. —L. *commotionem*, acc. of *com-motio* ; see motion (below).

emotion. (L.) Coined from L. *emotus*, pp. of *e-mouere*, to move away or much.

mob (1), a disorderly crowd. (L.) A contraction of *mobile uulgus*, i.e. fickle crowd. Both *mob* and *mobile* were in use, in the same sense, A.D. 1692-5.—L. *mobile*, neut. of *mobilis*, moveable, fickle; shoit for *mouibilis**.—L. *mouere*, to move.

mobile, easily moved. (F.—L.) F. *mobile.*—L. *mobilis* (above).

moment. (F. — L.) F. *moment.*—L. *momentum*, a movement; hence an instant of time ; short for *mouimentum**. — L. *mouere*, to move. **Doublets**, *momentum*, *movement*.

motion. (F. — L.) F. *motion.* — L. *motionem*, acc. of *motio*, movement.—L. *motus*, pp. of *mouere*, to move.

motive. (F. — L.) O. F. *motif*, 'a moving reason;' Cot.—Low L. *motiuus*, moving.—L. *mot-us*, pp. of *mouere*, to move.

motor. (L.) L. *mot-or*, a mover.

mutiny. (F.—L.) Formed from the old verb to *mutine*; Haml. iii. 4. 83.— O. F. *mutiner*, 'to mutine;' Cot.—O. F. *mutin*, tumultuous.—O. F. *meute*, a sedition; Low L. *mota*, a pack of hounds (= mod. F. *meute*). — L. *mota* (lit. moved, hence, a movement, bustle), fem. of *motus*, pp. of *mouere*, to move. Cf. mod. F. *émeute*.

promote, to advance, further. (L.) L. *promot-us*, pp. of *pro-mouere*, to move forward.

remote, distant. (L.) L. *remotus*, pp. of *re-mouere*, to remove (below). Or from O. F. *remot*, m. *remote*, f. 'remote, removed,' Cot.; from L. pp. *remotus*.

remove. (F.—L.) O. F. *remouvoir*, Cot. See **Re-** and **Move**.

Mow (1), to cut grass. (E.) M. E. *mowen*, pt. t. *mew*. A. S. *máwan*, to mow.+Du. *maaijen*, Dan. *meie*, G. *mähen*. Allied to Gk. ἀ-μά-ω, I reap, L. *me-t-ere*, to reap. (√ MA.)

mead (2), a meadow. (E.) So called because 'mowed.' M. E. *mede*. A. S. *mǽd*, a mead. Allied to prov. E. *math*, a mowing, as in *aftermath*.—A.S. *máwan*, to mow. Cf. G. *mahd*, a mowing, M. H. G. *mát*, a mowing, a mead, M. H. G. *matte*, a meadow, Swiss *matt*, a meadow (as in *Zermatt, Andermatt*).

meadow. (E.) This fuller form is due to the A.S. *mǽdu* (stem *mǽdw-*), a meadow.—A. S. *mǽd*, a mead. See also *moth*.

Mow (2), a heap, pile of hay or corn. (E.) M. E. *mowe*, A. S. *múga*, a mow. + Icel. *múga*, a swathe, also a crowd. Cf. Skt. *mav, mú*, to bind.

Mow (3), a grimace; *obsolete*. (F. — O. Du.) F. *moue*, 'a moe, or mouth;' Cot.—O. Du. *mouwe*, the protruded under-lip, in making a grimace (Oudemans). Allied to **Mock**, **Mop** (2).

Much; see **May** (1).

Mucilage; see **Mucus**.

Muck, filth. (Scand.) M. E. *muck.*— Icel. *myki*, dung; *moka*, to shovel dung out of a stable; Dan. *møg*, dung. ¶ Not allied to A. S. *meox*, dung.

Muck, Amuck, a term applied to malicious rage. (Malay.) Only in phr. 'to run amuck,' where *amuck* is all one word ; yet Dryden actually has 'runs *an Indian muck*,' Hind and Panther, iii. 1188. To *run amuck* = to run about in a rage.— Malay *ámuk*, 'rushing in a state of fienzy to the commission of indiscriminate murder ;' Marsden.

Mucus, slimy fluid. (L.) L. *mucus*, slime. + Gk. μύκος, discharge from the nose; μύκης, snuff of a wick.—√ MUK, to cast away; Skt. *much*, L. *mungere*, Gk. ἀπο-μύσσειν, to cast or wipe away.

mucilage, a slimy substance, gum. (F.—L.) F. *mucilage.*—L. *mucilago* (stem *mucilagin-*), mouldy moisture (4th cent.) —L. *mucus* (above).

Mud, wet soft earth, mire. (O Low G.) M. E. *mud* (not common). Not in A. S.— O. Low G. *mudde*, mud ; O. Swed. *modd*, mud (Ihre).+Bavarian *mott*, peat ; whence E. *moat*, q. v. Cf. also Icel. *móða*, mud ; Russ. *mytite*, to disturb, whence *myte*, a muddy place.

mother (3), lees, mouldiness. (O. Low G.) Properly *mudder*, but altered by confusion with M. E. *moder*, a mother. — O. Du. *modder*, mud or mire, also the lees, dregs, or 'the mother of wine and beer,' Hexham. + G. *moder*, mud, mould, mouldering decay ; which is actually sometimes called *mutter* (lit. mother). Extended from the word above.

muddle, to confuse. (O. Low G.) Lit. to dabble in mud ; frequentative from *mud*. 'Muddle, to rout with the bill, as geese and ducks do; also, to make tipsy and unfit for business ;' Kersey.+Dan. *muddre*, to stir up mud, from *mudder*, mud.

Muezzin, a Mohammedan crier of the hour of prayer. (Arab.) Arab. *mu-azzin*, *mu-zin*, the public crier, who assembles people to prayers. — Arab. *azan*, the call to prayers ; *uzn*, the ear.

Muff (1), a warm, soft cover for the hands. (Scand.) Formerly *muffe*; Minsheu. — O. Swed. *muff* (Ihre); Dan. *muffe*, a muff. Oldest sense 'sleeve.' + Du. *mof*, muff; O. Du. *mouwe*, a sleeve; G. *muff*; M. H. G. *mowe*, a wide hanging sleeve.

muffle, to cover up warmly. (F. — O. Low. G.) 'I *muffyll*;' Palsgrave. 'A *muffle*;' Levins (1570). — O. F. *mofle*, *moufle*, a kind of muff or mitten. — O. Du. *moffel*, a muff, mitten; dimin. of Du. *mof*, a muff (above).

Muff (2), a simpleton. (E.) Lit. 'a mumbler,' or indistinct speaker; hence a stupid fellow. Cf. prov. E. *muff*, *muffle*, to mumble; also *moffle*, *maffle*. + Du. *muffen*, to dote; prov. G. *muffen*, to be sulky. Allied to **Mumble**.

Muffle; see Muff (1).

Mufti, a magistrate. (Arab.) Arab. *muftí*, a magistrate. Allied to Arab. *fatwá*, a judgment, doom, sentence. ¶ The phr. *in mufti* means in a civilian costume, not in military dress.

Mug. (C.) (In Levins, 1570.) Prob. Celtic. — Irish *mugan*, a mug; *mucog*, a cup.

Muggy, damp and close. (Scand.) From Icel. *mugga*, soft drizzling mist; whence *mugguveðr*, muggy, misty weather. Cf. Dan. *muggen*, musty, mouldy, *mugne*, to grow musty. Perhaps allied to **Muck.**

Mugwort; see **Midge.**

Mulberry. (L. *and* E.) M. E. *moolbery*. Here the *l*, as is so often the case, stands for an older *r*, and M. E. *oo* answers to A. S. *ó*, as usual. Thus the prefix *mool-* is the same as A. S. *mór-*, in *mór-beám*, a mulberry tree. Again, the A. S. *mór-* is borrowed from L. *mōrus*, a mulberry-tree. The word *berry* is E.; see **Berry.** Cf. also Gk. μῶρον, μόρον, a mulberry, μορέα, a mulberry-tree. ¶ Similarly, G. *maulbeere*, a mulberry, is from L. *morus* and G. *beere*. **Der.** *syca-more*, q. v.

murrey, dark red; *obsolete*. (F. — L.) In Palsgrave. — O. F. *morée*, 'a kind of murrey, or dark red colour;' Cot. [Cf. Ital. *morato*, mulberry-coloured.] — L. *morus*, a mulberry.

Mulct, a fine. (L.) L. *mulcta*, a fine; also spelt *multa*. **Der.** *mulct*, verb.

Mule. (L.) A.S. *mul*. — L. *mūlus*, a mule.+Gk. μύκλος, an ass; μύκλα, a black stripe on an ass.

mulatto, one of mixed breed. (Span. — L.) Span. *mulato*, the same as *muleto*, a young mule, a mulatto. — L. *mulus*, mule.

Mulled; see Mould (1).

Mullein, verbascum. (E.) M. E. *mollyn*. A.S. *molegn*, mullein. (Cf. A. S. *holegn*, holly, whence prov. E. *hollin*, holly.) β.

Prob. named because good against moths; one kind is *Verbascum blattaria*, or moth-mullein); from Goth. *malo*, a moth, Dan. *möl*, a moth.

Mullet (1), a fish. (F. — L.) M. E. *molet*, *mulet*. — O. F. *mulet*; Cot. Dimin. from L. *mullus*, the red mullet.

Mullet (2), a five-pointed star; see Molar.

Mullion, an upright division between lights of windows. (F. — L.) A corruption of *munnion*, which occurs with the same sense. The lit. sense is 'stump,' because the *mullion* is, properly, the stump or lower part of the division below the tracery. — F. *moignon*, a stump. (Cf. E. *trunnion* = F. *troignon*, dimin. of F. *tronc* = Ital. *tronco*). — O. F. *moing*, maimed; the equivalent of Ital. *monco*, also *manco*, maimed. — L. *mancus*, maimed. Cf. Bret. *mouñ*, *moñ*, maimed, also occurring in the forms *mañk*, *moñk*, *moñs*. Also Span. *muñon*, the stump of an arm or leg; &c.

Multangular, &c.; see Multitude.

Multitude. (F. — L.) F. *multitude*. — L. *multitudinem*, acc. of *multitudo*, a multitude. — L. *multus*, many, much. Hence *mult-angular*, *multi-lateral*, &c.

multifarious. (L.) L. *multifarius*, manifold; the orig. sense seems to be 'many-speaking,' i.e. speaking on many subjects. — L. *multi-*, for *multus*, many; *fari*, to speak; see Fate.

multiply. (F. — L.) F. *multiplier*. — L. *multiplicare*. — L. *multiplic-*, from *multiplex*, many-fold; cf. *plic aris*, to fold. See Plait.

Mum! silence! (E.) M. E. *mom*, *mum*, to express the least sound made with closed lips. Cf. L. *mu*, Gk. μῦ (the same).

mumble, to speak indistinctly. (E.) Put for *mumm-le*. M. E. *momelen*, *mamelen*, to speak indistinctly; frequent. form due to M. E. *mom*, mum (above).

mummer, a masker, buffoon. (F. — Du.) O. F. *mommeur*, 'a mummer, one that goes a-mumming;' Cot. — O. Du. *mommen*, to go a-mumming; cf. *mom-aensicht*, a mummer's mask; Low. G. *mumme*, a mask. β. The word is imitative, from the sound *mum* or *mom*, used by nurses to frighten or amuse children, at the same time pretending to cover their faces. Cf. G. *mummel*, a bug-bear. **Der.** *mummer-y*, O. F. *mommerie*.

mump, to mumble, sulk, beg. (Du.) A *mumper* was a cant term for a beggar. —

Du. *mompen*, to mump, cheat (Sewel) ; cf. *mommelen*, *mompelen*, to mumble (Hexham). Thus *mump* is merely an emphatic form of *mum*, O. Du. *mommen*, to say mum, also to mask. Cf. Goth. *bi-mampjan*, to deride ; likewise of imitative origin.

mumps. (Du.) 'To have the *mumps*' or 'to be in the *mumps*' was to be sulky or sullen ; hence it was transferred to the disease which gave one a sullen appearance. From *mump* (above).

Mumble, Mummer; see Mum.

Mummy. (F. — Ital. — Pers.) O. F. *mumie*, a mummy. — Ital. *mummia*. — Pers. *mumáyin*, a mummy, embalmed body. — Pers. *móm*, wax, much used in embalming.

Mump, Mumps; see Mum.

Munch, to chew. (E.) M. E. *monchen* (Chaucer). Doubtless an imitative word, like *mumble*. ¶ It cannot be from F. *manger* (= L. *manducare*).

Mundane, worldly. (F. — L.) M. E. *mondain*. — F. *mondain*. — L. *mundanus*, adj. from *mundus*, the world (lit. order). — L. *mundus*, clean, adorned ; cf. Skt. *mand*, to adorn. (√ MAND.)

supramundane. (L.) L. *supra*, above ; *mundus* ; the world.

Municipal. (F. — L.) F. *municipal*. — L. *municipalis*, relating to a township. — L. *municipium*, a township which had the rights of Roman citizenship, whilst retaining its own laws. — L. *municip-*, stem of *municeps*, a free citizen, one who undertakes duties. — L. *muni-*, for *munus*, obligation, duty ; *capere*, to take. (√ MU.)

munificence, liberality. (F. — L.) F. *munificence*. — L. *munificentia*; formed from *munificus*, bountiful. — L. *muni-*, for *munus*, a duty, also a present ; *-fic-*, for *facere*, to make.

remunerate, to recompence. (L.) From pp. of *remunerare*, *remunerari*, to reward. — L. *re-*, again ; *munerari*, to discharge an office, from *muner-*, stem of *munus*, an office (above).

Muniment, a defence, title-deed. (F. — L.) F. *muniment*. — L. *munimentum*, a defence. — L. *munire*, to fortify ; put for *mœnire* *. — L. *mœnia*, neut. pl. walls, ramparts, defences. (√ MU.)

ammunition, store for defence. (F. — L.) From O. F. *amunition*, a soldiers' corruption, due to putting *l'amunition* for *la munition* (Littré). See below.

munition. (F. — L.) F. *munition*. — L. acc. *munitionem*, a defending. — L.

munitus, pp. of *munire* (above). Der. *am-munition* (above).

Munnion, old form of Mullion, q. v.

Mural. (F. — L.) F. *mural*. — L. *muralis*, belonging to a wall. — L. *murus*, a wall. Allied to Muniment. (√ MU.)

immure. (F. — L.) Put for *emmure*. — F. *emmurer*, to shut up in prison, lit. to enclose with a wall. — L. *im-* (= *in*), in ; *murus*, a wall.

Murder, Murther. (E.) M. E. *mordre*, *morthre*. A. S. *morðor*. + Goth. *maurthr*. β. We also find A. S. *morð*, Icel. *morð*, G. *mord*, death, cognate with L. *mors* (stem *mort-*) ; see Mortal.

Muriatic, briny. (L.) L. *muriaticus*, lying in brine. — L. *muria*, brine, salt liquor.

Muricated, prickly. (L.) L. *muricatus*, prickly. — L. *muric-*, stem of *murex*, a prickly fish, a spike.

Murky, Mirky. (E.) The *-y* is a modern addition. M. E. *mirke*, *merke*. A. S. *murc*, *myrce*, *mirce*, dark. + Icel. *myrkr*, Dan. Swed. *mörk*, dark, mirky.

Murmur, sub. (F. — L.) F. *murmure*. — L. *murmur*, a murmur; *murmurare*, to murmur. + Skt. *marmara*, rustling sound of wind. A reduplicated form; cf. G. *murren*, Icel. *murra*, to murmur. Of imitative origin.

Murrain; see Mortal.

Murrey; see Mulberry.

Murrion; see Morion.

Muscadel; see Musk.

Muscle (1), the fleshy part of the body. (F. — L.) F. *muscle*. — L. *musculum*, acc. of *musculus*, (1) a little mouse, (2) a muscle, from its creeping appearance when moved. Dimin. of L. *mus*, a mouse ; see Mouse. (Cf. F. *souris*, (1) mouse, (2) muscle).

muscle (2), **mussel**, a shell-fish. (L.) In earlier use. M. E. *muscle*, A. S. *muxle*, *muscle* (Wright), a muscle (fish). — L. *musculus*, a sea-muscle, also a little mouse (above).

niche, a recess in a wall for a statue. (F. — Ital. — L.) F. *niche*. — Ital. *nicchia*, a niche, a shell-like recess in a wall. — Ital. *nicchio*, a shell, also a nitch (Florio). — L. *mitulum*, *mytilum*, acc. of *mitulus*, *mytilus*, a sea-muscle. 'Derived in the same way as Ital. *secchia* from *situla*, a bucket, and *vecchio* from *uetulus*, old ; as to the change of initial, cf. Ital. *nespola* with L. *mespilum*, a medlar ;' Diez. We also find L. *mutulus*, a sea-muscle ; double dim. of *mu-s*, a mouse.

Muscoid, moss-like. (L. *with* Gk. *suffix*.)

L. *musco-*, crude form of *muscus*, moss; and Gk. suffix -ειδης, like, from εἶδος, form. See Moss.

Muse (1), to meditate. (F.–L.) M. E. *musen*. – F. *muser*, 'to muse, dreame;' Cot. – O. F. *muse**, the mouth; for which see muzzle (below). The image is that of a dog scenting the air when in doubt as to the scent; cf. Ital. *musare*, to muse, also to gape about, ' to hould ones muzle or snout in the aire,' Florio; from Ital. *muso*, snout.

amuse, to divert. (F. – L.) F. *amuser*, 'to amuse, make to muse or think of, to gaze at;' Cot. – F. *a* (= L. *ad*), to, at; O. F. *muser*, to gaze at, stare at, muse; see above.

muzzle, snout. (F. – L.) M. E. *mosel*. – O. F. *mosel** (not found), also *musel* (Burguy), later *museau*, 'muzzle;' Cot. Diez shews that the orig. F. torm was *morsel* (still preserved in Bret. *morzeel* or *muzel*, a muzzle, forms borrowed from O. F.). This O. F. *morsel* is a dimin. from Low L. *morsus*, a morsel, also a snout, beak. – L. *morsus*, a bite; from *morsus*, pp. of *mordere*, to bite. See Mordacity. Cf. Ital. *muso*, snout, *morso*, a snaffle (Florio).

Muse (2), a goddess of the arts. (F.–L. – Gk.) F. *muse*. – L. *musa*. – Gk. μοῦσα, a muse.

mosaic-work, ornamental work made with small pieces of marble, &c. (F. – L. – Gk.) O. F. *mosaïque*, 'mosaical work;' Cot. – Low L. *musaicus**, adj., an extended form from L. *musæum opus*, mosaic work. – Late Gk. μουσεῖον, mosaic work, lit. artistic, neut. of μουσεῖος, belonging to the muses, artistic. – Gk. μοῦσα, a muse.

museum. (L. – Gk.) L. *museum*. – Gk. μουσεῖον, temple of the muses, a study, a school. – Gk. μοῦσα, a muse.

music. (F. – L. – Gk.) M.E. *musik*. – F. *musique*. – L. *musica*. – Gk. μουσική, musical art, fem. of μουσικός, belonging to the muses. – Gk. μοῦσα, a muse.

Museum; see Muse (2).

Mushroom; see Moss.

Music; see Muse (2).

Musit, a small gap in a hedge. (F.) O. F. *musette*, 'a little hole;' Cot. Dimin. of O. F. *musse*, a secret corner. – F. *musser*, to hide. See Mich. Root unknown.

Musk, a perfume. (F. – L. – Pers. – Skt.) F. *musc*. – L. *muscum*, acc. of *muscus*. – Pers. *musk*, *misk*. – Skt. *mushka*, a testicle; because musk was obtained from a bag be-

hind the musk-deer's navel. Lit. 'thief;' from *mush*, to steal. See Mouse.

muscadel, muscatel, muscadine. (F. – Ital. – L. – Pers. – Skt.) O. F. *muscadel*. – O. Ital. *moscadello*, *moscatello*, *moscatino*, names of wines, from their perfume. – O. Ital. *moscato*, scented with musk. – O. Ital. *musco*, musk. – L. *muscum* (above). And see Nutmeg.

Musket; see Mosquito.

Muslin. (F. – Ital. – Syriac.) F. *mousseline*. – Ital. *mussolino*, dimin. of *mussolo*, muslin. – Syriac *Mosul*, a city in Kurdistan, whence it first came. Arab. *Mawsil* (the same).

Musquito; see Mosquito.

Mussel; see Muscle (2).

Mussulman; see Moslem.

Must (1), part of a verb implying 'obligation.' (E.) Only the pt. t. remains, which is now also used as a present. M. E. *mot*, *moot*, pres. t., I am able, I am free to, I ought; pt. t. *moste*, *muste*, I was able, I ought. A. S. *ic mót*, pres. t.; *ic móste*, I must, pt. t.; as if from an infin. *mótan**. **+** O. Sax. *mótan*, pr. t. *ik mót*, pt. t. *ik mósta*; Du. *moeten*, to be obliged; Swed. *måste*, I must, both as pres. and pt. tense (whence the E. use); G. *müssen*, pr. t. *ich muss*, pt. t. *ich musste*; Goth. pr. t. *ik mot*, pt. t. *ik mosta*.

Must (2), new wine. (L.) M. E. *must*, A. S. *must*. – L. *mustum*, new wine; neut. of *mustus*, fresh, new.

moist. (F. – L.) M. E. *moiste*, often with the sense 'fresh;' Ch. C. T. 459, 12249. – O. F. *moiste*, later *moïte*. – L. *musteus*, new. – L. *mustum*, *mustus* (above). Der. *moist-ure*, O. F. *moisteur*.

mustard. (F. – L.; *with* Teut. *suffix*.) M. E. *mostard*. – O. F. *mostarde* (F. *moutarde*). Cf. Ital. *mostarda*. It took its name from being mixed with *must* or vinegar (Littré). – L. *mustum*, must; with suffix *-ard* (= G. *hart*).

musty, mouldy, damp. (L.) A doublet of *moisty*, used by Chaucer in the sense of 'new,' but by Ascham in the sense of 'moist.' – L. *musteus* (above). Prob. confused with O. F. *moisi*, 'mouldy, musty, fusty,' Cot.; from which, however, it cannot possibly be derived.

Mustachio; see Moustache.

Mustard, Musty; see Must (2).

Muster; see Monition.

Mutable. (L.) M. E. *mutable*. – L. *mutabilis*, changeable. – L. *mutare*, to change. (Prob. for *mouitare**, from *mouere*, to move; and so allied to **Move**.)

commute, to exchange. (L.) L. *commutare*, to exchange with.

mew (3), a cage for hawks, &c. (F.– L.) The pl. *mews* now means a range of stabling, because the royal stables were rebuilt (A. D. 1534) in a place where the royal falcons had been kept (Stow). M. E. *mewe*, *mue*, a cage where hawks were kept when moulting.–O. F. *mue*, a moulting, also a mew for hawks. – F. *muer*, to change, moult.–L. *mutare*, to change. **Der.** *mew-s*, as above.

moult, to cast feathers, as birds. (L.) The *l* is intrusive. M. E. *mouten*.–L. *mutare*.

mutual. (F. – L.) O. F. *mutuël*. Extended from L. *mutuus*, mutual, reciprocal, orig. 'exchanged.'–L. *mutare*.

permutation. (F.–L.) F. *permutation*.–L. acc. *permutationem*, a changing. –L. *permutatus*, pp. of *per-mutare*, to change thoroughly.

transmutation. (F.–L.) F. *transmutation*.–L. acc. *transmutationem*.–L. *transmutatus*, pp. of *trans-mutare*, to change over, shift, transmute.

Mute (1), dumb. (F.–L.) M. E. *muet*. – F. *muet*. – L. *mutum*, acc. of *mutus*, dumb. Cf. Skt. *múka*, dumb. (✓MU.)

Mute (2), to dung, as birds; see **Smelt**.

Mutilate. (L.) From pp. of L. *mutilare*, to maim.–L. *mutilus*, maimed. + Gk. μύτιλος, μίτυλος, curtailed, docked.

Mutiny; see **Move**.

Mutter, to murmur. (E.) M. E. *muttren*, *moteren*. A frequentative verb, from a base *mut-*, to express inarticulate mumbling. So also L. *mutire*, to mutter, prov. G. *mustern*, to whisper.

Mutton. (F. – L.?) M. E. *motoun*.– O F. *moton* (F. *mouton*), a sheep; Low L. *multo*, a sheep. Cf. Ital. *montone* (for *moltone**), a sheep. Prob. of Latin origin, whence also Irish and Manx *molt*, Gael.

mult, W. *mollt*, a wether sheep. Thus Diez cites Prov. *mout*, Como *mot*, Grisons *mutt*, castrated, and derives all from L. *mutilus*, maimed.

Mutual; see **Mutable**.

Muzzle; see **Muse** (1).

My; see **Me**.

Myriad. (Gk.) Gk. μυριάδ-, stem of μυριάς, the number of 10,000.–Gk. μυρίος, numberless.

Myrmidon. (L. – Gk.) Gen. in pl. *Myrmidons*. – L. *Myrmidones*, pl. – Gk. Μυρμιδόνες, pl. a warlike people of Thessaly, formerly in Ægina (Homer).

Myrrh. (F. – L. – Gk.–Arab.) M. E. *mirre*. – O. F. *mirre* (11th cent.); F. *myrrhe*.–L. *myrrha*.–Gk. μύρρα.–Arab. *murr*, (1) bitter, (2) myrrh, named from its bitterness. + Heb. *mór*, bitter.

Myrtle. (F. – L. – Gk. – Pers.) O. F. *myrtil*, dimin. of *myrte*, *meurte*, the myrtle-tree.–L. *murtus*, *myrtus*.–Gk. μύρτος.– Pers. *múrd*, the myrtle.

Mystery (1), a secret rite. (L.–Gk.) M. E. *mysterie*. – L. *mysterium*. – Gk. μυστήριον (Rom. xvi. 25). – Gk. μύστης, one who is initiated.–Gk. μύειν, to close the eyes; μῦ, a slight sound with closed lips. (✓MU, to bind.)

mystic, secret, allegorical. (F.–L.– Gk.) F. *mystique*. – L. *mysticus*. – Gk. μυστικός, mystic.–Gk. μύστης, fem. μύστις, one who is initiated (above).

mystify. (F. – Gk. *and* L.) F. *mystifier*, a modern and ill-coined word; coined from Gk. μυστι-κός, mystic, and F. *-fier* = L. *-ficare*, for *facere*, to make.

Mystery (2), **Mistery**, a trade, handicraft; see **Minor**.

Myth, a fable. (Gk.) Gk. μῦθος, a fable.–Gk. μῦ, a slight saying, a word, speech, tale. (✓MU.)

mythology. (F. – L. – Gk.) F. *mythologie*.–L. *mythologia*.–Gk. μυθολογία, legendary lore.–Gk. μῦθο-s, a fable; λέγειν, to tell.

N.

Nab, to seize. (Scand.) From Swed. *nappa*, Dan. *nappe*, to catch, snatch at, nab.

Nabob, an Indian prince. (Hindi. – Arab.) Hindi *nawáb* or *nawwáb*, orig. a pl. sb., but used in the sing. as a title of honour. Pl. of Arab. *náïb*, a vice-gerent, deputy, vice-roy. Cf. Arab. *nawb*, supplying the place of another.

Nadir, the point of the sky opposite the zenith. (Arab.) Arab. *nazír*, short for *nazíru's 'samt*, the nadir; lit. 'corresponding to the zenith.'–Arab. *nazír*, alike, corresponding to; *as'samt*, the azimuth, also the zenith. See **Azimuth**, **Zenith**. (The *z* is here the 17th letter of the Arab. alphabet.)

Nag (1), a little horse; see **Neigh.**

Nag (2), to worry, tease; see **Gnaw.**

Naiad, a water-nymph. (L. – Gk.) L. *naiad-*, stem of *naias*. – Gk. ναιάς, a water-nymph. – Gk. νάειν, to flow. (√ SNU.)

Nail. (E.) M. E. *nayl.* A. S. *nægel.*+ Du. *nagel*, Dan. *nagle*, Swed. *nagel*, G. *nagel*; Icel. *nagl*, the human nail, *nagli*, a nail or spike. β. The Teut. type is NAGLA, i.e. gnawer, scratcher, or piercer; see **Gnaw.** Allied to Lithuan. *nagas*, a claw, Russ. *nogote*, a nail, Skt. *nakha*, (for *nagha**), nail of the finger or toe (√ NAGH). ¶ But Gk. ὄνυξ, L. *unguis*, Irish *ionga*, a nail, seem to come from a √ ANGH, perhaps a variant of the root above.

Naive; see **Natal.**

Naked. (E.) A. S. *nacod.*+Du. *naakt*, G. *nackt*, Goth. *nakwaths*, Icel. *naktr*; also Dan. *nögen*, Swed. *naken*, Icel. *nakinn*. All these are pp. forms, from a verb *nake*, to strip, which actually occurs in Chaucer, tr. of Boethius, l. 4288. Allied to Skt. *nagna*, Russ. *nagoi*, L. *nudus*, Irish *nochd*, W. *noeth*, stripped, bare. (√ NAG, to strip.) See *nude.*

Name. (E.) A.S. *nama.*+Du. *naam*, Icel. *nafn*, *namn*, Dan. *navn*, Swed. *namn*, Goth. *namo*, G. *name*. Further allied to L. *nomen* or *gnomen*, a name; Gk. ὄνομα, οὔνομα (for ὄ-γνομαν*), Skt. *náman* (for *jnáman**); from √ GNA, to know. See **Know.**

  surname. (F. – L.; *and* E.) F. *sur*, L. *super*, above, over; and E. *name.*

Nankeen, Nankin, a kind of cotton cloth. (China.) So called from *Nankin*, in China.

Nap (1), a short sleep. (E.) M. E. *nappen*, verb, to doze. A.S. *hnæppian*, verb, to doze. Allied to A. S. *hnipian*, to bend oneself, droop, Icel. *hnipna*, to droop.

Nap (2), rough surface of cloth. (C.) Formerly *nop*; see **Knap.**

Nape; see **Knap.**

Napery, table-linen; see **Map.**

Naphtha. (L. – Gk. – Arab.) L. *naphtha*. – Gk. νάφθα. – Arab. *naft*, *nift*, naphtha, bitumen.

Napkin; see **Map.**

Narcissus; see **Narcotic.**

Narcotic, producing stupor. (F. – Gk.) F. *narcotique*. – Gk. ναρκωτικός, benumbing. – Gk. ναρκόω, I benumb; ναρκάω, I grow numb. – Gk. νάρκη, numbness, orig. con-traction; put for σνάρκη, i. e. contraction. See **Snare.**

narcissus, a flower. (L. – Gk.) L. *narcissus*. – Gk. νάρκισσος; named from its *narcotic* properties.

Nard, an unguent. (F. – L. – Gk. – Pers. – Skt.) F. *nard.* – L. *nardus*. – Gk. νάρδος, Mk. xiv. 3. – Pers. *nard.* – Skt. *nalada*, the Indian spikenard. – Skt. *nal*, to smell. Der. *spike-nard.*

Narration. (F. – L.) F. *narration.* – L. acc. *narrationem*, a tale. – L. *narratus*, pp. of *narrare*, to relate, lit. to make known. – L. *narus*, *gnarus*, knowing, acquainted with. – √ GNA, to know; see **Know.**

Narrow. (E.) M. E. *narowe*, *narewe*, *narwe*. A.S. *nearu*, narrow, closely drawn. Allied to **Snare, Nervo, Narcotic.** ¶ Not allied to *near.*

Narwhal, sea-unicorn. (Scand.) Dan. Swed. *narhval*; Icel. *náhvalr*, a narwhal. The lit. sense is 'corpse-whale;' the fish being (often) of a pallid colour. – Icel. *ná-r*, corpse; *hvalr*, whale.

Nasal; see **Nose.**

Nascent; see **Natal.**

Nasturtium; see **Nose.**

Nasty. (Scand.) Formerly also *nasky*; see *Mau-lave* in Cot. Put for *nasxky*, an initial *s* being lost. – Swed. dial. *naskug*, nasty, dirty, also spelt *snaskig*; Swed. *snuskig*, nasty. – Swed. dial. *snaska*, to eat like a pig, be slovenly; Dan. *snaske*, to eat like a pig. + Low G. *nask*, nasty; Norw. *nask*, greedy, *naska*, to champ. Allied to **Snatch.**

Natal, belonging to one's birth. (F. – L.) F. *natal* (O. F. *nöel*). – L. *natalis.* – L. *natus* (for *gnatus*), born (cf. Gk. κασί-γνητος, a blood relation); pp. of *nasci*, to be born. – √ GAN, to beget. See **Kin.**

  cognate. (L.) L. *co-gnatus*, allied by birth. – L. *co-* (for *cum*), together; *gnatus*, born, old form of *natus.*

  impregnate, to render pregnant. (L.) From pp. of L. *imprægnare*, to impregnate. – L. *im-* (for *in*), in; *prægnare**, for which see **pregnant** (below).

  innate, in-born. (L.) L. *innatus*, in-born. – L. *in*, in; *natus*, born; see **Natal.**

  naive, artless. (F. – L.) F. *naïve*, fem. of *naïf*, native, natural. – L. *natiuus*, native. – L. *natus*, born; see **Natal.**

  nascent, springing up. (L.) L. *nascent-*, stem of pres. pt. of *nasci*, to be born, arise, spring up, inceptive verb with pp. *natus* (above).

nation. (F. — L.) F. *nation.* — L. *nationem*, acc. of *natio*, a nation. — L. *natus*, born.

native. (F. — L.) F. *natif*, 'native;' Cot. — L. *natiuus*, natural. — L. *natus*, born.

nature. (F. — L.) F. *nature.* — L. *natura*, nature. — L. *natus*, born.

pregnant, fruitful, with child. (F. — L.) O. F. *pregnant*, 'pregnant, pithy;' Cot. — L. *prægnantem*, acc. of *prægnans*, pregnant. *Prægnans* has the form of a pres. part. of an obs. verb *prægnare**, to be before a birth, to be about to bear. — L. *præ*, before; *gnare**, to bear, of which the pp. *gnatus* or *natus* is used as the pp. of *nasci*, to be born.

preternatural. (L.) From L. *præter*, beyond; and *natural*, adj. from *nature*.

supernatural. (L.) From L. *super*, beyond, and *natural*, adj. from *nature*.

Nation, Native, Nature; see Natal.

Naught; see No (1).

Nauseous, Nautical; see Nave (2).

Nautilus, Naval; see Nave (2).

Nave (1), the hub of a wheel. (E.) M. E. *naue* (*u*=*v*). A.S. *nafu, nafa.* ✠ Du. *naaf*, Icel. *nöf*, Dan. *nav*, Swed. *naf*, G. *nabe*; Skt. *nábhi*, the nave of a wheel, navel, centre, boss, from *nabh*, to burst out. (✓ NABH.)

auger. (E.) Formerly *nauger*, a tool for boring holes. — A. S. *nafegár*, an auger, lit. nave-piercer, for boring holes in the nave of a wheel. — A. S. *nafa*, a nave; *gár*, a piercer, that which gores; see Gore (3).

navel. (E.) M. E. *nauel* (*u*=*v*); A.S. *nafela*, navel; dimin. of *nafa*, nave (or boss) of a wheel (above). ✠ Du. *navel*, Icel. *nafli*, Dan. *navle*, Swed. *nafle*, G. *nabel*; all dimin. forms; see above.

Nave (2), the body of a church. (F. — L.) F. *nef*, a ship, also the body of a church; by the common similitude which likened Christ's church to a ship. — L. *nauem*, acc. of *nauis*, a ship. ✠ Gk. *ναῦς*, a ship, Skt. *nau*. (✓ SNU.)

nauseous. (L. — Gk.) L. *nauseosus*, adj., from *nausea*, sea-sickness. — Gk. *ναυσία*, sea-sickness. — Gk. *ναῦς*, a ship.

nautical. (L. — Gk.) From L. *nauticus*, nautical. — Gk. *ναυτικός*, pertaining to ships. — Gk. *ναῦ-s*, a ship.

nautilus, a shell-fish. (L. — Gk.) L. *nautilus*. — Gk. *ναυτίλος*, a sea-man; also the nautilus (from its sailing). — Gk. *ναῦ-s*, ship.

naval. (F. — L.) F. *naval.* — L. *naualis*, belonging to ships. — L. *nauis*, a ship.

navigable, that can be traversed by ships. (F. — L.) F. *navigable.* — L. *nauigabilis.* — L. *nauigare*, to navigate. — L. *naui-*, crude form of *nauis*, a ship; *-igare*, for *agere*, to drive.

navigation. (F. — L.) F. *navigation*, sailing. — L. acc. *nauigationem*; from pp. of L. *nauigare* (above).

navy, a fleet. (F. — L.) M. E. *navie.* — O. F. *navie*, orig. a single ship. — L. *nauia*, a vessel. — L. *naui-s*, a ship.

Nay; see No (1).

Nazarite, a Jew who made vows of abstinence, &c. (Heb.; *with* Gk. *suffix*.) Heb. *názar*, to separate oneself, vow, abstain; with suffix *-ite* (= L. *-ita*, Gk. *-ιτης*).

Neap; see Nip.

Near; see Nigh.

Neat (1), black cattle, an ox. (E.) M.E. *neet*, both sing. and pl. A.S. *neát*, pl. *neát*, cattle. ✠ Icel. *naut*, pl. *naut*, cattle; M.H.G. *nôz, noss*, cattle. β. So named from their usefulness and employment; from pt. t. of A.S. *neótan, niótan*, to use, employ; cf. Icel. *njóta*, G. *geniessen*, Goth. *niutan*, to enjoy, get benefit from. Cf. Lithuan. *naudà*, usefulness, Skt. *nand*, to be pleased. (✓ NUD.) Der. *neat-herd*.

Neat (2), tidy. (F. — L.) F. *net*, masc., *nette*, fem., neat, pure. — L. *nitidus*, shining, neat. — L. *nitere*, to shine.

net (2), clear of all charges. (F. — L.) F. *net*, pure; hence, free (above).

Neb, beak, bill, nose; see Snap.

Nebula, a little cloud. (L.) L. *nebula.* ✠ Gk. *νεφέλη*, dimin. of *νέφος*, cloud, mist; Skt. *nabhas*, sky, æther, from *nabh*, to burst (from the bursting of rain-clouds). (✓ NABH.) See Nave (1).

Necessary. (F. — L.) O. F. *necessaire.* — L. *necessarius*, needful. — L. *necesse*, neut. adj., necessary. Perhaps allied to *nancisci*, to get.

Neck. (E.) M.E. *nekke.* A.S. *hnecca*, neck, orig. nape of the neck. ✠ Du. *nek*, Icel. *hnakki*, Dan. *nakke*, Swed. *nacke*, G. *nacken*, O. H. G. *hnach*, nape of the neck, back of the head. β. Orig. sense 'bump' or projection; allied to F. *nuque*, nape of the neck, and to E. Knuckle. See Nape.

Necromancy, divination by communion with the dead. (F. — L. — Gk.) M. E. *nigromancie* (since altered). — O. F. *nigromance*, 'nigromancy, conjuring, the black art;'

Cot. — Low L. *nigromantia*, corrupt form of L. *necromantia*. — Gk. νεκρομαντεία, necromancy. — Gk. νεκρό-s, a corpse; *μαντεία*, prophetic power. β. Gk. νεκρός is from νέκυς, a corpse; cf. L. *necare*, to kill. (√ NAK.) Gk. *μαντεία* is from μάντις, a -seer, lit. thinker. (√ MAN.) ¶ *Necromancy* was called 'the black art' owing to a popular etymology from L. *niger*, black; cf. the Low L. *nigromantia*.

Nectar. (L. — Gk.) L. *nectar*. — Gk. νέκταρ, the drink of the gods.

Need. (E.) M. E. *need*. A. S. *néd, niéd, nýd*, orig. compulsion. + Du. *nood*, Icel. *nauð*, Dan. Swed. *nöd*, Goth. *nauths*, G. *noth*. Allied to Russ. *nyjda*, need, *nydite*, to force; Skt. *nud*, to drive. (√ NU.)

Needle; see **Snare**.

Neese; see **Sneeze.**

Nefarious; see **Fate.**

Nogation, denial. (F. — L.) F. *negation*. — L. acc. *negationem*, denial. — L. *negatus*, pp. of *negare*, to deny; opposed to *aiere*, to affirm. Due to *ne*, not; and some form akin to *aiere*, to affirm; see **No** (1). *Aiere* is allied to Gk. ἠμί, I say; Skt. *ah*, to speak. (√ AGH.)

abnegate. (L.) From pp. of L. *ab-negare*, to deny.

deny. (F. — L.) M. E. *denien*. — O. F. *denier*, earlier form *deneier*. — L. *de-negare*, to deny fully.

renegade, renegado. (Span. — L.) Span. *renegado*, an apostate, one who has denied the faith; orig. pp. of *renegar*, to forsake the faith. — L. *re*, again; *negare*, to deny.

runagate, a vagabond. (F. — L.) A corruption of M. E. *renegat*, an apostate, villain; Ch. C. T. 5353. [The corruption was due to a popular etymology from *runne a gate* = run on the road, hence, to be a vagabond.] — O. F. *renegat*, 'a renegadoe;' Cot. — Low L. *renegatus*, pp. of *renegare*, to deny again, forsake the faith. — L. *re*, again; *negare*.

Neglect, Negligence; see **Legend.**

Negotiate, to do business. (L.) From pp. of L. *negotiare*, to do business. — L. *negotium*, business; compounded of *nec*, not, and *otium*, leisure.

Negro; see **Nigrescent.**

Negus. (E.) A beverage invented by Colonel *Negus* (one of a Norfolk family) in the time of Queen Anne.

Neif, Neaf, the fist. (Scand.) M. E. *neue* (*u* = *v*), dat. case. — Icel. *hnefi*, fist;

Swed. *näfve*, Dan. *næve*. Lit. 'closed' hand; allied to Gk. κνάμπτειν, to crook, bend.

Neigh. (E.) M. E. *neзen*. A. S. *hnégan*, to neigh; an imitative word. + Icel. *gneggja*, *hneggja*, Swed. *gnägga*, Dan. *gnegge*, O. Du. *neyen*, to neigh.

nag (1), a horse. (O. Low G.) M. E. *nagge*. — O. Du. *negghe, negge*, a small horse, lit. 'neigher.' From the verb above.

Neighbour; see **Nigh** and **Boor.**

Neither; see **No** (1).

Nemesis; see **Nomad.**

Neology, Neophyte, Neoteric; see **Now.**

Nepenthe, Nepenthes, a drug which lulled sorrow. (Gk.) Gk. νηπενθές, an epithet of a soothing drug (in Homer); neut. of νηπενθής, free from sorrow. — Gk. νη-, neg. prefix; πένθος, grief, allied to πάθος. See **No** (1) and **Pathos.**

Nephew. (F. — L.) M. E. *neueu* (— *neveu*). — O. F. *neveu*, 'a nephew;' Cot. — L. *nepotem*, acc. of *nepos*, a grandson, also a nephew. + Skt. *napát*, a grandson; A. S. *nefa*, a nephew; G. *neffe*, nephew. **Der.** *nepot-ism*, favouritism to relations, from L. *nepot-*, stem of *nepos*.

niece. (F. — L.) M. E. *nece, neyce*. — O. F. *niece* (F. *nièce*). — Low L. *neptia*, a niece. — L. *neptis*, a grand-daughter, niece; used as fem. of L. *nepos* (above).

Nereid, a sea-nymph. (L. — Gk.) L. *Nereid-*, stem of *Nereis*. — Gk. Νηρεΐs, a daughter of *Nereus* (Gk. Νηρεύς), an ancient sea-god. — Gk. νηρός, wet. (√ SNU.)

aneroid, dry, applied to a barometer having no liquid mercury in it. (Gk.) Coined from Gk. ἀ-, not; νηρό-s, wet; εἶδος, form, kind.

Nerve; see **Snare.**

Nesh, tender, soft. (E.) M. E. *nesh*. A. S. *hnæsce, hnesce*, soft. + Goth. *hnaskwus*, soft, tender.

Ness, a promontory. (E.) Seen in *Sheer-ness*, &c. A. S. *næss*, headland. + Icel. *nes*, Dan. *næs*, Swed. *näs*. Perhaps allied to **Nose.**

Nest. (E.) M. E. and A. S. *nest*. + Du. *nest*, Swed. *näste*, G. *nest*, Bret. *neiz*, Irish and Gael. *nead*, L. *nīdus* (for *nis-dus**), Lithuan. *lizdas* (for *nizdas**), Skt. *nída*, a nest, a den. β. Orig. 'a place to sit in.' Explained as short for **ni-sed-os*, a place in which to sit down; cf. Skt. *ni-sad*, to sit down. See **Sit. Der.** *nest-le*, frequent. form, orig. 'to frequent a nest' or resort; *nest-l-ing*.

Net (1), an implement for catching fish. (E.) A. S. *net*, *nett*. **+** Du. *net*, Icel. Dan. *net*, Swed. *nät*, Goth. *nati*, G. *netz*. Prob. allied to Skt. *nada*, a river.

Net (2), clear of all charges; see **Neat** (2).

Nether, lower. (E.) M. E. *nethere*. A. S. *neoðera, neoðra*, nether; a comp. adj. due to *niðer*, adv., downward, also a compar. form. To be divided as *neo-ðera, ni-ðer*, the suffix *-ðer* being comparative, as in *o-ther, nei-ther* (cf. Gk. *-τερος*, Skt. *-tara*). We find Skt. *ni-tarám*, adv., excessively, continually, grammatically a comp. form from *ni*, downward, into. **+** Icel. *neðri*, adj., *neðarr*, adv.; Dan. *neder-* (in comp.), whence *ned*, downward; Swed. *nedre*, G. *nieder*, nether. Der. *nether-most*, corruption of A. S. *niðemesta* (= *ni-ðe-m-est-a*); here *ni* (i. e. down) is the base, *-ðe-m* = Aryan *-ta-ma* (as in L. *op-ṭi-mus*), and *-est* is the usual A. S. superlative suffix.

beneath. (E.) M. E. *benethe*. A. S. *beneoðan*, prep. below. **—** A. S. *be-*, by; *neoðan*, adv. below, an unoriginal form suggested by *neoðera*, nether.

Nettle. (E.) M. E. *netle*. A. S. *netele, netle*, a dimin. form. **+** Du. *netel*, Dan. *nelde* (for *nedle**), Swed. *nässla* (for *nätla**), G. *nessel*. The simple form appears in O. H. G. *nazza*, Gk. *κνίδη*, a nettle, allied to *κναδ-άλλειν*, to scratch. Orig. sense 'scratcher' or 'stinger.' (Base HNAT = Aryan KNAD.)

nit, egg of a louse; a louse. (E.) M. E. *nite*, a nit, also a louse; A.S. *hnitu*. Orig. that which attacks or stings, from A.S. *hnítan*, to gore (Icel. *hníta*, to strike). **+** Du. *neet*, Icel. *nitr*, Dan. *gnid*, Swed. *gnet*, G. *niss*, Russ. *gnida*, a nit, Gk. *κόνις* (stem *κονίδ-*) (Base HNIT, from HNAT.)

Neuralgia; see **Snare**.

Neuter, Never; see **No** (1).

New; see **Now**.

Newel; see **Nucleus**.

Newfangled, News; see **Now**.

Newt, a kind of lizard. (E.) The initial *n* is unoriginal; *a newt* stands for *an ewt*. M. E. *newte*; also *ewte*, which is a contraction of M. E. *evete*. **—** A. S. *efeta*, a lizard. Orig. sense 'water-animal.' The base *ef-* = Skt. *ap*, water, Lithuan. *uppis*, a stream; cf. Lithuan. *uppitakis*, adj., that which goes in the water, as sb., a trout.

Next; see **Nigh**.

Nib; see **Snap**.

Nibble; see **Nip**.

Nice, fastidious, delicious. (F. **—** L.) M. E. *nice*, foolish, simple, later fastidious, and lastly delicious. **—** O. F. *nice*, lazy, simple; orig. ignorant. **—** L. *nescium*, acc. of *nescius*, ignorant. **—** L. *ne*, not; *sci-re*, to know. See **No** (1) and **Science**.

Niche; see **Muscle**.

Nick (1), a small notch; see **Notch**.

Nick (2), the devil. (E.) A name taken from our old mythology. A. S. *nicor*, a water-sprite, hobgoblin. **+** Icel. *nykr*, Dan. *nök, nisse*, Swed. *näcken*, G. *nix*, a water-goblin.

Nickel, a grayish white metal. (G. **—** Gk.?) G. *nickel*, nickel; *kupfernickel*, nickel of copper. *Kupfer-nickel* meant 'copper of Nicholas or Nichol,' a name given in derision, as it was thought to be a base ore of copper (Webster). If so, then *nickel* is from Gk. *Νικόλαος*, Nicholas (Acts vi. 5). ¶ Doubtful.

Nicknack; see **Knickknack**.

Nickname; see **Eke**.

Nicotian, belonging to tobacco. (F.) O. F. *Nicotiane*, 'Nicotian, tobacco, first sent into France by *Nicot* in 1560;' Cot. *Nicot* is a personal name.

Niece; see **Nephew**.

Niggard, a miser. (Scand.) M. E. *nigard*; where the suffix *-ard* is of F. origin (= O. H. G. *hart*, hard). We also find M. E. *nigun*, a niggard, and *niggish*, adj., stingy. **—** Icel. *hnöggr*, niggardly, Swed. *njugg*, niggardly, scanty.

Nigh. (E.) M. E. *neh, neih, ney*. A. S. *nedh, néh*, nigh; adj., adv., and prep. **+** Du. *na*, adv., Icel. *ná-* (as in *ná-búi*, a neighbour), Goth. *nehw, nehwa*, adv., G. *nahe*, adj., *nach*, prep., nigh. Closely allied to Goth. *ganohs*, sufficient, and to E. **Enough**. The sense is 'that which reaches to,' or 'that which suffices.' (√NAK.)

near, nigh. (E.) Now used as a positive, but orig. the comparative of *nigh*. [The form *nearer* is a double comparative.] M. E. *nerre*, adj., *ner*, adv., nigher; A. S. *neár*, comparative adv. from *neáh*, nigh. **+** Icel. *nær*, adv., both positive and comparative, orig. the latter.

neighbour. (E.) M. E. *neighebour*; A. S. *neáhgebúr* or *neáhbúr*. **—** A. S. *neáh*, nigh; *búr*, or *gebúr*, a husbandman, the same word as Du. *boer*, a boor. See **Boor**. **+** G. *nachbar*, M. H. G. *náchbúr*; from *nách*, nigh, *búr*, a husbandman.

next, nighest. (E.) M. E. *next* or

nehest, superl. of *neh*, nigh; A. S. *nêhst*, superl. of *nêh*, *nedh*, nigh.

Night. (E.) M. E. *night*, *niht*. A. S. *niht*, *neht*, *neaht*.+Du. G. *nacht*, Icel. *nátt*, Dan. *nat*, Swed. *natt*, Goth. *nahts*.+W. *nos*, Irish *nochd*, Lithuan. *naktis*, Russ. *noche*, L. *nox* (stem *noct-*), Gk. νύξ (stem νυκτ-), Skt. *nakta*. Lit. 'dead' time; cf. Skt. *nashta*, lost, invisible, dead; L. *necare*, to kill. (√NAK.)

benighted. (E.) Pp. of rare verb *be-night*, to obscure.

nightingale. (E.) M. E. *nightingale*, earlier *nightegale* (the *n* having been inserted); A. S. *nihtegale*. − A. S. *nihte*, gen. of *niht*, night; *gale*, a singer, from *galan*, to sing. Lit. 'singer by night.' So also Du. *nachtegaal*, Dan. *nattergal*, Swed. *näktergal*, G. *nachtigall*, O. H. G. *nahtagala*. See **Yell.**

nightmare, an incubus. (E.) M. E. *nightemare*. From A. S. *niht*, night; *mara*, a nightmare, incubus, lit. 'a crusher,' from √MAR, to crush. See **Mar.** [*Mara* is quite distinct from A. S. *mere*, a mare, but the two have been confused in Du. *nacht-merrie*, a nightmare.]+Icel. *mara*, Swed. *mara*, Dan. *mare*, Low G. *moor*, O. H. G. *mara*, *mar*; all with the sense of incubus or crushing weight on the breast.

nightshade, a plant. (E.) A. S. *niht-scadu*. − A. S. *niht*, night; *scadu*, shade; prob. because thought to be evil, and loving night.

nocturn, a service of the church. (F.− L.) F. *nocturne*, a nocturn; orig. nocturnal. − Low L. *nocturna*, a nocturn; fem. of L. *nocturnus*, nocturnal. Put for *nocttur-nus* *; from *noct-*, crude form of *nox*, night.

Nigrescent, growing black. (L.) From stem of pres. pt. of *nigrescere*, to grow black, inceptive of *nigrere*, to be black. − L. *nigr-*, for *niger*, black. Lit. 'night-like;' cf. Skt. *niç*, night, allied to *nakta*, night; see **Night.**

negro. (Span. − L.) Span. *negro*. − L. *nigrum*, acc. of *niger*, black.

Nimble, active. (E.) M. E. *nimel*; the *b* is excrescent. Lit. 'ready to catch;' from A. S. *nim-an*, to catch, take, seize; with suffix *-ol*, as in *sprǽc-ol*, talkative. We actually find A. S. *numol* or *numul*, taking, seizing, or quick at taking. Cf. Icel. *nema*, Goth. *niman*, G. *nehmen*, to take. (√NAM.)

benumb. (E.) M. E. *benome*, orig. a pp. with the sense of 'benumbed' or 'deprived of.' − A. S. *be-*, prefix, lit. 'by;' *numen*, pp. of *niman*, to take; see below.

numb. (E.) M. E. *nome*, *nomen*, pp. seized, taken, caught with, overpowered, deprived of sensation. Pp. of M. E. *nimen* (A. S. *niman*), to take; see **Nimble.**+ Icel. *numinn*, bereft, pp. of *nema*, to take.

Nine. (E.) M. E. *nine*, where the final *-e* is a pl. suffix, and *nin-* is for *nizen*, nine (Layamon). A. S. *nigon*, *nigen*, nine.+ Du. *negen*, Icel. *níu*, Dan. *ni*, Sw. *nio*, G. *neun*, Goth. *niun*, W. *naw*, Ir. *naoi*, L. *nouem*, Gk. ἐννέα (=ἐ-νέϜ-α), Skt. *navan*, nine.

nones, the 9th day before the ides. (L.) From L. *nona*, ninth (i. e. ninth day), fem. of *nōnus*, ninth. Put for *nouim-us* *; from *nouem*, nine.

noon, mid-day. (L.) Orig. the 9th hour or 3 P.M., but afterwards the time of the church-service called *nones* was shifted to mid-day. We find A. S. *nón-tíd* (lit. noon-tide), the ninth hour, Mk. xv. 33. − L. *nona*, i. e. ninth hour, fem. of *nōnus*, ninth (above).

November. (L.) L. *Nouember*, the ninth month of the Roman year. − L. *nouem*, nine.

nuncheon, a luncheon. (Hybrid; L. and E.) The ending is confused with that of *luncheon*. M. E. *nonechenche* (for *none-schenche*), Riley, Memorials of London, p. 265; lit. a 'noon-drink,' to accompany the *nonemete* or 'noon-meat.' − M. E. *none*, noon; *schenche*, a pouring out of drink. − A. S. *nón*, noon (of L. origin, as above); *scencan*, to pour out drink. β. The A. S. *scencan* is lit. 'to pour out through a pipe;' derived from A. S. *scanc*, a shank, hollow bone, pipe; see **Shank.**

Ninny, a simpleton. (Ital.) Ital. *ninno*, a child (Diez). Cf. Span. *niño*, a child, one of little experience. − Ital. *ninna*, a lullaby, nurse's song to lull children to sleep, also written *nanna*. Of imitative origin.

Nip. (E.) M. E. *nippen*, put for *knippen*; see G. Douglas, Prol. to Æn. xii. l. 94. Not in A. S. + Du. *knijpen*, to pinch, *knippen*, to snap; Dan. *knibe*, Sw. *knipa*, G. *kneifen*, *kneipen*, to pinch. Also Lithuan. *žnybti*, *žnypti*, to nip. (Base KNIB or KNIP.)

knife. (E.) M. E. *knif*, pl. *kniues* (with *u* = *v*). A. S. *cníf*, a knife, lit. an instrument for nipping or cutting off; see above. **+** Du. *knijf*, Icel. *knífr*, Dan. *kniv*, Swed. *knif*, prov. G. *kneif*. (Cf. F. *canif*, from G.)

neap, scanty, very low ; said of a tide. (E.) M. E. *neep*; A. S. *nép*. A. S. *nép* stands for *hnép*, as shewn by Icel. *hneppr* or *neppr*, scanty. Cf. also Dan. *knap*, scanty, strait, narrow, *knap* or *neppe*, adv., scarcely. Orig. sense 'pinched.' Allied to **Nip.**

nibble. (E.) Lit. ' to nip often ; ' the frequent. of *nip*, to pinch off the end of grass, &c. **+** Low G. *nibbeln*, *knibbeln*, to nibble, to gnaw slightly. (Cf. *dibble* from *dip*.)

Nipple ; see **Snap.**

Nit ; see **Nettle.**

Nitre. (F. – L. – Gk. – Arab.) F. *nitre*. – L. *nitrum*. – Gk. νίτρον. – Arab. *nitrún*, *natrún*, natron, native alkaline salt. (*Nitre* and *natron* are doublets, but applied to different substances.) Der. *nitro-gen*, that which produces nitre, from γεν-, base of γίγνειν, to produce.

No (1), a word of refusal or denial. (E.) M. E. *no*; A. S. *ná*, *no*, adv., never, no. – A. S. *ne*, not ; *á*, ever (a word superseded by *aye*, which is of Scand. origin). β. With A. S. *ne*, not, cf. Goth. *ni*, Russ. *ne*, Irish, Gael. W. *ni*, L. *ne* (in *non-ne*), Skt. *na*, not ; all from a base NA, not.

naught, nought. (E.) M. E. *naught*. A. S. *náwiht*, also *náht*. – A. S. *ná*, not (above) ; *wiht*, a whit ; see **Whit.** Der. *naught-y* (lit. naught-like, worthless). Doublet, *not*.

nay. (Scand.) M. E. *nay*. – Icel. *nei*, Dan. *nei*, Swed. *nej*, nay. Negative of **Aye**, q. v.

neither. (E.) M. E. *nether*, *nother*, *nowther*, *nawther*. – A. S. *náwðer*, contr. form of *náhwæðer*, neither. – A. S. *ná*, not (above) ; *hwæðer*, whether. Thus *neither* = *no-whether*. See **Either** (which also contains *whether*). ¶ It should rather be *nother*, but has been influenced by *either*. Doublet, *nor*.

neuter. (L.) L. *neuter*, neither ; hence, sex-less. – L. *ne*, not ; *uter*, whether ; see **Whether.** Der. *neutr-al*, &c.

never. (E.) M. E. *neuer* (*u* = *v*). A. S. *næfre*. – A. S. *ne*, not ; *æfre*, ever ; see **Ever.**

no (2), none. (E.) Short for *none* (below). Der. *no-body*, i.e. none body ; it took the place of M. E. *no man*. So also *no-thing*.

non-, prefix, not. (L.) L. *non*, not ; orig. not one. – L. *ne*, not ; *unum*, one.

nonage. (L. *and* F. – L.) I. e. *non-age*, minority. So also *non-conforming*, *non-descript*, *non-entity*, *non-juror*, *non-sense*, *non-suit*.

none. (E.) M. E. *noon*, *non*. A. S. *nán*. – A. S. *ne*, not ; *án*, one. Hence *no*, as in *no-thing*, *no-body*, by loss of final *n*.

nonpareil, matchless. (F. – L.) F. *non*, not ; *pareil*, equal. – L. *non*, not ; Low L. *pariculus*, equal, double dimin. from *par*, equal.

nonplus. (L.) ' To be at a *nonplus*,' to be in perplexity, not to be able to proceed. – L. *non*, not ; *plus*, more, further.

nor. (E.) M. E. *nor*, short for *nother*, neither ; see **neither** (above).

not (1), a word expressing denial. (E.) M. E. *not*, short form of *nought* ; see **naught** (above).

not (2), I know not, *or* he knows not. (E.) *Obsolete*. M. E. *not*, *noot*. A. S. *nát*. – A. S. *ne*, not ; *wát*, I know, *or* he knows ; see **Wit.**

nothing. (E.) Short for *no thing* ; see **none** (above).

notwithstanding. (E.) M. E. *nought withstonding*, Gower, C. A. ii. 181. From *naught* and *withstand*.

nought, the same as **naught** (above).

noway, noways. (E.) The older form is *nowayes*. – A. S. *nánes weges*, by no way, the gen. case used adverbially. See **none** (above) and **Way.**

nowhere. (E.) A. S. *náhwær*. – A. S. *ná*, not ; *hwær*, where. See **No** (1) and **Where.**

nowise. (E.) Short for *in no wise*, M. E. *on none wise* ; where *none* is dat. of M. E. *noon*, none, and *wise* is dat. of *wise*, a way, from A. S. *wíse*, a way. See **none** (above) and **Wise, sb.**

null, invalid. (L.) L. *nullus*, none. – L. *ne*, not ; *ullus*, any, short for *unulus**, dimin. of *unus*, one. ¶ Perhaps (F. – L.). **No** (2), none ; see **No** (1).

Noble. (F. – L.) F. *noble*. – L. *nobilem*, acc. of *nobilis*, well-known. Put for *gno-bilis**. – L. *gno-*, base of *noscere* (i. e. *gnos-cere*), to know ; allied to E. **Know.** Der. *nobil-i-ty*, O. F. *nobilitet*, L. acc. *nobilita-tem*. Also *i-gnoble* (below).

acquaint. (F. – L.) M. E. *acqueynten*, earlier *acointen*. – O. F. *acointer*, *acointier*, to acquaint with. – Low L. *adcognitare* (Brachet). – L. *ad*, to ; *cognitus*, pp. of *co-gnoscere*, to know.

annotate, to make notes on. (L.) From pp. of L. *annotare*, to make notes on. — L. *an-* (for *ad*), to, on; *notare*, to mark, from *nota*; see note (below).

binomial, consisting of two terms. (L.) Badly coined from L. *bi-*, double; *nom-en*, a name; see noun (below).

cognisance, knowledge, a badge. (F. — L.) Formerly *conisaunce*. — O. F. *connoissance*, knowledge; later *cognoissance*. — O. F. *connoissant*, pres. pt. of O. F. *conostre*, to know. — L. *cognoscere*, to know. — L. *co-* (= *cum*), together, fully; *gnoscere*, to know.

cognition, perception. (L.) From L. *cognitio*. — L. *cognitus*, pp. of *cognoscere* (above).

cognomen, a surname. (L.) L. *co-gnomen*, a surname. — L. *co-* (*cum*), with; *gnomen* = *nomen*, a name; see noun (below).

connoisseur, a critical judge. (F. — L.) F. *connaisseur*, formerly *connoisseur*, a knowing one. — O. F. *connoiss-ant*, pres. pt. of O. F. *conostre*; see **cognisance** above.

denominate. (L.) From pp. of L. *denominare*, to name. — L. *de*, down; *nominare*, to name, from *nomin-*, stem of *nomen*, a name; see noun (below).

denote. (F. — L.) F. *denoter*. — L. *denotare*, to mark out. — L. *de*, down; *notare*, to mark, from *nota*, a mark. See note (below).

ignoble. (F. — L.) F. *ignoble*, not noble. — L. *i-gnobilis*, where *i-* = *in*, not; see **Noble** (above).

ignominy, disgrace. (F. — L.) F. *ignominie*. — L. *ignominia*. — L. *i-* (for *in*), not; *gnomin-*, stem of *gnomen*, old form of *nomen*, name, fame; see noun (below).

ignore, to disregard. (F. — L.) F. *ignorer*. — L. *ignorare*, not to know. — L. *i-* (for *in*), not; and base *gno-*, as in *gnoscere* = *noscere*, to know. Der. *ignor-ant*, *-ance*; also *ignoramus*, lit. we are ignorant of that, an old law-term.

incognito, lit. unknown. (Ital. — L.) Ital. *incognito*, unknown. — L. *in-cognitus*, not known; see **cognition** (above).

nomenclator, one who names things. (L.) L. *nomenclator*, lit. 'name-caller.' — L. *nomen*, name; *calare*, to call; see **Calends**.

nominal. (F. — L.) F. *nominal*. — L. *nominalis*, nominal; belonging to a name.

— L. *nomin-*, crude form of *nomen*, a name; see noun (below).

nominate. (L.) From pp. of L. *nominare*, to name. — L. *nomin-*, crude form of *nomen*; see noun (below).

notable. (F. — L.) F. *notable*. — L. *notabilis*, remarkable. — L. *notare*, to mark. — L. *nota*, a mark; see note (below).

notary. (F. — L.) O. F. *notaire*. — L. acc. *notarium* (from *notarius*), one who makes notes, a scrivener. — L. *nota*, a note; see note (below).

note, a mark. (F. — L.) F. *note*. — L. *nota*, a mark, lit. that which a thing is known. Put for *gnôta**, and allied to *nôtus*, known, pp. of *noscere*. (For the short *o*, cf. L. *cognitus* = *cognôtus*.) Der. *not-at-ion*, from L. *notatio*, from pp. *notatus*; and see *not-able*, *not-ary* above.

notice. (F. — L.) F. *notice*. — L. *notitia*, a being known, knowledge. — L. *notus*, pp. of *noscere*, to know.

notify. (F. — L.) F. *notifier*. — L. *notificare*, to make known. — L. *noti-*, for *notus*, known; *-ficare*, for *facere*, to make.

notion. (F. — L.) F. *notion*. — L. acc. *notionem*, an investigation, a notion. — L. *notus*, pp. of *noscere*, to know.

notorious. (L.) From L. *notorius*, manifest. — L. *nôtor*, a voucher, witness. — L. pp. *notus*, known. Der. *notori-e-ty*, O. F. *notorieté* (Cot.).

noun, the name of a thing. (F. — L.) O. F. *noun*, *non*, *nun* (F. *nom*), a name. — L. *nomen*, a name (= *gno-men**); from (*g*)*noscere*, to know.

pronoun. (F. — L.) Coined from L. *pro*, for; and E. *noun*. Suggested by L. *pronomen*, a pronoun.

quaint, neat, odd. (F. — L.) M. E. *queint*, also *quoint*, *coint*, commonly with the sense of 'famous.' — O. F. *coint*, 'quaint, compt, neat, fine;' Cot. — L. *cognitus*, well-known, pp. of *cognoscere*, to know; see **cognisance** (above). Confused with L. *comptus*, neat, pp. of *cômere*, to adorn (= *co-imere* = *con-emere*); esp. in F., but the M. E. word keeps to the L. *cognitus*. Der. *ac-quaint* (above).

recognise. (F. — L.) Formed from the sb. *recognisance* (Chaucer, C. T. 13260). — O. F. *recoignisance*, an acknowledgment. — O. F. *recognis-ant*, pres. part. of *recognoistre* (F. *reconnaître*). — L. *re-co-gnoscere*, to know again. See **cognisance** (above). Der. *recognit-ion* (from L. pp. *recognit-us*).

reconnoitre, to survey. (F. — L.) O. F.

recognoistre, ' to recognise, to take a precise view of:' Cot. See above.

renown, fame. (F. = L.) Put for *renowm.* M. E. *renoun,* also *renomee, renommee* (3 syllables). = F. *renom,* also *renommé,* renown; we also find O. F. *renon* (12th cent.). Cf. Port. *renome,* Span. *renombre,* renown. = F. *re-,* again; *nom,* a name (also *nonmé,* pp. of *nommer,* to name). = L. *re-,* again; *nomen,* a name; see **noun** (above).

Nobody; see **No** (1).

Nock, old form of **Notch.**

Nocturn; see **Night.**

Nod. (E.) M. E. *nodden.* Not in A S.; but the orig. form began with *hn.* The orig. sense was to push, beat, shake. Cf. Icel. *hnyðja,* a rammer for beating turf; O. H. G. *hnôton,* to shake. (Base HNUD.) Allied to **Knock, Nudge.**

Noddle, the head; see **Knot.**

Node, a knot. (L.) L. *nodus,* a knot. Put for *gnōdus**; cognate with **Knot.**

denouement, the undoing of a knot. (F. = L.) F. *dénouement,* sb., from *dénouer,* to undo a knot. = L. *dis-,* apart; *nodus,* a knot.

Noggin, a wooden cup; see **Knack.**

Noise. (F. = L. = Gk. ?) M. E. *noise.* = F. *noise,* O. F. *nose,* a debate, quarrel, noise. Cf. Prov. *noisa, nausa, nueiza.* β. Diez holds that it can only be derived from L. *nausea,* sea-sickness, disgust, hence annoyance, &c.; the L. word being borrowed from Gk. See **Nausea.** γ. Some attempt to derive it from L. *noxia,* harm, put for *noxa,* harm; see **Noxious.** (Disputed; see Diez, Scheler, Littré.) Der. *nois-y.*

Noisome; see **Odium.**

Nomad, wandering. (Gk.) Gk. *νομαδ-,* stem of *νομάs,* roaming in search of pasture. = Gk. *νομόs,* a pasture, allotted abode. = Gk. *νέμειν,* to assign. (√NAM.)

nemesis. (L. = Gk.) L. *nemesis.* = Gk. *νέμεσις,* allotment, retribution, vengeance. = Gk. *νέμειν,* to distribute.

numismatic, relating to coins. (L. = Gk.) Coined from L. *numismat-,* stem of *numisma,* current coin. = Gk. *νόμισμα,* a custom, also current coin. = Gk. *νομίζειν,* to adopt, use as coin. = Gk. *νόμος,* usage. = Gk. *νέμειν,* to distribute. Here belongs the suffix *-nomy,* as in *astro-nomy,* &c.

Nomenclator, Nominal; see **Noble.**

Non-, *prefix,* not; see **No** (1).

Nonce; see **One.**

Nones; see **Nine.**

Nonpareil, Nonplus; see **No** (1).

Nook. (C.) M. E. *nok;* Lowl. Sc. *neuk.* = Irish and Gael. *niuc,* a corner, nook.

Noon; see **Nine.**

Noose, a slip-knot. (F. = L. ?) In Beaumont and Fletcher. Orig. doubtful; perhaps from O. F. *nous,* pl. of *nou* (mod. F. *nœud*), a knot. = L. *nodus,* a knot. Wedgwood cites Languedoc *nous-couren,* a running knot, *nouzelut,* knotty. It can hardly be from W. *nais,* Gael. *nasg,* Irish *nasc,* Bret. *nask,* a band, tie.

Nor; see **No** (1).

Normal, according to rule. (L.) L. *normalis,* adj. = L. *norma,* a carpenter's square, rule, pattern. For *gnorima**; allied to **Gnomon.** (√GNA.)

enormous, great beyond measure. (F. = L.) Formed from *enorm* (obsolete). = F. *enorme,* huge. = L. *enormis,* out of rule, huge. = L. *e,* out; *norma,* rule.

Norman, Norse; see **North.**

North. (E.) A. S. *norð.* + Du. *noord,* Icel. *norðr,* Dan. Swed. G. *nord.* (Root unknown.)

norse. (Scand.) Short for *Norsk,* the Norw. and Dan. spelling of Norse. Icel. *norskr,* Norse. Short for *North-isk,* i. e. *North-ish.*

northern. (E.) A. S. *norðern;* cognate with O. H. G. *nordaróni,* lit. 'north-running,' i. e. coming from the north. Thus the suffix *-ern* is allied to **Run.** Der. *north-er-ly,* put for *north-ern-ly.*

norman. (F. = Scand.) O. F. *Normand.* = Dan. *Normand;* Icel. *Norðmaðr* (= *Norðmannr*), pl. *Norðmenn.* Lit. ' North-man.'

Nose. (E.) M. E. *nose.* A. S. *nósu.* + Du. *neus,* Icel. *nös,* Dan. *næse,* Swed. *näsa,* G. *nase,* Russ. *nos',* Lithuan. *nosis,* L. *nasus,* Skt. *nâsâ.* Root uncertain. Der. *nose-gay;* cf. prov. E. *gay,* a painted picture in a book, from *gay,* adj.

nasal. (F. = L.) F. *nasal.* = Low L. *nasalis,* belonging to the nose. = L. *nasus,* nose.

nasturtium, a flower. (L.) Lit. ' nose-wring;' from the sharp smell. = L. *nasturtium,* cress; better spelt *nasturcium.* = L. *nas-us,* nose; *torquere,* to twist, torment; see **Torment.**

nostril. (E.) *Nostril* = *nose-thrill* or *nose-thirl.* M. E. *nosethirl;* A. S. *nósðyrl.* = A. S. *nós-u,* nose; *ðyrel,* a perforation, orifice; see **Thrill.**

nozzle, a snout. (E.) Formerly *nozle*; dimin. of *nose*.

nuzzle, to thrust the nose in. (E.) Formerly *nousle, nosyll*; a frequent. verb; from *nose*, sb. Cf. Swed. *nosa*, to smell to.

Nosology, science of disease. (Gk.) Gk. νόσο-s, disease; -λογία, from λόγος, discourse, from λέγειν, to speak.

Nostril; see Nose.

Nostrum, a quack medicine. (L.) L. *nostrum*, lit. 'our own,' i.e. a special drug peculiar to the seller. Neut. of *noster*, ours. — L. *nos*, we. Cf. Skt. *nas*, us.

Not (1), **Not** (2); see No (1).

Notable, Notary; see Noble.

Notch, Nock, an indentation. (O. Low G.) M. E. *nokke*. — O. Du. *nock*, a notch in the head of an arrow; O. Swed. *nocka*, a notch; Swed. dial. *nokke, nokk*. ¶ The O. Ital. *nocca*, a nock, is of Teut. origin.

nick (1), a small notch. (O. Low G.) *Nick* is an attenuated form of *nock*, the old form of *notch* (above). So also *tip* from *top*.

Note, Notice; see Noble.

Nothing; see No (1).

Notify, Notion, Notorious; see Noble.

Notwithstanding; see No (1).

Nouch; see Ouch.

Nought; see No (1).

Noun; see Noble.

Nourish; see Nutriment.

Novel, Novice; see Now.

November; see Nine.

Now. (E.) M. E. *now, nou, nu*; A.S. *nú*. **+** Du. *nu*, Icel. *nú*, Dan. Swed. O. H. G. Goth. *nu*, Skt. *nu, nú*. Cf. Gk. νῦ-ν, L. *nu-nc*.

innovate, to introduce something new. (E.) From pp. of L. *innouare*, to renew, make new. — L. *in*, in; *nouus*, new; see novel (below).

neology, the introduction of new phrases. (Gk.) Gk. νέο-s, new; -λογία, from λόγος, discourse, from λέγειν, to speak; see new (below).

neophyte, a novice. (L. — Gk.) L. *neophytus*. — Gk. νεόφυτος, lit. new planted, hence, a novice. — Gk. νέο-s, new; φυτ-όν, a plant, φυτ-ός, grown, from φύειν, to grow, cause to grow, allied to Be.

neoteric, novel. (L. — Gk.) L. *neotericus*. — Gk. νεωτερικός, novel. — Gk. νεώτερος, comparative of νέος, new; see new (below).

new. (E.) M. E. *newe*; A. S. *niwe*,

neowe. **+** Du. *nieuw*, Icel. *nýr*, Dan. Swed. *ny*, Goth. *niujis*, G. *neu*, L. *nouus*, W. *newydd*, Irish and Gael. *nuadh*, Lithuan. *naujas*, Russ. *novuii*, Gk. νέος, Skt. *nava*, new. Cf. Skt. *nútana*, new. All from base NU, i.e. *now*; *new* means 'that which is now,' recent.

newfangled, fond of novelty. (E.) The *d* has been added. M. E. *newefangel*, i.e. fond of what is new. Compounded of *newe*, new, and *fangel*, ready to catch, from A. S. *fangen*, pp. of *fón*, to catch. The suffix *-el* is the same as in A. S. *sprec-ol*, fond of speaking, talkative, &c. See Fang.

news, tidings. (E.) Formerly *newes*, s. pl., lit. new things, first used about A. D. 1500. It is a translation of F. *nouvelles*, news, pl. of O. F. *novel*, new.

novel. (F. — L.) O. F. *novel* (F. *nouveau*). — L. *nouellus*, new, dimin. of *nouus*, new. See new (above). Der. *novel-ty*, from O. F. *noveliteit*, from L. acc. *nouellitatem*, newness.

novice, a beginner. (F. — L.) F. *novice*. — L. *nouicius, nouitius*, new, fresh, a novice. — L. *nouus*, new. Der. *noviti-ate*, from F. *novitiat*, 'the estate of a novice,' Cot.; from Low L. *nouitiatus*, sb.

renew. (L. and E.) From L. *re-* again; and E. new.

renovate. (L.) From L. *renouatus*, pp. of *renouare*, to renew. — L. *re-*, again; *nouus*, new.

Noway, Noways, Nowhere, Nowise; see No (1).

Noxious. (L.) L. *noxius*, hurtful. — L. *noxa*, hurt. — L. *nocere*, to hurt; cf. *nex*, destruction. (√NAK.)

innocent. (F. — L.) F. *innocent*. — L. *innocent-*, stem of *innocens*, harmless. — L. *in*, not; *nocens*, pres. pt. of *nocere*, to hurt.

innocuous. (L.) L. *innocuus*, harmless. — L. *in*, not; *nocere*, to hurt.

nuisance. (F. — L.) F. *nuisance*, a hurt. — F. *nuisant*, hurtful; pres. pt. of *nuire*, to hurt. — L. *nocere*, to hurt.

obnoxious, offensive. (L.) Formerly in the sense of 'liable to.' — L. *obnoxius*, liable to; also, hurtful. — L. *ob*, against; *noxius*, hurtful.

Nozzle; see Nose.

Nucleus, core. (L.) L. *nucleus*, small nut, kernel. — L. *nuc-*, stem of *nux*, a nut. ¶ Not allied to E. *nut*.

newel, the upright column round which

a circular staircase winds. (F.−L.) Formerly *nuell.*−O. F. *nual* (12th cent.), later *noyau*, 'the stone of a plumme, the nuell or spindle of a winding staire;' Cot.−L. *nucale*, neut. of *nucalis*, lit. belonging to a nut; hence a kernel or stone of a plum. −L. *nuc-*, stem of *nux*, a nut. ¶ Named from its *central* position.

Nudge; see **Knack.**

Nude, naked. (L.) L. *nūdus*, bare; put for *nugdus* *. Allied to **Naked.**

denude, to lay bare. (L.) L. *de-nudare*, to make fully bare.−L. *de*, fully; *nudare*, vb., from *nudus*, adj.

Nugatory, trifling, vain. (L.) L. *nugatorius*, adj. from *nugator*, a trifler. − L. *nugatus*, pp. of *nugari*, to trifle. − L. pl. *nugæ*, trifles.

Nugget, a lump of metal. (E.) Formerly *niggot*; see Trench, Eng. Past and Present. Prob. a corruption of *ningot*, put for *ingot*; see **Ingot.**

Nuisance; see **Noxious.**

Null; see **No** (1).

Numb; see **Nimble.**

Number. (F. − L.) F. *nombre.* − L. *numerum*, acc. of *numerus*, a number. Allied to **Nomad.** (√ NAM.) Der. *out-number.*

enumerate. (L.) From pp. of L. *enumerare*, to reckon up.−L. *e*, out, fully; *numerare*, vb., from *numerus*, number.

numeral. (L.) From L. *numeralis*, belonging to number.−L. *numerus.*

numeration. (F.−L.) F. *numeration.* −L. acc. *numerationem*, a numbering.− L. *numeratus*, pp. of *numerare*, to number. −L. *numerus*, a number.

numerous. (F. − L.) F. *numereux* (Cot.). − L. *numerosus*, adj., from *numerus*, sb., a number.

supernumerary. (F.−L.) F. *supernumeraire* (Cot.). − L. *super-numerarius*, excessive in number.

Numismatic; see **Nomad.**

Nun. (L.) M. E. and A.S. *nunne.* − Low L. *nunna*, *nonna*, a nun; orig. a title of respect; oldest sense, 'mother.' It answers to L. *nonnus*, father, also a monk. + Gk. *νάννη*, aunt; Skt. *naná*, mother, a familiar word used by children. Formed like *ma-ma*, *da-da* (*daddy*), and the like. Der. *nunn-er-y*, from O. F. *nonnerie*, which from O. F. *nonne* = Low L. *nonna.*

Nuncheon; see **Nine.**

Nuncio, a messenger. (Ital.−L.) Ital. *nuncio.* − L. *nuntium*, acc. of *nuntius*, a

bringer of tidings. Prob. for *nouentius* *, a bringer of news, from *nouus*, new.

announce. (F. − L.) F. *annoncer.* − L. *annuntiare*, to announce. − L. *an-* (= *ad*), to; *nuntiare*, to bring tidings, from *nuntius* (above).

annunciation. (L.) Directly from L. *annunciatio*, announcement. − L. *annunciatus*, pp. of *annuntiare* (above).

denounce. (F.−L.) O. F. *denoncer.* −L. *denuntiare*, to declare.−L. *de*, down, fully; *nuntiare*, to tell (above). Der. *denunciat-ion*, from L. pp. *denunciatus.*

enunciate. (L.) From pp. of L. *e-nunciare*, to utter, declare fully.

pronounce. (F. − L.) F. *prononcer.* − L. *pro-nuntiare*, to pronounce, lit. tell forth. Der. *pronunciat-ion*, from L. pp. *pronuntiatus.*

renounce. (F.−L.) F. *renoncer.*−L. *re-nuntiare*, to bring back a report, also to disclaim, renounce. Der. *renunciat-ion*, from L. pp. *renuntiatus.*

Nuncupative, declared by word of mouth. (F.−L.) F. *nuncupatif* (Cot.).− Low L. *nuncupatiuus*, nominal.−L. *nuncupatus*, pp. of *nuncupare*, to call by name. Perhaps from L. *nomen*, name; *capere*, to take.

Nuptial. (F. − L.) F. *nuptial.* − L. *nuptialis*, belonging to a marriage. − L. *nuptiæ*, s. pl. a wedding. − L. *nupta*, a bride; fem. of pp. of *nubere*, to marry, lit. 'to veil.' Allied to **Nebula.**

connubial. (L.) L. *connubialis*, relating to marriage.−L. *con-* (*cum*), with; *nubere*, to marry.

nymph. (F.−L.−Gk.) F. *nymphe.* −L. *nympha.*−Gk. *νύμφη*, a bride, lit. 'a veiled one;' allied to L. *nupta* (above).

Nurse, Nurture; see **Nutriment.**

Nut. (E.) M. E. *note*, *nute*; A. S. *hnutu*. + Du. *noot*, Icel. *hnot*, Swed. *nöt*, Dan. *nöd*, G. *nuss.* Cf. Lithuan. *kandǔlas*, a kernel, from *kando*, I bite. ¶ Not allied to L. *nux.* Der. *nut-hatch*, i. e. nut-hacker; see **Hatch** (3).

nutmeg, the musk-nut. (E.; *and* F. − L. − Pers. − Skt.) M. E. *notemuge*, later *nutmegge*. Here *-muge* is from O.F. *muge*, musk, from L. *muscum*, acc. of *muscus*, musk; see **Musk.** Cf. O. F. *muguette*, a nutmeg; also called *noix muscade*, Span. *nuez moscada*, Ital. *noce moscada*, Low L. *muscata*, nutmeg.

Nutation, a nodding. (L.) From L. *nutatio*, a nodding. − L. *nutare*, to nod, frequent. of *nuere*, to nod. **+** Gk. νεύειν, to nod.. (Base NU.)

innuendo, an indirect hint. (L.) Not to be spelt *inuendo*. From L. *innuendo*, by intimating;·gerund of *innuere*, to nod towards, intimate. **–** L. *in*, in, at; *nuere*, to nod.

Nutriment, food. (L.) L. *nutrimentum*, food.**–**L. *nutrire*, to nourish, suckle, feed.

nourish. (F.–L.) M. E. *norisen.* **–** O. F. *noris-*, stem of pres. pt. of *norir* (F. *nourrir*), to nourish.**–**L. *nutrire* (above).

nurse. (F.–L.) Contracted from M. E. *norice, nurice.* **–** O. F. *norrice* (F. *nourrice*). **–** L. *nutricem*, acc. of *nutrix*, a nurse. **–** L. *nutrire*, to nourish.

nurture. (F.–L.) M. E. *norture.* **–** O. F. *noriture* (F. *nourriture*).**–**L. *nutritura*, nourishment; from *nutritus*, pp. of *nutrire*, to nourish.

nutritious. (L.) L. *nutritius*, better *nutricius*, adj., nourishing. **–** L. *nutrici-*, crude form of *nutrix*, a nurse (above).

nutritive. (F. **–** L.) F. *nutritif.* Formed with F. suffix *-if* (L. *-iuus*), from *nutritus*, pp. of *nutrire*.

Nuzzle; see Nose.

Nylghau, a kind of antelope. (Pers.) Pers. *nīlgāw*, a nylghau, lit. 'blue cow.' **–** Pers. *nil*, blue; *gāw*, a cow, allied to E. *cow.*

Nymph; see Nuptial.

O.

O (1), **Oh**, interjection. (E.) M. E. *o*; not in A. S.**+**Du. Dan. Swed. G. Goth. L. *o*; Gk. ὦ, ὤ. There is no reason for distinguishing between *o* and *oh.*

O (2), a circle. (E.) So called because the letter *o* is of a circular shape.

Oaf; see Elf.

Oak. (E.) M. E. *ook*; A. S. *āc.* **+** Du. Icel. *eik*; Dan. *eeg*, *eg*, Swed. *ek*, G. *eiche*; Lithuan. *auźolas.* ¶ Not allied to *acorn.*

Oakum, tow; see Comb.

Oar. (E.) M. E. *ore*; A. S. *ār.***+**Icel. *ár*, Dan. *aare*, Swed *åra.* Further allied to Gk. ἐρ-ετής, oarsman, ἐρ-ετμός=L. *rēmus*, oar; Lithuan. *ir-klas*, an oar, *ir-ti*, to row, Skt. *ar-itra*, a paddle, rudder. (√AR.) See Row.

Oasis. (L.–Gk.–Egypt.) L. *oasis.* **–** Gk. ὄασις, αὔασις, a fertile islet in the Libyan desert. Of Egypt. origin; cf. Coptic *ouahe*, an oasis, a dwelling-place, *oulh*, to dwell (Peyron).

Oast, Oast-house, a kiln for drying hops. (E.) M. E. *oost, ost.* A. S. *āst*, a kiln, drying-house.**+**Du. *eest*, O. Du. *ast* (the same). Allied to Gk. αἶθος, a burning heat. (√IDH.)

Oath. (E.) M. E. *ooth, oth.* A. S. *āð.* **+**Du. *eed*, Icel. *eiðr*, Dan. Swed. *ed*, Goth. *aiths*, G. *eid*, O. H. G. *eit.*

Oats. (E.) M. E. *otes*, pl. A. S. *āta,●* sing., pl. *ātan.* Allied to Icel. *eitill*, a nodule in stone, Norw. *eitel*, a gland, knot, nodule, Russ. *iadro*, a kernel, ball, Gk. οἶδος, a swelling. From the swollen shape. (√ID.)

Ob-, *prefix.* (L.) It changes to *oc-* before *c*, *of-* before *f*, *op-* before *p*. L. *ob*, with very variable senses, as towards, at, before, upon, over, about, near. Cf. Lithuan. *apē*, near.

Obdurate; see Dure.

Obedient, Obeisance; see Audience.

Obelisk; see Obolus.

Obese, fat; see Edible.

Obey; see Audience.

Obfuscate; see Fuscous.

Obit; see Itinerant.

Object; see Jet (1).

Objurgation; see Jury.

Oblate, Oblation; see Tolerate.

Oblige; see Ligament.

Oblique, slanting, perverse. (F. **–** L.) F. *oblique.***–**L. *obliquus, oblicus*, slanting, sideways, awry.**–**L. *ob*; *liquis*, oblique (a rare word). The orig. sense of *liquis* is 'bent;' cf. Russ. *luka*, a bend, Lithuan. *lenkti*, to bend. (√LAK.)

Obliterate; see Liniment.

Oblivion. (F.–L.) F. *oblivion.* **–** L. acc. *obliuionem*, forgetfulness. **–** L. *obliuisci*, to forget. Perhaps from *ob*, over; *liuescere* *, to grow livid or dark, from base of *liu-idus*, livid; see Livid.

Oblong; see Long (1).

Obloquy; see Loquacious.

Obnoxious; see Noxious.

Oboe; see hautboy, under Altitude.

Obolus, a small Gk. coin. (L.–Gk.) L. *obolus.***–**Gk. ὀβολός, a small coin, perhaps orig. in the shape of a spike or nail; allied to Gk. ὀβελός, a spit.

obelisk. (F. – L. – Gk.) O. F. *obelisque*. – L. *obeliscum*, acc. of *obeliscus*. – Gk. ὀβελίσκος, a pointed spit; hence a thin pointed pillar; dimin. of ὀβελός, a spit.

Obscene. (L.) L. *obscenus*, *obscænus*, *obscænus*, repulsive, foul. Etym. doubtful.

Obscure, dimin. (F. – L.) F. *obscur*. – L. *obscurus*, dark, lit. 'covered over.' – L. *ob*; and *-scurus*, i.e. covered; cf. Skt. *sku*, to cover. (√ SKU.)

Obsequies, Obsequious; see Sequence.

Observe; see Serve.

Obsolescent, going out of use. (L.) From pres. pt. of L. *obsolescere*, to grow old, inceptive form of *obsolere*, to decay. Doubtful; perhaps from L. *ob*, against; *solere*, to be wont.

obsolete. (L.) L. *obsoletus*, pp. of *obsolere* (above).

Obstacle, Obstetric, Obstinate; see State.

Obstreperous, clamorous. (L.) L. *obstreperus*, clamorous. – L. *ob*, against, near; *strepere*, to rattle.

Obstriction; see Stringent.

Obstruct; see Structure.

Obtain; see Tenable.

Obtrude; see Intrude.

Obtuse; see Contuse.

Obverse; see Verse.

Obviate, Obvious; see Viaduct.

Occasion, Occident; see Cadence.

Occiput; see Capital.

Occult; see Cell.

Occupy; see Capacious.

Occur; see Current.

Ocean. (F. – L. – Gk.) O. F. *ocean*. – L. *oceanum*, acc. of *oceanus*. – Gk. ὠκεανός, the great stream supposed to encompass the earth.

Ocelot, a quadruped. (Mexican.) Mexican *ocelotl*, a tiger; applied by Buffon to the ocelot.

Ochre, a fine clay, commonly yellow. (F. – L. – Gk.) O. F. *ocre*, 'oker;' Cot. – L. *ochra*. – Gk. ὤχρα, yellow ochre; from its pale colour. – Gk. ὠχρός, pale, wan.

Octagon, Octangular, &c.; see Octave.

Octave. (F. – L. – Gk.) Lit. 'eighth;' hence, eight days after a festival, eight notes in music. – F. *octave*, an octave (Cot.). – L. *octaua*, fem. of *octauus*, eighth. – L. *octo*, eight. + Gk. ὀκτώ, eight; cognate with E. **Eight**.

octagon, a plane 8-sided figure. (Gk.)

From Gk. ὀκτά, for ὀκτώ, eight; γων-ιά, an angle, der. from γόνυ, knee; see **Knee**.

octahedron, a solid 8-sided figure. (Gk.) From ὀκτά, for ὀκτώ, eight; ἕδρα, a base, from the base ἑδ-, to sit; see **Sit**.

octangular, having eight angles. (L.) From L. *oct-o*, eight; *angulus*, angle.

octant, the aspect of two planets when distant by the eighth part of a circle. (L.) L. *octant*, stem *octans*, an instrument for measuring the eighth of a circle. – L. *oct-o*, eight.

October. (L.) L. *October*, the eighth month of the Roman year. – L. *octo*, eight.

octogenarian, one who is eighty years old. (L.) From L. *octogenarius*, belonging to eighty. – L. *octogeni*, eighty each, distributive form of *octoginta*, eighty. – L. *octo*, eight; *-ginta*, short for *decinta**, a derivative of *decem*, ten.

octosyllabic. (L. – Gk.) L. *octosyllabicus*, having eight syllables. – Gk. ὀκτώ, eight; συλλαβή, a syllable; see **Syllable**.

Ocular. (L.) L. *ocularis*, belonging to the eye. – L. *oculus*, eye; cognate with E. **Eye**.

binocular, having two eyes. (L.) From L. *bin-i*, double; *oculus*, eye.

inoculate. (L.) In old authors it means 'to engraft.' – L. *inoculatus*, pp. of *inoculare*, to engraft, insert a graft. – L. *in*, in; *oculus*, an eye, also a bud of a plant.

monocular, one-eyed. (Gk. *and* L.) From Gk. μόν-ος, sole; L. *oculus*, eye. See **Mono-**, prefix.

Odd, not even, strange. (Scand.) M. E. *odde*. – Icel. *oddi*, a triangle, a point of land; metaphorically (from the triangle), an odd number (orig. *three*); hence also the phr. *standask í odda*, to stand (or be) at odds, to quarrel; *oddamaðr*, the odd man, third man who gives a casting vote, *oddatala*, an odd number. Allied to *oddr*, a point of a weapon (put for *ordr* *). + A. S. *ord*, point of a sword, point; Dan. *od*, a point, Swed. *udda*, odd, *udde*, a point; G. *ort*, a place, M. H. G. *ort*, extreme point. (√ WAS, to cut.)

Ode, a song. (F. – L. – Gk.) F. *ode*. – L. *oda*, *ode*. – Gk. ᾠδή, a song; for ἀοιδή, a song. – Gk. ἀείδειν, to sing. Allied to Skt. *vad*, to speak. (√ WAD.)

epode. (F. – L. – Gk.) O. F. *epode*. – L. *epodos*. – Gk. ἐπῳδός, an epode, something sung after. – Gk. ἐπ-ί, upon, after; ἀείδειν, to sing.

monody. (Gk.) Gk. μονῳδία, a solo,

a lament. — Gk. μόν-os, alone ; ῷδή, a song.

palinode, a recantation, in song. (F. — L. — Gk.) F. *palinodie* (Cot.). — L. *palinodia.* — Gk. παλινῳδία, a recantation, esp. of an ode. — Gk. πάλιν, back, again; ῷδή, an ode.

parody. (L. — Gk.) L. *parodia.* — Gk. παρῳδία, also παρῳδή, a song sung beside (i. e. in imitation of) another. — Gk. παρ-ά, beside ; ῷδή, an ode.

prosody. (F. — L. — Gk.) F. *prosodie.* — L. *prosodia.* — Gk. προσῳδία, a song sung to an instrument, a tone, accent, prosody (or laws of verse). — Gk. πρός, to, accompanying ; ῷδή, an ode. And see *comedy, melody, psalmody, rhapsody, tragedy.*

Odium, hatred. (L.) L. *odium,* sb. — L. *odi,* I hate ; an old pt. tense used as present. Allied to Gk. ὠθεῖν, to push away, Skt. *vadh,* to strike. (√WADH.)

annoy, to vex. (F. — L.) M. E. *anoien, anuien.* — O. F. *anoier, anuier,* to annoy. — O. F. *anoi, anui* (F. *ennui*), vexation. Cf. Span. *enojo,* O. Venetian *inodio,* vexation. — L. *in odio,* lit. in hatred, common in the Low. L. phr. *in odio habui,* lit. I had in hatred, I was annoyed with ; cf. L. *in odio esse, in odio uenire,* to incur hatred. — L. *in,* in ; *odio,* abl. of *odium,* hatred (above).

ennui. (F. — L.) Mod. F. *ennui,* annoyance ; O. F. *anoi* (as above).

noisome, annoying, troublesome. (F. — L.; *with* E. *suffix.*) Formed from M. E. *noy,* annoyance ; with E. suffix -*some.* This M. E. *noy* is short for M. E. *anoy, anoi.* — O. F. *anoi,* vexation (above).

Odour. (F. — L.) M. E. *odour.* — F. *odeur.* — L. *odorem,* acc. of *odor,* scent. Cf. Gk. ὄζειν (= ὄδ-γειν), to smell. (√AD.) Der. *odorous,* from L. *odorus,* by throwing back the accent.

olfactory, relating to smell. (L.) L. *olfactorius,* adj., from L. *olfactor,* one who smells, *olfactus,* a smelling. — L. *olfactus,* pp. of *olfacere, olefacere,* to scent. — L. *olĕ-re,* to smell ; *facere,* to make, cause. This L. *olere* is put for *odere*, whence *od-or,* scent ; cf. L. *lacruma* for *dacruma.*

osmium, a metal. (Gk.) The oxide has a disagreeable smell. — Gk. ὀσμή, ὀδμή, a smell. — Gk. ὄζειν, to smell (above).

ozone, a substance perceived by its smell in the air after electric discharges. (Gk.) Gk. ὄζων, smelling ; pres. pt. of ὄζειν (above).

redolent, fragrant. (F. — L.) F. *redo-*

lent. — L. *redolent-,* stem of pres. pt. of *redolere,* to emit odour. — L. *red-,* again ; *olēre,* for *odēre ,* to be odorous (above).

Of, from, &c. (E.) M. E. *of ;* A. S. *of.* + Du. Icel. Swed. Dan. Goth. *af ;* G. *ab,* O. H. G. *aba ;* L. *ab,* Gk. ἀπό, Skt. *apa,* away. (Base AP.)

a-, (6), prefix. (F. — L.; *or* L.) In *a-bate,* the prefix is F. *a,* for L. *ab,* from. In *a-vert,* the prefix is L. *a* (for *ab*).

ab- (1), prefix. (L.) L. *ab ;* also *a, abs.* ¶ Distinct from *ab-* (for *ad*) in *ab-breviate.*

apo-, prefix. (Gk.) Gk. ἀπό, from (above).

off, away from. (E.) Another spelling of *of.* M. E. *of ;* as in 'Smiteth *of* my hed' = smite *off* my head ; Ch. C. T. 784.

offing, the part of the visible sea remote from the shore. (E.) Merely formed from *off* (above) with the noun-suffix -*ing.*

Off ; see **Of.**

Offal, waste meat. (E.) M. E. *offal,* falling remnants, chips of wood, &c. From *off* and *fall.* + Du. *afval,* windfall, offal ; Dan. *affald,* a fall off, offal ; G. *abfall ;* all similarly compounded.

Offend ; see **Defend.**

Offer ; see **Fertile.**

Office ; see **Optative.**

Offing ; see **Off.**

Offscouring. (E.) From *off* and *scour.* So also *off-set, off-shoot, off-spring.*

Oft, Often ; see **Over.**

Ogee, Ogive, a double curve. (F. — Span. — Arab.) ' An *ogiue* or *ogee,* a wreath, circlet, or round band in architecture,' Minsheu. An *ogee* arch is a pointed arch, with doubly-curved sides. — O. F. *augive, ogive,* an ogive or ogee (Cot.). — Span. *auge,* highest point ; from the pointed top of Moorish arches, which have doubly-curved sides. — Arab. *áwj,* summit. Der. *ogiv-al,* adj. (also written *ogee-fall* !). See p. 579.

Ogle, to glance at. (Du.) A frequent. form of Du. *oogen,* ' to cast sheeps eyes upon one,' Hexham. (Cf. Low G. *oegeln,* to ogle, from *oegen,* to look at.) — Du. *ooge,* eye ; cognate with E. **Eye.**

Ogre, a monster. (F. — Span. — L.) F. *ogre.* — Span. *ogro,* O. Span. *huergo, huerco, uerco,* cognate with Ital. *orco,* a hobgoblin, demon (Diez). — L. *orcum,* acc. of *orcus,* (1) the abode of the dead, (2) the god of the infernal regions, Orcus, Pluto. Minsheu gives O. Span. *huerco,* hell. Der. *ogr-ess,* F. *ogresse.*

Oh ; see **O** (1).

Oil ; see **Olive.**

Ointment; see **Unguent**.

Old. (E.) M. E. *old.* A. S. *eald.* **+** Du. *oud* (for *old**), G. *alt*, Goth. *altheis.* Allied to -*ultus*, in L. *ad-ultus*, grown up. (√ AL.)

alderman. (E.) A. S. *ealdorman*, lit. *elder-man*; see **elder** (below.)

eld, old age. (E.) M. E. *elde*, old age; A. S. *yldu*, antiquity, from *eald*, old.

elder, older. (E.) Both as adj. and sb. A. S. *yldra*, elder, adj.; comparative of *eald*, old. Also A. S. *ealdor*, an elder, sb.; from *eald*, old, with suffix -*or*.

eldest. (E.) A. S. *yldesta*, superl. of *eald*, old.

Oleaginous; see **Olive**.

Oleander, the rose-bay-tree. (F. — Low L.) O. F. *oleandre*, rose-bay-tree (Cot.). The same as Ital. *oleandro*, Span. *eloendro* (Minsheu), Port. *eloendro, loendro*; all variously corrupted from Low L. *lorandrum* (Isidore). It seems to have been confused with *oleaster*. Perhaps Low L. *lorandrum* stands for *lauro-dendrum**, from L. *laurus*, laurel, and Gk. δένδρον, a tree; but this wants confirmation.

Oleaster; see **Olive**.

Olfactory; see **Odour**.

Oligarchy; see **Arch-** (1).

Olio, a mixture, medley. (Span. — L.) A mistaken form for *olia*, intended to represent Span. *olla* (pronounced *olya*), a round earthen pot, also an olio, esp. in phrase *olla podrida*, a hodge-podge. — L. *olla*, O. Lat. *aula*, a pot.

Olive. (F. — L. — Gk.) F. *olive.* — L. *oliua.* — Gk. ἐλαία, an olive-tree. (√ RI.)

oil. (F. — L. — Gk.) M. E. *oile.* — O. F. *oile* (F. *huile*). — L. *oleum.* — Gk. ἔλαιον, oil; cf. ἐλαία, an olive-tree.

oleaginous. (L. — Gk.) L. *oleaginus*, oily; adj., from *oleum*, oil (above).

oleaster, wild olive. (L. — Gk.) L. *oleaster*, Rom. xi. 17; formed from *olea*, an olive-tree. — Gk. ἐλαία, an olive-tree.

Ombre, a game at cards; see **Human**.

Omega, the end. (Gk.) Gk. ὦ, called ὦ μέγα, i. e. great *o*, long *o*; which is the *last* letter of the Gk. alphabet, as opposed to *alpha*, the *first* letter. Μέγα is neut. of μέγας, great, allied to E. **Mickle**.

Omelet, a pan-cake, chiefly of eggs. (F. — L.) F. *omelette, aumelette* (Cot.). These are from O. F. *amelette*, but this again was preceded by the forms *alemette, alemelle* (Scheler). The sense of *alemelle* was 'a thin plate,' still preserved in F.

alumelle, sheathing of a ship. Roquefort gives O. F. *alemele*, blade of a knife; thus the *omelet* was named from its shape, that of a 'thin plate' of metal. β. Lastly *l'alemelle* is a corruption of *la lemelle*, the correct form. — L. *lamella*, a thin plate, properly of metal; dimin. of *lamina*, a thin plate; see **Lamina**. ¶ See this clearly traced by Scheler and Littré.

Omen, a sign of a future event. (L.) L. *omen*; O. Lat. *osmen*.

abominate. (L.) From pp. of L. *abominari*, lit. to turn away from that which is of ill omen. — L. *ab*, away; *omen*, an omen.

Omit; see **Missile**.

Omni-, prefix. (L.) L. *omnis*, all. Der. *omni-potent*, all-powerful; *omni-present*, everywhere present; *omni-scient*, all-knowing; *omni-vorous*, all-devouring; see **Potent**, **Present**, **Science**, **Voracious**.

omnibus, a public vehicle. (L.) So called because intended for the use of all. — L. *omnibus*, for all; dat. pl. of *omnis*. ¶ Commonly shortened to *bus*.

On. (E.) M. E. *on*; A. S. *on*. **+** Du. *aan*, Icel. *á*, Dan. *an*, Swed. *å*, G. *an*, Goth. *ana*, Gk. ἀνά, Russ. *na*. (Aryan form ANA.) Allied to **In**.

ana-, prefix. (Gk.) Gk. ἀνά, on, up, &c. Shortened to *an-* in *an-eurism*.

Once; see **One**.

Once, sometimes for **Ounce** (2).

One (1), single, sole. (E.) M. E. *oon.* A. S. *án*, one. **+** Du. *een*, Icel. *einn*, Dan. *een*, Swed. *en*, G. *ein*, Goth. *ains*, W. *un*, Irish and Gael. *aon*, L. *unus*, O. L. *oinos*, Gk. *οἰνός*, one. (Aryan AINA, one.)

a, short for *an*; see **an** (below).

a- (12), prefix. (E.) In the word *a-pace*, put for *one pace*, the prefix *a* is short for *an*, the indef. article, the same word as *one*.

alone. (E.) M. E. *al one, al oon*, written apart; here *al*, adv., means 'entirely,' and *oon* is the M. E. form of *one*. (*Alone = all one*.)

an, a. (E.) Used as indef. article; from A. S. *án*, one, similarly used. (Thus *an* is the same word as *one*.) *A* is a shortened form of *an*, first used about A.D. 1200.

anon, immediately. (E.) M. E. *anon, anoon*; also *onan*. A. S. *on án*, lit. 'in one moment.' — A. S. *on*, on, in; *án*, one.

any. (E.) M. E. *ani, oni, æni*, &c.; A. S. *ænig*, any; formed with A. S. suffix -*ig* (E. -*y*) from *án*, one. **+** Du. *eenig*, any, from *een*; one; G. *einiger*, from *ein*, one.

atone, to set at one, to reconcile. (E.) Made up from the words *at* and *one*, and due to the frequent use of the phrase *at oon*, at one (i. e. reconciled) in Middle English. *Al at on* = all agreed; Rob. of Glouc. p. 113. Tyndall has *atonemaker*, i. e. reconciler, Works, p. 158. Der. *atonement*, i. e. *at-one-ment*; we actually find the word *onement*, reconciliation, in old authors.

aught, the same as **ought** (below).

lone. (E.) Short for *alone*, the initial *a* being dropped, as in *mend, vanguard*, &c. See **alone** (above). Der. *lone-ly*.

nonce. (E.) In phr. *for the nonce*, M. E. *for then anes*. Here *then* is for A.S. *ðám*, dat. of the def. article; *anes*, once, here treated as a sb., is properly an adverb; see **once** (below). The sense is ' for the once,' i. e. for the occasion.

once. (E.) M. E. *ones*; A.S. *ánes*, adv., once. Orig. gen. case (masc. and neut.) of *án*, one; the gen. case was used adverbially, as in *need-s, twi-ce, thri-ce*.

one (2), a person, spoken of indefinitely. (E.) In the phrase ' *one* says,' *one* means 'a single person.' It is merely a peculiar use of the ordinary word *one*. ¶ Not F *on*.

only. (E.) M. E. *oonli*, adj. and adv.; A.S. *ánlíc*, adj., unique, lit. ' one-like.' — A. S. *án*, one; *líc*, like.

ought, anything. (E.) M. E. *ouȝt*, *ought*, also spelt *aught, awiht*, &c. (mod. E. *aught*). — A. S. *áwiht*, aught. — A.S. *á*, short for *án*, one; *wiht*, a whit; see **Whit**. (Thus *ought*=*one whit*.)

Onerous, burdensome. (F. — L.) F. *onereux*. — L. *onerosus*, adj. — L. *oner-*, stem of *onus*, a burden.

exonerate. (L.) From pp. of L. *exonerare*, to free from a burden; *onerare* is from *oner-*, stem of *onus*.

Onion; see **Unity**.

Only; see **One**.

Onomatopoeia, name-making, the formation of a word with a resemblance in sound to the thing signified. (Gk.) Gk. *ὀνοματοποιία*, the making of a name. — Gk. *ὀνοματο-*, crude form of *ὄνομα*, a name; and *ποιεῖν*, to make; see **Name** and **Poem**.

anonymous, nameless. (Gk.) Gk. *ἀνώνυμος*, nameless. — Gk. *ἀνα*, neg. prefix; and *ὄνομα*, name (the long *ω* = *a* + *o*).

homonymous, like in sound, but differing in sense. (L. — Gk.) L. *homonymus.*

— Gk. *ὁμώνυμος*, having the same name. — Gk. *ὁμό-s*, same; *ὄνομα*, name. See **Same**. Der. *homonym*, F. *homonyme*, from L. *homonymus.*

metonymy, the putting of one word for another. (L. — Gk.) L. *metonymia.* — Gk. *μετωνυμία*, change of name. — Gk. *μετά*, implying ' change ;' *ὄνομα*, name.

paronymous, allied in origin; alike in sound. (Gk.) Gk. *παρώνυμος*, formed from another word by a slight change. — Gk. *παρά*, beside; *ὄνυμα*, a name. Der. *paronom-as-ia*, a slight change in a word's meaning, from Gk. *παρωνυμασία*, better *παρονυμασία*.

synonym. (F. — L. — Gk.) F. *synonime*. — L. (pl.) *synonyma*, lit. synonyms; from the adj. *synonymus*, synonymous, having the same sense as another word. — Gk. *συνώνυμος*, of like meaning. — Gk. *σύν*, together; *ὄνομα*, a name. Der. *synonymous*, from L. *synonymus*; *synonymy*, from L. *synonymia*, Gk. *συνωνυμία*, likeness of name.

Onset, an assault. (E.) Due to the phr. *set on !* i. e. attack ! From *on* and *set*.

Onslaught, an attack. (E.) From *on* and M. E. *slaht*, A.S. *sleaht*, a stroke, blow, formed from *sleán*, to strike; see **Slay**.

Onward, Onwards. (E.) From *on* and *-ward, -wards*; see **Toward**.

Onyx, a kind of agate. (L. — Gk.) L. *onyx*. — Gk. *ὄνυξ*, a nail; a veined gem, onyx, from its resemblance to the finger-nail. See **Nail**.

Oolite; see p. 579.

Ooze, moisture, soft mud. (E.) Formerly *wose*; M. E. *wose*. A.S. *wáse, wós*, moisture, juice. + Icel. *vás*, wetness; O. H. G. *waso*, sod, turf. Der. *ooze*, verb.

Opacity; see **Opaque**.

Opal, a gem. (F. — L.) F. *opale*. — L. *opalus*, an opal. Cf. Gk. *ὀπάλλιος*, an opal; Skt. *upala*, a stone, gem.

Opaque. (F. — L.) F. *opaque*. — L. *opacum*, acc. of *opacus*, dark, obscure. Der. *opac-i-ty*, from F. *opacité*, L. acc. *opacitatem*.

Open, unclosed; see **Up**.

Opera; see below.

Operate. (L.) From pp. of L. *operari*, to work. — L. *opera*, work; allied to L. *opus* (stem *oper-*), work, toil. + Skt. *apas*, work. (√AP.)

co-operate. (L.) From pp. of L. *cooperari*, to work with.

inure, to habituate. (F. — I.) Also

spelt *enure*, but *inure* is better, since the word arose from the phrase *in ure*, i. e. in operation, in work, in employment, formerly common. Here *in* is the E. prep. *in*; *ure* is from O. F. *eure*, also spelt *uevre*, *ovre*, work, action; from L. *opera*, work. (Cf. *man-ure* = *man-œuvre*.) See also *manure*, *manœuvre*.

Ophidian, relating to serpents. (Gk.) From Gk. ὀφιδι-*, an imaginary form wrongly supposed to be the crude form of ὄφις, a serpent.

ophicleide, a musical instrument. (F.—Gk.) Lit. a 'key-serpent;' because made by adding *keys* to an old musical instrument called a *serpent* (from its twisted shape).—Gk. ὄφι-s, a serpent; κλειδ-, stem of κλείς, a key.

Ophthalmia; see Optic.

Opinion. (F.—L.) F. *opinion.*—L. *opinionem*, acc. of *opinio*, a supposition.—L. *opinari*, to suppose, opine.—L. *opinus*, thinking, expecting; only in *nec-opinus*, *in-opinus*, unexpected. Allied to *ap-isci*, to obtain, comprehend; see Apt, Optative. (√AP.) Der. *opine*, F. *opiner*, L. *opinari* (above).

Opium. (L.—Gk.) L. *opium.*—Gk. ὄπιον, poppy-juice.—Gk. ὀπός, sap.

Opossum, a quadruped. (W. Indian.) —W. Indian *opassom*; in the language of the Indians of Virginia.

Oppidan. (L.) L. *oppidanus*, belonging to a town.—L. *oppidum*, a town; O. Lat. *oppedum*.

Opponent; see Position.

Opportune; see Port (2).

Oppose; see Pose.

Opposite; see Position.

Oppress; see Press.

Opprobrious. (L.) From L. *opprobriosus*, full of reproach.—L. *opprobrium*, reproach.—L. *op-* (for *ob*), on, upon; *pro-brum*, disgrace.

Oppugn; see Pugilism.

Optative, wishing. (F.—L.) Chiefly as the name of a mood.—F. *optatif.*—L. *optatiuus*, expressive of a wish. — L. *optatus*, pp. of *optare*, to wish. Allied to *ap-isci*, to obtain; cf. Skt. *áp, ap*, to obtain, get. (√AP.)

adopt. (L.) L. *adoptare*, to adopt, choose.—L. *ad*, to, for; *optare*, to wish.

copious, ample. (F.—L.) O. F. *copieux.*—L. *copiosus*, plentiful.—L. *cōpia*, plenty; put for *co-opia.*—L. *co-* (for *cum*), together; *op-*, base of *op-es*, wealth. Cf. *in-opia*, want.

copy. (F.—L.) M. E. *copy*, abundance; the mod. sense is due to the multiplication of an original by means of *copies.*—O. F. *copie*, abundance; also a copy.—L. *copia*, plenty (above).

office, duty. (F.—L.) F. *office.*—L. *officium*, duty; lit. 'doing of a service;' contr. from *opificium.*—L. *opi-*, crude form of *opes*, wealth; *facere*, to do; see below. Der. *offic-er*, F. *officier*, Low L. *officiarius*; *offic-i-ous*, F. *officieux*, L. *officiosus*.

optimism, the doctrine that all is for the best. (L.) From L. *optim-us*, choicest, best; with suffix *-ism* (Gk. *-ισμος*). L. *op-ti-mus* is a superl. form from a base *op-* (i. e. choice); cf. *optare*, to wish.

option, choice. (F.—L.) F. *option.*—L. *optionem*, acc. of *optio*, choice. Allied to L. *optare*, to wish (above).

opulent, wealthy. (F.—L.) F. *opulent.*—L. *opulentus*, wealthy.—L. *op-*, base of *opes*, wealth. Cf. Skt. *apnas*, wealth.

Optic, relating to the sight. (F.—Gk.) F. *optique.* — Gk. ὀπτικός, belonging to the sight; cf. ὀπτήρ, a spy. From the base οπ- (for οκ-) seen in Ionic ὄπ-ωπ-α, I have seen, ὄψ-ομαι, I shall see; cf. L. *oc-ulus*, the eye. See Eye. (√AK.)

autopsy, personal inspection. (Gk.) Gk. αὐτοψία, a seeing with one's own eyes. — Gk. αὐτ-ός, self; and ὄψις, sight.

catoptric, relating to optical reflection. (Gk.) Gk. κατοπτρικός, reflexive. — Gk. κάτοπτρον, a mirror.—Gk. κατ-ά, down, inward; ὄπτ-ομαι, I see.

dioptrics, the science of the refraction of light. (Gk.) Gk. τά διοπτρικά, dioptrics.—Gk. διοπτρικός, relating to the δίοπ-τρα, an optical instrument for taking heights, &c.—Gk. δι-ά, through; ὄπτ-ομαι, I see.

ophthalmia, inflammation of the eye. Gk. ὀφθαλμία.—Gk. ὀφθαλμός, the eye, put for ὀπταλμός *; cf. Doric ὀπτίλος, the eye. —Gk. ὄπτ-ομαι, I see.

synopsis, a general view. (L.—Gk.) L. *synopsis.* — Gk. σύνοψις, a seeing all together.—Gk. σύν, together; ὄψις, sight. Der. *synoptic-al*, from Gk. adj. συνοπτικός.

Or (1), conjunction, offering an alternative; see Either.

Or (2), ere; see Ere.

Or (3), gold; see Aureate.

Oracle; see Oral.

Oral, spoken. (L.) Coined from L. *or-*, stem of *os*, the mouth.+Skt. *ásya*, mouth, *ánana*, mouth. (√AN.)

adore. (L.) L. *adorare*, to pray to. —

L. *ad*, to; *orare*, to pray, from *or*-, stem of *os*, the mouth.

inexorable. (F. – L.) F. *inexorable.* – L. *inexorabilis*, that cannot be moved by intreaty. – L. *in*-, not; *ex-orare*, to gain by intreaty.

oracle. (F. – L.) F. *oracle.* – L. *oraculum*, a divine announcement; double dimin. formed from *ora-re*, to pray (above).

oration. (F. – L.) F. *oration.* – L. acc. *orationem.* – L. *oratus*, pp. of *orare*, to pray; see **adore** (above).

orator. (F. – L.) Formerly *oratour.* – F. *orateur.* – L. *oratōrem*, acc. of *orator*, a speaker. – L. *oratus*, pp. of *orare*, to pray, to speak (above).

orifice. (F. – L.) F. *orifice*, a small opening. – L. *orificium*, an opening, lit. 'making of a mouth.' – L. *ori*-, crude form of *os*, mouth; *facere*, to make.

orison, a prayer. (F. – L.) O. F. *orison, oreison* (F. *oraison*). – L. *orationem*, acc. of *oratio*, a prayer; see **oration** (above).

osculate, to kiss. (L.) From pp. of L. *osculari*, to kiss. – L. *osculum*, a little mouth, pretty mouth; double dimin. of *os*, the mouth.

peroration. (F. – L.) F. *peroration.* – L. *perorationem*, acc. of *peroratio*, the close of a speech. – L. *peroratus*, pp. of *perorare*, to complete a speech. – L. *per*, through; *orare*, to speak (above).

Orang-outang, a large ape. (Malay.) Malay *órang útan*, lit. 'wild man.' – Malay *órang*, a man; *útan, hútan*, woods, wilds of a country, wild.

Orange. (F. – Ital. – Pers.) O. F. *orenge* (F. *orange*). Put for *narenge**, but the initial *n* was lost (in Italian), and then *arenge* became *orenge* by a popular etymology from *or*, gold. Cf. Span. *naranja*, an orange. – Ital. *arancio*, an orange. – Pers. *náranj, nárinj, nárang*, an orange. Allied to Pers. *nár*, a pomegranate.

Oration, Orator; see **Oral.**

Orb. (F. – L.) F. *orbe.* – L. *orbem*, acc. of *orbis*, a circle, sphere.

exorbitant, extravagant. (F. – L.) F. *exorbitant.* – L. *exorbitant*-, stem of pres. pt. of *exorbitare*, to fly out of a track. – L. *ex*, out; *orbita*, a track (below).

orbit. (L.) L. *orbita*, a track, circuit; formed with suffix *-ta* from *orbi*-, crude form of *orbis*, an orb, circle.

Orchard; see **Wort.**

Orchestra. (L. – Gk.) L. *orchestra.* –

Gk. ὀρχήστρα, an orchestra; which, in the Attic theatre, was a space on which the chorus danced. – Gk. ὀρχέομαι, I dance.

Orchis, a plant. (L. – Gk.) L. *orchis.* – Gk. ὄρχις, a testicle, a plant with roots of testicular shape. **Der.** *orchid*, a false form, since the gen. case of ὄρχις is ὀρχέως.

Ordain; see **Order.**

Ordeal; see **Deal.**

Order. (F. – L.) F. *ordre*, O. F. *ordine.* – L. *ordinem*, acc. of *ordo*, order. Perhaps allied to **Origin. Der.** *dis-order*.

co-ordinate. (L.) L. *co* (for *cum*), together; *ordinatus*, arranged, pp. of *ordinare*; see **ordain** (below).

extraordinary (L.) L. *extra-ordinarius*, beyond what is ordinary, rare.

inordinate. (L.) L. *in*-, not; *ordinatus*, ordered, controlled, pp. of *ordinare*; see **ordain** (below).

ordain, to set in order. (F. – L.) M. E. *ordeinen.* – O. F. *ordener* (later *ordonner*). – L. *ordinare*, to set in order. – L. *ordin*-, crude form of *ordo*, order. **Der.** *pre-ordain.*

ordinal, shewing the order. (L.) L. *ordinalis*, adj., in order. – L. *ordin*-, crude form of *ordo*, order.

ordinance. (F. – L.) F. *ordinance.* – Low L. *ordinantia*, a command. – L. *ordinant*-, pres. pt. of *ordinare* (above).

ordinary. (F. – L.) F. *ordinaire.* – L. *ordinarius*, regular (as sb., an overseer). – L. *ordin*-, crude form of *ordo*, order. **Der.** *ordinary*, sb.

ordination. (L.) From L. *ordinatio*, an ordinance, also ordination. – L. *ordinatus*, pp. of *ordinare*, to ordain.

ordnance, artillery. (F. – L.) Formerly *ordinance*; it had reference to the *bore* or *size* of the cannon, and was thence transferred to the cannon itself; see **ordinance.**

primordial, original. (F. – L.) F. *primordial.* – L. *primordialis*, original. – L. *primordium*, origin. – L. *prim-us*, first; *ordiri*, to begin, allied to *ordo*, order. See **Primo.**

subordinate, of lower rank. (L.) Coined, with suffix *-ate* (L. *-atus*), from L. *sub ordinem*, under the rank. – L. *sub*, under; *ordinem*, acc. of *ordo*, order.

Ordure; see **Horrid.**

Ore. (E.) M. E. *or*; A. S. *ár*, ore. It seems to be another form of A. S. *ár*, brass, bronze. **+** Icel. *eir*, O. H. G. *ér*,

Goth. *aiz*, brass; L. *æs*, ore, bronze. Cf.
Skt. *ayas*, iron.

Organ. (F. – L. – Gk.) F. *organe.* – L.
organum, an implement. – Gk. ὄργανον, an
implement; allied to ἔργον, work; see
Work.

orgies, sacred rites, revelry. (F. – L. –
Gk.) F. *orgies.* – L. *orgia*, sb. pl. a festival
in honour of Bacchus, orgies. – Gk. ὄργια,
sb. pl., orgies, rites, from sing. ὄργιον, a
sacred act; allied to ἔργον, work.

Oriel; see **Aureate**.

Orient, eastern. (F. – L.) F. *orient.* –
L. *orient-*, stem of *oriens*, rising, the east;
orig. pres. pt. of *oriri*, to rise, begin. +
Skt. *ri*, to rise. (√AR.)

abortion. (L.) From L. *abortio*, an
untimely birth. – L. *abortus*, pp. of *aboriri*,
to fail. – L. *ab*, away; *oriri*, to arise, grow.

origin. (F. – L.) F. *origine.* – L. *ori-
ginem*, acc. of *origo*, a beginning. – L.
oriri, to rise.

Orifice; see **Oral**.

Oriflamme; see **Aureate**.

Origan, wild marjoram. (F. – L. – Gk.)
F. *origan.* – L. *origanum.* – Gk. ὀρίγανον,
lit. 'mountain-pride.' – Gk. ὀρῐ = ὀρει-, crude
form of ὄρος, a mountain; γάνος, beauty,
ornament.

Origin; see **Orient**.

Oriole; see **Aureate**.

Orison; see **Oral**.

Orlop; see **Leap**.

Ormolu; see **Aureate**.

Ornament. (F. – L.) M. E. *ornament.*
– F. *ornement.* – L. *ornamentum*, an
adornment. – L. *ornare*, to adorn. Allied
to Skt. *varna*, colour, beauty, from *vri*, to
cover. (√WAR.)

adorn. (L.) L. *adornare*, to deck. –
L. *ad*, to, on; *ornare*, to adorn.

ornate. (L.) From pp. of L. *ornare*,
to adorn.

suborn, to procure secretly, bribe. (F.
– L.) F. *suborner.* – L. *subornare.* – L.
sub, secretly; *ornare*, to furnish, properly
to adorn.

Ornithology, the science of birds.
(Gk.) Gk. ὄρνιθο-, crude form of ὄρνις, a
bird; -λογία, from λόγος, a discourse,
λέγειν, to speak. Allied to A.S. *earn*, an
eagle, named from its soaring; cf. Gk.
ὄρνυμι, I stir up, rouse. (√AR.)

ornithorhyncus, an Australian animal. (Gk.) Named from the resemblance
of its snout to a duck's bill. – Gk. ὀρνιθο-,
for ὄρνις, bird; ῥύγχος, a snout.

Orphan. (L. – Gk.) L. *orphanus.* –
Gk. ὀρφανός, destitute; John, xiv. 18.
Allied to L. *orbus*, destitute.

Orpiment, Orpine; see **Aureate**.

Orrery, an apparatus for illustrating the
motion of the planets. (Ireland.) Con-
structed at the expense of Charles Boyle,
earl of *Orrery*, about 1715. *Orrery* is a
barony in co. Cork, Ireland.

Orris; see **Iris**.

Ort; see **Eat**.

Orthodox, of the right faith. (L. – Gk.)
Late L. *orthodoxus.* – Gk. ὀρθόδοξος, of the
right opinion. – Gk. ὀρθό-s, upright, right;
δόξα, an opinion, from δοκεῖν, to seem.

orthoepy, correct pronunciation. (Gk.)
From Gk. ὀρθοέπεια, orthoepy. – Gk. ὀρθό-s,
right; ἔπ-ος, a word; see **Epic**.

Orthography, correct writing. (F. – L.
– Gk.) M. E. *ortographie.* – F. *ortographie.*
– L. *orthographia.* – Gk. ὀρθογραφία. – Gk.
ὀρθό-s, right; γράφειν, to write.

Orthopterous, lit. straight - winged.
(Gk.) Gk. ὀρθό-s, straight; πτερόν, a wing.

Ortolan, a bird. (F. – Ital. – L.) O. F.
hortolan. – O. Ital. *hortolano*, a gardener,
also an *ortolan*, lit. 'haunter of gardens.' –
L. *hortulanus*, a gardener. – L. *hortulus*,
dimin. of *hortus*, a garden; allied to **Yard**.

Orts; see **Eat**.

Oscillate, to swing. (L.) From pp. of
L. *oscillare*, to swing. – L. *oscillum*, a
swing.

Osculate; see **Oral**.

Osier. (F. – Low L. – Gk.) F. *osier*, 'the
ozier, red withy, water-willow tree;' Cot.
Allied to Low L. *osariæ*, *ausariæ*, osier-
beds (9th cent.). – Gk. οἶσος, an osier.
(√WI.)

Osmium; see **Odour**.

Osprey; see **Osseous**.

Osseous, bony. (L.) L. *osseus*, bony. –
L. *oss-*, stem of *os*, a bone. Cf. Gk. ὀστέον,
Skt. *asthi*, a bone.

osprey, the fish-hawk. (L.) A corruption of *ossifrage*, the older name for the
bird. – L. *ossifragus, ossifraga*, an osprey. –
L. *ossifragus*, bone-breaking; (from its
strength). – L. *ossi-*, crude form of *os*, bone;
frag-, base of *frangere*, to break.

ossifrage. (L.) In Levit. xi. 13; see
above.

ossify, to turn to bone. (F. – L.) From
L. *ossi-*, crude form of *os*, bone; F. *-fier*,
for L. *-ficare*, to make, from *facere*, to
make. Der. *ossific-at-ion*.

osteology, science of the bones. (Gk.)

Gk. ὀστέο-ν, a bone (above); -λογία, from λόγος, a discourse, λέγειν, to speak.

Ostensible, Ostentation; see Tend (1).

Osteology; see **Osseous**.

Ostler; see hostler, under Host (1).

Ostracise; see **Oyster**.

Ostrich; see **Aviary**.

Other, second, different. (E.) M. E. *other*; A. S. *ôðer*, other, second. **+** Du. *ander*, Icel. *annarr* (for *antharr**), Dan. *anden*, Swed. *andra*, G. *ander*, Goth. *anthar*, Lithuan. *antras*, L. *alter* (for *anter**), Skt. *antara*, other. In Skt. *an-tara*, the suffix is the usual comparative suffix (as in Gk. σοφώ-τερος, wiser). All from Aryan ANA, this, he. Thus the orig. sense is 'beyond this,' i. e. second.

Otter; see **Water**.

Otto, the same as **Attar**.

Ottoman, a low stuffed seat. (F. — Turk.) F. *ottomane*, an ottoman, sofa. — F. *Ottoman*, Turkish. So named from *Othman* or *Osman*, founder of the Turkish empire.

Ouch, Nouch, the socket of a precious stone, ornament. (F. — O. H. G.) Usually *ouch*, yet *nouch* is the true form. M. E. *nouche*. — O. F. *nouche*, *nosche*, *nusche*, a buckle, clasp, bracelet (Burguy); Low L. *nusca*. — M. H. G. *nuske*, O. H. G. *nusca*, a buckle, clasp, brooch.

Ought (1), pt. t. of **Owe**, q. v.

Ought (2), anything; see One.

Ounce (1), twelfth part of a pound. (F. — L.) M. E. *unce*. — O. F. *unce* (F. *once*). — L. *uncia*, (1) an ounce, (2) an inch. Allied to Gk. ὄγκος, mass, weight.

inch. (L.) M. E. *inche*; A. S. *ynce*. — L. *uncia*, an inch. See Inch.

Ounce (2), **Once**, a kind of lynx. (F. — Pers.?) F. *once*, an ounce. Cf. Port. *onça*, Span. *onza*, Ital. *lonza*, an ounce. Prob. Ital. *lonza* stands for *l'onza*, since we also find Ital. *onza*, an ounce (Florio, 1598). Perhaps a nasalised form from Pers. *yúz*, a panther, pard, lynx, esp. those used (like the ounce) in hunting deer.

Our; see **Us**.

Ourang-outang; see **Orang-outang**.

Ousel, a kind of thrush. (E.) M. E. *osel*. A. S. *ôsle*. (Put for *ansle** or *amsle**, like A. S. *ôðer*=Goth. *anthar*.)**+**G. *amsel*, O. H. G. *amsala*, an ousel.

Oust, to eject. (F. — L.) O. F. *oster*, 'to remove;' Cot. (F. *ôter*). Of disputed origin; some derive it from *obstare*, which does not suit the sense; Diez suggests L.

haustare*, a derivative of *haurire* (pp. *haustus*), to draw water. Cf. E. *ex-haust*; and L. *exhaurire*, used in the sense 'to remove.'

Out, without, abroad. (E.) M. E. *oute*, *ute*, adv. A. S. *úte*, *útan*, adv., out, without; formed (with adv. suffix -*e* or -*an*) from A. S. *út*, adv. out, from. **+** Du. *uit*, Icel. *út*, Dan. *ud*, Swed. *ut*, G. *aus*, Goth. *ut* (= A. S. *út*), *uta* (= A. S. *úte*), *utana* (= A. S. *útan*); Skt. *ud*, up, out. (Aryan UD.) ¶ Hence numerous compounds, such as *out-balance*, *out-bid*, *out-break*, presenting no difficulty.

about. (E.) M. E. *abuten*; A. S. *âbútan*, for *onbútan* (also found). — A. S. *on*, on, at; *bútan*, outside, without, contr. from *be-útan*, which is compounded of *be*, by, and *útan*, adv., without. (*About* = *on-by-out*, i e. on the outside.)

but (1), prep. and conj., except. (E.) M. E. *bute*, *buten*. A. S. *bútan*, conj., except; prep., besides, without; orig. an adv. meaning 'outside.' See **about** (above). **+** Du. *buiten*, except.

outer, comp. form; see utter (below).

outmost; see utmost (below).

outward. (E.) A.S. *úteweard*, out-ward. — A.S. *úte*, out; *weard*, -ward; see **Toward**.

utmost. (E.) A popular corruption of M. E. *outemest* (Rich. Coer de Lion, 2931), by confusion with *most*. A.S. *útemest*, formed with double superl. suffix -*m-est* from A.S. *úte*, out.

utter, outer. (E.) M. E. *utter*. A. S. *úttor*, which occurs as well as *útor*; both are comparative forms of *út*, out. Der. *utter*, verb.

Outlaw. (Scand.) M. E. *outlawe*. — Icel. *útlâgi*, an outlaw, lit. out of (beyond) the law. — Icel. *út*, out; *lög*, law; see Out and **Law**.

Outlet. (E.) M. E. *utlete*, lit. 'a letting out.' — A. S. *út*, out; *lâtan*, to let.

Outrage; see **Ultra-**.

Outrigger. (E. *and* Scand.) A projecting spar for extending sails, a projecting rowlock for an oar, a boat with projecting rowlocks. From Out and **Rig**.

Outward; see Out.

Oval, egg-shaped. (F. — L.) F. *oval*. Formed with suffix -*al* (= L. -*alis*) from L. *ouum*, an egg. **+** Gk. ᾠόν, an egg. β. L. *ouum* and G. ᾠόν are from a common base AWI, appearing in L. *auis*, a bird; see **Aviary**. And see **Egg**. Der. *ov-ar-y*,

Low L. *ouaria*, the part of the body in which eggs are formed in birds; *ovi-form*, egg-shaped; *ovi-parous*, from L. *oui-parus*, egg-producing (see **Parent**).

Ovation, a lesser Roman triumph. (F. ‑ L.) F. *ouation.* ‑ L. acc. *ouationem*, from *ouatio*, a shouting, exultation. ‑ L. *ouatus*, pp. of *ouare*, to shout. **+** Gk. αὔειν, to shout.

Oven. (E.) M. E. *ouen* (= *oven*). A.S. *ofen, ofn.*+Du. *oven*, Icel. *ofn, omn* (also *ogn*), Swed. *ugn*, G. *ofen*, Goth. *auhns*. (The common base is UHNA.)

Over, above, across. (E.) M. E. *ouer* (= *over*). A.S. *ofer.*+Du. *over*, Icel. *yfir, ofr*, Dan. *over*, Swed. *öfver*, G. *über*, Goth. *ufar*, Gk. ὑπέρ, L. *s-uper*; Skt. *upari*, above. The Aryan form is UPARI, locative case of UPARA, upper (Skt. *upara*, L. *s-uperus*, A. S. *yfera*). This is a comparative form from Aryan UPA (Skt. *upa*, near, on, under; Gk. ὑπό, L. *s-ub*, Goth. *uf*, under; E. *-ove* in *ab-ove*). Closely allied to **Up**. (The senses 'over' and 'under' are curiously mixed.) ¶ Hence a large number of compounds beginning with *over*, which present no difficulty.

oft, often, frequently. (E.) A.S. *oft*; whence M. E. *ofte*, with added *-e*, and lastly *ofte-n* with added *-n.*+Icel. *oft*, Dan. *ofte*, Swed. *ofta*, G. *oft*, Goth. *ufta*; answering in form to Gk. ὕπατος, highest; a superlative form allied to the comp. form *over*. From the notion of what is over or excessive, we pass to that of frequency.

Overt, open, public. (F. ‑ L.) O. F. *overt* (later *ouvert*), pp. of *ovrir* (later *ouvrir*), to open. The etymology is disputed; Diez suggests that *ovrir* is a shortened form of O. F. *a-ovrir, a-uvrir* (Livre des Rois), answering to Prov. *adubrir*, to open. The latter can be resolved into L. *ad, de, operire*, where *ad* is a mere prefix, and *de-operire* is to uncover. Littré considers *ovrir* as put for *avrir*, i.e. L. *aperire*, to open. β. We may consider *overt* as due to confusion between *operire* and *aperire*, both difficult words, and prob. related. Perhaps *a-perire* = *ab-perire**, to uncover, and *operire* = *ob-perire**, to cover up, where *-perire* is allied to L. *parare*, to prepare, get ready.

overture, a proposal, beginning. (F. ‑ L.) O. F. *overture*, latter *ouverture*, an opening, from' O. F. *overt*, open (above).

Oviform, Oviparous; see **Oval**.

Owe, to possess; hence, to possess another's property, be in debt, be obliged. (E.) M. E. *aȝen, awen, owen*, orig. 'to possess'; hence to be obliged to do, to be in debt. A.S. *ágan*, to have, possess (whence long *o* from A. S. *á*, and *w* for *g*). +Icel. *eiga*, to possess, have, be bound, own; Dan. *eie*, Swed. *äga*, O. H. G. *eigan*, Goth. *aigan*, to possess. Allied to Skt. *iç*, to possess (√IK.)

ought. (E.) The pres. tense of A. S. *ágan* is *ic áh*, really an old pt. tense; hence was formed the pt. t. *áhte*, M. E. *ahte, aughte, oughte*, mod. E. *ought*.

owing, in phr. *owing to* = due to, because of. (E.) Orig. pres. pt. of *owe*, verb.

own (1), possessed by any one, peculiar to oneself. (E.) M. E. *aȝen, awen, owen*, contracted to *own* by loss of *e*. A. S. *ágen*, own, orig. pp. of *ágan*, to possess; see **Owe** (above). **+** Icel. *eigin*, Dan. Swed. *egen*.

own (2), to possess. (E.) M. E. *aȝnien, ahnien, ahnen, ohnen*. A.S. *ágnian*, to appropriate, claim as one's own; causal verb, from A.S. *ágen*, own (above).+Icel. *eigna*, to claim as one's own; from *eigin*, own. **Der.** *own-er*.

Owl, a bird. (E.) M. E. *oule*. A.S. *úle.*+Du. *uil*, Icel. *ugla*, Dan. *ugle*, Swed. *ugla*, G. *eule*, O.H.G. *hiuweld*, *úwela*. Allied to L. *ulula*, Skt. *ulukâ*, an owl. The sense is 'howler,' from the imitative √UL, to howl; cf. L. *ululare*, to howl. See **Howl**.

Own (1), **Own** (2); see **Owe**.

Own (3), to grant, allow. (E.) Much confused with *own* (2), yet of different origin. M. E. *unnen*, to grant; A. S. *unnan*, to grant. The pres. t. is A.S. *ic an*, M. E. *ich an* or *ich on*, I own, grant.+Icel. *unna*, to grant, pres. t. *ek ann*; O. Sax. *gi-unnan*, G. *gönnen*, O. H. G. *gi-unnan*, to grant.

Ox. (E.) M. E. *ox, oxe*, pl. *oxen*; A.S. *oxa*, pl. *oxan.*+Du. *os*, Icel. *uxi, oxi*, Dan. Swed. *oxe*, G. *ochse, ochs*, Goth. *auhsa, auhsus*, W. *ych*; Skt. *ukshan*, an ox, bull (lit. impregnater). The Skt. *ukshan* is derived from Skt. *uksh*, to sprinkle. (√WAG.)

oxlip, a flower. (E.) A.S. *oxanslyppe*, orig. an ox-slop, piece of ox-dung (a coarse name, like some other plant-names). ‑ A. S. *oxan*, gen. case of *oxa*, ox; *slyppe*, a slop; see **Slop**. (So also *cow-slip* = *cow-slop*).

Oxalis, Oxide; see **Oxygen**.

Oxlip; see **Ox**.

Oxygen, a gas often found in acid compounds. (Gk.) Lit. ' acid-generator.' — Gk. ὀξύ-s, sharp, acid; γεν-, to produce, base of γίγνομαι, I am born. (√ AK and √ GAN.)   Allied to Acid.

oxalis, wood-sorrel. (L. — Gk.) L. *oxalis*. — Gk. ὀξαλίς, (1) sour wine, (2) sorrel; from its sourness. — Gk. ὀξύς, acid (above).

oxide, a compound of oxygen with a non-acid base. (Gk.) Coined from *ox-* (for *oxy-*, as in *oxy-gen*), and *-ide*, Gk. -ειδής, like.   See Oxygen.

oxymel, a mixture of honey and vinegar. (L. — Gk.) L. *oxymeli*. — Gk. ὀξύμελι. — Gk. ὀξύ-s, sharp, acid; μέλι, honey; see Mellifluous.

oxytone, having an acute accent on the last syllable. (Gk.)   Gk. ὀξύτονος,

shrill toned. — Gk. ὀξύ-s, sharp; τόνος, a tone; see Tone.

paroxysm. (F. — L. — Gk.) F. *paroxisme*. — L. *paroxysmus*. — Gk. παροξυσμός, irritation, the fit of a disease. — Gk. παροξύνειν, to irritate. — Gk. παρ-ά, beside; ὀξύνειν, to sharpen, from ὀξύς, sharp.

Oyer, Oyez; see Audience.

Oyster. (F. — L. — Gk.) M. E. *oistre*. — O. F. *oistre* (F. *huître*). — L. *ostrea*; also. *ostreum*. — Gk. ὄστρεον, an oyster; named from its hard shell. — Gk. ὀστέον, a bone, shell; see Osseous.

ostracise, to banish by a vote written on a potsherd. (Gk.) Gk. ὀστρακίζειν, to ostracise. — Gk. ὄστρακον, a potsherd, tile, voting-tablet, orig. a shell. — Gk. ὄστρεον, an oyster, orig. a shell.

Ozone; see Odour.

PA–PE.

Pabulum; see Pastor.
Pace; see Patent.
Pacha; see Pasha.
Pachydermatous; see Derm.
Pacify; see Pact.
Pack, a bundle. (C.?) Of Celtic origin; cf. Gael. *pac*, a pack, also a mob (whence E. *pack* of rascals), *pac*, verb, to pack; Irish *pac*, a pack, *pacaigim*, I pack up; Brel. *pak*, a pack. (Hence also Icel. *pakki*, Dan. *pakke*, Swed. *packa*, Du. *pak*, G. *pack*.) Allied to Skt. *paç*, to fasten, L. *pangere*; see Pact. (√ PAK.) Der. *pack-age*, with F. suffix *-age* (as in *bagg-age*); *pack-et*, from O. F. *paquet*, a packet, bundle, dimin. form from Low G. *pakk*, O. Du. *pack*, or from Bret. *pak* (above). ¶ Perhaps Latin.

Pact, a contract. (L.) L. *pactum*, an agreement. — L. *pactus*, pp. of *pacisci* to agree, inceptive form of *pacĕre*, to agree. Allied to *pangere*, to fasten, fix; Skt. *paç*, to bind, Gk. πήγνυμι, I fasten. And see Fadge. (√ PAK.)

appease. (F. — L.) M. E. *apaisen*. — O. F. *apaisier* (F. *apaiser*), to pacify, bring to a peace. — O. F. *a pais*, to a peace. — L. *ad pacem*, to a peace; see peace (below).

compact (1), adj., fastened together, fitted, close, firm. (F. — L.) O.F. *compacte*. — L. *compactus*, fitted together, pp. of *compingere*. — L. *com-* (=cum), together; *pangere*, to fasten.

compact (2), sb., a bargain, agreement. (L.) L. *compactum*, sb. — L. *compactus*, pp. of

compacisci, to agree with. — L. *com-* (*cum*), with; *pacisci*, to make a bargain (above).

impact, a striking against. (L.) L. *impactus*, pp. of *impingere*, to impinge (below).

impinge, to strike against. (L.) L. *impingere*, to strike against. — L. *im-* (*in*), on, upon; *pangere*, to fasten, also to strike.

pacify. (F. — L.) F. *pacifier*. — L. *pacificare*, to make peace. — L. *paci-*, crude form of *pax*, peace; *-ficare*, for *facere*, to make; see peace (below).

page (2), one side of the leaf of a book. (F. — L.) F. *page*. — L. *pāgina*, a page, leaf. Orig. a leaf; and named from the fastening together of strips of papyrus to form a leaf. — L. *pag-*, base of *pangere*, to fasten (pp. *pac-tus* = *pag-tus*).

pageant, an exhibition, spectacle. (Low L. — L.) Orig. the moveable scaffold on which the old 'mysteries' were acted. M. E. *pagent* (Prompt. Parv.); formed, with excrescent *t* after *n*, from Low L. *pagina*, a scaffold, stage for shews, made of wooden planks. — L. *pagina*, a page of a book, also a plank of wood. Named from being fastened together; see page (2). Der. *pageant-r-y*.

pale (1), a stake, limit. (F. — L.) M. E. *paal*. — F. *pal*, ' a pale, stake;' Cot. — L. *pālus*, a stake. Put for *pag-lus**; from *pag-*, base of *pangere*, to fasten, fix. ¶ The heraldic *pale* is the same word; so is *pole* (1).

palette, a small slab on which painters mix colours. (F. — Ital. — L.) F. *palette*, orig. a flat blade, spatula, a flat saucer, and lastly, a palette. — Ital. *paletta*, a flat blade, spatula; dimin. of *pala*, a spade. — L. *pāla*, a spade, shovel, flat-bladed 'peel' for putting bread into an oven. Orig. a spade for planting. — L. *pag-*, base of *pangere*, to fasten, also to plant.

palisade. (F. — L.) F. *palissade*, a row of pales. — F. *paliss-er*, to enclose with pales. — F. *palis*, a pale, extended from *pal*, a pale; see **pale** (1) above.

pallet (2), an instrument used by potters, also by gilders; also a palette. (F. — Ital. — L.) It is a flat-bladed instrument for spreading plasters, gilding, &c.; and is only another spelling of **palette** (above).

pay (1), to discharge a debt. (F. — L.) M. E. *paien.* — O. F. *paier, paer* (F. *payer*), to pay, to content. — L. *pacare*, to pacify; in late Lat., to pay a debt. — L. *pac-*, stem of *pax*, peace; see **peace** (below).

peace. (F. — L.) M. E. *pais.* — O. F. *pais* (F. *paix*). — L. *pacem*, acc. of *pax*, peace, orig. a compact. — L. *pac-*, as in *pacisci*, to make a bargain; see **Pact**.

peculate, to pilfer. (L.) From pp. of L. *peculari*, to appropriate to one's own use. Formed as if from *peculum**, put for *peculium*, private property; see below.

peculiar, one's own, particular. (F. — L.) F. *peculier.* — L. *peculiaris*, one's own. — L. *peculium*, private property; closely allied to *pecunia*, money; see below.

pecuniary. (F. — L.) F. *pecuniaire.* — L. *pecuniarius*, relating to money or property. — L. *pecunia*, property. — L. *pecu-a*, neut. pl., cattle of all kinds, property; pl. of *pecus*, cattle. Cf. Skt. *paçu*, cattle, lit. that which is fastened up, i. e. domestic cattle; from *paç*, to fasten. (√PAK.)

peel (3), a fire-shovel. (F. — L.) Once a common word. — F. *pelle*, older form *pale*, a fire-shovel. — L. *pala*; see **palette** (above).

pell-mell, confusedly. (F. — L.) O. F. *pesle-mesle*, 'pell-mell, confusedly;' Cot. Spelt *pellemelle* in the XIIIth cent. (mod. F. *pêle-mêle*). Lit. 'stirred up with a fire-shovel.' — F. *pelle*, a fire-shovel; O. F. *mesler*, to mix up; see **peel** (3) above, and **Medley**.

pole (1), a large stake. (L.) M. E. *pole*, formed (by usual change of *á* to long *o*) from A.S. *pál*, a pale, pole. — L. *pālus*, a stake; see **pale** (1) above.

propagate. (L.) From pp. of L. *propagare*, to peg down, propagate by layers,

produce; allied to *propages, propago*, a layer, and from the same source as *compages*, a joining together. — L. *pro*, forth; *pag-*, base of *pangere*, to fasten, set (hence to peg down a layer). **Der.** *propag-and-ist*, a coined word from the name of the society entitled *Congregatio de propagandá fide*, constituted at Rome, A.D. 1622. And see **Prune** (1).

repay. (F. — L.) O. F. *repayer.* — O. F. *re-* (L. *re-*), back; *payer*, to pay; see **pay**.

Pad (1), a soft cushion. (Scand. — C.? *or* C.?) Also in the sense of 'saddle' (Levins, 1570); also in the sense of 'bundle' (Halliwell). The same word as *pod*, orig. a bag; see below. **Dér.** *pad*, verb.

pod, a husk. (Scand. — C.? *or* C.?) Orig. a leather bottle, a bag; a *pad* is a stuffed bag, a cushion. — Swed. dial. *pude*, a cushion; Dan. *pude*, a cushion. — Gael. *put*, a large buoy, inflated sheep-skin. (Or from the Celtic directly.)

pudding, an intestine filled with meat, a sausage; hence, a sort kind of meat, made of flour, eggs, &c. (C.) Of Celtic origin; cf. Irish *putog*, a pudding, Gael. *putag*; W. *poten*, a paunch, a pudding; Corn. *pot*, a bag, pudding. β. Further allied to W. *pwtyn*, a short round body, Gael. *put*, a large buoy, inflated skin; all (apparently) from a base PUT, to swell out, as in Swed. dial. *puta*, to be inflated. Cf. E. *pout*.

Pad (2), a thief on the high road; see **Path**.

Paddle (1), to finger, dabble; see **Pat** (1).

Paddle (2), a little spade; see **Spade**.

Paddock (1), a toad. (Scand.) M. E. *paddok*, dimin. of M. E. *padde*, a toad. — Icel. *padda*, Swed. *padda*, Dan. *padde*, a toad, frog. ✛ Du. *padde, pad.* Lit. 'jerker,' i.e. 'jumper;' cf. Gk. σφοδρός, active, Skt. *spand*, to vibrate, whence *sparça-spanda*, a frog. (√SPAD.)

Paddock (2), a small enclosure; see **Park**.

Padlock, a loose-hanging lock. (E.?) A lock for hampers, &c.; prob. coined by adding *lock* to ·prov. E. *pad*, a pannier (Norfolk). This word is also written *ped*; see **Pedlar**.

Pæan, a hymn to Apollo. (L. — Gk.) L. *pæan.* — Gk. Παιάν, Παιών, (1) Pæan, Pæon, physician of the gods, (2) Apollo, (3) a hymn to Apollo.

peony, pæony, a flower. (F. — L. — Gk.) Altered to suit the Lat. spelling.

M. E. *pione.* — O. F. *pione* (F. *pivoine*). — L. *pæonia*, medicinal, from its supposed virtues; fem. of *Pæonius*, belonging to *Pæon* (as above).

Pædobaptism; see Pedagogue.

Pagan, a countryman; hence, a heathen. (L.) L. *paganus*, (1) a villager, (2) a pagan, because the rustic people remained longest unconverted. — L. *paganus*, adj., rustic. — L. *pagus*, a village, district, canton. Supposed to be from *pag-*, base of *pangere*, to fasten; as being marked out by fixed limits; see Pact.

paynim, **painim**, a pagan. (F. — L.) 'The *paynim* bold;' F. Q. i. 4. 41. M. E. *paynim*, a pagan; but this sense is due to a singular mistake. A *paynim* is properly not a *man*, but a *country* or district, and is identical with *paganism*, formerly used to mean heathendom, or the country of pagans. Rightly used in King Horn, 803, to mean 'heathen lands.' — O. F. *paienisme*, lit. paganism; Low L. *paganismus*. Formed with suffix *-ismus*, from L. *pagan-us*, a pagan.

peasant. (F. — L.) O. F. *paisant*, another form of O. F. *paisan*, a peasant; (cf. Ital. *paisano*, Span. *paesano*, a com-patriot). Formed with suffix *-an* (L. *anus*), from O. F. *pais* (F. *pays*), a country (cf. Ital. *paese*, Span. *pais*, Port. *pais*, a country). — Low L. *pagense*, neut. of *pagensis*, belonging to a village. — L. *pagus*, a village, district.

Page (1), a boy attending a person of rank. (F. — Low L. — L. ?) M. E. *page*. — F. *page*. — Low L. *pagium*, acc. of *pagius*, a servant. Cf. Span. *page*, Port. *pagem*, Ital. *paggio*, a page. Etym. disputed; but prob. *pagius* is a mere variant of *pagensis*, belonging to a village; from L. *pagus*, a village, district; see Pagan. β. Diez thinks that Ital. *paggio* was formed from Gk. παιδίον, a little boy, dimin. of παῖς, a boy. This does not account for Port. *pagem*, which certainly points to L. *pagensis*. (See Diez, Littré, Scheler.)

Page (2), one side of a leaf; see Pact.

Pageant; see Pact.

Pagoda, an Indian idol's temple. (Port. — Pers.) From Port. *pagoda*, *pagode*, a pagoda. — Pers. *but-kadah*, an idol-temple. — Pers. *but*, idol, image; *kadah*, habitation. (The initial Pers. letter is sometimes rendered by *p*, as in Devic's Supp. to Littré.)

Pail; see Patent.

Pain. (F. — L.) M. E. *peine.* — F. *peine*,

a pain, a penalty. — L. *pæna*, punishment, penalty, pain. + Gk. ποινή, penalty.

impunity. (F. — L.) F. *impunité.* — L. acc. *impunitatem*, acc. of *impunitas*, impunity. — L. *impuni-s*, without punishment. — L. *im-* (= *in-*), not; *pæna*, punishment.

penal. (F. — L.) O. F. *penal*, 'penall;' Cot. — L. *pœnalis*, belonging to punishment. — L. *pæna*, punishment.

penance. (F. — L.) O. F. *penance*, older form *penéance*. — L. *pœnitentia*, penitence. — L. *pœnitent-*; see below.

penitent. (F. — L.) O. F. *penitent.* — L. *pœnitent-*, stem of pres. pt. of *pœnitere*, to cause to repent, frequent. form of *pœnire* = *punire*, to punish. — L. *pæna*, penalty.

pine (2), to suffer pain, waste away. (L.) M. E. *pinen*, to suffer, more frequently, to torment; a verb formed from M. E. *pine*, torment. — A. S. *pín*, pain; borrowed from L. *pæna*, pain.

punch (2), to beat, bruise. (F. — L.) Short for *punish*; M. E. *punchen*, *punischen*, are equivalent words (Prompt. Parv.). See below.

punish. (F. — L.) M. E. *punischen.* — F. *puniss-*, stem of pres. pt. of *punir*, to punish. — L. *punire*, to punish. — L. *pæna*, penalty.

repent, to rue. (F. — L.) F. *repentir*, to repent. — L. *re-*, again; *pœnitere*, to cause to repent; see penitent (above).

repine. (L.) Compounded of L. *re-*, again; and *pine*, to fret; see pine (above).

subpœna, a writ commanding attendance under a penalty. (L.) L. *sub*, under; *pænâ*, abl. of *pæna*, a penalty.

Paint; see Picture.

Painter, a rope for mooring a boat. (F. — L. — Gk.) Assimilated to *painter*, one who paints; orig. M. E. *panter*, a noose, esp. for catching birds. — O. F. *pantiere*, a snare for birds, a large net for catching many at once. — L. *panther*, a hunting-net for catching wild beasts. — Gk. πάνθηρος, adj., catching all sorts. — Gk. πᾶν, neut. of πᾶς, every; θήρ, a wild beast. See Pan- and Deer. (And see *panther*.)

Pair; see Par.

Palace. (F. — L.) M. E. *palais.* — F. *palais.* — L. *palatium*, orig. a building on the *Palatine* hill at Rome; esp. a palace of Nero on this hill. The *Palatine* hill is supposed to have been named from *Pales*, a pastoral divinity, the goddess who protected flocks; her name means 'protector.'

Cf. Skt. *pála*, a guardian, from *pá*, to protect. (√ PA.)

paladin. (F. – Ital. – L.) F. *paladin*, a knight of the round table. – Ital. *paladino*, a warrior; orig. a knight of the *palace* or royal household. – L. *palatinus* (below).

palatine. (F. – L.) In phr. 'count *palatine*;' the proper sense is 'pertaining to the palace or royal household.' – L. *palatinus*, (1) the name of a hill at Rome, (2) belonging to a palace; see **Palace** (above).

Palanquin, Palankeen, a light litter in which travellers are borne on men's shoulders. (Hind. – Skt.) Cf. F. *palanquin*, Port. *palanquim*, a palankeen. All from Hindustani *palang*, a bed, bedstead (Forbes); also spelt *pálki*, and (in the Carnatic) *pallakki* (Wilson); Pali *palanki*, a palankeen (Yule). – Skt. *paryanka* (Prakrit *pallanka*), a couch-bed, bed. Apparently named from being wrapped about one. – Skt. *pari* (= Gk. περί), round, about; *anka*, a hook, also the flank.

Palate. (F. – L.) O. F. *palat*. – L. *palatum*, the palate, roof of the mouth.

Palatine; see **Palace.**

Palaver; see **Parable.**

Pale (1), a stake; see **Pact.**

Pale (2), wan. (F. – L.) O. F. *palle*, *pale*, later *pasle* (F. *pâle*). – L. *pallidus*, pale. Allied to **Fallow.**

pallid. (L.) L. *pallidus*, pale (above).

pallor. (L.) L. *pallor*, paleness. – L. *pallere*, to be pale.

Palæography, the study of ancient modes of writing. (Gk.) – Gk. παλαιό-s, old, from πάλαι, adv., long ago; γράφ-ειν, to write.

palæology, archæology. (Gk.) From Gk. παλαιό-s, old; -λογια, discourse, from λόγος, a word, λέγειν, to speak.

palæontology, the science of fossils, &c. (Gk.) From Gk. παλαιό-s, old; ὄντο-, crude form of ὤν, existing; -λογία, discourse, from λόγος, a word, λέγειν, to speak.

Palestra, a wrestling-school. (L. – Gk.) L. *palæstra.* – Gk. παλαίστρα, a wrestling-school. – Gk. παλαίειν, to wrestle. – Gk. πάλη, wrestling. Allied to πάλλειν, σπαίρειν, to quiver. (√SPAR.)

Paletot, a loose garment. (F. – Du.) Mod. F. *paletot*, formerly spelt *palletoc*, a sort of coat. – O. Du. *paltroc*, also *palsrock*, a coat, jacket (Oudemans). We find M. E. *paletoke* (also from Dutch), used of a dress

worn by soldiers, knights, and kings, and usually made of silk or velvet. I have little doubt that the orig. sense is 'palace-coat,' i. e. court-dress. – O. Du. *pals*, a palace; O. Du. *roc* (= G. *rock*, O. H. G. *hroch*), a coat. Cf. O. Du. *palsgrave*, G. *pfalzgraf*, E. *palgrave* (lit. count of the palace). See **Palace.**

Palette; see **Pact.**

Palfrey. (F. – Low L.) M. E. *palefrai*, *palfrei*. – O. F. *palefrei* (F, *palefroi*). – Low L. *paraveredus*, lit. 'an extra post-horse' (White). – Low L. *para-* (Gk. παρά), beside, hence, extra; *ueredus*, a post-horse, courier's horse. β. Perhaps *ueredus* stands for *uehe-redus*[*], i. e. carriage-drawer, from L. *uehere*, to carry, draw, and L. *rheda*, a four-wheeled carriage (said to be a Gaulish word; cf. W. *rhedu*, to run, *rhe*, swift). ¶ Cf. Du. *paard*, G. *pferd*, a horse, both derived from *paraveredus*.

Palimpsest, a MS. which has been twice written on, the first writing being partly erased. (Gk.) Gk. παλίμψηστον, a palimpsest, neut. of παλίμψηστος, scraped again (to renew the surface). – Gk. πάλιμ-, for πάλιν, again; ψηστός, scraped, from ψάειν, to rub.

Palindrome, a word or sentence that is the same whether read forwards or backwards. (Gk.) Such a word is *madam*. – Gk. παλίνδρομος, running back again. – Gk. πάλιν, again; δρόμος, a running, from δραμεῖν, to run; see **Dromedary.**

Palinode; see **Ode.**

Palisade; see **Pact.**

Pall (1), a cloak, mantle, shroud. (L.) A. S. *pæll.* – L. *palla*, a mantle; cf. *pallium*, a coverlet.

palliate, to cloak, excuse. (L.) From L. *palliatus*, covered as with a cloak. – L. *pallium*, a coverlet, cloak.

Pall (2), to become vapid. (F. – L.) *Pall* seems to be nothing but a shortened form of *appal*, formerly used in just the same sense. Palsgrave has *palle* and *appalle*, both in the sense of losing colour by standing as drink does; also 'I *palle*, I fade.' See further below.

appal. (F. – L.) The transitive sense is late; the M. E. *appalled* meant 'faded in look,' or 'rendered pale'; cf. Chaucer, C. T. 10679. – O. F. *appalir, apalir,* to grow pale; also to make pale (Cot.). 'I *appalle*, as drinke dothe, whan it leseth his colour'; Palsgrave. – O. F. *a* (= L. *ad*), prefix; O. F. *palle*, pale. See **Pale.** ¶ Not of Celtic origin.

Palladium, a safeguard of liberty. (L. —Gk.) L. *Palladium*; Virg. Æn. ii. 166, 183.—Gk. Παλλάδιον, the statue of Pallas on which the safety of Troy depended.— Gk. Παλλάς (stem Παλλαδ-), Pallas, an epithet of Athene.

Pallet (1), a kind of mattress, properly one of straw. (F.—L.) M. E. *paillet*.— F. *paillet*, a heap of straw, given by Littré as a provincial word.—F. *paille*, straw.— L. *palea*, straw, chaff. + Gk. πάλη, fine meal; Skt. *palâla*, straw.

palliasse, a straw mattress. (F.—L.) F. *paillasse* (with *ll* mouillés), a straw-bed; spelt *paillace* in Cotgrave. — F. *paille*, straw; with suffix -*ace* (=L. -*aceus*). —L. *palea* (above).

Pallet (2); see **Pact**.

Palliasse; see **Pallet** (1).

Palliate; see **Pall** (1).

Pallid, Pallor; see **Pale** (2).

Pall-mall; see **Mall** (2).

Palm (1), inner part of the hand. (F.— L.); also (2) a tree (L.). The sense of 'flat hand' is the older, the tree being named from its flat spreading leaves, which bear some resemblance to the hand spread out. But the sense of 'tree' is the older in English, occurring already as A. S. *palm*, borrowed from L. *palma*, a palm-tree. β. To this spelling the M. E. *paume*, palm of the hand, has been accommodated, though it was orig. borrowed from F. *paume*, also from L. *palma*, the palm of the hand. + Gk. παλάμη, the palm of the hand; A. S. *folm*, the same. Der. *palm-ate*, *palm-ist-r-y*; also *palm-er*, M. E. *palm-ere*, one who bore a palm-branch in memory of having been to the Holy Land; hence a *palmer* or *palmer-worm*, a sort of caterpillar, supposed to be so named from its wandering about.

Palpable, that can be felt. (F.—L.) F. *palpable* (Littré, Palsgrave).—L. *palpabilis*, that may be felt. — L. *palpare*, to feel, *palpari*, to handle. The orig. sense was 'to quiver;' cf. *palp-ebra*, the eye-lid, and *palpitare* (below). Allied to Skt. *sphal*, to quiver. (√SPAR.)

palpitate, to throb. (L.) From pp. of L. *palpitare*, to throb; frequent. of *palpare*, orig. to quiver (as above).

Palsy; see **Paralysis**.

Palter, to dodge, shuffle, equivocate. (Scand.) Spelt *paulter* in Cotgrave, s. v. *harceler*. The orig. sense is to haggle, to haggle over such worthless stuff as is called

paltrie in Lowland Scotch. More literally, it is 'to deal in rags;' see further below.

paltry, worthless. (Scand.) Lowland Sc. *paltrie* is a sb., meaning trash; so also Norfolk *paltry*, 'rubbise, refuse,' Forby. But both sb. and adj. are from an old sb. *palter*, rags, which is still preserved in Danish and Swedish. — Swed. *paltor*, rags, pl. of *palta*, a rag, tatter; Dan. *pialter*, rags, pl. of *pialt*, a rag. [This plural in -*er* (or -*or*) is seen in English in M. E. *child-er*, children, *breth-er*, brothers.] β. We find the adj. itself in Low G. *paltrig*, ragged, from *palte*, a rag, piece torn off a cloth; and in prov. G. *palterig*, paltry, from *palter* (pl. *paltern*), a rag (Flügel). We find also O. Du. *palt*, a fragment, Friesic *palt*, a rag. Cf. G. *spalten*, to split.

Pampas, plains in S. America. (Peruvian). The final *s* is the Span. pl. suffix.— Peruvian *pampa*, a plain.

Pamper; see **Pap** (1).

Pamphlet, a small book. (F.?—L.?— Gk.?) Spelt *pamflet*, Test. of Love, pt. iii, near the end. Etym. quite uncertain. We find F. *pamphile*, the knave of clubs, from the Gk. name *Pamphilus*; similarly, I should suppose that there was a F. form *pam-filet**, or Low L. *pamphiletus**, coined from L. *Pamphila* (of Gk. origin), the name of a female historian of the first century, who wrote numerous *epitomes* of history. We find Low Lat. *panfletus*.

Pan. (L.) M. E. *panne*. A. S. *panne*, a pan, broad shallow vessel. Borrowed from British; cf. Irish *panna*, W. *pan*, a pan; Low L. *panna*, a pan. These are clearly corrupted forms of L. *patina*, a shallow bowl, pan, bason. See **pail**, under **Patent**. Der. *pan-cake*.

Pan-, *prefix*, all. (Gk.) Gk. πᾶν, neut. of πᾶς, all.

Panacea, a universal remedy. (L.—Gk.) L. *panacea*. — Gk. πανάκεια, a universal remedy; allied to πανακής, all-healing.— Gk. πᾶν, all (above); ἀκέομαι, I heal, ἄκος, a remedy.

Pancreas, a fleshy gland, commonly called sweet-bread. (L.—Gk.) L. *pancreas*. —Gk. πάγκρεας, sweet-bread; lit. 'all flesh,' from its softness.—Gk. πᾶν, all; κρέας, flesh. See **Pan-** and **Carnal**.

Pandect, a digest. (F. — L. — Gk.) Usually in pl. *pandects*. — O. F. *pandectes*, pl. (Cot.)—L. *pandecta*, the title of a collection of laws made by order of Justinian; also (in sing.) *pandectes*. — Gk. πανδέκται, pandects; from Gk. πανδέκτης, all-receiving, comprehensive. – Gk. πᾶν, all; δέχομαι, I receive. See Pan and Digit.

Pandemonium. (Gk.) The home of all the demons. – Gk. πᾶν, all; δαίμονι-, for δαίμων, a demon; see Pan- and Demon.

Pander, Pandar, a pimp.' (L. – Gk.) L. *Pandarus.* – Gk. Πάνδαρος, a personal name; the name of the man who procured for Troilus the favour of Chryseis. The *name* is from Homer; but the *story* belongs to medieval romance.

Pane, a patch of cloth, plate of glass. (F. – L.) M. E. *pane*, a portion. – F. *pan*, 'a pane, piece, or pannell;' Cot. – L. *pannum*, acc. of *pannus*, a cloth, rag, patch. Allied to **Vane.**

counterpane (2), counterpart of a deed. (F. – L.) O. F. *contrepan, contrepant*; Cot. – F. *contre* (L. *contra*), over against; *pan*, a pledge; see **pawn** (below).

panel, pannel, a board with a surrounding frame, &c. (F. – L.) M. E. *panel*, (1) a piece of cloth, sort of saddle, (2) a schedule containing jurors' names; the general sense being 'little piece.' – O. F. *panel* (later *paneau*), 'a pannel of wainscot, of a saddle,' &c.; Cot. – Low L. *panellus*, dimin. of *pannus*, a cloth; see **Pane.** Der. *em-panel, im-panel*, to put upon a panel, enroll jurors' names.

panicle, a form of inflorescence. (L.) L. *panicula*, a tuft; double dimin. of *panus*, the thread wound round the bobbin of a shuttle. (Gk. πῆνος.) Allied to L. *pannus*, cloth; see **Pane** (above).

pawn (1), a pledge. (F. – L.) F. *pan*, 'a pane, piece, panel, also a pawn, gage, skirt of a gown, pane of a hose,' &c.; Cot. – L. *pannum*, acc. of *pannus*, a cloth; see **Pane** above, which is the same word. β. The explanation is, that the readiest pledge to leave was a piece of clothing; cf. Span. *paños*, clothes. The Du. *pand*, G. *pfand*, O. H. G. *phant*, a pledge, are early borrowings from L. *pannus*, with excrescent *d* or *t* after *n*. Der. *im-pawn*, to put in pledge, to pledge; *pawn*, verb.

penny. (L.; *with* E. *suffix.*) M. E. *peni*; pl. *penies*, contracted form *pens* (whence mod. E. *pence*). A. S. *pening*, a penny; later form *penig*, whence M. E. *peni*. The oldest form is *pending* (Thorpe, Diplomatarium, p. 471); formed with E. suffix -*ing* from the base *pand**. β. This base is the same word as Du. *pand*, a pawn, pledge; G. *pfand*, O. H. G. *pfant*,

not Teutonic, but borrowed from L. *pannus*; see **pawn** (1) above. The lit. sense is 'little pledge,' i. e. a token, coin. + Du. *penning*, Icel. *penningr*, Dan. Swed. *penning*; G. *pfennig*, O. H. G. *phantinc*, dimin. of *pfant*; all similarly formed.

Panegyric. (L. – Gk.) L. *panegyricus*, a eulogy; from L. *panegyricus*, adj. – Gk. πανηγυρικός, fit for a full assembly, festive, solemn; hence applied to a festival oration. – Gk. πᾶν, all; ἄγυρι-s, Æolic form of ἀγορά, a gathering, a crowd.

Panel; see **Pane.**

Pang, a violent pain, throe; see **Prong.**

Panic, extreme fright. (Gk.) Gk. τὸ πανικόν, Panic fear, supposed to be inspired by the god Pan. – Gk. πανικός, adj., from Πάν, Pan, a rural god of Arcadia. Cf. Russ. *pan'*, Lithuan. *ponas*, a lord. (√PA.)

Panicle, Pannel; see **Pane.**

Pannier; see **Pantry.**

Panoply, complete armour. (Gk.) Gk. πανοπλία, full armour. – Gk. πᾶν, all; ὅπλ-α, arms, armour, pl. of ὅπλον, an implement. – Gk. ἕπω, I am busy about; allied to **Sequence.** And see **Pan-.**

Panorama, a kind of large picture. (Gk.) Lit. 'a view all round.' – Gk. πᾶν, all; ὅραμα, a view, from ὁράω, I see. See **Pan-** and **Wary.**

Pansy; see **Pendant.**

Pant, to breathe hard. (E. ?) M. E. *panten*, to pant (15th cent.); apparently an E. word. The O. F. *pantais* (Sherwood, index to Cotgrave) meant 'shortness of breath, in hawks,' and was a term in hawking; but it may have been of E. origin. So also O. F. *pantois*, short-winded, F. *panteler*, to pant. The Devonshire word is *pank*, prob. of imitative origin; cf. Low G. *pinkepanken*, to hammer, *pinkepank*, clang of hammers. ¶ Hardly from W. *pantu*, which does not mean to press (Diez), but to sink in, indent.

Pantaloon (1), a ridiculous character, buffoon. (F. – Ital. – Gk.) F. *pantalon.* – Ital. *pantalone*, a buffoon; from the personal name *Pantaleone*, common in Venice, St. *Pantaleone* being the patron-saint of Venice. Prob. from Gk. πανταλέων, lit. 'all-lion,' a Gk. personal name. – Gk. παντα-, all; λέων, lion.

pantaloons, a kind of trousers. (F. – Ital. – Gk.) F. *pantalon*, so called because worn by Venetians. – Ital. *pantalone*, a Venetian; see above.

Pantheism, the doctrine that the universe is God. (Gk.) From **Pan-** and **Theism**; see below.

pantheon. (L. – Gk.) L. *pantheon.* – Gk. πάνθειον, a temple consecrated to all the gods. – Gk. πᾶν, all; θεῖος, divine, from θεός, god.

Panther, a quadruped. (F. – L. – Gk.) M. E. *pantere.* – O. F. *panthere.* – L. *panthera*, *panther.* – Gk. πάνθηρ, a panther; prob. of Skt. origin. ¶ A supposed derivation from πᾶν, all, θήρ, a beast, gave rise to numerous fables.

Pantomine, a dumb actor; later, a dumb show. (F. – L. – Gk.) F. *panto-mime*, an actor of many parts in one play. L. *pantomimus.* – Gk. παντόμιμος, all-imitating, a pantomimic actor. – Gk. παντο-, crude form of πᾶς, all; μῖμος, a mime, imitator; see Pan- and **Mimic**.

Pantry. (F. – L.) M. E. *pantrie.* – O. F. *paneterie.* – Low L. *panetaria*, *panitaria*, a place where bread is made or kept. – Low L. *paneta*, one who makes bread. – L. *pan-is*, bread, food. (√PA.)

appanage, provision for a dependent, &c. (F. – L.) A law term. – O. F. *appanage* (F. *apanage*), properly a provision for maintenance; see Cotgrave and Brachet. – O. F. *apaner*, to nourish, lit. to supply with bread; Low L. *apanare.* – O. F. *a* (for L. *ad*), to, for; *pain*, bread, from L. *panem*, acc. of *panis*, bread.

pannier, a bread-basket. (F. – L.) M. E. *panier.* – F. *panier.* – L. *panarium*, a bread-basket. – L. *panis*, bread. See also **Company**.

Pap (1), food for infants. (E.) '*Pap-mete* for chylder;' Prompt. Parv. (A.D. 1440). Cf. M. E. *pappe*, only in the sense of 'breast.' Of infantine origin, due to the repetition of *pa, pa*, in calling for food; cf. L. *papa, pappa*, the word by which infants call for food. So also Du. *pap*, G. *pappe*, pap; Dan. *pap*, Swed. *papp*, paste-board. Cf. Pap (2), **Papa**.

pamper, to glut. (O. Low G.) Frequent. from Low G. *pampen*, to cram. – Low G. *pampe*, broth, pap, nasalised form of *pappe*, pap.

pap (2), a teat, breast. (Scand.) M. E. *pappe.* – O. Swed. *papp*, the breast; changed, in mod. Swedish, to *patt*. So also Swed. dial. *pappe*, N. Fries. *pap*, *papp*, Lithuan. *pápas*, the breast. The same as Pap (1); and due to the infant's call for food.

Papa, father. (F. – L.) Not found in old books; rather, borrowed from F. *papa.* – L. *papa*, found as a Roman cognomen. Cf. L. *pappas*, a tutor, borrowed from Gk. πάππας, papa; Homer, Od. vi. 57. Due to the repetition of *pa, pa*; see Pap (1).

papal, belonging to the pope. (F. – L. – Gk.) F. *papal.* – Low L. *papalis*, adj., from L. *papa*, a bishop, spiritual father. – Gk. πάπα, πάππα, vocative of πάπας, πάππας, papa, father (above).

pope, the father of a church, bishop of Rome. (L. – Gk.) M. E. *pope*; formed from A. S. *pápa*, pope, by the usual change from *á* to long *o.* – L. *papa*, pope, father; see papal (above).

Paper; see Papyrus.

Papilionaceous; see Pavilion.

Papillary, belonging to or resembling nipples or teats, warty. (L.) From L. *papilla*, a small pustule, nipple, teat; dimin. of *papula*, a pustule. ᐩ Lithuan. *pápas*, a teat, *pampti*, to swell out; Gk. πομφός, bubble, blister. (√PAP, to swell out.) See Pimple.

Papyrus. (L. – Gk. – Egyptian?) L. *papyrus.* – Gk. πάπυρος, an Egyptian rush or flag, of which a writing material was made. Prob. of Egyptian origin.

paper. (L. – Gk. – Egyptian?) M. E. *paper*; directly from L. *papyrus* (above).

papier-maché, paper made into pulp, moulded, dried, and japanned. (F. – L.) F. *papier*, paper, from L. acc. *papyrum*; F. *maché*, lit. chewed, pp. of *macher*, L. *masticare*, to chew. See **Masticate**.

Par, equal value. (L.) L. *par*, equal. Perhaps allied to **Pare**.

apparel, to clothe. (F. – L.) M. E. *aparailen.* – O. F. *aparailler*, to dress, apparel. – O. F. *a*, to; *pareiller, parailler*, to assort, to put like things with like, arrange, from *pareil*, like, similar. – L. *ad*, to; Low L. *pariculus*, similar, formed from L. *par*, equal.

compeer, an associate. (F. – L.) M. E. *comper.* – F. *com-*, together; O. F. *per*, a peer, equal. – L. *com-* (*cum*), together; *par*, equal; see **peer** (below).

disparage, to offer indignity, lower in rank or esteem. (F. – L.) M. E. *desparagen.* – O. F. *desparager.* – O. F. *des-*, apart; *parage*, rank. – L. *dis-*, apart; Low L. *paraticum*, society, rank, equality of rank, from L. *par*, equal.

disparity. (L.) From L. *dis-*, apart; and E. *parity*, equality, from L. *par*, equal. Suggested by L. *dispar*, unequal.

pair, two equal or like things. (F. — L.) M. E. *peire.* — F. *paire,* 'a pair;' Cot. — F. *pair,* 'like, equal;' id. — L. *parem,* acc. of *par,* equal.

parity, equality. (F. — L.) F. *parité.* — L. *paritatem,* acc. of *paritas,* equality. — L. *par,* equal.

peer (1), an equal. (F. — L.) The twelve *peers* of France were of *equal* rank. M. E. *pere, per.* — O. F. *per, peer,* later *pair,* a peer ; or as adj. equal. — L. *parem,* acc. of *par,* equal. Der. *peer-less.*

prial, three of a sort, at cards. (F. — L.) A corruption of *pair-royal*; (see Nares).

umpire, an arbitrator. (F. — L.) Formerly *numpire*; M. E. *nompere.* The lit. sense is the unequal, or odd (third) man, who decides between two others. — O. F. *nompair,* 'odde,' Cot.; older form *nomper.* — L. *non,* not; *par,* equal.

Para-, prefix. (Gk.) Gk. παρά, beside. Allied to Skt. *pará,* away, from, L. *per,* through, and to E. *for-* in *for-give.* (√PAR.)

Parable. (F. — L. — Gk.) M. E. *parabole.* — O. F. *parabole.* — L. *parabola,* Mark, iv. 2. — Gk. παραβολή, a comparison, a parable. — Gk. παραβάλλειν, to cast or put beside, to compare. — Gk. παρά, beside; βάλλειν, to cast; see Balustrade.

palaver. (Port. — L. — Gk.) A parley. — Port. *palavra,* a word, parole. — L. *parabola* (above).

parabola, a certain plane curve. (L. — Gk.) L. *parabola.* — Gk. παραβολή, the conic section made by a plane *parallel* to the surface of the cone; see **Parable.**

parley. (F. — L. — Gk.) F. *parler,* sb. speech, talk, a parley. — F. *parler,* verb, to speak. — Low L. *parabolare,* to talk. — L. *parabola*; see **Parable** (above).

parliament. (F. — L. — Gk.; *with* F. *suffix.*) M. E. *parlement.* [We also find Low L. *parliamentum,* corresponding to our spelling *parliament.*] — F. *parlement,* 'a speaking, parleying, a supreme court;' Cot. — F. *parler,* to speak (as above); with F. suffix -*ment* (= L. -*mentum*).

parlour. (F. — L. — Gk.) M. E. *parlour, parlur.* — O. F. *parleor,* later *parloir,* a parlour, lit. a room for conversation. — F. *parl-er,* to speak; with suffix -*eor* = L. -*atorium*; so that *parlour* answers to a Low L. form *parabolatorium** (not found), a place to talk in. (Cf. F. *dortoir* = L. *dormitorium.*) See above.

parole. (F. — L. — Gk.) F. *parole,* a word, esp. a promise; the same word as

Prov. *paraula,* Span. *palabra* (= *parabla**), Port. *palavra.* — Low L. *parabola,* a discourse; L. *parabola,* a parable. See **Parable** above.

Parachute; see **Pare.**

Paraclete, the Comforter. (L. — Gk.) L. *paracletus.* — Gk. παράκλητος, called to one's aid, the Comforter (John, xiv. 16.) — Gk. παρακαλεῖν, to call to one's aid. — Gk. παρά, beside; καλεῖν, to call.

Parade; see **Pare.**

Paradigm, an example, model. (F. — L. — Gk.) F. *paradigme.* — L. *paradigma.* — Gk. παράδειγμα, a pattern, model, example of declension. — Gk. παρά, beside; δείκνυμι, I point out, show. See **Diction.**

Paradise. (F. — L. — Gk. — Pers.) F. *paradis.* — L. *paradisus.* — Gk. παράδεισος, a park, pleasure-ground; an oriental word, and now ascertained to be of Pers. origin. — O. Pers. (Zend) *pairidaéza,* an enclosure, place walled in. — O. Pers. *pairi* (= Gk. περί), around; *diz* (= Skt. *dih*), to mould, form, shape (hence to form a wall of earth). √DHIGH; see **Dike.**

parvis, a porch, room over a porch. (F. — L. — Gk. — Pers.) O. F. *parvis,* a porch, outer court before a house or church. — Low L. *paravisus,* corruption of *paradisus,* a church-porch, outer court, paradise.

Paradox. (F. — L. — Gk.) F. *paradoxe.* — L. *paradoxum,* neut. of *paradoxus,* adj. — Gk. παράδοξος, contrary to received opinion. — Gk. παρά, beside; δόξα, opinion, from δοκεῖν, to seem; see **Dogma.**

Paraffine. (F. — L.) Named from its having but small affinity with an alkali. — F. *paraffine.* — L. *par-um,* little; *affinis,* having affinity; see **Affinity.**

Paragoge, the addition of a letter at the end of a word. (L.) [Thus, in *tyran-t,* the final letter is *paragogic.*] — L. *paragoge.* — Gk. παραγωγή, a leading by or past, alteration. — Gk. παράγειν, to lead past. — Gk. παρ-ά, beyond; ἄγειν, to lead; see **Agent.**

Paragon. (F. — Span. — L.) F. *paragon.* — Span. *paragon,* a model of excellence. This singular word owes its origin to two prepositions, united in one phrase. — Span. *para con,* in comparison with, as in *para con el,* in comparison with him. — Span. *para,* itself a compound prep., answering to O. Span. *pora,* from L. *pro ad* (Diez); *con,* from L. *cum,* with. Thus it really results from three L. preps., viz. *pro, ad, cum.*

Paragraph, a short passage of a book.

(F. — L. — Gk.) Actually corrupted, in the 15th century, into *pargrafte*, *pylcrafte*, and *pilcrow* ! — F. *paragraphe*. — Low L. *paragraphum*, acc. of *paragraphus*. — Gk. παράγραφος, a line or stroke in the margin, a paragraph-mark ; hence the paragraph itself. — Gk. παρά, beside ; γράφειν, to write ; see **Graphic**. (N. B. The *pilcrow* or paragraph mark is now printed ¶.)

Parallax, the difference between the real and apparent places of a star. (Gk.) Gk. παράλλαξις, alternation, change ; also parallax (in modern science). — Gk. παραλλάσσειν, to make things alternate. — Gk. παρά, beside ; ἀλλάσσειν, to change, alter, from ἄλλος, other ; see **Alien**.

Parallel, side by side, similar. (F. — L. — Gk.) O. F. *parallele*, Cot. — L. *parallelus*. — Gk. παράλληλος, parallel, beside each other. — Gk. παρ-ά, beside ; ἀλλήλος*, one another, only in the gen. dat. and acc. plural. β. The crude form ἀλλήλο- stands for ἄλλ' ἄλλο-, a reduplicated form, lit. 'the other the other' or 'one another ;' from Gk. ἄλλος, other ; see **Alien**.

parallelogram. (F. — L. — Gk.) O.F. *paralelograme*, Cot. — L. *parallelogrammum*. — Gk. παραλληλόγραμμον, a figure contained by two pairs of parallel lines. — Gk. παράλληλο-ς, parallel (above) ; γράμμα, a line, from γράφειν, to write.

parallelopiped. (L. — Gk.) So written ; a mistake for *parallelepiped*. — L. *parallelepipedum*. — Gk. παραλληλεπίπεδον, a body formed by parallel surfaces. — Gk. παράλληλο-s, parallel ; ἐπίπεδον, a plane surface, neut. of ἐπίπεδος, on the ground, from ἐπί, upon, and πέδον, the ground.

Paralogism, a conclusion unwarranted by the premises. (F. — L. — Gk.) F. *paralogisme*. — L. *paralogismus*. — Gk. παραλογισμός, a false reckoning or conclusion. — Gk. παραλογίζομαι, I misreckon. — Gk. παρά, beside, amiss ; λογίζομαι, I reckon, from λόγος, reason ; see **Logic**.

Paralysis. (L. — Gk.) L. *paralysis*. — Gk. παράλυσις, a loosening aside, disabling of nerves, paralysis or palsy. — Gk. παραλύειν, to loosen aside. — Gk. παρά, beside ; λύειν, to loosen, allied to **Lose**. Der. *paralyse*, from F. *paralyser*, verb formed from F. sb. *paralysie*, paralysis. Also *paralytic*, from Gk. παραλυτικός, afflicted with palsy.

palsy. (F. — L. — Gk.) M. E. *palesy*, fuller form *parlesy*. — F. *paralysie*. — L. *paralysin*, acc. of *paralysis* (above).

Paramatta, a fabric like merino. (New S. Wales.) So named from *Paramatta*, a town near Sydney, New South Wales.

Paramount ; see **Mount**.

Paramour ; see **Amatory**.

Parapet ; see **Pare**.

Paraphernalia, ornaments. (L. — Gk.) Properly the property which a bride possesses beyond her dowry. Formed by adding L. neut. pl. suffix -*alia* to Low L. *paraphern-a*, the property of a bride over and above her dower. — Gk. παράφερνα, that which a bride brings beyond her dower. — Gk. παρά, beside ; φερνή, that which is brought, from φέρειν, to bring, allied to E. **Bear** (1).

Paraphrase. (F. — L. — Gk.) O. F. *paraphrase*. — L. *paraphrasin*, acc. of *paraphrasis*. — Gk. παράφρασις, a paraphrase, free translation. — Gk. παρά, beside ; φράσις, a phrase, from φράζειν, to speak ; see **Phrase**.

Paraquito, Parakeet, a little parrot. (Span.) Span. *periquito*, a little parrot, dimin. of *perico*, a parrot. Diez supposes *perico* to be a nickname, meaning 'little Peter,' dimin. of *Pedro*, Peter. See **Parrot**.

Parasite. (F. — L. — Gk.) F. *parasite*. — L. *parasitus*. — Gk. παράσιτος, eating beside another at his table, a flatterer, toad-eater. — Gk. παρά, beside ; σῖτος, wheat, food. Orig. in a good sense ; see Gk. Lex.

Parasol ; see **Pare**.

Parboil ; see **Bull** (2).

Parcel ; see **Part**.

Parch, to scorch. (F. — L.) Very difficult. M. E. *parchen*, to parch. Prob the same as M. E. *perchen*, to pierce, an occasional form of *percen*, to pierce. This is the most likely solution ; in fact, a careful examination of M. E. *perchen* fairly proves the point. It was at first used in the sense 'to pierce with cold,' and was afterwards transferred to express the effects of heat. We still say '*piercing* cold.' See Milton, P. L. ii. 594. — F. *percer*, to pierce. See **Pierce**.

Parchment. (F. — L. — Gk.) M. E. *perchemin*. — F. *parchemin*. — L. *pergamina*, parchment ; fem. of L. *Pergamenus*, belonging to Pergamos (where parchment was first invented). — Gk. περγαμηνή, parchment, from Πέργαμος, Πέργαμον, Pergamus, in Mysia of Asia Minor.

Pard, a panther, leopard. (L. — Gk.) L. *pardus*. — Gk. πάρδος. An Eastern word ;

cf. Pers. *párs*, a pard; Skt. *pridáku*, a leopard. Der. *leo-pard, camelo-pard*.

Pardon; see Date (1).

Pare, to shave off. (F. – L.) M.E. *paren.* – F. *parer*, to deck, trim, pare. – L. *parare*, to get ready, prepare. (√ PAR.)

apparatus, gear. (L.) L. *apparatus*, preparation. – L. *apparatus*, pp. of *apparare*, to prepare for. – L. *ap-* (for *ad*), for; *parare*, to get ready.

compare, to set together, so as to examine likeness or difference. (F. – L.) F. *comparer.* – L. *comparare*, to adjust, set together. – L. *com-* (*cum*), together; *parare*, to get ready.

emperor, a ruler. (F. – L.) O. F. *empereor.* – L. *imperatorem*, acc. of *imperator*, a ruler. – L. *imperare*, to rule. – L. *im-* (for *in*), upon, over; *parare*, to make ready, order. Der. *empr-ess*.

empire. (F. – L.) F. *empire.* – L. *imperium*, command. – L. *im-* (*in*), upon, over; *parare*, to make ready.

imperative. (F. – L.) F. *imperatif*, imperious. – L. *imperatiuus*, due to a command. – L. *imperatum*, a command; neut. of *imperatus*, pp. of *imperare*; see emperor (above).

imperial. (F. – L.) O. F. *emperial*, later *imperial.* – L. *imperialis*, belonging to an empire. – L. *imperium*, an empire; see empire (above).

parachute, an apparatus for breaking a fall from a balloon. (F. – L.) F. *parachute*, put for *par' à chute*, lit. that which parries or guards against a fall. – F. *parer*, to deck, also to guard against; *à*, prep., to, against; *chute*, a fall. Here *parer* = L. *parare*; *à* = L. *ad*; and *chute* is allied to Ital. *caduto*, fallen, from L. *cadere*, to fall.

parade, display. (F. – Span. – L.) F. *parade*, a show, also 'a stop on horseback,' Cot. The latter sense was the earliest in French. – Span. *parada*, a stop, halt, from *parar*, verb, to halt, also to get ready. – L. *parare*, to get ready. The sense 'display' was due to the F. verb *parer*, to deck, trim, from the same L. *parare*.

parapet, a rampart, breast-high. (F. – Ital. – L.) F. *parapet.* – Ital. *parapetto*, a wall breast-high; lit. 'guarding the breast.' – Ital. *parare*, to adorn, also to guard, parry; *petto*, breast. – L. *parare*; *pectus*, the breast.

parasol, a sun-shade. (F. – Port. – L.) F. *parasol*, 'an umbrello;' Cot. – Port.

parasol, an umbrella to keep off the sun's heat. – Port. *para-r*, to ward off; *sol*, sun. See **parry** (below) and **Solar**.

parry, to ward off. (F. – L.) F. *paré*, sb., used as equivalent to Ital. *parata*, a defence, guard. – F. *parer*, to prepare, also to guard, ward off. – L. *parare*.

prepare. (F. – L.) F. *préparer*; Cot. – L. *prae-parare*, to make ready beforehand.

rampart. (F. – L.) Also spelt *rampire, rampier, rampar.* – O. F. *rempart*, *rempar*, a rampart of a fort. – O. F. *remparer*, to put again into a state of defence. – L. *re-*, again; *im-* (*in*), in; *parare*, to get ready.

repair (1), to restore, amend. (F. – L.) F. *réparer.* – L. *re-parare*, to recover, repair, make ready anew. Der. *repar-able*, F. *reparable*, L. *reparabilis*; *repar-at-ion*, F. *reparation*.

separate, to keep apart. (L.) L. *separatus*, pp. of *separare*, to sever. – L. *se-*, apart; *parare*, to get ready, set. Der. *separate*, adj., kept apart (not so old as the verb).

sever, to separate. (F. – L.) O. F. *sevrer.* – L. *separare*, to separate (above). Der. *dissever*.

several, adj. (F. – L.) O. F. *several.* – Low L. *separale*, a thing set apart. – L. *separare*, to separate (above).

Paregoric, assuaging pain. (L. – Gk.) L. *paregoricus*, assuaging. – Gk. παρηγορικός, addressing, encouraging, soothing. – Gk. παρηγορεῖν, to address. – Gk. παρά, beside, ἀγορά, an assembly; whence also ἀγορεύειν, to address an assembly.

Parent. (F. – L.) F. *parent*, a kinsman. – L. *parent-*, stem of *parens*, a parent, lit. one who produces. – L. *parere*, to produce. (√ PAR.)

appear, to become visible. (F. – L.) M.E. *apperen.* – O. F. *apparoir, aparoir.* – L. *apparère*, to appear. – L. *ap-* (*ad*), to, forth; *parère*, to come in sight, a secondary verb from *parère*, to produce, put forth. Der. *appar-it-ion, appar-ent*, &c., from L. *apparere*.

parturient, about to produce young. (L.) L. *parturient-*, stem of pres. pt. of *parturire*, to be ready to produce young. – L. *partur-us*, fut. part. of *parère*, to produce. Der. *partur-it-ion*, F. *parturition*, L. acc. *parturitionem*, from *parturitus*, pp. of *parturire*.

repertory, a treasury. (F. – L.) F.

repertoire. – L. *repertorium,* an inventory.
– L. *repertor,* a finder, discoverer. – L.
reperire, to find out. – L. *re-,* again; *parire*
(Ennius), usually *parere,* to produce; see
Parent (above).

transparent. (F. – L.) F. *transparent,* 'clear-shining;' Cot. – L. *trans,*
through; *parent-,* stem of pres. pt. of
parēre, to appear; see **appear** (above).

Parenthesis; see **Theme.**

Parget, to plaister a wall. (L.?) Perhaps obsolete; once common. M. E. *par-
geten,* fuller form *spargetten,* also *sparchen;*
Prompt. Parv. (1440). Perhaps from L.
spargitare, frequent. of *spargere,* to sprinkle;
see **Sparse.** β. Or from L. *paries,* a wall
(some say). If so, the *s* of *spargetten* =
O. F. *es-,* L. *ex.*

Parhelion, a mock sun. (L. – Gk.) L.
parhelion. – Gk. παρήλιον, neut. of παρήλιος,
beside the sun. – Gk. παρ-ά, beside; ἥλιος,
sun; see **Heliacal.**

Parian, belonging to Paros. (Gk.) *Paros*
is an island in the Ægean sea.

Parietal, forming the walls, applied to
two bones in the front of the skull. (L.)
L. *parietalis,* belonging to a wall. – L.
pariet-, stem of *paries,* a wall. Supposed
to mean 'that which goes round;' from
par-, equivalent to Gk. περί, Skt. *pari,*
round about, and *i-re,* to go.

pellitory (1), **paritory,** a wild flower
that grows on walls. (F. – L.) *Pellitory*
is for *paritory.* M. E. *paritorie.* – O. F.
paritoire, 'pellitory;' Cot. – L. *parietaria,*
pellitory; fem. of *parietarius,* belonging to
walls. – L. *pariet-,* stem of *paries* (above).

Parish. (F. – L. – Gk.) M. E. *parische.*
– F. *paroisse.* – L. *parœcia.* – Gk. παροικία,
a neighbourhood; hence, an ecclesiastical
district. – Gk. πάροικος, neighbouring. – Gk.
παρ-ά, near; οἶκος, house, abode, allied to
Vicinage. Der. *parishion-er,* formed by
adding *-er* (needlessly) to M. E. *parisshen*
= O. F. *paroissien,* a parishioner.

parochial. (L. – Gk.) L. *parochialis.*
– L. *parochia,* same as *parœcia* (above).

Parity; see **Par.**

Park, an enclosed ground. (E.) *Park* =
O. F. *parc,* is a F. spelling; but the word
is really E., being a contraction of M. E.
parrok, an enclosure, A. S. *pearruc, pearroc*
(the same). The A. S. *pearroc* is formed,
with dimin. suffix *-oc* (as in *bull-ock*) from
A. S. *sparran,* to enclose, lock, fasten.
This loss of initial *s* is seen in the use of
M. E. *sparren* and *parren* as equivalent

forms, in the same sense. (Cf. G. *sperren,*
to shut.) The verb, meaning 'to fasten
with a *spar* or bar,' is formed from the sb.
Spar (1), q. v. β. The word is common
to Teutonic tongues; as in Du. *perk,* Swed.
Dan. *park,* G. *pferch,* whence not only F.
parc, Ital. *parco,* Span. *parque,* but also
Irish and Gael. *pairc,* W. *park* and *parwg*
(= E. *parrok*), Bret. *park.*

paddock (2), a small enclosure. (E.)
Not an old word; used by Evelyn; a cor-
ruption of M. E. *parrok,* spelt *parrocke* in
Palsgrave. (So also *poddish* for *porridge.*)

Parley, Parliament, Parlour; see
Parable.

Parlous; see **Peril.**

Parochial; see **Parish.**

Parody; see **Ode.**

Parole; see **Parable.**

Paronymous; see **Onomatopœia.**

Paroxysm; see **Oxygen.**

Parricide; see **Paternal.**

Parrot. (F. – L. – Gk.) F. *perrot,* of
which the lit. sense is 'little Peter,' given
to the bird as a nickname; see Cotgrave.
Also written *Pierrot,* both forms being from
Pierre, Peter. – L. *Petrum,* acc. of *Petrus,*
Peter. – Gk. πέτρος, a stone, rock; also Peter.
Der. F. *perroquet,* borrowed from Span.
perichito or *periquito,* dimin. of *Perico,*
Peter; see **Paraquito.** ¶ The F. word
is prob. imitated or borrowed from Span.
or Portuguese.

Parry; see **Pare.**

Parse; see **Part.**

Parsee, an adherent of the old Persian
religion, in India. (Pers.) Pers. *pársí,* a
Persian. – Pers. *Párs,* Persia.

peach (1), a fruit. (F. – L. – Pers.)
M. E. *peche.* – O. F. *pesche,* a peach. – L.
persicum, a peach; so called from growing
on the *Persica arbor,* Persian tree. – Pers.
Párs, Persia.

Parsimony, frugality. (F. – L.) F.
parsimonie (Minsheu). – L. *parsimonia,*
better *parcimonia.* – L. *parci-,* for *parcus,*
sparing; with suffix *-monia* (Aryan *-man-
ya*). Allied to *parcere,* to spare. L. *parcus*
is allied to Gk. σπαρνός, scarce, rare, and
to E. *spare.*

Parsley. (F. – L. – Gk.) Formerly
persely. – F. *persil;* older form *peresil.* –
L. *petroselinum.* – Gk. πετροσέλινον, rock
parsley. – Gk. πέτρο-ς, rock, stone; σέλινον,
a kind of parsley; see **Celery.**

Parsnep, Parsnip. (F. – L.) Formerly
parsnep, and still better *pasneppe,* as in

Palsgrave; the *r* being intrusive. — O. F. *pastenaque*, a parsnip (by dropping *t*, and change of *qu* to *p*, as in Gk. πέμπε = L. *quinque*). — L. *pastinaca*, a parsnep; orig. a root dug up. — L. *pastinare*, to dig up. — L. *pastinum*, a two-pronged dibble. ¶ The suffix -*nep* was assimilated to that of *turnep*.

Parson; see **Sound** (3).

Part. (F. — L.) F. *part*. — L. *partem*, acc. of *pars*, a part. Orig. 'a share,' that which is provided; from the same base as *re-per-ire* and *par-are*; see **Pare**. **Der.** *part*, verb.

apart, aside. (F. — L.) F. *à part*, apart, alone, singly; Cot. — L. *ad partem*, lit. to the one part or side, apart. — L. *ad*, to; *partem*, acc. of *pars*, a part.

apartment, a separate room. (F. — Ital. — L.) F. *appartement*. — Ital. *appartamento*, lit. separation. — Ital. *appartare*, to withdraw. — Ital. *a parte*, apart. — L. *ad partem*; see above.

apportion. (F. — L.) F. *apportioner*, to portion out to. — F. *ap-* (put for *a* before *p*, in imitation of L. *ap-* = *ad*), to; *portion*, a portion; see **portion** (below).

compartment. (F. — L.) F. *compartiment*, a partition; Cot. — F. *compartir*, to divide into equal parts; Low L. *compartire*. — L. *com-* (*cum*), together; *partire*, to part, from *parti-*, crude form of *pars*, a part.

depart. (F. — L.) O. F. *departir*, to divide, to part from. — L. *de*, from; *partire* (above).

impart. (F. — L.) O. F. *impartir*. — L. *impartire*, *impertire*, to give a share to. — L. *im-* (= *in*), to, upon; *partire* (above).

parcel. (F. — L.) M. E. *parcel*. — F. *parcelle*, a small piece or part. — Low L. *particella*, only preserved in Ital. *particella*, a small part. Dimin. of L. *particula*; see **particle** (below).

parse, to tell the parts of speech. (L.) To *parse* is to tell 'quæ *pars* orationis,' i.e. what part of speech a word is. — L. *pars*, a part.

partake. (F. — L.; *and* Scand.) Put for *part-take*, i. e. take part. Wyclif has *part-takynge*, 1 Cor. x. 16 (earlier version). See **Part** and **Take**.

partial. (F. — L.) F. *partial*. — Low L. *partialis*, referring to a part only. — L. *parti-*, crude form of *pars*, a part.

participate. (L.) From pp. of L. *participare*, to take a part. — L. *particip-*, stem of *particeps*, sharing in. — L. *parti-*,

crude form of *pars*, a part; *capere*, to take.

participle. (F. — L.) The *l* is an E. insertion, as in *syllable*. — F. *participe*. — L. *participium*, a participle; supposed to partake of the nature both of an adjectival sb. and a verb. — L. *participi-*, crude form of *particeps*, sharing in; see above.

particle. (F. — L.) F. *particule* (16th cent.) — L. *particula*, double dimin. from *parti-*, crude form of *pars*, a part.

partisan (1), an adherent of a party. (F. — Ital. — L.) F. *partisan*. — Ital. *partigiano*, a partner; answering to a Low L. form *partitianus*. — L. *partitus*, pp. of *partiri*, to part, divide. — L. *parti-*, crude form of *pars*, a part.

partition. (F. — L.) F. *partition*. — L. acc. *partitionem*, a sharing, partition. — L. *partitus*; see above.

partner. (F. — L.) A curious corruption of M. E. *parcener*, frequently misread and misprinted as *partener*, by the common confusion between *c* and *t* in MSS. — O. F. *parsonnier*, 'a partener, or co-parcener;' Cot. — Low L. *partitionarius*, not found, though the shorter form *partionarius* occurs. — L. *partition-em*, acc. of *partitio*, a sharing, share; see **partition** (above).

party. (F. — L.) M. E. *partie*, usually 'a part.' — O. F. *partie*, a part, a party; Cot. — L. *partita*, fem. of *partitus*, pp. of *partiri*, to divide.

portion. (F. — L.) F. *portion*. — L. acc. *portionem*, a share, from *portio*; closely allied to *parti-*, crude form of *pars*, a part.

proportion. (F. — L.) F. *proportion*. — L. acc. *proportionem*, from *proportio*, comparative relation. — L. *pro*, before, in relation to; *portio*, a portion; see above.

repartee, a witty reply. (F. — L.) F. *repartie*, 'a reply;' Cot. Orig. fem. of *reparti*, pp. of *repartir*, to re-divide, to answer thrust with thrust, to reply. — F. *re-*, again; *partir*, to part, also to rush, dart off, burst out laughing. — L. *re-*, again; *partire*, to share, from crude form of *pars*, a part.

Partake; see **Part**.

Parterre; see **Terrace**.

Partial, Participate; see **Part**.

Participle, Particle; see **Part**.

Partisan (1), an adherent of a party; see **Part**.

Partisan (2), **Partizan**, a halberd. (F. — O. H. G.) F. *pertuisane*, 'a partisan, or leading-staffe;' Cot. O. F. *pourtisaine*

(15th cent.); Ital. *partegiana*, 'a partesan, iauelin ;' Florio. [The F. *pertuisane* is an accommodated spelling, to make it look like F. *pertuiser*, to pierce through (due to L. *per-tundere*).] β. Apparently from O.H.G. *partá*, M. H. G. *barte*, a battle-axe; see Halberd ; but the suffix seems due to some confusion with Low L. *partizare*, to divide, or with Ital. *partigiano*, a partner.

Partition, Partner ; see Part.

Partridge, a bird. (F.–L.–Gk.) M. E. *pertriche.*–F. *perdrix*, where the second *r* is intrusive.–L. *perdicem*, acc. of *perdix*. –Gk. πέρδιξ, a partridge.

Parturient ; see Parent.

Party ; see Part.

Parvenu ; see Venture.

Parvis ; see Paradise.

Pasch, the Passover. (L.–Gk.–Heb.) A. S. *pascha.* – L. *pascha.* – Gk. πάσχα.– Heb. *pesakh*, a passing over ; the passover ; Exod. xii. 11.–Heb. *pásakh*, he passed over.

Pash, to dash. (Scand.) Swed. dial. *paska*, to dabble in water, Norweg. *baska*, to dabble in water, tumble, work hard ; the same as Dan. *baske*, to slap, *baxes*, to box, Norw. *baksa*, to box; see Box (3), of which it is a mere variant. And see Plash.

Pasha, Pacha (Pers.) Also *bashaw*. Pers. *báshá, bádsháh*, a governor of a province, great lord ; the same as *pádsháh*, a prince, great lord ; lit. 'protecting the king.' –Pers. *pád*, protecting ; *sháh*, king. See Bezoar and Shah.

Pasquin, Pasquinade, a lampoon. (F. – Ital.) (Formerly also *pasquil*=F. *pasquille*.) – F. *pasquin* (whence *pasquinade*), a pasquin, lampoon.–Ital. *Pasquino*, 'a statue in Rome on whom all libels are fathered;' Florio. From the name of a cobbler at Rome, whose stall was frequented by gossips; his name was transferred to a statue found near his stall at his death, on which the wits of the time secretly affixed lampoons; see Haydn.

Pass. Passage ; see Patent.

Passion, Passive ; see Patient.

Passport ; see Patent.

Paste. (F. – L. – Gk.) O. F. *paste* (F. *pâte*).–Late L. *pasta*, paste. – Gk. παστή, a mess of food ; orig. fem. of παστός, besprinkled, salted ; from πάσσειν, to sprinkle. The orig. sense was ' a salted mess of food.' Der. *past-y*, M. E. *pastee*, O.F. *pasté* (F. *pâté*), a pasty ; *past-r-y*, orig. a room in which pasties were kept (cf. *pantry, buttery*).

patty, a little pie. (F. – L. – Gk.) Mod. F. *pâté*; O. F. *pasté*, a pasty (see above).

Pastel ; see Pastor.

Pastern, Pastille ; see Pastor.

Pastime ; see Patent.

Pastor, a shepherd. (L.) L. *pastor*, a shepherd, lit. 'feeder.'–L. *pastum*, supine of *pascere*, to feed, an inceptive verb; pp. *pa-ui*. (√ PA.) Der. *pastor-al*, F. *pastoral*.

pabulum. (L.) L. *pabulum*, food ; formed with suffix *-bulum*, from *pa-ui*, pt. of *pascere*, to feed (above).

pastel, a coloured crayon. (F.–Ital.– L.) An artist's term.–F. *pastel*, 'a pastel, crayon ;' Hamilton. – Ital. *pastello*, a pastel.–L. *pastillum*, a little loaf or roll ; the pastel being named from being shaped like a roll. Dimin. of *pastus*, food.–L. *pastus*, pp. of *pascere*, to feed. ¶ *Not* allied to *paste* ; see *pastille* below.

pastern. (F.–L.) Formerly *pastron* ; Palsgrave. – O. F. *pasturon*, 'the pastern of a horse;' Cot. (F. *pâturon*.) So called because a horse at *pasture* was tethered by the *pastern* ; the tether itself was called *pasture* in O. French. – O. F. *pasture*, pasture ; see pasture below.

pastille, a small cone of aromatic substances, to be burnt in a room. (F.–L.) F. *pastille*, a little lump or loaf; see Cotgrave. – L. *pastillum*, a little loaf; dimin. of *pastus*, food ; see pastel (above).

pasture. (F. – L.) O. F. *pasture*, a feeding.–L. *pastura*, a feeding.–L. *pastus*, pp. of *pascere*, to feed.

pester. (F.–L.) Formerly to encumber, clog ; and short for *impester*. – O. F. *empestrer*, 'to pester, intangle, incumber ;' Cot. (F. *empêtrer*.) Orig. 'to hobble a horse at pasture.' – Low L. *im-* (*in*), on, upon ; *pastorium*, a clog, for a horse at pasture.–L. *pastus*, pp. of *pascere*, to feed.

repast, a meal. (F.–L.) O. F. *repast*, later *repas.*–L. *re-*, again ; *pastum*, acc. of *pastus*, food, from *pascere*, to feed.

Pat (1), to strike lightly. (E.) In Bacon, Nat. Hist. § 62. Most likely the same word as A. S. *plættan*, to strike ; by loss of *l* as in *patch* (1). Cf. Swed. dial. *pjätta*, to pat, *plätta*, to tap (Rietz) ; Bavarian *patzen*, to pat.

paddle (1), to finger, dabble in water. (E.) Formerly to finger, handle ; Haml. iii. 4. 185; Oth. ii. 1. 259. It stands for *pattle*, frequent. of *pat*; see below. Cf. Low G. *pladdern*, to paddle.

patter, to strike frequently, as hail. (E.) A frequentative of *pat*; see above. Cf. prov. E. (Lonsdale) *pattle*, to pat gently.

Pat (2), a small lump of butter. (C.) Irish *pait*, a hump, lump, *paiteog*, a small lump of butter; Gael. *pait*, *paiteag* (the same).

Pat (3), quite to the purpose. (E.) Due to a peculiar use of *pat*, to strike, tap; see Pat (1). 'It will fall [happen] *pat*;' Mid. N. Dr. v. 188. The sense is due to a curious confusion with Du. *pas*, pat, fit, G. *pass*, pat, fit; not true Teut. words, but borrowed from F. *se passer*, to be contented, make shift; cf. E. *pass*.

Patch (1), a piece sewn on a garment, a plot of ground. (O. Low G.) M. E. *pacche*. But *patch* stands for *platch*, by loss of *l*; '*Platch*, a large spot, a patch, a piece of cloth sewn on to a garment to repair it;' Dial. of Banffshire, by W. Gregor. — Low G. *plakke*, *plakk*, (1) a spot, (2) a patch, (3) a patch or plot of ground; cf. Du. *plek*, a patch of ground. Allied to Goth. *plats*, a patch, Mark, ii. 21, where Wycliffe has *pacche*; also to A.S. *plæca*, prov. E. *plek*, a patch of ground. (√ PLAG.)

patch (2), a paltry fellow. (O. Low G.) Temp. iii. 2. 71. *Patch* meant a fool or jester, from the parti-coloured or patch-like dress; Wolsey had two fools so named (Nares). The same word as *patch* (1). Der. *patch-ock*, a clown, a dimin. form, Spenser, View of Ireland, Globe ed., p. 636, col. 2; spelt *pajock*, Hamlet, iii. 2.

Pate, the head; see **Plate**.

Paten; see **Patent**.

Patent, open, public; as sb., an official document conferring a privilege. (F. — L.) M. E. *patente*, a patent; so called because *open* to general inspection. — O. F. *patent* (fem. *patente*), patent, wide open. — L. *patent-*, stem of pr. pt. of *patere*, to lie open. Cf. Gk. πετάννυμι, I spread out. (√ PAT.)

compass. (F. — L.) F. *compas*, a circuit, circle, limit; also a pair of compasses. — Low L. *compassus*, a circuit. — L. *com-* (*cum*), with; *passus*, a pace, step, passage, route; so that *compassus* = a route that joins together, circuit. See pace (below). Der. *compass*, verb; *compasses*, s. pl., an instrument for drawing circles.

expand. (L.) L. *expandere* (pp. *expansus*), to spread out. — L. *ex*, out; *pand-*

ere, to spread out; causal from *patēre*, to lie open. Der. *expanse*.

pace, a step. (F. — L.) M. E. *pas*. — F. *pas*. — L. *passum*, acc. of *passus*, a step, pace, lit. a stretch, distance between the feet in walking. — L. *passus*, pp. of *pandere*, to stretch; see above.

pail. (F. — L.) M. E. *paile*. — O. F. *paele*, a kind of pan (13th cent.). — L. *patella*, a small pan, dish for cooking; dimin. of *patera*, flat dish, saucer. Allied to Gk. πατάνη, a flat dish; see paten (below). β. But now better explained as (E.). From A. S. *pægel*, a pail; formerly misprinted *wægel*. See Anglia, viii. 450.

pass, to move onward. (F. — L.) M. E. *passen*. — F. *passer*. — Low L. *passare*, to pass. — L. *passus*, a step; see pace (above). β. Diez takes Low L. *passare* to be the frequent. form of *pandere*, to stretch; it comes to much the same thing.

passage. (F. — L.) F. *passage*. — Low L. *passaticum*, a right of passage. — Low L. *passare*; see above.

passport. (F. — L.) F. *passeport*, written permission to pass through a gate, &c. — F. *passer*, to pass; *porte*, gate, from L. *porta*; see Port (3).

pastime. (F. — L.; *and* E.) From *pass* and *time*.

paten. (F. — L. — Gk.) O. F. *patene* (Cot.). — L. *patina*, *patena*, a flat dish. — Gk. πατάνη, a flat (open) dish. See Pan.

surpass. (F. — L.) F. *surpasser*, to excel. — F. *sur* (L. *super*), beyond; *passer*, to pass; see pass (above).

trespass. (F. — L.) F. *trespasser*, to exceed, pass beyond (hence, in E., to sin). — F. *tres-*, L. *trans*, beyond; *passer*, to pass; see pass (above).

Paternal. (F. — L.) F. *paternel*. — Low L. *paternalis*, fatherly. — L. *paternus*, fatherly. — L. *pater*, father. Lit. 'guardian;' formed with suffix *-ter* of the agent from √ PA, to feed, guard. See Father.

expatriate. (L.) From pp. of Low L. *expatriare*, to banish. — L. *ex*, out of; *patria*, native country, from *patri-*, crude form of *pater*, father.

parricide, (1) the murderer of a father; (2) murder of a father. (F. — L; *or* L.) The former is the orig. sense, and answers to F. *parricide*, L. *parricida*, a murderer of a father. — L. *parri-*, for *patri-*, crude form of *pater*; *cædere*, to kill (whence *-cida*, a slayer). **2**. The second sense is directly from L. *parricidium*, the murder of a father, from the same sb. and verb.

patois, a vulgar dialect of French. (F. −L.) F. *patois*, country talk; which stands for an older form *patrois* (Diez, Littré). − Low L. *patriensis*, a native; hence, belonging to the natives. − L. *patria*, native country.−L. *patri-*, crude form of *pater*, a father.

patriarch. (F.−L.−Gk.) O. F. *patriarche*. − L. *patriarcha*. − Gk. πατριάρχης, chief of a race or tribe.−Gk. πατρι-ά, a race; ἄρχειν, to rule. See Arch- (*prefix*).

patrician, a Roman nobleman. (L.) Formed with suffix *-an*, from L. *patricius*, noble; a descendant of the *patres*, i. e. senators or fathers of the state.

patrimony. (F. − L.) M. E. *patrimonie.*−F. *patrimoine.*−L. *patrimonium*, an inheritance.−L. *patri-*, crude form of *pater*, father; with suffix *-monium* (Aryan *-man-ya*).

patriot. (F. − Low L. − Gk.) O. F. *patriote.*−Low L. *patriota.*−Gk. πατριώτης, properly a fellow-countryman.−Gk. πατριά, a race, from πατρι-, for πατήρ, a father. ¶ The mod. sense of *patriot* arose in *French*.

patristic, pertaining to the fathers of the church. (F.−L.) F. *patristique* (Littré). Coined from L. *patri-*, crude form of *pater*, a father. (Ill coined; *-ist-* being Greek.)

patron. (F.−L.) F. *patron.*−L. *patronum*, acc. of *patronus*, a protector; extended from *patr-*, stem of *pater*, father.

patronymic. (F. − L. − Gk.) O. F. *patronymique.* − L. *patronymicus.* − Gk, πατρωνυμικός, belonging to the father's name. − Gk. πατρωνυμία, a name taken from the father.−Gk. πατρο-, for πατήρ, a father; ὄνυμα, a name; see Name.

pattern, an example, model to work by. (F.−L.) M. E. *patron*; (the old spelling).−F. *patron*, 'a patron .. also a pattern, sample;' Cot. See patron (above).

repair (2), to resort to. (F.−L.) F. *repairer*, to haunt; Cot. Older form *repairier* (Burguy).−L. *repatriare*, to repair to one's own country.−L. *re-*, back; *patria*, native country, from *patri-*, crude form of *pater*, a father.

Path, a way, track. (E.) A.S. *pað*, *paδ*, a path.+Du. *pad*, G. *pfad*; L. *pons* (crude form *ponti-*), a path, way, also a bridge; Gk. πάτος, Skt. *patha*.

pad (2), a thief on the high road. (Du.) We now say *foot-pad*. Formerly a *padder*, one who goes on the *pad*, i. e. foot-path. −

Du. *pad*, a path; see above. (Many cant words are Dutch.) **Der.** *pad*, a nag, orig. *pad-nag*, a road-nag.

Pathos. (Gk.) Gk. πάθος, suffering, emotion.−Gk. παθεῖν, used as 2 aor. infin. of πάσχειν, to suffer. Allied to πό-θος, a yearning, πέν-θος, grief, πόν-ος, work. (√SPA.) Allied to **Patient. Der.** *path-et-ic*, from O. F. *pathetique*, L. *patheticus* −Gk. παθητικός, extended from παθητός, subject to suffering.

antipathy. (Gk.) From Gk. ἀντιπά-θεια, antipathy, lit. 'a suffering (feeling strongly) against.' − Gk. ἀντί, against; παθεῖν, to suffer.

apathy. (Gk.) From Gk. ἀπάθεια, want of feeling.−Gk. ἀ-, not; παθεῖν, to suffer.

sympathy. (Gk.) From Gk, συμπά-θεια, fellow-feeling. − Gk. συμ-, for σύν, with; παθεῖν, to suffer.

Patient. (F. − L.) O. F. *patient.* − L. *patient-*, stem of pres. pt. of *pati*, to suffer. Allied to Pathos. (√SPA.) **Der.** *patience*, F. *patience*, L. *patientia*.

compassion. (F.−L.) F. *compassion.* −L. *compassionem*, acc. of *compassio*, sympathy.−L. *com- (cum)*, with; *passio*, suffering; see passion (below).

compatible. (F.−L.) F. *compatible*, 'compatible, concurrable;' Cot.−Low L. *compatibilis*, adj., used of a benefice which could be held together with another.−L. *compati*, to endure together with.−L. *com- (cum)*, with; *pati*, to endure.

passion. (F. − L.) F. *passion.* − L. *passionem*, acc. of *passio*, (properly) suffering.−L. *passus*, pp. of *pati*, to suffer.

passive. (F.−L.) F. *passif.*−L. *passiuus*, suffering.−L. *passus* (above).

Patois, Patriarch; see **Paternal**. **Patrician, Patrimony**; see **Paternal**. **Patriot, Patristic**; see **Paternal**.

Patrol, a going of the rounds in a garrison. (F. − Teut.) O.F. *patrouille*, 'a still night-watch in warre;' Cot. Lit. a tramping about; from O. F. *patrouiller*, to paddle in water, the same word (but with inserted *r*) as *patouiller*, to paddle or dabble in with the feet. Formed from O. F. *pate* (F. *patte*), the paw or foot of a beast. From a Teut. source; cf. G. *patsche*, an instrument for striking the hand, *patsch-fuss*, web foot of a bird; *patschen*, to strike, dabble, walk awkwardly; Bavarian *patzen*, to pat; see Pat (1). ¶ Hence also Span. *pata*, paw, *patullar*, to run through mud, *patrullar*, to patrol, Ital. *pattuglia*, a patrol (without the inserted *r*).

patten, a clog. (F. – Teut.) Formerly *paten*. – F. *patin*, a patten, 'also a footstall of a pillar;' Cot. – O. F. *pate* (F. *patte*), a paw or foot of a beast, 'also a foot-stall of a pillar;' Cot. Of Teut. origin; see above.

Patron, Patronymic; see **Paternal.**

Patten; see **Patrol.**

Patter; see **Pat** (1).

Pattern; see **Paternal.**

Patty; see **Paste.**

Paucity, fewness. (F. – L.) F. *paucité*. – L. *paucitatem*, acc. of *paucitas*, fewness. – L. *paucus*, few; allied to **Few.**

Paunch. (F. – L.) O. F. *panche, pance*. – L. *panticem*, acc. of *pantex*, belly, paunch.

Pauper. (L.) L. *pauper*, poor. *Pau-* is allied to *paucus*, few; *-per*, to L. *parare*, to provide. Lit. 'providing little,' i. e. having little.

impoverish. (F. – L.) Corrupted from O. F. *appovris-*, stem of pres. pt. of *appovrir*, to impoverish. – F. *ap-* (= L. *ad*), towards; O. F. *povre*, poor (below).

poor. (F. – L.) From M. E. *poure* (really *povre*), poor. – O. F. *povre*, poor. – L. *pauperem*, acc. of *pauper*; see **Pauper** above.

poverty. (F. – L.) M. E. *pouertee* (= *povertee*). – O. F. *poverte*, later *povreté*, poverty (F. *pauvreté*). – L. *paupertatem*, acc. of *paupertas*, poverty. – L. *pauper*, poor.

Pause, a stop. (F. – L. – Gk.) F. *pause*. – Late L. *pausa*. – Gk. παῦσις, a pause, ceasing. – Gk. παύειν, to make to cease; παύεσθαι, to cease. **Doublet,** *pose*, q. v.

Pave. (F. – L.) M. E. *pauen* (= *paven*). – F. *paver*, to pave. – L. *pauare* *, corrupt form of L. *pauire*, to beat, strike, ram, tread down. + Gk. παίειν, to strike; cf. Skt. *pavi*, thunder-bolt. (√ PU.) **Der.** *pavement*, F. *pavement*, L. *pauimentum*, a hard floor, from *pauire*, to ram; also *pav-i-or* (cf. *law-y-er*), from O. F. *paveur*, 'a paver,' Cot.

Pavilion. (F. – L.) M. E. *pavilon*. – F. *pavillon*, a tent; so called because spread out like the wings of a butterfly. – L. *papilionem*, acc. of *papilio*, (1) a butterfly, (2) a tent. Name from fluttering; allied to **Palpitate.**

papilionaceous, having a winged corolla resembling a butterfly. (L.) Coined,

with suffix *-aceus*, from L. *papilion-*, crude form of *papilio*, a butterfly (above).

Pavise, a large shield. (F.) Also spelt *pavese, pavish, pauice, pauys, paues*. – F. *pavois*, 'a great shield;' Low L. *pavensis*. (Span. *paves*; Ital. *pavese, pavesce*, Florio.) Of uncertain origin; perhaps from the city of *Pavia*, in Italy.

Paw. (F. – Lat. *or* Teut. ?) M. E. *pawe, powe*, a paw. – O. F. *poe* (also *pote*), a paw; the same as Prov. *pauta*, Catalan *pota*, a paw. Perhaps from Low G. *pote*, Du. *poot* (whence G. *pfote*), a paw. Or all from an imitative root; cf. F. *patte*.

Pawl, a short bar, as a catch to a windlass. (L.) W. *pawl*, a pole, stake, bar; borrowed from L. *palus*, a stake. See **pale** (1), under **Pact.**

Pawn (1), a pledge; see **Pane.**

Pawn (2), a piece at chess; see **Pedal.**

Paxwax, strong tendon in the neck of animals. (E.) M. E. *paxwax*, also *fexwax*, the latter being the right form. – A. S. *feax*, *fex*, hair; *weaxan*, to grow. Thus the lit. sense is 'hair-growth,' because it is where the growth of hair ends; for the same reason, it is called *haarwachs* in German.

Pay (1), to discharge a debt; see **Pact.**

Pay (2), to pitch a ship's seam; see **Pitch** (1).

Paynim; see **Pagan.**

Pea, a vegetable. (L.) Formerly *pease, pese;* M. E. *pese*, pl. *pesen* or *peses*. A. S. *pisa*, pl. *pisan*. – L. *pisum*, a pea. + Gk. πίσος, a pea. (√ PIS.)

Peace; see **Pact.**

Peach (1), a fruit; see **Parsee.**

Peach (2), short for M. E. *apechen*, to impeach; see **Pedal.**

Peacock. (L. – Gk. – Pers. – Tamil; *and* E.) M. E. *pecok, pocok;* where *cok* = E. *cock*. We also find M. E. *po*, A. S. *pawe*, borrowed from L. *pauo* (whence Du. *paauw*, G. *pfau*, F. *paon*). Borrowed from Gk. ταώς, for ταϝῶς, a peacock; the change from τ to ρ being due to the word being ill understood, as it was foreign both to L. and Gk. – Pers. *táwus, táus*, a peacock. – O. Tamil *tókei, tógei*, a peacock; see M. Müller, Lect. on Lang. i. 233 (8th ed.). ¶ Better *pocock*, which is still a surname.

Pea-jacket, a coarse thick jacket. (Du. *and* F.) The prefix *pea-* is borrowed from Du. *pij, pije*, a coat of a coarse woollen stuff; Hexham has O. Du. *pije*, 'a piegowne, rough gowne, such as seamen weare.' The same as Low G. *pije*. Cf. Swed. dial. *pade*, a coat, also spelt *paje*, *paja, pait*; Goth. *paida*, a coat, M. Il. G. *pfeit*, a shirt.

Peak. (C. — L. ?) M. E. *pec*. — Irish *peac*, a sharp-pointed thing; cf. Gael. *beic*, a point, nib, beak of a bird. Prob. from L. *spica*.

beak. (F. — C. — L. ?) M. E. *beke*. — F. *bec*; Low L. *beccus*. — Bret. *bék*, a beak; Gael. *beic*; W. *pig*.

bicker, to skirmish. (C.) Frequentative of M. E. *biken*, to skirmish, *beken*, to peck. — W. *hicra*, to bicker, properly to keep pecking. — W. *pig*, a pike, beak of a bird.

peck (1), to strike with the beak, to pick up. (C. — L.) M. E. *pekken*, used as equivalent to *pikken*, to pick or peck up. A mere variant of *pick*; see below.

peg, a wooden pin. (Scand. — C. — L. ?) M. E. *pegge*. — Dan. *pig*, spike, from *pik*, a pike; Swed. *pigg*, spike, from *pik*, a pike. Cf. also Corn. *peg*, a prick; W. *pig*, a peak, point. All these words are prob. ultimately of Lat. origin; see **Peak.**

pick, to peck, pierce, also to pluck, &c. (C. — L.) The sense 'to cull flowers' goes back to the notion of picking them out as a bird would with its beak; *pick* and *peck* are mere variants; cf. M. E. *pikken, pekken,* used as equivalent words, Ch. C. T. Group B. 4157. Of Celtic origin. — Irish *pioc*, Gael. *pioc*, to pick, nibble, pluck, peck; W. *pigo*, to pick, peck, prick, choose; Corn. *piga*, to prick.

pickadill, piccadill, a piece set round the edge of a garment, a collar. (F. — Span. — L.) Obsolete; but preserved in *Piccadilly*, a street in London, named from a certain house, which was 'a famous ordinary near St. James's;' see Blount and Nares. — F. *piccadille*; pl. *piccadilles*, 'the several pieces fastened together about the brimme of the collar of a doublet;' Cot. Formed, with Span. dimin. suffix -*illo*, from Span. *picado*, pp. of *picar*, to puncture; cf. Span. *picadura*, a puncture, an ornamental gusset in clothes. — Span. *pica*, a pike (hence a pricking instrument); a word of Latin origin; see **pike** (below).

pickaxe. (F. — L.) Not an *axe* at all, but a corruption of M. E. *pikois, pikeis*, a mattock. — O. F. *picois*, later *picquois*, a mattock. — O. F. *piquer*, to pierce, thrust into. — F. *pic*, a 'pick' or kind of mattock. — Bret. *pic*, a pick; cf. W. *pig*, a point, pike, Irish *piocaid*, a mattock; see **pike** (below).

picket, a peg for fastening horses, a small outpost. (F. — L.) F. *piquet, picquet*, a little pickaxe, a peg thrust in the ground. Dimin. of F. *pic* (above).

pike, a sharp-pointed weapon, a fish. (L.) M. E. *pike*, a peaked staff, *pic*, a spike; also M. E. *pike*, a fish, named from its sharply pointed jaws. — Irish *pice*, a pike, fork, Gael. *pic*, W. *pig*, Bret. *pik*, pike, point, pickaxe. The same word as *pick*, sb. a mattock, and short for *spike*; see **Spike.** Der. *pik-er-el*, a young pike (fish); *pike-staff*, corruption o. *piked-staff*, i. e. staff armed with a pike or spike.

pip (3), a spot on cards. (F. — L.) A corruption of *pick*, formerly a spade at cards. — F. *pique*, a spade at cards; the same as **pique** (below).

pique, wounded pride. (F. — L.) O. F. *picque, pique*, 'a pike, pike-man; also a pike [pique], debate, quarrel,' Cot. The same word as *pike* (above); lit. 'a piercer,' that which pierces. Der. *pique*, verb, *piqu-ant*, pres. part. of F. *piquer*, verb.

piquet, a game at cards. (F. — L.) F. *piquet*, lit. 'a little contest;' dimin. of F. *pique*, a debate, contest; see above. ¶ Littré says *piquet* was named from its inventor; even if so, the ultimate etymology remains the same.

pitch (2), to throw, fall headlong, fix a camp. (L.) A weakened form of *pick*, to throw, Cor. i. 1. 204, esp. to throw a *pike* or dart; also to plunge a sharp *peg* or *spike* into the ground for fixing tents. M. E. *picchen*, pt. t. *pihte* (later *pight*). — W. *pigo*, to prick; see **pick** and **pike** (above).

Peal, short for *appeal*; see **Pulsate.**

Pean; see **Pæan.**

Pear, a fruit. (L.) A S. *pera, pere*. — L. *pirum*, a pear (whence also Ital. *pera*).

perry. (F. — L.) F. *poiré*, 'perry, drink made of pears;' Cot. Formed with suffix -*é* (= L. -*atus*, made of) from F. *poire*, a pear. — L. *pirum*, a pear. ¶ O. F. *perey*.

Pearl. (F. — L.) M. E. *perle*. — F. *perle*, 'a pearl, a berrie;' Cot. Of disputed origin; we find also Ital., Span., Prov. *perla*, Port. *perola, perla*; Low L. *perula* (7th cent.). Prob. put for L. *pirula**, i. e. a little pear, from L. *pirum*, a pear; cf. Span. *perilla*, (1) a little pear, (2) a pear-shaped ornament, O. Ital. *perolo*, a little button on a cap. Perhaps suggested by the various senses of L. *bacca*, (1) a berry, (2) olive-berry, (3) round fruit, (4) a pearl (Horace). See **Purl** (2).

Pearl-barley. (F. − L.; *and* E.) F. *orge perlé*, pearl-barley (Hamilton); but this seems to be a corruption of *orge pelé*, 'pilled barley,' Cot. See **Peel** (1).

Peasant; see **Pagan**.

Peat, a kind of turf for fuel. (E.) · The true form is *beat*. [The change from *b* to *p* is very rare, but occurs again in *purse*.] '*Beat*, the roots and soil subjected to the operation of *burning beat*, i. e. sod-burning;' E. Dial. Soc. Glossary, B. 6. So called because used as fuel, for *beeting*, i.e. mending the fire; from M. E. *beten*, to replenish a fire, Chaucer, C. T. 2255.− A. S. *bétan*, to amend.− A. S. *bót*, a remedy, advantage; see **Boot** (2).

Pebble. (E.) A. S. *papol-stán*, a pebble-stone.

Peccable, Peccadillo; see **Peccant**.

Peccant, sinning. (F.−L.) First used in phr. '*peccant* humours.' − F. *peccant*, sinning; *l'humeur peccante*, corrupt humour; Cot. − L. *peccant-*, stem of pres. pt. of *peccare*, to sin.

peccable, liable to sin. (L.) Coined as if from L. *peccabilis**, from *peccare*.

peccadillo. (Span. − L.) Span. *peca-dillo*, a slight fault; dimin. of *pecado*, a sin.− L. *peccatum*, a sin.− L. *peccatus*, pp. of *peccare*, to sin.

Peccary, a quadruped. (F.−S. American.) F. *pécari*, a peccary (Buffon). Prob. from *pachira*, the name given to the peccary in Oronoko (Clavigero, Hist. Mexico).

Peck (1), to pick, snap up; see **Peak**.

Peck (2), a dry measure, 2 gallons. (C. ?) M. E. *pekke*, a peck. An obscure word; but it can hardly be other than a sb. derived from the verb *pekken*, to peck or snap up. *Peck* merely means 'a quantity;' cf. 'a *peck* of troubles;' also prov. E. *peck*, meat, victuals. So also F. *picotin*, a peck (measure), from *picoter*, to peck as a bird; see therefore **peck** (1); s. v. **Peak**.

Pectinal, lit. comb-like. (L.) From L. *pectin-*, stem of *pecten*, a comb. − L. *pectere*, to comb. + Gk. πεκτεῖν, to comb, from πέκειν, to comb. (√PAK.)

Pectoral, belonging to the chest. (F.− L.) F. *pectoral*. − L. *pectoralis*, adj., from *pector-*, stem of *pectus*, the breast.

expectorate. (L.) From pp. of L. *expectorare*, to expel from the breast. − L. *ex*, out of; *pector-*, stem of *pectus*.

poitrel, peitrel, armour for a horse's breast. (F.−L.) O. F. *poitral*; Cot.− L. *pectorale*, neut. of *pectoralis* (above).

Peculate, Peculiar, Pecuniary; see **Pact**.

Pedagogue, a teacher. (F.−L.−Gk.) F. *pedagogue*.−L. *pædagogus*.−Gk. παιδα-γωγός, a slave who led a boy to school; hence, a tutor.−Gk. παιδ-, stem of παῖς, a boy; ἀγωγός, leading, from ἄγειν, to lead. The Gk. παῖς = παϝις (*pauis*), allied to L. *puer*, a boy. (√PU.)

pedobaptism, infant baptism. (Gk.) From Gk. παιδο-, crude form of παῖς, a boy; and *baptism*.

Pedal, belonging to the foot. (L.) The *pedal* keys in an organ are acted on by the feet.−L. *pedalis*, belonging to the foot.− L. *ped-*, stem of *pes*, foot. + A. S. *fót*, foot. See **Foot**.

biped. (L.) L. *biped-*, stem of *bipes*, two-footed.−L. *bi-*, double; *pes*, a foot; see **Bi-**.

despatch, dispatch. (F.−L.) The orig. sense was 'to remove a hindrance.' Better spelling, *despatch*.−O. F. *despecher* (F. *dépêcher*), to hasten, despatch.−O. F. *des-* (L. *dis-*), apart, away; *-pescher*, to hinder. This O. F. *-pescher* occurs only in *despescher* (oldest form *despeecher*) and *impescher*, answering to Low L. *dispedicare** and *impedicare*, of which the latter occurs with the sense 'to put hindrances in the way;' both from L. *pedica*, a fetter, clog, which is from L. *ped-*, stem of *pes*, a foot. See **impeach** (below).

expedite. (L.) From pp. of L. *expedire*, to extricate the foot, release, get ready.−L. *ex*, out; *ped-*, stem of *pes*, foot.

impeach, to charge with a crime. (F −L.) The original sense was 'to hinder;' as, 'to *impeach* and stop their breath,' Holland, tr. of Pliny, b. xi. c. 3.−O. F. *empescher*, 'to hinder, stop, bar, impeach;' Cot. Older spelling *empeëscher*, where the *s* is adventitious. Littré and Scheler connect it with Prov. *empedegar*, and derive all the forms from Low L. *impedicare*, to fetter.− L. *im-* (for *in*), on, upon; *pedica*, a fetter, from *pedi-*, crude form of *pes*, a foot. β. At the same time, the Span. *empachar*, Ital. *impacciare*, to delay, are from a Low L. frequent. form of L. *impingere* (pp. *impactus*), to bind, fasten; see **Pact**. These two sets of words may have been confused. See **despatch** (above).

impede, to obstruct. (L.) From L. *impedire*, to entangle the feet, obstruct.− L. *im-* (=*in*), in; *pedi-*, crude form of *pes*, foot. Der. *impedi-ment*.

pawn (2), a piece at chess. (F.—L.) M. E. *paune, poune, poun.*—O. F. *paon,* a pawn (Roquefort), also *poon* (Littré); but the proper form is *peon* (Burguy), agreeing with Span. *peon,* a foot-soldier, pawn, Ital. *pedone,* a foot-soldier, *pedona,* a pawn (Florio).—Low L. *pedonem,* acc. of *pedo,* a foot-soldier.—L. *ped-,* stem of *pes,* foot. ¶ The O. F. *paon* is the same word; cf. F. *faon* (E. *fawn*), from Low L. *fetonem,* shewing the same substitution of *a* for *e*; there is no need to connect it with F. *paon,* a peacock, as Littré does, ignoring the Ital. and Span. words.

peach (2), to inform against. (F.—L.) Short for M. E. *apechen,* to impeach, a variant of *impechen,* to impeach, by the substitution of prefix *a-* (L. *ad*) for *im-* (L. *in*). See **impeach** (above).

pedestal. (Span.—Ital.—L. *and* G.) Span. *pedestal,* 'the base of a pillar,' Minsheu. Not a Span. word, but wholly borrowed from Ital. *piedestallo,* 'a footstall or treshall [threshold] of a door;' Florio. Clumsily compounded from L. *pedem,* acc. of *pes,* a foot; and G. *stall,* a stall; see **Stall.**

pedestrian. (L.) Properly an adj.; from L. *pedestri-,* crude form of *pedester,* one who goes on foot. Put for *pedit-ter*,* from *pedit-,* stem of *pedes,* one who goes on foot; with suffix *-ter* (Aryan *-tar*). *Ped-it-* is from *ped-* stem of *pes,* foot; and *it-um,* supine of *ire,* to go.

pedicel, pedicle, the foot-stalk of fruit. (F.—L.) *Pedicel* is from mod. F. *pédicelle;* but *pedicle* (olden and better) from O. F. *pedicule,* a leaf-stalk; Cot.—L. *pediculus,* little foot, foot-stalk, pedicle; double dimin. of *pedi-,* crude form of *pes,* foot.

pediment, an ornament finishing the front of a building. (L.) Better *pedament,* as the only L. word like it is *pedamentum,* a stake or prop, with which vines are supported. The sense seems to be due to the allied word *pedatura,* a prop, also (in Low L.) a space, site; since a pediment does, in fact, enclose a space which was often ornamented with sculpture. History obscure. Form of the word from L. *pedare,* to prop; from *ped-,* stem of *pes,* a foot.

piepowder court, a summary court of justice formerly held at court. (F.—L.) The E. *piepowder* is a corruption of O. F. *pied pouldré,* i. e. dusty foot. The court was called, in Latin, *Curia pedis pulver-*

azati, the court of the dusty foot, from the dusty feet of the suitors.—F. *pied,* foot, from L. *pedem,* acc. of *pes;* O. F. *pouldre,* pp. of *pouldrer,* to cover with dust, from *pouldre,* dust; see **powder,** under **Pulverise.**

pioneer, a soldier who clears the way before an army. (F. — L.) Formerly *pioner.* — F. *pionnier,* O. F. *peonier,* a pioneer; a mere extension of F. *pion,* O. F. *peon,* a foot-soldier, but esp. applied to sappers and miners. See further under **pawn** (2).

quadruped. (L.) L. *quadrupedus,* four-footed; *quadruped-,* stem of *quadrupes, quadripes,* four-footed.—L. *quadru-s,* four times; *pes,* a foot; see **Quadrant.**

Pedant. (F.—Ital.—Gk.?) F. *pedant.* —Ital. *pedante,* 'a pedante, or a schoolmaster, the same as *pedagogo;*' Florio. The suffix *-ante* is a pres. participial form; the stem *ped-* is prob. the same as in Ital. *pedagogo,* and therefore due to Gk. παιδεύειν, to instruct; see **Pedagogue.** Prob. confused with Ital. *pedare,* to tramp about, from L. *ped-,* stem of *pes,* foot.

Peddle; see **Pedlar.**

Pedestal, Pedestrian, Pedicel; see **Pedal.**

Pedigree. (F.?) Old spellings *pedegree* (1627); *pedigrew* (1570); *petygrewe* (1530). Also, in Prompt. Parv. (1440) *pedegru, petygru,* with slight variations, explained by 'lyne of kynrede and awncetrye, *Stemma, in Scalis.*' Etym. unknown; prob. F.; guesses wild, and unsatisfactory.

Pediment; see **Pedal.**

Pedlar, Pedler, Peddler, a dealer in small wares. (Scand.? *or* C.?) The old word was usually *peddare, pedder,* a man who hawked about fish in baskets called *peds,* or occasionally *pads.* See *Pedde* in Prompt. Parv.; Norfolk *ped* (Forby); Lowl. Sc. *peddir,* a pedlar (Jamieson). The orig. sense was prob. 'bag,' and the word is to be identified with *pad* and *pod;* see **Pad** (1).

peddle, to deal in small wares. (Scand.? *or* C.?) Coined from the sb. *pedlar,* later form of *peddar,* as explained above.

piddling, trifling. (Scand.? *or* C.?) From the verb *piddle,* to trifle (Ascham); allied to *peddle* (above). But also spelt *pittle, pettle.*—Swed. dial. *pittla,* to pick at.

Pedobaptism; see **Pedagogue.**

Peel (1), to strip off skin; see **Pell.**

Peel (2), to pillage; see **Pill** (2).

Peel (3), a fire-shovel; see **Pact**.

Peep (1), to chirp; see **Pipe**.

Peep (2), to look through a narrow aperture. (F. − L.) Palsgrave has: 'I peke or prie, *Ie pipe hors*;' i.e. I peep out. Thus *peep* is directly from F. *piper*, lit. to pipe, but also used in the sense to peep. The explanation is, probably, that the fowler, engaged in catching birds, hid himself in a bush, and *peeped out*, as represented in a MS. Cot. gives F. *piper*, 'to whistle, chirp like a bird, cousen, deceive, cheat, beguile;' *pipée*, 'the peeping or chirping of small birds, counterfeited by a bird-catcher, also a counterfeit shew;' *pipe*, 'a bird-call.' The F. *piper* is from L. *pipare*, *pipire*, to chirp; see **Pipe**.

Peer (1), an equal; see **Par**.

Peer (2), to look narrowly, pry. (O. Low G.) M. E. *piren.* − Low G. *piren*, to look closely, in which *l* is lost after *p*; the full form is *pliren*, to peer, orig. to draw the eye-lids together, so as to look closely. +Swed. *plira*, Dan. *plire*, to blink. See **Blear-eyed**.

pry, to peer. (O. Low G.) M. E. *prien*; put for *piren*, by the shifting of *r* so common in E., as in *bird*=M. E. *brid*, *bride*=M. E. *burd*. See above.

Peer (3), to appear. (F. − L.) Short for *appear*, just as M. E. *peren* is short for *apperen*; see **appear**, s. v. **Parent**.

Peevish, fretful, whimpering. (E.) M. E. *peuisch, peyuesshe*; also *pevych, pevage*, uncouth, perverse (G. Douglas). Orig. 'making a plaintive cry;' from Lowl. Sc. *peu*, to make a plaintive noise, E. *pew-* in *pewet*, a bird. See **Pewet**. So also F. *piauler*, to chirp, *pule*, whence E. *pule*, to whimper. For the suffix, cf. *thiev-ish*, *mop-ish*.

Peewit; see **Pewet**.

Peg; see **Peak**.

Pelf, lucre, booty. (F. − L. ?) M. E. *pelfyr, pelfrey*, Spolium; Prompt. Parv. − O. F. *pelfre*, booty, spoil; allied to *pelfrer*, to pilfer (Roquefort). Prob. allied to O. F. *piller*, to rob, L. *pilare*, to plunder; see **Pill** (2). ¶ But the whole word has not been explained. Cf. O. F. *pilfeier*, to rob (Roquefort).

pilfer. (F. − L. ?) O. F. *pelfrer*, to rob, pilfer. − O. F. *pelfre*, plunder; see above.

Pelican. (F. − L. − Gk.) F. *pelican.* − L. *pelicanus*, *pelecanus.* − Gk. πελεκάν, πελεκᾶς, wood-pecker, also a water-bird. Named from its large bill, as the woodpecker was named from its pecking. − Gk. πελεκάω, I hew with an axe, peck. − Gk. πελεκύς, an axe. +Skt. *paraçu*, an axe.

Pelisse; see **Pell**.

Pell, a skin. (F. − L.) M. E. *pell, pel.* − O. F. *pel* (F. *peau*). − L. *pellem*, acc. of *pellis*, a skin. See **Fell** (2).

peel (1), to strip off skin. (F. − L.) From F. *peler*, 'to unskin;' Cot. (Cf. O. Ital. *pellare*, 'to unskin;' Florio). − O. F. *pel*, skin (above). ¶ But this verb was confused with F. *piller*; see **Pill** (2). And even of F. *peler* some senses are due to L. *pilare*, to deprive of hair, from *pilus*, hair.

pelisse, a silk habit. (F. − L.) Formerly a furred robe. − F. *pelisse*, *pelice*, 'a skin of fur;' Cot. − L. *pellicea*, fem. of *pelliceus*, made of skins. − L. *pellis*, a skin.

pellicle, a thin film. (F. − L.) F. *pellicule.* − L. *pellicula*, a small skin; dimin. of *pellis*, a skin.

pelt (2), a skin, esp. of a sheep. (F. − L.) M. E. *pelt*, a shortened form of *peltry*, skins, *peltry-ware*, dealing in skins. − O. F. *pelleterie*, the trade of a skinner. − O. F. *pelletier*, a skinner. Formed (like *bijoutier*, with suffix *-tier* = L. *-tarius*) from O. F. *pel*, a skin. − L. *pellis*.

pilch. (L.) Orig. a warm fur garment. M. E. *pilche*. A. S. *pylce*. − L. *pellicea*; see **pelisse** (above).

pillion. (C. − L.) Irish *pilliun*, *pillin*, a pack-saddle; Gael. *pillean*, *pillin*, a pack-saddle, cloth put under a rustic saddle. − Irish *pill*, a covering, *peall*, a skin; Gael. *peall*, a skin, coverlet. − L. *pellis*, a skin.

plaid. (C. − L.) Gael. (and Irish) *plaide*, a blanket, plaid. Short for *peallaid*, a sheep-skin. − Gael. (and Irish) *peall*, a skin; both from L. *pellis*, a skin.

surplice. (F. − L.) F. *surplis*; Cot. − Low L. *superpelliceum*, a surplice. − L. *super*, over; *pelliceus*, made of skins; see **pelisse** (above).

Pellet; see **Pile** (1).

Pellitory (1), **Paritory**, a wild flower; see **Parietal**.

Pellitory (2), **Pelleter**, the plant pyrethrum; see **Pyre**.

Pell-mell; see **Peak**.

Pellucid; see **Lucid**.

Pelt (1), to throw; see **Pulsate**.

Pelt (2), a skin; see **Pell**.

Pelvis, the bony cavity in the lower part of the abdomen. (L.) L. *peluis*, a base, hence the pelvis.

Pen (1), to enclose; see Pen (2).

Pen (2), an instrument for writing. (F. –L.) O. F. *penne.* – L. *penna,* a feather; O. L. *pesna* (for *petna* *). From √PAT, to fly. See **Feather.**

pen (1), to shut up. (L.) M. E. *pennen.* A. S. *pennan,* only in the comp. *on-pennan,* to un-pen, unfasten. *Pennan* is properly to fasten with a *pin* or peg; cf. Low G. *pennen,* to bolt a door, from *penn,* a pin or peg; see **pin** (below).

pennon, pennant. (F. – L.) M. E. *penon, penoun.* – O. F. *pennon,* 'a flag, streamer; also the feather of an arrow;' Cot. – L. *penna,* wing, feather (hence a plume, standard).

pin, a peg, &c. (L.) M. E. *pinne,* a peg. Perhaps A. S. *pinn,* a pen, style for writing (unauthorised). We find also Irish *pinne,* Gael. *pinne,* a pin, peg, spigot; W. *pin,* pin, style, pen; Du. *pin,* pin, peg, Swed. *pinne,* a peg, Dan. *pind,* a (pointed) stick, Icel. *pinni,* a pin, G. *penn,* a peg. All from L. *pinna,* variant of *penna,* a feather, pen, fin, pinnacle; Late L. *penna,* a probe.

pinion, joint of a wing. (F. – L.) F. *pignon,* a gable-end; Cot. But the sense of *pinion* was no doubt sometimes given to F. *pignon,* since we find Span. *piñon* with the sense of 'pinion,' and O.F. *pignon,* a pennon on a lance. [Again, the mod. F. *pignon* has the sense of E. *pinion,* a small wheel working with teeth into another; in which case the derivation is from L. *pinna,* the float of a water-wheel.] – L. *pinna,* variant of *penna,* a feather; Low L. *pinna,* a peak. See **Pen** above.

pinnacle. (F. – L.) F. *pinacle,* Cot. – L. *pinnaculum,* a pinnacle (Mat. iv. 5). Double dimin. of Low L. *pinna,* a peak, L. *pinna,* a feather, &c. See above.

pinnate, feather-like. (L.) L. *pinnatus,* feathered. – L. *pinna,* for *penna,* a feather.

Penal, Penance; see **Pain.**

Pencil. (F. – L.) The old sense was a small hair-brush for painting. – O. F. *pincel,* later *pinceau,* 'a pensill, brush;' Cot. – L. *penecillus,* a small tail, painter's brush; dimin. of *peniculus,* which is a double dimin. of *penis,* a tail.

Pendant, anything hanging, a hanging ornament. (F. – L.) F. *pendant,* a pendant. – F. *pendant,* pres. pt. of *pendre,* to hang. – L. *pendēre,* to hang; allied to *pendĕre,* to weigh. (√SPAND, SPAD.) Der.

pend-ent, hanging, Latinised form of F. *pendant;* *pend-ing,* Anglicised form of F. *pendant,* during.

append, to add afterwards. (F. – L.) Formerly intransitive. M. E. *apenden,* to depend on, belong to. – O. F. *apendre,* depend on. – F. *a,* to; *pendre,* to hang. – L. *ad,* to; *pendere.* Der. *append-ix.*

compendious, brief. (L.) L. *compendiosus,* adj., from *compendium,* an abridgment, lit. a saving, sparing of expense. – L. *com-* (*cum*), with; *pendĕre,* to weigh, esteem of value.

compensate. (L.) From pp. of L. *compensare,* to weigh one thing against another. – L. *com-* (*cum*), together; *pensare,* to weigh, frequent. of *pendĕre,* to weigh (pp. *pensus*).

counterpoise. (F. – L.) From *counter* and *poise;* see **poise** (below).

depend. (F. – L.) F. *dependre,* to depend, hang on; Cot. – L. *dependere,* to hang down or from. – L. *de,* down, from; *pendēre,* to hang.

dispense. (F. – L.) O. F. *dispenser,* to dispense with. – L. *dispensare,* to weigh out, frequent. form of *dispendere,* to weigh out. – L. *dis-,* apart; *pendĕre,* to weigh.

expend, to spend. (L.) L. *expendĕre,* to weigh out, lay out. – L. *ex,* out; *pendĕre,* to weigh. Der. *expense,* from L. *expensa,* money spent, fem. of pp. *expensus;* *expendit-ure,* from Low L. *expenditus,* a false form of the pp. *expensus.*

impend, to hang over. (L.) L. *impendēre,* to hang over. – L. *im-* (for *in*), on, over; *pendēre,* to hang.

pansy, heart's-ease. (F. – L.) F. *pensée,* 'a thought; also, the flower paunsie;' Cot. (It is the flower of thought or remembrance.) Prop. fem. of pp. of F. *penser,* to think. – L. *pensare,* to weigh, ponder, frequent. of *pendere,* to weigh.

pendulous. (L.) L. *pendulus,* hanging. – L. *pendēre,* to hang.

pendulum. (L.) L. *pendulum,* neut. of adj. *pendulus* (above).

pensile, suspended. (F. – L.) F. *pensil;* Cot. – L. *pensilis,* pendent; from *pendēre,* to hang.

pension. (F. – L.) F. *pension.* – L. *pensionem,* acc. of *pensio,* a payment. – L. *pensus,* pp. of *pendēre,* to weigh, weigh out money, pay.

pensive. (F. – L.) M. E. *pensif.* – F. *pensif,* thoughtful. – F. *penser,* to think; see **pansy** (above).

penthouse, a shed projecting from a building. (F. – L.) Formerly *pentice,* whence it is corrupted. – O. F. *apentis, appentis,* 'a penthouse;' Cot. – L. *appendicium,* an appendage, allied to *appendix* (the same). – L. *ap-* (*ad'*), to; *pendēre,* to hang.

pentroof, a roof with a slope on one side only. (F. – L.; *and* E.) This has affected the sense of *penthouse,* though they mean quite different things. Here *pent* is from F. *pente,* a slope, formed from F. *pendre,* to hang. – L. *pendēre.*

perpendicular. (F. – L.) F. *perpendiculaire.* – L. *perpendicularis,* according to the plumb-line. – L. *perpendiculum,* a plummet, for careful measurement. – L. *perpendere,* to weigh or measure carefully. – L. *per,* thoroughly; *pendēre,* to weigh.

poise, to balance, weigh. (F. – L.) M. E. *poisen, peisen.* – O. F. *peiser, poiser;* later *peser,* to weigh. Allied to O. F. *pois, peis,* a weight (now misspelt *poids,* from a notion of its being derived from L. *pondus,* which is *not* the case). – Low L. *pensum, pensa,* a portion, weight; L. *pensum,* a portion weighed out to spinners, a task. – L. *pensus,* pp. of *pendēre,* to weigh.

ponder, to weigh in the mind, consider. (L.) L. *ponderare,* to weigh. – L. *ponder-,* stem of *pondus,* a weight. – L. *pendēre,* to weigh.

pound (1), a weight, a sovereign. (L.) Orig. a weight. M. E. *pund.* A. S. *pund,* pl. *pund.* – L. *pondo,* a weight, used as an indeclinable sb., though orig. meaning 'by weight;' allied to *pondus,* a weight (above).

prepense, premeditated. (F. – L.) F. *pre-,* beforehand; *penser,* to think. – L. *præ,* beforehand; *pensare,* to weigh, ponder, intens. form of *pendēre,* to weigh.

preponderate. (L.) From pp. of L. *præponderare,* to outweigh. – L. *præ,* before; *ponderare,* to weigh; see ponder (above).

propensity, an inclination. (L.) Coined from L. *propensus,* hanging forward, inclining towards; pp. of *pro-pendēre,* to hang forwards.

recompense, to reward. (F. – L.) F. *recompenser,* 'to recompence;' Cot. – L. *re-,* again, *compensare,* to compensate; see **compensate** (above).

spencer, a short over-jacket. (F. – L.) Named after Earl *Spencer,* died 1845. The name is from M. E. *spenser,* also *despenser.*

– O. F. *despencier,* a spender, a caterer, clerk of a kitchen; Cot. – O. F. *despenser,* to spend; frequent. of *despendre.* – L. *dispendere,* to weigh out, pay. – L. *dis-,* apart; *pendēre,* to weigh.

spend. (L.) A. S. *spendan,* to spend. Shortened from L. *dispendere,* to spend, waste, consume. We find Low L. *spendium* for *dispendium, spensa* for *dispensa;* also *spendibilis moneta,* money for expenses (A.D. 922). So also Ital. *spendere,* to spend, *spendio* (= L. *dispendium*), expense. – L. *dis-,* away, apart; *pendēre,* to weigh out, pay.

suspend. (F. – L.) F. *suspendre.* – L. *suspendere* (pp. *suspensus*), to hang up. – L. *sus-* (for *subs-*), extension of *sub,* under; *pendēre,* to hang. Der. *suspense, suspension.*

Pendulous, Pendulum; see **Pendant.**

Penetrate. (L.) From pp. of L. *penetrare,* to pierce into. Compounded of *pene-,* base of *penes,* with, *peni-tus,* within, with which cf. *penus,* the inner part of a sanctuary; and *-trare* (as in *in-trare*), to pass over, allied to Skt. *tri,* to cross.

Penguin, Pinguin, a bird. (C. ?) 'In a tract printed in 1588, we read that Sir F. Drake gave a certain island the name of *Penguin Island* in 1587, from the penguins found there. The word appears to be W. *pen gwyn,* i. e. white head.' If so, it must first have been given to another bird, such as the auk (the puffin is common in Anglesey), since the penguin's head is black.

Peninsula. (L.) L. *peninsula,* a piece of land nearly an island. – L. *pene, pæne,* almost; *insula,* an island. So also *penultimate,* almost the last, last but one; *pen-umbra,* partial shadow.

Penitent; see **Pain.**

Pennon, Pennant; see **Pen** (2).

Penny; see **Pane.**

Penny-royal, a herb. (F. – L.) A singular corruption of the old name *pulial royal.* Cotgrave translates F. *pulege* by 'penny royall, puliall royall.' Again, the old name is due to L. *puleium regium,* a name given to the plant from its supposed efficacy against fleas (cf. E. *flea-bane*). From L. *pulex,* a flea; *regius,* royal.

Pensile, Pension, Pensive; see **Pendent.**

Pent, for *penned,* pp. of **Pen** (1), q.v.

Pentagon, a plane five-sided figure. (F. – L. – Gk.) F. *pentagone.* – L. *pentagonus,* adj., pentagonal. – Gk. πεντάγωνος, pentagonal; neut. πεντάγωνον, a pentagon. — Gk. πεντά, old form of πεντέ, five; γωνία, an angle, from γόνυ, a knee; see Knee. And see Five.

pentameter, a verse of five metres. (L. — Gk.) L. pentameter. — Gk. πεντά-μετρος.—Gk. πεντά, old form of πεντέ, five; μέτρον, a metre.

pentateuch, the five books of Moses. (L. — Gk.) L. pentateuchus. — Gk. πεντά, five (above); τεῦχος, a tool, also a book.

pentecost, Whitsuntide; orig. a Jewish festival on the 50th day after the Passover. (L.—Gk.) L. pentecoste. — Gk. πεντηκοστή, Pentecost, Acts, ii. 1; fem. of πεντηκοστός, fiftieth. — Gk. πεντήκοντα, fifty.

Penthouse, Pentroof; see Pendant.

Penultimate, Penumbra; see Peninsula.

Penury, want. (F. — L.) F. penurie. — L. penuria, want, need. + Gk. πενία, σπανία, need.

Peony; see Pæan.

People; see Popular.

Pepper. (L.—Gk.—Skt.) A. S. pipor. — L. piper. — Gk. πέπερι. — Skt. pippala, (1) holy fig-tree, (2) long pepper; pippalī, the fruit of pippala.

Pepsine, one of the constituents of gastric juice. (F.—Gk.) Mod. F. pepsine. — Gk. πέψ-, fut. of πέπτειν, to cook. (√PAK.)

Per-, prefix, through. (L.; or F. — L.) L. per, through; whence F. per-, par-, prefix. Allied to Gk. παρά, beside; Skt. pará, away, forth, param, beyond; E. from. (√PAR.)

Perambulate; see Amble.

Perceive; see Capacious.

Perch (1), a rod for a bird to sit on; a measure. (F.—L.) F. perche.—L. pertica, a rod, bar.

Perch (2), a fish. (F. — L. — Gk.) F. perche. — L. perca. — Gk. πέρκη, a perch; from the dark marks.—Gk. πέρκος, πέρκνος, spotted, blackish; cf. Skt. priçni, spotted, pied, from spriç, to sprinkle.

Percolate; see Colander.

Percussion; see Quash.

Perdition; see Date (1).

Peregrination; see Agriculture.

Peremptory; see Exempt.

Perennial; see Annals.

Perfect; see Fact.

Perfidious; see Faith.

Perfoliate; see Foliage.

Perforate. (L.) From pp. of L. per-

forare, to bore through; where forare is cognate with E. Bore, q. v.

Perform; see Furnish.

Perfume; see Fume.

Perfunctory; see Function.

Perhaps; see Hap.

Peri, a fairy. (Pers.) Pers. parī, a fairy. Lit. 'winged;' from Pers. par, a wing, feather. (√PAT.)

Peri-, prefix, round. (Gk.) Gk. περί, around, about. + Skt. pari, round about. Allied to per-, prefix. (√PAR.)

Pericardium, the sac surrounding the heart. (L. — Gk.) L. pericardium. — Gk. περικάρδιον.—Gk. περί, around; καρδία, the heart; see Heart.

Pericarp, a seed - vessel. (Gk.) Gk. περικάρπιον, shell of fruit. — Gk. περί, around; καρπός, fruit; see Harvest.

Pericranium; see Cranium.

Perigee; see Geography.

Perihelion; see Heliacal.

Peril, danger. (F. — L.) F. peril. — L. periclum, periculum, danger, lit. 'a trial.' — L. periri, to try; an obsolete verb, of which the pp. peritus is common. Allied to Gk. πειράω, I try, περάω, I pass through, and to E. fare; see Fare. (√PAR.) Der. peril-ous.

experience, knowledge due to trial. (F.—L.) O.F. experience.—L. experientia, a proof, trial. — L. experient-, stem of pres. pt. of ex-periri, to make a thorough trial of (above). Der. experi-ment, F. experiment, L. experimentum, a trial.

expert, experienced. (F.—L.) O F. expert. — L. expertus, pp. of ex-periri, to experience (above).

parlous. (F.—L.) Short for peril-ous.

Perimeter; see Metre.

Period, time of a circuit, epoch, perfect sentence. (F. — L. — Gk.) F. periode, a perfect sentence. — L. periodus.—Gk. περί-οδος, a going round, circuit, complete sentence. — Gk. περί, round; ὁδός, a way; see Exodus. ¶ The sense of 'circuit' is directly from Gk.

Peripatetic, a walking about. (L. — Gk.) L. peripateticus.—Gk. περιπατητικός, given to walking about, esp. while disputing; a name given to followers of Aristotle.—Gk. περιπατέω, I walk about.—Gk. περί, about; πατέω, I walk, from πάτος, a path, cognate with E. Path, q. v.

Periphery, circumference. (L. — Gk.) L. periferia, peripheria. — Gk. περιφέρεια, the circumference of a circle. — Gk. περί,

around ; φέρειν, to carry, cognate with E.
Bear, verb.

Periphrasis; see **Phrase**.

Perish; see **Itinerant**.

Periwig; see **Pile** (3).

Periwinkle (1), a plant. (L.) Formed,
with suffixed -*le* and inserted *i*, from M. E.
pervenke, a periwinkle; A. S. *peruincæ.* —
L. *peruinca*, a periwinkle; also called *uinca*
peruinca, a name doubtless orig. given to
some twining plant. — L. *per*, through,
thoroughly; *uincire*, to bind; allied to
Withy. (✓ WI.)

Periwinkle (2), a small univalve mollusc. (Hyb.) A corrupt form, due to confusion with the word above. The best name
is simply *winkle*; see **Winkle**. Properly
peniwinkle, Halliwell; A. S. *pinewincla*, a
periwinkle, or sea-snail. ¶ The A. S. *pine*-
is from L. *pina*, a mussel.

Perjure; see **Jury**.

Perk, to make smart or trim. (W.) W.
perc, compact, trim; *percu*, to smarten,
trim; *percus*, smart.

pert, saucy. (C.) M. E. *pert*, another
form of *perk*, adj., smart, proud, Spenser,
Shep. Kal. Feb. l. 8. See above. ¶ But
in some cases *pert* is short for *apert*; for
which see **Malapert**. The two sources
were confused.

Permanent; see **Mansion**.

Permeate, to pervade, pass through
small openings. (L.) From pp. of L. *per-*
meare, to pass through. — J., *per*, through;
meare, to pass, go, allied to *migrare*, to
migrate.

congè, congee, leave to depart. (F. —
L.) F. *congé*, ' leave, dismission;' Cot.
O. F. *congie, cunge, congiet* (Burguy); the
same as Prov. *comjat*. — Low L. *comiatus*,
leave, permission (8th cent.); the same as
L. *commeatus*, a travelling together, also
leave of absence. — L. *com-* (*cum*), together;
meatus, a course, from pp. of *meare*, to go.

Permit; see **Missile**.

Permutation; see **Mutable**.

Pernicious, hurtful. (F. — L.) F. *per-*
nicieux. — L. *perniciosus*, destructive. — L.
pernicies, destruction. — L. *per*, thoroughly;
nici-, put for *neci-*, crude form of *nex*,
slaughter; see **Internecine**.

Peroration; see **Oral**.

Perpendicular; see **Pendant**.

Perpetrate. (L.) From pp. of L. *per-*
petrare, to perform thoroughly. — L. *per*,
thoroughly; *patrare*, to accomplish; allied
to *potens*, powerful; see **Potent**.

Perpetual. (F. — L.) M. E. *perpetuel*.
— F. *perpetuel*. — L. *perpetualis*, universal ;
in later use, permanent. — L. *perpetuus*,
continuous, constant, perpetual. — L. *perpet-*,
stem of *perpes*, lasting throughout, continuous. — L. *per*, through; *pet-*, weakened
form of ✓ PAT, to go, appearing in Gk.
πάτος, a path, πατεῖν, to tread. Thus the
orig. sense is ' going through,' with reference to a continuous path. See **Path**.

Perplex; see **Ply**.

Perquisite; see **Query**.

Perry; see **Pear**.

Persecute; see **Sequence**.

Persevere; see **Severe**.

Persist; see **State**.

Person; see **Sound** (3).

Perspective; see **Species**.

Perspicacity, Perspicuous; see
Species.

Perspiration; see **Spirit**.

Persuade; see **Suasion**.

Pert, forward, saucy; see **Perk**.

Pertain, Pertinacity; see **Tenable**.

Perturb; see **Turbid**.

Peruke; see **Pile** (3).

Peruse; see **Use**.

Pervade; see **Evade**.

Pervert; see **Verse**.

Pervicacious, wilful. (L.) Coined
from L. *peruicaci-*, crude form of *peruicax*,
wilful; allied to *peruicus*, stubborn. Perhaps from *per*, through; and *ui-s*, strength;
see **Violate**.

Pervious; see **Viaduct**.

Pessimist, one who complains that all
is for the worst. (L.) Coined from L.
pessim-us, worst; superl. connected with
peior, worse; see **Impair**.

Pest. (F. — L.) F. *peste*. — L. *pestem*,
acc. of *pestis*, a plague.

pestiferous. (L.) L. *pestiferus*, or *pes-*
tifer, plague-bringing. — L. *pesti-s*, plague;
ferre, to bring.

pestilent. (F. — L.) F. *pestilent*. — L.
pestilent-, stem of *pestilens*, hurtful; formed
as if from a verb *pestilere**, from *pestilis*,
pestilential. — L. *pesti-*, crude form of *pestis*.

Pester; see **Pastor**.

Pestilent; see **Pest**.

Pestle; see **Pistil**.

Pet (1), a tame animal, a child treated
fondly. (C.) Formerly *peat*. — Irish *peat*,
sb., a pet ; adj., petted; Gael. *peata*, a pet,
a tame animal.

pet (2), a fit of peevishness. (C.) We
also find *pettish*, capricious, i.e. like a *pet*

or spoilt child; see above. Hence the phr.
'to take *pet*,' or 'to take the *pet*,' i.e. to
act like a spoilt child; and finally *pet*, sb.,
a fit of wilfulness.

Petal. (Gk.) Gk. πέταλον, a leaf (hence
petal of a flower); neut. of πέταλος, spread
out, flat. + L. *patulus*, spreading; from
patere, to spread. (√ PAT.)

Petard, an explosive war-engine. (F. —
L.) F. *petard, petart*, 'a petard or pe-
tarre;' Cot. Lit. 'explosive.' Formed
with suffix -*art* (= G. *hart*, hard, common
as a suffix) from F. *peter*, to break wind. —
F. *pet*, a breaking wind, slight explosion. —
L. *peditum*, neut. of *peditus*, pp. of *pēdere*
(for *perdere**), to break wind. + Gk. πέρ-
δειν, Skt. *pard*, Icel. *freta*, G. *furzen*.
(√ PARD.)

Petiolo, footstalk of a leaf. (F. — L.)
F. *pétiole.* — L. *petiolum*, acc. of *petiolus*,
little stalk. β. Perhaps for *pediolus**; the
usual derivation is from *pedi-*, crude form
of *pes*, a foot; see **Pedal.**

Petition. (F. — L.) F. *petition*; Cot.
— L. acc. *petitionem*, from *petitio*, a
suit. — L. *petitus*, pp. of *petere*, to at-
tuck, to beseech, ask; orig. to fall on.
(√ PAT.)

appetite. (F. — L.) O. F. *appetit, appetite.* — L. *appetitus*, an appetite, lit. 'an
assault upon.' — L. *appetere*, to attack. — L.
ap- (*ad*), to; *petere*, to attack.

competent. (F. — L.) F. *competent*;
orig. pres. part. of *competer*, to be sufficient for. — L. *competere*, to be sufficient for.
— L. *com-* (*cum*), with; *petere*, to seek.

competitor. (L.) L. *competitor*, a
rival candidate. — L. *com-* (*cum*), with;
petitor, a seeker, from *petitus*, pp. of *petere*,
to seek. **Der.** *compete*, verb, from L.
competere.

impetus. (L.) L. *impetus*, lit. 'a falling on;' a rush, attack. — L. *im-* (*in*), on;
petere, to fall, fly, seek.

petulant. (L.) L. *petulant-*, stem of
petulans, forward, pert, ready to attack. —
L. *petere*, to attack.

repeat. (F. — L.) Formerly *repete.* —
F. *repeter*, Cot. — L. *re-petere*, to attack
again, reseek, repeat. **Der.** *repet-it-ion*.

Petrel, a bird. (F. — G. — L. — Gk.)
Formerly *peterel.* — F.*pétrel, pétérel*; formed
as a dimin. of *Pêtre*, i.e. Peter, and the
allusion is to the action of the bird,
which seems, like St. Peter, to walk on the
sea. The F. form of Peter is *Pierre*;
Pêtre is borrowed from G. *Peter*, Peter;

the G. name for the bird being *Peters-
vogel* (= Peter's-fowl, Peter's-bird). — L.
Petrus. — Gk. πέτρος, a stone, Peter
(John, i. 42).

petrify, to turn into stone. (F. — Gk.
and L.) F. *petrifier*; as if from a L.
*petrificare**, not used. — L. *petri-*, for *petra*,
a rock; *facere*, to make. The L. *petra* is
borrowed from Gk. πέτρα, a rock; cf.
πέτρος, a stone.

petroleum, rock-oil. (L. — Gk.) Coined
from L. *petr-a*, rock; *oleum*, oil. — Gk.
πέτρα, rock; ἔλαιον, oil; see **Oil.**

pier, a mass of stone-work. (F. — L. —
Gk.) M. E. *pere.* — O. F. *piere* (F. *pierre*),
a stone. — L. *petra.* — Gk. πέτρα, a rock,
stone.

samphire, a herb. (F. — L. *and* Gk.)
Spelt *sampier* in Baret (1580). — F. *saint
Pierre*, St. Peter; whence *herbe de saint
Pierre*, samphire. — L. *sanctum*, acc. of
sanctus, holy; *Petrum*, acc. of *Petrus*,
Peter; see **petrel** (above).

Petronel, a horse-pistol. (F. — Span. —
L.) F. *petrinal*, 'a petronell, or horseman's
piece;' Cot. Said to have been invented
in the Pyrenees; and almost certainly
derived from Span. *petrina*, a belt, a girdle
(hence a horseman's belt for attaching a
petronel). Allied to Span. *petral*, a poitrel;
and named from going round the breast. —
L. *pector-*, stem of *pectus*, the breast. See
Pectoral.

Petty, small. (F. — C.) M. E. *petit.* —
F. *petit*, small. Diez derives this from a
Celtic base *pit*, finely pointed, which he
finds represented by W. *pid*, a tapering
point. Cf. Ital. *piccolo*, small, from a
Celtic base *pic*, seen in W. *pig*, a point,
peak. **Der.** *petti-fogger*, where *fogger* is
from O. Du. *focker*, 'a monopole, or an
engrosser of wares and commodities;'
Hexham.

Petulant; see **Petition.**

Pew. (F. — L. — Gk.) O. F. *pui*, an
elevated space; *puye*, an open gallery with
rails (hence applied to an enclosed space
or to a raised desk to kneel at). — L.
podium, a balcony, esp. near the arena,
where distinguished persons sat. (So E.
pew meant a place for distinguished persons
in church.) — Gk. πόδιον, a little foot
(whence the senses of foot-stool, gallery to
sit in, &c., must have been evolved, since
there can be no doubt as to the identity of
the L. and Gk. words). — Gk. ποδί-, crude
form of πούς, foot. See **Foot.** ¶ Cf.

Du. *puye*, 'a pue,' Hexham; borrowed from F. *puye*.

Pewet, Peewit, the lapwing. (E.) Also *puet* (Phillips). Named from its plaintive cry; see **Peevish.**

Pewter. (F. – E.?) M. E. *pewtir*. – O. F. *peutre, peautre, piautre*, a kind of metal (Roquefort). It stands for *peltre**, and is akin to Span *peltre*, Ital. *peltro*, pewter. Diez remarks that the Ital. *peltro* is believed to be derived from English, which he rejects, but only on the ground that *pewter* could not become *peltro*. However, *peltro* is probably (like F. *peutre*), an adaptation of E. *spelter*; see **Spelter.**

PH.

Ph. Initial *ph* is distinct from *p*, and has the sound of *f*; it represents the Gk. φ, almost every word beginning with *ph* being of Gk. origin. The only exceptions are *philibeg*, better *fillibeg*, which is Gaelic, and *Pharisee*, really of Hebrew origin, but coming to us through Greek.

Phaeton, a kind of carriage. (F. – L. – Gk.) F. *phaéton*; occurring A.D. 1792. – L. *Phaethon.* – Gk. Φαέθων, son of Helios, and driver of the chariot of the sun; lit. 'shining,' being pres. part. of φαέθειν, to shine. – Gk. φάειν, to shine. See **Phantom.** (√ BHA.)

Phalanx. (L. – Gk.) L. *phalanx.* – Gk. φάλαγξ, a battalion.

Phantasm; see below.

Phantom. (F. – L. – Gk.) M. E. *fantome.* – O. F. *fantosme.* – L. *phantasma.* – Gk. φάντασμα, a vision, spectre, lit. apparition. – Gk. φαντάζειν, to display. – Gk. φαν-, as in φαίνειν (= φάν-γειν), to shew, lit. to cause to shine; whence φάντης*, one who shews (as in ἱερο-φάντης). – Gk. φά-ειν, to shine. **+** Skt. *bhá*, to shine. (√ BHA.)

diaphanous, transparent. (Gk.) Gk. διαφαν-ής, transparent. – Gk. διά, through; φαν-, in φαίνειν, to shew, appear.

epiphany, Twelfth Day. (F. – L. – Gk.) F. *epiphanie.* – L. *epiphania.* – Gk. ἐπιφάνια, manifestation; orig. neut. pl. of ἐπιφάνιος, manifest, but used as equivalent to ἐπιφάνεια, sb. – Gk. ἐπιφαίνειν, to shew forth. – Gk. ἐπί, to; φαίνειν, to shew.

fancy. (F. – L. – Gk.) Short for M. E. *fantasie.* – O. F. *fantasie.* – Low L. *phantasia.* – Gk. φαντασία, a making visible (hence, imagination). – Gk. φαντάζειν, to display; see **Phantom** (above).

fantastic. (Gk.) Gk. φανταστικός, able to represent or shew. – Gk. φαντάζειν, to display (above).

fantasy; longer form of **fancy** (above).

phenomenon, a remarkable appearance. (L. – Gk.) L. *phænomenon.* – Gk. φαινόμενον, pl. φαινόμενα, an appearance, neut. of pass. part. of φαίνειν, to shew (pass. φαίνομαι, I appear). And see **Hierophant, Sycophant.**

Pharisee, one of a religious school among the Jews. (L. – Gk. – Heb.) L. *phariseus, pharisæus.* – Gk.φαρισαῖος, Matt. ix. 11, lit. 'one who separates himself from men.' – Heb. *párash*, to separate.

Pharmacy. (F. – L. – Gk.) M. E. *fermacy.* – O. F. *farmacie*, later *pharmacie*. – L. *pharmacia.* – Gk. φαρμακεία, knowledge of drugs. – Gk. φάρμακον, a drug. β. Perhaps named from bringing help; from φάρειν, Doric for φέρειν, to bring.

Pharynx. (L. – Gk.) L. *pharynx.* – Gk. φάρυγξ, the joint opening of the gullet and wind-pipe, a cleft, a bore; allied to φάραγξ, a chasm. From the root φαρ-, to bore; see **Bore** (1). (√ BHAR.)

Phase, Phasis, an appearance. (L. – Gk.) Late L. *phasis*, pl. *phases*. – Gk. φάσις, an appearance; from base φα-, to shine; cf. φά-ος, light. (√ BHA.) β. The Gk. φάσις also means 'a saying, declaration,' in which sense it is connected with φημί, I speak, declare, from √ BHA, to speak. This root is perhaps ultimately identical with √ BHA, to shine.

emphasis, stress of voice. (L. – Gk.) L. *emphasis.* – Gk. ἔμφασις, a declaration, emphasis. – Gk. ἐμ- (ἐν), in; φάσις, an appearance, also a declaration, as explained above.

Pheasant, a bird. (F. – L. – Gk.) Formed with excrescent *t* (after *n*) from M.E. *fesaun*, a pheasant. – O. F. *faisan*. – L. *phasiana*, a pheasant; put for *Phasiana auis*, Phasian bird. – Gk. φασιανός, a pheasant, lit. Phasian, i. e. coming from the river *Phasis* in Colchis.

Phenix, Phœnix. (L. – Gk.) L. *phœnix.* – Gk. φοῖνιξ, a phœnix (Herod. ii. 73). Perhaps named from its bright colour, like that produced by the *Phœnician* dye.

Phenomenon; see Phantom.

Phial, Vial. (F. – L. – Gk.) Formerly *vial, viall, viol,* altered to *phial* in modern editions of Shakespeare. – O. F. *phiole,* 'a violl,' Cot. (Mod. F. *fiole*). – L. *phiala.* – Gk. φιάλη, a broad, flat, shallow cup or bowl (now applied to a small bottle).

Philanthropy, love of mankind. (L. – Gk.) L. *philanthropia.* – Gk. φιλανθρωπία, benevolence. – Gk. φιλάνθρωπος, loving mankind. – Gk. φιλ-, for φίλος, friendly, kind ; ἄνθρωπος, a man.

philharmonic, loving music. (Gk.) From Gk. φίλ-ος, friendly, fond of ; and L. *harmoni-a* = Gk. ἁρμονία, harmony ; see Harmony.

philippic, a discourse full of invective. (L. – Gk.) L. *Philippicum,* pl. *Philippica,* used to denote the celebrated orations of Demosthenes against Philip. – Gk. φίλιππος, Philip ; lit. ' a lover of horses.' – Gk. φίλ-ος, fond of ; ἵππος, a horse.

philology, study of languages. (L. – Gk.) L. *philologia.* – Gk. φιλολογία, love of discourse, love of literature and language. – Gk. φιλόλογος, fond of discourse ; also, a student of literature and language. – Gk. φίλο-ς, fond of ; λόγος, discourse, from λέγειν, to speak.

philosophy, love of wisdom. (F. – L. – Gk.) M. E. *philosophie.* – F. *philosophie.* – L. *philosophia.* – Gk. φιλοσοφία, love of wisdom. – Gk. φιλόσοφος, loving knowledge. – Gk. φίλο-s, fond of ; σοφός, skilful, σοφία, skill ; see Sophist. Der. *philosoph-er,* by adding *r* to M. E. *philosophe,* which represents F. *philosophe,* L. *philosophus,* Gk. φιλόσοφος.

philtre, a love potion. (F. – L. – Gk.) F. *philtre.* – L. *philtrum.* – Gk. φίλτρον, a love charm, love potion, drink to make one love. – Gk. φίλ-ος, dear ; -τρον (Aryan -*tar*), denoting the agent.

Philibeg, a kilt ; see Fillibeg.

Phlebotomy, blood-letting. (F. – L. – Gk.) F. *phlebotomie.* – L. *phlebotomia.* – Gk. φλεβοτομία, blood-letting, lit. cutting of a vein. – Gk. φλεβο-, crude form of φλέψ, a vein ; τομός, cutting, from τέμνειν, to cut ; see Tome.

fleam, a kind of lancet. (F. – L. – Gk.) F. *flamme,* a fleam ; Hamilton. – Low L. *flevotomum, phlebotomum,* a lancet. – Gk. φλεβοτόμον, a lancet. – Gk. φλεβο-, crude form of φλέψ, a vein ; τομ-, for ταμ-, base of τέμνειν, to cut. Hence also M. H. G. *fliedeme,* Du. *vlijm,* a fleam ; the F. form

is due to loss of the syllable -*vo*- in Low L. *fle'tomum,* and subsequent abbreviation (as in E. *plane* for L. *platanum*).

Phlegm, slimy matter in the throat, sluggishness. (F. – L. – Gk.) The use of the term was due to the supposed influence of the 'four humours ;' phlegm causing a sluggish or 'phlegmatic' temperament. – F. *phlegme.* – L. *phlegma.* – Gk. φλέγμα (base φλεγματ-), (1) a flame, (2) inflammation, (3) viscous humour, phlegm. – Gk. φλέγειν, to burn.+L. *flag-rare,* to burn ; see Flame. Der. *phlegmat-ic,* from base φλεγματ-.

phlox, a flower. (Gk.) It means 'flame,' from its colour. – Gk. φλόξ, flame. – Gk. φλέγ-ειν, to burn (above).

Phocine, belonging to the family of seals. (L. – Gk.) From L. *phoca,* a seal. – Gk. φώκη, a seal.

Phœnix; see Phenix.

Phonetic, representing sounds. (Gk.) From Gk. φωνητικός, belonging to speaking. – Gk. φωνέω, I produce a sound. – Gk. φωνή, a sound ; cf. φημί, I speak. (√BHA.) Der. *phono-graph, -logy,* &c.

anthem. (L. – Gk.) Formerly *antem.* A.S. *antefn.* – Late L. *antiphona,* an anthem. – Gk. ἀντίφωνα, considered as fem. sing., but really neut. pl. of ἀντίφωνος, sounding in response to ; from the alternate singing of the half-choirs. – Gk. ἀντί, over against ; φωνή, voice, sound.

antiphon. (L. – Gk.) Low L. *antiphona,* an anthem or antiphon ; see above.

symphony, (F. – L. – Gk.) F. *symphonie,* Cot. – L. *symphonia.* – Gk. συμφωνία, music (Luke xv. 25). – Gk. σύμφωνος, harmonious. – Gk. συμ-, for σύν, together ; φωνή, sound.

Phosphorus. (L. – Gk.) L. *phosphorus.* – G. φωσφόρος, light-bringing, i.e. producing light. – Gk. φῶς, light (= φάος, light), from base φα-, to shine ; -φορος, bringing, from φέρειν, to bring. (√BHA and √BHAR.)

photography. (Gk.) From Gk. φωτο-, crude form of φῶς, light (above) ; and γράφειν, to write.

Phrase. (F. – L. – Gk.) F. *phrase.* – L. *phrasem,* acc. of *phrasis.* – Gk. φράσις, a speaking, a speech, phrase. – Gk. φράζειν (= φράδ-γειν), to speak ; cf. φραδής, shrewd. Der. *anti-phrasis, meta-phrase, peri-phrasis, para-phrase* ; with prefixes *anti-, meta-, peri-, para-.*

Phrenology, science of the functions of the mind. (Gk.) From Gk. φρενό-, crude form of φρήν, mind; -λογία, from λόγος, a discourse, from λέγειν, to speak.

Phthisis, consumption of the lungs. (L. – Gk.) L. *phthisis.* – Gk. φθίσις, consumption, decay. – Gk. φθίνειν, to decay, wane. Cf. Skt. *kshi*, to destroy, *kshitis*, decay. **Der.** *phthisic*, properly an adj., from L. *phthisicus*, adj., consumptive; but used as a sb. (= L. *phthisica*), with the same sense as *phthisis*; often called and spelt *tisic*.

Phylactery, an amulet, amongst the Jews. (F. – L. – Gk.) M. E. *filaterie*, Wyclif. – O. F. *filatere, filatiere* (Littré); mod. F. *phylactère.* – L. *phylacterium.* – Gk. φυλακτήριον, a preservative; Matt. xxiii. 5. – Gk. φυλακτήρ, a guardian. – Gk. φυλάσσειν, to guard; φύλαξ, a guard.

Physic. (F. – L. – Gk.) Orig. the healing art; hence, medicine. – O. F. *phisique*, science of medicine; also, natural philosophy. – L. *physica*, natural science. – Gk. φυσική, fem. of φυσικός, natural, physical. – Gk. φύσι-s, nature, being. – Gk. φύ-ειν, to produce.+Skt. *bhú*, to be; L. *fore*;

E. *be*. (√BHU.) **Der.** *physic-s*; *physic-i-an*; &c.

metaphysics, the science of mind. (L. – Gk.) Formerly also *metaphysic.* – L. *metaphysica*, neut. pl. metaphysics. – Gk. μετὰ τὰ φυσικά, after physics; because the study was supposed to follow that of physics or natural science.

physiognomy, visage, expression of features. (F. – L. – Gk.) M. E. *fisnomie*, *visnomie.* – O. F. *phisonomie*, later *physiognomie*, a knowledge of a man's character by his features; hence features, expression. Formed as if from L. *physiognomia**, but really from the longer form *physiognomonia.* – Gk. φυσιογνωμονία, the art of reading the features; sometimes φυσιογνωμία. – Gk. φυσιογνώμων, adj., judging character. – Gk. φυσιο-, for φύσις, nature; γνώμων, an interpreter; see **Gnomon.**

physiology, the science of nature. (F. – L. – Gk.) F. *physiologie*; Cot. – L. *physiologia.* – Gk. φυσιολογία, an enquiry into the nature of things. – Gk. φυσιο-, for φύσις, nature; -λογία, from λόγος, a discourse, from λέγειν, to speak.

PI–PY.

Piacular; see **Pious.**
Pianoforte; see **Plain.**
Piastre, a coin; see **Plate.**
Piazza; see **Plate.**
Pibroch; see **Pipe.**
Pica; see **Pie** (1).
Piccadill, Pickadill; see **Peak.**
Pick, Pickaxe, Picket; see **Peak.**
Pickle, a liquid in which substances are preserved. (E.?) M. E. *pikil, pykyl*; Prompt. Parv. Probably from *pickle*, frequent. of *pick*, in the sense to pick out or 'cleanse;' with reference to the. gutting or cleansing of the fish with which the operation of pickling is begun. We find M. E. *pykelynge*, 'purgulacio,' derived from '*pykyn*, or clensyn, or cullyn owte the onclene, *purgo, purgulo, segrego*;' Prompt. Parv. See **Pick**, orig. of Celtic origin. β. We also find Du. *pekel*, pickle; which some have derived from the name of the supposed inventor of pickling, whose name is variously given as *Beukeler, Böckel*, and *Pökel*; a story in which it is hard to believe.

Picnic. (E.) Found in F. as early as

1740, and in Swedish before 1788; but borrowed in those languages from English. Origin obscure. *Pic* is prob. from *pick*, in the sense to nibble; cf. slang E. *peck*, food, *peckish*, hungry. *Nic* is for *knick*, a trifle; another name for a picnic was *nick-nack* (Foote, Nabob, act 1).

Picture. (L.) L. *pictura*, properly the art of painting. – L. *pictus*, pp. of *pingere*, to paint. Allied to Skt. *piñj*, to dye, colour. (√PIG or PIK.)

depict. (L.) Formerly used as a pp. – L. *depictus*, pp. of *de-pingere*, to depict, lit. paint down or fully.

paint. (F. – L.) M. E. *peinten*, verb. – F. *peint*, -pp. of *peindre*, to paint. – L. *pingere*, to paint.

pigment. (L.) L. *pigmentum*, colouring matter. – L. *pig-*, base of *pingere*.

pimento, all-spice. (Port. – L.) Also *pimenta.* – Port. *pimenta*, pimento. The same as O. F. *piment*, a spiced drink. – L. *pigmentum*, (1) a pigment, (2) the juice of plants; see **pigment.**

pint, a measure for liquids. (F. – Span. – L.) F. *pinte.* – Span. *pinta*, a spot, mark, pint. Named from being a marked part of a larger vessel. – L. *picta*, fem. of *pictus*, painted, marked, pp. of *pingere*, to paint. So also Span. *pintura* = a picture.

Piddle, to trifle; see **Pedlar**.

Pie (1), a magpie; unsorted printer's type. (F. – L.) The unsorted type is called *pie*, or *pi*, short for *pica*, from the common use of pica-type; see below. The magpie is M. E. *pie*. – F. *pie*. – L. *pica*, a magpie. Cf. L. *picus*, wood-pecker, Skt. *pika*, Indian cuckoo, Gk. σπίζα, a finch. Orig. sense probably 'chirper;' cf. L. *pipire*, to chirp, Gk. σπίζειν.

pie (2), a book which ordered the manner of performing divine service. (F. – L.) Here *pie* is (as above) a F. form of L. *pica*, which was an old name for the Ordinale; so called from the confused appearance of the black-letter type on white paper, resembling a magpie. Certain sizes of type are still called *pica*.

piebald, of various colours, in patches. (F. – L.; *and* C.) Compounded of *pie*, a magpie, and *bald*; see **Bald**. The old sense of *bald*, or *ball'd*, is streaked, from W. *bal*, having a white streak on the forehead, said of a horse. Cf. *skew-bald*.

pie (3), a pasty. (F. – L.) F. *pie*, a broiled remnant of a shoulder of mutton (Littré); the same word.

Piece. (F. – L.?) M. E. *pece*, *piece*. – O. F. *piece*; F. *pièce*. Cf. Ital. *pezza*. Span. *pieza*, Prov. *pessa*, *pesa*, Port. *peça*, a piece; Low L. *petium*, a piece of land (A. D. 730). Origin uncertain; Scheler draws attention to the use of Low L. *pedica* in the sense of 'piece of land;' which suggests a derivation from L. *pedi-*, crude form of *pes*, a foot. Cf. **Petiole**.

apiece, in a separate share. (E.; *and* F. – L.?) Put for *on piece*, i. e. in a piece; cf. *a-sleep* = *on sleep*, i. e. in sleep.

piece-meal. (F. – L.?; *and* E.) M. E. *pece-mele*, by pieces at a time. The M. E. suffix *-mele*, lit. 'by bits,' occurs in other compounds, and is also spelt *-melum*; from A. S. *mælum*, dat. pl. of *mæl*, a portion; see **Meal** (2).

Piepowder Court; see **Pedal**.

Pier, a mass of stone-work; see **Petrel**.

Pierce. (F. – L.?) M. E. *percen*. – F. *percer*; generally thought to be contracted from O. F. *pertuisier*, to pierce, lit. to make a hole. – O. F. *pertuis*, a hole (Ital. *pertugio*). The O. F. *pertuis* (like Ital. *pertugio*), answers to a Low L. *pertusium* *,

extended from L. *pertusus*, pp. of *pertundere*, to thrust through, pierce. (Ennius has *latu' pertudit hasta* = the spear pierced his side; White.) – L. *per*, through; *tundere*, to beat; see **Contuse**.

Piety; see **Pious**.

Pig. (E.?) M. E. *pigge*. A. S. *pecg* (in a charter of Swinford, copied into the Liber Albus at Wells; Earle). + Du. *bigge*; Low G. *bigge*, a pig, a little child; cf. Dan. *pige*, Swed. *pige*, Icel. *pika*, a girl. ¶ Certain masses of molten metal are called *sows* and *pigs*; hence *pig-iron*.

Pigeon; see **Pipe**.

Piggin, a small wooden vessel. (C.) Gael. *pigean*, a pitcher, jar; dimin. of *pige*, *pigeadh*, an earthen jar; Irish *pigin*, small pail, *pighead*, earthen jar; W. *picyn*, a piggin.

Pight, old form of *pitched*; see **Peak**.

Pigment; see **Picture**.

Pigmy; see **Pygmy**.

Pike; see **Peak**.

Pilaster; see **Pile** (2).

Pilch; see **Pell**.

Pilchard, a fish. (C.) Formerly *pilcher*. – Irish *pilseir*, a pilchard. Cf. W. *pilcod*, minnows.

Pilcrow, a curious corruption of **Paragraph**, q. v.

Pile (1), a tumour, lit. a ball. (L.) Only in the pl. *piles*. – L. *pila*, a ball.

pellet, a little ball. (F. – L.) M. E. *pelet*. – O. F. *pelote*, a tennis-ball. Dimin. from L. *pila*, a ball.

piles. (L.) Small tumours. See **Pile** (1) above.

pill (1), a little ball of medicine. (F. – L.) Short for *pilule*. – F. *pilule*, 'a pill;' Cot. – L. *pilula*, a little ball, globule; dimin. of *pila*, a ball.

platoon, a company of men. (F. – L.) F. *peloton*, a tennis-ball, also a group of men, a platoon. Dimin. of O. F. *pelote*, a tennis-ball; see **pellet** (above).

Pile (2), a pillar, heap, stake. (L.) M. E. *pile*; A. S. *pil*. – L. *pila*, a pillar, a pier of stone. The sense of stake is due to L. *pilum*, a javelin. ¶ The heraldic *pile* is a sharp stake. In the phrase *cross and pile* (of money), answering to the modern 'head and tail' (rather, *tail and head*), the *pile* took its name from the *pile* or short pillar on which the coin rested when struck; see Cotgrave, s.v. *pile*.

pilaster, a square pillar. (F. – Ital. – L.) F. *pilastre*. – Ital. *pilastro*, 'a pilaster, small piller;' Florio.—Ital. *pila*, 'a flat-sided pillar;' id.—L. *pila*, a pillar.

pillar. (F.—L.) M.E. *piler*.—O.F. *piler*, later *pilier*. (Span. *pilar*.)—Low L. *pilare*, a pillar.—L. *pila*, pillar, pier.

Pile (3), a hair, fibre of wool. (L.) L. *pilus*, a hair. Der. *three-piled*, L. L. L. v. 2. 407.

depilatory, removing hair. (L.) Formed, in imitation of O. F. *depilatoire* (Cot.), from a Low L. adj. *depilatorius**, not found. —L. *de*, away; *pilare*, to pluck away hair, from *pilus*, hair.

periwig, a peruke. (Du.—F.—Ital.—L.) Formerly *perwigge*, *perwicke* (Minsheu). This is a Du. form, from O. Du. *peruyk*, 'a perwig;' Sewel.—F. *perruque*; see below.

perruque. (F.—Ital.—L.) In use in the 17th cent.; *periwig* being earlier (in English).—F. *perruque*.—Ital. *parruca*, O. Ital. *parucca*, 'a periwig,' Florio; also spelt *perucca*, id. The same as Port. *peruca*, Span. *peluca*, Sardinian *pilucca*, orig. a mass of hair, and allied to O. Ital. *piluccare*, 'to pick or pull out haires or feathers one by one;' Florio. From Ital. *pelo*, hair.—L. *pilum*, acc. of *pilus*, a hair.

plush. (F.—L.) F. *peluche*, 'shag, plush;' Cot. The same as Span. *pelusa*, nap, Ital. *peluzzo*, soft down. All from a Low L. form *pilucius**, hairy, not found.—L. *pilus*, hair.

wig. (Du.—F.—Ital.—L.) Short for *periwig*, which see (above).

Piles; see **Pile** (1).

Pilfer; see **Pelf.**

Pilgrim; see **Agriculture.**

Pill (1), a globule; see **Pile** (1).

Pill (2), to plunder. (F.—L.) Also spelt *peel*; and, conversely, *peel*, to strip, is spelt *pill*; the words have been confused, but are really different; see **peel** (2) below. M. E. *pillen*, to plunder.—F. *piller*.—L. *pilare*, to plunder, pillage, not common. Prob. distinct from *pilare*, to deprive of hair. Der. *pill-age*, F. *pillage*.

compile. (F.—L.) O. F. *compiler*.— L. *compilare*, to plunder, pillage, rob; so that the word had, at first, a sinister meaning.—L. *com-* (*cum*), with; *pilare*, to rob.

peel (2), to pillage. (F.—L.) In Milton, P. L. iv. 136. Distinct from *peel*, to strip; another spelling of *pill* (above).

Pillage; see **Pill** (2).

Pillar; see **Pile** (2).

Pillion; see **Pell.**

Pillory. (F.) F. *pilori*, 'a pillory;' Cot. Of unknown origin; other remarkable variants occur, viz. Port. *pelourinho*, Prov. *espitlori*, Low L. *pilloricum*, *spiliorium*. There has clearly been a loss of initial *s*. Prob. from L. *specere*, to see.

Pillow. (L.) M.E. *pilwe*; A.S. *pyle*; both from L. *puluinus*, a cushion, pillow, bolster; whence also Du. *peuluw*, G. *pfühl*.

Pilot, one who conducts ships in and out of harbour. (F.—Du.) O.F. *pilot* (Cot.); F. *pilote*.—O. F. *piloter*, to take soundings (Palsgrave).—O. Du. *peilloot* (mod. Du. *peillood*, but *loot* for *lood* occurs in Hexham's O. Du. Dict.), a sounding-lead.—O. Du. *peylen*, contracted form of *pegelen*, to guage, from the sb. *pegel*, a guage; and O. Du. *loot*, mod. Du. *lood* (cf. G. *loth*), cognate with E. *lead*, a lead or plummet for sounding; see **Lead** (2). β. The form *pegel* is, however, rather Danish than Dutch; the Du. word seems borrowed from Dan. *pægel*, a half-pint measure, in which depths were measured by pegs in the side.—Dan. *pege*, to point; allied to Swed. *peka*, to point (and perhaps to E. *peg* and *peak*).

Pimento; see **Picture.**

Pimp; see **Pipe.**

Pimpernel, a flower. (F.—L.) O. F. *pimpernelle* (F. *pimprenelle*). Cf. Span. *pimpinela*, Ital. *pimpinella*. Diez considers these words to be borrowed from L. *bipinella* = *bipennula*, a dimin. of *bipennis*, i. e. double-winged. The pimpernel was confused with burnet (Prior), and the latter has from two to four scale-like bracts at the base of the calyx (Johns). If this be right, we refer the word to L. *bi-*, double; *penna*, a wing.

Pimple. (L.) A nasalised form of A.S. *pipel* (Cockayne). [The alleged A. S. *pinpel* is Lye's misprint for *winpel*!] Prob. not an E. word, but borrowed from L. *papula*, a pimple. Cf. Gk. πομφός, bubble, blister, Lithuan. *pampti*, to swell. Orig. sense 'swelling.' Note also Skt. *piplu*, a mole or freckle; F. *pompette*, 'a pumple or pimple on the nose or chin,' Cot.; and perhaps W. *pwmp*, a bump. (✓PAP.)

Pin; see **Pen** (2).

Pinch. (F.—C.?) F. *pincer*. A nasalised form of O. Ital. *pizzare*, Span. *pizcar*, to nip; cf. Ital. *pinzo*, a sting, goad. The orig. sense seems to have been a slight prick with a sharp-pointed instrument, from a Celtic base *pit*, a point, seen in W. *pid*, a tapering point. Hence also Du. *pitsen*, to pinch (Hexham). See **Petty**. Der. *pinch-ers* or *pinc-ers*; cf. F. *pinces*, 'a pair of pinchers;' Cot.

Pinchbeck, a metal. (Pers. name.) From the inventor, Mr. Chr. *Pinchbeck*, in the 18th century. From *Pinchbeck*, Lincolnsh.

Pindar, Pinner; see Pound (2).

Pine (1), a tree; see **Pitch** (1).

Pine (2), to waste away; see **Pain**.

Pinfold; see Pound (2).

Pinion; see Pen (2).

Pink (1), to pierce, prick. (C. − L. ?) M. E. *pinken*, to prick. A nasalised form of *pick*, in the sense 'to peck,' from a Celtic source; cf. Gael. and Irish *pioc*, W. *pigo*, Corn. *piga*, to prick, sting; see **pick**, s. v. **Peak**. We may note E. *pink*, to cut round holes or eyes in silk cloth (Bailey), as equivalent to O. F. *piquer*, the same (Cotgrave). ¶ Not from A. S. *pyngan*, M. E. *pingen*, to prick, which is borrowed from L. *pungere*.

Pink (2), half-shut, applied to the eyes. (Du. − C. − L.) Obsolete; cf. '*pink* eyne,' Antony, ii. 7. 121. − O. Du. *pincken* (also *pinck-oogen*), to shut the eyes (Hexham). The notion is that of narrowing, bringing to a point or peak, making small; from a Celtic source; see **Peak**. Cf. prov. E. *pink*, a very small fish, minnow.

Pink (3), the name of a flower, and of a colour. (C. − L.) As in *violet, mauve*, the name of the colour is due to that of the flower. The flower is named from the delicately cut or *peaked* edges of the petals; see **Pink** (1). β. Similarly, F. *pince*, a pink, is from F. *pincer*, to pinch, nip; but F. *pince* and E. *pink* are not the same word; their ultimate source is, however, much the same; see **Pinch**.

Pink (4), a kind of boat. (Du.) See Nares. Short for O. Du. *espincke*, also written *pincke*, 'a pinke, or a small fisher's boat,' Hexham. The same word as Icel. *espingr*, Swed. *esping*, a long boat; named from Icel. *espi*, aspen-wood, O. Du. *espe*, an aspen-tree. See **Aspen**.

Pink-eyed, having small eyes; see Pink (2).

Pinnace; see Pitch (1).

Pinnacle, Pinnate; see Pen (2).

Pint; see Picture.

Pioneer; see Pedal.

Piony, the same as Peony.

Pious. (F. − L.) F. *pieux*; O. F. *pius*, taken directly from L. *pius*, holy, devout (not from a form *piosus* *).

expiate. (L.) From pp. of L. *expiare*, to atone for fully. − L. *ex*, fully ; *piare*, to propitiate, from *pius*, devout.

piacular, expiatory. (L.) L. *piacularis*, adj., from *piaculum*, an expiation. − L. *piare*, to propitiate (above).

piety. (F. − L.) F. *piété*. − L. *pietatem*, acc. of *pietas*, devoutness. − L. *pius*, devout.

pity. (F. − L.) M. E. *pitee*. − O. F. *pite, pitet* (12th cent.). − L. *pietatem* (above). Doublet, *piety*. Der. *pite-ous*, put for M. E. *pitous*, from O. F. *piteus* = Low L. *pietosus*, merciful.

Pip (1), a disease of fowls. (F. − L.) M. E. *pippe*. − O. F. *pepie*, 'pip;' Cot. (Span. *pepita*, Port. *pevide*, Ital. *pipita*.) − L. *pituita*, phlegm, rheum, also the pip (whence first *pivita*, and afterwards *pipita*). Hence also Du. *pip*; Swed. *pipp*, &c. β. L. *pituita* is from a verbal stem *pitu-* = *sputu-*, from *sputus*, pp. of *spuere*, to spit out. Allied to **Spew**.

Pip (2), the seed of fruit. (F. − L. − Gk.) Short for *pippin* or *pepin*, the old name. − F. *pepin*, a pip. Allied to Span. *pepita*, a pip [quite distinct from *pepita*, pip in fowls]; and prob. to Span. *pepino*, a cucumber. β. There seems to be no doubt that *pepin* was first applied to the remarkable seeds of the cucumber and melon ; and is derived from L. *pepo*, a melon, borrowed from Gk. πέπων, a melon. γ. This Gk. πέπων was orig. an adj., signifying 'ripened' or 'ripe; from πέπτειν, to cook, to ripen, allied to Skt. *pach*, L. *coquere*, to cook. See **Cook**.

pippin, a kind of tart apple. (F. − L. − Gk.) Named from seed-pips ; the old sense of *pippin* was a pip; see above. 'Perhaps an apple raised from the pip or seed ;' Wedgwood. (So Arnold's Chron.)

Pip (3), a spot on cards; see **Peak**.

Pipe, a musical instrument formed of a long tube; hence a tube. (E.) M. E. *pipe*. A. S. *pipe*. An imitative word. So also Irish and Gael. *piob*, Irish *pib*, W. *pib* ; Du. *pijp*, Icel. *pipa*, Swed. *pipa*, Dan. *pibe*, G. *pfeife*. Also L. *pipire*, Gk. πιπίζειν, to chirp. From the cry *pi-pi* of a young bird.

peep (1), to chirp, cry like a chicken. (F. − L.) M. E. *pipen*. − O. F. *piper*, also *pepier*, to chirp as a bird. − L. *pipare*, *pipire*, to chirp (above). See also Peep (2).

pibroch, a martial tune. (Gael.) Gael.

piobaireachd, a pipe-tune, tune on the bag-pipe. — Gael. *piobair*, a piper. — Gael. *piob*, a pipe (above).

pigeon, a bird. (F. — L.) F. *pigeon*, a pigeon, a dove. — L. *pipionem*, acc. of *pipio*, lit. 'chirper.' — L. *pipire*, to chirp (above).

pimp, a pandar. (F. — L.) Orig. a smartly dressed fellow. — F. *pimper*, to dress up smartly. A nasalised form of F. *piper*, to pipe, also to beguile, cheat; cf. also Prov. *pimpar*, to render elegant, from *pimpa*, sb. (equivalent to F. *pipeau*) meaning (1) a pipe, (2) a bird-call, (3) a snare; besides which, F. *piper* meant to excel in a thing. Note also F. *pimpant*, smart, spruce; and see Littré. — L. *pipare*, to chirp (hence to pipe).

pipkin, a small earthen pot. (E.) A dimin. (with suffix -*kin*) of E. *pipe*, in the sense of cask. This particular sense of *pipe* may have been imported; it occurs both in F. and Du.; see *pipe* in Cotgrave, *pijpe* in Hexham.

pivot, a pin on which a wheel, &c. turns. (F. — Ital. — Low L.) F. *pivot*. Formed, with dimin. suffix -*ot*, from Ital. *piva*, a pipe, weakened form of *pipa*, a pipe. The Ital. *piva* meant (1) a pipe, (2) a tube with fine bore, (3) a solid peg. — Low L. *pipa*, a pipe; allied to L. *pipare*, to chirp; see **Pipe** (above).

Pipkin; see **Pipe**.

Pippin; see **Pip** (2).

Pique, Piquet; see **Peak**.

Pirate. (F. — L. — Gk.) F. *pirate*. — L. *pirata*. — Gk. πειρατής, one who attempts, one who attacks, a pirate. — Gk. πειράω, I attempt. — Gk. πεῖρα, an attempt. (√ PAR.)

Pirogue, a sort of canoe. (F. — W. Indian.) F. *pirogue* (Span. *piragua*). From the native W. Indian name; said to be Caribbean.

Pirouette, a whirling round, quick turn. (F.) F. *pirouette*, 'a whirling about, also a whirligig;' Cot. Dimin. of the Guernsey word *piroue*, a little wheel or whirligig (Métivier). Confused in spelling with F. *roue* (L. *rota*) a wheel; but clearly allied to M. E. *pirie*, a whirlwind or great storm, *pirle*, *prille*, a child's whirligig; cf. also F. *birrasque*, a tempest at sea, caused by whirlwinds (Cot.). All from the imitative word *pirr* or *birr*, as in Scotch *pirr*, a gentle wind, Icel. *byrr*, wind, E. *birr*, *buzz*, *purr*. From the whirring sound.

Pisces, the Fish. (L.) L. *pisces*, pl. of *piscis*, a fish; cognate with E. **Fish**, q. v.

Pish! (E.) Of imitative origin; beginning with expulsion of breath, and ending in a hiss.

Pismire; see **Piss**.

Piss. (F.) F. *pisser*; supposed to be a Romance word, and of imitative origin.

pismire, an ant. (F. *and* Scand.) The old name of the ant; from the strong urinous smell of an anthill. The first syllable is from F. *pisser* (above). β. The second is M. E. *mire*, an ant; from Swed. *myra*, Dan. *myre*, Icel. *maurr*, an ant. This word for 'ant' is widely spread; cf. Irish *moirbh*, W. *mor-grugyn*, Russ. *muravei*, Gk. μύρμηξ, an ant; Corn. *murrian*, ants.

Pistachio, Pistacho, the nut of a certain tree. (Span. — L. — Gk. — Pers.) Span. *pistacho*. — L. *pistacium*. — Gk. πιστάκιον, a nut of the tree called πιστάκη. — Pers. *pistah*, the pistachio nut.

Pistil, in a flower. (L.) Named from the resemblance in shape to the pestle of a mortar. — L. *pistillum*, a small pestle, dimin. of an obsolete form *pistrum**, a pestle. — L. *pistum*, supine of *pinsere*, to pound. + Gk. πτίσσειν, Skt. *pish*, to pound. (√ PIS.)

pestle. (F. — L.) M. E. *pestel*. — O. F. *pestel*, later *pesteil* (Cot.). — L. *pistillum* (above).

piston. (F. — Ital. — L.) F. *piston*, 'a pestell,' Cot.; also a piston. — Ital. *pistone*, a piston; *pestone*, a large pestle. — Ital. *pestare*, Late L. *pistare*, to pound. — L. *pistus*, pp. of *pinsere*, to pound.

Pistol, a small hand-gun. (F. — Ital.) F. *pistole*. — Ital. *pistola*, 'a dag or pistoll;' Florio. We also find O. Ital. *pistolese*, 'a great dagger,' in Florio; and it is agreed that the name was first applied to a dagger, and thence transferred to the pistol, which even in E. was at first called a *dag* (F. *dague*, a dagger). A pistol is to a gun what a dagger is to a sword. β. The Ital. *pistolese* (= Low L. *pistolensis*) means ' belonging to Pistola;' so also Ital. *pistola* is from *Pistola*, now called *Pistoja*, a town in Tuscany, near Florence. The Old Lat. name of the town was *Pistoria*.

pistole, a gold coin of Spain. (F. — Ital.) The name, however, is not Spanish, but French, and the coins were at first called *pistolets*. The name is of jocular origin. — F. *pistolet*, a little pistol, also a pistolet; Cot. Diez explains that the crowns of Spain, being reduced to a smaller size than the French crowns, were called *pistolets*, and the smallest *pistolets* were called *bidets*; cf. F. *bidet*, 'a small pistoll;' Cot. — F. *pistole*, a pistol; see above.

Piston; see **Pistil**.

Pit. (L.) M. E. *pit*, *put*; A. S. *pyt.* — L. *puteus*, a well, pit (Luke, xiv. 5). Perhaps a spring of pure water, from L. *putus*, pure, allied to *purus*; see **Pure**. Der. *pit*, verb, to set in competition, from the setting of cocks to fight in a *pit*.

Pitapat. (E.) A reduplication of *pat*, weakened to *pit* in the first instance.

Pitch (1), a black sticky substance. (L.) M. E. *pich*; older form *pik*; A. S. *pic.* — L. *pic-*, stem of *pix*, pitch. **+** Gk. πίσσα (for πίκ-γα), Lithuan. *pikkis*, pitch.

pay (2), to pitch the seam of a ship. (Span. — L.) Span. *pega*, a varnish of pitch; *empegar*, to pitch. Here *empegar* is from L. *picare*, to pitch (with prefix *em-* = L. *in*). — L. *pic-*, stem of *pix*, pitch. ¶ The M. E. word for 'pitch' is *peis*, *peys*, from O. F. *pois*, pitch, from L. acc. *picem*.

pine (1), a tree. (L.) A. S. *pin.* — L. *pinus*, a pine; put for *pic-nus**. — L. *pic-*, stem of *pix*, pitch. Thus *pine* = pitch-tree.

pinnace. (F. — Ital. — L.) F. *pinasse*, 'the pitch-tree; also a pinnace;' Cot. — O. Ital. *pinaccia*, a pinnace (Florio). So named because made of pine. — L. *pinus*, a pine.

Pitch (2), to throw; see **Peak**.

Pitcher; see **Beaker**.

Pith. (E.) M. E. *pithe*. A. S. *piða*, pith. **+** Du. *pit*, O. Du. *pitte*, Low G. *peddik*.

Pittance, a dole. (F.) M. E. *pitaunce*. — F. *pitance*, 'meat, food, victuall of all sorts, bread and drinke excepted;' Cot. Cf. Span *pitanza*; Ital. *pietanza* (which is prob. corrupted by a supposed connection with *pietà*, pity); also Span. *pitar*, to distribute or dole out allowances. β. Ducange explains Low L. *pictantia* as a pittance, orig. a dole of the value of a *picta*, which was a very small coin issued by the counts of Poitiers (Pictava). If this be right, the etymology is from *Pictava*, Poitiers.

Pity; see **Pious**.

Pivot; see **Pipe**.

Placable; see **Please**.

Placard. (F. — Du.) F. *placard*, *plaquard*, 'a placard, inscription set up; also rough-cast on walls;' Cot. — F.

plaquer, to rough-cast; also to stick or paste on; Cot. — F. *plaque*, a flat ingot or bar, flat plate. — Du. *plak*, a ferula, a slice (hence, a thin plate); whence *plakken*, to glue or fasten up, formerly 'to plaister,' Hexham.

Place; see **Plate**.

Placenta; see **Plain**.

Placid; see **Please**.

Plagiary. (F. — L.) F. *plagiaire*, one who kidnaps; also 'a book-theef;' Cot. — L. *plagiarius*, a kidnapper. — L. *plagium*, kidnapping; *plagiare*, to ensnare. — L. *plaga*, a net. *Plaga* is for *placa**, from √ PLAK, to weave; see **Plait**.

Plague. (L.) M. E. *plage.* — L. *plaga*, a stroke, blow, injury, disaster. **+** Gk. πληγή, a blow, plague, Rev. xvi. 21; from πλήσσειν (= πλήκ-γειν), to strike; cf. L. *plangere*, to strike. (√ PLAK.)

apoplexy. (Low L. — Gk.) Low L. *apoplexia.* — Gk. ἀποπληξία, stupor, apoplexy. — Gk. ἀποπλήσσειν, to cripple by a stroke. — Gk. ἀπό, off; πλήσσειν, to strike (above).

complain. (F. — L.) O. F. *complaindre.* — Low L. *complangere*, to bewail. — L. *com-* (*cum*), with; *plangere*, to bewail, lit. to strike, beat the breast.

plaint, a lament. (F. — L.) M. E. *pleinte.* — O. F. *pleinte.* — Low L. *plancta*, allied to L. *planctus*, lamentation. — L. *planctus*, pp. of *plangere* (above).

plaintiff. (F. — L.) M. E. *plaintif.* — F. *plaintif*, 'a plaintiff;' Cot. Formed with suffix -*if* (L. -*iuus*), from *planctus*, pp. of *plangere* (above).

plaintive. (F. — L.) F. *plaintive*, fem. of F. *plaintif* (above).

Plaice; see **Plate**.

Plaid; see **Pell**.

Plain, flat, evident. (F. — L.) F. *plain.* — L. *planus*, flat. *Plānus* stands for *placnus**; cf. Gk. πλάξ (stem πλακ-), a flat place. (Base PLAK, flat.)

esplanade, a level space. (F. — Ital. — L.) O. F. *esplanade*, 'a planing, levelling, evenning of ways;' Cot. Formed from O. F. *esplaner*, to level; the suffix being due to an imitation of Ital. *spianata*, an esplanade, a levelled way, from *spianare*, to level. — L. *explanare*, to level. — L. *ex*, out; *planare*, to level, from *planus*, flat.

explain. (F. — L.) O. F. *explaner*, Cot. — L. *explanare*, to make plain. — L. *ex*, thoroughly; *planare*, to make plain, lit. to flatten, from *planus*, flat.

pianoforte, piano. (Ital. — L.) So called from producing *soft* and *loud* effects. — Ital. *piano*, soft; *forte*, strong, loud. — L. *planus*, level (hence smooth, soft); *fortis*, strong; see Force.

placenta, a substance in the womb. (L.) L. *placenta*, lit. a flat cake. **+** Gk. πλακοῦς, a flat cake, from πλάξ, a flat surface; see Plain.

plan. (F. — L.) F. *plan*, 'the ground-plat of a building;' Cot. — F. *plan*, flat; later form of O. F. *plain*. — L. *planum*, acc. of *planus*, flat. Properly, a drawing (for a building) on a flat surface.

plane (1), a level surface. (F. — L.) F. *plane*, fem. of *plan*, flat (above). — L. *plana*, fem. of *planus*, flat.

plane (2), a tool; also to render a surface level. (F. — L.) M. E. *plane*, a tool. — F. *plane*. — Late L. *plana*, a tool for planing. 2. We find also M. E. *planen*, to plane. — F. *planer*. — L. *planare*, to plane (White). — L. *planus*, flat.

planisphere, a sphere projected on a plane. (L. *and* Gk.) From L. *planus*, flat; E. *sphere*, of Gk. origin; see Sphere.

plank, a board. (L.) M. E. *planke*. — L. *planca*, a flat board. Nasalised from the base *plac-*, flat; see Plain, Placenta (above).

Plaint, Plaintiff, Plaintive; see Plague.

Plait; see Ply.

Plan, Plane; see Plain.

Plane (3), a tree; see Plate.

Planet. (F. — L. — Gk.) M. E. *planete*. — O. F. *planete*. — L. *planeta*. — Gk. πλανήτης, a wanderer; also πλανής, a wanderer; the pl. πλάνητες means the wandering stars or planets. — Gk. πλανάομαι, I wander. — Gk. πλάνη, wandering. Perhaps for πάλνη; cf. L. *palari*, to wander.

Plane-tree; see Plate.

Planisphere, Plank; see Plain.

Plant, Plantain, Plantigrade; see Plate.

Plash (1), a puddle, shallow pool. (O. Low G.) M. E. *plasche*. — O. Du. *plasch*, a plash, pool; *plasschen in 't water*, to plash or plunge in the water; Hexham. Cf. also G. *platschen*, Dan. *pladske* (for *platske**), Swed. *plaska* (for *platska**), to dabble; from the base PLAT, to strike, seen in A. S. *plættan* or *plættian*, to strike; see Pat. Compare *plod*.

Plash (2), to pleach; see Ply.

Plaster, Plastic; see Plate.

Plat (1), **Plot**, a patch of ground; see Plot.

Plat (2), to plait; see Ply.

Platane, a plane-tree. (L.) L. *platanus*.

Plate, a thin piece of metal, flat dish. (F. — Gk.) M. E. *plate*. — O. F. *plate*; properly the fem. of *plat*, flat. Cf. Low L. *plata*, a lamina, plate of metal; Span. *plata*, plate, silver; but the Span. word was borrowed from French. — Gk. πλατύς, flat, broad; whence also Du. Dan. *plat*, G. Swed. *platt*, flat. **+** Lithuan. *platus*, broad; Skt. *prithus*, large. (√PRAT.)

pate, the head. (F. — G. — Gk.) M. E. *pate*; the etymology is disguised by loss of *l*; *pate* stands for *plate*, i. e. the crown of the head. — O. F. *pate*, not recorded in the special sense of 'head,' but explained by 'plate' in Cotgrave. — G. *platte*, a plate, a bald pate, in vulgar language, the head (Flügel); M. H. G. *plate*, a plate, shaven pate; Low L. *platta*, the clerical tonsure. All from Gk. πλατύς, flat, broad (above).

piastre. (F. — Ital. — L. — Gk.) F. *piastre*. — Ital. *piastra*, plate of metal, also a piastre or coin; allied to Ital. *piastro*, a plaster, Low L. *plastreus*, made of plaster. — L. *emplastrum*, a plaster; see plaster (below).

piazza. (Ital. — L. — Gk.) Ital. *piazza*, a market-place, chief street. — L. *platea*; see place (below).

place. (F. — L. — Gk.) F. *place*. — L. *platea*, a broad way, a courtyard. — Gk. πλατεῖα, a broad way; fem. of πλατύς, broad. **¶** A *place* was orig. a courtyard or square, a piazza.

plaice, a fish. (F. — L.) O. F. *plaïs*. — L. *platessa*, a plaice; so called from its flatness. From the base *plat-*, as seen in Gk. πλατύς, flat, broad.

plane (3), a tree. (F. — L. — Gk.) M. E. *plane*. — F. *plane*. — L. *platanum*, acc. of *platanus*, a plane. — Gk. πλάτανος, a plane; named from its spreading form. — Gk. πλατύς, wide.

plant. (L.) M. E. *plante*. A. S. *plante*. — L. *planta*, a plant; properly, a spreading sucker or shoot. From the base *plat-*; see plaice (above).

plantain. (F. — L.) F. *plantain*. — L. *plantaginem*, acc. of *plantago*, a plantain. Named from its spreading leaf; allied to plant (above).

plantigrade, walking on the sole of the foot. (L.) From *planti-*, for *planta*, the sole or *flat* part of the foot; *grad-i*, to walk. *Planta* is from the base *plat-*, flat; see **plant, plaice**.

plaster. (L. — Gk.) M. E. *plastre*; A. S. *plaster.* [Also spelt *plaister* = O. F. *plaistre.*] — L. *emplastrum*, a plaster for wounds, the first syllable being dropped. — Gk. ἔμπλαυτρον, a plaster, a form used by Galen instead of ἔμπλαστον, a plaster, neut. of ἔμπλαστος, daubed on or over. — Gk. ἐμπλάσσειν, to daub on. — Gk. ἐμ- (for ἐν), on; πλάσσειν, to mould, form in clay or wax. Here πλάσσειν = πλατ-γειν *, orig. to spread flat, from πλατύς, flat.

plastic. (L. — Gk.) L. *plasticus.* — Gk. πλαυτικός, fit for moulding. — Gk. πλάσσειν, to mould (above).

plateau, a flat space. (F. — Gk.) F. *plateau*, for O. F. *platel*, a small plate; dimin. of *plat*, a plate. — F. *plat*, flat. — Gk. πλατύς, broad; see **Plate** (above).

platform, a flat surface, level scaffolding; formerly, a ground-plan, plan. (F. — Gk. *and* L.) F. *plateforme*, 'a platform, modell;' Cot. — F. *plate*, fem. of *plat*, flat; *forme*, form. See above; and see **Form**.

platina, a metal. (Span. — F. — Gk.) Span. *platina*; named from its silvery appearance. — Span. *plata*, silver. — O. F. *plate*, hammered plate, also silver plate; see **Plate** (above).

platitude. (F. — Gk.) F. *platitude*, flatness, insipidity. Coined from F. *plat*, flat; see **Plate** (above).

platter, a flat plate. (F. — Gk.) M. E. *plater.* — O. F. *platel*, a plate (with change from *l* to *r*); dimin. of *plat*, a plate; see **plateau** (above).

replace. (F. — L. *and* Gk.) From *re-* (F. *re-*, L. *re-*), again, and **place** (above).

supplant. (F. — L.) F. *supplanter.* — L. *supplantare*, to trip up. — L. *sup-* (*sub*) under; *planta*, the sole of the foot.

transplant. (F. — L.) F. *transplanter.* — L. *trans-plantare*, to plant in a new place; see **plant** (above).

Plateau, Platform; see **Plate**.

Platina, Platitude; see **Plate**.

Platoon; see **Pile** (1).

Platter; see **Plate**.

Plaudit, applause. (L.) Due to mis-reading L. *plaudite* as if it were an E. word, with silent *e*. Formerly *plaudite* or *plaudity*. — L. *plaudite*, clap your hands; 2 pers. pl. imp. of *plaudere* (also *plodere*), to applaud.

applaud. (L.) L. *applaudere*, to applaud, pp. *applausus* (whence E. *applause*). — L. *ap-* (for *ad*), to, at; *plaudere* (above).

explode, to drive away noisily, burst. (F. — L.) O. F. *exploder*, 'to explode, publicly to disgrace or drive out;' Cot. — L. *explodere*, pp. *explosus*, to drive off the stage by noise (the old sense in E.). — L. *ex*, away; *plodere, plaudere*, to clap hands. Der. *explos-ive, -ion.*

plausible. (L.) L. *plausibilis*, praiseworthy. — L. *plausi-*, for *plausus*, pp. of *plaudere*, to clap; with suffix *-bilis*.

Play, a game. (E.; *perhaps* L.) M. E. *play.* A. S. *plega*, a game, sport; also (commonly), a fight, battle. Cf. A. S. *plegian*, to strike, clap; *plegian mid handum*, to clap hands. β. I suspect this to be merely a borrowed word, from L. *plaga*, a stroke; see **Plague**. ¶ Some connect it with *plight*; which is doubtful.

Plea; see **Please**.

Pleach, Plash; see **Ply**.

Plead; see **Please**.

Please. (F. — L.) M. E. *plesen.* — O. F. *plesir, plaisir*, to please (F. *plaire*). — L. *placere*, to please. Allied to *placare*, to appease. Perhaps allied to **Pray**. Der. *pleas-ant*, from O. F. *plesant*, pleasing, pres. pt. of *plesir*; also *dis-please.*

complacent. (L.) From stem of pres. pt. of *com-placere*, to please.

complaisant. (F. — L.) F. *complaisant*, obsequious, pres. part. of *complaire*, to please. — L. *com-placere*, to please.

placable. (L.) L. *placabilis*, easy to be appeased. — L. *placare*, to appease.

placid. (F. — L.) F. *placide*, 'calm;' Cot. — L. *placidus*, pleasing, gentle. — L. *placere*, to please.

plea, an excuse. (F. — L.) M. E. *plee, play.* — O. F. *ple, plai*, occasional forms of O. F. *plait, plaid*, a plea. — Low L. *placitum*, a decree, sentence, &c. (with numerous meanings), orig. a decision, that which has seemed good. — L. *placitum*, neut. of *placitus*, pp. of *placere*, to please.

plead. (F. — L.) M. E. *pleden.* — O. F. *plaider*, to plead, argue. — O. F. *plaid*, a plea; see **plea** above.

pleasure. (F. — L.) An E. spelling of F. *plaisir*, pleasure (like E. *leisure* for F. *loisir*). This F. sb. is merely the infin. mood used substantively. — L. *placere*; see **Please.**

Pleat, Plait; see **Ply**.

Plebeian, vulgar. (F. — L.) O. F. *plebeien* (F. *plébéien*); formed, with suffix *-en* (L. *-anus*) from L. *plebeius*, adj., from *plebes*, more commonly *plebs*, the people.

Orig. 'a crowd;' allied to *plerique*, many, and to **Plenary**. (√PAR.)

Pledge, a security, surety. (F. − L.) M. E. *plegge*, a hostage, security. − O. F. *plege*, a surety (F. *pleige*). Allied to O. F. *plevir*, later *pleuvir*, to warrant. The O. F. *plevir* answers to L. *præbere*, to afford; and O. F. *plege* to a Lat. form *præbium** (Diez). So also Prov. *plevizo* = L. *præbitio*, a provision. See further under **Prebend**. ¶ This etymology has much in its favour; we cannot derive O. F. *plege* from L. *prædium* or *præs*, a pledge.

replevy, to return detained goods on a pledge to try the right in a suit. (F. − L.) F. *re-* (L. *re-*), again; *plevir*, to be surety (above).

Pleiocene, Pleistocene; see **Pleonasm**.

Plenary, full. (Low L. − L.) Low L. *plenarius*, entire. − L. *plenus*, full. ✛ Gk. πλέ-ως, full. (√PAR.)

accomplish. (F. − L.) M. E. *accomplisen*. − O. F. *acomplis-*, stem of pres. pt. of *acomplir*, to complete. − L. *ad*, to; *complere*, to fulfil; see **complete** (below).

complement. (L.) L. *complementum*, that which completes. − L. *complere* (below).

complete, perfect. (L.) L. *completus*, pp. of *complere*, to fulfil. − L. *com-* (*cum*), together; *plere*, to fill. Allied to *ple-nus*, full.

compliance, compliant; formed with suffixes *-ance, -ant*, from the verb to *comply*, which, however, is not of F. origin; see **comply** (below).

compline. (F. − L.) M. E. *complin*, the last church-service of the day; it is orig. an adj. (like *gold-en* from *gold*), and stands for *complin song*; the sb. is *complie* (Ancren Riwle). − O. F. *complie*, (mod. F. *complies*, which is pl.), compline. − Low L. *completa*, fem. of *completus*, complete; because it completed the day's service; see **complete** (above).

compliment. (F. − Ital. − L.) F. *compliment*. − Ital. *complimento*, compliment, civility. − Ital. *complire*, to fill up, to suit. − L. *com-plere*, to fill up; see **complete** (above).

comply, to yield, agree, accord. (Ital. − L.) It has no doubt been supposed to be allied to *ply* (whence *compliant*, by analogy with *pliant*), but is quite distinct, and of Ital. origin. − Ital. *complire*, to fill up, fulfil, to suit, also 'to use compliments,

ceremonies, or kind offices and offers;' Florio. Cf. Span. *complir*, to fulfil, satisfy. − L. *complere*, to fill up; see **complete** (above.) Cf. *supply* (below.)

depletion. (L.) '*Depletion*, an emptying;' Blount. Formed, in imitation of *repletion*, from L. *depletus*, pp. of *deplere*, to empty. − L. *de*, away; *plere*, to fill.

expletive. (L.) L. *expletiuus*, filling up. − L. *expletus*, pp. of *ex-plere*, to fill up.

implement, a tool. (Low L. − L.) Low L. *implementum*, an accomplishing; hence, means for accomplishing. − L. *implere*, to fill in, execute. − L. *im-* (for *in*), in; *plere*, to fill.

plenipotentiary, having full powers. (L.) Coined from L. *pleni-*, for *pleno-*, crude form of *plenus*, full; and *potenti-*, crude form of *potens*, powerful; see **Potent**.

plenitude, fulness. (F. − L.) F. *plenitude*. − L. *plenitudo*, fulness. − L. *pleni-*, for *plenus*, full; with suffix *-tudo*.

plenty, abundance. (F. − L.) M. E. *plentee*. − O. F. *plente*, *plentet*. − L. *plenitatem*, acc. of *plenitas*, fulness. − L. *pleni-*, for *plenus*, full. Der. *plenteous*, M. E. *plenteus*, often spelt *plentivous*, from O. F. *plentivose* (Burguy); from O. F. *plentif*, answering to Low L. form *plenitiuus*.

replenish. (F. − L.) O. F. *repleniss-*, stem of pres. pt. of *replenir*, to fill up again; now obsolete. − L. *re-*, again; Low L. *plenire**, from L. *plenus*, full.

replete, full. (F. − L.) F. *replet*, masc.; *replete*, fem., full. − L. *repletus*, filled up; pp. of *re-plere*, to fill again.

supplement. (F. − L.) F. *supplément*; Cot. − L. *supplementum*, a filling up. − L. *supplere*, to fill up. − L. *sup-* (*sub*), up; *plere*, to fill.

supply. (F. − L.) Formerly *supploy* (Levins). − F. *suppléer*, to supply; Cot. − L. *supplere*, to fill up (above).

Plenitude, Plenty; see **Plenary**.

Pleonasm. (L. − Gk.) L. *pleonasmus*. − Gk. πλεονασμός, abundance. − Gk. πλεονάζειν, to abound, lit. to be more. − Gk. πλέον, neut. of πλέων, πλείων, more, comparative of πλέως, full. ✛ L. *plenus*, full. See **Plenary**.

pleiocene, more recent, **pleistocene**, most recent. (Gk.) From Gk. πλείω-ν, more, or πλεῖστο-s, most; and καινός, recent, new. Πλείων, πλεῖστος are comp. and superl. of πλέως, full.

Plethora, excessive fulness, esp. of blood. (L. — Gk.) L. *plethōra*. — Gk. πληθώρη, fulness. — Gk. πλῆθ-ος, a throng, crowd; allied to πλήρης, full.

Pleurisy, inflammation of the *pleura*, or membrane which covers the lungs. (F. — L. — Gk.) F. *pleuresie*. — L. *pleurīsis*; also *pleuritis*. — Gk. πλευρῖτις, pleurisy. — Gk. πλευρά, a rib, side, pleura. Der. *pleurit-ic*, from πλευρῖτ-ις; *pleuro-pneumonia*, inflammation of pleura and lungs, from πνεύμων, a lung; see Pneumatic.

Pliable, Pliant; see Ply.

Plight (1), pledge; hence, as vb., to pledge. (E.) M. E. *pliht*, danger, also engagement, pledge. A. S. *pliht*, risk, danger. Formed, with suffix *-t* (Aryan *-ta*), from the A. S. strong verb *plión*, pt. t. *pleah*, to risk; cf. A. S. *plió*, danger. + O. Du. *plicht*, duty, debt, use; *plegen*, to be accustomed; G. *pflicht*, duty, from O. H. G. *plegan*, to promise or engage to do. Der. *plight*, verb, A. S. *plihtan*, weak verb, from *pliht*, sb.

Plight (2), to fold; as sb., a fold, also state, condition. M. E. *plite*. See Ply.

Plinth, the lowest part of the base of a column. (F. — L. — Gk.; *or* L. — Gk.) F. *plinthe*. — L. *plinthus*. — Gk. πλίνθος, a brick, tile, plinth. Allied to **Flint**.

Plod. (C.) Orig. to splash through water or mud; hence, to trudge on laboriously, toil onward. From M. E. *plod*, a puddle. — Irish *plod*, *plodan*, a pool; *plodach*, a puddle, whence *plodanachd*, paddling in water; Gael. *plod*, *plodan*, a pool. Perhaps allied to **Plash** (1).

Plot (1), a conspiracy; see Ply.

Plot (2), **Plat**, a small piece of ground. (E.) A. S. *plot*, a plot of ground; Cockayne's Leechdoms, iii. 286. Allied to Goth. *plats*, a patch, and a mere variant of Patch, q. v. Cf. prov. E. *pleck*, a place, *plock*, a small meadow.

Plough. (Scand. — C. ?) M. E. *plouh*, *plow*; also A. S. *ploh*, rare, and borrowed. — Icel. *plógr*, a plough (also prob. a borrowed word); Swed. *plog*, Dan. *plov*. So also O. Fries. *ploch*, G. *pflug*; (Lithuan. *plugas*, Russ. *pluge* are borrowed from Teutonic). β. But Grimm has grave doubts as to its being a true Teut. word; I suspect it to be Celtic, from Gael. *ploc*, a block of wood, stump of a tree (hence, a primitive plough); see Block.

Plover; see Pluvial.

Pluck, to snatch. (E.) M. E. *plukken*.

A. S. *pluccian*, Matt. xii. 1.+Du. *plukken*, Icel. *plokka*, *plukka* (perhaps borrowed), Dan. *plukke*, Swed. *plocka*, G. *pflücken*. (Base PLUK.) ¶ A Teut. word; obviously, A. S. *pluccian* cannot be borrowed from Ital. *piluccare* (!), as some think. Der. *pluck*, sb., a butcher's term for the heart, liver, and lights of an animal, whence mod. E. *pluck*, courage, *plucky*, adj.

Plug; see Block.

Plum; see Prune (2).

Plumage; see Plume.

Plumb, a lead on a string, as a plummet. (F. — L.) Formerly *plomb*; M. E. *plom*. — F. *plomb*, 'lead, a plummet;' Cot. — L. *plumbum*, lead. Cf. Gk. μόλυβος, μόλυβδος, lead. Der. *plumb*, verb, to sound a depth; *plumb-er*, sb., F. *plombier*.

plumbago, blacklead. (L.) L. *plumbago*, a kind of leaden ore. — L. *plumbum*.

plummet. (F. — L.) M. E. *plommet*. — F. *plombet*; dimin. of *plomb*, lead; see Plumb (above).

plump (2), straight downward. (F. — L.) Formerly *plum*, *plumb*; Milton, P. L. ii. 933. — F. *à plomb*, downright (cf. Ital. *cadere a piombo*, to fall plump, lit. like lead). — F. *plomb*, lead (above). Der. *plump*, verb, to fall heavily down; so also G. *plumpen*, Swed. *plumpa*, &c., to fall plump, are all due to L. *plumbum*, lead.

plunge. (F. — L.) F. *plonger*, 'to plunge, dive;' Cot. Formed from a Low L. *plumbicare* *, not found, but verified by Picard *plonquer*, to plunge; see Diez, s. v. *piombare*. A frequentative form from L. *plumbum*, lead; cf. Ital. *piombare*, to throw, hurl, fall heavily like lead, from *piombo*, lead.

Plumbago; see Plumb.

Plume. (F. — L.) F. *plume*. — L. *pluma*, a small feather, down. (√ PLU, to float.)

plumage. (F. — L.) F. *plumage*, 'feathers;' Cot. — F. *plume* (above).

Plummet; see Plumb.

Plump (1), full, round, fleshy. (E. *or* O. Low G.) M. E. *plomp*, rude, clownish; also *plump*, sb., a cluster or clump. The word seems to be E., as the prov. E. *plim*, to swell out, is the radical verb; hence *plump*, i. e. swollen out. Cf. *plump*, to swell (Nares).+O. Du. *plomp*, clownish, dull (a metaphorical use, from the notion of thickness); Swed. Dan. G. *plump*, clumsy, blunt, coarse. Der. *plump-er*, a kind of vote (to *swell out* a candidate's chances against all the rest).

Plump (2), straight downward ; see **Plumb.**

Plunder, to pillage. (G.) G. *plündern,* to steal trash, to pillage ; from *plunder,* sb., trumpery, trash, baggage, lumber.+O. Du. *plunderen, plonderen,* to pillage ; connected with Low G. *plunnen, plunden,* rags, worthless household stuff. Hence to *plunder* is to strip a house even of its least valuable contents.

Plunge ; see **Plumb.**

Pluperfect ; see **Plural.**

Plural. (F. – L.) M. E. *plural.* – O. F. *plurel* (F. *pluriel*). – L. *pluralis,* plural, expressive of *more* than one. Allied to Gk. πλείων, more, πλέως, full ; and to **Plenary.** (√ PAR.)

pluperfect. (L.) Englished from L. *plusquamperfectum,* by giving to *plus* the F. pronunciation, and dropping *quam.* The lit. sense is 'more than perfect,' applied to a tense. – L. *plus,* more ; *quam,* than ; *perfectum,* perfect.

plurisy, superabundance. (L. ; *mis-formed.*) Shak. uses *plurisy* to express plethora ; so also Massinger and Ford. Formed from L. *pluri-,* crude form of *plus,* more, by an extraordinary (prob. a jocular) confusion with *pleurisy.*

surplus. (F. – L.) F. *surplus,* 'an over-plus ;' Cot. – L. *super,* above ; *plus,* more.

Plush ; see **Pile** (3).

Pluvial, rainy. (F. – L.) F. *pluvial.* – L. *pluuialis,* rainy. – L. *pluuia,* rain. – L. *plu-it,* it rains. (√ PLU.)

plover, a bird. (F. – L.) M. E. *plover.* – O. F. *plovier,* later *pluvier.* Formed from Low L. *pluuiarius *,* equivalent to L. *pluuialis,* rainy (above). These birds were said to be most seen and caught in a rainy season ; whence also the G. name *regenpfeifer* (rain-piper).

Ply. (F. – L.) M. E. *plien,* to bend, to mould as wax (hence, to toil at). – F. *plier,* 'to fold, plait, ply, bend ;' Cot. – L. *plicare,* to fold. + Gk. πλέκειν, Russ. *pleste,* G. *flechten,* to weave, plait. (√ PLAK.) Der. *pli-ant,* bending, from F. *pliant,* pres. pt. of *plier* ; *pli-ers* or *ply-ers,* pincers for bending wire ; *pli-able* (F. *pliable*).

accomplice. (F. – L.) An extension, by prefixing F. *a* (= L. *ad*), of the older form *complice.* – F. *complice,* 'a complice, confederate ;' Cot. – L. acc. *complicem,* from *complex,* an accomplice ; lit. 'interwoven ;' see **complex** (below).

apply. (F. – L.) O. F. *aplier* (Roquefort). – L. *applicare,* to join to, turn or apply to. – L. *ap-* (*ad*), to ; *plicare,* to fold, twine. **Der.** *applic-at-ion,* from pp. *applicatus* ; also *mis-apply.*

complexion. (F. – L.) F. *complexion,* appearance. – L. *complexionem,* acc. of *complexio,* a comprehending, compass, habit of .body, complexion, – L. *complexus,* pp. of *complecti,* to surround, entwine. – L. *com-* (*cum*), together ; *plectere,* to plait ; see **pleach** (below).

complex. (L.) L. *complex,* interwoven, intricate. – L. *com-* (*cum*), together ; and *-plex* (stem *-plic-*), woven, as in *du-plex,* allied to *plic-are,* to twine.

complicate. (L.) From pp. of L. *complicare,* to render complex. – L. *complex* (stem *complic-*), complex (above).

complicity. (F. – L.) F. *complicité,* 'a bad confederacy ;' Cot. – F. *complice,* a confederate ; see **accomplice** (above).

deploy, to open out, extend. (F. – L.) F. *déployer,* to unroll, unfold ; O. F. *des-ploier,* to unfold. – L. *dis-,* apart ; *plicare,* to fold.

display. (F. – L.) O. F. *despleier, desploier,* to unfold, shew. – L. *dis-,* apart ; *plicare,* to fold.

employ. (F. – L.) O. F. *employer,* to employ. – L. *implicare,* to implicate (hence employ) ; see **implicate** below.

explicate, to explain. (L.) From pp. of L. *explicare,* to unfold, explain. – L. *ex,* out ; *plicare,* to fold.

explicit. (L.) L. *explicitus,* old pp. of *ex-plicare,* to unfold, make plain.

exploit. (F. – L.) M. E. *esploit,* success, Gower, C. A. ii. 258. – O. F. *esploit,* revenue, profit ; later, an exploit, act. – L. *explicitum,* a thing settled, ended, or displayed ; neut. of *explicitus* (above). Cf. Low L. *explicta,* revenue.

implicate. (L.) From pp. of L. *implicare,* to involve. – L. *im-* (*in*), in ; *plicare,* to fold.

implicit. (L.) L. *implicitus,* old pp. of *implicare* (above).

imply. (F. – L.) Coined from L. *im-* (*in*), and *ply* ; as if from a F. *implier ** ; but the F. form was *impliquer,* still earlier *emploier* (whence E. *employ*). See **Ply** (above).

perplex. (F. – L.) *Perplexed,* pp., was first in use. – F. *perplex,* 'perplexed, intangled ;' Cot. – L. *perplexus,* entangled, interwoven. – L. *per,* thoroughly ; *plexus,* entangled, pp. of *plectere,* to weave; see **plait** (below).

plait. (F. — L.) From M. E. *plait,* sb., a fold. — O. F. *pleit, ploit, plet,* a fold (F. *pli*). — L. *plicatum,* neut. of *plicatus,* pp. of *plicare,* to fold; see **Ply** (above).

plash (2), the same as **pleach** (below).

pleach, plash, to intertwine boughs in a hedge. (F. — L.) M. E. *plechen.* — O. F. *plessier,* later *plesser,* 'to plash, plait young branches.' &c.; Cot. — Low L. *plessa,* a thicket of woven boughs; put for *plectia *.* — L. *plectere,* to weave; extended from base PLAK, to weave, whence also *plicare,* to fold.

pleat, another form of **plait** (above).

pliant. (F. — L.) F. *pliant,* pres. pt. of *plier,* to bend; see **Ply** (above).

plight (2), a fold, to fold. (F. — L.) Orig. a sb. 'With many a folded *plight,* F. Q. ii. 3. 26. Misspelt for *plite*; Chaucer has *pliten,* to fold, Troil. ii. 697; *plite,* state, C. T. 10209. It is the fem. form of *plait.* — O. F. *plite.* — L. *plicita.*

plot (1), a conspiracy. (F. — L.) Short for *complot*; for the loss of *com-,* cf. *fence* for *defence, sport* for *disport,* &c. — F. *complot,* 'a complot, conspiracy;' Cot. Diez rightly derives this from L. *complicitum,* neut. of *complicitus,* pp. of *complicare,* to complicate, involve, entangle; see **complicate** (above).

reply. (F. — L.) M. E. *replien.* — O. F. *replier,* the old form afterwards replaced by the 'learned' form *repliquer,* to reply. — L. *re-plicare,* lit. to fold back; as a law term, to reply. **Der.** *replica,* a repetition, from Ital. *replica,* a sb. due to *replicare,* to repeat, reply.

splay, to slope, in architecture; to dislocate a bone. (F. — L.) In both senses, it can be proved to be a contraction for **display** (above). **Der.** *splay-footed.*

supple. (F. — L.) M. E. *souple.* — F. *souple, soupple,* pliant. — L. *supplicem,* acc. of *supplex,* with the old sense of 'bending under.' — L. *sup-* (*sub*), under.; *plic-,* as seen in *plic-are,* to fold.

suppliant. (F. — L.) F. *suppliant,* pres. pt. of *supplier,* to pray humbly. — L. *supplicare*; see below.

supplicate. (L.) From pp. of L. *supplicare,* to beseech. — L. *supplic-,* stem of *supplex,* bending under or down, beseeching; see **supple** (above).

¶ From the same root we also have *sim-ple, sim-plic-ity, dou-ble, du-plic-ate,*

tre-ble, tri-ple, tri-plic-ity, quadru-ple, multi-ple, &c.

Pneumatic. (Gk.) Gk. πνευματικός, relating to wind or air. — Gk. πνεῦμα (stem πνευματ-), wind, air. — Gk. πνέειν, to blow. Allied to **Neese.**

pneumonia. (Gk.) Gk. πνευμονία, disease of the lungs. — Gk. πνευμον-, stem of πνεύμων (also πλεύμων), a lung. — Gk. πνέειν, to blow, breathe.

pulmonary, affecting the lungs. (L.) L. *pulmonarius,* affecting the lungs. — L. *pulmon-,* stem of *pulmo,* a lung. *Pulmo* = Gk. πλεύμων, variant of πνεύμων (above).

Poach (1), to dress eggs. (F. — O. Low G.?) Formerly *poch.* — F. *pocher*; Cot. gives '*œuf poché,* a potched (poached) egg.' The orig. sense was prob. 'a pouched' egg, i. e. an egg so dressed as to preserve it in the form of a pouch. — F. *poche,* a pouch; see **pouch,** s. v. **Poke** (1). See Scheler's explanation.

Poach (2), to intrude into preserves. (F. — O. Low G.) F. *pocher*; Cot. explains *pocher le labeur d'autruy* by 'to poch into, or incroach upon, another man's imploiment, practise, or trade.' The old sense was to put into a pouch, poke, or bag (Littré); cf. mod. E. to *bag,* to *pocket.* — F. *poche,* a bag; see **pouch,** s. v. **Poke** (1).

Pock (1), a pustule. (E.; *perhaps* C.) *Small pox* = small *pocks,* where *pocks* is pl. of *pock.* M. E. *pokke,* a pock, pl. *pokkes.* A. S. *poc,* a pustule. + Du. *pock,* G. *pocke,* a pock. β. Prob. of Celtic origin, and allied to *poke* (1), a bag; cf. Gael. *pucaid,* a pimple, Irish *pucoid,* a pustule, *pucadh,* a swelling up, Gael. *poc,* to become like a bag.

Pocket; see **Poke** (1).

Pod; see **Pad** (1).

Poem. (F. — L. — Gk.) F. *poëme,* Cot. — L. *poema.* — Gk. ποίημα, a work, composition, poem. — Gk. ποιεῖν, to make.

poesy. (F. — L. — Gk.) M. E. *poesie.* — F. *poësie.* — L. *poësin,* acc. of *poësis,* poetry. — Gk. ποίησις, a composition, poem. — Gk. ποιεῖν, to make.

poet. (F. — L. — Gk.) F. *poëte.* — L. *poeta.* — Gk. ποιητής, a maker. — Gk. ποιεῖ-ν, to make; with suffix -της of the agent.

posy. (F. — L. — Gk.) In all its senses, it is short for *poesy.* It meant a short poem, esp. a short motto in verse on knives and rings, Hamlet, iii. 2. 162; hence it meant a nosegay, because the flowers chosen for it enigmatically represented a posy or motto,

It even meant a collection of precious stones, forming a motto; Chambers, Look of Days, i. 221.

Poignant, Point; see **Pungent**.

Poise; see **Pendant**.

Poison; see **Potable**.

Poitrel, Peitrel; see **Pectoral**.

Poke (1), a bag, pouch. (C.) M. E. *poke.* — Irish *poc*, Gael. *poca*, a bag. Cf. Icel. *poki*, O. Du. *poke*, a bag, prob. borrowed from Celtic; also Icel. *pungr*, A. S. *pung*, a pouch.

pocket, a small pouch. (F. — C.) M. E. *poket*. Dimin. of O. Norman *poque* (Norman dial. *pouque*, Métivier), the same as F. *poche*, a pocket, pouch. — O. Du. *poke*, a bag (Hexham); prob. borrowed from Celtic.

pouch. (F. — C.) M. E. *pouche.* — O. F. *pouche*, variant of *poche*; see above.

pucker, to gather into folds. (C.) Particularly used of the folds in the top of a *poke* or bag, when gathered together by drawing the string tight. So also Ital. *saccolare*, to pucker, from *sacco*, a. sack; and E. *purse*, as 'to *purse* up the brows.' From **Poke** (1) above.

Poke (2), to thrust, push. (C.) M. E. *poken, pukken.* — Irish *poc*, a blow, kick; Corn. *poc*, a shove, Gael. *puc*, to push. (Cf. W. *pwtio*, to push, whence North E. *pote*, to kick.) — √ PUK, to thrust; see **Pungent**.

Pole (1), a stake. (L.) See **Pact**.

Pole (2), a pivot, end of earth's axis. (F. — L. — Gk.) F. *pol.* — L. *polum*, acc. of *polus.* — Gk. πόλος, a pivot, hinge. — Gk. πέλειν, to be in motion; allied to κέλομαι, κέλλω, I urge on. (√ KAR.)

Pole-axe, a kind of axe; see **Poll**.

Polecat, a kind of weasel. (Hybrid.) M. E. *polcat*; where *cat* is the ordinary word; but the origin of *pol-* is doubtful. β. Guesses are: (1) a Polish cat (unlikely, as it is in Chaucer); (2) a *pool-cat*, which is unsatisfactory; (3) from O. F. *pulent*, stinking = L. *purulentus*, the same (unlikely; wrong vowel); (4) from F. *poule*, a hen, because the *pole-cat* slays capons; see Chaucer, C. T. 12789. Cf. the pronunciation of *poul-try*. This is best.

Polemical, warlike. (Gk.) From Gk. πολεμικός, warlike. — Gk. πόλεμος, war. Cf. Zend *par*, to fight, Lith. *perti*, to strike, Russ. *prate*, to resist. (√ PAR.)

Police. (F. — L. — Gk.) F. *police*, orig. civil government. — L. *politīa.* — Gk. πολιτεία, polity, government. — Gk. πολίτης, a citizen. — Gk. πόλις, a state, city.

Orig. a crowd; cf. Skt. *purī*, a town. (√ PAR.) **Der.** *polic-y.* O. F. *policie* = L. *politia*; *polit-ic*, from Gk. πολιτικός, adj. **Der.** *acro-polis, metro-polis, cosmo-polite.*

Policy, a writing or contract of insurance; see **Poly-**.

Polish, to make smooth. (F. — L.) F. *poliss-*, stem of pres. pt. of *polir.* — L. *polire*, to make smooth. Prob. allied to **Liniment**, *po-* being an old prefix.

interpolate. (L.) From pp. of L. *interpolare*, to furbish up, patch, interpolate. — L. *interpolus, interpolis*, polished up. — L. *inter*, in between; *polire*, to polish.

polite. (L.) L. *politus*, polished; pp. of *polire*, to make smooth (above).

Polka, a dance. (Bohemian?) Said to have been first danced by a Bohemian peasant-girl in 1831, and to have been named *polka* at Prague in 1835. — Bohemian *pulka*, half; from the half-step prevalent in it (Webster). ¶ Rather, from Pol. *Polka*, a Polish woman.

Poll, the head, esp. the back part. (O. Low G. — C.) Hence it means also a register of heads or persons, a voting-place, &c. M. E. *pol*, a poll; *pol bi pol*, head by head, separately. — O. Du. *polle, pol, bol*, 'head or pate,' Hexham; Low G. *polle*; Swed. dial. *pull*, Dan. *puld* (for *pull*). As initial *p* and *k* are occasionally interchangeable, it is the same as O. Swed. *kull, kulle*, crown of the head, whence *kulla*, to poll or shave off the hair; Icel. *kollr*, top, shaven crown. Of Celtic origin. — Irish *coll*, head, neck; W. *col*, peak, top; cf. L. *corona*, a crown, Gk. κορυφή, summit, κάρα, head, κάρ, hair of the head. **Der.** *poll*, to cut off the hair of the head. Also *pole-axe*, formerly *poll-ax* (Ch.), O. Low G. *pollexe*, i.e. head-axe. Also *poll-ard*, a tree that is polled. And see **Kill**.

Pollock, Pollack, a fish. (C.) Irish *pullog*, a pollock; Gael. *pollag*, a whiting.

Pollen. (L.) L. *pollen, pollis*, fine flour. Cf. Gk. πάλη, fine sifted meal, πάλλειν, to shake.

Pollute. (L.) L. *pollutus*, pp. of *polluere*, to defile. Orig. to wash over, as a flooded river. — L. *pol-*, allied to O. Lat. *por-*, towards; *luere*, to wash; see **Lave**.

Polony, a Bologna sausage. (Ital.) Ital. *Bologna*, where they were made (Evelyn).

Poltroon, a dastard, lazy fellow. (F. — Ital. — G.) F. *poltron*, a sluggard; Cot. — Ital. *poltro*, a varlet, coward, sluggard; cf. *poltrare*, to lie in bed. — Ital. *poltro*, a

bed, couch. — G. *polster*, a bolster, cushion,
quilt; the same as E. **Bolster**, q. v. A
poltroon is a *bolster-man*, a lie-a-bed.
Poly-, many. (L. — Gk.) L. *poly-*. — Gk.
πολύ-, crude form of πολύς, much.+Skt.
puru, much. Allied to **Full**.

policy, a warrant for money in the
funds, a contract of insurance. (F. — Low
L. — Gk.) Confused with *policy*, from
police, with which it has nothing to do. —
F. *police* (Hamilton). — Late L. *politicum*,
polecticum, corruptions of *polyptychum*, a
register (a common word; Ducange). — Gk.
πολύπτυχον, a piece of writing in many
folds, hence a long register; orig. neut. of
πολύπτυχος, having many folds. — Gk. πολύ-,
much; πτυχο-, crude form of πτύξ, a fold,
leaf, layer, connected with πτύσσειν, to
fold up.

polyanthus, a flower. (L. — Gk.) L.
polyanthus. — Gk. πολύανθος, many-flowered.
— Gk. πολύ-, many; άνθος, flower.

polygamy. (F. — L. — Gk.) F. *poly-
gamie*. — L. *polygamia*. — Gk. πολυγαμία, a
marrying of many wives. — Gk. πολύ-, much;
-γαμία, from γάμος, marriage.

polyglot, speaking many languages.
(Gk.) Gk. πολύ-, much, many; γλῶττα=
γλῶσσα, tongue, language; see **Gloss**.

polygon, a many-sided plane figure.
(Gk.) Gk. πολύ-, many; γωνία, an angle,
from γόνυ, a knee.

polyhedron, a many-sided solid figure.
(Gk.) Gk. πολύ-, many; -έδρον, for έδρα, a
base, from έδειν, to sit; see **Sit**.

polynomial. (Gk. *and* L.) Coined to
go with *bi-nomial*. — Gk. πολύ-, many; L.
nomen, a name, term.

polypus, an animal with many feet.
(L. — Gk.) L. *polypus*. — Gk. πολύπους,
many-footed. — Gk. πολύ-, many; πούς, foot.

polysyllable. (Gk.) From *poly-* and
syllable.

polytheism. (Gk.) From *poly-* and
theism.

Pomade, Pommade. (F. — Ital. — L.)
F. *pommade*, pomatum; so called because
orig. made of apples. — Ital. *pomada*, *pomata*,
'a pomado to supple one's lips, lip-salve,'
Florio. — Ital. *pomo*, an apple. — L. *pomum*,
an apple, fruit.

pomegranate. (F. — L.) O. F. *pome
grenate* (also turned into *pome de grenate*
by confusion of the sense); the same as
Ital. *pomo granato*. — L. *pomum*, an apple;
granatum, full of seeds, from *granum*, a
grain, seed; see **Grain**.

pommel, a knob. (F. — L.) M. E.
pomel, a boss. — O. F. *pomel* (later *pom-
meau*), a pommel; lit. 'small apple.'
Dimin. from L. *pomum*, an apple.

Pomp. (F. — L. — Gk.) F. *pompe*. — L.
pompa. — Gk. πομπή, a sending, escorting,
solemn procession. — Gk. πέμπειν, to send.

pump (2), a thin-soled shoe. (F. — L.
— Gk.) So called because used for *pomp*
or ornament; cf. F. *à pied de plomb et de
pompe*, with a slow and stately gait; Cot.

Pond; see **Pound** (2).
Ponder; see **Pendant**.
Ponent; see **Position**.
Poniard; see **Pugilism**.

Pontiff. (F. — L.) F. *pontif*. — L. *ponti-
ficem*, acc. of *pontifex*, a Roman high-priest;
lit. 'a path-maker' or 'road-maker,' but
the reason for the name is not known.
— L. *ponti-*, crude form of *pons*, a path,
a bridge; *facere*, to make; see **Path**.
(√PAT.)

pontoon. (F. — Ital. — L.) F. *ponton*.
— Ital. *pontone*, a large bridge; augmentative of *ponte*, a bridge. — L. *pontem*, acc.
of *pons*, a path, a bridge.

punt (1), a flat-bottomed boat. (L.)
A. S. *punt*. — L. *ponto*, a punt, also a
pontoon; see above.

Pony. (C.) Gael. *poniadh*, a little
horse, a pony. Also vulgar Irish *poni*,
perhaps borrowed from English.

Poodle, a dog. (G.) G. *pudel*, a poodle;
Low G. *pudel*, *pudel-hund*, allied to Low G.
pudeln, to waddle, used of fat persons and
short-legged animals. Cf. Low G. *pudel-
dikk*, unsteady on the feet, *puddig*, thick.
Allied to **Pudding**.

Pooh. (Scand.) Icel. *pú*, pooh. Allied
to **Puff**.

Pool (1), a small body of water. (L.)
M. E. *pol*, *pool*. A. S. *pól*, Irish *poll*, *pull*,
a hole, pit; Gael. *poll*, a hole, pit, bog,
pool; W. *pwll*, Corn. *pol*, Manx *poyl*, Bret.
poull, a pool. All from late L. *padulis*
(Ital. *padule*), a marsh.

Pool (2), receptacle for the stakes at
cards. (F. — L.) F. *poule*, (1) a hen, (2) a
pool, at various games; the stakes being
the eggs to be got from the hen. — Low L.
pulla, a hen; fem. of *pullus*, a young
animal; see **Foal**. (√PU.)

poult, a chicken. (F. — L.) M. E.
pulte. — F. *poulet*, a chicken; dimin. of
poule, a hen (above). Der. *poult-er*, afterwards extended to *poult-er-er*; *poult-r-y* (for
poult-er-y).

pullet. (F.—L.) M. E. *polete.*—O. F. *polete,* later *poulette,* fem. of F. *poulet,* a chicken (above).

Poop. (F.—L.) F. *poupe, pouppe.*—L. *puppim,* acc. of *puppis,* hinder part of a ship.

Poor; see **Pauper.**

Pop. (E.) 'To *poppe,* coniectare;' Levins. Of imitative origin; allied to M. E. *poupen,* to blow a horn; also to Puff.

Pope; see **Papa.**

Popinjay, orig. a parrot. (F.—Bavarian *and* L.; *with modified suffix.*) M. E. *popingay,* also spelt *papeiay* (= *papejay*). The *n* is inserted as in *passe-n-ger, messe-n-ger.*—O. F. *papegai,* 'a parrot or popinjay;' Cot. Cf. Span. *papagayo,* Port. *papagaio,* a parrot. β. But there is also O. F. *papegau,* a parrot (13th cent.), Ital. *papagallo,* a parrot, lit. 'a talking cock;' and this is the older form. [The change was due to the substitution of *jay* (F. *gai, geai*) for 'cock,' because the jay seemed to come nearer than a cock to the nature of a parrot.]— Bavarian *pappel,* a parrot, from *pappeln,* to chatter (= E. *babble*); and L. *gallus,* a cock. Cf. Lowl. Sc. *bubblyjock* (i.e. babble-jack), a turkey-cock.

Poplar, a tree. (F.—L.) O. F. *poplier*; F. *peuplier.* Formed with suffix *-ier* (= L. *-arius*) from O. F. *pople**, later *peuple,* a poplar.—L. *populum,* acc. of *pōpulus,* a poplar. Named from its trembling leaves; *pōpulus* = *palpulus**; cf. *palpitare,* to tremble; see **Palpitate.**

Poplin. (F.) F. *popeline,* a fabric; at first called *papeline,* A. D. 1667 (Littré). Perhaps named from *Poppeling* or *Popper-ingen,* near Ypres, in W. Flanders. See N. and Q. 6 S. vi. 305.

Poppy. (L.) A. S. *popig*; borrowed from L. *papauer,* a poppy (with loss of *-er*).

Populace; see below.

Popular. (F.—L.) F. *populaire.*—L. *popularis,* adj., from *populus,* the people. (√ PAR.)

depopulate. (L.) From pp. of L. *de-populare,* to lay waste, lit. deprive of people or inhabitants.

people. (F.—L.) M. E. *people, poeple.* —O. F. *pueple*; F. *peuple.*—L. *populum,* acc. of *populus,* people.

populace. (F.—Ital.—L.) F. *popu-lace.* — Ital. *popolazzo, popolaccio,* 'the grosse, vile, common people;' Florio. — Ital. *popolo,* people. — L. acc. *populum.* ¶ The suffix *-accio* is depreciatory.

public. (F. — L.) F. *public,* masc., *publique,* fem.; Cot. — L. *publicus,* belonging to the people; short for *populicus**. —L. *populus,* the people.

publican. (L.) M. E. *publican.* — L. *publicanus,* a tax-gatherer, Luke. iii. 12; orig. an adj., belonging to the public revenue.—L. *publicus* (above).

publication. (F.—L.) F. *publication.* — L. acc. *publicationem.*—L. *publicatus,* pp. of *publicare,* to make public. — L. *publicus,* public.

publish. (F.—L.) M. E. *publishen.* An irregular formation; founded on F. *publier,* to publish.—L. *publicare* (above).

Porcelain; see **Pork.**

Porch; see **Port** (2).

Porcine, Porcupine; see **Pork.**

Pore (1), a minute hole in the skin. (F. —L.—Gk.) F. *pore.*—L. *porum,* acc. of *porus.*— Gk. πόρος, a passage, pore. Allied to **Fare.** (√ PAR.)

Pore (2), to look steadily, gaze long. (Scand.—C.) M. E. *poren.*—Swed. dial. *pora, pura, pȧra,* to work slowly and gradually, to do anything slowly (Rietz). Cf. Low G. *purren,* to poke about, clean out a hole, Du. *porren,* to poke. The idea seems to be that of poking about slowly, hence to *pore over* a thing, be slow about it. β. Prob. of Celtic origin; cf. Gael. *purr,* to push, thrust, drive, urge; Irish *purraim,* I thrust, push.

Pork. (F.—L.) F. *porc.* — L. *porcum,* acc. of *porcus,* a pig. + Lithuan. *parszas,* W. *porch,* Irish *orc* (with usual loss of *p*), A. S. *fearh,* a pig (whence E. *farrow*).

porcelain. (F. — Ital. — L.) Named from the resemblance of its polished surface to that of the univalve shell with the same name. — F. *porcelaine, pourcelaine,* 'the purple-fish, the Venus-shell;' Cot.—Ital. *porcellana,* 'the purple-fish, a kind of fine earth, whereof they make .. *porcellan* dishes;' Florio. β. The shell is named from the curved shape of its upper surface, like a pig's back. — Ital. *porcella,* a pig, dimin. of *porco,* a hog, pig.—L. *porcum,* acc. of *porcus,* a pig.

porcupine. (F.—L.) M. E. *porkepyn* (3 syllables).—O. F. *porc espin,* Palsgrave; (now called *porcépic*). So also Span. *puerco espin,* Ital. *porco spinoso.*—O. F. *porc,* a pig; *espin,* by-form of *espine,* a spine, prickle.—L. *porc-um,* acc. of *porcus*; *spina,* a thorn; see **Spine.** ¶ But mod. F. *porcépic* was formerly *porc espi,* derived from *spica*, spike, not *spina*, a thorn. We also find E. *porpin*, short for *porkepin*; whence *porpint*, altered to *porpoint*, *porkpoint*; whence *porpent-ine*; all these forms occur.

porpoise, porpess. (F.—L.) M.E. *porpeys.*—O. F. *porpeis*, a porpoise; now obsolete, and replaced by *marsouin*, borrowed from G. *meer-schwein* (mere-swine). Put for *porc-peis.**—L. *porc-um*, acc. of *porcus*, a pig; *piscem*, acc. of *piscis*, a fish.

Porphyry; see Purple.

Porridge. (F.—C.—L.) Another form of *pottage*, which first became *poddige* (as preserved in Craven *poddish*) and afterwards *porridge*, just as the Southern E. *errish* is corrupted from *eddish* (A. S. *edisc*), stubble. Similarly, *pottanger* (Palsgrave) was the old form of *porringer*. See p. 366, col. 2, last line.

porringer. (F.—L.; *with* E. *suffix*.) Formed from *porrige* (= *porridge*) by inserted *n*, as in *messenger*; with E. suffix *-er*. It means a small dish for porridge.

Port (1), demeanour. (F.—L.) M.E. *port.*—F. *port*, 'the carriage, or demeanor of a man;' Cot. A sb. due to the verb *porter*, to carry. — L. *portare*, to carry. Allied to Fare. (√PAR.) Der. *port*, verb, as 'to *port* arms;' *port-ed*, P. L. iv. 980. Also *port-er*, a bearer of a burden, substituted for M. E. *portour*, from F. *porteur*. Hence *porter*, the name of a strong malt-liquor, so called from being the favourite drink of London *porters*. Also *port-folio*, a case large enough to carry *folio* paper in (cf. F. *porte-feuille*), *port-manteau*, F. *portmanteau*; see **Mantle, Mantua**; *port-ly, port-li-ness*.

comport, to suit, behave. (F.—L.) F. *se comporter*, to behave.—L. *com-* (*cum*), together; *portare*, to carry.

deport. (F.—L.) O. F. *deporter*, to bear, endure; *se deporter*, to forbear, quiet oneself.—L. *de-portare*, to carry down, remove; with extended senses in Low Latin. Der. *deportment*, O. F. *deportment*, behaviour. ¶ Prob. confused with *disport*, at any rate in French.

disport. (F.—L.) M. E. *disporten*, to amuse.—O. F. *se desporter*, to amuse oneself, orig. to cease from labour; later *de-porter*, and confused with the word above. —L. *dis-*, away; *portare*, to carry (hence, to remove oneself from or cease from labour).

export. (L.) L. *ex-portare*, to carry away.

import. (F.—L.; *or* L.) In two senses: (1) to signify.—F. *importer*, to signify.—L. *importare*, to import, bring in, introduce, cause; (2) to bring in from abroad; directly from the same L. *importare*.—L. *im-* (*in*), in; *portare*, to bring. Der. *import-ant*, i. e. importing much.

importable, intolerable; *obsolete*. (F. —L.) F. *importable*. — L. *importabilis*, that cannot be borne.—L. *im-* (*in*), not; *portare*, to bear.

porter (1), a carrier; (3) a liquor; see Port (1) above.

portesse, portous, a breviary. (F.— L.) M. E. *portous, porthors*.—O. F. *porte-hors*, a translation of the Latin name *porti-forium*.—F. *porter*, to carry; *hors*, forth (O. F. *fors*).—L. *portare*, to carry; *foris*, abroad.

purport, to imply. (F.—L.) O. F. *purporter, pourporter*, to declare, inform (hence, imply); we also find *purport*, sb., tenour (Roquefort).—O. F. *pur*, F. *pour*, from L. *pro*, according to; *porter*, to carry, bring, from L. *portare*. For the sense, cf. *import*.

report. (F.—L.) M. E. *reporten*.—F. *reporter*, to carry back, tell.—L. *re-portare*, to carry back.

sport, mirth. (F.—L.) Short for *dis-port, desport*; (so also *splay* for *display*). The verb is M. E. *disporten*, to amuse; see **disport** (above).

support. (F.—L.) M. E. *supporten*. —F. *supporter*.—L. *supportare*, to carry to a place; in Late L., to endure.—L. *sup-* (*sub*), near; *portare*, to carry.

transport. (F.—L.) F. *transporter*, 'to carry or convey over;' Cot.—L. *transportare*, to carry across.

Port (2), a harbour. (L.) M. E. *port*. A. S. *port.*—L. *portus*, a harbour. Closely allied to **port** (3) below.

importune, to molest. (F.—L.) From M. E. *importune*, adj., troublesome. — F. *importun*, 'importunate;' Cot. — L. *importunus*, unfit, unsuitable, troublesome. Orig. 'hard of access;' from L. *im-* (*in*), not; *portus*, access, a harbour. Der. *importun-ate*.

opportune, timely. (F.—L.) F. *op-portun*.—L. *opportunus*, convenient, seasonable, lit. 'near the harbour,' or 'easy of access.'—L. *op-* (*ob*), near; *portus*, access, harbour.

porch. (F.—L.) F. *porche*.—L. *por-ticum*, acc. of *porticus*, a gallery, porch;

formed, with suffix *-icus*, from L. *porta*, a
door; see **port** (3).

port (3), a gate, entrance. (F. – L.) F.
porte. – L. *porta*, a gate. Allied to Gk.
πόρος, a ford, way, and to E. **Fare**. Der.
port-er, F. *portier*, L. *portarius*; *port-al*,
O. F. *portal*, Low L. *portale*.

port (4), a dark wine. (Port. – L.) Short
for *Oporto wine.* – Port. *o porto*, i. e. the
harbour; where *o* is the def. art. (= Span.
lo = L. *illum*), and *porto* is from L. *portum*,
acc. of *portus*, a harbour.

portcullis. (F. – L.) M. E. *portcolise*.
– O. F. *porte coleïce* (13th cent.), later *porte
coulisse*, or *coulisse*, a portcullis, lit. sliding
door. – L. *porta*, a door; Low L. *colaticius* *,
not found, from *colatus*, pp. of *colare*, to
flow, glide, slide; see **Colander**.

porte, the Turkish government. (F. – L.)
The *Sublime Porte* is a F. translation of
Babi Ali, the chief office of the Ottoman
government, lit. 'high gate;' (Arab. *bâb*,
gate, *ally*, high). – F. *porte*, a gate. – L.
porta, gate; see **port** (3) above.

porter (2), a gate-keeper; see **port**
(3) above.

portico. (Ital. – L.) Ital. *portico.* – L.
porticum, acc. of *porticus*; see **porch**
(above).

Port (3), a gate; (4) wine; see **Port** (2).
Portcullis, **Porte**; see **Port** (2).
Portend; see **Tend** (1).
Porter (1), a carrier; see **Port** (1).
Porter (2), a gate-keeper; see **Port** (2).
Porter (3), a kind of beer; see **Port** (1).
Portesse, a breviary; see **Port** (1).
Portico; see **Port** (2).
Portion; see **Part**.
Portly; see **Port** (1).
Portrait, **Portray**; see **Trace** (1).
Pose (1), a position, attitude. (F. – L.
– Gk.) Modern; but important. – F. *pose*,
attitude. – F. *poser*, to place, set. – Low L.
pausare, to cease; also to cause to rest
(and so put for L. *ponere*, the sense of
which it took up). – L. *pausa*, a pause. –
Gk. παῦσις, a pause. – Gk. παύειν, to make
to cease; παύεσθαι, to cease. ¶ One of
the most remarkable facts in F. etymology
is the extraordinary substitution whereby
Low L. *pausare*, coming to mean 'to
cause to rest,' usurped the place of L.
ponere, to place, with which it has *no etymological connection*. This it did so ef-
fectually as to restrict F. *pondre* (= L.
ponere) to the sole sense 'to lay eggs,'
whilst in all compounds it thrust it aside,

so that *compausare* (F. *composer*) usurped the
place of L. *componere*, and so on throughout. But note that, on the other hand,
the sb. *position* (with all derivatives) is
veritably derived from L. *ponere*; see **Position**; see **repose** (below).

appose; see **pose** (2) below.

compose. (F. – L. *and* Gk.) F. *composer*, to compound, make; Cot. – F. *com-
(L. cum*), together; and F. *poser*, to put,
of Gk. origin, as shewn above.

decompose; from *de-*, prefix, and *compose* above.

depose. (F. – L. *and* Gk.) O. F. *de-
poser*, to displace. – O. F. *de-* (L. *de*), from;
and F. *poser*, to place, of Gk. origin, as
above.

dispose. (F. – L. *and* Gk.) O. F. *dis-
poser*, to arrange. – O. F. *dis-* (L. *dis-*),
apart; F. *poser*, to place (above).

expose. (F. – L. *and* Gk.) O. F. *ex-
poser*, to lay out. – O. F. *ex-* (L. *ex*), out;
F. *poser*, to place, lay (above).

impose. (F. – L. *and* Gk.) F. *im-
poser*, to lay upon. – F. *im-* (L. *in*), upon;
F. *poser*, to lay (above).

interpose. (F. – L. *and* Gk.) F. *in-
terposer*, to put between. – L. *inter*, between; F. *poser*, to put (above).

oppose. (F. – L. *and* Gk.) F. *opposer*,
to withstand. – L. *op-* (for *ob*) against; F.
poser, to place (above).

pose (2), to puzzle by questions. (F. –
L. *and* Gk.) M. E. *apposen*, to question;
not really = F. *apposer*, but a corruption of
M. E. *opposen*, to oppose, hence, to cross-
question; see **oppose** above. ¶ Confused
with *appose*, because of *apposite*, for which
see position.

propose. (F. – L. *and* Gk.) F. *proposer*, lit. to place before. – L. *pro*, before;
F. *poser*, to place (above).

purpose (1), to intend. (F. – L. *and*
Gk.) O. F. *purposer*, a variant of *proposer*,
to propose, intend; see above. (F. *pur-* =
L. *pro*.)

puzzle, a difficult question. (F. – L.
and Gk.) Orig. a sb., and short for *op-
posal*, spelt both *opposayle* and *apposayle* in
Lydgate, with the sense of question. These
are coined words, from the verb *oppose*, like
deni-al from *deny*, &c. See **pose** (2) above.

repose. (F. – L. *and* Gk.) F. *reposer*,
to rest, pause; Low L. *repausare*, to pause,
rest. – L. *re-*, again; *pausare*, to pause,
from *pausa*, sb., due to Gk. παῦσις, a
pause. ¶ Important; this is the verb

which seems to have given rise to *poser* and its compounds.

suppose. (F.—L. *and* Gk.) F. *supposer*, to imagine.—L. *sup-* (*sub*), under, near; F. *poser*, to place, put (above).

transpose. (F. — L. *and* Gk.) F. *transposer*, to transpose, remove.—L. *trans*, across; F. *poser*, to put (above).

Position. (F. — L.) F. *position*. — L. *positionem*, acc. of *positio*, a placing. — L. *positus*, pp. of *ponere*, to place. β. *Ponere* is for *po-sinere*, where *po-* stands for an old prep. (*port*), and *sinere* is to allow; see Site. ¶ Quite distinct from *pose* (1); all the compounds of *ponere* belong here, as below.

apposite. (L.) Chiefly in the phrase '*apposite* answers,' i. e. suitable answers, made to a *poser* or *opposer*, i. e. an examiner. (Hence the verb to *oppose*, to question, was frequently corrupted to *appose*.)—L. *appositus*, suitable; pp. of *apponere*, to put near.—L. *ap-* (*ad*), to; *ponere*, to put.

component, composing. (L.) L. *component-*, stem of pres. pt. of *componere*, to compose.—L. *com-* (*cum*), together; *ponere*, to put.

composition. (F. — L.) F. *composition.*—L. acc. *compositionem*, acc. of *compositio*, a putting together.—L. *compositus*, pp. of L. *com-ponere* (above).

compost, a mixture. (F. — Ital. — L.) O. F. *composte.*—Ital. *composta*, a mixture. —L. *composita*, fem. of *compositus*, pp. of *com-ponere* (above).

compound. (L.) The *d* is excrescent; M. E. *compounen.*—L. *com-ponere*, to compound, put together (above).

deponent, one who testifies. (L.) L. *deponent-*, stem of *deponere*, to lay down, also (in late L.) to testify. — L. *de*, down; *ponere*, to lay.

deposit, verb. (F. — L.) F. *depositer*, to entrust. — L. *depositum*, a thing laid down, neut. of pp. of *deponere* (above).

deposition. (F.—L.) O. F. *deposition.* — L. acc. *depositionem*, a depositing. — L. *depositus*, pp. of *deponere*, to lay down (above).

depot, a store. (F. — L.) F. *dépôt*. O. F. *depost.* — L. *depositum*, a thing laid down (hence, stored); neut. of *depositus* (above).

disposition. (F.—L.) F. *disposition.* —L. acc. *dispositionem*, a setting in order. —L. *dispositus*, pp. of *dis-ponere*, to set in various places, to arrange.

exponent. (L.) L. *exponent-*, stem of pres. pt. of *ex-ponere*, to expound, indicate.

exposition. (F. — L.) F. *exposition.* —L. acc. *expositionem.* — L. *expositus*, pp. of *ex-ponere*, to set forth, expound.

expound. (L.) The *d* is excrescent. M. E. *expounen.* — O. F. *espondre*, to explain.—L. *ex-ponere*, to set forth, explain.

imposition. (F. — L.) F. *imposition.* — L. acc. *impositionem*, a laying on. — L. *impositus*, pp. of *imponere*, to lay on.—L. *im-* (*in*), on ; *ponere*, to lay.

impost. (F.—L.) F. *impost*, a tax.— L. pp. *impositus* (above).

impostor. (L.) L. *impostor*, a deceiver ; from L. *imponere* (above).

interposition. (F.—L.) F. *interposition.* — L. acc. *interpositionem*, a putting between. — L. *interpositus*, pp. of *interponere*, to put between. — L. *inter*, between ; *ponere*, to put.

juxtaposition. (L. *and* F. — L.) Coined from L. *iuxta*, near; and *position*. See Joust.

opponent. (L.) L. *opponent-*, stem of pres. part. of *opponere* (below).

opposite. (F. — L.) F. *opposite.* — L. *oppositus*, pp. of *opponere*, to set against. — L. *op-* (*ob*), against; *ponere*, to set.

ponent, western. (F. — L.) F. *ponent*, 'the west ;' Cot.—L. *ponent-*, stem of pres. pt. of *ponere*, to lay, hence to set (as the sun).

positive. (F. — L.) F. *positif.* — L. *positiuus*, settled.—L. *posit-us*, pp. of *ponere*, to set, settle.

post (1), a stake set in the ground. (L.) M. E. *post* ; A. S. *post.* — L. *postis*, a post ; i. e. something firmly fixed.—L. *postus*, short for *positus*, pp. of *ponere*, to set.

post (2), a military station, a public letter-carrier, stage on a road. (F. — L.) Orig. a military post ; then a fixed place on a line of road, a station ; then a stage, also a traveller who used relays of horses, &c.—F. *poste*, masc., a carrier, messenger ; fem. posting, a riding post.—Low L. *postus*, fem. *posta*, a post, station.—L. *positus*, pp. of *ponere*, to place.

postillion. (F. — Ital. — L.) F. *postillon.*—Ital. *postiglione*, a post-boy.—Ital. *posta*, a post; with suffix *-iglione* = L. *-ilionem.* See post (2) above.

postpone, to put off. (L.) L. *postponere*, to put after, delay.—L. *post*, after ; *ponere*, to put.

posture. (F. — L.) F. *posture.* — L.

positura, arrangement. — L. *positus*, pp. of *ponere*, to put.

preposition. (F.—L.) O. F. *preposition.* — L. acc. *præpositionem*, a setting before ; a preposition (in grammar). — L. *præ-positus*, pp. of *præ-ponere*, to set before.

proposition. (F.—L.) F. *proposition.* —L. acc. *propositionem*, a statement.—L. *propositus*, pp. of *proponere*, to put forth. —L. *pro*, forth ; *ponere*, to put.

propound. (L.) The *d* is excrescent; formerly *propoune*, *propone*. — L. *proponere* (above).

provost, a prefect. (F. — L.) O. F. *provost*, variant of *prevost*, 'the provost or president of a college ;' Cot. — L. *præpositum*, acc. of *præpositus*, a prefect, one set over. — L. *præponere*, to set over. — L. *præ*, before ; *ponere*, to put.

purpose (2), intention. (F.—L.) M.E. *purpos*. — O. F. *pourpos*, a variant of *propos*, a purpose. — L. *propositum*, a thing proposed, neut. of pp. of *pro-ponere*.

repository, a storehouse. (F. — L.) F. *repositoire*, a store-house. — L. *repositorium*.—L. *repositus*, pp. of *re-ponere*, to lay up, store.

supposition. (F.—L.) F. *supposition*. —L. acc. *suppositionem*. — L. *suppositus*, pp. of *supponere*, to suppose.—L. *sup-* (*sub*), near ; *ponere*, to place.

transposition. (F.—L.) F. *transposition*.—L. acc. *transpositionem*.—L. *transpositus*, pp. of *transponere*, to transpose. — L. *trans*, across ; *ponere*, to put.

Positive ; see Position.

Posse ; see Potent.

Possess ; see Sedentary.

Posset, a warm curdled drink. (C.) M. E. *possyt*. — Irish *pusoid*, a posset ; W. *posel*, curdled milk, posset.

Possible ; see Potent.

Post (1) and (2) ; see Position.

Post-, prefix. (L.) L. *post*, after, behind. Cf. Skt. *paçchát*, behind ; abl. sing. of Vedic adj. *paçcha*, behind.

post-date ; from *post* and *date*.

posterior, hinder. (L.) L. *posterior*, comp. of *posterus*, coming after. — L. *post*, after. **Der.** *posterior-s*, i.e. posterior parts.

posterity. (F.—L.) F. *posterité*.—L. *posteritatem*, acc. of *posteritas*, futurity, posterity.—L. *posteri-*, for *posterus*, coming after.

postern. (F.—L.) O.F. *posterle*, also spelt *posterne* (by change of *l* to *n*) ; later *poterne*, ' a back-door to a fort ;' Cot. —

L. *posterula*, a small back-door. — L. *posterus*, behind.

posthumous, postumous. (L.) L. *postumus*, the latest-born ; hence, as sb., a posthumous child. Written *posthumus* from an absurd popular etymology from *post humum*, forced into the impossible sense of ' after the father is in the ground or buried ;' hence F. *posthume*, Port. *posthumo* ; but Span. and Ital. *postumo* are right. β. L. *postumus* = *post-tu-mus*, a superl. form of *post*, behind ; cf. *op-tu-mus*, best.

postil, an explanatory note or commentary on the Bible. (F.—L.) F. *postille*.— Low L. *postilla*, a marginal note in a Bible. Derived by Ducange from L. *post illa uerba*, i.e. after those words, because the glosses were added afterwards.

post-meridian, pomeridian, belonging to the afternoon. (L.) L. *pomeridianus*, also *postmeridianus*, the same.— L. *post*, after ; *meridianus*, adj., from *meridies*, noon ; see **Meridian.**

post-mortem. (L.) L. *post*, after ; *mortem*, acc. of *mors*, death.

post-obit. (L.) L. *post*, after ; *obitum*, acc. of *obitus*, death.

preposterous. (L.) L. *præposterus*, inverted, hind side before.—L. *præ*, before ; *posterus*, later, coming after.

puisne, puny. (F.—L.) *Puny* is for *puisne*, a law-term, implying inferior in rank.—O. F. *puisné*, ' puny, younger, born after ;' Cot. — L. *post natus*, born after ; see **Natal.**

Posterior, &c. ; see Post-.

Postillion ; see Position.

Postpone ; see Position.

Postscript ; see Scribe.

Postulate, a self-evident proposition. (L.) L. *postulatum*, a thing demanded (and granted) ; neut. of pp. of *postulare*, to demand. Allied to *poscere*, to ask.

expostulate. (L.) From pp. of L. *ex-postulare*, to demand earnestly.

Posture ; see Position.

Posy ; see Poem.

Pot. (C.—L.) M. E. *pot*. Irish *pota*, Gael. *poit*, W. *pot*, Bret. *pôd* ; whence also F. *pot*, Du. *pot*, &c. A drinking-vessel ; cf. Irish *pot-aim*, I drink, borr. from L. *potare* ; see **Potable.** (√PA.)

potash. (C. *and* E.) From *pot* and *ash* ; ash obtained by burning vegetable substances in a pot. Latinised as *potassa* ; whence *potass-ium.*

pottage. (F. — C.) M. E. *potage.*—F.

potage ; formed with F. suffix -*age* (L. -*aticum*), from F. *pot*, of Celtic origin.

pottle. (F. – C.) M. E. *potel.* – O. F. *potel*, a small pot, small measure ; dimin. of F. *pot*, a pot (above).

potwalloper. (C. *and* E.) Lit. ' one who boils a pot ; ' hence a voter who has a vote because he can boil a pot on his own fire. *Wallop*, to boil, is the same word as **Gallop**, q. v.

putty. (F. – C.) O. F. *potée*, calcined tin, also putty ; orig. a pot-ful (of broken bits of metal) ; cf. O. F. *pottein*, broken bits of metal, *pottin*, solder. All from F. *pot*, a pot ; of Celtic origin.

Potable, drinkable. (F. – L.) F. *potable.* – L. *potabilis*, drinkable. – L. *potare*, to drink ; *potus*, drunken. + Skt. *pá*, to drink, Irish *pot-aim*, I drink.   (√ PĀ.)

poison. (F. – L.) F. *poison*, poison. – L. *potionem*, acc. of *potio*, a draught, esp. a poisonous draught ; see below.

potation. (L.) From L. *potatio*, a drinking. – L. *potatus*, pp. of *potare*, to drink.

potion. (F. – L.) F. *potion.* – L. *potionem*, acc. of *potio*, a draught. – L. *potare*, to drink ; see **Potable.**

Potash ; see **Pot.**

Potation ; see **Potable.**

Potato. (Span. – Hayti.) Span. *patata*, a potato. – Hayti *batata*, the same.

Potch, to thrust ; see **Poke** (2).

Potent. (L.) L. *potent-*, stem of *potens*, powerful, pres. part. of *posse*, to be able ; *possum*, I am able. *Possum* is short for *poti-sum**, from *potis*, powerful, orig. ' a lord ; ' allied to Skt. *pati*, a master, lord, Lithuan. *patis*, Russ. -*pode* in *gos-pode*, lord. Skt. *pati* is lit. ' feeder,' from *pa*, to feed. (√ PĀ.) Allied to **Pastor.** Der. *omnipotent.*

posse. (L.) L. *posse*, infin. to be able ; used as sb., meaning ' power.'

possible. (F. – L.) F. *possible.* – L. *possibilis*. Put for *potibilis**; see **Potent** (above).

power. (F. – L.) M. E. *poer* ; later *po-w-er*, the *w* being inserted. – O. F. *poer* (mod. F. *pouvoir*), to be able ; hence, as sb., power. – Low L. *potere*, to be able ; the same as L. *posse*, to be able.

puissant, mighty. (F. – L.) F. *puissant*, powerful. Cf. Ital. *possente*, powerful. From *possent-*, stem of a barbarous L. *possens**, substituted for L. *potens*, powerful.

Pother ; see **Put.**

Potion ; see **Potable.**

Pottage ; see **Pot.**

Potter ; see **Put.**

Pottle, Potwalloper ; see **Pot.**

Pouch ; see **Poke** (1).

Poult, Poultry ; see **Pool** (2).

Poultice. (L.) Gascoigne has the pl. *pultesses* (Steel Glas, 997) ; this is really a double plural, as *pultes* is a pl. form. – L. *pultes*, pl. of *puls*, a thick pap, or pap-like substance. + Gk. πόλτος, porridge.

Pounce (1), to dart on ; see **Pungent.**

Pounce (2), fine powder ; see **Spume.**

Pound (1), a weight ; see **Pendant.**

Pound (2), an enclosure for strayed cattle. (E.) M. E. *pond*. A. S. *pund*, an enclosure.

pindar, pinner, an impounder. (E.) Formed with suffix -*er* of the agent from A. S. *pyndan*, to pen up. – A. S. *pund*, an enclosure. ¶ Not allied to *pen* (1).

pinfold, a pound. (E.) Put for *pind-fold*; (also spelt *pond-fold*). – A. S. *pyndan*, to pen up ; (or *pund*, an enclosure ;) and *fold.*

pond. (E.) M. E. *pond*, variant of *pound*, an enclosure ; it means a pool formed by damming up water. See **Pound** (2) above. Cf. Irish *pont*, (1) a pound, (2) a pond.

Pound (3), to bruise in a mortar. (E.) The *d* is excrescent. M. E. *pounen*. – A. S. *punian*, to pound.

pun. (E.) Orig. to pound ; hence to pound words, beat them into new senses, hammer at forced similes. Shak. has *pun* = to pound, Troil. ii. 1. 42. – A. S. *punian* (above).

Pour. (C.) M. E. *pouren*, esp. used with *out*. The orig. sense was prob. to ' jerk ' or ' throw ' water out of a vessel. Of Celtic origin ; cf. W. *bwrw*, to cast, throw, rain ; *bwrw gwlaw*, to rain, lit. ' to cast rain ; ' Gael. and Irish *purr*, to push, thrust, drive, urge.

Pourtray ; see **Portray**, s. v. **Traco** (1).

Pout (1), to sulk. (C.) W. *pwdu*, to pout, to be sullen ; (whence perhaps F. *bouder*, to pout, and E. *boud-oir*).

pout (2), a fish. (C.) A. S. *æle-pútan*, pl. eel-pouts. The fish has the power of inflating a membrane above the eyes ; hence *pout* = *pout-er* ; see above.

Poverty ; see **Pauper.**

Powder ; see **Pulverise.**

Power ; see **Potent.**

Pox ; see **Pock.**

Practice. (F. – L. – Gk.) From M. E. *praktike*, of which it is a weakened form. – F. *practique*, practice. – L. *practica*, fem. of *practicus*. – Gk. πρακτικός, fit for business; whence ἡ πρακτική, practical science, experience. – Gk. πράσσειν (= πράκ-γειν, to do, accomplish. (√PAR.) Der. *practise*, verb; *practition-er*, formed by needlessly adding *-er* to the older term *practician*, from O. F. *practicien*, 'a practicer in law;' Cot.

pragmatic. (F. – L. – Gk.) F. *pragmatique*, belonging to business. – L. *pragmaticus*. – Gk. πραγματικός, skilled in business. – Gk. πραγματ-, stem of πρᾶγμα (= πρακ-μα), a deed, thing done.

Prætor, Pretor; see Itinerant.

Pragmatic; see Practice.

Prairie, an extensive meadow. (F. – L.) F. *prairie*, a meadow. – Low L. *prataria*, meadow-land. – L. *pratum*, a meadow, flat land. (√PRAT.)

Praise; see Precious.

Prance; see Prank (1).

Prank (1), to deck, adorn. (E.) M. E. *pranken*, to trim; allied to obs. E. *prink*, to trim (Nares). *Prink* is a nasalised form of *prick*; cf. Lowl. Sc. *preek*, to be spruce, *prick - me - dainty*, finical, *prink*, *primp*, to deck, to prick. *Prank* is an allied form to these; see further under **Prick.** So also O. Du. *proncken*, to display one's dress, *pronckepinken*, *pronckeprinken*, to glitter in a fine dress; G. Dan. Swed. *prunk*, show, parade; O. Du. *pryken*, to make a shew.

prance. (E.) M. E. *prancen*, *prauncen*, used of a horse; it means to make a shew, shew off; closely allied to M. E. *pranken*, to trim. So also O. Du. *pronken*, to make a show, to strut about.

prank (2), a trick. (E.) An act done to shew off, a trick to make people stare; allied to **Prank** (1).

Prate. (Scand.) M. E. *praten.* – O. Swed. *prata*, Dan. *prate*, to prate, talk; cf. Swed. Dan. *prat*, talk. + O. Du. *praten*, to prate, Du. *praat*, talk. **Der.** *pratt-le*, the frequentative form.

Prawn. (Origin unknown.) M. E. *prane*, Prompt. Parv. Perhaps (through a lost F. form) from L. *perna*, a sea-mussel; cf. O. Ital. *parnocchie*, 'a fish called shrimps or praunes;' Florio.

Pray; see Precarious.

Pre-, beforehand. (L.; *or* F. – L.) F. *pre-*, L. *pre-*, *præ-*, from L. *præ*, prep.,

before. Put for *prai**, a locative case; closely allied to **Pro-**. ¶ Hence numerous compounds, many of which, like *precaution*, are of obvious origin.

Preach; see Diction.

Prebend; see Habit.

Precarious. (L.) L. *precarius*, obtained by prayer or as a favour, doubtful, precarious. – L. *precari*, to pray. – L. *prec-*, stem of *prex*, a prayer. + Skt. *pracch*, G. *fragen*, to ask. (√PARK.)

deprecate. (L.) From pp. of L. *deprecari*, to pray against, pray to remove. – L. *de*, away; *precari* (above).

imprecate. (L.) From pp. of L. *imprecari*, to call down upon by prayer. – L. *im-* (*in*), upon; *precari* (above).

pray. (F. – L.) M. E. *preyen*. – O. F. *preier* (F. *prier*). – L. *precari* (above). Der. *pray-er*, M. E. *preiere*, O. F. *preiere*, from L. *precaria*, fem. of *precarius*, adj.; see **Precarious** (above).

Precaution; see Caveat.

Precede; see Cede.

Precentor; see Cant (1).

Precept; see Capacious.

Precinct; see Cincture.

Precious. (F. – L.) O. F. *precieus* (F. *prétieux*). – L. *pretiosus*, valuable. – L. *pretium*, price, value. Allied to Skt. *pana* (i. e. *parna**), wages, price; Gk. πέρ-νημι, I sell. (√PAR, to buy.)

appraise. (F. – L.) M. E. *apreisen*, to value. – O. F. *apreiser* (spelt *apretier* in Roquefort). – O. F. *a-*, prefix; *preiser*, to value, from *preis*, value, price. – L. *ad*, at; *pretium*, a price.

appreciate. (L.) From pp. of L. *appretiare*, to value at a price. – L. *ap-* (*ad*) at; *pretium*, a price.

depreciate. (L.) From pp. of L. *depretiare*, to lower the price of. – L. *de*, down; *pretium*, price.

praise. (F. – L.) O. F. *preis*, price, value, merit (hence, tribute to merit). – L. *pretium*, price, value. Der. *dis-praise*.

price. (F. – L.) M. E. *pris*. – O. F. *pris*, by-form of O. F. *preis* (above).

prize (2), to value highly. (F. – L.) M. E. *prisen*. – F. *priser*, to esteem; Cot. – O. F. *pris*, a price, value; see **price** (above)

Precipice; see Capital (1).

Precise; see Cæsura.

Preclude; see Clause.

Precocious; see Cook.

Precursor; see Current.

Predatory, given to plundering. (L.)

L. *prædatorius*, plundering. – L. *prædator*, a plunderer. – L. *prædari*, to plunder. – L. *præda*, booty. β. *Præda* probably = *præhed-a**, that which is seized beforehand; from' *præ*, before, and *hed-*, base of *hendere*, to seize, get; see Get. (So also *prendere* = *pre-hendere*.) γ. Otherwise, L. *præda* = Irish *spreidh*, cattle, W. *praidd*, flock, herd, booty, prey.

depredate. (L.) From pp. of L. *deprædari*, to plunder. – L. *de*, fully; *prædari*, to rob (above).

prey, sb. (F. – L.) O. F. *preie* (F. *proie*). – L. *præda* (above). Der. *prey*, vb.

Predecessor; see Cede.

Predicate, Predict; see Diction.

Predilection; see Legend.

Preface; see Fate.

Prefect; see Fact.

Prefer; see Fertile.

Prefigure; see Figure.

Pregnant; see Natal.

Prehensile, adapted for grasping. (L.) Coined with suffix *-ile* (L. *-ilis*) from L. *prehens-us*, pp. of *prehendere*, *prendere*, to lay hold of. – L. *præ*, before; obsolete *hendere*, to grasp, cognate with E. Get, q. v.

apprehend. (L.) L. *apprehendere*, orig. to lay hold of. – L. *ap-* (*ad*), to, at; *prehendere*, to grasp (above).

apprentice. (F. – L.) From a dialectal F. form, such as the Walloon *apprentiche*, imported hither from the Low Countries; the proper O. F. form being *aprentif*. The Walloon *apprentiche* (Prov. *apprentiz*, Span. *aprendiz*) is from Low L. *apprenticius*, a learner of a trade, a novice. – Low L. *apprendere*, to learn; short for L. *apprehendere*, to lay hold of (above).

apprise, to inform. (F. – L.) From the M. E. sb. *apprise*, information, teaching. – O. F. *apprise*, instruction. – O. F. *appris*, *apris*, pp. of *aprendre*, to learn. – Low L. *apprendere* (above).

comprehend. (L.) L. *com-prehendere*, to grasp; where *com-* = *cum*, together.

comprise. (F. – L.) O. F. *compris*, later *comprins*, pp. comprised, comprehended. – F. *comprendre*, to comprehend. – L. *comprehendere* (above).

enterprise. (F. – L.) O. F. *entreprise*, later *enterprinse*, an enterprise. – O. F. *enterpris*, pp. of *enterprendre*, to undertake. – Low L. *interprendere*. – L. *inter*, among; *prendere*, short for *prehendere*, to lay hold of.

impregnable. (F. – L.) The *g* is inserted. – O. F. *imprenable*, 'impregnable;' Cot. – O. F. *im-* (= L. *in*), not; F. *prendre*, from L. *prehendere*, to take, seize.

imprison. (F. – L.) Put for *emprison*. – O. F. *emprisonner*, to imprison. – O. F. *em-* (= L. *in*), in; *prison*, a prison (below).

prentice, short for apprentice (above).

prise, prize, a lever. (F. – L.) ' *Prise*, a lever;' Halliwell. Hence ' to *prise* open a box,' or corruptly, ' to *pry* open.' – F. *prise*, a grasp, tight hold (hence, leverage). Orig. fem. of *pris*, pp. of *prendre*, to grasp. – L. *prehendere*, to grasp.

prison. (F. – L.) O. F. *prisun*, F. *prison*; cf. Ital. *prigione*, a prison. – L. acc. *prensionem*, acc. of *prensio*, a seizing, seizure. – L. *prensus*, for *prehensus*, pp. of *prehendere*, to seize.

prize (1), a thing captured from the enemy or won in a lottery. (F. – L.) F. *prise*, a seizure, also, a prize; see prise (above).

prize (3), the same as **prise** (above).

reprehend, to reprove. (L.) L. *reprehendere*, to hold back, check, blame. – L. *re-*, back; *prehendere*, to seize, to hold.

reprisal. (F. – Ital. – L.) O. F. *presaille*, a taking or seizing on, a reprisal. [The change of vowel is due to obs. verb *reprise*, to seize in return, from F. *repris*, pp. of *reprendre* = L. *reprehendere*, (here) to seize again.] – Ital. *ripresaglia*, booty. – Ital. *ripresa*, a taking again; fem. of *ripreso*, pp. of *riprendere*, to reprehend, also to retake. – L. *re-prehendere* (above).

surprise, sb. (F. – L.) O. F. *sorprise*, *surprise*, a taking unawares. Fem. of *sorpris*, pp. of *sorprendre*, *surprendre*, to surprise. – L. *super*, upon; *prehendere*, to seize.

Prejudge, Prejudice; see Judge.

Prelate; see Tolerate.

Preliminary; see Limit.

Prelude; see Ludicrous.

Premature; see Pre- and Mature.

Premier; see Prime (1).

Premise, Premiss; see Missile.

Premium; see Exempt.

Premonish; see Monition.

Prentice; see Prehensile.

Prepare; see Pare.

Prepense, Preponderate; see Pendant.

Preposition; see Position.

Preposterous; see Post-.

Prerogative; see Rogation.

Presage; see Sagacious.

Presbyter. (L.—Gk.) L. *presbyter.*—
Gk. πρεσβύτερος, an elder; orig. elder,
comparative of πρέσβυς, old.

priest. (L.—Gk.) M. E. *preest*; A.S.
preóst. Contracted (like O. F. *prestre*)
from L. *presbyter* (above). Cf. '*Prester*
John.'

Prescience; see **Science.**

Prescribe; see **Scribe.**

Presence, Present; see **Sooth.**

Presentiment; see **Sense.**

Preserve; see **Serve.**

Preside; see **Sedentary.**

Press (1), to squeeze. (F.—L.) M. E.
pressen.—F. *presser.*—L. *pressare*, frequent.
of *premere* (pp. *pressus*), to press. Der.
press, sb.; *press-ure.*

compress. (L.) L. *compressare*, to
oppress.—L. *com-* (*cum*), together; *pressare* (above).

depress. (L.) From L. *depressus*, pp.
of *de-primere*, to press down.

express, adj., exactly stated. (F.—L.)
O. F. *expres.*—L. *expressus*, distinct; pp. of
ex-primere, to press out. Der. *express*,
verb.

impress. (L.) L. *impressare*, frequent.
of *imprimere*, to press upon.—L. *im-* (*in*),
on; *premere*, to press.

imprint. (F.—L.) The verb, in Sir
T. More, is formed as if from *im-* and
print; but *print* itself is short for *emprint.*
—O. F. *empreinte*, 'a stamp, print;' Cot.
Orig. fem. of pp. of *empreindre*, 'to print,
stamp;' id.—L. *imprimere*, to impress,
press upon (above). See **print** (below).

oppress. (F. — L.) F. *oppresser.* —
Low L. *oppressare*, frequent. of L. *opprimere*,
to oppress.—L. *op-* (*ob*), near; *premere*, to
press.

print, sb. (F. — L.) M. E. *printe*,
prente, preinte; short for *empreinte*, borrowed from O. F. *empreinte*, 'a stamp,
print;' Cot. See **imprint** (above). Der.
print, verb; *re-print.*

repress. (F.—L.) From F. *re-*, again,
and *presser*, to press; but used with sense
of L. *re-primere*, to press back, check.

reprimand. (F.—L.) F. *réprimande*,
formerly *reprimende*, 'a reproof;' Cot.—
L. *reprimenda*, a thing that ought to be
repressed; hence, a check. Fem. of fut.
part. pass. of *reprimere*, to repress (above).

sprain, vb. (F.—L.) Formed from
O. F. *espreindre*, 'to press, wring,' Cot.;
(just as *strain* is from O. F. *estreindre.*
Mod. F. *épreindre*).—L. *exprimere*, to press

out (whence *espreindre*, put for *espreimre*,
by change of *m* to *n*, with excrescent *d*).
—L. *ex*, out; *premere*, to press. Der.
sprain, sb.

suppress. (L.) From L. *suppressus*,
pp. of *supprimere*, to suppress.—L. *sup-*
(*sub*), under; *premere*, to press.

Press (2), to hire men for service,. make
men serve as sailors, &c.; see **State.** Der.
press-gang.

Prestige; see **Distinguish.**

Presume; see **Exempt.**

Pretend; see **Tend** (1).

Preter-, *prefix.* (L.) L. *præter*, beyond;
comp. form of *præ*, before; see **Pre-.**

Preterite; see **Itinerant.**

Pretermit; see **Missile.**

Preternatural; see **Natal.**

Pretext; see **Text.**

Pretty. (C. — L. — Gk.) M. E. *prati*;
A. S. *prætig, prættig*, orig. deceitful, tricky;
hence clever, cunning, the usual M. E.
sense. Formed with suffix *-ig* from
A. S. *præt*, deceit, trickery. Cf. Lowl.
Sc. *pratty, pretty*, tricky, from *prat*,
a trick (G. Douglas). Borr. from W.
praith, an act, deed, Corn. *prat*, a trick;
or rather from the O. Brit. form of
Low L. *practica*, a deed, plot. See
Practice.

Prevail; see **Valid.**

Prevaricate; see **Varicose.**

Prevent; see **Venture.**

Previous; see **Viaduct.**

Prey; see **Predatory.**

Prial; see **Par.**

Price; see **Precious.**

Prick. (E.) M. E. *prikke, prike*, sb.
A. S. *pricu, prica*, a point, prick, dot.+
O. Du. *prick*, a prickle, Dan. *prik*, Swed.
prick, a dot, mark. β. Allied to Irish
sprichar, a sting, Skt. *prish*, to sprinkle,
prishata, speckled, also a dot; and to
E. **Sprinkle.** Orig. sense 'a small spot,'
as caused by sprinkling; hence a tiny
wound. Der. *prick*, verb; *prick-le*, sb.

Pride; see **Proud.**

Priest; see **Presbyter.**

Prim; see **Prime.**

Prime (1), first, chief. (F. — L.) F.
prime, properly 'prime,' the first canonical
hour. — L. *prima*, fem. of *primus*, first.
Primus is for *pro-imus* *, superl. from *pro*,
forth, forward. So also A. S. *for-ma*, first,
from *fore*; see **Former, Pro-.** So also
Gk. πρῶ-τος, first, from πρό; Skt. *pra-ta-
ma*, first. Der. *prim-ary, prim-ate*, O. F.

primat, L. acc. *primatem*, from *primas*, a chief man.

premier. (F. – L.) F. *premier*, first. – L. *primarium*, acc. of *primarius*, chief. – L. *primus*, first.

prim, neat. (F. – L.) O. F. *prim*, masc., *prime*, fem., prime, forward, also *prime*, masc. and fem., thin, slender, small, as *cheveux primes*, 'smooth or delicate hair;' Cot. The sense is first-grown, small, delicate. ¶ The word was perhaps confused with *prink*, to deck; see **Prank**.

prime (2), to make a gun quite ready. (F. – L.) Cf. *prime*, to trim trees; *prime*, first position in fencing; and esp. the phr. 'to put into *prime* order.' A peculiar use of *prime* (1).

primero, an old game at cards. (Span. – L.) Span. *primero*, lit. 'first.' – L. *primarius*; see **premier** (above).

primeval. (L.) Coined from L. *primus*, first; *æuum*, age; cf. L. *primæuus*, primeval.

primitive. (F. – L.) F. *primitif*. – L. *primitiuus*, earliest of its kind. – L. *primus*, first.

primogeniture. (F. – L.) O.F. *primogeniture*, 'the being eldest;' Cot. – L. *primogenitus*, first-born. – L. *primo-*, crude form of *primus*, first; *genitus*, pp. of *gignere* (base *gan*), to beget, produce; see **Genus**.

primrose. (F. – L.) F. *prime rose*, first rose; L. *prima rosa*; such is the obvious and popular etymology; but, historically, *primrose* is a substitution for M. E. *primerole*, a primrose. Dimin. of Low L. *primula*, a primrose (still preserved in Span. *primula*, the same). Again, *primula* is a derivative of *primus*, first. ¶ The word *rose* has, accordingly, nothing to do with *primrose*, except by popular blunder.

prince. (F. – L.) F. *prince*. – L. *principem*, acc. of *princeps*, a chief, lit. 'taking the first place.' – L. *prin-*, for *prim-us*, first; *capere*, to take; see **Capital**.

principal. (F. – L.) F. *principal*. – L. *principalis*, chief. – L. *princip-*, stem of *princeps*, a chief (above).

principle. (F. – L.) The *l* is an E. addition, as in *syllable*. – F. *principe*, a principle, maxim; orig. beginning. – L. *principium*, a beginning. – L. *principi-*, crude form of *princeps*, taking the first place; see **prince** (above).

prior (1), former. (L.) L. *prior*, former.

Put for *pro-ior* *, comp. of *pro*; see **prime** (above).

prior (2), head of a priory. (F. – L.) M. E. *priour*. – F. *prieur*. – L. *priorem*, acc. of *prior*, former, hence, a superior; see above.

pristine, ancient. (F. – L.) O. F. *pristine*. – L. *pristinus*, ancient; allied to *pris-cus*, former, and to *prior*, *prime*. ¶ See also *privet*.

Primero, Primeval, &c.; see **Prime**.
Primordial; see **Order**.
Primrose, Prince; see **Prime**.
Principal, Principle; see **Prime**.
Print; see **Press**.
Prior (1) and (2); see **Prime**.
Prise, a lever; see **Prehensile**.

Prism. (L. – Gk.) L. *prisma*. – Gk. πρίσμα (stem πρισματ-), a prism; lit. a piece sawn off. – Gk. πρίζειν, to saw; cf. πρίειν, to saw. Der. *prismat-ic*.

Prison; see **Prehensile**.
Pristine; see **Prime**.

Private. (L.) L. *priuatus*, apart; pp. of *priuare*, to bereave. – L. *priuus*, single; lit. put forward, sundered from the rest. It stands for *prai-uus* *, from *prai*, old form of *præ*, before; see **Pre-**.

deprive. (L.) Low L. *depriuare*, to deprive of office, degrade. – L. *de*, fully; *priuare*, to deprive (above).

privilege. (F. – L.) O. F. *privilege*. – L. *priuilegium*, (1) a bill against a person, (2) an ordinance in favour of one, a privilege. – L. *priui-*, for *priuus*, single; *legi-*, crude form of *lex*, law.

privy, private. (F. – L.) O. F. *prive* (F. *privé*), private. – L. *priuatus* (above).

Privet, a shrub. (F.? – L.?) *Privet* seems to be a corruption of *primet*, which also means a primrose; confusion between the plants arose from the L. *ligustrum* being applied to both. We also find, for privet, the names *prim*, *primprint*, *primprivet*; where *print* is short for *primet* (*prim't*), and *primprint* stands for *prim-prim-et*. Prob. named from being formally cnt and trimmed; cf. *prime*, to cut trees (Halliwell). See **prim**, under **Prime** (1). *Primet*, a primrose, is likewise from *prime*.

Privilege, Privy; see **Private**.
Prize (1), a thing won; see **Prehensile**.
Prize (2), to value; see **Precious**.
Prize (3), to open a box; see **Prehensile**.

Pro-, prefix. (L. or Gk.; or F. – L.) L. *prŏ-*, prefix, before; whence *prō* (= *prod*), an abl. form, used as a prep. Also Gk. πρo-, prefix; πρό, prep., before; cf. Skt. *pra*, before, away. Der. *pre-*, prefix; *pri-or, pri-me, pri-vate, prow, pro-vost*, &c.

Proa, a small ship. (Malay.) Malay *praü, práu*, a general term for small ships.

Probable. (F. — L.) F. *probable*. — L. *probabilis*, that may be proved. — L. *probare*, to test, prove, orig. to try the goodness. — L. *probus*, good, excellent.

approbation. (F. — L.) F. *approba-tion*. — L. acc. *approbationem*, approval. — L. *approbatus*, pp. of *approbare*, to approve (below).

approve. (F. — L.) O. F. *approver*. — L. *approbare*, to approve. — L. *ap-* (*ad*), to; *probare*, to test, try, esteem as good. Der. *approv-al*. Der. *dis-approve*.

disprove. (F. — L.) O. F. *des-* (L. *dis-*), apart, away; *prover*, to prove; see prove (below).

improve. (F. — L.) A coined word, formerly used as equivalent, or nearly so, to *approve*. From L. *im-* (*in*); and O. F. *prover*, from L. *probare*; see prove (below).

probation. (F. — L.) F. *probation*. — L. acc. *probationem*, a trial, proof. — L. *probatus*, pp. of *probare*, to test; see Pro-bable (above).

probe. (L.) A coined word; cf. Late L. *proba*, a proof. — L. *probare*, to test; see above.

probity. (F. — L.) F. *probité*, honesty. L. *probitatem*, acc. of *probitas*, honesty. — L. *probus*, honest, excellent.

proof, a test, evidence. (F. — L.) For-merly *profe* (1551). M. E. *preef, preove*. — F. *preuve*, a trial; Cot. — Late L. *proba*, a proof. — L. *probare*, to test (above).

prove, to test, demonstrate. (F. — L.) The usual old sense is to *test*, as in 'the exception *proves* (tests) the rule,' a transla-tion of L. *exceptio probat regulam*. — O. F. *prover*, later *prouver*, ' to prove, try, essay, verifie;' Cot. — L. *probare*, to test, try the goodness of. — L. *probus*, excellent.

reprieve. (F. — L.) Really the same word as *reprove*, but nearer to M. E. *re-preven*, to reject, put aside, disallow; 'to *reprieve* a sentence' is to disallow it; see reprove (below).

reprobate. (L.) L. *reprobatus*, re-proved, rejected; pp. of *re-probare*, to re-ject upon trial. — L. *re-*, back; *probare*, to test.

reprove. (F. — L.) M. E. *reproven*,

also *repreven*. — O. F. *reprover* (F. *réprou-ver*), to reprove, condemn. — L. *reprobare* (above).

Probation, Probe, Probity; see Pro-bable.

Problem. (F. — L. — Gk.) O. F. *prob-leme*; F. *problème*. — L. *problema*. — Gk. πρόβλημα, a thing thrown forward, or put forward as a question for discussion. — Gk. πρό, forward; βλῆμα, a casting, from βάλ-λειν, to cast.

Proboscis. (L. — Gk.) L. *proboscis*. — Gk. προβοσκίς, an elephant's trunk or ' feeder.' — Gk. πρό, in front; βόσκειν, to feed; see Botany.

Proceed; see Cede.

Proclaim; see Claim.

Proclivity; see Acclivity.

Procrastinate, to postpone. (L.) From pp. of L. *procrastinare*, to delay, put off till the morrow. — L. *pro*, forward, off; *crastinus*, belonging to the morrow, from *cras*, morrow.

Procreate; see Create.

Proctor; see Cure.

Procumbent; see Covey.

Procure; see Cure.

Prodigal; see Agent.

Prodigy. (F. — L.) Englished from F. *prodige*, a prodigy, wonder. — L. *prodigium*, a token, portent. β. Perhaps for *prod-agium**, i. e. a saying beforehand, from *prod* (*prō*), before, and *agium**, a saying, as in *ad-agium*; see Adage.

Produce; see Duke.

Proem. (F. — L. — Gk.) O. F. *proëme*, ' a proem, preface;' Cot. — L. *prooemium*. — Gk. προοίμιον, an introduction. — Gk. πρό, before; οἶμος, a way, path, from √ I, to go.

Profane; see Fane.

Profess; see Fame.

Proffer; see Fertile.

Proficient; see Fact.

Profile; see File (1).

Profit; see Fact.

Profligate. (L.) L. *profligatus*, cast down, abandoned, dissolute; pp. of *profli-gare*, to dash down. — L. *pro*, forward; *fligere*, to strike, dash. See Afflict. (√ BHLAGH.)

Profound; see Fund.

Profuse; see Fuse (1).

Prog; see Prowl.

Progenitor, Progeny; see Genus.

Prognostic; see Gnome.

Programme; see Graphic.

Progress; see Grade.

Prohibit; see Habit.

Project; see Jet (1).

Prolate; see Tolerate.

Prolepsis, anticipation. (L. – Gk.) L. *prolepsis*. – Gk. πρόληψις, lit. a taking beforehand. – Gk. πρό, before; λῆψις, a seizing, from λήψ-ομαι, fut. of λαμβάνειν, to seize. See **Catalepsy**.

Prolific. (F. – L.) F. *prolifique*, fruitful. – L. *proli-*, crude form of *prōles*, offspring; *-ficus*, from *facere*, to make. L. *prōles* = *pro-oles*, from *pro*, before, and *olēre* *, to grow, whence *ad-olescere*, to grow up. See **Adult**.

Prolix. (F: – L.) F. *prolixe*. – L. *prolixus*, extended. Lit. 'that which has flowed forth' or beyond bounds; from *pro*, forth, *liquere*, *liqui*, to flow. See **Liquid**.

Prolocutor; see **Loquacious**.

Prologue; see **Logic**.

Prolong; see **Long** (1).

Promenade; see **Menace**.

Prominent; see **Eminent**.

Promiscuous; see **Miscellaneous**.

Promise; see **Missile**.

Promontory, a headland. (L.) L. *promontorium*, a ridge, headland. Prob. from *prominere*, to jut out; see prominent, s. v. **Eminent**; and cf. **Mount**.

Promote; see **Move**.

Prompt; see **Exempt**.

Promulgate. (L.) From pp. of *promulgare*, to publish. (Of unknown origin.)

Prone. (F. – L.) F. *prone*. – L. *pronum*, acc. of *pronus*, inclined forwards. *Prōnus* prob. stands for *prouonus* *, from *pro*, forward; cf. Gk. πρηνής (= πραϝανός), headlong, Skt. *pravana*, inclined to, prone.

Prong, spike of a fork. (C.) Spelt *prongue* in Levins (1570). A nasalised form of the root seen in W. *procio*, to thrust, stab, poke, Gael. *brog*, to stimulate, stir, goad; cf. prov. E. *prog*, to prick, thrust.

pang, a sharp pain. (C.) Spelt '*prange* of love;' Court of Love, l. 1150 (ed. 1561); M. E. *pronge*, a throc, a woman's pang (Prompt. Parv.). The sense is 'a sharp stab,' a prick; see above. ¶ The loss of *r* may have been suggested by prov. F. *poigne*, a grip; cf. O. F. *empoigner*, to grip (Cot.), allied to F. *poing*, the fist, L. *pugnus*. Cf. *speak* for *spreak*.

Pronoun; see **Noble**.

Pronounce; see **Nuncio**.

Proof; see **Probable**.

Prop. (C.) M. E. *proppe*. – Irish *propa*, Gael. *prop*, a prop, support.

Propagate; see **Pact**.

Propel; see **Pulsate**.

Propensity; see **Pendant**.

Proper, one's own, peculiar, suitable. (F. – L.) M. E. *propre*. – F. *propre*. – L. *proprium*, acc. of *proprius*, one's own. Prob. akin to *prope*, near.

appropriate. (L.) From pp. of L. *appropriare*, to make one's own. – L. *ap-* (*ad*), to; *proprius*, one's own.

impropriate, to appropriate to private use. (L.) Coined from L. *im-* (*in*), in; *propriare*, to appropriate, from *proprius*, one's own.

property. (F. – L.) M. E. *propertee*. – O. F. *properté*, property (Littré), also propriety, fitness. – L. *proprietatem*, acc. of *proprietas*, property, ownership; also propriety of terms. – L. *proprius*, one's own.

propriety. (F. – L.) F. *propriété*, a property, also 'a comely assortment,' Cot. – L. acc. *proprietatem* (above).

Prophet. (F. – L. – Gk.) O. F. *prophete*. – L. *propheta*. – Gk. προφήτης, one who declares, an expounder, a prophet. – Gk. πρό, publicly, lit. before; φη-μί, I speak; with suffix -της of the agent. (√BHA.) Allied to **Fame**.

prophecy. (F. – L. – Gk.) M. E. *prophecie*, sb. – O. F. *prophecie*, variant of *prophetie*, a prophecy. – L. *prophetia*. – Gk. προφητεία, a prediction. – Gk. προφήτης, a prophet (above). Der. *prophesy*, vb.

Propinquity, nearness. (L.) Englished from L. *propinquitas*, nearness. – L. *propinquus*, near. – L. *prope*, adv., near.

approach. (F. – L.) M. E. *approchen*, *aprochen*. – O. F. *aprochier*, to approach. – L. *appropiare*, to draw near to. – L. *ap-* (*ad*), to; *prope*, near.

approximate. (L.) From pp. of L. *approximare*, to draw near to. – L. *ap-* (*ad*), to; *proximus*, very near, superl. from *prope*, near.

proximity. (F. – L.) F. *proximité*. – L. *proximitatem*, acc. of *proximitas*, nearness. – L. *proximus*, very near; a superl. form from *prope*, near.

reproach. (F. – L.) F. *reprocher*, to reproach. Cf. Span. *reprochar*, Prov. *repropchar*, to reproach; answering to a Low L. *repropiare* *, not found, to bring near to, impute to, reproach. – L. *re-*, again; *propi-us*, nearer, comp. of *prope*, near. (A translation of L. *obicere* (*objicere*), to bring near or cast before one, to reproach.)

Propitious, favourable. (L.) L. *propitius*, favourable. Prob. a term in augury, with the sense 'flying forwards.'—L. *pro*, forward; *petere*, to seek, orig. to fly. See Petition. Der. *propitiate*, from pp. of L. *propitiare*, to render propitious.

Proportion; see Part.

Propose; see Pose (1).

Proposition, Propound; see Position.

Propriety; see Proper.

Prorogue; see Rogation.

Pros-, towards. (Gk.) Gk. πρός, towards; fuller form προτί, extended from πρό, before. + Skt. *prati*, towards, from *pra*, before. See Pro-.

Proscenium; see Scene.

Proscribe; see Scribe.

Prose; see Verse.

Prosecute; see Sequence.

Proselyte, a convert. (F.—L.—Gk.) O. F. *proselite*. — L. *proselytum*, acc. of *proselytus*.—Gk. προσήλυτος, one who has come to a place, a stranger, a convert to Judaism; Acts, ii. 10.—Gk. προσέρχομαι, I approach, 2 aor. προσῆλθον (=προσήλυθον).—Gk. πρός, to; ἔρχομαι, I come.

Prosody; see Ode.

Prosopopœia, personification. (L.—Gk.) L. *prosopopœia*.—Gk. προσωποποιία personification.—Gk. προσωποποιεῖν, to personify.—Gk. πρόσωπο-ν, a face, a person; ποιεῖν, to make. Πρόσωπον is from πρός, towards, and ὤπ-, stem of ὤψ, face, appearance. See Pros-, Optic, and Poem.

Prospect; see Species.

Prosperous; see Desperate.

Prostitute; see State.

Prostrate; see Stratum.

Protean. (L.—Gk.) From L. *Prote-us*, a sea-god who often changed his form. — Gk. Πρωτεύς, a sea-god.

Protect; see Tegument.

Protest; see Testament.

Prothalamium. (L. — Gk.) Late L. *prothalamium**. — Gk. προθαλάμιον*, a song written before a marriage; a coined word.—Gk. πρό, before; θάλαμος, a bedroom, bride-chamber. Coined to accompany *Epithalamium*, q. v.

Protocol, the first draught of a document. (F.—L.—Gk.) O. F. *protocole*, 'the first draught or copy of a deed.—Low L. *protocollum*. — Late Gk. πρωτόκολλον, explained by Scheler to mean orig. a first leaf, glued on to MSS., in order to register

by whom the MS. was written, &c. By a decree of Justinian, certain MSS. were to be thus accompanied by a fly-leaf. It means 'first glued on,' i. e. fastened on at the beginning.—Gk. πρῶτο-s, first; κολλᾷν, to glue, from κόλλα, glue. Πρῶτος is a superl. form from πρό, before; see Pro-.

protomartyr. (F.—L.—Gk.) F. *protomartyre*.—Late L. *protomartyr*. — Gk.πρωτόμαρτυρ, lit. 'first martyr.'—Gk. πρῶτος, first (above); μάρτυρ, a martyr; see Martyr.

prototype. (F.—L.—Gk.) F. *prototype*.—L. acc. *prototypum*.—Gk. πρωτότυπον, a prototype, neut. of πρωτότυπος, according to the first form.—Gk. πρῶτο-s, first (above); τύπος, a type; see Type.

Protract; see Trace (1).

Protrude; see Intrude.

Protuberant; see Tuber.

Proud. (E.) M. E. *prud*, later *proud*; older form *prut*. A. S. *prút*, proud; whence the Icel. *prúðr*, proud, is supposed to have been borrowed.' Cf. Dan. *prud*, stately.

pride. (E.) M. E. *pride, prude*. A.S. *prýte*, pride; regularly formed (by the usual change from *ú* to *ý*) from A.S. *prút*, proud.

Prove; see Probable.

Provender; see Habit.

Proverb; see Verb.

Provide; see Vision.

Province. (F.—L.) F. *province*.—L. *prouincia*, a territory, conquest. (Of doubtful origin.)

Provision; see Vision.

Provoke; see Vocal.

Provost; see Position.

Prow, front part of a ship. (F.—L.—Gk.) O. F. *prouĕ* (F. *proue*), prow. Cf. Ital. *prua, proda.*—L. *prōra*, a prow; the 2nd *r* disappearing to avoid the double trill.—Gk. πρῷρα (for πρώι-ρα), the prow.—Gk. πρωί, in front (usually early), an old locative form allied to πρό-, before. See Pro-.

Prowess, bravery. (F. — L.) M. E. *prowes, pruesse.*—O. F. *prouesse*, prowess; formed with suffix *-esse* (= L. *-itia*) from O. F. *prou* (F. *preux*), valiant. β. Etym. disputed; we also find O. F. *prod, prud*,fem. *prode, prude*; Prov. *pros*, Ital. *prode*. Also O.F. *prou*, sb., advantage, whence M. E. *prow*, advantage. Although O. F. *prod* was used to translate L. *probus*, the spelling with *d* shews there is no connection.

γ. Scheler explains it from L. *prod-*, as occurring in *prod-esse*, to benefit; so that *prod* was taken to mean 'for the benefit of;' and we even find F. *prou* used as an adverb, as in *prou*, 'much, greatly, enough;' Cot. *Prod* is an ablative form of *prō*, before; and is the same as L. *prō*, for.

prude, a woman of affected modesty. (F. – L.) F. *prude*, *preude*, orig. in a good sense, chaste; fem. of F. *preux*, O.F. *prou*, excellent (above).

Prowl. (C.?) M.E. *prollen*, to search after continually. 'I *prolle*, I go here and there to seke a thyng:' Palsgrave. I take it to stand for *prokle* * or *proggle* *, a frequentative form from *proke*, to thrust or poke, *progue*, to go a-begging. See *proke*, *prolle* in Halliwell; *prog*, *progue*, *prowl* in Todd's Johnson and Nares. Prob. from W. *procio*, to thrust, stab, poke, confused with L. *procare*, to ask; we also find M.E. *prokken*, to demand, Swed. *pracka*, to go begging, G. *prachern*, to beg; also vulgar E. *prog*, provisions, i.e. that which is got by *progging* or searching or begging about. All these words are somewhat obscure. ¶ Certainly *not* allied to L. *præda*, F. *prvie*, which became *prey* in English.

Proximity; see **Propinquity**.

Proxy; see **Cure**.

Prude; see **Prowess**.

Prudent; see **Vision**.

Prune (1), to trim trees. (F.? – L.?) Very difficult. M.E. *proinen*, *prunen*, to dress oneself up smartly, trim; Gascoigne has *proyne*, to prune off shoots. Prob. from a provincial form of F. *provigner* (also spelt *preugner*, *progner*, Littré), 'to plant or set a stocke, staulke, slip, or sucker,' Cot.; hence the sense to clear off or to trim off suckers, stalks, &c. This verb is from F. *provin*, O.F. *provain*, a sucker. – L. *propaginem*, acc. of *propago*, a layer, a sucker. See **propagate**, s.v. **Pact.**

Prune (2), a plum. (F. – L. – Gk.) F. *prune*. – L. *prunum*. – Gk. προῦνον, shorter form of προὖμνον, a plum.

plum. (L. – Gk.) A.S. *plúme*, a plum; formed (by change of *r* to *l*) from L. *prunum* (above).

prunella, **prunello**, a strong woollen stuff, orig. of a *dark* colour. (F. – L. – Gk.) F' *prunelle*, a sloe; (with ref. to the colour); whence *prunella* is a Latinised form. Dimin. of F. *prune* (above).

Prurient. (L.) L. *prurient-*, stem of

pres. pt. of *prurire*, to itch, orig. to burn. Allied to E. **Freeze**.

Pry; see **Peer** (2).

Psalm. (L. – Gk.) M.E. *psalm*, formerly *salm*. A.S. *sealm*. – L. *psalmus*. – Gk. ψαλμός, a touching, twitching the strings of a harp; also a song, psalm. – Gk. ψάλλειν, to touch, twitch, twang a harp. Cf. ἀσπαίρειν, to pant, Skt. *sphur*, to tremble, throb. (√SPAR.) Der. *psalmod-y*, F. *psalmodie*, L. *psalmodia*, Gk. ψαλμῳδία, a singing to the harp, from ᾠδή, a song; see **Ode**.

psaltery, a stringed instrument. (F. – L. – Gk.) O.F. *psalterie* (12th cent.) – L. *psalterium*. – Gk. ψαλτήριον, a kind of harp. – Gk. ψαλτήρ, a harper. – Gk. ψάλ-λειν, to twang a harp; with suffix -τηρ of the agent. **Der.** *psalter*, O.F. *psaltier*, a book of psalms, L. *psalterium*, (1) a psaltery, (2) a psalter.

Pseudonym. (F. – Gk.) F. *pseudo-nyme* (1772). – Gk. ψευδώνυμος, adj., called by a false name. – Gk. ψεῦδο-ς, falsehood (ψευδής, false); ὄνυμα, a name; (ω = οο).

Pshaw, interjection. (E.) An imitative word; cf. *pish*, *pooh*.

Psychical, pertaining to the soul. (L. – Gk.) From L. *psychicus*. – Gk. ψυχικός, belonging to the soul or life. – Gk. ψυχή, soul, life, orig. breath. – Gk. ψύχειν, to blow. Cf. Skt. *phút*, the sound of blowing. (√SPU.)

metempsychosis, transmigration of souls. (Gk.) Gk. μετεμψύχωσις. – Gk. μετεμψυχόω, I make the soul pass from one body to another. – Gk. μετ-ά, denoting 'change'; ἐμ-, for ἐν, in, into; ψυχ-ή, the soul.

psychology. (Gk.) Gk. ψυχο-, for ψυχή, soul, life; -λογία, from λόγος, a discourse, from λέγειν, to speak.

Ptarmigan, a bird. (Gael.) Gael. *tarmachan*; Irish *tarmochan*.

Puberty. (F. – L.) F. *puberté*, youth. – L. *pubertatem*, acc. of *pubertas*, age of maturity. – L. *pubes*, the signs of manhood, hair. Allied to *pu-pus*, *pu-er*, a boy. (√PU.) **Der.** *pubescence*, sb. due to *pubescent-*, stem of pres. pt. of *pubescere*, to arrive at puberty.

Public, Publican; see **Popular**.

Publication, Publish; see **Popular**.

Puce, the name of a colour. (F. – L.) Lit. 'flea-colour.' – F. *puce*, a flea; *couleur puce*, puce; O.F. *pulce*. – L. *pulicem*, acc. of *pulex*, a flea. ¶ Not the same as *puke*, which (as meaning a colour) remains un-explained.

Puck. (C.) M. E. *pouke.*—Irish *puca,* an elf, sprite; W. *pwca, pwci.*+Icel. *púki,* an imp; G. *spuk,* a hobgoblin.

pug, a monkey, a kind of dog. (C.) Orig. an imp, or little demon (Ben Jonson). Weakened form of *puck* above. ' A *pug-dog* is a dog with a short monkey-like face;' Wedgwood. And see **Bug.**

Pucker; see **Poke** (1).

Pudding; see **Pad.**

Puddle (1), a small dirty pool. (C.) M. E. *podel.* Prob. for *plodel*,* like E. *bubble* for *blubble.*—Irish *plodach,* puddle, mire, *plodan,* a small pool, Gael. *plodan,* a small pool. All from Irish and Gael. *plod,* a pool, standing water. Prob. borrowed from L. acc. *paludem,* a marsh. Cf. **Pool** (1).

puddle (2), to make thick or muddy. (C.) From the sb. above. Cf. Irish and Gael. *plodanachd,* paddling in water, from *plodan,* a small pool.

Puerile. (F.—L.) F. *pueril* (16th cent.). —L. *puerilis,* boyish.—L. *puer,* a boy. (√ PU.)

puerperal, relating to child-birth. (L.) From L. *puerpera,* fem. adj., bearing a child.—L. *puer,* child; *parere,* to bear; see **Parent.**

Puff, to blow. (E.) M. E. *puffen;* of imitative origin.+G. *puffen,* to puff, pop, Dan. *puffe,* to pop, Swed. *puffa,* to crack, push; W. *pwff,* a puff. Allied to **Pop, Pooh.**

puffin, a bird. (E.) From its *puffed out* appearance, or from its swelling beak.

Pug; see **Puck.**

Pugilism. (L.) From L. *pugil,* a boxer. Allied to L. *pugnus,* Gk. πυγ-μή, the fist; and to E. **Fist.**

impugn. (F.—L.) F. *impugner.*—L. *impugnare,* to fight against.—L. *im-* (for *in*), against; *pugnare,* to fight, from *pugnus,* a fist.

oppugn, to resist. (F.—L.) F. *op-pugner.* — L. *oppugnare.* — L. *op-* (*ob*), against; *pugnare,* to fight (above).

poniard. (F.—L.; *with* G. *suffix.*) F. *poignard,* a dagger.—F. *poing* (O. F. *poign*), the fist; with suffix *·ard* = G. *hart* (lit. hard). (So also Ital. *pugnale,* a poniard, from *pugno,* fist; Span. *puñal,* a poniard, from *puño,* fist, handful, hilt.)—L. *pugnus,* fist.

pugnacious. (L.) Coined from L. *pugnaci-,* crude form of *pugnax,* combative. — L. *pugnare,* to fight. — L. *pugnus,* the fist.

repugnant. (F. — L.) F. *repugnant,* pres. pt. of *repugner,* ' to repugne, thwart;' Cot.—L. *re-pugnare,* to fight against.

Puisne; see **Post-.**

Puissant; see **Potent.**

Puke, to vomit. (E.?) Prob. for *spuke*,* or *spewk*,* an extended form of *spew.* Cf. G. *spucken,* to spit.

Pule, to chirp, to whimper. (F.—L.) F. *piauler,* ' to cheep as a young bird, to pule or howle;' Cot. Cf. Ital. *pigolare,* to chirp, moan. Imitative words; allied to L. *pipi-lare, pipare,* to chirp; see **Pipe.**

Pull. (E.) M. E. *pullen;* A. S. *pullian,* to pull, pluck.+Low G. *pulen,* to pick, pinch, pull, pluck, tear. Perhaps allied (with loss of initial *s*), to L. *pellere.* See **Pulsate.**

Pullet; see **Pool** (2).

Pulley. (F. — L.) M. E. *poliue* (= *polivè,* riming with *drivè*), Ch.; also *poleyne,* Prompt. Parv. The latter form is from F. *poulain,* ' a fole, a colt, also the rope wherewith wine is let down into a seller [cellar], a pulley-rope;' Cot.—Low L. *pul-lanus,* a colt.—L. *pullus,* a young animal; see **pullet,** s. v. **Pool** (2). So also E. *pulley* answers to mod. F. *poulie.* β. The trans-ference of sense causes no difficulty; thus F. *poutre,* a filly, also means a beam, and F. *chèvre,* a goat, also means a kind of crane; the names of animals are applied to contriv-ances for exerting force. Cf. also Low L. *polanus,* a pulley or pulley-rope, also a kind of sledge. ¶ Diez derives E. *pulley* from F. *poulie* and then, conversely, F. *poulie,* from E. *pull.* This is very unlikely; there is nothing to connect *pulley* with *pull;* and indeed, the old spellings (*poleyn,* a pulley, *pullen,* to pull) separate the words from each other.

Pulmonary; see **Pneumatic.**

Pulp. (F. — L.) F. *pulpe.* — L. *pulpa,* pulp of fruit, pith.

Pulpit. (F. — L.) O. F. *pulpite.* — L. *pulpitum,* a scaffold, stage for actors.

Pulsate, to throb. (L.) From pp. of L. *pulsare,* to throb, beat; frequent. form of *pellere* (pp. *pulsus*), to drive. Cf. Skt. *sphar, sphur,* to throb. (√ SPAR.)

appeal. (F. — L.) M. E. *appelen, apelen.* — O. F. *apeler.* — L. *appellare,* to address, call upon; intensive form of *ap-pellere,* to drive to, incline towards.—L. *ap-* (*ad*), to; *pellere,* to drive.

appellant. (F. — L.) F. *appellant,* pres. pt. of *appeller,* to call upon, appeal; also spelt *appeler.* — L. *appellare* (above).

compel. (L.) L. *com-pellere,* to compel, lit. to drive together. Der. *compuls-ion,* from pp. *compuls-us.*

dispel. (L.) L. *dis-pellere,* to drive away, disperse.

expel. (L.) L. *ex-pellere,* to drive out. Der. *expulsion,* O. F. *expulsion,* L. acc. *expulsionem,* from pp. *expuls-us.*

impel. (L.) L. *im-pellere,* to urge on. Der. *impulse,* from pp. *impulsus.*

interpellation. (F. — L.) F. *interpellation.* — L. acc. *interpellationem.* — L. *interpellatus,* pp. of *interpellare,* to drive between, to hinder, interrupt. — L. *inter,* between; *pellere,* to drive.

peal, a loud sound, chime of bells, noise of a trumpet. (F. — L.) A shortened form of *appeal,* O. F. *apel, appel;* Cot. gives *appel,* pl. *appeaux,* 'chimes.' Note also M. E. *apel,* an old term in hunting music (Halliwell); this we now call a *peal.* The prefix *a-* was prob. mistaken for the E. indef. article. The O. F. *apel* is from O. F. *apeler,* verb; see **appeal** (above).

pelt (1), to throw, cast. (L.) M. E. *pelten,* also *pilten, pulten,* to thrust, cast. The forms *pilten, pulten,* answer to an A. S. form *pyltan* *, not found, but it must have been in use. — L. *pultare,* to beat, strike, knock; the L. *u* being represented by A. S. *y,* precisely as in A. S. *pyt* for L. *puteus* (E. *pit*). *Pultare* (like *pulsare*) is an iterative form of *pellere,* to drive.

propel, to urge forward. (L.) L. *pro-pellere,* to drive forward. Der. *propuls-ion,* from pp. *propulsus.*

pulse (1), a throb. (F. — L.) F. *pouls,* 'the pulse;' Cot. — L. *pulsum,* acc. of *pulsus,* the beating of the pulse. — L. *pulsus,* pp. of *pellere.*

pursy, short-winded. (F. — L.) M. E. *purcy,* also *purcyf* (Palsgrave). — O. F. *pourcif* (Palsgrave), variant of *poulsif,* 'pursie, short-winded,' Cot. — O. F. *poulser,* F. *pousser,* to push, also to gasp for breath; see **push** (below).

push. (F. — L.) M. E. *possen, pussen.* — O. F. *pousser, poulser,* to push, thrust. — L. *pulsare,* to beat, thrust, frequent. of *pellere,* to drive.

repeal. (F. — L.) Altered from O. F. *rapeler,* F. *rappeler,* to repeal. — O. F. *re-* (L. *re-*); *apeler,* later *appeler,* to appeal. See **appeal** (above). *Repeal = re-appeal.*

repel. (L.) L. *re-pellere,* to drive back. Der. *repulse,* from pp. *repulsus.*

Pulse (1), a throb, vibration; see **Pulsate.**

Pulse (2), grain or seed of beans, pease, &c. (L.) M. E. *puls.* L. *puls,* a thick pap or pottage made of meal, pulse, &c. (hence applied to the pulse itself). Der. *poultice,* q. v.

Pulverise. (F. — L.) F. *pulveriser;* Cot. — Late L. *puluerizare,* to reduce to dust, L. *puluerare,* the same. — L. *puluer-* stem of *puluis,* dust. (Prob. allied to *pul-sus,* pp. of *pellere,* to drive about.)

powder. (F. — L.) M. E. *poudre.* — F. *poudre,* O. F. *poldre, puldre.* Formed with excrescent *d* from L. *puluerem,* acc. of *puluis,* dust.

Puma, a quadruped. (Peruvian.) Peruv. *puma.*

Pumice; see **Spume.**

Pummel, the same as *pommel;* see **Pomade.**

Pump (1), a machine for raising water. (F. — Teut. — L.) M. E. *pumpe.* — F. *pompe.* — G. *pumpe,* also spelt *plumpe,* which is the older and fuller form. Cf. prov. G. *plumpen,* to pump. β. The G. *plumpen* also means to plump, fall plump, move suddenly and violently, from the plunging action of the piston. It is therefore allied to E. **Plump** (2), and to **Plumb,** and is ultimately of Latin origin. γ. We even find prov. E. *plump,* to pump, Corn. *plumpy,* to pump; cf. F. *plomber,* to sound with a plummet; and cf. **Plunge.** We also find Du. *pomp,* Swed. *pump,* Dan. *pompe,* Russ. *pompa,* a pump, all borrowed words; and (the weakened forms) Span. and Port. *bomba,* a pump.

Pump (2), a thin-soled shoe; see **Pomp.**

Pumpion, Pumpkin, a kind of gourd. (F. — L. — Gk.) The old forms are *pumpion* and *pompon.* — F. *pompon,* 'a pumpion or melon;' Cot. — L. *peponem,* acc. of *pepo,* a large melon. — Gk. πεπων, a kind of melon, eaten quite ripe. — Gk. πεπων, mellow, from πεπ-τειν, to ripen; see **Cook.** ¶ The insertion of *m* before *p* causes no difficulty.

Pun; see **Pound** (3).

Punch (1), to perforate; see **Pungent.**

Punch (2), to beat; see **punish,** s. v. **Pain.**

Punch (3), a beverage. (Hindi. — Skt.) So called from consisting of *five* ingredients, spirit, water, lemon-juice, sugar, spice; introduced from India, by way of Goa; mentioned A.D. 1669. — Hindi *panch*, five. — Skt. *pañchan*, five. See **Five**. ¶ The Hindi and Skt. short *a* is pronounced like E. *u* in *mud*; it occurs again in *pundit*.

Punch (4), a short, hump-backed fellow in a puppet-show. (Ital.—L.) A contraction for *Punchinello*, which occurs A.D. 1666 (Nares). This is a corruption of Ital. *pulcinello* (by the change of *l* to *n*, the Ital. *ci* being sounded as E. *chi*). *Pulcinello* is the droll clown in Neapolitan comedy; we also find Ital. *pulcinella*, 'punch, buffoon,' Meadows. A dimin. form of Ital. *pulcino*, a young chicken; cf. *pulcella*, a young girl; from L. *pullus*, the young of any animal, allied to *puer*, a boy. See **Pullet**. The lit. sense of *pulcinello* is little chicken; thence, a little boy, a puppet. ¶ Confused with prov. E. *punch*, short, fat, which is allied to **Bunch**. *Judy* is for *Judith*, once a common name.

Puncheon (1), a punch, for perforating; see **Pungent**.

Puncheon (2), a cask. (F.—L.?) From O. F. *poinson*, 'a bodkin, also a puncheon [steel tool], also a stamp, mark, print, or seale; also, a wine-vessell;' Cot. This is a difficult word; but I conclude that the O. F. *poinson* (F. *poinçon*) remains the same word in all its senses, and that the cask was named from the 'mark, print, or seale' upon it, which was made with a *puncheon* or stamp. See **puncheon** (1), s. v. **Pungent**. ¶ So also *hogshead* = *oxhead*, a stamped mark. Ital. *punzone* means both puncheon or bodkin, and puncheon or wine-vessel.

Punchinello; see **Punch** (4).

Punctate, **Punctilio**; see **Pungent**.

Punctual, **Punctuate**, **Puncture**; see **Pungent**.

Pundit, a learned man. (Skt.) Skt. *pandita* (with cerebral *nd*), adj., learned, sb., a wise man, scholar. — Skt. *pand*, to heap up or together. See **Punch** (3).

Pungent. (L.) L. *pungent-*, stem of pres. pt. of *pungere*, to prick, pt. t. *pu-pug-i*, pp. *punctus*. (Base PUG, PUK.)

appoint. (F. — L.) M. E. *apointen*. — O. F. *apointer*, to prepare, arrange, settle. —Low L. *appunctare*, to repair, appoint, settle a dispute; Ducange. — L. *ap-* (*ad*); Low L. *punctare*, to mark by a point, from Low L. *puncta*, a prick, fem. of *punctus*, pp.; see **point** (below). Der. *disappoint*.

counterpoint, the composing of music in parts. (F. — L.) O. F. *contrepoinct*, 'a

ground or plain song, in music;' Cot. The lit. sense is *point against point*, from the *points* or dots which represented musical notes, and were placed on staves over or against each other in compositions in two or more parts. — F. *contre*, against; *point*, a point; see **point** (below).

compunction, remorse. (F.—L.) O.F. *compunction*. — Low L. acc. *compunctionem*. —L. *compunctus*, pp. of *compungi*, to feel remorse, pass. of *compungere*, to prick. — L. *com-* (*cum*); *pungere*, to prick.

expunge. (L.) L. *ex-pungere*, to prick out, blot out. In MSS., *expunction* of a word is denoted by *dots under it*. Der. *expunct-ion*.

poignant. (F. — L.) F. *poignant*, stinging, pres. part. of *poindre*, to prick. — L. *pungere*, to prick.

point. (F. — L.) M. E. *point*. — F. *point*, *poinct*, a point, prick. — L. *punctum*; orig. neut. of *punctus*, pp. of *pungere*, to prick.

'pounce (1), to seize with the claws. (F. — L.) Orig. a term in hawking; a hawk's claws were termed *pounces*. A *pounce* is also a punch or stamp (Nares); a *pounson* or *punsoun* was a dagger (Barbour). Formed as if from an O. F. verb *poncer**, to pierce, not recorded, though we find Span. *punchar*, to pierce, and the sb. *puncha*, a prickle (the exact equivalent of E. *pounce*, a hawk's talon). The Span. *punchar* answers to a Low L. *punctiare**, not found, but regularly formed from L. *punctus*, pp. of *pungere*.

punch (1), to perforate. (F.—L.) M. E. *punchen*, to prick; which seems to have been coined from the sb. *punchion*, *punchon*, *punsoun*, a dagger, awl. See below.

puncheon (1), a punch or awl. (F.— L.) M. E. *punchon*, *punsoun*. — O. F. *poinson*, 'a bodkin, also a puncheon, a stamp,' &c.; Cot. Cf. Span. *punzon*, a punch, Ital. *punzone*, a punch, bodkin, also a wine-barrel. — L. *punctionem*, acc. of *punctio*, a pricking, puncture. The gender of this word was changed from fem. to masc., whilst at the same time the sense was changed from 'pricking' to ' pricker.' — L. *punctus*, pp. of *pungere*, to prick. See also **Puncheon** (2).

punctate, punctured. (L.) Coined from L. *punct-um*, a print; with suffix -*ate* (L. -*atus*).

punctilio. (Span. — L.) Span. *puntillo*, a nice point of honour; dimin. of *punto*, a point. – L. *punctum*, a point; see point (above).

punctual. (F. – L.) F. *ponctuel*, 'punctuall;' Cot. – Low L. *punctualis*. – L. *punctu-m*, a point; see point (above).

punctuate. (L.) From pp. of Low L. *punctuare*, to determine, define. – L. *punctu-m*, a point (above).

puncture. (L.) L. *punctura*, a prick. – L. *punctus*, pp. of *pungere*, to prick.

punt (2), to play at a game at cards called basset. (F. – Span. – L.) F. *ponte*, a punt, a punter, *ponter*, to punt. – Span. *punto*, a point, also a pip at cards. – L. *punctum*, a point.

Punish; see **Pain**.

Punkah, a large fan. (Hindi. – Skt.) Hind. *pankhá*, a fan; allied to *pankha*, a wing, feather, *paksha*, a wing. Allied to Skt. *paksha*, a wing. Cf. Pers. *pankan*, a sieve, a fan.

Punt (1), a flat-bottomed boat; see **Pontiff**.

Punt (2), to play at basset; see **Pungent**.

Puny; see **Post-**.

Pupa, a chrysalis. (L.) L. *pupa*, a girl, doll, puppet (hence, undeveloped insect). Fem. of *pupus*, a boy; allied to *putus*, *puer*, a boy. (√PU.)

pupil (1), a scholar, ward. (F. – L.) O. F. *pupile*, F. *pupille* (masc.). – L. *pupillum*, acc. of *pupillus*, an orphan-boy, ward; dimin. of *pupus*, a boy (above).

pupil (2), the central spot of the eye. (F. – L.) F. *pupille* (fem.). – L. *pupilla*, a little girl, also pupil (name due to the small images seen in the pupil). Fem. of *pupillus* (above).

puppet. (F. – L.) M. E. *popet*. – O. F. *poupette*, 'a little baby, puppet;' Cot. Dimin. of L. *pupa*; see **Pupa** (above).

puppy, (1) a whelp; (2) a dandy. (F. – L.) 1. F. *poupée*, 'a baby, a puppet;' Cot. Here 'baby' really means 'doll,' but it is clear that, in E., the term was applied to the young of an animal, esp. of a dog. The F. *poupée* (as if = L. *pupata**) is a derivative of L. *pupa*; see **Pupa** (above). 2. In the sense of 'dandy,' *puppy* represents O. F. *poupin*, *popin*, spruce, trim (as if = L. *pupinus**); from the same source. Der. *pup*, short for *puppy*.

Pur-, *prefix*. (F. – L.) O. F. *pur-*, F. *pour-*, F. *pour*, for; a curious variation of L. *pro*, for. Thus *pur-* and *pro-* are equivalent; and *pur-vey*, *pro-vide* are doublets.

Purblind. (F. – L. *and* E.) Orig. *pure-blind*, i. e. wholly blind, M. E. *pur blind*, Rob. of Glouc. p. 376. See **Pure** and **Blind**. It afterwards came to mean partly blind, prob. through confusion with the verb to *pore*, as Sir T. Elyot writes *pore-blind*. (Similarly *parboil*, to boil thoroughly, came to mean to boil partially.) *Pure* = wholly, Tw. Nt., v. 86.

Purchase; see **Capacious**.

Pure. (F. – L.) F. *pur*, masc., *pure*, fem., pure. – L. *purus*, pure. Cf. Skt. *pû*, to purify. (√PU.)

expurgate. (L.) From pp. of L. *expurgare*, to purify thoroughly. – L. *ex*, thoroughly; *purgare*, to purge, purify; see purge (below).

purge. (F. – L.) F. *purger*. – L. *purgare*, to purify. L. *purgare* = *pur-igare* (Plautus). – L. *pur-us*, pure; *agere*, to make.

purify. (F. – L.) F. *purifier*. – L. *purificare*, to make pure. – L. *puri-*, for *purus*, pure; *facere*, to make. Der. *purific-at-ion*.

puritan. (L.) A barbarous word, to designate one who aimed at great *purity* of life; see below.

purity. (F. – L.) M. E. *puretee*. – F. *pureté*, 'purity;' Cot. – L. acc. *puritatem*, pureness. – L. *purus*, pure.

spurge, a plant. (F. – L.) Named from its corroding (and so cleansing away) warts. – O. F. *spurge*, *espurge*. – O. F. *espurger*, to purge away. – L. *ex-purgare*, to cleanse away; see purge (above).

Purl (1), to flow with a murmuring sound. (Scand.) Swed. *porla*, to purl, bubble as a stream; a frequent. form from a base *pur-*, imitative of the sound. See **Purr**, **Pirouette**.

Purl (2), spiced beer. (F. – L.) In Phillips, ed. 1706. But it should be *pearl*. It was a term in cookery; thus *sucre perlé* is sugar boiled twice, *bouillon perlé*, jelly-broth. Cf. G. *perlen*, to pearl, rise in small bubbles like pearls. See **Pearl**.

Purl (3), to form an edging on lace, &c.; see **File** (1).

Purl (4), to upset. (E.) Better *pirl*; from M. E. *pirle*, a whirligig, formed by the frequent. suffix *-l* from the imitative word *pirr*, to whirl. See **Purr**, **Pirouette**. So also Ital. *pirlare*, 'to twirle round;' Florio. See **Purl** (1).

Purlieu, the border of a forest, &c. (F. – L.) Formerly *pourallee*, altered to *purlieu* by confusion with F. *lieu*, a place;

also spelt *purley*. The F. *pourallee* (O. F. *puralee*) is a sort of translation of Low L. *perambulatio*, which meant 'all that ground near any forest, which, being made forest by Henry II., Rich. I., or king John, were (*sic*) by *perambulations* granted by Henry III., severed again from the same;' Manwood's Forest Laws. The etymology is from O. F. *pur* (F. *pour*) = L. *pro*, and O. F. *alee*, a going, for which see **Alley.**

Purloin; see **Long** (1).

Purple. (F.–L.–Gk.) M. E. *purpre* (with *r* for *l*).–O. F. *porpre*, later *pourpre*, purple. – L. *purpura*, the purple-fish. – Gk. πορφύρα, the purple-fish; cf. Gk. πορφύρεος, purple, orig. an epithet of the surging sea.–Gk. πορφύρειν, reduplicated form of φύρειν, to mix up, stir violently, allied to L. *furere*, whence E. **Fury.**

porphyry. (F. – L. – Gk.) M. E. *porphurie*, answering to an O. F. form *porphyrie**, which Cotgrave gives only in the form *porphyre*.–L. *porphyrites*.–Gk. πορφυρίτης, porphyry, a hard rock named from its purple colour.–Gk. πορφύρα, the purple-fish (above).

Purport; see **Port** (1).

Purpose (1), to intend ; see **Pose.**

Purpose (2), intention ; see **Position.**

Purr, Pur. (E.) An imitative word for various sounds, chiefly of the murmuring of a cat. Cf. Scotch *pirr*, a gentle wind ; E. *buzz* ; Irish *burburus*, a gurgling sound. See **Purl** (1), **Purl** (4), and **Pirouette.**

Purse. (F.–L.–Gk.) M. E. *purs*; also *pors*; also *burs*.–O. F. *borse*, later *bourse*, a purse.–Low L. *bursa*, a purse.– Gk. βύρση, a hide, skin ; of which purses were made. ¶ For the unusual change from *b* to *p*, cf. *gossip*, *peat*. Der. *purse*, verb, to wrinkle up, like a purse drawn together.

bursar. (Low L.–Gk.) Low L. *bursarius*, a purse-bearer.–Low L. *bursa* (above).

disburse. (F.–L. *and* Gk.) O. F. *desbourser*, to take out of a purse.–O. F. *des-* (= L. *dis-*), away ; F. *bourse* (above).

reimburse, to refund. (F.–L. *and* Gk.) Adapted from F. *rembourser* by substituting L. *re-im-* for F. *rem-* (with the same force). –L. *re-*, again ; *im-*, for *in*, in ; F. *bourse*, a purse (above).

Purslain, Purslane, a herb. (F.–L.) M. E. *purslane*.–O. F. *porcelaine*, *pourcelaine*, purslane ; Cot. Formed from L. *porcilaca*, purslain (Pliny); usually spelt *portulaca*.

Pursue; see **Sequence.**

Pursy; see **Pulsate.**

Purtenance; see **Tenable.**

Purulent; see **Pus.**

Purvey; sée **Vision.**

Pus, white matter from a sore. (L.) L. *pus* (gen. *puris*), pus. ✛ Gk. πύον, matter ; Skt. *púya*, pus, from *púy*, to stink. (✓PU.)

purulent. (F.–L.) F. *purulent*.–L. *purulentus*, full of matter.–L. *pur-*, stem of *pus*.

Push; see **Pulsate.**

Pusillanimous. (L.) L. *pusillanimus*, mean-spirited; also *pusillanimis*. – L. *pusill-us*, mean, small ; *animus*, courage. *Pusillus* is dimin. of *pusus*, small, allied to *puer*, a boy; see **Puerile** and **Animate.** (✓PU ; ✓AN.)

Puss, a cat, hare. (E.) Prob. an imitative word, from the spitting of the cat. We find also Du. *poes*, Low G. *puus*, *puus-katte*, Swed. dial. *pus*, Irish and Gael. *pus.* And even S. Tamil *pusei*, a cat ; *pusha* in the Cashgar dialect of Affghan. Lith. *puz*, a word to call a cat.

Pustule. (F. – L.) F. *pustule*. – L. *pustula*, longer form of *pusula*, a blister, pimple. Allied to Gk. φυσαλίς, a bladder, φυσάω, I blow. (✓SPU, to blow.)

Put. (C.) M. E. *putten* ; A. S. *potian*. –Gael. *put*, to push, thrust ; W. *pwtio*, Corn. *poot*, to push, kick.

pother, a bustle, confusion. (C.) Also *pudder.* The same as **potter** (below).

potter. (C.) To *potter* is to poke about, hence to stir, confuse, disorder, also to do a thing inefficiently ; so also *pother*, to poke, disorder (Bailey, Halliwell). These are frequentative forms of *put*, to thrust ; see above. Cf. Du. *poteren*, 'to search one thoroughly,' Hexham ; *peuteren*, to fumble, poke about ; words of C. origin.

Putative, reputed. (F.–L.) F. *putatif.* –L. *putatiuus*, presumptive.–L. *putatus*, pp. of *putare*, to think, suppose. The orig. sense was to make clean, then to make clear, to come to a clear result.–L. *putus*, clean. (✓PU.)

account. (F.–L.) M. E. *accompten*, *accounten*. – O. F. *acompter*, *aconter*, to account. – O. F. *a* ; *compter*, *conter*, to count ; see count (below).

amputate. (L.) From pp. of L. *amputare*, to cut off round about.–L. *am-*, short for *amb-*, *ambi-*, round about; *putare*, to cleanse, also to lop or prune trees.

compute. (L.) L. *computare*, to reckon.—L. *com-* (*cum*), together; *putare*, to think.

count (2), to reckon. (F. — L.) F. *conter*, formerly also *compter*.—L. *computare*, to compute; see above.

depute. (F.—L.) F. *deputer*; Cot.—L. *deputare*, to cut off, also to impute, destine.—L. *de*, down; *putare*, to cut off, orig. to cleanse. **Der.** *deput-y*, O. F. *deputé*, one deputed, pp. of *deputer*.

discount, verb. (F. — L.) Formerly *discompt.* — O. F. *descompter*, to reckon back or off.—O. F. *des-* (L. *dis-*), away; *compter*, to count; see **count** (above).

dispute. (F. — L.) F. *disputer.* — L. *disputare*, to argue. — L. *dis-*, apart; *putare*, to think.

impute. (F. — L.) F. *imputer.* — L. *imputare*, to ascribe. — L. *im-* (*in*), towards; *putare*, to reckon.

recount. (F.—L.) F. *raconter*, to tell, relate.—F. *re-* (L. *re-*), again; *aconter*, to account; see **account** (above). *Recount* = *re-account*.

repute. (F. — L.) F. *reputer.* — L. *reputare*, to repute (lit. reconsider).—L. *re-*, again; *putare*, to think.

Putrid. (F. — L.) F. *putride.* — L. *putridus*, stinking.—L. *putri-*, crude form of *puter*, *putris*, rotten; *putrere*, to be rotten. — L. *putere*, to stink. See **Pus**. (√PU.)

putrefy. (F.—L.) F. *putrefier*; formed as if from L. *putrificare**; but the true L. forms are *putrefacere*, to make putrid, *putrefieri*, to become putrid.—L. *putri-s*, putrid; *facere*, to make.

Puttock, a kite, hawk. (F.—L.; *and* E.) From *poot*; cf. *sparrow-hawk*. Prov. E. *poot*, a chicken, *pout*, young of game; the same as *poult*, which is short for *pullet*. See under **pool** (2). The suffix *-ock* is a diminutive; or, more probably, a corruption of *hawk*.

Putty; see **Pot**.

Puzzle; see **Pose** (1).

Pygmy. (F.—L.—Gk.) F. *pygmé*, adj., dwarflike; Cot.—L. *pygmæus*, adj., dwarflike; from pl. *Pygmæi*, the race of Pygmies.—Gk. Πυγμαῖοι, pygmies, fabulous dwarfs of the length of a πυγμή, i.e. about 13½ in., from the elbow to the knuckles or fist.—Gk. πυγμή, a fist; see **Pugilist**.

Pylorus. (L.—Gk.) L. *pylorus*.—Gk. πυλωρός, the lower orifice of the stomach, entrance to the intestines; orig. a gatekeeper. — Gk. πύλ-η, a gate; οὖρος, a keeper, watcher.

Pyramid. (L.—Gk.) Formerly *pyramis*. — L. *pyramis* (stem *pyramid-*). — Gk. πυραμίς (stem πυραμιδ-), a pyramid. Prob. of Egyptian origin.

Pyre. (L.—Gk.) L. *pyra.*—Gk. πύρα, a funeral pile.—Gk. πῦρ, fire; allied to E. **Fire**.

pellitory (2), **pelleter**, the plant pyrethrum. (Span. — L. — Gk.) Span. *pelitre*.—L. *pyrethrum*.—Gk. πύρεθρον, a hot spicy plant.—Gk. πῦρ, fire.

pyrites. (L.—Gk.) L. *pyrites*.—Gk. πυρίτης, a flint, pyrites; orig. an adj., belonging to fire.—Gk. πῦρ, fire.

pyrotechnic, belonging to fireworks. (Gk.) Coined from Gk. πυρο-, crude form of πῦρ, fire; τεχνικός, artistic, from τέχνη, an art; see **Technical**.

Pyx. (L. — Gk.) Shortened from L. *pyxis*, a box.—Gk. πυξίς, a box. — Gk. πύξος, box-wood; named from its close grain. — Gk. πυκνός, dense. (√ PAK.) Allied to **Box** (1), **Box** (2).

bushel, a measure. (F. — L. — Gk.) M. E. *bushel.* — O. F. *boissel.* — Low L. *buscellus*, *bussellus*, a bushel. — Low L. *bussulus*, a small box. — Low L. *bussida*, a form of *buxida*, acc. of *buxis*, a box. — Gk. πυξίς, a box (above).

Q.

Quack (1), to make a noise as a duck. (E.) M. E. *queke*, as a duck's cry; an imitative word. + Du. *kwaken*, G. *quaken*, Icel. *kvaka*, Dan. *qvække*, to croak, quack. Cf. L. *coaxare*, to croak, Gk. κόαξ, a croaking.

quack (2), to cry up a nostrum. (E.) Merely a particular use of the word above; to cackle, prate, sing the praises of a nostrum, to pretend to medical skill. **Der.** *quack-salver*, i.e. a *quack* who cries up his *salves* or ointments, from Du. *kwakzalver*, a quacksalver, from *kwakzalven*, verb, to puff up salves.

quail (2), a bird. (F. — Low L. — Low G.)

M. E. *quaille.* — O. F. *quaille,* F. *caille.* —
Low L. *quaquila,* a quail. — O. Du. *quackel,*
a quail. — O. Du. *quacken,* Du. *kwaken,* to
quack (above). From the noise which the
bird makes.

Quadragesima, Quadrangle, Quadrant; see **Quadrate.**

Quadrate. (L.) L. *quadratus,* pp. of
quadrare, to make square. — L. *quadrus,*
square. Put for *quaterus*,* from *quatuor,*
four; see **Four.**

quadragesima, forty days of Lent.
(L.) L. *quadragesima,* lit. fortieth; fem.
of *quadragesimus*; older form *quadragensimus,* fortieth = *quadragentimus*.* — L.
quadraginta, forty. — L. *quadr-us,* square,
fourfold; *-ginta,* short for *deginta* = decinta*,* tenth, from *decem,* ten.

quadrangle. (F. — L.) F. *quadrangle.*
— L. *quadrangulum,* sb., neut. of *quadrangulus,* four - cornered. — L. *quadr-us,*
square; *angulus,* angle. See **Angle** (1).

quadrant. (L.) M. E. *quadrant.* — L.
quadrant-, stem of *quadrans,* sb., a fourth
part. Extended from L. *quadrus,* belonging to four.

quadrennial. (L.) Put for *quadriennial,* adj. — L. *quadriennium,* a space
of four years. — L. *quadri-,* for *quadrus,*
belonging to four; *annus,* a year; see
Annals.

quadrilateral. (L.) L. *quadrilaterus,* four-sided. — L. *quadrus* (above); *later-,*
stem of *latus,* a side. See **Lateral.**

quadrille. (F. — Span. — L.) Formerly
a game at cards for four. — F. *quadrille,*
(1) fem., a troop of horses; (2) masc., a
game at cards. The former answers to
Ital. *quadriglia,* O. Ital. *squadriglia,* a
troop; but the latter to Span. *cuadrillo,* a
small square, allied to *cuadrilla,* a meeting of four persons. — Span. *cuadra,* a
square. — L. *quadra,* fem. of *quadrus*
(above).

quadrillion, a million raised to the
fourth power. (L.) Coined by prefixing
quadr- (for L. *quadrus*) to *-illion,* which
is *m-illion* without the *m.*

quadroon. (Span. — L.) For *quartroon.*
— Span. *cuarteron,* the child of a creole
and a Spaniard; one who is, in a fourth
part, a black; also a fourth part. — Span.
cuarto, a fourth part. — L. *quartum,* acc. of
quartus, fourth; see **quartern** (below).

quadruped; see **Pedal.**

quadruple. (F. — L.) F. *quadruple.*
— L. *quadruplum,* acc. of *quadruplus,* fourfold. — L. *quadru-s,* four times; *-plus,*
signifying 'fold;' see **Double.**

quarantine. (F. — L.) O. F. *quarantine,* usually *quarantaine,* a space of forty
days. — F. *quarante,* forty. — L. *quadraginta,* forty; see **quadragesima** (above).

quarrel (2), a square-headed cross-bow
bolt. (F. — L.) M. E. *quarel.* — O. F. *quarrel,*
later *quarreau,* a diamond, square tile,
cross-bow bolt. — Low L. *quadrellus,* a
quarrel. — L. *quadrus,* square (above).

quarry (1), a place where stones are
dug. (F. — L.) Formerly *quarrer*; M. E.
quarrere, a place where stones are squared.
— O. F. *quarriere,* a quarry; F. *carrière.* —
Low L. *quadraria,* a quarry for *squared*
stones. — L. *quadrare,* to square. — L. *quadrus,* square. ¶ The sense was suggested
by L. *quadratarius,* a stone-squarer, also a
stone-cutter (merely).

quart, the fourth of a gallon. (F. — L.)
M. E. *quarte.* — F. *quarte.* — L. *quarta* (i. e.
pars), a fourth part; fem. of *quartus,* fourth.
Apparently short for *quatur-tus*.* — L.
quatuor, four.

quartan. (F. — L.) F. *quartaine,* recurring on the fourth day (said of a fever).
— L. *quartana* (*febris*), a quartan fever;
fem. of *quartanus,* belonging to the fourth.
— L. *quartus,* fourth (above).

quarter. (F. — L.) M. E. *quarter.* —
O. F. *quarter, quartier.* — L. *quartarius,*
fourth part. — L. *quartus,* fourth.

quartern, fourth of a pint. (F. — L.)
Short for *quarteron.* M. E. *quarteroun.* —
O. F. *quarteron,* a quartern. — Low L.
quarteronem, acc. of *quartero,* a fourth
part. — Low L. *quarterus,* from L. *quartus,*
fourth.

quartet, quartette. (Ital. — L.) Ital.
quartetto (*quartette* is a F. spelling); dimin.
of *quarto,* fourth. — L. *quartus.*

quarto, having the sheet folded into
four leaves. (L.) From L. phr. *in quarto,*
in a fourth part; where *quarto* is abl. of
quartus, fourth.

quaternary, consisting of fours. (F.
— L.) F. *quaternaire.* — L. *quaternarius.*
L. *quaterni,* pl. four at a time. — L. *quatuor,*
four.

quaternion. (L.) L. *quaternion-,*
stem of *quaternio,* a band of four men;
Acts, xii. 4. — L. *quaterni,* pl.; see above.

quatrain. (F. — L.) F. *quatrain,* a
stanza of four lines. — F. *quatre,* four. — L.
quatuor, four.

quire (1), a collection of sheets of

paper. (F. – L.) Spelt *cwaer* in the Ancren Riwle. – O. F. *quaier* (13th cent.), later *quayer, cayer*; mod. F. *cahiér*. – Low L. *quaternum*, a collection of four leaves (we find Low L. *quaternus* also, glossed by O.F. *quaer* in Wright's Voc. i. 116); whence also Ital. *quaderno*, a quire. [The suffix *-num* is lost as in F. *enfer* from L. *infernum*.] – L. *quatuor*, four. ¶ Not from L. *quaternio*, which could not thus suffer loss of the acc. termination *-nionem*.

squad, a small troop. (F. – Ital. – L.) O. F. *esquadre, escadre*. – Ital. *squadra*, a squadron; see **squaro** (below).

squadron. (F. – Ital. – L.) O. F. *esquadron*. – Ital. *squadrone*; augmentative of *squadra* (above).

square. (F. – L.) M. E. *square*. – O. F. *esquarré*, squared; *esquarre*, a square, squareness. Cf. Ital. *squadrare*, to square; *squadra*, a square, also a squadron of men (orig. a square). All from Low L. *ex-quadrare**, not found, but a mere intensive (with prefix *ex*) of L. *quadrare*, to square. – L. *quadrus*, four-cornered; see **Quadrate** (above).

squire (2), a square, carpenter's rule. (F. – L.) M. E. *squire*. – O. F. *esquierre*; mod. F. *équerre*. A variant of O. F. *esquarre*; see **square** (above).

Quadrennial, Quadrilateral, Quadrille, Quadrillion, Quadroon, Quadruped, Quadruple; see above.

Quaff, to drink in large draughts. (C.) Here *ff* stands for guttural *ch*, as in *quach*, i. e. to drink out of a *quach* or cup, usually called *quaich, quech, queff* in Lowland Scotch. – Irish and Gael. *cuach*, a cup, bowl.

Quagga, a quadruped. (Hottentot.) Said to be a Hottentot imitative word, from the barking noise made by the animal.

Quagmire; see **Quake**.

Quail (1), to cower. (E.) M. E. *quelen*, to die. A.S. *cwelan* (pt. t. *cwæl*), to die; whence *ácwelen*, to die utterly. + Du. *quelen*, O. H. G. *quelan*, to pine. (Base KWAL.) Cf. A. S. *cwalu*, destruction, Icel. *kvöl*, Dan. Swed. *qval*, G. *qual*, agony. ¶ Distinct from prov. E. *quail*, to coagulate, from O. F. *coailler* (F. *cailler*), from L. *coagulare*.

qualm. (E.) M. E. *qualm*, usually 'a pestilence.' A. S. *cwealm*, pestilence. – A. S. *cwæl*, pt. t. of *cwelan* (above). + Du. *kwalm*, Dan. *qvalm*, Swed. *qvalm*, G. *qualm*, suffocating vapour; Dan. *qvalme*, nausea (whence the mod. E. sense).

quell, to subdue. (E.) M. E. *quellen*, to kill. A. S. *cwellan*, to kill; causal of *cwelan* (above). + Du. *kwellen*, Icel. *kvelja*, Swed. *qvälja*, Dan. *qvæle*, to torment, choke; all causal forms.

Quail (2); see **Quack**.

Quaint; see **Noble**.

Quake. (E.) M. E. *quaken, cwakien*. A.S. *cwacian*, to quake; cf. *cweccan*, to wag. Orig. 'to give life to,' set in motion; allied to **Quick**. (Base KWAK.) Der. *Quak-er* (A.D. 1650); see Haydn.

quagmire. (E.) Spelt *quake-mire* in Stanihurst; i. e. quaking bog.

Quality. (F. – L.) M. E. *qualitee*. – F. *qualité*. – L. *qualitatem*, acc. of *qualitas*, sort, kind. – L. *quali-s*, of what sort. Allied to E. **Which**.

qualify. (F. – L.) F. *qualifier*. – Low L. *qualificare*, to endue with a quality. – L. *quali-s*, of what sort; *facere*, to make.

Qualm; see **Quail** (1).

Quandary, an evil plight. (Scand.) Corruption of M. E. *wandreth*, evil plight, peril, adversity; (cf. Scottish *quhar* for *whar*, where; prov. M. E. *squete* for *swete*, sweet.) – Icel. *vandræði*, difficulty, trouble. – Icel. *vand-r*, difficult; with suffix *-ræði* (= E. *-red* in *hat-red*). – Icel. *vann*, pt. t. of *vinna*, to toil; see **Win**. So also O. Swed. *wandräde*, difficulty, from *wand*, difficult.

Quantity. (F. – L.) M. E. *quantitee*. – F. *quantité*. – L. *quantitatem*, acc. of *quantitas*, quantity. – L. *quanti-*, for *quantus*, how much. Allied to Gk. πόσος (Ion. κόσος), how much; and to E. **Who**.

Quarantine; see **Quadrate**.

Quarrel (1), a dispute; see **Querulous**.

Quarrel (2), cross-bow bolt; see **Quadrate**.

Quarry (1), a place for digging stones; see **Quadrate**.

Quarry (2), heap of game; see p. 94, col. 2.

Quart, Quartan, &c.; see **Quadrate**.

Quartz, a mineral. (G.) G. *quarz*, rock-crystal.

Quash. (F. – L.) M. E. *quaschen*. – O. F. *quasser*, later *casser*, to break, quash. – L. *quassare*, to shatter; frequent. of *quatere* (supine *quassum*), to shake.

concussion. (F. – L.) F. *concussion*. – L. *concussionem*, acc. of *concussio*, a violent shaking. – L. *concussus*, acc. of *concutere*, to shake together. – L. *con-*, for *cum*, together; *quatere*, to shake.

discuss. (L.) M. E. *discussed*, pp.

driven away. — L. *discussus*, pp. of *discutere*, to shake asunder ; in late L., to discuss. — L. *dis-*, apart ; *quatere*, to shake.

percussion. (L.) From L. *percussio*, a striking. — L. *percussus*, pp. of *percutere*, to strike. — L. *per*, through ; *quatere*, to strike. **Der**. *re-percussion*.

rescue. (F. — L.) M. E. *rescouen*. — O. F. *rescourre*, to rescue, save. (The same word as Ital. *riscuotere*.) — Low L. *rescutere* (A.D. 1308) ; which stands for *re-excutere*, to drive away again. — L. *re-*, again ; *ex*, away ; *quatere*, to shake.

Quassia, a South-American tree. (Personal name.) Named by Linnæus (like *dahl-ia* from *Dahl*) from *Quassi*, a negro, who pointed out the use of the bark as a tonic. *Quassi* is a common negro name.

Quaternary, **Quaternion**, **Quatrain** ; see **Quadrate**.

Quaver. (E.) Frequent. of *quave*, M. E. *quauen* (*u=v*), to quake. Allied to M. E. *quappen*, to throb, palpitate. (Base KWAP, allied to KWAK.) See **Quake**. **Der**. *quaver*, sb., a note in music, orig. a trill, shake. And see *quiver* (1).

Quay, a wharf. (F. — C.) Formerly *kay*, *key* ; M. E. *key*, *keye*. — O. F. *quay* (F. *quai*), 'the key of a haven ;' Cot. — Bret. *kaé*, an enclosure, W. *cae*, an enclosure, hedge. (Phil. Soc. Trans. 1869, p. 254.)

Quean ; see **Queen**.

Queasy. (Scand.) M. E. *quaysy*, *queysy*, causing or feeling nausea. — Norweg. *kveis*, sickness after a debauch ; Icel. *iðra-kveisa*, colic ; Swed. dial. *kvesa*, soreness, blister, pimple. Cf. Swed. *kväsa*, to bruise ; A. S. *tó-cwísan*, to crush ; Goth. *kwistjan*, to destroy.

Queen. (E.) Also spelt *quean*, which spelling is restricted to the use of the word in a bad sense ; but the words are one. M. E. *queen*, in both senses. A. S. *cwén*, a woman. + Du. *kween*, a barren woman or cow ; Icel. *kván*, wife, *kona*, woman ; Dan. *qvinde*, woman, *kone*, wife ; Swed. *qvinna*, a female, *kona*, a quean ; Goth. *kwens*, *kweins*, *kwino*, woman, O. H. G. *quená* ; Gk. γυνή, Skt. *jani*, a wife. (√GAN.) Doublet, *quean*.

Queer. (Low G.) A cant word. — Low G. *queer*, across, *quere*, obliquity. In Awdelay's Fraternity of Vagabonds, p. 4, 'a *quire* fellow ' is one who has just come out of prison ; cf. Low G. *in der quere liggen*, to lie across, lie queerly. So also

G. *quer*, transverse ; *querkopf*, a queer fellow.

Quell ; see **Quail** (1).

Quench. (E.) M. E. *quenchen*. A. S. *cwencan*, to extinguish ; causal of A. S. *cwincan* (pt. t. *cwanc*), to go out, be extinguished. Lengthened from A. S. *cwínan* (pt. t. *cwán*), to go out, be extinguished. Cf. O. Fries. *kwinka*, to be extinguished.

Querimonious ; see **Querulous**.

Quern, **Kern**, a handmill for grinding grain. (E.) M. E. *querne*. A. S. *cweorn*, *cwyrn* ; orig. 'that which grinds.' + Du. *kweern*, Icel. *kvern*, Dan. *quærn*, Swed. *qvarn*, Goth. *kwairnus*. Cf. Gk. γύρις, fine meal. (√GAR, to grind.)

Querulous, fretful. (L.) L. *querulus*, full of complaints. — L. *queri*, to complain. (√KWAS.) See **Wheeze**.

cry. (F. — L.) M. E. *crien*. — F. *crier*. (Fuller forms occur in Ital. *gridare*, Span. *gridar*, Port. *gritar*.) — L. *quiritare*, to shriek, cry, lament (Brachet). Frequent. of L. *queri*, to lament. ·

decry, to condemn. (F. — L.) O. F. *descrier*, to cry down, disparage. — O. F. *des-* = L. *dis-*, implying the reversal of an act, and here opposed to ' cry up ;' *crier*, to cry (above).

quarrel (1), a dispute. (F. — L.) M. E. *querele*. — O. F. *querele*, later *querelle*. — L. *querela*, a complaint. — L. *queri*, to complain.

querimonious, fretful. (L.) From L. *querimonia*, a complaint. — L. *queri*, to complain ; with Aryan suffixes *-man-ya*.

Query, an enquiry. (L.) Put for *quære*, i. e. enquire thou. — L. *quære*, imp. sing. 2. pers. of *quærere*, to seek (put for *quæs-ere* *, as in L. *quæso*, I beg). Cf. Skt. *chi*, to search.

acquire. (L.) L. *acquirere*, to get, obtain. — L. *ac-*, for *ad*; to ; *quærere*, to seek. **Der**. *acquisit-ion* ; from pp. *acquisitus*.

conquer. (F. — L.) M. E. *conqueren*. — O. F. *conquerre*. — L. *conquirere*, to seek after, go in quest of; in late L., to conquer. — L. *con-* (*cum*), with ; *quærere*, to seek. **Der**. *conquest*, M. E. *conqueste*, from Low L. *conquisitum*, neut. of *conquisitus*, pp. of *conquirere*.

disquisition, an investigation. (L.) From L. *disquisitio*, a search into. — L. *disquisitus*, pp. of *disquirere*, to examine. L. *dis-*, apart ; *quærere*, to seek.

enquire. (F. — L.) M. E. *enqueren* ;

QUEST.   QUILL.   **385**

altered from *enquere* to *enquire* to make it look more like Latin; and afterwards to *inquire*, to make it look still more so. — O. F. *enquerre, enquerir.* — L. *inquirere,* to seek into. — L. *in,* in; *quærere,* to seek. **Der.** *enquir-y,* often turned into *inquiry*; *enquest* (now *inquest*), from O. F. *enqueste,* L. *inquisita (res),* a thing enquired into.

exquisite, sought out, excellent. (L.) L. *exquisitus,* pp. of *exquirere,* to seek out. — L. *ex,* out; *quærere,* to seek.

inquest, later spelling of M. E. *enqueste*; see **enquire.**

inquire, late spelling of **enquire**; see above.

inquisition. (F. — L.) F. *inquisition.* — L. acc. *inquisitionem,* a search into. — L. *inquisitus,* pp. of *inquirere*; see enquire (above).

perquisite, a small gain. (L.) Low L. *perquisitum,* an extra profit above the yearly rent, arising from fines, waifs, &c.; neut. of *perquisitus,* pp. of *perquirere,* to seek after thoroughly. — L. *per,* thoroughly; *quærere,* to seek.

quest, a search. (F. — L.) O. F. *queste*; F. *quête.* — L. *quæsita (res),* a thing sought; fem. of pp. of *quærere.*

question. (F. — L.) F. *question.* — L. acc. *quæstionem,* an enquiry. — L. *quæsere,* old form of *quærere,* to seek.

request. (F. — L.) O. F. *requeste.* — L. *requisita,* a thing asked, fem. of pp. of *requirere,* to ask back. — L. *re-*; and *quærere,* to seek.

require. (F. — L.) M. E. *requeren,* altered to *requiren.* — O. F. *requerir.* — L. *requirere* (above). **Der.** *requis-ite,* from pp. *requisitus.*

Quest, Question; see **Query.**

Queue; see **Caudal.**

Quibble; see **Quip.**

Quick, living, lively. (E.) M. E. *quik.* A. S. *cwic.*+Du. *kwik,* Icel. *kvikr,* Dan. *qvik,* Swed. *qvick*; extension from the older form in Goth. *kwius,* living; cf. L. *uiuus,* Lith. *gywas,* Russ. *jivoi,* alive; Skt. *jív,* to live. (√GIW.)

quicken. (E.) M. E. *quiknen,* orig. to become alive. — A. S. *cwic,* alive.

Quid; see **Cud.**

Quiddity, a nicety, cavil. (L.) Low L. *quidditas,* the nature of a thing. — L. *quid,* what; i. e. what is it? Neut. of *quis,* who; see **Who.**

quillet, a sly trick in argument. (L.)

Short for L. *quidlibet,* anything you choose. — L. *quid,* anything; *libet,* it pleases (you).

Quiet, adj. (L.) L. *quietus,* quiet; orig. pp. of *quiere*,* only used in the inceptive form *quiescere,* to be still. Cf. *quies,* rest. Allied to Gk. κεῖμαι, I rest; Skt. *çí,* to lie still. (√KI.) **Der.** *quiet,* sb. and vb.; *quietus,* sb.; *quiescent,* from stem of pres. pt. of *quiescere.*

acquiesce. (L.) L. *acquiescere,* to rest in. — L. *ac-,* for *ad,* to; *quiescere,* to rest

acquit. (F. — L.) M. E. *aquiten.* — O. F. *aquiter,* to settle a claim; Low L. *acquietare.* — L. *ac-* (for *ad*), to; *quietare,* vb., formed from *quietus,* discharged, free, orig. at rest. See quit (below).

coy. (F. — L.) O. F. *coi,* oldest form *coit,* quiet, still; spelt *coy, quoy,* in Cotgrave. — L. *quietus,* still.

decoy, to allure. (L.; *and* F. — L.) Coined by prefixing L. *de,* down, to O. F. *coi,* quiet, E. *coy* (above). ¶ No doubt the verb to *coy* (older than *de-coy*) took a new sense by confusion with Du. *kooi,* a cage, called a *coy* in Norfolk, with the sense 'decoy' for birds; but M. E. *coyen,* to blandish, occurs in the Prompt. Parv., and Spenser uses *accoy,* F. Q. iv. 8. 59. As for the Du. *kooi,* O. Du. *koye* (Hexham), it appears to be from L. *cauea,* a cage; see **cage,** p. 73, l. 9.

quit, freed, free. (F. — L.) Orig. an adj., as in '*quit* claim.' M. E. *quyt, quit,* also *quyte,* free; adj. — O. F. *quite,* discharged, released, freed. — L. *quietum,* acc. of *quietus,* at rest, hence, free. Thus *quit* is short for *quiet.* **Der.** *quit,* verb, F. *quitter,* O. F. *quiter,* from the adj.; hence *quitt-ance,* O. F. *quitance,* Low. L. *quietantia*; *ac-quit* (above).

quite. (F. — L.) M. E. *quite*; an adverbial use of the M. E. adj. *quite,* free, now spelt *quit*; see above.

requiem. (L.) The Mass for the Dead was called *requiem,* because it began 'Requiem æternam dona eis.' — L. *requiem,* acc. of *requies,* repose. — L. *re-*; *quies,* rest.

requite. (F. — L.) Also spelt *requit,* Temp. iii. 3. 71. From *re-* and *quit*; see quit (above).

Quill (1), a feather, pen. (F. — O. H. G.) M. E. *quille.* '*Quylle,* a stalk, Calamus;' Prompt. Parv. *Quill* also means the faucet of a barrel, or a reed to wind yarn on. This is a difficult and doubtful word; it would seem that the bird's quill was named from its tapering shape, like that of the

conical pin used in the game of kails or
kayles (see **Kails**). – O. F. *quille*, ' a keyle, a
big peg or pin of wood ; ' Cot. [A distinct
word from F. *quille*, a keel.] – O. H. G.
kegil, G. *kegel*, a nine-pin, skittle, cone,
bobbin. (The sense of ' bobbin ' accounts
for the E. *quill*, a reed to wind yarn on.)

Quill (2), to pleat a ruff. (F. – O. H. G. ;
or L.) Etym. doubtful; either (1) so
called from being folded over quills or
reeds; see **Quill** (1). Or (2) allied to
the Guernsey word *enquiller*, to pleat
(Métivier); derived by Métivier from O. F.
cuillir, to gather, collect (L. *colligere*).
This latter derivation is far from being
convincing ; the difference between *quiller*
and *cuillir* is considerable, the conjugation
being different. Surely *enquiller* must be
related to F. *quille* (above).

Quillet ; see **Quiddity**.

Quilt, a bed-cover, &c. (F. – L.) M. E.
quilte. – O. F. *cuilte*, a quilt (12th cent.),
also spelt *cotre, coutre*. – L. *culcita, culcitra*,
a cushion, mattress, pillow, quilt ; the latter
form gave O. F. *cotre*.

counterpane (1), a coverlet for a bed.
(F. – L.) A corrupted form ; it stands for
counterpoint, as in Shak. – O. F. *contrepoinct*, the back stitch or quilting stitch,
also a quilt; Cot. β. Thus named, by a
popular etymology, from a fancied connection with O. F. *contrepoincter*, to work the
back-stitch (from *contre* = L. *contra*). But
really connected with O. F. *coutrepoincter*,
to quilt (also in Cotgrave). In fact, *contrepoinct* is a corruption of *coutrepoinct, coute-
point*, a counterpane. – L. *culcita puncta*, a
counterpane, a stitched quilt (see Ducange).
– L. *culcita*, a quilt ; *puncta*, fem. of *punctus*, pp. of *pungere*, to prick.

cushion. (F. – L.) M. E. *quisshen*. –
O. F. *coissin, coussin*, a cushion. – Low L.
culcitinum*, not found, but regularly formed
from *culcita*, a cushion (above).

Quinary ; see **Quinquagesima**.

Quince. (F. – L. – Gk.) Formerly
quence, quyns. (Cf. O. F. *coignasse*, ' the
greatest kind of quince,' Cot.) Merely the
pl. form of M. E. *quyne, coine*, or *coin*,
a quince. – O. F. *coin*, F. *coing*, a quince.
(The same as Prov. *codoing*, Ital. *cotogna*,
a quince.) – L. *cydonium*, a quince ; (the
Ital. *cotogna* being from L. *cydonia*.) – Gk.
κυδώνιον μῆλον, a quince, lit. a Cydonian
apple. – Gk. Κυδωνία, Κυδωνίς, Cydonia,
one of the chief cities of Crete.

Quincunx ; see **Quinquagesima**.

Quinine, extract of Peruvian bark. (F.
– Peruv.) F. *quinine*, formed with suffix
-ine (L. *-ina*), from F. *quina*, Peruvian
bark. – Peruvian *kina*, or *kina-kina*, said
to mean ' bark,' esp. that which we call
Peruvian bark.

Quinquagesima. (L.) L. *quinquagesima* (*dies*), fiftieth (day); fem. of *quin-
quagesimus*, fiftieth. – L. *quinqua-*, for *quinque*, five, allied to E. **Five** ; *-gesimus*, put for
-gensimus *, *-censimus* *, *-centimus* *, short
for *decentimus* *, tenth, from *decem*, ten.

quinary, consisting of fives. (L.) L.
quinarius, arranged by fives. – L. *quini*,
five at a time. Put for *quinc-ni* *, from
quinque, five.

quincunx, an arrangement by fives
(L.) Applied to trees arranged like the
spots on the side of a die marked 5 ; L.
quincunx. – L. *quinque*, five; *uncia*, an
ounce, small mark, spot on a die ; see
uncial, under **Inch**. ¶ So also *quinqu-
angular*, having five angles; *quinqui-ennial*,
lasting 5 years.

quintuple, five-fold. (F. – L.) F.
quintuple. – L. *quintuplus* *, a coined
word. – L. *quintu-s*, fifth, from *quinque*;
-plus, i. e. *-fold*; see **Double**.

Quinsy ; see **Cynic**.

Quintain. (F. – L.) F. *quintaine*, a
post with arms, for beginners to tilt at.
The form of the word is such that it must
be allied to L. *quintana*, a street in the
camp, which separated the *fifth* maniple
from the sixth ; where was the market and
business-place of the camp. Doubtless
this public place was also the scene of
martial exercises and trials of skill; the
Low L. *quintana* means (1) a quintain,
also (2) a part of a street (space) where
carriages could pass. – L. *quintanus*, from
quintus, fifth. Put for *quinc-tus* *, from
quinque, five.

Quintal ; see **Cent**.

Quintessence ; see **Essence**.

Quintuple ; see **Quinquagesima**.

Quip, a taunt, cavil. (L.) Formerly
quippy ; Drant's Horace, bk. ii. sat. 1. –
L. *quipfe*, forsooth (ironical).

quibble. (C.) Dimin. of *quib*, a quip
(Coles); which is a weakened form of *quip*.

Quire (1), of paper ; see **Quadrate**.

Quire (2), a band of singers ; see **Chorus**.

Quirk, a cavil. (C.) Prob. for *quirt*. –
W. *chwired*, a quirk, piece of craft, from
chwiori, to turn briskly ; cf. *chwyr-nu*, to
whir, buzz. Cf. Gael. *cuireid*, a turn,

wile, trick, which (however) Macleod refers to *car*, to turn. Prob. allied to **Whir.**

Quit, Quite; see **Quiet.**

Quiver (1), to shiver. (E.) Allied to obsolete adj. *quiver*, full of motion, brisk; A. S. *cwifer*, in the comp. adv. *cwifer-lîce*, eagerly. Cf. O. Du. *kuiven*, *kuiveren*, to quiver (Kilian).

Quiver (2), a case for arrows. (F.— O. H. G.) O. F. *cuivre*, *cuevre*, *couire*, a quiver. — O. H. G. *kohhar* (G. *köcher*), a quiver.+A. S. *cocer*, a quiver.

Quixotic. (Span.) Named from *Don Quixote* or *Quijote*, a novel by Cervantes.

Quoif; the same as **Coif.**

Quoin; see **Coin.**

Quoit, Coit, a ring of iron for throwing at a mark. (F. — L.?) M. E. *coite*, *coyte*; cf. Lowl. Sc. *coit*, to push about, justle. Prob. from O. F. *coiter*, to press, push, hasten, incite, instigate (which prob. also had the sense 'to hurl'). Of doubtful origin; perhaps from L. *coactare*, to force, from *coactus*, pp. of *cogere*, to compel; see **Cogent.**

Quorum. (L.) It was usual to nominate members of a committee, *of whom* (*quorum*) a certain number must be present to form a meeting.—L. *quorum*, of whom; gen. pl. of *qui*, who. Allied to **Who.**

Quota, a share. (Ital.—L.) Ital. *quota*, a share. — L. *quota* (*pars*), how great a part; fem. of *quotus*, how great. — L. *quot*, how many; allied to *qui*, who; see **Who.**

quote. (F.—L.) Formerly also *cote.*— O. F. *quoter*, *coter*, to quote. — Low L. *quotare*, to mark off into chapters and verses, for references; hence, to give a reference. — L. *quotus*, how many, how much, with allusion to chapters, &c.; see above.

quotidian, daily. (F. — L.) F. *quotidien.* — L. *quotidianus*, daily. — L. *quoti-*, for *quotus*, how many; *dies*, a day. Thus *quotidianus* = on however many a day, on any day, daily.

quotient. (F.—L.; *or* L.) F. *quotient*, the part which falls to each man's share; Cot. — L. *quotient-**, the imaginary stem of L. *quotiens*, how many times, which is really indeclinable. — L. *quot*, how many (above).

Quoth, he says, he said. (E.) Properly a pt. t.; also as pres. t. M. E. *quoth*, *quod.* — A. S. *cwæð*, pt. t. of *cweðan*, to say. + Icel. *kvað*, pt. t. of *kveða*, to say. Allied to Skt. *gad*, to speak. (√ GA.)

bequeath. (E.) A. S. *bicweðan*, to declare. — A. S. *bi-*, by (E. *by*); *cweðan*, to say.

bequest. (E.) M. E. *biqueste* (rare); the correct form being *bequide.* From A. S. *be-*, *bi-* (E. *by*); *cwide*, a saying, from *cweðan*, to say. Cf. A. S. *bicweðan*, to bequeath. ¶ Clearly *bequest* is a corrupt form, due to confusing A. S. *cwide*, a saying, with *quest*, a word of F. origin, occurring in *in-quest*, *re-quest*, as well as in the simple form; see quest, s. v. **Query.**

Quotidian, Quotient; see **Quota.**

R.

Rabbet, to cut the edges of boards, to fit them; see **Beat.**

Rabbi, Rabbin, sir. (L.—Gk.—Heb.) L. *rabbi*, John i. 38.—Gk. *ῥαββί.*—Heb. *rabbi*, literally 'my master.' — Heb. *rab*, great; as sb., master; and *î*, my.—Heb. root *râbab*, to be great. (The form *rabbin* is French.)

Rabbit. (O. Low G.?) M. E. *rabet.* Dimin. of an older form only found in O. Du. *robbe*, a rabbit. Cf. Span. and Port. *rabo*, tail, hind quarters; *rabear*, to wag the tail. ¶ The true E. name is *cony.*

Rabble. (O. Low G.) From the noise made by a crowd.—O. Du. *rabbelen*, to chatter; prov. G. *rabbeln*, to chatter (Flügel). The suffix *-le* gives a frequenta-

tive force; *rabble* = that which keeps on making a noise. Cf. Gk. *ῥαβάσσειν*, to make a noise.

rapparee, an Irish robber. (Irish.) Irish *rapaire*, a noisy fellow, sloven, robber, thief; cf. *rapal*, noise, *rapach*, noisy. Cf. Gael. *rapair*, a noisy fellow.

Rabid, mad. (L.) L. *rabidus*, mad. — L. *rabere*, to rage, rave. (√ RABH.)

rage. (F.—L.) F. *rage.* — L. *rabiem*, acc. of *rabies*, rage.—L. *rabere*, to rage. And see **Rave.**

Raca. (Chaldee.) Matt. v. 22. Chaldee *rêkâ*, worthless; hence, foolish.

Raccoon, Racoon. (N. American Indian.) Spelt *rackoon* in Bailey (1735). The native W. Indian name. '*Arathkone*, a beast like a fox;' glossary of Indian

Words subjoined to A Historie of Travaile into Virginia, by W. Strachey (pub. by the Hackluyt Soc. in 1849).

Race (1), a swift course. (E.) M. E. *rees, rase.* A. S. *rǽs,* a swift course. + Icel. *rás.* Cf. Skt. *rish,* to flow. (√ ARS, to flow.)

Race (2), a family. (F. – O. H. G.) F. *race.* – O. H. G. *reiza,* a line, stroke, mark (hence a line or lineage). + Icel. *reitr,* a scratch, from *ríta,* to scratch, write ; see **Write.** ¶ Perhaps confused with L. *radix,* from which, however, the F. *race* cannot have been derived (Diez).

racy, of strong flavour, spirited. (F. – O. H. G.; *with* E. *suffix.*) *Rac-y* = indicative of its *race,* due to its breed.

Race (3), a root ; see **Radix.**

Raceme, a cluster. (F. – L.) F. *racème.* – L. *racemum,* acc. of *racemus,* a cluster.

raisin. (F. – L.) M. E. *reisin.* – O. F. *raisin,* a grape; also a bunch. – L. *racemum* (above).

Rack (1), a grating above a manger, instrument of torture ; see **Reach.**

Rack (2), light vapoury clouds ; see **Wreak.**

Rack (3), to pour off liquor, to clear it from dregs or lees. (F. – L. ?) Minsheu (1627) speaks of '*rackt* wines.' – F. *raqué*; whence *vin raqué,* 'small, or corse wine, squeezed from the dregs of the grapes, already drained of all their best moisture ;' Cot. Cf. Span. *rascon,* sour; *rascar,* to scrape. Prob. of L. origin ; see **Rascal.**

Rack (4), another spelling of *wrack,* i. e. wreck ; see **Wreak.**

Rack (5); see **Arrack.**

Rack (6), a neck of mutton. (E.) – A. S. *hracca,* neck (Somner). We also find (7) *rack,* for *reck,* to care; (8) *rack,* to relate, from A. S. *reccan,* to reckon; (9) *rack,* a pace of a horse, i. e. a *rocking* pace; see **Rock** (2). Also *rack* (10), a track, cart-rut. from Icel. *reka,* to drive; see **Wreak.**

Racket (1), **Raquet,** a bat with a net-work blade. (F. – Span. – Arab.) M. E. *raket*; borrowed from O. F. – Span. *raqueta,* a racket, battle-dore. – Arab. *ráhat,* the palm of the hand (hence the game of fives, which preceded rackets). To this day. tennis is called in F. *paume,* i. e. palm of the hand, though now played with bats.

Racket (2). a noise. (C.) Gael. *racaid,* a noise ; Irish *racan,* noise. – Gael. *rac,* to make a noise like geese or ducks. Of imitative origin ; cf *rattle.*

Racoon ; see **Raccoon.**

Racy ; see **Race** (2).

Radical, Radish ; see **Radix.**

Radius, a ray. (L.) L. *radius,* a ray.

irradiate. (L.) From pp. of L. *irradiare,* to shine upon. – L. *ir-,* for *in,* on ; *radiare,* to shine, from *radius,* a ray.

radiant. (L.) From stem of pres. pt. of L. *radiare,* to shine. – L. *radius,* ray.

ray. (F. – L.) O. F. *raye* ; F. *raie.* – L. *radium,* acc. of *radius,* a ray.

Radix, a root. (L.) L. *radix* (stem *radic-*), a root. + Gk. ῥάδιξ, a branch, rod. See **Wort.** Der. *radic-al.*

eradicate. (L.) From pp. of L. *eradicare,* to root out. – L. *e,* out ; *radicare,* to root, from *radic-,* stem of *radix,* root.

race (3), a root. (F. – L.) 'A *race* of ginger;' Wint. Ta. iv. 3. 50. – O. F. *raïs, raiz,* a root. – L. *radicem,* acc. of *radix.*

radish. (F. – Prov. – L.) F. *radis* (not a true F. word, but borrowed from Provençal). – Prov. *raditz,* a root. – L. *radicem* ; see above.

rash (3), to pull, tear violently. (F. – L.) '*Rashing* off helmes ;' F. Q. v. 3. 8. M. E. *aracen,* afterwards shortened to *racen.* – O. F. *esracer* (F. *arracher*), to root up, pull away violently. – L. *exradicare,* to root out. – L. *ex,* out ; *radicare* ; see **eradicate** (above).

Raffle ; see **Rape** (1).

Raft. (Scand.) M. E. *raft,* a spar, beam ; orig. sense 'rafter.' – Icel. *raptr* (*raftr*), a rafter, beam (where the final *r* is merely the sign of the nom. case); Dan. *raft,* a rafter, a beam. Extended from Icel. *ráf, ræfr,* a roof, cognate with O. H. G. *rávo,* a spar. rafter. Allied to Gk. ὄροφος, a roof. ¶ Not the same as A. S. *hróf,* a roof.

rafter, a beam to support a roof. (E.) A. S. *ræfter.* An extension of the word above.

Rag. (E.) M. E. *ragge.* We only find A. S. *raggie,* rough, shaggy ; formed from a sb. *ragge**. + Swed. *ragg,* rough hair, whence *raggig,* shaggy ; Icel. *rögg.* shaggi-ness, *raggaðr,* shaggy. Orig. sense 'shaggi-ness,' whence the notion of untidiness. ¶ The resemblance to Gk. ῥάκος, a shred of cloth, is purely accidental (for Gk. κ = E. *h*). Der. *rag-stone,* i. e. rugged stone ; *rag-wort,* i.e. ragged plant.

Rage ; see **Rabid.**

Ragout ; see **Gust** (2).

Raid ; see **Ride.**

Rail (1), a bar. (O. Low G.) M. E. *rail*. Not found in A. S. Through O. F. *reille*, from a Low G. form *regel* (cf. *hail* (1), *nail*, *rain*). — Low G. *regel*, a rail, cross-bar; Swed. *regel*, a bar, bolt. + G. *riegel*, O. H. G. *rigil*, a bar, bolt, orig. a latch of a door. This O. H. G. *rigil* is from O. H. G. *rîhan*, to fasten (G. *reihen*, to put in a row, connect). Allied to Skt. *lekha* (for *rekha*), a line, stroke. (√RIK.)

Rail (2), to brawl, scold; see **Rase**.

Rail (3), a bird; see **Rattle**.

Rail (4), part of a woman's night-dress. (E.) See Halliwell and Palsgrave. M. E. *reȝel*. — A. S. *hrægl*, *hregl*, swaddling-clothes. + O. Fries. *hreil*, *reil*, O. H. G. *hregil*, a garment.

Raiment. (F. — L. *and* Scand.; *with* F. suffix.) Short for *arrai-ment*; see **Array**.

Rain. (E.) M. E. *rein*. A. S. *regn*, also *rén* (by contraction). + Du. *regen*, Icel. Dan. Swed. *regn*, G. *regen*, Goth. *rign*, rain. Cf. L. *rigare*, to moisten.

Raindeer; see **Reindeer**.

Raise; see **Rise**.

Raisin; see **Raceme**.

Rajah; see **Regent**.

Rake (1), an implement. (E.) A. S. *raca*, a rake. + Icel. *reka*, a shovel, Dan. *rage*, a poker, Swed. *raka*, an oven-rake, G. *rechen*, a rake. Allied to Goth. *rikan* (pt. t. *rak*), to collect, heap up. (√RAG.) Der. *rake*, verb.

Rake (2), a dissolute man. (Scand.) M. E. *rakel*, rash; oddly corrupted to *rakehell* (Trench, Nares); finally shortened to *rake*. — Swed. dial. *rakkel*, a vagabond, from *raka*, to run hastily, O. Swed. *racka*, to run about. So also Icel. *reikall*, vagabond, from *reika*, to wander.

Rake (3), a nautical term; see **Reach**.

Rakehell, a vagabond; see **Rake** (2).

Rally (1), to reassemble; see **Ligament**.

Rally (2), to banter; see **Rase**.

Ram. (E.) A. S. *ram*. + Du. *ram*, G. *ramm*. Cf. Skt. *ram*, to sport, &c.; *rati*, passion. Der. *ram*, verb, to but, push, thrust; *ram-rod*.

Ramble; see **Roam**.

Ramify. (F. — L.) F. *ramifier*, to put forth branches (hence, to branch off). — L. *rami-*, for *ramus*, a branch, bough; *-ficare*, for *facere*, to make.

Ramp, Romp, to bound, leap; properly to climb, scramble, rear; also to sport boisterously. (F. — Teut.) M. E. *rampen*, to rage; cf. *ramp-ant* (F. *ramp-*

ant), rearing, said of a lion. — F. *ramper*, 'to creep, run, crawle, climb;' Cot. Orig. sense 'to clamber;' cf. Ital. *rampare*, to clutch, *rampa*, a claw, grip. The Ital. *rampare* (Prov. *rapar*) is a nasalised form from Low G. *rappen*, to snatch hastily, Dan. *rappe*, to hasten; cf. G. *raffen*, to snatch. See **Rape** (1).

Rampart; see **Pare**.

Ramsons, broad-leaved garlic. (E.) A double plural; put for *rams-en-s*. Here *ramsen* = A. S. *hramsan*, ramsons; a pl. form, from a sing. *hramsa*. + Swed. *rams-lök* (*lök* = leek); Dan. *rams*; Lithuan. *kremusze*, wild garlic; Irish *creamh*, garlic, Gk. κρόμυον, an onion.

Rancid. (L.) L. *rancidus*, rancid. — L. *rancere*, to stink.

rancour. (F. — L.) M. E. *rancour*. — F. *rancour*. — L. *rancorem*, acc. of *rancor*, spite, orig. rancidness. — L. *rancere* (above).

Random, said or done at hazard. (F. — Teut.) M. E. *randon*; esp. in phr. *in randon*, in great haste. — O. F. *randon*, the force and swiftness of a great stream; whence phr. *à randon*, in great haste, with impetuosity. Hence *randonner*, to run swiftly. So also Span. *de rendon*, *de rondon*, rashly, impetuously. — G. *rand*, a brim, edge, verge, margin; whence Ital. *a randa*, with difficulty, exactly (lit. near the verge). Cf. G. *bis am rande voll*, full to the brim. The sense of F. *randon* has reference to the force of a *full* or *brimming* river. + A. S. *rand*, Icel. *rönd*, Dan. *rand*, rim, verge; Swed. *rand*, a stripe.

Range; see **Ring**.

Rank (1), a row, class, order; see **Ring**.

Rank (2), adj., coarse in growth; see **Reach** (1).

Rankle; see p. 393, col. 1.

Ransack. (Scand.) Icel. *rannsaka*, to search a house, ransack; Swed. *ransaka*, Dan. *ransage*. — Icel. *rann*, a house, abode; *sak*, base of *sœkja*, to seek. The Icel. *rann* stands for *rasn* *, and is the same as A. S. *ræsn*, a plank, beam, Goth. *razn*, a house. See **Seek**.

Ransom; see **Exempt**.

Rant. (Du.) O. Du. *ranten*, to dote, be enraged. + G. *ranzen*, to toss about, make a noise.

Ranunculus. (L.) L. *ranunculus*, a little frog; also, a plant. Double dimin. of *rāna*, a frog, put for *rac-na* *, i.e. croaker. Cf. L. *raccare*, to growl.

rennet (2), a sweet kind of apple. (F.

—L.) Formerly spelt *renate*, from an odd notion that it was derived from L. *renatus*, born again ! — F. *reinette, rainette*, a rennet ; the same as *rainette*, a little frog; from the speckled skin. Dimin. of F. *raine*, a frog. — L. *rana* (above).

Rap (1), to strike smartly; a smart stroke. (Scand.) Dan. *rap*, a rap, tap; Swed. *rapp*, a blow ; Swed. *rappa*, to beat. Of imitative origin ; allied to **Rattle**.

Rap (2), to seize hastily; see **Rape** (1).

Rapacious ; see **Rapid**.

Rape (1), a seizing by force. (Scand.) M. E. *rape*, haste, hurry. The word has been affected by a popular etymology connecting it with L. *rapere*, to which it is unrelated; see **rapt** (below). The M. E. *rape*, hurry, haste, is a common word; see Chaucer's lines to Adam Scrivener. — Icel. *hrap*, ruin, falling down, *hrapaðr*, a hurry, *hrapa*, to hasten ; Swed. *rapp*, Dan. *rap*, quick ; see **rap** (2) below. Der. *rape*, verb.

raffle, a kind of lottery. (F. — G.) M. E. *rafle*, a game at dice. — F. *rafle*, *raffle*, a game at three dice. — F. *rafler*, to snatch up. — G. *raffeln*, to snatch up ; frequent. of *raffen*, to snatch away, carry off hastily. See below.

rap (2), to snatch, seize hastily. (Scand.) M. E. *rapen*, to hasten, act hastily. — Icel. *hrapa*, to fall, tumble, hasten, hurry; Swed. *rappa*, to seize, snatch, Dan. *rappe*, to make haste ; Swed. *rapp*, Dan. *rap*, quick, brisk. + G. *raffen*, to snatch. ¶ Chiefly in the phrase to *rap* and *rend*, corruption of *ráp* and *renne* = 'seize and plunder;' where *renne* is from Icel. *ræna*, to plunder, from *rán*, plunder.

rapt, carried away. (E.; *confused with* L.) Put for *rapped*, pp. of *rap*, to hurry, carry away; 'What thus *raps* you?' Cymb. i. 6. 51. But it was soon confused, by a popular etymology, with L. *raptus*, pp. of *rapere*, to seize, with which it had no orig. connection ; and very soon it was always spelt *rapt*, and believed to be the equivalent of *raptus*, and to belong to nothing else ; see Milton, P. L. iii. 522.

Rape (2), a plant. (L.) M. E. *rape*. — L. *rapa*, *rapum*, a turnip, a rape.+Gk. *ῥάπυς*, a turnip, *ῥαφανίς*, a radish ; Russ. *riepa*, a turnip.

Rape (3), a division of a county, in Sussex. (Scand.) Icel. *hreppr*, a district; prob. orig. a share. — Icel. *hreppa*, to catch ; cf. A. S. *hreppan*, to lay hold of.

Rapid. (F. — L.) F. *rapide*. — L. *rapidus*,

quick, lit. snatching away. — L. *rapere*, to snatch. + Gk. *ἁρπάζειν*, to seize ; whence E. *harpy*.

rapacious. (L.) Coined from L. *rapaci-*, crude form of *rapax*, grasping. — L. *rapere*, to grasp.

rapine. (F. — L.) F. *rapine*, 'rapine, ravine ;' Cot. — L. *rapina*, robbery, plunder. — L. *rapere*, to seize.

raptorial. (L.) Used of birds of prey. — L. *raptori-*, crude form of *raptor*, one who seizes. — L. *rapere*, to seize.

rapture. (L.) Coined, as if from L. *raptura* *, from L. *raptus*, pp. of *rapere*.

ravage, sb., plunder. (F. — L.) F. *ravage*, 'ravage ;' Cot. — L. *ravir*, to bear away suddenly. — L. *rapere*.

raven (2), to plunder, to devour. (F. — L.) Better spelt *ravin*. From M. E. *ravine*, sb., plunder. — O. F. *ravine*, rapidity, impetuosity (oldest sense 'plunder,' as in L.). — L. *rapina*, plunder ; see **rapine** (above).

ravine, a hollow gorge. (F. — L.) F. *ravine*, a hollow worn by floods, also a great flood ; O. F. *ravine* (above).

ravish, to seize with violence. (F. — L.) M. E. *rauischen*. — F. *raviss-*, stem of pres. pt. of *ravir*, to ravish. — L. *rapere*, to seize.

Rapier, Rappee, see **Rasp**.

Rapine ; see **Rapid**.

Rapparee ; see **Rabble**.

Rapt ; see **Rape** (1).

Raptorial, Rapture ; see **Rapid**.

Rare. (F. — L.) F. *rare*. — L. *rarum*, acc. of *rarus*, rare.

Rascal, a knave, villain. (F. — L.) M. E. *raskaille*, the common herd. It was a term of the chase ; certain animals, not worth hunting, were so called. The hart, till he was six years old, was accounted *rascayle*. The O. F. word must also have been spelt *rascaille* *, clearly the same word as mod. F. *racaille*, 'the rascality or base or rascall sort, the scumme, dregs, offals, outcasts of any company,' Cot. Due to an O. F. word cognate with Prov. Span. Port. *rascare*, to scrape ; the orig. sense being 'scrapings.' All from a Low L. *rasicare* *, a frequent. form from *rasum*, supine of *radere*, to scrape ; see **Rase**.

Rase, Raze, to scrape, efface. (F. — L.) M. E. *rasen*, to scrape. — F. *raser*. — Low L. *rasare*, to graze, to demolish. — L. *rasum*, supine of *radere*, to scrape. Allied to **Rodent**.

abrade. (L.) L. *ab-radere*, to scrape off. **Der.** *abras-ion*, from pp. *abrasus*.

erase. (L.) L. *erasus*, pp. of *e-radere*, to scratch out.

rail (2), to brawl, scold. (F.–L.) F. *railler*, to deride. Cf. Span. *rallar*, to scrape, to molest, vex; Port. *ralar*, to scrape; corresponding to a Low L. type *radulare**. – L. *radere*, to scrape, graze. Der. *raill-er-y*, F. *raillerie*, banter.

rally (2), to banter. (F.–Teut.) We also find the sb. *rallery*, 'pleasant drolling,' Phillips, ed. 1710. This is, of course, another spelling of *raillery*; and *rally* is merely another form of *rail* (2), somewhat closer in form to F. *railler* (above).

rash (2), a slight eruption on the body. (F.–L.) O. F. *rasche*, *rasque*; F. *rache*. The same as Prov. *rasca*, the itch. So called from the wish to scratch it; cf. Prov. *rascar*, to scratch, equivalent to a Low L. *rasicare**. – L. *rasum*, supine of *radere*, to scrape. See **Rascal**.

rasorial. (L.) L. *rasori-*, crude form of *rasor*, one who scrapes. – L. *rasum*, supine of *radere*, to scrape.

raze, the same as **Rase** (above).

razor. (F.–L.) F. *rasoir*, a razor, lit. a shaver. – F. *raser*, to shave; see **Rase** (above).

Rash (1), headstrong. (Scand.) M. E. *rash*, *rasch*. – Dan. Swed. *rask*, quick, rash; Icel. *röskr*, vigorous.+Du. *rasch*, G. *rasch*. Cf. Skt. *ricch*, to go, to attack; Gk. ὄρνυμι, I excite. (√AR.)

rasher, a thin slice of broiled bacon. (Scand.) '*Rasher* on the coales, quasi *rashly* or hastily roasted,' Minsheu. This is right; cf. '*Rashed*, burnt in cooking, by being too hastily dressed;' Halliwell.

Rash (2), a slight eruption; see **Rase**.

Rash (3), to pull violently; see **Radix**.

Rasher; see **Rash** (1).

Rasorial; see **Rase**.

Rasp, verb. (F. – O. H. G.) M. E. *raspen*. – O. F. *rasper* (F. *râper*). – O. H. G. *raspôn*, whence G. *raspeln*, to rasp. Cf. O. H. G. *hrespan*, to rake together.

rapier, a light narrow sword. (F.– Span.– O. H. G.) F. *rapiere*; it was considered as Spanish. '*Rapiere*, Spanische sworde;' Palsgrave. No doubt *rapiere* stands for *raspiere**, a name given in contempt, meaning 'a rasper' or poker; hence it was called 'a *proking-spit* of Spaine;' Nares. – Span. *raspadera*, a raker. – Span. *raspar*, to rasp, scratch. – O. H. G. *raspôn* (above). ¶ So Diez; Littré rejects this solution, but unadvisedly.

rappee, a kind of snuff. (F. – Teut.) F. *râpé*, lit. rasped, reduced to powder; pp. of *râper*, to rasp; see **Rasp** (above).

rasp-berry, a kind of fruit. (F.– O. H. G.; *and* E.) Formerly called *raspis*, *raspes*, but this is merely a pl. form used as a singular. Named from its roughness. So also Ital. *raspo*, a rasp, also a raspberry.

Rat. (E.) M. E. *rat*. A.S. *ræt*.+O. Du. *ratte*, Du. *rat*, Dan. *rotte*, Swed. *råtta*, G. *ratte*, *ratz*; Low G. *ratus*, *rato* (whence F. *rat*).+Irish and Gael. *radan*, Bret. *raz*; cf. Skt. *rada*, a tooth, an elephant; *vajra-rada*, a hog. (√RAD.) Der. *rat*, verb, to desert one's party, as rats are said to leave a falling house.

ratten, to take away a workman's tools for offending the trades' union. (F.–Low L. – Teut.) *Ratten* is the Hallamshire (Sheffield) word for a rat; hence applied to working secret mischief, which is attributed to rats. 'I have been *rattened*; I had just put a new cat-gut band on my lathe, and last night the *rats* have carried it off;' N. and Q. 3. S. xii. 192. M. E. *raton*, a rat.– F. *raton*, dimin. of F. *rat* (above).

Ratafia; see **Arrack**.

Ratch, a rack with teeth; see **Reach**.

Rate (1), a proportion, standard, tax. (F.–L.) O. F. *rate*, price, value. – L. *ratus*, determined, fixed, settled, pp. of *reor*, I think, judge, deem.

arraign. (F. – L.) M. E. *arainen*. – O. F. *aranier*, *areisnier*, to speak to, discourse with, cite, arraign.–O. F. *a* (L. *ad*), to; *reisner*, *reisoner*, to reason, from O. F. *reson*, *raison*, reason, advice; see **reason** (below).

ratify. (F.–L.) F. *ratifier*.–Low L. *ratificare*, to confirm. – L. *rati-*, for *ratus*, settled; *-ficare*, from *facere*, to make.

ratio. (L.) L. *ratio*, calculation. – L. *ratus*, pp. of *reor*, I think, deem.

ration, rate or allowance of provisions. (F.–L.) F. *ration*. – L. *rationem*, acc. of *ratio* (above).

reason. (F.–L.) M. E. *resoun*, *reisun*. –O. F. *reison* (F. *raison*). – L. *rationem*, acc. of *ratio*, calculation, reason (above).

Rate (2), to scold, chide. (F.–L.) M. E. *raten*, Ch. C. T. 3463; *araten*, to reprove. Also spelt *retten*, *aretten*.–O.F. *aretter*, to impute.–L. *ad*, to; and *reputare*, to count. See **Repute**. ¶ Not from *rate* (1).

Rath, early; **Rather**, sooner. (E.) *Rather* is the compar. of *rath*, early, soon.

A. S. *hraðe*, adv., quickly, *hræð*, adj., quick, swift; hence *hraðor*, sooner.+Icel. *hraðr*, swift; M. H. G. *rad*, *hrad*, quick.

Ratify, Ratio, Ration; see **Rate** (1).

Ratlines, Ratlins, Rattlings, the small transverse ropes crossing the shrouds of a ship. (E.; *and* F. **- L.**) It seems to be *rat-lines*, a jocular name, as if affording ladders for the rats to get up by. ¶ The Du. name is *weeflijn*, i.e. web-line. There is a Dan. *ratline*, but it means a tiller-rope, from *rat*, a wheel.

Rattan, a Malacca cane. (Malay.) Also spelt *ratan* (Johnson). **-** Malay *rótan*, the rattan-cane.

Ratten; see **Rat.**

Rattle, to clatter. (E.) M. E. *ratelen*. A. S. *hrætelan* *, only preserved in A. S. *hrætele, hrætelwyrt*, rattle-wort, a plant which derives its name from the rattling of the seeds in the capsules. **+** Du. *ratelen*, G. *rasseln*, to rattle; allied to Gk. κροτεῖν, to knock, make to rattle. (√KRAT.)

rail (3), a bird. (F. **-** Teut.) O. F. *rasle*, 'a rayle,' Cot. (F. *râle*). **-** O. Du. *rallen*, short for O. Du. *ratelen*, to rattle. (From its cry.)

Raught, pt. t. of **Reach,** q. v.

Ravage; see **Rapid.**

Rave. (F. **-** L.) M. E. *raven*. **-** O. F. *râver*, cited by Diez, s. v. *rêver*, as a Lorraine word; hence the derivative *ravasser*, 'to rave, talk idly;' Cot. Allied to Span. *rabiar*, to rave, a verb formed from the sb. *rabia*, rage, allied to L. *rabies*, rage. **-** L. *rabere*, to rage; see **Rabid.** ¶ This is the solution given by Diez, and the best.

revery. (F. **-** L.) F. *rêverie*, a raving, a vain fancy, a revery. **-** F. *rêver*, formerly *resver, râver*, to rave.

Ravel, to untwist, unweave, entangle. (O. Du.) The orig. sense has reference to the untwisting of a string or woven texture, the ends of threads of which become afterwards entangled. To *unravel* is to disentangle; to *ravel out* is to unweave. **-** O. Du. *ravelen*, to ravel; mod. Du. *rafelen*, to fray out, unweave; Low G. *reffeln*, to fray out. Of unknown origin; perhaps connected with G. *raffen*, to snatch; cf. G. *raffel*, an iron rake, grate of flax. ¶ The Du. *ravelen*, to dote (from O. F. *râver*, see **Rave**), is a different word. Der. *un-ravel*.

Ravelin, a detached work in fortification, with two embankments raised before the counterscarp. (F. **-** Ital.) F. *ravelin*. **-** O. Ital. *ravellino, revellino* (Ital. *rivel-*

lino), a ravelin. Orig. unknown; thought to be from L. *re-*, back; *uallum*, a rampart.

Raven (1), a bird. (E.) M. E. *raven*. A. S. *hræfn, hrefn*.+Du. *raaf*, Icel. *hrafn*, Dan. *ravn*, G. *rabe*. Named from its cry; cf. L. *crepare*, to rattle. (√KRAP.)

Raven (2), to plunder, devour, **Ravine, Ravish;** see **Rapid.**

Raw. (E.) M. E. *raw*. A. S. *hreáw, hræw*. **+** Du. *raauw*, Icel. *hrár*, Dan. *raa*, Swed. *rå*, O. H. G. *ráo*, G. *roh*. Allied to L. *crudus*, raw, Skt. *krúra*, sore, cruel, hard. (√KRU.)

Ray (1); see **Radius.**

Ray (2), a fish. (F. **-** L.) O. F. *raye*, F. *raie*. **-** L. *raia*, a ray. β. L. *rāia = ragya **, cognate with G. *roche*, a ray, a roach; see **Roach.**

Rayah, a person, not a Mahometan, who pays the capitation-tax, a word in use in Turkey. (Arab.) It may be explained as 'subject,' though the orig. sense is 'a flock,' or pastured cattle. **-** Arab. *ra'iyah, ra'iyat*, a flock; from *ra'i*, feeding, pasturing, *ra'y*, pasturing, tending flocks.

ryot, the same. (Arab.) Arab. *ra'iyat* (above).

Raze, Razor; see **Rase.**

Re-, Red- *prefix*, again. (F. **-** L.; *or* L.) L. *re-, red-*; commonly the former, except in *red-eem, red-olent, red-dition*. ¶ Hence a large number of compounds, such as *re-address, re-arrange*, which cause no difficulty.

Reach (1), to attain. (E.) M. E. *rechen*, pt. t. *raghte, raughte*, pp. *raught*. **-** A. S. *rǽcan, rǽcean*, pt. t. *rǽhte*. **+** O. Friesic *reka*, G. *reichen*. The A. S. *rǽcan* (= *raikian*) seems to mean 'to get into one's power,' and is allied to the sb. *rīce*, power, answering to Goth. *reiki*, power, authority. Still more closely allied to the sb. *ge-rǽc*, occasion, due time; this would give the orig. sense 'to seize an opportunity;' it comes to much the same thing. The Teut. base is RAK = Aryan RAG, to rule; see **Regent.** Der. *reach*, sb., which also means 'a stretch in a river.'

rack (1), a grating above a manger, an instrument of torture. (E.) In some senses the word is doubtless English; cf. M. E. *rekke*, a rack for hay. In the particular sense 'to torture.' it may have been borrowed from O. Du. *racken*, to rack, to torture. The radical sense of *rack* is to extend, stretch out, and it is closely allied to **Reach** (above); hence, as sb., *rack* is a straight bar (cf. G. *rack*, a rail, bar);

hence, a frame-work, such as the bars in a grating above a manger, a frame-work used for torture, a bar with teeth in which a cog-wheel can work. *On the rack* = in great anxiety ; a *rack-rent* is a rent stretched to its full value, or nearly so. Allied words are Icel. *rakkr*, straight, *rekkja*, to strain, O. Du. *racken*, to stretch, reach out, to rack ; Swed. *rak*, straight, G. *rack*, a rack, rail, *recken*, to stretch ; esp. Low G. *rakk*, a shelf, as in E. *plate-rack*. ¶ *Rack* is used in more senses than any other E. word ; see *rack* (2), *rack* (3), &c.

rake (3), the projection of the extremities of a ship beyond the keel, the inclination of a mast from the perpendicular. (Scand.) 'In sea-language, the *rake of a ship* is so much of her hull or main body, as hangs over both the ends of her keel ;.' Phillips (1710). Evidently from *rake*, vb., to reach, extend (Halliwell). — Swed. dial. *raka*, to reach, *raka fram*, to reach over, project ; Dan. *rage*, to project, jut out. Allied to **Reach**.

rank (2), coarse in growth, very fertile ; also rancid. (E.) The sense 'rancid' is due to confusion with O. F. *rance*, 'musty,' Cot., which is from L. *rancidus*. But M. E. *rank* means strong, forward ; from A.S. *ranc*, strong, proud, forward. ✛ Du. *rank*, lank, slender (like things of quick growth) ; Icel. *rakkr* (for *rankr**), straight, slender, Swed. *rank*, long and thin, Dan. *rank*. erect. A nasalised form of Teut. base RAK, to stretch, to make straight. (√ RAG.)

rankle, to fester. (F. — L.) Doubtless confused with *rank* (2) above. But prob. of F. origin ; Anglo-F. *rancler*, *arancler*, to fester. — L. *rancere*, to stink. See **Rancid**.

ratch, a rack or bar with teeth. (E.) A weakened form of *rack* (1) above, in the sense of 'bar with teeth ;' hence it came to mean a kind of a toothed wheel. **Der.** *ratch-et*, in watch-work, 'the small teeth at the bottom of the fusee or barrel that stop it in winding up.'

Reach (2), to try to vomit ; see **Retch**.

Read. (E.) M. E. *reden*. A. S. *rǽdan*, to discern, advise, read ; pt. t. *rǽdde*, pp. *gerǽd*. — A. S. *rǽd*, counsel. — A. S. *rǽdan* (strong verb) to advise, persuade ; with the remarkable pt. t. *reórd*. This verb is allied to Goth. *garedan*, to provide, Icel. *ráða* (pt. t. *réð*), to advise, G. *rathen* (pt. t. *rieth*), to advise. (Teut. base RAD ; root RADH.)

riddle (1), an enigma. (E.) Properly *riddles* ; and the pl. should be *riddles-es*. M. E. *redels*. — A.S. *rǽdelse*, pl. *rǽdelsan*, a riddle, ambiguity, something requiring explanation. — A. S. *rǽdan*, to discern, explain (above). ✛ Dan. *raadsel* (for *raad-se-la*, by inversion of the suffixes) ; G. *räthsel*, a riddle. ¶ We still say *to read a riddle*, i.e. to explain it.

Ready ; see **Ride**.

Real (1), actual. (F. — L. ; *or* L.) Either from O. F. *real* (F. *réel*), or directly from Low L. *realis*, belonging to the thing itself. — L. *res*, a thing.

rebus, a representation of a word by pictures. (L.) Thus *Bolton* was represented by pictures of a *bolt* and a *tun*. — L. *rebus*, by things, i.e. by means of things ; abl. pl. of *res*, a thing.

republic. (F. — L.) F. *republique*, 'the commonwealth ;' Cot. — L. *respublica*, a republic. — L. *res*, a matter, state ; *publica*, fem. of *publicus*, public.

Real (2), a small coin ; see **Regent**.

Realgar, red orpiment. (F. — Span. — Arab.) F. *réalgar*. — Span. *rejalgar*. — Arab. *rahj al-ghár*, powder of the mine, mineral powder. — Arab. *rahj*, powder ; *al*, the ; *ghár*, a cavern, mine.

Realm ; see **Regent**.

Ream. (F. — Span. — Arab.) M. E. *reeme*. — O. F. *raime* (F. *rame*), a ream or bundle of paper. — Span. *resma*, a ream. — Arab. *rismat* (pl. *rizam*), a bundle.

Reap. (E.) M. E. *repen* (pt. t. *rep*, pp. *ropen*). A.S. *rípan, rýpan*, with the possible form *répan*, since *i* (*ý*) stands for *é*, when *é* is a mutation of *eá* (*eó*) ; cf. A.S. *ríp, rýp*, a reaping, harvest. Allied to Du. *rapen*, to reap, gather, G. *raufen*, to pluck, Goth. *raupjan*, to pluck ; and to **Reave**.

ripe. (E.) M. E. *ripe*. A. S. *rípe*, fit for reaping ; cf. *ríp*, harvest. — A. S. *rípan*, to reap. ✛ Du. *rijp*, G. *reif*, ripe.

Rear (1), to raise ; see **Rise**.

Rear (2), the back part. (F. — L.) M. E. *rere*, chiefly in adv. *arere*, *arrere*, in the rear. — O. F. *riere*, backward ; whence *ariere* (F. *arrière*), behind, backward. — L. *retro*, backward ; whence *ad retro* = F. *arrière*. See **Retro-**.

arrears, sb. pl. (F. — L.) From M. E. *arere*, adv., in the rear ; see above. ¶ What we now call *arrears* answers to M. E. *arerages*, s. pl. formed from M. E. *arere* with F. suffix *-age*.

rearward, the rear-guard. (F. — L.

and G.) The old spelling is *rereward,* M. E. *rerewarde,* short for *arere-warde,* i. e. guard in the rear. See **Rear** (2) and **Ward.**

reredos, a screen at the back of a thing, esp. of an altar. (F.—L.) From M. E. *rere,* rear; and F. *dos,* back, from L. *dorsum,* back. ¶ Tautological.

rereward ; see rearward (above).

Rear (3), insufficiently cooked. (E.) M. E. *rere.* A. S. *hrér,* half-cooked.

Rearmouse ; see Reremouse.

Rearward ; see **Rear** (2).

Reason ; see **Rate** (1).

Reave, to rob. (E.) M. E. *reuen* (=*reven*) ; pt. t. *rafte, refte,* pp. *raft, reft.* A. S. *reáfian,* to despoil, lit. to strip.— A. S. *reáf,* clothing, a robe, spoil, plunder. — A. S. *reáf,* pt. t. of strong verb *reófan,* to deprive.+Icel. *raufa,* to reave, from sb. *rauf,* spoil, which from *rauf,* pt. t. of *rjúfa,* to break up, violate ; G. *rauben,* to rob, from *raub,* plunder. (√RUP.)

bereave. (E.) A. S. *bireáfian.*—A. S. *bi-,* prefix ; *reáfian,* to despoil (above). Der. *be-reft,* short for M. E. *bereued,* pp. of *bereuen* (*bereven*), to bereave.

rob. (F.—O. H. G.) M. E. *robben.*— O. F. *robber,* more commonly *rober,* to disrobe, spoil, strip off clothing, plunder. — F. *robe,* a robe ; see below.

robe. (F.—O. H. G.) F. *robe,* formerly also *robbe.*—M. H. G. *roub,* O. H. G. *raup* (G. *raub*), booty, spoil ; hence, a garment taken from the slain, clothing.+ A. S. *reáf,* Icel. *rauf,* sb. (above). Der. *dis-robe.*

rover, a pirate. (Du.) M. E. *rover.*— Du. *roover,* a robber, pirate, thief. — Du. *rooven,* to rob.—Du. *roof,* spoil. + A. S. *reáf,* Icel. *rauf,* G. *raub,* spoil (above). Der. *rove,* verb, to wander ; evolved from the sb.

rubbish, broken stones, waste matter, refuse. (F. — O. H. G.) M. E. *robows, robeux,* Prompt. Parv. ; pl. of an old form *robel*,* clearly represented by mod. E. *rubble* ; see below. ¶ *Rubbish* is, in fact, a corrupt form of the old plural of *rubble.*

rubble, broken stones, rubbish. (F.— O. H. G.) ' *Rubble,* or *rubbish* of old houses ;' Baret (1580). This answers exactly to an old form *robel*,* O. F. *robel*,* only found in the pl. *robeux.* ' A grete loode of *robeux* ;' cited by Way in Prompt. Parv. Obviously the dimin. of F. *robe* in the sense of ' trash,' so well preserved in

the cognate Ital. *roba,* ' a gowne, a robe, wealth, goods, geare, trash, pelfe,' Florio. Cf. Ital. *robaccia,* old goods, rubbish ; *robiccia,* trifles, rubbish ; from *roba.* See *robe* (above).

Rebate ; see **Batter** (1).

Rebeck, a three-stringed fiddle. (F.— Ital.—Arab.) O. F. *rebec,* also spelt *rebebe.* —Ital. *ribecca,* also *ribebba,* a rebeck.— Arab. *rabáb, rabába,* a rebeck. (Devic.)

Rebel ; see Dual.

Rebound ; see Boom (1).

Rebuff, a repulse. (Ital.) In Milton, P. L. xi. 936. — Ital. *rebuffo, ribuffo,* a check.—Ital. *ribuffare,* ' to check, chide ;' Florio.—Ital. *ri-* (L. *re-*) back ; *buffare,* a word of imitative origin, like E. *puff*; see Puff.

Rebuke, to reprove. (F.—L.) M. E. *rebuken.*—O. F. *rebouquer,* later *reboucher,* to blunt a weapon ; metaphorically, to put aside a request.—F. *re-,* back ; *bouquer,* later *boucher,* to obstruct, stop the mouth, shut up, also to hoodwink (hence to blunt), formed from *bouque,* Picard form of F. *bouche,* the mouth.—L. *re-,* back ; *bucca,* the puffed cheek (later, the mouth). Thus to *rebuke* is to stop one's mouth, obstruct.

Rebus ; see **Real** (1).

Rebut ; see **Beat.**

Recall, Recant ; see **Call, Cant** (1).

Recede ; see Cede.

Receive ; see Capacious.

Recent. (F.—L.) O. F. *recent* (F. *récent*).—L. *recent-,* stem of *recens,* fresh, new, orig. ' beginning anew.'—L. *re-,* again ; *-cent-,* a stem prob. allied to Russ. *po-cin-ate,* to begin.

Receptacle ; see Capacious.

Recess ; see Cede.

Recipe, Recipient ; see Capacious.

Reciprocal. (L.) From L. *reciprocus,* returning, alternating. Of unknown origin.

Recite ; see Cite.

Reck, to regard. (E.) M. E. *rekken.* A. S. *récan,* to care (put for *rócian*).* Formed from a sb. with base *róc-,* care, which exists in the cognate M. H. G. *ruoch,* O. H. G. *ruoh,* care, heed, whence the M. H. G. *ruochen,* O. H. G. *róhhjan,* to reck. Der. *reck-less,* A. S. *réce-leás* ; cf. Du. *roekeloos,* reckless.

Reckon. (E.) M. E. *rekenen.* A. S. *ge-recenian,* to explain ; allied to *ge-reccan, reccan,* to rule, order, direct, explain, ordain, tell.+Du. *rekenen* ; Icel. *reikna,* to reckon, allied to Icel. *rekja*, to trace out; Dan. *regne*, Swed. *räkna*; G. *rechnen*, allied to M. H. G. *rechen*. O. H. G.· *rachjan*, to declare, tell. β. All secondary verbs; from the sb. seen in Icel. *rök*, neut. pl., a reason, ground, origin, O. H. G. *rahha*, a thing, subject. (√RAG.)

Reclaim; see Claim.

Recline; see Incline.

Recluse; see Clause.

Recognise; see Noble.

Recoil, verb. (F.–L.) M. E. *recoilen*. –F. *reculer*, 'to recoyle, retire;' Cot. Lit. to go backwards.–F. *re-*, back; *cul*, the hinder parts.–L. *re-*, back; *culum*, acc. of *culus*, the hinder parts.

Recollect; see Legend.

Recommend; see Mandate.

Recompense; see Pendant.

Reconcile; see Calends.

Recondite, secret. (L.) L. *reconditus*, put away, hidden, secret; pp. of *recondere*, to put back again.–L. *re-*, back; *condere*, to put together. The L. *condere* (pt. t. *condidi*) is from *con-* (*cum*), with, and *dare* (pt. t. *dedi*), to give, used in composition with the force of 'put.' See Date (1).

Reconnoitre; see Noble.

Record; see Cordial.

Recount; see Putative.

Recoup; see Coppice.

Recourse; see Current.

Recover. (F.–L.) O. F. *recovrer, recuvrer* (F. *recouvrer*).–L. *recuperare*, to recover, also to recruit oneself. A difficult word; perhaps orig. 'to make good again,' from Sabine *cuprus*, good, of which the orig. sense may have been 'desirable,' from L. *cupere*, to desire.

recuperative, tending to recover. (L.) L. *recuperatiuus*, (properly) recoverable.–L. *recuperare* (above).

Recreant; see Creed.

Recreation; see Create.

Recriminate; see Crime.

Recruit; see Crescent.

Rectangle, Rectify, &c. ; see Regent.

Recumbent; see Covoy.

Recuperative; see Recover.

Recur; see Current.

Recusant; see Cause.

Red. (E.) M. E. *reed* (with long vowel). A. S. *réad*.+Du. *rood*, Icel. *rauðr*, Dan. Swed. *röd*, G. *roth*, Goth. *rauds*. Also Gk. ἐρυθρός, Irish and Gael. *ruath*, W. *rhudd*, L. *ruber* (for *rudher* *), red; allied to Skt. *rudhira*, blood. Note also the

Icel. strong verb *rjóða* (pt. t. *rauð*), to redden; A. S. *reóðan*, to redden.

rust. (E.) A. S. *rust*, rust; orig. redness. Allied to A. S. *rudu*, ruddiness, and *redd*, red.+Du. *roest*, Dan. *rust*, Swed. G. *rost*.

Reddition; see Date (1).

Redeem; see Exempt.

Redintegration; see Tangent.

Redolent; see Odour.

Redoubt; see Duke.

Redoubtable; see Dual.

Rodound; see Undulate.

Redress; see dress, p. 396, col. 2.

Reduce; see Duke.

Redundant; see Undulate.

Reechy; see Reek.

Reed. (E.) M. E. *reed*. A. S. *hreód*, a reed.+Du. *riet*; G. *riet, ried*.

Reef (1), a ridge of rocks; see Rive.

Reef (2), a portion of a sail; see Rive.

Reek, vapour. (E.) M. E. *reke*. A. S. *réc*, vapour.–A. S. *reác*, pt. t. of *reócan* (strong verb), to reek, smoke. (Base RUK.) + Du. *rook*, Icel. *reykr*, Swed. *rök*, Dan. *rög*, G. *rauch*; cf. Icel. *rjúka*, (pt. t. *rauk*), G. *riechen*, to smoke, reek. Orig. 'dimness;' cf. Skt. *raja, rajas*, dimness, *rajani*, night, *ranj*, to dye.

reechy, dirty. (E.) Lit. 'smoky;' weakened form of *reeky*; cf. Low Sc. *reekie*, smoky.

Reel (1), a small spindle for winding yarn. (E.) M. E. *rele*; A. S. *hreol*, a reel. + Icel. *hræll, ræll*, a weaver's rod or sley.

Reel (2), a Highland dance. (Gael.) Gael. *righil*, a reel.

Reeve (1), to pass the end of a rope through a hole; see Rive.

Reeve (2), an officer, steward. (E.) A. S. *geréfa*, an officer; orig. sense 'famous;' formed (by usual change from *ó* to *é*) from A. S. *róf*, active, excellent, famous. Cf. O. Sax. *róf*, famous. ¶ *Not* allied to G. *graf*. Der. *borough-reeve*; *port-reeve*; *sheriff*, q. v.

Refection; see Fact.

Refel; see Fallible.

Refer; see Fertile.

Refine; see Final.

Reflect; see Flexible.

Reform; see Form.

Refract; see Fragile.

Refrain (1), to restrain, forbear. (F.–L.) M. E. *refreinen*. – F. *refrener*, to repress; Cot. – L. *refrenare*, to bridle, hold in with a bit. — L. *re-*, back; *frenum*, a bit, curb. The orig. sense of *frenum* is 'holder' or 'keeper,' from √DHAR, to support, maintain; cf. Skt. *dhri*, to support, L. *firmus*, firm. ¶ Prob. sometimes confused with O. F. *refreindre*, 'to bridle,' Cot.; this is from L. *refringere* (i. e. *re-frangere*), to break back.

Refrain (2), the burden of a song; see **Fragile.**

Refresh; see **Fresh.**

Refrigerate; see **Frigid.**

Reft; see **Reave.**

Refuge; see **Fugitive.**

Refulgent; see **Fulgent.**

Refund, Refuse, Refute; see **Fuse** (1).

Regain; see **Gain.**

Regal, Regalia; see **Regent.**

Regale, to entertain. (F. — L. ?) F. *régaler*, to entertain (Littré). . [Not allied to *regal*, as Cotgrave suggests.] The same as Span. *regalar*, to make much of, pamper; orig. to melt (Diez). Diez derives it from L. *regelare* to melt, thaw; from L. *re-*, back, *gelare*, to freeze (see **Gelid**). But Scheler connects F. *régaler* with O. F. *galer*, to rejoice, which is preferable; see **Gala.**

Regard; see **Ward.**

Regatta. (Ital.) Orig. a strife, contention, hence a race, rowing match. — Ital. *regatta, rigatta*, 'a strife for the maistrie;' Florio. — O. Ital. *rigattare*, to wrangle, to haggle as a huckster does. So also Span. *rigatear*, to haggle, retail provisions, to rival in sailing. Doubtless these stand for Ital. *recatare*, Span. *recatear*, to retail; lit. 'to cater again;' from L. *re-* and *captare*, to catch, procure. See **Re-** and **Cater.**

Regenerate; see **Genus.**

Regent. (F. — L.) F. *regent*, a regent, vice-gerent. — L. *regent-*, stem of pres. pt. of *regere*, to rule. Allied to Gk. ὀρέγειν, to stretch, Goth. *uf-rakjan*, to stretch out, Skt. *rij*, to stretch, *ráj*, to govern. (√RAG.) See **Right.**

address, vb. (F. — L.) F. *adresser*. — F. *a*, to; *dresser*, to direct, dress; see **dress** (below).

adroit. (F. — L.) F. *adroit*, dexterous. — F. *à droit*, rightfully. — F. *à* (L. *ad*), to; Low L. *directum*, right, justice, neut. of *directus*; see **direct** (below).

alert. (F. — Ital. — L.) F. *alerte*; formerly *allerte*, and (in Rabelais) *a l'erte*, i. e.

on the watch. — Ital. *all'erta*, on the watch; from the phr. *stare all'erta*, to stand erect, be on one's guard. — Ital. *alla* (for *a la*), at the, on the; *erta*, fem. of *erto*, erect. — L. *ad*, to, at; *illam*, fem. acc. of *ille*, he; *erectam*, fem. acc. of *erectus*, erect; see **erect** (below).

correct. (L.) L. *correctus*, pp. of *corrigere*, to correct. — L. *cor-* (for *con-* = *cum*), together; *regere*, to rule.

direct, adj. (L.) L. *directus*, pp. of *dirigere*, to direct. — L. *di-*, for *dis-*, apart; *regere*, to rule.

dirge. (L.) Formerly *dirige*; from the first word of the anthem ' *dirige*, Dominus meus,' Ps. v. 8; in the office for the dead. — L. *dirige*, direct thou; 2 p. imper. sing. of *dirigere* (above).

dress. (F. — L.) O. F. *dresser, drescer*, to erect, set up, dress; answering to a Low L. form *directiare**. — L. *directus*, pp. of *dirigere*, to direct; see **direct** (above).

erect, adj. (L.) L. *erectus*, upright; pp. of *erigere*, to set up straight. — L. *e*, out, up; *regere*, to make straight, rule.

escort, a guide, guard. (F. — Ital. — L.) O. F. *escorte*. — Ital. *scorta*, a guide; fem. of *scorgere*, to see, perceive, guide (orig. to set right). — L. *ex*, entirely; *corrigere*, to correct; see **correct** (above).

insurgent. (L.) L. *insurgent-*, stem of pres. pt. of *insurgere*, to rise up or on, to rebel. — L. *in*, on; *surgere*, to rise; see **surge** (below).

insurrection. (L.) From L. *insurrectio*. — L. *insurrectus*, pp. of *insurgere*, to rebel (above).

interregnum. (L.) L. *inter*; between; *regnum*, a reign, rule, from *regere*.

rajah, prince. (Skt.) Skt. *rdja*, the form used in compounds in place of *rájan*, a king. Cognate with L. *rex*; see **regal** (below).

real (2), a small Spanish coin. (Span. — L.) Span. *real*, lit. a 'royal' coin. — L. *regalis*; see **regal** (below).

realm. (F. — L.) M. E. *roialme, realme*. — O. F. *realme* (F. *royaume*), a kingdom; answering to a Low L. *regalimen**. — L. *regalis*, royal; see **regal** (below).

rectangle, a four-sided right-angled figure. (F. — L.) F. *rectangle*, a right angle (Cot.). — L. *rectangulus*, having a right angle. — L. *rect-us*, right; *angulus*, an angle. *Rectus* was orig. the pp. of *regere*, to rule.

rectify. (F. − L.) F. *rectifier.* − Low L. *rectificare*, to make right. − L. *recti-*, for *rectus* (above); *-ficare*, for *facere*, to make.

rectilineal, rectilinear. (L.) From L. *rectiline-us*, formed by straight lines. − L. *recti-*, for *rectus*, straight; *linea*, a line. L. *rectus* was orig. pp. of *regere*.

rectitude. (F. − L.) F. *rectitude.* − L. *rectitudo*, uprightness. − L. *rectus*, straight, upright (above).

regal. (F. − L.) F. *regal*, royal (Cot.) − L. *regalis*, adj., from *reg-*, stem of *rex*, a king. − L. *regere*, to rule. Der. *regal-ia*, insignia of a king; neut. pl. of *regalis*.

regicide, slayer of a king; slaying of a king. (F. − L.) F. *regicide* (Minsheu). − L. *regi-*, crude form of *rex*, king, from *regere*; *-cida*, a slayer, from *cædere*, to slay. Otherwise; from L. *regi-* (as before); *-cidium*, a slaying, from *cædere*.

regimen. (L.) L. *regimen*, guidance. − L. *regere*, to rule, direct.

regiment. (F. − L.) F. *regiment*, 'a regiment of souldiers,' Cot. O. F. *regiment*, a government. − L. *regimentum*, rule, government. − L. *regere*, to rule.

region. (F. − L.) F. *region*, − L. *regionem*, acc. of *regio*, territory. − L. *regere*, to rule, govern.

regnant, reigning. (L.) L. *regnant-*, stem. of pres. pt. of *regnare*, to reign. − L. *regnum*, kingdom. − L. *regere*, to rule.

regular. (L.) L. *regularis*, according to rule. − L. *regula*, a rule. − L. *regere*.

reign, sb. (F. − L.) M. E. *regne.* − F. *regne.* − L. *regnum*, kingdom. − L. *regere*.

resource. (F. − L.) O. F. *resource*, later *ressource*, 'a new source,' Cot. − F. *re-*, again; *source*, source; see **source** (below).

resurrection. (F. − L.) O. F. *resurrection.* − L. acc. *resurrectionem.* − L. *resurrectus*, pp. of *re-surgere*, to rise again.

royal. (F. − L.) M. E. *real*, *roial.* − O. F. *real*, *roial* (F. *royal*). − L. *regalis*, royal; see **regal** (above).

rule, sb. (F. − L.) M. E. *reule*, *riwle.* − O. F. *riule*, *reule* (F. *règle*). − L. *regula*, a rule. − L. *regere*, to rule.

sortie. (F. − L.) F. *sortie*, a going forth; fem. of *sorti*, pp. of *sortir*, to sally forth. Cf. Span. *surtida*, a sortie, from O. Span. *surtir*, to rise. β. F. *sortir*, Span. *surtir*, answer to a Low L. form *surrectire**, to rise up. − L. *surrectum*, supine of *surgere*, to rise up; see **surge** (below).

The contraction of *surrectire** to F. *sortir* is proved to be correct by Ital. *sorto*, occurring as pp. of *sorgere*, to rise.

source. (F. − L.) M. E. *sours.* − O. F. *sorse*, *surse* (F. *source*), a source. Here *sorse* is fem. of *sors*, old pp. of O. F. *sordre* (F. *sourdre*), to rise. − L. *surgere*, to rise; see **surge** (below).

surge. (L.) Coined directly from L. *surgere*, to rise (pp. *surrectus*). Short for *surrigere**, as the pp. shews. − L. *sur-* (*sub*), up; *regere*, to rule, direct.

unruly, disregarding restraint. (E.; and F. − L.) From *un-*, prefix, and *rule*; with suffix *-y*; a coined word. See **rule** (above). ¶ Not from M. E. *unro*, restlessness. Fabyan has *unruled*.

Regicide, Regimen; see **Regent**.
Regiment, Region; see **Regent**.
Register; see **Gerund**.
Regnant; see **Regent**.
Regress; see **Grade**.
Regret, sorrow (F. − L. *and* O. Low G. ?) F. *regret*, grief; *regretter*, to lament (Cot.). Oldest form of the verb, *regrater*. Of disputed origin; see Scheler. The most likely solution is that which derives O. F. *regrater* from L. *re-*, again, and the Low G. verb which appears in Goth. *gretan*, to weep, Icel. *gráta*, Swed. *gråta*, Dan. *græde*, A. S. *grǽtan*, Lowl. Sc. *greit*, to weep, bewail. See **Greet** (2). Cf. 'I mone as a chylde doth for the wantyng of his nourse or mother, *je regrete*;' Palsgrave.
Regular; see **Regent**.
Rehearse; see **Hearse**.
Reign; see **Regent**.
Reimburse; see **Purse**.
Rein; see **Tenable**.
Reindeer, Raindeer, a kind of deer. (Scand. − Lapp.; *and* E.) M. E. *raynedere*. Formed by adding *deer* (see **Deer**) to Icel. *hreinn*, a reindeer; cf. O. Swed. *ren*, a reindeer. (We also find A. S. *hrán*, Dan. *rensdyr*, Du. *rendier*, G. *rennthier*, all due to O. Swed. *ren*.) β. Diez refers us to Lapp *raingo*, but this is merely a bad spelling of Swed. *renko*, i. e. rein-cow. The true Lapp word is *påtso*, a reindeer, which happens to be constantly used in company with Lapp *reino*, a pasturage, which was wrongly applied by the Swedes to the animal itself. Cf. Lapp *påtsoit warin reinohet*, to pasture reindeer on the fells; and similar sentences in Ihre, Lexicon Lapponicum, p. 374.

Reins, the lower part of the back. (F. – L.) O. F. *reins.* – L. *renes,* pl., kidneys, reins.

renal. (F. – L.) F. *renal.* – L. *renalis,* adj., formed from *renes,* s. pl. (above).

Reject; see **Jet** (1).

Rejoice; see **Gaud.**

Rejoin; see **Join.**

Relapse; see **Lapse.**

Relate; see **Tolerate.**

Relax; see **Lax.**

Relay (1), a set of fresh dogs or horses, a fresh supply. (F. – L. ?) Orig. used of dogs and horses. – F. *relais,* a relay; *chiens de relais, cheveaux de relais,* dogs or horses kept in reserve; Cot. The orig. sense is 'a rest,' and *chiens de relais* are dogs kept at rest; cf. *à relais* 'at rest, that is not used;' Cot. Probably from L. *relaxare,* to loosen, let loose, allow to rest; see **Lax.** Cf. Italian *cani di rilasso,* dogs kept in reserve (late edition of Florio by Torriano, 1688).

Relay (2), to lay again; from *re-* and *lay.*

Release; see **Lax.**

Relegate; see **Legal.**

Relent; see **Lenient.**

Relevant; see **Levity.**

Relic, Relict; see **Licence.**

Relieve; see **Levity.**

Religion. (F. – L.) F. *religion*; Cot. – L. acc. *religionem,* from *religio,* piety; allied to *religens,* fearing the gods, pious. *Re-ligens* is the opposite of *neg-ligens,* negligent; see **Neglect.** Allied also to Gk. ἀλέγειν, to reverence. ¶ Referred to L. *religare,* to bind, by Lewis and Short.

Relinquish, Reliquary; see **Licence.**

Relish; see **Lick.**

Reluctant. (L.) From stem of pres. pt. of *reluctare, reluctari,* to struggle against. – L. *re-,* back ; *luctari,* to struggle, from *lucta,* a wrestling. Allied to Gk. λυγ-ίζειν, to bend, writhe in wrestling; Skt. *ruj,* to bend, break. (√RUG.)

Rely; see **Lie** (1).

Remain; see **Mansion.**

Remand; see **Mandate.**

Remark; see **Mark.**

Remedy; see **Medicine.**

Remember; see **Memory.**

Remind; see **Mind.**

Reminiscence; see **Memory.**

Remit; see **Missile.**

Remnant; see **Mansion.**

Remonstrate; see **Monster.**

Remorse; see **Mordacity.**

Remote; see **Move.**

Remount; see **Mount** (2).

Remove; see **Move.**

Remunerate; see **Municipal.**

Renal; see **Reins.**

Renard; see **Reynard.**

Rencounter, Rencontre; see **Contra.**

Rend. (E.) M. E. *renden.* A. S. *hrendan,* to cut or tear down. Allied to Skt. *krit,* to cut; L. *cre-na* (for *cret-na*), a cranny. (√KART.) **Der.** *rent,* sb., from pp. *rent.*

Render, Rendezvous; see **Date** (1).

Renegade; see **Negation.**

Renew; see **Now.**

Rennet (1), that which curdles milk; see **Run.**

Rennet (2), an apple; see **Ranunculus.**

Renounce; see **Nuncio.**

Renovate; see **Now.**

Renown; see **Noble.**

Rent (1), a tear; see **Rend.**

Rent (2), annual payment; see **Date** (1).

Renunciation; see **Nuncio.**

Repair (1), to renew; see **Pare.**

Repair (2), to resort; see **Paternal.**

Repartee; see **Part.**

Repast; see **Pastor.**

Repay; see **Pact.**

Repeal; see **Pulsate.**

Repeat; see **Petition.**

Repel; see **Pulsate.**

Repent; see **Pain.**

Repercussion; see **Quash.**

Repertory; see **Parent.**

Repine; see **Pain.**

Replace; see **Plate.**

Replenish, Replete; see **Plenary.**

Replevy; see **Pledge.**

Reply; see **Ply.**

Report; see **Port** (1).

Repose; see **Pose** (1).

Repository; see **Position.**

Reprehend; see **Prehensile.**

Represent; see **Sooth.**

Repress; see **Press.**

Reprieve; see **Probable.**

Reprimand; see **Press.**

Reprisal; see **Prehensile.**

Reproach; see **Propinquity.**

Reprobate, Reprove; see **Probable.**

Reptile, crawling; usually, as a sb. (F. – L.) F. *reptile,* 'crawling;' Cot. – L. *reptilem,* acc. of *reptilis,* creeping. – L. *rept-us,* pp. of *repere,* to creep. + Lithuan. *rep loti,* to creep. Allied to **Serpent.**

surreptitious. (L.) L. *surreptitius*, better *surrepticius*, done stealthily. — L. *surreptum*, supine of *surrepere*, to creep under or upon. — L. *sur-* (*sub*), under; *rep-ere* (above).

Republic; see **Real** (1).

Repudiate. (L.) From pp. of L. *re-pudiare*, to reject. — L. *repudium*, a casting off, rejection of what one is ashamed of. — L. *re-*, away; *pud-*, base of *pudere*, to feel shame, cf. *pudor*, shame.

Repugnant; see **Pugilism**.

Repulse; see **Pulsate**.

Repute; see **Putative**.

Request, **Require**; see **Query**.

Requiem, **Requite**; see **Quiet**.

Reredos; see **Rear** (2).

Reremouse, Rearmouse, a bat. (E.) A. S. *hrēremús*, a bat; from the flapping of its wings. — A. S. *hréran*, to agitate, from *hrór*, motion, allied to *hrór*, adj., quick; *mús*, a mouse. Cf. prov. E. *flitter-mouse*, a flutter-mouse or bat.

Rereward; see **Rear** (2).

Rescind, to repeal. (F. — L.) F. *re-scinder*, to cancel; Cot. L. *re-scindere*, to cut off, annul. — L. *re-*, back; *scindere*, to cut. Allied to **Schism**. (√SKID.)

abscind, to cut off. (L.) L *ab-scindere*, to cut off.

abscissa. (L.) Fem. of *abscissus*, cut off; pp. of *abscindere*.

Rescript; see **Scribe**.

Rescue; see **Quash**.

Research; see **Circle**.

Resemble; see **Similar**.

Resent; see **Sense**.

Reserve; see **Serve**.

Reside, Residue; see **Sedentary**.

Resign; see **Sign**.

Resilient; see **Salient**.

Resin, Rosin. (F. — L. — Gk.) M. E. *recyn, recine*. — O. F. *resine*, 'rosin;' Cot. — L. *rēsīna*, Jer. li. 8 (Vulgate). — Gk. ῥητίνα, resin, gum from trees. (For the interchange of *s* and *t*, cf. L. *tu* with Gk. σύ, thou.)

Resist; see **State**.

Resolute, Resolve; see **Solve**.

Resonant; see **Sound** (3).

Resort; see **Sort**.

Resound; see **Sound** (3).

Resource; see **Regent**.

Respect, Respite; see **Species**.

Respire; see **Spirit**.

Resplendent; see **Splendour**.

Respond; see **Sponsor**.

Rest (1), repose. (E.) A. S. *rest, ræst,* rest. + Du. *rust*, Dan. Swed. *rast,* Icel. *röst* (the distance between two resting-places), Goth. *rasta* (a stage), O. H. G. *rasta*, rest. Allied to Skt. *ra-ti*, pleasure, Gk. ἐρωή, rest. (√RA.)

Rest (2), to remain, be left over; see **State**.

Restaurant; see **Store**.

Restitution, Restive; see **State**.

Restore; see **Store**.

Restrain, Restrict; see **Stringent**.

Result; see **Salient**.

Resume; see **Exempt**.

Resurrection; see **Regent**.

Resuscitate; see **Cite**.

Retail; see **Tailor**.

Retain; see **Tenable**.

Retaliate, to repay. (L.) From pp. of L. *retaliare*, to requite; allied to *talio*, retaliation in kind, as in *lex talionis*, the law of retaliation.

Retard; see **Tardy**.

Retch, Reach, to try to vomit. (E.) A. S. *hrǽcan*, to try to vomit. — A. S. *hréc*, a cough, allied to *hráca*, the throat (G. *rachen*). Allied to Gk. κράζειν = κράγ-γειν, to croak.

Retention; see retain, p. 496. col. 2.

Reticent; see **Tacit**.

Reticule. (F. — L.) F. *réticule*, a net for the hair, a reticule. — L. *reticulum*, a little net; double dimin. of *rete*, a net.

retina, the innermost coating of the eye. (L.) So called because resembling network. Coined from *reti-*, crude form of *rete*, a net.

Retinue; see **Tenable**.

Retire; see **Tier**.

Retort; see **Torture**.

Retract, Retreat; see **Trace** (1)

Retrench; see **Trench**.

Retribution; see **Tribe**.

Retrieve; see **Trover**.

Retro-, backwards. (L.) L. *retro*, backwards; a comparative form from *re-* or *red-*, back. See **Rear** (2).

Retrocession; see **Cede**.

Retrograde; see **Grade**.

Retrospect; see **Species**.

Return; see **Turn**.

Reveal; see **Vehicle**.

Reveille; see **Vigil**.

Revel, a noisy feast. (F. — L.) M. E. *reuel* (*revel*), sb. — O. F. *revel*, pride, rebellion, sport, jest, disturbance, disorder (Roquefort). — O. F. *reveler*, to rebel, hence.

to riot. — L. *rebellare*, to rebel; see **Rebel**.
Der. *revell-er*; whence *revel-r-y*.

Revenge; see **Vindicate**.

Revenue; see **Venture**.

Reverberate. (L.) From pp. of L.
reuerberare, to beat back (hence, to re-
echo). — L. *re-*, back; *uerberare*, to beat,
from *uerber*, a scourge.

Revere. (F. — L.) O. F. *reverer* (F.
révérer), to reverence. — L. *reuereri*, tò
revere, stand in awe of. — L. *re-*, again;
uereri, to fear, feel awe, allied to E.
Wary. Der. *reverence*, F. *reverence*, L.
reuerentia.

Reverie, Revery; see **Rave**.

Reverse, Revert; see **Verse**.

Review; see **Vision**.

Revile; see **Vile**.

Revise, Revisit; see **Vision**.

Revive; see **Victuals**.

Revoke; see **Vocal**.

Revolt, Revolve; see **Voluble**.

Revulsion; see **Convulse**.

Reward; see **Ward**.

Reynard, Renard, a fox. (F. — Teut.)
O. F. *renard, regnard* (F. *rénard*). — Low G.
(Old Flemish) *Reinaerde*, the name given
to the fox in the celebrated O. Flemish epic
so called. . Cognate with O. H. G. *Regin-
hart*, lit. ' strong in counsel;' from O. H. G.
regin, ragin, counsel, and *hart* (E. *hard*),
strong.

Rhapsody. (F. — L. — Gk.) F. *rapsodie*,
Cot. — L. *rhapsodia*. — Gk. *ῥαψῳδία*, the re-
citing of epic poetry, part of an epic poem,
a rhapsody, tirade. — Gk. *ῥαψῳδός*, one who
strings (lit. stitches) songs together, a
reciter of epic poetry. — Gk. *ῥαψ-*, stem of
fut. of *ῥάπτειν*, to stitch together, fasten together; *ῳδή*, an ode; see **Ode**.

Rhetoric. (F. — L. — Gk.) F. *rhetorique*;
Cot. — L. *rhetorica*, i.e. *rhetorica ars*, the
art of rhetoric; fem of *rhetoricus*, adj. —
Gk. *ῥητορικός*, rhetorical; adj. from *ῥήτωρ*,
an orator, speaker. — Gk. *εἴρειν*, to speak
(pt. t. *εἴ-ρη-κα*). Allied to **Verb**.

Rheum. (F. — L. — Gk.) F. *rheume*. —
L. *rheuma*. — Gk. *ῥεῦμα* (stem *ῥευματ-*), a
flow, flux, rheum. — Gk. *ῥεύ-σομαι*, fut. of
ῥέειν, to flow. + Skt. *sru*, to flow. (√
SRU.) Der. *rheumat-ic*.

diarrhoea. (L. — Gk.) L. *diarrhœa*. —
Gk. *διάρροια*, lit. ' a flowing through.' —
Gk. *διαρρέειν*, to flow through. — Gk. *διά*,
through; *ῥέειν*, to flow.

rhythm. (F. — L. — Gk.) F. *rithme*,
Cot. L. *rhythmus*. — Gk. *ῥυθμός*, mea-

sured motion, time, measure. — Gk. *ῥέειν*,
to flow.

Rhinoceros. (L. — Gk.) L. *rhinoceros*.
— Gk. *ῥινόκερως*, lit. ' nose-horn.' — Gk. *ῥινο-*,
crude form of *ῥίς*, nose; *κέρας*, a horn.

Rhododendron; see **Rose**.

Rhodomontade; see **Rodomontade**.

Rhomb, Rhombus. (L. — Gk.) L.
rhombus (F. *rhombe*). — Gk. *ῥόμβος*, a thing
twirled round, whirling spindle, a thing
in the shape of a whirling spindle, a four-
sided figure with equal sides but unequal
angles. — Gk. *ῥέμβειν*, to revolve. See also
Rumb.

Rhubarb. (F. — Low L. — Gk.) O. F.
rheubarbe; F. *rhubarbe*. — Low L. *rheu-
barbarum* (= *rheum barbarum*). — Gk.
ῥῆον βάρβαρον, rhubarb; lit. ' Rheum from
the barbarian country.' Gk. *ῥῆον* is an
adj. from *ῥά*, the rha-plant, rhubarb, which
was also called *Rha Ponticum*. *Rha*
took its name from the river *Rha*, i. e. the
Volga.

Rhumb; see **Rumb**.

Rhyme; see **Rime** (1).

Rhythm; see **Rheum**.

Rib. (E.) M. E. *ribbe*. A.S. *ribb*. +
Du. *rib*, Icel. *rif*, Swed. *ref-been* (rib-bone),
Dan. *rib-been*, G. *rippe*, Russ. *rebro*.

Ribald. (F. — Teut.) M. E. *ribald*,
ribaud. — O. F. *ribald*; F. *ribaut*. — Low L.
ribaldus, a ruffian; cf. Low L. *ribalda*, a
prostitute. Of Teut. origin. — O. H. G.
hrípá, M. H. G. *ríbe*, a prostitute; cf. O. F.
riber, to toy with a female. The suffix *-ald*
is due to O. H. G. *walt*, power.

Riband, Ribbon. (C.) Not allied to
band; the final *d* is excrescent. M. E.
riban. — Irish *ribin*, a ribbon, from *ribe*, a
flake, hair, ribbon; Gael. *ribean*, a ribbon,
fillet, from *rib, ribe*, a hair, rag, clout,
tatter; W. *rhibin*, a streak, from *rhib*, a
streak.

Rice. (F. — Ital. — L. — Gk. — O.Pers.) O.F.
ris, rice; F. *riz*. — Ital. *riso*. — L. *oryza*. —
Gk. *ὄρυζα, ὄρυζον*, rice, grain. From an
O. Pers. form, preserved in the Pushto
(Afghan) *wrijzey, wrijey*, rice; *wrijza'h*, a
grain of rice (Raverty). Hence also Arab.
uruzz, ruzz, Span. *arroz*, rice.

Rich. (E.) M. E. *riche*. A.S. *ríce*,
rich, powerful. (Cf. E. *pitch* from A.S.
pic). + Du. *rijk*, Icel. *ríkr*, Swed. *rik*, Dan.
rig, Goth. *reiks*, G. *reich*. Allied to **Regent**. ¶ The F. *riche* is from M.H.G.
ríche (G. *reich*); but the E. word is independent of the F. form. See below.

riches. (F. – O. H. G.) M. E. *richesse*, a sing. sb. ; the pl. being *richesses.* – F. *richesse*, wealth. – M. H. G. *riche* (G. *reich*), rich ; cognate with A. S. *ríce* (above).

rix-dollar, a coin. (Du. – G.) Du. *rijks-daalder*, a rix-dollar. – G. *reichsthaler*, a dollar of the empire. – G. *reichs*, gen. case of *reich*, empire, allied to G. *reich*, rich ; and *thaler*, a dollar ; see **Dollar.**

Rick. (E.) *Rick* is for *reek* or *hreek* ; M. E. *reek*. A. S. *hreác*, a heap, a rick ; also *hrýcca*, a rick. + Icel. *hraukr*, a rick.

ruck (2), a heap, small pile. (Scand.) O. Swed. *ruka*, Icel. *hraukr*, a rick, heap.

Rickets; see **Wring.**

Ricochet, the rebound of a cannon-ball. (F.) F. *ricochet*, ' the sport of skimming a thin stone on the water, called a Duck and a Drake ; ' Cot. Origin unknown.

Rid, to free. (E.) M. E. *ridden.* A. S. *hreddan*, to snatch away, deliver. + O. Fries. *hredda*, Du. *redden*, Dan. *redde*, Swed. *rädde*, G. *retten*.

Riddle (1), an enigma ; see **Read.**

Riddle (2), a large sieve. (E.) M. E. *ridil.* A. S. *hridder*, a vessel for winnowing corn ; the suffixed *-er* and *-il* (-*la*) being equivalent. + Irish *creathair*, Gael. *criathar* ; from Irish and Gael. *crath*, to shake. Cf. Gk. κραδάειν, to shake. Orig. sense ' shaker.'

Ride. (E.) M. E. *riden*, pt. t. *rood*, pp. *riden.* A. S. *rídan*, pt. t. *rád*, pp. *riden.* + Du. *rijden*, Icel. *ríða*, Dan. *ride*, Swed. *rida*, G. *reiten.*

array, verb. (F. – L. *and* Scand.) O. F. *arraier*, to array. – O. F. *arrai*, *arroi*, preparation. – L. *ad* (becoming *ar-* before *r*), to, for ; Swed. *reda*, Dan. *rede*, order, Icel. *reiða*, tackle, *reiði*, implements, all allied to A. S. *ráede*, ready ; see **ready** (below).

curry ; see under **Curry** (1).

raid. (Scand.) Icel. *reið*, a riding, a road. – Icel. *ríða*, to ride.

raiment. (F. – L. *and* Scand.) Short for *array-ment* ; see **array** (above).

ready. (E.) M. E. *redi.* A. S. *ráede*, ready ; orig. ' equipped for riding,' or ' prepared for a raid.' – A. S. *ráed-on*, pt. t. pl. of *rídan*, to ride.

road. (E.) M. E. *roode*, *rode* (both for ships and horses). – A. S. *rád*, a road, also a raid. – A. S. *rád.* pt. t. of *rídan*, to ride.

Ridge. (E.) M. E. *rigge*, *rugge.* A. S. *hrycg*, the back of a man or beast. + Du. *rug*, back, ridge, Dan. *ryg*, Swed. *rygg*, Icel. *hryggr*, G. *rücken*, O. H. G. *hrucki.*

rig (3), a ridge. (E.) M. E. *rigge* (above).

Ridiculous. (L.) L. *ridiculus*, laughable. – L. *ridere*, to laugh.

deride. (L.) L. *de-ridere*, to laugh down, laugh at. **Der.** *deris-ive*, from pp. *derisus.*

risible. (F. – L.) F. *risible.* – L. *risibilis*, laughable. – L. *risus*, pp. of *ridere*, to laugh.

Riding; see **Three.**

Rife. (Scand.) M. E. *rif.* – Icel. *rífr*, munificent, abundant ; O. Swed. *rif*, rife. + O. Du. *rijf*, abundant ; Low G. *rive*, abundant, munificent, extravagant. Cf. Icel. *reifa*, to bestow.

Riff-raff; see **Rifle** (1).

Rifle (1), to spoil, plunder. (F. – Teut.) F. *rifler*, 'to rifle, spoile ; ' Cot. Formed, with frequentative *-l-*, from Icel. *hrífa*, *rífa*, to catch, grapple, grasp, allied to which is Icel. *hrífs*, plunder. (√ KARP.)

riff-raff, refuse. (F. – Teut.) M. E. *rif and raf*, things of small value, hence every bit. – F. *rif et raf*, every bit ; also spelt *rifle et rafle*, ' Il ne lui lairra *rif ny raf*, he will strip him of all ; ' Cot. Here *rif* or *rifle* is a thing of small value, from *rifler*, to rifle, ransack ; and *rafle* is from O. F. *raffler*, to rifle, ravage. Both are words of Teut. origin, drawn together by their sound, though of different origin F. *rifler* is from Icel. *hrífa* (above) ; F. *raffler* is from G. *raffen*, to seize ; see **Rape** (1).

Rifle (2), a kind of musket ; see **Rive.**

Rift; see **Rive.**

Rig (1), to fit up a ship. (Scand.) Spelt *rygge* in Palsgrave. – Norweg. *rigga*, to bind up, wrap round, also to rig a ship ; *rigg* sb., rigging. Cf. Swed. dial. *rigga på*, to harness a horse.

Rig (2), a frolic ; see **Wring.**

Rig (3), a ridge ; see **Ridge.**

Right. (E.) M. E. *right.* A. S. *riht.* + Du. *regt*, Icel. *réttr* (for *réhtr**), Dan. *ret*, Swed. *rät*, G. *recht*, O. H. G. *reht*, Goth. *raihts*; L. *rectus.* See **Reg-nt.** (√ RAG.)

righteous. (E.) Corruption of M. E. *rightwis* ; A. S. *rihtwís*, i. e. wise as to what is right. – A. S. *riht*, right ; *wís*, wise.

Rigid. (L.) L. *rigidus*, stiff. – L. *rigere*, to be stiff. Prob. orig. ' to be straight ; ' cf. L. *rectus*, straight.

Rigmarole. (Scand. ; *and* F. – L.) Well known to be a corruption of *ragman-roll*, orig. a deed with many signatures, a long list of names; hence, a long stupid story. Lit. 'coward's roll.'— Icel. *ragmenni*, a coward, from *ragr*, a coward, and *maðr* (= *mannr*), a man; with the addition of *roll*, for which see **Roll**. The Icel. *ragr* seems to be the same as Icel. *argr*, a coward, A. S. *earg*.

Rile : see **Roil**.

Rill, a streamlet. (O. Low G.) Prob. from O. Low G. *rille*, E. Friesic *rille*, a streamlet. Apparently for **ridele, *rithele* ; cf. A. S. *rîðe*, a stream; Low G. *ride*, a stream.

Rim. (E.) M. E. *rim*. A. S. *rima*, a verge, edge. Perhaps borrowed from W. *rhim, rhimp, rhimyn*, a rim, edge.

Rime (1), verse, poetry, &c. (E.) Usually absurdly misspelt *rhyme*, by confusion with (Gk.) *rhythm*, but this error is not found before A. D. 1550. M. E. *rime*. A. S. *rîm*, number, reckoning (hence rime, from the numerical regularity of verse).+Du. *rijm*, Icel. *rima*, Dan. *riim*, Swed. *rim*, G. *reim*, O. H. G. *rim* (whence Ital. Span. Port. *rima*, F. *rime*) ; Irish *rimh*, W. *rhif*. Prob. allied to Gk. ἀριθμός, number, Irish and Gael. *aireamh*, W. *eirif*, number. (√AR ?)

Rime (2), hoarfrost. (E.) Put for *hrime*. A. S. *hrîm*, hoarfrost. + Du. *rijm*, Icel. *hrîm*, Dan. *riim*, Swed. *rim*. Allied to G. *reif*, hoar-frost, Gk. κρυμ-ός, κρύ-ος, frost ; see **Crystal**.

Rind. (E.) M. E. *rind, rinde*. A. S. *rinde*, bark of a tree, crust (of bread).+ O. Du. and G. *rinde*, bark.

Ring (1), a circle. (E.) M. E. *ring*. A. S. *hring*.+Du. *ring*, Low G. *ring, rink*, Icel. *hringr*, Swed. Dan. G. *ring*, O. H. G. *hrinc* ; Gk. κρίκος, κίρκος, L. *circus*, Russ. *krug'* ; Skt. *chakra*, a wheel, ring.

arrange. (F.—L. and O. H. G.) M. E. *arayngen*.—O. F. *arengier*, to put into a rank.—O. F. *a* (L. *ad*), to ; *rangier, renger*, to range ; see **range** (below).

derange. (F.—L. and O. H. G.) F. *déranger*, to disarrange ; formerly *desranger*. —L. *dis-*, apart ; O. F. *rangier*, to range ; see **range** (below).

harangue. (F. — O. H. G.) O. F. *harangue*, an oration. The same as Span. *arenga*, Ital. *aringa*. Orig. a speech made in the midst of a *ring* of people ; as shewn by Ital. *aringo*, an arena, lists, also a pulpit. — O. H. G. *hrinc* (G. *ring*), a ring, ring of

people, an arena, circus, lists. Cognate with A. S. *hring*, a ring.

range. (F.—O. H. G.) The sense ' to rove' arose from the trooping about of ranks of armed men.—F. *ranger* (O. F. *renger*), to' range, rank, order, array, lit. ' to put into a rank.'—F. *rang* (O. F. *reng*), a rank (below).

rank (1), a row, line of soldiers, class. (F.—O. H. G.) M. E. *reng, renk*.—O. F. *reng* (F. *rang*), a rank, row, list, range.— O. H. G. *hrinc*, a ring, ring of men, hence a row or rank of men.

rink, a course for the game of curling, &c. (E.) A peculiar pronunciation of *ring*, in the sense of *prize-ring*, &c. Cf. Low G. *rink*, a ring.

Ring (2), to sound a bell. (E.) M. E. *ringen*. A. S. *hringan*, to clash, ring ; a *weak* verb, as it is also in all Teut. tongues except English, which has pt. t. *rang*, by analogy with *sang* from *sing*.+Du. *ringen*, Icel. *hringja*, Dan. *ringe*, Swed. *ringa*. Cf. Icel. *hrang*, a din, L. *clangor*.

Rinse. (F. — Scand.) O. F. *rinser*, ' to reinse linnen clothes ;' Cot. — Icel. *hreinsa*, to cleanse, from *hreinn*, clean ; Dan. *rense*, from *reen* ; Swed. *rensa*, from *ren*. Cf. also G. *rein*, Goth. *hrains*, pure, clean.

Riot. (F.—O. H. G. ?) F. *riote*, a brawling. The same as Prov. *riota*, Ital. *riotta*, dispute, strife. Perhaps for *rivote* * ; from O. H. G. *rîben* (G. *reiben*), to grate, rub, hence to provoke. Perhaps allied to **Ribald**.

Rip ; see **Rive**.

Ripe ; see **Reap**.

Ripple (1), to pluck seeds from stalks of flax ; see **Rive**.

Ripple (2), to cause or shew wrinkles on the surface, said of water. (E.) A late word; variant of *rimple*, to wrinkle, to ripple. M. E. *rimplen*, to wrinkle.—A. S. *hrympelle*, a wrinkle.—A. S. *hrumpen, ge-hrumpen*, pp. of strong verb *hrimpan*, to wrinkle ; of which the only trace is the pp. *gerumpen* (late spelling of *gehrumpen*). So also O. Du. *rimpel*, a wrinkle, *rimpelen*, to wrinkle; O. H. G. *hrimfen*, M. H. G. *rimpfen* (cf. G. *rümpfen*), to crook, bend, wrinkle. (Teut. base HARP, answering to Aryan KARP, as in Gk. κάρφειν, to wrinkle.)

rumple. (E.) The M. E. form is *rimplen*, to rimple. *Rimple* and *rumple* are from the same verb, viz., A. S. *hrimpan* (pp. *gehrumpen*), to wrinkle ; see above.+ Du. *rompelen, rompen*, to wrinkle ; *rom-*

pel, rimpel, a wrinkle; G. *rümpfen,* to wrinkle.

Ripple (3), to scratch slightly; see **Rive**.

Rise. (E.) M. E. *risen.* A. S. *rîsan,* pt. t. *râs,* pp. *risen.* + Du. *rijzen,* orig. to move, also to fall (just contrary to the E. sense); Icel. *rîsa* ; O. H. G. *rîsan,* to move up or down, to rise, to fall; Goth. *ur-reisan,* to arise. (Base RIS, to slip away; cf. Skt. *rî,* to distil.)

arise. (E.) A. S. *ârîsan.* – A. S. *â-,* prefix; *rîsan,* to rise. + Goth. *ur-reisan* (for *us-reisan*), to arise. See A- (4).

raise. (Scand.) M. E. *reisen.* – Icel. *reisa,* to make to rise, causal of *rîsa,* to rise; so also Dan. *reise,* Swed. *resa,* to raise. See **Rise** (above).

rear (1), to raise. (E.) M. E. *reren.* A. S. *ræran,* to rear; put for *ræsan* *, and the exact equivalent of Icel. *reisa* (above). Causal form of *rîsan,* to rise.

Risible; see **Ridiculous.**

Risk. (F. – Span. – L.) F. *risque,* peril; Cot. Orig. a maritime word. – Span. *risco,* a steep abrupt rock; whence the sense of 'peril,' as shewn by Span. *arriesgar,* O. Span. *arriscar,* to venture into danger (lit. to go against a rock). The orig. sense of *risco* is cut off, sheer, like a sharp rock. – L. *resecare,* to cut back, cut off short (curiously verified by the use of the Como word *resega,* a saw, also risk; Diez). – L. *re-,* back; *secare,* to cut; see **Section.** (See further in Diez.)

Rite, Rival; see **Rivulet.**

Rive, to tear. (Scand.) M. E. *riuen* (*u=v*). – Icel. *rîfa,* pt. t. *rîf,* pp. *rifinn* (= E. *riven*), to rive; Dan. *rive,* Swed. *rifva,* + Du. *rijven,* to grate, G. *reiben,* to grate, rub. Cf. Gk. ἐρείπειν, to dash down, ἐρείκειν, to rive; Lithuan. *rėkti,* to cut.

reef (1), a ridge of rocks. (Du.) Formerly *riff.* – Du. *rif,* a reef. + Icel. *rif,* a reef, allied to *rifa,* a fissure, rift; Dan. *rev,* a sand-bank (*revle,* a shoal, *revne,* to split), Swed. *refva,* a cleft, gap. The orig. sense is 'rift' or gap (in the sea).

reef (2), a portion of a sail. (Du.) M. E. *riff.* – Du. *reef,* 'a riff in a sail,' Sewel; O. Du. *rif, rift,* a reef. + Icel. *rif,* a reef in a sail, also a reef or rock; Dan. *reb,* Swed. *ref,* reef. Orig. a 'rift,' i. e. a strip or shred of a sail.

reeve (1), to pass a rope through a ring. (Du.) Du. *reven,* to reeve. – Du. *reef,* a reef in a sail; because a reeved rope is used for reefing; see above.

rifle (2), a kind of musket. (Scand.) Short for *rifled gun,* from the verb *rifle,* to groove. – Dan. *rifle,* to rifle, groove, frequent. of *rive,* to rive, to tear; hence *rifle,* a groove, *riffel,* a rifled gun; Swed. *reffla,* to rifle, from *rifva,* to scratch, groove, grate, tear. So also G. *riefe,* a furrow; *riefen,* to rifle. See **Rive.**

rift. (Scand.) Dan. *rift,* rift, rent. – Dan. *rive,* to tear. Cf. Icel. *ript,* a breach of contract. See **Rive.**

rip. (Scand.) M. E. *ripen,* to grope, search into; *rypen vp,* to seek out (cf. E. *rip up*). – Norweg. *ripa,* to scratch, Swed. dial. *ripa,* to scratch, pluck asunder (like E. *rip open*); Dan. *oprippe,* to rip up; Swed. *repa up,* to rip up, *repa,* to scratch. Allied to Icel. *rîfa,* to rive; *rîfa upp,* to pull up, *rîfa aptr,* to rip up. Allied to *rive.*

ripple (1), to pluck the seeds from flax-stalks. (Scand.) M. E. *ripplen, ripelen,* to ripple; from the sb. *ripple,* a flax-comb (Jamieson). Formed, with suffix -*le,* of the agent, from Swed. *repa,* to ripple flax, orig. to scratch, rip; see **rip** (above). + Du. *repelen,* to ripple, from *repel,* a ripple, from *repen,* to beat flax; G. *riffeln,* to ripple, from *riffel,* a ripple.

ripple (3), to graze slightly. (Scand.) '*Ripple,* rescindere;' Levins (1570). Frequentative of *rip* (above).

rivel, to wrinkle. (E.) M. E. *riuelen* (*u=v*). A. S. *ge-riflian,* to wrinkle; a frequent. form from Icel. *rîfa,* to rive; see **Rive** (above).

River. (F. – L.) M. E. *riuer* (*u=v*). – O. F. *riviere.* (F. *rivière.*) The same as Span. *ribera,* a shore, strand, sea-coast, Ital. *riviera,* shore, bank, also a river; Low L. *riparia,* (1) shore, bank, (2) river. – Low L. *riparius,* belonging to a shore. – L. *ripa,* shore, bank. The special sense may have been due to some confusion with L. *riuus* (see **River** above).

arrive. (F. – L.) F. *arriver* – Low L. *arripare, adripare,* to come to shore, land. – L. *ad,* to; *ripa,* shore, bank. **Der.** *arriv-al.*

Rivet. (F. – Scand.) F. *rivet,* 'the welt of a shoe,' Cot.; also a rivet (Littré). – F. *river,* to rivet, clench, fasten back. – Icel. *rîfa,* to tack, sew loosely together; *rîfa saman,* to stitch together. Cf. Shetland *riv,* to sew coarsely, Aberdeen *riv,* to rivet.

Rivulet. (L.) Dimin. from L. *riuulus,* a small stream; dimin. of *riuus,* a stream lit. ' flowing.' Cf. Skt. *ri*, to distil, ooze. Cf. Ital. *rivoletto* ('Torriano).

derive. (F. — L.) O. F. *deriver*, to derive, also to drain. — L. *deriuare*, to drain off water. — L. *de*, from; *riuus*, a stream.

rite. (L.) L. *ritus*, a custom. **+** Skt. *riti*, a going, way, usage; from *ri*, to go, flow. (✓ RI.) Der. *ritu-al*, from *ritu-*, crude form of *ritus*.

rival. (F. — L.) F. *rival.* — L. *riualis*, sb., one who uses the same brook as another, a near neighbour, a rival. — L. *riuus*, a stream.

Rix-dollar; see **Rich.**

Roach, a fish. (E.) M. E. *roche.* A. S. *-eohhe, reohche.* **+** Du. *rog,* a ray, O. Du. *roch,* a skate; Dan. *rokke,* Swed. *rocka,* a ray; G. *roche,* a roach, ray; L. *rāia* (for *ragia* *), a ray. Doublet, *ray* (2).

Road; see **Ride.**

Roam. (E.) M. E. *romen*; also *ramen* (Layamon). Allied to A. S. *á-réman,* to spread out (usually explained to lift up); prov. E. *rame, raim, rawm,* to stretch, spread about, roam, ramble. Cf. A. S. *rómigan* (sense doultful). We also find O. Du. *ramen,* to stretch, Du. *ramen,* to aim, plan, O. Sax. *rómón,* to aim at, O. Fries. *ramia,* to strive after, O. H. G. *rámén,* to strive after. Orig. to stretch out after, strive after, aim at; hence to spread, roam, ramble. The particular sense was prob. influenced by confusion with M. E. *Rome-rennere,* a runner to Rome, pilgrim; cf. Ital. *Romeo,* one who goes to Rome, a pilgrim.

ramble. (E.) Frequentative of M. E. *ramen,* prov. E. *rame,* to spread abroad, sprawl; hence, to gad about. The *b* is excrescent, and *ramble* is for prov. E. *rammle,* to ramble (Whitby Glossary).

Roan. (F.) O. F. *rouën*; ' *cheval rouën,* a roan horse;' Cot. Mod. F. *rouan.* Span. *ruano, Ital. rovano, roano* (Florio). Prob. the Ital. *rovano* stands for a Low L. type *rufanus* *, i. e. reddish, extended from O. Ital. *rufo,* L. *rufus,* red. ¶ Sometimes derived from the town of *Rouen,* with which Ital. *rovano* can have nothing to do.

Roan-tree, Rowan-tree, the mountain ash. (Scand.) Spelt *roun-tree, roan-tree, rowan-tree* in Jamieson. — Swed. *rönn,* O. Swed. *runn, rönn,* roan-tree; Dan. *rön,* Icel. *reynir,* the same. Cf. L. *ornus,* the same.

Roar. (E.) M. E. *roren.* A. S. *rárian,*

to bellow. **+** M. H. G. *réren.* Cf. Skt. *rá,* to bellow. Of imitative origin. (✓ RA.)

Roast. (F. — G.?) M. E. *rosten.* — O. F. *rostir,* 'to rost;' Cot. (F. *rôtir*). — G. *rösten,* to roast, *rost,* a grate, gridiron. β. Or the word may be Celtic; Irish *rost,* roast meat, Gael. *rost, roist,* W. *rhostio,* Bret. *rosta,* to roast; in this case, the O. F. *rostir* is from Bret. *rosta,* and the G. word is of Celtic origin.

Rob, Robe; see **Reave.**

Robin. (F. — O. H. G.) F. *Robin,* proper name; pet name for *Robert.* — O.H.G. *Ruodperht* (G. *Ruprecht,* i. e. Rupert). Lit. ' fame-bright,' illustrious in fame. — O.H.G. *ruod-,* allied to Icel. *hróthr,* fame; O.H.G. *perht* = E. *bright.* See **Hobgoblin.**

Robust. (F. — L.) F. *robuste.* — L. *robustus,* strong. — O. L. *robus* (L. *robur*), strength. **+** Skt. *rabhas,* force; from *rabh,* to seize. (✓ RABH.)

corroborate. (L.) From pp. of L. *corroborare,* to strengthen. — L. *cor-,* for *con-* (*cum*), with; *robor-,* stem of *robur,* strength.

Roc, a huge bird. (Pers.) Pers. *rukh,* the name of a huge bird; also a hero.

Rock (1), a large mass of stone. (F. — C.?) O. F. *roke* (13th cent.), commonly *roche,* a rock. The same as Prov. *roca,* Span. *roca,* Port. *roca, rocha,* Ital. *rocca, roccia,* a rock. — Irish and Gael. *roc,* a rock; Bret. *roch* (with guttural *ch,* shewing that the Bret. word is Celtic). β. But Gael. *roc* is said to be borrowed from E.; and the origin is disputed; Diez suggests a Low L. *rupica** to account for Ital. *rocca,* and a Low L. *rupea** to account for F. *roche* (which will not explain O. F. *roke*); as if from L. *rupes,* a rock.

Rock (2), to shake, totter. (Scand.) M. E. *rokken.* — Dan. *rokke,* to rock, shake, Swed. *rockera,* to rock about. Allied to Dan. *rykke,* to pull, *ryk,* a pull; Icel. *rykkr,* a hasty pull. **+** G. *ruck,* a pull, jolt. (Base RUK.)

Rock (3), a distaff. (Scand.) Icel. *rokkr,* Swed. *rock,* Dan. *rok,* a distaff. **+** G. *rocken.*

rocket (1), a kind of fire-work. (Ital. — G.) O. Ital. *rocchetto,* 'a bobbin to wind silk upon; a squib or wild fier;' Florio. So named from its shape, resembling that of a bobbin or a distaff. — M. H. G. *rocke,* G. *rocken,* a distaff.

Rocket (1); see above.

Rocket (2), a plant. (F. — Ital. — L.) F.

roquette. — Ital. *ruchetta*, dimin. of *ruca*, garden-rocket. — L. *eruca*, a sort of cole-wort.

Rod (E.); see **Rood**.

Rodent, gnawing. (L.) From stem of pres. part. of *rodere*, to gnaw. Allied to **Rase**.

corrode. (F. — L.) F. *corroder*. — L. *corrodere*, to gnaw to pieces. — L. *cor*- (for *con-* = *cum*), with; *rodere*, to gnaw. **Der.** *corrosive*, from pp. *corrosus*.

erode. (F. — L.) F. *eroder*. — L. *erodere*, to eat away. — L. *e*, away; *rodere*, to gnaw.

rostrum. (L.) L. *rostrum*, a beak; pl. *rostra*, a pulpit for speakers in the forum, adorned with beaks of ships taken from the Antiates. Put for *rod-trum**. — L. *rodere*, to gnaw, to peck.

Rodomontade, vain boasting. (F. — Ital.) F. *rodomontade*. — Ital. *rodomontada*, a boast. Due to the boastful character of *Rodomonte*, in the Orlando Furioso of Ariosto, b. xiv.

Roe (1), a female deer. (E.) M. E. *ro*. A. S. *ráh*. + Icel. *rá*, Dan. *raa*, Swed. *rå*, Du. *ree*, G. *reh*. **Der.** *roe-buck*.

Roe (2), spawn. (Scand.) Put for *roan*; the final *n* was dropped, being mistaken for the pl. suffix, as in *shoon* for shoes, *eyne* for eyes. M. E. *rowne*. — Icel. *hrogn*, Dan. *rogn*, Swed. *rom*, roe. + G. *rogen*, roe. Cf. Gk. ῥοκή, a round pebble.

Rogation. (F. — L.) F. *rogation*. — L. acc. *rogationem*, a supplication. — L. *rogatus*, pp. of *rogare*, to ask.

abrogate. (L.) From pp. of L. *abrogare*, to repeal a law. — L. *ab*, away; *rogare*, to ask, propose a law.

arrogate. (L.) From pp. of L. *arrogare*, to ask, adopt, attribute to, add to. — L. *ar*- (for *ad*), to; *rogare*, to ask. **Der.** *arrogant*, from the pres. pt.

derogate. (L.) From pp. of L. *derogare*, to repeal a law, detract from. — L. *de*, away; *rogare*, to ask, propose a law.

interrogate. (L.) From pp. of L. *interrogare*, to question. — L. *inter*, thoroughly; *rogare*, to ask.

prerogative. (F. — L.) O. F. *prerogative*, a privilege. — L. *prærogatiua*, a previous choice, preference, privilege. — L. *præ*, before; *rogare*, to ask.

prorogue. (F. — L.) F. *proroger*. — L. *prorogare*, to propose an extension of office, lit. to ask publicly; hence, to defer. — L. *pro*, publicly; *rogare*, to ask.

supererogation. (L.) Low L. *super-* *erogatio*, that which is done beyond what is due. — L. *supererogare*, to pay out in excess. — L. *super*, beyond; *e*, out; *rogare*, to ask. (The L. *erogare* = to lay out, expend.)

surrogate, a substitute. (L.) L. *surrogatus*, pp. of *surrogare*, to elect in place of another. — L. *sur*- (for *sub*), in place of; *rogare*, to ask, elect.

Rogue, (F. — C.) F. *rogue*, 'arrogant, proud, presumptuous, rude. surly;' Cot. Cf. E. *rogu-ish*, saucy. The orig. sense was a surly fellow; hence a vagabond. — Bret. *rok*, *rog*, arrogant, proud, haughty, brusque. Cf. Irish and Gael. *rucas*, pride.

Roil, Rile, to vex. (F. ? — L. ?) The old word *roil* meant (1) to disturb, vex, (2) to wander about. — O. F. *roeler*, another form of O. F. *roler*, to roll; whence the senses to roll about, disturb, or to rove about. See **Roll**. (So Stratmann.)

Roistering; see **Rustic**.

Roll; see **Rotary**.

Romance. (F. — L.) O. F. *romans*, a romance. This form is due to late L. adv. *romanice*, as in the phr. *romanice loqui* = F. *parler romans*, to speak Romance, i. e. the vulgar Latin dialect of every-day life, as distinguished from book-Latin. *Romanice*, i. e. Roman-like, is from L. *Romanus*, Roman. — L. *Roma*, Rome.

romaunt. (F. — L.) O. F. *romant*, an occasional form of O. F. *roman*, also spelt *romans*, a romance; see above. **Der.** *romant-ic*.

Romp; see **Ramp**.

Rondeau; see **Rotary**.

Rood, the cross; a measure of land. (E.) The same word as *rod*, which is shortened from M. E. *rood* (also *rod*), a rood, a rod. Both *rood* and *rod* are used as measures, though the former is restricted to square measure, and the latter to linear; both senses are due to the use of a rod for measurement. A. S. *ród*, a gallows, cross, properly a rod or pole. + Du. *roede*, rod, perch, wand; G. *ruthe*, a rod of land; L. *rudis*, a rod, staff. Cf. Skt. *nyag-rodha*, lit. 'growing downwards,' the Indian fig-tree; where *rodha* is from √RUDH (Skt. *ruh*), to grow. *Rood* or *rod* was orig. 'a shoot,' hence a branch, pole.

Roof. (E.) M. E. *rof*. A. S. *hróf*. + Du. *roef*, a cabin, Icel. *hróf*, a shed; Russ. *krov'*, a roof.

Rook (1), a kind of crow. (E.) M. E. *rook*. A. S. *hróc*. + Icel. *hrókr*, Dan.

raage, Swed. *roka,* Irish and Gael. *rocas,*
M. H. G. *ruoch.* Lit. 'croaker;' cf. Goth.
hrukjan, to crow as a cock, Skt. *kruç,* to
cry out, Gael. *roc,* to croak.

Rook (2), a castle, at chess. (F. — Pers.)
M. E. *rook.* — F. *roc.* — Pers. *rokh,* a rook.
Said to have meant 'warrior.'

Room, space, a chamber. (E.) The old
meaning is space, place. M. E. *roum.*
A. S. *rúm*; 'næfdon *rúm*' = they had no
room, Luke, ii. 7. We also find adj. *rúm,*
spacious. **+** Du. *ruim,* adj., spacious,
ruim, sb., room; Icel. *rúmr,* spacious;
rúm, space, Dan. and Swed. *rum,* adj. and
sb.; Goth. *rums,* adj. and sb., G. *raum,*
sb. Allied to L. *rus,* open country. **Der.**
roomy, adj., used for M. E. *roum,* adj.

rummage, to search thoroughly. (E.;
with F. *suffix.*) Due to the sb. *roomage,*
i. e. stowage; whence *roomage, romage,* vb.,
to find room for close packing of things in
a ship, also *rummage,* to clear a ship's
hold, also to search narrowly (Phillips).

Roost, sb. (E.) M. E. *roost,* a perch for
fowls. A. S. *hróst,* the same. **+** O. Du.
roest, a hen-roost. Cf. Lowl. Sc. *roost,* the
inside of a roof; the orig. *roost* was on the
rafters inside a roof. Allied to Icel. *hrót,*
Goth. *hrot,* a roof. **Der.** *roost,* vb.

Root (1), **Root** (2); see **Wort.**

Rope. (E.) M. E. *roop.* A. S. *ráp.* **+**
Du. *reep,* Icel. *reip,* Swed. *rep,* Dan. *reb*;
G. *reif,* circle, hoop, ring, sometimes a
rope. **Der.** *rop-y,* stringy, glutinous.

Rose (L. — Gk. — Arab.) A. S. *róse.* —
L. *rosa*; borrowed from Gk. *ῥόδον,* a rose
(whence a form *ῥοδία* * = *rosa*); Æolic
βρόδον. — Arab. *ward,* a rose. **Der.** *rhododendron* (Gk. *δένδρον,* a tree).

Rosemary. (F. — L.) M. E. *rosmarin.*
— O. F. *rosmarin.* — L. *rosmarinus, ros-
marinum,* rosemary, lit. sea-dew; called
ros maris in Ovid. — L. *ros,* dew; *marinus,*
marine. Named from some fancied connection with sea-spray; altered to *rosemary*
(as if for *rose of Mary*).

Rosin; see **Resin.**

Rostrum; see **Rodent.**

Rot. (E.) A weak verb; the proper pp.
is *rotted,* but *rotten* is commoner, which is
a Scand. form (see below). M. E. *roten,*
pp. *roted.* A. S. *rotian,* pp. *rotod.* **+** Du.
rotten, to rot.

rotten, putrid. (Scand.) M. E. *roten.*
— Icel. *rotinn,* Swed. *rutten,* Dan. *raaden,*
rotten. The Icel. *rotinn* is the pp. of a
lost verb (base RUT), to decay.

Rotary, turning like a wheel. (L.)
Formed from L. *rota,* a wheel. **+** Gael.
and Irish *roth,* W. *rhod,* Lithuan. *ratas,* G.
rad, a wheel. Cf. Skt. *ratha,* a chariot,
car, from *ri,* to go. (√ AR.) **Der.**
rotate, from pp. of L. *rotare,* to turn round.

comptroller, another spelling of *controller*; see below.

control, sb. (F. — L.) *Control* is short
for *contre-roll,* old form of *counter-roll.* —
O. F. *contre-role,* a duplicate register, used
to verify the official or first-made roll. — '
O. F. *contre,* over against; *role,* a roll. —
L. *contra,* against; *rotulus,* a roll; see
roll (below).

roll, vb. (F. — L.) M. E. *rollen.* —
O. F. *roler,* F. *rouler.* — Low L. *rotulare,*
to revolve, roll. — L. *rotula,* a little wheel;
dimin. of *rota,* a wheel. **Der.** *roll,* sb.,
O. F. *role,* L. *rotulus.*

rondeau. (F. — L.) F. *rondeau,* a
kind of poem, O. F. *rondel*; see **roundel**
(below).

rotundity. (F. — L.) F. *rotondité.* —
L. *rotunditatem,* acc. of *rotunditas,* roundness. — L. *rotundus,* round; see **round**
(below).

roué. (F. — L.) F. *roué,* lit. broken on
the wheel; hence a profligate, supposed to
merit that punishment. Pp. of *rouer,* to
turn round (L. *rotare*). — F. *roue,* a wheel.
— L. *rota,* a wheel.

rouleau. (F. — L.) F. *rouleau,* a roll
of paper; hence, a roll of coins in paper.
Dimin. of O. F. *role,* later *roule,* a roll;
see roll (above).

roulette, a game of chance. (F. — L.)
F. *roulette,* a ball which rolls on a turning
table; fem. of *roulet,* dimin. of *roule,* a
roll; see above.

round. (F. — L.) O. F. *roönd,* F. *rond.*
— L. *rotundus,* round. — L. *rota,* a wheel.

roundel, a kind of ballad. (F. — L.)
O. F. *rondel,* later *rondeau,* a poem
containing a line which recurs or comes
round again. — F. *rond,* round; see
above.

roundelay. (F. — L.) F. *rondelet,*
dimin. of O. F. *rondel* above. See **roundel.**
¶ Prob. confused, in spelling, with E. *lay,*
a song.

rowel. (F. — L.) F. *rouelle,* a little
wheel (on a bit or a spur). — Low L.
rotella, dimin. of *rota,* a wheel.

rundlet, runlet, a small barrel. (F. —
L.) Formerly *roundlet*; dimin. of O. F.
rondele, a little barrel, named from its

roundness.— F. *rond*, round; see round (above).

surround. (F. – L.) Confused with *round*. Orig. *suround*, i. e. 'to overflow.' – O. F. *suronder*. – L. *super-undare*.

Rote (1), routine; see **Rupture.**

Rote (2), a kind of fiddle; see **Crowd** (2).

Rotten; see **Rot.**

Rotundity; see **Rotary.**

Rouble, Ruble, a Russian coin. (Russ.) Russ. *ruble*, a rouble, 100 copecks; orig. ' piece cut off.' — Russ. *rubite*, to cut.

Roué; see **Rotary.**

Rouge; see **Ruby.**

Rough. (E.) M. E. *rough, rugh, row, ruh,* &c. A. S. *rúh*, rough, hairy; also *rúw.*+Du. *ruig*, O. Du. *ru*, Dan. *ru*, Low G. *ruug*, O. H. G. *rúh*, G. *rauh*. Cf. Lithuan. *raukas*, a fold, *rukti*, to wrinkle. ¶ Distinct from *raw.*

rug. (Scand.) Swed. *rugg*, rough entangled hair. Orig. ' rough;' cf. Du. *ruig*, Low G. *ruug*, rough (above).

rugged. (Scand.) M. E. *rugged*; also *ruggy*, Ch. C. T. 2885. The latter is from Swed. *ruggig*, rough, hairy. — Swed. *rugg*, rough entangled hair (above).

Rouleau, Roulette; see **Rotary.**

Roun, Round, to whisper; see **Rune.**

Round, Roundel; see **Rotary.**

Rouse (1), to excite, to wake up. (Scand.) A term of the chase; when a hart rushed out of its covert, it was said to *rouse*. M. E. *rusen*, to rush out. — Swed. *rusa*, to rush, *ruse frem*, to rush forward; Dan. *ruse*, to rush. Cf. A. S. *hreósan*, to rush, to fall down quickly. (Base HRUS.)

arouse. (Scand.) Formed from *rouse* by prefixing *a-*. This prefix was clearly suggested by that of *a-rise*; see **A-** (4).

rush (1), to move swiftly forward. (Scand.) M. E. *ruschen*. — O. Swed. *ruska*, to rush, also to shake. Extension of O. Swed. *rusa*, to rush; see above. Cf. Dan. *ruske*, to shake, pull, twitch.

rustle. (Scand.) Frequent. of Swed. *rusta*, to stir, make a noise, a variant of O. Swed. *ruska*, to shake, rush; see above. Cf. G. *rauschen, ruschen*, to rustle, to rush.

Rouse (2), a drinking-bout. (Scand.) In Shak. — Swed. *rus*, drunkenness, Dan. *ruus*, intoxication; Dan. *sove rusen ud* = to sleep out a rouse, to sleep oneself sober. + Du. *roes*, drunkenness. Prob. allied to East Friesic *rúse*, noise, uproar, ' row;' *rúsen*, to make a noise; G. *rausch*, a

drunken fit. (Really a *Danish* word; such a bout being called ' the Danish *rowza*.')

row (3), an uproar. (Scand.) Put for *rouse*; for loss of final *s*, cf. *pea, cherry, sherry, shay* (*chaise*), &c.

Rout, a defeat, a crowd; see **Rupture.**

Route, Routine; see **Rupture.**

Rover; see **Reave.**

Row (1), a line, rank. (E.) M. E. *rowe*. — A. S. *ráw, ráwe, ráwe,* a row; *hegeráwe,* a hedge-row. ¶ Distinct from Du. *rij,* G. *reihe.*

Row (2), to propel with oars. (E.) M. E. *rowen.* — A. S. *rówan,* to row. + Du. *roeijen,* Icel. *róa,* Swed. *ro,* Dan. *roe,* M. H. G. *ruejen.* Allied to Skt. *aritra,* a paddle, rudder, Lithuan. *irti,* to row; Gk. ἐρ-ετμός, a paddle, oar. (√AR.)

rudder. (E.) M. E. *roder, rother.* A. S. *róðer,* a paddle. Here *róðer* = rowing implement; from *ráw-an,* to row. (Paddles preceded rudders.) + Du. *roer* (for *roder*), an oar, rudder; Swed. *roder, ror*; Dan. *ror*; G. *ruder.*

Row (3), an uproar; see **Rouse** (2).

Rowan-tree; see **Roan-tree.**

Rowel; see **Rotary.**

Royal; see **Regent.**

Rub. (C.) M. E. *rubben.* — Gael. *rub,* to rub, Irish *rubadh,* a rubbing, W. *rhwbio,* to rub. ¶ Not allied to G. *reiben,* for which see **Rive.**

Rubbish, Rubble; see **Reave.**

Rubric; see below.

Ruby, a red gem. (F. – L.) O. F. *rubi, rubis*; F. *rubis* (where *s* is the old sign of the nom. case). Cf. Span. *rubi, rubin,* Port. *rubim,* Ital. *rubino.* — Low L. *rubinus,* a ruby; from its colour. — L. *ruber,* red; *rubere,* to be red. Allied to L. *rufus,* red; and to E. **Red.**

erubescent. (L.) L. *erubescent-,* stem of pres. pt. of *erubescere,* to grow red. — L. *e,* out, much; *rubescere,* to grow red, inceptive form of *rubere,* to be red.

rouge, red paint. (F. – L.) F. *rouge,* red. — L. *rubeus,* red; (whence F. *rouge,* like F. *rage* from L. *rabies*). Allied to L. *ruber, rufus,* red.

rubicund, ruddy. (F. – L.) F. *rubicunde.* — L. *rubicundus,* very red. — L. *ruber,* red.

rubric, a direction printed in red. (F. – L.) F. *rubrique.* — L. *rubrica,* red earth; also a title written in red. — L. *rubro-,* crude form of *ruber,* red.

Ruck (1), a fold, crease. (Scand.) Icel. *hrukka,* a wrinkle; cf. *hrokkin,* curled, pp of *hrökkva*, to recoil, give way, curl. Cf. Swed. *rynka*, Dan. *rynke*, a wrinkle; Du. *kreuk*, a fold, crease, W. *crych*, a wrinkle. See **Crook**.

Ruck (2), a heap; see **Rick**.

Rudder; see **Row** (2).

Ruddock, a red-breast. (E.) A.S. *rud-duc*. Perhaps from Celtic; cf. W. *rhud-dog*, Corn. *ruddoc*, a red-breast.

Ruddy. (E.) M.E. *rody*; answering to A.S. *rudig**, not found; formed from A.S. *rud-on*, pt. t. pl. of *reódan*, to redden, a strong verb, whence also A.S. *reád*, red; see **Red**.

Rude. (F. – L.) F. *rude*. – L. *rudem*, acc. of *rudis*, rough, raw, rude.

erudite, learned. (L.) L. *eruditus*, pp. of *erudire*, to free from rudeness, to teach. – L. *e*, from; *rudis*, rude.

rudiment. (F. – L.) F. *rudiment*. – L. *rudimentum*, a thing in the first rough state, a first attempt. – L. *rudi-s*, rude.

Rue (1), to be sorry for. (E.) M.E. *rewen*. A.S. *hreówan* (pt. t. *hreáw*). + O. Sax. *hrewan*, O.H.G. *hriuwan*, G. *reuen*. Cf. Icel. *hryggr*, grieved, *hrygð*, ruth. Allied to L. *crudelis*, cruel, harsh, *crudus*, raw. (√KRU.)

ruth, pity. (Scand.) M.E. *reuthe*. – Icel. *hrygð*, *hrygð*, ruth, sorrow. Allied to A.S. *hreówan*, to rue (above).

Rue (2), a plant. (F. – L. – Gk.) F. *rue*. – L. *ruta*. – Gk. ῥυτή, rue.

Ruff (1), a kind of frill. (E.) 'Ruffe of a shirt;' Levins (1570). So called from its uneven surface; the root appears in A.S. *redfan*, to reave (pt. t. pl. *ruf-on*), Icel. *rjúfa* (pt. t. *rauf*), to break, rip, break a hole in. (√RUP.) This is verified by Lithuan. *rupas*, uneven, rugged, *ruple*, rough bark of trees, with which cf. *ruffle* (1) below. Also Icel. *rúfinn*, rough, uncombed.

ruffle (1), to disorder a dress. (E.) M.E. *ruffelen*, to entangle, run into knots. Allied to **Ruff** (1) above.+O. Du. *ruyffelen*, to ruffle, wrinkle, *ruyffel*, a wrinkle, a crumple; Lithuan. *ruple*, rough bark on old trees. Der. *ruffle*, sb.

Ruff (2), the name of a bird. (E.?) Said to be named from the male having a *ruff* round its neck in the breeding season. But the female is called a *reeve*, which points to formation by vowel-change from some different source.

Ruff (3), a fish. (E.?) M.E. *ruffe*. Origin unknown.

Ruffian; see **Ruffle** (2).

Ruffle; see **Ruff** (1).

Ruffle (2), to bluster, be turbulent. (O. Du.) Obsolete. *Rufflers* were cheating bullies, highwaymen, lawless or violent men (Nares). – O. Du. *roffelen*, *roffen*, to pandar; Low G. *ruffeln*, to pandar, *ruffeler*, a pimp, intriguant; Dan. *ruffer*, a pandar. A *ruffler* and a *ruffian* are much the same.

ruffian, a bully. (F. – Teut.) O.F. *rufien*, *ruffien*, 'a bawd, pandar;' Cot.– O. Du. *roffen*, to pandar (above).

Rug, Rugged; see **Rough**.

Rugose, full of wrinkles. (L.) L. *rugosus*, adj., from *ruga*, a wrinkle. Der. *corrugate*, L. pp. *cor-rugatus* (*cor-* = *con-*).

Ruin. (F. – L.) F. *ruine*. – L. *ruina*, overthrow. – L. *ruere*, to rush, fall down.

Rule; see **Regent**.

Rum (1), a spirituous liquor. (F. – Teut.) Called *rumbo* in Smollet, Per. Pickle, c. ii. and c. ix; this is short for the sailor's word *rumbowling*, grog. Orig. called *Rumbullion* in Barbadoes, A.D. 1651; from Devonsh. *rumbullion*, uproar, rumpus. Founded on F. *ramper*. See **Ramp**.

Rum (2), strange, queer. (Hindi.) 'Rum, gallant, a cant word;' Bailey (1735). *Rum* really means 'Gypsy;' hence 'good' from a Gypsy point of view, but 'suspicious' from an outsider's point of view. Hence *rome bouze*, *rum booze*, good wine. *Rom* means 'a husband, a Gypsy;' *rómmani*, adj., Gypsy. This Gypsy word *rom* answers to Hindi *dom* (with initial cerebral *d*, confused with *r*), a man of low caste; Skt. *domba*, 'a man of low caste, who gains his livelihood by singing and dancing;' Benfey.

Rumb, Rhumb, a line for directing a ship's course on a chart; a point of the compass. (F. – Span. – L. – Gk.) See *Rumb* in Phillips. – F. *rumb*, 'a romb, or point of the compasse, a line drawn directly from wind to wind in a compasse, traversboord, or sea-card;' Cot. – Span. (and Port.) *rumbo*, a ship's course (represented by spiral lines on a globe). – L. *rhombum*, acc. of *rhombus*, a magician's circle, a rhombus. – Gk. ῥόμβος, a top, a magic wheel, whirling motion; also a rhombus. See **Rhomb**. *Rhomb* meant revolution of the sphere, Milton, P. L. viii. 134; hence whirling or spiral lines, &c. ¶ No connection with Du. *ruim*, which merely means room or space, or sometimes the hold of a ship, i. e. its room or capacity for stowage.

Rumble, to make a low, heavy sound. (E.) Prov. E. *rommle, rummle*; M. E. *romblen* (with excrescent *b*). Frequent. form, meaning ' to repeat the sound *rum* ;' cf. L. *rumor*, a rumour; Skt. *ru*, to hum. See **Rumour. +** Du. *rommelen*, Dan. *rumle*, to rumble, buzz.

Ruminate. (L.) From pp. of L. *ruminare*, to chew the cud, ruminate. **—** L. *rumin-*, stem of *rūmen*, the throat, gullet. Put for *rug-men**, allied to L. *rug-ire*, to roar, bray. (√RU.) See **Rumour.**

Rummage; see **Room.**

Rummer, a sort of drinking-glass. (Du. **—** G. **—** L. ?) Used for Rhenish wine. ' Rhenish *rummers* ;' Dryden. **—** Du. *roemer, romer*, a wine-glass; Low G. *römer*, a large wine-glass. **—** G. *römer*, a rummer; also ' Roman.' I am told that the glasses were so called because used in former times in the *Römersaal* at Frankfort, when they drank the new emperor's health. If so, it is from L. *Roma*, Rome.

Rumour. (F. **—** L.) M. E. *rumour*. **—** F. *rumeur*. **—** L. acc. *rumorem*, from *rumor*, a noise, murmur. Cf. L. *rumitare*, to spread reports. **—** √ RU, to make a humming noise. See **Rumble.**

Rump. (Scand.) M. E. *rumpe*. **—** Icel. *rumpr*, Swed. *rumpa*, Dan. *rumpe*. **+** Du. *rompe*, ' the bulke of a body or corps, or a body without a head ;' Hexham.

Rumple, to wrinkle; see **Ripple** (2).

Run. (E.) M. E. *rinnen*, pt. t. *ran*, pp. *runnen, ronnen* ; A.S. *rinnan*, pt. t. *rann*, pp. *gerunnen*; also found in the transposed form *irnan*, pt. t. *arn*. **+** Du. *rennen*, Icel. *renna*, Dan. *rinde*, Swed. *rinna*, Goth. *rinnan*, G. *rennen*. Allied to Skt. *rinomi*, I go, rise, rí, to go; L. *or-iri*, to rise. (√AR.)

rennet (1), the prepared inner membrane of a calf's stomach, used to make milk coagulate. (E.) M. E. *renet*; from M. E. *rennen*, to run; prov. E. *run*, to congeal, coagulate. See above. Hence *rennet* is also called *runnet* (Pegge's Kenticisms); also *erning* (Derbyshire), from A. S. *irnan*, to run. So also O. Du. *rinsel, runsel, renninge*, ' curds, or milk-runnet,' from *rinnen*, ' to presse, curdle;' Hexham. Cf. G. *rinnen*, to run, curdle, coagulate.

Runagate; see **Negation.**

Rundlet, Runlet; see **Rotary.**

Rune, one of the old characters used for incised inscriptions. (E.) M. E. *rune*, counsel. A. S. *rún*, a rune, mystery, secret conference, whisper. Orig. sense ' whisper' or murmur, hence a mystery, lastly an incised character, because writing was a secret known to few. **—** √RU, to buzz. **+**Goth. *runa*, O. H. G. *rún*, a secret, counsel. Allied to **Rumour.**

roun, round, to whisper. (E.) Shak. has *round*, with excrescent *d*. M. E. *rounen*. **—** A.S. *rúnian*, to whisper. **—** A. S. *rún*, a whisper (above).**+**G *raunen*, to whisper; from O. H. G. *rún* (above).

Rung, a round of a ladder. (E.) M. E. *ronge*, a stake. A. S. *hrung*, a stake of a cart, beam or spar.**+**O. Du. *ronge*, a beam of a plough; Icel. *röng*, rib in a ship; G. *runge*, a pin, a bolt; Goth. *hrugga* (= *hrunga*), a staff. Perhaps allied to **Ring.** The sense seems to be ' rounded stick.'

Rupee, an Indian coin. (Hind. **—**Skt.) Hindustáni *rúpiyah*, a rupee. **—**Skt. *rúpya*, handsome, also (as sb.) silver. **—**Skt. *rúpa*, beauty.

Rupture. (F. **—**L.) F. *rupture*. **—**L. *ruptura*, a breakage. **—**L. *rupt-us*, pp. of *rumpere*, to break (pt. t. *rupi*). Allied to **Reave.** (√RUP.)

abrupt. (L.) L. *abruptus*, pp. of *abrumpere*, to break off. **—**L. *ab*, off ; *rumpere*, to break.

corrupt. (L.) L. *corruptus*, pp. of *corrumpere*, to break wholly, corrupt. **—** L. *cor-* (for *con-* = *cum*), together; *rumpere*.

disruption. (L.) From L. *disruptio, diruptio*, a breaking asunder. **—** L. *disruptus, diruptus*, pp. of *dis-rumpere, di-rumpere*, to break apart.

eruption. (L.) From L. *eruptio*, a breaking out. **—**L. *eruptus*, pp. of *e-rumpere*, to break out.

interruption. (F. **—**L.) F. *interruption*. **—**L. acc. *interruptionem*, a breaking into. **—**L. *interruptus*, pp. of *inter-rumpere*, to break into.

irruption. (F. **—**L.) F. *irruption*, ' a forcible entry ;' Cot. **—**L. acc. *irruptionem*, a breaking into. **—** L. *ir-* (for *in*), into; *ruptus*, pp. of *rumpere*, to break.

rote (1), routine, repetition. (F. **—**L.) M. E. *bi rote*, with repetition, by heart; lit. in a beaten track. **—**O. F. *rote* (F. *route*), a way, a beaten track. See **route** (below).

rout, (1) a defeat, (2) a troop or crowd. (F. **—**L.) F. *route*, ' a rowt, defeature; also a rowt, herd, flock, troope; also a rutt, way, path;' Cot.—L. *rupta*, pp. of *ruptus*, broken; from *rumpere*. This L. *rupta* came to mean (1) a defeat, flying mass of broken troops; (2) a fragment of an army, a troop; (3) a way broken or cut through a forest, a way, route.

route, a way, course. (F.—L.) F. *route*, a way, route; see the word above.

routine, a beaten track. (F.—L.) F. *routine*, usual course; lit. small path. Dimin. of F. *route* (above).

rut (1), a track left by a wheel. (F.—L.) F. *route*, 'a rutt, way;' Cot. See rout (above).

Rural; see Rustic.

Ruse; see Cause.

Rush (1), to move swiftly forward; see Rouse (1).

Rush (2), a plant. (E. *or* L.) M. E. *rusche, rische, resche.* A. S. *risce, resce,* a rush (better form *rysce**). + Du. G. *rusch,* rush, reed, small brushwood. Perhaps merely borrowed from L. *ruscum,* butcher's broom. **Der.** *bul-rush* (prob. for *bole-rush,* round-stemmed rush); cf. *bull-weed,* i. e. bole-weed, knapweed.

Rusk. (Span.) Span. *rosca de mar,* sea-rusks, a kind of biscuit; *rosca,* a roll (twist) of bread. Cf. Port. *rosca,* the winding of a snake. Origin unknown.

Russet. (F.—L.) M. E. *russet.* — F. *rousset,* 'russet, ruddy;' Cot. Dimin. of F. *roux* (fem. *rousse*), reddish.—L. *russus,*

reddish. Put for *rudh-tus**, from the base appearing in Gk. *ἐ-ρυθ-ρός*, red; see Red.

Rust; see Red.

Rustic. (F.—L.) F. *rustique.*—L. *rusticus,* belonging to the country.—L. *rus,* the country. Cf. Russ. *raviina,* a plain, Zend *ravan,* a plain.

roistering, turbulent. (F.—L.) From the sb. *roister,* a bully, turbulent fellow.— F. *rustre,* 'a ruffin, royster, sawcie fellow,' Cot. By-form of O. F. *ruste,* a rustic, the *r* being epenthetic.—L. *rusticum,* acc. of *rusticus,* rustic.

rural, belonging to the country. (F.—L.) F. *rural.*—L. *ruralis,* adj.—L. *rur-,* stem of *rus,* country.

Rustle; see Rouse (1).

Rut (1), a track left by a wheel; see Rupture.

Rut (2), to copulate, as deer. (F.—L.) M. E. *rutien,* to rut; from *rut,* sb.—F. *rut, ruit,* 'the rut of deer or boars.'—L. *rugitum,* acc. of *rugitus,* the roaring of lions; hence, the noise made by deer in rut-time. —L. *rugire,* to roar (whence F. *ruir*).— √RU, to make a noise; see Rumour.

Ruth; see Rue (1).

Rye. (E.) M. E. *reye.* A. S. *ryge,* rye. + Du. *rogge,* Icel. *rúgr,* Dan. *rug,* Swed. *råg,* G. *roggen,* O. H. G. *rocco.* Cf. Russ. *roje,* rye; Lithuan. *ruggei,* pl. sb., rye.

Ryot; the same as Rayah, q. v.

S.

Sabaoth, hosts. (Heb.) Heb. *tsevā'ôth,* armies; pl. of *tsává',* an army.—Heb. *tsává',* to go forth as a soldier.

Sabbath. (L. — Gk. — Heb.) M. E. *sabat.* — L. *sabbatum.* — Gk. *σάββατον.* — Heb. *shabbáth,* rest, sabbath, sabbath-day. —Heb. *shábath,* to rest.

Sable, an animal. (F.—Slavonic.) O.F. *sable.* — Russ. *sobole,* the sable; also a furtippet. ¶ As black sable was best liked, the word *sable* also means 'black.'

Sabre, Saber. (F. — G. — Hungarian.) F. *sabre.*—G. *säbel,* a falchion.—Hungarian *szablya,* a sabre; cf. *szabo,* a cutter, *szabni,* to cut.

Saccharine; see Sugar.

Sacerdotal; see Sacred.

Sack (1), a bag. (L. — Gk. — Heb. — Egyptian?) M. E. *sak.* A. S. *sacc.* — L. *saccus.* — Gk. *σάκκος.* — Heb. *saq,* sack-cloth,

a sack for corn. Prob. of Egyptian origin; cf. Coptic *sok,* sack-cloth (Peyron). From Heb. *saq* are borrowed Du. *zak,* G. *sack,* &c.

sack (2), to plunder. (F. — L., &c.) From the sb. *sack,* pillage. — F. *sac,* ruin, spoil. From the use of a *sack* in removing plunder; prob. in a metaphorical sense. From Low L. *saccare,* to put into a bag; Low L. *saccus,* a garment, a purse, L. *saccus,* a sack; see above.

sackbut, a kind of wind-instrument. (F.—Span.—Heb. *and* Tent.) F. *saquebute,* a sackbut. — Span. *sacabuche,* a tube used as a pump; also, a sackbut, trombone. Lit. 'that which exhausts the chest,' from the exertion used. — Span. *sacar,* to draw out, exhaust, the same as F. *sacquer,* to draw out hastily, lit. to draw out of a sack, from Heb. *saq* (above); *buche,* maw, stomach, chest, from O. H. G. *bózo*, a bunch, allied to O. H. G. *bózen*, to beat (Diez).

satchel, a small bag. (F. – L., &c.) O. F. *sachel*, a little bag. – L. *saccellum*, acc. of *saccellus*, dimin. of *saccus*, a sack (above).

Sack (3), the name of an old Spanish wine. (F. – L.) Formerly also *seck*, meaning a ' dry ' wine. – F. *sec*, dry; *vin sec*, sack. Cf. Span. *seco*, dry. – L. *siccum*, acc. of *siccus*, dry.

desiccate, to dry up. (L.) From pp. of L. *desiccare*, to drain dry. – L. *de*, away; *siccare*, to dry, from *siccus*.

Sackbut; see **Sack** (1).

Sacred. (F. – L.) *Sacred* is the pp. of M. E. *sacren*, to consecrate, render holy; a verb now obsolete. – F. *sacrer*, to consecrate. – L. *sacrare*, to consecrate. – L. *sacr-*, stem of *sacer*, holy. From base *sac-* of L. *sancire*, to make holy. (√SAK.)

consecrate. (L.) From pp. of L. *consecrare*, to render sacred. – L. *con-* (*cum*), with, wholly; *sacrare*, to consecrate.

desecrate. (L.) From pp. of L. *desecrare*, to profane.

execrate. (L.) From pp. of L. *execrari*, put for *exsecrari*, to curse greatly. – L. *ex*, greatly; *sacrare*, to consecrate, also to declare accursed.

sacerdotal. (F. – L.) F. *sacerdotal*. – L. *sacerdotalis*, belonging to a priest. – L. *sacerdot-*, stem of *sacerdos*, a priest, lit. ' presenter of offerings or sacred gifts ' (Corssen). – L. *sacer*, sacred; *dare*, to give. Cf. *dos* (stem *dot-*), a dowry, from the same verb.

sacrament. (L.) L. *sacramentum*, an engagement, military oath, vow; in late L., a sacrament. – L. *sacrare*, to render sacred. – L. *sacr-*, stem of *sacer*, sacred.

sacrifice. (F. – L.) F. *sacrifice*. – L. *sacrificium*, lit. a rendering sacred; cf. *sacrificare*, to sacrifice. – L. *sacri-*, for *sacer*, sacred; *facere*, to make.

sacrilege. (F. – L.) F. *sacrilege*. – L. *sacrilegium*, the stealing of sacred things. – L. *sacri-*, for *sacer*, sacred; *legere*, to gather, steal; see **Legend**.

sacristan, **sexton**. (F. – L.) *Sacristan* is rare; it is commonly *sexton*, M. E. *sextein*, orig. a keeper of the sacred vestments, afterwards a grave-digger. – F. *sacristain*, ' a sexton or vestry-keeper; ' Cot. Extended from Low L. *sacrista*, a sacristan. – L. *sacr-*, stem of *sacer*.

saint. (F. – L.) M. E. *seint*, *saint*. –

F. *saint*. – L. *sanctum*, acc. of *sanctus*, holy. – L. *sanctus*, pp. of *sancire*, to render sacred; see **Sacred** (above).

sanctify. (F. – L.) F. *sanctifier*. – L. *sanctificare*, to make holy. – L. *sanctus*, holy; *-ficare*, for *facere*, to make.

sanctimony. (F. – L.) F. *sanctimonie*. – L. *sanctimonia*, holiness. – L. *sanctus*, holy; see **saint** (above).

sanction. (F. – L.) F. *sanction*. – L. *sanctionem*, acc. of *sanctio*, a rendering sacred. – L. *sanctus*, pp. of *sancire*, to render sacred. See **Sacred**.

sanctity. (F. – L.) F. *sanctité*. – L. acc. *sanctitatem*, from *sanctitas*, holiness. – L. *sanctus*, holy (above).

sanctuary. (F. – L.) M. E. *seintuarie*, a shrine. – O. F. *saintuarie* (F. *sanctuaire*). – L. *sanctuarium*, a shrine. – L. *sanctus*, holy (above).

Sad. (E.) The orig. sense was sated; hence tired, grieved. A. S. *sæd*, sated, satiated. + O. Sax. *sad*, Icel. *saddr*, Goth. *saths*, G. *satt*, sated, full. Allied to **Sate**, **Satiate**.

Saddle. (E.) M. E. *sadel*. A. S. *sadol*. + Du. *zadel*, Icel. *söðull*, Swed. Dan. *sadel*, G. *sattel*, O. H. G. *satul*. The same as Russ. *siedlo*, L. *sella* (put for *sedla* *, from *sedere*, to sit). The sense is ' seat; ' the form of the word is abnormal, the true E. word being *settle*. It may have come to us from the Slavonic. Allied to **Sit**, q.v.

Sadducee. (L. – Gk. – Heb.) L. pl. *Sadducæi*. – Gk. pl. Σαδδουκαῖοι. – Heb. pl. *tsedûkîm*; pl. of *tsádôq*, just, righteous. – Heb. *tsádaq*, to be just. The name was really derived from *Tsádôq* (*Zadok*), the founder of the sect, whose name meant ' the just.'

Safe; see **Salvation**.

Saffron, a plant. (F. – Arab.) F. *safran*, *saffran*. – Arab. *za'farán*, saffron.

Sag, to droop. (Scand.) M. E. *saggen*. – Swed. *sacka*, to settle, sink down; cf. Dan. *sakke*, to have stern-way; Low G. *sakke*, to settle (as dregs). Perhaps allied to **Sink**.

Saga; see **Say** (1).

Sagacious. (L.) From L. *sagaci-*, crude form of *sagax*, of quick perception. – L. *sagire*, to perceive by the senses.

presage. (F. – L.) O. F. *presage*. – L. *præsagium*, a divining beforehand. – L. *præ-sagire*, to perceive beforehand.

Sage (1), wise; see **Sapid**.

Sage (2), a plant; see **Salvation**.

Sagittarius. (L.) L. *sagittarius*, an archer. – L. *sagitta*, an arrow.

Sago, a starch. (Malay.) Malay *ságu*, *ságú*, sago, pith of a tree named *rumbiya*.

Sail, sb. (E.) M. E. *seil*. A. S. *segel*, *segl*, a sail. ╋ Du. *zeil*, Icel. *segl*, Dan. *seil*, Swed. G. *segel*. Lit. 'that which endures or resists the wind;' cf. Skt. *sah*, to bear, undergo, be able to resist. (√SAGH.)

Saint; see **Sacred**.

Sake. (E.) M. E. *sake*, purpose, cause. A. S. *sacu*, strife, dispute, crime, law-suit; orig. 'contention.' Cf. Goth. *sakan* (pt. t. *sók*), to contend. ╋ Du. *zaak*, matter, affair, business; Icel. *sök*, a charge, crime; Dan. *sag*, Swed. *sak*, G. *sache*.

Salaam, Salam. (Arab.) Arab. *salám*, saluting, wishing peace; a salutation. – Arab. *salm*, saluting. ╋ Heb. *shelám*, peace, from *shálam*, to be safe.

Salad; see **Salt**.

Salamander, a reptile. (F. – L. – Gk.) F. *salamandre*. – L. *salamandra*. – Gk. σαλαμάνδρα, a kind of lizard. Of Eastern origin; cf. Pers. *samandar*, a salamander.

Salary; see **Salt**.

Sale. (Scand.) M. E. *sale*. – Icel. *sala*, fem., *sal*, neut., a sale, bargain; Swed. *salu*, Dan. *salg*. Orig. sense 'delivery,' or 'a handing over;' allied to Lithuan. *sulyti*, to proffer, *pa-sula*, an offer.

sell (1), to deliver for money. (E.) A. S. *sellan*, *sillan*, *syllan*, to hand over, deliver; a secondary verb, derived from the sb. above. ╋ Icel. *selja*, Dan. *sælge*, Swed. *sälja*, O. H. G. and Goth. *saljan*, to hand over, offer.

Salic, Salique. (F. – O. H. G.) F. *Salique*, belonging to the Salic tribe. This was a Frankish tribe, prob. named from the river *Sala* (now Yssel). Cf. Skt. *salila*, water, from *sri*, to flow. (√SAR.)

Salient. (L.) From pres. pt. of L. *salire*, to leap, spring forward. Allied to Skt. *sri*, to flow, *sari*, water-fall, Gk. ἅλλομαι, I leap. (√SAR.)

assail. (F. – L.) O. F. *assailler*, *asaillir*, to attack (L. *assilire*). – L. *ad*, to; *salire*, to leap, rush forth.

assault. (F. – L.) O. F. *assalt*. – L. *ad*, to; *saltus*, a leap, attack, from *saltus*, pp. of *salire*, to leap.

desultory, jumping from one thing to another. (L.) L. *desultorius*, orig. the horse of a *desultor*; hence, inconstant. – L. *desultor*, one who leaps down, or from

horse to horse. – L. *desultus*, pp. of *desilere*, to leap down. – L. *de*, down; *salire*.

exult, to leap for joy. (L.) L. *exultare*, better spelt *exsultare*, to leap up, exult. – L. *exsultus*, pp. of *exsilere*, to leap out. – L. *ex*, out; *salire*, to leap.

insult. (F. – L.) F. *insulter*. – L. *insultare*, to leap upon, scoff at, insult; frequent. of *insilere*, to leap upon. – L. *in*, on; *salire*, to leap.

resilient. (L.) L. *resilient-*, stem of pres. part. of *resilire*, to leap back. – L. *re-*, back; *salire*, to leap.

result, verb. (F. – L.) O. F. *resulter*, 'to rebound or leap back; also to rise of, come out of;' Cot. – L. *resultare*, to rebound; frequent. of *resilere* (above).

sally. (F. – L.) M. E. *salien*. – F. *saillir*, to issue forth; also to leap. – L. *salire*, to leap. Der. *sally*, sb. = F. *saillie*, a sally, from the fem. of pp. *sailli*.

salmon. (F. – L.) M. E. *salmon*, *saumon*. – O. F. *saumon* (for *salmon**). – L. *salmonem*, acc. of *salmo*, a salmon. Lit. 'a leaper.' – L. *salire*, to leap.

saltire, in heraldry, a St. Andrew's cross. (F. – L.) A cross in this position (X). – F. *saultoir*, St. Andrew's cross (Cot.). Also O. F. *sautoir*, orig. a stirrup of a triangular shape △; the cross being named from the position of the stirrup's sides. – Low L. *saltatorium*, a stirrup. – L. *saltatorius*, belonging to leaping or springing; suitable for mounting a horse. – L. *saltator*, a leaper. – L. *saltare*, frequent. of *salire*, to leap.

saltation, dancing. (L.) Rare; from L. *saltatio*, a dancing. – L. *saltatus*, pp. of *saltare*, to dance, frequent. of *salire*.

Saline; see **Salt**.

Saliva. (L.) L. *saliua*, spittle. ╋ Gk. σίαλον, Russ. *slina*, spittle. Allied to **Slime**.

Sallet, a kind of helmet. (F. – Ital. – L.) Corruption of O. F. *salade*, a sallet, headpiece. – Ital. *celata*, a helmet. – L. *cælata* (*cassis*), an ornamented helmet. – L. *cælatus*, pp. of *cælare*, to engrave, ornament (steel). – L. *cælum*, a chisel, graver. Allied to *cædere*, to cut.

Sallow (1), **Sally,** a kind of willow. (E.) M. E. *salwe*. – A. S. *sealg-*, stem of *sealh*, a willow. Named from growing near the water; cf. Skt. *salila*, *saras*, *sari*, water, *sarasiya*, a lotus. ╋ Icel. *selja*, Swed. *sälg*, *sälj*, Dan. *selje*, G. *sahl-weide*, O. H. G. *salahá*, L. *salix*, Gael. *saileach*, Irish *sail*, *saileach*, W. *helyg* (pl.), Gk. ἑλίκη, a willow. (√SAR.)

Sallow (2), pale, wan. (E.) M. E. *salow.* A. S. *salu,* sallow. **+** Du. *zaluw,* Icel. *sölr,* O. H. G. *salo,* tawny (whence F. *sale,* dirty).

Sally; see **Salient.**

Salmagundi; see **Salt.**

Salmon; see **Salient.**

Saloon. (F.—O. H. G.) F. *salon,* large room. — F. *salle,* room. — O. H. G. *sal* (G. *saal*), an abode, hall, room. **+** Icel. *salr,* A. S. *sæl, sele,* hall. Orig. 'an abode;' cf. Goth. *saljan,* to dwell.

Salt. (E.) M. E. *salt.* A. S. *sealt,* both adj. and sb. Orig. an adj., as in *sealt wæter,* salt (i. e. salted) water. So also Icel. *saltr,* Dan. Swed. *salt,* Du. *zout,* W. *hallt,* all adjectives, from a form SAL-TA, salted, answering to L. *sal-sus,* salted. The true sb. form appears in L. *sal,* Gk. ἅλς, Russ. *sole,* W. *hal,* Skt. *sara,* salt. The Skt. *sara* also means the coagulum of curds or milk, from *sri,* to go, flow. (√SAR.)

salad. (F. — Ital. — L.) F. *salade.* — O. Ital. *salata,* a salad of herbs; lit. 'salted;' fem. of *salato,* salted, pickled, pp. of *salare,* to salt. — Ital. *sal. sale,* salt. — L. *sal,* salt.

salary, stipend. (F. — L.) F. *salaire.* — L. *salarium,* orig. salt-money, given to soldiers to buy salt. — L. *sal,* salt.

saline. (F.—L.) F. *salin,* fem. *saline,* adj. — L. *salinus,* as in *salinæ,* salt-pits. — L. *sal,* salt.

salmagundi, a seasoned hodge-podge. (F. — Ital.—L.) F. *salmigondis,* spelt *salmagondin* in Cotgrave, who describes the dish. Orig. 'seasoned salt-meats.' — Ital. *salami,* pl. of *salame,* salt-meat, from L. *sal,* salt; *conditi,* pl. of *condito,* seasoned, savoury, from L. *conditus,* pp. of *condire,* to pickle, season.

salt-cellar. (E.; *and* F. — L.) Put for *salt-sellar* or *salt-selar,* where *selar* is an old word for 'salt-holder;' so that the prefix *salt* is superfluous. O. F. *salicre,* 'a salt-seller;' Cot. — L. *salarium,* salt-cellar (in late L.); from L. *salarius,* adj., belonging to salt. — L. *sal,* salt. See **salary** (above).

salt-petre, nitre. (E.; *and* F. — L. *and* Gk.) Put for O. F. *salpestre,* salt-petre (Cot.). — L. *sal petræ,* salt of the rock. — L. *sal,* salt; Gk. πέτρα, a rock; see **Petrify.**

sauce. (F. — L.) F. *sauce.* — L. *salsa,* a thing salted; fem. of *salsus,* salted. See **Salt. Der.** *sauc-er,* orig. a vessel for sauce; *sauc-y,* full of sauce, pungent.

sausage. (F.—L.) F. *saucisse.*—Low L. *salcitia,* L. *salsicium,* a sausage, of *salted* or seasoned meat.—L. *salsus,* salted. — L. *sal,* salt.

souse, pickle. (F. — L.) Merely another spelling of sauce (above). Hence *souse,* vb., to immerse, orig. to plunge in brine.

Saltation, Saltire; see **Salient.**

Salubrious, Salutary, Salute, Salvage; see **Salvation.**

Salvation. (F.—L.) F. *salvation.*—L. acc. *saluationem,* acc. of *saluatio,* a saving. — L. *saluatus,* pp. of *saluare,* to save.— L. *saluus,* safe. Allied to **Serve.** (√SAR.)

safe. (F. — L.) M. E. *sauf.* — F. *sauf,* safe.—L. *saluum,* acc. of *saluus,* safe.

sage (2), a plant. (F. — L.) M. E. *sauge.* — O. F. *sauge.* — L. *saluia,* sage; from its supposed healing virtues. — L. *saluus,* safe, hale, sound.

salubrious. (L.) From L. *salūbris,* healthful. Put for *salut-bris*,* i. e. health-bringing.—L. *salut-,* stem of *salus,* health; *-bris,* bringing, from √BHAR, to bear, bring. This suffix also appears as *-fer;* hence also *salutifer,* health-bringing.

salutary. (F.— L.) F. *salutaire.*—L. *salutaris,* healthful. — L. *salut-,* stem of *salus,* health; allied to *saluus,* hale.

salute. (L.) L. *salutare,* to wish health to, to greet.—L. *salut-* (above).

salvage. (F. — L.) O. F. *salvage,* lit. 'a saving.' — O. F. *salver,* F. *sauver,* to save.—L. *saluare,* to save.—L. *saluus.*

salver, a plate on which anything is presented. (Span. — L.) Put for Span. *salva,* a salver, a plate on which anything is presented; it also means the previous tasting of viands before they are served up. — Span. *salvar,* to save, free from risk, to taste the food or drink of nobles to save them from poison. — L. *saluare,* to save (below). ¶ A *salver* (*salva*) is properly a plate or tray on which drink was presented to the taster, and then to the drinker of a health; cf. Span. *hacer la salva,* to drink one's health.

save. (F. — L.) M. E. *sauuen* (= *sauven*). — F. *sauver.*—L. *saluare,* to save.

Salve, ointment. (E.) A. S. *sealf.*

Same. (E.) M. E. *same.* A. S. *same,* only as adv., as in *swá same swá men,* the same as men, just like men. The adj. use is Scand.; from Icel. *samr*, Dan. Swed. *samme*, the same. **+** O. H. G. *sam*, adj., *sama*, adv.; Goth. *sama*, the same (cf. *samana*, together), Russ. *samuii*, Gk. ὁμός, Skt. *sama*, same. Allied to Skt. *sam*, with, together, L. *simul*, together, *similis*, like.

Samite, a rich silk stuff. (F. **—** L. **—** Gk.) O. F. *samit*. **—** Low L. *examitum*. **—** Late Gk. ἑξάμιτον, a stuff woven with six kinds of thread. **—** Gk. ἑξ, six; μίτος, a thread of the woof. See **Dimity**.

Samphire; see **Petrel**.

Sample; see **Exempt**.

Sanatory; see **Sane**.

Sanctify, Sanctimony; see **Sacred**.

Sand. (E.) A. S. *sand*. **+** Du. *zand*; Icel. *sandr*; Swed. Dan. G. *sand*.

Sandal, shoe. (F. **—** L. **—** Gk.) F. *sandale*. **—** L. *sandalium*. **—** Gk. σανδάλιον, dimin. of σάνδαλον, a wooden sole bound on to the feet with straps. Cf. Pers. *sandal*, a sandal.

Sandal-wood. (F. **—** Pers. **—** Skt.) F. *sandal*. **—** Pers. *chandal*, *chandan*. **—** Skt. *chandana*, sandal, the tree. **—** Skt. *chand*, to shine.

Sandwich. (E.) Named from John Montague, 4th Earl of *Sandwich*, died 1792, who used to have *sandwiches* brought to him at the gaming-table. **—** A. S. *Sandwíc*, Sandwich, a town in Kent.

Sane. (L.) L. *sanus*, of sound mind. Allied to Gk. σάος, σῶς, sound.

sanatory. (L.) From L. *sanator*, a healer. **—** L. *sanare*, to heal. **—** L. *sanus*.

Sanguine. (F. **—** L.) F. *sanguin*, bloody, of a sanguine complexion. **—** L. *sanguineus*, adj., from *sanguin-*, stem of *sanguis*, blood.

consanguineous. (L.) L. *consanguineus*, related by blood. **—** L. *con-* (*cum*), together; *sanguin-*, stem of *sanguis*, blood.

Sanhedrim. (Heb. **—** Gk.) Late Heb. *sanhedrîn*, borrowed from Gk. συνέδριον, a council; lit. a sitting together. **—** Gk. σύν, together; ἕδρα, a seat, from ἕζομαι, I sit; see **Sit**.

Sans. (F. **—** L.) F. *sans*, without; O. F. *sens*. **—** L. *sine*, without. **—** L. *si ne*, if not, except.

Sanskrit. (Skt.) Skt. *sanskrita*, lit. ' symmetrically formed.' **—** Skt. *sam*, together; *krita*, made, from *kri*, to make.

Sap (1), juice of plants. (E.) A. S. *sæp*. **+** O. Du. *sap*, O. H. G. *saf*, G. *saft*. Cf. Gk. ὀπός, L. *sucus*, Irish *sug*, Russ. *sok'*, sap.

Sap (2), to undermine. (F. **—** Low L. **—** Gk.?) O. F. *sapper*, F. *saper*. **—** O. F. *sappe* (F. *sape*), a kind of hoe. (Cf. Span. *zapa*, Ital. *zappa*, mattock). **—** Low L. *sapa*, a hoe. Prob. from Gk. σκαπάνη, a hoe; from σκάπτειν, to dig.

Sapid, savoury. (L.) Rare. L. *sapidus*, savoury. **—** L. *sapere*, to taste; also to be wise.

insipid. (L.) L. *insipidus*. **—** L. *in*, not; *sapidus*, savoury.

sage (1), wise. (F. **—** L.) F. *sage*. **—** Low L. *sabius**, put for L. *sapius*, whence *nesapius*, unwise (Petronius). **—** L. *sapere*, to be wise.

sapience. (F. **—** L.) F. *sapience*. **—** L. *sapientia*, wisdom. **—** L. *sapient-*, stem of pres. pt. of *sapere*, to be wise.

savour. (F. **—** L.) O. F. *savour*, later *saveur*. **—** L. *saporem*, acc. of *sapor*, taste. **—** L. *sapere*, to be aware.

Saponaceous; see **Soap**.

Sapphic, a kind of metre. (L. **—** Gk.) L. *sapphicus*, belonging to Sappho. **—** Gk. Σαπφώ, Sappho of Lesbos, died about 592 B.C.

Sapphire. (F. **—** L. **—** Gk. **—** Heb.) F. *saphir*. **—** L. *sapphirus*. **—** Gk. σάπφειρος, a sapphire. **—** Heb. *sappîr* (with initial *samech*), a sapphire. Cf. Pers. *saffir*, sapphire.

Saraband. (F. **—** Span. **—** Pers.) F. *sarabande*, a Spanish dance. **—** Span. *zarabanda*, a dance of Moorish origin. **—** Pers. *sarband*, lit. ' a fillet for fastening a lady's head-dress.' **—** Pers. *sar*, head; *band*, band.

Saracen. (L. **—** Arab.) L. *saracenus*, lit. one of the Eastern people. **—** Arab. *sharqíy*, eastern. **—** Arab. *sharq*, east, rising sun. **—** Arab. root *sharaqa*, it rose.

sarcenet, sarsnet, a thin silk. (F. **—** L. **—** Arab.) O. F. *sarcenet*, a stuff made by the Saracens. **—** Low L. *saracenicum*, sarcenet. **—** L. *Saracenus*, Saracen (above).

sirocco, a hot wind. (Ital. **—** Arab.) Ital. *sirocco*, south-east wind. **—** Arab. *sharq*, east (above).

Sarcasm, a sneer. (F. **—** L. **—** Gk.) F. *sarcasme*. **—** L. *sarcasmus*. **—** Gk. σαρκασμός, a sneer. **—** Gk. σαρκάζειν, to tear flesh, to bite the lips in rage, to sneer. **—** Gk. σαρκ-, stem of σάρξ, flesh. **Der.** *sarcastic*, Gk. σαρκαστικός, sneering.

sarcophagus. (L. **—** Gk.) L. *sarcophagus*, a stone tomb; made of a lime-stone which was supposed to consume the corpse (Pliny). **—** Gk. σαρκοφάγος, flesh-consuming; hence lime-stone. **—** Gk. σαρκο-, crude form of σάρξ, flesh; φαγεῖν, to eat.

Sarcenet; see **Saracen**.

Sardine (1), small fish. (F.–L.–Gk.) F. *sardine*.–L. *sardina, sarda*.–Gk. σαρδίνη, σάρδα, a kind of fish; perhaps named from Σάρδω, Sardinia.

Sardine (2), a gem. (L.–Gk.) L. *sardinus* *, equivalent to Gk. σαρδίνος, Rev. iv. 3. Named from *Sardis*, in Asia Minor (Pliny).

sardonyx, a gem. (L.–Gk.) L. *sardonyx*.–Gk. σαρδόνυξ, i e. Sardian onyx. –Gk. σαρδ-, for Σάρδεις, Sardis; ὄνυξ, onyx. See **Onyx**.

Sardonic, sneering. (F.–L.–Gk.) F. *sardonique*, usually *sardonien*, in phrase *ris sardonien*, 'a forced or carelesse mirth;' Cot.–L. *Sardonicus*, usually *Sardonius*.–Gk. σαρδόνιος, said to be derived from σαρδόνιον, a plant of Sardinia (Σάρδω), which was said to screw up the face of the eater; Virgil, Ecl. vii. 41. See **Sardine** (1).

Sarsaparilla. (Span.) Span. *zarzaparilla*, a plant. Span. *zarza* means 'bramble,' probably from Basque *sartzia*, a bramble; *parilla* or *parrilla* is properly a dimin. of *parra*, a trained vine.

Sarsnet; see **Saracen**.

Sash (1), a frame for glass; see **Capacious**.

Sash (2), a scarf, girdle. (Pers.) Formerly *shash*. Pers. *shast*, of which one meaning is 'a girdle worn by the fire-worshippers;' also spelt *shest*.

Sassafras; see **Saxifrage**.

Satan. (Heb.) Heb. *sátán*, an enemy. –Heb. root *sátan*, to persecute.

Satchel; see **Sack**.

Sate, Satiate. (L.) *Sate* is from *sated*, used as a short form of *satiate* in the sense of 'satisfied.' (Suggested by L. *sat* for *satis*; *satur*, full.)–L. *satiatus*, pp. of *satiare*, to sate, fill full.–L. *sat, satis*, sufficient; *satur*, full. Allied to **Sad**. Der. *satiety*, F. *satieté*, from L. acc. *satietatem*, fulness.

assets, effects of a deceased debtor. (F. –L.) F. *assez* (pron. *assets* in O. F.), sufficient (to pay with).–L. *ad satis*, up to what is enough.

satire (F.–L.) F. *satire*.–L. *satira, satura*, a species of poetry; orig. 'a medley.' Derived from *satura lanx*, a full dish, dish full of mixed ingredients; where *satura* is fem. of *satur*, full.

satisfy. (F.–L.) O. F. *satisfier* (later *satisfaire*). Formed as if from Low L. *satis-*

ficare *, substituted for L. *satisfacere*, lit. ' to make enough.'–L. *satis*, enough; *facere*, to make. Der. *satisfact-ion*, from pp. *satisfactus*.

saturate. (L.) From pp. of L. *saturare*, to fill full.–L. *satur*, full.

soil (3), to feed cattle with green grass, to fatten with feeding. (F.–L.) O. F. *saoler*, later *saouler*, to glut, satiate (F. *soûler*).–O. F. *saol*, full, cloyed.–L. *satullus*, filled with food.–L. *satur*, full.

Satellite. (F.–L.) F. *satellite*, 'a sergeant, catchpole;' Cot.–L. *satellitem*, acc. of *satelles*, an attendant.

Satin. (F.–L.) F. *satin*. (Ital. *setino*, Port. *setim*.)–Low L. *satinus, setinus*, satin.–Low L. *seta*, silk; L. *seta*, a bristle, a hair.

seton, an artificial irritation under the skin. (F.–L.) F. *séton*, in use in the 16th century; the orig. sense is 'a thread.' Formed (as if from Low L. *seto* *), from L. *seta*, a bristle, stiff hair.

Satire, Satisfy; see **Sate**.

Satrap, a Persian viceroy. (F.–L.–Gk.–Pers.) F. *satrape*.–L. *satrapam*, acc. of *satrapes*.–Gk. σατράπης.–Zend (Ο Pers.) *shôithra-paiti*, ruler of a region.– Zend. *shôithra*, a region; *paiti*, chief. Cf Skt. *kshetra*, a field, region; *pati*, a lord.

Saturate; see **Sate**.

Saturnine. (F.–L.) O. F. *saturnin* (usually *Saturnien*), under the influence of the malign planet Saturn; hence, melancholy.–L. *Saturnus*, Saturn; lit. 'the sower;' from *satum*, supine of *serere*, to sow. See **Season**.

saturday. (L. and E.) A.S. *Sæterdæg*, also *Sætern-dæg*, i. e. Saturn's day.– L. *Saturnus*, Saturn; A.S. *dæg*, a day.

Satyr. (F.–L.–Gk.) F. *satyre*.–L. *satyrus*.–Gk. σάτυρος, a satyr, a sylvan god.

Sauce, Saucer, Saucy; see **Salt**.

Saunter. (F. ?) Origin unknown.

Saurian, one of the lizard tribe. (Gk.) From Gk. σαύρα, σαῦρος, a lizard.

Sausage; see **Salt**.

Sauterne, a wine. (F.) From *Sauterne* in France, department of Gironde.

Savage; see **Silvan**.

Savanna, a meadow-plain. (Span.–L.–Gk.) Span. *sabana* (with *b* as *v*), a sheet for a bed, large cloth, large plain (from the appearance of a plain covered with snow).–L. *sabanum*, a linen cloth.– Gk. σάβανον, a linen cloth, towel.

Save; see **Salvation**.

Saveloy; see **Cerebral**.

Savin, Savine, Sabine, a shrub. (L.) L. *sabina*; orig. *Sabina herba*, a Sabine herb. The *Sabines* were a people of central Italy.

Savour; see **Sapid**.

Savoy, a kind of cabbage. (F.) Brought from the dukedom of *Savoy*.

Saw (1), a cutting instrument. (E.) M.E. *sawe*. A.S. *saga*, lit. a cutter; from Teut. base SAG = √ SAK, to cut. + Du. *zaag*, Icel. *sög*, Dan. *sav*, Swed. *såg*, G. *säge*. See **Secant**. Der. *see-saw*, a reduplicated form.

Saw (2), a saying; see **Say**.

Saxifrage, a plant. (F. – L.) F. *saxifrage*. – L. *saxifraga*, spleen-wort; so named because it was supposed to break stones in the bladder. – L. *saxi-*, for *saxum*, a stone; *frag-*, base of *frangere*, to break.

sassafras, a kind of laurel. (F. – Span. – L.) F. *sassafras*. – Span. *sasafras*, from O. Span. *sassafragia*, the herb saxifrage; sassafras was so named from being supposed to possess the like virtue. – L. *saxifraga* (above).

Say (1), to speak. (E.) M.E. *seggen*. A.S. *secgan*, pt. t. *sægde*, pp. *gesægd*. + Du. *zeggen*, Icel. *segja*, Dan. *sige*, Swed. *säga*, G. *sagen*, O.H.G. *sekjan*. Cf. Lithuan. *sakyti*, to say.

saga, a tale. (Scand.) Icel. *saga*, a tale; cf. Icel. *segja*, to say (above).

saw (2), a saying. (E.) M.E. *sawe*. A.S. *sagu*, a saying; cf. A.S. *secgan*, to say.

Say (2), a kind of serge. (F. – L. – Gk.) O.F. *saie*, say. (Cf. Span. *saya*, *sayo*, a tunic; *sayete*, a thin stuff.) So called because used for making a kind of coat called in Latin *saga*, *sagum*, or *sagus*; Low L. *sagum*, (1) a mantle, (2) a kind of cloth. – Gk. σάγος, a soldier's mantle; so called from hanging down. Cf. Skt. *sajj*, *sañj*, to adhere, hang down from.

Say (3), to essay; short for *assay* or *essay*; see **Essay**.

Scab. (E.) A.S. *scæb*, *sceb*, scab, itch. + Dan. Swed. *skab*, G. *schabe*. Lit. 'something that is scratched;' cf. L. *scabere*, to scratch, *scabies*, itch. See **Shave**.

shabby, mean. (E.) Also *shabbed*; *shabby* and *shabbed* are the same as *scabby* and *scabbed*. For the sense, cf. *scurvy* (= *scurfy*).

Scabbard. (F. – Teut.) M.E. *scaubert*,

scauberk, *scaberke*, a scabbard; answering to an O.F. *escauberc**, not found. The F. form is made up of O.F. *escale*, a scale, husk, case; and *-berc*, a protection, as in O.F. *hau-berc*, *hal-berc*, a hauberk. – O.H.G. *scala*, a scale, husk, case; *bergan*, to hide, protect. Thus *scabbard* = *scauberk* = *scale-berk*, with the reduplicated sense of 'cover-cover,' or protecting case. See **Scale** (1) and **Hauberk**.

Scaffold; see **Capacious**.

Scald (1), to burn; see **Caldron**.

Scald (2), scabby; see **Skill**.

Scald (3), a poet; see **Scold**.

Scale (1), shell, husk, flake; see **Skill**.

Scale (2), a bowl or dish of a balance; see **Skill**.

Scale (3), a ladder, gradation; see **Scan**.

Scalene. (L. – Gk.) L. *scalenus*, adj. – Gk. σκαληνός, scalene, uneven. Allied to σκελλός, crook-legged, halting; cf. σκαίρειν, to skip.

Scall, a scab; see **Skill**.

Scallop, Scalp; see **Skill**.

Scalpel, a small sharp knife. (L.) L. *scalpellum*, dimin. of *scalprum*, a knife. – L. *scalpere*, to cut. (√ SKARP.)

Scammony, a cathartic gum-resin. (F. – L. – Gk.) O.F. *scammonie*. – L. *scammonia*. – Gk. σκαμμωνία, σκαμωνία, scammony, a kind of bind-weed.

Scamp, Scamper; see **Camp**.

Scan. (L.) Short for *scand*; the *d* was prob. mistaken for the pp. suffix *-ed*. – L. *scandere*, to climb; also, to scan a verse. + Skt. *skand*, to spring up. (√ SKAND.)

ascend. (L.) L. *ascendere*, to climb up. – L. *ad*, to; *scandere*, to climb. Der. *ascens-ion*, from pp. *ascensus*.

condescend. (F. – L.) F. *condescendre*. – Low L. *condescendere*, to grant (lit. to descend with). – L. *con-* (*cum*), with; *descendere* (below). Der. *condescens-ion*.

descend. (F. – L.) F. *descendre*; Cot. – L. *descendere*, lit. to climb down. – L. *de*, down; *scandere*. Der. *descent*, from O.F. *descente*, a sudden fall, verbal sb. from *descendre*.

escalade, a scaling of walls. (F. – Span. – L.) F. *escalade*. – Span. *escalado*, *escalada*, a scaling; from *escalar*, to scale. – Span. *escala*, a ladder. – L. *scala*; see scale below.

scale (3), a ladder, gradation. (L.) L. *scala*, a ladder. L. *scā-la* = *scad-la**; from *scad-*, base of *scandere*, to climb.

scandal. (F. – L. – Gk.) F. *scandale.* – L. *scandalum.* – Gk. σκάνδαλον, a snare ; also a scandal, offence, stumbling-block. Orig. the spring of a trap, the stick which sprang up when the trap was shut, and on which the bait was placed ; usually called σκανδάληθρον. – √SKAND, to spring up.

scansion. (L.) From L. *scansio,* a scanning. – L. *scansus,* pp. of *scandere.*

slander, scandal. (F. – L. – Gk.) M. E. *sclandre, sclaundre.* – O. F. *esclandre,* scandal. The oldest O. F. form was *scandele,* whence *escandle, escandre,* and finally *esclandre,* with inserted *l.* It is merely another form of *scandal* (above).

transcend. (L.) L. *transcendere,* to climb over, to surpass. – L. *tran-,* for *trans,* beyond ; *scandere,* to climb.

Scandal, Scansion ; see **Scan.**

Scant, adj. (Scand.) M. E. *skant,* insufficient. – Icel. *skamt,* neut. of *skammr,* short, brief ; whence *skamta,* to dole out (hence to scant or stint) ; Icel. *skamtr,* a dole. In Norwegian, *nt* appears for *mt,* as in *skant,* a dole, *skanta,* to measure closely. **Der.** *scant-y.*

Scantling ; see **Cant** (2).

Scapegoat ; see **Cape** (1).

Scapular, belonging to the shoulder-blades. (L.) Low L. *scapularis,* adj., from *scapulæ,* pl. shoulder-blades. Prob. allied to *scapus,* a shaft, stem, stalk. **Der.** *scapular-y,* a kind of scarf, F. *scapulaire,* Low L. *scapulare.*

Scar (1). mark of a wound. (F. – L. – Gk.) O. F. *escare.* – L. *eschara,* a scar, esp. of a burn. – Gk. ἐσχάρα, a hearth, fire-place, scar of a burn.

Scar (2), **Scaur,** a rock ; see **Shear.**

Scaramouch ; see **Skirmish.**

Scarce ; see **Excerpt.**

Scare ; see **Shear.**

Scarf (1), a light piece of dress thrown over the shoulders ; see **Sharp.**

Scarf (2), to join pieces of timber ; see **Sharp.**

Scarify ; see **Shear.**

Scarlet. (F. – Pers.) O. F. *escarlate,* scarlet. (Span. *escarlata,* Ital. *scarlatto.*) – Pers. *saqalât, siqalât, suqlât,* scarlet cloth. Orig. the name of a stuff, which was often of a scarlet colour. ¶ Hence Pers. *saqlatûn,* scarlet cloth, whence M. E. *ciclatoun* (Chaucer). The Turkish *iskerlat,* scarlet, is merely borrowed from Ital. *scarlatto* (Zenker).

Scarp ; see **Sharp.**

Scathe, to harm. (E.) A.S. *sceaðan,* pt. t. *scôd,* + Icel. *skaða,* Swed. *skada,* Dan. *skade,* G. Du. *schaden,* Goth. *gaskathjan* (pt. t. *gaskoth*). Allied to Skt. *kshata,* wounded, pp. of *kshan,* to wound ; *kshati,* hurting. (√ SKA.) **Der.** *scathe,* sb., A. S. *sceaða.*

Scatter. (E.) M. E. *scateren.* A. S. *scateran.* + Gk. σκεδ-άννυμι, I sprinkle, σκέδ-ασις, a scattering ; Skt. *kshad,* to cut. (√SKA.)

shatter. (E.) M. E. *schateren,* to scatter, to dash as a falling stream ; hence to break in pieces. A. S. *scateran* (above).

Scavenger ; see **Show.**

Scene. (L. – Gk.) L. *scena, scæna* (whence also F. *scene*). – Gk. σκηνή, a sheltered place, tent, stage, scene. Allied to **Shade.** (√SKA.)

proscenium, the front part of a stage. (L. – Gk.) L. *proscenium.* – Gk. προσκήνιον, the place before the stage (or scene). – Gk. πρό, before ; σκηνή, a scene.

Scent ; see **Sense.**

Sceptic ; see **Species.**

Sceptre. (F. – L. – Gk.) F. *sceptre.* – L. *sceptrum.* – Gk. σκῆπτρον, a staff to lean on, a sceptre. – Gk. σκήπτειν, to prop ; also to hurl. + Skt. *kshap,* to throw. (√SKAP.)

Schedule ; see **Schism.**

Scheme. (L. – Gk.) Formerly *schema.* – L. *schema.* – Gk. σχῆμα, form, appearance, also used as a term in rhetoric. – Gk. σχή-σω, fut. of ἔχ-ειν, to hold, have (base σεχ-). Cf. Skt. *sah,* to bear. (√ SAGH.)

Schism. (F. – L. – Gk.) F. *schisme.* – L. *schisma.* – Gk. σχίσμα, a rent, split, schism. – Gk. σχίζειν (base σχιδ-), to cleave. + L. *scindere,* Skt. *chhid,* to cut. (√SKID.)

schedule. (F. – L. ; *or* F. – L. – Gk.) Formerly *scedule.* – O. F. *schedule, cedule,* 'a schedule, scroll ;' Cot. – L. *schedula,* a small leaf of paper ; dimin. of *scheda* (or *scida*), a strip of papyrus-bark. Either from L. *scid-,* base of *scindere,* to cut ; or borrowed from Gk. σχίδη, a cleft piece of wood, from σχίζειν, to cleave.

schist, slate-rock. (Gk.) Gk. σχίστος, easily cleft. – Gk. σχίζειν, to cleave.

squill. (F. – L. – Gk.) F. *squille,* 'squill, sea-onion ;' Cot. – L. *squilla, scilla.* – Gk. σκίλλα, a squill ; also σχῖνος. Put for σκιδ-λα*, from easily splitting into scales. – Gk. σχίζειν, to split.

School. (L.–Gk.) M. E. *scole*. A. S. *scólu* (with lengthened *o*). – L. *schola*. – Gk. σχολή, rest, leisure, employment of leisure time, also a school. Orig. ' a pause ; ' from the base σχο- =σχα-, base of ἔχειν, to hold ; see **Scheme.** (√SAGH.) Der. *schol-ar*, A. S. *scólere* ; *scholi-ast*, from Gk. σχολιαστής, a commentator.

shoal (1), a multitude of fishes, a troop, crowd. (L.) Spelt *shole* in Spenser ; M. E. *scole*, a school, hence, a troop, throng, crowd ; see above. ¶ The sailor's phrase ' a *school* of fish ' exhibits the same word ; it also appears as *scull*, Troil. v. 5. 22.

Schooner ; see **Shun.**

Sciatic, pertaining to the hip-joint. (F. – L. – Gk.) F. *sciatique*, adj. – L. *sciaticus*, corruption of L. *ischiadicus*, subject to gout in the hips. – Gk. ἰσχιαδικός, subject to pains in the loins. – Gk. ἰσχιαδ-, stem of ἰσχιάς, pain in the loins. – Gk. ἰσχίον, the socket in which the thigh-bone turns. Der. *sciatic-a*, fem. of L. adj. *sciaticus*.

Science. (F. – L.) F. *science*. – L. *scientia*, knowledge. – L. *scient-*, stem of pres. pt. of *scire*, to know, orig. to discern. Allied to **Skill.**

ascititious, incidental. (L.) Coined, as if from L. *ascititius**, from *ascitus*, pp. of *asciscere*, or *adsciscere*, to receive, learn. – L. *ad*, to ; *sciscere*, to learn, inceptive form of *scire*, to know.

conscience. (F. – L.) F. *conscience*. – L. *conscientia*, consciousness. – L. *con-* (for *cum*), with ; *scientia*, knowledge ; see science above. Der. *conscionable*, an ill-contrived word, used as a contraction of *conscience-able*, or instead of *conscible**, which would have been the proper formation from *conscire*.

conscious. (L.) For L. *conscius*, aware. – L. *conscire*, to be aware of.

prescience. (F. – L.) O. F. *prescience*. – L. *præ-scientia*, foreknowledge.

sciolist. (L.) Formed, with suffix -*ist*, from L. *sciol-us*, a smatterer. – L. *sci-re*, to know.

Scimetar, Cimetar. (F. *or* Ital. – Pers. ?) F. *cimeterre*, ' a scymitar ; ' Cot. Cf. Ital. *scimitarra*, ' a simitar,' Florio. Prob. from Pers. *shimshír*, *shamshír*, ' a cimeter,' Rich. Dict. p. 909. Lit. lion's claw. – Pers. *sham*, nail, claw ; *shér*, lion.

Scintillation. (F. – L.) F. *scintillation*. – L. acc. *scintillationem*, a sparkling. – L. *scintillare*, to sparkle. – L. *scintilla*, a spark.

stencil, to paint in figures by help of a

pierced plate. (F. – L.) Prob. from O. F. *estinceller*, to sparkle, also to cover with stars. – O. F. *estincelle*, a spark. – L. *scintilla*, a spark.

tinsel, gaudy ornament. (F. – L.) From O. F. *estincelle*, a spark, a star-like ornament ; see above.

Sciolist ; see **Science.**

Scion ; see **Secant.**

Scirrhous, pertaining to a hard swelling. (L. – Gk.) From L. *scirrhus*, sb. a late form. used for *scirrhoma*, a hard swelling. – Gk. σκίρρος, σκῖρος, σκίρρωμα, a hard swelling. – Gk. σκιρός, hard.

Scissors. (F. – L.) Falsely spelt, and not from *scindere*, to cut. M. E. *sisoures, cisoures*. – O. F. *cisoires*, shears ; used instead of *ciseaux*, ' sizars,' Cot. The latter is the pl. of O. F. *cisel*, chisel ; see **Chisel.** Both words are due to L. *cædere*, to cut ; see **Cæsura.** ¶ No doubt the word was confused with L. *scissor*, which properly means ' a tailor,' from L. *scindere*, to cut.

Scoff. (O. Low G.) M. E. *skof*. – O. Fries. *schof*, a scoff. ✛ Icel. *skaup, skop*, mockery. Cf. O. Du. *schoppen, schobben*, to scoff, Icel. *skopa*, to scoff. The orig. sense was prob. ' a rub ' or ' a shove ; ' see **Shove.**

Scold. (O. Low G.) M. E. *scolden*. Formed from Du. *schold*, pt. t. of *scheldan*, to scold. Cf. G. *schelten*, to scold. Allied to Icel. *skjalla*, (pt. t. *skal*, pp. *skollinn*), G. *schallen*, Swed. *skalla*, to resound.

scald (3), a poet. (Scand.) Icel. *skáld*, a poet ; orig. ' loud talker ' or ' declaimer.' – Icel. *skjalla*, to resound (pt. t. *skal*).

Scollop ; see **Skill.**

Sconce, (1) and (2) ; see **Abscond.**

Scoop. (Scand.) M. E. *scope*, sb. – Swed. *skopa*, a scoop. ✛ O. Du. *schoepe, schuppe*, a scoop, shovel ; Dan. *skuffe*, G. *schüppe*, a shovel. Cf. Gk. σκύφος, a cup, σκάφος, a hollow vessel, from σκάπτειν, to dig.

Scope. (Ital. – Gk.) Ital. *scopo*, a mark to shoot at, scope ; Florio. – Gk. σκοπός, a mark, a watcher ; allied to Gk. σκέπτομαι, I see, spy, which is cognate with L. *specere* ; see **Species.**

bishop. (L. – Gk.) A. S. *bisceop*. – L. *episcopus*. – Gk. ἐπίσκοπος, a bishop ; lit. ' overseer.' – Gk. ἐπί, upon ; σκοπός, one that watches ; see above. Der. *bishop-ric* ; where *ric* = A. S. *ríce*, dominion, allied to **Rich.**

episcopal. (F. — L. — Gk.)   O. F. *episcopal.* — L. *episcopalis*, adj., from *episcopus* (above).

Scorbutic, afflicted with scurvy. (Low L. — Low G.)   From Low L. *scorbutus*, scurvy; Latinised from Low G. *schorbock*, *schärbuuk*, scurvy; O. Du. *scheurbuyck*, scurvy. The name is due to some confusion, as the lit. sense of O. Du. *scheurbuyck* is 'rupture of the belly,' from *scheuren*, to tear, and *buyck* (mod. Du. *buik*), the belly.

Scorch. (F. — L.)   O. F. *escorcher*, *escorcer*, lit. to flay (Ital. *scorticare*). — L. *ex*, off; *cortic-*, stem of *cortex*, bark, rind, husk. ¶ Or (Scand.) — Norweg. *skrekka*, to shrink.

Score; see **Shear**.

Scoria, slag. (L. — Gk.)   L. *scoria*. — Gk. σκωρία, dross, scum. — Gk. σκῶρ, dung, ordure. ╋A. S. *sceurn*, dung.

Scorn. (F. — O. H. G.)   M. E. *scorn*. — O. F. *escarn*, derision. — O. H. G. *skern*, mockery, scurrility.

Scorpion. (F. — L. — Gk.)   F. *scorpion*. — L. *scorpionem*, acc. of *scorpio*, the same as *scorpius*. — Gk. σκορπίος, a scorpion, also a prickly sea-fish. (√SKARP.)   See **Sharp**.

Scotch, to cut with narrow incisions. (Scand.)   *Scotch*, sb., is a slight cut, such as was inflicted by a *scutcher* or riding-whip; see Cotgrave, s. v. *verge*. From prov. E. *scutch*, to beat slightly, dress flax. — Norweg. *skoka*, *skuku*, a swingle for beating flax; allied to Swed. *skäkta*, to beat flax.

Scot-free; see **Shoot**.

Scoundrel. (E.)   Lit. 'a loathsome fellow;' and put for *scunner-el*, where -*el* is an agential suffix. From Lowl. Scotch *scunner*, *sconner*, to loathe, also (formerly) to shrink through fear, act as a coward; so that *scunner-el* = one who shrinks, a coward. See Barbour, Bruce, xvii. 651. The verb *scunner* is the frequentative of A. S. *scun-ian*, to shun; see **Shun**.

Scour; see **Cure**.

Scourge; see **Cuirass**.

Scout (1), a spy; see **Audience**.

Scout (2), to ridicule an idea. (Scand.) Allied to Lowl. Scotch *scout*, to pour out a liquid forcibly, to *shoot* it out. — Icel. *skúta*, *skúti*, a taunt; cf. *skot-yrði*, scoffs. — Icel. *skut-*, stem of pt. t. pl. of *skjóta*, to shoot. Cf. Swed. *skjuta*, (1) to shoot, (2) to shove; *skjuta skulden på*, to thrust the blame on; Dan. *skyde*, to shoot, thrust (blame on), repel. See **Shoot**.

Scowl. (Scand.)   M. E. *scoulen*. — Dan. *skule*, to scowl, cast down the eyes; allied to Low G. *schulen*, to hide oneself, prov. G. *schulen*, to hide the eyes, look slily, peep. Allied to Dan. *skiul*, shelter, Icel. *skjól*, shelter, cover. See **Sheal**.

sculk. (Scand.)   M. E. *skulken*. — Dan. *skulke*, to sculk, slink; Swed. *skolka*, to play the truant. Allied to Icel. *skolla*, to sculk, keep aloof, and *skjól*, shelter, cover (above).

Scrabble; see **Sharp**.

Scraggy; see **Shrink**.

Scramble, Scrap, Scrape; see **Sharp**.

Scratch. (Scand.)   Due to the confusion of M. E. *skratten*, to scratch, with M. E. *cracchen*, to scratch. β. M. E. *skratten* stands for *skarten**, an extended form from Icel. *sker-a*, to shear, cut, and means 'to cut slightly,' to scrape. The word *scrape* is a similar formation from the same root SKAR, to cut; see **Shear**. γ. M. E. *cracchen* stands for *kratsen**. — Swed. *kratsa*, to scrape, *krats*, a scraper. — Swed. *kratta*, to rake, scrape; from a base KART, an extension of √KAR, to cut. δ. The roots SKAR and KAR are identical; cf Gk. κείρειν, to shear, A. S. *sceran*; see **Shear**. And see **Grate** (2).

Scrawl. (E.)   A contraction of *scrabble*, to write carelessly, which see under **Sharp**. ¶ Confused with M. E. *scraulen*, to crawl, a form of *crawl* with prefix *s* (= O. F. *es-* = L. *ex*) used with an intensive force.

Scream. (Scand.)   M. E. *scremen*. — Icel. *skræma*, Swed. *skräma*, Dan. *skramme*, to scare; orig. to cry aloud. Cf. Swed. *skrän*, a scream. Allied to **Screech** and **Shriek**.

Screech. (Scand.)   M. E. *scriken*. — Icel. *skrækja*, to shriek, Swed. *skrika*, to shriek; Dan. *skrige*, ╋ Gael. *sgreach*, to shriek; W. *ysgrechio*, to scream.

shriek. (Scand.)   Another form of *screech*; from M. E. *scriken* (above).

shrike, the butcher-bird. (Scand.) Icel. *skríkja*, a shrike, lit. 'shricker.' — Icel. *skríkja*, to titter, orig. to shriek, and allied to Icel. *skrækja* (above).

Screen. (F. — Teut.)   M. E. *scren*. — O. F. *escran*, 'a skreen,' Cot. (Mod. F. *écran*.)   Derived by Diez from G. *schragen*, a trestle, stack of wood; cf. also G. *schranne*, a railing, *schranke*, a barrier. β. In the sense of 'coarse sieve,' it is the same word; so called because it *screens* (or wards off) the coarser particles, and prevents them from coming through.

Screw (1). (F. − L. *or* Teut. ?) Formerly *scrue.* − O. F. *escroue,* 'a scrue;' Cot. (F. *écrou.*) Origin doubtful; Diez derives it from L. *scrobem,* acc. of *scrobs,* a ditch, also a hole. Or perhaps from Du. *schroef,* Icel. *skrúfa,* Swed. *skruf,* Dan. *skrue,* a screw, which appear to be from √SKRU, to cut. Cf. G. *schraube,* a screw.

Screw (2), a vicious horse. (E.) The same word as *shrew,* q. v.

Scribble; see **Scribe**.

Scribe. (L.) L. *scriba,* a writer. − L. *scribere,* to write, orig. to scratch or cut slightly. (√SKARBH.)

ascribe. (L.) L. *ascribere,* to write down to one's account. − L. *a-,* for *ad,* to; *scribere,* to write.

circumscribe. (L.) L. *circum-scribere,* to write or draw around, to limit.

conscript. (L.) L. *conscriptus,* enrolled; pp. of *con-scribere,* to write down together.

describe. (L.) L. *de-scribere,* to write down, describe fully; pp. *descriptus* (whence *description*).

descry. (F. − L.) M. E. *descryen,* to discern. − O. F. *descrire,* short form of O. F. *descrivre,* to describe. − L. *describere* (above).

inscribe. (L.) L. *in-scribere,* to write in or upon; pp. *inscriptus* (whence *inscription*).

postscript. (L.) L. *postscriptum,* that which is written after. − L. *post,* after; *scriptum,* neut. of pp. of *scribere,* to write.

prescribe. (L.) L. *præ-scribere,* to write beforehand, prescribe; pp. *præscriptus* (whence *prescription*).

proscribe. (L.) L. *pro-scribere,* lit. to write publicly; pp. *proscriptus* (whence *proscription*).

rescript. (F. − L.) O. F. *rescript,* a reply in writing. − L. *rescriptum,* neut. of pp. of *re-scribere,* to write back.

scribble. (L.; *with* E. *suffix.*) Formed from *scribe* with frequent. suffix *-le*; the suffix giving it a verbal force.

scrip (2), a piece of writing; the same word as *script* (below).

script. (F. − L.) O. F. *escript,* 'a writing.' − L. *scriptum,* neut. of pp. of *scribere,* to write.

scripture. (F. − L.) M. E. *scripture,* a writing. − O. F. *escripture.* − L. *scriptura,* a writing. − L. *scriptus,* pp. of *scribere,* to write.

scrivener. (F. − L.) Formerly a *scriven*; the suffix *-er,* of the agent, is an E. addition. M. E. *scriuein.* − O. F. *escrivain.* − Low L. *scribanum,* acc. of *scribanus,* a notary. − L. *scribere,* to write.

subscribe. (L.) L. *sub-scribere,* to write (one's name) under; pp. *subscriptus* (whence *subscription*).

superscription. (F. − L.) F. *superscription*; Cot. − L. acc. *superscriptionem.* − L. *superscriptus,* pp. of *super-scribere,* to write above or over.

transcribe. (L.) L. *transcribere,* to copy out from one book into another. − L. *trans,* across, over; *scribere,* to write. Der. *transcript,* from neut. of pp. *transcriptus*; also *transcript-ion.*

Scrimmage; see **Skirmish**.

Scrip (1), a small bag; see **Sharp**.

Scrip (2), **Script, Scripture, Scrivener**; see **Scribe**.

Scrofula. (L.) L. *scrofula,* a little pig; whence the pl. *scrofulæ,* used in the sense of scrofulous swellings; perhaps from the swollen appearance of the glands. Dimin. of *scrofa,* a breeding sow, lit. a digger; from the habit of swine; cf. L. *scrobs,* a ditch. (√SKARBH.)

Scroll; see **Shroud**.

Scrub; see **Shrub** (1).

Scruple. (F. − L.) F. *scrupule,* 'a little sharp stone .. in a mans shooe,' Cot.; hence a hindrance, perplexity, doubt, also a small weight. − L. *scrupulum,* acc. of *scrupulus,* a sharp stone, dimin. of *scrupus* (the same). From √SKRU, allied to √SKAR, to cut.

Scrutiny. (L.) L. *scrutinium,* a careful enquiry. − L. *scrutari,* to search into carefully, as if among broken pieces. − L. *scruta,* s. pl., broken pieces.

inscrutable, that cannot be scrutinised. (F. − L.) F. *inscrutable.* − L. *inscrutabilis.* − L. *in,* not; *scrutari,* to scrutinise.

Scud; see **Shoot**.

Scuffle; see **Shove**.

Sculk; see **Scowl**.

Scull (1), the cranium; see **Skill**.

Scull (2), a light oar; see **Skill**.

Scull (3), a shoal of fish; see **School**.

Scullery; see **Swill**.

Scullion, a kitchen menial. (F. − L.) Not allied to *scullery* (except in popular use). The true sense is a dish-clout, a name transferred to the maid who used it; just as *mawkin* meant both 'maid' and 'dish-clout.' − O. F. *escouillon,* 'a dish-clout, a maukin ;' Cot. The same word as Span. *escobillon*, a sponge for cannon, formed from *escobilla*, dimin. of *escoba*, a brush, broom. —L. *scopa*, used in pl. *scopæ*, a broom or brush made of small twigs.

Sculpture. (F.—L.) F. *sculpture.*—L. *sculptura*, sculpture, lit. a cutting. — L. *sculptus*, pp. of *sculpere*, to cut, carve ; allied to *scalpere*, to cut. (√ SKARP.)

Scum. (Scand.) Dan. *skum*, froth ; Swed. *skum*, froth. + G. *schaum* (as in *meer-schaum*). (√ SKU, to cover.)

skim, to take off scum. (Scand.) Dan. *skumme*, Swed. *skumma*, to skim ; from *skum*, scum. The E. verb preserves the true vowel-change ; cf. *fill* from *full*.

Scupper. (F.) So named because the water seems to be spit forth from it. —O.F. *escopir*, *escupir*, to spit out ; so also Span. and Prov. *escupir*. Apparently from Du. *schoppen*, to scoop away, *schup*, a scoop, shovel. (Yet the Du. name is *spiegat*, lit. 'spit-hole.' Perhaps O.F. *escopir* = L. *ex-spuere*.)

Scurf. (E.) A.S. *scurf*, scurf, *sceorfa*, scurf, scab. — A. S. *scurf-*, stem of pp. of *sceorfan*, to scrape. Allied to Sculptura. Cf. Swed. *skorf*, Dan. *skurw*, G. *schorf*, scurf.

scurvy, adj. (E.) The same word as *scurf-y*, afflicted with scurf, scabby. Hence as sb., the name of a disease.

Scurrile, buffoon-like. (L.) L. *scurrilis*, adj., from *scurra*, a buffoon.

Scurvy ; see Scurf.

Scutch ; see Scotch.

Scutcheon ; see Escutcheon.

Scutiform. (F.—L.) O. F. *scutiforme*, shaped like a shield. —L. *scuti-*, put for crude form of *scutum*, shield ; *forma*, form.

Scuttle (1), a shallow basket or vessel. (L.) A.S. *scutel*, a vessel. —L. *scutella*, a small tray, dimin. of *scutra*, a tray. Prob. allied to *scutum*, a shield, cover.

skillet, a small pot. (F. — L.) Formerly *skellet*. — O. F. *escuellette*, 'a little dish ;' Cot. Dimin. of O. F. *escuelle*, a dish. — L. *scutella* (above).

Scuttle (2), an opening in a ship's hatchway ; see Shoot.

Scuttle (3), to hurry along ; see Shoot.

Scythe. (E.) M.E. *sithe*. A.S. *síðe* ; oldest form *sigðe*. Lit. 'cutter ;' from √ SAK, to cut. + Du. *zeis* ; Icel. *sigðr*, *sigð* ; Low G. *seged*, *segd* ; O. H. G. *segensa*, G. *sense*.

Se-, away, apart. (L.) L. *se-*, prefix ; full form *sed*, without.

Sea. (E.) M.E. *see*. A.S. *sǽ*, sea, lake. + Du. *zee* ; Icel. *sær* ; Dan. *sö* ; Swed. *sjö* ; G. *see* ; Goth. *saiws*.

Seal (1), a stamp ; see Sign.

Seal (2), a sea-calf. (E.) M. E. *sele*. A.S. *seolh*. + Icel. *selr* ; Dan. *sæl* ; Swed. *själ*.

Seam, Seamstress ; see Sew.

Sear, Sere, withered. (E.) M.E. *sere*, A.S. *seár*, dry ; *seárian*, to dry up. + O. Du. *sore*, Du. *zoor*, Low G. *soor*. (√ SUS.)

sorrel (2), of a reddish-brown colour. (F. — Teut.) A dimin. form from O. F. *sor*, F. *saur*, sorrel of colour. —Low G. *soor*, sear, dried up, withered (as above).

Search ; see Circle. Der. *re-search*.

Season. (F.—L.) M. E. *seson*. —O. F. *seson*, *seison*, *saison*. (Cf. Span. *sazon*, O. Prov. *sadons*, *sasos*, Bartsch.) — Low L. *sationem*, acc. of *satio*, sowing-time, i. e. spring, regarded as the chief season for preparing crops. —L. *satus*, pp. of *serere*, to sow. ¶ The Span. word is *estacion*, Ital. *stagione* ; from acc. of L. *statio*, a station, hence a stage (period).

Seat ; see Sit.

Secant, a line that cuts another, or that cuts a circle. (L.) From *secant-*, stem of pres. pt. of *secare*, to cut. (√ SAK.)

bisect. (L.) From L. *bi-*, short for *bis*, twice ; and *sect-um*, supine of *secare*, to cut.

dissect. (L.) L. *dissectus*, pp. of *dissecare*, to cut asunder.

insect. (F. — L.) F. *insecte*. —L. *insectum*, lit. 'a thing cut into,' i. e. nearly divided, from the shape. —L. *insectus*, pp. of *in-secare*, to cut into.

intersect. (L.) L. *intersectus*, pp. of *inter-secare*, to cut between or apart.

scion. (F.—L.) M.E. *sioun*. —O.F. *cion*, F. *scion*, 'a scion, shoot ;' Cot. Orig. 'a cutting.' —O.F. *sier*, F. *scier*, to cut. — L. *secare*, to cut.

section. (F. — L.) F. *section*. — L. *sectionem*, acc. of *sectio*, a cutting. — L. *sectus*, pp. of *secare*, to cut.

segment. (L.) L. *segmentum*, a piece cut off ; put for *sec-mentum**. —L. *secare*, to cut.

sickle. (L.) A.S. *sicol*. — L. *secula*, a sickle, cutter. —L. *sec-are*, to cut.

trisect. (L.) Coined from L. *tri-*, in three parts ; and *sect-um*, supine of *secare*, to cut.

Secede ; see Cede.

Seclude; see Clause.

Second; see Sequence.

Sacret, Secretary; see Concern.

Sect; see Sequence.

Section; see Secant.

Secular. (F.—L.) M. E. *seculere.*—O.F. *seculier*, 'secular, temporall;' Cot. — L. *secularis*, secular, worldly.—L. *sæculum*, a generation, an age, the world.

Secure; see Cure.

Sedan-chair. (F.) Named from *Sedan*, a town in France. Cf. F. *sedan*, cloth made at Sedan (Littré).

Sedate; see Sedentary.

Sedentary. (F.—L.) F. *sédentaire.*—L. *sedentarius*, ever sitting.—L. *sedent*-, pres. pt. of *sedere*, to sit. (√SAD.)

assess, to fix a tax. (L.) Coined from L. sb. *assessor*, one who adjusted taxes; orig. a judge's assistant, one who sat by him.—L. *assessus*, pp. of *assidere*, to sit near (below). See **assize** (1) below.

assiduous. (L.) L. *assiduus*, sitting down to, constant, unremitted.—L. *assidere*, to sit near.—L. *as*-, for *ad*, to, near; *sedere*, to sit.

assize (1), a session of a court of justice. (F.—L.) M. E. *assise.*—O.F. *assis, assise*, an assembly of judges; also a tax, an impost. Properly a pp. of O.F. *asseoir*, to sit near, assist a judge.—L. *assidere*, to sit near, also to impose a tax. See above.

assize (2), a fixed quantity or dimension. (F.—L.) O.F. *assise*, a tax, impost; the Low L. *assisa* (the same word) was also used in the sense of a fixed allowance of provisions. The same word as the above.

dissident. (L.) L. *dissident*-, stem of pres. pt. of *dissidere*, to sit apart, to disagree.—L. *dis*-, apart; *sedere*, to sit.

excise (1), a duty, tax. (Du. — F. — L.) A misspelling of O. Du. *aksiis* or *aksys*, excise, corr. from O.F. *assise*, a tax. ¶ Or = O.F. *accise**, a score.—L. *accisus*, pp. of *accidere*, to cut into, to score.

hostage. (F. — L.) O.F. *hostage*, a hostage; the same as Ital. *ostaggio*, O. Prov. *ostatje*. We also find Ital. *statico*, a hostage; and both *ostaggio* and *statico* answer to a Low L. form *obsidaticus**, regularly formed from Low L. *obsidatus*, the condition of a hostage. — L. *obsid-*, stem of *obses*, a hostage, one who remains behind with the enemy. — L. *obsidere*, to stay.—L. *ob*, at, on, near; *sedere*, to sit.

insidious. (F.—L.) F. *insidieux*, deceitful. — L. *insidiosus*, treacherous. — L.

insidiæ, pl. troops of men who lie in wait, also cunning wiles.—L. *insidere*, to lie in wait, lit. 'to sit in.'—L. *in*, in; *sedere*, to sit.

possess. (L.) L. *possessus*, pp. of *possidere*, to possess. The orig. sense was 'to remain near.'—O. Lat. *port*, a prep. answering to Gk. ποτί or πρός, near; *sedere*, to sit.

preside. (F. — L.) O. F. *presider*, to preside, govern.—L. *præ-sidere*, to sit before, preside over. Der. *presid-ent*.

reside. (F.—L.) O. F. *resider*, to reside, stay.—L. *re-sidere*, to sit or remain behind.

residue. (F.—L.) O. F. *residu.*—L. *residuum*, a remainder, neut. of *residuus*, remaining.—L. *residere* (above).

sedate, quiet. (L.) L. *sedatus*, pp. of *sedare*, to settle or make calm, causal of *sedere*, to sit.

sediment. (F. — L.) O.F. *sediment.* —L. *sedimentum*, a settling (of dregs).— L. *sedere*, to sit, settle.

see (2), seat of a bishop. (F. — L.) M. E. *se.*—O. F. *sed, se*, seat.—L. *sedem*, acc. of *sedes*, a seat. —L. *sedere*, to sit.

sell (2), a saddle. (F.—L.) O. F. *selle*, seat, saddle.—L. *sella*, seat; put for *sed-la**. —L. *sedere*, to sit.

session. (F.—L.) F. *session.*—L. *sessionem*, acc. of *sessio*, a sitting.—L. *sessus*, pp. of *sedere*.

sizar, a scholar admitted at lower fees, at Cambridge, than a pensioner. (F.—L.) Named from *size*, formerly a farthing's-worth of bread or drink (Blount). *Size* is short for *assize*, an allowance of provisions; see **assize** (1).

size (1), an allowance of food; hence, generally, magnitude. (F.—L.) Short for *assize*; see **assize** (1).

size (2), weak glue. (Ital.—L.) Ital. *sisa*, 'syse or glew,' Florio. Short for *assisa*, size. So called from making colours lie flat. — O. Ital. *assisare*, 'to sute [suit] well;' Florio. — Ital. *assiso*, pp. of *assidere*, to situate.—L. *assidere*, lit. to sit near.— L. *as*- (for *ad*), near; *sedere*, to sit.

subside. (L.) L. *subsidĕre*, to settle down. — L. *sub*, under, down; *sidere*, to settle, allied to *sedere*, to sit.

subsidy. (F. — L.) F. *subside*, of which an older form was prob. *subsidie**. — L. *subsidium*, a body of troops in reserve, assistance; lit. that which sits in reserve. — L. *sub*, under, in reserve; *sedere*, to sit. Der. *subsidi-ary*, from L. adj. *subsidiarius*.

supersede. (F. – L.) O. F. *superseder*, to leave off, desist (hence to suspend or defer a matter). – L. *supersedere*, to sit upon, to preside over, refrain, desist from. – L. *super*, upon ; *sedere*, to sit. **Der.** *supersession* (from pp. *supersessus*).

surcease, to cease, cause to cease. (F. – L.) Not allied to *cease* (except in popular etymology). A corruption of O. F. *sursis*, masc., *sursise*, fem., 'surceased, intermitted ;' Cot. This word was also used as a sb., to signify 'delay;' hence *surcease*, vb., to delay. *Sursis* is the pp. of O. F. *surseoir*, 'to surcease, delay,' Cot. – L. *supersedere*, to desist from, hence to delay proceedings ; see **supersede** (above).

Sedge. (E.) M. E. *segge*. – A. S. *secg*, sedge ; lit. 'cutter,' i. e. sword-grass; from the shape. (√ SAK, to cut.)

Sediment ; see **Sedentary**.

Sedition ; see **Itinerant**.

Seduce ; see **Duke**.

Sedulous, diligent. (L.) L. *sēdulus*, diligent.

See (1), to perceive by the eye. (E.) M. E. *seen*, *sen*. A. S. *seón* ; pt. t. *seáh*, pp. *gesegen*. + Du. *zien* ; Icel. *sjá* ; Dan. *see* ; Swed. *se* ; G. *sehen* ; Goth. *saihwan*, pt. t. *sahw*. **Der.** *seer*, i. e. see-er.

sight. (E.) M. E. *sight*. A. S. *siht*, *gesiht*, commonly *gesihð*. From A. S. *ge-seg-en*, pp. of *seón*, to see (above). + Du. *gezigt* ; Dan. *sigte* ; Swed. *sigt* ; G. *sicht*.

See (2) ; see **Sedentary**.

Seed ; see **Sow** (1).

Seek. (E.) M. E. *seken*. A. S. *sécan*, to seek, strive after. A causal form, as if from *sóc* * = Goth. *sok*, pt. t. of *sakan*, to strive. Closely allied to **Sake.** + Du. *zoeken* ; Icel. *sækja*, *sœkja* ; Dan. *söge* ; Swed. *söka* ; G. *suchen*.

beseech. (E.) M. E. *besechen*, *biseken*. – M. E. *be-* (prefix) ; *seken*, to seek (above).

Seel, to close up the eyes. (F. – L.) O. F. *siller*, ' to seal up the eie-lids;' Cot. Also spelt *ciller*. – O. F. *cil*, eye-lid. – L. *cilium*, eye-lid, eye-lash ; lit. 'a covering.' Cf. L. *domi-cilium* ; and *celare*, to hide. (√ KAL.)

Seem. (E.) M. E. *semen*. A. S. *séman*, to satisfy, conciliate (hence, to suit, a sense due to the adj. *seemly* ; see below). + Icel. *sæma*, to honour, bear with, conform to, allied to *sæmr*, fit, *sóma*, to befit, also to *samr*, same. See **Same.**

beseem. (E.) M E. *besemen*, to befit.

– M. E. *be-*, prefix ; *semen*, to seem (above).

seemly, fit. (Scand.) M. E. *semlich*. – Icel. *sæmiligr*, seemly. – Icel. *sæmr*, fit ; with suffix *-ligr*, like (-ly). – Icel. *sama*, to beseem, cognate with Goth. *samjan*, to please, lit. ' to be the same,' agree with. – Icel. *samr*, same ; see **Same.**

Seer ; see **See.**

Seesaw. (E.) A reduplicated form ; from the verb *to saw*. From the motion of a sawyer. See **Saw** (1).

Seethe, to boil. (E.) Pt. *sod*; pp. *sodden*. M. E. *sethen*, pt. t. *seeth* (pl. *soden*), pp. *soden*. A. S. *seóðan*, pt. t. *seáð*, pp. *soden*. + Icel. *sjóða*, pt. t. *sauð* ; Dan. *syde* ; Swed. *sjuda* ; G. *sieden*. Allied to Goth. *sauths*, a burnt-offering, Icel. *svíða*, to burn, singe.

sod. (E.) So called from the *sodden* appearance of soft turf in wet places. The connection with the verb *to seethe* appears clearly in Du. *zode*, sod, green turf, O. Du. *zode*, seething, also sod ; G. *sode*, sod, *sod*, bubbling up of boiling water. Cf. also A. S. *seáð*, a well, pit, from *seáð*, pt. t. of *seóðan*, to seethe ; O. Fries. *satha*, sod, *sath*, a well.

suds. (E.) The proper sense is 'things sodden ;' pl. of *sud*, which is derived from A. S. *sod-en*, pp. of *seóðan*, to seethe. Cf. prov. E. *sudded*, flooded ; O. Du. *zode*, a seething, boiling.

Segment ; see **Secant.**

Segregate ; see **Gregarious.**

Seignior ; see **Senate.**

Seize ; see **Sit.**

Solah, a pause. (Heb.) Supposed to mean 'a pause;' from Heb. *sáláh*, to rest.

Seldom. (E.) A.S. *seldum*, *seldan*, *sel don*, seldom, lit. at rare times, from *seld*, adj., rare, strange. Allied to Goth. *ana-silan*, L. *silere*, to be silent (hence to wonder). + Du. *zelden*, Icel. *sjaldan*, Dan. *sielden*, Swed. *sällan*, G. *selten*, adv., seldom. See **Silent.**

Select ; see **Legend.**

Self. (E.) A.S. *self*, also *seolf*, *sylf*, self. + Du. *zelf* ; Icel. *sjálfr* ; Dan. *selv* ; Swed. *sjelf* ; Goth. *silba* ; G. *selbe*, *selb-st*.

selvage. (Du.) Lit. 'self-edge.' – O. Du. *selfegge*, selvage. – O. Du. *self*, self ; *egge*, edge. Mod. Du. *zelfkant*, selvage ; from *zelf*, self, *kant*, edge.

Sell (1) ; see **Sale.**

Sell (2), a saddle ; see **Sedentary.**

Selvage ; see **Self.**

Semblance; see **Similar**.

Semi-, half. (L.) L. *semi-*, half. **+** Gk. ἡμι-, half; A.S. *sám*, half; Skt. *sámi*, half = *sámyá*, old instr. case of *sámya*, equality, from *sama*, even, same. Allied to **Same**. Der. *semi-breve*, &c.

Seminal, relating to seed. (F.—L.) F. *seminal*.—L. *seminalis*, relating to seed.— L. *semin-*, stem of *semen*, seed.—L. *se-ui*, pt. t. of *serere*, to sow. See **Sow** (1).

disseminate. (L.) From pp. of L. *disseminare*, to scatter seed.—L. *dis-*, apart; *seminare*, to sow, from *semin-*, crude form of *semen*, seed.

seminary. (L.) L. *seminarium*, a seed-garden, seed-plot (hence a place of education).—L. *semin-* (above).

Sempiternal, everlasting. (L.) F. *sempiternel*. — L. *sempitern-us*, everlasting. — L. *sempi-*, for *semper*, always; with suffix *-ter-nus*. β. L. *semper* = *sama-per* *; where *sama* = Skt. *sama*, same (cf. L. *semi-*), and *per* means 'through.'

Sempster; see **Sew** (1).

Senary; see **Six**.

Senate, a council of elders. (F.—L.) F. *senat.*—L. *senatum*, acc. of *senatus*, council of elders. — L. *sen-ex*, old, *sen-ium*, old age. Cf. O. Gk. ἕνος, old, Goth. *sineigs*, W. *hen*, O. Skt. *sana*, old.

seignior. (F. — L.) O. F. *seigneur*, lord. — L. *seniorem*, acc. of *senior*; see **senior** (below).

seneschal, a steward. (F. — Teut.) O. F. *seneschal*. Orig. sense ' old servant.' — Goth. *sin-s*, old (only preserved in superl. *sin-ista*, eldest); *skalks*, a servant. Cf. **Marshal**.

senile, old. (L.) L. *senilis*, old. — L. *sen-ex*, old.

senior. (L.) L. *senior*, older; comp. of *senex*, old.

signor. (Ital. — L.) Ital. *signore*, sir. — L. acc. *seniorem*; see **seignior**.

sir, sire. (F. — L.) *Sir* is short for *sire*. — F. *sire*, sir. — L. *senior*, older, elder; (the word *seignior* being from the acc. *seniorem*). *Sire* is a weakened form of O. F. *senre* = L. *senior*.

sirrah. (Icel.—F.—L.) Icel. (and prob. O. Danish) *síra*, sirrah, a term of contempt, but at first used in a good sense; i. e. sir (13th cent.). — O. F. *sire*, Prov. *sira*, sir. — L. *senior*; see **sir** (above).

surly, proud, churlish. (F.—L.; *with* E. *suffix*.) Formerly *serly* (Levins); also *syrly*, Spenser, Shep. Kal. July, 203. Put

for *sir-like*, i. e. domineering. See **sir** (above).

Send. (E.) A.S. *sendan.*+Du. *zenden*; Icel. *senda*; Dan. *sende*; Swed. *sända*; Goth. *sandjan*; G. *senden*.

Sendal, Cendal, a rich thin silken stuff. (F.—Low L.—Skt.) O.F. *sendal*; Low L. *cendalum*, *cindadus*, *cindatus*, &c. So called because brought from India. — Skt. *sindhu*, the Indus, also Scinde. — Skt. *syand*, to flow; see **Indigo**.

Seneschal, Senile, Senior; see **Senate**.

Senna. (Ital. — Arab.) Ital. *sena* (Florio). — Arab. *saná*, senna.

Sennight; short for *seven night*, a week.

Sense. (F.—L.) F. *sens*, 'sence;' Cot. — L. *sensum*, acc. of *sensus*, feeling. — L. *sensus*, pp. of *sentire*, to feel, perceive.

assent. (F. — L.) O. F. *assentir*. — L. *assentire*, to assent, agree to.—L. *as-* (for *ad*), to; *sentire*, to feel, perceive.

consent. (F.—L.) F. *consentir*. — L. *consentire*, to agree to.—L. *con-* (for *cum*), with; *sentire*, to feel.

dissent. (L.) L. *dissentire* (pp. *dissensus*), to differ in opinion.—L. *dis-*, apart; *sentire*, to feel, think. Der. *dissens-ion*, from the pp. *dissensus*.

presentiment. (F. — L.) O. F. *presentiment*, 'a fore-feeling;' Cot.—L. *præsenti-re* to feel beforehand.

resent. (F. — L.) F. *se resentir* (or *ressentir*), to have a deep sense of. — L. *re-*, again; *sentire*, to feel. Der. *resentment*.

scent, vb. (F. — L.) A false spelling for *sent*, as in Hamlet, i. 5. 58 (ed. 1623). — F. *sentir*, 'to feel, sent;' Cot.—L. *sentire*, to feel, perceive.

sensual. (L.) Late L. *sensualis*, endowed with feeling.—L. *sensu-s*, feeling.— L. *sensus*, pp. of *sentire*, to feel.

sentence. (F. — L.) F. *sentence*. — L. *sententia*, a way of thinking; put for *sentientia* *.—L. *senti-re*, to feel, think.

sentiment. (F.—L.) M. E. *sentement*. — O. F. *sentement*; as if from a Low L. *sentimentum* *.—L. *sentire* (above).

Sensual, Sentence, Sentiment; see **Sense**.

Sentinel. (F.—Ital.—L.?) F. *sentinelle*. —Ital. *sentinella*, 'a watch, a sentinell;' Florio. Supposed to be equivalent to L. *sentinator*, one who pumps bilge-water out of a ship (which requires constant attention).—L. *sentina*, the hold of a ship. Cf.

O. Ital. *sentina*, 'a sinke, a companie of lewde rascals, the pumpe of a ship;' Florio. (Doubtful; much disputed.)

sentry. (F. — Ital. — L.?) An E. corruption of *sentinel*, which seems to have been connected, in popular etymology, with F. *sentier*, a path, extended from O. F. *sente* = L. *semita*, a path. ¶ There is nothing to show that *sentry* is a correct form; it occurs, spelt *sentrie*, in Minsheu (1627).

Separate; see **Pare**.

Sepoy. (Pers.) Pers. *sipáhí* (pronounced nearly as *sepoy*), a horseman, soldier. — Pers. *sipáh, sipah*, an army.

Sept, a clan; see **Sequence**.

September. (L.) L. *September*, the seventh month of the Roman year. — L. *septem*, seven. See **Seven**.

septenary. (L.) L. *septenarius*, consisting of seven. — L. *septeni*, pl. seven apiece. — L. *septem*, seven.

septennial. (L.) From L. *septennium*, a period of seven years. — L. *septennis*, adj., of seven years. — L. *sept-em*, seven; *annus*, year.

septuagesima. (L.) Lit. 'seventieth (day).' — L. *septuagesima* (*dies*), seventieth (day), fem. of *septuagesimus*, seventieth. — L. *septuaginta*, seventy. — L. *septua-*, due to *septem*, seven; *-ginta* = *-cinta*, short for *decinta* *, tenth, from *decem*, ten.

Sepulchre. (F. — L.) O. F. *sepulcre*. — L. *sepulcrum*, ill-spelt *sepulchrum*, a tomb. — L. *sepul-tus*, pp. of *sepelire*, to bury. Der. *sepult-ure*, from *sepultus*.

Sequel; see **Sequence**.

Sequence. (F. — L.) F. *sequence*, a sequence. — L. *sequentia*, sb., a following; from pres. pt. of *sequi*, to follow. (√SAK.)

associate. (L.) From pp. of L. *as-sociare*, to join to. — L. *as-* (for *ad-*), to; *sociare*, to join, associate. — L. *socius*, a companion; see *sociable* (below).

consecutive. (F. — L.) F. *consecutif*, Cot. — L. *consecut-us*, pp. of *con-sequi*, to follow together; with suffix *-if* (L. *-iuus*).

consequent. (L.) L. *consequent-*, stem of pres. pt. of *consequi* (above).

dissociate. (L.) From the pp. of L. *dis-sociare*, to separate from.

ensue. (F. — L.) O. F. *ensuir*, to follow after. — L. *in-sequi*, to follow upon.

execute. (F. — L.) O. F. *executer*. — L. *executus, exsecutus*, pp. of *ex-sequi*, to follow out, pursue, perform.

exequies. (F. — L.) O. F. *exeques*,

'funerals;' Cot. — L. *exsequias*, acc. pl. of *exsequiæ*, funeral obsequies, lit. 'followings.' — L. *exsequi* (above).

intrinsic, inherent. (F. — L.) O. F. *intrinseque*, 'inward;' Cot. — L. *intrinse-cus*, lit. 'following inwards.' — L. *intr-a*, within; *in*, in; *sec-us*, lit. following, from *sequi*, to follow.

obsequies. (F. — L.) O. F. *obseques*, 'obsequies;' Cot. — L. *obsequias*, acc. of *obsequiæ*, funeral rites, lit. followings. — L. *obsequi*, to follow near, comply with. — L. *ob*, near; *sequi*, to follow.

obsequious. (F. — L.) O. F. *obsequieux*; Cot. — L. *obsequiosus*, full of compliance. — L. *obsequium*, compliance. — L. *obsequi*, to comply with (above).

persecute. (F. — L.) F. *persecuter*, vb. — L. *persecutus*, pp. of *per-sequi*, to pursue.

prosecute. (L.) From L. *prosecutus*, pp. of *pro-sequi*, to pursue.

pursue. (F. — L.) O. F. *porsuir, pursuir, poursuir*; mod. F. *poursuivre*, to pursue. — O. F. *por, pur* = L. *pro*; and *suir* = L. *sequi*, to follow. Der. *pursu-ant*, from the pres. pt. of O. F. *pursuir*; *pursuiv-ant*, from the pres. pt. of *poursuivre*; *pursuit*, from F. *poursuite*, fem. sb., answering to L. *prosecuta*, fem. of the pp.

second. (F. — L.) O. F. *second*. — L. *secundus*, second, next following. — L. *sequi*, to follow.

sect. (F. — L.) F. *secte*, 'a sect or faction;' Cot. — Low L. *secta*, a set of people, a suit of clothes, a suit at law. — L. *sec-* (as in *sec-undus*), base of *sequi*, to follow. ¶ Sense obscured by confusion with *secare*, to cut.

sept, a clan. (F. — L.) Used in the 16th cent. as synonymous with *sect*, of which it is a corruption or variant. So also Prov. *cepte*, a sect.

sequel. (F. — L.) O. F. *sequele*, 'a sequell;' Cot. — L. *sequela*, a result. — L. *sequi*, to follow.

sequester. (F. — L.) F. *sequestrer*, to sequester or lay aside. — L. *sequestrare*, to surrender, lay aside. — L. *sequester*, a mediator, trustee, agent. Prob. orig. 'a follower.' — L. *sequi*, to follow.

sociable. (F. — L.) F. *sociable*. — L. *sociabilis*, companionable. — L. *socia-re*, to accompany. — L. *socius*, companion, follower; allied to L. *sequi*, to follow. (√SAK.) Der. *as-sociate, dis-sociate*.

social. (L.) L. *socialis*, adj., from *socius* (above).

society. (F. – L.) F. *société.* – L. acc. *societatem*, from nom. *societas*, fellowship. – L. *socius*, a companion; see **sociable.**

subsequent. (L.) From stem of pres. pt. of *sub-sequi*, to follow close after.

sue. (F. – L.) M. E. *suen*, *sewen*. – O. F. *sevre*, *suir* (F. *suivre*), to follow. – Low L. *sequere*, to follow, used for L. *sequi*, to follow. Der. *en-sue* (above), *pur-sue* (above).

suit. (F. – L.) F. *suite*, a pursuit, suit at law, also a suite or 'following.' – Low L. *secta*, a following, a sect, a suite, a suit at law, suit of clothes, set, &c.; see **sect** (above).

suite. (F. – L.) F. *suite*; see above.

Sequester; see **Sequence.**

Sequin, a gold coin. (F. – Ital. – Arab.) F. *sequin*; Cot. – Ital. *zecchino*, a Venetian coin. – Ital. *zecca*, a mint; Florio. – Arab. *sikkat* (pron. *sikkah*), a die for coins.

Seraglio. (Ital. – L.) Misused in E.; the true sense is merely 'enclosure;' but it was confused with Pers. *saráy* or *serái*, a palace, king's court, seraglio. Really from Ital. *serraglio*, an enclosure; formed with suffix *-aglio* (= L. *-aculum*) from Low L. *serare*, to bar, to bolt, shut in. – L. *sera*, a bar, bolt. – L. *serere*, to join together; see **Series.**

Seraph. (Heb.) Coined from the pl. form *seraphim*. – Heb. *seráphím*, s. pl., seraphs, lit. exalted ones (Gesenius).

Sere; see **Sear.**

Serecloth; see **Cerecloth.**

Serene. (L.) L. *serenus*, bright, clear. Allied to Gk. σέλας, brightness, σελήνη, moon. (√ SWAR.)

serenade. (F. – Ital. – L.) F. *serenade.* – Ital. *serenata*, music beneath a lady's window; orig. fem. of pp. of *serenare*, to make clear or to cheer, to be merry. – L. *serenus*, bright.

Serf; see **Serve.**

Serge; see **Silk.**

Sergeant; see **Serve.**

Series, a row. (L.) L. *series*, a row. – L. *serere*, to join or bind together (pp. *sertus*). – Gk. εἴρειν, to bind. (√ SWAR.)

assert. (L.) From L. *assertus*, pp. of *asserere*, to add to, claim, assert. – L. *as-* (for *ad*), to; *serere*, to join, connect.

concert. (F. – Ital. – L.) Often confused with *consort* in old writers. – F. *concerter*, 'to consort, or agree together;' Cot. – Ital. *concertare*, to concert, contrive, adjust; cf. *concerto*, sb., agreement. Also

(better) spelt *consertare*, to adjust, *conserto*, sb., concert, or (as pp.) interwoven. – L. pp. *consertus*, joined together. – L. *con-serere*, to join together. Cf. L. *serta corona*, a wreathed garland. ¶ The Ital. forms shew that it was confused with L. *con-certare*, to contend, struggle together. Der. *concert*, sb., *concert-ina.*

desert (1), a waste. (F. – L.) O. F. *desert*, a wilderness. – L. *desertus*, waste; pp. of *deserere*, to desert, abandon. – L. *de*, away (negative); *serere*, to join.

dissertation, a treatise. (L.) From L. *dissertatio*, a debate. – L. *dissertatus*, pp. of *dissertare*, to debate; frequent. of *dis-serere*, to disjoin, discuss. – L. *dis-*, apart; *serere*, to join.

exert. (L.) Lit. 'to struggle forth,' or 'put forth.' L. *exertus*, better spelt *ex-sertus*, thrust forth; pp. of *exserere*, to thrust out. – L. *ex*, out; *serere*, to join, to put.

insert. (L.) From L. *insertus*, pp. of *inserere*, to introduce, put in. – L. *in*, in; *serere*, to join, put.

serried, crowded together. (F. – L.) F. *serrer*, to compact, press close, to lock. – Low L. *serare*, to bolt. – L. *sera*, a bolt. – L. *serere*, to join. And see **Seraglio.**

Serious. (F. – L.) O. F. *serieux.* – Low L. *seriosus*, serious. – L. *sērius*, grave, earnest. Cf. G. *schwer*, heavy.

Sermon. (F. – L.) F. *sermon.* – L. *sermonem*, acc. of *sermo*, a speech, discourse.

Serous; see **Serum.**

Serpent. (F. – L.) F. *serpent.* – L. *serpentem*, acc. of *serpens*, a serpent; orig. pres. pt. of *serpere*, to creep. (√ SARP.)

Serrated, notched like a saw. (L.) L. *serratus*, notched like a saw. – L. *serra*, a saw. Prob. for *sec-ra** ; from *secare*, to cut.

Serried; see **Series.**

Serum, whey. (L.) L. *serum*, whey, serum. + Gk. ὀρός, whey. (√ SAR, to flow.) Der. *ser-ous*, adj.

Serve. (F. – L.) F. *servir.* – L. *seruire*, to serve. Allied to *seruus*, a slave; *seruare*, to keep, protect. (√ SAR, to protect.) Der. *serv-ant*, from pres. pt. of F. *servir*; *serv-ice*, F. *service*, L. *seruitium*; *serv-ile*, L. *seruilis*; *serv-itude*, F. *servi-tude*, L. acc. *seruitudinem*.

conserve, vb. (F. – L.) F. *conserver.* – L. *conseruare*, to preserve. – L. *con-* (for *cum*), fully; *seruare*, to keep. Der. *conserve*, vb.; *conserv-atory*, &c.

desert (2), merit. (F. – L.) O. F. *deserte*, lit. a thing deserved, pp. of *deservir*, to deserve; see below.

deserve. (F. – L.) O. F. *deservir*. – L. *deseruire*, to serve fully; in late Lat., to deserve.– L. *de*, fully; *seruire*, to serve.

dessert. (F. – L.) O. F. *dessert*, the last course at dinner.– O. F. *desservir*, to do ill service to; also, to take away the courses at dinner.– O. F. *des-* = L. *dis-*, away; *seruire*, to serve.

disservice, ill service. (F. – L.) F. *desservice.* – O. F. *des-* = L. *dis-*, apart, ill; *service*, service. See **Serve** (above).

observe. (F. – L.) O. F. *observer.* – L. *obseruare*, to take notice of, mark.– L. *ob*, near; *seruare*, to keep, heed.

preserve. (F. – L.) O. F. *preserver*, to preserve.– L. *præ*, beforehand; *seruare*, to keep.

reserve. (F. – L.) O. F. *reserver.* – L. *re-seruare*, to keep back.

reservoir. (F. – L.) F. *reservoir.* – Low L. *reseruatorium*, a store-house.– L. *reserua-re*, to reserve.

serf. (F. – L.) F. *serf*, a servant.– L. *seruum*, acc. of *seruus*, a slave.

sergeant, serjeant. (F. – L.) M. E. *sergeaunt, sergant.* – O. F. *sergant, serjant*, an officer. – Low L. *seruientem*, acc. of *seruiens*, an officer; orig. pres. pt. of *seruire*, to serve.

subserve. (L.) L. *sub-seruire*, to serve under another.

Session; see **Sedentary.**

Set; see **Sit.**

Seton; see **Satin.**

Settoo, Settle; see **Sit.**

Seven. (E.) A.S. *seofon*, seven. + Du. *zeven*; Icel. *sjö, sjau*; Dan. *syv*; Swed. *sju*; G. *sieben*; Goth. *sibun*; L. *septem*; Gk. *ἑπτά*; W. *saith*; Irish *seacht*; Russ. *seme*; Lith. *septyni*; Skt. *saptan.* **Der.** *seven-teen*, A.S. *seofontýne*; *seven-ty*, A.S. *hund-seofontig* (*hund* being dropped); *seven-th.*

Sever, Several; see **Pare.**

Severe. (F. – L.) O. F. *severe.* – L. *seuerus*, severe, serious, grave. **Der.** *sever-ity*, F. *severité.*

asseverate. (L.) L. *asseueratus*, pp. of *asseuerare*, to speak in earnest.– L. *as-*, (for *ad*), to; *seuerus*, earnest.

persevere. (F. – L.) Formerly *persé-ver.* – O. F. *perseverer.* – L. *perseuerare*, to persist in a thing. – L. *per*, thoroughly; *seuerus*, earnest.

Sew (1), to fasten with thread. (E.) M. E. *sowen, sewen.* A. S. *siwian*, to sew. + Icel. *sýja*; Dan. *sye*; Swed. *sy*; O. H. G. *siwan*; Goth. *siujan*; L. *suere*; Lith. *suti*; Russ. *shite*; Skt. *siv.* (√ SIW.)

seam. (E.) A. S. *sedm.* + Icel. *saumr*; G. *saum*; Du. *zoom*; Dan. Swed. *söm.* (Base SAUMA; from √ SU = √ SIW.)

seamstress, sempstress. (E.; *with* F. *suffix.*) A. S. *sédmestre*, a seamstress; with suffix *-ess* (= F. *-esse* = Gk. *-ισσα*).– A. S. *sedm*, a seam (above); with suffix *-es-tre*; see **Spinster.**

Sew (2), to follow; the same as **Sue;** see **Sequence.**

Sewer (1), a large drain. (F. – L.) Frequently spelt *shore.* Formed, with suffix *-er* (of the agent), from the verb *sew*, to dry, to drain (Tusser). We also find *sew*, sb., a drain. Short tor *essewe*.*– O. F. *essuier, esuer*, to dry, dry up. – L. *ex-succare, exsucare*, to dry up, deprive of moisture.– L. *ex*, out; *sucus*, moisture, allied to *sugere*, to suck. See **Suck.** We also find O. F. *essuier*, sb., a sewer, which answers exactly to the E. sb. ¶ Or from O. F. *seuwiere* = L. *ex-aquaria.*

Sewer (2), the officer who formerly set and tasted dishes, &c. (E.) '*Seware, at mete*, Depositor, dapifer, sepulator;' Prompt. Parv. From M. E. *sewen*, to set meat, bring in dishes, &c.; a verb formed from M. E. *sew*, sb., pottage, sauce, boiled meat, &c.– A. S. *seaw*, juice. ¶ Not allied to any F. word.

Sex. (F. – L.) F. *sexe.* – L. *sexum*, acc. of *sexus*, sex. Perhaps orig. 'division;' from *sec-are*, to cut. **Der.** *sex-u-al*, L. *sexualis.*

Sexagenary. (L.) L. *sexagenarius*, belonging to sixty. – L. *sexageni*, sixty each; distribute form of *sexaginta*, sixty. – L. *sex*, six; and *-ginta* = *-cinta**, for *decinta**, tenth, from *decem*, ten. See **Six.**

bissextile, a name for leap-year. (L.) Low L. *bissextilis annus*, bissextile year.– L. *bissextus*, an intercalary day; so called because the intercalated day (formerly Feb. 24) was called the *sixth* of the calends of March; there being thus two days with the same name. – L. *bis*, twice; *sextus*, sixth.

sexagesima. (L.) L. *sexagesima* (*dies*), i.e. sixtieth (day); fem. of *sexagesimus*, sixtieth, ordinal form of *sexaginta*, sixty.

sexennial. (L.) From L. *sexennium*,

a period of six years. – L. *sex*, six; *annus*, a year.

sextant, the sixth part of a circle. (L.) L. *sextant-*, stem of *sextans*, a sixth part. – L. *sext-us*, sixth, from *sex*, six; with suffix *-ans*, like that of a pres. pt. of a verb in *-are*.

sextuple, sixfold. (L.) Coined from *sextu-s*, sixth; with suffix *-ple* (as in *quadru-ple*), answering to L. *-plic-*, stem of *-plex*, as seen in *du-plex*, *com-plex*.

Sexton; see **Sacristan**.

Sextuple; see **Sexagenary**.

Shabby; see **Scab**.

Shackle; see **Shake**.

Shad, a fish. (E.) A.S. *sceadd*. + Prov. G. *schade*, a shad; cf. Irish *sgadan*, a herring; W. *ysgadan*, pl., herrings.

Shade, Shadow. (E.) M.E. *shade*, *shadue*. A.S. *scæd*, shade, neut. sb.; *sceadu*, shadow, fem. sb. + Du. *schaduw*, Goth. *skadus*, shadow; G. *schatten*, Irish *sgath*, shade; Gk. σκότος, σκοτία, gloom. (√ SKA, to cover.)

shed (2), a slight shelter, hut. (E.) O. Kentish *shed* (written *ssed*), shade; a dialectal form (Ayenbite of Inwyt).

Shaft; see **Shave**.

Shag, rough hair. (E.) A.S. *sceacga*, hair. + Icel. *skegg*, Swed. *skägg*, a beard, Dan. *skjæg*, beard, awn, wattle; from Icel. *skaga*, to jut out. The orig. sense is 'roughness.' Der. *shagg-y*, adj. *Shag* tobacco is rough tobacco.

Shagreen, a rough-grained leather. (F. – Turkish.) F. *chagrin*. It was orig. made of the skin of the *back* of the horse or mule. – Turk. *sághrī*, *saghrī*, back of a horse, shagreen. See **Chagrin**.

Shah, king of Persia. (Pers.) Pers. *sháh*, a king. See **Check**. Der. *pa-sha*.

Shake. (E.) A.S. *sceacan*, *scacan*, pt. t. *scóc*, pp. *scacen*. + Icel. *skaka*, Sw. *skaka*, Dan. *skage*; Skt. *khaj*, to move to and fro. (√ SKAG.)

shackle. (E.) A.S. *sceacul*, bond, fetter; orig. a loose bond; from its *shaking* about. + Icel. *skökull*, pole of a carriage, from *skaka*; Swed. *skakel*, loose shaft of a carriage; Dan. *skagle*, the same. Cf. Swed. dial. *skak*, a chain.

shank, lower part of the leg. (E.) A.S. *sceanca*, *scanca*, bone of the leg; named from its motion in running; lit. 'runner.' – A.S. *sceacan*, to shake, also to run, flee, hasten. + Du. *schonk*, Dan. *skank*, Swed. *skank*, Low G. *schake*, leg.

shock (1), a violent shake. (F. – Teut.) M. E. *schokken*, to shock, jolt. – F. *choc*, a shock; *choquer*, to give a shock. – O. H. G. *scoc*, a shock, shaking movement. Cf. A. S. *scóc*, pt. t. of *sceacan*, to shake.

shock (2), a pile of sheaves of corn. (O. Low G.) M. E. *schokke*. – O. Du. *schocke*, a shock, cock, heap; so called from being tossed together. – O. Du. *schocken*, to jolt, shock, cock, heap up; see above.

shog, to jog on. (C.) W. *ysgogi*, to wag, shake; *ysgog*, a quick motion, jolt. Allied to A. S. *sceacan*, to shake. See **Jog**.

skink, to serve out wine. (E.) M. E. *schenchen*, *skenken*. A.S. *scencan*, to pour out; orig. to draw off through a pipe. – A. S. *scanc*, a shank, shank-bone, hollow bone (hence, a pipe). So also Du. *schenken*, Icel. *skenkja*, Dan. *skienke*, G. *schenken*, to skink. See **Nunchion**.

Shako, a military cap. (F. – Hung.) F. *shako*. – Hungarian *csako*, a cap, shako; spelt *tsákó* in Dankovsky's Magyar Lexicon, p. 900.

Shale; see **Skill**.

Shall. (E.) A.S. *sceal*, I shall, I must; pt. t. *sceolde*, I should, ought. The orig. sense was 'to owe,' to be liable for; cf. Lith. *skilti*, to owe, be liable. + Icel. *skal*, pt. t. *skyldi*; Sw. *skall*; Dan. *skal*; Du. *zal*; G. *soll*; Goth. *skal*, infin. *skulan*.

Shalloon, a light woollen stuff. (F.) From *Chalons*, in France, E. of Paris.

Shallop, a light boat. (F. – Span.) F. *chaloupe*. – Span. *chalupa*, 'a flat-bottomed boat,' Minsheu (1623). Prob. of American origin. See **Sloop**.

Shallot, Shalot, a kind of onion. (F. – L. – Gk.) O. F. *eschalote*, variant of *escalogne*, a shallot. – L. *ascalonia*, a shallot; fem. of *Ascalonius*, belonging to Ascalon. – Gk. Ἀσκάλων, Ascalon; a chief city of the Philistines. Of Phœnician origin.

Shallow. (Scand.) M. E. *schalowe*, also found as *schold*, *schald*, Barbour, Bruce, ix. 354. – Icel. *skálgr*, oblique, awry; hence sloping, shelving, as a shore. Cf. Swed. dial. *skjalg*, oblique, slant; G. *scheel*, *schel*, oblique; Gk. σκολιός, crooked, awry. And see **Scalene**.

shoal (2), shallow, a sandbank. (Scand.) Orig. an adj., meaning 'shallow,' formerly *shole*, and (with excrescent *d*) *shold* or *shald* (as above). – Icel. *skálgr*, oblique, awry; see above. See also **Shelve**.

Shalm; see **Shawm**.

Sham; see **Shame**.

Shamble, to walk awkwardly; see **Camp**.

Shambles. (L.) Orig. stalls on which butchers expose meat for sale; pl. of *shamble*, a bench, butcher's bench or stall. A. S. *scamel*, a stool. — L. *scamellum*, a stool, little bench; allied to *scamnum*, step, bench, *scabellum*, foot-stool. Orig. sense 'a prop;' cf. L. *scapus*, shaft, stem, stalk; Gk. σκῆπτειν. (√ SKAP.)

Shame. (E.) A. S. *sceamu*, *scamu*. + Icel. *skömm*; Dan. Sw. *skam*; G. *scham*. Allied to Goth. *skanda*, shame, Skt. *kshan*, to wound. (√ SKA.)

ashamed. (E.) A. S. *áscamod*, pp. of *áscamian*, to put to shame. — A. S. *á-*, extremely; *scamian*, to shame, from *scamu*, shame. β. Or for A. S. *ofscamod*, with the same sense (with prefix *of-*, off, very).

sham. (E.) Northern E. *sham*, a shame, disgrace (hence, trick). ' Wheea's *sham* is it '= whose fault is it? Whitby Glossary. Cf. Icel. *skömm* (stem *skamm-*), shame, disgrace, outrage.

shamefaced, modest. (E.) Corruption of M. E. *shamefast*, modest. — A. S. *sceamfæst*, lit. firm in shame, i.e. in modesty. — A. S. *scamu*, shame, modesty; *fæst*, fast, firm; see **Fast**.

Shammy, Shamoy; see **Chamois**.

Shampoo. (Hind.) Hindustani *chámpná*, to join, to stuff, press, thrust in, shampoo; from the kneading or pressure used in the operation.

Shamrock. (C.) Irish *seamrog*, trefoil, dimin. of *seamar*, trefoil; Gael. *seamrag*.

Shank; see **Shake**.

Shape, vb. (E.) A. S. *sceapan*, *scapan*, pt. t. *scóp*, pp. *scapen*; we also find *sceppan*, *scippan*, weak verb. + Icel. *skapa*, Swed. *skapa*, Dan. *skabe*, G. *schaffen*. Allied to **Shave**.

ship. (E.) A. S. *scip*. — A. S. *scippan*, to make, from *scapan*, to shape. + Du. *schif*, Icel. *skip*, Dan. *skib*, Swed. *skepp*, Goth. *skip*, G. *schiff*.

skiff. (F. — M. H. G.) F. *esquif*, ' a skiffe, little boat;' Cot. — M. H. G. *skif*, G. *schiff*, a ship. Cf. G. *schaffen*, to shape; see **ship** (above).

skipper. (Du.) Du. *schipper*, a mariner. — Du. *schip*, a ship; cognate with E. *ship*; see **ship** (above).

Shard; see **Shear**.

Share (1) and (2); see **Shear**.

Shark. (L. ? — Gk. ?) In Shak.; not an old word. Supposed to be derived from L. *carcharus*, a kind of dog-fish (perhaps through an O. F. form, not now found). — Gk. καρχαρίας, a kind of shark; from its sharp teeth. — Gk. κάρχαρος, jagged (as teeth). Cf. Skt. *karkara*, hard. Der. *shark-ing*, voracious, prowling; *shark up*, to snap up; also *shirk*, better *sherk*, another spelling of *shark*, verb, to act as a shark, to prowl, cheat, avoid, slink from.

Sharp. (E.) A. S. *scearp*. + Du. *scherp*, Icel. *skarpr*, Swed. Dan. *skarp*, G. *scharf*. Allied to L. *scalpere*, to cut, Gk. σκορπίος, scorpion. (√ SKARP.)

counterscarp, exterior slope of a ditch. (F. — L. *and* Teut.) F. *contrescarpe*; Cot. — F. *contre*, over against; *escarpe*, a scarp. See **Counter**, and **scarp** (below).

escarpment. (F. — Ital. — Teut.) Formed from F. *escarpe*, a scarp; with suffix *-ment* (L. *-mentum*); see **scarp** (below).

scarf (1), a light piece of dress. (E.) The orig. sense is merely 'shred' or 'scrap' of stuff. A. S. *scearfe*, a piece; *scearfian*, to shred. + Du. *scherf*, a shred; G. *scherbe*, a pot-sherd. (Base *skarf* = √ SKARP.) β. The particular sense is due to O. F. *escharpe*, a scarf, really the same word, answering to O. Du. *schärpe*, a scrip, variant of Du. *scherf* (as above).

scarf (2), to join timber together. (Scand.) Swed. *skarf*, a scarf, seam, joint. + Bavarian *scharben*, to cut a notch in timber, G. *scharben*, to cut small. Cf. Dan. *skarre*, to scarf, Icel. *skör*, a rim, edge, scarf, joint in planking. (√ SKARP, extension of √ SKAR.) See **Shear**.

scarp. (F. — Ital. — Teut.) F. *escarpe*. — Ital. *scarpa*, 'a curtein of a wall;' so called because cut *sharp*, i. e. steep. — O. H. G. *scharf*, *scharpf*, sharp; see **Sharp**.

scrabble, to scrawl. (E.) Lit. 'to scratch or scrape;' put for prov. E. *scrapple*, frequent. of *scrape*.

scramble. (E.) Nasalised form of prov. E. *scrabble*, to scramble, allied to *scraffle*, to scramble, *scrapple*, to grub about; frequentatives of *scrape*, prov. E. *scrap*, to scrape.

scrap. (Scand.) Icel. *skrap*, scraps, trifles, lit. *scrapings*. — Icel. *skrapa*, to scrape.

scrape. (Scand.) Orig. to scratch with something *sharp*. — Icel. *skrapa*, Swed. *skrapa*, Dan. *skrabe*, to scrape. + Du. *schrapen*; A. S. *scearpian*, to scarify, from *scearp*, sharp.

scrip (1), a small bag. (Scand.) Icel. *skreppa*, Swed. *skräppa*, a scrip. Orig. sense 'scrap,' because made of a scrap of stuff; cf. G. *scherbe*, a shred.

Shatter; see **Scatter**.

Shave. (E.) A. S. *sceafan, scafan*, pt. t. *scóf*, pp. *scafen*. + Du. *schaven*; Icel. *skafa*; Swed. *skafva*, Dan. *skave*, Goth. *skaban*, G. *schaben*.+Lith. *skapoti*, to shave, cut, L. *scabere*, to scratch, scrape, Gk. σκάπτειν, to dig. (√SKAP.)

shaft. (E.) A. S. *sceaft*, shaft of a spear; from being *shaven* smooth. — A. S. *scaf-en*, pp. of *scafan*, to shave. + Icel. *skapt, skaft*, Dan. Sw. *skaft*, G. *schaft*, Du. *schacht* (for *schaft*).

Shaw, thicket. (E.) A. S. *scaga*.+Icel. *skógr*, a shaw, wood; Swed. *skog*, Dan. *skov*. Cf. Skt. *sku*, to cover.

Shawl. (Pers.) Pers. *shál* (pron. *shawl*), a shawl, mantle.

Shawm, Shalm, a musical instrument. (F. – L. – Gk.) O. F. *chalemie*, a reed pipe; allied to *chaume*, a straw. – L. *calamus*, a reed. – Gk. κάλαμος, a reed. See **Haulm**.

She. (E.) M. E. *sche*. A. S. *seó*, used as fem. of def. article, but in the Northumb. dialect as dem. pronoun. Fem. of *se*, orig. 'he;' cognate with Goth. *sa*, that. + Du. *zij*, G. *sie*; Icel. *sú, sjá*, fem. of *sá*, that; Goth. *so*, fem. of *sa*, that; Gk. ή, fem. of ό; Skt. *sá*, she, fem. of *sas*, he. (See p. 579.)

Sheaf; see **Shove**.

Sheal, a temporary summer hut. (Scand.) Also spelt *shiel, shielin, sheelin*. – Icel. *skjól*, a shelter, cover, Dan. Swed. *skjul*, a shed; Icel. *skýli*, a shed. Cf. Skt. *sku*, to cover.

Shear. (E.) A. S. *sceran*, pt. t. *scær*, pp. *scoren*.+Du. *scheren*, Icel. *skera*, Dan. *skære*, G. *scheren*, to shear; Gk. κείρειν, to cut. (√SKAR.)

jeer. (Du.) From Du. phrase *den gek scheeren*, lit. to shear the fool, hence to jeer at one; hence the word *gekscheeren*, or simply *scheeren*, to jeer. Now spelt *scheren*.

scar (2), **scaur**, a rock. (Scand.) M.E. *scarre*. – Icel. *sker*, a skerry, isolated rock; Dan. *skiær*, Swed. *skär*. So called because cut off from the main land; see **share** (below).

scare. (Scand.) M. E. *skerren*, to scare; from *skerre*, adj., timid, shy. – Icel. *skjarr*, timid, shy; allied to *skirrask*, to shun, lit. to sheer off; see **sheer** (2) below.

scarify. (F. – L. – Gk.) F. *scarifier*. – L. *scarificare*, to scarify, scratch open;

from *scarifare*, to scarify. – Gk. σκαριφάομαι, I scratch. – Gk. σκάριφος, a sharp pointed instrument. Allied to **Shear**.

score. (E.) M. E. *score*, properly a cut; hence twenty, denoted by a long cut on a cut stick. A. S. *scor*, a score. – A. S. *scor-en*, pp. of *sceran*, to shear.+Icel. *skor*, Swed. *skåra*, Dan. *skaar*, score, cut.

shard, sherd, fragment. (E.) A. S. *sceard*, a fragment; lit. 'cut thing.' – A. S. *scær*, pt. t. of *sceran*, to shear. Cf. Icel. *skarð*, a notch. Der. *pot-sherd*.

share (1), a portion. (E.) A. S. *scearu*, a share, part. – A. S. *scær*, pt. t. of *sceran*, to share.

share (2), a plough-share. (E.) A. S. *scear*, plough-share. – A. S. *scær* (as above).

sheer (2), to deviate from one's course. (Du.) Du. *scheren*, to shear, cut, withdraw, go away; *scheerje van hier*, sheer off! (Sewel).

sherd; see **shard** (above).

shirt. (Scand.) M. E. *shirte, shurte*. – Icel. *skyrta*, a shirt, kind of kirtle; Swed. *skjorta*, Dan. *skiorte*. So called because *short*. – Icel. *skortr*, shortness; see **Short**.

shore (1), strand of a lake or sea. (E.) M. E. *schore*. A. S. *score* (Somner); cf. A. S. *scoren clif*, a shorn cliff, precipice. – A. S. *scor-en*, pp. of *sceran*, to shear.

shore (2), **shoar**, a prop. (Scand.) M. E. *schore*. – Icel. *skorða*, a prop, stay, esp. under a boat; *skorða*, vb., to underprop, shore up; Norweg. *skorda, skora*, prop; Swed. dial. *skåre*, a piece of cut wood. So called because *shorn* or cut off of a suitable length. – Icel. *skor-inn*, pp. of *skera*, to shear.

short. (E.) A. S. *sceort*, short; lit. 'cut off.' – A. S. *scor-en*, pp. of *sceran*, to shear. Cf. Icel. *skortr*, shortness, O. H. G. *scurz*, short, L. *curtus*, short (whence E. *curt*).

skirt. (Scand.) M. E. *skyrt*. – Icel. *skyrta*, a shirt, kind of kirtle; see **shirt** (above). A doublet of *shirt*, but restricted to the lower part of a garment.

Sheath; see **Shed** (1).

Shed (1), to part, pour, spill. (E.) Orig. 'to separate.' A. S. *sceádan, scádan*, pt. t. *scéd*, pp. *scáden*, to shed; whence M. E. *scheden*, weak verb (with long *e*, but the *e* has been shortened). + Goth. *skaidan*, G. *scheiden*, to part. (Base SKID.)

sheath. (E.) A. S. *scéð, scæð*, a sheath, orig. that which separates, hence a husk, shell, pod. + Du. *scheede*, Dan.

skede, Swed. *skida*, G. *scheide*, a sheath; Icel. *skeiðir*, fem. pl., a sheath (lit. things that separate or open). Der. *sheathe*, verb.

shide, a thin piece of board. (E.) A. S. *scíde*, a billet of wood; from the base of the verb *to shed*. + Icel. *skíð*, G. *scheit*, a billet.

skid. (Scand.) Orig. a thin slip of wood, to put under a wheel. — Swed. *skid*, a wooden shoe or sole; Icel. *skíð*, a billet of wood; see above. See also **Shoddy**.

Shed (2), a hut; see **Shade**.

Sheen, fairness. (E.) See **Show**.

Sheep. (E.) A. S. *sceáp*, *scép*; pl. the same. + Du. *schaap*, G. *schaf*. Cf. Polish *skop*, a wether, from Church Slavonic *skopiti*, to castrate.

shepherd. (E.) A. S. *sceáphyrde*, a keeper of sheep; see **Herd** (2). Der. *shepherd-ess*.

Sheer (1), bright, pure, perpendicular. (Scand.) A *sheer* descent is a clear (unbroken) one. M. E. *shere*, bright. — Icel. *skærr*, Dan. *skær*, sheer, bright. Allied to Icel. *skírr*, A. S. *scír*, bright; from the base of the verb *to shine*; see **Shine**. Der. *Sheer-Thursday*, the day before Good Friday; cf. Icel. *skíra*, to cleanse, baptise.

Sheer (2), to deviate; see **Shear**.

Sheet; see **Shoot**.

Sheik, a chief. (Arab.) Arab. *sheikh*, an elder, chief; orig. sense 'old.'

Shekel, a Jewish weight and coin. (Heb.) Heb. *sheqel*, a shekel (weight). — Heb. *shâqal*, to weigh.

Shekinah. (Heb.) It signifies the visible presence of God; lit. 'dwelling.' — Heb. *shekínâh*, dwelling. — Heb. *shâkan*, to dwell.

Sheldrake. (E.) Put for *sheld-drake*, variegated or spotted drake. '*Sheld*, flecked, party-coloured;' Coles (1684). M. E. *sheld* is a shield; and the allusion is to the ornamentation of shields. Cf. A. S. *scild*, a shield, used also of part of a bird's plumage (Grein). So also Icel. *skjöldungr*, a sheldrake, *skjöldóttr*, dappled, from *skjöld*, a shield. See **Shield**.

Shelf. (E.) M. E. *schelfe*, *shelfe*. A. S. *scylfe*, plank, shelf. Orig. a thin piece, flake; allied to *shell* and *skill*. + Low G. *schelfe*, a shelf, *schelfern*, to flake off; Du. *schelpe*, G. *schelfe*, a shell, husk.

Shell; see **Skill**.

Shelter; see **Shield**.

Shelve, to slope down. (Scand.) Not

allied to *shelf*. Florio translates O. Ital. *stralare* by 'to shelve or go aside, aslope, awry.' The *v* stands for a guttural. — Icel. *skelgja-sk* (where *-sk = sik*, oneself), to come askew. — Icel. *skálgr*, wry, oblique, (hence sloping). See **Shallow**.

Shepherd; see **Sheep**.

Sherbet, a drink. (Arab.) Arab. *sharbat*, a drink, draught, sherbet, syrup. — Arab. root *shariba*, he drank.

shrub (2), a drink, chiefly made with rum. (Arab.) Arab. *shirb*, *shurb*, a drink. — Arab. root. *shariba* (above).

syrup, **sirup**. (F. — Span. — Arab.) F. *syrop*. — Span. *xarope*, a drink. — Arab. *sharáb*, *shuráb*, wine, beverage, syrup. — Arab. root *shariba* (above).

Sherd; see **Shear**.

Sheriff; see **Shire**.

Shorry. (Span. — L.) Formerly *sherris*. — Span. *Xeres*, a town in Spain, near Cadiz. — L. *Cæsaris*, gen. case of *Cæsar*, proper name (Dozy).

Shew; see **Show**.

Shibboleth, a test-word. (Heb.) Heb. *shibbóleth*, an ear of corn, also a river; see Judges, xii. 6.

Shide, a thin piece of board; see **Shed** (1).

Shield. (E.) A. S. *scild*, *sceld*. + Du. *schild*, Icel. *skjöldr*, Dan. *skiöld*, Swed. *skold*, Goth. *skildus*, G. *schild*.

shelter. (E.) A curious corruption of M. E. *sheldtrume*, a body of guards or troops, a squadron; frequently spelt *sheltron*, *sheltrun*; it came to mean a guard or protection of any kind, perhaps through confusion with *sheal*, q. v. — A. S. *scildtruma*, lit. 'shield-troop,' a guard. — A. S. *scild*, shield; *truma*, a band of men.

Shieling; see **Sheal**.

Shift. (E.) M. E. *schiften*, to divide, change, shift, remove; orig. 'to divide.' A. S. *sciftan*, to divide. + Icel. *skipta* (for *skifta*), to divide, part, shift, change; Swed. *skifta*, Dan. *skifte*, the same. Allied to Icel. *skífa*, to cut into slices, *skífa*, a slice, prov. E. *shive*, a slice, *sheave*, a wheel of a pulley. See **Shiver** (2).

Shilling. (E.) A. S. *scilling*. + Du. *schelling*; Icel. *skillingr*; Dan. Swed. *skilling*; Goth. *skilliggs* (for *skillings**); G. *schilling*. β. The suffix *-l-ing* is a double diminutive; the base is SKIL, to divide; see **Skill**. Reason for the name uncertain; but cf. Swed. *skiljemynt*, Dan. *skillemynt*, small change, small money.

Shimmer, to glimmer. (E.) A. S. *scimrian,* frequent. form of *scíman, scímian,* to shine, allied to *scínan,* to shine; see **Shine.** + Du. *schemeren*; Swed. *skimra*; G. *schimmern.* Cf. O. H. G. *scímo,* a bright light, Icel. *skími,* a gleam.

Shin. (E.) A. S. *scina*; whence *scin-bán,* shin-bone. + Du. *scheen*; G. *schiene,* also a splint; Swed. *sken-ben,* Dan. *skinne-been,* shin-bone. Orig. sense perhaps 'thin slice,' from the sharp edge in front. See **Skin.**

Shine. (E.) A. S. *scínan,* pt. t. *scán,* pp. *scinen.* + Du. *schijnen,* Icel. *skína*; Dan. *skinne*; Swed. *skina*; Goth. *skeinan*; G. *scheinen.* (Base SKI.)

Shingle (1), a wooden tile. (L.) M. E. *shingle,* corruption of *shindle*,* as shewn by the corresponding G. *schindel,* a shingle, splint, thin piece of wood. — L. *scindula,* another spelling of *scandula,* a shingle.— L. *scindere,* to cleave. (Base SKID, weak form of √SKAD, to cleave, whence L. *scandula.*) Cf. Skt. *chhid,* to cut.

Shingle (2), coarse round gravel on the sea-shore. (Scand.) Corruption of Norweg. *singl* or *singling,* coarse gravel, shingle, named from the crunching or ringing noise made by walking on it.— Norweg. *singla,* to ring, tinkle, Swed. dial. *singla* (the same); frequent. form of Swed. dial. *singa,* the same word as E. *sing*; see **Sing.**

Shingles. (F.—L.) Put for *singles* or *sengles,* pl. of the old word *sengle,* a girth; the disease encircling the body like a belt. — O. F. *cengle, sangle,* 'a girth, a sengle;' Cot.—L. *cingulum,* a belt.—L. *cingere,* to surround; see **Cincture.**

Ship; see **Shape.**

Shire. (E.) A. S. *scír, scíre,* a shire, province; orig. 'employment, care.' Cf. A. S. *scírian,* to appoint, allot. ¶ Not allied to **Shear.**

sheriff. (E.) Put for *shire-reeve.* A. S. *scír-geréfa,* a shire - reeve; see **Reeve.** Der. *sheriff-al-ty,* usually spelt *shrievalty.*

Shirk; see **Shark.**

Shirt; see **Shear.**

Shittah-tree, Shittim-wood. (Heb.) *Shittim* is a pl. form.—Heb. *shittáh,* pl. *shittím,* a kind of acacia (the *t* is *teth*).

Shive, Sheave; see **Shiver** (2).

Shiver (1), to tremble. (Scand.) Formerly *shever,* in Baret (1580); M. E. *chiueren, cheueren (chiveren, cheveren),* where *ch* stands for earlier *k,* so that the orig. form was *kiveren*,* which I suppose

to be merely the Scand. form of E. *quiver,* and a frequentative of Icel. *kippa,* to pull, snatch, quiver convulsively, Swed. dial. *kippa,* to snatch, twitch. Cf. Icel. *kona* for E. *queen.* See **Quiver.** ¶ The spelling with *sh* was due to confusion with the word below.

Shiver (2), a splinter, small piece of wood. (Scand.) A *shiver* is a small piece; hence *to shiver,* to break in pieces. Again, *shiver* is the dimin. of *shive,* a thin slice, the same as prov. E. *sheave,* a thin disc of wood, wheel of a pulley. — Icel. *skífa,* a slice. + Du. *schijf,* Dan. *skive,* Swed. *skifva,* G. *scheibe,* a slice. Cf. G. *schiefer,* a slate, splinter, shiver. (Base SKIB, weak form of SKAB, to shave.) See **Shave.**

skewer. (Scand.) Formerly *skiver,* old form of *shiver,* i. e. a splint, a wooden pin. — Icel. *skífa,* a slice; see above.

Shoal (1), a crowd; see **School.**

Shoal (2), a sand-bank; see **Shallow.**

Shoar, a prop; see **shore** (2), under **Shear.**

Shock (1), a violent shake; see **Shake.**

Shock (2), a pile of sheaves; see **Shake.**

Shock (3), a rough-coated dog. (E.) Supposed to be a variant of **Shag,** q. v. *Shock-headed* is rough-headed, with shaggy hair.

Shoddy, a material obtained from tearing into fibres loose woollen goods. (E.) Probably so called because made of stuff *shed* or thrown off in spinning wool. Cf. M. E. *schode,* the parting of the hair; from A. S. *sceádan,* to part. See **Shed** (1).

Shoe. (E.) M. E. *scho.* A. S. *sceó*; pl. *gescý* or *sceón.* + Du. *schoen*; Icel. *skór*; Swed. and Dan. *sko*; Goth. *skohs*; G. *schuh.* Cf. Skt. *sku,* to cover.

Shog; see **Shake.**

Shoot. (E.) A. S. *scótian,* to dart; secondary verb, from the primary A. S. verb *sceótan,* pt. t. *sceát,* pp. *scoten,* of which only the pp. *shotten* is preserved (in the phrase *shotten herring* = a herring that has lost its roe). + Du. *schieten*; Icel. *skjóta*; Dan. *skyde*; Sw. *skjuta*; G. *schiessen.* (Base SKUT.) Cf. Skt. *skund,* to jump, go by leaps, *skand,* to jump, ascend.

scot-free, free from payment. (E.) A. S. *scot,* payment, esp. a contribution to a common fund, into which it is *shot.* — A. S. *scot-en,* pp. of *sceótan,* to shoot. + Du. *schot* (whence O. F. *escot,* a tavern-score); Icel. *skot,* a shot, a contribution; G. *schoss,* a shot, a scot.

scud, to run quickly. (Scand.) Dan. *skyde*, to shoot; *skyde over stevn*, lit. 'to shoot over the stem,' to scud along; *skudsteen*, a stone quoit, called in Scotch a *scudding-stane*. See **Shoot.**

scuttle (2), an opening in a hatchway of a ship. (F. — Span. — Teut.) O. F. *escoutille*, scuttle. — Span. *escotilla*, the hole in the hatch of a ship. — Span. *escotar*, to cut a hole, orig. to cut a hole in a garment to fit the neck or bosom. — Span. *escote*, the sloping of a jacket,'&c. — Du. *schoot*, lap, bosom; see **sheet** (above). **Der.** *scuttle*, verb, to sink a ship by making holes in it.

scuttle (3), to hurry along. (Scand.) The same as prov. E. *scuddle* (Bailey), frequent. of *scud* (above).

sheet. (E.) M. E. *schete.* A. S. *scête*, *scýte*, a sheet; also *scéat*, a corner, nook, fold of a garment, corner of a sail, hence a *sheet* or rope fastened to a corner of a sail. — A. S. *scéat*, pp. of *scéotan*, to shoot, hence to jut out. The orig. sense of *sheet* was 'projection,' hence ' corner,' &c. ♣ Icel. *skaut*, corner, sheet of a sail; Swed. *skot* (the same); Du. *schoot*, shoot, sprig, sheet; Goth. *skauts*, hem of a garment; G. *schooss*, flap of a coat, lap, bosom.

shot. (E.) M. E. *schot.* A. S. *ge-sceot*, implements for shooting. — A. S. *scot-en*, pp. of *scéotan*, to shoot. ♣ Icel. *skot*, Du. *schot*, a shot, shooting; G. *schoss*, *schuss*, a shot.

shut. (E.) M. E. *shutten, shitten.* A. S. *scyttan*, to shut; to fasten a door with a bolt (called a *shuttle*). We still say ' to *shoot* a bolt.' The A. S. *scyttan* is a weak verb; from *scut-*, base of pt. t. pl. of *scéotan*, to shoot. ♣ Du. *schutten*, G. *schützen* (similarly formed). See below.

shuttle. (E.) So called from being *shot* across the threads in weaving. M. E. *schitel*, also a bolt of a door. Formed, with suffix *-el* of the agent, from A. S. *scut-*, base of pt. t. pl. of *scéotan*, to shoot. ♣ Dan. *skytte, skyttel*, a shuttle. **Der.** *shuttle-cock*; from its being *shot* backwards and forwards like a *shuttle*, and because furnished with feathers.

skittish. (Scand.) From Lowl. Scotch *skit*, to flounce, caper about. This is a secondary verb, of Scand. origin, from the verb *to shoot*. — Swed. dial. *skytta, skyttla*, to run about, *skutta, skötta*, to leap about; from Swed. *skjuta*, to shoot. Cf. Swed. *skytt*, Icel. *skyti*, a marksman; whence the verb *to skit* in the sense to aim at or

reflect upon a person, and the sb. *skit*, an oblique taunt.

skittles, a game. (Scand.) Formerly *skittle-pins*; so called because *shot* at by a *skittle* or projectile. — Dan. *skyttel*, a shuttle; Icel. *skutill*, a projectile, harpoon, bolt of a door. — Icel. *skut-*, base of pt. t. pl. of *skjóta*, to shoot; see **Shoot.**

Shop. (E.) A. S. *sceoppa*, a stall, booth. Allied to *scypen*, a pen for cattle. ♣ Low G. *schup*, a shed; G. *schuppen*, a shed, covert (whence O. F. *eschoppe*, a shop). Cf. Gk. σκέπας, a cover.

Shore (1), sea-strand; see **Shear.**

Shore (2), **Shoar**, a prop; see **Shear.**

Shore (3), a sewer; see **Sewer.**

Short; see **Shear.**

Shot; see **Shoot.**

Shoulder. (E.) A. S. *sculder, sculdor.* ♣ Du. *schouder*, Swed. *skuldra*, Dan. *skulder*, G. *schulter.*

Shout. (Unknown). M. E. *shouten*; Chaucer, Troil. ii. 614. Etym. unknown; cf. Icel. *skúta, skúti*, a taunt.

Shove. (E.) M. E. *shouen.* A. S. *scofian*, weak verb, allied to *scúfan*, pt. t. *scéaf*, pp. *scofen*, to shove. ♣ Icel. *skúfa*; Dan. *skuffe*, Swed. *skuffa*, Du. *schuiven*, G. *schieben* (pt. t. *schob*); Goth. *skiuban*. Cf. Skt. *ksubh*, to become agitated, *kshobha*, agitation.

scuffle. (Scand.) The frequentative of Swed. *skuffa*, to push, shove, jog (above). Cf. O. Du. *schuffelen*, to drive on, also to run or shuffle off, from *schuiven*, to shove.

sheaf. (E.) M. E. *scheef.* A. S. *scéaf*, a sheaf, pile of corn shoved together. — A. S. *scéaf*, pt. t. of *scúfan*, to shove. So also Du. *schoof*, Icel. *skauf*, G. *schaub*, sheaf.

shovel. (E.) A. S. *scofel*, a shovel, for lifting and shoving. — A. S. *scof-en*, pp. of *scúfan* (above). **Der.** *shovel-er*, a kind of duck.

shuffle. (Scand.) The frequentative of Swed. *skuffa*, to push, shove; another form of *scuffle.*

Show, Shew. (E.) M. E. *schewen*, vb. A. S. *sceawian*, to see, behold; later, to make to see, point out, show. ♣ Du. *schouwen*, Dan. *skue*, G. *schauen*, to behold. (√ SKU, SKAW.) **Der.** *show*, sb.; *shewbread.*

scavenger. (E.; *with* F. *suffix.*) Formerly *scavager*; the *n* is intrusive. The sense has much changed; a *scavager* was an officer who took custom upon the *scavage*, i.e. the display of goods for sale, and who also had to attend to cleansing

the streets for that purpose. *Scavage =
shew-age*, a barbarous word, with F. suffix
-age (= L. *-aticum*), from A. S. *sceawian*,
to shew.

sheen, fairness, splendour. (E.) M. E.
schene, adj., fair. A. S. *scéne, sceóne, scýne*,
fair, showy; allied to *sceawian*, to show,
see. + O. Sax. *scóni*, adj.; Du. *schoon*, adj.;
G. *schön*, adj.; Goth. *skauns*, beautiful.
¶ Not really allied to *shine*.

Shower. (E.) M. E. *schour*. A. S.
scúr. + Du. *schoer*; Icel. *skúr*; Swed.
skur; Goth. *skura*, a storm; G. *schauer*,
O. H. G. *scúr*. Prob. allied to L. *obscurus*, dark, and to E. *sky*.

Shred; see **Shroud**.

Shrew, a scold. (E.) M. E. *shrewe*,
adj., applied to both sexes, wicked, bad.
Also spelt *screwe*. A. S. *screáwa*, a shrew-
mouse, fabled to have a very venomous bite.
Lit. ' biter;' from Teut. base SKRU; to
cut; see **Shroud**. So also prov. G.
scher-maus, a mole, lit. 'shear-mouse,'
from G. *scheren*, to cut. Der. *shrew*, to
curse, talk like a shrew; also *screw* (2), q. v.

beshrew. (E.) M. E. *bi-schrewen*, to
imprecate a curse on. From *schrewe*, adj.,
wicked; with prefix *bi-*.

shrewd, malicious, cunning. (E.) The
old sense is 'malicious.' M. E. *schrewed*,
accursed, depraved, hence malicious; pp.
of *schrewen*, to curse, from the adj. *schrewe*,
malicious.

shrew-mouse, an animal like a mouse.
(E.) A. S. *screáwa*; see **Shrew** (above).

Shriek; see **Screech**.

Shrievalty; see **Sheriff**, under **Shire**.

Shrift; see **Shrove-tide**.

Shrike; see **Screech**.

Shrill. (Scand.) M. E. *shril*; Lowl.
Scotch *skirl*, a shrill cry, *skirl*, to cry
aloud. — Norweg. *skryla, skræla*, to cry
shrilly. Cf. Low G. *schrell*, G. *schrill*,
shrill; A. S. *scralletan*, to cry aloud. From
a base SKRAL, strengthened form of
SKAL, to resound, whence Icel. *skella* (pt.
t. *skall*), G. *er-schallen*, to resound, also
M. E. *shil*, shrill. Allied to **Scold**.

Shrimp. (E.) M. E. *shrimp*; cf. Lowl.
Scotch *scrimp*, to straiten, *scrimpit*, dwarf-
ish. A parallel form to *shrink*; cf. A. S.
scrimman, to shrink. See the traces of O.
Swed. *skrimpa*, strong verb, to contract, in
mod. Swed. dialects (Rietz). See **Shrink**.

Shrine. (L.) A. S. *scrín*, a box. — L.
scrinium, chest, box.

Shrink. (E.) A. S. *scrincan*, pt. t.

scranc, pp. *scruncen*, to contract, shrivel
up. + O. Du. *schrinken*, to shrink, grow
smaller; Swed. *skrynka*, a wrinkle. Allied
to **Shrimp, Shrivel, Shrug**.

scraggy, lean, rough. (Scand.) The
same as M. E. *scroggy*, covered with thin
straggling bushes. From prov. E. *scrag*, a
forked branch, lean person, *scrog*, a stunted
bush. — Swed. dial. *skraka*, a great dry tree,
long lean man; allied to Swed. dial. *skrokk*,
anything shrunken, *skrukka*, to shrink
together, *skrugeg*, crooked. All from
Norweg. strong verb *skrekka*, to shrink
(pt. t. *skrakk*), which stands for *skrenka**,
by assimilation, and is cognate with A. S.
scrincan, to shrink.

Shrive; see **Shrove-tide**.

Shrivel. (Scand.) A frequentative form
from a base *shriv-*, which is to be traced
in O. Northumb. *screpa*, to pine away,
Norweg. *skrypa*, to waste, Swed. dial.
skryyp, to shorten, contract, Swed. *skröplig*,
feeble, Dan. *skröbelig*, infirm; cf. Icel.
skrjupr, brittle, frail. Allied to **Shrimp**.

Shroud. (E.) A. S. *scrúd*, garment,
clothing. + Icel. *skrúð*, ornament, shrouds
of a ship; Dan. and Swed. *skrud*, dress,
attire. Orig. a 'shred' of stuff, a piece cut
or torn off; cf. G. *schrot*, a cut, a piece,
schroten, to cut, saw; Goth. *dis-skreitan*, to
tear to shreds; A.S. *screáde* (= mod. E. *shred*).

scroll, a roll of paper. (F. — Teut.)
Dimin. (with suffix *-l*) of M. E. *scrowe*, a
scroll. — O. F. *escroue*, 'a scrowle,' Cot. —
O. Du. *schroode*, a shred, strip, slip of
paper; allied to **shroud** (above).

Shrove-tide, Shrove-Tuesday. (E.)
The time for *shrift* or confession. The sb.
shrove is formed from *shrove*, pt. t. of the
verb to *shrive* (M. E. *schriuen*, pt. t.
shroof). — A. S. *scrifan*, to shrive, impose a
penance, pt. t. *scráf*. The pt. t. *scráf* was
merely formed by analogy with *dráf*, from
drífan, snáð, from *sníðan*, &c.; it is not
a Teut. verb, but borrowed from L. *scribere*, to write, draw up a law, hence, to
impose a penance (whence also G. *schrei-
ben*, pt. t. *schrieb*, to write). See **Scribe**.

shrift, confession. (E.) A. S. *scrift*,
confession, prescribed penance. — L. *scriptus*, pp. of *scribere*; see above.

Shrub (1), a low dwarf tree. (E.) A. S.
scrob, a shrub. Cf. prov. E. *shruff*, light
rubbish wood, *scroff*, refuse of wood. Prob.
allied to *shrimp*; from the stunted manner
of growth.

scrub, to rub hard. (E.) M. E. *scrobben*,

to **scrub** (orig. to rub with a branch of a shrub); from A. S. *scrob*, a shrub. Cf. E. *broom*, from the shrub so called; Lowl. Scotch *scrubber*, 'a handful of heath tied tightly together for cleaning culinary utensils;' Jamieson. **Der.** *scrubb-y*, mean, orig. shrubby, stunted.

Shrub (2); see **Sherbet**.

Shrug. (Scand.) The old sense is to shrink, shrink up. — Dan. *skrugge, skrukke*, to stoop, Swed. dial. *skrukka, skruga*, to huddle oneself together, allied to *skrinka*, to shrink. See **Shrink**.

Shudder. (O. Low G.) M. E. *schoderen, schuderen*. A frequentative verb. — O. Sax. *skuddian*, to shake; O. Du. *schudden*, to shake, tremble.

Shuffle; see **Shove**.

Shun. (E.) M. E. *shunien, shonien*. A. S. *scúnian*, to shun, avoid; orig. sense, to hurry away, hasten. Cf. Icel. *skunda, skynda*, Swed. *skynda sig*, Dan. *skynde*, to hasten, hurry, speed.

schooner. (E.) Properly *scooner*, but spelt as if derived from Dutch, which is not the case, the Du. *schooner* being of E. origin. First called a *scooner* in 1713, when the first schooner was so named in Gloucester, Massachusetts, from the remark that 'she *scoons*,' i. e. glides swiftly. This verb is the Clydesdale *scon* or *scoon*, to glide swiftly, applied to stones with which one makes 'ducks and drakes' in the water. — A. S. *scúnian*, to shun, orig. to speed, scud along.

shunt. (Scand.) Prov. E. *shunt*, to turn aside; M. E. *shunten*, to start aside, put for *shunden**. — Icel. *skunda*, to speed; see **Shun**.

Shut, Shuttle, Shuttle-cock; see **Shoot**.

Shy. (Scand.) M. E. *skyg*, scrupulous, shunning evil. (Also *shey, sceouh*, said of a shy horse; which answers to A. S. *sceóh*, timid.) — Dan. *sky*, shy; Swed. *skygg*, skittish, shy, coy. Allied to G. *scheu*, timid, shy, M. H. G. *schiech*, the same.

eschew, to shun. (F. — O. H. G.) M. E. *eschewen*. — O. F. *eschever*, to shun. — O. H. G. *sciuhan*, to frighten, also to fear. — O. H. G. and M. H. G. *schiech, schich*, shy, timid (above).

Sib, related. (E.) A. S. *sibb*, akin to; see **Gossip**.

Sibilant, hissing. (L.) L. *sibilant-*, stem of pres. pt. t. of *sibilare*, to hiss. — L. *sibilus*, hissing.

Sibyl. (L. — Gk.) L. *Sibylla*. — Gk. Σίβυλλα, a Sibyl or prophetess.

Sick. (E.) M. E. *sik, sek*. A. S. *seóc*.+ Du. *ziek*; Icel. *siúkr*; Dan. *syg*; Swed. *sjuk*; G. *siech*; Goth. *siuks*, which is from Goth. *siukan*, to be ill, pt. t. *sauk* (strong verb).

Sicker, Siker; see **Cure**.

Sickle; see **Secant**.

Side. (E.) M. E. *side*. A. S. *síde*, side; allied to A. S. *síd*, long, wide. + Du. *zijde*; Icel. *síða*; Dan. *side*; Swed. *sida*; G. *seite*.

aside. (E.) Put for *on side*.

beside. (E.) A. S. *be sídan*, by the side of; where *sídan* is dat. of *síde*, side. **Der.** *beside-s*, with adverbial suffix *-s*.

sidesmen. (E.) Officers chosen to assist a churchwarden; also called *sidemen*, i. e. men at one's side. Cf. L. *assessor*, one who sits besides another.

Sidereal, starry. (L.) Put for *sideral*, from L. *sideralis*, relating to the stars. — L. *sider-*, stem of *sidus*, a star.

consider. (F. — L.) F. *considerer*. — L. *considerare*, to consider, orig. to contemplate the stars. — L. *con-* (*cum*), together; *sider-*, stem of *sidus*, a star.

Siege. (F. — L.) The orig. sense was 'seat,' or 'a sitting down,' esp. in order to besiege a town — O. F. *siege*, a seat, throne; F. *siège*. Not immediately from L. *sedes*, but from a verb *sieger**, suggested by *assieger*, to besiege, answering to Low L. *assediare*, to besiege. — Low L. *assedium*, a siege; put for L. *obsidium*, a siege; both words being due to L. *sedere*, to sit; see **Sedentary**. **Der.** *be-siege*, with E. prefix.

Sienna, a pigment. (Ital.) Made from earth of *Sienna*, a place in Tuscany.

Sieve. (E.) M. E. *sive*. A. S. *sife*; oldest spelling *sibi* (8th cent.).+ Du. *zeef*; G. *sieb*. Perhaps orig. made of rushes; cf. prov. E. *seave*, a rush, Icel. *sef*, Swed. *säf*, Dan. *siv*, a rush.

sift. (E.) A. S. *siftan*, to sift. — A. S. *sife*, a sieve. + Du. *ziften*, to sift, *zift*, a sieve; from *zeef*, a sieve.

Sigh. (E.) M. E. *sighen*, also *syken*. A. S. *sícan*, to sigh, pt. t. *sác*, pp. *sicen*. Cf. Swed. *sukka*, Dan. *sukke*, to sigh, groan.

Sight; see **See** (1).

Sign. (F. — L.) O. F. *signe*. — L. *signum*, a mark. **Der.** *sign*, verb; *sign-at-ure*, from the pp. of the L. verb *signare*, to sign.

ancient (2), a banner, standard-bearer.

(F.–L.) Put for *ancien*, a corruption of O. F. *enseigne*; see **ensign** below.

assign. (F.–L.) O. F. *assigner.*–L. *assignare*, to assign, mark out to.–L. *as-* (for *ad*), to; *signare*, to mark, from *signum*.

consign. (F.–L.) F. *consigner.*–L. *consignare*, to attest, register, record, remark.–L. *con-* (for *cum*), together; *signare*, to mark; see above.

countersign, to attest by signing in addition. (F.–L.) F. *contresigner*, 'to subsigne;' Cot.–F. *contre*, over against; *signer*, to sign; see **Counter**.

design, verb. (F.–L.) O. F. *designer*, to denote, to design.–L. *designare*, to denote, mark down.–L. *de*, down; *signare*, to mark, from *signum*. Der. *design-ate*.

ensign. (F.–L.) O. F. *ensigne*, more commonly *enseigne*, 'a sign, ensigne, standard;' Cot.–Low L. *insigna*, L. *insigne*, a standard.–L. *insignis*, remarkable. –L. *in*, upon; *signum*, a mark; i.e. 'with a mark on it.'

insignia. (L.) L. *insignia*, marks of office; pl. of *insigne*, which is the neuter of *insignis* (above).

resign, to yield up. (F.–L.) F. *resigner.* – L. *resignare*, to unseal, annul, resign.–L. *re-*, back; *signare*, to sign, from *signum*, a sign, mark.

seal (1), a stamp. (F.–L.) M. E. *seel.* – O. F. *seel*, a signet (F. *sceau*). – L. *sigillum*, a seal, mark; dimin. form allied to *signum*, a mark. Der. *seal*, verb.

signal. (F.–L.) F. *signal.*–Low L. *signale*, sb., neut. of L. *signalis*, belonging to a sign. – L. *signum*, a sign.

signet. (F.–L.) F. *signet*; dimin. of F. *signe*; see **Sign** (above).

signify. (F.–L.) F. *signifier*, to betoken. – L. *significare*, to shew by signs. – L. *signi-*, for crude form of *signum*, a sign; *-ficare*, for *facere*, to make.

Signal, Signet, Signify; see **Sign**. **Signor;** see **Senate**.

Silence. (F.–L.) F. *silence.*–L. *silentia*, silence.–L. *silent-*, stem of pres. pt. of *silere*, to be silent. Der. *silent*, from L. *silent-*, stem of *silens*, pres. pt. of *silere*.

Silex, flint. (L.) L. *silex* (stem *silic-*), flint. Der. *silic-a*.

Silhouette. (F.) This meagre form of portrait, made by tracing the outline of a shadow, was named (in derision) after Etienne de *Silhouette*, French minister of finance in 1759.

Silk. (L.–Gk.–Chinese?.) A. S. *seolc*.

–L. *sericum*, silk; neut. of *Sericus*, belonging to the *Seres*. – Gk. Σῆρες, pl., Chinese. This name is perhaps from Chinese *se*, *sei*, silk.

serge. (F.–L.–Gk. – Chinese?.) F. *serge*, a silken stuff.–L. *serica*, fem. of *sericus*, silken, the same as *Sericus* (above).

Sill, base of a door. (E.) A. S. *syl*, a base, support. + Icel. *syll*, *svill*, a sill; Swed. *syll*, Swed. dial. *svill*; Dan. *syld*; G. *schwelle*, sill, threshold. Lit. 'a swell' or swelling; from the rise in the doorway caused by the beam used as a sill. See **Swell**. Der. *ground-sill*, spelt *grunsel* in Milton, P. L. i. 460.

Sillabub, a mixture of wine with milk, &c. (E. *and* Scand.) Formerly *sillibouk*, which perhaps stood for *swill-bouk* or rather *swell-bouk*, i. e. swell-belly; where *bouk* is from Icel. *búkr*, the belly. Cf. Icel. *sylgr*, a drink, allied to *sulla*, to swill; also O. Du. *swelbuyck*, 'a windie dropsie,' Hexham. ¶ Former part of the word doubtful; latter part certain.

Silly. (E.) Orig. 'timely;' then happy, lucky, blessed, innocent; lastly, simple, foolish. A. S. *sǽlig*, *gesǽlig*, timely. – A. S. *sǽl*, time, season, happiness. + Du. *zalig*, Icel. *sæll*, Swed. *säll*, G. *selig*, blest, happy; Goth. *sels*, good. Allied to O. Lat. *sollus*, favourable, L. *saluus*, safe; see **Safe**.

Silt. (Scand.) Formed, with participial suffix *-t*, from the verb *sile*, to drain.– Swed. *sila*, to drain, strain, filter; *sil*, a filter. Cf. Icel. *sía*, Dan. *sie*, A. S. *sthan*, to filter; allied to A. S. *sígan*, to let drop, Skt. *sich*, to discharge, Gk. ἰκ-μάς, moisture. (√SIK.)

Silvan, Sylvan. (L.) The spelling with *y* is bad.–L. *siluanus*, belonging to a wood.–L. *silua*, a wood.+Gk. ὕλη, a wood (connection with *silua* doubtful).

savage. (F. – L.) M. E. *sauage.*– O. F. *savaige*, *salvage* (F. *sauvage*). – L. *siluaticus*, belonging to a wood, wild.– L. *silua*, a wood.

Silver. (E.) A. S. *seolfor* (for *silfor* *), like *meolc* for *milc* *).+Du. *zilver*; Icel. *silfr*; Dan. *sölv*; Swed. *silfver*; G. *silber*; Goth. *silubr*; Russ. *serebro*; Lith. *sidâbras*. Perhaps named from its whiteness; cf. L. *sidus*, a star, Lith. *swidus*, bright.

Similar. (F.–L.) F. *similaire*; as if from L. *similaris* *, extended from *similis*, like. Allied to *simul*, together, and to E. **Same**.

assemble. (F. – L.) O. F. *assembler.* – Low L. *assimulare*, to collect (different from L. *assimulare*, to feign.) – L. *as-*, for *ad*, to; *simul*, together.

assimilate. (L.) From pp. of L. *assimilare*, to make like. – L. *as-*, for *ad*, to; *similis*, like.

dissemble. (F. – L.) O. F. *dis-* (= L. *dis-*), apart; *sembler*, to seem, appear; cf. O. F. *dissimuler*, to dissemble. – L. *dis-*, apart, away; *simulare*, to pretend; cf. L. *dissimulare*, to pretend that a thing is not. See **simulate** (below).

dissimilar, unlike. (F. – L.) O. F. *dissimilaire.* – O. F. *dis-* (= L. *dis-*, apart); and *similaire*; see **Similar**.

dissimilitude, dissimulation; from L. *dis-*, apart, and **similitude, simulation**.

resemble. (F. – L.) O. F. *resembler.* – O. F. *re-*, again; *sembler*, to seem, be like. – L. *re-*, again; *simulare*, to make like. See **Simulate** (below).

semblance, appearance. (F. – L.) O.F. *semblance*, appearance. – F. *sembler*, to seem. – L. *similare*, *simulare*; see **simulate** (below).

simile. (L.) L. *simile*, a comparison, a like thing; neut. of *similis*, like.

similitude. (F. – L.) F. *similitude.* – L. acc. *similitudinem*, likeness. – L. *similis*, like.

simulate. (L.) From pp. of L. *simulare*, also *similare*, to make like. – L. *similis*, like; *simul*, together.

simultaneous. (L.) Late L. *simultaneus*; coined from L. *simult-im*, at the same time. – L. *simul*, together.

Simile, Similitude; see **Similar**.

Simious, monkey-like. (L.) From L. *simia*, an ape. – L. *simus* (Gk. σιμός), flat-nosed.

Simmer. (E.) A frequentative form, from the base *sim*, to express the sound of gentle boiling. Cf. Dan. *summe*, G. *summen*, Swed. dial. *summa*, to hum, buzz.

Simnel, a kind of rich cake. (F. – L.) O. F. *simenel*; Low L. *siminellus*, bread of fine flour; also called *simella* in Low L. – L. *simila*, wheat-flour of the finest quantity; whence *siminellus*, put for *similellus**.

Simony, traffic in ecclesiastical preferment. (F. – L. – Gk. – Heb.) F. *simonie*; Low L. *simonia*. Named from *Simon Magus* (Acts viii. 18). – Gk. Σίμων, Simon. – Heb. *Shim'ôn*, Simeon; lit. one who hears. – Heb. root *shâma'*, he heard.

Simoom. (Arab.) Arab. *samûm*, a sultry pestilential wind; from its poisonous nature. – Arab. root *samma*, he poisoned.

Simper, to smirk. (Scand.) From Scand.; cf. Norw. *semper*, fine, smart; Dan. dial. *semper, simper*, affected, coy, prudish; O. Swed. *semper*, one who affectedly refrains from eating. Formed from O. Swed. *sipp*, *simp*, an affected woman, Swed. *sipp*, adj., finical, prim. All from the notion of *sipping*, or taking only a little at a time; hence, prudish, affected, coy, &c. Cf. Low G. *sipp*, prim, *den Mund* sipp *trekken*, to make a small mouth. See **sip**, under **Sup**.

Simple. (F. – L.) F. *simple.* – L. *simplicem*, acc. of *simplex*, lit. 'one-fold.' – L. *sim-*, from the base *sama**, the same (appearing also in *sin-guli*, one by one, *sem-el*, once, *sim-ul*, together); and *plic-*, from *plicare*, to fold; see **Same** and **Ply**. Der. *simplicity*, F. *simplicité*, from L. acc. *simplicitatem*; *simpli-fy*, to make simple.

simpleton. (F. – L.) I. e. *simple-t-on*, with double suffix; formed with F. suffix *-on* from F. *simplet*, a simple person, fem. *simplette*, 'a simple wench.' Cot. – F. *simple*, simple; with suffixed *-t*. (So also *musk-et-oon*.)

Simulate, Simultaneous; see **Similar**.

Sin. (E.) A. S. *syn, sinn, senn.* + Du. *zonde*; Icel. *synd, synð*; Dan. Swed. *synd*; G. *sünde*, O. H. G. *suntja*. Thus the A. S. word has lost a final *d*, and E. *sin* stands for *sind*. Allied to L. *sons* (stem *sont-*), guilty, sinful; which again is allied to the pres. pt. of the Aryan root AS, to be. 'Language regards the *guilty* man as the man *who it was*;' Curtius. See **Sooth**. Der. *sin*, verb.

Since. (E.) Written for *sins*, which is short for M. E. *sithens*, since. This is formed, with adverbial suffix *-s*, from M. E. *sithen*, since, a modification of A. S. *stð ðám*, after that, also written *siððan*. β. The A. S. *stð* was orig. an adj., meaning 'late,' then later, after; cf. Goth. *seithus*, late, *seithu*, adv., late. The A. S. *ðám* is the dat. (neuter) of the definite article or demonst. pronoun. The G. *seitdem*, since, is precisely the A. S. *siððan*.

Sincere. (F. – L.) O. F. *sincere.* – L. *sincerus*, pure, sincere. Der. *sincerity*, from F. *sincerité*, from L. acc. *sinceritatem*.

Sinciput; see **Capital**.

Sinder, the true spelling of **Cinder**, q. v.

Sine. (L.) From L. *sinus*, a bosom, a fold, a curve; peculiarly used. See **Sinus**

Sinecure; see Cure.

Sinew. (E.) M. E. *sinewe.* A. S. *sinu.* +Du. *zenuw*; Dan. *sene*; Swed. *sena*; G. *sehne*; also Icel. *sin.* Lit. 'that which binds;' cf. Skt. *si,* to bind.

Sing. (E.) A. S. *singan,* orig. to sing, resound; pt. t. *sang,* pp. *sungen.* Of imitative origin.+Du. *zingen*; Icel. *syngja*; Dan. *synge*; Swed. *sjunga*; Goth. *siggwan* (for *singwan**); G. *singen.*

singe, to scorch. (E.) Put for *senge*; M. E. *sengen.* A. S. *sengan,* to singe; lit. 'to make to sing,' from the hissing of a burning log, &c. Causal of *singan,* to sing (above).+Du. *zengen,* G. *sengen,* causal verbs, similarly formed.

song. (E.) M. E. *song.* A. S. *sang.*— A. S. *sang,* pt. t. of *singan.*+Du. *zang*; Icel. *söngr*; Swed. *sång*; Dan. and G. *sang*; Goth. *saggws* (for *sangws*).

songster. (E.) A. S. *sangystre, sangestre,* a singer.—A. S. *sang,* pt. t. of *singan,* to sing; with double suffix *-es-tre* of the agent. **Der.** *songstr-ess,* with. F. suffix.

Single. (L.) L. *singulus,* single, separate, in late Latin; in classical Latin, we have only *singuli,* pl., one by one. Allied to **Simple,** q. v. (M. E. and O. F. *sengle.*)

singular. (F.—L.) M. E. *singuler.*— F. *singulier.* — L. *singularis,* single. — L. *singuli,* pl., one by one (above).

Sinister. (L.) L. *sinister,* on the left hand, inauspicious.

Sink. (E.) Properly intransitive; the transitive form should be *senk* or *sench*; cf. *drench* from *drink.* — A. S. *sincan,* intrans., pt. t. *sanc,* pp. *suncen.* + Du. *zinken*; Icel. *sökkva* (for *sönkva*); Dan. *synke*; Swed. *sjunka*; G. *sinken*; Goth. *sigkwan* (for *singkwan*). β. For the trans. form, cf. A. S. *sencan,* to cause to sink, G. *senken.* **Der.** *sink,* orig. a place into which filth *sank* or was collected; Cor. i. 1. 126.

Sinus, a bay, gulf, &c. (L.) L. *sinus,* a bosom, bend, bay, fold. Now only used in the form *sine,* in mathematics. **Der.** *sinuous,* L. *sinuosus,* full of curves.

insinuate. (L.) From pp. of L. *insinuare,* to introduce by winding or bending. — L. *in,* into; *sinus,* a bend.

Sinople, green. (F.—L.—Gk.) F. *sinople,* 'green;' Cot.—Low L. *sinopis,* greenish, also reddish; L. *sinopis,* red ochre. — Gk. σινωπίς, σινωπική, a red earth found in Cappadocia, and imported from *Sinope,* on the Black Sea.

Sip; see Sup.

Siphon. (F.—L.—Gk.) F. *siphon.*—L. *siphonem,* acc. of *sipho,* a siphon, bent pipe for drawing off liquids. — Gk. σίφων, a small pipe or reed.

Sippet; see Sup.

Sir, Sire; see Senate.

Siren. (L.—Gk.) L. *siren.*—Gk. σειρήν, a nymph who enticed sea-men to destruction by her magic song; allied to σύριγξ, a pipe; see Syringe.

Sirloin, for Surloin; see Lumbar.

Sirname, for Surname; see Name.

Sirocco; see Saracen.

Sirrah; see Senate.

Sir-reverence. (L.) Put for *save-reverence,* a translation of L. *salud reuer-entid,* i. e. reverence to you being preserved, or, by your leave. — L. *salud,* abl. fem. of *saluus,* safe; and *reuerentid,* abl. of *reuerentia.*

Sirup; see Sherbet.

Siskin, a song-bird. (Dan.) Dan. *sisgen,* a siskin; Swed. *siska.* It means 'chirper;' cf. Swed. dial. *sisa,* to make a noise like a wood-grouse, Du. *sissen,* to hiss.

Sister. (Scand.) A Scand. form.—Icel. *systir,* Swed. *syster,* Dan. *söster.* + A. S. *sweostor*; Du. *zuster*; Goth. *swistar*; G. *schwester.* Further allied to L. *soror* (for *sosor**); Skt. *svasri.* **Der.** *cousin,* q. v.

Sit. (E.) A. S. *sittan,* pt. t. *sæt,* pp. *seten.*+Du. *zitten*; Icel. *sitja*; Dan. *sidde*; Swed. *sitta*; Goth. *sittan*; G. *sitzen.*+L. *sedere*; Gk. ἕζομαι, I sit; Skt. *sad.* See **Sedentary.** (√SAD.)

beset. (E.) A. S. *bisettan,* to surround. —A. S. *bi,* by, around; *settan,* to set; see **set** (below).

saddle; see Saddle (in separate article).

seat, sb. (Scand.) Icel. *sæti,* a seat; Swed. *säte*; Dan. *sæde.*—Icel. *sat,* pt. t. of *sitja,* to sit (above). **Der.** *seat,* vb.

seize, to grasp. (F.—O. H. G.) M. E. *seysen, saisen,* a law term, to put one in *seisin* or possession of a thing, also, to take possession; hence, to seize, take. — O. F. *saisir, seisir,* to put in possession of, to take possession.—O. H. G. *sazzan, sezzan,* to set, put, place, hence, to put in possession of; the same as G. *setzen,* to set. See **set** (below). **Der.** *seis-in,* O. F. *seisine, saisine,* from the verb *saisir.*

set. (E.) A. S. *settan,* to set, make to sit; causal of *sittan,* to sit (derived from the pt. t. *sæt*).+Icel. *setja*; Dan. *sætte*;

Swed. *sätte*; G. *setzen*; Du. *zetten*; Goth. *satjan*; all causal forms.

settee, a seat with a long back; apparently an arbitrary variation of *settle*, sb., which see below.

settle (1), a long bench with a high back. (E.) A. S. *setl*, a seat.+Goth. *sitls*; G. *sessel*; L. *sella* (for *sed-la* *). See **sell** (2), under **Sedentary**.

settle (2), to fix, adjust. (E.) Two distinct words have been confused. 1. A.S. *setlan*, to fix; lit. to take a seat, settle down as in a seat, from A.S. *setl*, a seat; see above. 2. In the phrase ' to *settle* a dispute' it is a totally different word, and put for M. E. *sahtlen*, to reconcile, A.S. *sahtlian*, to reconcile.—A.S. *saht*, reconciliation.—A.S. *sacan*, to contend, strive, dispute; whence also E. **Sake**, q. v.

Site. (F.—L.) F. *site*, *sit*.—L. *situm*, acc. of *situs*, a site, place.—L. *situs*, pp. of *sinere*, to let, suffer, permit; the orig. sense seems to have been to place. Hence **Position**, q. v.

situate. (L.) Low L. *situatus*, pp. of *situare*, to place.—L. *situ-*, crude form of *situs*, a place. Der. *situat-ion*.

Sith, since. (E.) Short for M. E. *sithen*; see **Since**.

Six. (E.) A. S. *six*.+ Icel., Dan., and Swed. *sex*; G. *sechs*; Goth. *saihs*; Russ. *sheste*; W. *chwech*; Gael. and Irish *se*; L. *sex*; Gk. *ἕξ*; Lith. *szeszi*; Pers. *shash*; Skt. *shash*. Der. *six-th*, M. E. *sixte*, A. S. *six-ta*; *six-ty*, A. S. *sixtig*. See **Sexagenarian**.

senary, belonging to six. (L.) L. *senarius*, adj., from *seni*, six apiece; put for *sex-ni* *.—L. *sex*, six (above).

Sizar; see **Sedentary**.

Size (1) and (2); see **Sedentary**.

Skain, Skene, Skein, a dagger, knife. (Irish.) Irish and Gael. *sgian*, a knife; W. *ysgien*, a cutting instrument. Cf. W. *ysgi*, a cutting off. (√SKI, to cut.) Der. *skains-mate* (Shak.); unless it be from *skein*, q. v.

Skate (1), a large flat fish. (Scand.—L.) M. E. *scate*.—Icel. *skata*; Norw. *skata*.—L. *squatus*, a skate. Cf. Irish *sgat*, a skate.

Skate (2), **Scate**, a frame with a steel blade, for sliding on ice. (Du.) Properly *skates*; the *s* being dropped because *skates* looked like a pl. form. Formerly called *scatches* (another form of *skateses*, pl.).—Du. *schaatsen*, skates, a pl. form, from a sing. *schaats*, whence *schaatsryder*, a skate-rider, **skater**. It appears to be allied to Low G.

schake, a shank, leg, cognate with E. **Shank**. Thus *scatches* or *skates* are 'shanks,' contrivances for lengthening the stride; cf. F. *échasse*, a stilt, also from Du. *schaats*.

Skein, Skain, a knot (or quantity) of thread or silk. (C.) M. E. *skeyne*, a quantity of yarn.—Irish *sgainne*, a fissure, flaw, also a skein or clue of thread; Gael. *sgeinnidh*, flax, thread. β. Apparently as much as is contained in a single piece, from break to break.—Irish *sgainim*, I cleave; Gael. *sgain*, to rend apart. Der. (probably) *skains-mates*, companions (Shak.), as if associated in winding yarn.

Skeleton. (Gk.) Gk. *σκελετόν*, a dried body; neut. of *σκελετός*, dried.—Gk. *σκέλλειν*, to dry, parch.

Skeptic; see **Sceptic**.

Sketch. (Du.—Ital.—L.—Gk.) Du. *schets*, a draught, sketch.—Ital. *schizzo*, a first rough draught.—L. *schedium*, a thing made hastily; from *schedius*, adj., hastily made.—Gk. *σχέδιος*, sudden; allied to *σχεδόν*, near; from the base *σχε-*, to hold. Allied to **Scheme**.

Skew. (O. Low G.) M. E. *skewen*, verb, to turn aside.—O. Du. *schuwen*, *schouwen*, to avoid, shun; Low. G. *schuwen*, *schouen*, to avoid.+O. H. G. *sciuhen*, G. *scheuen*, to avoid; from *scheu*, adj., shy. Thus *to skew* is to turn aside, like a shying horse, and is derived from the adj. appearing in E. *shy*. See **Shy**. Der. *askew*, i. e. *on the skew*.

skewbald, piebald. (O. Low G. *and* C.) Marked in a *skew* or irregular manner; see **Bald**. Cf. *pie-bald*.

Skewer; see **Shiver** (2).

Skid; see **Shed** (1).

Skiff; see **Shape**.

Skill, discernment, tact. (Scand.) M. E. *skil*, often in the sense of 'reason.'—Icel. *skil*, a distinction; cf. *skilja*, to part, separate, distinguish; Dan. *skiel*, Swed. *skäl*, reason; Dan. *skille*, Swed. *skilja*, to separate. Allied to Lith. *skelti*, to cleave; Swed. *skala*, to peel. (√SKAL = √SKAR, to cut.) Der. *skill*, verb, as in phr. ' it *skills* not,' i. e. makes no difference; from Icel. *skilja*, often used impersonally, with the sense ' it differs.'

scald (2), scabby. (Scand.) For *scalled*, i. e. afflicted with the *scall*; see **scall** (below).

scale (1), a shell, a flake. (E.) M. E. *scale*. A.S. *sceale*, *scale*, a shell, husk, scale.+Dan. and Swed. *skal*, a shell, pod;

G. *schale*, shell, husk (whence O. F. *escale*, F. *écale*, with which the E. word may have been confused). (√SKAL = √SKAR.)

scale (2), a bowl or dish of a balance. (E.) Formerly also *scole*. A. S. *scále*, a scale of a balance.+Icel. *skál*, Dan. *skaal*, Swed. *skál*, bowl; Du. *schaal*, scale, bowl; G. *schale*, cup, dish, bowl; allied to **scale** (1).

scall, scab on the skin. (Scand.) From Icel. *skalli*, a bald head; orig. a peeled head. Cf. Swed. *skallig*, bald, from *skala*, to peel. Allied to Swed. *skal*, a husk; see **scale** (1). Der. *scald* (2) = *scalled*, afflicted with scall.

scallop, **scollop**, a kind of shell-fish. (F. − Teut.) M. E. *skalop*. − O. F. *escalope*, a shell. − O. Du. *schelpe* (Du. *schelp*), a shell, especially a scallop-shell.+G. *schelfe*, a husk. Allied to *scale* (1), *shell*, &c. Der. *scallop*, verb, to cut an edge into scallop-like curves.

scalp. (O. Low G.) M. E. *scalp*. − O. Du. *schelpe*, a shell (hence, skull). See above. Cf. O. Swed. *skalp*, a sheath; also O. Ital. *scalpo*, the scalp, a word borrowed from Teutonic.

scull (1), **skull**, the cranium. (Scand.) M. E. *skulle*, *scolle*. Named from its bowl-like shape. − Icel. *skál*, Dan. *skaal*, Swed. *skál*, bowl, basin; see **scale** (2).

scull (2), a small light oar. (Scand.) Named from the slightly hollowed blades, like the dish of a balance. − Icel. *skál*, a hollow; Swed. *skálig*, concave. See **scull** (1). Der. *scull*, verb, to use sculls.

shale, a slaty rock. (G.) G. *schale*, a shell, peel, scale; whence *schal-gebirge*, a mountain formed of thin strata. Cognate with E. *scale* (1).

shell. (E.) M. E. *shelle*, sb. A.S. *scell*, *scyll*.+Du. *schel*; Icel. *skel*; Goth. *skalja*, a tile. The sense is 'thin flake;' cf. Swed. *skala*, to peel. Der. *shell*, verb.

skull; see **scull** (1) above.

Skillet; see **Scuttle** (1).

Skim; see **Scum**.

Skin. (Scand.) Icel. *skinn*, Swed. *skinn*, Dan. *skind*, skin. Cf. G. *schinden*, to skin, flay; also W. *cen*, skin, *ysgen*, dandriff.

Skink; see **Shake**.

Skip. (C.) M. E. *skippen*. − Irish *sgiob*, to snatch; Gael. *sgiab*, to move suddenly, twitch; W. *ysgipio*, to snatch away, *ysgip*, a quick snatch, twitch, *cipio*, to snatch, *cip*, a quick pull. Cf. Skt. *kship*, to throw, move quickly, *kshipra*, adj., quick.

Skipper; see **Shape**.

Skirmish. (F. − O. H. G.) Also spelt *scrimmage*. M. E. *scarmishe*. − O. F. *escarmouche*, 'a skirmish, bickering;' Cot. − O. H. G. *skerman*, to defend, fight, also spelt *scirman*. − O. H. G. *scirm* (G. *schirm*), a shield, screen, shelter, guard, defence. To *skirmish* is, properly, to fight behind cover, hence to advance to fight under shelter. β. The change of vowel from the O. F. *a* to E. *i* was due to the fact that we had previously borrowed the M. E. word *skirmen*, to skirmish, from the O. F. *eskermir* (later *escrimer*), to fence, fight; this is from O. H. G. *scirman*, as above.

scaramouch, a buffoon. (F. − Ital. − O. H. G.) From *Scaramoche*, a famous Italian zany who acted in England in 1673 (Blount). Also called *Scaramouche*, which was the F. spelling; but his real name was *Scaramuccia*, of which the lit. sense is 'a skirmish,' being the same word as the O. F. *escarmouche* (above).

Skirt; see **Shear**.

Skittish, **Skittles**; see **Shoot**.

Skulk; see **Scowl**.

Skunk, a quadruped. (N. American Indian.) Said to be from the Abenaki *seganku*, a skunk; this is a dialect of Algonquin (Lower Canada).

Sky. (Scand.) M. E. *skye*, a cloud. − Icel. *ský*, a cloud; Dan. Swed. *sky*, a cloud. Allied to A. S. *scúa*, shade; Skt. *sku*, to cover. (√SKU.)

Slab (1), a thin slip of timber or stone. (Scand.) M. E. *slab*. Put for *slap* *; allied to prov. E. *slape*, slippery. − Icel. *sleppa* (pt. t. *slapp*), to slip; Norweg. *sleip*, adj., slippery, *sleip*, sb., a smooth piece of timber for dragging anything over, esp. used of pieces of timber used for the foundation of a road, the same as North. E. *slab*, 'the outside plank of a piece of timber, when sawn into boards,' Ray. Such a *slab* could be used for roads, being smooth on one (the upper) side. β. Hence we explain *sleeper* (for rails), as forming a *slape* or smooth foundation; cf. Norfolk *slaper*, *sleeper*, the trunk of a tree cut short, M. E. *slepir*, slippery. Cf. also O. Du. *slippen*, (1) to slip, (2) to slit. See **Slip**.

Slab (2), slimy. (C.) The same as prov. E. *slabby*, sloppy, dirty. − Irish *slab*, *slaib*, Gael. *slaib*, mire, mud. Cf. Icel. *slepja*, slime. See **Slop**.

Slabber, to slaver. (O. Low G.) Frequentative of O. Du. *slabben*, to slaver, to

lap, sup, or lick up; Low G. *slabbern*,
slubbern, to slabber, lap, slip, frequent. of
slabben, to lap.+G. *schlabbern*, *schlabben*,
to lap, to slabber. Cf. prov. E. *slap*, to
lick up food, eat quickly.

slaver, to slabber. (Scand.) Icel.
slafra, to slaver; cognate with Low G.
slabbern (above). **Der.** *slaver*, sb., from
Icel. *slafr*, *slefa*, slaver.

slobber, slubber, to do carelessly, to
sully. (Scand.) Dan. *slubbre*, to slabber;
Swed. dial. *slubbra*, to slubber, slobber, be
disorderly, frequent. of Swed. dial. *slubba*,
to mix liquids carelessly, to be careless.+
Du. *slobberen*, to sup up; Low G. *slubbern*, to lap, sip.

Slack. (E.) M. E. *slak*. A. S. *sleac*,
slack, slow.+Icel. *slakr*; Swed. Dan. *slak*;
prov. G. *schlak*, slack, loose. Orig. sense
' fluid ;' see below.

slag, dross, scoria. (Swed.) Swed. *slagg*,
dross of metal; so called from flowing
over when fused. Cf. Icel. *slagna*, to flow
over, *slag*, *slagi*, wet, damp, water pene-
trating walls. It is a weakened form of
slack, as seen by G. *schlacke*, ' dross, slacks,
sediment,' Flügel; *schlackern*, to trickle,
schluck, slack, drossy, sloppy; Low G.
slakke, slag. Orig. sense ' fluid ;' cf. Skt.
srij, to let loose, let flow, effuse, shed.

slake, to slacken, quench, wet. (E.)
A. S. *sleacian*, to grow slack; *sleccan*, to
grow slack (hence, to make slack, slacken).
−A.S. *sleac*, slack; see **Slack**.+Icel.*slökva*
(pp. *slokinn*), to slake; Swed. *släcka*, to
quench, allay, slake, from *slak*, adj.

Slam. (Scand.) Norweg. *slemba*, *slemma*,
to smack, bang, slam a door; Swed. dial.
slämma, to push hastily; Icel. *slamra*, to slam.
Cf. Swed. *slammer*, a noise. Allied to **Slap**.

Slander; see **Scan**.

Slang, vulgar language; see **Sling**.

Slant, to slope. (Scand.) M. E. *slenten*,
to slope, glide. −Swed. dial. *slenta*, *slänta*,
causal of *slinta* (pt. t. *slant*), to slide, slip
with the foot; Swed. *slinta*, to slip, glance
aside. The E. adj. *slant*, sloping, answers
to Swed. dial. *slant*, slippery. Allied to
Slide; and cf. **Slink**.

aslant, i. e. *on the slant*.

Slap. (E. ?) M. E. *slappe*, a smart blow;
prob. an imitative word; allied to **Slam**.
+Low G. *slapp*, sound of a blow, a slap;
G. *schlapp*, interj., slap ! *schlappe*, sb., a
slap, *schlappen*, to slap. **Der.** *slap-bang*,
violently.

Slash, Slate; see **Slit**.

Slattern, an untidy woman. (Scand.)
From prov. E. *slatter*, to waste, to be untidy, to throw about; frequent. of *slat*, to
dash or throw about.−Icel. *sletta*, to slap,
dab, dash liquids about; Norweg. *sletta*, to
fling about, jerk; Icel. *sletta*, sb., a dab,
spot of ink. Allied to Norweg. *slett*, a
blow; A. S. *gesleht*, a smiting, from *sleán*,
to smite; it is therefore allied to **Slay**.
¶ *Slut* is quite distinct.

sleet. (Scand.) M. E. *sleet*. − Norw.
sletta, sleet; so named from dashing in
one's face.−Norweg. *sletta*, to fling, Icel.
sletta, to slap, dab; see above. Cf. York-
shire *slat*, a spot, slattery, wet.

Slaughter; see **Slay** (1).

Slave. (F.−G.−Slavonic.) F. *esclave*.
−G. *sklave*, M. H. G. *slave*, a slave.−G.
Slave, a Slavonian captive, a slave. In
Slavonic, the name *Slave* meant 'intelligible,'
from Church-Slav. (and Russ.) *slovo*, a word.
−Church-Slav. *slu-ti*, to be named.

Slaver; see **Slabber**.

Slay (1), to kill. (E.) Orig. to smite.
M. E. *sleen*.−A. S. *sleán* (contracted form
of *slahan*), to smite, pt. t. *slóh*, pp. *slegen*.+
Du. *slaan*; Icel. *slá*; Dan. *slaae*; Swed.
slå; Goth. *slahan*; G. *schlagen*. (Teut.
base SLAH.)

slaughter, sb. (Scand.) M. E. *slaghter*.
−Icel. *slátr*, slaughter, whence *slátra*, to
slaughter cattle. The A. S. form is *sleaht*,
whence M. E. *slaught*.+Du. Dan. *slagt*, G.
schlacht; from the base of **Slay** (above).

slay (2), **sley**, a weaver's reed. (E.)
A. S. *slá*, also *slahæ*; so called from *striking* the web together.−A. S. *sleán* (=*slahan*), to strike; see **Slay** (1).

sledge-hammer. (E.) A reduplicated
form; a *sledge* means ' a hammer.'−A.S.
slecge, a heavy hammer, smiter. − A. S.
sleg-en, pp. of *sleán*, to smite.+Du. *slegge*,
slei, Swed. *slägga*, Icel. *sleggja*, a sledge or
heavy hammer.

sleight, dexterity. (Scand.) Put for
sleighth ; M. E. *sleighthe*. − Icel. *slægð*, sly-
ness, cunning.−Icel. *slagr*, sly. So also
Swed. *slögd*, dexterity, from *slög*, dexterous.

sly, cunning. (Scand.) M. E. *slie*. −
Icel. *slægr*, sly, cunning; Swed. *slug*; Dan.
siug, *slu*; G. *schlau*. We also find Swed.
slög, dexterous, Icel. *slægr*, kicking (as a
horse). Allied to **Slay**; cf. G. *verschlagen*,
cunning, crafty, sly. Orig. ' dexterous with
the hammer.' See also **Slattern**, **Sleet**.

Slay (2); see under **Slay** (1).

Sleave, **Sleave-silk**, soft floss silk.

(Scand.) 'Ravelled *sleave*,' i. e. tangled loose silk. — Dan. *slöife*, a loose knot, Swed. *sleif*, a knot of ribbon.+Low G. *slöpe, slepe*, a slip-knot, from *slepen*, to slip ; G. *schleife*, a loop, slip-knot, from *schleifen*, to slip. Allied to **Slip**. Cf. G. *schlaff*, Low G. *slapp*, loose, slack.

Sled, Sleigh, Sledge ; see **Slide**.

Sledge-hammer ; see **Slay** (1).

Sleek, Slick, smooth, glossy. (Scand.) M. E. *slyk, slike*. — Icel. *slikr*, sleek, smooth. Allied to Du. *slijk*, G. *schlick*, grease ; from the Low G. strong verb *sliken* (pt. t. *sleek*, pp. *sleken*) = G. *schleichen* (pt. t. *slich*), to slink, crawl, move as if through mire ; see **Slink**. Orig. sense 'greasy,' like soft mud.

Sleep, vb. (E.) A. S. *slæpan, slépan*, pt. t. *slép*.+Du. *slapen* ; Goth. *slepan* ; G. *schlafen*, to sleep. The sb. is A. S. *slǽp*, Du. *slaap*, Goth. *sleps*, G. *schlaf*, O. H. G. *sláf*, orig. 'drowsiness ;' allied to Low G. *slapp*, G. *schlaff*, lax, loose, flabby, unbent, relaxed (as in sleep) ; also to Icel. *sleppr*, slippery, and to E. **Slip**. Cf. E. *sleepy*, i. e. inactive.

Sleeper, a block of wood under rails ; see **Slab** (1).

Sleet ; see **Slattern**.

Sleeve. (E.) A. S. *sléfe, sléf*, a sleeve ; also spelt *slýfe, slýf*.+O. Du. *sloove*, a veil, cover ; G. *schlaube*, husk, shell, allied to M. H. G. *sloufen*, to let slip, cover, causal of M. H. G. *sliefen*, O. H. G. *slífan*, to slip. Cf. Goth. *sliupan* (pt. t. *slaup*, pp. *slupans*), to slip, creep into. Certainly allied to *slip*, from the *slipping* of the sleeve on and off, in dressing and undressing. See **Slip**, and **Slop** (2).

Sleigh ; see **Slide**.

Sleight ; see **Slay** (1).

Slender ; see **Slide**.

Slice ; see **Slit**.

Slick ; see **Sleek**.

Slide, vb. (E.) A. S. *slídan*, pt. t. *slád*, pp. *sliden*. Cf. also A. S. *slidor*, slippery, G. *schlitten*, a sledge. Also Irish and Gael. *slaod*, to slide, Lith. *slídus*, slippery. *Sli-de* and *sli-p* are from the same root ; cf. Skt. *sri*, to flow, *sriti*, gliding. (✔ SAR.)

sled, a sledge. (Scand.) M. E. *slede*. — Icel. *sleði*, Dan. *slæde*, Swed. *slede*, a sledge. + Du. *slede*, G. *schlitten*, a sledge. From the verb *to slide* (above).

sledge. (Scand.) This is a corrupt form ; apparently put for *sleds*, pl. of *sled*.

sleigh. (Scand.) An ill-spelt word ; there is no final guttural. — Norweg. *slee*, short for *slede*, a sledge ; so also Du. *sleekoets*, put for *sledekoets*, lit. 'a sledge-coach.'

slender, thin, feeble. (O. Low G.) M. E. *slendre*. — O. Du. *slinder*, slender, thin ; as sb., a water-snake, named from its gliding or trailing. — O. Du. *slinderen*, also *slidderen*, to drag, train along, trail ; Low G. *slindern*, to slide on the ice (whence Low G. *slender*, a trailing. gown). Nasalised forms from the verb *to slide*. (See note.)

Slight, adj. (O. Low G.) M. E. *slight*, orig. sense even or flat, as of a thing beaten flat ; then plain, smooth, simple, trivial, &c. — O. Du. *slicht*, even, plain, *slecht*, slight, simple, vile ; cf. *slichten*, 'to slight, to make even or plaine,' Hexham. + O. Low G. *slight*, even, simple, bad ; Icel. *sléttr*, flat, smooth, trivial ; Dan. *slet*, level, bad ; Swed. *slät*, smooth, worthless, slight ; Goth. *slaihts*, smooth ; G. *schlicht*, smooth, plain, homely. Orig. 'beaten flat,' or 'beaten' (i.e. worsted, weak). Allied to **Slay** (1).

Slim. (Du.) Orig. sense 'sloping ;' thence weak, poor, thin, bad, slight ; prov. E. *slim*, crafty. — O. Du. *slim*, awry, crafty.+ Dan. Swed. *slem*, worthless ; Icel. *slæmr*, vile ; G. *schlimm*, bad, cunning. Cf. prov. E. *slam*, the slope of a hill, tall and lean. Prob. from the same root as *slip, slide, slender*.

Slime. (E.) A. S. *slím*. + Du. *slijm* ; Icel. *slím* ; Swed. *slem* ; Dan. *sliim* ; G. *schleim* ; Russ. *slina*, saliva, *slize*, slime. Cf. L. *saliua*, Gk. σίαλον, spittle.

Sling, vb. (E.) A. S. *slingan*, pt. t. *slang*, pp. *slungen*.+Icel. *slyngva, slöngva* ; G. *schlingen*, to wind, twist, sling. Der. *sling*, sb.

slang, vulgar language. (Scand.). Norweg. *sleng*, a slinging, a device, a burthen of a song, *slengja*, to sling, *slengja kjeften*, to slang, abuse (lit. 'to sling the jaw'), *slengjenamn*, a slang-name, *slengjeord*, a slang word, insulting word. All from *slengja*, to sling, causal form from the Icel. *slöng*, pt. t. of *slyngva* (above).

Slink. (E.) A. S. *slincan*, to creep ; nasalised form of A. S. *slican* * (not found), which is cognate with Low G. *sliken*, to creep (pt. t. *sleek*, pp. *sleken*), and G. *schleichen*, to creep (pt. t. *schlich*). + Lith. *slinkti*, to creep. Allied to **Sleek** ; also to *sli-p, sli-de, sli-ng*.

Slip. (E.) A weak verb ; due to A. S. *slipan*, pt. t. *sláp*, pp. *slipen*, to slip, glide. We also find A. S. *sleópan, slúpan*, pt. t.

sleap, pp. *slopen*.+Du. *slippen*, Icel. *sleppa*, Swed. *slippa*, G. *schliefen*, all weak verbs; also Icel. *sleppa* (pt. t. *slapp*), Dan. *slippe*, strong verbs; also Goth. *sliupan*, pt. t. *slaup*, pp. *slupans*, to slip or creep into. All from √SARP, to glide; see **Serpent**. Der. *slipp-er*, a loose shoe easily slipped on; *slipper-y*, from A. S. *slipor*, slippery, with added *-y*. And see *sleeve*.

slop (1), a puddle. (E.) M. E. *sloppe*, a pool. — A. S. *sloppe*, *slyppe*, the sloppy droppings of a cow, as in *cū-sloppe* (cow-slip); also A. S. *slype*, a viscid substance. Orig. sense 'a slippery place;' cf. Icel. *slöp*, slimy offal of fish, *slepja*, slime, Irish *slaib*, mire. See further below.

slop (2), a loose garment. (Scand.) M. E. *sloppe*. — Icel. *sloppr*, a slop, long loose gown. — Icel. *slupp*-, stem of pt. t. pl. of *sleppa*, to slip. So named from its trailing on the ground. So also Dan. *slæb*, a train, from *slæbe*, to trail; G. *schleppe*, train, *schleppen*, to trail. Compare **Sleeve**.

slope, an incline. (E.) M. E. *slope*; *a-slope*, on the slope, ready to slip. — A. S. *sláp*, pt. t. of *slīpan*, to slip. Cf. prov. E. *slape*, slippery, from Icel. *sleipr*, slippery.

sloven. (Du.) O. Du. *slof*, *sloef*, a sloven, with M. E. suffix *-ein* (= F. *-ain*, L. *-anus*); Du. *slof*, careless; *slof*. sb., neglect, an old slipper. The base is Low G. *slup*-, as seen in Goth. *slup-ans*, pp. of *sliupan*, to slip. Cf. Irish *slapach*, slovenly.

Slit. (E.) M. E. *slitten*, weak verb; from *sliten*, strong verb. — A. S. *slītan*, to slit, rend; pt. t. *slát*, pp. *sliten*. + Icel. *slíta*, Swed. *slita*, Dan. *slide*, to rend; Du. *slijten*, to wear out; O. H. G. *slīzan*, G. *schleissen*, to slit, *schlitzen*, to slice. Cf. Skt. *sridh*, to injure.

eclat. (F. — O. H. G.) F. *éclat*, splendour; lit. 'a bursting forth.' — F. *éclater*, to burst forth; O. F. *s'esclater*, to burst. — O. H. G. *schleizan*, deriv. of *schlīzan*, to slit, burst (above).

slash. (F. — O. H. G.) M. E. *slashen*. We also find *slish*. — O. F. *esclecher*, *esclischer*, *esclescher*, to dismember, sever, disunite; *esclesche*, a severing (Roquefort). — O. H. G. *slīzan*, *schlīzan*, to split, rend, destroy (above).

slate. (F. — O. H. G.) M. E. *slat*, *sclat*. — O. F. *esclat*, a splinter, slice of wood, &c. (hence a thin slice of slate). — O. F. *esclater*, to split, burst, shiver; see **eclat** (above).

slice, sb. (F. — O. H. G.) M. E. *slice*, *sclice*. — O. F. *esclice*, a splinter, shiver, piece

of split wood. — O. F. *esclicer*, to slit. — O. H. G. *sclīzan*, *slīzan*, to slit; see **Slit**. Der. *slice*, verb.

Sliver, a splinter, twig. (E.) M. E. *sliver*, dimin. of prov. E. *slive*, a slice, chip; from M. E. *sliuen* (*sliven*), to cleave. — A. S. *slīfan*, to cleave, pt. t. *sláf*. A parallel form to A. S. *slītan*, pt. t. *slát*; see **Slit**.

Slobber; see under **Slabber**.

Sloe. (E.) M. E. *slo*. A. S. *slá*, pl. *slán*. + Du. *slee*, O. Du. *sleeu*; Dan. *slaaen*; Swed. *slån*; G. *schlehe*, pl. *schlehen*; O. H. G. *sléhá*. + Lith. *slywa*, a plum, Russ. *sliva*, a plum. β. Named from its tartness; cf. O. Du. *sleeuw*, sharp, tart, *sleeuwigheydt der Tanden*, a setting of the teeth on edge; the same word as Du. *sleeuw*, slow, used in another relation. See **Slow**.

Slogan, war-cry. (Gael.) Gael. *sιuagh-ghairm*, the signal for battle, lit. ' cry of the host.' — Gael. *sluagh*, host, army; *gairm*, outcry, from *gairm*, to cry out.

Sloop, a ship. (Du.) Du. *sloep*, O. Du. *sloepe*, a sloop. Etym. doubtful; the Du. *sloep* appears to be merely borrowed from O. F. *chaloupe*, a shallop; see **Shallop**. If so, the word is not Teutonic, and cannot be connected with the verb *to slip* (as Diez suggests).

Slop (1) and (2); see **Slip**.

Slope; see **Slip**.

Slot (1), a bolt of a door, bar. (O. Low G.) Du. *slot*, a lock, fastening. — Du. *slot*-, stem of pp. of *sluiten*, to shut; so also Low G. *slot*, a bar, from *sluten*, to shut. We find also Swed. *sluta*, G. *schliessen*, O. H. G. *sliozan*, to shut. Allied to L. *claudere*, to shut; see **Clause**. (√SKLU.)

Slot (2), track of a deer. (Scand.) Also spelt *sleuth*; M. E. *sleuth*, *sloth*. — Icel. *slóð*, a track or trail. Allied to **Sled** and **Slide**.

Sloth; see **Slow**.

Slouch, to have a clownish look or gait. (Scand.) From *slouch*, sb., a great lubberly fellow (Phillips). — Icel. *slókr*, a slouching fellow; allied to *slakr*, slack. Cf. Swed. *sloka*, to droop, *slokig*, hanging, slouching; Dan. *slugöret*, having drooping ears. See **Slack**.

slug, to be inactive. (Scand.) M. E. *sluggen*, vb., *slugge*, adj., slothful. — Dan. *slug*, weakened form of *sluk*, appearing in *slugöret*, *sluköret*, having drooping ears; Norweg. *sloka*, to slouch, Swed. *sloka*, to droop. Note also Low G. *slukkern*, *slakkern*, to be loose. *slukk*, melancholy, downcast. All allied to **Slack**. **Der**. *slugg-ard*, with F. suffix *-ard* (= O. H. G. *-hart*, cognate with E. *hard*).

Slough (1), a muddy pool, mire. (C.) M. E. *slogh*, *slough*. A. S. *slóh* (stem *slóg-*), a slough. — Irish *sloc*, a pit, hollow, allied to *slugpholl*, a whirl-pool. — Irish *slugaim*, I swallow up. So also Gael. *sloc*, pit, pool, *slugan*, a gulf; from *sluig*, to swallow up. Allied to Swed. *sluka*, G. *schlucken*, to swallow.

Slough (2), the cast skin of a snake, &c.; the dead part which separates from a sore. (Scand.) Pronounced *sluf*. M. E. *slouh*, *slughe*, *slouȝe*, skin of a snake. The corresponding word appears in Swed. dialects as *slug* (Rietz), which is prob. allied to G. *slauch*, a skin, bag, also the gullet, and so to G. *schlucken*, to swallow; see **Slough** (1). ¶ There is also a Swed. dial. *sluv*, a covering, answering to Low G. *sluwe*, a husk, O. Du. *sloove*, a veil, skin, allied to E. **Sleeve**, and the verb **Slip**. But if the connection of *slough* with G. *schlauch* be real, these words are wholly unrelated. (A difficult word.)

Sloven; see **Slip**.

Slow. (E.) A. S. *sláw*, slow. + Du. *slee*, Icel. *sljór*; Dan. *slöv*, Swed. *slö*, blunt, dull.

sloth. (E.) Lit. 'slowness.' A. S. *sláwð*, sloth, slowness. — A. S. *sláw*, slow. **Der**. *sloth*, an animal; *sloth-ful*.

Slow-worm. (E.) In popular etymology, it is 'a slow worm,' but the true sense is 'slay-worm,' the snake that strikes. A. S. *slá-wyrm*; where *slá* (for *slaha**) means 'striker,' from *sleán*, to strike. This is clearer from Swed. *slå* or *ormslå*, a slow-worm, where *orm* = E. *worm*, and *slå* is 'striker,' from *slå*, to strike; so also Norw. *ormslo*, a slow-worm, also called *slo*, from *slaa*, to strike. ¶ Distinct from A. S. *sleáw*, Swed. *slö*, slow; as shewn by the vowels.

Slubber; see **Slabber**.

Slug; see **Slouch**.

Sluice; see **Clause**.

Slumber, verb. (E.) The *b* is excrescent. M. E. *slumeren*, frequent. of M. E. *slumen*, to slumber, from *slume*, sb., slumber. — A. S. *sluma*, sb., slumber. + Du. *sluimeren*; Dan. *slumre*, frequent. of *slumme*, to slumber; Swed. *slumra*, vb.; G. *schlummern*, vb. Perhaps allied to Lith. *snudis*, a slumberer, Russ. *sno-vidtse*, a dreamer.

Slut. (Scand.) M. E. *slutte*. — Icel. *slöttr*, a heavy, loglike fellow; Swed. dial. *slåta*, a slut, *slåter*, an idler; Norw. *slott*, an idler, Dan. *slatte*, a slut. — Icel. *slota*, to droop, Norw. *sluta*, to droop; allied to Dan. *slat*, *slatten*, loose, flabby. From *slot-*, stem of pp. of Norw. *sletta* (strong verb), to dangle, drift, idle about (Aasen). β. Further allied to Du. *slodde*, a slut, and to the verb *to slide*. Cf. Irish *slaodaire*, a lazy person, from *slaod*, to slide.

Sly; see **Slay** (1).

Smack (1), taste. (E.) M. E. *smak*. A. S. *smæc*, taste, flavour; whence *smecgan*, to taste. + O. Du. *smaeck*, Dan. *smag*, Swed. *smak*, G. *geschmack*, taste. **Der**. *smack*, verb, to taste.

Smack (2), a sounding blow. (E.?) Confused with the word above, but really distinct; prob. of imitative origin. Allied to Swed. *smacka*, to smack, Swed. dial. *smakka*, to throw down noisily, *smäkka*, to hit smartly; Du. *smak*, a loud noise, G. *schmatzen*, to smack, fell a tree.

smash. (Scand.) Swed. dial. *smaske*, to kiss with a sounding smack; *smask*, a slight report, noise; *smiska*, to slap. The form *smaske* is for *smakse**, as in Low G. *smaksen*, to kiss with a smack. Extended from the base SMAK, with addition of *s*; see above.

Smack (3), a fishing-boat. (Du.) O. Du. *smacke*, Du. *smak*, a smack, hoy.+ Dan. *smakke*. Generally thought to stand for *snack*, allied to *snake*; cf. A. S. *snacc*, a smack, small vessel; Icel. *snekkja*, a smack, so named from its snake-like motion in the water. So also Dan. *snekke* (1) a snail, (2) a vessel or smack. See **Snake**, **Sneak**.

Small. (E.) A. S. *smæl*.+ Du. Dan. Swed. *smal*, narrow, thin; Goth. *smals*, small; G. *schmal*, thin. Allied to Icel. *smár*, Dan. *smaa*, Swed. *små*, small; cf. Gk. σμικρός, small; L. *macer*, thin.

smallage, celery. (E.; *and* F. — L.) Put for *small ache*; from F. *ache*, parsley = L. *apium*, parsley.

Smalt; see **Smelt** (1).

Smaragdus; see **Emerald**.

Smart, to feel pain. (E.) M. E. *smerten*. A. S. *smeortan*.+Du. *smarten*, Dan. *smerte*, Swed. *smärta*, G. *schmerzen*. Also allied to L. *mordere*, to bite; Skt. *mrid*, to rub, grind, crush. **Der**. *smart*, sb.; *smart*, adj., painful, also pungent, brisk, lively.

Smash; see **Smack** (2).

Smattering, sb. (Scand.) M. E. *smateren*, to make a noise; hence, to prate, talk ignorantly. — Swed. *smattra*, to clatter, variant of Swed. *snattra*, to chatter. **+** Dan. *snaddre*, to jabber, G. *schnattern*, to prate, chatter. **β**. Further allied to Dan. *snakke*, G. *schnacken*, to prate, Swed. *snack*, Dan. *snak*, G. *schnack*, talk, twaddle. Allied to **Smack** (2).

Smear. (E.) A. S. *smerien*, to smear. **—** A. S. *smeru*, fat; *smere*, fatness. So also Icel. *smyrja*, Dan. *smöre*, Swed. *smörja*, G. *schmieren*, to smear; from Du. *smeer*, Dan. Swed. *smör*, G. *schmeer*, fat, grease. Cf. Lith. *smarsas*, fat; Gk. μύρον, un-guent; Gk. σμά-ειν, to rub, wipe. (√ SMA.) And see **Smelt** (1).

smirch, to besmear. (E.) Weakened form of *smer-k*, extended from M. E. *smer-en*, to smear; see **Smear**.

Smell, odour. (E.) M. E. *smel*, *smul*. Allied to Du. *smeulen*, Low G. *smelen*, to smoulder; also to A. S. *smoran* or *smorian*, to smother, suffocate. Der. *smell*, vb.

smother, sb. (E.) Put for *smorther*; M. E. *smorther*, a suffocating smoke, lit. 'that which stifles;' formed (with suffix *-ther* of the agent) from A. S. *smor-ian*, to stifle, smother.

smoulder, vb. (E.) M. E. *smolderen*, vb.; from M. E. *smolder*, sb., a stifling smoke. *Smol-der* = *smol-ther* * = *smor-ther*, M. E. form of *smother*; see above. Cf. Dan. *smul*, dust.

Smelt (1), to fuse ore. (Scand.) Dan. *smelte*, to smelt; Swed. *smälta*, to smelt. (Properly a Swed. word.) **+** O. Du. *smilten*, *smelten*, G. *schmelzen*, to smelt. Orig. sense 'to become oily' or 'become soft;' from O. Du. *smalt*, grease, melted butter, O. H. G. *smalz*, fat, grease; allied to Lith. *smarsas*, fat, Goth. *smairthr*, fat. Allied to **Smear**.

mute (2), to dung; used of birds. (F. — O. Low G.) O. F. *mutir*, 'to mute as a hawke;' Cot. Short for O. F. *esmeutir*, the same; oldest spelling *esmeltir*. — O. Du. *smelten*, *smilten*, to smelt, to liquefy; also to mute (Hexham).

smalt, blue enamel. (Ital. — O. H. G.) Ital. *smalto*, enamel. — O. H. G. *smalzjan*, G. *schmelzen*, to smelt; from the method of preparation. See also **Enamel**.

Smelt (2), a fish. (E.) A. S. *smelt.* **+** Dan. *smelt*, Norw. *smelta*. Perhaps the sense is 'smooth;' cf. A. S. *smeolt*, *smylt*, serene, smooth (as the sea).

Smile, vb. (Scand.) Swed. *smila*, to smile, smirk; Dan. *smile*. **+** M. H. G.

smielen, *smiren*; L. *mirari*, to wonder at; Skt. *smi*, to smile. (√ SMI.)

smirk. (E.) A. S. *smercian*, to smile. Cf. M. H. G. *smiren*, the same as M. H. G. *smielen*, to smile (above).

Smirch; see **Smear**.

Smirk; see **Smile**.

Smite. (E.) A. S. *smítan*, pt. t. *smát*, pp. *smiten*. **+** Du. *smijten*; Dan. *smide*, to fling; G. *schmeissen*, to smite, fling, cast; O. H. G. *smízan*, to throw, stroke, smear. Cf. Goth. *bismeitan*, to besmear. **β**. The orig. sense was to 'smear' or rub over, as in Gothic; cf. O. Swed. *smita*, to smite, *smeta*, to smear; Skt. *meda*, fat, from *mid*, to be unctuous. 'To rub over' seems to have been a sarcastic expression for 'to beat;' we find *well anoynted* = well beaten, Romance of Partenay, l. 5653. (√ SMID.)

smudge. (Scand.) Dan. *smuds*, smut, dirt; see below.

smut, a spot of dirt or soot. (Scand.) Formerly *smutch*, put for *smuts**. — Swed. *smuts*, smut, dirt, Dan. *smuds*, smut; whence Swed. *smutsa*, Dan. *smudse*, to soil. **+** G. *schmutz*, dirt; *schmutzen*, to smudge. **β**. Allied to Swed. *smet*, grease, filth, *smitta*, to bedaub, infect; A. S. *smittian*, to spot, *besmítan*, to defile. All from base of the verb *to smite* (above).

Smith; see **Smooth**.

Smock, a woman's shirt. (E.) M. E. *smok*. A. S. *smoc*. Put for *smog**. — A. S. *smog-en*, pp. of *smeógan*, *smúgan*, to creep into. So called because 'crept into,' or put over the head. Cf. Shetland *smook*, to draw on a glove or stocking. **+** Icel. *smokkr*, a smock; from *smog-inn*, pp. of *smjúga*, to creep through a hole, to put on a garment over the head. Cf. O. Swed. *smog*, a round hole for the head.

smug, neat, spruce. (Scand.) Formerly *smoog*, *smug*; weakened form of *smuk**. — Dan. *smuk*, pretty, fine, fair; O. Swed. *smuck*, elegant, fair. **+** Low G. *smuk*, neat, trim; G. *schmuck*, trim, spruce; cf. *schmücken*, to adorn, M. H. G. *schmucken*, to clothe, adorn, also to withdraw to a place of security, derived from the M. H. G. strong verb *smiegen*, to creep into, cognate with A. S. *smeógan*, *smúgan*, to creep (above). **β**. Thus *smug* meant 'dressed' or 'trim;' allied to *smock*, attire (above).

smuggle, to import or export secretly. (Scand.) Dan. *smugle*, to smuggle; cf. *i smug*, secretly, *smug-handel*, contraband trade; Swed. *smuga*, a lurking-hole, Icel.

smuga, a hole to creep through. ▬ Icel. *smug-u*, pt. t. pl. of *smjúga*, to creep, creep through a hole, cognate with A. S. *smúgan*, to creep (above).

Smoke, sb. (E.)   A. S. *smoca*. ▬ A. S. *smoc-en*, pp. of strong verb *smeócan* (pt. t. *smeác*), to smoke, reek. + Du. *smook*, sb. ; G. *schmauch*, sb.   Perhaps allied to Irish *smuid*, smoke, *much*, smoke, W. *mwg*, smoke.   Der. *smoke*, verb, from A. S. *smoc-igan*, weak verb.

Smooth, adj. (E.)   M. E. *smoothe* ; also *smethe*.   A. S. *sméðe*, Northumb. *smoeðe*, sometimes *smöðe*, smooth.   The orig. sense was ' flattened with the hammer,' or ' forged ; ' from a lost strong verb *smíðan*, to forge (pt. t. *smáð**, pp. *smiðen**); the form *smooth* being due to the pt. t. *smáð**. This supposed strong verb still exists in the cognate Swed. dial. *smida*, to forge, pt. t. *smed*, pp. *smiden* (Rietz); cf. Dan. *smede*, to forge, *smidig*, malleable, supple, soft.   Further allied to G. *geschmeidig*, malleable, smooth, Du. *smijdig*, malleable. Der. *smoothe*, verb.

smith. (E.)   A. S. *smíð*, a worker with the hammer. ▬ A. S. *smíð-en**, pp. of lost strong verb *smíðan** (see above). + Du. *smid* ; Icel. *smiðr* ; Dan. Swed. *smed* ; G. *schmied* ; Goth. *smitha*.   Cf. Dan. *smede*, Swed. *smida*, to forge ; Icel. *smíð*, smith's work, from an Icel. lost strong verb cognate with Swed. dial. *smida* (above).   Der. *smith-y*, A. S. *smiððe* (Icel. *smiðja*).

Smother, Smoulder ; see **Smell**.

Smug, Smuggle ; see **Smock**.

Smudge, Smut ; see **Smite**.

Snack ; see **Snatch**.

Snaffle ; see **Snap**.

Snag, a short branch, knot on a stick, abrupt projection. (C.)   A sb. from prov. E. *snag*, to trim, cut small branches from a tree. ▬ Gael. *snaigh*, to hew, cut down, trim trees ; Irish *snaigh*, a hewing, cutting.

Snail, Snake ; see **Sneak**.

Snap, verb. (Du.)   Du. *snappen*, to snap, snatch. + Dan. *snappe*, Swed. *snappa*, G. *schnappen*.   (Base SNAP, allied to SNAK.)   See **Snatch**.

neb, beak, nose. (E.)   M. E. *neb*, face. A. S. *nebb*, face. + Du. *neb*, bill, nib, mouth ; Icel. *nef*, nose ; Dan. *næb* ; Swed. *näbb*. β. Put for *sneb** ; cf. Du. *sneb*, bill, beak ; G. *schneppe*, nozzle ; G. *schnabel*, bill, M. H. G. *snabel*, from M. H. G. *snaben*, to snap. γ. Hence *sneb* is for *snep** ; from the verb *to snap*.

nib, point of a pen. (E.)   Another form of *neb* ; see above.

nipple, a teat. (E.)   Formerly *neble* (Palsgrave) ; dimin. of *nib* or *neb* ; see above.   Der. *nipple-wort*.

snaffle. (Du.)   Put for *snaffle-piece*, i. e. nose-piece. ▬ Du. *snavel*, a horse's muzzle ; O. Du. *snavel, snabel*, bill, snout.   Dimin. of O. Du. *snabbe, snebbe*, bill, beak, lit. ' snapper ; ' put for *snappe**, from O. Du. *snappen*, to snap up ; see **Snap**.

snip, vb. (Du.)   Du. *snippen*, to snip, clip ; weakened form of *snappen*, to snap, intercept ; see **Snap.** + G. *schnippen*, to snap ; allied to *schnappen*. ¶ Prob. confused with **Nip**.   Der. *snip*, sb. ; *snipp-et*, a small piece.

snipe, a bird. (Scand.)   M. E. *snype*. ▬ Icel. *snípa*, a snipe ; Dan. *sneppe*, a snipe ; Swed. *snäppa*, a sand-piper. + Du. *snip, snep*, O. Du. *snippe, sneppe* ; G. *schnepfe*. It means 'a snapper ;' cf. O. Du. *snebbe*, beak, lit. snapper. ¶ See also **Snub**.

Snare, a noose. (E.)   A. S. *snear*, cord, string, noose. + Du. *snaar*, a string ; Icel. *snara* ; Dan. *snare* ; Swed. *snara* ; O. H. G. *snarahha*, a noose. β. The O. H. G. *snarahha* shews an orig. final guttural ; the sb. is from a strong verb, seen in M. H. G. *snerhen*, to twist tightly ; from a base SNARH = Aryan √SNARK, whence Gk. νάρκη, cramp ; see **Narcissus**.   Cf. √SNAR, to twist, wind ; see **nerve** (below). γ. All from √SNA, to wind, spin ; whence L. *nere*, to spin, Skt. *snása*, sinew, tendon.

enervate. (L.)   From pp. of L. *eneruare*, to deprive of nerve or strength. ▬ L. *e*, out of ; *neruus*, a nerve ; see **nerve** (below).

needle. (E.)   Also *neeld* ; M. E. *nedle*, also *nelde*.   A. S. *nædel*. + Du. *naald* (for *naadl**) ; Icel. *nál* ; Dan. *naal* ; Swed. *nål* ; G. *nadel* ; Goth. *nethla*. β. All from a Teut. type NÂ-THLA, i. e. sew-er, from NA, to sew, as in G. *nähen*, to sew, L. *nere*, Gk. νήθειν, νέειν, to spin ; and NA is for √SNA, as in Irish *snathad*, a needle, *snathaim*, I string together, *snaidhe*, thread, A. S. *snear*, string, snare.   See **Snare**.

nerve. (F. ▬ L.)   F. *nerf* ; Cot. ▬ L. *neruum*, acc. of *neruus*, a sinew. + Gk. νεῦρον, a sinew, string ; G. *schnur*, a string, cord, tie.   Allied to **Snare**.

neuralgia, pain in the nerves. (Gk.) From Gk. νεῦρ-ον, a nerve, and ἀλγ-ος, pain ; with suffix -ια.   The Gk. νεῦρον is cognate with L. *neruus*; see **nerve** (above).

Snarl; see **Sneer**.

Snatch. (E.) M. E. *snacchen*, as if from *snakken**; cf. Lowland Sc. *snak*, a snap of the jaws.+Du. *snakken*, to gasp. (Base SNAK, parallel to SNAP.) See **Snap**. Der. *snack*, sb., a portion, lit. 'a bit snatched up,' a hasty meal, a share; *to go snacks* = to go shares. Also prov. E. *sneck*, snap or latch of a door.

Sneak. (E.) M. E. *sniken*. A. S. *snícan*, to creep.+Icel. *snik-inn*, hankering after, from a lost strong verb; Swed. dial. *snika* (pt. t. *snek*), to hanker after; Dan. *sniga sig*, to sneak, slink.+Gael. and Irish *snaig*, *snaigh*, to creep.

snail. (E.) M. E. *snayle*. A. S. *snægl*, *snegel*, a snail; dimin. of *snaga**, put for *snaca*, a snake, creeping thing. + Swed *snäcka*, G. *schnecke*, a snail; Icel. *snigill*, Dan. *snegl*. See below.

snake. (E.) A. S. *snaca*, a snake (perhaps orig. *snáca*).+Icel. *snákr*, *snókr*; Dan. *snog*; Swed. *snok*.+Skt. *nága*, a snake. Orig. 'a creeper;' allied to **Sneak** (above).

Sneap, to pinch, check; see **Snub**.

Sneer, to scoff. (Scand.) M. E. *sneren*. —Dan. *snærre*, to grin like a dog, shew one's teeth at a person; allied to **snarl**. (Base SNAR.)

snarl, vb. (E. ?) Frequentative form of *snar*, to shew one's teeth like a dog, spelt *snarre* in Palsgrave. Not found in A. S.; but cf. O. Du. *snarren*, 'to brawl, to scold, or to snarle,' Hexham. + G. *schnarren*, to growl, snarl. And see **Sneer** (above).

snore, vb. (E.) M. E. *snoren*; cf. A. S. *snora*, sb., a snoring, snore.+O. Du. *snorren*, to grumble, allied to *snarren* (above).

snort, vb. (Scand.) M. E. *snorten*, to snore; put for *snorken**. —Dan. *snorke*, to snort; Swed. *snorka*, to threaten (orig. to fume, be angry). + Du. *snorken*; G. *schnarchen*. (Base SNAR, longer form of SNAR.) See **Sneer** (above).

Sneeze, vb. (E.) M. E. *snesen*; Chaucer has *fnesen* (Cant. Tales, H. 62), of which *snesen* is a modification. A. S. *fneósan*, to sneeze; whence *fnæst*, a puff.+Du. *fniezen*; Swed. *fnysa*; Dan. *fnyse*. (Base FNUS, parallel form to HNUS; see below.)

neese, **neeze**, to sneeze, puff. (E.) M. E. *nesen*; not in A. S.+Du. *niezen*,

to sneeze; O. Icel. *hniósja*; Dan. *nyse*; Swed. *nysa*; G. *niezen*. (Base HNUS.)

Sniff, to scent. (Scand.) M. E. *sneuien* (*snevien*). —Icel. *sneffja**, to sniff, a lost verb, whence *snaf̄ōr*, sharp-scented; Dan. *snive*, to sniff; cf. Swed. *snyfta*, to sob. Allied to Icel. *snippa*, *snapa*, to sniff.

snivel, to keep on sniffing, whimper. (Scand.) Formerly *sneevle*, *snevil*. M. E. *sneuelen* (*snevelen*); frequentative of M. E. *sneuien* (*snevien*), to sniff (above).

snuff (1), to sniff, smell. (Du.) From O. Du. *snuffen*, *snuyven* (Du. *snuiven*), 'to snuffe out the filth out of one's nose,' Hexham; Du. *snuf*, smelling, scent.+Swed. *snufva*, a catarrh, *snufven*, a sniff, scent; G. *schnupfen*, a catarrh, *schnupfen*, to take snuff. Cf. also Icel. *snippa*, to sniff, *snoppa*, a snout. Perhaps allied to **Snout**. Der. *snuff*, powdered tobacco; also *snuff-le*, Swed. dial. *snöfla*, Dan. *snövle* (prov. G. *schnuffeln*, *schnüffeln*).

Snip, **Snipe**; see **Snap**.

Snite; see **Snout**.

Snivel; see **Sniff**.

Snob; see **Snub**.

Snood, a fillet, ribbon. (E.) A. S. *snód*, a fillet; orig. 'a twist,' wreath. Cf. Icel. *snúa*, Dan. *snoe*, Swed. *sno*, to twist, twine; Icel. *snúðr*, a twist.

Snore, **Snort**; see **Sneer**.

Snot; see **Snout**.

Snout. (Scand.) M. E. *snoute*.—Swed. *snut*, snout, muzzle; Dan. *snude*. + Du. *snuit*; G. *schnauze*. Cf. Dan. *snue*, to sniff, prov. G. *schnau*, snout, beak. Allied to **Sniff**. (Base SNU, to snuff up, sniff.)

snite (1), to wipe the nose. (Scand.) Icel. *snýta*, Swed. *snyta*, Dan. *snyde*, to snite.—Swed. *snut*, Dan. *snude*, snout (above).

snite (2), a snipe. (E.) M. E. *snite*. A. S. *sníte*, a snite or snipe. Allied to **Snout**; from his long bill.

snot, mucus from the nose. (E. ?) M. E. *snotte*. Not in A. S.+O. Fries. *snotte*; Du. Dan. *snot*. Allied to **snite** (1) above.

Snow. (E.) A. S. *snáw*. + Du. *sneeuw*, Icel. *snær*, Dan. *snee*, Swed. *snö*, Goth. *snaiws*, G. *schnee*. + Lith. *snégas*, Russ. *snieg'*, L. *nix* (gen. *niuis*), Gk. acc. *νίφα*, Irish *sneachd*, W. *nyf*. (Teut. base SNIW, for SNIG; √SNIGH.) Cf. Lith. *snigti*, to snow, L. *ningit*, it snows.

Snub, to check, reprimand. (Scand.) Also *sneb*, *snib*. M. E. *snibben*. — Dan. *snibbe*, to reprimand; Swed. *snubba*, Icel. *snubba*, to snub, chide. Orig. to 'snip off' the end of a thing; cf. Icel. *snubbótr*, snubbed, nipped, with the tip cut off; *snupra*, to snub. β. Allied to obs. E. *sneap*, to pinch, nip, answering to Icel. *sneypa*, to castrate, also to disgrace, snub; Swed. *snöpa*, to castrate, *snubba*, to clip off. Allied to **Snap**, and **Snip**. Der. *snub-nosed*, i. e. with a short or stumpy nose, as if with the end cut off.

snob. (Scand.) Prov. E. *snob*, a vulgar person, also, a journey-man shoemaker, *snap*, a lad, servant, usually in a ludicrous sense; Lowl. Sc. *snab*, a cobbler's boy.— Icel. *snápr*, a dolt, with the notion of impostor, a boaster, used as a by-word; Swed. dial.*snópp*, a boy, anything stumpy.—Swed. dial. *snóppa*, to cut off, make stumpy; and see **Snub**. Cf. Swed. *snopen*, ashamed.

snuff (2), to snip off the top of a candle-wick. (Scand.) M. E. *snuffen*, to snuff out a candle; cf. *snoffe*, sb., the snuff of a candle. Put for *snuppen**; cf. prov. E. *snop*, to eat off, as cattle do young shoots.—Swed. dial. *snóppa*, to snip off, snuff a candle; Dan. *snubbe*, to nip off. See **Snub** (above). Der. *snuff*, sb.

Snubnosed; see **Snub**.

Snuff (1), to sniff up; see **Sniff**.

Snuff (2), to snuff a candle; see **Snub**.

Snug. (Scand.) Cf. prov. E. *snug*, tidy, trimmed up; *snog*, the same. — Icel. *snöggr*, smooth, said of wool or hair; O. Swed. *snygg*, short-haired, trimmed, Swed. *snygg*, cleanly, neat, genteel; Dan. *snög*, *snök*, neat, smart. Orig. 'trimmed;' hence neat, smart, tidy, comfortable. β. From a verb seen in Norweg. and Swed. dial. *snikka*, to cut, do joiner's work, prov. E. *snick*, *snig*, to notch, cut. Cf. **Snag**.

So. (E.) M. E. *so*. A. S. *swá*. + Du. *zoo*, Icel. *svá*, *svo*, *so*; Dan. *saa*, Swed. *så*, G. *so*, Goth. *swa*. β. From a case of Aryan SWA, one's own; cf. L. *suus*, Skt. *sva*, one's own. Lit. 'in one's own way.'

Soak; see **Suck**.

Soap. (E.) M. E. *sope*. A. S. *sápe*. + Du. *zeep*, Icel. *sápa*, Dan. *sæbe*, Swed. *såpa*, G. *seife*. Perhaps L. *sapo* (whence F. *savon*, &c.) was borrowed from Teutonic; the true L. (cognate) word seems to be *sebum*, tallow, grease.

saponaceous, soapy. (L.) Coined, as if from L. *saponaceus**, from L. *saponem*, acc. of *sapo*, soap (Pliny).

Soar. (F.—L.) M. E. *soren*.—F. *essorer*, to expose to air; also, 'to sore up,' Cot.— Low L. *exaurare** (not found), to expose

to air.—L. *ex*, out; *aura*, breeze, air. Perhaps L. *aura* was borrowed from Gk. αὔρα, a breeze; in any case, it is formed with suffix -*ra* (of the agent) from √ AW, to blow. See **Air**.

Sob, vb. (E.) M. E. *sobben*, answering to A. S. *seófian*, to lament. + G. *seufzen*, to sigh, O. H. G. *suftón*, to sob, O. H. G. *súft*, a sigh, sob; all from O. H. G. *súfan*, to sup, sup up. Allied to **Sup**. Der. *sob*, sb.

Sober; see **Ebriety**.

Sobriquet, Soubriquet, a nickname. (F.—L. *and* C.) F. *sobriquet*, 'surname, nickname, a jeast broken on a man;' Cot. He also spells it *sotbriquet*, *soubriquet*. From O. F. *soubzbriquet*, a chuck under the chin (14th cent.); hence, a quip, an affront, a nickname. Here O. F. *soubz*, F. *sous*, is from L. *sub*, under; *briquet* is the same word as E. *brisket*; see **Brisket**. The Norman *bruchet* meant the bole of the throat, breast-bone in birds; whence *fouler sus l'bruchet*, to seize by the throat. 'Percussit super mentonem faciendo dictum *le soubriquet*;' A. D. 1335. See Hericher, Norm. Gloss., and Littré.

Soc, Socage; see **Soke**.

Sociable, Society; see **Sequence**.

Sock. (L.) A. S. *socc*. — L. *soccus*, a light shoe, slipper, sock, buskin of a comedian.

socket. (F.—L.) O. F. *soket* (Roquefort), dimin. of O. F. *soc**, later F. *souche*, a stump or stock of a tree; the same as Ital. *zocco*, stump of a tree, Span. *zoco*, Port. *socco*, wooden shoe or clog, mod. F. *socque*, a clog. β. All from L. *soccus*, sock, shoe, hence, a wooden shoe or clog (and hence a block of wood, stump, &c.). Note F. *socle*, a plinth, pedestal, Ital. *zoccolo* (1) a plinth, (2) a wooden shoe. I conclude that *socket* is a dimin. of *sock*, notwithstanding the change in sense; cf. E. *shoe*, a kind of socket, as a term in machinery (Webster).

Sod, turf; see **Seethe**.

Sodden; see **Seethe**.

Soda; see **Solid**.

Soder, or Solder; see **Solid**.

Sodomy. (F. — L. — Gk. — Heb.) F. *sodomie*, a sin imputed to the inhabitants of Sodom. — F. *Sodome*, Sodom. — L. *Sodoma*. — Gk. Σόδομα. — Heb. *Sedóm*; said to mean 'burning.'

Sofa. (Arab.) Arab. *suffat*, *suffah*, 'a sopha;' Rich. Dict. p. 936.—Arab. root *saffa*, to draw up in line, to put a seat to a saddle; ibid.

Soft. (E.) A. S. *sófte*; also *séfte* (by modification). **+** O. Sax. *sáfto*, adv., softly; G. *sanft*, soft; O. H. G. *samfto*, adv., gently; Du. *zacht*, for *zaft* (whence G. *sacht*). Der. *soft-en*.

Soil (1), ground; see **Sole** (1).

Soil (2), to defile; see **Sow** (2).

Soil (3), to fatten; see **Sate**.

Soirée, an evening party. (F.—L.) F. *soirée*, evening; hence, an evening party. Cf. Ital. *serata*, evening.—L. *sēr-us*, late in the day (whence Ital. *sera*, F. *soir*, evening); with suffix *-ata* (—F. *-ée*). See **Diary**.

Sojourn; see **Diary**.

Soke, Soc, a franchise, land held by socage. (E.) The A. S. *sacu* meant 'a contention,' a 'law-suit'; whence the Law term *sac*, the power of hearing suits and administering justice within a certain precinct. The A. S. *sócn* meant 'investigation,' or 'a seeking into'; whence the Law term *sóc* or *soke*, the right of hearing disputes and inquiring into complaints, also, the precinct within which such right was exercised; see Blount, Spelman, Ellis, Thorpe, Schmid. β. Etymologically, *sac* (A.S. *sacu*) is the same word as **Sake**, q. v. *Soke* (A.S. *sóc*) is the exercise of judicial power; and *soken* (A. S. *sócn*, *sócen*) is an inquiry; both allied to E. *seek*, and derived from A. S. *sóc*, pt. t. of *sacan*, to contend; see **Seek**. Der. *soc-age*, a barbarous law term made by adding F. *-age* (L. *-aticum*) to A.S. *sóc*. (The *o* is long.)

Solace, a relief. (F.—L.) M. E. *solas*.—O. F. *solaz* (where *z* = *ts*).—L. *solatium*, a comfort.—L. *solatus*, pp. of *solari*, to console. (Others give the sb. as *solacium*, from the same verb.) Allied to *saluare*, *seruare*, to keep. (√SAR.) Der. *solace*, vb.

console. (F. — L.) F. *consoler*. — L. *consolari*, to comfort.—L. *con-* (for *cum*) with; *solari*, to comfort (above).

disconsolate. (L.) Low L. *disconsolatus*, comfortless. — L. *dis-*, apart; *consolatus*, pp. of *consolari* (above).

Solan-goose, a bird. (Scand. *and* E.) The E. *goose* is an addition.—Icel. *súlan*, lit. 'the gannet,' where *-n* stands for the definite article; def. form of Icel. *súla*, a gannet, solan goose; Norweg. *sula*, the same.

Solar, belonging to the sun. (L.) L.

solaris, solar. — L. *sol*, sun. **+** Icel. *sól*, Goth. *sauil*, Lith. *sáule*, W. *haul*, Irish *sul*, Gk. σείριος, the dog-star; Skt. *sura*, *súra*, *swar*, sun, splendour. (√SWAR.) Allied to **Serene**.

solstice. (F. — L.) F. *solstice*. — L. *solstitium*, the solstice; lit. a point (in the ecliptic) at which the sun seems to stand still.—L. *sol*, the sun; *stit-um*, put for *statum*, supine of *sistere*, to make to stand still, from *stare*, to stand.

Solder, Soldier; see **Solid**.

Sole (1), under side of foot or shoe. (L.) A. S. *sole*. — L. *solea*, sole of the foot, or of a shoe. — L. *solum*, the ground.

exile, banishment. (F. — L.) O. F. *exil*, 'an exile, banishment;' Cot.—L. *exilium*, better *exsilium*, banishment.—L. *exsul*, a banished man, one driven from his native soil.—L. *ex*, out of; *solum*, soil, ground (above). ¶ But now gen. der. from L. *salire*, to leap, run.

soil (1), ground, country. (F. — L.) M. E. *soile*.—O. F. *soel*, *suel*, later *sueil*, threshold of a door.—Late L. *solea*, soil, ground (by confusion with L. *solum*, ground); L. *solea*, a sandal, sole, timber on which wattled walls are built. Allied to L. *solum*, ground; whence F. *sol*, soil, ground (from which, however, the E. word cannot be directly derived).

sole (2), a fish. (F.—L.) M. E. *sole*.— F. *sole*, sole; Cot.—L. *solea*, sole of the foot; also, the sole-fish. The sole of the foot is the type of flatness.

Sole (3), alone. (F.—L.) O. F. *sol* (F. *seul*).—L. *sōlus*, alone. Prob. the same word as O. Lat. *sollus*, entire, complete (in itself). See **Solemn**.

desolate, solitary. (L.) L. *desolatus*, forsaken; pp. of *desolare*, to forsake.—L. *de*, fully; *solare*, to make lonely, from *solus* (above).

solitary. (F.—L.) M. E. *solitarie*.—O. F. *solitarie**, orig. form of *solitaire*. — L. *solitarius*, solitary. Short for *solitarius**, from *solitat-*, stem of *solitas*, loneliness.—L. *solus*, alone.

solitude. (F. — L.) F. *solitude*. — L. *solitudo*. — L. *soli-*, for *solo-*, from *solus*, alone; and suffix *-tudo*.

solo. (Ital.—L.) From Ital. *solo*, alone. —L. *solus*, alone.

sullen, morose. (F.—L.) Orig. solitary, hating company; M. E. *soleine*, which also meant a mess of food for *one* person. —

O. F. *solain*, lonely; only given in Roquefort as a pittance for a religious person (i. e. for *one* person). It answers to a Low L. *solanus**, not found; cf. O. F. *soltain*, solitary, answering to a Low L. *solitaneus**. — L. *solus*, alone.

Solecism, impropriety in speaking or writing. (F. — L. — Gk.) O. F. *soloecisme*; Cot. — L. *solæcismus*. — Gk. σολοικισμός, a solecism. — Gk. σολοικίζειν, to speak incorrectly. — Gk. σόλοικος, speaking incorrectly, like an inhabitant of Σόλοι (*Soloi*) in Cilicia, where the Gk. dialect was corruptly spoken. **Der.** *solecist*, sb.

Solemn. (F. — L.) M. E. *solempne*. — O. F. *solempne*. — L. *solemnem*, acc. of *solemnis*, older forms *solennis*, *sollennis*, annual, occurring yearly like a religious rite, religious, solemn. — L. *sollus*, entire, complete; *annus*, a year. Hence *solemn* = returning at the end of a complete year. The O. Lat. *sollus* = Gk. ὅλος, entire, Skt. *sarva*, all, entire. **Der.** *solemn-ity*, *-ise*.

Sol-fa, to sing the notes of the gamut. (L.) It means to sing the notes by the names *si*, *la*, *sol*, *fa*, *mi*, *re*, *ut* (where, for *ut*, *do* is now used). These names are of L. origin; see **Gamut**. **Der.** *solfeggio*, from Ital. *solfeggio*, the singing of the gamut; also *sol-mi-sation*, coined from *sol* and *mi*.

Solicit. (F. — L.) F. *soliciter*. — L. *sollicitare*, to agitate, arouse, urge, solicit. — L. *sollicitus*, lit. wholly agitated. — L. *solli-*, for *sollo-*, crude form of *sollus*, whole ; *citus*, aroused, pp. of *ciere*, to shake, excite. See **Solemn** and **Cite**. **Der.** *solicitous*, for L. *sollicitus*; *solicit-ude*, F. *solicitude*, from L. *solicitudo*, anxiety.

Solid. (F. — L.) F. *solide*. — L. *solidum*, acc. of *solidus*, firm. Allied to O. Lat. *sollus*, whole; see **Solemn**. **Der.** *solid-ar-i-ty*, 'a word which we owe to the F. communists, and which signifies a fellowship in gain and loss, a being, so to speak, all in the same bottom,' Trench. Also *solid-i-fy*, from F. *solidifier*, to render solid.

consolidate. (L.) From pp. of L. *con-solidare*, to render solid. — L. *con-* (*cum*), together ; *solidare*, to make solid, from *solidus*. **Der.** *consols*, a familiar abbreviation for *consolidated annuities*.

soda. (Ital. — L.) Ital. *soda*, O. Ital. *soda*, 'a kind of fearne ashes whereof they make glasses;' Florio. Fem. of Ital. *sodo*, 'solide, tough ;' ibid. (Similarly O. F.

soulde, glasswort, answers to L. *solida*; prob. from the hardness of the products obtained from glasswort.) — L. *solidus*, solid, hard. **Der.** *sod-ium*, a coined word.

soder, solder, a firm cement from fusible metals. (F. — L.) Formerly *soder*, *sowder*, sometimes *soulder* ; pronounced sod'ur. — O. F. *soudure*, also *souldure*, 'a souldering, and particularly the knot of soulder which fastens the led [lead] of a glasse window ;' Cot. (Mod. F. *soudure*.) — O. F. *souder*, *soulder*, to consolidate, make firm. — L. *solidare*, to make firm. — L.*solidus*, firm.

soldier. (F. — L.) M. E. *sodiour*, *soudiour*, *souldier*. — O. F. *soldier*, *soudoier*, *souldoyer*, one who fights for pay ; Low L. *soldarius*. — Low L. *soldum*, pay. — Low L. *solidus*, a piece of money (whence O. F. *sol*, F. *sou*); orig. 'a solid piece.' — L. *solidus*, solid ; cf. E. 'hard cash.'

soliped, an animal with uncloven hoof. (L.) Short for *solidiped*. — L. *solidiped-*, stem of *solidipes*, solid-hoofed (Pliny). — L. *solidi-*, for *solidus*, solid ; *pes*, a foot; see **Foot**.

sou. (F. — L.) F. *sou*, O. F. *sol*, a coin. — Low L. *solidus*, solid, also a coin; cf. *l. s. d.*, i. e. *libræ*, *solidi*, *denarii*.

Soliloquy ; see **Loquacious**.

Soliped ; see **Solid**.

Solitary, Solitude, Solo; see **Sole** (3).

Solmisation ; see **Solfa**.

Solstice ; see **Solar**.

Soluble, Solution ; see **Solve**.

Solve. (L.) L. *soluere*, to loosen, relax, explain ; pp. *solutus*. — L. *so-*, for *se-*, apart ; *luere*, to loosen, allied to Gk. λύ-ειν, to set free, and to E. **Lose**. **Der.** *solvent*, from the stem of the pres. pt.

absolute, unrestrained, complete. (L.) L *absolutus*, pp. of *absoluere*, to set free ; see below.

absolve. (L.) L. *absoluere*, to set free. — L. *ab*, away ; *soluere*, to loosen. **Der.** *absolut-ion* (from pp. *absolutus*).

dissolute. (L.) L. *dissolutus*, licentious ; pp. of L. *dissoluere* (below).

dissolve. (L.) L. *dissoluere*, to dissolve, loosen, relax. — L. *dis-*, apart ; *soluere*, to loosen. **Der.** *dissolut-ion* (from pp. *dissolutus*).

resolute. (L.) L. *resolutus*, pp. of *resoluere* (below).

resolve. (L.) L. *resoluere*, to loosen, melt ; hence to separate into parts (also, to decide, resolve). – L. *re-*, back ; *soluere*, to loosen. **Der.** *resolut-ion* (from pp. *resolutus*).

soluble. (F. – L.) F. *soluble*. – L. *solubilis*, dissolvable. – L *solu-*, base of *solu-tus*, pp. of *soluere* ; with suffix *-bilis*.

solution. (F. – L.) F. *solution*. – L. *solutionem*, acc. of *solutio*, a loosing. – L. *solut-us*, pp. of *soluere*, to loosen, solve.

Sombre, gloomy. (F. – L.) F. *sombre*, gloomy. Cf. Port. and Span. *sombrio*, gloomy, from Port. and Span. *sombra*, shade. Diez refers these to L. *umbra*, shade, with prefix *sub* ; cf. Prov. *sotz-ombrar*, to shade. Littré refers them to L. *umbra*, shade, with prefix *ex*. Either solution seems possible ; the latter is the simpler. See **Umbrage.**

Some. (E.) A.S. *sum*, some one, a certain one, one ; pl. *sume*, some. + Icel. *sumr*, Goth. *sums*, O. H. G. *sum*, some one ; Dan *somme*, pl., Swed. *somlige*, pl., some. Allied to **Same. Der.** *some-body*, *-thing*, *-time*, *-times* (where *-s* is an adverbial suffix).

-some, suffix. (E.) A.S. *-sum*, as in *wyn-sum* = E. *win-some*. Cf. G. *lang-sam*, slow. Here the orig. form was SAMA, identical with Teut. SAMA, same ; see **Same.**

Somersault, Somerset. (F. – Ital. – L.) F. *soubresault*, 'a sobresault or summersault, an active trick in tumbling ;' Cot. – Ital. *soprasalto*. – Ital. *sopra*, above, over ; *salto*, a leap. – L. *supra*, above, over ; *saltum*, acc. of *saltus*, a leap, from pp. of L. *salire*, to leap ; see **Salient.**

Somnambulist, one who walks in his sleep. (L.) Coined (with suffix *-ist* = L. *-ista* = Gk. *-ιστης*, as in *bapt-ist*) from L. *somn-us*, sleep, and *ambulare*, to walk. See below, and see **Amble.**

Somniferous, causing sleep. (L.) L. *somnifer*, sleep-bringing ; with suffix *-ous*. – L. *somni-*, for *somno-*, for *somnus*, sleep ; *-fer*, bringing, from *ferre*, to bring. β. The L. *somnus* is for *sopnus* *, allied to L. *sopor*, sleep, Skt. *svapna*, sleep. (√ SWAP.)

somnolence. (F. – L.) F. *somnolence*. – L. *somnolentia*, sleepiness. – L. *somnolentus*, sleepy. – L. *somno-*, for *somnus*, sleep (above) ; with suffix *-lentus*.

Son. (E.) M.E. *sone*. A.S. *sunu*. + Du. *zoon* ; Icel. *sunr*, Dan. *sön*, Swed. *son*, G. *sohn*, Goth. *sunus*, Lith. *sunus*, Russ. *suin'*, Gk. *υίός* (for *συίος* *) ; Skt. *súnu*, from Skt. *su*, *sú*, beget. (√ SU.) See **Sun.**

Sonata ; see **Sound** (3).

Song ; see **Sing.**

Sonnet, Sonorous ; see **Sound** (3).

Soon. (E.) M.E. *sone*. A.S. *sóna*. + O. Fries., O. Sax., O. H. G. *sán* ; Goth. *suns*, immediately.

Soot. (E.) A.S. *sót*. + Icel. *sót*, Swed. *sot*, Dan. *sod*. + Lith. *sódis*, soot.

Sooth, true. (E.) A.S. *sóð*, true ; whence *sóð*, neut. sb. the truth. [The A.S. *sóð* stands for *sanð* * ; the long *o* is due to loss of *n*.] + Icel. *sannr* (for *sanðr* *), Swed. *sann*, Dan. *sand*. β. All from Teut. base SANTHA, short for AS-ANTHA, lit. being, that which is, from √ AS, to be. Allied to L. *sens*, being, as in *ab-sens* (stem *ab-sent-*), *præ-sens* (stem *præ-sent*) ; Skt. *sat* (for *sant* *), true. See **Essence** and **Are** ; also **Sin. Der.** *for-sooth*, i. e. for a truth ; *sooth-say*, to say truth.

absent. (L.) L. *absent-*, stem of *absens*, i. e. being away ; see above.

present (1), near at hand. (F. – L.) O. F. *present*. – L. *præsent-*, stem of *præsens*, i. e. being in front or near ; see above. **Der.** *present-ly* ; *presence*, sb., O. F. *presence*, L. *præsentia*.

present (2), to give. (F. – L.) O. F. *presenter*. – L. *præsentare*, to place before, hold out, offer. – L. *præsent-*, stem of *præsens* (above). **Der.** *present*, sb., a gift.

represent. (F. – L.) O. F. *representer*. – L. *re-præsentare*, to bring before again, exhibit ; see **present** (2) above.

soothe. (E.) The orig. sense was to assent to as being true, hence to say yes to, humour, flatter, approve of. ' Is 't good to *soothe* him in these contraries ?' Com. Errors, iv. 4. 82. M. E. *soðien*, to confirm, verify. A.S. *ge-sóðian*, to confirm, prove to be true. – A. S. *sóð*, true ; see **Sooth.**

soothsay. (E.) To say sooth, i. e. tell truth, predict.

Sop ; see **Sup.**

Sophist, a captious reasoner. (F. – L. – Gk.) Usually *sophister* in old authors, but the final *r* is unoriginal. – O. F. *sophiste*. – Low L. *sophista*. – Gk. *σοφιστής*, a skilful man, also a Sophist, teacher of arts for money (see Liddell). – Gk. *σοφίζειν*, to instruct. – Gk. *σοφός*, wise ; allied to *σαφής*, of a keen taste, clear, sure. Allied to **Sapient. Der.** *sophist-r-y*, *sophist-ic* (Gk. *σοφιστικός*) ; *sophis-m* (Gk. *σόφισμα*, a device).

Soporiferous, inducing sleep. (L.) From L. *soporifer*, sleep-bringing ; by adding

-ous. — L. *sopori-*, crude form of *sopor*, sleep ; *-fer*, bringing, from *ferre*, to bring. The L. *sopor* is cognate with Skt. *svap-na*, sleep (from *svap*, to sleep), Gk. ὕπνος, sleep, A. S. *swefen*, a dream. (√SWAP.)

soporific, causing sleep. (L.) L. *sopori-* (above); and *-fic*, for *facere*, to make, cause.

Soprano ; see **Sub-**, prefix.

Sorcery ; see **Sort**.

Sordid, dirty, vile. (F. — L.) F. *sordide*. — L. *sordidus*, dirty. — L. *sordi-*, crude form of *sordes*, dirt. Allied to **Swarthy**.

Sore, adj. (E.) M. E. *sor*. A. S. *sár*, painful.+Du. *zeer*, Icel. *sárr*, Swed. *sår*, O. H. G. *sér*, wounded, painful ; cf. G. *sehr*, sorely, very, *versehren*, to wound. Der. *sore*, sb., neuter of adj. *sár*.

sorry, sore in mind, aggrieved. (E.) M. E. *sory*. A. S. *sárig*, adj., sorry, sad, sore in mind ; from *sár*, sore.+Du. *zeerig*, Swed. *sårig*, sore, full of sores, words which preserve the orig. sense. ¶ Spelt with two *r*'s by confusion with *sorrow*, with which it was not originally connected.

Sorrel (1), a plant ; see **Sour**.

Sorrel (2), reddish-brown ; see **Sear**.

Sorrow, grief. (E.) M. E. *sorwe*, *sorȝe*. A. S. *sorge*, gen. dat. and acc. of *sorh*, *sorg*, sorrow, anxiety.+Du. *zorg*, Icel. *sorg*, Dan. Swed. *sorg*, G. *sorge*, Goth. *saurga*, care, grief. Cf. Lith. *sirgti*, to be ill, suffer. ¶ Not allied to *sore* or *sorry*, though the present sense and spelling of *sorry* shews confusion with it.

Sorry ; see **Sore**.

Sort, a kind. (F. — L.) F. *sorte*, fem., sort, kind ; allied to F. *sort*, masc., luck, fate. — L. *sortem*, acc. of *sors*, lot. Perhaps allied to **Series**.

assort. (F. — L.) O. F. *assortir*, to sort, assort, match (15th century). — O. F. *as-* (=L. *as-*, for L. *ad*), to ; *sort-*, stem of L. *sors*, lot.

consort. (L.) Low L. *consortia*, a company ; L. *consort-*, stem of *consors*, one who shares property with another, a neighbour. — L. *con-* (for *cum*), together ; *sort-*, stem of *sors*, a lot, share.

resort, to betake oneself to. (F. — L.) O. F. *resortir*, *ressortir*, ' to issue, goe forth againe, resort ;' Cot. Orig. a law term ; to appeal. — Low L. *resortire*, to be subject to a tribunal ; cf. *resortiri*, to return to any one. — L. *re-*, again ; *sortiri*, to obtain ; so that *re-sortiri*, is to re-obtain, gain by appeal. — L. *re-*, again ; *sorti-*, crude form of *sors*, a lot.

sorcery. (F. — L.) O. F. *sorcerie*, casting of lots, magic. — O. F. *sorcier*, a sorcerer. — Low L. *sortiarius*, a teller of fortunes by lots, sorcerer. — L. *sorti-*, crude form of *sors*, a lot.

Sortie ; see **Regent**.

Sot, a stupid fellow, drunkard. (F. — C. ?) M. E. *sot* (Ancren Riwle). — O. F. *sot* (fem. *sotte*), sottish. Origin doubtful ; perhaps Celtic. Cf. Bret. *sôt*, *sôd*, stupid ; Irish *suthaire*, a dunce.

besot. (E. *and* F.) From *sot* ; with E. prefix *be-*.

Sou ; see **Solid**.

Soubriquet ; see **Sobriquet**.

Sough, a sighing sound. (Scand.) Icel. *súgr*, a rushing sound. We also find M. E. *swough*, from the allied A. S. *swógan*, to resound. Compare *sigh*.

Soul. (E.) A. S. *sáwel*, *sáwl*.+Du. *ziel*, Icel. *sála*, *sál*, Dan. *siæl*, Swed. *själ*, G. *seele*, Goth. *saiwala*.

Sound (1), adj., healthy. (E.) M. E. *sound*. A. S. *sund*. + Du. *gezond* ; Swed. Dan. *sund* ; G. *gesund*. Perhaps allied to *sane*.

Sound (2), strait of the sea. (E.) M. E. *sound*. A. S. *sund*, (1) a swimming, (2) power to swim, (3) a strait of the sea, that could be swum across.+Icel. Dan. Swed. G. *sund*. Doubtless put for *swomd* *, and derived from *swum-*, stem of pp. of *swim-man*, to swim. See **Swim**. Der. *sound*, swimming-bladder of a fish, another use of the same word.

Sound (3), a noise. (F. — L.) The final *d* is added. M. E. *soun*. — F. *son*. — L. *sonum*, acc. of *sonus*, a sound.+Skt. *svana*, sound. (√SWAN.)

assonant. (L.) L. *assonant-*, acc. of *assonans*, sounding like ; pres. pt. of *assonare*, to respond to. — L. *as-* (for *ad-*), to ; *sonare*, to sound, from *sonus*, sound.

consonant, agreeing to. (F. — L.) F. *consonant*, accordant ; Cot. — L. *consonant-*, stem of pres. pt. of *con-sonare*, to sound together ; see above.

dissonant. (F. — L.) O. F. *dissonant* ; Cot. — L. *dissonant-*, stem of pres. pt. of *dis-sonare*, to be unlike in sound ; see **asso-nant** above.

parson. (F. — L.) M. E. *persone*, which also means *person*. It is certain that *parson* = *person* ; see Low L. *persona*, a person of rank, a choir-master, curate, parson (Ducange). See below. ¶ Blackstone gives the right etymology, but the wrong reason; the Low L. *persona* was applied to rank or dignity, and had nothing to do with a fanciful embodiment of the church in the parson's person! Der. *parson-age*.

person. (F. – L.) M.E.*persone,persoune.* – O. F. *persone*, F. *personne.* – L. *persōna*, a mask used by an actor, a personage, character played by an actor, a person. – L. *persōnare*, to sound through; the large-mouthed mask of the actor was named from the voice sounding through it. – L. *per*, through; *sonare*, to sound, from *sonus*, sound.

resonant. (L.) From stem of pres. pt. of L. *re-sonare*, to sound back, echo, resound.

resound. (F. – L.) O. F. *resonner* (12th cent.). – L. *resonare* (above).

sonata. (Ital. – L.) Ital. *sonata*, a sounding, a sonata. From the fem. of pp. of Ital. *sonare*, to sound. – L. *sonare*, to sound, from *sonus*, sound.

sonnet. (F. – Ital. – L.) F. *sonnet.* – Ital. *sonetto*, a sonnet, canzonet; dimin. of *sono*, a sound, tune. – L. *sonum*, acc. of *sonus*, a sound. Der. *sonnet-eer*, Ital. *sonettiere*, a sonnet-writer.

sonorous. (L.) L. *sonōrus*, loud-sounding. – L. *sonōr-*, stem of *sonor*, sound, noise. – L. *sonare*, to sound. – L. *sonus*, sound.

unison, concord. (F. – L.) F. *unisson.* – L. *unisonum*, acc. of *unisonus*, having a like sound. – L. *uni-*, for *uno-*, crude form of *unus*, one; *sonus*, a sound.

Sound (4), to measure depth of water. (F. – Scand.) In Palsgrave. – F. *sonder*, to sound the depth of. – Icel. Dan. and Swed. *sund*, a strait, narrow channel. Cf. A. S. *sund-gyrd*, a sounding-rod, *sund-line*, a sounding-line; see Sound (2). ¶ This is my solution; Diez derives F. *sonder* from a supposed L. *sub-undare**, to go under the water; but Span. *sonda* means a sound or channel as well as a sounding-line.

Soup; see Sup.

Sour. (E.) A. S. *súr.* + Du. *zuur*, Icel. *súrr*, Dan. *suur*, Swed. *sur*, G. *sauer*. + W. *sur*, sour, Lith. *surus*, salt; Russ. *surovuii*, raw, coarse, harsh, rough.

sorrel (1), a plant. (F. – M. H. G.) O. F. *sorel* (F. *surelle*). – M. H. G. *súr* (G. *sauer*), sour; from its taste. So also A. S. *súre*, sorrel, from *súr*, sour.

Source; see Regent.

Souse, pickle; see Salt.

South. (E.) A. S. *súð.* + Du. *zuid*; Icel. *suðr*, also *sunnr*, south (cf. *suðreyjar*, lit. southern islands, Sodor, the Hebrides); Dan. Swed. *syd*, Swed. *sunnan*, the south; O. H. G. *sund*, G. *süd*. β. The Teut. type is SUNTHA, south; certainly allied to Sun, q. v. Lit. 'the sunned quarter.' Der. *south-ern*, lit. 'running from the south;' cf. O. H. G. *sundrôni*, southern, put for *sunda-rôni*, running from the south.

Souvenir; see Venture.

Sovereign; see Sub-, *prefix.*

Sow (1), to scatter seed. (E.) A. S. *sáwan*, pt. t. *seów*, pp. *sáwen*. + Du. *zaaijen*, Icel. *sá*, Dan. *saae*, Swed. *sá*, O. H. G. *sáwen*, G. *säen*, Goth. *saian*. + W. *hau*, Lith. *seti*, Russ. *sieiate*, L. *serere* (pt. t. *se-ui*, pp. *sa-tum*), to sow. (√SA, to cast.)

seed. (E.) A. S. *sǽd*, seed. – A. S. *sáwan*, to sow. + Du. *zaad*, Icel. *sæði*, *sáð*, Dan. *sǽd*, Swed. *säd*, G. *saat*.

Sow (2), a female pig. (E.) Also applied to oblong pieces of melted metal, whence smaller pieces branch out, called *pigs*. M. E. *sowe*. A. S. *sugu*, also *sú*. + Du. *zog*, Icel. *sýr*, Dan. *so*, Swed. *so*, *sugga*, G. *sau*. + W. *hwch*, Irish *suig*, L. *sus*, Gk. *ῦs*, *σῦs*, a sow; Zend *hu*, a boar. Lit. 'producer,' from the prolific nature of the sow. (√SU, to produce.)

soil (2), to defile. (F. – L.) M. E. *soilen*. [Not allied to M. E. *sulen*, E. *sully*.] – O. F. *soillier*, F. *souiller*, to soil; *se souiller*, to wallow as a sow. – O. F. *soil*, *souil*, 'the soile of a wild boare, the mire wherein he hath wallowed;' Cot. [Cf. Prov. *sulhar*, to soil, *solh*, mire, *sulha*, a sow; plainly from L. *sucula*, a young sow, dimin. of *sus*, a sow.] – L. *suillus*, adj., belonging to swine. – L. *sus*, a sow. Der. *soil*, sb., a stain; quite distinct from *soil*, ground.

swine, a sow, pig, pigs. (E.) M. E. *swin*, both sing. and pl. A. S. *swin*, a pig; pl. *swin*, swine. + Du. *swijn*, a swine, hog; Icel. *svín*, pl. *svín*, Dan. *sviin*, pl. *sviin*, Swed. *svin*, G. *schwein*, O. H. G. *swin*; Goth. *swein*, neut. sb. sing. So also Russ. *svineya*, a swine, *svinka*, a pig, *svinoi*, swinish. All orig. adjectival forms, like L. *suinus* (Varro), related to swine, formed from *sui-*, crude form of *sus*, a sow.

Soy, a sauce. (Japanese.) Also *sooja*, 'which has been corrupted into *soy*;' Eng. Cycl. Japanese *shôyu*, soy, sauce; though the name is now given to the bean (*Dolichos soja*) whence *soy* is made.

Spa, a place where is a spring of mineral water. (Belgium.) Named after *Spa*, S.W. of Liège, in Belgium.

Space. (F. – L.) F. *espace.* – L. *spatium*, a space; 'lit. that which is drawn out.' (√SPA, to draw out.) Cf. Gk. σπά-ειν, to draw. **Der.** *spac-i-ous*.

expatiate. (L.) From pp. of L. *expatiari*, better *exspatiari*, to wander. – L. *ex*, out; *spatiari*, to roam, from *spatium*, space.

Spade. (E.) A. S. *spædu*, *spada*, a spade. + Du. *spade*, Icel. *spaði*, Dan. Swed. *spade*, G. *spate*, *spaten*; Gk. σπάθη, broad blade, sword-blade, spathe of a flower. (whence L. *spatha*, F. *épée*). From its flat surface. (√SPA, to draw out.) **Der.** *spaddle*, a paddle; *spad-ille*, ace of spades, F. *spadille*, Span. *espadilla*, small sword, ace of spades, dimin. of Span. *spada*, a spade (= L. *spatha* = Gk. σπάθη).

epaulet, a shoulder-knot. (F. – L. – Gk.) F. *épaulette*; dimin. from *épaule* (O. F. *espaule*), a shoulder. – Late L. *spatula*, shoulder-blade; L. *spatula*, a broad blade; see **spatula** below.

espalier, lattice-work for training trees. (F. – Ital. – L. – Gk.) O. F. *espallier* ; Cot. – Ital. *spalliera*, back of a chair, support, espalier. – Ital. *spalla*, shoulder. – L. *spatula*; see **epaulet** above.

paddle (2), a little spade, esp. to clean a plough with. (E.) Formerly *spaddle*; dimin. of *spade*.

spatula, a broad-bladed knife for spreading plaisters. (L. – Gk.) L. *spatula*, dimin. of *spatha*. – Gk. σπάθη, a broad blade.

Spalpeen, a mean fellow. (Irish.) Irish *spailpin*, a mean fellow; from *spailp*, a beau, also, self-conceit; Gael. *spailpean*, from *spailp*; cf. Gael. *spailp*, to strut.

Span, to measure, grasp. (E.) M. E. *spannen*. A. S. *spannan*, to bind, pt. t. *spénn*; *gespannan*, to bind, connect. + O. H. G. *spannan*, to extend, connect; Du. *spannen*, to span, stretch, put horses to, Dan. *spænde*, Swed. *spände*, to stretch, span, buckle; Icel. *spenna*, to clasp. Allied to **Space** and **Spin.** (√SPA.) **Der.** *span*, sb., stretch of the hand, 9 inches in space. ¶ For *span-new*, see under **Spoon.**

Spangle. (E.) M. E. *spangel*, dimin. of *spang*, a metal fastening (hence, small shining ornament). A. S. *spange*, a metal

clasp. + O. Du. *spange*, a thin plate of metal; G. *spange*, brooch, clasp, buckle. Allied to Lith. *spingèti*, to glitter (Schleicher).

Spaniel. (F. – Span. – L.) M. E. *spaniel*, *spaneʒeole*. – O. F. *espagneul*, a spaniel, Spanish dog. – Span. *Español*, Spanish. – Span *España*, Spain. – L. *Hispania*, Spain.

Spank, to slap, move quickly. (E.) We also have *spanker*, a large active man or animal; *spanking*, large, lusty. An E. word. + Low G. *spakkern*, *spenkern*, to run and spring about quickly. From a base SPAK, significant of quick action. **Der.** *spank-er*, an after-sail in a barque.

Span-new; see **Spoon.**

Spar (1), a beam, bar. (E.) M. E. *sparre*. The A. S. sb. is vouched for by the derived verb *sparrian*, to fasten a door with a bar. + Du. *spar*, Icel. *sparri*, Dan. Swed. *sparre*; O. H. G. *sparro*, G. *sparren*, spar, bar. Also Irish and Gael. *sparr*, beam. Allied to **Spear.** **Der.** *spar*, verb, to fasten a door. And see *park*.

Spar (2), a mineral. (E.) A. S. *spær-stán*, a spar-stone. Cf. G. *sparkalk*, plaster. ¶ Distinct from G. *spat*, *spath*, spar.

Spar (3), to box, wrangle. (F. – Teut.) Used of fighting-cocks. – O. F. *esparer*, 'to fling or yerk out with the heels;' Cot. – Low G. *sparre*, sb., a struggling, striving; G. *sich sperren*, to struggle against, resist, oppose. Allied to Skt. *sphur*, to throb, struggle; Gk. σπαίρειν, ἀσπαίρειν, to struggle convulsively; Russ. *sporite*, to quarrel, wrangle. (√SPAR.)

Spare, frugal, lean. (E.) A. S. *spær*, spare; whence *sparian*, verb, to spare. + Icel. *sparr*, Dan. *spar-som*, Swed. *spar-sam*, G. *spär-lich*, thrifty; Gk. σπαρνός, rare. (√ SPAR, to scatter.) **Der.** *spar-ing*, *spare-rib*; *spare*, verb, from A. S. *sparian* (above).

Spark (1), a small particle of fire. (E.) A. S. *spearca*. + O. Du. *sparcke*; Low G. *sparke*. So called from the crackling of a fire-brand, which throws out sparks; cf. Icel. *spraka*, to crackle, Lith. *spragéti*, to crackle like burning fire-wood, Gk. σφάραγος, a crackling. (√SPARG, from √SPAR, to quiver.)

Spark (2), a gay young fellow. (Scand.) The same as Wiltsh. *sprack*, lively. – Icel. *sparkr*, sprightly, also *sprækr*; Swed. dial. *spräker*, *spräk*, *spräg*, talkative. Orig.

'noisy;' see **Spark** (1). **Der.** *sprag*, i. e. *sprack*, used by Sir Hugh, Merry Wives, iv. 1. 84.

Sparrow. (E.) A. S. *spearwa*. + Icel. *spörr*, Dan. *spurv*, Swed. *sparf*, O. H. G. *sparo*, G. *sper-ling*. Lit. 'flutterer;' from √SPAR, to quiver. **Der.** *sparrow-hawk*; and see *spavin*.

Sparse, thinly scattered. (L.) L. *sparsus*, pp. of *spargere*, to scatter, sprinkle. Cf. Skt. *sṛiç*, to sprinkle. (√SPARG, from √SPAR, to scatter; Gk. σπείρειν.)

asperse, to cast calumny upon. (L.) From L. *aspersus*, pp. of *aspergere*, to besprinkle.—L. *a-* (for *ad*); *spargere*, to scatter.

disperse, to scatter abroad. (L.) From L. pp. *dispersus*, pp. of *dispergere*, to scatter abroad.—L. *di-* (for *dis-*), apart; *spargere*, to scatter.

intersperse. (L.) From L. *interspersus*, pp. of *interspergere*, to sprinkle amongst.—L. *inter*, among; *spargere*, to scatter.

Spasm. (F.—L.—Gk.) F. *spasme*, the cramp.—L. *spasmum*, acc. of *spasmus*.— Gk. σπασμός, a spasm.—Gk. σπάειν, to draw, pluck. (√SPA.) **Der.** *spasm-od-ic*, from Gk. σπασμώδης, convulsive.

Spat, young of shell-fish; see **Spit** (2).

Spate, a river-flood. (C.) Irish *speid*, a great river-flood; (a similar word must have existed in Gaelic, but Macleod and Dewar do not record it).

Spatter; see **Spit** (2).

Spatula; see **Spade.**

Spavin, a swelling near the joints of horses, producing lameness. (F.—Teut.) M. E. *spaveyne*.—O. F. *esparvain*, 'a spavin in the leg of a horse;' Cot. The same as Span. *esparavan*, (1) a sparrow-hawk; (2) spavin; answering to a Low L. adj. *sparvanus*, belonging to a sparrow, parallel to Low L. *sparvarius*, a sparrow-hawk, lit. belonging to sparrows. Thus the lit. sense is 'sparrow-like,' from the hopping or sparrow-like motion of a horse afflicted with spavin. Derived from O. H. G. *sparwe*, a sparrow, cognate with E. **Sparrow**, q. v. ¶ Generally explained as 'sparrow-hawk-like,' contrary to grammar and sense.

Spaw, the same as **Spa,** q. v.

Spawn, the eggs of fish or frogs. (F.— L.) From M. E. *spawnen, spanen*, to spawn, as fishes; Prompt. Parv. Put for *spaund*, with loss of *d*. See Wright's Voc. i. 164;

N. & Q. 6 S v. 465.—O. F. *espandre*, 'to shed, spill, pour out, scatter abroad in great abundance:' Cot.—L. *expandere*, to spread out, shed abroad; see **expand**, under **Patent.**

Speak. (E.) M. E. *speken*, but (before A. D. 1200) *spreken*; the word has lost an *r*. Late A. S. *specan*, A. S. *sprecan*, pt. t. *spræc*, pp. *sprecen*. + Du. *spreken*; G. *sprechen*, pt. t. *sprach*. All from Teut. base SPRAK, to make a noise, as in Icel. *spraka*, to crackle; see **Spark** (1).

bespeak. (E.) From *speak*, with E. prefix *be-*.

speech. (E.) M. E. *speche*. A. S. *spǽc*, earlier form *sprǽc*, speech.—A. S. *sprecan*, to speak (above). + Du. *spraak*, G. *sprache*, speech.

spokesman. (E.) In Shak. Two Gent. ii. 1, 152. Oddly formed from *spoke*, pt. t. of *speak*, instead of from the infin. *speak*; for the *s*, cf. *hunt-s-man*, *sport-s-man*.

Spear. (E.) M. E. and A. S. *spere*. + Du. *speer*, Icel. *spjör*, Dan. *spær*, G. *speer*; L. *sparus*, a small missile-weapon, dart. Prob. allied to *spar*, a beam, bar (hence, a pole). See **Spar** (1).

Special; see **Species.**

Species, a kind. (L.) L. *species*, look, appearance, kind, sort.—L. *specere*, to look, see. + O. H. G. *spehōn*, G. *spähen*, to spy. + Gk. σκέπτομαι, I look. + Skt. *paç, paç*, to spy. (√SPAK, to see.)

aspect. (L.) L. *aspectus*, look.—L. *aspectus*, pp. of *aspicere*, to look.—L. *a-* (for *ad*), to, at; *specere*, to look.

circumspect, prudent. (L.) L. *circumspectus*, prudent; orig. pp. of *circumspicere*, to look around.

conspicuous. (L.) L. *conspicuus*, visible.—L. *con spicere*, to see thoroughly.

despise, to contemn. (F.—L.) M. E. *despisen*.—O. F. *despis-*, used as the stem of the pres. part. and pres. t. pl. of the verb *despire*, to despise, look down upon.—L. *despicere*, to look down, look down on. **Der.** *despic-able*, from L. *despic-ere*.

despite, spite, hatred. (F.—L.) M. E. *despit*.—O. F. *despit*, 'despight, spight;' Cot.—L. *despectus*, contempt:—L. *despectus*, pp. of *de-spicere*, to despise (above).

especial. (F.—L.) O. F. *especial*.—L. *specialis*, belong to a special kind.—L. *species*, a kind.

espy, to spy, see. (F.—O. H. G.) M. E. *espien*.—O. F. *espier*.—O. H. G. *spehōn*

(G. *spähen*), to spy ; see **Species** (above).

Der. *espi-on-age,* F. *espionnage,* from O. F. *espion,* a spy, borrowed from Ital. *spione,* a spy, from O. H. G. *spehôn,* to spy.

expect. (L.) L. *expectare,* better *exspectare,* to look for anxiously. ― L. *ex,* thoroughly ; *spectare,* to look ; see **spectacle** (below).

inspect. (L.) L. *inspectare,* to observe ; frequent. of *in-spicere,* to look into.

introspection. (L.) From L. *introspectio,* a looking into. ― L. *intro-,* within, *spect-us,* pp. of *specere,* to look.

perspective. (F. ― L.) F. *perspective,* ' the optike art ;' Cot. ― L. *perspectiua,* the art of inspecting ; orig. fem. of *perspectiuus,* looking through. ― L. *perspectus,* pp. of *per-spicere,* to look through.

perspicacity, keenness of sight. (F. ― L.) F. *perspicacité.* ― L. acc. *perspicacitatem,* sharp-sightedness. ― L. *perspicaci-,* crude form of *perspicax,* sharp-sighted. ― L. *per-spicere,* to see through.

perspicuous, clear. (L.) L. *perspicuus,* clear. ― L. *per-spicere,* to see through.

prospect. (L.) L. *prospectus,* a view. ― L. *prospectus,* pp. of *pro-spicere,* to look forward. **Der.** *prospectus* = L. *prospectus,* a view.

respect, sb. (F. ― L.) F. *respect,* ' respect, regard ;' Cot. ― L. *respectum,* acc. of *respectus,* a looking at. ― L. *respectus,* pp. of *re-spicere,* to look at, look back upon. **Der.** *respect,* verb ; *respect-able, respect-ive* ; also *dis-respect.*

respite, delay, reprieve. (F. ― L.) O. F. *respit,* a respite. Orig. sense regard, respect had to a suit on the part of a judge. ― L. acc. *respectum,* respect ; see above.

retrospect. (L.) From L. *retrospectus,* (unused) pp. of *retro-spicere,* to look back.

sceptic. (F. ― L. ― Gk.) F. *sceptique.* ― L. *scepticus.* ― Gk. σκεπτικός, thoughtful, inquiring ; pl. σκεπτικοί, the Sceptics, followers of Pyrrho (3rd century). ― Gk. σκέπτομαι, I consider ; see **Species** (above).

scope ; see **Scope** (separately).

special. (F. ― L.) Short for *especial* ; see **especial** (above).

specie, money in gold or silver. (L.) Evolved as a sb. from the old word *species,* ' money paid by tale,' Phillips ; prob. by confusion with L. abl. *specie,* as if *paid in specie* = paid in visible coin.

specify. (F. ― L.) O. F. *specifier,* to particularise. ― L. *specificare.* ― L. *specificus,* specific, particular. ― L. *speci-es* ; kind ; *-fic-,* for *facere,* to make.

specimen. (L.) L. *specimen,* an example, something shown. ― L. *speci-,* for *specere,* to see ; with suffix *-men.*

specious, showy. (F. ― L.) O. F. *specieux,* fair. ― L. *speciosus,* fair to see. ― L. *speci-,* for *specere,* to see ; with suffix *-osus.*

spectacle. (F. ― L.) F. *spectacle,* a sight. ― L. *spectaculum,* a show. ― L. *spectare,* to behold, frequentative of *specere,* to see.

spectator. (L.) L. *spectator,* a beholder. ― L. *specta-re,* to see ; with suffix *-tor.* ― L. *spect-um,* supine of *specere,* to see.

spectre. (F. ― L.) F. *spectre,* ' an image, ghost ;' Cot. ― L. *spectrum,* a vision. ― L. *spec-ere,* to see.

specular. (L.) L. *specularis,* belonging to a mirror. ― L. *speculum,* a mirror. ― L. *spec-ere,* to see. ¶ But Milton uses it with reference to L. *specula,* a watch-tower ; also from *spec-ere* ; see below.

speculate. (L.) From pp. of L. *speculari,* to behold. ― L. *specula,* a watch-tower. ― L. *spec-ere,* to see. **Der.** *speculat-ion, -ive.*

spice. (F. ― L.) M. E. *spice,* formerly used also in the sense of *species* or kind. ― O. F. *espice,* spice. ― L. *speciem,* acc. of *species,* a kind, which in late L. meant also a spice, drug.

spite. (F. ― L.) M. E. *spyt, spite.* Merely short for *despite,* by loss of the first syllable (as in *fence* for *de-fence*). See **despite** (above). **Der.** *spite-ful.*

spy, to see. (F. ― O. H. G.) Short for *espy* ; see **espy** (above). **Der.** *spy,* sb.

suspect. (F. ― L.) M. E. *suspect,* orig. a pp. with the sense suspected or suspicious. ― F. *suspect,* suspected. ― L. *suspectus,* pp. of *suspicere,* to suspect, lit. ' to look under,' mistrust. ― L. *su-* (for *sus-, subs-*), under ; *specere,* to look.

suspicion. (F. ― L.) M. E. *suspecion.* ― O. F. *suspezion,* suspicion ; later *souspeçon,* Cot. (mod. F. *soupçon.*) ― L. *suspicionem,* acc. of *suspicio,* suspicion. ― L. *suspicere,* to suspect (above).

transpicuous, transparent. (L.) Coined, as if from L. *transpicuus* *, from *transpicere,* to see through. ― L. *tran-,* for *trans,* beyond ; *specere,* to look. Compare *perspicuous.* See also **Auspice, Frontispiece, Scope.**

Specify, Specimen, Specious ; see **Species.**

Speck, a small spot. (E.) A. S. *specca,* a spot, mark. Allied to Low G. *spakig,*

spotted with wet, *spaken*, to spot with wet;
O. Du. *spickelen*, to speckle, frequentative
of O. Du. *spicken*, to spit. Cf. G. *spucken*,
tᴏ spit. *Speck* is 'that which spots,' from
Teut. base SPAK, to spit. (So also *spot*,
from *spit*.) Der. *speck-le*, a little speck;
speck-le, verb.

**Spectacle, Spectator, Spectre, Spe-
cular**; see **Species**.

Speech; see **Speak**.

Speed, success, velocity. (E.) A. S. *spéd*,
haste, success. Put for *spódi**, by the
usual change from *ó* to *é*. ‒ A.S. *spówan*,
to succeed. + Du. *spoed*, speed ; O. H. G.
spuot, *spôt*, success, from *spuon*, to succeed.
Allied to Skt. *sphíti*, increase, prosperity,
from *spháy*, to enlarge. (√ SPA.) Der.
speed, vb., A. S. *spédan*, from *spéd*, sb.

Speir, to ask ; see **Spur**.

Spelicans ; see **Spell** (4).

Spell (1), an incantation. (E.) M. E.
spel. A.S. *spel*, *spell*, a saying, story, narrative ; hence a form of words, spell. + Icel.
spjall, a saying ; O. H. G. *spel*, narrative ;
Goth. *spill*, fable.

spell (2), to tell the names of letters of
a word. (E.) M. E. *spellen*, to spell, to
tell. A. S. *spellian*, to tell, recount. ‒ A.S.
spell, a story (above). + Du. *spellen*, to spell,
M. H. G. *spellen*, to relate ; Goth. *spillon*,
to narrate. ¶ Or else from *spell* (4), a
splinter, because a splinter of wood was
used as a pointer, to assist in spelling
words ; we find *speldren*, to spell, even in
the Ormulum, from *spelder*, a splinter.

Spell (3), a turn of work. (E.) From
A. S. *spelian*, to supply another's room, to
act or be proxy for. Allied to Du. *spelen*,
Icel. *spila*, G. *spielen*, to act a part, play a
game ; from the sb. appearing as Du. Swed.
spel, Icel. Dan. *spil*, G. *spiel*, a game.

Spell (4), **Spill**, a thin slip of wood, slip
of paper. (E.) Formerly *speld*, but afterwards confused with **spell** (2), q. v. M. E.
speld, a splinter. A.S. *speld*, a torch, spill
to light a candle. Orig. a splinter ; from
Teut. base SPALD, to cleave ; cf. G.
spalten, to cleave; see **spill** (2) below. + Du.
speld, a pin, splinter; Icel. *speld*, a square
tablet, orig. thin piece of board, *spilda*, a
slice; M. H. G. *spelte*, a splinter. Cf.
Shetland *speld*, to split.

spelicans, thin slips of wood. (Du.)
O. Du. *spelleken*, a small pin; dimin. of
O. Du. *spelle* (Du. *speld*), a splinter (above).

spill (1), a slip of paper for lighting
candles ; see **Spell** (4) above.

spill (2), to destroy, shed. (E.) (Not
allied to *spoil*.) M. E. *spillen*, to destroy,
mar ; also, to perish. A. S. *spillan*, *spildan*,
to destroy. ‒ A. S. *spild*, destruction ; orig.
'a hewing in pieces,' and allied to **Spell**
(4), above.

Spelt, a kind of corn. (E.) A. S. *spelt*,
corn. + Du. *spelt*, G. *spelz* ; cf. G. *spelze*,
chaff, shell, beard of ear of corn. Prob.
allied to *split*, and *spell* (4). .

Spelter, pewter, zinc. (E. ?) In Blount
(1674). Prob. E. ; cf. Low G. *spialter*,
pewter ; Du. *spiauter*. ¶ This seems to
be the original of Pewter, q. v.

Spencer, Spend; see **Pendant**.

Sperm, spawn, spermaceti. (F. ‒ L. ‒
Gk.) M. E. *sperme*. ‒ F. *sperme*, 'sperm,
seed ;' Cot. ‒ L. *sperma*. ‒ Gk. σπέρμα. ‒
Gk. σπείρειν, to sow; orig. to scatter with
a jerk of the hand. (√ SPAR.) Der.
sperm-at-ic (Gk. σπερματικός); *spermaceti*,
L. *sperma-ceti*, i.e. sperm of the whale ; see
Cetaceous.

sporadic, scattered here and there. (Gk.)
Gk. σποραδικός, scattered. ‒ Gk. σποραδ-,
stem of σποράς, scattered. ‒ Gk. σπείρειν,
to scatter.

. **spore**. (Gk.) Gk. σπόρος, seed-time;
also a seed. ‒ Gk. σπείρειν, to sow.

Spew, Spue. (E.) A. S. *spíwan*, pt. t.
spáw, pp. *spiwen*, to vomit. + Du. *spuuwen*,
Icel. *spýja*, Dan. *spye*, Swed. *spy*, G. *speien*,
Goth. *speiwan*, L. *spuere*, Lith. *spjauti* ;
Gk. πτύειν (for σπύειν *), to spit. (√ SPU.)
Allied to *pip* (1), *puke* (1), *spit* (2).

Sphere, a globe, ball. (F. ‒ L. ‒ Gk.)
M. E. *spere*. ‒ O. F. *espere*, later *sphere*. ‒ L.
sphæra. ‒ Gk. σφαῖρα, a ball. Lit. ‘that
which is tossed about ;’ cf. Gk. σπείρειν, to
toss about, scatter. (√ SPAR.)

Sphinx. (L. ‒ Gk.) L. *sphinx*. ‒ Gk.
σφίγξ (gen. σφιγγός), lit. ‘the strangler,’
because the Sphinx strangled travellers who
could not solve her riddles. ‒ Gk. σφίγγειν,
to throttle. [The legend is Egyptian.]

Spice; see **Species**.

Spick and Span-new, quite new.
(Scand.) Lit. ‘spike and spoon-new,’
where *spike* is a point, nail, and *spoon* is a
chip ; hence, new as a spike or nail just
made, or a chip just cut off. See **Spike**
and **Spoon**.

Spider; see **Spin**.

Spigot; see **Spike**.

Spike. (L.) L. *spica*, an ear of corn, a
point, a pike. Cf. Irish *pice*, Gael. *pic*,
W. *pig*, a peak, pike ; see **Pike**. β. The

Du. *spijker*, a nail, Icel. *spik*, &c., are borrowed from L.

spigot. (C. – L.) M. E. *spigot*, a peg for a cask. – Irish and Gael. *spiocaid*, a spigot ; dimin. of Irish *spice*, a spike, long nail, peg. Borrowed from L. *spica* (above).

spikenard. (L. ; *and* F. – L. – Gk. – Pers. – Skt.) Put for *spiked nard* (L. *nardus spicatus*), i. e. nard furnished with spikes, in allusion to the mode of growth. And see **Nard**.

spoke, a bar of a wheel. (E.) A. S. *spáca*, a spoke. + Du. *speek*, a spoke, G. *speiche*, prov. G. *spache*, a spoke. Allied to (perhaps formed from) L. *spica* (above).

Spill (1), a splinter, chip ; see **Spell** (4).

Spill (2), to mar, shed ; see **Spell** (4).

Spin, to draw out threads. (E.) A. S. *spinnan*, pt. t. *spann*, pp. *spunnen*.+Du. *spinnen*, Icel. Swed. *spinna*, Dan. *spinde*, G. *spinnen*, Goth. *spinnan*. Allied to Gk. σπά-ειν, to draw out. (√ SPA.) See also **Span**.

spider. (E.) M. E. *spither*, *spiðre*. Not found in A. S., but = a form *spinther**, whence (by loss of *n* before *th*, as in *tooth*, *other*) we should have *spiðer*, the exact equivalent of the M. E. form. Formed from the verb to *spin* with suffix *-ther* (Aryan *-tar*) of the agent, as in *fa-ther*. Cf. prov. E. *spinner*, a spider.+Du. *spin*, Dan. *spinder*, Swed. *spinnel*, G. *spinne*, spider or spinner.

spindle. (E.) The *d* is excrescent after *n*. M. E. *spinel*, also *spindele*. A. S. *spinl*, i. e. 'spinner,' from *spinnen*, to spin. + O. Du. *spille* (for *spinle* *), G. *spindel* (with excrescent *d*). Der. *spindl-y*, thin like a spindle ; *spindle-tree* (Euonymus) formerly used for spindles and skewers.

spinster, orig. a woman who spins. (E.) M. E. *spinnestere*. From A. S. *spinnan*, to spin ; with A. S. suffix *-estre* (E. *-ster*). β. This suffix is a compound one (*-es-tre*), compounded of the Aryan suffixes *-as* and *-tar*, as in Low L. *poet-as-ter*, L. *ole-as-ter*. It was used in A. S. (as in Du.) solely with reference to the feminine gender, but this restricted usage was soon set aside in a great many M. E. words. Cf. Du. *spinster*, a spinster, *zangster*, a female singer ; also E. *seamstress* (i. e. *seam-ster-ess*), *songstress* (i. e. *song-ster-ess*), where the F. fem. suffix *-ess* is superadded.

Spinach, Spinage ; see **Spine**.

Spindle ; see **Spin**.

Spine, a prickle. (F. – L.) O. F. *espine*, a thorn. – L. *spina*, a thorn, prickle ; also the back-bone. Allied to **Spike**. ¶ Observe that in the sense of 'back-bone' the word is Latin.

spinach, spinage, a vegetable. (Ital. – L.) *Spinage* is a weakened form of *spinach*. – Ital. *spinace* (pronounced *speen-aachai*), 'the hearbe spinage,' Florio. Formed (as if from Low L. *spinaceus**) from *spina*, a thorn, because the fruit is sometimes very prickly ; so also Span. *espinaca*. ¶ Or (F. – Span. – Arab. – Pers.) O. F. *espinace*. – Span. *espinaca*. – Arab. *isfándj* (Devic).

spinet, a kind of musical instrument. (F. – Ital. – L.) So called because struck by a *spine* or pointed quill. O. F. *espinette*. – Ital. *spinetta*, a spinet, also a prickle ; dimin. of *spina*, a thorn. – L. *spina*.

spinny, a thicket. (F. – L.) O. F. *espinoye*, 'a thicket, grove, a thorny plot ;' Cot. F. *épinaie*. – L. *spinetum*, a thicket of thorns. – L. *spina*, a thorn.

Spink, a finch. (Scand.) M. E. *spink*. – Swed. dial. *spink*, a sparrow ; *gull-spink*, a gold-finch ; Norw. *spikke* (for *spinke* *), small bird. + Gk. σπίγγος, a finch, i. e. 'chirper ;' from σπίζειν, to chirp. From the sound of chirping or piping ; cf. Lith. *speng-ti*, to resound. **Doublet,** *finch*.

Spinney, Spinny ; see **Spine**.

Spinster ; see **Spin**.

Spiracle ; see **Spirit**.

Spire (1), a tapering body, sprout, steeple. (E.) A. S. *spir*, spike, stalk. + Icel. *spira*, spar, stilt, Dan. *spire*, germ, sprout, Swed. *spira*, a pistil, G. *spiere*, a spar. Perhaps allied to *spike* and *spine*. ¶ Distinct from **Spire** (2).

Spire (2), a coil, wreath. (F. – L.) F. *spire*. – L. *spira*, a coil, twist, wreath.+Gk. σπεῖρα, a coil ; allied to σπυρίς, a basket. (√ SPAR.) Der. *spir-al*, F. *spiral*, L. *spiralis*.

Spirit. (F. – L.) M. E. *spirit*. – O. F. *espirit*, later *esprit*. – L. acc. *spiritum*, from *spiritus*, breath. – L. *spirare*, to breathe.

aspire. (F. – L.) F. *aspirer*, to breathe, covet, aspire to. – L. *aspirare*, lit. to breathe towards. – L. *a-* (for *ad*), to ; *spirare*, to breathe. Der. *aspir-ate*, to pronounce with a full breathing.

conspire. (F. – L.) F. *conspirer*. – L. *con-spirare*, to blow together, combine, plot.

expire. (F. – L.) O. F. *expirer*. – L.

expirare, exspirare, to breathe out, die.—
L. *ex,* out ; *spirare,* to breathe.

inspire. (F.—L.) O. F. *enspirer,* also
inspirer (Cot.).—L. *in-spirare,* to breathe
into.

perspiration, a sweating. (F. — L.)
F. *perspiration.* — Late L. acc. *perspira-
tionem,* lit. a breathing through.—L. *per-
spirare,* to breathe through.

respire, to breathe, take rest. (F.—L.)
F. *respirer.*—L. *re-spirare,* to breathe again
or back.

spiracle. (F. — L.) F. *spiracle,* 'a
breathing-hole ;' Cot.—L. *spiraculum,* air
hole.—L. *spirare,* to breathe.

sprightly, spritely. (F. — L.; *with*
E. *suffix.*) *Sprightly* is a false spelling ;
see below.

sprite, a spirit. (F. — L.) The false
spelling *spright* is common, and is retained
in the adj. *sprightly.* M. E. *sprit, sprite.*
— F. *esprit,* the spirit ; hence, a spirit. —
L. *spiritum,* acc. of *spiritus; see* Spirit
above.

transpire, to ooze out. (L.) From
L. *tran-,* for *trans,* through ; *spirare,* to
breathe.

Spirt; see spurt, under Sprout.

Spit (1), a skewer, iron prong for roasting meat. (E.) M. E. *spite.* A. S. *spitu,*
a spit. + Du. *spit,* Dan. *spid,* Swed. *spett,*
M. H. G. *spiz;* G. *spitze,* point, top. Prob.
allied to **Spike.** Cf. W. *pid,* a tapering
point.

Spit (2), to eject from the mouth. (E.)
M. E. *spitten.* A. S. *spittan ;* also *spætan,*
pt. t. *spátte,* to spit. + Icel. *spýta,* Dan.
spytte, Swed. *spotta,* G. *spützen* (cf. G.
spucken). Allied to **Spew.** (Base SPUT;
√ SPU.) Der. *spittle,* formerly *spettle,*
spatil, spotil, A. S. *spátl.*

spat, young of shell-fish. (E.) Formed,
like *spot,* from the notion of *spitting* or
ejecting ; see spot (below).

spatter, to besprinkle. (E.) The usual
sense is *be-spot,* and it is a frequentative of
spot, verb ; see spot (below).

spot, a blot, mark made by wet. (E.)
M. E. *spot.* Allied to M. E. *spotil,* A. S.
spátl, spittle. From the notion of spitting ;
a *spot* is a thing spat out, a blot, wet
mark. + Du. *spat,* a speck, *spatten,* to be-
spot ; Swed. *spott,* spittle, *spotta,* to spit ;
Dan. *spætte,* a spot. Cf. **Speck.**

Spite; see Species.

Spittle (1), saliva ; see Spit (2).

Spittle (2), a hospital ; see Host (1).

Splash, to dash water about. (Scand.)
Coined, by prefixing *s-* (= O. F. *es-,* L. *ex*)
used for emphasis, to *plash,* used in the
same sense (White Kennett). — Swed.
plaska, to splash, short for *platska**, as
shewn under **Plash** (1) ; Dan. *pladske,* to
splash. Cf. Swed. dial. *plätta,* to tap, pat.
See **Pat.**

Splay; see Ply.

Spleen. (L. — Gk.) M. E. *splen.* —
L. *splen.* — Gk. σπλήν, the spleen. +Skt.
plihan ; L. *lien.* Der. *splen-etic.*

Splendour. (F.—L.) F. *splendeur.*—
L. *splendorem,* acc. of *splendor,* brightness.
—L. *splendere,* to shine. **Der.** *re-splendent.*

Spleuchan, a tobacco-pouch. (Gael.)
Gael. *spliuchan,* Irish *spliuchan,* a pouch.

Splice; see Split.

Splint, Splent; see Split.

Split. (Scand.) Dan. *splitte,* to split,
Swed. dial. *splitta,* to disentangle or sepa-
rate yarn.+Du. *splijten,* G. *spleissen.* Al-
lied to Dan. *split,* Du. *spleet,* a split, rent,
G. *spleisse,* a splinter. From Teut. base
SPALT, variant of SPALD, to cleave ; see
Spell (4).

splice. (Du.) O. Du. *splissen,* to in-
terweave rope-ends ; so named from *splitting* the rope-ends beforehand ; from Du.
splitsen, to splice (really an older form).
Formed by adding *s* to the base of Du.
splijten, O. Du. *spleten, splitten,* to split.+
Dan. *splidse,* to splice (put for *splitse**) ;
from *splitte,* to split ; Swed. *splissa,* G.
splissen, to splice. Der. *splice,* sb.

splint, splent, a thin piece of split
wood. (Scand.) Formerly *splent.* — Swed.
splint, a kind of spike, a forelock (flat
iron peg) ; Dan. *splint,* a splinter.—Swed.
splinta, to splinter, from Swed. dial. *splitta,*
to split, Dan. *splitte,* to split.

Splutter, to speak hastily and confusedly.
(Scand.) Put for *sprutter,* frequentative of
sprout, the orig. form of *spout ;* see **Spout.**

Spurt. It means 'to keep on *spouting*
out ;' *spout* being formerly used (as now)
in the sense 'to talk.' 'Pray, *spout* some
French ;' Beaum. and Fletcher, Coxcomb,
iv. 4. Cf. Low G. *sprutten,* to spout, spurt.

Spoil, to plunder. (F. — L.) M. E.
spoilen.—F. *spolier,* 'to spoile ;' Cot.—L.
spoliare, to strip off spoil. — L. *spolium,*
spoil, booty ; orig. skin stripped off, dress
of a slain warrior. Cf. Gk. σκῦλον, spoil.
Der. *spoil,* sb.; *spoliation,* from L. pp.
spoliatus.

despoil. (F.—L.) O. F. *despoiller* (F.

dépouiller), to despoil. — L. *de-spoliare*, to plunder.

Spoke; see **Spike**.

Spokesman; see **Speak**.

Spoliation; see **Spoil**.

Spondee. (L. – Gk.) The metrical foot marked (– –). — L. *spondæus*. — Gk. σπον-δεῖος, a spondee, used for solemn melodies at treaties or truces. — Gk. σπονδαί, a solemn treaty, truce; pl. of σπονδή, a drink-offering, libation to the gods. — Gk. σπένδειν, to pour out. Der. *sponda-ic*.

Sponge. (F. – L. – Gk.) O. F. *esponge* (F. *éponge*). – L. *spongia*. – Gk. σπογγιά, a sponge; also σπόγγος (Attic σφόγγος). + L. *fungus*, a fungus (from its spongy nature). Prob. allied to **Swamp**.

spunk, tinder; a match, spark, spirit, mettle. (C. – L. – Gk.) Orig. ' tinder.' – Gael. and Irish *sponc*, sponge, spongy wood, tinder. – L. *spongia* (above).

Sponsor. (L.) L. *sponsor*, a surety. – L. *sponsus*, pp. of *spondere*, to promise. Prob. allied to Gk. σπονδαί, a truce.

correspond. (L.) Coined from L. *cor-* (for *con-*, *cum*), together; and *respond* (below).

despond. (L.) L. *despondere*, (1) to promise fully, (2) to give up, lose (hence to despair). — L. *de*, (1) fully, (2) away; *spondere*, to promise.

espouse. (F. – L.) O. F. *espouser*, to espouse, wed. — O. F. *espouse*, a spouse. — L. *sponsa*, a betrothed woman; cf. *sponsus*, a betrothed man. – L. *sponsus*, pp. of *spondere*, to promise.

respond. (F. – L.) O. F. *respondre*. – L. *respondere* (pp. *responsus*), to answer. – L. *re-*, back; *spondere*, to promise. Der. *response*, from O. F. *response*, an answer, from L. *responsum*, neut. of pp. *responsus*.

spouse. (F. – L.) From O. F. *espouse*, a spouse; see **espouse** (above).

Spontaneous. (L.) L. *spontaneus*, willing. – L. *spont-*, as seen in abl. *sponte*, of one's own accord, from a lost nom. *spons**. Perhaps allied to Skt. *chhand*, to please.

Spool, a reel for winding yarn on. (O. Low G.) M. E. *spole*. – O. Du. *spoele*, Du. *spoel*, a spool, quill; Low G. *spole*. + Swed. *spole*, Dan. *spole*, G. *spule*, spool, bobbin.

Spoom; see **Spume**.

Spoon, an instrument for supping liquids. (E.) M. E. *spon*. A. S. *spón*, a chip, splinter of wood (which was the orig. spoon). + Du. *spaan*, Icel. *spánn*, *spónn*, Dan. *spaan*, Swed. *spån*, G. *span*, a chip.

span-new, quite new. (Scand.) M. E. *span-newe*. – Icel. *spánnýr*, *spánýr*, span-new, lit. 'new as a chip.' — Icel. *spánn*, a chip, shaving, spoon; *nýr*, new. See above.

Sporadic, **Spore**; see **Sperm**.

Sporran. (Gael.) Gael. *sporan*, a purse, pouch worn with the kilt; Irish *sparan*, the same.

Sport; see **Port** (1).

Spot; see **Spit** (2).

Spouse; see **Sponsor**.

Spout, to squirt out, rush out as a liquid out of a pipe. (Scand.) This word (like *speak*) has lost an *r*; it stands for *sprout*; the *r* is also preserved in *spurt*, with nearly the same sense as *spout*. — Swed. *sputa*, occasionally used for *spruta*, to squirt, spout, spurt; *spruta*, sb., a syringe, squirt; Dan. *sprude*, to spout, spurt; Du. *spuiten*, to spout, *spuit*, a squirt (with lost *r*, as in E.); Low G. *sputtern*, *sprutten*, to spout. See **Sprout**, **Spurt**. β. The loss of *r* was prob. due to confusion with *spit*.

sputter. (Scand.) The frequentative of *spout* (above). It means 'to keep on spouting out;' hence to speak rapidly and indistinctly. ¶ Distinct from *spatter* and *spit*.

Sprack, **Sprag**; see **Spark** (2).

Sprain; see **Press**.

Sprat, a small fish. (Du.) M. E. *sprot*. — Du. *sprot*, a sprat; also a sprout or sprig of a tree. ' *Sprat*, a small fish, considered as the fry of the herring;' Wedgwood. Allied to *sprout*, with the sense of ' fry,' or young ones. See **Sprout**.

Sprawl, to toss about the limbs. (Scand.) M. E. *spraulen*. Short for *sprattle* or *sprottle*; cf. North E. *sprottle*, to struggle. — Swed. *sprattla*, dialectally *spralla*, to sprawl; Dan. *sprætte*, *sprælle*, to sprawl, flounder, toss the limbs about. + Du. *spartelen*, to flutter, wrestle. (Base SPART, from √ SPAR, to quiver.) See **Spar** (3).

Spray (1), foam tossed with the wind. (Du.?) A late word, given in Bailey's Dict. (1745). Of uncertain origin. Perhaps from Du. *spreiden*, to spread, scatter. Cf. Norw. *spreie*, used for *spreida*, to spread; Low G. *spreen* (for *spreden*).

Spray (2), sprig of a tree. (Scand.) Dan. *sprag*, a sprig; Swed. dial. *spragg*, the same; Icel. *sprek*, a stick. Allied to Lith. *sproga*, a spray of a tree, also a rift, from *sprog-ti*, to crackle, split, sprout, bud; Icel. *spraka*, to crackle. See **Spark** (1), **Sprig**.

Spread. (E.) A. S. *sprædan*, to extend.

+ Du. *spreiden*, Low G. *spreden*, G. *sprei-ten*; cf. Swed. *sprida*, Dan. *sprede*, to spread. Allied to **Sprout, Sprit**.

Spree, a frolic. (C.) Irish *spre*, a spark, flash, animation, spirit; *spraic*, vigour.

Sprig. (E.) M. E. *sprigge*. A. S. *sprec* (Somner). **+** Icel. *sprek*, a stick; Low G. *sprikk*, stick, twig. Allied to **Spray** (2).

Sprightly; see **Spirit**.

Spring, verb. (E.) A. S. *springan*, *sprincan*, pt. t. *sprang*, *spranc*, pp. *sprungen*. **+** Du. G. *springen*, Swed. *springa*, Dan. *springe*; Icel. *springa*, to burst, split. β. Orig. sense 'to split or crack,' as when we say that a cricket-bat is *sprung*; or to *spring* (i.e. burst) a mine. Allied to Lith. *sprog-ti*, to crack; also to **Spark** (1), **Speak**. (√SPARG.) Der. *spring*, sb., a leap, also a burst out of water, also the budding time of year, also a crack in a mast; *springe*, a snare made with a flexible (springing) rod.

sprinkle. (E.) Formerly *sprenkle*, frequentative of A. S. *sprencan*, *sprengan*, to sprinkle, scatter abroad; causal of A. S. *sprincan*, *springan*, to spring (above). **+** Du. *sprenkelen*, frequent. of *sprengen*, the causal of *springen*; G. *sprenkeln*, frequent. of *sprengen*, to scatter, to spring a mine, causal of *springen*.

Sprit; see **Sprout**.

Sprite; see **Spirit**.

Sprout, to germinate. (O. Low G.) M. E. *spruten*. [Not from A. S. *spreótan*, nor from A. S. *sprýtan*.] **–** O. Fries. *spruta*, strong verb, pp. *spruten*, to sprout; Low G. *spruten*, *sprotten*, to sprout. **+** Du. *spruiten*, G. *spriessen* (pt. t. *spross*). β. Allied to A. S. *spreótan*, pt. t. *spreát*, pp. *sproten*, to sprout; also to Icel. *spretta*, to spurt, spout (pt. t. *spratt*), prov. G. *spratzen*, to crackle, burst with heat. (Base SPRAT, allied to SPRAK, to burst; see **Speak**.) γ. The cognate Swed. *spruta* means to spout out water, and is the original of E. *spout*; see **Spout**.

sprit, a spar extending a fore-and-aft sail. (E.) M. E. *spret*, a pole. A. S. *spreót*, a pole; orig. a sprout, shoot, branch of a tree. **–** A. S. *spreótan*, to sprout (above).

spurt (1), **spirt**, to spout out. (E.) The older sense is to germinate. *Spurt* stands for *sprut*; M.E. *sprutten*, to sprout or shoot. A.S. *spryttan*, to produce as a sprout or shoot; causal form from A.S. *spreótan*, to sprout. See **Sprout**. And see **Spout**.

spurt (2), a violent exertion. (Scand.)

Formerly *spirt*. **–** Icel. *sprettr*, a spurt, spring, bound, run. **–** Icel. *spretta* (pt. t. *spratt*), to start, spring; also to sprout, to spout.

Spruce, fine, smart. (F. **–** G.) Hall's Chronicle tells us that a particular kind of fashionable dress was that in which men 'were appareyled after the manner of *Prussia* or *Spruce*;' see Richardson's Dict. M. E. *spruce*, Prussia, P. Plowman, C. vii. 279, B. xiii. 393; also written (more usually) *pruce*. **–** O. F. *Pruce* (F. *Prusse*), Prussia. **–** G. *Preussen*, Prussia. See **Spruce-beer**.

Spruce-beer, a kind of beer. (G.; *confused with* F. *and* E.) Originally called in German *sprossen-bier*, i. e. 'sprouts-beer,' obtained from the young sprouts of the black spruce fir. **–** G. *sprossen*, pl. of *spross*, a sprout (from *spriessen*, to sprout); and *bier*, cognate with E. *beer*; see **Sprout** and **Beer**. β. But the word was Englished as *Spruce-beer*, i. e. Prussian beer, where *Spruce* meant *Prussia*; see **Spruce** above. So also *spruce fir* meant Prussian fir; and *spruce leather* meant Prussian leather.

Spry, active. (Scand.) Swed. dial. *sprygg*, very active, skittish; allied to Swed. dial. *spräg*, *spräk*, spirited, mettlesome. See **Sprack**, **Spark** (2).

Spue; see **Spew**.

Spume, foam. (L.) L. *spuma*, foam. Cf. Skt. *phena*, A.S. *fám*, foam.

pounce (2), fine powder. (F. **–** L.) F. *ponce*; '*pierre ponce*, a pumis stone;' Cot. **–** L. *pumicem*, acc. of *pumex*, pumice; see below.

pumice. (L.) A.S. *pumic-stán*, pumice stone. **–** L. *pumic-*, stem of *pumex*, pumice. Put for *spumex* *, i. e. foam-like stone, from its appearance. **–** L. *spuma*, foam.

spoom, to run before the wind. (L.) Lit. 'to throw up *spume* or foam.' **–** L. *spuma*, foam.

Spunk, tinder, &c.; see **Sponge**.

Spur. (E.) M. E. *spure*. A. S. *spura*, *spora*, a spur. **+** Du. *spoor*, a spur, also a track; Icel. *spori*, Dan. *spore*, Swed. *sporre*, G. *sporn*, spur. (√SPAR.) See **Spar** (3). The orig. sense is 'kicker;' from its use on the heel; cf. Lith. *spir-ti*, to kick.

speir, to ask. (E.) Northern E. A. S. *spyrian*, to ask, track out. **–** A. S. *spor*, a foot-track; allied to *spora*, a spur (above). **+** Icel. *spyrja*, G. *spüren*.

spoor, a trail. (Du.) Du. *spoor*; see **Spur.** **+** A. S. *spor*, a foot-track (above).

spurn. (E.) M. E. *spurnen*, to kick

against, hence to reject. A. S. *speornan*, *gespornan*, to kick against (pt. t. *spearn*, pp. *spornen*). Allied to **Spur.** + Icel. *sperna* (pt. t. *sparn*) ; L. *spernere*, to despise, a cognate form, not one from which the E. word is merely borrowed. (Base SPARN ; √ SPAR.)

Spurge, a plant ; see **Pure.**

Spurious. (L.) L. *spurius*, false.

Spurn ; see **Spur.**

Spurry, a plant. (F. – G.) O. F. *spurrie*, 'spurry or frank, a Dutch [German] herb ;' Cot. Of Teut. origin ; cf. G. *spörgel*, *spergel*, *spark*, spurry.

Spurt (1), **Spirt,** to jet out ; see **Sprout.**

Spurt (2), a violent exertion ; see **Sprout.**

Sputter ; see **Spout.**

Spy ; see **Species.**

Squab, (1) to fall plump, (2) a sofa, a young bird. (Scand.) See *squab, squob* in Halliwell. And see *squab*, to fall plump, *squab*, with a sudden fall, in Johnson. **1.** From Swed. dial. *sqvapp*, a word imitative of a splash ; cf. G. *schwapp*, a slap, E. *swap*, to strike. **2.** From Swed. dial. *sqvabb*, loose or fat flesh, *sqvabba*, a fat woman, *sqvabbig*, flabby ; from the verb appearing in Norw. *sqvapa*, to tremble, shake, allied to M. E. *quappen*, to throb, and E. *quaver* ; see **Quaver.** Cf. Icel. *kvap*, jelly, jelly-like things.

squabble, to wrangle. (Scand.) Swed. dial. *skvabbel*, a dispute. – Swed. dial. *skvappa*, to chide, lit. make a splashing, from the sb. *skvapp, sqvapp*, a splash. Cf. Prov. E. *swabble*, to squabble, allied to *swab*, to splash over, *swap*, to strike.

Squad, Squadron ; see **Quadrate.**

Squalid. (L.) L. *squalidus*, rough, dirty. – L. *squalere*, to be rough, parched, dirty. Der. *squal-or*, sb.

Squall, to cry out. (Scand.) Swed. *sqvala*, to gush out violently, *sqval*, a rush of water, *sqval-regn*, a violent shower of rain (E. *squall*, sb., a burst of rain) ; Dan. *sqvaldre*, to clamour, *sqvalder*, clamour, noisy talk ; Swed. dial. *skvala*, to gush out, cry out, chatter. + Gael. *sgal*, a loud cry, sound of high wind ; allied to G. *schallen*, Icel. *skella* (pt. t. *skall*), to resound. (Base SKAL.)

Squander, to dissipate. (Scand.) Orig. to disperse, scatter abroad ; Dryden, Annus Mirabilis, st. 67. Nasalised form of Lowl. Sc. *squatter*, to splash water about, scatter, squander, prov. E. *swatter*, to throw water about. These are frequentatives from Dan.

sqvatte, to splash, spurt, also to squander ; Swed. *sqvätta*, to squirt, Icel. *skvetta*, to squirt out water. The *d* appears in O. Du. *swadderen*, to dabble in water ; Swed. dial. *skvadra*, to gush out of a hole (as water). Cf. *scatter* and *squirt.*

Square ; see **Quadrate.**

Squash, to crush. (F. – L.) O. F. *esquacher*, to crush, also spelt *escacher*, 'to squash ;' Cot. (Mod. F. *écacher*.) The F. *cacher* answers to Sardinian *cattare* = L. *co-actare*, to constrain, force, press. The prefix *es* = L. *ex*, extremely. β. Thus the etymology is from L. *ex* ; and *coactare*, formed from *coact-us*, pp. of *cogere* (= *co-agere*), to drive together. See **Ex-** and **Cogent ;** also **Con-** and **Agent. Der.** *squash*, sb., an unripe peascod.

squat, to cower. (F. – L.) Lit. to lie flat, as if pressed down ; the old sense is to press down, squash. M. E. *squatten*, to crush flat. – O. F. *esquatir*, to flatten, crush. – O. F. *es-* (= L. *ex*), extremely ; *quatir*, to press down. Diez shews that O. F. *quatir* is a derivative of L. *coactus*, pp. of *cogere*, to press, compel ; see above.

Squaw, a female. (W. Indian.) Massachusetts *squa, eshqua*, Naragansett *squáws*, a female (Webster).

Squeak, to cry out shrilly. (Scand.) Swed. *sqväka*, to croak ; Norw. *skvaka*, to cackle ; Icel. *skvakka*, to sound like water shaken in a bottle. Allied to **Quack.**

squeal. (Scand.) Swed. *sqväla*, Norw. *skvella*, to squeal. Used (instead of *squeakle**) as a frequentative of *squeak*, and applied to a continuous cry.

Squeamish ; see **Swim** (2).

Squeeze, to crush, press tightly. (E.) The prefixed *s* is due to O. F. *es-* (= L. *ex*), very ; *queeze* = M. E. *queisen*, to squeeze. This M. E. *queisen* is from A. S. *cwisan*, *cwýsan*, also *cwésan*, to crush. Allied to Goth. *kwistjan*, to destroy, Swed. *qväsa*, to squeeze, bruise, G. *quetschen*, to squash, bruise.

Squib, (1) a paper tube, with combustibles ; (2) a lampoon. (Scand.) **1.** *Squibs* were sometimes fastened slightly to a rope, so as to run along it like a rocket ; whence the name. From M. E. *squippen*, *swippen*, to move swiftly, fly, sweep, dash. – Icel. *svipa*, to flash, dart, *svipr*, a swift movement ; Norw. *svipa*, to run swiftly. Allied to **Sweep, Swift. 2.** A *squib* also means a political lampoon, but was formerly applied, not to the *lampoon itself*, but to the *writer* of it ; see Tatler, no. 88,

Nov. 1, 1709. A *squib* thus meant a fire-work, a flashy fellow, making a noise, but doing no harm. *Squib* also means child's squirt, from its shooting out water instead of fire.

Squill; see **Schism.**

Squinancy, old spelling of *quinsy*; see **Cynic.**

Squint, to look askew. (Scand.) The same as prov. E. (Suffolk) *squink*, to wink. — Swed. *svinka*, to shrink, flinch (whence the notion of looking aside), nasalised form of *svika*, to balk, flinch, fail; cf. O. Swed. *svinka*, to beguile. ¶ This is the most probable account of a difficult word.

Squire (1), the same as **Esquire.**

Squire (2), a carpenter's rule; see **Quadrate.**

Squirrel. (F. − L. − Gk.) M.E. *squirel, scurel.* − O. F. *escurel* (F. *écureuil*). − Low L. *scurellus*, a squirrel; put for *sciurellus**, dimin. of *sciurus*, a squirrel. − Gk. σκίουρος, a squirrel; lit. 'a shadow-tail,' from his bushy tail. − Gk. σκί-α, shadow; οὑρά, tail.

Squirt, sb. (Scand.) The *r* appears to be intrusive; allied to prov. E. *squitter*, to squirt, and *squitter*, diarrhœa. − Swed. dial. *skvittär*, to sprinkle all round, frequentative of *skwitta*, to squirt, Swed. *sqvätta*, to squirt. Cf. Dan. *sqvatte*, to splash. Allied to **Squander.**

Stab. (C.) Irish *stob-aim*, I stab; Gael. *stob*, to fix a stake in the ground, from *stob*, a stake, pointed iron or stick, stub. Allied to **Staff,** q. v. **Der.** *stab*, sb.

Stable, Stablish; see **State.**

Stack; see **Stick** (1).

Staff. (E.) A.S. *stæf*; pl. *stafas*, staves. **+** Du. *staf*, Icel. *stafr*, Dan. *stab*, *stav*, Swed. *staf*, G. *stab*; Gael. *stob*, a stake, stump. Allied to Skt. *sthâpaya*, to place, set (set up a post), causal of *sthâ*, to stand. (√STA.)

stave, piece of a cask, part of a piece of music. (E.) Merely another form of *staff*, due to M. E. dat. sing. *staue* (*stave*) and pl. *staues* (*staves*). Cf. Icel. *stafr*, a staff, a stave; Dan. *stav*, staff, *stave*, stave.

stem (1), trunk of a tree. (E.) M.E. *stem.* A.S. *stæfn, stefn, stemn,* (1) stem of a tree, (2) stem or prow of a vessel; also spelt *stæfna, stefna.* Formed, with suffix *-na,* from A.S. *stæf,* a staff, prop; a *stem* of a tree being the staff or support of it, and a *stem* of a vessel being the upright post in front of it. **+** Du. *stam,* trunk,

steven, prow; Icel. *stafn, stamn,* stem of vessel, *stofn,* trunk; Dan. *stamme,* trunk, *stævn,* prow; Swed. *stam,* trunk, *stäf,* prow, *fram-stam,* fore-stem, *bak-stam,* back-stem, stern; G. *stamm,* trunk, *vorder steven,* prow-post, stem, *hinter steven,* stern-post.

stem (2), prow of a vessel. (E.) The same word as the preceding.

stem (3), to check, stop. (E.) From *stem* (1), the stem of a tree; from the throwing of a tree-trunk into a river, which checks the current. So Icel. *stemma,* Dan. *stemme,* to dam up, from *stamme,* trunk; G. *stammen,* to fell trees, dam up water.

Stag; see **Stair.**

Stage; see **State.**

Stagger; see **Stick** (1).

Stagnate, to cease to flow. (L.) From L. *stagnatus,* pp. of *stagnare,* to be still, cease to flow. − L. *stagnum,* a still pool, a stank; see **stank** (below). **Der.** *stagnant,* from stem of pres. pt. of *stagnare.*

stanch, staunch, to stop a flow of blood. (F. − L.) O. F. *estancher,* to stanch. − Low L. *stancare,* to stanch, a variant of late L. *stagnare,* to stanch, the same as L. *stagnare,* to cease to flow (above). **Der.** *stanch,* adj., firm, sound, not leaky.

stank, a pool, tank. (F. − L.) An old word; once common. − O. F. *estang,* a pond. (The same as Prov. *estanc,* Span. *estanque,* Port. *tanque,* a pond, pool.) − L. *stagnum,* a pool of stagnant or standing water. Put for *stac-num**, allied to Skt. *stak,* resist (hence to be firm or still). (Base STAK, from √STA.)

tank, a pool. (Port. − L.) Port. *tanque,* cognate with Span. *estanque,* O. F. *estang* (above).

Staid; see **Stay** (1).

Stain; see **Tinge.**

Stair, a step up. (E.) M.E. *steir, steyer.* A.S. *stæger,* a stair, step; lit. a step to climb by. − A.S. *stâg* (also *stâh*), pt. t. of *stîgan,* to climb. **+** Du. *steiger,* a stair, Icel. *stegi,* step, Swed. *stege,* ladder, Dan. *stige;* ladder, G. *steg,* a path; from Du. *stijgen,* Icel. *stîga,* Swed. *stiga,* Dan. *stige,* G. *steigen,* to mount, climb. Allied to Skt. *stigh,* to ascend, Gk. στείχειν. (√STIGH.)

stag, a male deer. (Scand.) Also applied (in dialects) to a male animal generally. − Icel. *steggr, steggi,* a he-bird, drake, tom-cat. Lit. 'mounter;' from Icel. *stîga,* to mount. Spelt *stugga;* Laws of Cnut.

stile (1), a set of steps for climbing over. (E.) M.E. *stile.* A.S. *stigel,* a stile.

— A. S. *stig-en*, pp. of *stígan*, to climb; with suffix -*el* of the agent.

stirrup. (E.) Put for *sty-rope*, i. e. a rope to mount by; the orig. stirrup was a looped rope for mounting into the saddle. M. E. *stirop.* A. S. *stí-ráp, stig-ráp.* — A.S. *stig-en*, pp. of *stígan*, to mount; *ráp*, a rope; see **Rope.**

sty (1), enclosure for swine. (E.) M.E. *stie.* A. S. *stígo*, a sty, a pen for cattle.+ Icel. *stía, stí*, sty, kennel, Swed. *stia*, pig-sty, pen for geese, Swed. dial. *sti, steg*, pen for swine, goats, or sheep, G. *steige*, pen, chicken-coop. β. Certainly from √STIGH, to ascend; though the reason is not clear; but cf. Gk. στοῖχος, a row, file of soldiers, also a row of poles with hunting-nets into which game was driven, i. e. a pen or *sty.*

sty (2), small tumour on the eye-lid. (E.) The A. S. name was *stígend*, lit. 'rising;' from the pres. pt. of *stígan*, to ascend, climb, rise. Short for *stígend edge*, lit. 'rising eye;' which, being ill understood, was corrupted into M. E. *styanye*, as if it meant 'sty on eye;' after which -*anye* was dropped, and the word *sty* was the result.+Low G. *stieg, stige*, sty on the eye; from *stigen*, to rise.

Staithe; see **Stead.**

Stake; see **Stick** (1).

Stalactite, a kind of crystal hanging from the roof of some caverns. (Gk.) Formed, with suffix -*ite* (Gk. -ιτης), from σταλακτ-ός, trickling. — Gk. σταλάζειν (= σταλάγ-γειν), to drip; from σταλάειν, to drip. (Base STAL, to be still; √STA.)

stalagmite, a cone of carbonate of lime on the floor of some caverns. (Gk.) Gk. στάλαγμ-α, a drop; with suffix -*ite* (Gk. -ιτης). — Gk. σταλάζειν (above).

Stale (1), too long kept; see **Stall.**

Stale (2), a snare; see **Steal.**

Stale (3), a handle; see **Stall.**

Stalk (1) and (2); see **Stall.**

Stall, a standing-place for cattle, &c. (E.) M. E. *stal.* A. S. *steal, stæl*, station, stall. + Du. *stal*, Icel. *stallr*, Dan. *stald*, Swed. *stall*, G. *stall*; Lith. *stalas*, a table; Skt. *sthála*, firm ground, from *sthá*, to stand. (Base STAL; √STA.)

stale (1), too long kept, vapid, trite. (Scand.) *Stale*, as a sb., means urine of cattle or horses. — Swed. *stalla*, to put into a stall, also to stale (as cattle); Dan *stalde*, to stall-feed, *stalle*, to stale (as horses). — Swed. *stall*, Dan. *stald*, a stable, stall. *Stale* is that which reminds one of

the stable, tainted, &c. β. In one sense, we may explain *stale* (in the case of unsold provisions) as 'too long exposed to sale.' — O. F. *estaler*, to display wares on stalls; from *estal*, a stall. — G. *stall*, a stall (above). It comes to much the same thing.

stale (3), **steal**, the handle of anything. (E.) M. E. *stele.* A. S. *stæl, stel*, stalk, stem. + Du. *steel*, stalk, stem, handle; G. *stiel*, stalk, handle. Allied to *still* and *stall*; the *stale* being that by which the tool is held firm and unmoved.

stalk (1), a stem. (E.) M. E. *stalke*, of which one sense is the side-piece (stem) of a ladder. A dimin. form, with suffix -*k*, from A. S. *stæl, stel*, a stalk; see **stale** (3) above.+Icel. *stilkr*, Swed. *stjelk*, Dan. *stilk*, stalk; Gk. στέλεχος, stem of a tree, στελεόν, a handle.

stalk (2), to stride. (E.) M. E. *stalken.* A. S. *stælcan*, to walk warily; allied to *stealc*, high.+Dan. *stalke*, to stalk. The notion is that of walking on *stalks* or lengthened legs, i. e. on tip-toe and cautiously, lifting the feet high. See **stalk** (1) above. Der. *stalk-ing-horse*, a horse for stalking game; see Halliwell.

stallion, an entire horse. (F. — O. H. G.) M. E. *stalon.* — O. F. *estalon* (F. *étalon*), a stallion; so called because kept in a *stall* and not made to work. — O. H. G. *stal* (G. *stall*), a stall, stable; see **Stall** (above).

still (1), motionless. (E.) M. E. *stille.* A.S. *stille*, still; allied to *stillan*, verb, to remain in a place or stall. — A. S. *steal, stæl*, a stall, place; see **Stall** (above).+ Du. *stil*, still, *stillen*, to be still, *stellen*, to place, from *stal*, a stall; Dan. *stille*, Swed. *stilla*, G. *still*, still; Dan. *stille*, to still, also to place, Swed. *stilla*, to quiet, G. *stillen*, to still, *stellen*, to place; Dan. *stald*, Swed. G. *stall*, a stall. *Still* is to be explained from Teut. base STELLYA, to put into a stall or place, to make still, from the sb. *stall*; and means 'brought to a resting-place.' Der. *still*, adv., A. S. *stille*, continually, ever.

Stalwart, sturdy. (E.) For *stalworth.* M. E. *stalworth, stelewurðe, stealewurðe, stalewurðe.* A.S. *stælwyrðe*, pl., serviceable (said of ships); A. S. Chron. an. 896. β. We find A. S. *gestælan* used as short for *gestæðelian.* Hence Sievers explains the form *stæl-* or *stæl-* as being short for *staðel*, a foundation. Thus *stæl-wyrðe* is for *stǽðel-wyrðe, lit. ' foundation-worthy,' i. e. firmly fixed, firm, constant. γ. Leo explains it as stall-worthy, i. e. worthy of a stall or place, which is hardly intelligible, and does not suit the M. E. forms.

Stamen; see State.

Stamin, Tamine, Taminy, Tammy, a kind of stuff; see State.

Stammer, to stutter. (E.) M. E. stameren, vb.; from A. S. stamer, stamur, adj., stammering. The suffix -er- is adjectival, expressing ' disposed to;' thus stam-er = disposed to come to a stand-still, from a base STAM, extended from √STA, to stand, remain fixed. + Du. stameren, stamelen, Icel. stamma, Dan. stamme, Swed. stamma, G. stammern, stammeln, to stammer; Icel. stamr, O. H. G. stam, Goth. stamms, adj., stammering.

Stamp, to tread heavily, to pound. (E.) M. E. stampen. A. S. stempan. + Du. stampen, Icel. stuppa, Swed. stampa, Dan. stampe, G. stampfen; also Gk. στέμβειν, to stamp, Skt. stambh, to make firm, stop, make hard, stamba, stambha, a post. Allied to Step. (√STABH; from √STA.)

stampede, a panic. (Span. – Teut.) Stampede is a sudden panic, causing cattle to take to flight and run for many miles; any sudden flight due to panic. – Span. (and Port.) estampido, a crash, sudden sound of anything bursting or falling. Formed as if from a verb estampir *, akin to estampar, to stamp. The reference appears to be to the noise made by the blows of a pestle upon a mortar. Of Teut. origin; see above.

Stanch, Staunch; see Stagnate.

Stanchion, a support, beam, bar. (F. – L.) O. F. estançon, estanson, ' a prop, stay;' Cot. Not derived from the O. F. estancher, to prop (allied to E. stanch), but a diminutive of O. F. estance, a situation, condition, also a stanchion (Scheler). – Low L. stantia, a chamber, a house, lit. ' that which stands firm.' – L. stant-, stem of pres. pt. of stare, to stand. See State. ¶ But the word may have been confused with O. F. estancher, to prop (as above), which is the same word as estancher, to staunch; for which see Stanch. The root is the same either way. (√STA.)

Stand. (E.) A. S. standen, pt. t. stód, pp. standen. +Icel. standa, Goth. standan; Du. staan (pt. t. stond); Swed. stå (pt. t. stod); G. stehen (pt. t. stand). All from

base STAND. + L. stare; Gk. ἔστην, I stood, Russ. stoiate, Skt. sthá, to stand. (√STA.) For allied words, see State. Der. stand, sb.; standish, put for stand-dish, a standing dish for pen and ink.

standard. (F. – O. H. G.) O. F. estandart, a standard or ensign, a standard measure. The flag was a large one, on a fixed (standing) pole. – O. H. G. stand-an, to stand; with suffix -art (= O. H. G. hart, a suffix, orig. the same as hart, adj., hard). ¶ Cf. Span. estandarte, a standard; O. Du, standaert, ' a standard or a great trophie, a pillar, column, mill-post' (Hexham), evidently from the verb stand. The O. F. estendard, Ital. stendardo are modified forms, as if from L. extendere, to spread out.

understand. (E.) A. S. understandan, lit. to stand under or among, hence, to comprehend (like L. intel-ligere). – A. S. under, under; standan, to stand.

withstand. (E.) A. S. wiðstandan, to resist, lit. stand against. – A. S. wið, against; standan, to stand; see With.

Stang, a pole; see Sting.

Stank, a pool; see Stagnate.

Stannary, relating to tin-mines. (L.) Low L. stannaria, a tin-mine. – L. stannum, tin.

Stanza; see State.

Staple, (1) and (2); see Step.

Star. (E.) M. E. sterre. A. S. steorra. +Du. ster; O. H. G. sterro. Cf. Icel. stjarna, Dan. stjarne, Swed. stjerna, Goth. stairno; also L. stella (for ster-ula *), Gk. ἀστήρ, Corn. steren, W. seren, Skt. tárá. Orig. sense 'sprinkler' of light; from √STAR, to sprinkle (Max Müller).

Starboard; see Steer (2).

Starch; see Stark.

Stare (1), to gaze fixedly. (E.) A. S. starian; from a Teut. adj. STARA, fixed, appearing in G. starr, fixed; cf. Skt. sthira, fixed, allied to sthá, to stand. (√STA.) +Icel. stara, stira, to stare; Swed. stirra, Dan. stirre, to stare. ¶ Hence ' staring hair' is ' stiff-standing hair.'

stare (2), to glitter. (E.) M. E. staren; whence staring colours = bright colours. The same word as stare (1); from the glittering of staring eyes.

Stark, stiff, rigid, entire. (E.) A. S. stearc, stiff, strong. +Du. sterk, Icel. sterkr, Dan. stærk, Swed. G. stark. Orig. ' rigid,' from the sense of stretched tight; allied to Stretch. Der. stark, adv., as in stark mad.

starch. (E.) *Starch* is stuff that stiffens; from the adj. *stark* above. Cf. G. *stärke*, (1) strength, (2) starch; from *stark*, adj.

Stark-naked, quite naked. (E.) An ingenious substitution for M. E. *start-naked*, lit. ' tail naked,' i. e. with the hinder parts exposed, but used in the sense of wholly naked. From A. S. *steort*, a tail; as in *red-start*, i. e. red-tail, a bird.+Du. *stert*, Icel. *stertr*, Dan. *stiert*, Swed. *stjert*, G. *sterz*, a tail.

Starling. (E.) M. E. *sterling*, double dimin. of M. E. *stare*, a starling.—A. S. *stær*, a starling.+Icel. *starri*, *stari*, Dan. *stær*, Swed. *stare*, G. *staar*, L. *sturnus*.

Start, to move suddenly. (E.) M. E. *sterten*; pt. t. *stirte* (Havelok, 873), *sturte*, *storte* (Layamon, 23951). Allied to Du. *storten*, to precipitate, fall, rush, G. *stürzen*; also to O. Du. *steerten*, to flee, run away, which prob. meant 'to turn tail,' or 'shew the tail,' hence to turn over suddenly, and is allied to A. S. *steort*, a tail. See **Stark-naked**.

Starve. (E.) M. E. *steruen* (*sterven*), to die (without reference to the means of death). A. S. *steorfan*, pt. t. *stearf*, pp. *storfen*, to die; whence *sterfan*, to kill (weak verb). + Du. *sterven*, G. *sterben*. (Base STARB.) Der. *starve-l-ing*, double dimin., expressive of contempt; *starv-ation*, an ill-coined hybrid word, introduced from the North about 1775.

State, a standing, position, condition, &c. (F.–L.) O. F. *estat*.–L. *statum*, acc. of *status*, condition.–L. *status*, pp. of *stare*, to stand.+Gk. ἔστην, I stood; Skt. *sthā*, to stand; cognate with E. *stand*. (√STA.)

arrest, to stop. (F.–L.) O. F. *arester* (F. *arrêter*), to stay.—O. F. *a* (= L. *ad*), to; L. *restare*, to stay, from *re-*, and *stare*; see rest (2) below.

assist. (F.–L.) F. *assister*. – L. *as-sistere*, to step to, approach, assist. – L. *as-* (for *ad*), to; *sistere*, to place, stand, from *stare*, to stand.

circumstance. (L.) From L. *cir-cumstantia*, lit. a standing around, also an attribute, circumstance (influenced by F. *circonstance*). – L. *circumstant-*, stem of pres. pt. of *circum-stare*, to stand round.

consist. (F.–L.) F. *consister*, to consist, rest, abide, &c.–L. *consistere*, to stand together, consist.–L. *con-* (for *cum*), together; *sistere*, from *stare*.

constant, firm. (F.–L.) F. *constant*.

—L. *constant-*, stem of *constans*, firm; orig. pres. pt. of *con-stare*, to stand together.

constitute. (L.) L. *constitutus*, pp. of *constituere*, to cause to stand together, establish. — L. *con-* (*cum*), together; *statuere*, causal of *stare* (pp. *status*), to stand.

contrast, vb. (F.–L.) F. *contraster*, to strive, contend against (hence to be in opposition to, &c.).–Low L. *contra-stare*, to stand against.

cost. (F. – L.) M. E. *costen*. — O. F. *coster* (F. *coûter*), to cost.—L. *con-stare*, to stand together, last, also to cost.

desist. (F. – L.) O. F. *desister*, to cease.—L. *desistere*, to put away, also to desist.—L. *de*, away; *sistere*, to put, from *stare*.

destine. (F.–L.) O. F. *destiner*, to ordain.—L. *destinare*, to destine, ordain.— L. *destina*, a prop, support.—L. *de*, down; and *stina**, a prop, derivative from √ STA, to stand. See *obstinate* (below).

destitute. (L.) L. *destitutus*, left alone; pp. of *destituere*, to place alone.— L. *de*, away; *statuere*, to place, causal of *stare*.

distant. (F. – L.) O. F. *distant*.–L. *distantem*, acc. of *distans*, pres. pt. of *di-stare*, to stand apart.

establish. (F.–L.) M. E. *establissen*.— O. F. *establiss-*, base of pres. pt. of *establir*, to establish.–L. *stabilire*, to establish.–L. *stabilis*, firm; see stable (1) below.

estate. (F. – L.) O. F. *estat.* – L. *statum*, acc. of *status*, state; see **State** above.

exist, to continue to be. (L.) L. *ex-istere*, better *exsistere*, to come forth, arise, be.–L. *ex*, out; *sistere*, to set, stand, from *stare*.

extant, existing. (L.) Late L. *extant-*, stem of *extans*, for *exstans*, pres. pt. of *ex-stare*, to stand forth, exist.

insist. (F.–L.) F. *insister*.–L. *in-sistere*, to set foot on, persist.–L. *in*, in; *sistere*, to set, stand, from *stare*.

instance. (F.–L.) F. *instance*, 'instance, urgency;' Cot. – L. *instantia*, a being near, urgency.–L. *instant-*, stem of pres. pt. of *in-stare*, to be at hand, to urge.

institute. (L.) L. *institutus*, pp. of *instituere*, to set, establish.–L. *in*, in; *statuere*, to place, causal of *stare* (pp. *statum*).

interstice. (F.–L.) F. *interstice*.—

L. *interstitium*, an interval of space. – L. *inter*, between ; *stătus*, pp. of *sistere*, to place, from *stare*, to stand.

obstacle. (F. – L.) F. *obstacle.* – L. *obstaculum*, a hindrance. – L. *ob*, against ; -*staculum*, double dimin. from *sta-re*, to stand.

obstetric, pertaining to midwifery. (L.) L. *obstetricius*, adj., from *obstetrici*-, crude form of *obstetrix*, a midwife; lit. an assistant, stander near. – L. *ob*, near; with fem. suffix -*trix* (of the agent).

obstinate. (L.) L. *obstinatus*, resolute ; pp. of *obstinare*, to set about, be resolved on. – L. *ob*, near ; and *stina**, a prop, from √ STA. See **destine** (above).

persist. (F. – L.) F. *persister.* – L. *persistere*, to continue, persist. – L. *per*, through ; *sistere*, to stand, from *stare*.

press (2), to hire men for service. (F. – L.) *Press* is a corruption of the old word *prest*, ready ; whence *prest-money*, ready money advanced to a man hired for service, earnest money ; also *imprest*, a verb (now *impress*), to give a man earnest money. When it became common to use *compulsion* to *force* men into service, it was confused with the verb to *press*. *Prest money* was money lent. – O. F. *prester* (F. *prêter*), to lend, advance money. – L. *præ-stare*, to stand forward, also to come forward, provide, furnish, give, offer. Der. *press-gang*, *im-press*, *im-press-ment*.

prostitute. (L.) L. *prostitutus*, pp. of *prostituere*, to expose openly, prostitute. – L. *pro*, forth ; *statuere*, to place, causal of *stare*.

resist. (F. – L.) O. F. *resister.* – L. *resistere*, to stand back, withstand. – L. *re-*, back ; *sistere*, to stand, from *stare*.

rest (2), to remain, be left over. (F. – L.) F. *rester*, to remain. – L. *re-stare*, to stop behind, remain. ¶ Distinct from *rest* (1), repose.

restitution. (F. – L.) F. *restitution.* – L. *restitutionem*, acc. of *restitutio*, a restoring. – L. *restitutus*, pp. of *restituere*, to restore. – L. *re-*, again ; *statuere*, to place, causal of *stare*, to stand.

restive. (F. – L.) Confused with *restless*, but it really means stubborn, refusing to move. – F. *restif*, 'restie, stubborn, drawing backward ;' Cot. – F. *rester*, to remain ; see **rest** (2) above. ¶ Hence E. *rusty* in the phr. *to turn rusty* = to be stubborn.

stable (1), a stall for horses. (F. – L.)

O. F. *estable*, a stable. – L. *stabulum*, a stall. – L. *stare*, to stand still.

stable (2), firm. (F. – L.) O. F. *estable* – L. *stabilis*, firm. – L. *stare*.

stablish. (F. – L.) Short for **establish** (above).

stage. (F. – L.) O. F. *estage*, 'a story, stage, loft, also a dwelling-house ;' Cot. [Hence it meant a stopping-place on a journey, or the distance between stopping-places.] Cf. Prov. *estatge*, a dwelling-place ; answering to a Low L. form *statt-cum**, a dwelling-place. – L. *stat-um*, supine of *stare*.

stamen, male organ of a flower. (L.) Lit. 'a thread.' – L. *stamen*, the warp *standing up* in an upright loom. – L. *stare*, to stand. Der. *stamina*, orig. pl. of *stamen*, lit. threads, in a warp, firm texture.

stamin, a kind of stuff. (F. – L.) M. E. *stamin*. – O. F. *estamine*, ' the stuff tamine ;' Cot. – L. *stamineus*, consisting of threads. – L. *stamin*-, stem of *stamen*, a thread (above).

stanza. (Ital. – L.) Ital. *stanza*, O. Ital. *stantia*, 'a lodging, chamber, dwelling, also stance or staffe of verses ;' Florio. So called from the stop or pause at the end of it. – Low L. *stantia*, an abode. – L. *stant-*, stem of pres. pt. of *stare*.

station. (F. – L.) F. *station.* – L. *stationem*, acc. of *statio*, a standing still. – L. *status*, pp. of *stare*. Der. *station-er*, orig. a bookseller who had a *station* or stall in a market-place ; hence *station-er-y*, things sold by a *stationer*. Also *station-ary*, adj.

statist, a statesman, politician. (F. – L. ; *with* Gk. suffix.) Coined from *state* by adding -*ist* (L. -*ista*, Gk. -ιστης).

statue. (F. – L.) O. F. *statue* (trisyllabic). – L. *statua*, a standing image. – L. *statu-*, crude form of *status*, a position, standing. – L. *status*, pp. of *stare*.

stature, height. (F. – L.) F. *stature.* – L. *statura*, an upright posture, height. – L. *status*, pp. of *stare*.

status, condition. (L.) L. *status* ; see **State** (above).

statute. (F. – L.) F. *statut.* – L. *statutum*, a statute ; neut. of *statutus*, pp. of *statuere*, to place, set, causal of *stare*.

subsist, to live, continue. (F. – L.) F. *subsister*, ' to subsist ;' Cot. – L. *subsistere*, to stay, abide. – L. *sub*, near to ; *sistere*, to stand, from *stare*, to stand.

substance. (F. – L.) F. *substance.* –
L. *substantia*, substance, essence. – L. *substant-*, stem of pres. pt. of *substare*, to exist,
lit. 'to stand near or beneath.' – L. *sub*,
near ; *stare*, to stand. Der. *substanti-al* ;
also *substant-ive*, F. *substantif*, L. *substantiuus*, self-existent, used of the verb *esse*,
and afterwards applied, as a grammatical
term, to nouns substantive.

substitute, sb. (F. – L.) F. *substitut*,
a substitute. – L. *substitutus*, pp. of *substituere*, to put in stead of. – L. *sub*, near, instead of ; *statuere*, to put, causal of *stare*,
to stand.

superstition. (F. – L.) F. *superstition.*
– L. acc. *superstitionem*, a standing near a
thing, amazement, dread, religious awe,
scruple. – L. *superstiti-*, crude form of
superstes, one who stands near, a witness.
– L. *super*, above, near ; *stătum*, supine
of *sistere*, to stand, from *stare*, to stand.

transubstantiation, the doctrine that
the bread and wine in the Eucharist are
changed into Christ's body and blood. (F.
– L.) F. *transsubstantiation.* – Late L. acc.
transubstantiationem ; see Hildebert of
Tours (died 1134), sermon 93. – Late L.
transubstantiatus, pp. of *transubstantiare* ;
coined from *trans*, across (implying change)
and *substantia*, substance ; see **substance**
(above).

Statics, the science treating of bodies at
rest. (Gk.) From Gk. στατικός, at a standstill ; ἡ στατική, statics. – Gk. στατ-ός,
placed, standing ; verbal adj. from στα-,
base of ἵστημι, I place, stand. (√STA.)

apostasy. (F. – L. – Gk.) F. *apostasie* ; Low L. *apostasia.* – Gk. ἀποστασία,
late form of ἀπόστασις, revolt, lit. 'a standing away from.' – Gk. ἀπό, off, away ;
στάσις, a standing, from στα-, base of ἵστημι
(above).

apostate. (F. – L. – Gk.) O. F. *apostate, apostat.* – Low L. *apostata.* – Gk. ἀποστάτης, a deserter, apostate. – Gk. ἀπό, off ;
-στάτης, standing, from στα- (above).

ecstasy. (F. – L. – Gk.) Englished from
O. F. *ecstase.* – Low L. *ecstasis*, a trance. –
Gk. ἔκστασις, displacement ; also, a trance.
– Gk. ἐκ, out ; στάσις, a standing ; see
apostasy (above).

system, method. (L. – Gk.) XVII
cent. – L. *systema.* – Gk. σύστημα, a complex whole put together, a system. – Gk.
σύ-ν, together ; στῆ-ναι, to stand, from
ἵστημι, I stand.

Station, Statist, Statue ; see **State**

Stature, Status, Statute ; see **State.**

Staunch ; see **Stagnate.**

Stave ; see **Staff.**

Stay (1), to remain, prop, delay. (F. –
O. Du.) O. F. *estayer*, 'to prop, stay ; '
Cot. – O. F. *estaye*, sb. fem. 'a prop, stay ; '
id. – O. Du. *stade* or *staeye*, 'a prop, stay ; '
Hexham ; O. Flem. *staey*, a prop. Allied
to E. **Stead.** The loss of *d* between two
vowels is not uncommon in Dutch, as in
broer, brother, *teer* (for *teder*), tender.

staid, grave. (F. – O. Du.) Put for
stay'd, pp. of *stay*, verb, to support, make
steady.

stays, a bodice. (F. – O. Du.) Merely
a pl. of *stay*, a support. (So also *bodice* =
bodies.)

Stay (2), a rope supporting a mast. (E.)
A. S. *stæg*, a stay. + Du. *stag*, Icel. Dan.
Swed. G. *stag.* Der. *stay-sail.*

Stead. (E.) M. E. *stede.* A. S. *stede*, a
place. + Du. *stad*, a town, Icel. *staðr*, *staða*,
a place ; Dan. Swed. *stad*, town, Dan. *sted*,
place ; G. *stadt, statt*, town, place, Goth.
staths, place. Allied to L. *statio*, a station.
(√STA.) Der. *home-stead, bed-stead.*

bestead. (Scand.) Chiefly as a pp. –
Dan. *bestedt*, placed, bestead ; with the
same use as in E. – Dan. *be-* (= E. *be-*, by) ;
sted, a place ; with pp. suffix -*t*.

instead. (E.) For *in stead*, i.e. in the
place.

staithe, a landing-place. (E.) A. S.
stæð, *steð*, bank, shore. + Icel. *stöð*, harbour, roadstead. Allied to **Stead.**

steadfast. (E.) A. S. *stedefæst*, firm
in its place. – A. S. *stede*, place ; *fæst*,
firm ; see **Fast.** + O. Du. *stedevast*, Icel.
staðfastr, Dan. *stadfast.*

steady, firm. (E.) M. E. *stedy.* A. S
stæððig, steady. – A. S. *stæð*, stead, bank ;
see **staithe** (above). + O. Du. *stedigh*, Icel
stöðugr, Dan. *stadig*, Swed. *stadig* ; G
stätig, continual, from *statt*, a place.

stith, an anvil. (Scand.) M. E. *stith.*
– Icel. *steði*, an anvil ; allied to *staðr*, a
fixed place ; named from its firmness. +
Swed. *städ*, an anvil. Der. *stith-y*, properly a smithy, also an anvil.

Steak ; see **Stick** (1).

Steal. (E.) A. S. *stelan*, pt. t. *stæl*, pp.
stolen. + Du. *stelen*, Icel. *stela*, Dan. *stiæle*,
Swed. *stjäla*, G. *stehlen*, Goth. *stilan.* Cf.
Gk. στέλλειν, to put away.

stale (2), a snare. (E.) M. E. *stale*,
theft, a trap. A. S. *stalu*, theft. – A. S.
stæl, pt. t. of *stelan*, to steal.

Steam, sb. (E.) M. E. *steem*. A. S. *steám*, vapour, smell, smoke. + Du. *stoom*. Der. *steam*, vb.

Steed, a horse; see **Stud** (1).

Steel. (E.) M. E. *steel*. A. S. *stél**, *stéle**; but only found as *style*, steel, which is a late spelling. + Du. *staal*, Icel. *stál*, Dan. *staal*, Swed. *stål*, G. *stahl*, O. H. G. *stahal*. The O. H. G. *stah-al* shews the root to be STAK, as in Skt. *stak*, to resist, Lithuan. *stok-as*, a stake. Named from its firm resistance. Der. *steel*, vb., A. S. *stýlan* (Icel. *stæla*).

steelyard. (E.) Orig. the *yard* in London where *steel* was sold by German merchants (Stow); hence a weighing machine used in this yard; now generally misunderstood as meaning a yard or bar of steel.

Steep (1), precipitous. (E.) M. E. *steep*. A. S. *steáp*, steep, high. + Icel. *steypðr*, steep, lofty. Allied to *Stoop*, whence the notion of sloping down, or tilted up; cf. Swed. *stupande*, sloping; Norweg. *stupa*, to fall, *stup*, a steep cliff. See **Stoop**.

steeple. (E.) A. S. *stýpel*, a lofty tower, later *stepel*; so called from its height. — A. S. *steáp*, steep, high (with regular change from *ed* to *ý*).

Steep (2), to soak; see **Stoop** (1).

Steeple; see **Steep** (1).

Steer (1), a young ox. (E.) A. S. *steór*. + Du. G. *stier*, a bull, Icel *stjórr*, Goth. *stiur*; L. *taurus* (for *staurus**), Gk. *ταῦρος* (for *σταῦρος**); Russ. *tur'*, W. *tarw*. β. The sense is merely 'full-grown' or 'large,' as in Skt. *sthúla* (for *sthúra*), great, large, powerful, *sthúra*, a man, *sthúrin*, a pack-horse; so also A. S. *stór*, Icel. *stórr*, Dan. Swed. *stor*, large. (√STU; for √STA.) Der. *stir-k*, a bullock, A. S. *stýr-ic* (with vowel-change from *eó* to *ý*.)

Steer (2), to guide. (E.) M. E. *steren*. A. S. *steóran*, *stýran*, to steer. + Du. *sturen*, Icel. *stýra*, Dan. *styre*, Swed. *styra*, G. *steuern*, to steer; Goth. *stiurjan*, to confirm. β. Weak verb; from the sb. appearing in M. E. *stere*, Du. *stuur*, Icel. *stýri*, G. *steuer*, a rudder, still retained in *star-board*; see **star-board** (below).

star-board, the right side of a ship. (E.) M. E. *sterebourde*. A. S. *steórbord*, i.e. steer-board, the side on which the steersman stood; in the first instance, he probably used a paddle, not a helm. Cf. Icel. *á stjórn*, at the helm, or on the starboard side. — A. S. *steór*, a rudder or paddle

to steer with; *bord*, board, border, edge or side; see **Board**. The O. H. G. *stiura* means a prop, staff, paddle, rudder, allied to Icel. *staurr*, a post, stake, Gk. *σταυρός*, an upright pole or stake. (√STU, allied to √STA.) + Du. *stuurboord*, Icel. *stjórnborði*, Dan. Swed. *styrbord*; all similarly compounded.

stern (2), hind part of a vessel. (Scand.) Icel. *stjórn*, a steering, steerage, helm; hence a name for the hind part of a vessel. From Icel. *stjór-i*, a steerer, allied to E. *steer* (2).

Stellar. (L.) L. *stellaris*, starry. — L *stella*, star; short for *ster-ula**, a dimin. form allied to E. **Star**.

constellation. (F. — L.) F. *constellation*. — L. acc. *constellationem*, cluster of stars. — L. *con-* (*cum*), together; *stella*, star.

Stem (1), (2), and (3); see **Staff**.

Stench; see **Stink**.

Stencil; see **Scintillation**.

Stenography, shorthand writing (Gk.) From Gk. *στενό-ς*, narrow, close; *γράφ-ειν*, to write.

Stentorian, extremely loud. (Gk.) From Gk. *Στέντωρ*, Stentor, a Greek at Troy, with a loud voice (Homer). — Gk. *στέν-ειν*, to groan; with suffix *-τωρ*. (√STAN.) See **Stun**.

Step, a pace, degree, foot-print. (E.) M. E. *steppe*. A. S. *stæpe*. — A. S. *stapan*, to go, advance; pt. t. *stóp*, pp. *stapen*; whence *steppan*, weak verb, which corresponds better to the mod. E. word. Cf. Du. *stap*, G. *stapfe*, a footstep; Russ. *stopa*, a step; Skt. *stambh*, to make firm. (√STABH, from √STA.) See also **Stamp**.

staple (1), a loop of iron. (E.) A. S. *stapul*. Orig. sense a prop, something that holds firm. — A. S. *stapan*, strong verb, to step, tread firmly. + Du. *stapel*, staple, stocks, a pile; Dan. *stabel*, Swed. *stapel*; G. *staffel*, a step, *stapel*, a staple (below).

staple (2), a chief commodity of a place. (F. — Low G.) The sense has changed; it formerly meant a chief market, with reference to the place where things were most sold. — O. F. *estaple*, 'a staple, a mart or general market, a publique storehouse;' Cot. (F. *étape*.) — Low G. *stapel*, a heap; hence a heap laid in order, store, store-house; the same word as **staple** (1). The Du. *stapel* means (1) a staple, (2) the stocks, (3) a pile or heap. All from the notion of fixity or firmness.

Stepchild. (E.) A.S. *steópcild*; where *cild* = E. *child*; see Child. We also find A. S. *steópbearn*, step - bairn, stepchild, *steópfæder*, stepfather, *steópmóder*, stepmother, &c. β. The sense of *steóp* is 'orphaned,' and *steópcild* is the oldest compound; we find A. S. *ásteápte*, pl., made orphans, also O. H. G. *stiufan*, to deprive of parents.+Du. *stiefkind*, stepchild; Icel. *stjúpbarn*, step-bairn; Swed. *styfbarn*; G. *stiefkind*.

Steppe, a large plain. (Russ.) Russ. *stepe*, a waste, heath, steppe.

Stereoscope, an optical instrument for giving an appearance of solidity. (Gk.) From Gk. *στερεό-s*, solid, stiff; *σκοπ-εῖν*, to behold.

   stereotype, a solid plate for printing. (Gk.) Gk.*στερεό-s*, hard, solid; and *type*, q.v.

Sterile. (F. — L.) O. F. *sterile*. — L. *sterilem*, acc. of *sterilis*, barren.

Sterling; see East.

Stern (1), severe, austere. (E.) M. E. *sterne*. A. S. *styrne*, stern (which should rather be spelt *sturn*). Allied to Du. *stuursch*, stern, Swed. *stursk*, refractory; Goth. *andstaurran*, to murmur against.

Stern (2); see Steer (2).

Sternutation, sneezing. (L.) L. *sternutatio*, a sneezing. — L. *sternutatus*, pp. of *sternutare*, to sneeze, frequentative of *sternuere*, to sneeze. Allied to Gk. *πτάρ-νυσθαι*, to sneeze.

Stertorous, snoring. (L.) Coined from L. *stertere*, to snore.

Stethoscope, the tube used in auscultation, as applied to the chest. (Gk.) Lit. 'chest - examiner.' — Gk. *στῆθο-s*, chest; *σκοπ-εῖν*, to consider.

Stevedore; see Stipulation.

Stew, to boil slowly. (F. — Teut.) M. E. *stuwen*, orig. to bathe; formed from the old sb. *stew* in the sense of bath or hothouse (as it was called); the pl. *stews* generally meant brothels. An Anglicised form of O. F. *estuve*, a stew, stove, hothouse (F. *étuve*). — O. H. G. *stupá*, a hot room for a bath (mod. G. *stube*, a chamber). Allied to Stove, q. v.

Steward. (E.) A. S. *stíweard*, *stíward*, a steward. Lit. 'a sty-ward:' from A.S. *stigo*, a sty, *weard*, a ward. The orig. sense was one who looked after the domestic animals, and gave them their food; hence, one who provides for his master's table, or who superintends household affairs. We also find *stíwita*, *stigwita*, a

steward, with the same prefix. See sty (1), under Stair; and Ward.

Stick (1), to stab, pierce, thrust in, adhere. (E.) The orig. sense was to sting, pierce, stab, fasten into a thing; hence, to be thrust into a thing, to adhere. Two verbs are confused in mod. E., viz. (1) *stick*, to pierce; (2) *stick*, to be fixed in. α. We find (1) M. E. *steken*, strong verb, to pierce, pt. t. *stak*, pp. *steken*, *stiken*; answering to an A. S. *stecan**, pt. t. *stæc**, pp. *stecen** (not found); cognate with Low G. *steken* (pt. t. *stak*, pp. *steken*), G. *stechen* (pt. t. *stach*, pp. *gestochen*). Further allied to Gk. *στίζειν* (= *στίγ-γειν*), to prick, L. *instigare*, to prick, Skt. *tij*, to be sharp; and to E. **Sting.** (√ STAG, STIG.) β. We also find (2) A. S. *stician*, pt. *sticode*, weak verb; allied to Icel. *stika*, to drive piles, Swed. *stikka*, Dan. *stikke*, to stab, sting, G. *stecken*, to stick, set, also to stick fast, remain.

   etiquette, ceremony. (F. — G.) F. *étiquette*, a label, ticket, also a form of introduction. — O. F. *etiquet* (for *estiquet*), 'a little note, such as is *stuck up* on the gate of a court,' &c.; Cot. — G. *stecken*, to stick, put, set, fix; allied to G. *stechen*, to stick, pierce (above); see ticket (below).

   stack, a large pile of wood, &c. (Scand.) M. E. *stak*. — Icel. *stakkr*, a stack of hay; *stakka*, a stump (as in our chimney-stack); Swed. *stack*, a rick, heap, stack; Dan. *stak*. The sense is 'a pile,' that which is *stuck* up. Allied to stake (below).

   stagger, to reel, vacillate. (Scand.) A weakened form of *stacker*, M. E. *stakeren*. — Icel. *stakra*, to push, to stagger; frequentative of *staka*, to punt, push. Allied to Icel. *stjaki*, a punt-pole; and to stake (below).

   stake, a post, strong stick. (E.) M. E. *stake*. A. S. *staca*, a stake. From the Teut. base STAK, to pierce, appearing in G. *stach*, pt. t. of *stechen*, to stick, pierce; see Stick (1) (above).

   steak, a slice of meat for cooking. (Scand.) M. E. *steike*. — Icel. *steik*, a steak; so called from being stuck on a wooden peg, and roasted before the fire.— Icel. *steikja*, to roast, on a spit or peg. Allied to Icel. *stika*, a stick; and to Stick (1). + Swed. *stek*, roast meat, *steka*, to roast; allied to *stick*, a prick, *sticka*, to stick, stab; Dan. *steg*, a roast, *ad vende steg*, to turn the spit. Cf. G. *anstecken*, to put on a spit, *anstechen*, to pierce.

stick (2), a small branch of a tree. (E.) M. E. *stikke.* A. S. *sticca,* a stick, peg, nail. So called from its piercing or sticking into anything; the orig. sense being 'peg,' then a small bit of a tree. Allied to **Stick** (1) above. **+** Icel. *stika,* a stick.

stickleback, a small fish. (E.) So called from the *stickles* or small prickles on its back. *Stick-le* is dimin. of *stick* (2).

stitch, a pain in the side, a passing through stuff of a needle and thread. (E.) M. E. *stiche.* A. S. *stice,* a pricking sensation.—A. S. *stician,* to prick, pierce.

stoccado, stoccata, a thrust in fencing. (Ital. — Teut.) *Stoccado* is an accommodated form, as if it were Spanish.— Ital. *stoccata,* 'a foyne, thrust,' Florio. — Ital. *stocco,* 'a short sword, a tuck,' Florio; with pp. suffix *-ata.* — G. *stock,* a stick, staff, trunk, stump; cognate with E. **stock** (below).

stock, a post, &c. (E.) The sense is a thing *stuck* or fixed, hence a post, trunk, stem, a fixed store, fund, capital, cattle, trunk, butt-end of a gun, &c. A. S. *stocc,* stock, post. Formed as if from an A. S. pp. *stocen*,* pp. of a strong verb *stecan*,* as noted s. v. **Stick** (1) above. **+** G. *stock,* O. H. G. *stoch,* from *gestochen,* pp. of *stechen,* to stick, pierce; Du. *stok,* Icel. *stokkr,* Dan. *stok,* Swed. *stock.*

stockade, a breastwork formed of stakes. (E.; *with* F. *suffix.*) Coined in imitation of F. *estocade,* which only meant a thrust in fencing. From E. *stock* (above).

stocking. (E.) *Stocking* is a dimin. form of *stock,* used as short for *nether-stock.* 'Un bas des chausses, *a stocking, or nether-stock;*' Cot. The clothing of the lower part of the body consisted of a single garment, called *hose,* in F. *chausses.* It was afterwards cut in two at the knees, and divided into *upper-stocks,* and *nether-stocks* or *stockings.* In this case, *stock* means a piece or stump, a piece cut off; see **stock** (above).

stoker, one who tends a fire. (Du.) Orig. used to mean one who looked after a fire in a brew-house (Phillips). — Du. *stoker,* 'a kindler, or setter on fire,' Hexham. — Du. *stoken,* to kindle a fire, stir a fire.— Du. *stok,* to stack, stick (hence, a poker for a fire). Cognate with **stock.** (above).

tick (5), credit. (F. — G.) Short for *ticket;* Nares shews that to take things

without immediate payment was to take *on ticket,* afterwards shortened to *on tick;* see below.

ticket, a bill stuck up, a marked card. (F. — G.) O. F. *etiquet,* 'a little note, bill, or ticket, esp. such as is *stuck up* on the gate of a court;' Cot. — G. *stecken,* to stick, stick, up, fix; cognate with E. *stick.*

tuck (2), a rapier. (F. — Ital. — G.) F. *estoc,* 'the stock of a tree, a rapier, a tuck;' Cot. — Ital. *stocco,* a truncheon, rapier, tuck; Florio. — G. *stock,* a stock, stump, &c.; see **stock, stoccado** (above).

Stick (2), a staff, twig; see **Stick** (1).

Stickleback, a fish; see **Stick** (1).

Stickler, one who parts combatants, or settles disputes between two who are fighting. (E.) Now only used of one who insists on etiquette or persists in an opinion. Corruption of M. E. *stightlen, stightilen,* to dispose, order, arrange, govern, subdue; commonly used of a steward who arranged matters, acting as a master of ceremonies. See Will. of Palerne, 1199, 2899, 3281, 3841, 5379; Destruction of Troy, 117, 1997, 2193, 13282, &c. This M. E. *stightlen* is a frequentative of A. S. *stihtan, stihtian,* to control. Cognate with O. Du. *stichten,* to build, impose a law; Dan. *stifte,* to institute, Swed. *stifta, stikta,* G. *stiften,* to found, institute.

Stiff. (E.) M. E. *stif.* A. S. *stif,* stiff. **+** Du. *stijf,* Dan. *stiv,* Swed. *styf.* Allied to Lith. *stiprus,* strong, *stip-ti,* to be stiff, L. *stipes,* a stem; also to E. **Staff.**

stifle. (Scand.; *confused with* F. — L.) Icel. *stifla,* to dam up, choke. Norweg. *stivla,* to stop, hem in, lit. to stiffen; *stivra,* to stiffen; frequentatives of Norw. *stiva,* Dan. *stive,* to stiffen. All from the adj. above. Confused with O. F. *estiver,* to pack tight, stive; see **stevedore.**

Stigmatise. (F. — Gk.) F. *stigmatiser,* to brand with a hot iron, defame. — Gk. στιγματίζειν, to mark, brand. — Gk. στιγματ-, base of στίγμα, a prick, mark, brand. — Gk. στίζειν (= στίγ-γειν), to prick. Allied to **Stick** (1). (√STIG.)

Stile (1), a set of steps; see **Stair.**

Stile (2), the correct spelling of **Style** (1), q. v.

Stiletto; see **Style** (1).

Still (1), calm; see **Stall.**

Still (2), to distil, trickle down. (L.; *or* F. — L.) In some cases, it represents L. *stillare,* to fall in drops; more often, it is short for *distil* (below).

distil. (F. – L.) O. F. *distiller.* – L. *distillare*, *destillare*, to drop or trickle down. – L. *de*, down; *stillare*, to drop, from *stilla*, a drop.

instil. (F. – L.) F. *instiller.* – L. *instillare*, to pour in by drops. – L. *in*, in; *stillare*, to drop (above).

still (3), sb., an apparatus for distilling. (L.) Short for M. E. *stillatorie*, a still, from *stillat-us*, pp. of *stillare* (above).

Stilt. (Scand.) M. E. *stilte*. – Swed. *stylta*, Dan. *stylte*, a stilt; Dan. *stylte*, to walk on stilts. + Du. *stelt*; G. *stelze*, a stilt; O. H. G. *stelza*, prop, crutch. Allied to **Stalk** (1). Also to Gk. στήλη, a column; orig. sense a high post, upright pole.

Stimulate. (L.) From pp. of L. *stimulare*, to prick forward. – L. *stimulus*, a goad (put for *stig-mulus**). Allied to **Stick** (1) and **Stigmatise.** (√STIG.)

instigate, to urge on. (L.) From pp. of *instigare*, to goad on. – L. *in*, on; and base STIG, to prick; cf. L. *stinguere*, to prick; see **Distinguish.**

Sting. (E.) A. S. *stingan*, pt. t. *stang*, pp. *stungen*. + Icel. *stinga*, Swed. *stinga*, Dan. *stinge*. Nasalised form of **Stick** (1).

stang, a pole, stake. (Scand.) M. E. *stange.* – Icel. *stöng* (gen. *stangar*), a pole, stake; Dan. *stang*, Swed. *stång*, Du. *stang*, G. *stange*. From the pt. t. of the verb *to sting* (above).

stingy, mean. (E.) The same as Norfolk *stingy* (pronounced *stin-ji*), nipping, unkindly, ill-humoured. Merely the adj. from *sting*, sb., which is pronounced *stinj* in Wiltshire. So also Swed. *sticken*, pettish, fretful, from *sticka*, to sting.

Stink. (E.) A. S. *stincan*, pt. t. *stanc*, pp. *stuncen*. + Du. *stinken*, Icel. *stökkva* (pt. t. *stökk*), Dan. *stinke*, Swed. *stinka*, G. *stinken*; Goth. *stiggkwan* (for *stingkwan*), to smite, strike, thrust. The orig. sense seems to have been 'to strike against;' hence to strike against the sense of smell.

stench, sb. (E.) A. S. *stenc*, a strong smell, often in the sense of fragrance. – A. S. *stanc*, pt. t. of *stincan* (above). + G. *stank*.

Stint; see **Stunted.**

Stipend; see **Stipulation.**

Stipple, to engrave by means of small dots. (Du.) Du. *stippelen*, to speckle, dot over. – Du. *stippel*, a speckle; dimin. of *stip*, a point. Allied to **Stab.**

Stipulation, a contract. (F. – L.) F.

stipulation. – L. acc. *stipulationem*, a covenant. – L. *stipulatus*, pp. of *stipulari*, to settle an agreement. – O. Lat. *stipulus*, firm, fast; allied to *stipes*, a post. (√STAP, from √STA.) ¶ Not from *stipula*, a straw, though this is an allied word, dimin. of *stipes*.

constipate. (L.) From pp. of L. *constipare*, to join closely, press together.

costive. (F. – L.) From O. F. *costevé* = L. *constipatus*, constipated. See *constiper* in Littré.

stevedore, one who stows a cargo. (Span. – L.) Span. *estivador*, a wool-packer; hence a stower of wool for exportation, and generally, one who stows a cargo. – Span. *estivar*, to compress wool, to stow a cargo. – L. *stipare*, to press together. Cf. Span. *estiva*, O. F. *estive*, stowage; Ital. *stiva*, ballast.

stipend, salary. (L.) L. *stipendium*, a tax, tribute; put for *stipi-pendium**, a payment in money. – L. *stipi-*, crude form of *stips*, small coin; *pendere*, to weigh out, pay; see **Pendant.** β. *Stips* is supposed to mean 'pile of money;' from *stipare*, to heap together; cf. *stipes*, a post (perhaps a pile).

Stir. (E.) M. E. *stiren*, *sturen*. A. S. *styrian*, to move, stir. Allied to Icel. *styrr*, a stir, Du. *storen*, Swed. *störa*, G. *stören*, to disturb, O. H. G. *stören*, to scatter, destroy, disturb. Further allied to L. *sternere*, to scatter. (√STAR.)

storm. (E.) A. S. *storm*, storm; lit. 'that which lays low.' + Icel. *stormr*, Du. Swed. Dan. *storm*, G. *sturm*. From the same root as E. *stir* and L. *sternere*; see above.

sturgeon, a fish. (F. – O. H. G.) O. F. *estourgeon*, *esturgeon*; Low L. acc. *sturionem*, from nom. *sturio*. – O. H. G. *sturjo*, *sturo*, a sturgeon; lit. 'a stirrer,' because it stirs up mud by floundering at the bottom of the water. – O. H. G. *stören*, to spread, stir (G. *stören*) ; see **Stir** (above). + A. S. *styria*, *stiriga*, a stirrer, a sturgeon, from *stirian*, to stir; Swed. Dan. *stör*, sturgeon, from Swed. *störa*, to stir.

Stirk; see **Steer** (1).

Stirrup; see **Stair.**

Stitch; see **Stick** (1).

Stith, an anvil; see **Stead.**

Stiver, a Dutch penny. (Du.) Du. *stuiver*, a small coin. Perhaps orig. 'atom' or small piece; cf. G. *stüber*, a stiver, which appears to be related to G. *stieben*, to fly about, be scattered, *staub*, dust, *stäubchen*, an atom.

Stoat, an animal. (Scand.) *Stoat* also means a stallion (Bailey); M. E. *stot*, a stoat, stallion, bullock. It was, in fact, like *stag*, a general name for a male animal. — Icel. *stútr*, a bull, Swed. *stut*, Dan. *stud*, a bull, Swed. dial. *stut*, a young ox, young man; Norw. *stut*, a bullock, an ox-horn. Orig. 'a pusher,' hence ox-horn, strong creature, male. Allied to Du. *stooten*, to push (whence *stooter*, stallion), Swed. *stöta*, Dan. *stöde*, G. *stossen*, Goth: *stautan*, to push. (Base STUT.)

Stoccado, Stoccata; see **Stick** (1).

Stock, Stockade, Stocking; see **Stick** (1).

Stoic. (L. — Gk.) L. *Stoicus*. — Gk. Στωϊκός, a Stoic; lit. 'belonging to a colonnade, because Zeno taught under a colonnade at Athens.— Gk. στοά (Attic στωά), a colonnade, row of pillars. (√ STA.)

Stoker; see **Stick** (1).

Stole, long robe, scarf. (L. — Gk.) L. *stola.*— Gk. στολή, equipment, robe, stole. — Gk. στέλλειν, to equip. Allied to **Stall**.

diastole, dilatation of the heart. (Gk.) Gk. διαστολή, a drawing asunder, dilatation. — Gk. διαστέλλειν, to put aside or apart. — Gk. διά, apart; στέλλειν, to place, put.

epistle, a letter. (F. — L. — Gk.) O. F. *epistle*, also *epistre*. — L. *epistola*. — Gk. ἐπιστολή, message, letter.— Gk. ἐπιστέλλειν, to send to.— Gk. ἐπί, to; στέλλειν, to equip, send.

systole, contraction of the heart, shortening of a syllable. (Gk.) Gk. συστολή, a drawing together. — Gk. συστέλλειν, to draw together. — Gk. σύ-ν, together; στέλλειν, to place, put. See also **Apostle**.

Stolid, stupid. (L.) L. *stolidus*, firm, stock-like, stupid. Allied to **Stultify**, and to **Stall**.

Stomach. (F. — L. — Gk.) M. E. *stomak*. — O. F. *estomac.*— L. acc. *stomachum.*— Gk. στόμαχος, mouth, gullet, stomach; dimin. of στόμα, mouth.

Stone. (E.) M. E. *stoon*. A.S. *stán.*+ Du. *steen*, Icel. *steinn*, Dan. Swed. *sten*, G. *stein*, Goth. *stains*. Cf. Gk. στία, a stone.

Stool. (E.) M. E. *stool*. A. S. *stól*, seat. + Du. *stoel*, Icel. *stóll*, Dan. Swed. *stol*, Goth. *stols*, seat, chair; G. *stuhl*, chair, pillar; Russ. *stol'*, table. Lith. *stálas*,

table. Lit. 'that which stands firm;' cf. Gk. στή-λη, pillar. (√ STA.)

Stoop (1), to lean forward. (E.) A. S. *stúpian.* + O. Du. *stuypen*, O. Icel. *stúpa*, to stoop; Swed. *stupa*, to tilt, fall. Allied to **Steep** (1).

steep (2), to soak in a liquid. (Scand.) M. E. *stepen*, Icel. *steypa*, to make to stoop, overturn, pour out liquids, cast metals (hence to pour water over grain or steep it); causal of *stúpa*, to stoop (above); so also Swed. *stöpa*, to cast metals, steep corn, Dan. *stöbe*, the same.

Stoop (2), a beaker; see **Stoup**.

Stop. (L.) Not E., but L. M. E. *stoppen*, A. S. *stoppian*, to stop up; so also Du. *stoppen*, to stop, stuff, cram, Swed. *stoppa*, Dan. *stoppe*, G. *stopfen*, Ital. *stoppare*, to stop up with tow, Low L. *stupare*, to stop up with tow, cram, stop. All from L. *stupa, stuppa*, coarse part of flax, hards, oakum, tow. Cf. Gk. στύπη, στύππη, the same; Skt. *stumbh*, to stop. Allied to **Stub, Stupid, Stump**. Der. *stopp-le*, i.e. stopper.

estop. (F. — L.) A law term; to stop, impede. — O. F. *estoper*; Low L. *stupare* (above).

Storax, a resinous gum. (L. — Gk.) L. *storax, styrax.*— Gk. στύραξ.

Store, sb. (F. — L.) M. E. *stor, stoor*, provisions. — O. F. *estor*, a nuptial gift; *estoire*, store, provisions; Low L. *staurum*, the same as *instaurum*, store. — L. *instaurare*, to construct, build, restore; Low L. *instaurare*, to provide necessaries. — L. *in*, in; *staurare*, to set up, place; also found in *re-staurare*, to restore. From an adj. *staurus* * = Skt. *sthávara*, fixed; cf. Gk. σταυρός, an upright pole. (√ STA.) Der. *store*, verb, O. F. *estorer*, from Low L. *staurare* * = *instaurare*.

restaurant. (F. — L.) Mod. F. *restaurant*, lit. 'restoring;' pres. pt. of *restaurer*, to restore, refresh (below).

restore. (F. — L.) O. F. *restorer*, also *restaurer.*— L. *restaurare*, to restore.— L. *re-*, again; *staurare**; see **Store**.

story (2), set of rooms on a level or flat. (F. — L.) Orig. merely 'a building' or 'thing built.' — O. F. *estorée*, a thing built; fem. of pp. of *estorer*, to build.— Low L. *staurare**, put for L. *instaurare*, to construct, build, &c. See **Store**. Der. *clere-story*, i.e. clear-story, story lighted with windows, as distinct from *blind-story*.

Stork, bird. (E.) A. S. *storc*. + Du. *stork*, Icel. *storkr*, Dan. Swed. G. *stork*. Cf. Gk. τόργος, large bird. Prob. allied to **Stalk** (2); cf. A. S. *stealc*, high; also to **Stark**.

Storm; see **Stir**.

Story (1), a narrative; see **History**.

Story (2), set of rooms; see **Store**.

Stot, stallion, bullock; see **Stoat**.

Stoup, Stoop, flagon. (Scand.) M. E. *stope*. — Icel. *staup*, a knobby lump, also a stoup; Swed. *stop*, three pints.+A. S. *stéap*, a cup; Du. *stoop*, a gallon; G. *stauf*, a cup. Orig. a lump, mass; properly a mass of molten metal; cf. Icel. *steypa*, to cast metals; see **steep** (2), under **Stoop**.

Stout. (F. — O. Low G.) M. E. *stout*. — O. F. *estout*, stout, bold. — O. Du. *stolt*, *stout*, stout, bold; — Low G. *stolt*, A. S. *stolt*, the same. + G. *stolz*, proud. Allied to **Stolid**. **Der.** *stout*, sb., a strong beer.

Stove. (E.) A. S. *stofa*.+O. Du. *stove*, 'a stewe, hot-house, or a baine,' Hexham; Low G. *stove*. + Icel. *stofa, stufa*, a bathing-room with a stove; G. *stube*, a room.

stew, vb. (F. — Teut.) The verb was formed from the sb. *stew*, orig. a bath, hot-house; pl. *stews*, a brothel. The sb. was commonly used in the pl. *stues, stewes, stuwes*, &c., various spellings of O. F. *estuves*, 'stews, stoves, or hot-houses;' Cot. Mod. F. *étuve*. — O. H. G. *stupá*, a hot room for a bath (G. *stube*, a room); cognate with O. Du. *stove* (above). **Der.** *stew*, sb., stewed meat.

Stover, food for cattle. (F. — L.?) In Shak.; M. E. *stouer* (*stover*), necessaries. — O. F. *estover, estovoir*, necessaries; orig. the infin. mood of a verb which was used impersonally with the sense 'it is necessary.' Perhaps from L. *studere*, to endeavour.

Stow, to pack away. (E.) M. E. *stowen*, lit. to put in a place. — A. S. *stów*, a place. +Icel. *eld-sto*, fire place; Lit. *stowa*, place where one stands, from *stóti*, to stand. (√STA.)

bestow. (E.) From *stow*, with prefix *be*-.

Straddle; see **Stride**.

Straggle. (E.) Formerly *stragle*. Put for *strackle*; cf. prov. E. *strackle-brained*, thoughtless. Frequentative of M. E. *straken*, to roam, wander; P. Plowman's Crede, 82. Allied to **Strike**, q. v.

Straight; see **Stretch**.

Strain, Strait; see **Stringent**.

Strand (1). shore. (E.) A. S. *strand*.+

Icel. *strönd* (gen. *strandar*), margin, edge; Dan. Swed. G. *strand*.

Strand (2), thread of a rope. (Du.) The final *d* is added. — Du. *streen*, a skein, hank of thread. + G. *strähne*, a skein, hank. (Prob. allied to *stretch* and *string*.)

Strange; see **Exterior**.

Strangle, to choke. (F. — L. — Gk.) O. F. *estrangler*. — L. *strangulare*. — Gk. στραγγαλύειν, στραγγαλίζειν, to strangle. — Gk. στραγγάλη, a halter. — Gk. στραγγός, twisted. Allied to **String** and **Stretch** (√STARG.)

strangury. (L. — Gk.) L. *stranguria*. — Gk. στραγγουρία, retention of urine, when it falls by drops. — Gk. στραγγ-, base of στράγξ, a drop, that which oozes out (allied to στραγγός, twisted); οὖρ-ον, urine.

Strap. (L.) Prov. E. *strop*; A. S. *stropp*. — L. *struppus*, strap, thong, fillet. Allied to Gk. στρόφος, a twisted band; see **Strophe**. (Hence also F. *étrope*.)

strop, a piece of leather, for sharpening razors. (L.) A. S. *stropp*, a strap; see **Strap** (above).

Strappado. (Ital. — Teut.) A modified form of *strappata* (just as *stoccado* was used for *stoccata*). — Ital. *strappata*, a pulling, a wringing, the strappado. — Ital. *strappare*, to pull, wring. — H. G. (Swiss) *strapfen*, to pull tight, allied to G. *straff*, tight. ¶ Perhaps not really Teutonic, but borrowed from L. *struppus*; see **Strap**.

Stratagem. (F. — L. — Gk.) O. F. *stratageme*. — L. *strategema*. — Gk. στρατήγημα, the device of a general. — Gk. στρατηγός, general, leader. — Gk. στρατ-ός, army (orig. camp, allied to L. *stratus*, see below); ἄγ-ειν, to lead.

Stratum. (L.) L. *stratum*, a layer, that which is spread flat; neut. of *stratus*, pp. of *sternere*, to spread. + Gk. στόρνυμι, I spread out. (√STAR.)

consternation. (F. — L.) F. *consternation*. — L. acc. *consternationem*, fright. — L. *consternatus*, pp. of *consternare*, to frighten; intensive form of *consternere*, to bestrew, throw down. — L. *con-* (*cum*), together; *sternere*, to strew.

prostrate. (L.) L. *prostratus*, pp. of *pro-sternere*, to throw forward on the ground. **Der.** *prostrat-ion*.

stray, to wander. (F. — L.) O. F. *estraier*, to wander; orig. to rove about the streets or ways. Cf. Prov. *estradier*, a wanderer in the streets, one who strays, from Prov. *estrada* (= O. F. *estree*), a street;

O. Ital. *stradiotto*, a wanderer, from *strada*, street. — L. *strata*, a street ; see below. Der. *stray*, *estray*, sb.

street. (L.) A. S. *strǽt.* — L. *strata*, i. e. *strata uia*, a paved way ; *strata* being fem. of pp. of *sternere*, to strew, pave.

Straw, sb. (E.) A. S. *streaw*, *streow*, *stred.*+Du. *stroo*, Icel. *strá*, Dan. *straa*, Swed. *strå*, G. *stroh*. Allied to L. *stramen*, straw. Lit. ' what is scattered ;' see **Stratum.** (√STAR.)

straw-berry. (E.) A. S. *strédberige*, straw-berry ; from the resemblance of its runners to straws.

strew, straw, vb. (E.) M. E. *strewen.* A. S. *streowian*, to strew, lit. scatter straw. — A. S. *streaw*, straw. + Du. *strooijen*, to strew ; from *stroo*, straw. Der. *be-strew.*

Stray ; see **Stratum.**

Streak ; see **Strike.**

Stream. (E.) A. S. *stréam.*+Du. *stroom*, Icel. *straumr*, Swed. Dan. *ström*, G. *straum.* Allied to Russ. *struia*, Irish *sroth*, a stream. All from √SRU, to flow, which in Teut. and Russ. became STRU ; cf. Skt. *sru*, Gk. *ῥέειν*, to flow.

Street ; see **Stratum.**

Strength ; see **Strong.**

Strenuous. (L.) L. *strenuus*, vigorous, active.+Gk. στρηνής, strong, στερεός, firm.

Stress ; see **Stringent.**

Stretch. (E.) M. E. *strecchen.* — A. S. *streccan*, pt. t. *strehte*, pp. *streht.* Formed as a causal verb from A. S. *strec*, *strǽc*, violent, strong, variant of A. S. *stearc*, strong ; see **Stark.** Thus *stretch* = to make stiff or hard, as in straining a cord.+Du. *strekken*, Dan. *strække*, Swed. *sträcka* ; G. *strecken*, from *strack*, adj., straight. Allied to **Stringent.** (√STARG.)

straight. (E.) M. E. *streijt*, orig. pp. of M. E. *strecchen*, to stretch ; A. S. *streht*, pp. of *streccan* (above). Der. *straight*, adv., M. E. *streijt* ; *straight-way* ; *straight-en.*

Strew ; see **Straw.**

Stricken ; see **Strike.**

Strict ; see **Stringent.**

Stride, vb. (E.) M. E. *striden*, pt. t. *strade*, *strood.* A. S. *strídan*, to strive, also to stride, pt. t. *stráď.* So also Low G. *striden* (pt. t. *streed*), to strive, to stride ; Du. *strijden*, G. *streiten*, Dan. *stride*, strong verbs, to strive, contend ; Icel. *stríða*, Swed. *strida*, weak verbs, to strive. β. The orig. sense was ' to contend,' hence to take long steps (as if in contention with another). Der. *be-stride.*

straddle. (E.) Formerly *striddle* (Levins) ; frequentative of *stride.*

strife. (F. — Scand.) O. F. *estrif*, strife. — Icel. *stríð*, strife, contention. Cf. O. Sax. and O. Fries. *stríd*, strife. From the verb **Stride** (above).

strive. (F. — Scand.) M. E. *striuen* (*striven*), properly a weak verb. — O. F. *estriver*, to strive. — O. F. *estrif*, strife (above).

Strike, to hit. (E.) M. E. *striken*, orig. to proceed, advance, to flow ; hence used of smooth swift motion, to strike with a rod or sword. The verb is strong ; pt. t. *strak*, pp. *striken* ; the phrase ' *stricken* in years' meant ' *advanced* in years.' A. S. *strícan*, to go, proceed, advance swiftly and smoothly ; pt. t. *stríc*, pp. *stricen.* + Du. *strijken*, to smooth, rub, stroke, spread, strike ; G. *streichen*, the same. Cf. Icel. *strjúka*, to stroke, rub, wipe, strike ; Swed. *stryka*, Dan. *stryge*, the same. Allied to L. *stringere*, to graze, touch lightly with a swift motion. Der. *strike*, sb., the name of a measure, orig. an instrument with a straight edge for levelling (striking off) a measure of grain.

streak, a line or long mark. (Scand.) M. E. *streke.* — Swed. *strek*, a dash, streak, line ; Dan. *streg*, the same.+Goth. *striks*, a stroke with the pen ; A. S. *strica*, a line (whence M. E. *strike*).

stroke (1), a blow. (E.) M. E. *strook.* — A. S. *stríc*, pt. t. of *strícan*, to strike.

stroke (2), to rub gently. (E.) M. E. *stroken.* A. S. *strácian*, to stroke ; a causal verb, from *stríc*, pt. t. of *strícan* (above). Cf. G. *streicheln*, to stroke, from *streichen*, to rub.

String ; see **Strong.**

Stringent. (L.) L. *stringent-*, stem of pres. pt. of *stringere*, to draw tight, compress, urge ; pp. *strictus.* Allied to **Strong.**

astriction. (L.) From L. *astrictio*, a drawing together. — L. *astrictus*, pp. of *astringere* (below).

astringent. (L.) From stem of pres. pt. of *astringere*, to bind or draw closely together. — L. *a-* (for *ad*), to ; *stringere*, tc draw tight.

constrain, to compel. (F. — L.) O. F. *constraindre*, later *contraindre.* — L. *constringere*, to bind together, fetter.

distrain. (F. — L.) O. F. *destraindre*, to strain, press, vex extremely (hence to seize goods for debt). — L. *di-stringere*, tc pull asunder.

distress, calamity. (F. — L.) O. F. *destresse*, oldest form *destrece*. A verbal sb. from a Low L. *districtiare* * (not used), regularly formed from L. *districtus*, pp. of *distringere*, to pull asunder (in late L. to punish, afflict); see above.

district, a region. (F. — L.) O. F. *district*. — Low L. *districtus*, territory wherein a lord has power to distrain (Ducange). — L. *districtus*, pp. of *di-stringere*.

obstriction, obligation. (L.) Coined from L. *obstrictus*, pp. of *ob-stringere*, to bind, fasten.

restrain. (F. — L.) O. F. *restraindre* (F. *restreindre*), to restrain. — L. *re-stringere*, to draw back tightly, bind back. Der. *restraint*, from O. F. *restrainte*, fem. of pp. of *restraindre*.

restrict. (L.) From L. *restrictus*, pp. of *re-stringere*, to bind back.

strain. (F. — L.) O. F. *estraindre*, ' to wring hard;' Cot. — L. *stringere*, to draw tight.

strait, adj. (F. — L.) M. E. *streit*. — O. F. *estreit* (F. *étroit*), narrow, strict. — L. *strictum*, acc. of *strictus*; see **strict** (below).

stress, strain. (F. — L.) Sometimes short for *distress*; see **distress** (above). Otherwise, from O. F. *estrecir*, *estroissir*, to straiten, pinch, contract. This answers to a Low L. *strictiare* * (not used), regularly formed from L. *strictus* (below).

strict. (L.) L. *strictus*, pp. of *stringere*, to tighten, draw together, &c.

Strip. (E.) M. E. *stripen*. A. S. *strȳpan*, to plunder, strip. + Du. *stroopen*, to plunder, *strippen*, to strip off leaves, *strepen*, to stripe. Der. *strip*, sb., a piece stripped off.

stripe. (Du.) Orig. a streak; M. E. *stripe*; not an old word; prob. a weaver's term. — O. Du. *strijpe*, a stripe in cloth; Du. *streep*; Low G. *stripe*, a stripe or strip. + G. *streif*. From the notion of flaying; the O. Du. *stroopen* meant to flay; hence *strijpe*, a strip, mark of a lash, a stripe.

stripling. (E.) A double dimin. from *strip*; hence a lad as thin as a *strip*, a growing lad not yet filled out.

Strive; see **Stride**.

Stroke, (1) and (2); see **Strike**.

Stroll, to wander. (Scand.) Formerly *stroule*, *stroyle*. (A contracted form, as if for *strugle* *.) Frequentative of Dan. *stryge*, to stroll, Swed. *stryka*, to stroke, also to ramble. Allied to **Strike**; cf. M. E. *striken*, to go, proceed, wander.

Strong. (E.) A. S. *strang*, *strong*. + Du. *streng*, Icel. *strangr*, Dan. *streng*, Swed. *sträng*; G. *streng*, strict. Nasalised form of **Stark**. Cf. Gk. στραγγός, tightly twisted.

strength. (E.) A. S. *strengðu*. — A. S *strang*, strong.

string. (E.) A. S. *strenge*, cord; from its being tightly twisted. — A. S. *strang*, strong, violent. Cf. Gk. στραγγαλή, a halter; from στραγγός, tightly twisted. + Du. *streng*, string, from *streng*, severe; so also Icel. *strengr*, Dan. *stræng*, Swed. *sträng*, G. *strang*, cord, string.

Strop; see **Strap**.

Strophe, part of a poem or dance. (Gk.) Gk. στροφή, a turning; the turning of the chorus, dancing to one side of the orchestra, or the strain sung during this evolution; the *strophe*, to which the *antistrophe* answers. — Gk. στρέφειν, to turn.

antistrophe. (Gk.) Gk. ἀντιστροφή, a return of the chorus (see above). — Gk. ἀντί, over against; στροφή, a strophe.

apostrophe. (L. — Gk.) L. *apostrophe*. — Gk. ἀποστροφή, a turning away, the mark called an apostrophe; in rhetoric, a turning away to address one person only. — Gk. ἀπό, away; στρέφειν, to turn. See also **Catastrophe**.

Strow; see **strew**, under **Straw**.

Structure. (F. — L.) F. *structure*. — L. *structura*, a structure. — L. *structus*, pp. of *struere*, to build, orig. to heap together. Allied to **Stratum**.

construct. (L.) From L. *constructus*, pp. of *construere* (below).

construe. (L.) L. *construere*, to heap together, build, also to construe a passage. — L. *con-* (*cum*), together; *struere*, to pile, build. Der. *mis-construe*.

destroy. (F. — L.) M. E. *destroien*. — O. F. *destruire*. — L. *de-struere*, to pull down, unbuild, overthrow (pp. *destructus*). Der. *destruct-ion* (from the pp.).

instruct. (L.) From L. *instructus*, pp. of *in-struere*, to build into, instruct.

instrument. (F. — L.) F. *instrument*. — L. *instrumentum*, an implement, tool. — L. *instruere* (above); with suffix *-mentum*.

obstruct. (L.) From L. *obstructus*, pp. of *ob-struere*, to build in the way of anything, lit. build against.

superstructure. (L.) From L. *super*, above; and **Structure**.

Struggle, vb. (Scand.) M. E. *strogelen*; a weakened form of *strokelen* *, not found.

A frequentative verb; from Icel. *strok-*, stem of *strokinn*, pp. of *strjúka*, to strike, beat, flog (hence, to use violence); cf. Icel. *strokka*, to churn with a hand-churn (called *strokkr*) made with an upright shaft which is worked up and down. Note also Swed. *stryka*, to strike, Dan. *stryge*, to strike, to stroke; the weakening from *k* to *g* being common in Danish.

Strum, to thrum on a piano. -(Scand.) An imitative word, put for *sthrum* *. Made by prefixing an intensive *s*- (= O. F. *es*- = L. *ex*), very, to Thrum. q. v.

Strumpet. (F. – L.) M. E. *strompet*. The *m* is an E. insertion; it stands for *stropet* * or *strupet* *. The *-et* is a F. dimin. suffix. – O. F. *strupe*, variant of O. F. *stupre*, concubinage. – L. *stuprum*, dishonour, violation. Cf. also Ital. *struprare*, the same as *stuprare*, to ravish; Span. *estrupar*, the same as *estuprar*.

Strut (1), to walk about pompously. (Scand.) M.E. *strouten*, to spread or swell out. – Dan. *strutte*, *strude*, to strut; cf. Norw. *strut*, a spout that sticks out, a nozzle. The orig. sense seems to be 'to stick out stiffly;' cf. Icel. *strútr*, a hood sticking out like a horn; Low G. *strutt*, rigid. + G. *strotzen*, to strut, be puffed up; cf. *strauss*, a tuft, bunch.

strut (2), a support for a rafter. (Scand.) Orig. a stiff piece of wood; from *strut*, to stick out or up. Cf. Icel. *strútr*, Low G. *strutt* (above).

Strychnine. (Gk.) From Gk. στρύχνος, nightshade, poison; with F. suffix *-ine*.

Stub, stump of a tree. (E.) A. S. *styb*, a stub. + Du. *stobbe*, Icel. *stubbi*, Dan. *stub*, Swed. *stubbe*. Cf. Gk. στύπος, a stump, Skt. *stambh*, to make firm, set fast. (√ STUP; from √ STA.)

stubble. (F. – O. H. G.) M. E. *stobil*, *stoble*. – O. F. *estouble*, *estuble*. – O. H. G. *stupfilá*, G. *stoppel*, stubble. + Du. *stoppel*, stubble; L. *stipula*, dimin. of *stipes*.

stubborn. (E.) M. E. *stoburn*, *stiborn*; also *stibornesse*, *stybornesse*, stubbornness, for which Palsgrave has *stubblenesse*. The final *n* is due to misunderstanding *stibornesse* as *stiborn-nesse*; or, in any case, has been added; cf. *bitter-n*, *slatter-n*. *Stubor**, *stibor** represent an A. S. form *styb-or**, not found, but of perfectly regular form; *-or* being a common adj. suffix, as in *bit-or*, bitter. From A.S. *styb*, a stub. Thus *stubborn* = stock-like, not easily moved, like an old stub or stump.

stump. (Scand.) M. E. *stumpe*. – Icel. *stumpr*, Swed. Dan. *stump*, stump, end, bit. + Du. *stomp*, G. *stumpf*. Cf. Skt. *stambha*, a post, stem, Icel. *stúfr*, a stump. A nasalised form of *stub*.

Stucco. (Ital. – O. H. G.) Ital. *stucco*, hardened, encrusted; stucco. – O. H. G. *stucchi*, a crust; G. *stück*, a piece, patch. Allied to Stock.

Stud (1), a collection of breeding-horses and mares. (E.) M. E. *stood*. A.S. *stód*, a stud; orig. an establishment or herd in a stall. + Icel. *stóð*, Dan. *stod*, G. *gestüt*. Cf. Russ. *stado*, a herd or drove, Lith. *stodas*, a drove of horses. (√ STA.) Der. *stud-horse*.

steed. (E.) M. E. *stede*. A. S. *stéda*, a stud-horse, stallion, war-horse. – A. S. *stód*, a stud (with the usual change from *ó* to *é*). + G. *stute*, a stud-mare; Icel. *stóð-hestr*, stud-horse, *stóðmerr*, stud-mare.

Stud (2), a rivet, large-headed nail, &c. (E.) Also a stout post, prop; hence a projection, boss, support. – A. S. *studu*, *stuþu*, a post. + Icel. *stoð*, Swed. *stöd*, a post; Dan. *stöd*, stub, stump. (√ STU, allied to √ STA.)

Student. (L.) From L. *student-*, stem of pres. pt. of *studere*, to be busy about, to study.

study, sb. (F. – L.) M. E. *studie*. – O. F. *estudie* (F. *étude*). – L. *studium*, zeal, study. Cf. Gk. σπουδή, zeal. Der. *studio*, Ital. *studio*, a school, from L. *studium*.

Stuff, materials. (F.–L.) O.F. *estoffe*, 'stuffe;' Cot. – L. *stupa*, *stuppa*, the coarse part of flax, hards, tow; the pronunciation of this L. word being Germanised before it passed into French (Diez). Cf. G. *stoff*, stuff, materials. β. The sense of the L. word is better preserved in the verb *to stuff*, i. e. to cram, to stop up, G. *stopfen*, to fill, stuff, quilt, from Low L. *stuppare*, to stop up; whence also E. Stop, q. v.

stuffy, close, stifling. (F. – L.) From O. F. *estouffer*, to choke (F. *étouffer*). The same as O. F. *estoffer*, to stuff or cram up. – O. F. *estoffe*, stuff (above). ¶ So Scheler, disputing the suggestion of Diez, who needlessly goes to the Gk. τῦφος, smoke, mist, in order to explain *estoffe*.

Stultify. (L.) Coined, with suffix *-fy* (F. *-fier*, L. *-ficare*), from L. *stulti-* = *stulto-*, crude form of *stultus*, foolish. Allied to Stolid.

Stumble, vb. (Scand.) The *b* is excrescent. M. E. *stomblen*, *stomelen*, *stum-*

len ; also *stomeren*. – Icel. *stumra*, Norw. *stumra*, to stumble; Swed. dial. *stambla*, *stomla*, *stammra*, to stumble, falter. Practically a doublet of *stammer*, with reference to hesitation of the step instead of the speech; see **Stammer**.

Stump; see **Stub**.

Stun, to make a loud din, to amaze, esp. with a blow. (E.) M. E. *stonien*. – A. S. *stunian*, to make a din. – A. S. *stun*, a din. + Icel. *stynr*, a groan; G. *stöhnen*, to groan, Gk. στέν-ειν, to groan; Skt. *stan*, to sound, to thunder. (√STAN.) Der. *astony, astound*; see **Astonish**.

Stunted, hindered in growth. (E.) From A. S. *stunt*, adj., dull, obtuse, stupid, orig. 'short;' hence, metaphorically, short of wit; also not well grown; but the peculiar sense is Scand. + Icel. *stuttr* (for *stuntr* *), short, stunted; O. Swed. *stunt*, cut short.

stint, to limit, restrain, cut short. (E.) Orig. 'to shorten.' M. E. *stintan* (also *stentan*). A. S. *styntan*, in *for-styntan*, properly 'to make dull;' formed from A. S. *stunt*, stupid, by vowel-change from *u* to *y*. The peculiar sense is Scand. + Icel. *stytta* (for *stynta* *), to shorten, from *stuttr*, short, stunted; Swed. dial. *stynta*, to shorten, from *stunt*, small, short. See above.

Stupefy, Stupendous; see **Stupid**.

Stupid. (F. – L.) F. *stupide*. – L. *stupidus*, senseless. – L. *stupere*, to be amazed. Cf. Skt. *stambh*, to stupefy, make immoveable; also *sthápaya*, to set, place firmly, from *sthá*, to stand. (√STA.)

stupefy. (F. – L.) F. *stupéfier*; due to *stupéfait*, pp., made directly from L. *stupefactus*, made stupid. – L. *stupe-re*, to be stupid; *factus*, pp. of *facere*, to make.

stupendous. (L.) L. *stupendus*, amazing, to be wondered at, fut. pass. part. of *stupere*, to be amazed.

Sturdy. (F. – L.?) It formerly meant rash or reckless; hence, brave, bold M. E. *sturdi*, *stordy*, rash. – O. F. *estourdi*, amazed, also rash, heedless; pp. of *estourdir*, 'to amaze;' Cot. (Mod. F. *étourdir*, Ital. *stordire*, to stun, amaze.) β. Explained by Diez from a Low L. form *extorpidire* *, to numb, render senseless. If so, it is from L. *ex*, out, thoroughly; and L. *torpidus*, dull. See **Torpid**.

Sturgeon; see **Stir**.

Stutter. (Scand.) Frequentative of *stut*, once common in the same sense.

'I *stutte*, I can nat speake my wordes redyly;' Palsgrave. M. E. *stoten*. – Icel. *stauta*, to beat, strike, also to stutter; Swed. *stöta*, Dan. *stöde*, to strike against. + G. *stossen*; Goth. *stautan*, to strike. Orig. 'to strike against,' to trip. (√STUD.)

Sty, (1) and (2); see **Stair**.

Style (1), a pointed tool for writing, a mode of writing. (F. – L.) It should be *stile*, as it is not 'Gk. M. E. *stile*. – F. *stile, style*, 'a stile, manner of indicting;' Cot. – L. *stilus*, an iron pin for writing; a way of writing. Lit. 'a pricker.' Allied to **Stimulate**. (√STIG.)

stiletto, a small dagger. (Ital. – L.) Ital. *stiletto*, a dagger; dimin. of O. Ital. *stilo*, a dagger. – L. *stilum*, acc. of *stilus*, an iron pin (above).

Style (2), the middle part of the pistil of a flower; gnomon of a dial. (Gk.) Gk. στῦλος, a pillar, long upright body like a pillar; allied to στήλη, a pillar. (√STU, by-form of √STA.)

Styptic, astringent. (F. – L. – Gk.) F. *styptique*. – L. *stypticus*. – Gk. στυπτικός, astringent. – Gk. στύφειν, to contract, draw together, to be astringent; orig. to make firm; allied to στύπος, a stump, stem, block.

Suasion, advice. (F. – L.) F. *suasion*. – L. acc. *suasionem*; from *suasio*, persuasion. – L. *suasus*, pp. of *suadere*, to persuade, lit. 'to make sweet.' – L. *suadus*, persuasive; allied to *suāuis* (= *suaduis* *), sweet. See **Sweet**.

assuage. (F. – L.) O. F. *asuager*, *asoager*, to soften, appease; (Prov. *asuaviar*). – F. *a* (= L. *ad*), to; and L. *suauis*, sweet.

dissuade. (F. – L.) O. F. *dissuader*; Cot. – L. *dissuadere*, to persuade from. – L. *dis-*, apart; *suadere*, to persuade; see **Suasion**.

persuade. (F. – L.) F. *persuader*. – L. *per-suadere*, to advise thoroughly, succeed in advising.

suave, pleasant. (F. – L.) F. *suave*; Cot. – L. *suavis*, sweet.

Sub-, *prefix*. (L., or F. – L.) L. (and F.) *sub-*, prefix. Orig. form *sup* *; whence the comparative form *sup-er*, above, allied to Skt. *upari*, above. *Sub* seems to have meant 'close to ;' hence it came to mean both just above, above, and just below, below; it is cognate with E. **Up**, q. v., also with Gk. ὑπό; see **Hypo-**. ¶ *Sub* becomes *suc-* before *c*, *suf-* before *f*, *sug-* before *g*, *sum-* before *m*, *sup-* before *p*, *sur-* before *r*; and see **sus-** (below).

consummate. (L.) From pp. of L. *con-summare*, to bring into one sum, to perfect. — L. *con- (cum)*, together; *summa*, a sum (below).

soprano. (Ital. — L.) Ital. *soprano*, supreme; highest voice in music. — Low L. *superanus*, chief; see sovereign (below).

sovereign. (F. — L.) M. E. *souerain* (*soverain*). — O. F. *soverain*, later *souverain*, princely, chief. — Low L. *superanus*, chief. — L. *super*, above; see super- (below).

sum, amount, total. (F. — L.) M. E. *summe*. — F. *somme*. — L. *summa*, sum, chief part, amount; orig. fem. of *summus* (= *sup-mus* *), highest, superl. form from *sub* (= *sup* *), above. Der. *summ-ar-y*, sb., from F. *sommaire*, 'a summary,' Cot., from L. *summarium*, a summary.

summit, top. (F. — L.) F. *sommet*, top. Dimin. of O. F. *som*, top of a hill. — L. *summum*, highest point, neut. of *summus*, highest; see sum (above).

super-, *prefix*. (L.) L. *super*, above; cf. L. *superus*, upper. Comparative form of *sub* (*sup* *). + Gk. ὑπέρ, above; from ὑπό, above; Skt. *upari*, above, locative case of *upara*, upper, comparative of *upa*, near, close to.

superior. (F. — L.) Formerly *superiour*. — F. *superieur*. — L. *superiorem*, acc. of *superior*, higher; comparative from *superus*, high, which is itself an old comparative form from *sub* (*sup* *).

supernal. (F. — L.) F. *supernel*, 'supernall;' Cot. Answering to a Low L. *supernalis* *, from L. *supern-us*, upper; from *super*, above; see super- (above).

supine, on one's back, lazy. (L.) L. *supinus*, lying on one's back. — L. *sup* *, orig. form of *sub*, up; with suffix *-inus*.

supra-, *prefix*, above. (L.) L. *supra*, above, adv. and prep.; short for *superâ*, abl. fem. of *superus*, upper: see super- (above). Der. *supra-mundane*.

supreme. (F. — L.) F. *suprême*. — L. *supremus*, highest. Put for *supra-i-mus* *, from a form *supera* (= L. *superus*, upper), with Aryan suffixes *-ya* and *-ma*. See super- (above).

sur- (2), *prefix*. (F. — L.) F. *sur*, above. — L. *super*, above. See super- (above).

sus-, *prefix*. (L.) L. *sus-*, prefix; put for *subs* *, extended form of *sub*, under.

suzerain, a feudal lord. (F. — L.) F. *suzerain*, 'sovereign, yet subaltern;' Cot. A coined word, made from F. *sus* = L. *susum* or *sursum*, above; so that F.

suzerain answers to a Low L. *suseranus* * or *surseranus* *. β. The L. *sursum* = *suuorsum* *, lit. turned upwards; from *su-* = *sub*, up, and *uorsum* = *uersum*, neut. of pp. of *uertere*, to turn.

Subaltern; see Alien.

Subaqueous; see Aquatic.

Subdivide; see Divide.

Subdue; see Duke.

Subjacent, Subject; see Jet (1).

Subjoin, Subjugate, Subjunctive; see Join.

Sublime. (F. — L.) F. *sublime*. — L. *sublimis*, lofty, raised on high. (Origin doubtful.)

Sublunar; see Lucid.

Submerge; see Merge.

Submit; see Missile.

Subordinate; see Order.

Suborn; see Ornament.

Subpœna; see Pain.

Subscribe; see Scribe.

Subsequent; see Sequence.

Subserve; see Serve.

Subside, Subsidy; see Sedentary.

Subsist, Substance; see State.

Substitute; see State.

Subtend; see Tend (1).

Subterfuge; see Fugitive.

Subterranean; see Terrace.

Subtle; see Text.

Subtract; see Trace (1).

Suburbs; see Urbane.

Subvert; see Verse.

Succeed; see Cede.

Succinct; see Cincture.

Succory; see Chicory.

Succour; see Current.

Succulent, juicy. (F. — L.) F. *succulent*. — L. *suculentus*, *succulentus*, full of juice. — L. *sucu-s*, *succu-s*, juice; with suffix *-lentus*. + Gk. ὀπός, juice. See Suck, Opium.

Succumb; see Covey.

Such, of a like kind. (E.) M. E. *swulc*, *swilc*, *swich*, *such*. A. S. *swylc*. + O. Sax. *sulic*, Du. *zulk*, Icel. *slíkr*, Dan. *slig*, Swed. *slik*, G. *solch*, Goth. *swaleiks*. β. The Goth. *swaleiks* is from *swa*, so, and *leiks*, like; hence *such* = *so-like*; see So and Like.

Suck. (E.) M. E. *souken*. A. S. *súcan*, pt. t. *seác*, pp. *socen*. [There is an A. S. by-form *súgan*; cognate with Icel. *súga*, Dan. *suge*, Swed. *suga*, G. *saugen*.] β. The A. S. *súcan* is cognate with L. *sugere*, W. *sugno*, Gael. *sug*, to suck; W. *sug*, Irish *sugh*, Gael. *sugh*, juice; cf. L. *sucus*, juice; see Succulent.

soak. (E.) It also means to suck up,

imbibe. M. E. *soken,* (1) to suck, (2) to soak. A. S. *súcan,* to suck, to soak. See **Suck.** Cf. W. *swga,* soaked, *sugno,* to suck.

suction. (F. — L.) F. *suction.* Formed (as if from L. *suctio**) from L. *suctus,* pp. of *sugere,* to soak.

Sudatory, a sweating bath. (L.) L. *sudatorium,* a sweating-bath; neut. of *sudatorius,* serving for sweating. — L. *sudatori-,* crude form of *sudator,* a sweater. — L. *suda-re,* to sweat; with suffix *-tor.* Cognate with E. **Sweat.**

exude. (L.) From L. *exudare,* better *ex-sudare,* to sweat out, distil.

sudorific. (F. — L.) F. *sudorifique,* causing sweat. — L. *sudorificus,* the same. — L. *sudori-,* crude form of *sud-or,* sweat, allied to *sudare,* to sweat; *-ficus,* making, from *facere,* to make.

Sudden; see **Itinerant.**

Suds; see **Seethe.**

Sue; see **Sequence.**

Suet. (F. — L.) M. E. *suet.* Formed, with dimin. suffix *-et,* from O. F. *seu, suis* (F. *suif*), suet, fat. — L. *sebum, seuum,* tallow, suet, grease.

Suffer; see **Fertile.**

Suffice; see **Fact.**

Suffix; see **Fix.**

Suffocate. (L.) From pp. of L. *suffocare,* to choke; lit. to put under the throat. — L. *suf-* (for *sub*), under; *fauc-,* stem of *fauc-es,* sb. pl., gullet, throat.

Suffrage, a vote. (F. — L.) F. *suffrage.* — L. *suffragium,* a vote, suffrage.

Suffusion; see **Fuse** (1).

Sugar. (F. — Span. — Arab. — Pers. — Skt.) F. *sucre.* — Span. *azucar.* — Arab. *assokkar*; put for *al,* the, *sokkar, sakkar,* sugar. — Pers. *shakar.* — Skt. *çarkará,* gravel, also candied sugar. Prob. allied to Skt. *karkara,* hard.

saccharine. (F. — L. — Gk. — Skt.) F. *saccharin,* adj., from L. *saccharon,* sugar. — Gk. σάκχαρον. — Skt. *çarkará* (above).

Suggestion; see **Gerund.**

Suicide, self-murder; one who dies by his own hand. (F. — L.) A word coined *in England* (before A.D. 1750), but on a F. model; the F. *suicide,* oddly enough, was borrowed from us. Like *homicide,* the word has a double meaning, (1) answering to L. *suicidium *,* from L. *sui,* of himself, and *-cidium,* a slaying, from *cædere,* to slay; (2) = L. *suicida *,* from L. *sui,* of himself, and *-cida,* a slayer. See **Cæsura.**

Suit, Suite; see **Sequence.**

Sulcated, furrowed. (L.) L. *sulcatus,* pp. of *sulcare,* to furrow. — L. *sulcus,* a furrow.

Sulky, obstinate, silently sullen. (E.) Not an old form, but deduced from the sb. *sulkiness,* by dropping *-ness.* However, *sulkiness* is itself a corrupt form, standing for *sulken-ness,* formed by adding *-ness* to the adj. *sulken.* This appears as A. S. *solcen,* slothful, remiss; chiefly in the comp. *á-solcen,* also *be-solcen,* with a like sense. The sb. *ásolcennes,* sloth, disgust, sulkiness, is quite a common word. β. Further, *solcen* was the pp. of a strong verb *seolcan* (pt. t. *sealc*), to be slothful or to stupefy.

Sullen; see **Sole** (3).

Sully, to tarnish, spot. (E.) M. E. *sulien.* A. S. *sylian,* to sully, defile, lit. to bemire. Formed (with the usual change from *o* to *y*) from A. S. *sol,* mud, mire. ✛ Swed. *söla,* to bemire, Dan. *söle,* Goth. *bisauljan,* G. *sühlen*; from the sb. appearing as Dan. *söl,* G. *suhle,* M. H. G. *sol,* mire. ¶ Not allied to the verb *to soil,* with which it is doubtless often confused.

Sulphur. (L. — Skt. ?) L. *sulphur.* Perhaps borrowed from Skt. *çulvári,* sulphur.

Sultan. (F. — Arab.) F. *sultan.* — Arab. *sultán,* victorious, also a ruler, prince. Der. *sultan-a,* from Ital. *sultana,* fem. of *sultano,* sultan, from Arab. *sultán.*

Sultry, Sweltry, very hot and oppressive. (E.) *Sweltry* is the older form, and is short for *swelter-y,* from the verb to *swelter* (M. E. *swelteren, swalteren*). Again, *swelter* is a frequentative form from M. E. *swelten,* to swoon, faint, die. — A. S. *sweltan,* to die. ✛ Icel. *svelta* (pt. t. *svalt*), Dan. *sulte,* Swed. *svälta,* Goth. *swiltan,* to die.

Sum; see **Sub-.**

Sumach, a tree. (F. — Span. — Arab.) F. *sumac,* also *sumach.* — Span. *zumaque.* — Arab. *summâq,* a species of shrub, sumach.

Summer (1), hot season. (E.) M. E. *somer, sumer.* A. S. *sumer, sumor.* ✛ Du. *zomer,* Icel. *sumar*; Dan. *sommer,* Swed. *sommar,* G. *sommer,* O. H. G. *sumar.* Further allied to O. Welsh *ham,* W. *haf,* Zend *hama,* summer, Skt. *samá,* a year.

Summer (2), a beam; see **Sumpter.**

Summerset; see **Somersault.**

Summit; see **Sub-.**

Summon; see **Monition.**

Sumpter, a pack-horse. (F. — Low L. — Gk.) *Sumpter* is an extension from M. E. *somer,* a pack-horse, which must be first considered. β. M. E. *somer* is from O. F. *somier, sommier, sumer,* a pack-horse, the same as Low L. *sagmarius*, corruptly *salma-rius*, a pack-horse. — Gk. σάγμα, a pack-sad-dle. — Gk. σάττειν (base σακ-), to pack, fasten on a load, orig. to fasten. γ. Hence E. *sumpter*, which orig. meant (not a pack-horse, but) a pack-horse-driver, baggage-carrier. — O. F. *sommetier*, a pack-horse-driver; answering to a Low L. *sagmatarius**. — Gk. σαγματ-, stem of σάγμα (above). δ. The old word *summer*, a beam, was so called from its bearing a great weight, and is the same as M. E. *somer* (above). Hence E. *bressomer*, familiar form of *breast-summer*, a beam placed breast-wise, to support a superin-cumbent wall. ¶ I explain *sumpter* in K. Lear, ii. 4. 219, as meaning 'pack-horse-driver;' a man, not a horse.

Sumptuary, Sumptuous; see **Exempt.**

Sun. (E.) M. E. *sonne.* A. S. *sunne*, fem. sb. + Du. *zon*, G. *sonne*, Goth. *sunno*, all feminine; Goth. *sunna*, masc. Cf. L. *so-l*, Skt. *su-rya*, the sun. Lit. ' that which begets ' or produces. (√SU.) **Der.** *south*, q. v.

Sunder, to divide. (E.) A. S. *syndrian, sundrian*, to put asunder. — A. S. *sundor*, adv, asunder, apart. + Icel. *sundra*, Dan. *söndre*, Swed. *söndra*, G. *sondern*, to sunder; from Icel. *sundr*, Dan. Swed. *sönder*, adv., apart, G. *sonder*, adj., separate. (Base SUND; root unknown.)

Sup, to imbibe, lap up. (E.) M. E. *soupen*. A. S. *súpan* (pt. t. *seáp*, pp. *sopen*), to sup, drink in. Parallel form to **Suck**. + Du. *zuipen*, Icel. *súpa*, Swed. *supa*, O. H. G. *súfan* (Base SUP.)

sip, vb. (E.) M. E. *sippen*. It answers to an A. S. *syppan**, regular causal form from A. S. *súpan*, to sup. **Der.** *sip*, sb.

sippet, a little sop. (E.) Dimin. of *sop*, with vowel-change (from *o* to *y* = *i*).

sop, sb. (E.) M. E. *soppe*. It answers to an A. S. *soppa**, regularly formed from *sop-en*, pp. of *súpan*, to sup. Cf. Icel. *soppa*, a. sop; from *sop-inn*, pp. of *súpa*, to sup. **Der.** *milk-sop*.

soup. (F. — Teut.) F. *soupe.* — O. Du. *sop, zop*, broth; *soppe, zoppe*, a sop; Icel. Swed. *soppa*, a sop. See above.

supper. (F. — Teut.) M. E. *soper.* — O. F. *soper* (F. *souper*), a supper. It is the infin. mood used as a sb. — O. F. *soper*, to sup (F. *souper*). — Low G. *supen*, Icel. *súpa*, Swed. *supa*, to sup. See **Sup.**

Super-, prefix; see **Sub-.**

Superannuate; see **Annals.**

Superb. (F. — L.) F. *superbe.* — L. *superbus*, proud; one who thinks himself above others. — L. *super*, above. See super-, under **Sub-.**

Supercargo; see **Car.**

Supercilious, disdainful. (L.) From L. *supercili-um*, (1) an eye-brow, (2) haughtiness, as expressed by raising the eye-brows. — L. *super*, above; *cilium*, eye-lid, lit. 'covering' of the eye. Cf. L. *celare*, to hide; see **Cell.**

Supererogation; see **Rogation.**

Superficies; see **Face.**

Superfine; see **Final.**

Superfluous, excessive. (L.) L. *super-fluus*, overflowing. — L. *super*, over; *fluere*, to flow; see **Fluent.** **Der.** *superflui-ty*, F. *superfluité*, from L. acc. *superfluitatem.*

Superinduce; see **Duke.**

Superintend; see **Tend** (1).

Superior; see **Sub-.**

Superlative; see **Tolerate.**

Supernumerary; see **Number.**

Superscription; see **Scribe.**

Supersede; see **Sedentary.**

Superstition; see **State.**

Superstructure; see **Structure.**

Supervene; see **Venture.**

Supervise; see **Vision.**

Supine; see **Sub-.**

Supper; see **Sup.**

Supplant. (F. — L.) F. *supplanter.* — L. *supplantare*, to put something under the sole of the foot, trip up, overthrow. — L. *sup-* (= *sub*), under; *planta*, sole; see plant, under **Plate.**

Supple; see **Ply.**

Supplement; see **Plenary.**

Suppliant, Supplicate; see **Ply.**

Supply; see **Plenary.**

Support; see **Port** (1).

Suppose; see **Pose** (1).

Supposition; see **Position.**

Suppress; see **Press** (1).

Suppurate; see **Pus.**

Supra-, *prefix*; see **Sub-.**

Supreme; see **Sub-.**

Sur- (1), *prefix*. (L.) Put for *sub* before *r*; only in *sur-reptitious, sur-rogate.*

Sur- (2), *prefix*. (F. — L.) See **Sub-.**

Surcease; see **Sedentary.**

Surcharge; see **Car.**

Surd, having no rational root. (L.) L. *surdus*, deaf; hence, deaf to reason, irrational. *Surdus* also means dirty, and is allied to **Sordid.**

absurd, ridiculous. (L.) L. *absurdus*,

contrary to reason, inharmonious. ─ L. *ab*, away; *surdus*, dim, indistinct, harsh in sound, deaf.

Sure; see **Cure**.

Surf, the foam of the waves on the shore. (E.) The *r* is intrusive; spelt *suffe*, with the sense of 'rush,' in Hackluyt's Voyages, ed. 1598, vol. ii. pt. i. 227: 'The *suffe* of the sea [sweep or rush of the inflowing wave] setteth her [a raft's] lading dry on the land.' I suppose *suffe* to be the same as '*sough* of the sea,' also spelt *souf*, *souch* in Jamieson. M. E. *swough*, from *swoughen*, *swowen*, to make a rushing noise. ─ A. S. *swógan*, to make a rushing noise; see **Swoon**.

Surface; see **Face**.

Surfeit; see **Fact**.

Surge, the swell of waves. (L.) '*Surge* of the see, *uague*;' Palsgrave. Coined directly from L. *surgere* (=*sur-rigere*, i. e. *sub-regere*), to rise; see **Regent**.

Surgeon, Surgery; see **Chirography**.

Surloin; see **Lumbar**.

Surly; see **Senate**.

Surmise; see **Missile**.

Surmount; see **Mount**.

Surname; see **Name**.

Surpass; see **Patent**.

Surplice; see **Pell**.

Surplus; see **Plural**.

Surprise; see **Prehensile**.

Surrebutter. (F. ─ L. *and* O. H. G.) A legal term, meaning an answer or reply to a *rebut*. From F. *sur* (L. *super*), upon, in reply to; and F. *rebouter*, to rebut, the infin. mood being used as a sb. See **rebut**, under **Beat**. And see **Surrejoinder**.

Surrender; see **Date** (1).

Surrejoinder. (F. ─ L.) A *rejoinder* in reply. 'The plaintiff may answer him by a *rejoinder*; upon which the defendant may *rebut*; and the plaintiff may answer him by a *surrebutter*;' Blackstone, Comment. b. iii. c. 20. From F. *sur*, upon, in reply to; and F. *rejoindre*, to rejoin, used as a sb. See **Rejoin**, under **Join**.

Surreptitious; see **Reptile**.

Surrogate; see **Rogation**.

Surround; see p. 407, col. 1.

Surtout; see **Total**.

Surveillance; see **Vigil**.

Survey; see **Vision**.

Survive; see **Victuals**.

Sus-, *prefix*; see **Sub-**.

Susceptible; see **Capacious**.

Suspect; see **Species**.

Suspend; see **Pendant**.

Suspicion; see **Species**.

Sustain; see **Tenable**.

Sutler, one who sells provisions in a camp. (Du.) Du. *soetelaar* (Sewel); usually *zoetelaar*; O. Du. *zoetelaer*, 'a scullion, a sutler, or a victualler,' Hexham. Orig. a scullion, drudge, menial who does dirty work; formed with suffix -*aar* (=E. -*er*) from *zoetelen*, 'to sullie,' Hexham. Cognate with Low G. *suddeln*, Dan. *sudle*, G. *sudeln*, to sully, daub. All these are frequentative forms, with suffix -*el*- or -*l*-; from Swed. *sudda*, to daub, stain, soil. Allied to Icel. *suddi*, steam from cooking, drizzling rain, *suddaligr*, wet and dank, *soð*, broth in which meat has been sodden; all from Icel. *sjóða*, to seethe. Further allied to E. *suds*, and to the verb **Seethe**, q. v.

Suture, a seam. (F.─L.) F. *suture*. ─ L. *sutura*. ─ L. *sutus*, pp. of *suere*, to sew; see **Sew**.

Suttee. (Skt.) Skt. *satí*, a true or virtuous wife, a term applied to a widow who immolates herself on the funeral pile of her husband; hence (incorrectly) the burning of a widow. Skt. *satí* = *santí*, fem. of *sant*, being, existing, true, right, virtuous; pres. pt. of *as*, to be. (√AS.) See **Sooth**.

Suzerain; see **Sub-**.

Swabber. (Du.) Older than *swab*, verb. ─ Du. *zwabber*, 'a swabber, the drudge of a ship;' Sewel. Cf. Du. *zwabberen*, to drudge. ✛ Swed. *svab*, a fire-brush, *svabla*, to swab; Dan. *svabre*, to swab; G. *schwabber*, a swabber. Cf. also Norw. *svabba*, to splash about. Allied to **Swap**, **Swoop**, **Sweep**.

Swaddle; see **Swath**.

Swagger; see **Sway**.

Swain. (Scand.) Icel. *sveinn*, a boy, lad, servant; Swed. *sven*, Dan. *svend*, a swain, servant. ✛ Low G. *sween*; O. H. G. *suein*, *suén*, A. S. *swán*. Allied to Goth. *swinths*, strong.

Swallow (1), a bird. (E.) A. S. *swalewe*. ✛ Du. *zwaluw*, Icel. *svala*, Dan. *svale*, Swed. *svala*, G. *schwalbe*. Cf. O. Du. *swalpen*, 'to flote, tosse, beate against with waves,' Hexham. It means 'tosser,' or mover to and fro; from its flight.

Swallow (2), to absorb. (E.) M. E. *swolwen*, *swolჳhen*. A secondary verb, from A. S. *swolg-en*, pp. of *swelgan*, to swallow, strong verb. ✛ Du. *zwelgen*,

Icel. *svelgja*, Dan. *svælge*, Swed. *svälja*, G. *schwelgen*, to swallow. Der. *ground-sel*, q. v.

Swamp; see Swim (1).

Swan. (E.) A. S. *swan*. + Du. *zwaan*, Icel. *svanr*, Dan. *svane*, Swed. *svan*, G. *schwan*.

Swap, to strike. (E.) M. E. *swappen*, to strike; also, to go swiftly. Allied to **Sweep, Swoop.** It means 'to strike with a sweeping stroke.'

Sward. (E.) It orig. meant skin, rind, or covering. .A. S. *sweard*, the skin of bacon, rind. *Green-sward* is the grassy covering of the land, green turf. + Du. *zwoord*, rind of bacon; Icel. *svörðr*, skin, sward, *grassvördr*, green - sward; Dan. *flesksvär*, flesh - sward, *grönsværd*, green-sward; G. *schwarte*, rind, bark, skin.

Swarm. (E.) A. S. *swearm*; lit. 'that which hums;' from √SWAR, to hum, buzz, as in Skt. *svri*, to sound, *svara*, voice, L. *susurrus*, a hum. + Du. *zwerm*, Icel. *svarmr*, Dan. *sværm*, Swed. *svärm*, G. *schwarm*. Cf. Lith. *surma*, a pipe.

Swart, Swarthy. (E.) The proper form was *swart*, afterwards *swarth*, whence *swarth-y*. M. E. *swart*. A. S. *sweart*. + Du. *zwart*, Icel. *svartr*, Dan. *sort*, Swed. *svart*, G. *schwartz*, Goth. *swarts*. Allied to L. *sordidus*, dirty. Orig. sense 'blackened by heat.' (√SWAR, to glow.)

Swash, to strike forcibly. (Scand.) Cf. Swed. dial. *svasska*, to make a swashing noise, as when one walks with water in the shoes. It stands for *svak-sa*; cf. Norweg. *svakka*, to make a noise like water under the feet. Prov. E. *swack*, a blow, fall, *swacking*, crushing, huge.

Swath, a row of mown grass. (E.) A. S. *swaðu*, a track, foot-track, trace. + Du. *zwad*, *zwade*, a swath (Sewel); G. *schwad*. The sense of 'mown grass' is original; cf. Low G. *swad*, a swath, *swade*, a scythe. The earliest meaning seems to have been 'shred' or 'slice;' cf. Norweg. *swada*, vb., act. and neut. to shred or slice off, to flake off.

swaddle, to swathe an infant. (E.) Formerly *swadle*, *swadell*; put for *swathel*. It means to wrap in a swaddling-band, which was called a *swathel* or *swethel*. — A. S. *sweðel*, a swaddling-band; lit. 'that which swathes;' see below.

swathe, to enwrap, bandage. (E.) M. E. *swathen*. A. S. *sweðian*, to enwrap. — A. S. *swaðu*, (1) as much grass as is mown at once, (2) a shred of cloth

used as a bandage; orig. a 'shred;' see Swath.

Sway, to swing, incline, rule over. (Scand.) M. E. *sweyen*. — Icel. *sveigja*, to bend aside, swing a distaff, *sveggja*, to make to sway or swing. Causal form from a lost verb *svíga**, to bend, whence *svigna*, to give way, *svigi*, a bending switch; this verb is preserved in Swed. dial. *sviga* (pt. t. *sveg*), to bend; cf. Swed. *svag*, weak (pliant). Cf. also Dan. *svaie*, Du. *zwaaijen*, to sway, swing, brandish. Allied to **Swing.** (Base SWAG.)

swagger. (Scand.) Frequentative of *swag*, to sway from side to side. 'I *swagge*, as a fatte persons belly *swaggeth* as he goth;' Palsgrave. *Swag* = *sway*; see Sway.

switch, a pliant rod. (Du.) Put for *swich*, weakened form of *swick*. — O. Du. *swick*, 'a swich, or a whip;' Hexham. — O. Du. *swicken*, 'to totter or to waggle;' id. A *switch* is a pliant rod; the base is SWIK, weakened form of SWAK, which appears (nasalised) in Du. *swanken*, to bend, and in O. Du. *swanck*, a switch. The base SWAK is parallel to SWAG, appearing in Sway (above); hence Norw. *svige*, *sveg*, a switch, Icel. *sveigr*, *svigi*, a switch. And see Swink.

Swear. (E.) M. E. *sweren*. A. S. *swerian*, pt. t. *swór*, pp. *sworen*, to swear; also as weak verb, to speak, declare. + Du. *zweren*, Icel. *sverja*, Dan. *sværge*, Swed. *svärja*, G. *schwören*. Allied to Goth. *swaran*, Icel. *svara*, to answer. Orig. 'to speak loudly;' cf. Skt. *svara*, sound, voice. See Swarm. (√SWAR.)

answer, to reply. (E.) A. S. *andswerian*, *andswarian*, to answer, speak in reply. — A. S. *and-*, against, in reply; *swerian*, to speak, to swear. The A. S. *and-* = G. *ant-* (in *ant-worten*) = Gk. *ἀντί*; see Anti-.

Sweat, sb. and vb. (E.) M. E. *swote*, sweat, sb.; whence *sweten*, to sweat. A. S. *swát*, sb.; whence *swǽtan*, vb. The A. S. *swǽtan* became M. E. *sweten*, and should be mod. E. *swet*, the vowel being shortened; similarly A. S. *lǽtan* = M. E. *leten* = mod. E. *let*. The spelling *sweat* is thoroughly bad. The sb. should be *swote*, but has been modified to agree with the verb. + Du. *zweet*, sb.; Icel. *sveiti*, Dan. *sved*, Swed. *svett*, G. *schweiss*; Skt. *sveda*, sweat, from *svid*, to sweat. (√SWID.) See Suda-tory.

Sweep; see **Swoop**.

Sweet. (E.) M. E. *swete*, with by-forms *swote*, *sote*. A. S. *swéte*, sweet. + O. Sax. *swóti*, Du. *zoet*, Icel. *sœtr*, Dan. *söd*, Swed. *söt*, G. *süsz*, O. H. G. *suozi*. β. The Teut. type is SWOTYA, from a base SWAT = Aryan √ SWAD, to please; whence Skt. *svad, svád*, to taste, eat, please, *svádu*, sweet, Gk. ἡδύς, L. *suāuis*. See **Suave**.

sweetheart. (E.) M. E. *swete herte*, lit. sweet heart, i. e. dear love; see Chaucer, Troil. iii. 1181, 1210, and last line.

Swell. (E.) M. E. *swellen*, pt. t. *swal*. A. S. *swellan*, pt. t. *sweall*, pp. *swollen*.+ Du. *zwellen*, Icel. *svella*, Swed. *svälla*, G. *schwellen*. (Base SWAL, to toss, boil up, swell.) See **Swallow** (1).

Swelter; see **Sultry**.

Swerve, to turn aside. (E.) M. E. *sweruen* (*swerven*). A. S. *sweorfan*, pt. t. *swearf*, pp. *sworfen*, to rub, file, polish (hence to move swiftly to and fro, to turn aside in moving).+Du. *zwerven*, to swerve, wander, riot, rove; O. Sax. *swerban*, to wipe; O. Fries. *swerva*, to creep; Icel. *sverfa* (pt. t. *svarf*), to file; Goth. *biswairban*, to wipe. β. The particular sense appears in Dan. dial. *svirre*, to move to and fro, to swerve, to turn aside; cf. Dan. *svirre*, to whirl round, *svire*, to revel, *svarre*, *svarbe*, to turn in a lathe, Swed. *svirra*, to murmur, *svarfva*, to turn in a lathe. From √ SWAR, to hum (see **Swarm**); whence the senses to whirl, to work to and fro, wipe, rub, file, go to and fro, wander, swerve; from the sounds made by rapid motion. *Swerving* is due to rapid motion; see **Swirl**.

Swift. (E.) A. S. *swift*. Put for *swipt**, from Teut. base SWIP, to move swiftly; cf. Icel. *svipa*, to swoop, flash, whip, *svipall*, shifty, *svipligr*, swift, G. *schweifen*, to move along, &c. See **Squib** and **Swivel**.

Swill, to wash dishes, drink greedily. (E.) M. E. *swilien*. A. S. *swilian*, to wash. From a Teut. base SKWAL; cf. Swed. *sqvala*, to gush, *sqval*, a gush, wash of water, *sqvalor*, washings, swill. Hence M. E. *squyler*, a washer of dishes; also Icel. *skyla*, Dan. *skylle*, to swill, rinse, wash, *skyllevand*, dish-water, G. *spülen* (for *squülen**), to swill, rinse. Der. *swill*, sb., hog's-wash; whence *swill*, verb, to drink like a pig, Rich. III, v. 2. 9.

scullery, a place for swilling dishes, &c. (E.) The suffix -*y* (= F. -*ie*) is the same as in *butter-y, pantr-y*. *Sculler* is a remarkable variant of *swiller*, due to Scand. influence. It was formerly spelt *squylerey*, and a menial who washed dishes was called a *squyllare* or *squyler*. This spelling was due to Swed. *sqvalor*, washings; whilst the Icel. *skyla*, Dan. *skylle*, to rinse (and perhaps some confusion with *scullion*) caused a change from *squillery* to *scullery*. Examples of these changes are plentiful. See **Swill** above. ¶ Not allied to *scullion*.

Swim (1), to move about in water. (E.) A. S. *swimman*, pt. t. *swamm*.+Du. *zwemmen*, Icel. *svimma*, Dan. *svömme*, Swed. *simma*; G. *schwimmen*. (Base SWAM.) Cf. Skt. *sū*, to impel.

swamp. (Scand.) Not an old word. The *p* is excrescent. — Dan. Swed. *svamp*, a sponge, fungus; (hence applied to swampy ground, which seems to be exclusively an E. use). + M. H. G. *swam*, *swamp*, G. *schwamm*, a sponge, fungus; Du. *zwam*, Goth. *swamms*, sponge; Low G. *swamm*, *swamp*, fungus; A. S. *swam*, fungus. All from √ SWAM, to swim. β. Further allied to Gk. σομφός, spongy, Goth. *swumsl*, a swamp; and even to **Sponge**. We find also prov. E. *swank*, *swang*, a swamp; and as E. *swank*: E. *swamp* :: Gk. σπόγγος : Gk. σομφός.

Swim (2), to be dizzy. (E.) From M. E. *swime*, a dizziness. A. S. *swíma*, a swoon, swimming in the head. + Icel. *svimi*, dizziness, Dan. *svimle*, to be giddy, *besvime*, to swoon; Swed. *svimma*, to be dizzy, *svindel*, dizziness. β. A. S. *swíma = swin-ma**; the real base is SWIN; hence Swed. *svindel*, G. *schwin-del*, dizziness; Swed. *för-svinna*, to disappear, Icel. *svina*, to subside (as a swelling). The orig. notion is that of failure, giving way, subsidence, &c.; see **swindler** (below).

squeamish, over-nice. (Scand.; *with* F. *suffix*.) *Squamish*, Baret (1580). M. E. *skeymous, sweymous*; Prompt. Parv.; *skoymus*, disdainful. Formed, with suffix -*ous* (= O. F. -*eus* = L. -*osum*), from M. E. *sweem*, vertigo, dizziness, swoon; *swem*, a sore grief. The word meant 'overcome with dizziness,' faint, hence expressing distaste or disgust at, over-nice, fastidious. — Icel. *sveimr*, a bustle, a stir; Norw. *sveim*, a hovering about, a sudden sickness, dizziness. Allied to Icel. *svimi*, a swimming in the head, Swed. *swimning*, a swoon, Dan. *svimmel*, giddiness, dizziness, *svime*, a fainting fit. See above. ¶ Prob. confused with *qualmish*; but *qualm* is from a totally different source; see **Quell**.

swindler, a cheat. (G.) XVIII cent. – G. *schwindler*, an extravagant projector, a swindler. – G. *schwindeln*, to be dizzy, act thoughtlessly. – G. *schwinden*, to decay, sink, vanish, fail. **+** A.S. *swindan*, pt. t. *swand*, to languish.

Swine; see **Sow** (2).

Swing. (E.) M. E. *swingen*, pt. t. *swang*, pp. *swungen*. A.S. *swingan*, pt. t. *swang*, pp. *swungen*, to scourge, also to fly, flutter, flap with the wings. **+** Swed. *svinga*, Dan. *svinge*, to swing, whirl; G. *schwingen*. (Base SWANG, nasalised form of SWAG.) Allied to **Sway**.

swinge, to beat, whip. (E.) M. E. *swengen*. A.S. *swengan*, to shake, toss; *sweng*, a blow; the causal form of **Swing**. Orig. ' to flourish a whip.'

swingle, a staff for dressing flax. (E.) M. E. *swinglen*, to beat flax; *swingle*, a swingle. This answers to an A.S. *swingel**, lit. beater, from *swingan*, to beat; see **Swing**. Cf. A.S. *swingele*, a scourging.

swingle-tree, the bar that swings at the heels of harnessed horses. (E.) M. E. *swingle-tre*. – M. E. *swingle*, a beater, but lit. 'a swinger,' or that which swings; *tre*, a piece of wood; see **Tree**.

Swink, to toil. (E.) Obsolete; once very common. A. S. *swincan*, pt. t. *swanc*, pp. *swuncen*, to labour, work hard. From the violent action; allied to **Swing**.

Swirl, to whirl in an eddy. (Scand.) Norweg. *svirla*, to whirl round; frequent. of *sverra* (=Dan. *svirre*), to whirl, orig. to hum. See **Swerve**.

Switch; see **Sway**.

Swivel, a link turning on a pin or neck. (E.) Spelt *swiuell* in Minsheu (1627); formed, with suffix *-el* of the agent, from A. S. *swifan*, to move quickly, revolve. Allied to **Swift**. Lit. sense ' that which readily revolves.'

Swoon, to faint. (E.) M. E. *swounen*, *swoghenen*, *swowenen*, to swoon. Formed (with formative *n*, giving a passive sense, as in Goth. verbs in *-nan*) from M. E. *swowen*, *swoghen*, to swoon, to sigh deeply. This is a weak verb, closely allied to A.S. *swógan*, to move or sweep along noisily, to sough, to sigh as the wind, a strong verb, of which the pp. *geswógen* occurs with the actual sense of 'in a swoon.' 'Se læg *geswógen*' = he lay in a swoon, Ælfric's Hom. ii. 336. So also A. S.

geswówung, a swooning, A. S. Leechdoms, ii. 176, l. 13. Cf. Low G. *swögen*, to sigh, *swugten*, to swoon. Allied to **Sough**, q. v. ¶ No connection with G. *schwinden*, for which see **Swim** (2).

Swoop, vb. (E.) M. E. *swopen*, usually in the sense to sweep. A. S. *swópan*, to sweep along, rush, swoop; also, to sweep (pt. t. *sweóp*, pp. *swápen*). **+** Icel. *sveipa*, to sweep, swoop; *sópa*, to sweep; G. *schweifen*, to rove. (Base SWAIP, from SWIP, weakened form of √SWAP, to move forcibly; Lith. *sup-ti*, to swing, toss, rock a cradle.) Allied to **Swift**.

sweep, verb. (E.) M. E. *swepen*. A weak verb, answering to A.S. *swápan**, not used, the regular causal form of A.S. *swápan*, to swoop (above).

Sword. (E.) M. E. *swerd*. A.S. *sweord*. **+** Du. *zwaard*, Icel. *sverð*, Dan. *sværd*, Swed. *svärd*, G. *schwert*. Lit. 'wounder;' cf. Skt. *svṛ*, to hurt, kill; G. *schwer*, painful. (√SWAR.)

Sybarite, an effeminate person. (L. – Gk.) L. *Sybarites*. – Gk. Συβαρίτης, an inhabitant of *Sybaris*, a town named from the river *Sybaris*, on which it was situated; in Lucania, Lower Italy.

Sycamine, a tree. (L. – Gk. – Heb.?) L. *sycaminus*. – Gk. συκάμινος; Luke, xvii. 6. Prob. a Gk. adaptation of Heb. *shiqmím*, pl. of *shiqmáh*, a sycamore; that it has been confused with *sycamore* is obvious.

Sycamore, a tree. (L. – Gk.) Better *sycomore*. – L. *sycomorus*. – Gk. συκόμορος, lit. 'fig-mulberry.' – Gk. σῦκο-ν, fig; μόρον, a mulberry.

Sycophant. (L. – Gk.) L. *sycophanta*, an informer, parasite. – Gk. συκοφάντης, lit. ' fig-shewer,' also an informer, a false adviser. [Etymology certain, but the reason for the peculiar use is unknown; perhaps fig-shewer = one who points outs figs to another, a parasite. The usual explanation, ' informer against those who exported sacred figs from Attica,' is wholly unauthorised.] – Gk. σῦκο-ν, a fig; *-φαντης*, lit. ' shewer,' from φαίνειν, to shew. See **Hierophant**.

Syllable. (F. – L. – Gk.) The third *l* is intrusive. M E. *sillable*. – O. F. *sillabe*, also *sillable*. – L. *syllaba*. **=** Gk. συλλαβή, a syllable, lit. 'holding together,' so much of a word as makes a single sound or element. – Gk. συλ-, for σύν, together; λαβ-, base of λαμβάνειν, to- take, seize. (√RABH.)

Syllogism; see **Logic**.

Sylph, an imaginary being inhabiting the air. (F. – Gk.) F. *sylphe*. – Gk. σίλφη, a kind of worm or grub (Aristotle). On this word it would seem that Paracelsus formed the name *sylphe*; he also used the names *gnome*, *salamander*, and *nymph* (all of *Greek* origin), to signify, respectively, a genius of earth, fire, and water. Hence the form *sylph-id*, a false form, but only explicable on the hypothesis of a Greek origin; as if from a nom. σιλφις * (base σιλφιδ-). ¶ Littré's explanation, that *sylph* is of Gaulish origin, seems to me futile; Paracelsus could hardly know Gaulish.

Sylvan, misspelling of Silvan.

Symbol, a sign. (F. – L. – Gk.) F. *symbole*. – L. *symbolum*. – Gk. σύμβολον, a token, pledge, a sign by which one infers a thing. – Gk. συμβάλλειν, to throw together, compare, infer. – Gk. συμ- (σύν), together; βάλλειν, to throw.

Symmetry; see Metre.

Sympathy; see Pathos.

Symphony; see Phonetic.

Symposium, a merry feast. (L. – Gk.) L. *symposium*. – Gk. συμπόσιον, a drinking-party, banquet. – Gk. συμ- (for σύν), together; πο-, base of πέ-πω-κα, I drank, πό-σις, a drink. See Potable.

Symptom, an indication of disease. (F. – L. – Gk.) Properly a medical term. – F. *symptome*; Cot. – L. *symptoma*. – Gk. σύμπτωμα, a casualty, anything that befals one. – Gk. συμπίπτειν, to fall in with. – Gk. συμ- (σύν), together; πίπτειν, to fall. (√ PAT.)

Syn-, *prefix*. (L. – Gk.; *or* F. – L. – Gk.) A Latinised spelling of Gk. σύν, together. It becomes *syl-* before *l*; *sym-* before *b, m, p, ph*; and *sy-* before *s* or *z*.

Synæresis; see Heresy.

Synagogue. (F. – L. – Gk.) F. *synagogue*. – L. *synagoga*. – Gk. συναγωγή, a bringing together; congregation. – G. σύν, together: ἀγωγή, a bringing, from ἄγειν, to bring, drive. (√ AG.)

Synalœpha, a coalescence of two syllables into one. (L. – Gk.) L. *synalœpha*.

– Gk. συναλοιφή, lit. a melting together. – Gk. σύν, together; ἀλείφειν, to anoint. Cf. Skt. *lip*, to besmear, anoint. (√ RIP.)

Synchronism; see Chronicle.

Syncopate, to contract a word. (L. – Gk.) From pp. of L. *syncopare*, of which the usual sense is 'to swoon.' – L. *syncope*, *syncopa*, a swoon; also, syncope. – Gk. συγκοπή, a cutting short, syncope, loss of strength. – Gk. συγ- (written for σύν, together, before κ); κοπ-, base of κόπτειν, to cut. (√ SKAP.)

Syndic. (F. – L. – Gk.) F. *syndic*, 'a syndick, censor, controller of manners;' Cot. – L. *syndicus*. – Gk. σύνδικος, adj., helping in a court of justice; as sb., a syndic. – Gk. σύν, together; δίκη, justice. Allied to Diction. (√ DIK.)

Synecdoche, a figure of speech whereby a part is put for the whole. (L. – Gk.) L. *synecdoche*. – Gk. συνεκδοχή, lit. a receiving together. – Gk. σύν, together; ἐκδέχομαι, I receive, from ἐκ, out, and δέχομαι, I receive. (√ DAK.)

Synod. (F. – L. – G.) F. *synode*. – L. *synodum*, acc. of *synodus*. – Gk. σύνοδος, a coming together, a meeting. – Gk. σύν, together; ὁδός, a way, a coming. (√ SAD.)

Synonym; see Onomatopœia.

Synopsis; see Optic.

Syntax; see Tactics.

Synthesis; see Theme.

Syphon, Syren; see Siphon, Siren.

Syringe. (F. – L. – Gk.) F. *syringue*, 'a siringe, squirt;' Cot. – L. *syringem*, acc. of *syrinx*, a reed, pipe, tube. – Gk. σῦριγξ, a reed, pipe, shepherd's pipe, whistle. From the humming or piping noise; see Swarm. (√ SWAR.) Der. *syring-a*, a flowering shrub, so named because the stems were used for making Turkish pipes.

Syrup, Sirup; see Sherbet.

System; see Statics.

Systole; see Stole.

Syzygy, conjunction. (Gk.) Gk. συζυγία, conjunction. – Gk. σύζυγος, conjoined. – Gk. σύ-ν, together; ζυγ-, base of ζεύγνυμι, I join; see Yoke. (√ YUG.)

T.

Tabard, a herald's coat. (F. – L. – Gk.?) M. E. *tabard*. – O. F. *tabart, tabard*, a kind of coat. Etym. unknown; perhaps from L. *tapet-*, stem of *tapete*, hangings, painted cloths, whence also E. *tippet*. See Tapestry.

Tabby, a kind of waved silk. (F. – Span. – Arab.) A *tabby* cat is one marked like the silk. – F. *tabis* (15th cent.). – Span. *tabi*, a silken stuff; O. Span. *attabi*. – Arab. '*utábi*, a rich waved silk. It was the name of a quarter in Bagdad where the silk was made; named after prince *Attab*, great-grandson of Omeyya. (See Dozy and Devic.) **Der.** *tabi-net*, explained in Webster as 'a more delicate kind of tabby.'

Tabernacle; see Tavern.

Tabid. (L.) L. *tabidus*, wasting away. — L. *tabere*, to waste away, languish.

Table. (F. — L.) F. *table.* — L. *tabula*, a plank, flat board, table. Lit. 'extended' or flat; cf. Skt. *tata*, stretched out. (√TA, or TAN, to stretch.) **Der.** *tabul-ate*, *tabul-ar*, from L. *tabula*; *tabl-eau*, from F. *tableau*, dimin. of F. *table*.

entablature. (F. — L.) F. *entablature*, 'the intablature;' Cot. Properly 'something laid flat,' and, though now applied to the part of a building surmounting the columns, orig. applied to a pedestal or flooring. — L. *in*, upon; *tabulatum*, board-work, a flooring, from *tabula*, a plank (above).

tafferel, taffrail, upper part of the stern of a ship. (Du. — L.) Du. *tafereel*, a panel, a picture, a tablet or board. Put for *tafel-eel* *, dimin. of Du. *tafel*, a table; cf. G. *täfelei*, boarded work, from G. *tafel*, a table. — L. *tabula*, a table, plank, board. ¶ The spelling *taffrail* points to confusion with *rail*.

Taboo, Tabu, to forbid the use of. (Polynesian.) *Taboo* is a prohibition in great force in the islands of the Pacific; cf. 'the *Tabu*, or interdict;' Kotzebue, Voyage, 1830, ii. 178. New Zealand *tapu*; Solomon Islands *tambu*.

Tabour, Tabor, a small drum. (F. — Span. — Arab.) F. *tabour* (mod. F. *tambour*). — Span. *tambor*, *atambor* (where *a* = *al*, the Arab. def. article). — Arab. *tambúr*, 'a kind of lute or guitar with a long neck, and six brass strings, also a drum.' Prob. of imitative origin; cf. Arab. *tabbál*, a drummer. **Der.** *tabour-et* or *tabret*, a dimin. form.

tambour, a small drum-like frame, for embroidering. (F. — Span. — Arab.) F. *tambour*, a tambour, also a drum; see above.

tambourine. (F. — Span. — Arab.) F. *tambourin*, a tabour, dimin. of F. *tambour*, a tabour or drum; see Tabour.

Tabular, Tabulate; see Table.

Tache (1), a fastening; see Tack.

Tache (2), a blemish; see Tack.

Tacit, silent. (L.) L. *tacitus*, silent. — L. *tacere*, to be silent. + Goth. *thahan*, Icel. *þegja*, to be silent. **Der.** *tacit-urn*, F. *taciturne*, L. *taciturnus*, silent; *tacit-urnity*, F. *taciturnité*, L. acc. *taciturnitatem*, silence.

reticent, silent. (L.) From stem of pres. pt. of L. *reticere*, to be very silent. — L. *re-*; and *tacere*, to be silent.

Tack, a small nail, a fastening; also to fasten. (C.) M. E. *takke*, *tak*, a fastening; *takken*, to fasten together. — Irish *taca*, pin, peg, nail, fastening; Gael. *tacaid*, tack, peg; Bret. *tach*, a nail, *tacha*, to fasten. β. Hence a *tack* or rope fastening a sail; also the verb *tack*, to sew slightly. (Prob. from √STAG, and allied to Take and Tangent.)

attach. (F. — C.) O. F. *attacher*, to attach, fasten. — O. F. *a*, for L. *ad*, to; Bret. *tacha*, to fasten, from *tach*, a tack, nail (above). **Der.** *attach-ment*.

attack. (F. — C.) F. *attaquer*, to assault. A dialectal form of *attacher*; see above.

detach. (F. — C.) F. *détacher*, to unfasten. — F. *dé* = O. F. *des-* = L. *dis-*, apart; Bret. *tacha*, to fasten (above). **Der.** *detach-ment*.

tache (1), a fastening. (C.) 'A *tache*, a buckle, a claspe;' Baret (1580), s. v. *Claspe*. A weakened form of *tack*, like *church* for *kirk*; see Tack.

tache (2), a blemish. (C.) M. E. *tache*, also *tecche*, a bad habit, blemish, vice, caprice, behaviour. — O. F. *tache*, 'a spot, staine, reproach;' Cot. Also spelt *taiche*, *teche*, *teque*, *tek*, a natural quality, esp. a vice, ill habit; mod. F. *tache*, a stain. Cf. Ital. *tacca*, notch, cut, defect, stain; Port. and Span. *tacha*, tack, small nail, defect, flaw, crack. Either the sense of 'nail' has been transferred to that of 'scratch,' or (which is more likely), the sense of scratch, defect, flaw, comes directly from √STAG, to stick, sting, pierce, &c. See *tetchy* (below).

tetchy, techy, fretful, peevish, touchy. (F. — C.) The sense is full of freaks, whims, or caprices; from *tetch*, M. E. *teche*, *tecche*, *tache*, a bad habit, whim; see *tache* (2) above. ¶ This is the word which is now corrupted to *touchy*, as if sensitive to the touch.

Tackle; see Take.

Tact; see Tangent.

Tactics, the art of manœuvring forces. (Gk.) Gk. τακτικά, neut. pl., tactics. — Gk. τακτικός, adj., fit for arranging. — Gk. τακτός, arranged, ordered; verbal adj. of τάσσειν (base τακ-), to arrange, order. **Der.** *tactic-ian*.

syntax. (L. — Gk.) L. *syntaxis*. —

Gk σύνταξις, arrangement; hence, arrangement of words.—Gk. σύν, together; τάξις, order, from τάσσειν, to arrange.

taxidermy, the art of stuffing the skins of animals. (Gk.)   From Gk. τάξι-ς, order (above); δέρμ-α, a skin, from δέρ-ειν, to flay, cognate with **Tear** (1).

Tadpole; see **Toad.**

Tafferel, Taffrail; see **Table.**

Taffeta, Taffety, a thin silk stuff. (F. —Ital.—Pers.)   F. *taffetas,* 'taffata;' Cot. —Ital. *taffetà,* 'taffeta;' Florio.—Pers. *táftah,* twisted, woven, taffeta.—Pers. *táftan,* to twist, spin, curl.

Tag, a point of metal at the end of a lace, &c. (Scand.)   'An aglet or *tag* of a poynt;' Baret (1580).— Swed. *tagg,* a prickle, point, tooth.+Low. G. *takk,* point, tooth.   Prob. of Celtic origin; see **Tack.**   Der. *tag-rag,* for *tag and rag*=every appendage and shred.

Tail (1), hairy appendage, appendage. (E.)   M. E. *tayl.*   A. S. *tægel, tægl,* a tail.+Icel. *tagl,* Swed. *tagel,* hair of mane or tail; Goth. *tagl,* hair; G. *zagel,* a tail.   Root uncertain.

Tail (2); see under **Tailor.**

Tailor. (F.—L.)   Properly 'a cutter,' or cutter out.   M. E. *taylor.*—O. F. *tailleor,* later *tailleur,* 'a cutter;' Cot.—F. *tailler,* to cut. — F. *taille,* a slitting, an incision.—L. *talea,* a thin rod, stick, slip; an agricultural term for a slip or layer (Diez).

detail, a small part. (F.—L.)   O. F. *detail,* 'a peece-mealing, also retaile, or a selling by parcels;' Cot.—O. F. *detailler,* to cut into pieces.—O. F. *de-* (=L. *de-*), down, fully; *tailler,* to cut; see above.   Der. *detail,* verb (which is from the sb. in E., though in F. it is the other way).

entail, to bestow as a heritage. (F.—L.)   Orig. to cut into; also to abridge, to limit; hence to limit in a peculiar legal way.   Spelt *entayle* in Levins (1570); M. E. *entailen,* to cut, carve.—O. F. *en-tailler,* to carve, grave.—F. *en-* (=L. *in*), in; *tailler,* to cut; see **Tailor.** And see **tail** (2) below.

intaglio, a kind of carved work. (Ital. —L.)   Ital. *intaglio,* a sculpture, carving. —Ital. *intagliare,* to cut into.—Ital. *in* (= L. *in*), in; *tagliare* = Low L. *taleare,* to cut twigs, to cut, from *talea,* a slip, twig.

retail, sb. (F.—L.)   *To sell by retail* is to sell by small pieces.—O. F. *retail,* a shred, paring, small piece.—O. F. *retailler,*

to shred, cut small.—O. F. *re-* (=L. *re-*), again; *tailler,* to cut; see **Tailor.**

tail (2), the term applied to an estate which is limited to certain heirs. (F.—L.)   Better spelt *taille*; see Todd's Johnson.— F. *taille,* a cutting, &c.; the same word as **tally** (below).   And see **entail** (above).

tally, a stick notched so as to match another stick; an exact match. (F.—L.)   M. E. *taille,* a tally; for keeping accounts. —F. *taille,* a notch, cut, incision, cutting; also a tally, or score kept on a piece of stick by notches. —L. *talea,* a slip of wood; see **Tailor.**   ¶ The final *-y* in *tall-y* is due to the frequent use of F. *taillé,* pp., to signify 'notched;' cf. *lev-y, jur-y, pun-y,* where *-y* = F. *-é.*

Taint; see **Tinge.**

Take. (Scand.)   M. E. *taken,* pt. t. *tok,* pp. *taken.* — Icel. *taka,* pt. t. *tók,* pp. *tekinn,* to lay hold of, seize, grasp, take; Swed. *taga,* O. Swed. *taka,* Dan. *tage.* + Goth. *tekan,* to touch; cognate with L. *tangere*; see **Tangent.** (√STAG.)

betake. (E. *and* Scand.)   M. E. *betaken,* to deliver, hand over, commit.   Formed from M. E. *taken,* to take (often to deliver); with E. prefix *be-* = A. S. *be-, bi*; see **By.**

tackle, equipment, gear, tools. (Scand.)   M. E. *takel.*—Swed. and O. Swed. *tackel,* tackle of a ship; Dan. *takkel,* tackle, whence *takle,* to rig. Cf. Du. *takel,* a pulley, *takelen,* to rig. The suffix *-el* denotes the agent; *tack-le* is that which *takes* or grasps, from its holding the masts firmly.—Icel. *taka,* to grasp, seize, &c., also to take (above).   ¶ The W. *tacl,* a tool, is either borrowed from M. E. *takel,* or it may be cognate; the root being STAG.

undertake, to take upon oneself, attempt. (E. *and* Scand.)   M. E. *undertaken,* compounded of *under* and M. E. *taken,* to take.   Der. *undertak-er,* lit. one who takes a business in hand; Oth. iv. 1. 224.

Talc, a mineral. (F.—Span.—Arab.)   F. *talc.*—Span. *talco.*—Arab. *talq,* talc, mica.

Tale, a number, a narrative. (E.)   M. E. *tale.*   A. S. *talu,* a number, also a narrative. + Du. *taal,* speech; Icel. *tal,* speech, *tala,* number; Dan. *tale,* speech, Swed. *tal,* number, speech, G. *zahl,* number.   Perhaps related to Skt. *dri,* to consider, *â-dara,* regard, care.

tell, to count, narrate. (E.)   A. S. *tellan,* pt. t. *tealde,* pp. *teald*; a weak verb.

—A. S. *talu*, number, narrative (above).
+ Du. *tellen*, Icel. *telja*, Dan. *tælle*, Swed.
tälja, G. *zählen*; all from the sbs. above.
Talent. (F. **—L. —**Gk.) The sense of
'ability' is from the parable; Matt. xxv.
F. *talent*, 'a talent in money; also will,
desire;' Cot. **—**L. *talentum.* **—** Gk. τάλαν-
τον, a balance, weight, sum of money,
talent. Named from being lifted and
weighed; cf. Skt. *tul*, L. *tollere*, to lift,
Gk. τάλ-ας, sustaining. (√TAL.) Allied
to **Tolerate. Der.** *talent-ed*, in use before
A. D. 1700.

Talisman, a spell. (Span. — Arab. — Gk.)
Span., *talisman*, a magical character. —
Arab. *tilsamán*, pl. of *tilsam*, *tilism*, a
talisman, magical image. — Late Gk.
τέλεσμα, mystery, initiation; Gk. τέλεσμα,
a payment; τελεσμός, an accomplishment.
— Gk. τελέειν, to accomplish, end. **—** Gk.
τέλος, end; also initiation into a mystery.
Cf. Skt. *trí*, to pass over, fulfil, *tara*, a
passage, a spell. (√TAR.)

Talk. (Scand. — Lith.) Connected with
tell and *tale* in popular etymology; but
wrongly. M. E. *talken.* **—** Swed. *tolka*,
Dan. *tolke*, Icel. *túlka*, to interpret, explain,
plead. — Swed. Dan. *tolk*, Icel. *túlkr*, an
interpreter, speaker; M. H. G. *tolk*, the
same. — Lithuanian *tulkas*, an interpreter;
tulkóti, to interpret; *per tulkas kalbéti*, to
preach by means of an interpreter. Prob.
allied to Skt. *tark*, to suppose, speak.
¶ The only Lithuanian word in English;
due to some intercourse between the
Scandinavians and Lithuanians by means
of an *interpreter*.

Tall, high in stature, lofty. (E. *or* C.?)
M. E. *tal*, which meant seemly, elegant;
it also means obedient, good, obsequious,
valiant, bold, great. Allied to A. S. *tæl*,
appearing in *leóf-tæl*, friendly, *un-tala*, bad
(Northumb. Gospels, Matt. xxvii. 23).
The sense of *tæl* seems to have been good
or excellent; allied to A. S. *teala*, *tela*,
adv., well, excellently. So also Goth.
un-tals, indocile, uninstructed, from which
we infer *tals*, docile, allied to Goth. *gatils*,
suitable, A. S. *til*, fit, good, excellent (a
common word), whence E. *till*, verb. See
Till (1). β. But in the particular sense of
'lofty' (almost the only sense left in the
mod. E. *tall*), the word may be Celtic; cf.
W. *tal*, high, Corn. *tal*, high; Corn. *tal*
carn, the high rock. It is remarkable that
Irish *talla* means 'meet, fit, proper, just.'
(A difficult word.)

Tallow. (O. Low G.) M. E. *talgh.* **—**
O. Du. *talgh*, *talch*, tallow; Du. *talk*, Low
G. *talg*; Dan. Swed. *talg*; Icel. *tólgr*, *tólg*,
tólk. So also G. *talg*, tallow (apparently
borrowed from Low G).

Tally; see **Tailor.**

Talmud, the body of Hebrew laws, with
comments. (Chaldee.) Chaldee *talmúd*,
instruction, doctrine; cf. Heb. *talmíd*, a
scholar, from *lámad*, to learn, *limmad*, to
teach.

Talon. (F. **—**L.) Particularly used of
a hawk's hind claw and toe. **—** F. *talon*, a
heel. **—** Low L. *talonem*, acc. of *talo*, heel.
— L. *talus*, heel.

Tamarind. (F. **—** Span. **—** Arab. *and*
Pers.) F. *tamarind.* **—** Span. *tamarindo.*
— Arab. *tamr*, a ripe date; *Hind*, India.
Lit. 'Indian date.' β. The Arab. *tamr* is
allied to Heb. *támár*, a palm tree; *Hind*
is borrowed from Pers. (which turns *s* into
h), and is derived from Skt. *sindhu*, the
river Indus. See **Indigo.**

Tamarisk, a tree. (L.) L. *tamariscus*,
also *tamarix*, *tamarice.* **+** Skt. *tamálaka*,
a tree with a dark bark; allied to *tamas*,
darkness.

Tambour, Tambourine; see **Tabour.**

Tame, adj. (E.) M. E. *tame.* A. S.
tam, tame; whence *tamian*, *temian*, to
tame. **+** Du. *tam*, Icel. *tamr*, Swed.
Dan. *tam*, G. *zahm.* Allied to L. *domare*,
Skt. *dam*, Gk. δαμάειν, to tame. (√DAM.)
See **Daunt.**

Tammy, Tamine; the same as **Stamin.**

Tamper; see **Temper.**

Tampion, a plug; see **Tap (1).**

Tan. (F. **—** Bret.) From F. *tan*, 'the
bark of a young oak, wherewith leather is
tanned;' Cot. **—** Bret. *tann*, an oak, also
tan. (The G. *tanne*, fir-tree, is prob.
borrowed from Celtic.) **Der.** *tan*, verb,
&c.; *tan-ling*, Cymb. iv. 4. 29.

tawny. (F. **—**C.) Put for *tanny*; spelt
tenny in heraldry. '*Tanny* coloure, or
tawny;' Prompt. Parv. **—** F. *tanné*, tawny;
lit. tanned; pp. of *tanner*, to tan. **—** F. *tan*,
sb., tan (above).

Tandem. (L.) L. *tandem*, at length;
applied to two horses harnessed *at length*.
A University joke.

Tang (1), a strong taste; see **Tongs.**

Tang (2), to make a shrill sound. (E.)
To *tang* is to ring out; an imitative word;
allied to *tinker*, *tingle*, *twang.*

Tang (3), part of a knife-blade; see
Tongs.

Tang (4), seaweed; see **Tangle**.

Tangent. (L.) From L. *tangent-*, touching, stem of pres. pt. of *tangere* (base *tag*), to touch; pp. *tactus.* **+** Gk. base ταγ-, as in τεταγών, having taken; Goth. *tekan*, to touch; Icel. *taka*, to take. (√STAG.) Allied to **Take, Tack**.

attain. (F. - L.) M. E. *atteinen.* - O. F. *ateindre, ataindre*, to reach to. - L. *attingere*, to attain. - L. *at-*, for *ad*, to; *tangere*, to touch.

attainder. (F.-L.) From the O. F. *ateindre*, verb, to convict; used substantively; see above.

attaint, to convict. (F. - L.) From M. E. *atteynt, ateynt*, convicted, whence the verb has been evolved; orig. pp. of *atteinen*, to reach to, also to convict. - O. F. *ateindre* (above). ¶ In no way allied to *taint*.

contact, sb. (L.) L. *contactus*, a touching. - L. *contactus*, pp. of *con-tingere*, to touch closely.

contagion. (F.-L.) F. *contagion.* - L. *contagionem*, acc. of *contagio*, a touching, hence contagion. - L. *con-* (=*cum*), with; *tag-*, base of *tangere*, to touch.

contaminate. (L.) From pp. of L. *contaminare*, to defile. - L. *contamin-*, stem of *contāmen*, contagion; which stands for *contagmen**. - L. *con-* (=*cum*); *tag-*, base of *tangere*, to touch.

contiguous. (L.) L. *contiguus*, that may be touched, near. - L. *contig-*, base of *contingere*, to touch (below).

contingent, dependent on. (L.) From stem of pres. pt. of *contingere*, to touch, relate to. - L. *con-* (=*cum*); *tangere*, to touch.

entire. (F.-L.) O. F. *entier*, whole. - L. *integrum*, acc. of *integer* (below).

integer, a whole number. (L.) L. *integer*, whole, entire; lit. untouched, i. e. unharmed. - L. *in-*, not; *tag-*, base of *tangere*, to touch.

redintegration, renovation. (L.) From L. *redintegratio*, restoration. - L. *red-*, again; *integer*, whole, entire (above).

tact. (L.) L. *tactus*, touch; hence, delicacy. - L. *tactus*, pp. of *tangere*, to touch.

tangible. (F. - L.) F. *tangible.*-L. *tangibilis*, touchable. - L. *tangere*, to touch.

task, sb. (F.-L.) Lit. a tax. M. E. *taske.* - O. F. *tasque, tasche*, a task (mod. F. *tâche*).-Low L. *tasca*, a tax, another

form of Low L. *taxa*, a tax.-L. *taxare* (below).

taste. (F.-L.) Orig. to handle, feel, the usual sense of M. E. *tasten.*-O. F. *taster*, to handle, feel, taste. Cf. Low L. *taxta*, a probe for wounds; which proves that O. F. *taster* answers to a Low L. *taxitare**, iterative form of *taxare*, to feel, handle (Gellius). Again *taxare* (= *tactare**) is an intensive form of L. *tangere* (pp. *tactus*).

tax, sb. (F.-L.) M. E. *taxe.* = F. *taxe.* = F. *taxer*, to tax.-L. *taxare*, to handle, value, appraise, tax. Put for *tactare**; from *tactum*, supine of *tangere*, to touch.

Tangle, to knot confusedly. (Scand.) Spelt *tangell* in Palsgrave. To *tangle* is 'to keep twisting together like seaweed;' a frequentative verb from North. E. *tang*, sea-weed.-Dan. *tang*, Swed. *tång*, Icel. þang, kelp or bladder-wrack, a sea-weed (whence the idea of confused heap); cf. Icel. þöngull, sea-weed. So also prov. E. *tangle*, sea-weed; Norman F. *tangon*, a kind of sea-weed (*Fucus flagelliformis*, Métivier). Der. *en-tangle*, with F. prefix *en-* (=L. *in*).

Tanist, a presumptive heir to a prince. (Irish.) Irish *tanaiste*, apparent heir. - Irish *tanaise*, second in rank (Rhŷs).

Tank; see **Stagnate**.

Tankard. (F. - L. - Gk. ?) O. F. *tanquard*, a tankard (Rabelais). Orig. uncertain; the suffix -*ard* is common in French. Perhaps from L. *cantharus*, a tankard, from Gk. κάνθαρος, the same.

Tansy, a plant. (F. - Low L. - Gk.) M. E. *tansaye, tansey.* - O. F. *tanasie, tanaisie*; earlier form *athanasie, atanasie*. (Cf. O. Ital. *atanasia*, Port. *atanasia*, tansy.)-Low L. *athanasia**, merely the Latinised form of Gk. ἀθανασία, immortality. Cf. O. Ital. *atanato* (lit. immortal), the rose-campion; Florio. Prob. from its supposed virtue, and its use in medicine. - Gk. ἀθάνατος, immortal. - Gk. ἀ-, not; θαν-εῖν, 2 aor. of θνήσκειν, to die.

Tantalise. (Gk.) Formed with F. suffix -*iser* (=L. -*izare*=Gk. -ιζειν), from Gk. Τάνταλος, Tantalus, in allusion to his story. The fable was that he was placed up to his chin in water, which fled from his lips whenever he desired to drink; Tantalus is the sun, that evaporates water. The name means 'enduring;' from √TAL, to endure.

Tantamount. (F.-L.) First used as

a verb, with the sense 'to amount to as much.'—F. *tant*, so much, as much, from L. *tantum*, neut. of *tantus*, so great; and E. *amount* (of F. origin); see Amount.

Tap (1), to knock gently. (F.—Teut.) F. *taper*, *tapper*, 'to tap, hit, bob;' Cot.—Low G. *tappen*, to grope, fumble, *tapp*, *tappe*, fist, paw, a blow; Icel. *tapsa*, to tap. Prob. of imitative origin; cf. Russ. *topate*, to stamp with the foot, Arab. *tabl*, a drum; E. *dub-a-dub*.

tip (2), to tilt. (Scand.) Generally in the phrase *tip up*, or *tip over*; a weakened form of *tap*. Cf. *tip and run*, i. e. tap and run (a game); *tip for tap*, blow for blow (Bullinger's Works, i. 283), now *tit for tat*. —Swed. *tippa*, to tap, tip, strike gently, touch lightly. Cf. Icel. *tapsa*, to tap.

tipple, to drink habitually. (Scand.) —Norweg. *tipla*, to tipple; frequent. of *tippa*, to drip from a point or tip.—Norw. *tipp*, a tip; cognate with *tip* (1), p. 515, col. 1. (Misplaced.)

tipsy. (Scand.) Formed from *tip* with suffix -*sy*, as in *trick-sy*, &c.; see tip (2) above.

Tap (2), a short pipe to draw liquor from a cask, a plug. (E.) M. E. *tappe*. A.S. *tæppe* *, not found; but we find A. S. *tappere*, one who taps casks.+Du. *tap*, Icel. *tappi*, Dan. *tap*, a tap; Swed. *tapp*, a tap, handful, wisp, G. *zapfen*, a tap. β. The orig. idea was prob. a tuft or wisp of something, to stop a hole with; cf. Swed. *tapp* (above), and G. *zopf*, a top of a tree, a tuft of hair, Icel. *toppr*, a tuft or lock of hair. Allied to Top and Tuft. Der. *tap-root*; *tap-ster*, A. S. *tæppestre*, a fem. form of *tæppere* (above).

tampion, a kind of plug. (F.—Teut.) F. *tampon*, bung, stopple; nasalised form of F. *tapon*, the same. Formed (with suffix -*on*) from F. *taper*, *tapper*, to stop with a bung (a Picard word).—Du. *tap*, a bung, tap; Low G. *tappe*, the same.

Tape; see Tapestry.

Taper (1), a small wax candle. (C.?) M. E. *taper*. A. S. *tapor*, *taper*. Prob. of Celtic origin; from Irish *tapar*, a taper, W. *tampr*, a taper, torch. Cf. Skt. *tapas*, fire, *tap*, to shine. Perhaps allied to Tepid.

taper (2), long and slender. (C.?) *Taper* means *taper-like*, shaped like the tapers used in churches, which were sometimes thinner at the top. Holland has: 'taper-wise, sharp-pointed in the top;' tr. of

Pliny, xvi. 16. See above. ¶ The A. S. *tæper-ax*, a kind of axe, is unallied; cf. Russ. *topor'*, an axe.

Tapestry. (F.—L.—Gk.) A corruption of the old form *tapisserie*.—F. *tapisserie*, tapestry.—F. *tapisser*, to furnish with tapestry.—F. *tapis*, tapestry hangings; Low L. *tapecius*.—L. *tapete*, cloth, hangings.—Gk. ταπητ-, stem of τάπης, a carpet, woollen rug. Cf. Pers. *tabastah*, a fringed carpet.

tape. (L.—Gk.) M. E. *tape*, also *tappe*. A. S. *tæppe*, a tape, a fillet; closely allied to A.S. *tæppet*, a tippet. The A.S. pl. *tæppan* probably meant strips of stuff or cloth. Borrowed from L. *tapete*, cloth; see above.

tippet. (L.—Gk.) M. E. *tipet*, *tepet*. A.S. *tæppet*, a tippet.—L. *tapete*, cloth (above).

Tapioca. (Brazilian.) Brazilian *tipioka*, the poisonous juice which issues from the root of the cassava when pressed (Littré); hence tapioca, which is also prepared from the root of the cassava.

Tapir, a quadruped. (Brazilian.) Brazilian *tapy'ra*, a tapir (Mahn).

Tar. (E.) M.E. *terre*. A.S. *teoru*, tar; also spelt *teru*, *tyrwa*.+Du. *teer*, Icel. *tjara*, Dan. *tiære*, Swed. *tjära*. β. Cf. also Icel. *tyri*, resinous wood; allied to Lithuan. *darwa*, *derwa*, resinous wood, particularly the parts of the fir-tree that readily burn, also to Russ. *drevo*, a tree, *derevo*, wood, timber, W. *derw*, an oaktree, and E. *tree*. Orig. sense 'wood,' esp. resinous wood for fuel; hence resin from such wood. Allied to Tree. ¶ For *tar* = sailor, see below.

tarpauling, a cover of tarred canvas. (E. *and* L.) It means *tarred pauling* or *tarred palling*; a *palling* is a covering, from the verb *pall*, to cover. This verb is from *pall*, sb., a cover; see Pall. Der. *tarpaulin*, an old name for a sailor (Smollett), now abbreviated to *tar*.

Taraxacum, the dandelion. (Arab.) From Arab. *tarasacon*, explained as a kind of succory, Pers. *tarkhashqún*, wild endive; Latinised as *taraxacon*, in Avicenna. (Devic; supp. to Littré.)

Tardy. (F.—L.) F. *tardif*, tardy. (Cf. Ital. *tardivo*, tardy.) From L. *tardus*, slow; with suffix -*iuus*. Allied to *terere*, to rub, also to waste time. See Trite.

retard, to delay. (F.—L.) F. *retarder*, to hinder.—L. *retardare*, to delay.—L. *re*-, again; *tardare*, to make slow, from *tardus*, slow.

Tare (1), a plant. (E.) M. E. *tare*. Not in A.S.; but peculiar to English. Prob. from the verb *to tear*; cf. prov. E. *tearing*, great, rough, *tare*, brisk.

Tare (2), an allowance. (F. ─ Span. ─ Arab.) F. *tare*, loss, waste in merchandise. ─ Span. *tara*, tare, allowance in weight. Lit. ' what is thrown away.' ─ Arab. *tarha*, what is thrown away, detriment (Devic); *tirh*, *turrah*, thrown away. ─ Arab. root *taraha*, he threw prostrate, threw down.

Target, a small shield, &c. (E.; *with* F. *suffix*.) Formerly also *tergat*; the *-et* is the F. dimin. suffix. ─ A. S. *targe*, a targe, shield.✛Icel. *targa*, a target; O.H.G. *zarga*, a frame, side of a vessel, wall, G. *zarge*, frame, case, side, border. (The F. *targe*, Span. *tarja*, &c., are of Teut. origin.) Cf. Lith. *darżas*, enclosure, border, halo round the moon. ¶ Distinct from Arab. *darkat*, *darakat*, a shield, whence Port. and Span. *adarga*, a small square target.

Targum, a Chaldee paraphrase of the Old Testament. (Chaldee.) Chaldee *targûm*, an interpretation. ─ Chal. *targém*, to interpret. Cf. Arab. *tarjumán*, an interpreter; see **Dragoman**.

Tariff. (F. ─ Span. ─ Arab.) F. *tariffe*, a casting of accounts. ─ Span. *tarifa*, a list of prices, book of rates. ─ Arab. *ta'ríf*, giving information, notification (because a tariff gives notice). ─ Arab. *'arf*, knowing, knowledge. ─ Arab. root *'arafa*, he knew.

Tarn, a pool.' (Scand.) M. E. *terne*. ─ Icel. *tjörn* (gen. *tjarnar*), a tarn, pool; Swed. dial. *tjärn*, *tärn*, a pool without an outlet.

Tarnish. (F. ─ O. H. G.) F. *terniss-*, stem of pres. pt. of *se ternir*, to become dim, lose lustre (Cot.). ─ M. H. G. *ternen*, O.H.G. *tarnjan*, to obscure, darken.✛A. S. *dernan*, *dyrnan*, to hide, from *derne*, *dyrne*, adj., secret; cf. O. Sax. *derni*, hidden, secret; Gk. θάλαμος, a secret chamber, lurking-place. (✓DHAR.)

Tarpauling; see **Tar**.

Tarragon, a plant; see **Dragon**.

Tarry. (E.; *confused with* F. ─ L.) The present form is due to confusion of M. E. *targen*, to delay, tarry, with M. E. *tarien*, to irritate. α. M. E. *targen*, to delay. ─ O. F. *targer*, to tarry, delay; answering to a Low L. form *tardicare* *. ─ L. *tardus*, slow; see **Tardy**. β. M. E. *tarien*, to irritate, provoke, also to tire; hence to hinder, delay. [This is the true

source of the word, though its meaning has been affected and fixed by the F. *targer*.] ─ A. S. *tergan*, to vex, provoke; closely allied to tire (4); see **Tear** (1).

Tart (1), acrid; see **Tear** (1).

Tart (2), a small pie; see **Torture**.

Tartan, a wollen stuff. (F. ─ Span. ─ L. ?) F. *tiretaine*, ' linsie-wolsie, or a kind therof, worn ordinarily by the French peasants;' Cot. ─ Span. *tiritaña*, a thin woollen stuff; so named from its flimsiness. ─ Span. *tiritar*, to shiver, shake with cold. Doubtless from a lost Latin verb, allied to Gk. ταρταρίζειν, to shake with cold; see **Tartar** (3).

Tartar (1), an acid salt in casks, a concretion on the teeth. (F. ─ Low. L. ─ Arab.) A term due to the alchemists; called *sal tartre*, or *tartre*, in Chaucer. ─ F. *tartre*, 'tartar,' Cot.; Low L. *tartarum*. ─ Arab. *durd*, dregs, sediment, tartar of wine; *durdíy*, dregs. Cf. Arab. *darad*, a shedding of teeth; which Devic connects with tartar on the teeth.

Tartar (2), a native of Tartary. (Tatar.) A perverse spelling of *Tatar*, owing to a popular etymology which regarded Tatars as let loose out of *Tartarus* or hell (see below). From *Tátar*, a Tatar, or inhabitant of Tatary (as it should be spelt).

Tartar (3), Tartarus, hell. (L. ─ Gk.) ' The gates of *Tartar* ;' Tw. Nt. ii. 5. 225. ─ L. *Tartarus*. ─ Gk. Τάρταρος, Tartarus, the infernal regions; conceived to be a place of extreme cold; cf. Gk. ταρταρίζειν, to shiver with cold.

Task; see **Tangent**.

Tassel (1), a bunch of silk, &c., as an ornament. (F. ─ L.) M. E. *tassel*. ─ O. F. *tassel*, an ornament, clasp; also a piece of square stuff (cf. Ital. *tassello*, a square, a collar of a cloak). ─ L. *taxillum*, acc. of *taxillus*, a small die; dimin. of *tālus*, a knuckle-bone, a die made of a knuckle-bone. *Tālus = tax-lus**, as shewn by the dimin. *taxillus*, and means a bone cut or squared; cf. Skt. *taksh*, to hew, prepare, make. (✓TAK.) ¶ The application to a · tassel is curious; a wood-cut at p. 272 of Guillim's Display of Heraldry (1660) shews a tassel ornamented with strings and dots; these strings divide it into squares, each of which (having a dot in the middle) resembles *an ace on a die*.

Tassel (2); the same as **Tercel**; see **Tri-**.

Taste; see **Tangent**.

Tatter, a shred. (Scand.) Also spelt *totter*. ─ Icel. *töturr*; pl. *tötrar*, *töttrar*, rags, tatters; Norweg. *totror, tottrur,* also *taltrar,* pl. rags, tatters. + Low G. *taltern,* rags; *taltrig,* ragged. Thus *tatter* stands for *talter*; the *lt* became *tt* by the assimilation so common in Icelandic. I suppose the orig. sense was 'that which flaps or flutters about,' and that it is closely allied to *totter,* q. v.

Tattle, vb. (E.) M. E. *tatelen, totelen, tateren,* to tattle, prattle. We also find M. E. *titeren,* to tattle, whence mod. E. *tittle,* in the phrase *tittle-tattle.* *Tattle* and *tittle* are frequentative forms, from a base TAT or TIT, expressive of the iteration of the syllables *ta, ta, ta,* or *ti, ti, ti,* to indicate constant prattling. So also Du. *tateren,* to stammer, E. *taratantara,* the sound of a trumpet, Low G. *titetatein,* to tittle-tattle, *taat-goos,* a gabbling goose, a chatterer; Ital. *tattamella, chat,* prattle. Der. *tittle,* weakened form of *tattle,* as above; whence *tittle-tattle.*

titter, to giggle. (E.) The same as M. E. *titeren,* to prattle; from a repetition of the syllable *ti,* which was also used to indicate laughter, as in the word *te-hee* (in Chaucer). See also *twitter* and *twaddle.*

Tattoo (1), the beat of a drum recalling soldiers to their quarters. (Du. *or* Low G.) Formerly *taptoo* (Phillips); used as early as A. D. 1663. — Du. *taptoe,* tattoo. — Du. *tap,* a tap; *toe,* to, i. e. shut, closed. Due to the phrase appearing in Low G. *tappen to slaan,* lit. 'to strike a tap to,' a proverbial phrase (like E. *shut up*) signifying to close, conclude; esp. used of closing the taps of the public-houses, at the sound of the drum. So also G. *zapfenstreich,* the tattoo, is lit. 'tap-stroke;' and Low G. *tappenslag,* the tattoo, is lit. 'tap-shutting.' β. The Du. *tap* is cognate with E. *tap*; and Du. *toe* with E. *to,* prep. See Tap and To.

Tattoo (2), to mark the skin with figures, by pricking in colouring matter. (Tahitian.) See Cook's First Voyage, b. i. c. 17, b. iii. c. 9. — Tahitian *tatau,* tattoo-marks; derived from *ta,* a mark (Littré).

Taunt; see Tenable.

Taurus. (L.) L. *taurus,* a bull. — Gk. ταῦρος; A. S. *steór.* See Steer (1).

Taut; see Tight.

Tautology. (F. — Gk.) L. *tautologia.* — Gk. ταυτολογία, a repetition of what has been said already. — Gk. ταυτολόγος, repeating what has been said. — Gk. ταυτό, short for τὸ αὐτό or τὸ αὐτόν, the same thing; -λογος, speaking, from λέγειν, to speak.

Tavern. (F. — L.) F. *taverne.* — L. *taberna,* a hut, orig. a hut of boards; a tavern. Allied to L. *ta-bula,* a plank, board; see Table. (√ TA = TAN.)

tabernacle. (F. — L.) F. *tabernacle.* — L. *tabernaculum,* a tent; double dimin. of *taberna,* a booth.

Taw, Tew, to prepare skins, curry; also to toil. (E.) M. E. *tawen, tewan.* A. S. *tawian,* to prepare, dress, get ready; also, to scourge. Cf. A. S. *getawe,* implements. + Du. *touwen,* to curry leather; O. H. G. *sawjan,* to make, prepare; Goth. *taujan,* to do, cause. (Base TAU; from √ DU, to work; Max Müller, tr. of Rig-Veda, i. 63, 191.)

team, a family, set, animals harnessed in a row. (E.) M. E. *tem, teem.* A. S. *teám,* a family, offspring. + Du. *toom,* a rein (from the notion of reducing to order); Low G. *toom,* offspring, also a rein; Icel. *taumr,* a rein; Dan. *tömme,* Swed. *töm,* a rein; G. *zaum,* a bridle, from O. H. G. *zawjan,* to cause, prepare (above).

teem (1), to be prolific. (E.) M. E. *temen,* to teem, a verb formed from the sb. *tem,* progeny (above).

tool. (E.) M. E. *tol, tool.* A. S. *tól, tohl,* a tool. + Icel. *tól,* neut. pl. tools. Lit. an implement for working with; from Teut. base TU = √ DU, to work. Cf. Zend *du,* to do, work. See Taw above.

tow (2), coarse part of hemp. (E.) M. E. *tow.* A. S. *tow,* occuring in *tow-líc weorc,* material for spinning, lit. 'tow-like stuff,' and in *tow-hús,* a tow-house, house for spinning. Orig. the *operation,* not the *material*; cf. A. S. *getawa,* implements. Allied to A. S. *tawian,* to prepare, work; see Taw (above). + O. Du. *touw,* tow, *touwen,* to tan leather, *touwe,* a weaver's implement; Icel. *tó,* a tuft of wool for spinning.

Tawdry, showy, gaudy. (E.) Formerly used in the phrase *tawdry lace,* which meant lace bought at *St. Awdry's* fair, held in the Isle of Ely (and elsewhere) on St. Awdry's day, Oct. 17. *Tawdry* is a familiar contraction of *St. Awdry.* β. Again *Awdry* is a popular form of *Etheldrida,* the Latinised form of the A. S. female name *Æþeldryð* or *Æþelþryð.* It means 'noble strength;' from A. S. *æðel* or *æþel,* noble, and *þryð* or *þrýðu,* strength. Cf. Icel. *þrúðr,* the name of a goddess; and the suffix in *Ger-trude,* a name of O. H. G. origin.

Tawny; see Tan.

Tax; see Tangent.

Taxidermy; see Tactics.

Tea. (Chinese.) Spelt *tee* in Pepys' Diary, Sept. 28, 1660; *cha* in Blount (1674). From the Amoy pronunciation (*té*) of the Chinese name for the plant, which is (in other parts of the empire) called *ch'a* or *ts'a*; Williams, Chin. Dict. p. 5; Douglas, Chin. Dict. of the Amoy vernacular, p. 481. Hence Ital. *cia*, tea; F. *thé*, G. *thee*, Malay *téh*, tea.

Teach; see Token.

Teak, a tree. (Malayálam.) Malayálam *tékka*, the teak-tree; Tamil *tékku*, the same (H. H. Wilson).

Teal; see Till (1).

Team; see Taw.

Tear (1), to rend. (E.) M. E. *teren*. A.S. *teran*, pt. t. *tær*, pp. *toren*. ✛ Goth. *ga-tairan*, to break, destroy; Lith. *dir-ti*, to flay, Gk. δέρ-ειν, to flay; Russ. *dra-te*, to tear; Zend *dar*, to cut; Skt. *dṛi*, to burst. (√ DAR.) Cf. also G. *zehren* (weak verb).

tart (1), acrid, sharp, severe. (E.) A.S. *teart*, tart, severe; lit. tearing, i.e. bitter. − A. S. *tær*, pt. t. of *teran*, to tear.

tire (1), to exhaust. (E.) M. E. *tirien*, *teorien*. A.S. *teorian*, (1) to be tired, (2) to tire; weak verb, due to A.S. *teran*, to tear.

tire (4), to tear a prey, as is done by predatory birds. (E.) M.E. *tiren*, to tear a prey. A. S. *tirigan*, to provoke, vex, irritate; but orig. to tear. Derivative of A. S. *teran*, to tear. (See also Tarry.)

Tear (2), a drop of fluid from the eye. (E.) M. E. *tere*. A.S. *teár*, *tár*. ✛ Icel. *tár*, Dan. *taar*, *taare*, Swed. *tår*, Goth. *tagr*, O. H. G. *zahar* (pl. *zahere*, whence mod. G. *zähre*). ✛ O. Lat. *dacrima*, L. *lacrima*, Gk. δάκρυ, δάκρυμα, W. *dagr*, a tear. β. All from √ DAK, to bite, Gk. δάκ-νειν, Skt. *daç*, from the notion still preserved in the phrase *bitter* (i.e. *biting*) *tears*.

train-oil. (Du.; *and* F. − L. − Gk.) For *oil*, see Oil. Formerly *trane-oyle* or *trane*. − O. Du. *traen*, 'trayne-oyle made of the fat of whales; also a tear, liquor pressed out by the fire;' Hexham. The orig. sense is 'tear;' then drops forced out in boiling blubber, &c. Mod. Du. *traan*, a tear, G. *trähne*. The G. *trähne* is really a pl. form = M. H. G. *trähene*, pl. of *trahen*, a tear, closely allied to M. H. G. *zaher* (put for *taher**), a tear. Similarly, Du. *traan*

is allied to Dan. *taar*, a tear, and to E. *tear* (above).

Tease; see Touse.

Teasel; see Touse.

Teat, nipple of the female breast. (E.) Also *tit*. M. E. *tete*; also *tette*, *titte*. A.S. *tit*, a teat; pl. *tittas*. ✛ O. Du. *titte*; G. *zitze*. Cf. also F. *tette*, Span. *teta*, Ital. *tetta*, all of Teut. origin. Also W. *didi*, *did*, a teat. (As if from an Aryan base DI.) ¶ Distinct from W. *teth*, G. *tütte*, Gk. τίτθη, τιτθός, a teat, which appear to be allied to Skt. *dhe*, to suck, Goth. *daddjan*, to suckle.

Teazle, i.e. teasel; see Touse.

Technical. (Gk.) Formed with suffix -*al* (= L. -*alis*) from Gk. τεχνικός, belonging to the arts. − Gk. τέχνη, art, allied to **architect.** (F. − L. − Gk.) F. *architecte*. − L. *architectus*, the same as *architecton*. − Gk. ἀρχιτέκτων, a chief builder or artificer. − Gk. ἀρχι-, chief (see Archi-); τέκτων, a carpenter, builder. (See also Text.)

Ted, to spread mown grass. (Scand.) Icel. *teðja*, to spread manure; from *tað*, manure; cf. *taða*, hay grown in a well-manured field, *töðu-verk*, hay-making, lit. 'ted-work.' So also Norw. *tedja*, Swed. dial. *täda*, to spread manure; from *tad*, manure. ✛ Bavarian *zetten*, to strew; G. *ver-zetteln*, to scatter.

Tedious. (L.) L. *tædiosus*, irksome. − L. *tædium*, irksomeness. − L. *tædet*, it irks one. (We also use *tedium*, sb.)

Teem (1), to be prolific; see Taw.

Teem (2), to think fit. (E.) Rare, and obsolete. (E.) See *Teem* in Halliwell. Cf. the A. S. suffix -*týme*, -*téme*, fit, in *luf-téme*, love-befitting, pleasant, *wiðer-týme*, unbefitting. Related to Goth. *gatiman* (pt. t. *gatam*), to suit, agree with; and allied to E. Tame. Cf. G. *ziemen*, to be fit, *ziemlich*, passable; Du. *betamen*, to beseem, &c.

beteem. (E.) It means to think fit, hence to permit, to allow; Mids. Nt. Dr. i. 1. 131; Hamlet, i. 2. 141. From *teem* (above), with prefix *be-*.

Teem (3), to empty; see Toom.

Teen, vexation, grief. (E.) M. E. *tene*. A. S. *teóna*, accusation, vexation. − A. S. *teón*, contracted form of *tíhan*, to accuse. ✛ Goth. *gateihan*, to tell, make known; G. *zeihen*, to accuse; L. *dicare*, to make known. Allied to Diction. (√ DIK.) ¶ *Teen* means a making known, public accusation, reproach, injury, vexation, grief.

Teetotaller, a total abstainer. (F. – L.; *with* E. *prefix and suffix.*) *Tee-total* is an emphasised form of **Total,** q. v. The word originated with R. Turner, of Preston, who, at a temperance meeting about 1833, asserted that nothing but *te-te-total* will do; see the Staunch Teetotaller, ed. by J. Livesey, of Preston, Jan. 1867. (Haydn.)

Teetotum, Totum, a spinning toy. (L.) Formerly *totum* (Ash, 1775, Phillips, 1706). So called from the side formerly marked *T*, which signified *totum*, i. e. all the stake, from L. *totum*, neut. of *totus*, the whole; see **Total.** Hence the name *totum*, or *T- totum*.

Tegument, a covering. (L.) L. *tegumentum*, a covering. – L. *tegere,* to cover. +Gk. στέγειν, Skt. *sthag,* to cover. Allied to **Thatch.** (√ STAG.)

detect. (L.) From L. *detectus,* pp. of *de-tegere,* to uncover, expose.

integument. (L.) L. *integumentum,* a covering, skin. – L. *in,* upon; *tegere,* to cover.

protect. (L.) From L. *protectus,* pp. of *pro-tegere,* to protect; lit. cover in front.

tile. (L.) M. E. *tile,* contracted form of A. S. *tigele,* a tile. – L. *tegula,* a tile. – L. *tegere,* to cover.

toga. (L.) L. *toga,* a mantle, lit. covering. – L. *tegere,* to cover.

Teil-tree, a linden tree. (F. – L.; *and* E.) O. F. *teil,* the inner bark of a lime-tree (mod. F. *tille*). – L. *tilia,* a lime-tree; also, the inner bark of a lime-tree.

Telegraph. (Gk.) Modern. From Gk. τῆλε, afar; γράφειν, to write. **Der.** *tele-gram,* coined to express 'telegraphic message;' from γράμμα, a written character.

telescope. (Gk.) From Gk. τῆλε, afar; σκοπεῖν, to behold. See **Scope.**

Tell; see Tale.

Telluric, belonging to earth. (L.) From L. *telluri-,* crude form of *tellus,* earth. **Der.** *telluri-um,* a rare metal.

Temerity. (F. – L.) F. *temerité.* – L. acc. *temeritatem,* rashness. – L. *temerus**, rash, only found in the adv. *temere,* rashly. Orig. sense of *temere* was 'in the dark;' cf. Skt. *tamas,* gloom.

Temper, vb. (F. – L.) M. E. *tempren.* – F. *temperer,* to temper. – L. *temperare,* to apportion, regulate, qualify. Allied to *temperi, tempori,* adv., seasonably, and to *tempus,* time; see **Temporal.**

attemper. (F. – L.) O. F. *atemprer,* to modify. – O. F. *a* (= L. *ad*), to; *temprer, temperer,* to temper (above).

distemper (1), to derange the temperament of body or mind. (F. – L.) M. E. *distemperen.* – O. F. *destemprer,* to derange. – O. F. *des-* (= L. *dis-*), apart; *temprer* (mod. F. *tremper*), from L. *temperare.*

distemper (2), a kind of painting. (F. – L.) O. F. *destemprer,* later *destremper,* 'to soake, steepe, moisten, make fluid, liquid, or thin;' Cot. The same word as the above.

tamper, to meddle, practise upon. (F. – L.) The same word as *temper,* used actively, but in a bad sense; 'to influence in a bad way.'

Tempest; see Temporal.

Temple (1), a fane. (L.) A.S. *templ, tempel.* – L. *templum,* a temple. + Gk. τέμενος, a sacred enclosure, piece of ground cut off; allied to τέμνειν, to cut. (√TAM.) **Der.** *templ-ar,* Low L. *templarius.*

contemplate. (L.) From pp. of *contemplari,* to observe, consider, prob. used at first of augurs who frequented the temples. – L. *con-* (= *cum*); *templum,* a temple.

Temple (2), flat portion of the side of the head above the cheek-bone. (F. – L.) M. E. *templis,* pl. – O. F. *temples,* pl., the temples (mod. F. *tempes*). – L. *tempora,* pl., the temples. **Der.** *tempor-al,* adj., belonging to the temples.

Temporal (1), worldly, secular. (F. – L.) M. E. *temporal.* – O. F. *temporal, temporel,* adj. – L. *temporalis,* temporal. – L. *tempor-,* crude form of *tempus,* time.

contemporaneous. (L.) L. *contemporaneus,* adj., at the same time. – L. *con-* (*cum*), with; *tempor-,* stem of *tempus,* time.

contemporary. (L.) L. *con-,* with; and L. *temporarius,* temporary, adj., from *tempor-,* stem of *tempus,* time.

extempore. (L.) From L. *ex tempore,* at the moment. – L. *ex,* from, out of; *tempore,* abl. of *tempus,* time.

tempest. (F. – L.) O. F. *tempeste* (F. *tempête*), a storm; answering to a Low L. *tempesta,* fem. of Low L. *tempestus,* adj., which was used instead of L. *tempestas,* season, fit time, weather, also bad weather, storm. Allied to L. *tempus,* time (above).

tense (1), part of a verb, indicating time of action. (F. – L.) M. E. *temps,* Chaucer, C. T. 16343. – F. *temps,* time (also O. F. *tens*). – L. *tempus,* time, also a tense.

Temporal (2), belonging to the temples; see **Temple** (2).

Tempt; see **Tenable**.

Ten. (E.) A. S. *tén*, also *týn*, *teón*, ten. + Du. *tien*, Icel. *tíu*, Dan. *ti*, Swed. *tio*, Goth. *taihun*, G. *zehn*, L. *decem*, Gk. δέκα, Lith. *déssimtis*, Russ. *desiate*, W. *deg*, Irish and Gael. *deich*, Pers. *dah*, Skt. *daçan*. (Aryan DAKAN.)

tenth. (E.) M. E. *tenþe*, due to confusion of A. S. *teóða*, tenth, with Icel. *tíundi*, tenth; the true E. word is *tithe*.

tithe, a tenth part. (E.) M. E. *tithe*, also *tethe*. A. S. *teóða*, tenth; put for *teon-ða**, (*n* being lost) from A. S. *teón* or *týn*, ten.

Tenable, that can be held. (F.–L.) F. *tenable*, 'holdable,' Cot.–F. *tenir*, to hold. –L. *tenere*, to hold, keep; orig. to extend. +Skt. *tan*, to extend, stretch. (√ TAN.)

abstain. (F.–L.) O. F. *abstener* (F. *abstiner*).–L. *abstinere*, to refrain from. – L. *abs*, from ; *tenere*, to hold. Der. *abstinence*, F. *abstinence*, from L. *abstinentia*, sb.

appertain. (F.–L.) O. F. *apartenir* (F. *appartenir*), to belong to.–F. *a* (=L. *ad*), to; *pertinere*, to belong; see **pertain** (below).

appurtenance. (F.–L.) O. F. *apurtenaunce*, *apartenance*, that which belongs to.–O. F. *apartenir*, to belong to (above).

attempt. (F.–L.) O. F. *atempter*, to undertake.–L. *attentare*, to attempt.– L. *at*- (for *ad*), to; *tentare*, to try; see **tempt** (below).

contain. (F.–L.) O. F. *contenir*.– L. *con-tinere*, to hold together, contain; pp. *contentus*.

content, adj. (F.–L.) F. *content*, satisfied. – L. *contentus*, content; pp. of *continere* (above). Der. *dis-content*.

continent. (F.–L.) F. *continent*, adj., moderate. – L. *continent*-, stem of pres. pt. of *continere*; see **contain** (above).

continue. (F.–L.) F. *continuer*. – L. *continuare*, to continue. – L. *continuus* (below). Der. *dis-continue*.

continuous. (L.) L. *continuus*, lit. holding together. – L. *con-tinere*, to hold together, contain.

countenance. (F.–L.) O. F. *contenance*, gesture, demeanour; also look, visage. – L. *continentia*, continence, which in late L. meant 'gesture, demeanour.'– L. *continent*-, stem of pres. pt. of *continere*; see **continent** (above). Der. *dis-countenance*, vb.

countertenor. (F.–Ital.–L.) O. F. *contreteneur*; Cot. – Ital. *contratenore*, a countertenor, the highest adult male voice. –Ital. *contra*, against, over against; *tenore*, a tenor; see **tenor** (below).

detain. (F.–L.) O. F. *detenir*. –L. *de-tinere*, to hold back; pp. *detentus*. Der. *detent-ion* (from the pp.).

entertain. (F.–L.) O. F. *entretenir*. –Low L. *inter-tenere*, to entertain, lit. 'to hold or keep among.'

impertinent, not pertinent. (F.–L.) From F. *im-*=L. *im-* (for *in-*), not; and *pertinent* (below).

obtain. (F.–L.) F. *obtenir*. – L. *obtinere*, to hold, obtain. – L. *ob*, near; *tenere*, to hold.

pertain. (F.–L.) M. E. *partenen*. – O. F. *partenir*. – L. *per-tinere*, to extend through to, belong.

pertinacity. (F.–L.) F. *pertinacité* (16th cent.). Coined, with suffix -*té*=L. -*tatem*, from L. *pertinaci*-, crude form of *pertinax*, very tenacious. – L. *per*, thorough; *tenax*, tenacious, from *tenere*, to hold.

pertinent. (F.–L.) F. *pertinent*.– L. *pertinent*-, stem of pres. pt. of *pertinere*, to belong to, relate to; see **pertain** (above).

purtenance. (F.–L.) Short for M. E. *apurtenance*; see **appurtenance** (above).

rein. (F.–L.) M. E. *reine*.–O. F. *reine*, rein of a bridle. (The same as Ital. *redina*, Span. *rienda*, transposed form of *redina*.)–Low L. *retina**, not found, but easily coined from L. *retinere*, to hold back (whence L. *retinaculum*, a rein). See below.

retain. (F.–L.) F. *retenir*.–L. *retinere*, to hold back; pp. *retentus*. Der. *retent-ion* (from the pp.).

retinue. (F.–L.) M. E. *retenue*.– O. F. *retenue*, a body of retainers; fem. of *retenu*, pp. of *retenir* (above).

sustain. (F.–L.) M. E. *susteinen*.– O. F. *sustenir*, *sostenir* (F. *soutenir*).–L. *sustinere*, to uphold.–L. *sus*- (for *subs*-), up; *tenere*, to hold. Der. *sustenance*, O. F. *sustenance*, L. *sustinentia*, sb. ; *sustentation*, from L. *sustentatio*, maintenance, from *sustentare*, frequentative of *sustinere*.

taunt, vb. (F.–L.) O. F. *tanter*, occasional form of *tenter*, 'to tempt, prove, essay, suggest, provoke, or move unto evill ;' Cot. – L. *tentare*, to try, prove, attack, assail, &c. ; see **tempt** (below).

¶ The meaning seems to have been affected

by F. *tancer* (formerly also *tencer*), to check, taunt, reprove; this is closely allied, being equivalent to a Low L. form *tenti-are**, due to *tentum*, supine of *tenere*.

tempt. (F.–L.) O. F. *tempter*, later *tenter*, to tempt, prove. – L. *temptare*, *tentare*, to handle, try the strength of, assail, tempt; frequentative of *tenere* (pp. *tentus*), to hold.

tenacious. (L.) Coined from L. *tenaci-*, crude form of *tenax*, holding fast. – L. *tenere*, to hold.

tenacity. (F.–L.) F. *tenacité.* – L. *tenacitatem*, acc. of *tenacitas*, a holding firm. – L. *tenaci-* (above).

tenant. (F.–L.) F. *tenant*, holding, pres. pt. of *tenir*. – L. *tenere*, to hold. Der. *lieu-tenant*, q. v.

tenement, a holding. (F.–L.) F. *tenement.* – Low L. *tenementum*, a fief. – L. *tenere*, to hold.

tenet. (L.) L. *tenet*, he holds; 3rd pers. sing. pres. of *tenere*. (Cf. *habitat*, *exit*.)

tenon. (F.–L.) F. *tenon*, ‘a tenon, the end of a rafter put into a morteise;’ Cot. So called because it *holds fast*. – F. *tenir*, to hold fast. – L. *tenere*, to hold.

tenor. (F. – L.) Formerly (better) *tenour*. M. F. *tenour*, import. – F. *teneur*, import, content of a matter. – L. *tenorem*, acc. of *tenor*, a holding on; a course, tenor of a law. – L. *tenere*, to hold. ¶ The sense of *tenor* in music (Ital. *tenore*) is due to the notion of holding or continuing the dominant note (Scheler).

tent (2), a roll of lint used to dilate a wound. (F.–L.) M. E. *tente.* – F. *tente*; Cot. A verbal sb from F. *tenter* = L. *tentare*, to try, prove, probe. Cf. Span. *tienta*, a probe. See **tempt** (above).

tentacle, feeler of an insect. (L.) Coined from L. *tenta-re*, to feel; with suffix *-cu-lum*; see **tempt** (above).

tentative. (L.) L. *tentatiuus*, adj., trying, tentative. – L. *tentare*, to try; see **tempt** (above).

tenure. (F.–L.) F. *tenure.* – Low L. *tenura*, a holding (of land). – L. *tenere*, to hold. See also **Tend**, **Lieutenant**, **Maintain**.

Tenacious, Tenant; see **Tenable**.

Tench, a fish. (F.–L.) O. F. *tenche* (F. *tanche*). – L. *tinca*, a tench. Prob. ‘nibbler;’ cf. *tinea*, a moth.

Tend (1), to aim at, move towards, incline, bend to. (F.–L.) F. *tendre.* – L. *tendere*, to stretch, extend, direct, tender.

Allied to *tenere*, to hold; see **Tenable**. (✓ TAN.) Der. *tend-enc-y*, formed by adding *-y* to the obsolete sb. *tendence*, coined from the stem of the pres. part.

attend. (F. – L.) O. F. *atendre*, to wait. – L. *attendere* (pp. *attentus*), to stretch towards, give heed to. – L. *at-* (for *ad*), to; *tendere*, to stretch. Der. *attention* (from the pp.); *attent*, adj., 2 Chron. vi. 40, vii. 15.

contend. (F.–L.) F. *contendre.* – L. *con-tendere*, to stretch out, exert, fight. Der. *content-ion* (from the pp.).

distend. (L.) L. *dis-tendere*, to stretch apart. Der. *distent-ion* (from the pp.).

extend. (L.) M. E. *extenden.* – L. *ex-tendere*, to stretch out; pp. *extensus*. Der. *extens-ion*, *-ive* (from the pp.); also *ex-tent*, sb. (as if from a pp. *extentus*).

intend. (F. – L.) M. E. *entenden.* – F. *entendre.* – L. *in-tendere*, to stretch to, bend or apply the mind to, design.

intense. (L.) L. *intensus*, stretched out, pp. of *intendere* (above).

intent, design. (F.–L.) M. E. *entente.* – F. *entente*, intention; participial sb. from F. *entendre*, to intend; see **intend** (above).

intent, adj. (L.) L. *intentus*, bent on; pp. of *intendere*; see **intend** (above).

ostensible. (L.) Coined from *ostensi-* = *ostenso-*, crude form of *ostensus*, pp. of *ostendere*, to shew; with suffix *-bilis*. See below.

ostentation. (F.–L.) F. *ostentation.* – L. *ostentationem*, acc. of *ostentatio*, display. – L. *ostentatus*, pp. of *ostentare*, intensive form of *ostendere*, to shew, lit. stretch before. – L. *os-* (for *ob-s-*, lengthened from *ob*), near, before; *tendere*, to stretch.

portend. (L.) L. *portendere*, to predict; lit. to stretch out towards, point out. – L. *por-* (O. Lat. *port-*), towards; *tendere*, to stretch. Der. *portent*, O. F. *portent*, L. *portentum*, neut. of pp. of *portendere*.

pretend. (F.–L.) O. F. *pretendre.* – L. *præ-tendere*, to spread before, hold out as an excuse, allege, pretend. Der. *pretence*, misspelt for *pretense*, from late L. *prætensus*, used for L. *prætentus*, pp. of *prætendere*.

subtend. (L.) L. *sub-tendere*, to stretch or extend beneath.

superintendent, an overseer. (F.– L.) F. *superintendant*; Cot. – L. *superin-dent-*, stem of pres. pt. of *super-intendere*, to superintend. – L. *super*, above; *inten-*

dere, to apply the mind to; see **intend** (above).

tend (2), to take care of. (F.‒L.) A docked form of **attend** (above).

tender (2), to proffer, offer, shew. (F.‒ L.) F. *tendre*, ' to tend, .. also to tender or offer unto ;' Cot.‒L. *tendere*, to stretch out.

tender (3), a small vessel that attends a larger, a coal-carriage attached to a loco- motive engine. (F.‒L.) Short for *attend- er*, i. e. attendant on ; see **attend** (above).

tendon. (F.‒L.) F. *tendon*, ' a ten- don, or taile of a muscle;' Cot. From a Low L. form *tendo**, gen. *tendonis* and *tendinis* ; cf. Span. *tendon*, Ital. *tendine*, a tendon. Lit. ' stretcher.' ‒ L. *tendere*, to stretch.

tense (2), tightly strained. (L.) L. *tensus*, pp. of *tendere*, to stretch. Der. *tense-ness*, with E. suffix.

tension, the act of straining, a strain. (F.‒L.) F. *tension*, used in 16th cent. ‒L. *tensionem*, acc. of *tensio*, a stretching. ‒L. *tens-um*, supine of *tendere*. So also *tens-or*, a coined word.

tent (1), a pavilion. (F.‒L.) F. *tente*. ‒Low L. *tenta*, a tent; fem. of L. *tentus*, pp. of *tendere*, to stretch, spread out.

tent (4), heed, attention. (F. ‒ L.) Lowl. Sc. *take tent*. Short for *attent*, i.e. *attention*.

tenter, a frame for stretching cloth. (F.‒L.) Properly *tenture*; but a vb. *tent* was coined, and from it a sb. *tenter*, which supplanted M. E. *tenture*.‒F. *tenture*, a stretching.‒L. *tentura*, a stretching.‒L. *tentus*, pp. of *tendere*, to stretch. Der. *tenter-hook*.

toise, a measure, 6 ft. 4½ in. (F.‒L.) F. *toise*, ' a fadome ;' Cot.‒L. *tensa*, fem. of *tensus*, pp. of *tendere*, to stretch (reach).

Tend (2) ; see **Tend** (1).

Tender (1), soft, delicate. (F.‒L.) F. *tendre*.‒L. *tenerum*, acc. of *tener*, tender, orig. thin ; allied to *tenuis*, thin. (√ TAN.) Der. *tender*, vb., to regard fondly, a word more or less confused with *tender* (2); whence *tender*, sb., regard, care, K. Lear, i. 4. 230.

tendril. (F.‒L.) From O. F. *tendril- lons*, pl. ' tendrells ;' Cot. ; or from an O. F. *tendrille**, not recorded. We also find O. F. *tendron*, ' a tender fellow, also a tendrell ;' Cot.‒F. *tendre*, tender (above).

Tender (2), to offer; see **Tend** (1).

Tender (3), a small vessel, &c., **Ten- don** ; see **Tend** (1).

Tendril; see **Tender** (1).

Tenebrous, Tenebrious, gloomy. (F. ‒ L.) F. *tenebreux*. ‒ L. *tenebrosus*, gloomy.‒L. *tenebræ*, pl., darkness. Allied to Skt. *tamas*, gloom. . (√ TAM.) See **Dim**.

Tenement, Tenet; see **Tenable**.

Tennis. (F.‒L.?) Etymology practi- cally unknown. M. E. *tenise* (accented on *i*); Gower, Balade to Henry IV., st. 63 ; also *teneis, teneys*. Low L. *tenisia, teniludium*. I suspect a derivation from O. F. *tenies*, pl. of *tenie*, ' a fillet, head-band ; . . also a kind of brow or juttying [projection] on a pillar;' Cot. This O. F. *tenie*=L. *tænia* (Gk. ταινία), a band, fillet. Perhaps from the band across the court. ¶ Usually derived from F. *tenez* (= L. *tenete*), *imagined* to mean ' take this,' and to be ejaculated by the player in serving ; a pure guess, like the one above.

Tenon, Tenor; see **Tenable**.

Tense (1), part of a verb ; see **Tem- poral** (1).

Tense (2), tightly strained ; see **Tend** (1).

Tent (1), a pavilion; see **Tend** (1).

Tent (2), roll of lint ; see **Tenable**.

Tent (3), a wine ; see **Tinge**.

Tent (4), care, heed ; see **Tend** (1).

Tentacle, Tentative; see **Tenable**.

Tenter ; see **Tend** (1).

Tenuity, thinness. (F.‒L.) F. *tenuité*. ‒L. *tenuitatem*, acc. of *tenuitas*, thinness. ‒L. *tenui-s*, thin ; lit. ' stretched out.' Allied to **Thin**. (√ TAN.)

attenuate. (L.) From pp. of L. *atten- uare*, to make thin.‒L. *at-* (for *ad*), to; *tenu-is*, thin.

extenuate. (L.) From pp. of.L. *ex- tenuare*, to thin, reduce, palliate.‒L. *ex* ; out, very ; *tenu-is*, thin.

Tenure ; see **Tenable**.

Tepid. (L.) L. *tepidus*, warm. ‒ L. *tepere*, to be warm.+Skt. *tap*, to be warm, Russ. *topite*, to heat. (√ TAP.)

Teraphim, idols, household gods. (Heb.) Heb. *teráphím*, s. pl., images connected with magical rites.

Terce, the same as **Tierce**; see **Tri-**.

Tercel, Tassel, the male of any hawk; see **Tri-**.

Terebinth, turpentine-tree. (L.‒Gk.) L. *terebinthus*.‒Gk. τερέβινθος, the turpen- tine-tree.

turpentine, exudation from the tere- binth. (F.‒L.‒Gk.) F. *turbentine* ; Cot. ‒L. *terebinthus* (above).

Tergiversation, a subterfuge, fickleness. (F.—L.) F. *tergiversation.*—L. *tergiuersationem*, acc. of *tergiuersatio*, a subterfuge.—L. *tergiuersatus*, pp. of *tergiuersari*, to turn one's back, turn right round, shuffle.—L. *tergi-*, for crude form of *tergum*, the back; and *uersari*, to turn about, pass. of *uersare*, frequent. of *uertere*, to turn; see **Verse.**

Term. (F.—L.) M. E. *terme.*—F. *terme.* —L. *terminum*, acc. of *terminus*, boundary, limit. +Gk. τέρμα, limit; Skt. *trí*, to pass over. (√ TAR.)

determine. (F.—L.) O. F. *determiner.* —L. *determinare*, to bound, end.—L. *de*, down, fully; *terminare*, to bound, from *terminus* (above). Der. *pre-determine.*

exterminate. (L.) From pp. of L. *exterminare*, to put or drive beyond bounds. —L. *ex*, out; *terminus*, boundary.

termination. (F. — L.) F. *termination.*—L. acc. *terminationem*, a bounding, ending.—L. *terminatus*, pp. of *terminare*, to bound, end.—L. *terminus*, boundary.

terminus, end. (L.) L. *terminus* (above).

Termagant. (F. — Ital. — L.) M.E. *Termagant*, a (supposed) Saracen idol, hence a ranting character in old moralities [plays], and finally a scolding woman.—O. F. *Tervagant, Tervagan*, a (supposed) Saracen idol.—Ital. *Trivigante*, the same (Ariosto, xii. 59). Probably for *Trivagante*, the moon, wandering under the three names of *Selene* (or *Luna*) in heaven, *Artemis* (*Diana*) in earth, *Persephone* (*Proserpina*) in the lower world.—L. *ter*, thrice; *uagant-*, stem of pres. pt. of *uagari*, to wander.

Termination, Terminus; see **Term.**

Tern, a bird. (Scand.) Dan. *terne*, *tærne*, Swed. *tärna*, Icel. *þerna*, a tern.

Ternary; see **Tri-.**

Terrace. (F. — Ital. — L.) F. *terrace*, *terrasse*, a terrace, platform, plat. — Ital. *terraccia, terrazza*, a terrace, long mound of earth.—Ital. *terra*, earth.—L. *terra*, earth. β. *Terra = tersa* *, i. e. dry ground; allied to Gk. τέρσεσθαι, to dry up. (√ TARS.)

inter. (F. — L.) M.E. *enterren.* — F. *enterrer*, to bury.—Low L. *interrare*, to put into the ground. — L. *in*, in; *terra*, ground. Der. *inter-ment*, F. *enterrement.*

parterre. (F.—L.) F. *parterre*, an even piece of garden-ground. — F. *par terre*, along the ground.—L. *per terram*, along the ground.

subterranean, subterraneous. (L.)

From L. *subterraneus*, underground.—L. *sub*, under; *terra*, ground.

terreen, tureen, a large bowl for soup. (F.—L.) Both spellings are bad; *terrine* would be better.—F. *terrine*, an earthen pan.—L. *terr-a*, earth; with suffix *-inus.*

terrene, earthly. (L.) L. *terrenus*, earthly.—L. *terra*, earth.

terrestrial. (L.) From L. *terrestri-s*, earthly; with suffix *-alis.* Put for *terrens-tris* *; from *terra*, earth.

terrier (1), a kind of dog. (F.—L.) M. E. *terrere*, a 'burrow-dog,' one who pursues rabbits, &c. at their holes.—F. *terrier*, 'the hole, berry, or earth of a conny [rabbit] or fox; also, a little hillock;' Cot.—Low L. *terrarium*, a little hillock, mound (burrow).—L. *terra*, earth.

terrier (2), a register of landed property. (F.—L.) F. *papier terrier*, a roll of tenants' names, &c.—Low L. *terrarius*, as in *terrarius liber*, a book wherein landed property is described.—L. *terra*, land.

territory, domain. (F.—L.) F. *territoire*, a territory. — L. *territorium*, a domain, land round a town. — L. *terra*, land; formed as if from a sb. with crude form *territori-*, i. e. possessor of land.

tureen, the same as **torreon** (above). And see **turmeric.**

Terreen, Terrene, Terrestrial; see **Terrace.**

Terrible; see **Terror.**

Terrier (1) and (2); see **Terrace.**

Terrific; see **Terror.**

Territory; see **Terrace.**

Terror, dread. (F.—L.) Formerly also *terrour.*—F. *terreur.*—L. *terrorem*, acc. of *terror*, dread.—L. *terrere*, to scare, make afraid, orig. to tremble. Cf. Skt. *tras*, to tremble, be afraid; Lith. *triszēti*, to tremble, Russ. *triasti*, to shiver.

deter. (L.) L. *deterrere*, to frighten from.—L. *de*, from; *terrere*, to frighten. Der. *deterr-ent.*

terrible. (F. — L.) F. *terrible.* — L. *terribilis*, causing terror.—L. *terrere*, to frighten.

terrific. (L.) L. *terrificus*, causing terror.—L. *terri-*, in *terri-tus*, pp. of *terrere*, to frighten; *-ficus*, causing, from *facere*, to make.

Terse, concise, neat. (L.) L. *tersus*, wiped off, clean, neat, pure, nice, terse; pp. of *tergere*, to wipe, wipe dry, polish a stone.

Tertian, Tertiary; see **Tri-.**

Tesselated. (L.) L. *tessellatus*, checkered, furnished with small square stones (as a pavement). — L. *tessella*, a small square piece of stone, little cube; dimin. of *tessera*, a die (to play with), small cube. ¶ Root uncertain; *not* from Gk. τέσσαρες, four.

Test, a pot in which metals are tried, a trial, proof. (F. — L.) M. E. *test*, a pot or vessel used in alchemy. — O. F. *test* (F. *têt*), a test, in chemistry; answering to a Low L. *testum**, not found. Closely allied to O. F. *teste* (F. *tête*), a pot-sherd, a skull, answering to Low L. *testa*, a vessel used in alchemy. So also Ital. *testo*, a test, melting-pot, *testa*, an earthen pot, pot-sherd, skull, head, burnt tile or brick. All due to L. *testa*, a piece of baked earthenware, potsherd, shell, skull. *Testa = tersta**, i. e. dried, baked, allied to *terra* (= *tersa**), dry ground; from √TARS, to dry.

testaceous, having a hard shell. (L.) L. *testaceus*, having a shell. — L. *testa*, tile, shell, &c.

tester, a sixpence; flat canopy over a bed or pulpit. (F. — L.) Mod. E. *tizzie*, a sixpence; the *tester*, *testern*, or *testoon* was named from the head upon it (of Louis XII of France); in England *all* coins bore the head, so that our use of the term was borrowed. — F. *teston*, 'a testoon, piece of silver worth xviij*d*. sterling;' Cot. — O. F. *teste*, a head. — L. *testa*, tile, skull. ¶ So also a *tester* for a bed is from O. F. *testiere*, 'a head-piece,' Cot.; from O. F. *teste* (as before).

testy, fretful. (F. — L.) F. *testu*, 'heady;' Cot. — O. F. *teste*, the head; see **tester** (above).

Testament. (F. — L.) F. *testament*, a will. — L. *testamentum*, a will. — L. *testa-ri*, to be a witness. — L. *testis*, a witness. Der. *in-testate*, i. e. without a will; *testa-tor*, one who makes a will, fem. *testa-trix*.

attest. (L.) L. *attestari*, to be witness to. — L. *at-* (= *ad*), to; *testari*, to be witness (above).

contest, vb. (F. — L.) F. *contester*. — L. *contestari*, to call to witness; hence, to argue, &c. — L. *con-* (*cum*), together; *testari*, to witness. Der. *contest*, sb.

detest. (F. — L.) O. F. *detester*, to loathe. — L. *detestari*, to execrate, imprecate evil by calling down the gods to witness. — L. *de*, down; *testari*, to witness (above).

intestate, without a will. (L.) L. *in-*testatus, that has made no will. — L. *in*, not; *testatus*, pp. of *testari*, to make a will.

protest. (F. — L.) F. *protester*. — L. *protestari*, to protest, bear public witness. — L. *pro*, forth, in public; *testari*, to witness (above).

testify. (F. — L.) F. *testifier*. — L. *testificari*, to bear witness. — L. *testi-s*, a witness; *-ficari*, for *facere*, to make.

testimony. (L.) L. *testimonium*, evidence. — L. *testi-s*, a witness; with Aryan suffixes *-man-ya*.

Tester; see **Test**.

Testicle. (F. — L.) F. *testicule*. — L. *testiculum*, acc. of *testiculus*, dimin. of *testis*, a testicle. Prob. considered as a witness of manhood, and the same word as *testis*, a witness.

Testify, Testimony; see **Testament**.

Testy; see **Test**.

Tetchy, Techy, touchy; see **Tack**.

Tether, a rope for fastening up. (C.) Formerly written *tedder*. M. E. *tedir*. — Gael. *teadhair*, a tether; *taod*, a halter, hair rope, chain, cable; *taodan*, little cord; Irish *tead*, *teud*, cord, rope, *teidin*, small rope, cord; W. *tid*, a chain; Manx *tead*, *teid*, a rope. Cf. W. *tedu*, to stretch; Skt. *tantu*, a thread, from *tan*, to stretch. (√TA?) β. We find also Icel. *tjöðr*, a tether, Low G. *tider*, Swed. *tjuder*, Dan. *töir*, prob. all of Celtic origin.

Tetragon, a figure with four angles. (F. — L. — Gk.) F. *tetragone*, adj., four-cornered. — L. *tetragonus*, adj. — Gk. τετρά-γωνος, four-cornered. — Gk. τέτρα- (for τέτραρα-), prefix allied to τέτταρες, Attic form of τέσσαρες, four, cognate with E. Four; and γωνία, an angle, from γόνυ, a knee, cognate with E. Knee. Der.

tetrahedron, a solid figure contained by four equilateral triangles. (Gk.) Gk. τέτρα- (as above); ἔδρον, from ἔδρα, a base, which from ἔδ-ειν, to sit; see **Sit**.

tetrarch; see **Arch-**, *prefix*.

tetrasyllable, a word of four syllables. (F. — L. — Gk.) Coined from Gk. τέτρα-, four (as above); and συλλαβή, a syllable. Cf. F. *tetrasyllabe*, L. *tetrasyllabus*, Gk. τετρασύλλαβος, of four syllables.

trapezium, an irregular four-sided figure. (L. — Gk.) L. *trapezium*. — Gk. τραπέζιον, a small table, also a trapezium. Dimin. of τράπεζα, a table, shortened form of τετρα-πέζα*, i. e. a four-footed bench. — Gk. τέτρα-, four (see **Tetragon**); πέζα, foot, allied to πούς (stem ποδ-), a foot; see **Foot**. Der. *trapeze*, F. *trapèze*, a swing in the shape of a trapezium, as thus: △. From L. *trapezium*, (above).

Tetter, a cutaneous disease. (E.) M. E. *teter*. A.S. *teter*, a kind of itch. Cf. G. *zittermal*, a tetter. Allied to Icel. *titra*, G. *zittern*, to tremble (with the notion of rapid rubbing). β. Perhaps further allied to Bret. *daroueden*, W. *tarwden* (whence F. *dartre*), Skt. *dadru*, a tetter.

Teutonic. (L. – Gothic.) L. *Teutonicus*, adj., from *Teutones*, s. pl., the Teutons, a people of Germany; lit. 'men of the nation,' or 'the people.' – Goth. *thiuda*, a people, nation (or from a dialectal variant of this word). See **Dutch**.

Text. (F. – L.) M. E. *texte*. – F. *texte*, a text, subject of a book. – L. *textum*, a thing woven, fabric, style of an author, text of a book. – L. *textus*, woven, pp. of *texere*, to weave. + Skt. *taksh*, to cut wood, to prepare. Further allied to **Tactics**. (√ TAK.)

context. (L.) L. *contextus*, a joining together, order (hence, context of a book). – L. *con-* (*cum*), together; *textus*, pp. of *texere*, to weave.

pretext. (F. – L.) O.F. *pretexte*, a pretext. – L. *prætextum*, a pretext; orig.

neut. of *prætextus*, pp. of *præ-texere*, lit. to weave in front.

subtle. (F. – L.) Formerly *sotil, sotel*; the *b* was a later insertion, and is never sounded. – O. F. *sotil, soutil*, later *subtil*. – L. *subtilem*, acc. of *subtilis*, fine, thin, accurate, subtle. The orig. sense of *subtilis* was 'finely woven;' from L. *sub*, under, closely, and *tela*, a web, for which see **toil** (2) below. Der. *subtle-ty*, M. E. *soteltee*, from O. F. *sotilleté*, subtlety, from L. acc. *subtilitatem*.

textile. (L.) L. *textilis*, woven. – L. *textus*, pp. of *texere*, to weave.

texture. (F. – L.) F. *texture*, 'a texture, web;' Cot. – L. *textura*, a web. – L. *textus*, pp. of *texere*, to weave.

tissue. (F. – L.) F. *tissu*, 'a ribbon, fillet, or headband of woven stuffe;' Cot. Also *tissu*, masc., *tissue*, fem., woven; old pp. of *tistre* (mod. F. *tisser*), to weave. – L. *texere*, to weave.

toil (2), a net, snare. (F. – L.) F. *toile*, cloth; pl. *toiles*, toils, snares for wild beasts. – L. *tela*, a web, thing woven; put for *tex-la* *, from *texere*, to weave.

toilet, toilette. (F. – L.) F. *toilette*, 'a toylet, the stuff which drapers lap about their cloths, a bag to put nightgowns in;' Cot. – F. *toile*, a cloth (above).

TH.

Th. This is distinct from *t*, and should have a distinct symbol. Formerly, the A. S. þ and ð were used (but indiscriminately) to denote *both* the sounds now denoted by *th*. When þ degenerated into a symbol closely resembling *y*, *y* was at last substituted for it; hence we find *yᵉ* and *yᵗ* used, by early printers, for *the, that*; it is needless (I hope) to remark that *yᵉ man* was never *pronounced* as *ye man* in the middle ages.

I here use ð for A. S. words, and ð or *th* for M. E. words, beginning with the sound of *th* in *that*; and þ for A. S. and M. E. words beginning with the sound of *th* in *thin*. Observe these facts. (1) Initial *th* is always pronounced as in *thin* except (*a*) in words allied to *that*; and (*b*) in words allied to *thou*. (2) In the middle of a word, it is pronounced as *th* in *thin*, except when *e* follows; compare *breath* with *breathe*; an exception is *smooth*. (3) No word beginning with *th* (except *thurible*,

formed on a *Greek* base) is of *Latin* origin; some (easily known) are *Greek*; *thummim* is *Hebrew*; all the rest are *English*.

Than; see **That**.

Thane; see **Thee** (2).

Thank; see **Think**.

That. (E.) M. E. *that*. A.S. *ðæt*, orig. neuter of a demonstrative pronoun, also used as neuter of the definite article. The corresponding masc. form is *ðe*, but this is rarely used, *se* being commonly used instead. We thus have A. S. masc. *ðe*, fem. *ðeó*, neut. *ðæt*, from the Teut. pronominal base THA = Aryan TA, meaning 'he' or 'that.' The suffix -*t* is merely the sign of the neut. gender, like Lat. -*d* in *i-d, illu-d, istu-d, qui-d.* β. The full declension is as follows. SING. NOM. *ðe, ðeó, ðæt* [usually replaced by *se, seó, ðæt*]; GEN. *ðæs, ðære, ðæs*; DAT. *ðám, ðære, ðám*; ACC. *ðone, ðá, ðæt*; INSTRUMENTAL (for all genders) *ðý*. PLURAL: NOM. AND ACC. *ðá*; GEN. *ðæra*; DAT. *ðám.* + Du. *de*, the, *dat*, that;

Icel. *þat*, the; Dan. *den*, neut. *det*, the; Swed. *den*, neut. *det*, this.; G. *der*, *die*, *das*, the, *dass*, that; Goth. *thata*, neut. of def. article.+Lith. *tas*, *ta*, that; Russ. *tote*, *ta*, *to*, that; Gk. *τό*, neut. of def. art.; Skt. *tat*, it, that; L. *-te*, *-ta*, *-tud* (in *is-te*, *is-ta*, *is-tud*).

than, conj. (E.) Frequently written *then*, and orig. the same word as *then*. M. E. *thanne*, *thonne*. A. S. *ðonne*, than. Closely allied to A. S. *ðone*, acc. masc. of the def. art.; see **That**, § β.+Du. *dan*; G. *dann*, *denn*. Cf. L. *tum*.

the (1), def. art. (E.) M. E. *the*. A. S. *ðe*, rarely used as nom. masc. of def. art., but common as an indeclinable relative; see **That**, § β.

the (2), in what (or that) degree. (E.) Only in such phrases as '*the* more, *the* merrier.' This is the *instrumental case* of the def. art. M. E. *the*; A. S. *ðý*; see **That**, § β.+Goth. *the*, Icel. *því*, *þí*, inst. case of art. or dem. pronoun.

their, belonging to them. (Scand.) M. E. *thair*.—Icel. *þeirra*, of them, used as gen. pl. of *hann*, he, but really the gen. pl. of the def. article, as shewn by A. S. *þára*; see **That**, § β.

them, objective case of *they*. (Scand.) Really an old dat. case.—Icel. *þeim*, dat. of *þeir*, they; see **they** (below).+A. S. *þám*, dat. pl. of def. art.; see **That**, § β.

then. (E.) Frequently written *than* in old books, and originally identical with it; see **than** (above).

thence. (E.) M. E. *thennes* (dissyllabic); whence *thens*, by contraction, later written *thence*. The *s* is an adverbial suffix; earlier forms were *thenne*, *thanne*, in which a final *n* has been lost.—A. S. *ðanan*, thence; formed from base *ða-* with the repeated suffix *-na-na*. The base *ða* = Teut. base THA; see **That**.+G. *dannen*, thence; from base *da-*.

there (1), in that place. (E.) M. E. *ther*, *thar*. A. S. *ðær*, *ðer*. The suffix *-r* seems to be due to a locative case of the Aryan suffix *-ra*, as in Skt. *upa-ri*, Gk. *ὑπέ-ρ*. The base is Teut. base THA; see **That**.+Du. *daar*, Icel. *þar*, Dan. Swed. *der*, Goth. *thar*, G. *da*. Compare **Here**, **Where**.

there-, *only as a prefix*. (E.) In *thereby*, *there-in*, *there-of*, &c. Here *there-* answers to A. S. *ðære*, dat. fem. of def. art.; hence *there-fore* = A. S. *fore ðære*, i. e. because of the thing or reason, where some

fem. sb. is understood. Hence the word compounded with *there-* is *always à preposition*; as, for instance, *-after*, *-at*, *-by*, *-from*, *-in*, *-of*, *-on*, *-to*, *-unto*, *-upon*, *-with*.

these. (E.) Orig. the same word as *those*, of which it was, at first, only a dialectal variant. See **those** (below).

they. (Scand.) Chiefly in the Northern dialect; M. E. *thai* (gen. *thair*, dat. and acc. *thaim*, *tham*). This usage is Scand., not E., as in A. S. these words are only used as pl. of def. art.—Icel. *þeir*, nom. pl., they; *þeirra*, gen. pl., their; *þeim*, dat. pl., them. So also Dan. Swed. *de*, they, *dem*, them; Dan. *deres*, Swed. *deras*, their, theirs.+A. S. *þá*, nom. pl. of def. art.; gen. *þára*; dat. *þám*; see **That**, § β.

this. (E.) M. E. *this*, *thes*; pl. *these*, *thuse*, *thos*, &c., the forms *these* and *those* being both used as plurals of *this*; the plural of *that* being *tho*. Gradually *these* became the settled pl. of *this*, whilst *those* supplanted *tho* as pl. of *that*.—A. S. *ðes*, *ðeós*, *ðis*, this; pl. *ðás* (= *these*), *ðás* (= those), either form being used. [M. E. *tho* answers to A. S. *ðá*, pl. of def. art.; see **That**, § β.] β. *This* (A. S. *ðe-s*) is an emphatic form, due to joining the pronom. bases THA and SA.+Du. *deze*, Icel. *þessi*, G. *dieser*.

thither. (E.) M. E. *thider*. A. S. *ðider*.+Icel. *þaðra*; Goth. *thathro*; cf. Skt. *tatra*, there, thither. Formed from Teut. base THA (Aryan TA) with a suffix which is supposed to be the instrumental case of a comparative in *-ta-ra*.

those. (E.) Originally a mere variant of *these*, which see above.

though. (E.) M. E. *thogh*. A. S. *ðeáh*, *ðéh*.+Du. *doch*, yet, but; Icel. *þó*, Dan. *dog*, Swed. *dock*, G. *doch*, Goth. *thauh*. All from Teut. base THA, that, with suffix *-UH*, used in Gothic as a demonstrative suffix (like L. *-ce* in *hic-ce*). The sense is 'with respect to that in particular.'

thus. (E.) M. E. *thus*. A. S. *ðus*; prob. the same as *ðýs*, instrumental case of *ðes*, this; see **this** (above).+O. Fries. and O. Sax. *thus*; Du. *dus*.

Thatch, sb. (E.) M. E. *þak*. A. S. *þæc*, thatch; whence *þeccan*, to thatch.+Du. *dak*, sb., whence *dekken*, verb (whence E. *deck* is borrowed); Icel. *þak*, sb., Dan. *tag*, Swed. *tak*, G. *dach*.+Gk. *τέγος*, *στέγος*, a roof, Irish *teagh*, Gael. *teach*, *tigh*, W. *ty*, a house. (√STAG.) Allied to **Tegument**; and see **Tight**.

Thaw, verb. (E.) A. S. *þawian, þawan,* a weak verb, from a lost sb.+Du. *dooijen,* to thaw, from *dooi,* thaw; Icel. *þeyja,* from *þá,* sb.; Dan. *töe,* Swed. *töa.* Cf. G. *verdauen,* to digest, concoct; *thauen,* to thaw. ¶ *Not* allied to *dew.*

The (1), def. art.; see **That.**

The (2), in what (or that) degree; see **That.**

Theatre. (F. – L. – Gk.) F. *theatre;* Cot. – L. *theatrum.* – Gk. θέατρον, a place for seeing shows. – Gk. θεάομαι, I see.

amphitheatre. (Gk.) Gk. ἀμφιθέατρον, a theatre with seats all round the arena. – Gk. ἀμφί, around; θέατρον, a theatre (above).

theorem. (L. – Gk.) L. *theorema.* – Gk. θεώρημα, a spectacle; a subject for contemplation, theorem. – Gk. θεωρεῖν, to behold. – Gk. θεωρός, a spectator. – Gk. θεάομαι, I see (above).

theory. (F. – L. – Gk.) F. *theorie,* 'theory;' Cot. – L. *theoria.* – Gk. θεωρία, a beholding, contemplation, speculation. – Gk. θεωρός, a spectator (above).

Thee (1), acc. of **Thou,** q. v.

Thee (2), to prosper, thrive. (E.) Obsolete. M. E. *theen.* – A. S. *þeón, þión,* pt. t. *þedh,* pp. *þogen,* to thrive; allied to *þíhan,* to increase, pt. t. *þáh,* pp. *þigen.* + Goth. *theihan,* to thrive, increase; G. *gedeihen;* Du. *gedijen;* Lith. *tikti,* to be worth, to suffice, *tekti,* to fall to the lot of. (√TAK.)

thane, a dignitary among the English. (E.) M. E. *þein.* A. S. *þegen, þegn, þén,* a thane. Lit. 'mature' or 'grown up.' – A. S. *þigen,* pp. of *þíhan,* to increase (above). + Icel. *þegn;* G. *degen,* a warrior, from *gedigen,* pp. of M. H. G. *díhen* (G. *gedeihen*), to grow up, become mature; Gk. τέκνον, a child. ¶ *Not* allied to G. *dienen,* to serve.

Theft; see **Thief.**

Their; see **That.**

Theism, belief in a God. (Gk.) Coined, with suffix *-ism* (Gk. *-ισμος*), from Gk. θε-ός, a god.

apotheosis, deification. (Gk.) Gk. ἀποθέωσις, deification. – Gk. ἀποθεόω, I deify, lit. 'set aside as a god.' – Gk. ἀπό, away; θεός, a god.

atheism. (Gk.) Coined from Gk. ἄθεος, denying the gods, without a god. – Gk. ἀ-, negative prefix; θέος, a god.

enthusiasm, inspiration. (Gk.) Gk. ἐνθουσιασμός, inspiration. – Gk. ἐνθουσιάζω, I am inspired. – Gk. ἔνθους, for ἔνθεος, full

of the god, having a god within, inspired. – Gk. ἐν, in; θεός, a god.

theocracy. (Gk.) See **Aristocracy.**

theogony. (L. – Gk.) L. *theogonia.* – Gk. θεογονία, the origin of the gods. – Gk. θεό-s, a god; -γονία, origin, from γεν-, base of γίγνομαι, I become; see **Genus.**

theology. (F. – L. – Gk.) M. E. *theologie.* – F. *theologie;* Cot. – L. *theologia.* – Gk. θεολογία, a speaking about God. – Gk. θεολόγος, adj., speaking about God. – Gk. θεό-s, a god; λέγειν, to speak.

theurgy, supernatural agency. (L. – Gk.) L. *theurgia.* – Gk. θεουργία, divine work, magic. – Gk. θεό-s, a god; ἔργ-ον, a work, cognate with E. **Work.**

Them; see **That.**

Theme. (F. – L. – Gk.) M. E. *teme.* – O. F. *teme,* later *theme,* 'a theam;' Cot. – L. *thema.* – Gk. θέμα, that which is laid down, a theme for argument. – Gk. base θε-, to place; τί-θη-μι, I place. + Skt. *dhâ,* to put; see Do (1). (√DHA.)

anathema, a curse. (L. – Gk.) L. *anathema.* – Gk. ἀνάθεμα, a thing devoted or accursed. – Gk. ἀνατίθημι, I devote. – Gk. ἀνά, up; τίθημι, I place, set (above). Der. *anathemat-ise* (from stem ἀναθεματ-).

antithesis. (Gk.) Gk. ἀντίθεσις, an opposition, a setting opposite. – Gk. ἀντί, against; θέσις, a setting; see **thesis** (below).

apothecary. (Low L. – Gk.) M. E. *apotecarie,* also *potecarie.* – Low L. *apothecarius, apotecarius.* – L. *apotheca,* a storehouse, shop. – Gk. ἀποθήκη, a store-house. – Gk. ἀπό, away; τί-θη-μι, I put.

epithet. (L. – Gk.) L. *epitheton.* – Gk. ἐπίθετον, an epithet; neut. of ἐπίθετος, added. – Gk. ἐπί, besides; θε-, base of τίθημι, I place.

hypothesis. (L. – Gk.) L. *hypothesis.* – Gk. ὑπόθεσις, a placing under, a supposition. – Gk. ὑπό, under; θέσις, a placing; see **thesis** (below).

metathesis. (L. – Gk.) L. *metathesis.* – Gk. μετάθεσις, transposition. – Gk. μετά, implying 'change;' θέσις, a placing; see **thesis** (below).

parenthesis. (Gk.) Gk. παρένθεσις, an insertion, a putting in beside. – Gk. παρ-ά, beside; ἐν, in; θέσις, a placing; see **thesis** (below).

synthesis. (L. – Gk.) L. *synthesis.* – Gk. σύνθεσις, a putting together. – Gk. σύν, together; θέσις, a placing; see **thesis** (below). Der. *synthet-ic-al,* from Gk. συνθετικός, skilled in putting together.

thesaurus. (L. – Gk.) See treasure (below).

thesis. (L. – Gk.) L. *thesis.* – Gk. θέσις, a thing laid down, a proposition. – Gk. θε-, base of τίθημι, I place. Der. *apo-thesis, para-thesis, pros-thesis, pro-thesis,* all rare words, with prefixes ἀπό, παρά, πρός, πρό respectively; also *anti-thesis, hypo-thesis, meta-thesis, par-en-thesis, syn-thesis* (explained above).

treasure. (F. – L. – Gk.) The former *r* is intrusive. M. E. *tresor.* – O. F. *tresor* (F. *trésor*); the same as Ital. *tesoro,* Span. *tesoro.* – L. *thesaurum,* acc. of *thesaurus.* – Gk. θησαυρός, a treasure, store, hoard. – Gk. base θη-, θησ-, as in τί-θη-μι, I place, store up, fut. θήσ-ω; (the suffixes are not clear). Der. *treasur-y,* short for *treasure-ry,* O. F. *tresorerie.*

Then, Thence ; see That.

Theocracy ; see Aristocracy.

Theodolite, an instrument used in surveying. (Unknown.) Generally said to be Greek, for which there is no evidence. All the explanations are worthless. Formerly *theodelitus,* meaning 'a circle with a graduated border'; used A.D. 1571.

Theogony, Theology ; see Theism.

Theorem, Theory ; see Theatre.

Therapeutic, pertaining to the healing art. (F. – L. – Gk.) F. *therapeutique,* healing; Cot. – L. *therapeutica* (*ars*), the healing art; fem. of *therapeuticus.* – Gk. θεραπευτικός, tending. – Gk. θεραπεύω, an attendant. – Gk. θεραπεύειν, to wait on. – Gk. θεραπ-, stem of θέραψ, an assistant. From √ DHAR, to maintain, support; cf. Skt. *dhri,* to maintain, bear.

There ; see That.

Thermometer, an instrument for measuring the temperature. (Gk.) From Gk. θερμό-s, warm, allied to Skt. *gharma,* warm ; and μέτρον, a measurer ; see Metre.

Thesaurus ; see Theme.

These ; see That.

Thesis ; see Theme.

Theurgy ; see Theism.

Thews, pl. sb., sinews, manners. (E.) *Thews* in Shak. means sinews or strength ; but M. E. *thewes* almost always means habits or manners. A.S. *þeawas,* pl. of *þew,* habit, custom, demeanour (orig. sense 'strength'). + O. Sax. *thau,* custom. Cf. Skt. *tu,* to be strong, *tuvi-* (prefix), greatly. (√ TU.)

They ; see That.

Thick. (E.) M. E. *þikke.* A. S. *þicce.*

---

thick. + O. Sax. *thikki,* Du. *dik,* Icel. *þykkr,* Dan. *tyk,* Swed. *tjok, tjock* ; G. *dick.* Perhaps allied to Gael. and Irish *tiugh,* fat, thick, W. *tew,* thick, plump.

thicket. (E.) A. S. *þiccet,* i. e. a thick set of bushes, &c.

Thief. (E.) Pl. *thieves.* M. E. *þeef,* pl. *þeues.* A. S. *þeóf,* pl. *þeófas.* + Du. *dief,* Icel. *þjófr,* Dan. *tyv,* Swed. *tjuf,* G. *dieb,* Goth. *thiubs.* Perhaps allied to Lith. *tupěti,* to squat down (hence, to hide one-self).

theft. (E.) Put for *thefth.* M. E. *þefte.* A. S. *þiefðe, þeófðe,* theft. – A. S. *þeóf,* a thief. + Icel. *þýfð,* O. Fries. *thiufthe.*

Thigh. (E.) M. E. *þih.* A. S. *þeó, þeóh,* thigh. + Du. *dij,* Icel. *þjó,* thigh, rump, O. H. G. *deoh.* The orig. sense is 'thick or plump part'; allied to Lith. *tùk-ti,* to become fat, Russ. *tuch-nite,* to fatten. (Base TUK ; √ TU.)

Thill, shaft of a cart. (E.) Also spelt *fill* ; whence *fill-horse.* M. E. *þille.* A. S. *þille,* slip of wood, thin board, plank, thin pole. + Icel. *þilja,* plank, G. *diele,* plank, board. Doublet, *deal,* a thin board.

Thimble ; see Thumb.

Thin. (E.) M. E. *þinne.* A. S. *þynne* + Du. *dun,* Icel. *þunnr,* Dan. *tynd* (for *tynn* *), Swed. *tunn,* G. *dünn.* + W. *teneu,* Gael. Irish *tana,* Russ. *tonkii,* L. *tenuis,* Gk. ταναός, Skt. *tanu.* Lit. 'stretched out.' (√ TAN.)

Thine, Thy ; see Thou.

Thing. (E.) A. S. *þing, þinc, þincg.* + Du. G. *ding* ; Icel. *þing,* a thing, also an assembling, meeting, council (so also Dan. Swed. *ting*). Prob. allied to Lith. *těkti* (pres. t. *tenk-ù*), to fall to one's share, suffice ; *tìk-ti,* to suit, fit, *tik-ras,* fit, right. Perhaps from √ TAK, to fit, prepare; if so, a thing is 'what is prepared' or made, an object. Der. *hus-tings,* q. v.

Think. (E.) M. E. *þenken,* to think; orig. distinct from the impers. vb. *þinken,* to seem, for which see methinks (below). [But confusion between the two was easy and common. The pt. t. of M. E. *þenken* should have been *thoghte,* and of M. E. *þinken* should have been *thughte* ; both were merged in the form *thoughte,* mod. E. *thought.*] – A. S. *þencan, þencean,* to think, pt. t. *þohte.* A weak verb ; allied to A. S. *þanc,* a thought, also a thank ; see thank (below). + Icel. *þekkja,* Dan. *tænke,* Swed. *tänka,* G. *denken* (pt. t. *dachte*) ; Goth.

thagkian, i.e. *thankian** (pt. t. *thahta*).
Der. *be-think*, with prefix *be-* = *by*.

methinks. (E.) Lit. 'it seems to me;'
here *me* is the dat. case, and *thinks* is an
impers. verb, M. E. *þinken*, to seem. A. S.
me þynceð, it seems to me; from *þyncan*,
to seem. + O. Sax. *thuncian*, Icel. *þykkja*,
Goth. *thugkjan*, i.e. *thunkjan**, G. *dünken*,
to seem. A secondary verb, allied to A. S.
þanc, a thought; see below.

thank, thanks. (E.) M. E. *þank*, a
thought, kindly remembrance, goodwill;
hence *thanks*, pl. expressions of goodwill.
A. S. *þanc*, *þonc*, sb., thought, favour, content, thank. + Du. *dank*, Icel. *þökk*, Dan.
tak, Swed. *tack*, Goth. *thagks*, i. e. *thanks**,
remembrance, thank. From a Teut. base
THAK, to think, suppose; cf. O. Lat.
tongēre, to think, to know, Lith. *tikéti*, to
believe. (Root TAG, prob. allied to √
TAK.) Der. *thank*, verb.

thought, sb. (E.) Better *thoght*. M. E.
þoght. A. S. *þoht*, *ge-þoht*, a thought, lit.
thing thought of. − A. S. *þoht*, pp. of
þencan, to think; see **Think.** + Icel.
þótti, *þóttr*; G. *gedacht*, from *gedacht*, pp.
of *denken*.

Third; see **Three.**

Thirl, to pierce; see **Through.**

Thirst, sb. (E.) Lit. 'dryness.' M. E.
þurst. A. S. *þurst*, *þyrst*, thirst; whence
þyrstan, verb, to thirst. + Du. *dorst*, Icel.
þorsti, Dan. *törst*, Swed. *törst*, G. *durst*,
Goth. *thaurstei*. β. The Goth. *thaurstei*
is from *thaurs-ans*, pp. of *thairsan* (pt. t.
thars), to be dry; with suffix *-tei*. This is
cognate with Gk. τέρσεσθαι, to become
dry. Skt. *trish*, to thirst; *tarsha*, thirst.
(√ TARS.) Allied to **Terrace** and **Torrid.**

Thirteen, Thirty; see **Three.**

This; see **That.**

Thistle. (E.) M. E. *þistil*. A. S. *þistel*.
+ Du. *distel*, Icel. *þistill*, Dan. *tidsel*, Swed.
tistel, G. *distel*. Lit. 'tearer,' from base
THINS, to pull; cf. Goth. *at-thinsan*, to
pull towards one, O. H. G. *thinsan*, to pull
forcibly, to tear. (Base TANS; √ TAN.)

Thither; see **That.**

Thole (1), **Thowl,** a peg to steady an
oar. (E.) M. E. *thol*. A. S. *þol* (8th cent.).
+ Du. *dol*; Icel. *þollr*, young tree, wooden
peg, thole; Dan. *tol*; Swed. *tall*, pine-tree;
Norw. *tall*, *toll*, fir-tree, *toll*, a thole. Orig.
sense 'tree' or 'young tree;' hence a bit of
fir-wood for a peg. ¶ Not allied to *thill*.

Thole (2), to endure. M. E. *þolien*.
A. S. *þolian*, to suffer, endure. + Icel. *þola*,

Dan. *taale*, Swed. *tåla*, O. H. G. *doltn*
(whence G. *geduld*, patience), Goth. *thulan*.
+L. *tollere, tolerare*. (√ TAL.)

Thong; see **Twinge.**

Thorax. (L. − Gk.) L. *thorax*. − Gk.
θώραξ, a breast-plate; also the breast, chest.
Lit. 'defender;' cf. Skt. *dháraka*, a trunk
to protect clothes, from *dhri*, to keep. (√
DHAR.)

Thorn. (E.) A. S. *þorn*. + Du. *doorn*,
Icel. *þorn*, Dan. *tiörn*, Swed. *törne*, G.
dorn, Goth. *thaurnus*. + Russ. *tërn'*, the
black-thorn; Polish *tarn*, a thorn. Lit.
'piercer.' (√ TAR.)

Thorough; see **Through.**

Thorp, Thorpe, a village. (E.) A. S.
þorp, a village.+Du. *dorp*, Icel. *þorp*, Dan.
Swed. *torp*, G. *dorf*, Goth. *þaurp*, a field.
Cf. Lith. *troba*, a building, house, Irish
treabh, village, W. *tref*, hamlet. Perhaps
orig. 'a farm;' cf. Gael. *treabh*, to till.

Those; see **That.**

Thou. (E.) A. S. *ðú*, thou. + Icel. *þú*,
Goth. *thu*, Dan. Swed. G. *du*. + Irish and
Gael. *tu*, W. *ti*; L. *tu*, Russ. *tui*; Gk. σύ,
τύ, Pers. *tú*, Skt. *tvam*. (Base TU.)

thee. (E.) A. S. *ðé*, dat. and acc. of
ðú, thou.

thine, thy. (E.) M. E. *thin*, shortened
to *thy* before a following consonant. A. S.
ðín, thy, possessive pronoun, declined as
an adj. − A. S. *ðín*, gen. case of *ðú*, thou.
+ Icel. *þinn*, Dan. Swed. *din*, G. *dein*,
Goth. *theins*. Der. *thy-self* (=*thine self*).

Though; see **That.**

Thought; see **Think.**

Thousand. (E.) M. E. *þousand*. A. S.
þúsend. + Du. *duizend*, Icel. *þúsund*, *þús-
hund*, *þúshundrað*; Dan. *tusind*, Swed.
tusen, G. *tausend*, Goth. *thusundi*. Cf. also
Lith. *tukstantis*, Russ. *tuisiacha*, a thousand.
¶ Not yet explained; in Icel. *þús-hund*, the
syllable *hund* = A. S. *hund*, a hundred.

Thowl; see **Thole** (1).

Thrall, a slave. (Scand.) O. Northumb.
ðral, borrowed from Norse. − Icel. *þræll*,
a thrall, serf; Dan. *træl*, Swed. *träl*. Cognate with O. H. G. *drigil*, a thrall, serf;
lit. 'a runner,' i. e. one who runs on mes-
sages. From base of Goth. *thragjan*, A. S.
þrægian, to run; cognate with Gk. τρέχειν,
to run. (√ TARGH, to run.) ¶ The
'etymology' from *thrill* is impossible. Der.
thral-dom, Icel. *þrældómr*.

Thrash, Thresh. (E.) *Thresh* is
older; M. E. *þreshen*, for *þershen*. − A. S.
þerscan, to thrash (strong verb). + Du.

dorschen, Icel. þreskja, Dan. *tærske*, Swed. tröska, G. *dreschen*, Goth. *thriskan* (pt. t. *thrask*). Orig. to rattle, make a din or rattling noise ; cf. Russ. *tresk-ate*, to crackle, burst, *tresk'*, a crash, O. Slav. *troska*, stroke of lightning. Prob. first used of thunder, then of the noise of the flail.

threshold, a piece of wood or stone under an entrance-door. (E.) *Thresh-old* = *thresh-wold*, lit. the piece of wood threshed or beaten by the tread of the foot. M. E. *preshwold*. A. S. *perscwald*, late *perscold*. — A. S. *persc-an*, to thresh ; *wald*, *weald*, wood, a piece of wood ; see **Wold**. +Icel. *preskjölder*, threshold ; from *preskj-a*, to thresh, *völlr*, wood.

Thrasonical, vain-glorious. (L. — Gk.) Coined from *Thrasoni-*, crude form of *Thraso*, the name of a bragging soldier in Terence's Eunuchus. Evidently from Gk. θρασ-ύς, bold, spirited ; allied to **Dare** (1). (√ DHARS.)

Thrave, a number of sheaves of wheat. (Scand.) M. E. *praue*, *preue* (*thrave*, *threve*). — Icel. *prefi*, a thrave ; Dan. *trave*, a score of sheaves ; Swed. *trafve*, a pile of wood. Orig. 'a handful' or 'armful.' — Icel. *prífa*, to seize, grasp (pt. t. *preif*). See **Thrive**.

Thread ; see **Throw**.

Threat, sb. (E.) M. E. *pret*. A. S. *predt*, a crowd, crush of people, also great pressure, calamity, trouble, threat. — A. S. *predt*, pt. t. of *predtan*, to afflict, vex, urge. + Goth. *us-thriutan*, to vex greatly, G. *verdriessen*, to vex. + Russ. *trudite*, to make one work, urge, vex ; L. *trudere*, to push, crowd, urge. (Base TRUD, TRU ; √ TAR.) Der. *threat-en*, verb.

Three. (E.) M. E. *pre*. A. S. *preó*, *prió*, *prý*, *prí*, three.+Du. *drie*, Icel. *prír*, Dan. *tre*, Swed. *tre*, Goth. *threis*, G. *drei*. + Irish, Gael. and W. *tri*, Russ. *tri*, L. *tres* (neut. *tri-a*), Gk. τρεῖς (neut. τρί-α), Lith. *trys*, Skt. *tri*. (Base TRI.) Perhaps 'going beyond,' or 'complete ;' cf. Skt. *trí*, to go beyond, complete.

riding, one of the three divisions of the county of York. (Scand.) Put for *thriding* (*North - riding = North - thriding*). — Icel. *pridjungr*, the third part of a thing, third part of a shire. — Icel. *priði*, third. — Icel. *prír*, three. So also Norweg. *tridjung*, a third part.

third. (E.) Put for *thrid*. M. E. *pridde*, *pride*. A. S. *pridda*, third. — A. S. *preó*, three. + Du. *derde*, Icel. *priði*, Dan.

tredie, Swed. *tredje*, G. *dritte*, Goth. *thridja*, W. *tryde*, Russ. *tretii*, L. *tertius*, Gk. τρί-τος, Skt. *tritja*.

thirteen. (E.) M. E. *prettene*. A. S. *preótýne*. — A. S. *preó*, three ; *týn*, ten ; with pl. suffix *-e*. + Du. *dertien*, Icel. *prettán*, Dan. *tretten*, Swed. *tretton*, G. *dreizehn*.

thirty. (E.) M. E. *pritti*. A.S. *pritig*, *prittig*. — A. S. *prí*, *preó*, three ; *-tig*, suffix denoting 'ten ;' see **Ten**. + Du. *dertig*, Icel. *prjátíu*, Dan. *tredive*, Swed. *trettio*, G. *dreizsig*.

thrice. (E.) For *thris*, contr. form of M. E. *priës*, *pryës* (dissyllabic), where the suffix *-s* is adverbial (orig. mark of gen. case). Earlier form *prië*. — A. S. *priwa*, thrice. — A. S. *prí*, three.

Threnody, a lament. (Gk.) Gk. θρην-ῳδία, a lamenting. — Gk. θρῆν-ος, a wailing, from θρέ-ομαι, I cry aloud ; ῳδή, ode ; see **Ode**.

Thresh ; see **Thrash**.

Threshold ; see **Thrash**.

Thrice ; see **Three**.

Thrid, a thread ; see **Throw**.

Thrift ; see **Thrive**.

Thrill ; see **Through**.

Thrive. (Scand.) M.E. *priuen* (*thriven*), pt. t. *praf*, *prof*, pp. *priuen*. — Icel. *prífa* (pt. t. *preif*, pp. *prifinn*), to clutch, grasp, grip, seize ; hence *prífask* (with suffixed *-sk* = *-sik*, self), lit. to seize for oneself, to thrive. + Dan. *trives*, Swed. *trifvas*, reflex. verb, to thrive.

thrift, frugality. (Scand.) M. E. *prift*. — Icel. *prift*, thrift ; also *prif*, the same. — Icel. *prif-inn*, pp. of *prifa* (above). Cf. Norw. *trivelse*, prosperity.

Throat, the gullet. (E.) M. E. *prote*. A.S. *prote*, *prota*, *protu*, throat.+ O. H. G. *drozzá*, whence G. *drossel*, throat, throttle. Initial *s* seems to be lost ; cf. Du. *strot*, O. Du. *stroot*, *stroote*, the throat, gullet ; Ital. *strozza*, the gullet (a word of Teut. origin). We also find Swed. *strupe*, Dan. *strube*, the throat.

throttle, the wind-pipe. (E.) Dimin. of *throat*. Der. *throttle*, verb, to press on the wind-pipe. See **Thropple**.

Throb, to beat forcibly, as the heart. (E.) M. E. *probben*, to throb. Allied to Russ. *trepete*, palpitation, throbbing ; L. *trepidus*, trembling. See **Trepidation**.

Throe, a pang. (E.) M. E. *prowe*. A. S. *pred*, short for *predw*, a rebuke, affliction, threat, evil, pain. — A. S. *predw*, pt. t. of *preówan*, to afflict severely (from the pp.

þrowen of which verb are þrowian, to suffer, þrowung, martyrdom). + Icel. þrá, a throe ; M. H. G. drô, drowe, a threat (whence G. drohen, to threaten). Cf. Russ. trytite, to nip, pinch, gall. (√ TRU, from √ TAR.)

Throne. (F. – L. – Gk.) Formerly trone (Wyclif). – O. F. trone (F. trône). – L. thronum, acc. of thronus. – Gk. θρόνος, a seat ; lit. a support. (√ DHAR.)

dethrone. (F. – L. and Gk.) O. F. desthroner, 'to unthrone ;' Cot. – O. F. des- = L. dis-, apart ; L. thronus = Gk. θρόνος (above).

Throng, a great crowd of people. (L.) M. E. þrong. A.S. ge-þrang, a throng. – A.S. þrang, pt. t. of þringan, to crowd, press. + Du. drang, Icel. þröng, G. drang, a throng. Allied to Lith. trenk-ti, to jolt, push. (Aryan base TRANK ; from √ TARK.) Der. throng, verb.

Thropple, Thrapple, wind-pipe. (E.) Thropple is a parallel form to throttle, with the same sense ; cf. Swed. strupe, Dan. strube, the throat, Icel. strjúpi, the spurting or bleeding trunk, when the head is cut off. See Throttle.

Throstle, the song-thrush. (E.) M. E. þrostel. A.S. þrostle, a throstle. + M. H. G. trostel, of which a varying form is troschel (G. drossel). Throstle is a variant of throshel (M. E. thrusshil, Prompt. Parv.), dimin. of Thrush (1).

Throttle ; see Throat.

Through, prep. (E.) M. E. þurh. A.S. þurh, O. Northumb. þerh. + Du. door, G. durch, O.H.G. durh, Goth. thairh, through. β. The Goth. thairh, through, is allied to thairko, a hole ; from √ TAR, to bore. Cf. Irish tar, beyond, through, tri, through ; L. tr-ans, across ; Skt. tiras, through, from trí, to pass over. Der. through-out, cognate with G. durchaus, the same.

drill (1), to pierce, to train soldiers. (Du.) Borrowed from Du. drillen, to drill, to bore, to turn round, shake, brandish, drill soldiers, form to arms. Cognate with E. thrill, to pierce ; see thrill (below).

thorough. (E.) Merely a later form of the prep. through, spelt þoru in Havelok, and þuruh in the Ancren Riwle. It became an adverb, whence thoroughly, adv., with added suffix. And hence, finally, thorough, adj.

thrill, thirl, to pierce. (E.) The old sense of thrill was to pierce ; also spelt thirl, which is an older spelling. M. E. þirlen, þrillen. A.S. þyrlian, to pierce ; shorter form of þyrelian, the same ; lit. ' to

make a hole.' – A.S. þyrel, a hole ; orig. an adj. with the sense 'pierced,' and put for þyrh-el*, as shewn by the cognate M. H. G. durchel, pierced. Derived from A. S. þurh, through (with change of u to y), just as M. H.G. durchel is from G. durch, through. See Through.

trill (2), to turn round and round. (Scand.) Perhaps obsolete. M. E. trillen, Chaucer, C. T. 10630. – Swed. trilla, Dan. trille, to roll, turn round ; the same as Du. drillen ; see drill (1) above.

trill (3), to trickle, roll. (Scand.) Merely a particular use of the word above. Perhaps confused with trickle.

Throw, to cast, hurl. (E.) M.E. þrowen, pt. t. þrew, pp. þrowen. A.S. þráwan, to twist, hurl, whirl ; pt. t. þreów, pp. þráwen. [The orig. sense, to twist, is preserved in thread.] Allied to Du. draaijen, to twist, whirl ; G. drehen, to turn ; L. torquere, to twist ; cf. Skt. tarku, a spindle. (√ TARK.)

thread. (E.) M. E. þreed, þred. A.S. þrǽd, thread ; lit. ' that which is twisted.' – A. S. þráwan, to twist (with the usual change from á to ǽ, and loss of w). + Du. draad, Icel. þráðr, Dan. traad, Swed. tråd, thread ; G. draht, drath, wire.

thrid, a thread. (E.) Another spelling of thread (Dryden, Hind and Panther, iii. 278).

Thrum (1), the tufted end of a weaver's thread. (Scand.) M. E. þrum. – Icel. þrömr (gen. þramar), the edge, verge, brim of a thing (hence the edge of a web) ; Norw. tröm, tram, trumm, edge, brim ; Swed. dial. trumm, tröm, a stump, the end of a log. + O. Du. drom, thread on a weaver's shuttle ; G. trumm, end, thrum, stump of a tree. + Gk. τέρμα, end ; L. terminus ; see Term.

Thrum (2), to play noisily. (Scand.) Icel. þruma, to rattle, thunder ; Swed. trumma, to beat, drum ; cf. Dan. tromme, a drum. See Drum.

Thrush (1), a bird. (E.) M. E. þrusch. A.S. þrysce, a thrush. + O. H. G. drosca, a thrush ; whence G. drossel. β. We also find Icel. þröstr, Swed. trast, A.S. þrost-le, a thrush ; allied to L. turdus, turda, a thrush, Lith. strazdas, strazda, a thrush. Cf. L. stur-nus, a starling.

Thrush (2), a disease marked by small ulcerations in the mouth. (Scand.) In Phillips (1706). Orig. 'a dryness ;' or lit. 'dryishness.' Formed by adding Icel. suffix -sk (= -ish or -ishness) to Icel. þurr, dry, as proved by Dan. *tröske*, Swed. *torsk*, Swed. dial. *trôsk*, the thrush; forms which are to be compared with Dan. *törke*, Swed. *törka*, Icel. *þurka*, drought, and with M. E. *thurst*, thirst. A parallel form to Thirst, q. v.

Thrust, vb. (Scand.) M. E. *þrusten*, *þristen.* — Icel. *þrýsta*, to thrust, press, compel. Allied to Threaten, and to L. *trudere*, to thrust.

Thud, a dull sound of a blow. (E.) Used by G. Douglas and Burns. A. S. *þóden*, a whirlwind. From the same root (STU) as *thump*, *type*, and L. *tundere*.

Thug, an assassin. (Hindustani.) Hind. *thag*, *thug* (with cerebral *th*), a cheat, knave, a robber who strangles travellers; Maráthi *thak*, *thag*, a thug (H. H. Wilson).

Thumb. (E.) M. E. *þombe*; with excrescent *b*. A. S. *þuma* or *þúma*, the thumb. + Du. *duim*, Swed. *tumme*, G. *daumen*. Lit. 'the *thick* finger;' from √ TU, to grow large. See Tumid.

thimble. (E.) M. E. *þimbil*; formed (with excrescent *b*) from A. S. *þýmel*, a thumb-stall. — A. S. *þúma*, thumb (with the usual change from *ú* to *ý*).

Thummim, perfection. (Heb.) *Urim and thummim* = light and perfection; though the forms are, strictly, plural. — Heb. *tummím*, pl. of *tóm*, perfection, truth. — Heb. root *támam*, to be perfect.

Thump, vb. (E.) Allied to Icel. *dumpa*, to thump, Swed. dial. *dompa*, to thump, *dumpa*, to make a noise. Cf. *tympanum*.

Thunder, sb. (E.) For *thuner*; the *d* is excrescent. M. E. *þoner*. A. S. *þunor*. — A. S. *þunian*, to rattle, thunder; cf. *geþun*, a loud noise. + Du. *donder*; Icel. *þórr* (for *þonr*), Thor, god of thunder; G. *donner.* + L. *tonare*, to thunder, Skt. *tan*, to sound. β. We further find A. S. *tonian* to thunder, which points to loss of initial *s*, appearing in Skt. *stan*, to sound, thunder, sigh, *stanita*, thunder, and in E. *stun*. (√ STAN.)

thursday. (E.; *confused with* Scand.) *Thur* is a corruption of M. E. *thuner*, thunder, by confusion with *Thor*, which had the same sense. M. E. *þurs-day*, *þors-day*. A. S. *þunres dæg*, Thursday. — A. S. *þunres*, gen. of *þunor*, thunder; *dæg*, day.

Confused with Icel. *þórsdagr*, Thursday; from *þórs*, gen. of *þórr*, Thor, and *dagr*, a day. So also Du. *Donderdag*, Swed. Dan. *Torsdag*, G. *Donnerstag*.

Thurible, a censer. (L. — Gk.) English from L. *thuribulum*, *turibulum*, a vessel for holding incense. — L. *thuri-*, *turi-*, crude form of *thus*, *tus*, frankincense; with suffix *-bulum* (as in *fundi-bulum*, from *fundere*). L. *thus* is borrowed from Gk. *θύος*, incense. — Gk. *θύ-ειν*, to burn a sacrifice. Allied to Fume. (√ DHU.) See Thyme.

Thursday; see Thunder.

Thus; see That.

Thwack, Whack, to beat. (E.) A variant of M. E. *þakken*, to stroke, from A. S. *þaccian*, to stroke (a horse). Jocularly used. + Icel. *þjökka*, to thwack, thump.

Thwart, transversely, transverse. (Scand.) Properly an adv.; afterwards an adj.; lastly, a verb. M. E. *thwert*, *thwart*, across. — Icel. *þvert*, neut. of *þverr*, adj., perverse, adverse. Used adverbially in phrases such as *um þvert*, across, athwart, *taka þvert*, to take athwart, to deny flatly. β. The Icel. *þverr*, adj., is cognate with A. S. *þweorh*, perverse, transverse, Dan. *tvær*, transverse (whence *tvært*, adv., across), Swed. *tvär*, across (whence *tvärt*, adv., rudely), Du. *dwars*, Goth. *thwairhs*, cross, G. *zwerch*, adv., across, awry. Allied to Twirl.

Thwite, to cut. (E.) Obsolete. A. S. *þwítan*, pt. t. *þwát*, pp. *þwiten*, to cut.

whittle (1), to pare or cut with a knife. From the obsolete sb. *whittle*, a knife, the same as M. E. *þwitel*, a knife, lit. 'a cutter.' — A. S. *þwítan*, to cut (above).

whittle (2), to sharpen. (E.) Used as a slang term; 'well *whittled*' = thoroughly drunk. Lit. sharpened like a *whittle* or knife; see Whittle (1) above. Doubtless confused with *whet*, to sharpen, which is quite a different word.

Thy; see Thou.

Thyme, a plant. (F. — L. — Gk.) The *th* is pronounced as *t*, because borrowed from French. M. E. *tyme.* — F. *thym*, 'the herb time;' Cot. — L. *thymum*, acc. of *thymus.* — Gk. *θύμος*, *θύμον*, thyme, from its sweet smell. — Gk. *θύος*, incense; see Thurible. (√ DHU.)

TI–TY.

Tiara, a wreathed ornament for the head. (L. — Gk. — Pers.) L. *tiara.* — Gk. *τιάρα*, *τιάρας*, a Persian head-dress. Doubtless of Pers. origin. Cf. Pers. *táj*, a diadem;

tájwar, wearing a crown.

Tibia, the large bone of the leg. (L.) L. *tibia*, shin-bone.

Tic, a twitching of the muscles. (F. —

Teut.) F. *tic*, a twitching ; *tic douloureux*, painful twitching, a nervous disease. Formerly F. *ticq*, *tiquet*, a disease suddenly seizing a horse (Cot.). Cf. Ital. *ticchio*, a vicious habit, caprice. Most likely allied to G. *zucken*, to twitch, shrug, Low G. *tukken*, to twitch ; with which cf. G. *zug*, a draught, *siehen*, to draw (Scheler). See Tick (4).

Tick (1), a small insect infesting dogs, sheep, &c. (E.) M. E. *tyke*, *teke* ; not in A. S. [The F. *tique* is borrowed from Teutonic.]+O. Du. *teke*, Low G. *teke*, *täke*, G. *zäcke*, *zecke* (whence Ital. *zecca*). Orig. sense ' biter ' or ' stinger ;' from √ STAG, to pierce, sting, whence also Goth. *tekan*, to touch, Icel. *taka*, to take ; see Take.

Tick (2), cover of a feather-bed. (L. — Gk.) M. E. *teke*, 14th cent. Englished from L. *teca*, *theca*, a case (whence F. *taie*). — Gk. θήκη, a case to put a thing in. — Gk. θη-, base of τίθημι, I put, put away.

Tick (3), to beat as a watch. (E.) An imitative word, like *click* ; perhaps suggested by Tick (4). Cf. G. *ticktak*, pit-a-pat.

Tick (4), to touch lightly. (E.) M. E. *teck*, a light touch ; whence the game called *tick* or *tig*, in which children try to touch each other. Not in A. S.+Du. *tik*, a touch, pat, tick, *tikken*, to tick, pat ; Low G. *tikk*, a light touch. A weakened form of the base TAK, to touch ; see Take.

tickle. (E.) M. E. *tikelen* ; frequentative form from the base *tik*-, to touch lightly ; see Tick (4). It means ' to keep on touching lightly.' Hence also M. E. *tikel*, unstable, ticklish, easily moved by a touch ; mod. E. *ticklish*, unstable.

Tick (5), credit, Ticket ; see Stick (1).

Tickle ; see Tick (4).

Tide. (E.) M. E. *tide*. A. S. *tíd*, time, hour, season. + Du. *tijd*, Icel. *tíð*, Dan. Swed. *tid*, G. *zeit*. Lit. an allotted time, appointed season ; cf. Skt. *day*, to allot, Gk. δαίομαι, I assign. (√ DA.) Allied to Time. Der. *tide-waiter*, an officer who *waits* for arrival of vessels with the *tide*, to secure payment of duties.

tidings. (Scand.) M. E. *tidinde*, later *tidinge*, afterwards *tidings*. — Icel. *tíðindi*. neut. pl. tidings, news ; orig. ' things that happen.' From a pres. pt *tíðandi** of a verb *tíða**, to happen, only found in the cognate A. S. *tídan*, to happen. — Icel. *tíð*, sb. time ; just as A. S. *tídan* is from *tíd*, time.+Dan. *tidende*, tidings, Du. *tijding*, G. *zeitung*.

tidy, seasonable, neat. (E.) M. E. *tidy*, seasonable, from M. E. *tid* or *tide*, time ; see Tide.+Du. *tijdig*, Dan. Swed. *tidig*, G. *zeitig*, timely.

Tie ; see Tow (1).

Tier, a rank, row. (F. — Teut.) Formerly *tire*, a better spelling ; Florio explains Ital. *tiro* by ' a *tyre* of ordinance.' — F. *tire*, ' a draught, pull, .. also a *tire* ; a stroke, hit, reach, gate, course, or continuance of a course ;' Cot. [Cf. Span. *tiro*, a set of mules ; Ital. *tiro*, ' a shoot, shot, tire, reach, .. a stones caste, a *tyre* of ordinance ;' Florio (1598).] — F. *tirer*, to draw, drag, pull, &c. The orig. sense was to tear or pull violently ; from the verb appearing as Goth. *tairan*, E. *tear* ; see Tear (1). ¶ I find no evidence for connecting it with O. F. *tiere*, a row, rank, though there may have been some confusion ; the A. S. *tíer*, occurring but once, is an obscure and doubtful word, and has nothing to do with it, that I can see.

retire. (F. — Teut.) O. F. *retirer*, ' to retire, withdraw ;' Cot. — F. *re*-, back ; *tirer*, to pull ; see Tier (above).

tirade, a strain of reproof. (F. — Ital. — Teut.) F. *tirade*, lit. ' a lengthening out.' — Ital. *tirata*, a drawing, a pulling. — Ital. *tirare*, to pull, draw, pluck ; the same as F. *tirer* ; see Tier.

tire (5), a train. (F. — Teut.) Only in Spenser, F. Q. i. 4. 35. Coined from F. *tirer*, to draw ; see above, and see Tier.

Tierce, Terce ; see Tri-.

Tiger. (F. — L. — Gk. — Pers.) M. E. *tigre*. — F. *tigre*. — L. *tigrem*, acc. of *tigris*, a tiger. — Gk. τίγρις. — Zend (O. Pers.) *tighri*, an arrow (hence a tiger, from its swiftness, also the river *Tigris*, from its swiftness) ; mod. Pers. *tír*, an arrow, the river Tigris.

Tight, tighten, sharp ; allied to Skt. *tigma*, sharp, from *tij*, to be sharp. (√ STAG.)

Tight. (Scand.) Properly *thight* ; but, as both Dan. and Swed. put *t* for *th*, it easily became *tight*. Prov. E. *thite*, tight, close, compact ; M. E. *tiȝt*, also *þiȝt*, *thyht*. — Icel. *þéttr*, tight, esp. water-tight ; Swed. *tät*, close, tight, solid, compact ; Dan. *tæt*, tight, close, compact, taut, water-tight. M. E. *tiȝt* shews the old guttural ; the Icel. *þéttr* is for *þehtr**, as shewn by Du. *digt*, G. *dicht*, tight ; orig. ' thatched ' or ' covered in,' hence ' water-tight.' Cognate with L. *tectus*, Gk. στεκτός (in ά-στεκτος), thatched, covered in. See Thatch. (√ STAG.)

taut. (Dan.) Dan. *tæt*, tight, close, taut (above).

Tike, a dog, low fellow. (Scand.) M. E. *tike.* — Icel. *tík*, Swed. *tik*, a bitch.

Tile; see Tegument.

Till (1), to cultivate. (E.) M. E. *tilien.* A. S. *tilian*, to labour, endeavour, strive after, to till land. Orig. to aim at excellence. — A.S. *til*, good, excellent, profitable; *til*, sb. goodness. + Du. *telen*, to breed, cultivate, till; G. *zielen*, to aim at, from O. H. G. *zil*, a mark. Der. *til-th*, A. S. *tilð*, a crop, cultivation.

teal, a bird. (E.) M. E. *tele* (13th cent.); not in A. S.+Du. *teling*, a generation, production, also teal; from *telen*, to breed (above). The orig. sense was merely 'a brood' or 'a flock,' and its use as a specific term was accidental; we still use *teal* as a pl. form.

till (2), to the time when. (Scand.) M. E. *til*; chiefly in the Northern dialect; O. Northumb. *til*, Matt. xxvi. 31. — Icel. *til*, Dan. *til*, Swed. *till*, prep., to. Orig. a case (perhaps acc. sing.) of Icel. *tili*, *tlli*, aim, bent; hence used to express purpose or direction towards; cognate with O. H. G. *zil*, aim, mark (above).

Till (3), a drawer for money. (E.) The proper sense is 'drawer,' something that can be pulled out. Dryden has *tiller* in this sense, tr. of Juvenal, vi. 384. From M. E. *tillen*, to draw, draw out, also to allure; also spelt *tullen*. A. S. *tyllan*, only in the comp. *for-tyllan*, to draw aside, lead astray.+Du. *tillen*, to heave, lift up, Low G. *tillen*, to lift, move, Swed. dial. *tille*, to lay hold of.

tiller, the handle of a rudder. (E.) Prov. E. *tiller*, a handle, lit. 'puller.' From M. E. *tillen*, to draw, pull (above).

Tilt (1), the covering of a cart. (E.) M. E. *teld*, later *telt*, the same. A. S. *teld*, a tent. The final *t* was due to the cognate Dan. *telt*, Swed. *tält*, a tent.+O. Du. *telde*, Icel. *tjald*, G. *zelt*. Perhaps orig. 'skin;' cf. Gk. δέρος, a skin.

Tilt (2), to cause to heel over, to joust in a tourney. (E.) Orig. sense 'to totter;' hence to cause to totter, to upset, tilt over, upset an enemy in a tourney. M. E. *tilten*, *tylten*, to totter, be unsteady; answering to an A. S. *tyltan* * (not found), regularly formed (by change from *ea* to *y*) from A. S. *tealt*, adj., unsteady, unstable.+Icel. *tölta*, to amble; Swed. *tulta*, to waddle; G. *zelt*, an ambling pace. Der. *tilt*, sb.

toddle, to walk unsteadily. (E.) The same as Lowl. Sc. *tottle*, to walk with short steps, and equivalent to E. *totter*; see below.

totter, to be unsteady. (E.) Put for *tolter*, a form occurring in Clare's Village Minstrel; cf. Lowl. Sc. *tolter*, adj. and adv., unsteady (not a *verb*, as Jamieson says). *Tolter*, as a vb., is a frequentative of M. E. *tulten*, to tilt, be unsteady (above); and is just the same as A. S. *tealtrian*, to totter, from the adj. *tealt*, unsteady. + O. Du. *touteren* (= *tolteren* *), to tremble.

Tilth; see Till (1).

Timber, wood for building. (E.) A. S. *timber*, material to build with; put for *timer* * (the *b* being excrescent). + Icel. *timbr*, Dan. *tömmer*, Swed. *timmer*, G. *zimmer*. Cf. Goth. *timrjan*, to build. From Teut. base TAM, to build. (√DAM.)

Timbrel, a kind of tambourine; see Type.

Time. (E.) M. E. *time*. A. S. *tíma*. + Icel. *tími*, Dan. *time*, Swed. *timme*. From the same root as Tide.

Timid. (F. — L.) F. *timide*. — L. *timidus*, fearful. — L. *timere*, to fear. Allied to Skt. *tam*, to choke, *tamas*, darkness. (√TAM.)

intimidate. (L.) From pp. of Low L. *intimidare*, to frighten. — L. *in*, intensive prefix; *timidus*, timid.

timorous. (L.) Coined, with suffix *-ous*, from L. *timor*, fear. — L. *timere*, to fear.

Tin. (E.) A. S. *tin*. + Du. *tin*, Icel. *tin*, Dan. *tin*, Swed. *tenn*, G. *zinn*. ¶ Distinct from L. *stannum*.

Tincture; see Tinge.

Tind, to light or kindle. (E.) Also spelt *tine*; nearly obsolete. M. E. *tenden*. A. S. *tendan*, to kindle. + Dan. *tænde*, Swed. *tända*, Goth. *tandjan*. (From a lost strong verb *tindan* *, making pt. t. *tand* *, pp. *tunden* *.)

tinder. (E.) M. E. *tinder*, more commonly *tunder*, *tondre*. A. S. *tyndre*, anything for kindling fires from a spark. (From pp. *tunden* * of lost verb *tindan* *; see above.) + Icel. *tundr*; cf. *tandri*, fire; Dan. *tönder*, Swed. *tunder*, G. *zunder*, tinder.

Tine, the tooth or spike of a fork or harrow. (E.) Formerly *tind*. M. E. *tind*. A. S. *tind*. + Icel. *tindr*, Swed. *tinne*, tooth of a rake. Prob. allied to Skt. *danta*, a tooth, and to Tooth.

Tinge, to dye. (L.) L. *tingere*, pp.

tinctus, to dye. **+** Gk. τέγγειν, to wet, dye; see tint.

distain. (F.—L.) M. E. *disteinen*.—O. F. *desteindre*, to distain, take away colour. **—** O. F. *des-* = L. *dis-*, away; *tingere*, to dye.

stain, vb. (F.—L.) Short for **distain** (above). 'I *stayne* a thynge, *Je destayns*;' Palsgrave. The orig. sense was to dim the colour of a thing. **Der.** *stain*, sb.

taint, sb. (F.—L.) F. *teint, teinct*, 'a stain;' Cot.—F. *teint*, pp. of *teindre*, to tinge.—L. *tingere*, to dye.

tent (3), a wine. (Span.—L.) From Span. *vino tinto*, a deep-coloured (lit. tinted) wine. **—** L. *tinctus*, pp. of *tingere*, to dye.

tincture. (L.) L. *tinctura*, a dyeing. **—** L. *tinctus*, pp. of *tingere*, to dye.

tint, a tinge of colour. (L.) Formerly *tinct*. Spenser has *tinct* = dyed. **—** L. *tinctus*, pp. of *tingere*, to dye.

Tingle; see **Tinker.**

Tinker. (E.) M. E. *tinkere*. So called because he makes a *tinking* sound, in the mending of metal pots, &c. From M. E. *tinken*, to ring or tinkle; Wyclif, 1 Cor. xiii. 1. Of imitative origin; cf. O. Du. *tinge-tangen*, to tingle, *tintelen*, to tinkle, L. *tinnire*, to tinkle, ring, *tintinnum*, a tinkling.

tingle. (E.) M. E. *tinglen*, a weakened form of *tinklen*, to tinkle, which, again, is a frequentative form of M. E. *tinken*, to tink (above), of which a weaker form is *ting*. 'To *ting*, tinnire; *tingil*, tinnire;' Levins (1570). The orig. sense was to ring, then to vibrate, thrill, to feel a sense of vibration as when a bell is rung.

tinkle, to jingle. (E.) Frequentative of M. E. *tinken*, to ring; see **Tinker.**

Tint; see **Tinge.**

Tinsel; see **Scintillation.**

Tiny, very small. (E.) Preceded, in Shakespeare, by the word *little*; as, 'a *little tiny* boy,' 'my *little tiny* thief,' 'pretty *little tiny* kickshaws.' Also spelt *teeny*; as '*teeny*, (1) tiny, (2) fretful, peevish, fractious;' Halliwell. From *teen*, sb., anger, peevishness; so that the orig. sense of *little tiny* was 'little fractious,' applied to a child or pet, and the orig. sinister sense was lost sight of. See **Teen.** Cf. *pet*, a dear child, with *pettish*, peevish. **¶** This seems the simplest solution.

Tip (1), the extreme top; see **Top.**

Tip (2), to tilt; see **Tap** (1).

Tippet; see **Tapestry.**

Tipple; see p. 491, col. 1, l. 20.

Tipsy; see **Tap** (1).

Tirade; see **Tier.**

Tire (1), to exhaust; see **Tear** (1).

Tire (2), to deck; see **Attire.**

Tire (3), a hoop of iron that binds the fellies of wheels. (F.—Teut. ?) '*Tire*, the ornament of womens heads, the iron band of a cart-wheel,' Phillips, ed. 1706. Prob. identical with *tire*, a woman's head-dress. *Tire* meant to deck, also to arrange. Palsgrave has: 'I *tyer* an egge, *Je accoustre*; I *tyer* with garmentes,' &c. See tire (2), s. v. **Attire.**

Tiro (4), to tear a prey; see **Tear** (1).

Tire (5), a train; see **Tier.**

Tiro, Tyro, a novice. (L.) L. *tiro*, a novice, recruit. **¶** The usual spelling with *y* is absurd.

Tisic; see **Phthisis.**

Tissue; see **Text.**

Tit, a small horse or child. (Scand.) Icel. *tittr*, a tit, bird; Norw. *tita*, a little bird. Orig. 'something small;' cf. prov. E. *titty*, small.

titlark. (Scand. *and* E.) Lit. 'small lark;' from **tit** and **lark.**

titmouse, a kind of small bird. (Scand. *and* E.) Not connected with *mouse*; the true pl. should be *titmouses*, but *titmice* is used, by confusion with *mice*. M. E. *titmose*. Compounded of *tit*, small (see **Tit**); and A. S. *máse*, a name for several small birds, e.g. A. S. *fræc-máse, colmáse, swic-máse*, all names of birds. **+** Du. *mees*, G. *meise*, a titmouse, small bird. The sense of A. S. *máse* was also probably 'small;' from √MI, to diminish.

Titan, the sun-god. (L. **—** Gk.) L. *Titan*.—Gk. Τιτάν, the sun-god. **+** Skt. *tithá*, fire. (√ TITH, to burn.) **Der.** *titan-ic*.

Tit for tat, blow for blow. (Scand.) A corruption of *tip for tap*, where *tip* is a slight tap (Bullinger, Works, i. 283).

Tithe; see **Ten.**

Titillation, a tickling. (F. **—** L.) F. *titillation*.—L. acc. *titillationem*, a tickling. **—** L. *titillatus*, pp. of *titillare*, to tickle.

Titlark; see **Tit.**

Title. (F. **—** L.) M. E. *title*. **—** O. F. *title* (F. *titre*).—L. *titulum*, acc. of *titulus*, a superscription on a tomb, altar. Cf. Gk. τιμή, honour. **Der.** *titul-ar*, from F. *titulaire*, titular.

tittle, a jot. (F.—L.) M. E. *titel*.—O. F. *title*, a title; also *titre, tiltre*, 'a tittle, a small line drawn over an abridged word, also a title;' Cot.—L. *titulum*, acc. of *titulus*, a title. β. In late Latin *titulus* must have meant a mark over a word, as shewn by O. F. *title* (above).

Titmouse; see **Tit.**

Titter; see **Tattle.**

Tittle; see **Title.**

Tittle-tattle, prattle; see **Tattle.**

To. (E.) M. E. *to*. A. S. *tô*. + Du. *toe*, G. *zu*, Goth. *du*, Russ. *do*, to, up to. Cf. Gk. -δε, towards.

to- (2), *prefix*, to. (E.) Only in *to-day*, *to-gether*, *to-morrow*, *to-night*, *to-ward*; and in the obsolete M. E. *to-name*, nickname, and a few other words. See below.

to-day, this day. (E.) Compounded of *to*, prep., and *day*; *to* being formerly used in the sense of 'for.' Thus A. S. *tô dæge* = for the day, to-day; *dæge* being the dat. of *dæg*, day. So also *to-night*, *to-morrow*.

too. (E.) The same word as *to*, prep.; used adverbially.

To- (1), *prefix*, in twain, asunder, to pieces. (E.) Only retained in the phrase *all to-brake* = utterly broke asunder, Judges ix. 53. The M. E. phrase *al to-brake* meant wholly brake-asunder, the *al* being adverbial, and *to-brake* the pt. t. of *tobreken*, to break asunder. But about A.D. 1500, it was mistakenly written *all-to brake*, as if *all-to* meant 'altogether,' and *brake* was separate from *to*; and later writers much confused the matter, which is still often wrongly explained. The A. S. *tô-*, prefix, was very common, as in *tôbrecan*, to break asunder, *tôblâwan*, to blow asunder; cognate with O. Friesic *to-*, *te-*, O. H. G. *zar-*, G. *zer-*, signifying 'asunder.' Further cognate with L. *dis-*, apart; see **Dis-.**

To- (2), *prefix*; see **To.**

Toad. (E.) M. E. *tode*. A. S. *tádige*, *tádie*, a toad.

tadpole. (E. *and* C.) Lit. a *toad* which is nearly all *poll* or head; from its shape; see **Poll.** Formerly called a *bull-head*, which was also the name of a small fish with a large head.

toad-eater. (E.) Formerly a companion or assistant to a mountebank, who pretended to eat toads, swallow fire, &c.; now shortened to *toady*.

Toast, (1) and (2); see **Torrid.**

Tobacco. (Span.—Hayti.) Span. *tabaco*. A word taken from the language of Hayti (Clavigero, Hist. of Mexico).

Tocsin; see **Touch.**

Tod, a bush, a measure of wool, a fox. (Scand.) Icel. *toddi*, a tod of wool, bit, piece (the fox being named *tod* from his bushy tail).+G. *zotte*, *zote*, a tuft of hair, anything shaggy.

Today; see **To.**

Toddle; see **Tilt** (2).

Toddy. (Hindustani.) Hind. *tári*, *tádi*, 'vulgarly toddy, juice or sap of the palmyra-tree,' &c.; H. H. Wilson. —Hind. *tár*, a palm-tree, palmyra-tree. ¶ The *r* has a peculiar sound, which has come to be represented by *d* in English.

Toe. (E.) A. S. *tá*, pl. *tán*. A contracted form, standing for *táhe**.+Du. *teen*, Icel. *tá*, Dan. *taa*, Swed. *tå*, G. *zehe*; O. H. G. *zéhá*, a toe, also a finger. Allied to **Digit.**

Toft; see **Tuft** (2).

Toga; see **Tegument.**

Together; see **Gather.**

Toil (1), labour; to labour. (F.—Teut.?) M. E. *toil*, disturbance, tumult; *toilen*, to pull about (the sense having somewhat altered).—O. F. *touiller*, to entangle, shuffle together, mix confusedly, trouble, &c.; see Cotgrave. Prob. from a frequentative form of O. H. G. *zucchen* (G. *zucken*), to twitch, pull quickly; cf. O. H. G. *zocchón*, to pull, tear, snatch away, *zogón*, to tear, pull; all derivatives from O. H. G. *zîhan* (G. *ziehen*), to pull; see **Tow** (1). ¶ *Toil* is often derived from O. Du. *tuylen*, to till or manure land, but it is impossible to explain it from this source; the M. E. usage is completely at variance with this view.

Toil (2), a snare; see **Text.**

Toilet, Toilette; see **Text.**

Toise; see **Tend** (1).

Tokay, a wine. (Hungary.) From *Tokay*, a town in Hungary, E. N. E. from Pesth.

Token. (E.) M. E. *token*. A. S. *tácen*, *tácn*.—A. S. *teáh* (=*táh**), pt. t. of *tîhan*, usually *teón*, to point out, indicate, hence to accuse, criminate. + Du. *teeken*, Icel. *tákn*, *teikn*, Dan. *tegn*, Swed. *tecken*, G. *zeichen*, Goth. *taikns*. All from Teut. base TIH = √DIK, whence L. *in-dic-are*, to point out. See **Diction.**

betoken. (E.) Formed from *token* with prefix *be-* = A. S. *be-*, *bi*, by.

teach. (E.) M. E. *techen*. A. S. *tǽcan*, to shew how to do, shew, pt. t. *tǽhte*, pp. *tǽht*. Formed (with usual change from *d* to *é*) from *tác-*, base of *tác-en*, a token, also appearing as *teáh*, pt. t. of *tîhan* (above).

Tolerate. (L.) From pp. of L. *tolerare*,

to put up with; allied to *tollere*, to lift,
bear, take.+Skt. *tul*, to lift, Gk. τλῆ-ναι,
to suffer, A. S. *þolian*, to endure. (√TAR,
TAL.) β. From L. *tlatum*, supine of *tollere*, usually written *latum*, are formed numerous derivatives, such as *ab-lat-ive*, *collat-
-ion*, *di-late*, *e-late*, *ob-late*, &c.; see below.

ablative; see Ablative.

collation, a comparison; formerly, a
conference. (F. ‒ L.) O. F. *collation*, a
conference. ‒ L. acc. *collationem*, a bringing
together, a conferring. ‒ L. *collatum*, supine
in use with the verb *conferre*, to bring together (but from a different root). ‒ L. *col-
* (for *con- =cum*), together; *latum*, supine
of *tollere*, to take, bear. See above.

correlate, to relate or refer mutually.
(L.) Coined from L. *cor-* (*=cum*), together; and **relate** (below).

delay, sb. (F. ‒ L.) O. F. *delai*, delay
(The same as Ital. *dilata*, delay.) ‒ L.
dilata, fem. of *dilatus*, deferred, put off.
‒ L. *di-* (*=dis-*), apart; *latus*, borne, carried, pp. of *tollere* (above).

dilate. (F. ‒ L.) O. F. *dilater*, to widen.
‒ L. *dilatus*, spread abroad; the same as
dilatus, deferred; see **delay** (above).

elate, lifted up, proud. (L.) L. *elatus*,
lifted up. ‒ L. *e*, out; *latus*, pp. of *tollere*,
to lift.

extol. (L.) L. *extollere*, to lift or
raise up. ‒ L. *ex*, out, up; *tollere*, to lift.

oblate, widened at the sides. (L.) L.
oblatus, spread out (at the sides). ‒ L. *ob*,
towards; *latus*, borne, carried out, pp. of
tollere, to bear.

oblation, an offering. (F. ‒ L.) F.
oblation, an offering; Cot. ‒ L. acc. *obla-
tionem*, acc. of *oblatio*, an offering. ‒ L.
oblatus, used as pp. of *offerre*, to offer (but
from a different root); see oblate (above).

prelate, a church dignitary. (F. ‒ L.)
O. F. *prelat*. ‒ L. *prælatus*, set above; used
as pp. of *præferre*, to prefer (but from a
different root). ‒ L. *præ*, before; *latus*,
borne, set, pp. of *tollere*, to lift, bear.

prolate, extended in the direction of
the polar axis. (L.) L. *prolatus*, extended.
‒ L. *pro*, forward; *latus*, carried, pp. of
tollere, to lift, bear.

relate, to describe, tell. (F. ‒ L.) F. *re-
later*, 'to relate;' Cot. ‒ Low L. *relatare*,
to relate. ‒ L. *relatus*, used as pp. of *referre*,
to relate (but from a different root). ‒ L. *re-*,
again; *latus*, borne, pp. of *tollere*, to bear.

superlative. (F. ‒ L.) F. *superlatif*,
Cot. ‒ L. *superlatiuus*, as a grammatical

term. ‒ L. *superlatus*, excessive, lit. ' borne
beyond.' ‒ L. *super*, beyond; *latus*, pp. of
tollere, to bear.

translate. (F. ‒ L.) F. *translater*,
Cot. ‒ Low L. *translatare*, to translate
(12th cent.). ‒ L. *translatus*, transferred;
used as pp. of *transferre* (but from a different root). ‒ L. *trans*, across, beyond;
latus, borne, pp. of *ferre*, to bear. See
also Atlas, Legislate, Talent.

Toll (1), a tax. (E.) M. E. *tol*. A. S.
toll, tribute. +Du. *tol*, Icel. *tollr*, Dan. *told*
(for *toll**), Swed. *tull*, G. *zoll*. Prob. allied
to Tale. ¶ There is no reason for sup-
posing it due to Gk. τελώνιον, a toll-house;
the word is prob. truly Teutonic, and if so,
a cognate Gk. word would begin with *d*.

Toll (2), to pull a bell, sound as a bell.
(E.) The old use was ' to *toll* a bell,' i. e.
to pull it; from M. E. *tollen*, to stir, draw,
pull, allied to *tullen*, to entice, allure, and
prob. to A. S. *fortyllan*, to allure; see
Till (3).

Tolu, a kind of resin. (S. America.) Said
to be named from *Tolu*, a place on the
N. W. coast of New Granada, S. America.

Tom, pet name for Thomas. (L. ‒ Gk. ‒
Heb.) M. E. *Thomme*. ‒ L. *Thomas*. ‒ Gk.
Θωμᾶς, Thomas. From Heb. *thoma*, a twin.

tomboy, a rude girl. (L. ‒ Gk. ‒ Heb.;
and O. Low G.) From Tom and Boy.

tomtit, a small bird. (L. ‒ Gk. ‒ Heb.;
and Scand.) From Tom and Tit.

Tomahawk, a light war-hatchet. (W.
Indian.) Algonkin *tomehagen*, Mohegan
tumnahegan, Delaware *tamoihecan*, a war-
hatchet (Webster).

Tomato, a love-apple. (Span. ‒ Mexican.?) Span. (and Port.) *tomate*. ‒ Mexican
tomatl, a tomato (Littré).

Tomb. (F. ‒ L. ‒ Gk.) F. *tombe*. ‒ L.
tumba. ‒ Gk. τύμβος*, put for τύμβος, a
tomb. Allied to Tumulus.

Tomboy; see Tom.

Tome, a volume. (F. ‒ L. ‒ Gk.) F.
tome. ‒ L. acc. *tomum*. ‒ Gk. τόμος, a section, a volume. ‒ Gk. τέμνειν, to cut.
Allied to Tonsure. (√TAM or TAN.)

anatomy. (F. ‒ L. ‒ Gk.) F. *ana-
tomie*. ‒ L. *anatomia*. ‒ Gk. ἀνατομία, the
same as ἀνατομή, dissection. ‒ Gk. ἀνατέμ-
νειν, to cut up. ‒ Gk. ἀνά, up; τέμνειν,
to cut.

atom. (F. ‒ L. ‒ Gk.) F. *atome* (Cot.)
‒ L. *atomus*. ‒ Gk. ἄτομος, sb., an indivisi-
ble particle; allied to ἄτομος, adj., indivisi-
ble. ‒ Gk. ἀ-, not; τέμνειν, to cut, divide.

entomology. (Gk.) From Gk. *ἔντομο-ν*, an insect; neut. of *ἔντομο-s*, cut into, so called from the very thin middle part (see **Insect**).—Gk. *ἐν*, in; *τέμνειν*, to cut.

epitome. (L.—Gk.) L. *epitome.*—Gk. *ἐπιτομή*, a surface-incision, also an abridgment.—Gk. *ἐπί*, upon; *τέμνειν.* to cut. Cf. **Lithotomy, Phlebotomy.**

Tomorrow; see to-day, under To.

Tomtit; see Tom.

Ton, Tun, a large barrel, great weight. (L.) M. E. *tonne*, a large barrel, hence a great weight. A. S. *tunne*, a barrel. So also Du. *ton*, Icel. Swed. *tunna*, Dan. *tönde*, tun, cask; G. *tonne*, cask, weight; Gael. and Irish *tunna*, W. *tynell*, tun, barrel. All from Low L. *tunna*, a cask (9th cent.). Prob. allied to L. *tinea, tina, tinum*, a wine-vessel, cask.

tunnel. (F. — L.) O. F. *tonnel* (later *tonneau*), a tun, great vessel; hence a tunnel (or trap) for partridges, which was an arched tunnel of wire, strengthened by *hoops* at intervals (whence the name). It came to mean any kind of tunnel or shaft, e. g. the shaft or pipe of a chimney, &c. Dimin. from Low L. *tunna* (above).

Tone. (F.—L.—Gk.) F. *ton.* — L. acc. *tonum.* — Gk. *τόνος*, a thing stretched, a string, note, tone.—Gk. *τείνειν*, to stretch. + Skt. *tan*, to stretch. (√TAN.)

attune, to bring to a like tune. (L. *and* L. — Gk.) From L. *at-* (=*ad*), to; and E. tune (below).

diatonic, proceeding by tones. (Gk.) Gk. *διατονικός*, from *διάτονος* (lit. stretched out), diatonic. — Gk. *διατείνειν*, to stretch out. — Gk. *διά*, out, thoroughly; *τείνειν*, to stretch.

intone, to chant. (L. *and* Gk.) Low L. *intonare*, to sing according to tone.—L. *in*, in; Gk. *τόνος*, a tone. ¶ Occasionally confused with L. *intonare*, to thunder forth, a pure Latin word.

tonic. (Gk.) Lit. 'giving tone.'—Late Gk. *τονικός*, adj., from *τόνος* (above).

tune, tone, melody. (F. — L. — Gk.) M. E. *tune.* — F. *ton*, 'a tune, or sound;' Cot. See **Tone.**

Tongs, s. pl. (E.) M. E. *tonge, tange*, sing. sb.; the pl. is due to the *two* arms of the instrument. A. S. *tange*, a pair of tongs, pincers; also *tang*.+Du. *tang*, Icel. *töng* (pl. *tangir*), Dan. *tang*, Swed. *tång*, G. *zange*. Orig. sense 'a biter' or 'nipper;' from √DAK, to bite.

tang (1), a strong taste. (Du.) O. Du.

tanger, sharp, biting to the taste; lit. pinching. — Du. *tang*, a pair of pincers (above).

tang (3), tongue of a buckle, the part of a knife which goes into the haft. (Scand.) Icel. *tangi*, tang of a knife, which is *nipped* by the handle; allied to *töng*, tongs (above).

Tongue. (E.) M. E. *tunge, tonge.* A. S. *tunge.* + Icel. Swed. *tunga*, Dan. *tunge*, Du. *tong*, G. *zunge*, Goth. *tuggo* (=*tungo**). + O. Lat. *dingua* (L. *lingua*), Irish *teanga* (for *denga**), a tongue. Root uncertain. Allied to **Lingual.**

Tonic; see **Tone.**

Tonight; see to-day, under To.

Tonsil. (F. — L.) F. *tonsille*; Cot.— L. *tonsilla*, a sharp pointed pole for mooring boats; pl. *tonsillæ*, the tonsils (the reason is not clear). Dimin. of *tonsa*, an oar.

Tonsure. (F. — L.) F. *tonsure.* — L. *tonsura*, a clipping. — L. *tonsus*, pp. of *tondere*, to shear, clip. Cf. Gk. *τένδειν*, to gnaw; see **Tome.**

Tontine, a kind of lottery. (F. — Ital.) F. *tontine.* Named from Laurence *Tonti*, a Neapolitan (about A.D. 1653).

Too; see To.

Tool; see Taw.

Toom, empty. (Scand.) M. E. *tom*, *toom.*—Icel. *tómr*, Swed. Dan. *tom*, empty.

teem (3), to empty. (Scand.) Icel. *tœma*, Dan. *tömme*, Swed. *tömma*, verb; from the adj. above. And see **Tuft** (2).

Toot (1), to peep, spy; see **Tout.**

Toot (2), to blow a horn. (O. Low G.) Spelt *tute* in Levins (1570).—O. Du. *tuyten*, 'to sound a cornet,' Hexham; cf. Du. *toethoren*, a toot-horn, bugle.+Swed. *tjuta*, Dan. *tude*, to howl, to toot ; Icel. *þjóta* (pt. t. *þaut*), to resound, blow a horn; A. S. *þeótan*, to howl; cf. Goth. *thut-haurn*, a trumpet. (√TUD.) Allied to **Thud.**

Tooth. (E.) A.S. *tóð*, pl. *téð* and *tóðas.* (The long *o* is due to loss of *n*; *tóð* = *tanth.*) + Du. *tand*, Icel. *tönn*, Dan. *tand*, Swed. *tand*, G. *zahn*, O. H. G. *zand*, Goth. *tunthus.*+L. *dens* (stem *dent*-), Lith. *dantis*, W. *dant*, Skt. *danta*, Gk. *ὀδούς* (stem *ὀδόντ-*). All participial forms; orig. sense either 'dividing,' from √DA, or 'eating,' from √AD; according as *δ* in Gk. *ὀδόντ-* is unoriginal or original.

Top (1), summit. (E.) M.E. *top.* A.S. *top.* + Du. *top*; Icel. *toppr*, tuft, top; Dan. *top*, tuft, crest, top; Swed. *topp*, summit; G. *zopf*, tuft, top. Allied to **Tap** (of a cask). Der. *topp-le*, to be top-heavy, tumble over.

tip (1). (E.) A weakened form of *top*. M. E. *tip*. + Du. Swed. Dan. *tip*, Low G. *tip*; cf. G. *zipfel*, a small tip. **Der.** *tip*, verb, chiefly in pp. *tipped*, i. e. furnished with a silver top or iron spike; whence *tipped-staff*, later *tipstaff*, an officer with a tipped staff.

top (2), a child's toy. (E.) M. E. *top*; so called because sharpened to a tip or top, on which it is spun. Cf. O. Du. *top*, (1) summit, (2) child's top.

topsyturvy. (E.) Formerly *top-turvy*, *topsydturvy*, *topsy-tervy* (1528). Hardly for *top-side-turvy*, where *top-side* = upper side; for *topsyterny* is the older form. Just as *upside down* was formerly *upsodown*, so *topsyterny* prob. = *top so tervy*. *Tervy* may be from A. S. *torfian*, to throw, cast; M.E. *torvien*, to throw (Layamon, 16703). But much doubt remains. ¶ Explained *topside t'other way* by late writers, where *t'other way* is a false gloss.

Topaz, a gem. (F. — L. — Gk.) F. *topase*. — L. *topazus*, *topazion*. — Gk. τόπαζος, τοπάζιον, a topaz. Prob. from its brightness; cf. Skt. *tapa*, illuminating. ¶ Pliny derives it from an island called *Topazos*, in the Red Sea, the position of which is 'conjectural;' from Gk. τοπάζειν, to conjecture. This is 'conjectural' indeed.

Toper, a great drinker. (F. *or* Ital. — Teut. ?) Certainly allied to F. *tôper*, to cover a stake, a term in dice-playing; whence *tôpe*, interjection (short for *je tôpe*, I accept your offer) in the sense 'agreed!' Also used as a term in drinking; cf. O. Ital. *topa*, in dicing, agreed! throw! also (in drinking), I pledge you! Cf. Span. *topar*, to butt, strike, accept a bet. Of Teut. origin; from the *striking* of hands or of glasses together, as in Ital. *intoppare*, to strike against an obstacle. Cf. E. *tap*, *top*, *tup*, which appear to be from an imitative root meaning to strike; the W. *topi* means 'to gore with the horns.' (Form of root STAP?)

Topic. (F. — L. — Gk.) F. *topiques*, 'topicks, books or places of logical invention.' — L. *topica*, s. pl., title of a work by Aristotle. — Gk. τοπικά (the same), neut. pl. of τοπικός, local, relating to τόποι or common-places. — Gk. τόπος, a place.

topography. (F. — L. — Gk.) F. *topographie*. — L. *topographia*. — Gk. τοπο-γραφία, description of a place. — Gk. τόπο-s, a place; γράφ-ειν, to describe.

Topple; see under Top (1).

Topsyturvy; see Top (1).
Torch; see Torture.
Torment, Tormentil; see Torture.
Tornado; see Turn.
Torpedo; see below.
Torpid, sluggish. (L.) L. *torpidus*, benumbed. — L. *torpere*, to be numb or stiff; orig. to be sated; cf. Skt. *trip*, to be sated; τέρπειν, to satisfy. (√TARP.)

torpedo. (L.) L. *torpedo*, numbness; also a cramp-fish (which electrifies or numbs). — L. *torpere* (above).

Torrent; see below.
Torrid. (F. — L.) F. *torride*. — L. *torridus*, scorched. — L. *torrere*, to be dry. + Gk. τέρσεσθαι, to become dry. (√TARS.)

toast (1), scorched bread. (F. — L.) O. F. *tostée*, a toast of bread; orig. pp. fem. — L. *tosta*, pp. fem. of *torrere*, to parch (above).

toast (2), a person whose health is drunk. (F. — L.) The reference is to the *toast* usually put in stirrup-cups, &c., in drinking healths; see the story in the Tatler, no. 24, June 4, 1709 (Todd).

torrent. (F. — L.) F. *torrent*. — L. acc. *torrentem*, a raging stream; from *torrens*, raging, impetuous, boiling, hot; orig. pres. pt. of *torrere*, to heat.

Torsion; see Torture.
Torso, trunk of a statue. (Ital. — L. — Gk.) Ital. *torso*, stump, trunk, stalk. — L. *thyrsus*, stalk, stem. — Gk. θύρσος, a stalk, rod, thyrsus.

Tortoise, Tortuous; see Torture.
Torture. (F. — L.) F. *torture*. — L. *tortura*, torture, wringing pain. — L. *tortus*, pp. of *torquere*, to twist, wring, whirl. Allied to **Throw**. (√TARK.)

contort. (L.) L. *contortus*, pp. of *con-torquere*, to twist together.

distort. (L.) L. *distortus*, pp. of *dis-torquere*, to twist aside.

extort. (L.) L. *extortus*, pp. of *ex-torquere*, to twist out, wring out.

retort, a censure returned; tube for distilling. (F. — L.) F. *retorte*, a retort; lit. a thing twisted back. — F. *retorte*, fem. of *retort*, pp. of *retordre*, to twist back. — L. *re-torquere*, to twist back.

tart (2), a small pie. (F. — L.) M. E. *tarte*. — O. F. *tarte*, 'a tart;' Cot. Named from being twisted up; the same as F. *tourte*, a tart, Ital. *tartera*, *torta*, a pie or tart, Span. *torta*, a round cake. — L. *torta*, fem. of *tortus*, pp. of *torquere* (above).

torch. (F. — L.) M. E. *torche*. — F.

torche, a torch, also a wreath, wreathed wisp or piece of tow, Low L. *tortia*, a torch, twist. — L. *tortus*, pp. of *torquere*, to twist.

torment. (F. — L.) O. F. *torment* (F. *tourment*). — L. *tormentum*, an engine for throwing stones, or for inflicting torture. Formed with suffix *-mentum* from *tor-*, put for *torc-*, base of *torquere*, to twist, hurl.

tormentil, a herb. (F. — L.) F. *tormentille*. Said to be so called from its relieving tooth-ache. — O. F. *torment*, torment, pain (above).

torsion. (F. — L.) F. *torsion*, 'a wresting;' Cot. — L. acc. *torsionem*, a wringing. — L. *tors-i*, pt. t. of *torquere*, to twist.

tortoise. (F. — L.) M. E. *tortuce, tortu, tortoise*. The form is Southern French; cf. Prov. *tortesa*, a tortoise; the M. E. *tortu* answers to F. *tortue*, a tortoise. So named from the twisted feet; cf. O. F. *tortis*, crooked. All due to L. *tortus*, pp. of *torquere*, to twist.

tortuous. (F. — L.) M. E. *tortuos*. — F. *tortueux*. — L. *tortuosus*, crooked. — L. *tortus*, pp. of *torquere*, to twist.

trousers, trowsers. (F. — L.) The latter *r* is modern; put for the old word *trowses*, or *trouses*, breeches. — F. *trousses*, s. pl. breeches, trunk-hose. A jocular term, signifying 'cases' or 'coverings,' pl. of *trousse*, a bundle, case, quiver. — F. *trousser*, to truss, pack, gird, tuck up, &c.; see truss (below).

trousseau, a package; bride's outfit. (F. — L.) F. *trousseau*, a little bundle; dimin. of *trousse*, a bundle, a pack; from O. F. *trousser*, to pack; see below.

truss, to pack, fasten up. (F. — L.) O. F. *trusser*, also *torser* (later *trousser*), to pack up; orig. to twist together; answering to a Low L. *tortiare**. — L. *tortus*, pp. of *torquere*, to twist. Compare torch (above).

Tory. (Irish.) First used about 1680 in the political sense. The Irish State Papers, Jan. 24, 1656, mention 'tories and other lawless persons.' — Irish *toiridhe*, *tor, toruighe*, lit. a (hostile) pursuer, also a searcher (hence, a plunderer); cf. *toireacht*, pursuit, search, &c. — Irish *toirighim*, I fancy, I pursue, search closely. Cf. Gael. *toir*, pursuit, search; &c.

Tose; see Touse.

Toss, to jerk. (W.) W. *tosio*, to jerk, toss; *tos*, a quick jerk, toss.

Total. (F. — L.) F. *total*. — Low L.

totalis, adj.; extended from L. *totus*, entire, orig. 'very great.' (√TU.)

surtout. (F. — L.) From F. *sur tout*, lit. 'over all.' — L. *super*, over; *totum*, acc. of *totus*, all. And see Teetotaller, Teetotum.

Totter; see Tilt (2).

Toucan, a bird. (F. — Brazil.) F. *toucan*; a Brazilian word (Littré).

Touch. (F. — Teut.) F. *toucher*. (Also O. F. *toquer*, to knock or strike against; Ital. *toccare*, to touch, strike, smite.) — O. H. G. *zucchen*, G. *zucken*, to twitch, draw with a quick motion. A secondary verb, due to O. H. G. *ziohan* (G. *ziehen*), cognate with Goth. *tiuhan*, L. *ducere*, to draw, lead. (√DUK.) See Tow (1).

tocsin, sound of an alarm-bell. (F. — Teut. *and* L.) O. F. *toquesing* (F. *tocsin*), an alarm-bell, or its sound. Lit. 'striking of the signal-bell.' — O. F. *toqu-er*, to strike, touch; O. F. *sing* (mod. F. *signe*), a sign, a signal; see Sign.

tucket, a flourish on a trumpet. (Ital. — Teut.) Ital. *toccata*, a prelude, tolling of a bell, a tucket; a striking. — Ital. *toccata*, fem. of pp. of *toccare*, to strike, touch; see Touch.

Touchwood. (Low G. ?) *Wood* is superfluous; *touch* is for M. E. *tache*, tinder for receiving sparks (P. Plowman, B. xvii. 245). Perhaps from Low G. *takk*, Du. *tak*, twig, bough; so that *taches* are 'dried sticks.' See Tag, Tack.

Touchy, corruption of Tetchy, q. v.

Tough. (E.) M. E. *tough*. A. S. *tóh*, tough. + Du. *taai*, flexible, pliant, viscous, tough; G. *zähe*, O. H. G. *zähe*, tough, tenacious. Perhaps allied to Goth. *tahjan*, to rend (orig. to bite = Gk. δάκνειν); as being that which resists biting, hard to bite.

Tour; see Turn.

Tournament, Tourniquet; see Turn.

Touse, Tose, to pull about, tear. (E.) M. E. *tosen*, to pull, orig. to tease wool. [Cf. mod. E. *Towzer*, a dog's name, lit. 'tearer.'] This answers to an A. S. *túsan**, *túsian**, only found in the modified form *túsan* (below).

tease, to card wool, to vex, plague. (E.) M. E. *taisen*; (more commonly, *tosen*). A. S. *túsan*, to pluck, pull, modified from an older form *túsian**, not recorded, but the original of M. E. *tosen*. + O. Du. *teesen*, to pluck wool; Dan. *tæse*, Bavarian *zaisen* (Schmeller).

teasel, a plant. (E.) M. E. *tesel*,

A. S. *tǽsl*, *tǽsel*, lit. 'teaser,' from its use in teasing wool.—A. S. *tǽsan*, to tease.

tussle, to scuffle. (E.) The same as *tousle*, to disorder; frequent. of *touse*, to pull about.

Tout, to solicit custom. (E.) M. E. *toten*, orig. to peep about, hence to be on the look-out for custom. A. S. *tótian*, to project, stick out (hence, peep out). Cf. Icel. *tota*, *túta*, peak, Dan. *tude*, spout, Swed. *tut*, point, muzzle, &c. ¶ Not allied in any way to Toot (2).

Tow (1), to tug along. (E.) M. E. *towen*, *toȝen*. Not in A. S.; but we find A. S. *toh-line*, a tow-line, towing-rope.— A. S. *tog-en*, pp. of *teóhan*, *teón*, to pull, draw. + G. *ziehen*, Goth. *tiuhan*, L. *ducere*, to draw. (√DUK.)

tie, vb. (E.) M. E. *tiȝen*, *teyen*, to tie; an unoriginal verb, from the sb. *teye*, a tie, band.—A. S. *teág*, *teáh*, *týge*, a rope.—A. S. *tug-on*, pt. t. pl. of *teóhan*, to pull (above). Cf. Icel. *taug*, a tie, *tygill*, a string.

tuck (1), to gather in a dress. (O. Low G.) M. E. *tukken*.—Low G. *tukken*, to pull up, draw up, tuck up, also to entice (=O. Du. *tocken*, to entice). Formed from the same base as *tug* (below). + G. *zucken*, to twitch up; see Tough.

tug, vb. (O. Low G.) M. E. *toggen*.— O. Du. *tocken*, *tucken*, to entice; Low G. *tukken*, to pull up, draw up. From the base appearing in A. S. *tug-on*, pt. t. pl. of *teóhan*, to pull; see tie (above).

Tow (2), coarse part of hemp; see Taw.

Toward, **Towards**. (E.) M. E. *towardes*, formed by adding *-es* (genitive suffix used adverbially) to M. E. *toward*. The A. S. *tóweard* is usually an adj., with the sense 'future, about to come'; *tóweardes* was a prep., usually put after its case.— A. S. *tó*, too; *-weard*, in the direction of, cognate with Icel. *-verðr*, M. H. G. *-wert*, Goth. *-wairths*, and allied to L. *uersus*, towards. β. All these suffixes are derivatives of the verb appearing in E. as *worth*, to become; see Worth (2). The same suffix appears in *after-ward*, *in-ward*, &c.; the lit. sense is 'that which has become' or 'that which is made to be,' or 'that which is turned;' hence *in-ward* = turned in, *to-ward*, turned to, &c.

Towel. (F.—O. H. G.) M. E. *towaille*. — F. *touaille*, 'a towel;' Cot. O. F. *toaille* (Low L. *toacula*, Span. *toalla*, Ital. *tovaglia*). — O. H. G. *twahilla*, *dwahilla* (G. *zwehle*), a towel.—O. H. G. *twahan*, to

wash.+A.S. *þweán* (= *þwahan*), Icel. *þvá*; Dan. *toe*, Goth. *thwahan*, to wash.

Tower. (F.—L.) O. F. *tur* (later *tour*). —L. *turrem*, acc. of *turris*, a tower.+Gk. τύρσις, τύρρις, a tower, bastion; cf. Gael. *torr*, conical hill, tower, castle.

turret. (F. — L.) F. *tourette*; Cot. Dimin. of O. F. *tur*, F. *tour* (above).

Town. (E.) M. E. *toun*, an enclosure, town. A. S. *tún*, a fence, farm, town.+ Du. *tuin*, fence, Icel. *tún*, enclosure, homestead, G. *zaun*, hedge. + Irish and Gael. *dun*, a fortress, W. *din*, a hill-fort. Cf. Irish *dur*, L. *durus*, firm.

Toxicology, the science which investigates poisons. (Gk.) From Gk. τοξικό-ν, poison for arrows (from τόξον, a bow); -λογία, from λέγειν, to discourse. β. Τόξον is from √TAKS, to hew, shape, extended from √TAK, to cut; see Tactics.

Toy, sb. (Du.) Du. *tuig*, tools, utensils, implements, stuff, refuse, trash; whence *speel-tuig*, playthings, toys, lit. 'stuff to play with.' Hence the phrase *op de tuy houden*, 'to hold with a toy,' to amuse, toy with one; O. Du. *tuyg*, 'silver chains with a knife, cizzars, pincushion, &c. as women wear,' Sewel. + Icel. *tygi*, gear, Dan. *töi*, gear, *lege-töi*, a plaything, toy, Swed. *tyg*, gear, trash, G. *zeug*, stuff, trash, G. *spielzeug*, playthings. β. Perhaps the orig. sense was 'spoil;' cf. Icel. *toga af*, to strip off; the form allies it with Tow (1). (√DUK.) ¶ As to the sound, cf. *hoy* = Flemish *hui*.

Trace (1), a track, foot-print. (F.—L.) F. *trace*, 'trace, path, tract;' Cot. A verbal sb. from F. *tracer*, to trace, follow, also spelt *trasser*, to trace out, delineate. The same as Ital. *tracciare*, Span. *trazar*, to trace out, plan, sketch. These answer to a Low L. *tractiare**, formed from *tractus*, pp. of *trahere*, to draw, originally to drag violently. Cf. Gk. θράσσειν (= τράχ-γειν*), to trouble, θραγ-μός, a crash. (√TARGH.) ¶ Not allied to E. *draw*.

abstract. (L.) L. *abstractus*, pp. of *abs-trahere*, to draw away.

attract. (L.) From L. *attractus*, pp. of *attrahere*, to attract.—L. *at-* (= *ad*), to; *trahere*, to draw.

contract (1), to draw together. (L.) L. *contractus*, pp. of *con-trahere*, to draw together.

contract (2), a bargain. (F.—L.) F. *contract*; Cot.—L. *contractus*, sb., a drawing together, a bargain. — L. *contractus*, pp. (above).

detraction. (L.) From L. *detractio*, a withdrawal ; hence a taking away of one's credit. — L. *detractus*, pp. of *de-trahere*, to take away, also to disparage.

distract, vb. (L.) From L. *distractus*, pp. of *dis-trahere*, to draw apart.

entreat. (F. — L.) O. F. *entraiter*, to treat of. — F. *en* (= L. *in*), in, concerning ; F. *traiter* = L. *tractare*, to handle, treat ; see **treat** (below).

extract, vb. (L.) L. *extractus*, pp. of *ex-trahere*, to draw out.

portrait. (F. — L.) O. F. *pourtraict*, 'a pourtrait ;' Cot. — O. F. *pourtraict, pourtrait*, pp. of *pourtraire*, to portray (below).

portray, pourtray. (F. — L.) M. E. *pourtraien*. — O. F. *portraire, pourtraire*, to portray. — Low L. *protrahere*, to depict ; L. *pro-trahere*, to draw forward, to reveal.

protract. (L.) From L. *protractus*, pp. of *pro-trahere*, to draw forward, also to extend, prolong.

retract. (F. — L.) O. F. *retracter*, 'to revoke ;' Cot. — L. *retractare*, frequent. of *re-trahere*, to draw back.

retreat, sb. (F. — L.) M. E. *retrete*. — O. F. *retrete*, later *retraite*, a retreat, fem. of *retret*, pp. of *retraire*, to withdraw. — L. *re-trahere*, to draw back.

subtract. (L.) L. *subtractus*, pp. of *sub-trahere*, to draw away underneath, to subtract.

trace (2), one of the straps by which a vehicle is drawn. (F. — L.) M. E. *traice, trace*, which Palsgrave explains by O. F. *trays* ; this is a plural form — mod. F. *traits*, pl. of *trait*. — O. F. *trays*, later *traits, traicts*, pl. of *traict*, explained by Cotgrave as 'a teame-trace or trait.' Thus *trace = traits* ; see **trait** (below).

tract (1), a continued duration. a region. (L.) L. *tractus*, a drawing out, course, region. — L. *tractus*, pp. of *trahere*, to draw.

tract (2), a short treatise. (L.) Short for *tractate*, now little used. — L. *tractatus*, a tractate, treatise, tract. — L. *tractatus*, pp. of *tractare*, to handle ; see **treat** (below).

tractable. (L.) L. *tractabilis*, manageable. — L. *tractare*, to handle, frequent. of *trahere* (pp. *tractus*), to draw.

trail, verb. (F. — L.) M. E. *trailen*, to draw along ; from *traile*, sb., a train of a dress. — O. F. *traail* = Low L. *trahale*, a train of a dress (Wright's Vocab. i. 134). From L. *traha*, a sledge ; from *trahere*, to draw.

trailbaston, a law term. (F. — L.) Anglo-F. *traylbastoun*, a term applied to certain lawless men. It meant 'trail-stick' or 'stick-carryer.' Fully explained in Wright's Polit. Songs, p. 383 ; but constantly misinterpreted. The *justices of traylbaston* were appointed by Edw. I. to try them. From *trail*, vb. (above) ; and O. F. *baston*, a stick. See **Baton**.

train, sb. and vb. (F. — L.) M. E. *train*, sb., *trainen*, vb. — F. *train*, a great man's retinue ; *traine*, a sledge ; *trainer*, to trail along (Cot.). — Low L. *trahinare*, to drag along. — L. *trahere*, to draw. **Der.** *train-band*, corruption of *train'd-band*.

trait, a feature. (F. — L.) F. *trait*, a line, stroke ; Cot. — F. *trait*, pp. of *traire*, to draw. — L. *trahere*, to draw.

treat, vb. (F. — L.) F. *traiter*. — L. *tractare*, to handle ; pp. of *trahere* (pp. *tractus*), to draw.

treatise. (F. — L.) M. E. *tretis*. — O. F. *tretis, traitis*, a thing well handled or nicely made ; answering to a Low L. form *tractitius* *. — F. *traiter*, to treat (above).

treaty. (F. — L.) M. E. *tretee*. — O. F. *traite* [i. e. *traité*], a treaty, pp. of *traiter*, to treat (above).

Trace (2), strap of a vehicle ; see **Trace** (1).

Trachea, wind-pipe. (L. — Gk.) L. *trachea*. — Gk. τραχεῖα, lit. 'the rough,' from the rings of gristle round it ; fem. of τραχύς, rough.

Track, a course. (F. — Teut.) Distinct from *trace*. — F. *trac*, 'a track, beaten way ;' Cot. — Du. *trek*, a draught ; *trekken*, to draw, pull, tow, travel, march, &c. Allied to O. H. G. strong verb *trehhan*, to scrape, shove, draw. ¶ In no way allied to **Trace** (1).

treachery. (F. — Teut.) M. E. *trecherie, tricherie*. — F. *tricherie*, treachery ; Cot. — O. F. *tricher, trecher, trichier*, to trick ; cf. Ital. *treccare*, to cheat. — M. H. G. *trechen*, to draw, pull, tow (hence to entice, delude) ; see **trick** (below).

trick (1), a stratagem. (Du.) XIV cent. — Du. *trek*, a trick, also a lineament, the same word as Du. *trek*, a pull, draught, line. — Du. *trekken*, to pull ; cf. M. H. G. *trechen* (above). Cf. Du. *streek*, G. *streich*, a stroke, trick. ¶ The change from *e* to *i* was due to M. E. *trichen*, to play the traitor ; see **treachery** (above).

trick (2), to deck out. (Du.) From the sb. *trick* above, which also meant a neat contrivance, a toy, trifle, &c.

trick (3), to delineate a coat of arms. (Du.) Du. *trekken.* to draw, also to delineate, trick, or sketch out.

trigger. (Du.) Formerly *tricker.*—Du. *trekker,* a trigger; lit. ' that which draws or pulls.'—Du. *trekken,* to pull.

Tract (1) and (2), **Tractable** ; see **Trace** (1).

Trade; see **Tread.**

Tradition; see **Date** (1).

Traduce; see **Duke.**

Traffic, vb. (F.—L.) F. *trafiquer,* ' to traffick ;' Cot. Cf. Ital. *trafficare,* Span. *traficar, trafagar,* Port. *traficar, trafeguear,* to traffic. β. Origin uncertain ; but cf. O. Port. *trasfegar,* to traffic, also to decant wine (Diez). This points a derivation from L. *trans,* across ; and Low L. *vicare*,* to exchange, a vb. formed from L. *uicis,* change (the Low L. *v* becoming *f,* as in F. *fois* from L. *uicis*). ¶ Not from *trans* and *facere* (Scheler), because the suffix *-ficare* becomes *-fier* in French. See **Trans-** and **Vicar.**

Tragedy. (F.—L.—Gk.) F. *tragedie.* —L. *tragœdia.*—Gk. τραγῳδία, a tragedy ; lit. ' a goat-song ; ' prob. because a goat (as the spoiler of the vines) was sacrificed to Dionysus.—Gk. τραγῳδός, a tragic singer; lit. ' goat-singer.'—Gk. τράγ-ος, a he-goat; ᾠδός, a singer, contracted from ἀοιδός ; see **Ode.** Der. *trag-ic,* F. *tragique,* L. *tragicus,* Gk. τραγικός, lit. ' goatish.'

Trail, Trailbaston, Train ; see **Trace** (1).

Train-oil; see **Tear** (2).

Trait; see **Trace** (1).

Traitor, one who betrays. (F.—L.) O. F. *traitor.*—L. *traditorem,* acc. of *traditor,* one who betrays.—L. *tradere,* to betray; see **Date** (1).

betray. (F.—L.; *with* E. *prefix.*) From *be-,* prefix; and O.F. *traïr* (F. *trahir*), to deliver up, from L. *tradere.* ¶ The prefix *be-* was due to confusion with *bewray.*

Trajectory; see **Jet** (1).

Tram, a coal-waggon, car on rails. (Scand.) The words *dram-road* and *tram-road* occur as early as A.D. 1794; we even find *tram* in a will dated 1555 (Surtees Soc. Public. xxxviii. 37). The same as Lowl. Sc. *tram,* shaft of a cart, beam, bar, prov. E. *tram,* a milk-bench (orig. a log of wood). The *tram-road* was prob. at first a log-road, then a rail-road on sleepers.— Swed. dial. *tromm,* log, stock of a tree, also a summer-sledge; O. Swed. *trắm, trum,*

piece of a cut tree. Orig. sense a beam, shaft, bar, log; then a shaft of a cart, a sledge; cf. Low G. *traam,* a beam, handle of a wheel-barrow; O. H. G. *dram, tram,* O. Du. *drom,* a beam, O. Icel. *þram.* Prob. orig. the same as *thrum,* an end, bit; see **Thrum** (1). ¶ The ' derivation ' from *Outram* (about 1800) is ridiculous; it ignores the accent, and contradicts the history.

Trammel. (F.—L.) M. E. *tramaile.* — F. *tramail,* ' a tramell, or a net for partridges;' Cot. (Mod. F. *trémail,* Ital. *tramaglio.*)—Low L. *tramacula, tramagula* (Lex Salica). Prob. from L. *tri-,* threefold, and *macula,* a mesh, net (Diez). ¶ The Span. form *trasmallo* is corrupt.

Tramontane; see **Mount** (1).

Tramp, vb. (E.) M. E. *trampen* ; not in A.S. ✝Low G. and G. *trampen,* Dan. *trampe,* Swed. *trampa,* to tramp, tread; Goth. *ana-trimpan* (pt. t. *ana-tramp*), to tread on. Nasalised form of base TRAP; see **Trap** (1).

trample. (E.) M. E. *trampelen,* frequent. of M. E. *trampen* (above).

Tram-way; see **Tram.**

Trance; see **Itinerant.**

Tranquil. (F.—L.) F. *tranquille,* calm.—L. *tranquillus,* at rest.—L. *tran-,* for *trans,* beyond (hence extremely); and the base *qui-,* to rest, whence also *qui-es,* rest. See **Quiet.**

Trans-, *prefix.* (L.) L. *trans,* beyond, across, over. Orig. pres. pt. of a verb *trare** (whence *in-trare*), to pass over; cf. Skt. *trí,* to pass over. (√ TAR.) ¶ It occurs as *trans-, tran-,* and *tra-.*

Transact; see **Agent.**

Transalpine; see **Alp.**

Transcend; see **Scan.**

Transcribe; see **Scribe.**

Transept. (L.) Lit. cross-enclosure.— L. *tran-,* for *trans,* across ; *septum,* enclosure, orig. neut. of pp. of *sepire,* to enclose, from *sæpes,* a hedge. Cf. Gk. σηκός, a pen, fold.

Transfer; see **Fertile.**

Transfigure, -fix, -form, -fuse; see **Figure, Fix, Form, Fuse** (1).

Transgression; see **Grade.**

Transient, Transit; see **Itinerant.**

Translate; see **Tolerate.**

Translucent; see **Lucid.**

Transmigration; see **Migrate.**

Transmit; see **Missile.**

Transmute; see **Mutable.**

Transom, a thwart-piece across a double

window, lintel, cross-beam. (L.) Corruption of L. *transtrum*, a transom (Vitruvius). — L. *trans*, across; *-trum*, suffix (as in *aratrum*, that which ploughs, a plough).

Transparent; see **Parent**.

Transpicuous; see **Species**.

Transpire; see **Spirit**.

Transplant; see **Plate**.

Transport; see **Port** (1).

Transpose; see **Pose** (1).

Transposition; see **Position**.

Transubstantiation; see **State**.

Transverse; see **Verse**.

Trap (1), a snare, gin. .(E.) M. E. *trappe*. A. S. *treppe*, a trap (cf. F. *trappe*, of Teut. origin). **+** O. Du. *trappe*, mousetrap; O. H. G. *trapo*. Orig. sense 'step;' a *trap* is that on which an animal steps, or puts its foot. Cf. Du. *trappen*, to tread, *trap*, a stair, step, kick, Swed. *trappa*, a stair. Allied to **Tramp**. Cf. Span. *trampa*, a trap. Der. *trap*, vb.; *trap-door*, *trap-bat*.

trap (3), a kind of igneous rock. (Scand.) Swed. *trappa*, a stair, *trapp*, trap-rock; Dan. *trappe*, stair. *trap*, trap-rock. So called from its appearance; its tabular masses seem to rise in steps.

trapan, trepan (2), to ensnare. (F. — O. H. G.) Formerly *trapan*. — O. F. *trappan*, *trapant*, a snare, trap (Roquefort). Prob. for *trapant**, pres. pt. of O. F. *traper*, *trapper*, to trap (from which it is, in any case, derived). — F. *trappe*, a trap. — O. H. G. *trapo*, a trap (above).

Trap (2), to adorn, deck. (F. — Teut.) M. E. *trapped*, decked; from M. E. *trappe*, trappings of a horse, &c. From an O. F. *trap**, not recorded, but the same as F. *drap*, cloth, as proved by Low L. *trapus*, cloth, Span. Port. *trapo*, a cloth, clout. This is a High German form, with *t* for Low G. *d*; compare G. *treffen*, to hit, with Swed. *drabba*, to hit. See **Drape**. Der. *trapp-ings*, s. pl.

Trap (3), a kind of rock; see **Trap** (1).

Trapan; see **Trap** (1).

Trapezium, Trapeze; see **Tetragon**.

Trappings; see **Trap** (2).

Trash, refuse. (Scand.) The orig. sense was bits of broken sticks found under trees; '*trash* and short sticks,' Evelyn. — Icel. *tros*, rubbish, twigs used for fuel; Norweg. *tros*, fallen twigs, half-rotten branches easily broken; Swed. *trasa*, a rag, tatter, Swed. dial. *trås*, a heap of sticks. Derived from the Swed. dial. phrase *slå i tras*, to break in pieces, the same as Swed. *slå in kras*, to

break in pieces; so that *tr* stands for *kr*, just as Icel. *trani* means a crane (see Crano). — Swed. *krasa*, Dan. *krase*, to crash, break; see **Crash**. *Trash* means 'crashings,' i. e. bits readily *cracked* off, dry twigs that break with a *crash* or snap.

Travail; see **Trave**.

Trave, a shackle. (F. — L.) A *trave* was a frame of rails for confining unruly horses. — O. F. *traf*, a beam, later *tref* (Cot.). — L. *trabem*, acc. of *trabs*, a beam. Der. *archi-trave*, q. v.

travail, toil. (F. — L.) F. *travail*, toil, labour. The same as Ital. *travaglio*, Span. *trabajo*, Port. *trabalho*, toil, labour; orig. an obstacle, impediment, clog, as Span. *trabajo*. It also meant a pen for cattle, a trave for horses; cf. F. *en-traver*, to shackle or fetter (Cotgrave). β. It answers to a Low L. *travaculum**, from a verb *travare**, to shackle, occurring in Span. *trabar*, to shackle, fetter, clog. All from L. *trab-em*, acc. of *trabs*, *trabes*, a beam.

travel, to journey. (F. — L.) The same word as *travail*; from the toil of travelling in olden times.

Traverse; see **Verse**.

Travesty; see **Vest**.

Trawl, to fish with a drag-net. (F. — Teut.) O. F. *trauler*, to go hither and thither (Roquefort); also spelt *troller*, mod. F. *trôler*; see below.

troll, to roll, sing a catch, fish for pike. (F. — Teut.) M. E. *trollen*, to roll; *to troll a catch* is to sing it irregularly (see below); *to troll a bowl* is to circulate it; *to troll* is also to draw hither and thither. — O. F. *troller*, which Cotgrave explains by 'hounds to *trowle*, raunge, or hunt out of order;' O. F. *trauler*, to run or draw hither and thither; mod. F. *trôler*. — G. *trollen*, to roll, troll. **+**Du. *drollen*, Low G. *drulen*, to roll, troll. Prob. allied to **Trill** (2). ¶ Distinct from *trail*.

Tray, a shallow vessel. (E.) M. E. *treye*. A. S. *treg*, a tray (=L. *alueolum*, misprinted *alucolum*, Wright's Voc. i. 290). Perhaps allied to **Trough**.

Treachery; see **Track**.

Treacle. (F. — L. — Gk.) Formerly a medicament; the mod. *treacle* is named from resembling it in appearance. M. E. *triacle*, a sovereign remedy. — F. *triacle*, also spelt *theriaque* (the *l* being unoriginal, as in *syllable*). — L. *theriaca*, an antidote against poisons, esp. venomous bites. — Gk. θηριακὰ φάρμακα, s. pl., antidotes against the bites of wild beasts. — Gk. θηριακός, belonging to a wild beast. — Gk. θηρίον, a wild animal. — Gk. θήρ, a wild beast, cognate with E. **Deer.**

Tread, vb. (E.) M. E. *treden.* A. S. *tredan,* pt. t. *trœd,* pp. *treden.*+Du. *treden,* G. *treten.* We also find Icel. *troða,* pt. t. *traö,* pp. *troðinn* (which accounts for E. *trodden*); Dan. *trœde,* Swed. *tråda,* Goth. *trudan* (pt. t. *trath*). Allied to **Trap** (1), **Tramp**; cf. Skt. *drd, dru,* to run. (√ DRA.) **Der.** *tread-le,* a thing to tread on (in a lathe).

trade. (E.) The old sense was 'path;' hence a beaten track, regular business. M. E. *tred.* — A. S. *trœd,* pt. t. of *tredan,* to tread (above). **Der.** *trade-wind,* a wind that keeps a beaten track, or blows always in the same direction.

Treason; see **Date** (1).

Treasure; see **Theme.**

Treat; see **Trace** (1).

Treble; see **Tri-.**

Treddle, put for **Treadle**; see **Tread.**

Tree. (E.) M. E. *tree, tre* (which also means dead wood, timber). A. S. *treó, treow,* a tree, timber. + Icel. *tré,* Dan. *trœ*; Swed. *trä,* timber, also *träd,* a tree (put for *trä-et,* lit. the wood, with post-positive article). + Goth. *triu.* + Russ. *drevo,* a tree, W. *derw,* an oak, Irish *darag,* Gk. δρῦς, oak, Skt. *dru,* wood; Skt. *dâru,* a kind of pine.. **Der.** *tree-nail,* a wooden peg.

Trefoil; see **Foliage.**

Trellis, lattice-work. (F. — L.) M. E. *trelis.* — F. *treillis,* 'a trellis;' Cot. — F. *treiller,* to lattice. — F. *treille,* a latticed frame. — Low L. *trichila, tricla,* an arbour.

Tremble. (F. — L.) F. *trembler.* — Low L. *tremulare.* — L. *tremulus,* adj., trembling. — L. *tremere,* to tremble. + Lith. *trim-ti,* Gk. τρέμ-ειν, to tremble. (√ TRAM.) **Der.** *trem-or,* L. *tremor,* a trembling; *tremulous,* L. *tremulus* (above); *tremendous,* L. *tremendus,* lit. to be feared, fut. pass. pt. of *tremere,* to fear.

Trench, vb. (F. — L.?) M. E. *trenche.* — O. F. *trencher,* verb, 'to cut, carve, slice, hew,' Cot. Now spelt *trancher.* β. Etym. much disputed; perhaps allied to L. *truncare,* to lop, from *truncus,* a log. **Der.** *trench-ant,* cutting, from the pres. part. of *trencher*; also *trench-er,* a wooden plate, to cut things on, O. F. *trencheoir.*

retrench. (F. — L.?) O. F. *retrencher,* 'to curtall, diminish;' Cot. — L. *re-,* back; and F. *trencher,* to cut (above).

Trend, to bend away, said of direction. (E.)˙ M. E. *trenden,* to roll, turn round. Allied to A. S. *trendel,* a circle round the sun, a ring; Dan. Swed. *trind,* round.

trundle, to roll. (E.) Cf. *trundle-bed,* a bed running on wheels; *trundle-tail,* a round tail of a dog. — A. S. *trunden**, pp. of a lost verb *trindan**, to roll (pt. t. *trand**); whence also A. S. *win-tryndel,* a little round shield. The *i* appears in Dan. Swed. *trind,* round; the *a,* modified to *e,* appears in M. E. *trenden,* to turn, roll, secondary verb from *trand**, pt. t. of *trindan**. Cf. also O. Fries. *trund,* round.

Trental; see **Tri-.**

Trepan (1), a small saw for removing a piece of a broken skull. (F. — L. — Gk.) F. *trepan.* — Low L. *trepanum.* — Gk. τρύπανον, an augur, borer; also a trepan. — Gk. τρυπᾶν, to bore. — Gk. τρύπα, τρύπη, a hole. — Gk. τρέπειν, to turn, bore; see **Trope.**

Trepan (2), to ensnare; see **Trap** (1).

Trepidation. (F. — L.) F. *trepidation.* — L. acc. *trepidationem,* a trembling. — L. *trepidatus,* pp. of *trepidare,* to tremble. — L. *trepidus,* trembling, agitated. — O. Lat. *trapara,* to turn round, cognate with Gk. τρέπειν, to turn; see **Trope.** (√ TARK.)

intrepid. (L.) L. *in-trepidus,* fearless, not alarmed.

Trespass; see **Patent.**

Tress, Tressure; see **Tri-.**

Trestle, Tressel, a support for a table. (F. — L.) O. F. *trestel,* later *tresteau,* 'a tresle for a table,' Cot. (Mod F. *tréteau.*) — Low L. *transtellum**, the same as L. *transtillum,* dimin. of *transtrum,* a crossbeam. See **Transom.** ¶ For *tres-* = L. *trans,* cf. *tres-pass.*

Tret. (F. — L.) *Tret,* 'an allowance made for the waste, which is always 4 in every 104 pounds;' Phillips. It prob. meant an allowance for waste in transport. — F. *traite,* 'a draught, .. also a transportation, shipping over, and an imposition upon commodities;' Cot. — L. *tracta,* fem. of *tractus,* pp. of *trahere,* to draw; see **Trace** (1). Cf. O. Ital. *tratta,* 'leaue to transport merchandise;' Florio.

Trey; see **Tri-** (below).

Tri-, relating to three. (L.) L. *tri-,* three times; allied to *tres* (neut. *tri-a*), three. Allied to **Three.** So also Gk. τρι-, prefix; from τρεῖς (neut. τρί-α), three.

tercel, the male of the hawk. (F. — L.) Also (corruptly) *tassel.* M. E. *tercel*; dimin. *tercelet.* — O. F. *tiercel**, only recorded in the dimin. *tiercelet*, 'the tassell, or male of any kind of hawk ; so tearmed because he is, commonly, a third part lesse then the female ;' Cot. [Another alleged reason is, that every third bird hatched was, in popular opinion, sure to be a male.] So also Ital. *terzolo*, 'a tassel gentle of a hawke ;' Florio. — O. F. *tiers, tierce*, third ; see tierce (below).

ternary. (L.) L. *ternarius*, consisting of three. — L. *terni*, pl. by threes. — L. *ter*, three times ; *tres*, three.

tertian, recurring every third day. (F. — L.) F. *tertiane*, a tertian ague. — L. *tertiana*, fem. of *tertianus*, tertian. — L. *tertius*, third. — L. *ter*, thrice, *tres*, three.

tertiary. (L.) L. *tertiarius*, containing a third part ; used to mean belonging to the third. — L. *tertius*, third (above).

tierce, terce. (F. — L.) It meant a third hour, a third of a pipe or cask, a third card, a third thrust (in fencing). — O. F. *tiers, tierce*, third. — L. *tertius*, third. — L. *ter*, thrice ; *tres*, three.

treble, threefold. (F. — L.) O. F. *treble*. — L. *triplum*, acc. of *triplus*, threefold ; see triple (below).

trental, a set of thirty masses for the dead. (F. — L.) O. F. *trentel, trental* (Roquefort). — F. *trente*, thirty. — L. *triginta*, thirty. — L. *tri-*, thrice ; *-ginta*, short for *decinta**, tenth.

tress, a plait of hair, ringlet. (F. — Gk.) M. E. *tresse*. — F. *tresse*, a tress ; *tresser*, to braid hair. The same as Ital. *treccia*, a braid, plait, Span. *trenza*. — Low L. *tricia*, variant of *trica*, a plait. — Gk. τρίχα, in three parts, threefold ; from a common way of plaiting hair (Diez). — Gk. τρι-, thrice (above).

tressure, an heraldic border. (F. — Gk.) Formed, with F. suffix *-ure*, from F. *tresser*, to plait. — F. *tresse*, a plait (above).

trey, three. (F. — L.) O. F. *treis*. — L. *tres*, three.

triad, the union of three. (F. — L. — Gk.) F. *triade*, Cot. — L. *triad-*, stem of *trias*, a triad. — Gk. τριάς, triad. — Gk. τρι-, thrice (above).

triangle. (F. — L.) F. *triangle*. — L. *triangulum*, sb. ; neut. of *triangulus*, three-angled. — L. *tri-*, thrice ; *angulus*, an angle ; see Angle.

tribrach, a metrical foot containing 3 short syllables. (L. — Gk.) L. *tribrachys*. — Gk. τρίβραχυς. — Gk. τρι-, three ; βραχύς, short.

tricentenary. (L.) Coined from L. *tri-* and Centenary, q. v.

tricolor. (F. — L.) F. *tricolore*, put for *drapeau tricolore*, three-coloured flag. — F. *tricolor*, the three-coloured amaranth. — L. *tri-*, three ; *color-*, stem of *color*, colour.

trident. (F. — L.) F. *trident*. — L. *tridentem*, acc. of *tridens*, a three-pronged spear. — L. *tri-*, three ; *dens*, tooth, prong.

triennial. (L.) Coined from L. *triennium*, a period of three years. — L. *tri-*, three ; *annus*, year.

trifoliate, three-leaved. (L.) From L. *tri-*, three ; *foli-um*, leaf.

triform, having a triple form. (L.) L. *triformis*. — L. *tri-*, three ; *form-a*, form.

triglyph, a three-grooved tablet. (L. — Gk.) L. *triglyphus*. — Gk. τρίγλυφος, a triglyph ; lit. 'thrice-cloven.' — Gk. τρι-, thrice ; γλύφειν, to carve, groove.

trigonometry. (Gk.) 'Measurement of triangles.' — Gk. τρίγωνο-ν, a triangle ; *-μετρια*, measurement, from μέτρον, a measure. Gk. τρίγωνον is from τρι-, three ; γων-ία, angle, allied to γόνυ, knee.

trihedron, a figure having three bases. (Gk.) From Gk. τρι-, three ; ἕδρον, ἕδρα, a base, from ἕδ-ειν, to sit, rest.

trilateral, trilingual, triliteral. (L.) From L. *tri-*, three ; and *lateral*, &c.

trillion. (F. — L.) A coined word ; short for *tri-million* ; see Billion.

trinity. (F. — L.) M. E. *trinitee*. — O. F. *trinite*. — L. acc. *trinitatem*, a triad. — L. *trinus*, pl. *trini*, by threes. — L. *tri-*, thrice, three.

trio. (Ital. — L.) Ital. *trio*, music in three parts. — L. *tri-*, three.

triple, three-fold. (F. — L.) F. *triple*. — L. *triplum*, acc. of *triplus*, threefold. — L. *tri-*, three ; *-plus*, allied to *plenus*, full. See Double.

triplicate, threefold. (L.) From pp. of L. *triplicare*, to treble. — L. *tri-*, three ; *plicare*, to weave, fold ; see Ply.

tripod. (L. — Gk.) L. *tripod-*, stem of *tripus*. — Gk. τρίπους (stem τριποδ-), a tripod, three-footed brass kettle, three-legged table. — Gk. τρι-, three ; πούς, foot ; see Foot.

trireme, galley with three banks of oars. (L.) L. *triremis*, having three banks of oars. — L. *tri-*, three ; *remus*, oar.

trisect; see Section.

triumvir. (L.) One of three men associated in an office. L. pl. *triumuiri*, three men, evolved from the gen. pl. *trium* *uirorum*, belonging to three men. — L. *trium*, gen. pl. of *tres*, three; *uirorum*, gen. pl. of *uir*, a man; see Virile.

trivet, trevet, a three-footed support. (F.—L.) Spelt *trevid* (1493). — F. *trepied*, *tripied*, 'a trevet,' Cot. — L. *tripedem*, acc. of *tripes*, having three feet. — L. *tri-*, three; *pes*, a foot. Cf. **tripod** (above).

trivial, common. (F.—L.) F. *trivial*. — L. *triuialis*, belonging to three cross-roads, that which may be picked up anywhere, common. — L. *triuia*, a place where three roads meet. — L. *tri-*, three; *uia*, a way.

Trial; see **try**, under **Trite**.

Triangle; see **Tri-**.

Tribe, a race. (F.—L.) F. *tribu*, 'a tribe;' Cot. — L. *tribu-*, crude form of *tribus*, a tribe. Said to have been one of the *three* original families in Rome. — I. *tri-*, three; *-hus*, family (?), allied to Gk. φυ-λή, a tribe.

attribute. (L.) From pp. of L. *attribuere*, to assign. — L. *at-* (*ad*), to; *tribuere*; see **tribute** (below).

contribute. (L.) From pp. of L. *contribuere*, to contribute, lit. pay together; see **tribute** (below).

distribute, to allot, deal out. (L.) From pp. of L. *dis-tribuere*, to deal out, allot separately.

retribution. (F. — L.) F. *retribution*. — L. acc. *retributionem*, requital. — L. *retributus*, pp. of *re-tribuere*, to pay back.

tribune. (F.—L.) M. E. *tribun*. — F. *tribun*. — L. *tribunum*, acc. of *tribunus*, lit. the chief officer of a tribe. — L. *tribus*, a tribe (above).

tribute, sb. (F.—L.) M. E. *tribut*. — F. *tribut*, tribute. — L. *tributum*, tribute, lit. a thing paid; neut. of pp. of *tribuere*, to assign to a tribe, to assign, pay. — L. *tribu-s*, a tribe.

Tribrach; see **Tri-**.

Tribulation; see **Trite**.

Tribune, Tribute; see **Tribe**.

Trice (1), a short space of time. (Span.) In the phr. *in a trice*. — Span. *en un tris*, in a trice, in an instant; from *tris*, the noise made by the cracking of glass, a crack, an instant. So also Port. *triz*, cracking of glass, a crash, crack, instant; *en hum triz*, in a trice. Prob. of imitative origin; but see **Trash**.

Trice (2), **Trise**, to haul up, hoist. (Scand.) M. E. *trisen*, to hoist sail (orig. with a pulley). — Swed. *trissa*, a pulley,

triss, spritsail-brace; Dan. *tridse*, a pulley, *tridse*, verb, to trice. From the base *trid-*, to turn, as in Dan. *trid-se*, a pulley (above). Allied to **Trend, Trundle.**

Tricentenary; see **Tri-**.

Trick, (1), (2), and (3); see **Track.**

Trickle, verb. (E.) M. E. *triklen*, short for *striklen*, *strikelen*, to trickle, frequentative of M. E. *striken*, to flow (Spec. of English, ed. Morris and Skeat, p. 48, l. 21). — A. S. *strican*, to flow, a particular use of *strican*, to strike; see **Strike**. Cf. **streak**, and G. *streichen*. ¶ The loss of *s* occurs again in *trick* (1), &c.; and was due to confusion with *trill* (2).

Tricolor, Trident, Triennial; see **Tri-**.

Trifle. (F.—L.) M. E. *trufle, trefle*, rarely *trifle*. — O. F. *trufle*, mockery, raillery, a little jest, dimin. of *truffe*, a gibe, jest (Cot.). Properly a truffle, a thing of small worth; the O. F. *truffe* also means a truffle (Cot.). See **truffle**, under **Tuber.**

Trifoliate, Triform; see **Tri-**.

Trigger; see **Track.**

Triglyph, Trigonometry, &c.; see **Tri-**.

Trill (1), to shake, quaver. (Ital.) In music. — Ital. *trillare*, to trill, shake; *trillo*, sb., a shake. A imitative word, like Span. *trinar*, to trill.

Trill (2), to turn round and round; see **Through.**

Trill (3), to trickle; see **Through.**

Trillion; see **Tri-**.

Trim, verb. (E.) M. E. *trimen, trumen*. A. S. *trymian, trymman*, to set firm, to strengthen, set in order, prepare, array. Formed (by usual change of *u* to *y*) from A. S. *trum*, adj., firm, strong. Der. *trim*, sb.; *be-trim.*

Trinity; see **Tri-**.

Trinket (1), a small ornament. (F.—L.?) M. E. *trenket*, a shoemaker's knife; also spelt *trynket* (Palsgrave). Tusser speaks of 'trinkets and tooles.' Hence it seems to have meant a toy-knife, such as ladies wore on chains; and, generally, a small ornament. Prob. from an O. F. *trenquer**, to cut, byform of *trencher*, to cut; cf. Span. *trinchar*, Ital. *trinciare*, to cut, carve. See **Trench**. ¶ Doubtful.

Trinket (2), **Trinquet**, the highest sail of a ship. (F. — Span. — Du.?) F. *trinquet*, the highest sail; Cot. — Span. *trinquete*, a trinket. Allied to Span. *trincar*, to keep close to the wind, *trincar los* *cabos*, to fasten the rope-ends. ‒ Span. *trinca*, a rope for lashing fast. Minsheu has *poner la vela a la trinca*, to put a ship that the edges of the sails may be to the wind. β. Perhaps from O. Du. *strick*, a noose, *stricken*, to tie running knots. ¶ Section β is doubtful.

Trio; see **Tri-**.

Trip, vb. (E.) M. E. *trippen*, to step lightly. A weakened form of the base TRAP, to tread; see **Trap** (1) and **Tramp**. +Du. *trippen*, *trappen*, to tread on; *trippelen*, to trip, dance; Swed. *trippa*, Dan. *trippe*, to trip, tread lightly.

Tripe. (C.) M. E. *tripe*. ‒ Irish *triopas*, s. pl. entrails, tripes; W. *tripa*, intestines; Bret. *stripen*, tripe, pl. *stripou*, intestines. Hence also F. *tripe*, Span. and Port. *tripa*, Ital. *trippa*, tripe.

Triple, Triplicate; see **Tri-**.

Tripod, Trireme; see **Tri-**.

Trisect; see **Section**.

Trist; see **Tryst**; p. 526, col. 1.

Trite. (L.) L. *tritus*, worn, pp. of *terere*, to rub, wear away. + Russ. *terete*, Lith. *triti*, to rub. (√ TAR.)

attrition. (F. ‒ L.) F. *attrition*. ‒ L. acc. *attritionem*, a rubbing or wearing away. ‒ L. *attritus*, pp. of *atterere*, to rub away. ‒ L. *at-* (*ad*); *terere*, to rub.

contrite. (L.) L. *contritus*, thoroughly bruised; hence, penitent; pp. of L. *conterere*, to rub together, bruise.

detriment. (F.‒L.) O. F. *detriment*. ‒ L. *detrimentum*, loss; lit. 'a rubbing away.' ‒ L. *detri-tus*, pp. of *de-terere*, to rub down; with suffix *-mentum*.

tribulation. (F.‒L.) F. *tribulation*. ‒L. acc. *tribulationem*, affliction. ‒ L. *tribulatus*, pp. of *tribulare*, to rub out corn; hence, to afflict. ‒ L. *tribulum*, a sledge for rubbing out corn, consisting of a wooden frame with iron spikes beneath it. ‒ L. *tri-*, base of *tri-tus*, pp. of *terere*, to rub; with suffix *-bulum*, denoting the agent.

triturate. (F.‒L.) From pp. of L. *triturare*, to rub down, thrash, grind. ‒ L. *tritura*, a rubbing. ‒ L. *tritus*, pp. of *terere*, to rub.

try, to select, test, examine, &c. (F.‒ L.) M. E. *trien*, to select, pick out, choose. The same as Prov. *triar*, to separate corn from the straw, also to choose. ‒ Low L. *tritare*, to thresh. ‒ L. *tritus*, pp. of *terere*, to rub. It meant to thresh, separate, purify, cull, pick, &c. **Der.** *tri-al*.

Triton, a sea-god. (L. ‒ Gk.) L. *triton*.

‒ Gk. Τρίτων, a Triton. Cf. Skt. *trita*, the name of a deity.

Triturate; see **Trite**.

Triumph. (F. ‒ L.) O. F. *triumphe*, later *triomphe*. ‒ L. *triumphum*, acc. of *triumphus*, a public rejoicing for a victory. +Gk. θρίαμβος, a hymn to Bacchus.

trump (2), one of a leading suit of cards. (F.‒L.) Well known to be a corruption of *triumph*; see Latimer's Sermons, and Nares. ‒ F. *triomphe*, 'the card-game called ruffe, or trump; also the ruffe or trump at it;' Cot. See above.

Triumvir, Trivet; see **Tri-**.

Trivial; see **Tri-**.

Trochee. (L. ‒ Gk.) L. *trochæus*. ‒ Gk. τροχαῖος, running; also the tripping foot which consists of a long syllable followed by a short one. ‒ Gk. τρέχειν, to run.

truck (2), a small wheel, low-wheeled vehicle. (L. ‒ Gk.) Modified from L. *trochus*, a wheel. ‒ Gk. τροχός, a runner, wheel, disc. ‒ Gk. τρέχειν, to run. **Der.** *truckle-bed*, a bed on little wheels, where *truckle* = L. *trochlea*, a little wheel.

truckle, to submit servilely to another. (L. ‒ Gk.) From the phrase to *truckle under*, due to the old custom of putting a *truckle-bed* under a larger one; the truckle-bed being occupied by a servant, pupil, or inferior. It originated in University slang, from L. *trochlea* (as above).

Troglodyte, a dweller in a cave. (F. ‒ Gk.) F. *troglodyte*. ‒ Gk. τρωγλοδύτης, one who creeps into holes, a cave-dweller. ‒ Gk. τρωγλο-, put for τρώγλη, a hole, cave; δύειν, to enter. β. Τρώγλη is from τρώγειν, to gnaw, bite, gnaw a hole; δύειν is from √ DU, to go, advance, Skt *du*, to go, move.

trout. (L. ‒ Gk.) A. S. *truht*. ‒ L. *tructa*. ‒ Gk. τρώκτης, a nibbler, also a fish with sharp teeth. ‒ Gk. τρώγειν (above). Lit. 'nibbler.'

Troll; see **Trawl**.

Trombone; see **Trump** (1).

Tron, a weighing-machine. (F. ‒ L.) O. F. *trone*, a weighing-machine; Low L. *trona* (Ducange). ‒ L. *trutina*, a pair of scales. Cf. Gk. τρυτάνη, tongue of a balance, pair of scales. **Der.** *tron-age*.

Troop, a crew. (F. ‒ L.?) F. *troupe*; Low L. *tropus*. Also Span. *tropa*, O. Ital. *troppa*. Origin doubtful; but prob. due to L. *turba*, a crowd (Diez). See **Trouble**.

Trope, a figure of speech. (L. ‒ Gk.) L. *tropus*. ‒ Gk. τρόπος, a turn, a trope. ‒

Gk. τρέπειν, to turn.+L. *torquere*, to twist, turn. (√TARK.)

trophy. (F. – L. – Gk.) F. *trophée*, 'a trophee;' Cot. – L. *tropæum*, a sign of victory. – Gk. τροπαῖον, a trophy, monument of an enemy's *defeat*. Neut. of τροπαῖος, belonging to a defeat. – Gk. τροπή, a return, putting to flight of an enemy. – Gk. τρέπειν, to turn.

tropic. (F. – L. – Gk.) M.:E. *tropik.* –F. *tropique*, 'a tropick;' Cot. – L. *tropicum*, acc. of *tropicus*, tropical. – Gk. τροπικός, belonging to a turn; the *tropic* is the point where the sun appears to turn from N. to S., or from S. to N. in the zodiac. – Gk. τρόπος, a turn; see Trope (above). And see Trepan (1), Trover.

Trot, verb. (F. – L.) F. *trotter*; O. F. *troter.* We also find O. F. *trotier*, Low L. *trotarius*, a trotter, messenger, supposed to be from L. *tolutarius*, going at a trot. –L. *tolutim*, adv., at a trot; lit. 'liftingly,' i.e. lifting the feet. –L. *tollere*, to lift; see Tolerate. (So Diez, Scheler, and Littré.)

Troth; see True.

Troubadour; see Trover.

Trouble, verb. (F. – L.) F. *troubler*, O. F. *trubler.* It answers to a Low L. *turbulare**, a verb made from L. *turbula*, a disorderly group, dimin. of L. *turba*, a crowd. Cf. Gk. τύρβη, disorder, throng, Skt. *tvar, tur*, to hasten. See Turbid.

Trough. (E.) M. E. *trogh.* A. S. *troh, trog,* a hollow vessel, trough. + Du. Icel. G. *trog,* Dan. *trug,* Swed. *tråg.*

Trounce; see Trunk.

Trousers, Trousseau; see Torture.

Trout, a fish; see Troglodyte.

Trover, an action at law arising out of the finding of goods. (F. – L. – Gk.) O. F. *trover* (F. *trouver*), to find; orig. to devise, invent, make up poetry. The same as Prov. *trobar,* Port. Span. *trovar,* Ital. *trovare,* to versify. β. Since Ital. *v* and Prov. *b* arise from L. *p*, the corresponding Low L. form must have been *tropare**, to versify. – L. *tropus,* a trope; Late L. *tropus,* a song, manner of singing. – Gk. τρόπος, a trope, also a mode in music. See Trope.

contrive. (F. – L. *and* Gk.) A corrupt spelling; M. E. *controuen, contreuen* (= *controven, contreven*). – O. F. *controver,* to find, find out (Bartsch). – O. F. *con-* (= L *con-*, for *cum*); O. F. *trover,* to find (above).

retrieve, to recover. (F. – L. *and* Gk.) Formerly *retreve.* – O. F. *retreuver,* also

retrover, later *retrouver,* to find again. – L. *re-,* again; O. F. *trover,* to find (above).

troubadour. (Prov. – L. – Gk.) A F. modification of Prov. *trobador,* also *trobaire,* a troubadour, inventor of songs or verses. Here *trobador* answers to a Low L. acc. *tropatorem** (= Ital.*trovatore,* Span.*trovador*); whilst *trobaire* (F. *trouvère*) answers to a Low L. *troparius**. Both from the verb *tropare** (as seen in Ital. *trovare,* Span. *trovar,* Prov. *trobar*); see Trover (above).

Trow; see True.

Trowel. (F. – L.) M. E. *truel.* – F. *truelle,* O. F. *truele;* Low L. *truella,* a trowel. Dimin. of L. *trua,* a stirring-spoon, skimmer, ladle (hence a trowel, from the shape).

Trowsers; see Torture.

Troy-weight. (F. *and* E.) Orig. a weight used at the fair of *Troyes,* a town in France, S. E. of Paris. See Arnold's Chronicle, ed. 1811, pp. 108, 191; Haydn, Dict. of Dates, &c.

Truant, an idler. (F. – C.) F. *truand,* a beggar; *truand,* adj., beggarly; Cot. (The same as Span. *truhan,* Port. *truhão,* a buffoon, jester.) – W. *truan,* wretched, a wretch; Bret. *truek,* a beggar; Gael. *truaghan,* a wretch, miserable creature. Cf. W. *tru,* wretched, Corn. *troc,* wretched, Irish *trogha,* Gael. *truagh,* miserable, &c.

Truce; see True.

Truck (1), to barter, exchange. (F. – Span. – Gk.?) M. E. *trukken.* – F. *troquer,* 'to truck, barter;' Cot. – Span. *trocar,* to barter.' Cf. Ital. *truccare,* 'to truck, barter, to skud away;' Florio (1598). Origin disputed; the sense 'skud away' is clearly due to Gk. τρόχος, a course, from τρέχειν, to run; see Truck (2), under Trochee.

Truck (2), a small wheel, wheeled car; see Trochee.

Truckle; see Trochee.

Truculent, barbarous. (F. – L.) F. *truculent.* – L. acc. *truculentum,* cruel. – L. *truc-,* stem of *trux,* fierce, wild.

Trudge, to march heavily. (Scand. ?) Perhaps orig. to walk in heavy shoes; from Swed. dial. *truga, trudja,* a snowshoe; Norw. *truga,* Icel. *þruga,* a snowshoe, a large flat frame worn by men to prevent them sinking in snow. ¶ Uncertain. It can hardly be from O. Ital. *truccare,* 'to trudge, skud away,' Florio; for which see Truck (1).

True, firm, certain. (E.) M. E. *trewe.* A. S. *tréowe, trýwe,* true. Orig. 'believed;' allied to O. Prussian *druwit,* to believe

(Fick). **+** Du. *trouw*, Icel. *tryggr*, *trúr*, Dan. *tro*, Swed. *trogen*, G. *treu*, Goth. *triggws*, true. Cf. Goth. *trauan*, to believe, trust, be persuaded.

betroth. (E.) From *troth*; with prefix *be-* (= E. *by*).

troth. (E.) Merely a variant of *truth*.

trow, to believe, suppose. (E.) M. E. *trowen.* A. S. *tréowian*, to trow; a secondary verb formed from the sb. *tréowa*, trust, which again is from the adj. *tréowe*, true, (above).+Icel. *trúa*, to trow, from *trúr*, true; Dan. *troe*, to trow, from *tro*, sb., truth, adj., true.

truce. (E.) Ill spelt; it should rather be *trews*, i. e. pledges; it is the pl. of *trew*, a pledge of truth, from the adj. *true*. (This is proved by the M. E. forms.) — A.S. *tréowa*, *trúwa*, a compact, pledge, faith.— A.S. *tréowe*, true.

trust. (Scand.) M. E. *trust*. — Icel. *traust*, trust, protection, firmness; Dan. Swed. *tröst*, consolation.+G. *trost*, consolation, Goth. *trausti*, a covenant. From the same base as *true*.

truth, troth. (E.) M. E. *trewthe*, *trouthe*; A.S. *tréowðu*, truth.— true; see true (above).+Icel. *tryggð*, truth.

tryst, trist, an appointment to meet. (Scand.) See Jamieson; properly ' a pledge.' M. E. *trist*, *tryst*, trust. Cf. Icel. *treysta*, to rely on, confirm; from *traust*, trust; see trust (above).

Truffle; see Tuber.

Trull, a worthless woman. (G.) G. *trulle*, *trolle*, a trull. Cognate with O. Du. *drol*, a jester, Icel. *troll*, a merry elf; see Droll. Lit. 'a merry companion.'

Trump (1), a trumpet. (F.—L.?) M. E. *trumpe*, *trompe*.—F. *trompe*, 'a trump;' Cot. Cf. Span. *trompa*, Ital. *tromba*. The Ital. *tromba* is a nasalised form answering to a Low L. *truba**, which (though not found in L.) is clearly the same as Lithuan. *truba*, a horn, Russ. *truba*, a tube, trumpet. The Lat. form is *tuba*; see Tube.

trombone. (Ital.—L.?) Ital. *trombone*, a trombone, augmentative form of Ital. *tromba*, a trumpet (above).

trumpery, nonsense. (F. — L. ?) F. *tromperie*, 'a wile, fraud;' Cot. —F. *tromper*, to deceive; orig. to play the trumpet, whence the phrase *se tromper de quelqu'un*, to play with any one, amuse oneself at their expense.—F. *trompe*, trump (above).

trumpet. (F. — L. ?) F. *trompette*, dimin. of *trompe* (above).

Trump (2); see **Triumph.**

Trumpery, Trumpet; see Trump (1).

Truncate, Truncheon; see Trunk.

Trundle; see Trend.

Trunk, stem of a tree, &c. (F.—L.) F. *tronc*, trunk.—L. *truncum*, acc. of *truncus*, trunk, stem, bit cut off.—L. *truncus*, adj., cut off, maimed. Prob. from *torquere*, to twist, hence to twist off; cf. *torculum*, a press. Der. *trunk-hose*, i. e. *trunk'd-hose*, knee-breeches, breeches cut short.

trounce, to beat. (F.—L.) To beat with a great stick. — O. F. *tronche*, a great piece of timber, allied to *tronc*, a trunk (above); see truncheon (below).

truncate, to cut off short. (L.) From pp. of L. *truncare*, to cut off.—L. *truncus*, a stump.

truncheon. (F.—L.) M. E. *tronchoun*. —O. F. *tronson*, *tronchon*, a little stick; dimin. of *tronc*, a trunk; see Trunk (above). Mod. F. *tronçon*.

trunnion, one of the projecting stumps on each side of a cannon, on which it rests in the carriage. (F.—L.) F. *trognon*, a stump; dimin. of *tron*, a stump, which is a shortened form of *tronc*, a trunk.

Trunk (2), of an elephant. (F.—L. ?) Corruption of F. *trompe*; see Trump (1).

Truss; see Torture.

Trust, Truth, Tryst; see True.

Try; see Trite.

Tub, a small cask. (O. Low G.) M. E. *tubbe*. —O. Du. *tobbe*, a tub; Low G. *tubbe*, a tub.

Tube. (F. — L.) F. *tube*. — L. *tubum*, acc. of *tubus*, a tube, pipe; akin to *tuba*, a trumpet. Der. *tub-ul-ar*, from L. *tubulus*, dimin. of *tubus*. And see Trump (1).

Tuber, a rounded root. (L.) L. *tuber*, a bump, tumour, also a truffle. Lit. 'swelling;' allied to **Tumid. Der.** *tuber-cle*, a little swelling.

protuberant. (L.) From stem of pres. pt. of *pro-tuberare*, to bulge out.— L. *pro*, forward; *tuber*, a swelling.

truffle. (F.—L.) F. *truffle*, also *truffe*, a round edible fungus, found underground. Span. *trufa*, a truffle. The F. *truffe*, Span. *trufa*, answer to L. pl. *tubera*, truffles, whence was formed a F. fem. sb. *tufre**, easily altered to *truffe*. We also find Ital. *tartufo*, a truffle = L. *terræ tuber*, i.e. truffle of the earth. And see **Trifle**.

Tuck (1), to fold or gather together a dress; see Tow (1).

Tuck (2), a rapier; see Stick (1).

Tucket; see Touch.

Tuesday. (E.) A.S. *Tiwes dæg*, the day of *Tiw*, the god of war.+Icel. *Týs dagr*, the day of *Týr*; Dan. *Tirsdag*, Swed. *Tisdag*, G. *Dienstag*, O. H. G. *Zies tac*, the day of *Ziu*, god of war. β. The A.S. *Tiw*, Icel. *Týr*, O. H. G. *Ziu* is the same name as L. *Ju-* in *Ju-piter*, Gk. Ζεύς, Skt. *Dyaus*, and means 'the shining one.' (√ DIW.)

Tuft (1), a crest, knot. (F. – Teut.) M. E. *tuft*, but the final *t* is excrescent; prov. E. *tuff*, a tuft. – F. *touffe*, a tuft or lock of hair. – G. *zopf*, a weft of hair, tuft, pigtail; Icel. *toppr*, a top, tuft, or lock of hair; O. Du. *top*, a tuft. ¶ W. *twff* is borrowed from E., and preserves the correct form.

Tuft (2), **Toft**, a plantation, a green knoll. (Scand.) In the sense of 'plantation,' this word has been confused with *tuft* (1); the F. *touffe de bois* = 'tuft of trees;' Cot. But in the sense of 'green knoll,' it is the M. E. *toft*, a knoll. – Icel. *topt* (pronounced *toft*), also *tupt, toft, tomt*, a knoll, toft, clearing, cleared space; the orig. spelling was *tomt*. – Icel. *tômt, tomt*, neut. of *tômr*, empty; see **Toom**. So also Swed. *tomt*, a toft, neuter of *tom*, empty, clear; Norw. *tuft, tomt*, toft, clearing.

Tug; see Tow (1).

Tuition. (F. – L.) F. *tuition*. – L. acc. *tuitionem*, protection. – L. *tuitus*, pp. of *tueri*, to guard, protect.

intuition. (L.) Formed, by analogy, from L. *intuitus*, pp. of *in-tueri*, to look upon. – L. *in*, upon; *tueri*, to watch.

tutelage, guardianship. (L.; *with* F. *suffix.*) From L. *tutel-a*, protection; with F. suffix *-age* (= L. *-aticum*). – L. *tut-us*, short for *tuitus* (above).

tutelar. (L.) L. *tutelaris*, protecting. – L. *tut-us*, short for *tuitus* (above).

tutor. (L.) L. *tutor*, a guardian, tutor. – L. *tut-us* (above).

Tulip; see Turban.

Tumble, vb. (E.) M. E. *tumblen*; frequent. of *tomben, tumben*, to tumble. – A. S. *tumbian*, to turn heels over head, dance. + Du. *tuimelen*, G. *taumeln, tummeln*; O. H. G. *tûmôn*, to turn over and over (whence F. *tomber*); Dan. *tumle*. β. Initial *s* is lost; it is the same word as **Stumble**, q. v. **Der.** *tumbler*, sb. (1) an acrobat, (2) a glass without a foot, which could only be set down when empty; *tumb-r-el*, a cart that falls over, O. F. *tumbrel*, from F. *tomber*, to tumble, fall over.

Tumefy; see Tumid.

Tumid. (L.) L. *tumidus*, swollen. – L. *tumere*, to swell. Cf. Gk. τύλη, a swelling. (√ TU.) **Der.** *tum-our*, F. *tumeur*, from L. acc. *tumorem*, a swelling.

intumescence, a swelling. (F. – L.) F. *intumescence*. From stem of pres. pt of L. *intumescere*, to begin to swell. – L. *in*, very; *tumescere*, inceptive form of *tumere*, to swell.

tumefy, to cause to swell. (F. – L.) F. *tumefier*; Cot. – Low L. *tumeficare*[*], put for L. *tumefacere*, to make to swell. – L. *tume-re*, to swell; *facere*, to make.

tumult. (F. – L.) F. *tumulte*. – L. acc. *tumultum*, an uproar. – L. *tumere*, to swell, surge up.

tumulus. (L.) L. *tumulus*, a mound. – L. *tumere*, to swell. And see **Tomb**.

Tun; see Ton.

Tune; see Tone.

Tungsten, a heavy metal. (Swed.) Swed. *tungsten*, lit. 'heavy stone.' – Swed. *tung*, heavy; *sten*, stone. Swed. *tung* = Icel. *þungr*, heavy, from √ TU, to swell, be strong; *sten* is cognate with E. *stone*.

Tunic. (L.) A. S. *tunica*. – L. *tunica*, an under-garment. **Der.** *tunic-le, tunicat-ed*.

Tunnel; see Ton.

Tunny, a fish. (F. – L. – Gk.) F. *thon*; Cot. – L. *thunnum*, acc. of *thunnus*. – Gk. θύννος, θῦνος, a tunny. Lit. 'the darter.' – Gk. θύνειν, allied to θύειν, to rush along (√ DHU.)

Turban. (F. – Ital. – Turk. – Pers. – Hind.) Formerly *turbant, turribant, turband*; also *tolipant, tulipant, tulibant*. – F. *turbant, turban*, a turban; Cot. – Ital. *turbante*, 'a turbant;' Florio. – Turk. *tulbend*, vulgar form of *dulbend*, a turban. – Pers. *dulband*, a turban. – Hind. *dulband*, a turban.

tulip, a flower. (F. – Ital. – Turk. – Pers. – Hind.) F. *tulippe*, also *tulipan*, a tulip; so called from its likeness to a turban. – Ital. *tulipa, tulipano*, a tulip. – Turk. *tulbend*, a turban (above).

Turbid. (L.) L. *turbidus*, disturbed. – L. *turbare*, to disturb. – L. *turba*, a crowd, confused mass of people. See **Trouble**.

disturb. (F. – L.) M. E. *distourben*. – L. *dis-turbare*, to drive asunder, disturb.

perturb. (F. – L.) F. *perturber*; Cot. – L. *per-turbare*, to disturb thoroughly.

turbulent. (F. – L.) F. *turbulent*. – L. *turbulentus*, full of commotion. – L. *turbare*, to disturb; see **Turbid.**

Turbot. (F.—L.) F. *turbot*, a fish.—
Low L. *turbo*, a turbot ; L. *turbo*, a spindle,
reel ; from its rhomboidal shape. So also
L. *rhombus*, a spindle, rhombus, turbot.

Tureen ; see **Terrace**.

Turf. (E.) M. E. *turf*, pl. *turues*
(*turves*). A. S. *turf*.+Du. *turf*, Icel. *torf*,
sod, peat ; Dan. *törv*, Swed. *torf*, O. H. G.
zurba. Cf. Skt. *darbha*, a matted grass,
from *dṛibh*, to bind.

Turgid. (L.) L. *turgidus*, swollen.—
L. *turgere*, to swell out.

Turkey. (F.—Tatar.) Called a *Turkey*
cock, or a cock of *India*, from the notion
that it came from *Turkey* or from India ;
so also G. *Calecutische hahn*, a turkey-
cock, is lit. a cock of Calicut. (It really
came from the New World.) From F.
Turquie, Turkey.—F. *Turc*, a Turk.—
Tatar *Turk*, a Turk ; orig. an adj. meaning
'brave.' ¶ The usual Turkish word for
'Turk' is '*Osmanlí*.

turquoise, turkis, a gem. (F.—Ital
—Tatar.) F. *turquoise*; orig. fem. of *Tur-
quois*, Turkish.—Ital. *Turchesa* a torquoise,
or Turkish stone.—Tatar *Turk*, a Turk.

Turmeric. (F.—L.) F. *terre-mérite*,
turmeric (Littré ; s. v. *Curcuma*).—L.
terra merita, apparently 'excellent earth.'
—L. *terra*, earth ; *merita*, fem. of *meritus*,
pp. of *mereri*, to deserve. ¶ But *terra
merita* is prob. a barbarous corruption ;
perhaps of the Arab. name *kurkum*?

Turmoil, sb. (F.?—L.?) Formerly
turmoyl ; probably a corrupt form, the
latter part of the word being assimilated
to *moil*, q. v. ; and the former part to
turn. Prob. from F. *tremouille*. 'the
hopper of a mill,' also called *trameul*
(Cotgrave) ; also spelt *tremoie*, *tremuye*
(Roquefort). (The form *trameul* is sufficiently near.) β. So named from being in
continual motion.—L. *tremere*, to tremble,
shake. Cf. prov. E. *tremmle*, to tremble.

Turn, verb. (F.—L.) M. E. *turnen*,
tournen.—F. *tourner*, O. F. *torner*.—L.
tornare, to turn in a lathe.—L. *tornus*, a
lathe.+Gk. τόρνος, a tool to draw circles
with ; allied to τορός, piercing, L. *terere*, to
rub, bore. (√ TAR.) Der. *turn*, sb.

attorney. (F.—L.) M. E. *attourneye*.
—O. F. *atorne* [i. e. *atorné*], pp. of *atorner*,
to direct, prepare, transact business.—F. *a*
(=L. *ad*), to ; O. F. *torner*, to turn (above).

contour, an outline. (F.—L.) F. *contour*, orig. the environs of a town, suburb.
—F. *contourner*, 'to compasse about,'

Cot. ; lit. to turn round together.—F. *con-
(=L. *con-*, for *cum*), together ; O. F.
torner, to turn.

detour, a winding way. (F.—L.) F.
détour, a circuit ; verbal sb. from F.
détourner, to turn aside.—F. *dé-* (=L *dis-*),
aside, apart ; *tourner*, to turn (above).

return, vb. (F.—L.) F. *retourner* (Cot.).
—F. *re-* (=L. *re-*), back ; *tourner*, to turn.

tornado, a hurricane. (Span.—L.)
Properly *tornada*, 'i. e. a return, or turning
about, a sudden storm at sea ;' Blount.—
Span. *tornada*, a return, turn about ; orig.
fem. of pp. of *tornar*, to turn.—L. *tornare*,
to turn (above).

tour, a circuit. (F.—L.) Lit. 'a turn.'
—F. *tour*, lit. a turn ; verbal sb. from F.
tourner, to turn ; see **Turn**.

tournament. (F.—L.) M. E. *turne-
ment*.—O. F. *tornoiement*, a tournament
(Burguy). — O. F. *tournoier*, to joust. —
O. F. *tornoi, tornei*, a tourney, joust ; lit. a
turning about.—O. F. *torner*, to turn ; see
Turn.

tourney. (F.—L.) O. F. *tornei* (above).

tourniquet. (F.—L.) F. *tourniquet*, lit.
' that which turns about ;' a name given to
a stick turned round to tighten a bandage,
to stop a flow of blood.—F. *tourner*, to
turn (above).

turnpike. (F.—L. ; *and* C.) Formerly a name given to the old-fashioned
turn-stile, which revolved on the top of a
post. From **Turn** and **Pike**.

Turnip, Turnep, a plant. (F.—L. ;
and L.) The latter part of the word is
M. E. *nepe*, a turnip, A. S. *nǽp*, borrowed
from L. *nāpus*, a kind of turnip ; cf. Irish
and Gael. *neip*, a turnip. β. The former
part appears to be F. *tour* in the sense of
' wheel,' to signify its round shape ; it looks
as if it had been turned. A turner's wheel
was formerly called a *turn* in English, and
tour in French. See **Turn**.

Turpentine ; see **Terebinth**.

Turpitude ; (F.—L.) F. *turpitude*.—L.
turpitudo, baseness.—L. *turpis*, base.

Turquoise ; see **Turkey**.

Turret ; see **Tower**.

Turtle (1), a turtle-dove. (L.) A. S.
turtle ; formed, by change of *r* to *l*, from
from L. *turtur*, a turtle (whence also G.
turtel, Ital. *tortora, tortola*). An imitative
word ; due to a repetition of *tur*, used to
express the coo of a pigeon.

turtle (2), the sea-tortoise. (L.) English sailors, ill understanding the Port.

tartaruga, Span. *tortuga*, a tortoise or sea-turtle, turned these words into *turtle*. The Span. and Port. words are allied to **Tortoise**.

Tush, an exclamation of impatience. (E.) Formerly *twish*, an expression of disgust. Cf. *pish* and *tut*.

Tusk. (E.) A.S. *tusc*, usually spelt *tux*, also *twux*, a tusk. Prob. for *twisc**, as if 'a double tooth;' from A.S. *twis*, double, allied to *twá*, two. See **Two**.

Tussle; see **Touse**.

Tut, an exclamation of impatience. (E.) Cf. F. *trut* (the same); and cf. *tush*.

Tutelar, Tutelage, Tutor; see **Tuition**.

Twaddle, to tattle. (E.) Formerly *twattle*, a collateral form of *tattle*.

Twain; see **Two**.

Twang, to sound with a sharp noise. (E.) A collateral form of *tang*; see **Tang** (2).

Tweak, to twitch, pinch. (E.) M. E. *twikken*, answering to an A.S. form *twiccan**, whence A.S. *twicca*, as in A.S. *angel-twicca*, a hook-twitcher, the name of a worm used as a bait.+Low G. *twikken*, G. *zwicken*, to pinch.

twinkle. (E.) A.S. *twinclian*, to twinkle; a frequentative form of *twink*, appearing in M. E. *twinken*, to blink, wink. Again, this is a nasalised form of M. E. *twikken*, to twitch (hence to quiver); see above and below.

twinkling. (E.) M. E. *twinkeling*, the twitching of an eye.—M. E. *twinkelen*, to wink; the same word as E. *twinkle*.

twitch, to pluck. (E.) M. E. *twicchen*, a weakened form of *twikken*, to tweak (above).

Tweezers, nippers. (F.—Teut.; *with E. suffix*.) A surgeon's box of instruments was formerly called *a tweese*, whence small surgical instruments were called *tweezes*, a form afterwards turned into *tweezers*, and used of small nippers in particular. β. Again, the word *tweese* was really at first *twees*, the plural of *twee* or *etwee*, a surgical case; *etwee* being merely an Englished form of O. F. *estuy*, F. *étui*.—O. F. *estuy*, 'a sheath, case, a case of little instruments, now commonly termed an *ettwee*;' Cot. γ. The O. F. *estuy* is the same as Span. *estuche*, Port. *estojo*, O. Ital. *stuccio*, *stucchio*, 'a little pocket-case with cizors, pen-knife, and such trifles in them' (*sic*); Florio.—M. H. G. *stúche* (prov. G. *stauch*), a cuff,

a short and narrow muff (hence a case). ¶ Etymology quite clear; *estuy* became *etwee*, *twee*, then *twees*, then *tweeses*, and lastly *tweezers*, which might be explained as 'instruments belonging to a *tweese*.'

Twelve; **Twenty**; see **Two**.

Twibill, Twice, Twig (1); see **Two**.

Twig (2), to comprehend. (C.) Irish *tuig-im*, I understand; Gael. *tuig*, to understand.

Twilight, Twill; see **Two**.

Twin, Twine; see **Two**.

Twinge, to nip. (E.) M. E. *twingen*, orig. a strong verb, to nip, pain. Not in A.S.; but in O. Friesic *twinga*, *thwinga* (pt. t. *twang*), to constrain.+Dan. *tvinge*, Swed. *tvinga*, Icel. *þvinga*, to force, constrain; Du. *dwingen*, G. *zwingen*. β. The M. E. *twengen*, to twinge, answers better to the mod. E. word; this is a secondary form, from the strong verb *twingen* above. Allied to Lith. *twenk-ti*, to dam up, Skt. *tañch*, to contract. (√ TANK, or TAK.)

thong, a strip of leather. (E.) Put for *thwong*. M. E. *thwong*, a thong; A.S. *þwang*, a thong. Orig. 'a twist,' or twisted string, hence a string, cord, thong, strip of leather.—O. Friesic *thwang**, variant of *twang*, pt. t. of *thwingan* or *twingan* (above).

Twinkle; see **Tweak**.

Twirl, to turn rapidly round. (E.) It stands for *thwirl* (like *twinge* for *thwinge*). Frequentative of A.S. *þweran*, to turn, whence *þwiril*, the handle of a churn. Cognate with O. H. G. *tweran*, *dweran*, to whirl round, and with L. *terere*, to bore. (√ TAR.) β. The frequent. form appears also in Du. *dwarlen*, to twirl, *dwarlwind*, a whirlwind; cf. Low G. *dweerwind*, a whirlwind.

Twist; see **Two**.

Twit; see **Wit** (1)

Twitch; see **Tweak**.

Twitter, vb. (E.) Frequentative from a base *twit*; allied to *titter*, *tattle*, and *twaddle*; all of imitative origin.+G. *zwitschern*, to twitter; Du. *kwetteren*, Dan. *qviddre*, Swed. *qvittra*.

Two, Twain. (E.) The A.S. forms shew that the difference between *two* and *twain* was orig. one of gender only. A.S. *twegen*, masc., two (M. E. *tweien*, *twein*, E. *twain*); *twá*, fem., two; neut. *twá* or *tu*, two.+Du. *twee*, Icel. *tveir*, Dan. *to*, Swed. *tvá*, *tu*, Goth. *twai*, G. *zwei* (also *zween*, masc.), Irish *da*, Gael. *da*, *do*, W. *dau*, Russ. *dva*, Lith. *dwi*, L. *duo* (whence

F. *deux*, E. *deuce*), Gk. δύο, Skt. *dva, dwa*. (Aryan form DWA.) Cf. also L. *bi-, bis*, twice; and the prefixes *di-, dia-, dis-*. Der. *a-two*, i. e. *on two* = in two.

between. (E.) A. S. *betweónan*, between; also *betweónum*. — A. S. *be*, by; *tweónum*, dat. pl. of *tweón*, double, twain, formed from *twá*, two (above).

betwixt. (E.) M. E. *betwixe*; to which *t* was afterwards added. — A. S. *betweohs, betweoh*, betwixt. — A. S. *be*, by; *tweoh = twih*, double, from *twá*, two. Cf. G. *zwischen*, betwixt; allied to *zwei*, two.

twelve. (E.) M. E. *twelf*, whence *twelf-e*, a pl. form, also written *twelue* (= *twelve*). A. S. *twelf, twelfe*.+O. Fries. *twilif*, Du. *twaalf*, Icel. *tólf*, Dan. *tolv*, Swed. *tolf*, G. *zwölf*, O. H. G. *zwelif*, Goth. *twalif*. β. The Goth. *twa-lif* is composed of *twa*, two; and *lif*, the equivalent in *sense* to the Lithuan. *-lika*, occurring in *dwy-lika*, twelve. Again, the suffix *-lika* is allied to Lithuan. *lekas*, remaining, left over, from *lik-ti*, to remain. So also Goth. *-lif* is allied to A. S. *lifian*, to remain. Hence *twa-lif* = two over ten, i. e. twelve. Der. *twelf-th*, put for *twelft* = A. S. *twelfta*, twelfth; *twelvemonth* = M. E. *twelfmonthe*.

twenty. (E.) A. S. *twentig*. — A. S. *twen = twén*, short for *twegen*, twain; and *-tig*, suffix allied to Goth. *tigjus* and E. *ten*. +Goth. *twaitigjus*, Du. *twintig*, Icel. *tuttugu*, G. *zwanzig*; all similarly formed.

twibill, twybill, a two-edged bill. (E.) M. E. *twibil*. A. S. *twíbill*. — A. S. *twí-*, double; *bill*, a bill; see **twice** (below).

twice. (E.) M. E. *twiës* (dissyllabic). A. S. *twíges*, a late form, put for the older *twíwa*, twice. — A. S. *twí-*, double (the same as L. *bi-*, Gk. δι-, Skt. *dvi*); allied to *twá*, two.

twig (1), a shoot of a tree. (E.) A. S. *twíg* (pl. *twígu*), a twig; orig. the fork of a branch, and named from being double, the small shoot branching off from the larger one. — A. S. *twí-*, double; see above. +Du. *twijg*, G. *zweig*. Cf. G. *zwiesel*, a forked branch.

twilight. (E.) M. E. *twilight*. The prefix *twi-* (A. S. *twí-*) is lit 'double' (see **twice** above); but is here used rather in the sense of doubtful or half; cf. L. *dubius*, doubtful, from *duo*, two.+G. *zwielicht*, O. Du. *tweelicht*; similarly compounded.

twill. (Low G.) Low G. *twillen*, to make double; cf. *twill*, a forked branch.

Allied to Swed. Dan. *tvilling*, a twin. The word has reference to a peculiar method of doubling the warp-threads, or taking two of them together; this gives an appearance of diagonal lines, in textile fabrics. From A. S. *twí-*, double (above).

twin. (E.) A. S. *ge-twinne*, twins.+ Icel. *tvinnr*, in pairs; Lithuan. *dwini*, twins; cf. L. *bini*, two at a time. From the A. S. *twí-*, double; the *-n* gives a distributive force, as in L. *bi-n-i*, two at a time.

twine, vb. (E.) M. E. *twinen*, to twist together. From A. S. *twín*, sb., a twisted or doubled thread. — A. S. *twí-*, double; see **twice** (above).+Du. *twijn*, sb., a twist, twine, Icel. *tvinni*, twine; Swed. *tvinntråd*, twine-thread.

twist, vb. (E.) M. E. *twisten*, vb. formed from A. S. *twist*, sb., a rope or twisted cord. — A. S. *twí-*, double; with suffix *-st*, as in *bla-st* from *blow*. The Du. *twist*, Dan. Swed. *tvist*, G. *zwist*, mean 'discord,' which is another sense of the same word; so also M. E. *twist*, a twig or fork of a branch; Icel. *tvistr*, the deuce, in card-playing.

Tympanum; see **Type**.

Type. (F. — L. — Gk.) F. *type* (Sherwood). — L. *typum*, acc. of *typus*. — Gk. τύπος, a blow, mark of a blow, stamp, impress, mark, mould, type, &c. — Gk. τυπ-, base of τύπτειν, to strike. Cf. Skt. *tup, tump*, to hurt; also L. *tundere*, Gk. στυφ-ελίζειν, to strike. (√STUP.) Der. *typ-ic*, Gk. τυπικός; whence *typic-al*, &c.

antitype. (Gk.) Gk. ἀντίτυπον; 1 Pet. iii. 21; neut. of ἀντίτυπος, adj., formed according to a model. — Gk. ἀντί, over against; τύπος, type.

archetype, the original type. (F. — L. — Gk.) F. *archetype*, 'a principall type;' Cot. — L. *archetypum*, the original pattern. — Gk. ἀρχέτυπον, a model; neut. of ἀρχέτυπος, stamped as a model. — Gk. ἀρχε- = ἀρχι-, prefix (see **Archi-**); τύπος, a type.

timbrel. (F. — L. — Gk.) Dimin. of M. E. *timbre*, a small tambourine. — O. F. *timbre, tymbre*, a timbrel. — L. *tympanum*, a drum; see below.

tympanum, the hollow part of the ear, &c. (L. — Gk.) L. *tympanum*, a drum, tympanum. — Gk. τύμπανον, a drum, roller; the same as τύπανον, a drum. — Gk. τυπ-, base of τύπτειν, to strike. Der. *tym-pany*, Gk. τυμπανίας, a dropsy in which the belly is tightly stretched, as a drum.

Typhoon, a violent whirlwind. (Chinese.)

A modern word; it is a Chinese word meaning 'a great wind.' — Chinese *ta*, great; *fâng* (in Canton *fung*), wind, whence *ta fung*, a gale, a typhoon (Williams). ¶ *Tyfoon* would be better; *typhoon* is due to confusion with the old word *typhon* (not uncommon in old authors), from Gk. τυφῶν, better τυφώς, a whirlwind. The close accidental coincidence of these words in sense and form is very remarkable, as Whitney notes.

Typhus, a kind of fever. (L. — Gk.) L. *typhus*. — Gk. τῦφος, smoke, mist; also stupor, esp. if arising from fever; *typhus fever* = stupor-fever. — Gk. τύφειν, to smoke. Cf. Skt. *dhûp*, to fumigate. (√DHU.) Der. *typho-id*, i. e. typhus-like, from εἶδος, resemblance.

Tyrant. (F. — L. — Gk.) The *t* is added. O. F. *tiran*, also *tyrant*. — L. *tyrannum*, acc. of *tyrannus*, a tyrant. — Gk. τύραννος, a lord, sovereign, master; orig. in a good sense. Der. *tyrann-y*, F. *tyrannie*, L. *tyrannia*, Gk. τυραννία, sovereignty.

Tyro, misspelling of **Tiro**, q. v.

U.

Ubiquity, omnipresence. (F. — L.) F. *ubiquité*, 'an ubiquity;' Cot. As if from L. acc. *ubiquitatem* *, a being everywhere; a coined word. — L. *ubique*, everywhere. — L. *ubi*, where; with suffix *-que*, allied to L. *quis*, who. Der. *ubiquit-ous*.

Udder. (E.) A. S. *úder*, an udder. + O. Du. *uder*, Du. *uijer*, Icel. *júgr* (for *júdr* *), Swed. *jufver*, *jur*, Dan. *yver*; G. *euter*, O. H. G. *úter*.+Gael. and Irish *uth*, L. *uber*, Gk. οὖθαρ, Skt. *ûdhar*, *ûdhan*, an udder. Root unknown.

Ugly, frightful. (Scand.) M. E. *ugly*, *uglike*. — Icel. *uggligr*, fearful, dreadful. — Icel. *ugg-r*, fear; *-ligr* = A. S. *-líc*, like. Allied to Icel. *ugga*, to fear, *ógn*, terror, *ógna*, to threaten; also to Goth. *ogan*, to fear, *ogjan*, to terrify, *agis*, terror, Icel. *agi*, terror, and E. **Awe.** Der. *ugli-ness*.

Uhlan, Ulan, a lancer. (G. — Polish. — Turkish.) G. *uhlan*, a lancer. — Pol. *ułan*, a lancer. Borrowed (according to Mahn) from Turk *oglán*, a youth, lad.

Ukase, an edict. (F. — Russ.) F. *ukase*. — Russ. *ykaz*', an edict; cf. *ykazate*, to indicate, shew, order, prescribe. — Russ. *y-*, prefix; *kazate*, to shew.

Ulcer, a dangerous sore. (F. — L.) F. *ulcère*. — L. *ulcer-*, stem of *ulcus*, a sore.+ Gk. ἕλκος, a wound, sore.

Ullage, the unfilled part of a cask. (F. — L. — Gk.) '*Ullage of a cask*, that which it wants of being full;' Phillips. — O F. *eullage*, a filling up. — O. F. *eullier*, to fill a cask up to the bung. Cotgrave spells it *oeiller*, and the sb. as *oeillage*. Lit. 'to oil,' from the adding of a little oil to prevent evaporation. From O. F. *oile*, oil. See Oil.

Ulterior, Ultimate; see **Ultra-**.

Ultra-, beyond. (L.) L. *ultra*, beyond, adv. and prep. Orig. fem. abl. of O. Lat. *ulter*, adj.; really a comparative form (with suffix *-ter*) from the base *ul-*, allied to O. Lat. *ollus*, that, *olle* (*ille*), he.

antepenultima, the last syllable but two in a word. (L.) L. *ante*, before; *pænultima*, fem. adj., last but one, from *pæn-e*, almost, *ultima*, last.

outrage. (F. — L.) F. *outrage*, earlier form *oltrage*, excessive violence. (Cf. Ital. *oltraggio*.) — O. F. *oltre*, F. *outre*, beyond; with suffix *-age* (= L. *-aticum*). — L. *ultra*, beyond.

penultima; see antepenultima.

ulterior, further. (L.) L. *ulterior*, further; comp. of O. L. *ulter*, adj. (above).

ultimate, furthest. (L.) L. *ultimatus*, pp. of *ultimare*, to be at the last. — L. *ultimus*, last; *ul-ti-mus* being a double superl. form from the base *ul* ; see **Ultra** (above).

ultramarine, beyond sea; as sb., sky-blue. (Span. — L.) Span. *ultramarino*, beyond sea; also a blue colour. — L. *ultra*, beyond; *mar-e*, sea; and suffix *-inus*; see **Marine.**

ultramontane, beyond the Alps. (F. — Ital. — L.) F. *ultramontain*. — Ital. *oltramontano*. — L. *ultra*, beyond; *mont-em*, acc., a mountain; with suffix *-anus*; see **Mountain.**

ultramundane, beyond the world. (L.) L. *ultra*, beyond; *mundanus*, worldly, from *mundus*, world; see **Mundane.**

utterance (2), extremity. (F. — L.) F. *outrance*, extremity. — F. *outre*, beyond. — L. *ultra*, beyond; see **Ultra-** (above).

Umbel, Umber; see **Umbrage.**

Umbilical, pertaining to the navel. (F. — L.) F. *umbilical*, adj., from *umbilic*, navel (Cot.). — L. *umbilicum*, acc. of *um-*

bilicus, navel, middle, centre.+Gk. ὀμφαλός, navel. Initial *n* has been lost; cf. Skt. *nábhi*, navel; see **Nave** (1).

Umbrage, shade of trees; offence. (F. — L.) Properly 'shadow;' hence, shadow or suspicion of injury. — F. *ombrage, umbrage*, shade, also suspicion. — F. *ombre*, shadow (with suffix *-age* = L. *-aticum*). — L. *umbra*, shadow.

adumbrate. (L.) From pp. of L. *adumbrare*, to cast shadow over, shadow forth. — L. *ad*, to; *umbra*, shadow.

umbel, an umbrella-like form of a flower. (L.) L. *umbella*, a parasol; dimin. of *umbra*, a shade.

umber. (F. — Ital. — Lat.) F. *ombre*, short for *terre d'ombre*, lit. 'earth of shadow,' a brown earth used for shadowing in paintings. — Ital. *terra d'ombra*, lit. earth of shadow. — L. *terra*, earth; *de*, of; *umbra*, shadow.

umbrella. (Ital. — L.) Ital. *umbrella, ombrella*, a parasol; dimin. of Ital. *ombra*, a shade. — L. *umbra*, a shade.

Umpire. (F. — L.) Put for *numpire*, the old form of the word; M. E. *nompere, noumpere*, also *nounpere, nounpier*, P. Plowman, B. v. 337. — O. F. *nomper* *, later *nompair*, peerless, odd (Cot.); earliest form *nonper* (Roquefort). Used, like L. *impar*, in the sense of arbitrator; the lit. sense is unequal, odd, hence a third man called in to arbitrate, a 'non-peer.' — O. F. *non*, not; O. F. *per, pair*, a peer. See **Non-**; also **peer-**, under **Par**. ¶ There is no doubt as to this result.

Un- (1), neg. prefix. (E.) Prefixed to sbs., adjs., and advs. (Distinct from *un-* (2) below.) A. S. *un-*, neg. prefix.+Du. *on-*, Icel. *ó-, ú-*, Dan. *u-*, Swed. *o-*, Goth. *un-*, G. *un-*, W. *an-*, L. *in-*, Gk. *ἀν-, ἀ-*, orig. *ἀνα-*, Zend. *ana-*, Pers. *ná-*, Skt. *an-*. β. The Aryan form seems to have been ANA; whence also L. *ne*, and Gk. *νη-*, Goth. *ni-*, Russ. *ne-*, Gael. *neo-*, negative prefixes. γ. Readily prefixed to a large number of words; a few of these, such as *un-couth*, of which the simple form is not used, will be found below.

Un- (2), verbal prefix, expressing the reversal of an action. (E.) Quite distinct from *un-* (1) above; only used with verbs. Thus *to un-lock* = to reverse locking, to open that which was closed by locking. A. S. *un-*.+Du. *ont-*, G. *ent-*, O. H. G. *ant-*, Goth. *and-* (as in *and-bindan*, to unbind). Precisely the same as E. *an-* in *an-swer*,

A. S. *and-*, Gk. ἀντι-; see **Anti-**. ¶ In the case of *past participles*, the prefix is ambiguous; thus *un-bound* may either mean 'not bound,' with prefix *un-* (1), or may mean 'undone' or released, with prefix *un-* (2).

Un- (3), prefix. (O. Low G.) Only in *un-to, un-til*, which see.

Unanimous; see **Unity**.

Unaneled, without having received extreme unction. (E.; *and* L. — Gk.) In Hamlet, i. 5. 77. Lit. 'un-on-oiled.' — A. S. *un-*, not; *on* (M. E. *an*), on, upon; *eled*, pp. of *elan*, to oil, verb from *ele*, sb., oil. The A. S. *ele*, oil, is borrowed from L. *oleum*, Gk. ἔλαιον, oil; see **Oil**.

Uncial; see **Inch**.

Uncle. (F. — L.) M. E. *uncle*. — F. *oncle*. — L. *auunculum*, acc. of *auunculus*, a mother's brother, lit. 'little grandfather;' dimin. of *auus*, a grandfather.

Uncouth, strange; see **Can** (1).

Unction; see **Unguent**.

Under, beneath. (E.) A. S. *under*.+Du. *onder*, Icel. *undir*, Dan. Swed. *under*, Goth. *undar*, G. *unter*, under. Common as a prefix.

undern, a certain period of the day. (E.) The time denoted differed at different periods. The A. S. *undern* meant the third hour, about 9 a. m.; later, it meant about 11 a. m.; and, still later, the afternoon, in which sense it survives in prov. E. *aunder, aandorn, orndorns, doundrins*, &c. +Icel. *undorn*, M. H. G. *untarn*, Goth. *undaurni*; the lit. sense being merely 'intervening period.' Derived from A. S. *under*, with the sense 'among' or 'between,' like G. *unter*.

Understand; see **Stand**.

Undertake; see **Take**.

Undulate, to wave. (L.) From pp. of L. *undulare*, to fluctuate. — L. *undula**, dimin. of *unda*, a wave. + A. S. *ýð* (for *unð**), wave; Icel. *unnr*. Allied to **Wet** and **Water**; cf. Skt. *und*, to wet, Lith. *wandŭ*, water.

abound. (F. — L.) F. *abonder*. — L. *abundare*, to overflow. — L. *ab*, away; *unda*, wave.

abundance. (F. — L.) M. E. *aboundance*. — O. F. *abondance*. — L. *abundantia*, plenty. — L. *abundant-*, stem of pres. pt. of *abundare* (above).

inundation. (F. — L.) Imitated from F. *inondation*. — L. *inundationem*, acc. of *inundatio*, an overflowing. — L. *inundare*, to overflow. — L. *in*, upon, over; *unda*, a wave.

redound. (F.—L.) F. *redonder.* — L. *redundare,* to overflow. — L. *red-,* again, back; *unda,* a wave.

redundant. (L.) From stem of pres. pt. of L. *redundare* (above).

superabound. (F.—L.) From *super-* and *abound;* see **abound** (above). Der. *superabund-ant;* see **abundant** (above).

Uneath, scarcely, with difficulty. (E.) Obsolete. M. E. *uneþe.* A. S. *uneðe,* adv., from adj. *uneðe,* difficult. — A. S. *un-,* not; *eðe, eð,* easy; the orig. sense being waste, empty, hence easy to occupy. Cf. O. Sax. *ôði,* easy; G. *öde,* waste, deserted. Icel. *auðr,* empty, Goth. *auths, authis,* desert, waste; also L. *otium,* leisure.

Ungainly, awkward. (Scand.; *with* E. suffix.) Formed by adding *-ly* to M. E. *ungein,* inconvenient. — A. S. *un-,* not; Icel. *gagn,* ready, serviceable, convenient, allied to *gegna,* to meet, suit, *gegn,* against, and to E. **Again.** Cf. Icel. *ô-gegn,* ungainly.

Unguent, ointment. (L.) L. *unguentum,* ointment. — L. *unguent-,* stem of pres. pt. of *ungere,* to anoint. + Skt. *añj,* to smear. (√AG, ANG.)

anoint. (F. — L.) M. E. *anoint,* used as a pp. = anointed. — O. F. *enoint,* pp. of *enoindre,* to anoint. — O. F. *en* (=L. *in*), upon; *oindre,* to smear (= L. *ungere* above).

ointment. (F. — L.) The former *t* is due to confusion with *anoint;* the M. E. form is *oinement.* — O. F. *oignement,* an anointing, also an unguent. —O. F. *oigne-r,* the same as *oindre,* to anoint (=L. *ungere*); with suffix *-ment.*

unction. (F. — L.) F. *onction.* — L. *unctionem,* acc. of *unctio,* an anointing. — L. *unct-us,* pp. of *ungere,* to anoint. Der. *unctu-ous,* Low L. *unctu-osus.*

Unicorn; see **Corn** (2), or **Unity.**

Uniform, Union, &c.; see **Unity.**

Unity, oneness. (F.—L.) M. E. *unitee.* — F. *unité* (*unité*). — L. *unitatem,* acc. of *unitas,* unity. — L. *uni-,* for *uno-,* crude form of *unus,* one, cognate with **One.**

annul. (L.) L. *annullare,* to bring to nothing. — L. *an-* (for *ad*), to; *nullus,* no one; see **null** (below).

null, of no force. (L.) L. *nullus,* for *ne ullus,* not any; where *ullus,* any, is short for *unulus*,* from *unus,* one.

onion, a plant. (F.—L.) F. *oignon.* — L. *unionem,* acc. of *unio;* see **union** (2) below.

unanimous, of one mind. (L.) L.

unanimus, of one mind. — L. *un-us,* one; *animus,* mind. See **Animal.**

unicorn. (F. — L.) F. *unicorne,* a fabulous one-horned animal. — L. *unicornem,* acc. of *unicornis,* one-horned. — L. *uni-,* for *unus;* *corn-u,* a horn. See **Horn.**

uniform, adj. (F. — L.) F. *uniforme.* — L. *uniformem,* acc. of *uniformis,* having one form. — L. *uni-,* for *unus,* one; *form-a,* form; see **Form.**

union (1), concord. (F.—L.) F. *union.* — L. acc. *unionem,* oneness. — L. *uni-,* for *uno-,* crude form of *unus,* one.

union (2), a large pearl. (F.—L.) The same word as the above; the L. *unio* means oneness, also a single pearl of a large size, also a kind of onion.

unique. (F. — L.) F. *unique,* single. — L. *unicum,* acc. of *unicus,* single. — L. *uni-,* for *unus,* one.

unison; see **Sound** (3).

unit. (F. — L.) Formed by dropping the final *-y* of *unity.* ' *Unit, Unite,* or *Unity,* in arithmetic, the first significant figure, or number 1,' &c.; Phillips; see **Unity** (above).

unite. (L.) L. *unitus,* pp. of *unire,* to unite. — L. *uni-,* for *unus,* one.

universal. (F. — L.) F. *universel,* O. F. *universal.* — L. *uniuersalis,* belonging to the whole. — L. *uniuersus,* turned into one, combined into a whole. — L. *uni-,* for *unus,* one; *uersus,* pp. of *uertere,* to turn; see **Verse.** Der. *univers-ity,* F. *université,* from L. acc. *uniuersitatem.*

univocal, having but one meaning. (L.) From L. *uniuoc-us,* univocal; with suffix *-alis.*— L. *uni-,* for *unus,* one; *uoc-,* stem of *uox,* voice, sense; see **Voice.**

Unkempt; see **Comb.**

Unless, if not, except. (E.) Formerly *on les,* or *lesse,* in the phrase *on lesse that,* i.e. in less than, on a less supposition than. Thus *un-* here stands for *on.* See **On** and **Less.**

Unruly; see **Regent.**

Until; see below.

Unto, even to. (O. Low G.) M. E. *unto* (not in A. S.). Put for *und-to;* where *to* is the usual prep., and *und* is the O. Fries. *und, ont,* Goth. *und,* O. Sax. *und,* unto; whence O. Sax. *un-tô,* unto. This prefix is common in A. S. in the form *ôð,* wherein *n* is dropped; so that A. S. *ôð* : Goth. *und* :: A. S. *tôð* : Goth. *tunthus* (tooth). Origin obscure, perhaps orig. identical with **Un-** (2).

until. (O. Low G. *and* Scand.) The

same word as above, with the substitution of Icel. *til*, to, for E. *to*. See **Till**.

Up. (E.) M. E. *vp*, *up*; A.S. *up*, *upp*, adv. **+** Du. *op*, Icel. *upp*, Dan. *op*, Swed. *upp*, Goth. *iup*, G. *auf*, O. H. G. *úf*. Allied to L. *s-ub*, Gk. *ὑπό*, Skt. *upa*, near, on, under. See **Over**.

    above. (E.) A. S. *ábufan*, above. **–** A.S. *á*, for *an*=*on*, on; *be*, by; *ufan*, upward. We find also *be-ufan*, above, without the prefix *á*. The A. S. *ufan* is cognate with G. *oben*, and is extended from Goth. *uf*, allied to Goth. *iup*, up. Cf. Goth. *uf-ar* = E. over.

    open, unclosed. (E.) The verb is from the adj. *open*, which is sometimes shortened to *ope* (Coriol. i. 4. 43). A.S. *open*, adj., open, lit. 'that which is lifted up,' from the lifting of a tent-door. **–** A. S. *up*, up. **+** Du. *open*, adj., from *op*, up; Icel. *opinn*, from *upp*; Swed. *öppen*, from *upp*; G. *offen*, from *auf*, O. H. G. *úf*. Der. *open*, verb, A. S. *openian*, to make open.

    upon. (E.) A.S. *uppon*, upon. **–** A.S. *upp*, up; *on*, on.**+**Icel. *upp á*, upon; Swed. *på*, Dan. *paa* (contracted forms).

Upas, the poison-tree of Java. (Malay.) Malay *úpas*, a poisonous juice; *púhn úpas*, upas-tree (*púhn*=tree).

Upbraid, to reproach. (E.) M. E. *vpbreiden*, to reproach.**–**A.S. *up*, up, upon, on; *bregdan*, to braid, weave, also to lay hold of, seize. The orig. sense seems to have been to lay hold of, hence to attack, accuse, &c. The A. S. *bregdan*, also = E. *braid*, to weave; so that *-braid* in *up-braid* is the usual verb *braid*, used in a special sense. So also Dan. *be-breide* (lit. be-braid), to upbraid.

Upholsterer; see **Hold**.

Upon; see **Up**.

Uproar, tumult. (Du.) The spelling shews confusion with E. *roar*.**–** Du. *oproer*, 'uprore, tumult;' Hexham. **–** Du. *op*, up; *roeren*, to excite, stir, move; so that *oproer* =a stirring up, commotion. **+** Swed. *upp-ror*, Dan. *uprör*, G. *aufruhr*. β. The verb is Du. *roeren*, Swed. *röra*, Dan. *röre*, G. *rühren*, A. S. *hréran*, to stir; see **Reremouse**. The A. S. *hréran* is from *hrór*, adj., active, busy.

Upsidedown. (E.) From *up*, *side*, and *down*. But the M. E. form was *up-so-doun*, i. e. 'up as it were down.'

Upstart, sb. (E.) From *upstart*, verb; to start up; Spenser, F. Q. i. 1. 16. See **Start**.

Upwards; see **Up** and **-ward**, suffix.

Urbane, courteous. (L.) L. *urbanus*, belonging to a city.**–** L. *urb-s*, a city. Der. *urban*, doublet of *urbane*; *urban-i-ty*, F. *urbanité*, from L. acc. *urbanitatem*, courteousness.

    suburb. (L.) L. *suburbium*, suburb. **–**L. *sub*, near; *urbi-*, crude form of *urbs*, a town. Der. *suburb-an*.

Urchin, a hedgehog, goblin, imp, small child. (F.–L.) Orig. hedgehog (Tempest, i. 2. 326); hence, goblin, imp, small child; it being supposed that some imps took a hedgehog's shape; see **Hag**.–O. F. *ireçon*, *eriçon*, *herisson*, a hedgehog; formed with suffix *-on* (= L. *-onem*) from L. *ericius*, a hedgehog, lengthened form of *ēr* (gen. *ēri-s*), a hedgehog. **+** Gk. χήρ, hedgehog. Lit. 'bristly;' cf. L. *horrere*. (√ GHAR.)

Ure, practise, use. (F.–L.) Obsolete, except in *in-ure*, *man-ure*. (Distinct from *use*.)–O. F. *eure*, *uevre*, *ovre*, work, action. **–**L. *opera*, work: see **Operate**.

Urge. (L.) L *urgere*, to urge, drive. Allied to **Wreak**. (√ WARG.) Der. *urg-ent*, from stem of pres. part.

Urim. (Heb.) Heb. *úrím*, lights; pl. of *úr*, light. See **Thummim**.

Urine. (F.–L.) F. *urine*.–L. *urina*. **+**Gk. *οὖρον*, urine; Skt. *vári*, *vár*, water; Icel. *úr*, drizzling rain; A. S. *wer*, sea. Orig. 'water.'

    diuretic, provoking discharge of urine. (F.–L.–Gk.) O. F. *diuretique*; Cot.**–** L. *diureticus*.–Gk. διουρητικός.**–** Gk. διουρέειν, to pass urine. **–** Gk. δι-ά, through; οὖρον (above).

Urn. (F.–L.) M. E. *urne*.**–** F. *urne*. **–**L. *urna*, urn.

Us. (E.) A.S. *ús*, dat. pl. of *wé*, we; *ús*, *úsic*, acc. pl. of *wé*.**+**Du. *ons*, Icel. *oss*, Swed. *oss*, Dan. *os*, G. *uns*; Goth. *uns*, *unsis*, dat. and acc. pl.

    our. (E.) A.S. *úre*, of us; gen. pl. of *wé*, we. This gen. pl. became a poss. pron., and was regularly declined as such; *úre* stands for *ús-ere* * = Goth. *unsara*, gen. pl. of Goth. *weis*, we. Der. *our-s*, A. S. *úres*; *our-self*, *our-selves*.

Use, sb. '(F.–L.) M. E. *use*, *vse*.–O.F. *us*, use, usage.–L. *usum*, acc. of *usus*, use. **–**L. *usus*, pp. of *uti*, to use. Cf. Skt. *úta*, pp. of *av*, to please, to be satisfied. (√ AW.) Der. *use*, vb., F. *user*, Low L. *usare*, frequent. of L. *uti*, to use; *us-age*, F. *usage*; *usu-al*, L. *usualis*, adj., from *usu-*, crude form of *usus*, use; &c.

abuse. (F. – L.) F. *abuser*, to use amiss. – L. *abus-us*, pp. of *abuti*, to use amiss. – L. *ab*, away, from, hence, amiss ; *uti*, to use. So also *dis-use, mis-use, ill-use*.

peruse. (F. – L.) The orig. sense was ' to use up,' to go through thoroughly ; hence to examine thoroughly or all over, to survey ; the only difficulty in the word is in its change of sense. From *per-*, thoroughly ; and *use*. ¶ Certain.

usurp, to seize to one's own use. (F. – L.) F. *usurper*. – L. *usurpare*, to employ, acquire ; also, to usurp. β. Clearly derived from *us-us*, use, but the rest of the word is obscure ; perhaps from *usum rumpere*, to break a user, hence to assert a right to (Key, Roby) ; others suggest *usu-rapere*, to seize to one's own use.

usury. (F. – L.) M. E. *usurye, usure.* – F. *usure*, usury, the occupation of a thing. – L. *usura*, use, enjoyment, interest, usury. – L. *usu-s*, pp. of *uti*, to use.

utensil. (F. – L.) F. *utensile*, sb. – L. *utensilis*, adj., fit for use ; whence *utensilia*, neut. pl. utensils. Put. for *utent-tilis**, from the stem of pres. pt. of *uti*, to use.

utilise. (F. – L.) F. *utiliser*, a modern word ; coined from *util-e*, useful, with suffix *-ise* (Gk. -ιζειν). – L. *utilis*, useful. – L. *uti*, to use.

utility. (F. – L.) F. *utilité*. – L. acc. *utilitatem*, from nom. *utilitas*, usefulness. – L. *utili-s*, useful. – L. *uti*, to use.

Usher, a door-keeper. (F. – L.) M. E. *uschere, ussher.* – O. F. *ussier, uissier*, later *huissier*, ' an usher, or door-keeper ;' Cot.

– L. *ostiarium*, acc. of *ostiarius*, a door-keeper. – L. *ostium*, a door. Extended from L. *os*, mouth ; see **Oral.**

Usquebaugh ; see **Whiskey.**

Usurp, Usury ; see **Use.**

Ut, the first note of the musical scale. (L.) L. *ut.* See **Gamut.**

Utas, the octave of a feast. (F. – L.) *Utas* is a Norman F. word corresponding to O. F. *oitauues*, pl. of *oitauue*, octave, eighth day. – L. *octaua* (*dies*), eighth day ; fem. of *octauus*, eighth. – L. *octo*, eight. See **Octave**

Utensil ; see **Use.**

Uterine, born by the same mother of a different father. (F. – L.) F. *uterin*, ' of the womb, born of one mother ;' Cot. – L. *uterinus*, born of one mother. – L. *uterus*, womb.

Utilise, Utility ; see **Use.**

Utmost, Utter ; see **Out.**

Utopian. (Gk.) An adj. due to Sir T. More's description of *Utopia*, an imaginary island, situate *nowhere*. – Gk. οὐ, not ; τόπος, a place ; see **Topic.**

Utterance (1), an uttering. (E. ; *with* F. *suffix*.) From the verb *to utter*, frequent. of M. E. *outen*, A. S. *útian*, to put out. – A. S. *út*, out. See **Out.**

Utterance (2), extremity ; see **Ultra-.**

Uvula. (L.) Late L. *uvula*, dimin. of L. *uua*, a grape, a cluster, also the uvula.

Uxorious, excessively fond of a wife. (L.) L. *uxorius*, fond of a wife. – L. *uxori-*, crude form of *uxor*, a wife. Allied to Skt. *vaçá*, a wife, fem. of *vaça*, subdued.

V.

V. In Middle-English, *v* is commonly written as *u* in the MSS. ; conversely, *v* is put for *u* in a few words, chiefly *vp, vnder, vnto, vs, vse*, and the prefix *vn-*.

Vacation. (F. – L.) F. *vacation.* – L. acc. *uacationem*, leisure. – L. *uacatus*, pp. of *uacare*, to be empty or at leisure.

evacuate. (L.) From pp. of L. *euacu-are*, to empty. – L. *e*, out ; *uacuus*, empty (below).

vacuum. (L.) L. *uacuum*, an empty space ; neut. of *uacuus*, empty. – L. *uacare*, to be empty.

Vaccinate. (L.) Coined as if from pp. of *vaccinare**, to inoculate. – L. *uaccinus*, belonging to cows. – L. *uacca*, a cow. Lit.

' a lowing animal ;' cf. Skt. *vâç*, to cry, low. (√ WAK.) ¶ First used about 1798.

Vacillation. (F. – L.) F. *vacillation*, ' a reeling, staggering ;' Cot. – L. *uacilla-tionem*, acc. of *uacillatio*, a reeling, wavering. – L. *uacillatus*, pp. of *uacillare*, to reel. Cf. Skt. *vank*, to go tortuously, *vakra*, bent. Allied to **Wag, Weigh.**

Vacuum ; see **Vacation.**

Vade, to wither ; see **Fatuous.**

Vagabond, Vagary, Vagrant ; see under **Vague.**

Vague, unsettled. (F. – L.) F. *vague*, wandering ; *vaguer*, to wander. – L. *uagus*, wandering ; whence *uagari*, to wander. Allied to **Vacillate.**

extravagant. (F. — L.) F. *extravagant*. — Low. L. *extrauagant-*, stem of *extrauagans*, extravagant, lit. wandering beyond. — L. *extra*, beyond ; *uagans*, pres. pt. of *uagari*, to wander.

vagabond. (F. — L.) F. *vagabond*, 'a vagabond;' Cot. — L. *vagabundus*, adj., strolling about. — L. *uaga-ri*, to wander (above) ; with suffix *-bundus*.

vagary. (L.) Also *vagare* (trisyllabic; Stanyhurst) ; orig. used as a verb ; cf. F. *vaguer*, 'to wander, vagary;' Cot. — L. *uagari*, to wander (above).

vagrant. (F.—G.) A. F. *wakerant*, a vagrant. — M. H. G. *welkern*, to walk about. ¶ Confused with L. *uagari*.

Vail (1), the same as **Veil**.

Vail (2), to lower ; see **Valley**.

Vail (3), a gift to a servant ; see **Valid**.

Vain. (F. — L.) F. *vain*. — L. *uanum*, acc. of *uanus*, empty, vain. Probably *uānus = uac-nus**, allied to **Vacation**.

evanescent. (L.) From stem of pres. pt. of L. *euanescere*, to vanish away. — L. *e*, away ; *uanescere*, to vanish ; see below.

vanish. (F. — L.) M. E. *vanissen*, *vanisshen*. Derived from an O. F. verb *vanir**, with pres. pt. *vanissant**, but the verb is only recorded in the compound *envanir*, to vanish (12th cent.) ; see *évanouir* in Littré. Cf. Ital. *svanire*, to vanish (where *s* = L. *ex*). — L. *uanescere*, to vanish, lit. to become empty. — L. *uanus*, empty.

vanity. (F. — L.) F. *vanité*. — L. *uanitatem*, acc. of *uanitas*, emptiness. — L. *uanus*, vain, empty.

vaunt. (F.—L.) F. *se vanter*, to boast. — Low L. *uanitare*, to speak vanity, flatter ; (F. *se vanter* = to flatter oneself). A frequentative form from *uanus*, vain.

Vair, a kind of fur ; see **Various**.

Valance, a fringe of drapery, now applied to a part of the bed-hangings. (F.—L.) Chaucer has 'a litel kerchief of *valence*;' Assembly of Foules, 272. Prob. named from *Valence* in France, near Lyons (still famous for silks). — L. *Ualentia*, a name given to several towns, evidently with the sense of 'strong.' — L. *ualent-*, stem of pres. pt. of *ualere*, to be strong ; see **Valid**. ¶ Johnson derives it from *Valentia* in Spain ; but was it ever famous for silk ?

Vale, a valley ; see **Valley**.

Valediction, Valentine, Valerian ; see **Valid**.

Valet; see **Vassal**.

Valetudinary; see **Valid**.

Valhalla, the hall of the slain. (Scand.) Icel. *valhöll* (gen. *valhallar*), lit. the hall of the slain. — Icel. *valr*, the slain, slaughter ; *höll*, *hall*, a hall ; see **Hall**.

Valiant ; see **Valid**.

Valid, having force. (F.—L.) F. *valide*. — L. *ualidus*, strong. — L. *ualere*, to be strong.

avail. (F.—L.) M. E. *auailen* (= *availen*). Compounded of F. *a* (=L. *ad*), to ; O. F. *valoir*, *valer*, to be of use, from L. *ualere*, to be strong.

convalesce. (L.) L. *conualescere*, to begin to grow well ; an inceptive form. — L. *con-* (=*cum*), with ; *ualere* (above).

countervail. (F.—L.) M. E. *contrevailen*. — O. F. *contrevaloir*, to avail against. — O. F. *contre*, against ; *valoir*, to avail. — L. *contra*, against ; *ualere*, to be strong.

prevail. (F.—L.) O. F. *prevaloir*, to prevail. — L. *præualere*, to have great power. — L. *præ*, before, excessive ; *ualere*, to be strong. **Der.** *prevalent*, from L. *præualent-*, stem of pres. pt. of *præualere*, to prevail.

vail (3), a gift to a servant. (F.—L.) A headless form of *avail*, sb., in the sense of profit, help (Palsgrave). From *avail*, verb (above).

valediction, a farewell. (L.) Formed from L. *ualedictus*, pp. of *ualedicere*, to say farewell. — L. *uale*, farewell ; *dicere*, to say. β. L. *uale*, lit. 'be strong,' is the 2 pers. sing. imp. of *ualere*, to be strong.

valentine. (F.—L.) Named from *St. Valentine's* day, Feb. 14. — F. *Valentin*. — L. *Ualentinus*. — L. *ualenti-*, crude form of pres. pt. of *ualere*, to be strong.

valerian. (F. — L.) F. *valeriane*, valerian ; a flower. — Late L. *ualeriana*, valerian. Fem. of *Ualerianus*, prob. a personal name ; derived from L. *ualere*, to be strong.

valetudinary. (F.—L.) F. *valetudinaire*, sickly. — L. *ualetudinarius*, sickly. — L. *ualětudin-*, stem of *ualetudo*, health (whether good or bad). — L. *uale-re*, to be strong.

valiant, brave. (F.—L.) F. *vaillant*, valiant ; O. F. *valant*, pres. pt. of F. *valoir*, to profit. — L. *ualere*, to be strong.

valour. (F.—L.) O. F. *valor*, *valur*, *valeur*, value, worthiness. — L. *ualorem*.

acc. of *ualor*, worth. – L. *ualere*, to be strong, to be worth.

value. (F. – L.) F. *valuē*, fem. 'value;' Cot. Fem. of *valu*, pp. of *valoir*, to be worth. – L. *ualere*, to be worth.

Valise, a travelling-bag. (F.) F. *valise*, 'a male [mail], wallet;' Cot. The same as Ital. *valigia*; and corrupted in German to *felleisen*. β. Etym. unknown; Diez supposes it to be founded on L. *uidulus*, a leathern travelling-trunk. Devic suggests Pers. *walíchah*, a large sack, or Arab. *walíhat*, a corn-sack.

Valley. (F. – L.) M. E. *vale*, *valeie*. – O. F. *valee* (F. *vallée*), a valley; parallel to Ital. *vallata*, a valley, which appears to mean, literally, 'formed like a valley.' Formed with suffix *-ee* (= L. *-ata*), from F. *val*, a vale; which is from L. *uallem*, acc. of *uallis*, a vale. Cf. Gk. ἕλος, wet, low ground.

avalanche. (F. – L.) F. *avalanche*, the descent of snow into a valley. – F. *avaler*, to swallow; but the old sense was 'to let fall down.' – F. *aval*, downward, lit. 'to the valley.' – F. *a* (= L. *ad*), to; *val*, vale (below).

vail (2), to lower. (F. – L.) From O. F. *avaler*, to let fall down (above).

vale, a valley. (F. – L.) M. E. *val*. – F. *val*. – L. *uallem*, acc. of *uallis*.

Valour, Value; see **Valid**.

Valve. (F. – L.) F. *valve*, 'a foulding, or two-leaved door, or window;' Cot. – L. *ualua*, sing. of *ualuæ*, the leaves of a folding-door. Allied to L. *uoluere*, to revolve; see **Voluble**.

bivalve. (F. – L.) F. *bivalve*, bivalve, both adj. and sb. – L. *bi-*, double; *ualua*, a leaf of a folding door.

Vamp; see **Van** (1).

Vampire. (F. – G. – Servian.) F. *vampire*. – G. *vampyr*. – Servian *vampir*, *wampira*, a blood-sucker, a supposed ghost that sucked men's blood.

Van (1), the front of an army. (F. – L.) Short for *van-guard*, which stands for M. E. *vantwarde*. – O. F. *avant-wàrde*, later *avant-garde*, 'the vanguard of an army;' Cot. – F. *avant*, before; O. F. *warde*, a guard; see **Advance** and **Guard** or **Ward**.

vamp, the fore-part of a shoe. (F. – L.) Short for M. E. *vampay*, also *vaumpe*, a vamp. – F. *avant-pied*, 'the part of the foot that's next to the toes.' – F. *avant*, before; *pied*, foot, from L. acc. *pedem*.

Van (2), the same as **Fan**.

Van (3); see **Caravan**.

Vandal, a barbarian. (L. – G.) L. *Uandalus*, a Vandal, one of the tribe of *Uandali*, i. e. 'wanderers.' – G. *wandeln*, to wander; cognate with E. **Wander**.

Vane, a weather-cock. (E.) Formerly also *fane*. A. S. *fana*, a small flag.✝ Du. *vaan*, Icel. *fáni*, Dan. *fane*, Swed. Goth. *fana*, G. *fahne*. Orig. a bit of cloth; allied to L. *pannus*, a cloth; see **Pane**.

Vanguard; see **Van** (1).

Vanilla, a plant. (Span. – L.) Misspelt for Span. *vainilla*, a small pod, or capsule (which is the orig. sense). Dimin. of Span. *vaina*, a scabbard, a pod. – L. *uagina*, scabbard, sheath, pod.

Vanish, Vanity; see **Vain**.

Vanquish; see **Victor**.

Vantage. (F. – L.) Short for M. E. *avantage*; see **advantage**, under **Advance**.

Vapid; see **Vapour**.

Vapour, mist. (F. – L.) F. *vapeur*. – L. *uapōrem*, acc. of *uapor*, vapour. L. *uapor*, stands for *cuapor**, allied to Lith. *kwápas*, breath, Gk. καπνός, smoke; Lith. *kwépti*, to breathe. (√ KWAP.)

evaporate. (L.) From pp. of L. *euaporare*, to pass off in vapour. – L. *e*, out; *uapor*, vapour.

vapid, insipid. (L.) L. *uapidus*, stale, flat, said of wine. – L. *uappa*, vapid or palled wine; wine that has emitted its vapour or strength; allied to *uapor* (above).

Varicose, permanently dilated, as a vein. (L.) L. *uaricosus*. – L. *uaric-*, stem of *uarix*, a dilated vein; named from its crooked appearance. – L. *uarus*, crooked.

divaricate, to fork, diverge. (L.) From pp. of L. *diuaricare*, to spread apart. – L. *di-*, for *dis-*, apart; *uaricus*, straddling, from *uarus*, crooked.

prevaricate. (L.) From pp. of L. *præuaricari*, to straddle, hence to swerve, shuffle, shift, quibble. – L. *præ*, before, excessively; *uaric-us*, straddling (above).

Variegate, Variety; see **Various**.

Various. (L.) L. *uarius*, variegated, diverse, manifold. **Der.** *varie-ty*, F. *variété*, from L. acc. *uarietatem*, variety.

meniver, minever, a kind of fur. (F. – L.) M. E. *meniuer* (*meniver*). – O. F. *menu ver*, *menu vair*, miniver; lit. 'little vair.' – O. F. *menu*, small, from L. *minutus*, small; *vair*, a fur; (below).

vair, a kind of fur. (F. – L.) F. *vair*, 'a rich fur;' Cot. – L. *uarius*, variegated. **Der.** *vair-y* (in heraldry), from F. *vairé*, 'diversified with argent and azure;' Cot. Hence *meni-ver* (= F. *menu vair*), above.

variegate. (L.) From pp. of L. *uariegare*, to make of various colours. = L. *uarie*, adv., of divers colours; *-gare*, due to *agere*, to drive, to make.

vary. (F. = L.) F. *varier*. = L. *uariare*, to vary. = L. *uarius*, various (above).

Varlet; see **Vassal.**

Varnish; see **Vision.**

Vary; see **Various.**

Vascular; see **Vase.**

Vase. (F. = L.) F. *vase*, a vessel. = L. *uasum*, allied to *uas*, a vessel. Allied to Skt. *vâsana*, a receptacle, cover. (√WAS.)

extravasate. (L.) Coined from *extra*, beyond; *uas*, a vessel; with suffix *-ate*.

vascular. (L.) From L. *uasculum*, a small vessel; double dimin. of *uas* (above).

vessel. (F. = L.) M. E. *vessel*. = O. F. *vaissel*, a vessel, ship, later *vaisseau*, a vessel (of any kind). = L. *uascellum*, a small vase or urn; dimin. of *uas* (above).

Vassal, a dependent. (F. = C.) M. E. *vassal*. = F. *vassal*, 'a vassall, subject, tenant;' Cot. The orig. sense is 'servant;' Low L. *uassallus*; extended from Low L. *uassus*, *uasus*, a servant. = Bret. *gwaz*, a servant, vassal; W. Corn. *gwas*, youth, servant.

valet. (F. = C.) F. *valet*, 'a groom;' Cot. The same word as *varlet* (below).

varlet. (F. = C.) O. F. *varlet*, 'a groom, stripling, youth;' Cot. An older spelling was *vaslet*, dimin. of O. F. *vassal*, a vassal (above). The successive spellings were *vaslet*, *varlet*, *valet*.

Vast. (F. = L.) F. *vaste*. = L. *uastus*, vast, great, of large extent; see **waste** (below).

devastate. (L.) From pp. of L. *deuastare*, to lay waste. = L. *de*, down; *uastare*, to lay waste, from adj. *uastus*.

waste, desert, unused. (F. = O. H. G. = L.) M. E. *wast*. = O. F. *wast*, in the phrase *faire wast*, to lay waste (Roquefort); whence mod. F. *gâter* (= *gaster* = *waster*). = O.H.G. *wastę*, sb., a waste, *wasten*, to lay waste. Borrowed from L. *uastus*, waste, desolate, also vast, *uastare*, to lay waste. β. It is remarkable that we also find A.S. *wéste*, O. H. G. *wuosti*, waste; these forms are not *borrowed* from Latin, but are cognate. (Aryan type, WASTA; root unknown.)

Vat, a large vessel for liquors. (E.) M. E. *vat* (Southern); also *fat* (Northern). A.S. *fæt*, a vessel, cask. + Du. *vat*, Icel.

fat, Dan. *fad*, Swed. *fat*, G. *fass*. Lit 'that which contains;' cf. Du. *vatten*, to catch, contain, G. *fassen*, to seize, contain.

fat (2), a vat. (E.) A dialectal (Northern) form of *vat*. Der. *wine-fat*.

Vaudeville. (F.) F. *vaudeville*, orig. a country ballad; 'so tearmed of *Vaudevire*, a Norman town, wherein Olivier Bassel [or Basselin], the first inventor of them, lived;' Cot. Basselin was a Norman poet, whose songs were named after his native valley, the *Val de Vire*; *Vire* is in Normandy, S. of Bayeux.

Vault, (1) and (2); see **Voluble.**

Vaunt; see **Vain.**

Vaward, another spelling of *vanward* or *vanguard*; see **Van** (1).

Veal. (F. = L.) O. F. *veel*, a calf. = L. *uitellum*, acc. of *uitellus*, dimin. of *uitulus*, a calf. + Gk. ἰταλός, a calf; Skt. *vatsa*, a calf, properly 'a yearling,' from Skt. *vatsa*, Gk. ἔτος, a year. Allied to **Veteran.**

vellum. (F. = L.) M. E. *velim*. = O. F. *velin* (F. *vélin*). = Low L. *uitulinium*, or *pellis uitulina*, vellum, calf's skin. = L. *uitulinus*, adj., from *uitulus*, a calf.

Veda, knowledge; one of the ancient sacred Skt. books. (Skt.) Skt. *veda*, lit. knowledge. = Skt. *vid*, to know; allied to **Wit.**

Vedette, Vidette; see **Vigil.**

Veer. (F. = L.) F. *virer*, to turn, veer; allied to F. *virole*, a ferrule, and to Low L. *uirola*, a ring to bind anything, answering to L. *uiriola*, dimin. of *uiria*, armlet, large ring. Also allied to *environ* (below). All from √WI, to twist, wind round, as in L. *ui-ere*, to bind, wind round. Cf. also F. *virolet*, 'a boy's wind-mill;' Cot. From the same root are **Ferrule** and **Withy.**

environ, to surround. (F. = L.) O. F. *environner*, to surround. = F. *environ*, round about. = F. *en* (= L. *in*), in; *virer*, to turn, veer; see above.

Vegetable. (F. = L.) F. *vegetable*, adj., 'vegetable, fit or able to live;' Cot. This is the old sense. = L. *uegetabilis*, full of life, animating. = L. *uegetare*, to quicken, enliven. = L. *uegetus*, lively. = L. *uegere*, to quicken, arouse. Allied to **Vigorous.** Der. *vegetat-ion*, F. *vegetation* (Cot.).

Vehement; see **Vehicle.**

Vehicle. (L.) L. *uehiculum*, a carriage. = L. *uehere*, to carry, convey. + Skt. *vah*, to carry. Allied to **Weigh.** (√WAGH.)

convex. (L.) L. *conuexus*, arched, vaulted; orig. pp. of *conuehere*, to bring together. — L. *con-* (for *cum*), together; *uehere*, to carry, bring.

inveigh, to attack with words, rail. (L.) From L. *inuehere*, to carry into or to, to introduce, attack, inveigh against.— L. *in*, against; *uehere*, to bring. β. The etymology is verified by the use of E. *invective*, borrowed from F. *invective*, 'an invective;' Cot.; from L. *inuectiuus*, adj., scolding, due to *inuectus*, pp. of *inuehere*.

reveal. (F. — L.) F. *reveler*, 'to reveale;' Cot. — L. *reuelare*, to draw back a veil. — L. *re-*, back; *uelum*, veil; see **veil** (below).

vehement, passionate. (F.—L.) F. *vehement* (Cot.). — L. *uehement-*, stem of *uehemens*, passionate; lit. 'carried out of one's mind.' β. *Uehe-* has been explained as 'out of the way,' equivalent to some case of Skt. *vaha*, a way; from *vah*, to carry. In any case, it is clearly allied to *uehere* (above).

veil, sb. (F. — L.) O. F. *veile*, later *voile*.— L. *uelum*, a sail; also a cloth. Lit. 'propeller' of a ship; from *uehere*, to carry along.

vein. (F.—L.) F. *veine*.—L. *uēna*, a vein. Lit. 'conveyer' of the blood.—L. *uehere*, to carry.

venesection, blood-letting. (L.) L. *uenæ*, of a vein, gen. of *uena*; and *section*.

venous, belonging to a vein. (L.) L. *uenosus*, adj., from *uena*, a vein.

vex, to harass. (F.—L.) F. *vexer.*— L. *uexare*, to vex; orig. intensive form of *uehere* (pt. t. *uex-i*). And see **Viaduct**.

Veil, Vein; see **Vehement**.

Vellum; see **Veal**.

Velocity. (F. — L.) F. *velocité*, swiftness. — L. acc. *uelocitatem*. — L. *ueloci-*, crude form of *uelox*, swift. Allied to **Volatile**. **Der.** *veloci-pede*, lit. 'swift-foot,' coined from L. *ueloci-* (above), and L. *ped-*, stem of *pes*, a foot.

Velvet. (Ital. — L.) M. E. *velouette*, *velouet*; Spenser has *vellet*. — O. Ital. *veluto* (Ital. *velluto*), velvet; answering to a Low L. *uillutus* *, shaggy, by-form of L. *uillosus*, shaggy. — L. *uillus*, shaggy hair; allied to *uellus*, fleece, and to E. **Wool**.

Venal. (F. — L.) F. *venal*, saleable. — L. *uenalis*, saleable.—L. *uēnus*, *uēnum*, sale. Put for *ues-nus* *, *ues-num* *, allied to Skt. *vasna*, price, *vasu*, wealth. **Der.** *venal-ity*.

vend, to sell. (F.—L.) F. *vendre.*—L. *uendere*, to sell; short for *uenundare*, lit. to give or offer for sale, also written *uenum dare.*—L. *uenum*, sale; *dare*, to give.

vent (2), sale, utterance. (F. — L.) Formerly common.—F. *vente*, sale, selling. —F. *vendre.*—L. *uendere* (above).

Veneer; see **Furnish**.

Venerable; see below.

Venereal. (L.) Coined from L. *uenereus*, *ueneri-us*, pertaining to Venus or love. —L. *ueneri-*, crude form of *uenus*, love. Allied to Skt. *van*, to love, honour.

venerable. (F.—L.) F. *venerable.*— L. *uenerabilis*, to be reverenced. — L. *uenera-ri*, to reverence.—L. *uener-*, stem of *uenus*, love. **Der.** *venerat-ion*, from pp. of *uenerari*.

Venery, hunting; see **Venison**.

Venesection; see **Vehicle**.

Venew, Venue; see **Venture**.

Vengeance; see **Vindicate**.

Venial. (F. — L.) O. F. *venial*. — L. *uenialis*, pardonable.—L. *uenia*, pardon; also grace, favour. Allied to **Venereal**.

Venison. (F. — L.) M. E. *veneison.* — O. F. *veneisun*, later *venaison*, 'venison, flesh of beasts of chase;' Cot.—L. *uenationem*, acc. of *uenatio*, the chase, also game.—L. *uenatus*, pp. of *uenari*, to hunt.

venery, hunting. (F.—L.) F. *venerie*, 'hunting;' Cot.—O. F. *vener*, to hunt.— L. *uenari*.

Venom. (F.—L.) M. E. *venim*.—O. F. *venim* (F. *venin*).—L. *uenenum*, poison.

Venous; see **Vehicle**.

Vent (1), an air-hole, flue. (F. — L.) '*A vent*, meatus, porus; *To vent*, aperire, euacuare;' Levins. Doubtless influenced by a popular etymology from F. *vent*, wind; but the true sense was fissure, aperture. Formerly *fent*. '*Fent* of a gowne, *fente*;' Palsgrave.—F. *fente*, 'a cleft, rift;' Cot.—F. *fendre*, to cleave.—L. *findere*, to cleave. See **Fissure**. **Der.** *vent*, verb, Temp. ii. 2. 111; certainly confused with F. *vent*, wind; see **Vent** (3).

Vent (2), sale; see **Venal**. Sometimes confused with the words above and below.

Vent (3), to snuff up air, breathe, expose to air, (F.—L.) See Spenser, Shep. Kal. Feb. 75; F. Q. iii. 1. 42. The word was prob. solely due to a misuse of, and confusion with, the two words above; but the popular etymology is obvious.—F. *vent*, wind.—L. *uentum*, acc. of *uentus*, wind; cognate with **Wind** (1). **Der.** *vent-age*, air-hole, Hamlet, iii. 2. 373.

ventail, lower half of the moveable part of a helmet. (F. — L.) M. E. *auentaile* (with prefix *a* = F. *a* = L. *ad*). — F. *ventaille*, 'breathing-part of a helmet;' Cot. — F. *venter*, to puff; with suffix *-aille* (= L. *-aculum*). — F. *vent*, wind (above).

ventilate. (L.) From pp. of L. *uentilare*, to blow, winnow. From an unused adj. *uentilus* *, due to *uentus*, wind.

Ventral, belonging to the belly. (L.) L. *uentralis*, adj., from *uenter*, the belly.

ventricle. (F. — L.) F. *ventricule*, 'the ventricle, the place wherein the meat sent from the stomack is digested;' Cot. — L. *uentriculum*, acc. of *uentriculus*, stomach, ventricle, double dimin. of *uenter*, belly.

ventriloquist. (L.) Coined from L. *uentriloqu-us*, lit. speaking from (or in) the belly. — L. *uentri-*, crude form of *uenter* (above) ; *loqui*, to speak. See **Loquacious.**

Venture, sb. (F. — L.) A headless form of M. E. *auenture* (*aventure*), an adventure, chance. — F. *aventure*, a chance, occurrence. — L. *aduentura*, fem. of *aduenturus* about to happen. — L. *ad*, to ; *uenturus*, fut. pt. of *uenire*, to come. Cognate with E. **Come.** (✓ GAM.) Doublet, *adventure*.

advent, approach. (L.) L. *aduentus*, approach. — L. *aduentus*, pp. of *aduenire*, to approach. — L. *ad*, to; *uenire*, to come.

adventure. (F. — L.) Formerly spelt *aventure* ; the F. prefix *a-* was needlessly turned into the L. *ad-*; see **Venture** (above). Der. *adventure*, verb ; *per-adventure*, i. e. by chance, where the prefix should rather be *par* (F. *par*, L. *per*).

avenue. (F. — L.) F. *avenue*, *advenue*, access ; hence an approach to a house (esp. one shaded by trees). — F. *avenir*, to come to. — L. *ad*, to ; *uenire*, to come.

contravene, to hinder. (L.) Low L. *contrauenire*, to oppose; to break a law. — L. *contra*, against ; *uenire*, to come.

convene, to assemble. (F. — L.) F. *convenir*, to assemble. — L. *con-uenire*, to come together.

convenient, suitable. (F. — L.) From stem of L. *conueniens*, suitable ; orig. pres. pt. of *con-uenire*, to come together, suit.

convent. (L.) L. *conuentus*, an assembly. — L. *conuentus*, pp. of *con-uenire*.

convention. (F. — L.) F. *convention*, 'a compact;' Cot. — L. acc. *conuentionem*, a meeting, compact. — L. *conuentus*, pp. of *con-uenire*, to come together, meet.

covenant, agreement. (F. — L.) O. F. *covenant*, also *convenant*, agreement. — O. F. *convenant*, pres. pt. of *convenir*, to assemble, agree. — L. *conuenire* (above).

event, result. (L.) L. *euentus*, *euentum*, sb. — L. *euentus*, pp. of *e-uenire*, to come out, result.

intervene, to come between. (F. — L.) F. *intervenir*; Cot. — L. *inter-uenire*, to come between.

invent. (F. — L.) F. *inventer*, to devise. — L. *inuentus*, pp. of *in-uenire*, to come upon, find out. Der. *invent-ion*, &c.

parvenu, an upstart. (F. — L.) F. *parvenu*, lit. one who has arrived, hence, one who has thrived. Pp. of *parvenir*, to arrive, thrive. — L. *per-uenire*, to arrive, come through.

prevent. (L.) The old meaning was ' to go before;' cf. O. F. *prevenir*, ' to prevent, anticipate, forestall ;' Cot. — L. *præuentus*, pp. of *præ-uenire*, to go before.

revenue, income. (F. — L.) O. F. *revenuē*, 'revenue, rent;' Cot. Fem. of *revenu*, pp. of *revenir*, to come back. — F. *re-*, back ; *venir*, to come. — L. *re-*, back; *uenire*, to come.

souvenir. (F. — L.) F. *souvenir*, sb., a remembrance ; merely the verb *souvenir*, to remember, used as a sb. — L. *sub-uenire*, to occur to one's mind.

supervene. (L.) L. *super-uenire*, to come upon or over, to follow, occur.

venew, venue, veney, (1) a turn or bout or thrust in fencing ; (2) a locality. (F. — L.) F. *venuē*, 'a coming, a *venny* in fencing, turn, trick;' Cot. Lit. a coming, home-thrust; fem. of *venu*, pp. of *venir*, to come. — L. *uenire*, to come. 2. As a law-term, *venue* is the same word, and signifies a place of arrival, locality. ¶ Apparently confused by Blackstone with O. F. *visne*, vicinity (from L. *uicinia*).

Venue ; see **venew**, under **Venture.**

Veracious ; see **Very.**

Veranda, Verandah, a covered balcony. (Port. — Span. — L.) Port. *varanda*. — O. Span. *varanda*, a stair-railing ; in Pedro de Alcala (1505). — Span. *vara*, a rod, rail. — L. *uara*, a forked pole. Cf. L. *uarus*, crooked. Hence also was borrowed Skt. *varanda*, a portico, which is quite a modern word. See *veranda* in Yule.

Verb, the word ; the chief word in a sentence. (F. — L.) F. *verbe*. — L. *uerbum*, a word. Put for *uerdhum* *, cognate with

E. **Word. Der.** *verb-iage*, F. *verbiage*, from O. F. *verboier*, to talk.

adverb. (L.) Used to qualify a verb. — L. *ad*, to ; *uerbum*, a word, verb.

proverb. (F. — L.) F. *proverbe*. — L. *prouerbium*, a common saying. — L. *pro*, publicly ; *uerb-um*, a word.

Verbena. (L.) L. *uerbena*, orig. a sacred bough ; afterwards, vervain. Allied to *uerber*, twig, shoot, rod.

vervain. (F. — L.) F. *verveine*, 'vervaine ;' Cot. — L. *uerbena* (above).

Verdant, flourishing. (F. — L.) F. *verdant*, pres. pt. of *verdir*, to flourish. — O. F. *verd*, green. — L. *uiridis*, green. Der. *verdure*, F. *verdure*, lit. greenness.

farthingale, fardingale, a hooped petticoat. (F. — Span. — L.) O. F. *verdugalle*, 'a vardingall ;' Cot. — Span. *verdugado*, a farthingale, lit. 'provided with hoops.' — Span. *verdugo*, young shoot of a tree, rod, hoop. — Span. *verde*, green. — L. *uiridis*, green.

verdigris, rust of bronze. (F. — L. ?) F. *verd de gris*, 'verdigrease, Spanish green ;' Cot. Spelt *verte grez* in the 13th cent. (Littré). *Verte grez* is lit. 'green grit,' a substitution (as I think) for O. F. *verderis*, 'verdigrease,' Cot. (the correct form). — Low L. *uiride æris*, verdigris ; the usual name in alchemy ; lit. 'green of brass.' — L. *uiride*, neut. of *uiridis*, green ; *æris*, gen. of *æs*, brass, bronze.

verjuice. (F. — L.) F. *verjus*, verjuice ; lit. 'green juice.' — O.F. *verd*, green (above); *jus*, juice; see **Juice.**

vert, green. (F. — L.) F. *vert*, O. F. *verd* (above).

viridity, greenness. (L.) L. *uiriditas*, greenness. — L. *uiridis*, green.

Verdict; see **Very.**

Verdigris; see **Verdant.**

Verge (1), a wand of office, edge, brink. (F. — L.) Distinct from *verge* (2) below. M. E. *verge*, a wand, rod, yard (in measure). — F. *verge*, 'a rod, wand, yard, hoope, ring, rood of land ;' Cot. From the sense of rod it came to mean hoop, ring (hence, edge) ; the sense of edge also easily followed from the Law-term *verge*, i. e. limit of jurisdiction. — L. *uirga*, a rod, pliant twig. Der. *verg-er*, a rod-bearer, macebearer, F. *verger*, L. *uirgarius*.

Verge (2), to tend towards. (L.) L. *uergere*, to bend, tend, incline towards, incline. Allied to *ualgus*, bent, Skt. *vrijana*, crooked. (√WARG.) ¶ The phrase 'to

be on the *verge* of' is quite distinct, and belongs to **Verge** (1).

converge. (L.) Coined from L. *con-* (*cum*), together ; and *verge*.

diverge. (L.) Coined from L. *di-* (for *dis-*), apart ; and *verge*.

Verify, Verisimilitude, Verity ; see **Very.**

Verjuice; see **Verdant.**

Vermicelli, Vermicular, Vermilion ; see **Vermin.**

Vermin. (F. — L.) F. *vermine*, vermine ; applied to obnoxious insects, &c. As if from a Lat. adj. *uerminus* *, formed from *uermi-*, crude form of *uermis*, a worm ; cognate with E. **Worm.**

vermicelli. (Ital. — L.) Ital. *vermicelli*, lit. 'little worms;' from the shape. Pl. of *vermicello*, dimin. of *verme*, a worm. — L. *uermem*, acc. of *uermis*, a worm.

vermicular, pertaining to a worm. (L.) From L. *uermiculus*, a little worm ; dimin. of *uermis*, a worm.

vermilion. (F. — L.) F. *vermillon*, 'a little worm, vermilion ;' Cot. — F. *vermeil*, vermilion. — L. *uermiculus*, dimin. of *uermis* (above). ¶ So named from the cochineal insect, by confusion with *crimson* ; but *vermilion* is generally made from red lead.

Vernacular, native. (L.) From L. *uernacul-us*, adj., native ; lit. belonging to a home-born slave. — L. *uerna*, a homeborn slave. Lit. 'dweller;' cf. Skt. *vas*, to dwell.

Vernal. (L.) L. *uernalis*, extended from *uernus*, belonging to spring. — L. *uer*, spring. + Gk. ἔαρ, Russ. *vesna*, Icel. *vár*, Dan. *vaar*, Swed. *vår*, spring ; the time of increasing brightness. Cf. Skt. *vasanta*, spring, *ush*, to burn, glow.

Vernier, a kind of scale, for fine measurement. (F.) Invented by *P. Vernier*, died Sept. 14, 1637.

Verse. (L.) M. E. *vers, fers* (Ormulum) ; A. S. *fers*. — L. *uersus*, a turning, course, row, line of poetry. — L. *uersus*, pp. of *uertere*, to turn. Allied to **Worth** (1). (√WART.) Der. *vers-ed*, imitated from L. *uersatus*, pp. of *uersari*, pass. of frequent. of *uertere* ; *vers-at-ile*, quickly turning, F. *versatil* (Cot.), L. *uersatilis*, versatile, also from L. pp. *uersatus*.

adverse. (F. — L.) O. F. *advers*, often *avers* (F. *averse*), adverse to. — L. *aduersus*, turned towards, also opposed to ; pp. of

aduertere, to turn to. — L. *ad*, to ; *uertere*, to turn. **Der.** *advers-ary*, *advers-ity*.

advert, to turn to, regard. (L.) L. *ad-uertere*, to turn to. **Der.** *in-advert-ent*, not regarding.

advertise. (F.—L.) From the stem of O. F. *advertiss-ant*, *avertiss-ant*, pres. pt. of *advertir*, *avertir*, to inform, certify. — L. *aduertere* (above).

avert. (L.) L. *a-uertere*, to turn away. **Der.** *averse*, from L. pp. *auersus*.

controversy. (L.) From L. *controuersia*, a quarrel. — L. *controuersus*, opposed.—L. *contro-*, for *contra*, against ; *uersus*, pp. of *uertere*, to turn.

converse. (F.—L.) F. *converser*, to associate with ; Cot. — L. *conuersari*, to live with.—L. *con-* (*cum*), with ; *uersari*, to dwell (lit. turn oneself about), orig. pass. of frequent. of *uertere*, to turn.

convert. (L.) L. *con-uertere*, to turn wholly, change.

divers, diverse, various. (F. — L.) O. F. *divers*, masc., *diverse*, fem., 'divers, differing ;' Cot. — L. *diuersus*, various ; orig. pp. of *diuertere*, to turn asunder, separate, divert (below).

divert. (F.—L.) O. F. *divertir*, 'to divert, alter ;' Cot.—L. *di-uertere*, to turn aside. **Der.** *divers-ion*, from pp. *diuersus*.

divorce. (F.—L.) O. F. *divorce*.—L. *diuortium*, a separation.—L. *diuortere*, the same as *diuertere*, to turn aside, separate (above).

inverso, opposite. (F.—L.) M. E. *invers.*—O. F. *invers.*—L. *inuersus*, pp. of *inuertere* (below).

invert. (L.) L. *in-uertere*, to turn towards or up, to invert.

obverse, lit. turned *towards* one, used of the face of a coin. (L.) L. *obuersus*, pp. of *ob-uertere*, to turn towards.

pervert. (F.—L.) F. *pervertir*. — L. *per-uertere*, to overturn, ruin, corrupt, pervert. **Der.** *perverse*, from pp. *peruersus*.

prose. (F.—L.) F. *prose*.—L. *prōsa*, put for *prorsa oratio*, direct speech ; hence, unimbellished speech ; fem. of *prorsus*, forward, short for *prouersus*, lit. turned forward.—L. *pro*, forward ; *uersus*, pp. of *uertere*, to turn.

reverse. (F. — L.) M. E. *reuers* (*revers*).—O. F. *revers.* — L. *reuersus*, lit. turned backward ; pp. of *re-uertere*, to turn backward.

revert. (F.—L.) O. F. *revertir*, 'to re-vert, returne ;' Cot.—L. *re-uertere* (above).

subvert. (F.—L.) F. *subvertir*; Cot. — L. *sub-uertere*, to turn upside down, overthrow. **Der.** *subvers-ion*, from pp. *subuers-us*.

transverse. (L.) L. *transuersus*, turned across, laid across ; pp. of *trans-uertere*, to turn across.

traverse, laid across. (F.—L.) F. *travers*, masc., *traverse*, fem. 'crosse-wise ;' Cot. — L. *transuersus*, transverse (above). **Der.** *traverse*, verb, F. *traverser*, 'to thwart or go overthwart,' Cot.

versify. (F. — L.) F. *versifier*. — L. *uersificare*, to make verses.—L. *uersi-*, for *uersus*, a verse ; *-ficare*, for *facere*, to make. **Der.** *versificat-ion*, from pp. *uersificatus*.

version. (F.—L.) F. *version*.—Low L. *uersionem*, acc. of *uersio*, a version, translation.—L. *uersus*, pp. of *uertere*, to turn.

vertebra. (L.) L. *uertebra*, a joint, vertebra.—L. *uertere*, to turn.

vertex, top. (L.) L. *uertex*, top, pole of the sky (which is the turning-point of the stars), but afterwards the zenith. — L. *uertere*, to turn. **Der.** *vertic-al*, F. *vertical*, from L. *uerticalis*, vertical, which from *uertic-*, stem of *uertex*, top.

vertigo, giddiness. (L.) L. *uertigo*, giddiness.—L. *uertere*, to turn.

vortex, a whirlpool. (L.) L. *uortex*, also *uertex*, whirlpool. — L. *uertere*, to turn.

Versify, Version; see **Verse**.

Verst, a Russian measure of length. (Russ.) Russ. *versta*, 3500 English feet.

Vert; see **Verdant**.

Vertebra, Vertex, Vertigo; see **Verse**.

Vervain; see **Verbena**.

Very, true. (F.—L.) M. E. *verrai.*—O. F. *verai* (F. *vrai*), true. Cf. Prov. *verai*, true. It answers to a Low L. type *ueracus* *, allied to L. *uerax*, true. — L. *uerus*, true, credible (whence O. F. *voir*).

aver. (F.—L.) F. *averer*. — Low L. *auerare*, *aduerare*, to affirm to be true. — L. *ad*, to ; *uerum*, truth, neut. of *uerus*, true.

veracious, truthful. (L.) From L. *ueraci-*, crude form of *uerax*, true. — L. *uerus*, true.

verdict. (F.—L.) M. E. *verdit* (the correct form). — O. F. *verdit* (F. *verdict*). — L. *uere dictum*, truly said ; whence Low L. *ueredictum*, true saying, verdict. — L.

uere, adv., from *uerus*, true; *dictum*, neut. of *dictus*, pp. of *dicere*, to say.

verify. (F.—L.) F. *verifier*; Cot.— L. *uerificare*, to make true.—L. *ueri-*, for *uerus*, true; *-ficare*, for *facere*, to make.

verisimilitude, likelihood. (F.—L.) F. *verisimilitude.* — L. *uerisimilitudo.* — L. *ueri similis*, like the truth.—L. *ueri*, gen. of *uerum*, the truth, orig. neuter of *uerus*, true; *similis*, like.

verity, truth. (F.—L.) F. *verité.*— L. *ueritatem*, acc. of *ueritas*, truth.—L. *ueri-* = *uero-*, crude form of *uerus*, true.

Vesicle, a small tumour or cell. (L.) L. *uesicula*, dimin. of *uesica*, a bladder.

Vesper. (L.) M. E. *vesper*, the evening-star (Gower). — L. *uesper*, evening-star, evening; *uespera*, even-tide. Hence O. F. *vespre* (F. *vêpre*), evening, and *vespres*, vespers, even-song.+Gk. ἕσπερος, adj. and sb., evening; Lith. *wákaras*, evening, Russ. *vecher'*, evening; allied to Skt. *vasati*, night, and to E. **West**.

Vessel; see **Vase**.

Vest, a garment. (L.) L. *uestis*, a garment, clothing.+Goth. *wasti*, clothing; cf. Gk. ἕν-νυμι (=Fεσ-νυμι), I clothe, ἐσ-θής, clothing, Skt. *vas*, to put on clothes. (√WAS.)

divest. (L.) Low L. *diuestire*, the same as L. *deuestire*, to strip off clothes. — L. *di-* (for *dis-*), apart; *uestire*, to clothe, from *uestis*, clothing.

invest. (F.—L.) F. *investir.* — L. *in-uestire*, to clothe in or with.

travesty. (F. — L.) Orig. a pp., borrowed from F. *travesti*, disguised, pp. of *se travestir*, to change one's apparel. — F. *tra-* (L. *trans*), implying 'change;' *vestir*, to clothe, from L. *uestire*, to clothe.

vestment. (F.—L.) M. E. *vestiment.* — O. F. *uestiment* (F. *vêtement*). — L. *uestimentum*, clothing. — L. *uestire*, to clothe.

vestry. (F.—L.) Altered from O. F. *vestiaire*, 'vestry;' Cot.—L. *uestiarium*, a wardrobe; neut. of *uestiarius*, adj., from *uestis*, a robe.

vesture. (F.—L.) O. F. *vesture.*— Low L. *uestitura*, clothing.—L. *uestire*, to clothe.

Vestal. (F.—L.) F. *Vestal*, a Vestal virgin. — L. *Uestalis*, belonging to a Vestal, also a priestess of Vesta.—L. *Uesta*, Vesta, goddess of fire and purity.+Gk. ἐστία, goddess of the domestic hearth; cf. Skt. *ush*, to burn. (√WAS.)

Vestibule. (L.) L. *uestibulum*, a fore-court; lit. 'separated from the abode.'— L. *ue-*, separate from; *stabulum*, an abode; see **stable**, under **State**. L. *ue-* = Skt. *vi-*, apart, allied to L. *duo*, two.

Vestige. (F. — L.) F. *vestige*, a step, foot-track.—L. *uestigium*, foot-track.

investigate. (L.) From pp. of L. *inuestigare*, to track out. — L. *in*, in, upon; *uestigare*, to trace, allied to *uestigium*, a foot-track (above).

Vestment, Vesture; see **Vest**.

Vetch, a plant. (F. — L.) Also *fitch*. M. E. *feche* (of which the Southern form would be *veche*).—O. F. *veche*, *vesse*, *vesce*, vetch. — L. *uicia*, a vetch; lit. 'twiner,' from its tendrils; cf. *vimen*, a pliant twig. (√WI.)

fitch, a spelling of *vetch* (above).

Veteran. (L.) L. *ueteranus*, experienced; as sb., a veteran.—L. *ueter-*, stem of *uetus*, old, lit. 'advanced in years.' Cf. Gk. ἔτος, Skt. *vatsa*, a year.

inveterate. (L.) L. *inueteratus*, pp. of *inueterare*, to retain for a long time. — L. *in*, in; *ueter-*, stem of *uetus*, old (above).

votorinary. (L.) L. *ueterinarius*, of or belonging to beasts of burden; as sb., a cattle-doctor. — L. *ueterinus*, belonging to beasts of burden. The L. *ueterina* meant an animal at least a year old, one that had passed its first year; from the base *vat-*, meaning year (above). See **Wether**.

Veto, a prohibition. (L.) L. *ueto*, I forbid.

Vex; see **Vehicle**.

Viaduct. (L.) L. *uia ducta*, a road conducted across (a river, &c.).—L. *uia*, a way, road; *ducta*, fem. of pp. of *ducere*, to carry, conduct. L. *uia*, formerly *uea* = Skt. *vaha*, a road; from L. *uehere* = Skt. *vah*, to carry; see **Vehicle, Way**.

convey, convoy, vb. (F.—L.) M.E. *conueien*, *conuoien* (*conveien*, *convoien*), to convey, also to convoy. — O. F. *conveier*, *convoier*, to convey, convoy, accompany on the way.—Low L. *conuiare*, to accompany. —L. *con-* (*cum*), with; *uia*, way.

deviate. (L.) From pp. of L. *deuiare*, to go out of the way. — L. *de*, from; *uia*, way.

devious. (L.) L. *deuius*, going out of the way.—L. *de*, from; *uia*, way.

envoy. (F. — L.) O. F. *envoy*, a sending. — O. F. *envoier*, earliest form *entveier*, to send. — O. F. *ent-*, away (from L. *inde*, thence); O. F. *veier* = L. *uiare*, to travel, from *uia*, a way.

impervious, impassable. (L.) L. *imperuius*, impassable. — L. *im-*, for *in-*, not ; *peruius* ; see **pervious** (below).

invoice, a particular account of goods sent out. (F.—L.) A corruption of *envois*, an English pl. of F. *envoi*, O. F. *envoy*, a sending ; see **envoy** (above).

obviate. (L.) From pp. of L. *obuiare*, to meet in the way, to prevent. — L. *ob*, over against ; *uia*, way.

obvious. (L.) L. *obuius*, lying in the way, evident. — L. *ob*, over against ; *uia*, the way.

pervious, penetrable. (L.) L. *peruius*, passable. — L. *per*, through ; *uia*, a way.

previous. (L.) L. *præuius*, on the way before, going before. — L. *præ*, before ; *uia*, way.

voyage. (F.—L.) M. E. *viage*, *veage*. — O. F. *veiage*, later *voyage*. — L. *uiaticum*, properly provisions for a journey. — L. *uiaticus*, belonging to a journey. — L. *uia*, a way. ¶ See also **Trivial**.

Vial, Phial, a small bottle. (F.—L.— Gk.) M. E. *viole*. — O. F. *viole*, *fiole*. — L. *phiala*. — Gk. φιάλη, a shallow cup or bowl.

Viands ; see **Victuals**.

Vibrate. (L.) From pp. of L. *uibrare*, to swing, shake. ✛Skt. *vip*, to throw. (√ WIP.)

Vicar. (F. — L.) F. *vicaire*, a deputy. — L. *uicarius*, a deputy, orig. an adj., deputed, put in place of. — L. *uic-*, stem of *uicis*, a turn, change, succession. (√WIK.)

vice-gerent. (F. — L.) F. *vicegerent*, a deputy ; Cot. — L. *uice*, in place of ; *gerent-*, stem of pres. pt. of *gerere*, to carry on, rule ; see **Gesture**. ¶ So also *vice-admiral*, *vice-roy* (from F. *roi*, L. *regem*, king), *vice-regal*.

vicissitude. (L.) L. *uicissitudo*, change. Allied to *uicissim*, by turns.— L. *uic-is* (genitive), a change.

viscount. (F. — L.) The usual old spelling was *vicounte* (and the *s* is not pronounced even at this day).— F. *vicomte*, 'a vicount, at first the deputy of an earl ;' Cot. O. F. *viscomte* (12th cent.).—L. *uice*, in place of ; *comitem*, acc. of *comes*, a count ; see **Count** (1).

Vice (1), a fault. (F. — L.) F. *vice*. — L. *uitium*, blemish, fault. Der. *vic-i-ous*, F. *vicieux*, L. *uitiosus*, faulty ; *viti-ate*, from pp. of L. *uitiare*, to injure.

vituperation, blame. (F. — L.) F. *vituperation*. — L. acc. *uituperationem*. — L. *uituperatus*, pp. of *uituperare*, to blame, lit. 'to prepare (or find) a blemish.'— L. *uitu-*, for *uiti-*, base of *uitium*, a vice, fault ; *parare*, to prepare, provide.

Vice (2), an instrument for holding things firmly. (F.—L.) M. E. *vice*, orig. ' a screw,' because tightened by a screw. — F. *vis*, 'vice, a winding-staire ;' Cot. O. F. *viz*.— L. *uitis*, a vine, bryony, lit. ' that which winds or twines.' (√ WI.)

Vice-gerent ; see **Vicar**.

Vicinage, neighbourhood. (F.—L.) Altered F. from *voisinage*, neighbourhood.—F. *voisin*, near.—L. *uicinus*, near, lit. ' belonging to the same street.' — L. *uicus*, a village, street ; see **Wick** (2).

Vicissitude ; see **Vicar**.

Victim. (F.—L.) F. *victime*.—L. *uictima*, a victim.

Victor. (L.) L. *uictor*, a conqueror.— L. *uict-um*, supine of *uincere*, to conquer (pt. t. *uic-i*). (√ WIK.) Der. *victor-y*, F. *victorie*, L. *uictoria*.

convince. (L.) L. *conuincere*, to overcome by proof. — L. *con-* (*cum*), with; *uincere*, to conquer. Der. *convict*, verb and sb., from *conuictus*, pp. of *conuincere*.

evict. (L.) Formerly, to evince. — L. *euictus*, pp. of *euincere* (below).

evince. (L.) L. *euincere*, to overcome; hence to prove beyond doubt. — L. *e*, out, thoroughly ; *uincere*, to conquer.

invincible. (L.) L. *in-*, not ; *uincibilis*, easily overcome, from *uincere*, to conquer.

vanquish. (F. — L.) M. E. *venkisen*, *venquishen*.—O. F. *veinquiss-*, stem of pres. pt. of *veinquir*, occurring in the 14th cent. as a collateral form of *veincre*, to conquer (F. *vaincre*). — L. *uincere*, to conquer.

Victuals. (F. — L.) Pl. of *victual*, pedantic spelling of M. E. *vitaille*, provisions. — O. F. *vitaille*, usually in pl. *vitailles*, victuals.—L. neut. pl. *uictualia*, provisions; from *uictualis*, belonging to nourishment. —L. *uictu-*, crude form of *uictus*, food.— L. *uictus*, pp. of *uiuere*, to live ; allied to *uiuus*, living, and to E. **Quick**. Cf. Skt. *jîv*, to live. (√ GIW.)

convivial. (L.) Coined as adj. from L. *conuiui-um*, a feast. — L. *con-* (*cum*), together ; *uiuere*, to live (hence eat).

revive. (F. — L.) F. *revivre*. — L. *reuiuere*, to live again, revive.

survive. (F. — L.) F. *survivre*, to outlive. — L. *super-uiuere*, to live beyond, outlive.

viands, food. (F. — L.) Pl. of *viand*. — F. *viande*, food. — L. *uiuenda*, neut. pl. provisions, food; from fut. pass. part. of *uiuere*, to live.

viper. (F. — L.) F. *vipere*. — L. *uipera*, a viper. Lit. 'that produces living young;' short for *uiuipara*, fem. of *uiuiparus*, producing living young; see **viviparous** (below).

vital. (F. — L.) F. *vital*. — L. *uitalis*, belong to life. — L. *uita*, life; allied to *uiuere*, to live.

vivacity. (F. — L.) F. *vivacité*, liveliness. — L. *uiuacitatem*, acc. of *uiuacitas*, liveliness. — L. *uiuaci-*, crude form of *uiuax*, tenacious of life. — L. *uiuere*, to live.

vivid (L.) L. *uiuidus*, lively. — L. *uiuere*, to live.

vivify. (F. — L.) F. *vivifier*, to quicken. — L. *uiuificare*, to quicken. — L. *uiui-*, for *uiuus*, living; *-ficare*, for *facere*, to make.

viviparous. (L.) L. *uiuiparus*, producing living young. — L. *uiui-*, for *uiuus*, living; *parere*, to produce.

vivisection. (L.) Coined from L. *uiui-* (above); and *section*.

wyvern, wivern, a two-legged dragon, in heraldry. (F. — L.) The final *n* is added, as in *bitter-n*. M. E. *wiuere* (*wivere*), a serpent. — O. F. *wivre* (F. *givre*), a viper. — L. *uipera*, a viper; see **viper** (above).

Videlicet; see **Vision**.

Vidette; see **Vigil**.

Vie, to contend for superiority. (F. — L.) M. E. *vien*, a contracted form of *envien*, to vie, contend for superiority. (Cf. *fence* for *defence*, *story* for *history*, &c.). — O. F. *envier* (*au ieu*), 'to vie;' Cot. The lit. sense of O. F. *envier* was to invite [quite distinct from *envier*, to envy], esp. used in gaming in the sense 'to open a game by staking a certain sum;' precisely as Span. *envidar*, Ital. *invitare*, to invite, to vie, or propose a stake. — L. *inuitare*, to invite (of which *vie* is thus seen to be a doublet). See **Invite**. ¶ The sense was to stake a sum to draw on or invite a game, then to wager, bet against, contend, strive for the upper hand.

View; see **Vision**.

Vigil. (F. — L.) Lit. 'a watching.' F. *vigile*, 'a vigile, eve of a holy day;' Cot. — L. *uigilia*, a watch. — L. *uigil*, awake. —

L. *uigere*, to be lively. (√WAG.) Der. *vigil-ant*, F. *vigilant*, from stem of pres. pt. of L. *uigilare*, to watch.

invigorate, to give vigour to. (L.) From pp. of L. *inuigorare*, to give vigour to. — L. *in*, towards; *uigor*, vigour.

reveille, an alarum at break of day. (F. — L.) From F. *réveil*, a reveillee, O. F. *resveil*, 'a hunt's-up, or morning-song for a new married wife, the day after the marriage;' Cot. (The E. *reveillee* is a trisyllable, and probably answers to the infinitive mood *réveiller*, used substantively.) — F. *re-*, again; O. F. *esveiller*, to waken. — L. *re-*, again; *ex*, out, greatly; *uigilare*, to watch.

surveillance, inspection. (F. — L.) F. *surveillance*, superintendence. — F. *surveillant*, pres. pt. of *surveiller*, to superintend. — L. *super*, over; *uigilare*, to watch.

vedette, vidette, a cavalry sentinel. (F. — Ital. — L.) F. *vedette*, a sentinel. — Ital. *vedetta*, a horse-sentry; formerly a watch-tower. A corruption of Ital. *veletta*, a watch-tower; prob. by confusion with *vedere*, to see. Dimin. of Ital. *veglia*, a watching, vigil. — L. *uigilia*, a vigil, watch.

vigour, energy. (F. — L.) O. F. *vigur*, *vigor*, vigour. — L. *uigorem*, acc. of *uigor*, liveliness. — L. *uigere*, to be lively.

Vignette; see **Wine**.

Vigour; see **Vigil**.

Viking, a Northern pirate. (Scand.) Icel. *víkingr*, a pirate, free-booter, rover. Lit. 'a creek-dweller,' one of the men who haunted the bays and creeks. — Icel. *vík*, creek, inlet, bay; with suffix *-ingr*, i. e. 'son of,' or belonging to. — Icel. *víkja*, to turn, veer, trend, recede. Allied to **Weak**.

Vile. (F. — L.) F. *vil*, fem. *vile*, base. — L. *uilis*, base, mean.

revile, (F. — L.) M. E. *reuilen* (= *revilen*). Coined by prefixing F. *re-* (= L. *re-*), again, to O. F. *aviler*, 'to make vile or cheap;' Cot. This verb is from F. *a* (= L. *ad*); and F. *vil* (L. *uilis*), cheap.

Villa. (L.) L. *uilla*, a farm-house, lit. 'small village.' Short for *uicula* *, dimin. of *uicus*, a village. See **Wick** (2).

village. (F. — L.) F. *village*. — L. *uillaticus*, adj., belonging to a farm-house. — L. *uilla* (above). .

villain. (F. — L.) M. E. *vilein*. — O. F. *vilein*, servile; as sb., a bondman, slave, villain. — Low L. *uillanus*, orig. a farm-servant, hence a slave, serf, villain. — L.

uilla, a farm-house. **Der.** *villain-y*, O. F. *vilenie, vilanie*, servitude, baseness.

Vinculum, a link. (L.) L. *uinculum*, a bond, fetter. — L. *uincire*, to bind.

Vindicate. (L.) From pp. of L. *uindicare*, to arrogate, lay claim to. — L. *uindic-*, stem of *uindex*, a claimant, lit. ' one who expresses a desire.' — L. *uin-*, signifying ' desire,' allied to *uenia*, favour, permission ; *dic-*, base of *dicare*, to appoint, *dicere*, to say.

avenge. (F. — L.) O. F. *avengier*, to avenge. — F. *a* (L. *ad*), to ; *vengier*, to avenge, from L. *uindicare*, to lay claim to, also to avenge (above).

revenge. (F. — L.) O. F. *revenger*, later *revencher*, to avenge oneself. (F. *revancher*.) — F. *re-* (= L. *re-*), again ; O. F. *vengier, venger*, from L. *uindicare*.

vengeance. (F. — L.) F. *vengeance*, ' vengeance ;' Cot. — F. *venger*, to avenge. — L. *uindicare*.

vindictive. (F. — L.) Shortened from F. *vindicatif*, ' revenging ;' Cot. From L. *uindicatus*, pp. of *uindicare*, to avenge ; with suffix *-iuus*. See **Vindicate** (above).

Vine, Vinegar ; see **Wine**.

Vinewed, mouldy. (E.) Also *finewed, fenowed* (Nares). From A.S. *fineged*, pp. of *finegian*, to become mouldy. — A.S. *finig*, mouldy (Joshua, ix. 5). The right form seems to be *fenig*, answering to M. E. *fenny*, dirty, vile, also used to mean ' mouldy,' adj. from A.S. *fenn*, mire, the same word as mod. E. *fen* ; see **Fen**.

Vintage, Vintner ; see **Wine**.

Viol. (F. — L.) F. *viole, violle*, ' a violin ;' Cot. The same as Ital. Span. *viola*, Port. *viula, viola*. — Low L. *vidula, vitula*, a viol (Diez). — L. *uitulari*, to celebrate a festival, keep holiday ; prob. orig. to sacrifice a calf. — L. *uitulus*, a calf ; see **Veal**. And see **Fiddle**.

violin. (Ital. — L.) Ital. *violino*, dimin. of Ital. *viola*, a viol (above).

violoncello. (Ital. — L.) Ital. *violoncello*, dimin of *violone*, a bass-viol, which is an augmentative form of *viola*, a viol (above).

Violate. (L.) From pp. of L. *uiolare*, to treat with force, violate. Formed as if from an adj. *uiolus* *, due to *ui-s*, force.

violent. (F. — L.) F. *violent*. — L. *uiolentus*, full of might. Formed as if from an adj. *uiolus* * (above).

Violet, a flower. (F. — L.) F. *violet*, m., *violette*, f. (Cot.). Dimin. of F. *viole*, ' a

gilliflower ;' Cot. — L. *uiola*, a violet. **+** Gk. *ïov*, a violet. **Der.** *violet*, adj.

Violin, Violoncello ; see **Viol**.

Viper ; see **Victuals**.

Virago ; see **Virile**.

Virgin. (F. — L.) O. F. *virgine*. — L. *uirginem*, acc. of *uirgo*, a maid. **Der.** *virgin-als*, the name of a musical instrument, played upon by *virgins*.

Viridity ; see **Verdant**.

Virile, manly. (F. — L.) F. *viril*, ' manly ;' Cot. — L. *uirilis*, adj., from *uir*, a man. Allied to **Hero**.

virago (L.) L. *uirago*, a manlike woman. — L. *uir*, a man.

virtue. (F. — L.) M. E. *vertu*. — F. *vertu*. — L. *uirtutem*, acc. of *uirtus*, manly excellence. — L. *uir*, a man.

virtuoso. (Ital. — L.) Ital. *virtuoso*, one skilled in the fine arts, orig. ' virtuous.' — Ital. *virtù*, shortened form of *virtute*, virtue, also, a love of the fine arts. — L. *uirtutem* (above).

Virulent. (F. — L.) F. *virulent*. — L. *uirulentus*, full of poison. — L. *uirus*, poison. **+** Gk. *íós*, Skt. *visha*, poison.

Visage, Visard ; see **Vision**.

Viscid, sticky, clammy. (L.) L. *uiscidus*, sticky, clammy. — L. *uiscum*, mistletoe, birdlime. **+** Gk. *ίxós*, mistletoe.

viscera, entrails. (L.) L. *uiscera*, neut. pl. entrails ; allied to **Viscid** (above). **Der.** *e-viscer-ate*, to remove the entrails.

Viscount ; see **Vicar**.

Visier ; see **Vizier**.

Visible ; see under **Vision**.

Vision. (F. — L.) F. *vision*. — L. *uisionem*, acc. of *uisio*, sight. — L. *uisus*, pp. of *uidere*, to see. **+** Gk. *ίδεîν*, to see ; Skt. *vid*, to know. Allied to **Wit**. (√ WID.)

advice. (F. — L.) M. E. *auis* (*avis*), without *d.* — O. F. *avis*, an opinion ; orig. a compound word, put for *a vis*, i. e. according to my opinion. — L. *ad*, according to ; *uisum*, that which has seemed good to one, orig. neut. of *uisus*, pp. of *uidere*, to see.

advise. (F. — L.) M. E. *aduisen*, also *auisen* (*avisen*), without *d.* — O. F. *aviser*, to be of opinion. — O. F. *avis* (above).

envy, sb. (F. — L.) M. E. *enuie* (*envie*). — O. F. *envie*. — L. *inuidia*, envy ; see invidious (below).

evident. (F. — L.) O. F. *evident*. — L. *euident-*, stem of *euidens*, visible, pres. pt. of *e-uidere*, to see clearly.

improvise. (F. — Ital. — L.) F. *im-*

proviser. – Ital. *improvvisare*, to sing extemporaneous verses. – Ital. *improvviso*, sudden, unprovided for. – L. *improuisus*, unforeseen. – L. *im-*, for *in-*, not; *pro*, before; *uisus*, pp. of *uidere*, to see.

invidious (L.) From L. *inuidiosus*, causing odium or envy. – L. *inuidia*, envy. – L. *inuidere*, to envy, lit. to look upon (in a bad sense). – L. *in*, upon; *uidere*, to look.

provide. (L.) L. *prouidere* (pp. *prouisus*), to foresee, act with foresight. – L. *pro*, before; *uidere*, to see. Der. *provident*, *provis-ion*.

proviso. (L.) From the L. phrase *prouiso quod*, it being provided that; where *prouiso* is abl. of *prouisus*, pp. of *prouidere*; see **provide** (above).

prudent. (F. – L.) F. *prudent.* – L. *prudentem*, acc. of *prūdens*, short for *prŏuidens*, foreseeing, pres. pt. of *prouidere*, to foresee (above).

purvey. (F. – L.) M. E. *purueien*, *porueien* (*purveien*, *porveien*), to provide. – O. F. *porvoir* (F. *pourvoir*), to provide. – L. *pro-uidere*, to foresee, provide.

review, verb. (F. – L.) To view again; from *re-* and *view*.

revise. (F. – L.) F. *reviser.* – L. *reuisere*, to look back on, revisit. – L. *re-*, again; *uisere*, to survey, from *uisus*, pp. of *uidere*, to see.

revisit. (F. – L.) From *re-* and *visit.*

supervise. (L.) L. *super*, above, over; *visere*, to survey; see **revise** (above).

survey. (F. – L.) F. *sur*, over; O. F. *veër* (later *veoir*), to see. – L. *super*, over; *uidere*, to see.

varnish. (F. – L.) F. *vernis*, 'varnish;' Cot. Orig. an adj. from *verni*, pp. of O. F. *vernir*, to glaze, polish. – Low L. *uitrinus*, glassy. – L. *uitrum*, glass; see **vitreous** (below).

videlicet, viz., namely. (L.) In old MSS. and books, the abbreviation for *et* resembled *ʓ*; hence *niet* (short for *videlicet*) was misread as *viz*. – L. *uidelicet*, short for *uidere licet*, it is possible to see, it is evident, hence, to wit, namely. – L. *uidere*, to see; *licet*, it is allowable; see **Licence.**

view, sb. (F. – L.) F. *veuē*, 'a view, sight;' Cot. Fem. of *veu*, pp. of O. F. *veoir* (F. *voir*), to see. – L. *uidere*, to see.

visage, look, face. (F. – L.) F. *visage*, face, look. – F. *vis*, visage; with suffix *-age* (– L. *-aticum*). – L. *uisum*, acc. of

uisus, sight, afterwards look, face. – L. *uisus*, pp. of *uidere*, to see.

visard, the same as **visor** (below).

visible. (F. – L.) F. *visible.* – L. *uisibilis*, that can be seen. – L. *uis-us*, pp. of *uidere*, to see.

visit. (F. – L.) F. *visiter.* – L. *uisitare*, to visit, go to see, frequent. of *uisere*, to behold; from *uisus*, pp. of *uidere*.

visor, visard, vizor. (F. – L.) The *d* is added. M. E. *visere.* – F. *visiere*, 'the viser, or sight of a helmet;' Cot. Formed from F. *vis*, the face; see **visage** (above). A *visor* also meant a mask, from its covering the face; Cotgrave has '*faux visage*, a maske, or vizard.'

vista. (Ital. – L.) Ital. *vista*, lit. a view. – Ital. *vista*, fem. of *visto*, seen, a by-form of *veduto*, pp. of *vedere*, to see. – L. *uidere*, to see.

visual. (F. – L.) F. *visual.* – L. *uisualis*, belonging to the sight. – L. *uisu-*, crude form. of *uisus*, sight. – L. *uisus*, pp. of *uidere*, to see.

vitreous. (L.) L. *uitreus*, *uitrius*, glassy. – L. *uitri-*, for *uitro-*, crude form of *uitrum*, glass. The *i* in *uitrum* was originally long; so that *uitrum* = *uid-trum**. – L. *uidere*, to see.

vitriol. (F. – L.) F. *vitriol*, 'vitrioll;' Cot. Said to be so called from its transparency. – Low L. *uitriolus** = L. *uitreolus*, glassy. – L. *uitreus*, glassy. – L. *uitrum*, glass (above).

Visit, Visor; see **Vision.**

Vista, Visual; see **Vision.**

Vital; see **Victuals.**

Vitiate; see **Vice** (1).

Vitreous, Vitriol; see **Vision.**

Vituperation; see **Vice** (1).

Vivacity, Vivid, Vivify; see **Victuals.**

Viviparous, Vivisection; see **Victuals.**

Vixen; see **Fox.**

Viz.; see videlicet, under **Vision.**

Vizard; see **visor**, under **Vision.**

Vizier, Visier, a councillor of state. (Arab.) Arab. *wazîr*, a counsellor of state; orig. a porter, one who bears the burden of state affairs. – Arab. root *wazara*, to bear a burden, sustain.

alguazil, a police officer. (Span. – Arab.) Span. *alguazil.* – Arab. *al*, the; *wazîr*, a vizier, officer.

Vocable; see **Vocal.**

Vocal, uttering sound. (F. – L.) F. *vocal.* – L. *uocalis*, adj., from *uoc-*, stem of *uox*, voice, sound. + Gk. ἔπος, a word; Skt. *vachas*, speech, from *vach*, to speak. (✓WAK.)

advocate, sb. (F. – L.) O. F. *advocat*, 'an advocate;' Cot. – L. *aduocatus*, an advocate, one 'called upon' to plead. – L. *aduocatus*, pp. of *ad-uocare*, to call to, call upon.

advowson. (F. – L.) O. F. *advouson*, patronage; hence the right of presentation to a benefice (Roquefort). – Low L. *aduocationem*, acc. of *aduocatio*, patronage. – Low L. *aduocatus*, a patron; the same as L. *aduocatus*, an advocate.

avocation. (L.) From L. *auocatio*, a calling away of the attention, hence a diversion, amusement; afterwards used in the sense of employment. – L. *auocatus*, pp. of *a-uocare*, to call away.

avouch. (F. – L.) M. E. *avouchen*. Formed by prefixing *a-* (= F. *a*, L. *ad*) to M. E. *vouchen*, to vouch; see **vouch** (below).

convoke. (L.) L. *con-uocare*, to call · together.

evoke. (L.) L. *e-uocare*, to call forth.

invocation. (F. – L.) F. *invocation*. – L. *inuocationem*, acc. of *inuocatio*, a calling upon. – L. *inuocatus*, pp. of *in-uocare*, to call upon.

invoke. (F. – L.) F. *invoquer*. – L. *in-uocare*, to call upon.

provoke. (F. – L.) F. *provoquer*; Cot. – L. *pro-uocare*, to call forth.

revoke. (F. – L.) O. F. *revocquer* (F. *révoquer*). – L. *re-uocare*, to recall.

vocable, a term, word. (F. – L.) F. *vocable*. – L. *uocabulum*, an appellation, name. – L. *uocare*, to call. – L. *uoc-*, stem of *uox*, voice, name. **Der.** *vocabulary*, from Low L. *uocabularium*, a list of words.

vocation. (F. – L.) F. *vocation*. – L. acc. *uocationem*, a calling, invitation. – L. *uocatus*, pp. of *uocare*, to call.

vociferation. (F. – L.) F. *vociferation*. – L. acc. *uociferationem*, an outcry. – L. *uociferatus*, pp. of *uociferari*, to lift up the voice, cry aloud. – L. *uoci-*, crude form of *uox*, voice; *fer-re*, to bear, carry, cognate with E. *bear*.

voice. (F. – L.) M. E. *vois*. O. F. *vois* (F. *voix*). – L. *uocem*, acc. of *uox*, voice, sound.

vouch, to warrant. (F. – L.) O. F. *voucher*, 'to vouch, cite, pray in aid in a suit;' Cot. – L. *uocare*, to call, call upon, summon. – L. *uoc-*, stem of *uox*, voice.

vouchsafe. (F. – L.) Formerly *vouch safe*, i. e. warrant as safe; from *vouch* and *safe*.

vowel. (F. – L.) F. *voyelle*, 'a vowell;' Cot. – L. *uocalem*, acc. of *uocalis* (*litera*), a vowel. vocal letter; see **Vocal.**

Vogue, mode, fashion. (F. – Ital. – Teut.) Formerly *vogue* meant sway, authority, power. – F. *vogue*, 'vogue, sway, power; a cleer passage, as of a ship in a broad sea;' Cot. Orig. 'sway of a ship,' verbal sb. of F. *voguer*, 'to saile forth;' id. – Ital. *voga*, sb., stroke of an oar, *vogare*, to row in a galley. – G. *wogen*, to fluctuate, be in motion on the sea. – G. *woge*, a wave. Allied to **Wag, Weigh.**

Voice; see **Vocal.**

Void, empty. (F. – L.) O. F. *voide* (F. *vide*). – L. *uiduum*, acc. of *uiduus*, bereft; hence, waste, empty. Allied to **Widow.**

avoid, to shun. (F. – L.) M. E. *auoiden* (*avoiden*), to make empty. – O. F. *esvuidier*, *esveudier*, to empty out, dissipate. – O. F. *es-* (= L. *ex*), out; *vuidier*, *voidier*, to empty = L. *uiduare*, from *uiduus*. ¶ This word seems to have suffered an extraordinary confusion with F. *éviter*, to avoid (L. *e-uitare*), with which it had no etymological connection; the M. E. *avoiden* commonly means 'to empty;' hence, to get out of the way.

devoid, quite void. (F. – L.) M. E. *deuoid*; due to *deuoided*, pp. of *deuoiden*, to empty. – O. F. *desvuidier*, *desvoidier*, to empty out. – O. F. *des-* (= L. *dis-*); *voidier*, to empty, from L. *uiduare*.

Volant, flying. (F. – L.) F. *volant*, pres. pt. of *voler*, to fly. – L. *uolare*, to fly. Cf. Skt. *val*, to hasten, move to and fro.

volatile. (F. – L.) F. *volatil*, 'flying;' Cot. – L. *uolatilis*, flying. – L. *uolatus*, flight. – L. *uolare*, to fly.

volley. (F. – L.) F. *volée*, a flight;' Cot Hence, a flight of shot. – L. *uolata*, fem. of pp. of *uolare*, to fly.

Volcano, a burning mountain. (Ital. – L.) Ital. *volcano*, a volcano. – L. *Uolcanum*, acc. of *Uolcanus*, *Uulcanus*, Vulcan, god of fire, fire. Allied to Skt. *ulká*, a firebrand, meteor; G. *wallen*, to boil.

vulcanise, to combine caoutchouc with sulphur by heat. (L) Coined, with suffix *-ise*, from *Vulcan*, god of fire, fire (above). **Der.** *vulcan-ite*, vulcanised caoutchouc.

Volition; see **Voluntary.**

Volley; see **Volant.**

Volt; see **vault** (2), under **Voluble.**

Voltaic, originated by Volta. (Ital.)

From *A. Volta*, of Como, died March 6, 1826.

Voluble, fluent. (F. – L.) F. *voluble*, 'voluble, easily rolled, glib ;' Cot. – L. *uolubilis*, easily turned about. – L. *uolu-*, as in *uolu-tus*, pp. of *uoluere*, to roll ; with suffix *-bilis*. ✛ Goth. *walwjan*, Gk. ἐλύειν, to roll ; allied to Russ. *valite*, to roll, Skt. *vara*, a circle. (√ WAR.)

circumvolve. (L.) L. *circum-uoluere*, to roll round, surround.

convolve. (L.) L. *con-uoluere*, to roll together, writhe about. Der. *convolut-ion*, from pp. *conuolutus* ; *convolv ul us*, L. *conuoluulus*, a twining plant.

devolve. (L.) L. *de-uoluere*, to roll down, bring or transfer to. ¶ The old sense of *devolve* was 'to transfer.'

evolve. (L.) L. *e-uoluere*, to unroll, disclose. Der. *evolut-ion*, from pp. *euolutus*.

involve. (F. – L.) F. *involuer*, 'to involve ;' Cot – L. *in-uoluere*, to roll in, roll up. Der. *involut-ion*, *involute* ; from pp. *inuolutus*.

revolt, a rebellion. (F. – Ital. – L.) F. *revolte*, 'a revolt ;' Cot. – O. Ital. *revolta* (Ital. *rivolta*), a revolt ; fem. of *revolto*, turned, overthrown, pp. of *revolvere*, to turn, roll back, overturn. – L. *re-uoluere*, to roll back (below).

revolve. (L.) L. *re-uoluere*, to turn again, revolve. Der. *revolut-ion*, from pp. *reuolutus*.

vault (1), an arched roof, cellar. (F.– L.) For *vaut* ; the *l* was needlessly inserted. M. E. *voute*, *vowte*, *vawte*, *vaute*. – F. *voute* (also *voulte*, with inserted *l*), 'a vault, arch, a vaulted roof ;' Cot. O. F. *volte*, a vault (whence the later form *voute*, mod F. *voûte*) ; this is the fem. of O. F. *volt*, vaulted, lit. bent, bowed, the same as Ital. *volta*. – L. *uoltus*, an abbreviation for *uolutus*, pp. of *uoluere*, to roll, turn round. Thus a *vault* meant a 'bowed' roof, hence a chamber with bowed roof, a cellar which has an arched roof.

vault (2), to bound, leap. (F. – Ital. – L.) F. *volter*, 'to vault ;' Cot. – F. *volte*, a round, turn, tumbler's gambol. – Ital. *volta*, a sudden turn ; the same word as *volta*, a vault (above).

volt, another spelling of **vault** (2) (above).

volume, a roll, a book. (F. – L.) F. *volume*. – L. *uolumen*, a roll, scroll ; hence, a book on a parchment roll. – L. *uolu-*, as in *uolu-tus*, pp. of *uoluere*, to roll.

volute, a spiral scroll on a capital. (F. – L.) F. *volute* (Cot.). – L. *uoluta*, a volute ; fem. of *uolutus*, pp. of *uoluere*.

Volume ; see **Voluble**.

Voluntary. (F. – L.) F. *voluntaire*, *volontaire*. – L. *uoluntarius*, willing. – L. *uoluntas*, free will. – L. *uoluns* *, by-form of *uolens*, willing, from *uelle*, to wish, *uolo*, I wish. ✛Gk. βούλομαι, I will ; Skt *vri*, to choose, select. Allied to **Will**. (√ WAR.)

volition. (F. – L.) F. *volition*. – Low L. *uolitionem*, acc of *uolitio* *, volition (not found, but prob. a term of the schools). – L. *uolo*, I wish.

voluptuous. (F. – L.) F. *voluptueux*, Cot. – L. *uoluptuosus*, addicted to, or full of pleasure. – L. *uolupt-as*, pleasure. – L. *uolup*, *uolupe*, adv., agreeably. – L. *uol-o*, I wish.

Volute ; see **Voluble**.

Vomit, sb. (L.) L. *uomitus*, a vomiting ; whence *uomitare*, to vomit. – L. *uomitus*, pp. of *uomere*, to vomit. ✛ Gk. ἐμεῖν, Skt. *vam*, to vomit. (√ WAM.)

Voracity. (F. – L.) F. *voracité*. – L. *voracitatem*, acc. of *uoracitas*, hungriness. – L. *uoraci-*, crude form of *uorax*, greedy to devour. – L. *uorare*, to devour. – L. *-uorus*, devouring, as in *carni-uorus*, flesh-eating. Allied to Skt. *-gara*, as in *aja-gara*, goat-devouring ; Gk. βορός, gluttonous. (√ GAR.)

devour. (F. – L.) O. F. *devorer*. – L. *de-uorare*, to consume, eat up.

Vortex ; see **Verse**.

Vote, sb. (L.) L. *uotum*, a wish ; orig. a vow. – L. *uotum*, neut. of *uotus*, pp. of *uouere*, to vow. Der. *vot-ive*, L. *uotiuus*, promised by a vow ; *vot-ary*, a coined word, like *votaress*, *votress*.

devote, verb. (L.) L. *deuotus*, pp. of *de-uouere*, to devote, vow fully.

devout. (F. – L.) M. E. *deuot* (*devot*), also spelt *devoute*. – O. F. *devot*, devoted. – L. *deuotus* (above).

vow, sb. (F. – L.) M. E. *vow*, *vou*. – O. F. *vou*, *vo* (F. *vœu*), a vow. – L. *uotum*, a vow (above). ¶ Hence the M. E. *avow*, sb., common in the sense of 'vow,' Chaucer, C. T. 2239, 2416 ; and hence the verb *avow*, to vow. Yet *avow* commonly answers to L. *aduocare*, and is a doublet of *avouch* ; see avouch, under **Vocal**.

Vouch, Vouchsafe ; see Vocal.

Vow ; see Vote.

Vowel ; see Vocal.

Voyage; see **Viaduct**.

Vulcanise; see **Volcanic**.

Vulgar. (F. — L.) F. *vulgaire*. — L. *uulgaris*, belonging to the common people. — L. *uulgus*, *uolgus*, the common people; a throng, crowd. + Skt. *varga*, a troop, *vraja*, a flock, multitude, from *vrij*, to exclude. (√ WARG.) Der. *vulgar-ity*; also *vulgate*, the E. name for the L. version of the Bible known as the *editio uulgata*, where *uulgata* is fem. of pp. of *uulgare*, to publish.

     divulge. (F. — L.) F. *divulguer*, 'to divulge, reveal;' Cot. — L. *di-uulgare*, to

publish abroad. — L. *di-*, for *dis-*, apart; *uulgare*, to publish, from *uulgus* (above).

Vulnerable. (L.) L. *uulnerabilis*, liable to injury. — L. *uulnerare*, to wound. — L. *uulner-*, crude form of *uulnus*, a wound. Allied to *uellere*, to pluck, tear. + Skt. *vrana*, a wound, fracture. (√ WAR.)

Vulpine, fox-like. (F. — L.) F. *vulpin*; Cot. — L. *uulpinus*, fox-like. — L. *uulpi-*, crude form of *uulpes*, a fox.

Vulture. (L.) L. *uultur*, a vulture; lit. 'tearer.' — L. *uul-*, as in *uul-si*, pt. t. of *uellere*, to pluck, tear. Allied to **Vulnerable**.

WA-WE.

Wabble, Wobble; see **Whap**.

Wacke, a kind of soft rock. (G.) G. *wacke*, a stone consisting of quartz, sand, and mica.

Wad, a small bundle of stuff, little mass of tow. (Scand.) Swed. *vadd*, wadding, O. Swed. *wad*, clothing, stuff, Icel. *vað-mál*, wadmal, a plain woollen stuff. + G. *watte*, wadding, wad; *wat*, cloth (whence F. *ouate*, &c.). Allied to **Weed** (2). Der. *wadd-ing*, *wad-mal*.

Waddle; see **Wade**.

Wade, to walk slowly, esp. through water. (E.) A. S. *wadan*, pt. t. *wód*, to wade, go. + Du. *waden*, Icel. *vaða*, pt. *vóð*, to wade; Icel. *vað*, a ford; Dan. *vade*, Swed. *vada*, O. H. G. *watan*, to wade, go. Further allied to L. *uadum* (for *uadhum**), a ford, *uadere*, to go, Skt. *gádha*, shallow.

     waddle, to walk clumsily. (E.) Frequentative of *wade* (above).

Wafer. (F. — O. Low G.) M. E. *wafre*. — O. F. *waufre* (F. *gaufre*), a wafer. — O. Du. *waeffel*, a wafer (Du. *wafel*); Low G. *wafel*; G. *waffel*, wafer.

Waft; see **Wave** (1).

Wag; see **Weigh**.

Wage, Wager; see **Wed**.

Waggle, Waggon, Wagtail; see **Weigh**.

Waif; see **Waive**.

Wail; see **Wo**.

Wain, Wainscot; see **Weigh**.

Waist; see **Wax** (1).

Wait, sb. and vb.; see **Wake** (1).

Waive, to relinquish a claim. (F. — Scand.) M. E. *waiuen*, *weiuen* (*waiven*, *weiven*), to set aside, shun, push aside,

remove. — O. F. *waiver**, only recorded in the later form *guesver*, 'to waive, refuse, abandon, give over, surrender, resigne;' Cot. Low L. *waviare*, to waive. — Icel. *veifa*, to vibrate, move about, move loosely to and fro (whence the sense of 'let go' seems to have been evolved). Allied to **Vibrate**. (√ WIP.) ¶ Distinct from *wave*.

     waif, sb., a thing abandoned, a thing found astray. (F. — Scand.) M. E. *waif*, *weif*; pl. *wayues*, *weyues* (*wayves*, *weyves*). — O. F. *waif*, later *gaif*, pl. *waives*, *gaives*; *choses gaives*, 'weifes, things forsaken, or lost;' Cot. — Icel. *veif*, anything moving or flapping about (applied, e. g. to the fin of a seal); *veifa*, to vibrate, move about (above).

Wake (1), to be brisk, cease from sleep. (E.) M. E. *waken*, pt. t. *wook*; properly intransitive; whence the weak verb *waken*, pt. t. *waked*, to cause to wake, rouse. A. S. *wacan*, to arise, come to life, be born, pt. t. *wóc*, pp. *wacen*, whence *wacian*, weak verb, to wake, watch, pt. t. *wacode*. + Goth. *wakan* (pt. t. *wok*), *wakjan* (pt. t. *wakida*); Du. *waken*, Icel. *vaka*, Dan. *vaage*, Swed. *vaka*, G. *wachen*. Der. *wake*, sb., a vigil, A. S. *wacu*.

     await. (F. — L. *and* O. H. G.) O. F. *awaiter*, *awaitier*, to wait for. — O. F. *a* (= L. *ad*), for; *waitier*, to wait; see *wait* vb. (below).

     bivouac. (F. — G.) F. *bivouac*, orig. *bivac*. — G. *beiwache*, a keeping watch. — G. *bei*, near (= E. *by*); *wachen*, to watch (above).

     wait, sb. (F. — O. H. G.) Orig. a watchman, sentinel, afterwards one who is

awake at night, a night-musician. — O. F.
waite, a guard, watchman; later *guet*. —
O. H. G. *wahta*, a watch-man, orig. a
watch, a guard, a being awake.—O. H. G.
wahhen (G. *wachen*), to be awake (above).
¶ Also used in the phr. *to lie in wait*.

wait, vb. (F.—O. H. G.) O. F. *waiter*,
waitier, *gaiter*, later *guetter*, to watch,
wait. — O. F. *waite*, a watchman, a watching (above).

waken, to awake. (E.) Now usually
transitive, but orig. *intransitive only*, in
the sense 'to become awake.' M. E.
waknen, *wakenen*. A.S. *wæcnan*, to be
aroused, be born; intrans. form from
wacan; to wake (above). ¶ The verbal
suffix *-en* has now usually a *transitive*
force; the M. E. suffix *-n-en* is properly
intransitive, as in Gothic. Cf. Goth.
gawaknan, Swed. *vakna*, Dan: *vaagne*, to
become awake. Der. *a-waken*, where the
prefix *a-* = A.S. *á-*; see A- (4).

watch, sb. (E.) M.E. *wacche*; A.S.
wæcce, a watch, guard. — A. S. *wacan*, to
wake (above). Der. *watch*, vb., M. E.
wacchen, A. S. *wacian*, weak verb.

Wake (2), the track of a ship. (Scand.)
In Norfolk, a *wake* means a space of un-
frozen water in a frozen tarn or 'broad.'
The proper sense is an opening in ice,
passage through ice, hence a track of a
ship through a frozen sea, or a track generally. — Icel. *vak-*, stem of *vök*, a hole,
opening in ice; Swed. *vak*, Norweg. *vok*
(the same). Hence Norweg. *vekkja*, Dan.
vaage, to cut a passage for ships through
ice. The orig. sense was 'a wet place.'—
Icel. *vökr*, wet (Lowl. Scotch *wak*); cf.
Du. *wak*, moist. Gk. ὑγρός, wet.

Waken; see **Wake** (1).

Wale, Weal, the mark of a blow. (E.)
M. E. *wale*. A. S. *walu*, a weal; orig. 'a
rod.'+O. Fries. *walu*, rod, wand, Icel. *völr*,
a round stick, Goth. *walus*, a staff. Cf.
Russ. *val'*, a cylinder, *valiate*, to roll. β.
The sense of rod or beam is preserved in
gun-wale, the plank along the edge of
a ship . protecting the guns. Doublet,
goal, q.v.

Walk, vb. (E.) M. E. *walken*, pt. t.
welk, pp. *walken*. A. S. *wealcan*, pt. t.
weólc, pp. *wealcan*, to roll, toss oneself
about, rove about; hence, generally, to
ramble, walk. + O. Du. *walcken*, to press,
full cloth, Swed. *valka*, to roll, full, work,
Dan. *valke* (same), G. *walken*, to full.
Allied to L. *uergere*, to bend, turn, incline.

(√ WARG, extension of WAR, to turn,
roll.)

Wall. (L.) A.S. *weall*, borrowed from
L. *uallum*, a rampart, orig. a row of stakes.
— L. *uallus*, a stake, palisade, lit. pro-
tection. Cf. Skt. *vri*, to cover, surround.
(√ WAR.)

circumvallation. (L.) Formed from
pp. of L. *circumuallare*, to surround with a
rampart. — L. *circum*, around; *uallum*, a
rampart.

interval. (F. — L.) O. F. *intervalle*.
— L. *interuallum*, lit. the space between
the rampart of a camp and the soldier's
tents. — L. *inter*, between; *uallum*, rampart.

Wallet; see **Wattle**.

Wall-eyed, with diseased eyes. (Scand.)
'*Glauciolus*, an horse with a *waule eye*;'
Cooper (1565).— Icel. *valdeygðr*, corruption
of *vagleygr*, wall-eyed, said of a horse.—
Icel. *vagl*, a beam, also a beam in the eye,
disease of the eye; *eygðr*, *eygr*, eyed, from
auga, eye, cognate with E. *eye*. The Icel.
vagl is the same as Swed. *vagel*, a perch,
roost, sty in the eye, Norw. *vagl*, a hen-
roost.

Wallop; see **Potwalloper**.

Wallow. (E.) M. E. *walwen*. A.S.
wealwian, to roll round. Cognate with L.
uoluere, to roll; see **Voluble**.

Walnut. (E.) Lit. 'a foreign nut.' A.S.
wealh, foreign; *hnut*, a nut.+Du. *walnoot*,
Icel. *valhnot*, Dan. *valnöd*, Swed. *valnöt*,
G. *wallnusz*. β. The A.S. *wealh* makes
the pl. *wealas*, foreigners, which is the
mod. E. *Wales* (now applied to the country
itself); cognate with O. H. G. *walah*,
a foreigner, whence G. *Wälsch*, foreign,
Italian.

Walrus; see **Whale**.

Waltz; see **Welter**.

Wampum, small beads, used as money.
(N. American Indian.) W. Indian *wampum*; from the Massachusetts *wômpi*, Delaware *wâpi*, white (Mahn).

Wan, colourless. (E.) M. E. *wan*. A.S.
wann, *wonn*, dark, black, colourless; now
applied to *pale* objects deficient in colour.
¶ Prob. allied to *win*; not to be connected with *wane* (as the A.S. form shews).

Wand, Wander; see **Wind** (2).

Wane, to decrease (as the moon). to
fail. (E.) A.S. *wanian*, to wane, decrease.
— A.S. *wan*, *won*, deficient. + Icel. *vana*,
vb., from *vanr*, deficient. Cf. Goth. *wans*,
lacking, Skt. *úna*, wanting. (√ WA.)

wanion. (E.) In the phr. *with a wanion,* i. e. with ill-luck. I believe *wanion* = North E. *waniand,* waning, pres. pt. of M. E. *wanien,* to wane; see **Wane** (above). Sir T. More (Works, p. 306) writes *in the waniand,* which I explain to mean 'in the waning of the moon,' i. e. with ill-luck; see Brand, Popular Antiq. on *The Moon.* (So also Wedgwood.)

want, lack. (Scand.) M. E. *want,* first used as an adj., signifying 'deficient.' — Icel. *vant,* neut. of *vanr,* adj., lacking, which was formerly used with a gen. case following; as, *var þeim vettugis vant,* there was lacking to them of nothing, i. e. they wanted nothing. The Icel. *vanr* = A. S. *wan*; see **Wane** (above). Der. *want,* vb., Icel. *vanta,* from the adj. *vanr.*

wanton, unrestrained. (E.) M. E. *wantoun,* unrestrained, not educated; full form *wantowen.* — M. E. *wan-,* prefix, lacking, a neg. prefix (from A. S. *wan,* lacking); *towen* = A. S. *togen,* pp. of *teón,* to draw, to educate. See **Wane** and **Tow** (1).

Wapentake; see **Weapon.**

War. (E.) M. E. *werre.* A. S. *werre,* A. S. Chron. an. 1119. Also *war*; we find: 'armorum oneribus, quod Angli *war-scot* dicunt,' Laws of Cnut, De Foresta, § 9. (Not common, the usual A. S. words being *wig, hild, winn, guð.*) + O. Du. *werre,* war, whence *werren,* to embroil; Ó. H. G. *werra,* broil, confusion, strife (whence O. F. *werre,* F. *guerre*). (Base WARR, for WARS; allied to **Worse.**) Der. *war-fare,* i. e. war-expedition; from A. S. *faran,* to go.

guerilla, guerrilla, irregular warfare. (Span. — O. H. G.) Span. *guerrilla,* a skirmish, lit. 'little war;' dimin. of *guerra,* war. — O. H. G. *werra,* war (above).

warrior. (F. — O. H. G.) M. E. *werriour.* — O. F. *werreiur*,* old spelling of O. F. *guerreiur,* a warrior. — O. F. *werreier*, *guerreier,* to make war (whence E. *warray* in Spenser, F. Q. i. 5. 48, ii. 10. 21). — O. F. *werre, guerre,* war. — O. H. G. *werra,* war (above).

Warble; see **Whirl.**

Ward, a guard, watch, &c. (E.) M. E. *ward.* A. S. *weard,* masc., a guard, watchman, defender; also *weard,* fem., a guarding, protection, defence. Allied to **Wary.** (Base WAR.) + Icel. *vörðr,* (1) a watchman, (2) a watching; G. *wart,* Goth. *-wards* in *daura-wards,* a door-keeper. Der. *ward,* verb, *ward-er,* sb.; also *bear-ward, steward,* &c.

award, vb. (F. — L. *and* O. H. G.) M. E. *awarden.* — O. F. *eswardeir, esgardeir,* to examine, adjudge. — O. F. *es-* (= L. *ex*), out; O. F. *warder,* to ward, guard; see **guard** (below).

guard, vb. (F. — · O. H. G.) O. F. *garder,* earliest form *warder,* to guard. — O. H. G. *warten,* M. H. G. *warden,* to watch; cognate with A. S. *weardian,* to watch, from *weard,* sb.; see **Ward.** Der. *guard-ian*; see **Warden** (below).

regard, vb. (F. — L. *and* O. H. G.) F. *regarder,* to look, look at, view. — L. *re-,* back; F. *garder,* to guard; see **guard** (above).

reward, vb. (F. — L. *and* O. H. G.) O. F. *rewarder,* later spelling *regarder*; see **regard** (above).

warden, (1) a guardian, (2) a kind of *keeping* pear. (F. — O. H. G.) M. E. *wardein.* — O. F. *wardein*,* old spelling of *gardein, gardain,* Low L. *guardianus,* a guardian. — O. F. *warder,* later *garder,* to guard; with L. suffix *-ianus*; see **guard** (above).

wardrobe. (F. — G.) M. E. *warderobe.* — O. F. *warderobe,* later *garderobe,* a guardrobe, i. e. place for keeping robes. See **guard** (above), and **Robe.**

Ware (1), merchandise; see **Wary.**

Ware (2), aware; see **Wary.**

Wariness; see **Wary.**

Warison; see **Warrant.**

Warlock; a wizard. (E.) M. E. *warloghe,* a wicked one, the devil; *warlawe,* a deceiver. — A. S. *wǽrloga,* a traitor, perfidious man, liar, truce-breaker; (hence, a witch, wizard). Lit. 'liar against the truth.' — A. S. *wǽr,* truth (cognate with L. *uerum,* truth); *loga,* a liar, from *log-en,* pp. of *ledgan,* to lie. See **Verity** and **Lie** (2).

Warm. (E.) A. S. *wearm.* + Du. G. *warm,* Icel. *varmr,* Dan. Swed. *varm.* β. Allied to Russ. *varite,* to boil, scorch, L. *uulcanus,* fire. (√WAR.)

Warn; see **Wary.**

Warp, sb. (E.) M. E. *warp.* A. S. *wearp,* a warp, in weaving. — A. S. *wearp,* pt. t. of *weorpan* (strong verb), to cast, throw, hence, to throw the shuttle. + Icel. *varp,* a throwing, from *varp,* pt. t. of *verpa,* to throw; Swed. *varp,* a warp; O. H. G. *warf* (G. *werfte*), from *warf,* pt. t. of *werfen,* to throw. (Base WARP.) Der. *warp,* verb, from Icel. *varpa,* to throw, cast (hence, to twist out of shape); this mod. E. *warp* is a secondary (weak) verb, not the same as A. S. *weorpan*. So also Swed. *varpa*, Dan. *varpe*, to warp a ship, from Swed. *varp*, the draught of a net. And see **Wrap**.

Warrant, sb. (F.—O. H. G.) M. E. *warant*. — O. F. *warant, guarant*, later *garant*, ' a warrant ;' Cot. The form *warant* is that of the pres. pt., with the sense ' protecting.' — O. H. G. *warjan, werjan* (G. *wehren*), to protect, lit. ' to heed.'— O. H. G. *wara*, heed, care. Allied to **Wary**. Der. *warrant*, verb; *warrant-y*, O. F. *warantie*, orig. fem. of pp. of *warantir*, to warrant; see **guarantee** (below).

guarantee, sb. (F.—O. H. G.) Formerly *guarantȳ* or *garanty*, which are better spellings.—O. F. *garantie, garrantie*, a warranty; fem. of pp. of *garantir*, to warrant.—O. F. *garant, warant*, a warrant; see **warrant** (above). Der. *guarantee*, verb.

warison, warisoun, protection, reward. (F.—O. H. G.) M. E. *warisoun*, protection (the true sense); more common in the sense of reward or help; it also meant recovery from illness or healing. —O. F. *warison, garison*, surety, safety, provision, healing. —O. F. *warir*, to protect, heal.—O. H. G. *warjan, werjan*, to protect; see **Warrant**.

warren, sb. (F. — O. H. G.) M. E. *wareine*.—O. F. *warenne, varenne*, later *garenne*, ' a warren of conies,' Cot.; Low L. *warenna*, a preserve for hares, &c.— O. H. G. *warjan*, to protect, preserve (above). And see **Garret**.

Wart. (E.) M. E. *werte*, A. S. *wearte*, a wart.+ Du. *wrat*, Icel. *varta*, Dan. *vorte*, Swed. *vårta*, G. *warze*. Orig. ' growth ' or ' excrescence ;' allied to **Wort** (1).

Wary, Ware, cautious. (E.) M. E. *war*; *war-y* is a rather late form, with added -y (as in *murk-y*). A. S. *wær*, cautious. + Icel. *varr*, Dan. Swed. *var*, Goth. *wars*. Cf. G. *gewahr*, aware. Allied to Skt. *var-man*, armour, from *vri*, to cover; also to Gk. ὁρ-άω, I perceive, L. *uer-eri*, to regard, dread. (√WAR.) Der. *wari-ness*.

aware. (E.) A corruption of M. E. *iwar, ywar*, aware (common); from A. S. *gewær*, aware. — A. S. *ge-*, a common prefix, not altering the sense; *wær*, ware, wary; see **Wary** (above).

beware. (E.) Now written as *one* word; but merely short for *be ware*, i. e. be wary or cautious; see **Wary** (above).

ware (1), merchandise. (E.) M. E. *ware*. A. S. *waru* (L. *merx*; Wright). The orig. sense was prob. ' valuables,' and the word is allied to A. S. *waru*, protection, guard, custody. + Icel. *vara*, Dan. *vare*, Swed. *vara*, Du. *waar*, G. *waare*, a commodity; allied to Dan. *vare*, Swed. *vara*, G. *wahre*, care.

ware (2), aware. (E.) See Acts iv. 16. M. E. *war*; A. S. *wær*, cautious. (The true form, whence *wary* was made by adding -y.) See **Wary** (above).

warn. (E.) A. S. *wearnian, warnian*, (1) to take heed, which is the usual sense, (2) to warn. From the sb. *wearn*, refusal, denial, orig. a guarding of oneself. Allied to **Wary** (above). + Icel. *varna*, to warn off, from *vörn*, a defence; Swed. *varna*, G. *warnen*. Der. *fore-warn*, *pre-warn*.

weir, wear, a dam. (E.) M. E. *wer*; A. S. *wer*; allied to *werian*, to defend, protect, also to dam up. Allied to *wær*, wary. + Icel. *vörr*, a fenced-in landing-place; G. *wehr*, a defence, *mühlwehr*, a mill-dam.

Was, pt. t. of the verb *to be*. (E.) M. E. *was*, pl. *weren*. A. S. *wæs*, I was; he was; *wære*, thou wast; pl. *wæron*, were; subjunctive sing. *wære*, pl. *wæron*. Mod. E. substitutes *wast* for the A. S. *wære* in the indicative, and *wert* for the same in the subjunctive; both are late forms. β. The infin. is A. S. *wesan*, to be; cognate with Du. *wezen*, Icel. *vera*, Dan. *være*, Swed. *vara*, Goth. *wisan*, to be, dwell, remain; Skt. *vas*, to dwell. (√WAS, to dwell.) γ. The form *was* answers to Icel. *var*, Du. *was*, Dan. Swed. *var*, G. *war*, Goth. *was*; and the pl. *were* to Icel. *várum, várut, váru*, Du. G. *waren*, Swed. *voro*, Goth. *wesum, wesuth, wesun*.

wassail. (E.) M. E. *wasseyl, wassayl*, orig. a drinking of a health, from the Northern E. *wæs hál*, answering to A. S. *wes hál*, lit. ' be whole,' a form of wishing good health. Here *wes* is imperative sing. of *wesan*, to be; and *hál* is the same as mod. E. *whole*. The dialectal form *hæl* is the same as mod. E. *hale* (doublet of *whole*). See **Hale** (1).

Wash, vb. (E.) M. E. *waschen*, pt. t. *wessh*. A. S. *wascan*, pt. t. *wósc, wóx*, pp. *wascen*. + Du. *wasschen*, Icel. Swed. *vaska*, Dan. *vaske*, G. *waschen* (pt. t. *wusch*). Allied (in my opinion) to Skt. *uksh*, to sprinkle, to wet.

Wasp. (E.) Prov. E. *waps, wops*; A. S. *wæps*. + G. *wespe*, L. *uespa*; Lith. *wapsà*, a gad-fly; Russ. *osa*, a wasp.

Wassail; see **Was** or **Hale** (1).

Waste; see **Vast**.

Watch; see **Wake** (1).

Water, sb. (E.) A. S. *wæter*. **+** Du. *water*, G. *wasser*. Allied to Icel. *vatn*, Dan. *vand*, Swed. *vatten*, Goth. *wato*, Russ. *voda*, Gk. *ὕδωρ*, L. *unda*, Lith. *wandů*, Skt. *udan*, water. All from √WAD, to wet. **Der.** *water*, vb.

otter. (E.) M. E. *oter*, A. S. *otor*. **+** Du. *otter*, Icel. *otr*, Dan. *odder*, Swed. *utter*, G. *otter*, Russ. *vuidra*, Lith. *udra*; also Gk. *ὕδρα*, a hydra, water-snake. Allied to *water*; compare Gk. *ὕδρα*, hydra, with *ὕδωρ*, water. The sense is 'dweller in the water.' Doublet, *hydra*, q. v.

wet, moist. (E.) M. E. *wet*, *weet*; A. S. *wæt*, wet. **+** Icel. *vátr*, Dan. *vaad*, Swed. *vắt*, wet. Allied to **Water** (above). **Der.** *wet*, vb., A. S. *wætan*.

Wattle, a flexible rod, hurdle; fleshy part under the throat of a cock or turkey. (E.) The orig. sense was something twined or woven together; hence a hurdle, a bag of woven stuff, a bag on a cock's neck. M. E. *watel*, a bag; A. S. *watel*, *watul*, a hurdle. Base WAT; from √WA, to bind.

wallet, a bag, budget. (E.) M. E. *walet*, a corruption of M. E. *watel*, a wattle, also a bag. In P. Plowman, C. xi. 269, where some MSS. express 'bag-full' by *watel-ful*, others have *walet-ful*. Again, Shakespeare has *wallets* for bags of flesh upon the neck (Temp. iii. 3. 46), which is the same as *wattles*. Further, cf. O. Du. *waetsack*, G. *watsack*, *wadsack*, a wallet, where *wat-* answers to the base of A. S. *wat-el*.

Wave (1), to fluctuate. (E.) M. E. *wauen*. A. S. *wafian*, esp. in the sense to wonder at or waver in mind; the lit. sense appears in the adj. *wæfre*, wavering, restless. Cf. Icel. *vafra*, *vafla*, to waver; *vafl*, hesitation. **Der.** *wave*, sb., from the verb above (not the same word as M. E. *wawe*, a wave, which is allied to *wag*).

waft. (E.) Put for *waff*, like *graft* for *graff*. Again, *waff* is the same as *wave*, in the sense 'to beckon by waving something'; see Merch. Ven. v. 11.

waver, vb. (E.) M. E. *waueren* (*waveren*), to wander about.—A. S. *wæfre*, restless, wandering. **+** Icel. *vafra*, to waver; see above.

Wax (1), to grow. (E.) M. E. *waxen*, pt. t. *wox*, *wex*, pp. *woxen*, *waxen*. A. S. *weaxan*, pt. t. *weóx*, pp. *geweaxen*. **+** Du. *wassen*, Icel. *vaxa*, Dan. *væxe*, Swed.

växa, G. *wachsen*, Goth. *wahsjan*, pt. t. *wohs*. Further allied to Gk. *αὐξάνειν*, Skt. *vaksh*, to wax, grow. (Base WAKS, extended from √WAG, to be strong.) Allied to **Eke**, **Augment**.

waist. (E.) M. E. *wast*, waist; lit. 'the growth' of a man, or the part of the body where size and strength are developed. The same word as M. E. *wacst*, strength, answering to an A. S. form *wæxt**, not found, but nearly allied to A. S. *wæstme*, growth.—A. S. *weaxan*, to grow. **+** Goth. *wahstus*, growth, increase, stature; Icel. *vöxtr*, stature, shape. **Der.** *waist-coat*.

Wax (2), a substance made by bees. (E.) M. E. *wax*; A. S. *weax*.**+**Du. *was*, Icel. Swed. *vax*, Dan. *vox*, G. *wachs*, Russ. *vosk'*, Lith. *waszkas*.

Way. (E.) M. E. *wey*, *way*. A. S. *weg*. **+**Du. *weg*, Icel. *vegr*, Dan. *vei*, Swed. *väg*, G. *weg*, Goth. *wigs*. **+** Lith. *weźa*, the track of a cart; L. *uia*; Skt. *vaha*, a way, from *vah*, to carry. See **Weigh**. (√ WAGH.) **Der.** *al-way*, *al-ways*, see **All**; *way-faring*, i. e. faring on the way, A. S. *weg-férend*, where *férend* is the pres. pt. of *féran*, to travel; *way-lay*, *way-worn*.

away. (E.) M. E. *awei*. A. S. *onweg*, away.—A. S. *on*, on; *weg*, way.

wayward, perverse. (E.) M. E. *weiward*, headless form of M. E. *aweiward*, adv. in a direction away from a thing; from M. E. *awei*, away, and *-ward*, suffix. See **away** (above).

We, pl. of the 1st pers. pronoun. (E.) M. E. *we*. A. S. *wé*. **+** Du. *wij*; Icel. *vér*, Dan. Swed. *vi*; G. *wir*; Goth. *weis*.

Weak. (Scand.) The Scand. form has ousted M. E. *wook*, A. S. *wác*, weak. *Weak* is from Icel. *veikr*, Swed. *vek*, weak; Dan. *veg*, pliant. **—** Icel. *veik*, pt. t. of *víkja*, to turn aside; cognate with A. S. *wác*, pt. t. of *wícan*, to give way. (Base WIK.) Allied to **Wick** (1) and **Wicker**.

Weal; see **Will** (1).

Weald, a wooded region, an open country. (E.) Two words have been confused, viz. *wild* and *wold* (or *wald*). The M. E. *wald* or *wæld* became *weld* and *weeld*; Caxton speaks of 'the *weeld*' of Kent. See further under **Wold**. But Shakespeare and Lyly speak of 'the *wilde*' of Kent; see **Wild**.

Wealth; see **Will** (1).

Wean; see **Win**.

Weapon. (E.) M. E. *wepen*. A. S. *wǽpen*, a weapon. **+** Du. *wapen*, Icel.

vápn, Dan. *vaaben*, Swed. *vapen*, G. *waffe*; Goth. *wepna*, neut. pl. weapons. Allied to A. S. *wǽpman*, a full grown-man, a male.

wapentake, a district. (Scand.) M. E. *wapentake*. A. S. *wǽpengetǽce*, not an E. word, but borrowed from Icel. *vápnatak*, lit. a weapon-touching, hence, a vote of consent so expressed, and, finally, the district governed by a man whose authority was confirmed by the touching of weapons. See Thorpe, Ancient Laws, i. 455. − Icel. *vápna*, gen. pl. of *vápn*, a weapon; and *tak*, a touching, grasping, allied to **Take**.

Wear (1), to wear clothes, to consume by use. (E.) M. E. *weren*, pt. t. *wered*. A. S. *werian* (pt. t. *werode*).+Icel. *verja*, O. H. G. *werian*, to wear; Goth. *wasjan*, to clothe. (√WAS, to clothe.) ¶ All the senses of *wear* can be deduced from the sense of carrying clothes on the body; hence it means to consume or use up by wear, to destroy, efface. The pt. t. *wore* is modern. Not allied to A. S. *werian*, to defend, which is a different word.

Wear (2) a weir; see **weir**, under **Wary**.

Wear (3), to veer a ship; the same as **Veer**, q. v.

Weary, exhausted, tired. (E.) M. E. *weri*. A. S. *wérig*, tired.−A. S. *wórian*, to tramp about, wander, travel.−A. S. *wór*, a moor, swampy place (tedious to tramp over).+O. Sax. *wórig*, O. H. G. *wórag*, weary. (The change from *ó* to *é* is quite regular.) ¶ Not allied to *wear* (1).

Weasand; see **Wheeze**.

Weasel. (E.) M. E. *wesel*, *wesele*. A. S. *wesle*, a weasel.+Du. *wezel*, Icel. *vísla*, Dan. *væsel*, Swed. *vessla*, G. *wiesel*. Perhaps allied to **Wizen**; from its thinness.

Weather. (E.) M. E. *weder*; A. S. *weder*. (The *th* seems due to Icel. *veðr*.) +Du. *weder*, Icel. *veðr*, Dan. *veir*; Swed. *väder*, wind, weather; G. *wetter*. Allied to G. *gewitter*, a storm, Icel. *land-viðri*, a land-wind; Russ. *vietr'*, wind, breeze, Lith. *wétra*, storm. Allied to **Wind** (1).

weather-beaten, **weather-bitten**. (E.) Both forms seem to be correct. The former means 'beaten by the weather,' from *beat*. The latter means 'bitten by the weather,' from *bite*, and occurs in Wint. Tale, v. 2. 60; derived from Swed. *väder-biten*, lit. bitten by the weather.

wither. (E.) Orig. trans.; M. E. *widren*, *wederen*, to expose to weather.

Weave. (E.) M. E. *weuen* (*weven*).

A. S. *wefan*, pt. t. *wæf*, pp. *wefen*.+Du. *weven*, Icel. *vefa*, Dan. *væve*, Swed. *vefva*, G. *weben*. (Base WAB=√WABH.)

web. (E.) A. S. *webb*, a web; from *wæf*, pt. t. of *wefan* (above).+Du. *web*, Icel. *vefr*, Dan. *væv*, Swed. *väf*, G. *gewebe*.

weft. (E.) A. S. *weft*, *wefta*, the threads woven across the warp; from A. S. *wæf*, pt. t. of *wefan*, to weave.+ Icel. *veftr*.

woof, the weft. (E.) This curious word is a corruption of M. E. *oof*, the *w* being prefixed owing to a popular etymology from *weave* (which is true, but not in the way which popular etymologists would understand). The M. E. *oof* is a contraction of A. S. *ówef*, the woof. − A. S. *ó*, contraction of *on*, upon; *wef*, a sb. due to *wæf*, pt. t. of *wefan*, to weave.

Wed, vb. (E.) M. E. *wedden*. A. S. *weddian*, lit. to pledge, engage; hence to betroth. − A. S. *wed*, a pledge. + O. Du. *wedde*, Icel. *veð*, Swed. *vad*, G. *wette*, Goth. *wadi*, a pledge, wager. Allied to L. *uas* (gen. *uad-is*), a pledge, Gk. ἄ-εθλον (=ἄ-ϝεθ-λον), the prize of a contest; Skt. *vadhú*, a bride. (√WADH.)

wage, a gage, pledge; pl. **wages**, pay for service. (F.−Teut.) M. E. *wage*, pl. *wages*. − O. F. *wage*, later *gage*, a gage, pledge; hence, a stipulated payment. A verbal sb. from O. F. *wager*, to pledge, Low L. *wadiare*.−Goth. *wadi*, a pledge (above). Der. *wage*, vb., as in *to wage war*, orig. to declare (or pledge oneself to) war.

wager, a bet. (F.−Teut.) M. E. *wager*, *wajour*. − O. F. *wageure*, later *gageure*, 'a wager;' Cot.−Low L. *wadiatura*, from *wadiare*, to pledge (above). Der. *wager*, vb. See also **Gage** (1).

wedlock, marriage. (E.) A. S. *wedlác*, lit. a pledge, pledging. − A. S. *wed*, a pledge; *lác*, a sport, also, a gift, and often used as a mere suffix. See **Lark** (2).

Wodge. (E.) M. E. *wegge*. A. S. *wecg*. +Du. *wig*, Icel. *veggr*, Dan. *vægge*, Swed. *vigg*, M. H. G. *wecke*, a wedge; G. *wecke*, a kind of wedge-shaped loaf. Lit. 'a mover,' from its effect in splitting trees; allied to **Wag**. (√WAGH.)

Wedlock; see **Wed**.

Wednesday. (E.) M. E. *wednesday*. A. S. *wódnesdæg*, Woden's day. (The change from *ó* to M. E. *é* is quite regular.) + Du. *woensdag*, Icel. *óðinsdagr*, Swed.

Dan. *onsdag*; all meaning 'Woden's (or Odin's) day.' β. The name *Wóden* signifies 'furious;' from A. S. *wód*, mad, furious (= Icel. *óðr*, Goth. *wods*). See **Wood** (2). *Woden* was identified with L. *Mercurius*.

Wee, tiny. (Scand.?) M. E. *we*, only as sb., in the phrase 'a litel *we*' = a little bit, a little way. I have little hesitation in assuming the O. Northern E. *we*, a way, space, to be the same as Dan. *vei*, a way, cognate with E. **Way**, q. v. Cf. North. E. *way-bit*, also *wee-bit*, a small space. ¶ Certainly not allied to G. *wenig*, little.

Weed (1), a noxious plant. (E.) M. E. *weed*; A. S. *weód*, *wiód*, a weed. + O. Saxon *wiod*. Root unknown.

Weed (2), a garment. (E.) M. E. *wede*. A. S. *wǽde*, neuter, *wǽd*, fem., a garment. + O. Fries. *wede*, O. Sax. *wádi*; Icel. *váð*, a piece of stuff, cloth; O. H. G. *wát*, *wót*, clothing, armour. Lit. 'something that binds' or is wrapped round; cf. Goth. *ga-widan* (pt. t. *ga-wath*), O. H. G. *wetan*, to bind together, Zend *vadh*, to clothe.

Week. (E.) M. E. *weke*, *wike*; A. S. *wice*, *wicu*, a week. (There was a later A. S. *wucu*, a week, which became M. E. *wouke*, a week, and is obsolete.) + Du. *week*, Icel. *vika*, Swed. *vecka*, O. H. G. *wecha*, *wehha* (mod. G. *woche*). We also once find Goth. *wiko*, in the sense of order or succession (Luke i. 8), answering to L. *ordine* (not to *uicis*). The orig. sense seems to have been 'succession,' series; cf. Icel. *víkja*, to turn, return; see **Weak**.

Ween; see **Win**.

Weep. (E.) M. E. *wepen*, pt. t. *weep*, *wep*. A. S. *wépan*, pt. t. *weóp*, to cry aloud, raise an outcry. — A. S. *wóp*, a clamour, outcry (by the usual change from *ó* to *é*). + O. Sax. *wópian*. vb., from *wóp*, outcry; Icel. *æpa*, to shout, from *óp*, outcry. Allied to Russ. *vopite*, to sob, lament. Cf. Skt. *vác̣*, to cry, howl. ¶ Not allied to *whoop*.

Weet; see **Wit** (1).

Weevil, a small beetle. (E.) M. E. *weuel*, *wiuel* (*wevel*, *wivel*); A. S. *wifel*, *wibil*.+Icel. *yfill*, O. Du. *wevel*, O. H. G. *wibil*. A dimin. form; from A. S. *wibba*, a beetle; of which the orig. sense was prob. 'wriggler' or 'flutterer.' Cf. Lith. *wábalas*, a chafer, winged insect.

Weft; see **Weave**.

Weigh. (E.) M. E. *weghen*. A. S. *wegan*, pt. t. *wæg*, to carry, bear; also, to move; also to raise, lift (cf. to *weigh*

anchor); to weigh. + Du. *wegen*; Icel. *vega*, to move, lift; Dan. *veie*, Swed. *väga*; G. *wegen*, to move, *wiegen*, to rock, *wägen*, to weigh. Allied to L. *uehere*, Skt. *vah*, to carry. (✓ WAGH.)

wag. (Scand.) M. E. *waggen*. — O. Swed. *wagga*, Swed. *vagga*, to wag, sway, rock. Cognate with A. S. *wagian* (= M. E. *wawen*), to wag, which is a secondary verb derived from A. S. *wæg*, pt. t. of *wegan* (above). Similarly, the Swed. *vagga* is a secondary verb, from Icel. *vag-*, base of *vega*, to weigh (above). Der. *wag-tail*.

waggle, to wag frequently. (Scand.) Frequent. form of **wag** (above).

wagon, **waggon**. (Du.) XVI cent. Borrowed from Du. *wagen*, a wagon; which is cognate with **wain** (below).

wain, a waggon. (E.) M. E. *wain*, *wayn*; formed (by the usual change of *æg* to *ay*) from A. S. *wægn*, a wain; we also find A. S. *wǽn*, a contracted form. — A. S. *wæg*, pt. t. of *wegan*, to carry; see **Weigh** (above). (Thus *wain* = vehicle.) + Du. *wagen* (whence E. *wagon*), Icel. *vagn*, Dan. *vogn*, Swed. *vagn*, G. *wagen*.

wainscot, panelled boards on walls of rooms. (Du.) XIV cent. — Du. *wagenschot*, 'wainscot;' Hexham. As if from Du. *wagen*, a wain; but really a corruption of O. Du. *waeghe-schot*, wall-boarding; from O. Du. *waeg* (Du. *weeg*, A. S. *wáh*) a wall, and *schot*, 'a wainscot, partition,' &c., Sewel, or 'a closure of boards,' Hexham. It came to mean boards for covering walls, hence, boards for panel-work, oak-panelling, wainscot in general. The Du. *schot* is cognate with E. *scot* and *shot*. (Misplaced.)

weight. (E.) M. E. *weght*, *wight*. A.S. *wiht*, *gewiht*, weight. + Du. *gewigt*, Icel. *vætt*, Dan. *vægt*, Swed. *vigt*, G. *gewicht*.

wey, a heavy weight; from two to three cwt. (E.) M. E. *wege*. A. S. *wǽge*, a weight. — A. S. *wǽg-*, stem of pt. t. pl. of *wegan*, to weigh.

Weir, **Wear**, a mill-dam; see **Wary**.

Weird; see **Worth** (2).

Welcome; see **Will** (1).

Weld (1); to beat metal together; see **Well** (2).

Weld (2), dyer's weed. (E.) M. E. *welde*, *wolde*; Lowl. Sc. *wald*. Apparently an E. word. ¶ Quite distinct from *woad*.

Welfare; see **Will** (1).

Welkin, sky, clouds. (E.) M. E. *welkin*, more commonly *welkne*, *welkene*, *welken*, *wolken.* — A. S. *wolcnu,* clouds, pl. of *wolcen,* a cloud.+O. Sax. *wolkan,* G. *wolke,* a cloud. ¶ The suggested connection with A. S. *wealcan,* to roll, is not proven.

Well (1) ; see **Will** (1).

Well (2), a spring, fount. (E.) M. E. *welle* ; A.S. *wella,* a spring. — A. S. *weallan* (pt. t. *weóll*), to well up, boil (but the mod. E. *well,* vb., is derived from the secondary verb *wellan* or *wyllan,* with the same sense). + Icel. *vell,* ebullition, from *vella,* to boil (pt. t. *vall*) ; Du. *wel,* a spring ; Dan. *væld* ; G. *welle,* a wave, surge, from *wallen,* to boil. Further allied to Skt. *val,* to move to and fro, Russ. *valiate,* to roll. Also allied to **Warm.** (√WAL=WAR.) Der. *well,* vb., as above.

weld (1), to beat metal together. (Swed.) The *d* is excrescent after *l;* the word is Swedish, from the iron-works there. — Swed. *välla,* orig. to well, now only in the sense to weld iron; cf. Dan. *vælde,* to well up (with excrescent *d,* as in English). Cognate with E. *well,* vb.

Wellaway ; see **Wo.**

Welsh, pertaining to Wales. (E.) M.E. *walsh,* foreign. A. S. *wælisc, welisc,* foreign. Formed, with suffix *-isc* (E. *-ish*) and vowel-change, from A. S. *wealh,* a foreigner. See **Walnut.**

Welt. (C.) The old sense seems to be border, hem, fringe. M. E. *welte.* — W. *gwald,* a hem, welt, *gwaltes,* the welt of a shoe ; *gwaldu,* to welt, hem ; allied to Gael. *balt,* welt, border, belt, Irish *balt* (same). It seems thus to be allied to **Belt.**

Welter, to wallow, roll about. (E.) Formerly also *walter. Walter, welter,* are frequentatives from M. E. *walten,* to roll over, tumble, turn over. — A. S. *wealtan* (strong verb), to roll over.+Icel. *velta* (pt. t. *valt*), to roll, Dan. *vælte,* to overturn ; Swed. *vältra,* to welter, frequent. of *välta,* to roll; G. *wälzen,* to roll, welter, from

walzen, to roll. Cf. Goth. *us-waltjan,* to subvert. (Base WALT, from √ WAR.)

waltz, a dance. (G.) Short for G. *walzer,* a waltz (with *z* sounded as *ts*). — G. *walzen,* to roll, revolve ; see above.

Wen, a tumour. (E.) A.S. *wenn.* + Du. *wen* ; Low G. *ween.* Prob. allied to Goth. *winnan,* to suffer, *wunns,* affliction; the Goth. *winnan* is the same as A. S. *winnan,* to toil, to win (whence E. *win*). See **Win.**

Wench. (E.) M. E. *wenche,* earlier form *wenchel,* a child, (male or female). — A. S. *winclo,* s. pl., children (of either sex). Allied to A. S. *wencel,* weak, *wancol,* tottery (hence weak, infantine). From the base WANK, seen in G. *wanken,* to totter, M. H. G. *wenken,* to render unsteady. Allied to **Wink.**

Wend, Went; see **Wind** (2).

Were, pl. of **Was,** q. v.

Werwolf, a man-wolf. (E.) A. S. *were-wulf,* a werwolf, the devil. — A. S. *wer,* a man; *wulf,* a wolf.+G. *währwolf,* M.H.G. *werwolf,* a man-wolf ; from M. H. G. *wer,* a man, and *wolf.* (Hence O. F. *garoul,* F. *garou,* now *loupgarou,* i.e. wolf-werwolf.) See **Virile.** ¶ It was supposed that fierce men were turned into wolves; cf. Gk. λυκάνθρωπος, i.e. wolf-man.

West. (E.) A. S. *west,* adv., westward; *west-dæl,* west part or quarter. + Du. *west,* Icel. *vestr,* Dan. Swed. *vest,* G. *west.* Allied to Skt. *vasta,* a house, *vasati,* dwelling-place, night; from *vas,* to dwell. The supposed place of abode of the sun at night. (√ WAS.)

Wet; see **Water.**

Wether, a castrated ram. (E.) A. S. *weðer.*+O. Sax. *wethar, withar,* Icel. *veðr,* Dan. *væder,* Swed. *vädur,* G. *widder,* Goth. *withrus,* a lamb. Lit. ' a yearling ;' allied to **Veal.**

Wey; see **Weigh.**

WH.

Wh. This is distinct from *w.* The mod. E. *wh* answers to A. S. *hw,* Icel. *hv,* L. *qu,* Aryan *kw.*

Whack, to beat ; see **Thwack.**

Whale. (E.) M. E. *whal, qual.* A. S. *hwæl.*+Du. *walvisch* (whale-fish), G. *wallfisch,* Icel. *hvalr,* Dan. Swed. *hval.* It also

meant a porpoise, grampus, &c. The sense is 'roller;' from the rolling of porpoises. Allied to **Wheel.**

walrus, a large seal. (Du. — Scand.) Du. *walrus.* — Swed. *vallross,* Dan. *hvalros,* a morse; lit. a 'whale-horse;' the same as A. S. *hors-hwæl,* a morse, horse-whale.

— Swed. *vall*, Dan. *hval*, a whale; Icel. *hross*, a horse. Said to be named from the neighing sound made by the animal.

Whap, to beat, flutter. (E.) Also *whop*, *wap*, *wop*. M. E. *quappen*, to palpitate, throb. From a base KWAP, to throb; see **Quaver**. Cf. also W. *chwap*, a sudden stroke, *chwapio*, to strike, slap.

wabble, wobble, to reel, move unsteadily. (E.) Frequentative of *wap*, *whap*, to flutter (Halliwell); see above.+Low G. *wabbeln*, *quabbeln*, to palpitate, to wabble.

Wharf (1), a place for landing goods. (E.) A. S. *hwerf*, a dam or bank to keep out water (Thorpe, Diplomatarium, pp. 361, 381); *mere-hwearf*, sea-shore (Grein).— A. S. *hwearf*, pt. t. of *hweorfan*, to turn, turn about. β. This difficult word, with a great range of senses, meant a turning, reversion, turning-place, space, dam, shore, dockyard, as proved by the cognate words, viz. Du. *werf*, Icel. *hvarf*, Dan. *værft*, Swed. *varf*, O. Swed. *hwarf*, &c. The A. S. *hweorfan* answers to Goth. *hwairban*, to turn oneself about, walk, Icel. *hverfa*, to turn. (Base HWARB.) Allied to **Curve**. ¶ *Not* allied to G. *werfen*, to throw. Der. *wharf-inger*, for *wharfager*; with inserted *n*, as in *messenger*, *passenger*.

Wharf (2), bank of a river. (E.) In Shak. Hamlet, i. 5. 33. Cf. A. S. *mere-hwearf*, sea-shore (Grein); it is the same word as **Wharf** (1).

What; see **Who**.

Wheal (1), a pimple. (E.) Distinct from *weal*, *wale*, a mark of a blow. Perhaps from A. S. *hwéle*, a wheal (Somner). Cf. W. *chwiler*, a maggot, wheal, pimple. ¶ Difficult and doubtful.

whelk (2), a small pimple. (E.) M. E. *whelke*, Chaucer, C. T. 634. Dimin. of *wheal* (above).

Wheal (2), a mine. (C.) A Cornish word. — Corn. *hwel*, a work, a mine. Cf. W. *chwel*, a course, a turn.

Wheat; see **White**.

Wheedle. (G. ?) In Blount, ed. 1674; who connects it (quite unsatisfactorily) with W. *chwedla*, to gossip, *chwedl*, a fable, tale. But perhaps from G. *wedeln*, to wag the tail, to fan (hence, probably, to flatter). This is from the sb. *wedel*, a fan, tail, O. H. G. *wadol*, a tail. ¶ Doubtful.

Wheel. (E.) A. S. *hwéol*, shorter form of *hweowol*, a wheel; also spelt *hweohl*. + Icel. *hjól*, Dan. *hiul*, Swed. *hjul*.

Wheeze. (E.) A. S. *hwésan* or *hwǽsan*

(pt. t. *hwebs*), to wheeze. Cf. Icel. *hvæsa*, Dan. *hvæse*, to hiss, to wheeze. Allied to Skt. *çvas*, to breathe hard, sigh, L. *quer-i* (pp. *ques-tus*), to complain. (√ KWAS.) Cf. E. *whis-tle*, *whis-per*.

weasand, wesand, the wind-pipe. (E.) A. S. *wásend*, the gullet; but the mod. E. *wesand* answers rather to a by-form *wǽsend**. The orig. sense probably was 'the wheezing thing,' the wind-pipe; put for *hwǽsend*, pres. pt. of *hwǽsan*, to wheeze (above).

Whelk (1), a mollusc with a spiral shell. (E.) Ill spelt; it should be *welk* or *wilk*. M. E. *wilk*; A. S. *wiloc*, later *weoluc*, *weluc*. Named from its convoluted shell; cf. A. S. *wealcan*, to roll, walk; see **Walk**. Der. *whelk'd*, i. e. convoluted, K. Lear, iv. 6. 71; spelt *wealk'd* in the first folio.

Whelk (2); see **Wheal** (1).

Whelm, to overturn, cover over by something that is turned over, to overwhelm, submerge. (Scand.) M. E. *whelmen*, to turn a hollow vessel upside down (Palsgrave), to turn over; Lowl. Sc. *quhemle*, *whommle*, *whamle*, to turn upside down. Closely related to M. E. *wheluen* (*whelven*) and *ouerwheluen* (*overwhelven*), used in the same sense. β. The only difficulty is to explain the final -*m*; this is due to the fact that *whelm*, verb, is really formed from a sb. *whelm*, standing for *hwelf-m*, the *f* being dropped because unpronounceable. This appears from O. Swed. *hwalma*, to cock hay, derived from the sb. *hwalm*, a hay-cock; where *hwalm* is for *hwalfm**, being derived from O. Swed. *hwalf*, an arch, vault, *hwälfwa*, to arch over (make into a rounded shape). Thus the suffix -*m* is substantival (as in *doo-m*, *bloo-m*, &c.), and the Teut. base is HWALB, to become convex (M. H. G. *welben*, pt. t. *walb*), the derivatives of which appear in A. S. *hwealf*, adj., convex, sb., a vault, Icel. *hválf*, *hólf*, a vault, *hválfa*, *hólfa*, to 'whelve' or turn upside down, G. *wölben*, to arch over. γ. We thus trace the following forms, viz. base HWALB, to swell out, become convex; Icel. *hvelfa*, to vault, turn a round vessel upside down; hence *whelm*, sb., a thing made convex, *whelm*, vb., to make convex, turn a round vessel over, capsize. Forby remarks that *whelm*, in the E. Anglian dialect, signifies 'to turn a tub or other vessel upside down, whether to cover anything with it or not.' Der. *over-whelm*.

Whelp, a puppy. (E.) A. S. *hwelp*, sb.

+ Du. *welp*, Icel. *hvelpr*, Dan. *hvalp*, Swed. *valp*, M. H. G. *welf*. Root unknown.

When, Whence, Where; see Who.

Wherry, a shallow, light boat. (Scand.) The word, in Scand. dialects, signifies crank, easily turned. — Icel. *hverfr*, shifty, crank (said of a ship); Norw. *kwerv*, crank, unsteady, quick (said of a boat). — Icel. *hverfa* (pt. t. *hvarf*), to turn. See **Whirl**.

Whet. (E.) M. E. *whetten*. A. S. *hwettan*, to sharpen. — A. S. *hwæt*, keen, bold, brave. **+** Du. *wetten*, Icel. *hvetja*, Swed. *vättja*, G. *wetzen*, to sharpen, en courage; from O. Sax. *hvat*, Icel. *hvatr*, bold, O. H. G. *hwas*, sharp. **Der.** *whetstone*, A. S. *hwetstán*.

Whether; see Who.

Whey. (E.) M. E. *whey*. A. S. *hwǽg*, whey. **+** Du. *hui*, *wei*. Cf. W. *chwig*, whey fermented with sour herbs.

Which; see Who.

Whiff, sb., a puff. (E.) M. E. *weffe*, vapour. An imitative word, like *puff*, *fife*. **+** W. *chwiff*, a puff, *chwaff*, a gust; Dan. *vift*, a puff, gust. Cf. A.S. *hwíða*, a breeze.

whiffle, to blow in gusts, veer as the wind. (E.) Frequentative of *whiff*, to puff. **Der.** *whiffl-er*, a piper, fifer, hence one who goes first in a procession.

Whig. (E. ?) See Todd's Johnson and Nares. *Whig* is a shortened form of *whiggamor*, applied to certain Scotchmen who came from the west to buy corn at Leith; from the word *whiggam*, employed by these men in driving their horses. A march to Edinburgh made by Argyle was called 'the *whiggamor's* inroad,' and afterwards those who were opposed to the court came to be called *whigs*. (Burnet, Own Times, b. i.) The Glossary to Sir W. Scott's novels has : '*whigamore*, a great whig; *whigging*, jogging rudely, urging forward.' To *whig awa* is to jog on briskly. I suppose that the *h* is intrusive, and that these words are allied to Lowl. Sc. *wiggle*, to move about, and to A. S. *wecgan*, to move, agitate, move along. See **Weigh**.

While, a time. (E.) A. S. *hwíl*, sb., a pause, a time. **+** Icel. *hvíla*, a place of rest; Dan. *hvile*, rest; Swed. *hvila*, rest; G. *weile*, Goth. *hweila*, a time. Prob. allied to L. *qui-es*, rest. (**√** KI.) **Der.** *while*, adv.; *whiles*, M. E. *whiles*, adv. (with gen. suffix -*es*); whence *whils-t*, with added *t* (as in *amongs-t*, *amids-t*); also *whil-om*,

formerly, from A. S. *hwílum*, dat. pl. of *hwíl*, a time. Also *mean-while*, see **Mean** (3); also *whiling-time*, the waiting a little time before dinner (Spectator, no. 448), whence the phrase *to while away time*, probably with some thought of confusion with *wile*.

Whim, a freak. (Scand.) Skelton has *whim-wham*. — Icel. *hvima*, to wander with the eyes, as a silly person; Norw. *kvima*, to whisk about, trifle. Cf. Swed. dial. *hvimmerkantig*, giddy in the head. **Der.** *whimsey*, a whim, from the allied Norw. *kvimsa*, Swed. dial. *hvimsa*, Dan. *vimse*, to be giddy, skip or whisk about.

wimble(2), active. (Scand.) In Spenser, Shep. Kal. March, 91. — Swed. dial. *vimmla*. to be giddy or skittish, frequent. of Swed. dial. *vima*, to be giddy, allied to Icel. *vim*, giddiness. Compare **Whim** (above).

Whimper, to whine. (E.) The same as Lowland Sc. *whimmer*, to whimper, frequentative of *whim*, another form of *whine*; see **Whine**. ' [They] wil *whympe* and *whine*;' Latimer, Seven Sermons, ed. Arber, p. 77.

Whin, gorse. (C.) M. E. *whynne*, *quyn*. — W. *chwyn*, weeds; cf. Bret. *chouenna* (with guttural *ch*), to weed.

Whine, vb. (E.) A. S. *hwínan*, to whine. **+** Icel. *hvína*, Swed. *hvina*, Dan. *hvine*, to whir, whiz, whine. Cf. Icel. *kveina*, to wail, Goth. *kwainon*, to mourn, Skt. *kvan*, to buzz. **Der.** *whimp-er*, q. v.

Whip, to move quickly, to flog. (E.) M. E *whippen*, to overlay a cord by rapidly binding the twine round it, *whippe*, a scourge. From the sense of rapid movement. **+** Du. *wippen*, to skip, formerly to shake; Low G. *wippen*, to bob up and down; Dan *vippe*, to see-saw, bob; Swed. *vippa*, to wag, jerk; G. *wippen*, to move up and down, see-saw, jerk. (I find no very early authority for the *h*.) **Der.** *whip*, sb.

whipple-tree, a swing-bar for traces. (E.) The sense is 'piece of swinging-wood,' composed of *tree* (as in *axle-tree*) and the verb *whipple*, frequent. of *whip*, to move about quickly, to see-saw (above).

Whir, to buzz. (Scand.) An imitative word, like *whiz*. — Dan. *hvirre*, to whirl, twirl; Swed. dial. *hvirra*, to whirl. Allied to **Whirl**.

Whirl. (Scand.) M. E. *whirlen*. A contraction for *whirf-le* *, frequent. of M. E. *wherfen*, to turn. — Icel. *hvirfla*, to whirl; frequent. of *hverfa* (pt. t. *hvarf*), to turn round; Dan. *hvirvle*, Swed. *hvirfla*, O. Du. *wervelen*, to whirl; G. *wirbeln*, to whirl, to warble. (Base HWARB.) Allied to **Wharf**. **Der.** *whirl-wind*, from Icel. *hvirfilvindr*, Dan. *hvirvelvind*, Swed. *hvirfvelvind*, a whirlwind; also *whirl-pool*; *whirl-i-gig* (see **Gig**).

warble, to sing as a bird. (F. ‒ O. H. G.) M. E. *werbelen, werbelen*. ‒ O. F. *werbler* (Burguy). ‒ M. H. G. *werbelen*, old spelling of G. *wirbeln*, to whirl, run round, warble (above).

Whisk, to move or sweep quickly. (Scand.) The *h* is intrusive. It is properly *wisk*, orig. to wipe, brush, sweep, esp. with a quick motion, as when using a light brush; the *h* was due to confusion with *whiz, whir, whirl*, &c. ‒ Dan. *viske*, to wipe, rub, sponge, from *visk*, a wisp, rubber; Swed. *viska*, to wipe, also to wag (or whisk) the tail, from *viska*, 'a whisk, a small broom,' Widegren; Icel. *visk*, a wisp of hay, something to wipe with, a rubber. ✦ G. *wischen*, 'to wipe, wisk, rub,' Flügel; from the sb. *wisch*, 'a whisk, clout,' id. β. The sb. which thus appears as Icel. *visk*, Swed. *viska*, G. *wisch*, meant orig. 'a washer;' from the Teut. base WASK, to wash; see **Wash**. **Der.** *whisk-er*, from the likeness to a small brush. 'Nestor *brush'd* her with his *whisk-ers*;' Dryden, Troilus, iv. 2. Also *whisk-y*, a light gig, easily *whisked* along.

Whisky, Whiskey, a spirit. (Gaelic.) Gaelic *uisge-beatha*, water of life, whiskey; the latter element being dropped; see below.

usquebaugh. (Irish.) Irish *uisge beatha*, usquebaugh, whiskey. ‒ Irish *uisge*, water; *beatha*, life, allied to Gk. βίος, life.

Whisper, vb. (E.) M. E. *whisperen*. O. Northumb. *hwisprian*, to murmur, Luke, xix. 7, John, vii. 12. ✦ O. Du. *wisperen, wispelen*, G. *wispeln*. Cf. also Icel. *hvískra*, Swed. *hviska*, Dan. *hviske*, to whisper. (Base HWIS.) Allied to **Wheeze** and **Hiss**.

whistle, vb. (E.) A. S. *hwistlian*, as in *hwistlere*, a whistler, piper. ✦ Icel. *hvísla*, to whisper; Dan. *hvisle*, to hiss, whistle; Swed. *hvissla*, to whistle. (Base HWIS.) See above.

Whist; see **Hiss**.

Whistle; see **Whisper**.

Whit; see **Wight** (1).

White. (E.) M. E. *whit*. A. S. *hwít*. ✦ Du. *wit*, Icel. *hvítr*, Dan. *hvid*, Swed. *hvit*, Goth. *hweits*, G. *weiss*. Allied to Skt. *çveta*, white, from *çvit*, to shine, to be white; also to Russ. *svietite*, to shine. (√KWI.) **Der.** *whit-ing*, a fish with delicate white flesh, also ground chalk; also *whit-ster*, a whitener, bleacher.

wheat. (E.) M. E. *whete*. A.S. *hwǽte*, wheat; named from the whiteness of the meal; see **White** (above). ✦ Du. *weite, weit*, Icel. *hveiti*, Dan. *hvede*, Swed. *hvete*, Goth. *hwaiteis*, G. *weizen*. **Der.** *wheat-en*, adj., A.S. *hwǽten*.

whit-sunday. (E.) Lit. *white Sunday*, as is perfectly certain from the A. S. name *hwíta sunnan-dæg*, Icel. *hvítasunnudagr*, Norwegian *kvittsunndag*; these are *facts*, though constantly denied by the lovers of paradoxical and far-fetched etymologies. The difficulty lies *only* in the reason for the name. 'The great festivals, Yule, Easter, and Pentecost, but esp. the two latter, were the great seasons for christening; in the Roman Catholic church, especially Easter, whence in Roman usage the Sunday after Easter was called *Dominica in Albis*; but in the Northern churches, perhaps owing to the cold weather at Easter-time, Pentecost . . seems to have been esp. appointed for christening and for ordination; hence the following week was called the Holy Week, Icel. *Helga Vika*;' Icel. Dict. The case is parallel to that of *noon*, which at first meant 9th hour, or 3 P.M., but was afterwards *shifted*. So also in other cases. **Der.** *Whitsun-week*, short for *Whitsun-day's week* (Icel. *hvítasunnudags-vika*); *Whitsun-tide*, short for *Whitsunday-tide*.

whittle (3), a blanket. (E.) M. E. *whitel*; A. S. *hwítel*. Named from its white colour. ‒ A. S. *hwít*, white.

Whither; see **Who**.

Whitlow, a painful swelling on the fingers. (Scand.) Corruption of *whickflaw*, a whitlow (Halliwell); where *whick* is the Northern pronunciation of *quick*, i. e. the sensitive part of the finger round the nail; Icel. *kvika*. *Flaw* is the Swed. *flaga*, a flaw, crack, breach, flake. See **Quick** and **Flaw**. The sense is 'crack near the quick,' hence a painful sore, afterwards a painful swelling. It was corrupted first to *whitflaw* (Holland), and afterwards to *whitlow*; by confusion with *white*. 'Paronychia, a *whitflaw*;' Wiseman, Surgery, b. i. c. 11.

Whitsunday; see **White**.

Whittle, (1) and (2); see **Thwite**.

Whittle (3), a blanket; see **White**.

Whiz, to hiss. (E.) 'The woods do *whizz*;' Surrey, tr. of Æneid, b. ii. An imitative word; allied to **Hiss** and **Wheeze**. + Icel. *hvissa*, to hiss.

Who, pronoun. (E.) Formerly *who*, *what*, *which*, were interrogative pronouns. *Which*, *whose*, *whom*, occur as *relatives* as early as the end of the 12th century, but *who*, as a *relative*, is not found before the 14th century. (Morris.) A. S. *hwá*, who; neuter, *hwæt*, what; gen. *hwæs*, whose; dat. *hwám*, to whom; acc. masc. and fem. *hwone*, whom [obsolete], neut. *hwæt*, what; instrumental *hwí*, in what way, how, why. + Du. *wie*, Icel. *hverr*, Dan. *hvo*, Swed. *hvem*, G. *wer*, Goth. *hwas*, Irish *co*, L. *quis*, Lith. *kas*, Skt. *kas*. (Base KA = Teut. HWA.)

how. (E.) M. E. *hou*, *hu*; A. S. *hú*. Prob. only another form of A. S. *hwí*, why; see **why**. + O. Fries. *hu*, Du. *hoe*. Cf. Goth. *hwaiwa*, how.

what. (E.) A. S. *hwæt*, neut. of *hwá*.

when. (E.) M. E. *whan*; A. S. *hwænne*, *hwonne*, when. + O. Du. *wan*, G. *wann*, Goth. *hwan*. Prob. allied to Goth. *hwana*, A. S. *hwone*, acc. masc. of Goth. *hwas*, A. S. *hwá*, who.

whence. (E.) M. E. *whennes*, older form *whanene*.—A. S. *hwanan*, whence; closely allied to **when** (above).

where. (E.) M. E. *wher*; A. S. *hwær*, *hwar*, where; allied to *hwá*, who. + Du. *wâar*, Icel. *hvar*, Dan. *hvor*, Swed. *hvar*, G. *war*- (in *war-um*), Goth. *hwar*.

whether, which of two. (E.) See Matt. xxvii. 21. A. S. *hwæðer*, which of two; formed with comparative suffix *-ðer* (Aryan *-tara*) from the base of *who*. + Icel. *hvárr*, M. H. G. *weder*, Goth. *hwathar*, Lith. *katras*, L. *uter*, Gk. κότερος, πότερος, Skt. *katara*.

which. (E.) M. E. *which*; *quhilk*

(Barbour). A. S. *hwilc*, *hwelc*, which; short for *hwí-líc*, lit. 'why-like,' i. e. how like, in what way like.—A. S. *hwí*, how, instrumental case of *hwá*, who; *líc*, like; see **Why** and **Like**. + O. Sax. *hwilik*, O. Fries. *hwelik*, Du. *welk*, Icel. *hvílíkr*, Dan. Swed. *hvilken*, G. *welcher*, O. H. G. *hwelih*. Cf. L. *qualis*.

whither. (E.) M. E. *whider*. A. S. *hwider*, *hwæder*, whither. + Goth. *hwadre*. Cf. *hither*, *thither*.

why. (E.) M. E. *whi*; for *whi* = on what account (common). A. S. *hwí*, in what way, instrumental case of *hwá*, who; see **Who** (above).

Whole; see **Hale** (1).

Whoop, to shout. (F. – Teut.) The initial *w* is unoriginal; formerly *hoop*. M. E. *houpen*. – F. *houper*, 'to hoop unto;' Cot. Of Teut. origin; cf. Goth. *hwopjan*, to boast (Romans ix. 8). Der. *whooping-cough* or *hooping-cough*.

hubbub. (F. = Teut.) Formerly also *whoobub*, a confused noise. *Hubbub* = *hoop-hoop*, reduplication of *hoop*. *Whoobub* = *whoop-hoop*.

Whore, sb. (Scand.) The *w* is unoriginal. M. E. *hore*. – Icel. *hóra*, an adulteress, fem. of *hórr*, an adulterer; Dan. *hore*, Swed. *hora*. + Du. *hoer*, G. *hure*, O. H. G. *huora*; Goth. *hors*, masc., an adulterer. Allied to Polish *kurwa*, Church-Slavonic *kuruva*, an adulteress. Prob. also to L. *cárus*, loving, Skt. *kámaga*, a lascivious woman (from *kam*, to love). ¶ Certainly not allied to *hire*!

Whorl. (E.) The same as *wharl*, a piece of bone placed on a spindle to twist it by. The likeness between a *wharl* on a spindle and a *whorl* of leaves is sufficiently close. Contraction of M. E. *wharvel*, *whorvil*; from A. S. *hweorfa*, a wharl. – A. S. *hweorfan*, to turn; see **Wharf**, **Whirl**. + O. Du. *worvel*, a wharl; *worvelen*, to twist or twine.

Why; see **Who**.

WI – WY.

Wick (1), a twist of threads for a lamp. (E.) M. E. *wicke*, *weyke*, *wueke*. A. S. *weoca*, a wick. + O. Du. *wiecke*; Low G. *weke*, lint; Dan. *væge*, Swed. *veke*, a wick. Orig. sense 'pliant' or 'soft;' allied to **Weak**. The A. S. *wác*, weak, and *weoca* (= *wica**), a wick, are both from *wic-en*, pp.

of *wícan*, to give way. Cf. O. Du. *weeck*, soft, Dan. *veg*, pliant, Norw. *vik*, a bend, a skein of thread, Swed. *vek*, soft, *vekna*, to soften, G. *weich*, soft, pliant. Hence the sense is 'a bit of soft stuff,' such as lint, &c.

Wick (2), a town. (L.) A. S. *wíc*;

borrowed from L. *uicus*, a village. See
Vicinity.

Wick (3), **Wich**, a creek, bay, salt-pit.
(Scand.) Icel. *vík*, a small creek, inlet,
bay; see **Viking.**

Wicked; see **Wit** (1).

Wicker, made of twigs. (E. *or* Scand.)
M. E. *wiker*, a pliant twig, properly a sb.
— A. S. *wic-en*, pp. of *wícan*, to give way,
bend, ply; see **Weak. +** Dan. dial. *vegre*,
a pliant rod, allied to Dan. *veg*, pliant,
weak; Swed. dial. *vekare*, *vikker*, willow,
from Swed. *veka*, to bend, ply. See
witch-elm (below).

wicket, a small gate. (F. — Scand.)
M. E. *wiket.* — O. F. *wiket** (the right form),
also written *wisket* (with intrusive *s*) and
viguet; mod. F. *guichet*; Walloon *wichet.*
Formed, with F. dimin. suffix *-et*, from
Icel. *vik-inn*, pp. of the strong verb *víkja*,
to move. turn, veer. Cf. Swed. *vicka*, to
wag, *vika*, to turn away, A. S. *wícan*, to
give way. Lit. ' a small thing that easily
turns;' esp. used of a small door, easily
opened, made within a large gate. **Der.**
wicket (at cricket), which was at first ' a
small gate,' being made 2 feet wide by 1
foot high (A.D. 1700).

witch-elm, wych-elm. (E.) M. E.
wiche. A. S. *wice.* The sense is ' bending,' or drooping; from the pendulous
branches. — A. S. *wic-en*, pp. of *wícan*, to
bend; see **Wicker.**

Wide. (E.) A. S. *wíd.* **+** Du. *wijd*,
Icel. *víðr*, Swed. Dan. *vid*, G. *weit.* Perhaps ' separated;' cf. Skt. *vedha*, piercing,
breaking through; *vedhana*, perforation,
also *depth.* **Der.** *wid-th*, XVI cent.; put
for the old word *wide-ness.*

Widgeon, a bird. (F. — L. ?) Spelt
wigion in Levins (1570). — O. F. *wigeon**,
later *vigeon*, a whistling duck (Littré). Prob.
from L. *uipionem*, acc. of *uipio*, a kind of
small crane (Pliny, x. 49).

Widow. (E.) M. E. *widewe*; A. S.
widwe, *widuwe.* **+** Du. *weduwe*. G. *wittwe*,
Goth. *widuwo.* Further allied to L. *uidua*,
fem. of *uiduus*, bereft of, deprived of; W.
gweddw, Russ. *vdova*, Skt. *vidhavá*, a
widow. The root seems to be WIDH, as
in Skt. *vidh*, to lack (St. Petersburg Dict.
vi. 1070). **¶** The supposed etymology of
Skt. *vidhavá* (from *vi*, without, *dhava*, a
husband) is disproved by all the cognate
forms. See **Void. Der.** *widow-er*, M. E.
widewer, coined from *widow* by adding *-er*;
so also G. *wittwer.*

Wield. (E.) M. E. *welden*, to govern,
possess, manage. A. S. *geweldan*, *gewyldan*,
to have power over. This is a weak verb,
due to A. S. *wealdan* (pt. t. *weóld*), to have
power over, govern, rule, possess. **+** Icel.
valda, G. *walten*, Goth. *waldan*, to govern;
allied to Lith. *waldyti*, Russ. *vladiete*, to
rule, possess. From the same root as
Valid.

Wife. (E.) A. S. *wíf*, a woman, neut.
sb. with pl. *wíf* (unchanged). **+** Du. *wijf*,
Icel. *víf*, Dan. *viv*, G. *weib*, O. H. G. *wíp*,
a woman. Root obscure; certainly not
allied to *weave* (A. S. *wefan*), as the fable
runs.

woman. (E.) A curious corruption of
A. S. *wífman*, lit. wife-man, the word *man*
being formerly applied to both sexes. This
word became *wimman*, pl. *wimmen*, in the
10th century, and this pl. is still in use in
spoken English. In the 12th century, it
became *wumman* (just as A. S. *widu*
became *wudu*, see **Wood**), whence prov.
E. *wumman* [wum·un] ; and finally *woman.*
¶ Cf. *leman* from A. S. *leófman*, *Lammas*
from A. S. *hláfmæsse*; see **Leman,**
Lammas.

Wig; see **Pile** (3).

Wight (1), a person, creature. (E.)
M. E. *wight*, *wiȝt.* A. S. *wiht*, a creature,
animal, person, thing (very common).**+**Du.
wicht, a child; Icel. *vættr*; Dan. *vætte*, an
elf; G. *wicht*, Goth. *waihts*, fem. a wight,
waiht. neut. a whit. **β.** The Teut. type is
WEHTI, i. e. ' something moving,' a moving object indistinctly seen. — A. S. *wegan*,
to move; see **Weigh.**

whit, a thing, particle. (E.) The *h* is
misplaced; *whit* is put for *wiht*, the same
as *wight*, a person, also a thing, bit, whit.—
A. S. *wiht*, a wight, a thing. bit; see above.
Der. *aught* = A. S. *áwiht*, one whit;
whence *n-aught*, *n-ot.*

Wight (2), nimble, strong. (Scand.) In
Spenser, Shep. Kal., March, 91. M. E.
wight, valiant. — Icel. *vígr*, fit for war,
neut. *vígt*, serviceable (accounting for the
final *t*), Swed. *vig*, nimble, *vigt*, adv.,
nimbly. From Icel. *víg* (= A. S. *wíg*),
war. — Icel. *vega*, to fight, smite; cf. Goth.
weigan (pt. t. *waih*), to fight, strive.

Wigwam, an Indian hut. (N. Amer
Indian.) Algonquin (or Massachusetts)
wêk, his house; this word, with possessive
and locative affixes, becomes *wékou-om-ut*,
in his house; whence E. *weekwam* or *wigwam* (Webster).

Wild, Wilderness; see **Will** (1).

Wile, a trick. (E.) M. E. *wile*; A. S. *wil*, *wile*, a wile. + Icel. *vél*, *væl*, an artifice. Cf. Lithuan. *wilti*, to deceive.

guile, a wile. (F. – O. Low G.) O. F. *guile*. From A. S. *wil*, Icel. *vel*, *væl*, a trick, guile (above). **Der.** *be-guile*, vb., with E. prefix *be-* (= *by*).

Wilful; see **Will** (1) below.

Will (1), to desire, be willing. (E.) M. E. *willen*, pt. t. *wolde*; A. S. *willan*, *wyllan*, to wish, be willing; pres. *wyle*, *wile* (2 p. *wilt*), pt. t. *wolde*. + Du. *willen*, Icel. *vilja*, Dan. *ville*, Swed. *vilja*, Goth. *wiljan* (pt. t. *wilda*), G. *wollen* (pres. *will*, pt. t. *wollte*), Lithuan. *weliti*, L. *uelle* (pres. *uolo*), Gk. βούλομαι, I will, wish, Skt. *vri*, to choose. (√WAR.) **Der.** *will-ing*, orig. a pres. part. Also *willy-nilly*, answering both to *will I*, *nill I*, and to *will he*, *nill he*; from A. S. *nillan*, short for *ne willan*, not to wish (= L. *nolle*, not to wish).

bewilder, to perplex. (E.) Made by prefixing E. *be-* (= *by*) to M. E. *wildern*, a wilderness; the sense is 'to lead astray;' see **wilderness** (below).

weal, sb. (E.) M. E. *wele*; A. S. *wela*, weal, prosperity. – A. S. *wel*, adv., well; see **well** (below). + Dan. *vel*, Swed. *väl*, G. *wohl*, welfare.

wealth, riches. (E.) M. E. *welthe*; not in A. S. Extended from M. E. *wele*, prosperity (above). + Du. *weelde*, luxury.

welcome. (Scand.) Put for *well come*. – Icel. *velkominn*, welcome, lit. well come. – Icel. *vel*, well; *kominn*, pp. of *koma*, to come. So also Dan. *velkommen*, Swed. *välkommen*, welcome. ⁋ Distinct from A. S. *wilcuma*, one who comes at another's pleasure; where *cuma* is 'a comer,' from *cuman*, to come.

welfare. (E.) M. E. *welfare*. – M. E. *wel*, well; *fare* = A. S. *faru*, a faring, lit. a journey, from A. S. *faran*, to fare; see **Fare**.

well (1), excellently. (E.) M. E. *wel*; A. S. *wel*, orig. 'agreeably to a wish;' allied to *will*, sb. and vb. + Du. *wel*, Icel. *vel*, Dan. *vel*, Swed. *väl*, Goth. *waila*, G. *wohl*, well.

wild. (E.) M. E. *wilde*; A. S. *wild*, wild, untamed. + Du. *wild*; Icel. *villr*, wild, also astray, bewildered, confused; Dan. Swed. *vild*, G. *wild*, Goth. *wiltheis*. β. The Goth. *wil-theis* is formed with a pp. suffix from *wil-*, base of *wiljan*, to will,

wish, and means 'actuated by will;' so also Icel. *villr*, wandering at will, whence Lowl. Sc. *will*, astray. Cf. W. *gwyllt*, wild, allied to W. *gwyllys*, the will.

wilderness, a waste place. (E.) M. E. *wildernesse*, Layamon, 30335; it stands for *wildern-nesse* *. We also find M. E. *wilderne*, a desert, formed, with adj. suffix *-n* from A. S. *wilder*, a wild animal; so that *wildern* = belonging to wild animals, hence, a waste place. The A. S. *wilder* is short for *wild deór*, a wild animal; see **Deer**. **Der.** *be-wil-der*.

wilful. (E.) M. E. *wilful*; formed with suffix *-ful* from M. E. *wil-le*, will; see **will** (2) below.

will (2), sb., desire. (E.) M. E. *wille*, A. S. *willa*, sb. – A. S. *willan*, to will; see **Will** (1) above. + Du. *wil*, Icel. *vili*, Dan. *villie*, Swed. *vilja*, G. *wille*, Russ. *volia*.

Willow. (E.) M. E. *wilow*, *wilwe*; A. S. *welig*. + Du. *wilg*, Low G. *wilge*.

Wimberry; see **Wine**.

Wimble (1), a gimlet. (Scand.) M. E. *wimbil*. – Dan. *vimmel*, a boring-tool; of which the orig. form was probably *vimpel* * or *wimpel* *, as it seems to be parallel to Dan. *vindel*, as seen in *vindeltrappe*, a spiral staircase. Cf. G. *wendeltreppe*, a spiral staircase, *wendelbohrer*, a wimble or augur. Prob. allied to **Wind** (2). Cf. O. Du. *wemelen*, 'to pearce or bore with a wimble;' Hexham.

gimlet, gimblet. (F. – G.) O. F. *gimbelet* 'a gimlet or pearcer;' Cot. Of M. H. G. origin; formed from a base WIMP, parallel to WIND, to turn or wind; cf. mod. G. *wendel-bohrer*, a wimble (above). Note also Icel. *vindla*, to wind up, *vindill*, a wisp.

Wimble (2), active; see **Whim**.

Wimple, a covering for the neck. (E.) M. E. *wimpel*; A. S. *winpel*, a wimple. + Du. *wimpel*, a streamer, pendant; Icel. *vimpill*, Dan. Swed. *vimpel*, G. *winpel*, a pennon. β. The lit. sense is 'that which binds round,' hence a veil; from Teut. base WIP, to bind round; see **Wisp**.

gimp, a kind of trimming, made of twisted silk, cotton, or wool. (F. – O.H.G.) See Bailey's Dict. vol. ii., ed. 1731. Named from some resemblance to the folds of a wimple. – O. F. *guimpe*, a nun's wimple; also *guimple* (see index to Cotgrave, s. v. *wimple*). – O. H. G. *wimpal*, a light robe; G. *wimpel*, a streamer; see above. ⁋ Prob. confused with F. *guipure*, a thread of silk lace; from the Teut. base WIP, to twist or bind; (wimple being from the same base). Perhaps we may derive gimp directly from the base; but it must still be a F. form, and of O. H. G. origin.

Win, to gain by labour, earn. (E.) M. E. winnen, pt. t. wan, won, pp. wonnen. A. S. winnan, to fight, struggle, try to get, labour, suffer; pt. t. wann, pp. wunnen.+ Du. winnen, Icel. vinna, Dan. vinde, Swed. vinna; G. gewinnen, O. H. G. winan, to fight, strive, earn; Goth. winnan, to suffer. Allied to Skt. van, to beg, ask for, honour; L. uenerari, to honour, uenus, desire. (√ WAN.)

wean, to accustom a child to bread and meat, to reconcile to a new custom. (E.) We also use the word, less properly, in the sense, 'to disaccustom,' because a child that is weaned to meat is also being weaned from the breast. M. E. wenen; A. S. wenian, to accustom; áwenian, to wean away or disaccustom. From a sb. wana*, custom, only found in the cognate Icel. vani, custom, O. H. G. gi-wona, custom. Allied to wont (below). + Du. wennen, to accustom, afwennen, to wean from; Dan. vænne, Swed. vänja, G. gewöhnen, to accustom; Dan. vænne fra, Swed. vänja af, G. entwöhnen, to wean from.

ween, to suppose, think. (E.). M. E. wenen. A. S. wénan, to imagine.—A. S. wén, sb., expectation; orig. 'a striving after.' Allied to Win (above). + Du. wanen, Icel. vána, G. wähnen, Goth. wenjan, to expect, fancy; from Du. waan, Icel. ván, G. wahn, Goth. wens, expectation, conjecture, orig. 'a striving after.'

winsome, pleasant. (E.) A. S. wynsum, delightful; formed with suffix -sum from wyn, joy. Again, wyn is formed (by vowel-change of u to y) from wun-, stem of pp. of winnan, to desire, win.

wont, used, accustomed. (E.) Properly the pp. of won, to dwell, remain, be used to; it came to be used as an adj., and then as a sb.; and, its origin being forgotten, the pp. suffix -ed was again added, producing a form wont-ed = won-ed-ed! Chaucer has woned, i. e. wont, as a pp.; C. T. 8215; Troilus, i. 511. Pp. of M. E. wonien, A. S. wunian, to dwell, be used to. —M. E. wone, A. S. wuna, sb., custom, use, wont.—A. S. wun-, base of pp. of winnan, to strive after; see Win above. Wont is a habit due to continual endeavour. Cf. Icel. vanr, adj., accustomed, vani, a

usage; G. gewohnt, wont, pp. of wohnen, to dwell. Der. wont, sb., put for M. E. wone, usage (by confusion); hence wont, verb, wont-ed, accustomed. And see Wish, Wound.

Winberry; see Wine.

Wince, to flinch; see Wink.

Winch, sb., a crank; see Wink.

Wind (1), air in motion. (E.) M. E. wind; A. S. wind. + Du. wind, Icel. vindr, Dan. Swed. vind, G. wind, Goth. winds. Further cognate with W. gwynt, L. uentus, wind. Orig. a pres. part., with the sense of 'blowing.' From √ WA, to blow; whence also Skt. vá, to blow, vátas, wind, Goth. waian, to blow, Russ. vieiate, to blow, vieter', wind, Lithuan. wêjas, wind. From the same root is E. weather, q.v. Der. wind, to blow a horn, pt. t. and pp. winded, Much Ado, i. 1. 243, often oddly corrupted to wound! Also wind-fall, wind-mill, &c.

window. (Scand.) Orig. sense 'wind-eye,' an eye or hole for the admission of air and light. M. E. windowe, windohe, windoge. — Icel. vindauga, a window; lit. 'wind-eye.' — Icel. vindr, wind; auga, eye; see Eye. ¶ Butler has windore, a corrupted form, as if for wind-door.

winnow. (E.) M. E. windewen, winewen, to winnow. A. S. windwian, to winnow, expose to wind. — A. S. wind, wind. So also L. uentilare, from uentus.

Wind (2), to turn round, twist. (E.) M. E. winden, pt. t. wand, wond, pp. wunden. A. S. windan, pt. t. wand, pp. wunden. + Du. winden, Icel. vinda, Dan. vinde, Swed. vinda (to squint), G. winden, Goth. windan (in bi-windan). From base WAND, to wind or bind.

wand, a slender rod. (Scand.) M. E. wand. — Icel. vöndr (gen. vand-ar), a switch; O. Swed. wand; Dan. vaand. + Goth. wandus, a rod, orig. a pliant stick; from wand, pt. t. of windan, to wind, bind. From the use of wands in wicker-work.

wander, to ramble. (E.) A. S. wandrian, to wander; used as frequentative of wend, to go, but formed from wand, pt. t. of windan, to wind; see wend (below).+ Du. wandelen, G. wandeln.

wend, to go. (E.) Little used except in the pt. t. went (used as pt. t. of to go). M. E. wenden; A S. wendan, to turn, also to turn oneself, proceed, go. The pt. t. wende became wente, and finally went. Causal of A. S. windan, to wind (above).+

Du. *wenden*, Icel. *venda*, Dan. *vende*, Swed. *vända*, Goth. *wandjan*, G. *wenden*, to turn; all causal forms.

went. (E.) See above.

windlass (1), a machine with a turning axis. (Scand.) A corruption (due to confusion with the word below) of M. E. *windas*, a windlass; Chaucer, C. T. 10498, &c. — Icel. *vindáss*, a windlass. — Icel. *vind-a*, to wind; *áss*, a pole, rounded beam. ✠ Du. *windas*, O. Du. *windaes*, a windlass. β. Here O. Du. *aes*, Icel. *áss*, is cognate with Goth. *ans*, a beam (distinct from Du. *as*, O. Du. *asse*, an axis).

windlass (2), a circuit. (Hybrid; E.; and F. — L.) Formerly *windlasse*; Hamlet, ii. 1. 65; &c. Put for *wind-lace*, a winding course; from *wind*, vb., and *lace*, a snare, twisted string, twist, the same word as mod. E. *lace*; see **Lace**.

wonder, sb. (E.) A.S. *wundor*, a portent, wonder. Orig. a thing from which one turns aside in awe; allied to A.S. *wandian*, to turn aside from, to respect, revere, M. E. *wonden*, to conceal through fear, flatter, turn from. — A.S. *wund-en*, pp. of A.S. *windan*, to wind; the verb *wandian* being from the pt. t. *wand*.

wondrous, wonderful. (E.) A corruption of the old word *wonders*, wondrous, orig. an adv., but also an adj. '*Wonders* dere' = wondrously dear; '*wonders* men' = wonderful men. *Wonders* was formed by adding the adv. suffix *-s* (orig. a gen. case) to the M. E. *wonder*, adj., wonderful, Chaucer, C. T. 455. This adj. is short for *wonderly*, adj. = A.S. *wunderlic*, wonderful, the *ly* being dropped because it seemed like an adverbial ending.

Window; see **Wind** (1).

Wine (L.) A. S. *win*, wine; borrowed from L. *uinum*, wine (whence also G. *wein*, &c.). ✠ Gk. *οἶνος*, wine; *οἴνη*, a vine, The Gk. *οἴνη* is from √ WI, to wind, twist, twine (see **Withy**); from the twining growth. Cf. Lith. *apwynys*, hop-tendril, Skt. *nénis*, a braid of hair.

vignette, a small engraving with ornamented border. (F. — L.) First applied to borders in which wine-leaves and tendrils were introduced; XVII cent. — F. *vignette*, a little vine; pl. *vignettes*, 'branchlike flourishes;' Cot. Dimin. of F. *vigne*, a vine; see **vine** (below).

vine. (F. — L.) F. *vigne*. — L. *uinea*, a vineyard; in late L. (apparently) a vine. Fem. of L. *uineus*, adj., from *uinum*, wine

(above). **Der.** *vine-yard*, substituted for A. S. *win-geard*, a vineyard, lit. 'wine-yard.' See **Yard** (1).

vinegar; see under **Acid**.

vintage. (F. — L.) Corruption of M. E. *vindage*, *vendage*; by confusion with *vint-ner*. — F. *vendange*, *vendenge*, a vintage. — L. *uindemia*, a vintage. — L. *uin-um*, wine, grapes; *-demia*, a taking away, from *dēmere*, to take away. *Demere* = *de-imere* *, from *emere*, to take.

vintner. (F. — L.) M. E. *vintener*, altered form of earlier *vineter*, *viniter*. — F. *vinetier*, 'a vintner;' Cot. — Low L. *uinetarius*, a wine-seller. — L. *uinetum*, a vineyard. — L. *uinum*, grapes, wine.

wimberry, winberry (L. and E.) A. S. *winberie*, *winberige*, a grape, lit. a wine-berry. — A.S. *win*, from L. *uinum*, wine, *berige*, a berry; see **Berry**.

Wing. (Scand.) M. E. *winge*, *wenge*. — Icel. *vængr*, a wing; Dan. Swed. *vinge*. Lit. 'wagger' or flapper; nasalised form from the base WIG, as in Goth. *gawigan*, to shake (pt. t. *gawag*). Allied to **Wag**.

Wink, to move the eyelids quickly. (E.) 1. M. E. *winken*, pt. t. *winkede*. — A.S. *wincian*, to wink. 2. But we also find *winken*, strong verb, pt. t. *wank*, *wonk*, shewing that there was also a strong A. S. verb *wincan* * (pt. t. *wanc* *, pp. *gewuncen* *), whence A. S. *wanc-ol*, wavering, and other forms. ✠ O. Du. *wincken*, *wencken*, to wink; *wanck*, sb., a twinkling of an eye, an instant; Icel. *vanka*, to wink; Dan. *vinke*, Swed. *vinka*, to beckon; G. *winken*, to nod. β. All from Teut. base WANK, nasalised from √ WAK, as in L. *uacillare*, to totter, Skt. *vañch*, to go, pass over, of which the causal form means to avoid. Orig. sense 'to move aside.'

wince. (F. — M. H. G.) M. E. *wincen*. — O. F. *wincir* *, necessarily the old form of *guinchir*, to wriggle, writhe aside (Cot.); also spelt *guenchir*, *ganchir*. — M. H. G. *wenken*, to wince, start aside. ═ M. H. G. *wank*, pt. t. of *winken*, to move aside, nod, beckon (above).

winch, the crank of an axle. (E.) M. E. *winche*; prov. E. *wink*; A. S. *wince*, a winch, orig. a bent handle. Cf. A.S. *wincel*, a corner, lit. bend; from the strong verb *wincan* * (above). So also Lithuan. *winge*, a bend or turn of a river or road.

winkle, a kind of shell-fish. (E.) A. S. *wincle*, a winkle. Named from the convoluted shell; allied to *wince*, a winch, orig. a bend, turn (above). See also **Wench.**

Winnow; see **Wind** (1).

Winsome, pleasant; see **Win.**

Winter. (E.) A. S. *winter*, a winter, also a year. + Du. *winter*, Icel. *vetr*, Dan. Swed. *vinter*, G. *winter*, Goth. *wintrus*. Prob. 'wet season,' and allied to **Wet**; cf. Lith. *wandû*, water, Skt. *und*, to wet.

Wipe. (E.) A. S. *wípian*, to wipe; orig. to rub with a wisp of straw. From a sb. *wip* *, only preserved in the Low G. *wiep*, a wisp of straw. Allied to **Wisp.**

Wire. (E.) A. S. *wír*, a wire. + Icel. *vírr*, wire; cf. Swed. *vire*, to twist; O.H.G. *wiara*, an ornament of (twisted) gold; L. *uiriæ*, armlets of metal; Lithuan. *wëla*, iron-wire. Lit. 'a twist;' from √ WI, to wind, twist; see **Withy.** And see **Ferrule.**

Wis; see **Wit** (1).

Wise (1), knowing; see **Wit** (1).

Wise (2), manner, way; see **Wit** (1).

Wiseacre; see **Wit** (1).

Wish, verb. (E.) M. E. *wischen.* A. S. *wýscan*, to wish; formed (by the usual change from *u* to *ý*) from A. S. *wúsc*, sb., a wish (obsolete). β. This A. S. *wúsc* stands for *wunsc* *, cognate with O. Du. *wunsch*, Icel. *ósk*, G. *wunsch*, O. H. G. *wunsc*, a wish; whence are derived Icel. *æskja*, G. *wünschen*, to wish. Allied to Skt. *vânksh*, *vânch*, to wish, a desiderative form from *van*, to ask. Similarly the E. word is a desiderative form from √ WAN, to desire, whence E. *win*; see **Win.** Der. *wish-ful*; and see *wistful.*

Wisp, a small bundle of straw or hay. (E.) M. E. *wisp*, also *wips*, which is the older form; connected with the verb *to wipe.* Allied to Low G. *wiep*, Norweg. *vippa*, a wisp, Swed. dial. *vipp*, a little sheaf or bundle, Goth. *waips*, a crown (orig. a twisted wreath). Lit. 'a rubber;' cf. Dan. *vippe*, to see-saw, go to and fro, Swed. *vippa*, G. *wippen*, to go up and down, see-saw. Named from the vibratory motion in rubbing; see **Vibrate.**

Wist, knew; see **Wit** (1).

Wistful, eager. (E.) The history of the word shews it to be a substitution for *wishful*, 3 Hen. VI, iii. 1. 14; which is from *wish*, sb., with suffix *-ful*. β. But it seems to have been confused with *wistly*, a word used by Shakespeare in place of M. E. *wisly*, certainly, verily, exactly, formerly a common word; see Chaucer,

C. T. 1865, 3992, &c. This M. E. word is from Icel. *viss*, certain (distinct from, yet allied to, *víss*, wise); allied to Icel. *vita*, to know; see **Wit** (1).

Wit (1), to know. (E.) The parts of this verb are often ill understood and wrongly given. M. E. infin. *witen*; pres. t. *I wot*, with 3 p. *he wot* (later *wotteth*), and 2 p. *thou wost* (later *wottest*), pl. *witen*; pt. t. *wiste*, pp. *wist.* A.S. *witan*; pres. t. *ic wát*, *þú wást*, *he wát*, pl. *witon*; pt. t. *wiste*, also *wisse*, pl. *wiston*; pp. *wist.* Gerund *tó witanne* (mod. E. *to wit*). + Du. *weten*, Icel. *vita*, Dan. *vide*, Swed. *veta*, G. *wissen*, Goth. *witan*, to know. Further allied to L. *uidere*, to see, Gk. ἰδεῖν, to see (pt. t. οἶδα = I *wot*, I know), Skt. *vid*, to see. (√ WID.)

bewitch. (E.) M. E. *bewicchen.* = A.S. *be-*, prefix (E. *by*); *wiccian*, to use witchcraft, from *wicce*, a witch; see **witch** (below).

disguise, vb. (F. – L. *and* O. H. G.) O. F. *desguiser*, to disguise. – O. F. *des-* = L. *dis-*, apart; and *guise*, guise (below). Lit. 'to change the guise of.'

guise, way, wise. (F. – O. H. G.) M. E. *gise*, *guise.* – O. F. *guise*, way, wise, manner. – O. H. G. *wísa* (G. *weise*), a wise; cognate with **wise** (2) below.

twit, to remind of a fault. (E.) Shortened from M. E. *atwiten*, to reproach. – A.S. *ætwítan*, to twit, reproach. – A.S. *æt*, at, upon; *wítan*, to blame, orig. to observe, hence to observe what is amiss. β. This A.S. *wítan* answers to Goth. *weitjan*, to observe, allied to Goth. *witan*, to know; see **Wit** (1) above.

weet, to know. (E.) Another spelling of Wit (1) above; used by Spenser, F. Q., i. 3. 6; &c.

wicked. (E.) Orig. a pp., with the sense 'rendered evil,' from the obsolete adj. *wikke*, evil. This adj. answers to A. S. *wicca*, a wizard; see **witch** (below). Thus *wicked* = rendered witch-like.

wise (1), discreet, learned. (E.) A. S. *wís*, wise. + Du. *wijs*, Icel. *víss*, Dan. *viis*, Swed. *vis*, G. *weise*, wise. Clearly allied to A.S. and Goth. *witan*, to know; prob. the orig. form was *witsa* *, whence *wísa* * by loss of *t* and consequent lengthening of *i*; where *wísa* * is the standard Teutonic form. Der. *wis-dom*, A.S. *wís-dóm.*

wise (2), manner, way. (E.) M. E. *wise*; A.S. *wíse*, way. Orig. sense 'wise-ness' or skill; from *wíse*, adj., wise (above). **+** Du. *wijs*, Dan. *viis*, Swed. *vis*, G. *weise*, sb. **Der.** *like-wise* (i. e. in like wise); *other-wise*. **Doublet**, *guise*.

wiseacre. (Du. **–** G.) Borrowed from O. Du. *wijs-segger*, supposed to mean a wise sayer, sooth-sayer. **–** G. *weissager*, supposed to mean wise sayer. β. But the G. word is really a corruption of O. H. G. *wizagô*, a prophet, seer; from O. H. G. *wizan*, to see. The cognate A. S. word is *wîtega*, a prophet, seer; from A. S. *wîtan*, to see. β. The verbs *wizan*, *wîtan*, are cognate with L. *uidere*, to see; and closely allied to A. S. *witan*, to know; see Wit (1) above.

wis; see **ywis** (below).

wit (2), sb., knowledge, &c. (E.) M. E. *wit*; A. S. *wit*, knowledge. **–** A. S. *witan*, to know; see Wit (1). **+** Icel. *vit*, Dan. *vid*, Swed. *vett*, G. *witz*, wit.

witch. (E.) M. E. *wicche*, both masc. and fem., a wizard, a witch; A. S. *wicca*, masc., *wicce*, fem. Here *wicce* is the fem. of *wicca*; and *wicca* is a corruption of *wîtga*, commonly used as a short form of *wîtega*, a prophet, seer, also a magician, sorcerer. **–** A. S. *witan*, to see, allied to *witan*, to know. Similarly Icel. *vitki*, a wizard, is from *vita*, to know. **Der.** *be-witch*, verb (above).

witness, testimony. (E.) Properly an abstract sb. A. S. *witnes*, testimony. **–** A. S. *wit-an*, to know, with suffix *-nes*; thus the orig. sense was 'knowledge' or 'consciousness.' Cf. Icel. *vitna*, Dan. *vidne*, to testify. **Der.** *witness*, vb.

wizard, wisard. (F. **–** Teut.) M. E. *wisard*. **–** O. F. *wischard**, necessarily the orig. form of O. F. *guischard*, *guiscart*, sagacious. **–** Icel. *vizk-r*, clever, sagacious, knowing (where *-r* is merely the suffix of the nom. case); with F. suffix *-ard* **=** G. *hart*, hard, strong, confirmed in (as in numerous other words). β. The Icel. *vizkr* is a contracted form of *vitskr*; from *vit-a*, to know, with suffix *-sk-* (**=** E. *-ish*). Hence *wiz-ard* **=** *witt-ish-ard*.

ywis, certainly. (E.) M. E. *ywis*, *iwis*, adv., certainly. A. S. *gewis*, adj., certain; which came to be used adverbially. Allied to Wit (1) above. **+** Du. *gewis*, adj. and adv., certain, certainly; Icel. Swed. *viss*, Dan. *vis*, certain; Dan. *vist*, Swed. *visst*, certainly; G. *gewiss*, certainly. ¶ The adv. *iwis* is often printed *Iwis* or *I wis*; whence (by confusion of *i* (**=** A. S. *ge-*) with the first personal pronoun), the

supposed verb *wis*, to know, has been evolved; but it is a fiction of editors. Distinct from M. E. *wissen*, to shew, a causal verb.

Witch-elm, Wych-elm; see **Wicker**.

With. (E.) A. S. *wið*, by, near, among; it also means 'against,' as in mod. E. *with-stand*, *with-say*. **+** Icel. *við*, against, by, at; Dan. *ved*, Swed. *vid*, near, by, at. **Der.** *with-al*, from M. E. *with*, with, *alle*, dat. case of *al*, all; *with-in*, A. S. *wiðinnan*; *with-out*, A. S. *wiðûtan*. Hence also *with-draw*, *with-hold*, *with-say*, *with-stand*; and see below.

withers, the ridge between the shoulder-blades of a horse. (E.) So called because it is the part which a horse *opposes* to his load, or on which the stress of the collar comes in drawing. **–** A. S. *wiðer*, against; *wiðre*, resistance; extended from A. S. *wið*, against (above). Cf. G. *widerrist*, withers of a horse; from *wider*, old spelling of *wieder*, against, and *rist*, an elevated part.

Withdraw. (E.) From *with*, i. e. towards oneself; and *draw*. Hence *with-draw-ing-room*, a retiring-room, now oddly contracted to *drawing-room* !

Withe; see **Withy**.

Wither; see **Weather**.

Withers; see **With**.

Withhold. (E.) From *with*, i. e. back, towards oneself; and *hold*.

Within, Without; see **With**.

Withsay, to contradict. (E.) From *with*, in the sense 'against ;' and *say*.

Withstand, to resist. (E.) From *with*, in the sense 'against ;' and *stand*.

Withy, Withe, a flexible twig. (E.) M. E. *wiði*; A. S. *wiðig*, a willow. Named from its flexibility; from √ WI, to twine, plait, as in L. *ui-ere*, Russ. *vite*, to twine. **+** O. Du. *weede*, hop-plant (twiner); Icel. *viðja*, a withy, *við*, a withe, *viðir*, a willow; Dan. *vidie*, Swed. *vide*, willow; G. *weide*, willow. Cf. L. *ui-men*, a twig, *ui-tis*, a vine, *ui-num*, vine (orig. twining plant).

Witness; see **Wit** (1).

Wittol, a cuckold. (E.) Formerly supposed to mean 'wit-all ;' also thought to represent A. S. *witol*, knowing, wise, from *witan*, to know. There is no foundation for this, as the word is not used in the M. E. period. Bp. Hall writes *witwal*; i. e. *wittol* is the same as *witwall*, or *woodwale*, the name of a bird. Florio (ed. 1598) explains

Ital. *godano* by 'the bird called a *witwal* or *woodwall*;' and in a later edition, 'a *wittal* or *woodwale*.' If this be so, we may be sure that allusions were made to the *woodwale* similar to those endless allusions to the *cuckoo* which produced the word *cuckold*. See **Woodwale.**

Wivern; see **Victuals.**

Wizard, Wisard; see **Wit** (1).

Wizen, to shrivel or dry up. (E.) M. E. *wisenen,* to become shrivelled; O. Northumb. *wisnian,* to become dry, John xv. 6; we find also A. S. *for-wisnian,* to dry up. ✛ Icel. *visna,* to wither, formed from the old pp. *visinn,* wizened, occurring also as Dan. and Swed. *vissen.* This is a pp. of a lost strong verb, from a base WIS, to dry up.

Wo, Woe. (E.) M. E. *wo*; A. S. *wá,* interj. and adv.; *weá,* wo, sb. ✛ Du. *vee,* interj. and sb.; Icel. *vei,* Dan. *vee,* Swed. *ve,* G. *weh,* Goth. *wai,* interj.; also Dan. *vee,* G. *weh,* sb. Allied to L. *uæ,* wo! Orig. an exclamation; hence a cry of pain, &c. Der. *wo-begone,* i.e. wo-surrounded, from M. E. *begon,* pp. of *begon* = A. S. *begán,* to surround, lit. to go round about; from A. S. *be-* (= E. *by*), and *gán,* to go. Also *wo worth,* i. e. wo be to; see **Worth.**

bewail. (E. *and* Scand.) M. E. *biwailen, bewailen.* From the prefix *be-, bi-* (A. S. *bi-*), and M. E. *wailen,* to wail; see **wail** (below).

wellaway, an exclamation of sorrow. (E.) M. E. *weilawey*; also *wa la wa.* It stands for *wei la wei* or *wa la wa.* A. S. *wá lá wá,* lit. wo! lo! wo!—A. S. *wá,* wo; *lá,* lo; *wá,* wo. ¶ Early misunderstood, and turned into *wellaway,* and even into *welladay,* Merry Wives, iii. 3. 106.

wail, to lament. (Scand.) M. E. *weilen.* —Icel. *væla* (formerly *wæla*), to wail; also spelt *vála, vola.* Lit. 'to cry wo;' from *væ, vei,* interj., wo! See **Wo** (above).

Woad, a plant, used for dyeing. (E.) M. E. *wod, wood.* A. S. *wád, waad,* woad. ✛ Du. *weede,* Dan. *vaid, veid,* Swed. *veide,* G. *waid,* M. H. G. *weit* (whence O. F. *waide,* mod. F. *guède*). Allied to L. *uitrum,* woad. ¶ Distinct from *weld* (2).

Wold, a down, plain open country. (E.) M. E. *wold, wald.* A. S. *weald, wald,* a wood, forest (hence waste ground, and finally open country, as in Icelandic). ✛ O. Sax. and O. Fries. *wald,* a wood; G. *wald*; O. H. G. *walt,* a wood; Icel. *völlr,*

gen. *vallar* (= *valdar* *), a field, plain. The same as **Weald.**

Wolf. (E.) M. E. *wolf,* pl. *wolues* (= *wolves*). A. S. *wulf,* pl. *wulfas.* ✛ Du. G. *wolf,* Icel. *úlfr,* Dan. *ulv,* Swed. *ulf,* Goth. *wulfs.* Futher allied to Lith. *wilkas,* Russ. *volk',* Gk. λύκος, L. *lupus,* Skt. *vrika,* a wolf. Orig. form WALKA, i. e. 'tearer;' from √ WARK, to tear; cf. Skt. *vraçch,* to tear, Lith. *wilkti,* to pull. Der. *wolv-er-ene,* a coined word.

Woman. (E.) See **Wife.**

Womb. (E.) Lowl. Sc. *wame,* the belly. M. E. *wombe, wambe.* A. S. *wamb, womb,* the belly.✛Du. *wam,* belly of a fish; Icel. *vömb,* Dan. *vom,* Swed. *vámb, vámm,* G. *wampe, wamme,* Goth. *wamba,* the belly.

Wombat, a marsupial mammal. (Australian.) A corruption of *womback* or *wombach,* the native Australian name. (Collins, New South Wales, 1802; Bewick, Quadrupeds.)

Won, to dwell, remain. (E.) M. E. *wonen,* A. S. *wunian,* to dwell; see **wont,** under **Win.**

Wonder, Wondrous; see **Wind** (2).

Wont; see **Win.**

Woo, to court. (E.) M. E. *woʒen, wowen.* A. S. *wógian,* to woo; lit. to incline, bend towards oneself.—A. S. *wóg-,* stem of *wóh,* bent, crooked. Allied to Goth. *wahs,* bent (in *un-wahs,* unbent); Skt. *vakra,* crooked. (√ WAK.)

Wood (1), timber, forest. (E.) M. E. *wode.* A. S. *wudu,* of which the orig. form was *widu,* wood.✛Icel. *viðr,* a tree, wood; Dan. Swed. *ved*; O. H. G. *witu.* Cf. Irish *fiodh,* a wood, tree; W. *gwydd,* trees. Perhaps allied to **Withy.** Der. *wood-en, -y, -ed.*

woodruff, a plant. (E.) M. E. *wodruffe.* A. S. *wuderofe, wudurofe,* woodruff. Perhaps named from the *ruff* or whorl of leaves round the stem.

woodwale, a bird. (E.) Also called *witwall, wittal.* M. E. *wodewale,* perhaps a woodpecker. From A. S. *wudu,* a wood; the form *wittwall* being due to A. S. *widu,* older form of *wudu.* The sense of *-wale* is not known. ✛ O. Du. *weduwael,* a kind of yellow bird; M. H. G. *witewal,* an oriole. (Cf. **Wittol.**)

Wood (2), mad, furious. (E.) In Mids. Nt. Dr. ii. 1. 192. M. E. *wod.* A. S. *wód,* mad, raging. ✛ Icel. *óðr,* Goth. *wods,* frantic. Cf. G. *wuth,* madness. Perhaps allied to L. *uates*, a prophet, one filled with divine frenzy. Hence the name *Woden*; see **Wednesday**.

Woodruff, Woodwale; see **Wood**(1).

Woof; see **Weave**.

Wool. (E.) M. E. *wolle.* A. S. *wull, wul.*+Du. *wol*, Icel. *ull*, Dan. *uld*, Swed. *ull*, G. *wolle*, Goth. *wulla*, wool. Allied to Lith. *wilna*, Russ. *volna*, Skt. *úrná*, wool; L. *uellus*, fleece. Lit. ' covering,' hence a fleece; the Skt. *úrná* being derived from *vri*, to cover. (√WAR.)

woolward, clothed in wool only, for penance. (E.) See L. L. L. v. 2. 717. M. E. *wolleward*, lit. with the skin towards (against) the wool. From *wool* and *-ward*, suffix. See **Toward**.

Word. (E.) A. S. *word.*+Du. *woord*, Icel. *orð*, Dan. Swed. *ord*, G. *wort*, Goth. *waurd*; Lith. *wardas*, a name; L. *uerbum* (base *uardh*), a word. Lit. 'a thing spoken;' from √WAR, to speak; cf. Gk. εἴρειν, to speak. **Doublet**, *verb*.

Work, sb. (E.) M. E. *werk.* A. S. *weorc, werc.*+Du. *werk*, Icel. *verk*, Dan. *vark*, Swed. *verk*, G. *werk*. Further allied to Gk. ἔργον, work, ἔοργα, I have wrought, Zend. *vareza*, a working, Pers. *warz*, gain. (√WARG.) **Der.** *work*, verb, A. S. *wyrcan* (by vowel-change from *eo* to *y*).

wright, a workman. (E.) M. E. *wrighte.* A. S. *wyrhta*, a worker.—A. S. *wyrht*, a deed, work; formed with suffix *-t* from *wyrcan*, to work. — A. S. *weorc*, work, sb. (as above). **Der.** *cart-wright, ship-wright, wheel-wright.*

World. (E.) M. E. *werld.* A. S. *weoruld, weorold.*+Du. *wereld*, Icel. *veröld*, Dan. *verden* (where *-en* is the article), Swed. *verld*, G. *welt*, M. H. G. *werlt*, O. H. G. *weralt.* β. The lit. sense is 'age of man' or 'course of man's life,' hence a life-time, course of life, experience of life, &c. The component parts are A. S. *wer* (Icel. *verr*, O. H. G. *wer*, Goth. *wair*), a man; and A. S. *yldo* (Icel. *öld*, an age; see **Virile** and **eld** (under **Old**).

Worm. (E.) M. E. *worm.* A. S. *wyrm*, a worm, snake.+Du. *worm*, Icel. *ormr*, Dan. Swed. *orm*, G. *wurm*, Goth. *waurms*; also L. *uermis*, a worm. Prob. allied also to Skt. *krimi*, Lith. *kirmis*, a worm, Irish *cruimh*, a maggot; also to E. *vermin*, *carmine* and *crimson.* See Curtius, ii. 173.

Wormwood, a bitter plant. (E.) A corrupted form, the word having no real reference either to *worm* or to *wood.*

M. E. *wermode*, later *wormwod.* A. S. *wermód.*+Du. *wermoet*, G. *wermuth.* β. The lit. sense is *ware-mood*, i. e. preserver of the mind, from a supposed belief in its virtues; just as hellebore was called *wédeberge*, i. e. preservative against madness. From A. S. *wer-ian*, to defend; *mód*, mood, mind. See **Wary** and **Mood** (1).

Worry, to harass. (E.). M. E. *wirien, worowen*, orig. to strangle, and used of the worrying of sheep by dogs or wolves. A. S. *wyrgan*, only in comp. *áwyrgan*, to harm. + Du. *worgen*, O. Fries. *wergia*, *wirgia*, G. *würgen*, to strangle, suffocate. Allied to A. S. *wyrigan*, to curse, M. E. *warien.* β. Formed (by change of *ea* to *y*) from the sb. appearing in A. S. *wearg*, an outlaw, a wolf, Icel. *vargr*, an outlaw, a wolf, an accursed person. Allied to M. H. G. *wergen*, in comp. *irwergen* (= *erwergen*), a strong verb, to choke, throttle, strangle. (√WARGH, to choke.)

Worse, comparative adj. and adv., more bad. (E.) M. E. *wurs, wers*, adv., *wurse, werse*, adj.; A. S. *wyrs*, adv., *wyrsa*, adj., worse.+ O. Sax. *wirs*, adv., *wirsa*, adj.; Icel. *verr*, adv., *verri*, adj.; Dan. *værre*, Swed. *värre*, adj.; M. H. G. *wirs*, adv., *wirser*, adj.; Goth. *wairs*, adv., *wairsiza*, adj. β. The common Teut. type is WERS-ISA, where -ISA is the comparative suffix, and the base is WARS, to twist, entangle, confuse; cf. O. H. G. *werran*, G. *wirren*, to twist, entangle; see **War**. *Worse* does duty for *wors-er*, and *worst* for *wors-est.* **Der.** *worse*, sb., *wors-en*, vb.

worst, superlative. (E.) A.S. *wyrst*, adv., *wyrsta*, contracted form of *wyrsesta*, adj., which also occurs as *wyrresta*, Matt. xii. 45.+O. Sax. *wirsista*, adj.; Icel. *verst*, adv., *verstr*, adj.; Dan. *værst*, Swed. *värst*, O. H. G. *wirsist.*

Worship; see **Worth** (1).

Worst; see **Worse**.

Worsted, twisted yarn. (E.) M. E. *worsted*, Chaucer, C. T. 264. Named from the town of *Worsted*, in Norfolk. *Worsted* stands for *Worth-stead*; from *Worth*, an estate, and *stead*, a place.

Wort (1), a plant. (E.) M. E. *wort.* A.S. *wyrt*, a wort, plant, herb. + O. Sax. *wurt*, Icel. *urt, jurt*, Dan. *urt*, Swed. *ört*, G. *wurz*, Goth. *waurts*. Allied to L. *radix*, Gk. ῥίζα (= Ϝρίδ-ya), W. *gwreiddyn*, a root.

orchard. (E.) M. E. *orchard.* A. S.

orceard, older forms *ortgeard, wyrtgeard,* i. e. wort-yard; compounded of *wort* and *yard,* i. e. a herb-garden, which is the old sense. **+** Dan. *urtgaard,* Swed. *örtegård,* Goth. *aurtigards,* a garden, similarly compounded. See **yard** (1).

root (1), lowest part of a plant. (Scand.) M. E: *rote.* **—** Icel. *rót,* Swed. *rot,* Dan. *rod,* a root. Put for *vrót* = vórt*,* and allied to Goth. *waurts,* a root, A. S. *wyrt,* a wort, a root; the initial *v* being dropped, as is usual in Icelandic in the combination *vr.* See below.

root (2), **rout,** vb., to grub up, as a hog. (E.) A. S. *wrótan,* to grub up; whence prov. E. *wrout,* the same. **+** O. Du. *wroeten,* the same; Icel. *róta,* to grub up, from *rót,* sb., a root. From the sb. above. So also Dan. *rode,* to root up, from *rod,* a root.

wort (2), an infusion of malt, new beer. (E.) M. E. *wort* or *worte.* A. S. *wyrte,* in the compound *max-wyrte,* lit. mash-wort, an infusion of worts. **—** A. S. *wyrt,* a wort; see **Wort** (1).**+**Icel. *virtr,* Norweg. *vyrt, vört,* Swed. *vört,* G. *bier-würze,* beer-wort.

Wort (2); see above.

Worth (1), adj., deserving of; sb., desert, value. (E.) M. E. *wurth, worth.* A. S. *weorð, wurð,* adj., honourable; sb., value. **+** Du. *waard,* adj., *waarde,* sb.; Icel. *verðr,* adj., *verð,* sb.; Dan. *værd,* adj. and sb.; Swed. *värd,* adj., *värde,* sb.; G. *werth,* adj. and sb.; Goth. *wairths,* adj. and sb. β. Teut. type WERTHA, adj., valuable : from √WAR, to guard, keep. Allied to **Ware** (1) and **Wary.** Der. *worth-y,* adj., suggested by Icel. *verðugr,* worthy; *worth-less.*

worship, sb. (E.) Short for *worthship.* A. S. *weorðscipe, wyrðscipe,* honour. **—** A. S. *weorð, wyrð,* adj., honourable; with suffix *-scipe* (E. *-ship*), allied to E. *shape.* Der. *worship,* verb.

Worth (2), to become, to be, to befall. (E.) In phr. *wo worth the day* = wo be to the day. M. E. *worthen,* to become. A. S. *weorðan,* to become, pt. t. *wearð,* pl. *wurdon.* **+** Du. *worden,* pt. t. *werd;* Icel. *verða,* pt. t. *varð;* Dan. *vorde;* Swed. *varda;* G. *werden;* Goth. *wairthan,* to become, pt. t. *warth.* β. All from Teut. base WARTH, to become = √ WART, to turn; cf. L. *uertere,* to turn, *uerti,* to turn to, become. See **Verse.**

weird, fate, destiny. (E.) Properly a

sb.; also used as adj. M. E. *wirde, wyrde.* A. S. *wyrd, wird,* fate, destiny, one of the Fates; lit. 'that which happens.' **—** A. S. *wurd-on,* pt. t. pl. of *weorðan,* to become, take place, happen (above). **+** Icel. *urðr,* fate; from *urð-,* stem of pt. t. pl. of *verða.*

Wot, I know, or he knows; see **Wit** (1).

Would; see **Will** (1).

Wound, a hurt. (E.) A. S. *wund.* **+** Du. *wond, wonde,* Icel. *und,* Dan. *vunde,* G. *wunde,* sb. We also find G. *wund,* Goth. *wunds,* wounded, harmed; from the pp. of the strong verb which appears as A. S. *winnan* (pp. *wunnen*), to fight, struggle, win. See **Win.** (√ WAN.) Der. *wound,* verb, A. S. *wundian.*

Wrack, sea-weed, ruin; see **Wreak.**

Wraith, an apparition. (Scand.) Lowl. Sc. *wraith,* Ayrshire *warth,* the supposed apparition of one's guardian angel : see Jamieson. **—** Icel. *vörðr* (gen. *varðar*), a guardian. **—** Icel. *varða,* to guard ; see **Ward.** Cf. Icel. *varða, varði,* a beacon, a pile of stones to warn a way-farer, Norweg. *varde,* a beacon, *vardyvle* (= ward-evil ?), a guardian or attendant spirit, or wraith.

Wrangle; see **Wring.**

Wrap, to enfold. (E.) M. E. *wrappen;* also spelt *wlappen,* whence **Lap** (3). Prov. E. *warp,* to wrap up, also to weave ; clearly a derivative of **Warp.** Perhaps due to the folding together of a fishing-net ; cf. Icel. *varp,* the cast of a net, *varpa,* a cast, also the net itself, *skóvarp,* the binding of a shoe, lit. 'shoe-warp.' **Doublet,** *lap* (3). Cf. *en-velop, de-velop.*

Wrath; see **Writhe.**

Wreak, to revenge. (E.) M. E. *wreken.* A. S. *wrecan,* pt. *wræc,* pp. *wrecen,* to wreak, revenge, punish, orig. to drive, urge, impel.**+**Du. *wreken;* Icel. *reka,* pt. t. *rak,* to drive, thrust, repel, wreak ; G. *rächen,* to avenge ; Goth. *wrikan,* to persecute. β. Allied to Lith. *wargti,* to suffer affliction, Russ. *vrag',* a foe, persecutor ; and to **Urge** and **Verge** (2). (√ WARG.)

rack (2), light vapoury clouds, mist. (Scand.) See Hamlet, ii. 2. 506 ; Antony, iv. 14. 10. M. E. *rak.* **—** Icel. *rek,* drift, motion, a thing drifted ; cf. *skýrek,* the rack or drifting clouds. **—** Icel. *reka,* to drive, thrust, toss (above). Cf. Swed. *skippet vräker* = the ship drifts.

rack (4), the same as *wrack;* in the phr. 'to go to *rack* and *ruin*;' see **wrack** (below).

wrack, a kind of sea-weed; shipwreck, ruin. (E.) Lit. 'that which is cast ashore;' well shewn by mod. F. *varech*, (1) sea-weed cast ashore, (2) pieces of a wrecked ship cast ashore; this F. word being borrowed from English. M.E. *wrak*, a wreck; a peculiar use of A.S. *wræc*, exile, expulsion. — A.S. *wræc*, pt. t. of *wrecan*, to drive, urge, wreak; see **Wreak** (above). + Du. *wrak*, sb., a wreck. adj., broken; Icel. *rek*, anything drifted ashore; Dan. *vrag*, Swed. *vrak*, wreck, trash. Cf. Du. *wraken*, Dan. *vrage*, to reject.

wrack, ruin, remains of what is wrecked. (E.) Formerly *wrack*; the same as **wrack** (above).

wretch, a miserable creature. (E.) Lit. 'outcast.' M.E. *wrecche*. A.S. *wrecca*, an outcast, an exile. — A.S. *wræc*, pt. t. of *wrecan*, to drive, urge, hence to exile; see **Wreak** (above). Cf. Lithuan. *wargas*, misery. Der. *wretch-ed*, i.e. made like a wretch.

Wreath; see **Writhe**.

Wren, a small bird. (E.) M.E. *wrenne*. A.S. *wrenna*, *wrænna*, a wren; lit. 'lascivious bird.' — A.S. *wræne*, lascivious. Allied to Dan. *vrinsk*, proud, Swed. *vrensk*, not castrated (said of horses), M.H.G. *reinno*, *wrenno*, a stallion. β. All from a base WRIN, to neigh (as a horse), squeal (as a pig); hence, to chirp (as a sparrow); cf. Norweg. *rina*, to whine, squeal, Icel. *hrína* (pt. t. *hrein*), to whine, squeal, &c., applied to cocks, dogs, swine, horses, &c. Hence Icel. *rindill*, a wren.

Wrench; see **Wring**.

Wrest, **Wrestle**; see **Writhe**.

Wretch; see **Wreak**.

Wretchlessness, the same as *recklessness*; see **Reck**.

Wriggle; see **Wring**.

Wright; see **Work**.

Wring, to twist. (E.) M.E. *wringen*. A.S. *wringan*, pt. t. *wrang*, pp. *wrungen*, to press, compress, strain, wring. + Du. *wringen*; G. *ringen* (pt. t. *rang*), to wrestle, to wring, turn. Allied to **Wry** and **Wreak**; cf. L. *uergere*, to bend, Skt. *vrij*, to bend.

rickets, a disease of children, accompanied by softness of the bones and great weakness. (E.) A prov. E. word first noticed about A.D. 1620; whence the medical term *rachitis* was coined about 1650, with a punning allusion to Gk. ῥάχις, the spine. Cf. prov. E. *rickety*, i.e. tottery,

weak, unstable. Formed from M.E. *wrikken*, to twist, wrest, still in use in the phrase 'to wrick one's ancle.' Allied to A.S. *wringan*, to twist (above); and see **Wry** (below). Cf. Du. *wrikken*, to be rickety.

rig (2), a frolic, prank. (E.?) We also find *rig*, to be wanton; *riggish*, wanton. Put for *wrig*, and allied to *wriggle*; see **Wriggle** (below). Cf. Du. *wrikken*, to stir to and fro, *wriggelen*, to wriggle; and see **rickets** (above). '

wrangle, verb. (E.) M.E. *wranglen*, to wrestle, also to dispute. Frequentative of *wring*, formed from the A.S. pt. t. *wrang*; see **Wring** (above). Thus the sense was to keep on twisting or urging; hence to wrestle or argue vehemently. Cf. Dan. *vringle*, to twist, entangle. Der. *wrangle*, sb.; *wrangl-er*, a disputant in the schools (at Cambridge), now applied to a first-class-man in the mathematical tripos.

wrench, a twist, sprain. (E.) M.E. *wrenche*, only in the metaphorical sense of perversion, deceit. A.S. *wrence*, *wrenc*, guile, fraud, orig. crookedness or perversion, lit. 'a twist.' Allied to A.S. *wringan*, to wring, twist; see **wrinkle** (below). Der. *wrench*, verb.

wriggle, vb. (E.) Frequentative of *wrig*, to move about, Skelton, Elinour Rumming, 176; which is a weakened form of M.E. *wrikken*, to twist; we actually find A.S. *wrigian*, but this passed into the form *wry*. + Du. *wriggelen*, to wriggle, frequent. of *wrikken*, to move or stir to and fro; Dan. *vrikke*, to wriggle, Swed. *vricka*, to turn to and fro. See **rickets** (above), and **wry** (below).

wrinkle (1), a small ridge or unevenness on a surface. (E.) M.E. *wrinkel*. Evidently allied to A.S. *wringan*, to twist. The lit. sense is 'a little twist,' causing unevenness. + O Du. *winckel*, a wrinkle, allied to *wringen*, to twist; Dan. *rynke*, Swed. *rynka*, a wrinkle, forms due to the pp. of an old strong verb. Der. *wrinkle*, vb.

wrinkle (2), a hint. (E.) Lit. 'a small trick;' dimin. of A.S. *wrenc*, a trick; see **wrench** (above).

wrong, perverted, bad. (E.) M.E. *wrong*. A.S. *wrang*, a wrong, sb.; orig. an adj. — A.S. *wrang*, pt. t. of *wringan*, to wring, wrest, pervert. + Du. *wrang*, acid, sour (because acids *wring* the mouth); Icel. *rangr*, awry, wrong; Dan. *vrang*,

Swed. *vrång*, perverse. **Der.** *wrong*, verb.

wry, twisted, turned aside. (E.) From the M. E. *wrien*, verb, to twist, bend aside; A. S. *wrigian*, to drive, impel, incline towards. Cf. Goth. *wraikws*, crooked, Skt. *vrij*, to bend. See **wriggle** (above). **Der.** *a-wry*, put for *on wry*, Barbour, Bruce, 4. 705.

Wrinkle, (1) and (2); see **Wring**.

Wrist; see **Writhe**.

Write. (E.) The orig. sense was 'to score,' i. e. to scratch the surface of wood with a knife. M. E. *writen*, pt. t. *wroot*, pp. *writen* (with short *i*). A. S. *writan*, pt. t. *wrát*, pp. *writen*.+O. Sax. *writan*, to cut, write; Du. *rijten*, to tear; Icel. *ríta*, to scratch, write; Swed. *rita*, to draw; G. *reissen*, to cut, tear. Allied to Skt. *vardh*, to cut, *vrana*, a wound, *vraçch*, to tear. (√WAR, to tear.) **Der.** *writ*, sb., A. S. *gewrit*, from the pp. *writen*.

Writhe. (E.) M. E. *writhen*, pt. t. *wroth*, pp. *writhen* (with short *i*). A. S. *wríðan*, pt. t. *wráð*, pp. *wriðen*, to twist about.+Icel. *ríða*, Dan. *vride*, Swed. *vrida*, to wring, twist, turn. Cf. Lat. *uertere*, to turn. (√WART, to turn.)

wrath, anger. (E.) M. E. *wraththe*. O. Northumb. *wræððo*. – A. S. *wráð*, adj., wroth; see **wroth** (below).+Icel. *reiði*, Dan. Swed. *vrede*, sb., wrath; from Icel. *reiðr*, Dan. Swed. *vred*, adj., wroth.

wreath, a garland. (E.) M. E. *wrethe*. A. S. *wræð*, a twisted band, bandage, fillet. Formed (with vowel-change of *á* to *æ*) from *wráð*, pt. t. of *wríðan*, to writhe, twist. **Der.** *wreathe*, verb.

wrest, to distort. (E.) M. E. *wresten*. A. S. *wræstan*, to twist forcibly. From *wræst*, adj., firm, strong (orig. tightly strung or twisted); which stands for *wræðst**, formed with the suffix *-st* (as in *bla-st*) and vowel-change of *á* to *æ*, from *wráð*, pt. t. of *wríðan*, to twist. Cf. Icel. *reista*, to wrest, Dan. *vriste*, to wrest.

wrestle. (E.) M. E. *wrestlen*. A. S. *wræstlian*, to wrestle; frequentative of *wræstan*, to wrest, twist about; see above. +O. Du. *wrastelen*, *worstelen*, to struggle, wrestle.

wrist. (E.) M. E. *wrist*, *wirst*. A. S. *wrist*, also called *handwrist*, i. e. that which turns the hand about. Put for *wrið-st**, and formed (like *wrest*) with suffix *-st* from *wrið-en*, pp. of *wríðan*, to writhe, twist about.+Low G. *wrist*; Icel. *rist*, instep, from *rið-inn*, pp. of *ríða*, to twist; Dan. Swed. *vrist*, instep, from *vride* or *vrida*, to twist; G. *rist*, instep, wrist.

wroth, angry. (E.) A.S. *wráð*; from *wráð*, pt. t. of *wríðan*, to writhe.

Wrong, Wry; see **Wring**.

Wych-elm; see **Wicker**.

Wyvern, Wivern; see **Victuals**.

X.

Xebec, a small three-masted vessel. (Span. – Turk.) Span. *xabeque*. – Turk. *sumbaki*, a kind of ship. Cf. Pers. *sumbuk*, Arab. *sumbúk*, a small boat, a pinnace. (Devic.)

Y.

Y- prefix. (E.) In *y-clept*, *y-wis*. M. E. *y-, i-*; A. S. *ge-*, a common prefix. This prefix appears as *e-* in *e-nough*, and as *a-* in *a-ware*. + Du. G. *ge-*, prefix; Goth. *ga-*, prefix. Cf. Gk. *-γέ*, enclitic, Skt. *ha*, an emphatic particle.

Yacht. (Du.) Du. *jagt*, O. Du. *jacht*, a swift boat. Cf. Du. *jagten*, O. Du. *jachten*, to speed, hunt; *jacht*, a hunting. – Du. *jagen*, to hunt, chase.+G. *jagen*, to hunt. Perhaps allied to G. *jähe*, quick, and to **Gay** and **Go**.

Yam, a large esculent tuber. (Port.) Port. *inhame*, a yam (Littré). Remoter origin unknown; but not European.

Yankee, a citizen of New England, or of the United States. (Scand. ?) In use in Boston, 1765. Dr. Wm. Gordon, in his Hist. of the American War, ed. 1789, vol. i. pp. 324, 325, says it was a favourite cant word in Cambridge, Mass., as early as 1713, and that it meant 'excellent,' as 'a *yankee* good horse.' The word may have spread from the students through New England, and have thence obtained a wider currency. It appears to be the same as Lowl. Sc. *yankie*, a sharp, clever, forward woman; cf. Lowl. Sc. *yanker*, an agile girl, an incessant talker, a smart stroke, *yank*, a jerk, smart blow, *yanking*, active (Jamieson). We also find *yank*, to jerk, noted by Buckland (Log of a Naturalist, 1876, p. 130) as an American word. β. Thus *yank-y* is quick, spry, from *yank*, to jerk; and *yank* is a nasalised form of Lowl. Sc. *yack*, to talk fast, *yaike*, a blow. Of Scand. origin; cf. Swed. dial. *jakka*, to rove about, Swed. *jaga*, to hunt, Icel. *jaga*, to move about. So also Du. G. *jagen*, to hunt. See Yacht.

Yap; see Yelp.

Yard (1), an enclosed space. (E.) M.E. *yerd*. A.S. *geard*, an enclosure, court.+ Icel. *garðr* (whence E. *garth*), Dan. Du. *gaard*, Swed. *gård*, G. *garten*, a garden; Russ. *gorod'*, a town; L. *hortus*, a garden; Gk. χόρτος, a court-yard. β. The Aryan form is GHARTA, lit. 'a place surrounded or enclosed.' (√GHAR, to seize, enclose.) Allied to Gird (1). Doublets, *garden, garth*. Der. *court-yard, orchard* (= *wort-yard*).

Yard (2), a rod, 36 inches, cross-bar on a mast. (E.) M.E. *ȝerde, yerde*, a stick, rod. A.S. *gyrd, gierd*, a rod.+Du. *garde*, a twig, rod, G. *gerte*, a switch. Allied to O.H.G. *gart*, Icel. *gaddr*, Goth. *gazds*, a goad.

gird (2), to jest at, jibe. (E.) A peculiar use of M.E. *girden*, to strike with a rod, to pierce. From M.E. *gerde, yerde*, a rod; see yard (above). To *gird at* = to strike at, jest at; a *gird* is a cut, sarcasm; Tam. Shrew, v. 2. 48.

gride, to pierce, cut through. (E.) See Spenser, F.Q. ii. 8. 36. A metathesis of *gird*, M.E. *girden*, to strike, pierce; see gird (2) above.

jerk. (E.) Formerly 'to lash.' Cotgrave explains F. *fouetter* by 'to scourge, lash, *yerk*, or *jerke*.' We also find *jert*, with the sense of *gird* or taunt. Cotgrave explains *attainte* by 'a gentle nip, quip, or *jert*, a sleight *gird*.' The words *jerk, jert, gird* appear to be all connected; see gird (2) above.

Yare, ready. (E.) M.E. *ȝare, yare*, ready. A.S. *gearu, gearo*, ready, quick, prompt.+Du. *gaar*, done, dressed (as meat); Icel. *gerr*, perfect; O.H.G. *garo*, ready; cf. G. *gar*, adv., wholly. Allied to Gear.

yarrow, the plant milfoil. (E.) M.E. *yarowe, yarwe*. A.S. *gæruwe, gearuwe, gearwe*, yarrow. Lit. 'that which dresses,' or puts in order, or cures; from the old belief in its curative properties as a healer of wounds. — A.S. *gearwian*, to make ready (hence, to heal). — A.S. *gearu*, ready

(above). So also G. *garbe*, yarrow; cf. G. *gerben*, to dress leather.

Yarn. (E.) M.E. *yarn*. A.S. *gearn*, thread.+Du. *garen*, Icel. Dan. Swed. G. *garn*. Allied to Gk. χορδή, a cord, orig. a string of gut; cf. Icel. *garnir*, guts. See Cord, Chord.

Yarrow; see Yare.

Yaw, to go unsteadily, as a ship. (Scand.) Norw. *gaga*, to bend backwards, esp. used of the neck of a bird; *gag*, adj., bent back, said of a knife not set straight in the haft; Icel. *gagr*, bent back. Cf. Bavarian *gagen*, to move unsteadily. Perhaps allied to Go; it seems to be a reduplicated form.

Yawl (1), a small boat. (Du.) Du. *jol*, a yawl, a Jutland boat.+Dan. *jolle*, Swed. *julle*, a yawl. Root unknown.

jolly-boat. (Scand. and E.) Here *jolly* is a mere E. adaptation of Dan. *jolle*, a yawl (above); the addition of *boat* is needless.

Yawl (2), to howl; see Yell.

Yawn, to gape. (E.) Formerly *yane*. M.E. *ganien*, also *gonen*. A.S. *gánian*, to yawn. — A.S. *gán*, pt. t. of *ginan*, strong verb, to gape widely.+Icel. *gina*, to gape, pt. t. *gein*; cf. Gk. χαίνειν, to gape. Allied to L. *hiare*, to gape, Gk. χάος, a yawning gulf; see Hiatus and Chaos. (√GHI.)

Ye. (E.) M.E. *ye, ȝe*, nom.; *your, ȝour*, gen.; *you, ȝou, yow*, dat. and acc. pl. A.S. *ge*, nom. ye; *eówer*, gen. of you; *eów*, to you, you, dat. and acc.+ Du. *gij*, ye, *u*, you; Icel. *ér, ier*, ye, *yðar*, your, *yðr*, you; Dan. Swed. *i*, ye, you; G. *ihr*; Goth. *jus*, ye, *izwara*, your, *izwis*, you. β. The common Aryan base is VU; whence Lith. *jus*, ye; Gk. ὑ-μεῖς, ye, Skt. *yú-yam*, ye.

you. (E.) Properly the dat. and acc. of *ye*; see above.

your. (E.) M.E. *your*. A.S. *eówer*, your; orig. gen. pl. of *ge*, ye; see Ye (above). Der. *your-s*, M.E. *youres*, from A.S. *eówres*, gen. sing. masc. and neut. of *eówer*, your, possessive pronoun.

Yea, verily. (E.) This is the simple affirmative; *yes* is a strengthened form, often accompanied by an oath in our early writers. M.E. *ye*. A.S. *ge*, yea.+Du. Dan. Swed. G. *ja*, Icel. *já*, Goth. *ja, jai*. Allied to Goth. *jah*, A.S. *ge*, also, and; and to Skt. *ya*, Gk. ὅς, who, which were originally demonstrative pronouns. The orig. sense was 'in that way,' just so.

yes. (E.) A strengthened form of *yea*.
M. E. *yis, yus.* A. S. *gise, gese,* yes.
Prob. short for *geá sý,* i. e. yea, let it be
so; where *ged,* yea, is explained above, and
sý, let it be, is the imperative form from
the √AS, to be.

Yean, Ean, to bring forth young. (E.)
Here the prefixed *y-* answers to the A. S.
prefix *ge-.* A. S. *eánian,* to ean; *ge-eánian,*
to yean. We find *ge-eáne eówa* = the ewes
great with young, Gen. xxxiii. 13. There
can be little doubt that *ge-eáne* is here put
for *ge-eácne* *, i. e. pregnant; where *eácne*
is pl. of *eácen,* pregnant, lit. increased.
Allied to **Eke** (1). Thus to *yean* simply
means 'to be pregnant.' Der. *yean-ling,*
a new-born lamb.

Year. (E.) M. E. *ȝeer, yeer,* often
unaltered in the plural (hence ' a *two-year*
old colt'). A. S. *geár, gér,* a year, pl.
geár.+Du. *jaar,* Icel. *ár,* Dan. *aar,* Swed.
år, G. *jahr,* Goth. *jer.* Further allied to
Gk. ὥρος, a season, year, ὥρα, season, hour;
Skt. *ýdtu,* time. Lit. 'that which passes.'
(√YA, to pass; from √I, to go.)

yore, formerly. (E.) M. E. *yore.* A. S.
geára, adv., formerly; lit. ' of years, during
years,' orig. gen. pl. of *gedr,* a year (above).

Yearn (1), to long for. (E.) M. E.
yernen. A. S. *gyrnan,* to yearn, be desirous. – A. S. *georn,* adj., desirous (with
vowel-change of *eo* to *y*).+Icel. *girna,* to
desire, from *gjarn,* eager; Goth. *gairnjan,*
to long for, from *gairns,* desirous. β.
Again, the adj. is from the verb appearing
in O. H. G. *gerón,* G. *be-gehren,* to long
for; allied to Gk. χαίρειν, to rejoice, χαρά,
joy, Skt. *hary,* to desire. (√GHAR.)

Yearn (2), to grieve. (E.) Also spelt
earn, ern; Hen. V., ii. 3. 3, ii. 3. 6; Jul.
Cæs. ii. 2. 129; Merry Wives, iii. 5. 45;
Rich. II. v. 5. 56; Hen. V. iv. 3. 26. A
corruption of *yerm, erm,* M. E. *ermen,* to
grieve (Chaucer, C. T. 12246); the prefixed
y- being due to A. S. prefix *ge-,* as in the
case of *yean.* From A.S. *yrman,* to grieve,
also *ge-yrman,* to grieve, be miserable. –
A. S. *earm,* adj., poor, miserable, wretched
(with vowel-change from *ea* to *y*). Cf.
Du. *arm,* Icel. *armr,* Dan. Swed. G. *arm,*
Goth. *arms,* wretched.

Yeast. (E.) M. E. *yeest, yest.* A. S.
gist, gyst, yeast.+Du. *gest.* Icel. *jast, jastr,*
Swed. *jäst,* Dan. *gier,* G. *gäscht, gischt.*
All from the √YAS, to ferment, appearing in O. H. G. *jesan,* G. *gähren,* to
ferment; Gk. ζέειν, to boil, ζεστός, fervent.

See **Zeal.** Der. *yeast-y* or *yest-y,* frothy,
Hamlet, v. 2. 199.

Yede, went. (E.) M. E. *yede, ȝede*;
also *eode.* A. S. *ge-eode,* also *eode,* went,
only in the pt. t.; where *eo-* stands, by
rule, for original *i.* (√I, to go; cf. Lat.
ire, to go.) So also Goth. *i-ddja,* went;
from the same root. ¶ Not allied to *go.*

Yelk; see **Yellow.**

Yell. (E.) M. E. *yellen.* A. S. *gellan,*
gyllan, to cry out, resound.+Du. *gillen,*
Icel. *gella,* also *gjalla* (pt. t. *gall*), Dan.
giælle, gialde, Swed. *gälla,* G. *gellen,* to
ring, resound. Allied to Icel. *gala,* pt t.
gól, to sing, O. H. G. *galan*; A. S. *galan,*
pt. t. *gól,* whence E. *nightin-gale.*
(√GHAR, to sound.)

yawl (2), to howl. (Scand.) Also *yole,*
yowl (Halliwell). M. E. *goulen, ȝaulen.*–
Icel. *gaula,* Norw. *gaula,* to low, bellow,
roar. Allied to *yell.*

Yellow. (E.) M. E. *yelwe, yelu.* A. S.
geolo, geolu, yellow. + Du. *geel,* G. *gelb.*
Allied to L. *heluus,* light yellow, Gk. χλόη,
young verdure of trees. Further allied to
Green, Gall (1).

yellow-hammer, yellow-ammer,
a song-bird. (E.) The *h* is an ignorant
insertion; *ammer* answers to A. S. *amore,*
a small bird.+O. Du. *emmerick,* a yellow-
ammer, G. *gelbammer, goldammer,* yellow-
ammer or gold-ammer, *emmerling,* the
same. β. The prob. sense is 'chirper;'
from a base AM, seen in Skt. *am,* to
sound, Icel. *emja,* to howl, G. *jammer,*
lamentation.

yolk, yelk, yellow part of an egg.
(E.) M. E. *yolke, yelke.* A. S. *geoleca,*
the yolk, lit. 'yellow part.'–A. S. *geolu,*
yellow (above).

Yelp, to bark shrilly. (E.) M. E. *yel-*
pen, also to boast. A. S. *gilpan, gielpan,*
pt. t. *gealp,* pp. *golpen,* to boast, exult,
talk noisily.+Icel. *gjálpa,* to yelp. Allied
to **Yell.**

yap, to yelp. (Scand.) The same as
yaup, Lowl. Sc. form of *yelp.* – Icel.
gjálpa, to yelp (above); whence also F.
japper, to yap.

Yeoman. (E.) M. E. *yoman,* also
yeman. It appears to answer to an A.S.
gáman * (not found), with a variant *gǽ-*
man *; these would become *yoman, yeman*
in M. E. These words are cleared up by
the existence of O. Fries. *gaman,* a vil
lager, from *ga,* a village, and *man,* a man;
so also O. Du. *goymannen,* arbitrators

appointed to decide disputes, from O. Du. *gouve*, a hamlet (Hexham). Cf. also G. *gau*, a province, Goth. *gawi*, a district. ¶ As to the vowel-sounds, cf. E. *deal*, *dole*, answering to A. S. *dǽl*, *dál*; also *ere*, *or*, answering to A. S. *ǽr*, *ár*; also *yore*, as compared with *year*. Many solutions have been proposed of this difficult word.

Yerk, the same as **jerk**; see **Yard** (2).

Yea; see **Yea**.

Yesterday. (E.) M. E. *yisterdai*; from A. S. *geostra*, *giestra*, *gystra* (yester-), and *dæg*, a day.+Du. *gisteren*, *dag van gister*, G. *gestern*, Goth. *gistradagis*. β. *Yester-* answers to Lat. *hester-* in *hes-ter-nus*, adj., belonging to yesterday; where again the syllable *hes-* is cognate with Icel. *gær*, Dan. *gaar*, Swed. *går*, Lat. *her-i*, Gk. χθές, Skt. *hyas*, yesterday. The suffix *-ter* is comparative, as in *in-ter-ior*, *ex-ter-ior*, &c. γ. The E. *yester-* answers to an Aryan type GHYAS-TRA, of which the prob. sense was 'the morning beyond;' where GHYAS signifies 'morning.'

Yet. (E.) M. E. *yet*, *yit*. A. S. *git*, *get*, *giet*, moreover. + O. Fries. *ieta*, *ita*, M. H. G. *iezuo*, *ieze*, yet; cf. G. *jetz-t*, now. β. The M. H. G. *ie-zuo* is compounded of *ie-*, and *zuo* = A. S. *tó*, too; hence A. S. *get* is prob. short for *ge tó*, i.e. 'and also,' moreover; see **Yea** and **Too**.

Yew, a tree. (E.) M. E. *ew*. A. S. *iw*. +Du. *ijf*, Icel. *ýr*, G. *eibe*, O. H. G. *iwa*, yew. Perhaps of Celtic origin; we also find Irish *iubhar*, Gael. *iubhar*, *iughar*, W. *yw*, *ywen*, Corn. *hivin*, Bret. *ivin*, a yew. ¶ *Not* allied to *ivy*.

Yex, to hiccough. (E.) M. E. *yexen*, *yesken*. A. S. *giscian*, to sob, sigh. Prob. allied to L. *hiscere*, to yawn, *hiare*, to yawn; see **Yawn**. (√GHI.)

Yield. (E.) M. E. *gelden*, *yelden*, pt. t. *yald*, pp. *yolden*, to pay; hence, to yield up. A. S. *gieldan*, *gildan*, pt. t. *geald*, pp. *golden*, to pay, give up.+Du. *gelden*, Icel. *gjalda*, Dan. *gielde*, to pay; Swed. *gälla*, to be worth; G. *gelten*, pt. t. *galt*, to be worth; Goth. *fra-gildan*, to pay back. (Base GALD.)

guild, **gild**, a kind of club. (E.) M. E. *gilde*, *3ilde*. Cf. A. S. *gegilda*, a member of a club; formed from A. S. *gild*, a payment.—A. S. *gildan*, to pay.+Du. *gild*, a gild; Icel. *gildi*, payment, a gild; G. *gilde*, a gild; Goth. *gild*, tribute-money. **Der.** *guild-hall*, better *gild-hall*.

Yoke, sb. (E.) M. E. *yok*. A. S. *geoc*, *gioc*, *ioc*, a yoke for oxen.+Du. *juk*, Icel. *ok*, Dan. *aag*, Swed. *ok*, Goth. *juk*, G. *joch*, W. *iau*, L. *iugum*, Russ. *igo*, Lith. *jungas*, Gk. ζύγον, Skt. *yuga*, a yoke, a couple. Lit. 'that which joins;' all from √YUG, to join. See **Join**. **Der.** *yoke*, verb.

Yolk; see **Yellow**.

Yon, adj., at a distance. (E.) M. E. *yon*, *3on*. A. S. *geon*, yon; Ælfred, tr. of Gregory's Past. Care, ed. Sweet, p. 443.+ Icel. *enn*, the, orig. that, often mis-written *hinn*; Goth. *jains*, G. *jener*, yon, that. β. From the Aryan pronominal base YA, that; with suffix -NA; cf. Skt. *ya*, who, orig. that; Gk. ὅς (for *yós*). From the same base are *ye-a*, *ye-s*, *ye-t*. **Der.** *yond-er*, M. E. *yonder*, adv.; cf. Goth. *jaindre*, adv., yonder, there.

beyond. (E.) M. E. *beyonde*. A. S. *begeondan*, beyond.—A. S. *be-*, for *be* or *bi*, by; and *geond*, prep. across, beyond, from *geon*, yon.

Yore; see **Year**.

You, **Your**; see **Ye**.

Young. (E.) M. E. *yong*, *yung*. A. S. *geong*, *giung*, *iung*, young. + Du. *jong*, Icel. *ungr*, *jungr*, Dan. Swed. *ung*, G. *jung*, Goth. *juggs* (written for *jungs**). β. These forms answer to Lat. *iuuencus*, a young animal, heifer, W. *ieuanc*, young; other forms (without the final guttural) occur in L. *iuuenis*, Lith. *jaunas*, Skt. *yuvan*, young, Russ. *iunuii*, young. **Der.** *young-ling*, *young-ster*; also *youn-ker*, borrowed from Du. *jonker*, *jonkheer*, i.e. young sir, compounded of *jong*, young, and *heer*, sir, a lord.

youth. (E.) M. E. *youthe*; earlier *3uweðe*, *3u3eðe*, youth. A. S. *gióguð*, *geóguð*, youth. [The middle *g* became *w*, and then disappeared.] Put for *geong-uð**, the *ó* standing for *on* as in *tóð* (Goth. *tunthus*), tooth, *gós* (G. *gans*), goose.+ O. Sax. *juguð*, Du. *jeugd*, G. *jugend*, all contracted forms from the same base *jung* = young. Thus *you-th* = *young-th*; indeed the M. E. *yongðe* occasionally occurs.

Yule, Christmas. (E.) M. E. *3ole*, *yole*. A. S. *iula*, *geóla*; also *geól*, *gehhol*. December was called *se ǽrra geóla*, the former yule; and January *se æftera geóla*, the latter yule. β. The most likely solution is that it meant 'a time of revelry,' being connected with M. E. *youlen*, *yollen*, to cry out or yawl; see **Yawl**. We actually find A. S. *gýlan*, to make merry, keep festival (Grein); also G. *jolen, johlen, jodeln,* to sing in a high-pitched voice, Du. *joelen,* to revel. ¶ The attempt to connect this word with *wheel* is perfectly futile, and explains nothing.

jolly. (F.–Scand.) M. E. *ioly,* earliest form *iolif.* – O. F. *jolif,* later *joli,* 'jolly, gay, trim, fine;' Cot. Orig. sense 'festive.' – Icel. *jól,* a great feast in the heathen time; cognate with A. S. *geóla,* yule (above).

Ywis, certainly. (E.) M. E. *ywis, iwis;* often written *Iwis, I-wis,* in MSS., whence, by a singular error, the fictitious verb *wis,* to know, has been evolved by lexicographers, though unknown to our old MSS. A. S. *gewis,* adj. certain, which came to be used as an adverb. β. Here the *ge-* is a mere prefix; see **Y-** (above); the adj., *wis,* certain, is allied to **Wise** and **Wit,** verb.+ Du. *gewis,* adj. and adv., certain, certainly; G. *gewiss,* certainly; Icel. *viss,* certain, Dan. *vis,* Swed. *viss,* certain; Dan. *vist,* Swed. *visst,* certainly.

Z.

Zany, a buffoon. (Ital. – Gk. – Heb.) O. Ital. *Zane,* Ital. *Zanni,* a familiar form of *Giovanni,* John; used to mean 'a sillie John, a gull, a noddie, clowne, foole, simple fellowe in a plaie,' Florio. – Gk. Ἰωάννης, John. – Heb. *Yókhánán,* i. e. the Lord graciously gave. – Heb. *Yó,* the Lord; *khánan,* to shew mercy.

Zeal. (F. – L. – Gk.) Formerly *zele.* – F. *zele,* 'zeale;' Cot. (Mod. F. *zèle.*) – L. *zelum,* acc. of *zelus,* zeal. – Gk. ζῆλος, ardour. Put for ζέσ-λος *; cf. ζέσ-ις, a boiling, seething; ζέειν, to boil. From √ YAS, to seethe, ferment; see **Yeast.** Der. *zeal-ot,* F. *zelote,* 'zealous,' Cot.; from L. *zelotes,* Gk. ζηλωτής, a zealot. ∙

jealous. (F. – L. – Gk.) M. E. *jalous, gelus.* – O. F. *jalous* (later *jaloux.*) – Low L. *zelosus,* full of zeal. – L. *zelus,* zeal (above). Der. *jealous-y,* F. *jalousie.*

Zebra. (Port. – Ethiopian.) Port. *zebra* (Span. *cebra, zebra*). The animal is S. African; according to Littré, the word is of Ethiopian origin.

Zedoary, an E. Indian root resembling ginger. (F. – Low L. – Pers.) F. *zedoaire,* Cot. – Low L. *zedoaria.* – Pers. *zadwár, zidwár,* zedoary; also spelt *jadwár.* ¶ The O. F. form was *citouart, citoual, citoal;* whence M.E. *cetewale,* Chaucer, C.T. 13691.

Zenith. (F. – Span. – Arab.) M. E. *senyth.* – O. F. *cenith;* F. *zenith.* – Span. *zenit,* O. Span. *zenith.* – Arab. *samt,* a way, road, path, tract, quarter; whence *samt-ur-ras,* the zenith, vertical point of the heavens; also *as-samt,* an azimuth. β. *Samt* was pronounced *semt,* of which Span. *zenit* is a corruption; again, *samt* is here short for *samt-ur-ras* or *semt-er-ras* (as above), lit. the way overhead, from *ras,* the head. See **Azimuth.**

Zephyr. (F. – L. – Gk.) F. *zephyre,* the west wind. – L. *zephyrum,* acc. of *zephyrus,* the west wind. – Gk. ζέφυρος, the west wind. Allied to ζόφος, darkness, gloom, the dark quarter, west.

Zero; see **Cipher.**

Zest. (F. – L. – Gk.) Formerly a chip of orange or lemon-peel, used for flavouring drinks; hence, something that gives a relish, or simply a relish. – F. *zest,* 'the thick skin whereby the kernell of a walnut is divided,' Cot.; hence, a slice of lemon-peel. – L. *schistus, schistos,* lit. cleft, divided. – Gk. σχιστός, divided. – Gk. σχίζειν, to cleave; see **Schism.**

Zigzag, having sharp, quick turns. (F. – G.) F. *zigzag.* – G. *zickzack,* a zigzag; *zickzack segeln,* to tack, in sailing. β. I think that *zickzack,* clearly reduplicated from *zack,* answers to a *tack* in sailing; since G. *z* corresponds to Low G. *t.*

Zinc, a metal. (G.) G. *zink,* zinc; of uncertain origin. Perhaps allied to *zinn,* tin; and meaning 'tin-like.'

Zodiac; see **Zoology.**

Zone, a belt. (F. – L. – Gk.) F. *zone.* – L. *zona.* – Gk. ζώνη, a girdle; put for ζωσ-νη *. – Gk. ζώννυμι (= ζωσ-νυμι), I gird. Cf. Lith. *jósta,* a girdle, from *jósti,* to gird. (√YAS.)

Zoology. (Gk.) Coined from Gk. ζῷο-ν, a living creature, animal; and -λογία, allied to λόγος, discourse, from λέγειν, to speak. β. Gk. ζῷον is neut. of ζῶος, living; allied to ζωή, life, ζάειν, ζῆν, to live. Supposed to be allied to Zend *ji,* to live. (√GI.)

azote, nitrogen. (Gk.) So called because destructive to animal life. – Gk. ἀ-, negative prefix; ζωτικός, preserving life, from ζω-ή, life.

zodiac, an imaginary belt in the heavens, containing the twelve *signs*. (F. – L. – Gk.) F. *zodiaque*. – L. *zodiacus*. – Gk. ζωδιακός, sb., the zodiacal circle ; so called from containing the twelve constellations chiefly represented by animals. – Gk. ζωδιακός, adj., belonging to animals. – Gk. ζῴδιον, a small animal ; dimin. of ζῷον, a living creature (above).

zoophyte. (F. – Gk.) F. *zoophyte.* – Gk. ζωόφυτον, a living being ; an animal-plant. – Gk. ζωό-s, living ; φυτόν, a plant, that which has grown, from φύειν, to produce, grow, from √BHU, to exist. See Be.

Zymotic, a term applied to diseases, in which a poison works through the body like a ferment. (Gk.) Gk. ζυμωτικός, causing to ferment. – Gk. ζυμόω, I cause to ferment. – Gk. ζύμη, leaven. Allied to L. *ius*, broth ; see Juice.

CORRECTIONS AND NOTES.

[Some of the etymologies given in the preceding pages will require modification when the history of the words treated of becomes more accurately known. I add here such corrections and improvements as have hitherto occurred to me.—W.W.S.]

Angel. The A. S. form is *engel*, from Latin. Afterwards altered by F. and L. influence.

Anneal. Perhaps the A. S. words should be *onǽlan* and *ǽlan*, with long *æ*. Yet see Fick, i. 100.

Backgammon. Strutt suggests that, after all, this word merely means 'back-game,' because the pieces taken off are put back to the starting-point. This seems the best solution, and makes the word E. — A.S. *bæc*, back; *gamen*, game. Cf. Du. *verkeeren*, to pervert; also to play at ticktack (a kind of backgammon); Sewel.

Bamboo. Canarese *banbu*, bamboo.

Bedlam. Bethlehem means 'house of bread.'—Heb. *beth*, house; *lekhem*, bread (*kh* = G. *ch*).

Bid (2). *Bid*, to command, has entirely taken the place of *bid* (1), to pray, from which it has borrowed all its forms. Hence, strictly, this *bid* (2) is actually derived from A.S. *biddan*, to pray, though it preserves the sense of A. S. *beódan*. See **Bid** (1).

Bizarre. The Basque *bizar* means a beard; hence the Span. *bizarro*, valiant, may have been derived, by the idiom which makes the Span. *hombre de bigote* mean a man of spirit; for *bigote* means a moustache.

Boast. M. E. *bost*, *boost*, means (1) noise, (2) pride, boast. Cf. Swed. *pust*, a puff of wind. Prob. E.; from a root PUS, to blow. Cf. Lithuan. *pús-ti*, to blow.

Bode, s. v. Bid (2), p. 38. Add: *bod*, sb., is from *bod-en*, pp. of *beódan*, to bid; so also Icel. *boð*, sb., is from *boð-inn*, pp. of Icel. *bjóða*, to bid.

Bolt, s. v. Bulge, p. 55. The A. S. *bolt* also occurs in the sense of cross-bow bolt.

Boon. When *boon* is used as a sb., as in 'a great *boon*,' it answers to F. *bon*, sb.—L. *bonum*, sb., orig. neut. of *bonus*, adj., good.

Boult, to sift meal. Explained under Bolt (2), p. 44, col. 2.

Bowline. See Bow (4), under Bough, p. 47.

Bungalow. The Bengalee word is *bánglá*, a thatched cottage; from *Banga*, Bengal.

Calm. Cf. Prov. *calma*, heat; Low Lat. *cauma*, heat, Job xxx. 30 (Vulgate).

Camlet. The Arab. *khamlat* is in no way allied to *camel*, but is from Arab. *khaml*, pile, plush, a carpet with a long pile, a cushion on a saddle. The confusion arose from the fact that camel's hair was *sometimes* used for making camlet.

Cant (1). Probably borrowed, like many other cant words, from the Netherlands. Walloon *canter*, to sing.—L. *cantare*. Cf. *re-cant*.

Cark. The W. *carc*, anxiety, was borrowed from M. E. *kark*. The Anglo-F. *kark* is the F. *charge*, and meant a burden, weight, cargo. So also Anglo-F. *sorkarker*, to overload, lit. surcharge; *deskarker*, to unload, discharge. 'A *karke* of peper,' a load of pepper.

Chapel (p. 66). Others say that *capella* meant a canopy, a recess in a chapel for an altar (Diefenbach).

Check. Really (F. — Arab. — Pers.). O. F. *eschec*, *eschac*; a form due to the Arab. pronunciation (almost as *shág*) of the Pers. *sháh*.

Chill. West Saxon *ciele*, *cyle*; oldest form *celi*. From the strong verb appearing in Icel. *kala*, to freeze, pt. t. *kól*, pp. *kalinn*. *Cool* is from the pt. t. of the same verb.

Clot. We also find A. S. *clot*, a mass, clot; in the dat. pl. *clottum*.

Clove (1). M. E. *cloue*, as well as *clow*. Prob. the *u* was misread as meaning *v*.

Coddle. *Coddle* = castrate, Beaum. and Fletcher, *Philaster*, v. 4. 31. But *caddle* = O. F. *cadeler*, to pamper. — O. F. *cadel*, a coddled child. — L. acc *catellum*, a whelp; dimin. of *catulus*, a whelp. — L. *catus*, a cat. See **Cat**.

Consent. See under **Sense**, p. 424, col. 2.

Cool. See note upon **Chill** (above).

Cowl (1). It is probable that A.S. *cufle* and Icel. *kufl* are mere borrowings (through the British) from L. *cucullus*, a cowl. Cf. Irish *cochal*, a cowl.

Cricket (2), p. 101, col. 2. Otherwise, named from *cricket*, a small stool, used in playing stool-ball (a game). Orig. a small crutch or perch; see **crutch**, p. 102, l. 15 (It makes little difference).

Cross, s. v. **Crook**, p. 101. The M.E. *crois* and M.E. *cros* are distinct words; *crois* (from O. F. *crois*) is obsolete; but *cros*, still in use, is Provençal. It occurs in Gaimar's Chronicle, l. 2833 (A.D. 1150), and perhaps earlier.

Cruet. Anglo-F. *cruet*, dimin. of O. F. *cruye*, a pitcher of stone-ware. — Du. *kruik*, a crock; see **Crook**.

Crusade, s. v. **Crook**, p. 102. Perhaps borrowed immediately from Provençal.

Distribute. See under **Tribe**, p. 523, col. 1.

Dot. The sbs. are from the pp. *dott-in* of Icel. *detta*, pt. t. *datt*, to drop. Orig. sense a drop, something let fall.

Duty, p. 190, col. 2. Anglo-F. *duete*, debt, obligation; Liber Albus, p. 211.

Entertain. See under **Tenable**, p. 496, col. 2.

Fledge. The M.E. *flegge*, also *fligge*, comes nearer to A.S. *flycge*, ready to fly, if this be a true A.S. word.

Foam. The A.S. *fám* answers rather to M.H.G. *feim*, Russ. *piena*, Skt. *phena*, foam.

Frampold. Add: the suffix *-fol* is from W. *ffol*, foolish.

Furze. The comparison with Gael. *preas* is doubtful.

Gang (2), to go. See under **Go**, p. 179.

Glitter. Read: M.E. *gliteren*, to shine; frequent. of A.S. *glitian*, to shine. + Icel. *glitra*, &c.

Ham: Add: cf. Icel. *höm*, haunch of a horse; Du. *ham*, the ham.

Howl. Add: so also Du. *huilen*, Icel. *ýla*, Dan. *hyle*, Swed. *yla*, to howl.

Hussif. The M.E. name was *nedyl-hows*, i.e needle-house (Wülcker).

Impertinent. See under **Tenable**, p. 496, col. 2.

Ingrate. See under **Grace**, p. 182, col. 1.

Invincible. See under **Victor**, p. 544, col. 2.

Iron-mould; see **mould** (3), s. v.

Mole (1), p. 290.

Jeer. Cf. G. *scheren*, 'to shear, fleece, poll, lop, cheat, plague, tease;' Flügel.

Jenneting. (F. — L. — Gk. — Heb.) Prob. for *jeanneton*; a dimin. from F. *pomme de S Jean*, an early apple, called in Italian *melo de San Giovanni*, i. e. St. John's apple. So called because, in France and Italy, it ripened about June 24, St. John's day. So also, there is an early pear, called *Amiré Joannet* or *Jeanette*, or *petit St. Jean*; G. *Johannisbirn*. F. *Jean* = Lat. acc. *Iohannem*, from Gk. Ἰωάννης, John. — Heb. *Yóhánán*, the grace of the Lord.

Knave. This may be E.; both A.S. *cn-apa* and A.S. *cn-yht* (knight) may be allied to A. S. *cyn*, kin.

Law, p. 248, col. 1. The history and use of the word shew that it is rather Scand. than E.

Leak. Cf. 'þæt hlece scip,' the leaky ship (Ælfred).

Lewd. Note the great change in sense.

Linnet. Perhaps directly from L.; we find A.S. *linet-wige*, a linnet (whence Lowl. Sc. *lintwhite*); lit. 'flax-hopper.' From L. *linum*, flax; the portion *wige*, hopper, being dropped.

Lissom. See under **Lithe**, p. 253, col. 2.

Ogee. Prob. Arab. *áwj* is not a true Arab. word, but from Gk. ἀπόγαιον, the apogee.

One (1). Already written *won* in M.E. See Guy of Warwick, ed. Zupitza, note to l. 7927.

Oolite, a kind of limestone. (F. — Gk.) F. *oolithe* (with *th* sounded as *t*). — Gk. ᾠό-ν, egg; λίθ-ος, stone. Lit. 'egg-stone.' See **Oval**.

Rock (1). We actually find A.S. *stán-rocca*, gen. pl., to translate L. *scopulorum*. This may have been borrowed from Celtic. At any rate, it is strong evidence against a Latin origin.

She. The A.S. *seó*, Icel. *sjá*, answers to Skt. *syá*, fem. of *syas*, that. Prob. from Aryan SA, he; YA, that.

Slender. Really (F. — O.Du.). O. F. *esclendre* (Palsgrave). — O.Du. *slinder*.

Trunk (2), of an elephant. Corrupted from F. *trompe*, 'a trump; also, the snowt of an elephant;' Cotgrave.

Wine. Some think that Gk. οἶνος is not of Aryan origin; cf. Heb *yayin*, wine; Ethiopic *wein*, *wain*, wine.

APPENDIX.

I. LIST OF PREFIXES.

THE following is a list of the principal prefixes in English, shewing their origin. It is perhaps, not quite exhaustive, but contains nearly all of any consequence. For further information, see the etymologies of the words *a-down*, &c., in the Dictionary.

A- (1), in a-down. (E.) See **Of.**

A- (2), in a-foot. (E.) See **On.**

A- (3), in a-long. (E.) See **An-** (5).

A- (4), in a-rise. (E.) A.S. *á-*, intensive prefix to verbs. **+** Goth. *us-, ur-*; G. *er-*.

A- (5), in a-chieve. (F.**–**L.) See **Ad-**.

A- (6), in a-vert. (L.) See **Ab-**.

A- (7), in a-mend. (F.**–**L.) See **Ex-** (1).

A- (8), in a-las. (F.**–**L.) O. F. *a-*; from L. *ah!* interj.

A- (9), in a-byss. (Gk.) See **An-** (2).

A- (10), in a-do. (E.) For *at do*.

A- (11), in a-ware. (E.) M. E. *i-, y-*; A.S. *ge-*, prefix. See **Y-**.

A- (12), in a-pace. (E.) For *a pace*; *a* for *an*, indef. art.

A- (13), in a-vast. (Du.) Du. *hou vast*, hold fast.

A- (14), in a-pricot. (Arab.) Arab. *al*, def. art. See **Al-** (3).

Ab- (1); ab-dicate, ab-undance. (L.; *or* F.**–**L.) L. *ab*, from. Lengthened to *abs-* in *abs-cond*; cf. Gk. *ἄψ*, perhaps orig. a gen. case. **+** E. *of*; Gk. *ἀπό*; Skt. *apa*, away from. See **Apo-, Of.** This prefix also appears as *a-, adv-, av-, v-*; ex. a-vert, adv-ance, av-aunt, v-anguard.

Ab- (2); ab-breviate. (L.) Put for L. *ad*; see **Ad-**.

Abs-; abs-cond, abs-tain. (L.; *or* F.**–**L.) L. *abs-*, extended form of *ab*; see **Ab-** (1).

Ac-; see **Ad-**.

Ad-; ad-apt, ad-dress. (L.; *or* F.**–**L.) L. *ad*, to, at, for.**+**Goth. *at*, A.S. *æt*, E. *at*. This prefix appears as *a-, ab-, ac-, ad-, af-, ag-, al-, an-, ap-, ar-, as-, at-*; ex.: a-chieve, ab-breviate, ac-cede, ad-mire, af-fix, ag-gress, al-lude, an-nex, ap-pend, ar-rogate, as-sign, at-tract.

Adv-; see **Ab-** (1).

Af-; see **Ad-**.

After-. (E.) E. *after*, prep.; A.S. *æfter*.

Ag-; see **Ad-**.

Al- (1); see **Ad-**.

Al- (2); al-ligator. (Span. **–** L.) Span. *el*, def. art. **–** L. *ille*, he. See **L-** (2).

Al- (3); al-cohol. (Arab.) Arab. *al*, def. art. This also appears as *a-, ar-, as-, el-, l-*. Ex.: a-pricot, ar-tichoke, as-sagai, el-ixir, l-ute.

Am- (1); am-bush. (F.**–**L.) F. *em-*.**–** L. *im-*, for *in*, prep.; see **In-** (2).

Am- (2); am-brosia. (Gk.) See **An-** (2).

Am- (3); am-bassador; see **An-** (5).

Ambi-, Amb-; ambi-dextrous; ambition. (L.; *or* F.**–**L.) L. *ambi-*, on both sides, around.**+**Gk. *ἀμφί*. See below.

Amphi-. (Gk.) Gk. *ἀμφί*, on both sides, around.**+**L. *ambi-*; see **Ambi-**.

An- (1); see **Ad-**.

An- (2), **A-** (9), negative prefix. (Gk.) Gk. *ἀν-, ἀ-*, neg. prefix. Hence *am-* in ambrosia; *a-* in a-byss.**+**L. *in-*, E. *un-*; see **In-** (3), **Un-** (1).

An- (3); see **Ana-**.

An- (4); an-oint. (F.**–**L.) For F. *en-*. **–** L. *in*, prep.; see **In-** (2).

An- (5); an-swer. (E.) A.S. *and-*, in reply to, opposite to.**+**Goth. *and-*; Du. *ent-*; G. *ent-*; Gk. *ἀντί*. Shortened to *a-* in a-long; appearing as *e-* in e-lope, as *am-* in am-bassador, and as *em-* in embassy; the same as *un-* in verbs. See **Anti-, Un-** (2).

An- (6); an-cestor. (F.**–**L.) See **Ante-**.

Ana-, An- (3); ana-gram, an-eurism. (Gk.) Gk. *ἀνά*, upon, on, up.**+**A. S. *on*, Goth. *ana*. See **On-**.

Anci-; anci-ent. (F.**–**L.) See **Ante-**.

Ann-; ann-eal. (E.) See **Anneal** in the Dict.

Ant-; ant-agonist. (Gk.) See **Anti-**.

Ante-. (L.) L. *ante*, before. Also *anti-, anci-, an-*; as in anti-cipate, anci-ent, an-cestor.

Anth-; anth-em. (Gk.) See below.

Anti- (1), **Ant-**. (Gk.) Gk. *ἀντί*, against, opposite to. Also *ant-, anth-*, as in antagonist, anth-em. See An- (5), Un- (2).

Anti- (2); see **Ante-**.

Ap-; ap-pend; see **Ad-**.

Aph-; aph-æresis; see below.

Apo-. (Gk.) Hence *aph-* in aph-æresis. Gk. ἀπό, from, off. **+** L. *ab*; A. S. *of*; see **Ab-** (1), **Of**.

Ar- (1); see **Ad-**.

Ar- (2); ar-tichoke; see **Al-** (3).

Arch-, Archi-, Arche- ; arch-bishop, arch-angel, archi-tect, arche-type. (Gk.) Gk. ἀρχι-, chief. **–** Gk. ἄρχειν, to be first.

As- (1); as-sign; see **Ad-**.

As- (2); as-sagai; see **Al-** (3).

At-; see **Ad-**.

Auto-, Auth-, self. (Gk.) Gk. αὐτό-s, self. Hence *auth-* in auth-entic; *eff-* in eff-endi.

Av- ; av-aunt. (F.–L.) F. *av-* ; from L. *ab*; see **Ab-** (1).

Ba-; ba-lance; see **Bi-**.

Be-. (E.) A. S. *be-, bi-,* the same as *bt,* by, prep. ; E. *by*.

Bi-, double. (L.) L. *bi-,* double, from an earlier form *dui-,* related to *duo,* two. **+** Gk. δι-, double, allied to δύω, two; Skt. *dwi-,* allied to *dva,* two ; E. *twi-* in twi-bill. Hence F. *bi-* in bi-as, F. *ba-* in ba-lance ; and see below.

Bin-; bin-ocular. (L.) L. *bin-i,* distributive form allied to *bi-* above.

Bis-; bis-cuit. (F.–L.) F. *bis,* L. *bis,* twice ; extended from *bi-* (above). Cf. E. *twice* ; see **Dis-**.

C-; c-lutch. (E.) A. S. *ge-,* prefix. See **Y-**.

Cat-; cat-echism; see **Cata-**.

Cath-; cath-olic ; see below.

Cata-, down. (Gk.) Gk. κατά, down, downwards. Hence *cat-, cath-,* in cat-echism, cath-olic.

Circum-, round. (L.) L. *circum,* around, prep. Hence *circu-* in circu-it.

Co-; see **Com-**.

Col-; see **Com-**.

Com-. (L. or F.–L.) L. *com-,* together, used in composition for *cum,* prep. together. **+** Gk. σύν, together ; see **Syn-**. It appears as *co-, col-, com-, con-, cor-, coun-*; ex.: co-agulate, col-lect, com-mute, con-nect, cor-rode, coun-cil. Also as *co-* in co-uch, co-st; *cu-* in cu-stom; *cur-* in cur-ry (1). ¶ *Combustion* is for com-bustion.

Con-; con-nect; see **Com-**.

Contra-, against. (L.) L. *contra,* against.

Becomes *contro-* in contro-versy; loses final *a* in Ital. contr-alto. Hence F. *contre,* against, as in contr-ol ; but the F. form is usually written *counter* in English. Hence also *countr-y*.

Cor-; cor-rode; see **Com-**.

Coun- ; coun-cil; see **Com-**.

Counter-. (F.–L.) See **Contra-**.

Cu-; cu-stom ; see **Com-**.

Cur-; cur-ry (1) ; see **Com-**.

D-; d-affodil; see **De-** (1).

De- (1); de-scend, de-bate. (L.; *or* F.– L.) L. *de,* down, downward. Used with an oppositive sense in de-form; with an intensive sense in de-clare, &c. Changed to *di-* in di-stil. Distinct from the prefix below.

De- (2); de-feat. (F.–L.) F. *dé-,* O. F. *des-,* from L. *dis-,* apart; see **Dis-**. Distinct from the prefix above.

De- (3); de-vil ; see **Dia-**.

Dea-; dea-con; see **Dia-**.

Demi-, half. (F.–L.) F. *demi.*–L. *dimidius,* half; see **Demi-** in Dict.

Des-; des-cant; see **Dis-**.

Di- (1), double. (Gk.) Gk. δι-, double, allied to δίς, twice, and δύο, two; see **Bi-**. Ex. di-lemma.

Di- (2), apart, away. (L.) See **Dis-**.

Di- (3); di-stil; see **De-** (1).

Dia-. (Gk.) Gk. διά, through, between, apart; allied to **Di-** (1). Shortened to *di-* in di-æresis; appearing as *de-, dea-,* in de-vil, dea-con.

Dif-; see **Dis-**.

Dis-, apart, away. (L.; *or* F.–L.) L. *dis-,* apart, in two, another form of *bis-,* double ; *dis-* and *bis-* are variants from an older form *duis-,* double, also used in the sense in two, apart ; see **Bis-**. *Dis-* becomes *des-* in O. French, also *dé-* in later F.; but the O. F. *des-* is sometimes altered to *dis-,* as in dis-cover. The various forms are *di-, dif-, dis-, des-, de-,* and even *s* ; as in di-verge, dif-fuse, dis-pel, des-cant, de-feat, de-luge, s-pend.

Dou- ; dou-ble ; see **Duo-**.

Duo-, Du-, two, double. (L.) L. *duo,* two ; cognate with E. *two.* Only in duo-decimo, duo-denum ; shortened to *du-* in du-al, du-plicate, &c. Appearing as *dou-* in dou-ble, dou-bt.

Dys-, badly. (Gk.) Gk. δύς, badly, with difficulty. Some connect it with **To-** (2).

E- (1); e-normous ; see **Ex-** (1).

E- (2); e-nough; see Y-.

E- (3); e-lope. (Du.) Du. *ent-*, away; cognate with A. S. *and-* ; see An- (5).

E- (4); e-squire. (F.) This *e-* is a F. addition, of purely phonetic value, due to the difficulty which was experienced in pronouncing initial *sq-*, *sc-*, *st-*, *sp-*. So also in e-scutcheon, e-state, e-special; to which add e-schew.

Ec- ; ec-logue. (Gk.) Gk. ἐκ, also ἐξ, out.+ L. *ex*, Lithuan. *isz*, Russ. *iz'*, out; see Ex- (1). Also *el-*, *ex-*, as in el-lipse, ex-odus.

Eff- ; see Ex- (1).

Eff- ; eff-endi; see Auto-.

El- (1) ; el-lipse ; see Ec-.

El- (2) ; el-ixir ; see Al- (3).

Em- (1); em-brace. (F. — L.) F. *em-* ; L. *im-*, for *in* ; see In- (2).

Em- (2); em-piric ; see En- (2).

Em- (3); em-bassy ; see An- (5).

En- (1); en-close. (F.—L.) F. *en-* ; L. *in-* ; see In- (2).

En- (2); en-ergy. (Gk.) Gk. ἐν, in.+L. *in* ; A.S. *in*. See Em- (2), In- (1), In- (2).

En- (3); en-emy. (F. — L.) Negative prefix; see In- (3).

Endo-, within. (Gk.) Gk. ἔνδο-ν, within; extended from ἐν, in ; see En- (2), and Ind-.

Enter- ; enter-tain. (F. — L.) F. *entre.* = L. *inter*, among ; see Inter-. Shortened to *entr-* in entr-ails.

Ep-, Eph- ; see below.

Epi-, upon. (Gk.) Gk. ἐπί, upon. + Skt. *api* ; allied to L. *ob-*. See Ob-. It appears as *ep-*, *eph-*, in ep-och, eph-emeral.

Es- ; es-cape ; see Ex- (1).

Eso-, within. (Gk.) Gk. ἔσω, within ; from ἐς, εἰς, into.

Eu-, well. (Gk.) Gk. εὖ, well ; neut. of ἐύς, good, orig. ' real ;' for ἐσ-ύς *, from √ AS, to be. Written *ev-* in ev-angelist.

Ev- ; ev-angelist ; see Eu-.

Ex- (1), out of, very. (L. ; *or* F. — L.) L. *ex*, also *e*, out of; also used intensively. +Gk. ἐξ, ἐκ, out. See Ec-, and see below. It appears as *a-*, *e-*, *ef-*, *es-*, *ex-*, *iss-*, *s-*, in a-mend, e-normous, ef-fect, es-cape, ex-tend, iss-ue, s-ample.

Ex- (2), out of, away. (Gk.) Gk. ἐξ, out ; as in ex-odus. See above.

Exo-, without. (Gk.) Gk. ἔξω, outside, without ; adv. from ἐξ, out (above).

Extra-, beyond. (L.) A comparative abl. form, from L. *ex*, out ; see Ex- (1). Cf. *exter-* in exter-ior, exter-nal. It appears also as *stra-* in stra-nge.

For- (1), in place of. (E.) E. *for*, prep.; in *for-as-much*, *for-ever*, which might just as well be written as separate words instead of compounds. Allied to Per-, Pro-.

For- (2) ; for-give. (E.) A. S. *for-*, intensive prefix. + Icel. *for-*, Dan. *for-*, Swed. *för-*, Du. G. *ver-*, Goth. *fra-*, Skt. *pará-*.

For- (3); for-feit. (F. — L.) F. *for-*, prefix. = L. *foris*, outside, out of doors. Also in *for-close*, sometimes spelt *fore-close*.

For- (4); for-ward ; see Forth-.

Fore- (1), before. (E.) A. S. *fore*, for, before, prep. ; *fore*, adv. Allied to For- (1).

Fore- (2); fore-go. (E.) A bad spelling of *for-go* ; see For- (2).

Forth-. (E.) Only in *forth-with*. A. S. *forð*, forth.+Gk. πρός, Skt. *prati*, towards ; O. Lat. *port-* ; see Por- (1).

Fro- ; fro-ward. (E.) Short for *from*.

Gain-, against. (E.) A. S. *gegn*, against. Ex. gain-say.

Hemi-, half. (Gk.) Gk. ἡμι-, half. + L. *semi-*, half ; see Semi-. Shortened to *me-* in me-grim.

Hetero-, other. (Gk.) Gk. ἕτερο-s, other.

Holo-, entire. (Gk.) Gk. ὅλο-s, entire.

Homo-, same. (Gk.) Gk. ὁμό-s, same; cognate with E. *same*. Lengthened to *homœo-*, like, in homœo-pathy.

Hyper-, above, beyond. (Gk.) Gk. ὑπέρ, above ; see Over-.

Hypo-, Hyph-, Hyp-. (Gk.) Gk. ὑπό, under.+L. *sub*, under ; see Sub-. Hence *hyph-* in hyph-en ; *hyp-* in hyp-allage.

I- ; i-gnoble ; see In- (3).

Il- (1); il-lude ; see In- (2).

Il- (2) ; il-legal ; see In- (3).

Im- (1); im-bed ; see In- (1).

Im- (2); im-mure, im-merge ; see In- (2).

Im- (3); im-mortal ; see In- (3).

In- (1); in-born. (E.) A.S. *in*, prep. It also becomes *im-* before *b* and *p* ; as in im-bed, im-park. See below.

In- (2); in-clude. (L. ; *or* F. — L.) L. *in*, in.+Gk. ἐν, in ; A.S. *in*. En- (2). It appears as *am-*, *an-*, *em-*, *en-*, *il-*, *im-*, *in-*, *ir-*, in am-bush, an-oint, em-brace, en-close, il-lude, im-mure, in-clude, ir-ritate.

In- (3), negative prefix. (L.) L. *in-*, neg. prefix.+Gk. ἀν-, ἀ-, neg. prefix ; E. *un-*, before nouns. See **An-** (2), **A-** (9), **Un-** (1). It appears as *en-*, *i-*, *il-*, *im-*, *in-*, *ir-*, in en-emy, i-gnoble, il-legal, im-mortal, in-firm, ir-regular.

Ind-; ind-igent. (L.) O. Lat. *ind-o*, within.+Gk. ἔνδον, within; see **Endo-**.

Intel-; see below.

Inter-, between. (L.) L. *inter*, between. A comparative form, allied to L. *inter-ior*, within; cf. L. *inter-nus*, internal. It appears as *intel-* in intel-lect, *enter-* in enter-tain; and cf. entr-ails. Closely allied are L. *intro-*, within, *intra-*, within.

Intra-, within; see **Inter-**.

Intro-, within; see **Inter-**.

-Ir- (1); ir-ritate; see **In-** (2).

Ir- (2); ir-regular; see **In-** (3).

Iss-; iss-ue. (F.−L.) F. *iss-*, from L. *ex*; see **Ex-** (1).

Juxta-, near. (L.) L. *iuxta*, near.

L- (1); l-one. (E.) Short for *all*; l-one = al-one.

L- (2); l-ouver. (F.−L.) F. *l'*, for *le*, def. art.−L. *ille*, he, that. See **Al-** (2).

L- (3); l-ute. (Arab.) Short for Arab. *al*, the, def. art. See **Al-** (3).

Male-, **Mal-**, **Mau-**, badly. (L.; or F.−L.) L. *male*, badly, ill; whence F. *mal*, which becomes also *mau-* in mau-gre.

Me-; me-grim; see **Hemi-**.

Meta-, **Meth-**, **Met-**, among, with, after; also used to imply change. (Gk.) Gk. μετά, among, with, after.+A. S. *mid*, G. *mit*, Goth. *mith*, with. It appears also as *meth-* in meth-od, *met-* in met-eor.

Min-; min-ster; see **Mono-**.

Mis- (1); mis-deed; mis-take. (E. *and* Scand.) A. S. *mis-*, wrongly, amiss.+ Icel. Dan. Du. *mis-*; Swed. *miss-*; Goth. *missa-*, wrongly. Allied to *miss*, vb.

Mis- (2), badly, ill. (F.−L.) O. F. *mes-*, from L. *minus*, less; used in a depreciatory sense. Appearing in mis-adventure, mis-alliance, mis-chance, mischief. Quite distinct from **Mis-** (1).

Mono-, **Mon-**, single. (Gk.) Gk. μόνο-s, single, sole, alone. Hence *mon-k*, *min-ster*.

Multi-, **Mult-**, many. (L.; or F.−L.) From L. *multus*, much, many.

N (1); n-ewt, n-uncle. (E.) *A newt = an ewt*, where the prefixed *n* is due to the indef. article. *My nuncle = mine uncle*, where the *n* is due to the possessive pronoun. In *n-once*, the prefixed *n* is due to the dat. case of the def. article, as shewn.

N- (2), negative prefix. (E. *or* L.) In *n-one*, the prefixed *n* is due to A. S. *ne*, not. In *n-ull*, it is due to the cognate L. *ne*, not. See **Ne-**.

Ne-, **Neg-**. (L.) L. *ne*, not; *nec* (whence *neg-* in neg-ligere), not, short for *ne-que*, nor, not. In ne-farious, neg-ation, neglect, neg-otiate, ne-uter. See **N-** (2).

Non-, not. (L.; *or* F.−L.) L. *non*, not; short for *ne unum*, not one; see above. It appears as *um-* in um-pire, put for *numpire*.

O-; o-mit; see **Ob-**.

Ob-. (L.; *or* F.−L.) L. *ob*, near; allied to Gk. ἐπί, upon, near; Skt. *api*, moreover, Lith. *apê*, near. See **Epi-**. The force of *ob-* is very variable; it appears as *o-*, *ob-*, *oc-*, *of-*, *op-*, also as extended to *os* (for *obs*?) in o-mit, oblong, oc-cur, of-fer, op-press, os-tensible

Oc-; oc-cur; see **Ob-**.

Of- (1); of-fal. (E.) A.S. *of*, of, off, away. This word is invariably written *off* in composition, except in the case of *offal*, where its use would have brought three *f*'s together.+L. *ab*, Gk. ἀπό; see **Ab-** (1), **Apo-**. It appears as *a-* in a-down.

Of- (2); of-fer; see **Ob-**.

Off-; see **Of-** (1).

On-, on, upon. (E.) A.S. *on*, on. + Gk. ἀνά. From a pronominal base. See **Ana-**. It often appears as *a-*, as in a-foot, asleep, &c.

Op-; op-press; see **Ob-**.

Or- (1); or-deal, or-ts. (E.) A.S. *or-*; cognate with Du. *oor-*, O. Sax. and G. *ur-*, Goth. *us*, away, out of.

Or- (2); or-lop. (Du.) Short for Du. *over*, cognate with E. *over*; see **Over-**.

Os-; os-tensible; see **Ob-**.

Out-. (E.) A.S. *út*, E. *out*, prep.+Goth. *ut*, G. *aus*, Skt. *ud*, out. Shortened to utt- in utt-er.

Outr-; outr-age. (F.−L.) F. *outre* = L. *ultra*, beyond; see **Ultra-**.

Over-. (E.) A.S. *ofer*, E. *over*, prep.+ Goth. *ufar*, L. *s-uper*, Gk. ὑπέρ, Skt. *upari*, above. A comparative form from **Up**, q. v. See **Hyper-**, **Super-**, **Or-** (2).

Pa-; pa-lsy; see **Para-**.

Palin-, Palim-, again. (Gk.) Gk. πάλιν, back, again. It becomes *palim-* in palim-psest.

Pan-, Panto-, all. (Gk.) Gk. πᾶν, neut. of πᾶς, all; παντο-, crude form of the same, occurring in panto-mime.

Par- (1); par-son; see **Per-**.

Par- (2); par-ody; see **Para-**.

Para-, beside. (Gk.) Gk. παρά, beside. Allied to E. *for*, L. *per*, also to Gk. περί. See **Per-, Peri-**, and **For-** (1). It becomes *pa-* in pa-lsy, *par-* in par-ody. ¶ Quite distinct from *para-* in para-chute, para-pet, para-sol, from F. *parer*.

Para- (2); para-dise. Zend *pairi* = Gk. περί.

Pel-; pel-lucid; see **Per-**.

Pen-; pen-insula. (L.) L. *pæn-e*, almost.

Per-, through. (L.; *or* F. – L.) L. *per*, through. Allied to **Para-** and **For-** (1). It appears also as *par-* in par-son, par-don; as *pel-* in pel-lucid; and as *pil-* in pil-grim.

Peri-, around. (Gk.) Gk. περί, around.+Skt. *pari*, round about. Allied to **Para-**, &c.

Pil-; pil-grim; see **Per-**.

Po-; po-sition; see **Por-**.

Pol-; pol-lute; see **Por-**.

Poly-, many. (Gk.) Written for Gk. πολύ-, crude form of πολύ-s, much, many. Allied to E. *full*.

Por- (1); por-tend. (L.) L. *por-*, from O. Lat. *port*, prep., signifying towards, forth; cognate with Gk. πρός, towards, Skt. *prati*, towards, and E. *forth*. It appears as *po-, pol-, por-, pos-*, in po-sition, pol-lute, por-tend, pos-sess.

Por- (2); por-trait; see **Pro-** (1).

Pos-; pos-sess; see **Por-**.

Post-, after. (L.) L. *post*, after, behind. Hence F. *puis*, appearing as *pu-* in pu-ny.

Pour-; pour-tray; see **Pro-**.

Pr- (1); pr-ison; see **Pre-**.

Pr- (2); pr-udent; see **Pro-** (1).

Pre-, Præ-, before. (L.) L. *pre-*, for *præ*, prep., before; put for *prai* *, an old locative case. Allied to **Pro-**. This prefix occurs also in pr-ison; and is curiously changed to *pro-* in pro-vost.

Preter-, beyond. (L.) L. *præter*, beyond; comparative form of *præ*, before.

Pro- (1), before, instead of. (L.; *or* F. – L.) L. *prŏ-*, before, in front, used as a prefix; also L. *prō*, put for *prod*, abl. case used as a preposition, which appears in *prod-igal*. Allied to Gk. πρό, before, Skt. *pra*, before, away; also to E. *for*. See below; and see **For-** (1). It ap-

pears also as *prof-, pour-, por-, pur-, pr-*, in prof-fer, pour-tray, por-trait, pur-vey, pr-udent; where *pour-, por-, pur-* are due to the F. form *pour*.

Pro- (2), before. (Gk.) Gk. πρό, before; cognate with **Pro-** (1). In pro-logue, pro-phet, pro-scenium, pro-thalamium.

Pro- (3); pro-vost; see **Pre-**.

Prod-; prod-igal; see **Pro-** (1).

Prof-; prof-fer; see **Pro-** (1).

Pros-, in addition, towards. (Gk.) Gk. πρός, towards. Allied to **Forth-** and **Por-** (1).

Proto-, Prot-, first. (Gk.) From Gk. πρῶτο-s, first; superl. form of πρό, before; see **Pro-** (2). Shortened to *prot-* in prot-oxide.

Pu-; pu-ny; see **Post-**.

Pur-; pur-vey. (F. – L.) See **Pro-** (1).

R-; r-ally; see **Re-**.

Ra-; ra-bbet; see **Re-**.

Re-, Red-, again. (L.) L. *re-*, *red-* (only in composition), again, back. *Red-* occurs in red-eem, red-olent, red-ound, red-undant, red-dition; and is changed to *ren-* in ren-der, ren-t. In re-ly, re-mind, re-new, it is prefixed to purely E. words; and in re-call, re-cast, to words of Scand. origin. It appears as *r-* in r-ally (1); and as *ra-* in ra-gout. **2.** *Re-* is frequently prefixed to other prefixes, sometimes coalesce with it, so that these words require care. For example, rabbet = re-a-but; rampart = re-em-part; cf. also re-ad-apt, re-col-lect, re-con-cile, re-sur-rection, &c.

Rear-; see **Retro-**.

Red-, Ren-; see **Re-** (above).

Rere-; rere-ward; see **Retro-**.

Retro-, backwards, behind. (L.) L. *retro-*, backwards, back again; a comparative form from *re-*, back; see **Re-**. The prefixes *rear-, rere-*, in rear-guard, rere-ward, are due to L. *retro*, and are of F. origin.

S- (1); s-ober, s-ure; see **Se-**.

S- (2); s-pend; see **Dis-**.

S- (3); s-ample; see **Ex-** (1).

S- (4); s-ombre; see **Sub-**.

Sans-, without. (F. – L.) F. *sans*, without. – L. *sine*, without; see **Sine-**.

Se-, Sed-, away, apart. (L.) L. *se-*, apart; O. Lat. *sed-*, apart, which is probably retained in sed-ition. The orig. sense was probably 'by oneself.' It appears as *s-* in s-ober, s-ure.

Semi-, half. (**L.**) L. *semi-*, half. **+** Gk.
ἡμί-, half; see **Hemi-**.

Sine-, without. (**L.**) L. *sine*, without;
lit. if not.—L. *si*, if; *ne*, not. Hence F.
sans, without.

So-; so-journ; see **Sub-**.

Sover-, **Sopr-**; see **Super-**.

Stra-; stra-nge; see **Extra-**.

Su-; su-spect; see **Sub-**.

Sub-, under. (**L.**) L. *sub*, under, (sometimes) up. Allied to Gk. ὑπό, under;
Skt. *upa*, near, under; also to E. *up* and
of. See **Hypo-**, **Of-**, **Up-**. *Sub* also appears as *s-*, *so-*, *su-*, *suc-*, *suf-*, *sug-*, *sum-*,
sup-, *sur-*, in s-ombre, so-journ, su-spect,
suc-ceed, suf-fuse, sug-gest, sum-mon,
sup-press, sur-rogate. It is also extended
to *sus-* (for *subs-*); as in sus-pend.

Subter-, beneath. (**L.**) L. *subter*, beneath; comparative form from *sub*, under. See **Sub-**.

Suc-, **Suf-**, **Sug-**, **Sum-**, **Sup-**; see
Sub-.

Super-, above, over. (**L.**) L. *super*,
above; comparative form of L. *sub*,
under, also up.**+**Gk. ὑπέρ, over, beyond;
A.S. *ofer*, E. *over*. See **Hyper-**, **Over-**;
also **Sub-**. Hence *supra*, beyond, orig.
abl. feminine. Also *sover-* in sover-eign,
which is a F. form; and *sopr-* in sopr-ano,
which is an Ital. form. Also F. *sur-* =
L. *super*.

Supra-, beyond; see above.

Sur- (1); sur-rogate; see **Sub-**.

Sur- (2); sur-face; see **Super-**.

Sus-; sus-pend; see **Sub-**.

Sy-, **Syl-**, **Sym-**; see **Syn-**.

Syn-, with, together with. (**Gk.**) Gk.
σύν, with. Allied to L. *cum*, with; see
Com-. It appears as *sy-*, *syl-*, *sym-*, and
syn-, in sy-stem, syl-logism, sym-metry,
syn-tax.

T- (1); t-wit. (**E.**) *Twit* is from A.S.
æt-witan, to twit, reproach; thus *t-* is
here put for E. *at*.

T- (2); t-awdry. (**F.—L.**) *Tawdry* is for
Saint Awdry; thus *t-* is here the final
letter of *sain-t*.

T- (3); t-autology. (**Gk.**) Here *t-* represents Gk. τό, neuter of def. article.

Thorough-, through. (**E.**) Merely another
form of E. *through*.

To- (1), to-day. (**E.**) A.S. *tó*, to.

To- (2), intensive prefix. (**E.**) Obsolete,
except in *to-brake*. A.S. *tó-*, apart,
asunder; prob. cognate with L. *dis-*,

apart. See **Dis-**. ¶ Some connect it
with Gk. δύς-; see **Dys-**.

Tra-, **Tran-**; see below.

Trans-, beyond. (**L.**) L. *trans*, beyond.
Shortened to *tran-* in tran-scend; and
to *tra-* in tra-duce, tra-verse, &c. Hence
F. *tres-*, occurring in tres-pass; and *tre-*
in tre-ason.

Tre- (1), **Tres-**. (**F.—L.**) See above.

Tre- (2); tre-ble. (**F.—L.**) See below.

Tri- (1), thrice. (**L.**) L. *tri-*, thrice;
allied to *tres*, three. Hence tri-ple, treble, &c.

Tri- (2), thrice. (**Gk.**) Gk. τρι-, thrice; allied
to τρία, neut. of τρεῖς, three. Hence trigonometry, &c.

Twi-, double, doubtful. (**E.**) A.S. *twi-*,
double; allied to *twá*, two. Hence twi-
bill, twi-light.

Ultra-, beyond. (**L.**) L. *ultra*, beyond;
orig. abl. fem. of O. Lat. *ulter*, adj., appearing in *ulter-ior*, which see in Dict.
Hence F. *outre*, beyond, appearing in
outr-age; also in E. utter-ance (2), corruption of F. *outr-ance*.

Um-; um-pire; see **Non-**.

Un- (1), negative prefix to nouns, &c. (**E.**)
A.S. *un-*, not; cognate with L. *in-*, not,
Gk. ἀν-, not. See **An-** (2), **In-** (3).

Un- (2), verbal prefix, signifying the reversal of an action. (**E.**) A.S. *un-*,
verbal prefix; cognate with Du. *ont-*,
ent-, G. *ent-*, O. H. G. *ant-*, Goth. *and-*.
The same as E. *an-* in an-swer; see
An- (5), **Anti-**.

Un- (3); un-til, un-to. (**O. Low G.**) See
un-to in Dict., p. 533.

Un- (4), **Uni-**, one. (**L.**) L *un-us*, one;
whence uni-vocal, with one voice; unanimous, of one mind; &c. Cognate
with E. *one*.

Under-. (**E.**) A.S. *under*, E. *under*, prep.

Up-. (**E.**) A.S. *up*, E. *up*, prep. Allied
to Of, Sub-, Hypo-.

Utt-. (**E.**) See **Out**.

Utter-. (**F.—L.**) Only in *utter-ance* (2).
F. *outre*, L. *ultra*; see **Ultra-**.

V-; v-an. (**F.—L.**) See **Ab-** (1).

Ve-, apart from (**L.**) L. *ue-*, apart from;
prob. allied to L. *bi-* and *duo*, two. Only
in ve-stibule, and (possibly) in ve-stige.

Vice-, **Vis-**, in place of. (**L.**; *or* **F.—L.**)
L. *uice*, in place of, whence O. F. *vis*,
the same. The latter appears only in
vis-count.

With-, against. (E.) A. S. *wið*, against; the sense is preserved in with-stand. In with-hold, with-draw, it signifies 'back.'

Y-; y-wis, y-clept. (E.) A. S. *ge-*, prefix; M. E. *i-*, *y-*. This prefix appears as *a-* in a-ware, as *c-* in c-lutch, and as *e-* in e-nough. See **A-** (11), **E-** (2).

II. SUFFIXES.

THE number of suffixes in modern English is so great, and the forms of several, especially in words derived through the French from Latin, are so variable, that an attempt to exhibit them all would tend to confusion. The best account of their origin is to be found in Schleicher, Compendium der Vergleichenden Grammatik der Indo-germanischen Sprachen. An account of Anglo-Saxon suffixes is given at p. 119 of March, Comparative Grammar of the Anglo-Saxon Language. Lists of Anglo-Saxon words, arranged according to their suffixes, are given in Loth, Etymologische Angel-saechsischenglische Grammatik, Elberfeld, 1870. The best simple account of English suffixes in general is that given in Morris, Historical Outlines of English Accidence, pp. 212-221, 229-242; to which the reader is particularly referred. See also Koch, Historische Grammatik der Englischen Sprache, vol. iii. pt. 1, pp. 29-76. Schleicher has clearly established the fact that the Aryan languages abound in suffixes, each of which was originally intended slightly to modify the meaning of the root to which it was added, so as to express the radical idea in a new relation. The force of many of these must, even at an early period, have been slight, and in many instances it is difficult to trace it; but in some instances it is still clear, and the form of the suffix is then of great service. The difference between *lov-er*, *lov-ed*, and *lov-ing* is well marked, and readily understood. One of the most remarkable points is that most Aryan languages delighted in adding suffix to suffix, so that words are not uncommon in which two or more suffixes occur, each repeating, it may be, the sense of that which preceded it. Double diminutives, such as *parti-c-le*, i.e. a little little part, are sufficiently common. The Lat. superl. suffix *-is-si-mus* (Aryan *-yans-ta-ma*) is a simple example of the use of a treble suffix, which really expresses no more than is expressed by *-mus* alone in the word *pri-mus*. The principal Aryan suffixes, as given by Schleicher, are these: *-a*, *-i*, *-u*, *-ya*, *-wa*[1], *-ma*, *-ra* (later form *-la*), *-an*, *-ana*, *-na*, *-ni*, *-nu*, *-ta*, *-tar* or *-tra*, *-ti*, *-tu*, *-dhi*, *-ant* or *-nt*, *-as*, *-ka*. But these can be readily compounded, so as to form new suffixes; so that from *-ma-na* was formed *-man* (as in E. *no-min-al*), and from *-ma-na-ta* or *-man-ta* was formed *-manta* (as in E. *argu-ment*). Besides these, we must notice the comparative suffix *-yans*, occurring in various degraded shapes; hence the Gk. μεῖζον-, greater, put for μέγ-yον, the *s* being dropped. This suffix usually occurs in combination, as in *-yans-ta*, Gk. -ιστο-, superl. suffix; *-yans-ta-ma*, Lat. *is-si-mus* (for *-is-ti-mus* *), already noted. The combinations *-ta-ra*, *-ta-ta* occur in the Gk. -τερο-, -τατο-, the usual suffixes of the comparative and superlative degrees.

One common error with regard to suffixes should be guarded against, namely, that of mis-dividing a word so as to give the suffix a false shape. This is extremely common in such words as *logi-c*, *civi-c*, *belli-c-ose*, where the suffix is commonly spoken of as being *-ic* or *-ic-ose*. This error occurs, for instance, in the elaborate book on English Affixes by S. S. Haldemann, published at Philadelphia in 1865; a work which is of considerable use as containing a very full account, with numerous examples, of suffixes and prefixes. But the author does not seem to have understood the matter rightly, and indulges in some of the most extraordinary freaks, actually deriving *musk* from 'Welsh *mus* (from *mw*, that is forward, and *ws*, that is impulsive), that starts out, an effluvium;' p. 74. The truth is that *civi-c* (Lat. *ciuicus*) is derived from Lat. *ciui-*, crude form of *ciuis*, a citizen, with the suffix *-cus* (Aryan -KA); and *logi-c* is from Gk. λογικός, from λογι-, put for λόγο-, crude form of λόγος, a discourse, with the suffix -κος (Aryan -KA) as before. Compare Lat. *ciui-tas*, Gk. λογο-μαχία. *Belli-c-ose*, Lat. *bellicosus*, is from Lat. *belli-*, put for *bello-*, crude form of *bellum*, war, with suffix *-c-ōsus*

---

[1] Schleicher writes *-ja* for *-ya*, *-va* for *-wa*, in the usual German fashion.

(Aryan *-ka-wan-ta*, altered to *-ka-wan-sa*; Schleicher, § 218). Of course, words in *-i-c* are so numerous that *-ic* has come to be regarded as a suffix at the present day, so that we do not hesitate to form *Volta-ic* as an adjective of *Volta*; but this is English misuse, not Latin etymology. Moreover, since both *-i-* and *-ka* are Aryan suffixes, such a suffix as *-ι-κος*, *-i-cus*, is *possible* both in Greek and Latin; but it does not occur in the particular words above cited, and we must therefore be careful to distinguish between a suffixed vowel and an essential part of a stem, if we desire to understand the matter clearly.

One more word of warning may perhaps suffice. If we wish to understand a suffix, we must employ comparative philology, and not consider English as an absolutely isolated language, with laws different from those of other languages of the Aryan family. Thus the *-th* in *tru-th* is the *-ð* of A. S. *treów-ð*, gen. case *treów-ðe*, fem. sb. This suffix answers to that seen in Goth. *gabaur-ths*, birth, gen. case *gabaur-thais*, fem. sb., belonging to the *-i-*stem declension of Gothic strong substantives. The true suffix is therefore to be expressed as Goth. *-thi*, cognate with Aryan *-ti*, so extremely common in Latin; cf. *do-ti-*, dowry, *men-ti-*, mind, *mor-ti-*, death, *mes-si-* (= *met-ti-*), harvest, that which is mown. Hence, when Horne Tooke gave his famous etymology of *truth* as being 'that which a man *troweth*,' he did in reality suggest that the *-ti-* in Lat. *mor-ti-* is identical with the *-t* in *mori-t-ur* or in *ama-t*; in other words, it was a mere whim.

III. LIST OF ARYAN ROOTS.

The following is a brief list of the forms of the Aryan roots which appear in English. By an Aryan root is meant a short monosyllabic base which occurs in more than one, and frequently in several, of the Aryan languages. These languages are usually divided into seven groups, viz. Indian, Persian, Celtic, Græco-Latin, Teutonic, Slavonic, and Lettic (to which belongs Lithuanian). As far as English is concerned, the most important languages belonging to these groups are (1) Sanskrit, belonging to the Indian group; (2) Greek; (3) Latin; and (4) Anglo-Saxon, Icelandic, and Old High-German, all belonging to the Teutonic group. Old Slavonic and Lithuanian are also often very helpful in explaining the forms and significations of the roots. An example of a Teutonic base is BAR, to bear, appearing in A. S. *bær*, pt. t. of *beran*, to bear, and in the Gothic *bar*, pt. t. of *bairan*, to bear. Now a comparison of this base with the forms occurring in Skt. *bhar*, Gk. φέρ-ειν, Lat. *fer-re*, to bear (which three can all be reduced to a common original of the form BHAR), shews us that the base which in the Teutonic languages appears as BAR is found in what may be called the 'classical' languages in the form BHAR; the only difference being in the initial letter. Further comparison between the Teutonic and classical languages shews that several hundred roots exist in which the same phenomenon occurs, and hence Grimm was enabled to demonstrate that the forms of the roots vary in different Aryan languages according to a regular law, now usually known as 'Grimm's law.' It is sufficient to state here that, if Gothic, Anglo-Saxon, and Icelandic spellings be adopted as the basis of 'English' or 'Teutonic' roots, and Sanskrit spellings be adopted as the basis of 'classical' roots, then the following changes occur initially.

English.	g	k(c)	h	d	t	th	b	p	f
Sanskrit.	gh	g	k	dh	d	t	bh	.	p

In the lower line a blank will be observed below E. *p*. It is usually said that E. *p* answers to Skt. *b*, but there is no proof of this; and my own impression is that it answers (abnormally) to Skt. *p*, which in some cases did not turn into E. *f*, as the regular law requires.

The following list of roots is a bare enumeration of them, with an account of the double forms. Such as are printed in thick type, as **AK**, are 'classical' or primitive Aryan forms; such as are printed in other capitals, as AH, are 'English' or primitive Teutonic forms. It must further be observed that similar *sound-shiftings* occur when the letters are *final* as well as *initial*; but the case of the initial letters was mentioned first, as being the easiest to follow. It may also be noted here that a primitive R frequently passes into L, even at an early period; of this, a considerable number of examples might readily be adduced. For a much fuller account of these roots, with illustrative examples, the student is referred to my larger Etymological Dictionary.

☞ The roots are arranged according to the alphabetical order of the Sanskrit alphabet, by help of which we obtain an Aryan alphabet, as follows: a, i, u, ai, au; k, g, gh; t, d, dh, n; p, b, bh, m; y, r, l, w; s. If this arrangement causes any trouble in finding a root, the reader has only to consult the index appended to the list, which is arranged in the usual English order. See p. 597.

1. √ **AK** (= √ AH), to pierce, to be sharp, to be quick.

2. √ **AK** (= √ AH), to see.

3. √ **AK**, to be dark.

4. √ **AK**, or **ANK** (= √ AH or ANG), to bend.

5. √ **AG** (= √ AK), to drive, urge, conduct, ache.

6. √ **AGH**, to say, speak.

7. √ **AGH**, to be in want.

8. √ **AGH** or **ANGH** (= √ AG or ANG), to choke, strangle, compress, afflict.

9. √ **AD** (= √ AT), to eat.

10. √ **AD**, to smell.

11. √ **AN**, to breathe.

12. Base **ANA**, this, that; demonstrative pronoun.

¶ For √ **ANK** and √ **ANGH**, see nos. 4 and 8.

13. √ **ANG**, to anoint, smear.

14. √ **AP**, to seize, attain, bind; to work.

15. √ **AM**, to take.

16. √ **AR**, sometimes **AL**, to raise, move, go.

17. √ **AR**, to drive, to row; probably the same as the root above.

18. √ **AR**, to plough.

19. √ **AR**, to gain, acquire, fit; the same as √ **RA**, to fit; see no. 288.

20. √ **ARK**, to protect, keep safe.

21. √ **ARK**, to shine.

22. √ **ARG**, to shine.

23. √ **ARS**, to flow, glide swiftly.

24. √ **AL**, for original **AR**, to burn.

¶ For another √ **AL**, see no. 16.

25. √ **AW**, to be pleased, be satisfied.

26. √ **AW**, to blow; the same as √ **WA**, to blow; see no. 330.

27. √ **AS**, to breathe, live, exist, be.

28. √ **AS**, to throw, leave (or reject).

29. Pron. base **I**, indicating the 3rd person; orig. demonstrative.

30. √ **I**, to go.

31. √ **IK** (= √ IG), to possess, own.

32. √ **ID** (= √ IT), to swell.

33. √ **IDH** (= √ ID), to kindle.

34. √ **IS**, to glide, move swiftly.

35. √ **IS**, to be vigorous.

36. √ **IS**, to seek, wish for.

¶ √ **UG**, (1) to be wet, (2) to be strong; see nos. 336, 337.

¶ √ **UD**, to wet; see no. 339.

37. √ **UL**, to howl.

38. √ **US**, to burn; see also no. 364.

39. Base **KA** (= HWA), interrogative pronoun.

40. √ **KA**, also **KI** (= √ HI), to sharpen. See no. 70.

41. √ **KAK** (= √ HAH), to laugh, cackle, make a noise, quack (onomatopoetic).

42. √ **KAK** (= √ HAG), to surround, gird.

43. √ **KAK**, or **KANK** (= √ HAH or HANG), to hang, to waver.

44. √ **KAT** (= √ HATH), to cover, protect.

45. √ **KAD** (= √ HAT), to fall, go away.

a. Skt. *çad*, to fall, causal *çâd-aya*, to drive; Lat. *cad-ere*, to fall, *ced-ere*, to go away; A. S. *hat-ian*, to hate (orig. to drive away).

β. Another variation from the same root occurs in the Skt. *çât-aya*, to fell, throw down, *çat-ru*, hatred; A.S. *heaδ-o*, war; Goth. *hinth-an* (pt. t. *hanth*, pp. *hunthans*), to hunt after, catch, *hand-us*, the hand.

46. √ **KAN**, to ring, sing.

¶ For √ **KANK**, see no. 43.

47. √ **KAP** (= √ HAF), to contain, hold, seize, grasp.

48. √ **KAP**, or **KAMP**, to move to and fro, to bend, vibrate, &c.

49. √ **KAM** (= √ HAM), to bend.

50. √ **KAM**, to love; orig. form, **KA**.

¶ For √ **KAMP**, see no. 48.

51. √ **KAR**, to make.

52. √ **KAR**, or **KAL** (= √ HAR), to move, speed, run.

53. √ **KAR** (= √ HAL), to project, stand up (?).

54. √**KAR** (= √ HAR), to hurt, destroy.

55. √**KAR** (= √HAR), to be hard or rough; also in the form **KARK**.

56. √ **KAR** (= √HAR), to curve, or to roll.

57. √**KAR** (= √HAR), to burn.

58. √**KAR**, or **KAL** (= √HAL), to cry out, exclaim, call.

59. √**KARK** (= √KRAK, KLAK, HLAH, HRANG), to make a loud noise, crack, clack, laugh, ring.

¶ For another √**KARK**, see no. 55.

60. √**KART**(= √HRAD, HRAND), to cut, rend.

61. √ **KART** (= √ HARTH), to weave, plait.

62. √**KARD** (= √HART), to swing about, jump.

63. √**KARM** (= √HARM), to be tired.

64. √ **KAL** (= √ HAL), to hide, cover.

¶ For another √**KAL**, see no. 52.

65. √ **KALP** (= √HALP), to assist, help.

66. √**KAS**, to praise, report, speak.

67. √**KAS**, to bound along, speed.

68. √**KAS**, to cough, wheeze.

69. Base **KI** (= HI); pronominal base, weakened from the base KA, who.

70. √**KI** (= √HI), to excite, stir, rouse, sharpen.

71. √**KI**, to search.

72. √ **KI** (=√ HI), to lie down, repose.

73. √ **KIT** (= √HID), to perceive.

74. √ **KU**, to swell out; hence (1) to take in, contain, be hollow, (2) to be strong.

75. √**KU** (= √HU), to beat, strike, hew.

76. √**KUK** (= √HUH), to bend, bow out.

77. √ **KUDH** (= √ HUD), to hide.

78. √**KUP**, or **KUBH**(=√HUP), to go up and down, bend oneself (to lie down), to be crooked.

79. √ **KNAD**, or **KNID** (= √ HNAT or HNIT), to bite, scratch, sting.

80. √**KRI**, or **KLI** (= √HLI), to cling to, lean against, incline.

81. √**KRU**, or **KLU** (= √HLU), to hear.

82. √**KRU** (= √ HRU), to be hard, stiff. or sore.

¶ For roots **KLI** and **KLU**, see nos. 80, 81.

83. √**KWAP**, to breathe out, to reek.

84. √**KWAS** (= √HWAS), to sigh, wheeze, pant.

85. √**KWI** (= √HWI), to shine; only found in the extended forms **KWID**, **KWIT** (= √ HWIT), to be white.

86. √**GA** or **GAM** (= √KWAM), to come, to go, walk, proceed.

87. √**GA**, to beget, produce, of which the more usual form is **GAN** (= √KAN, to produce, allied to KI, to produce, cause to germinate).

88. √**GAN** (= √KAN), to know; also occurring as **GNA** (= KNA).

89. √**GABH**, to be deep, to dip.

90. √**GABH**, to snap, bite, gape.

¶ For √**GAM**, see no. 86.

91. √**GAR** (= √KAR or KAL), to cry out, make a creaking noise, crow, chirp, call.

92. √**GAR**, to devour, swallow, eat or drink greedily (also as **GWAR**).

93. √**GAR**, to assemble.

94. √**GAR** (= √ KAR), to grind, orig. to crumble, esp. with age.

95. √**GAR**, to oppress; perhaps the same as the root above.

96. √**GAR**, to fall; in the form **GAL**.

97. √**GARDH** (= √ GRAD), to strive after, to be greedy.

98. √**GARBH** (= √ GRAP), to grip, seize.

99. √**GAL** (= √KAL), to freeze, be cold.

¶ For another √**GAL**, see no. 96.

100. √**GAS**, to bring, heap together.

101. √**GI**, to overpower, win.

102. √ **GIW** (= √KWI), perhaps orig. **GI**, to live.

103. √**GU** (= √KU), to bellow, to low.

104. √**GU** (= √ KU), to drive.

105. √**GUS** (= √KUS), to choose, taste.

¶ For √**GNA**, to know, see no. 88.

106. √**GHA** (= √GA), to gape, yawn; also, to separate from, leave; see also no. 119.

107. √**GHAD**(=√GAT),to seize, get.

108. √**GHAN**(= √GAN), to strike.

109. Base **GHAM-A** (= GAM-A), earth.

110. √**GHAR** (= √GAR, or GLA), to glow, to shine.

111. √**GHAR**(= √GRA or GAL), to be yellow or green; orig. to glow. See no. 110.

112. √GHAR (= √GAR), to rejoice, be merry, orig. to glow; also, to yearn. See no. 110.

113. √GHAR (= √GAR), to seize, grasp, hold, contain.

114. √GHAR (= √GAR), to bend or wind about (?).

115. √GHAR (= √GAR), to yell, sing loudly.

116. √GHAR, weaker form GHRI (= GRI), to rub, grind; hence, to besmear.

117. √GHARS, to bristle, to be rough; extended from √GHAR, to rub, to be rough. See no. 116.

118. √GHAS (= √GAS, GAR), to wound, strike.

119. √GHI (= √GI), to yawn; weaker form of √GHA, to yawn; see no. 106.

120. √GHID (= √GID), perhaps, to sport, skip.

121. √GHU (= √GU), to pour; whence also √GHU-D, to pour, √GHU-S, to gush.

122. √GHAIS (= √GAIS), to stick, adhere.

123. √TA, to stretch; more commonly TAN; see no. 127.

124. √TAK (whence √THANK), to fit, prepare, make, produce, generate, succeed; lengthened form TAKS, to hew, to prepare, to weave.

125. √TAK (= √THAH), to be silent.

126. √TAK (= √THAH), to thaw; orig. to run, flow.

127. √TAN (= √THAN), to stretch; see √TA above.

¶ √TAN, to thunder; short for STAN; see no. 422.

128. √TANK (= √THANG), to contract, compress.

129. √TAP, to glow.

130. √TAM, to choke, stifle; also to be choked, or breathless, to fear.

131. √TAM or TAN, to cut; hence, to gnaw.

132. √TAR (= √THAR), to pass over or through, to attain to; also to go through, to penetrate or bore, to rub, to turn.

133. √TAR, to tremble; usually in the longer forms TARM or TARS.

134. √TAR or TAL (= √THAL), to lift, endure, suffer.

135. √TARK (= √THARH), to twist, turn round, torture, press. Extension of √TAR, to pass through (no. 132).

136. √TARG, to gnaw; extension of √TAR, to bore (no. 132).

137. √TARGH, to pull, draw violently.

138. √TARP, to be satiated, enjoy; hence, to be gorged or torpid. (But Fick separates these senses.)

139. √TARS (= √THARS), to be dry, to thirst.

¶ For √TAL, to lift, see no. 134.

140. √TITH, to burn.

141. √TU (= √THU), to swell, be strong or large.

¶ √TUD, to strike; put for √STUD, to strike; see no. 431.

142. √TWAK (= √THWAH), to dip, to wash.

143. √DA, to give.

¶ The pt. t. of Lat. dare is dedi; hence verbs like con-dere (pt. t. con-didi) are to be considered as compounds of dare, but they seem to have taken up the sense of √DHA, to place, put, on which account they are frequently referred to that root. The form shews that they should rather be referred hither; the other root being rightly represented in Latin only by facere and its compounds.

144. √DA (= √TA), to distribute, appoint; weaker form DI (= √TI).

145. √DA, to know; whence √DAK, to teach, of which a weaker form is √DIK (= √TIH), to shew.

146. √DA, to bind.

147. √DAK (= √TAH, TANG), to take, hold.

148. √DAK, to honour, think good or fit.

149. √DAK (= √TAH), to bite, to pain.

¶ For another √DAK, see no. 145.

150. √DAM (= √TAM), to tame.

151. √DAM (= √TAM), to build.

152. √DAR (= √TAR), to tear, rend, rive.

153. √DAR, to sleep.

154. √DAR, to do.

155. √DAR, also DAL (= √TAL), to see, consider, regard, purpose; hence √DAR-K, to see.

156. √DARBH, to knit or bind together.

¶ For √DAL, see no. 155.

157. √DI, to hasten.

¶ For another √DI, see no. 144.

¶ √DIK, to shew; see no. 145.

158. √DIW (= √TIW), to shine.

159. √DU (= √TU), to work, toil.

160. √**DU**, to go, to enter; whence √**DUK** (= √TUH), to lead, conduct.

161. √**DRA**, to run; whence √**DRAM**, to run, and √**DRAP**, to run, flow; also √TRAP, to tramp, √TRAD, to tread.

162. √**DHA** (= √DA), to place, set, put, do.

☞ See note to √**DA**. to give; no. 143.

163. √**DHA** (= √DA), to suck.

164. √**DHAN**, to strike.

165. √**DHAR** (= √DAR or DAL), to support, sustain, maintain, hold, keep. Hence is √**DHARGH** (no. 166).

166. √**DHARGH**, to make firm, fasten, hold, drag; extended from √**DHAR**, to hold (above).

167. √**DHARS** (= √DARS), to dare; extension of √**DHAR**, to maintain; see no. 165.

168. √**DHIGH** (= √DIG), to smear, knead, mould, form.

169. √**DHU** (= √DU), to shake, agitate, fan into flame.

170. √**DHUGH** (= √DUG), to milk; also to yield milk, to be serviceable or strong.

171. √**DHUP** (= √DUP, DUF), to render smoky, dusty, or misty; extended from √**DHU**, to shake (no. 169).

172. √**DHRAN** (= √DRAN), to drone, make a droning sound; shorter form √**DHRA**.

173. √**DHWAR** (= √DWAL), to rush forth, bend, fell, stupefy, deceive.

174. √**DHWAS** (= √DWAS), to fall, to perish.

175. √**NAK** (= √NAH), to be lost, perish, die.

176. √**NAK** (= √NAH), to reach, attain.

177. √**NAG** (= √NAK), to lay bare.

178. √**NAGH** (= √NAG), to bite, scratch, gnaw, pierce.

179. √**NAGH**, to bind, connect.

180. √**NAD**, later form **NUD** (= √NUT), to enjoy, profit by.

181. √**NABH** (√NAB), to swell, burst, injure; also appearing in the form **AMBH**.

182. √**NAM**, to allot, count out, portion out, share, take.

183. √**NAS**, to go to, to visit, repair to.

184. √**NIK**, to let fall, to wink.

185. Base **NU**, now; of pronominal origin.

¶ √**NUD**, to enjoy; see √**NAD** (180).

186. √**PA** (= √FA), to feed, nourish, protect; extended form **PAT** (= FAD).

187. √**PA**, weakened forms **PI** and **BI**, to drink.

188. √**PAK** (= √FAH or FAG), to bind, fasten, fix, hold fast.

189. √**PAK**, to cook, to ripen (perhaps originally **KAK**).

190. √**PAK** (= √FAH), to pluck, to comb; metaphorically, to fight.

191. √**PAT** (= √FATH), to fall, fly, seek or fly to, find or light upon.

192. √**PAT** (= √FATH), to spread out, lie flat or open.

193. √**PAT** (= √PATH, abnormally), to go.

194. √**PAD** (= √FAT), to go, bring, fetch, hold.

195. √**PAP**, also **PAMP**, to swell out, grow round.

196. √**PAR** (= √FAR), to fare, advance, travel, go through, experience.

197. √**PAR**, more commonly **PAL** (= √FAL), to fill.

198. √**PAR**, to produce, afford, prepare, share.

199. √**PAR**, to be busy, to barter.

200. √**PARK**, usually **PRAK** (= √FRAH), to pray, ask, demand.

201. √**PARD** (= √FART), to explode slightly.

202. √**PAL** (= √FAL), to cover (?).

¶ For another √**PAL**, see no. 197.

203. √**PI** (= √FI), to hate.

204. √**PI**, to swell, be fat.

205. √**PI**, to pipe, chirp, of imitative origin; in the reduplicated form **PIP**.

206. √**PIK**, weaker form **PIG**, to prick, cut, adorn, deck, paint.

207. √**PIS**, to pound.

208. √**PU** (= √FU), to purify, cleanse, make clear or evident.

209. √**PU** (= √FU), to beget, produce.

210. √**PU**, to strike.

211. √**PU** (= √FU), to stink, to be foul.

212. √**PUK**, weaker form **PUG**, to strike, pierce, prick.

213. √**PUT**, to push, to swell out (?). (Doubtful; tentative only; see note to **pudding**, s. v. **Pad** (1), p. 322).

214. Base **PAU** (= FAU), little, which Fick connects with √**PU**, to beget; the sense of 'little' being connected with that of 'young.' See no. 209.

215. √**PRAK**, commonly **PLAK**

(= √FLAH), to plait, weave, fold to-gether.

¶ For another √PRAK, see no. 200.

216. √PRAT, usually PLAT, to spread out, extend.

☞ There seems to have been a by-form PLAD, answering to E. *flat*; cf. also *plat* (1), *plot*. We also require another variant PLAK, to account for *plac-enta, plank,* and *plain.*

217. √PRI (= √FRI), to love.

218. √PRU, to spring up, jump; the same as √PLU below, no. 221.

219. √PRUS (= √FRUS), to burn; also to freeze.

220. √PLAK, weaker form PLAG (= √FLAK), to strike.

221. √PLU, for earlier PRU (= √ FLU), to fly, swim, float, flow; see no. 218.

222. √BUK, to bellow, snort, puff; of imitative origin.

223. √BHA, to shine; whence the secondary roots BHAK, BHAN, BHAW, and BHAS, as noted below.

A. √BHA, to shine.
B. √BHAK, to shine.
C. √BHAN, to shew.
D. √BHAW, to glow.
E. √BHAS; Skt. *bhás,* to shine, ap-pear.

224. √BHA, also √BHAN (= √ BAN), to speak clearly, proclaim. Pro-bably orig. the same root as the preceding.

225. √BHA, usually BHABH (= √BAB), to tremble.

226. √BHA, or BHAN (= √BAN), to kill.

¶ For √BHAK, to shine, see no. 223.

227. √BHAG (= √BAK), to portion out, to eat.

228. √BHAG (= √BAK), to bake, roast.

229. √BHAG (= √BAK), to go to, flee, turn one's back.

230. √BHADH (= √BAD); also BHANDH (= BAND), to bind; weak-ened form BHIDH, to bind (Curtius).

¶ For √BHAN, (1) to shine, (2) to speak, see nos. 223, 224.

¶ For √BHABH, to tremble, see no. 225.

231. √BHAR (= √BAR), to bear, carry.

232. √BHAR (= √BAR), to bore, to cut.

233. √BHARK or BHRAK, to shut in, stop up, cram; of which there

seems to have been a variant BHARGH (= √BARG), to protect.

234. √BHARK (= √BARH, BRAH), to shine. Allied to √BHARG, to shine; see below, no. 235.

235. √BHARG, usually BHALG or BHLAG (= √BLAK), to shine, burn.

236. √BHARB, to eat.

237. √BHARS (= √BARS or BRAS), to be stiff or bristling.

238. √BHAL (= √BAL), to re-sound; extended from √BHA, to speak: see above, no. 224.

¶ √BHALG, to shine; see no. 235.

239. √BHALGH (= √BALG), to bulge, to swell out.

¶ For √BHAW and BHAS, to shine; see no. 223.

240. √BHID (= √BIT), to cleave. bite.

241. √BHIDH, to trust; orig. to bind; weakened form of √BHADH, which see (no. 230).

242. √BHU (= √BU), to grow, be-come, be, dwell, build.

243. √BHUG (= √BUK), collateral form BHRUG (= BRUK), to enjoy, use.

244. √BHUGH (= √BUG), to bow, bend, turn about.

245. √BHUDH (= √BUD), to awake, to admonish, inform, bid; also, to become aware of, to search, to ask.

246. √BHUR (= √BUR, BAR), to be active, boil, burn, rage.

247. √BHRAG (= √BRAK), to break.

248. √BHRAM, to hum, to whirl, be confused, straggle.

249. √BHLA (= √BLA), to blow, puff, spout forth.

250. √BHLA (= √BLA), to flow forth, blow as a flower, bloom, flourish. (Prob. orig. identical with the preceding.)

251. √BHLAGH (= √BLAG), to strike, beat.

252. √MA, to measure, shape, ad-measure, compare; hence √MAD (= √ MAT), to mete.

253. √MA, to think, more commonly MAN; hence also √MADH, to learn, to heal.

254. √MA, to mow.

¶ √MA, to diminish; see √MI below (no. 270).

255. √MAK, to have power, be great, strong or able, to assist; appearing also in the varying forms MAGH (= √MAG) and

MAG (= MAK). The various bases are much commingled.

256. √MAK (=√MAH), to pound, to knead, macerate.

¶ For the root **MAGH** or **MAG**, see no. 255.

257. √MAT, to whirl, turn, throw, spin.

258. √MAD, to drip, to flow.

259. √MAD (= √MAT), to chew; perhaps orig. to wet, and the same as the root above.

¶ For the √MADH, to learn, heal; see no. 253.

260. √MAN, to remain; orig. to think, to wish, dwell upon, stay, and the same as the √MA above; see no. 253.

261 √MAN, to project.

262. √MAND, to adorn.

263. √MAR, also **MAL**, to grind, rub, kill, die; also, to make dirty. For extensions of this root, see nos. 266-269.

264. √MAR, to shine; whence √ MARK (= √MARG), to glimmer.

265. √MAR or **MUR**, to rustle, murmur; of imitative origin. See √MU (no. 276).

266. √MARK, to touch rub slightly, stroke, seize; see no. 263.

267. √MARG (=√MALK) to rub gently, wipe, stroke, milk. Extension of √MAR; see no. 263.

268. √MARD (=√MALT), to rub down, crush, melt. An extension of √ MAR; see no. 263.

269. √MARDH (= √MALD), to be soft, moist, or wet. An extension of √ MAR, to grind; see no. 263.

¶ For √MAL, to grind, see no. 263.

270. √MI, to diminish; prob. from an earlier form **MA**. Hence Teut. base MIT, to cut.

271. √MI, to go.

272. √MIK (= √MIH), to mix.

273. √MIGH (= √MIG), to sprinkle, wet.

274. √MIT (=√MID), to exchange.

275. √MU, to bind, close, shut up, enclose.

276. √MU, to utter a slight suppressed sound, to utter a deep sound, to low, to mutter; see no. 265.

277. √MU, to move, push, strip off.

278. √MUK, to loosen, dismiss, shed, cast away.

¶ √MUR, to murmur; the same as √MAR, to rustle; see no. 265.

279. √MUS, to steal.

280. Pronominal base **YA**; originally demonstrative, meaning 'that.'

281. √YA, to go; secondary form from I, to go; for which see above; no. 30. Hence √YAK, to cause to go away, to throw (Curtius).

282. √YAG, to worship.

283. √YAS, to ferment, seethe.

284. √YAS, to gird (with long *a*).

285. √YU, to keep back, defend, help(?). So Fick, i. 732, who refers hither Skt. *yu-van*, Lat. *iu-uenis*, young, and all kindred words. But Curtius (i. 285) and Vaniček refer Lat. *iu-uars* and *iu-uenis* to √DIW, to shine, connecting them with Lat. *Iu-piter*. Neither theory seems quite clear.

286. √YU, to bind together, to mix; whence √YUG, to join, for which see below.

287. √YUG (= √YUK), to join, yoke; an extension of √YU, to bind (see above).

288. √RA, to fit; the same as √ AR, to gain, fit; see no. 19.

289. √RA, to rest, to be delighted, to love. Hence √LAS, which see below; no. 324.

290. √RA, also **LA**, to resound, bellow, roar; extended form **RAS**. See also √ RAK, no. 292; and see no. 304.

291. √RA, another form of √AR, to go, or to drive. ☞ Fick gives the root the sense of to fit, thus making it the same as √AR, to fit. It seems much simpler to connect *ratis* and *rota* with the sense 'to go, drive, or run.'

292. √RAK, also **LAK**, to croak, to speak.

293. √RAG (= √RAK), to stretch, stretch out, reach, make straight, rule.

294. √ RAG (= √ RAK), also **LAG**, to collect; hence to put together, to read. Hence no. 323.

295. √RAG (=√RAK), also **LAG**, to reck, heed, care for.

296. √ RAGH, nasalised form **RANGH** or **LANGH** (= √LANG), to spring forward, jump.

297. √RAD (= √RAT), to split, gnaw, scratch.

298. √RADH, or **LADH**, to quit, leave, forsake.

299. √RADH (= √RAD), to assist, advise, interpret, read.

300. √RAP, to cover, roof over.

301. √RAP, to snatch, seize: usually

regarded as a variant of the commoner √ RUP, no. 315; and see no. 321.

302. √ RAB or LAB (= √ LAP), to droop, hang down, slip, glide, fall.

303. √ RABH (= √ RAB), also LABH (= LAB), to seize, lay hold of, work, be vehement; of which the original form was ARBH (= ARB).

304. √ RABH (= √ RAB), to make a noise; extended from √ RA, to resound; no. 290.

305. √ RI, also LI, to pour, distil, melt, flow. Hence √ LIK, to melt, flow.

306. √ RIK (= √ RIH), to scratch, furrow, tear. See also no. 309.

307. √ RIK, also LIK (= √ LIH), to leave, grant, lend.

308. √ RIGH, also LIGH (= √ LIG), to lick.

309. √ RIP (= √ RIF), to break, rive. A variant of √ RIK, to scratch; see no. 306.

310. √ RU, to sound, cry out, bray, yell; whence the extended form RUG, to bellow.

311. √ RUK, also LUK (= √ LUH), to shine.

312. √ RUG, or LUG (= √ LUK), to break, bend, treat harshly, make to mourn; to pull, lug.

313. √ RUDH (= √ RUD), to redden, to be red.

314. √ RUDH or LUDH (= √ LUD), to grow.

315. √ RUP (= √ RUB), also LUP, to break, tear, seize, pluck, rob. See √ RAP, no. 301; and √ LAP, no. 321.

¶ √ LA, to low; the same as √ RA, to resound; see no. 290.

316. √ LAK, to bend, depress.

¶ √ LAK, to speak; see √ RAK, to speak (no. 292).

317. √ LAG, to be lax, to be slack or languid.

¶ √ LAG, to collect; see √ RAG, to collect (no. 294).

¶ √ LAG, to reck; see √ RAG, to reck (no. 295).

318. √ LAGH (= √ LAG), to lie down.

319. √ LAD (= √ LAT), to let, let go, make slow.

¶ √ LADH, to quit; see no. 298.

¶ √ LANGH, to spring forward; see no. 296.

320. √ LAP, weakened form LAB, to lick, lap up.

321. √ LAP, to peel; parallel form LUP. See √ RUP above; no. 315.

322. √ LAP, to shine.

¶ √ LAB, to droop; see no. 302.

¶ √ LABH, to seize; see no. 303.

323. √ LAS, to pick out, glean; from √ LAG, to collect; no. 294. This root is probably due to an extension of Teutonic √ LAK to LAKS, with subsequent loss of *k*; see Curtius, i. 454.

324. √ LAS, to yearn or lust after, desire. Probably an extension of √ RA, to rest, love; no. 289.

¶ √ LI or LIK, to flow; see no. 305.

¶ √ LIK, to leave; see no. 307.

¶ √ LIGH, to lick; see no. 308.

325. √ LIP, for older RIP, to smear, to cleave; an extension of √ RI or LI, to flow; no. 305.

¶ √ LIBH, to desire; see no. 329.

326. √ LU, to wash, cleanse, expiate.

327. √ LU, to cut off, separate, loosen; whence Teut. √ LUS, to be loose, to lose.

328. √ LU, to gain, acquire as spoil.

¶ √ LUK, to shine; see no. 311.

¶ √ LUG, to break; see no. 312.

¶ √ LUDH, to grow; see no. 314.

¶ √ LUP, to break; see no. 315.

¶ √ LUS, to be loose; see no. 327.

329. √ LUBH (= √ LUB), to desire, love; also in the weakened form LIBH.

330. √ WA, to breathe, blow; the same as √ AW, to blow; see no. 26.

331. √ WA, to bind, plait, weave; commoner in the weakened form WI, to bind; see no. 366. And see nos. 343, 347.

332. √ WA, to fail, lack, be wanting.

333. √ WAK, to cry out; hence to speak.

334. √ WAK (= √ WAH), weaker form WAG (= √ WAK), to bend, swerve, go crookedly, totter, nod, wink.

335. √ WAK, to wish, desire, be willing.

336. √ WAG (= √ WAK), or UG (= √ UK), to be strong, vigorous, or watchful, to wake; hence the extended form WAKS (= WAHS), to wax, to grow.

337. √ WAG or UG (= √ WAK), to wet, to be moist; whence the extended form WAKS or UKS (= √ UHS), to sprinkle.

338. √ WAGH (= √ WAG), to carry, to remove, to wag.

339. √ WAD (= √ WAT), also UD, to well or gush out, to moisten, to wet.

340. √ WAD, to speak, recite, sing.

341. √WADH (= √WAD), to carry home, to wed a bride, to take home a pledge; hence to pledge.

342. √WADH, to strike, kill, thrust away, hate.

343. √WADH (= √WAD), to bind, wind round; extension of √WA, to bind; see no. 331.

344. √WAN, to honour, love, also to strive to get, to try to win; whence the desiderative √WANSK; see no. 346.

345. √WAN, to hurt, to wound. Orig. to attack, strive to get; merely a particular use of the verb above, as shewn by the A.S. *winnan* and Icel. *vinna*.

346. √WANSK, to wish; desiderative form of √WAN, to try to win; see no. 344 above.

347. √WABH (= √WAB), to weave; extended from √WA, to plait, see no. 331.

348. √WAM, to spit out, to vomit.

349. √WAR, also WAL, to choose, to like, to will; hence, to believe.

350. √WAR, to speak, inform.

351. √WAR, also WAL, to cover, surround, protect, guard, be wary, observe, see.

352. √WAR, also WAL, to wind, turn, roll; hence, to well up, as a spring. Orig. the same as WAR, to cover, surround (above); and see nos. 358, 359.

353. √WAR, also WAL, to drag, tear, pluck, wound; see also √WARK below, no. 355.

354. √WAR, also WAL, to be warm, to be hot, to boil. Compare √ WAR, to wind (no. 352).

355. √WARK, also WALK, to drag, tear, rend; extended from √WAR, to drag (no. 353). ☞ Fick refers Gk. ῥήγ-νυμι, I break, to this root; it certainly seems distinct from L. *frangere* = E. *break*.

356. √WARG (= √WARK), to press, urge, shut in, bend, oppress, irk.

357. √WARG (= √WARK), to work. Prob. the same as no. 356.

358. √WARGH (= √WARG), to choke, strangle, worry. Extended from √ WAR, to wind, turn, twist (no. 352).

359. √WART (= √WARTH), to turn, turn oneself. to become, to be. Extended from √WAR, to turn (no. 352).

360. √WARDH, to grow, increase.

361. √WARP, to throw.

¶ For √WAL, with various meanings,

see nos. 349, 351-354; and for √WALK, see no. 355.

362. √WAS, to clothe, to put on clothes.

363. √WAS, to dwell, to live, to be. Prob. orig. the same root as the above.

364. √WAS, to shine; US, to burn; see no. 38.

365. √WAS, to cut.

366. √WI, to wind, bind, plait, weave; weakened form of √WA, to weave (no. 331). Hence √WIK, to bind; see no. 368.

367. √WI, to go, to drive; extended form WIT (= √WITH), to drive.

368. √WIK, to bind, fasten; extended from √WI, to bind (no. 366).

369. √WIK, to come, come to, enter.

370. √WIK, to separate, remove, give way, change, yield; by-form WIG (= √ WIK), to yield, bend aside.

371. √WIK (= √WIG), to fight, to conquer, vanquish.

372. √WID (= √WIT), to see, observe; hence, to know.

373. √WIDH (= √WID), to pierce, perforate, break through.

374. √WIP (= √WIB), to tremble, vibrate, shake.

¶ Pronominal base SA, he; see base SAM (no. 384).

375. √SA, to sow, strew, scatter.

376. √SAK, to follow, accompany.

377. √SAK, to cut, cleave, sever; also found in the form SKA; see no. 396.

378. √SAK, weaker form SAG, to fasten; also to cleave to, hang down from.

379. √SAK, to say.

380. √SAGH (= √SAG), to bear, endure, hold, hold in, restrain.

381. Base SAT, full; perhaps from a root SA, to sate.

382. √SAD (= √SAT), to sit.

383. √SAD, to go, travel.

384. Base SAM, also found as SA- (at the beginning of a word), together, together with. From the pronominal base SA, he, this one.

385. √SAR, to string, bind; a better form is √SWAR, which see (no. 458).

386. √SAR, also SAL, to go, hasten, flow, spring forward. See nos. 388, 451.

387. √SAR, also SAL, to keep, preserve, make safe, keep whole and sound.

388. √SARP (= √SALB), to slip along, glide, creep. Extended from √ SAR, to flow (no. 386).

¶ √SAL, (1) to flow, (2) to preserve; see nos. 386, 387.

389. √SIK (= √SIH), to wet, to pour out.

390. √SIW or SU, to sew, stitch together.

391. √SU, to generate, produce.

392. √SU or SWA, to drive, to toss; whence √SWAL, to agitate, boil up, swell; √SWAP, to move swiftly; also Teut. √SWAM, to swim, Teut. √SWAG, to sway; and Teut. √SWANG, to swing.

393. √SUK, also SUG (= √SUK), to flow, to cause to flow, to suck. (The root shews *both* forms.)

394. √SUS, to dry, wither.

395. √SKA, to cover, shade, hide.

396. √SKA, variant of √SAK, to cut (no. 377); hence √SKAN, to dig; and see nos. 398, 402, 403, 406, 409, 411, 416.

397. √SKAG (= √SKAK), to shake.

398. √SKAD (= √SKAT), to cleave, scatter, commoner in the weakened form SKID, which see below; no. 411. Extended from √SKA, to cut (no. 396).

399. √SKAD (= √SKAT), to cover; extension of √SKA, to cover (no. 395).

400. √SKAND, to spring, spring up, climb.

401. √SKAND, to shine, glow.

402. √SKAP, to hew, to cut, to chop; an extension from √SKA, to cut (no. 396).

403. √SKAP (= √SKAP or SKAB), to dig, scrape, shave, shape; probably orig. the same as the preceding.

404. √SKAP, to throw, to prop up.

405. √SKAR, to move hither and thither, to jump, hop, stagger or go crookedly.

406. √SKAR or SKAL, to shear, cut, cleave, scratch, dig. See no. 396.

407. √SKAR, to separate, discern, sift.

408. √SKAR or SKAL, to resound, make a noise; whence Teut. base SKRI, to scream.

409. √SKARP or SKALP, to cut; lengthened form of √SKAR, to cut.

¶ √SKAL, (1) to cleave, (2) to resound; see nos. 406, 408.

410. √SKAW, to look, see, perceive, beware of.

411. √SKID, to cleave, part; weakened form of √SKAD, to separate; see no. 398. ¶ Fick separates *cædere* from *scindere*, assigning to the former a root SKIDH; this seems quite needless, see Curtius, i. 306.

412. √SKU, to cover; see no. 395.

413. √SKU, also extended to SKUT (= √SKUD), to move, shake, fly, fall, drop.

414. √SKUD (= √SKUT), or SKUND, to spring out, jut out, project, shoot out, shoot; weakened form of √SKAND, to spring (no. 400).

415. √SKUBH (= √SKUB), to become agitated, be shaken; hence to push, shove. Extended from √SKU, to move (no. 413).

416. √SKUR, also √SKRU, to cut, scratch, furrow, flay, weakened form of √SKAR, to cut (no. 406).

417. √SKLU, to shut (given by Fick under KLU).

418. √STA, to stand, whence various extended forms; see the roots STAK, STAP, STABH, STAR, STU. Hence also the Teutonic bases STAM, to stop, STAD, to stand fast.

419. √STAK, also STAG (= √ STAK), to stick or stand fast; extension of √STA, to stand (no. 418). ¶ The E. *stock* is better derived from √STAG, to thrust (no. 421).

420. √STAG (= √STAK), to cover, thatch, roof over.

421. √STAG (= √STAK, STANK, STANG), to thrust against, to touch, also to smite, strike against, smell, stink, sting, pierce. See also √STIG (no. 428).

422. √STAN, to make a loud noise, stun, thunder.

423. √STAP (= √STAB), to cause to stand, make firm. Extended from √STA, to stand, no. 418.

424. √STABH (= √STAP), to stem, stop, prop, orig. to make firm; hence to stamp, step firmly. Extended from √STA, to stand, no. 418.

425. √STAR, to strew, spread out; also found in the forms STRA, STLA, STRU. And see no. 427.

426. √STAR or STAL, to be firm, also set, place; extended from √STA, to stand, which see; no. 418.

427. √STARG, STRAG, to stretch tight; variants STRIG and STRUG. Extended from √STAR, to spread out, no. 425.

428. √STIG (= √STIK), to stick or pierce, to sting, prick; weakened form of √STAG, to sting; no. 421.

429. √STIGH (= √STIG), to stride, to climb.

430. √STU, to make firm, set, stop, weaker form of √STA, to stand (no. 418); whence √STUP, to set fast.

431. √STU, to strike; extended forms STUD, to strike, beat, and STUP, to beat.

432. √SNA, by-form SNU, to bathe, swim, float, flow.

433. √SNA, to bind together, fasten, especially with string or thread. Often given as NA; but see Curtius, i. 393.

434. √SNAR, to twist, draw tight; longer form SNARK (= √SNARH), to twist, entwine, make a noose. Extended from √SNA, to bind (above).

435. √SNIGH (= √SNIG, also SNIW), to wet, to snow.

¶ SNU, to bathe; see no. 432.

436. √SPA or SPAN, to draw out, extend, increase; to have room, to prosper; to stretch, to pain; to spin.

437. √SPAK, to spy, see, observe, behold.

438. √SPAG or SPANG, to make a loud clear noise.

439. √SPAD or SPAND, to jerk, sling, swing.

¶ For roots SPAN, SPANG, SPAND, see nos. 436, 438, 439.

440. √SPAR, also SPAL, to quiver, jerk, struggle, kick, flutter; see nos. 442, 443.

441. √SPARK, to sprinkle, to be-spot, to scatter.

442. √SPARG, to crack, split, crackle, spring; an extension of √SPAR, to quiver (no. 440).

443. √SPAL, to stumble, to fall. Originally identical with √SPAR, to quiver (no. 440).

¶ For √SPAL, to quiver, see no. 440.

444. √SPU, to blow, puff.

445. √SPU, SPIW, to spit out.

446. √SMA, to rub, stroke; longer form SMAR, to rub over, smear, wipe.

447. √SMAR, to remember, record.

448. √SMARD, to pain, cause to smart.

449. √SMARD or SMALD (= √SMALT), to melt as butter, become oily, to melt. Extended from √SMAR, to smear (no. 446).

450. √SMIL, to smile, to wonder at.

451. √SRU, also STRU, to flow, stream. Allied to √SAR, to flow (no. 386).

¶ For roots SWA, SWAL, SWAP, and the Teutonic bases SWAM, SWAG, SWANG, see no. 392.

452. √SWAD (= √SWAT), to please, to be sweet, esp. to the taste.

453. √SWAN, to resound, sound.

454. √SWAP (= √SWAB), to sleep, slumber.

455. √SWAP, to move swiftly, cast, throw, strew; weakened form SWIP, to sweep.

¶ For root SWAP, to move swiftly, and the Teut. √SWAM, to swim; see √SU, to toss (no. 392).

456. √SWAR, to murmur, hum, buzz, speak. Of imitative origin.

457. √SWAR, also SWAL, to shine, glow, burn.

458. √SWAR, sometimes given as SAR, to string, to bind; also to hang by a string, to swing. See no. 385.

459. √SWARBH, to sup up, ab-sorb.

460. √SWAL, to toss, agitate, swell; extended from √SU (no. 392).

¶ For roots SWAL, (1) to swell, (2) to glow, see nos. 392, 457.

461. √SWID (= √SWIT), to sweat.

BRIEF INDEX TO THE ABOVE ROOTS.

The following Index is merely a guide for finding the place, and does not enumerate all the forms.

da, da-, 143-156.
dha, dha-, 162-167.
dhigh, 168.
dhran, 172.
dhu, dhu-, 169-171.
dhw-, 173, 174.
di, di-, 157, 158.
dra, dra-, 161.
du, 159, 160.
ga, ga-, 86-100.
gha, gha-, 106-118.
ghais, 122.
ghi, ghi-, 119, 120.
ghri, 116.
ghu, 121.
gi, giw, 101, 102.

gna, 88.
gu, gus, 103-105.
i, i-, 29-36.
ka, ka-, 39-68.
ki, ki-, 69-73.
knad, 79.
kr-, 80-82.
ku, ku-, 74-78.
kw-, 83-85.
la-, 316-324.
lip, 325.
lu, lu-, 326-329.
ma, ma-, 252-269.
mi, mi-, 270-274.
mu, mu-, 275-279.
na, na-, 175-183.

nik, 184.
nu, 185.
pa, pa-, 186-202.
pau, 214.
pi, pi-, 203-207.
pl-, 220, 221.
pr-, 215-219.
pu, pu-, 208-213.
ra, ra-, 288-304.
ri, ri-, 305-309.
ru, ru-, 310-315.
sa, sa-, 375-388.
sik, siw, 389, 390.
sk-, 395-417.
sm-, 446-450.
sn-, 432-435.

sp-, 436-445.
sru, 451.
st-, 418-431.
su, su-, 391-394.
sw-, 452-461.
ta, ta-, 123-139.
tith, 140.
tu, twak, 141, 142.
ud, 339.
ug, 336, 337.
ul, 37.
us, 38, 364.
wa, wa-, 330-365.
wi, wi-, 366-374.
ya, ya-, 280-284.
yu, yug, 285-287.

IV. HOMONYMS.

HOMONYMS are words which, though spelt alike, differ considerably in meaning. They may be divided into two classes: (*a*) homonyms from entirely different roots, or at any rate by no means closely connected; (*b*) homonyms from the same root, not differing very widely in origin. Those which belong to the latter class are distinguished by being printed in italics. For further information, see the Dictionary.

abide, allow, an, ancient, angle, arch, arm, art, as, ay.

baggage, bale, *balk*, ball, band, bang, bank, barb, bark, barm, barnacle, barrow, base, bass, baste, bat, *bate*, batten, *batter*, bauble, bay, *beam*, bear, beaver, beck, beetle, bid, bile, bill, billet, *bit*, blanch, blaze, blazon, *bleak*, blot, blow, boil, boom, boot, *bore*, botch, bottle, bound, bourn, bow, bowl, *box*, brake, brawl, bray, *braze*, breeze, *brief*, broil, brook, budge, buffer, buffet, *bug*, bugle, bulk, bull, bump, bunting, burden, *bury*, bush, busk, buss, but, butt.

cab, cabbage, calf, can, cant, cape, caper, *capital*, card, carousal, carp, case, chap, *char*, chase, chink, chop, chuck, cleave, *close*, clove, *club*, clutter, cob, cobble, cock, cockle, cocoa, cod, codling, 'cog, coil, colon, *compact*, con, *contract*, cope, corn, corporal, cotton, count, counterpane, *court*, cow, cowl, crab, *crank*, crease, cricket, croup, crowd, cuff, culver, *cunning*, curry, cypress.

dab, dam, dare, date, *deal*, *defer*, defile, *demean*, desert, deuce, die, *diet*, *distemper*, do, dock, don, down, dowse, drab, dredge, drill, *drone*, duck, dudgeon, dun.

ear, earnest, egg, *eke*, elder, embattle, emboss, entrance, exact, excise.

fair, *fast*, fat, fawn, fell, ferret, feud, file, *fine*, fit, flag, *fleet*, flock, flounce, *flounder*, flue, fluke, flush, foil, fold, *font*, for (for-), force, fore-arm, forego, foster, found, *fount*, *fratricide*, fray, freak, fret, frieze, frog, fry, full, fuse, fusee, fusil, *fust*.

gad, gage, *gain*, gall, gammon, *gang*, gantlet, gar, garb, *gender*, gill, gin, gird, glede, glib, gloss, gore, gout, grail, grate, grave, graze, greaves, greet, *gull*, gum, gust.

hack, *hackle*, haggard, *haggle*, hail, hale, hamper, *handy*, harrier, hatch, hawk, heel, helm, hem, herd, hernshaw, hey-day, *hide*, hind, hip, hob, *hobby*, hock, hold, hoop, hop, hope, host, how, hoy, hue, *hull*, *hum*. il-, im-, in-, (prefixes), *incense*, *incontinent*, indue, *interest*, *intimate*, ir- (*prefix*).

jack, jade, *jam*, jar, jet, *jib*, *job*, *jump*, junk, just.

kedge, keel, kennel, kern, *kind*, kindle, kit, knoll.

lac, *lack*, *lade*, lake, lama, lap, lark, *lash*, last, lathe, lawn, lay, lead, league, *lean*, lease, leave, leech, *let*, lie, lift, light, lighten, *like*, limb, limber, lime, *limp*, ling, link, list, litter, *live*, lock, log, *long*, loom, loon, low, lower, lumber, lurch, lustre, lute.

mace, mail, *main, mall*, mangle, march, *mark*, maroon, mass, mast, match, mate, *matter*, may, mead, meal, mean, meet, mere, mess, mew, *might*, milt, mine, mint, mis-, miss, *mite*, mob, mole, mood, moor, mop, *mortar*, mother, mould, *mount*, mow, muff, mullet, *muscle*, muse, must, mute, mystery.

nag, nap, nave, neat, net, nick, *no*, not.

O, *one*, or, ought, ounce, own.

pad, paddle, paddock, page, pale, pall, pallet, *pap*, partisan, pat, *patch*, pawn, pay, peach, *peck*, peel, peep, peer, pellitory, pelt, pen, perch, periwinkle, *pet*, pie, pile, pill, pine, *pink*, pip, pitch, plane, plash, plat, plight, plot, plump, poach, poke, pole, pool, pore, *port, porter*, pose, post, pounce, pound, pout, *prunk, present*, press, *prime, prior*, prize, prune, *puddle*, puke, pulse, pump, punch, puncheon, punt, *pupil, puppy*, purl, purpose.

quack, quail, quarrel, quarry, quill, quire, quiver.

race, rack, racket, rail, rake, rally, rank, rap, rape, rash, rate, raven, ray, reach, real, rear, *reef*, reel, reeve, refrain, relay, rennet, rent, repair, rest, riddle, rifle, rig, rime, ring, ripple, rock, rocket, roe, rook, *root*,

rote, rouse, row, ruck, rue, ruff, ruffle, rum, rush, rut.

sack, sage, sallow, sap, sardine, sash, saw, say, scald, scale, scar, scarf, *sconce*, scout, screw, scrip, scull, scuttle, seal, seam, see, sell, settle, sew, sewer, *share*, shed, sheer, shingle, shiver, shoal, shock, shore, *shrew*, shrub, *size*, skate, slab, *slay*, slop, slot, smack, smelt, *snite*, snuff, soil, sole, sorrel, sound, sow, *spark*, spell, spill, spire, spit, spittle, spray, *spurt*, squire, stale, *stalk, staple, stare*, stay, *stem*, stern, *stick*, stile, still, stoop, story, strand, *stroke*, *strut*, stud, *sty*, style, summer, swallow, swim.

tache, tail, tang, tap, *taper*, tare, tart, tartar, tassel, tattoo, tear, teem, temple, temporal, *tend*, tender, tense, tent, *terrier*, *the*, thee, *there* (*there*-), thole, thrum, thrush, tick, till, tilt, tip, tire, to-, *toast*, toll, toll, toot, top, tow, *trace, tract*, trap, trepan, trice, *trick*, trill, trinket, truck, trump, tuck, tuft, turtle, twig.

un-, *union, utter*, utterance.

vail, van, *vault*, vent, verge, vice.

wake, *ware*, wax, weed, weld, well, wharf, wheal, wick, wight, *will*, wimble, wind, windlass, *wise, wit*, wood, *wort*, worth, *wrinkle*.

yard, yawl, yearn.

V. LIST OF DOUBLETS.

Doublets are words which, though apparently differing in form, are nevertheless, from an etymological point of view, one and the same, or only differ in some unimportant suffix. Thus *aggrieve* is from L. *aggrauare*; whilst *aggravate*, though really from the pp. *aggrauatus*, is nevertheless used as a verb, precisely as *aggrieve* is used, though the senses of the words have been differentiated. In the following list, each pair of doublets is entered only *once*, to save space.

abbreviate—abridge.
aggrieve—aggravate.
ait—eyot.
alarm—alarum.
allocate—allow (1).
amiable—amicable.
ancient (2)—ensign.
announce—annunciate.
ant—emmet.
anthem—antiphon.
antic—antique.
appeal, *sb.*—peal.
appear—peer (3).
appraise—appreciate.

apprentice—prentice.
aptitude—attitude.
arbour—harbour.
arc—arch (1).
army—armada.
arrack—rack (5).
assay—essay.
assemble—assimilate.
assess—assize, *vb.*
attach—attack.

balm—balsam.
barb (1)—beard.
base—basis.

baton—batten (2).
bawd—bold.
beak—peak; *and see* pike.
beaker—pitcher.
beef—cow.
beldam—belladonna.
bench—bank (1), bank (2).
benison—benediction.
blame—blaspheme.
blare—blase (2).
block—plug.
boss—botch (2).
bound (2)—bourn (1).
bower—byre.

box (2) –pyx, bush (2).
breve—brief.
briar—furze?
brother—friar.
brown—bruin.
bug—puck, pug.

cadence—chance.
caitiff—captive.
caldron, cauldron — chaldron.
calumny—challenge.
camera—chamber.
cancer—canker.
card (1)—chart, carte.
case (2)—chase (3) ; cash.
cask—casque.
castigate—chasten.
catch—chase (1).
cattle—chattels, capital (2).
cavalier—chevalier.
cavalry—chivalry.
cave—cage.
cell—hall.
chaise—chair.
chalk—calx.
champaign—campaign.
channel—canal, kennel.
chant—cant (1).
chapiter—capital (3).
chariot—cart.
chateau—castle.
check, sb.—shah.
chicory—succory.
chief—head.
chieftain –captain.
chirurgeon—surgeon.
choir—chorus, quire (2).
choler—cholera.
chord—cord.
chuck (1)—shock (1).
church—kirk.
cipher—zero.
cithern—guitar.
clause—close, sb.
climate—clime.
clough—cleft.
coffer—coffin.
coin—coign, quoin.
cole—kail.
collect—cull.
collocate—couch.
comfit—confect.
commend—command.
complacent – complaisant.
complete, vb.—comply.
compost – composite.

comprehend—comprise.
compute—count (2).
conduct, sb.—conduit.
cone—hone.
confound—confuse.
construe—construct.
convey—convoy.
cool—gelid.
core—heart.
corn (1)—grain.
corn (2)—horn.
costume - custom.
cot, cote—coat.
couple, vb.—copulate.
coy—quiet, quit, quite.
crape—crisp.
crate—hurdle.
crevice—crevasse.
crimson—carmine.
crook—cross.
crop—croup (2).
crypt—grot.
cud—quid.
cue—queue.
curricle—curriculum.

dace—dart.
dainty—dignity.
dame—dam, donna, duenna.
date (2)—dactyl.
dauphin—dolphin.
deck—thatch.
defence—fence.
defend—fend.
delay—dilate.
dell—dale.
dent—dint.
deploy—display.
depot—deposit, sb.
descry—describe.
desiderate—desire, vb.
despite—spite.
deuce (1)—two.
devilish—diabolic.
diaper—jasper.
die (2)—dado.
dimple—dingle.
direct—dress.
dish—disc, desk, dais.
display—splay.
disport—sport.
distain—stain.
ditto—dictum.
diurnal—journal.
doge—duke.
dole—deal, sb.
doom— -dom (suffix).

dray—dredge (1).
drill—thrill, thirl.
dropsy—hydropsy.
due—debt.
dune—down (2).

eatable—edible.
éclat—slate.
emerald—smaragdus.
emerods—hemorrhoids.
employ—imply, implicate.
endow—endue.
engine—gin (2).
entire—integer.
envious—invidious.
enwrap—envelop.
escape—scape.
escutcheon—scutcheon.
especial—special.
espy—spy.
esquire—squire (1).
establish—stablish.
estate—state, status.
etiquette—ticket.
evil—ill.
example—ensample, sample.
exemplar—sampler.
extraneous—strange.

fabric—forge, sb.
fact—feat.
faculty—facility.
fan—van (1).
fancy—fantasy, phantasy.
fashion—faction.
fat (2)—vat.
feeble—foible.
fell (2)—pell.
feud (2)—fief.
feverfew—febrifuge.
fiddle—viol.
fife—pipe, peep (1).
finch—spink.
finite—fine (1).
fitch—vetch.
flag (4)—flake.
flame—phlegm.
flower—flour.
flue (1)—flute.
flush (1)—flux.
foam—spume.
font (1)—fount.
foremost—prime.
fragile—frail.
fray (1)—affray.
fro—from.
fungus—sponge.

fur—fodder.
furl—fardel.
fusee (1)—fusil (1).

gabble—jabber.
gad (1)—goad, ged.
gaffer—grandfather.
gage (1)—wage.
gambado—gambol.
game—gammon (2).
gaol—jail.
gaud—joy.
gay—jay.
gear—garb (1).
genteel—gentle, gentile.
genus—kin.
germ—germen.
gig—jig.
gird (2)—gride.
girdle—girth.
goal—weal, wale.
granary—garner.
grisly—gruesome.
grove—groove.
guarantee, *sb.*—warranty.
guard—ward.
guardian—warden.
guest—host (2).
gulle—wile.
guise—wise (2).
gullet—gully.
gust (2)—gusto.
guy—guide, *sb.*
gypsy—Egyptian.
hale (1)—whole.
hamper (2)—hanaper.
harangue—ring, rank (1).
hash—hatch (3).
hautboy—oboe.
heap—hope (2).
helix—volute.
hemi-—semi-.
history—story (1).
hoop (2)—whoop.
hospital — hostel, hotel, spital.
human—humane.
hurl—hurtle.
hyacinth—jacinth.
hydra—otter.
hyper-—super-.
hypo-—sub-.

illumine—limn.
imbrue—imbue.
inapt—inept.
inch—ounce (1).

indite—indict.
influence—influenza.
innocuous—innoxious.
invite—vie.
invoke—invocate.
iota—jot.
isolate—insulate.

jealous—zealous.
jeer—sheer (2).
joint—junta, junto.
jointure—juncture.
jut—jet (1).

kith—kit (3).
knoll (1)—knuckle.
knot—node.

label—lapel, lappet.
lac (1)—lake (2).
lace—lasso.
lair—leaguer; *also* layer.
lake (1)—loch, lough.
lap (3)—wrap.
launch, lanch—lance, *verb.*
leal—loyal, legal.
lection—lesson.
levy—levee.
lieu—locus.
limb (2)—limbo.
lineal—linear.
liquor—liqueur.
listen—lurk.
load—lade (1).
lobby—lodge.
locust—lobster.
lone—alone.

madam—madonna.
major—mayor.
male—masculine.
malediction—malison.
mangle (2)—mangonel.
manœuvre—manure.
mar—moor (2).
march (1)—mark (1), marque.
margin—margent, marge.
marish—marsh.
mash, *sb.*—mess (2).
mauve—mallow.
maxim—maximum.
mean (3)—mizen.
memory—memoir.
mentor—monitor.
metal—mettle.
milt (2)—milk.

minim—minimum.
minster—monastery.
mint (1)—money.
mister—master.
mob (1)—mobile, moveable.
mode—mood (2).
mohair—moire.
moment—momentum, movement.
monster—muster.
morrow—morn.
moslem—mussulman.
mould (1)—mulled.
musket—mosquito.

naive—native.
naked—nude.
name—noun.
naught, nought—not.
neither—nor.
nucleus—newel.

obedience—obeisance.
octave—utas.
of—off.
onion—union (2).
ordinance—ordnance.
orpiment—orpine.
osprey—ossifrage.
otto—attar.
outer—utter (1).
overplus—surplus.

paddle (1)—patter.
paddle (2)—spatula.
paddock (2)—park.
pain, *vb.*—pine (2).
paladin—palatine.
pale (2)—pallid.
palette—pallet (2).
paper—papyrus.
paradise—parvis.
paralysis—palsy.
parole—parable, parle, palaver.
parson—person.
pass—pace.
pastel—pastille.
pate—plate.
paten—pan.
patron—pattern.
pause—pose.
pawn (1)—pane, vane.
paynim—paganism.
peer (2)—pry.
pelisse—pilch.
pellitory (1)—paritory.

pen (2) — pin.
penance — penitence.
peregrine — pilgrim.
peruke — periwig, wig.
phantasm — phantom.
piazza — place.
pick — peck (1), pitch (*verb*).
picket — piquet.
piety — pity.
pigment — pimento.
pistil — pestle.
pistol — pistole.
plaintiff — plaintive.
plait — pleat, plight (2).
plan — plain, plane (1).
plateau — platter.
plum — prune (2).
poignant — pungent.
point — punt (2).
poison — potion.
poke (1) — pouch.
pole (1) — pale (1), pawl.
pomade, pommade — pomatum.
pomp — pump (2).
poor — pauper.
pope — papa.
porch — portico.
posy — poesy.
potent — puissant.
poult — pullet.
pounce (1) — punch (1).
pounce (2) — pumice.
pound (2) — pond.
pound (3) — pun, *vb*.
power — posse.
praise — price.
preach — predicate.
premier — primero.
priest — presbyter.
private — privy.
probe, *sb*. — proof.
proctor — procurator.
prolong — purloin.
prosecute — pursue.
provide — purvey.
provident — prudent.
puny — puisne.
purl (3) — profile.
purpose (1) — propose.

quartern — quadroon.
queen — quean.

raceme — raisin.
rack (1) — ratch.
radix — radish, race (3), root (1), wort (1).

raid — road.
rail (2) — rally (2).
raise — rear (1).
rake (3) — reach.
ramp — romp.
ransom — redemption.
rapine — ravine, raven (2).
rase — raze.
ratio — ration, reason.
ray (1) — radius.
rayah — ryot.
rear-ward — rear-guard.
reave — rob.
reconnaissance — recognisance.
regal — royal.
relic — relique.
renegade — runagate.
renew — renovate.
reprieve — reprove.
residue — residuum.
respect — respite.
revenge — revindicate.
reward — regard.
rhomb, rhombus — rumb.
ridge — rig (3).
rod — rood.
rondeau — roundel.
rote (1) — route, rout, rut.
round — rotund.
rouse (2) — row (3).
rover — robber.

sack (1) — sac.
sacristan — sexton.
saliva — slime.
saw (2) — saga.
saxifrage — sassafrass.
scabby — shabby.
scale (1) — shale.
scandal — slander.
scar (2), scaur — share.
scarf (1) — scrip, scrap.
scatter — shatter.
school — shoal, scull (3).
scot(free) — shot.
scratch — grate (2).
screech — shriek.
screw (2) — shrew.
scuttle (1) — skillet.
sect, sept — suite, suit.
separate — sever.
sergeant, serjeant — servant.
settle (1) — sell (2), saddle.
shamble — scamper.
shawm, shalm — haulm.
shed (2) — shade.

shirt — skirt.
shred — screed.
shrew (1) — screw (2).
shrub (2) — syrup.
shuffle — scuffle.
sicker, siker — secure, sure.
sine — sinus.
sir, sire — senior, seignior, señor, signor.
skewer — shiver (2).
skiff — ship.
skirmish — scrimmage, scaramouch.
slabber — slaver.
sloop — shallop ?.
snivel — snuffle.
snub — snuff (2).
soil (1) — sole (1), sole (2).
sop — soup.
soprano — sovereign.
souse — sauce.
species — spice.
spell (4) — spill (1).
spend — dispend.
spirit — sprite, spright.
spoor — spur.
spray (2) — sprig (*perhaps* asparagus).
sprit — sprout, *sb*.
sprout, *vb*. — spout.
spry — sprack.
squall — squeal.
squire (2) — square.
stank — tank.
stave — staff.
stock — tuck (2).
stove — stew, *sb*.
strait — strict.
strap — strop.
superficies — surface.
supersede — surcease.
suppliant supplicant.
sweep — swoop.

tabor — tambour.
tache (1) — tack.
taint — tent (3), tint.
tamper — temper.
task — tax.
taunt — tempt, tent (2).
tawny — tenny.
tease — touse, tose.
tend (1) — tender (2).
tense (2) — toise.
tercel — tassel (2).
thread — thrid.
tight — taut.

tithe—tenth.
to—too.
ton—tun.
tone—tune.
tour—turn.
track—trick (1).
tract (1)—trait.
tradition—treason.
treachery—trickery.
trifle—truffle.
tripod—trivet.
triumph—trump (2).
troth—truth.
tuck (1)—tug, touch.

tulip—turban.

umbel—umbrella.
unity—unit.
ure—opera.

vade—fade.
valet—varlet.
vast—waste.
veal—wether.
veneer—furnish.
venew, veney—venue.
verb—word.
vertex—vortex.

viaticum—voyage.
viper—wyvern, wivern.
visor—vizard.
vizier, visier—alguazil.
vocal—vowel.

wain—wagon, waggon.
wattle—wallet.
weet—wit (1).
whirl—warble.
wight (1)—whit.
wold—weald.
wrack—wreck, rack (4).

yelp—yap.

VI. DISTRIBUTION OF WORDS ACCORDING TO THE LANGUAGES FROM WHICH THEY ARE DERIVED.

The Dictionary shews from what language each word is derived, as far as its etymology is at present ascertained. The largest classes of words are the following.

1. Words of purely ENGLISH origin, most of which are found in Anglo-Saxon, or are words of imitative origin.

2. Words of SCANDINAVIAN or OLD DANISH origin, due to the frequent incursions of the Danes, many of whom permanently settled in England. Their speech was closely allied to the oldest English as represented by Anglo-Saxon.

3. Words of CELTIC origin, due to the ancient Britons. The English frequently took to themselves British wives, which led to their adoption of several Celtic words. These are, however, less numerous than we might perhaps at first expect them to be.

4. Words of LATIN origin; borrowed (1) from Latin directly; (2) through the medium of French. Both these classes of words are very large. Here also may be included words of Low Latin origin, i.e. borrowed from the debased or rustic Latin, which employed words not to be found in the best classical authors.

5. Words of GREEK origin; borrowed (1) from Greek directly; (2) through the medium of Latin; (3) through the medium of Latin, and afterwards of French; (4) through the medium of French (the word not being used in Latin).

6. HYBRID WORDS, made up from two different languages. Such a word is *bankrupt*, *bank* being of Teutonic, but -*rupt* of Latin origin. Words of this character are rather numerous, but their component parts are, in most cases, easily accounted for.

Words *strictly* belonging to the above classes are numerous, and will not be further noticed here. But there are also other smaller classes of words which are here brought particularly under the reader's notice.

Before proceeding to enumerate these, a few remarks upon some of the classes already mentioned may be useful.

1. ENGLISH. Amongst these we must include:

Place-names: canter, carronade, dunce, galloway. *Personal name*: kit-cat.

Also two words that seem to have been originally English, and to have been re-borrowed.

French from English: pewter.
Portuguese from English: dodo (?).

2. SCANDINAVIAN; see p. 603.   We must also include the following:

Icelandic: geysir.

Swedish: dahlia, flounce(1), flounder (2), gantlet (gantlope), kink, slag, tungsten.

Danish: backgammon?, cam, floe, fog, jib (1), jib (2), jolly-boat, siskin.

Norwegian: lemming (leming).

French from Scandinavian: abet, barbed, bet, bigot, blemish, bondage, brandish, brasier (brazier), braze (1), bun, equip, flotsam (*Law* F.), frisk, frown, gauntlet, grate (2), grimace, grudge, haberdasher, hale (2), haul, hue (2), jib (3), jolly, locket, Norman, rinse, rivet, sound (4), strife, strive, waif, waive, wicket.

Dutch from Scandinavian: furlough, walrus.

French from Dutch from Scandinavian: droll.

Russian from Scandinavian (cf. Swedish *knut*): knout.

French from Low Latin from Scandinavian: forage.

3. CELTIC; see p. 603.   Amongst these we must also include the following:

Welsh: bragget, clutter (3), coracle, cromlech, crowd (2), crumpet, flannel, flimsy, flummery, hawk (3), maggot, metheglin, perk, toss?.

Gaelic: brose, capercailzie, cateran, clan, claymore, fillibeg (philibeg), gillie, gowan, loch, mackintosh, pibroch, plaid, ptarmigan, reel (2), slogan, spleuchan, sporran, whiskey.

Irish: gallow-glass, kern (1) (kerne), lough, orrery, rapparee, skain (skene), spalpeen, tanist, Tory, usquebaugh.

French from Celtic (or Breton): attach, attack, baggage (1), baggage (2), bar, barrel, barrier, basin, basenet (basnet), beak, billet (2), billiards, bobbin?, boudoir?, bound (2), bourn (1), brail, branch, brave, bray (2), bribe, brisket, bruit, budge (2), budget, car, carcanet, career, carol, carpenter, carry, caul, cloak (cloke), gaff, garter, gobbet, gobble (*with* E. *suffix*), gravel, grebe, harness, hurl (*with* E. *suffix*), hurt, hurtle (*with* E. *suffix*), javelin, job (2), lay (2), lias, lockram, maim (2)?, mavis, mutton?, petty?, pickaxe, picket, pip (3), pique, piquet, pottage, pottle, pouch, putty, quay, rock (1)?, rogue, sot?, tan, tawny, tetchy (techy, touchy), truant, valet, varlet, vassal.

Spanish from Celtic: bravado, gabardine (gaberdine), galliard, garrote (garrotte).

French from Spanish from Celtic: piccadill (pickadill).   *Perhaps* barricade.

Italian from Celtic: bravo, caricature.

French from Italian from Celtic: barracks.

French from Latin from Celtic: carrack, charge, chariot, league (2).

French from Low Latin from Celtic: felon?.

Spanish from Low Latin from Celtic: cargo.

Dutch from Celtic: knap, pink (2), plug.

Old Low German from Celtic: poll.

French from Low German from Celtic: packet.

Scandinavian from Celtic: peck (1), peck (2), peg, pore (2).

French from German from Celtic: gable, rote (2).

4. Words of LATIN origin; see p. 603.   We must also include the following:

Low Latin from French from Latin: crenellate.

Norman-French from Latin: fitz, indefeasible.

Dutch from French from Latin: cruise, domineer, excise (1), flout, sconce (1).

German from French from Latin: cashier.

French from Low Latin from Latin: cadet, identity, mastiff, menagerie, menial, page (1).

Italian from Low Latin from Latin: falchion.

French from Italian from Low Latin from Latin: medal.

Provençal from Latin: cross, crusade.

French from Provençal from Latin: barnacles, corsair.

Italian from Latin: allegro, askance, attitude, belladonna, breve, broccoli, canto, canzonet, caper (1), casino, cicerone, comply, contraband, contralto, cupola, curvet, dado, dilettante, ditto, doge, duel, duet, ferret (2), floss, grampus, granite, gurgle, incognito, influenza, infuriate, intaglio, isolate, Jerusalem artichoke, junket, lagoon (lagune), lava, levant, macaroni (maccaroni), madonna, malaria, manifesto, marmot, Martello tower, mezzotinto, miniature, monkey, motto, nuncio, opera, pianoforte, piano, portico, profile, punch (4), punchinello, quartet (quartette), quota, redoubt, semibreve, seraglio, signor (signior), size (2), soda, solo, sonata, soprano, stanza, stiletto, trio, trombone?, umbrella, velvet, vermicelli, vista, volcano.

French from Italian from Latin: alarm (alarum), alert, apartment, arcade, artisan, auburn, battalion, bulletin, cab (1), cabbage (1), cape (2), capriole, carnival, cascade, casque, cassock, cavalcade, cavalier, cavalry, citadel, colonel, colonnade, compliment, compost, concert, concordat, corporal (1), corridor, cortege, costume, countertenor, cuirass, douche, ducat, escort, esplanade, facade, florin, fracas, fugue, gabion, gambol, improvise, incarnadine, infantry, lavender, lutestring, macaroon?, manage, manege, mien, mizen, (mizzen), model, motet, musket, niche, ortolan, paladin, palette, pallet (2), parapet, partisan (1), pastel, peruke, pilaster, pinnace, piston, pomade (pommade), pontoon, populace, porcelain, postillion, preconcert, reprisal, revolt, rocket (2), salad, sallet, salmagundi, saveloy (cervelas), scamper, sentinel?, sentry?, somersault (somerset), sonnet, spinet, squad, squadron, termagant, terrace, tramontane, ultramontane, umber, vault (2), vedette (vidette). *Also* carnation.

Dutch from French from Italian from Latin: periwig, shamble (*verb*), wig.

German from Italian from Latin: barouche.

Spanish from Latin: alligator, armada, armadillo, booby, capsize, carbonado, cask, commodore, comrade, cork, courtesan, disembogue, domino, don (2), duenna, dulcimer, flotilla, funambulist, gambado, grandee, hidalgo, jade (2), junta, junto, lasso, manchineel, matador, merino, mosquito (musquito), negro, olio, pay (2), peccadillo, primero, punctilio, quadroon,

real (2), renegade (renegado), salver, sherry, stevedore, tent (3), tornado, ultramarine, vanilla, verandah.

French from Spanish from Latin: calenture, creole, doubloon, escalade, farthingale (fardingale), grenade, ogre, ombre, parade, paragon, petronel, pint, punt (2), quadrille, risk, sassafras, spaniel, tartan?.

Portuguese from Latin: binnacle, caste, junk (2), moidore, molasses, pimento, port (4), tank.

French from Portuguese from Latin: corvette, fetich (fetish), parasol.

Dutch from Latin: buoy, tafferel (taffrail).

Old Dutch from Latin: chop (2).

Scandinavian from Latin: cake, skate (1).

Scandinavian from English from Latin: kindle.

German from Latin: drilling.

French from Old High German from Latin: waste.

French from Teutonic from Latin: pump (1)?.

Dutch from German from Latin: rummer?.

Celtic from Latin: ingle, pot, spigot.

Russian from Latin: czar.

French from Portuguese from Arabic from Greek from Latin: apricot.

French from Spanish from Arabic from Latin: quintal.

Low Latin: baboon, barrister, campaniform, cap, capital (3), dominion, edible, elongate, elucidate, embassy, fine (2), flask, flavour, funeral, grate (1), hoax, hocus-pocus, implement, indent, intimidate, pageant, plenary, proxy.

French from Low Latin: abase, ballet, barbican, bargain, bass (1), bittern, borage, burden (2), burl, camlet, canton, cape (1), cope (1), cygnet, felon?, ferret (1), festival, flagon, frock, gash, gauge (gage), gouge, hutch, oleander, palfrey.

French from Provençal from Low Latin: ballad.

French from Italian from Low Latin: basement, bassoon, pivot.

French from Spanish from Low Latin: caparison.

5. Words of GREEK origin; see p. 603. We must also include the following:

Low Latin from Latin from Greek: intone.

Italian from Latin from Greek: ba-

lustrade, grotto, madrigal, orris, piazza, torso.

French from Italian from Latin from

Greek: canopy, cornice, espalier, germander, grotesque, piastre.

Dutch from Italian from Latin from Greek: sketch.

Spanish from Latin from Greek: buffalo, cochineal, morris, pellitory (2) (pelleter), savanna (savannah).

French from Spanish from Latin from Greek: maroon (2), rumb (rhumb).

Portuguese from Latin from Greek: cockroach, palaver.

French from Portuguese from Latin from Greek: marmalade.

Provençal from Latin from Greek: troubadour.

Old Low German from Latin from Greek: beaker.

Old Dutch from Latin from Greek: gittern.

French from German from Latin from Greek: petrel (peterel).

Celtic from Latin from Greek: pretty, spunk.

Low Latin from Greek: apoplexy, apothecary, bursar, cartulary, catapult, chamomile (camomile), comb (coomb), hulk, imp, impracticable, intoxicate, lectern (lecturn), magnesia, pericranium.

French from Low Latin from Greek: acolyte, allegory, almanac, anchoret (anchorite), apostasy, apostate, bottle (1), butler, buttery, bushel, calender, calm, carbine, card (1), carte, catalogue, cauterise, celandine, chronicle, clergy, climacter, climate, clinical, cockatrice, dome, embrocation, fleam, galoche, liturgy, lobe, mangonel, patriot, pitcher, policy.

Dutch from Low Latin from Greek: dock (3), mangle (2).

Spanish from French from Greek: platina.

Italian from Greek: archipelago, barytone, bombast, catacomb, gondola, scope?

French from Italian from Greek: baluster, banisters, cartridge (cartouche), emery, galligaskins, manganese?, moustache (mustache), pantaloon (1), pantaloons, pedant ?.

French from Provençal from Italian from Greek: dredge (2).

French from Spanish from Greek: truck (1).

German from Greek: cobalt, nickel ?.

French from German from Greek: pate.

Spanish from Arabic from Greek: talisman.

Portuguese from Spanish from Arabic from Greek: albatross.

French from Spanish from Arabic from Greek: alembic, limbeck.

French from Arabic from Greek: alchemy, carat.

Spanish from Persian from Greek: tarragon.

Hebrew from Greek: sanhedrim.

Turkish from Greek: effendi.

Scandinavian from English from Greek: kirk.

6. Words of HYBRID origin cannot very well be classed, from the nature of the case; see p. 603. To the above six classes we may add these following.

7. Words of OLD LOW GERMAN origin. The following words I call 'Old Low German' for want of a better name. Many of them may be truly English, but are not to be found in Anglo-Saxon. Some may be Friesic. Others may yet be found in Anglo-Saxon. Others were probably borrowed from the Netherlands at an early period, but it is difficult to assign the date. The list will require future revision, when the history of some at least may be more definitely settled.

Botch (1), bounce, boy, brake (1), brake (2), bulk (2), bully, bumble-bee, cough, curl, dog, doxy, duck (3), flounder (1), fob, girl, groat, hawk (2), hawker, kails, kit (1), knurr, knur, lack (1), lack (2), lash (2), loll, loon (1) (lown), luck, mazer, mud, muddle, nag (1), nick (1), notch (nock), ort (orts), pamper, patch (1), patch (2), peer (2), plash (1), plump?, pry, queer, rabbit?, rabble, rail (1), scalp, scoff, scold, shock (2), shudder, skew, slabber, slender, slight, slot (1), snot, spool, sprout, tallow, toot (2), tub, tuck (1), tug, un- (3), unto.

French from Old Low German: antler?, border, brick, broider, choice, chuck (1), cratch, dace, dandy?, dart, fur, garment, garnish, garrison, goal, gruel, guile, hamlet, heinous, hobby (1), hobby-horse, hobby (2), jangle, lampoon, marish, massacre, muffle, mute (2), poach (1)?, poach (2)?, pocket (or C.), pulley (or F. from L.), stout, supper, wafer. *Perhaps* paw.

Low Latin from Old Low German: badge.

French from Low Latin from Old Low German: filter.

To the above may also be added the following words, which do not seem to have been in very early use:

Fluke (2), huckaback, touch - wood, twill.

French from Low German: fudge, staple (2), tampion.

Low Latin from Low German: scorbutic.

French from Low Latin from Low German: quail (2).

8. Words borrowed from DUTCH.

Ahoy, aloof, anker, avast, bale (3), ballast, belay, beleaguer, bluff, blunderbuss, boom (2), boor, bouse (boose), brabble, brack, brackish, brandy, bruin, bum-boat, bumpkin, burgomaster, bush (2), buskin, caboose, cant (2), clamp, clinker, cope (2), dapper, delf, derrick, doit, doll ?, dot, drill (1), duck (4), duffel, easel, elope, flout, fop, frolic, fumble, gallippot, gas, glib (1), golf, groove, growl, gruff, guelder-rose, gulp, hackle (1), hatchel, hackle (2), heckle, heyday (1), hoarding, hold (2), holland, holster, hop (2), hope (2), hottentot, hoy (1), hoy (2), hustle, isinglass, jeer, jerkin, kilderkin, kink, kipper, knapsack, land-grave, landscape, lash (1), leaguer, ledger, lighter, link (2), linstock (lintstock), litmus, loiter, manikin (manakin), margrave, marline, measles, minikin, minx ?, mob (2), moor (2), mop (2), mope, morass, mump, mumps, ogle, orlop, pad (2), pickle (*or* E. ?), pink (4), quacksalver, rant, reef (1), reef (2), reeve (1), rover, ruffle, selvage (selvedge), sheer (2), skate (2) (scate), skipper, slim, sloop, sloven, smack (3), snaffle, snap, snip, snuff (1), spelicans, splice, spoor, sprat, stipple, stiver, stoker, stove, strand (2) ?, stripe, sutler, swab, switch, tang (1), tattoo (1), toy, trick (1), trick (2), trick (3), trigger, uproar, wagon (waggon), wainscot, yacht, yawl (1).

Old Dutch: crants, deck, dell, firkin, foist, hogshead, hoiden (hoyden), hoist, huckster, lollard, lop, mite (1), ravel.

Named from towns in Flanders or Belgium: cambric, spa.

French from Dutch (or Old Dutch): arquebus, clique, cracknel, cresset, cruet, dredge (1), drug, drugget, fitchet, frieze (1), friz (frizz), hackbut, hackney, hack, hoarding, hotch-pot (hodge-podge), mow (3), mummer, paletot, pilot ?, placard, staid, stay (1).

French from Old Flemish: gallop.

French from Spanish from Dutch ?: trinket (2), *or* trinquet.

Spanish from English from Dutch: filibuster.

9. Words borrowed from GERMAN. from German is very small.)

(The number of words borrowed *directly*

Bismuth, Dutch, feldspar, fuchsia, fugleman, gneiss, hock (2), huzzah, landau, maulstick, meerschaum, mesmerise (*with* F. *suffix*), plunder, poodle, quartz, shale, swindler, trull, wacke, waltz, wheedle ?, zinc.

To these add (from *Old German*): buss (1); also *German from French from Old High German*: veneer.

German (*Moravian*) *personal name*: camellia.

Dutch from German: dollar, etch, rixdollar, wiseacre.

French from German: allegiance, allure, band (2), bandy, bank (2), banner, banneret, banquet, bastard, bawd, bawdy, belfry, bistre ?, bivouac, blanket, blazon (2), botch (2), brach, bray (1), brunette, burnish, carouse, carousal (1), chamois, coat, coterie, cricket (1), etiquette, fauteuil, gaiety, garret, gimlet (gimblet), grumble, haggard (1), hash, hatch (3), hatchet, haversack, hoe, housings, Huguenot, lansquenet, latten, lattice, lecher, list (2), lobby ?, lumber (1), marque (letters of), marquee, mignonette, mitten ?, motley, popinjay (*with modified suffix*), raffle, roast ?, shammy (shamoy), spruce, spurry, ticket, wardrobe, zigzag.

Italian from German: rocket (1).

French from Italian from German: burin, canteen, group, poltroon, tuck (2).

Latin from German: Vandal.

Low Latin from German: lobby ?, morganatic.

Low Latin from French from German : hamper (2) (*also* hanaper).

French from Low Latin from German : brush, lodge, marchioness, marquis, mason ?.

MIDDLE HIGH GERMAN : bugle (2).

French from Middle High German : bale (1), beadle, brewis, browze, bruise ?, buckram, burgess, butcher, butt (1), butt (2), buttock (*with* E. *suffix*), button, coif, cotillon (cotillion), demarcation (demarkation), gaiter, gallant, gay, gonfanon (gonfalon), grape, grapnel, grapple, grisette, grizzly, grizzled (*with* E. *suffix*), halberd (halbert), jig, marquetry, quoif, rebut (*with* L. *prefix*), sorrel (1), skiff, warble, warden (1), warden (2), wince.

FRENCH FROM OLD HIGH GERMAN : arrange, await, award, baldric, ball (2), balloon, ballot, banish, baron, baste (3), bastile, blanch (1), blank, boot (1), boss, bottle (2), brawn, bream, chamberlain, chine, cray-fish (craw-fish), dance, eclat, enamel, ermine, eschew, espy, fief, fife, filbert, frank, franchise, franklin, freight, furbish, furnish, garb (1), garb (2), garden, gimp, guarantee (guaranty), guard, guise,

habergeon, hanseatic, harangue, harbinger, hardy, haubeck, haunch, herald, heron, hob (2), hut, jay, liege, mail (2), marshal, minion, mushroom, ouch (nouch), partisan (2) (partizan) ?, perform (*with* L. *prefix*), quill (1), quill (2) (*or* L.), quiver (2), race (2), racy (*with* E. *suffix*), range, rank (1), rasp, rasp-berry (*and* E.), riches, riot ?, rob, robe, robin, rochet, rubbish, rubble, Salic (Salique), saloon, scorn, seize, skirmish, slash ?, slate, slice, spy, stallion, standard, stubble, tarnish, towel, warrant, wait.

French from Low Latin from Old High German : abandon, ambassador, equerry, frank, install (instal), sturgeon, warren.

Low Latin from Old High German : faldstool.

Spanish from Old High German : guerilla (guerrilla).

French from Spanish from Old High German : rapier.

Italian from Old High German : bandit, fresco, smalt, stucco ; *from German* : halt (2).

French from Italian from Old High German : decant.

French from Austrian : cravat.

10. Other words of indeterminate TEUTONIC origin. *Teutonic* is here used as a *general* term, to shew that the following words (derived through French, Spanish, &c.) cannot quite certainly be referred to a *definite* Teutonic dialect, though clearly belonging to the Teutonic family.

French from Teutonic : bacon, bourd ?, brawl (2), broil (1), burgeon, cantle, crochet, crosier, crotchet, croup (2), crupper, crush, darnel ?, guide, hoop (2), hubbub, huge ?, label, moat, mock, moraine, patrol, patten, rail (3), rally (2), ramp, random, rappee, retire, reynard (renard), ribald, riff-raff, rifle (1), romp, ruffian, scabbard, scallop (scollop), screen ?, scroll, seneschal, shock (1), sorrel (2), soup, spar (3), spavin, stew, tap (1), tic, tier, tire (2), tire (3), tire (5), toil (1) ?, touch, track, trap (2), trawl, treachery, trepan (2) (trapan), tuft (1), troll, wage, wager, warison, whoop, wizard (wisard).

Spanish from-Teutonic : guy (guy-rope), stampede.

French from Spanish from Teutonic : scuttle (2).

Italian from Teutonic : balcony, loto (lotto), stoccado (stoccata), strappado, tucket. *Perhaps* bunion.

French from Italian from Teutonic : bagatelle, bronze, escarpment (*with* L. *suffix*), scaramouch, scarp, tirade, vogue.

Low Latin from Teutonic : allodial, feud (2), feudal.

French from Low Latin from Teutonic : ambush, bouquet, fief, marten, ratten.

Spanish from Low Latin from Teutonic : ambuscade.

Latin from Gothic : Teutonic.

11. Words of indeterminate ROMANCE origin. The *Romance* languages, which include French, Italian, Spanish, and Portuguese, are, strictly speaking, unoriginal, but we cannot always trace them. A large number of terms belonging to these languages are derived from *Latin, Greek, Celtic*, &c. Those in this section are words of which the origin is local or obscure.

French : abash, aery, air (2), andiron, arras, artesian, baboon, banter ?, barren,

barter, bass (1), baton (batoon), batten (2), battlement, bayonet, beaver (2), beguine, bevel, bice, bijou, blond, blouse, brattice, breeze (1), breeze (2), broil (2), buffer (1), buffer (2), buffet (1), buffet (2), buffoon, burganet (burgonet), busk (2), buttress, cabbage (2), caliber (calibre), calipers, caliver, champagne, cheval-de-frise, chicanery, chiffonier, cockade, curlew, davit, dine, disease, drab (2), drape, dupe, ease, embattle (1), embattle (2), emblazon, emboss (1), emboss (2), embrasure, embroider, embroil, entice, entrench, fribble, frieze (2), frippery, furbelow, galley, galliot, gallon, garland, gasconade, gavotte, gibbet, giblets, gill (3), gingham, gobelin, gormandize, gourmand, graze (1)?, greaves (2), grouse, guillotine, guzzle, harass, haricot (1), haricot (2), harlequin, harlot, harridan, haunt, jack (2), jacket, jostle, lawn (2), lees, loach, loo, lozenge, magnolia, maraud, martin, martinet, martingale, martlet, mich, mortise, musit, Nicotian, pamphlet?, pavise, pedigree?, pillory, pinch, pinchbeck (*personal name*), pirouette, piss, pittance, poplin, ricochet, roan, sauterne, savoy, scupper, sedan-chair, shalloon, silhouette, toper (*or* Ital.), valise, vaudeville, vernier.

Dutch from French: harpoon.

French from Provençal: charade.

Italian: andante, cameo, cock (4), galvanism, imbroglio, mantua, milliner?, ninny, polony, rebuff, regatta, sienna, trill, voltaic.

French from Italian: bastion, bauble (2), bergamot, brigade, brigand, brigantine, brig, brusque, burlesque, bust, caprice, capuchin, carousal (2), casemate, charlatan, frigate, gala, gallery, gallias, gazette, gusset, maroon (1), pasquin, pasquinade, pistol, pistole, ravelin, rodomontade, theorbo, tontine.

Spanish: anchovy, banana, bastinado, battledoor, bilbo, bilboes, brocade, cigar, cinchona (chinchona), embargo, filigree, galleon, galloon?, imbargo, paraquito, quixotic, rusk, sarsaparilla, trice (1).

French from Spanish: barricade, bizarre, capstan, caracole, cordwainer, morion (murrion), shallop.

Portuguese: cocoa (1), dodo, emu, yam.

12. Words of SLAVONIC origin. This is a general term, including Russian, Polish, Bohemian, Servian, &c.

French from Slavonic: sable.

French from German from Slavonic: calash, slave.

Dutch from Slavonic: eland.

Polish: polka.

German from Bohemian: howitzer.

French from German from Servian: vampire.

Russian: drosky, morse, rouble (ruble), steppe, verst.

French from Russian: ukase.

13. A word of LITHUANIAN origin. Curiously enough, there is only *one* English word which can be traced to Lithuanian, and the introduction of it into English is due to the fact that it had been borrowed from that language by the Danes. The word is *talk*.

14. Words of PERSIAN origin.

Persian: bang (2), barbican?, bashaw, bazaar, caravan, caravansary, dervis (dervish), divan, durbar, firman, ghoul, houri, jackal, jasmine (jessamine), Lascar, mohur, nylghau, Parsee, pasha (pacha, pashaw, bashaw), peri, sash (2), sepoy, shah, shawl, van (3).

Hindustani from Persian: zamindar, zanana.

Greek from Persian: cinnabar (cinoper).

Latin from Greek from Persian: asparagus, gypsum, laudanum, Magi, tiara?.

French from Latin from Greek from Persian: caper (2), jujube, magic, myrtle, paradise, parvis, satrap, tiger.

French from Italian from Latin from Greek from O. Persian: rice.

Spanish from Latin from Greek from Persian: pistachio (pistacho).

French from Latin from Persian: peach (1).

French from Low Latin from Persian: zedoary.

Italian from Persian: scimetar (cimeter)?.

French from Italian from Persian: carcase (carcass), jargonelle, mummy, orange, rebeck, taffeta (taffety).

French from Spanish from Persian: julep, saraband.

Portuguese from Persian: pagoda, veranda (verandah)?.

French from Portuguese from Persian: bezoar.

French from Persian: check, checker (chequer), checkers (chequers), chess, exchequer, jar (2), lemon, lime (3), ounce (2)?, rook (2), scarlet.

Dutch from Persian: gherkin.

Low Latin from Arabic from Persian: borax.

French from Spanish from Arabic from Persian: hazard, tabour (tabor)?, tambour?, tambourine?. *Perhaps* spinach.

Spanish from Turkish from Persian: lilac.

French from Arabic from Persian: azure.

15. Words of SANSKRIT origin.

Sanskrit: avatar, banyan, brahmin (brahman), champak, pundit, rajah, Sanskrit, suttee, Veda.

Latin from Greek from Sanskrit: hemp, pepper.

French from Latin from Greek from Sanskrit: beryl, brilliant, ginger, mace (2), saccharine.

French from Latin from Greek from Persian from Sanskrit: nard.

French from Spanish from Latin from Greek from Persian from Sanskrit: indigo.

French from Latin from Persian from Sanskrit: musk.

French from Italian from Latin from Persian from Sanskrit: muscadel (muscatel), muscadine.

Latin from Sanskrit: sulphur?.

French from Low Latin from Sanskrit: sendal (cendal).

Persian from Sanskrit: lac (1).

French from Portuguese from Persian from Sanskrit: lacquer (lacker).

French from Persian from Sanskrit: lake (2), sandal (wood).

French from Spanish from Arabic from Persian from Sanskrit: sugar.

Arabic from Sanskrit: kermes.

French from Arabic from Sanskrit: crimson.

French from Italian from Arabic from Sanskrit: candy.

Hebrew from Sanskrit: algum.

Hindi from Sanskrit: loot, pawnee, punch (3), punkah, rajpoot, rupee.

Hindustani from Sanskrit: chintz, jungle, lac (2), palanquin.

Bengali from Sanskrit: jute.

Malay from Sanskrit: paddy.

Portuguese from Malay from Sanskrit: mandarin.

16. Words of MAGYAR or HUNGARIAN origin. (This language does not belong to the Aryan family.)

Hungarian: hussar, tokay.

French from Hungarian: shako.

French from German from Hungarian: sabre.

17. Words of TURKISH origin. (This language does not belong to the Aryan family.)

Turkish: bey, caftan, chouse, dey, horde, ketch, turkey.

French from Turkish: janisary, ottoman, shagreen (*and perhaps* chagrin).

French from Italian from Turkish: caviare, turquoise.

Spanish from Turkish: xebec.

German from Polish from Turkish: uhlan.

18. Words of SEMITIC origin. The principal Semitic languages are Hebrew, Arabic, Chaldee, Syriac, &c.; the borrowed words in English being somewhat numerous.

Hebrew: alleluia (allelujah), bdellium, behemoth, cab (2), cherub, cinnamon, corban, ephod, gopher, hallelujah, hin, homer, Jehovah, jug, log (3), Messiah, Nazarite (*with* Gk. *suffix*), Sabaoth, Satan, Selah, seraph, shekel, Shekinah (Shechinah), shibboleth, shittah (tree), shittim (wood), teraphim, thummim, urim.

Greek from Hebrew: alphabet, delta, hosanna, iota.

Latin from Greek from Hebrew: amen, cassia, cumin (cummin), Jacobite, Jesus, jot, Levite, manna, Pasch, Pharisee, rabbi (rabbin), sabbath, Sadducee, sycamine?, Tom. *Also* balsam?, jordan.

French from Latin from Greek from

Hebrew: camel, cider, ebony, elephant, Hebrew, hyssop, jack (1), Jacobin, Jew, jockey, lazar, maudlin, sapphire, simony, sodomy. *Also* balm?, jenneting?

French from Spanish from Latin from Greek from Hebrew: Jesuit.

Italian from Greek from Hebrew: zany.

Latin from Hebrew: leviathan.

French from Latin from Hebrew: jubilee.

French from Hebrew: cabal.

French from places in Palestine: bedlam, gauze.

Syriac: Maranatha.

Latin from Greek from Syriac: abbot, damask, mammon.

French from Latin from Greek from Syriac: abbess, abbey, damson.

French from Italian from Syriac: muslin.

Chaldee: raca, talmud, targum.

Arabic: alkali, alkoran, arrack, attar (of roses), azimuth, carob-tree, elixir, emir, harem, hegira, hookah (hooka), houdah (howdah), jerboa, koran, Mahometan (Mohammedan), moonshee, moslem, muezzin, mufti, nadir, otto, rack (5), rayah, ryot, salaam (salam), sheik, sherbet, shrub (2), simoon, sofa, taraxacum, visier (vizier).

Latin from Greek from Arabic: naphtha, rose.

French from Latin from Greek from Arabic: jasper, myrrh, nitre.

French from Italian from Latin from Greek from Arabic: diaper.

Spanish from Greek from Arabic: dragoman.

French from Latin from Arabic: amulet, chemise, sarcenet (sarsnet).

Low Latin from Arabic: algebra, saracen.

French from Low Latin from Arabic: camlet, tartar (1).

Italian from Arabic: artichoke, felucca, senna, sirocco,

French from Italian from Arabic: alcove, arabesque, magazine, sequin, zero.

Spanish from Arabic: alguazil, arsenal, bonito, calabash?, caraway (carraway), carmine, maravedi, minaret.

French from Spanish from Arabic: amber, cotton (1), fanfare, galingale, garble, garbage, genet, jennet (gennet), lackey (lacquey), mask (masque), masquerade, mosque, ogee (ogive), racket (1) (raquet), realgar, ream, sumach, syrup (sirup), tabby, talc, tare (2), tariff, zenith.

Portuguese from Arabic: assagai, calabash?.

French from Portuguese from Arabic: albatross (*but ultimately Greek*).

French from Arabic: admiral, alcohol, assassin, barberry (berberry), bedouin, calif (caliph), cipher, civet, fardel?, furl?, gazelle, lute (1), Mamaluke (Mameluke), mattress, mohair (moire), saffron, sultan.

Persian from Arabic: mussulman.

French from Persian from Arabic: mate (2).

Turkish from Arabic: coffee, giaour.

Hindi from Arabic: nabob.

Italian from Malay from Arabic: monsoon.

19. Words of ASIATIC origin, but NEITHER ARYAN NOR SEMITIC.

Hindustani: anna, bangle, cowry, shampoo, thug, toddy.

French from Italian from Turkish from Persian from Hindustani: tulip, turban.

E. Indian place-names: calico, cashmere, (kerseymere).

Hindi: rum (2).

French from Low Latin from Hindi: bonnet.

Bengali: tomtom.

Persian from Bengali: bungalow.

Marathi: pice.

Canarese: areca.

Portuguese from Malayalim: betel.

Malayalim: teak.

Tamil: catamaran, coolie, curry (2), pariah.

Malay: bamboo [perhaps *Canarese*], caddy, cassowary, cockatoo, crease (2) *or* creese, dugong, gong, gutta-percha, lory (lury), mango, muck (amuck), orangoutang, proa (prow), rattan, sago, upas.

French from Malay: ratafia.

French from Arabic from Malay: camphor.

Chinese: china, Chinese, nankeen, tea, typhoon.

Portuguese from Chinese: junk (1).

Latin from Greek from Chinese: silk.

French from Latin from Greek from Chinese: serge.

Japanese: japan, soy.

Portuguese from Japanese: bonze.

Java: bantam.
Annamese: gamboge.
Russian from Tatar: cossack, mammoth.
Persian from Tatar: khan, tartar (2).
Mongolian: mogul.

Thibetan: lama (1).
Australian: kangaroo, paramatta, wombat.
Tahitian: tattoo (2).
Polynesian: taboo.

20. Words derived from various AFRICAN languages.

Hebrew from Egyptian: ephah.
Latin from Greek from Hebrew from Egyptian: sack (1).
French from Latin from Greek from Hebrew from Egyptian: sack (2), satchel.
Latin from Greek from Egyptian: ammonia, ibis, oasis, paper?, papyrus?.
French from Latin from Greek from Egyptian: barge, bark (1), gum (2), gypsy.
French from Spanish from Arabic from Egyptian: giraffe?.

French from Italian from Low Latin from Egyptian: fustian.
French from Barbary: barb (2).
Morocco: morocco.
Portuguese from Ethiopian: zebra?.
West African: baobab, canary, chimpanzee, guinea ; *also* gorilla (Old African).
Hottentot: gnu, quagga.
From a negro name: quassia.

21. Words derived from various AMERICAN languages.

North-American Indian: hominy, moccasin (mocassin), moose, opossum, racoon (raccoon), skunk, squaw, tomahawk, wampum, wigwam.
Mexican: jalap, ocelot.
Spanish from Mexican: cacao, chocolate, copal, tomato?.
Spanish from Hayti: guaiacum, maize, manatee, potato, tobacco.
Caribbean (or other West Indian languages): hammock, macaw.
Spanish from West Indian: cannibal, canoe, guava, iguana, hurricane.

French from West Indian: buccaneer, caoutchouc, pirogue.
Peruvian: jerked (beef), llama, pampas, puma.
Spanish from Peruvian: alpaca, condor, guano.
French from Peruvian: quinine.
Brazilian: jaguar, tapioca, tapir.
Portuguese from Brazilian: ipecacuanha.
French from Brazilian: toucan.
South American: mahogany, tolu.
French from South American: peccary.

SUPPLEMENT.

[I here give some additional words, not accounted for in the preceding pages.]

Aborigines, indigenous inhabitants. (L.) L. *aborigines*, the nations which, previous to historical record, drove out the Siouli (Lewis and Short). Coined from L. *ab origine*, from the beginning; where *origine* is the abl. of *origo* (Virgil, Æn. i. 642).

Accolade, the dubbing of a knight. (F. —Ital.—L.) F. *accollade*, in Cotgrave, ed. 1660; lit. an embrace round the neck, then a salutation, light tap with a sword in dubbing a knight.—Ital. *accolata*, fem. of pp. of *accollare*, to embrace about the neck (Florio).—L. *ac-*, for *ad*, to, about; *collum*, the neck.

Accordion, a musical instrument. (Ital. —L.) From Ital. *accord-are*, to accord, to tune an instrument; with suffix *-ion* (as in *clar-ion*).—Low L. *accordare*, to agree.— L. *ac-*, for *ad*, to; *cord-*, stem of *cor*, the heart. See **accord**, p. 94, col. 2.

Adipose, fatty. (L.—Gk.) Late L. *adiposus*, fatty.—L. *adip-*, stem of *adeps*, sb., fat. Borrowed from Gk. ἄλειφα, fat.— Gk. ἀλείφειν, to anoint. (√ RIP.)

Adit, access to a mine. (L.) L. *adit-us*, approach, entrance.—L. *adit-um*, supine of *ad-ire*, to go to.—L. *ad*, to; *ire*, to go.

Aerolite, a meteoric stone. (Gk.) Put for *aerolith*, which was also once in use.— Gk. ἀερο-, from ἀήρ, air; λίθ-ος, a stone.

Aeronaut, a balloonist. (F. — Gk.) F. *aéronaute*.—Gk. ἀερο-, from ἀήρ, air; ναύτ-ης, a sailor, from ναῦς, a ship.

Affreightment, the hiring of a vessel to convey cargo. (F.—L. *and* G.) An E. spelling of F. *affretement*, now written *affrètement*, the hiring of a ship.—F. *affreter* (now *affréter*), to hire a ship.—L. *af-*, for *ad-*, prefix; and F. *fret*, the freight of a ship. See **Fraught**, p. 161.

Aftermath, a second crop of mown grass. (E.) Here *math* means 'a mowing;' a derivative from **Mow**. Allied to **Mead**. Cf. G. *mahd*, a mowing; *nachmahd*, aftermath.

Aga, Agha, a chief officer. (Turk.) Turk. *aghá*, master.

Agistment, the pasturage of cattle by agreement. (F.—L.) From the F. vb. *agister*, to assign a resting-place.—F. *a* (L. *ad*), to; and O.F. *giste*, a couch, lodging. See **Gist**, p. 226, col. 1.

Agnate, allied. (L.) L. *agnatus*, allied; pp. of *agnasci* = *ad-gnasci*. — L. *ad*, to; *gnasci*, to be born, usually spelt *nasci*.— √ GAN, to beget.

Agraffe, a kind of clasp. (F.—O.H.G.) F. *agrafe*; also *agraphe* (in Cotgrave), a hook, clasp; *agrafer*, to clasp. The verb is from F. *a* (=Lat. *ad*), to; and M.H.G. *krapfe*, O.H.G. *chrapho*, a hook. See **Grape**.

Agrimony, a plant. (F. — L. — Gk.) M.E. *agremoine*.—O.F. *agrimonie*; Cot. —Low L. *agrimonia*, for L. *argemonia*. So called because supposed to cure white spots in the eye.—L. *argema*, a spot in the eye.— Gk. ἄργεμον, the same.—Gk. ἀργός, white.

Air (2), an affected manner. (F.) F. *aire*, mien. The same as Ital. *aria*, mien. See **Debonair** and **Malaria**.

Airt, a point of the compass. (Gael.) Gael. *uird*, a height, a quarter or point of the compass; *ard*, a height. Cf. O. Irish *aird*, a point, limit.

Aitch-bone, the rump-bone. (Hyb.; F.—L. *and* E.) Orig. spelt *nache-bone*.— O.F. *nache*, sing. of *naches*, the buttocks; and E. *bone*. *Naches*=Low L. *naticas*, acc. of *naticæ*, dimin. of L. *nates*, the buttocks.

Alcayde, a judge; see **Cadi** (below).

Alimony, money allowed for a wife's support upon her separation from her husband. (L.) L. *alimonia*, nourishment. —L. *alere*, to nourish; see **Aliment**.

Aline, Align, to range in a line. (F. —L.) Adapted from mod. F. *aligner*, to range in a line. From the phr. *à ligne*, into line.—L. *ad*, to; *linea*, a line. See **Line**. (*Aline* is the better spelling for the E. word.)

Along (2); in phr. *all along of you*, &c. (E.) Corruption of M.E. *ilong*, Layamon,

15502.— A.S. *gelang*, as in *on ǒǎm gelang*, along of that.— A.S. *ge-*, prefix; *lang*, long.

Altruism, regard for others. (Ital.— L.; *with* Gk. *suffix*.) Coined from Ital. *altrui*, another, others, a form of *altro*, another, when preceded by a preposition. Orig. a dat. case.— L. *alteri huic*, to this other; datives of *alter*, other, and *hic*, this.

Ameer, the same as **Emir**, p. 134.

Ana, Anna, a sixteenth of a rupee. (Hind.) Hind. *ána*, a sixteenth part, esp. of a rupee. (H. H. Wilson.)

Anaconda, a large serpent. (Ceylon.) Now used of a S. American boa; but at first applied to a large snake in Ceylon. The Tamil *ánaikondra* means 'having killed an elephant' (Yule).

Anæmia, bloodlessness. (L.— Gk.) A Latinised form of Gk. ἀναιμία, want of blood.— Gk. ἀν-, not; αἷμα, blood.

Aniline, a substance which furnishes a number of dyes. (F.— Span.— Arab.— Pers.) Formed, with suffix *-ine*, from *anil*, a dye-stuff.— F. *anil*.— Span. *añil*, azure.— Arab. *an-níl*; put for *al-níl*, where *al* is the def. art., and *níl* is borrowed from Pers. *níl*, blue, or the indigo-plant.

Apparitor, an officer who attends magistrates to execute their orders; an officer who serves the process of a spiritual court. (L.) L. *apparitor*, an attendant, lictor.— L. *apparere*, to appear as attendant, wait on. See **Appear**.

Appoggiatura, a grace-note or passing tone prefixed, as a support, to an essential note of a melody. (Ital.— L. *and* Gk.) Ital. *appoggiatura*, lit. a support.— Ital. *appoggiare*, to lean upon.— Ital. *ap-* (for *ad*), to, upon; *poggio*, a place to stand or lean on, &c.— L. *ad*, to; *podium*, an elevated place, a balcony, from Gk. πόδιον. See **Pew**, p. 345.

Archimandrite. (L.— Gk.) L. *archimandrita*, a chief or principal of monks, an abbot.— Late Gk. ἀρχιμανδρίτης, the same.— Gk. ἀρχι-, chief; μάνδρα, an enclosure, fold, afterwards a monastery. See **Arch-** and **Madrigal**.

Areca, a genus of palms. (Canarese.) Canarese *adika*, *adike*, areca-nut; the cerebral *d* being mistaken for *r*. Accented on the first syllable.

Assagai, Assegai. (Port.— Moorish.) Introduced into Africa by the Portuguese. — Port. *azagaia*, a dart, javelin.— Arab. *al*, the (def. art.); O. Span. *zagaya*, a dart, a word of Moorish origin; see **Lancegay**.

Assart, the offence of grubbing up trees and destroying the coverts of a forest. (F. —L.) From F. *essarter*, to grub up, clear ground of shrubs.— L. *ex*, out, thoroughly; Low L. *sartare*, frequent. of L. *sarrire*, *sarire*, to grub up weeds.

Assoil, to absolve, acquit. (F.— L.) M.E. *assoilen*.— O.F. *assoldre*, *asoldre*, to absolve; which makes pres. sing. subj. *assoile*.— L. *absoluere*, to absolve.— L. *ab*, from; *soluere*, to loosen. See **Solve**, p. 450. Doublet, *absolve*.

Atabal, a kettle-drum. (Span.— Arab.) Span. *atabal*.— Arab. *a* (for *al*, def. article); *tabl*, a drum.

Ataghan; see **Yataghan** (below).

Atoll, a group of coral islands forming a ring. (Maldive Islands.) 'We derive the expression from the Maldive islands . . . where the form of the word is *atolu*. It is prob. connected with the Singhalese prep. *átul*, 'inside.' (Yule.)

Auk, a sea-bird. (Scand.) Swed. *alka*; Icel. *alka*, *álka*, an auk.

Auto-da-fe. (Port.— L.) Lit. 'decree of faith;' a judgment of the Inquisition, also, the execution of such judgment, when the decree or sentence is read to the victims.— Port. *auto*, action, decree; *da*, short for *de a*, of the; *fé*, faith. [The Span. form is *auto de fé*, without the article *la* = Port. *a*.] — L. *actum*, acc. of *actus*, act, deed; *de*, prep.; *illa*, fem. of *ille*, he; *fidem*, acc. of *fides*, faith.

Avadavat, a finch-like E. Indian bird. (Arab. *and* Pers.) Formerly *amadavat* (Murray); or *amudavad*, N. and Q. 6 S. ii. 198. Named from the city of *Ahmedabad*, whence they were imported.— Arab. *Ahmed*, a proper name; Pers. *ábád*, a city.

Ayah, a native waiting-maid, in India. (Port.— L.) Port. *aia*, a nurse, governess (fem. of *aio*, a tutor). Prob. from L. *auia*, a grandmother.— L. *auus*, a grandfather.

Bakshish, Backsheesh, a present, small gratuity. (Pers.) Pers. *bakhshísh*, a gratuity; from *bakhshídan*, to give; *baksh*, a share, portion. Cf. Zend *baksh*, to distribute.

Balas-ruby, a variety of ruby, of a pale rose, red, or orange colour. (F.— Low L.— Arab.— Pers.) Formerly *balais*, — F. *balais*; Low L. *balascus*, *balascius*.— Arab. *balakhsh*, a ruby (Devic).— Pers. *badakhshí*, a ruby; named from Badakhshan, N. of the river **Amoo** (Oxus).

Baldachin (*pronounced* bauldakin *or* baldakin), a canopy over an altar, throne, &c. (F. *or* Ital. — Arab.) F. *baldaquin*; Ital. *baldacchino*, a canopy, tester, orig. hangings or tapestry made at Bagdad. — Ital. *Baldacco*, Bagdad.—Arab. *Baghdád*, Bagdad.

Bandanna, a silk handkerchief with white spots. (Hind.) Hind. *bándhnú*, 'a mode of dyeing in which the cloth is tied in different places, to prevent the parts tied from receiving the dye . . . a kind of silk cloth;' Shakespear's Hind. Dict.

Bandicoot, a large Indian rat. (Telugu.) Telugu *pandi-kokku*, lit. pig-rat (Yule).

Bangle, a kind of bracelet. (Hind.) Hind. *bangri*, a bracelet, bangle. (H. H. Wilson.)

Banjo, a six-stringed musical instrument. (Ital. — Gk.) A negro corruption of *bandore*, *bandora*, or *pandore*. — Ital. *pandora*, a musical instrument, usually with three strings. — Gk. πανδοῦρα, the same. Perhaps of Egypt. origin.

Banshee, a female spirit supposed to warn families of a death. (Gael.) Gael. *beanshith*, a banshee. — Gael. *bean*, a woman; *sith*, a fairy.

Barbican (addit. to p. 29). Col. Yule suggests that this word represents the Pers. *báb-khána*, 'gate-house,' a name actually inscribed on a double-towered gate-way in Cawnpore. From Arab. *báb*, gate; and Pers. *khána*, a house.

Barrator, one who incites to quarrels and lawsuits. (F.) Formerly *barratour*, *baratour*; from M.E. *barat*, strife, deceit. — F. *barat*, 'cheating, deceit, guile, also a barter,' Cotgrave. Allied to Barter.

Bashaw, the old form of Pasha, p. 333.

Basil (2), the hide of a sheep tanned. (F. — Span. — Arab.) M.E. *basen*, *bazein*. — F. *basane*, O.F. *basanne*. — Span. *badana*, a dressed sheep-skin.—Arab. *bitánat*, the [inner] lining of a garment, for which basil-leather was used. — Arab. root *batana*, to cover, hide.

Basnet, Bassinet, a kind of light helmet. (F. — C.) M. E. *basinet*. — O. F. *bacinet*, *bassinet*, a small bason, also a basnet or head-piece. Dimin. of Basin.

Bavin, a faggot. (F.) Prov. E. (Wilts.) *bavin*, a faggot; hence, as adj., soon kindled and burnt out, 1 Hen. IV. iii. 2. 61.— O.F. *baffe*, a faggot, bundle (Godefroy, Roquefort). Remoter origin unknown.

Beaver (3), **Bever**, a short intermediate repast. (F. — L.) M. E. *beuer*

(= *bever*). — O. F. *beivre*, a drink; substantival use of O.F. *bevre*, *beivre*, to drink. — L. *bibere*, to drink.

Bedell. From the Latinised form (*bedellus*), of O.F. and M.E. *bedel*; see **Beadle**, s.v. Bid (2), p. 38.

Begum, in the E. Indies, a lady of the highest rank. (Pers. — Turk. *and* Arab.) Pers. *begum*, a queen, lady of rank; lit. 'mother of the governor.'—Turk. *beg*, *bey*, a bey, governor; Arab. *um*, *umm*, mother.

Bend, an oblique band, in heraldry. (F. — G.) O.F. *bende*, also *bande*, a band; see Cotgrave. The same word as F. *bande*, a band of men; see Band (2), s.v. Bind, p. 39.

Benzoin, a resinous substance. (F. — Span. — Arab.) F. *benjoin*, 'gum benzoin or gum benjamin;' Cotgrave. — Span. *benjui*. The Span. *la benjui* seems to have been substituted for the Arab. name, *lubán jáwí*, lit. frankincense of Java.

Besant, Bezant, a gold circle, in heraldry. (F. — L. — Gk.) Intended to represent a gold coin of Byzantium. — O.F. *besant*, 'an ancient gold coin;' Cot. — L. *Byzantium*. — Gk. Βυζάντιον, the old name of Constantinople.

Bever, a potation; see Beaver (3) above.

Bezique, a game at cards. (F. — Pers.) F. *bisique* (with *g*); also *bésy* (Littré). The first form = Pers. *bázíchi*, sport, a game; the second = Pers. *bází*, play. — Pers. *bázídan*, to play.

Bezonian, a beggarly fellow. (F. — O.H.G.) In 2 Hen. IV. v. 3. 118. Formerly *bisonian*; made by adding E. *-ian* to F. *bisogne*, spelt *bisongne*, in Cotgrave, 'a filthe knave . . . bisonian.'—O.H.G. *bi-*, prefix, E. *be-*; *sunna*, lawful excuse, necessity; cf. Goth. *sunja*, truth, sooth. From the sense of 'necessity' came the sense of 'necessitous' for the adj. *bisogne*; hence, further, it came to mean needy, poor, beggarly. Cf. F. *besoin*, *soin*. See Essoin (below).

Biggen, a night-cap. (F.) O.F. *beguin*, 'a biggin for a child;' Cot. Named from the caps worn by beguines; see Beguine.

Blindman's buff; see Buff below.

Board (2), to go on board a ship, to accost. (F. — Teut.) The sb. *board* is E., but the verb, formerly spelt *borde*, *bord*, is short for *aborde*, used by Palsgrave. — F. *aborder*, 'to approach, accost, abboord, or lay aboord;' Cot. — F. *a*, to (L. *ad*); *bord*, edge, brim, side of a ship, from Icel. *bord*, Du. *boord*, side of a ship. See Board.

Bohea, a kind of tea. (Chinese.) So named from the *Bohea* hills; the mountain called *Bou-y* is situated in the province of *Fokien* or *Fukian*, on the S.E. coast of China.

Bolus, a large pill. (L.—Gk.) Low L. *bōlus* (not L. *bŏlus*), a Latinised form of Gk. βῶλος, a clod, lump.

Bonito, a fish of the tunny kind. (Span. —Arab.) Span. *bonito.*—Arab. *baynīs*, a bonito. (The final *s* here is a letter which is properly sounded as E. *th*.)

Boomerang, a wooden missile, implement. (Australian.) Corrupted from a native Australian word.

Botargo, a cake made of the roe of the sea-mullet. (Ital.—Arab.) Ital. *botargo*, pl. *botarghe*; see Florio and Torriano.— Arab. *butarkha*, botargo; given by Devic. Supposed to be composed of *bu*, Coptic def. article, and Gk. τάριχος, dried fish (Journ. des Savants, Jan. 1848, p. 45).

Bout (2), in phr. a drinking-*bout*, or a *bout* of foul weather. (F.—O.H.G.) The E. *by bouts* answers to F. *par boutées*, 'by fits or pushes, now and then;' Cot.—F. *bouter*, to thrust, to butt. See Butt (1).

Bow-line. (Scand.) *Not* so called because it keeps a ship's sail *bowed* (for it rather keeps it straight), but so called because fastened to the side of the sail.—Icel. *bóg-lína*, lit. 'side-line,' a line fastened to the side or 'shoulder' of a sail.—Icel. *bóg-r*, shoulder, side, also bow of a ship; *lína*, line. Allied to Bough and Bow (4); but not to Bow (1).

Boycott, to combine with others in refusing to have dealings with any one. (E.) From the treatment accorded to Capt. *Boycott*, of Lough Mask House, co. Mayo, Ireland, in Dec. 1880.

Brae, an acclivity, slope of a hill. (Gael.) Gael. *braigh*, top, upper part; hence, higher part of a hill.

Braid, full of deceit. (E.) In All's Well, iv. 2. 73, *braid* is short for *braided*, i. e. full of *braids* or tricks. M.E. *braid*, trick, deceit.—A.S. *brægd*, deceit; cf. A.S. *brægd*, pt. t. of *bregdan*, to draw out, weave, knit, braid.

Brassart, the piece of armour which protected the upper part of the arm. (F.— L.) F. *brassart* (Cotg.), *brassard* (Littré); also *brassal*. Formed with suffix -*ard* from F. *bras*, arm. *Bras* is formed from O.F. *brasse*, later form of *brace.*—L. *brachia*, pl., the two arms. See Brace, p. 48.

Breach, a rupture. (F.—M.H.G.?) Said, at p. 50, to be E. But M.E. *breche* may have been borrowed from O.F. *breche* (F. *brèche*), a breach.—M.H.G. *brechen*, to break; cognate with A.S. *brecan*.

Bromine, a chemical element. (Gk.) Named from its ill odour. Formed, with suffix -*ine*, from Gk. βρῶμ-ος, a stink.

Brougham, a kind of carriage. (Personal name.) Date 1839. Named after the first Lord Brougham.

Buff, in **Blindman's buff**. (F.) Formerly *blindman-buff*, a game; in which game boys used to *buffet* one (who was blinded) on the back, without being caught, if possible. From O.F. *bufe*, F. *buffe*, a buffet, blow. See Buffet (1), p. 54.

Bugloss, a plant. (F.—L.—Gk.) Lit. 'ox-tongue.'—F. *buglosse.*—L. *buglossa*; also *buglossus.*—Gk.βούγλωσσος, ox-tongue; from the shape of the leaves.—Gk. βοῦ-s, ox; γλῶσσ-α, tongue.

Bulbul, a nightingale. (Pers.) Pers. *bulbul*, a bird with a melodious voice, resembling the nightingale. Of imitative origin.

Bulrush; see Rush (2), p. 410.

Burke, to murder by suffocation; to murder, stifle. (Personal name.) From the name of *Burke*, an Irishman who committed murders by suffocation; executed at Edinburgh, Jan. 28, 1829.

Burnet, a plant. (F.—O.H.G.) Low L. *burneta.*—O.F. *brunete*, the name of a flower: *burnette, brunette*, a kind of dark brown cloth, also a brunette. See Brunette, p. 53, bottom of col. 1.

Burnouse, Burnoose, an upper cloak worn by the Arabs. (F.—Arab.) F. *burnous, bournous.*—Arab. *burnus*, a kind of high-crowned cap, worn formerly in Barbary and Spain; whence Span. *al-bornoz*, a kind of cloak with a hood.

Butty, a companion or partner in a work. (Scand.; or F.—Scand.) Shortened from *boty-felowe* or *booty-fellow*, one who shares booty with others. From *boty*, old spelling of *booty* = F. *butin*, booty. Of Low G. or Scand. origin; see Booty, p. 46.

Cacique, a W. Indian chief. (Span. —W. Indian.) Span. *cacique*, an Indian prince. From the old language of Hayti.

Caddis, a kind of worsted lace or tape. (F.) In Wint. Tale, iv. 4. 208. M.E. *cadas*, explained by *bombicinium* in Prompt. Parv.; (hence Irish *cadas*, caddis). Though usually explained as being 'of worsted,' I suppose it was orig. of coarse silk. — F. *cadarce*, 'the coursest part of silke, whereof sleave is made;' Cot. Span. *cadarzo*, coarse, entangled silk, that cannot be spun on a reel; Port. *cadarço*, a coarse silk. Origin unknown; *probably* Eastern. Der. *caddis-worm*, from the caddis-like shape of the case of the larva.

Cadi, a judge. (Arab.) Arab. *qádí, qází*, a cadi or cazi, a judge. Hence Span. *al-calde*, the judge; where *al* is the Arab. def. article.

Calender, a kind of wandering monk. (F. — Pers.) F. *calender*. — Pers. *qalandar*, a kind of wandering Muhammadan monk, who abandons everything and retires from the world.

Callet, Callat, a worthless woman. (F. — Low L. — Low G.) In Oth. iv. 2. 121. — F. *caillette*, lit. a little quail; dimin. of *caille*, a quail, also a woman. Littré gives *caille coiffée*, femme galante. See **Quail**, p. 381, last line.

Calthrop, Caltrap, a star-thistle, a ball with spikes for annoying cavalry. (L. *and* Teut.) M.E. *kalketrappe*, A.S. *calcetrappe*, a star-thistle. Coined from L. *calci-*, crude form of *calx*, the heel; and the Teutonic word *trap*. Lit. 'heel-trap;' see **Trap**. So also F. *chaussetrappe*, the same.

Calumet, a kind of pipe for tobacco. (F. — L. — Gk.) F. *calumet*, a pipe; dimin. of *calumeau*, or *chalumeau*, a pipe. — L. *calamus*, a reed. — Gk. κάλαμος, a reed. See **Shawm**, p. 430.

Cannon, at billiards. (F. — Span.) A corruption of *carrom*, shortened form of F. *caramboler*, v., to make a cannon at billiards, to touch two other balls with one's own; see Hoyle's Games. Orig. sense, to touch the red ball; whence *caramboler*, to cannon (as above) and *carambolage*, sb., a cannon. — Span. *carambola*, a manner of playing at billiards, a device, trick, cheat. Origin unknown.

Canon (2), a dignitary of the church. (F. — L. — Gk.) M.E. *canun, canoun*. — O.F. *canogne*, now *chanoine*. — Lat. *canonicum*, acc. of *canonicus*, adj., one on the church-roll or list. — L. *canon*, the church-roll. See **Canon**, p. 63, col. 2.

Cantle, a piece. (F. — Low L. — L. — Gk.) M.E. *cantel*. — O.F. *cantel* (mod. F. *chanteau*), a piece, bit. — Low Lat. *cantellus*, dimin. from L. *canthus* = Gk. κάνθος, the corner of the eye, the felloe of a wheel.

Carafe, a glass water-bottle. (F. — Span. — Arab.) F. *carafe*. — Span. *garrafa*, a cooler, vessel to cool wines in. — Arab. *ghiráf*, draughts of water; Arab. root *gharf, gharaf*, to draw water. (Dozy, Devic.) ¶ Or from Pers. *qarába*, a large flagon.

Carboy, a large glass bottle, protected by wicker-work. (Arab.?) Pers. *qarába*, a large flagon; which is prob. of Arab. origin. Cf. Pers. and Arab. *qirbah*, a water-skin, water-bottle.

Carkanet. See **Carcanet**, p. 68.

Caroche, a kind of coach. (F. — Ital. — C.) Obsolete; but the present sense of *carriage* is due to it. — F. *caroche*, variant of *carosse*, 'a carosse or caroach;' Cot. — Ital. *carroccia, carrozza*, a chariot. Extended from Ital. *carro*, a car. See **Car**, p. 67.

Cashew-nut, the nut of a W. and E. Indian tree. (F. — Brazilian?) *Cashew* is a corruption of F. *acajou*, which is said to be from the native Brazilian name *acajaba* or *acajaiba*. (Mahn, Littré.)

Cassava, a plant. (Span. — Hayti.) Span. *casabe*; also *cazavi*, 'the bread made in the W. Indies, of the fruit called the *yuca*;' Pineda. It properly means a bread made from the root of the manioc; said to be from the Hayti *casabbi*, with the same sense. See R. Eden's Works, ed. Arber, p. 175. See **Tapioca**, p. 491.

Castanets, instruments used for making a snapping noise. (F. — Span. — L. — Gk.) F. *castagnettes*, 'finger-knackers, wherewith players make a pretty noise in some dances;' Cot. — Span. *castañetas*, castanets; pl. of *castañeta*, a snapping noise resembling the cracking of roasted chestnuts. — Span. *castaña*, a chestnut. — Lat. *castanea*, the chestnut-tree. Cf. χάσταρος, a chestnut, see **Chestnut**.

Catafalque, a temporary canopy or scaffold, used in funeral solemnities. (F. — L. *and* Teut.) F. *catafalque*; Span. and Ital. *catafalco*. See further under the doublet **Scaffold**, p. 65, bottom of col. 2.

Catamaran (addit. to p. 71). From Tamil *kaṭṭu*, binding; *maram*, wood (Yule).

Catenary, belonging to a chain; used of the curve in which a chain hangs. (L.) From L. *catena*, a chain; see **Chain**.

Cateran, a Highland robber. (Gael.) From Gael. *ceatharnach*, a soldier, fighting man. — Gael. and Irish *cath*, battle; cf. W.

cad, battle. ¶ The word *kern* is the same word, from Irish *ceatharnach*, in which the *th* and *ch* are hardly sounded.

Cater-cousin, a remote relation, good friend. (F. – L.) Spelt *quater-cousin*, Coles (1684). Lit. 'fourth cousin;' cf. '*cater-point*, in dice, the number four;' Bailey. – O.F. *catre*, four, from L. *quatuor*, four; and **Cousin**.

Cates, provision. (F. – L.) So called because provided by the *catour*, mod. E. *cater-er*; see **cater**, s. v. **Capacious**, p. 65. '*Cater*, a steward, a provider of *cates*;' Baret (1580).

Caucus, a name applied to certain political meetings. (American Indian?) Said to be from an Algonkin word meaning to speak, to counsel, whence *kaw-kaw-wus*, a counsellor. 'Their elders, called *caw-cawwassoughes*;' Capt. Smith's Works, ed. Arber, p. 347. '*Caucorouse*, which is captaine;' id. p. 377. ¶ This is more likely than the entirely unsupported story about *caulkers*' meetings.

Cave in. (O. Low G.) Properly to *calve in*, a phrase introduced by Du. navvies. Cf. W. Flanders *inkalven*, to cave in; E. Friesic *kalfen*, to calve as a cow, also to cave in. The falling portion of earth is compared to a calf dropped by a cow.

Cayman, an American alligator. (Caribbean.) Also *caiman*. The spelling *cayman* is Spanish. – Caribbean *acayúman* (Littré).

Celt (1), a name originally given to the Gauls. (C.) Cæsar calls the Gauls *Celtæ*; the word probably meant 'warriors;' cf. Icel. *hildr*, war; Lith. *kalti*, to strike; L. *per-cellere*, to strike through, beat down (Rhys).

Celt (2), a primitive chisel or axe. (Low L.) Low L. *celtis*, assumed nom. of the abl. *celte* (= with a chisel), in the Vulgate Version of Job xix. 24. But this reading is due to some error, and there seems to be no such word in Latin.

Cess, limit, measure. (F. – L.) In 1 Hen. IV. ii. 1. 8. Orig. a tax, rate, rating, assessment; see Spenser, State of Ireland, Globe ed., p. 643, col. 2. From *cess*, verb, to rate; which is short for **Assess**.

Chablis, a white wine. (F.) From *Chablis*, 12 mi. E. of Auxerre, in the department of Yonne, France.

Champak, a tree. (Skt.) Skt. *champaka*, the champak.

Châtelaine; see under **Castle**, p. 71.

Chaudron, entrails. (F.) Macb. iv. 1. 33. The *r* is inserted by confusion with F. *chaudron*, a caldron. – O.F. *chaudun*, older forms *caudun, caldun*, entrails (Godefroy). Cf. G. *kaldaunen*, entrails; from Mid. Low G. *kaldune*, the same. Thought to be of Celtic origin; cf. W. *coludd*, pl. *coluddion*, entrails; and perhaps Gael. *caolan*, the same.

Cheeta, Cheetah, the hunting leopard, a leopard used for the chase. (Hind. – Skt.) Hind. *chítá*. – Skt. *chitra*, spotted; also visible, clear. – Skt. *chit*, to perceive. See **Chintz**, p. 79.

Cheroot, a cigar. (Tamil.) Tamil *shuruṭṭu*, a roll; hence, a roll of tobacco (Yule).

Cheveril, kid leather. (F. – L.) O.F. *chevrel* (mod. F. *chevreau*), a kid; kid leather. Dimin. of O.F. *chevre*, F. *chèvre*, a goat, kid. – L. *capram*, acc. of *capra*, a she-goat.

Chevron, an ordinary, in heraldry, resembling two rafters of a house. (F. – L.) Most likely meant to represent the saddle-peak. – F. *chevron*, 'a kid, a chevron in building, a rafter;' Cot. Augmentative form of *chevre*, a she-goat. – L. *capra*, a she-goat; see **Caper** (1). Cf. L. *capreolus*, which, in the same way, means a prop.

Chibouk, a Turkish pipe. (Turk.) Turk. *chibúk, chybúk*, a stick, tube, pipe (Zenker, p. 349).

Chinchilla, a small rodent animal. (Span. – L.) Span. *chinchilla*, lit. 'a little bug,' as if from its smell; but undeservedly so named. – Span. *chinche*, a bug. – L. *cimicem*, acc. of *cimex*, a bug.

Chinchona; the same as **Cinchona**, p. 81.

Chopine, a high-heeled shoe. (F. – Span.) In Hamlet, ii. 2. 447; for *chapine*. – O.F. *chapin*; later *chappin* (Cotgrave). – Span. *chapin*, a clog with a cork sole, woman's shoe, high cork shoe. Perhaps from Span. *chapa*, which seems orig. to have meant a covering, and to be the same word as E. *cape*.

Chutny, a kind of hot relish. (Hind.) Hind. *chatní* (Yule).

Cid, lit. a chief or commander. (Span. – Arab.) Usually a title of Roderigo Diaz, the national hero of Spain. – Arab. *sayyid*, a lord, a prince; Richardson's Dict., p. 864.

Cistvaen, a British monument. (L. *and* W.) W. *cistfaen*, a stone chest, monument made with four upright stones, and a fifth on the top.—W. *cist*, a chest (from L. *cista*) ; and *maen*, a stone.

Clachan, a small village with a church. (Gael.) Gael. *clachan*, (1) a circle of stones, (2) a small rude church, (3) a small village with a church.—Gael. *clach*, a stone. So also Irish *clachan*, a hamlet ; *clach*, a stone.

Cleat, a piece of iron for strengthening the soles of shoes; a piece of wood or iron to fasten ropes to. (E.) M.E. *clete*, a wedge ; also *clite*, *clote*, a lump. Allied to **Clot**.

Clerestory, a story in a church, furnished with windows. (F.—L.) Old spelling of *clear-story*. The triforium below is sometimes called the *blind-story*. See **Story** (2).

Clove (3), a denomination of weight. (F.—L.) Spelt *clous* (pl.) in Anglo-F., and *clauos* (acc. pl.) in Lat. ; Liber Custumarum, pp. 63, 107. Low L. *clauus*, a lump, quantity ; L. *clauus*, a nail. The same word as **Clove** (1), p. 85, col. 2.

Cobra, a hooded snake. (Port.—L.) Port. *cobra*, also *cobra de capello*, i. e. snake with a hood.—L. *colubra*, snake ; *de*, of ; *capellum*, acc. of *capellus*, hat, hood, dimin. of *capu*, a cape. See Notes and Queries, 7 S. ii. 205.

Coca, a Peruvian plant. (Span.—Peruv.) Span. *coca*—Peruv. *cuca* ; Garcilasso, Peru, bk. 8. c. 15. Distinct both from *cocoa* (or *coco*) and *cacao*.

Cockroach. (Span.—L.—Gk. ?) Span. *cucaracha*, a wood-louse, cockroach. Cf. Span. *cuco*, a kind of caterpillar. Perhaps from L. *coccum*, a berry ; Gk. κόκκος.

Coistrel, a mean fellow. (F.—L.) Put for *coustrel*, the older form (Palsgrave). An E. adaptation of F. *coustillier*, an armour-bearer, groom, lackey ; lit. 'one who carries a poiñard.'—F. *coustille*, a poniard ; variant of O.F. *coustel*, better *coutel*, a knife.—L. *cultellum*, acc. of *cultellus*, a knife ; dimin. of *culter*. See **Coulter**, p. 96, col. 1.

Colleen, a girl. (Irish.) Irish *cailin*, a girl ; dimin. of *caile*, a country-woman. Gael. *cailin*, dimin. of *caile*.

Collie, Colly, a kind of shepherd's dog. (C.) Formerly *coaly*, *coley*.—Gael. *cuilean*, *cuilein*, a whelp, puppy. Perhaps from Gael. *cu*, a dog.

Colporteur, a hawker of wares. (F.—L.) Lit. 'one who carries wares on his neck;' F. *colporteur*.—F. *colporter*, to carry

on the neck.—F. *col*, neck ; *porter*, to carry. —L. *collum*, neck ; *portare*, to carry.

Colza oil, a lamp-oil made from the seeds of a variety of cabbage. (F.—L. *and* Du.) F. *colza*, better *colzat*.—Du. *koolzaad*, rape-seed, cabbage-seed.—Du. *kool* (borrowed from L. *caulis*), cole, cabbage; and Du. *zaad* = E. *seed*.

Comfrey, a plant. (F.—L.) O.F. *cumfirie*: Low L. *cumfiria* ; corruptions of Low Lat. *confirma*, comfrey, a name given to the plant from its supposed healing powers.—L. *con-firmare*, to make firm, to strengthen.

Complot, a conspiracy; see **plot** (1), p. 359, col. 1.

Consent; see under **Sense**, p. 424, col. 2.

Conundrum. (Unknown.) Formerly used in the sense of whim, crotchet, or hoax. Possibly a corruption of L. *conandum*, a thing to be attempted, problem ; like *quillet* for *quidlibet*. (A guess.)

Co-parcener, a co-partner. (F.—L.) *Parcener* is the true old spelling of *partner* ; see p. 332, col. 2.

Copeck, a small Russian coin, worth less than ½d. ; a hundredth part of a rouble. (Russ.) Russ. *kopieika*. See **Rouble**, p. 407.

Coronach, a dirge. (Gael.) Gael. *coranach*, a dirge, lit. 'a howling together.'—Gael. *comh-* (L. *cum*), together ; *ranaich*, a howling, from the verb *ran*, to howl, cry, roar.

Corral, an enclosure for animals, pen. (Span.—L.) Span. *corral*, a court, yard, enclosure.—Span. *corro*, a circle, a ring of people met to see a show. From the phrase *correr toros*, to hold a bull-fight, lit. to run bulls.—L. *currere*, to run. See **Kraal** (below), p. 625.

Corrie (Gael.) Gael. *coire*, a circular hollow surrounded with hills, a mountain dell.

Cosy, Cozy, comfortable, snugly sheltered. (C.) Lowland Scotch *cosie*, *cozie* (Burns) ; Gael. *cosach*, *cosaguch*, abounding in recesses; also snug, sheltered.—Gael. *cos*, a hollow, recess, cave ; Irish *cuas*, a cave.

Coupon, an interest warrant attached to transferable bonds which is cut off to be presented for payment. (F.—L.—Gk.) F. *coupon*, a piece cut off, a coupon.—F. *couper*, to cut, slash.—F. *coup*, a blow.—Low L. *colpus*, short for *colaphus*, a blow.—Gk. κόλαφος, a blow on the ear.

Covin, secret agreement, fraud; a law-term. (F. – L.) M.E. *covine*. – O.F. *covine*, agreement. – O.F. *covenir*, to assemble, agree. – L. *con-uenire*, to come together. See **Convene**, **Covenant**, p. 540.

Creel, an angler's osier basket. (Gael.) Mod. Gael. has only the dimin. *craidhleag*, a basket, a creel. From O. Irish *criol*, a coffer (Windisch).

Crewel, worsted yarn, slightly twisted. (Du.?) Formerly *crule* (Palsgrave; s.v. *Caddas*). – Du. *krul*, a curl; *krullen*, 'to curl, crisp, wind, turn;' Sewel. Bailey defines *crewel* as 'two-twisted worsted.' See **Curl**.

Cringle, an iron ring. (Scand.) Icel. *kringla*, a circle; cf. *kringar*, pl., the pullies of a drag-net. Allied to Du. *kring*, a circle, Swed. *kring*, prep., around; also to **Crinkle**, **Crank** (1), and **Cringe**.

Crumpet, a kind of soft bread-cake. (W.) Prob. from W. *crempog* (also *crammwyth*), a pancake, a fritter.

Crusty, ill-tempered. (E.) Prob. for *cursty*, i. e. curst-like; *curst* signifies ill-tempered, not only in Shak., but in Cursor Mundi, l. 19201. *Curst* is the pp. of *curse*, vb., from *curse*, sb.

Cubeb, a spicy berry. (F. – Span. – Arab.) F. *cubebe*, in Cotgrave. – Span. *cubeba*. – Arab. *kabábat*, pl. *kabábah*, cubeb, an aromatic.

Cuisse, a piece of armour for the thighs. (F. – L.) Pl. *cuisses*, 1 Hen. IV. iv. 1. 105. – F. *cuisse*, thigh. – L. *coxa*, hip.

Dacoit, a robber. (Hind.) Hind. *ḍakait*, a robber belonging to an armed gang (Yule). Der. *dacoit-y*, robbery.

Dado. (Ital. – L.) Formerly used of the die, or square part in the middle of the pedestal of a column; afterwards applied to the part of an apartment between the plinth and the impost moulding. O. Ital. *dado*, a die; see **die** (2), s.v. **Date** (1); p. 109, col. 1.

Daft, foolish; see **Deft** (below).

Davit (p. 110). Spelt *Dauid* in Capt. Smith's Works, ed. Arber, p. 793.

Dawk, transport by relays of men and horses. (Hind.) Hind. *ḍāk*, post, transport, &c. (Yule).

Daywoman, dairy-woman. (Scand. *and* E.) In Shak. L. L. L. i. 2. 137. The addition of *woman* is needless. *Day* = M.E. *deye* = Icel. *deigja*, a maid; esp. a dairy-maid; see **Dairy**, s.v. **Dike**, p. 118, col. 1.

December. (L.) *December*, orig. the name of the *tenth* month. – L. *decem*, ten.

Deft, neat, dexterous. (E.) M.E. *deft*, *daft*. A.S. *dæft*, as seen in *ge-dæfte*, mild, gentle, meek; *ge-dæftlíce*, fitly, seasonably; *dæftan*, to prepare. From A.S. *ge-daf-en*, fit, pp. of a lost strong verb *dafan*.

Demijohn, a glass vessel, enclosed in wickerwork. (F. – Pers.) Corruption of F. *dame-jeanne*, again corrupted from Arab. *damjána*, a large glass vessel. So named from the Pers. town of Damghan, in Khorassan, celebrated for glass-works.

Derrick, a kind of crane. (Du.) Orig. the gallows; and named from a Dutch hangman; see T. Dekker, Seven Deadly Sins of London, ed. Arber, p. 17. – Du. *Dierryk*, *Dirk*, *Diederik*; answering to G. *Dietrich*, A.S. *þeódríc*, 'chief of the people.'

Dingle, a deep valley. (E.) M.E. *dingle*, a depth, hollow. Dimin. of A.S. *ding*, a dark prison (Grein).

Dingy (with -hard *g*), a small boat. (Bengali.) Beng. *dingy*, a small boat; 'it has become legitimately incorporated in the vocabulary of the British Navy, as the name of the smallest ship's boat' (Yule).

Dittany, a plant. (F. – L. – Gk.) M.E. *ditane*, *ditany*. – O.F. *dictame*, 'ditany;' Cotgrave. – L. *dictamnum*, acc. of *dictamnum* or *dictamnus*. – Gk. δίκταμνον, δίκταμνος; named from *Dicte*, in Crete.

Dolmen, a monument of two upright stones, with a third across them. (Bret. – L. *and* C.) Bret. *dolmen*, lit. 'table-stone;' Legonidec. – Bret. *dol*, also *tol*, *taol*, a table (from L. *tabula*); and *men*, a stone.

Dornick, a kind of cloth; *obsolete*. (Flemish.) Named from Flem. *Dornick*, better known by the F. name of *Tournay* (Lat. *Tornacus*).

Dory, a fish. (F. – L.) Spelt *doree* in Holland, tr. of Pliny, b. 32, c. 11; Anglo-F. *dore*. – Low L. *dorea*, *doracus*; Latinised from F. *d'or*, of gold (L. *de auro*), from its colour. 'Gustum *doreæ* quæ nomen sumpsit ab auro;' A. Neckam, De Laudibus, pt. iii. l. 561. Nicknamed *John dory* by E. sailors.

Duds, shabby clothes. (Scand.) Formerly *dudes* (with long *u*); cf. the mod. E. deriv. *dowd-y*. – Icel. *dúði*, swaddling clothes, wraps. Prob. from Icel. *dúa* (pt. t. *dúði*), to shake about.

Duffer, a stupid person. (Scand.) Lowl. Sc. *dowfart*, formed with suffix *-art* from the adj. *dowf*, stupid, dull; lit. 'deaf.' — Icel. *dauf-r*, deaf; see **Deaf.**

Eanling, a lamb. (E.) *Eanling* is from the verb *ean*, which is *y-ean* without the prefix *y-* (= A.S. *ge*). See **Yean,** p. 574.

Écarté, a game at cards. (F.—L. and Gk.) In this game, cards may be *discarded* and exchanged; hence the name.—F. *écarté*, discarded, pp. of *écarter*, to discard.—L. *ex*, out, away; F. *carte* ═ Low L. *carta*, from Gk. χάρτη, a leaf of paper, hence a card.

Eery, timid, affected by fears, melancholy, strange. (E.) See Jamieson. M.E. *ary*, *arh*, *arey*, *arye*, *erye*, timid; spelt *eri* in Cursor Mundi, 17685.—A.S. *earg*, *earh*, timid, cowardly. Cf. Icel. *argr*, *ragr*; G. *arg*.

Egret, the lesser white heron. (F.— O.H.G.) O.F. *egrette*, *aigrette*, dimin. of a form *aigre** (whence also Prov. *aigr-on*, O.F. *hair-on*, E. *her-on*).—O.H.G. *heigir*, *heiger*, a heron. See **Heron.**

Eisel, vinegar. (F.—L.) In Shak. M.E. *eisel*, *eisil*, *uisil*.—O.F. *aisil*, *eisil*, also *aisi*, vinegar (Godefroy). *Aisil* appears to be a lengthened form of *aisi*.—Low L. *acitus*, bitter; closely related to L. *acetum*, vinegar. The Goth. *akeit*, vinegar, A.S. *ecid*, G. *essig*, seem to be due to Low L. *acitum* rather than *acetum*.

Elecampane, a plant. (F.—L.) Short for F. *enule-campane*.—L. *inula campana*, elecampane. Here *campana* prob. means wild, growing in the fields; from L. *campus*, a field.

Eloign, Eloin, to remove and keep at a distance, to withdraw. (F.—L.) O.F. *esloigner*, to remove, keep away.—O.F. *es*, away; *loing* (F. *loin*), far off.—L. *ex*, away; *longe*, adv. far off.

Emblements, the produce of sown lands, crops which a tenant may cut after the determination of his tenancy. (F.—L.) From O.F. *embleër*, *emblaër*, *emblader* (F. *emblaver*), to sow with corn.—Low Lat. *imbladare*, to sow.—L. *im-*, for *in*, in; Low L. *bladum* ═ L. *ablatum*, a crop, corn, lit. 'what is carried away.'

Embonpoint, plumpness of person. (F.—L.) F. *embonpoint*, plumpness. For *en bon point*, in good case.—L. *in*, in ; *bonum*, neut. of *bonus*, good ; *punctum*, point.

Emprise, enterprise; see **Imprese.**

Endue (2), to clothe. (L.) A corrup-

tion of *indue*; as in '*endue* thy ministers with righteousness.'—L. *induere*, to clothe. See **Indue** (2).

Engrailed, indented with curved lines; in heraldry. (F.—L. and Teut.) O.F. *engresle*, pp. of *engresler*, to engrail.—O.F. *en*, in ; *gresle* (F. *grêle*), hail.—L. *in*, in ; and G. *gries*, grit. See **Grail** (3).

Ensilage, the storing of grain, &c., underground. (F.—Span.—L. and Gk.) F. *ensilage*.—Span. *ensilar*, to store up underground.—Span. *en*, in ; *silo*, a pit for storing grain.—L. *in*, in ; *sirus*, borrowed from Gk. σιρός, a pit for storing grain.

Epergne, an ornamental stand for the centre of a table. (F.—L. and G.) F. *épergne*, commonly spelt *épargne*, lit. thriftiness, sparingness. So called from the method of ornamentation ; the F. *taille d'épargne* is applied to a sort of ornamentation in which certain parts are cut away and filled in with enamel, leaving the design *in relief*, i. e. *spared* or left uncut. See Littré and Cotgrave (s. v. *espargne*).—F. *épargner*. O.F. *espargner*, *espergner*, to spare.—G. *sparen*, to spare ; see **Spare.**

Escrow, a deed delivered on condition. (F.—Teut.) M.E. *scroue*, *scrow*; the orig. word of which *scro-ll* is the diminutive. See **Scroll,** s. v. **Shroud,** p. 434, col. 2.

Escuage, a pecuniary satisfaction in lieu of feudal service. (F.—L.) O.F. *escuage* ═ Low L. *scutagium*. Formed with suffix *-age* from O.F. *escu*, a shield ; because *escuage* was first paid in lieu of service in the field.—L. *scutum*, a shield.

Essoin, an excuse for not appearing in court. (F.—L. and Teut.) O.F. *essoine*, *exoine*, 'an essoine, or excuse ;' Cot.— O.F. *es-* (L. *ex*), very, as an intensive prefix; O.F. *soine* (cf. F. *soin*), Low Lat. *sunnia*, from O.H.G. *sunna*, lawful excuse.

Estop, to bar. (F.—L.) The same as **Stop.**

Estovers, supplies of various necessaries. (F.—L.) I.e. *stovers*, pl. of *stover*; see **Stover,** p. 474.

Estreat, a true copy, in law. (F.—L.) Lit. 'extract.' O.F. *estrete*, fem. of pp. of *estraire*, to extract.—L. *extracta*, fem. of pp. of *extrahere*; see **Extract,** p. 518, col. 1.

Eucalyptus, a genus of trees, including the blue gum-tree. (Gk.) Latinised from Gk. εὖ, well ; καλυπτός, covered, surrounded. The reference is to the hood protecting the stamens.

Exergue, the small space left beneath the base-line of a subject engraved on a coin. (F.—Gk.) The final *-ue* is not pronounced; cf. *prologue*, &c. —F. *exergue*, so called because lying 'out of the work.' —Gk. *ἐξ*, out of; *ἔργον*, work.

Exsequies: see **Exequies**, p. 425, bottom of col. 1.

Eyas, a nestling. (F.—L.) For *nias*; due to putting *an eyas* for *a nias*.—F. *niais*, a nestling; Cot. He also gives *niard*, whence *faulcon niard*, 'a nias falcon.' Cp. Ital. *nidiace*, or *nidaso falcone*, 'an eyase-hawk, a young hawk taken out of her nest;' Torriano. Formed as if from Low Lat. *nidacem**, acc. of *nidax**, adj. from L. *nidus*, a nest.

Fandango, a Spanish dance. (Span.) Span. *fandango*, 'a dance used in the W. Indies;' Pineda (1740).

Faquir, Fakir, an Oriental religious mendicant. (F.—Arab.) F. *faquir, fakir*. —Arab. *faqîr*, one of a religious order of mendicants; lit. 'poor, indigent;' Richardson's Dict. p. 1096.

Feeze, Feaze, Pheeze. (E.) Properly 'to put to flight, drive away, chase away, harass, worry;' often misexplained by 'whip.' M.E. *fesen*; A.S. *fésian*, by-form of *fýsian*, to drive away quickly, chase.— A.S. *fús*, quick, prompt.

Fellah, a peasant. (Arab.) Pl. *fellahin*. —Arab. *fellâh, fallâh*, a farmer, peasant. —Arab. root *falah*, to plough, till.

Fenugreek, a plant. (F.—L.) F. *fenugrec*.—L. *fænum Græcum*, lit. Greek hay.

Fess, a horizontal band in heraldry. (F. —L.) O.F. *fesse* (Roquefort); mod. F. *fasce*, a fess.—L. *fascia*, a girth; allied to *fascis*, a bundle; see **Fascine**.

Feuter, to lay spear in rest. (F.—Teut.) From M.E. *feuter*, a rest for a spear.—O.F. *feutre*, older *feltre*, a piece of felt, also a rest (prob. at first felted) for the lance. Cp. Ital. *feltro*, felt. Of Teut. origin; see **Felt**, p. 147.

Feuterer, a dog-keeper. (F.—Low L. —C.) In Ben Jonson, Every Man out of his Humour, ii. 1; see Nares. Older spelling *veuterer*, put for *veutr-er*.—O.F. *veutre*, mod. F. *vautre*, a mongrel between a hound and a mastiff.—Low Lat. acc. *veltrum*; allied to L. *vertaga, vertagra*, grey-hound. Said to be Celtic; cf. Cornish *guilter*, a mastiff.

Fez, a red Turkish cap, without a brim.

(F. — Morocco.) F. and Turk. *fez*, a cap; so called because made at Fez, in Morocco.

File, to defile. (E.) A.S. *fýlan*, to make foul.—A.S. *fúl*, foul. See **Defile** (1), p. 112.

Fills, used for *thills*. (E.) See **Thill**.

Fiord, a sea-loch, deep inlet of the sea. (Scand.) Norw. *fjord*, Dan. *fiord, fjord*; Icel. *fjörðr*. See **Frith**, p. 145, top of col. 2.

Firm (2), a partnership. (Port.—L.) The proper sense is 'signature' of the house or (as we call it) the firm.—Port. *firma*; a signature; a firm.—Port. *firmar*, to confirm, sign.—L. *firmare*, to make firm. —L. *firmus*, firm.

Flawn, a kind of custard. (F.—O.H.G.) M.E. *flaun*.—F. *flan*, O.F. *flaon*, a flawn; (cf. Span. *flaon*, Ital. *fiadone*).—O.H.G. *flado*, a broad flat cake; G. *fladen*. From Dan. *flad*, Icel. *flatr*, flat.

Fly, a vehicle. (E.) A name given to a kind of four-wheeled vehicle drawn by men at Brighton, in 1816. Called *fly-coach* in 1818 (Scott, Heart Midl. ch. 1). From *fly*, v.

Forejudge, to deprive a man of a thing by the judgment of a court. (F.—L.) Better spelt *forjudge*.—F. *forjuger*, to judge amiss, to dispossess of.—O.F. *for-=fors* (L. *foris*), out of, outside; *juger*, to judge.

Fosset, a spigot; see **faucet**, p. 144, col. 1, near the bottom.

Franion, a gay idle companion. (F.— L.) For F. *fainéant*, 'an idle luske; lewd companion;' Cotgrave.—F. *fait néant*, he does nothing.—L. *facit*, he does; *ne*, not; *entem*, acc. of *ens*, being, substance.

Frankalmoign, the name of the tenure by which most church-lands are held. (F. —O.H.G. *and* L.—Gk.) Lit. 'free alms.' —F. *franc*, free; Anglo-F. *almoine* = O.F. *almosne*, alms. See **Frank** and **Almoner**.

Free-booter, a rover, pirate. (Du.) Borrowed from Du. *vrijbuiter*, a free-booter, robber.—Du. *vrijbuiten*, to rob; *vrijbuit*, plunder, lit. 'free booty.' Du. *vrij* = E. *free*. And see **Booty**, p. 46.

Frith, an enclosure, forest, wood. (E.) Obsolescent; M.E. *frith*, peace, also enclosure, park, &c. Cf. W. *ffridd*, park, forest, which is borrowed from M.E.— A.S. *frið*, peace; *friðu*, peace, security, asylum. Cf. Icel. *friðr*, Dan. Swed. *fred*, Du. *vrede*, G. *friede*, peace.

Fritillary, a plant. (L.) So named because the flower was thought to resemble a dice-box. — L. *fritillus*, a dice-box.

Fritter away, to diminish, waste. (F. — L.) Merely a derivative from *fritter*, sb., p. 164, bottom of col. 1. A *fritter* meant (1) a kind of pancake, (2) a fragment; hence *fritter*, vb., to cut up into fragments for frying, to break up, &c.

Fylfot, a peculiarly formed cross. (E.) The word probably means ' four-footed.' The A.S. *feówer*, four, when used in composition, occurs as *fiðer* and *fiðr*. Cf. Swed. *fyrfotad*, four-footed. The change from *r* to *l* is common.

Galingale, the pungent root of a plant. (F. — Span. — Arab.) M.E. *galingale*. — O.F. *garingal* (also no doubt *galingal*, though not so recorded). — Span. *galanga*, galingale. — Arab. *khalanján*, galingale; said to be of Pers. origin.

Gallowglas, Galloglas, a heavy-armed foot-soldier. (Irish.) Irish *galloglach*, a servant, a galloglas. — Irish *gall*, a foreigner, an Englishman; *oglach*, a youth, servant, soldier (from *óg*, young). It meant 'an English servitor,' as explained by Spenser, View of the State of Ireland, Globe ed. p. 640. (See N. and Q. 6 S. x. 145.) ¶ A shorter account at p. 169.

Galore, in plenty. (C.) Irish *goleor*, Gael. *gu leor, gu leoir*, sufficiently. Formed from Irish and Gael. *leor*, sufficient, by prefixing *go* or *gu*, used to turn an adj. into an adverb.

Galt, Gault, clay and marl. (Scand.) Norweg. *gald*, hard ground, a place where ground is trodden hard; Icel. *gald*, hardtrodden snow.

Gang (2), to go; see under **Go**, p. 179.

Garb, a wheatsheaf, in heraldry. (F. — O.H.G.) Picard *garbe*, F. *gerbe*, a sheaf. — O.H.G. *garba* (G. *garbe*), a sheaf. Lit. 'what is grabbed' or caught up into a bundle by grasping. Cf. E. *grab*, Swed. *grabba*, to grasp; Skt. *grah*, Vedic *grabh*, to seize. (Also, more shortly, at p. 170.)

Gavial, the crocodile of the Ganges. (F. — Hind.) F. *gavial* (a corrupt form). — Hind. *ghariyál*, a crocodile.

Geck, a dupe. (Du.) In Tw. Nt. v. 351. — Du. *gek*, formerly *geck*, a fool, sot; cf. G. *Geck*, the same.+Dan. *gjek*, fool; Icel. *gikkr*, a pert, rude person. ¶ Not to be confused with A.S. *géac*, cuckoo; nor with *gowk*; nor with *gawky*.

Gecko, a nocturnal lizard. (Malay.)

Also F. *gecko*. — Malay *ghékoq*, a gecko; so named from an imitation of its cry (Devic).

Germander. (F. — Ital. — L. — Gk.) F. *germandrée*, germander. — Ital. *calamandrea*, germander (by change of *l* to *r*). A corrupt form from L. *chamædrys*, germander. — Gk. χαμαίδρυς, germander; lit. 'ground-tree,' i. e. low tree. — Gk. χαμαί, on the ground; δρῦς, tree.

Ghaut, a landing-place, quay, way down to a river; mountain-pass. (Hind.) Hind. *ghát*. See Yule.

Ghoo, boiled or clarified butter. (Hind. Skt.) Hind. *ghí*. — Skt. *ghṛta*, clarified butter; orig. pp. of *ghṛ*, to sprinkle.

Gillie, a boy, page. (C.) Gael. *gille*, *giolla*, Irish *giolla*, boy, lad.

Giron, Gyron, in heraldry, the eighth part of a shield, made by drawing a diagonal line from the top corner to the centre, and from the centre horizontally towards the same side; a right-angled triangle. (F. — O.H.G.) F. *giron*, a giron (Littré). — O.H.G. *gêrun*, acc. of *gêro*, a lance, spear; M.H.G. *gêre*, a gore or gusset in a garment, a triangular piece. — O.H.G. *gêr*, a spear, cognate with A.S. *gár*, a spear. See **Gore** (2), p. 181. (Diez, Schade.)

Gladden, Gladen, a plant; *Iris pseudacorus*. (L.) A.S. *glædene*; borrowed from L. *gladiolus*, a sword-lily. Dimin. of L. *gladius*, a sword.

Glamour, see **Gramarye** (below).

Glanders, glandular swellings. (F. — L.) O.F. *glandres*, pl. — Lat. pl. acc. *glandulas*, swollen glands; see **Gland**, p. 176.

Gleek (1), a scoff, jest. (Scand.) Also a glance of the eye; see Nares. Sc. *glaik*, a glance of the eye. The same as Sc. *laik*, play; with prefix *g*-=A.S. prefix *ge*-; cf. Icel. *glíkr*, like, with A.S. *líc*, like. — Icel. *leikr*, a game, sport. — Icel. *leika*, to play, sport, put a trick upon; Swed. *leka*, Dan. *lege*.+A.S. *ge-lácan*, to delude; *ge-lác*, sb., play.

Gleek (2), a game at cards. (F. — G.) See Nares. — O.F. *glic*, a game at cards; Nares, Roquefort. Lit. sense 'hazard, luck.' — G. *glück*, luck; see **Luck**.

Gloaming, twilight. (E.) Merely the Scot. form of *glooming*, i. e. the time of becoming dusk; see **Gloom**, p. 178, col. 1.

Gramarye, magic. (F. — L. — Gk.) M.E. *gramery*, skill in grammar, and hence skill in magic. — O.F. *gramaire*, grammar; see **Grammar**. ¶ The word *glamour* is a mere corruption of *gramarye* or *grammar*, meaning (1) grammar, (2) magic.

Greengage, a green plum. Named from Sir W. *Gage*, of Hengrave Hall, near Bury, before A.D. 1725. There is also a *blue Gage*, a *yellow Gage*, and a *purple Gage*.

Grilse, the young salmon on its first return from the sea to fresh water. (Scand.?) Said to be a corruption of Dan. *graalax*, Swed. *grålax*, lit. 'grey salmon;' from Dan. *graa*, Swed. *grå*, gray; and Dan. Swed. Icel. *lax*, G. *lachs*, a salmon.

Grise, Grize, a step. (F. – L.) Also spelt *greece, greese*, &c. The proper spelling is *grees*, and the proper sense is 'a flight of steps,' though often used as meaning a single step. *Grees* is the pl. of M.E. *gree, gre*, a step. – O.F. *gre*, a step (Roquefort); cf. F. *de-gré*, E. *de-gree*. – L. *gradus*, a step. Der. Prov. E. (Norf.) *grissens*, steps = *gree-s-en-s*, a treble plural.

Gromwell, a plant. (F. – L.) Formerly *gromelle, grumelle, gromel, grumel*. – O.F. *grumel* (F. *grumeau*), a clot, pellet ; dimin. of F. *grume*, a grain. – L. *grumulus*, a little hillock, hence a grain ; dimin. of *grumus*, a hillock. Named from its hard, stony, grain-like seeds.

Guanaco, a kind of Peruvian sheep. (Span. – Peruv.) Span. *guanaco* (Pineda). – Peruv. *huanacu*, a wild sheep.

Guilder, a Du. coin. (Du. – G.) Corruption of Du. *gulden*, a guilder; borrowed from G. *gulden*, *gülden*, a coin at first made of *gold*. – G. *gold*, gold.

Gunny, a coarse kind of sacking. (Hind. – Skt.) Hind. and Mahratti *gon, gonî*, a sack, sacking. – Skt. *gonî*, a sack (Yule).

Gyron ; see Giron.

Hacienda, a farm, estate, farm-house. (Span. – L.) Span. *hacienda*, an estate, orig. employment. The *c* is pronounced as *th* in *thin*. – L. *facienda*, things to be done ; neut. pl. of fut. pass. part. of *facere*, to do.

Hadji, Hajji, one who has performed the pilgrimage to Mecca. (Arab.) Arab. *hájí*, 'a Christian who has performed the pilgrimage to Jerusalem, or a Muhammedan [who has performed] that to Mecca;' Rich. Dict. p. 549.

Haggis, a dish of sheep's entrails, chopped up, seasoned, and boiled in the sheep's maw. (E.; *with* F. *suffix*.) M.E. *hagas, hageis, hakeys* ; coined with F. suffix *-ace*, from the E. verb to *hack*, Lowland Sc. *hag*,

to chop up. (The Gael. *taigeis* is merely a corruption of the E. word.)

Hardock, Hordock, the corn-bluebottle ; *Centaurea cyanus*. (E.) *Hardokes*, pl., is the reading in K. Lear, iv. 4. 4, ed. 1623 ; the quartos have *hordocks*. The same as *haudod*, used in Fitzherbert's Husbandry to mean the corn-bluebottle ; see Glossary, and pref. p. xxx. Mr. Wright (note to K. Lear) shows that *hardhake* means the *Centaurea nigra*. Both plants were called, indifferently, *knobweed, knotweed*, and *loggerheads*. Named from the hardness of the head of the *Centaurea nigra* ; for which reason it was also called *iron-weed, iron-heads*, &c. See Plant-names, by Britten and Holland.

Hashish, Hasheesh, an intoxicating drink. (Arab.) See under **Assassin**, p. 20.

Henna, a paste used for dyeing the nails, &c., of an orange hue. (Arab.) Arab. *hinná-a, hind*, or *hinna-at*, the dyeing or colouring shrub (*Lawsonia inermis*); Rich. Dict. p. 582.

Hobbledehoy, a lad approaching manhood. (F.) I believe this to be precisely O.F. *hobel de hoi*, a vulgar rascal of to-day. *Hobel* is the dimin. of O.F. *hobe*, an inferior kind of hawk, a hobby ; constantly used as a term of contempt. See **Hobby** (2), p. 208, col. 1. O.F. *hoi* (F. *hui*) is from L. *hodie*, to-day.

Hordock; see **Hardock**.

Hornblende, a mineral. (G.) Named from its horn-like cleavage and glittering appearance. G. *hornblende*. – G. *horn*, horn; *blenden*, to blind, to dazzle, from *blind*, blind.

Hox, to hamstring ; put for *hocks*, which is corrupted from *hock*. See **Hough**, p. 209, col. 2.

Imam, Imaum, a Muhammedan priest. (Arab.) Arab. *imám*, a chief, prelate, priest.

Imbroglio, intrigue, perplexity. (Ital.) Ital. *imbroglio*, perplexity. – Ital. *imbrogliare*, to entangle. – Ital. *im-*, for *in*, in; *broglio*, a broil, confusion ; see **Broil** (2).

Imprese, an heraldic device, with a motto. (Ital. – L.) In Rich. II. iii. 1. 25. Also spelt *Impresa* (Nares). – Ital. *impresa*, 'an imprese, an embleme'; also, an enterprise;' Florio. Fem. of *impreso*, undertaken (hence, adopted), pp. of *imprendere*, to undertake. – L. *in*, in ; *prehendere*, to lay hold of. **Doublet**; *emprise*, an enterprise, Spenser, F. Q. ii. 4. 12; from F. *emprise*, fem. pp. of *emprendre*, to undertake (Cotgrave).

Inch, an island. (Gael.) Gael. *innis*, an island.+Irish *innis*; W. *ynys*.

Incony, very pretty, very sweet, very dear. (E.) For *in-conny*. *In* is an intensive prefix; cf. M.E. *inly*, extremely; *conny*, or *canny* is North E., meaning skilful, wary, gentle, excellent, &c. Formed from E. *can*, I know; cf. Icel. *kunnigr*, knowing, wise. ' *Conny*, *Canny*, pretty, or bonny;' E. D. S., Gloss. B. 1.

Invecked, Invected, in heraldry, indented with successive cusps. (L.) Lit. ' carried in.'—L. *inuectus*, pp. of *in-uehero*, to carry inwards.

Inveigle (addit. to p. 221). It precisely answers to Anglo-F. *enveoglir*, to blind, in Will. of Wadington's Manuel des Peches, l. 10639. This is a mere (ignorant) variant of F. *aveugler*, to blind; like *imposthume* for *apostume*.

Ironmould; see **Mould** (3), s.v. **Mole** (1), p. 290, col. 1.

Islam; see **Moslem**, p. 294, col. 1.

Jaggery, a coarse brown sugar. (Canarese.—Skt.) A corruption of Canarese *sharkare*, unrefined sugar; H. H. Wilson.—Skt. *çarkarâ*; see **sugar**, p. 480.

Jape, to mock, jest, befool. (F.—Scand.) Obsolete. M.E. *japen*. — F. *gaber*, ' to mock, flout, gull.' Cotgrave; O.F. *gap*, mockery (Roquefort). — Icel. *gabba*, to mock. See **Gabble**.

Jereed, a wooden javelin used in mock fights. (Arab.) Arab. *jarid*, a palmbranch stripped of its leaves, a lance.

Joss, a Chinese idol. (Port.—L.) Not Chinese, but corrupted from Port. *Deos*, God. Cognate with Span. *Dios*, God, O.F. *deus*. — L. *Deus*, nom., God. See **Deuce**, s. v. **Deity**, p. 113, col. 1.

Juggernaut, the name of an Indian idol. (Skt.) Skt. *jagannâtha*, lord of the universe, monarch of the world (Benfey, p. 465). — Skt. *jagat*, world; *nâtha*, protector, lord.

Jute, a substance resembling hemp. (Bengali—Skt.) Bengali *jût*, the fibres of the bark of the *Corchorus olitorius*; named from its shaggy appearance. — Skt. *jata* (with cerebral *t*), matted hair, as worn by ascetics; also applied to the fibrous roots of the banyan, which descend from the branches.

Jutty, a projection. (F.—L.) For *jetty*; see **jut**, p. 226, col. 2. **Der.** *jutty*, v., to project beyond.

Kecksies, hemlocks. (C.) For *hecks-es*; and *kecks* is also written *kex*. See **Kex**, p. 231, col. 1.

Keelhaul. (Scand. *and* E.) Also *keelhale*, ' to punish in the seaman's way, by dragging the criminal under water on one side of the ship and up again on the other;' Johnson. From *keel* and *haul* or *hale*.

Kestrel, a base kind of hawk. (F.—L.) Put for *kesrel*; the *t* is excrescent, as in *whils-t*, &c.—O.F. *quercerelle*, 'a kastrell;' Cotgrave. Dimin. of O.F. *quercelle*, the same.—L. *querquedula*, a kind of teal.

Khedive, a prince. (F.—Pers.) F. *khédive*.—Pers. *khadîw, khidîw*, a great prince, sovereign; *khidêwî*, the khedive, vice-roy of Egypt. Cf. Pers. *khodâ*, God.

Kiddle, a kind of weir formed of basketwork placed in a river to catch fish (O.F.). Anglo-F. *kidel*, pl. *kideux*.—O.F. *cuidel* (Godefroy); later form *quideau*, ' a wicker engine whereby fish is caught;' Cotgrave. Low L. *kidellus*.

Kiosk, a small pavilion. (Turk.—Pers.) F. *kiosque*. — Turk. *kushk, köshk* (pronounced with *k* as *ki*), a kiosk.—Pers. *kûshk*, a palace, villa, portico.

Kraal, an enclosure, a collection of huts, an African village. (Du.—Port.—L.) Du. *kraal*, an African village.—Port. *curral*, an enclosure; the same word as Span. *corral*. See **Corral**, p. 619.

Lanner, Lanneret, a kind of falcon. (F.—L.) F. *lanier*, 'a lanner;' Cotg.—L. *laniarius*, a butcher, one that tears and rends.—L. *laniare*, to rend. **Der.** Hence *lanyard*, F. *lanière*, a thong; i. e. a thong for a lanner.

Last. (E.) In the phr. *at last*, the word *last* is the sb., meaning foot-track, &c.; see **Last** (2). This is shown by the usage in A.S. and Icel.; it meant at first ' on the track;' but is now used as if *last* were the superlative of *late*. (But the mod. phr. *at last* may have originated independently.)

Launch, a large ship's boat. (Span.) Span. *lancha*, ' the pinnace of a ship;' Pineda (1740). Port. *lancha*, the same. Origin doubtful.

Levin, lightning. (E. ?) M.E. *leyfnyng*, lightning; Wrt. Voc. 735.42. Prob. E.; but not found in A.S. Cf. Icel. *leiptr* (pronounced *leiftr*), lightning; Swed. dial. *lygna, lyvna, ljuna*, lightning; Swed. *ljunga*, to lighten; Goth. *lauhmuni*,

lightning. Apparently from the same root as E. *light*, sb.

Library. Not from L. *librarium*, as said in former editions, but from Low L. *libraria*, fem., with the same sense. Hence also Span. *libreria*, Port. *livraria*, Ital. *libreria, libraria.* Florio (1598) has Ital. *libraria*, 'a librarie.'

Lilt, to sing, dance. (Scand.) M.E. *lilting-horn*, horn to dance to. Formed (with added -*t*) from Norweg. *lilla*, to sing in a high tone, O. Swed. *lylla*, to lull to sleep. Allied to **Lull.**

Limehound, a dog in a leash. (Hybrid; F.–L., *and* E.) Short for *liam-hound*, used by Turberville. The M.E. *liam* or *lyam* means 'a leash.'– O.F. *liem*, now spelt *lien*, a band. – L. *ligamen*, a tie. See **Lien**; p. 249, col. 2.

Lither, pestilent, stagnant, dull. (E.) In 1 Hen. VI. iv. 7. 21, '*lither* sky' means pestilent or dull lower air; cf. '*luther* eir,' pestilent air, P. Pl., C. xvi. 220. M.E. *luther, lither.*– A.S. *lȳðer*, evil, idle, sickly, dull. Not to be confused with *lithe*, pliant.

Llano, a level steppe or plain. (Span.– L.) Commoner in the pl. *llanos.*– Span. *llano*, pl. *llanos*, a plain; from *llano*, adj., plain, flat,– L. *planus*, flat.

Lofty, high. (Scand.) Lit. 'in the air, airy;' from *loft*, sb.; p. 255.

Lorimer, a maker of horses' bits, spurs, &c. (F.– L.) Also *loriner.*–O.F. *lorimier*, later *lormier*, 'a spurrier;' Cotgrave. Put for *lorinier**. – O.F. *lorein, lorain*, rein, bridle, bit. – Low L. *lorenum, loranum*, a rein, bit.– L. *lorum*, thong.

Losel, Lorel, a worthless fellow, reprobate. (E.) One devoted to perdition. From A.S. *los*, destruction, *los-ian*, to lose, also to perish. From the strong verb *léosan*, to lose, pp. *lor-en* (for original *los-en). *Lor-el* is formed from the base *lor-* of the pp. in use, and *los-el* from the equivalent and original base of the same. For the suffix, cf. A.S. *wac-ol*, watchful.

Luce, the pike; a fish. (F.– Low L. –Gk.) Lit. 'wolf-fish.'– F. *lucs, lus*, a pike; Cot.– Low L. *lucius*, a pike.–Gk. λύκος, a wolf; also a (ravenous) fish. Cf. 'Pyke, fysche, *dentrix, lucius, lupus*;' Prompt. Parv. 'Luce, fysche, *lucius*;' id.

Lym, a lime-hound : K. Lear, iii. 6. 72. Short for **Limehound** (above).

Madeira, a sort of wine. (Port.–L.)

Named from the isle of *Madeira*, i. e. 'the well-wooded.'– Port. *madeira*, wood, timber. – L. *materia*, stuff, wood, timber. See **Matter** (1).

Mail (Black), a forced tribute. (F.–L.) *Mail* is a Scottish term for rent. *Black-mail* or *black rent* is the rent paid in cattle, as distinct from *white money* or silver.– F. *maille*, 'a French halfpenny;' Cotgrave. O.F. *meaille, maaille.*– Low L. *medalia*, lit. 'medal.' See **Medal.**

Mainour. (F.–L.) In the phr. 'taken with the mainour' or 'taken in the manner;' i. e. caught in the act. Anglo-F. *meinoure*, *mainoure.*–O.F. *maineuvre*, lit. manœuvre; hence, act. See **Manœuvre**, p. 270, col. 1.

Malkin, a kitchen-wench. (F.–O.H.G.) *Malkin* is for *Mald-kin*, the dimin. of *Mald, Mold*, or *Maud*, i. e. *Matilda*. See **Grimalkin**, p. 186. ¶Not the dimin. of *Mary*; cf. 'Malkyne, or Mawt, Molt, Mawde, *Matildis, Matilda*;' Prompt. Parv.

Mallecho, malefaction, mischief. (Span. –L.) Hamlet, iii. 2. 147.–Span. *malhecho*, 'misdone; an euill deed;' Minsheu.–Span. *mal*, ill; *hecho*, done, pp. of *hacer*, to do. –L. *male*, ill; *factus*, pp. of *facere*, to do.

Manchineel, a tree. (Span.–L.) So called from its apple-like fruit. – Span. *manzanillo*, a little apple-tree, the manchineel tree; dimin. of Span. *manzana*, an apple.–L. *Matiana*, fem. of *Matianus*, adj., the epithet of a kind of apple; lit. 'Matian.'– L. *Matius*, the name of a Roman gens.

Manciple, a purveyor, esp. for a college. (F.–L.) M.E. *manciple*, with inserted *l.* –O.F. *mancipe*, a slave; cf. O. Ital. *mancipio*, a slave, farmer, manciple.–L. *mancipium*, a slave; orig. 'possession.'– L. *mancip-*, base of *manceps*, a taker in hand. –L. *man-us*, hand; *cap-ere*, to take.

Mandolin, a guitar. (F.– Ital.– Gk.) F. *mandoline.* –Ital. *mandolino*, dimin. of *mandola, mandora*, a kind of guitar. Put for Ital. *pandora.* See further under **Banjo** (above), p. 615.

Mangel-wurzel, (properly) a kind of beet. (G.) Corrupted from G. *mangold-wurzel*, lit. 'beet-root.' – G. *mangold* (M.H.G. *mangolt*), beet (of unknown origin); *wurzel*, root, allied to E. *wort* (1).

Mango (addit. to p. 268). The Malay word is of Tamil origin.– Tamil *mán-káy*, i. e. '*mán*-fruit,' the tree being *mám-arum*, i. e. '*mán*-tree' (Yule).

Mangrove. (Hybrid; Malay *and* E.) 'A sort of trees called *mangroves*;' Eng. Garner, vii. 371; A.D. 1689. Put, as I suppose, for *mang-groves*, from the peculiar growth in groves or thickets. — Malay *manggi-manggi*, the name for the tree.

Marchpane, a sweet cake, made with almonds and sugar. (F. — Ital.) O.F.*marse-pain*; now *massepain*. — Ital. *marciapane*, *marzapane*, a marchpane; Florio. Origin of *marcia* unexplained, but prob. from a proper name: *pane* = Lat. acc. *panem*, bread.

Martello tower, a watch-tower. (Ital. — L.; *and* F. — L.) So called because the watch-men gave the alarm by striking a bell with a hammer; see Ariosto, Orlando, x. 51; xiv. 100. From Ital. *martello*, a hammer; Low L. *martellus*. Dimin. of *martus** = L. *marcus*, a hammer.

Martingale (addit. to p. 273). It is probable that Littré is wrong. The F. *martingale* answers to Span. *al-martaga*, 'a kinde of headstall for a horse, trimmed, gilt, and embroidered;' Minsheu (1623); where *al.* is merely the Arab. def. article. The sb. may be derived from Arab. *rataqa*, in the sense 'to cause to go with a short step;' see Yule. I find Arab. *rataka* given by Richardson as a verbal root, whence *ratak*, going with a short quick step.

Maund, a basket. (E.) A.S. *mand*, a basket; in a MS. of the eighth century. + Du. *mand*; prov. G. *mand, mande, manne* (whence F. *manne*).

Mavourneen, my darling. (Irish.) From Irish *mo*, my; and *mhuirnin*, mutated form of *muirnin*, darling, from *muirn*, affection. (*Mh* = *v*.)

Mazurka, a dance. (Pol.) From Pol. *Mazurka*, lit. a woman of Massovia or Mazovia, a province of Poland containing Warsaw. Similarly, *polka* means 'a Polish woman;' and secondly, a dance.

Methylated, used of spirits of wine when mixed with methyl to make it undrinkable. (L. — Gk.) Formed with suffix *-ated* from *methyl*, meaning a gas procured by the destructive distillation of wood. *Methyl* is a latinised spelling of Gk. μεθ' (= μετά, after, by means of), followed by ὕλη, wood.

Minx (addit. to p. 284, col. 2, bottom). The Low G. *minsk*, a man (like G. *Mensch*), can be used as a neuter. It then signifies precisely 'minx,' as a term of mild reproach.

Mishna, a digest of Jewish traditions. (Heb.) Heb. *mishnah*, a repetition, a second part. — Heb. root *shánáh*, to repeat.

Misty (2), doubtful, ambiguous, as applied to language. (F. — L. — Gk.) In the phrases '*misty* language' and '*mistiness* of language,' *misty* is not from E. *mist*, but is short for *mystic*; see Palmer, Folk-Etymology. See **Mystic,** p. 300, col. 2.

Mongoose; see **Mungoose** (below).

Moonshee, a secretary, interpreter. (Arab.) Arab. *munshi*, a secretary, a language-master or tutor.

Mouldy, musty. (Scand.) Orig. distinct from *mould*, ground; also from mould as used in *iron-mould*. Formed from the sb. *mould*, mustiness, in which the final *d* is excrescent. From the M.E. verb *moulen*, to grow musty; formerly very common, and much used in the pp. *mouled*. — Icel. *mygla*, to grow musty. — Icel. *mugga*, mustiness. See **Muggy.** Thus *mould* is 'mugginess' in this use. So also Swed. *mögla*, to grow mouldy; *mögel*, mouldiness.

Moy, a piece of money. (F. — Port. — L.) In Henry V. iv. 4. 14. Not short for *moidore*, but precisely the *moi* alone; *moidore* = *moi d'or* is obviously a F. pronunciation of Port. *moeda d'ouro*, lit. 'money of gold.' — Port. *moeda*, money. — Lat. *moneta*, money.

Mulligatawny, a hot soup. (Tamil.) Tamil *milagu-tannír*, lit. 'pepper-water;' Yule.

Mungoose, a kind of ichneumon. (Telugu.) Telugu *mangísu*; 'Jerdon gives *mangús*, however, as a Deccani and Mahratti word;' Yule.

Mustang, a wild horse of the prairies. (Span. — L.) Span. *mesteño* (with *ñ* as *ny*), belonging to the graziers (who catch them). — Span. *mesta*, a body of proprietors of cattle, a company of graziers. — L. *mixta*, fem. of pp. of *miscere*, to mingle. Cf. Span. *mestura*, a mixture.

Naker, a kettle-drum. (Arab.) Arab. *naqqárah*, a kettle-drum; see Palmer's Pers. Dict. col. 659.

Nargileh, Nargili, Nargile. (Pers.) A pipe or smoking-apparatus in which the smoke is passed through water. — Pers. *nárjíl*, a cocoa-nut, because these pipes were originally made with a cocoa-nut, which held the water (Devic).

Natron, native carbonate of soda. (Arab.) A doublet of *nitre*: see **Nitre,** p. 306.

Nautch, a kind of ballet-dance by women. (Hind. – Prakrit – Skt.) Hind. (and Mahratti) *nách*, a dance; Prakrit *nachcha*. – Skt. *nrtya*, dancing, acting; orig. fut. pass. part. of *nrt*, to dance, to act. Der. *nautch-girl*, a dancing girl (Yule).

Navvy, a labourer employed on railways, &c. (L.) Short for *navigator*, formerly used to mean a labourer employed on canals for *navigation*; first used, according to Haydn, about 1830.

Nihilist, a member of a revolutionary secret society, esp. in Russia. (L.) Etymologically, one who denies real existence. – L. *nihil*, nothing.

Nincompoop, a simpleton. (L.) Thought to be a corruption of L. *non compos* (*mentis*), not sound in mind.

Nizam, the title of a ruler in the Deccan, in Hindustan. (Pers. – Arab.) From the Arab. *niḍhám*, government, which the Persians pronounce as *nizám*. Though the proper sense is 'government,' in the phrase *nizám-'l-mulk* it is used as a title, meaning 'governor of the empire.' – Arab. root *nazama*, he arranged or ordered. (Devic, Richardson.)

Nole, Noule, Nowl, head. (E.) See Nares. Mid. Nt. Dr. iii. 2. 17. For *knoll*. Cf. Swed. *knöl*, a knob, and prov. E. *nob* (for *knob*), head. See **Knoll**, p. 233, col. 1.

Nonchalant, careless. (E. – L.) F. *nonchalant*, careless; pres. pt. of O.F. *nonchaloir*, to be careless about. – O.F. *non*, not; *chaloir*, to glow, hence to be hot over, take care for. – L. *non*, not; *calere*, to glow.

Nullah, a water-course, bed of a torrent. (Hind.) Hind. *nála*, a water-course (Yule).

Oca, the name of a certain edible root. (Peruvian.) Peruv. *occa*, the same.

Octoroon, the offspring of a white person and a quadroon. (L.) One who is, in an eighth part, a black. Coined from L. *octo*, eight; in imitation of *quadroon*.

Odalisque, a female slave in a Turkish harem. (F. – Turk.) F. *odalisque*; better *odalique* (Devic). – Turk. *odaliq*, a chambermaid. – Turk. *oda*, a chamber.

Omrah, a prince, lord. (Arab.) 'Aigrettes by *omrahs* worn;' Scott, Vis. of Don Roderick, st. 31. *Omrah* is properly a plural, like **Nabob**, q. v. – Arab. *umará*,

pl. of *amír*, a prince, emir; see **Emir**, p. 134. Cf. the Arab. title *amíru'l-umará*, prince of princes.

Orc, Ork, a large marine animal; a narwhal, or grampus. (L.) See Nares. – L. *orca*, perhaps the narwhal (Pliny).

Orgulous, proud. (F. – O. H. G.) Also *orgillous*; M. E. *orgeilus*; Anglo-F. *orguyllous*. – O.F. *orguillus*, later *orgueilleux*, proud. – O. F. *orguil*, F. *orgueil*, pride. From O.H.G. *urguol*, remarkable, notable (Graff).

Orle, a kind of fillet, in heraldry, &c. (F. – L.) F. *orle*, a hem, narrow border. – Low L. *orla*, a border, edge; dimin. of L. *ora*, border, edge, margin.

Ouphe, an elf, fairy. (E.) Mer. Wives, iv. 4. 49. A variant of *oaf* = *elf*. See oaf, s. v. **Elf**, p. 132.

Paddy, rice in the husk. (Malay. – Skt.) Malay *pádí*, rice in the husk. – Skt. *bhakta*, (properly) boiled rice, food. Orig. pp. of *bhaj*, to divide, possess, &c.

Pale, in heraldry, a broad central stripe down a shield. (F. – L.) The same word as *pale*, a stake. – F. *pal*. – L. *palus*.

Pannage, food of swine in woods. (F. – L.) Anglo-F. *panage*. – O. F. *pasnage*, 'pawnage, mastage, monie for feeding of swine with mast;' Cotgrave. From a Low L. type *pastionaticum**. – Low L. *pastionare*, to feed on mast, as swine. – L. *pastion-*, stem of *pastio*, grazing, used in Low L. to mean right of pannage. – L. *past-um*, supine of *pascere*, to feed.

Paramatta (addit. to p. 329). Properly spelt *Parramatta*; the lit. sense is 'place of eels;' where *parra* represents eels, and *matta*, place. *Parramatta* is also the name of the river; *Cabramatta*, ten miles off, is not a river.

Pariah, an outcast. (Tamil.) Tamil *paraiyan*, corruptly *pariah*, Malayálim *parayan*, a man of low caste, performing the lowest menial services; one of his duties is to beat the village drum (called *parai* in Tamil), whence, probably, the appellation of the caste. (H. H. Wilson.)

Pavin, Pavan, a stately Spanish dance. (F. – Span. L. – Gk. – Tamil.) F. *pavane*. – Span. *pavana*, a grave dance (see *Pavan* in Nares). Prob. from a Low L. *pavanus, peacock-like, from the row of stately dancers (Scheler); cf. Span. *pava*, a peahen, a turkey, *pavada*, a flock of turkeys, *pavo*, adj., like a peacock (whence

pavonear, to walk with affected gravity).
— L. *pauus*, earlier *pauo*, a peacock.
See **Peacock**, p. 336.

Pawnee, drink. (Hind. — Skt.) Hind.
páni, water. — Skt. *pánīya*, allied to *pána*,
a beverage. — Skt. *pá*, to drink. (√PA.)

Peel (4), a small castle. (F. — L.) M. E.
pel, *pile*, a castle; cf. mod. E. *pile*, an
edifice. — F. *pile*, a mass, heap. — L. *pila*, a
pier of stone.

Pheeze. See **Feeze**, p. 622.

Pice, a small copper coin. (Maráthi.)
Maráthi *paisá*, a copper coin; sometimes
rated at four to the anna, or sixty-four to
the rupee.

Pillau, Pilaf, a dish of meat or fowl,
boiled with rice and spices. (Pers.) Pers.
pilāv, *pilav*, a dish made of rice and meat;
Palmer.

Polo, a game. (Balti.) 'It comes from
Balti; *polo* being properly, in the language
of that region, the ball used in the game;'
Yule. Balti is in the high valley of the
Indus.

Polypus, Polyp, an aquatic animal of
the radiate type. (L. — Gk.) L. *polypus*.
— Gk. πολύπους, many-footed. — Gk. πολύ-s,
many; πούς, a foot. ¶ F. *polype*, Ital. and
Span. *polipo*, L. *polypūs* (gen. *polypi*); all
false forms, due to treating the Lat. ending
-pūs as if were *-p-ūs*.

Pomander, a globe-shaped box or case
for holding perfumes. (Span. — L.) Accented on the *first* syllable; see Nares.
Evidently from Span. *poma*, a pomander
(Minsheu); Pineda gives *poma*, 'a little
small box full of holes to carry perfumes
in to smell to, also a pomander.' The
suffix seems to be Span. *-andero*, as in
viv-andero, a sutler, *hil-andero*, a spinner,
a rope-walk; or *-anda*, as in *bar-anda*, a
railing. The box was named from its
shape; cf. Span. *pomo*, an apple, also the
globe held by a king at his coronation.
— L. *pomum*, an apple. Cf. also *pom-ade*,
in which the suffix is equivalent to L.
-ata, pp. fem.; and see **Verandah**.
¶ The usual forced etymology from an
imaginary F. *pomme d'ambre* is, to me,
incredible.

Pose (3), a cold in the head. (C.) In
Chaucer. A.S. *geposu*, a cough (where
ge- is a mere prefix). Borrowed from W.
pas, a cough; allied to Irish *casachdas*,
a cough, Skt. *kás*, to cough. (√KAS.)

Prig (1), to steal. (E.) Cant *prygge*, to
ride, ride off with a horse which a man has

to take care of; *prigger of prauncers*, a
horse-stealer; see Harman's Caveat, pp. 42,
43, and p. 84, col. 3. Modification of
prick, to spur, to ride; Spenser, F. Q. i.
1. 1. See **Prick**.

Prig (2), a pert, pragmatical fellow. (E.)
From the verb to *prick*, in the sense to
trim, adorn, dress up. Lowl. Sc. *prig-
me-dainty*, *prick-me-dainty*, a prig. See
above.

Proletarian, a citizen of the lowest
class, useful only by producing children.
(L.) From L. *proletarius*, one who served
the state by help of his children only.
— L. *proles*, offspring. — L. *pro*, forth; *alere*, to nourish.

Prosthetic, prefixed. (Gk.) Modern;
as if for Gk. προσθετικός, lit. disposed to
add; allied to Gk. πρόσθε-ros, added, put
to. — Gk. πρός, to; θε-τός, placed, put,
verbal adj. from the base θε-, to place. See
Theme, p. 503.

Puggry, Puggery, a scarf round the
hat. (Hind.) Hind. *pagrí*, a turban; Yule.

Purim, an annual Jewish festival; the
feast of lots. (Heb.) Heb. *púrím*, lots;
pl. of *púr*, a lot. See Esther ix. 26.

Purview, a proviso. (F. — L.) Now
applied to the enacting part of a statute;
so called because it orig. began with *purveu
est*, it is provided. — O.F. *porveu*, pp. of
O.F. *porvoir* (F. *pourvoir*), to provide. —
L. *pro-uidere*, to provide. See **Purvey**,
p. 547, col. 1.

Rajpoot, a prince. (Hind. — Skt.) Hind.
rajpút, a prince; lit. 'son of a rajah.' —
Skt. *ráj-á*, a king; *putra*, son.

Raki, arrack. (Turk.) Turk. *ráqí*, arrack. — Arab. *'araq*, arrack; see **Arrack**,
p. 18.

Ramadan, a great Mohammedan fast.
(Arab.) So called because kept in the ninth
month, named *Ramadan*. — Arab. *ramadán*,
pronounced *ramazán* in Turkish and Arabic.
As it is in the ninth month of the lunar
year, it may take place in any season; but
it is supposed to have been originally held
in the hot season. The word implies ' con-
suming fire;' from Arab. root *ramada*, it
was hot. (Devic, Richardson.)

Razzia, a sudden raid. (F. — Algiers.)
F. *razzia*, *razia*; borrowed from the Alger-
ine *razia*, which is a peculiar pronunciation
of Arab. *gházía*, a raid, expedition against
infidels (Devic). — Arab. *ghází*, a hero, a
leader of an expedition.

Redgum, a disease of infants. (E.) M.E. *reed gounde*, lit. 'red matter' (of a sore); Prompt. Parv. From A.S. *réad*, red; *gund*, matter of a sore.

Reveille (addit. to p. 545, col. 2). When E. *reveillee* is used as a trisyllable, it represents F. *reveillez*, wake ye, imper. plural. The E. word is also spelt *reveillez*; Brand, Pop. Antiq. ed. Ellis, ii. 176.

Rob, a conserve of fruit. (F. – Span. – Arab.) F. *rob*, 'the juice of black whortleberries preserved;' Cot. – Span. *rob*, thickened juice of fruit with honey. – Arab. *rubb*, 'a decoction of the juice of citrons and other fruits, inspissated juice, rob;' Richardson.

Rochet, a fine white linen robe, like a surplice, worn by bishops. (F. – M.H.G.) F. *rochet*, 'a frock; a prelate's rochet;' Cot. – M H.G. *roc* (G. *rock*), a frock, coat. ✚Du. *rok*, O. Fries. *rokk*, the same.

Rowan-tree, the mountain-ash. (Scand.) The word *tree* is E. *Rowan*, also spelt *roan*, is from the Dan. *rön*, Swed. *rönn*, the mountain-ash; Icel. *reynir* (the same). ¶ The Icel. *reynir* also means 'a trier, examiner;' from *reyna*, to prove, try, which verb is derived by vowel-change from *raun*, trial, experiment. *If* these two words (*reynir*) are connected, it may relate to the fact that twigs of the rowan-tree were considered as a counter-charm against witchcraft, and so made proof of the witch.

Rowlock, Rollock, Rullock, the place of support for an oar. (E.) Spelt *orlok* in the Liber Albus, pp. 235, 237. A corruption of *oar-lock*. – A.S. *árloc*, a rowlock. – A.S. *ár*, oar; *loc*, cognate with G. *loch*, a hole. The orig. rowlocks were actual holes, and were called also *oar-holes*.

Ruff, a game at cards. (F.) A modification of F. *ronfle*, 'hand-ruffe, at cards,' Cotgrave; *jouer à la ronfle*, 'to play at hand-ruffe, also to snore,' id. Cf. Ital. *ronfa*, ruff; *ronfare*, to snort, to trump at cards. Of imitative origin.

Sahib, sir, master; a title. (Hind. – Arab.) Hind. *sáhib*. – Arab. *sáhib*, lord, master. The initial letter is *sdd*; the third is the sixth of the Arab. alphabet.

Saker, a kind of falcon; a small piece of artillery. (F. – Span. – Arab.) (The gun was called after the falcon; cf. *musket*.) – F. *sacre*, 'a saker; the hawk, and the artillery so called;' Cot. – Span. *sacre*, a saker (in both senses). – Arab. *saqr*, a hawk (with initial *sdd*). Engelmann has shown

that the word is not of Lat. origin, as said by Diez (Devic).

Sambo, the offspring of a negro and mulatto. (Span. – L. – Gk.) Span. *zambo*, formerly *çambo* (Pineda), bandy-legged; also as sb., a sambo (in contempt). – Late L. *scambus*. – Gk. σκαμβός, crooked, said of the legs. Perhaps allied to σκάζειν, to halt.

Sandblind, half blind. (E.) In Shakespeare; a corruption of *sam-blind*, half blind. The prefix = A.S. *sám-*, half, which is cognate with L. *semi-*, Gk. ἡμι-; see Semi-, Hemi-.

Sardius, a gem. (L. – Gk.) Rev. xxi. 20. – L. *sardius* (Vulgate). – Gk. σάρδιος, σάρδιον, a gem of Sardis.

Saunter. (F. – L.) Prob. for O.F. *s'auntrer*, to adventure oneself. I find mention of a man 'qe *sauntre* en ewe,' who ventures on the water, who goes to sea; Year-book of 11 Edw. III. p. 619. O.F. *auntrer* is the same as *adventurer*; see adventure, p. 540, col. 1.

Scallion, a plant allied to garlic. (F. – L. – Gk. – Phœnician.) O.F. *escalogne*, a scallion; see further under Shallot.

Scrannel, thin, weakly, wretched. (Scand.) In Milton, Lycidas, 124. Prov. E. *scranny*, thin, lean; *scrannel*, a lean person (Lincolnshire). – Swed. dial. *skran*, weak; Norweg. *skran*, thin, lean, dry; Dan. *skranten*, sickly, weakly. Cf. Swed. dial. and Norw. *skrinn*, thin, lean, weak, dry. Allied to *shrink*.

Scroyles, rascals. (F. – L.) In K. John, ii. 1. 373. – O.F. *escroelles*, later *escrouelles*, 'the king's evil,' i.e. scrofula; Cot. – Low L. *scrofellæ* *(not found); dimin. of *scrofula*; see Scrofula, p. 420. Transferred, as a term of abuse, from the disease to the person said to be afflicted with it.

Seam (2), a horse-load. (Low L. – Gk.) M.E. *seem*, A.S. *seám*. Borrowed (like G. *saum*) from Low L. *sauma*, corrupt form of *sagma*, a horse-load, pack. – Gk. σάγμα, a pack-saddle. See Sumpter.

Seine, a large fishing-net. (F. – L. – Gk.) F. *seine*. – L. *sagena*. – Gk. σαγήνη, a large fishing-net. Allied to σαγίς, a wallet, σαγή, trappings, and σάττειν (= σάκ-γειν), to pack, load.

Sennet, a signal-call on a trumpet. (F. – L.) See Nares; and Wright's note to K. Lear, i. 1. 23. Also spelt *sinet*. – O.F. *sinet*, *signet*, presumably 'a signal;' dimin. of F. *signe*, a sign, a mark, note. – L. *signum*; see Sign.

Sepal, a leaf or division of the calyx of a flower. (F.—L.) F. *sépale*, a sepal. Coined to pair off with F. *pétale*, a petal, by taking part of the Lat. adj. *separ*, separate, and adding the same suffix -*ale* (Littré). Thus *sep-al* is, as it were, short for *separ-al*, where *separ-* is allied to L. *separare*, to separate. See **Separate.**

Serai, a palace. (Pers.) Pers. *serái*; see **Seraglio,** p. 426, col. 1.

Seraskier, a Turkish general. (F.— Turk.—Pers. *and* Arab.) F. *séraskier*, *sérasquier*.—Turk. *ser'asker*, chief of the army, with a light sound of *i* after the *k.*— Pers. *sar*, head (with initial *sin*); and *Arab.* '*askar*, an army (Devic).

Service-tree, a kind of wild pear-tree. (L. *and* E.) *Service* is a corruption of *serv-ĕs* (dissyllabic), the M.E. plural of *serf* or *serve*, the name of the fruit. A.S. *syrf*, *syrfe*, the fruit of the service-tree; *syrf-tréow*, a service tree (more correctly sirf-tree).—L. *sorbus*, the tree; *sorbum*, the fruit of the same.

Set. When we speak of a *set* of things, this is a variant of *sect* or *sept*. The Low Latin word is *secta*, common in old wills.

Shaddock, a large species of orange. (E.) Named from Captain *Shaddock*, who first introduced it into the West Indies from China, early in the eighteenth century.

Shillelagh, an oaken stick used as a cudgel. (Irish.) Named from *Shillelagh*, a barony in Wicklow famous for oaks. It means 'descendants of Elach;' from Irish *siol*, seed, descendants.

Siesta, orig. a noon-day nap. (Span.— L.) Span. *siesta*, the hottest part of the day, the time for a nap, gen. from one to three o'clock. But orig. the sixth hour, or noon.—L. *sexta* (*hora*), sixth hour, noon; fem. of *sextus*, sixth.—L. *sex*, six.

Skellum, a cheat. (Du.) See Nares Du. *schelm*, a rogue, villain; the Du. *sch* being rendered (as in *landscape*) by *sk = sc.* +G. *schelm*; O.H.G. *scelmo*, a pestilence, carrion, worthless rogue.

Skua, a gull, bird. (Scand.) Icel. *skúfr*, *skúmr*, the skua, or brown gull. Prob. from the colour. Cf. Icel. *skúmi*, dusk; Swed. and Norweg. *skum*, dusky, dull (of the weather); dusky (in colour).

Sleuth-hound, a slot-hound; see **Slot** (2), p. 443, col. 2.

Slug-horn, a battle-cry. (C.) Ignorantly used by Chatterton to mean a sort of *horn*; but really Old Sc. *slogorne*, an old corruption of *slogan*, a war-cry. See **Slogan,** p. 443, col. 2.

Slur, to contaminate, pass over lightly with slight notice. (Scand.) The orig. sense is to trail in mud, draggle; hence, to pass over slightingly.—Icel. *slóra*, to trail; contr. form of *slobra*, to drag or trail oneself along.—Icel. *sloð*, a trail; see **Slot** (2), p. 443. Cf. Swed. dial. *slöra*, to be negligent; Norweg. *slörs*, to be negligent, slur, sully, *slöde*, *slöe*, to draggle, *slöda*, *slöe*, a trail. ¶ Practically, a *th* is lost; as if for *slother*＊.

Spade, at cards. (Span.—L.—Gk.) A substitution for the Span. *espada*, meaning (1) a sword, (2) a spade at cards. See under **Spade,** p. 454, col. 1.

Sparkle, a small spark. (E.) Dimin. of **Spark** (1), p. 454, col. 2. Hence *sparkle*, verb, to throw out sparkles, to glitter. Cf. Du. *sparkelen*, to sparkle. Or the form *spark-le* may be verbal and frequentative.

Spoor, a foot-trail; see p. 461, col. 2, near the bottom.

Stearine, one of the proximate principles of animal fat. (F.—Gk.) F. *stéarine*; formed, with suffix -*ine*, from Gk. *stéap*, tallow, hardened fat. Allied to Gk. *sta-tós*, standing; see **Statics.**

Steatite, a soft magnesian rock with a soapy feel. (F.—Gk.) Formed with suffix -*ite*, from Gk. *stéar*- as in *stéat-os*, gen. of *stéap*, tallow, fat. See above.

Strain (2), descent, lineage, birth. (E.) *Strain* in Shak.; *strene* in Spenser. M.E. *streen*, Chaucer, C.T., Cl. Tale, 157. A.S. *stréon*, strength, product; whence, *strynan*, to beget.

Strath, a flat valley. (C.) Gael. *srath*, a valley with a river, low-lying country beside a river; Irish *srath*, *sratha*, the bottom of a valley, fields beside a river. Cf. Irish *sroth*, a stream.

Swan-hopping, taking up swans to mark them. (E.) The usual explanation, that it stands for *swan-upping*, is right. See old tract on *upping* in Hone, Every-day Book, ii. 958. From the prep. *up.*

Swarth, a quantity of grass cut down at one stroke of the scythe. (E.) In Tw. Nt. ii. 3. 162. An error for *swath*, as in Troil. v. 5. 25. See **Swath,** p. 483.

Taboo, Tabu, to forbid the use of. (Polynesian.) The verb is formed from the sb. *taboo*, which is the E. pronunciation of New Zealand *tapu*, a prohibition or interdict;

pronounced *tambu* in the Solomon Islands. Kotzebue mentions the '*Tabu*,' or interdict,' in his New Voyage Round the World, London, 1830, ii. 178. ¶ Not in any way connected with the custom of *te pi*, as erroneously said in former editions.

Tapioca (addit. to p. 491). The Brazilian *tipi-óca* means 'dregs squeezed out;' from *tipi*, residue, dregs; and the verbal root *og*, *ók*, to take by force, pull, pluck off, hence to squeeze (Cavalcanti).

Tar (2), a sailor; see Tarpauling, p. 491.

Tarre, to incite, set on. (E.) In Shak. Hamlet, ii. 2. 370. M. E. *tarien*, to irritate, provoke.—A.S. *tergan*, to vex, provoke. See **Tarry**, p. 492.

Tenny, a colour in heraldry. (F.—C.) The same as *tawny* or *tanny*; see tawny, s. v. Tan.

Thwaite, a clearing. (Scand.) Common in place-names. Icel. *þveit*, a paddock, orig. a clearing in woods, a cutting.—Icel. *þvíta**, not found, but=A.S. *þwítan*, to cut. See Thwite, p. 508.

Tibert, a cat. (Low G.) Purposely confused with *Tybalt* in 'Romeo, iii. 1. 80. *Tibert* is the name of the cat in 'Reynard the Fox' (Caxton).

Tiff (1), to deck, dress out. (F.—O. Low G.) M.E. *tiffen*.—O.E. *tiffer*, *tifer* (more commonly *atiffer*), 'to deck, trim, adorn;' Cotg.—O. Du. *tippen*, to cut, clip, cut off the *tip* of the hair. See Tip (1), p. 515, col. 1.

Tiff (2), a pet, fit of ill-humour; also liquor, drink. (Scand.) Orig. 'a sniff;' hence (1) a pet, (2) a sup or draught of beer.—Norweg. *tev*, a drawing in of the breath, sniff; *teva*, to sniff; Swed. dial. *täv*, smell, taste; Icel. *þefa*, to sniff.

Tiffin, luncheon. (Scand.) Anglo-Indian; orig. Northern English *tiffin*, i.e. *tiffing*, sipping, eating and drinking out of due season. From *tiff*, a draught of beer. See above.

Tine, to kindle; see Tind, p. 510.

Tomtom, a kind of drum. (Bengáli.) Bengáli *tantan*, vulgarly *tomtom*, a small drum. Prob. named from the sound.

Torque, a collar of twisted gold. (F.—L.) F. *torque*, in Littré.—L. *torquem*, acc. of *torques*, a twisted collar, a torque.—L. *torquere*, to twist. See Torture.

Tourmaline, the name of a mineral. (F.—Cingalese.) F. *tourmaline*. Formed from the native name in Ceylon, where it is said to be called *tournamal* (*turnamal*?);

Webster. If so, it seems to stand for *tournamal-ine*.

Tripos, an honour examination at Cambridge. (L.—Gk.) Better spelt *tripus*, as in An Eng. Garner, vii. 267 (1670). It was orig. applied to a certain M.A. chosen at a commencement to make an ingenious satirical speech; hence the later *triposverses*, i.e. facetious Latin verses on the reverse side of which the *tripos-lists* were printed. Thus the orig. reference was (not to the *three* classes, but) to the three-legged stool used by the *Tripus*, who was also called a *Prævaricator*, or (at Oxford) a *Terræ filius*; and the lists were named from the verses which took the place of the speech delivered by the M.A. on the *tripus*.

Tucker, a fuller. (F.—O. Low G.) M.E. *touker*, lit. 'beater.' O.F. *touker*, *toquer*, to beat; variant of *toucher*, to touch. See Tocsin, p. 516, col. 2. *Tuck* of drum = beat of drum.

Tulle, a kind of silk open-work or lace. (F.) Named from *Tulle*, the chief town in the department of Corrèze (France), where it was first made (Littré).

Turbary, a right of digging turf, or a place for digging it. (Low L.—O.H.G.) Low L. *turbaria*, the same.—O.H.G. *turba*, older form of *zurba*, turf.+A.S. *turf*. See Turf, p. 528.

Twire, to peep out. (E.) In Shak. Son. 28. Only recorded in the cognate M.H.G. form *zwieren*, to peep out (Schade). ¶ Nares is wrong in citing *twire*=*twitter* from Chaucer; the true reading is *twitreth*.

Use (2), profit, benefit. (F.—L.) When *use* is employed, legally, in the sense of 'benefit,' it is a modernised spelling of the Anglo-F. form of the Lat. *opus*, employment, need. We find the Anglo-F. spellings *oes*, *oeps*, *uoes*; O.F. *oes*, *eus*, *ues*.

Utis, festival merriment; see Utas, p. 535.

Vambrace, **Vantbrace**, armour for the fore-arm. (F.—L.) The word simply means 'fore-arm.' It is short for *avantbrace*.—F. *avant-bras*, 'a vambrace, armour for an arm; also, the part of the arm which extends from the elbow to the wrist;' Cotgrave. (The latter is the orig. sense.) —F. *avant*, before; *bras*, the arm.—L. *ab*, *ante*, from before, in front; *brachium*, arm (which gave O.F. *brace*, arm; see Scheler). See Van (1) and Vamp. ¶ Similarly, armour for the upper part of the arm was called a *rere-brace*, i. e. rear-brace.

Vamplate, another name for a vambrace. (F. – L. *and* Gk.) From F. *avant*, in front, fore; and *plate*. See above.

Veney, a bout at fencing; see **Venew**, s.v. **Venture**, p. 540, col. 2.

Wacke, a rock allied to basalt. (G.) G. *wacke*, wacke; M.H.G. *wacke*, O.H.G. *waggo*, a kind of flint.

Wallah, lit. an agent. (Hind.) H. H. Wilson explains Hind. *wálá* as one who is charged with doing any duty; Yule says it is practically an adj. suffix, like the L. *-arius* (or E. *-er*); orig. an agent, doer, &c. See *Competition-wallah* in Yule; we may explain this as *competition-er* = *competitor*.

Wear a ship; the same as **Veer**, p. 538.

Whinyard, a kind of sword. (Scand.) Lit. *whine-yard*, where *yard* means rod, or (more likely) is a mere suffix (*-i-ard*). – Icel. *hvin-a*, to whizz, whistle through the air like a weapon; the same word as E. *whine*, but used in a different way. Cf. also E. *whinny*; and Lowl. Sc. *whing-er*, a whinyard, from the verb *whinge*, an extension of *whine*.

Whortle-berry, the bilberry. (E.) Miswritten for *wortleberry*. – A.S. *wyrtil*, a small shrub, dimin. of *wort*; and E. *berry*. See **Wort** (1), p. 569. ¶ Not from A.S. *heort-berige* = hart-berry.

Woon, a governor, officer. (Burmese.) Burm. *wun*, a governor or officer of administration; lit. 'a burden,' hence presumably 'the bearer of the burden;' Yule, p. 867. See **Vizier** for the sense, p. 547, col. 2.

Wourali, Ourali, Oorali, Ourari, Curari, a resinous substance, used for poisoning arrows. (Guiana.) From '*ourali*, written also *wourali, urali, urari, curare,* &c., according to the pronunciation of the various tribes;' W. H. Brett, Indian Tribes of Guiana, 1868, p. 140.

Yak, an animal. (Thibet.) Thibetan *ɣyaɡ*, a male yak, where the symbol γ is used to denote a peculiar Thibetan sound; H. A. Jäschke, Dict. p. 668.

Yataghan, Ataghan, a dagger-like sabre, with doubly curved blade. (Turk.) Turk. *yátághán*, the same; Zenker's Dict. pp. 947, 958.

Yucca, a genus of American liliaceous plants. (Span. – Caribbean?) Span. *yuca*, said to be a word of Caribbean origin.

Zamindar, Zemindar, a land-holder. (Hind. – Pers.) Hind. *zamíndár*, a land-holder. – Pers. *zamín*, earth, land; *dár*, holding, possessing.

Zanana, Zenana, the female apartments. (Hind. – Pers.) Hind. *sanána*, the women's apartments. – Pers. *zanán*, women; pl. of *zan*, a woman, which is cognate with E. **Queen**.

Zariba, Zareeba, an enclosure, slight defence. (Arab.) Used in newspapers with reference to the war in the Soudan. – Arab. *zaríbat*, 'a fold, a pen, an enclosure for cattle; den or haunt of wild beasts; lurking-place for a hunter;' Rich. Dict. p. 775.

Zend, an ancient Persian dialect. (Zend.) Properly the translation into the Pahlevi language of the *Avesta*, or Zoroastrian scriptures; but commonly used to denote the language, an ancient Persian dialect, in which the *Avesta* is written. It is supposed that *Avesta* means the 'text,' and *Zend* the 'commentary' or 'explanation.' The word *zend* is mod. Persian (Palmer); also written *zand* (Richardson); and corresponds to Zend *zaiñti*, knowledge, information, appearing in the compounds *ā-zaiñti, paiti-zaiñti*, knowledge, and answering to the Skt. form *jañti** (not found), from the Aryan root GAN, to know (Fick, i. 67, 321). See **Can** (1), p. 62. β. *Avesta* has been explained as meaning 'the settled' text (Skt. *ava-sthita*, from *ava-sthá*, to be firm: root STA); or, otherwise, as meaning 'that which is proclaimed or made known' (cf. Skt. *á-vid*, to report: root WID). See Max Müller, Lectures, 8th ed. i. 237.

Zouave, one of a body of soldiers in the French service, orig. Arabs. (N. African.) N. African *Zouaoua*, a tribe of Kabyles living among the Jurjura mountains in Algeria.